2001

2001

WOMEN IN WORLD HISTORY

A Biographical Encyclopedia

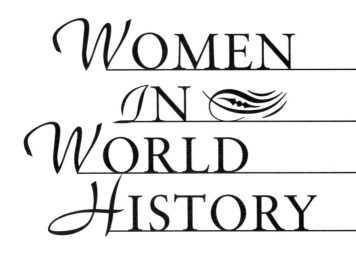

WOMEN IN WORLD HISTORY

A Biographical Encyclopedia

VOLUME
15
Sul-Vica

Anne Commire, Editor
Deborah Klezmer, Associate Editor

YORKIN PUBLICATIONS

GALE GROUP
™
THOMSON LEARNING

Detroit • New York • San Diego • San Francisco
Boston • New Haven, Conn. • Waterville, Maine
London • Munich

Yorkin Publications

Anne Commire, *Editor*
Deborah Klezmer, *Associate Editor*
Barbara Morgan, *Assistant Editor*

Eileen O'Pasek, Gail Schermer, Patricia Coombs, James Fox,
Catherine Cappelli, Karen Rikkers, *Editorial Assistants*
Karen Walker, *Assistant for Genealogical Charts*

Special acknowledgment is due to Peg Yorkin who made this project possible.

Thanks also to Karin and John Haag, Bob Schermer, and to
the Gale Group staff, in particular Dedria Bryfonski, Linda Hubbard, John Schmittroth, Cynthia Baldwin,
Tracey Rowens, Randy Bassett, Christine O'Bryan, Rebecca Parks, and especially Sharon Malinowski.

The Gale Group

Sharon Malinowski, *Senior Editor*
Rebecca Parks, *Editor*
Laura Brandau, *Assistant Editor*
Linda S. Hubbard, *Managing Editor*

Margaret A. Chamberlain, *Permissions Specialist*
Mary K. Grimes, *Image Cataloger*

Mary Beth Trimper, *Production Director*
Evi Seoud, *Assistant Production Manager*

Cynthia Baldwin, *Product Design Manager*
Tracey Rowens, *Cover and Page Designer*
Michael Logusz, *Graphic Artist*

Barbara Yarrow, *Graphic Services Manager*
Randy Bassett, *Image Database Supervisor*
Dan Newell, *Imaging Specialist*
Christine O'Bryan, *Graphics Desktop Publisher*
Dan Bono and Ryan Cartmill, *Technical Support*

Library of Congress Catalog Card Number 99-24692
A CIP record is available from the British Library

ISBN 0-7876-4074-3
Printed in the United States of America.

Library of Congress Cataloging-in-Publication Data

Women in world history : a biographical encyclopedia / Anne Commire, editor, Deborah Klezmer, associate editor.
    p. cm.
Includes bibliographical references and index.
ISBN 0-7876-3736-X (set) — ISBN 0-7876-6436-7 (v.13). —
ISBN 0-7876-4073-5 (v. 14) — ISBN 0-7876-4074-3 (v.15) — ISBN 0-7876-4075-1 (v.16) — ISBN 0-7876-4076-X (v.17)
    1. Women—History Encyclopedias.2. Women—Biography Encyclopedias.
I. Commire, Anne. II. Klezmer, Deborah.
    HQ1115.W6 1999   99-24692
    920.72'03—DC21

10 9 8 7 6 5 4 3 2 1

addressed her dead father in the essay, and also dedicated it to him, expressing her hopes that the essay might perpetuate his name in the same way as if she had been a son to carry on the family line. She remained a loyal, fiercely dedicated, and proud Jew until her death in 1641.

SOURCES:

Henry, Sondra, and Emily Taitz. *Written Out of History: Our Jewish Foremothers.* NY: Biblio Press, 1990.

B. Kimberly Taylor, freelance writer, New York, New York

Sullam, Sara Coppia (1590–1641)

Italian Renaissance figure. Name variations: Sara Copio Sullam. Born Sara Coppia or Copio in Venice, Italy, in 1590; died in 1641; was able to read Latin, Greek, Spanish, Hebrew, and Italian by age 15; married Joseph Sullam.

Sara Coppia Sullam typified the cultural achievements of Renaissance Italy; although she was born in 1590 and raised in the humble ghetto regions of Venice, she was able to read five languages by the time she was 15. She could perform on the lute and harpsichord, and was known as a gifted poet, although very little of her work has survived. After her marriage to Joseph Sullam, a wealthy Jewish man, she turned their home into one of the most popular literary salons in Venice, frequented by Jews and Gentiles alike. She often entertained the most distinguished people of the era in Venice by reading her own poetry and performing music. Her prominence in Venetian cultural life made her a desirable prospect for conversion to Christianity, but she rejected all attempts to turn her away from Judaism.

Despite her steadfast devotion to her faith, Sullam found herself the victim of rumors that she did not believe in the immortality of the soul. To defend her position and religious beliefs, she wrote a pamphlet in 1621 titled *Manifesto of Sara Coppia Sullam, Jewess, in which she refutes the opinion denying immortality of the soul, falsely attributed to her by Sr. Bonifaccio.* As a demonstration of her belief in immortality, she

Sullavan, Margaret (1911–1960)

American actress, known for her moving performance in Three Comrades *and her light touch in* The Shop Around the Corner. *Born Margaret Brooke Sullavan on May 16, 1911, in Norfolk, Virginia; died on January 1, 1960, of an overdose of barbiturates; daughter of Cornelius H. Sullivan (a broker) and Garland (Council) Sullavan; attended Miss Turnbull's Norfolk Tutoring School for Girls; attended the Walter Herron Taylor School, St. George's, and Chatham Episcopal Institute; attended Sullins College, Bristol, Virginia; married Henry Fonda (an actor), in 1930 (divorced within a year); married William Wyler (a director), in 1934 (divorced 1936); married Leland Hayward (a producer-agent), in 1936 (divorced); married a businessman; children: daughters, Brooke Hayward (an author) and Bridget Hayward.*

Selected theater: made stage debut as Isabella Parry in Strictly Dishonorable *(1930); made Broadway debut in* A Modern Virgin *(1931); appeared as Paula Jordan in* Dinner at Eight *(1932), Terry Randall in* Stage Door *(1936), Sally in* The Voice of the Turtle *(1943), Hester Collyer in* The Deep Blue Sea *(1952);* Sabrina Fair *(1953);* Janus *(1955).*

Selected filmography: Only Yesterday *(1933);* Little Man What Now? *(1934);* The Good Fairy *(1935);* So Red the Rose *(1935);* Next Time We Love *(1936);* The Moon's Our Home *(1936);* Three Comrades *(1938);* The Shopworn Angel *(1938);* The Shining Hour *(1938);* The Shop Around the Corner *(1940);* The Mortal Storm *(1940);* Back Street *(1941);* So Ends Our Night *(1941);* Appointment for Love *(1941);* Cry Havoc *(1943);* No Sad Songs for Me *(1950).*

A magnetic and versatile actress who was successful on both stage and screen, Margaret Sullavan is remembered primarily for her wrenching performance as Robert Taylor's tubercular wife in the film *Three Comrades* (1938), and for her portrayal of the struggling young actress in John van Druten's stage play *The Voice of the Turtle* (1943), for which she won the New

York Drama Critics' award. Never happy with the business of making movies, Sullavan turned her back on Hollywood at the height of her success, but continued to work on stage, although advancing deafness made it necessary for her to read lips in order to continue to perform.

Sullavan was born in 1911 in Norfolk, Virginia, the daughter of **Garland Sullavan** and Cornelius H. Sullivan, a successful financial broker. High spirited as a child, she was sent to a variety of strict private schools but never lost her willfulness. Her love of acting began with recitations in the family parlor at the age of six and continued throughout her school days, although her mother and father strongly disapproved of the stage as a career. At 17, having compromised with her parents, she went off to Boston, ostensibly to study dance, but after three weeks she transferred to drama school, supporting herself by clerking in a local department store. In the summer of 1928, she joined the University Players Guild, a group of students from Harvard, Princeton, and Smith College who produced plays on Cape Cod. Sullavan left after the first season to return home for her coming-out party, but returned the following season, more determined than ever to become an actress. In 1930, she was chosen to play Isabella Perry in the Southern company of *Strictly Dishonorable*, her first substantial role to date. That year, she also married Henry Fonda, then a fellow actor in the Guild. The marriage lasted less than a year.

In 1931, Sullavan made her Broadway debut in the leading role of *A Modern Virgin*, an ill-fated play that lasted for only 29 performances. Over the course of the next two years, she appeared in four more doomed productions, although her reputation as an actress continued to grow. In 1933, she replaced **Marguerite Churchill** in the role of Paula Jordan in the hit play *Dinner at Eight*. During the run, she signed a three-year contract with Universal Pictures, with the provision that she have summers free to work in the theater. From the onset, however, Sullavan was less than enthralled about acting in films, largely because she felt she had yet to prove herself as a stage actress. "Acting in the movies is just like ditch-digging," she told one executive. (After viewing the rushes of her first film *Only Yesterday*, she reportedly offered the studio $2,500 to release her from contract.) Though Sullavan may have been a problem to the studio heads, she absolutely delighted moviegoers.

While filming her third movie, *The Good Fairy* (1933), Sullavan married her director William Wyler. Their romance was the result of a series of disagreements between the two which culminated in a dinner engagement and a subsequent meeting of the minds. The union lasted until 1936, when Sullavan's movie contract expired and she returned to New York to play a small role in the Broadway play *Stage Door*. During the run of the show, she married her Hollywood agent Leland Hayward and moved back to California. Following a brief hiatus, during which time her two children, Brooke and Bridget, were born, she returned to the screen under a six-film deal Hayward had arranged for her at MGM. Friends reported at the time that her happy married life had changed Sullavan. "She is much calmer, softer, and is completely domesticated," said one.

Sullavan's later films were slightly more weighty and allowed her to extend her range. Notable was her touching performance in *Three Comrades* (1938), for which she won the New York Drama Critics' Best Actress award and the *Picturegoer* Gold Medal. One of her best comic roles ("a performance of impish and infinite delicacy," according to David Shipman) was in *The Shop Around the Corner* (1940), co-starring James Stewart and directed by Ernst Lubitsch. In 1942, after filming *Cry Havoc* (1943), Sullavan returned to Broadway to play Sally, a young actress who falls in love with an army sergeant on leave, in *The Voice of the Turtle*, a play in which she had also invested some money. Howard Barnes of the New York *Herald Tribune* proclaimed her portrayal "impeccably right . . . little short of magnificent. . . . She reads her lines and plays her business so aptly that there is no questioning the fact that she is the finest actress of our day in the theater." After a considerable run, the play went to London in 1947, but failed to repeat its American success. It was later made into a movie with *Eleanor Parker.

In 1950, Sullavan returned to films for the final time, to play a young woman dying of cancer in *No Sad Songs for Me*. Her stage career flourished, however, with performances in *The Deep Blue Sea* (1952), *Sabrina Fair* (1953), and *Janus* (1954). Along the way, she divorced Hayward and married a businessman. In 1960, depressed by the prognosis of her encroaching deafness, the actress took her own life by consuming an overdose of barbiturates. In 1977, Sullavan's daughter **Brooke Hayward** published the bestselling *Haywire* (1977), about herself, her mother, and her father.

SOURCES:
Boardman, Gerald. *The Oxford Companion to American Theatre*. NY: Oxford University Press, 1984.

Katz, Ephraim. *The Film Encyclopedia*. NY: HarperCollins, 1994.
Rothe, Anna, ed. *Current Biography 1944*. NY: H.W. Wilson, 1944.
Shipman, David. *The Great Movie Stars: The Golden Years*. Boston, MA: Little, Brown, 1995.

Barbara Morgan,
Melrose, Massachusetts

Sullerot, Evelyne (1924—)

French sociologist and journalist. Born Evelyne Annie Henriette Pasteur on October 10, 1924, in Montrouge, France; daughter of André Pasteur and Georgette (Roustain) Pasteur; educated at Compiègne, Royan and Uzès, and then at the universities of Paris and Aix-en-Provence; married François Sullerot, in 1946; children: three sons and one daughter.

Co-founded the French Family Planning Association (1955); served as an advisor to the United Nations, the International Labour Organization, and the European Economic Community; authored several books on women's issues.

Evelyne Sullerot was born in 1924 in Montrouge, France. She studied at Compiègne, Royan and Uzès, and took courses at the universities of Paris and Aix-en-Provence. After her 1946 marriage to François Sullerot, she taught for two years in the first of what would be a series of increasingly prestigious teaching posts. In the mid-1960s, Sullerot was a teacher at the French Press Institute, as well as a professor at the Free University of Brussels and head of the Faculty of Letters at the University of Paris.

Her teaching positions aside, Sullerot earned renown as the co-founder in 1955 of the French Family Planning Movement. Sullerot expertly combined her interests in feminism and sociology as secretary-general of the organization from 1955 to 1958, after which she became honorary president. Her expertise in women's issues resulted in an impressive body of published work, as well as advisory posts to the United Nations, the European Economic Community, and the International Labour Organization. In addition, she became a member of the French Economic and Social Council.

Sullerot's traditional feminist philosophies flavored her numerous books, including *La vie des femmes* (1964), *Demain les femmes* (1965), *Histoire et sociologie du travail féminin* (1968), *La femme dans le monde moderne* (1970), *Les françaises aux travail* (1973), *Histoire et mythologie de l'amour* (1976), and *L'âge de travailler* (1986). Sullerot focused much of her attention on

Opposite page
Margaret Sullavan

the impact of women's professional activities on family structures and trends in industrial societies.

SOURCES:

Buck, Claire, ed. *The Bloomsbury Guide to Women's Literature*. NY: Prentice Hall, 1992.

International Who's Who of Women. 2nd ed. London: Europa Publications, 1997.

Uglow, Jennifer S., comp. and ed. *The International Dictionary of Women's Biography*. NY: Continuum, 1982.

B. Kimberly Taylor, freelance writer,
New York, New York

Sullivan, Annie (1866–1936).

See Keller, Helen for sidebar on Anne Sullivan Macy.

Sullivan, Mrs. Cornelius (1877–1939).

See Sullivan, Mary Quinn.

Sullivan, Kathryn (b. 1951).

See Astronauts: Women in Space.

Sullivan, Leonor Kretzer

ℒeonor
𝒦retzer
𝒮ullivan

(1902–1988)

U.S. congressional representative. Born Leonor Kretzer on August 21, 1902, in St. Louis, Missouri; died in St. Louis on September 1, 1988; daughter of Frederick William and Nora (Jostrand) Kretzer; attended public and private schools in St. Louis; attended Washington University; married John Berchmans Sullivan (a legislator and politician), on December 27, 1941 (died January 1951).

Leonor Sullivan was born Leonor Kretzer in St. Louis, Missouri, in 1902. After attending both private and public schools, she attended night classes at Washington University. She also taught business and accounting classes in addition to directing the St. Louis Comptometer School. Upon her marriage in 1941 to John B. Sullivan, U.S. representative of the 11th District in Missouri, she entered the world of politics as his campaign manager and administrative aide from 1942 until his death in 1951. She then diverted her administrative energies to supporting Missouri congressional representative Theodore Irving. No longer content with staying in the political background, Sullivan resigned her position in May 1952, to run for the Democratic congressional nomination in her own right. Two years later, despite the unwelcoming political climate for women, she defeated incumbent Claude I. Bakewell, who had been appointed to serve out her husband's term, to win that seat in the 82nd Congress.

The victory made Leonor Sullivan the only woman representative from Missouri. She earned a reputation as a defender of consumers, and worked throughout her nearly 25-year career in Congress to protect the American public from hazardous substances, harmful cosmetics, food-color additives, and tainted meat. Beyond consumer health issues, Sullivan was instrumental in the passage of the 1968 Consumer Credit Protection Act, which mandated "truth in lending," in which lenders are required to give customers information about the cost of credit. The act had special significance for women, as it gave them the right to obtain credit under their own names.

Sullivan also championed the interests of the poor through her attempts to revive a surplus food-stamp program that the government had offered between 1939 and 1943. Although the legislation initially was rejected in 1957 and again in 1959, Sullivan's persistence was rewarded when a permanent food-stamp program won approval from Congress in 1964. Once again, women—the primary providers of meals in families—benefited from her legislative efforts; as recipients, they could select food from grocery shelves rather than be forced to accept the government's agricultural surplus. Her service in these causes and as a member of the Committee on Banking and Currency, the Committee on

Merchant Marine and Fisheries, and the Joint Committee on Defense Production won her re-election 12 times. The 74-year-old declined to run in the 1977 campaign, but accomplished passage of the 1976 Fishery and Conservation Management Act, which declared a 200-mile fisheries conservation zone off U.S. shores. Richard A. Gephardt succeeded to her seat. Sullivan returned to her native St. Louis and lived there until her death, at age 86, on September 1, 1988.

SOURCES:

Office of the Historian. *Women in Congress, 1917–1990*. Commission on the Bicentenary of the U.S. House of Representatives, 1991.

Weatherford, Doris. *American Women's History*. NY: Prentice Hall, 1994.

B. Kimberly Taylor, freelance writer, New York, New York

Sullivan, Mary Quinn (1877–1939)

Art collector who was one of the founders of the Museum of Modern Art in New York City. Name variations: Mrs. Cornelius Sullivan. Born Mary Josephine Quinn in Indianapolis, Indiana, on November 24, 1877; died on December 5, 1939; eldest daughter of Thomas Quinn and Anne (Gleason) Quinn; attended Shortridge High School; studied at the Pratt Institute in New York City; studied at the Slade School for Fine Art of University College, London; married Cornelius Joseph Sullivan (an attorney and art collector), on November 21, 1917 (died 1932); no children.

Mary Quinn Sullivan was the eldest of eight children of Thomas and **Anne Quinn** of Indianapolis, Indiana; both parents were descended from Irish Roman Catholic families. Thomas had settled in the Indianapolis area 20 years prior to Mary's birth in 1877, and made a living as a farmer just outside the city. The Quinn children were raised in an atmosphere conducive to the free development of their talents, and Mary enjoyed her first training in art at the Shortridge High School. She enrolled at the Pratt Institute in New York City in 1899 and within two years had completed her studies and was working as a drawing instructor at a school in Queens. The New York City Board of Education then selected her to travel to Europe in 1902 to observe art schools there. While in France and Italy, Mary particularly appreciated Impressionist and Post-Impressionist paintings. Upon her return home, she assumed greater responsibilities as the supervisor of drawing for the city-wide network of elementary schools, and secretary of the New York High School Teachers' Association. Although by 1909 she had ascended professionally

to the head of the art department of DeWitt Clinton High School, she resigned that position to acquire additional training. In 1910, she entered the program at the Slade School of Fine Art, which was attached to the University College in London. This resulted in a post as instructor of design and household arts and sciences at her alma mater, Pratt Institute. In 1914, she contributed a textbook, *Planning and Furnishing the Home: Practical and Economical Suggestions for the Homemaker*, to the school and also provided occupational therapists with art training during World War I.

In 1917, Mary resigned from her position at Pratt and married New York attorney and art collector Cornelius Joseph Sullivan. Together, they collected rare paintings and entertained a wide circle of diverse friends at their home in Astoria, Queens. Among the works they purchased by modern artists were Paul Cézanne's *Madame Cézanne*, Henri de Toulouse-Lautrec's *Woman in the Garden of Mr. Forest*, George Rouault's *Crucifixion*, Amedeo Modigliani's *Sculptured Head of a Woman*, and a Picasso. The Sullivan collection also included 16th-century works, as well as silver and furniture.

Mary Sullivan's friends in the art world encouraged her to foster art through donations and active collecting. Her association with ✿▶ **Katherine Dreier** and ✿▶ **Margaret Dreier Robins**, both noted suffragists and settlement-house workers, led to her interest in modern art, which was reinforced by her relationships with prominent art collectors and patrons such as ✿▶ **Lillie Bliss** and **Abby Aldrich Rockefeller*. Artist Arthur B. Davies persuaded Sullivan and Bliss to donate funds to the landmark Armory Show of 1913.

Sullivan's circle of art-patron friends generated the concept of the Museum of Modern Art in the mid-1920s, although specific action was not taken until after Davies' death in 1928. Sullivan was among the seven trustees to sign the charter for the museum, housed in a New York brownstone, in 1929. Its first exhibition, *Cézanne, Gauguin, Seurat, van Gogh*, opened to the public in November of that year. The museum moved to more permanent quarters in 1932, and managed to survive the rocky financial times of the Depression through generous funding from Sullivan and others. In addition to her work as a trustee, Sullivan chaired the extension and furnishing committees for new galleries. Cornelius Sullivan was equally invested in the museum's success, using his skills in the legal profession to act as counsel to the museum. In 1933, the year after he died, Mary Sullivan re-

◀✿
Katherine Dreier and ***Margaret Dreier Robins***. *See Dreier Sisters.*

◀✿
Bliss, Lillie*. See Rockefeller, Abby Aldrich for sidebar.*

signed as trustee, but accepted a position as honorary trustee for life in 1935. Although firmly ensconced in New York, Sullivan also devoted her energy to develop the artistic environment of her hometown of Indianapolis by founding the Gamboliers' Society, designed to purchase art for the John Herron Art Institute.

During the last ten years of her life, Sullivan was involved in gallery work, presenting solo shows for such artists as Peter Hurd in her own gallery on East 56th Street, and setting up a small, two-room gallery within the larger gallery owned by **Lois Shaw**. Just two years before her death she auctioned off her husband's extensive collection, possibly because of precarious financial circumstances, and poor health necessitated the closing of her gallery in 1939. While preparing to auction off her own art collection—numbering around 200 pieces—Sullivan succumbed to a combination of pleurisy and diabetes on December 5, 1939. Already scheduled for the following day, the auction revealed Sullivan's keen judgment and refined taste in art with she had amassed an impressive collection over her lifetime. Her longtime friend Abby Aldrich Rockefeller purchased a Modigliani and an André Derain for the permanent collection of the Museum of Modern Art in Sullivan's memory.

SOURCES:

James, Edward T., ed. *Notable American Women, 1607–1950.* Cambridge, MA: The Belknap Press of Harvard University, 1971.

B. Kimberly Taylor, freelance writer, New York, New York

Sullivan, Maxine (1911–1987)

African-American singer who was famous for her rendition of the Scottish folk song "Loch Lomond." Name variations: Marietta Williams. Born Marietta Williams in Homestead, Pennsylvania, on May 13, 1911; died on April 7, 1987, in New York City; trained as a nurse in the 1950s; married John Kirby (a bandleader), in 1938 (divorced 1941); married Cliff Jackson (a pianist), in 1950 (died 1970); children: Paula Morris and Orville Williams.

Selected discography: "Loch Lomond" (1937); "I'm Coming, Virginia" (1937); "Annie Laurie" (1937); "Blue Skies" (1937); "Nice Work If You Can Get It" (1937); "St. Louis Blues" (1938); "When Your Lover Has Gone/ My Ideal" (1942); The Complete Charlie Shavers with Maxine Sullivan (1956); The Queen (1981); The Great Songs of the Cotton Club by Harold Arlen and Ted Koehler (1984); Uptown (1985).

Selected theater and film: appeared in the Hollywood film musicals Going Places *(opposite Louis Armstrong) and* St. Louis Blues *(both 1938); appeared on Broadway in* Swingin' the Dream *(1939).*

Born Marietta Williams in Homestead, Pennsylvania, in 1911, Maxine Sullivan grew up in a home filled with music. Her father and uncles all played musical instruments, and she began singing at home when she was very young. Her grandmother encouraged the six-year-old child to sing at a local library show, and as she grew into her teens, she was performing in organized groups, including her uncle's band, the Red Hot Peppers. Sullivan made her professional debut at a small Pittsburgh speakeasy. Her soft voice was perfectly suited to the acoustics of the Benjamin Harrison Literary Club, a popular place to hear the leading jazz artists of the 1930s. Pianist **Gladys Mosier** heard Sullivan perform there and recommended her to pianist and arranger Claude Thornhill in 1936.

Sullivan moved to New York City, and after an audition was hired at the famous Onyx Club as an intermission entertainer earning $40 a week, with Mosier and Thornhill as her managers. Sullivan's light voice was well suited to classic folk songs, which she adapted to a swinging beat. On August 6, 1937, she recorded the Thornhill-arranged "I'm Coming, Virginia," "Annie Laurie," "Blue Skies," and "Loch Lomond." Backed by the John Kirby Quintet on "Loch Lomond," Sullivan attracted national attention. Although some radio stations did not like swing renditions of classic tunes, other stations responded to public demand and played Sullivan's recording of the Scottish folk song. As a result, her weekly salary at the Onyx soared to $80 and eventually to $150.

In addition to marrying bandleader Kirby in 1938, Sullivan also performed in two Hollywood films that year. She appeared opposite Louis Armstrong and Ronald Reagan in *Going Places,* and with *Dorothy Lamour and Lloyd Nolan in *St. Louis Blues.* The year 1939 took her to Broadway with Louis Armstrong and Benny Goodman in *Swingin' the Dream,* a jazz version of *A Midsummer Night's Dream.* She also included in her repertoire such pop tunes as "I've Got the World on a String," "Wrap Your Troubles in Dreams," and "I Got a Right to Sing the Blues." Sullivan and Kirby worked together on her radio show, "Flow Gently, Sweet Rhythm," a CBS-produced broadcast that aired for two years and frequently offered jazz versions of classical music. However, while Sullivan and Kirby's careers were experiencing increasing success, their marriage disintegrated, and they divorced in 1941. After touring with the Benny Carter orchestra, Sullivan launched a solo act, performing in the late 1940s with Johnny Long and Glenn Miller before returning to New York City for six years at Le Ruban Bleu and four years at the Village Vanguard.

In 1950, Sullivan married stride pianist Cliff Jackson, and she retired six years later to devote more time to her family. She was active in local school board activities and became president of the Parent-Teachers Association of P.S. 136 in the Bronx. She also trained as a nurse, spending time working as a health counselor. In 1956, she purchased a building in the South Bronx and established a community center called the House That Jazz Built, dedicated to her husband, supported by memberships and grants, and administered with the help of senior citizens. Tired of touring, Sullivan occasionally performed at local clubs with jazz musicians such as Bobby Hackett, Charlie Shavers, Earl Hines, and Bob Wilber. In 1979, she earned a Tony Award nomination for her performance in the Broadway musical *My Old Friends*. Despite failing health, Sullivan appeared at jazz festivals around the world and recorded 11 albums, all of which were well received and which earned her Grammy nominations in 1982, 1985, and 1986.

After a career of more than 50 years, Sullivan suffered a seizure on April 1, 1987, and died six days later. Conflicting reports as to the cause of death indicate that she died either from heart failure or lung cancer.

SOURCES:

Kernfeld, Barry, ed. *The New Grove Dictionary of Jazz.* NY: St. Martin's Press, 1988, 1994.

Smith, Jessie Carney, ed. *Notable Black American Women, Book II.* Detroit, MI: Gale Research, 1996.

B. Kimberly Taylor, freelance writer,
New York, New York

Sulner, Hanna (c. 1918–1999)

Hungarian document analyst and handwriting expert.
Born Hanna Fischof in Budapest, Hungary, around 1918; died in New York City on January 5, 1999; daughter of Professor Julius Fischof (a handwriting analyst); studied criminology, earned special degree to teach document examination; married Laszlo Sulner (a handwriting analyst), in November 1947 (died 1950); children: one son, Andrew (a document expert).

Studied handwriting analysis with father from age 16; took over father's handwriting analysis work (1944); drawn into Communist government plot to frame Cardinal Jozsèf Mindszenty (c. 1947); de-nounced trial after escaping to Vienna (1949); published Disputed Documents (1966).

One of the world's leading authorities in the field of handwriting analysis, Hanna Sulner spent her life analyzing and authenticating documents, many of them at issue in important legal cases. She was born Hanna Fischof around 1918 in Budapest, Hungary, where her father, Professor Julius Fischof, an expert on handwriting and document analysis, settled after World War I. Hanna began working and studying with him when she was 16 years old. She also studied criminology and obtained a special degree that qualified her to teach document examination at the University of Budapest school of law. When her father died in 1944, she took over his work and professional position as the official handwriting and documentation expert for the Hungarian courts, police, and military. Known as a meticulous professional, she soon inherited his reputation as well.

Laszlo Sulner joined the office in 1946, and the two were married the following year. Gradually, without at first being aware of it, the couple became a party to the plot to discredit Cardinal Jozsèf Mindszenty. The cardinal was a fervent anti-Communist and staunch enemy of the Soviet-backed Hungarian government's Communist police state. As primate of the largely Roman Catholic country, however, he was a highly influential personality and much respected, and so could not be summarily jailed or executed as many others were. The government's solution was an elaborate frame-up that included falsified documents proving, among other charges, treason.

Laszlo forged the majority of the documents purported to be either written or signed by the cardinal, but Hanna was also fully involved; their cooperation came under the threat of death, and they felt they had no choice. In 1949, Mindszenty was convicted of treason during a three-day trial in which the documents forged by the Sulners and by police who had been trained by Laszlo were prime evidence. As the trial was drawing to a close, the Sulners escaped to Austria on February 6, 1949. Four days later in Vienna, they publicly denounced the trial as a fraud and displayed microfilm of the forged documents on which they had worked.

The next year, Laszlo died in Paris at age 30. The cause was listed as heart disease, but Hanna insisted that he had been poisoned by Communist agents. She fled to the United States with her infant son, and resumed her career in New York City. Sulner was a much sought-after expert witness, and was well known for being unusually particular about the quality of photocopies made of documents she was asked to examine, insisting on the help of her own expert assistants. She published many articles about document analysis and a 1966 handbook, considered to be authoritative, titled *Disputed Documents*.

SOURCES:
"Hanna F. Sulner, 81, Expert Drawn into Mindszenty Plot," in *The New York Times*. January 19, 1999.

Malinda Mayer, writer and editor,
Falmouth, Massachusetts

Sulpicia I (fl. 1st c. BCE)

Roman poet. Flourished in the 1st century BCE.

Sulpicia I moved in the cultural circle surrounding the Roman M. Valerius Messalla Corvinus, patron of poets Ovid and Tibullus. There is some debate as to whether she was also his niece. Sulpicia authored six elegiac poems that survived with the works of Tibullus. According to *An Encyclopedia of Continental Women Writers*, although the poems total only 40 lines, they represent the sole example of work by the *docta puellae* (educated female companions of the elegists), and were greatly admired by modernist poet Ezra Pound. In these brief lines, Sulpicia I professes her love for a man named Cerinthus and boasts that her poetry made him love her. She also touched on other common love-related themes including infidelity and the pain of love.

SOURCES:
Buck, Claire, ed. *The Bloomsbury Guide to Women's Literature*. NY: Prentice Hall, 1992.
Wilson, Katharina M., ed. *An Encyclopedia of Continental Women Writers*. Vol. 2. NY: Garland, 1991.

B. Kimberly Taylor, freelance writer,
New York, New York

Sulpicia II (fl. 1st c. CE)

Roman poet. Flourished in the 1st century CE; married Calenus.

Nothing is known of Sulpicia II's life except what was written about her by the Roman poet Martial toward the end of the 1st century. Apparently she wrote graphic lyric poems celebrating her love for her husband Calenus, and Martial compared her favorably to the famous *Sappho. Scholars believe that two somewhat garbled lines of poetry published in an ancient commentary on Juvenal are all that is left of her work. A satire of about 70 lines in hexameter verse about the expulsion of philosophers from Rome by the emperor Domitian (1st century CE) has also been tentatively attributed to her.

SOURCES:
Buck, Claire, ed. *The Bloomsbury Guide to Women's Literature*. NY: Prentice Hall, 1992.
Wilson, Katharina M., ed. *An Encyclopedia of Continental Women Writers*. Vol. 2. NY: Garland, 1991.

B. Kimberly Taylor, freelance writer,
New York, New York

Sulzberger, I.O. (1892–1990)

American civic leader who oversaw the development of The New York Times *in the course of her lifetime. Name variations: Iphigene Ochs; Iphigene Ochs Sulzberger; Mrs. Arthur H. Sulzberger. Born Iphigene Bertha Ochs on September 19, 1892, in Tennessee; died of respiratory failure on February 26, 1990, in Stamford, Connecticut; daughter of Adolph Ochs (a newspaper publisher) and Iphigenia (Wise) Ochs (the daughter of Isaac Mayer Wise, a rabbi and founder of American Reform Judaism); attended Dr. Sachs School for Girls and Benjamin-Dean School, both in Manhattan, New York; attended Barnard College; married Arthur Sulzberger (president and publisher of* The New York Times*), on November 17, 1917 (died 1968); children: Marian Sulzberger Heiskell (b. 1918); Ruth Sulzberger Holmberg (b. 1921); Judith P. Sulzberger (b. 1923); Arthur Sulzberger (b. 1926).*

I.O. Sulzberger was born Iphigene Ochs in Tennessee in 1892, into a Jewish family already involved in the newspaper business. Her father Adolph Ochs controlled *The Chattanooga Times*, and at the time of Iphigene's birth was lobbying for small newspapers' participation in the Associated Press. Her mother **Iphigenia Wise Ochs** was the daughter of Isaac Mayer Wise, a rabbi in Cincinnati who founded American Reform Judiasm. Known as "If" or "Iffy" within the close-knit family circle, Sulzberger was schooled at home until the age of eight. Her relationship with her father Adolph proved pivotal to her own interest in the newspaper business, particularly after he purchased the faltering *New York Times* and moved the family to New York in 1896. Sulzberger then began her formal studies at Dr. Sachs School for Girls and the Benjamin-Dean School, both in Manhattan. In 1910, she attended Barnard College. In addition to her classes, she also received an extensive education in the arts on trips with her mother to New York's museums, and with her family to Europe.

Sulzberger's education in the newspaper business began when her father took her to the paper's offices, although he disapproved of the interest in journalism she cultivated during her years at Barnard College. He did, however, challenge her to think with balanced reason and to cling to factual accuracy—two qualities mirrored in the paper that she would oversee. At Barnard, Iphigene met Arthur Hays Sulzberger, who was engaged in military training in preparation for service in World War I. Although he was due to be shipped overseas, she married him in a ceremony at her parents' home on November 17, 1917. The war ended before Arthur was called to service abroad, and the pair made their home in New York, where Arthur joined his father-in-law at *The Times*.

Adolph Ochs' death in 1935 propelled both Sulzbergers to prominent leadership positions at *The Times*. Her father's will made them trustees of the paper, while Arthur also became president and publisher. True to her father's wishes, I.O. Sulzberger remained on the sidelines when it came to running the paper, except for a stint as director of special events during World War II when she coordinated programs to assist the war effort. She was also a tireless worker in civic affairs, concentrating on the conservation of public parks and education. Her activism began in college with her work in the Henry Street Settlement, the Jewish Big Sisters Program, and the Cedar Knolls School for disturbed children.

Sulzberger's service to New York's parks began in 1928 when she joined the Parks Association. As president of the volunteer group after 1934, she was instrumental in winning funding for a chess and checkers house in Central Park as well as the restoration of the Joseph Rodman Drake Park in the Bronx. She eventually became chair of the group in 1950, as well as honorary chair of the Central Park Conservancy, a fundraising group dedicated to the improvement of Central Park. The New York Botanical Garden in the Bronx also benefited from Sulzberger's commitment to parks beautification. The institution's partnership with a nearby high school to train student gardeners found a vigorous supporter in Sulzberger, for which she was honored with its distinguished service award in 1965.

Sulzberger's interest in children's education led her to foster similar programs at the Metropolitan Museum of Art which were designed to teach young people how to restore furniture and paintings, as well as a cooperative program in which high school students alternated classroom studies with on-the-job training. She put her fund-raising skills to the test for her alma mater, Barnard College, during the school's drive to build what would become the Adele Lehman Hall-Wollman Library, dedicated in 1960. This was one of many projects Sulzberger saw to

completion as a lifelong trustee of the school. She also acted as trustee and served on the boards of several other educational institutions, including the Hebrew Union College-Jewish Institute of Religion, the University of Chattanooga and the Cedar Knolls School. The wealth of honorary doctorates she received from other schools—including one from the Bishop College of Dallas, a black school to which she had made substantial donations—proved her impact on children's education.

Although she was a woman of many interests, Sulzberger's most exotic project was her support of Richard E. Byrd's exploration of Antarctica. He expressed his gratitude by christening both a body of water and a mountain after her. Sulzberger Bay and Mount Iphigene are both located near Marie Byrd Land.

Known as the "matriarch of *The New York Times*," Sulzberger remained a constant in the leadership of the paper as management shifted from her husband to her son-in-law, Orvil E. Dry-

I.O.
Sulzberger

foos, who became president in 1957. Four years later, Arthur Sulzberger also relinquished the position of publisher to Dryfoos, although he remained as chair. A stroke in the years before Arthur's death in 1968 necessitated his nearly total reliance on Iphigene. Dryfoos having died in 1963, the paper was now in the hands of Arthur Ochs Sulzberger, the only son among the Sulzbergers' four children. Joining their mother as directors at *The Times* were her daughters **Marian Sulzberger Heiskell**, **Ruth Sulzberger Holmberg** and Dr. **Judith P. Sulzberger**. Having served as the quiet "conscience" of the paper for over 70 years, I.O. Sulzberger died in her sleep of respiratory failure on February 26, 1990, at age 97.

SOURCES:

The New York Times Biographical Service. February 1990.
Weatherford, Doris. *American Women's History.* NY: Prentice Hall, 1994.

B. Kimberly Taylor, freelance writer,
New York, New York

Sumac, Yma (1927—)

Peruvian-born singer who was noted for her incredible range of four octaves. Born Emperatriz Chavarri on September 10, 1927, in the highland village of Ichocan, Peru; sixth child of Imma (Sumack Emilia Atahualpa) Chavarri and Sixto Chavarri; attended the Instituto de Santa Teresa, a Catholic school for girls in Lima; married Moises Vivanco (a musician and composer), on June 6, 1942 (divorced 1958); children: one son, Papuchka ("Charlie").

Peruvian singer Yma Sumac, whose four-octave vocal range and exotic repertoire brought her world renown during the 1950s and 1960s, was born Emperatriz Chavarri in a small mountain town north of Lima, Peru. A participant in local festivals as a child, she was discovered by a government official who passed news of her remarkable voice on to Moises Vivanco, a musician, composer, and the director of the Peruvian National Board of Broadcasting, who took over management of her singing career. Sumac became part of his performing troupe, Moises' Compañia, and with them made her radio debut early in 1942. She and Vivanco were married that same year, after which they toured with the troupe in Rio de Janeiro, Buenos Aires, and Mexico City. In 1946, after paring down the troupe considerably, Vivanco and Sumac, along with her cousin **Cholita Rivero**, arrived in New York, where they began performing as the Inca Taky Trio.

Sumac was not the immediate success in the United States that her husband had hoped. Bookings were few and far between, and the couple endured four lean years, during which Sumac gave birth to her son, Papuchka ("Charlie"). Sumac's break came when a promoter from Capitol Records saw her perform in a New York nightclub and was intrigued by her unique voice and repertoire. In 1950, Capitol produced her first album, *Voice of Xtabay*, which featured melodies in the Quechua Indian language and was an instant bestseller (as were subsequent albums *Mambo* and *Legend of the Sun Virgins*). With Sumac's first successful recording came a flood of creative publicity surrounding her background. She was described variously as a Brooklynite who spelled her name Amy Camus backwards, and as an authentic Inca princess. One particularly imaginative writer proclaimed her one of the chosen "Golden Virgins," a sun worshiper, whose singing was controlled by Indian sorcerers who evoked the spirits of birds and jaguars from her throat.

Sumac went on to play an Arabian princess in the Broadway musical *Flahooley* (1951) and also appeared in two Hollywood films: *Secret of the Incas* (1954) and *Omar Khayyam* (1957). She performed in concert at the Hollywood Bowl, Constitution Hall in Washington, and New York's Carnegie Hall, among other venues. Her repertoire, composed mostly by her husband, included ancient Andean folk themes as well as arias from *The Magic Flute*, *Lakmé*, and *La Traviata*. In performance, the singer accentuated her exotic appearance, dressing in native costume and bedecking herself in heavy Peruvian silver and gold jewelry. Reviewing her concert at Carnegie Hall for the *New York Herald Tribune* (February 18, 1954), Virgil Thomson found her voice beautiful and her technique impeccable. "She sings very low and warm, very high and bird-like; and her middle range is no less lovely than the extremes of her scale. That scale is very close to four octaves, but it is in no way inhuman or outlandish in sound."

In 1957, Sumac went through a well-publicized divorce from her husband, after which her career went into decline. She toured Europe during the 1960s, but an American comeback in 1968 never materialized. A 1972 recording of rock 'n' roll also failed, as did an attempt at country-western. After a number of years spent living and occasionally performing in Peru, Sumac (an American citizen since 1955) returned to the U.S., where she now lives in the Los Angeles area. She gave several concerts in New York and San Francisco during the 1980s, and acted in a revival of Stephen Sondheim's *Follies* in Long Beach, California, in early 1990. In 1997, then almost 70, Sumac performed at the Montreal International Jazz Festival.

Yma Sumac

SOURCES:
Candee, Marjorie Dent, ed. *Current Biography Yearbook 1955*. NY: H.W. Wilson, 1955.
Lamparski, Richard. *Whatever Became of . . . ?* 4th series. NY: Crown, 1973.

Barbara Morgan,
Melrose, Massachusetts

Summerskill, Edith (1901–1980)

English politician, doctor, and author who, as a member of Parliament (1938–55), successfully campaigned for a wide array of women's rights. Name variations: Baroness Summerskill. Born Edith Clara Summerskill on April 19, 1901, in London; died in 1980; daughter of William Summerskill (a physician and radical politician) and Edith Summerskill; educated at Eltham Hill Grammar School and King's College, London; studied at Charing Cross Hospital; married (Edward) Jeffrey Samuel (a physician), in 1924 or 1925; children: Michael Summerskill and Shirley Summerskill (both elected to use their mother's maiden name).

Edith Summerskill was born on April 19, 1901, in London, England, the daughter of William and **Edith Summerskill**. One of her earliest influences was her father, whose pro-feminist and radical political stands once led him to stand for Parliament as an Independent candidate. Also a physician, William took his young daughter with him on visits to patients, and passed on to her not only a love of the profession but also a firm belief in preventative medicine. Although women comprised only 4% of Britain's physicians, Summerskill followed her father into medicine. She studied at King's College in London and finished her studies with hands-on experience at Charing Cross Hospital. After qualifying as a physician at age 23 and becoming a member of the Royal College of Surgeons and a licentiate of the Royal College of Physicians, she married fellow physician E. Jeffrey Samuel and started a medical practice with him.

Summerskill's work as a doctor among London's poor population further cemented in her mind the importance of preventing, rather than just treating, disease. While attending to patients suffering from rickets caused by malnutrition and those ill with tuberculosis from drinking tainted milk, she became involved with the Socialist Medical Association, a group of doctors dedicated to the establishment of a free national health service. She served as its vice-president for many years, but the association's lack of influence impressed on Summerskill the importance of gaining entrance into the political arena in order to exact real change.

Summerskill first became involved in politics in 1931, as a member of the maternity and child welfare committee in London; she was especially concerned about the high maternal mortality rate due to unhygienic conditions. Three years later, she won her first of many political campaigns as a Labour candidate when she made a surprise showing in the Conservative stronghold of Middlesex to win a seat on the county council. While retaining this position, she ran in national campaigns for Parliament in Putney and Lancashire, although she was unsuccessful until she defeated the Conservative candidate in a by-election in West Fulham in 1938.

Summerskill's entrance into the House of Commons was notable in that she represented the advancement of women in two professions formerly believed to "men's work": medicine and politics. As a member of Parliament, Summerskill became a vocal advocate of the causes for which she fought in her medical practice, and her support of women's rights in the areas of equal pay, birth control, and property rights were mixed with more radical ideas such as wages for housework, a just tax on prostitution, and legal rights in polygamous marriages. Although she was a controversial figure, her expertise on women's issues led to an international reputation, as Spain, Italy, the Soviet Union and the United States invited her to examine their welfare and maternity services. Believing that with equal rights comes equal responsibility, during World War II Summerskill encouraged women to join with men in learning to use weapons in the event of an invasion of England through the establishment of the Women's Home Defence Movement in 1939. Taking this idea a step further, she campaigned for women's admission into Britain's Home Guard and achieved this goal in 1943. Her expanding role in national and international politics necessitated her resignation from her county council seat in Middlesex in 1941.

In the years immediately following the war, Summerskill showed no signs of slowing down her activities. Appointed as under-secretary at the Ministry of Food in 1945, she was finally able to strike a blow against the tuberculosis-spreading tainted milk she had campaigned against earlier in her career with the passage of the 1949 Clean Milk Act, which she hailed as her finest achievement. She gained a more prestigious appointment in 1950 when she was named Minister of National Insurance, becoming the first married woman to reach a Cabinet ranking (two single women had preceded her in Cabinet positions). However, the Labour government fell out of favor the following year, forcing her into a quick exit from this post. In the short time she had in power, Summerskill had pioneered legislative efforts to win compensation for workers suffering from industrial injuries or diseases.

This political setback increased Summerskill's role in her own party. Having served as a member of the Labour Party's National Executive Committee since 1944, she became its chair in 1954. Becoming the representative from Warrington the following year, she made social security a special cause as a member of the shadow cabinet (opposition) until 1957. In 1961, Summerskill was honored with a life peerage, becoming Baroness Summerskill of Kenwood, which gained her entrance into the House of Lords. Five years later, she was made a Companion of Honour.

Summerskill continued to battle on behalf of women's rights in the House of Lords, particularly as president of the Married Women's Association. She won significant victories for women in the area of property rights with the passage of the Married Women's Property Act (1964) and the Matrimonial Homes Act (1967). In the interests of national health, she also opposed smoking and sought to make professional boxing illegal. She published *Babies Without Tears* in 1941, a book with a pro-anesthesia stance; *The Ignoble Art*, which explained her position on boxing, in 1956; *Letters to My Daughter* in 1957; and *A Woman's World* in 1967. Her daughter **Shirley Summerskill** carried on her mother's activism by also becoming a doctor and an influential Labour MP. Edith Summerskill spent her later years touring the world and instigating important political changes for women in Britain before her death in 1980.

SOURCES:

The Concise Dictionary of National Biography. Oxford: Oxford University Press, 1992.

Moritz, Charles, ed. *Current Biography Yearbook 1963.* NY: H.W. Wilson, 1963.

Uglow, Jennifer S., comp. and ed. *The International Dictionary of Women's Biography.* NY: Continuum, 1982.

B. Kimberly Taylor, freelance writer, New York, New York

Summitt, Pat (1952—)

American basketball player and coach. Name variations: Pat Head; Patricia Summitt. Born Patricia Sue Head in Henrietta, Tennessee, on June 14, 1952; fourth of five children of Richard Head and Hazel (Albright) Head; University of Tennessee at Martin, B.S., 1974; University of Tennessee at Knoxville, M.A.; married Ralph B. Summitt (a bank president), in 1980; children: son Ross Tyler (b. September 21, 1990).

While a student at University of Tennessee-Martin, led the Lady Pacers to a 64–29 record over four years and had most career points (1,405), most career free throws (361), and most points in a season (530 in 1971–72); coached the Olympic gold-medal team (1984); as head coach of the University of Tennessee Lady Vols, had a career record of 759–153 at the end of the 2000–2001 season; won six NCAA titles (1987, 1989, 1991, 1996, 1997, 1998) and had appeared in all 20 NCAA tournaments as of 2001; was the first female coach to receive the John Bunn Award given by the Basketball Hall of Fame (1990); inducted into the International Women's Sports Hall of Fame (1990); finished the 1997–1998 season with a perfect 39–0 record and was named coach of the year by the Associated Press (1998); inducted into the Basketball Hall of Fame (2000); was named Naismith College Basketball Women's Coach of the Century (2001).

When Patricia Summitt's parents learned that Clarksville High had no girls' basketball team, they simply picked up and moved. The young athlete had always loved the sport; she and her three brothers played for hours on a makeshift court in the hayloft of their dairy barn. "There was never a sense of boys' basketball as opposed to girls' basketball," she said. "It was just basketball." Summitt soon made her mark as a member of the varsity squad at Cheatham County High School in Ashland City, Tennessee. In 1970, she enrolled at the University of Tennessee at Martin (UTM), one of the few institutions then offering women's basketball. She led the team to a spot in the first Association of Intercollegiate Athletics for Women (AIAW) national basketball championships in 1972. A year later, she was captain of the American team that won a silver medal at the World University Games in Moscow. Summitt was also a member of the U.S. Olympic team that played in the inaugural Olympic women's basketball tournament, in which the Americans came in second to the Soviets. A knee injury forced her to stay on the bench her senior year, but by that time she had already established several records which have yet to be broken.

After receiving her bachelor's degree in physical education, Summitt decided to go on for her master's degree at the University of Tennessee in Knoxville (UTK); as a graduate assistant, she was

Pat Summitt

made head coach of the women's basketball team in 1974. That first season, she had 16 wins and 8 losses with a team whose members had never really played the sport (she was also driving the team bus). Fundamentals, conditioning, and teamwork all had to be learned. But Summitt excelled at motivation, and by 1977 UTK placed third in the national championships.

Coach Summitt soon made her mark. She guided the U.S. Junior National Team to a gold medal in their first international competition in 1977 and a gold medal at the Pan American Games in Mexico City. By 1980, she was assistant coach of the U.S. women's Olympic team. Four years later, she was head coach; her team included *Lynette Woodard, *Teresa Edwards, *Anne Donovan, and *Cheryl Miller. At the Los Angeles Olympic Games in 1984, she was the only woman among the world's basketball coaches and quickly established her authority when her team won the gold medal. "In training camp, Pat would push us past the point where we didn't think we had anything left," wrote her former Olympic player *Nancy Lieberman-Cline. "She taught us that our bodies wouldn't quit if our minds didn't quit. Pat's practices were so tough that the games seemed like cake." Said Summitt, "I don't mind being tough because my dad was tough. I don't mind showing affection because my mother showed affection."

As coach for over 27 years at UTK, Summitt has worked her magic. She has been the third winningest active coach in the NCAA. She was awarded Coach of the Year by the Women's Basketball Coaches Association in 1983; Naismith Coach of the Year in 1987 and 1989 and Coach of the Century in 2001; and was the first woman to be given the John Bunn Award by the Basketball Hall of Fame in 1989. In 1990, Summitt was inducted into the International Women's Sports Hall of Fame; in 2000, she was inducted in the Basketball Hall of Fame, along with fellow inductee Isiah Thomas.

As a player and coach, Pat Summitt has been integral in making women's basketball into a popular spectator sport. Games at UTK average 10,000 spectators each. Fans love to watch the quick and powerful women on the court who win more often than not. As of 2001, under her leadership, the Lady Vols have won six NCAA National Collegiate Women's Basketball championships (1987, 1989, 1991, 1996, 1997, 1998), with no end in sight. She has also written two books, *Reach for the Summitt* and *Raise the Roof*. The woman who drove the team bus now has a team car, makes a hefty salary, and has her own radio show.

SOURCES:

Lay, Nancy. *The Summitt Season*. Champaign, IL: Leisure Press, 1989.

Lieberman-Cline, Nancy, with Debby Jennings. *Lady Magic: The Autobiography of Nancy Lieberman-Cline*. NY: Sagamore, 1991.

Woolum, Janet. *Outstanding Women Athletes: Who They Are and How They Influenced Sports in America*. Phoenix, AZ: Oryx, 1992.

Karin L. Haag, freelance writer, Athens, Georgia

Sumner, Helen Laura (1876–1933).

See Woodbury, Helen Sumner.

Sumner, Jessie (1898–1994)

U.S. Republican congressional representative whose eight years in Congress were marked by her fiscal conservatism, her opposition to U.S. involvement in World War II, and her conviction that the Soviet Union would politically influence the countries it liberated. Born in Milford, Illinois, on July 17, 1898; died in Watseka, Illinois, on August 10, 1994; daughter of A.T. Sumner and Elizabeth (Gillan) Sumner; graduated from Girton School in Winnetka, Illinois, 1916; Smith College, degree in economics, 1920; studied law at the University of Chicago, Columbia University, Oxford University, and the University of Wisconsin, and studied at the School of Commerce at New York University.

Jessie Sumner was born in 1898, the daughter of **Elizabeth Gillan Sumner** and A.T. Sumner, an Illinois banker, and the granddaughter of a pioneer with extensive land holdings numbering into the thousands of acres. Growing up in Milford, Illinois, about 88 miles south of Chicago, she went to area schools, including the private Girton School in Winnetka from which she graduated in 1916. Although she attended the University of Chicago in the course of her study of law, Sumner spent most of her college years at various institutions out of state, beginning with Smith College, from which she graduated in 1920. Deciding upon a law career, she took classes at Columbia University and Oxford University in England, as well as the University of Wisconsin and the School of Commerce at New York University. Admitted to the bar in 1923, she entered practice in Chicago that year and became a member of several law and political organizations, among them the Chicago Bar Association, the Illinois Women's Bar Association, the National Women Lawyer's Association, the Business and Professional Women's Club, the National Women's Republican Club, and the National Federation of Women's Clubs. After briefly working in the New York banking district prior to the economic crash that precipitated the Great Depression, she returned to her hometown of Milford to continue her law practice in 1932.

A catalytic event in Sumner's life was the kidnaping of her brother by bank robbers, and her role in the subsequent prosecution of those responsible. The conviction inspired in Sumner thoughts of becoming a state's attorney, but her campaign for the post was unsuccessful. However, she was elected to finish the rest of her uncle's term as judge of Iroquois County in 1937, after his unexpected death earlier that year. The election made her the first female judge in the state of Illinois, and she capitalized on the publicity in her 1938 bid for a seat in the U.S. House of Representatives. As a Republican in the predominantly Republican 18th District, she overcame her Democratic opponent, James A. Meeks, on an anti-New Deal platform.

Sumner's eight years in Congress were marked by her fiscal conservatism and her vigorous opposition to U.S. involvement in World War II. Although a member of the Committee on Banking and Currency by virtue of her banking experience, she devoted much of her time to a losing battle to halt military and diplomatic initiatives that would increase the United States' role in world affairs. She entered office a year after the passage of the Neutrality Act, which was considered the peak of popularity for isolationist sentiment, but found herself increasingly alone in her non-interventionist stance as the years progressed. Prior to America's entrance into the war, she voted with the minority against the expansion of the Navy, the lifting of the arms embargo, and the creation of reciprocal trade agreements with other nations. She argued against the Burke-Wadsworth Selective Service bill for military training by pointing out that the German war machine had an advantage of several years' build-up which the United States could not hope to equal. She was highly critical of President Franklin Roosevelt, referring to him disparagingly as "Papa Roosevelt"; she felt that he conducted much of his foreign policy in secret, and she also accused him of mismanaging funds earmarked for national defense.

With the U.S. entrance into the war after the Japanese attack on Pearl Harbor in 1941, Sumner became equally vocal regarding her distrust of American allies Great Britain and the Soviet Union. The latter was a special target of Sumner's cynicism, as she saw little difference between Hitler and Stalin. In fact, she opposed the invasion of the western coast of Europe because she did not want to relieve the Soviet Union—under pressure from Germany on the eastern front—by engaging

Jessie Sumner

Germany in a two-front war. She was convinced that the war was not worth the million American lives she predicted such an invasion would cost. As the war progressed, she became increasingly concerned that the Soviet Union would politically influence the countries it liberated. Neither did Great Britain escape her critical notice as she felt that British leaders tried to contain the authority of American military leaders George C. Marshall and General Douglas MacArthur. Sumner's lack of confidence in the European powers inspired her attempts to limit the U.S. government's participation in the international organizations which arose as the end of the war neared. She argued against endorsing U.S. involvement in the formation and funding of international relief organizations such as the United Nations Relief and Rehabilitation Administration. In June 1945, she declared the U.S. entry into the World Bank and the International Monetary Fund to be the worst fraud in American history. The United Nations was another target, as leading the way to what Sumner termed a "world super-state."

Increasingly marginalized in Congress because of her unpopular isolationist stance, Sumner still managed a few legislative victories, most of them related to her conservative fiscal policies. She secured an amendment to a $20 billion naval appropriations bill which prohibited the use of parties, champagne, or gifts during the launching of new ships in 1942. She also found unexpected allies in Democrats and liberal Republicans when the women legislators joined together in a rare inter-party stand to demand that the Appropriations Committee ease the child-care burden of women war workers in factories; Sumner later reversed her support of child-care services in favor of cost-cutting initiatives. One of her female colleagues, *Clare Boothe Luce, teamed with Sumner to defeat the Ruml-Carlson plan to revise the tax system in order to ease the financial burden on American taxpayers in 1943. She likewise opposed a demobilization bill which sought to secure unemployment compensation for war-time workers in 1944.

Even though she garnered little support for her war-related policies in Congress, Sumner had the backing of her constituents and of the anti-Roosevelt, isolationist *Chicago Tribune*. She was re-elected to her fourth term in November 1944, but decided against seeking renomination in 1946. Upon her retirement from Congress, Sumner once again returned to Milford to resume her position as vice-president of the bank her father had founded, the Sumner National Bank. In 1966, she became president of the bank, holding that position until her death on August 10, 1994, in Watseka, Illinois.

SOURCES:
Office of the Historian. *Women in Congress, 1917–1990.* Commission on the Bicentenary of the U.S. House of Representatives, 1991.
Rothe, Anna, ed. *Current Biography, 1945.* NY: H.W. Wilson, 1945.

B. Kimberly Taylor, freelance writer, New York, New York

Sunderland, countess of.

See Sidney, Dorothy (1617–1684).
See Churchill, Sarah Jennings for sidebar on Anne Churchill (1684–1716).

Sung.

See Song.

Sunnichild (d. 741)

*Bavarian princess. Name variations: Suanehilde; possibly Kunehilda. Died in 741; possibly daughter of Theodebert, duke of Bavaria, and *Folcheid; sister of*

*Guntrud of Bavaria; became second wife of Charles Martel, mayor of Austrasia and Neustria (r. 714–741), in 725; children: Grifo; daughter *Chiltrud; and possibly *Adeloga Martel.*

Sun Yat-sen, Mme. (1893–1981).

See Song Sisters for Song Qingling.

Supervia, Conchita (1895–1936)

Spanish mezzo-soprano. Name variations: Lady Rubenstein. Born on December 9, 1895, in Barcelona, Spain; died in childbirth on March 30, 1936, in London, England; studied at the Colegio de las Damas Negras in Barcelona; married Sir Ben Rubenstein, in 1931; children: two, including son George.

Debuted in Buenos Aires in Bretón's Los amantes de Teruel *(1910); sang with the Chicago Opera (1915–16); debuted at Teatro alla Scala (1924); made London debut at Covent Garden in Rossini's* La Cenerentola *(1934).*

Conchita Supervia, born of an old Andalusian family in Barcelona in 1895, began studying singing at age 10. At 15, she made her operatic debut with a traveling Spanish company in Buenos Aires, singing the part of an old woman, and she was the youngest singer ever to have professionally sung Octavian, in the Rome premiere of Richard Strauss' *Der Rosenkavalier*. Supervia assisted the conductor Vittorio Gui in reviving Rossini's bel canto operas. Known especially for her Carmen, Supervia was the first contralto, as opposed to a soprano, to be regarded as a prima donna. She possessed a kind of magnetism which would not be seen again on opera stages until the arrival of *Maria Callas, and her singing and acting were both superb. Supervia could also be volatile; she once sued Covent Garden (1934) for omitting one of her performances and made her point, settling out of court. Supervia became Lady Rubenstein after her marriage in 1934 and had one son, George. She died at age 40, at the height of her powers, giving birth to a second child. Supervia appeared in the screen version of *La Bohème* and in the British film *Evensong*, starring *Evelyn Laye (1934).

John Haag, Athens, Georgia

Supremes, The (1964–1977)

Popular Motown group of the 1960s. Originally called "The Primettes" when first organized in 1959 by Florence Ballard and Mary Wilson, girlhood

friends who had grown up together in a Detroit housing project. Diana Ross soon joined the group, which eventually recorded their first song for Berry Gordy's Motown Records in 1964, when the group's name was changed to "The Supremes."

Recording of "Where Did Our Love Go" was their first song to reach Billboard magazine's Top 100; had seven #1 hits and were rarely out of the Top Ten (1965–69); group's name was changed to "Diana Ross and The Supremes" (1967), leading to Florence Ballard's withdrawal and replacement; group gave their last performance as "Diana Ross and The Supremes" (1970), after which Ross left the group to pursue a solo career while Mary Wilson continued to tour and record with various replacement singers until the group was disbanded (1977).

Partial discography (albums only, all on Motown): Meet the Supremes (1963); A Bit of Liverpool (1964); Where Did Our Love Go (1965); The Supremes at the Copa (1965); More Hits by The Supremes (1965); I Hear a Symphony (1966); Supremes a Go Go (1966); The Supremes Sing Holland-Dozier-Holland (1967); The Supremes Sing Rodgers & Hart (1967); Diana Ross and The Supremes Greatest Hits Vols. 1 and 2 (1967); Reflections (1968); Love Child (1968); Diana Ross and The Supremes Join the Temptations (1968); T.C.B. (1968); Live at the Talk of the Town (1968); Let the Sunshine In (1969); Cream of the Crop (1969); Diana Ross and The Supremes Greatest Hits Vol. 3 (1969); Farewell, New Ways But Love Stays (1970); The Magnificent Seven (w/ The Four Tops) (1970); Dynamite (1971); Floy Joy (1972); Baby Love (1973); Anthology (1974); High Energy (1976); Supremes (1976); Supremes at Their Best (1978); Stoned Love (1979); Superstar Series, Vol. 1, Greatest Hits (featuring Mary Wilson, 1981).

Singles: "Your Heart Belongs to Me" (1964); "Baby Love" (1964); "Come See about Me" (1964); "Stop! In the Name of Love" (1965); "Back in My Arms Again" (1965); "Nothing But Heartaches" (1965); "I Hear a Symphony" (1965); "My World Is Empty Without You" (1966); "Love Is Like an Itching in My Heart" (1966); "You Can't Hurry Love" (1966); "You Keep Me Hangin' On" (1966); "Love Is Here and Now You're Gone" (1967); "The Happening" (1967); "Reflections" (1967); "In and Out of Love" (1967); "Love Child" (1968); "Someday We'll Be Together" (1969).

Ballard, Florence (1943–1976). Born in Detroit, Michigan, on June 30, 1943; died of a heart attack in 1976; eighth of thirteen children of Lurlee Ballard; married Tommy Chapman (separated 1973); children: three daughters, including Lisa Marie.

Ross, Diana (1944—). Born Diane Ross in Detroit, Michigan, on March 26, 1944; daughter of Fred Earl Ross and Ernestine (Moten) Ross (d. 1984); graduated from Cass Technical High School, 1962; married Robert Silberstein, Jr., in 1971 (divorced 1976); married Arne Naess (a shipping magnate), in 1985; children: (first marriage) three daughters, Rhonda Suzanne, Tracee Joy (b. 1972), and Chudney Lane (b. 1975); (second marriage) Ross and Evan.

Films: Lady Sings the Blues (1972); Mahogany (1975); The Wiz (1978).

Wilson, Mary (1944—). Born in Greenville, Mississippi, on March 6, 1944; daughter of Johnnie Mae Wilson (d. 1999) and Sam Wilson; from age three to age nine, thought her mother's younger sister I.V. Pippin was her mother; at age 57, got her associate's degree in arts, New York University, 2001; married Pedro Ferrer; children: daughter Turkessa.

It did not seem the most auspicious beginning for a career in the rough and tumble music world. In a smoky Detroit union hall one night in 1959, during a raucous party for the rank and file of one of the United Auto Workers' locals, four girls stepped uncertainly onto the stage in their first professional engagement. The name chosen for them by their manager was The Primettes, a sister group to the act that had preceded them, the all-male Primes. After three numbers marked by cautious harmony and some rudimentary choreography, the Primettes left the stage to scattered applause. Those who, years later, would remember the performance as the birth of one of the world's most famous female groups would recall less the girls' music than their clean-cut wardrobe—white pleated skirts, white sweaters, white bobby sox and white gym shoes.

The four were all friends from Detroit's Brewster Housing Projects, one of the largest government-financed apartment complexes in Detroit, and almost entirely inhabited by African-American families who had left the poor, rural South to look for work on the assembly lines of Detroit's automobile factories. Mary Wilson had been born in Greenville, Mississippi, on March 6, 1944, but the other three girls had all come into the world in the projects. Florence Ballard, born in June 1943, was the eighth of thirteen children; Diane Ross was the second of six and was the same age as Mary, having been born on March 26, 1944. The fourth Primette, **Betty Travis** (sources variously give her last name as McGlown, Horton, or Anderson), had also been born that year.

The idea for a singing group was Ballard's, although all the girls had been singing in church choirs or at family functions for as long as anyone could remember. It was one of the first things Ballard mentioned to Mary Wilson when the two met at a local talent show in which both were appearing in 1958. Both girls were fans of Freddy Limon and the Teenagers, whom they had seen on the "Ed Sullivan Show," and both were envious of the Franklin girls (**Erma, Carolyn** and **Aretha Franklin**) who were already forming a group and were often featured in the choir at church on Sundays.

*B*aby, baby, where did our love go?

—The Supremes

It seemed too good to be true when, early in 1959, Flo excitedly told Mary that she had been asked by The Primes' manager, Milton Jenkins, to form an all-girl counterpart to his most successful act. Jenkins was known up and down Detroit's Hastings Street, where all the best clubs and restaurants were, for his flashy wardrobe and bright red 1958 Cadillac. Jenkins had adapted the style of urban white "doo-wop" groups for black audiences, and the Primes were his first big success. The invitation to audition for him had come by way of one of the Prime's members, who was dating Betty Travis and had told her of Jenkins' idea for the Primettes. Needing a fourth singer to match their all-male counterparts, the three girls—Florence, Mary, and Betty—were joined by Diane (later Diana) Ross, the girlfriend of another of The Primes.

Arriving at Jenkins' hotel room without thinking to prepare an audition piece beforehand, Ballard suggested Ray Charles' "Night Time (Is the Right Time for Love)." "Without having had a minute of rehearsal . . . we all fell into our parts, and we sounded wonderful," Mary Wilson remembered many years later. Jenkins must have agreed for, shortly afterward, The Primettes made their debut down at the union hall. Over the next year, The Primettes played a series of "sock hops," dances organized and emceed by local disc jockeys, and it soon became clear to everyone that it was Florence Ballard's energy and powerful, clear voice that gave the group life. "Singing was Flo's ticket out" of the projects, Mary Wilson once noted, "and so The Primettes became her life. Everyone who heard us agreed that Flo was the best." Diana Ross would be equally complimentary about Mary Wilson, who, she said, "fit so well with Florence and me. She carried the exact sound just between the two of us that blended all our voices together . . . so that we were like one voice."

Betty Travis left the group early on, her mother feeling she should spend more time at her school-

work, and was replaced by **Barbara Martin** as The Primettes began to work particularly hard at choreographing a series of coordinated gestures and movements that in time became smooth enough to seem almost spontaneous. By 1960, the girls were confident enough of their act to enter that year's Detroit-Windsor Freedom Festival's amateur talent contest, sponsored by radio stations in the Motor City and across the Detroit River in Windsor, Ontario. The Primettes were deemed the best female group at the Festival. The win led to the most important decision of their fledgling career—to audition for Berry Gordy's Motown Records.

Like Marvin Jenkins, Gordy—a former boxer, auto worker, and songwriter—had begun by promoting a single act, The Five Stars, a group of friends for whom he wrote and produced. In 1959, the year The Primettes were formed, Gordy had persuaded United Artists to distribute his artists under Gordy's new Tamla label; by 1960, he had moved into larger quarters in a house on Detroit's West Grand Boulevard that he called "Hitsville USA." Gordy's genius was in sensing that mainstream American audiences, black and white, were ready for a more pop-oriented, rhythm and blues sound—a sound that became synonymous during the coming decade with the new label he created for it, Motown (from Detroit's nickname, "Motor Town"). At the time The Primettes came to him for an audition, in the late summer of 1960, Motown already had made a name for itself with such artists as ***Mary Wells** and Smokey Robinson. (It was Robinson who arranged their audition with Gordy.) "I sensed that his mind was clicking every moment, even when he was talking to us," Wilson remembered of her first meeting with Gordy. "If you were smart, you knew that there was something going on behind his smile."

Gordy turned the group down, telling them to finish high school before coming back. But he wasn't about to get rid of The Primettes so easily. "Berry Gordy was not the only one who knew what he wanted," Diana Ross wrote many years later. "I have never been able to take no for an answer, and he had definitely not seen the last of me." As a way of keeping themselves in Gordy's thoughts, the girls took to hanging around the studios after school every day, contributing the occasional handclaps or "oohs" to the backup work on various Motown records.

During the next few months, The Primettes survived what could have been several fatal setbacks. First, Barbara Martin announced she was leaving the group to marry, nearly leading to its disintegration before Ross convinced Wilson and Ballard to continue as a threesome. The intensive rehearsals needed to rework the groups' harmonies and choreography nearly collapsed when Florence mysteriously failed to appear, even at school. It was not until several days had passed that Wilson and Ross learned that Ballard had been raped by a new boyfriend, a trauma from which both girls later said Florence never fully recovered. To compound the group's troubles, a recording contract that they had signed with a new company—Flick Records, for its Lu-Pine label—came to nothing when the company's distributor was indicted in the payola scandal that rocked the radio and record industry at the time. The records they recorded for Lu-Pine in the fall of 1960 were not released until 1968 and are highly prized by collectors.

Late in 1960, The Primettes once again auditioned for Gordy, getting as far as recording "I Want a Guy" for him before Gordy once again declined to sign them. This time, however, Gordy put the girls under the tutelage of Smokey Robinson, who worked with them on their material and presentation. Finally, in January 1961, Gordy offered them a contract on the condition

The Supremes (Florence Ballard, Mary Wilson, and Diana Ross).

they come up with a new name. Everything from "The Darleens" to "The Jewelettes" to "The Sweet P's" was tried before Ballard's favorite name, "The Supremes," finally prevailed.

Gordy's contract with his new group was the standard one he offered all his eager young acts, and one that in later years would lead to legal action from many of them, including Mary Wilson. Gordy took care to present each of the girls with individual contracts, as well as one for the group as a whole, and exercised total creative and financial control. The Supremes were paid no salaries, their income being strictly from a small allowance and from royalties which amounted to two cents for every record sold—a lump sum which was then split between the girls. In addition, Gordy was allowed to deduct from royalties any advances he made to promote the act. (Mary Wilson once estimated the girls each made some $5,000 for every million records sold.) Only Motown was authorized under the contracts to dismiss group members or hire new ones, and only Motown had authority over material and arrangements. Motown was, in effect, the sole manager, agent, accountant, and financial adviser for The Supremes, who never saw standard accounting sheets or the tax returns Motown filed on their behalf. "In truth," Wilson later said, "few of us knew anything at all about the business and fewer still knew to have legal counsel for any business dealings or contracts."

The group's new life as The Supremes did not at first seem destined for success. Motown released their demo recording of "I Want a Guy" on its Tamla label to little notice in 1961. The group's next eight records—including their first record on the Motown label, 1962's "Your Heart Belongs to Me"—barely made it onto *Billboard*'s Top 100. During these early years, each of the girls took turns singing lead—Ballard on the more upbeat numbers, Ross on the slower, sensitive love songs, and Wilson on the ballads.

By 1963, now ages 19 and 20, the women were known around Motown as "the no-hit Supremes," although the taunts subsided somewhat after their "When the Lovelight Starts Shining in Your Eyes" made *Billboard*'s Top 20 in October of that year. The women were as surprised as everybody else when they were included on Dick Clark's "Caravan of Stars" national tour as a warm-up act for the major talent. Also to everyone's astonishment, the song The Supremes recorded just before leaving on the tour, "Where Did Our Love Go," rocketed to #1 and made them instant stars on Clark's tour. The song had been written for them by the same team that had

given them their Top 20 hit the year before, the songwriters Brian and Eddie Holland and Lamont Dozier. Holland-Dozier-Holland were responsible for "the Motown sound," characterized by heavy percussion overlaid with filigrees of guitars, strings, horns, and backup vocals. "Where Did Our Love Go," with Ross singing lead, is remembered for its thumping drum-tambourine-handclap beat and the "baby, baby" back vocal supplied by Ballard and Wilson. None of the women cared much for the song that marked the beginning of their rise to stardom.

From 1964 on, it seemed as if nothing could stand in their way. No less than four consecutive #1 hits followed—"Baby Love," "Come See about Me," "Stop! In the Name of Love," and "Back in My Arms Again"—all within one year and all written by Holland-Dozier-Holland. The Supremes were as popular on stage as they were on record, especially when Gordy went to work on their wardrobe and dressed them identically in sequined, full-length gowns, full-length white gloves, high-heeled shoes and elaborate, piled hairdos which never budged during the careful choreography designed for each number. The Supremes became Motown's leading ambassadors for Berry Gordy's goal of bridging the gap between black and white audiences in the United States, and presenting Europeans, who were fascinated by the act during several tours of England and the Continent, with a glossy, sophisticated image of African-American culture. By the mid-1960s, only The Beatles and Elvis Presley could command greater crowds at live concerts.

On stage, The Supremes presented a seamless image of sisterhood. Ross did most of the chatter between songs, although Ballard became a crowd pleaser with her sassy comments that put the lie to Ross' insistence on characterizing her as "the quiet one." During Ross' solo of "You're Nobody Till Somebody Loves You," with its line "Gold won't bring you happiness," Flo would bring down the house by interrupting "Give me that gold, girl, and I'll do my *own* shoppin'!"; or, when Ross told an audience whose male portion obviously appreciated her slim figure that "Thin is in," Flo shot back, "But, honey, fat is where it's *at*!" By 1965, in fact, it was obvious that Ballard was putting on weight at an alarming rate, although Motown assiduously hid from the public Florence's increasingly serious drinking problem, the tensions which were growing within the group, and the fact that Ross had become Gordy's lover.

Berry Gordy had long realized that it was Ross' voice and stage presence that was the most commercial of the three women, making their relationship a sometimes stormy combination of the personal and professional. Ross later characterized him as "an incomparable visionary, a dynamite character, and a special human being," but to the other two women, The Supremes was becoming a Ross-Gordy franchise. "Seeing Diane and Berry together," Mary Wilson once wrote, "I never knew exactly who was directing whom; when changes occurred, we never knew which one of them had instigated them." Ballard, who saw herself as The Supremes' creator, was especially hurt by Gordy's favoritism and often showed up drunk for recording sessions and live appearances, in which she was replaced frequently by **Marlene Barrow** ("and frankly few people . . . were ever the wiser," Wilson drily noted). The quarrels between Ballard and Gordy were made only more bitter and acrimonious when Gordy announced in early 1967 that the group's name would be changed to "Diana Ross and The Supremes," Ross explaining the change in her first name from Diane to Diana by saying there had been a typographical error on her birth certificate. "The name change was not my idea," Ross insisted, claiming it was "all in the natural scheme of things." She noted that the press had long been singling her out and even blamed fans for playing favorites with each of the women and pitting them against one another.

Ballard, however, had begun to suspect that Ross was intent on breaking up the group and pursuing a solo career. To her, the name change was the first step in The Supremes' demise. Her threats to expose Gordy's financial practices only made matters worse. "You'll be sorry you messed with me, Berry Gordy," she was once heard telling him. "I know a lot about you, more than you think. And don't you forget it." Mary Wilson, the group's peacemaker, tried her best to hold the group together. "I saw the group as something bigger and more important than any one of us. I was content to play on the team. Diane didn't feel that way about things, and her attitude was obvious to everyone we worked with." At the time the name change was announced, Ross occupied a separate dressing room on tour and arrived separately at each venue, often in Gordy's company. Matters came to a head almost as soon as Motown had publicly announced the name change early in 1967, when Ballard arrived drunk for a concert in Las Vegas and so overweight that her costume could barely contain her. Wilson and Ross went on without her, announcing that Florence had had to be hospitalized for exhaustion, but it is probable that Gordy fired Ballard once and for all from The

Supremes that night. She was replaced by **Cindy Birdsong**, who had been appearing with **Patti Labelle** and the Bluebelles, another Motown act.

A further upheaval in The Supremes' fortunes came that year, when Holland-Dozier-Holland left Motown to start their own record company. Although The Supremes never left the charts, with hits by other composers like "I'm Gonna Make You Love Me," "Love Child," and "Someday We'll Be Together," they turned increasingly to cover versions of old standards with such album titles as *We Remember Sam Cooke* and *The Supremes Sing Rodgers & Hart*. Gordy also increased their television exposure. They were frequent guests on "The Ed Sullivan Show" from 1965 to 1969 and appeared on the special "TCB (Takin' Care of Business)" with Gordy's most successful male group, The Temptations (some of whose members had come from the old Primes). The women hosted their own weekly television show, "Hollywood Palace," for one season and even appeared as nuns in an episode of "Tarzan," a network series of the time.

By the end of the decade, rumors that Diana Ross would be leaving The Supremes were widespread, especially when she appeared alone on "The *Dinah Shore* Show" in 1969. It came as no surprise when the announcement was officially made in December of that year. Diana Ross gave her last performance with The Supremes in Las Vegas on January 14, 1970. "If she hadn't left the group, something would have had to change," Mary Wilson wrote some years later, although she claimed to see the change as a beginning, not an end. "This was . . . not the end of The Supremes," she said, "but the end of the dream Diane, Flo and I had shared. After years of hard work, I was embarking on another wonderful adventure. I had been blessed to have been in The Supremes the first time; now it could happen all over again." Diana Ross, however, characterized her departure in less philosophical terms, claiming some 20 years later that "the girls treated me very badly. They had gone against me with a vengeance. They were so blinded by jealousy that they never stopped to think . . . that our records were selling because of my sound."

(In the summer of 2000, amidst much hype, Ross mounted a Diana Ross and The Supremes "Return to Love" reunion tour, in which neither Wilson nor Birdsong participated because they were offered some $3 million each in comparison to her $15–20 million paycheck. Ticket prices were as high as $250. Fans stayed away from the ersatz "reunion" in droves, and the tour was cancelled after a month.)

For a time, after **Jean Terrell** replaced Ross, it seemed as if Wilson's hopes for a rejuvenated Supremes might be realized. The new Supremes had two Top Ten hits during the first year of their existence, "Stoned Love" and "Everybody Has the Right to Love," along with an appearance on a television special with The Four Tops, another Motown group, with whom they also recorded two albums. "The Supremes give not the slightest indication of missing Diana Ross," wrote one reviewer in *The Los Angeles Times* in 1970, "or that in their reorganization they are riding any other crest but the one set aside for superstars." But such a glowing assessment proved to be premature, for personnel changes took their toll on the group's stability. Cindy Birdsong left the group for a year, and eventually departed completely and was replaced by **Susaye Greene**; while Jean Terrell quit in 1973 and was replaced by **Sherrie Payne**. The strain was evident in the fact that no new Supremes albums were released from the end of 1973 to the summer of 1975. "These personnel changes haven't helped our situation at all," Wilson admitted to a reporter in 1974. "Motown's waiting to see whether we're stable before they let us record another album." There were some more albums and appearances in the next few years, but even Wilson, the last of the original Supremes, eventually had to give up. The Supremes were officially disbanded in 1977, with Motown legally preventing Wilson from using the name for her new solo act, except as "Mary Wilson of The Supremes." In 1988, in a testament to the influence of a group that hadn't existed for more than ten years, The Supremes were inducted into the Rock and Roll Hall of Fame.

During the 1970s, while Wilson was struggling to keep The Supremes alive and Ross was becoming an international celebrity as a solo act and as an actress, Florence Ballard's fortunes had declined precipitously. "Florence was always on a totally negative trip," Ross once told a reporter. "She wanted to be a victim. When she left The Supremes and the money stopped coming in, it really messed up her head." By 1975, after the birth of three children and an estrangement from her husband, Ballard was living in Detroit on $270 in monthly welfare payments and was in danger of having her modest house on Buena Vista Avenue placed in foreclosure. Ross, who claimed to have tried to contact Ballard over the years only to be rebuffed by Flo's family, told friends that she had unsuccessfully attempted to get a check to Florence to save her home but had been forced to void it when Florence's husband had demanded it be made out to

him. Wilson had tried to do her part, too, arranging for Florence to visit her in Los Angeles in August 1975 and bringing her on stage during one of The Supremes' shows, Florence standing in a soft blue spotlight to receive the cheers of fans who still remembered her. Other efforts to help Ballard were not forthcoming, from any other Motown artists or from Gordy himself. Florence was forced to give up her house and move in with a sister.

Returning to Detroit after the appearance in Los Angeles, Ballard had apparently decided to try and heal wounds that had been festering for eight years and called Ross. "It was a very strange call," Diana remembered. "She said she was ready to go back singing." A few days after the call, Ballard received what she described as "an unexplained cash settlement" of $50,000, which may have been a gift from Ross or a settlement from a long-standing court action she had pursued against an attorney who had once represented her in a suit against Motown over royalties. With the money, she purchased a new home and a Cadillac. Barely two months later, in February 1976, Florence Ballard died of a heart attack which doctors said had been brought on by her high blood pressure and by medication she had been taking to lose weight. Her mother thought differently. "I think she died of a broken heart," **Lurlee Ballard** said.

Both Ross and Wilson attended Ballard's funeral, to which Berry Gordy made sure to send most of the top Motown acts. Ross caused a stir during the service by asking Wilson to join her in a silent prayer at Ballard's coffin while flashbulbs popped and TV cameras rolled. After the crowds and reporters dispersed, Wilson followed the hearse to Detroit's Memorial Park and marked the loss of a girlfriend's dream by throwing a single rose on top of the coffin. Except for Ballard's immediate family and a few close friends, Mary was alone as Florence was finally laid to rest. Diana had already left.

SOURCES:

De Beer, Frans. "Supremes Biography," published by the Diana Ross Fan Club, undated.

Ross, Diana. *Secrets of a Sparrow*. NY: Villard, 1993.

Stambler, Irwin, ed. *Encyclopedia of Pop, Rock and Soul.* Rev. ed. NY: St. Martin's Press, 1974.

Taborelli, J. Randy. *Call Her Miss Ross*. Secaucus, NJ: Carol Publishing, 1989.

Wilson, Mary. *Dreamgirl*. NY: St. Martin's Press, 1986.

RELATED MEDIA:

Dreamgirls, loosely based on The Supremes, starring **Jennifer Holliday**, **Sheryl Lee Ralph**, and **Loretta Devine**, opened on Broadway at the Imperial Theater, December 20, 1981, directed and choreographed by Michael Bennett, book and lyrics by

Tom Eyen, costumes by **Theoni V. Aldredge**, lighting by *****Tharon Musser**.

Norman Powers, writer-producer,
Chelsea Lane Productions,
New York, New York

Surratt, Mary E. (c. 1820–1865)

American woman hanged, despite little evidence of guilt, for involvement in Lincoln's assassination. Name variations: Mrs. Surratt; also seen as Mary Seurat. Born Mary Eugenia Jenkins near Waterloo, Prince George's County, Maryland, around 1820 (some sources cite 1817, others 1823); hanged in Washington, D.C., on July 7, 1865; third child and first daughter of Samuel Isaac Jenkins; attended Miss Winifred Martin's Catholic Girls' School in Alexandria, Virginia; married John Harrison Surratt (a farmer), in 1835 (died 1862); children: Isaac Douglas Surratt (b. 1841); Anna Eugenia Surratt (b. 1843); John Harrison Surratt (b. 1844, who became a secret dispatch rider for the Confederacy).

Mary E. Surratt, wittingly or unwittingly, became involved in the conspiracy to assassinate Abraham Lincoln. In 1862, Surratt moved to Washington and opened a boarding house, which became the meeting place of John Wilkes Booth, her son John H. Surratt, and other conspirators as they plotted to kill President Lincoln, Secretary of State William Henry Seward, and other members of the government. After studying for the priesthood, John Surratt had become a spy for the Confederacy and was a friend of Booth's. Following Lincoln's death, Mary Surratt was arrested and, along with three of Booth's accomplices, was tried and convicted by a military commission appointed by President Andrew Johnson. The sentence of death by hanging was carried out in Washington, D.C., on July 7, 1865. During the trial, doubts as to Surratt's guilt were expressed, and a long controversy in the press followed, the weight of opinion inclining in her favor. Whether she was guilty or not, most historians believe that Surratt was convicted and given the death sentence on flimsy evidence. Ironically, her son John, who had taken an active part in the plot, escaped to Canada. Brought back in 1866, he was tried the following year. But the case was *nolle prosequi*—the government did not have enough evidence to secure indictment—and he went free in 1868.

Born around 1820 near Waterloo, Maryland, Mary Eugenia Jenkins was raised by her mother (name unknown) after the death of her father Samuel Isaac Jenkins. She attended Miss

Winifred Martin's Catholic Girls' School in Virginia and converted to Roman Catholicism, to which she remained faithful even during an era of intense anti-Catholic feeling. She was in her teens when she married farmer John H. Surratt, and they settled on his inherited farm near Glensboro, Maryland, eventually raising three children: Isaac, Anna, and John. The destruction of their farm by a fire forced John Surratt into work as a railroad contractor until he was able to buy 1,200 acres in Prince George's County in 1840. Although the purchase put the family deeply in debt, it was successful enough to allow the Surratts to build a tavern and store at the crossroads ten miles southeast of Washington, D.C. The area eventually became known as Surrattsville, later changed to Clinton.

Mary E. Surratt

Around the time of the Civil War, the Surratts experienced a series of catastrophes which led to the family's financial ruin. By 1857, half of their land had been sold or rented, and their property was further reduced when their slaves ran away and Union forces raided the farm. The family itself had its ranks divided when Surratt's son Isaac joined Confederate forces in the South; her other son, John, left for St. Charles' College near Baltimore; and her husband died in 1862. John returned home to assume his father's position as postmaster of Surrattsville, but this, too, was stripped away when a Republican took the post a year later.

Left without income, Mary Surratt moved to Washington, D.C. There she opened a boarding-house on October 1, 1864, which benefited from a good location. Her son John joined her there that December, while maintaining his covert activities as a Confederate courier. Among his circle of Confederate associates was the famed actor John Wilkes Booth, who included John Surratt in his plan to kidnap President Abraham Lincoln and hold him as ransom for the release of Confederate prisoners. Although she was apparently unaware of the plot, Mary Surratt's boarding-house became one of the meeting places for the conspirators. The group aborted an attempt to kidnap the president in March 1865, and the collapse of the Confederacy a month later brought a halt to further kidnapping plans. Booth, however, decided to assassinate Lincoln as a way of avenging the South. Most of his friends left him at this point, including John Surratt, but Booth was able to retain several accomplices in what became a mounted attack on the presidential hierarchy.

On the night of April 14, 1865, Booth fatally shot Lincoln at Ford's Theater and later was himself shot and killed while evading capture. Fellow conspirator George Atzerodt did not carry out his assignment to kill Vice-President Andrew Johnson. Lewis Powell (or Payne by some accounts), who was to assassinate Secretary of State William Seward, the man third in line for the presidency, stabbed but did not kill his victim in his home that same night. The consequences of the devastating attacks were swift and no less forceful than the outraged reaction from the American public. The police arrested the major players quickly, and also took into custody Mary Surratt and her daughter **Anna Surratt**. Mary had just returned from Surrattsville the night of the murder. Her son John escaped to Canada.

Speculation abounded that the attack had been orchestrated by Confederate officials in an attempt to claim by subterfuge what they lost in the war. A military tribunal, hastily arranged, focused on eight people. Mary Surratt was the only woman among them, and appeared to be a special target of the prosecutors, who withheld evidence—such as Booth's diary—which might have exonerated her. During the course of the trial, which lasted less than two months, Surratt was not allowed to testify on her behalf. Although the testimony of some of the accused regarding her involvement was apparently coerced by federal authorities eager to convict, Powell's assertion that Surratt was innocent of the whole affair was ignored.

The evidence against Surratt was circumstantial at best. In an attempt to collect money to pay the mortgage on her property in Surrattsville, she had made two trips to an area known for being sympathetic to the South shortly before the attacks, and, in the course of the second trip, had delivered a package from Booth to one of her tenants, John Lloyd. This scant proof of her guilt, coupled with the role her boardinghouse played as a meeting place for the conspirators, was enough for the tribunal to convict her. Of the eight suspects, the tribunal gave four of them prison sentences and condemned the other four to be hanged, Surratt among them. Her lawyers learned about the verdict by reading it in the newspapers.

On July 7, 1865, Surratt joined the three men also sentenced to die on a scaffold in the courtyard of the Old Penitentiary Building. Powell continued to proclaim Surratt's innocence even at that final hour, but to no avail. All four were hanged before a solemn crowd. It was said that a majority of the members of the military commission had signed a petition for clemency to President Johnson, but that the petition had been withheld from his knowledge. This allegation was vigorously denied. However, as the shock over the president's death dissipated, Surratt's conviction came under scrutiny, particularly with the return of her son John from Canada in 1867. His trial differed from his mother's in that it was not tinged with vengeful emotions, and he gained release from prison in 1868 after the majority of the jury voted to acquit him.

Mary Surratt's conviction has inspired speculation as to why prosecutors went to such lengths to portray her guilt. Undoubtedly, the shock of a presidential assassination and the resulting pressure to convict with speed and severity were major factors, particularly coming so closely on the heels of the end of the Civil War. At a time when the emotions of every American citizen were the most strained, Surratt became a target of anti-Confederate hysteria. Some historians have also noted that aspects of Surratt's life apart from her politics may have negatively influenced the tribunal, specifically her Roman Catholic faith and the fact that she was a businesswoman. As a conciliatory gesture, authorities allowed Surratt's daughter Anna to give her mother's remains a proper burial in Mount Olivet Cemetery in Washington, D.C.

SOURCES:
James, Edward T., ed. *Notable American Women, 1607–1950*. Cambridge, MA: The Belknap Press of Harvard University, 1971.
McHenry, Robert, ed. *Famous American Women*. NY: Dover, 1980.
Read, Phyllis J., and Bernard L. Witlieb. *The Book of Women's Firsts*. NY: Random House, 1992.
Weatherford, Doris. *American Women's History*. NY: Prentice Hall, 1994.

B. Kimberly Taylor, freelance writer, New York, New York

Surrey, countess of.

See Isabel of Vermandois (d. before 1147).
See Isabel de Warrenne (c. 1137–1203).
See Marshall, Maud (d. 1248).
See Isabella of Angoulême for sidebar on Alice le Brun (d. 1255).
See Joan de Vere (fl. 1280s).
See Tylney, Elizabeth (d. 1497).
See Tylney, Agnes (1476–1545).

Susan of Powys (fl. 1100s)

Queen of Powys. Flourished in the 1100s; daughter of Gruffydd ap Cynan, king of Gwynedd, and *Angharad (d. 1162); married Madog ap Maredudd, king of Powys; children: four, including *Marared (mother of Llywelyn II the Great, Ruler of All Wales).

Susann, Jacqueline (1921–1974)

Popular American author who wrote the bestseller Valley of the Dolls. Born in Philadelphia, Pennsylvania, on August 20, 1921; died of cancer in New York City on September 21, 1974; daughter of Robert Susann (a portrait painter) and Rose (Jans) Susann (a teacher); educated in Philadelphia public schools; married Irving Mansfield (a press agent and radio-television producer), in 1939; children: one son, Guy (b. 1946).

Selected writings: Every Night, Josephine! *(1963);* Valley of the Dolls *(1966);* The Love Machine *(1969);* Once Is Not Enough *(1973);* Dolores *(1976);* Yargo *(1979).*

Jacqueline Susann made her mark in the literary world with decidedly un-literary material. Using her show-business background, she drew on her personal relationships and experiences to produce wildly popular novels that were generally reviled by book critics as trashy and one-dimensional. Susann's flair for the dramatic—evinced in both her personal life and her narrative style—overcame the negative reviews to capture the interest of millions of readers. At the time of her death in 1974, her 1966 novel *Valley of the Dolls* was ranked as the bestselling book of all time by the *Guinness Book of Records.*

Jacqueline Susann was born on August 20, 1921, in Philadelphia, Pennsylvania, the daughter of **Rose Jans Susann**, a teacher, and Robert Susann. As she grew up, Jacqueline developed an especially close relationship to her father, a portrait painter who counted Supreme Court justices and sports figures among his clients. Her academic career was marked by her lackluster performance in Philadelphia's public schools, which may have helped convince her parents to let her try her hand at acting in New York rather than attend college. The young woman had an insatiable desire for fame, and enjoyed moderate success in her 20-year career as a model and actress, appearing in 21 plays and on television in dramatic productions, panel shows, and commercials. However, the closest she came to genuine accolades was being named as television's best-dressed woman several times.

Susann's 1962 diagnosis of breast cancer may have influenced her decision to change careers. After undergoing a mastectomy and chemotherapy and cobalt treatments, she made a pact with God for another ten years of life in which to realize her passionate dream of becoming famous. Aware that her acting career would not provide the fame she sought, Susann turned to writing—a profession she had previously dabbled in by writing the play *Lovely Me* in 1946. As a preview of her later work, the play was popular even though critics panned it, and concerned the dark side of Hollywood and Broadway. In 1963, she published her first book, *Every Night, Josephine!*. The book, about her own life as seen through the eyes of her beloved poodle Josephine, originally sold close to 40,000 copies. An ambitious self-promoter, Susann embarked on an unprecedented publicity tour, often appearing with Josephine in matching outfits. She enjoyed publicity, as did her husband of nearly 25 years, Irving Mansfield, who was both a press agent and a producer. The pair's celebrity even found them as the guests of honor at a tea party thrown by the Duke and *Duchess of Windsor.

Although the sales for *Every Night, Josephine!* were significant, the success of Susann's first book would never approach that of her second, *Valley of the Dolls*, in 1966. The story about rich, beautiful, and self-destructive women was steamy enough to attract attention on its own (some critics called it pornographic), but Susann ensured its visibility by mounting another promotional publicity blitz. Although the critics universally panned the novel, the gossipy, glamorous narrative, combined with the publicity generated on her tour, kept it at the #1 spot on *The New York Times* bestseller list for a record 28 consecutive weeks. Strong sales made it the all-time bestseller—topping 20 million copies sold by the time of Susann's death in 1974.

Michael Goldberg notes that *Valley of the Dolls* added something new to the potboiler genre: "Susann combined her inside knowledge of the dark side of show business with her moral outrage against the drugs and alcohol to which she was addicted to produce a curiously compelling hybrid. The titillating story, which centered on the lives of the rich and famous, was at bottom a morality play." Although also referring to pretty girls, "dolls" was Susann's slang term for the pills consumed by the book's main characters. Although Susann insisted that the show-business women in the story were purely fictional creations, many readers drew parallels between the characters and Susann's own associates, including *Judy Garland, *Ethel Merman, and Susann herself. Naturally, plans for a movie version quickly took hold, and *Valley of the Dolls* hit

America's movie screens the following year. Like the book, the movie—starring *Susan Hayward, Barbara Parkins, Patty Duke, and *Sharon Tate—was a resounding success, grossing over $70 million. It is now considered a camp classic.

Susann had found her milieu, and produced two more novels in the same vein in the next seven years. In 1969, she released *The Love Machine*, which also had several self-destructive female characters who revolve around the book's main character, ambitious television tycoon Robin Stone. Like the dual meaning of "dolls," this book's title refers to both Stone—apparently based on Susann's own father—and the television industry. Featuring all the sex and glitz of its predecessor, *The Love Machine* also picked up *Valley*'s morality as the swinging Stone reforms his abusive ways to settle down with the movie-star heroine. Although the cachet of her name alone could have sold the book, Susann continued her vigorous promotion efforts. She reportedly flew to publicity events in a chartered plane with "The Love Machine" painted on the fuselage. This book, too, enjoyed vast success, staying on the bestseller list for 21 weeks.

The Love Machine was followed in 1973 by *Once Is Not Enough*, which also proved extremely popular, keeping the #1 spot for nine weeks. Perhaps again drawing on her relationship with her father, Susann featured a female character who cannot emotionally separate from her producer-gambler dad in the midst of a plot brimming with lust, assaults, and melodramatic accidents. Both this and *The Love Machine* followed in *Valley*'s footsteps by becoming a pricey movie with big box-office returns.

Although needled by negative criticism throughout her writing career, Susann dismissed the derisive assessment of her literary talent. According to *People* magazine, she once said: "I write for women who read me on the goddamn subways. They want to press their noses against the windows of other people's houses and get a look at parties they'll never be invited to, the dresses they'll never get to wear, the lives they'll never live." The incredible royalties generated by her books funded an equally extravagant lifestyle for Susann and her husband. Dining out every night at New York's best restaurants and living in posh hotel suites, Susann appeared to be at the peak of happiness. However, her success was marred by two secrets she kept from even her closest friends. Susann had given birth to a son, Guy, in 1946, and felt that his autism may have been the result of her drug and alcohol abuse during that time. She and Irving institutionalized the boy when he was still a toddler. Although Susann and Irving consistently visited him, few of their friends even knew the couple had a child, and those who did were led to believe that he was away at boarding school or hospitalized with asthma. Susann was equally reticent about her 12-year struggle with cancer, of which few were aware until it had reached advanced stages in 1974. Susann succumbed to it at Doctors Hospital in Manhattan on September 21, 1974.

Two of Susann's books were published posthumously, *Dolores* (1976) and *Yargo* (1979). *Dolores*, a fictionalized account of John F. Kennedy's assassination, drew some comments for Susann's brash comparisons between herself and *Jacqueline Kennedy, the other famous "Jackie" of the day. *Yargo*, a novel of romance and science fiction, had been written in the 1950s. In 1982, *Valley of the Dolls* went out of print, but experienced a revival 15 years later along with an increase of interest in Susann herself. Along with plans for a sequel to the film, the end of the 1990s saw Susann's biography, *Lovely Me: The Life of Jacqueline Susann*, become a television movie in 1998, starring Michele Lee. In 2000, the movie *Isn't She Great*, starring Bette Midler as Susann and Nathan Lane as Irving, opened to disappointing reviews and spent only one week in theaters.

SOURCES:
Buck, Claire, ed. *The Bloomsbury Guide to Women's Literature*. NY: Prentice Hall, 1992.
Current Biography Yearbook. NY: H.W. Wilson, 1972.
Garraty, John A., and Mark C. Carnes, eds. *American National Biography*. NY: Oxford University Press, 1999.
Goldberg, Michael. "Jacqueline Susann," in *Dictionary of American Biography*. Edited by Kenneth T. Jackson. NY: Scribner, n.d.
McHenry, Robert, ed. *Famous American Women*. NY: Dover, 1980.
People Weekly. October 27, 1997, pp. 59–62.
Publishers Weekly. September 22, 1997, p. 24.
TV Guide. December 5, 1998, pp. 5–6.

Jo Anne Meginnes, freelance writer, Brookfield, Vermont

Susanna (fl. 6th c. BCE)

Biblical woman. Name variations: Susannah. Flourished around the 6th century BCE; daughter of Hikiah; married Joakim.

According to versions of the Book of Daniel, Susanna was the daughter of Hikiah, and the wife of Joakim. She was reputedly raised in Babylon during the period of the Hebrews' captivity, and is alleged to have been beautiful and devout according to the law of Moses. Her husband was said to have been rich and to have owned a fine home with a garden, in which it was customary for the Jews of Babylon to meet in order to dispense with community business, mostly of a legal nature. As our sources have it, it was customary for a court to meet in the coolness of Joakim's garden during the morning hours. These sessions were presided over by two elders (selected annually), who broke off their proceedings at noon so that the participants could return to their respective homes for their midday meals. Once the day's legal business had been completed, Susanna made it her habit to enjoy the privacy of this same garden.

One year, two lecherous elders are said to have taken note of Susanna's perambulations, which they began to follow regularly from hidden locations. Since Susanna believed herself to be alone, she made no effort to conceal her beauty while traversing her garden, although she otherwise would have done so in the presence of men who were not of her family. Having the opportunity to gaze upon Susanna's beauty, these elders came to be overcome with lust, but were for some time afraid to admit their desires because of their sense of shame. Eventually, one hot day each of the elderly voyeurs announced that he was going home to dine. On this day, however, neither had any intention of doing so, as each had resolved to return to the garden so as to assault Susanna. The two, however, confronted each other before encountering Susanna, and both were forced to confess to their lust. As they were doing so in their hidden outpost, Susanna emerged from her house with her maids. Announcing that it was her intention to bathe, Susanna required of her maids that they return to the house and fetch the soap and olive oil that would be required for her ablution.

This opportunity emboldened the elders to confront Susanna and to demand from her sexual favors, threatening that if she would not consent to do so they would accuse her of arranging a tryst with a handsome youth. They added they would testify to the fact that it was for that purpose that Susanna had dismissed her maids. Susanna was on the horns of a dilemma: the penalty for adultery was death, but could she afford to refuse their lewd advances, since it was unlikely that her testimony would outweigh those of two legal pillars of the community, even if, ironically, they were accusing her of crimes which they, and not she, longed to commit? Being pure of mind, Susanna could not consent to their blackmail, thinking it a far better thing to confront false testimony than to commit the reputed sin. She shouted out for help, only to have the two elders respond in kind. Their din quickly drew Susan-

na's household into the garden, where the elders made their false accusation. Thus confronted, Susanna was tried, unveiled, before her family. During the proceedings, the elders claimed that they had caught her and her lover in the act, but that her lover, being young and robust, had escaped. They then professed that they had been unable to obtain from Susanna the name of her paramour.

Appalled by the accusations of the elders, those present at the hearing hastily condemned Susanna to death. At that moment she is said to have prayed, with the result that God inspired the young prophet Daniel to protest the undo dispatch of the trial. After Daniel's intercession, it was agreed that the trial should be reopened. Daniel separated the two elders and interrogated them in isolation about their testimony. His one question to each was: under what tree did Susanna's tryst occur? The first replied, "under a clove tree," while the second stated, "under a yew tree." The discrepancy of their testimonies came to prove that the elders were lying, with the result that it was they, and not Susanna, who were put to death.

The historicity of the Book of Daniel is largely discounted today, with most scholars arguing that the work as we have it is a product of the 2nd century BCE, rather than a 6th-century BCE work written by a historical Daniel. Another problem with the historicity of the story as it stands is that it is not found in the Hebrew text of Daniel, although it is in both the Septuagint and Theodotion. Protestant Christians include this story among the Bible's Apocrypha, while Catholics officially attribute it the canonical Book of Daniel. Regardless of the narrative's historicity, it serves as an interesting morality tale, with a threat against the Hebrews arising not from some foreign source, but from within the community itself. Famous among the many paintings of Susanna are those rendered by Rembrandt and *Artemisia Gentileschi, both called *Susanna and the Elders.*

William S. Greenwalt,
Professor of Classical History,
Santa Clara University, Santa Clara, California

Susanne de Bourbonne (1491–1521).
See Louise of Savoy for sidebar on Suzanne of Bourbon.

Suslova, Nadezhda (1845–1916).
See Liubatovich, Olga for sidebar.

Sussex, countess of.
See Howard, Elizabeth (d. 1534).
See Villiers, Barbara for sidebar on Anne Palmer (1661–1722).

Süssmuth, Rita (1937—)

German academic and politician who rose through the ranks of the Christian Democratic Union Party to become the German Parliament's president in 1988. Name variations: Rita Sussmuth; Rita Suessmuth. *Born on February 17, 1937, in Wuppertal, Germany; educated at universities of Münster, Tübingen, and Paris; married Hans Süssmuth (a professor); children: one daughter.*

Born on February 17, 1937, in Wuppertal, Germany, Rita Süssmuth studied at universities in Münster, Tübingen, and Paris. She then taught at several German universities, including those at Stuttgart and Osnabrück from 1963 to 1966, the Pädagogische Hochschule Ruhr from 1966 to 1969 (to which she returned in 1971), and the University of Dortmund in 1980.

Aligning herself with the Christian Democratic Union Party, Süssmuth rose through the ranks and worked on several governmental committees on women, children, marriage, and family affairs throughout the 1970s and 1980s. She served as the director of the research institute Frau und Gesellschaft (Women and Society) in Hanover before assuming the role of chair of the Christian Democratic Union Women's Association in 1986, and minister of Youth, Family Affairs, Women and Health the following year.

In 1987, Süssmuth joined the Bundestag, the German equivalent of Parliament, and became its president in 1988. She headed the governing body until the close of the 20th century. A persuasive advocate of social justice, she often defended politically disdained perspectives on controversial issues. She also questioned the leadership within her own party and continued in her efforts to advance women's issues. Following the end of her presidency of the Bundestag, she continued in politics as the parliamentary deputy for the Christian Democratic Union, visiting Slovakia to lecture on European unification.

SOURCES:

Drost, Harry. *What's What and Who's Who in Europe.* NY: Simon & Schuster, 1995.
International Who's Who, 1998–99. Europa Publications, n.d.
The Johns Hopkins Gazette. May 18, 1998.

Jo Anne Meginnes, freelance writer, Brookfield, Vermont

Sutcliff, Rosemary (1920–1992)

English novelist and children's writer. Born on December 14, 1920, in West Clandon, Surrey, England; died on July 23, 1992; daughter of a naval officer; educated privately and at Bideford School of Art, 1935–39.

Selected fiction for adults: Lady in Waiting *(1956);* The Rider of the White Horse *(1959);* Sword at Sunset *(1963);* The Flowers of Adonis *(1969);* Blood and Sand *(1987).*

Selected fiction for children and young adults: The Chronicles of Robin Hood *(1950);* The Armourer's House *(1951);* Brother Dusty-Feet *(1952);* Simon *(1953);* The Eagle of the Ninth *(1954);* Outcast *(1955);* The Shield Ring *(1956);* The Silver Branch *(1957);* Warrior Scarlet *(1958);* The Bridge-Builders *(1959);* The Lantern Bearers *(1959);* Knight's Fee *(1960);* Dawn Wind *(1961);* The Mark of the Horse Lord *(1965);* The Chief's Daughter *(1967);* A Circlet of Oak Leaves *(1968);* The Witch's Brat *(1970);* The Truce of the Games *(1971);* Heather, Oak, and Olive: Three Stories *(1972);* The Capricorn Bracelet *(1973);* The Changeling *(1974);* We Lived in Drumfyvie *(1975);* Blood Feud *(1976);* Shifting Sands *(1977);* Sun Horse, Moon Horse *(1977);* Song for a Dark Queen *(1978);* Frontier Wolf *(1980);* Three Legions: A Trilogy *(1980);* Eagle's Egg *(1981);* Bonnie Dundee *(1983);* Flame-Coloured Taffeta *(1985);* The Roundabout Horse *(1986);* Little Hound Found *(1989);* A Little Dog Like You *(1990);* The Shining Company *(1990);* The Minstrel and the Dragon Pup *(1993).*

Selected nonfiction for children and young adults: The Chronicles of Robin Hood *(1950);* The Queen Elizabeth Story *(1950);* Houses and History *(1960);* Beowulf *(1961, also issued as* Dragon Slayer: The Story of Beowulf *[1966]);* The Hound of Ulster *(Cuchulain Saga, 1963);* Heroes and History *(1965);* A Saxon Settler *(1965);* The High Deeds of Finn MacCool *(1967);* Tristan and Iseult *(1971);* The Light Beyond the Forest: The Quest for the Holy Grail *(1979);* The Sword and the Circle: King Arthur and the Knights of the Round Table *(1981);* The Road to Camlann: The Death of King Arthur *(1981);* Black Ships before Troy *(1993).*

Selected other: Rudyard Kipling *(1960);* Ghost Story *(screenplay, 1975); (editor, with* **Monica Dickens***)* Is Anyone There? *(1978);* Blue Remembered Hills *(autobiography, 1983);* Mary Bedell *(play, 1986).*

Born in England on December 14, 1920, Rosemary Sutcliff was only two years old when she contracted the physically debilitating Still's disease, an arthritic condition that ultimately restricted her to a wheelchair. She was schooled at home by her mother, who often read aloud to her, and was particularly captivated by the legends of King Arthur and Robin Hood, the tales of Rudyard Kipling, and especially the true stories of adventure told to her by her naval officer father. Sutcliff did not receive formal schooling until she was nine and her family settled in Devon, but she left school at age 14 to study painting at the Bideford School of Art. Prevented, however, by her disability from working on any project larger than the miniatures at which she excelled, she turned to writing as a creative outlet.

Steeped in the history and archaeology of ancient Britain, Sutcliff felt a particular fondness for the Roman period. "I think that I am happiest of all in Roman Britain," she said in a 1986 interview with Raymond H. Thompson. "I feel very much at home there." Although her first efforts involved the retelling of the British legend of Robin Hood, she produced her breakthrough work in 1954 with *The Eagle of the Ninth*. Set in Roman times, it describes the journey of former centurion Marcus Aquila to recover the eagle standard of his father's 9th Hispana Legion after the legion vanished mysteriously in the country north of Hadrian's Wall. Presented by the BBC on its "Children's Hour" series, the work was followed by other novels that focused on later generations of the Aquila family, including *The Silver Branch* (1957), *The Lantern Bearers* (1959), and *Frontier Wolf* (1980).

Sutcliff's historical novels are set in times of violent upheaval in which warring nations must inevitably adapt to changing political landscapes. Within this larger framework, Sutcliff frequently positions a character who must also adapt to personal upheaval. A common theme is that of a young boy's initiation into manhood, often as an orphan surviving among strangers. *Outcast*, written in 1955, chronicles the struggles of the orphan Beric to adapt in the warring world of early Roman Britain. Similarly, the leading figures of *The Shield Ring* (1955) are orphans caught in the attempts of Viking settlers to combat a Norman invasion in England's Lake District. In *Dawn Wind* (1962), the young Owain slowly comes to terms with life in an Anglo-Saxon world after the death of his family.

Sutcliff's distinguished retelling of traditional British and Celtic hero tales, which also emphasize endurance and heroic struggle against great odds, include stories of Beowulf, Finn MacCool, Cuchulain, Robin Hood, Tristan and Iseult, and King Arthur. Convinced of the historical existence of King Arthur, Sutcliff began to write a trilogy about him in 1979 with *The Light Beyond the Forest: The Quest for the Holy Grail*. In 1981, she completed the series with *The Sword and the Circle: King Arthur and the Knights of the Round Table* and *The Road to*

Camlann: The Death of King Arthur. Researching the known history of the Dark Ages, Sutcliff worked what she believed to be true about Arthurian legend into this setting. "It was very strange because I have never written a book which was so possessive," Sutcliff told Thompson about beginning this series. "It was extraordinary—almost frightening. It took me about 18 months to write, and it absolutely rode me throughout the entire time." Feeling almost possessed by the character of Arthur and the male experience throughout the writing of the series, she also admitted that it took her a long time to return to what she described as "getting back into a woman's skin" after its completion.

Although some of Sutcliff's work focuses on female protagonists, such as the tragic tale of Boadicea (*Boudica) in *Song for a Dark Queen* in 1978, the traditional domestic roles that were open to women of the ancient world held little interest for her. With a keen understanding of military tactics, Sutcliff cast most of her central characters as male, especially soldiers. However, as Thompson points out, the soldiers in Sutcliff's work often experience a softening or a deepening sensitivity to the human condition. Sutcliff seldom evoked the element of romantic love in her work, preferring instead to explore deep and enduring friendships and familial ties within the context of conflicting loyalties.

Considered one of the most important writers of historical fiction for young people, Sutcliff told Thompson that her books "are for children of all ages, from nine to ninety." Despite the scant documentation of the early historical eras of which she wrote, Sutcliff set the standard for the genre with the depth of her research and the power of her artistic ingenuity. Her skill at vivifying the past and its physical and political landscapes in more than 50 books earned her several Carnegie Medal commendations—Britain's highest award for young adult fiction—and numerous "notable book" honors by the American Library Association. In addition, she was named a fellow of the Royal Society of Literature in 1982. She recalled her own early years of struggle and physical impairment in a 1983 autobiography, *Blue Remembered Hills*. Named an officer in 1975 and then a commander of the Order of the British Empire in 1992, Rosemary Sutcliff died on July 23 of that year.

SOURCES:

Buck, Claire, ed. *The Bloomsbury Guide to Women's Literature*. NY: Prentice Hall, 1992.
Contemporary Popular Writers. Detroit, MI: St. James Press, 1997.
Meek, Margaret. *Rosemary Sutcliff*. NY: Walck, 1962.

St. James Guide to Young Adult Writers. 2nd ed. Detroit, MI: St. James Press, 1999.

Shattock, Joanne. *The Oxford Guide to British Women Writers.* Oxford University Press, 1993.

Thompson, Raymond H. "Interview with Rosemary Sutcliff [1986]," in *Interviews with Authors of Modern Arthurian Literature.*

Jo Anne Meginnes, freelance writer, Brookfield, Vermont

Sutherland, duchess of.

See Leveson-Gower, Harriet Elizabeth Georgiana (1806–1868).

Sutherland, Efua (1924–1996)

Prominent Ghanaian poet, author, theater director and filmmaker who also held academic and government positions sponsoring the development of the arts in her newly independent country. Name variations: *Efua Nyankoma; Efua Theodora Morgue; Efua Theodora Sutherland. Born on June 27, 1924, in Cape Coast, in the British colony of the Gold Coast; died on January 2, 1996; attended St. Monica's School and Training College, the Gold Coast; Homerton College, Cambridge University, B.A., and School of Oriental and African Studies, University of London; married William Sutherland, in 1954; children: Esi Reiter Sutherland; Muriel Amowi Sutherland; Ralph Gyan Sutherland.*

Returned to the Gold Coast (1951); was a teacher at St. Monica's School (1951–54); after the Gold Coast became the independent state of Ghana, organized Ghana Society of Writers (1957); began publication of literary magazine Okyeame (Spokesman, 1959); founded Ghana Experimental Players (1958); founded Ghana Drama Studio (1961); appointed Research Fellow in Literature and Drama, University of Ghana (1963); made first visit to Atwia (1964); completed story house at village of Atwia (1966); founded Kusum Players (1968).

Major works: (drama) Edufa (1962), Foriwa *(1962),* The Marriage of Anansewa *(1975); (prose)* The Roadmakers *(1961),* Playtime in Africa *(1962),* New Life at Kyerefaso *(1964).*

Efua Sutherland devoted her career to promoting African art forms. Along with her work as a teacher and radio broadcaster, this Ghanaian intellectual wrote short stories, plays, and poems; she also led the way in creating numerous organizations and projects to develop African writing and African theater. Sutherland wrote both in English and in Akan (or Twi), one of the languages of her African homeland. She

was known primarily as a playwright, and her most significant works, notes critic J. Nkukaki Amankulor of the University of Nigeria, "show her development within the European dramatic tradition as well as her determination to create a new dramatic aesthetic . . . [for] a truly African theater." While some of her work was directed toward an adult audience, her other writings were intended for African children.

Using the traditional storytelling format by which African folklore has been transmitted, in her three major plays Sutherland worked to create appropriate dramatic forms for her newly independent country. Some critics see her writing as primarily didactic, aiming at teaching her audience lessons in both traditional morality as well as the skills to cope with a changing environment. Others note how Sutherland's dramas demonstrate her strong interest in exploring and criticizing the role of women in African society. William B. Branch, for example, claims that Sutherland is not "an authentic, dyed-in-the-wool, crusading feminist." But he goes on to insist that "there is nevertheless a sense of warning implicit in Sutherland's dramas . . . that there must be meaningful change in relationships between men and women on this planet, and soon." **Gay Wilentz**, a feminist critic, finds that Sutherland's dramas show the dominant role that women have played in handing down African traditions from generation to generation.

The future writer was born Efua Theodora on June 27, 1924, at Cape Coast, a coastal town in the British colony of the Gold Coast. Some sources give her family name as Morgue. Her parents were Christian and urbanized, but they were members of the Fante tribe of the Akan language group. Sutherland's first name, Efua, was the customary name for female children of the tribe born on a Friday. She received two additional names that symbolized her dual heritage. In accordance with Fante custom, eight days after her birth she was given a name taken from one of her ancestors, Nyankoma. At her Christian baptism, she was given the name Theodora. Both mean "Gift of God."

The young girl obtained her education on two continents. After graduating from St. Monica's School and Training College at Mampong in the Ashanti region of the Gold Coast, she continued her studies in England. One of the first African women to attend Cambridge University, she studied there at Homerton College and took a B.A. degree; she continued her education abroad at the School of Oriental and African Studies at the University of London. At age 27, she returned to Ghana to start a career in secondary education. She taught first at the Fijai Secondary School at Sekondi and subsequently at her alma mater, St. Monica's at Mampong. In 1954, the young teacher married William Sutherland, an African-American and an official of an international relief organization. The couple went on to create a family with three children: Esi Reiter, Muriel Amowi, and Ralph Gyan.

Sutherland's early years as a teacher coincided with dramatic events in her homeland. In 1957, Great Britain ended its century-old control over the Gold Coast, and the newly independent country took the name Ghana. It was the first of Africa's sub-Saharan states to see the end of European rule and to achieve independence. Although there were a number of urban centers along the coast such as Accra and Cape Coast, the vast majority of Ghana's population lived in rural villages in the interior.

Once she had settled back in Ghana, Sutherland took up the cause of promoting African literature in written form. This was a departure from the continent's tradition of maintaining cultural products in the form of oral works. In conformity with that tradition, even educated Africans tended to link written literature with Western forms and ideas. The absence of a compelling written literature reflecting their own heritage served to discourage most Africans from any extensive reading effort.

Sutherland took on the problem both as a writer and as an organizer. She began to write in 1951, later recalling that she became dissatisfied with the materials available for the first group of children she was assigned to teach. In 1957, Sutherland made another effort to remedy the situation by founding the Ghana Society of Writers. Progress came slowly, and her determination was renewed when, in 1958, an exhibit Sutherland put on showed the complete absence of such English-language works by Ghanaian authors. At that time, she commented to a friend, "When the first children's book by a Ghanaian is published I shall die happy." She put herself to the task and her own children's book, *Playtime in Africa*, appeared in 1962. "Dedicated to the Children of the New Africa," as she put it, the book was illustrated with 40 photographs by Willis E. Bell. It presented African children with pictures of their peers at play in a variety of outdoor settings.

As a literary pioneer, the young teacher struck off in an even more novel direction in developing a theatrical movement in her native country. While Ghana had a tradition of public storytelling and dramatic performances at festi-

vals and funerals, there was nothing on the order of formal theater. Sutherland changed that by sponsoring adult theatrical productions and also by creating a children's theater program. The government of Ghana provided some financial support for her endeavors, and she also received help from such sources as the Rockefeller Foundation. Thus, Sutherland was able to create a theatrical center, the Ghana Drama Studio, in the national capital at Accra. Its first full production studio, an outdoor auditorium, opened in 1961. Characteristically, Sutherland had studied the Ghanaian tradition of outdoor social occasions and storytelling and decided that the Drama Studio should continue along these lines.

In 1959, she and fellow members of the Ghana Society of Writers were aided by the Ministry of Information in creating a literary magazine. Entitled *Okyeame* (meaning a chief's official speaker), this publication was intended to promote creative writing among members of Ghana's population. Another step in Sutherland's career came in 1963 when she was appointed Research Fellow in Literature and Drama at the Institute of African Studies of the University of Ghana. In her new role, she was able to train young actors and playwrights. Moreover, in her official capacity, she toured many remote areas of the country in search of Ghanaian oral literature.

Sutherland applied her prodigious energies to the study of Ghanaian folklore. "I'm on a voyage of discovery," she said. "I'm discovering my own people." In Ghanaian society, funerals were the occasion for public entertainment to accompany the vigil for the deceased. She attended these and other traditional ceremonies. Sutherland's quest for folk tales led her to the small, impoverished Fante village of Atwia, with a population of 700, in the Central Region of Ghana. She stayed four months on her initial visit in 1964. The village was famous for its storytelling, but the visitor was particularly impressed by the community's determination to provide its children with an elementary education. Nonetheless, most of its youngsters departed for Ghana's cities once they reached their teenage years. With the aid of the village elders, Sutherland moved to revitalize the small community's cultural life, beginning with the construction of a village theater. Said Sutherland, "I have had a long-standing hunch that the educated African had better *get with* the uneducated communities which form the bulk of his society in every African country at present."

Sutherland contributed money from her research funds to buy building materials, and the villagers themselves provided the labor. Soon, emigrants from the village who had settled in urban Ghana returned to contribute their skills as masons and carpenters. During the construction, Sutherland brought University of Ghana students from the departments of literature and drama to the village for visits. The seminars in which they participated gave the villagers in this remote setting an indication of what the finished theater would add to their community. In June 1966, the community theater was completed. It received the Fante name Kodzidan (The Story House). An initial performance a month later attracted all the participants in the International Music Festival Conference then being held at Accra.

With Sutherland taking the lead, Atwia began an economic as well as a cultural revival. The exodus of teenagers from the village slowed as new developments such as a theater ensemble and a corn mill for processing grain made Atwia a lively center for the surrounding area. For Sutherland, the entire Atwia adventure was an important lesson for the urban inhabitants of Ghana and other parts of Africa. They could now see how to revitalize the uneducated communities around them.

In a 1968 interview, Sutherland reflected on her own need to learn about "hidden areas . . . important areas of Ghanaian life, which I just wasn't in touch with." Her forays into the countryside had given this city-bred intellectual a new perspective on her nation's life: "I've just made a very concentrated effort to make it untrue that I do not know my people and I know them now." That same year, Sutherland founded the Kusum Players (Kusum Agoromba). This group of professional actors with its home at the Ghana Drama Studio toured the country presenting plays to groups of various ages. Most of the plays it performed were by Sutherland and several were in the Akan language.

Sutherland responded with dismay to an interviewer's questions in 1972 as to whether "you are the pivot around which all the drama in Accra circulates." Nonetheless, she admitted to managing several plays at the Drama Studio, while also organizing poetry readings and editing *Okyeame*. At the same time, she remained active in promoting experimental village theaters. "I somehow get the energy to do it," she said. "I suppose it is a sense of joy that I have in doing it that keeps me going." She was the first well-known media personality in Ghana, working in both radio and television.

In that 1968 interview, Sutherland expressed her hope that her work would help spread English in Ghana. She regretted that

Ghanaians "don't wear the language comfortably," and thus productions in Akan reached a much higher standard. Nonetheless, she looked forward to the day when Ghana would be a bilingual society.

Sutherland's own writing in Akan reached a high level of maturity by the early 1960s. In 1962, two important plays appeared. *Edufa* stressed social relations in African society, while *Foriwa* placed a greater emphasis on political developments. Some critics have noted incorrectly that the plays were written in English and misdate their appearance as occurring in 1967. In fact, the two received their debuts in 1962, almost certainly in Akan, and were first performed in English in 1967.

The somber work *Edufa* borrowed themes from Euripides' *Alcestis* to dramatize the story of a man facing oracles' predictions of his death. He responds to this crisis by trying to put his father in the path of destiny, but, by mistake, it is Edufa's wife who takes his place. Notwithstanding the European roots of the story, Sutherland drew on traditional African beliefs in the role of oracles to make the play meaningful to a Ghanaian audience. In her use of a chorus, she mingled African and European elements. The dramatic device came from the traditions of Greek drama, but, composed of village women, this element placed the drama within the environment of a typical African rural community.

Sutherland also made Edufa, the central male character of the play, into what Lloyd Brown calls a representative of "the new elite of educated and wealthy men who have adopted the worst features of Western culture." As Brown points out, Edufa is presented with an opportunity to save his wife by "joining the entire family . . . in a collective beseeching of the gods." But he is too selfish and too divorced from traditional African values "of family and religion" to take this path. On the other hand, his wife Ampoma displays an African tradition of sharing and self-sacrifice that her coldly materialistic and egotistic husband has abandoned. But, in Brown's view, Sutherland also uses Ampoma for the larger purpose of criticizing women's role in African society. In a key passage, Ampoma declares that women conceal and restrict their desires and expressions, "preventing the heart from beating out its greatness." At the same time, the presence of a secondary character, an alienated poet and intellectual named Senchi, reemphasizes the Westernization of African society and Sutherland's desire to incorporate that change into her work.

That same year, in the more political drama *Foriwa*, she presented a work with a very different tone. Here Sutherland investigated in charming fashion the problem of bringing new knowledge to an African community. This work drew more heavily than *Edufa* on what Brown calls "the indigenous forms and conventions of the dramatist's own culture." In the play, several characters join in a successful effort to revive and reinvigorate the traditional beliefs of an African village. A four-branched tree set in the midst of the village and devoted to the gods stands present throughout the play. It represents healthy continuity, and the ability to grow on the basis of a lengthy past. Similarly, the wandering young university graduate Labaran joins forces with the town's queen-mother and her daughter Foriwa to seize "a dormant vitality . . . waiting to be released from static and unproductive notions of tradition." By making two women into agents of change, Sutherland again presented a critique of the basic forms of African society.

In 1975, in what Amankulor calls "Sutherland's most valuable contribution to Ghanaian drama and theater," *The Marriage of Anansewa*, the playwright developed a new dramatic form that drew upon African traditions. As in *Foriwa*, the tone of the work is light-hearted and playful. The drama's action halts for a number of musical intervals in which the performers converse with the audience. These interludes create a community between the players and the observers, allowing for a running commentary about the action taking place on the stage. Such a dramatic format drew upon the "spider (Ananse) stories" of Ghanaian tradition.

At a time when traditional values and modern needs have come into conflict, she has helped Africans, literate and illiterate, adapt to change creatively, by giving them outlets for self-expression and also encouraging a deeper sense of community and purpose.

—Louise Crane

The play's plot tells how an African villager, Ananse, places his daughter before a number of suitors. Having drawn gifts from all, he must announce the girl's death to avoid the inevitable confrontation with a group of disappointed would-be sons-in-law. One suitor, however, insists on taking responsibility for the girl's funeral even though custom places no such burden on him. As a consequence, Ananse must arrange his daughter's miraculous return from the dead and her betrothal to this pillar of generosity. The play thus shows Sutherland's continuing interest in African traditions and the possibility of renewing them in a creative way. Meanwhile, the audience is presented with a positive view of the age-old ceremonies through which Ananse's daughter Anansewa is initiated into adulthood.

As her country's most renowned dramatist, Sutherland traveled abroad to spread word about her work, notably in the United States. In the 1980s, she served as chair of the Ghanaian National Commission on Education. In that capacity, Sutherland was an advocate for increased government expenditures on education, since, as she noted, "money cannot be used for anything better than to ensure that society is well founded on children who are the base."

Efua Sutherland died at the age of 71 on January 2, 1996. In her obituary in *The Guardian*, **Margaret Busby** observed that "she held a special place [in the life of her country] having been the dominant presence in theater there for more than three decades." Her government honored her by naming one of the capital city's parks the Efua Sutherland Children's Park.

SOURCES:

Branch, William B., ed. *Crosswinds: An Anthology of Black Dramatists in the Diaspora*. Bloomington, IN: Indiana University Press, 1993.

Brown, Lloyd W. *Women Writers in Black Africa*. Westport, CT: Greenwood Press, 1981.

Crane, Louise. *Ms. Africa: Profiles of Modern African Women*. Philadelphia, PA: J.B. Lippincott, 1973.

Fister, Barbara. *Third World Women's Literatures: A Dictionary and Guide to Materials in English*. Westport, CT: Greenwood Press, 1995.

Jones, Eldred Durosimi, ed. *Women in African Literature Today*. London: James Curry, 1987.

McFarland, Daniel Miles. *Historical Dictionary of Ghana*. Metuchen, NJ: Scarecrow, 1985.

Owomoyela, Oyekan, ed. *A History of Twentieth-Century African Literatures*. Lincoln, NE: University of Nebraska Press, 1993.

Pieterse, Cosmo, and Dennis Duerden, eds. *African Writers Talking: A Collection of Radio Interviews*. NY: Africana Publishing, 1972.

"Reaching Out to Young Africa," in *The Guardian*. January 27, 1996.

Serafin, Steven R., comp. and ed. *Modern Black Writers*. Supplement. NY: Continuum, 1995.

Wilentz, Gay. *Binding Cultures: Black Women Writers in Africa and the Diaspora*. Bloomington, IN: Indiana University Press, 1992.

SUGGESTED READING:

Holloway, Karla F.C. *Moorings & Metaphors: Figures of Culture and Gender in Black Women's Literature*. New Brunswick, NJ: Rutgers University Press, 1992.

Pellow, Deborah, and Naomi Chazan. *Ghana: Coping with Uncertainty*. Boulder, CO: Westview Press, 1986.

Neil M. Heyman, Professor of History,
San Diego State University,
San Diego, California

Opposite page
Joan Sutherland

Sutherland, Joan (1926—)

Australian-born singer, particularly renowned for her work in bel canto operas, who became one of the most celebrated opera stars of the 20th century. Name variations: Dame Joan Sutherland. Pronunciation: SUH-thur-land. Born on November 7, 1926, in Sydney, Australia; daughter of William Sutherland (a tailor and businessman) and Muriel (Alston) Sutherland; attended St. Catherine's School, Waverly, Australia; Metropolitan Secretarial School, Sydney; Rathbone School of Dramatic Art, Sydney; Covent Garden Opera school, London; married Richard Bonynge, on October 16, 1954, in Ladbroke Grove, Great Britain; children: one son, Adam.

Made public debut as singer in chorus of Bach's Christmas Oratorio (1946); made solo debut the same year in concert performances of Henry Purcell's Dido and Aeneas and Handel's Acis and Galatea; won Mobil Quest Vocal Contest (1950); moved to London (1951); hired by Covent Garden Opera, London (1952); debuted at Paris Opera (1960); debuted at La Scala Opera in Milan, Italy, and New York City's Metropolitan Opera (1961); triumphed in her first return tour of her native Australia (1965); named Dame Commander of the British Empire (1979); named "Australian of the Year" (1989); retired from performing (1990).

Notable roles: Lucia in Gaetano Donizetti's Lucia di Lammermoor; Donna Anna in Wolfgang Amadeus Mozart's Don Giovanni; Alcina in George Friedrich Handel's Alcina; Amina in Vincenzo Bellini's La Sonnambula (her favorite role); Elvira in Bellini's I Puritani; Norma in Bellini's Norma; Marie in Donizetti's La Fille du Regiment.

"Success is one thing, sustaining it is something else," Dame Joan Sutherland wrote in her autobiography. One of the premier opera sopranos of the 20th century, Sutherland, who was raised in an Australian family impoverished after the death of her father, overcame numerous obstacles to reach the pinnacle of the world of international opera. In order to stay there, she had to struggle with still more obstacles, battling constant health problems while she maintained the globe-hopping schedule typical of opera stars in the late 20th century.

Sutherland's roots were in Australia. Her father William Sutherland, a Scottish immigrant to Australia at age 22, became a respected businessman in Sydney, running a tailor shop. His first marriage, to his cousin **Clara McDonald**, produced four children. After Clara died during an influenza outbreak in 1919, he married Muriel Alston, who gave birth to two children,

Sutherland's sister **Barbara** in 1922 and Joan in 1926. At a birth weight of more than 11 pounds, Joan was described by her mother as a "plump baby with a sunny disposition." As she grew, she was described as having a "big boned frame" like Muriel.

Some of Joan Sutherland's early memories were of hearing her mother sing. A mezzo-soprano who would "have made an opera singer," **Muriel Sutherland** was urged, in her youth, to move to Europe in order to study in London or Paris. Although she chose to stay in Australia, she practiced singing nearly every day, even as a mother. As young as age three, Sutherland loved to sit next to her mother at the piano while Muriel sang. Joan tried to sing along, and it was said that by age seven she knew arias from operas such as Giacomo Meyerbeer's *Les Huguenots* and Donizetti's **Lucrezia Borgia*.

From the family's home, with its beautiful view, she "could see the sparkling waters of Sydney harbor," Sutherland later reminisced, "and those unreal blue skies." The family frequently went swimming at a nearby beach. When William's business was adversely affected by the Depression, so that even the lawyers and physicians among his customers fell behind in paying for their tailor-made suits, the family struggled to keep the beach house. When Joan was six years old, her father collapsed on the beach while returning from a swim and died from a massive heart attack. He left behind two mortgages on the family house and a stack of uncollected bills. Only then was the family forced to move. The children of her father's first marriage, three girls and a boy, chose to establish their own household. Barbara, Joan, and Muriel moved to live with a maternal grandmother at Woollahra.

In 1934, Joan and Barbara were sent by their mother to St. Catherine's, a school for girls in Waverly. Their tuition was paid for by scholarships, including an endowment from a local Freemasons organization to which their father had belonged. Although she felt gauche and overweight as a teenager and was embarrassed by her frequent bouts with infected sinuses, Sutherland showed some interest in performing in school plays. She admired the young American singer and motion-picture actress *Deanne Durbin* and the opera singer *Grace Moore*. She talked of appearing one day on the stage of Covent Garden, the main London opera house.

Yet Sutherland was often denied the lead roles in school plays because of her size, and she was devastated to be told that she could not remain in the school choir because her voice

drowned out the others. Muriel, who feared that her daughter's voice could be ruined if it were "forced" prematurely, would not even allow her to have private voice lessons until she was 18.

Sutherland attended Metropolitan Secretarial College after leaving St. Catherine's, and during World War II became a typist at Sydney University, where she transcribed military-related reports on radios, weather forecasting, and missiles. She volunteered to work at military canteens in her spare time. For awhile it appeared that her half-brother Jim was missing in action, but the family was relieved when word came that he was, instead, a prisoner of war. The family did experience tragedy after the war, when Barbara Sutherland, believing herself to be a schizophrenic, committed suicide by jumping from a cliff.

In 1945, Sutherland pushed her mother into allowing her to enter a national vocal music contest, created by voice teachers John and **Ada Dickens**, which offered free music lessons to the winner. With Muriel as accompanist, Joan sang arias from Camille Saint-Saen's *Samson and Delilah*. Although she appeared in a shapeless dress, with poorly done hair and makeup, the judges were impressed with the power and richness of her voice, and she was declared the winner.

The Dickenses worked with Sutherland, attempting to extend the upper range of her voice by putting her through endless repetitions of scales. At their suggestion, she began to learn French, and an elocution teacher worked to rid her of her Australian accent. She was also enrolled in the Rathbone Academy of Dramatic Art, where teachers tried to overcome her self-consciousness about her size, telling her, "On stage, small people look small. Tall people fill the stage."

Sutherland made her debut as a singer in 1946, when she performed in the chorus for a presentation of Bach's *Christmas Oratorio*. Her solo debut quickly followed the next year, as she performed, to good reviews, in concert performances of Henry Purcell's *Dido and Aeneas* and George Friedrich Handel's *Acis and Galatea*. In order to gain further performing experience, Sutherland joined amateur music clubs, including the Affiliated Music Clubs of New South Wales, which gave performances in an assortment of Australian cities. She also attended a variety of other musical events, including performances by the Sydney Symphony Orchestra. At one of the orchestra's performances, she met a young music student named Richard Bonynge. Although he was four years younger, they became friends. It was the beginning of a relationship that would make Bonynge, in one writer's

words, both her staunchest defender and her severest critic.

Sutherland began entering music contests which offered cash prizes, with the thought that she might accumulate enough money to study in Europe. Although she was disappointed that she came in fourth in the Vacuum Oil contest of 1949, she won first place the next year in the Mobil Quest contest. Part of the prize was a stipend to allow her to tour much of Australia, giving concerts in selected cities. By 1951, Sutherland had saved enough money to move to Great Britain. Not only did her mother go along, but so did Bonynge, who enrolled in the Royal College of Music in London.

At first, things did not go well in Britain for Sutherland. She was able to secure an audition at Covent Garden, the main London opera house. But she was not hired, and the administrator who held her audition wrote that although she had a nice "ring" to her voice, she had "very little gifts by nature." To prepare for a future audition, she enrolled in the company's opera school. She made a negative impression on some of her teachers, partly because of her self-consciousness and partly because of her notoriously poor memory: she was unable to remember all the words at her first public recital. She also had not learned to move around the stage in a graceful or dignified way, and she would sometimes bend her knees to appear shorter than she was. One of her teachers, Edward Downes, secretly tried to have her dismissed from the opera school because he considered her clumsy and incapable of direction.

Bonynge, who began taking an interest in Sutherland's career, frequently argued with both Sutherland and her mother. Muriel envisioned her daughter as a dramatic soprano of great power, and she wanted Joan to practice Wagnerian music. Bonynge, who had been influenced by the recordings of reigning opera diva *Maria Callas, wanted Sutherland to sing the bel canto operas of the early 19th-century composers Giacchino Rossini and Bellini. Meaning, literally, "beautiful singing," bel canto is a demanding style featuring expressive and spectacular vocals. With its emphasis on rapid runs and florid musical passages, usually written for lead sopranos, it is often described as "coloratura" singing. Bonynge conceded that bel canto was not an easy path for Sutherland to take, describing it as a "vocal circus . . . [where] . . . the singers have to tread the high wire. . . . [T]hey are doing vocal gymnastics . . . and there is always an element of doubt whether they will make it." But he worked to convince Sutherland that she could be at least the equal of the two most famous operatic sopranos of the 1950s and 1960s, Callas and *Renata Tebaldi.

To extend Sutherland's range, Bonynge would position her so that she could not see his hands on the piano keys, then begin other scales higher and higher up, without telling her what he was doing. Muriel feared that Bonynge's ideas would be the ruination of her daughter's voice, and even Joan had her doubts. "We fought like cats and dogs over it," she said. "It took Richard three years to convince me to stop singing Wagner and start singing the early nineteenth century operas by Rossini and Donizetti." Bonynge responded, "I learned as much from her as she learned from me."

The debate between Bonynge and Muriel Sutherland occurred because Joan's voice, a large voice with an expanding range, was difficult to classify. It had become evident, as one critic would write, that her voice could "carry over the orchestra." Was she a lyric soprano suited to Handel or Mozart, or a dramatic soprano whose talents lay in heroic Wagnerian roles? Or did her talents lie in between, in the bel canto operas which demanded both an agile voice and extraordinary stamina? It would take time for both Richard and Muriel to realize that Sutherland's most outstanding virtue as a singer was her versatility. She would be distinctive among 20th-century operatic sopranos for the extraordinary range of music she could sing well. It was a gift she shared with Callas.

Sutherland appeared in the periodic productions of the Covent Garden opera school, and she also earned enough money to help pay her tuition by appearing in the school's opera radio productions. She held three auditions for Covent Garden staff members, but she was not hired into the opera's "stable" of regular singers until after her fourth audition, in 1952.

In her early appearances with the opera's company, her extraordinary abilities, as well as the need for her to work on certain areas, became apparent. Her first appearances in opera school productions included roles in Mozart's *The Magic Flute* and *Don Giovanni*. Her appearance in *The Magic Flute* drew a review which noted that she was a "dramatic soprano" capable of singing "either Italian or Wagnerian" roles. But the reviewer also noted that she had "much to learn about style."

Like many aspiring opera singers, Sutherland had discovered that she produced the most musically pure singing when she was allowed to stand motionless on stage, as if in concert-hall performance of an opera. Callas, however, had forever ended that possibility; although Callas' voice was sometimes criticized as thin in her highest range, her formidable acting ability had made her a groundbreaking soprano. Callas had integrated singing and acting, and her emphasis was on performance as much as music. The result was performances often described as "mesmerizing" or "compelling." In the world of opera, it was generally conceded that Callas had raised the standards of opera "acting" to new heights.

When Muriel returned to Australia in 1953, Richard moved into their London-area house with Joan; they were married in 1954. Bonynge worked with Sutherland to convince her that she could both sing and move dramatically across the stage at the same time. He argued that her very size would make her appear unusually dramatic on the huge stages of opera houses. Bonynge assumed a major role in shaping Sutherland's career, insisting that she had to show "dignity" even when appearing in public outside of an opera house. He wanted no news photographers to catch her eating an ice cream cone. He is given credit for convincing Sutherland to lose weight—eventually some 40 pounds—and to change her bleached blonde hair to red, which would become her "signature" look on stage.

Sutherland's dramatic coach, Norman Ayrton, also worked to make her into a singing actress. He taught opera as the art of movement and "concentration" on stage, and he was frank and direct in criticizing the way Sutherland moved across a stage. In rehearsing one scene, he told her that while she was supposed to be a young girl overcome by grief, she moved about the stage as if she were the captain of a hockey team.

If anyone has claims to be the Singer of the Century, it is surely Joan. And yet here is an artist who, from first to last, has kept her sense of wonder, of gratitude, taking nothing for granted, the last person to give herself the sort of airs assumed by far too many leading singers.

—Edward Greenfield

Sutherland's operatic performances of the 1950s began to establish her famed versatility. She appeared in three different roles in Jacques Offenbach's *The Tales of Hoffmann*. Her appearance in Carl Maria von Weber's *Der Freitschutz* in 1954 drew critical praise for her "ravishing" voice, and when she appeared in Vancouver, Canada, in 1958 in a production of

Mozart's *Don Giovanni*, guest conductor Bruno Walter called her the "the best Donna Anna I have ever heard."

One of her early performances as a Covent Garden regular was a small part in the bel canto opera *Norma*, by Bellini. The title role was sung by Callas, and Sutherland had the opportunity to observe firsthand the extent to which Callas drove herself for perfection, even to the point of exhaustion. Callas talked to Sutherland during rehearsals, encouraging her to experiment with bel canto operas. When Sutherland performed the lead role of *Lucia di Lammermoor* at Covent Garden in 1959, Callas attended one of the rehearsals. They were photographed together, with Callas telling Sutherland in the presence of the press, "You were wonderful, just wonderful." Sutherland later said of Callas: "She gave me the inspiration to join her at the beginning of my career and she never failed to encourage what I tried to do."

For Sutherland's performance as Lucia, the Italian producer Franco Zeffirelli was brought in to help her with stage movements. One of the first things he did was to try to rid her of the habit of "thrashing her hands on stage." While noting that she had triumphed in lighter fare such as *The Tales of Hoffmann* and *The Magic Flute*, he worked at transforming her from a comic to a tragic actress, trying to suppress, on stage, her naturally mischievous but self-effacing personality. In a 1957 production of Guiseppe Verdi's *Otello*, in which she played Desdemona, he convinced her that she could move across the stage "gracefully and with dignity."

Sutherland's Lucia became the basis for her debuts at the three other world-class opera houses, besides Covent Garden: Paris (1960); La Scala in Milan, Italy (1961); and the Metropolitan Opera in New York City (also 1961). Thus, within ten years of arriving in Britain, Sutherland had successfully debuted at the four major opera houses of the world. When she appeared in Zeffirelli's production of Handel's *Alcina* in Venice in 1960, the roaring crowd began to shout "*e stupenda*" ("she is stupendous"), leading to the nickname "La Stupenda." Now in demand, she began a 30-year, globe-trotting career.

Not everything was easy. Sutherland found herself in a hasty and ill-prepared production of *La Traviata* at Covent Garden in 1960, when audience members complained that they could clearly hear the sound of the prompters. Her appearance in *I Puritani* at the Glyndebourne Festival in Scotland the same year was praised for "exquisite" singing, but her first presentation of *La Sonnambula* at that same festival was not a success (although she would enjoy great success with it later).

Although Sutherland's debut at the Metropolitan Opera in 1961 was a triumph—she was called a "supreme technician" whose "spectacular" and "phenomenal" singing made her the "new queen of song"—Sutherland and Bonynge had a difficult working relationship with the director of the opera, Sir Rudolf Bing. Bing at first refused to deal with Bonynge as Sutherland's manager, insisting on dealing with Sutherland herself. He initially resisted Sutherland's demands that she be given the right of approval over parts of the production, including costuming and her choice of conductor, although he admitted to Bonynge, "With a voice like your wife's, you could get away with murder."

The newly confident Sutherland began to insist that she appear in opera productions on her own terms. In preparing for her triumphant debut in Verdi's *La Traviata* at the Metropolitan Opera—which one music critic hailed as "possibly the best heard in this house"—she argued with Bing over the costumes that he wanted her to wear. When Bing insisted, "It is a matter of taste, Miss Sutherland," she replied, "Yes, Mr. Bing, yours or mine."

Sutherland's success came despite continual health problems, including nearly constant recurrences of the sinus problems and ear infections that had plagued her since childhood. During one performance, she had to turn away from the audience when an ear abscess burst on stage while she was singing a high E-flat. Following laborious procedures to cap her teeth, she began to complain of pains in her knees, which started to swell on stage during one performance. At one opera recording session, she was forced to sit, and sing sitting, through the entire session. Doctors eventually diagnosed a form of rheumatism brought on by infections in her capped teeth, making it necessary for her to go through the capping process again.

Her determination and gallantry in performing under less than ideal conditions became legendary. When word arrived of her mother's death only a few hours before a concert performance in New York City, she gave her performance before flying to Australia. A fall on stage aggravated a spinal arthritis condition in 1962, when she was rehearsing for a performance of Giacomo Meyerbeer's *Les Huguenots*. Although forced to wear an uncomfortable metal corset, she insisted on doing something few modern sopranos have agreed to do—to make a stage entrance while riding a horse, as called for in the opera's libretto.

There was growing recognition of the uniqueness of her voice. One critic, noting that bel canto required many rapid note changes and singing in the "high stratosphere" of notes, marveled that her voice, under stress, became "golden" rather than "brittle." Her voice, it was said, had a warmth of tone more characteristic of dramatic sopranos than coloraturas. Yet she gained some of her greatest fame in bel canto coloratura roles, producing a "beautifully even trill, not a wobble" that one critic said resembled the sound of a flute. Another claimed she had the "most beautiful trill in the world." She was known for the accuracy of her rapid arpeggios, or runs, and for exact phrasing even in such rapid vocalizing.

As Sutherland aged, she did not lose her voice: it became darker and richer, rather than thinning out. She became a "singing actress" praised by one critic for "keeping [me] sitting on the edge of the seat" with the "ravishing beauty" of her voice, the ease with which she executed difficult musical passages, and her convincing portrayal of a woman "tormented" by "love, hate, bitterness, and despair."

International recognition followed. In 1961, she was named Commander of the Order of the British Empire. She received many honorary doctorates, including ones from Aberdeen University and the University of Liverpool. In 1975, she was named Companion of the Order of Australia, the highest honor in the new Australian system of honors which replaced the older British system of awards in her native country. The award recognized her "service to Australia and to humanity at large." When Nicaragua honored the 15 greatest opera singers of all time with a series of stamps in 1975, she was included. In 1979, she was named Dame Commander of the British empire (DBE), the second Australian to be honored (the first being *Nellie Melba in 1918). Joan was named "Australian of the Year" in 1989, and a performing arts center was named after her in Penrith.

The maturing and internationally renowned soprano had her share of tiffs with conductors. Early in her career, she had a heated disagreement with Rafael Kubelik over which parts should be sung and which parts should be spoken in Georges Bizet's opera *Carmen*. Although Bizet had called for a large amount of spoken dialogue, Sutherland, who still had traces of her Australian accent, resisted. As usual, Bonynge played the role of negotiator for, and defender of, his wife. When guest conduct Nello Santi refused to change tempos that made Sutherland uncomfortable during rehearsals in 1961, Sutherland, with Bonynge's support, eventually walked out of the theater and left the production.

At times such as these, she sometimes was given unfavorable coverage in some of the newspapers in her native Australia, but she gloried at the overwhelming reception she received during a concert tour of Australia in 1965. It was her first return to her native country in 14 years. At her initial performance, the audience gave her some 20 curtain calls.

The ever-present Bonynge had a much more difficult time establishing his own career as a conductor. Sutherland insisted that he be the conductor for a large portion of her recordings, numbering some 100, most of which were done with the British recording company Decca. But Bonynge was often denied recognition as being a musical specialist in his own right. There were disconcerting incidents. Sutherland insisted that he be the conductor for her highly successful appearance as Lucia at Hamburg in 1971. The orchestra resisted taking directions from Bonynge, however, and he was booed when he came onstage to take his bows. He shook his fist in anger and refused to join the rest of the cast in taking bows.

By 1975, Bonynge had gained considerable recognition as the most eminent contemporary authority on bel canto operas, and during that year he began conducting at the Metropolitan Opera and elsewhere on his own, without the presence of Sutherland. Although the Bonynges had spent increasing amounts of their free time at their villa in Switzerland—where they socialized with, among others, their neighbor Noel Coward—they purchased a house near Sydney after Bonynge was named musical director of the Sydney Opera, succeeding Edward Downes. Sutherland defended both her husband and herself, criticizing "aristocratic conductors who . . . [do not] understand music," and she added that when she and other women opera singers complained, "we are told sarcastically that we are behaving like prima donnas. I say, 'Long live prima donnas.'"

The decade of the 1970s marked the most active period of her career, as she journeyed around the globe for opera and concert performances. At age 50, she admitted to feeling a "little long in the tooth" for some roles, but her asking price for each appearance, estimated at between $5,000 and $10,000, made her one of the two most highly paid opera singers of the decade. She had become, claimed her husband, "the singer with the widest repertoire of any singer who has ever lived." Her international reputation had risen to the point that she could begin to become a mentor to lesser-known singers. One whom she "sponsored" in early recordings was the emerging tenor Luciano Pavarotti.

Sutherland chose to retire in 1990, making her final appearances in the Sydney Opera House in *Les Huguenots*, followed by a gala appearance at Covent Garden in which she sang duets with Pavarotti and *Marilyn Horne. In retirement, Sutherland found herself in demand as a judge in music contests around the globe, and her travel schedule was hardly diminished. Approaching her 70th birthday, she observed: "There is no sense of my being retired. Now my function in life appears to be that of judging how others sing, as opposed to being judged myself."

SOURCES:

Adams, Brian. *La Stupenda: A Biography of Joan Suther-land.* London: Hutchinson, 1980.

Braddon, Russell. *Joan Sutherland.* NY: St. Martin's Press, 1962.

Major, Norma. *Joan Sutherland.* Introduction by Dame Joan Sutherland. London: Queen Anne Press, 1987.

Sutherland, Joan. *A Prima Donna's Progress: The Autobi-ography of Joan Sutherland.* Washington, DC: Regnery, 1997.

SUGGESTED READING:

Bonynge, Richard. *Joan Sutherland and Richard Bonynge: With the Australian Opera.* Newark, NJ: Gordon & Breach, 1990.

Mackenzie, Barbara and Findlay. *Singers of Australia from Melba to Sutherland.* Melbourne: Lands-downe, 1967.

May, Robin. *A Companion to the Opera.* London: Lut-terworth, 1977.

Sutherland, Joan. *The Joan Sutherland Album.* Newark, NJ: Gordon & Breach, 1986.

COLLECTIONS:

Material relating to Sutherland is included in the Bonynge archives in Les Avants, Switzerland; in the archives of individual opera houses, particularly Covent Garden and the New York Metropolitan Opera; in the Sydney Opera House Trust Library; and in the archives of the BBC.

Niles Holt, Professor of History,
Illinois State University,
Normal-Bloomington, Illinois

Sutherland, Lucy Stuart (1903–1980)

Australian-born English historian and administrator. Name variations: Dame Lucy Sutherland. Born Lucy Stuart Sutherland in Geelong, Australia, on June 21, 1903; died at her home in Oxford, England, on August 20, 1980; daughter of Alexander Charles Suther-land (a mining engineer) and Margaret Mabel (Goddard) Sutherland; educated at Roedean School and the University of Witwatersrand in South Africa; graduat-ed from Somerville College, Oxford; never married.

Born in 1903 in Geelong, Australia, the only daughter of Alexander and **Margaret Goddard**

Sutherland, Lucy Stuart Sutherland spent most of her young life in South Africa. She attended the Roedean School in Johannesburg and later the University of Witwatersrand, where she earned a scholarship to Somerville College of Oxford University. In addition to her excellent scholarly work in history, in 1926 Sutherland became the first woman to address the Oxford Union in a speech supporting women's colleges. Upon graduating a year later, she accepted a po-sition as a tutor at Somerville, which led quickly to a tutorial fellowship.

Although a noted scholar of 18th-century history, Sutherland accepted a principalship in the Board of Trade in 1941, in the early years of World War II, rising to the rank of assistant sec-retary by 1945. She returned to Oxford in 1945 and was considered for the post of principal at both Somerville and Lady Margaret Hall, ac-cepting the latter. Sutherland found great satis-faction in this role as the school doubled in size under her administration, including the con-struction of several new buildings. Her promi-nence within the Oxford community increased when she became the pro-vice-chancellor of the university from 1961 to 1969, the first woman to assume such a position. Other British univer-sities recognized her accomplishments with hon-orary degrees. She retired in 1971.

Sutherland's historical interests focused pri-marily on prominent institutions in the 18th cen-tury. Her publications include *The East India Company in Eighteenth Century Politics* (1952) and a significant study of Oxford University dur-ing that time period, on which she worked during the last decade of her life. She also edited part of *The Correspondence of Edmund Burke* in 1960, and cooperated in the preparation of *History of Parliament.* Sutherland was named a Comman-der of the British Empire (CBE) in 1947, a Dame of the British Empire (DBE) in 1969, and received a fellowship at the British Academy in 1954. She died at her home on August 20, 1980.

SOURCES:

The Dictionary of National Biography, 1971–1980. Lord Blake and C.S. Nicholls, eds. Oxford: Oxford Uni-versity Press, 1986.

Jo Anne Meginnes, freelance writer,
Brookfield, Vermont

Sutherland, Margaret (1897–1984)

Australian composer. Born Margaret Ada Sutherland in Adelaide, South Australia, on November 20, 1897; died in Melbourne on August 12, 1984; daughter of Alice (Bowen) Sutherland and George Sutherland (leader writer on The Age); attended Marshall Hall

Conservatorium; married Dr. Norman Albiston, in 1926 (divorced 1948); children: two.

Selected works: Pavan (1938); Prelude and Jig *(1939);* Suite on a Theme of Purcell *(1939); Concertino (1939); Concerto (1945); Rondel (1945); Adagio (1946); Threesome (1947); Ballad Overature (1948); Bush Ballad (1950);* The Haunted Hills *(1950);* Open Air Piece *(1953);* Violin Concerto *(1954); Concerto Grosso (1955); Outdoor Overature (1958);* Three Temperaments *(1958); Movement (1959); Concertante (1961); Fantasy (1962).*

Margaret Sutherland's career documents what all composers, especially women, endure as they struggle to gain recognition. She was born in Adelaide, South Australia, in 1897. In 1914, she received a scholarship to study at the Marshall Hall Conservatorium. She also studied with Edward Goll and Fritz Hart, and the Belgian conductor and violinist Henri Verbrugghen provided opportunities for Sutherland to hear live music, particularly chamber music. When she was 19, he invited her to go to Sydney to perform Beethoven's G major Piano Concerto. In 1923, Sutherland went to Europe for further study with Arnold Bax in London. While there, she composed her Sonata for Violin and Piano which Bax considered the best he had ever heard written by a woman. After two years' study in London, Paris, and Vienna, she returned to Australia in 1925. Sutherland would struggle for the next four decades. There was little interest in new music in Australia, making it particularly difficult for her compositions to be heard. Friends arranged performances of her music at small gatherings in Melbourne. Sutherland married in 1926 and had two children. For the next decade, she taught at the Melbourne Conservatory as well as privately. She did not compose much during this time although she continued to perform in chamber groups.

In 1935, ten years after she wrote it, her Sonata for Violin and Piano was published. That same year, she completed *Suite on a Theme of Purcell,* a work that received many performances under the direction of George Szell. In 1937, she composed *Dithyramb.* String Quartet, *House Quartet, Pavan for Orchestra, The Soldier,* and *Prelude for Jig* followed. During World War II, Sutherland arranged mid-day concerts of works of modern Australian composers which were sponsored by the Red Cross. Although the Australian Broadcasting Company could have broadcast the concerts, they were ignored. As an active member of the Council for Education, Music, and the Arts, Sutherland worked tirelessly to reform music education in her country, which

she felt lacked creativity. In 1943, she determined to set aside land for the Victoria Arts Center, collecting over 40,000 signatures to implement the project. The Center was completed in 1982.

After Sutherland's divorce in 1948, she began a creative period in her life during which she composed nine orchestral works, twelve chamber works, a chamber opera, and many smaller pieces. Also that year, Boosey and Hawkes agreed to publish her Concerto for String Orchestra which she had submitted under the name "M. Sutherland." The offer was withdrawn, however, when the publisher discovered the "M." stood for Margaret. When this work was performed in 1958, *The Sydney Herald News* noted on February 17, "Another concerto for strings by Margaret Sutherland of Melbourne was not out of place in this august company." When her *Fantasy for Violin and Orchestra* did not win the Composers Competition Concert in Sydney in 1958, some were critical of the judges, as they considered hers to be "a far more finished and solidly inspired composition" than the winning piece. *The Haunted Hills,* which premiered in 1951, was recorded by the Melbourne Symphony Orchestra, as was her orchestral suite, *Three Temperaments,* composed in 1958. The Australian Broadcasting Company recorded 19 of Sutherland's orchestral and chamber works, although not all were widely available.

In the 1950s, Sutherland organized the Camerata Society, a chamber group dedicated to performing Australian music. It was no easy feat to assure that younger Australian composers would have an opportunity to have their music performed. In 1965, she collaborated with Lady **Maie Casey** on *The Young Kabbarli,* a chamber opera based on the life of *****Daisy May Bates,** a pioneer worker among the Aborigines. This work was the first Australian opera to be recorded in Australia. Toward the end of her life, Sutherland's compositions finally began to gain the recognition long denied her. At age 70, she received her first commission, and the University of Melbourne awarded her an honorary doctorate. At age 73, she was made an Officer of the British Empire Order. For her 75th birthday, a week of celebrations marked her accomplishments. During that celebration, Dr. H.C. Coombs, chair of the Australian Council for the Arts, noted: "Dr. Sutherland was one of the first practicing artists to proclaim the need for a unified vision of the arts. [She was] also in the very front ranks of those who ventured to be identified unequivocally as a modern Australian composer." Sutherland lived to be 87 and her contributions were increasingly recognized. Said James Murdock, "If

Alfred Hill is the Father of Australian music, then Margaret Sutherland is the Matriarch."

SOURCES:

LePage, Jane Weiner. *Women Composers, Conductors, and Musicians of the Twentieth Century.* Vol. III. Metuchen, NJ: Scarecrow, 1988, pp. 250–263.

John Haag, Associate Professor of History, University of Georgia, Athens, Georgia

Sutherland, Nellie (1864–1943).

See Glyn, Elinor.

Sutter, Linda (1941–1995).

See Messick, Dale for sidebar.

Suttner, Bertha von (1843–1914)

Austrian baroness whose antiwar novel Die Waffen Nieder! *became a bestseller in late 19th-century Europe, laying the basis for peace societies in central Europe and winning the Nobel Peace Prize for its author, the first woman so honored. Pronunciation: SOOT-ner. Name variations: Countess Kinsky; Baroness von Suttner. Born Bertha Felicie Sophie Kinsky in Prague on June 9, 1843; died on June 21, 1914; daughter of Count Franz Joseph Kinsky von Wehinitz and Tettau (a field marshal in the Austrian army) and Countess Sophie Wilhelmina Kinsky (the daughter of a cavalry captain); educated by governesses and relatives; married Baron Arthur von Suttner (1850–1902, a novelist), on June 12, 1876; no children.*

Served as private secretary to Alfred Nobel (1876); lived with husband in the Caucasus section of Russia (1876–85); published first major book, Das Maschinenzeitalter *(The Machine Age, spring 1889); published* Die Waffen Nieder! *(late 1889); co-founded the journal* Die Waffen Nieder! *with the pacifist Alfred Fried (1892), title changed to* Friedens-Warte *(1899); founded the Austrian Peace Society (1891); attended the Hague Peace Congresses (1899 and 1908); visited the United States, partly to secure funding for peace activities (1904 and 1911); won the Nobel Peace Prize (1905).*

Selected publications: Das Maschinenzeitalter *(Zurich: Verlags-Magazin, 1889);* Die Waffen Nieder! Eine Lebensgeschichte *(Dresden: E. Pierson, 1889, translated into English as* Lay Down Your Arms!, *1905);* Memoiren *(Stuttgart: Deutsche Verlags-Anstalt, 1901).*

During the late 19th century, when a German magazine asked its readers to name the most famous women of the age, second and third place went to two thespians: France's *Sarah Bernhardt and Italy's *Eleonora Duse. The winner,

however, was the Austrian Baroness Bertha von Suttner, whose antiwar novel *Die Waffen Nieder!* (*Lay Down Your Arms!*) would have an impact in Europe equivalent to the influence of *Harriet Beecher Stowe's *Uncle Tom's Cabin* in the United States. A bestseller in the late 19th century, *Die Waffen Nieder!* would, in 1905, move the Swedish committee to select her as the first woman to receive the Nobel Peace Prize.

Ironically, Bertha von Suttner had been born in 1843 into an Austrian family, the Kinskys, with a long history of military service. Although her father died before she was born, she was well aware of his long and distinguished service as a field marshal and member of the imperial cavalry in the Austrian army. Her mother's side of the family also featured a string of Austrian soldiers.

The young Bertha had a male guardian who was also a soldier. He was Friedrich, landgraf (count) of Fuerstenberg, whom she affectionately called "Fritzerl." A high civil servant, he was from one of the loftiest aristocratic families in Austria. He was also a devoutly religious man whom the adult Bertha remembered as someone who never failed to miss mass or a "church festival," but she also remembered him as someone who traveled little and never left the borders of Austria.

Although she was born into the ranks of privilege, von Suttner never felt at home among the Austrian nobility. In that highly stratified aristocracy, it was whispered that her mother's family ranked much lower than her father's. While her father's family, the Kinskys, traced their lineage back to Bohemian counts of the 12th century, that lineage was not ancient enough to position it among the most prestigious noble lines of the Austrian Empire. In her memoirs, von Suttner recalled frequently seeing her mother Countess **Sophie Wilhelmina Kinsky** sitting alone at social gatherings of the Austrian elite.

The young Bertha was taught by her mother to ignore such social pressures and to fulfill her life's ambitions in her own way. She remembered her mother's beautiful singing voice, but she also recalled her mother's bitterness that her own parents had not supported her desire to take singing lessons and become an opera singer.

Von Suttner's knowledge of the world outside Austria was greatly enlarged by her cousin, Elvira. Elvira and her mother, "Aunt Tante," came to live with the Kinskys when Bertha was 11. Elvira shared with Bertha her knowledge of Shakespeare, of the German historian Friedrich Hegel, and of the German philosopher Immanuel Kant. The foursome frequently traveled to Venice, Vienna, and Rome, and during these trips von Suttner would study music and Elvira would practice writing dramas and poems.

In one way, the trips proved a major influence on von Suttner. Aunt Tante and Sophie Kinsky, who shared a love of gambling, lost much of the family fortune in the casinos of Europe. Not only was Sophie reduced to living on a meager widow's pension, but there was now not enough money to provide a dowry for her daughter. Spinsterhood, a dreaded fate in late 19th-century Europe, loomed as a possibility. Although von Suttner was engaged twice, marriage did not result. The first was ended by the man's family, who considered Bertha too old for their son; the second engagement ended when her fiancé died of illness while aboard a ship at sea.

Prodded by her mother, Bertha sought employment as a governess and eventually accepted a position to the four daughters of the von Suttner family of Harmannsdorf, Austria. Although she was not asked to be governess to the family's two sons, one of the them, Arthur, was attracted to her, despite the fact that he was nearly eight years younger. Bertha gave him no encouragement, but when the young man's mother discovered him one night standing at the open door of Bertha's bedroom, talking with her, she insisted that Bertha give up the governess position and leave the household.

Seeking new employment, Bertha responded to an ad which appeared in a Viennese newspaper: "A very wealthy, cultured elderly gentlemen living in Paris, desires to find a lady of mature years, familiar with languages, as secretary to and manager to his household." The "elderly gentlemen" who placed the ad proved to be Alfred Nobel, the 43-year-old dynamite maker and magnate, who invited von Suttner to his Paris home for an interview and immediately hired her as head housekeeper and private secretary. She was intrigued by his personality, saying, "It was a rare pleasure to talk with him about the world and its people . . . as well as its problems."

Von Suttner was also impressed by Nobel's commitment to world peace, although she was less certain about his ideas on how to end war. Nobel insisted that it was "nonsense to demand immediate and total disarmament as a path of peace," since "the road to peace leads only through the graveyard." He lamented that "my explosives lack sufficient effectiveness to end war," and he predicted that war would not be abolished until "it is just as deadly for women and children as for troops at the front." Europe's armaments race would end only when the day

came that "any two army corps can destroy each other in a second."

Within a week of her arrival in Paris, she received a telegram from Arthur von Suttner proposing marriage. "I cannot live without you," it read. Bertha responded with an identical reply, and quickly returned to Austria. Since his family continued to oppose their marriage—Bertha was 33 and Arthur was 26—the couple decided to marry secretly, in a provincial chapel near Vienna.

Knowing that they were not going to be welcomed by his family, they decided to leave Austria, moving instead to the Caucasus section of Russia, near the border with the Ottoman Empire (Turkey). Bertha's family had friends in that area, and it was thought that one of them might secure for Arthur a position in the government of the Russian tsar, Alexander II. They settled in the Caucasus with "a mixture of adventurousness and hope."

The job never materialized, and Bertha and Arthur struggled to make a living; he gave German lessons to eager Russians, and she taught piano. When war broke out in 1877 between Russia and Turkey, Arthur discovered that Austrian newspapers would pay him for sending them letters about the war, written from the viewpoint of an Austrian who was actually living near the fighting. Eventually, he began to write full articles for pay, generally for both newspapers and magazines. Von Suttner helped her husband and, in time, began writing articles of her own.

In 1885, Arthur's parents asked the couple to come back to Austria. They returned, not as wayward children but as financially independent adults. But von Suttner found the atmosphere of the family mansion at Harmannsdorf to be stifling and dull. "I am no stranger to loneliness," she wrote, "but family life here is the most tedious imaginable." To pass the time, she continued her writing, and in early 1889 produced her first novel, *Das Maschinenzeitalter* (*The Machine Age*). It consisted of imaginary lectures by an observer, living in the future, who commented on conditions at the second half of the 19th century. In it, von Suttner—who listed her name as *Jemand* (German for *someone*) because she feared that potential readers might pass over a book written by a woman—criticized the narrowness of opinions in her time, as well as the exaggerated nationalisms, the double standards of morality for men and women, and the need to emancipate women from outdated conventions. The book set the tone for much of her subsequent writings, which she summarized as directed against the "enemies of mankind, brutality and lies."

To von Suttner, the topic of war was a logical one for her next novel. She had lived through, and remembered, wars in 1859 (Italy and Austria), 1864 (the German states and Denmark), 1866 (Austria and Prussia), and 1870–71 (France and Prussia). When she and Arthur occasionally journeyed to Paris to visit Alfred Nobel, she noticed the frequent talk of war with Germany. She became convinced that the German chancellor Otto von Bismarck was promoting talk of war with France as a way to convince the German Reichstag, a parliamentary body, to increase the military budget.

By the time *Das Maschinenzeitalter* appeared, she had already begun writing a novel entitled *Die Waffen Nieder!* (*Lay Down Your Arms!*). In her research for the novel, she read newspaper accounts of recent wars, interviewed veterans, and read government documents. The fact that the novel was told from the viewpoint of a suffering woman would prove to be the basis for much of its popular appeal. *Die Waffen Nieder!* described the experiences of a woman, Martha Althaus, during the wars of 1859, 1864, 1866, and 1870–71. Of aristocratic birth (like Bertha), Martha loses her first husband in the Italian-Austrian war of 1859. Lamenting the "uselessness of sacrificed lives," Martha sees her second husband, an Austrian army officer, go off to war with Prussia in 1866.

When, in a dream, she thinks that she hears him call for help, she wanders through the battlefields of Europe, looking for his body. This portion of the novel gave von Suttner the opportunity to describe graphically the aftermath of battles, including the piles of dead bodies. Suffering a nervous breakdown, Martha returns home, where she finds her husband, alive. The two commit themselves to fight for peace with the same vigor that soldiers pursued war. "Who takes up a mission and works for it, must give up his life for it, even if he realizes how little one person can be responsible for the success of a cause," von Suttner argued. The novel, in its conclusion, asserts that "when millions find satisfaction in seeing the triumph of peace, the fortifications of war will fall to pieces. Millions will join us."

Publisher after publisher rejected the novel. One wrote her that it was impossible to publish such an antiwar novel "in our military state." When the book was finally published, however, it was a quick success. Twelve editions appeared in the first six years, and it was quickly translated into eight European languages. Nobel wrote von Suttner that her book should appear "in 2,000 tongues and should be pub-

lished, read, and thought over in each one of them." He termed her an "Amazon who is vigorously waging war against war." When she moved to take advantage of the book's popularity by establishing an Austrian peace society in 1891, he sent her 2,000 francs and a completed membership application. The book also stimulated the formation of civic and regional peace societies in Germany.

In her continuing correspondence with Nobel, von Suttner worked to convince him to leave money in his will to establish a prize for individuals and organizations working for peace. Nobel had planned to leave money to reward significant scientific work, but he was intrigued by von Suttner's ideas and wrote asking her to "instruct me and convince me . . . and I will do great things for your movement." Von Suttner was the individual most responsible for convincing him to add a peace prize to his planned endowments.

By the time of *Die Waffen Nieder!*, von Suttner's pacifism had begun to diverge considerably from Nobel's conviction that an arms race might lead to peace and that his weapons would bring a more rapid end to war than her peace congresses. She maintained that military weapons always seem to acquire new lives, and their only purpose is to cause death. She sought a "new world order open to all national states." "Do not tell me," she proclaimed, "that a unified Europe is a mad dream; it is the only salvation." Her friend Alfred Fried observed that she could have lived a lazy life of luxury, but chose, instead, to brave ridicule as a "naive woman" because she thought that "peace is more important than any one government."

Die Waffen Nieder! made her a celebrity at international conferences and peace meetings, where she was at ease in dealing with European diplomats and generals. Only the Germans snubbed her, she complained. She also noted that "as a woman" she was frequently not invited to men-only dinners honoring other prominent pacifists of the day. Nevertheless, she became a prized speaker at the meetings of peace organizations.

Fried noted that she was often invited to speak not because of her speaking style, but because of her ideas and her sincerity. He reported that she spoke quite undramatically—in too low a voice, he said—but in a regal, almost matronly manner. He added, however, that he thought her "regal manner" was partly the result of her tendency, because of nearsightedness, to point her head slightly upward so that she could more easily read from her speaking notes.

Since women were forbidden by Austrian law to serve in the Austrian government, she chose, in the years from 1890 until her death, to become heavily involved in a variety of peace organizations and conferences, including the International Arbitration and Peace Society in London, founded in 1880 by Hogsdon Pratt; the War and Peace Museum in Lucerne, Switzerland, whose opening she attended with Arthur; the Berne Peace Congress of 1892; and the Interplanetary Union, which laid a basis for the later League of Nations. Together with Fried, she founded the pacifist journal *Die Waffen Nieder!*

in 1892; its name was changed to *Friedens-Warte* (Peace Watch) in 1899.

Although she attended both Hague Peace Conferences of 1899 and 1908, she complained that the agenda had been set by diplomats and professional military men. She called for a third conference which would exclude anyone who "profited from war" or whose career was related to war.

Arthur died in 1902. One of their last joint activities was the founding of the League against anti-Semitism. They had both been horrified by the Dreyfus Affair in France, in which a French

Bertha
von
Suttner

Jew, a military officer, had been accused of treason and imprisoned on Devil's Island. When they heard acquaintances make statements like "Dreyfus belongs on Devil's Island, and all the Jews along with him," they became convinced that the charges against Dreyfus were motivated by anti-Semitism rather than fact. Arthur ran the organization on a day-to-day basis, while Bertha wrote publicity for the organization in which she attacked prominent European anti-Semites such as the French Count Joseph de Gobineau and the German writer Houston Stewart Chamberlain. She accused them of being "superpatriots touting the superiority of a single race."

She especially regretted her husband's absence when, in 1905, a telegram arrived from Oslo, Norway. Since the telegram had "charges due," she dismissed the delivery man without accepting it. Having second thoughts, she immediately called him back, and read: "Dearest Madam: It is a great pleasure to inform you that at its session today the Nobel committee decided to honor you with its peace prize." She traveled to Oslo to receive the prize on April 18, 1906. In her address at the ceremony, she called for an international organization of nations to arrange for, and monitor, world peace, and for "international standards of behavior for nations."

Now an international celebrity, von Suttner visited the United States twice, in 1904 and (for a lecture tour) in 1911. She received the accolades of American President Theodore Roosevelt, a fellow Nobel laureate who told her, "World Peace is coming, without a doubt, it is coming." In turn, she praised "the wealth, the splendor, and the unbounded possibilities of the American nation." She returned to Europe with some of that wealth; the Carnegie Peace Foundation, founded by the industrial magnate Andrew Carnegie, awarded her a lifelong pension as a reward for her work for peace.

The early years of the 20th century alarmed her. She complained that the major European nations were involved in an arms race in which new weapons would be introduced purely for the purpose of terrorizing the enemy. In an article entitled "The Militarization of the Air," she warned that the newly invented airplane would become a weapon of terror, making women and children vulnerable to attack even if they were located well behind battle lines. She also saw the seeds of a terror weapon in scientific work on radium. While not anticipating the atomic bomb, she did warn that future wars would use "radium rays" which would have "terrible effects" on soldiers.

Her thoughts on future weapons were not the only area where she proved to be a prophet.

She worried about the continual wars, in the early years of the 20th century, between the new nations of the Balkan peninsula. She condemned the "cheap sentimentalism" of journalists and soldiers who found the Balkans Wars to be "fascinating and exhilarating." When she died in 1914, her death came less than ten days before the event that would start World War I—the assassination, in the Balkan city of Sarajevo, of the heir to the throne of her native Austria.

SOURCES:

Kempf, Beatrix. *Suffragette for Peace: The Life of Bertha von Suttner*. Trans. by R.W. Last. London: Oswald Wolff, 1972.

Lengyel, Emil. *And All Her Paths were Peace: The Life of Bertha von Suttner*. Nashville, TN: Thomas Nelson, 1975.

Suttner, Bertha von. *Memoiren*. Stuttgart: Deutsche Verlags-Anstalt, 1901.

SUGGESTED READING:

*Pauli, Hertha. *Cry of the Heart: The Story of Bertha von Suttner*. Trans. by Richard and Clara Winston. NY: Ives Washburn, 1957.

Playne, Caroline E. *Bertha von Suttner and the Struggle to Avert the World War*. London: George Allen & Unwin, 1936.

COLLECTIONS:

Many of the papers of Bertha von Suttner are held in the Library of the United Nations in Geneva, Switzerland. Much of her correspondence with Alfred Nobel is housed in the Nobel Foundation at Stockholm, Sweden.

Niles Holt, Professor of History, Illinois State University, Normal-Bloomington, Illinois

Sutton, Carol (1933–1985)

First woman to head the news staff of a major American daily newspaper (1974). Born June 29, 1933, in St. Louis, Missouri; died of cancer on February 19, 1985, in Louisville, Kentucky; graduated from University of Missouri School of Journalism (Columbia) in 1955; married Charles Whaley (a communications director); children: Carrie and Kate.

Hired as secretary at Courier-Journal *in Kentucky (1955), and within a year promoted to reporter; named editor of women's section (1963); became managing editor (1974); promoted to assistant to the publisher of* Courier-Journal *and* Louisville Times *(1976); was senior editor of* Courier-Journal *and* Louisville Times *(1979–85).*

Carol Sutton was born in 1933 in St. Louis, Missouri, and grew up in the area. Upon her 1955 graduation from the University of Missouri's School of Journalism in Columbia, she applied for a job as a reporter at the Louisville, Kentucky, *Courier-Journal*. She was offered a secretarial position instead, but she accepted it and earned a promotion to reporter before she had been there a year.

Although most women reporters in the 1950s found themselves relegated to covering stories on fashion and society, Sutton distinguished herself in a wide range of challenging topics, including natural disasters and politics. An innovative editor of the *Courier-Journal*'s women's section beginning in 1963, she renamed it "Today's Living" and included coverage of such crucial issues as poverty and abortion. When she was promoted to managing editor of the paper in 1974, she became the first woman in history to head the news staff of a major American daily, and *Time* magazine carried her photograph on its cover. In her new post, Sutton continued to demonstrate the intensity and integrity that had marked her successful stint as a reporter and section editor. In 1975, the *Courier-Journal*'s photographic coverage of a school desegregation crisis won the Pulitzer Prize. She became assistant to the publisher of the jointly operated *Courier-Journal* and *Louisville Times* in 1976, ascending to the position of senior editor of these two newspapers' separate editorial staffs in 1979. In this post, Sutton was instrumental in attracting minority reporters to her papers and became a role model to the next generation of women journalists.

In addition to serving as chair of the Pulitzer Prize juries from 1975 to 1976, Sutton was a member of the selection committee of Harvard University's Nieman Fellows journalism award. She died of cancer in Louisville on February 19, 1985, age 51.

SOURCES:
The New York Times Biographical Service. February 1985.
Read, Phyllis J., and Bernard L. Witlieb. *The Book of Women's Firsts.* NY: Random House, 1992.

Jo Anne Meginnes, freelance writer,
Brookfield, Vermont

Sutton, May (1887–1975)

American tennis champion who was the youngest national champion in history before Mo Connolly, and Wimbledon's first foreign champion. Name variations: *May Sutton Bundy. Born May Godfray Sutton in Plymouth, England, on September 25, 1887 (some sources wrongly cite 1886); died on October 4, 1975, in Santa Monica, California; youngest of seven children of Adolphus Sutton (a British naval officer); sister of tennis players Ethel Sutton, Adele Sutton, Florence Sutton, and Violet Sutton; married Thomas Bundy (a tennis star), in 1912; children: four, three sons and daughter Dorothy Bundy Cheney (also a tennis player).*

Won U.S. singles championship (1904 and 1907); won Wimbledon championship (1905 and 1907).

Once referred to as the grand dowager of tennis, May Sutton was born in 1887 in Plymouth, England, and came to the United States on her father's sailboat when she was six. She grew up in Pasadena, California, on a ten-acre ranch. Her other sisters—**Ethel, Adele, Florence,** and **Violet Sutton**—were all avid tennis players, battling each other daily on the family's clay court, prompting the later comment, "It takes a Sutton to beat a Sutton." Between 1899 and 1915, every singles title in the Southern California championships was claimed by a Sutton sister. Adele and Florence would play well into advanced age.

In 1900, at age 13, May won the Southern California Women's championship. Four years later, she won the Women's Singles at the U.S. National championships, without losing a set. At 17, she would hold the record as the youngest national champion in history until **Maureen Connolly* began her reign at age 16 in 1951. In 1905, Sutton became the first American to win Wimbledon, beating the ever-graceful British champion **Dorothea Lambert Chambers* on Centre Court. In 1906, in a repeat matchup, Chambers took the title. The following year, Sutton beat Chambers once more for another Wimbledon championship.

The intense, square-jawed Sutton was an aggressive opponent with a topspin forehand, writes **Billie Jean King* in *You Have Come a Long Way:* "May did not look like the former champions and she did not play like them, either. Instead of slicing the ball on her forehand side with an open racket face, May pounded it. . . . Unlike her eastern counterparts, [she] dressed for the game, not the show. Her dresses hung just above her ankles, and the sleeves of her oversize shirts (some thought they belonged to her father) were pushed up to the elbows to allow her freedom of movement. Although most women were wearing only loose-fitting corsets at that time, it is questionable whether May, at 160 pounds, wore any kind of corset at all."

In 1912, Sutton married National Men's Doubles champion Thomas Bundy. Their daughter ⚘➤ **Dorothy Bundy Cheney** would become the first American woman to win the Australian championship (1938). After time off to raise a family, May Sutton returned to the game in 1921, still ranked 4th in the country. At age 41, she once again played at Wimbledon and made it to the singles semifinals before losing. Sutton turned professional in 1930 and devoted the next 34 years to teaching.

Barbara Morgan,
Melrose, Massachusetts

*See sidebar
on the
following page*

❧▶ Cheney, Dorothy Bundy (1917—)

American tennis player. Name variations: Dodo. *Born in 1917; daughter of *May Sutton (1887–1975) and Thomas Bundy (both tennis players).*

Ranked sixth in the world in 1946, Dorothy Cheney won 11 straight Women's Hard Court Singles titles between 1957 and 1967 and has won over 170 national senior championships. At age 80, she received the Southern California Tennis Association Lifetime Achievement Award.

Suyin, Han (b. 1917).

See Han Suyin.

Suzanne of Bavaria (1502–1543)

Margravine of Brandenburg. Born on April 2, 1502; died on April 23, 1543; daughter of Albert IV the Wise (1447–1508), duke of Bavaria (r. 1465–1508); married Casimir, margrave of Brandenburg, on August 24, 1518; children: Marie of Brandenburg-Kulmbach (b. 1519).

Suzanne of Bourbon (1491–1521).

See Louise of Savoy for sidebar.

Suze, Henriette de Coligny, comtesse de la (1618–1683).

See Coligny, Henriette de.

Suzman, Helen (1917—)

South African parliamentary opponent of apartheid who championed human rights and the rule of law. Pronunciation: Sooz-man. Born Helen Gavronsky on November 7, 1917, in Germiston, South Africa; daughter of Samuel Gavronsky (a self-made businessman) and Frieda (David) Gavronsky; educated at St. George's School, Parktown Convent, and University of the Witwatersrand (B.Commerce, 1941); married Moses Meyer (Mosie) Suzman (a physician), on August 13, 1937; children: Frances Suzman; Patricia Suzman.

Elected to South African Parliament (March 1953); retired from Parliament (June 1989), age 71.

Writings: (memoirs) In No Uncertain Terms (Jonathan Ball, 1993).

Helen Suzman was born in a small mining town ten miles southeast of Johannesburg, in South Africa's Transvaal, on November 7, 1917, the day of the Russian Revolution. Her father had emigrated to South Africa from a *shtetl* (vil-

lage) on the border of Lithuania and Latvia. She was educated at non-Jewish schools in Johannesburg, to which the family moved, but remained a member of the Jewish community. Her major subjects at the University of the Witwatersrand were economics and economic history, and after the birth of her daughters, she agreed to return to the University to teach in its economic history department, first as a tutor and then as a temporary lecturer.

Her study of economic history, and especially of the implications of the country's migrant labor system, on which she collected material which was submitted to the government-appointed Native Laws Commission by the South African Institute of Race Relations, encouraged her to make politics her career, to help bring about a more just economic and political order.

After the shocking defeat of the United Party (UP) in the 1948 general election, Suzman became increasingly active in organizing for the party in northern Johannesburg and in its Women's Council. She first came to public attention in 1952 as a leading figure in Women's Action, an organization to mobilize women against the Nationalist government. Later that year, she agreed, somewhat reluctantly, given her family responsibilities and job, to stand for nomination for the parliamentary seat of Houghton, a safe UP constituency which embraced the most prosperous of Johannesburg's northern suburbs. She won the nomination, in part because of her honesty in saying that she did not know the answer to certain questions put to her, and in the 1953 general election was returned as a member of the House of Assembly.

Suzman was member of Parliament (MP) for Houghton from 1953 to 1989. As Parliament met in Cape Town, she had to stay there for up to six months each year, though her home remained in Hyde Park, Johannesburg. As an opposition member, she believed her main role was to hold the government to account. In the particular circumstances of South Africa at that time, she used the platform which Parliament provided to speak out against the horrors of apartheid, to draw public attention to those horrors, and to try to help its victims. She also campaigned on behalf of women's rights: her first speech in Parliament, where for six years she was the only woman among 166 MPs, was in the debate on the Matrimonial Affairs Bill, an early milestone on the road to legal equality for women. She continued to fight for such equality, making major contributions in Parliament in 1975, 1984, and 1988, and pleading for the participation of more women at the first meeting of the Convention for a Democratic South Africa (CODESA) in 1991.

In her early years in Parliament, this small, attractive, vivacious woman joined the small group of UP MPs who sought to wean the party away from support for social and political segregation. Like others on the liberal wing of the party, she found herself waging constant battles against conservatives in the party caucus. The UP opposed separate education for Africans, the removal of Africans from the western areas of Johannesburg, and the further entrenchment of the policy of reserving certain jobs for whites, but was often hesitant to criticize the National Party (NP) government. Suzman's first act of defiance came when the party in 1953 initially supported the Separate Amenities Bill, which provided for racial segregation in public places. After the UP lost the 1958 general election, she and other liberal MPs were blamed for the party's defeat, and the new leader of the party aligned himself with its conservative majority.

At the 1959 party congress in Bloemfontein, Suzman was one of the group of MPs who resigned from the UP in disgust when it voted against the grant of more land to Africans. This group then formed a new party, the Progressive Party (PP), which opposed racial segregation root and branch and stood for a democratic political order, though in its early years one which included the old idea of a qualified color-blind franchise. In those years, it gained a small black membership, but because of legislation passed in 1968 it was forced to become a whites-only party. To those who called upon it then to dissolve itself, it argued that it should continue to work for nonracialism even if it could have no black members.

In 1959, the PP MPs immediately came under pressure to resign their seats and fight elections for the new party. It was clear, however, that few if any would win such elections, and so they all agreed not to resign. Suzman found herself one of an initial 12 members of the new party in Parliament. When a general election was fought in 1961, she was the only one to be returned to Parliament, thanks to a superb election campaign in her Houghton constituency. Her majority was only 564 votes. In the further general elections of 1966 and 1970, she was also the only member of her party to be returned. For 13 years, she was the only Progressive MP.

These were Suzman's most testing and finest years. At this time, it came to be said of her that she was in effect the entire parliamentary opposition, for the feeble UP offered little or no resistance as many key apartheid laws were enacted, and Suzman was left to battle alone. A journalist, asked in the mid-1960s for proof that South Africa was not a police state, replied that the proof was the English-language press and Helen Suzman.

In Parliament, she was called a "communist" and "saboteur" and not infrequently subjected to anti-Semitic and sexist remarks. Only someone as tough as she was could have continued and could have won the respect even of some of her bitterest opponents. In her memoirs, she calls her chief enemies, the three prime ministers H.F. Verwoerd, John Vorster and P.W. Botha, "as nasty a trio as you could encounter in your worst nightmares." She was in the House of Assembly when Verwoerd was stabbed to death by a parliamentary messenger in 1966; in a fit of rage, P.W. Botha, then a minister, turned on her and blamed her for the assassination. She continued to infuriate Botha, who in 1972 said she represented "all those people who break laws and want to banish order."

Whenever I am downhearted and depressed at the course of events in South Africa, I have only to think of Helen Suzman and of all she has done and endured and achieved to feel a resurgence of confidence, determination and faith.

—Harry Oppenheimer

There was a certain irony in the fact that a regime so authoritarian as the NP had enough respect for the parliamentary system that it allowed Suzman to oppose to the extent that she did. Perhaps being a woman helped her sometimes to get her way, though she was to say that she did not think it did. But above all it was her sheer tenacity and determination, along with her patent integrity and honesty, which enabled her to achieve so much. Her spirit was caught in the title she chose for the memoirs she wrote in her retirement: *In No Uncertain Terms*.

As Parliament in the worst years of apartheid became little more than a rubber stamp for the government, Suzman used the tradition of question time to expose as much as she could of what the government was doing. During each session of Parliament, she asked on average about 200 questions, far more than anyone else. In her hundreds of speeches, always incisive and clear, her special targets were the injustices of migrant labor, forced removals, and the Group Areas Act.

Her training in economics gave her an excellent grasp of fiscal issues. No one in Parliament argued more forcefully that the continuation of apartheid was incompatible with economic growth. No one argued more ably that apartheid was not only a crime but also an economic blunder. She never had any sympathy for the socialist solutions advanced by extra-parliamentary anti-apartheid groups on the extreme left: she continued to believe in the merits of a market-driven economy, and enjoyed close and cordial relations with Harry Oppenheimer of the Anglo American Corporation and other representatives of big business.

Though Suzman never stopped an apartheid act from being enacted, for decades her presence in Parliament and her voice of protest represented a spark of hope amid darkness for many people. That she continued to express liberal views and defend liberal values from the platform of Parliament helped keep those values alive, until they revived as apartheid began to fall apart.

Suzman enjoyed a close relationship with her constituents, and Houghton once again became a safe seat as her electorate increasingly recognized the value of the role she was playing. After every parliamentary session, she presented a full report back on her work and an assessment of the current scene. But she also saw herself as having a wider constituency, embracing the great majority who because of apartheid were not represented in Parliament, and she championed human rights outside as well as inside the walls of Parliament.

At the time of the 1960 post-Sharpeville state of emergency, she paid her first visit to a jail to see how political prisoners were being treated, and after that she made such visits to jails whenever she could. She was highly critical of the "90 day" detention law which Vorster pushed through Parliament in the early 1960s. Towards the end of that decade, she visited some of the areas from which Africans were being forcibly removed, because of the government's influx control and Bantustan policies, then raised the issue in Parliament. In 1967, she made the first of her visits to the political prisoners on Robben Island, a visit which led directly to an improvement in conditions in the prison. She met Nelson Mandela on average once every four years after that, and continued to press for his release from jail. Suzman also visited his wife three times when **Winnie Madikizela-Mandela** was banished to the Orange Free State.

In September 1977, Suzman attended the funeral of Steve Biko of the Black Consciousness movement, and the following March was asked to speak at the funeral of Robert Sobukwe of the Pan Africanist Congress. In attending these memorial services, she expressed her solidarity with those struggling against apartheid and her protest against the measures taken by the government to silence leaders of the black majority. She was a strong opponent of the new tricameral constitution of 1983, primarily because it excluded the African majority.

It was not until the 1974 general election that she was once again joined in Parliament by other Progressives, when six others were elected, to her immense satisfaction. With colleagues to help her, Suzman took a less prominent role. Not a strategist, and never officially leader of her party, she worked well as part of a team and never sought the leadership, though she remained the best-known and most revered Progressive. In 1975, her party merged with a break-away from the UP and became the Progressive Reform Party, later the Progressive Federal Party (PFP). In 1977, it replaced the UP as the official (largest) opposition.

Because she believed that Parliament provided an important platform for attacking government policy, she found it difficult to forgive the brilliant Frederick van Zyl Slabbert, the PFP leader, when in February 1986 he suddenly decided to resign from Parliament and the party. The following year the far-right Conservative Party took over as the official opposition. Shortly before Suzman retired from Parliament, there was yet another merger, when the Progressives were absorbed in a new Democratic Party (DP). Initially, she had mixed feelings about the new party, for she did not like the way the merger took place, but after her retirement she continued to work for the DP and served on its delegation to CODESA, the multiparty negotiating forum, in December 1991.

From the late 1970s, measures began to be passed for which she had long campaigned, including the lifting of restrictions on African trade unions in 1979; the abolition of the pass laws in 1986; and the improvement of prison conditions. And gradually she won praise even from Nationalists for her parliamentary skills, her debating ability and witty repartee across the floor of the House, and for advocating policies which they eventually took over. After her retirement, her portrait was hung in the corridors of Parliament, the only non-Cabinet minister to be so honored. The eminent historian **Phyllis Lewsen** has with justice called her South Africa's greatest parliamentarian.

A woman of great political courage, Helen Suzman stuck to what she believed. Having bat-

Helen
Suzman

tled apartheid ideologues for so long, in the 1980s she found herself opposed from a different quarter, when Archbishop Desmond Tutu and many Africans condemned her opposition to sanctions. She insisted on taking a firm stand against economic sanctions and divestment from South Africa, arguing that such measures would not help those they were intended to help. Instead, they would increase unemployment and poverty and destroy the economy. By pulling out of the country, American business would, she said, lose its positive influence. Nor did she believe that such measures would help end apartheid. In the event, however, while the economy was probably damaged less than she feared, economic measures, and in particular financial sanctions, did play a major role in forcing the government to change course at the end of the 1980s.

While vilified by the government in South Africa, she began to receive high honors abroad for her fight for human dignity and civil rights in her country. In June 1973, Oxford University made her a honorary doctor of civil laws, and many other universities granted her similar honors. In 1980, she received the Medal of Honor from the mayor of New York City, and in 1983 an award by the International League of Human Rights. Of South Africans of this century, only General Jan Smuts, Archbishop Tutu, and Nelson Mandela were more honored internationally. Yet she remained modest about her achievements and was happy to be known simply as "Helen."

Her critics on the left said that by serving in Parliament she helped legitimize the system, and some called on her and other Progressives to walk out. She was even on occasion lumped with other whites as part of the white minority oppressive regime. Her totally convincing reply was that she used the parliamentary process to expose the injustices of apartheid and to try to keep alive democratic values. Nelson Mandela, in a foreword for her memoirs, said that her role in opposing apartheid had to be applauded.

Well groomed and elegant, and a sparking conversationalist, Helen Suzman remained active in public life in retirement. She had often lectured abroad about her country, and she continued to do this. She collected more awards—perhaps most notably, she was invested as a Dame of the British Empire by Queen *Elizabeth II in October 1989, the only foreign citizen to be so honored. Suzman served as president of the Institute of Race Relations from 1990, her memoirs were published to considerable acclaim in 1993, and at the end of that year she was appointed a member of the vitally important Independent Electoral Commission, which Parliament set up to oversee the April 1994 general election and ensure that it was free and fair.

SOURCES:
Lee, R., ed. *Values Alive: A Tribute to Helen Suzman.* Johannesburg: Jonathan Ball, n.d. [1990].
Lewsen, P., ed. *Helen Suzman: The Solo Years.* Johannesburg: Jonathan Ball and A.D. Donker, 1991.
Strangewayes-Booth, J. *A Cricket in the Thorn Tree: Helen Suzman and the Progressive Party.* Johannesburg: Hutchinson, 1976.
Suzman, Helen. *In No Uncertain Terms.* Johannesburg: Jonathan Ball, 1993.

SUGGESTED READING:
Slabbert, F. van Zyl. *The Last White Parliament.* Johannesburg: Jonathan Ball and Hans Strydom, 1985.
Swart, R. *Progressive Odyssey.* Cape Town: Human and Rousseau, 1991.

COLLECTIONS:
Suzman papers are in the University of the Witwatersrand Library, Johannesburg.

Christopher Saunders,
Associate Professor in History,
University of Cape Town,
Cape Town, South Africa

Svartz, Helga (1890–1964).

See Martinson, Moa.

Svetla, Caroline (1830–1899)

Czech author and feminist who was one her nation's most influential writers in the 19th century. Name variations: Karolina Svetla or Karolína Světlá; Johanna Mužáková or Johanna Muzakova; Johanna Rotová. Born Johanna Rotová on February 24, 1830, in Prague; died on September 7, 1899; married Petr Mužák (a teacher).

Selected writings: The Cross by the Stream *(1868);* A Village Novel *(1869).*

Caroline Svetla, the pseudonym of Johanna Rotová, was born into the family of a wealthy German-Czech merchant in Prague in 1830. She married fellow Czech patriot and teacher Petr Mužák—taking her name from his home village of Světlá—but apparently had more in common with influential Czech writer Jan Neruda, whose lover she became later in life. Like Neruda, in the 1860s and 1870s Svetla was a prominent member of the Máj circle of Czech writers, led by **Karen Hynek Mácha**, who sought to create a revolutionary literature based on their own liberal views and political nationalism.

Svetla first published her writings in Máj journals, and she devoted much of her career to composing tales of the Prague middle class or stories about the rural lifestyle of those living in the mountains of northern Bohemia. Referring to Svetla as a "strong and even austere moralist, an ardent patriot, a feminist, a liberal thinker, a lover of the mountains and simple peasants," the *Columbia Dictionary of Modern European Literature* suggests a comparison with George Eliot (*Mary Anne Evans**). However, critics of her work among the next generation of Czech writers found it excessively romantic and didactic, especially its unrealistic and artificial plots that often involved conflicted young women. Her stories about the inhabitants of the Ještěd Mountains enjoyed wide readership nevertheless. Later generations of critics perceived an underlying complexity to her writing, recognizing that she used the well-preserved folklore and customs of this region as a backdrop to contemporary moral problems. For example, as noted by Claire Buck, in Svetla's popular novel of 1868, *The Cross by the Stream*, an intelligent village girl tries to expiate a family curse by subduing an aristocratic brute, thus signifying that servitude was needless. From a literary perspective, critics tend to consider *A Village Novel*, written in 1869, as her most successful work. In it, according to the *Reader's Encyclopedia of Eastern European Literature*, three women attempt to shape the ideal man. The man's wife represents "pagan materialism," his lover "pure emotion, Nature, Protestantism," and his mother "reason, severe Catholicism." The mother wins and the man earns the respect of his community at the expense of his mental and emotional well-being.

In her later years, Svetla wrote political stories about the revolutions of 1848. She also founded the first serious Czech women's association, the Women's Work Club, in 1871. Four years later, she suffered from nearly total blindness and, for the remainder of her life, had to dictate her work to a niece. Credited with introducing poetic realism to Czech literature, Svetla is regarded as the most influential female Czech prose writer of the 19th century after *Božena Němcová. She died in Prague in 1899.

SOURCES:
Buck, Claire, ed. *The Bloomsbury Guide to Women's Literature*. NY: Prentice Hall, 1992.
Columbia Dictionary of Modern European Literature. Horatio Smith, gen. ed. NY: Columbia University Press, 1947.
Pynsent, Robert B., ed. *Reader's Encyclopedia of Eastern European Literature*. NY: HarperCollins, 1993.
Wilson, Katharina M., ed. *An Encyclopedia of Continental Women Writers*. NY: Garland, 1991.

Jo Anne Meginnes, freelance writer, Brookfield, Vermont

Svilova, Elizaveta (1900–1975)

Soviet filmmaker. Born in 1900; died in 1975; married Dziga Vertov (d. 1954), a documentary filmmaker.

Member of the Kino-eye group; collaborated on Vertov's films Man with a Movie Camera *(1929),* Enthusiasm *(1930), and* Three Songs of Lenin *(1934); won Stalin Prize for her 1946 film* Fascist Atrocities.

Selected films: About Transport *(1939);* They Learn at the Collective Farms *(1939);* The Roof of the World *(1940);* The Chusovaia River *(1940);* The Oath of the Young *(1943);* Born by the Storm *(1945);* The Parade of the Youth *(1946);* Fascist Atrocities *(1946);* People's Trial *(1946);* The Slavonic Congress in Belgrade *(1947).*

Elizaveta Svilova, a film editor in post-tsarist Russia, was the wife and uncredited collaborator of Dziga Vertov, the man considered the "father" of Soviet documentary. Svilova and Vertov were both members of the influential Kino-eye group, dedicated to a formalist technique of film editing known as Soviet montage. Svilova and other montage theorists explored the way film cutting could reconstruct and reinterpret reality, experimenting with the ways editing could create new meanings by the use of close-ups, angles, movement within the frame, light and shade, and film speed. Svilova's interests lay in reediting documentary footage, much like *Esther Shub. She believed that "documentary material is life" and perceived the traditional narrative fictional film as constrained by leaden theatrical conventions, in stark contrast to the vivid immediacy of the proletarian newsreel.

Svilova's work as editor, assistant, and co-director in collaboration with Vertov produced such classic documentaries as 1929's *Man with a Movie Camera*, a landmark in experimental cinema. The film chronicles one day in the life of a movie cinematographer, played by Vertov's brother Mikhail Kaufman, as he photographs life in the city. The creative team of Vertov, Kaufman and Svilova, who also performed in the film, was known within their circle as "The Council of Three." Other famous and important films directed by Vertov with the help of Svilova include *Enthusiasm* (1930) and *Three Songs of Lenin* (1934).

During a period of unemployment in the 1930s, Vertov relied on Svilova's work as a film editor to support them until they once again found employment together as documentarists. At the same time, Svilova created her own important films, including the 1946 film *Fascist Atrocities* which garnered her the Stalin Prize for editing. *Fascist Atrocities* was actually used as evidence in the Nuremberg trials, the proceedings of which Svilova covered in another film, *People's Trial* (1946). From her husband's death in 1954 until her own in 1975, Svilova was active in the publication and dissemination of his theoretical work, maintaining archival prints of Vertov's work and ensuring that his legacy—unlike hers—would not be forgotten.

SOURCES:
Foster, Gwendolyn A., ed. *Women Film Directors: An International Bio-Critical Dictionary*. Westport, CT: Greenwood, 1995.

Paula Morris, D.Phil., Brooklyn, New York

Svolou, Maria (d. 1976)

Greek feminist, Communist, and anti-Nazi activist during World War II. Died in 1976; married Alexander Svolous (a law professor).

Editor of magazine Woman's Struggle; sent into exile for political views (1936–40, 1948); twice elected member of Parliament representing Greek Leftist Party.

At a young age, Maria Svolou became an active member of the women's movement in Greece. She worked tirelessly for feminist causes in the role of secretary of the League for Women's Rights, writing and campaigning about the inequality experienced by Greek women, fighting against prostitution, and advocating the creation of evening schools for working women. As inspector of labor in the Ministry of Economics, Svolou was able to draw attention to the poverty of many working-class women and the abysmal standards of their housing and working conditions.

In addition to her feminist activism, Svolou was an outspoken advocate of the peace movement and, from 1911 to 1936, was in the forefront of anti-fascist politics. As editor of the magazine *Woman's Struggle*, Svolou was a social commentator who lectured on the important issues of the day. This public expression of her left-wing politics resulted in exile. She and her husband, law professor Alexander Svolous, were driven out of Greece from 1936 to 1940 during General Ioannis Metaxa's dictatorship.

In 1940, Svolou returned to public service in Greece, working as a volunteer nurse during the Greek-Albanian War and then in the Red Cross, organizing communal meals for needy children suffering under German occupation during World War II. Her anti-fascist beliefs inspired her to join the resistance movement, and she spent a year as a member of the National Council, the independent government convened in the mountains of free Greece. The end of German occupation was followed by civil war in Greece. Svolou's Communist sympathies again resulted in exile in 1948. Upon her return, however, she was twice elected member of Parliament for the Greek Leftist Party, and served as a member of its Central Committee.

SOURCES:

Uglow, Jennifer S., comp. and ed. *The International Dictionary of Women's Biography.* NY: Continuum, 1982.

SUGGESTED READING:

Hart, Janet. *New Voices in the Nation: Women and the Greek Resistance, 1941–1964.* Ithaca, NY: Cornell University Press, 1996.

Paula Morris, D.Phil.,
Brooklyn, New York

Swain, Clara A. (1834–1910)

American medical missionary to India who founded the first hospital for women there. Born Clara Swain on July 18, 1834, in Elmira, New York; died on December 25, 1910, in Castile, New York; tenth and youngest child of John Swain and Clarissa (Seavey) Swain; attended public schools in Castile, New York, Female Seminary in Canandaigua, New York, and Castile Sanitarium; graduated from the Woman's Medical College of Pennsylvania, 1869; never married; no children.

Clara Swain was born in 1834 in Elmira, New York, and grew up in Castile, in the Genesee River Valley. After taking her teaching certificate, she spent her early 20s working in area schools. In 1865, following a three-year course of medical training at the deeply spiritual Castile Sanitarium, run by Dr. **Cornelia A. Greene**, Swain began medical study at the Woman's Medical College of Pennsylvania in Philadelphia. After graduating in 1869, Swain responded to an appeal for a woman to undertake medical care and instruction for girls in an orphanage and women in seclusion in Bareilly, northwest India. Recommended and endorsed by her instructors, Swain was sponsored by the Woman's Foreign Missionary Society of the Methodist Episcopal Church. She sailed for India on November 3, 1869, along with another Methodist, *Isabella Thoburn, arriving in Bareilly on January 20, 1870. In an effort to both recruit assistants and educate local women about medical concerns specific to women, she began lectures in anatomy, physiology, and materia medica to a class of 17, 14 from the orphanage and 3 young married women. In three years, 13 had passed the exams allowing them to practice in "all ordinary diseases."

In 1871, the Nawab of Rampore donated the land located next to the Methodist Mission in Bareilly for the building of a women's hospital. A dispensary was completed on this site in May 1873 and the first women's hospital in India was opened in January 1874, designed so that women in seclusion could come without breaking caste rules. Overworked, Swain returned to Castile in 1876 to recover her health, but in 1879, even though she was still less than robust, she went back to Bareilly. At the request of Rajputana, the rajah of Khetri, in 1885 Swain became the court appointed physician for his wife, the rani, and the women of his palace. She continued in this position for the remainder of her time in India, interrupted only by a visit to the States on furlough in 1888. In 1896, Swain retired from active missionary service and returned to her family home in Castile, New York. In 1907–08, during the Jubilee Celebration of the Methodist mission to India, Swain returned for an extended visit. She spent her last years in Castile at the home of **Mary T. Greene**, niece and successor of Cornelia Greene, and died there on Christmas Day, 1910. Recognized as the first female missionary physician to minister especially to woman and children, Swain not only established better health care for women in India but also provided them with educational and employment opportunities as well. The Clara Swain Hospital, greatly enlarged and now open to women and men, is still operating in Bareilly.

SOURCES:
Hoskins, Robert. *Mrs. Clara A. Swain, M.D., First Medical Missionary to the Women of the Orient.* Boston, MA: Woman's Foreign Missionary Society of the Methodist Episcopal Church, 1912.

Wilson, Dorothy Clarke. *Palace of Healing: The Story of Dr. Clara Swain, First Woman Missionary Doctor, and the Hospital She Founded.* NY: McGraw-Hill, 1968.

SUGGESTED READING:
Swain, Clara A. *A Glimpse of India.* Women in American Protestant religion, 1800–1930 series. NY: Garland, 1987.

COLLECTIONS:
Some papers relating to Swain's mission, including a copy of her manuscript *A Glimpse of India*, which represents the bulk of her letters from India, are housed in the Schlesinger Library of Radcliffe College.

Amanda Carson Banks,
Vanderbilt Divinity School,
Nashville, Tennessee

Swallow, Ellen Henrietta (1842–1911).

See Richards, Ellen Henrietta.

Swanborough, Baroness (1894–1971).

See Isaacs, Stella.

Swan of Lichfield (1742–1809).

See Seward, Anna.

Swanson, Gloria (1897–1983)

Silent film star whose lasting legacy was her outsized performance as the ex-movie queen in the 1950 classic Sunset Boulevard. *Born Gloria May Josephine Swenson on March 27, 1897 (though her autobiography claims 1899), in Chicago, Illinois; died on April 4, 1983; daughter of Adelaide (Klanowski) Swenson and Joseph Theodore Swenson; married Wallace Beery (an actor), in 1916 (divorced 1919); married Herbert K. Somborn, in 1920 (divorced 1925); married Henri, Marquis de la Falaise de la Coudraye, in 1925 (divorced 1930); married Michael Farmer (an Irish*

sportsman), on August 16, 1931 (divorced 1934); married William N. Davey (an investment broker), in 1945 (divorced 1945); married William Dufty, in 1976; children: (second marriage) **Gloria Somborn Anderson** *(b. 1920); (fourth marriage)* **Michele Farmer** *(b. 1932); (adopted) Joseph Swanson.*

Made first film (1914); made first film in which she was billed by name, The Fable of Elvira and Farina and the Meal Ticket *(1915); gave other notable performances in* The Danger Girl *(1916), in which she drove a racing car and did her own stunts,* Teddy at the Throttle *(1917), in which she was tied to a railroad track and slipped into a hole between the rails at the last moment while a steam train rolled over her,* Shifting Sands *(1918), an anti-German propaganda film during World War I,* Don't Change Your Husband *(1919), the first of her films directed by Cecil B. De Mille,* Beyond the Rocks, *which co-starred Rudolph Valentino,* Madame Sans-Gêne *(1925), the first American feature film shot abroad on location (in France),* The Love of Sunya *(1927), the first film she produced,* Sadie Thompson *(1928), source of one of her many run-ins with the censorious Hays Office but also of her first Oscar nomination,* The Trespasser *(1929), her first talkie, in which she also sang songs, and source of her second Oscar nomination,* Father Takes a Wife *(1941), her only film between 1934 and 1950—a commercial failure,* Sunset Boulevard *(1950), her masterpiece, which unwittingly traced her own fall from silent star; published her autobiography* Swanson on Swanson *(1980).*

Selected filmography: appeared in many film shorts (1915–17); made at least 70 films, including Society for Sale *(1918);* Her Decision *(1918);* You Can't Believe Everything *(1918);* Everywoman's Husband *(1918);* Shifting Sands *(1918);* Station Content *(1918);* Secret Code *(1918);* Wife or Country *(1918);* Don't Change Your Husband *(1919);* For Better for Worse *(1919);* Male and Female *(1919);* Why Change Your Wife? *(1920);* Something to Think About *(1920);* The Great Moment *(1921);* The Affairs of Anatol *(1921);* Under the Lash *(1921);* Don't Tell Everything *(1921);* Her Husband's Trademark *(1922);* Beyond the Rocks *(1922);* Her Gilded Cage *(1922);* The Impossible Mrs. Bellew *(1922);* My American Wife *(1923);* (cameo) Hollywood *(1923);* Prodigal Daughters *(1923);* Bluebeard's Eighth Wife *(1923);* Zaza *(1923);* The Humming Bird *(1924);* A Society Scandal *(1924);* Manhandled *(1924);* Her Love Story *(1924);* Wages of Virtue *(1924);* Madame Sans-Gêne *(1925);* The Coast of Folly *(1925);* Stage Struck *(1925);* The Untamed Lady *(1926);* Fine Manners *(1926);* The Love of Sunya *(1927);* Sadie Thompson

(1928); Queen Kelly *(1928);* The Trespasser *(1929);* What a Widow! *(UA, 1930);* Indiscreet *(UA, 1931);* Tonight or Never *(UA, 1931);* Perfect Understanding *(UA, 1933);* Music in the Air *(Fox, 1934);* Father Takes a Wife *(RKO, 1941);* Sunset Boulevard *(Par., 1950);* Three for Bedroom C *(WB, 1952);* Mio Figlio Nerone *(Nero's Mistress, 1956);* Airport 1975 *(1974).*

Gloria Swanson was one of the most successful silent film actresses and an early Hollywood millionaire. Married six times and linked romantically (or rather, erotically) with dozens of other men, she brought an electric charge of sexy glamour to the screen and helped create the public image of the passionate movie star's larger-than-life existence. Cranky and eccentric in her private life, eating a salt-free vegetarian diet of lentils and seaweed, she consummated her acting life in Billy Wilder's classic film *Sunset Boulevard* (1950), which showed the sad, mad decline of a star like herself.

She was born in 1897 to an army family, the daughter of **Adelaide Swenson** and Joseph Swenson. Her father's work meant that her parents were often separated, and eventually divorced. She lived with her mother but kept in touch with her father when he was stationed nearby, growing up chiefly in Chicago but also for periods in Key West, Florida, and Puerto Rico. She took voice and art lessons at the urging of her ambitious mother, and since she lived near the Essanay Film Company, she began to visit the film lot as a teenager where filmmakers noticed her striking dark looks. Gloria got several bit parts in early silent comedies before the First World War and was hired as a regular actor in 1914 for $3.25 per week. Most of her initial films no longer exist; early directors, who often knocked them off in a day or two, saw them as short-term money-spinners and failed to anticipate the day when film historians would seek out remaining copies.

While working on one of her earliest films, *Sweedie Goes to College,* Swanson met Wallace Beery, soon to be her first husband. They both went to Hollywood, which was quickly becoming the center of the rapidly growing film industry, and starred together in several silent melodramas at Mack Sennett's Keystone studio. In *Teddy at the Throttle,* they enacted the classic scene of the villain tying the young innocent across the railroad tracks before an onrushing express train. Swanson married Beery when he was about 30 and she was 17, but almost at once regretted it. He beat her severely. In her autobiography, she described their wedding night as a rape, adding that when he found she was pregnant he made her drink an abortifacient medicine.

Another early Hollywood companion was Charlie Chaplin, who told her, after doing some experimental scenes, that she lacked the temperament and style for slapstick comedy, that she was immune to custard pies. She specialized, rather, in playing the lofty and aloof young woman who could be moved to pity or admiration by an honorable gesture. As film historian **Molly Haskell** noted, however:

> Alternating with her woman-of-the-world roles, she often played unspoiled ingenues. In Allan Dwan's *Stage Struck* she played a goofy, gracefully incompetent waitress in a greasy spoon who makes halfhearted attempts to efface herself while her boyfriend moons over the visiting actress—the posturing, arrogant prima donna, the whirlwind of conceited womanhood she herself would be playing some years later.

Leaving Sennett, Swanson moved in 1919 to another growing studio, Paramount, and made a favorable impression on the director Cecil B. De Mille. He turned her into a major star over the next few years in such domestic dramas as *Don't Change Your Husband* and *The Affairs of Anatol.* "She was usually the wife in these films and her gowns were sensational," writes Lawrence Quirk. "She made the boudoir and even the bathroom matters of breathless concern to millions of female fans who couldn't get enough of her clothes, her man problems, and her resolutions of assorted on-screen marital dilemmas." In one of these Paramount films, *Beyond the Rocks* (1922), her leading man was Rudolph Valentino. The script, by ***Elinor Glyn,** a popular British romantic novelist, squeezed the maximum of sentimental drama out of the situation, in which Swanson was unhappily married to an old bore but was in love with a handsome lord (Valentino). She nobly renounced him but then her husband conveniently died while exploring Arabia, leaving her free to fall swooning into Valentino's embrace.

With a second husband, Herbert Somborn, who was a movie promoter and owner of a chain of "Brown Derby" restaurants, she gave birth to a child, Gloria, in 1920, but this marriage foundered almost as rapidly as her first. Already renowned for extramarital escapades and now suing for a second divorce, Swanson posed a problem for Paramount Studios. Hollywood had suffered bad publicity from the Fatty J. Arbuckle scandal, when the comedy star allegedly raped a movie fan with a bottle, which led to her death from internal injuries. The studios were

eager to allay charges that movies encouraged licentious behavior and that the stars themselves were immoral. The owners and directors foresaw that if they did not police themselves they would suffer intrusive censorship from state or federal government agencies. Eventually, Hollywood wrote a formal "Production Code" and established a clearinghouse, the "Hays Office," to monitor all new productions, showing them to the Catholic Legion of Decency before sending them out on general release. The Code kept some sex out of the films but hardly out of the stars' lives, though after Swanson's second divorce her contract did include a "morals clause" which terminated her salary if her extramarital affairs became public. Swanson, despite escalating threats and embarrassments, ultimately went through six husbands and dozens of affairs but benefited from an indulgent publicity press which hyped her virtues and suppressed most news of her vices.

$\mathcal{S}$wanson, like Joan Crawford after her, was one of those emblematic (and aggressively adaptable) figures in whom we see reflected the changing tastes of a decade. Her image altered considerably until it became frozen for posterity as the imperious prima-donna-past-her-prime of *Sunset Boulevard*. In her earliest films she was just the opposite: a dippy, half-witted trouper who would rather hover in the wings than steal the spotlight.

—Molly Haskell

Her third husband was the Marquis Henri de la Falaise, a French hero of World War I whom she met in Paris while filming *Madame Sans-Gêne* and married in 1925 in Passy town hall. Finding herself pregnant and knowing that giving birth seven months after marriage would put another severe dent in her image, she had another abortion. The doctor bungled the operation, and she almost died from the blood-poisoning it caused. Fans waited anxiously for the outcome and gave her a hero's welcome when she got back to America, not knowing the cause of her sudden postnuptial illness. In her autobiography, she wrote that after her triumphal return to Hollywood, stage managed for maximum drama by the studios, she told her mother, "It's the saddest night of my life. I'm just twenty six. Where do I go from here?"

Since 1923, enjoying an income of $7,000 per week, she had worked less in Hollywood than at the Astoria studios in New York. Her contract with Paramount ended in 1926, and although the studio's owners, Jesse Lasky and Adolf Zukor, offered her a million dollars per year to renew it, she decided to join United Artists and try making films over which she had more artistic control. After some early failures, which quickly ate into the fortune she had made as a studio actress, she made a hit with *Sadie Thompson*, adapted from the Somerset Maugham short story "Rain." In it, she plays a prostitute trying to escape from her past. She is raped by a hypocritical evangelical minister who has pretended to be reforming her morals. The story required intricate negotiations with the censors but finally appeared to glowing reviews. (The film would spawn a succession of remakes, including *Rain* [1932] starring *Joan Crawford and *Miss Sadie Thompson* [1953] with *Rita Hayworth.)

Swanson's business partner in the late 1920s was Joseph P. Kennedy, later America's ambassador to England and father of the future president. Himself a notorious womanizer, he and Swanson began a torrid love affair which caused more trouble among Hollywood's moral guardians. In her breathlessly melodramatic autobiography, Swanson described their first tryst:

> He moved so quickly that neither of us could speak. With one hand he held the back of my head, with the other he stroked my body and pulled at my kimono. He kept insisting in a drawn out moan, "No longer, no longer. Now." He was like a roped horse, rough, arduous, racing to be free. After a hasty climax he lay beside me, stroking my hair. Apart from his guilty, passionate mutterings he had still said nothing cogent.

William O'Connell, archbishop of Boston, at one point asked Swanson to leave Kennedy, who was a prominent member of his flock, but Swanson retorted that the archbishop should be berating Kennedy, not her, since she wasn't even a Catholic. The affair lasted from 1927 to 1930 when Kennedy left both Swanson and Hollywood, apparently having made far more money from the partnership than she.

These years of the late 1920s brought the first talking films to the public, which led to the fall of some stars and the rise of others. An unsuitable voice did not matter in the silents but could now be a disabling factor. Swanson, however, made a smooth transition from silents to talkies and said that claims of a traumatic change in the business were a fuss about nothing. Trained as a singer in childhood, she sang several songs in *The Trespasser*, her first film with a soundtrack. It was an immense commercial success and won her an Oscar nomination.

She could not follow up on the success of *The Trespasser*, however, and several subsequent films flopped. She spent much of 1931 and 1932 in London, where she met and married an Irish adventurer, Michael Farmer. They had a daughter, Michele, in 1932 and Swanson even put Farmer into a film which she financed and directed, *A Perfect Understanding*. The other male lead was Laurence Olivier, but he was not yet a major star and this film also led to financial losses. By 1934, divorced for the fourth time and involved in another love affair with a married man, this time the actor Herbert Marshall, she began to find parts difficult to obtain, and many prominent Hollywood figures now ostracized her for her public adultery. She was 35, had been in a series of financial fiascos, and seemed to cause more trouble than the studios could recoup in profits. As a result, she spent the next seven years out of films, watching a new generation of younger actors and actresses rise to stardom. In one of the few understated passages of her autobiography, she observed: "In many ways I had not been fortunate in my choice of men, particularly in the area of money. In all four marriages I had footed all the bills and now most of the money I had made was gone."

To recover some of her losses, she now began a business, helping to finance inventors. Named Multiprises, it had offices in Rockefeller Center, New York, and began to trade in eccentric possibilities like durable luminous paint. Some of the inventors she met were refugees from Nazi Germany, and by pulling the right strings she was able to expedite their exit visas from Germany and establish them in America. In the factory she bought in the New York borough of Queens, one of the inventors, Leopold Karniol, created a process for making plastic buttons; another, Anton Kratky, improved on carbide-steel cutting tools, both of which inventions proved useful to the American economy as it geared up for the Second World War. A brief return to films in 1941 led only to another flop, and at the start of the war it seemed unlikely that Swanson had any future in Hollywood.

Meanwhile, she was busy working as a stage actress, raising her three children (two daughters and an adopted son), and making radio appearances. She campaigned for Wendell Willkie during the 1940 election and worked in theater through most of the war years. Her fifth husband, William Davey, was an alcoholic who went through a complete personality transformation between his sober and drunken periods. Within a month that marriage too was over. Swanson was embarrassed to have a fifth divorce to her credit but in the late 1940s she adapted to the newest entertainment medium by

From the movie Sunset Boulevard, starring William Holden and Gloria Swanson.

starring in a television show, "The Gloria Swanson Hour." Though it ran successfully for six months, she decided that at $350 a week the pay was too poor and the work too exhausting.

In 1950, her spectacular return in *Sunset Boulevard* was all the more striking because of her steady decline from stardom in the previous 16 years. The story of a former Hollywood star who has aged, turned ugly, and gone slightly crazy (Molly Haskell describes her as "a gargoyle of vanity and manipulation" with "all the grace and dignity of a weasel in heat"), and her inability to come to terms with her fall from greatness, carried at least an element of biographical truth. Directed by Billy Wilder and co-starring William Holden as a scriptwriter whom the Swanson character murders in a jealous rage when she thinks he is about to desert her, *Sunset Boulevard* secured her an Oscar nomination. Wrote James Agee, a leading critic of the 1940s and 1950s, "Miss Swanson, required to play a hundred percent grotesque, plays it not just to the hilt but right up to the armpit, by which I mean magnificently."

Swanson reappeared on television in the 1950s and 1960s but spent more time on the stage in New York where she remained a popular draw. After *Sunset Boulevard*, other directors wanted to recast her as the faded former star going steadily crazy, but she had an understandable reluctance to fall in with their plans. Her last film was the shabby sensation *Airport 1975* by which time the simple fact that she was in a film at all drew more press notice than any quality to her acting. She wrote her "kiss-and-tell" autobiography, *Swanson on Swanson* (1980), and lived to see it sell tens of thousands of copies before dying in her sleep at the age of 84 in 1983.

SOURCES:

Agee, James. *Agee on Film: Reviews and Comments.* Boston, MA: 1958.
Haskell, Molly. *From Reverence to Rape: The Treatment of Women in the Movies.* NY: 1974.
Quirk, Lawrence J. *The Films of Gloria Swanson.* Secaucus, NJ: Citadel Press, 1984.
Swanson, Gloria. *Swanson on Swanson.* NY: Random House, 1980.

SUGGESTED READING:

Brownlow, Kevin. *Behind the Mask of Innocence.* NY: 1990.
Hirsch, Foster. *Acting Hollywood Style.* NY: 1991.
Walker, Alexander. *The Shattered Silents.* London: 1978.

Patrick Allitt, Professor of History, Emory University, Atlanta, Georgia

Swanson, Pipsan Saarinen

(1905–1979)

Finnish-American interior, glassware and textile designer. Name variations: Pipsan Saarinen; Pipsan Saari-nen-Swanson; Eva Lisa Saarinen Swanson. Born Eva Lisa Saarinen on March 3, 1905, in Finland; died in October 1979 in Michigan; daughter of architect Eliel Saarinen (1873–1950) and sculptor Loja (Gesellius) Saarinen (1879–1968); sister of architect Eero Saarinen (1910–1961); sister-in-law of *Aline B. Saarinen (1914–1972); married Robert Swanson (an architect).

Pipsan Saarinen was born in 1905 into an influential family of artists and architects. Her father Eliel Saarinen was the foremost architect of his generation in Finland; her mother *Loja Saarinen was a sculptor. Eero Saarinen, her only sibling, was to become one of the most important architects of the 20th century, known for his innovative work in Europe and the United States, including the CBS building in New York City (known as "Black Rock") and the St. Louis Arch (the Jefferson National Expansion Memorial).

Pipsan moved to the United States with her family in 1923, after studying weaving and other crafts in Helsinki. Her father designed the Cranbrook Academy of Art in Bloomfield Hills, Michigan, and moved his family there in 1925. The work of the academy became focal in their lives. Eliel Saarinen was president of the academy until 1948, and Pipsan taught there until 1935. By this time married to architect Robert Swanson (who would briefly go into partnership with both her father and brother), Pipsan left Cranbrook in order to head the interior design department at her husband's office.

A designer in the tradition of Scandinavian modernism, Pipsan brought a cutting-edge contemporary sensibility to the traditional craft elements of her work, emphasizing clean lines and simplicity. She specialized in furniture, textile and glassware design, and also served as a color consultant to various companies, including Barwick Mills, Goodall Fabrics, and the Pittsburgh Plate Glass Company. Many of Pipsan Swanson's designs were exhibited, and she won numerous awards for excellence.

Paula Morris, D.Phil., Brooklyn, New York

Swanwick, Anna (1813–1899)

British translator, feminist, and philanthropist. Born in Liverpool, England, on June 22, 1813; died, age 86, at Tunbridge Wells, Kent, on November 2, 1899; youngest daughter of John Swanwick.

Anna Swanwick was born in Liverpool in 1813. She was educated at home and at a fashionable boarding school but was dissatisfied with her schooling, which stressed the proper skills for women. In 1839, Swanwick journeyed to Berlin to study German, Greek, and Hebrew. On her return to London in 1843, she took up mathematics. Swanwick's first volume of translations, *Selections from the Dramas of Goethe and Schiller*, appeared in 1843. In 1847, she published a translation of Schiller's *Jungfrau von Orleans*; this was followed by *Faust, Tasso, Iphigenie* and *Egmont* (1850). In 1878, she published a complete translation of both parts of *Faust* in blank verse (illustrated by Retch) which ranked as one of the best, ran through several editions, and was included in Bohn's series of foreign classics in English. Swanwick then turned her attention to translating from the Greek. In 1865, she published a blank verse translation of Aeschylus' *Trilogy* (1865), followed by a complete edition of Aeschylus, illustrated by Flaxman (1873).

Though chiefly remembered for her translations, Swanwick also published original prose: *Books, our Best Friends and Deadliest Foes* (1886); *An Utopian Dream and How it May Be Realized* (1888); *Poets, the Interpreters of their Age* (1892); and *Evolution and the Religion of the Future* (1894).

Along with a large circle of noted friends, including Crabb Robinson, Robert Browning, Alfred, Lord Tennyson, and James Martineau, Swanwick was also involved in social and philanthropic movements. In 1861, she signed John Stuart Mill's petition to Parliament for women's enfranchisement. She also led in the crusade to open universities to women and helped found Girton College, Cambridge, and Somerville Hall, Oxford. Swanwick was awarded a LL.D. from the University of Aberdeen.

SUGGESTED READING:
Bruce, M.L. *Anna Swanwick: A Memoir*, 1904.

Swarthout, Gladys (1904–1969)

American mezzo soprano. Born on December 25, 1904, in Deepwater, Missouri; died on July 7, 1969, in Florence, Italy; daughter of Frank Leslie Swarthout and Ruth (Wonser) Swarthout; graduated from Bush Conservatory of Music in Chicago, doctorate in music, 1923; married Harry Richmond Kern, on March 22, 1925 (died October 20, 1931); married Frank M. Chapman, Jr., in 1932 (died 1966); no children.

Sang with Chicago Civic Opera Company, Ravinia Park Opera Company and Metropolitan Opera House; star of radio shows and movie musicals; wrote memoirs, Come Soon, Tomorrow *(1945).*

Selected filmography: Rose of the Rancho *(1936);* Give Us This Night *(1936);* Champagne Waltz *(1937);* To Have and to Hold *(1937);* Romance in the Dark *(1938);* Ambush *(1939, only non-singing role).*

Gladys Swarthout, born in 1904 in the Ozark mining town of Deepwater, Missouri, had an unusually large and mature voice as a child. While a 13-year-old student at Central High in Kansas City, she auditioned for and won the post of contralto soloist in a church choir by posing as a 19-year-old. Her poise as a teenaged singer was remarkable, and at her first recital she impressed a wealthy Kansas City family so much that they decided to finance her career.

By the time she received her doctorate in music in 1923 from the Bush Conservatory of Music in Chicago, Swarthout was an accomplished concert singer, having given recitals throughout the United States, often performing with her older sister **Roma Swarthout**. Gladys

Gladys Swarthout

made her operatic debut with the Chicago Civic Opera Company in the 1924–25 season, singing 22 roles in 50 performances, more than any other singer in the company. After a successful stint with the Ravinia Park Opera Company in Chicago in the late 1920s, Swarthout made her debut at the Metropolitan Opera House in New York on November 15, 1929. She sang the part of La Cieca in *La Gioconda*, which would be one of her best-known roles. Swarthout quickly became one of the company's leading mezzo-sopranos, featured in the American premiere of *Sadko* and taking over many roles from the retiring **Marion Telva**. With a repertoire of over 25 operas, she excelled in *Mignon* and *Carmen* but was also celebrated for her performances in *Norma*, *Peter Ibbetson* and *La Forza del Destino*.

A chic, attractive woman, often featured on "best-dressed" lists, Swarthout spent much of the late 1930s in Hollywood as Paramount's answer to MGM's **Jeanette MacDonald*. The publicity attending her films brought Swarthout to a much larger audience, but her films were not huge hits, despite such co-stars as Fred MacMurray (in 1937's *To Have and to Hold*). She made her final film, *Ambush*, in 1939.

Swarthout's talents were better suited to radio, a branch of her career that also began in the 1930s. She appeared on such programs as the "Chase and Sanborn Hour," "Caravan," and "Ford Sunday Evening," and had her own mixed musical program on WEAF in New York City. Beginning in the late 1930s, critics named her "Number-One Female Singer of Classics" on the radio for five successive years. Radio helped Swarthout's fame spread. She published a book of memoirs, *Come Soon, Tomorrow*, in 1945. Her concerts and recordings were popular successes. But although she was pleasing to listen to and look at, some critics attacked her lack of intensity of feeling and expression, which was believed to limit her dramatic abilities on the opera stage.

Swarthout married Frank Chapman in 1932—the year after the death of her first husband Harry Richmond Kern—and he gave up his own career as a singer to act as her manager. In 1957, a year after undergoing heart surgery, Swarthout retired from the stage. She eventually moved with Chapman to a villa in Florence, Italy, where she died in 1969.

SOURCES:
Ewen, David, ed. *Living Musicians*. NY: H.W. Wilson, 1940.
Lamparski, Richard. *Whatever Became of . . . ?* NY: Crown, 1967.

Paula Morris, D.Phil.,
Brooklyn, New York

Sweden, queen of.

𝓑lanche
𝓢weet

W O M E N   I N   W O R L D   H I S T O R Y

See Désirée (1777–1860).
See Frederica Dorothea of Baden (1781–1826).
See Josephine Beauharnais (1807–1876).
See Louise of the Netherlands (1828–1871).
See Sophia of Nassau (1836–1913).
See Victoria of Baden (1862–1930).
See Louise Mountbatten (1889–1965).
See Silvia Sommerlath (b. 1943).

Sweden, regent of.
See Margaret I of Denmark (1353–1412).

Sweeney, Mrs.
See Margaret (d. 1993), duchess of Argyll.

Sweet, Blanche (1895–1986)

American silent-film actress. Born on June 18, 1895, in Chicago, Illinois; died in 1986; married Marshall "Mickey" Neilan (a director), in 1922 (divorced 1929); married Raymond Hackett (an actor), in 1936 (died 1958).

Selected filmography: The Lonedale Operator *(1911);* The Painted Lady *(1912);* Judith of Bethulia *(1913);* Home, Sweet Home *(1914);* The Avenging Conscience *(1914);* The Warrens of Virginia *(1915);* The Unpardonable Sin *(1919);* Quincy Adams Sawyer *(1922);* Anna Christie *(1923);* Tess of the D'Urbervilles *(1924);* The Sporting Venus *(1925);* Showgirl in Hollywood *(1930).*

Blanche Sweet was born in Chicago in 1895, the daughter of theatrical parents. She began her stage career as a small child and was a seasoned veteran by the time she began her film career in 1909. Sweet was to become one of the earliest and greatest silent actresses. She worked for Biograph on 14th Street in Manhattan and, along with *Mary Pickford, became D.W. Griffith's first major dramatic star. Sweet, who did not have the delicate image of many of her contemporaries, played feisty, determined heroines rather than fragile girls. Her most memorable roles for Griffith were in two of his landmark films, *The Lonedale Operator* (1911) and—with *Lillian and *Dorothy Gish in supporting roles—1913's *Judith of Bethulia*, Griffith's most ambitious production before *The Birth of a Nation*.

Around 1915, Sweet left Griffith for Famous Players-Lasky, to star for Cecil B. De Mille and work for her first husband, director Marshall Neilan, whom she married in 1922 and divorced in 1929. Neilan, known as Mickey, directed many famous films of the silent era, including the Mary Pickford version of *Rebecca of Sunnybrook Farm* (1917). Sweet made over

70 films, but her best performances were in the title role of the first screen adaptation of *Anna Christie* (1923) and in 1924's *Tess of the D'Urbervilles*, directed by Neilan.

Sweet's career declined with the end of the silent-picture era. She made only three "talkies" (all in 1930, singing as well as speaking in two of the films) before retiring to a successful vaudeville career, often reprising scenes from her films. She toured the United States in the early 1930s with an act called "Sweet and Lovely." Sweet married again in 1936, to her stage co-star, screen veteran Raymond Hackett. They met on the MGM lot and first performed together in the 1935 play *The Party's Over*, going on to tour hit plays from Broadway around the country. After Hackett died in 1958, Sweet left Los Angeles and returned to New York, where her career had begun, and made a brief comeback in some small movie roles in the late 1950s. She died in 1986.

SOURCES:

Katz, Ephraim. *The Film Encyclopedia.* NY: Harper-Collins, 1994.

Lamparski, Richard. *Whatever Became of . . . ?* NY: Crown, 1967.

Slide, Anthony. *Silent Portraits: Stars of the Silent Screen in Historic Photographs.* Vestal, NY: Vestal Press, 1989.

Paula Morris, D.Phil.,
Brooklyn, New York

Sweet, Winifred (1863–1936).
See Black, Winifred Sweet.

Swenson, May (1913–1989)

Major American poet who presented much of her imaginative and sensual poetry using vivid visual patterns. Born on May 28, 1913 (often mistakenly given as 1919); died of a heart attack at Bethany Beach, Delaware, on December 4, 1989; daughter of Dan Arthur Swenson and Margaret (Hellberg) Swenson, members of a Mormon family of Swedish immigrants, in Logan, Utah; attended Utah State Agricultural College (later Utah State University), 1930–34; never married; lived with Rozanne R. Knudson; no children.

Moved to New York (1936); had initial stay at Yaddo writers' colony (1950); published her first volume of poetry (1954); became editor at New Directions Press (1956); received Guggenheim fellowship (1959); received Amy Lowell fellowship for travel in Europe (1960); received Ford Foundation fellowship (1965); resigned from New Directions Press (1966); was poet-in-residence at Purdue University (1966–67); received Rockefeller Foundation award, began relationship with Rozanne Knudson (1967); received Lucy Martin Donnelly fellowship from Bryn

Mawr College (1968); elected to National Institute of Arts and Letters (1970); received Academy of American Poets fellowship (1979); participated in Rosalynn Carter's White House Salute to Poetry and American Poets (1980); received Bollingen Prize in Poetry from Yale University (1981); wrote and delivered Phi Beta Kappa poem at Harvard University commencement ceremony (1982); received MacArthur Foundation fellowship, received honorary degree from Utah State University (1987); gave Theodore Roethke reading at the University of Washington (1989); posthumous publication of her collection The Love Poems of May Swenson *(1991); posthumous publication of her collection of poems,* Nature *(1994).*

Major works—poetry: Another Animal *(1954);* Cage of Spines *(1958);* To Mix with Time *(1963);* Poems to Solve *(1966);* Half Sun Half Sleep *(1967);* Iconographs *(1970);* In Other Words *(1987);* The Love Poems of May Swenson *(1991);* Nature *(1994). Prose:* Made with Words *(1998). Drama:* The Floor *(1966).*

With the appearance of her first volume of verse in 1954, May Swenson established herself as one of America's leading poets. Over the course of her career, she wrote between 800 and 900 poems and published 450 in 11 volumes of poetry, along with prose and translations. Two final volumes were published posthumously. She was deeply influenced by the poets *Marianne Moore and *Elizabeth Bishop from whom she absorbed the principles of close observation and verbal precision. Swenson's own poetic voice, however, had a more unruly element than that to be found in the work of these mentors. Grace Schulman has summarized Swenson's literary work by noting that "the voice of May Swenson combines the directness of intimate speech and the urgency of prayer."

At times Swenson took up unlikely themes for her poetry, including the space program and the experiences of its astronauts. But she wrote poems describing nature as well. These sometimes contained what critic Edward Hirsch called "appropriate sexual metaphors, resonances and overtones." Her love poetry, however, was filled with an even stronger strain of sexual energy. In addition to the sensuality of her imagery, she became well known for her talent in presenting poetry in the visual shape of the theme she was pursuing. As Swenson herself said, she wanted "to cause an instant object-to-eye encounter with each poem before it is read word-for-word." First producing the poem itself, Swenson only then developed the shapes ("iconographs" as she called them) since, "the painting must be major,

not the frame." In the view of critic Anthony Hecht, Swenson, in striving for visual effects in her poetry, put herself into "an elect coterie of writers that would include e.e. cummings and Guillaume Apollinaire." Swenson's work also included extensive critical writing, prose stories, translations, and children's books.

May Swenson was born the eldest of ten children to a Mormon family in Logan, Utah, on May 28, 1913. The Swenson parents were Swedish immigrants. May's father Dan Arthur Swenson had immigrated in 1894, and he met May's mother **Margaret Hellberg Swenson** when he returned to Sweden as a Mormon missionary. Dan Swenson attended the Utah Agricultural College (later Utah State University) and went on to become a professor of mechanical engineering there. The language of the Swenson home was Swedish, and the young girl did not begin speaking English until she entered primary school. Early pictures of her show May as a child and young teenager dressed in Swedish clothing with her hair braided in the style of her parents' homeland.

May Swenson wrote both poetry and prose as a child. It was the literary hero of her early years, Edgar Allan Poe, who inspired her to think of writing in several literary genres. She later recalled that her writing stemmed partly from being an unsocial person in a large family; she escaped into solitude and there, in her loneliness, she wrote to amuse herself. One of her first works of prose, a story entitled "Christmas Day," was published in the Logan High School newspaper in 1929. Swenson attended the Utah State Agricultural College from 1930 to 1934; there she published her first poem in *The Scribble*, the college's literary magazine. At college, she became increasingly detached from her family's Mormon heritage. After receiving a degree in English and art, Swenson remained in Utah for a year, working at a Salt Lake City newspaper. According to some sources, she was a reporter; according to others, she spent the year selling advertising. In 1936, she and an older cousin moved to New York, where the rest of her life was centered. Nonetheless, much of her poetry reflected her early life in the West and her continuing love of the outdoors.

In New York, Swenson was unable to find the work she desired as a newspaper reporter, and instead she took positions as a writer's helper, ghostwriter, and editor for others. For a year, she did research for the Writers' Project of President Franklin Roosevelt's Works Progress Administration (WPA). There her job involved interviewing

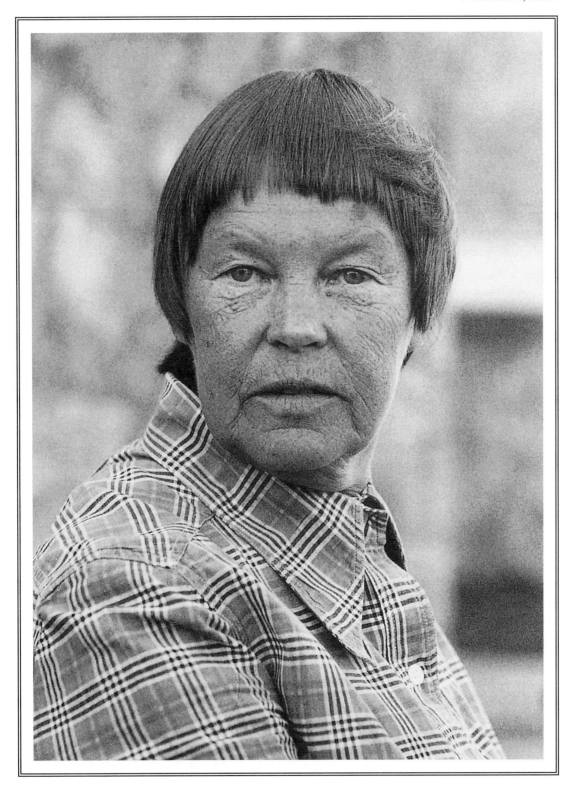

May
Swenson

members of the New York City working class. Her financial situation was so precarious that she and a young Czech immigrant whom she had interviewed, **Anca Vrbovska,** combined their meager resources and shared a succession of small apartments for several years. Some students of Swenson's life indicate that a romantic liaison developed between the two women.

Swenson worked for several publications in the drug industry between 1942 and 1949, writing poetry in her spare time. She advanced from typist to editor and speechwriter as she became more established. In 1949, she took the daring step of leaving this stable employment. With a reserve of $1,000, she planned to devote a year entirely to her poetry and the task of getting her work published. Her plan succeeded, and her poetry began to appear in *The Saturday Review of Literature* and *New Directions 11*. After numerous rejections, her work was accepted for the stellar outlet of the time, *The New Yorker*. The editor-in-chief of *New Directions*, James Laughlin, put her on his staff with the onerous tasks of reading manuscripts and writing rejection letters. She went on to become an editor for the magazine in 1956, a position that she gave up ten years later when her fame as a poet was established.

An early sign of her promise as a poet came when she reached the finals of the Yale Series of Younger Poets publication competition, and in 1950 she was invited to the Yaddo retreat near Saratoga, a gathering point for writers and other artists. There Swenson wrote a number of short stories, including one, "Appearances," set in a writers' colony. At Yaddo, she also began a longstanding friendship with the established poet Elizabeth Bishop. Their correspondence stretched from 1950 until Bishop's death in 1979. Initially Swenson played the role of apprentice poet receiving advice from an elder, but, in time, the two became equally confident in constructively criticizing the other's work.

> *May Swenson was that rarest of literary creatures in our century, an authentic poet of celebration and praise. An Orpheus fulfilled.*
>
> —Edward Hirsch

An important measure of success came for Swenson in May 1953 when John Hall Wheelock, the editor for Charles Scribner's Sons, accepted *Another Animal*, a collection of her work, for publication. In January 1956 at the Poetry Center in New York City, she gave her first public reading of her verse. Nonetheless, she remained dependent on various secretarial jobs to support herself until she could save enough money for a few months of concentrated literary production. As her friend and fellow poet *Mona Van Duyn put it, "May was one of the most unmaterialistic people I know. Nunlike, she warmed and fed herself primarily with writing."

Another Animal set down many of the themes Swenson would explore throughout her career as a poet. Swenson "dwells on the living body with an immediacy that heightens the dread of its loss," writes Schulman. She presents a series of "insistent, unanswerable questions" about life

and its possibilities. She also showed her incessant curiosity about such disparate topics as technology and nature. Moreover, in this earliest of her works, she began to experiment with shapes, putting her poems on the page in patterns that gave a visual expression to her ideas. These typographical devices often gave a dramatic force to her writing by splitting her poems or putting them in striking shapes. She employed this technique throughout her career. "[W]ith their profiles, or space patterns, or other graphic emphases," wrote Swenson, such poems "signal that they are to be seen as well as read and heard, I suppose."

In 1958, she published *A Cage of Spines*, her second collection of verse, and Swenson's growing eminence as a poet permitted her to supplement her always scant income with a reading tour that included an engagement at her alma mater, Utah State; she also read her work in San Francisco and Berkeley. Swenson found such public appearances a trial, and she never managed to bring her nervousness completely under control. Two grants, a Guggenheim Foundation fellowship and an *Amy Lowell Travelling Scholarship, freed her making such awkward public appearances, and the Lowell Scholarship facilitated a visit to Europe. With her roommate **Pearl Schwartz**, she toured France, Spain, and Italy, camping out in order to extend their stay.

With a growing literary reputation, Swenson was now offered a number of visiting professorships at institutions of higher learning. In the academic year 1966–67, she became poet in residence at Purdue University. Her persistent shyness in front of an audience made her a reluctant teacher, and she was also skeptical about the possibility of teaching students how to write poetry. Nonetheless, she took on that task at the Indiana university, informing her students at their first class, "I can't teach anyone how to write poetry but I can try to teach why the writing of poetry can't be taught." At Purdue, Swenson met **Rozanne "Zan" Knudson**, a member of the English faculty, and, in 1967, the two began a romantic friendship that lasted for the final decades of Swenson's life. After Swenson's year in Indiana was over, they bought a New York summer cottage in the small town of Sea Cliff on the north shore of Long Island.

Swenson continued to take on short teaching stints. In 1972, she taught a poetry workshop at her alma mater, Utah State University, partly to be near her siblings and old college friends in the stressful months after the death of her mother. She went on to teach at the University of Lethbridge in Canada, the Riverside campus of the

University of California, and the Greensboro campus of the University of North Carolina. In the 1960s and early 1970s, Swenson's long-standing facility with the Swedish language gave her the opportunity to translate the works of such Swedish poets as Ingemar Gustafson, Erick Lindegren, and Thomas Tranströmer.

The decade of the 1980s brought the once obscure and financially pinched poet both a wave of public recognition and a novel burst of affluence. In January 1980, at the invitation of first lady *Rosalynn Carter, Swenson joined more than 200 other poets who were received at the White House in "A Salute to Poetry and American Poets." The following year, she received the Bollingen Prize for poetry from Yale University, joining such eminent earlier winners as Wallace Stevens and Robert Frost. In 1982, she spoke at Harvard University's commencement ceremony, delivering the Phi Beta Kappa poem she had been asked to write for the occasion. In June 1987, she returned to Utah to receive an honorary doctorate from her alma mater, Utah State University. While she was still on campus she learned that the MacArthur Foundation had chosen her for a fellowship, one of its so-called "genius" awards, in the amount of $380,000. Characteristically, she gave much of the money away to her nieces and nephews; then, she and her companion Rozanne Knudson took advantage of this unusual burst of affluence to travel to New Zealand.

In an interview given in 1978, Swenson defined the originality of her poetry. She said she felt no need to follow the contemporary trends for women writers in making psychological confessions or presenting social commentary. Instead, she wrote about nature, broadly conceived. "For me, nature includes everything: the entire universe, the city, the country, the human mind, human creatures, and the animal creatures." In her view, "Real poets don't follow the trend. . . . They may be leading the trend, but they aren't hooked up to it."

In an interview for the *Los Angeles Times* conducted in August 1989, five months before her death, Swenson noted how youth had promoted her productivity as a poet. Thus the wisdom of old age had not turned out to be a benefit to her writing, since "the best poetry has its roots in the subconscious to a great degree." She could, with greater effort, overcome her decreasing energy and the inevitable complexities of adult life. Nonetheless, she said, "Youth, naiveté, reliance on instinct more than learning and method, a sense of freedom and play, even trust in randomness is necessary to the making of a poem."

Many critics find that Swenson's originality comes especially from those poems in shapes that create a visual image as a frame for her words and thoughts. White lines and curves move through much of her verse to make the form of her poem mirror the patterns of the real world. In *Iconographs*, her 1970 collection of verse, each of the 46 poems in the volume has a special shape incorporating angles, dramatic spacings, and curves. Swenson stated specifically that she wished "to make an existence in space, as well as time, for the poem."

She began *Iconographs* with a particularly striking and powerful poem entitled "Bleeding," a dialogue between the knife and the wound that it was creating. By using spaces in the text of the poem to slash the page, Swenson jolted the reader with a powerful image of a cut literally curving through the work's 44 lines. This was at a time when American women poets were writing extensively about bodily sensations, and some critics found the poem a powerful feminist statement. Nonetheless, it has been noted that "Bleeding" has no specific references to gender and could easily refer to pain and sickness in general as well as a knife cutting a male victim. In "Feel Me," another poem in *Iconographs*, Swenson explored and expressed her feelings upon the recent death of her father. Once again, she used a visual technique with devastating force, with spaces creating a diagonal line from the upper left hand to the lower right hand corner to present a picture of fracture and loss.

Swenson died of a heart attack at her winter home in Bethany Beach, Delaware, on December 4, 1989. She had been ill for some time with asthma and high blood pressure. Her body was returned to her home state for burial in Logan City. A measure of her obscurity was the confusion in various obituaries over her age and the size of the award she had received from her MacArthur fellowship. Some American newspapers listed her year of birth as 1919 and recorded her arrival in New York in 1949, ten years after the fact. Some listed her most prestigious award as bringing her $130,000, little more than one third of the actual sum she received.

Since only half of her poems had appeared in print during her lifetime, new works by Swenson continued to be published after her death, including *The Love Poems of May Swenson* in 1991 and *Nature* in 1994. The volume of love poems brought together 55 poems that had been written between 1938 and 1987. The poems, 13 of which had never appeared in print, were complex pieces that drew on both male and female imagery to express what Grace Schulman has called "intense love between women, written at time when that genre was rare in poetry. . . . the sexual love she dramatizes so brilliantly is Sapphic." Notes Edward Hirsch: "The birds, and especially the bees, have never been so slyly deployed." Rereading Swenson's larger body of work in the light of this new volume, Hirsch noted that "it becomes increasingly evident that a large number of Swenson's radiant nature poems are also love poems." *Nature* was described by one critic as "a dazzling posthumous collection of nature poems by a poet who epitomized the art of awareness." It presented 182 of Swenson's works including 10 poems published for the first time and another 19 that had not yet appeared in book form.

SOURCES:

Gilbert, Sandra M., and Susan Gubar, eds. *Shakespeare's Sisters: Feminist Essays on Women Poets.* Bloomington, IN: Indiana University Press, 1979.

Knudson, R.R., and Suzanne Bigelow. *May Swenson: A Poet's Life in Photos.* Logan, UT: Utah State University Press, 1996.

"May Swenson: Selected and edited by Anthony Hecht," in *The Wilson Quarterly.* Vol. 21. Winter 1997, pp. 105–112.

Schulman, Grace. "Life's Miracles: The Poetry of May Swenson," in *The American Poetry Review.* Vol. 23. September–October 1994, pp. 9–13.

Swenson, May. *Made with Words.* Edited by Gardener McFall. Ann Arbor, MI: University of Michigan Press, 1998.

Van Duyn, Mona. "Important Witness to the World," in *Parnassus: Poetry in Review.* Vol. 16, no. 1. August 1990, pp. 154–156.

SUGGESTED READING:

Greiner, Donald, ed. *American Poets Since World War II.* Part 2: L–Z. Detroit, MI: Gale Research, 1980.

Howard, Richard. *Alone with America: Essays on the Art of Poetry in the United States Since 1950.* NY: Atheneum, 1969.

Zona, Kirstin Hotelling. "A 'Dangerous Game of Change': Images of Desire in the Love Poems of May Swenson," in *Twentieth Century Literature.* Vol. 44, pt. 2. Summer 1998, pp. 219–241.

Neil M. Heyman,
Professor of History,
San Diego State University,
San Diego, California

Anne
Sophie
Swetchine

Swetchine, Anne Sophie

(1782–1857)

Russian mystic, writer, and social leader. Pronunciation: SVYEE-chen. Name variations: Madame Swetchine. Born Anne Sophie Soymanof, Soymonoff, or Soymanov in Moscow, Russia, in 1782; died in 1857; married General Swetchine, in 1799.

Anne Sophie Swetchine was born Anne Sophie Soymanov in Moscow in 1782. At 17, she married a general, a quiet, inoffensive man who was 25 years her senior. Anne was small and plain, yet said to be possessed of such spiritual beauty and charm that she won the admiration and worship of many friends. Madame Swetchine came under the influence of Joseph de Maistre and converted to Roman Catholicism in 1815. Settling in Paris the following year, she fostered her religious leanings by maintaining a private chapel (a rare Church indulgence) and a salon famed not only for its courtesy and brilliance but for its spiritual atmosphere. The salon flourished until her death. Swetchine's *Life and Works*, marked by mysticism, was published posthumously by M. de Falloux in two volumes in 1860 (the best known writings of which are *Old Age* and *Resignation*), followed by two volumes of her *Letters* in 1861.

Swindler, Mary Hamilton

(1884–1967)

American archaeologist. Born Mary Hamilton Swindler on January 3, 1884, in Bloomington, Indi-

ana; died on January 16, 1967, in Haverford, Pennsylvania; daughter of Harrison T. Swindler and Ida Hamilton Swindler; University of Indiana at Bloomington, A.B., 1905, A.M. in Greek, 1906; Bryn Mawr College, Ph.D., 1912; never married; no children.

Wrote Ancient Painting *(1929); was the first woman editor-in-chief of* American Journal of Archaeology *(1932–46); awarded an LL.D. from Indiana University (1941); received the Achievement Award of the American Association of University Women (1951) and the prize of the American Council of Learned Scholars (1959); was a fellow of both the Royal Society of the Arts, London, and the German Archaeological Institute.*

Mary Hamilton Swindler, born in 1884 in Bloomington, Indiana, to **Ida Hamilton Swindler** and Harrison Swindler, a merchant, was to become one of the most influential classical archaeologists in the United States. She studied Greek, played basketball, and acted in college productions at the University of Indiana, and was awarded an A.M. in 1906. Later that year, she moved to Bryn Mawr College in Pennsylvania, remaining there nearly all her life and helping to make it a distinguished archaeological center.

In 1909, the ❧➤ **Mary E. Garrett** European fellowship took Swindler to Berlin and Athens, where she studied at the American School of Classical Studies (to which she returned to teach in 1938). This exposure to sites, monuments and museums inspired her to later found a museum at Bryn Mawr and to raise an annual fellowship for Bryn Mawr students to study abroad. Swindler earned her Ph.D. in 1912 and became a professor of classical archaeology in 1931. She returned to her dissertation topic, Cretan culture, in her major published work *Ancient Painting* (1929), a richly descriptive, groundbreaking book on art from Paleolithic cave paintings to early Christian catacombs. Swindler's reputation was enhanced by her editorship from 1932 to 1946 of the *American Journal of Archaeology*, which she improved and expanded. The first woman to be editor-in-chief, Swindler transformed the journal into a truly international publication.

Swindler was an enormously respected and quietly charismatic scholar and teacher, with a direct, humorous manner. She challenged and inspired her students at Bryn Mawr and the other colleges at which she taught—the University of Pennsylvania and the University of Michigan—after retiring from Bryn Mawr on an inadequate pension in 1949. Swindler began a second major work, which would have been called "The Beginnings of Greek Art," but a heavy workload and poor health prevented her from completing it. She died of bronchopneumonia in Haverford, Pennsylvania, in 1967.

SOURCES:
Read, Phyllis J., and Bernard L. Witlieb. *The Book of Women's Firsts.* NY: Random House, 1992.
Sicherman, Barbara, and Carol Hurd Green, eds. *Notable American Women: The Modern Period.* Cambridge, MA: Belknap Press of Harvard University, 1980.

Paula Morris, D.Phil.,
Brooklyn, New York

Swinford, Catherine (c. 1350–1403).

See Beaufort, Joan (c. 1379–1440) for sidebar.

Swisshelm, Jane Grey (1815–1884)

*American newspaper publisher, abolitionist and suffragist. Name variations: Jane Grey Cannon. Born on December 6, 1815, in Wilkensburg, near Pittsburgh, Pennsylvania; died in Pennsylvania in 1884; daughter of Thomas Cannon and Marcy (Scott) Cannon; studied briefly at Edgeworth Boarding School, Braddock's Field, Pennsylvania; largely self-educated; married James Swisshelm, in 1836 (divorced 1857); children: one daughter, **Mary Henrietta Swisshelm** (b. 1851).*

Started newspapers in Pennsylvania, Minnesota and Washington, D.C.; wrote memoir, Reminiscences of Half a Century *(1880).*

Jane Grey Swisshelm was born Jane Grey Cannon in Wilkensburg, a small frontier town in Pennsylvania, in 1815. Her Scottish-Irish parents, merchant Thomas Cannon and **Marcy Scott Cannon**, had seven children, but only Jane and her sister **Elizabeth Cannon** survived into adulthood. Raised a strict Presbyterian, Jane was largely self-educated, spending just six weeks at the Edgeworth Boarding School in Braddock's Field, Pennsylvania. After her father died when she was seven, she taught lacemaking to help the family finances, becoming a schoolteacher at the age of 14.

In 1836, against the advice of her mother, she married James Swisshelm, a devout Methodist and domineering, manipulative man. Life with him and his mother was so difficult that for a time early in her marriage Swisshelm lived in self-imposed exile in a hut on her mother-in-law's property. The couple moved to Louisville, and while her husband's business ventures failed, her own thrived; Swisshelm built a successful corset-making business and, back in Pennsylvania after nursing her dying mother for a year, taught at a female seminary in Butler. During this period of

❧➤
Garrett, Mary E.
See Thomas, M. Carey for sidebar.

separation from her husband, Swisshelm's love of reading and natural talent as a writer inspired her to publish anonymous articles in a local newspaper. Returning to married life and her husband's family farm outside Pittsburgh, Swisshelm began her career in journalism by contributing stories, poems and articles to Philadelphia and Pittsburgh newspapers.

With the help of her mentor Robert M. Riddle, editor of the *Pittsburgh Commercial Journal*, Swisshelm launched her own paper, the *Saturday Visiter* [sic], in Pittsburgh in 1848. In order to finance this venture, Swisshelm used the proceeds from the sale of her mother's house. Her husband's demand that this money be turned over to him motivated Swisshelm to join *Lucretia Mott and **Mary A. Grew** in lobbying the Pennsylvania legislature; in 1848, the right of married women to own property became law.

Juggling the demands of motherhood (her only child, Mary Henrietta, known as Nettie, was born in 1851) and her newspaper work, Swisshelm became known nationally for her editorials among proponents of the abolitionist cause. She also published practical advice (in her "Letters to Country Girls" series) and advocated equal education and property rights for women, though she resisted affiliation with any of the suffrage movement's organizations. Horace Greeley, editor of the *New-York Daily Tribune*, hired her as the first woman correspondent in Washington, representing both his paper and her own. On her 1850 visit to the capital, Swisshelm discovered that women were barred from the Senate Press Gallery. After successfully campaigning for equal rights for women reporters, Swisshelm became ensnared in Washington gossip; an unsubstantiated report she ran in the *Visiter* (alleging that presidential nominee Daniel Webster had fathered interracial children) compromised her relationship with Greeley and the *Tribune*, and she returned to Pennsylvania.

Swisshelm's marriage was very unhappy. She later described it as 20 years "without the legal right to be alone one hour." Her husband and mother-in-law coerced her into

Jane Grey Swisshelm

giving up painting and reading, and Swisshelm's natural independence of spirit was progressively crushed. Not content with forbidding her to read any book except the Bible, her husband even tried to sue Marcy Scott Cannon's estate for the time his wife had spent nursing her. In 1857, Swisshelm left him and was divorced for desertion. Selling her paper, she and her daughter moved to Minnesota, where she had family, and began publishing another anti-slavery paper, the *St. Cloud Visitor*. Her press was destroyed by political opponents led by hard-line Democrat General Sylvanus B. Lowry, the paper's financial backer, who disagreed with her abolitionist views and her support for the candidacy of Republican presidential candidate Abraham Lincoln. Undeterred, Swisshelm closed the paper and re-launched it as the *St. Cloud Democrat*.

An energetic speaker, Swisshelm addressed the Minnesota house in 1860 and its senate in 1862 on abolition and women's rights. The wit and intelligence of her editorials and speeches won her respect, but the strength and radical nature of her opinions made her a controversial figure. "Millions of women in this country are condemned to the most menial drudgery," she wrote. "But let one aspire to use her mental powers—and O! What a fainting fit Mr. Propriety has taken! Just to think that 'one of the deah creatures' should forsake the woman's sphere." While she championed the rights of African-Americans, Swisshelm's opinions on Native Americans were more in keeping with populist views of the day. She once referred to them as "lazy, impudent beggars." When the Sioux attacked prairie settlements during the Civil War and 38 of their leaders were hanged in retribution, Swisshelm, on a lecture tour of the East, argued in favor of even more severe punitive measures; ironically, her first attempts at journalism in the 1840s had been articles condemning capital punishment.

In 1863, Swisshelm ended a lecture tour in Washington, D.C., and decided to stay there, selling her Minnesota paper. She served as a nurse in military hospitals and was offered a clerkship in the War Department. In 1865, she began a third newspaper, the *Reconstructionist*, but her differences with Andrew Johnson's administration cost Swisshelm her clerkship and led to the paper's bankruptcy, a failure repeated in 1866 after the launch of her "liberal sheet" *The Wasp*. Advised by friends *Mary Todd Lincoln and Secretary of War Edwin McMasters Stanton, Swisshelm sued for a share of her late ex-husband's estate and retreated from public life to her native Pennsylvania.

A small, pretty woman, Swisshelm was an idealist and activist who was often perceived as an eccentric. Still active in public speaking even after her retirement, she became a thorn in the side of the National Woman Suffrage Association (NWSA), and was tolerated rather than welcomed on its finance committee in 1877. Feisty to the end, and regarded as a maverick by many in the women's suffrage movement, Swisshelm was critical of the NWSA in her memoir, *Reminiscences of Half a Century*, published in 1880. She died in 1884 and was buried in her native Pittsburgh.

SOURCES:

Belford, Barbara. *Brilliant Bylines*. NY: Columbia University Press, 1986.

Edgerly, Lois Stiles, ed. and comp. *Give Her This Day: A Daybook of Women's Words*. Gardiner, ME: Tilbury House, 1990.

Weatherford, Doris. *American Women's History*. NY: Prentice Hall, 1994.

Woodward, Helen Beal. *The Bold Women*. NY: Farrar, Straus, 1953.

Paula Morris, D.Phil.,
Brooklyn, New York

Switzer, Kathy (b. 1947).

See Samuelson, Joan Benoit for sidebar.

Switzer, Mary E. (1900–1971)

Director of the Office of Vocational Rehabilitation who revolutionized the vocational rehabilitation of the disabled in America. Born Mary Elizabeth Switzer on February 16, 1900, in Newton Upper Falls, Massachusetts; died on October 16, 1971, in Washington, D.C.; daughter of Julius F. Switzer and Margaret (Moore) Switzer; studied at public schools; Radcliffe College, A.B. in international law, 1921; never married; no children; lifelong companion of Isabella Stevenson Diamond.

As director of the Office of Vocational Rehabilitation, held one of the highest appointive offices in the U.S. government; awards include the President's Certificate of Merit, President's Award of the National Rehabilitation Association (1955), Albert Lasker Award (1960), and numerous honorary doctorates, including degrees from Tufts University and Boston University.

Mary Switzer, the oldest of two daughters, was born in 1900 in Newton Upper Falls, Massachusetts, to manual worker Julius F. Switzer and **Margaret Moore Switzer**. By age 11, Switzer was a virtual orphan: her father had left the family, and her mother had died. She and her sister were raised as Roman Catholics by two maternal aunts and "Uncle Mike" Moore, a machinist, Irish patriot, woman's suffragist and socialist who was an important early influence. From her aunts and uncle, Switzer learned the value of hard work and was encouraged into public service.

Switzer attended public schools, graduating from Newton Classical High School in 1917. She won a scholarship to Radcliffe, helping to support herself with a variety of jobs. Switzer found college a stimulating experience, and she was one of the founders of the reformist Inter-Collegiate Liberal League. She was the first undergraduate at Radcliffe to major in international law, receiving her A.B. in 1921, and moved to Washington, D.C., after graduation. Her first government post there was with the District of Columbia Minimum Wage Board, where she met **Isabella Stevenson Diamond**, with whom she subsequently lived all her life. Diamond, she later wrote, taught her "the advantage of a balanced life" with "interests as broad as life is . . . and the way to organize life to enjoy all."

The first dozen years of her career were quiet, while she served as executive secretary of the Women's International League for Peace and Freedom and then entered the federal civil service. In 1922, she became a junior economist in the Treasury Department and was assigned the task of reporting on current affairs for Secretary Andrew W. Mellon and President Herbert Hoover. In 1934 her career took off when the assistant secretary of the treasury, *****Josephine Roche**, assigned her to oversee the U.S. Public Health Service. Switzer helped to consolidate health and welfare programs into the Federal Security Agency (FSA), which later became the Department of Health, Education and Welfare and is now the Department of Health and Human Services. She received the President's Certificate of Merit for her war work in the highly confidential War Research Service and the Procurement and Assignment Service for medical personnel. She went on to help set up the World Health Organization, demonstrating a gift for hard work and organization that won her much prestige, influence and respect.

Switzer's appointment as director of the Office of Vocational Rehabilitation (OVR) in 1950 placed her in one of the highest positions ever given to a woman in the federal government. The OVR had been established in 1920 to award state grants for the vocational rehabilitation of disabled people. Switzer infused the moribund program with dynamic energy and vision, creating a single focus for all private organizations and state and federal agencies: to assist all disabled people in finding satisfying work. At the time she took the post, the number of rehabilitated individuals returning to the work force was 56,000 a year; in ten years, Switzer had increased that number to over 88,000. She also transformed the program by including in its ranks those with severe disabilities who would have been rejected for rehabilitation prior to her tenure, including those with mental illnesses or retardation. Switzer was possibly inspired in this field of work because of contact early in her career with **Tracy Copp**, a pioneer in equal opportunities for the disabled. Largely as a result of Switzer's dogged dedication, Congress passed the landmark Vocational Rehabilitation Act in 1954, funding research, training for specialists, and the construction of rehabilitation centers. The International Society for the Welfare of Cripples honored her with medicine's highest award, the Albert Lasker Award, in 1960 for her efforts on behalf of the disabled. She was the first woman to receive this prestigious honor.

Switzer, who once described herself as a "dedicated bureaucrat," had excellent political skills which helped her survive numerous administrations. She retired in 1970, after serving as administrator of the Social and Rehabilitation Service in the Department of Health, Education and Welfare, and died of cancer in Washington the following year.

SOURCES:

Current Biography Yearbook. NY: H.W. Wilson, 1962.

Sicherman, Barbara, and Carol Hurd Green, eds. *Notable American Women: The Modern Period.* Cambridge, MA: Belknap Press of Harvard University, 1980.

Paula Morris, D.Phil.,
Brooklyn, New York

Swoopes, Sheryl (1971—)

African-American basketball player. Born on March 25, 1971, in Brownsfield, Texas; attended South Plains Junior College; graduated from Texas Tech in Lubbock; married Eric Jackson; children: son Jordan Eric Jackson (b. 1997).

First woman to have her own athletic shoe named for her (Nike "Air Swoopes"); led the Texas Tech Lady Rangers to the NCAA championship (1993), setting an NCAA record in the process for most points scored by any basketball player (47) in Final Four history; won gold medal in Atlanta Olympics (1996); was a founding player in the Women's National Basketball Association (WNBA); *led the Houston Comets to three straight WNBA championships beginning with the inaugural season (1997); won gold medal in Sydney Olympics (2000).*

Born in 1971, Sheryl Swoopes grew up in the small town of Brownsfield in West Texas and spent most of her spare time in childhood playing basketball with her brothers. Already a towering six feet tall in high school, she was recruited by the women's basketball team at University of Texas in Austin, the state's premier team. Swoopes' time in Austin lasted only four days. Homesick, she returned to Brownsfield to attend South Plains Junior College, where she was named Junior College Player of the Year. In 1991, she transferred to a nearby college, Texas Tech in Lubbock, leading its team, the Lady Rangers, to the National Collegiate Athletic Association (NCAA) Final Four in 1993. In the NCAA championship final, Swoopes scored 47 points, more than any other player, male or female, in NCAA finals history, to bring her team the victory.

That performance brought Swoopes awards (including National Player of the Year) and a considerable amount of media attention, but the absence of a professional basketball league for women in the United States forced her move to Italy in order to play professionally. After she spent a few months playing in Bari, in southern Italy, a contract dispute resulted in her departure from the Italian team. She returned to the United States and did volunteer coaching at Texas Tech for a time. In 1994, she landed a spot with the U.S. women's basketball team, competing in the world basketball championships and the Goodwill Games. Team USA was undefeated in its pre-Olympic tournaments and, as a member of the 1996 United States Olympic team, Swoopes won the expected gold medal at the Atlanta Olympic Games.

In June 1997, by now married to Eric Jackson, she gave birth to her first child, Jordan Eric Jackson, and was back on the court six weeks later—this time in one of the new women's professional basketball leagues in the United States, the Women's National Basketball Association (WNBA). That season she took her team, the Houston Comets, to a league championship, a feat the team repeated in 1998 and 1999. Swoopes was also named to the All-WNBA First Team in 1998, the same year she was second on the Comets team in scoring, three-point percentage, rebounds and steals. At the 2000 Olympics in Sydney, Australia, she and her teammates—including *Lisa Leslie, *Dawn Staley, and *Teresa Edwards—wrested the gold medal from the Australian women's team with a score of 76–54. In

Sheryl
Swoopes

addition to her other awards and achievements, Swoopes is the first woman to have an athletic shoe named after her (Nike's "Air Swoopes").

SOURCES:
The Day [New London, CT]. August 14, 1997.

Johnson, Anne Janette. *Great Women in Sports*. Detroit, MI: Visible Ink, 1998.
People Weekly. January 27, 1997; December 29, 1997.
Sports Illustrated: Womensport. Spring 1997.

Paula Morris, D.Phil,
Brooklyn, New York

Swynford, Catherine (c. 1350–1403).

See Beaufort, Joan (c. 1379–1440) for sidebar.

Sybil (fl. 1030).

See Elflaed.

Sybil of Conversano (d. 1103)

Duchess of Normandy. Name variations: Sybilla. Died in February 1103 at Rouen, France; buried at Caen Cathedral, Normandy, France; daughter of Geoffrey, count of Conversano; married Robert II (some cite III) Curthose (c. 1054–1134), duke of Normandy (r. 1087–1106), in 1100, in Apulia, Italy; children: William III the Clito (1101–1128), count of Flanders (r. 1127–1128); Henry of Normandy (b. 1102).

Sybilla (d. 1122)

*Queen of Scots. Born around 1092, in Domfront, Normandy; died on July 12, 1122, at Loch Tay, Scotland; buried at Dunfermline Abbey, Fife, Scotland; illegitimate daughter of Henry I, king of England (r. 1100–1135), and *Sybilla Corbert; married Alexander I (1078–1124), king of Scots (r. 1107–1124), around 1107; children: Malcolm, earl of Ross (b. around 1110).*

Sybilla of Anjou (1112–1165)

*Countess of Boulogne. Countess of Flanders (very briefly). Name variations: Sybilla de Gatinais; Sybil of Anjou. Born in 1112 (some sources cite 1114 or 1116); died in 1165 at the Abbey of St. Lazarus, in Bethlehem, Israel; interred at the abbey; daughter of Fulk V the Younger, count of Anjou and king of Jerusalem, and *Ermentrude (d. 1126), countess of Maine; married William III the Clito (1101–1128), count of Flanders (r. 1127–1128), in 1123 (annulled 1124); married Theodore of Alsace, count of Flanders, in 1134; children: (second marriage) Philip of Alsace, count of Flanders (r. 1157–1191); Matthew I, count of Boulogne (d. 1173); *Margaret of Alsace (c. 1135–1194). Eventually, Sybilla took the veil in the Abbey of St. Lazarus in Bethlehem. William III the Clito's second wife was *Joan of Montferrat (d. 1127).*

Sybilla of Brandenburg (fl. 1500)

*Duchess of Juliers. Flourished around 1500; married William III (or IV), duke of Juliers (Jülich) and Berg; children: *Maria of Julich-Berg (mother of *Anne of Cleves).*

Sybilla of Cleves (1514–1554)

*Sister of Anne of Cleves. Born in 1514; died in 1554; daughter of John III, duke of Cleves (r. 1521–1539), and *Maria of Julich-Berg; sister of *Anne of Cleves (who married Henry VIII, king of England); married John Frederick I, elector of Saxony.*

Sybilla of Saxe-Coburg-Gotha (1908–1972)

*Duchess of Westerbotten. Name variations: Sibylla; Sibylla Saxe-Coburg; princess Wettin. Born Sybilla Calma Mary Alice Bathildis Feodore on January 18, 1908, in Gotha, Thuringia, Germany; died on November 28, 1972, in Stockholm, Sweden; daughter of Charles Edward Saxe-Coburg, 2nd duke of Albany, and *Victoria Adelaide of Schleswig-Holstein (1885–1970); married Gustav Adolphus, duke of Westerbotten, on October 19, 1932; children: *Margaret Bernadotte (b. 1934, who married John Ambler); *Birgitta of Sweden (b. 1937, who married Johann Georg of Hohenzollern); *Desiree Bernadotte (b. 1938, who married Niclas Silferschiöld); *Christina Bernadotte (b. 1943); Charles also known as Carl XVI Gustavus (b. 1946), king of Sweden (r. 1973—).*

Syers, Madge Cave (1881–1917)

British figure skater. Name variations: Madge Syers-Cave. Born Madeline Cave in England in 1881; died in September 1917; married Edgar W. Syers (her coach).

Was the first woman to enter the world championship (1902), winning second and causing skating officials to create a special competition for women; won women's Olympic figure skating gold medal and a bronze in the pairs with husband-coach Edgar Syers (1908).

Born in England in 1881, Madge Cave was an excellent swimmer and equestrian; she also loved skating and was quite successful in skating figures. Her coach, Edgar W. Syers, introduced young Madge to the less rigid Austrian International style. Skating had been practiced in Europe since the Middle Ages, particularly in the Netherlands, where frozen canals were perfect for the sport. After the execution of Charles I in England, his exiled son Charles II brought skating back with him when he returned to claim the English throne. The English developed the shorter blade which made figure skating possible. The Austrians invented "waltzing" on the ice, free skating or the modern skating now so popular.

Madge Syers was trained in traditional English figure skating, but she adapted very well to free skating, winning the first English national pairs competition in 1899. In 1900, she placed second in international pairs events. Competing with her coach, the talented skater eventually married him, and the couple continued competition individually and together. Sometimes they competed against each other.

In 1902, Madge Syers entered the all-male world championship, the only woman ever to do so. There were no rules against a women entering the competition, so she was allowed to compete. She came in second to Ulrich Salchow, the great skater from Sweden who had invented the jump named after him. The next year officials closed the competition to women, but Syers had made an important point and a women's world championship was established in 1906. To no one's surprise Madge Syers won the 1906 women's championship, repeating her victory in 1907. In the meantime, she won the first singles championship in Britain in 1903 and defended it against her husband in 1904. In the 1908 London Olympics, Syers won the first gold medal in women's singles and a bronze in pairs with her husband. At age 35, Syers died of heart disease. She was inducted into the Figure Skating Hall of Fame.

SOURCES:

Markel, Robert, Nancy Brooks, and Susan Markel. *For the Record. Women in Sports.* NY: World Almanac, 1985.

Karin Loewen Haag,
Athens, Georgia

Sylva, Carmen (1843–1916).
See Elizabeth of Wied.

Symborska, Wislawa (b. 1923).
See Szymborska, Wislawa.

Synadene of Byzantium (c. 1050–?)

Queen of Hungary. Name variations: Sophia or Zsofia. Born around 1050; death date unknown; married Geza I, king of Hungary (r. 1074–1077); children: Coloman or Koloman (1070–1114), king of Hungary (r. 1095–1114); Almos, duke of Croatia (who married Ingeborg of Sweden).

Syntyche

Biblical woman. Pronunciation: SIN-tih-keh.

Syntyche and **Euodia**, who were members of the church of Philippi, and may have also been deaconesses, had an argument, at which time the apostle Paul beseeched them to "be of the same mind in the Lord."

Syria, queen of.
See Laodice I (c. 285–c. 236 BCE).
See Mavia (c. 350–c. 430 CE).

Syro-Phoenician

Biblical woman. Pronunciation: sigh-row feh-KNEE-shun.

Syro-Phoenician was a Gentile woman from Phoenicia, a nation that had been incorporated into the Roman province of Syria (thus the name Syro-Phoenician), who brought her afflicted daughter to Jesus to be healed. Although she was not of the Jewish nation, she believed that Jesus could heal. He tested her by silence, refusal, and reproach, but she stood firm in her faith, and her petition was granted.

Szabó, Herma (b. 1902).
See Planck-Szabó, Herma.

Szabo, Violette (1921–1945)

British secret agent in France during World War II. Name variations: (code name) Louise. Born Violette Reine Elizabeth Bushell (some sources cite Bushnell) on June 26, 1921 (some sources cite 1918), in Paris, France; executed at Ravensbrück concentration camp sometime between January 25 and February 5, 1945 (some sources cite January 26); daughter of Charles Bushell (an Englishman who operated a fleet of tourist taxis) and a French mother (name unknown); educated mostly in London; married Etienne Michel René Szabo (a French soldier), in August 1940 (killed in action on October 24, 1942); children: daughter Tania (b. June 8, 1942).

Awarded the George Cross for courage for her work in Normandy and around Limoges (1946); awarded the Croix de Guerre (1947).

During World War II, British agent Violette Szabo single-handedly held off a Nazi SS infantry regiment so her partner, a local leader of the Maquis, could escape with information important to the Allies. Captured and sent to Paris for interrogation, she never revealed the identity of any of her contacts. She was tortured in Nazi prisons, then sent with two other women agents to Ravensbrück concentration camp in Germany, where all three were executed.

Violette Szabo was born Violette Bushell in Paris in 1921. Her father Charles Bushnell, an Englishman who operated a fleet of tourist taxis, and her French mother, whose name is unknown, had met while Charles was serving in World War I. Szabo was raised in London, speaking French with her mother and English with her father and friends. She was a cyclist and a good gymnast, and excelled at athletic games and feats requiring muscular strength. Her father taught her to shoot at carnival shooting galleries. After finishing school, Szabo became a hairdresser's assistant and later worked in a large department store. Apolitical, she did not take the war against Hitler seriously until the tragedy was brought home when her mother's homeland of France fell.

On Bastille Day, July 14, 1940, there was a parade in London of the Free French Army. Mrs. Bushell, who drove an ambulance for the Women's Transport Service of the First Aid Nursing Yeomanry (FANYs), sent Violette to find a French soldier to bring home for dinner. Five weeks after Etienne Michel René Szabo accepted the invitation, he and Violette were married. Their wedding ceremony, however, was interrupted by an air raid, and their honeymoon lasted only a few days. Etienne then sailed with his regiment to North Africa. Violette saw him only once more, for a week in Liverpool where he had been sent for a short vacation. After he flew back to Cairo, she joined the Auxiliary Transport Service (ATS), a women's branch of the British Army. In April 1942, she took a leave to prepare for the arrival of her daughter, **Tania Szabo**, who was born on June 8 in Paddington. Violette wrote her husband regularly, but she had no news of him until that October, when she learned that he had been killed while advancing against General Erwin Rommel's forces at El Alamein in North Africa. Along with bringing her shock and grief, the news of his death intensified her hatred of the Nazis and of the terror and destruction they were spreading across Europe.

Szabo now wanted a more direct role in the war, as a spy. Because she was bilingual, she was the perfect candidate, much valued by the British War Office, but her enthusiasm almost worked against her. The life of a spy requires a person who can handle the dull as well as dangerous and highly confidential work. Some sources say she was approached to become an agent, while others say she applied to the Special Operations Executive (SOE). Szabo was offered a desk job, but she held out for an agent's assignment. Accepted as an agent, she was officially commissioned as an ensign in the FANYs while secretly

being trained for sabotage and parachute jumping. Even her parents did not know of her true assignment. Slim, beautiful and high-spirited, with natural athletic ability and a rugged physical constitution, Szabo excelled. She was taught holds and grips for unarmed combat, and proved outstanding at weapons training, becoming an expert with Bren and Sten guns. She told her training officer, **Peggy Minchin**, she would be happy to die fighting if only she could take some Germans with her. During this time, however, she twisted her ankle at parachute training school, and it was never strong after that.

Szabo undertook her first mission in France in May 1944, when she traveled as a courier from Paris to Rouen tracing uncaptured members of a Rouen-based Resistance group that had been uncovered and broken up. Successful, she returned to England after about six weeks of work. In early June, she parachuted into occupied Paris. Her mission was to coordinate groups of French Resistance spies with the local underground leader, whose code name was "Anastasia"; her orders were to protect him at all costs. After successfully completing one mission, they ran into a Gestapo patrol from an SS infantry regiment on its way to reinforce German divisions. Szabo and Anastasia left their car and ran. The Germans shot Violette in the arm, but she continued to run, turning and firing at them from her Sten gun until her weak ankle gave out. Though Anastasia tried to help her, she insisted that he escape. While he did so, she stood and emptied her magazine at the Germans, who had been joined by reinforcements. Other accounts have Szabo keeping the Nazis at bay with her rapid-firing machine gun, moving from window to window in a small house as she covered her partner's escape.

Anastasia hid in a woodpile. Szabo fired until she ran out of ammunition and the Germans closed in. They took her biting and kicking to an officer who stood near Anastasia's hiding place. When the officer offered her a cigarette, she spat in his face. Without discovering the Maquis leader, the Nazis took Szabo to a jail in Limoges. Though she was interrogated for hours, she never revealed the information they wanted. They then sent her to Fresne, the notorious prison near Paris, where she was placed under heavy guard, interrogated and tortured.

In August 1944, while the Allies were approaching Paris, the Nazis evacuated their prisoners and deported them to concentration camps in Germany. Szabo was one of twelve women who were chained in pairs and sent on a week's journey by night train. Several male SOE officers were also on that train, including a good friend of Szabo's, with whom she spoke. That British officer survived the war, and reported what she had told him to SOE. During the journey, the train was attacked by British forces and the Germans fled to try to defend themselves. With another woman chained to her, Szabo dragged herself through the corridor with bottles of water for the men agents who were going mad with thirst. Seventeen Germans were killed in the air attack. The train was put out of commission and the prisoners were held in stables for the night.

Finally, Szabo and the other women prisoners arrived at Ravensbrück, the most feared women's concentration camp, where *Odette Sansom was also imprisoned. There they were met by jackbooted women guards wielding whips. Illness, beatings and torture were common at Ravensbrück. Prisoners shared bunks infested with lice, and the smell of death from the crematoriums was everywhere. They were forced to labor from dawn to dusk on starvation rations, building roads or working in the fields or in the war factories. Twice, Szabo was caught trying to escape and sent to solitary confinement, where she was whipped. In the cold of winter, she was sent with two other SOE agents, **Danielle Bloch** and **Lilian V. Rolfe**, to a site 300 miles away and forced to cut down trees to prepare the land for an aerodrome. Danielle Bloch (codenamed "Ambrosia") was Jewish and consequently a target for the Nazis. She had worked with the French Resistance before escaping to Britain and joining the SOE. After training, she returned to the Paris Sector on March 3, 1944. Acting as a courier, she carried out much useful work until the group was betrayed on June 19, 1944, and she was captured during a Gestapo raid on one of the group's hideouts. Lilian V. Rolfe (codenamed "Nadine") was a tall, dark young woman with an English father and a French mother. Brought up in Brazil, she had been living in Surrey when she joined the SOE, and arrived in the field on April 6, 1944, to act as a wireless (radio) operator. She was captured by a group of Germans who had not been looking for her but took her into custody after questioning.

Szabo, Bloch and Rolfe were sent back to Ravensbrück a few months before the German surrender. There, sometime between January 25 and February 5, 1945, Szabo was executed with a bullet to the back of the neck. Bloch and Rolfe were killed the same way.

After the war, their friend Vera Atkins traveled to Germany to search the prisons and the

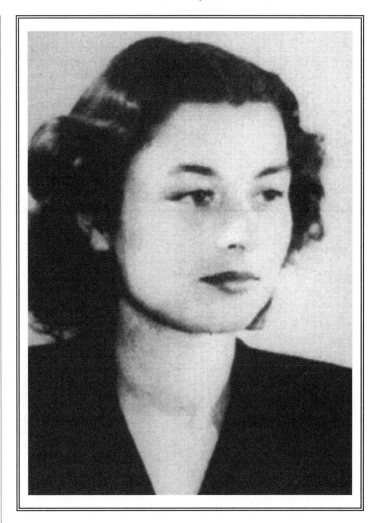

Violette Szabo

camps for any information on the women's fate. For many weeks, she interviewed hundreds of people connected with the Nazi concentration camps, building up a dossier of evidence which was used at the war trials. Among the men she interviewed was Johann Schwarzhuber, second-in-command at Ravensbrück, who was later hanged. His statement to Atkins read:

> One evening, towards 1900 hours they (Lilian, Danielle, Violette) were called out and taken to the cemetery yard by the crematorium. Camp Commandant Suhren made these arrangements. He read out the order for their shooting. . . . I was myself present. The shooting was done by Schult with a small caliber gun through the back of the neck. They were brought forward singly by Corporal Schenk. Death was certified by Dr K Trommer. The corpses were removed singly by internees who were employed in the crematorium, and burnt. The clothes were burnt with the bodies.
>
> I accompanied the three women in the crematorium yard. A female overseer was also present and was sent back when we

reached the crematorium. Zappe stood guard over them while they were waiting to be shot.

All three were very brave and I was deeply moved, Suhren was also impressed by the bearing of these women. He was annoyed that the Gestapo did not themselves carry out these shootings.

In all, 50 SOE women agents were sent to France. Fifteen were captured by the Nazis, two of those fifteen escaped and only Odette Sansom survived. Violette Szabo was awarded the George Cross, Britain's highest civilian award, in 1946. The following year, France awarded her the Croix de Guerre, its highest honor. In 1981, a commemorative blue plaque was placed on the home in London where Szabo had lived with her parents and daughter; it reads in part, "Secret Agent lived here. She gave her life for the French Resistance." The United Kingdom also issued a postage stamp in her honor in 1995, and in June 2000, the house in Wormelow, Herefordshire, where Szabo often visited her aunt and uncle opened as the Violette Szabo Museum.

SOURCES:

Fraser, Antonia, ed. *Heroes and Heroines.* London: Weidenfeld & Nicolson, 1980.

Gleeson, James Joseph. *They Feared No Evil: The Woman Agents of Britain's Secret Armies 1939–45.* London: R. Hale, 1976.

Mahoney, M.H. *Women in Espionage: A Biographical Dictionary.* Santa Barbara, CA, 1993.

Minney, R.J. *Carve Her Name with Pride.* London, 1956.

RELATED MEDIA:

Carve Her Name with Pride (119 min. British film), starring Paul Scholfield and **Virginia McKenna** as Szabo, based on the book by R.J. Minney, produced by Rank, 1958.

Susan Slosberg,
Adjunct Professor of Public Relations,
Baruch College, The City University of New York,
New York, New York

Szarvady, Wilhelmine Clauss
(1834–1907).

See Clauss-Szárvady, Wilhelmina.

Szatkowska, Zofia or Zofdja de
(1890–1968).

See Kossak, Zofia.

Szczucka, Zofia (1890–1968).

See Kossak, Zofia.

Szenes, Chana (1921–1944).

See Senesh, Hannah.

Szenes, Katalin (b. 1899).

See Senesh, Hannah for sidebar.

Szewinska, Irena (1946—)

Polish track star who won seven Olympic medals, three of them gold. Name variations: Irene Kirszenstein; Irena Kirszenstein-Szewinska; Irena Szewinska-Kirszenstein. Born Irena Kirszenstein in Leningrad, USSR (now Russia), on May 24, 1946; married Junusz Szewinski (a runner who became her coach), in 1967; children: son Andrzej (b. February 1970).

Won medals in each of the four Olympics in which she competed, a feat no man or woman had ever accomplished: won silver in long jump, silver in 200 meters, gold in 4x100-meter relay in Tokyo Olympics (1964), won bronze in 100 meters, gold in 200 meters in Mexico City Olympics (1968), won bronze in 200 meters in Munich Olympics (1972), won gold in 400 meters in Montreal (1976); became the first woman to break 50 seconds in the 400 meters when she ran that race in 49.9 seconds (1974).

Irena Szewinska was born Irena Kirszenstein in Leningrad, USSR, in 1946. In September 1939, her parents had fled the Nazi invasion of Poland; had they not, they would have perished like millions of other Jews. Shortly after their daughter's birth, they returned to Warsaw. Irena was an athletic child, and her mother encouraged her to join a local sports club, where she became a sprinter and long jumper. Szewinska was a member of the Polish national team at the 1964 Tokyo Olympics, coming from out of nowhere to win a silver medal in the 200-meter run (setting a European record of 23.1 seconds), another silver in the long jump (establishing a national record of 21'7½"), and a gold medal in the 400-meter relay (during which the Polish relay team also clocked a world record). By the time Szewinska returned home, she had become a Polish superstar.

In 1965, Szewinska tied the world record with 11.1 seconds in the 100 meters, defeated two American Olympic champions in the 100 and 200 meters, broke the world record in the 200 meters with a race of 22.7 seconds, and was named Poland's Athlete of the Year. The Poles loved this sprinter whose athletic feats drew international attention. In Warsaw, Szewinska was often stopped on the streets for her autograph and songs were written in her honor. Her face became familiar in magazines and newspapers. This was particularly gratifying to the Jewish Szewinska, who was painfully aware of the virulent anti-Semitism that had had such devastating results in Europe. She enjoyed representing her country.

In the European championships in Budapest in 1966, Szewinska won gold medals in the 200 meters, long jump, and 400-meter relay as well as a silver medal in the 100 meters. *World Sport*, a British magazine, enhanced her international reputation when she was chosen Sportswoman of the Year. In 1967, Irena married Junusz Szewinski, who was once a runner and had become her coach. In the 1968 Olympics in Mexico City, she won a gold in the 200 meters, setting a new world record of 22.5 seconds. She also won a bronze in the 100 meters.

After the 1968 Olympics, Szewinska began to tire of running competitively and decided to take a well-deserved rest. After a year, she returned to training, feeling better mentally and physically. In February 1970, her son Andrzej was born, and she felt pregnancy and childbirth had improved her performance. She won bronze medals in the 200 meters at the 1971 European championships and at the 1972 Munich Olympics.

Szewinska then decided to concentrate on the 400-meter race, having devoted much of her career to the 100 and 200 meters. In 1974, she became the first woman to break the 50 seconds barrier, running the 400 meters in 49.9 seconds. This marked the beginning of a comeback. *Renate Stecher, a young East German, had begun to dominate the track. When Szewinska defeated Stecher in the European championship's 100- and 200-meter events, chopping a tenth of a second from her 200-meter world mark, there was no question about her prominence. United Press International voted Szewinska Sportswoman of 1974 and *Track and Field News* named her woman athlete of the year.

In the 1976 Montreal Olympics, she won her seventh Olympic medal, a gold in the 400 meters. More important, Szewinska's time was 49.29, lowering her own world record by almost half a second. Because so many women athletes from Eastern bloc countries performed so ably, Szewinska was asked if her athletic feats represented a triumph for Communism. She replied, "I know the people from Poland were very happy to see the Polish flag flying the highest. But I run because it gives me great pleasure and satisfaction. I run for me." In 1977, Szewinska won the 400 meters in the Düsseldorf World championship in 49.0 seconds, a new world record.

Competing in the 1980 Olympics, Irena Szewinska wanted to be the first person to win a total of eight Olympic medals, but this was not to be. At 34, she was one of the older competitors, and she returned home without a medal. Her career had been incredible, however. Szewinska won a total of seven Olympic medals, three of them gold, and ten European medals,

Irena Szewinska

five of them gold. She had been one of the best in her field for over 16 years.

SOURCES:

Condon, Robert J. *Great Women Athletes of the 20th Century*. Jefferson, NC: McFarland, 1991.

Slater, Robert. *Great Jews in Sports*. Middle Village, NY: Jonathan David, 1983.

Karin L. Haag, freelance writer, Athens, Georgia

Szold, Henrietta (1860–1945)

Fiercely practical founder of Hadassah, the Women's Zionist Organization of America, who established a comprehensive network of public health services in pre-Israel Palestine. Pronunciation: Zold. Born Henrietta Szold on December 21, 1860, in Baltimore, Maryland; died on February 13, 1945, in Palestine; daughter of Benjamin Szold (a rabbi of Oheb Shalom Congregation, Baltimore, Maryland) and Sophie Schaar Szold; attended Western Female High School, Baltimore, 1877, and Jewish Theological Seminary, New York, 1902–05; never married.

Became a Baltimore correspondent for the New York Jewish Messenger *(1877); taught at Misses Adams' French and English School for Girls, Baltimore (1878–92); worked as editor and translator, Jewish Publication Society of America (1888–1916); founded Russian night school, Baltimore (1889–93); was a founding member of Zionist Association of Baltimore (1893); made first visit to Palestine (1909); was honorary secretary for Jewish Agricultural Station, Palestine, and Federation of American Zionists (1910); founded Hadassah, Women's Zionist Organization of America, New York (1912), and was president (1912–26); helped organize American Zionist Medical Unit (1916); was executive in charge of Health and Education, World Zionist Organization (1927–30); awarded honorary Doctor of Hebrew Letters, Jewish Institute of Religion (1930); elected member of Vaad Leumi (General Jewish Council), Palestine (1931–33); served as director, Department of Social Welfare, Vaad Leumi, Palestine (1932–37); served as director, Youth Aliyah (1933–45); established Children's Foundation in Palestine (1941); awarded honorary Doctor of Humanities, Boston University (1944).*

Henrietta Szold's first visit to Palestine in 1909 galvanized her Zionism. In 1881, Russian immigrants had introduced her to the philosophy that only creation of a national homeland could guarantee preservation of Jewish history, culture, language—and lives. During her tour of Palestine with her mother nearly 30 years later, she moved from philosophy to action. Szold was startled by the stark contrast between magnificent religious sites and the squalid living conditions endured by 600,000 Christian, Muslim, and Jewish residents. Only 12 Jewish doctors attended to the medical needs of 80,000 Jews. The first Jewish hospital had opened in 1854, but the number had increased to only four by the time of Szold's visit. Most Jews relied on folk remedies and amulets. If these failed, they sought the counsel not of doctors but of druggists who prescribed questionable cures. Palestine had no organized medical association to control standards and no central health agency to educate the population about causes and cures of widespread diseases. Szold wrote to her sisters, "There is so much strife, so much misery, so much to make the heart ache." Just before returning to the United States, Szold visited the Evelina de Rothschild School for Girls. Inside the school, regular visits from an eye doctor prevented the spread of trachoma. Outside, flies swarmed around other children's diseased eyes. The discrepancy proved

to Szold that Palestine needed intensive public health education and modern medical care. Her mother reportedly encouraged her, "Here is work for you. Your group ought to do practical work in Palestine." On February 24, 1912, Szold took her mother's advice. She transformed her "group"—an informal circle of Jewish women studying Zionist philosophy—into the first chapter of Hadassah, the Women's Zionist Organization of America. Szold mobilized Hadassah to establish comprehensive public health services in Palestine, laying the groundwork for what would become the most advanced medical system in the Middle East.

Henrietta Szold was born on December 21, 1860, the first of eight daughters of Rabbi Benjamin Szold and **Sophie Schaar Szold** who had named her after *Henriette Herz, a German Jew famous for her command of languages and her literary salon. Szold's parents had immigrated from Hungary to Baltimore, Maryland, only the year before, and Benjamin had become the rabbi of Oheb Shalom, a German-speaking congregation. But Harriet was born just four months before the Civil War erupted in the United States, and the Szolds struggled under tremendous inflation, shortages, and political uncertainty. During the war, Sophie Szold gave birth to two more daughters, Estella and Rebecca, neither of whom survived their first year. After the war, the Szolds had five more daughters: **Rachel** (b. 1865), **Sadie** (b. 1868), Johanna (b. 1871), **Bertha** (b. 1873) and **Adele** (b. 1876). Only Rachel, Bertha, Adele and Henrietta survived to mature adulthood.

Despite such tragedy, the Szolds encouraged their daughters' intellectual pursuits. Henrietta worked as her father's secretary and translator at Oheb Shalom, and he often discussed religion, politics and literature with her. In 1877, she graduated first in her class from Western Female High School. Less than a year later, she began teaching French, German, and Algebra at a local girls' finishing school, the Misses Adams' English and French School for Girls. During her 14-year tenure there, she also took on private students and taught religious classes at Oheb Shalom Congregation.

Teaching was just one outlet for her intellect. In 1877, the weekly *New York Jewish Messenger* hired her to report on events in Baltimore. Her column appeared under the pen name Shulamith. The newspaper later asked her to write general commentary on Jewish life. In 1888, Szold began volunteering for the Jewish Publication Society of America (JPS). A nonprof-

it educational association, the JPS depended on volunteers to translate Jewish literature from Yiddish, Hebrew, German, and French. For the next five years, she worked from her home in Baltimore, translating and editing texts through the mail.

Szold might have been satisfied with a quiet career as a teacher and writer, but international events in 1881 changed her perspective. The Russian Revolution touched off a massive immigration of Russian Jews. In Baltimore, as in many other American cities, the existing Jewish population was mostly German. The increasingly successful members of this community were well assimilated in American culture and many were uncomfortable with the Russians' poverty and their overtly "foreign" language, clothing and habits. Despite their reservations, German-Jewish leaders established charities to assist the immigrants.

Rabbi Szold was among the many religious leaders who met the immigrants as they arrived at the port of Baltimore. Unlike most others, however, he often brought the Russian newcomers into his home. Henrietta accompanied her father to the docks and found jobs for the immigrants in Jewish-owned shops and businesses. In her father's study, she participated in their passionate discussions of literature, poetry, and Zionism. She strongly supported their efforts to become self-sufficient. In a *Baltimore Sun* editorial, she described the immigrants as "cultured, intelligent men and women, abreast of the times, speaking and reading several foreign languages and versed in history and literature. They need merely a vehicle in which to convey to their fellow workers an idea of their inner worth."

In that spirit, she helped the Russian-organized Hebrew Literary Society establish a night school in 1889. She gathered donations and rented two back rooms on the second floor of a store. Society members refurbished the space for classrooms and collected school supplies. During the first semester, 150 Russian immigrants registered for classes in English and American history. Students who could paid 30 cents a month in tuition, soon enabling Szold to offer $15 a month to teachers. In just three years, enrollment was up to 708 Russian, German and Polish immigrants—Jews and non-Jews alike.

In the fall of 1893, members of the Hebrew Literary Society organized the Zionist Association of Baltimore. Szold and her father became founding members, and she soon began public advocacy of Zionism. She gave her first lecture in 1896 at a meeting of the local chapter of the National Council of Jewish Women. In 1899, she attended the second annual conference of the Federation of American Zionists, held in Baltimore, and was chosen as an honorary member of the executive committee.

Henrietta Szold's dedication to Zionism took root quickly, but it grew slowly. The Szold household underwent difficult changes in the last decade of the 19th century. Her sister Sadie died of pneumonia, and her father lost his job. In December 1891, Oheb Shalom congregation voted to replace Rabbi Szold. Although he was satisfied with the congregation's decision, Henrietta was troubled. She wrote to her sister, Bertha, "I cannot yet reconcile myself to the thought that the congregation is going to go its own way, and not look up to Papa as a guide."

More changes followed. That spring, the JPS offered Henrietta a full-time job in Philadelphia. With great trepidation, she resigned from her teaching positions and moved out of the Szold home for the first time. Her duties included public relations, editing, advertising and translation. She had no typewriter, no assistant and a small, sparsely furnished office. Szold was not averse to the hard work and long hours, but she found living away from home difficult. She left Philadelphia when her father became ill in 1895, taking her work to Baltimore. She edited and translated JPS books until 1916. Her name appears in *The American Jewish Yearbook*, a massive *History of the Jews* and other volumes.

Benjamin Szold died during the summer of 1902, and Henrietta was nearly immobilized with grief. She decided to edit and publish his papers in an effort to keep alive their intellectual partnership, but she thought the project required better knowledge of the Talmud. At a time when Jewish women were excluded from formal religious study and practice, she appealed for admission to the Jewish Theological Seminary in New York City. The Seminary opened in the fall of 1902, staffed by scholars well educated in Orthodoxy but open to Reform—a theological balance that would later become Conservative Judaism. Szold had met Dr. Solomon Schecter, a rabbinical professor from Cambridge, England, who was president of the school, and he strongly supported her application. The Seminary admitted her in 1903 as a special student. She was the first woman to study there.

In New York, she continued to explore Zionism, attending regular meetings of the Federation of American Zionists. In 1905, she met Judah Magnes, an unabashedly Zionist rabbi at the head of the staunchly anti-Zionist Temple Emanu-El. In 1907, he invited her to join his secretary's study circle. Similar groups of Jewish women had been organized across New York to discuss Zionism. Although she was twice the age of most members, Szold joined the Hadassah Study Circle. She deepened her intellectual commitment to Palestine through her interaction with men like Magnes and a growing circle of women Zionists.

At the same time, Szold became increasingly bored in her formal classes, since she was more familiar with Talmudic study than she had assumed.

In fact, she had a great deal to offer the Seminary professors, many of whom spoke little or no English. She organized classes to help them, and scholars like Louis Ginzberg began looking to her as a teacher. Szold and Ginzberg developed a strong attachment. Szold stopped attending classes at the Seminary in 1905 without completing her father's work, and focused on her professional—and personal—relationship with Ginzberg. She worked with him on his book *Geonica*, translated his lecture notes and, for the JPS, edited his masterpiece, *The Legends of the Jews*. Ginzberg married another woman in 1908. Disappointed, Szold asked the JPS to assign another editor to his work. She took a leave of absence, and she and her mother began their six-month tour of Europe and the Middle East in June 1909.

Although her reasons for leaving the country were personal, the journey proved crucial in her political development. In November 1909, she wrote, "The result is that I am still a Zionist, that I think Zionism is a more difficult aim to realize than I ever did before, and, finally, that I am more than ever convinced that if not Zionism, than nothing—then extinction for the Jew." At first, she channeled her new energies into work for the Federation of American Zionists. She was elected its honorary secretary in 1910 and began organizing the group's financial records. She wrote to Schechter, "I cannot flatter myself that I am doing Zionist work; cleaning up other people's Aegean stables is too far removed from Jewish ideal hopes." In the early months of 1911, she resigned her position, determined to organize American women for practical work in Palestine.

In February 1912, she began working with **Emma Gottheil** and a committee of women from New York study circles to formally organize women Zionists. Attracted by an invitation to establish a group for "the promotion of Jewish enterprises in Palestine and the fostering of Jewish ideals," 38 women attended the organizational meeting on February 24. In the vestry of Temple Emanu-El, they drew up by-laws, naming their organization the Daughters of Zion and their chapter Hadassah. Henrietta Szold, who had been elected president, asked members to decide on a project they could begin in Palestine. They all agreed on the dire need for a public health program, including maternal care and a visiting nurse system. At the organization's first board meeting on April 4, however, they voted to wait until they had at least 300 members before initiating a project.

But Henrietta Szold did not wait. She met with Nathan Straus (brother-in-law of *Ida **Straus**) in December 1912. Straus, a well-known public health advocate and department store magnate, had recently established a prenatal care center in Jerusalem. He told Szold he would pay travel expenses and four months' salary for one nurse if the Daughters of Zion could support her for two years in Palestine. There was one condition: the nurse had to be ready to leave for Palestine with his family on January 18, 1913. Szold calculated that her group needed to raise $2,400 to hold up their end of the bargain.

On January 1, she called an emergency board meeting. Her organization had only 157 members and $542 in dues, and the board doubted they could meet Straus' challenge. Nonetheless, they began working. Lobbying among non-Zionist Jewish organizations in Chicago, founding member **Eva Leon** quickly raised enough money to support two nurses: **Rose Kaplan** from Mount Sinai and **Rachel Landy**, a non-Zionist from Cleveland.

On January 18, Eva Leon, Nathan Straus, his wife **Lina Gutherz Straus**, and the nurses left for Palestine to establish a settlement house. Szold left for a speaking tour of Baltimore, Washington, D.C., Cincinnati, Chicago, Boston, Philadelphia and other cities where she successfully organized new chapters of the Daughters of Zion. By February 1913, she had collected enough money to affiliate with the Federation of American Zionists. The Daughters of Zion held their first national convention in June 1914 and formally changed their name to Hadassah.

Sending the nurses to Palestine was Szold's first victory for Hadassah, but the real work had only just begun. Kaplan and Landy set up a settlement house and struggled to establish a visiting nurse program in Palestine. In 1914, Dr. **Helena Kagan** arrived there from Switzerland, determined to set up maternal and child-care centers. All three women encountered resistance from doctors and patients unaccustomed to women practicing medicine. Together, the three established a maternal-care clinic and increased trachoma prevention in the schools.

With the outbreak of World War I, Palestine was cut off from supplies and communications. Hadassah urged the nurses to return home, but both shifted their efforts to refugee camps in Egypt. Palestine was increasingly devastated by disease and starvation. Rose Kaplan became ill herself. She returned home for cancer treatments in February 1915, and Rachel Landy followed that fall. Dr. Kagan remained in Jerusalem, repeatedly writing to Hadassah for assistance. Their responses never reached her.

As the situation became more desperate, the World Zionist Organization in Copenhagen called for the establishment of an emergency medical unit. In 1916, they asked the Provisional Executive Committee for General Zionist Affairs in New York to establish an American Zionist Medical Unit (AZMU). The Federation of American Zionists—of which Hadassah was an auxiliary—took on the project, and Louis Brandeis brought the idea directly to Henrietta Szold.

Szold agreed that Hadassah would send ten doctors and two nurses and medical supplies to Palestine, assuming the cost of $25,000. Hadassah's Board of Directors believed they were getting in over their heads, but Szold persisted. As war escalated, the cost of the AZMU venture multiplied; it was up to $100,000 by the fall of 1917. Szold made fundraising tours throughout the Eastern United States. Hadassah chapters rolled bandages and organized fundraising projects. Eva Leon negotiated for support from the Joint Distribution Committee, a non-Zionist umbrella organization of American Jewish charities.

Of course, money was not the only problem Hadassah faced. The entire mission was a tangle of diplomacy and red tape. The United States, keeping a watchful eye on the war in Europe, was unwilling to send supply ships or military transport to Palestine. Visas for medical personnel were impossible to obtain because Turkish Palestine was part of the enemy Ottoman Empire. The United States entered the war in April 1917, and Zionists began negotiating to send the Unit to Palestine on allied British military ships.

Henrietta Szold balked at the idea of sending the AZMU into Palestine on the backs of soldiers. While many American Jews were expressing their support for the war and aligning themselves with American allies, Szold, Rabbi Judah Magnes and others had become vocal pacifists. In January 1917, just months before the United States entered the war, Szold joined the People's Council of America for Peace and Democracy. "I am anti-war, and anti-this-war and anti-all wars," she explained.

Her Zionist peers feared she was obstructing both the progress of the AZMU and the larger purpose of Zionism. Jewish people must participate in an allied victory, they argued, in order to negotiate the establishment of a Jewish Nation in the postwar Middle East. They urged Szold to reconsider. She staged a brief protest and considered resigning from Hadassah. Ultimately, she decided to remain in the Zionist circle to combat famine and disease in war-torn Palestine. She regretfully resigned from the People's Council in October.

On November 2, 1917, the British government issued the Balfour Declaration, formally supporting the establishment of a Jewish state in Palestine. Arab riots broke out almost immediately, requiring seven more months of military planning and diplomacy before Hadassah's AZMU could embark. In June 1918, 44 Americans arrived in Palestine, blue Stars of David on their medical uniforms. Szold remained in the United States for nearly two more years, raising more money for the Unit.

But the AZMU proved worth the expense. The school hygiene, maternal and child care and nurse training programs the Unit established were firmly rooted in Palestine by 1919—and Hadassah with them. In 1929, Szold wrote, "The Hadassah Medical Organization came into this country as a war relief organization and remained in the land as a peace organization." Indeed, the Unit enabled Hadassah to lay the groundwork of an impressive network of services. In February 1919, Hadassah established a nursing school and began translating medical textbooks into Hebrew for the students. The first class graduated in 1921, just in time to begin replacing the AZMU nurses who had begun pulling out of Palestine.

Henrietta Szold finally moved to Palestine in 1920 and began overseeing the daily operation of Hadassah projects. Despite its enormous victories, Hadassah struggled for more than a decade after the war. European Jewish immigration to Palestine increased steadily while donations and funding decreased dramatically. The World Zionist Organization cut Hadassah's budget by two-thirds. Most American Jews lost interest in Zionism when the Balfour Declaration did not immediately result in a Jewish state, and membership in Hadassah and other American organizations dwindled. In Palestine, Henrietta Szold struggled under the weight of unpaid bills for everything from electricity to groceries and medical supplies. She was often unable to pay salaries. Even a $20,000 donation from Nathan Straus covered only 25% of their debts. In 1932, she wrote to Edgar Behrend, "I confess that I am beginning to think that the time for retirement from such intensive, straining activity as I have been drawn into has arrived. I confess to homesickness, too. On the other hand, when I begin to plan the retreat, I feel like a deserter."

Henrietta Szold was beginning to prepare for her retirement to Baltimore in 1931, but she was elected to the seven-member executive committee of the Vaad Leumi, Palestine's Jewish Assembly. As a member of the Vaad Leumi, she assisted in transferring responsibility for health and educational projects from Zionist groups to local Jewish community organizations. She also took the lead in establishing a central social service bureau. The Vaad Leumi envisioned the bureau as an information clearinghouse, but Szold helped them plan a more modern department of Social Welfare, staffed by social workers and supported by a corps of volunteers. Initially funded by a grant from the American-based Palestine Endowment Fund, the Department opened three social work facilities in 1932, and Szold ran them until 1937.

Social workers and other services proved crucial as immigrants streamed into Palestine. By 1932, economic depression in Germany had exposed latent anti-Semitism, and Jews were looking for a way to leave the country. In Berlin, *Recha Freier began Youth Aliyah, an organization established to help Jewish children escape to Palestine. At first, Szold was skeptical of the plan. She feared that Palestine was ill-prepared to meet the needs of a massive influx of immigrants—especially children who would require supervision. History made her fears irrelevant. In 1933, Adolf Hitler rose to power, and over 30,000 German refugees streamed into Palestine, more than three times the 1932 number.

Szold visited Berlin in 1933, unprepared for the overt and vengeful anti-Semitism she witnessed. Still full of doubt about Palestine's ability to care for young refugees, she took charge of the Youth Aliyah bureau in Palestine. She adopted a plan developed by Chaim Arlosoroff—similar to one Freier had suggested—for housing almost 3,000 children in kibbutzim, boarding schools and children's villages. Once she had a plan, Szold began the arduous task of obtaining visas. The British refused to issue immigration permits for the children unless Szold could prove there were resources to support them for two years. Szold collected enough evidence to obtain the first 350 permits in late 1933. When the first Youth Aliyah children arrived in Palestine on February 19, 1934, Szold met them at the dock in Haifa and greeted each by name, a tradition she maintained with each new wave of young refugees.

As Szold was struggling to obtain visas and arrange housing and education for the children, Hadassah was staging a fight of its own—for independence. In 1933, Hadassah had dissolved its affiliation with the male Federation of American Zionists (FAZ). In 1935, it initiated a controversial struggle for sole control of Youth Aliyah fundraising in the United States. Its desire for autonomy directly challenged World Zionist Congress efforts to eliminate division in the Zionist agenda and competition for funds. A heated battle ensued between Hadassah and organizations like the American Palestine Campaign and the Zionist Organization of America (formerly FAZ). In January 1936, they reached a compromise. As Youth Aliyah's exclusive American agent, Hadassah agreed to focus fundraising efforts on women and credit the United Palestine Appeal with any money it raised.

Hadassah's bid for independence foreshadowed a split between the organization and its founder. Henrietta Szold openly advocated peace between Jews and Arabs in Palestine. In 1936, she wrote, "The fears of the Arabs are not groundless. Our peaceful endeavors in our own behalf are undeniably pressing them to the wall." Most Zionists did not share Szold's compassion for the Arabs whose terrorist attacks against Jews had escalated in the 20 years since the Balfour Declaration. In 1937, she was booed at the World Zionist Conference. "I am not pleading for justice to the Arabs alone," she said. "I am pleading for justice to ourselves, to our principles, the sacred principles for which our martyrs gave their blood."

In 1942, Szold, Judah Magnes and others founded Ihud—Unity—an organization dedicated to planning a bi-national Arab-Jewish state in Palestine. At the same time, American Jews began to renew their support for the Zionist agenda. At the Biltmore Conference in 1942 and the American Jewish Conference in 1943, they demanded the establishment of an independent Jewish state. Heated letters flew back and forth between Hadassah leaders in New York and Szold in Palestine. In the end, Hadassah aligned with the American Jewish agenda, stopping just short of denouncing Szold. In Palestine, Jewish newspapers were more overt, demanding her expulsion from Zionist groups.

In 1917, she had given into similar pressure, putting aside her public support of pacifism. This time, she ignored her critics and focused on her work. As World War II raged, Youth Aliyah children arriving in Palestine were increasingly malnourished, exhausted, and emotionally scarred. She dedicated the remainder of her life to meeting their needs. In 1941, just three years before her death, she established a Children's Bureau through the Vaad Leumi, providing the initial funding with $70,000 from her own savings. Later renamed Mosad Szold, the bureau ensured all children equal access to social and educational services. Although she lived to see a healthy nation emerging out of the third world country of Palestine, Henrietta Szold did not live to see the establishment of the State of Israel. She died in Palestine in 1944.

SOURCES:
Dash, Joan. *Summoned to Jerusalem: The Life of Henrietta Szold.* NY: Harper and Row, 1979.
Geller, Lawrence D. *The Henrietta Szold Papers in the Hadassah Archives, 1875–1965.* NY: Hadassah, the Women's Zionist Organization of America, 1982.
Levin, Alexandra, ed. *Henrietta Szold and Youth Aliyah: Family Letters, 1934–1944.* NY: Herzl Press, 1986.
———. *The Szolds of Lombard Street: A Baltimore Family, 1859–1909.* Philadelphia, PA: Jewish Publication Society of America, 1960.
Levin, Marlin. *Balm in Gilead: The Story of Hadassah.* NY: Schocken, 1973.

SUGGESTED READING:
Fineman, Irving. *Woman of Valor: The Story of Henrietta Szold.* NY: Simon and Schuster, 1961.
Gidal, Nachum T. *Henrietta Szold: The Saga of an American Woman.* NY: Gefen, 1996.
Lowenthal, Marvin. *Henrietta Szold: Life and Letters.* NY: Viking, 1942.

RELATED MEDIA:
Kessler, Barry, Curator. "Daughter of Zion: Henrietta Szold, An American Jewish Womanhood." Traveling exhibit. Jewish Historical Society of Maryland. Baltimore, MD, 1995.

COLLECTIONS:
The Henrietta Szold Papers, Hadassah Archives, Hadassah, the Women's Zionist Organization of America, New York City.

Denise D. Meringolo, Curator,
Jewish Historical Society of Greater Washington,
Washington, D.C.

Szönyi, Erzsebet (1924—)

Hungarian composer, choral conductor, pianist, and lecturer known throughout the world for her work in music education. Name variations: Szoenyi. Born in Budapest, Hungary, on April 25, 1924; studied with Nadia Boulanger.

Erzsebet Szönyi was born in Budapest, Hungary, in 1924. From 1942 to 1947, she studied at the Liszt Academy with Janos Viski and Ernö Szegedi. Upon graduation, she won a scholarship to the Paris Conservatoire to study with *Nadia Boulanger, Tony Aubin, and Olivier Messiaen. Szönyi won the conservatoire's prix de composition in 1948, then returned to Budapest where she taught at the Ferenc Liszt Academy, becoming director of the academy's school of music in 1960. She also won the Liszt (1947) and Erkel (1959) prizes. Around 1950, Szönyi began composing opera, beginning with *Dalma* in 1952. She also composed works for

children, such as the ballets *Garden Tale* (1949) and *The Cricket and the Ants* (1953). This interest in works for children led her to collaborate closely with Zoltan Kodaly, the great Hungarian composer, in order to successfully implement his ideas for music education in Hungary's schools. Szönyi was soon known as an international expert on musical education for children. She became supervisor of Hungarian music conservatories in 1951 and served on the board of directors of the International Society for Music Education. Szönyi was a prolific composer with over 100 works for orchestra, voice, piano, and theater. She also wrote several volumes translated into English, German, and Japanese about teaching music to young children.

SOURCES:
Cohen, Aaron I. *International Encyclopedia of Women Composers.* 2 vols. NY: Books & Music (USA), 1987.
Sadie, Stanley, ed. *New Grove Dictionary of Music and Musicians.* 20 vols. NY: Macmillan, 1980.

John Haag,
Athens, Georgia

Szumowska, Antoinette
(1868–1938)

Polish pianist. Born in Lublin, Poland, on February 22, 1868; died in Rumson, New Jersey, on August 18, 1938; married Joseph Adamowski (a cellist), in 1896.

Antoinette Szumowska began her formal piano studies at the Warsaw Conservatory with the noted teacher Aleksander Michailowski (1851–1938). She then continued her education with Ignace Jan Paderewski in Paris from 1890 through 1895, making her Paris debut in 1891. In 1892, George Bernard Shaw reviewed one of her London recitals, noting that she played "beautifully and intelligently." In 1895, she settled in the United States, where the bulk of her career was spent as the pianist of the Adamowski Trio (whose cellist she married), a group that garnered an enviable reputation for excellence in chamber music. She also taught privately and at the New England Conservatory; the Puerto Rican pianist Jesus Maria Sanroma (1902–1984) was among her most accomplished students.

John Haag,
Athens, Georgia

Szymanowska, Maria Agata
(1789–1831)

Polish composer, pianist, and teacher known especially for her nocturnes. Name variations: Szymanowski; Shimanovskaya. Born Maria Agata

Wolowska in Warsaw, Poland, on December 14, 1789; died of cholera in St. Petersburg, Russia, on July 24, 1831; married Theophilus Jozef Szymanowski (a Polish landowner), in 1810 (divorced 1820); children: three, including daughter **Celina Szymanowska,** *who married Adam Mickiewicz, the poet.*

By the 1830s, Romantic music combined with the piano had become the rage throughout Europe and America. Throughout the 19th century, a number of women became famous concert pianists, including *Clara Schumann and *Teresa Carreño. Many of these artists wrote their own compositions so that audiences could buy their sheet music to play at home. In the age before phonograph recordings, tapes, and CDs, sheet music guaranteed a more widespread audience, as well as additional revenue. With the growth of the European middle class, pianos became common, so the market for sheet music grew. It was this market Maria Agata Szymanowska exploited.

Born Maria Agata Wolowska in Warsaw in 1789, Szymanowska was the first Polish pianist to gain a European reputation. Although her parents were not musical, they had seen to it that their daughter acquired the best education Warsaw could provide. She toured continental Europe in 1810, the same year she married. Her husband, landowner Theophilus Jozef Szymanowski, did not support her concert career, so Szymanowska left him, taking their three children with her. From 1820, she sustained her family through her concerts and compositions.

The great German writer Johann Wolfgang von Goethe was infatuated with Szymanowska; she was one of the aging Olympian's last passions. He considered her playing superior to that of the reigning virtuoso Hummel, describing her performing as "incredible," and wrote his *Aussöhnung* for her. Robert Schumann also had a very high opinion of her Etudes. Szymanowska was appointed pianist to the Russian imperial court in 1822 and won the admiration of Russian intellectuals, including the poet Alexander Pushkin and the composer Mikhail Glinka.

As a composer, Szymanowska was sometimes called "the feminine John Field," after the Irish-born inventor of the nocturne. Her mazurkas were derived from folk music while the nocturnes sometimes resembled those of Field, though some are clearly superior, including the one in B-flat, which Frédéric Chopin knew well. Szymanowska was one of the first composers to use Polish dance forms such as the mazurka and polonaise as the basis for her compositions. She used these forms in nocturnes, waltzes, and etudes which were known and played throughout Europe; anyone with a piano could more or less duplicate the sound. Szymanowska's use of Polish folk music had an enormous influence on the young Chopin who used this concept in his own works. As a composer and artist, Szymanowska was quite the rage, paving the way for other Polish musicians who would play their music on concert stages throughout the world.

SOURCES:

Cohen, Aaron I. *International Encyclopedia of Women Composers.* 2 vols. NY: Books & Music (USA), 1987.

John Haag,
Athens, Georgia

Szymborska, Wislawa (1923—)

Polish poet, essayist and translator—one of the leading poets, and the leading woman poet—in post-World-War-II Poland, who won the 1996 Nobel Prize for Literature. Name variations: Wisława Szymborska; Wislawa Symborska; (pseudonym) Stanczykowna. Pronunciation: Vee-SWAH-vah Shim-BOR-skah. Born on July 2, 1923, in Prowent-Bnin, Poland; daughter of Wincenty Szymborski and Anna (Rottermund) Szymborska; attended schools in Cracow (Kraków); attended a Polish underground school during German occupation in World War II; granted an undergraduate degree from the Jagiellonian University, Cracow; married Adam Wlodek or Włodek (divorced); married Kornel Flipowicz (also seen as Filipowicz), a poet and prose writer (died 1990).

Published first poem in a supplement to Dziennik Polski *(Polish Daily, 1945); published some 30 poems in the* Daily *(1945–48); worked on the staff of the literary newspaper* Życie Literackie *(Literary Life, 1952–81); criticized for writing elitist poetry, in violation of Socialist Realism, when she attempted to publish her first book of poems (1948); accepted Stalinist-era Socialist Realism and criticized Western countries in* Dlatego żyjemy *(That's Why We Live (1952) and* Pytania zadawane sobie *(Questioning Oneself, 1954); repudiated Socialist Realism in* Wołanie do Yeti *(Calling Out to Yeti, 1957); completely omitted pre-1956 poems from her collected works of poetry,* Poezje *(Poetry, 1970); emerged as a mature poet with* Sto pociech *(A Hundred Laughs, 1967); received the Goethe Award (1991); received the Polish PEN Poetry award (1996); received the Nobel Prize for Literature (1996).*

Selected writings: What We Live For *(1952);* Questions Put to Myself *(1954);* Wołanie do Yeti

(Calling Out to Yeti, 1957); Salt (1962); Wiersze wybrane (Selected Poems, 1964); Sto pociech (A Hundred Laughs, 1967); Poezje (Poetry, 1970); Wielka liczba (A Great Number, 1976); Nothing Twice (1980); Ludzie na moście (People on a Bridge, 1986); Koniec i początek (The End and the Beginning, 1993); Widok z ziarnkiem piasku (View with a Grain of Sand, 1996).

Wislawa Szymborska, the leading woman poet in Poland in the 20th century, is a native of a country which has been the focus of much upheaval and tragic events in the last two centuries. Victimized by three powerful neighboring states which divided its land among themselves in the late 1700s, Poland did not exist as a separate, single polity in the 19th century. Although it was restored to its status as a single nation at the end of World War I—in what Polish poets saw as the rebirth of their country—Poland was the first country to be invaded by German troops in World War II. Freed from the Nazi terror by victorious Soviet troops, Poland came under the control of a Soviet-controlled bureaucracy.

/Her poetry] with ironic precision allows the historical and biological context to come to light in fragments of human reality.

—**Nobel Prize committee**

Throughout these catastrophes, Polish poets have represented a continuation of Poland in a cultural guise, even when there was no "Poland" on the map. But they have also carried the burden of speaking for their nation, and especially of speaking for those who perished. Despite these difficulties, the second half of the 20th century proved to be a renaissance of Polish poetry, so much so that a writer for *The New York Times* has spoken of the "greatness of Polish poetry at the end of the 20th century [which has] much to do with its philosophical and ethical seriousness." Polish poetry, he added, has "come to be admired by other poets during the past 20 years or so for its immense intellectual sophistication, its lucid rejection of tyranny and its humane and democratic values."

Prominent in this renaissance has been Szymborska, considered not only Poland's most eminent woman poet of the 20th century but also one of its three greatest poets of the century, the other two being Tadeusz Różewicz and Zbigniew Herbert. Szymborska belongs to the generation of Polish poets who were tempered in the horrors of the Nazi occupation, when the leaders of Poland's cultural life were largely driven underground by the Nazi control of Poland. Some perished, such as the poets Tadeusz Gajcy and Krzysztof Baczyński, who died in the Warsaw uprising against Nazi rule in 1944. It is estimated that Poland lost almost a fifth of its population during this period.

Freed by liberating Soviet armies, Poland became a Communist country in the aftermath of the war, and Szymborska's generation also experienced the rigors of this period. Under the dictums of the Communist government's policy of Socialist Realism, the writings of Polish intellectuals were expected to contribute to the building of a socialist society, were expected to be written in a way that made them "accessible" to the masses, and were expected to be "politically constructive" rather than negative toward the regime.

Polish intellectuals, who sometimes bore guilt at being survivors of the Nazi era and keenly felt the burden of speaking in place of those who had not survived, responded in various ways to the demands of the new Communist regime. During this period, some, such as Herbert and Miron Białoszewski, went into "internal emigration," neither writing nor saying anything that might be construed as political. Some, like Czeslaw Miłosz, went into exile in the West, and others, such as Konstanty Gałczyński, returned to Poland, wrote poetry, and were disappointed that they failed to gain any kind of official recognition from the government.

Szymborska chose a different path. Born in 1923 in Bnin, near the city of Posnan, in central west Poland, and named after Poland's largest river, the Wisla, she was eight years old when her family moved to Cracow. She would become a lifelong citizen of that city. Her first attempts at poetry were encouraged by her father, who gave her money for each poem. She was in her early teens when World War II began and in her early 20s when it came to an end. Szymborska attended illegal, underground classes during the Nazi occupation of Poland and eventually received her degree from Jagiellonian University, specializing in sociology and Polish language studies. Her first poem to be published, "I Seek the Word," appeared in 1945 in a supplement to a Polish newspaper, the *Polish Daily* (*Dziennik Polski*), where she eventually published some 30 poems, many of which expressed sorrow for the tribulations of her country and expressed guilt over those who had perished in the Nazi occupation.

In 1952, Szymborska joined the staff of a literary newspaper, *Życie Literackie* (*Literary Life*), and remained with the newspaper until 1981, working as its poetry editor and writing a column. From 1967 through 1972, she also published more than 130 book reviews, mostly in the same newspaper, evaluating a diverse mix of books on topics which ranged from music and psychology to do-it-yourself.

A slow writer who has emphasized quality over quantity—one writer has called her the "least prolific of the major poets of our time"—Szymborska has often released a new book of poetry only about every five to seven years. While she has been a careful writer by choice, events in her early career also made her cautious. In 1948, her first attempt at producing a book of poetry—basically taken from the poems that she had published in the *Polish Daily*—was rejected by the Communist regime. It was said that the poems were too elitist to be accessible to the average worker, and the topics of the poems were said too personal and not universal in scope. A campaign was mounted against her that included even demonstrations by schoolchildren.

Rather than go into "internal exile" or flee the country, Szymborska chose to accept the Stalinist-era, Socialist Realist dictums—sincerely, she said later—and her first two books of poetry, *Dlatego żyjemy* (*That's Why We Live*, 1952) and *Pytania zdawane sobie* (*Questioning Oneself*, 1954) were filled with themes that met the Communist party's approval: suspicion of the West, an emphasis on the need for peace, and praise for the building of a new workers' society. Among the poems published in these volumes was "Old Working Woman," in which an old woman speaks of the suffering she has endured under the capitalist system, including being fired because she was pregnant; "From Korea," which is presented as an eyewitness account of an American soldier putting out the eyes of a Korean civilian; and "Her Soldier," which condemns the release of war criminals from American, British or French military prisons. "Most of my generation got into Communist ideology at about the same time," she later told a newspaper interviewer. "They had entered Communism as a group, but had to find their own way out."

The quality of Szymborska's poetry in these volumes is considered mediocre at best, and she later in effect disavowed these poems by including only nine in an edition of her collected poems entitled *Wiersze wybrane* (*Selected Poems*, 1964), and by including none at all in another retrospective collection, entitled *Poezje* (*Poetry*, 1970). "When I was young, I had a moment of believing in Communist doctrine," she subsequently told an interviewer. "I wanted to save the world through Communism. Quite soon I understood that it doesn't work, but I've never pretended that it didn't happen to me."

Following the "thaw" year of 1956, Szymborska broke with Socialist Realism when she published a volume of poetry entitled *Wołanie do Yeti* (*Calling Out to Yeti*, 1957). In these poems, the Yeti or Abominable Snowman is compared to Communism, or possibly to Joseph Stalin himself, in apparent references to institutions and individuals who, like the Yeti, provide neither humane direction nor comfort for artists and poets. Included in the volume is her groundbreaking poem "Rehabilitation," in which she strove to explain why so many writers had followed government dictums for an area—literature—that was properly the realm of individuals and not institutions. Regarding her earlier acquiescence in Communist artistic standards, Szymborska noted, "Since 1955, I haven't written a single poem using 'we,' only 'I.' I decided that I had to do something with myself, and my own problems. I wanted to make my own thoughts orderly. I finished speaking on anyone's behalf but my own."

Since the appearance of *Calling Out to Yeti*, Szymborska has occasionally dealt with political themes but generally has chosen to keep politics and poetry separate. The mature Szymborska has said in an interview that she largely relinquished political themes because she is not certain that poetry can adequately deal with them. When she commented on the Vietnam War in "Vietnam," the poem never specified the nationality or political beliefs of an American interrogator but focused instead on sympathy for the victims of misfortune and suffering.

Szymborska has shown greater willingness to comment on political developments which have affected individuals whom she has known. In "Rehabilitation," she deals with the case of the Hungarian Communist leader Laslo Rajk, who was executed on a charge of treason in 1948, during a Soviet campaign against the independent-minded Communist government of Yugoslavia. "Rehabilitation" cites the case as an example of human beings' willingness to destroy the reputation of others. It especially condemned attempts to wipe Rajk's name off the history books, pretending that he had never existed. In this poem, Szymborska also expressed deep sorrow that she had, at the time, believed that such accused individuals were really traitors. Central to this poem is a sense of frustration that the world of poetry cannot rectify injustices; in the realm of politics, poets are sometimes helpless.

Only on a few occasions has Szymborska been politically active. In the late 1970s, she joined a movement to block attempts to amend to the Polish constitution of 1952 in ways that would have created closer ties with the Soviet government. She has also been a participant in the Flying University movement in Poland, consisting of courses which are intended to correct "Communist distortions" of Polish society and history.

Combined, the Nazi and Soviet periods in Poland caused Polish poets to re-examine their roles, raising questions about the goals and practical effects of poetry. Szymborska seems to believe that the disasters of the recent past demand a "simpler, very brash language," making it necessary to have a "poetry without artifice" or without elevated language. She is suspicious of poems that rest only on descriptions of beautiful scenes, faked emotion, or sentimentality. Her style has been described as concise, "terse," and "ironic" rather than passionate. She loves puns, and her poems often explore what is possible with the use of language.

Calling Out to Yeti and her next volume of poems, *Sto pociech* (*A Hundred Laughs*, 1967), marked her emergence as an individual, indeed iconoclastic, poet who is difficult to classify, and even to place in what is often called the "Polish school of poetry." Her post-Stalinist era poems have been quite different from her early work and are generally characterized by an assertion of the autonomy of the individual against threats from determinism, from utopian systems, and from collectivist ideas. Generally starting from simple observations, her poems often explore contradictions in human thought and social life, using a tone of irony that has been described as "ironic moralism." The themes of many of her poems are the earth itself, the creation of it, and the objects on it. The poems often celebrate life and the creative process, asserting that humans are part of a phenomenon that is nature—a grand, wonderful, intriguing world that should elicit praise, wonderment, and astonishment.

Much of Szymborska's poetry deals with deep philosophical questions in witty ways. One of her best-known poems in *Calling Out to Yeti*, entitled "Two Monkeys by Bruegel," works on two levels. Two monkeys speak intelligently of the history of humanity, and find it to be depressing. As the poem progresses, it becomes clear that these are supposed to be the same two animals portrayed in the famous Bruegel painting, kept in chains by humans and considered to be a lower life form than humans. "Any Event" examines the uselessness and futility of language, providing a long list of words which are used to substitute for a true understanding of things. Words, particularly explanations which are contradictory, can pretend to be truth.

When Poland was under martial law during the 1980s, Szymborska published in a Polish exile journal in Paris, and her work also appeared in the underground press in Poland under the pseudonym Stanczykowna. The name appears to be a reference to the most famous court jester in Polish history, Stanczyk, who had the reputation of being able to recite unwelcome truths while seeming to play the clown.

The range of her poems has been astonishing, from the question whether humans can stop the flow of time ("People on a Bridge"); whether humans are really better adapted to nature than creatures, like dinosaurs, that have become extinct ("A Dinosaur's Skeleton"); of how real is reality ("Reality Riddle"); to the question of life after death ("Elegiac Account"). Animals have frequently been a major theme in her poems. "Seen from Above" argues that animals are not on earth for man to use or misuse, and that even the death of a beetle should be given respect. In some of her work, memory and dreams are presented as being essentially the same thing, because both are seen as attempts to regain things that are lost in the past (as in her poems "Memory at Last" and "In Praise of Dreams"). A frequent theme in her poems is a focus on the dark side of human beings, such as the human urge for self-destruction ("Discovery"); terrorism ("The Terrorist: He Watches"), the ability of human beings to become savages ("The Hunger Camp near Jaslo"); or the use of drugs to combat despair and feelings of abandonment ("Advertisement").

Noting that she was trained in the scientific method, Szymborska has said that in preparation for much of her poetry, she reads a wide variety of material, ranging from books on the sciences to travel books. Subjects for her poems, she insists, are never lacking. Her goal is to make each of her poems distinctive and different from the others that she writes, and she spends a large amount of time shaping them. What she wants to avoid, she confesses, is being the kind of person who spends an entire lifetime essentially writing the same poem over and over, each time trying to improve on the previous attempt. Her later poetry, which has tended more toward free verse, has also carried a tone of skepticism, a mocking tone which humorously balances out the very serious subjects that she often explores. For many of her readers, according to one writer, her poems represent a kind of "joy arising from the play of intellect and the imagination."

Szymborska's poems are tempered by a kind of rationality that is lacking in the work of many other Polish poets, some of whose verses harken back to the Romantic school of the 19th century, with its emotional descriptions of patriotism or religion. Her outlook has been compared to the Enlightenment, the historical period preceding Romanticism which is sometimes termed the "age of reason." Yet attempts to compare Szymborska's work to the Enlightenment have also been challenged by critics who point out that her poetry is usually imbued with wit and feelings and is certainly not "academic" in tone.

Many of her poems since 1957 have used a woman's viewpoint to make philosophical observations about nature and human emotions such as loneliness or isolation, and historical figures such as *Mary Stuart do appear in her work, but very few of her poems clearly advocate feminism. One of the best-known exceptions is "Portrait of a Woman," which praises women's ingenuity and ability to adapt. Generally, however, since Polish grammar identifies the gender of the speaker, it is clear the speaker in many of her poems is a woman character. "Should someone classify my work as 'women's work,' I would not be too upset," she told an interviewer, "but I am not concerned to make an issue out of this fact."

Some of her later poetry has been lyric poetry celebrating love, although even here Szymborska has included philosophical questions, such as the inevitability of some degree of "emotional distance" between two humans, even if lovers. Some critics think, however, that her most successful love poems have been ones which gently mock the subject, such as "Buffo," in which one of the lovers speculates on how they would be viewed 100 years later and wonders if actors might stage a comedy based on their relationship.

As Szymborska's reputation grew during the 1960s and 1970s, sales of her books increased. *Wielka liczba* (*A Great Number*, 1976) sold some 10,000 copies in Poland. Szymborska has also occasionally translated French poetry, and although she has reportedly written short stories, she has not published them. Szymborska's awards, from both within and outside of Poland, have included the Gold Cross of Merit, the Order of Polonia Restituta, the Goethe award, the Herder Award, and the Polish PEN club award.

Szymborska's poetry has appeared in foreign editions, in Russian, Czech, French, German, Dutch, Hungarian, and English. Selections of her poems were also translated into Swedish and published in volumes in 1980 and 1989. It is believed that these translations helped bring Szymborska's work to the attention of the Swedish Academy and may have contributed to her eventual selection as a Nobel laureate.

When it was announced in 1996 that Szymborska had won the Nobel Prize for Literature, newspaper reporters who were eager to interview Szymborska had difficulty locating the reclusive poet, who has seldom been willing to discuss details of her personal life. Ensconced in a small town named Zakopane in the mountains of Poland, she managed to elude most of the press and spent her time in seclusion crafting her Nobel acceptance speech. Szymborska dislikes the public spotlight, a fact that has moved one writer to dub her the "*Greta Garbo of Poland."

When Szymborska became a Nobel laureate—the fifth Pole to win the literature award—there was recognition in her native country that her poetry has moved beyond Polish issues and increasingly has dealt with universal themes. In the view of Piotr Sommer, a fellow Polish poet, giving the Nobel prize to her means giving it to a poet who has not tried to be put on any "special 'Polish pedestal.'" Yet Szymborska chose to return much of her prize money to her native country, telling reporters that she planned to donate the entire sum, exceeding $1 million, to charity.

In her Nobel acceptance speech, Szymborska noted that when she travels, government officials and other travelers generally act unbelieving or even alarmed when they discover that they are talking with a poet. Speculating that philosophers "probably get the same reaction," Szymborska noted that few films are produced about poets, but there are "very many" motion pictures about great scientists or artists, and that there are even "spectacular" films about painters.

In the case of poets, Szymborska added, there is nothing very inspiring about seeing them at work. A poet "sits down or sprawls across a sofa," or stares around the room, looking at a wall or ceiling, and then after a while writes down a few lines. "Who could stand to sit and watch such a process?," she asked. Worse, Szymborska insisted, was the fact that once a word has "hit the page," the poet starts to think that the answer is makeshift, and the poems, often the object of "self-dissatisfaction" by their creators, are eventually "frozen in time" and clipped together by "literary historians" who call them a writer's "oeuvres."

At the end of her acceptance speech, Szymborska noted that the "wonder of the world" is central to her poetry. "Our world is astonishing," even if the unlimited size of the universe scares people, or the limits of human ability depress people, or the suffering of "people, animals, or even plants" causes bitterness. Therefore, she predicted, there will always be work for poets.

SOURCES:

Gajer, Ewa. "Polish Poet Wislawa Szymborska," in *Hecate: A Women's Interdisciplinary Journal.* Vol. 23, no. 1, 1997, pp. 140–142.

Levine, Madeline G. *Contemporary Polish Poetry 1925–1972.* Boston, MA: Twayne, 1981.

Szymborska, Wislawa. *People on a Bridge: Poems.* Introduced and translated by Adam Czerniawski. London and Boston: Forest Books, 1996.

———. *Poems: New and Collected, 1957–1997.* Translated from the Polish by Stanislaw Baranczak and Clare Cavanagh. NY: Harcourt Brace, 1998.

———. *Sounds, Feeling, Thoughts: Seventy Poems.* Translated and introduced by Magnus J. Krynski and Robert A. Maguire. Princeton, NJ: Princeton University Press, 1981.

———. *View with a Grain of Sand.* Translated by Stanislaw Baranczak and Clare Cavanagh. NY: Harcourt Brace, 1995.

SUGGESTED READING:

Baranczak, Stanislaw, and Clare Cavanagh, eds. and trans. *Polish Poetry of the Last Two Decades of Communist Rule: Spoiling Cannibals' Fun.* Evanston, IL: Northwestern University Press, 1991.

Czerniawski, Adam, ed. *The Mature Laurel.* Chester Spring, PA: Dufour, 1991.

COLLECTIONS:

Other than Szymborska's own selections of poems for her two collections, *Wiersze wybrane* (*Selected Poems,* 1964) and *Poezje* (*Poetry,* 1970), there are also untranslated versions of her book reviews in *Lektury nadobowiazkowe* (*Recommended Reading,* Cracow: Wydawnictwo Literackie, 1973).

Niles Holt, Professor of History,
Illinois State University,
Normal, Illinois

Taba, Hilda (1902–1967)

Estonian-American author, professor, and curriculum development specialist. Born on December 7, 1902, in Estonia; died of peritonitis on July 6, 1967, in Burlingame, California; daughter of Robert Taba (a teacher and farmer) and Liisa (Leht) Taba; University of Tartu, Estonia, B.A., 1926; Bryn Mawr College, M.A., 1927; Columbia University, Ph.D., 1933.

Hilda Taba was born in 1902 in southeastern Estonia, one of nine children. Although her mother had attended only elementary school, her father had attained a secondary education and taught school. Both parents worked the family farm on land received as partial remuneration for teaching. Assisted by scholarships, all their children attended college.

Taba graduated with a bachelor's degree in 1926 from the University of Tartu in Estonia and came to the United States under a scholarship to attend Bryn Mawr College. She received a master's degree in education and psychology in 1927, and then went on to study at Teachers College, Columbia University, where she earned a Ph.D. in 1933. Her dissertation, *Dynamics of Education: A Methodology of Progressive Educational Thought*, acknowledged indebtedness to her mentors, prominent philosophers of the day such as John Dewey, and laid out the theories and techniques that she later developed.

Taba taught school for two years in Estonia, but returned to the United States and became in-

volved in an eight-year project of the Progressive Education Association to extend the group's theories to the secondary level without compromising students' chances of attending colleges which operated under more traditional guidelines. At the outset of this study, Taba began as director of curriculum research at one of the participating schools, New York City's Dalton School, and later became a staff associate, evaluating student development in the 30 schools involved in the study. As a result of this work, she was appointed assistant professor at Ohio State University in 1936 and at the University of Chicago in 1938.

Taba took a leave from the University of Chicago from 1945 to 1948 and directed a joint education project sponsored by the American Council on Education and financed by the National Conference of Christians and Jews. The intent of this project was to study intergroup relations from the perspective of race, religion, and ethnic background and to analyze the progress of these students through revision of teaching materials and methods. She continued this work as director of the Center for Intergroup Education at the University of Chicago from 1948 to 1951. Taba directed experimental programs in human relations, developed curricula, and educated teachers in these concepts. She also wrote numerous books and articles based on the research gained from these projects.

In 1951, Taba was appointed professor of education at San Francisco State College. There, she wrote her most important book, *Curriculum Development: Theory and Practice* (1962), which described a systematic approach to curriculum planning and design. In it, she advocated beginning with classroom units developed by teachers and from that creating a plan for the overall curriculum. This inverted the traditional sequence of events that had begun with an overall plan, and also brought classroom teachers into the development process.

After this, she served as director of many federally funded projects, working with teachers and school districts. Research on teaching methods and the way children think resulted in *Teachers' Handbook for Elementary Social Studies* (1967), which taught how to use specific facts to lead to generalizations. In conjunction with the work, she developed an elementary school-level social studies curriculum that utilized this approach to improve students' skills in critical thinking. As a direct result, the Taba Program in Social Science, a series of textbooks for grades one through eight, was published in the 1970s.

An energetic person with an astute intellect, Taba was particularly interested in travel, music, the theater, gardening, and reading. She was also a prodigious writer and innovative educator, writing or co-authoring nearly two dozen books, and her pioneering work influenced those who followed her in the field of curriculum development. Although many of her ideas have been surpassed, in 1976 she was posthumously named one of the 12 greatest people in the history of curriculum development by the Association for Supervision and Curriculum Development. Taba died of peritonitis in Burlingame, California, on July 6, 1967.

SOURCES:

Sicherman, Barbara, and Carol Hurd Green, eds. *Notable American Women: The Modern Period.* Cambridge, MA: The Belknap Press of Harvard University, 1980.

Martha Jones, M.L.S.,
Natick, Massachusetts

Tabei, Junko (1939—)

Japanese mountaineer who was the first woman to climb Mt. Everest. Born Junko Ishibashi in Miharu Machi, in the Fukushima prefecture, Japan, in 1939; graduated from Showa Women's College, Tokyo,

Junko Tabei

1962; married Masanobu Tabei (a mountaineer), in 1959; children: daughter Noriko (b. 1972); son Shinya (b. 1978).

Made first all-female ascent of Central Buttress on Tanigawa-Dake (1965); was the first woman to climb Mt. Everest (1975).

Junko Tabei was born Junko Ishibashi in Miharu Machi, in the Fukushima prefecture of Japan, in 1939. While on school holiday at age ten, in a spirit of youthful independence, she climbed Yumoto (6,562 ft.). But the exuberant escapade was rare, since Tabei had an unhappy childhood and adolescence, hampered by societal restrictions. Then, just before college graduation, she began climbing once more. "[I]t was like some vital organ in my body had started to function again. This was the real me and I discovered myself by climbing mountains. I felt a great sense of freedom."

In 1962, she joined the Hakurei Mountaineering Club and found a job with the Japanese Physics Society, editing the *Journal of European Physics.* She trained on the highest mountain in Japan, Fuji (12,388 ft.), practicing how to break a fall with her ice axe. At 22, she climbed Goryu Dake and was soon out-climbing her companions. She then changed to a more demanding seven-member club, Rhyu ho toko. In 1956, she and **Rumie Saso** made the first all-female winter ascent of the Central Buttress (Ichino-kura) on Tanigawa-Dake. Saso was later killed on another expedition while trying to save her falling second.

In March 1970, Tabei joined an all-women expedition, which included and was led by **Eiko Miyuzaki** (Mrs. Eiko Hisano), to climb Annapurna III (24,787 ft.) in the Himalayas. Of the eight climbers and one doctor, Tabei alone reached the summit on May 19th.

In 1975, she (as climbing leader) and Miyuzaki (as overall leader) planned an attack on Mt. Everest, but when they sought backing from the Japanese business community, they were told it was folly. Everest was the highest mountain in the world, said the business leaders; it was subject to frequent storms, and there was a race against time because of the coming monsoons. Ten women attempting to climb Mt. Everest would undoubtedly fail. Finally, a newspaper and television station underwrote the venture, but the budget was lean. In 1973, an Italian expedition had cost £600,000; the 1974 Japanese Mountain Association assailed the mountain with the help of £200,000. Tabei's group had amassed only £86,000.

Despite this, the women proceeded, though they had to deal with a shortage of jumars, a mechanical device that aids climbing up fixed ropes; instead, they had to climb hand-over-hand. On May 3, 1975, having retreated to Camp II because of worsening weather, Tabei and her tentmates were awakened by an avalanche. When the sherpas dug them out, Tabei's legs were badly bruised and her hips stretched from being pulled out. The television crew began to write off the attempt, and there was mounting pressure on Tabei to abandon the cause. They had lost valuable time and the monsoons would soon start. But after three days, Tabei began to walk again. On May 10, she and Sherpa Sirdar Ang Tschering started up the mountain once more. By May 16th, they were preparing to attack the summit. Wrote Birkett and Peascod in *Women Climbing:*

> Deep powder snow made the going very arduous. After reaching the South (lesser) summit they followed the ridge, which became increasingly knife-edged, to the technical crux, the Hillary step (a small, but very steep snow couloir, named after its first ascensionist, Edmund Hillary). The crest of the ridge was too narrow to walk on, so they traversed below it on one side, using the edge itself as a handhold. . . . A slip here would have been fatal, but soon the Hillary step was reached. . . . Resting many times, taking only one step at a time, she willed that there would be a last step. The sherpa's words: "Tabei San, this is the top," were just reward.

Thus, on May 16, 1975, Junko Tabei became the first woman to stand at the summit of Mt. Everest. She was 36. "Thank Goodness I don't have to go any higher," she joked. That same year, **Phanthog**, a Tibetan woman, followed. Japanese climber **Yasuko Namba** (1949–1996), the next woman to reach the top of Everest, died on the descent in the blizzard of 1996 that claimed seven other lives. It was one of the worst disasters in the history of Everest climbs.

SOURCES:

Birkett, Bill, and Bill Peascod. *Women Climbing: 200 Years of Achievement.* London: A&C Black, 1989.
Tabei, Junko. *Everest Mother.* Shinco-Sha, 1982.
Unsworth, Walt. *Everest.* Allen Lane, 1981.

Taber, Gladys (1899–1980)

American poet, novelist, short-story writer, essayist, and columnist. Born Gladys Leonae Bagg on April 12 (though most sources cite April 12, the Social Security Index cites April 24), 1899, in Colorado Springs, Colorado; died on March 11, 1980, in Hyannis, Massachusetts; daughter of Rufus Mather Bagg and Grace Sibyl (Raybold) Bagg; Wellesley College, B.A., 1920;

Lawrence College, M.A., 1921; graduate study at Columbia University, 1931–33; married Frank Albion Taber, Jr., in 1922; children: **Constance Anne Taber.**

Selected fiction: Late Climbs the Sun *(1934);* Tomorrow May Be Fair *(1935);* The Evergreen Tree *(1937);* A Star to Steer By *(1938);* Long Tails and Short *(short stories, 1938);* This Is for Always *(1938);* Nurse in Blue *(1943);* The Heart Has April Too *(1944);* Give Us This Day *(1944);* Give Me the Stars *(1945);* The Family on Maple Street *(1946);* Daisy and Dobbin: Two Little Seahorses *(juvenile, 1948);* When Dogs Meet People *(short stories, 1952);* Spring Harvest *(1959);* One Dozen and One *(short stories, 1966).*

Selected nonfiction: Harvest at Stillmeadow *(1940);* Especially Spaniels *(1945);* Stillmeadow Kitchen *(1947); (with Ruth Kistner)* Flower Arranging for the American Home *(1947);* The Book of Stillmeadow *(1948);* Especially Father *(1949);* The First Book of Dogs *(juvenile, 1949);* The First Book of Cats *(juvenile, 1950);* Stillmeadow Seasons *(1950); (with Barbara Webster)* Stillmeadow and Sugarbridge *(1953);* Stillmeadow Daybook *(1955);* Mrs. Daffodil *(1957);* What Cooks at Stillmeadow: The Favorite Recipes of Gladys Taber *(1958);* Stillmeadow Sampler *(1959);* The Stillmeadow Road *(1962);* Another Path *(1963);* Gladys Taber's Stillmeadow Cookbook *(1965);* Especially Dogs . . . Especially at Stillmeadow *(1968);* Flower Arranging *(1969);* Amber: A Very Personal Cat *(1970);* My Own Cape Cod *(1971);* My Own Cookbook: From Stillmeadow and Cape Cod *(1972);* Country Chronicle *(1974);* The Best of Stillmeadow: A Treasury of Country Living *(1976);* Harvest of Yesterdays *(autobiography, 1976);* Conversations with Amber *(1978);* Still Cove Journal *(1981).*

Selected other writings: Lady of the Moon *(play, 1928);* Lyonnesse *(poetry, 1929).*

Gladys Taber was born in 1899 in Colorado Springs, Colorado, the second daughter of **Grace Raybold Bagg** and Rufus Mather Bagg, a descendant of a Massachusetts Puritan family that included both Cotton and Increase Mather. Taber began writing early, penning a historical novel at age nine and poetry at ten. She attended Appleton High School in Appleton, Wisconsin, before receiving a bachelor's degree at Wellesley College in 1920. Upon graduation, she returned home to Appleton, where she taught English at Lawrence College while earning a master's degree there in 1921. She married a fellow teacher, Frank Albion Taber, Jr., in 1922 and gave birth to daughter Constance. Though she became a freelance writer in 1932, Taber also taught English at Randolph Macon Women's College in

Lynchburg, Virginia, during the academic year 1925–26, and creative writing at Columbia University from 1936 to 1943.

She published a collection of poetry, *Lyonnesse*, in 1926, and her first novel *Late Climbs the Sun* (1934) was favorably reviewed in *The New York Times*. By then the Tabers, with Gladys' sister and her sister's two children, had moved to Stillmeadow, a 17th-century farmhouse in the Connecticut countryside, which would become her inspiration for numerous books and articles about country living. The early years on the farm were lean and full of hard work, including keeping a large garden and raising cocker spaniels, all of which was recounted in her books. *Harvest at Stillmeadow* (1940) was her initial collection of essays on day-to-day country living, working, and meditation, and included her observations on life. *The Book of Stillmeadow* (1948) and *Stillmeadow Seasons* (1950) followed. Taber also published books on such topics as raising cocker spaniels and flower arranging, as well as cookbooks, historical and romance novels, and children's books. *Especially Father* (1949) is a biography of her impetuous father.

In addition to contributing more than 200 short stories to periodicals in the United States and abroad, Taber wrote columns for women's magazines. From 1938 to 1958, she wrote "Diary of Domesticity" for the *Ladies' Home Journal*, where she also served as an assistant editor from 1946 to 1958, and after that authored "Butternut Wisdom" for *Family Circle*. Taber published her autobiography *Harvest of Yesterdays* in 1976. She died on March 11, 1980, in Hyannis, Massachusetts; a book about her home on Cape Cod, Massachusetts, *Still Cove Journal* (1981), was published posthumously.

SOURCES:
Contemporary Authors New Revision Series. Vol. 4. Detroit, MI: Gale Research, 1981.
Current Biography. NY: H.W. Wilson, 1952.

Martha Jones, M.L.S.,
Natick, Massachusetts

Taber, Mrs. Robert (1866–1950).

See Marlowe, Julia.

Tabitha (fl. 37 CE).

See Dorcas.

Tabouis, Geneviève (1892–1985)

French columnist, one of the first women to achieve international distinction as a journalist, who was read throughout Europe and America between WWI and WWII and despised by Hitler. Name variations: Genevieve Tabouis; Cassandra. Pronunciation: JAWN-vee-ev Tah-BOO-ee. Born Geneviève Rapatel Le Quesne on February 23, 1892, in Paris, France; died on September 22, 1985, in Paris; daughter of Fernand Le Quesne (a well-known artist) and a mother of the French upper class named Cambon; attended convent schools; spent three years at the Sorbonne and the School of Archaeology at the Louvre; married Robert Tabouis, in 1916; children: one daughter; one son.

First book, on ancient history, interrupted by World War I (1914); gained favorable reputation for journalistic work (after 1924); became foreign news editor for L'Oeuvre (1932); with Germany's invasion of France, escaped to U.S. (1939); founded and published French language magazine, Pour la Victoire, in New York (1940–45); returned to Paris (1945); for service to France, made an Officier de la Légion d'honneur and awarded Commandeur de l'orde national du Mérite.

Publications: Nebuchadnezzar; Private Life of Tutankhamen; Solomon; Blackmail or War; Perfidious Albion—Entente Cordiale; A Life of Jules Cambon; (memoirs) They Called Me Cassandra (1942); (memoirs) Vingt ans de 'suspense' diplomatique.

Throughout the 1930s, as Adolf Hitler proceeded with his ruthless, systematic takeover of Germany and the establishment of the Third Reich, one journalist writing for a leading European newspaper turned out column after column describing his motives and methods, which sent der Führer into a rage. Throughout the Western world there were many willing to credit Hitler with accomplishing something of a miracle in the way he had brought Germany back from the terrible defeat of World War I. The British lauded his ability to bring order out of chaos, Americans were ready to praise his suppression of dangerous leftists and Communists, and even the French were willing to acknowledge that at least the trains in the German Reich ran on time. So how was it that one obstinate Frenchwoman, writing for a leading French daily, could be such a thorn in his side? Week after week, she not only attributed the worst possible motives to his political moves, but anticipated his actions in ways that sometimes disrupted his carefully laid plans. There were times her predictions proved so uncannily accurate, Hitler began to believe that she could read his mind.

Except for family connections, there was not much in the early life of Geneviève Tabouis to indicate what she would become. She was born Geneviève Le Quesne on February 23, 1892, in

Paris, France, the daughter of an artist, Fernand Le Quesne, and an upperclass French woman named Cambon whose family was active in government service. Two of Tabouis' uncles, Paul and Jules Cambon, were well-known diplomats. (Jules Cambon was the French ambassador to Germany.) Geneviève was educated in a convent, where she reported she "didn't learn very much." By age 15, she had raised silkworms and kept a frog, when history and poetry began to supersede her earlier enthusiasms. She studied for three years at the Sorbonne, then attended the school of archaeology at the Louvre, where she took courses in Egyptology, hieroglyphics, Egyptian literature, and Assyrian architecture. Egypt interested her most, and she called it "the most feminist country in history." When she learned how to write a letter in hieroglyphs to her favorite dancing partner, she considered the achievement one of the happiest of her life.

She was at work on a book on ancient history in August 1914 when the outbreak of World War I intervened. Shortly afterward, she met Robert Tabouis, who later became administrator of French radio, and they married in 1916. After the birth of two children, a son and daughter, Tabouis had no plans for pursuing a career, but she did follow politics with increasing interest and attended political debates in the Chamber of Deputies.

Through her uncles, Tabouis became acquainted with a number of important political figures, and it was Jules Cambon who recognized the literary flair in letters written by his niece. With his encouragement, she began to write short, amusing articles describing events and personalities for the newspaper, and her connections gave her access to good subjects. In her first major interview, however, inexperience with the ways of diplomacy nearly led her into disaster. She was in Geneva, where she spoke with the German foreign secretary, Herr Schubert, and simply wrote down everything that he told her, causing a furor when the article reached print. She learned a great deal about the art of discretion from the incident, while continuing to build her contacts, particularly in diplomatic circles.

At the end of WWI, the world of European diplomacy Tabouis had chosen to cover was in great turmoil. Older empires had been replaced by smaller nation-states, the right-wing Fascists were struggling against the left-wing Communists, and after 1929 Europe was further destabilized by the onset of the Great Depression. While many were ready to maintain peace at all costs, others wanted urgently to reject capitalism and embrace Communism, and the political atmosphere was ripe for the rise of figures of strong leadership. Thus Benito Mussolini took over the government in Italy, Adolf Hitler rose to power in Germany, and Joseph Stalin ruled the Soviet Union with an iron hand. Across the continent of Europe, the future of democracy looked bleak.

By the 1930s, Tabouis was a columnist for *L'Oeuvre*, an outstanding leftist French daily. Both an idealist and a realist, she was a passionate fighter for peace, and an ardent supporter of the new League of Nations, founded with the intention of preventing future wars. Tabouis was not a pacifist, however, and despite her close association with her uncles, she placed little faith in the effectiveness of diplomacy. In her writings, she became one of the first voices raised against the threat of the growing movement in Germany known as National Socialism. Reviewing the recent history of France, she judged that her country traditionally underestimated its opponents, a failing which had cost dearly in 1870, when Germany's Bismarck had taken over France's regions of Alsace and Lorraine. The Germans had invaded France again in 1914, and Tabouis now feared France would fall to the Germans a third time.

Geneviève Tabouis

Compiling her stories out of her glittering Paris apartment, Tabouis kept three secretaries hard at work through long hours. Her intimate, chatty stories made good copy, and were read by virtually everyone. It was a rare week when one of her predictions did not rock a foreign office somewhere on the Continent. Quick to use the latest in technology, she made long-distance telephone lines invaluable to her work, and thought nothing of flying off to track down a story long before airplane use became commonplace.

As a woman in journalism, Tabouis experienced considerable discrimination. At the start of her career, she signed her articles G.R. Tabouis, and wrote in the masculine to disguise her gender. Later she wrote, "[I]n France men don't much like being under the orders of a woman," and she was deeply angered by one publisher who turned down a manuscript of hers, saying, "Your book, Madame, is very good. It's a terrible pity you're not a man. I should like to publish it." Nor was she appeased when her tutor, M. Reinach, the famous Hellenist scholar, explained the publisher's behavior: "It's a sort of homage which men pay to women. It shows in their hearts they fear a woman's mind and her work." In 1932, she was made foreign news editor of *L'Oeuvre*, and her columns were syndicated throughout Europe, Great Britain, and the United States. Tabouis rarely appeared at the newspaper's editorial offices, however, continuing to work out of her home.

Madame Tabouis knew yesterday what I am now saying to you at a time I didn't know myself what I would say. But she knew it, this wisest of all women.

—Adolf Hitler

Outspoken as she was, Tabouis was not without critics. For one thing, she was willing to risk making predictions, and these did not always prove true. For example, after she had speculated that an alliance would be reached between the Soviet Union, France, England, Rumania, and Turkey, in 1939 Hitler and Stalin signed a non-aggression pact between Germany and the USSR that excluded the rest of Europe. But for every poor prediction there was one of deadly accuracy. History was to prove that her highly unpopular attacks on Hitler and Mussolini demonstrated an understanding of their warlike intentions that otherwise went unvoiced.

Tabouis returned to her historic interests in the writing of three books—*Nebuchadnezzar*, *Private Life of Tutankhamen*, and *Solomon*. Her works on politics and diplomacy included *Blackmail or War*, *Perfidious Albion—Entente Cordiale*, and *A Life of Jules Cambon*. "I can scarcely remember an evening when I haven't worked," she noted, "even over the weekends and at Christmas." The only form of relaxation she indicated to her readers was playing with her cats.

As the 1930s drew to a close, Tabouis' predictions proved to be all too exact. Hitler's armies first attacked Poland, then moved on to the Netherlands, Denmark, Norway, and France. In short order the Nazis controlled Western Europe and were moving to conquer the Soviet Union. Shortly before the German Army entered Paris, Tabouis fled for her life and eventually reached the U.S. Stripped of her citizenship by the occupying army, and tried for treason in absentia, she voiced her feelings in New York:

> Today, a refugee from my country, I am being tried for treason before a court at Riom. I am deprived of all rights, including the elementary right of defending myself. . . . But this is not my greatest misfortune. Today, after 16 years of incessant work in behalf of an ideal, I am compelled to acknowledge that all my efforts as a writer, teacher, and public speaker have utterly failed.

Throughout WWII, Tabouis published and wrote for *Pour la Victoire*, the weekly French-language magazine she had founded in New York; she also wrote *They Called Me Cassandra*, a memoir. In 1945, followed the Liberation, she returned to France, where she wrote her second memoir, *Vingt ans de 'suspense' diplomatique*, and remained active in journalism until a late age, although her influence was never again as great as it had been during the interwar years. Never willing to trust the Germans, she deeply opposed moves by President Charles de Gaulle to form a closer alliance between France and West Germany. Tabouis was honored for service to her country as an Officier de la Légion d'honneur and Commandeur de l'orde national du Mérite, and when she died on September 22, 1985, age 93, she was lauded as the "doyenne of French journalists."

SOURCES:

"Aunt Geneviève," in *Time*. Vol. 34, no. 24. December 11, 1939, pp. 58–59.

Bell, David S., *et al.*, eds. *Biographical Dictionary of French Political Leaders Since 1870*. NY: Harvester-Wheatsheaf, 1990.

Goebbels, Joseph. *Die Tagebücher von Joseph Goebbels*. Sämtliche Fragmente. Teil I. Aufzeichnungen 1924–1941, Band 3 (1.1.1937–31.12.1939). Munich: K.G. Saur, 1987, p. 298 (diary entry dated October 11, 1937).

"La Mort de Geneviève Tabouis," in *Le Monde*. September 24, 1985, p. 15.

Lazareff, Pierre. *Deadline. The Behind-the-Scenes Story of the Last Decade in France*. Trans. by David Partridge. NY: Random House, 1942.

"Mme Geneviève Tabouis," in *The Times* [London]. September 25, 1985, p. 14.

"Queen Journalist of Europe," in *Newsweek*. Vol. 16, no. 7. August 12, 1940, p. 53.

Tabouis, Geneviève. "Credo of a Frenchwoman," in *Current History and Forum*. Vol. 52, no. 1. September 1940, pp. 19–20.

———. *They Called Me Cassandra*. NY: Scribner, 1942.

———. "Were I American—," in *Independent Woman*. Vol. 19, no. 10. October 1940, pp. 319, 336.

Werner, Max. "Lady of the Press," in *The Living Age*. Vol. 351, no. 4442. November 1936, pp. 230–232.

Karin Loewen Haag,
freelance writer,
Athens, Georgia

Taeuber, Irene Barnes (1906–1974)

American demographer and first woman president of the Population Association of America. Born Irene Barnes on December 25, 1906, in Meadville, Missouri; died of pneumonia and emphysema on February 24, 1974, in Hyattsville, Maryland; daughter of Ninevah D. Barnes (a farmer and barber) and Lily (Keller) Barnes; University of Missouri, B.A., 1927; Northwestern University, M.A., 1928; University of Minnesota, Ph.D., 1931; married Conrad Taeuber (a demographer), in 1929; children: Richard Conrad (b. 1933); Karl Ernst (b. 1936).

Coedited the Population Association of America's Population Index; joined Princeton University's Office of Population Research (1936) and was appointed senior research demographer (1961); coauthored 16 books and monographs on demography and population; was the first woman elected to presidency of PAA (1953); researched Japanese population and published The Population of Japan *(1958), a landmark demographic analysis; was the first woman elected vice-president of International Union for the Scientific Study of Population (1961).*

Irene Barnes Taeuber was born in Meadville, Missouri, in 1906, the second of four children of Ninevah C. Barnes and **Lily Keller Barnes**. One younger brother died in infancy. Irene was closest to her mother Lily and maternal grandparents, who nursed her through scarlet fever in childhood. Ninevah was variously a farmer, a barber, and a justice of the peace, and was often absent from the family for periods of time, once for over a year.

Although Ninevah opposed his daughter's further education, Lily encouraged it, and upon graduation from high school, Irene attended Northeast Missouri State Teachers College for a year. Assisted by scholarships, she then transferred to the University of Missouri where she majored in sociology and received a B.A. in 1927. Influenced as well by the study of biology, Irene continued in the field of sociology, receiving an M.A. in 1928 from Northwestern University and a Ph.D. in 1931 from the University of Minnesota.

While in graduate school in 1929, Irene married Conrad Taeuber. They were research assistants together at the University of Wisconsin, where they gathered rural demographic statistics. Both then received appointments to Mt. Holyoke College's economics and sociology department, Irene as an instructor and Conrad as an assistant professor. In the early years of her marriage, Irene worked part-time in order to be with her two sons, who would also choose careers in fields related to demography.

In 1935, Taeuber began working with the Population Association of America in the preparation of a serial publication, a bibliography of recent articles on population. The next year Princeton University established the Office of Population Research (OPR) under the direction of Frank W. Notestein; there, Taeuber and **Louise K. Kiser** were co-editors of the *Population Index*, the successor of the original bibliographic serial. In addition to her career-long affiliation with the OPR, Taeuber also served as director of the Library of Congress census library project from 1941 to 1944, when she became head of the social demography section of the American Sociological Association. After Kiser's death in 1954, however, Taeuber wanted to devote more time to her own research and asked to be relieved of her duties with the *Population Index*. Working in a predominantly male field, Taeuber faced such challenges as receiving less clerical and research assistance than her male colleagues. While she maintained an international reputation with over 250 articles to her credit, it was not until 1961 that she was promoted to senior research demographer at the OPR, a position she would hold until her retirement in 1973.

During the mid-20th century, the field of demography grew as the U.S. government recognized the importance of population studies in formulating policies. The League of Nations had commissioned the OPR in 1939 to study future populations of Europe, and Taeuber was involved in this work and in the study of Asian populations. After World War II, she made several trips to Japan, developing a lifelong interest in that country. Although she did not understand the language, she could readily grasp Japanese statistical tables, and when her study *The Population of Japan* (1958) was published it was recognized as a landmark work of demography. It also prompted the Japanese government to begin its own program of demographic analysis.

Throughout her studies, Taeuber covered numerous countries, including Africa, Latin America, and Oceania. With her husband, she coauthored *The Changing Population of the United States* (1958) and *People of the United States in the Twentieth Century* (1971). In her work, she was interested in the cultural as well as the social and economic reasons for population trends. Her early fieldwork prompted several visits to rural villages, and she also stressed the roles of women and children in the studies in which she participated. At the time of her death, Taeuber had been working on population trends in China. Since little research had been undertaken in this field, it was information gathered later that confirmed her theory that China was bringing its fertility rate under control.

Taeuber was a consultant to many governmental and international organizations. She served also as president of the Population Association of America from 1953 to 1954 and vice-president of the International Union for the Scientific Study of Population from 1961 to 1965—the first woman elected to either of these positions. Taeuber received two honorary degrees and distinguished service medals from the universities of Missouri and Minnesota, and was visiting professor at Johns Hopkins University from 1961 to 1965. A careful and sensitive researcher, Taeuber was admired by her colleagues and students alike. She continued to work up until her death from pneumonia and emphysema at her home in Hyattsville, Maryland, on February 24, 1974.

SOURCES:

Read, Phyllis J., and Bernard L. Witlieb. *The Book of Women's Firsts*. NY: Random House, 1992.

Sicherman, Barbara, and Carol Hurd Green, eds. *Notable American Women: The Modern Period*. Cambridge, MA: The Belknap Press of Harvard University, 1980.

Martha Jones, M.L.S.,
Natick, Massachusetts

Taeuber-Arp, Sophie (1889–1943).

See Tauber-Arp, Sophie.

Taft, Helen Herron (1861–1943)

American first lady (1909–13), the primary force behind her husband's political career, whose influence in the White House was cut short by a debilitating stroke from which she never fully recovered. Name variations: Mrs. William Howard Taft; Nellie Taft. Born on June 2, 1861, in Cincinnati, Ohio; died on May 22, 1943, in Washington, D.C.; fourth of eleven children of John Williamson Herron (a lawyer) and Harriet (Collins) Herron; graduated from Miss Nourse's School; attended the University of Cincinnati; married William Howard Taft (1857–1930, 27th president of the United States), on June 19, 1886, in Cincinnati, Ohio; children: Robert Alphonso Taft (1889–1953, a senator from Ohio); Helen Herron Taft Manning (1891–1987, president of Bryn Mawr College); Charles Phelps Taft (1897–1983, a lawyer, civic leader, and mayor of Cincinnati).

To call Helen Herron Taft purposeful would not begin to do her justice. Many believe that it was her energy, motivation, and drive that propelled her husband into the presidency. Her plans began to take shape when she was just 17. After visiting the White House with her father, who at one time had been a law partner of Rutherford B. Hayes, she vowed that if she gave up plans to enter a convent and decided instead to get married, it would be to a man who would be president. William Howard Taft, as it turned out, was just that fellow.

Helen Herron Taft, known as Nellie, was born in 1861 in Cincinnati, Ohio, the daughter of John Williamson Herron and **Harriet Collins Herron**. Although she grew up in a family of eleven children, Helen was educated at a private girls' school where she studied languages and literature. Long hours were also spent practicing at the family piano. As a young woman, she longed for independence, but found career choices limited. Church work did not appeal, and a brief stint as a teacher was frustrating because the boys were so difficult to discipline. She considered a musical career, but questioned the depth of her talent. To bring meaning into what she thought might be too "frivolous" a life, she and a couple of friends established a Sunday afternoon salon to foster "brilliant discussion of topics intellectual and economic." Invited to attend was Helen's latest beau William Taft, a young attorney whom she had recently met at a sledding party.

William was an ardent suitor, but Helen turned down two of his proposals, complaining that he did not adequately value her opinions. After convincing her that he found her smarter, and prettier, than any other woman he knew, they finally married in June 1886. Returning to Cincinnati after a 100-day honeymoon, they settled into a new home, where first child Robert was born. William was appointed solicitor general in 1890 and a federal circuit judge in 1892. Helen had two more children, Helen and Charles, but found her life of quiet domesticity almost unbearable. She put her spare energy and musical talent into organizing and managing the Cincinnati Orchestra Association.

Another political door finally opened in 1899, when President William McKinley asked William Taft to head a commission to the Philippines. When her husband waffled, Helen urged him to accept. Eager for adventure, she packed up the children for what turned out to be a four-year stint, culminating in William's appointment as governor-general of the Philippines. Diplomatic duties, entertaining, and two world tours provided more than adequate training for the White House duties to come. In 1904, an invitation to William to join Theodore Roosevelt's Cabinet as secretary of war brought the Tafts back to the United States.

William was not enthralled with the political arena. He longed instead for a position on the Supreme Court, but Helen had made her opposition clear when Roosevelt mentioned the possibility of such an appointment while the Tafts were still in the Philippines. When another vacancy on the court appeared in 1906, Helen lost no time in arranging a meeting with Roosevelt to discuss her husband's future. Although it is not known exactly what took place behind closed doors, Roosevelt came away with a clear picture of "why the court appointment was not desired." William was hand picked by Roosevelt to run for the presidency on the Republican ticket in 1908; that November, he easily defeated William Jennings Bryan. On inauguration day, Helen Taft, in an unprecedented move, rode next to her husband in the inaugural parade down Pennsylvania Avenue. Since Roosevelt had already left Washington, the seat was vacant, and in every respect belonged to her.

Although Helen claimed that her active involvement in her husband's career ended when he became president, she continued to influence his decisions, especially at the beginning of his term. Often sitting in on important political discussions, she also accompanied him on political trips and golf outings. Their relationship was once described as that of "two men who are intimate chums." Helen additionally involved herself in every detail of managing the executive mansion. With hopes of economizing, she replaced the White House steward with a competent housekeeper. She insisted on comparison shopping and scrutinized every expenditure. Helen managed the Tafts' personal budget so well that after four years she had managed to set aside $100,000 for the family bank account.

Ironically, two months into her tenure as first lady, Helen suffered a stroke which affected the left side of her face and her speech. She never fully recovered, and her effectiveness was greatly diminished. With her husband's help, she learned to talk again, although her speech remained somewhat impaired. Eldest daughter **Helen Herron Taft Manning** acted as White House hostess during her mother's year-long recuperation.

Helen Herron Taft

After leaving the White House in 1913, the Tafts moved to New Haven, Connecticut, where William took a position as a law professor at Yale University. In 1921, his lifetime dream was finally realized when Warren G. Harding appointed him chief justice of the Supreme Court. William served nine years before his death in 1930. Helen survived her husband by 13 years, enjoying a fairly active retirement. She died at age 82 and was buried next to her husband at Arlington National Cemetery.

By far the most well received and permanent of Helen Taft's contributions to her nation was her plan to enhance Potomac Park with the planting of 3,500 cherry trees, which were donated by the mayor of Tokyo. The trees were planted in a design copied from Manila's Luneta, an oval drive with a bandstand at either end, serving as the city's meeting place. To this day, the annual blooming of the cherry blossoms lures tourists to the U.S. capital from around the world, a lasting memorial to Helen Herron Taft.

SOURCES:

Caroli, Betty Boyd. *First Ladies.* NY: Oxford University Press, 1987.

McConnell, Jane and Burt. *Our First Ladies: From *Martha Washington* to *Lady Bird Johnson.* NY: Thomas Y. Crowell, 1964.

Melick, Arden David. *Wives of the Presidents.* Maplewood, NJ: Hammond, 1977.

Paletta, LuAnn. *The World Almanac of First Ladies.* NY: World Almanac, 1990.

COLLECTIONS:
William Howard Taft Papers, Library of Congress.

Barbara Morgan,
Melrose, Massachusetts

Taft, Jessie (1882–1960)

*American psychologist and social services educator.
Born Julia Jessie Taft on June 24, 1882, in Dubuque,
Iowa; died from a stroke on June 7, 1960, in Philadelphia, Pennsylvania; daughter of Charles Chester Taft
(a wholesale fruit seller) and Amanda May (Farwell)
Taft; Drake University, B.A., 1904; University of
Chicago, Ph.B., 1905, Ph.D., 1913; companion of
Virginia Robinson (a psychologist and writer),
1912–1960; children: (adopted) two.*

The eldest of three daughters, Jessie Taft
was born in 1882 in Dubuque, Iowa, to Charles
and **Amanda Taft**. Except for a brief stint in
Florida, Jessie lived in Iowa throughout her
young adulthood. The Tafts enjoyed a comfortable middle-class existence, as Charles ran a successful wholesale fruit business. When Amanda
gradually lost her hearing and became increasingly detached from the family, Jessie developed
a close relationship with an aunt who had come
to live with them.

After graduating from high school, Taft received a B.A. from Drake University in 1904 and
a Ph.B. in 1905 from the University of Chicago.
She then taught mathematics, Latin, and German at the West Des Moines High School for
four years before returning to the University of
Chicago under a fellowship to work on her doctorate. Taft's years in Chicago profoundly affected her professional life. She studied philosophy
and psychology with George Herbert Mead,
James H. Tufts, and Addison W. Moore and was
particularly influenced by the writings of such
women as *Charlotte Perkins Gilman, *Ida Tarbell, and *Edith Abbott. While at the University
of Chicago, she also met **Virginia Robinson**,
who became her lifelong friend and companion,
professional colleague, and biographer. In 1913,
Taft earned a Ph.D., and two years later published her dissertation under the title *The
Woman's Movement from the Point of View of
Social Consciousness*. In it, she defined the need
to reconcile the social world of women with that
of a professional life.

While on leave from Chicago in 1912, Taft
had spent six months in New York City with
Robinson, interviewing women in prisons and
reformatories for a study initiated by *Katharine
Bement Davis**. After receiving her doctorate, she
returned and worked for Davis at the New York
State Reformatory for Women and then in 1915
became director of the Social Services Department of the New York State Charities Aid Association's Mental Hygiene Committee. There she
developed mental health programs for the state
of New York and carried a caseload at the New
York Hospital Mental Hygiene Clinic. She also
established the Farm School in New Jersey for
children who were having problems in school.

In 1918, Taft moved to Philadelphia, where
her professional reputation and expertise in social
work with children increased. She was appointed
director of the Seybert Institution's newly created
Department of Child Study, a shelter for children
awaiting placement. Her department was taken
over by the state in 1920 and Taft was able to expand the mental health services offered to children. She also established a training program for
staff, assisted in finding placement for children,
and counseled foster parents.

It was during this period that Taft developed her theories on foster care and adoption,
and the role of the social worker and agency in
the process. She was in demand to speak and
write on the subject, and her personal life influenced her professional opinions. She and Robinson, who had purchased a house together in
Flourtown, Pennsylvania, adopted two children.

Another major influence upon Taft's life occurred when she met Otto Rank in 1924 and underwent analysis with him in 1926. Her opportunity to apply his theories to her social work
came when, in 1934, she was appointed professor of social casework at the Pennsylvania
School of Social Work (later part of the University of Pennsylvania). There she worked with
Robinson until her retirement in 1950. Taft established the curriculum and influenced its practical philosophy, known as functionalism.

At this time a controversy arose in social
work education between the Freudian approach
to practice, which involved a diagnosis and treatment determined by the therapist, and the Pennsylvania School's functional approach, which offered assistance. Taft wrote extensively about
functionalism and its application to social work
education and in 1933 published *The Dynamics
of Therapy in a Controlled Relationship*. In addition to a two-volume translation of Rank's work,
Taft spent her retirement years working on a biography of Rank, which was published in 1958.
Straightforward in her relationships with others,
Taft strongly believed that a person's professional
self was the one of true value. She died of a
stroke in a Philadelphia hospital in 1960.

SOURCES:

Sicherman, Barbara, and Carol Hurd Green, eds. *Notable American Women: The Modern Period*. Cambridge, MA: The Belknap Press of Harvard University, 1980.

Martha Jones, M.L.S.,
Natick, Massachusetts

Tagaskouita (1656–1680).

See Tekakwitha, Kateri.

Taggard, Genevieve (1894–1948)

American poet. Born in Washington state on November 28, 1894; died on November 8, 1948, in New York City; daughter of Alta Gale (Arnold) Taggard and James Nelson Taggard (both schoolteachers); graduated fromm the University of California at Berkeley in 1920; married Robert L. Wolf (a writer), on March 21, 1921 (divorced 1934); married Kenneth Durant (who worked for Tass, the Soviet news agency), on March 10, 1935; children: (first marriage) Marcia Sarah Wolf (b. 1922).

Selected works: For Eager Lovers (NY: Selzer, 1922); Hawaiian Hilltop (San Francisco, CA: Wyckoff & Gelber, 1923); Words for the Chisel (NY: Knopf, 1926); Travelling Standing Still: Poems, 1918–1928 (NY: Knopf, 1928); Monologue for Mothers (Aside) (NY: Random House, 1929); The Life and Mind of Emily Dickinson (NY: Knopf, 1930); Remembering Vaughan in New England (NY: Arrow, 1933); Not Mine to Finish: Poems 1928–1934 (NY: Harper, 1934); Calling Western Union (NY: Harper, 1936); Collected Poems, 1918–1938 (NY: Harper, 1938); Long View (NY: Harper, 1942); A Part of Vermont (East Jamaica, VT: River Press, 1945); Slow Music (NY: Harper, 1946); (selected by Donald Angus) Origin: Hawaii (Honolulu: Angus, 1947); (edited by Taggard, George Sterling, and James Rorty) Continent's End: An Anthology of Contemporary California Poets (San Francisco, CA: Book Club of California, 1925); (edited by Taggard) May Days: An Anthology of Masses-Liberator Verse, 1912–1924 (NY: Boni & Liveright, 1925); (edited by Taggard) Circumference: Varieties of Metaphysical Verse, 1456–1928 (NY: Covici Friede, 1929); (edited by Taggard and Dudley Fitts) Ten Introductions: A Collection of Modern Verse (NY: Arrow, 1934).

Although Genevieve Taggard's poetry was well known in her time to both literary and popular audiences, her work as a poet is now largely forgotten, and she is best known as the author of *The Life and Mind of Emily Dickinson* (1930). A passionate, intuitive, and bold interpretation of the father-daughter relationship and of Dickinson's psychology, it proposed George Gould as Dickinson's mysterious lover and her father as a repressive villain. The book, well received when it was published but since superseded, was based on Taggard's acquaintance with people who remembered Dickinson, reinforced with meticulous scholarship. In addition to poetry and scholarly work, Taggard wrote short stories, reviews, essays, and articles on poetic theory, and edited literary journals and anthologies. In her prose work, she was a tireless crusader for more involvement—in liberal causes, in art, in life. Her first commitment was to the writing of poetry, however, and at her best, she produced some fine poems containing imagery still vivid today. Her writer friends included Wallace Stevens, who strongly influenced her work, especially her later poems. Yet Taggard's poems are only occasionally derivative, and her best poetry, on art, woman's experience, and social injustice, has much in common with the work of later poets such as *Sylvia Plath and especially *Adrienne Rich.

Taggard was born in 1894 to **Alta Arnold Taggard** and James Nelson Taggard, both schoolteachers in Waitsburg, Washington; the eldest of three children, she was the granddaughter of two Union soldiers. When she was two years old, the family moved to Hawaii. There her parents served as missionaries for the fundamentalist Disciples of Christ, and her father built up a public school at Kalihiwaena, near Honolulu. Taggard spent most of her childhood in Hawaii, where she grew up among her father's Hawaiian, Chinese, Japanese, and Portuguese students, and she developed a hearty dislike for American tourists. The Bible was the only book her parents allowed in the house ("I made Bible stories into fairy-tales," she wrote in 1927), but she read Keats and Ruskin secretly, and at school she learned Hawaiian legends. When the family made preparations to return to Waitsburg in 1905 (because her father was thought to have tuberculosis), one Hawaiian playmate told her, "Too bad you gotta be Haole [white]"—and later she wrote, "Off and on, I have thought so too, all my life." The family did not like Waitsburg, and in 1906 they came back to Hawaii, where they stayed until 1910, when James' ill-health once again drove them back to Waitsburg. They remained there, her father working a small pear farm for his brother, until 1912. The contrast between small-town rural America and the rich multiracial cosmopolitanism of Hawaii made a lasting impression on Genevieve: the cruel and brutal insensitivity she found in Waitsburg, where the Taggards lived the life of the rural poor, crystallized into a liberalism she later expressed through leftist poetry and commitment to liberal and proletarian causes. In 1934, she wrote that the time in Waitsburg had been "the active source of my convictions. It told us what to work against and what to work for." It is quite possible that the family's financial history also contributed to her political and feminist convictions: after many years of saving, her parents had accumulated $2,000, and it was earmarked to pay for Alta's college education, but when James' brother fell on hard times, the money went to him. With it he bought a farm in Waitsburg, became prosperous, but never repaid the loan: "my mother," Taggard later wrote, "went as nearly insane with rage as she could permit herself." Instead, he hired James, when he was forced to leave Hawaii, to work on his pear farm—and it was in those years that, in Genevieve's words, "used as my uncle's hired help and wearing his family's cast off clothing, we integrated ourselves into the single struggle to exist."

In 1906, when she was 12, she entered the missionary Punahou school and began to write poetry; her first published poem, "Mitchie-Gawa" (about American Indians) appeared in the school magazine, the *Oahuan*, in 1910. In Waitsburg, she was the editor of the high school paper, *Crimson and Gray*, and in 1914 (the year she became editor of the *Oahuan*), just three months before graduation, her father fell ill again, and she took over his teaching at his school. The family moved to California in the fall, and, with friends contributing $200 toward expenses, she entered the University of California at Berkeley. Since her father was now an invalid, Taggard and her mother (according to an account she published in 1927) became servants in a boardinghouse for Berkeley students; her studies interrupted by work, she took six years to graduate. She studied poetry with Witter Bynner at Berkeley, and in November 1915 her poem "Lani" was published by the San Francisco magazine *Overland*. In December 1919, *Harper's* published another of her poems, "An Hour on the Hill," and in her final year at Berkeley, she became the salaried editor of the college literary magazine, the *Occident*. Before her graduation she had become a socialist, familiar with radical-literary circles in San Francisco. "At the end of college," she told *Twentieth-Century Authors* (1942), "I called myself a Socialist in a rather vague way. Since then I have always been to the left of center. In those days Frank Norris and Jack London were still heard of as friends of friends. The great city of San Francisco taught me a good deal that I needed to know."

After Taggard graduated from Berkeley in 1920, Max Eastman, editor of the radical *Liberator*, arranged a job for her on the *Freeman*, and she moved to New York. There, she began publishing her work in such magazines as *Nation* and *Harriet Monroe*'s *Poetry*, and in such journals as *Liberator*. The job with the *Freeman* did not materialize, and she instead worked for the avant-garde publisher B.W. Huebsch. On March 21, 1921, she married Robert L. Wolf, a writer, and the following year had her only child, **Marcia Sarah Wolf**. Also in 1921, she joined with Maxwell Anderson and Padraic Colum to found and edit the *Measure: A Magazine of Verse*, which rapidly became quite prestigious but folded in 1926. In 1922, her first book, *For Eager Lovers*, was published. Reviewing it for the *Bookman*, **Grace Conkling** called Taggard "genuinely original in her musical effects. Her imagination is to be trusted." Louis Untermeyer, in the *Literary Review*, praised the book highly: "It is a woman speaking; straightforward, sensitive, intense. Instead of loose philosophizing there is a condensed clarity; instead of rhetoric we have revelation." Mark Van Doren, in the *Nation*, said that this first volume "places her among the considerable poets of contemporary America." The collection consists mostly of rhymed, personal poems about love and nature. A few, such as "Thirst," come close to the imagism of H.D. (*Hilda Doolittle), and others, such as "Twentieth Century Slave Gang," look forward to the theme of social injustice which dominates so many of her later poems.

In the 1920s, Taggard and Wolf both served as contributing editors to *New Masses*, but in a 1927 symposium she expressed her uneasiness with pressures to join the proletarian cause. No doubt her experiences, in childhood and youth, of intense sectarianism and of the social pressures inevitably attendant on the embracing of a "cause" led her to back off: hers was an independent cast of mind and personality.

Genevieve Taggard's poems were praised by such well-known writers as Edmund Wilson and Allen Tate, but they were often disparaged by the popular press. Her poems tend to reflect the best and worst of the intellectual currents of their times; the lyricism, focus on art, and concern for the image of the 1920s, and the 1930s social conscience and sense of place—but they make strongly individual statements as well. From her first poems published in the 1910s and 1920s to her last work in the 1940s, Taggard's writing evolved through a series of roughly defined stages, from rhymed poems of nature and love, through protest poetry, to the often experimental poems she wrote in the 1940s about art and women's experience. However, social protest was her overriding concern and it was her protest poetry which was most likely to draw unfavorable criticism from the popular press. *Time*, for instance, once described it as the work of a "worried, earnest, political nondescript."

In 1922, Taggard and her husband spent a year in San Francisco, where she gave courses in poetry and helped edit an anthology of California poems, *Continent's End*, in which she called for more honest involvement in social issues, and less artistic detachment among regional writers. In 1923, she published *Hawaiian Hilltop*, a small pamphlet of poems that show her development of a sense of place. That same year, she and her family settled in New Preston, Connecticut. Her anthology *May Days*, drawn from the pages of *New Masses* and the *Liberator* was published in 1925; it was followed in 1926 by *Words for the Chisel*, her first book to be widely read and reviewed with favorable notices in national and popular literary journals. Some of the poems in *Words for the Chisel* contain strong images from Taggard's Hawaiian childhood, while others deal with social inequities. The collection includes a number of sparse, economical poems about love and art, and shows a passion and political restraint not found in the earlier ones. *Katherine Anne Porter, herself politically sympathetic to Taggard's position, wrote in the *New York Herald Tribune* (April 18, 1926) that "this is poetry to be read for its own sake"; Joseph Auslander, in the *New York World*, talked of the "sovereign and dextrous craftsmanship"; and Allen Tate, in the *Nation* (April 28, 1926), praised the work as "intelligently sustained." He went on: "The artistic aim indicated by the title . . . would be pretentious, if it were not accurately realized. Only with excessive zeal could one discover a single failure in her three volumes of poetry." But he then sounded a note which would recur throughout Taggard's career, and possibly haunt her: "It is unfortunately true . . . that she has not yet produced a single perfect utterance." This was a remark that Leo Kennedy would echo in *Book Week* in 1946, while reviewing her collection *Slow Music*: "There is not a bad poem in the book . . . but it is like a shop window full of everything from children's toys to bull fighting equipment to hardware and tourist travel literature. I think that what I am regretting is the absence of a unified sensibility in these fine poems."

Travelling Standing Still (1928), a selection of previously published poems, brought further critical acclaim (though again with reservations)

from such critics as William Rose Benét and Edmund Wilson. Taggard next produced two brief pamphlets, *Monologue for Mothers (Aside)* (1929) and *Remembering Vaughan in New England* (1933), each containing a single poem, as well as her widely praised biography of *Emily Dickinson, published in 1930.

She had spent 1928 in Southern France, and in 1929 moved to New England, where she taught at Mt. Holyoke College for a year. A Guggenheim award in 1931 took her to Capri and Majorca with her daughter and sister **Ernestine Taggard**. In 1932, she began teaching at Bennington College in Vermont. Taggard divorced her husband in 1934, and the following year married Kenneth Durant, who worked for Tass, the Soviet news agency. She also left Bennington for a faculty position at Sarah Lawrence College, where she would teach until 1946. Taggard bought a farm, Gilfeather, at East Jamaica, Vermont, a few miles south of her grandfather's hometown of Londonderry. No farmer, she settled into a life of teaching and observing—and writing.

Not Mine to Finish: Poems 1928–1934, her next collection, was published in 1934. At the time, Taggard was fascinated by New England, which seemed to her to exemplify the best America had to offer. In contrast to New York, Vermont appeared to be unspoiled and humane. But two years later, as was apparent from her next collection, she had changed her mind. Instead of opportunity for self-realization amid natural beauty, New England came to mean exploitation and injustice. After witnessing the treatment of workers involved in the Vermont quarry workers' strike, she wrote in the introduction to 1936's *Calling Western Union*:

> I was wrong about Vermont. At first it looked to me the way it looks to the summer visitor who goes up there to get a rest. And then the facts contradicted my hope. I saw canned wood-chuck in the farmers' cellars. . . . I knew a man who worked in a furniture factory for ten cents an hour! I saw his starved wife and children. Slow starvation gives children starry eyes and delicate faces. . . . When they eat, the quarry workers eat potatoes and turnips. . . . And so I say I was wrong about Vermont.

This long introductory essay is considered by far the most vivid and evocative part of the book; Taggard describes her Hawaiian childhood, the disappointment of her return to the United States, and her unfulfilled search for a promising and just America. The poems, on the other hand, were more social protest than art, with such titles as "To an American Worker

Dying of Starvation," "Up State—Depression Summer," "Feeding the Children," and "Mass Song." A number of poems have rousing assertions as conclusions: "We must feed the children. Vote the strike!"; "I hope the people win"; "For my class I have come/ To walk city miles with many, my will in our work." Others express standard condemnations of middle-class complacency. Reviews were mixed at best.

After the publication of *Calling Western Union*, Taggard pursued various poetic interests. Her *Collected Poems* was published in 1938, with selections from her earliest work but an emphasis on the protest poems from the 1930s. She also worked with composers at putting poetry to music; in 1939 one of her poems, set to music by William Schuman, was sung at Carnegie Hall. Her last major collection, 1946's *Slow Music*, was a departure from the strident protest poems of the 1930s. With a kind of deliberate artificiality, impersonal and elegiac in tone, the poems focus on the colors of life and death; a color symbolism Taggard devised persists throughout the book. Her sister Ernestine had died in 1943, and Taggard herself soon would be all but confined to her home due to illness. She left Vermont only rarely, to receive medical treatment in New York. *Slow Music* shows Wallace Stevens' influence most clearly, but it is the earlier Stevens of *Harmonium* (1923) whose traces can most easily be found. According to the reviewer for *Kirkus Reviews*, the poetry is "sometimes fanciful, sometimes profound, brightly-hued and yet often obscure." Rolfe Humphries, in the *Nation* (March 8, 1947)—a usually sympathetic journal to which Taggard had contributed often—commented: "Miss Taggard's specialty is a peculiar kind of lyric, very frail, clear, disembodied; larksong descending from way up high in the pure air, or coming down from above the cloud. This is a difficult genre to sustain, or repeat; aiming at effects of innocence, of being 'natural,' Miss Taggard overdoes it a little."

As early as *Continent's End* (1925), she had deplored "the Longfellow-Whittier School—the Lo! here and Lo! there! school in American poetry—a school that never absorbed its environment, but always held it at arm's length in the gesture of a curio-lecturer," and in 1947 she published a book of regional poetry, *Origin: Hawaii*. She died in a New York hospital the following year.

SOURCES:

Kunitz, Stanley J., and Howard Haycraft, eds. *Twentieth Century Authors*. NY: H.W. Wilson, 1942.
Nation. April 28, 1926; March 8, 1947.
New Republic. October 21, 1936.
New York Herald Tribune. April 18, 1926.
Saturday Review of Literature. November 10, 1934.

COLLECTIONS:

Papers: Taggard's papers are in the Berg Collection at the New York Public Library and in the Taggard Archive at the Dartmouth College Library.

Freely adapted from **Janet McCann**,
Texas A&M University,
for *Dictionary of Literary Biography*,
Volume 45: American Poets, 1880–1945, First Series.
Edited by Peter Quartermain, University of British Columbia.
Gale Research, 1986, pp. 375–381

Tagliaferro, Magda (1893–1986)

Brazilian-French pianist, especially known for her performances of Fauré, who concertized into her 90s. Name variations: Magda Tagliafero. Born in Petropolis, Brazil, on January 19, 1893; died in Rio de Janeiro on September 9, 1986; her father was a French pianist of note.

Magda Tagliaferro was born in 1893 in Petropolis, Brazil, where her father, later a pianist of note, had been sent to as an engineer on a French government mission. She began her studies in Brazil and moved to Paris in 1906. In 1907, she won a first prize in the class of her teacher Antonin Marmontel. Another teacher, Alfred Cortot, helped the young pianist technically and artistically, and her Paris recital debut in 1908 was a success. In 1910, she accompanied the composer Gabriel Fauré on a tour, playing his *Ballade* with him at a second piano. Tagliaferro had one of the longest musical careers in history—over 75 years—and was still able to delight audiences when she was in her 90s. Her devotion to the delicate and fastidious music of Fauré never waned. In 1929, she made the first recording of his *Ballade* for Piano and Orchestra. In 1981, she made her last recording, in digital sound, of the same *Ballade* in its two-piano version (with Daniel Varsano). In 1939, the French government sponsored her on an extended tour of the Americas; she remained in the United States during World War II, resuming her career in Paris in 1949. Critics agreed that her performances of Fauré's aristocratic music were permeated with elegance and warmth. Her 1983 Carnegie Hall recital captivated listeners and critics with superbly clear articulation and phrasing. She also championed the works of living composers. In 1929, the Brazilian composer Heitor Villa-Lobos dedicated his *Momoprecoce* for Piano and Orchestra to her, and she gave the premiere performance. She often included the music of the Venezuelan-born French composer Reynaldo Hahn in her programs and made a recording of his Piano Concerto in the 1930s.

Throughout her career, she performed Hahn's charming Sonatina. Her students included Wladyslaw Kedra and *Cristina Ortiz.

SOURCES:

Dubal, David. *The Art of the Piano.* NY: Summit, 1989.

Slonimsky, Nicolas, ed. *Baker's Biographical Dictionary of Musicians.* 8th ed. NY: Schirmer, 1992.

Tagliaferro, Magda. *Quase tudo.* Rio de Janeiro: Nova Fronteira, 1979.

Timbrell, Charles. *French Pianism: An Historical Perspective.* White Plains, NY: Pro/Am Music Resources, 1992.

John Haag,
Athens, Georgia

Taglioni, Maria (1804–1884)

Italian ballerina who was one of the most acclaimed dancers of the Romantic period. Name variations: Marie Taglioni; countess de Voisins; countess of Voisins. Born in Stockholm, Sweden, on April 23, 1804; died in Marseilles, France, on April 23, 1884; only daughter and one of three children of Filippo Taglioni (1778–1871, a dancer and choreographer) and Sophia (Karsten) Taglioni; niece of Salvatore Taglioni (1780–1868, the principal dancer and ballet master at Naples); aunt of Maria Taglioni (1833–1891, also a ballet dancer); married Count Gilbert de Voisins, in 1832 (separated 1835); children: daughter Marie ("Nini," b. 1836); son Georges (b. 1843, father unknown).

"Legend has completely triumphed over fact," wrote the celebrated ballet historian André Levinson about famed ballerina Maria Taglioni, one of the most acclaimed dancers of the Romantic period. "A literary fiction has colored the truth regarding this great person; the lyrical outbursts of poets exalted the 'Sylphide' to the seventh heaven; the engravings which adorned *Keepsakes* masked her real features beneath a likeness of pure convention. The complex and private life of a human being is submerged under a monotonous and verbose phraseology, because mediocrity in literature had never sunk so low as during the aftermath of 1830." According to **Parmenia Migel**, much of the record on Taglioni was set straight by her biographer Léandre Vaillat, who had access to many of the ballerina's private papers in preparing his work. Migel's one complaint, however, is that Vaillat was so enamored of his subject that he too glossed over many of her imperfections.

Maria Taglioni was born into a great ballet family. Her father Filippo Taglioni was a renowned Italian dancer, choreographer, and ballet master and his brother Salvatore Taglioni was the principal dancer and ballet master at Naples for half a century. Maria's younger brother Paul was also a dancer and choreographer, and Paul's daughter **Maria Taglioni** (1833–1891) would have a dancing career prior to her marriage to Prince Joseph Windisch-Grätz in 1866. Maria's father Filippo was in Stockholm, Sweden, when he met and married Maria's mother **Sophia Karsten Taglioni**, the daughter of the leading opera singer Christoffer Karsten. Maria was born in Stockholm in April 1804 but grew up in Vienna (where her two brothers, Gustave and Paul, were born) and in Cassel, where Filippo served as ballet master until the Napoleonic wars made him decide to move his family to Paris. Maria was nearly 12 when she began studying ballet with her father's teacher. "She was a thin, stoop-shouldered, unprepossessing child, and it did not help matters that she often played hooky from class or failed to make a sufficient effort whenever she was present," writes Migel. At 17, when Maria was expected to make her debut, she simply was not ready, and Jean Aumer, the newly appointed ballet master at the Paris Opèra, suggested to Sophia Taglioni that her daughter might be better suited to dressmaking than dancing. In the meantime, Filippo, now serving as ballet master in Vienna, sent for his family and arranged for Maria to debut at the Kärnthner-Thor. When he realized that she was unprepared, he put her through a rigorous six-month training program which kept her on the brink of exhaustion.

On June 19, 1822, cured of her poor posture, and thoroughly schooled in the restraint, delicacy, and good taste demanded by her father, Taglioni made her debut in *La Réception d'une nymphe au temple de Terpsichore*, a ballet staged especially for the occasion. "For the first time that my daughter Maria appeared on the stage, she obtained the very greatest success," wrote Filippo in his journal. For the next year, Maria continued to dance in Vienna, gaining assurance and poise and observing such experienced dancers as **Amalia Brugnoli**, from whom she learned much about dancing on point.

After Vienna, Taglioni performed for three months in Munich and then went on to Stuttgart, where she received an even more enthusiastic reception. She spent three years there, the happiest of her career, although her father kept her hard at work, perfecting her point technique and her famed *ballonné* style. During the summer before her last year at Stuttgart, Maria, accompanied by her family, went to Paris to practice for her debut at the famed Paris Opéra. She would make six mandatory trial appearances with the Opéra before obtaining a contract, the first of which occurred on July 12, 1827. Dancing the *pas* in *Le Sicilien*, she was "a more than total success," as her father noted in his diary. By her sixth appearance, she had inspired some jealousy among the Opéra's personnel. (By one account, envious rivals scattered bits of soap on the stage before her entrance, hoping she might fall.) Over the course of the next two years, her popularity increased, culminating with her triumphant performance in the title role of *La Sylphide*, the ballet that from then on would be associated with her. Ushering in the Romantic era, the ballet is a fairy tale about a Scottish youth who sees and converses with a magical sylph-like creature invisible to everyone but himself. Coinciding with Taglioni's appearance in this important work was her signing of a six-year contract with the Opéra, at which time her father also became ballet master. Maria also celebrated another contract: her engagement to Count Gilbert de Voisins, who was considered a thoroughly worthless scoundrel by most everyone who knew him.

La Sylphide premiered on March 12, 1832, marking a number of production "firsts," including the introduction of a costume that would become standard for ballet dancers, the "romantic tutu." Designed for Taglioni by Eugène Lami, it consisted of a tight-fitting bodice, baring the neck and shoulders, and a bell-shaped light gauzy skirt reaching midway between knee and ankle to reveal pale tights and satin shoes, with a darned rather than blocked toe to support the foot on point. (Down through the years, the tutu has been adapted to various lengths, but has remained essentially the same.) The production also boasted a moonlit forest scene utilizing new gas reflectors, and the flight of dozens of sylphs, "flown" above the stage on invisible wires. It was Maria Taglioni's dancing, however, that inspired the most impassioned responses to the ballet. "Never before or since has there been such a gush of febrile, overwrought prose as that which flooded the Paris press from then on for years to come," writes Migel, who also quotes a few of the best: "The flight of birds or the airy passage of butterflies cannot be described in words; they must be seen. It is the same with Mlle Taglioni: language is powerless," or "She speaks to the soul; she makes one dream," or "To describe Marie Taglioni one would have to dip a hummingbird quill into the colors of the rainbow and inscribe it on the gauze wings of a butterfly." The ballerina particularly treasured a letter from one young man who upon seeing her dance was seemingly stricken with a fatal case of love sickness. "Farewell, farewell, beloved Marie. Your image, the image of Taglioni, will be close to me in the tomb."

Less than a month after the premiere, a cholera epidemic closed the ballet, and Taglioni fled Paris to perform in Berlin and in London, where on July 14, 1834, she married her count in a Protestant church ceremony. (Because the count's father disapproved of the marriage, the French civil ceremony was deferred until August 28, 1834, in Paris.) The groom, however, wearied of his bride quickly, and the couple separated after eight weeks. They reunited for a six-month period in 1835, but legally separately for good in 1844.

Shocked and upset by her husband's hasty departure, Taglioni then also faced some serious competition from *Fanny Elssler, who made her own debut at the Paris Opéra in September 1834. Several years younger than Maria, quite a bit prettier, and dancing in an appealing staccato style, Elssler stole much of the spotlight from Taglioni. Their rivalry, fueled in part by the partisanship of the critics, divided the public into two opposing camps—Taglionists and Elsslerists—and grew uglier as time went on.

In May 1835, following her brief reunion with her husband, Taglioni was laid up for six months with her famous "*mal au genou*," a mysterious knee ailment which baffled doctors. The following March, she gave birth to a daughter Maria ("Nini"). From that time forward, the ballet community took to referring to the pregnancy of a dancer as "*mal au genou*." In 1843, Maria gave birth to a second child, Georges, whose father is apparently unknown. He may have been the writer Eugène Demares, who helped Filippo create the ballet *La Fille du Danube* for the dancer, and was reported to be her lover, but Georges' paternity has never been verified.

La Fille du Danube, meant to counter Elssler's stunning performance in the *Le Diable boiteux*, received only mixed revues, making Taglioni more cranky and temperamental than usual. Meanwhile, new management at the Opéra was not as patient with her frequent knee problems and refusals to perform. In 1837, Maria left Paris for an appearance in St. Petersburg, accompanied by her family and her lover Eugène, who now also served as her agent, manager, and librettist.

Maria's Russian debut was recorded by Eugène as, "Immense, immense success! Incredible success! Such as has never been seen before." Audiences indeed went wild, and tributes to the ballerina flowed in, including gifts of jewels

from Tsar Nicholas I—diamond and emerald broaches and earrings, and a garland of diamond and turquoise forget-me-nots for her to wear in her hair. Following her first season, she was contracted for four more years, with time allotted for tours to Poland, Vienna, and London. For Taglioni, now at the peak of her success, even the specter of Fanny Elssler seemed remote and unimportant. Her perfect world was shattered, however, when Eugène fell ill and died within two weeks. Despite her overwhelming grief, the ballerina went on with her work, dancing the lead role in her father's *L'Ombre*, which told the story of the ghost of a young girl seeking her lost lover.

Taglioni left Russia in 1842. Now a wealthy woman, she invested in a house on the shore of Lake Como and in two palazzi in Venice, where she planned to retire. Before leaving the stage, however, she returned to Paris to perform in a revival of *La Sylphide*, which was reviewed by Théophile Gautier, then the city's leading ballet critic. He noted that age had not diminished Taglioni's performance.

> Always the same elegant and slender form, the same calm, intelligent, and modest features; not a single feather has fallen from her wing; not a hair has silvered beneath her chaplet of flowers! . . . What airiness! What rhythmic movements! What noble gestures! What poetic attitudes and, above all, what a sweet melancholy! What lack of restraint, yet how chaste!

Other critics were neither as verbose nor as kind, among them Albéric Second, who saw Maria perform in a revival of *L'Ombre*. "Don't speak to me anymore about your old Taglioni, that forty-six-year-old sylphide," he wrote, adding six years to the age of the ballerina, "who is always being thrown at other dancers, the way Molière is thrown at playwrights."

With retirement looming, and despite her turbulent temperament, Taglioni had apparently mellowed enough with age to agree to appear with three of her rival performers—*Carlotta Grisi, *Fanny Cerrito, and *Lucile Grahn—in *Pas de Quatre*, composed by Cesare Pugni and choreographed by Jules Perrot, and performed in London. Called "the greatest Terpsichorean exhibition that was ever known in Europe," the four ballerinas were welcomed with clapping and cheering that continued throughout the performance, and a barrage of bouquets, wreaths, and garlands that so littered the stage it became almost impossible to dance amid the clutter. On the heels of this success, Perrot and Pugni staged *Le Jugement de Pâris*, in which Taglioni danced the *Pas des Déeses* with Cerrito and Grahn.

Maria Taglioni retired from the stage in 1847, although her professional career was not yet ended. In 1859, she was confirmed as Inspectrice de la danse at the Paris Opéra, a position she retained until 1870, and as such taught advanced classes. (As a teacher, she became the mentor of ballerina *Emma Livry who died at an early age when her costume caught fire.)

As a result of some unwise financial speculations made by her father, Maria lost most of her fortune late in life, and was forced to move to London, where she established a school of dance and deportment. She lived on her own and remained socially active until 1880, when she went to live with her son Georges and his family in Marseilles. She died there four years later.

Maria Taglioni's influence upon ballet cannot be overstated. "She freed it from the lingering remnants of affectation, the artificial and stilted style of the 18th century," writes ballet historian Anatole Chujoy. "Her art invested ballet with a hitherto unknown quality of spirituality, emphasized by her technique, her prodigious elevation, and her ability to seemingly remain in the air at the highest point of ascent before descending."

SOURCES:

Chujoy, Anatole, and P.W. Manchester, eds. *The Dance Encyclopedia*. NY: Simon and Schuster, 1967.

Migel, Parmenia. *The Ballerinas: From the Court of Louis XIV to Pavlova*. NY: Macmillan, 1972.

Barbara Morgan,
Melrose, Massachusetts

Taia (c. 1400–1340 BCE).

See Tiy.

Tailleferre, Germaine (1892–1983)

French composer, a member of the famous group of modern musicians known as Les Six, who emancipated herself from the musical constraints of academic training to create lively, crisp, straightforward music that echoed jazz. Name variations: Germaine Tuillefere; Germaine Taileferre; Germaine Taillefesse. Pronunciation: Tal-e-fair. Born Germaine Marcelle Taillefesse on April 19, 1892, in Parc Saint-Maur, outside Paris; died on November 7, 1983, in Paris, at age 91; daughter of a Norman farmer and a pianist; admitted to the Paris Conservatoire, 1904; married Ralph Barton, in 1925 (divorced 1931); married Jean Lageat, in 1931; children: (second marriage) Françoise Lageat.

First admitted to the Paris Conservatoire (1904); forced by father to attend convent school (1906); reinstated at the conservatory (1914); proclaimed a musical protegee of Erik Satie (1917); was a member, with five other musicians, of group known as Les Six (1920–24); traveled to U.S. to perform and married Ralph Barton (1925); divorced Barton and married Lageat (1931); appeared in musical exhibit sponsored by the International Council of Music featuring Les Six (1952); honored with other members of Les Six at a celebration of their 35th anniversary in Paris (1954); awarded the Grand Prix Musical from the Académie des Beaux Arts (1973); awarded a second Grand Prix Musical by the City of Paris (1978).

In Paris in the 1920s, where Ernest Hemingway wrote novels, *Gertrude Stein held her salon, Jean Cocteau designed stage sets, and Pablo Picasso created his radically new paintings, there was a sense that anything could happen. In the Latin Quarter and up on Montparnasse, cafés were filled with patrons drawn from all over the world by the cultural ferment. On Saturday nights, at a club called Le Gaya near the Place de la Concorde, crowds were also gathering to hear the new music being played by a group of six musicians. On any given evening, the likes of the Prince of Wales, Artur Rubinstein, and Princess **Violette Murat** were in attendance at the club, while others clamored outside to get in. Among the six performers was one young woman, Germaine Tailleferre, whose compositions epitomize the magic of that creative period.

Born on April 19, 1892, in Parc Saint-Maur outside of Paris, Germaine Marcelle Taillefesse was the youngest of three girls and two boys. She came from sturdy Norman stock; her family had tilled the land of the region for generations. Her mother, a pianist, sensed Germaine's artistic ability early on. While she taught piano to her older daughters, Germaine would often stay close at hand, then go to her toy piano and pick out the piece she had heard. She was also deft at drawing and needlework. But her strict, conservative father, who could be cruel, bitterly opposed her musical education. Even so, her mother helped her to practice the piano while he was away, and in 1904 she arranged for her daughter to audition for one of the teachers at the Conservatoire de Paris, the most important musical academy in France. Germaine was accepted as a student and entered the conservatory at age 12, but her father's objections remained so vehement that in 1906 she was removed and sent to a convent school. Still, she had won a First prize and began to teach music to earn money for her own musical education.

At the end of her convent schooling, Germaine was reinstated at the conservatory and proved to be an extremely gifted student under the tutelage of Maurice Ravel, Claude Debussy, and Charles-Marie Widor. She became close to Ravel and made the acquaintance of Darius Milhaud, Arthur Honegger, and Georges Auric, who would one day join her in the group known as Les Six. In 1914, the onset of World War I caused many students to leave the conservatory; Widor's composition class was comprised of only Tailleferre, Milhaud, Honegger, and Henri Cliquet-Pleyel. Wrote Francis Poulenc, "How ravishing our Germaine was in 1917, with her school girl's satchel full of all the Conservatoire's first prizes! How kind and gentle she was! . . . [W]hat a charming and precious contribution her music makes!"

In 1917, Tailleferre's father died in an accident and her mother suffered from phlebitis. Germaine continued to teach to help support her family. On Saturday nights she would often go to Montmartre, where the small apartment of Milhaud was a gathering place for young composers, musicians, and poets. Evenings "chez Darius" expanded her creative horizons as she got to know young painters and poets as well as musicians. She became interested in Cubism and the music of Igor Stravinsky, whose ballet *The Rite of Spring* had caused an uproar in Paris when it was first performed in 1913. In 1917, she traveled to Spain, and returned with the intention of studying art, but she continued to give music lessons to support herself and her mother. Around this time she began to call herself Tailleferre rather than Taillefesse, because she liked the sound better.

May 18, 1917, was a landmark date in the artistic life of Paris, when Sergei Diaghilev's Ballets Russes performed *Parade*. Conceived by Jean Cocteau, with music by Erik Satie and sets

Germaine
Tailleferre

by Pablo Picasso, the new work took Paris by storm. Audiences loved the larger-than-life cubist costumes and the musical score which employed the sounds of typewriters, sirens, and airplanes. The creativity of the capricious, opinionated Satie attracted many young composers. When he heard Tailleferre reading through one of her own compositions for two pianos, he proclaimed her to be his *fille-musicale* and decided to include her music at the informal concerts he sponsored. Around this time Tailleferre also became a good friend of the pianist Artur Rubinstein, to whom she dedicated a *Quatuor*. Like Satie and others, Rubinstein appreciated Tailleferre's bold new style. Along with other young composers of the period, she demonstrated a need for "less ethereal music, closer to the realities of . . . daily life, for a cutting, biting music."

On November 11, 1918, WWI came to an end, and the seeds of modernism began to flourish. In Paris, change was suddenly everywhere. Cafés overflowed, automobiles crowded busy streets, and dresses rose above the knee, while artists and intellectuals believed that literature, art, and music must all be reshaped to fit a new dynamic. In this climate, Tailleferre and five friends found themselves at the helm of a brief musical movement. One evening in January 1920, a studio concert was held on the rue Huyghens. It was a small musical gathering typical of ones where young composers like Germaine had a chance to demonstrate their compositions. That evening the critic Henri Collet was in the audience and heard pieces by Georges Auric, Darius Milhaud, Louis Durey, Francis Poulenc, Arthur Honegger, and Germaine Tailleferre. Other than being young and French, the only force binding this group of composers was the fact that all were in the circle of Eric Satie. But articles by Collet soon appeared in *Comoedia* describing the works of Les Six, and creating a legend which changed the lives of all six performers. Although no philosophy or style bound them together, the friends decided to keep the name. As Auric said later, "Labels in concerts as in industry are very important. If one puts a label on a can of Coca-Cola, it sells much better than if one does not."

The label certainly helped to launch Tailleferre's career. Several of her compositions, including her String Quartet, *Images*, and *Jeu de plein air*, soon became well known. Some described her as a "princess" of modern music. Despite the tremendous attention she received, Tailleferre remained modest and shy, and somewhat overwhelmed by her newly glamorous mi-

lieu. She had little flair for the politics of success. To the displeasure of Satie, she remained friendly with Ravel, who encouraged her to enter competitions to win prize money that she badly needed, and she even became a milliner to augment her income. Her fame grew, meanwhile, as Les Six became the rage, and she completed *Ballade*, Sonata for Violin and Piano, and a ballet, *Le Marchand d'oiseaux*.

By 1924, the popularity of Les Six had peaked. The critics and the public, recognizing that the group was held together by no central theme, felt misled by the label and the composers themselves began to disclaim it, going on with their individual work. Another critic, Emile Vuillermos, wrote biting articles proclaiming that in the case of Les Six "publicity takes rank over art." But by this time Tailleferre had been invited to New York by the famous conductor Leopold Stokowski. On February 14, 1925, she performed her Sonata for Violin and Piano in New York's Aeolian Hall, and the following September she was performing in New York again when she met Ralph Barton, a famous caricaturist who spoke French fluently. Several years her senior, Barton soon proposed marriage, and she accepted.

It was Barton's fourth trip to the altar, and the marriage did not begin auspiciously. Largely because he did not want her to play or compose on a real instrument, Barton gave Tailleferre a player piano. In his mind, he had not married a musician; he had married a woman who could provide him with excellent French cuisine. The relationship did allow Tailleferre introduction to the talented and famous, including Charlie Chaplin, Sinclair Lewis, *Ethel Barrymore*, Somerset Maugham, *Loretta Young*, and Paul Morand. As well, some of her new works, including the orchestrated version of *Jeu de plein air* and a new Concertino for harp and orchestra, were performed in concert. The success rankled her husband, who announced he felt like "Monsieur Tailleferre," and his wife later described that period of her life by saying, "Yes, yes, yes, yes, yes. I married a well-known American who went mad."

In 1927, Barton decided they should move to Paris, and the couple's life began to stabilize. Tailleferre found it easier to work and composed *Deux Valses* for two pianos, *Pavane, Nocturne,* and *Finale* for orchestra, a Sicilienne and a Pastorale in A-flat. In 1929, she wrote *Six Chansons Françaises*, but in 1930, her mother, who had always been a great support, died. Her husband had begun to travel to and fro between New York and Paris, frequently seeing other women.

Not wishing to repeat her parents' confrontational relationship, Tailleferre remained conciliatory, which only enraged Barton, and she finally decided on a separation. On April 20, 1931, the divorce became final; one month later, on May 20, Barton committed suicide in New York, an event that was front-page news.

That same year Tailleferre married again. Her husband was a lawyer, Jean Lageat, and this marriage proved to be no happier than the first, since Lageat was also jealous of his wife and a serious illness aggravated his moods. Tailleferre gave birth to a daughter named **Françoise Lageat** and, to supplement the family income, began to write film music. She also composed an exuberant Overture, which many judge to be her finest piece. "I make music because I enjoy it," she said. "I know that it is not *grande musique*. It is light and gay music, which explains why sometimes I am compared to the *petits maîtres* of the 18th century, and I am very proud of this." In 1934, she wrote and performed her Concerto for Two Pianos, Chorus, and Orchestra.

Diagnosed with tuberculosis, Lageat was forced to spend three years in a Swiss sanitarium. Tailleferre accompanied him to Leysin, and her work suffered while she remained at his side. In 1936, she completed her Violin Concerto, and she continued to write film music. In 1937, she began a collaboration with Paul Valéry, the French poet, receiving a commission of 20,000 francs to compose a cantata using his lyric poetry. Recalling this happy time, Tailleferre described her walks with Valéry beneath the olive trees in the South of France. As they discussed the poem central to the work, "Narcisse," he would recite out loud while she would take down rhythmic dictation. The *Cantate du Narcisse* was performed in 1942 but never published. By this time Tailleferre and her daughter had followed her husband to New York to escape the Nazis. Germaine never felt at home in America, and she worried about family and friends in France. During those years she did not compose, but she did teach a few students. In 1948, when she returned to France, much had changed. Her home in Grasse had been occupied and pillaged by the Germans, and while trying to restore her household, she saw that her second marriage had become impossible. It would not end, however, until 1955.

In 1952, the International Council of Music sponsored an exhibit featuring manuscripts, stage sets, letters, and mementos of Les Six, and Tailleferre was drawn back to her early companions. On November 3, 1954, the 35th anniversary of the group was celebrated at the Théâtre des Champs-Élysées with a gala concert which drew 3,000 people to honor them. In 1955, Tailleferre bought a house in Saint-Tropez with her meager divorce settlement, and lived there with her granddaughter, Elvire, born to Françoise during a brief marriage. Raising the child and other family problems frequently kept her from work, but she still managed to compose. In the 1950s, she wrote a Second Sonata for violin and piano, a Sonata for harp, and a Concertino for flute, piano, and chamber orchestra. Her ballet *Parisiana* was first performed in 1953 in Copenhagen and again in 1954 at the Edinburgh Festival.

In 1961, Les Six, reduced to five by the death of Arthur Honegger, celebrated their 40th anniversary. Tailleferre continued to teach and to raise her adored young granddaughter. After the Paris riots in 1968, she joined the Communist Party to show sympathy with the students' cause. Because she never kept track of royalties or her music manuscripts, many of her works are incomplete or lost, and her life remained economically precarious. Six years before her death, however, friends formed an "Association Germaine Tailleferre" to look after her, and in 1973 she was awarded the Grand Prix Musical from the Académie des Beaux Arts. In 1978, she received a second Grand Prix Musical from the City of Paris. She continued to compose up to the time of her death, on November 7, 1983, at age 91—the last of Les Six.

SOURCES:
Brody, Elaine. *Paris. The Musical Kaleidoscope 1870–1925*. NY: George Braziller, 1987.
"Germaine Tailleferre," in *The Times* [London]. November 9, 1983, p. 16.
Harding, James. *The Ox on the Roof: Scenes from Musical Life in Paris in the Twenties*. London: Macdonald, 1972.
Mitgang, Laura. "Germaine Tailleferre: Before During and After *Les Six*," in Zaimont, Judith Lang, Catherine Overhauser, and Jane Gottlieb, Jane, eds., *The Musical Woman: An International Perspective*. Vol. II, 1984–1985. CT: Greenwood Press, 1987, pp. 177–221.
"La mort de Germaine Tailleferre. Compositeur au féminin," in *Le Monde*. November 9, 1983, p. 17.

Karin Loewen Haag,
freelance writer,
Athens, Georgia

Taimur, Aichat Asmat (1840–1902).

See Taymuriyya, 'A'isha 'Ismat al-.

Taisho empress (1885–1951).

See Sadako.

Tait, Agnes (c. 1897–1981)

American artist. Name variations: Mrs. William Mc-Nulty. Born around 1897 (some sources cite 1894) in Greenwich Village in New York City; died in 1981 in Santa Fe, New Mexico; educated at the National Academy of Design; married William McNulty (a journalist), in 1933.

Noted for decorative panels; active in a number of Depression-era federal art programs, for which she executed mural paintings and created Skating in Central Park; *selected to exhibit at the New York World's Fair (1939); later turned to printmaking and illustrating children's books.*

Born in Greenwich Village around 1897, Agnes Tait studied with Charles Hinton, Francis Jones, and Leon Kroll at the National Academy of Design in New York City. She initially distinguished herself as a creator of decorative panels of intricate friezes depicting trees with animals or flowers. In 1930, the United Fruit Company provided her with a grant to paint tropical scenes and portraits of Jamaicans and Haitians. Two years later, Florenz Ziegfeld commissioned her to paint a series of portraits of the cast of the Ziegfeld Follies. She had frequent exhibitions in New York until the beginning of the Great Depression, when she became involved in many of the art programs funded by the federal government as part of the New Deal.

In 1933, she married journalist William Mc-Nulty and that winter worked as an easel painter for the New York Public Works Art Project, where she executed one of her most well-known paintings, *Skating in Central Park* (1934). The work reflects many of the trends in art of this time, note Ann Sutherland Harris and Linda Nochlin. It has strong aspects of Tait's decorative style plus elements of the abstract. Bare tree limbs are silhouetted against the snow and sky while flattened figures circle the canvas. The strong patterns of the painting reflect what would become the American mural movement, which evolved out of the many relief projects for artists during the Depression and was made particularly famous by Thomas Hart Benton. According to Sutherland and Nochlin, the painting also reflects the new American primitive school of art in its inclusion of iconographic figures and its emphasis on placing American art and life in a historical context. The painting was eventually displayed in the Department of Labor building.

A member of the WPA's Federal Art Project, in 1937 Tait began to collaborate on the murals that decorate Bellevue Hospital. As well, *Olive Grove, Mallorca*, a decorative work of animals and figures in a landscape of trees, was selected for the Gallery of American Art Today at the New York World's Fair in 1939. In 1941, she received a commission to paint a mural frieze, *Fruits of the Land*, in the lobby of the U.S. Post Office in Laurinsburg, North Carolina.

After World War II, Tait moved to an artists' colony in Santa Fe, New Mexico, where she became interested in printmaking and the illustration of children's books. She illustrated *Peter and Penny of the Island* (1941), **Johanna Spyri's Heidi* (c. 1950) and *Paco's Miracle* (1961), among others. Tait died in Santa Fe in 1981.

SOURCES:

Harris, Ann Sutherland, and Linda Nochlin. *Women Artists: 1550–1950*. Los Angeles County Museum of Art and Alfred A. Knopf, 1976.

Martha Jones, M.L.S.,
Natick, Massachusetts

Taitu (c. 1850–1918).

See Taytu.

Tajolmolouk (1896–1981)

Queen of Iran. Name variations: HM Queen Tajolmolouk; HM The Empress Mother. Born Nimtaj Ayramlu on March 17, 1896; died in California in 1981; daughter of Brigadier General Tadfel Molouk; became second wife of Reza Shah Pahlavi, shah of Iran (r. 1925–1941, abdicated), in February 1915 (divorced April 1924); children: Shams Pahlavi (1917–1996); (twins) Muhammad Reza Pahlavi also known as Riza I Pahlavi, shah of Iran (r. 1941–1979, deposed), and *Asraf Pahlavi (1919—); Ali Reza Pahlavi (1921–1954). Reza Shah Pahlavi's first wife was his cousin Maryam Khanum (m. 1903); his third and fourth wives were Touran Amir Soleimani Saltaneh (1904–1995) and Queen Esmat.

Takako Doi (b. 1928).

See Doi, Takako.

Takamine Hideko (1924—)

Popular child actress, known as "the Japanese Shirley Temple," who in adulthood worked with Japan's most accomplished film directors, portraying a wide variety of roles. Name variations: Takama Yoshio. Pronunciation: Ta-ka-me-nay He-day-koe. Born Takama Yoshio in 1924 in Hakodate, Hokkaido, Japan; daughter of Hirayama Kinji (a restaurant owner); adopted by Hirayama Shige (her paternal aunt) and Ogino Ichiji (both of whom were benshi);

married Matsuyama Zenzo (a film director and screenwriter), in March 1955; no children.

Selected filmography: Tsuzurikata kyoshitsu *(Composition Class, 1938);* Nijushi no hitomi *(Twenty-four Eyes, 1954);* Na mo naku mazushiku utsukushiku *(Nameless, Poor, Beautiful, 1961).*

Selected writings: (autobiography) Watashi no tosei nikki *(1976).*

Takamine Hideko was born in Hakodate, Hokkaido, Japan, in 1924. Her early years were spent in her parents' restaurant, where she remembers being entertained by the geisha. Following the death of her mother, Hideko was raised by her aunt, who was a *benshi*, a professional narrator for silent films before the introduction of sound. When Hideko was five, her uncle took her to audition for the film *Mother*, in which she played her first role. Notes James O'Brien: "A winsome girl, she quickly became a popular child actress, affectionately known in her own country as 'the Japanese Shirley Temple.' Unlike Shirley Temple and most other child stars, Takamine Hideko managed to avoid the pitfalls that always seem to await the popular child performer trying to sustain a career beyond the period of natural charm and into adolescence." As a teenager, Hideko was a popular "pin-up girl," her photograph frequently sent as a gift to Japanese soldiers overseas. Following the war, she maintained her popularity with appearances in critically acclaimed films. In the 1970s, Hideko began writing her two-volume autobiography, *Watashi no tosei nikki*, which won a prestigious award for nonfiction. In it, she describes the ways in which serendipity, determination, and hard work enabled her to be a successful film actress.

SOURCES:
O'Brien, James. "Takamine Hideko: The Actress," in *Heroic With Grace: Legendary Women of Japan*. Chieko Mulhern, ed. Armonk, NY: M.E. Sharpe, 1991, pp. 265–296.

Linda L. Johnson,
Professor of History, Concordia College,
Moorhead, Minnesota

Takano-tenno (718–770).

See Kōken-Shōtoku.

Takaru, Princess (594–661).

See Kōgyoku-Saimei.

Talbert, Mary Morris (1866–1923)

African-American educator and civil-rights activist. Name variations: Mary Burnett Talbert. *Born Mary* Morris Burnett in Oberlin, Ohio, on September 17, 1866; died of coronary thrombosis in Buffalo, New York, on October 15, 1923; youngest of eight children of Cornelius J. Burnett and Caroline (Nichols) Burnett; Oberlin College, S.P. degree, 1886, B.A., 1894; married William Talbert (a city clerk and realtor), in 1891; children: **Sarah May Talbert** (who became an accomplished pianist and composer).

In 1887, when Mary Morris Talbert was hired as assistant principal of Bethel University, she became the first woman in the state to hold that position; by the following year, she was principal of Union High School in Little Rock. With her marriage to William Talbert, a successful city clerk and realtor, she moved to Buffalo and became active in the African-American community there; she was also a charter member in the highly active *Phillis Wheatley Club.

The Talberts were prominent in the black protest movement, founding the Michigan Avenue Baptist Church in 1892, and frequently sharing their home with reformers, including Booker T. Washington, W.E.B. Du Bois, and *Nannie Helen Burroughs. Talbert also worked regularly alongside fellow Oberlin alumnae *Anna J. Cooper and *Mary Church Terrell in the National Association of Colored Women (NACW); from 1916 to 1920, Talbert was its president.

In 1921, as vice-president of the National Association for the Advancement of Colored People (NAACP), Talbert took on a national crusade to support the Dyer Anti-Lynching Bill, raising much-needed funds to advertize the atrocities. She was the first woman to receive the coveted Spingarn Medal from the NAACP.

SOURCES:
Smith, Jessie Carney, ed. *Notable Black American Women*. Detroit, MI: Gale Research, 1992.

Talbot, Anne (d. 1440)

Duchess of Devon. Name variations: Anne Courtenay. Died on January 16, 1440; daughter of Richard Talbot, 4th lord Talbot, and **Ankaret Lestrange Talbot** *(1361–1413); married or associated with Hugh Courtenay, 4th earl of Devon; associated with John Botreaux; children: (with Hugh Courtenay) Thomas Courtenay (1414–1458), 5th earl of Devon.*

Talbot, Catherine (1721–1770)

English Bluestocking, essayist, and letter writer. Born in May 1721 in Berkshire, England; died on January 9, 1770, in London; daughter of Edward Talbot (archdeacon of Berkshire) and Mary (Martyn) Talbot; *never married; no children.*

Essayist Catherine Talbot was born in Berkshire, England, in 1721, the only child of **Mary Martyn Talbot** and Archdeacon Edward Talbot, who died a few months before her birth. Catherine and Mary were then taken in by the family of Edward Secker, bishop of Oxford and later archbishop of Canterbury, in whose home they would remain throughout most of Catherine's life. Secker tutored Talbot in modern languages, including German, Italian, and French, as well as in Latin; she was also taught geography and painting in addition to religious education. She put her excellent education, unusual for a woman of the 18th century, to use in composing moral essays and poetry.

Deeply devout, Talbot wrote treatises on scripture and other religious topics. Although she shared these with friends who admired her writing, she refused to allow the publication of all except one, which appeared in Samuel Johnson's *Rambler* in 1750. She was well known in London literary circles, and belonged to the group of well-educated women writers and scholars called the Bluestocking Circle. Talbot was also a prolific correspondent, and many of her letters to her Bluestocking friends have been preserved, including almost 30 years of letters to her closest friend, the poet *Elizabeth Carter. After suffering many years of ill health, Catherine Talbot died at age 49 of cancer. Carter arranged for the posthumous publication of Talbot's collected religious essays, entitled *Reflections on the Seven Days of the Week*. A second collection, *Essays on Various Subjects*, appeared in 1772. Her work also appeared in the 1792 anthology *The Athenian Letters*. Talbot's letters to Carter, for which she was best known in the 19th century, were collected and published by Carter's nephew in 1809.

SOURCES:

Myers, Silvia. *The Bluestocking Circle: Women, Friendship, and the Life of the Mind in Eighteenth-Century England*. NY: Oxford University Press, 1990.

Pennington, Montagu, ed. *A Series of Letters between Mrs. Elizabeth Carter and Catherine Talbot, from the year 1741 to 1770*. London: Rivington, 1809.

Shattock, Joanne. *The Oxford Guide to British Women Writers*. NY: Oxford University Press, 1993.

Laura York, M.A. in History, University of California, Riverside, California

Talbot, Elizabeth (d. 1487)

*Baroness Lisle. Died in 1487; daughter of John Talbot, 1st Viscount Lisle or L'Isle, and **Joan Chedder**; married Edward Grey, viscount L'Isle (r. 1483–1492); children: *Elizabeth Grey (fl. 1482–1530), 6th baroness Lisle; John Grey (b. 1480), 4th viscount Lisle; **Anne Grey** (who married Sir John Willoughby); **Margaret Grey** (who married Edward Stafford, 10th earl of Wiltshire).*

Talbot, Elizabeth (d. around 1506)

*Duchess of Norfolk. Name variations: Elizabeth Mowbray. Died around 1506; daughter of John Talbot (1384–1453), 1st earl of Shrewsbury (r. 1442–1453), and **Margaret Beauchamp** (1404–1467); married John Mowbray, 4th duke of Norfolk, before November 27, 1448; children: *Anne Mowbray (1472–1481).*

Talbot, Elizabeth (1518–1608)

Countess of Shrewsbury. Name variations: Bess of Hardwick; Bess of Hardwick Hall; Elizabeth of Hard-

Elizabeth Talbot (1518–1608)

*wick; Elizabeth Hardwick; Elizabeth Shrewsbury. Born in 1518 in Derbyshire, England; died on February 13, 1608 (some sources cite 1607); interred at Allhallows, Derby; fourth daughter and co-heiress of John Hardwick of Hardwick, Derbyshire, and **Elizabeth Leake**; married Robert Barlow, in 1532 (died 1533); married Sir William Cavendish, later 1st earl of Devonshire, in 1549 (died); married Sir William St. Loe (died); married George Talbot (1522–1591), 6th earl of Shrewsbury, on February 9, 1567 (separated 1583); children: (second marriage) Henry Cavendish (MP for Derby); William Cavendish (b. 1552), earl of Devonshire; Charles Cavendish; **Frances Cavendish**; Elizabeth Cavendish (d. 1582); Mary Talbot (d. 1632); grandchildren: Arabella Stuart.*

Renowned for her financial acuity, passion for building, and four shrewd marriages, Elizabeth Talbot, countess of Shrewsbury, was one of the wonders of the Elizabethan age. Widely called Bess of Hardwick, she was among the richest women in England (second only to the queen), and she knew how both to increase and to spend her money. The houses she built were grand mansions on a spectacular scale, and her masterpiece, Hardwick Hall in Derbyshire, is considered perhaps the finest extant house of the era. Lavishly windowed, its six towers prominently adorned with her initials wrought in stone three feet high, it contains a High Great Chamber (her favorite room) which Sacheverell Sitwell called "the most beautiful room, not in England alone, but in the whole of Europe." She was also an intimate of Queen *Elizabeth I, a longtime "custodian" of *Mary Stuart, queen of Scots, an occasional partner in court intrigue, a mother who assiduously promoted her children's interests, and an energetic businesswoman who did not suffer fools lightly.

She was born in 1518 in decidedly lesser circumstances, in a small manor house within sight of the land on which she would later build Hardwick Hall. The death while she was still young of her father, a respectable country squire, greatly damaged the family finances. At age 15, she married for the first time, and before she was 17 she was a widow in possession of her late husband's modest but helpful estate. After spending some years at court, where she readily adapted to the intricacies of social and political scheming, she married Sir William Cavendish in 1549. Cavendish, who was considerably older than his wife, had prospered mightily from his job of selling off and otherwise dealing with the properties Henry VIII seized from the Roman Catholic Church. They had six children, three

girls and three boys, and in 1552 William fulfilled Talbot's wish by purchasing Chatsworth, a Derbyshire estate with several thousand acres of land. With his assistance, she began her first major building project, a stone house that would take decades and much money to complete. When it was finally finished—long after the death of William, who had become the 1st earl of Devonshire—it was one of the most admired homes in the country, and became the Cavendish family seat. (Future generations would completely alter the house and grounds, building additions and changing the façade, and in particular filling the interior with an astonishing array of murals, furniture and artworks.)

Talbot was again a widow, this time with young children and William Cavendish's estate, when Elizabeth I came to the throne in 1558. Elizabeth previously had known and liked Talbot, and made her a lady-in-waiting at court. Some ten years later the queen would declare, "There is no Lady in this land that I better love and like," and Talbot retained her respect and (mostly) good will despite their ups and downs over the subsequent years. While at court, she met and married Sir William St. Loe, a captain of the Queen's Guard and another very wealthy man. Some of that wealth went towards the completion of Chatsworth House, and she inherited the rest of it after St. Loe died a few years into their marriage. Her final husband, whom she married on February 9, 1567, was George Talbot, earl of Shrewsbury. He was the richest of her husbands—indeed, perhaps the richest husband or bachelor in the land—and he possessed already a number of great country houses. He also possessed children. To keep his money in the family, they married their young children to each other: her daughter ❧➤ Mary Talbot wed his son Gilbert, and his daughter **Grace Cavendish** married her son Henry.

The newlyweds went to live at one of the earl's homes, Tutbury Castle in Staffordshire. In 1568, at the queen's pleasure, they found themselves with a long-term boarder: Mary Stuart, queen of Scots. Her "visit," complete with retinue and escape attempts, would last until 1584, three years before her execution. Talbot continued building Chatsworth and smaller houses with George's money, and negotiated excellent marriages for the rest of her children; all, that is, save for her daughter ❧➤ **Elizabeth Cavendish**. In 1574, much to Talbot's chagrin, George rashly arranged Elizabeth Cavendish's marriage to Mary Stuart's brother-in-law, Charles Stuart, 5th earl of Lennox. For that deed, Elizabeth Talbot joined *Margaret Douglas (1515–1578), mother of Charles, in the Tower of

Talbot, Mary. See *Stuart, Arabella for sidebar.*

Cavendish, Elizabeth. See *Stuart, Arabella for sidebar.*

London for three months. The queen apparently held no grudge against her, however, and did not remove Mary Stuart from Tutbury. After Charles Stuart's death in 1577, Elizabeth Cavendish moved back home with her mother. She brought with her her young daughter *Arabella Stuart, who would remain in Talbot's care after Elizabeth Cavendish died in 1582.

Talbot's prodigious spending had caused George much grief, a condition he was not shy about vocalizing, and in 1583 she left him to settle with her granddaughter at Chatsworth. The manor house on the estate had finally been finished, and there she supervised Arabella's education and interests (too closely for Arabella's liking) and, no doubt, dreamed of her next major building. Following her estranged husband's death in 1591, she inherited his fortune and began construction of Hardwick Hall. With near-unlimited resources at her disposal, she was able to ensure that it was built at a rapid clip (about nine years), three stories, six towers, long staircase from one end to the other, countless small-paned windows and all. Talbot lived at Hardwick House until her death in 1608. Nearly unchanged since that time, it is now maintained by the National Trust.

SOURCES AND SUGGESTED READING:
Durant, David N. *Bess of Hardwick: Portrait of an Elizabethan Dynast.* Weidenfeld & Nicolson, 1977.
Thorndike, Joseph J., Jr. *The Magnificent Builders.* NY: American Heritage, 1978.

Talbot, Elizabeth (1581–1651).

See Grey, Elizabeth.

Talbot, Marion (1858–1948)

American university dean, professor of household administration, and social reformer who cofounded the American Association of University Women. Born on July 31, 1858, in Thun, Switzerland; died of chronic myocarditis on October 20, 1948, in Chicago, Illinois; daughter of Israel Tisdale Talbot (a university dean) and Emily (Fairbanks) Talbot (an education reformer); educated in private schools; Boston University, B.A., 1880; Massachusetts Institute of Technology, B.S., 1888.

The eldest of six children (two of whom died in infancy), Marion Talbot was born in Thun, Switzerland, in 1858, while her parents were traveling in Europe. Her father Israel Talbot was a practitioner of homeopathic medicine and the first dean of the Boston University Medical School. Her mother **Emily Talbot** was an education reformer, a champion of college

preparatory courses for women who helped establish the Girls' Latin School in Boston. Marion grew up in Boston in an atmosphere of good works and social reform.

Because public secondary education for college preparation was not readily available to young women, Marion was educated privately at Chauncy Hall School and Girls' High School. She traveled abroad to study languages and was privately tutored in Greek and Latin. Conditionally admitted to Boston University, she earned a bachelor of arts degree in 1880. After college, Talbot traveled and became interested in a newly established field, the applied science of sanitation. Inspired by a family friend, *Ellen Swallow Richards, who was pioneering this field at the Massachusetts Institute of Technology (MIT), Talbot enrolled there in 1881. Although she left after one semester, she returned in 1884 and received a B.S. in 1888.

During this period, Talbot, her mother Emily, Richards, *Alice Freeman Palmer, and other women interested in the education of women organized the Association of Collegiate Alumnae to unite women dispersed throughout the nation, to establish standards for women's advanced education, and to provide fellowships for women graduate students. Talbot was the organization's first secretary and later president from 1895 to 1897. This organization eventually became the American Association of University Women.

Talbot was also interested in the application of science to the running of the home and was involved in the emerging field called domestic science. In 1887, she and Richards co-edited *Home Sanitation: A Manual for Housekeepers,* and in 1890, with the assistance of her friend Alice Palmer, she was appointed instructor in domestic science at Wellesley College.

In 1892, the president of the University of Chicago invited Palmer to create and direct a new program for women. She accepted under the condition that Talbot accompany and assist her. Thus Talbot became dean of undergraduate women and assistant professor of sanitary science in the department of social science and anthropology. In 1895, she was appointed associate professor, and four years later became dean of women for the university. In 1905, she was made a full professor in the department of household administration, which she created and which included **Alice Peloubet Norton** and *Sophonisba P. Breckinridge.

In her role as dean of women, Talbot was responsible for living conditions of the women students at the university, and she interpreted this as a mission to change the conventional life of women to include education for entering society. Society was defined by her as both the social obligations women assumed as well as the world at large, where educated women would participate toward its betterment. Talbot developed a system of dormitories organized as residential clubs for women. They had a director, a hospitality program, were self-governing, and emulated the attractions of a private home. To support these dormitory facilities, Talbot organized the Woman's Union in 1901 and a clubhouse with exercise facilities for women. While promoting living conditions for university women and objecting to academic discrimination based on gender, she firmly opposed the establishment of national sororities at the University of Chicago.

Talbot wrote in both her fields of interest, as an administrator of women's education and as a pioneer in the field of domestic science. Her writings combined science and reform. Her first published study, coauthored with Richards, was *Food as a Factor in Student Life* (1894), a practical study of diet in the women's dormitories. In *The Education of Women* (1910) and *The Modern Household* (1912), coauthored with Breckinridge, she critiqued the education of women in a changing technological society. Talbot believed that, although the home would always be the place for most women to exercise their influence on society, the traditional household was obsolete and efforts to perpetuate it useless. The modern household, according to Talbot, was a complex entity requiring the skills of a woman educated in administration and capable of exerting her influence upon the home—the central unit of society with a woman as its focal point.

In addition to her university responsibilities, Talbot participated in the Lake Placid conferences that led to the establishment of the Home Economics Association in 1908. Retiring in 1925, she served as acting president of Constantinople Woman's College in Turkey from 1927 to 1928 and from 1931 to 1932. She died in Chicago in 1948 of chronic myocarditis and was buried in Oak Woods Cemetery.

SOURCES:
James, Edward T., ed. *Notable American Women, 1607–1950*. Cambridge, MA: The Belknap Press of Harvard University, 1971.

Martha Jones, M.L.S.,
Natick, Massachusetts

Talbot, Mary (d. 1632).

See Stuart, Arabella for sidebar.

Talbot, Mary Anne (1778–1808)

British soldier and sailor. Name variations: Known as "The British Amazon." Born in 1778; died in 1808.

At age 14, Mary Anne Talbot became enamored of a British Army captain, by some accounts her husband, and followed him into the army. She joined the 82nd regiment of infantry, where she served in Flanders disguised as a drummer boy and a foot boy. With the army she served in the Caribbean city of Santo Domingo and in Valenciennes, France. At one point (some accounts indicate that it was due to the death of the captain, while others suggest it was due to his unpleasant behavior and not his death), she deserted the army and joined the navy as a "powder monkey"—a person who carried powder to the ship's guns. She also served as cabin boy on the *Le Sage* and on the *Brunswick* and was with Lord Howe during the war with France. During her service in the navy, Talbot was wounded in battle on June 1, 1794. Captured, she was imprisoned for 18 months. In 1796, her identity was discovered and her fighting career ended. She then became a servant for Robert S. Kirby, who wrote of her history in his 1804 work *Wonderful Museum*. Mary Anne Talbot died in 1808.

SOURCES:
The Concise Dictionary of National Biography. Oxford: Oxford University Press, 1992.
Macksey, Joan, and Kenneth Macksey. *The Book of Women's Achievements*. NY: Stein and Day, 1976.

Karina L. Kerr, M.A.,
Ypsilanti, Michigan

Tallchief, Maria (1925—)

Osage dancer, noted for many roles with the Ballet Russe de Monte Carlo and New York City Ballet, who was the first Native American to achieve the stature of prima ballerina in the United States. Name variations: Betty Marie Tall Chief. Born Elizabeth Marie Tall Chief on January 24, 1925, in Fairfax, Oklahoma; daughter of Alexander Tall Chief (a real estate investor) and Ruth (Porter) Tall Chief; sister of Marjorie Tallchief (b. 1927); graduated from Beverly Hills High School in California, 1942; married George Balanchine (the choreographer), in 1946 (annulled 1950); married Elmourza Natirboff (a charter plane pilot), in 1952 (divorced 1954); married Henry D. Paschen, Jr. (a construction company executive), in 1956; children: (third marriage) Elise Maria Paschen (b. 1959).

Moved with family to Los Angeles, California (1933); made first appearance as a soloist in Chopin Concerto, in Los Angeles (1940); toured as a member of the corps de ballet of the Ballet Russe de Monte

Carlo, then joined the company (1942); premiered two roles with the Ballet Russe (1946); joined husband George Balanchine at the Paris Opera, where she danced the role of Terpsichore in the premiere of Apollo *(1947); joined Ballet Society, soon renamed the New York City Ballet (1947); appeared in movie* The Million Dollar Mermaid *(1952); was the first Native American to achieve the rank of prima ballerina in the U.S. (1954); retired from New York City Ballet (1965); after period as artistic director for the Chicago Lyric Opera Ballet, co-founded Chicago City Ballet with her sister Marjorie Tallchief (1980).*

Notable roles: The ice-fairy queen in Le Baiser de la Fée *and Coquette in* Night Shadow, *for the Ballet Russe de Monte Carlo; Terpsichore in* Apollo, *for the Paris Opera Ballet; Eurydice in* Orpheus, *Firebird in* The Firebird, *the Swan Queen in* Swan Lake, *and the Sugar Plum Fairy in* The Nutcracker *for Ballet Society-New York City Ballet.*

Maria Tallchief's mother dreamed of her daughter becoming a concert pianist, and the child worked hard to please her, but ballet was what held her spellbound from the time of her first dance lessons at age four. Tallchief practiced the piano faithfully, mainly to get the music behind her so that she could spend more hours dancing. A music recital at age 12 demonstrated her true loyalties, when she arranged to play the piano for the first half of the program and dance for the second. Her musical training would in fact complement her dancing gifts as she rose through the ranks to become a world-renowned dancer and the first Native American prima ballerina in the United States.

She was born Elizabeth Marie Tall Chief on January 24, 1925, in Fairfax, Oklahoma, a small town on the Osage reservation. Her father Alexander Tall Chief was a real-estate investor whose grandfather had helped negotiate land agreements for the Osage people with the U.S. government in the late 19th century. Alexander's second wife **Ruth Porter Tall Chief** was of Dutch, Irish and Scottish ancestry, and the couple had three children: Maria (who was called Betty), *****Marjorie Tallchief**, two years younger, who would also become a dancer, and Gerald. The family lived in a large house in Fairfax, and the children considered the town their playground. A dance teacher came from Tulsa to give the Tallchief sisters lessons at home, and several buildings and businesses carried the family name.

Alexander and Ruth balanced each other. He was easygoing; she was strict. He was comfortable in Fairfax; she wanted to live in an area

that would offer more music and dance training opportunities for her daughters. In 1933, the family moved to Los Angeles, where famous dancers taught in Beverly Hills studios. The girls' first new teacher was horrified at the acrobatic nature of their training, as well as the fact that they had been allowed to dance *en pointe*—in hard toe shoes—at such an early age. While he immediately started them on a beginning study of movement, the piano lessons continued, emphasized by Ruth and tolerated by Maria.

While a student at Beverly Hills High School, Maria began studying dance under *****Bronislava Nijinska**, a former choreographer with the Ballet Russe and sister of the famed Russian dancer Vladislav Nijinsky. Ruth Tall Chief, intent on her daughters being well rounded, had insisted on their being schooled with students their own age. With her strong desire to please, Maria met her mother's high expectations; this penchant for hard work and perfection was to be the guiding principle of her career. The Tallchief sisters also studied with David Lichine and became friends with his wife, prima ballerina ❧ **Tatiana Riabouchinska**. In 1940, at age 15, Maria danced her first premiere role, in Nijinska's *Chopin Concerto;* Marjorie also appeared in the production, as did **Cyd Charisse**, who later became famous as a dancer and actress in film. When the Ballet Russe de Monte Carlo came through Los Angeles that year on its annual tour, Nijinska took the Tallchief sisters backstage. The company's director, who had visited Nijinska's studio and conducted classes in search of promising students, told Maria that the Ballet Russe might someday have a place for her, if she worked hard.

Tallchief graduated from high school in 1942. Her mother wanted her to go to college and wait for Marjorie to complete high school before the two considered joining a ballet company. That summer, Maria danced with the corps de ballet for the *****Judy Garland** film *Presenting Lily Mars*. On the day the job ended, Riabouchinska invited her to go to New York to try out for the Ballet Russe, where she might be able to dance until it was time to go to college. Arriving there, Tallchief found a place to live and took dance classes while waiting for an audition with the director of the Ballet Russe, who was preparing the company for a Canadian tour. World War II was then under way in Europe, and some Russian members of the company had been caught in America, unable to return to their country. In class, Maria generated interest among these highly trained dancers, including

❧▶
Riabouchinska, Tatiana. *See Toumanova, Tamara for sidebar.*

Maria
Tallchief

one who was manager of a rival dance company, Ballet Theater.

Finally, Maria had her audition, and was accepted into the corps of the Ballet Russe for its Canadian tour. Over the next several months, she learned the rigors of the life of a young corps dancer: traveling from place to place, constantly washing and repairing costumes, practicing long hours and then waiting for the word to perform or to return to the dressing room. She also learned that ballet had its political side, with a strict hierarchy of dancers within the company. Even among lowly corps members she observed the temperaments at work, the intense competition for roles, and the enmities for slights real and imagined. Meanwhile, she worked hard, learned new roles quickly, and was given some solo roles that brought her to the attention of the company's influential dancers. Friends in California had found Maria to be serious and sensitive but forthright, loyal and even merry once she gave her trust. In the intense atmosphere of the tour, however, Tallchief withdrew and gained a reputation for being aloof. She wrote in one of her daily letters home: "You cannot know what it is like to be the newest one in a ballet company. But I am learning and I see why things are as they are for me. Don't worry. I'll survive, no doubt. What matters is that I am dancing."

Tallchief had a mystery about her.

—Olga Maynard

Despite the cold Canadian weather and the frigid treatment from other dancers, Tallchief knew she would not be attending college at the end of the tour. Instead, she joined the corps of the Ballet Russe, and the issue then arose as to what to do about her name. In dance, the names of performers were closely associated with the history of the profession. Although ballet had originated in France, it had been dominated for many years by the influence of the great Russian dance schools and performers, and it was common practice among European and American dancers to enhance their careers with Russian-sounding names. At the Ballet Russe, the director now told several new members of the company, including Betty Marie Tall Chief, to take on names with "theatrical substance." One suggestion was to change Tall Chief to the Russian-sounding "Tallchieva." After long discussions with her friend and fellow dancer *Mia Slavenska, Betty Marie agreed to take the name Maria. She refused to give up her surname, consenting only to condensing it to the word Tallchief.

In the 1942 fall season, Tallchief continued to draw attention outside the ballet corps. In October, she danced a walk-on in *Rodeo*, choreographed by *Agnes de Mille, who called her performance "lyric, beautiful and evocative acting in the highest sense." But Tallchief yearned to dance the ballets of Nijinska, especially the *Concerto* she had performed in Los Angeles. It became her obsession to learn all the major roles, in all their variations. Continuing to study, practice, and "understudy everybody, even the understudies," she sometimes kept friendships at bay, and was resented by corps members who

thought her driven approach made them appear lazy. Lonely in this chilly environment, she only worked harder. Her thoughts were now centered completely on her career.

Following a tour, the Ballet Russe was scheduled to open in New York once more. On Christmas Eve, Tallchief learned that a ballerina had left the troupe, and there was a possibility that she herself might be the replacement in her beloved *Concerto*. She practiced feverishly for the next two days and was waiting in the wings when she was told that another dancer would perform the role. Back in her room, Tallchief wrote home of her disappointment and of the company politics that lay behind it. For days, the episode was the topic of gossip within the tight little world of ballet: it was said that prima ballerina *Alexandra Danilova had refused to dance with a corps girl, especially because Tallchief was "extraordinary . . . *en pointe*." At a New Year's Eve party, Danilova explained her position, in a way that Tallchief described as "very, very nice," and said she thought there might be a small role for her in another ballet, but the hurt remained. Meanwhile, she became even more obsessed with perfecting each of the major *Concerto* roles. She spent longer hours in rehearsal, lost sleep and weight, and fought off the colds making the rounds through the company that winter.

Her opportunity to perform in *Concerto* finally arrived in May 1943, when soloist **Nathalie Krassovska** hurt her foot. Tallchief, who still had a cold, tied her shoe ribbons and wiped her runny nose while waiting to go on. "As soon as I came off stage," she wrote, "Mme Slavenska was waiting, to tell me I had done wonderfully. Then came Mia. . . . Mme Danilova . . . smiled and said she wanted to congratulate me." Tallchief remained in *Concerto* through a tour of the New England states, but no changes were made in her billing or noted at performances. Krassovska left the company after the tour, and Tallchief's rise in status was indicated by the listing of her name in the ballet program. Her New York debut, at age 18, was well received by the critics, and when a friend told her that the American girls in the corps were bragging about her, she wrote to the family that this was the "best of all."

At the end of the season, Tallchief went home on vacation with an offer for a two-year contract with the Ballet Russe. Because she was still underage, her parents' signatures were required for the contract. Ruth Tall Chief refused to sign, having heard rumors that Krassovska planned to return to the company and that a new choreographer would be bringing in his own protegées. That autumn, Tallchief returned to the company expecting her chances to perform to be even slimmer. Indeed, with the changes wrought by recently hired choreographer George Balanchine, Tallchief received only one role for the season, until Nijinska returned and assigned her another. Balanchine had also been hired to choreograph a Broadway production, *Song of Norway*, for which he used the Ballet Russe corps on stage; Tallchief served as understudy to the prima ballerina. When the Ballet Russe left the show to mount its annual season, she refused an offer to stay behind on Broadway and take over the show's lead role. By this time, Marjorie had joined Ballet Theater, and the two drew attention not only because they were sisters but because they were Native Americans. As dancers, Maria was considered "symphonic" and an extraordinary technician, while Marjorie was admired for her flair and speed.

Though Maria still looked quite young and dressed like a schoolgirl, she had developed a repertoire and matured greatly as an artist; with her strength, technique and musicality, she was becoming what would eventually be known as the perfect Balanchine dancer. In 1946, Tallchief premiered two roles, the ice-fairy queen in *Le Baiser de la Fée* and the Coquette in *Night Shadow*. Late that summer, after he divorced *Vera Zorina, Tallchief quietly became Balanchine's fourth wife. Awed by the great choreographic genius, she could not imagine refusing him, despite their lack of an ordinary courtship. And Balanchine, while drawn to her potential as a dancer under his tutelage, was "also very taken by her Indian heritage," wrote one biographer. "It made him feel that in marrying her he was becoming really American."

Soon after the wedding, Balanchine resigned from the Ballet Russe to form his own company, Ballet Society. Remaining behind to fulfill her contract, Tallchief found that she lacked good new roles after his departure, although she nonetheless collected quite a following of fans on tour. Without Balanchine, however, the Ballet Russe deteriorated to a degree that shocked its audiences. As competition increased and many new young dancers came onto the scene, the company also fared badly in the competitive "ballet wars." In 1947, Balanchine accepted an invitation from the Paris Opera, and Tallchief made plans to join him that summer after her contract expired. Her dancing was better than ever, she had box-office appeal, and she was only one step away from the rank of ballerina. Friends were concerned, however, that Ballet Society would offer few opportunities for her to develop, and that the company itself would fail.

In May, Tallchief joined Balanchine in Paris and danced Terpsichore in *Apollo*. Making her international debut at age 22, she was the first American to dance with the Paris Opera Ballet since 1839, and she was a stunning success. The couple returned to New York for the 1948 season of Ballet Society, which changed its name to the New York City Ballet. That year, Tallchief received the annual Dance Magazine Award for her role as Eurydice in *Orpheus*. The season also saw the premiere of the ballet perhaps most associated with Maria Tallchief, Balanchine's *Firebird*, to music by Stravinsky. In November, clothed in the flame-colored costume of the Firebird, with crimson shoes and a feathered plume on her head, her arms and shoulders covered with gold-dust powder, she stunned both audiences and critics with her technique and fire, personifying the Russian folktale character. Amazement at her performance was universal, and controversy about the choreography added to the interest as audiences crowded into the company's theatrical home at City Center. Demand for tickets was so high that performances had to be added; the company made money for the first time. Although the New York City Ballet did not officially follow the old custom of ranking its dancers, Tallchief was now recognized as a full-fledged ballerina, onstage and off.

In 1951, Tallchief danced with Andrè Eglevsky, creating a dazzling new partnership for Balanchine's existing and new *pas de deux* roles. In both America and Europe, she continued to receive the highest accolades, dominating ballet headlines throughout the decade. After highly successful tours with the New York City Ballet and as a guest artist with Ballet Russe, she was firmly established, recognized internationally as the first prima ballerina. News reports emphasized her Russian imperial style of dance and her American, particularly Native American, origin. When New York City Ballet mounted a full-length production of *The Nutcracker* in 1954, she danced the role of the Sugar Plum Fairy; reviews noted her prima ballerina qualities, her "technical accomplishments . . . of secondary note to her authority and radiance."

During the 1950s, Tallchief's personal life remained generally unknown to the public. Her marriage to Balanchine was annulled in 1950, reportedly because she wanted children and he did not, and the two afterwards maintained a professional relationship at New York City Ballet. A marriage to charter airplane pilot Elmourza Natirboff ended in divorce in 1954. In 1956, she married Henry D. Paschen, Jr., a Chicago construction company executive; their daughter **Elise Maria Paschen** was born in January 1959.

Tallchief danced with the American Ballet Theater in 1960 before returning to the New York City Ballet. In 1963, she traveled to her hometown of Fairfax for a tribal celebration, in which she was conferred the honorary name Wa-Xthe-Thonba (Woman of Two Standards or Two Worlds), chosen by her grandmother. The Council of Fire paid tribute four years later with the Indian Achievement Award.

In 1965, just after the launch of the New York City Ballet's new season, Tallchief surprised the ballet world by announcing her retirement. "I got tired of people stopping me on the street to ask where I was dancing now," she remarked. "As I've said before, I don't mind being listed alphabetically but I do mind being treated alphabetically." She was 40 years old, and according to news accounts, Balanchine believed that 40 was the age at which a ballerina should retire. Nonetheless, for a time she continued to appear as a guest artist with American and international companies. Tallchief eventually became artistic director for the Chicago Lyric Opera Ballet. In 1980, with her sister Marjorie, she became a cofounder of the Chicago City Ballet. Years earlier, in 1965, the Capezio Dance Award perhaps best acknowledged the impact of Maria Tallchief on the world of dance: "[A]s an American ballerina, she has brought lustre to American ballet itself, contributing immeasurably in placing it on an equal aesthetic footing with the ballet standards of those European cultures which first nurtured the art of ballet."

SOURCES:
Champagne, Duane, ed. *The Native North American Almanac.* Detroit, MI: Gale Research, 1994.
Clarke, Mary, and David Vaughan, eds. *The Encyclopedia of Dance and Ballet.* NY: Putnam, 1977.
Cohen-Stratyner, Barbara Naomi. *Biographical Dictionary of Dance.* NY: Schirmer, 1982.
The Dance Encyclopedia. Compiled and edited by Anatole Chujoy and P.W. Manchester. NY: Simon and Schuster, 1967.
Erdrich, Heidi Ellen. *Maria Tallchief.* Illustrations by Rick Whipple. Austin, TX: Steck-Vaughn, 1993.
"I Cannot Wait," in *Newsweek.* October 25, 1965, p. 100.
Maynard, Olga. *Bird of Fire: The Story of Maria Tallchief.* NY: Dodd, Mead, 1961.
McHenry, Robert, ed. *Liberty's Women.* Springfield, MA: G.&C. Merriam, 1980.
Taper, Bernard. *Balanchine: A Biography.* NY: Macmillan, 1974.

SUGGESTED READING:
Balanchine, George. *Balanchine's Complete Stories of the Great Ballets.* Edited by Francis Mason. Drawings by **Marta Becket.** Garden City, NY: Doubleday, 1968.
De Leeuw, Adele. *Maria Tallchief: American Ballerina.* Champaign, IL: Garrard, 1971.
Myers, Elisabeth P. *Maria Tallchief: America's Prima Ballerina.* NY: Grosset and Dunlap, 1967.
Tallchief, Maria, with Larry Kaplan. *Maria Tallchief: America's Prima Ballerina.* NY: Henry Holt, 1997.
Tobias, Tobi. *Maria Tallchief.* NY: Crowell, 1970.

COLLECTIONS:
Dance Collection at the New York Public Library.

Margaret L. Meggs,
independent scholar,
Havre, Montana

Tallchief, Marjorie (1927—)

Osage Native American prima ballerina, noted for her romantic dance style, who became a co-founder of the Chicago City Ballet. Name variations: Marjorie Tall Chief; Marjorie Skibine. Born in Denver, Colorado, in 1927; daughter of Alexander Tall Chief (a real estate investor) and Ruth (Porter) Tall Chief; sister of Maria Tallchief (b. 1925); married George Skibine (a dancer), in 1947; children: Alex and George.

Danced with the Los Angeles Civic Opera Ballet, Ballet Theater, Original Ballet Russe, Grand Ballet du Marquis de Cuevas, Paris Opera, and the Ruth Page Chicago Opera Ballet; joined sister Maria Tallchief to co-found the Chicago City Ballet (1980); commemorated for lifetime achievement by President Bill Clinton at the Kennedy Center Honors (1996).

Marjorie Tallchief was born in Denver, Colorado, in 1927, the daughter of Alexander Tall Chief and **Ruth Porter Tall Chief.** As a girl, she loved acrobatic dancing so much that her mother feared she would become a circus trapeze artist. More lighthearted than her sister *Maria Tallchief, Marjorie was less intense about pursuing a dance career, but she studied with the famous choreographer *Bronislava Nijinska and danced with professional companies in Los Angeles during high school. In 1944, she became a member of the Ballet Theater in New York; while there, she received many invitations to dance in Broadway and Hollywood productions. She moved to Paris in 1947 to join the Grand Ballet du Marquis de Cuevas, and that July married her dance partner George Skibine. The couple would have two sons, Alex and George. Tallchief was a featured dancer of the Paris Opera from 1957 to 1962. She then danced in America with *Ruth Page's Chicago Opera Ballet and the Harkness Ballet before retiring in 1966 to take up dance teaching in Dallas, Texas. In 1980, she joined her sister Maria in co-founding the Chicago City Ballet. Wrote **Olga Maynard,** Marjorie Tallchief "was the personification of the pellucid classical style."

Margaret L. Meggs,
independent scholar,
Havre, Montana

Talley, Marion (1906–1983)

American opera singer. Born Marion Nevada Talley on December 20, 1906, in Nevada, Missouri; died on January 3, 1983, in Beverly Hills, California; daughter of Charles Marion Talley and Helen H. (Brown) Talley; attended school in Kansas City, Missouri; studied voice with Ottley Cranston in Kansas City and Frank LaForge in New York; also studied piano and violin; coached in opera and languages in Italy for one year; married Michael Baucheisen (a German pianist), on June 30, 1932 (annulled January 1933); married Adolph Eckstrom, on March 23, 1935.

The daughter of a telegraph operator, Marion Talley was born in 1906 in Nevada, Missouri, a small railroad town outside of Kansas City, where she grew up. Displaying musical talent at a young age, she began singing with the church choir when she was five years old. She studied piano and violin as a child and, impressed by her talents, local music lovers arranged a benefit concert, at which she sang, to help finance her career. The benefit earned $10,000.

In 1922, Talley moved to New York, where she studied with Frank LaForge. When her money ran out two years later, she returned to Kansas City and earned $13,000 by giving four concerts. She then traveled to Italy to further her musical studies, returning to the United States in 1925. Widely promoted as a great American singer from humble roots, she made her highly publicized Metropolitan Opera House debut on February 17, 1926. Thousands of opera fans waited in lines for tickets that sold for as much as $100. Her performance as Gilda in Verdi's *Rigoletto*, however, did not live up to the expectations of critics. She was considered a pleasant but not important soprano. Wrote Olin Downes: "She has a voice of uncommonly fresh and lovely quality. . . . However, she has not at the present the artistic knowledge to make the most of her gifts." That same year she also sang "Caro Nome" from *Rigoletto* in a film of the New York Philharmonic Symphony Orchestra, which was shown at the Warner Theater in New York City, making her the first woman to sing in a film. Talley remained with the Metropolitan Opera for three seasons and performed in several operas, including *Lucia, The Magic Flute,* and *Le Chant du Rossignol*; she also performed in many recitals.

After leaving the Metropolitan, Talley successfully ran a wheat farm in Colby, Kansas, for a few years. In 1934, she returned to music and began touring around the country, in addition to appearing on radio programs. In 1936, she appeared as a

feature singer in the movie *Follow Your Heart*. She also recorded arias by Rossini and Verdi as well as concert songs on the Victor label.

SOURCES:

Ewen, David, comp. and ed. *Living Musicians.* NY: H.W. Wilson, 1940.

Read, Phyllis J., and Bernard L. Witlieb. *The Book of Women's Firsts.* NY: Random House, 1992.

Karina L. Kerr, M.A.,
Ypsilanti, Michigan

Marion Talley

Tallien, Thérésa (1773–1835)

One of the most controversial women in French history, famed for her beauty, marriages, and liaisons, who intervened on behalf of supplicants during the Reign of Terror and was the queen of high society during the Thermidorean Reaction and the Directory.

Name variations: Theresa Tallien; Thérèsia Tallien; Thérèse or Teresa Cabarrus; Theresia de Tallien; Madame Jean-Lambert Tallien; formerly Marquise de Fontenay; later Comtesse de Riquet-Caraman and Princesse de Chimay. Pronunciation: tair-RAY-sya ka-BAR-oos tall-YEH. Born Juana-Maria-Ignacia-Teresa Cabarrus, later Jeanne-Marie-Ignace-Thérésa Cabarrus, on July 31, 1773, at the château of San Pedro de Carabanchel de Arriba, near Madrid; died at Chimay,

Belgium, of liver disease, and was buried at the Chimay parish church; daughter of François (Francisco) Cabarrus (1752–1810, a banker) and Maria-Antonia (Galabert) Cabarrus (1756–1827); educated in Paris at the Convent of the Presentation and the pension of Mme Leprince de Beaumont; married Marquis Jean-Jacques Devin de Fontenay, in 1788 (divorced 1793); married Jean-Lambert Tallien (1767–1820), in 1794 (divorced 1802); married Comte (François-) Joseph de Riquet-Caraman (b. 1771), later Prince de Chimay, in 1805; children: (with Fontenay) Théodore (Antoine-François-Julien-Théodore-Denis-Ignace, 1789–1815); (with Tallien) Rose-Thermidor-Laure-Joséphine Tallien, who eventually called herself Laure, then Joséphine (1795–1862); (with Gabriel-Julien Ouvrard, but surnamed Cabarrus) Clémence-Isaure (1800–1884), Jules-Joseph-Édouard, known as Édouard (1801–1862), Clarisse-Gabrielle-Thérésa, known as Clarisse (1802–1877), and Stéphanie-Caroline-Thérésa, known as Stéphanie (1803–1887); (with Prince Joseph de Chimay) Prince Joseph (1808–1866), Alphonse (1810–1866), Marie-Louise (1813–1814), and Marie-Louise-Thérésa-Valentine (1815–1876).

Was in Paris with her mother (1784–88); hosted a salon frequented by leading political figures (1788–93); in Bordeaux with Tallien, aided many people in avoiding trial or execution (1793–94); imprisoned in Paris and played a role in the fall of Robespierre (1794); was the leading social figure during the Thermidorean Reaction (1794–95); while mistress of Paul Barras, continued as leader of high society during the Directory (1795–99); was in Egypt and England (1798–1801); was mistress of "the richest man in France," Gabriel-Julien Ouvrard, but ostracized from court by Napoleon (1800–04); while married to the Prince de Chimay, continued to entertain notable figures, especially from the world of music, and engaged in numerous charitable activities (1805–35); resided principally in Belgium (1815–35).

Thérésa Tallien

Thérésa Tallien married for the first time well before she turned 15. Barely into adolescence, she was already a stunning beauty. Her physical attributes, in fact, lay at the root of her fortunes and misfortunes. Writers have made her the subject of a shelfful of fictionalized accounts. Any attempt to establish the truth about her continually confronts obstacles raised by her own often fanciful accounts and the legends, rumors, and innuendoes she inspired. Because so much of what was said about her—and for that matter was important about her—revolves around her private life, the unvarnished truth can never be known. And to return full circle, it was her beauty that kindled the imaginations of her contemporaries, spawning the tales that would shape her place in history.

She was born on July 31, 1773, near Madrid at the château of San Pedro de Carabanchel de Arriba. She and brothers Domingo-Vincente (b. 1774) and Francisco (1776–1794) were the children of François Cabarrus and **Maria-Antonia Galabert Cabarrus**. François was the elder son of Dominique Cabarrus (the Elder), a prosperous wholesale merchant (and a candidate for the nobility) in Bayonne, on the Spanish frontier, whose family had originated in Spanish Navarre. He sent François at age 18 to Valencia to learn Spanish and business. There he fell madly in love with Maria-Antonia, 16-year-old daughter of Antonio Galabert, Dominique Cabarrus' local agent (*correspondant*). Both families opposed a marriage, so the pair eloped. Facing an uncertain future, they were "rescued" by Maria's grandfather Don Pedro Galabert, who in the spring of 1773 made François manager of a neglected soap manufacturing operation at Carabanchel de Arriba. That summer their first child arrived and was baptized Juana-Maria-Ignacia-Teresa. (When she took French citizenship she became Jeanne-Marie-Ignace-Thérèse, but she always signed herself, and was called, "Thérésa" or "Thérésia.")

Very little about her life before her first marriage is known for certain. Family tradition, for example, holds that her mother's labor pains came on at a ball at the French embassy in Madrid; but this seems most unlikely because her parents plainly still lacked the requisite social standing to be invited. She is said to have spent her first three years with a peasant wetnurse, ignored by her parents. Growing up she was vivacious, impressionable, pretty, warm-voiced, and enjoyed being the center of attention.

François Cabarrus, not one to stay mired in a soap factory, soon discovered he had great talent in finance. He rose rapidly in high Madrid circles. After becoming a Spanish citizen in 1781, a year later, barely 30 years old, he became Charles III's chief financial advisor and received a charter to create the Banco de San Carlo, the direct ancestor of the Bank of Spain. It began operation on May 13, 1783. Possibly late that year or early in 1784, Thérésa, her mother, and probably her brothers went to Paris to begin her final education and the hunt for a husband.

It is impossible to establish a firm chronology of her education and social contacts before December 1787, when her father, back in Spain, received a letter about a projected marriage to Jean-Jacques Devin de Fontenay. She probably was educated by Benedictine sisters at the Convent of the Presentation on the Rue des Postes, and then at a well-known finishing school (*pension*) run by **Mme Leprince de Beaumont**, where she formed lifelong friendships with the future Mmes Champagny and Montalembert, and the writer *Sophie Gay (1776–1852). Gifted in the arts, Thérésa became a respectable practitioner of watercolor and especially music (piano, harp, guitar, and voice), which she loved with a passion.

It seems likely she returned to Spain at least once in these years. Allegedly, her mother's bachelor brother, Uncle Maximilien, aged 32, visited Carabanchel, fell in love with her, and sounded François about marriage. He roundly disapproved and sent her (back?) to Paris. While there, she and her mother were helped by the Le Couteulx de Noraye family and **Mme Boisgeloup de la Mancelière**, people prominent in financial and judicial circles. Invitations to balls, theaters, dinners, and soirées abounded. Thérésa's precocious beauty and gracious good humor won notice. There was Alexandre de Méréville (aged 26), son of Marquis Jean-Joseph de Laborde, with whom she had a brief summer's infatuation. There was also Marquis Charles-Louis Ducrest, brother of the writer Comtesse *Stéphanie de Genlis (1746–1830). He was a serious candidate, but his age (40) probably stood in the way. And the Prince de Listenay—but he was a rake.

It was Mme Boisgeloup who discovered Devin de Fontenay late in 1787. Aged 26, he was a member of the Parlement (High Court) of Paris, where his father, president of the Cour des Comptes (financial administration), also sat. Fontenay was short and not handsome but was described to François as witty, serious, and well mannered. Thérésa had little to say about the match, accepting it without feeling love or repugnance for her prospective mate. The financial arrangement, signed on February 2, 1788, showed her bringing 400,000 livres plus another 100,000 over ten years and three fine Paris residences François owned. Fontenay brought

830,926 livres plus 60,000 livres annually from the Parlement seat. (These were very large figures; ordinary workers earned only about a livre per day.) Soon after the marriage Fontenay bought a transmissible marquisate for 400,000 livres to solidify his somewhat shaky title.

On February 21, 1788, the pair married at the Church of Saint-Eustache before representatives of finance and the judiciary. It was agreed that until she was older they would live with his parents on the fashionable Île de Saint-Louis in the present Hôtel Chenizot. They also spent time at the family's Château de Fontenay-aux-Roses, in a Paris suburb near Sceaux. On May 2, 1789, Thérésa, not yet 16, had her first child, Théodore. The marriage, however, was already foundering. Fontenay proved to be a philanderer of the first order. Her childhood innocence had been speedily shattered. They stayed together for the sake of social acceptance, while Thérésa's mother reproached herself bitterly for hurrying her into marriage at such a tender age.

The Fontenays cut a large figure on the Paris social scene in the earliest years of the Revolution. They entertained numerous guests, among them the Marquis de La Fayette, writers Nicolas de Chamfort, Antoine Rivarol, Louis de Champcenetz, and the ducs de Monmorency and La Rochefoucauld-Liancourt. Thérésa's beauty soon was legendary, and remained so for decades. "When she entered a drawing room," recalled the composer Daniel-François Auber in old age, "she brought day and night with her—day for herself, night for the others." At 5'6", she was quite tall for that time, "a Diana the Huntress," as Mme *Henriette de La Tour du Pin put it in an oft-quoted description. "No human being," she went on, "has left the Creator's hand so beautiful." Her face was a perfect oval, her head somewhat small but well formed and crowned with ebony hair of the finest silk. She had large brown eyes, generous dark lashes and eyebrows, an "Irish" nose (slightly turned up at the end), a small mouth, small, sculptured red lips, brilliant teeth, a round chin, and very fair skin (whiteness was much prized). Her sculpted hands and arms were pleasantly fleshed out, neither fat nor thin, as was her attractive figure. She exuded robust health and youth, "uniting lovable French vivacity with Spanish voluptuousness," wrote Antoine Thibaudeau. Her every movement was a picture of grace, and her expression kind. "She exercised a charm which no word can express," said Mme de La Tour du Pin. Her slight foreign accent added an exotic touch, if one were necessary. Even those who maligned her for personal or political reasons denied neither her beauty nor her generosity of spirit (*bonté*). At a very young age and to all appearances without half trying, she was a phenomenon.

She and her husband kept close company with the early, moderate (constitutional monarchist) leaders of the Revolution. **Mme Charles de Lameth** was her good friend, and through her she mingled on intimate terms with the Lameth brothers, Charles, Alexandre (especially), and, to a lesser extent, Théodore, prominent soldier-politicians during the Estates-General and the Constituent Assembly (1789–91). She also numbered the Duc d'Aiguillon, Antoine Barnave, and the Comte de Mirabeau among her friends. It is said the latter two escorted her around the Bastille shortly after its fall. Other intimates included the brothers Félix and Louis Le Pelletier de Saint-Fargeaux. (She once described herself as "très liée" with the latter, who was famously assassinated—"martyred"—the day after Louis XVI's execution on January 21, 1793.) Progressive ideas from the Enlightenment attracted her. She joined the Loge Olympique of the Freemasons and the Club de 1789, founded by La Fayette, Abbé Sieyès, and the philosophe Condorcet. She also attended sittings of the Constituent Assembly and later the Legislative Assembly (1791–92) and the Convention (1792–95). Her husband—more from opportunism than conviction, one suspects—joined the (still moderate) Jacobin Club, where he made no waves. After the parlements were abolished, he tried to be elected a judge in December 1790 but won only seven votes in his best showing.

An interlude occurred late in 1789 when she and her husband traveled to Madrid so he could at last meet her father. Things turned out badly when a male companion he had brought along made a scandal at court. They returned early in 1790 with their marriage all but ended. More unhappiness followed when she learned on July 16 that her father had been arrested and imprisoned. After Charles IV had succeeded to the throne of Spain in 1788, his chief minister, Floridablanca, and some financiers jealous of her father's success brought about his arrest for malversion of funds. Thérésa was so upset that she beseeched La Fayette, commander of the National Guard, to invade Spain. He politely demurred.

Thérésa's social life continued apace. In April 1791, her name surfaced in the papers in an unfavorable light. Liberty of the press being exercised with abandon now, Paris was swamped with papers and pamphlets. As political tensions mounted in the spring of 1791, unbridled, libelous denunciations of one's foes be-

came more than ever the norm. Hence, Thérésa's connection to the constitutional monarchist faction made her fair game, especially for diehard royalists. On April 21, 1791, the royalist *Journal de la Cour et de la Ville* insinuated that she was offering more than wine and cake to her guests, and mentioned some names. *La Chronique scandaleuse* also weighed in. She protested to the editors in print. Whether her husband insisted on or wrote the letter is debated, although it seems clear he was becoming largely absent in her life.

It is impossible to say if this gossip held any truth. Had she been one of the myriad conquests of Mirabeau, the greatest early leader of the Revolution and now suddenly dead (April 2, 1791)? Or of Alexandre de Lameth? Or the Le Peletier de Saint-Fargeaux brothers? Or Condorcet? She was still only in her teens, was trusting, too often indiscreet, on the outs with her husband, and perpetually surrounded by awe-struck males. Moreover, the Jacobins' Republic of Virtue had not yet arrived to smother the licentiousness of the Ancien Régime. In short, the hyperventilating press scarcely needed more stimulation to conjure up visions of this delicious creature engaging in sexual romps with controversial figures, particularly one's political opponents.

As time went on she drifted leftward in her political opinions, and in the autumn of 1791 she broke with the Lameths because they had become more pro-monarchist. Nothing concrete is known about her activities from then until the ceremonial celebration on July 14, 1792 (the Fédération). The country was speeding into a storm. War had been declared (April 20) and the Prussians were invading. Chancellor Pasquier recalled in his memoirs encountering her at the Fédération and hearing her express fears about the future. Ironically, in light of later developments, she is said to have sat with Robespierre at the ceremonies and applauded him at the Jacobins on July 20 when he called for the French to rally in the face of looming disaster.

With the fall of the throne (August 10) and the convening of the Jacobin-dominated National Convention (September 20), her situation darkened. The Law of March 21, 1792, had made all foreign-born persons subject to surveillance by local watch committees, and she was feeling the pressure. Coincidentally, a law passed on September 20 legalized divorce. She and Fontenay wasted no time. They began proceedings on November 30, and the divorce became final on April 5, 1793. Her first thought now was to quit Paris, perhaps for Spain. She, her ex-husband, and little Théodore left for Bordeaux, arriving early in May. (Bourquin says Théodore stayed behind with his grandparents until they sent him to Bordeaux in early April 1794.) Fontenay, who wanted to flee to Martinique but was unable, soon took shelter in Normandy at Estimauville (Calvados), where he stayed until he returned to Bordeaux in March 1794 to go to America. Thérésa remained in Bordeaux even though she had a passport for Spain, probably made wary because France and Spain were now at war and her father was still in prison.

In Bordeaux, she lived with her great-uncle, Dominique Cabarrus (the Younger), and his son Jean Valère, prosperous shipowners. Nothing is known with absolute certainty about her activities before the approval of the Boyer-Fonfrède petition on November 13, 1793 (see below). There exists an oft-quoted tale of a trip, beginning by mid-June, to the spa at Bagnères in the Pyrenees. She was accompanied by a maternal uncle, Pierre-Vincent Galabert (aged 35), Édouard de Colbert (1774–1853), Baron Étienne-Auguste de Lamothe (1772–1836), and her 17-year-old brother Francisco. All, including her brother, were in love with her. On the way, at Langon, Colbert and Lamothe dueled over her attentions. Lamothe was wounded, so she stayed behind to nurse him. The others dispersed, while she and Lamothe spent a summer's idyll at Bagnères until he had to rejoin the army. (Lamothe, who left an amusing account of the affair, went on to become a general, as did Colbert.)

When Thérésa returned to Bordeaux, she felt obliged to move from her great-uncle's home. She took a vast second-floor apartment at the Hôtel Franklin. Meanwhile, Bordeaux had become locked in a struggle with the Convention in Paris, which was now dominated by left-leaning Jacobins (the "Mountaineers") and their Committee of Public Safety (CPS). The Mountaineers had expelled their rivals, the "Girondins," a group of moderates among whom were several from the department of the Gironde, which included Bordeaux. On October 16, four representatives-on-mission, armed with sweeping powers, and supported by a small force under General Guillaume Brune, entered Bordeaux and installed the Terror to bring the proud city to heel. Young Jean-Lambert Tallien took the lead.

On October 25, the representatives issued a decree saying anyone who solicited on behalf of detainees would be arrested. Yet, on November 13, the Surveillance Committee granted Thérésa's request for a release of the sequestered property of Mme **Justine Boyer-Fonfrède**, widow and sister of two Girondins guillotined in

Paris on October 31. Events would prove Thérésa was brave and good-hearted, but it is likely she had every reason to believe her request would be honored. On November 18, two agents of the CPS reported that Tallien was having "liaisons intimes" (whatever that may have meant) with Thérésa Cabarrus-Fontenay. She was arrested some time between November 30 and December 10 and imprisoned at the Fort du Hâ, but was quickly released (perhaps within hours) through Tallien's intervention. All details about this arrest—if it happened, although it seems probable—have disappeared.

> *When you go through a storm, you can't always choose the plank you cling to.*
>
> —Thérésa Tallien

The agents' letter apparently did not hurt Tallien, for he had many friends among the Mountaineers and knew too much about the horrifying Paris prison massacres of September 2–7, 1792, to be readily attacked by his enemies. He had risen rapidly. A tall, handsome man with blond curls, energetic, friendly, and capable of impassioned eloquence, he was the son of the butler of the Marquis de Bercy, who had paid for his education. Intending to be a notary, he found the Revolution opened doors to undreamed-of opportunities. He became a copyreader for Panckouke, a leading publisher; organized a fraternal society in the seething faubourg Saint-Antoine; founded (August 1791) a newspaper, *L'Ami des Citoyens*; became the leader of his Paris *section*, Lombards, and secretary of the Paris Commune (city government), which toppled the throne; was carried along (and hence implicated) in the September Massacres, in which he nevertheless saved some victims, notably Mme *Germaine de Staël*; was elected to the Convention (at 25 nearly its youngest member) by the department of Seine-et-Oise after Marat and Robespierre opposed him in Paris as an ideologically suspect climber; and in 1793 voted for the king's execution, implacably opposed the Girondins, and was appointed a representative-on-mission in the southwestern departments.

Such was the man who would give Thérésa Cabarrus the name by which she would be known to history. Had they met before he arrived in Bordeaux? Probably several times: at the Paris studio of *Elisabeth Vigée-Le Brun*, where she was posing for a portrait; at the home of Mme **Alexandre de Lameth**, where he delivered some proofs while she was visiting; and, most important, in September 1793 while he was inspecting in the Pyrenees (at Bagnères?). Mme de La Tour du Pin said Thérésa once told her he had done her a favor on that occasion (getting her brother Francisco transferred from a cavalry draft?). Did their "liaisons intimes" begin soon after Tallien entered Bordeaux on October 16? In any case, she plainly had enough influence to get the Boyer-Fonfréde petition approved, to intercede (it appears) to get Jean-Valère Cabarrus' sequestered property returned to him before her arrest, and to be released speedily once imprisoned. Whatever their relations to date, by mid-December it was public knowledge that they were lovers.

On December 10, 1793, Thérésa sat on the stage with Tallien at the Festival of Reason, thus making their liaison "official." Thereafter, they continually consorted in public, although she forbade him to move in with her. Her role, which became famous, was to mitigate the Terror through her influence over Tallien, who loved her for the rest of his life. He despised the Girondins and was harsh during his first months in Bordeaux. But executions fell off in January to 16 from 34 in December. In February, they sank to 10. Tallien returned to Paris on February 22, but numbers remained 10 or lower (none in May) until Thérésa left Bordeaux; they then rose to 21 in June and shot to 126 in July, after which the Terror ended. Grim as such figures are, they pale beside those recorded in many other locales. Thérésa's bravery, gentle presence, subtle influence, and countless intercessions to obtain passports or commute or remit sentences played a signal role in sparing Bordeaux the worst. A grateful citizenry cheered her in the streets, and Tallien himself became one of the few representatives around the country to win some popularity. He was mature enough to grasp that intimidation is more productive than outright repression. But the moderation of the Terror in Bordeaux also owed even more to the nature of the city's social makeup and mentality. Moderation seemed bred into its bones, murderous ideological passion alien to its soul. It was no coincidence that the moderates in the Convention had found leaders among the men from the Gironde.

From the outset, Tallien proved jealous. Apparently Thérésa was attracted to the dashing General Brune (later one of Napoleon's marshals), who lived a few steps from her place. Because he was often seen entering there, tongues wagged. Tallien got Paris to abolish Brune's command, and on December 22 he was ordered away. A decree from the Convention to hold a celebration honoring the retaking of Toulon from the British provided Tallien a chance to mollify Thérésa by letting her shine at the ceremony on December 30. He read the "Discours

sur l'Éducation" he had begged her to write for the occasion. Dazzling in a blue worsted riding habit with red velvet trimmings and yellow buttons, she basked in the public's admiration. Her essay abounded in the Rousseauistic platitudes of the hour, lauding simplicity, naturalness, and patriotism, and asserting that "children belong to the State before belonging to their parents." The Convention received it and sent it to the Education Committee for burial.

The most damaging charge made against Tallien and Thérésa has been that of avarice—that their famous "moderation" was no better than a racket which filled their pockets with money extorted from supplicants. If so, why didn't the supposed victims say so in their memoirs or, better still, to the CPS? Tallien's "crime," in Robespierre's eyes, was "moderatism"; if he had had evidence of peculation, he, the high priest of the Republic of Virtue, surely would have used it. Thérésa was independently wealthy, while Tallien never was, before or afterwards. The few known gifts they received were not regarded by the donors as extorted. The money from fines—which were substantial, in this commercial center—went by Tallien's own order to support the armies or public good works, huge sums, notably, to the hospice established at the former convent of the Benedictines at Saint-Croix.

Early in February 1794, Tallien removed the more hardline members of the two commissions running the Terror. After the CPS got word, he left on February 22 to defend himself in the Convention, which he did with great success. He supported Danton and the "Indulgents" against the Robespierrists, and during the Dantonists' final surge he served a term as president of the Convention (March 21–April 5). Ironically, his presidency witnessed the defeat and execution of the Dantonists. The Convention, overawed by Robespierre and Louis-Antoine de Saint-Just, approved—but with deepening uneasiness. If Danton could be reached, who might be next?

Tallien's sudden departure left Thérésa quite shaken. They had quarreled recently when he learned she had written to an old flame, Félix Le Pelletier de Saint-Fargeaux. But she did miss him and, especially, felt exposed as the Terror escalated nationally. She turned her charms on the sole remaining representative, Claude-Alexandre Ysabeau, and on a hotly Robespierrist inspector (April 1–24), Marc-Antoine Jullien. The latter resisted and once back in Paris reported on her unfavorably.

No sooner had Tallien left than her ex-husband arrived to settle money matters before emigrating to Martinique. The agreement (March 28) left her essentially with what she had brought to the marriage. Still, he asked for, and she gave him, all her jewels so he would have some liquid wealth. He did not thank her. The jewels she wore later during the Thermidorean period were probably these, repurchased by her father once he was released (1795) from his Spanish prison (says Bourquin), and not crown jewels stolen by Tallien after the September Massacres, as their enemies alleged.

To firm up her standing with the Jacobins, she wrote (perhaps with help) an "Address to the Convention on the Obligations [*engagements*] of Citizenesses," which was read on April 14 at the Club national de Bordeaux. It proposed for young unmarried women a kind of national service obligation to work in shelters for the poor and sick, and affirmed her desire to be among the first. It was no feminist tract, for it praised the domestic virtues and said women should be men's companions, not their competitors—orthodox Jacobin theses. A well-written piece, it was sent to the Convention, which voted it honors and sent it to the CPS and the Education committee, which filed it away. She also incorporated (April 2) a saltpeter works (for gunpowder) with Jean Martel, the 14-year-old son of a businessman needing to demonstrate his republican zeal. It was no fictional enterprise and operated after her flight.

She left Bordeaux on May 5 or 6 with a passport for Orléans. Despite the risk, she went on to Paris. The Convention had decreed (April 16) that all ex-nobles and foreign-born persons with whose countries France was at war must leave Paris, fortified places, and port cities. She left son Théodore with relatives and traveled with two servants and one Jean Guéry, a young man with the Cabarrus firm, to escort her. (Inevitably, insinuations have been made about Guéry.) After a brief stop in Paris, she went to Fontenay-aux-Roses, where Tallien furtively joined her for a few days. The local agent of the CPS spotted her, and on May 22 a warrant for her arrest went out.

After some murky intrigues involving double agents, the "femme Fontenay" was arrested at Versailles on the night of May 30–31 and brought to the Petite-Force prison in Paris. There she was strip-searched by eight leering jailers, given a filthy gown and her slip, and isolated in a windowless, vermin-infested cell. For 25 days, she recounted, she was not let out, nor was her straw changed or waste pail emptied. She took sick. According to a probably apocryphal story,

when someone asked Robespierre to ease her regime, he replied, "Well, once a day let her look in a mirror." Finally, she was allowed an hour a day in a sunlit room with others and eventually won more favors in return for sketching her jailers. Every day she felt a sickening fear when the warden read the names of those called before the Revolutionary Tribunal—and to almost certain death, because under the law of the 22nd Prairial II (June 10, 1794) the court could refuse to hear a defense, and death or release were the only verdicts allowed.

When Robespierre presented the 22nd Prairial law, he had stared at Tallien, who was shouted down when he objected. The key provision of the law removed the Convention deputies' immunity. Robespierre was planning to purge at least a half-dozen, Tallien and Joseph Fouché for certain. Why did he then delay? Little is known for certain, but it appears that even though he had had Tallien expelled from the Jacobins (June 14), he was leery of his support in some sectors of the Mountain and wanted an airtight case. Hence, Thérésa was not executed forthwith but instead pressured by promises of a release and a passport for her and her son if she would testify against him. She refused. With executions soaring in June and July (the "Great Terror"), events now moved to a climax.

A conspiracy against Robespierre took shape. Tallien, Fouché, Paul Barras, Stanislaus Fréron, and others (about a dozen, all Mountaineers) quietly stoked the deputies' fears that they might be on Robespierre's "list." Quarreling behind the scenes in the CPS aided their efforts. Robespierre, probably sensing that his hold was weakening, lay low until he made a great speech in the Convention on the 8th Thermidor (July 26) defending his policies and attacking unnamed conspirators. But he made a fatal tactical mistake when he refused to answer shouts from the floor to give names. This only confirmed the fears spread by the conspirators, who by now included Jean Collot d'Herbois and Jacques Billaud-Varenne of the CPS.

The showdown came the next day after a night of feverish activity. When Saint-Just, Robespierre's most reliable spokesman, his "prosecutor," went to the rostrum, it was now or never for the conspirators. Tallien instantly interrupted him on a vague point-of-order—Collot was presiding and allowed it—and proceeded to denounce him and Robespierre for "divisiveness." The atmosphere turned electric. Others followed Tallien to prevent Saint-Just, who seemed stunned, from speaking. They charged Robespierre with "tyranny" and "dictatorship." At a critical moment, when the debate threatened to wander into trivialities, Tallien intervened to refocus it. The drama reached its peak when Robespierre repeatedly tried to speak and was howled down by the now-stampeding Convention. Tallien melodramatically flourished a knife and cried that he intended to kill Robespierre if the Convention failed to act. Motions to arrest Robespierre and certain of his supporters were shouted through. After they escaped to the Paris City Hall and tried to raise a revolt, the Convention outlawed them. The Paris *sections* failed to rise, Convention forces led by Barras took the rebels captive, and the next day (July 28) they were dispatched to "the National Razor."

Thérésa played a role in this historical turning point and ever after took immense pride in it. But its true importance is disputable. Briefly, at some point while imprisoned she began to exchange letters with Tallien, doubtless with the connivance of the warden or a turnkey. For ink she used paint or her blood. On the 7th Thermidor (July 25), she wrote a letter which, unlike the others, has not survived and whose wording differs slightly in several reported versions. The best-known text runs as follows:

> The police administrator has left; he has just announced to me that tomorrow I shall go to the tribunal, that is to say, to the scaffold. That bears little resemblance to a dream I had this night. . . . Robespierre no longer existed and the prisons were opened. A brave man sufficed perhaps to bring it about; but thanks to your signal cowardice, there remains nobody who can enjoy such a benefit. Adieu.

Tallien replied, "Have as much prudence as I shall have courage, and above all stay cool." It is often said that Tallien, mortally afraid his mistress was about to die, now resolved to attack Robespierre immediately; that is, the letter in some manner triggered the events of the 9th Thermidor. When the story became known—not through Tallien, who never spoke of it and disliked talking about himself—the 21-year-old Thérésa was hailed by the public as their savior, "Notre Dame de Thermidor."

What to make of this story? There probably was a letter. That she called him a coward is disputed because at least one account by her does not mention it. What grounds did she have for such an accusation? Did he not tell her he was conspiring? Possibly, out of prudence. Maybe it was from desperation, in order to jolt him into action. Tallien (with Barras) played the leading public role on the 9th Thermidor. But the timing

of the showdown clearly had nothing to do with her letter. Robespierre's speech on the 8th had lit the fuse. Judging from a speech by Tallien himself on August 9, the choice of the 9th Thermidor seems to have depended on information fed to Fouché from inside the CPS about divisions which were isolating Robespierre. When Saint-Just rose to speak on the 9th, the die was cast, for the conspirators knew his customary role all too well. Tallien saw in a flash what was coming and rushed to the rostrum. Collot let him speak, and all unfolded from there.

As for Thérésa, she was not taken to the tribunal on the 8th as she had been told to expect. Nobody knows why. Did her letter influence the course of events? It was Tallien, after all, not another, who seized the initiative and assumed the mortal risk of belling the cat. Why doubt that his sure judgment and genuine eloquence during the harrowing debate were fueled not just by fear for his own skin (as was true of all the conspirators) but also by knowledge that his beloved Thérésa was in mortal danger? As she wrote to a friend several years later, "The 9th Thermidor, the most beautiful day of my life, because it was a bit [*un peu*] by my little hand that the guillotine was overthrown." Putting it that way, she spoke the truth.

From this point until Napoleon Bonaparte seized power on November 9, 1799, French politics were unsettled more than ever. The so-called Thermidorean Reaction lasted until October 26, 1795, when the Convention dissolved and was replaced by a new regime featuring a bicameral legislature and an executive of five men called Directors. (It was the Directory, so called, that Napoleon ended.) The country remained a republic but one continually threatened by unrepentant Jacobins on the left and resurgent monarchists on the right. The men in power kept the regime afloat by *basculement*, tilting to one side, then to another. To complicate matters, France was continually at war with a shifting coalition of enemies and experienced both victory and defeat in the fighting.

Tallien, now on the CPS (for a month), saw to Thérésa's early release, on the 12th Thermidor (July 30). She first spent some time reestablishing herself financially. Being property rich—although her ex-husband had sold off some without her consent—but cash poor, she sold personal effects. In mid-September, she went to Bordeaux to settle affairs and retrieve young Théodore. She took residence in Paris at 9, rue Saint-Georges off the rue Chausée-d'Antin. Although she and Tallien were seen everywhere together, they lived apart. On December 26, 1794, however, they married in a civil ceremony. Having learned from experience, she had had a rigorous marriage contract drawn—it looked as if she anticipated a divorce—which left her in complete control of her assets. Why did she marry him? Out of gratitude for twice saving her life? A sympathy inspired by shared danger? For protection from public attacks on her ("la Cabarrus," as she was called)? The fact that she was four months' pregnant? As she put it once, "When you go through a storm, you can't always choose the plank you cling to." Moreover, she was ambitious and felt drawn to powerful men. Tallien was a leading figure. Doubtless the pair anticipated a brilliant future.

Unfortunately, that prospect foundered in the tempests of the Thermidorean Reaction. While the Convention hesitated in the first weeks after Robespierre's fall, not knowing whether to end the Terror or continue it under new auspices, Tallien sensed that the public wanted it over. So he helped clear the air by denouncing it and the whole Jacobin Party (August 28)—for which he had to resign from the CPS. So deeply did he become involved in the anti-Jacobin movement, even (with Barras and especially Fréron) supporting gangs of overdressed young men, the "Jeunesse dorée" (Gilded Youth), to intimidate opponents, that reports circulated that he was in league with the monarchist émigrés. Still, when an émigré force landed and was crushed at Quiberon Bay (June 23–July 20, 1795), it was he who was sent, with Claude Blad, as a representative-on-mission to deal with it. He would have preferred to spare the prisoners, but the law required otherwise, and no promises had been made. Doubtless sensing, too, a need to burnish his republican credentials, he set in motion the drumhead trials and executions of 754 émigrés held over the next seven months. In the last weeks of the Convention, he tacked toward the Jacobins by calling (unsuccessfully) for nullification of the recent elections for the new legislative bodies because they reflected a conservative, possibly monarchist, revival. All in all, by the end of the Thermidorean Reaction, Tallien's political credit had sunk very low.

While Tallien's star waned, Thérésa's only burned brighter. Some time after their wedding they moved into a residence in her dowry, "La Chaumière" (The Cottage), which became famous as housing arguably the leading salon in Paris. (Borquin says they occupied "La Chaumière" in the spring of 1796.) "La Chaumière" was half-hidden amidst market gardens on a country lane, nowadays the rue Montaigne near the Champs-Élysées. She had it painted to look like a stage farm, with carefully imitated dilapidated bricks and woodwork and a roof of moss-grown thatch. The interior, however, while not large, was sumptuously furnished. Bankers, contractors, ex-nobles, generals, and deputies flocked to this reputedly most "political" of the salons. After years of Jacobin austerity, luxury and refinement reappeared—at least among the fortunate few, for the common people, victimized by galloping inflation, were enduring terrible deprivations during the winter of 1794–95, one of the coldest of the century. As if to mock Robespierre's Republic of Virtue, pre–1789-style indulgence ruled again. A dance craze swept society. The Thermidoreans probably were less immoral and licentious than has traditionally been alleged, but their reputation is not ill-deserved.

Thérésa Tallien constantly entertained or attended parties, balls, concerts, or the theater. Pregnancy seems not to have interfered all that much; she was at the Théâtre Feydeau when she went into labor with her daughter Rose-Thermidor-Laure-Joséphine Tallien, at first known as Thermidor, then Laure, then **Joséphine Tallien**, born May 17, 1795. She was the fashion pacesetter, introducing the "Grecian" style, which became the rage among "les Merveilleuses" (the Wonderfuls), a troop of trendy young women. It featured light fabrics, clinging robes secured with a belt fastened by a large cameo, light cashmere shawls, sandals, bare feet with toe rings, and wigs of every hue. Modifications became ever more daring. Victor de Broglie tells of seeing her arrive at the Ranelagh ballroom "dressed like Diana, bust semi-nude, shod in buskins and clothed, if one may use the word, in a tunic which did not go below the knees." Talleyrand once remarked of her, "One could not be more richly undressed." **Mme Hamelin**, not to be outdone, won her moment of fame by strolling topless from the Luxembourg to the Champs-Élysées, followed by a jeering crowd.

Frivolity abounded, causing vehement resentment among the hungry masses. The salons not only paraded the (often ill-gotten) wealth of their habitués, but also exerted huge political influence. Jaundiced observers have portrayed the times as subject to a greatly disproportionate influence of flighty, generally immoral women. The great historian Albert Mathiez once wrote, "The Revolution had destroyed these women's pleasures, diminished or threatened their fortunes, and changed their habits. How could they fail to loathe it?"

At first blush, Thérésa seems to fit this bill. Yet she did not "loathe" the Revolution per se, the freedoms it had brought, but only the bloodshed and brutality, the Revolution of the Terror, not of 1789. Frivolous her life was in many respects, yet for good reason she came to be called "Notre-Dame de Bon Secours" (Our Lady of Good Help). She answered a seemingly endless litany of pleas, especially from returned émigrés and ex-nobles but also from distressed souls of the humblest sort. Probably hundreds of prisoners owed her a debt for their release. She also worked to smooth relations between political opponents. No small part of her active social life, above all her salon, was a calculated effort to acquire influence which she could then use to help others. Moreover, her generosity extended even to showing no jealousy of other women's efforts, accomplishments, or beauty—no small virtue in that hothouse milieu. It is striking that one of her husband's most bitter foes, the deputy-memoirist Antoine Thibaudeau, wrote that "her rule [over society] dried many tears and, as far as I know, cost nobody anything."

By the summer of 1795, her marriage was dying. She later claimed that Tallien's role in the Quiberon affair caused her to become "disgusted" with one who had "too much blood on his hands." It may have been the last straw, anyhow. Tallien found himself reduced to a shadowy presence in society, tortured by jealousy which, she told a friend, once even led to threats to shoot her. By summer, too, she had become involved in a web of relationships that defies secure chronicling.

On August 6, 1794, Tallien had secured release from prison of a close acquaintance, one *Joséphine (Marie-Josèphe-Rose Tascher de la Pagerie), 31-year-old widow of General Alexandre de Beauharnais, recently executed. Thérésa and Joséphine (or Rose, as she was then called) became best friends; it was Joséphine who was chosen as baby Thermidor's godmother. At "La Chaumière," Joséphine met Paul Barras, an assiduous attender there. One day Barras brought along a strange-looking, somber, small, emaciated, bright-eyed young (aged 26) man with shoulder-length hair, Brigadier General Napoleon Bonaparte, currently vegetating in Paris while angling for a good assignment. (Barras had met him when he had been put in charge of the artillery at the siege of Toulon, where Barras was a representative-on-mission.) Thérésa took pity on him and had a tailor replace his shabby uniform with a fine outfit. Bonaparte had begun looking for a wife. Among others, the story goes, he approached Thérésa, who laughed him off with an out-of-character remark that she felt she "could do better." Fateful words. (Some claimed she

granted him "favors" anyway.) The rejection would one day haunt her.

Meanwhile, Joséphine had become Barras' mistress du jour, although Thérésa was never far from his view. On the 13th Vendémiaire III (October 5, 1795), events took a dramatic turn. To meet an uprising in Paris against the expiring Convention by sections stirred up by monarchist plotters, the Convention (as on the 9th Thermidor) appointed Barras commander of the defense. He in turn made Bonaparte in effect his second-in-command. At the critical moment, the young general smashed the uprising with well-sited artillery. The action catapulted him to prominence. As for Barras, he was elected one of the five Directors when the new regime debuted on October 26, and in short order became the dominant personality; of the five, he was the only one who lasted until Bonaparte overthrew the regime in November 1799.

Immediately after Vendémiaire, Bonaparte began to court Joséphine. Barras was tiring of her, and by January, at the latest, Thérésa had replaced her as mistress of Barras, then the most powerful man in France. On March 9, 1796, Bonaparte and Joséphine quietly married. As witnesses she chose her notary, the Talliens, and Barras—a piquant tableau.

Paul-François de Barras (1755–1829) was a ci-devant viscount and ex-army and naval officer blessed with extraordinary political instincts. Tall, handsome, vigorous, intelligent, with a grand seigneur's manners and presence, he habitually surrounded himself with beautiful young aristocratic women and (it was noted) handsome young men. He had married in 1791 but left after a few weeks to pursue a political career. In 1792, he won election to the Convention, which sent him and Fréron on mission to Toulon, where they (unlike Tallien) conducted a merciless repression. He was a gambler at the tables and in life, and an accomplished rake. Ambitious, venal, cynical, and amoral in excelsis, he attained similar heights as a lover of fine food, fast women, and the arts. Pleasure was his deity. And now to crown it all, he had the reputedly most beautiful woman in France for a mistress and as hostess for his ceaseless receptions, balls, and entertainments at "La Chaumière," the Luxembourg Palace (where the Directors resided), and his charming suburban Château de Grosbois, which had once belonged to Louis XVI's brother, the future Louis XVIII.

Directory society was a continuation of Thermidorean society on a grander scale and at a less frenetic pace. Thérésa, seconded by

Joséphine, the stunning *Juliette Récamier, and a squadron of blueblooded lovelies, starred at the Luxembourg Palace, to which she restored a luxurious éclat after the Revolutionary austerity had gutted it. She moved out of "La Chaumière" to reside at 21, rue Chausée-d'Antin, in the emerging Right Bank center of fashionable society, but spent most of her time as hostess for Barras at the Luxembourg and the Château de Grosbois when not visiting other homes, theaters, or ballrooms. These venues mixed ex-nobles, deputies, bureaucrats, service officers, and foreign dignitaries with bankers, artists, writers, musicians, army contractors, speculators, and sundry *nouveaux riches*—altogether the motleyest collection French high society had ever witnessed. Women were exceptionally visible. François Furet has observed that during these years between the religious and social prohibitions of the Old Regime and the Civil Code severities of Napoleon's empire, "women enjoyed a brief emancipation, revelling in the homage which the new society paid to feminine beauty and draping their bodies in scanty pseudo-classical garments."

Along with her strictly social role, Thérésa continued to answer pleas for help or favors. Most of her non-family correspondence consists of letters on behalf of others. Many years later she said her intention was to be useful to victims of all political opinions and that she felt she had nothing to fear from any party. Her motto was "Forget errors, pardon wrongs." Many came to her, of course, in order to reach Barras. She played no role in politics à la *Mme de Pompadour; her domain lay outside questions of policy. Rather, she was a dispenser of charities and a "fixer," someone to see who could drop words in the right places. She probably accepted money at times, her husband having none, but how much and under what circumstances is unknown. Certainly Barras kept her well supplied. She enjoyed spending yet also had a good head for finances. She loved money, Barras recalled, not for itself but for the pleasures it could get her.

At least once she appeared to overstep herself. Her father, out of prison and back in favor, turned up for two months in the summer of 1797, and after soundings was proposed by Spain in January 1798 as ambassador to France. Thérésa was delighted at the prospect, but her promotion of his candidacy hurt more than it helped. Talleyrand, the foreign minister, viewed her and her father as probable future intriguers, which he did not need, particularly because her royalist connections—the monarchists persistently courted her—promised trouble in the wake of the recent pro-Republican coup of the 18th Fructidor V (September 4, 1797). So the government politely evaded Spain's request by invoking a decree forbidding any French native to represent a foreign state in France. François returned to Spain, where he was richly consoled by being made minister of finance.

Thérésa loved the limelight, loved being applauded, admired, and courted. Not surprisingly, her celebrity reaped criticism and even hatred. A story goes that at a ball someone attached to the back of her gown a card reading "Respect national property." The press, as always, revelled in scurrilous rumors about "the New *Marie Antoinette," "Notre-Dame de Septembre" (recalling Tallien's link to the 1792 massacres), and "orgies" at "La Chaumière." When her liaison with Barras became obvious, a song went the rounds, "Ah! Ah! Madame Barras." A pamphlet signed "Belzébuth" appeared: "Letter from the Devil to the Greatest W. . . . in Paris. Do You Recognize Her?" She could hardly expect to escape unscathed, indeed, because the Directory was never popular—attacked from all sides, perpetually at war, exuding odors of corruption and license while the masses grappled with hunger and runaway inflation.

Tallien, meanwhile, limped along as a lowly deputy in the Council of Five Hundred. On February 26, 1797, Thérésa filed for divorce. He persuaded her to attempt a reconciliation, but it soon broke down. The stillborn son she delivered on December 20, 1797, probably was not Barras', as was assumed, but the fruit of this March reconciliation. At her friends' urging and because of her pregnancy and her father's candidacy for the ambassadorship, she allowed proceedings to stall. Misfortune dogged Tallien. The law of the 22nd Floréal VI (May 11, 1798) resulted in the nullification, for purely political reasons, of a number of recent elections, among them Tallien's. Unemployed now and desperate, he prevailed on Bonaparte to enroll him in the large civilian staff for the campaign in Egypt, departing on May 19. He may have hoped, too, that his absence would make Thérésa's heart grow fonder, and he wrote to her frequently. But it would be three years before that disastrous expedition ended and he could regain France. The wanderer found things considerably changed.

In January 1799, Thérésa and Barras had parted by mutual accord. The affair had worn thin, and Barras, his finger ever to the wind, had concluded that criticism of her had become dangerous to him, excess ballast. He was content, therefore, to drop her over the side into the waiting arms of a friend, "the richest man in France," Gabriel-Julian Ouvrard (1770–1846). Barras had smoothed the way. During a hunting party at Grosbois in late-1798, he had put her and Ouvrard in adjoining rooms. After the two separated from the others in the woods during the hunt and returned late, eyebrows went up. The new arrangement was inaugurated when in February 1799 she bought from Barras a splendid one-story Left Bank manse on the rue Babylone. Built by the Marquis de Barbançon, then owned by the Duc de Maine, it had been confiscated during the Revolution and bought by Barras. She added extensive gardens and furnished the place lavishly. Until his death in 1829, she and Barras remained on friendly terms.

Ouvrard, at 29 only three years older than she, had a wife (since 1795) who refused to leave her native Nantes for Paris. Charming, elegant, generous, and fairly handsome, he had rocketed to immense wealth by foreseeing the Revolution's ravenous appetite for paper. He bought and sold vast quantities and then, after hiding out in the army to escape charges of profiteering, returned to Paris following the 9th Thermidor to become active in business, foreign trade, and banking. In 1797, he became the navy's supplier-general and loaned ten million francs to the Directory.

Bonaparte's coup ending the Directory (November 9, 1799), sounded the knell for Thérésa Tallien's starring role in public life. She talked her way into the Luxembourg, which was surrounded by soldiers, to try to persuade Barras to resist, but he knew better. Bonaparte, who resented Ouvrard yet needed his wealth and competence, had him detained briefly in 1800 but soon called upon him to keep Paris supplied with wheat and then become supplier-general to the army, an obscenely lucrative commission. He would not, however, allow Thérésa entrée. He blamed her for Joséphine's misbehavior during his absences in Italy and Egypt, regarded her consorting with Barras as reprehensible, and, as noted, may have carried a grudge for her having put him down.

Almost nothing of a personal nature is known of her and Ouvrard's liaison, which lasted until 1804, save that they had four children. The pair lived on opposite banks of the Seine, entertained lavishly, and at the end parted with coolness but no obvious animosity, meeting mostly at weddings of their children, for whom he was a good father by the undemanding standards of the time. All the children bore her maiden name, Cabarrus. **Clémence Cabarrus**, born February 1, 1800, married Baron de Vaux, colonel in the

Royal Guard, but was widowed early and turned to charitable works, ending as Mother-Superior of the Congrégation de Saint-Louis; Édouard Cabarrus, born April 19, 1801, married **Adèle de Lesseps**, sister of the great engineer, and became a distinguished physician whose clientele included Alexandre Dumas, Balzac, Victor Hugo, Charles Gounod, and Emperor Napoleon III; **Clarisse Cabarrus**, born May 21, 1802, married a leading journalist, Achille-Ferdinand de Brunetière; and **Stéphanie Cabarrus**, born September 2, 1803, married Baron Amédée-Ferdinand Moisson de Vaux, of Normandy. Ouvrard, it seems, was a busy man; on September 7, 1801, his actual wife gave birth to a daughter.

As for poor Tallien, he regained France in April 1801 after being captured and released by the English only to learn that Thérésa was pregnant with her second child by Ouvrard and was resuming divorce proceedings. The divorce became final on April 8, 1802. They corresponded regularly until his death, mostly because of daughter Thermidor (now known as Joséphine). Thérésa habitually referred to him as "the friend par excellence." He was an affectionate father and helped as far as he could with his daughter's education. The elder Joséphine (after 1804, Empress), about his only remaining ally, paid her tuition at a *pension*. In April 1815, she married Comte Félix de Narbonne-Pelet, not rich but bearer of a fine name. Tallien lived on to a sad end. Napoleon spurned him because he had criticized his abandonment of the army in Egypt (1799), but he finally yielded to his pleas and named him (November 2, 1804) consul at Alicante, Spain. He fell very ill almost immediately and returned to France, where he lived on his modest salary until Napoleon's fall. Louis XVIII took pity on him (or sarcastically patronized this regicide) and granted him a small pension just before he died, all but destitute, on January 15, 1820.

Thérésa, her liaison with Ouvrard at an end, met Comte Joseph-Philippe de Riquet-Caraman late in 1804 at the salon of Germaine de Staël. They lost no time; the banns were published on January 6 and 13, 1805. Until the marriage, however, they were occupied with obtaining an annulment of her first marriage (the civil marriage with Tallien being a nullity in the eyes of the Church) and overcoming opposition from his family. At length, the archbishop of Paris, Cardinal de Belloy, decided the marriage had been "null and abusive" because of its speed and her age. The civil ceremony took place on August 3, and on August 18 a small religious service followed at the Saint-François-Xavier parish church in Paris. She was now Comtesse

Riquet-Caraman. A trip to Italy followed, partly on business connected with Joseph's inheritance, partly to try to persuade his outraged father to give them his blessing by obtaining that of the pope. The couple was well received in Venice, the courts of Florence and Naples, and by Pius VII, who duly blessed them. It did no good. Joseph's father died in 1807, unreconciled.

Joseph, two years her senior, came from an ancient noble family and had emigrated during the Terror. Tall and athletic, he was an imposing figure, refined, cultured (an excellent violinist), and upright in character. Soon, upon the death of a maternal uncle, he inherited the lands of Chimay, a former principality of the Holy Roman Empire located on the French border in the Belgian Ardennes (Hainault). Henceforth, he bore the courtesy title of Prince de Chimay, the principality having been annexed by France since 1795. In 1814, after Napoleon's fall, Chimay became part of the Kingdom of the Netherlands, which until 1830 included Belgium. François reluctantly changed his citizenship from French to Dutch, and in 1824 King William I of the Netherlands at last officially recognized Chimay's special status—thus legitimizing Thérésa's title of Princesse de Chimay.

The Château de Chimay had been unoccupied for two centuries. Pending its restoration, the couple resided at the rue Babylone manse and the Château de Menars, near Blois. Because of her exclusion from Napoleon's court during the Consulate (1800–04) and the Empire (1804–15), Thérésa's salon fell to the second tier, visited now mostly by longtime friends, foreign notables passing through, and artists and musicians. The Château de Chimay, too, became a favorite resort for the latter, among them composers Luigi Cherubini and Daniel-François Auber (who wrote an opera for her, *Jean de Couvin*, 1813, performed in her theater at the château); tenor Pierre Garat and the great Spanish mezzo-soprano *Maria Malibran (1803–36); violinists Charles de Bériot, Pierre Rode, and Pierre Baillot; pianist George Alexander Osbourne; poet Népomucène Lemercier; and painters Horace Vernet and Jean-Baptiste Isabey. The latter gave her lessons she used in painting excellent miniature portraits.

Napoleon, while in exile at St. Helena, recounted that Thérésa would meet him secretly at a masked ball every year and beg to be admitted to court, but he remained adamant. If you were Emperor, he retorted, would you admit a woman who had "two or three husbands and children by everybody?" One mistake can be ex-

cused, but a second, "and on and on?" She could not, of course, cite his own sexual transgressions, or those of his sisters *Carolina, *Elisa, and *Pauline Bonaparte. Moreover, he absolutely forbade Joséphine to see her, a gratuitous cruelty. After he divorced Joséphine (1810), however, they had a tearful reunion at Malmaison. Joséphine's early death (May 29, 1814) affected her greatly.

Thérésa had four children with Joseph: Prince Joseph de Chimay, born on August 20, 1808; Alphonse, born on June 16, 1810; Marie-Louise de Chimay, born on August 6, 1813 (died on January 14, 1814); and, at age 41, **Marie-Louise-Thérésa-Valentine de Chimay**, born on February 19, 1815. François did not adopt her six other children but treated them kindly as his own. Only a week before her lastborn arrived, her son Théodore, not yet 26, died (February 10). He had caused her much grief for years because of his gambling and incessant borrowing. Joséphine got him a post on General Junot's staff. Badly wounded, he retired to his paternal grandparents' Île-Saint-Louis home, where he had largely been raised, and soon died despite Thérésa's care.

At Chimay, she became a much-loved figure in this poverty-ridden region. "La Bonne Dame de Chimay" founded a 540-bed hospice and thread mill for the destitute, visited the poor and sick, gave money away, and furnished prizes for charity fairs and lotteries. "Doing good for others," she said, "is the sole happiness unmixed with pains that Heaven affords."

Her charitable labors helped her overcome the depression she suffered because of her exclusion (again) from court functions at The Hague by William I, a famously stubborn man. Her revolutionary past tracked her relentlessly through these years of political reaction. Joseph insisted, nevertheless, on fulfilling his court duties as chamberlain to the king and member of the First Chamber of the Estates-General. He and the children received invitations, but she did not. She spoke ill of nobody in public, but in private she wrote that this humiliation was a "moral assassination." She did not receive the support from her husband she might have expected and wrote that she felt useless and wanted to die. He became somber and morose, perhaps, she feared, seeing her as an obstacle to his advancement. "Tell me," she wrote in a pathetic letter, "that you do not regret having married me." In the end, she refused to be broken by her exclusion and by the calumnies to which she was becoming exposed in recently published memoirs:

"I have lived to this day," she wrote on July 25, 1829, "without having caused any tears to be shed, without having experienced a feeling of hatred or desire to take revenge; I want to die as I have lived."

For years she suffered from liver disease, which caused her belly to swell. Eleven childbirths, a dangerous proceeding in those times, also took a toll. She bled frequently. She visited spas at Plombières and Dieppe; while at Nice in October 1830 she experienced a crisis. It recurred in July 1834, and she declined thereafter. Near the end, her once-famous figure was swollen to the point of deformity. On January 15, 1835, she had herself carried to the terrace outside her room to savor the view one last time. That night at about 10 PM she died.

A huge crowd from around the region attended her funeral on the 19th. She was buried in the Old Cemetery in the center of town, but when it was closed her remains were transferred to the vault of the princes of Chimay beneath the choir of the parish church. In 1852 a monument was erected on the square containing four figures, three of princes of Chimay, one of her. The slab over the empty grave in the Old Cemetery contains a faint epitaph: "*Consoler, Secourir, Charmer, violà tout sa vie*" (To Console, to Aid, to Charm, that was her whole life).

Few persons have lived lives so representative of their times. "What a novel my life has been!" she declared in old age. Indeed. The decades of the French Revolution and the Napoleonic Empire remain some of the most event-filled passages in world history. "Though I have never been a queen," she observed, "I have lived for a time in a whirlwind not far different from that which surrounds a throne." As a woman, she was excluded from political power as such. Her gender limited her opportunities severely even though, as has been noted, the years when she was most in view saw European women experiencing more freedom than before or for a long time afterward. Men did the choosing. Without her legendary beauty she would not have drawn attention, for she possessed no truly extraordinary mind or abilities. A contemporary noted in 1821 that "she spoke well and knew how to be witty without seeking to appear so." But her wit left no *bons mots*. She was talented in music and painting, but never enough to overcome the prejudices against female artists. In her correspondence she seldom rose above banalities.

François Furet has cited Barras and Ouvrard as representative founders of the new union between power and finance which would mark the modern age. Thérésa Tallien linked them as a person, while her life in turn was representative of the life women experienced among men at the highest levels of society. She was thrust onto the grand stage when she was too young—much too young to be anything but dazzled by her easy victories over the crowd of men who coveted her. She was more a coquette than a *grande amoureuse*; she had no secret or passionate loves and wrote no burning love letters. In his memoirs, Baron de Frémilly described her as "a woman without a rudder, with a fragile heart and a Spanish temperament." Her beauty was her passport, the source of her rise, but also her burden, pushing her into situations which exposed her immaturity. She yielded to temptation too often, perhaps because "victory" was so easy. To her great credit, however, in the "whirlwind," enveloped by uncertainty and a society whose moral compass was swinging wildly, she remained in heart uncorrupted, a woman sincerely mourned by the legions she had helped in the course of a turbulent existence.

SOURCES:

Baczko, Bronislaw. *Ending the Terror: The French Revolution after Robespierre.* Trans. by Michel Petheram. Cambridge: Cambridge University Press, 1994.

Bourquin, Marie-Hélène. *Monsieur et Madame Tallien.* Paris: Perrin, 1987.

Castelnau, Jacques-Thomas de. *Madame Tallien, révolutionnaire, favorite, princesse.* Paris: Hachette: 1938.

Erlanger, Philippe. "Madame Tallien," in *Aventuriers et favorites.* Paris: Perrin, 1963, pp. 271–312.

Ferrus, Maurice. *Madame Tallien à Bordeaux pendant la Terreur.* Bordeaux: Feret, 1930.

Frénilly, M. de [Auguste-François]. *Recollections of Baron de Frénilly, Peer of France (1768–1828).* Edited by Arthur Chuquet. Trans. by Frederic Lees. NY: Putnam, 1909.

Furet, François. *French Revolution.* Trans. by Stephen Hardman. NY: Macmillan, 1970.

Gendron, François. *The Gilded Youth of Thermidor.* Trans. by James Cookson. Montréal: McGill-Queen's University Press, 1993.

Gilles, Christian. *Madame Tallien: La Reine du Directoire.* Biarritz: Atlantica, 1999.

Jumièges, Jean-Claude. *Madame Tallien, ou une femme dans la tourmente révolutionnaire.* Lausanne: Éd. Rencontre, 1967.

Kelly, Linda. *Women of the French Revolution.* London: Hamish Hamilton, 1987.

Knapton, Ernest John. *Empress Josephine.* Cambridge, MA: Harvard University Press, 1963.

Lenôtre, Georges. "Tallien in Old Age," in *Romances of the French Revolution.* 2 vols. Trans. by Frederic Lees. NY: Brentano's, 1909. Vol. I, pp. 139–149.

Lyons, Martyn. *France under the Directory.* Cambridge: Cambridge University Press, 1975.

Mathiez, Albert. *After Robespierre: The Thermidorean Reaction.* Trans. by Catherine Allison Phillips. NY: Alfred A. Knopf, 1931.

Matrat, Jean. *Robespierre, or The Tyranny of the Majority*. Trans. by Alan Kendall. NY: Scribner, 1974.

Mossiker, Frances. *Napoleon and Josephine: The Biography of a Marriage*. NY: Simon & Schuster, 1964.

Palmer, Robert Roswell. *Twelve Who Ruled: The Committee of Public Safety during the Terror*. Princeton, NJ: Princeton University Press, 1941.

Schom, Alan. *Napoleon Bonaparte*. NY: HarperCollins, 1997.

Sydenham, M. J. *The First French Republic, 1792–1804*. Berkeley, CA: University of California Press, 1973.

Waranoff, Denis. *The Thermidorean Regime and the Directory, 1794–1799*. Trans. by Julian Jackson. Cambridge: Cambridge University Press, 1984.

SUGGESTED READING:

Blanc, Olivier. *Last Letters: Prisons and Prisoners of the French Revolution, 1793–1794*. Trans. by Alan Sheridan. NY: Farrar, Straus & Giroux, 1987.

Bosher, J.F. *The French Revolution*. NY: W.W. Norton, 1988.

Brace, Richard M. *Bordeaux and the Gironde, 1789–1794*. Ithaca, NY: Cornell University Press, 1947.

Charles-Vallian, Thérèse. *Tallien, le mal-aimé de la Révolution*. Paris: J. Picollec, 1997.

Chimay, Gilone Le Veneur de Tuillère de, princesse de. *Madame Tallien, royaliste et révolutionnaire*. Paris: Plon, 1936.

Lefebvre, Georges. *The Thermidorians and The Directory: Two Phases of the French Revolution*. Trans. by Robert Baldick. NY: Random House, 1964.

Melzer, Sara E., and Leslie Rabine, eds. *Rebel Daughters: Women and the French Revolution*. NY: Oxford University Press, 1992.

Sokolnikova, Galina Osipova Serebriakova. *Nine Women, Drawn from the Epoch of the French Revolution*. Trans. by H.C. Stevens. NY: J. Cape & H. Smith, 1932.

Wilson, Robert McNair. *The Gypsy-Queen of Paris: Being the Story of Madame Tallien by Whom Robespierre Fell*. London: Chapman & Hall, 1934.

COLLECTIONS:

Chimay, Belgium: Archives of the Château de Chimay.

David S. Newhall,
Pottinger Distinguished Professor of History Emeritus,
Centre College, and author of
Clemenceau: A Life at War (1991)

Talma, Louise (1906–1996)

French-born American composer, first woman to win the Sibelius Award in composition, who was known as the dean of American women composers. Born in Arcachon, France, on October 31, 1906; died on August 13, 1996; attended Columbia University; studied at the Institute of Musical Art in New York under Howard Brockway, George Wedge, Helen Whily, and Percy Goetschius; studied piano with Isidor Philipp; studied under Nadia Boulanger at the Fontainebleau School of Music.

Born in Arcachon, France, in 1906, Louise Talma was reared by her mother, an operatic singer, after her father died in an accident. Talma studied at the Institute of Musical Art in New York under Howard Brockway, George Wedge, **Helen Whily**, and Percy Goetschius; she also studied piano with the renowned keyboard pedagogue Isidor Philipp. After attending Columbia University, she was at the Fontainebleau School of Music for 17 summers studying with ***Nadia Boulanger**, the teacher who taught Aaron Copland and Leonard Bernstein, and working as a teacher herself. Though she never imposed a style on her students, Boulanger was enormously enthusiastic about Igor Stravinsky's music. Inevitably, Stravinsky's work influenced Talma, while Boulanger renewed a desire in Talma to compose. Even though she had published no music, Talma applied for a Guggenheim fellowship at Boulanger's insistence. This advice proved fortuitous: Talma was the first woman to receive such a grant for composition.

Talma, who taught at Hunter College, composed many works. One of her most famous is her opera *The Alcestiad*, adapted from Thornton Wilder's play *Life in the Sun*. She had labored over the opera for five years and received a Senior Fulbright research grant in 1955–56 in order to spend ten months in Rome working on it. With Wilder's libretto, *Alcestiad* premiered on March 1, 1962, at Frankfurt-am-Main, making Talma the first American woman ever to have an opera staged at a major European opera house. That night, Wilder and Talma received a 20-minute ovation from the audience. Talma's pieces have been performed in recitals and concert halls throughout Europe and America. She was the first woman to be elected to the music department of the National Institute of Arts and Letters and the only American to teach at Fontainebleau in the summers during the late 1930s.

SOURCES:

Cohen, Aaron I. *International Encyclopedia of Women Composers*. 2 vols. NY: Books & Music (USA), 1987.

Page, Tim. "Gideon and Talma at 80—Composers and Neighbors," in *The New York Times Biographical Service*. October 1986, pp. 1276–1277.

John Haag,
Athens, Georgia

Talmadge, Constance (1898–1973)

American silent-film actress. Name variations: "Dutch." Born on April 19, 1898 (also seen as 1897, 1899, and 1900), in Brooklyn, New York; died on November 23, 1973, in Los Angeles, California; youngest daughter of Fred Talmadge and Margaret "Peg" Talmadge; sister of actresses Norma Talmadge (1893–1957) and Natalie Talmadge (1897–1969);

married John Pialoglou, also seen as John Pialogiou (a tobacco exporter); married Alistair McIntosh, also seen as Alistair MacIntosh (a captain in Her Majesty's Horse Guards); married Townsend Netcher (a department store tycoon); married Walter "Wally" Giblin (a Wall Street stockbroker; died).

Selected filmography: Buddy's First Call *(1914);* The Mysterious Lodger *(1914);* The Peacemaker *(1914);* In Bridal Attire *(1914);* In the Latin Quarter *(1914);* The Egyptian Mummy *(1914);* Billy's Wager *(1915);* The Green Cat *(1915);* The Master of His House *(1915);* The Lady of Shalott *(1915);* The Vanishing Vault *(1915);* Spades Are Trump *(1915);* Captivating Mary Carstairs *(1915);* The Missing Links *(1916);* The Matrimaniac *(1916);* Intolerance *(1916);* Betsy's Burglar *(1917);* Scandal *(1917);* The Honeymoon *(1917);* The Gray Chiffon Veil *(1918);* The Studio Girl *(1918);* A Pair of Silk Stockings *(1918);* A Lady's Name *(1918);* The Veiled Adventure *(1919);* The Fall of Babylon *(1919);* A Temperamental Wife *(1919);* A Virtuous Vamp *(1919);* Happiness a la Mode *(1919);* Two Weeks *(1920);* In Search of a Sinner *(1920);* The Love Expert *(1920);* The Perfect Woman *(1920);* Dangerous Business *(1920);* Mama's Affair *(1921);* Wedding Bells *(1921);* Lessons in Love *(1921);* Woman's Place *(1921);* The Primitive Lover *(1922);* Polly of the Follies *(1922);* East Is West *(1922);* Dulcy *(1923);* The Dangerous Maid *(1923);* The Goldfish *(1924);* Her Night of Romance *(1924);* Heart Trouble *(1924);* Learning to Love *(1925);* Her Sister from Paris *(1925);* Sybil *(1926);* The Duchess of Buffalo *(1926);* Venus of Venice *(1927);* Breakfast at Sunrise *(1927);* Venus *(1929).*

Constance Talmadge

The daughters of Fred and **Peg Talmadge**, a spunky, determined stage mother, silent film actresses *Norma, *Natalie, and Constance Talmadge were primed for the movie camera as soon as it became apparent that they were developing into beauties. The eldest, Norma, and the youngest, Constance, achieved stardom, although they never competed with each other. Norma, dark-haired and elegant, gained renown as the suffering heroine of melodrama, while blonde, athletic Constance (or "Dutch" as she was called) starred in sophisticated comedies. Skillfully managed by producer Joseph M. Schenck, who was married to Norma from 1916 to 1934, the sisters reached the height of their careers during the 1920s, but faded into obscurity with the advent of sound.

Constance entered films in 1914, and for two years played in comedy shorts opposite Billy Quirk. Her break came in 1916 when she was cast as the mischievous Mountain Girl in the Babylonian episode of D.W. Griffith's *Intolerance* (1916), a role which further showcased her athleticism and her natural talent for comedy. Around this time, Peg Talmadge convinced her new son-in-law to take over Constance's career as well as Norma's. Schenck subsequently starred Constance in a series of comedies, many of which were written by *Anita Loos and John Emerson, including *A Virtuous Vamp* (1919) and *Learning to Love* (1925). At the peak of her popularity, Constance made $6,000 a week and established the Constance Talmadge Film Company, which turned out 12 films over a six-year period. Her co-stars included Earle Foxe (*Honeymoon*, 1917), Ronald Colman (*Sybil*, 1926), and Chester Conklin (*Venus of Venice*, 1927). "Each film with Constance was a holiday," said silent actor Harrison Ford, who appeared in ten films with her through 1922. She "has a distinct gift for always keeping comedy on a high, sparkling plane, and she has created a wonderful screen personality." She made pictures for several studios, including Paramount, First National, and Selznick. However, most of her films were made with Joseph M. Schenck, her brother-in-law. Constance, ambivalent about her career from the start, retired from films in 1929 when talkies made their appearance.

Constance Talmadge's four husbands included a wealthy Greek tobacco importer; a British captain in His Majesty's Horse Guards; a department store tycoon; and her last, Walter Giblin, a Wall Street broker who died suddenly in 1964, leaving her a widow. According to Anita Loos, Constance remained on good terms with all of her ex-husbands, frequently hosting dinners for them and their current wives or significant others. In her later years, Constance battled a drinking problem and eventually withdrew to a suite at the Beverly Wilshire Hotel, where she lived in seclusion. The last of the Talmadge sisters, she died in 1973.

SOURCES:

Bawden, Liz-Anne. *The Oxford Companion to Film.* NY: Oxford University Press, 1976.

Katz, Ephraim. *The Film Encyclopedia.* 3rd ed. NY: HarperCollins, 1998.

Lamparski, Richard. *Whatever Became of . . . ?* NY: Crown, 1967.

Loos, Anita. *The Talmadge Girls: A Memoir.* NY: Viking, 1978.

Quinlan, David, ed. *The Film Lover's Companion.* Secaucus, NJ: Citadel, 1997.

Slide, Anthony. *Silent Portraits: Stars of the Silent Screen in Historic Photographs.* Vestal, NY: Vestal Press, 1989.

"Those Three Talmadge Girls!," in *Who's Who on the Screen.* Edited by Charles Donald Fix and Milton L. Silver. NY: Ross, 1929, pp. 101–104.

Karina L. Kerr, M.A.,
Ypsilanti, Michigan

Talmadge, Natalie (1897–1969)

American silent-film actress. Born in 1897 (some sources cite 1899) in Brooklyn, New York; died in 1969; middle daughter of Fred Talmadge and Margaret "Peg" Talmadge; sister of actresses Constance Talmadge (1898–1973) and Norma Talmadge (1893–1957); married Buster Keaton (the actor), in 1921 (divorced 1933); children: two sons.

Selected filmography: Isle of Conquest *(1919);* The Passion Flower *(1921);* Our Hospitality *(1923).*

Natalie Talmadge, the middle sister of *Norma and *Constance Talmadge, was born in 1897. Unlike her superstar sisters, Natalie was a reluctant actress, at first eschewing the profession to become the private secretary of Roscoe "Fatty" Arbuckle. Eventually, she began acting as well; however, she did not achieve her sisters' level of success. Performing small roles, usually in her sisters' films, she appeared in only two features in the 1920s. She is perhaps better known for having married Buster Keaton, in 1921. The two appeared together in *Our Hospitality* (1923) and two other films, but after that she spent her time supporting his career rather than pursuing her own. The couple had two sons before the marriage ended in divorce in 1933.

According to *Anita Loos in her memoir *The Talmadge Girls,* Natalie lacked the unpretentiousness of her two sisters, and following her marriage to Keaton "went Hollywood," presiding over a succession of showy houses which Loos called "burlesques of Hollywood bad taste." Natalie, who never remarried, spent her later years living in southern California, where she died in 1969, writes Loos, "through a sheer disinterest in living."

SOURCES:

Katz, Ephraim. *The Film Encyclopedia.* 3rd ed. NY: HarperCollins, 1998.

Loos, Anita. *The Talmadge Girls: A Memoir.* NY: Viking, 1978.

Quinlan, David, ed. *The Film Lover's Companion.* Secaucus, NJ: Citadel Press, 1997.

Slide, Anthony. *Silent Portraits: Stars of the Silent Screen in Historic Photographs.* Vestal, NY: Vestal Press, 1989.

"Those Three Talmadge Girls!," in *Who's Who on the Screen.* Ed. by Charles Donald Fix and Milton L. Silver. NY: Ross, 1929, pp. 101–104.

Karina L. Kerr, M.A.,
Ypsilanti, Michigan

Talmadge, Norma (1893–1957)

American silent-film actress. Born on May 26, 1893 (some sources cite 1895 and 1897), in Jersey City,

Natalie Talmadge

New Jersey (some sources cite Brooklyn, New York); died from a cerebral stroke due to complications from arthritis, pneumonia, and possibly drug abuse in Las Vegas, Nevada, on December 24, 1957; eldest daughter of Fred Talmadge and Margaret "Peg" Talmadge; sister of Constance Talmadge (1898–1973) and Natalie Talmadge (1897–1969); married Joseph M. Schenck (a film producer), in November 1916 (separated 1928, divorced 1934); married George Jessel (an actor, entertainer, and producer), in 1934 (divorced 1937 or 1939); married Carvel James (a physician), in 1946.

Selected filmography: A Broken Spell *(1910);* Dixie Mother *(1910);* Heart o' the Hill *(1910);* The Household Pest *(1910);* In Neighboring Kingdoms *(1910);* The Love of Chrysanthemum *(1910);* Murder by Proxy *(1910);* Uncle Tom's Cabin *(1910);* A Broken Spell *(1911);* The Child Crusoes *(1911);* The Convict's Child *(1911);* Forgotten *(1911);* The Four Poster Pets *(1911);* The General's Daughter *(1911);* Her Hero *(1911);* Her Sister's Children *(1911);* Nellie the Model *(1911);* Paola and Francesca *(1911);* The Sky Pilot *(1911);* A Tale of Two Cities *(1911);* The Thumb Print *(1911);* The Wildcat *(1911);* Captain Barnacle's Messmate *(1912);* Captain Barnacle's Reformer *(1912);* Captain Barnacle's Wolf *(1912);* The Extension Table *(1912);* Father's Hot Toddy *(1912);* The First Violin *(1912);* The Fortune in a Teacup *(1912);* His Official Appointment *(1912);* Lovesick Maidens of Cuddletown *(1912);* The Midget's Revenge *(1912);* Mr. Bolter's Sweetheart *(1912);* Mrs. Butler Buttles *(1912);* Mrs. 'Enry 'Awkins *(1912);* O'Hara Helps Cupid *(1912);* Omens and Oracles *(1912);* The Sphinx, or, Mrs. Carter's Necklace *(1912);* Squatter and Philosopher *(1912);* The Troublesome Step-daughters *(1912);* 'Arriet's Baby *(1913);* The Blue Rose *(1913);* Casey at the Bat *(1913);* Counsel for the Defense *(1913);* Country Barber *(1913);* The Doctor's Secret *(1913);* The Elopement at Home *(1913);* Extremities *(1913);* Fanny's Conspiracy *(1913);* Father's Hatband *(1913);* Getting Up a Practise *(1913);* He Fell in Love with His Mother-in-Law *(1913);* His Silver Bachelorhood *(1913);* His Little Page *(1913);* The Honorable Algernon *(1913);* Just Show People *(1913);* Keeping Husbands Home *(1913);* The Kiss of Retribution *(1913);* A Lady and Her Maid *(1913);* Let 'Em Quarrel *(1913);* O'Hara As a Guardian Angel *(1913);* O'Hara's Godchild *(1913);* Officer John Donovan *(1913);* An Old Man's Love Story *(1913);* The Other Woman *(1913);* Plot and Counterplot *(1913);* The Sacrifice of Kathleen *(1913);* The Silver Cigarette Case *(1913);* Sleuthing *(1913);* Solitaires *(1913);* Stenographer Troubles *(1913);* The Tables Turned *(1913);* Under the Daisies *(1913);* The Varasour Ball *(1913);* Wanted—A Strong Hand *(1913);* Cupid vs. Money *(1914);* The Curing of Myra May *(1914);* A Daughter of Israel *(1914);* Dorothy Danebridge *(1914);* Etta of the Footlights *(1914);* Fogg's Millions *(1914);* Goodbye Summer *(1914);* The Helpful Sisterhood *(1914);* The Hero *(1914);* The Hidden Letters *(1914);* John Rance—Gentleman *(1914);* The Loan Shark King *(1914);* Memories in Men's Souls *(1914);* Militant *(1914);* The Mill of Life *(1914);* Mr. Murphy's Wedding Present *(1914);* Old Reliable *(1914);* The Peacemaker *(1914);* Politics and the Press *(1914);* A Question of Clothes *(1914);* The Right of Way *(1914);* Sawdust and Salome *(1914);* Sunshine and Shadows *(1914);* Under False Colors *(1914);* A Wayward Daughter *(1914);* The Barrier of Faith *(1915);* The Battle Cry of Peace *(1915);* Captivating Mary Carstairs *(1915);* The Criminal *(1915);* A Daughter's Strange Inheritance *(1915);* Elsa's Brother *(1915);* Fortunes of a Composer *(1915);* Janet of the Chorus *(1915);* The Pillar of Flame *(1915);* The Children in the House *(1916);* The Crown Prince's Double *(1916);* The Devil's Needle *(1916);* Fifty-Fifty *(1916);* Going Straight *(1916);* The Honorable Algy *(1916);* Martha's Vindication *(1916);* The Missing Links *(1916);* The Social Secretary *(1916);* The Law of Compensation *(1917);* The Lone Wolf *(1917);* The Moth *(1917);* Panthea *(1917);* Poppy *(1917);* The Secret of the Storm Country *(1917);* By Right of Purchase *(1918);* De Luxe Annie *(1918);* The Forbidden City *(1918);* The Ghosts of Yesterday *(1918);* Her Only Way *(1918);* The Safety Curtain *(1918);* Salome *(1918);* The Heart of Wetona *(1919);* The Isle of Conquest *(1919);* The New Moon *(1919);* The Probation Wife *(1919);* The Way of a Woman *(1919);* The Branded Woman *(1920);* A Daughter of Two Worlds *(1920);* She Loves and Lies *(1920);* The Right of Way *(1920);* The Woman Gives *(1920);* Yes or No *(1920);* Love's Redemption *(1921);* The Passion Flower *(1921);* The Sign on the Door *(1921);* The Wonderful Thing *(1921);* Branded! *(1922);* The Eternal Flame *(1922);* Foolish Wives *(1922);* Smilin' Through *(1922);* Ashes of Vengeance *(1923);* Dust of Desire *(1923);* Sawdust *(1923);* Song of Love *(1923);* The Voice from the Minaret *(1923);* Within the Law *(1923);* In Hollywood with Potash and Perlmutter *(1924);* The Only Woman *(1924);* Secrets *(1924);* Graustark *(1925);* The Lady *(1925);* Kiki *(1926);* Camille *(1927);* The Dove *(1927);* Show People *(1928);* The Woman Disputed *(1928);* New York Nights *(1929);* Du Barry, Woman of Passion *(1930).*

Norma Talmadge, eldest of the acting Talmadge sisters, was born in 1893 in Jersey City,

New Jersey, although she reported her birth year variously as 1895 and 1897. Some sources indicate that she was born in Brooklyn, New York, where she attended school with her sisters *Constance and *Natalie Talmadge. When the girls came home from school, they would immediately descend into the cellar to dress up in clothing from other eras packed in the many trunks stored there. Under Norma's direction, they would enact the historical events that they had studied in school. While their father Fred had difficulty holding a job, their mother **Peg Talmadge** provided a steady income for the family by variously running a home laundry, teaching velvet painting, hawking her own line of cosmetics, and taking in boarders. Neglected by their father, the girls were raised by Peg, who insisted that her daughters call her by her given name, and who by all accounts was the epitome of the stage mother.

When Norma was 14, Peg got her a job modeling for illustrated song slides, and just three years later, in 1910, Norma made her debut at the Vitagraph Studio in nearby Flatbush. Her break came in 1911 with her performance in the original screen version of *A Tale of Two Cities*. While working at Vitagraph, Norma played a variety of roles, acquiring experience and exposure. After doing a film for National Film Corporation in California, Norma was signed, together with her sister Constance, by Triangle Studios. Most of Norma's early films were for Vitagraph and Triangle and exhibit more talent than skill as an actress, but she did attract the personal and professional attention Joseph M. Schenck, a prosperous film exhibitor who wanted to produce his own films. He established the Norma Talmadge Film Corporation in New York and released her films through First National and United Artists; in November 1916, they were married. A year later, they released their first film, *Panthea*, which met with enormous success, propelling Norma into stardom. Most notable among her films would be a series of melodramas, including *Smilin' Through* (1922), *Secrets* (1924), *Camille* (1927), and *The Dove* (1928).

Between the years 1917 and 1921, Norma appeared in about six films a year. Although these movies were predictable melodramas, she had become one of the most popular actresses on the screen—her nearest rival was her sister Constance—and was earning $8,000 a week. Schenck became head of United Artists in 1924, although Norma still needed to complete her contract with First National. Filming *Camille* (one of the numerous screen versions of the story

of *Alphonsine Plessis) for that studio, she fell in love with her co-star Gilbert Roland. In 1928, she separated from Schenck, who continued to manage her career, as well as that of her sister Constance, for a brief time. Although Schenck continued to pair the two lovers in films, the era of the "talkies" was approaching and the careers of both Norma and Roland were declining. Her limited range as an actress, as well as her strong Brooklyn accent, became apparent with the advent of sound and after starring in *New York Nights* (1929) and *Du Barry—Woman of Passion* (1930), based on the life of the 18th-century French courtesan *Jeanne Bécu du Barry, she retired from films with a large personal fortune. She had appeared in over 164 films.

Divorced from Schenck in 1934, Norma decided against marrying the younger Roland; instead, she wed stand-up entertainer George Jessel, but their relationship ended in divorce in 1937 or 1939. Around that time, Norma fell victim to arthritis, a painful condition which eventually made her dependent on drugs. It was her addiction, writes *Anita Loos, that brought about her third and final marriage, to a Beverly Hills' physician, Carvel James, whom she hoped would provide her with a steady supply of

Norma Talmadge

painkillers. She moved to Las Vegas, Nevada, in 1955. After years spent bedridden and in pain, Norma Talmadge died on Christmas Eve in 1957 from a cerebral stroke following pneumonia.

SOURCES:

Katz, Ephraim. *The Film Encyclopedia.* 3rd ed. NY: HarperCollins, 1998.

Loos, Anita. *The Talmadge Girls: A Memoir.* NY: Viking, 1978.

Quinlan, David, ed. *The Film Lover's Companion.* Secaucus, NJ: Citadel Press, 1997.

Slide, Anthony. *Silent Portraits: Stars of the Silent Screen in Historic Photographs.* Vestal, NY: Vestal Press, 1989.

"Those Three Talmadge Girls!," in *Who's Who on the Screen.* Ed. by Charles Donald Fix and Milton L. Silver. NY: Ross, 1929, pp. 101–104.

Karina L. Kerr, M.A.,
Ypsilanti, Michigan

Talvace, Adela (d. 1174)

Duchess of Salisbury. Name variations: Ala Talvas. Died on October 4, 1174; daughter of William Talvace, count of Ponthieu, and Helie Borel (b. 1080); married William de Warrenne (1119–1148), 3rd earl of Warrenne and Surrey (r. 1138–1148), a crusader who died in the Holy Land; married Patrick, 1st earl of Salisbury, in 1152; children: (first marriage) *Isabel de Warrenne (c. 1137–1203); Beatrice de Warrenne (first wife of Hubert de Burgh).

Tamar (fl. 1000 BCE)

Biblical woman. Flourished around 1000 BCE; daughter of King David and Maacah; sister of Absalom.

Tamar, who flourished around 1000 BCE, was the daughter of *Maacah and King David. Amnon, David's eldest son by another wife, *Ahinoam of Jezreel, was infatuated with Tamar, his beautiful half-sister, and schemed to be alone with her. He then raped her. Although furious, the king would not take retribution against his oldest son, but Tamar's brother Absalom was intent on revenge. After biding his time, he lured Amnon to a party and murdered him while Amnon was drunk. Absalom fled, but eventually David's general, Joab, persuaded David to let him return to Jerusalem. Absalom's gratitude was less them complete, however, for he soon rebelled against his father, declared himself king of Israel, and traveled around the country gathering recruits for a march on Jerusalem.

Tamar (fl. 1000 BCE)

Biblical woman. Flourished around 1000 BCE; daughter of Absalom.

Tamar was the only surviving daughter of Absalom, and the grandmother of Abijah (2 Sam. 14:27).

Tamar (fl. 1100 BCE).

See Ruth for sidebar.

Tamara (1160–1212)

Queen of the ancient kingdom of Georgia, renowned for the military exploits which increased her mountainous holdings from the Black to the Caspian seas, whose reign encompassed a flourishing of literature and the arts that marked the country's golden age. Name variations: Thamar; Tamara the Great. Born Tamara in 1160 in Georgia (the extensive Slavic kingdom east of the Black Sea in the Caucasus); died in Georgia in 1212 (some sources cite 1207); daughter of a princess of Osseti and George III, also known as Giorgi III (a descendant of Georgia's ruling Bagrationi line), king of Georgia; married George Bogolyubskoi, also seen as George Bogolyubski (a Kievan prince and son of Prince Andrew of Suzdal), in 1185 or 1187 (divorced 1188 or 1189); married David Soslan also seen as David Sosland, an Ossetian prince, in 1189 or 1190; children: (second marriage) son Giorgi (b. 1194), later George IV, king of Georgia; daughter Rusudani (b. 1195), later queen of Georgia.

Began rule as co-regent with her father (1178); assumed full power with his death (1184); defeated and banished first husband for his attempt to usurp her power (1191); quelled insurgents again (1193); defeated Bogolyubskoi for the last time (1200); during her reign, Georgia flourished culturally and economically, but decline set in not long after her death.

In the mountainous region dotted with old stone fortresses and early Christian churches that spans the area between the Black and Caspian seas, the ancient principality of Georgia has lain from earliest times at a crossroads of human history. Greeks and Romans came there to trade, and when the Ottoman Empire forced many of Georgia's neighbors to convert to Islam, its people held fast to their ancient form of Christianity. Near the end of the 12th century, the reign of Queen Tamara marked the country's golden age, with its capital at Tiflis, then one of the largest cities in the world, having a population of almost 100,000. Under Communist domination for most of the 20th century, Georgians remained staunch capitalists, trading and selling in most of the markets of the Soviet Union, even then demonstrating some of the same fierce independence that Queen Tamara came to symbolize in her day.

When Tamara came to power, she was the only remaining descendant in the Bagrationi line. Most of the kingdom had been unified by Bagrat III, who reigned from 975 to 1014, except for the capital city of Tiflis which was still in the hands of Muslim emirs. More than half a century after Bagrat's rule, Tamara's great-grandfather, David the Builder, conquered more territory, including Tiflis, during a rule lasting from 1089 to 1125. David was aided by European Crusaders, who had arrived in the Levant to recapture Jerusalem from the Seljuk Turks. While the Turks were defending themselves on that front, David won the brilliant victories that secured his lands.

The Georgian kingdom was structured along feudal lines that would change little until the 19th century. Nobles and members of the church held their domains in trust for the sovereign, in return for their allegiance to him in times of war. The country was divided into provinces ruled by dukes, or *erist'avs*, and the

Tamara

(1160–1212)

central administration was carried out by five *vazirs*, or ministers, including the chancellor (a position usually held by an archbishop), the war minister, the lord chamberlain, the chancellor of the exchequer, and the *atabag*, or lord high constable.

Tamara was the only legitimate child of a princess of the Caucasian kingdom of Osseti and King George III of Georgia. The fact that she was female meant that her father had to choose whether to name her as his successor or name a male who was not born into the ruling line of Georgia. King George chose to name Tamara, and implemented a sort of political campaign to ensure her acceptance by the Georgian nobility, church and military on his death.

During her reign . . . Georgia reached the height of its power, stretching from the Black Sea to the Caspian, and uniting under its throne countless different races in addition to the Georgians themselves.

—**Michael Pereira**

In 1178, after it became evident that there would be no more royal children, the king held a ceremony in which his daughter, only 18 years old, was declared "King of Kartli" and crowned co-ruler with him. This was a calculated move on George's part to convince his nobles that he wished Tamara to succeed him and that he believed she would be a competent ruler. During the coronation ritual, Tamara was named "Mountain of God" and received homage from the highest members of the church hierarchy as well as important nobles and military leaders. For the six remaining years of King George's life, Tamara acted as queen-regnant, sharing the responsibilities of rule.

On her father's death in 1184, Tamara assumed the throne as sole ruler of Georgia, and was crowned once more, to reaffirm her right to the succession. At the time of her succession, and throughout her long reign, Georgia was a large, prosperous kingdom stretching north to the Caucasus mountains and south to Armenia. Located between the Christian European west and the Islamic Middle East, it was a region constantly sought after by competing kingdoms and empires; added to its vulnerability in terms of geography was its constant state of internal warfare and civil strife, created by the warrior mentality and feudal government.

Tamara faced resistance to her rule from nobles in the country who wanted to limit royal power by setting up a legislative body with authority equal to that of the sovereign. The move was due in part to the resentment her father had aroused with arbitrary shows of favoritism, and paralleled what was going on in England at roughly the same time, when nobles enforced limits on the royal power of King John through their creation of the document known as the Magna Carta.

In Georgia, Queen Tamara was a much stronger and more practical ruler than King John. Through negotiation with the major feudal lords, she retained executive and legislative authority, although she was forced to consult with a council on affairs of state. Her struggle was due to the habits of fierce independence among her people, however, and not because she was a woman. Georgian women had always been accorded a high place in community life, and the people traditionally took pride in differentiating themselves from Muslims by their equal treatment of women as well as their acceptance of Christianity.

Only 24 years old, Tamara was kept under the guardianship of her aunt Rusudani, a particularly powerful influence during her reign. Rusudani was strong-minded and wily, and Tamara often turned to her for advice. History documents Tamara's many qualities of leadership: she was a good administrator, a steady soldier, and a careful diplomat, wise as well as pious, gentle, and humane. As queen, she was often described as forceful but maternal, and she was obeyed by her subjects out of love and respect—although to do otherwise would generally have been foolish.

Since Tamara was not a young woman by the standards of the time, it was important to secure an heir to the throne, so the nobles and Rusudani chose the queen's first husband. George Bogolyubski, son of Andrew of Suzdal, grand prince of Kiev, was an arrogant, selfish man. Following their marriage in 1187, Tamara was hard put to bear with her husband's constant drunken debauchery. She had been raised in the Orthodox Church of her parents, and created a court characterized by piety and austerity, two qualities Bogolyubski did not share. Although Tamara enjoyed popularity and the loyalty of most of her subjects, there were, not surprisingly, a number of Georgia's aristocrats who did not believe they should be ruled by a woman. Part of Tamara's motivation for marrying George was his military prowess, which he fostered by making continuous war on the Muslim peoples to the south. Tamara hoped his reputation would help shore up support for her reign among the military and nobility who might be inclined to rebel against a sole female ruler. However, George eventually became more of a liability than an asset, especially as a couple of years passed and Tamara remained childless. Apart from her personal dislike of George, the fact that the couple had no children after so long a time meant that Tamara had no real reason to keep him as her king-consort. Instead of choosing to have him punished for his misdemeanors, in 1187–88 she petitioned an assembly of bishops and nobles for a divorce, and exiled her ex-husband to Byzantium (Greece). The characteristically clement queen sent him off with many luxurious parting gifts.

Tamara married a second time soon after banishing George. This time the choice was her own, the noble David Sosland, an Ossetian prince from the same province as her mother. (Ossetia was a territory of the Georgian kingdom.) Tamara and David were a much more suitable couple, and in due time Tamara had two children: a son Giorgi or George, born in 1194, and a daughter ❧▸ **Rusudani**, born a year later. Not long after her second wedding in 1191, the queen faced the first serious opposition to her reign, led by none other than her exiled first husband. George Bogolyubski had traveled to Turkey, where he apparently convinced the sultan of Erzerum that together they could conquer Georgia. Only the eastern provinces rose to the queen's defense, and during the summer of 1191 her position was seriously threatened. Armies led by three insurgent nobles converged on Tiflis, and Bogolyubskoi was proclaimed king. He held the position only briefly, however, before Tamara's armies rose up defeated the three insurgents. The rebellion failed, despite considerable support from some of the nobility of western Georgia, after the queen herself led her army in two battles against the invading forces of her ex-husband. Despite his attempted coup, Tamara again treated Bogolyubski with leniency, and rather than having him put to death, released him into exile to Byzantium once more. Instead of being grateful for escaping with his life for a second time, the persistent Kievan prince tried to take the kingdom by force once again in 1200, and once again Tamara's troops defeated him and forced him from Georgia.

Tamara faced other internal threats to her throne after 1191, mostly from disaffected nobles eager to seek their own aggrandizement during the reign of a female monarch. However, she managed to put down every conspiracy and rebellion against her, although the constant threat led her to pursue aggressive military policies as a means of maintaining control. Like many queens, she showed herself to be adept at

❧▸ **Rusudani** (b. 1195)

Queen of Georgia. *Name variations: Russudan or Rusudan. Born in 1195 in Georgia (Russia); daughter of Queen Tamara (1160–1212) and David Soslan or Sosland; sister of Giorgi (b. 1194), later George IV, king of Georgia; children: son David Narin.*

The daughter of Queen *Tamara, Rusudani inherited the throne of Georgia in 1223, after the years of her brother George IV's reign had seen the kingdom start to fall from the pinnacle it reached under their mother. This was in large part due to George's inattention to policy and military matters, but the rising power of Genghis Khan and his Mongol hordes also wreaked havoc in the country. Rusudani, described as "unmarried but not a virgin queen," apparently was not much interested in statecraft, but she responded readily to military threats and opportunities. From 1225, she battled off and on for years with a prince of the Khwarizmians whose armies had claimed part of southern Georgia and occupied and sacked the capital city of Tiflis. Rusudani ruled from the city of Kutais until the Khwarizmian prince beat a hasty retreat from the approach of a Mongol army. The Mongols then turned to fight Persia, and the queen reoccupied Tiflis. She was forced to flee again in 1236 as the Mongols returned. This time they claimed the country for good, but it was not until 1243 that Rusudani formally agreed to Georgia's becoming a vassal state. By this time she was co-ruling with her young son David Narin, and the agreement with the Mongols, which allowed the Georgian government its autonomy in exchange for the payment of massive taxes, was meant to ensure that her son would inherit the whole of the country. The deal was not honored after Rusudani's death, however, and he inherited only a piece of it.

military strategy, and often rode into battle herself, a calculated move to motivate her troops to equal valor on the battlefield. Her policies were astonishingly successful in expanding her already extensive kingdom and gathering many important protectorates under Georgian rule.

During Tamara's reign, the great flowering of Georgian culture resulted in a golden age. The country's prosperity was unprecedented and its citizens felt a sense of unity and security they had never known before. Over half of its land was mountainous, and rich in minerals such as copper, iron, gold, and agate. Its precious metals had been fashioned for centuries into beautiful jewelry, and during Tamara's reign its artisans produced works of art in the form of necklaces, bracelets, and swords. Copper coins were minted using the monogram of the queen, and she became known, as sovereigns often do, for the construction carried out during her reign, including roads, bridges, a caravansary, fortresses, churches, and monasteries. More than a thousand years later, some of this architecture still attests to her power.

Music, painting, and literature also flourished under her rule. Some writings from the second half of the 12th century remain an important part of Georgia's heritage even today. Shota Rustaveli's saga *The Man in the Panther's Skin*, written during Tamara's reign, is considered one of the masterpieces of world literature. Dedicated to Tamara and her husband David, the work is written with classical clarity and characterized by lofty aspirations, heroic spirit, open-mindedness, and nobility of thought. Its heroine is the virtuous and gentle Nestan-Darejan, who rebels against a forced marriage and is forced to undergo imprisonment. Three knights swear to free her. Many have wondered if Tamara's own life did not inspire this literary work, which elevated Georgian poetry to new heights.

Within the complex and sophisticated social hierarchy and vast bureaucracy of the country, there were many court officials who served the queen in addition to her five vazirs. Some titles from that period gradually evolved into common Georgian surnames. Some known today which originated in large households include Amilakhvari (Master of the Royal Stables); Amirejibi (Master of the Chamber); and Meghvinetukhutsesi (Chief Wine Steward).

Throughout her reign, Tamara enjoyed the consistent loyalty and love of her subjects, who referred to her as their King Tamara, there apparently being no word for "queen" in the Georgian language. She died at the height of her power and popularity at age 53, and was deeply mourned by the Georgian people. Including her years as co-ruler, Tamara reigned for 34 years, greatly expanding her kingdom and increasing its prosperity; her memory is still preserved in Georgian culture, as she represents the pinnacle of the Georgian golden age.

Her son George IV, age 18, succeeded to the throne, and soon revealed an inaptitude for government as great as his mother's aptitude had been. Unconcerned with the lives of his subjects, he squandered his time with companions and refused to marry, leaving only an illegitimate child when he died young in 1223, a few years into his reign. The throne then went to Tamara's daughter Rusudani, who shared her brother's disinterest in the responsibilities of kingship. In 1236, she was forced to flee Georgia during the invasion of the armies of the great Mongolian leader Genghis Khan; leaderless and defenseless, the once-powerful kingdom of Georgia became only an addition to Genghis Khan's lists of conquered countries. Although its government remained autonomous, the country was forced to pay a heavy tribute, and taxation ruined the rural population while the towns declined. Beginning in 1403, there was a brief respite, but the growth of the Ottoman Empire put the Caucusus region under permanent Turkish influence. In 1801, Georgia was annexed by Russia, and it remained part of the Russian empire until the collapse of the Soviet Union in the late 20th century.

But in the land once ruled by Tamara, Georgians have never forgotten their golden age. Churches, fortresses, and palaces are still there to remind them of the kingdom which stretched from the Black Sea to the Caspian Sea, and *The Man in the Panther's Skin* recalls their era of greatness, while the queen of that era has come to symbolize all that was best in this mountainous nation and its people.

SOURCES:

Allen, W.E.D. *A History of the Georgian People.* NY: Barnes & Noble, 1971.

Daniel, Glyn. *The Georgians.* NY: Frederick A. Praeger, 1966.

Fraser, Antonia. "Lion of the Caucasus," in *The Warrior Queens.* NY: Alfred A. Knopf, 1989.

Lang, David Marshall. *The Last Years of the Georgian Monarchy 1658–1832.* NY: Columbia University Press, 1957.

Pereira, Michael. *Across the Caucusus.* London: Geoffrey Bles, 1973.

Uitz, Erika. *The Legend of Good Women: The Liberation of Women in Medieval Cities.* Wakefield, RI: Moyer Bell, 1988.

Wieczynski, Joseph L. *The Modern Encyclopedia of Russian and Soviet History.* Vol. 12. Academic International Press, 1979.

Karin Loewen Haag,
freelance writer,
Athens, Georgia

Tamiris (fl. 550–530 BCE)

Scythian queen. Name variations: Tamyris, Tomyris. Flourished between 550 and 530 BCE; warrior queen and ruler of the nomadic Massagetae tribe in Persia (now Iran), who lived beyond the lower Oxus River by the Aral Sea.

According to Herodotus, Tamiris spurned a marriage offer from Cyrus II the Great, founder of the great Persian Empire, who was after her kingdom along with her hand. In 530 BCE, though nearly 70, Cyrus campaigned in the distant northeastern part of his realm against Tamiris and the nomadic Massagatae and established an outpost on the Jaxartes River called Cyropolis (Cyreschata, modern Kurkath). With her son at the helm, Tamiris sent her armies to abort his invasion. When her son was slain, she led the army in his stead. Toward the end of July 530 BCE, she defeated Cyrus and he was killed in battle. On August 12, a text from Borsippa still bore the date "in the 9th year of Cyrus, of the King of the Lands," as news of the king's death had not yet reached Mesopotamia. But by August 31, the inscriptions at Babylon read, "Year of the beginning of the rule of Cambyses, of the King of the Lands." The body of the great monarch was transported about a thousand miles to be placed in his tomb at Pasargadae.

Tamiris, Helen (1902–1966)

American dancer and choreographer who contributed to a political outlook in modern dance and strived for communal support of the nascent art form. Name variations: Helen Becker. Pronunciation: Ta-MEER-iss. Born Helen Becker on April 24, 1902, in New York City; died of cancer on August 4, 1966, in New York City; only daughter and youngest of five children of Isor Becker (a tailor) and Rose (Simoneff) Becker (d. 1905, both Russian-Jewish immigrants); completed high school; married Daniel Nagrin, on September 3, 1943 (separated 1964); no children.

Made New York solo concert debut (1927); organized Dance Repertory Theater (1930–32); was a primary choreographer for Dance Project within the Federal Theater Project of the Works Progress Administration; served as the first president of the American Dance Association; choreographed for Broadway musicals (1940–50s); won Tony award for Touch and Go (1949).

Concert dances: "Subconscious" (1927); Manifesto (1927); Negro Spirituals (1929); Walt Whitman Suite (1934); Harvest 1935 (1935); How Long Brethren? (1937); Trojan Incident (1938); Adelante (1939); Dance for Walt Whitman (1958).

Selected theater: Annie Get Your Gun (1946); Inside USA (1948); Touch and Go (1949); Fanny (1954); Plain and Fancy (1955).

A tall woman with fiery red hair and dramatic features, Helen Tamiris became as notable for her political dynamism as for her appearances onstage, energizing the burgeoning modern-dance movement in America with her penchant for organizing and her concern for social issues. Her career as a dancer and choreographer encompassed various dance styles, from vaudeville to modern dance and the Broadway stage, and her captivating stage presence enlivened her performances, but it was ultimately her role as

an organizer that had the greater impact on the dance field. In 1927, at the beginning of her entree into modern dance, she wrote a self-titled "Manifesto" declaring the intentions that were to underlie her life's work:

> The dance of today is plagued with exotic gestures, mannerisms and ideas borrowed from literature, philosophy, sculpture and painting. Will people never rebel against artificialities, pseudo-romanticism and affected sophistication? The dance of today must have a dynamic tempo and be valid, precise, spontaneous, free, normal, natural and human.

Helen Becker was born on April 24, 1902, the daughter of Isor Becker and **Rose Simoneff Becker**, Russian-Jewish immigrants living on New York City's Lower East Side. The poverty, endless work of sewing sweatshops, and squalid living conditions of immigrant life indelibly shaped the children of the Becker family, as did the early death of their mother, when Helen was three. Along with two of her four brothers, Tamiris found solace in creativity. One brother became an artist and another a sculptor, while Helen began her dance career with classes at the Henry Street Settlement Playhouse (later known as the Neighborhood Playhouse). This remarkable institution, offering poor children opportunities to develop artistic skills, proved particularly successful in its program of dance classes, providing starts to a number of people, including Tamiris and *Anna Sokolow, who went on to professional dance careers. Classes in Interpretive Dancing and Character Dancing (later known as folk dancing) introduced young girls to the beauty and pleasures of movement and music. By the end of high school, Tamiris had decided to get out of the family house now populated by a stepmother and stepsisters and make dancing her life.

In 1920, Tamiris was hired for the corps de ballet of New York's Metropolitan Opera, where she was paid $12 per week. She stayed for three seasons. Because performance in the opera's ballet corps required more disciplined technique than she had learned, management provided her with three ballet classes per week along with her salary. The artificiality of ballet annoyed Tamiris, however, and pointe work prompted a later scornful remark, "Toe dancing. . . . Why not dance on the palms of the hands?" She soon developed a reputation as "wild Becker" for not keeping to the corps line, and for an exuberance that sometimes overtook others on the stage. The yearning to break out of ballet's restricting confines and to have the stage to herself were desires she would soon heed.

One benefit of the job at the Metropolitan Opera was that it allowed for summers off, during which she toured with other opera companies. On tour in South America, she became romantically involved with a South American writer who introduced her to political activism and new forms of literature and art. He also christened her with a new name from a poem about an ancient Persian queen: "Thou art *Tamiris, the ruthless queen who banishes all obstacles."

In 1923, Tamiris was 21 and still in the Metropolitan Opera corps when she attended a performance of the renowned modern dancer *Isadora Duncan at the Brooklyn Academy of Music. Duncan's presentation cemented Tamiris' break with ballet. Taking up classes at the Duncan school, she also recalled the lessons from the Henry Street Settlement, encouraging her to listen attentively to the music and move from the soul. Eventually Duncan's classes would inspire Tamiris to stop studying at schools and go out on her own.

But first the need to support herself led her to take various jobs with revues, where she earned far more money than with the opera (up to $125 a week). She grew increasingly dissatisfied, however, with being forced to be an entertaining spectacle. Each dance, she wrote in a draft of an autobiography, "was designed to astonish the audience—one surprise movement after another, like placing one brightly colored bead after another on a string with no relationship between them." What she longed to do was to create an entire program of meaningful dance.

On October 9, 1927, when Tamiris was 25, she at last made her debut as a soloist in modern dance to a sold-out audience at the Little Theater in Manhattan. Her program included 12 dances, ranging from the use of jazz music to the depiction of a circus, a piece inspired by Freud, entitled "Subconscious" and performed to Debussy, and one using no music at all. John Martin, the influential dance critic of *The New York Times*, gave the recital a mixed review; though he extolled her as a dancer of natural gifts, with long lines and a good sense of rhythm, he thought that she lacked technique. But reviewing her second concert, only a few months later, he placed her at the "forefront of the younger generation" of modern dancers, adding that she possessed a "warmth of style."

In the 1930s, while ceaseless accolades were paid to *Martha Graham, *Doris Humphrey and Charles Weidman, it was Tamiris who gave modern dance both a coherent social structure and a political voice. Her entrenched sense of mission, best displayed in her 1927 "Manifesto," placed her as a noticeable leader of the modern-dance movement, without her being its most talented progenitor. In 1930, just three years after her modern-dance debut, she organized the Dance Repertory Theater in an effort to combat the almost insurmountable costs of theatrical productions. Her idea was to have four leading modern dancers—Graham, Humphrey, Weidman and herself—perform on alternating nights for a week in a single theater. The benefits of this approach were to greatly reduce the cost of solo productions, consolidate the scattered audience of modern dance, and widen its support. The repertory company lasted for two seasons (with the addition of *Agnes de Mille in the 1931–32 season) but fell to the egoistic squabbles of the performers and the worsening economy of the Great Depression. In the next significant grouping of modern dancers, at the Bennington Summer School of Dance begun in 1934, Tamiris was not invited to participate. Why she was excluded remains obscure. Recalling the Bennington years for an oral history project, participants did not offer a definitive reason, but suggested a variety of reasons, including the belief that Tamiris did not measure up to the quality of a dancer like Graham, and that her political stances diminished the artistry of her work.

Despite the Bennington snub, Tamiris remained at the forefront of New York's modern-dance scene. In 1935, she was elected the first president of the Dance Association (renamed the American Dance Association in 1937). Before that, she served on the board of directors of the Concert Dancers' League, where she engaged in a battle to allow dance concerts on Sundays. Puritanical standards about the prurience of live performances still ruled the law books, making it illegal for plays, musical comedies, and dance to occur on Sunday, the Christian holy day. The fact that theaters were closed to regular performances made Sunday the only night some stages were available for smaller and less costly productions. The law was finally rescinded in 1932.

During the years of the Great Depression, Tamiris attempted to form a union of dancers, to help combat the greatly diminished opportunities for work. She was a strong supporter of the Dance Project of the WPA's Federal Theater Project, and choreographed works performed by the group. Later, during World War II, she worked again for the federal government, performing in a show presented by the U.S. Department of Agriculture, *It's Up to You*. In a bit of well-intended government propaganda, the USDA aimed to discourage people from buying illegal

items on the black market that were being rationed for the war; Tamiris danced as Porterhouse Lucy the Black-Market Steak. In 1944, she staged *The People's Bandwagon*, a revue for the reelection campaign of Franklin Roosevelt which utilized an interracial cast.

Throughout her career, Tamiris' strong advocacy for African-Americans distinguished her within the modern-dance movement. During the 1930s, other modern dancers ignored racial issues or treated them thematically in their choreography without actually employing black dancers. Tamiris included dances to Negro spiritual music as early as her second solo concert, in 1928, and such pieces became signatures of her repertory for the rest of her career. In 1936, she staged a piece of a larger work of hers for the Federal Theater Negro Ensemble, and *How Long Brethren?*, first staged in 1937, became an even more compelling achievement. Choreographed as part of the Dance Project of the Federal Theater Project, the show employed a large black chorus to sing seven songs of protest while dancers depicted the many injustices suffered by African-Americans. *How Long Brethren?* played to standing-room-only audiences, changing locations as the run was extended to several months.

The validity of modern dance is rooted in its ability to express modern problems and, further, to make modern audiences want to do something about them.

—Helen Tamiris

Like many others in the field during the 1930s, Tamiris used the nascent and expansive form of modern dance to create works making political statements. Artists and intellectuals of the 1930s frequently became politicized, particularly in debating the merits of socialism and communism. For many, the political awareness of the era was manifested in an artistic preoccupation with defining America and an American style for a particular art form. Louis Horst, the influential accompanist to many modern dancers "could not understand my insistence upon calling my dances American," wrote Tamiris. "To him it seemed paradoxical and inconsistent that I could speak of an American dance and a Universal dance in the same breath."

This combination, in fact, was exactly what she hoped to achieve. With her *Walt Whitman Suite* (1934), she showcased the problems facing Chinese laborers and African-Americans in the U.S. and ended with a more abstract plea for unity and peace, again at the forefront of putting African-Americans into such visions of America. From her *Negro Spirituals* to the multiracial cast of a Broadway revue entitled *Inside U.S.A.* (1948), she provided an integrated, diverse picture of America well before Jim Crow laws were outlawed in the South.

In 1944, at age 42, Tamiris ended her performing career. Concentrating on choreography, she became well known in the 1940–50s for her work in Broadway musicals. Bringing a modern dancer's sensibility to the meaning of movement (along with Agnes de Mille and *Hanya Holm), she gave a new importance to the role of the chore-

ographer in musicals. Her Broadway work included *Annie Get Your Gun* (1946), starring *Ethel Merman as *Annie Oakley, Fanny (1954), Plain and Fancy (1955) and Touch and Go (1949), for which she was awarded a Tony. Unencumbered by standards of art that had caused many modern dancers to disdain Broadway, she choreographed for musicals and demonstrated to actors how to better the rhythmical action of their bodies, and in doing so broadened the impact of dance.

In 1960, Tamiris came back to modern dance more fully, when she formed the Tamiris-Nagrin Dance Company with her husband Daniel Nagrin, whom she had married in 1946. The company lasted only a few years, as Nagrin and Tamiris separated in January 1964, but the return drew her back to promoting modern dance. She proposed a company similar to the earlier Dance Repertory Theater, but this one, the American Modern Dance Theater, was to be one group made up of leading stars and an ensemble instead of the fractious grouping of different companies. In 1963, she was also outspoken in berating the Ford Foundation for its massive $8 million grant to bolster ballet in the United States, while lending no support to modern dance. Tamiris correctly prophesied the formation of an audience that would provide continued financial security for ballet companies, while modern dance would be forced to struggle for survival and not even begin to attain the popularity and support allotted to ballet.

Tamiris remained involved in raising the status of African-Americans in dance. At a 1964 conference on "Creative Use of Minorities in Theater," she praised dance for the general acceptance of dancers of various ethnic backgrounds across the spectrum of companies, but she also accurately noted the problem that remained: training. African-Americans more typically ended up dancing in a jazz style because they were deprived of the opportunities to learn ballet or modern dance at a young age. In urging people to address this more subtle form of discrimination that relegated African-Americans to only a small selection of roles, her prescient perspective again mirrored trends in American society as a whole.

Dispirited by the tumultuous break with her husband and financially impoverished by medical bills, Tamiris lost her vivacious and defiant spirit in her last months. On August 4, 1966, at age 64, she died of cancer in a nursing home in the Bronx. Fittingly known as the "social conscience" of modern dance, she had added a commitment to social change to the passion of artistry, and left a legacy of moral purpose for other dancers to follow.

SOURCES:

Lloyd, Margaret. *The Borzoi Book of Modern Dance.* NY: Knopf, 1949.

Obituary, in *Dance Magazine.* September 1966, p. 6.

Schlundt, Christena L. *Tamiris: A Chronicle of Her Dance Career 1927–1955.* NY: New York Public Library-Astor, Lenox and Tilden Foundations, 1972.

Tamiris, Helen. "Tamiris in Her Own Voice: Draft of an Autobiography," in *Studies in Dance History.* Trans., ed. and annotated by Daniel Nagrin. Vol. 1, no. 1. Fall–Winter 1989.

SUGGESTED READING:

Jowitt, Deborah. *Time and the Dancing Image.* NY: William Morrow, 1988.

RELATED MEDIA:

Film excerpts of *Walt Whitman Suite, Negro Spirituals, Memoir, Women's Song* in the Dance Collection, Performing Arts Library, New York Public Library.

"Trailblazers of Modern Dance," WNET-NY's Great Performances: Dance in America Series, 1977.

COLLECTIONS:

Correspondence, papers, film clips, photographs in Helen Tamiris Collection, Dance Collection, Performing Arts Library, New York Public Library.

Julia L. Foulkes,
University of Massachusetts,
Amherst, Massachusetts

Tamyris (fl. 550–530 BCE).

See Tamiris.

Tanaka, Kinuyo (1910–1977)

Japanese actress and director. Born on November 23, 1910 (also seen as 1907 and December 29, 1909), in Shinomoseki, Japan; died on March 21, 1977; attended Tennoji Elementary School, Osaka, Japan; married Hiroshi Shimizu (a director), in 1929 (divorced); no children.

Selected filmography as actress: A Woman from the Genroku Era *(1924);* Ochimusha *(1925);* Torrent *(1926);* Intimate Dream *(1927);* Tales from a Land by the Sea *(1928);* The Village Bride *(1928);* I Graduated But . . . *(1929);* Oyosan *(1930);* I Flunked But . . . *(1931);* The Loyal Forty-Seven Ronin *(1932);* A Woman of Tokyo *(1933);* An Innocent Maid *(1935);* New Way *(1936);* The Tree of Love *(1937);* Woman of Osaka *(1940);* Musashi Miyamoto *(1944);* The Victory of Women *(1946);* The Love of the Actress Sumako *(1947);* Women of the Night *(1948);* My Love Has Been Burning *(1951);* Mother *(1952);* Life of Oharu *(1952);* Four Chimneys *(1953);* Ugetsu *(1953);* Sansho the Bailiff (The Bailiff, *1954);* Flowing *(1956);* Ballad of Narayama *(1958);* Equinox Flower *(1958);* Eternity of Love *(1961);* Lonely Lane *(1962);* Alone on the Pacific (My Enemy the Sea, *1963);* Red Beard *(1965);* Judo Champion *(1967);* Sandakan 8 *(1975);* Daichi no Komori-uta *(1976).*

Selected filmography as director: Love Letter *(also acted, 1953);* The Moon Rises *(also acted, 1955);* The Eternal Breasts *(also acted, 1955);* A Wandering Princess *(also acted, 1958);* Girls of the Night *(1961);* Love Under the Crucifix *(1962).*

The only woman film director to come out of Japan during the 1950s, Kinuyo Tanaka was a famous and respected actress before venturing behind the camera. In light of the conventional Japanese society of the 1950s, in which women's roles were strictly defined, her desire to stretch the boundaries was greeted with fierce opposition, and only through the most determined effort was she able to make six films. Faced with continued professional hostility and audience indifference, she finally abandoned her directoral pursuits and returned to acting.

Tanaka began her film career in the silent era and acted in more than 240 films, including Japan's first talkie and first color film. She won the Japan Kinema Jumpo Award for Best Actress for her work in *Ballad of Narayama* (1958) and the Best Actress Award at the Berlin Festival for *Sandakan 8* (1975). As an actress, she worked with some of Japan's most highly respected directors, among them Yasujiro Ozu and Kenji Mizoguchi. Tanaka was inspired to direct after learning that some American actresses, such as *Ida Lupino and *Claudette Colbert, were considering directoral projects; a visit to Hollywood in the winter of 1949 made her even more determined. Back home, however, Tanaka met with vehement opposition, particularly from the directors' union, then headed by Kenji Mizoguchi, who ironically had directed her in some of the era's most sensitive movies about women. A few within the ranks, however, were more supportive; Mikio Naruse served as a mentor by taking her on as an assistant director, and Keisuke Kinoshita and Yasujiro Ozu worked as scriptwriters for several of her projects.

According to Philip Kemp, Tanaka was not a particularly innovative director, but she brought a female sensitivity to previously established cinematic forms. "Women, who take the key roles in all her films, are treated not just with sympathy, but with a humorous affection rare in Japanese cinema of the period," he writes; he cites the spontaneous and warm father-daughter relationship in *The Moon Has Risen* (1955) and the relaxed natural interactions in *Love Under the Crucifix* (1962). All of Tanaka's films focus on women who must overcome prejudice in order to achieve their desired goals, and two of her films, *The Eternal Breasts*

(1955) and *Girls of the Night* (1961), were scripted by the noted feminist writer **Sukie Tanaka** (no relation). In Kemp's assessment, Tanaka's most remarkable film was *The Eternal Breasts*, based on the true story of a young woman poet (**Fumiko Nakashiro**), who is stricken with breast cancer. "Chilling, clinical images convey Fumiko's vulnerability and fear at the invasion of her body, first by the disease and then by a double mastectomy; while Tanaka celebrates the surge of sexuality her heroine experiences after the operation as a brief, defiant assertion of life and erotic joy in the face of approaching death."

Following the example of the heroine of her last directoral project, *Love under the Crucifix* (1962), who chooses death over a life out of her control, Tanaka opted to leave directing in 1962, with her dignity intact. The actress-director, who was married briefly to director Hiroshi Shimizu, continued to act in films until 1975. She died of a brain tumor on March 21, 1977.

SOURCES:

Katz, Ephraim. *The Film Encyclopedia*. NY: Harper-Collins, 1994.

Kemp, Philip. "Kinuyo Tanaka," in *The St. James Women Filmmakers Encyclopedia*. Edited by Amy L. Unterburger. Detroit, MI: Visible Ink, 1999.

Barbara Morgan,
Melrose, Massachusetts

Tanaquil (fl. late 7th–early 6th BCE)

Etruscan woman who was the reason her husband and her son-in-law became the first two Etruscan kings of Rome. Name variations: Caia Caecilia. Flourished between late 7th and early 6th BCE; died after 579 BCE; married Lucumo, later known as Lucius Tarquinius Priscus (or Tarquin); children: sons Lucius and Arruns; daughters (names unknown).

It cannot be known for certain whether the deeds attributed by much later sources to Tanaquil, a shadowy figure from Rome's regal period, are truly historical. Nevertheless, it is probable that she was a figure of history, and not merely of myth. She was probably from the Etruscan city of Tarquinii, and of noble birth. It is attested that she married Lucumo, one of two sons of a Demaratus, a wealthy Greek from Corinth who had settled in Tarquinii after being politically exiled from his native city. As the tale goes, Arruns, the second son of Demaratus, and then Demaratus himself, died in quick succession. Before he passed away, however, Arruns fathered a son by his wife, whose pregnancy never became known to her father-in-law before he expired. Thus, when Demaratus bequeathed his es-

tate, he did so only to Lucumo, who never shared any of it with his nephew, which he would have been forced to do had Demaratus known of the latter's existence. Such avarice was characteristic of Lucumo, as was ambition: two traits he held in common with Tanaquil, who is said to have been unwilling in marriage to endure any less lofty a level of material comfort or influence than she had known in the house of her father. Both husband and wife yearned for a social status which the citizens of Tarquinii were unwilling to grant them, because, although wealthy when he came to Tarquinii, Demaratus was a foreigner and was known to be of illegitimate birth. Hence, Lucumo was tainted by the liminality of his father.

Frustrated because her husband would never attain the honor that she wanted him to win in her native city, Tanaquil is said to have convinced Lucumo to emigrate to Rome, a younger city with a growing population where there would be room for an intrepid and ambitious man. Tanaquil is also alleged to have known that Rome already had been ruled by two kings of foreign birth, while the mother of the reigning monarch, Ancus Marcius, was non-Roman. Tradition has it that while Tanaquil and Lucumo were on the Janiculum (then not within Rome's limits) and about to enter the city for the first time, an eagle gently swooped down upon Lucumo in order to remove his hat, only to descend a second time to replace it on his head. Tanaquil is said to have been a gifted seer (the Romans believed the Etruscans to have been especially skilled in the reading of religious signs), who at this strange sequence of events joyously predicted that her husband was bound for greatness. Her reasons for doing so were as follows: the eagle (Jupiter's special bird) had approached Lucumo from an auspicious quadrant of the sky (probably from the right-front), it had seized his hat while not coming into contact with some baser part of his body, and had returned the hat to its appropriate place in an act of homage.

Thus came Lucumo and Tanaquil to Rome where they procured a home, and where in order to break from the past, Tanaquil convinced her husband to adopt a new name, which he did. Henceforth, Lucumo would be known as Lucius Tarquinius Priscus (or Tarquin). Rome's newest sensations ingratiated themselves with the local population through diplomatic speech, robust hospitality, and liberal beneficence. Their arrival so impressed the locals that it soon drew the attention of Rome's king. Ancus Marcius called Tarquin into his presence and was allegedly so affected by his deportment that he soon made it his habit to consult Tarquin on a number of topics, both public and private. Tarquin's stock rose with the king to the point that when he was on his deathbed (traditionally 617 BCE), he appointed Tarquin as the guardian of his two sons, both of whom were close to, but not quite yet at, the age of their majority. When Ancus Marcius died, Tarquin sent these would-be heirs on a hunting expedition while he canvassed the Roman Senate and people for the royal throne. (This is an eteliological story, for Tarquin was later believed to have established the model by which magistrates during the Republic campaigned for office.) Pointing out that Rome had known kings of foreign birth before, that he had held Ancus Marcius' confidence, that he had bestowed benefactions on most Romans since his arrival in their city, and that the former king's sons were still minors, Tarquin won the day and the throne. Goaded by Tanaquil, Tarquin had fulfilled the omen of greatness to come.

Among the accomplishments attributed to Tarquin were victories in war against several Latin cities and the Sabines, the drainage of the marshy lowlands which heretofore had prevented the isolated settlements on Rome's seven hills from meshing together into one continuous urban center, the fortification of the city with a wall of stone, and the foundation of what was to become Rome's most important temple, that dedicated to Jupiter "the Greatest and Best" on the Capitoline Hill.

Throughout all of her husband's reign, Tanaquil is said to have prodded his endeavors. More specifically, she is also alleged to have played the dominant role in the selection of Tarquin's successor, just as she had been germinal to his own accession. Although Tanaquil and Tarquin would eventually produce two sons—Lucius and Arruns—an omen recognized for what it was by Tanaquil proved decisive when it came to the issue of Tarquin's successor. It is said that one day a boy of servile status, although of noble birth, exhibited signs of future greatness. This child, Servius Tullius (578–535 BCE), was a son of the king (of the same name) of Corniculum, a town which Tarquin had subjected to Rome. In the process of this conquest, the elder Servius Tullius had been slain, and his pregnant wife captured. She was brought to Tarquin's palace, where her son was raised modestly, as befit one who was essentially war booty. One day this youth fell asleep in some public place, during which time his head was observed by many witnesses to have been engulfed in flames. The hue and cry which followed attracted the attention of the Roman king and queen. When Tanaquil arrived, a minion was about to fetch some water so as to douse the flames. Tanaquil forbade this action and commanded all to leave Servius Tullius alone until such time as he awoke by himself. Not long after, he is supposed to have done just that, at which time the fire was miraculously extinguished. Taking her husband aside, Tanaquil advised Tarquin to raise the boy as if he were a member of their own family. This was done, and Servius Tullius is said to have matured into the noblest "Roman" of his generation. Eventually, Tarquin—with Tanaquil's approval—married a daughter to Servius Tullius, who was thereafter favored in the succession.

After Tarquin had reigned for 38 years, and as it became increasingly clear that he intended to make Servius Tullius his successor, the bitter sons of Ancus Marcius, who felt that Tarquin had stolen their royal legacy from them, decided to take their revenge. It is maintained that they induced two shepherds to carry out the assassination of Tarquin so that they might challenge the ever more likely accession of Servius Tullius before his position became too entrenched to upset. These assassins staged a mock argument before the gates of the palace, and raised such a ruckus that it attracted the attention of Tarquin. Making an appearance as an arbiter of justice, Tarquin attempted to resolve the feigned dispute, but while he attended to the impassioned complaints of one of the parties, the other is said to have split his head in two with an axe.

Although the shepherds attempted an escape, both were captured by the king's lictors (guards and symbols of political authority) before they cleared the palace grounds. Amid the chaos that followed these actions, Tanaquil arrived to find her husband on the threshold of death. She assumed control of the situation by ordering the lictors to eject all of the witnesses to the assassination and by sealing off the palace grounds. Although she tried to save Tarquin's life, Tanaquil soon realized that her husband would die. Nevertheless, she is said to have decisively acted to procure Rome's political stability by ordering Servius Tullius to do as she commanded: to take vengeance upon his enemies, to protect her interests in a world which had been suddenly redefined, and to follow the "guidance" of the gods. Then, it is asserted that she went to a window on the second floor of the palace from which she could address the confused crowd of citizens which had begun to congregate before the closed palace gate. There, she asserted that the news was good: the king had been stunned by the blow of an attempted assassin, but he had survived and the prognosis for his recovery was good. All the same, she continued, Tarquin needed time for recovery. In the meantime, she added, he had decided to appoint Servius Tullius as his royal proxy. Tanaquil's son-in-law was thereafter bedecked in the royal robes-of-state, was escorted by the lictors who traditionally accompanied the king, and was set upon the accustomed royal chair, from which he began to sit in legal judgment and to act as king.

After a few days, the true fate of Tarquin became known throughout Rome, but Servius Tullius, with the consent of the Senate, continued to rule. The sons of Ancus Marcius, knowing about Servius Tullius' popularity and understanding that their agents had been captured alive, had already gone into self-imposed exile. Meanwhile, Tanaquil's sons, Lucius and Arruns, deprived of their mother's political support and bought off by marriages to the two daughters of Servius Tullius, saw fit to maintain low profiles and to postpone any ambitions either might have maintained towards the throne, at least for a time. (It is alleged that Lucius' first wife Tullia was a docile soul, while the *Tullia who married Arruns was cut more in the mold of Tanaquil. This second Tullia was said to have fretted over Arruns' lack of political ambition. Eventually she approached Lucius and offered herself as a political ally if each would first murder their current spouses. To this Lucius agreed, and after the gentle Tullia and Arruns had been removed from the scene, an unenthusiastic Servius Tullius, who was not aware of the murders, agreed to the marriage of the ambitious Tullia and Lucius. These later planned and carried out a coup against Servius Tullius, and eventually murdered him. The brazen Tullia is even said to have driven her chariot over the remains of her dead father. Years later, the rape of Roman matron *Lucretia by Tullia's and Lucius' son Sextus Tarquin would lead to the overthrow of Lucius' reign and the establishment of the Roman Republic.)

It is not unlikely that Tanaquil could have played a decisive role in the accessions of her husband and son-in-law, for women in Etruscan society, and to a certain extent in Roman, had much more freedom of action in both private and public affairs than did many of their counterparts in other ancient societies. Again, it is not known precisely how much of the material cited here is historical, although some of it likely is. Regardless, however Machiavellian Tanaquil's reputation might have been, during the historical period her liberality as a queen was revered for centuries after her death (after 579 BCE). So too were one of her girdles and the robe-of-state worn by Servius Tullius, both of which were said to have been woven by Tanaquil herself. Even so, by the 1st century of the common era, the name "Tanaquil" had become a readily accepted synonym for an "imperious woman."

William S. Greenwalt,
Professor of Classical History,
Santa Clara University,
Santa Clara, California

Tanaquille (d. 696)

Queen of the Franks. Died in 696; married Clovis III (680–695), king of all Franks (r. 691–695).

Tandy, Jessica (1909–1994)

British-born American actress of stage and screen whose later roles were notable for the grace she brought to her elderly characterizations. Born in London, England, on June 7, 1909; died of ovarian cancer at her home in Easton, Connecticut, on September 11, 1994; daughter of Harry Tandy (a rope manufacturer) and Jessie Helen (Horspool) Tandy; attended Dame Alice Owen's Girls School; trained at the Ben Greet Academy of Acting in London, 1924–27; married Jack Hawkins (an actor), in 1932 (divorced 1940); married Hume Cronyn (an actor), in 1942; children: (first marriage) Susan Hawkins (who married John Tettemer); (second marriage) Christopher Cronyn (b. 1943), **Tandy Cronyn** *(b. 1945, an actress).*

Selected theater: appeared as Ophelia opposite John Gielgud in Hamlet, *in London (1934); appeared as Blanche DuBois in* A Streetcar Named Desire *on Broadway (1947); worked in London and regional theaters, including the Guthrie in Minneapolis, Stratford (Connecticut) American Shakespeare Festival, Shaw Festival at Niagara on the Lake, and Stratford Festival in Ontario, Canada; starred opposite husband Hume Cronyn in* The Fourposter, The Physicists, A Delicate Balance, Noel Coward in Two Keys, The Gin Game, Foxfire, *and* The Petition.

Selected filmography: The Seventh Cross *(1944);* Forever Amber *(1947);* Light in the Forest *(1958);* The Birds *(1963);* Butley *(1974);* The World According to Garp *(1982);* The Bostonians *(1984);* Cocoon *(1985);* Driving Miss Daisy *(1990);* Fried Green Tomatoes *(1991);* Used People *(1992);* "The Story Lady" *(television movie, 1991).*

Television: nominated for an Emmy for her performance in Hallmark Hall of Fame's "To Dance with the White Dog," adapted by **Susan Cooper**, *CBS (1994).*

Once, when credited for "creating" the role of Blanche DuBois in Tennessee Williams' *A Streetcar Named Desire*, considered one of the

From the movie Driving Miss Daisy, *starring Jessica Tandy and Morgan Freeman.*

classic roles in American theater, Jessica Tandy replied: "A writer creates. An actor interprets. Sometimes an actor can find things in a part that even the author didn't know was there. But it was there. It was there." Starring opposite Marlon Brando, the British-born actress was Broad-way's original Blanche, and fellow cast member Karl Malden credited Tandy's professionalism for keeping the other actors in that production in line: "We used to kid about it but we meant it—she was like the mother hen, she was the real pro in that company. She really kept it together.

She did it with class. She said, 'It's time to go to work, let's go to work and get it over with,' and we did."

In an acting career that spanned six decades, Tandy became the winner of two Academy Awards and three *Antoinette Perry awards (Tonys), and was nominated for a television Emmy on the night of her death. Her most impressive accolades, however, came for her work on the stage.

Jessica Tandy was born in London, England, on June 7, 1909. Her father Harry Tandy, a businessman, died of cancer when she was 12; her mother Jessie Horspool Tandy worked several jobs to put her daughter through private school. After training at the Ben Greet Academy of Acting in London, Tandy made her professional debut in a play called The Manderson Girls in 1927, at a small theater in Soho; she was 23 when she first came to the attention of English audiences, in Children in Uniform, in 1932. That same year, she married English actor Jack Hawkins, who would be best known for his film performance in The Bridge on the River Kwai.

In 1940, after divorcing Hawkins, and to escape the war in England, Tandy emigrated to the United States with her daughter Susan Hawkins. New York had only a few bit parts to offer, so she paid the rent by working as a cipher clerk for the British embassy, and lent her voice to radio as Princess Nada in the serial "Mandrake the Magician." While in New York, she met actor Hume Cronyn, who claimed in his 1991 autobiography, A Terrible Liar, that he fell in love with her laugh: "I adored the way she made fun of me and the world in general. I was captivated by her sensitivity, talent, generosity to others, compassion, and of course her beauty and the fact that she seemed totally unaware of any of these qualities."

Married in 1942, Tandy and Cronyn moved to California, where both had contracts with film studios. But in Hollywood, Hume was more successful than his wife. "Nobody out there really took me seriously as an actress," recalled Tandy. "Hume really engineered my first significant parts in movies."

In 1946, at the Actors' Lab in Hollywood, Cronyn directed his wife in a one-act play titled Portrait of a Madonna, written by a hot young playwright with the unusual name of Tennessee Williams; The Glass Menagerie had just exploded onto Broadway, and Williams, who had been looking for his Blanche, found her in Jessica. A Streetcar Named Desire opened on Broadway in December 1947, and Tandy was a triumph, earning her first Tony as Best Actress for the role in 1948. Still neglected by the film industry, however, she saw the movie role go to actress *Vivien Leigh. It would take Hollywood another 40 years to discover Jessica Tandy.

Giving up on Hollywood, Tandy and Cronyn moved back East in the early 1950s, where they built a reputation for their collaborations on stage. Together, they starred in The Fourposter, The Physicists, A Delicate Balance, Noel Coward in Two Keys, The Gin Game, Foxfire, and The Petition. Tandy's work opposite Cronyn earned her Tonys for Best Actress in The Gin Game (1978) and in Foxfire (1983). She also appeared in a number of movies, usually in small character roles.

In 1989, Tandy was 80 when Hollywood offered a role opposite Morgan Freeman that was to make her famous. In Driving Miss Daisy, the screen adaptation of the play by Alfred Uhry, she played Daisy Werthan, a mid-century Southern belle "struggling to balance propriety and humanity," wrote Richard Corliss in Time magazine. For her performance, she won the Oscar as Best Actress of 1990. Her acceptance speech was the shortest on record. "Good for me," she said. Two years later, she followed that up with a second Oscar, for Best Supporting Actress in Fried Green Tomatoes.

"Few actresses had invested theatrical glamour with such elegance and intelligence as Jessica Tandy," wrote Corliss. When she accepted the first-ever Tony given for Lifetime Achievement in June 1994, "a hush fell on the heart of Broadway." Many in attendance knew that she had been battling ovarian cancer for five years. While acknowledging her award, writes Corliss, Tandy "wore her pain as gracefully as she had once donned Blanche's frilly frocks or Miss Daisy's housedress. Like the boldest modern actor, this classically trained lady was daring the audience to be a party to revelation: Look at me; see what's inside—the ache, the character, the beauty."

Jessica Tandy died at 6:00 AM on September 11, 1994, at age 85, her husband by her side. The night of her death, she was nominated for a television Emmy, along with her husband, for their mutual work on Hallmark Hall of Fame's "To Dance with the White Dog."

SOURCES:

Corliss, Richard. "The Last Leading Lady," in Time. September 26, 1994.

Kuchwara, Michael. "Stage and Screen Actress Jessica Tandy Dies at 85," in The Day [New London, CT]. September 12, 1994.

Tanguay, Eva (1878–1947)

French-Canadian-born American actress and vocalist who was known as the "I Don't Care Girl." Born on August 1, 1878, in Marbleton, Quebec, Canada; died on January 11, 1947, in Hollywood, California; daughter of Octave Tanguay and Adele (Pajean) Tanguay; married John Ford (a member of her acting troupe), on November 24, 1913 (divorced 1917); married Chandos Ksiazkewacz (also known as Allan Parado, a pianist), on July 22, 1927 (annulled).

Selected roles: appeared as Cedric Errol in Little Lord Fauntleroy, *Gabrielle de Chaulus in* My Lady *(1901), Phorisco in* The Chaperons *(1903), Claire de Lune in* The Office Boy *(1903), Carlotta Dashington in* The Sambo Girl *(The Blond in Black, 1904); appeared in* A Good Fellow *(1906),* The Follies of 1909 *(1909),* The Sun-Dodgers *(1912); appeared as Leona Tobasco in* Miss Tobasco *(1914), Phonette Duttier in* The Girl Who Smiles *(1916); also performed in several vaudeville tours.*

Eva Tanguay was born in 1878 in Marbleton, Quebec, Canada, but her family had moved to Holyoke, Massachusetts, by the time she was six. Her father died when she was young, leaving the Tanguays (two girls, two boys) in dire financial straits. However, when Tanguay was eight years old, she joined the Francesca Redding Company in the juvenile lead role of *Little Lord Fauntleroy* after the previous star fell ill while touring in Holyoke. Tanguay toured with the company for five years before receiving a small part in *The Merry World*. In 1901, she appeared at the Victoria Theater in New York in *My Lady*.

In 1903, she headlined in *The Office Boy* (with Frank Daniels) and *The Chaperones*. She also performed in musical comedies and vaudeville. Her songs included "I've Got to Be Crazy," "I Want Someone to Go Wild with Me," and "It's All Been Done Before but Not the Way I Do It"; another song became her theme and made her nationally famous as the "I Don't Care Girl." It was reported that she made as much as $3,500 for a one-week appearance, making her the best-paid vaudeville performer of the time. Possessing an animated stage personality, she reportedly could leave audiences with conflicting impressions of her. She had an "ability to command the unswerving attention of her audience," writes Albert F. McLean, Jr. Although one can understand how she "anticipated the flapper of the 1920s, especially in her unconventionality and her nervous desire to live," he adds, "there was a certain innocence beneath the surface crassness and aggressiveness, and a naive optimism" that infused her performances and songs.

Tanguay's personal life, however, was not as successful. She described her first marriage, to John Ford, as a joke—an impulse during an interlude in Ann Arbor, Michigan. Her second marriage, to her pianist Chandos Ksiazkewacz, was annulled on the grounds that he had given a false name when they married. Furthermore, her fortune—estimated at $2 million at one point—was completely lost due to overspending and real estate speculation. She also resented her public image as the "I Don't Care Girl."

During the 1920s, Tanguay's career was active, but by the 1930s her health was failing. In 1933, she had an eye operation to remove cataracts, and by 1937 she was unable to work due to arthritis. She retired to a small home in Hollywood where she lived her last 20 years in seclusion. At the age of 68 she died of a cerebral hemorrhage and was buried at the Hollywood Mausoleum.

SOURCES:

McLean, Albert F., Jr. "Eva Tanguay," in *Notable American Women, 1607–1950.* Edited by Edward T. James. Cambridge, MA: The Belknap Press of Harvard University, 1971.

Who Was Who in the Theater: 1912–1976. Detroit, MI: Gale Research, 1978.

RELATED MEDIA:

The I Don't Care Girl (78 min. film), starring *Mitzi Gaynor, David Wayne, and Oscar Levant, with a fleeting appearance by newcomer *Gwen Verdon, 20th Century-Fox, 1953.

Karina L. Kerr, M.A.,
Ypsilanti, Michigan

Tanguy, Katherine Sage (1898–1963).

See Sage, Kay.

Tangwystl (fl. 1180–1210)

*Paramour of King Llywelyn II the Great. Name variations: Tangwystyl Goch. Flourished around 1180 to 1210; married Ednyfed Fychan ap Kendrig, Lord of Brynffenigl; mistress and possibly later wife of Llywelyn II the Great (1173–1240), Ruler of All Wales; children: (with Ednyfed Fychan) many; (with Llywelyn) six, including Gruffydd, Lord of Lleyn (born before 1205–1244); *Gladys the Black (d. 1251); *Angharad; possibly *Ellen of Wales, countess of Huntingdon and Chester (d. 1253). Llywelyn II was married to *Joan of England (d. 1237), and there is some confusion between Joan of England and Tangwystl as to who had which children.*

Tania (1937–1967).

See Bunke, Tamara.

Tania (b. 1954).

See Hearst, Patricia Campbell.

Tanner, Beatrice or Stella (1865–1940).

See Campbell, Mrs. Patrick.

Tanning, Dorothea (1910—)

American Surrealist painter, graphic artist and sculptor. Name variations: Dorothea Tanning Ernst. Born in 1910 in Galesburg, Illinois; attended Knox College and the Art Institute of Chicago; married Max Ernst (an artist), in 1946 (died 1976).

Selected works: Children's Games *(1942);* Hotel du Pavot *(1942);* Birthday *(1942);* Self-Portrait *(1944);* Maternity *(1946);* Guardian Angels *(1946);* Max in a Blue Boat *(1946);* Eine Kleine Nachtmusik *(1946);* The Great Room *(1950–52);* Interior with Sudden Joy *(1951);* Family Portrait *(1954). Given a retrospective exhibition, Centre National d'Art Contemporain, France (1974).*

Dorothea Tanning was born in 1910 in Galesburg, Illinois, where she grew up. One of three daughters of Swedish parents, Tanning decided at age seven that she wanted to be an artist. According to *American Women Artists,* she was bored by school and retreated to the fantasy worlds of the children's classics in the public library. An insatiable reader, she particularly studied the illustrations of Arthur Rackham, Maxfield Parrish, and Sir John Tenniel. As she grew older, she found imaginative relief from Midwestern mores in books like Oscar Wilde's *The Picture of Dorian Gray* and Gustave Flaubert's *Salammbó,* as well as the gothic novels of *Mary Shelley and *Ann Radcliffe.

For two years, Tanning attended Knox College and then chose to study at the Art Institute of Chicago. After two weeks, she decided that she could learn more outside the classroom, so in 1936 she moved to New York. While there, she cultivated a bohemian lifestyle—reading everything from William Faulkner to the *Bhagavad Gita,* working odd jobs (including performing as an extra at the Metropolitan Opera), studying Hindu dance and philosophy, and painting. That first year in New York, she also attended the "Fantastic Art, Dada, and Surrealism" exhibition at the Museum of Modern Art, an experience that greatly influenced her. In 1939, she moved to Paris in search of the surrealist art community; however, the impending turmoil of World War II soon caused her to return to New York. Supporting herself as a draftswoman for advertising jobs, Tanning discovered that surrealism had become a vital movement in New York.

Tanning quickly became part of the surrealist circle of artists, a group that included among its members André Breton, Marcel Duchamp, André Masson, Yves Tanguy, *Kay Sage, Matta, Patrick Waldberg, and Max Ernst. Tanning also appeared in the surrealist film *Dreams That Money Can Buy* (1944–46), directed by Hans Richter. As well, she exhibited her work at the Julian Levy Gallery and created scenery and costume designs for the Ballet Russe de Monte Carlo and the New York City Ballet. In 1943, *Peggy Guggenheim (at the time married to Ernst) included Tanning in the exhibition "31 Women" at Art of This Century. Ernst, who was impressed with both Tanning and her work, divorced Guggenheim in 1946, and married Tanning in a double ceremony with Man Ray and Juliet Browner. That same year, the couple moved to Sedona, Arizona, the effects of which can be seen in the imagery of Tanning's paintings from that period. In 1952, the couple established permanent residency in France.

Meticulous in its realistic detail, Tanning's work also possesses a disturbing dreamlike quality often centered around the isolation of women or children. As noted in *American Women Artists,* Tanning has indicated that "she creates each of her paintings in a kind of ecstatic convulsion in which she gives herself up to chaos, dreams, and the liberating world of the imagination." After the early 1950s, her style became more diffuse and abstract, and in the late 1960s she began to work with soft sculptures.

Although she suffered early in her career from the perception that she was merely an extension of her more famous husband, Tanning is highly acclaimed throughout Europe where she was given a retrospective exhibition at the Centre National d'Art Contemporain in France in 1974. She also began to earn recognition in the United States as well, and her work generated much critical comment in New York when she returned to live there after Ernst's death in 1976. Her creations are held by numerous collections, including the Tate Gallery in London, the Georges Pompidou Center in Paris, the Menil Collection in Houston, and the Museum of Modern Art in New York. At age 90, Tanning enjoyed her first one-woman exhibition in America when the Philadelphia Museum of Art presented "Dorothea Tanning: Birthday and Beyond" from November 2000 until January 2001.

SOURCES:

Harrap's Illustrated Dictionary of Art and Artists. Kent, Eng.: Harrap's Reference, 1990.

Harris, Ann Sutherland, and Linda Nochlin. *Women Artists: 1550–1950.* Los Angeles County Museum of Art, 1976.

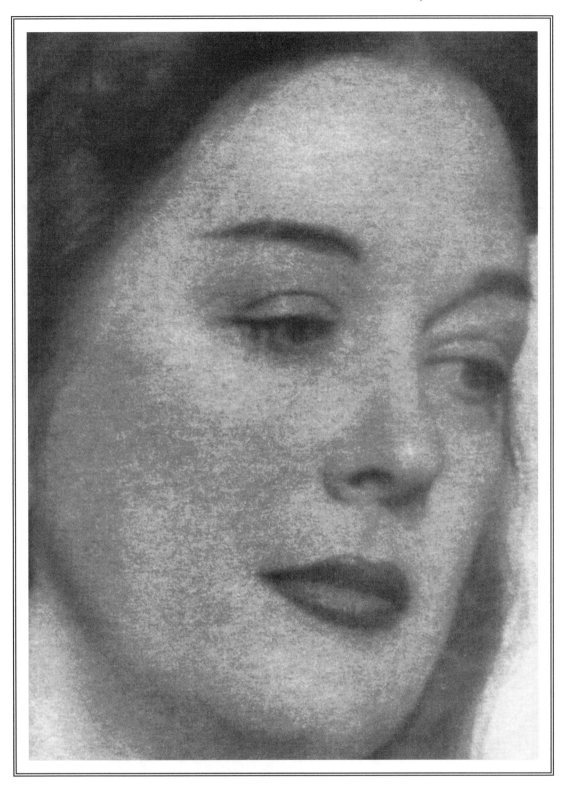

Dorothea
Tanning

Rubinstein, Charlotte Streifer. *American Women Artists from Early Indian Times to the Present.* Avon, 1982.

Karina L. Kerr, M.A.,
Ypsilanti, Michigan

Tao-Lao (1892–1938).

See Storni, Alfonsina.

Tappan, Caroline Sturgis
(1819–1888)

American transcendentalist poet. Name variations: Carrie Tappan; Caroline Sturgis. Born Caroline Sturgis in August 1819 in Boston, Massachusetts; died on

October 20, 1888, in Lenox, Massachusetts; daughter of William Sturgis (a sea captain and merchant) and Elizabeth Marston (Davis) Sturgis (daughter of Judge John Davis); sister of Ellen Sturgis Hooper (1812–1848); aunt of *Clover Adams (1843–1885); educated at home with her sisters; married William Aspinwall Tappan, on December 12, 1847; children: Ellen Sturgis Tappan (b. 1849); Mary Aspinwall Tappan (b. 1851).

❧▶
Hooper, Ellen Sturgis. See Adams, Clover for sidebar.

Born in 1819, Caroline "Carrie" Tappan grew up in Boston, Massachusetts, the fourth child in a family of five girls and one boy. Both of her parents were descended from old Cape Cod families. Her maternal grandfather John Davis was the U.S. district court judge for Massachusetts and the long-time president of the Massachusetts Historical Society. Like sisters ◀❧ **Ellen Sturgis Hooper** and **Susan Sturgis**, Caroline was educated at home and interested in literature. At age 13, she met ***Margaret Fuller**, whom she greatly admired. In 1835, when she was 16, Ralph Waldo Emerson was a guest in her parents' home. The following year marked the first of several extended visits that Tappan made with Fuller to the Emersons in Concord, and both Fuller and Emerson would continue to play an important role in her life.

When Fuller began her famous "Conversations" in the winter of 1839, Caroline and her sister Ellen were frequent attendees. After Emerson, Fuller, and other Transcendentalists began publishing the periodical *Dial* in 1840, Tappan contributed verse under the pseudonym "Z." She spent summers with the Emersons in Concord (Ralph was then married to **Lidian Jackson Emerson**) or with Fuller traveling the Great Lakes to Niagara and Fishkill-on-the-Hudson. In 1845, Tappan spent the summer as a boarder with Nathaniel and ***Sophia Peabody Hawthorne** in Concord. And sources suggest that it was Emerson who introduced her to her husband William Aspinwall Tappan, walking companion of Henry David Thoreau and the son of a wealthy New York merchant.

Married in 1847, William and Caroline had two daughters, Ellen (b. 1849) and Mary Aspinwall (b. 1851). They lived in Boston and spent their summers in the Berkshires. The "Little Red House," where Hawthorne wrote *The House of Seven Gables*, was situated on the Tappans' estate in Lenox, eventually renamed Tanglewood. The couple spent much of their time abroad, mostly in Italy, from the 1850s onward, eventually returning in 1885 to settle in Boston. Throughout her travels, Tappan wrote and published several children's books. Although her

contributions to the Transcendentalist movement were minor, she has been remembered for her close associations with its leaders. Caroline Tappan died at the age of 69 in Lenox.

SOURCES:
James, Edward T., ed. *Notable American Women, 1607–1950*. Cambridge, MA: The Belknap Press of Harvard University, 1971.

Karina L. Kerr, M.A.,
Ypsilanti, Michigan

Tappan, Eva March (1854–1930)

American teacher, children's author, and anthologist. Born on December 26, 1854, in Blackstone, Massachusetts; died from Parkinson's disease on January 29, 1930 (one source indicates January 30), in Worcester, Massachusetts; daughter of Edmund March Tappan (a minister) and Lucretia Logée Tappan (a teacher); educated in private schools; Vassar College, B.A., 1875; University of Pennsylvania, M.A., 1895, Ph.D., 1896.

Selected writings: Charles Lamb, the Man and the Author *(1896);* In the Days of Alfred the Great *(1900);* England's Story *(1901);* Old Ballads in Prose *(1901);* In the Days of Queen Elizabeth *(1902);* In the Days of Queen Victoria *(1903);* The Christ Story *(1903);* Robin Hood: His Book *(1903);* A Short History of America's Literature *(1906);* The Chaucer Story Book *(1908);* The Story of the Greek People *(1908);* Dixie Kitten *(1910);* When Knights Were Bold *(1912);* The House with the Silver Door *(1913);* Diggers in the Earth *(1916);* Ella: A Little Schoolgirl of the Sixties *(1923).*

Selected works as editor-compiler: Selections from Emerson *(1898);* American Hero Stories *(1906);* Folk Stories and Fables *(1907);* Myths from Many Lands *(1907);* The Children's Hour *(1907);* Stories of Legendary Heroes *(1907);* Poems and Rhymes *(1907);* A Friend in the Library *(15 vols., 1909);* The Book of Humor *(1916);* Adventures and Achievements *(1929).*

Eva March Tappan was born in Blackstone, Massachusetts, in 1854, the only child of Edmund March Tappan, a minister, and **Lucretia Logée Tappan**. In 1857, the family moved to Lawrence, Massachusetts, where Edmund had a pastorate. When he died three years later, Lucretia took a position as a teacher with the Smithville Seminary. While growing up, Eva, usually the youngest in her class, attended several private schools where her mother happened to be teaching, although she would have preferred to attend public school. In 1871, she started college at Vassar, where she was author of her class history and editor of the *Vassar Miscellany*. Elected to Phi Beta Kappa, Tappan received a bachelor's degree in 1875 and taught Latin and

German at Wheaton College in Massachusetts until 1880. She also was an associate principal at Raymond Academy in Camden, New Jersey, from 1884 to 1894. Tappan next attended the University of Pennsylvania, where she earned an M.A. in 1895 and a Ph.D. the following year, with a dissertation on the 17th-century English poet Nicholas Breton. In 1897, she began teaching English at the English High School in Worcester, Massachusetts, where she also directed school plays.

Tappan retired from teaching in 1904 to devote more time to writing, focusing on works for grade-school and high-school students. Many of her books were used in schools. Thoroughly researching her stories, Tappan brought to life kings and queens, knights, Greek and Roman societies, folk heroes, and historical and literary figures. She also translated folk tales from other countries and edited *The Children's Hour*, a 15-volume collection of literature, myths, and adventure and nature stories. Until 1928, she published a new book almost every year.

During World War I, Tappan worked as an assistant editor for the U.S. Food Administration. She was also a member of the Boston Authors' Club as well as the secretary for the Worcester Humane Society. Toward the end of her life, she suffered from growing deafness and lived in quiet retirement. Tappan died at age 75 from Parkinson's disease, and her ashes were buried in Bellevue Cemetery in Lawrence. To Vassar College, she bequeathed a generous scholarship fund for girls from Worcester County.

SOURCES:

James, Edward T., ed. *Notable American Women, 1607–1950*. Cambridge, MA: The Belknap Press of Harvard University, 1971.

Kunitz, Stanley J., and Howard Haycraft, eds. *Twentieth Century Authors*. NY: H.W. Wilson, 1942.

Karina L. Kerr, M.A.,
Ypsilanti, Michigan

Tarabotti, Arcangela (1604–1652)

Venetian Benedictine nun and writer known for her controversial pamphlets concerning the conditions of women. Name variations: (lay name) Elena Cassandra Tarabotti; (religious name) Suor or Sor (sister) Arcangela; (pseudonyms) Galerana Barcitotti and Galerana Baratotti (both involve acronyms of her name combined with puns of symbolic meaning: in Italian, galera ["prison"] and bara ["coffin"]). Pronunciation: Ark-AN-gel-a Tar-ra-BOT-ti. Born Elena Cassandra Tarabotti in Venice on February 24, 1604; died in Venice at the Sant'Anna in Castello monastery on February 28, 1652, age 48; daughter of Stefano Bernardi-no Tarabotti (a minor aristocrat) and Maria (Cadena) Tarabotti; never married; no children.

Became an educanda (boarder) in Sant'Anna monastery (1617); took the veil without vocation (September 8, 1620); made her religious profession (1623); five works published (1643–52).

Selected works: Il paradiso monacale (The Monastic Paradise, 1643), L'antisatira in risposta al "Lusso donnesco" satira menippea di Francesco Buoninsegni (The Antisatire answering "Womanish luxury," Menippean Satire by Francesco Buoninsegni, 1644, 2nd ed., 1646), Lettere familiari e di complimento (Informal and Greeting Letters, 1650), Che le donne siano della spezie degli uomini, difesa delle donne (Are Women of the same Species as Men? A Defence of Women, 1651, published in London, 1994); (posthumous works) La semplicità ingannata (Simplicity Tricked, 1654, formally placed on the Index of Forbidden Books in 1660), Inferno monacale (Monastic Hell, published in Turin, 1990); La tirannia paterna (Paternal Tyranny, first version of La semplicità ingannata, lost); (lost or planned works [only mentioned by Tarabotti; there is no historical evidence of their existence]): Il purgatorio delle mal maritate (Purgatory of Unhappily Married Women), Le contemplazioni dell'anima amante (Contemplating the Loving Soul), La via lasciata del Cielo (The Lost Way to Heaven), La luce monacale (Monastic Luminance).

In a remote part of Venice on September 8, 1620, at the poor and unadorned church of Sant'Anna in Castello monastery, 16-year-old Elena Cassandra Tarabotti assumed the brown cowl of the Benedictine order and submitted to the cutting of her hair by the mother superior, thus becoming Suor Arcangela. She knew she was leaving the outside world forever, because a ruling at the Council of Trent in 1563 had made all nuns subject to the papal law of strict enclosure. What she could not know was that within a relatively few years she would become widely known outside the convent walls with her writings on the condition of women. It is impossible to say if Tarabotti's destiny as a writer would have been the same had she married. Against the often-maintained theory that writing was once possible for women only within nunneries, there were two contemporaries of Tarabotti in the city of Venice, **Lucrezia Marinelli** (1571–1653) and *Sara Coppia Sullam (1590–1641), who were wives as well as authors of published treatises and novels. What we can say about Tarabotti is that her feelings about monastic life inspired the kind of deep analysis that only direct experience could give. And because her concerns remained separate from religious issues, her writings were generally outside the religious control of her spiritual father or confessor, as compared to the manipulations that sometimes affected the works of female saints. Her works are informed both by the particularity of her experience as an enclosed nun and by the similarity of women's limited experiences within society, a condition she bitterly denounced.

At the beginning of the 17th century, the Republic of the Serenissima, which included Venice, was still the leading maritime power of the Eastern Mediterranean and the most independent state on the Italian peninsula. Venice was a metropolis of 140,000 inhabitants, known around the world for its spice trade, golden thread fabrics, publishing houses and banks, and had been Europe's bridge to Eastern culture for centuries. Although its mainland possessions were stable, and the ruling patriciate had extended its dominions, estates, and investments, an era of decay had begun to set in. The terrible plague of 1630 killed almost a third of the population of Venice (the population of all Italy was shrunk from 13.3 million to 11.5 million), and its colonies, from the island of Cyprus to the shores of the Adriatic Sea, were being menaced by the Turks. The economic and commercial center of Europe was in fact slowly shifting to the Atlantic seaboard, and under the yoke of the gloomy Roman Catholic Church of the Counter Reformation, which was growing steadily in influence and control, Italy was ceding the role in culture, the arts and the sciences that had been its glory during the Renaissance.

In some ways, Tarabotti's life was affected by these circumstances as much as it was by the fact that she was a woman. To begin with, though contemporaries described her as fair (no portrait has come down to us), she was born a cripple, making it more than usually difficult—and costly—for her to acquire a husband. From the 14th to the 19th centuries, brides everywhere in Europe were expected to bring a substantial dowry, proportional to the status and wealth of their families, to a marriage. Elena Cassandra was the second child and the eldest of six girls, and no father in Venice would have been rich enough to provide weddings for six daughters. It is not clear if this large and barely well-off family belonged to the "citizens class," a sort of secondary patriciate whose ancestors had lived in Venice for centuries. Her father Stefano Bernardino Tarabotti, a "man expert in sea matters," may have been a shipowner and was certainly the owner of the family apartment. Probably, he was not as bad a person as his second

child seems to have thought, since he did manage to arrange for the marriages of two of her younger sisters, **Lorenzina Tarabotti (Pighetti)** and **Innocenza Tarabotti**. The three remaining Tarabotti girls went unmarried, however, an unusual fate among patrician and upper-class daughters, who generally entered a convent if they did not marry. After their mother **Maria Cadena Tarabotti**'s death, the Tarabotti "spinsters" were at the mercy of their brothers, and one of them, **Caterina Tarabotti**, a painter who had studied under the well-known *Padovanino*, did finally enter the Sant'Anna in Castello as a *pensionnaire*, long after her sister Elena's death.

Little is known about the early education of Elena Tarabotti or her sisters. If her older brother had a tutor, she may have had the opportunity to follow his lessons; this was often a girl's way to education. In her later literary works, Tarabotti declared that she was self-taught: "I know nothing for I came to live within the cloister at the age of 11, without having had the benefit of learning." Unlike the intellectual offerings of male monasteries, nunneries educated their charges in few skills beyond embroidery and reading (because, as nuns, they were required to read their prayers), a little Latin from the Religious Officio, and no writing. The elementary handwriting of Tarabotti's surviving letters is one indication of her educational limitations.

The record is unclear as to when Elena entered the Sant'Anna cloister as an *educanda* (boarder), either in 1615, as she later wrote, or 1617, according to the registries of the nunnery. It was not uncommon for girls first to enter a nunnery to be educated, and then to be persuaded by family necessity to stay there. In 1620, after Stefano had made a payment of 1,000 ducats to the Sant'Anna monastery as his daughter's spiritual dowry, she took her religious vows on the same day as her best friend, Suor **Regina Donà dalle Rose**. (At the time of Regina's death 30 years later, in 1650, Tarabotti would publish a moving "Compianto," describing the friendship shared by the two women up to 1645.) Tarabotti remained a novice, or probationary member of the religious community, until 1623, when she made her solemn vows of poverty, chastity and obedience, but she would never become an abbess or assume a position of leadership. Profession of vows usually occurred only one year after taking the veil, so the delay may have indicated bad health, lack of religious conviction, or even active resistance. As long as she remained a novice, it was still possible for Tarabotti to avoid the cloister. Although she left no record openly declaring that she had been forced by her parents into the monastic life, her writings include many allusions that indicate she disliked being a nun.

In the ensuing years, Tarabotti was seriously ill, and for a time it was feared she would not live. She remained in weakened health, and suffered throughout her life from a "tightness in her chest." This may have been tuberculosis, since she died younger than did most nuns. In her "Soliloquio a Dio" (Soliloquy to God), a sort of autobiography that she published as a preface to her first book, *The Monastic Paradise*, she recounts her life from the year 1620, describing a period of worldly interests, in which she knew "neither the excellence of religion, nor the obligation of a real nun," and committed "mental adulteries against God" which she explained as occurring because "in donning monastic dress, I did not respond to the voices of the Holy Spirit with the ardor I was supposed to." It is hard to reconstruct the facts of Tarabotti's life during this period: the archives offer no documentary evidence of any religious infraction or real scandal in the years 1620–30. Contemporaries like Father Angelico Aprosio describe her as a capricious, fashionable and elegant nun, following a practice typical among Venetian nuns, by which, according to Tarabotti, "at least a third of them are forced to enter the cloister." In her "Soliloquio," she also describes her conversion, due, in her words, to the visit made by the patriarch of Venice, Cardinal Cornaro, to Sant'Anna. From that date, in 1633, she describes herself as correct in her religion.

In discussing this complex and baroque author, it is important to differentiate between the historical facts and the deliberately constructed autobiography that Tarabotti often used in her works to give a credible image of herself. According to Benedetto Croce, Emilio Zanette and, lately, **Letizia Panizza**, who follow only Tarabotti's own declarations, the nun had an early period of rebellion during which she wrote her pamphlets *Monastic Hell* and *Paternal Tyranny* (which were too compromising to be published during her lifetime), denouncing why and how girls became unwilling nuns; following her conversion, she wrote *The Monastic Paradise*.

Reality seems to have been different: chronological proofs and textual analysis have led to modern consideration that her conversion (according to Conti Odorosio, Medioli and Gambier) was merely strategic. By this interpretation, Tarabotti, at age 39, probably decided to publish one of the works she had written, and chose the most decent and politically acceptable among her manuscripts to appear first in order

to pave the way for the publication of others. Unfortunately, we have no reasonable hypothesis regarding the origins and growth of her literary vocation up to that time, nor of the financial help she received in getting her works published, and so this scenario remains speculation. It is impossible to be certain about the identity of Tarabotti's first literary effort, for we know that *Paternal Tyranny* later became *Simplicity Tricked*, and it is probable that she reworked various essays at different times of her life.

> *You can only lose if you have lost liberty.*
> —**Arcangela Tarabotti**

Tarabotti was very aware, moreover, that some of her works were not publishable because they were "against the political, not the Catholic way of life." The themes she treated in her first public book, *The Monastic Paradise* (which she dedicated to Cardinal Cornaro), published in 1643, are exactly the same as those treated in *The Monastic Hell*: both state insistently that "voluntary inhabitants" consider "a convent Heaven," whereas "forced nuns feel all the pains of Hell in this life." Although she never tried to publish *Monastic Hell*, it seems that she allowed it to circulate as a manuscript, certainly after 1643 but probably before, which means it may well have been written before *Paradise*. Women are at the constant center of Tarabotti's examination, an unusual circumstance in those times; in all her pamphlets and essays, the political, social and economical condition of women are the only matters in which she shows concern. In 1644, the year after she printed her *Paradise*, Tarabotti published the *Antisatire* (written between 1638–44), in response to a contemporary controversy, defending women against the accusations of the Sienese writer Francesco Buoninsegni in his *Satire* (1638), who described women as vain and interested only in clothing. Tarabotti, in turn, accused men of being as fashionable as women and with less reason. In her last essay, in response to another literary controversy, Tarabotti claims that women are no less rational than men, providing refutation through the use of Biblical examples and quotations, according to the customary literary canon. According to Panizza, her *Difesa delle donne* (1652) was written between 1650 and 1652 but had to be published in an outlawed edition because the argument was too close to heresy.

Tarabotti dedicated two of her published works and one manuscript to the monastic condition of women. Her lucidity in analyzing the widespread phenomenon of the unwilling nun is

amazing: all the data she provides are historically confirmed. Moreover, because she personally
experienced the cloistered life, she provides an
unexpurgated picture of the interactions of the
sisters, the quality of their housing and meals,
and the suffering and joys of enclosure. As
Tarabotti points out in both *Monastic Hell* and
Simplicity Tricked—titles that eloquently state
her point of view—the destiny of upper- and
middle-class girls depended upon their fathers'
wealth and generosity. (Lower-class girls could
work to build up their own dowries.) In Venice,
it was common among nobles and merchants to
choose to marry off only their younger rather
than their elder daughters, thereby delaying the
expenditure of dowries as long as possible. The
"surplus" girls were forced to enter the cloister.
The latter destiny was the cheaper one, as
Tarabotti notes: a nun's spiritual dowry was
only 1,000 ducats, according to the strict laws of
the Republic, while the dowry a bride brought to
her groom ranged from 7,000 to 40,000 ducats.
Finally, the Venetian nobility, the Serenissima
State and the Church, pursuing a precise policy
of keeping the local nobility and privileged class
limited in size, ignored the Republic's laws re-
straining the amount of marital dowries, allowing the price to be driven up (and the rate of
marriages therefore driven down). Tarabotti denounced them: "You prefer to sacrifice your
daughters to the Reason of State, for, if all girls
would marry, the nobility would grow too large
and it would become impoverished by paying so
many dowries." Only reasonable dowries, less
ambitious weddings and the division of the patrimony in equal portions among both sons and
daughters would change the situation. Moreover, Tarabotti recognized women's enforced ignorance as an instrument of men's oppression:
"In prejudice of women, [you keep them] pur-
posely from studying, for, when they need it,
they do not know nor are they able to defend
themselves." She claimed the right for women to
study, even at the university level.

It is possible to reconstruct some of Tarabotti's relationships and connections through her
published *Lettere familiari e di complimento*
(1650). In the absence of a critical edition of this
work, however, the same cautions noted for her
autobiography also apply. For instance, Duke
Ferdinand of Parma, to whom she wrote a long
letter, never existed (the duke of that title had a
different name), whereas the "Very Illustrious
Mr. N" (for Nobody) of some letters is certainly
to be identified with her friend Father Angelico
Aprosio, who later became an enemy. Despite
these qualifications, Tarabotti's letters provide

significant information about her literary milieu:
among her correspondents were some members
of the Venetian *libertins érudits'* Academy of the
Incogniti, including Aprosio, who was a critic
and collector of rare books; Giovan Francesco
Loredan, a writer, member of the Council of the
Ten (one of the highest organs of the Republic),
and the powerful patrician to whom she dedicated her *Lettere*; Girolamo Brusoni, the writer and
former friar; and Giovan Francesco Busenello,
who was the librettist for Monteverdi.

Tarabotti also met many French travelers
who came to visit her at the parlatory of her
convent. (Because of an old law against espionage that was still in effect, nunneries were the
only place where Venetian patricians could meet
foreigners.) Through her friend Ambassador
Grémonville, who was in Venice in the years
1645–47, she was introduced to Gabriel Naudé,
the secretary of the French prime minister, and
even to France's Cardinal Mazarin. Both
Loredan and Grémonville can be considered
mentors and patrons: Loredan certainly introduced her to the publisher of *Antisatire*, Valvasense, who was the official "stampatore" of
the Incogniti Academy. Grémonville was certainly the French connection and force behind the
publication of *Simplicity Tricked* (1654), although it occurred after both their deaths. According to her published letters (mainly from the
last decade of her life), Tarabotti had few contacts with her own family after entering the
cloister, and out of the 253 letters in her episto-
lary, only 2 short communications are addressed
to her unmarried sisters. The only relative with
whom she remained in touch was the lawyer Giacomo Pighetti, who was a member of the Incogniti and married to her sister Lorenzina; seven of
her letters are addressed to him.

The particularly significant missing link involves the question of who and what influences
helped to raise Tarabotti from the cultural circumstances of an ordinary nun to the heights of
the informed and witty polemicist she became.
According to the quotations with which she saturated her essays, she could quote from the Bible
(even if, as one detractor noted, most of those
quotes came from her Religious Officio). She
also knew many poems, perhaps by heart; this
also was common among nuns, who avidly
sought out the masterpieces of Ariosto, Tasso
and Boiardo for entertainment, even if they were
prohibited by the Church as too worldly. Since
nunneries lacked the libraries filled with illuminated Latin treatises on theology, philosophy
and canon law that were preserved by male orders, the cultural level of the nuns was restricted

(except in comparison to the rest of world, where illiteracy was the norm). Tarabotti, however, quotes from Latin poets, the fathers of the Church and her contemporaries: undoubtedly, she owned a dictionary of quotations. Moreover, she must have had a close friend who sent her the compromising Incogniti books, or even Machiavelli and Aretino, that are discussed and quoted in her works.

When *The Monastic Paradise* appeared, it was immediately claimed that the book was not hers; no woman, it was assumed, could be capable of writing of such quality. Tarabotti took pride in her literary labors, which led to her membership in the international *Res publica literarum* toward the end of her career. That fame was the only comfort in her segregated life; even when she died at age 48 after a 15-day illness, on a cold winter day in 1652, she did not leave the convent. She was buried within the enclosure, a fate, as she often mentioned in her works, that befell all nuns.

Tarabotti's literary renown ended quickly. One century later she was remembered only for her polemical *Antisatire*, and as a woman writer she was regarded mostly as a curiosity. Today, however, her works are considered an important source on the condition of women's lives in the 17th century, while her personality, polemical style, wit and quick temper—all within the unwanted enclosure of the convent—have begun to make Tarabotti herself the object of historical research.

SOURCES:

Baratotti, Galerana (Arcangela Tarabotti). *La semplicità ingannata.* 1st ed. Leida: Gio Sambix (Jean et Daniel Elzevier), 1654, pp. 1–307.

Barcitotti, Galerana (Arcangela Tarabotti). *Che le donne siano della spetie degli uomini. Difesa delle donne contro Horatio Plata il traduttor di quei fogli che dicono "Le donne non esser della spetie degli uomini."* Norimbergh: Juvan Cherchenberger, 1651 (now Tarabotti, Arcangela, *Che le donne siano della spezie degli uomini* [Women are no less rational than men]. Edited with an introductory essay by Letizia Panizza. London: Institute of Romance Studies, University of London, 1994).

Chojnacki, Stanley. "Dowries and Kinsmen in Early Renaissance Venice," in *Journal of Interdisciplinary History 5.* 1975, pp. 571–600.

Conti Odorisio, Ginevra. *Donna e societa' nel Seicento.* Roma: Bulzoni, 1979.

Croce, Benedetto. *Nuovi saggi della letteratura del Seicento.* Bari: Laterza, 1931 (particularly Chap. XIII, "Donne letterate nel Seicento").

D.A.T. (Donna Arcangela Tarabotti). *Antisatira in risposta al Lusso donnesco, satira menippea di Francesco Buoninsegni.* 1st ed. Venezia: Valvasense, 1644.

Gambier, Madile. "Arcangela Tarabotti," in *Le stanze ritrovate. Antologia di scrittrici venete dal Quattrocento al Novecento.* Venezia: Eidos, 1991, pp. 117–125.

Medioli, Francesca. *"L'Inferno monacale" di Arcangela Tarabotti.* Torino: Rosenberg e Sellier, 1990.

Molmenti, Pompeo. *La storia di Venezia nella vita privata.* Bergamo: Istituto arti grafiche, 1908, vol. III.

Tarabotti, Arcangela. *Lettere familiari e di complimento.* Venezia: Guerigli, 1650.

———. *Paradiso monacale libri tre con un "Soliloquio a Dio."* Venezia: Oddoni, 1663 (1643).

Zanette, Emilio. *Suor Arcangela Tarabotti monaca del Seicento veneziano.* Roma-Venezia: Istituto per la collaborazione culturale, 1960.

SUGGESTED READING:

Cattaneo, Enrico. "Monacazioni forzate," in *Vita e processo di suor Virginia Maria de Leyva monaca di Monza.* Edited by Umberto Colombo. Milano: Garzanti, 1985, pp. 145–195.

Davis, James C. *A Venetian Family and its Fortune, 1500–1900: The Donà and the Conservation of Their Wealth.* Philadelphia, PA: American Philosophical Society, 1975.

Galilei, suor Maria Celeste. *Lettere al padre.* Edited by Giuliana Morandini. Torino: Editori La Rosa, 1983.

Lane, Frederic C. *Venice. A Maritime Republic.* Washington, DC: Johns Hopkins University Press, 1973 (It. trans. Torino, Einaudi, 1978).

Medioli, Francesca. "Monacations without vocation: a long term phenomenon," in *Culture, Society and Women in Renaissance Italy.* Edited by Letizia Panizza.

Molho, Anthony. "Tamquam vere mortua. Le professioni religiose femminili nella Firenze del tardo medioevo," in *Società e storia.* Vol. 43, 1989, pp. 1–44.

Rapp, Richard T. *Industry and Economic Decline In Seventeenth Century Venice.* Cambridge, MA: Harvard University Press, 1976.

Trexler, Richard. "Le célibat à la fin du Moyen Age: les religieuses de Florence," in *Annales E.S.C.* Vol. 27, 1972, pp. 1329–1350.

Zarri, Gabriella. "Monasteri femminili e città (secoli XV–XVIII)," in Chittolini, Miccoli, Giovanni, eds., *Storia d'Italia.* Vol. IX, *La Chiesa e il potere politico.* Torino: Einaudi, 1986, pp. 357–429.

COLLECTIONS:

Inferno monacale, in quarto manuscript on paper, pp. 1–124, located in a private collection in Venice.

Documents concerning Sant'Anna in Castello monastery are located in the State Archive of Venice, fondo (not catalogued): Suppressed religious congregations, Sant'Anna in Castello (1207–1804), buste 1–50.

Francesca Medioli, Ph.D., Bologna University, Italy, and author of *"L'Inferno monacale" di Arcangela Tarabotti* (Torino: Rosenberg e Sellier, 1990)

Tarbell, Ida (1857–1944)

American journalist and editor whose exposé of the Standard Oil Company made her name synonymous with the appellation muckraker. Name variations: (pseudonym) Iderem. Pronunciation: tar-BELL. Born Ida Minerva Tarbell on November 5, 1857, in Hatch Hollow, Erie County, Pennsylvania; died of pneumonia in a hospital in Bridgeport, Connecticut, on January 6, 1944; daughter of Franklin Sumner Tarbell (a carpenter) and Esther Ann (McCullough) Tarbell (a schoolteacher before marriage); Allegheny College, A.B., 1880, M.A., 1883; never married; no children.

Family moved to Rouseville, Cherry Creek Run, Pennsylvania (1860); moved to Titusville, Pennsylvania (1870); became preceptress, Union Seminary, Poland, Ohio; worked as associate editor, The Chautauquan (1883–91); was a student in France at the Sorbonne, Collège de France (1891–94); was an editor on staff and associate editor, McClure's Magazine (1894–1906); was associate editor, The American Magazine (1906–15); was a member of the women's committee, Council on National Defense (1917); was a member of President Woodrow Wilson's Industrial Conference (1919); was a member of President Warren G. Harding's Unemployment Conference (1921); was a member of the National Women's Committee for Mobilization of Human Needs (1933–36); posthumously inducted into the Women's Hall of Fame at Seneca Falls, New York (autumn 2000).

Selected publications: A Short Life of Napoleon Bonaparte *(1895);* Madame Roland: A Biographical Study *(1896); (with J. McCan Davis)* The Early Life of Napoleon Bonaparte *(1896);* The Early Life of Abraham Lincoln *(1896);* The Life of Abraham Lincoln *(2 vols., 1900);* Napoleon's Addresses *(1902);* History of the Standard Oil Company *(2 vols., 1904);* He Knew Lincoln *(1907);* Father Abraham *(1909);* The Tariff in Our Times *(1911);* Selections from the Letters, Speeches, and State Papers of Abraham Lincoln *(1911);* The Business of Being a Woman *(1912);* The Ways of Women *(1915);* New Ideals in Business: An Account of Their Practice and Their Effects Upon Men and Profits *(1916);* The Rising of the Tide: The Story of Sabinsport *(1919);* In Lincoln's Chair *(1920);* Boy Scouts' Life of Lincoln *(1921);* Peacemakers—Blessed or Otherwise: Observations, Reflections, and Irritations at an International Conference *(1922);* He Knew Lincoln, and Other Billy Brown Stories *(1924);* In the Footsteps of the Lincolns *(1924);* Life of Judge Gary: The Story of Steel *(1925);* A Reporter for Lincoln: The Story of Henry E. Wing, Soldier and Newspaperman *(1927);* Owen D. Young—A New Type of Industrial Leader *(1932);* The Nationalizing of Business, 1878–1898 *(1936);* Women at Work: A Tour Among Careers *(1939);* All in a Day's Work: An Autobiography *(1939).*

At age 43, Ida Tarbell was one of the most successful magazine writers in America. The author of well-received biographies of Napoleon and Lincoln, in the year 1901 she was running the editorial desk of *McClure's Magazine*, a leading monthly. Late that September, she journeyed to Europe on a special mission: to convince the journal's founder, Samuel Sidney McClure, of the need for a series of articles on John D. Rockefeller's Standard Oil Company. By then, Standard was the greatest oil conglomerate in the world, refining nearly 85% of the nation's crude oil, owning nearly 40,000 miles of pipeline, manufacturing over 86% of America's illuminating oil, and controlling the prices of the many varieties of petroleum.

McClure jumped at Tarbell's offer. Possessing an almost uncanny insight as to what most concerned his fellow citizens, "S.S."—as he always signed his name—knew that Americans were extremely disturbed about the new phenomenon of monopoly, popularly known as "the trust." Moreover, it was his own editor Tarbell, or as she signed herself "Iderem," who appeared so uniquely qualified to tell its tale. She had grown up in what was called the Oil Region of western Pennsylvania; she had lived only a few miles from the site where the first well was drilled; she had personally known most of Standard's earliest foes; her brother was currently an executive for Pure Oil, one of the few companies that had escaped Standard control; her father had made the very barrels used to contain the flow from the earliest gushes. It was a story, notes McClure biographer Peter Lyon, she could write "straight out of her gut."

Upon her return to America, Tarbell immediately started work. "I dream of the octopus by night and think of nothing else by day," she said. More than one person warned her, "Go ahead, and they will get you in the end." Her own father cautioned, "Don't do it, Ida—they will ruin the magazine." Yet, remaining undaunted, she was befriended by Standard vice president Henry H. Rogers, who had known her father in the early Pennsylvania days and who let her interview him frequently but secretly at Standard's New York headquarters. In the course of her research, she heard many reports of illegal railroad rebates made to Standard, but the "smoking gun" only appeared when a young Rockefeller employee confessed that he had been ordered to burn incriminating documents every month. Moreover, one embittered brother of John D.'s, Frank Rockefeller, covertly turned over papers he believed damning.

With the help of her research assistant John M. Siddell, Tarbell literally stalked John D. himself. Catching the 66-year-old executive at a Sunday service in Cleveland's Euclid Avenue Baptist Church, she noted: "There was an awful age in his face—the oldest man I had ever seen, I thought, but what power!" All in all, with his

Ida
Tarbell

"lipless mouth," "blank eyes," and head "swept of hair," "there was something indescribably repulsive about him."

Tarbell's first article, appearing in November 1902, was a bombshell, launching the most sensational serial ever to appear in an American magazine. The subsequent 18 issues of *McClure's* were equally provocative. Tarbell never denied what she called "the true greatness" of Standard Oil and would use such phrases as "perfection of organization," "ability and daring," "extraordinary intelligence and lucidity." Standard, she said, "was the most perfect business machine ever devised." But in general, her tale was a sordid one, full of ciphers, spies, arson, and kickbacks of all sorts, and some material was later shown to be exaggerated or fake. In fact, Tarbell biographer **Mary E. Tompkins** goes so far as to suggest that the means she used were "as questionable in journalism as were those she accused the Standard Oil Company of using in business." Tarbell later conceded: "The more intimately I went into the subject, the more hateful it became to me. No achievement on earth could justify those methods, I felt."

At one point, McClure wrote Tarbell, "You are today generally the most famous woman in America. You have achieved a great distinction. People universally speak of you with such a reverence that I am getting afraid of you." Commented Finley Peter Dunne's saloon-keeping Mr. Dooley, "Iderem's a lady but she has the punch!" Soon settlement organizer *Jane Addams was the only woman in America whose public stature equalled hers.

Not a word. Not a word about that misguided woman.
—John D. Rockefeller

Rockefeller privately referred to Tarbell as "that misguided woman" or, more flippantly, as "Ida Tarbarrel," but publicly the richest man in the nation presented a bold front. He told a reporter:

> All without foundations. The idea of the Standard forcing anyone to sell his refinery is absurd. The refineries wanted to sell to us, and nobody that has sold or worked with us but has made money, is glad he did so.

Tarbell's articles and her two-volume book, *A History of the Standard Oil Company* (1911), spelled disaster for the firm. Her findings were the object-lesson for many an editorial or sermon. In the West, where suspicions of Standard were particularly high, her name was a household word, and in Tulsa she was paraded through the streets as the "*Joan of Arc of the oil industry." A letter addressed to one "Ida M. Tarbell, Rockefeller Station, Hades" reached her promptly. According to the *New York World*, her work "gives us the same insight into the nature of trusts in general that the medical student gains of cancers from a scientific description of a typical case."

In May 1911, the Supreme Court gave the corporation six months to dissolve itself. Tarbell found the ruling a hollow one, for the 38 component parts of Standard maintained informal agreements and Rockefeller had not been sent to jail. The decision was significant, however, for now competitors had an even chance. Late in her life, a young historian asked her: "If you could rewrite your book today, what would you change?" "Not one word, young man, not one word," was the reply.

Ida Minerva Tarbell was born on November 5, 1857, in a log farmhouse in Hatch Hollow, Erie County, Pennsylvania; it belonged to her mother's parents. Her mother **Esther McCullough Tarbell** had been a schoolteacher before marriage. Her father Franklin Sumner Tarbell briefly homesteaded in Taylor County, Iowa, but was forced by the Panic of 1857 to return by foot to his native Pennsylvania, where he settled in Cherry Run. Teacher, farmer, carpenter—Franklin had been all of these. When, in 1859, oil was located near Titusville, Franklin took advantage of the discovery to establish the firm of Tarbell's Tanks, which employed scores of laborers and built wooden tanks holding 500 barrels of oil each. Ida's first real hometown was Rouseville, a dirty, violent settlement that combined the spirit of the California gold rush and the ethos of the Wild West. One observer remarked of the area, "Men think of oil, talk of oil, dream oil!" Living in a shanty close to her father's shop, Tarbell recalled that:

> All about us rose derricks, enginehouses and tanks; the earth about them was streaked and damp with the dumpings of the pumps, which brought up regularly the sand and clay and rock through which the drill had made its way. If oil was found, if the well flowed, every tree, every shrub, every bit of grass in the vicinity was coated with black grease and left to die. Tar and oil stained everything.

When oil was discovered at Pithole, ten miles from Rouseville, she recalled a "motley procession" of drifters traveling "on foot or horseback up the Valley of Cherry Run in full view from our house." In 1870, Franklin, by then a wealthy man, moved to Titusville, where he shifted an entire hotel from Pithole and turned it into the family mansion. Yet the oil producers soon felt themselves at the mercy of a strange new combine, the Rockefeller-controlled South Improvement Company, which made secret and illegal contracts with the Pennsylvania, New York Central, and Erie railroads. Franklin's fortunes fluctuated constantly, and the Tarbell household was suddenly filled with a tension young Ida never forgot. Later on, South Improvement drove Franklin's partner to suicide and Franklin had to assume the man's debts. Ida later wrote, "There was born in me a hatred of privilege—privilege of any sort."

Tarbell grew up in an intensely Methodist family, and even before adolescence, she "went forward" to be saved at an annual revival. However, she soon felt hypocritical about the matter, finding her conversion more a matter of prudence than piety. She also resolved never to wed, later summarizing her feeling by saying, "It would interfere with my plan; it would fetter my freedom. . . . When I was fourteen I was praying to God on my knees to keep me from marriage."

In 1876, after attending local public schools, Tarbell enrolled in Allegheny College in nearby Meadville. The only woman in her class of 40, she received her A.B. in 1880 and a master's degree three years later. The college turned her into what she called a "pantheistic evolutionist." Majoring in biology, she found Darwin's teachings the key to all creation.

Upon graduation, Tarbell taught at Union Seminary of Poland, Ohio. Her salary: $500 a year. Her tasks: the teaching of two classes each of Greek, Latin, French, and German, plus English, mathematics, geology, botany, geometry, and trigonometry. "It was a killing schedule for one person," she afterwards reported, and she resigned after two years.

From 1883 to 1891, Tarbell served on *The Chautauquan* magazine, published in Meadville as a correspondence school journal sponsored by the famous lecture movement located in Chautauqua, New York. Working up to 16 hours a day, she was coeditor in reality, though not in title. Possessing a circulation of 50,000, *The Chautauquan* supported such reformist causes as the eight-hour day, temperance, and the Knights of Labor. By this time, the budding journalist was over six feet tall, slim in figure, possessing long dark hair and clear eyes and bearing a wistful smile.

In 1891, Tarbell moved to Paris. She claimed she was "dying of respectability," but quite possibly she was smarting over the lack of promotion. Furthermore, she had long been fascinated by the role of women in the French Revolution, *Madame Roland in particular. Living modestly in the Latin Quarter and eating sparsely, she enrolled at the Sorbonne and the Collège de France while continuing her research at the Bibliothèque Nationale. To meet expenses, she would occasionally write articles on French life for such highly respected American periodicals as *Scribner's*.

In 1892, a Tarbell article on the paving of Paris came to the attention of S.S. McClure. "This girl can write," he said, and he made a point of stopping at her quarters in Paris. Soon she was interviewing Emile Zola, Alexandre Dumas, and Louis Pasteur—all for S.S.'s magazine.

In 1894, Tarbell moved to New York, there to work in *McClure's* editorial offices. Noting how obsessed the American public had become with Napoleon, S.S. asked her to supply the accompanying text to a famous collection of Napoleon prints owned by Gardiner Green Hubbard, a rich Bonaparte *aficionado* of Washington, D.C. Produced "on the gallop" within six weeks, her series was so successful that it became her first book: *A Short Life of Napoleon Bonaparte* (1895). If the volume were a bit episodic, jumping from one topic to another, it nonetheless gave a lively and accurate picture. A year later, her life of Madame Roland was published. It portrayed the stormy French revolutionary, who ended up on the guillotine, as motivated solely by love, thereby neglecting Roland's personal ambition, restless brilliance, and thirst for power.

McClure then shifted Tarbell's interest to Abraham Lincoln, a figure with whom S.S. was so enamored that he practically turned his editorial offices into a Lincoln research bureau. He issued a public appeal for Lincoln material, counting on Tarbell to track down the hundreds of replies to his request. At first Tarbell, whose heart still lay with the French Revolution, was unenthusiastic. "Out with you," he said to his star reporter. "Look, see, report." In 1895, she commenced four years of painstaking research in Kentucky, Illinois, and Washington. Lincoln biographer and former aide John G. Nicolay pooh-poohed her efforts, telling her outright, "You are invading my field." Yet her series on Lincoln's early life drove up *McClure's* circulation markedly, making it one of the nation's most important monthlies.

When, in 1900, her general Lincoln biography was published, she had gathered over 300 unpublished speeches and letters for the volume's appendix. She also was ghostwriter for the Civil War "recollections" of Charles A. Dana, editor of the *New York Sun* and once assistant to Secretary of War Edwin M. Stanton. Another project involved working on the memoirs of Carl Schurz from 1896 until the death of the politico in 1906.

Tarbell retained her interest in Lincoln throughout her entire life, eventually producing some ten books, including several for children. Sometimes she gullibly accepted fake claims, as when she argued that Lincoln's mother, *Nancy Hanks, was not born illegitimate. Sometimes she willingly went along with what was generally considered a legend, as when she supported the supposed romance of Lincoln and *Ann Rutledge. She made a real contribution, however, in stressing the positive side of Lincoln's frontier background and in uncovering innumerable facts. Lincoln biographer Benjamin P. Thomas called Tarbell "the pioneer scientific investigator" and Carl Sandburg praised her as the foremost Lincoln trailblazer.

Real fame came, however, with her exposé of Standard Oil, and ever after her name was associated with muckraking. In 1903, she—along with *McClure's* staffers Lincoln Steffens and Ray Stannard Baker—absolutely dominated American muckraking. She challenged President Theodore Roosevelt's comparison of her school of journalism with "the man with the muckrake" as described in John Bunyan's *Pilgrim's Progress*. The Bunyan figure, she claimed, was really raking in riches and was therefore one of the "malefactors of great wealth" whom Roosevelt himself had attacked. By then, writes Tarbell biographer **Kathleen Brady**, she had long been "the goddess of the Olympus which was *McClure's Magazine*" and S.S.'s most trusted ally.

Despite her own good fortune, Tarbell became increasingly disturbed by S.S.'s long stays overseas, personal philandering, and business schemes so wild that they included banks, life insurance companies, and a housing concern to be called "McClure's Ideal Settlement." Hence, in 1906, she joined with *McClure's* staffers John Phillips, Steffens, and Baker to purchase *The American Magazine*, which she helped staff until 1915. When S.S. heard the news, he mourned, "And you, too, Ida Tarbell." Although *The American* assumed a muckraking stance, it lacked the bite and liveliness of *McClure's*.

High on Tarbell's agenda was a series of articles, then a book, advocating lower tariffs. Personally advised by former president Grover Cleveland, she thought that low duties would reduce the power of monopoly. Checking every congressional debate and rate schedule, she turned a dull topic into a lively one. Indeed, President Woodrow Wilson was so impressed with her work that he asked her to serve on the Tariff Commission he established in 1916. Tarbell declined the offer, pleading lack of administrative experience, the inherent weakness of any such body, and her desire to remain in journalism.

Though bitterly hostile to Standard Oil, Tarbell was by no means an enemy of big business per se. Believing that the muckraking movement was more concerned with magazine circulation than what she called "the passion for facts," she wanted to inform the public that "there were leaders in practically every industry who regarded it not only as sound ethics but as sound economics to improve the lot of the worker." From 1912 to 1916, she spent the bulk of her time visiting factories throughout the nation. "I never saw a machine I did not want to run," she said. Espousing welfare capitalism, which she found "the Golden Rule in industry," she quickly became an advocate of Taylorism, that is, the "scientific management" techniques of Frederick W. Taylor, and of the industrial paternalism of Henry Ford. Her life of Judge Elbert H. Gary, board chair of United States Steel, was sheer eulogy. She presented U.S Steel as a "good trust," one which thought enough of its employees to design a stock-purchasing plan. Judge Gary had held workers to a 12-hour day and a 24-hour shift every fortnight and he was a strong foe of collective bargaining. In Tarbell's eyes, however, he epitomized "industrial statesmanship," and she even praised him for eliminating competition in the steel industry. Another eulogistic life, this one of Owen D. Young, portrayed her subject in such glowing terms that the board chair of General Electric appeared downright Lincolnesque in stature. When, in 1923, *Survey* magazine asked about the postwar views of prewar radicals, Tarbell denied ever having been a reformer at all.

In 1911, the publishers of *The American Magazine* sold control of their struggling venture to Crowell publishing, and most of the *McClure's* veterans disbanded. In 1915, Tarbell returned to freelance writing and professional lecturing, occupying herself in the latter vocation until 1922. By then in her 60s, she withstood a grueling schedule that sometimes involved Chatauqua speaking seven days a week, each time in a different city. The fact that she was showing the first signs of Parkinson's disease made life no easier.

Due to the influence of Stanford president David Starr Jordan, Tarbell had hoped to promote the peace movement, but as early as 1914 she foresaw full-scale United States participation in World War I. In April 1917, President Wilson appointed her to the Women's Committee of the Council of National Defense, where her particular focus lay in food conservation. She also served on the nation's wartime propaganda agency, George Creel's Committee on Public Information. Her one effort at writing a novel, *Rising of the Tide* (1919), was a failure. Although she could capture well the atmosphere of a small Midwestern town at war, she was weak at characterization, dialogue, and plot. After visiting the battle sites of the Great War for *Red Cross Magazine*, she returned as a crusader for U.S. membership in the League of Nations. At the same time, she rightly feared that the Paris Peace Conference, which she personally had attended, guaranteed a new global conflict. Upon hearing the terms presented to the Germans, she took to her bed and wept.

Unlike many reformist women, Tarbell saw suffrage as a peripheral issue. She wrote:

> The central fact of a woman's life, Nature's reason for her, is the child, his bearing and rearing. There is no escape from the divine order that her life must be built around this constraint, duty, or privilege, as she may please to consider it.

Furthermore, so she believed, competition with men directed women away from their vital most task, that of preserving domestic values, and the contest added to the breakdown of family life originally created by the industrial revolution. She later noted that her book *The Business of Being a Woman* (1912), in which she articulated such ideas, was "like a red flag to many of my militant friends." Additional Tarbell comments, such as the claim that women lacked the vision to attain greatness, led to a special opposition rally held in April 1912 at New York's Metropolitan Temple. Suffrage leader *Anna Howard Shaw, settlement worker *Florence Kelley, and author *Charlotte Perkins Gilman all voiced their displeasure. A while later, Jane Addams said, "There is some limitation to Ida Tarbell's mind," a comment that stung deeply.

Even in her 60s, Tarbell continued writing. In 1926, she offered *McCall's* readers an uncritical account of the Florida land boom. The same year, she reported for *McCall's* on Italy's new fascist regime. All about her, she found "rhythmic labor," "steady balance," and "orderly action." Impressed by dictator Benito Mussolini, whom she interviewed, she praised the sense of moral uplift she saw in his "world of work," though she predicted that one day he might overreach himself. She supported President Franklin D. Roosevelt's social security legislation, anti-speculation laws, and opposition to prohibition but found much of the New Deal too chaotic. As she said in 1939, on the topic of making the world better:

> I see no more promising path than each person sticking to the work which comes his way. . . . If the need for the moment is digging a ditch or washing the dishes, that is the greatest thing in the world for the moment. . . . It is by following this natural path that new and broader paths open to us.

In 1936, she contributed a volume on Gilded Age industrial life to the distinguished *History of American Life* series, edited by historians Arthur M. Schlesinger and Dixon Ryan Fox. She offered a highly competent survey and her introduction was particularly colorful.

Although Tarbell was accused of betraying her old ideas by her work on Gary, Young, and Mussolini, in reality she was always consistent. As noted by historian Otis Graham, Jr., and detected by colleague Lincoln Steffens decades earlier, she had always been fundamentally a conservative, whose admiration for titans of industry even predated her muckraking days. When she wrote in 1935 that America's hope lay in "discipline and the education of the individual to self-control and right doing," she was saying what she always believed. More reporter than analyst and formally untrained in economics, she remained a journalistic voice for middle-class America. Her work on Rockefeller and Lincoln retained scholarly respect long after her pot-boilers of the interwar period were ignored. *The New Yorker* called her memoirs, *All in a Day's Work*, "serenely charming in a way all their own." Ida Tarbell died on January 6, 1944.

SOURCES:

Brady, Kathleen. *Ida Tarbell: Portrait of a Muckraker.* NY: Putnam, 1984 (University of Pittsburgh Press, 1989).

Hamilton, Virginia der Veer. "The Gentlewoman and the Robber Baron," in *American Heritage.* Vol. XXI, no. 3. April 1970, pp. 78–86.

Tarbell, Ida M. *All in a Day's Work: An Autobiography.* NY: Macmillan, 1939.

Tompkins, Mary E. *Ida Tarbell.* NY: Twayne, 1974.

SUGGESTED READING:

Filler, Louis. *Crusaders for American Liberalism: The Story of the Muckrakers.* NY: Harcourt, Brace, 1939.

Graham, Otis L., Jr. *An Encore to Reform: The Old Progressives and the New Deal.* Oxford University Press, 1967.

Lyon, Peter. *Success Story: The Life and Times of S.S. McClure.* NY: Scribner, 1963.

Thomas, Benjamin P. *Portrait for Posterity: Lincoln and His Biographers.* Princeton, NJ: Rutgers University Press, 1947.

COLLECTIONS:

The papers of Ida Tarbell are located in Pelletier Library, Allegheny College, Meadville, Pennsylvania, and the Sophia Smith Collection, Smith College, Northampton, Massachusetts.

RELATED MEDIA:

"Our Plan" (VHS, 8 hrs., part 1 of 8 parts), in *The Prize: The Epic Quest for Oil, Money and Power*, Majestic Films, Ltd. and MICO, 1993.

Justus D. Doenecke,
Professor of History,
New College of the University of South Florida,
Sarasota, Florida

Tarkiainen, Maria (1880–1943).

See Jotuni, Maria.

Tarn, Pauline M. (1877–1909).

See Barney, Natalie Clifford for sidebar on Renée Vivien.

Taro, Gerda (1910–1937)

German-Jewish photojournalist, the first woman war photographer to die in combat, whose photographs of the Spanish Civil War brought powerful images to the attention of a public unable to fully grasp the growing menace of fascist aggression. Name variations: Gerda Pohorylle; Gerta Taro. Born in Stuttgart, Germany, on August 1, 1910; severely injured in an accident near the front lines near Brunete on July 25, 1937, and died in the Escorial military hospital on July 26, 1937; daughter of Heinrich (Hersch) Pohorylle and Gisela (Ghittel) Boral Pohorylle; had brothers Karl and Oskar; companion of Robert Capa (b. 1913, the photographer).

Gerda Taro lived a short, tragic life in a turbulent period of world history. Although she was born in Stuttgart, Germany, she was by no means typically German. Her parents Heinrich and **Gisela Pohorylle**, Polish Jews, were both born in Galicia, but moved from Galicia in Austrian Poland to Württemberg in southwestern Germany only a few years before her birth in search of a better life. Assisted by relatives who had arrived earlier, Heinrich began a modest egg business in the town of Reutlingen.

On August 1, 1910, their long-awaited first child was born. A daughter, she was named Gerda, and with the birth of two boys, Oskar in 1912 and Karl in 1914, the Pohorylle family was complete. Family happiness, however, was soon overshadowed by the events that transformed the world in the summer of 1914. Gerda's fourth birthday that August 1 was not a day of celebration but one of foreboding and apprehension, for it marked the start of the European conflict that in time became World War I. The Pohorylles' home region of Galicia was the site of bloody battles between the armies of tsarist Russia and Austria-Hungary. Soon, many thousands of Galician refugees would be crowding Berlin, Munich, Vienna and other cities. Wartime chaos and declining morale revived anti-Semitism which had not been as intense for decades, although the Pohorylle family, living as they did in relatively tolerant Württemberg, would be largely spared from these hatreds.

In 1916, Heinrich moved his family from Reutlingen to Stuttgart. By this time, Germany was suffering greatly from a war of attrition that placed immense burdens on civilians. As the war dragged on, the Pohorylles shared ever-increasing privations, which impacted on the great majority of Germans through rationing of bread, sugar, and milk. Taro and her brothers often went without milk for days or weeks at a time. In 1917, now pretty and bright, she was enrolled at Stuttgart's Königin-Charlotte-Realschule, the Württemberg capital's first "reformed" primary school for girls.

It was there that she first began to experience the phenomenon of *Anderssein*, of "being different." As Orthodox Jews, her family observed long-established traditions; thus, when Taro attended her school on Saturdays, the Jewish Sabbath, she could not fully participate in certain classroom activities. The reactions of her classmates varied, but many were puzzled by her "peculiar" behavior. When Gerda invited some of them to her home, which was extremely modest by German bourgeois standards, they became acutely aware of her otherness.

Whether their response was purely anti-Semitic in origin or not, some of Taro's classmates began seeing her as a member of a family of imperfectly assimilated *Ostjuden*, eastern Jews whose life was alien and essentially *undeutsch* ("un-German"). In the cruel ways of children, some teased and humiliated her. Taro began to deny her Jewish origins, which brought conflicting emotions, including those of shame, into her young life. Her childhood, however, was not all painful. She was regarded by her teachers and most of her classmates as a highly attractive, good student who found it easy to make friends.

Despite his relative poverty, Heinrich Pohorylle chose to remain in Germany, where he believed he would be able to raise his children in a civilized, tolerant milieu. Since his temperament resembled that of a dreamer and a Talmudic scholar rather than of an aggressive businessman, Heinrich's income as a traveling egg salesman remained modest, and his family's living standard remained precariously lower bourgeois. Help from the extended Pohorylle family, however, somehow always appeared in time to pluck Heinrich's family out of a crisis. In 1925, indeed, their situation brightened dramatically when Gerda's uncle Moritz decided to hire Heinrich as a permanent employee of his newly established egg business.

During these years, Taro continued to attend school, excelling both in the sciences and in foreign languages, English and French. By the time she entered her teens, she had become an extremely attractive young woman whose good looks began to turn young men's heads throughout Stuttgart. Her aunt Terra, who continued to spoil Gerda with presents and praise, began to look ahead to the time when Taro would be able to "make a good match." Gerda appeared to be quite content with these plans; she joined the "smart set" of Stuttgart by embracing the smoking habit, and by taking full advantage of the *Elizabeth Arden makeup kit she had been given by her always generous Tante Terra.

In 1927, after graduating from secondary school, Gerda received an even more munificent present from Aunt Terra when she was sent for a year's course at an exclusive Swiss finishing school, the Villa Florissant in Chamblandes-Pully, situated in a breathtaking location near Lausanne on Lake Geneva. Here, Taro further perfected her foreign language skills and displayed natural abilities in gymnastics, dancing and tennis. Known to her fellow students as "Poho," she had grown into a sociable young woman who laughed easily and had many friends. Upon her return to Stuttgart from Switzerland, Taro enrolled in a local business school to master the useful skills of stenography and typing.

For the next several years, she enjoyed life, making friends and finding in Hans Bote (known to all as "Pieter") her first love. Bote, a gentile, was a successful businessman more than a decade older than Gerda. Aunt Terra was deeply concerned that her niece might marry "Pieter," but to her great relief this did not happen. In 1929, the Pohorylle family moved to the city of Leipzig, where, with the generous financial backing of his Stuttgart family, Heinrich once again tried to find success in the egg business. In Leipzig, though she took courses in home economics and cooking, likely encouraged by the ubiquitous Tante Terra, Taro was also drawn into the increasingly tense political life of Weimar Germany. She befriended a number of individuals, Ruth Cerf, Dina Gelbke, and Erwin Ackerknecht among them, whose political views were militantly Communist but also often critical of the German Communist Party (KPD), which had become a bureaucratized Stalinist organization lacking a coherent strategy to counter the rapidly growing threat of Nazism.

Soon Gerda fell in love with Dina Gelbke's son Georg Kuritzkes, one of the leaders of Leipzig's left-wing youth movement. Although neither Gerda nor Georg ever joined the KPD, they supported its anti-Nazi militancy, and as members of Germany's threatened Jewish mi-nority both chose to participate in this struggle despite misgivings about overall KPD strategy. Along with Georg, Gerda attended anti-Nazi rallies and spent many hours typing documents, attending meetings, and distributing literature. In 1932, Georg's younger brother Soma was attacked and injured by two Nazi youths. Although found guilty, the two Nazis never served time in prison because of the birth of the Third Reich the following year.

Adolf Hitler became chancellor of Germany on January 30, 1933, and within weeks used the pretext of a non-existent "Communist plot" to imprison the nation by the end of March. Taro and her friends in Leipzig found that their city, too, quickly became subject to a dictatorial social order ruled by fear and insecurity. In the first weeks after the creation of the Hitler dictatorship, a strong resistance movement grew up in Leipzig and environs. Greta and her friends were active in this work, distributing anti-Nazi flyers and plastering the walls with posters.

Early in the morning of March 19, 1933, Taro was arrested and taken into "protective custody" (Schutzhaft). Fortunately, like her parents and brothers, she was a citizen of Poland, and after several anxious weeks, during which Polish diplomats interceded on her behalf, she was released on April 4. While in prison, Taro heard the screams of her colleagues while they were being beaten and tortured by Nazi brownshirts. Along with other women prisoners, Gerda signaled her unwillingness to bow to the forces of Nazi terror, but none of the women prisoners were physically injured.

Upon her release, Gerda discovered that anti-Jewish boycotts had virtually destroyed her father's business, which he now began to liquidate. In a Germany increasingly ruled by terror that made life for Jews and decent Germans a living hell, the Pohorylles decided to leave the country (they would eventually flee to Yugoslavia). Gerda, however, although she knew little about the country, decided to go to France. A friend from Stuttgart, Lies Levi, who was an active Social Democrat, had already found refuge in Paris some time earlier.

Taro arrived in Paris in the late autumn of 1933, virtually penniless but overjoyed to be in a country not ruled by Hitler. She was fortunate in that she spoke excellent French, and could also type, take shorthand and do bookkeeping. Fellow refugee Ruth Cerf found work as a domestic but was treated with disrespect and, after being fired, was reported to the immigration police by her middle-class ex-employers. Although poorly paid, Gerda soon became part of a German refugee network that met in cafés to discuss the political scene. By December 1933, she was working for psychoanalyst Dr. René Spitz, a student of Sigmund Freud. Through Spitz, Taro met the German refugee photographer Tim Gidal. Gidal, who had pioneered the new profession of photojournalism in Berlin in the 1920s, sparked Taro's interest in photographic journalism.

The first years Taro spent in Paris were not without pleasantries. Several times she visited her lover Georg for extended periods in Italy, where he was now studying medicine. A new love interest in Paris also appeared in Willi Chardack, another refugee from Leipzig. Gerda and her friends often sat and discussed current events for hours on end in the Café Capoulade, or sometimes at the Café Mephisto. After losing her job with Spitz, Taro supported herself for a while by selling newspapers on a Paris boulevard.

Her life changed dramatically in September 1934, when she met a young Hungarian photographer named André Friedmann (originally Endre Ernö, later to be known as Robert Capa), three years her junior. In 1932, Capa, who had fled Hungary for Berlin because of his left-wing politics, was sent by his employer to Copenhagen to photograph Leon Trotsky. Capa's dramatic and powerful photographs of Trotsky, which have become classics of photojournalism, appeared in print in the journal *Weltspiegel*, making the young Hungarian famous. Unfortunately, several months later, Hitler's accession to power forced him to flee to France. As a penniless leftist Jewish photojournalist, he arrived in Paris full of hope but with no solid prospects.

Soon after meeting the photographer, Gerda broke off her affair with Chardack and briefly moved in with Capa, who lived in a tiny hotel room in the Latin Quarter. He was often away for extended periods on photographic assignments, so during one of these Greta and a friend, **Lotte Rappaport**, sublet a small room in the apartment of Fred Stein, a German-Jewish refugee who, no longer able to practice law as he had done in Dresden, was now establishing himself as a photographer. It was here that Gerda began to learn the nuts and bolts of photography while working for Stein as a darkroom assistant. In October 1935, she found a job with the photographic agency Alliance Photo, which was successfully run by another refugee from Nazism, **Maria Eisner**. Now permanently employed, Taro found that her language skills stood her in good stead, and she learned rapidly about the business end of photojournalism. Although she was not always

faithful to him, and they went through dramatic but short-lived separations, Taro's relationship with Capa nevertheless had become a central fact of her private life, and they moved back in together. Increasingly assertive and confident of her abilities, she took charge of the happy-go-lucky Capa's often chaotic career. In February 1936, she was issued her first press pass.

As the couple became more confident in their skills, they decided to create new, improved names and images for themselves. To draw the attention of French editors, they chose to appear in new guises. These personas would be crafted from the pseudo-reality found in the fabled New World of America. André Friedmann was now Robert Capa, a name possibly derived from Hollywood's Frank Capra. Gerda Pohorylle emerged as Gerda Taro, perhaps inspired by some remote Italian villages she had once been enchanted by.

The great challenge that Capa and Taro were preparing for appeared much sooner than expected. In mid-July 1936, Republican Spain's democratically elected leftist government was threatened by a military coup led by Francisco Franco and other reactionaries. Franco's forces received substantial military backing from Hitler's Germany and Mussolini's Italy. Anti-fascists of various stripes as well as liberal democrats rallied to the cause of beleaguered Spain. Among them were Taro and Capa, who arrived in Barcelona on August 5, 1936. They immediately began taking photographs, preserving for history the courage of Spain's workers and peasants, men and women who were poorly armed and without military training.

Working sometimes together and sometimes at different areas of the front, Capa and Taro photographed not only soldiers, but also the hastily erected barricades these men and women had created in and around Barcelona. These dramatic photos were snapped up by news editors eager for images from the Spanish fighting, and appeared in the summer of 1936 in the *Züricher Illustrierte Zeitung* and in the French magazine *Vu*. Although they were in Spain professionally as photojournalists, both Taro and Capa also invested in the struggle of Spanish democracy against fascist aggression. As partisans in the war against Franco, Hitler, and Mussolini, they hoped that their photographs would not only inform the outside world but galvanize it politically. One of Taro's photographs of ill-equipped Spanish militia members appeared in the *Illustrated London News* under the caption, "Typical Defenders of the Spanish Republic." To secure her images, she often appeared with her

Gerda
Taro

Rolliflex in the midst of Republican soldiers, ignoring the bullets that flew from all directions.

Taro and Capa spent considerable time not only in the company of Spanish soldiers, but also with the "Volunteers for Liberty," units known collectively as the International Brigades. Coming to Spain illegally, the International Brigade volunteers, many of whom were Jewish Communists, risked their lives at the front to defeat the fascism they hated and feared. In Madrid, where the couple spent considerable time, they endured bombings by the German Nazi "volunteer" air squadron, the Condor Legion. As their photographs from Spain began appearing in the press, often the photographers were not properly credited. Even more astonishingly, their work sometimes appeared in magazines published in Nazi Germany. But the unauthorized dissemination of their efforts did not interest Taro and Capa. They were busy risking their lives to gather dramatic and persuasive images of a conflict that was changing the course of world history. Among the most moving photographs taken by Taro are not of soldiers but of Madrid's destroyed buildings, then-shocking documentation of the first city to be bombed. She was also able to capture on film one of the Spanish Republic's most heartening victories, the battle of Guadalajara in March 1937.

That summer, she commented to a colleague, British journalist Claud Cockburn, "how unfair it is, that we are still alive . . . when one thinks of how many truly great colleagues of ours have lost their lives in this offensive." On July 25, 1937, Taro invited another colleague, Canadian journalist Ted Allan, to join her on a visit to the front lines near Brunete. Soon after arriving in the combat zone, they found themselves in the midst of bombing attacks by German and Italian planes. Seeking shelter, she and Allan found a press car. Gerda was on its running board when a Republican tank, in retreat from the attack, went out of control and careened into their car. The tank bumped her from her perch, crushing her under its revolving lugs. From the other side of the car, Allan heard her screams but could do nothing, because he had been wounded himself. By the time he regained consciousness, Taro had been taken to the nearby British International Brigade 35th Division frontline hospital at the Escorial. On the way there, she had received a blood transfusion—a life-saving technique used for the first time during the Spanish Civil War—and remained conscious despite her wounds. Displaying "unbelievable courage," she was able to use her hands to hold her intestines inside her mutilated abdomen. But Gerda Taro died early the next morning, despite the efforts of doctors and nurses.

Her body was taken to Paris where on August 1, on what would have been her 27th birthday, Taro was buried after an impressive funeral. The service had been arranged by the French Communist Party, even though she had never joined it nor any other political organization. The guest list included numerous intellectual luminaries of the day, among them the Chilean poet Pablo Neruda. The total number of participants in the funeral may have been as high as 100,000, including a devastated Robert Capa who never seemed to stop crying during the long march to the Père-Lachaise cemetery. Alberto Giacometti designed her tomb, which was altered during the Nazi occupation to delete her name because the occupiers and their French collaborators appeared genuinely fearful of the growing myth of Gerda Taro as an antifascist *Joan of Arc.

In his 1938 book *Death in the Making*, which contains photographs by both him and Gerda Taro, Robert Capa wrote on the dedication page, "For Gerda Taro, who spent one year at the Spanish front, and who stayed on. R.C. Madrid, December 1937." In February 1938, an exhibition of Taro's Spanish photographs opened in New York City. From that point on, she would be romanticized and sometimes demonized as well, but rarely if ever objectively investigated. Taro's entire family was annihilated in the Holocaust. Her father and brothers had fled to Yugoslavia in the mid-1930s, but they met their deaths in German-occupied Serbia at an unknown time, most likely between August 1941 and March 1942. In effect, the Nazis had eradicated her entire family, then cleansed the Paris tomb of her name, as if in an attempt to eliminate all remaining traces of her existence. They did not succeed.

SOURCES:

Allan, Ted. *This Time a Better Earth: A Novel*. NY: William Morrow, 1939.

"The Camera Overseas: The Spanish War Kills Its First Woman Photographer," in *Life*. Vol. 3, no. 7. August 16, 1937, pp. 62–63.

Capa, Robert, and Gerda Taro. *Death in the Making*. Translated by Jay Allen. NY: Covici-Friede, 1938.

———. *Robert Capa: Cuadernos de Guerra en España (1936–1939)*. Valencia: Sala Parpalló, Diputación Provincial de Valencia, 1987.

Coleman, Catherine. "Women in the Civil War," in *Heart of Spain: Robert Capa's Photographs of the Spanish Civil War*. NY: Aperture Foundation, 1999, pp. 43–52, 174.

Córdova Iturburu, Cayetano. *España bajo el comando del pueblo*. Buenos Aires: Acento, 1938.

Denoyelle, Françoise. "Paris, Capitale Mondiale de la Photographie," in *Guerres Mondiales et Conflits Contemporains*. Vol. 43, no. 169, 1993, pp. 101–116.

Dogliani, Patrizia. "Fotografia ed Antifascismo negli Anni Trenti," in *Passato e Presente*. Vol. 19, 1989, pp. 127–154.

*Gellhorn, Martha. "Till Death Us Do Part," in *The Novellas of Martha Gellhorn*. NY: Alfred A. Knopf, 1993, pp. 269–309.

Gidal, Nachum T. "Jews in Photography," in Leo Baeck Institute. *Year Book XXXII*. London: Secker & Warburg, 1987, pp. 437–453.

Gidal, Tim. *Modern Photojournalism: Origin and Evolution, 1910–1933*. NY: Collier, 1973.

Görling, Reinhold. *Dinamita cerebral: Politischer Prozess und ästhetische Praxis im Spanischen Bürgerkrieg (1936–1939)*. Frankfurt am Main: K.D. Vervuert, 1986.

Guerrin, Michel. "Une exposition madrilene magnifie le myth de Robert Capa," in *Le Monde* [Paris]. March 2, 1999.

Ingendaay, Paul. "Der Krieg und die Würde des Menschen," in *Frankfurter Allgemeine Zeitung*. March 13, 1999, Menschen und Zeiten, p. VI.

Lewinski, Jorge. *The Camera at War: A History of War Photography from 1848 to the Present Day*. London: W.H. Allen, 1978.

Roth, Mitchel P. *Historical Dictionary of War Journalism*. Westport, CT: Greenwood Press, 1997.

Schaber, Irme. *Gerta Taro: Fotoreporterin im spanischen Bürgerkrieg: Eine Biografie.* 2nd ed. Marburg: Jonas, 1995.

Whelan, Richard. *Robert Capa: A Biography.* NY: Alfred A. Knopf, 1985.

Wyden, Peter. *The Passionate War: The Narrative History of the Spanish Civil War, 1936–1939.* NY: Simon and Schuster, 1983.

COLLECTIONS:

Robert Capa Papers, International Center of Photography, New York City.

John Haag,
Associate Professor of History,
University of Georgia,
Athens, Georgia

Tarrant, Margaret (1888–1959)

British illustrator and painter. Born Margaret Winifred Tarrant in 1888 in Battersea, south London, England; died on July 28, 1959; daughter of Percy Tarrant (a landscape painter and illustrator) and Sarah (Wyatt) Tarrant; studied art at Heatherley's School of Art, London, early 1920s; Guildford School of Art, 1935.

Selected illustrated books: Charles Kingsley's The Water-Babies *(1908);* Autumn Gleanings from the Poets *(1910);* Fairy Stories from Hans Christian Andersen *(1910); Charles Perrault's* Contes *(1910); Robert Browning's* The Pied Piper of Hamelin *(1912); M.A. Bigham's* Merry Animal Tales *(1913);* Nursery Rhymes *(1914); Marion St. John Adock's* The Littlest One *(1914) and* Knock Three Times! *(1917); F. Cole's* A Picture Birthday Book for Boys and Girls *(1915); Lewis Carroll's* Alice's Adventures in Wonderland *(1916); K. Howard's* The Little God *(1918); Robert Louis Stevenson's* Songs with Music from A Child's Garden of Verses *(1918); Harry Golding's* Verses for Children *(1918) and* Zoo Days *(1919); Robert Rudolph's* The Tookey and Alice Mary Tales *(1919);* Our Day *(1923);* Rhymes of Old Times *(1925); Marion St. John Webb's* The Forest Fairies, The House Fairies, The Insect Fairies, The Pond Fairies, The Sea Shore Fairies, The Wild-Fruit Fairies *(all 1925),* The Magic Lamplighter *(1926),* The Orchard Fairies, The Twilight Fairies, *and* The Seed Fairies *(all 1928); *Eleanor Farjeon's* An Alphabet of Magic *(1928);* Mother Goose: Nursery Rhymes *(1929); Harry Golding's* Fairy Tales *and* Our Animal Friends *(both 1930);* The Margaret Tarrant Birthday Book *(1932); B. Todd's* Magic Flowers *(1933);* Joan in Flowerland *(1935); M. Gann's* Dreamland Fairies *(1936); Margaret Tarrant's* Christmas Garland *(1942);* The Margaret Tarrant Nursery Rhyme Book *(1944);* The Margaret Tarrant Story Book *(1951); Katherine B. Bamfield's* The Story of Christmas *(1952).*

Margaret Tarrant was born in 1888 in Battersea, England, a suburb on London's south side. Her father Percy Tarrant, a well-known landscape painter and illustrator of books, magazines, and postcards, encouraged young Margaret to draw. As a child, she would use bed sheets to construct a tent and then display her drawings to her parents. The recipient of several awards from her Clapham High School art department, Margaret studied at Heatherley's School of Art in London to become a teacher before deciding instead to concentrate on watercolor painting and illustration.

At age 18, Tarrant did illustrations for publishers of Christmas cards; when she was 20, she illustrated Charles Kingsley's *The Water-Babies* (1908). After creating a series of paintings the following year for postcards that were published by C.W. Faulkner, she worked for various other publishers. Within the next four years, she illustrated at least 12 more books, including some of her own. Besides illustrations, she also created postcards, calendars, and silhouette designs, all of which were very popular. Her illustrations from *Nursery Rhymes* (1914) were reproduced as 48 postcards and sold extremely well. Her best-known painting, *The Piper of Dreams*, was also reproduced, selling thousands.

In 1920, she and **Marion St. John Webb** popularized the nursery theme "Flower Fairies." Tarrant had also become friends with children's book illustrator *Cicely Mary Barker, whose work influenced her own. During the 1920s and 1930s, her religious paintings became very popular. Tarrant had a long working relationship with the Medici Society, which sent her to Palestine in 1936 to gather additional subject material. The Medici Society also published several of her calendars, greeting cards, and large prints (such as *Sea Joy*), as well as many of her books and reproductions of her religious and fairy paintings. In addition to her watercolors and pen-and-ink drawings, Tarrant worked in graphite, creating several famous silhouette drawings.

After her parents' deaths in the mid-1930s, Tarrant returned for additional study at the Guildford School of Art, where she met fellow artist and lifelong friend **Molly Brett**. By 1953, her failing health and poor eyesight forced her to sell her home in Peaslake to live with her friend Brett. Tarrant died in 1959 and left her estate to 12 charities.

SOURCES:

Dalby, Richard. *The Golden Age of Children's Book Illustration.* NY: Gallery, 1991.

Grimes, Teresa, Judith Collins, and Oriana Baddeley. *Five Women Painters*. Great Britain: Lennard, 1989, pp. 19–20.

Karina L. Kerr, M.A.,
Ypsilanti, Michigan

Tarry, Ellen (1906—)

African-American writer. Born in 1906 in Birmingham, Alabama; attended Alabama State College for Negroes and Bank Street College Writers' Laboratory; children: Elizabeth.

Worked as a journalist, teacher, social worker, and writer; served as deputy assistant to the Regional Administrator for Equal Opportunity, Department of Housing and Urban Development; co-founded Friendship House (Chicago); worked for Archdiocese of New York.

*Selected works: (illustrated by Myrtle Sheldon) Janie Belle (Garden City Publishing, 1940); (illustrated by Oliver Harrington) Hezekiah Horton (Viking, 1942); (with Marie Hall Ets, illustrated by Alexander and Alexandra Alland) My Dog Rinty (Viking, 1946); (illustrated by Harrington) The Runaway Elephant (Viking, 1950); The Third Door: The Autobiography of an American Negro Woman (McKay, 1955, new edition with introduction by Nellie Y. McKay, University of Alabama Press, 1992); (illustrated by Donald Bolognese) *Katharine Drexel: Friend of the Neglected (Farrar, Straus, 1958); (illustrated by James Fox) Martin de Porres: Saint of the New World (Vision, 1963); Young Jim: The Early Years of James Weldon Johnson (Dodd, 1967); The Other Toussaint: A Modern Biography of Pierre Toussaint, a Post-Revolutionary Black (St. Paul Editions, 1981); Pierre Toussaint: Apostle of Old New York (Pauline Books, 1998). Author of weekly column, "Negroes of Note," in the* Birmingham Truth; *contributor to many Catholic periodicals.*

Ellen Tarry's writings have been heavily influenced by her involvement in the civil-rights movement. As a result, she became one of the first authors to use African-Americans as main characters in books for children. She began her writing career at the *Birmingham Truth* newspaper, for which she eventually became a reporter, columnist, and editorialist. After some years at the paper, she left the South for New York City. There she became part of a group of journalists and creative writers that included Claude McKay, James Weldon Johnson, Countee Cullen, and Langston Hughes. She also co-founded and worked at Friendship House, an interracial justice center in Harlem. It was there that she began a story hour for children in the neighborhood, using her young audiences to test out the stories she was writing. Her first published book, *Janie Belle* (1940), was soon followed by *Hezekiah Horton* (1942)—both notable for having African-American children as the main characters. The character of Hezekiah Horton was also featured in 1950's *The Runaway Elephant*.

My Dog Rinty, published in 1946, told in words and photos the story of a little boy whose troublesome dog becomes a valuable rat-hunter. Contemporary reviewers praised it first as a story of a boy and his dog, but many also noted with approval the way in which the author presented life in Harlem in a realistic, matter-of-fact style. "Showing the social range in a community, any community, from hardship to decency to comfort to luxury . . . indicating that the poor in old buildings live poorly; suggesting a concrete solution, that the buildings be replaced: all this was novel in a picturebook in 1946," notes Barbara Bader.

Perhaps Tarry's most significant book is her autobiography, *The Third Door: The Autobiography of an American Negro Woman*. The book, written in 1955, struck a determined and hopeful tone on the subject of civil rights. Reviewing a new edition of the book published in 1995, William L. Andrews noted, "Tarry is at pains to show what an African-American woman can do in alliance with fair-minded whites to bring about racial harmony and justice. For every recollection of discrimination and humiliation she suffered at the hands of bigots south and north, she gives her reader instances of successful interracial cooperation."

Tarry, who converted to Roman Catholicism as a young woman, also wrote biographies of two notable black Catholics: St. Martin de Porres, who lived in South America in the 17th century, and Pierre Toussaint, a Haitian slave who was brought to New York City by his owner around 1787. Toussaint eventually won his freedom, became wealthy, and bought the freedom of many other slaves. Known for his good works and piety, he became a leading citizen of Old New York. Tarry's research and writing on Toussaint were encouraged by a letter of Pontifical Blessing from Pope Paul VI. "Students and scholars from all over the United States have expressed interest in the life of this Haitian slave who became a respected citizen," wrote Tarry. "This book transformed me from being a writer to that of a resource person on the life and times of this man."

SOURCES AND SUGGESTED READING:

Bader, Barbara. *American Picturebooks from Noah's Ark to the Beast Within*. NY: Macmillan, 1976.

Children's Literature Review. Vol. 26. Detroit, MI: Gale Research, 1992.

Tarry, Ellen. "Autobiography," in *Something about the Author Autobiography Series.* Vol. 16. Detroit, MI: Gale Research, 1993.

———. *The Third Door: The Autobiography of an American Negro Woman.* McKay, 1955.

Tascher de la Pagerie, Marie-Josèphe (1763–1814).

See Josephine.

Tastu, Amable (1798–1885)

French poet. Born Sabine Casimire Amable Voïart in 1798 in Metz, France; died in 1885; married; children: one son.

Selected works: Poésies *(Poems, 1826);* Poésies nouvelles *(New Poems, 1834 or 1835);* Le Livre des enfants *(The Children's Book, 1836–37);* Tableau de la littérature italienne *(List of Italian Literature, 1843);* Tableau de la littérature allemande *(List of German Literature, 1844);* Voyage en France *(French Travel, 1845).*

The poetry of Amable Tastu, who was born Sabine Casimire Amable Voïart in 1798 in Metz, France, has been described as delicate, sentimental, sophisticated, and elevating. She was especially adept at writing elegiac poetry, and also wrote children's stories, educational texts, and literary criticism, and translated *Robinson Crusoe* into French in 1835. Her poetry led to her friendship with **Adelaïde de Dufrénoy** when Tastu's "Le Narcisse" (The Narcissus) was published in the *Mercure de France* (French Mercury) in 1816. Tastu worked in the book trade to support her family after her husband suffered financial problems with his printing business. Following his death, she traveled with her son, a diplomat, on his assignments to Cyprus, Baghdad, Belgrade, and Alexandria. With her sight beginning to fail, she returned to France in 1864.

Karina L. Kerr, M.A.,
Ypsilanti, Michigan

Tate, Phyllis (1911–1987)

British composer. Born in Gerrard's Cross, England, on April 6, 1911; died in 1987; studied at the Royal Conservatory of Music, 1928–32; married Alan Frank, in 1935; children: two.

Joined Composers' Guild (1959); served on the board of Performing Rights Society's Members' Fund, the first woman to do so (1976–81); received many commissions from important sponsors, including the BBC and the Royal Academy of Music; wrote Concerto for Saxophone and Strings *(1944), the opera* The Lodger, *based on the story of Jack the Ripper (1960), and* Serenade to Christmas *for soprano, chorus and orchestra (1972).*

Phyllis Tate, who mastered virtually all genres of music, had a long, successful career. She was particularly effective in setting words to music, and composed a number of works that not only impressed their premiere audiences but were able to find their way into the repertoire of major choral societies in Great Britain and other English-speaking countries. Tate composed relatively little purely orchestral music, but several of these works, including a 1933 Cello Concerto entitled *St. James Park—A Lakeside Reverie*, deserve to be revived. One of her most imaginative works, which fortunately has been recorded, is her 1968 work *Apparitions—Ballade for Tenor, Harmonica, String Quartet and Piano.* Also impressive and dramatically effective is Tate's 1976 work for narrator, soloists, chorus and orchestra, *St. Martha and the Dragon.* Tate was a champion of the economic interests of composers, serving from 1976 through 1981 as the first woman member of the board of the Performing Rights Society's Members' Fund.

John Haag,
Athens, Georgia

Tate, Sharon (1943–1969)

American actress who was murdered by the Manson Family. Born Sharon Marie Tate on January 24, 1943, in Dallas, Texas; murdered on August 9, 1969, in Beverly Hills, California; daughter of Paul Tate (a soldier) and Doris Tate; married Roman Polanski (a film director), on January 20, 1968.

Selected filmography: Adventures of a Young Man *(1961);* Barrabas *(1961);* The Wheeler Dealers *(1963);* The Americanization of Emily *(1964);* The Sandpiper *(1965);* Eye of the Devil *(1966);* The Fearless Vampire Killers *(1966);* Don't Make Waves *(1967);* Valley of the Dolls *(1967);* The Wrecking Crew *(1969);* The Thirteen Chairs *(12+1, 1970).*

Selected television appearances: "The Pat Boone Show," "Petticoat Junction," "Mr. Ed," "The Beverly Hillbillies" (1963–64), "The Man from U.N.C.L.E." (1965).

Selected documentaries: "All Eyes On Sharon Tate" (1966); "Ciao Federico Fellini Directs" (1969).

Called "generous-hearted" by those who knew her, Sharon Tate was born in 1943 in Dallas, Texas, the eldest of Paul and **Doris Tate's** three children. A beauty queen before graduating in 1961 from Vincenza American High School in Italy where her soldier-father was stationed, she appeared in her first film that year. In 1963, Tate auditioned for, and won, a part on the television situation comedy "Petticoat Junction," but the role was given to someone else when it was learned that *Playboy* magazine had published photographs of her. For the next two years, she studied acting, dancing, and singing, and performed small parts in television series such as "The Beverly Hillbillies," "Petticoat Junction," "The Man from U.N.C.L.E.," and "Mr. Ed." She also began to appear in films with recognized stars, such as **Julie Andrews** in *The Americanization of Emily* (1964), *****Elizabeth Taylor** in *The Sandpiper* (1965), and *****Deborah Kerr** in *Eye of the Devil* (1966). Roman Polanski then cast Tate in his comic horror film *The Fearless Vampire Killers* (1966), after which she returned to the United States from Italy to work with Tony Curtis in *Don't Make Waves* (1967). Her most important role, however, came that same year when she co-starred in an adaptation of *****Jacqueline Susann's** smash bestseller *Valley of the Dolls*. In 1969, Tate worked with Dean Martin in his final Matt Helm comedy *The Wrecking Crew* before receiving top billing in what would be her last film, *The Thirteen Chairs*, released in 1970.

Tate and Polanski were married in London in January 1968. When she became pregnant the following year, they rented a larger home, belonging to record producer Terry Melcher (son of *****Doris Day**) and his then girlfriend **Candice Bergen**. Upon completing *The Thirteen Chairs*, Tate joined Polanski at their London home. Unable to fly due to her advanced pregnancy, Tate sailed home on the *Queen *****Elizabeth II*; Polanski was to follow.

On August 9, 1969, two weeks before the baby was due, Tate was savagely murdered in her Beverly Hills home by members of Charles Manson's "Family." Four others shared her fate: coffee heiress **Abigail Folger**, her boyfriend Voyteck Frykowski, celebrity hair stylist Jay Sebring, and Steven E. Parent, a young man who was a friend of Polanski's 19-year-old caretaker. Parent, who met the killers in the driveway on his way home, was shot in his car. The other four were then herded into the living room by members of the "Manson Family," **Susan Atkins, Leslie Van Houten, Patricia Krenwinkel**, and Charles "Tex" Watson. They were forced onto the floor and tied up, Frykowski with a towel and the others with a single rope around their necks. Frykowski was the first to break loose, and in the ensuing chaos

all four died gruesomely, shot or stabbed. Folger's and Frykowski's bodies were found with multiple wounds outside, where they had been caught as they tried to escape. The bodies of Tate and Sebring were found in the living room. Tate had been the last to die; she had been stabbed repeatedly in the belly. Using her blood, the killers had written "pig" on a door. Charles Manson was not present during the murders (although he was present two days later at the nearby murders of Leno and **Rosemary LaBianca**), but he was the mastermind behind a twisted plot to incite race wars (helter-skelter) that would ultimately result in his becoming a supreme ruler. **Linda Kasabian**, another "Family" member who had served as a lookout during the murders, testified against Manson and the others after they were caught. They were found guilty and sentenced to death, but California repealed the death penalty after their trial. They are now serving life sentences and being rejected as they come up for parole.

SOURCES:

King, Greg. *Sharon Tate and the Manson Murders*. Barricade, 2000.

Kohn, George C. *Encyclopedia of American Scandal*. NY: Facts On File, 1989.

Walker, John, ed. *Halliwell's Filmgoer's and Video Viewer's Companion*. 10th ed. NY: HarperPerennial, 1993.

Karina L. Kerr, M.A.,
Ypsilanti, Michigan

Tatiana (1897–1918).

See Alexandra Feodorovna for sidebar.

Tauber-Arp, Sophie (1889–1943)

Swiss artist and member of the Dadaist movement who used purely geometric forms repeated many times against a plain background. Name variations: Sophie Taeuber or Sophie Taeuber-Arp; Sophie Täuber or Sophie Täuber-Arp. Born in 1889 in Davos, Switzerland; died following a heating accident in 1943 in Zurich, Switzerland; educated at Saint-Gall, Munich, and the Kunstgewerbeschule, Hamburg; also studied dancing with Rudolf von Laban; married Jean Arp (a sculptor), in 1921.

Born in Davos, Switzerland, Sophie Tauber trained in the decorative arts at Saint-Gall in Munich and at the Kunstgewerbeschule in Hamburg. In 1915, she joined the Schweizerischer Werkbund, where she met her future husband, the Alsatian sculptor Jean Arp. They were married in 1921.

Tauber-Arp taught weaving and embroidery from 1916 to 1929 at the School of Arts and

Crafts in Zurich. She also joined the Dadaists at the Café Voltaire in Zurich, mainly as a dancer but also collaborating with her husband on the café's abstract interior decorations. During this time she created theatrical sets, marionettes, stained glass, embroideries, collages, and furniture designs. She coauthored and published *Dessin et arts textiles* (1927), a book about decorative arts, and in 1937 founded a short-lived magazine on the subject.

Devoted to the decorative arts throughout her life, Tauber-Arp also became interested in abstract painting in 1915 and wood relief sculpture in 1931. According to *Women Artists: 1550–1950*, she was one of the first artists to recognize abstraction as a beginning point rather than an end result. With her husband, she created abstract designs in embroidery and weaving and experimented in torn-paper work from 1914 to 1918. Tauber-Arp's first abstract paintings were watercolors and drawings of rectangles and curved forms. She gradually reduced this to rectangles and triangles, culminating in the powerful large-scale *Triptych: Vertical-Horizontal Composition with Reciprocal Triangles* (1918). A year later, *Little Triptych, Free Vertical-Horizontal Rhythms, Cut and Pasted on a White Ground* (1919) employed a softer and more fluid approach.

In 1928, Tauber-Arp and her husband moved to a suburb of Paris, where she designed both the plans for their new house and the furnishings. She created further distinctive paintings came in the 1930s, using circular forms in both paintings and wood reliefs. **Nancy Heller** indicates that these circles, whether conical, segmented, or placed against rectangles, suggest space and movement with a subtle rhythm of color; their purely geometric forms hint at mathematical formulas. The relief sculptures featured bright colors and irregular edges, notes Heller. In them, the empty spaces were just as important as the solid areas.

In the 1930s, Tauber-Arp was associated with the Cercle et Carre group and the Abstraction-Creation group, both advocates of non-figural art. In 1940, during World War II, she and her husband left Paris and settled in Grasse until 1942, when they returned to Switzerland. The following year, Tauber-Arp died because of a faulty heating system in her bedroom.

SOURCES:

Harrap's Illustrated Dictionary of Art and Artists. Kent, GB: Harrap's Reference, 1990.

Harris, Ann Sutherland, and Linda Nochlin. *Women Artists: 1550–1950.* Los Angeles County Museum of Art, 1976.

Heller, Nancy G. *Women Artists: An Illustrated History.* NY: Abbeville Press, 1987.

Martha Jones, M.L.S.,
Natick, Massachusetts

Tauhida (d. 1932).

See Egyptian Singers and Entrepreneurs.

Tauseret (c. 1220–1188 BCE)

Wife of Egyptian pharaoh Seti II and briefly the ruler of the country in her own right (1196–1188 BCE). Name variations: Tausert; Twosret. Born around 1220 BCE; died in 1188 BCE; sister-wife of Seti II, king of Egypt; children: (stepson) Siptah.

The last legitimate member of the royal family of the brilliant 19th Dynasty of Egypt, Tauseret may have first enjoyed a joint rule with her brother-husband Seti II but then apparently attempted to assume the rulership of Egypt upon her husband's death. She constructed a large funerary temple for herself at ancient Thebes and a tomb in the Valley of the Kings, where no other woman of her dynasty was buried. For a time she was regent on behalf of her stepson, the young Siptah, who then ruled briefly by himself. Afterwards, she again ruled alone as a female pharaoh, but only for a short time. Her tomb was usurped by the founder of the 20th Dynasty, so she may have been overthrown. Indeed, the last years of the 19th Dynasty were remembered by the Egyptians for their breakdown of law and order.

Barbara S. Lesko,
Department of Egyptology,
Brown University,
Providence, Rhode Island

Taussig, Helen Brooke (1898–1986)

Renowned pediatric cardiologist and authority on congenital cardiac malformations who helped develop a surgical procedure that saved the lives of thousands of children. Pronunciation: TOE-sig. Born Helen Brooke Taussig on May 24, 1898, in Cambridge, Massachusetts; died in an automobile accident in Kennett Square, Pennsylvania, on May 21, 1986; daughter of Frank William Taussig (a professor of economics at Harvard University) and Edith (Guild) Taussig; graduated from the Cambridge School for Girls in 1917; attended Radcliffe College, 1917–19; graduated from the University of California at Berkeley, 1921; took graduate courses at Harvard University, 1921; studied and did research at Boston University, 1922–24; graduated from the Johns Hopkins University School of Medicine, 1927; never married; no children.

Honorary doctorates from 20 institutions, including Boston University School of Medicine (1948); Northwestern University (1951); Columbia University (1951); Women's Medical College of Pennsylvania (1951); University of Athens (Greece, 1956); Harvard University (1959); Göttingen University (Germany, 1960); University of Vienna (Austria, 1965); University of Massachusetts (1966); Jefferson Medical College and Medical Center (1967); Duke University (1968); Medical College of Wisconsin (1972).

Awards: more than 40 national and international awards, including Chevalier Légion d'Honneur (France, 1947); Passano Award (1948); American College of Chest Physicians, Honorary Medal (1953); Feltrinelli Prize (Italy, 1954); Albert Lasker Award (1954); ***Eleanor Roosevelt*** *Achievement Award (1957); American Heart Association Award of Merit (1957); Gairdner Foundation Award of Merit (Canada, 1959); American College of Cardiology Honorary Fellowship (1960); American Heart Association Gold Heart Award (1963); Medal of Freedom of the United States, presented by President Lyndon B. Johnson (September 14, 1964); American College of Cardiology, The Theodore and Susan Cummings Humanitarian Award (1965); Carl Ludwig Medal of Honor (Germany, 1967); The VII Interamerican Award of Merit (Peru, 1968); Presidential Medal of the Republic of Peru, presented by President Fernando Belaunde Terry (1968); American Pediatric Society Howland Award (1971); Tokyo Society of Medical Sciences and Faculty of Medicine Plaque (Japan, 1971); American College of Physicians Mastership (1972); American Heart Association, James B. Herrick Award of the Council of Clinical Cardiology (1974); The Johns Hopkins University Milton S. Eisenhower Gold Medal (1976); American College of Cardiology Presidential Citation (1980).*

Published first scientific article while in medical school (1925); was a fellow in cardiology and intern in pediatrics, Johns Hopkins Hospital (1927–29); was physician-in-charge, Harriet Lane Home Cardiac Clinic, Johns Hopkins Hospital (1930–63); first operated on a blue baby, Johns Hopkins Hospital (1944); became instructor in pediatrics, Johns Hopkins University School of Medicine (1930–46), associate professor of pediatrics (1946–59), professor of pediatrics (1959–63), professor emeritus (1963–86); published Congenital Malformations of the Heart *(NY: The Commonwealth Fund, 1947, rev. ed., 1960); was founding member of the Board of Pediatric Cardiology (1960); began investigation of birth deformities caused by thalidomide and other drugs (1962); served as president of the American Heart Association (1965–66); published 100 articles in scientific journals.*

More than any other person, Helen Brooke Taussig was responsible for the development of pediatric cardiology as a medical specialty. Before 1940, pediatricians knew little about the various congenital malformations of the infant heart. It was Taussig who developed the observations that helped differentiate malformations by their specific clinical signs. And she managed to do this despite two major inhibiting dysfunctions—loss of hearing that began after medical school and dyslexia that had plagued her since childhood.

She was born in 1898 in Cambridge, Massachusetts. As a child, she was humiliated in school by her dyslexia, since she was never able to read aloud in class with the same ease as other students. For Taussig, to read even a few lines was a struggle, and her instructors were not supportive. Because so little was known about dyslexia during the early 1900s, her teachers insisted that she could read if she really tried. At home, however, Helen was constantly encouraged by her father Frank Taussig, an eminent professor of economics at Harvard. She later recalled with gratitude that her father had never ridiculed her or told her she could do better, though after she failed reading and spelling several times, he privately feared she would not pass grade school. Once when Taussig became particularly discouraged, he cheered her with, "Helen, spelling is not logical. You're a very logical girl; no wonder you can't spell!" But Taussig had an ability to maintain an intense focus. Determined to overcome her impediment, she persevered, and her reading gradually improved; but reading would always remain a chore for her rather than a pleasure.

When Taussig, the youngest of four children, was 11 years old, her mother **Edith Guild Taussig** died of tuberculosis. Helen contracted a mild form of the disease and attended school only for half days over a two-year period. After Edith's death, Helen's bond with her father became even closer.

Every summer the Taussig family moved to a beach house overlooking Nantucket Sound in Cotuit on Cape Cod, where the children were encouraged to participate in outdoor activities, but only after they had spent the mornings studying. For the rest of her life, even when she had her own vacation home on the Cape, Taussig would continue to devote mornings to her studies. Guests were instructed to fix their own breakfasts and not to expect her to join them until lunch time.

After her graduation from the Cambridge School for Girls in 1917, Taussig enrolled in Radcliffe College, associated with Harvard,

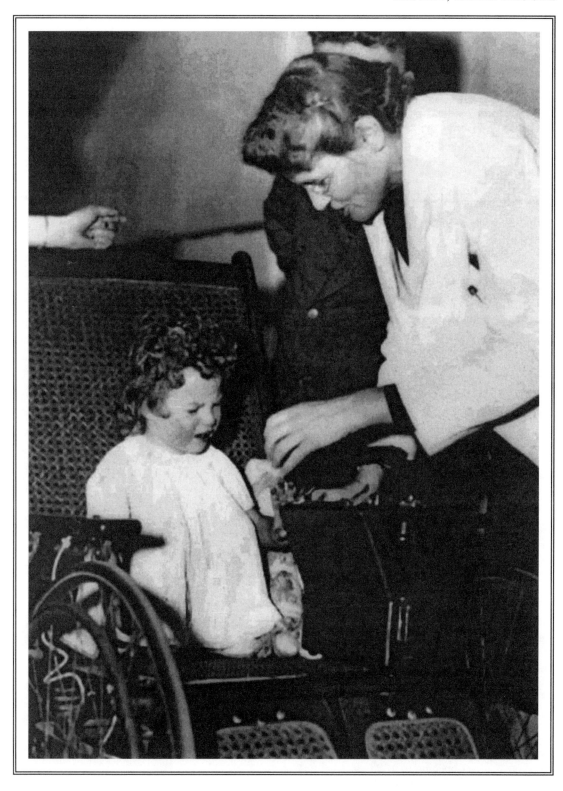

Helen B. Taussig with a "blue baby."

where she was known as Frank Taussig's daughter. During her two years there, she played in tennis tournaments and was on the varsity basketball team, but she was not particularly happy. After a trip to California with her father, she decided to transfer to the University of California at Berkeley where she would feel less in her father's shadow. The fact that Frank had remarried in 1918 and moved to Washington probably encouraged her desire for independence. Frank Taussig gave his permission for the transfer provided she finish her second year at Radcliffe.

When Helen graduated from the University of California in 1921, she was undecided about a career. Medicine was mildly appealing to her, but she had not taken the required premedical courses. Frank recommended public health as "a very good field for women" and suggested that she apply to the new School of Public Health at Harvard. But Harvard was not progressive in its admission policies, and women were not accepted as degree candidates. In an interview, Taussig was told by the dean of the School of Public Health that all students there "should have two years of medicine and then we will *permit* women to study but we will not *admit* them as candidates for degrees." Taussig made it clear to the dean that she considered such a proposal absurd. The interview did, however, strengthen her inclination to study medicine.

She began her medical studies at Harvard in 1921 when she was given special permission to take histology, provided that she sat apart from the male students in the lecture hall. During laboratory sessions with the microscope, she had to sit in another room where, she recalled, she "wouldn't contaminate" the men. (Harvard would not admit women as regular medical students until 1945.) Despite the school's policy of discrimination against women, Taussig's histology professor recognized her ability. Dr. Bremer urged her to enroll at Boston University where she could take other courses and receive credit for her work.

At Boston University, after her anatomy professor, Dr. Begg, suggested that she "get interested in one of the larger organs of the body" by studying the heart, Taussig spent hours meticulously dissecting beef hearts. Following months of careful experiments on heart tissue from humans and other mammals, she was the first to show that heart tissue from mammals would contract rhythmically, as did tissue from cold-blooded animals, when immersed in a special solution. Taussig reported these significant findings in her first scientific paper, published in 1925 in the *Journal of Physiology*.

It was Dr. Begg who suggested that Taussig apply to the Johns Hopkins Medical School in Baltimore, Maryland, where women had been accepted since its opening in 1893. When Begg mentioned that one letter from Harvard would get her in, Taussig asked Dr. Walter Cannon, a family friend and professor of physiology at Harvard, for a recommendation. Cannon wrote to Johns Hopkins: "I have had the opportunity to watch her work and if women were admitted to Harvard I would enthusiastically vote for her admission. As you are more liberal than we, I

hope you will admit her." Taussig was admitted in 1924 and graduated in 1927. She would spend her entire career at Johns Hopkins.

After two years as a fellow in cardiology and an intern in pediatrics, Helen Taussig came under the influence of Dr. Edwards A. Park, the new chair of pediatrics, who became her mentor. In 1930, when Park established a pediatric cardiac clinic at Johns Hopkins, he asked Taussig to be the director. Many children were brought to the clinic with complications from rheumatic fever. Others were cyanotic (blue babies) who struggled to breathe because their malformed hearts were not pumping enough blood to the lungs for it to become saturated with oxygen. Little could be done for the cyanotic children, but Taussig learned much from examining them.

The clinic was outfitted with a fluoroscope, a new device similar to an X-ray machine, that for the first time allowed imaging of cardiac abnormalities. While Taussig's tiny patients turned slowly in front of the fluoroscope tube, their beating hearts could be visualized for a few seconds at a time. When cyanotic children died, Taussig followed up by studying their hearts at autopsy, carefully correlating her findings with her clinical observations. Gradually, she began to discover that certain malformations created specific clinical signs and symptoms in children. This was a major step in the understanding of congenital malformations of the heart.

For a physician in 1930, especially a pediatrician needing to listen to the delicate sounds of a baby's abnormal heart, the stethoscope was indispensable. When Taussig began to lose her hearing in 1930 and realized that her ability to distinguish sounds with a stethoscope was diminished, it was a severe blow, because hearing aids were clumsy and inadequate. She confronted this obstacle squarely, however, by teaching herself to lip-read and training her fingers to "hear" by feeling vibrations. She practiced listening with her hands by placing them on cushions during radio concerts and feeling the amplified vibrations. At the clinic, she examined the children with her hands resting gently on their chests to feel the pulsations. As her skill increased, she often surprised her colleagues by detecting problems they had been unable to identify with the stethoscope.

Taussig was aided in her study of the heart by the work of Dr. *Maude Abbott*, a Canadian physician acknowledged during that period as the authority on congenitally malformed hearts. Taussig spent a short time in Toronto learning from Abbott, who generously shared her knowledge, showing Taussig her X-rays and autopsy specimens of various malformations.

As a result of her clinical findings and research, Taussig became convinced that a way should be found to surgically open a duct between the heart and lungs in cyanotic children so that sufficient blood could flow to the lungs for oxygenation. In 1939, a pediatric surgeon in Boston was considered a hero after he successfully operated to close a duct, called the ductus arteriosus, leading from the heart in a baby whose ductus had not closed naturally as it should have after birth. Taussig believed that if a ductus could be closed, then it might be possible to create an open ductus to carry blood to the lungs.

By the time Dr. Alfred Blalock came to the Johns Hopkins Hospital in 1941 as chair of the department of surgery, he had already performed three operations to close the ductus arteriosus. Taussig observed one such operation and told him: "I stand in awe and admiration of your surgical skill, but the really great day will come when you build a ductus for a cyanotic child, not when you tie off a ductus for a child who has a little too much blood going to his lungs." Replied Blalock: "When that day comes, this will seem like child's play."

Blalock was intrigued by Taussig's challenge and arranged for his male laboratory assistant, Vivien Thomas, to experiment with dogs to create an artificial ductus by joining two arteries. Anna, the first dog to undergo the Blalock-Taussig anastomosis, lived for years after the procedure and became a minor celebrity in Baltimore. Over the next two years, Thomas operated successfully on more than 200 dogs, often with Blalock observing. But before Blalock was able to experiment with the procedure unassisted by Thomas, Taussig presented the case of a child who was near death, struggling for air whenever she was removed from her oxygen tent. The Blalock-Taussig procedure was the child's only hope.

On November 29, 1944, 15-month-old **Eileen Saxon**, weighing just 9½ pounds, underwent the operation that Taussig had envisioned years before. She watched from the head of the operating table as Blalock and several associates created a new pathway to the lungs no larger than a matchstick. Two months later, after the child had recovered sufficiently to return home, the Blalock-Taussig procedure was performed on an 11-year-old girl, and in February 1945 a 9-year-old boy underwent the surgery. These three children were the subject of an article written by Blalock and Taussig that gave a detailed account of the procedure, noting that "each of the pa-

tients appears to be greatly benefitted." Denton Cooley, one of Blalock's young associates who assisted at the operations, later called the three operations "the dawn of heart surgery."

News of the operations spread throughout the world. Desperate parents besieged Taussig's clinic, sometimes arriving unexpectedly with their cyanotic children. After thorough examination, Taussig and her associates often decided that a cyanotic child would not benefit from surgery, but over the years she recommended more than 1,000 children to Blalock. When other surgeons began performing the procedure, at least 12,000 children were eventually saved before advances in cardiac surgery reduced the need for the Blalock-Taussig procedure. Years later, Taussig recalled the "great thrill" of "seeing a child change from blue to pink." Taussig kept in touch with many of her former patients, who usually went on to live healthy, productive lives. She considered "her babies" part of her extended family.

Taussig was responsible for attracting many young medical graduates to the field of pediatric cardiology, which she virtually created through her clinical work and her landmark textbook *Congenital Malformations of the Heart*, published in 1947. One of her former students later said that the book "provided the basis on which the discipline of pediatric cardiology was built." One pediatrician recalled that in the late 1940s he "held cardiac clinic with a stethoscope in one hand and Dr. Taussig's book in the other."

Students who trained with her as fellows for two years were known as the "Loyal Knights of Taussig," and they were indeed loyal to their mentor. The fellows became friends who supported her on her often difficult path as a women in the male medical establishment. She trained 123 men and women as pediatric cardiologists, and worked with many physicians from around the world who trained with her briefly. Every other year, Taussig held a reunion of all her fellows at her home in Baltimore or at Cape Cod, where they picnicked, played, reminisced, and held a two-day scientific program in pediatric cardiology. For Taussig, who never married, these former students were as much a part of her extended family as her former patients.

In the late 1940s, Taussig began to receive many honors. It pained her, however, that Blalock was elected to the prestigious National Academy of Sciences in 1945 and she was not. Taussig also felt discrimination at Johns Hopkins. She was not made an associate professor until 1946, two years after the first "blue baby" operation, and had to wait until 1959 to be made a full professor of pediatrics. After her retirement, she mentioned how disappointed she was that it took her so long to be promoted to the rank of professor. "A man would have had the promotion long before I got mine," she said. One of her former fellows wrote that "one cannot describe the real life of Helen Taussig without recalling the turmoil, the resentments, envy and bitterness that more than counterbalanced any recognition of her work. For many years she was constantly under siege, but she knew her course and fought back. She was aggressive, defensive, combative, sometimes triumphant and often defeated. She suffered." Most of the time, said another colleague, "she was a marvelous, gracious lady" who "demanded excellence." With sick children and their families, however, she was always patient and compassionate, and she impressed upon her fellows the importance of easing the burdens of the people who sought their help.

Taussig's influence expanded in 1962 after she took a short leave from Johns Hopkins to investigate an outbreak of severe birth defects in Germany. Many babies were being born with misshaped legs and flipperlike appendages for arms, a rare deformity known as phocomelia or "seal limb." Some investigators thought that an over-the-counter sedative and treatment for morning sickness called thalidomide might be the cause. After traveling through Germany and Great Britain, asking questions and studying the findings of other investigators, Taussig was soon convinced that thalidomide, taken between the 20th and 42nd day of pregnancy, interrupted limb development. Even one thalidomide tablet taken in this time period was enough to cause the deformity. Fortunately, Dr. **Frances O. Kelsey**, head of the Food and Drug Administration, had fought against approval of the drug in the United States. When Taussig returned home, she publicized her conclusions in scientific articles, in medical meetings, and before the Kefauver Committee in Congress. She was concerned not only about the effect of thalidomide but also about the possible effects of any drug that could result in birth defects. Her testimony helped ensure passage of legislation mandating careful testing of medications used during pregnancy.

Following her retirement from Johns Hopkins in 1963, at age 65, Taussig continued to be involved in activities that affected the welfare of children. As a prominent pediatric cardiologist, she promoted the public's awareness of this important medical specialty. In 1965, she became the first woman and the first pediatric cardiolo-

gist to be elected president of the American Heart Association. Over the next 20 years, she attended scientific meetings around the world, published over 40 scientific papers, and continued her research into the causes of malformations of the heart.

In the last years of her life, Taussig lived at a retirement home in Kennett Square, Pennsylvania, and studied cardiac malformations in wild birds at the Delaware Museum of Natural History. Her last paper, completed early in 1986, described her examination of the tiny hearts of warblers. Taussig was killed that year in an automobile accident on her way to cast a vote. One of her young colleagues summarized her final hour: "She died wanting to change the world."

SOURCES:

Baldwin, Joyce. *To Heal the Heart of a Child: Helen Taussig, M.D.* NY: Walker, 1992.

Gilbert, Lynn, and Gaylen Moore. *Particular Passions: Talks with Women Who Have Shaped Our Lives.* NY: Clarkson N. Potter, 1981, pp. 51–57.

McNamara, Dan G., James A. Manning, Mary Allen Engle, *et al.* "Helen Brooke Taussig: 1898 to 1986," in *Journal of the American College of Cardiology.* Vol. 10, 1987, pp. 662–671.

Neill, Catherine. "Profiles in Pediatrics II: Helen Brooke Taussig," in *The Journal of Pediatrics.* Vol. 125, 1994, pp. 499–502.

SUGGESTED READING:

Blalock, Alfred, and Helen B. Taussig. "The surgical treatment of malformations of the heart in which there is pulmonary stenosis or pulmonary atresia," in *Journal of the American Medical Association.* Vol. 128, 1945, pp. 189–202.

Morantz-Sanchez, Regina Markell. *Sympathy and Science: Women Physicians in American Medicine.* NY: Oxford University Press, 1985.

Nuland, Sherwin B. *Doctors: The Biography of Medicine.* NY: Alfred A. Knopf, 1988, pp. 422–456.

Walsh, Mary Roth. *Doctors Wanted: No Women Need Apply: Sexual Barriers in the Medical Profession, 1835–1975.* New Haven, CT: Yale University Press, 1979.

COLLECTIONS:

Correspondence and writings located in the Alan Mason Chesney Medical Archives of the Johns Hopkins Medical Institutions, Baltimore, Maryland.

Katherine G. Haskell,
freelance writer and medical editor,
Philadelphia, Pennsylvania

Tauti (c. 1850–1918).

See Taytu.

Tautphoeus, Baroness von (1807–1893)

Irish novelist. Name variations: Jemima Montgomery; Jemima Tautphoeus. Born Jemima Montgomery on

October 23, 1807, at Seaview, in County Donegal, Ireland; died on November 12, 1893; daughter of a landowner; educated at home; married Baron von Tautphoeus of Marquartstein (chamberlain to the king of Bavaria), in 1838 (died 1885); children: one son who also died in 1885.

Born the daughter of a landowner in 1807, at Seaview, in County Donegal, Ireland, Jemima Montgomery married Baron von Tautphoeus of Marquartstein, chamberlain to the king of Bavaria, in 1838. The baroness lived in Germany for the remainder of her life, authoring several novels that dealt with the manners and history of the Bavarian scene. Her principal works include *The Initials* (1850), which is considered her best; *Cyrilla* (1854); *Quits* (1857); and *At Odds* (1863). Her novels have been described as "delightful, brilliant, sympathetic, and full of charm," and serve as an accurate portrayal of their time.

Taylor, Ann and Jane
English writers.

Taylor, Ann (1782–1866). Name variations: Ann Gilbert; Mrs. Gilbert. Born on January 30, 1782, in London; died on December 20, 1866, in Nottingham; daughter of Reverend Isaac Taylor and Ann Martin Taylor (1757–1830, a writer); married Reverend Joseph Gilbert, in 1813; children: eight, including Josiah (b. 1814) and Joseph (b. 1817).

Taylor, Jane (1783–1824). Born on September 23, 1783, in London; died on April 12, 1824, in Ongar; daughter of Reverend Isaac Taylor and Ann Martin Taylor (1757–1830, a writer); never married; no children.

Sisters Ann and Jane Taylor were two of the most popular English writers for children of the early 19th century. Indeed, they shaped the way children's literature has been written ever since. Born in London, they were the eldest of five surviving children of Isaac Taylor, an engraver and later a Congregational minister, and *Ann Martin Taylor, later a published writer herself. The family was poor but the children were well educated at home by their parents in literature, art, mathematics, and the sciences. Between 1786 and 1811, the Taylors moved several times for economic reasons, finally settling in Ongar in 1811. Since he could not provide them with dowries, Isaac was determined that his daughters be able to support themselves, so they were apprenticed to him as engravers.

Despite long working hours, the sisters found time for writing poetry, short stories, plays, and word games, some of which were submitted to an annual Quaker journal, *Minor's Pocket Book*. In 1804, the publisher asked them to write a volume of children's verses, published in 1805 as *Original Poems for Infant Minds*. It became immensely popular in England, remaining in print continuously into the 1880s, and was translated and published abroad as well. The critical and commercial success of *Original Poems* stemmed from its fresh, often humorous verses which spoke to the experiences of children yet always conveyed a moral lesson. The most famous contribution was Ann's poem "My Mother," its sentimental view of middle-class motherhood making it one of the most reprinted and imitated poems of the century. The sisters' approach to moral teaching differed drastically from previous literature aimed at children, which was formal and prescriptive rather than engaging the young reader's imagination.

The success of their first volume led to additional books of poetry and reading primers, produced both individually and jointly, with occasional contributions from their father and brothers. The books often included Ann and Jane's engravings as illustrations. The bestselling *Rhymes for the Nursery*, published in 1806, included Jane's verse "Twinkle, twinkle, little star," still one of the best-known verses in English. The more somber *Hymns for Infant Minds*, published in 1811, found widespread acceptance in English Sunday schools as a teaching aid.

Ann Taylor married the Nonconformist Reverend Joseph Gilbert in 1813 and moved to Nottingham. The demands of marriage and motherhood—she had eight children—left Ann little time for writing, but she still contributed essays and reviews periodically to Christian journals, and published hymns. She composed a short biography on her husband after his death in 1853, and in her widowhood became a social activist, involved in the abolition movement and in the rehabilitation of former prostitutes. After Ann's death in 1866 at age 84, her son Joseph published her autobiography and some shorter religious essays.

Jane Taylor never married and remained a prolific author throughout her life. In 1812, she left her parents' home in Ongar and settled in Devon with her brother Isaac, who like their father was ordained a minister. In 1815, the critical success of her first novel, *Display*, established her reputation as an independent writer. Her works became more evangelical after a spiritual crisis in 1817, following her return to Ongar. Her health began to fail that year when she contracted cancer, but she continued to write

*A*nn (right)
and *J*ane
*T*aylor

and contributed essays on various moral themes to *Youth's Magazine* until 1822. Jane died at age 41 in 1824. Her brother Isaac edited a posthumous collection of her works as *Memoirs and Poetical Remains of the late Jane Taylor*, published in 1825.

SOURCES:

Shattock, Joanne. *The Oxford Guide to British Women Writers*. NY: Oxford University Press, 1993.

Stewart, Christina D. *The Taylors of Ongar: An Analytical Bio-bibliography*. NY: Garland, 1975.

Laura York, M.A. in History,
University of California, Riverside, California

Taylor, Ann Martin (1757–1830)

English writer. Name variations: Ann Martin. Born on June 20, 1757, in Kensington, England; died on June 4, 1830, in Ongar, England; married Reverend Isaac Taylor, in 1781; children: Ann Taylor (1782–1866); Jane Taylor (1783–1824); Isaac Taylor (b. 1787); Jefferys Taylor (b. 1792); Jemima Taylor (b. 1798); six who died young.

Ann Taylor, who is best known as the author of conduct books, was born in 1757 in Kensington to a middle-class family of converts to Methodism. Her intellectual gifts were encouraged by her schoolteachers and her parents, but her father's death in 1763 and her mother's two remarriages nearly ended her education. However, in 1781 she married Isaac Taylor, an engraver and book illustrator who was soon to become ordained as a Congregational minister, with whom she shared a love of learning. They had eleven children, of whom five survived to adulthood, all of them eventually to achieve fame as writers of religious and children's books. As their family grew, the Taylors were forced to move often—from London to Suffolk to Colchester—as the worsening economic situation in England decreased the amount of engraving work available. In 1811, they finally settled in Ongar where Isaac became pastor to the Methodist community there. Between them Ann and Isaac provided an excellent education to their large family, devising an original method of teaching which used materials they wrote themselves. When the children were away from home, Ann wrote to them often with advice on proper conduct and proper religious observance.

Although she believed that it was improper for women to be published authors, since a woman should devote herself to the care of her family, she allowed her two eldest daughters ❧▶ **Ann** and ❧▶ **Jane Taylor** to submit moral stories and poetry to a Quaker publisher. Their phenomenal literary success encouraged Ann to submit her letters of advice to the same publisher, hoping that her work could prove beneficial to other parents. In 1814, the letters were published to critical acclaim as *Maternal Solicitude*, with a preface by her daughter Ann. She also collaborated with Jane on *Correspondence between a Mother and Her Daughter at School*, a collection of fictional letters addressing moral conduct for young women. The popularity of this work led to *Practical Hints to Young Females* (1815) and *The Present of a Mistress to a Young Servant*, concerning the proper relationship between a middle-class woman and her servants and the management of an efficient household.

Despite her continuing poor health, in 1819 Ann published a fictional work, *The Family Mansion*. It was billed as "a tale" to distinguish it from a novel, since Ann believed novels to be frivolous and useless for the instruction of young people. Her second full-length work of fiction, like the first a bestseller, was *Retrospection* (1821).

Ann's last book was *Itinerary of a Traveller in the Wilderness*, a series of essays meditating on preparation for death and the afterlife. It appeared in 1825, after which she ceased to write because of her failing health. Isaac Taylor died in 1829; Ann survived him by less than a year, dying in 1830 at age 73. Many of her books remained in publication for more than 50 years after her death.

SOURCES:

Shattock, Joanne. *The Oxford Guide to British Women Writers*. NY: Oxford University Press, 1993.

Stewart, Christina D. *The Taylors of Ongar: An Analytical Bio-bibliography*. NY: Garland, 1975.

Laura York, M.A. in History, University of California, Riverside, California

Taylor, Anna Edson (c. 1858–c. 1921)

First person to survive going over Niagara Falls in a barrel. Name variations: Annie Taylor. Born around 1858; died around 1921.

On October 24, 1901, Anna Edson Taylor, a 43-year-old widow and schoolteacher from Bay City, Michigan, who could not swim, went over the 167' high Horseshoe Falls (on the Canadian side of Niagara Falls) in a 4½'x3" barrel. Taylor, who had a cooper build the conveyance, was protected by cushions inside the barrel, which was kept in an upright position by a blacksmith's anvil that weighed 100 pounds. A rubber hose connected to a small opening near the lid provided sufficient air to breathe.

The Pan American Exposition was in progress at the time and Niagara Falls was filled with tourists anxious to witness the event. Although the local coroner tried to dissuade Taylor from the attempt, she maintained that if the authorities tried to stop her, she would jump to her death over the Falls instead. The money that would reward her for going over the Falls was needed to pay off a debt.

The event began when a boat towed Taylor and the barrel to an area near Grass Island on the Niagara River. At 4:05 PM, the towing line was severed, and the barrel moved rapidly to-

❧
Taylor, Ann and *Jane Taylor.* See joint entry under Taylor, Ann and Jane.

ward the brink of the Falls. At 4:23 PM, the barrel balanced briefly at the top before plummeting over the precipice. It took a minute to resurface several hundred yards below the Falls and was recovered 17 minutes later and sawed open. Taylor, who had been knocked unconscious, was still dazed when she emerged, bleeding from a gash (some sources say on her forehead and others say behind her ear), and suffering bruises but no broken bones. When she was finally able to speak, she warned others against "the foolish thing I have done." Since then six men have attempted the same ride over the Falls, but only three have survived. Anna Edson Taylor died penniless at age 83.

SOURCES:

Felton, Bruce, and Mark Fowler. *Felton & Fowler's Famous Americans You Never Knew Existed.* NY: Stein and Day, 1979.

Griffin, Lynn, and Kelly McCann. *The Book of Women: 300 Notable Women History Passed By.* Holbrook, MA: Bob Adams, 1992.

Read, Phyllis J., and Bernard L. Witlieb. *The Book of Women's Firsts.* NY: Random House, 1992.

Karina L. Kerr, M.A.,
Ypsilanti, Michigan

Taylor, Betty (1916–1977)

Canadian athlete who ran the 60- and 80-meter hurdles. Born Elizabeth Taylor on February 22, 1916; died on February 2, 1977; raised in Hamilton, Ontario, Canada; attended McMaster University in Hamilton.

Betty Taylor began her career as one of Canada's leading track-and-field champions in 1930, at age 14. She competed in the Canadian women's track-and-field championships, held in conjunction with the British Empire Games in Hamilton, Ontario, and won the 60-meter hurdles event at the intermediate level. That August, as part of the Hamilton Olympic Club, Taylor competed in the junior category (because she was under 16) at the provincial championship meet and won the 60-meter hurdles with a time of 9.9 seconds, beating the intermediate time of 10.4 seconds. Prevented by the high cost of traveling from defending her Canadian title in 1931 at the championships held in Wetaskiwin, Alberta, she continued to compete for the Hamilton Olympic Club at meets around Ontario.

Taylor's first senior-level competition came in 1932 at the Canadian Olympic trials, where she finished second in the 80-meter hurdles finals. Although the team finished second overall at the Olympics, Taylor was eliminated in the preliminary heats. In the summer of 1933, however, she again rose to the top by winning the 80-

meter hurdles at the senior level at the nationals with a time of 12.4 seconds—more than a second faster than the previous year and 15 yards ahead of her nearest competitor.

In 1934, when Taylor was 18, she competed on the Canadian team at the British Empire Games and the Women's World Games, both held in London, England. During the trials, she and teammate **Roxy Atkins** tied and set a new Canadian record of 11.9 seconds for their event. At the Empire Games, Taylor won her preliminary heat and finished second in the final. During the Women's World Games, Taylor once again came in second, but ran the best race of her career. These races helped her to earn a reputation for being able to perform well under pressure against tough competition. Both Canadian and European critics praised her for her hurdling technique.

After returning to Canada, Taylor entered McMaster University in Hamilton on an athletic scholarship and became an honors student. While in college she participated in many sports, but also remained active in the Hamilton Olympic Club. In 1935, she again won the Canadian championship, coming from behind to beat Roxy Atkins. Defending her Ontario and national titles in 1936, she qualified for the Olympic team and was elected the team's captain. In Berlin, she was dubbed "Beautiful Betty" and once again performed well. In the semifinal heat she tied the world record of 11.7 seconds. However, in the finals, while in the lead, she was bumped by the hurdler in the lane next to her and knocked off stride. She managed to finish in the top four, a group so close together that the three medal winners were all given the same time. Although she was first thought to have placed fourth, a review of official photographs resulted in her winning the bronze medal.

In December 1936, Taylor was nominated for the Lou Marsh Trophy, an award for Canada's outstanding athlete, male or female, professional or amateur. Although she did not win this award, later that month she won the Canadian Press Award given by Canadian sportswriters. Also a winner of the Velma Springstead Memorial Trophy for the outstanding Canadian female athlete from the Women's Federation, Taylor was named the best Canadian female athlete of 1936. The last award during her career came in February 1937, when she was given the President's Prize by the Hamilton Olympic Club for being the club's outstanding athlete of 1936.

After receiving the award from her club, Taylor announced her retirement. Notes Cathy MacDonald: "During her tenure as Canada's premier hurdler [Taylor] continued the Canadian tradition of athletic excellence and was an important participant in the golden age of women's sport in Canada."

SOURCES:
MacDonald, Cathy. "Hamilton's Hurdler—Betty Taylor," in *Canadian Woman Studies*. Vol. 4, no. 3. Spring–May 1983, pp. 10–21.

Karina L. Kerr, M.A.,
Ypsilanti, Michigan

Taylor, Elizabeth (1912–1975)

English novelist and short-story writer. Born in Reading, Berkshire, England, on July 3, 1912; died of cancer on November 19, 1975; daughter of Oliver Coles and Elsie Coles; graduated from Abbey School, Reading, 1930; married John William Kendal Taylor (a manufacturer), in 1936; children: son Renny (b. 1937); daughter Joanna (b. 1941).

While husband was in Royal Air Force, lived in Scarborough, Yorkshire (1940–45); published first novel, At Mrs. Lippincote's (1945); last novel, Blaming, published posthumously (1976).

Selected works: At Mrs. Lippincote's (London: Davies, 1945); Palladian (London: Davies, 1946); A View of the Harbour (London: Davies, 1947); A Wreath of Roses (London: Davies, 1949); A Game of Hide-and-Seek (London: Davies, 1951); The Sleeping Beauty (London: Davies, 1953); Hester Lilly and Twelve Short Stories (London: Davies, 1954); Angel (London: Davies, 1957); The Blush and Other Stories (London: Davies, 1958); In a Summer Season (London: Davies, 1961); The Soul of Kindness (London: Chatto & Windus, 1964); A Dedicated Man and Other Stories (London: Chatto & Windus, 1965); Mossy Trotter (London: Chatto & Windus, 1967); The Wedding Group (London: Chatto & Windus, 1968); Mrs. Palfrey at the Claremont (London: Chatto & Windus, 1971); The Devastating Boys (London: Chatto & Windus, 1972); Blaming (London: Chatto & Windus, 1976).

The writer *Ivy Compton-Burnett described her friend Elizabeth Taylor as "a young woman who looks as if she never had to wash her gloves." Quiet dignity, "elegance and femininity" characterize Taylor both as a writer and a woman. Though little is known of her personal life, a great deal can be gleaned about her attitudes, interests, and views of the human condition from her twelve novels and four collections of short stories. She was unpretentious and pessimistic, loved few people, and did not believe in God. The daughter of Oliver and **Elsie Coles**, she was born on July 3, 1912, in Reading, Berkshire, England. After graduating from Abbey School in 1930, she worked as a governess and later as a librarian, married John William Kendal Taylor, who worked in the confectionery business, in 1936 and stopped working. In 1937, she gave birth to a son Renny, and in 1941 to a daughter Joanna. But behind the façade of quiet middle-class domesticity which characterized her public persona one finds a keen observer of human foibles, of the individual's desperate attempt to deal with isolation and loneliness.

When Taylor began writing in 1945, England was experiencing war-weariness, social upheaval, economic austerity, and an uncertain future. Contemporary writers strove to liberate literature "from the tyranny of a taste based on a world of wealth and leisure" that had defined "Englishness" in the years prior to World War II. Socialism, the "Welfare-State world," and the leveling of social classes "that aimed toward the lowest common denominator" promoted the rise of a working-class literature. The "angry young men" who railed against the class structure, and the smug, comfortable middle and upper-middle classes, were antithetical to the world Taylor chose to depict, to the world in which she lived.

Instead of dwelling on the drab conditions of life in the industrial areas of England, Taylor describes the lives of privileged classes who inhabit the Thames Valley, "an attractive—and very selective—part of England, the region she comes from and knows best." She writes about outwardly respectable, well-to-do, well-bred people, "a microcosm, a small section of English life" of which she was a member. Taylor regretted the mediocrity, the crass modernization that brought pollution, supermarkets, garish street lighting, and blocks of subsidized housing. So she ignored it and wrote about the people and places with which she was familiar. Like *Virginia Woolf, she preferred "books in which practically nothing happens" and emphasized the lives of her characters rather than plot or setting. Moreover, like one of her favorite authors, *Jane Austen (also an Abbey School graduate), Taylor was interested in domestic situations involving few characters.

Taylor's first two novels, *At Mrs. Lippincote's* and *Palladian*, are autobiographical; in the first, she describes the life of a woman (Julia) married to an RAF officer during World War II, trying to adjust to military life in northern England. Through Julia, Taylor evokes a mood of nostalgia and fear of the future in what she sees as a disintegrating, alien world. One of Taylor's central themes in all her writings is introduced here: "the theme of transition between two worlds," the genteel, complacent, and secure pre-1945 era that had been obliterated during the war, and the modern world shaken by social conflicts and economic austerity. Other common themes in her work include the failure of human relationships and loneliness. Julia and her husband Roddy do not "connect"; she resents being dependent on him, but lacks the spirit to challenge her situation. The plot of *Palladian* reveals Taylor's experiences while working as a governess: the story of a young woman who falls in love with her employ-

er. The characters are, however, vague and unconvincing, and the use of cliché and stereotypes, plus a weak ending, make this novel "disappointing," Florence Leclercq notes.

Taylor refused to reveal anything about her personal life, even to such close friends as Ivy Compton-Burnett and Robert Liddell; she maintained that she was "always disconcerted when I am asked for my life story, for nothing sensational, thank heavens, has ever happened. I dislike much travel or change of environment, and prefer the days . . . to come round almost the

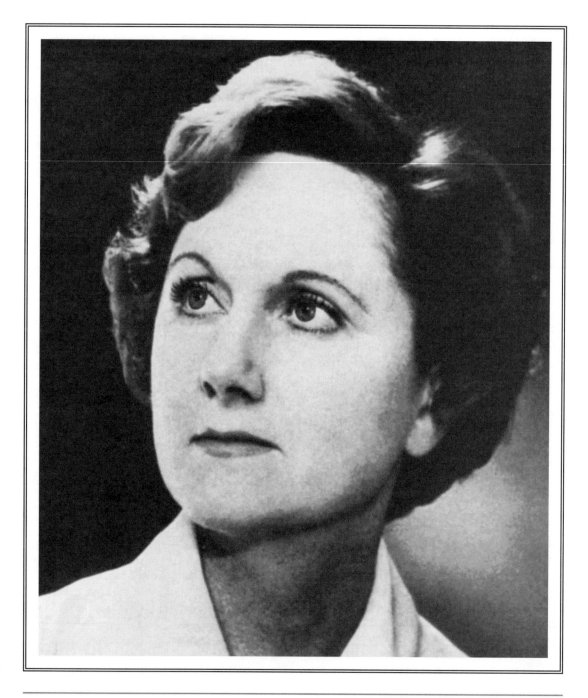

Elizabeth

Taylor

(1912–1975)

same, week after week." These attitudes are reflected in her work. Moreover, as she told Liddell, "I wouldn't describe anything that was not what I had gone through and understood myself—in my experience or out of my imagination and other people's words wouldn't do." Undoubtedly, her novels and short stories are windows into her inner self. Pessimism is pervasive in all her writing as she chronicles human failures, the "wasted lives" and "the uselessness of all human purposes, the vanity of men's efforts." Taylor herself chose a quiet, routine existence which allowed her to write. Liddell recalled that she "loved life indeed—but critically, fastidiously, and intelligently. She loved few people, but those very much." Elizabeth Taylor lived in, and wrote about, a restricted world of artists and writers and lonely men and women. But as she reveals, behind the walls of fine houses and gracious lifestyles, everyone suffers from loneliness, from self-imposed isolation, in "a closed world." This was Taylor's situation, for she, too, "avoided contact with the realities of the post-war world."

There appears to be a dark side to Taylor's personality—"her basic pessimism and lack of faith in human nature." Love, a sense of humor, and man's ability to survive are all one has in Taylor's world without God. To Taylor doing one's duty to oneself and others constituted morality. Her bleak view of humankind and the modern world did not, however, admit her to the ranks of the contemporary "angry" young writers in postwar Britain. Despite the grim, unsettled circumstances of post-1945 England, Taylor loved her native country: "It would be painful for me to consider living any other place. I find it so beautiful, harmonious and evocative, its landscape, style, tradition, even its climate." Taylor had the ability to ignore conditions outside of her own limited milieu in her life and her work. As one reviewer noted, "There is a peculiar and soothing Englishness about everything Mrs. Taylor writes." This accounts in large part for the success of her short stories that appeared in *The New Yorker*, *Harper's*, and *Harper's Bazaar* in the United States.

Elizabeth Taylor was not a part of the revival of realism in literature after 1945. Notes Leclercq, "Her lack of anger, failure to denounce class structure, her sympathy for the world she lives in, her gentleness, her quiet tone . . . have excluded her from the main drift of the contemporary English novel." But Taylor knew, and revealed, that behind the civilized, polite and mannered world she depicted, lurked the lonely individuals who through missed opportunities and wrong choices existed in quiet desperation. In *A Wreath of Roses*, the main character Frances is an artist whose pictures present a view of the world that is "ladylike and nostalgic, governessy, utterly lacking in ferocity, brutality, violence." Taylor's words could be applied to her own view. However, she was also aware "that beauty always hides ugliness, that underneath goodness lies evil." Her pessimism is seen when one of her characters admits, "Life's not simplicity. Not loving-kindness either. It's darkness and the terrible things we do to one another and to ourselves." Leclercq observes that Taylor "can be pitiless" in dealing with mankind.

It is striking that many of Taylor's main characters are creative artists and writers who fail to achieve fulfillment in their work or their lives. Their talents and efforts are never fully recognized, and despite their abilities, as one of Taylor's protagonists says, "in the things that really matter to us, we are entirely alone." Likewise, Taylor never "earned a literary reputation that would reflect the generally good reviews of her work," according to K.M. Stemmler. Kingsley Amis attributes her lack of recognition to her concentration on domestic life, what some critics labeled "women's" novels that were "frequently vilified." The writer **Anne Tyler** agrees with this assessment and points out that Taylor's work appeared at a time "when people spoke of 'women's novels' without so much as a set of quotation marks to excuse the phrase." Few knew the private side of Elizabeth Taylor, but she admitted that she gathered her subjects from personal observation, and as Tyler says, she "made it her business to explore the quirky underside of so-called civilization" and found "that the human soul is a remarkably dark and funny thing." And in her "delicate way, she could be absolutely savage." Taylor's "restraint and quietness" did not appeal to everyone. Her work is "within a certain tradition, about a certain class of people whom she knows well, about places she has lived all her life," writes Leclercq. But her writing is not "trivial." That Taylor wrote about what and who she knew lends an element of realism to her work and allows the reader a glimpse of the personality and life of the author.

Elizabeth Taylor traveled for only short periods outside of England. She drew her inspiration and her subjects closer to home. In 1948, she began corresponding with Robert Liddell, and visited him several times in Greece. After the "Colonels' Revolution" in 1967, Taylor refused to visit Greece under their regime. Later, she was "blacklisted" because she "said something disobliging in an interview" about this government, according to Liddell. But she and her husband John continued to visit Corsica, France, Crete, North Africa, and Istanbul.

During the 1970s, Taylor began to deal with the indignities and loneliness of the elderly. In *Mrs. Palfrey at the Claremont*, she creates an atmosphere of "resigned doom" among the residents of a retirement hotel in London. The old have nothing to give to society, and they are as dependent on others as children—one begins and ends one's life in a state of dependency. The old are redundant in a culture that worships youth. Taylor did not live long enough to endure the ravages of old age; in 1972, she contracted cancer which went into remission until the summer of 1975. She worked on her last novel, *Blaming*, until she died; it was published posthumously by her husband in 1976. In the final stages of the disease, she refused treatment that would have resulted in baldness: "I refuse to be a bed-ridden crone in a crooked wig," she wrote to Liddell. Elizabeth Taylor died on her "name-day," November 19, the feast day of St. *Elizabeth of Hungary.

SOURCES:

Leclercq, Florence. *Elizabeth Taylor*. Boston, MA: Twayne, 1985.

Liddell, Robert. *Elizabeth and Ivy*. London: Peter Owen, 1986.

Stemmler, K.M. "Elizabeth Taylor," in *Dictionary of Literary Biography*. Vol. 139. Detroit, MI: Gale Research, 1994, pp. 234–244.

SUGGESTED READING:

Amis, Kingsley. "At Mrs. Taylor's," in *Spectator*. June 14, 1957, p. 786.

Hicks, Granville. "Amour on the Thames," in *Saturday Review*. Vol. 44. January 21, 1961, p. 62.

Liddell, Robert. "Elizabeth Taylor," in *Contemporary Novelists*. Edited by James Vinson. NY: St. Martin's Press, 1972, pp. 1223–1225.

Wallace, Frances. "Elizabeth Taylor," in *Wilson Library Bulletin*. Vol. 22. April 1948, p. 580.

Jeanne A. Ojala,
Professor Emerita, Department of History,
University of Utah, Salt Lake City, Utah

Taylor, Elizabeth (1916–1977).

See Taylor, Betty.

Taylor, Elizabeth (1932—)

Academy Award-winning American actress who remains a respected and much-loved celebrity around the world, particularly after raising millions of dollars for AIDS research by lending her name and presence to fundraising events. Born on February 27, 1932, in London to American parents; daughter of Francis Taylor (an art dealer) and Sara (Warmbrodt)

*Taylor (who officially changed her name to Sara Sothern when she began acting in stock companies); married Conrad "Nicky" Hilton, Jr. (a hotelier), in 1950 (divorced 1951); married Michael Wilding (an actor), in 1952 (divorced 1957); married Michael Todd (a producer), in 1957 (died 1958); married Eddie Fisher (a singer), in 1959 (divorced 1964); married Richard Burton (an actor), in 1964 and 1975 (divorced 1973 and 1976); married John Warner (a senator), in 1976 (divorced 1982); married Larry Fortensky (a construction worker), in 1991 (divorced 1996); children: (second marriage) Michael Wilding, Jr. (b. 1953); Christopher Wilding (b. 1955); (third marriage) **Elizabeth Frances Todd** (b. 1957); (fifth marriage) adopted, **Maria Burton**.*

At outbreak of World War II (1939), moved with her parents to Los Angeles; made her screen debut (1942); while under contract to MGM, became as famous for her off-screen life as for her filmed work (1942–62); won her first Academy Award for her performance in Butterfield 8 *(1960); won second Academy Award for her work in* Who's Afraid of Virginia Woolf? *(1966); although later career has been less spectacular and marked by numerous health problems, remains a respected and much-loved celebrity around the world, particularly after raising millions of dollars for AIDS research by lending her name and presence to fundraising events; was the third recipient of the ***Marian Anderson** *Award for her work on behalf of AIDS awareness, research, and patient care (2000); was named a Dame of the Order of the British Empire by Queen ***Elizabeth II** *(2000).*

Selected filmography: There's One Born Every Minute *(1942);* Lassie Come Home *(1943);* Jane Eyre *(1944);* The White Cliffs of Dover *(1944);* National Velvet *(1944);* Courage of Lassie *(1946);* Cynthia *(1947);* Life with Father *(1947);* A Date with Judy *(1948);* Julia Misbehaves *(1948);* Little Women *(1949);* Conspirator *(1950);* The Big Hangover *(1950);* Father of the Bride *(1950); (unbilled cameo)* Quo Vadis *(1951);* Father's Little Dividend *(1951);* A Place in the Sun *(1951);* Callaway Went Thataway *(1951);* Love Is Better Than Ever *(1952);* Ivanhoe *(1952);* The Girl Who Had Everything *(1953);* Rhapsody *(1954);* Elephant Walk *(1954);* Beau Brummel *(1954);* The Last Time I Saw Paris *(1954);* Giant *(1956);* Raintree County *(1957);* Cat on a Hot Tin Roof *(1958);* Suddenly, Last Summer *(1959); (unbilled cameo)* Scent of Mystery *(1960);* Butterfield 8 *(1960);* Cleopatra *(1963);* The VIPs *(1963);* The Sandpiper *(1965);* Who's Afraid of Virginia Woolf? *(1966);* The Taming of the Shrew *(1967);* Doctor Faustus *(1967);* Reflections in a Golden Eye *(1967);* The Comedians

(1967); Boom! (1968); Secret Ceremony (1968); The Only Game in Town (1970); Under Milkwood (1971); Zee Zee & Co. (1972); Hammersmith Is Out (1972); Night Watch (1974); Ash Wednesday (1974); That's Entertainment (1974); The Driver's Seat (Identikit, 1974); The Blue Bird (1976); A Little Night Music (1977); Winter Kills (1979); The Mirror Crack'd (1980); (documentary, as narrator) Genocide (1981); Young Toscanini (1988); The Flintstones (1994); The Visit (1999). Television: "These Old Broads," starring Taylor, Joan Collins, Shirley MacLaine and Debbie Reynolds, written by Carrie Fisher and Elaine Pope, first aired on ABC in October 2000.

Elizabeth Taylor once ventured the opinion that her extraordinary career as a screen icon and public institution had been born from conflict. "Probably if there hadn't been a World War II," she told an interviewer, "I would have been a debutante . . . and married someone very secure and staid. I never would have become an actress." But it was the more personal turmoil of her private life that was responsible for her rise to fame as one of the world's most glamorous actresses.

Born in London to comfortably situated American parents on February 27, 1932, Taylor could very well have grown up as the proper young English woman she envisioned, although the luxuriant dark hair and the violet eyes that would become internationally famous were distinctly at odds with the usual pale beauty of English maidens. Neither her father Francis Taylor—an aristocratic art dealer with an equally aristocratic clientele drawn from the upper reaches of British society—nor her mother **Sara Taylor** envisioned anything but a normal, upper-class childhood for their daughter and their older son Howard, born three years earlier. Taylor grew up in the family's ivy-strewn brick house, Heathwood, in London's genteel Hampstead or, later, at their country cottage, Little Swallows, deep in the Kent countryside, where a patient pony named Betty provided Elizabeth with her first riding lessons. Dukes and duchesses, earls and countesses were family friends and provided an atmosphere of calm self-assurance that would serve Taylor well in years to come.

But there was show business in the family blood, for Sara (under the name Sara Sothern) had enjoyed in her younger days a brief reputation as an actress, particularly for her signature portrayal of a paralyzed young girl in a popular melodrama of the 1920s which had played to full houses on both Broadway and in London's West End. She had ended her stage career upon meeting Francis Taylor in New York and marrying him in 1926, but Sara still took a particular interest in the arts and saw to it that her daughter was enrolled in dancing classes at an early age. Thus it was that the duchess of York (now Queen Mother *Elizabeth Bowes-Lyon**) looked on in amusement at a dance recital while four-year-old Elizabeth Taylor flitted around the stage as a butterfly long past the end of her number, obliging her mother to run out from the wings to retrieve her. "It was a marvelous feeling on that stage," Taylor recalled years later. "The isolation, the hugeness, the feeling of space and no end to space—and then the applause bringing you back into focus, and noise rattling against your face."

Her parents chose a discreet private girls' school for the beginning of her formal education, unexpectedly cut short in her second year. Such were Francis Taylor's connections that a highly placed aide to Winston Churchill advised Francis early in 1939 to send his wife and children back to the United States, for war was sure to break out by that summer. While Francis supervised the closing of his London gallery, Sara and the children traveled the 6,000 miles to Pasadena, where Sara's father had settled. The Taylor children were forced to adapt to public grammar schools and quickly lost their British accents (although Taylor was always able to switch back and forth with ease). It was Francis' idea to open a gallery in Hollywood, where the closest thing America had to royalty might be willing to spend their money on fine art. Arriving in Los Angeles six months later, Francis soon found space in the lobby of Hollywood's elegant Chateau Elysee, and a home for his family in Beverly Hills.

During the Atlantic crossing with her mother, Elizabeth had seen her first film, *The Little Princess*, the film that convinced millions of American mothers that their own daughters could do just as well in the movies as *Shirley Temple (Black)*. Hollywood was overrun with such hopefuls when the Taylors arrived in town. Sara, with the stage actress' innate suspicion of the film business, carefully kept her daughter away. But with her husband's clients, including actors like Edward G. Robinson and directors like Billy Wilder and George Cukor, it was only a matter of time before the roving eyes of film studios looking for a rival to Shirley Temple settled on the dark-haired little girl with the startling violet eyes. Even gossip queen *Hedda Hopper*, who mentioned Francis Taylor's gallery and its sparkling clientele in her daily column, couldn't resist also mentioning the Taylors' beautiful little girl. Two years after leaving England, Elizabeth was signed to a standard seven-year contract by Universal in April 1941 and appeared briefly in a non-speaking role in a juvenile comedy called *There's One Born Every Minute* "firing elastic bands at fat ladies' bottoms," as Taylor remembered it years later. Her budding film career, however, was short-lived. Universal, deciding that she looked too serious and had none of Shirley's natural ebullience on screen, exercised its option to cancel the contract after the first year. "The kid has nothing," one studio director commented. It apparently did not occur to anyone that perhaps it was the material being offered that was to blame. Rival studio MGM, which Universal had beaten to the punch in signing Elizabeth, quickly stepped in with a film that suited her perfectly.

Production had already begun during the summer of 1942 on *Lassie Come Home*, adapted from Eric Knight's juvenile melodrama about a boy and his collie, when the child actress playing opposite Roddy McDowell developed an unforeseen problem. The intense lighting required to shoot color film in those days made the girl's eyes water terribly and filming had been shut down until a new, dry-eyed Priscilla could be found. Exactly how Taylor was given the role is the stuff of many Hollywood legends. Some say the film's producer, a friend of Francis Taylor's, happened to mention during an evening stroll that he needed a little girl who could handle a British accent; some say it was Francis who had been extolling his daughter's talents since the casting process had begun; some say it was because the wife of the film's director was the sister of Broadway's Edgar Selwyn, who had produced Sara's most famous play 20 years before and remembered his former star well. However it happened, Elizabeth was signed to a "test option"—essentially a freelance contract—at $100 a week for ten weeks, which was $150 less than was being paid to Lassie's trainer.

Although the film's real star (besides Lassie, of course) was 12-year-old Roddy McDowell, like Elizabeth a British expatriate sent to the safety of America during the war, Elizabeth's few scenes did not go unnoticed. The *Hollywood Reporter* noted that "Elizabeth Taylor looks like a comer," while the ever-watchful Hedda Hopper cooed that "Little Elizabeth Taylor is lovely." More important, Taylor's British-bred self-confidence and unexpected professionalism on the set were much remarked upon by her co-workers. McDowell later remembered that Elizabeth seemed "totally unaware of her beauty." Her mother, as impressed as anyone else, settled on a test of her daughter's talent by having her read the part she herself had

played so many years earlier on Broadway. "There sat my daughter playing perfectly the part of the child as I, a grown woman, had tried to do it," she later remembered. "It seemed she must have been in my head all those years I was acting." On the strength of her performance in *Lassie Come Home*, MGM offered a permanent contract, signed in January 1943, and again cast Taylor in a small part opposite McDowell in the wartime weeper *The White Cliffs of Dover*. But it was their next film together that would make Elizabeth Taylor a bona fide star.

The highly pitched emotionalism of her portrayal of Velvet Brown in 1944's *National Velvet* caught everyone unawares, and it was generally credited with keeping *Enid Bagnold's story of a young girl who rides her horse to victory in Britain's Grand National Steeplechase from sinking into tearful melodrama. "Whenever she speaks or thinks of horses," reported the London *Daily Telegraph*, "her strange azure eyes gleam and her whole frame trembles with the intensity of her passion." Equally intense was Taylor's preparation for the role. Production on the film was delayed for four months while she gained weight to make herself look older and more believable as a girl who disguises herself as a male jockey for the film's climactic race; and the spinal injuries she received in two falls during riding lessons before production began would plague her for the rest of her life. But when the film opened on Christmas Day, 1944, a normally reserved James Agee wrote that he had been "choked with a peculiar sort of adoration I might have felt if we were both in the same grade at primary school." MGM was quick to pick up on the connection the film encouraged in the public's mind between Elizabeth, horses, and animals in general. The collection of 22 chipmunks she tended during the shooting of a Lassie sequel, *Courage of Lassie*, was widely reported; and the studio publicity department quickly adapted a school essay Taylor had written about her favorite chipmunk into a children's book called *Nibbles and Me*.

By 1948, however, the nature-girl image was wearing thin. Taylor was now a strikingly beautiful 16 and was widely rumored to be Hollywood's next megastar, about to take her place with the likes of ◄ Joan Fontaine, *Barbara Stanwyck, and *Joan Crawford. On loanout to Warner Bros., Taylor had left her adolescence behind for good by playing the love interest in *Life with Father*, and had kissed a boy on the cheek for the first time on screen in MGM's own *Cynthia*. "She was beginning to be conscious in a very normal, teenage way of her own beauty,"

Fontaine, Joan.
See joint entry under de Havilland, Olivia and Joan Fontaine.

*Mary Astor, who played Elizabeth's mother in *Cynthia*, wrote in her memoirs. Both films had been released back to back in August and September 1947, prompting *Life* magazine to note: "Elizabeth Taylor has suddenly become Hollywood's most accomplished junior actress." MGM now began to promote the Junior Miss image, carefully arranging dates for their developing star and staging parties at which respectful young men squired her around the dance floor. One of them was her former co-star Roddy McDowell, photographed bowing to her, as if in recognition of her exalted new status.

MGM became anxious, however, when Taylor actually fell in love with one of her studio beaux, Glenn Davis, a West Point football hero of some national repute whom she dated while playing Amy in 1948's *Little Women*, the second screen version of the *Louisa May Alcott favorite. Amid rumors that the couple intended to announce their engagement, Taylor was packed off to England to shoot a political thriller, *Conspirator*, in which she was badly miscast as a housewife, even though she was still young enough to require a tutor on the set. But there was no doubt she was becoming a restless young

Elizabeth Taylor

woman. "Elizabeth gave me the feeling that she was tired of being watched [by her mother]," Victor Saville, the film's director, later said, although Sara wasn't the only one watching. Such was Taylor's fame that the end of her affair with Davis, and the announcement in June 1949 of her engagement to William Pawley, Jr., the son of a wealthy industrialist, were breathlessly reported in tabloids and fan magazines. Only three months later, the engagement was called off. Pawley would only say it was because of "circumstances beyond our control," but the annoyed public which took to calling her "Liz the Jilt" in print put the blame squarely on her shoulders for abandoning two men in less than six months. "Someone should administer a series of resounding smacks behind the bustle of her latest Paris creation," complained the *Sunday Pictorial* in London. "She is a living argument against employment of children in studios." It would not be the last time her romantic entanglements would overshadow her accomplishments on screen.

But all was temporarily forgiven with Taylor's radiant performance as the wealthy socialite Angela Vickers in *A Place in the Sun*, MGM's 1951 adaptation of Theodore Dreiser's *An American Tragedy*. She played opposite Montgomery Clift, an actor who would become almost a brother to her during his short, tragic life, and was directed by George Stevens. Both men were advocates of the emotional research and psychological analysis that were the hallmarks of so-called Method acting, and Elizabeth would later say that *A Place in the Sun* was the first film in which she had learned a craft, rather than exploited a talent. Stevens cast her, he said, because she was "the girl on the candybox cover, the beautiful girl in the yellow Cadillac convertible that every American boy thinks at one time or another he can marry," which is precisely what happens to Clift's George Eastman, with tragic results. "Miss Taylor reveals an understanding of passion and suffering that is electrifying," *Life* reported in its review of the film, while *The New Yorker* thought the film's "passionate and genuine romance avoids the bathos common to young love." So convincing was the on-screen relationship between Taylor and Clift that marriage rumors again began circulating, helped once again by MGM's publicity, which assiduously hid Clift's homosexuality from the public. "I never saw a girl more ripe for love and marriage than Elizabeth," burbled Hedda Hopper early in 1950. Hopper did not speculate who the intended husband might be even though her sources had given her a fair idea.

Taylor had been dating Conrad "Nicky" Hilton, Jr., the eldest son of the hotelier, for more than six months before the gossip columns got wind of the relationship. They had met through a mutual friend at Paramount as shooting was wrapping on *A Place in the Sun* in November 1949, but it wasn't until the spring of 1950, after Elizabeth had graduated from high school, that the 23-year-old Hilton told a reporter they would marry. At 18, Taylor naively felt prepared to settle down and raise a family, while Nick Hilton, then the manager of his father's Bel Air Hotel, was more interested in the fact he was marrying a movie star. Hilton did not count on the power MGM wielded over Taylor's life. The studio timed the wedding, on May 6, 1950, to coincide with the release of *Father of the Bride*, a domestic comedy in which Taylor played the role she was about to perform in real life. The marriage, close friends later said, was over before the couple left on a two-week European honeymoon. Frightened by her husband's sexual aggressiveness and his older, worldly circle of friends, Taylor looked tired and in ill health on her return. By the time she began work on a sequel to *Father of the Bride*, called *Father's Little Dividend*, in the late summer of 1950, she and Hilton had decided to separate. Formal divorce papers were filed late in the year as Taylor checked herself into a hospital under the name "Rebecca Jones," suffering from a nervous breakdown. "I was certainly a mixed up eighteen," Taylor confided to Hopper in an interview early in 1951, as she turned 19. When the columnist asked if she were happy, Elizabeth answered that she was, "but I am not nineteen happy."

Her six-month marriage to Nick Hilton, however, was merely the first of seven in Taylor's search for emotional security. Next in the line of succession was British actor Michael Wilding, whom Elizabeth met while shooting MGM's lavish adaptation of *Ivanhoe* in England. They were married in a civil ceremony in London on February 21, 1952, just a week shy of Taylor's 20th birthday. Once again, Elizabeth envisioned domestic bliss. "I just want to be with Michael and be his wife," she said. "He enjoys sitting home smoking his pipe, reading, painting. And that's what I intend doing—except smoking a pipe." And again, MGM intruded when it appeared it might lose its most popular female star to conjugal happiness. The studio offered Wilding a contract as a way to entice Taylor to remain in Hollywood and among its roster of talent. For a time, everyone was happy. Elizabeth had two sons—Michael, Jr. (b. 1953) and Christopher (b. 1955), both by Caesarean section; Wilding worked in several MGM pictures; and Taylor turned in another of her signature roles on loanout to Warner's in that studio's *Giant*, adapted from the *Edna Ferber novel and featuring the hottest male star of the time, James Dean. It was her second film for George Stevens, who drove her much harder than he had four years earlier in *A Place in the Sun* to make her transformation over the course of the film from an innocent Kentucky girl to a formidable Texas matron believable. After going on a crash diet before production began, Taylor developed severe headaches, stomach cramps, and thrombosis of the legs during the arduous shoot in the Texas countryside, although she and co-star Rock Hudson compensated by a good deal of drinking and carousing that formed the basis of a lifelong friendship. The tragedy of Dean's death in a motorcycle accident after completing his portions of the film affected Taylor so severely that she suffered another breakdown. It was her most difficult film to date, but is considered her finest work of the period.

Wilding's career, however, had not prospered in Hollywood. MGM declined to renew his contract when it expired in 1956, although Wilding seemed his usual debonair self during a weekend cruise with Taylor on the private yacht of Broadway impresario Michael Todd, then breaking into films with his extravagantly expensive adventure picture, *Around the World in Eighty Days*. Events moved swiftly after that weekend. Only weeks later, Taylor announced her separation from Wilding, and Todd proposed marriage and arranged for a Mexican divorce for Elizabeth in January 1957 that required no waiting period. Then Todd and Taylor married in Acapulco the following month, on February 2, 1957. Born Avrom Hirsh Goldbogen in Chicago, Todd was known for his brash, back-slapping business style, a fondness for private jets and opulent parties, and his lackadaisical financing. "I may be broke," he once said, "but I'm not poor." By all accounts, he and his new bride were deliriously happy. Taylor settled into what one observer thought was a "rich, contented opulence," traveling in elegant surroundings with her new husband and conspicuously displaying the new baubles he continually showered on her. In August 1957, Elizabeth presented Todd with a daughter, Elizabeth Frances, again delivered by Caesarean section. Todd, meanwhile, acted as her business manager with MGM, exploiting the studio's eagerness for Elizabeth to play Maggie in their production of Tennessee Williams' *Cat on a Hot Tin Roof* by announcing that his lawyers would cancel her contract if she were not al-

lowed to also appear in any film planned by his own film company. Taylor's only public appearance during 1957 was at the raucous party Todd threw for 18,000 at Madison Square Garden in October to mark the first anniversary of the release of *Around the World in Eighty Days*, which had been so wildly popular with the public that it was still showing in theaters across the country. As Taylor cut a huge birthday cake in front of a national television audience, the throngs below her on the floor of the arena degenerated into a free-for-all as gifts were tossed from bandwagons circling the floor and the champagne flowed. MGM was not amused.

Cat on a Hot Tin Roof began shooting during the winter of 1958, with Taylor playing opposite Burl Ives as Big Daddy and Paul Newman as his troubled son. The film's schedule did not allow Taylor to travel with Todd to New York in March for a weekend party being given in his honor; so a reluctant Todd departed on his private plane, Lucky Liz, on March 22 after telling his wife, "Without you, honey, I'd feel like half a pair of scissors." Hours later, word came that the plane had crashed in an ice storm over New Mexico and all on board had been killed. Production on the film was immediately shut down as Taylor was put under a doctor's care and heavily sedated. She had to be carried from the airplane that brought her to Todd's funeral in Chicago three days later, and seemed barely aware of her surroundings. But after several weeks, she returned to work on *Cat* because, she said, "Mike would have wanted me to." Somehow, she got through it. "When I was Maggie," she later said, "I could function. The rest of the time, I was a robot." Ironically, the first scene Taylor was required to play on her return to the set was one in which Maggie comforts Big Mama, who has just learned her husband will die of cancer. "I know what it's like to lose someone you love," Maggie says.

The public's sympathy for her, however, was short-lived when it was reported that Taylor had begun an affair with nightclub singer-turned-actor Eddie Fisher, whose friendship with Mike Todd had made him the go-between during Todd's whirlwind courtship of Elizabeth. Fisher was married to actress **Debbie Reynolds**—a marriage portrayed in print as a Hollywood dream come true. Privately, however, Fisher admitted, "We were married to the fan magazines, not to each other." The "Eddie-Debbie-Liz Biz," as the tabloid press dubbed it, became public just as *Cat on a Hot Tin Roof* was being released, making the film one of the highest-grossing pictures of 1958 and bringing Taylor her first Academy Award nomination. Fisher's Nevada divorce from Reynolds became final on May 12, 1959. The same day, he applied for a marriage license in Las Vegas and became Taylor's fourth husband in nine years.

Elizabeth's second Academy Award nomination quickly followed the first, for her work in another adaptation of a Tennessee Williams' play, *Suddenly, Last Summer*, shot in London during the summer of 1959 and released late that year. The film co-starred Montgomery Clift, then in the midst of his ultimately fatal struggle with drugs and alcohol, and was directed by Joseph Mankiewicz. Mankiewicz, impressed at the emotional range Taylor could summon without any formal training, thought she had a "tremendous primitive talent on which very few demands had been made." During the shoot, 20th Century-Fox producer Walter Wanger approached her about taking the title role in his next film, an overwrought, epic romantic adventure about those lovers of legend and myth, Marc Antony and *Cleopatra (VII). Elizabeth disliked the idea of playing a highly eroticized queen of the Nile almost as much as she did playing a high-priced call girl in the film MGM wanted as her next project, *Butterfield 8*, based on the John O'Hara novel. Both roles, Elizabeth thought, only seemed to reinforce the public's perception of her as a sexual adventurer. Almost jokingly, Taylor told Fox she'd accept *Cleopatra* for a million dollars, plus ten percent of the box office. In a sign of her growing power as a box-office draw, Fox agreed. It was the highest offer ever made to an American actress up to that time and the first element in a film project that would careen wildly out of control before its completion. Even Taylor would later call *Cleopatra* "the most bizarre piece of entertainment ever perpetrated."

She's probably the closest thing we have in America to royalty.
—Carole Bayer Sager

Meanwhile, MGM, to which Taylor was still under contract, had its own demands. Elizabeth would not be allowed to do *Cleopatra* and receive her million-dollar fee, it said, unless she first took on the role of the prostitute Gloria Wandrous in *Butterfield 8*, also to be directed by Mankiewicz. By now, however, Elizabeth had hit her stride as her own negotiator and demanded that the film be shot in New York and that Fisher be given the role of Gloria's sympathetic friend. Like Fox, MGM bowed to her demands and shooting began in January 1960 on the film Taylor later said she hated doing, but the one

that brought her her first Academy Award. Rumor had it that Elizabeth so disliked the completed film at its cast screening that she scrawled an obscenity across the screen in lipstick when it was over, much as Gloria writes the phrase "No Sale" across a bathroom mirror after a night of paid sex. Adding to Taylor's unhappiness was the fact that her marriage to Fisher was in trouble after less than a year. She admitted to Mankiewicz that she had only married Fisher as a way to "keep Mike alive"; Fisher, for his part, felt his career disappearing into the shadow of Taylor's, reducing him to chaperon of the growing collection of pets and luggage that made the move from Hollywood to London for *Cleopatra* a sort of royal progress.

Ominously, *Cleopatra* was shut down by the film's insurers in London when it became clear it was about to consume its entire budget after just two months of shooting. The film's original director was replaced with none other than Joe Mankiewicz, who immediately called for a new Marc Antony after screening the existing footage of Taylor and actor Stephen Boyd and deciding the requisite passion was lacking. The search for another Antony began as the film lurched back into production with scenes in which Antony did not appear, only to be shut down again when Taylor collapsed on the set and had to be rushed to the hospital for an emergency tracheotomy. She had been plagued by the flu since arriving in London and now, it was discovered, she had developed pneumonia. Production was halted from April 1961 until the following autumn, by which time the production had lost its studio space in London, moved to Rome, and had found its Marc Antony in Richard Burton, the fiery Welsh actor with the velvet voice who had just triumphantly appeared on Broadway in *Camelot*.

Burton had recorded in his diary some years earlier his first sight of Taylor lounging at a Hollywood pool party, noting indignantly that unlike most women, she ignored him. Now, however, the electricity between them was almost palpable. "Has anyone ever told you you're a very pretty girl?" Burton joked as they prepared to play their first scene together in Rome, for which he was terribly hung-over after another all-night drinking binge. Taylor thought he was "sweet and shaky." Mankiewicz and producer Wanger succeeded at first in keeping the budding romance between the two from public view, even though one crew member reported "they were so close you had to practically throw hot water on them to get them apart." "Le scandale," as Burton started calling it, had reached such heights by early 1962 (*Cleopatra* had now been in production for nearly two years) that his wife **Sybil Burton** left for New York to consult her lawyers; Eddie Fisher decamped for Los Angeles, never to return; the "chorus girl" from *Camelot* whom Burton had brought to Rome returned to the United States; and Taylor collapsed from nervous exhaustion and halted production yet again. With news that Fisher had filed for a divorce in April 1962, Hedda Hopper and ✤▶ **Louella Parsons** confided to their readers that Taylor had now broken up not only Burton's marriage, but her own as well. By the time *Cleopatra* finally wrapped in June 1962, destined to become one of Hollywood's most financially disastrous films, Burton and Taylor's lives and careers were inextricably entwined. Both appeared in 1963's *The V.I.Ps*, and Burton worked on his divorce settlement while living with Taylor in the villa they purchased in Puerta Vallarta, Mexico, the location for John Huston's production of *Night of the Iguana*, in which Richard starred.

They were finally married in Toronto, where Burton was touring in a production of *Hamlet*, on March 15, 1964. He quoted from the play's third act during his curtain call after the next performance, telling the audience: "We shall have no more marriages." But there would be many more films together, most notably 1965's *The Sandpiper*, in which Burton played a married minister who falls in love with single-mother Taylor; and 1966's *Who's Afraid of Virginia Woolf?*, a stunning adaptation of the Edward Albee play, directed by Mike Nichols. Taylor won her second Academy Award for her work as the foulmouthed harridan Martha, considered the crowning achievement of her screen career. One reviewer called it "the triumph of the shrew," for Taylor had done the impossible in dominating Burton on the screen. "He's not for me, that moon-faced chap beaten down by a woman," Burton felt obliged to tell a journalist who asked how closely he identified with the long-suffering George, but it seemed as if the strains that eventually ended their marriage began at this point. Even the couple's adoption of a little German girl they named Maria couldn't keep the marriage together. Burton's diaries from the late 1960s started to record a long list of arguments and drunken binges as the relationship began to unravel, as if it were unable to bear the pressure of two such formidable personalities. There were financial difficulties, too, for both Burton and Taylor enjoyed spending the millions they made together on their pictures. (Taylor, it was claimed, had earned a total of $7 million from *Cleopatra* alone.) By the early 1970s, Burton had been fired from

Tony Richardson's production of *Laughter in the Dark* because, Richardson said, the actor was incapable of playing his assigned role and repeatedly arrived late for his calls. Studio backing for the projects they undertook together began to disappear as more and more directors became wary of hiring Burton or Taylor, whose own career was affected by the decline of her husband's. The couple increasingly financed their own projects with backing from wealthy private investors, the two stars often working for a box-office percentage and expenses. Taylor's health remained problematical, including a hysterectomy in 1969; while Burton's drinking began to take its toll and his emotional health deteriorated when a beloved brother died from injuries suffered in an accident in Switzerland, where Burton had long had a home to escape British taxes.

Finally, in June 1973, Taylor released a handwritten note to the press announcing that she and Burton were separating. "Maybe we loved each other too much," she said. A formal divorce followed a year later, Taylor telling the Swiss court that life with Burton had become intolerable for her. It was with some surprise, then, that journalists flocked to South Africa barely a year later for the couple's second wedding. The lavish outdoor ceremony staged at a game preserve in October 1975 was the talk of the international press, Burton having reportedly given up alcohol to save his precarious health and telling Taylor he couldn't live without her. But their reunion lasted only until the following spring, by which time they had separated again and were in relationships with other lovers. After their second divorce, in the fall of 1976, both married their new paramours.

Taylor's sixth spouse not only had nothing to do with show business, but was a departure from his predecessors in that he was a reserved, old-line Virginian just building a career in politics, in which Elizabeth had begun taking an interest through her friendship with Henry Kissinger. She had appeared at the 1976 Democratic National Convention in support of Jimmy Carter, and shortly afterward attended a bicentennial reception at the British Embassy in Washington with John Warner, her assigned escort. Warner had been Richard Nixon's secretary of the navy and was considering a run for the Senate at the time he met Elizabeth, whom he found "exciting and stimulating"—somewhat of an understatement about a woman who had held Hollywood in thrall for 30 years. Taylor was particularly taken with Warner's 2,600-acre horse farm near Middleburg, Virginia, and his easy familiarity with the settled rhythms of a

✤▷
Parsons, Louella. *See joint entry under Hopper, Hedda and Louella Parsons.*

country gentlemen, so different from the up-heavals and restless wanderings of her past life. She fell in love with Warner, said one observer, because of "his roots, not his money." They were married in an outdoor ceremony on the grounds of Warner's farm on December 4, 1976. Taylor accepted little film work outside of a cameo or two and allowed her name and face to be used to advance Warner's ultimately success-ful campaign for the Senate, won by a narrow margin of just 5,000 votes. But a politician's wife was not a role for which Taylor felt suited. "There was no reason for me to get up," she later said. "I had nowhere to go. Later in the day, I'd rise, get dressed, then maybe read or watch television, or look at the walls, or do nothing." There were mounting frictions, too, between Taylor's independent spirit and Warn-er's aristocratic chauvinism. Taylor complained privately to Warner about his opposition to the Equal Rights Amendment, and openly contra-dicted him at a Republican Party forum when Warner spoke against women being eligible for the draft. Warner began to joke uneasily about his wife's "orneriness." By the time she traveled to England in 1979 to appear in the film adapta-tion of *Agatha Christie's The Mirror Crack'd, her enforced idleness and frustration were evi-dent in her ballooning weight, over 150 pounds by the time the production wrapped.

As another marriage headed for divorce, Elizabeth threw herself into a new challenge. Per-haps inspired by Burton's success in a Broadway revival of Camelot, Taylor announced that she would appear on the stage for the first time in her career. She chose to play *Lillian Hellman's cal-culating heroine Regina Giddens in a revival of The Little Foxes. There was perhaps a hint of her resentment toward Warner when she told jour-nalists she intended to play Regina as a victim of male domination, rather than as the villainess of more traditional interpretations. By the time the play opened on Broadway in May 1981, Tay-lor—now down to a slim 125 pounds—got a standing ovation at her first entrance and again when the curtain rang down. Critical reception was mixed, some reviewers complaining that Taylor's personality overshadowed the play itself, but it was precisely her reputation that ensured she played to full houses at every performance. Plans were now made to take the show to Lon-don, just as Taylor announced her separation from John Warner, leading to a divorce which be-came final in December 1982. (The gossip was that the last straw had been Warner's decision to sell his horse farm and move to the Watergate Hotel in Washington which, Taylor discovered to

her horror, did not accept pets.) London critics were less restrained in their comments when the show opened in the West End, one of them ven-turing the opinion that Elizabeth's emotions on stage "are signaled with a machete." Recalling Regina's line "The rich don't have to be subtle," the reviewer was of the opinion that "on this phi-losophy she has clearly based her entire perfor-mance." But by this time, Taylor was so enam-ored of the stage that she had formed the Elizabeth Taylor Repertory Company and had selected its next production, Noel Coward's Pri-vate Lives. Her co-star, she announced, would be none other than Richard Burton. Taylor had once again chosen material that reflected the tur-moil of her private life, seeing Coward's bitter-sweet comedy about two former lovers who try to rekindle their romance as a parable of her own state of affairs with Burton.

Burton, in perilous health and so weak that he could barely lift an arm above shoulder level, had visited her backstage during the West End run of the Hellman play and had attended her 50th birthday party. Elizabeth, in return, had paid a surprise visit to a benefit reading Burton gave of Dylan Thomas' Under Milkwood. But Burton scoffed at reporters' questions about whether he and Taylor would marry for a third time. "We don't need another one," he said. "We love each other with a passion so furious that we burn each other out." As if to prove his point, Burton, having divorced his young wife, took up with a production assistant on a multi-part television series he was then shooting.

Rehearsals in New York during March 1983 did not go well. Taylor had regained much of the weight she had lost for the Hellman play, while the pain medications she was taking for her back problems made it difficult for her to concentrate or remember lines. Burton, too, was weak and pale and had become blind in one eye. The curtain rose half an hour late on opening night, and no explanation was offered for a nearly hour-long intermission. The New York Times' Frank Rich wrote the next morning that Burton looked like "a tired millionaire steeling himself for an obligatory annual visit to an ac-countant"; the more caustic John Simon, noting that a line in the play describing Taylor's Aman-da as "running like a deer" had been cut, thought that "anything faster than a sumo wrestler is inconceivable." Taylor's dependence on alcohol and drugs to get her through the run of the show took its toll, leading to hospitaliza-tion before she rallied and took the show on tour in an attempt to recoup its losses. But the strain was too much. While Burton left to marry his production assistant, Taylor checked herself into California's *Betty Ford Clinic for substance abuse in December 1983.

By May 1984, her addictions had been cured, she had lost nearly 40 pounds, and she had written an inspirational book about her recovery, *Elizabeth Takes Off*. That same month, she visited Burton in London, where he was in the midst of production on what would be his last film, an adaptation of George Orwell's *1984*. It was their final meeting. In August, Burton suffered a massive cerebral hemorrhage at his home near Geneva and died hours later of a stroke. Taylor, in Los Angeles when she received word, collapsed from shock and was not present at Burton's funeral. But about two weeks later, at six o'clock on a rainy morning, she was escorted to the grave by bodyguards who shielded her from the glare of flashbulbs and television lights with their umbrellas. "It was one of the few moments Richard and I were alone," she later said. Such was her passion for him that more than ten years after his death, Taylor told journalist **Liz Smith** that she and Burton would have reunited a third time, despite Burton's denials. "Oh, I know it," Taylor said. "Absolutely, I was happy with him."

With Burton's death, it seemed, the old days and her old acquaintances were slipping away from her. Montgomery Clift had died of a drug overdose some years earlier; actor Peter Lawford, with whom she had acted in several pictures and who had struggled with her to overcome his own alcoholism at the Ford clinic, died of liver cancer in the same year as Burton. Her friendship with billionaire Malcolm Forbes, whose lavish 1989 party at his Moroccan estate Taylor attended, was cut short when he died just five months after they were photographed together at the affair. And Rock Hudson, with whom she had remained great friends since their days together in *Giant*, died from complications of AIDS in 1985. His passing led Taylor to call for increased AIDS research, when few were speaking out, and to chair the American Foundation for AIDS Research, raising $14 million by 1990.

Taylor's own health took another turn for the worse during the late 1980s, although she found time for several television mini-series and specials and to embark on a strenuous campaign to launch her perfume, Poison, in its famous amethyst bottle. She still suffered from painful spinal problems and by 1988 found herself back at the Betty Ford Clinic to deal with her dependency on painkillers and the return of her excessive drinking. Also in rehabilitation at the time

was a former truck driver and construction worker, Larry Fortensky, in whose company Taylor began appearing in public shortly after both had left the clinic. The courtship was interrupted by a dangerous viral infection in the spring of 1990 that put her in the hospital for weeks breathing with the aid of a ventilator amid rumors of her pending demise. "I have no plan to succumb," Taylor told reporters just before her release from the hospital. "I am a survivor."

She was well enough by early 1991 to have lost 30 pounds, to have stopped smoking, and to have begun a daily exercise regimen. "Oh, God, it's awful, I'm getting so pure," she joked after announcing her engagement to Fortensky, 39 years old and some 20 years her junior. She introduced him to her public during the media campaign for her new perfume, White Diamonds, and married him in a posh, $2 million wedding held at Michael Jackson's Never Land Ranch on October 6, 1991. Jackson served as best man. The 160 guests included everyone from Gregory Peck to **Liza Minnelli** to Henry Kissinger, all of whom were searched by 300 security guards while the press, barred from the ceremony, whirled overhead in a small army of helicopters. Fortensky remained very much in the background during their four years together, which ended in an amicable separation and divorce in 1996. "Larry and I both need our own space right now," was all Taylor would say, although she admitted that her continuing health problems, including hip replacement surgery, had placed a strain on the marriage. Then, in early 1997, just two days after attending a nationally televised 65th birthday party which raised $1 million for AIDS research, Taylor underwent surgery for a benign brain tumor.

True to form, she emerged triumphant. Her recovery was so complete that she was able to host both a Fourth of July party and a Labor Day celebration at her home, "walking around and entertaining everyone, quite jovial," as her doctor reported. She also found time that summer to fly to Istanbul for a benefit raising money for the children of Chechnya uprooted by ethnic wars and to attend two fundraisers in California for AIDS research. Taylor remains active in a number of charitable causes and still makes frequent public appearances. It is as if, one observer noted, she is constantly rediscovering and renewing herself. "I suppose when you find out what you've always wanted, that's not where the beginning begins," Taylor once told Truman Capote. "That's where the end starts."

SOURCES:

Smith, Liz. "Elizabeth Taylor Talks about . . . ," in *Good Housekeeping*. Vol. 225, no. 1. July 1997.

Walker, Alexander. *Elizabeth: The Life of Elizabeth Taylor*. NY: Grove Press, 1990.

SUGGESTED READING:

Heymann, C. David. *Liz: An Intimate Biography of Elizabeth Taylor*. Birch Lane, 1995.

Spoto, Donald. *A Passion for Life: The Biography of Elizabeth Taylor*. NY: HarperCollins, 1995.

Norman Powers,
writer-producer, Chelsea Lane Productions,
New York, New York

Taylor, Eva (1879–1966)

British science historian and geographer. Born Eva Germaine Rimington Taylor on June 22, 1879, in Highgate, England; died on July 5, 1966, in Wokingham, England; daughter of Charles Richard Taylor (a solicitor) and Emily Jane (Nelson) Taylor; educated at the Camden School for Girls and the North London Collegiate School for Girls; Royal Holloway College, B.S., 1903, D.Sc., 1929; studied at Oxford University; married; children: three sons (b. 1912, 1915, and 1919).

Selected writings: Tudor Geography, 1485–1583 *(1930);* Late Tudor and Early Stuart Geography, 1583–1650 *(1934);* The Mathematical Practitioners of Tudor and Stuart England *(1954);* The Haven-Finding Art: a history of navigation from Odysseus to Captain Cook *(1956);* The Mathematical Practitioners of Hanoverian England *(1966).*

Eminent historian and geographer Eva Taylor was born in England on June 22, 1879, to solicitor Charles Richard Taylor and **Emily Jane Nelson**. The youngest of the couple's three children, Eva suffered a childhood deprived of toys and pets after her mother ran away when Eva was only three. She overcame this hardship by developing a love of the natural world, particularly flowers and wild animals, which lasted throughout her lifetime.

Taylor began her education at home and then moved on to the Camden School for Girls and the North London Collegiate School for Girls. A scholarship student, she graduated with honors in chemistry from the Royal Holloway College in 1903, which led to appointments at two different girls' schools as a chemistry teacher. By 1906, Taylor was again a student herself, this time in geography at Oxford University, from which she earned a diploma with distinction. She remained at Oxford as a research assistant to A.J. Herbertson, the head of the geography school, from 1908 to 1910.

Taylor applied her education in geography as a mapmaker and textbook writer in London for the next six years, after which she resumed her teaching career as a lecturer at Clapham Training College for Teachers and at the Froebel Institute. She moved on to a lecturing post at East London College in 1920 and a similar post at Birkbeck College a year later. Birkbeck became her permanent academic home when she was appointed the school's chair of geography a year after earning her doctorate in 1929. A remarkable scholar, Taylor also enjoyed a brilliant reputation as a lecturer during her 15-year career at Birkbeck.

In 1930, she published *Tudor Geography, 1485–1583,* continuing the study with *Late Tudor and Early Stuart Geography, 1583–1650* in 1934. She also lent her leadership skills to committees beyond Birkbeck's walls by chairing the Royal Geographical Society committee on the distribution of the industrial population, and campaigned for the establishment of an atlas of Britain to aid in national and regional planning. She served her country during and immediately after World War II by contributing her expertise in geography to the Association for Planning and Regional Reconstruction. For her efforts, the Royal Geographical Society awarded her the Victoria Medal in 1947. Other organizations with which she was associated were the Hakluyt Society, the Institute of Navigation, the British Association for the Advancement of Science, and the Society of Nautical Research.

Taylor retired from Birkbeck in 1944, was elected one of the first fellows of Birkbeck College in 1960, and received a fellowship from the Royal Geographical Society in 1965. She also continued to publish scholarly works, including two volumes on historical mathematicians and one on navigation, in addition to numerous articles. Although a stroke suffered in 1964 limited her sight and movement, Taylor continued working well into her 80s, dying at Wokingham on July 5, 1966.

SOURCES:

The Concise Dictionary of National Biography. Oxford: Oxford University Press, 1992.

Williams, E.T., and C.S. Nicholls, eds. *The Dictionary of National Biography, 1961–1970.* Oxford: Oxford University Press, 1981.

Karina L. Kerr, M.A.,
Ypsilanti, Michigan

Taylor, Eva (1895–1977)

African-American singer, dancer, and radio show host. Name variations: Irene Gibbons; Catherine Henderson. Born Irene Gibbons on January 22, 1895, in St. Louis, Missouri; died of cancer on October 31, 1977, in Mineola, New York; daughter of Frank Gib-

bons and Julia (Evans) Gibbons; educated at Sumner High School in St. Louis; married Clarence Williams (a musician), on October 8, 1921 (died 1965); children: Clarence, Jr. (b. 1923); Spencer Patrick (b. 1926); Irene (b. 1928).

Selected recordings: (as Irene Gibbons) "My Pillow and Me" and "I'm Going Away Just to Wear You Off My Mind," "That Da Da Strain" and "Longing/ Let Me Forget"; (as Eva Taylor) "Original Charleston Strut/ If You Don't Know, I Know Who Will," "Shake That Thing/ Get It Fixed," and "Have You Ever Felt That Way?/ West End Blues"; (with the Charleston Chasers) "Ain't Misbehaving/ Moanin' Low" and "Turn On the Heat/ What Wouldn't I Do for That Man?"; (with Clarence Williams Trio) "Of All the Wrongs You've Done Me/ Everybody Loves My Baby" and "Mandy, Make Up Your Mind/ I'm a Little Blackbird Looking for a Bluebird."

Eva Taylor was born Irene Gibbons in 1895 in St. Louis, Missouri. When she was three, she began singing and dancing in vaudeville, performing with **Josephine Gassman** and Her Pickaninnies at St. Louis' Orpheum Theater. Later she toured with the troupe in the UnitedStates as well as in Europe, Australia, and New Zealand. In 1911, Taylor was in the chorus of the New York City production of Vera Violetta with Al Jolson. Returning to the Gassman troupe in 1914, she toured as a ballad singer and dancer.

After Taylor and bandleader Clarence Williams were married in 1921, they lived in New York City, where she performed in clubs and theaters, singing ballads and blues with her husband's group, the Clarence Williams Trio. In 1922, she appeared on stage in such shows as Queen of Hearts, Miller and Lyles' East Coast variety show Step On It, and Shuffle Along with ❧➤ **Florence Mills**, for whom Taylor understudied two years later in the musical revue Dixie to Broadway. From 1923 to 1930, Taylor sang at various venues around New York City, including the Apollo Theater, Carnegie Hall, Madison Square Garden, Lincoln Theater, the Savoy Ballroom, and the Harlem Casino. Other stage appearances included the musical revue Melodies of 1933, Mr. Jiggins of Jigginstown (1936), Bottomland and Miller and Lyles' Keep Shufflin'.

Taylor was also active in radio throughout the 1920s and 1930s, guesting on such programs as "Major Bowes Capitol Family Show" and "Soft Lights and Sweet Music." Her first radio appearance was in 1922 with her husband's trio on the "Musical Program," starring Vaughn De Leath ("The Original Radio Girl"). In 1929,

Taylor became the first black American female soloist to broadcast nationally and internationally. From 1932 to 1933, she hosted her own program, the "Eva Taylor, Crooner Show." As staff soloist at WEAF-WJZ, she often sang with the Knickerbockers Orchestra, but she also appeared on "Harlem" (with the Cab Calloway Orchestra), "The Eveready Hour" (with Nat Shilkret), "Atwater Kent Hour," "Slow River Show" (with *Lil Hardin Armstrong and the Clarence Williams Trio), and "Kraft Music Hall" (with the Paul Whiteman Orchestra).

During these years, Taylor recorded with her husband as well as others for the Black Swan, Okeh, Columbia, Edison, Victor, Velvetone, Vocalion, Bluebird, and ACR labels. She recorded under the names Eva Taylor, Irene Gibbons, and Catherine Henderson, and with such groups as the Charleston Chasers and the Riffers. She also wrote the song "May We Meet Again, Florence Mills."

Taylor stopped appearing professionally during World War II, performing instead at New York City hospitals for the Hospital Reserve Corps. In 1948, she sang at the *Bessie Smith Memorial Concert. Although less active musically during the 1950s and 1960s, she appeared on BBC radio in London with the Anglo-American Alliance Jazz Groups in 1967, recorded with the Anglo-American Boy Friends in Burnham, England, and appeared on television in New York City on the "Joe Franklin Show." During the 1970s, she appeared at the Overseas Press Club in New York City and at the Stampen Club in Stockholm, Sweden; as well, she performed in concert with the Sweet Peruna Jazz Band and Maggie's Blue Five group in Denmark and Sweden.

During Taylor's career, she had the opportunity to work with a number of notable performers, including Mills, Bessie Smith, *Ethel Waters, King Oliver, Al Jolson, Armand J. Piron, *Sara Martin, Lawrence Lomax, Clarence Todd, and Cab Calloway. Critics have suggested that her singing style was influenced by Katherine Henderson and *Sippie Wallace. Although she did not have a big voice, like some at the time, according to Brian Rust, "her rich and thrilling contralto" was "nevertheless ideally suited to all kinds of songs, flexible, warm, and human as its owner."

Taylor and Williams, who had three children, often performed together during their 44-year marriage which ended with his death in 1965. Eva Taylor died of cancer in New York, at age 82.

SOURCES:

Smith, Jessie Carney, ed. Notable Black American Women. Detroit, MI: Gale Research, 1992.

Karina L. Kerr, M.A.,
Ypsilanti, Michigan

➤❧
Mills, Florence.
See Women of
the Harlem
Renaissance.

Taylor, Florence M. (1879–1969)

British-born Australian architect, engineer, and publisher. Born Florence Mary Parsons in 1879 in Bristol, England; died on February 13, 1969; daughter of John Parsons (a government employee) and Eliza (Brooks) Parsons; educated at Sydney Technical College and University of Sydney Engineering School; married George Augustine Taylor, in 1907 (died 1928).

Together with husband, started the Building Publishing Company; published trade magazines, including The Australasian Engineer, Building *(later* Building, Lighting, and Engineering*),* The Commonwealth Home, *and* Construction.

Florence M. Taylor, the eldest of five girls, was born in England in 1879 but moved to Australia with her family in 1888. When she was 19, her father, a government employee, died, and she began working in an architect-engineer's office as a clerk. Deciding on a career of drafting, Taylor took night classes at the Sydney Technical College, later transferring to the University of Sydney. She initially failed her examinations at the college, and it took her eight years to finish school.

Taylor later became the chief draftsperson for John Burcham Clamp, the Diocesan architect, and was nominated by him in 1907 for associate membership in the New South Wales Institute of Architects. She was the first woman ever nominated for membership into this organization, but she was not admitted. That honor finally came in 1920, when she was admitted as Australia's first qualified female architect. Said Clamp, "She could design a place while an ordinary draftsman would be sharpening his pencil."

George Taylor, whom she married in 1907, was also an architect, and the couple shared many interests, including flying, which Florence mastered in 1909. Besides establishing a publishing company that produced 11 trade journals, they also helped to found the Town Planning Association of Australia in 1913. Their publishing company afforded them an opportunity not only to influence construction methods and materials but to focus on the need for urban planning. They were able to command the attention of the government and the public and in so doing were influential in promoting the interests of engineers, architects, and builders. For example, they organized support for Walter Burley Griffin's designs for Canberra through a petition of professionals.

When George died in 1928, Florence reduced the number of their company's publications to three: *Building* (renamed *Building, Lighting, and Engineering*), *Construction,* and *The Australasian Engineer.* However, she continued to conceive and execute ideas for the town, including a subway in Sydney, an airport in Newport, and an expressway to link the downtown area of Sydney with the suburbs. Under her guidance, the journals became a vital part of the engineering and architecture community.

Throughout her life, Taylor was actively involved in several organizations, including the Arts Club, the International Society of Australia, the Royal Empire Society, the Royal Aero Club of New South Wales, the Royal Society of Arts, and the Society of Women Writers. Although her unreserved questioning and criticism at times antagonized her contemporaries, she also gained their respect.

Taylor was honored by the naming of several design awards after her, including the Australian Institute of Metals' Florence M. Taylor medal and the plaque for distinguished service from the Master Builders' Association. In 1939, she was named Officer of the Order of the British Empire (OBE), and in 1961 was named Commander of the Order of the British Empire (CBE). That same year, ill health forced her to retire and live with her sister **Annis Parsons.** She died eight years later, on February 13, 1969.

SOURCES:
Radi, Heather, ed. *200 Australian Women.* Women's Redress Press, 1988.

Karina L. Kerr, M.A.,
Ypsilanti, Michigan

Taylor, Harriet (1807–1858)

English philosopher whose feminism influenced that of John Stuart Mill, her second husband. Name variations: Harriet Taylor Mill. Born Harriet Hardy in London, England, on October 8, 1807; died of lung congestion on November 3, 1858; daughter of Harriet (Hurst) Hardy and Thomas Hardy (a surgeon); educated at home by her father; married John Taylor (died of cancer, 1849); married John Stuart Mill (the philosopher) in London, in April 1851; children: (first marriage) two sons and a daughter, Helen Taylor (1831–1907).

Selected works: Letters to John Stuart Mill *(1851); "Enfranchisement of Women" in* Westminster Review *(July 1851); (collaborator with John Stuart Mill)* Principles of Political Economy *(1848) and* On Liberty *(1859); also wrote poetry.*

The philosophical work of Harriet Taylor was fostered by a group of Unitarian intellectuals which included the utilitarian philosopher

Harriet Taylor

John Stuart Mill. Mill was relentless in his praise of her and became her second husband. The ethical doctrine of utilitarianism, based on the idea that virtue is derived from utility, is used to support a liberal theory of politics in which the welfare of a community supersedes the freedom of individuals. The utilitarian journal, *The Westminster Review*, in which Taylor published her "Enfranchisement of Women" in July 1851, and the Unitarian journal, *Monthly Repository*, were forums for the political ideas of an intellectual group which included Thomas and *Jane Welsh Carlyle, William Johnson Fox, *Harriet Martineau, ❧ Eliza Flower, *Sarah Flower Adams, Southwood Smith, John Bowring,

and John Roebuck. Taylor is recognized not only for her philosophical treatments of marriage and of women's political equality, but also for her contributions to Mill's political writings, some of which she co-authored. Mill's praise of his wife in his autobiography is more than extraordinary. He presents her as a living goddess with near-perfect wisdom.

Born in London in 1807 into the lower aristocracy, Harriet was educated at home with her siblings by her father Thomas Hardy, a surgeon. It is likely that Harriet's strong personality and radical views made her an unconventional woman whom many people could not accept.

Flower, Eliza.
See Adams, Sarah Flower for sidebar.

Considered attractive and brilliant by some, she was more often derided as coarse and dull. She claimed that the only people who mattered to her were her two husbands, John Taylor and John Stuart Mill. She was close to Mill while still married to her first husband Taylor. Taylor recognized the love between Harriet and Mill, but asked that the formality of his marriage to her be preserved. For the 20 years while Harriet was married to Taylor, Mill lived with his mother and siblings. The frequent meetings between he and Harriet were not deterred by the gossip they inspired. Mill frequently dined at the Taylors' home when John Taylor was away, and Harriet traveled with him and her daughter *Helen Taylor along the English coast.

Although she had been working on them for some time, Harriet Taylor's philosophical writings began to appear in publication at the beginning of her friendship with Mill. She met him as part of a circle of Unitarian and utilitarian intellectuals, at a dinner party given by William Fox in 1830. John Stuart Mill, who took after his father James Mill (a colleague of Jeremy Bentham, founder of utilitarianism), became the most esteemed proponent of utilitarianism. At first, Harriet lauded him as a mentor, but as her own intellectual growth progressed she developed independent views, sometimes contrary to his in significant ways.

From 1840, she collaborated on almost everything that Mill wrote and, through "intelligently controverting" his ideas, further stimulated his intellectual work. Mill recognized her as the co-author of *The Principles of Political Economy* and *On Liberty* (although this assertion is disputed to some extent). Both Harriet and John claimed that he was the sole author cited because his established reputation would aid the success of the book; but it is apparent that Harriet's contribution was not made official because of the risk of scandal. She was then still married to John Taylor. Her husband had objected to the dedication of *Principles of Political Economy* to Harriet, and he wrote from his deathbed requesting that her authorship not be acknowledged. In *Principles*, published in 1848, Mill and Taylor argue that the individual liberty which is required by a just political system must come second to the solution of social problems. In *On Liberty* (1859), they expand on the concept of individual liberty, asserting that it should only be compromised to prevent injury to others; only the welfare of others within a community must take precedence over individual freedom.

Both Mill and Taylor were committed feminists. Her views, however, were more radical than

his, and for this reason the strong assertions made in the 1851 article "Enfranchisement of Women" are attributed to Taylor. Mill is credited solely as editor. Particularly concerned that women were educated only to "gain their living by marrying," Taylor argued in "Enfranchisement" that women have a right to both education and the self-development that comes with it, and she maintains that a woman's role as a wife or mother should not limit her pursuit of other careers. Equal education and equal access to employment, she argues, are integral to women's full political equality with men. While Mill too believed that a woman should be able to choose any career, he maintained that if her choice is to be a wife and mother then this contribution to the family is her career and thus she should not contribute economically or have the option of another career.

Taylor nursed her first husband for two months before he died of cancer in 1849. In April 1851, she married Mill, and they lived together on the outskirts of London. At this time, in recognition that his liberal ideals should extend to marriage, Mill issued a formal protest against the power conferred on the husband in the institution of marriage over "the freedom of action of the other party." He worked as a clerk and chief examiner at India House, where he would serve 35 years before his retirement in 1858.

Both Taylor and Mill suffered from poor health and on medical advice traveled frequently to warmer climates in France and Italy. After Mill's retirement, they left for the south of France and then Italy. During the journey, Harriet died of lung congestion on November 3, 1858. She was buried in Avignon cemetery in France, and Mill purchased a cottage close by so he could visit her grave almost every day. During the first few years in Avignon, with some help from Harriet's daughter Helen, he drafted *On the Subjection of Women*, a treatise which analyzes the political position of women and argues for securing their equality. *On the Subjection of Women* was the only feminist treatise written by a man for many centuries. Although the ideas expressed in this work were shared by many of Mill's intellectual friends, his relationship with Harriet Taylor likely inspired the writing. While Mill had always believed that women should be equal (and had in fact been taken into custody by the London police at the age of 17 for distributing birth-control information), Taylor made palpable for him the need for gender equality.

Mill argued that women were a subject class, different only from other slaves because the masters wish them to be willing slaves, and that their willingness is fostered by social conditioning. He lived in Avignon with his stepdaughter Helen for the rest of his life, except for a few years in the late 1860s when he served as a member of the English Parliament. While he was in the legislature, Mill was a speaker for the burgeoning women's suffrage movement. When he returned to Avignon, he revised the manuscript for *The Subjection of Women,* which was published in 1869.

SOURCES:

Kersey, Ethel M. *Women Philosophers: a Bio-critical Source Book.* NY: Greenwood Press, 1989.

Rossi, Alice S., ed. "Sentiment and Intellect," in *Essays on Sex Equality: John Stuart Mill and Harriet Taylor.* Chicago, IL: University of Chicago Press, 1970.

Scheir, Miriam, ed. *Feminism: The Essential Historical Writings.* NY: Random House, 1972.

Waithe, Mary Ellen, ed. *A History of Women Philosophers.* Boston, MA: Martinus Nijhoff, 1987–95.

SUGGESTED READING:

Borchard, Ruth. *John Stuart Mill, the Man.* London: Watts, 1957.

Hayek, F.A. *John Stuart Mill and Harriet Taylor: Their Friendship and Subsequent Marriage.* London: Routledge and Kegan Paul, 1951.

Mill, John Stuart. *Autobiography of John Stuart Mill.* NY: Columbia University Press, 1924.

Packe, Michael St. John. *The Life of John Stuart Mill.* London: Secker and Warburg, 1954.

Thomas, William. *Mill.* NY: Oxford University Press, 1985.

Catherine Hundleby, M.A. Philosophy,
University of Guelph,
Guelph, Ontario, Canada

Taylor, Harriette Deborah (1807–1874).

See Lacy, Harriette Deborah.

Taylor, Helen (1831–1907)

British suffragist and social reformer. Born in 1831; died in 1907 in Torquay, England; daughter of Harriet Taylor (1807–1858) and John Taylor; stepdaughter of John Stuart Mill (the philosopher and economist).

Helen Taylor was born in 1831, the daughter of John Taylor and philosopher *Harriet Taylor. She was already an adult when her mother married John Stuart Mill, the utilitarian philosopher, in 1851. John was devoted to her mother. After Mill's retirement in 1858, he and Harriet left for the south of France and then Italy, but Harriet died of lung congestion during the journey and was buried in Avignon cemetery. Helen joined Mill in Avignon, and together they produced *The Subjection of Women* (1869). She also edited the works of historian Henry Thomas Buckle in 1872 and Mill's autobiography in 1873. After Mill died that year, she moved to London and became involved in politics and social issues; she was considered a proficient public speaker. Taylor was a

member of the London School Board from 1876 to 1884 and helped to institute radical changes in London's industrial schools. She was also president of the Prisoners' Sustentation Fund. From 1880 to 1885, she vigorously opposed the Liberal government's policy of Irish coercion. She was a promoter of land nationalization, taxation of land values, and the women's suffrage movement. In 1881, she helped establish the Democratic Federation. She also campaigned for Parliament in North Camberwell but was denied the nomination in 1885. After that she removed to Avignon before returning to England in 1904. Taylor died at Torquay in 1907.

SOURCES:

The Concise Dictionary of National Biography. Oxford: Oxford University Press, 1992.

Karina L. Kerr, M.A.,
Ypsilanti, Michigan

Helen Taylor, with John Stuart Mill.

Taylor, Jane (1783–1824).

See joint entry under Taylor, Ann and Jane.

Taylor, Kamala (1924—)

British novelist who was one of the first women writers from the Indian subcontinent to achieve renown.

Name variations: Kamala Purnaiya Taylor; (pseudonym) Kamala Markandaya. Born in 1924 (one source cites 1923), in Chimakurti, India; graduated from the University of Madras; married; children: one daughter, Kim.

Selected writings: Nectar in a Sieve *(1954);* Some Inner Fury *(1955);* A Silence of Desire *(1960);* Possession *(1963);* A Handful of Rice *(1966);* The Coffer Dams *(1969);* The Nowhere Man *(1972);* Two Virgins *(1973);* The Golden Honeycomb *(1977);* Pleasure City *(1982, published as* Shalimar *in the U.S., 1983).*

Because of its wealth of natural resources, India was long considered the "jewel" in the colonial crown of the British Empire, which had first established a presence there in the 16th century, until gathering resentment and the political leadership of Indians like Mohandas Gandhi led to India's independence in 1947. Kamala Taylor, who was born into the Brahmin caste in Chimakurti, India, in 1924 and moved to England a year after independence, wrote a number of novels that reflect the historical and cultural links, and tensions, between England and India.

Nectar in a Sieve (1954), Taylor's first published novel, was the third she had written. Roundly praised, it launched her as a new voice in post-colonial English literature, was translated into 17 languages, and was named one of the American Library Association's Notable Books of 1955. Set in a farming village in India, *Nectar in a Sieve* depicts a world of great poverty in which political, economic, and social factors have not made death by starvation a thing of the past. Her second novel, *Some Inner Fury* (1955), introduced a theme that would become a mainstay of her fiction: the social and cultural conflicts between East and West, specifically between Indians and Britons. The book details a romance between an Indian woman and her English boyfriend during World War II; a great deal of it revolves around the significant "Quit India" campaign in which independence leaders pushed Britain to end its involvement with the Asian subcontinent. Like many Indians and Britons at the time, the characters in *Some Inner Fury* are divided over the issue.

What some critics consider her most fully realized novel, *A Silence of Desire* (1960), again portrays the dynamics of a world in which Western modernism and Eastern traditions uneasily co-exist; the story centers around an Indian immigrant and his ill wife's visits to a faith healer. *Possession* (1963) is set partly in London and tracks the relationship between an Indian artist and his aristocratic English patron. Though Tay-

lor has sometimes faced criticism—particularly from Indian scholars—for the perceived "unease" with which she writes of the poor, as well as for her reliance on more educated, middle-class immigrant characters, she nevertheless shows a willingness to delve into other facets of the immigrant experience. In *A Handful of Rice* (1966), she introduces readers to the crowded conditions of less affluent Indians sharing living quarters in London. Her 1972 novel *The Nowhere Man* portrays an elderly Indian immigrant, a London merchant, who becomes the target of discrimination and hate crimes.

Critics have noted that with her 1973 novel *Two Virgins*, Taylor introduced newer themes and more experimental prose. Since then, her novels have appeared less frequently, although she still writes as a freelance journalist. *Pleasure City*, published in 1982, concerns the friendship between a boy in an Indian fishing village and the junior executive of a massive, multinational company that builds a luxury resort nearby.

SOURCES:

Blain, Virginia, Patricia Clements, and Isobel Grundy. *The Feminist Companion to Literature in English.* New Haven, CT: Yale University Press, 1990.

The Bloomsbury Guide to Women's Literature. Edited by Claire Buck. NY: Prentice Hall, 1992.

Contemporary Novelists. 6th ed. Edited by Susan Windisch Brown. Detroit, MI: St. James Press, 1996.

Encyclopedia of World Literature in the 20th Century. Rev. ed. Edited by Leonard S. Klein. NY: Continuum, 1993.

Oxford Companion to English Literature. Rev. 5th ed. Edited by Margaret Drabble. Oxford: Oxford University Press, 1995.

Carol Brennan,
Grosse Pointe, Michigan

Taylor, Knox (1814–1835).

See Davis, Varina Howell for sidebar.

Taylor, Laurette (1884–1946)

American stage actress, considered one of the finest of the early 20th century, whose often troubled career ended in triumph with her creation of Amanda Wingfield in The Glass Menagerie. *Born Loretta Cooney on April 1, 1884, in New York City; died on December 7, 1946, in New York; first of three children of James Cooney and Elizabeth Cooney; married Charles A. Taylor (a producer), in 1901 (divorced 1910); married J. Hartley Manners (an English playwright), in 1911 (died 1928); children: (first marriage) Dwight (b. 1902); Marguerite (b. 1904).*

Made her professional stage debut (c. 1900); became the toast of Broadway for her work in The Girl in Waiting *(1910); secured her reputation in* Peg o' My Heart *(1912), in which she played for nearly three years; her career, built on a series of optimistic, simple-hearted characters, languished during the more cynical 1920s, forcing her retirement from the stage; returned briefly to the stage (late 1930s–early 1940s), most notably with her portrayal of Amanda Wingfield in the original production of Tennessee Williams'* The Glass Menagerie *(1945).*

Filmography: Peg o' My Heart *(1922);* Happiness *(1924);* One Night in Rome *(1924).*

It was a sad tale for a 12-year-old girl to tell, especially since Loretta Cooney's seventh-grade teacher had not been expecting such a melodramatic response to her request for a short biographical essay from each of her students. But on that spring day in 1896, Loretta moved everyone in the room to tears, including the teacher, with her poignant revelation that she was the result of an ill-fated but tender love affair between her mother and a Spanish count. "When you look into my mother's eyes," Loretta explained solemnly, "you may realize at times that she is longing for faraway Spain." The fact that it was all nonsense, or that it spread gossip around the neighborhood that her father was a cuckold, or that it threw her already fractious household into more turmoil, was of little consequence to Loretta. What counted was that she had held another audience captive with what James Cooney angrily referred to as his daughter's "imaginings."

Both James and **Elizabeth Cooney** were hard pressed to explain their eldest child's indefatigable dramatic flair. Elizabeth—like her husband, a first generation Irish American—was a hardworking dressmaker and milliner, while James was an unemployed harness and saddle-maker who alternated between fits of melancholy drinking and fervent Catholicism. The Cooneys were one of hundreds of Irish, German, and Italian families who had settled in the thriving Mount Morris Park section of New York City during the last half of the 19th century. Loretta's birth (with a caul, as the superstitious James always pointed out) on April 1, 1884, was followed by the births of two more children over the next four years, although neither of her younger siblings, Elizabeth and Edward, seemed to share their sister's theatrical orientation.

Both Loretta's father and grandmother—**Bridget Cooney**, who lived with her son and daughter-in-law—looked upon all "show people" as sinners and never set foot in a theater in their lives. But Loretta's mother, better educated

and less devout than her husband, loved the theater. She would often use the delivery of a just-finished dress as an excuse to take in the latest show at the Harlem Opera House, just across town. The inevitable friction between the conservative and the contemporary resulted in frequent outbursts, threats, and the occasional physical assault. "Mine was not a placid family," Taylor drily noted many years later.

It must have seemed to James that his wife was winning the war for his daughter's soul. The Spanish count incident was just one of many. There was the time Loretta, noticing that a French girl attracted a good deal of attention in the neighborhood, adopted a convincing French accent and the name "Laurice" until being sent home by her teacher; and there were her frequent expulsions from the public library for sobbing loudly and dramatically while reading her favorite authors—Dickens, Twain, and Sir Walter Scott. Then there were Loretta's famous "vestibule shows," staged in any handy public doorway or portico, complete with songs, dances, recitations, and costume changes behind a convenient stairwell. But it was the Spanish count story that got Taylor her start in show business.

Loretta's teacher tactfully suggested that singing and dancing lessons might help channel the girl's natural high spirits. Elizabeth, after the usual arguments from her husband, enrolled her daughter in classes with one Miss **Ida Whittington**, who lived conveniently just across the street. Whittington, a former vaudeville trouper, suggested Loretta change her first name to the more sophisticated Laurette, and printed up handbills announcing to a list of theatrical managers culled from the trades that "La Belle Laurette Will Give Imitations, Recitations, and Sing Songs." Just after Laurette's 13th birthday, she and Elizabeth were thrilled to be offered her first paying job on the stage, even if the appearance turned out to be in the industrial town of Lynn, Massachusetts. Taylor was booked for a week's engagement with a nickelodeon show, a low-brow form of variety show for which the admission was a nickel and the talent even cheaper. The audience was not impressed with Taylor's charms. Neither was the show's manager, who advised Laurette to stay off the stage. Nonetheless, the same New York agent found her another booking, this time in a storehouse on the docks of the little fishing village of Gloucester, Massachusetts. "It was a question of who smelled to high heaven the most," Taylor would later recall, "the audience or my act." Elizabeth, her artful fantasies of show business much abused, swore it was the end of a short-lived career. But Laurette wasn't so sure. When Taylor was expelled from high school for being, as the principal put it, "an intractable pupil," James promptly enrolled her in a secretarial school even as Miss Whittington continued to act as her unofficial show-business promoter. It was through Whittington that Laurette, now 15, made the casual acquaintance of Charles Alonzo Taylor, who was 34 at the time of their first meeting in 1899.

Charlie, who had spent most of his youth in the West as a railroad worker and newspaper reporter, was on the way to earning his title of the "Master of Melodrama" for a successful string of potboilers he had written, produced, and directed for the stage. No less than four of them were running, either in New York or on tour, when he paid a visit to his old friend Ida Whittington and stopped to ask directions from a gawky young girl with wide, dreamy eyes sitting on a stoop. A year later, the two met a second time when Charlie Taylor attended a vaudeville revue in Boston in which Laurette was appearing. This time he offered her the heroine's role in his new show, *King of the Opium Road*, and promised Elizabeth that her daughter would be chaperoned by an older woman who was also in the cast. But Elizabeth, suspicious of Charlie Taylor's motives, wrangled her own contract from him as a costume designer. James having by now abandoned her in a cloud of moral indignation, Elizabeth left her two younger children with a sister and took to the road with her daughter.

*A*rtists, to give their best to their creations, should be born without a sense of self-preservation.

—**Laurette Taylor**

As Laurette quickly discovered, Charlie Taylor's shows required physical stamina rather than polished acting skills, for his productions were more circus and spectacle than melodrama. In *King of the Opium Road*, which purported to be an inside look at the opium dens of San Francisco's Chinatown, Laurette was chased across the stage by evil henchmen and rescued by three acrobats standing on each other's shoulders, who retrieved her from the villain's second-story lair and carried her across the stage to another upper window where her rescuer awaited. Still, one local newspaper reporter along the tour's route noted that Laurette was "a beautiful and clever little soubrette whose work is praised by the most competent critics." It was obvious to Elizabeth that Charlie was attracted by more than Laurette's professional attributes, especially when he announced he'd written a new play especially for Laurette, *Child Wife*, about a young bride who is abducted by a lustful villain. Eliza-

beth raised the stakes this time, announcing she would return to New York and her two children only if Charlie married Laurette—an event which occurred early in 1901, just before *Child Wife* took to the road. Charlie was 36; Laurette, 16.

The show-business marriage was doomed almost from the start, for Laurette's childhood storytelling had now matured into a desire to be a great actress, while Charlie's purple prose and stage pyrotechnics had more to do with box-office receipts than artistic sensibilities. Ominously, *Child Wife* was his first flop, criticized in print for having "no shooting, no fireworks, and no red fire." The show died a merciful death on tour, Charlie announced he was broke, and Laurette that she was pregnant. Elizabeth paid their train fare back to New York, where Laurette gave birth to a son, Dwight, on New Year's Day, 1902.

Charlie recovered his fortunes by writing a string of four successful plays, in which Laurette galloped across the stage on a horse, jumped from moving trains, struggled through desert sandstorms, and engaged in shooting matches with a variety of villains, from whose clutches she was invariably rescued by a handsome lover. She quickly grew bored. Charlie became furious with her for changing his impossibly artificial dialogue, making the audience laugh with bits of impromptu stage business, and generally refusing to take her status as leading lady of the company seriously. "I had long observed," Taylor later recalled, "that leading women with an overwhelming sense of their dignity and importance lacked the human quality in their acting."

Laurette Taylor would one day become famous for this "human quality." It was born of sheer necessity, she said, for Charlie's repertory tours required his actors to learn a new play every week while the current production was on the boards. Laurette quickly discovered that it was better to concentrate on scene, character, and relationships during rehearsals, rather than mechanically learning lines, a task she would often save until the night before the play opened. When the curtain rose, Laurette was ready with a character which developed from beginning to end, one which interacted with the others on stage and actually seemed to be listening to them, as if hearing their words for the first time. It was an acting style which is now taken for granted, but which was at the time startlingly different from the florid, bombastic mannerisms that then ruled the stage. "She is delightfully natural and artless," one critic wrote of Taylor during her years with her husband's company, "and

Laurette
Taylor

apparently unconscious of her many attractions and the effect she is producing."

But Laurette was acutely conscious of the strains and tensions of a marriage as melodramatic as Charlie's stage creations, even after the birth of a daughter, **Marguerite Taylor**, in 1904. When Charlie lost a second fortune with a badly received show called *Scotty, King of the Desert Mines* (in which, this time, Laurette had to weather an on-stage train wreck, be carried away in a dog sled, and share the bill with a donkey named Slim), and then tried unsuccessfully to run a permanent theater in an old San Francisco church, Laurette and her two children moved back to New York in 1907, living with Elizabeth in a small apartment on the edge of the theater district.

Taylor arrived at a time when Broadway was turning away from the frivolity of the Gilded Age and discovering that audiences would pay to see more serious material. Still, it wasn't until a year after leaving Charlie that Laurette found work in a Chicago production of Ferenc Molnar's *The Devil*, which had been enjoying a successful run on Broadway. The Broadway company arrived in Chicago at the same time Taylor's company was opening its version of the play, and critics naturally compared the two leading ladies. One of them suggested that the Broadway company's ingenue see Laurette's performance "and learn the value of simplicity, the heartbreak of the valiant." Her work in Chicago received enough attention for the Shubert brothers to ask Laurette to audition for the lead in a new play they were mounting, written by a popular British playwright named J. Hartley Manners. The audition was Taylor's first meeting with the man who would transform her career and her life.

Manners—witty, cool-headed, and elegantly sophisticated—had been an actor on the London stage before embarking on a successful writing career in 1900. His earlier background is not well known, although Laurette must have appreciated a rumor current at the time that he was the illegitimate son of English nobility and had been raised in a Cockney household. Taylor was struck most of all by Manners' tranquility and gentlemanly grace, so unlike Charlie Taylor's fiery impetuosity. Manners said little during the audition, but must have been impressed enough to urge the Shuberts to give her the leading role in his new play, *The Great John Ganton*, which opened in tryouts in Chicago in 1909. The critics were mesmerized by her stage manner. "It has been suggested that perhaps this actress has not yet acquired a method," wrote one of them, "but when you note the excellence of her pauses . . . or when you listen with her while she listens with an eloquence more illuminating than a dozen sentences would be—then you are constrained to believe that hers is either an extraordinarily subtle method or an intuitive gift for expression that amounts to genius." Taylor arrived in triumph on Broadway with the show, the first of six plays in which she appeared during the next two years. Her "discovery" seemed to fade when two of those six closed out of town, although her work in a small role in the otherwise long-forgotten *Alias Jimmy Valentine* was praised by alert reviewers. During this period, Charlie arrived in New York demanding a reconciliation, a futile request considering he had abandoned his acting company a year earlier by running away to Canada with his leading lady. Laurette's response was to file for a divorce. From then on, she refused to talk about Charlie, only referring to him vaguely as "the manager" or "the producer" of her early career. She would, in fact, always claim he had died in 1910, the year of their divorce, although Charlie lived into his 70s and passed away in 1942.

Shortly after her divorce, Taylor appeared in another play written by J. Hartley Manners, *The Girl in Waiting*, rewritten especially for her from an earlier version. The comedy closed out of town, even Laurette admitting that she had not been ready for the sophisticated airs of the play's upper-class setting. "The play was obviously written by someone with a knowledge of inherited silverware," she once remarked, noting the social gulf between the cultured man from England and the Irish girl from Mount Morris Park. But the disparity proved no obstacle to the romance that was now growing between them, helped by a wealthy supporter of Manners who often invited them for weekend socials at her country home in Connecticut.

It was during these early days of their courtship that Manners gave Taylor the first draft of a new play about a Cockney maid who discovers she is the heir to the fortune of a wealthy, hitherto unknown uncle, and who transforms the icy reserve of her newly discovered aristocratic relatives with her warm-hearted good sense. Laurette disliked the play at first, bluntly telling Manners that his heroine rang untrue. During the summer of 1911, strolling through the Connecticut woods or rocking peacefully on a porch, Taylor told Manners about her own upbringing in a rowdy Irish-American household, and particularly about her grandmother Bridget. The quiet Manners listened closely, took notes, and rewrote the play to make the heroine an Irish colleen modeled on Bridget Cooney. The manuscript became Manners' marriage proposal to Taylor, for he presented it to her with a sapphire ring folded inside and the promise that they would marry as soon as *Peg o' My Heart*, as the play was now called, appeared on a stage. This proved to be more difficult than expected, all the leading producers of the day considering its relentlessly cheery heroine much too saccharine for sophisticated theatergoers.

Laurette, meanwhile, had been discovered yet again, for her work in 1911's *Seven Sisters*.

"Oh, what a jolly mixup!" enthused Chicago critic Ashton Stevens. "When she was a star, she wasn't; and now that she isn't, she is!" Taylor's next choice of role was born of the sheer necessity to work and earn a living, for she appeared in a Charlie Taylor-style melodrama called *The Bird of Paradise*, playing a Hawaiian princess who falls in love with a white man only to kill herself in the last act by throwing herself into a volcano. Her performance was noted mostly because of her grass skirt and bare feet, as well as her hula dance, all of which were considered quite scandalous at the time. During the show's run, Taylor asked the producer, Oliver Morosco, to read *Peg o' My Heart*, telling him of her engagement and its ruling condition. More out of kindness than anything else, Morosco bought the play from Manners for $500, later claiming it made him $5 million. Laurette Taylor and J. Hartley Manners were promptly married in the autumn of 1912.

Peg o' My Heart opened on Broadway in December as the inaugural presentation at the new Cort Theater on 48th Street. It remained there for the next 18 months, playing to packed houses and closing in the spring of 1914 only because Laurette was exhausted after starring in what became the longest-running dramatic play up to that time, with a total of 604 performances. "In ten minutes," wrote *New York Globe* critic Louis Sherwin on opening night, "she gave us more acting than we have been accustomed to seeing in ten months." The great *Sarah Bernhardt, who was given a private midmorning performance, predicted that Taylor would be the foremost American actress within five years. To Laurette's horror, she was especially praised for saving what was deemed a mediocre play. "Its color was not champagne, but sarsaparilla," as one wag put it. But Manners was delighted at her success and carefully guarded it. He personally oversaw the casting for the four road companies that were sent out in 1913, making sure that Laurette's name appeared on the top of all show bills in a special "role created by" category; and successfully sued the songwriters of the popular tune which shared the play's name, forcing them to remove Taylor's picture from the sheet music and preventing them from making claims that the song had anything to do with the production. By the time the show closed its New York run and opened a year's run in London in 1914, Manners was said to be making $10,000 a week in royalties. When the German zeppelin raids on London forced the show to close after more than 1,000 performances, Taylor wearily noted,

"We've made a lot of money, but even money gets very monotonous." Returning to New York, the couple bought a sumptuous home on fashionable Riverside Drive—the setting for their popular Sunday night theatrical suppers—and a country house in Easthampton which became a favorite retreat for Laurette.

Peg o' My Heart marked the beginning of a series of such collaborations and the most successful period in Taylor's career. Nearly always, her work was commended more than her husband's. ("Alas, poor Hartley!," *Ethel Barrymore once lamented. "Only the audience liked his plays.") The 1917 production of *The Harp of Life* ran for only three months, although Burns Mantle told his *New York Times* readers that "[Miss Taylor] is the mistress of a thousand tricks, but so perfect is her sense of the theater and so absolute her command of her art that trickery is the last charge her devoted audience will make against her." World War I had been raging in Europe for three years when the play opened, and Manners spent most of its brief run polishing and rehearsing Laurette in the fervently patriotic *Out There*, which opened two days before the United States declared war on Germany. For once, the critics reviewed the play as favorably as they did Taylor's performance as a Cockney maid who becomes a Red Cross nurse and goes off to war to serve her country. Her line "If *I* go, will *you* go?" was adopted by the government for use on its recruitment posters. The couples' first unmitigated failure was *The Wooing of Eve*, which Burns Mantle deemed "90% silly and uninteresting and only 10% Miss Taylor, which is its only charm." This was quickly followed by *Happiness*, with the typical Manners waif (in this case, a Brooklyn errand girl) who teaches her world-weary betters to look on the bright side. Although audiences continued to applaud her work enthusiastically in such roles, the critics were growing restless. "She has resources in feminine allure, poetic passion and in exalted tragedy," one of them complained, "which have remained dormant." But Taylor was fully aware of her debt to her husband. "When I met Hartley," she once wrote, "I had experience without discipline, confusion without understanding, nerves without balance. When Hartley was alive, I was kept like a very fine racehorse." Laurette stolidly overlooked Manners' growing fondness for alcohol, noting that it only made him more charming and debonair, and cherished their hours together, sharing a cocktail and discussing their next project. This turned out to be, in 1919, *One Night in Rome*, a confused tale of an Italian noblewoman who falls on hard times and turns to fortune-telling for a living. As usual, it was thumbs up for Laurette, thumbs down for the play, although it enjoyed a respectable Broadway run and moved to London for eight months in 1920.

Her one foray outside of a Manners-written part was a brief series of matinees in which she presented condensed versions of Shakespeare, notably *Romeo and Juliet*, *The Taming of the Shrew*, and *The Merchant of Venice*. Manners advised against it, but at her insistence produced and directed the series himself. While admiring for her courage, critics gently suggested she and the Bard were not the best of friends. "Shakespeare is dead," Taylor said when the series closed. "Long live Manners." Nor did she often venture away from the legitimate theater. Her three films were merely adaptations of her stage successes.

In 1921, Taylor recreated her best-loved role in a revival of *Peg o' My Heart* on a national tour, during which she and Manners were exposed to the excesses of the postwar Jazz Age. The genteel Manners was particularly disgusted with the drug and alcohol use and the free-wheeling morals that characterized the period. His answer was 1922's *The National Anthem*, which opened on New Year's Eve of that year. Laurette considered the play his finest, and her work as the young society girl destroyed by her descent into debauchery the best of her career. But Manners, formerly criticized for writing sticky-sweet Cinderella tales, was now taken to task for writing a hard-hitting tragedy. "It is an acrid sermon in four acts, aimed like a crudely pointed forefinger," complained Alexander Woolcott, who referred to its author as "the Reverend J. Hartley Manners." This time, audiences agreed and stayed away, closing the play in three months. It was an emotionally exhausting experience for Taylor, who often had to be led to her dressing room after the play's long closing scene in which her character, alone on the stage and realizing she is dying from an overdose, tries to telephone for help. "During the run of 'Anthem,' I lost my gaiety," she remembered. Stung by the criticism, she and Manners retired to Easthampton where the cocktail hour, it was rumored, grew longer and longer.

For the first time in nearly ten years, Taylor appeared in a play that had not been written by her husband. She served as her own playwright this time, adapting *Fannie Hurst*'s *Humoresque* and taking the lead role of Sarah Kantor. Once again Laurette was buffeted by unexpected criticism, this time from Jews who objected to an Irish actress playing a Jewish matron. Hurst herself came to Taylor's defense, as did a handful of

critics who considered her performance entirely believable and delicately crafted, but the play closed after only three weeks. Over the next five years, Taylor took on a variety of other roles, none of them written by Manners and none of them as well received. Manners, in fact, seemed unable to produce a new work. Deprived of the source of her greatest successes, Laurette turned increasingly to alcohol.

Friends were commenting on her increasingly erratic behavior by the mid-1920s, while Manners desperately tried to think of a concept for a new play that would rescue her from her addiction. Over his protests, Taylor starred in an American version of a play she had seen in Paris, *Her Cardboard Lover*, which opened on Broadway in 1926. Manners considered it a cheap, vulgar bedroom farce, and most critics agreed with him. "Peg o' My Heart would die of shame," one of them wrote, while a friend sent her a backstage note saying, "I don't like to see you in dirty plays, Peg!" Taylor exploded within earshot of the entire cast. "It's that Peg again!" she was heard to scream. "Will I never bury that girl?" Manners hurriedly patched together *The Comedienne*, based on a sketch he'd written years before, but it quickly closed in Chicago during tryouts. Another attempt, *Delicate Justice*, fared no better. Stories spread of Taylor's angry tongue-lashings of fellow cast members during rehearsals, while critics labeled Manners' story of a faith-healer "inane and sprawling," or "talky, odious and inept." It was the last play of her husband's in which Taylor would appear. After closing in *Zoe Akins' *The Furies* in 1928, Laurette entered a sanitarium for treatment of her disease.

Manners presented her with a new comedy on her release, but both of them knew Taylor was in no condition to appear on a stage. Not long afterward, the persistent "smoker's cough" that had plagued Manners for years was diagnosed as throat cancer, the disease that claimed his life in late 1928. "I'll be a fool without Hartley," Taylor told friends, "just a goddam fool!"

For the next four years, she disappeared from public view and into an alcoholic haze supported by the royalties from Manners' greatest gift to her, *Peg o' My Heart*. Her spending became so precipitous that her children took court action to attach the assets of the trust fund Manners had left their mother, which Taylor naturally saw as an attempt to steal all she had left of him. While relations with her children deteriorated, the friction seemed to revive her. Taylor gathered the strength to appear in public, causing a stir by testifying before a Congressional committee in 1932 against a bill proposing an excise tax on theater tickets. That same year, she accepted her first role since Manners' death, in a revival of J.M. Barrie's *Alice Sit by the Fire*. Critics and audiences alike were delighted with her return to the stage, *The New York Times*' Brooks Atkinson enthusing: "To have Miss Taylor back is a wondrous thing." But after the elation of being back on Broadway wore off, Taylor's drinking returned, and she began missing performances to such an extent that the show was closed early. The opening of a new play for which she was scheduled was first delayed, then canceled altogether, when it became public knowledge that her addiction had returned.

She disappeared from public life for another five years, emerging in 1937 to star in a summer-stock production of a play she had written herself, *At Marian's*, an autobiographical work about a recovering alcoholic. By now, alcoholism had begun to exact its debilitating physical cost. She grew increasingly ill and weak during the show's run, losing 45 pounds and developing severe anemia that required hospitalization. But there was yet another comeback in store for her, one that is still remembered with excitement by Broadway historians.

Ironically, it was an old show-business friend of Charlie Taylor's who suggested that Taylor appear in a planned 1939 revival of Sutton Vane's poignant *Outward Bound*, to be directed by Otto Preminger. Laurette appeared as the dowdy Mrs. Midget, one of a group of shipboard passengers who discover they have all died and are on their final passage to Eternity. The applause was so thunderous at Taylor's first entrance that the action had to be halted until it died down; and at the play's end, she was called back for 22 curtain calls. "Her playing is both modest and quiet," wrote Richard Watts in the *Times*. "It merely happens that she is one of the finest actresses in the world." Backstage, Taylor fell into the waiting arms of American Theater Wing president *Antoinette Perry, sobbing "Oh, Tony, it's back! The theater's back!"

The theater world waited expectantly for Taylor to select her next role from the many now offered to her, but she took her time. "Nothing but pipe-smoking, tobacco-chewing, horrible old women," she complained. After five years, she finally found the role which has preserved her reputation ever since—as the genteel Mrs. Amanda Wingfield in Tennessee Williams' memory play, *The Glass Menagerie*. The play opened at The Playhouse on 48th Street on March 30, 1945—

one day before Laurette's 61st birthday. Broadway was entranced by her delicate portrayal of a faded Southern belle who attempts to relive her girlhood by introducing her daughter to a "gentleman caller," destroying the daughter's romantic dreams when it is discovered the young man is married. As it had 25 years before, Taylor's completely natural stage presence electrified her audience. "There is a sense . . . of [Mrs. Wingfield] having been born out of a tradition, not out of a box," wrote *The New Republic*.

During the play's run, however, Taylor's physical condition seemed to weaken to the point where the curtain often had to be held some nights while she decided if she were strong enough to go on. Later in the show's run, Laurette would appear for the play's first act, then ask that her understudy finish the show. There were rumors, too, that Taylor had begun to drink again. By the time the show closed late in 1945, the understudy had been appearing nearly every night. Nonetheless, Taylor was awarded the coveted Critics Circle Award for Best Actress in 1946.

In June of that year, an operation to remove a benign growth on her vocal cords left her even weaker and confined to her bed. She received few visitors, save for her children, to whom she was by now reconciled. On the morning of December 7, 1946, Laurette Taylor died peacefully at home.

At the opening of *The Glass Menagerie*, one perceptive reviewer noted that watching Taylor's performance justified theater's existence long into the future. Indeed, her name is still reverently spoken by those who were fortunate enough to have seen her work and by those actors who learned from her. During rehearsals for *The Glass Menagerie*, one of the cast members complained of what seemed to be Taylor's disinterest. But it was only her usual, patient method of building a character at the expense of accurate line readings. Laurette was unruffled by the accusation. "How can you give it before it has grown inside?" she asked. In those few years after her long exile, Laurette Taylor had found herself again, and given generously.

SOURCES:

Atkinson, Brooks. *Broadway*. NY: Macmillan, 1970.
Courtney, Marguerite. *Laurette*. NY: Atheneum, 1968.

Norman Powers,
writer-producer, Chelsea Lane Productions,
New York, New York

Taylor, Lily Ross (1886–1969)

American classicist and educator who helped develop the influential 20th-century view of Roman political history and religion, including the areas of the Roman Republic's political structure and religious cults. Born on August 12, 1886, in Auburn, Alabama; died after being struck by a car on November 18, 1969, in Bryn Mawr, Pennsylvania; daughter of William Dana Taylor (a railway engineer and professor) and Mary (Ross) Taylor; educated at preparatory department of Pritchett College, Glasgow, Missouri, and at Madison High School; University of Wisconsin, A.B., 1906; attended the American Academy in Rome; Bryn Mawr College, Ph.D., 1912.

Selected works: Local Cults in Etruria (1932); The Divinity of the Roman Emperor (1931); Party Politics in the Age of Caesar (1949); The Voting Districts of the Roman Republic: The Thirty-five Urban and Rural Tribes (1960); Roman Voting Assemblies (1966).

Born in 1886 in Alabama, Lily Ross Taylor was the eldest of three children of William Dana Taylor and **Mary Ross Taylor**. Her mother died in 1895, and two years later her father, a well-known railway engineer, married **Annie L. McIntyre**, with whom he had three more children. William's work led the family around the country, before they eventually settled in Wisconsin in 1901. There her father was appointed a professor of railway engineering and Taylor attended high school and college.

Initially studying mathematics, Taylor realized from a course on Lucretius during her junior year that Roman studies interested her more. She graduated from the University of Wisconsin in 1906 and started graduate school at Bryn Mawr College that same year. From 1909 to 1910, she studied in Rome and then returned to Bryn Mawr to receive her Ph.D. in 1912. Her first book was her thesis, *The Cults of Ostia* (1912). That same year she became a Latin instructor at Vassar College, where she remained until 1927, eventually earning the title of professor.

In 1917, she became the first woman to receive a fellowship at the American Academy in Rome, although due to World War I, she left the academy for a few years to serve in the American Red Cross in Italy and the Balkans. She returned to the American academy in Rome in 1919 and remained there until 1920. Appointed professor and chair of the Latin department at Bryn Mawr in 1927, Taylor was named dean of the graduate school there in 1942. An excellent teacher, she was professionally acknowledged in 1952 with the *Life* Magazine Teachers Award.

In addition to teaching, Taylor was an associate editor for *Classical Philology* during the 1940s, and from 1943 to 1944 worked as a

principal social science analyst in the Office of Strategic Services in Washington, D.C. She was active in professional organizations as well, including the American Philological Association, for which she served as president in 1942, and the American Institute of Archeology, of which she was vice-president from 1935 to 1937. In 1947, she became the first woman appointed Sather Professor of Classics at the University of California. Her Sather Lectures were published in 1949 as *Party Politics in the Age of Caesar*.

In 1952, Taylor retired from Bryn Mawr to assume directorship of the Classical School of the American Academy in Rome, where she remained until 1955. Returning to Bryn Mawr, she lectured throughout the United States between 1956 and 1957 as a Phi Beta Kappa visiting scholar. In the late 1950s and early 1960s, she served as visiting professor at several universities, and also spent a year at Princeton University as a member of the Institute for Advanced Study. From 1964 to 1965, she was Jerome Lecturer at the American Academy in Rome and the University of Michigan.

A member of the American Philosophical Society and a fellow of the American Academy of Arts and Sciences, Taylor was honored with the Achievement Award of the American Association of University Women in 1952, the Citation for Distinguished Service from Bryn Mawr (awarded at the college's 75th anniversary) in 1960, the Award of Merit of the American Philological Association and the Cultori di Roma gold medal from the city of Rome, both in 1962. Throughout her life she was an enthusiastic traveler, and her fluency in Italian made Italy a favorite and rewarding place to visit. Taylor was killed by a hit-and-run driver in Bryn Mawr in 1969, at the age of 83.

SOURCES:
Sicherman, Barbara, and Carol Hurd Green, eds. *Notable American Women: The Modern Period.* Cambridge, MA: The Belknap Press of Harvard University, 1980.

Karina L. Kerr, M.A.,
Ypsilanti, Michigan

Taylor, Lucy Hobbs (1833–1910)

American who became the first woman with a dental degree in the world. Born Lucy Beaman Hobbs probably in Franklin County, rather than Clinton County, New York, on March 14, 1833; died in Lawrence, Kansas, on October 3, 1910; buried in the Oak Hill Cemetery, Lawrence, Kansas; daughter of Lucy (Beaman) Hobbs and Benjamin Hobbs; attended Franklin Academy, Malone, New York, 1845–49; Ohio College of Dental Surgery, D.D.S., 1866; married James Myr-

tle Taylor, in Chicago, Illinois, on April 24, 1867 (died December 14, 1886); no children.

Awards: member of the Iowa State Dental Society (1865) and the Illinois State Dental Society (1866); first female Noble Grand of Degree, Rebekah Lodge of the Independent Order of Odd Fellows, Lawrence, Kansas; Worthy Matron of the Adah Chapter of the Order of the Eastern Star, Lawrence, Kansas; president of the Republican Club, Lawrence, Kansas.

Enrolled at the Franklin Academy, Malone, New York (1845); graduated from the Franklin Academy (1849); moved to Cincinnati, Ohio (1859); was refused admission to Eclectic College of Medicine (1859); was refused admission to Ohio College of Dental Surgery (1859 and 1861); opened practice in Cincinnati (1861); opened practice in Bellevue, Iowa (1861); opened practice in McGregor, Iowa (1863); graduated from Ohio College of Dental Surgery (1866); was the first woman to address a state dental association (July 1866); moved to Chicago, Illinois (1866); elected to Illinois State Dental Society (1866); opened practice in Chicago (1866); moved to Lawrence, Kansas (December 1867); opened practice in Lawrence, Kansas (1867); joined Rebekah Lodge of the Independent Order of Odd Fellows (1871); joined Adah Chapter of Order of the Eastern Star (1875); went into semiretirement (1886); retired (1907).

Lucy Hobbs Taylor's original ambition was to became a medical doctor. For a woman in the mid-1800s, however, educational opportunities in medicine were almost non-existent. By 1830, a license was required to practice medicine in all but three states in America. Thus, medical colleges exercised increasing influence in the exclusion of women from the science. Nevertheless, Taylor demonstrated a strong determination to obtain medical training and enter some branch of the health-care professions.

Lucy Hobbs Taylor was born in a log cabin on March 14, 1833. Her place of birth is variously listed as Franklin or Clinton counties, New York. The seventh of ten children, she was the daughter of **Lucy Beaman Hobbs** and Benjamin Hobbs, who had moved from New England to New York several years previously. When Taylor was only ten years old, her mother died. Benjamin Hobbs subsequently married his sister-in-law **Hannah Beaman**, but Hannah too died suddenly shortly after the marriage. As a result, Lucy and her brother Thomas were enrolled at the Franklin Academy, a residential school in Malone, New York. There she received her formal education. Taylor proved a good student and graduated in 1849.

After graduating, Lucy Taylor took a teaching position at the public school in Brooklyn, Michigan, where she taught for ten years. When not teaching, she attended the local debating society, spelling bees, and sang in the choir. In Brooklyn, Taylor met the town physician and persuaded him to give her lessons in physiology and anatomy. At his suggestion, she attempted to enroll at the Eclectic College of Medicine in Cincinnati, Ohio, where it was reported that women were welcome as students. As **Caroline Bird** noted, the Eclectic College of Medicine was "one of the proprietary medical schools that amounted to diploma mills." Upon her arrival in Cincinnati in 1859, however, Taylor discovered that her application for admission had been denied due to her gender. Even though *Elizabeth Blackwell** had become the first American woman to receive a medical degree ten years previously, old prejudices still prevailed.

However, Charles A. Cleaveland, professor of materia medica and therapeutics at the Eclectic College of Medicine, agreed to tutor Taylor privately. He had been a salesman of medical equipment before being invited to teach at the college. When the private instruction which Taylor received from Cleaveland brought her no closer to her goal of becoming a doctor, he suggested that she pursue a career in dentistry, a field more accessible to women. Dentists were not required to make house calls, he told her, nor was it necessary to have a license to practice in the state of Ohio.

Contemporaries did not consider dentistry a profession. Instead, dentistry was thought of as a trade. Given the standards of oral hygiene at the time, this is hardly surprising. Writes Bird:

> Except in the cities, no one cared very much about the appearance of teeth, and if they rotted, almost anyone could pull them out. Like preachers and photographers, who sometimes pulled teeth on the side, early dentists served sparsely populated rural areas by travelling from town to town, carrying their tools with them. In the case of dentists, these were usually confined to a file, a few excavators, a vial of mercury, and silver coins to make fillings. Many people regarded dentists as little better than the patent medicine men who travelled the same routes.

At the time, Ohio dentists were attempting to organize a college of dentistry, similar to that of their medical colleagues. Schools of dentistry were not yet affiliated with universities and retained an independent status. Once founded, the Ohio College of Dental Surgery refused Taylor's request for admission.

After some persuasion, however, Jonathan Taft, dean of the college, agreed to teach Taylor privately for three months. For her part, Taylor found Taft "an earnest advocate of the right of women to study and pursue his profession." As well, she noted that Taft was a founder of the American Dental Association, and was "probably the most distinguished dentist who . . . ever practiced in Cincinnati." Having proved herself to Taft, Taylor was accepted as an apprentice to a dentist in private practice, Dr. Samuel Wardle, himself a graduate of the Ohio College of Dental Surgery. She had already approached several other dentists, including Dr. George Watt of Xenia, Ohio. Watt declined to take her on, as he wrote "for reasons beyond . . . control."

Years later, Taylor recalled in the third person the difficulty she faced in securing an apprenticeship. In the fall of 1859, there appeared in the western horizon a cloud "not as big as a man's hand, for it was the hand of a young girl, risen in appeal to man, . . . for the opportunity to enter a profession where she could earn her bread, not alone by the sweat of her brow, but by the use of her brain also. The cloud though small was portentous. It struck terror into the hearts of the community, especially the male portion of it. All innovations cause commotion. This was no exception. People were amazed when they learned that a young girl had so far forgotten her womanhood as to want to study dentistry."

[She] conquered prejudice and precedent and prepared the way for women to become practitioners of the science and art of dentistry.

—Ralph W. Edwards

From Wardle, Taylor learned the basics of dentistry, including the use of anaesthesia and the construction of false teeth. At night, she supported herself by taking in sewing. As well, she studied anatomy, hygiene, and physiology, while taking care of Wardle's office and the cleaning of his instruments. Taylor learned to extract teeth and to make fillings and dental impressions. Wardle, she noted, made it possible "for women to enter the profession. He was to us what Queen *Isabella [I] was to Columbus."

With her apprenticeship completed, Taylor again applied for admission to the Ohio College of Dental Surgery in March 1861. A student from Liberia also applied to the college. The resolution passed by the college spoke for itself. "By a vote of four against two neither women, nor men of African descent, would be received." As Taylor recalled:

There was not a college in the United States that would admit me, and no amount of persuasion could change their minds. So far as I know, I was the first woman who had ever taken instruction of a private tutor.

Undeterred, she took Wardle's advice, and opened her own office in Cincinnati. Competition was stiff. Within a few weeks of opening for business, she closed her doors. The onset of the Civil War deprived her of the clientele necessary to make her practice a success.

Taylor borrowed some money and set off for the West, opening an office in Bellevue, Iowa. The curiosity of the local population was aroused by the presence of a female dentist. In one year, she repaid the loan and saved $100, investing the profits in a dental chair. By her second year, Taylor had earned enough money to fully equip her office with modern dental instruments.

Seeking even greener pastures, she then moved to McGregor, Iowa, a thriving market town with saloons, gambling houses, and a steam ferry. The boomtown atmosphere translated into a prosperous practice. During her first year in McGregor, Taylor earned $3,000, not an inconsiderable sum for the time. As her reputation spread throughout the state, she was able to charge higher fees.

On July 19, 1865, Taylor was invited to a session of the newly incorporated Iowa State Dental Society by Dr. Luman Church Ingersoll, subsequently the first dean of dentistry at the State University of Iowa. In welcoming Taylor as a member of the society, Ingersoll declared:

The profession of dentistry . . . has nothing in its pursuits foreign to the instincts of women, and on the other hand, presents in almost every applicant for operations, a subject requiring a kind and benevolent consideration of the most refined and womanly nature.

Taylor was the first woman in American history to be recognized by such a body. Admission to the Iowa State Dental Society helped her gain acceptance with the conservative Ohio College of Dental Surgery in 1865. After six years of professional rejection, she was finally acknowledged by her peers. "I went to Iowa to commence practice," she recalled, "and was so successful that the dentists of the State insisted I should be allowed to attend the college. Their efforts prevailed, and I graduated from the Ohio Dental College at Cincinnati in the spring of 1866—the first woman in the world to take a diploma from a dental college."

Taylor was admitted to the senior class of the Ohio College of Dental Surgery. The course consisted of four months of study, a thesis on dental science, the construction of a pair of false teeth, and examinations. Wrote Professor Jonathan Taft:

> She was a woman of great energy and perseverance, studious in her habits, modest and unassuming; she had the respect and kind regard of every member of the class and faculty. As an operator she was not surpassed by her associates. Her opinion was asked and her assistance sought in difficult cases, almost daily by her fellow students. And though the class of which she was a member was one of the largest ever in attendance, it excelled all previous ones in good order and decorum—a condition largely due to the presence of a lady. In the final examination she was second to none.

On February 21, 1866, Lucy Taylor became the first woman in the world to become a Doctor of Dental Surgery. Dr. James Truman of the Pennsylvania College of Dental Surgery rejoiced that dentistry "welcomed a woman." The rejoicing was not universal, however. In the April 1866 issue of *The Dental Times*, Dr. George T. Baker wrote: "Should females be encouraged to enter the dental profession? I contend they should not.... The very form and structure of woman unfit her for its duties.... Its performance would, under certain circumstances, be attended with great danger."

While men debated the suitability of women as dentists, Taylor moved her practice to Chicago. In May 1866, she was elected to the Illinois State Dental Society. In July, she traveled to Burlington, Iowa, where she addressed the Iowa State Dental Society. In yet another first, Taylor became the first woman to lecture to a state dental association. Her paper dealt with the uses of mallet pressure, rather than hand pressure, in the filling of cavities.

In Chicago, Lucy met James Myrtle Taylor, a Civil War veteran who worked as a painter in the Chicago and Northwestern Railway maintenance shop. Following their marriage in 1867, James Taylor soon became his wife's apprentice, an interesting reversal of roles. It was common for wives to apprentice with their husbands in the trades, since it was a cost-effective way of bringing skilled hands into a family enterprise. James Taylor would learn his profession at minimal cost. As a man, it would be easy for him to become a licensed practitioner.

That November, Taylor sold her Chicago practice to Edmund Noyes, and the couple moved to Lawrence, Kansas, in December. New arrivals were pouring into the state, and dentists were much in demand. Taylor felt a particular affinity for the American frontier. As she wrote, "I am a New Yorker by birth, but I love my adopted country—the West." Together the Taylors opened

a practice. While James took male patients, Lucy catered to women and children; she also specialized in false teeth. The Taylors' business partnership was a profitable one, and their practice grew into one of the largest in the state of Kansas.

In 1886, Drs. J.M. and Lucy H. Taylor took "pleasure in announcing to their many friends, and patrons in Lawrence," that they were expanding their practice. "Associated with them in the dental profession," went the announcement, was "Dr. L.M. Mathews, of Ft. Scott, widely known to the profession, as one of the finest operators in the west ... equalled by few, and excelled by none in gold work, both operative and mechanical." The expansion of the practice, however, was not simply a business decision. The health of Taylor's husband had long been in decline. On December 14, 1886, James died, and Lucy Taylor went into semi-retirement. Though she continued to practice, she took only enough patients, as she commented, "to keep her out of mischief."

In later years, Taylor devoted much of her time to membership in the Rebekah Lodge of the Independent Order of Odd Fellows, and became the first female Noble Grand of Degree of the order. As well, she joined the Adah Chapter of the Order of the Eastern Star in 1875, and became the Worthy Matron of the Adah Chapter. Taylor was also elected president of Lawrence's Republican Club. Lucy Taylor never forgot the cause of women's suffrage, and engaged in fundraising efforts to better the lot of women.

At age 77, on October 3, 1910, Lucy Taylor died of a cerebral hemorrhage and was buried in the Oak Hill Cemetery in Lawrence, Kansas. At her funeral, former friends and patients alike recalled a woman known for her generosity and kindness of spirit. Lucy Hobbs Taylor blazed a trail for woman entering the dental profession. As she explained in a letter to *Matilda Joslyn Gage,* "You ask my reason for entering the profession. It was to be independent." She sought a career which offered more financial security and intellectual scope than those occupations which were traditionally reserved for women.

The example of Lucy Taylor elicited support from many quarters. By 1880, there were 61 female dentists practicing in the United States. In 1892, the Woman's Dental Association of the United States was founded. In 1896, Dr. James Truman introduced a resolution before a meeting of the American Dental Association, which read in part:

> In view of the successful results obtained in the education of women as dentists, we recommend to subordinate associations to

admit to full membership any woman duly qualified. . . . That in consultations, considerations of sex should be avoided; ability and moral character alone being the standard of judgment in all cases.

Lucy Taylor's entry into the profession of dentistry coincided with an increasing awareness among many Americans about the importance of oral hygiene. The science itself was making rapid advances. Gone were the days when itinerant dentists used silver coins as fillings. Gold fillings were increasingly employed, as was gutta percha for root canals. The theory of sterilization was gaining increasing acceptance, and orthodontia evolved into its modern form. Taylor recognized the changing nature of orthodontia and embraced it. She wrote:

The making of false teeth is not a mere mechanical operation. . . . This is the study of an artist; and a dentist, so far as it is required of him to imitate nature, should be as truly an artist as if he were a sculptor carving the feature in marbles.

Much like Elizabeth Blackwell in the field of medicine, Lucy Taylor held open the door for women to enter the field of dentistry. She applied for admission to the Ohio College of Dental Surgery on three separate occasions—in 1859, 1861, and 1865, when she was finally accepted. Her battle for equal opportunity is an example of stubbornness and courage. For her efforts, Lucy Taylor emerged, not only as a pioneer in her field, but as a highly skilled and conscientious health-care professional.

SOURCES:

Bird, Caroline. *Enterprising Women.* NY: W.W. Norton, 1976.

Edwards, Ralph W. "The First Woman Dentist—Lucy Hobbs Taylor, D.D.S. (1833–1910)," in *Bulletin of the History of Medicine.* Vol. 25, no. 3. Baltimore, MD: Johns Hopkins University Press, 1951.

Golemba, Beverly E. *Lesser-known Women.* Boulder, CO: Lynne Rienner, 1992.

*Stanton, Elizabeth Cady, *Susan B. Anthony, and Matilda Joslyn Gage, eds. *History of Woman Suffrage.* Vol. III. NY: Arno, 1969.

Stern, Madeleine B. *We the Women.* NY: Schulte, 1963.

SUGGESTED READING:

Stern, Madeleine B. "Taylor, Lucy Beaman Hobbs," in *Notable American Women, 1607–1950.* Edward T. James, ed. Cambridge, MA: The Belknap Press of Harvard University, 1971.

Hugh A. Stewart, M.A.,
University of Guelph,
Guelph, Ontario, Canada

❧▶

Taylor, Knox.

See Davis, Varina Howell for sidebar.

Taylor, Margaret Smith (1788–1852)

American first lady (1849–1850) who was an "invisible" presence in the White House. Name variations:

*Peggy Taylor. Born Margaret Mackall Smith on September 21, 1788, in Calvert County, Maryland; died on August 18, 1852, in Pascagoula, Mississippi; daughter of Walter Smith (a planter and veteran of the Revolutionary War) and Ann (Mackall) Smith; married Zachary Taylor (1784–1850, 12th president of the United States), on June 21, 1810, in Louisville, Kentucky; children: eight, including **Ann Mackall Taylor** (b. 1811); Sarah Knox Taylor (b. 1814, who married Jefferson Davis [1808–1889], later president of the Confederacy); **Octavia Pannill Taylor** (b. 1816); Margaret Smith Taylor (b. 1819); Mary Elizabeth Taylor Bliss (1824–1909); Richard Taylor (b. 1826).*

The story is told that Margaret "Peggy" Taylor considered her husband's presidential nomination in 1848 "a plot to deprive her of his society and shorten his life." She even prayed for his defeat. Nevertheless, "Old Rough and Ready" was victorious and Margaret was thrust into the White House, where she lived in seclusion on the second floor, amid rumors that she was uncultured "poor white of the wilds" and smoked a corn-cob pipe. In truth, she was Maryland gentry, the daughter of Walter Smith, a plantation heir and major in the Revolutionary War, and granddaughter, on her mother's side, of General James Mackall. As for the pipe, tobacco smoke made her quite ill.

Little is known of Margaret's early life. She was born in 1788 in Calvert County, Maryland. It is believed that she had two brothers and a sister, and that her mother **Ann Mackall Smith** died when Margaret was in her teens, leaving her in charge of the household. She met young Lieutenant Zachary Taylor in Kentucky, while visiting her sister, and they were wed in June 1810. Throughout most of their marriage, Margaret cheerfully followed her husband to various remote military garrisons. While he distinguished himself against Tecumseh, and in the Black Hawk and Seminole wars, she raised five daughters and a son in primitive and dangerous outposts. Two of the girls died of malaria in the Bayou country of Louisiana, where Zachary was transferred in 1819. The losses were devastating. When another son and daughter were born, the Taylors sent the children to live with relatives, rather than risk exposing them to further dangers. In 1835, their second daughter, ❧ Knox Taylor, also died of malaria, three months after eloping with Jefferson Davis, then a soldier under the command of her father and later president of the Confederacy.

In 1841, the Taylors finally settled on a plantation on the Mississippi, only to be parted again by the Mexican War. This time Margaret vowed that if her husband were spared, she would never set foot in society again. She kept her promise. In the White House, she welcomed the visits of friends and relatives in her private upstairs sitting room, ate with the family, and worshipped regularly at St. John's Episcopal Church. All official social functions, however, were presided over by her youngest daughter ❧▶ **Mary Elizabeth Bliss,** wife of Taylor's adjutant and secretary, William Bliss, or by *Varina Howell Davis, second wife of her former son-in-law Jefferson Davis.

Margaret's fears that the presidency would take her husband's life were not unfounded. Just over a year after assuming office, Zachary fell ill after a long exposure to the summer sun during a cornerstone-laying ceremony. He died five days later, on July 9, 1850. Margaret left Washington shortly after the funeral and never spoke of the White House again. She spent the last two years of her life surrounded by her children and grandchildren, and died at age 64. She is buried next to her husband in the Zachary Taylor National Cemetery in Louisville, Kentucky.

SOURCES:
Healy, Diana Dixon. *America's First Ladies: Private Lives of the Presidential Wives.* NY: Atheneum, 1988.
Klapthor, Margaret Brown. *The First Ladies.* Washington, DC: White House Historical Association, 1979.
Melick, Arden David. *Wives of the Presidents.* Maplewood, NJ: Hammond, 1977.
Paletta, LuAnn. *The World Almanac of First Ladies.* NY: World Almanac, 1990.

Barbara Morgan,
Melrose, Massachusetts

Taylor, Mary (1817–1893).

See Brontë Sisters for sidebar.

Taylor, Melanie Smith (1949—)

American equestrian in show jumping. Name variations: Melanie Ainsworth Smith. Born Melanie Ainsworth Smith in Litchfield, Connecticut, on September 23, 1949; married Lee Taylor (a polo player), in 1985.

Was the first American Grandprix Association Rider of the Year (1978); won the World Cup (1982); was on the first American equestrian team to win an Olympic gold medal in team jumping (1984); after retiring from competition, became a television commentator for equestrian events.

Melanie Smith Taylor, who up until 1985 won her titles under her maiden name of Melanie Ainsworth Smith, was fascinated by dressage, the

16th-century European art of training horses in precise movement in preparation for war. Women had not always been allowed to compete in this ancient sport and were restricted from Olympic equestrian competition until 1952. By the time Taylor began to compete in the 1970s, however, women were a familiar sight on the course. When she was first on the American Grandprix Association (AGA) tour in 1976, Taylor rode Radnor II and Val de Loire, the horse she rode while on the team that won the gold medal in 1979 in the Pan American Games.

Margaret Smith Taylor

An amazing partnership began, however, when Taylor mounted Calypso, a Dutch bay gelding. In 1979, she won the International Jumping Derby, and in 1980 was second in the World Cup final. That same year, she and Calypso won the Grand Prix of Paris and took the individual bronze medal at the Rotterdam Show Jumping Festival. Horse and rider continued in 1982, taking the American Invitational, the World Cup final, and the American Gold Cup.

> ❧▶ **Bliss, Mary Elizabeth** (1824–1909)
>
> *First daughter and White House hostess. Name variations: Betty Taylor; Betty Bliss. Born Mary Elizabeth Taylor in 1824; died in 1909; daughter of Margaret Smith Taylor (1788–1852) and Zachary Taylor (1784–1850, president of the United States); sister of *Knox Taylor; married William Wallace Smith Bliss (1815–1853, Zachary Taylor's adjutant and confidential secretary); married Philip Pendleton Dandridge; no children.*
>
> Mary Elizabeth Bliss, known as Betty, was the youngest of the Taylor daughters and functioned as social hostess for her mother *Margaret Smith Taylor. She was educated at a finishing school in Philadelphia and at age 25 married Lieutenant Colonel William Wallace Smith Bliss, who was an aide and confidential secretary to her father. Betty was a charming hostess, often called the "Wild Rose of the White House." After the death of her husband, she married Philip Pendleton Dandridge. She had no children by either marriage, and remained sympathetic to the Southern cause throughout her life. She died in 1909, at age 85.

In 1983, Taylor was on the U.S. team that won the Nations Cup and World Cup. In 1984, she and Calypso rested up for the Olympics. The American team consisted of Leslie Burr on Albany, Joe Fargis on Touch of Class, Conrad Homfeld on Abdullah, and Melanie Taylor on Calypso. "My goal always had been to win the team gold medal over the individual gold," she said.

> Though the individual event was very important to me, my dream had been realized in the team phase of the 1984 Olympics. August 7 was a day I will remember always. Calypso put in the round of his life on sheer heart and determination. We anchored the team with a clear performance in the first round, which brought us from the back to the front of the pack, going into the second round. The brilliant rides from my teammates kept us from needing to ride again. We already had won the gold medal.

For the first time in history, an American equestrian team won the gold medal in team jumping. The victory was decisive, due in part to Melanie Smith Taylor's clear round on Calypso.

SOURCES:

Markel, Robert, Nancy Brooks, and Susan Markel. *For the Record. Women in Sports.* NY: World Almanac, 1985.

Taylor, Melanie Smith. "Luck with a Lucky Boy," in *Riding for America: The United States Equestrian Team.* Edited by Nancy Jaffer. NY: Doubleday, 1990, pp. 24–29.

Karin Loewen Haag,
Athens, Georgia

Taylor, Sallie (1814–1835).

See Davis, Varina Howell for sidebar on Knox Taylor.

Taylor, Sarah Knox (1814–1835).

See Davis, Varina Howell for sidebar on Knox Taylor.

Taylor, Stella (1929—)

Long-distance swimmer. Born in 1929.

Stella Taylor, a former Catholic nun, became a long-distance swimmer and set several records, including records for swimming the English Channel, Loch Ness, and the straits between the Bahamas and Florida. Her greatest achievement happened at the age of 52 in Ft. Lauderdale, Florida. On a Tuesday in April 1982, at 10 PM, Taylor began swimming laps in the 55-yard pool at the International Swimming Hall of Fame; she remained in the pool until Friday afternoon at 3 PM—a total of 65 hours. She had traversed the length of the pool and back 3,120 times, an estimated 175 miles, which shattered her old record.

To sustain herself, Taylor had relied on a diet of honey, rice, egg salad, and cheese.

Karina L. Kerr, M.A.,
Ypsilanti, Michigan

Taylor, Susie King (1848–1912)

Author of Reminiscences of My Life in Camp, *the only Civil War memoir by an African-American woman veteran. Born Susie Baker on August 6, 1848, on the Isle of Wight off Savannah, Georgia; died on October 6, 1912, in Boston, Massachusetts; daughter of Raymond Baker and Hagar Ann (Reed) Baker (slaves on the Grest farm); married Sergeant Edward King, early 1860s (died in September 1866); married Russell L. Taylor, in 1879 (died c. 1902); children: (first marriage) one son (died 1898).*

Born a slave; escaped to freedom during the Civil War (April 1862); joined the First South Carolina Volunteers, later the 33rd U.S. Colored Troops, as a laundress, nurse, and teacher; was a teacher and house servant in Savannah, Georgia (1866–74); moved to Boston (1874); organized the Women's Relief Corps (1886); was president of local WRC (1893). Publications: Reminiscences of My Life in Camp *(1902).*

After four years of the bloodiest fighting in American history, Union troops captured Charleston in February 1865. South Carolina had been the first state to secede from the Union in 1861, and Fort Sumter in Charleston harbor was the scene of the initial battle. Among the Union troops entering the city were the men of the 33rd U.S. Colored Troops, and with them was 17-year-old Susie King (later Taylor), the nurse, teacher and laundress to Company E. As the departing Confederate troops set fire to the beautiful city, the Union troops, black and white, battled the blaze. Nevertheless, the civilian population of Charleston reviled the black soldiers, who had formerly been their slaves.

This was one of the most dramatic moments of the Civil War. For over 200 years, slave-owners had regarded their captive laborers as childlike inferiors, lacking the virtues of whites. This myth was shattered by the 180,000 African-American soldiers who shouldered arms for the Union. The sight of disciplined black troops turned the world upside down for pro-slavery Charleston residents. Susie King Taylor would record this event with customary restraint in her memoir *Reminiscences of My Life in Camp.*

Susie Baker was born a slave in 1848 on the Grest farm on the Isle of Wight, one of a chain of barrier islands off the Carolina and Georgia coast. Virtually all of what we know about Taylor's life comes from her memoir, and she says little about her own parents. Family legend was preserved through her grandmother **Dolly Reed**, a half-Indian woman born in 1820 who married Fortune Lambert Reed. Dolly's own grandmother lived 120 years and had seven children, five of whom died in the Revolutionary War.

Taylor was raised by her grandmother, who attended Mrs. Grest in Savannah. Slaves were forbidden to learn to read by law and custom, but some urban bondspeople were able to get an education despite this prohibition. As a child, Susie surreptitiously attended a school in the home of a free African-American woman; she "went every day about nine o'clock," wrote Taylor, "with her books wrapped in paper to prevent the police or white persons from seeing them." Later, a white playmate gave her some lessons, but only after Susie promised not to tell the girl's father about their studies. A white high-school student then instructed her further.

Taylor does not tell us how she first heard that the South had seceded from the Union, or that the Northerners were coming to put down the rebellion. There had been a huge celebration by secessionists in Savannah when Georgia left the Union, filling a square in the European-styled city. When Northern troops occupied the Sea Islands at the beginning of the Civil War, the whites told their slaves only that the Yankees planned to work them like oxen. But Taylor could read, and somehow managed to ascertain that the war might bring the end of slavery. At this early stage, however, the North was fighting only to restore the Union, not to abolish slavery.

In early April 1862, Union troops captured Fort Pulaski off the Georgia coast near Savannah: Taylor could hear the roar of the guns from miles away. When the Union general, David Hunter, declared that slaves within his lines would be declared free, she escaped with her uncle and his family, reaching St. Catherine Island about 25 miles south of the city. A Union gunboat removed a party of 30 African-Americans farther south to St. Simon's Island, where, Taylor wrote, "to my unbounded joy, I saw the 'Yankee.'"

The Northern officers soon learned that the 13-year-old girl could read and asked her to instruct the 40 children gathered on the island. In a few weeks, when books arrived from the North, Taylor taught the children by day and adults at night, "all of them so eager to learn to read, to read above all else." The escaped slaves heard rumors that the war would soon end, and that they might all be shipped to Liberia.

The situation on the Sea Islands was unique. These islands were 83% black and militarily undefended by the secessionists. When Union warships approached, many of the former slaveholders fled to the mainland, leaving behind their slaves and a rich cotton crop. Northern civilian antislavery activists came down to help organize farming on a free labor basis, and to teach. There were about 600 African-Americans on St. Simon's, and these were freed by the Union general as "contraband of war." Earlier in the conflict, President Abraham Lincoln had rebuked another Union general who followed this policy, but now Lincoln, driven by the logic of the war, let the order on the Sea Islands stand.

There was a military component to this new policy as well. When a few secessionists on St. Simon's, reinforced by a landing party, attacked some ex-slaves, the freed slaves regrouped, armed themselves, and fought back. General Hunter tried, without the backing of his superiors, to organize a black regiment, but the project was poorly planned and did not succeed. By August, however, Captain C.T. Trowbridge came to the islands to recruit black men for a regiment, the First South Carolina Volunteers, and in November, Thomas Wentworth Higginson, a militant abolitionist, became its colonel. Taylor joined this regiment, and after the war both the famous colonel and the unheralded washerwoman wrote accounts of their experience.

Susie King Taylor's story, though dramatic, is told in a matter-of-fact style. She was clearly a young woman of great courage and totally devoted to the cause of freedom. In several life-threatening situations she displayed the levelheadedness of a born leader. Her writing, too, is direct and unadorned. The picture that accompanies her book shows a beautiful woman of poise and dignity, with eyes that have seen sorrow. In an equal society, she might have been a professional nurse, teacher, or writer, but the prejudices of the time confined her choices.

The new regiment trained at Camp Saxton in Beaufort, South Carolina. There the men learned the complex maneuvering that characterized military training during the Civil War. Taylor was assigned to Company E, and of the ten companies in the regiment only one other seems to have had a woman in Susie's role The relations between the men and women sound mutually respectful in her account.

In 1862, when she was 14, she married Sergeant Edward King. In the style of the times, the writer Susie King Taylor kept her private life to herself and tells us little about her husband.

After the war, he tried to work as a carpenter, but whites kept him from practicing this skilled trade, and he worked instead as a longshoreman. He died soon after the war in September 1866, while Susie was pregnant. Nor does Taylor say much about her second husband, Russell L. Taylor, whom she married in Boston in 1879. He died about the time her book appeared in 1902. She writes little about her father or son, except to describe the latter's death in 1898. Her mother **Hagar Reed Baker**, however, acquired 700 acres of land near Savannah, a remarkable accomplishment for a freedwoman.

On January 1, 1863, a white South Carolinian, who had earlier freed his own slaves, read President Lincoln's Emancipation Proclamation to the assembled troops at Camp Saxton amid great feasting and rejoicing. While the Proclamation was limited in its scope, freeing rhetorically only those slaves it could not free physically, it laid the groundwork for the 13th Amendment that did end slavery. One soldier, who approached Higginson, confided that last year he had been a servant to a Confederate colonel, but now he was proud to be a soldier fighting for Emancipation.

[W]hen we read almost every day of what is being done to my race by some whites in the South, I sometimes ask, "Was the war in vain?"

—Susie King Taylor

While battling the Confederates, the regiment had to fight the Union as well. Black troops were paid only half the money given to white troops. In protest, the men refused the half-pay, a great sacrifice for those with families. Not until 1864 did they receive their full pay, including the money owed to them. Taylor, probably because her position was unofficial, received no pay for her service, and she wrote that she was happy simply to care for the men.

The First South Carolina Volunteers, later reorganized as the 33rd U.S. Colored Troops, fought bravely in 12 battles along the coast, from Jacksonville, Florida, to South Carolina. Higginson describes many of these clashes in detail, citing the steely determination of his men, who were fighting not only for the cause of freedom, but to destroy racist myths about African-Americans. Being a Civil War nurse took enormous courage. Taylor was never in combat, but she could disassemble, reassemble, and fire a musket. When wounded men returned to camp in great pain, the nurses had no effective anesthesia to offer. In this capacity, Susie met *Clara Barton, the celebrated Civil War nurse. Taylor found her to be cordial and dedicated to service.

Life in camp was not all battle and preparation. Given the limited supplies, Taylor did her best as a reading instructor. She also served a turn as cook, preparing vegetable soup and slapjacks of flour and water, and distributing salt beef and hard-tack biscuits. There was time for fun as well, and the drummer boys trained a pig to march in time with the soldiers. In the evenings, the regiment sometimes held "praise" meetings of prayer and revival.

Taylor had her own dramatic confrontation with death when a boat upon which she was traveling sank. Several passengers died in the disaster and the young nurse and a companion were rescued after four hours in the water at night. Years later, after the war, she suffered another shipwreck. Taylor describes both incidents with characteristic restraint.

When Higginson was wounded, he was replaced by Trowbridge, who led the company through the end of the war. The men fought the Confederates at Fort Gregg on James Island, where they endured many casualties. They took part in the capture of Charleston, and skirmished toward the end of the war with desperate bushwhackers. After the South surrendered in April 1865, the soldiers of Taylor's regiment were mustered out in February 1866.

After the war, the King family returned to Savannah, where Susie opened a school, since there were no schools for the African-American children. "I had twenty children at my school, and received $1.00 a month for each pupil. I also had a few older ones who came at night." When her husband died in 1866, and she was expecting her first child, she moved to the country for awhile, but, a city woman at heart, she soon returned to Savannah. Now there was a public school for black children, and Taylor struggled along financially as a teacher and later as a laundress for a white woman. After accompanying this woman on a journey to Boston, in 1874 Taylor moved to that city with the aid of a Boston family. Taylor most likely left the South to escape the new wave of oppression that descended upon the freedpeople. The brief period of Reconstruction, during which Northern armies occupied the South, was coming to a close. During this time, Southern blacks had gained and enjoyed some civil rights, but as the Southern states rejoined the Union, those rights were gradually lost.

In Boston, she worked in domestic service, married Russell L. Taylor in 1879, and probably

Susie
King
Taylor

lived in the West End black community. In 1886, she organized the Women's Relief Corps, a women's auxiliary to the Grand Army of the Republic, the Civil War Northern veterans' association. She became the local president in 1893, and prepared a census of the surviving black vet-

erans from her regiment. She also won a quilting award in 1898 that was probably a fund-raising effort for the veterans.

Taylor tells us little about her life in Boston, for her book is a Civil War memoir. That city had been the home of abolitionists before the war, and for awhile after it remained remarkably free of racial antagonism. "I have been in many states and cities, and in each I have looked for liberty and justice; . . . but it was not until I was within the borders of New England, and reached old Massachusetts, that I found it," she wrote. Boston's black community was small but vibrant, and the likelihood is that Taylor was an active member. In 1895, Boston's African-American women hosted the first convention of what later became the National Association of Colored Women. *Pauline E. Hopkins wrote for the nationally circulated *Colored American Magazine*. In 1898, the state dedicated a monument to African-American soldiers and their white officers who fought in the Massachusetts regiments. The fiery editor William Monroe Trotter demanded full civil and political rights in his weekly *Guardian* newspaper.

Taylor does not mention these various activities, but in a perceptive chapter titled "Thoughts on Present Conditions," she reflects on the injustices committed against black people. She is particularly concerned with lynching, which at that time was rampant and public throughout the South. Nor could she understand why the national government refused to intervene and put an end to the wave of terror directed against African-Americans. She decried the hypocrisy of a Confederate women's group that wanted to ban *Uncle Tom's Cabin*, the antislavery book by *Harriet Beecher Stowe that was being staged as a play, while they turned a blind eye toward lynchings occurring about twice weekly.

> I do not uphold my race when they do wrong. They ought to be punished, but the innocent are made to suffer as well as the guilty, and I hope the time will hasten when it will be stopped forever. . . . In this "land of the free" we are burned, tortured, and denied a fair trial, murdered for any imaginary wrong conceived in the brain of the negro-hating white man. There is no redress for us from a government which promised to protect all under its flag. It seems a mystery to me. They say, "One flag, one nation, one country indivisible." Is this true? Can we say this truthfully, when one race is allowed to burn, hang, and inflict the most horrible torture weekly, monthly, on another? No, we cannot sing "My country, 'tis of thee, Sweet land of Liberty!" It is hollow mockery.

In 1898, her son, an actor, fell ill while touring the South. Wrote Taylor in *Reminiscences of My Life in Camp*:

> On February 3, 1898, I was called to Shreveport, La., to the bedside of my son, who was very ill. He had been traveling on business when he fell ill, and had been sick two weeks when they sent to me. I tried to have him brought home to Boston, but they could not send him, as he was not able to sit and ride this long distance; on the sixth of February I left Boston to go to him. I reached Cincinnati on the eighth, where I took a train for the south. I asked a white man standing near—before I got my train what car I should take.
>
> "Take that one," he said, pointing to one.
>
> "But that is a smoking car!"
>
> "Well," he replied, "that is the car for colored people." I went to this car, and on entering it all my courage failed me. I have ridden in many coaches, but I was never in such as these. I wanted to return home again, but when I thought of my sick boy I said, "Well, others ride in these cars and I must do likewise," and tried to be resigned, for I wanted to reach my boy, as I did not know whether I should find him alive. . . .
>
> I got to Marion, Miss., at two o'clock in the morning, arrived at Vicksburg at noon, and at Shreveport about eight o'clock in the evening, and found my son just recovering from a severe hemorrhage. He was very anxious to come home, and I tried to secure a berth for him on a sleeper, but they would not sell me one, and he was not strong enough to travel otherwise. If I could only have gotten him to Cincinnati, I might have brought him home, but as I could not I was forced to let him remain where he was. It seemed very hard, when his father fought to protect the Union and our flag, yet his boy was denied, under this same flag, a berth to carry him home to die, because he was a Negro.

Her son remained behind and died alone.

On the way there and back, Taylor experienced the harassment of local whites, and even witnessed a hanging at Clarksdale, Mississippi. Somehow, she managed to keep up her hope for the future, without denying her disappointment in the present. She concluded her memoir with these words: "Justice we ask,—to be citizens of these United States, where so many of our people have shed their blood with their white comrades, that the stars and stripes should never be polluted."

SOURCES:

Higginson, Thomas Wentworth. *Army Life in a Black Regiment*. Boston, MA: Beacon Press, 1962 (first published in 1869).

Taylor, Susie King. *Reminiscences of My Life in Camp with the Thirty-Third U.S. Colored Troops, Late First South Carolina Volunteers: A Black Woman's Civil War Memories*. Edited by Patricia W. Romero (with new introduction by Willie Lee Rose). NY: Markus Weiner, 1988 (reprint of 1902 edition).

Wilson, Leslie. "Susie King Taylor," in *Notable Black American Women*. Edited by Jessie Carney Smith. Detroit, MI: Gale Research, 1992, pp. 1108–1113.

SUGGESTED READING:

Emilio, Luis F. *A Brave Black Regiment*. NY: Bantam, 1992 (first published in 1894).

Rose, Willie Lee. *Rehearsal for Reconstruction: The Port Royal Experiment*. Indianapolis, IN: Bobbs-Merrill, 1964.

RELATED MEDIA:

Glory (122 min. film), starring Matthew Broderick and Denzel Washington, released in 1989, concerns the Massachusetts 54th Regiment, which fought in the same area as the First South Carolina Volunteers.

Mark Schneider,
author of *Boston Confronts Jim Crow, 1890–1920*
(Northeastern University Press, 1997)

Taylor, Valerie (1935—)

Australian scuba diver and filmmaker. Born Valerie May Hughes in 1935 in Sydney, Australia; married Ron Taylor (an underwater filmmaker and photographer).

Valerie Taylor was born in 1935 and grew up near the water in Sydney, Australia. She first began swimming as therapy after a bout of poliomyelitis; she also started snorkeling and spearfishing at an early age. Taylor won the Australian women's scuba title in 1963 and the Australian Women's Spearfishing Open championship three times. She and her husband Ron Taylor gave up spearfishing for environmental reasons around 1968 and began to concentrate on underwater photography. Valerie was often photographed underwater by Ron, playing with sea animals.

The Taylors at first had difficulty attracting interest in their sea films, but signed an important contract in 1969 with Belgium University at Liege for six months of a scientific expedition to the Great Barrier Reef in Australia. Peter Gimbel later hired them to film his search for the great white shark, *Blue Water—White Death*. While in the Indian Ocean on this expedition, the Taylors had some hair-raising experiences. Once their shark cage was nearly lost when cables and tethers became entangled in shark-infested waters. Taylor was thankful for the quick thinking of the ship's sound man, who, she told Hillary Hauser, "had the captain maneuver the [ship] into position downstream and pick us up. Without his quick presence of mind we would probably still be going, drifting alone, tied to a whale 100 miles off the African Coast in the Indian Ocean."

Taylor is known for her ability to make herself part of the marine animal world. She will pet moray eels, feed barracudas, and play with octopi. Said Taylor: "I figure if I'm nice to them, they will be nice to me." A number of her encounters with sea creatures have been photographed or filmed. In *Blue Water—White Death* she is actually filmed while stroking the belly of the great white from her cage.

As a result of her skill and daring, Valerie has had starring roles in U.S. and foreign television series. In Australia, she was a guest star on the "Skippy the Bush Kangaroo" show, writing the episode herself. "Taylor's Innerspace," a television series shown in the U.S. and Australia, starred the Taylors. In 1974, they also filmed all the live shark segments for the box-office hit *Jaws*, director Steven Spielberg's adaptation of the Peter Benchley novel, which concerns an East Coast beach town terrorized by a shark with a taste for human flesh.

"I'm not as strong as a man," said Taylor, "which probably makes me not such a good diver. Technically, I'm hopeless, but I seen to have some sort of sixth sense about fish and other animals. I seem to know if I can approach a shark or if I should be out of the water. . . . Some people think I'm not afraid. Sometimes I'm awfully afraid, but I have a tremendous curiosity."

SOURCES:

Hauser, Hillary. *Women in Sports: Scuba Diving*. NY: Harvey House, 1976.

Oxford Companion to Australian Sport. Melbourne: Oxford University Press, 1992.

Sally A. Myers, Ph.D.,
freelance writer-editor

Taylor-Greenfield, Elizabeth
(c. 1819–1876).

See Greenfield, Elizabeth Taylor.

Taylor-Smith, Shelley (1961—)

Australian long-distance swimmer. Born in 1961 in Perth, Australia.

Born in Perth, Australia, in 1961, Shelley Taylor-Smith began setting local and state swimming records at the Surat Swim Club while still in her teens. After winning a scholarship to the University of Arkansas, she worked with coach Sam Freas, who encouraged her to perfect her long-distance swimming skills. She graduated with a degree in physical education and soon began setting marathon swimming records, breaking the women's four-mile time in 1983. At the Seal Beach 25-kilometer swim in 1985, she was the first woman to finish; she also won the Manhattan Island swim four times, setting a record in that event. From 1988 to 1990, she won the Australian marathon title. Her biggest accomplishment was winning the women's world marathon championship in Perth in 1991.

Sally A. Myers, Ph.D.,
freelance writer and editor

Taymuriyya, 'A'isha 'Ismat al-
(1840–1902)

Egyptian poet and essayist who advocated the education of women and was celebrated by later authors as one of the founders of feminist expression in Arabic. Name variations: 'A'isha Taymur; Aichat Asmat Taimur; Aisha Esmat al-Taymuriyya. Pronunciation: AY-sha IS-mat at-tay-moo-REE-a. Born in 1840 in Cairo, Egypt; died in Cairo in 1902; daughter of Isma'il Pasha Taymour (a Turkish notable of Kurdish origin who served as a government official in Egypt) and his Circassian concubine; began education in Turkish, Arabic, and Persian at home when quite young, stopped writing upon marriage and did not resume until after the death of her husband and father; married Mahmud Bey al-Islambuli (a Turkish notable), in 1854; children: daughter, Tawhida (died 1873, age 18).

Selected publications in Arabic include: Nata'ij al-Ahwal fi al-Aqwal wa-al-Af'al *(The Results of Circumstances in Words and Deeds, 1887);* Mir'at al-Ta'amul fi al-Umur *(The Mirror of Contemplation on Things, published during the last ten years of her life); and a collection of poetry,* Hilyat al-Tiraz *(Embroidered Ornaments, 1885. Also published a collection of Turkish poetry entitled* Shakufa *(Blossom).*

'A'isha al-Taymuriyya lived during an era of rapid social, economic, and political change that laid the foundation for a modern state in Egypt. The reforms that she witnessed would have a lasting effect on the position of women in Egyptian society, and she played a crucial role in this process. As the pace of modernization in Egypt accelerated and she tried to define her role in a changing world, 'A'isha al-Taymuriyya expressed her hopes and fears in prose and poetry. Thus, she became an icon for future generations of feminists.

When 'A'isha was born in 1840, Muhammad 'Ali Pasha (1805–1848) was the Ottoman governor of Egypt. Although Muhammad 'Ali ruled Egypt on behalf of the Ottoman sultan, he effectively established a hereditary dynasty and set in motion the process of modernization that would enable Egypt to emerge as an independent nation in the middle of the 20th century. He reorganized the Egyptian military along European lines, brought European advisors to Egypt, reformed the legal, educational, and health-care systems, and built factories. He also restructured the land-tenure system and improved irrigation, allowing the state to produce crops for export to Europe.

Muhammad 'Ali's reforms fostered a sense of national pride among Egyptians, and his government achieved de facto independence in 1833 when military victories against the Ottoman army forced the sultan to appoint his son, Ibrahim Pasha, governor of southern Anatolia and greater Syria. However, this independence was not destined to last. The Middle East was a major market for British exports, and Muhammad 'Ali's expansion into Syria had threatened British commerce in the region at a time when the European economy was weak. In response, the British initiated an aggressive export policy that was supported by the Ottoman sultan Mahmud II. In 1838, he signed a treaty with Britain that favored European commercial interests in the Middle East, and the next time fighting broke out between the Ottoman and Egyptian armies European forces came to the sultan's aid, forcing Muhammad 'Ali to pull out of Syria and frustrating his efforts at industrialization. By the middle of the 19th century, supplying raw materials to European industry was the basis of the Egyptian economy, and by 'A'isha al-Taymuriyya's death in 1902 the British had occupied Egypt for two decades.

Egypt did not achieve political or economic independence during 'A'isha al-Taymuriyya's lifetime, but modernization continued and contact between Egyptians and Europeans increased. The Cairo opera house that was built for the opening of the Suez Canal in 1869 brought a European art form to Egyptian audiences, improvements in transportation facilitated overseas travel, and journalism provided a public forum for exploring new ideas. In addition, a neighborhood called Isma'iliyya was established in Cairo where—for the first time in Egypt—wealthy people from different religious and ethnic backgrounds lived side by side (Badran, 1995).

'A'isha al-Taymuriyya was not the only Egyptian to struggle with issues of identity as she adapted to these changes. Throughout the 19th century, Egyptians were redefining themselves both as individuals and as a nation. They took pride in their shared history and rebelled against economic and political domination, but at the same time they adapted aspects of Ottoman and European culture. Defining their identity as Egyptians meant reconsidering what it meant to be men or women, Muslims or Christians, Turks or Arabs, and members of one nation in a rapidly changing world.

'A'isha
'Ismat al-
Taymuriyya

The Egyptian feminism that emerged in the 20th century had its roots in this process.

'A'isha al-Taymuriyya has been called the "mother of Egyptian feminism" because her work inspired later generations of feminist writers, but with the exception of her publications 'A'isha herself never ventured into the public sphere. 'A'isha was born to Isma'il Pasha Taymour, a Turkish notable of Kurdish origin who served as a government official in Egypt, and his Circassian concubine. She spent her childhood in the harem of her father's house, probably playing with her two sisters who were very close to her in age. 'A'isha also had a brother whose birth she celebrated in verse, but by the time he was born she had been married for several years and his childhood memories of her were vague. He described her as, "neither tall nor short, neither fair nor dark, and neither fat nor thin."

By her own account, as 'A'isha grew up she had no interest in learning weaving and embroidery from her mother. Instead, she was fascinated by language, by the stories the older women in the household told in the evening, and by the gatherings of literary men her father hosted. 'A'isha's favorite pastime was to hide with paper and pen and imitate the writers. This angered her mother, but her father supported her interest. She had started writing in Turkish (the language she spoke at home), and her father encouraged her to continue. He hired two teachers—one to teach her Persian, the other to instruct her in Arabic and the *Qur'an*—and he helped with her lessons himself. When she was still quite young, 'A'isha began to compose poetry, first in Persian and later in Arabic and Turkish, using traditional literary forms and metaphors to express her feelings.

> $\mathcal{W}$ere it possible for either male or female to exist in isolation, then the Knower of Secrets would have distinguished one to the exclusion of the other, and would not have put the favored one in need of the other.
>
> —'A'isha al-Taymuriyya

'A'isha dedicated herself to her education, but because of her gender she was restricted to studying at home. As part of Muhammad 'Ali's reform program, the Egyptian government had expressed interest in the education of girls in the early part of the 19th century. However, it was not until 1873 that the wife of one of Muhammad 'Ali's successors, **Tcheshme Hanim**, opened the Siyufiyya School—the first state school for girls. Even after this, it was some time before the education of girls outside of the domestic sphere became generally accepted in Egyptian society. Through the turn of the 20th century, upper-class families such as 'A'isha's preferred to educate their daughters at home. Frustrated by this segregation, 'A'isha idealized the position of women in European nations. She argued against the seclusion of Egyptian women in her essays, and she vented her anger in her poetry. At 13, she wrote, "If my tears water the earth I am not the one to be blamed, for I have suffered the fate of oppression at the hands of my fellow man."

While 'A'isha felt free to express her progressive views in her writing, her own lifestyle never challenged the sense of propriety that prevailed in her society. Her behavior was consistent with what people expected of an upper-class Egyptian woman during the second half of the 19th century. In 1854, at age 14, she was given in marriage to Mahmud Bey al-Islambuli, a Turkish notable like her father. In 1855, she gave birth to their only child, **Tawhida**, and in the years that followed 'A'isha gave up her literary work so that she could devote all of her energies to her family. 'A'isha's biographers have suggested that for a time she made Tawhida the focus of her life. 'A'isha herself remarked that as a child

Tawhida was different than she had been, showing an interest in knitting and running the household as well as in writing.

Tawhida's childhood was a joyful time for 'A'isha, but it ended abruptly and unexpectedly. Tawhida died in 1873 at the age of 18 from an unknown illness, and for 'A'isha the loss was almost unbearable. She wrote about her daughter's despair, "When she saw the hopelessness of the physician and his failure, her eyelids flowing with tears she said, 'Oh mother, the physician failed and the supporter that I hoped for in life passed me by!'"

Tawhida's death was the first of a series of losses for 'A'isha al-Taymuriyya. In 1882, her father died, followed by her husband only three years later, and 'A'isha turned to her writing for comfort. She published essays in the Egyptian press advocating education for girls and corresponded with other female intellectuals such as the Syrian poet **Warda al-Yaziji** (1838–1924). In addition, although she was already in her 40s, 'A'isha resumed her own education. During the last two decades of her life, she devoted herself to her poetry with new energy, studying grammar and metrics with two female professors, **Fatima al-Azhariyya** and **Sitita al-Tablawiyya**. Some of 'A'isha's poems eulogized friends and family members, some were romantic, and others had religious and moral themes.

During the final years of her life, 'A'isha al-Taymuriyya struggled with an inflammation of the eyes that made it difficult for her to write. She died in 1902.

SOURCES:

Badran, Margot. *Feminists, Islam, and Nation: Gender and the Making of Modern Egypt.* Princeton, NJ: Princeton University Press, 1995.

Booth, Marilyn. "Biography and Feminist Rhetoric in Early Twentieth Century Egypt: ***Mayy Ziyada**'s Studies of Three Women's Lives," in *Journal of Women's History.* Vol. 3, no. 2, 1991, pp. 38–64.

Opening the Gates: A Century of Arab Feminist Writing. Ed. by Margot Badran and Miriam Cook. Bloomington, IN: Indiana University Press, 1990.

al-Sayyid-Marsot, Afaf. *A Short History of Modern Egypt.* Cambridge: Cambridge University Press, 1985.

Tucker, Judith. "Problems in the Historiography of Women in the Middle East: The Case of Nineteenth Century Egypt," in *International Journal of Middle East Studies.* Vol. 15, no. 3, 1983, pp. 321–336.

Ziyadah, Mayy. *'A'isha Taymur: Sha'irat al-Tali'ah ['A'isha Taymur: A Vanguard Poet].* Cairo: Matba'at al-Muqtataf, 1926.

SUGGESTED READING:

Ahmad, Leila. *Women and Gender in Islam.* New Haven, CT: Yale University Press, 1992.

Kate Lang, Ph.D. in Near Eastern Languages, University of Chicago, Chicago, Illinois

Taytu (c. 1850–1918)

Empress of Ethiopia, an important contributor to the modernization of her country, who led troops in battle and devised strategies crucial in defeating the Italian army in 1896. Name variations: Taitu; Tauti; Queen of Shoa. Pronunciation: TIE-too. Born Taytu Betul Hayle Maryam, probably in 1850 or 1851, probably in Mahdere Maryam in Begemder, Ethiopia; died on February 11, 1918, in Addis Ababa; daughter of Betul (a warrior) and a mother whose second marriage was to a lay administrator of the monastery at Debre Mewi; married five times, the last, in April 1883, to Sahlé Maryam, who became Emperor Menelik II (or Menilek); no children.

Upon marriage to Sahlé Maryam, became queen of Shoa (1883); with husband's ascent to imperial throne, became empress of Ethiopia (1889); during the struggle against Italian armies, devised the strategy which defeated the fort at Adigrat (February 1896); led troops at the Battle of Adwa, Italy's final humiliating defeat (March 1, 1896); increased her power as regent after Menelik suffered a stroke (1906); lost the battle to guarantee the throne for a member of her own family after the death of Menelik (1913).

Dates of birth were not considered important in Ethiopia in the 19th century, so it is impossible to know exactly when Taytu Betul Hayle Maryam was born, although it was probably in 1850 or 1851. She belonged to a prominent family, descended from Emperor Susneyos (r. 1607–1632), and the most likely site of her birth was Mahdere Maryam, in the province of Begemder. There were two boys and two girls in the family, and Taytu was the third child. Her father, a warrior named Betul, died in 1853, of wounds sustained at the battle of Ayshal. After his death, her mother married a lay administrator of the monastery at Debre Mewi, where Taytu must have received her education, which was exceptional for an Ethiopian woman of that time. She could read and write Amharic, and knew Ge'ez, the language of the sacred texts handed down over centuries in one of the world's oldest Christian nations. Taytu also composed poetry, played chess, and performed on the begenna, or lyre.

Like most Ethiopian girls, Taytu made an abrupt transition from childhood into adulthood when she was married at age ten, to an officer in the army of Emperor Tewodros II. Sex was considered normal for Ethiopians of Taytu's age. Although the marriage bed was regarded by Ethiopians as an arena in which men conquered women, it was not unusual for Ethiopian women to marry several times or to take several lovers.

Taytu's first marriage started off badly, however. A few days after the ceremony, Tewodros put her husband in chains for some minor offense, and the young bride was forced to follow the army on foot, "chained at the wrist, grinding grain and cooking for the soldiers." This marriage eventually ended, and Taytu wed Kenyazmach Zikargatchew around 1881–82; he was the brother of the consort of Menelik (II), the king of Shoa. After her second husband beat her, Taytu announced she was going to visit her mother. When she left, a great deal of her abusive husband's property as well as many servants went with her. She never bothered with a divorce settlement, as she had, in effect, already profited considerably from the relationship.

Taytu married three more times before her final marriage, to Menelik. Although it was apparent by this time that she would never have children, her beauty and family connections made her a desirable match, and her union with Menelik II, beginning in April 1883, became one of history's most remarkable alliances. Born Sahlé Maryam, Menelik was heir to the throne of the Shoa (Shewa) kingdom in central Ethiopia, and had been battling Ethiopia's rulers for most of his life. His country had been virtually independent when in 1855 Tewodros II proclaimed himself emperor of Ethiopia and asserted control over the central part of the country. For the next ten years, Tewodros had held the young heir a prisoner at his court, until Menelik escaped, in 1865, and was proclaimed king of Shoa. The young king built Shoa into one of Ethiopia's strongest powers, seeking alliances with Europeans as well as within the country in order to acquire technical assistance and modern firearms. The Italians viewed Menelik as an ally, as did the French, who wanted use of his armies to stop the advance of the British into the southern Sudan. In 1885, when Italy occupied Ethiopia's Eritrean coast and began to push inland, Menelik remained neutral.

In 1889, after the death of Ethiopia's Emperor Yohannes, Menelik proclaimed himself emperor. Menelik wished to modernize his empire, and since their marriage, Taytu had become an increasingly valuable advisor. One of his first ventures was to build a new capital at Addis Ababa, on a site chosen by Taytu in 1886. Modern roads and bridges connected the new city with the rest of the empire, the tax system was reformed, a national currency was created, a postal system was instituted, and railways were built. Menelik also promoted secular education, established medical care, and founded a government press. By the turn of the century, telegraph and telephone lines stretched across the country and a national bank financed new enterprises.

Meanwhile, however, many internal factions vied for power, and Taytu was ever vigilant in protecting her husband's interests. When Menelik was away in battle at one point, a message from the soldiers of Weldya, the capital of Yejju, reached the empress, informing her that the city was about to be overrun by rebel troops led by Zegeye, and that Weldya's army was prepared to surrender. Their message read, "We are afraid, as there are not enough of us." Since most of the army was away under her husband's command, Taytu decided to make a show of will power and strength by sending a small force with 300 guns to Weldya, along with a proclamation which read:

> Take care that no dissension explodes between me and you. As for Zegeye, if I should hear that you permitted him to enter and govern Yejju, or even if I learn that you allowed him to drink water in Yejju from his cupped hand, we will become, you and I, mortal enemies.

Torn between their anxiety about a rebel leader and fear of crossing the powerful empress, the soldiers in Weldya rallied, defended the capital, and even captured some members of the rebel forces.

*R*eigned, aggrandized and made Ethiopia prosper.

—Chris Prouty

In 1889, Menelik signed a friendship pact with the Italians known as the Treaty of Ucciali. Drafted in both Amharic and Italian, the treaty was written in two distinct versions. In the Amharic text, Italy merely offered its services to Ethiopia as diplomatic intermediary with the outside world; but in the Italian version, Menelik later realized, the Ethiopian empire was now an Italian protectorate. Not surprisingly, these two very different versions soon led to war. Ethiopia had no intention of becoming a European colony.

When Menelik declared war, the Italians were not displeased, since Europeans had been victorious over native African armies for centuries. In Europe, an Italian victory was considered a foregone conclusion, but the strategists in Rome had failed to reckon with their foe. Ethiopia's dry and mountainous country provided perfect fighting terrain for those who knew it well, and the modern weapons Menelik had

stockpiled allowed his troops to meet the Italians on equal terms. Finally, the Ethiopian army numbered well over 100,000, while the Italians sent only 17,000 troops.

In early January 1896, Menelik decided to challenge a contingent of Italian forces holding the fort at Adigrat. The assault proved calamitous, as the Italians were able to rain fire down on the Ethiopian troops struggling up to the fort at the summit; by nightfall, some 500 Ethiopian casualties littered the slopes. Taytu, who had accompanied her husband on this military venture, then proposed a different strategy—cutting off the fort's water supply. On January 9, 900 men from the empress' contingent crept down the ravine and cut off the stream supplying the fort, then settled out of firing range to wait. By January 18, Major Galliano had sent out a message to Italian headquarters calling for reinforcements. "The fort resists, but we have only two rations of water left. Our fall is near." The fort soon surrendered, with no further casualties.

With his empress at his side, Menelik prepared for the final assault on the Italian troops in early spring. On March 1, 1896, the Battle of Adwa commenced, with Taytu in charge of organizing the defense perimeter, using her personal army of 5,000 men. Realizing that more than bullets would be required to win this engagement, the empress gathered 10–12,000 women and ordered them to collect and fill water jugs. Their duty was to provision the soldiers and care for the wounded, a strategy which proved of great worth in Ethiopia's arid climate. When the fighting began, Taytu rushed into the fray, calling to the troops, "Courage! Victory is ours! Strike!" It is reported that the "cannoneers to the right of where she stood fired so continuously that they succeeded in breaking the center of the enemy army." By 12:30 PM, the Battle of Adwa was over, at terrible cost to both sides. Casualties among the Ethiopian troops were between 10% and 15%, and among the Italians 50%. That night the empress returned to her tent and sat motionless on her throne, her face wet with tears.

The decisive defeat of Europeans at the hands of Ethiopian troops was a major news story throughout the world. On March 7, 1896, *The Spectator* commented: "The Italians have suffered a great disaster . . . greater than has ever occurred in modern times to white men in Africa." Photographs of Menelik and Empress Taytu appeared on front pages around the globe. Soon Taytu's name and the title "warrior queen" were synonymous. In the best tradition of yellow journalism, the press published fictional stories

Taytu

about the empress, re-
porting that she bathed in
the blood of virgin girls, and
blaming her for mutilations, for threatening to kill Italian officers taken as prisoners,
and even for starting the war itself. The Italians
remained convinced that Menelik would have
compromised except for his bloodthirsty consort, and no one outside Ethiopia seemed to recognize Taytu simply as a patriot fighting for the
freedom of her people.

Taytu had exercised great power since her
ascension to the throne. After the Battle of
Adwa, however, it was said that "nearly half of
Ethiopia is in the hands of her relatives." Over

the years the empress had
secured control of the country through nepotism, marriage
alliances, and accumulation of land
grants. Her brother, Ras Wele, controlled Tigray
and Yejju; her nephew, Ras Gugsa Wele, governed Begemder; Dejazmach Gesesse, another
nephew, ruled Semen and Wjolkit; Ras Wele
Giyorgis, her cousin's husband, controlled Keffa;
and these were only a few of her relatives in the
government. To maintain her power, Taytu also
used her considerable revenues to arm, clothe,
and feed her personal army.

Foreigners quickly noted Taytu's immense
power. Certainly Taytu controlled the day-to-

day operation of her country's government to a greater extent than royal contemporaries like Queen *Victoria. She was also more cynical than her husband about the foreigners who flocked to Addis Ababa seeking government contracts. Addressing such business interests, Taytu would pointedly ask, "Where will our poor country find the resources to satisfy the needs you create? Frankly do you think our people will be happier [with a railroad] than they are now?" Such hardheaded bargaining benefited the empire and gained the country international respect.

Menelik suffered a cerebral hemorrhage in 1906. Although he recovered, his physical strength declined, and Taytu increasingly assumed the powers of regent. On October 27, 1909, a second stroke left the emperor paralyzed and incapacitated, and a battle for succession ensued, as there was no immediate heir to the throne. In 1908, Menelik had designated his grandson, Iyasu V, as his successor, appointed a loyal regent, Tessema Nadew, and created a council of ministers. Now, however, Taytu sought to maintain her own power by placing one of her relations in line for the throne. When Menelik died in 1913, Iyasu was made emperor and Taytu retired from the court, her plans for further rule apparently defeated. Three years later, however, Iyasu was toppled and replaced by Taytu's long-favored successor, Menelik's daughter *Zauditu (1876–1930). Haile Selassie, who opposed Taytu, was appointed regent, a decision bitterly fought by the empress; when her further bid for power failed, she withdrew from imperial politics. Taytu died of heart failure on February 11, 1918. Zauditu lived until 1930, when she was succeeded by Haile Selassie, Ethiopia's last emperor.

Taytu lives on in memory, even in Italy, where expressions such as "Who does she think she is? Empress Taytu?" or "She is like Principessa Taytu" are testimonials to her imprint on the popular imagination. In Ethiopia, she is honored and remembered as a warrior, a modernizer, and a nationalist, a symbol of what can be achieved by the daring and brave.

SOURCES:

Marcus, Harold G. *The Life and Times of Menelik II: Ethiopia 1844–1913.* Oxford: Clarendon, 1975.

Prouty, Chris. *Empress Taytu and Menelik II: Ethiopia 1883–1910.* London: Ravens Educational and Development Services, 1986.

———, and Eugene Rosenfeld. *Historical Dictionary of Ethiopia.* London: Scarecrow, 1981.

Rosenfeld, Chris Prouty. *A Chronology of Menelik of Ethiopia.* East Lansing, MI: African Studies Center, 1976.

Sanderson, G.N. "The Foreign Policy of the Negus Menelik, 1896–1898," in *Journal of African History.* Vol. 4, 1964, pp. 87–97.

Williams, Larry, and Charles S. Finch. "The Great Queens of Ethiopia," in *Journal of African Civilizations.* Vol. 6, no. 1, 1984, pp. 12–35.

Karin Loewen Haag,
freelance writer,
Athens, Georgia

Tchernicheva, Lubov (1890–1976)

Russian-born British ballerina and ballet mistress who was one of Sergei Diaghilev's most brilliant dancers. Name variations: Liubov Pavlovna Chernysheva; Luba Tchernicheva. Born Lubov Pavlovna Tchernicheva in St. Petersburg, Russia, on September 17, 1890; died in Richmond, Surrey, England, on March 1, 1976; married Sergei Grigoriev (a stage and rehearsal director), in 1909 (died 1968).

A major figure in 20th-century classical ballet, Lubov Tchernicheva was born in St. Petersburg in 1890 and studied at that city's Imperial Ballet Academy, graduating in 1908. She joined the Maryinsky Theater and in 1909 married Sergei Grigoriev, the stage and rehearsal director. She and her husband moved to Paris in 1911 and joined the Ballets Russes company directed by the brilliant Sergei Diaghilev. Within a few years, Tchernicheva had become the company's leading dancer, comparable to *Tamara Karsavina. Where Karsavina projected warmth and voluptuousness, Tchernicheva was the embodiment of aristocratic aloofness, enigmatic elegance, and at times even icy sadism. Ballet critics were sometimes at a loss to describe her brilliance, noting simply that in such ballets as *Les Sylphides* she attained the state of "sweet melancholy which is the keynote of the ballet."

At home in the work of most of the great choreographers of her day, Tchernicheva was particularly distinguished in the repertory of Michel Fokine. In 1926, she took on the job of ballet mistress to Diaghilev's Ballets Russes. After the dissolution of this fabled company three years later, she looked for a new permanent position, finding it in 1932 with the Ballet Russe of Monte Carlo, formed by Colonel de Basil to fill the gap left by the demise of the Diaghilev ballet. Tchernicheva and her husband took on key roles. Innate physical endowments coupled with her intelligent use of her body enabled Tchernicheva to dance well past the retirement age of most ballerinas. After she had been dancing for more than three decades, many of her countless admirers affectionately referred to her as "Auntie Luba," not only as a sign of respect but also as a delicate allusion to her age. As late as 1937, she was brilliantly creating a new role, that of Francesca in David Lichine's *Francesca da Rimini*. Despite advancing years, she continued to dance and remained strikingly beautiful on stage, enjoying great success in such roles as Zobeide in *Scheherazade* and the Miller's wife in *The Three Cornered Hat*. Lubov Tchernicheva and her husband remained active in the de Basil company until it was disbanded in 1952.

Avoiding full retirement, Tchernicheva and her husband next concentrated on staging individual productions of great ballet classics from the Diaghilev repertory. Some of their highly praised productions included *The Firebird* (Sadler's Wells Ballet, 1954) and *Petrushka* (Royal Ballet, 1957). Incredibly, it was in 1959 that Tchernicheva made her last appearance on stage, creating the role of Lady Capulet in John Cranko's *Romeo and Juliet* at La Scala, Milan. Even after her husband died in 1968, she continued to teach at the Sadler's Wells Ballet and the London Festival Ballet. Always a strict disciplinarian, she was determined to maintain the ballet traditions of the imperial Russia that she had known in her youth. By the time Lubov Tchernicheva died in Richmond, Surrey, England, on March 1, 1976, her place in ballet history was secure.

SOURCES:

Beaumont, Cyril. *The Art of Lubov Tchernicheva*. London: C.W. Beaumont, 1921.

Koegler, Horst. *The Concise Oxford Dictionary of Ballet*. 2nd ed. Oxford: Oxford University Press, 1987.

"Lubov Tchernicheva: Celebrated ballet dancer," in *The Times* [London]. March 4, 1976, p. 16.

Woodcock, Sarah C. "Tchernicheva, Lubov," in Martha Bremser, ed., *International Dictionary of Ballet*. Vol. 2. Detroit, MI: St. James Press, 1993, pp. 1402–1405.

John Haag,
Associate Professor of History,
University of Georgia,
Athens, Georgia

Teale, Nellie (1900–1993)

American naturalist who collaborated with her husband Edwin Way Teale on a series of nature books that have been acclaimed as modern classics. Born Nellie Imogene Donovan in September 13, 1900, in Colorado Springs, Colorado; died of colon cancer in Windham, Connecticut, on July 18, 1993; educated at Earlham College, Richmond, Indiana; married Edwin Way Teale (1899–1980, the naturalist author), in 1923; children: David Allen Teale (killed in action in Germany, 1945).

Nellie Teale was an important contributor to the work of her husband, famous nature writer Edwin Way Teale. In a marriage of 57 years, the Teales became a powerful team, traveling great distances to observe and immerse themselves in the natural world, then creating some of the best books ever written in America on nature and its countless facets of beauty and mystery. Nellie Imogene Donovan was born in September 1900 in Colorado Springs, Colorado, and met Edwin Way Teale in the early 1920s, when both were English majors at Earlham College in Richmond, Indiana. "One afternoon, we were driving to Indianapolis," said Nellie, "and Edwin noticed the beautiful sunset. I had never been out with a man that had ever paid any attention to sunsets." Married in 1923, the couple moved to Wichita, Kansas, where Edwin taught public speaking and coached debating at Friends University. That year, they moved to New York City, where he received a master's degree in English from Columbia University. In 1925, the Teales also had their only child, a son they named David Allen. From 1928 through 1941, while Nellie was a mother and homemaker, Edwin worked as a feature writer on the staff of *Popular Science Monthly*, writing articles on all aspects of science and technology.

The Teales developed an insect garden near their home in Baldwin, on Long Island, which became the basis for Edwin's first book, 1937's *Grassroot Jungles*. A nature book of photographs with an accompanying text, *Grassroot Jungles* received a positive response from readers and critics because of its imaginative depiction of insects' lives, as well as the philosophical implications that humans might possibly gain from an encounter with this unusual sector of the natural world. In 1939 and 1940, three additional books by Edwin were released, *The Junior Book of Insects*, *The Boys' Book of Photography*, and *The Golden Throng*, the latter being a popular investigation of bees. Although he was 42 years old and not wealthy, in October 1941 Edwin resigned from the staff of *Popular Science Monthly* to begin living the sometimes perilous life of a freelance writer. Nellie became an essential participant in his work, as his researcher and in-house critic. Edwin sold articles and photographs to major periodicals, including *The Atlantic Monthly* and the *Illustrated London News*. In 1942, he published *New Horizons*, the story of the origin, development and purposes of their insect garden. With this volume, the Teale horizon expanded beyond insects, to include other fields of nature.

On March 16, 1945, during World War II, the couple's only child, David Allen Teale, was killed in combat while on reconnaissance patrol near the Moselle River in Germany. He was only 19 when he died, and his loss brought immeasurable grief to his parents. After "the awful years" of the war, Nellie and Edwin decided in early 1947 to travel from southern Florida to Maine in order to record the unfolding of spring, hoping to gather sufficient material to turn into a book. They began their trip in January in sub-tropical Florida and followed the spring north to the Canadian border, where after 17,000 miles of zig-zagging they reached their goal on June 21, 1947. When the book finally appeared in print in 1951 as *North with the Spring*, it turned out to be the first of a quartet of books on the different seasons across the American continent.

Three more books in the series, which ultimately came to be known as "The American Seasons," were researched and written over the next 15 years, with Nellie helping with editing. For *Autumn across America* (1956), the Teales traveled about 20,000 miles from Cape Cod to California. *Journey into Summer* (1960) was based on 19,000 miles covered in three months between New Hampshire's Franconia Notch and the summit of Pike's Peak in Colorado. The final book in the quartet, *Wandering through Winter*, appeared in 1965, by which time the couple had traveled 76,000 miles across the United States. *Wandering through Winter*, which won the 1966 Pulitzer Prize, was dedicated to the memory of David Allen Teale.

In 1959, the Teales sold their Long Island home and purchased a farm outside the village of Hampton, Connecticut. The couple lived in an 1806 Colonial Cape Cod house with pegged oak and chestnut beams and three huge fireplaces, on a property that was initially 79 acres of woods, pastures, and swamps. The land also contained two brooks, a mile of trails through the woods, and a waterfall. The Teales cut trails into the woods for observing birds and animals and named their property Trail Wood. Nellie was known to be a keen observer of the natural world, and it was said that she knew more about birds than her husband did. Later, they purchased additional acreage that brought the total property to 140 acres. The additional land boasted two more swamps, a cranberry bog, and an old carriage road. The land's varied topography inspired the Teales to create names evoking its different features, such as Far North Woods, Seven Springs Swamp, Witch Hazel Hill, Firefly Meadow, and Starfield.

According to Nellie, the spot she and her husband treasured the most was simply named Pond. Modeled after Walden Pond, it was excavated in the spring and summer of 1963 just southwest of their house, along a brook and natural hollow that contained a red maple swamp. As the pond began to fill, the couple watched a progression of plant, insect, and other wildlife settle into its new habitat. Cattails clustered along the banks, whirligig beetles and dragonflies traced zigzag patterns across the surface of the water. American bitterns and Canada geese rested at the pond for days at a time while on their southward migration. In his 1974 book *A Naturalist Buys an Old Farm*, Edwin described how "a smaller relative of the mink, a long-tailed weasel, made its appearance beneath the apple tree one day when Nellie was sitting motionless, absorbed in the activity of water spiders." Among Nellie Teale's many discoveries in the woods were beavers eagerly building a dam, which in time would serve to control the water level of the Pond. Fascinated by the activities they observed there, the Teales built a small screened-in house on the water's edge, where they sometimes picnicked and where Nellie read aloud the classics or mystery novels to her husband until the sun set. Years after Edwin's death in October 1980, Nellie Teale commented about her marriage and the 21 years they spent together at Trail Wood, "We always got along beautifully."

Shortly before he died, Edwin Way Teale arranged with the Connecticut Audubon Society to perpetuate Trail Wood as a wildlife sanctuary. (Nellie would also donate many of their books and letters to the Homer Babbidge Library of the University of Connecticut, which has a collection of Teale papers.) With Nellie having been granted life tenure in the farmhouse, the Trail Wood Audubon Sanctuary began to function in the early 1980s as one of the few remaining examples of an old Connecticut farm preserve. The administration of the property became the shared responsibility of the Connecticut Audubon Society and the Friends of Trail Wood, a group of local naturalists. Until her death in the summer of 1993, Nellie Teale continued to live in the old farmhouse at Trail Wood. To her last days, she remained a sharp-eyed naturalist and researcher who could mimic bird songs as well as identify mushrooms, plants, and insects. In her late 80s, she still enjoyed planting a wildflower garden with 25 varieties next to a sundial and the 100-year-old peony bush that had belonged to her husband's grandmother. Soft spoken and physically frail, with clear blue eyes and snow white hair, she could no longer walk the trails as she and her husband had once done, but in the evenings Nellie still relished sitting in the shade of a hickory tree in her back yard, listening avidly to the "warbling twitter of the woodcocks."

SOURCES:

Buell, Lawrence. "The Thoreauvian Pilgrimage: The Structure of an American Cult," in *American Literature*. Vol. 61, no. 2. May 1989, pp. 175–199.

Cevasco, George A. "Teale, Edwin Way," in Keir B. Sterling, *et al.*, eds., *Biographical Dictionary of American and Canadian Naturalists and Environmentalists*. Westport, CT: Greenwood Press, 1997, pp. 769–770.

Crist, Eileen. *Images of Animals: Anthropomorphism and Animal Mind*. Philadelphia, PA: Temple University Press, 1999.

———. "Naturalists' Portrayals of Animal Life: Engaging the Verstehen Approach," in *Social Studies of Science*. Vol. 26, no. 4. November 1996, pp. 799–838.

Dodd, Edward. *Of Nature, Time, and Teale: A Biographical Sketch of Edwin Way Teale*. NY: Dodd, Mead, 1966.

Hinchman, Lewis P., and Sandra K. Hinchman. "'Deep Ecology' and Revival of Natural Right," in *Western Political Quarterly*. Vol. 42, no. 3. September 1989, pp. 201–228.

Howe, Marvin. "Nellie I. Teale, 92; Naturalist Assisted In Acclaimed Books," in *The New York Times Biographical Service*. Vol. 24. July 1993, p. 1014.

Lawrence, Elizabeth Atwood. "Symbol of a Nation: The Bald Eagle in American Culture," in *Journal of American Culture*. Vol. 13, no. 1. Spring 1990, pp. 63–69.

Miller, David Stuart. "An Unfinished Pilgrimage: Edwin Way Teale and American Nature Writing," Ph.D. dissertation, University of Minnesota, 1982.

"Nellie Teale; Established Wildlife Sanctuary," in *The Hartford Courant*. July 20, 1993, p. B11.

Rierden, Andi. "The View from Trail Wood in Hampton: Author's Beloved Fields Remain His Memorial," in *The New York Times*. July 22, 1990, section 12 (Connecticut), p. 2.

Teale, Edwin Way. *The American Seasons*. 4 vols. NY: Dodd, Mead, 1981.

———. *Circle of the Seasons: The Journal of a Naturalist's Year*. NY: Dodd, Mead, 1953.

———. *Dune Boy: The Early Years of a Naturalist*. Rep. ed. Bloomington, IN: Indiana University Press, 1986.

———. *A Naturalist Buys an Old Farm*. NY: Dodd, Mead, 1974.

———. *A Walk Through the Year*. NY: Dodd, Mead, 1978.

Thorson, Robert M., and S.L. Harris. "How Natural are Inland Wetlands? An Example from the Trail Wood Audubon Sanctuary in Connecticut, USA," in *Environmental Management*. Vol. 15, no. 5. September–October 1991, pp. 675–687.

Wilson, David S. "The Flying Spider," in *Journal of the History of Ideas*. Vol. 32, no. 3. July–September 1971, pp. 447–458.

COLLECTIONS:

Edwin Way Teale Archives in the Homer Babbidge Library of the University of Connecticut, Storrs, Connecticut.

John Haag,
Associate Professor of History,
University of Georgia,
Athens, Georgia

Team USA: Women's Ice Hockey at Nagano

American team that won the gold medal at the first Olympics to feature women's ice hockey.

Bailey, Chris (1972—). Defenseman. *Name variations: (nickname) "Bails." Born on February 5, 1972, in Syracuse, New York; graduated from Marcellus High School, 1990; graduated from Providence College, 1994, with a degree in business management; lived in Marietta, New York.*

Named Most Valuable Player at the ECAC championship tournament (1994); four-time member of the U.S. Women's National Team (1994–97); named to the IIHF Pacific Women's Hockey championship All-Tournament Team and selected as the tournament's Outstanding Defensive Player (1995).

Quick-tempered, Chris Bailey played hockey at Providence College. She was named PC's Rookie of the Year in 1990–91, and earned All-Eastern College Athletic Conference honors as a junior and senior. She also played two years of soccer while in college. Bailey's father died when she was 13. "He never said I couldn't do anything," she said, "and he always was interested in everything I did. We went to so many games together."

Baker, Laurie (1976—). Forward. *Born on November 6, 1976; lived in Concord, Massachusetts.*

Blahoski, Alana (1974—). Forward. *Born on April 29, 1974; lived in St. Paul, Minnesota.*

Brown-Miller, Lisa (1966—). Forward. *Born on November 16, 1966, in Union Lake, Michigan; daughter of Jean Peters and Bob Brown; graduated from West Bloomfield (Michigan) High School; graduated from Providence College, 1988, with a degree in humanities; married John Miller (an engineer), in August 1995.*

Earned Eastern College Athletic Conference Coach of the Year honors (1991–92 season); served as head coach of the Princeton University women's ice hockey team (1991–96); named the ECAC Player of the Year and American Women's Hockey Coaches' Association Player of the Year following her senior campaign; played four years of hockey at Providence College; named Most Valuable Player of the U.S. Women's National Team (1992); member of the U.S. Women's National Team since its inception; played on six teams (1990, 1992, 1994, 1995, 1996, and 1997); member of the U.S. Women's Select Teams (1993, 1995, 1996, and 1997).

The oldest member of the U.S. women's Olympic ice hockey team and the smallest (5'1", 128 pounds), Lisa Brown-Miller was also the only married member of the USA Team. Wed to her engineer husband John in August 1995, she skipped her honeymoon to attend training camp. Brown-Miller was ready to hang up her skates years before hockey became an Olympic sport, but her husband convinced her she would regret it if she didn't give the Olympics a shot. After Nagano, Brown-Miller looked forward to starting a career, pursuing other sports, and finally spending some time with her husband. "Every time we're together, we're driving around looking at homes, wanting to get a dog," she said. "We just want to settle down and get on with things."

Bye, Karyn (1971—). Forward and assistant captain. Born on May 18, 1971, in River Falls, Wisconsin; daughter of Dorothy Bye and Charles Bye; graduated from River Falls High School, 1989; graduated from the University of New Hampshire, 1993, with a degree in physical education; received a graduate degree from Concordia University, Montreal, Canada.

Five-time member of the U.S. Women's National team (1992, 1994, 1995, 1996, and 1997); member of the U.S. Women's Select Teams (1993, 1995, 1996, and 1997); earned all-tournament honors and an Outstanding Performance Award for the U.S. at the Women's World championship (1994); named USA Today's Athlete of the Month (May 1995); named USA Hockey Women's Player of the Year (1995); captain at the IIHF Pacific Women's Hockey championship (1996).

As a high school student, Karyn Bye was a standout in softball and tennis as well as ice hockey, and was teammates with her brother Chris for one season when he was a senior and she was a sophomore.

Coyne, Colleen (1971—). Defenseman. Born on September 19, 1971; lived in East Falmouth, Massachusetts.

DeCosta, Sara (1977—). Goaltender. Name variations: (nickname) "D. C." Born on May 13, 1977; graduated from Toll Gate High School, 1996; attended Providence College; lived in Warwick, Rhode Island.

Member of the U.S. Women's National Junior Team (1995); member of the U.S. Women's National teams (1996).

At Toll Gate High School, Sara DeCosta was a backup goalie for two years before moving into a starting position during her final two years. She was the first woman ever to play in the Rhode Island Interscholastic League's championships, and earned the team's MVP award in 1995 and 1996.

Dunn, Tricia (1974—). Forward. Born on April 25, 1974; lived in Derry, New Hampshire.

Granato, Cammi (1971—). Forward and team captain. Born Catherine Granato on March 25, 1971, in Downers Grove, Illinois; lived in Manhattan Beach, California; sister of Tony Granato (hockey player for the San Jose Sharks); graduated from Downers Grove North High School; graduated from Providence College with a degree in social science, 1993; attended graduate school at Concordia University, Montreal, Canada.

Six-time member of the U.S. Women's National Team (1990, 1992, 1994–97); led U.S. in scoring at the IIHF Pacific Women's Hockey championship (1996); named Outstanding Forward at the Pacific Women's Hockey championship and received an Outstanding Player Award for the U.S. (1996); USA Hockey Women's Player of the Year Award (1996); captained the U.S. Women's National Team (1997); leading scorer at the Women's World championship (1997); earned a place on the Women's World championship All-Tournament Team; scored 256 goals in her career by the time of Nagano; scored first goal at Nagano.

One of the most recognized women hockey players in the U.S., Cammi Granato played on the boys' hockey team when she was in high school, and was also the MVP of her high school soccer and basketball teams. She was the leading goal-scorer of the Providence College hockey team (the Friars), and earned the ECAC Player of the Year Award in each of her final three years. When not competing for the U.S., Granato served as radio color commentator for the NHL's Los Angeles Kings on KRLA-AM, which she called "the hardest thing I've ever done. Hockey always came naturally and it was fun to push yourself to higher levels. This is kind of painful."

King, Katie (1975—). Forward. Name variations: (nickname) Kinger or Nitro. Born on May 24, 1975; lived in Salem, New Hampshire. Known for her power and speed.

Looney, Shelley (1972—). Forward. Born on January 21, 1972; lived in Trenton, Michigan.

Merz, Sue (1972—). Defenseman. Name variations: (nickname) Merphy. Born on April 10, 1972; lived in Greenwich, Connecticut; Olympic play: one goal, two assists.

Mleczko, A.J. (1975—). Forward. Born Allison Jaime Mleczko on June 14, 1975, in Nantucket, Massachusetts; daughter of Thomas Mleczko and Bambi Mleczko; graduated from the Taft School; attended Harvard University.

Earned first-team All-Ivy League honors (1994–95) and was a two-time ECAC Player of the Week; earned first-team All-Ivy League honors in junior year; was Harvard's lone All-Eastern College Athletic Conference selection (1994–95); led Harvard Crimson to a 22–1 record and the American Women's College Hockey Alliance National championship during her senior year; three-time member of the U.S. Women's National Team (1995, 1996, and 1997); member of the U.S. Women's Select Teams (1995, 1996, and 1997); named Patty Kazmaier Award winner for most outstanding player in women's intercollegiate hockey as well as the player of the year in the Ivy League and the ECAC (1999).

Mounsey, Tara (1978—). Defenseman. Born on March 12, 1978; lived in Concord, New Hampshire; graduated from Concord High School, 1986; attended Brown University.

Member of the U.S. Women's National Junior Team (1995); member of U.S. Women's Select Teams (1995 and 1996); won Outstanding Performance Award for the U.S. at the IIHF Pacific Women's Hockey championship (1996); two-time member of the U.S. Women's National Team (1996 and 1997).

In high school, Tara Mounsey captained her team to the 1996 New Hampshire State championship and was named the New Hampshire (Class L) Player of the Year (1995–96), the only woman ever to win that award. While attending Brown University, where she studied biology, Mounsey was the 1995–97 ECAC Rookie of the Year and was named to the ECAC Division I All-Star Team. She planned on pursuing a career as an orthopedic surgeon.

Movessian, Vicki (1972—). Defenseman. Born on November 6, 1972; lived in Lexington, Massachusetts.

Ruggiero, Angela (1980—). Defenseman. Name variations: (nickname) Rugger. Born on January 3, 1980; lived in Harrison, Michigan.

Schmidgall, Jenny (1979—). Forward. Born on January 12, 1979; lived in Edina, Minnesota.

Tueting, Sarah (1976—). Goaltender. Name variations: (nickname) Teeter. Born on April 26, 1976; daughter of William Tueting and Pat Tueting (a neuroscientist at the University of Illinois); lived in Winnetka, Illinois; graduated from New Trier High School; attended Dartmouth College.

Named Ivy League Rookie of the Year and Dartmouth's Rookie of the Year (1994–95); member of the

Team USA, 1998.

U.S. Women's National Select teams (1996); member of the U.S. Women's National Team (1997).

A music lover who plays the piano and cello, Sarah Tueting led the New Trier High School boys' hockey team to the state championship during her senior year and was named to the state all-star team. Having studied neurobiology at Dartmouth, she planned on a career in the medical field.

Ulion, Gretchen (1972—). Forward. *Born on May 4, 1972; lived in Marlborough, Connecticut; graduated from Loomis-Chaffee High School; graduated from Dartmouth College; received a master's degree in education.*

Set 11 Dartmouth and 4 Ivy League records during her college career; named Ivy League Player of the Year (1992–93 and 1993–94), and was Ivy League Player of the Year as a freshman; named to the New England Hockey Writers All-Star Team following her senior year; member of U.S. Women's Select Teams (1993, 1995, 1996, and 1997); three-time member of the U.S. Women's National Team (1994, 1995, and 1997).

Gretchen Ulion was a ninth-grade history and math teacher before the Olympics and planned to return to teaching.

Whyte, Sandra (1970—). Forward. *Born on August 24, 1970; graduated from Harvard University, 1992, with a degree in bio-anthropology; lived in Saugus, Massachusetts.*

Named Ivy League Player of the Year (1990–91 and 1991–92); five-time member of the U.S. Women's National Team (1992, 1994, 1995, 1996, and 1997); member of the U.S. Women's Select Teams (1993, 1995, 1996, and 1997).

Considered an Ivy League intellectual, Whyte explained her dedication to hockey as a matter of heart over intellect, but she had struggled with the decision to put her life on hold. "The last four years I have followed the lives of my college roommates as they progressed through medical school and law school," she wrote in a diary entry for USA Today. "I am awed by their accomplishments and cannot help but make comparisons as to the state of my own neglected career. Perhaps hockey is not the best way to make use of my expensive education, but oh how the Olympic rings pull at my heart."

In the mid-1980s, when Team USA players **Tara Mounsey** and **Allison Mleczko** were lacing up their first pairs of hockey skates and clutching sticks belonging to their brothers, the idea of a women's national hockey team was not even a glint in anyone's eye. Most young female players were forced to play with the boys, tucking their long hair under helmets and adopting assumed masculine names (thus, A.J. Mleczko, K.L. Bye). Many endured harassment from coaches and fellow players, or were subjected to jeers and insults from spectators. Indeed, all the women of Team USA told of the agonies of attempting to gain acceptance and recognition playing a "man's game." The struggles were all forgotten, however, on the night of February 17, 1998, at Big Hat Arena in Nagano, Japan, when the American women beat archrival **Canadian Women's National Ice Hockey Team** 3–1, winning the first-ever Olympic women's hockey tournament. Sticks flew, gloves scattered, and several of the women took a victory skate around the arena wrapped in an American flag. At the medal ceremony, team captain **Cammi Granato** broke down and wept into her hands. "When that medal went around my neck, I was so filled with emotion, I didn't even know how to handle it," she said later. "It's because of how much we've all worked and how much adversity we've all faced. It's that it all paid off—that all hits you at once." Even Canadian coach **Shannon Miller**, noted for her "clenched jaw," rough manner and unyielding drive to win, was moved to tears during the medal ceremony. "I couldn't believe an Olympic gold medal was being hung on a female hockey player's neck. I couldn't believe the impact that had on me."

From the formation of the first national team in 1990, women's hockey advanced at an amazingly rapid speed. Between 1990 and 1997, the number of women players registered with USA Hockey almost quadrupled, and the number of women's teams went from 149 to 910, although many of the women played on mixed-gender squads. The women's game differs from the men's in that it is slower and bars full-body checking, putting more emphasis on passing and stick handling. "There is no room for goons," said Granato. "Everyone's got to be skilled." Like women's basketball, it is more a game of finesse, more like the men's hockey games of yore. There is still plenty of physical contact, however, and the game has been known to get pretty rough. "Don't be misled by the no-checking rule," writes Mark Lasswell. "That just means the players get penalized for blatant bashing. 'Incidental contact' is allowed, and referees have been known to consider board-bending crunches incidental." **Erin Whitten**, a member of the U.S. Women's National Hockey Team and the first American woman to play hockey professionally, agrees that the women's game is one of finesse. "You have to find a way around the body checking so it tends to be a little more wide open, and then again a little more concentrated down by the goaltender," she told Phil Ponce. "There are a lot of close-in shots and a lot of rebounds."

Many of the 20 women on the 1998 team were long-time veterans of the national team and all of them had made incredible sacrifices for their sport. "I've postponed like everything," said forward **Sandra Whyte**, who has a college degree in bio-anthropology. "My boyfriend and I haven't been in the same state forever, it seems like. My college roommates, two of them are doctors and one's a lawyer. I don't even know what I want to be." **Lisa Brown-Miller**, who gave up a coaching job at Princeton to join the team, married in 1995, but was so busy training and touring that she did not have time for a honeymoon. **Angela Ruggiero**, the youngest member of the team, had to stockpile enough credits to be able to take off the fall and winter terms at prep school. On tour, she missed a morning

practice to take her SATs at a school near Boston; she also submitted her college admissions essay from the road, writing about the tour. "It's too bad they couldn't have waited a few more weeks," she said. "I could have written about the Olympics."

Team USA lived and toured together for five months before the Olympics, perfecting their game under the guidance of Ben Smith, who became their coach in June 1996. "He's our stability. He's our leader," said team captain Granato. "He made us stronger mentally and physically. He's made us better hockey players." Spending so much time together, the team bonded like a family. Off-ice activities included a Halloween outing to the Spooky World amusement park in western Massachusetts and a shopping spree in Osaka, where they were processed before heading to Nagano. Pranks were also a large part of downtime for the women. Tara Mounsey, who

---

❧ Canadian Women's National Ice Hockey Team (1998)

Botterill, Jennifer. Defenseman. Lived in Winnipeg, Manitoba; was Team Canada's youngest player at Nagano at age 18.

Brisson, Therese. Defenseman. Lived in Fredericton, New Brunswick; was inducted into the Concordia University Hall of Fame.

Campbell, Cassie. Defenseman. Lived in Brampton, Ontario; was a star at the University of Guelph.

Diduck, Judy. Defenseman. Lived in Sherwood Park, Alberta; is the younger sister of NHL defenseman Gerald Diduck.

Drolet, Nancy. Forward. Lived in Drummondville, Quebec; won three World championship gold medals with Canada.

Dupuis, Lori. Forward. Lived in Williamstown, Ontario; played at the University of Toronto.

Goyette, Danielle. Forward. Lived in St. Nazaire, Quebec; was a veteran of international competition.

Heaney, Geraldine. Defenseman. Lived in North York, Ontario; played in the first Women's World championship in 1990.

Hefford, Jayna. Forward. Lived in Kingston, Ontario; was the OWIAA Rookie of the Year with the University of Toronto.

Kellar, Becky. Defenseman. Lived in Hagarsville, Ontario; played four seasons at Brown University.

McCormack, Kathy. Forward. Lived in Fredericton, New Brunswick; played for the University of New Brunswick.

Nystrom, Karen. Forward. Lived in Scarborough, Ontario; played at Northeastern University in Boston.

Reddon, Lesley. Goaltender. Lived in Fredericton, New Brunswick; won four OWIAA championships at the University of Toronto.

Rheaume, Manon. Goaltender. Lived in Charlesbourg, Quebec; was the first woman to play professional hockey (see separate entry).

Schuler, Laura. Forward. Lived in Scarborough, Ontario; played at Northeastern University and the University of Toronto.

Smith, Fiona. Defenseman. Lived in Edam, Saskatchewan; played on a Canadian Senior Women's championship team.

St. Louis, France. Forward. Lived in St. Hubert, Quebec; at age 39, was the oldest Canadian hockey player in Nagano.

Sunohara, Vicki. Forward. Lived in Scarborough, Ontario; was an All-American at Northeastern University.

Wickenheiser, Hayley. Forward. Lived in Shaunavon, Saskatchewan; is a cousin of former NHL player Doug Wickenheiser.

Wilson, Stacy. Forward. Lived in Salisbury, New Brunswick; had represented Canada at every major international competition.

---

traveled with a Beanie Baby named Wrinkles and a Tigger doll, frequently entered the shower in her hotel room to find Tigger hanging from the showerhead, a shoelace tied around his neck. "Every time I get a chance, I'm terrorizing that thing," said Granato, who no doubt took a few jabs about her own traveling buddy, a bear named Jake.

Team USA's victory in Nagano was all the sweeter in light of their long-standing rivalry with the Canadians, who had won all four women's World championships dating back to 1990, leaving the U.S. in second place each time. In the four months leading up to the Olympics, however, the Americans won 7 of their 14 match-ups with Canada, giving rise to new hope. In their early Olympic matches, the team won grueling games over China, Sweden, Finland, and Japan to obtain their play-off position. Confronting Canada in the last game of the preliminary round (Canada, too, had already clinched a place in the gold-medal play-off), the U.S. rebounded from a 4–1 deficit in the third period to win the game 7–4. It was a gritty, controversial encounter which later prompted accusations from Canadian coach Shannon Miller that an unnamed U.S. player had made a remark about Canadian player **Danielle Goyette**'s father, who had died just before the Olympics. Sandra Whyte, who had confronted Goyette on the ice a few minutes earlier, took the heat for the remark and was forced to defend herself to the media. "I did make a comment to her but it was not about her father," she admitted. "What I said to her was not a nice thing. I was upset about something that happened in the game. But there's no excuse for me losing my temper." Coach Ben Smith defended Whyte, saying that none of his players would have made such a crude remark. "Our team sent a card to that player the other day, expressing our deepest sympathies," he said. "I know everybody signed it because I signed it myself."

The controversy made for an even more intense final game, which drew a record crowd of spectators. Ironically, Whyte assisted on the first two U.S. goals of the game (power-play goals by **Gretchen Ulion** and **Shelley Looney**). With 17 minutes left in the third period, and the U.S. still ahead 2–0, goalie **Sarah Tueting** blocked a shot by Canada's Danielle Goyette; two minutes later, Tueting had to block another shot. The Canadians, who were on the attack, finally broke through at 4:01 on a power play (Goyette), and the score was now 2–1. Minutes later, Tueting kicked away a potential game-tying shot, and the U.S. struggled to hold its lead. In the final

eight seconds of the game, Whyte intercepted a Canadian pass just outside her own blue line, then, slipping by a defender, made the 40-foot winning shot into an empty net. "I was thinking," she recalled later, "I have plenty of time. I better make sure it goes in." Seconds later, the Americans were tossing equipment into the air in a display reminiscent of the men's 1980 celebration following their win over the Russians at Lake Placid. At the medal ceremony, it was not only team captain Granato who could not stop crying. **Karyn Bye**, alternate captain and one of the team's leading scorers, also dissolved into tears. Brown-Miller, who received her medal after Bye, sobbed even harder. At the end of the ceremony, the players joined hands in a line at the middle of the rink as the national anthem was played. Tueting, whose brilliant play and 21 saves were invaluable to the team, was still beaming 90 minutes later. "It's beginning to sink in," she said, clutching flowers and wearing an Uncle Sam hat. "My cheeks still hurt from smiling so much."

As the glow of Nagano fades, the future of women's hockey remains uncertain. While some of the women of Team USA dream of a repeat gold-medal win at the Salt Lake City Winter Olympics in 2002, others have hung up their skates. Unable to return to multimillion dollar contracts with professional teams as their male counterparts do, they have moved on to other pursuits. As more women are drawn to the game, there may eventually be a talent pool large enough to support an NHL version of the Women's National Basketball Association (WNBA), but for now women's ice hockey remains an amateur sport.

SOURCES:

Gergen, Joe. "Prep Schooler Toughens USA," in *The Day* [New London, CT]. February 18, 1998.

——. "Whyte's Noise at Center Stage," in *The Day* [New London, CT]. February 18, 1998.

Herrmann, Mark. "The Fighting Words," in *The Day* [New London, CT]. February 16, 1998.

——. "Gold-Medal Guidance," in *The Day* [New London, CT]. February 17, 1998.

——. "Icy Relationships," in *The Day* [New London, CT]. February 15, 1998.

Lasswell, Mark. "Rink Ladies," in *TV Guide*. February 7, 1998.

Mondi, Lawrence. "A Game of Their Own," in *Time*. February 23, 1998.

Pucin, Diane. "U.S. women 'take their lives off hold,'" in *The Day* [New London, CT]. February 18, 1998.

Rosenberg, Debra, and Larry Reibstein. "Dreams and Nightmares," in *Newsweek*. March 2, 1998.

"She Shoots, She Scores!" *The News Hour with Jim Lehrer* (transcript). February 17, 1998.

"Sweet Victory at Nagano," in *The Day* [New London, CT]. February 25, 1998.

Whyte, Sandra. "Beyond the blue line: The women's ice hockey diary," in *USA Today*. November 24, 1998.

SUGGESTED READING:

Turco, Mary. *Crashing the Net: The U.S. Women's Olympic Ice Hockey Team and the Road to Gold.* NY: HarperCollins, 1999.

Barbara Morgan,
Melrose, Massachusetts

Teasdale, Sara (1884–1933)

American writer who was one of the foremost lyric poets in the early decades of the 20th century. Born in St. Louis, Missouri, on August 8, 1884; committed suicide in New York City on January 29, 1933; daughter of John Warren Teasdale (a wealthy businessman) and Mary Elizabeth (Willard) Teasdale; graduated from Hosmer Hall, 1903; married Ernest Filsinger (a St. Louis businessman), on December 19, 1914 (divorced in Reno, Nevada, September 5, 1929; he died in Shanghai, China, May 1937); no children.

Member of arts group, the Potters (1904–07); traveled to Europe and Near East (1905); published Sonnets to Duse *(1907); selected for membership in Poetry Society of America in New York (1910); moved to New York City (1916); won Poetry Society of America award (June 1917); awarded Columbia Poetry Prize (1918) and Brookes More Prize for poetry (1921).*

Selected works: Sonnets to Duse and Other Poems *(Boston: Poet Lore, 1907);* Helen of Troy and Other Poems *(NY: Putnam, 1911);* Rivers to the Sea *(NY: Macmillan, 1915);* Love Songs *(NY: Macmillan, 1917);* Flame and Shadow *(NY: Macmillan, 1920);* Dark of the Moon *(NY: Macmillan, 1926);* Stars To-Night, Verses Old and New for Boys and Girls *(NY: Macmillan, 1930);* Strange Victory *(NY: Macmillan, 1933);* The Collected Poems of Sara Teasdale *(NY: Macmillan, 1937); (ed. by William Drake)* Mirror of the Heart, Poems of Sara Teasdale *(NY: Macmillan, 1984).*

Other: (ed. by Teasdale) The Answering Voice: One Hundred Love Lyrics by Women *(Boston: Houghton Mifflin, 1917, enlarged ed., NY: Macmillan, 1928);* Rainbow Gold; Poems Old and New Selected for Girls and Boys by Sara Teasdale *(NY: Macmillan, 1922); Marguerite Wilkinson,* New Voices, *includes a contribution by Teasdale on writing lyric poetry (NY: Macmillan, 1936).*

"If I were only beautiful and a genius, what fun life would be," wrote Sara Teasdale. She was neither beautiful nor a genius, and she had little fun in life. She achieved success in the literary world, but personally foundered in a vain search for love and happiness. She was, however, "one of the great lyric poets of the English language," according to John Hall Wheelock. She was also shy, sensitive, physically frail, ambitious, and talented. Her Puritan background and Victorian upbringing burdened her with "crippling inhibitions that summed up the Victorian middle-class ideal of feminine propriety and refinement." Sara was pampered by her indulgent parents who kept her in a state of perpetual childhood until she was almost 30 years old. Only love and marriage, she believed, could free her from the oppressive restrictions imposed on her by her devout Baptist parents. Being torn between what she was and what she wanted to be created conflicts, and she "lived in contradictory worlds of feeling"; Sara's two selves, "Puritan and Pagan," never merged into a single personality. She accepted that a woman was to marry and live for her husband, but marriage "conflicted with the sense of being a free person in her own right." And William Drake claims: "In the end, the conflict cost her her life."

Sara was born in St. Louis, Missouri, in 1884 when her parents were already middle-aged; her father was 45, her mother 40. John Teasdale was a well-to-do businessman, and Sara adored him. Her mother **Mary Teasdale** was a strict Baptist and the dominant presence in the Teasdale household. The three other children, two boys and a girl, ranged in age from 19 to 14 at the time of Sara's birth. Teasdale was fond of her sister **Mamie Teasdale**, but never liked her brothers, George and John. The family home was large, comfortable, and secure, and Sara grew up in an adult world, never allowed to play with other children. She was considered frail, and each minor illness was treated as a medical crisis. Educated at home until age nine, she then attended prestigious girls' schools in St. Louis, first Mary Institute (founded by T.S. Eliot's grandfather) and Hosmer Hall which prepared young women for college. There was little chance that Teasdale's parents would have approved of higher education for their delicate girl, however. Medical experts claimed that if women "attempted to become educated their health would suffer" and "reduce them to unhealthy invalids and unfit childbearers." Moreover, girls were "never intended by the creator to undergo the stress and strain of higher education." Even without the rigors of higher education, Teasdale became a near-invalid and was plagued with ill health all her life.

Outwardly, Teasdale adhered to all the proprieties imposed on her by her pious mother, but she also lived a vivid, active inner life. Living "the life of a princess" with no responsibilities at home, she never learned to manage a household if she married, or to pursue a career and achieve financial independence, as if her life were to be a "perpetual childhood." Teasdale's life was orderly, regimented, and sanitized. She was a complex child, dreamy, yet practical, precocious, yet shy. And she was self-centered; her own needs were foremost in her insular world, and "it never entered her head to fit herself to others."

After graduating from Hosmer Hall in 1903, Sara and a few other young women formed a club called the Potters. She had been writing poetry for several years, and her enthusiastic, energetic friend **Williamina Parrish** encouraged her to publish some of her poems in their monthly magazine, *The Potter's Wheel*. The club promoted poetry and the fine arts above "the level of mundane reality." Serious intellectual discussions allowed Sara to have her work read and criticized. Even when she had achieved a literary reputation, she sought, and welcomed, advice and criticism from fellow poets. The Potters also provided an environment where she could establish friendships outside of the stifling atmosphere of the Teasdale family home. Sara's "aristocratic" ways at times amused her friends who called on her during designated "visiting hours" and "were announced by a maid" before Sara received them.

Women were central figures in Teasdale's life, beautiful, heroic women like Helen of Troy, the poet *Sappho, *Guinevere of Arthurian legend, and her female friends on whom she developed adolescent crushes. Since "feminine love" was considered "higher" than love between men and women, it was viewed as a harmless indulgence until one found the right man and married. In fact, Sara had never been exposed socially to men or boys, except for her father and brothers; consequently her budding sensuality was directed towards women.

The Teasdales traveled a great deal and spent each summer in Charlevoix on Lake Michigan. In 1905, Sara went abroad for the first time. With her mother she toured the Holy Land which was "miserable, filthy, poor, and diseased," and visited Egypt, Spain, Greece, Italy, France, and England. Her ancestors, paternal and maternal, were English, and Sara was proud of them: the founder of Concord, Massachusetts, in 1635, presidents of Harvard University, signers of the Declaration of Independence, legislators, judges, and clerics.

In 1906, Teasdale became a published writer. A prose sketch, "The Crystal Cup," appeared in William Morris Reedy's weekly, *The Mirror*, for which Sara was paid. A few months later, he published her poem "The Little Love." Reedy was "the H.L. Mencken of the Midwest," and Teasdale referred to him as her "literary God-father." Encouraged by the reception her work received, she began preparing a book of her poems for publication; 29 poems, which included many about the actress *Eleonora Duse, were issued by the Poet Lore Company in Boston. Sara's parents gave her $290 for the publication of 1,000 copies. She sent a copy to Arthur Symons, the English poet and critic, who praised her lyric poems in the *Saturday Review* (London) in October 1907. Teasdale never hesitated to promote her career and sent poems to major magazines, but only to those that paid for her work. This initial success led to plans for another book.

At age 23, Teasdale remained totally dependent on her parents, emotionally and financially. She questioned whether she could survive alone in the "real world." Her sheltered life and frequent illnesses often reduced her to "infantile helplessness." In one of her poems she queried, "How shall I sing of sunlight/ Who never saw the sun." Her horizons were expanded through correspondence with the stockbroker-poet John Myers O'Hara in New York City and Marion Cummings Stanley, a philosophy professor at the University of Arizona, whom she visited in 1908. Away from St. Louis and her family, Sara was more physically energetic and active, but on returning home she sank into depression, loneliness, and bouts of ill health. "Rest cures" in a sanitorium in Cromwell, Connecticut, brought little relief. Friends in St. Louis, including *Zoe Akins (later a playwright in New York) and the poet Orrick Johns introduced Teasdale to the rather risqué bohemian life in St. Louis that both shocked and attracted her. Unable to shed her puritanical inhibitions, she chose to adhere to social convention and find a husband to support her; she would have security while she pursued her literary career. Johns noted that Teasdale had "little existence outside of her poems," and she admitted, "I suppose my work is more truly I than I am myself."

In October 1910, the Poetry Society of America was founded in New York City; membership was by invitation only, and Teasdale was asked to join. To attend the meeting of the Society in February 1911, Sara, age 26, still had to obtain permission from her parents. "Waiting for love and fame," she arrived in New York in mid-January, an event that put an end to "the perpetual childhood and isolation of her home." Her book, *Helen of Troy and Other Poems*, had been accepted by Putnam in December 1910,

*S*ara
*T*easdale

and the title poem was read, and well received, at the Poetry Society meeting. She finally met O'Hara but was disappointed to find he was as shy and solitary as she was—and he was not in love with her as she mistakenly had believed. However, Teasdale found New York liberating, and she wrote "a flood of new poems" which included "Union Square" in which she describes the plight of a woman who wanted a man's love but could not initiate a relationship because "decent women" had to retain a pure, virginal image. Her lyric poems were based on her own emotions and experiences, she stated, and "Union Square" reflects her longings: "With the man I love who loves me not/ I walked in the street-lamps' flare—/ But oh, the girls who ask for love/ In the lights of Union Square."

Teasdale remained in New York for the March meeting of the Society. She had become friends with *Jessie Rittenhouse, a critic for *The New York Times Book Review*, who introduced Sara to members of the literary establishment. They remained friends throughout Teasdale's life. Home again in St. Louis, Sara became ill and chafed against her mother's rigid and overbearing control of her life. The stifling atmosphere did not affect Teasdale's literary production, however. She wrote a short story entitled "The Sentimentalist," using John Myers O'Hara as a character who rejects a woman's love. H.L. Mencken published it (her only prose piece) in *Smart Set* in April 1916. Her book, *Helen of Troy*, garnered praise from national magazines and newspapers and put her in contact with the poets Louis and **Jean Untermeyer**.

A second visit to New York in early 1912 brought an end to Sara's psychological attachment to St. Louis. Here she was a recognized talent, a woman, not a protected, obedient child. Only a passionate love was missing from her life as she laments in "Imeros," written in February 1912: "I am a woman who will live and die/ Without the one thing I have craved of God," and she pleads with God, "Send me not back to death unsatisfied." Melancholic thoughts did not diminish the pleasure she had during a four-month trip to Europe with Rittenhouse during the summer of 1912. And on the ship returning to New York, Teasdale fell in love with a charming Englishman, Stafford Hatfield. What he wanted or expected of her is not known, but Sara's reaction to commitment was not unexpected—she became ill and went home to St. Louis; as she described her reaction, "But I feared the onward surge,/ Like a coward I turned aside."

Teasdale dreaded the idea of being a spinster, an "old maid" who evoked the sympathy of family and friends. As she approached her 30th birthday, she was still dependent on her aging parents. She had no life or money of her own. She wanted a husband and had assumed that Hatfield's attentions meant he was in love with her. Once again she was disappointed, but she persevered. She now directed her sights to a young man whose poems she admired; John Hall Wheelock worked in Scribner's Book Store in New York (he was later an editor at Scribner's publishing house). Sara wrote him saying she wanted to meet him, a rather bold gesture on her part. And typically, she soon imagined herself in love. In January 1913, on a visit to New York, she went to the bookstore and found Wheelock was everything she wanted, handsome, talented, a gentleman, and unmarried. They began taking long walks together in the evening, but the passion Teasdale sought was not forthcoming. In New York, Sara was never lonely and made friends easily. *Harriet Monroe, the founder of *Poetry* magazine, became a lifelong friend. Surprisingly, Teasdale also enjoyed the companionship of the Communist activist John Reed. And then she met the poet Vachel Lindsay.

Like Teasdale, Lindsay was a Midwesterner, a passionate, productive poet whose fame was just beginning. He wrote to Sara, probably at the suggestion of their mutual friend Harriet Monroe. Lindsay urged Teasdale to leave New York, come home and write about St. Louis, to be "a poet of America"; New York was not America to him. He and Sara also were offspring of an intensely "puritanical evangelical Protestantism" which each found restrictive. Moreover, he still lived with his mother in Illinois "like an ungrown boy." But Teasdale identified with New York more than the Midwest, and when Lindsay visited her in St. Louis in 1914, he found the delicate, refined woman was also ambitious and strong willed. In spite of this, Lindsay fell in love with Teasdale, but the attraction was not reciprocated for Sara loved the evasive Wheelock.

Teasdale continued to attend Poetry Society meetings in New York and to socialize there. She was becoming more poised and self-confident, and her career was advancing. *Eunice Tietjens, a staff member of *Poetry* magazine in Chicago, visited Sara in the spring of 1914, and introduced her to a friend, St. Louis businessman Ernest Filsinger. He had read Teasdale's poetry and admired her work. He was "a man of culture, warmth, and deep sincerity" who knew several languages and had broad interests. When Filsinger fell in love with Teasdale, it created a dilemma for her. She loved Wheelock, was being pursued by Lindsay to marry him, and now Filsinger revealed his affection and intention to marry her. But Wheelock was actually in love with another woman, and Lindsay was unable to support a family. Teasdale needed a mature, self-assured man to provide her with financial and emotional stability.

As she confided to Tietjens, she did not love Filsinger, but she wanted to get married "for at bottom I am a mother more intensely than I am a lover." A rather strange self-portrait of a woman who knew nothing about children or about being a "lover." Ernest "idolized her to the point of letting her have her own way in everything," not unlike the pampered, indulgent life her parents had provided. Pragmatic considerations, not love, convinced Sara to accept his marriage proposal. As she wrote to Monroe, "I am doing what seems right to me. I may be all wrong, but I can't help it." Teasdale's decision was also dictated by social convention: she could not live with Lindsay as her lover. In a poem, she wrote, "I am a woman, I am weak,/ And custom leads me as one blind," a telling insight into her assessment of her life. Sara and Ernest were married in her parents' house in St. Louis on Saturday, December 19, 1914.

All Teasdale's friends liked Ernest, as did her parents and John Hall Wheelock who had urged her to marry Filsinger. If Sara had doubts about her marriage she did not vocalize them, but on December 4, she had written a poem entitled "I am Not Yours," a prophetic rendering of her future with Ernest. The couple settled in a hotel in St. Louis because Teasdale was preparing a book of poems for Macmillan; the title, *Rivers to the Sea*, was taken from a line in a poem by Wheelock. And domesticity was beyond Sara's ken. The reality of marriage was also setting in, and by the spring of 1915, she became ill as she had always done to avoid dealing with unpleasant situations. Sara respected Ernest, but she did not love him. She was determined to maintain her own identify; she wrote her sister-in-law, **Irma Filsinger**, that she did not want a "master" and that any man "who wants a woman's brain, soul, and body wants really only a slave." Indeed, to Sara her poetry and career were all important. In public she was the dutiful wife, but she and Ernest were companions, not lovers. Sex without love on her part was not satisfactory.

Outwardly happily married, Teasdale was at the pinnacle of her profession when she and Ernest attended the Poetry Society meeting in New York in January 1916. *Rivers to the Sea* was successful and received glowing reviews. She had begun preparing an anthology of love poems by women poets (*The Answering Voice*) which was accepted for publication by Houghton Mifflin in July. When Ernest's shoe-manufacturing business failed, he went to work for a textile firm in New York. On November 24, 1916, Sara left St. Louis permanently. She had a new book of poems ready for publication by December. Entitled *Love Songs*, the volume reflected her realization that "love was not attainable."

Sara Teasdale was now an acclaimed poet, and by the fall of 1917, she had three books in print which were selling well. In 1917, and again in 1918, she was awarded national poetry prizes which pleased her greatly. William Drake notes that she "was the first woman to gain a reputation as voicing a woman's point of view and emotions." Ill, depressed, and increasingly pessimistic, Teasdale began to withdraw into herself. Ernest was ambitious, driven to succeed, energetic, and active. He worked long hours and traveled extensively on business. A specialist on Latin American trade, he had written two books on the subject and spoke at numerous conferences. Teasdale's reaction was to accuse him of neglecting her. She renewed her friendship with Wheelock who was the subject of several of her published "love songs." When she drifted into deep depression, she left New York for lengthy rest cures; her black moods were not revealed in her poetry, however. As Wheelock declared, her poems were "a record of her experience," but "this record was symbolic rather than literal or confessional." Sara trusted Wheelock, and when she was pregnant in mid-1917, she asked his advice about an abortion, but he declined to give an opinion. She had an abortion, probably in August 1917.

Ernest continued to make month-long business trips abroad. Because of her illnesses, Sara remained alone at home. She developed a "secret obsessive fear of a threat to her marriage," perhaps another woman. Ernest was gregarious, enjoyed partying with friends, and even in New York often went out without his wife, but there was never any suggestion that he was unfaithful. To Teasdale, marriage was both "a safe haven" and a "prison." She missed Ernest when he was traveling, but his presence at home was an intrusion into her placid, routinized life. She accompanied Ernest to Cuba in December 1918, but not on his longer trips to Europe and South America. In the fall of 1919, she went to Santa Barbara alone, hoping the change would rejuvenate her. For several months, she worked on a new book of poems, *Flame and Shadow*, for Macmillan. She met William Butler Yeats whom she greatly admired, but avoided contact with the local residents. After returning to New York in mid-May 1920, she suffered from depression and became ever more reclusive, "more aloof and critical of poets she knew." The "new realism" poetry of Robert Frost, Vachel Lindsay, Carl Sandburg, Ezra Pound, and T.S. Eliot signaled a new era in literature, especially in academic circles, but Sara's lyrical verses were still popular with the reading public. *Flame and Shadow* had a second printing in late 1920. She won the Brookes More Prize for poetry, evidence that she was one of the most popular poets in America. Offered an honorary Doctor of Letters degree from Baylor University, she declined the honor. Her collection of poems for children, published in September 1922, was also an immediate success.

When Teasdale's father died in 1921, she experienced a sense of diminished identity. Obedience to social convention typified her choices and lifestyle. Always a "lady," she disparaged the writing of James Joyce as "coarse" and "as raw as I ever read," and disapproved of Ernest Hemingway's characters in *The Sun Also Rises*—without ever reading the book. According to Drake, Sara's Puritan upbringing had left her with inhibitions but not faith. Her love for Wheelock and increasing estrangement from Ernest drained her emotionally. She did travel with Ernest again to Cuba (1923) and to England (1925), but they spent more and more time apart. If Sara's life were poetry, Ernest sought refuge in work and travel. He provided her with a comfortable existence, and in addition, Teasdale's books sold well, providing her with a bit of necessary independence.

Sara also acquired a new friend, **Margaret Conklin**, a young college student who eventually became her literary executor. Margaret had written Sara asking for a photo for a former teacher who had fostered her love of poetry. When they met in the fall of 1916, Teasdale saw herself in the young woman, "What she had been." As Sara wrote, "I knew/ The self I was/ Came home with you." Without knowing it, Margaret became the daughter Teasdale never had. A trip to England with Conklin in 1927 delighted Sara. They remained close friends until Sara's death.

Convinced that Ernest was to blame for her unstable emotional state, Sara began to consider a divorce. She was concerned about her reputation and wanted to avoid gossip so she told only Conklin and Wheelock of her decision. When Ernest left for South Africa in May 1929, Teasdale went to Reno, Nevada, to obtain a divorce. She paid for her attorney's fees and did not ask Ernest for alimony. On June 1, Sara wrote to Ernest, informing him that their marriage was over. The divorce was granted in September on grounds of "extreme cruelty," that Ernest's neglect of her had affected her health. Back in New York, she announced to Wheelock, "I'm a free woman, I can do anything I want." Actually, Teasdale had always done what she wanted, and now as a free woman she experienced only loneliness and increased isolation. She became touchy and irritable and more self-absorbed. In order to earn money, she started to work on a critical and biographical introduction to the love poems of *Christina Rossetti, a project which developed into a biography, but was never completed.

In her mind, depression, ill health, and death were all that awaited her. Only after two years did she agree to see Ernest again, and she changed her will, leaving much of her substantial estate to him. Vachel Lindsay also visited her in mid-November 1931; in early December, she learned that he had committed suicide on December 4, by drinking a bottle of Lysol. On a research trip to England the following July, Teasdale contracted pneumonia in both lungs and returned to New York earlier than planned. She was also severely depressed, and friends tried to convince her to see a psychiatrist, but she refused. In the early hours of Sunday, January 29, 1933, Teasdale took a large cache of sleeping pills she had been collecting and lay in a tub of warm water. Newspapers reported that her death was accidental, but the medical examiner's findings refuted this. Morphine and phenobarbital were present in her system, and she had not drowned, facts not then made public.

John Hall Wheelock, who knew Teasdale so well, said, "The ordeal she went through seemed to have done something to her. . . . She cared supremely about her work [and] she was able to cry out in a way that was not just crying, but a real Beethoven cry." Sara Teasdale's ordeal was the unresolved conflict between her "warring selves," the "Puritan and Pagan or Spartan and Sybarite," as she described them. Her poignant plea to God to "send me not back to death unsatisfied" had gone unanswered.

SOURCES:

Drake, William. "Sara Teasdale," in *Dictionary of Literary Biography*. Vol. 45. Detroit, MI: Gale Research, 1983, pp. 396–405.

————. *Sara Teasdale: Woman & Poet*. San Francisco, CA: Harper & Row, 1979.

Schoen, Carol B. *Sara Teasdale*. Boston, MA: Twayne, 1986.

SUGGESTED READING:

Carpenter, Margaret Haley. *Sara Teasdale: A Biography*. NY: Schulte, 1960.

Gould, Jean. *American Women Poets*. NY: Dodd, Mead, 1980.

Monroe, Harriet. *A Poet's Life*. NY: Macmillan, 1938.

Sara Teasdale. Chicago, IL: Macmillan, 1930.

Walker, Cheryl. *Masks Outrageous and Austere: Culture, Psyche and Persona in Modern Women Poets*. Bloomington, IN: Indiana University Press, 1991.

COLLECTIONS:

Materials relating to Sara Teasdale are located in the Beinecke Rare Book and Manuscript Library of Yale University, the Missouri Historical Society in St. Louis, the Wellesley College Library, the University of Chicago Library, the Rollins College Library, and the library of the State University of New York at Buffalo.

Jeanne A. Ojala, Professor Emerita, Department of History, University of Utah, Salt Lake City, Utah

Teba, countess of.

See Eugénie (1826–1920).

Tebaldi, Renata (1922—)

Italian soprano who possessed one of the most beautiful voices of the mid-20th century. Born in Pesaro, Italy, on February 1, 1922; daughter of Giuseppina (Barbieri) Tebaldi and Teobaldo Tebaldi (a cellist); studied with Brancucci and Campogalliani at the Parma Conservatory, and with Carmen Melis and Giuseppe Pais at the Pesaro Conservatory; never married.

Debuted at Rovigo (1944); chosen by Toscanini to open at Teatro alla Scala (1946); debuted at Covent Garden (1950), San Francisco (1950), and Metropolitan Opera (1955).

Fated to be celebrated as one of the operatic world's greatest singers, to live in fame and wealth, Renata Tebaldi was born into poverty in 1922 in Pesaro, Italy. Even before her birth, her parents had separated, and it would be a long time before Renata learned that her cellist father Teobaldo Tebaldi was not dead but had abandoned her mother **Giuseppina Barbieri Tebaldi** for another woman. While an infant, Renata was taken by her mother and her maternal grandparents to live in Langhirano, a small town near Parma. She was deeply affected by her parents' failed marriage and became strongly attached to Giuseppina. At age three, Renata was stricken with polio. Although her right hip would continue to give her some trouble, she recovered, and while she was studying piano in Parma her teacher discovered that she had a voice with potential. When only 16 (but pretending she was 18), Tebaldi auditioned and was accepted by Parma's music conservatory.

During her second year there, she was invited to spend the Christmas season in Pesaro with her father's brother Valentino, who owned a small café. **Carmen Melis**, a famous former diva, often went there to buy pastries. Melis, though she had retired from the stage as a much-beloved *verismo* singer, now taught singing at the Pesaro conservatory. When Valentino told Melis about Renata's musical aspirations, the diva consented to listen to the young girl in her hotel suite. Very much the prima donna, Melis terrified Tebaldi. But, even though she was critical of Renata's manner of singing, Melis was quickly convinced that the voice had a lovely timbre and considerable potential. The next day, and indeed for the rest of her holiday, Tebaldi went to Melis for coaching. When she returned to Parma, her voice had improved so dramatically that her teachers found it difficult to believe that she was the same singer who had left town only a few weeks earlier.

Not long after, Tebaldi moved to Pesaro permanently in order to take classes with Melis, both at the conservatory and in private. As World War II began to affect Italy more and more, particularly because of frequent bombing raids, the Pesaro conservatory was closed, and Melis moved to the city of Como. Along with her mother, Renata relocated to the safer countryside, but continued to vocalize on her own even under worsening conditions. Teacher and student kept in touch as best they could, and in 1944 Melis informed Tebaldi that she had been able to arrange for her operatic debut in the small but significant role of Elena in Boïto's masterpiece, *Mefistofele*. Ten days before the performance in Rovigo, Tebaldi was able to meet with Melis for intensive study of the role. Melis "was perfectly marvelous," recalled Tebaldi; "she never left me, even in the wings of the theater, until the curtain went up. There I was on the couch, terrified. But la Signora was pleased with the results."

With Italy in chaos during the final phase of the war, Tebaldi had no further opportunities to sing in public, although she worked to perfect her technique for better days ahead. Her great opportunity came in 1946, when she appeared in the Trieste Opera in the role of Desdemona in Verdi's *Otello*. The newcomer was acclaimed, and as news of her talent spread, a music-starved Italy began to realize that a wonderful fresh voice was emerging. While performing in Brescia in 1946, Tebaldi was invited to audition at the fabled La Scala with the legendary Arturo Toscanini, who had just returned to Italy from the United States. Highly impressed, he chose her to perform in a gala concert of Verdi's *Te Deum*, to celebrate the reopening of the war-damaged opera house. As Tebaldi rehearsed, Toscanini said, "Ah, the voice of an angel." Virtually all in the audience that emotion-filled evening were overwhelmed by the celestial quality of Tebaldi's voice, and the "voice of an angel" tag would remain with her for the rest of her career.

Critics then and in later years described Tebaldi's voice in terms ranging from rich and warm to delicate, sumptuous, glowing, velvety, womanly—all virtues bound to capture a public that idolized her. As Schuyler Chapin has noted, it was a combination of all these qualities that made Tebaldi unique, "for whether she let fly with heroic splendor or scaled down to a shimmering pianissimo, she always honored the score with scrupulous care for dynamics." David

McKee has written of "the prodigious float" of Tebaldi's *piano* singing, and Harold Rosenthal's assessment was unstinting in its praise:

> Tebaldi possessed one of the most beautiful Italian voices of this century; she did not indulge in the overabundance of chest notes so dear to many Italian sopranos, and her *mezza voce* singing was a joy to hear. Early in her career her interpretations lacked dramatic conviction, but later they gave evidence of a heightened sense of drama, and the voice, which, in the years following her first London appearances, began to show some strain . . . again became as lovely as it originally was.

Soon after appearing under Toscanini's baton, in May 1947 Tebaldi made her La Scala stage debut in the starring role of Eva in Wagner's *Die Meistersinger von Nürnberg*, sung in Italian as *I maestri cantori*. Critics and audiences were equally ecstatic about the quality of her singing. In 1949, only five years after Tebaldi's debut, the British critic Lord Harewood, having heard Tebaldi in Florence sing the role of Pamira in a revival of Rossini's *L'assedio di Corinto*, reported in the journal *Ballet and Opera*: "she is probably the foremost lirico-dramatic soprano in the world." As Tebaldi's repertoire expanded, she went beyond standard Verdi and Puccini roles, displaying her mastery of title roles in such operas as *Andrea Chénier*, Catalani's *La Wally* (a Toscanini favorite), Spontini's *Olympia*, Handel's *Giulio Cesare*, and Verdi's rarely performed *Giovanna d'Arco*.

In 1950, Tebaldi became an international star with debuts at both London's Covent Garden and the San Francisco Opera, where she sang *Aïda*. At Covent Garden, she appeared as Desdemona on the opening night of the La Scala company's London season; during the same season, she also was heard in Verdi's *Requiem*. Tebaldi accepted the rigors of being an international opera star, often appearing in South American opera houses, where she was frequently compared with the great *Claudia Muzio, especially for her interpretation of Violetta.

Tebaldi made her Metropolitan Opera debut in 1955. The Met's authoritarian director, Rudolf Bing, would describe Tebaldi as an artist with "dimples of iron." Strong willed and even stubborn, she was by nature neither malicious nor unkind, but fate decreed that she and *Maria Callas would be seen as rivals by the media and by many, though by no means all, opera lovers. Tebaldi's long career unfolded during Callas' shorter but more intense career. Callas was seen as the wind of change while Tebaldi represented the more traditional school of singing. Callas also was known for reviving operas while Tebaldi was considered to perform the traditional repertoire. In fact, Tebaldi was a far more innovative singer than critics of the time often realized. She represented an opposite pole for a generation of operagoers who were forced to choose between her and Callas. Recordings, which span almost her entire career, reveal a youthful freshness and a power which could thrill audiences.

As early as 1950, Callas had shown signs of growing resentment at the then-reigning prima donna. By 1951, when both great singers were appearing at Rio de Janeiro's Municipal Opera House, the Greek diva's Tosca was booed, and Callas accused Tebaldi of having organized a cabal against her. When Tebaldi's first Milan appearance in *La Traviata* failed to impress audiences, Callas told the press, "Poor thing, I feel so sorry for her." Privately, Tebaldi commented to Lanfranco Rasponi: "Callas is flamboyant and thrives on this sort of thing. I am not, and I don't feel any need of this. I can stand on my accomplishments. I have my public and she has hers. There is enough space for both of us—to each her own." The Callas-Tebaldi "feud" hit its high (or low) point in 1956, when a *Time* cover story on Callas compared Callas' vocalism to champagne and Tebaldi's to Coca-Cola, with Callas adding that Tebaldi "has no spine." The result was a letter to the editor from Renata with the now-classic rejoinder: "She says I have no spine. That may be, but I have one thing she will never have—a heart."

A master of intrigue as well as a great artist, Maria Callas edged Tebaldi out at La Scala, but the evidence suggests that Tebaldi took these things in stride, shifting the focus of her activities from Europe to New York's Metropolitan Opera. She sang there regularly until 1972, giving more than 250 performances that are still fondly remembered by Manhattan's opera cognoscenti. In the mid-1960s, she suffered a vocal crisis that almost ended her career, but wisely withdrew from performing and after a year of restudying her vocal method came back at the top of her form. Tebaldi's fans remained devoted to her in the later years of her career when her voice began to betray some signs of decline. In her final appearances at the Met in 1973, she performed as Desdemona and Mistress Alice Ford in the two greatest Verdi operas, *Otello* and *Falstaff*. Three years later, in 1976, after a triumphant concert debut in the Soviet Union, Tebaldi retired from singing.

Still a beautiful woman in her 70s, Tebaldi lives elegantly in a sumptuous apartment in

Opposite page

*R*enata *T*ebaldi

Milan, surrounded by the mementos of her career. On the walls are autographs of Verdi, Puccini and other great Italian composers, as well as miniature paintings and photographs of herself in most of her favorite parts. On the piano are autographed photographs of Pope John Paul II and one of herself with President John F. Kennedy and *Jacqueline Kennedy. Asked how she spent her time, Tebaldi responded, "I am honored." Among her many honors have been the *Verdi d'Oro* award in 1973 and a new breed of rose named the Tebaldi Rose. Although opposed in principle to coaching because of what she felt was "the total lack of discipline existing today" among singers, Tebaldi did in fact spend time with a singer if she believed her talent to be extraordinary (as was the case with **Aprile Millo**).

After her own career ended, Tebaldi rarely if ever attended opera performances, being a critic of the "instant stars" of the final decades of the 20th century. ("Where are the big voices today? There are only tiny mosquitoes flying around," she declared to Rasponi.) Looking back with evident pleasure on her extraordinary achievements, she mused, "I don't have any kind of *cattivi pensieri*, any bad thoughts, only wonderful memories. My soul was so near to my singing, it was really an enjoyment for myself. . . . [W]hen you feel like that, it is possible to give to the audience."

SOURCES:

Ashbrook, William. "'Vissi d'arte': Perspectives on an Aria," in *Opera News*. Vol. 46, no. 6. December 5, 1981, p. 49.

Casanova, Carlamaria. *Renata Tebaldi: The Voice of an Angel*. Trans. and ed. by Connie Mandracchia DeCaro. Dallas, TX: Baskerville, 1995.

Chapin, Schuyler. *Sopranos, Mezzos, Tenors, Bassos, and Other Friends*. NY: Crown, 1995.

Christiansen, Rupert. *Prima Donna: A History*. NY: Penguin, 1986.

Forbes, Elizabeth. "Tebaldi: Wonderful Memories," in *Opera*. Vol. 42, no. 8. August 1991, pp. 883–885.

Giles, Patrick. "Real Live Tebaldi," in *Opera News*. Vol. 63, no. 8. February 1999, p. 79.

Graff, Yveta Synek. "Tosca Talks," in *Opera News*. Vol. 50, no. 9. January 18, 1986, pp. 18–23.

Harris, Kenn. *Renata Tebaldi: An Authorized Biography*. NY: Drake, 1974.

Lucano, Ralph V. "Tebaldi Festival," in *American Record Guide*. Vol. 61, no. 2. March–April 1998, pp. 277–278.

"Ludwig Lustig, Musicians' Representative, 94," in *The New York Times*. August 5, 1994, p. B6.

Mackay, Harper. "On the Double," in *Opera News*. Vol. 59, no. 4. October 1994, pp. 16–18, 20, 22.

McKee, David. "Tebaldi in *La Wally*," in *The Opera Quarterly*. Vol. 13, no. 3. Spring 1997, pp. 195–202.

Mordden, Ethan. *Demented: The World of the Opera Diva*. Simon & Schuster, 1990.

Panofsky, Walter. *Renata Tebaldi*. Berlin: Rembrandt, 1961.

Price, Walter. "Renata Resounding," in *Opera News*. Vol. 56, no. 10. February 1, 1992, pp. 16–18.

Rasponi, Lanfranco. *The Last Prima Donnas*. NY: Knopf, 1982.

Rosenthal, Harold D. *Great Singers of Today*. London: Caldor & Boyers, 1966.

———. *Sopranos of Today: Studies of Twenty-Five Opera Singers*. London: J. Calder, 1956.

Schonberg, Harold C. "Backward Glances," in *The Opera Quarterly*. Vol. 10, no. 4. Summer 1994, pp. 51–63.

Seroff, Victor. *Renata Tebaldi: The Woman and the Diva*. Rep. ed. Freeport, NY: Books for Libraries Press, 1970.

Stassinopoulos, Arianna. *Maria Callas: The Woman Behind the Legend*. NY: Ballantine, 1982.

Steane, J.B. *Singers of the Century*. Vol. 2. Portland, OR: Amadeus Press, 1998.

Tebaldi, Renata. "Prima Donnas" [letter to the editor], in *Time*. Vol. 68, no. 22. November 26, 1956, p. 10.

Tommasini, Anthony. "Beverly Peck Johnson, 96, Voice Teacher," in *The New York Times*. January 22, 2001, p. A18.

———. "Terence McEwen Dies at 69; Directed San Francisco Opera," in *The New York Times*. September 23, 1998, p. B12.

———. "Who's Queen of the Met? Her Fans Know Who," in *The New York Times*. December 13, 1995, p. C20.

Van Campen, Mariko. "New York Critics Review Maria Callas and Renata Tebaldi," M.A. thesis, University of British Columbia, 1977.

Willier, Stephen A. "Renata Tebaldi: The Voice of an Angel," in *The Opera Quarterly*. Vol. 13, no. 2. Winter 1996–1997, pp. 116–119.

John Haag,
Associate Professor of History,
University of Georgia,
Athens, Georgia

Teck, duchess of.

See Mary Adelaide (1833–1897).

Tecuichpo (d. 1551).

See Malinche for sidebar.

Teerlinc, Levina (c. 1520–1576)

Flemish artist who painted miniature portraits in Flanders and at the English court. Born Levina Benninck around 1520 (some sources cite 1515) in Bruges, Flanders (now a part of Belgium); died in 1576 in Stepney, England; daughter of Simon Benninck (a painter of miniatures and book illuminator); married; children: Marcus.

Works attributed to 16th-century miniature portrait painter Levina Teerlinc have been hard to document, but it is documented that she was both well known in her native Flanders and favored at the courts of several English kings and queens. She was born around 1520 in Bruges, the daughter of another miniature painter, and

achieved some fame in her own country before migrating to England around 1546 to accept an annuity from the court of Henry VIII. Teerlinc stayed at court for a number of years, working for Edward VI, *Mary I, and *Elizabeth I, whose portrait she first painted in 1551. She received expensive gifts from royalty, and she and her husband occupied a favored position at court. She became an English subject in 1566 and made her home in Stepney.

Teerlinc was the only Flemish miniature painter known to be at the English court between 1546 and the time of her death in 1576. She was also the most important miniaturist between the death of Hans Holbein the Younger in 1543 and the ascent of her successor, Nicolas Hilliard. Probably because she was a woman, her career was mostly overshadowed by that of Hilliard, who also found success in England. Although some works originally attributed to her have since been assigned to other artists, she probably painted an oval miniature showing an Elizabethan Maundy ceremony, which may have been a present from her to the queen. Other miniatures thought to be from her hand are *Portrait of a Young Woman* (1549), *Katherine, Countess of Hertford*, and a portrait of Elizabeth I in her coronation robes that dates to approximately 1559.

SOURCES:

Harris, Ann Sutherland, and Linda Nochlin. *Women Artists: 1550–1950*. Los Angeles County Museum of Art, 1976.

Sally A. Myers, Ph.D.,
freelance writer and editor

Teeters, Nancy Hays (1930—)

First woman on the board of governors of the Federal Reserve Bank. Born on July 29, 1930, in Marion, Indiana; Oberlin College, A.B., 1952; attended University of Michigan, M.A., 1954.

Born in 1930 in Marion, Indiana, Nancy Hays Teeters graduated from Oberlin College in Ohio with an A.B. degree in economics in 1952 and from the University of Michigan with an M.A. in economics in 1954. She was employed as a staff economist from 1957 to 1966 in the government finance section of the board of governors of the Federal Reserve System in Washington, D.C. Teeters served as an economist for the Bureau of the Budget from 1966 to 1970, and was a senior fellow of the Brookings Institute from 1970 to 1973. She and two other authors at Brookings wrote *Setting National Priorities: The*

1972 Budget in 1971, as well as similar documents for the 1973 and 1975 budgets.

From 1974 to 1975, Teeters served as president of the National Economists Club. She was also chief economist for the U.S. House of Representatives Committee on the Budget from 1974 to 1978. Tapped by President Jimmy Carter to serve as a member of the Federal Reserve's board of governors, Teeters held that post from 1978 to 1984, when she became vice-president and chief economist at IBM.

SOURCES:

Read, Phyllis J., and Bernard L. Witlieb. *The Book of Women's Firsts.* NY: Random House, 1992.

Sally A. Myers, Ph.D.,
freelance writer and editor

Teffi, N.A. (1872–1952)

Immensely popular Russian writer, best known for her comic short stories and feuilletons, who continued to enjoy a large readership even after emigrating from Russia in 1919. Name variations: *Nadezhda Aleksandrovna Teffi; Nadezhda Aleksandrovna Lokhvitskaia or Lokhvitskaya; Nadezhda Aleksandrovna Buchinskaia, Buchinskaya, or Buczynska; (pseudonym) Teffi.* Pronunciation: *Na-DYEZH-da A-lek-SAN-drov-na LOKH-vit-ska-ya TEF-fi. Born Nadezhda Aleksandrovna Lokhvitskaia in St. Petersburg, Russia, on May 9, 1872; died in Paris, France, on October 6, 1952; daughter of Aleksandr Lokhvitskii (a prominent St. Petersburg lawyer); mother's name unknown; sister of the poet Mirra Lokhvitskaia (1869–1905) and writers Varvara Lokhvitskaia and Elena Lokhvitskaia; married Vladislav Buchinskii, around 1890; children: daughter Valeriia (b. 1892); daughter Elena; son Jan.*

Gave birth to first of three children (1892); left husband Buchinskii (around 1900) and began a writing career in St. Petersburg; published her first poem (1901); served on the editorial staff of the journal The New Life (1905); published her first two books (1910); emigrated from Russia (1919); settled in Paris (1920).

Poetry: Seven Fires *(St. Petersburg, 1910);* The Salt of the Earth *(St. Petersburg, 1910);* Passion Flower *(Berlin, 1923);* Shamram: Poems of the East *(Berlin, 1923).*

Prose works: Humorous Tales *(2 vols., St. Petersburg, 1910–12);* And So It Became *(St. Petersburg, 1912);* Smoke Without Fire *(St. Petersburg, 1914);* Carousel *(St. Petersburg, 1914);* Nothing of the Sort *(St. Petersburg, 1915);* The Lifeless Beast *(St. Petersburg, 1916);* Evenings *(St. Petersburg, 1918);* Black Iris *(Stockholm, 1921);* The East and Other Stories *(Shang-*

hai, 1921); Treasures of the Earth *(Berlin, 1921);* The Quiet Backwater *(Paris, 1921);* So We Lived *(Stockholm, 1922);* Trot *(Berlin, 1923);* Nocturnal Day *(Prague, 1924);* A Slight of the Hand *(Moscow-Leningrad, 1926);* The Small City *(Paris, 1927);* Parisian Stories *(Moscow-Leningrad, 1927);* Tango of Death *(Moscow-Leningrad, 1927);* A Book—June *(Belgrade, 1931);* Reminiscences *(Paris, 1931);* An Adventure Novel *(Paris, 1932);* The Witch *(Berlin, 1936);* About Tenderness *(Paris, 1938);* Zigzag *(Paris, 1939);* All About Love *(Paris, n.d.);* Earthly Rainbow *(New York, 1952);* Prophet of the Past *(Moscow, 1967);* Stories *(Moscow, 1971);* Nostalgia *(Leningrad, 1989);* Humorous Tales *(Moscow, 1990).*

Plays: Eight Miniatures *(St. Petersburg, 1913);* Miniatures and Monologues *(St. Petersburg, 1915);* Plays *(Paris, 1934).*

Nadezhda Teffi was perhaps one of the most popular women writers in Russia at the turn of the century and in exile during the 1920s, 1930s, and 1940s. She began writing poetry in the Symbolist vein, following in the footsteps of her famous older sister ❧→ **Mirra Lokhvitskaia** (1869–1905), and gradually ex-

---

❧→ Lokhvitskaia, Mirra (1869–1905)

Russian poet and dramatist. Name variations: *Mariia; the Russian *Sappho. Born Mariia Aleksandrovna Lokhvitskaia in 1869; died from tuberculosis in 1905; daughter of Aleksandr Lokhvitskii, a prominent St. Petersburg lawyer; older sister of *N.A. Teffi (1872–1952), the writer; sister of writers* **Varvara Lokhvitskaia** *and* **Elena Lokhvitskaia**; *married in 1892; children: five.*

Between 1896 and 1904, Mirra Lokhvitskaia published five volumes of verse. Though married in 1892 and the mother of five, the charming and beautiful poet had a scandalous affair with Konstantin Bal'mont from 1896 to 1898 which in essence added to her popularity, as did her appearances at poetry readings. Lokhvitskaia's poetry "extended the terms that women poets could use in speaking of love to include overt sensuality [and] self-absorption," notes **Claire Buck**. Two of her books of poetry were awarded the coveted Pushkin prize, the first in 1896, the second posthumously in 1905. The poet also wrote three plays, *On the Road to the East, Immortal Love*, and *In nomine Domini*. "It is important to emphasize," notes Buck, "that in the early 20th century she was the standard against which other women poets were measured."

SOURCES:

Buck, Claire, ed. *Bloomsbury Guide to Women's Literature.* NY: Prentice Hall, 1992.

---

panded her repertoire to include short stories, feuilletons, plays, essays, memoirs, and a novel. Though her verse was perceived by critics as a pale imitation of *fin-de-siécle* poetry, her witty and laconic prose, which took the difficulties of daily life as its subject, was praised by Russian critics and readers alike. In fact, Teffi was so popular in Russia prior to the revolution that her name was used to sell perfume and candy. Unlike many Russian writers, Teffi did not see her creative impulses wane upon leaving Russia after the Bolshevik Revolution. Her ability to find humor in even the most trying circumstances of life in exile appealed to Russian readers who had also emigrated. Through her writings, Teffi became an unofficial spokesperson for the Russian émigré community. And, in this regard, she occupied a position in the émigré circles analogous to that of the Soviet humorist Mikhail Zoshchenko, who employed irony and wit to articulate the concerns of the "little man" in Soviet Russia in the 1920s and 1930s.

Teffi was born Nadezhda Aleksandrovna Lokhvitskaia into a half-Russian, half-French family in St. Petersburg on May 9, 1872. Her father belonged to an old Russian gentry family which had a long-standing relationship to the arts. Teffi's great-grandfather, Kondratii Lokhvitskii (1774–1830), was a Freemason during the reign of Alexander I and a writer of mystical poetry. Her father Aleksandr Lokhvitskii (1830–1884) was a prominent St. Petersburg lawyer and professor, who produced numerous books and articles on jurisprudence and served as editor of *The Judicial Times*. In addition to forging a prominent law career, Teffi's father became highly renowned for his oratory and repartee, and his witty sayings were frequently repeated throughout Russia. Teffi's mother (name unknown) was of French origin and also had creative inclinations. According to Teffi, her mother "loved poetry and was well acquainted with Russian and especially European classics."

In spite of the creativity on both the paternal and maternal sides, Teffi insists that the upbringing of her and her four siblings was rather traditional. "My childhood was spent in a large prosperous family. We were raised in the old manner, all in the very same way. [My parents] did not cope well with individuality and did not expect anything in particular from us." Nevertheless, the Lokhvitskiis managed to produce talented children. In fact, all four of the Lokhvitskiis' daughters distinguished themselves as creative writers. Teffi's eldest sister Mirra Lokhvitskaia established her reputation as a poet of note. Known as the "Russian *Sappho," be-

cause of her gender (rather than her sexual orientation), Mirra Lokhvitskaia received the prestigious Pushkin prize for her poetry twice, including once posthumously. Teffi's two younger sisters, **Varvara** and **Elena Lokhvitskaia**, also wrote. While they never achieved the fame of either Mirra or Nadezhda, they produced several sketches, which were published under the pen name "Miurgit," as well as plays which were performed at various theaters in St. Petersburg including the famous Petersburg comic theater, The Crooked Mirror. Teffi's elder brother Nikolai was the only child who did not forge a literary path for himself. He, instead, chose a military career. He became a general in the Russian army and commanded a regiment in France during World War I.

Teffi attended a gymnasium or secondary school in St. Petersburg and read widely in the Russian classics. As a child, she was enthralled with the works of Aleksandr Pushkin and Leo Tolstoy and even made a pilgrimage to Tolstoy's estate in Khamovniki, intending to request that Tolstoy not "kill off" Prince Bolkonsky in *War and Peace*. Gradually, Teffi's literary interests shifted from the 19th-century classics to the "new literature" of Russian Modernism known as Russian Symbolism. While still in secondary school, Teffi, together with her three sisters, began to write. Believing that it would create competitiveness if all of the sisters began publishing simultaneously, the Lokhvitskiis agreed that the younger sisters should enable the eldest sister Mirra to make her literary debut first. According to Teffi's younger sister, Elena, "Nadezhda would enter second and then I. And we agreed that we would not disrupt Mirra and only when she became famous and finally died would we have the right to publish our works. In the meantime we would write and preserve our works, at least . . . for prosperity." And, in keeping with this, Teffi did not fully launch her literary career until 1904, a little less than a year before the death of her sister Mirra.

Around 1890, Nadezhda Teffi married Vladislav Buchinskii, a Polish aristocrat and graduate of St. Petersburg University in law. Buchinskii became a judge in Tikhvin, where he and Teffi settled. In 1892, Teffi gave birth to a daughter, **Valeriia**, and around this same time, her husband abandoned his law career and moved the family to his estate in Mogilev. After the birth of a second daughter, **Elena**, and a son, Jan, Teffi left Buchinskii and began her career as a writer in St. Petersburg. Teffi published her first work, a poem, in 1901 under her maiden name Nadezhda Lokhvitskaia. She continued writing poetry but eventually expanded her literary enterprises to other genres including humorous plays, short stories, and feuilletons. By 1904, she was a regular contributor to the paper *Stock Market News* for which she wrote witty short sketches and stories that she began signing with the pseudonym "Teffi."

Teffi gave various etymologies for her pen name. In an interview early on in her literary career, she agreed with a journalist who proposed that the pseudonym "Teffi" had been derived from "Taffy," the name of the female character in a Rudyard Kipling story. Later, however, Teffi explained that she had, in fact, styled her pseudonym on the name of a silly friend of the family by the name of Steffi on the premise that fools are always lucky. Reluctant to offend her literary namesake, Teffi kept the true origin of her pen name concealed. Her decision to employ a pen name is interesting in and of itself. The surname "Teffi" not only has a foreign ring in Russian, but it is not gender-marked. In adopting this unmarked foreign-sounding surname, Teffi becomes part of a tradition of women writers in Russian Modernism who chose to employ exotic-sounding, gender-neutral or even masculine pen names to conceal their identity. Other writers include ❧▶ **Poliksena Solov'eva**, who employed the gender-neutral pseudonym Allegro, and *****Zinaida Gippius**, who used the playful masculine pseudonyms Anton Krainii (Anthony "The Extreme") and Tovarishch German (Comrade Herman) for her literary criticism.

In the years surrounding the 1905 Revolution, Teffi not only continued to write humorous short stories under her famous pen name, but she also took advantage of the loosening of censorship and began writing political satire. She even tried her hand at publishing, serving on the editorial board of the liberal journal *The New Life* along with other members of the literary avant-garde, including Maxim Gorky, Zinaida Gippius, *****Zinaida Vengerova**, and Nikolai Minsky. Teffi continued to serve on the journal's editorial staff until November 1905 when Lenin took control of the journal and decided to turn it into a Bolshevik party organ. Thereafter, Teffi's most important literary relationship was with the satirical journal *The Satyricon* (later known as *The New Satyricon*), which was opened in 1908 and featured other comic writers such as Arkady Averchenko. Unlike most of the other contributors of *The Satyricon*, Teffi did not base her humorous sketches on exaggerated characteristics or circumstances, but rather on daily occurrences that at first glance might seem serious. In addition to being a regular contributor to *The*

Satyricon, Teffi played an important role in the Petersburg comic theater, The Crooked Mirror, which was founded in 1908. Teffi's comedy *Love Across the Ages* was featured at the theater's opening night on December 6, 1908, along with a collective production, *The Days of Our Lives*, and V. Azov's *Authors*.

The year 1910 saw the release of Teffi's first two books with the publishing company Shipovnik (Dogrose), a turning point for her writing career. Her first, *Seven Fires*, consisted of 39 poems and one play on an oriental theme. The collection was written in a serious tone, much in the style of Russian Modernism. The reviews were mixed. The Symbolist poet and critic Valerii Briusov wrote:

> All poets from Heine to Blok . . . possess images, epithets, and devices which were copied by Miss Teffi and placed not without artifice into stanzas and new poems. Teffi calls her seven stones "Seven Fires": sapphire, amethyst, alexandrite, ruby, emerald, diamond, and topaz. But Miss Teffi's necklace is crafted from fake stones.

If Teffi's early attempts at poetry were denounced as "fake stones," her prose represented little gems. Her first volume of prose, *Humorous Stories*, published in 1910 was received with "immense success," wrote one biographer, "because the hearts of readers from eight to eighty [could] respond to them." Indeed, with the publication of her initial collection of humorous stories, Teffi seemed to have found her creative niche.

From 1911 and 1918, Teffi published six more major collections of comic stories which were well received by critics and readers alike. She also continued to publish in *The Satyricon* and became a regular contributor to the Moscow paper, *The Russian Word*. This period

---

❧▶ **Solov'eva, Poliksena** (1867–1924)

Russian writer. Name variations: Poliksena Solovieva or Solovieva; (pseudonym) Allegro. Born Poliksena Sergeevna Solov'eva in 1867; died in 1924; daughter of the president of Moscow University; sister of philosopher and theologian Vladimir Solov'ev or Soloviev (1853–1900); studied art and voice; lived with N.I. Manaseina (a children's writer).

Poliksena Solov'eva published her first poems in 1885. Ten years later, after moving to St. Petersburg and meeting *****Zinaida Gippius**, she published *Hoarfrost* under the pseudonym Allegro; the book won the Pushkin prize in 1908. With her companion **N.I. Manaseina**, a children's writer, Solov'eva published a highly respected children's magazine from 1906 to 1913.

marked the height of "Teffimania" in Russia. According to the Russian émigré writer Mark Aldanov, "Hardly any of the other writers in Russia have ever had as enormous a circle of readers as Teffi." He noted that although she published in the liberal press, "both Russias" read her and Tsar Nicholas II was one of her most devoted readers.

In the years directly preceding the revolution, however, Teffi abandoned the humorous tone that readers responded to so well. She not only began to write melancholic poetry, but she even adopted a more somber style in her short stories. In 1916, she published a volume of "serious" stories entitled *The Lifeless Beast* which were later reprinted in exile under the new title *The Quiet Backwater*. In the introduction to this collection, Teffi includes a warning to those readers expecting to find the old, witty Teffi: "In this collection there is much that is not humorous. I include this warning so that those of you seeking laughter and finding instead tears—the pearl of my soul—do not turn around and tear me to pieces."

I was born in St. Petersburg in the springtime and, as everyone knows, our Petersburg spring is extremely changeable. Now the sun is shining. Now it is raining. Therefore, like the pediment of a Greek theater, I also have two faces, one laughing and one weeping.

—N.A. Teffi

While Teffi, like many members of the Russian intelligentsia, was sympathetic toward the February Revolution, she did not support the Bolshevik Revolution. She left Russia in 1919, spending a short time in Kiev and Constantinople and eventually settling permanently in Paris. Teffi began her literary career anew as an émigré by publishing two of her poems in the February 1920 edition of the first Russian émigré journal, *Russia of the Future*. While many Russian writers found it difficult to continue producing works in exile, Teffi flourished as a writer. As the émigré writer Vladislav Khodasevich wrote in 1932, "Only Teffi and I continue to work. All of the other [Russian writers] republish old little things."

From 1920 to 1940, Teffi prepared 19 volumes of short stories (some of which were reprints) as well as two collections of poetry, a novel, memoirs, and a collection of plays. Two of her full-length plays, *A Moment of Fate* and *Nothing of the Sort*, were produced in Paris in 1937 and 1939 respectively. In addition, she wrote regularly for the Parisian émigré paper *The Latest News* as well as for its conservative

competitor *La Renaissance*. Though Teffi's works did not appear in Russia after the 1920s, she enjoyed a large readership in émigré circles throughout Europe and Asia. Collections of her short stories appeared in such places as Shanghai, Stockholm, Berlin, Prague, Belgrade, and New York as well as Paris.

Besides acquiring a substantial publishing record, Teffi occupied an important place in Russian cultural life in exile. She was one of the first members of the Russian émigré community to establish an active literary salon in Paris. Known for her generosity as well as her wit, she was frequently visited by Russian writers in need of support. In addition to running an influential salon, she also played a key role in organizing various foundations for Russian writers and artists. She helped to launch the Shaliapin Foundation which created the Herzen Library in Nice. She was also named a member of the "Real Russian Club" which regularly planned literary and artistic evenings. In addition, she was an active participant in the so-called Russian-French discussions which brought together French and Russian artists and writers for the free exchange of ideas. She was also named assistant director of the Organization of Russian Theatrical and Film Artists at the association's first meeting.

Teffi continued to be a productive member of the Russian literary and artistic community in the '30s and '40s, despite failing health. Because of her illness, she was unable to leave Paris before the German occupation and was forced to spend the war years there. Rumors circulated that Teffi had died in Paris during the war. She, however, survived the conflict and continued to work despite illness and poverty. Witnessing the demise of her contemporaries, Teffi was able to maintain a sense of humor. "All of my contemporaries are dying," she wrote, "but for some reason I keep on living. It is as if I am sitting in a dentist's waiting room. He calls the patients, clearly mixing up the order, but I feel awkward saying so, and sit, tired and spiteful." Teffi's turn finally came on October 6, 1952.

Though one of the most popular writers in turn-of-the-century Russia and in Paris in the 1920s and 1930s, Teffi was all but forgotten in Russia until the 1990s. While she continued to be published in the Soviet Union in the 1920s, she, along with many other émigré writers, was not published under Stalin's regime. Two small volumes of her stories were published in Moscow in 1967 and 1971, after the period of relaxation of censorship known as "The Thaw," and then she was promptly forgotten. Since the advent of Glasnost there has been a renewed interest in Teffi in Russia. In 1989, her memoirs were published in Leningrad, and in 1990 her first volume of prose, *Humorous Stories*, was published again in Moscow.

SOURCES:

Haber, Edythe C. "Nadezhda Teffi," in *Russian Literature Triquarterly*. Vol. 9, 1974, pp. 454–472.

———. "Predislovie" (Foreword) in *Gorodok: Novye rasskazy*. NY: Russica, 1982, pp. i–xiv.

———. "Teffi as a Miniaturist: An Examination of 'Ke fer?' and 'Slepaja'," in *Mnemozina: Studia Litteraria Russica in Honorem Vsevolod Setchkarev*. Joachim T. Baer and Norman W. Ingham, eds. Munich: Fink, 1974, pp. 163–170.

———. "Teffi's Adventure Novel," in *Studies in Russian Literature in Honor of Vsevelod Setchkarev*. J. Connolly and S. Ketchian, eds. Columbus, OH: Slavica, 1986, pp. 140–152.

Mamonova, Tat'iana. "Teffi: Light Humor," in *Russian Women's Studies: Essays on Sexism in Soviet Culture*. NY: Pergamon, 1989, pp. 106–111.

Neatrour, Elizabeth. "'Zhizn' smeetsia i plachet . . .' O sud'be i tvorchestve Teffi" ("'Life Laughs and Cries . . .' On the Fate and Work of Teffi"), in *Nostal'giia: Rasskazy; Vospominaniia*. N. Teffi. Moscow: Khudozhestvennaia literatura, 1989, pp. 3–18.

Nikolaev, D.D. "Zhemchuzhina russkogo iumora" (The Pearl of Russian Humor), in *Iumoristicheskye rasskazy*. N. Teffi. Moscow: Khudozhestvennaia literatura, 1990, pp. 3–18.

Pachmuss, Temira. *A Russian Cultural Revival: A Critical Anthology of Émigré Literature Before 1939*. Knoxville, TN: University of Tennessee Press, 1981, pp. 106–108.

———. *Women Writers in Russian Modernism: An Anthology*. Urbana, IL: University of Illinois Press, 1978, pp. 261–267.

Jenifer Presto,
Assistant Professor of Slavic Languages and Literatures,
University of Southern California,
Los Angeles, California

Tegakwitha (1656–1680).

See Tekakwitha, Kateri.

Tekahionwake (1861–1913).

See Johnson, E. Pauline.

Tekakwitha, Kateri (1656–1680)

*Mohawk who was the first native woman to be beatified by the Roman Catholic Church. Name variations: Tagaskouita; Tegakwitha; also known as Lily of the Mohawks, The Genevieve of New France, La Bonne Catherine, Katherine or Catherine Tekakwitha. Pronunciation: KAT-e-ree Tek-a-QUEE-ta. Born in 1656 at Ossernenon (now Auriesville, New York); died on April 17, 1680, at Caughnawaga, New France (near Montreal, Quebec, Canada); first child of Ken-*horonkwa (a Mohawk chief) *and* Kahenta; *given no formal education; never married; no children.*

On June 22, 1980, to the sounds of prayers in the Mohawk language, Pope John Paul II formally beatified a young native woman, Kateri Tekakwitha. She was the first native to be accorded this distinction, which in most cases leads to eventual canonization as a saint. The process of Kateri's beatification was unusual in that it occurred in a relatively short period of time. A joint Canadian-United States effort to have her candidacy accepted was launched as recently as 1939, and she passed the first stage, being named venerable, only four years later. The process was then delayed because Church authorities would accept only one of the two alleged miracles attributed to her. In 1979, however, the Vatican agreed to suspend this requirement and allowed Kateri to be beatified on the basis of numerous favors reputedly granted to those who had sought her intercession through prayer.

Kateri Tekakwitha was born sometime in 1656 at Ossernenon, a Mohawk settlement situated near the site of the present-day town of Auriesville, New York. Her father Kenhoronkwa was a prominent warrior and chief among the Mohawks. The latter formed the most easterly nation of the extensive Iroquois federation and were greatly feared because of their frequent raids north into New France (the name given to much of modern-day Quebec and Ontario). They were inveterate enemies of the French settlers in the region as well as the settlers' native allies the Hurons and the Algonquins. It was during one of these raids that Kateri's mother, an Algonquin called **Kahenta**, had been taken prisoner (probably by Kenhoronkwa himself) and forcefully taken to Ossernenon.

Kahenta had previously been converted to Christianity by the Jesuit priests at the small mission they had established at Trois-Rivières, New France. Like other Algonquin and Huron captives at Ossernenon, Kahenta was permitted to continue practicing her religious faith on condition that her rituals were conducted in private and that she made no attempt to convert other Mohawks. At that time, few Mohawks were Christians. The few that were had been inspired by the example of Father Isaac Jogues, a French Jesuit murdered near Ossernenon in 1646. There is some dispute in the sources regarding the extent of Kenhoronkwa's role in this atrocity. Whatever the truth, it is known that he refused to allow another Jesuit Father Lemoyne (who made several missions to the Mohawks' Christian captives between 1653 and 1658) to baptize his infant daughter.

When Kateri was about four years old, a devastating smallpox epidemic swept through the Mohawk nation. Within the space of three days, her father, mother, and infant brother all died, and Kateri did not fully escape the effects of the disease. The smallpox virus left her with both a severely disfigured face and very poor eyesight. It was perhaps the latter consequence which gave rise to her being called by the name Tekakwitha. A native child was normally endowed with a name that indicated something about the character or nature of that individual and, in the Mohawk dialect, "Tekakwitha" means "one who approaches, moving something before her." Given her poor eyesight, it is feasible to suggest that her name indicates something about her childhood need for some kind of walking aid.

Following her parents' deaths, Kateri was sent to live with her uncle (whose name has not been recorded) at Gandawagué about five miles from Ossernenon. Little is known about her life at Gandawagué. Her later Jesuit biographers suggested (on what basis it is not clear) that she was a shy, modest but attentive child who was instructed by her aunts in all the basic skills required of a native woman. In 1664, when she was about eight years of age, Kateri was given by her uncle in a juvenile betrothal. Such an arrangement, among the Mohawks, was one method of allying two families together but did not necessarily imply any future settlement between Kateri and her "husband."

[Kateri was] the new star of the new world.

—Francis Xavier de Charlevoix

In the autumn of 1666, the authorities in New France, tired of the constant raids by the Mohawks, sent a small expeditionary force under the command of Prouville de Tracy to subdue them. De Tracy besieged their main encampment at Tionnontogen and, when the Mohawks retreated without any serious resistance, went on to burn their other main settlements, including Ossernenon and Gandawagué. In July of the following year, a peace treaty was signed which included a provision that required the Mohawks to accept the presence of three Jesuit missionaries in their community. When Fathers Frémin, Bruyas, and Pierron arrived in September 1667 at a rebuilt Gandawagué, they were briefly accommodated in Kateri's uncle's lodge. Despite her young age, she was assigned the duty of furnishing the Jesuits' needs during their stay.

In his *History of New France* (published in 1732), another Jesuit priest, Father Francis Xavier de Charlevoix, suggested that the missionaries were so impressed by Kateri's piety that they made a special effort to instruct her in Catholic ritual. This story may be apocryphal because, over the next eight years, she gave no recorded, outward sign of wishing to embrace Catholicism. What is known is that during this period, Father Pierron, who had remained alone in charge of the Mohawk mission at Gandawagué, gradually managed to convert and baptize about half of the natives in the settlement. His task was complicated by occasional outbursts of anti-Christian sentiment (especially from young Mohawk warriors) and by the constant threat of raids on Gandawagué by another native group, the Mohegans. In response to one particularly ferocious raid in the summer of 1669, Kateri and her aunts moved to a safer site close to her former home at Caughnawaga. It was at this moment that her relatives made plans for her to marry.

Up until this time Kateri had always been submissive to the wishes of her family. When they informed her of their plans, however, she was appalled and stubbornly rejected any discussion of the idea (later in life she was to tell one of her spiritual advisors, Father Cholenec, "I hate marriage and am horrified at it"). Her family was deeply insulted by her refusal. Less, it must be stressed, because of her show of youthful rebellion, but, rather because of the effects her choice had on their lives due to the structure of Mohawk society. The Mohawk community was organized on particular matrilinear lines which meant that a bridegroom would become part of his new wife's family. For her aunts and uncle, a new young and strong husband for Kateri would have represented an economic guarantee against the vicissitudes of their old age.

In 1671, Father Pierron left Caughnawaga to take up a new appointment at the St. François Xavier mission located at the Saint-Louis (Lachine) rapids not far from Montreal. This mission, which had been founded some 30 years previously, was at that time one of the most important native Christian communities in North America. Although organized under the overall direction of Jesuit priests, the mission was effectively supervised by two native leaders; Togouiroui (also known as Kryn) and Louis Garonhiagué (known as Hot Ashes or Hot Powder—so-called because of his notoriously volatile temper). At some unknown date, an adopted sister of Kateri's had gone to live at the mission. This event, along with the increasingly numerous defections by other Mohawks to St. François Xavier from Caughnawaga and Gandawagué, greatly angered both Kateri's uncle and other native leaders.

In the summer of 1675, Father Jacques De Lamberville, who later became known among the Iroquois as the "Divine Man," arrived at Caughnawaga. Shortly after his arrival, Kateri revealed to him her desire to be baptized into the Catholic faith. Much to the opposition of her family and other members of the community, she was formally received into the Church on Easter day 1676 and given the name by which she is now popularly known, Kateri (Katherine).

Following Kateri's baptism, both her family and neighbors exerted a strong pressure that was designed to force her to recant her beliefs. Father Lamberville could do little to oppose this campaign and so, early the following year, advised Kateri to leave and travel to the St. François Xavier mission. By coincidence, Hot Ashes happened to be on a visit to Caughnawaga, and he readily agreed to assist in her flight. Following a hazardous journey, during which Kateri's uncle furiously pursued his niece threatening to kill her if he could, she arrived at the mission in the fall of 1677.

At the St. François Xavier mission, Kateri found refuge with **Anastasia Tegonhatsihongo**, an Algonquin native and a previous friend of her mother. Kateri and Anastasia quickly established a close rapport and their relationship was cemented by their mutual enthusiasm and devotion to the Catholic religion.

It was the normal practice among native converts to spend several years at the mission in spiritual training before being formally allowed to receive communion. The priests were so impressed by Kateri's evident piety and devotion to the faith, however, that they made a special decision to allow her to take communion on Christmas day 1677. This unusual distinction was complemented, a few months later, by her reception into the Confrérie de la Sainte-Famille, a pious and long-established association whose membership was almost invariably reserved for those who had been long adherents of the faith.

Throughout their relationship, the only recorded disruption between Kateri and Anastasia came when the latter pressed her friend to consider, once again, the prospect of marriage. Like Kateri's family earlier, Anastasia's motives in this regard were strictly practical. Two women living together alone in a hunter-gatherer society would have experienced on-going

Kateri
Tekakwitha

difficulties in providing those basic necessities required in order to survive. Despite her economic situation and the urgent entreaties of her friend, Kateri refused to even consider such a proposal. Marriage, for Kateri, was an institution that could only serve to distract and divert her from her principal duties in life, fidelity and obedience to the teachings of her spiritual advisors.

It was during this period that Kateri became aware of the life and work of ***Marguerite Bourgeoys**. Marguerite, the founder of a sect of nuns in Montreal, the Sisters of the Congregation of Notre Dame, carried out a variety of nursing and other charitable functions. Her example inspired Kateri to consider founding a new order of nuns that would be composed exclusively of native women dedicated to a contemplative life. Despite Kateri's enthusiasm for this project, Father Lamberville (who was now stationed at the St. François Xavier mission) strongly advised her to reexamine the feasibility of her idea. In the mid-18th century, the Catholic Church in New

France was neither willing nor able to take such a radical step and sanction the formation of a native order of nuns.

Despite this disappointment, Kateri persevered in the commitment to her faith. Although she was not permitted to become a nun, Lamberville and his superiors allowed her, in March 1679, to take a vow of perpetual chastity (one of the single most important professions which a nun is required to make). Following this affirmation, Kateri assumed a rigorously penitential lifestyle. She submitted herself to a variety of painful mortifications (flagellation, fasting, sleep deprivation and so forth). Although she was advised by the Jesuits to modify this painful regime, Kateri consistently refused to yield. It was because of this commitment that she soon became a figure of veneration among her fellow natives, Jesuit priests, and local French settlers. Inevitably, however, this strict lifestyle took a heavy toll on her already weak constitution.

Kateri, who was still only in her early 20s, gradually became so ill that she could no longer walk the short distance from her home to the local church. During her last months, she was racked by endless fevers and suffered constant pain. Eventually her health gave out completely and, as she lay dying, her small home became filled by her friends and neighbors who had come to revere her devotion. Kateri's last act was to exhort these visitors to follow the principles of Christian virtue.

Following her death, on April 17, 1680, Father Cholonec, one of her closest advisors, reported that her face, so severely marked in the past by the effects of the smallpox virus, had miraculously become "beautiful." In the years that followed, numerous intercessions and miracles were recorded by the faithful devotees at her shrine (Kateri's remains were buried in the small chapel of the St. François Xavier mission).

A short time later, Father Chauchetière painted a picture of Kateri (which for many years was displayed in the Church of St. Mary's, in Albany, New York). Chauchetière had a special interest in carrying out this project. Shortly after her death, he had found himself trapped by a violent storm in the church at St. François Xavier. As the walls of the church collapsed around him, Chauchetière, according to his own testimony, addressed a prayer to Kateri and managed to survive the danger. Thus began the cult of Kateri Tekakwitha.

SOURCES:
Béchard, Henri. *L'Héroïque Indienne Kateri Tekakwitha.* Montreal: Editions Fides, 1967.

Buehrle, Marie Cecelia. *Kateri of the Mohawks.* NY: All Saints Press, 1962.
Jodoin, Rachel. *Kateri Tekakwitha.* Outremount, Quebec: Lidec, 1983.
Martini, Teri. *Treasure of the Mohawks.* NY: St. Anthony Guild, 1962.
Walworth, Ellen. *The Lily of the Mohawks, 1656–1680.* Buffalo: Peter Paul and Brother, 1893.
SUGGESTED READING:
Anderson, Karen. *Chain Her by One Foot.* NY: Routledge, 1991.
Richter, Daniel K. *The Ordeal of the Long House.* Chapel Hill, NC: University of North Carolina Press, 1992.

Dave Baxter,
Department of Philosophy,
Wilfrid Laurier University,
Waterloo, Ontario, Canada

Tekakwitha, Katherine (1656–1680).
See Tekakwitha, Kateri.

Teles, Leonor (c. 1350–1386).
See Leonora Telles.

Telesilla (fl. 6th or 5th c. BCE)
Poet from Argos who defended her native city against the Spartan army. Name variations: Telessilla. Flourished in the 6th or 5th century BCE.

Sources written long after Telesilla's time credit her with the following accomplishment (Herodotus, her near contemporary, does not). Cleomenes, a Spartan king, invaded Argos and won a major battle. Many Argives died defending their land, and others fled in disarray to a religious sanctuary where they sought asylum only to be incinerated when Cleomenes set a sacred grove on fire. The losses suffered by the Argive army having been severe, Cleomenes approached Argos itself expecting little resistance. Led by Telesilla, however, the women of Argos organized their city's defense. Calling up slaves, old men and boys, Telesilla and her cohorts ordered them all onto the city's walls where they were meant to impress their oppressors by their numbers. Then, after scrounging up what arms and armor she could muster, Telesilla arrayed in military dress those Argive women who were mature enough to be convincing. Thereafter, she deployed them where she expected the Spartan attack to take place.

Approaching the Argive women thus positioned, the surprised Spartans arrayed for battle and then bellowed their famous war-cry, intending to reduce the Argives to panic. Nonetheless, the Argive women held their line. Coming to realize that they were confronting women, and conscious of the rebuke they would receive among the Greeks at large if they dared to butcher the women facing them, the Spartans withdrew from Argos with their mission unaccomplished. For the courage it took to organize her defense, Telesilla had a statue erected in her honor before a temple of Aphrodite in Argos. Because the statue is historical, so, probably, is the incident which is said to have led to its erection. This statue portrayed Telesilla as a poet with her published works strewn about her feet, while she, distracted from her muse, was in the act of securing a helmet on her head in preparation for battle.

William Greenwalt,
Associate Professor of Classical History,
Santa Clara University,
Santa Clara, California

Telkes, Maria (1900–1995)

Hungarian-born American physical chemist who investigated the practical uses of solar energy. Name variations: Maria de Telkes. Born Maria de Telkes on December 12, 1900, in Budapest, Hungary; died on December 2, 1995, in Budapest; daughter of Aladar de Telkes and Maria (Laban) de Telkes; naturalized U.S. citizen, 1937; Budapest University, B.A., 1920, Ph.D., 1924; never married; no children.

Maria Telkes, born Maria de Telkes in 1900 in Budapest, Hungary, developed her interest in science at an early age. In high school, she began to do extensive research on the sun and the possibilities of solar energy and learned to read the literature on the subject in four different languages. She received a number of academic prizes at Budapest University, from which she received a B.A. degree in 1920 and a Ph.D. in 1924. She taught physics in a Budapest school between 1923 and 1924.

On a visit to Cleveland, Ohio, in 1925, Telkes was invited to join the staff of the Cleveland Clinic Foundation. She continued her research as a biophysicist there until 1937, working for a time with Dr. George Crile on a series of experiments which led to the invention of a photoelectric mechanism for recording the energy of the human brain. She also collaborated with Crile on his book *Phenomena of Life*. After 1937, when she became a citizen of the United States, she was employed for two years as a research engineer at in the laboratories of Westinghouse Electrical and Manufacturing Company in East Pittsburgh, Pennsylvania.

The U.S. Office of Scientific Research and Development called upon Telkes to serve as civilian adviser during World War II. She developed a system for distilling fresh water from sea water, to be used on life rafts. In 1948, she applied some of the same technology to alleviate a water shortage in the Virgin Islands.

Telkes became a research associate in the solar energy conversion program at the Massachusetts Institute of Technology (MIT) in 1939. A solar-heated house designed by *Eleanor Raymond** was built on the estate of a donor **Amelia Peabody** in Dover, Massachusetts. Telkes not only planned the system to be used in the house, but also lived in it for several months to test the system's effectiveness. The key to this solar-power system was the use of sodium sulphate decahydrate, a compound which crystallizes and retains heat. According to subsequent tenants of the house, it maintained a steady temperature, winter and summer. Telkes presented her plan at meetings of the American Association for the Advancement of Science and at a forum sponsored by the *New York Herald Tribune*.

Telkes was the author of many scholarly articles on solar heating, thermoelectric generators and distillers, and electrical conductivity of solids and electrolytes. She did research at New York University, the University of Pennsylvania, and the University of Delaware. She continued

Maria
Telkes

experimenting, developing a solar-powered stove, and in the 1970s worked on an air-conditioning system which would store cool night air for use in the daytime. In 1977, she retired as a senior scientist at the University of Delaware but continued working as a consultant there into the 1990s. Ironically, she died in Budapest in 1995 on her first return visit since 1925.

SOURCES:

Current Biography. NY: H.W. Wilson, 1950.

Graham, Judith, ed. *Current Biography Yearbook.* NY: H.W. Wilson, 1996.

Sally A. Myers, Ph.D.,
freelance writer and editor

Telles, Leonora (c. 1350–1386).

See Leonora Telles.

Telles, Maria (d. 1379).

See Leonora Telles for sidebar.

Tellez, Dora Maria (1957—)

Nicaraguan revolutionary who participated in attempts to overthrow the government of Anastasio Somoza in the 1970s. Born in 1957 in Nicaragua; daughter of a government administrator and Maria Dora Tellez; studied medicine at the University of Leon.

Born in 1957 into an upper-middle-class home in Nicaragua, Dora Maria Tellez was bothered by the divisions among the social classes in her country from an early age. During the late 1960s, she became involved in the activities of the Sandinista National Liberation Front (FSLN), known as the Sandinistas, a revolutionary group opposed to the repressive government of Anastasio Somoza Debayle. After the earthquake which devastated Nicaragua in 1972, Tellez worked to alleviate suffering among the poor of Managua. At age 16 or 17, she was actively recruited by the FSLN and began to work for poor mountain people. After completing high school, she entered the University of Leon to study medicine.

In 1974, after an FSLN raid on the home of "Chema" Castillo, a high-level member of the Somoza government, repression against members of the revolutionary group and their families increased. Tellez went underground in 1976, as more and more political prisoners were taken. For a time she stayed in the mountains and then fled the country, leaving her family wondering about her safety. Not knowing if Dora Maria were dead, her mother was called several times to identify a body others believed to be that of Tellez.

In August 1978, following the assassination of Somoza opponent Pedro Joaquin Chamorro

(husband of *Violeta Chamorro), Tellez was "Commander Two" in the FSLN's occupation of the National Palace. She was one of the leaders who later took the city of Leon for the FSLN and became a hero to many who had opposed the Somoza government. By now the conflict between Somoza forces and the Sandinista guerrillas had grown into a full-scale civil war. Tellez told **Margaret Randall**, "Sandinism is our national identity. . . . It becomes an obsession—the people must rise up, they must."

Tellez recounts many horrific incidents that took place during the war. With no legal protections, innocent people were abducted, tortured, and killed by government forces. She told Randall: "It is impossible to see so much death and go on unaffected or unchanged by it. . . . We've had to live through things most people can't even imagine." After the FSLN assumed power in 1979, Tellez looked forward to assuming a political rather than a military role.

SOURCES:

Randall, Margaret, ed. *Sandino's Daughters: Testimonies of Nicaraguan Women in Struggle.* Vancouver, BC: New Star Books, 1981.

Sally A. Myers, Ph.D.,
freelance writer and editor

Tellez, Eleanor or Leonor (c. 1350–1386).

See Leonora Telles.

Tellez de Meneses, Eleanor (c. 1350–1386).

See Leonora Telles.

Tempest, Marie (1864–1942)

English actress who was hugely popular in both musical comedy and comic plays. Born Mary Susan Etherington on July 15, 1864, in London, England; died on October 14, 1942; educated at Midhurst and at a convent in Belgium; studied singing at the Royal Academy of Music, London; married Alfred E. Izard (divorced); married Cosmo Gordon-Lennox (an actor and playwright), in 1898 (died 1921); married William Graham Browne (an actor-director), in 1921 (died 1937); no children.

Selected theater: made London debut as Fiametta in Boccaccio *(Comedy Theater, May 1885); appeared as Lady Blanche in* The Fay o' Fire *(Opéra Comique, 1885), in the title role in* Erminie *(Comedy Theater, 1885); took over the title role in* Dorothy *(Prince of Wales Theater, 1887); appeared as Kitty in* The Red Hussar *(Lyric Theater, 1889); made New York debut in the same role (Palmer's Theater, August 1889); toured U.S. and Canada with the J.C. Duff Opera Co. (1890–91); appeared as Adam in* The Tyrolean *(Casi-*

no Theater, New York, 1891), O Mimosa San in The Geisha (Daly's Theater, London, 1896), in the title role in San Toy (Daly's Theater, 1899), as Nell Gwynn in English Nell (Prince of Wales Theater, 1900), in the title role in Peg Woffington (Prince of Wales Theater, 1901), as Becky Sharp in Vanity Fair (Prince of Wales Theater, 1901), as Kitty Silverton in The Marriage of Kitty (London and New York, 1903); toured America, Australia, and elsewhere (1914–22); appeared as Annabelle Leigh in Good Gracious, Annabelle (Duke of York's Theater, 1923), as Judith Bliss in Hay Fever (1925), as Angela Fane in The Cat's Cradle (Criterion Theater, 1926), in the title role in The First Mrs. Fraser (Haymarket Theater, 1929), as Fanny Cavendish in Theater Royal (Lyric Theater, 1934), as Georgia Leigh in Short Story (Queen's Theater, 1935), as Dora Randolph in Dear Octopus (Queen's Theater, 1938).

The celebrated English actress Marie Tempest first graced the stage as a singer in operas and musical comedies before taking up serious acting, at which she was also immensely successful, at age 36. Tempest's phenomenal popularity lay not so much in her creative genius, but in her unique ability to bring much of her own personality and temperament to the characters she portrayed. "She seems to radiate the joy of living," wrote a reviewer for the London Times upon seeing her performance in The Cat's Cradle in April 1926, "to drive it home to us by her mere presence, by the inspiring notes of her voice, and by the depth of worldly experience and indulgence for our human foibles in her glance. Briefly she is a perpetual refreshment and source of pleasure; something for which the theater exists and by which it triumphantly justifies its existence."

Born in London in 1864, Tempest was educated at Midhurst and at a convent in Belgium until age 16, when she took up the study of music, first in Paris and then at London's Royal Academy of Music. While still a student, she made her singing debut at St. James's Hall, and from that time on was hooked on performing. Taking her stage name from her godmother, Lady **Susan Vane-Tempest**, she began her career singing in the provinces, and made her London debut in May 1885, in the role of Fiametta in the comic opera Boccaccio. Critics unanimously praised her voice but were somewhat divided on the subject of her acting.

In February 1887, after leading roles in The Fay o' Fire, Erminie, and La Béarnaise, Tempest took over the title role in Dorothy from **Marion Hood**. She played the role for two years, then won great acclaim as Kitty Carroll in The Red

Hussar. Tempest made her American debut in that same role, opening at New York's Palmer Theater on August 5, 1889, to the delight of the critics. "It was a success and from the last notes of the song, Marie Tempest was received into the affections of New York theatergoers," wrote one. "After that the opera seemed to be a secondary consideration and the other players were but foils. Tempest only could fill the stage." The actress then toured the United States and Canada with the J.C. Duff Opera Company, taking roles in several well-known operas, including Arline in The Bohemian Girl, the title role in Mignon, and Mabel in The Pirates of Penzance. In October 1891, she returned to New York, where she was in constant demand for the next three years.

Back in London in 1895, Tempest began a five-year engagement at Daly's Theater, then under the management of George Edwardes. Now considered the queen of musical comedy, she was treated like royalty by Edwardes who insisted that she use the royal entrance rather than the stage door, and saw to it that a carriage wait-

Marie
Tempest

ed for her each evening after the show. Tempest also became the first actress to have her clothes designed by couturiers rather than theatrical designers. In 1898, she met and married actor and playwright Cosmo Gordon-Lennox, who also treated her like royalty, indulging her passion for shopping and redecorating. He introduced her to the world of literature and other intellectual pursuits. (Gordon-Lennox was Tempest's second husband; during her Royal Academy days, she had married and divorced Alfred Izard.)

In 1899, Tempest had a falling out with Edwardes over some long trousers he wanted her to wear for the title role in *San Toy*. She considered them tasteless and cut them into shorts before her first entrance, infuriating Edwardes and destroying their professional relationship. Not only did Tempest walk away from Daly's over the incident, but she turned her back on musical comedy as well. In August 1900, she entered the second phase of her career, opening as *Nell Gwynn** in *English Nell*, a play directed by Dion Boucicault, who also helped Tempest make the transition to straight plays. (She was serious about learning her craft, frequently spending an entire morning rehearsing simple stage business, like answering a phone or pouring a cup of tea.) Boucicault also directed Tempest in the title role in *Peg Woffington**, and as Becky Sharp in an adaptation of *Vanity Fair* (both 1901). In 1902, also under Boucicault's direction, she played Kitty Silverton in *The Marriage of Kitty*, which her husband had adapted from the French. The play, a huge success, marked the beginning of Tempest's eight-year relationship with producer Charles Frohman and remained in her repertoire for the next 30 years.

While Tempest was perfecting her acting technique and gaining a new reputation as a talented comedian, her marriage to Gordon-Lennox collapsed. In 1908, she met William Graham Browne, an aristocrat and actor six years her junior; their relationship is described by Eric Johns as the first deep friendship of her life. Their professional and personal association lasted 29 years, until Browne's death in 1937, although they did not marry until after Gordon-Lennox's death in 1921. Browne directed many of Tempest's productions, and encouraged her to further improve her acting. He also served as troubleshooter. "She was far from easy to work with," writes Johns, "and part of Willie's mission in life was to pour oil over troubled waters and keep the troupe together and in a reasonably happy frame of mind."

In September 1913, Tempest began a stint as manager of the Playhouse Theater in London, where she opened in the title role in *Mary Goes First*. With the outbreak of war in Europe, however, she soon went into debt. To keep afloat, she and Browne set off on a world tour which began in Toronto in October 1914, and over the course of the next eight years took them to New York, Chicago, Australia, New Zealand, South Africa, India, the Straits Settlements, China, Japan, the Philippines, and through the United States. Tempest returned to London's Duke of York's Theater in 1923, playing the role of Annabelle Leigh in *Good Gracious, Annabelle*, which had been warmly received on tour. The London audience, however, hated the play and hissed and booed their disapproval. "How long I stood there, leaning against the wings I do not know," she told her biographer Hector Bolitho. "Dimly I remember clapping my hands over my ears, trying to shut out that cruel noise. Able to bear it no longer, I rushed to my dressing room and closed the door behind me . . . after thirty-seven years as a trouper I had been booed for the first time and in London." Tempest also said that something in her died that night and that afterwards she never felt quite the same about her "dear public." To improve her frame of mind, she revived *The Marriage of Kitty*, and ran nearly a year in it.

It was not until her role as Judith Bliss in Noel Coward's *Hay Fever* (1925), a role written with her in mind, that Tempest had her next unqualified hit. "The most delightful thing of the evening was to see Miss Marie Tempest coming into her own again with a part which gave every scope for her really distinguished sense of comedy and her admirable technique," wrote the critic for *Punch*. She "moved the house to a storm of spontaneous applause by the exquisite singing of a little chanson d'amour, and it was in perfect voice—not a note strained or even thin." *Hay Fever* ran for 337 performances and was followed by *The Cat's Cradle* (1926), another solid hit for the actress.

Tempest continued to perform throughout the 1930s, celebrating her jubilee on May 28, 1935, with a special benefit performance at the Drury Lane Theater. She was made a Dame Commander of the British Empire (DBE) in 1937, which was also the year she lost Willie, a shattering blow from which she never fully recovered. Her last appearance on the London stage was as Dora Randolph in *Dodie Smith's *Dear Octopus*, a successful venture that ran for 373 performances. Glen Byam Shaw, who directed the 67-year-old actress in the play, was awed by her genius for stage business, particularly in a scene in which she was listening to her daughter's problems while setting the table for dinner. "As she listened she made table napkins into the shape of water lilies, but fitted each deft movement to the text, thus pointing the daughter's lines in the most apposite manner. It won a round of applause every night."

Tempest was rehearsing for another role, under the direction of Henry Kendall, when it became clear that she was unable to learn her lines and had to be let go. She took the news bravely, although her eyes were filled with tears as she awaited the taxi to take her home. She died within six weeks, on October 14, 1942. Noel Coward had once paid fitting tribute to Tempest: "When she steps on to a stage a certain magic occurs, and this magic is in itself unexplainable and belongs only to the very great."

SOURCES:
Hartnoll, Phyllis, and Peter Found. *The Concise Oxford Companion to the Theater.* Oxford: Oxford University Press, 1993.

Johns, Eric. *Dames of the Theatre.* New Rochelle, NY: Arlington House, 1974.

Morley, Sheridan. *The Great Stage Stars.* Australia: Angus & Robertson, 1980.

Barbara Morgan,
Melrose, Massachusetts

Temple, Dorothy (1627–1695).

See Osborne, Dorothy.

Temple, Shirley (b. 1928).

See Black, Shirley Temple.

Templeton, Fay (1865–1939)

American stage actress. Born on December 25, 1865, in Little Rock, Arkansas; died on October 3, 1939, in San Francisco, California; daughter of John Templeton and Alice (Vane) Templeton (both actors); married William H. "Billy" West, in 1883 (divorced 1883); possibly married Howell Osborn, in 1885; married William Joshua Patterson, on August 1, 1906 (died 1932).

Selected theatrical appearances: A Midsummer Night's Dream *(1873);* East Lynne *(1870s);* The Mascot, The Pirates of Penzance, *and* Monte Cristo, Junior *(1886);* The Corsair *(1888); (with Weber and Fields)* Hurly Burly *(1898); (with Weber and Fields)* Fiddle-dee-dee *(1900); (with Weber and Fields)* Twirly-Whirly *(1901);* Forty-five Minutes from Broadway *(1906);* H.M.S. Pinafore *(numerous appearances);* Roberta *(1933).*

The cliché "born in a trunk" certainly applies to Fay Templeton, who was born in 1865 in Little Rock while her theatrical parents were on tour in Arkansas. She made her first stage ap-

pearance as an infant, and by age five had her first speaking role. She appeared as Puck in Augustin Daly's production of *A Midsummer Night's Dream* and as Juliet in *Romeo and Juliet* before the age of ten. Other plays in which she performed in her early years included *Ellen Price Wood's melodrama *East Lynne* and several comic operas. A brief first marriage in 1883 to minstrel-show performer William H. (Billy) West ended in divorce after only a few months.

Templeton's career began to take flight around 1885, after she played the character of Gabriel in a revival of *Evangeline.* Critics during this period praised her for her acting, her singing, her comic talents, and her beauty. In 1886, she first appeared in London, and in 1888 she toured with the play *The Corsair,* earning lavish praise from critics and the public. For about seven years after this triumph, she seldom performed, instead traveling abroad with Howell Osborn, a wealthy New Yorker whom she claimed to have married. (No evidence exists for this claim, however.)

The famous vaudeville team of Joe Weber and Lew Fields enticed Templeton to join them in 1898 in their comedy *Hurly Burly.* Though Templeton could no longer play ingenue roles by this time, her voice had matured, and she was unequaled in her talent for mimicry. Another Weber and Fields musical, 1900's *Fiddle-dee-dee,* also made use of Templeton's talents. In that production, Templeton immortalized the song "Ma Blushin' Rosie" ("Rosie, You Are Ma Posie"). Two more Weber and Fields productions, *Hoity Toity* and *Twirly Whirly,* solidified Templeton's musical-comedy reputation. She was known for her contributions to Weber and Fields' burlesques of then-popular plays and for her imitations of other stars, such as *Lillian Russell and *Ethel Barrymore.

In 1903, Templeton starred in a musical, *The Runaways,* and reached the peak of her career playing the lead in George M. Cohan's *Forty-five Minutes from Broadway,* in which she sang "Mary is a Grand Old Name." By the time this successful play closed in 1907, she had married her third husband, William Joshua Patterson, a well-to-do contractor from Pittsburgh, where she resided for most of the rest of her life. For almost three decades following her marriage, she appeared frequently in the role of Buttercup in Gilbert and Sullivan's *H.M.S. Pinafore*—a role which suited her not only because of her talent but because of her increasing girth. Templeton also occasionally appeared with Weber and Fields and made many so-called "farewell appearances." After her husband's death in 1932, she was cast in a Hollywood film, *Broadway to Hollywood* (1933).

That same year, Templeton, now nearly 68, appeared as Aunt Minnie in Jerome Kern's *Roberta*. Because of her health and her enormous size, she played most of the role sitting down but still managed to tour with the company during the 1934–35 season. She moved from Pittsburgh to the Actors Fund Home in Englewood, New Jersey, in 1936, and later to a cousin's home in San Francisco, where she died in 1939. Those who remembered her work were generous with their praise after her death. A *New York Times* obituary noted, "They say there never was a better Buttercup."

SOURCES:

James, Edward T., ed. *Notable American Women, 1607–1950*. Cambridge, MA: The Belknap Press of Harvard University, 1971.

McHenry, Robert, ed. *Famous American Women*. NY: Dover, 1980.

The New York Times. October 4, 5, and 8, 1939.

Sally A. Myers, Ph.D.,
freelance writer and editor

Templeton, Rini (1935–1986)

American-born artist and social activist who used her talents to create art for the masses while living in Mexico. Born Lucille Corinne Templeton in Buffalo, New York, on July 1, 1935; died in Mexico City, Mexico, on June 15, 1986; daughter of Corinne (Flaacke) Templeton and Richard Templeton III; briefly married Alistair Graham (a Scottish musician), in 1956; married a Cuban artist in early 1960s (presumably divorced shortly thereafter); married John DePuy (a painter), on July 16, 1966 (separated by 1973).

Held first solo show at the TAA (Taos Art Association) Stables Gallery (an artists' cooperative) in Taos (November 1–14, 1969); worked in a loose alliance with a group of artists known as the Taos Moderns.

Rini Templeton was born in 1935 in Buffalo, New York, into a middle-class family who, she said, "took their children, as soon as they could walk, to the beach in the summer and the museum in the winter." During World War II, the Templetons moved to Washington, D.C., where her father worked for the Bureau of the Budget. In 1945, ten-year-old Rini's first public display of talent, a poem about V-E Day, was published in the Washington *Evening Star*.

In July 1946, the family moved to Chicago. Given an I.Q. test, Templeton scored so high officials were disbelieving, and the test was administered twice more. Because they were finally convinced of the results, Templeton received a full scholarship to the Laboratory School of the University of Chicago, a school primarily set up for faculty children; while there, she was editor of the Lab School newspaper, learned photography, and built her own darkroom. From 1947 to 1949, she was a "Quiz Kid" on NBC's popular radio—and later television—show. The program was built around a panel of prodigies who answered questions in various fields; Rini's areas of expertise were Shakespeare, music (especially opera), and baseball. In 1949, she published *Chicagoverse*, a collection of poems.

Templeton was a rebel early on. Though she completed all courses at the Lab School, she did not receive her degree because she refused to take physical education. From 1951 to 1952, she took graduate courses at the University of Chicago, where she was on the editorial board of the newspaper, *The Maroon*. The entire board, however, was blacklisted because of fallout from the workings of Senator Joseph McCarthy. Conflict with her parents caused her to move to a university dormitory. Then, in August 1952, the 17-year-old Templeton disappeared from home and hitchhiked through some 30 states, taking odd jobs like dishwashing. She was gone for almost 18 months. On her return, she apprenticed in the print shop of illustrator and printer Philip Reed.

With her "Quiz Kid" money, Templeton roamed Europe. Her sister **Jean Templeton** remembers seeing the 18-year-old off at a New York pier in mid-December 1953: "The day was cold and dreary when we went to the pier where she was to board the *Rotterdam*. . . . [A]s the ship pulled out . . . , I could see a lone figure up in the bow, silhouetted against the grey sky. It was Rini, alone, heading into the stormy sea." Templeton spent part of 1955–56 in Paris, lived that winter in Majorca, where she did her first known commercial art work, and in 1956 studied sculpture in England under Bernard Meadows at the Bath Academy, Corsham. She was also briefly married to a Scotsman. Returning home, she lived for a few months with an aunt before returning to her parents' home, where she set up a sculpture studio.

From 1958 to 1960, Templeton lived in Taos, New Mexico, working as art editor for the progressive newspaper *El Crepúsculo* (The Dawn) with **Mildred Tolbert**, Edward Abbey and others. She took the summer off to study sculpture with Harold Tovish at the Skowhegan School of Painting and Sculpture in Skowhegan,

Maine; she also studied printmaking at *La Esmeralda*, a highly respected workshop in Mexico City that would later be integrated into the National Institute of Fine Arts. She was taught etching by Isidoro Ocampo, and also studied in the Mexican state of Guerrero.

To celebrate the success of the Cuban Revolution, Templeton traveled to Cuba in January 1959 with a group of Mexican students. With the exception of a brief sojourn home to care for her convalescing mother, she remained in Cuba until November1964. She tutored in the Literacy Campaign, cut sugar cane, taught pottery making, helped found the Taller de Grabado de Catedral de La Habana (Havana Cathedral Printmaking Workshop), and published articles and letters defending the revolution in *The National Guardian* (1961–62).

While in Cuba her U.S. passport expired, impeding a return home. For the 1964 Christmas holidays, she met her parents in Montreal, Canada. The following year, her father pulled strings to bring his daughter back to the States, but Templeton was told she could not teach or speak about Cuba and could not make "any propaganda in favor of the revolution." Though Templeton was not anti-American, she was against big government and big business. She once told Rodolfo Lacy:

> When I was in Cuba, the Bay of Pigs invasion took place; the U.S. Ambassador told us Americans to leave, because he could not guarantee our security. A group of people, including myself, decided to stay and express our solidarity with the Cuban Revolution, and join the march against the invasion. I was the standard-bearer of our group, and I carried the U.S. flag through the streets of Havana as an expression of the people I belong to, who do not want war or exploitation in the world.

Moving to the Taos area, she became involved with Native American life and culture. The nomadic Templeton lived in a series of locations and homes, including that of painters Louis Riback and **Beatrice Mandelman**. In 1966, she married painter John DePuy; they set up housekeeping on Pilar Hill near Taos. "Rini had a shed where she welded her sculptures," wrote **Valentina Valdez**, a frequent visitor. "There was a little Coleman heater which didn't heat at all. I would go in there when Rini was working and maybe I would stay 15 or 20 minutes, then leave because it was freezing. Rini would work in there for hours."

In 1968–74, numerous exhibitions included the sculptures and silkscreens of Templeton and her husband. Working closely with the Chicano movement, she was staff artist for the newspapers *El Grito del Norte* and the *New Mexico Review*, and for the Rio Arriba People's Clinic and the Agricultural Cooperative of Tierra Amarilla. She also worked at the Taller Gráfico, a silkscreen plant in an old parochial school in the village of Los Ojos that produced calendars, cards and prints. Working late into the night, she would rise at dawn the next day. Templeton continued to print flyers and posters, placing them in strategic places throughout northern New Mexico. One of her heroes was Mexican engraver José Guadalupe Posada, who printed political satire against dictator Porfirio Díaz on cheap paper, selling them for a few centavos.

Turning away from sculpture, Templeton moved to Mexico City in late 1974, to study printmaking in a country known for its graphic tradition. She first stayed with Spanish photographer Manolo, then settled in San Jerónimo, on the outskirts of Mexico City. Since graphics could be mass produced (Templeton called it Xerox art), she felt it had a more immediate impact on people and could convey a cultural reality vividly and cheaply. Other art was an indulgence during difficult times; it was too costly to be made available to ordinary people. Said Templeton:

Rini Templeton

Sculpture seems to me to have a basically celebrative character—which I guess is why I love it, and always have one corner of hope of getting back to it someday. But it seems to me that in this particular time, in this continent, it is not really a time for celebration. At least not in any context I have been able to find, to make and place sculpture. There is a Uruguayan writer, Benedetti, who speaks of the "Art of Emergency." And in two senses: because our times are times of crisis, of emergency, and, says this writer, remember the other sense of the word, remember the verb To Emerge. Be aware that the people of our continent are emerging. Make what can be an art of emergence . . . . That says better than I could what I'm trying to do.

Templeton joined the Taller de la Gráfica Popular (TGP, Popular Graphic Workshop), started by Leopoldo Méndez during the 1930s, as well as the Taller de Arte e Ideologia (Art and Ideology Workshop) and *Punto Crítico* (Critical Point) magazine. Again she spent long periods of time in workshops. "It was quite normal to see her leave and come back 15 or 20 days later, in an old car where she seemed to carry everything she owned: a change of clothes, her work materials, some blankets and a little food," wrote fellow worker Reynaldo Olivares. "We were poor in those days but our work was intense."

*W*e must abandon all forms of cultural arrogance.

—**Rini Templeton**

Templeton made many trips back to the United States. Touring the West Coast, she proposed an exhibit on history of Mexico for Chicanos. She also designed the books *450 Years of Chicano History* for Chicano Communications Center and *Beyond the Border: Mexico and the U.S. Today*, and a translation of Mexican muralist David Alfaro Siqueiros' book *Como se pinta un mural* (How to Paint a Mural).

Still an activist, Templeton also traveled throughout Mexico to strikes and marches. Her unsigned drawings filled the publications of diverse movements. Invited by the Sandinista government, Templeton journeyed to Nicaragua in 1980 to train others in producing agit-prop materials.

Throughout the 1980s, Templeton worked for the homeless, and joined any group engaged in struggle: movements for labor, Chicano, land-grant, revolutionary, and social justice. Leaving San Jerónimo in late 1984, she moved to a rooftop room in Mexico City where she worked under the sky and from which she could see the mountains and the city. After the May Day

march of 1985 in Mexico City, the Mexican police pursued her for being "a foreigner participating in Mexican politics," but Templeton loved Mexico. In a May 28, 1981, letter concerning the death of Chicana leader **Magdalena Mora,** she wrote:

Magdalena is buried high on a Michoacán hillside, you can see the farms and towns, there are highways and mines, old *milpas* and high trees, mountains into the distance. Once dead, there is no better place that she could be. Except where she also is, in the hearts of us who had the joy to know her, and who now have the responsibility to carry forward her loving and combative spirit in the fight for the construction of socialism *sin fronteras.*

Out of the country during the 1985 Mexican earthquakes, Templeton returned to organize and fund raise. Her last trip to the United States was in 1986.

A tall woman with long, blonde hair and bangs, who spoke flawless Spanish, Rini Templeton was described as warm and loving, but intensely private. Though she would talk revolution and politics into the night, she was reticent when it came to family. After a 1985 family reunion in Hawaii, she wrote a friend that it was a good meeting: "Neruda said, don't forget the rocks." Because of an aversion to telephones, Templeton was known for her sudden disappearances and just as sudden returns. She was also an intrepid smoker of filterless Delicados who barely took time out for eating or sleeping; her self-imposed 16-hour work days took their toll.

On June 15, 1986, Rini Templeton's body was found in her room, where she had died suddenly and alone, days before, of natural causes: her heart had given out. Her ashes were kept at the U.S. Embassy, where she had so often stood outside in protest, then scattered in New Mexico. In Mexico City, a memorial was held on June 23 and the Rini Templeton Center of Graphic Documentation was established. After the Mexican earthquake, 400 apartments were given to earthquake victims. Units in the housing complex were named after Mexican heroes; one was named Rini Templeton. "Rini lived in an exciting era," noted **Enriqueta Vásquez,** "when history was for the making. . . . Chicanos were learning, teaching, experimenting and experiencing great change. We were on fire, alive, vibrant with a cause. It was a time of structuring a new tomorrow, and everybody or anybody was needed. It was an era of planting new seeds and the seeds were carried by many. Rini was such a carrier." Rini Templeton left behind sculptures, dozens of silkscreen prints, over 100 sketchbooks, over 9,000 drawings, and the oft-repeated saying, "Where there is life and struggle, there is Rini Templeton."

SOURCES:

El Arte de Rini Templeton: The Art of Rini Templeton. Foreword by John Nichols. Mexico, D.F.: Centro de Documentación Gráfica Rini Templeton; Seattle, WA: The Real Comet Press, n.d.

ten Boom, Corrie (1892–1983)

Dutch Evangelical who aided the underground during World War II, helping to save over 700 Jews from Nazi genocide, and spoke and wrote widely about her experiences and religious faith after the war. Born on April 15, 1892, in Haarlem, Holland; died on April 15, 1983, in Orange County, California; youngest daughter and one of four children (three girls and a boy) of Casper ten Boom (a watchmaker) and Cornelia ten Boom; attended Bible school; trained as a watchmaker, 1920–22; never married; no children.

One of four children of a Dutch watchmaker, Corrie ten Boom was born in 1892 and grew up in rooms above a clock shop in Haarlem, Holland, which had been opened in 1837 by her grandfather Willem and passed down to her father Casper. In addition to running their business, the ten Boom family were devout Christians who devoted themselves to social and religious causes within the community. Their house, called Béjé (short for Barteljorisstraat), was always open to anyone in need. Corrie, characterized as a rough-and-tumble, stubborn child, lost her mother in 1919. She attended Bible school and later trained as a watchmaker, becoming the first woman watchmaker licensed in Holland. In 1923, she organized the first girls' club in her community which later became part of the larger Triangle Club.

During the Nazi occupation in 1940, Corrie's brother Willem was the initial member of the family to became active in the underground rescue movement, but it was not long before the entire family was involved. "We had not planned our rescue work," Corrie said later. "People started coming to us, saying, 'The Gestapo is behind us,' and we took them in. Soon others followed." At any time, there were usually about six or seven people illegally housed with the ten Booms. Corrie became an organizer for the Haarlem underground, "the B group," which helped to locate other Dutch families brave enough to house the refugees. From 1943 to 1944, the ten Booms and their network of friends saved over 700 Jews, and protected scores of Dutch underground workers.

On February 28, 1944, the family was betrayed, and the Gestapo raided the house, conducting a systematic search. On that day, there were two Jewish men, two Jewish women, and two members of the Dutch underground hiding behind a false wall in Corrie's bedroom. They remained undiscovered, but Corrie and five other members of her family were arrested and taken to prison, as were some 15 of their friends who had come to the house throughout the day, unaware that the Gestapo waited inside. Although the house remained under guard, within two days the Resistance was able to rescue the hidden refugees, who had remained in silence within the cramped quarters with no water and very little food. All but one of them, a resistance worker, survived the war.

The ten Boom family was sent to Scheveningen Prison, where Casper, age 84, died ten days later. Corrie and her sister **Betsie ten Boom** were transferred first to Vught, then to Ravensbrück in Germany, where Betsie died in December 1944. Corrie survived and was released from the camp through a clerical error. (Corrie's nephew Kik also died in a prison camp during the war.

Corrie ten Boom

Her brother Willem was released from Scheveningen, but had already contracted tuberculosis of the spine, which he died of shortly after the war. Another sister **Nollie ten Boom**, who had been arrested with the rest of the family, survived along with Corrie.)

Corrie returned to Holland believing that her life was a gift from God. "There is no pit so deep that God's love is not deeper still," she often said. "God will give us the love to be able to forgive our enemies." In response to many invitations to share her experiences, she began a traveling ministry, taking her message to Christian groups and prisons in 60 countries over the next 32 years. Calling herself a "Tramp for the Lord," which also became the title of one of her books, she preached the Gospel of Jesus Christ, with an emphasis on forgiveness.

Her own spirit of forgiveness was tested in 1947, when, following a speaking engagement in Germany, she encountered one of the guards from Ravensbrück. Not recognizing her, he came forward following her talk and told her that he had become a Christian after the war. "I know that God has forgiven me for the cruel things I did there," he said, "but I would like to hear it from your lips as well." Remembering the horrors she and her sister had faced at Ravensbrück, Corrie wrestled with the decision to forgive him, which she called the most difficult thing she would ever have to do. "For I had to do it," she later explained, "I knew that. The message that God forgives has a prior condition: that we forgive those who have injured us." As she reached rather woodenly to take the hand that he proffered, she experienced a transformation. "The current started in my shoulder, raced down my arm, sprang into our joined hands," she wrote. "And then this healing warmth seemed to flood my whole being, bringing tears to my eyes. 'I forgive you, brother!' I cried. 'With all my heart.' For a long moment we grasped each other's hands, the former guard and the former prisoner. I had never known God's love so intensely as I did then." She returned to her travel with renewed commitment.

In addition to her travels, ten Boom was a prolific writer. In 1971, her book *The Hiding Place* became a bestseller. With the release of the movie in 1975, which starred ***Julie Harris**, she became a celebrity within the Evangelical community. Soon afterward, at age 84, she gave up her travels and settled in the United States, purchasing a modest home in Orange County, California. On August 23, 1978, ten Boom suffered a massive stroke which left her totally incapacitated. She survived until 1983, dying on her 91st birthday.

Corrie's memory, and that of her family, lives on at the ten Boom house, which is once again open to all as a museum. The ten Boom Clock and Watch shop has also been refurbished, and is overseen by a watchmaker who repairs watches on the premises. The family is also remembered at the Holocaust Museum in Jerusalem. There, in the Garden of Righteousness, Corrie ten Boom planted a tree in 1968, honoring the many Jewish lives her family saved.

SUGGESTED READING:
Carlson, Carole C. *Corrie ten Boom: Her Life, Her Faith.* Ravell, 1983.
Rosewell, Pamela (Moore). *Five Silent Years of Corrie ten Boom.* Zondervan, 1986.
Stamps, Ellen de Kroon. *My Years with Corrie.* Revell, 1978.
Wellman, Sam. *Corrie ten Boom.* Barbour, 1995.
RELATED MEDIA:
The Hiding Place (150 min. film), starring **Eileen Heckart**, Arthur O'Connell, Julie Harris as Betsie and **Jeannette Cliff** as Corrie, produced by World Wide, 1975.

Barbara Morgan,
Melrose, Massachusetts

Tencin, Claudine Alexandrine Guérin de (1685–1749).

See Salonnières for sidebar.

Teng (r. 105–121).

See Deng.

Teng Yingchao or Ying-ch'ao (1903–1992).

See Deng Yingchao.

Teng Yü-chih (b. 1900).

See Deng Yuzhi.

Teng, Teresa (1953–1995)

Taiwanese popular singer. Name variations: Little Teng. Born in 1953 in Taiwan; died of heart failure at age 43, after suffering an asthma attack, on May 8, 1995, in Chiang Mai, Thailand.

Born in Taiwan in 1953, pop singer Teresa Teng became a Chinese superstar after that nation became more open in the late 1970s. She was one of the first foreign artists to gain such a following, but Teng became a capitalist symbol in the eyes of the authorities. When her Mandarin love songs were banned in Beijing during the crackdowns throughout the 1980s, her records were smuggled in through Hong Kong. "It was said that 'Little Teng,'" noted *Time*, "was more popular than 'Old Deng' Xiaoping." When the cultural climate eased in China, her music again sold briskly. The songwriter Tsuo Hung-yun described her voice as "seven parts sweetness, three parts tears." Teresa Teng died suddenly after an asthma attack in 1995 in Chiang Mai, a northern resort city in Thailand, where she was on holiday.

Sally A. Myers, Ph.D.,
freelance writer and editor

Tennant, Eleanor.

See Connolly, Maureen for sidebar.

Tennant, Kylie (1912–1988)

Australian writer. Name variations: Kylie Tennant Rodd. Born Kathleen Tennant on March 12, 1912, in Manly, New South Wales, Australia; died on February 28, 1988, in Sydney, Australia; daughter of Thomas Walter Tennant and Kathleen (Tolhurst) Tennant; attended Brighton College and University of Sydney; married Lewis Charles Rodd (a schoolteacher and headmaster), on November 21, 1932 (died 1979); children: (daughter) Benison Rodd; John Laurence Rodd (died 1978).

Awards: S.H. Prior Memorial Prize for Tiburon *(1935) and* The Battlers *(1941); gold medal, Australian Literary Society for* The Battlers *(1941); fellowship from Commonwealth Literary Fund (1951); Commonwealth Jubilee Stage Play Award for* Tether a Dragon *(1952); Children's Book of the Year Award, Australian Children's Book Council (1960), for* All the Proud Tribesmen; *Officer of the Order of Australia (1980).*

Worked at various jobs (1928–32); full-time writer (1935–59); worked as journalist, editor, and publishing adviser (1959–69); full-time writer (1969–88); lecturer for Commonwealth Literary Fund (1957–58), member of advisory board (1961–73); member of board, Australian Aborigines Cooperatives; made appearances on Australian television and radio.

Selected novels: Tiburon *(originally serialized in* Bulletin, *1935, Endeavor Press, 1935);* Foveaux *(Gollancz, 1939);* The Battlers *(Macmillan, 1941);* Ride on, Stranger *(Macmillan, 1943);* Time Enough Later *(Macmillan, 1943);* Lost Haven *(Macmillan, 1946);* The Joyful Condemned *(St. Martin's, 1953, complete version published as* Tell Morning This, *Angus & Robertson, 1968);* The Honey Flow *(St. Martin's, 1956);* Tantavallon *(Macmillan, 1983).*

Short stories: (contributor) Edith M. Fry, ed., Tales by Australians *(British Authors' Press, 1939); (contributor) Cecil Mann, ed.,* Coast to Coast 1941 *(Angus & Robertson, 1941); (contributor) T. Inglis Moore, ed.,* Australia Writes *(Cheshire, 1953); (con-*

tributor) H.P. Heseltine, ed., Australian Idiom *(Cheshire, 1963); (general ed. and contributor)* Great Stories of Australia *(7 vols., St. Martin's, 1963–66); (general ed. and contributor)* Summer's Tales *(2 vols., St. Martin's, 1964–65);* Ma Jones and the Little White Cannibals *(collection, St. Martin's, 1967); (contributor)* The Cool Man and Other Contemporary Stories by Australian Authors *(Angus & Robertson, 1973).*

Nonfiction: Australia: Her Story; Notes on a Nation *(St. Martin's, 1953); (travelogue)* Speak You So Gently *(Gollancz, 1959); (with husband Lewis C. Rodd)* The Australian Essay *(Cheshire, 1968); (biography of Herbert Vere Evatt)* Evatt: Politics and Justice *(Angus & Robertson, 1970);* The Missing Heir: The Autobiography of Kylie Tennant *(Macmillan, 1986).*

Juveniles: John o' the Forest and Other Plays *(Macmillan, 1950);* The Bells of the City and Other Plays *(Macmillan, 1955);* The Bushrangers' Christmas Eve and Other Plays *(Macmillan, 1959);* All the Proud Tribesmen *(story, illustrated by Clem Seale, St. Martin's, 1959);* Trail Blazers of the Air *(stories, St. Martin's, 1966);* Tether a Dragon *(play, Associated Gener-*

*Kylie
Tennant*

al Publications, 1952); Long John Silver: The Story of the Film; Adapted by K. Tennant from the . . . Screenplay by Martin Rackin (Associated General Publications, 1954); The Man on the Headland (fictionalized biography, Angus & Robertson, 1971). Critic for Sydney Morning Herald. Australian literary advisor to Macmillan & Co.

A noted Australian author of social-realist fiction, Kylie Tennant wrote novels offering spirited and authentic portrayals of Australian life. Her award-winning 1935 first novel Tiburon, profiling a small town during the Depression, launched a prolific writing career that, in addition to nine more novels, saw her produce short stories, nonfiction, plays, and criticism. Noted for emphasizing the externals of human experience, Tennant's fiction abounds with authentic place descriptions, colorful characters, and fast-paced, witty dialogue. Although she often emerges as a reformer—Tennant's writings display an affinity for characters besieged by modern societal ills—at the same time she demonstrates a good-natured acceptance of some of life's harsher conditions. The obituary writer for the London Times noted that Tennant's "desire to improve society was at odds in her with her almost Brechtian celebration of its rougher elements and her conviction that human nature was not likely to change."

Tennant was born in Manly, New South Wales, in 1912, and originally named Kathleen. She acquired the name "Kylie"—an Australian Aborigine word for boomerang—during childhood, and kept it all of her life. Tennant left school at the age of 16, after which she took on a variety of jobs, including work for the Australian Broadcasting Commission, work as a salesgirl, and operating a chicken farm. For a year she attended the University of Sydney as a psychology student. In 1932, she hitchhiked and jumped trains throughout New South Wales, eventually ending up in the northern city of Coonabarabran where she married her husband. Three years later, Tiburon appeared, garnering critical praise for its authentic and lively depiction of the residents of a small New South Wales village living on handouts during the Great Depression. Tiburon won for its 23-year-old author the S.H. Prior Memorial Prize and, as the Times obituary writer notes, "a certain notoriety amongst the polite readership for its many swipes at things they held sacred, such as local politics and bureaucracy."

Throughout her writing career, Tennant was noted for the rigorous and thorough research she invested in her novels—often gained through firsthand experience. For The Battlers, she camped with vagabonds and migrant laborers, traveling across Australia in a cart. For The Joyful Condemned, Tennant lived among prostitutes and the slum inhabitants of Sydney—even managing to get herself thrown into jail. For other novels, she turned to technical tasks. Preparing for Lost Haven, she studied shipbuilding, and for The Honey Flow accompanied bee-keepers on their annual migrations through the blossoming eucalyptus trees of Australia. Tennant once commented that her preference was for people who existed on the margins of modern industrial society.

Critics praised Tennant's ability to portray authentically, with understanding and honesty, a spectrum of unordinary characters, locales, and situations. Regarding The Battlers, which profiles the lives of hobos, vagrants, and migrant workers, Lionel Bridge commented in Commonweal: "Here is a combination of the most unusual events happening to the most original characters in the strangest setting the American fiction audience is likely to be offered again." J.S. Southron in The New York Times praised both Tennant's control of her subject matter and its integrity: "There are enough stories in 'The Battlers' to have filled a novel twice the size in the hands of a less concise, less artistic writer. And there is the curious affection aroused in us for characters as unglamorous and devoid of showmanship as they are genuine. It is a book whose outstanding feature is the sort of strength that compels admiration." Klaus Lambrecht in the Saturday Review of Literature called The Battlers "a most appealing book" in that "there is humor in it and a bitter realism, tragedy and love, warmth and cruelty, and sensitive conception of a peculiar form of life." Tennant's third novel won her another S.H. Prior Memorial Prize, in addition to a gold medal from the Australian Literary Society.

Like The Battlers, Tennant's other novels were noted for empathetic and vigorous characterizations. In Ride on, Stranger, she tells of an Australian girl who leaves her family of seven "on a career of moderately healthy disillusionment among faith-healers, occultists, left-wings, aesthetes and others," according to a reviewer for the Times Literary Supplement. John Hampon in Spectator called Tennant a "lively gifted writer," who, in Ride on, Stranger, "handles the seamy side of life with robust vigour." The Times Literary Supplement reviewer added: "There is a good deal of fun in this sprawling, crowded story of uncultivated types in the Australian wilds and of excessively cultivated or freakish types in Sydney, and with the fun goes a certain hard honesty of sentiment that is frequently telling." Regarding the 1946 novel *Lost Haven*, Robert Traver noted in *Book Week* that Tennant displayed "a remarkable facility for figurative expression, the evocative phrase." He added that, although such "occasionally gets a trifle out of hand" and that "at times she pelts the reader with words," when Tennant "wants to—which is most of the time—she can write like an inspired demon."

One of Tennant's most praised works is the 1953 novel *The Joyful Condemned*, initially published in abridged form due to a paper shortage and fears of censorship backlash, and reissued 15 years later in its entirety as *Tell Morning This*. Tennant's longest novel, *The Joyful Condemned*, traces the lives of several working-class girls in wartime Sydney who indulge themselves in the worlds of the slums. Tennant "is remarkably skilful in conveying the helpless ignorance of such girls in [the] face of authority and their eagerness to escape from the gentility of middle-class life into the riotous freedom of their own world," noted a reviewer for the *Times Literary Supplement*. **Sylvia Stallings** wrote in the *New York Herald Tribune Book Review* that Tennant's "quick ear and eye bring home both the raciness of underworld speech and the curious beauty of the city at night, the searchlights 'working through the clouds like the fingers of a wool-classer through fleeces.' Her novel comes as a great wash of fresh air after the thin-blooded elegance of so many of her peers." Upon the novel's reissue as *Tell Morning This*, a reviewer for the *Times Literary Supplement* commented that the book was "told with clarity and honesty, and even, despite the bumpiness of much of the writing, a degree of poetic sensitivity."

In addition to her celebrated fiction, Tennant wrote in other genres, continuing to demonstrate thorough and thoughtful treatment of subject matter. *Australia: Her Story; Notes on a Nation* was praised by Fritz Stern in the *Saturday Review* as an "excellent example of popular history, an art which nowadays is too often neglected in favor of specialized treatises or historical novels which mistake life for lust." Tennant's 1970 biography of Herbert Vere Evatt, *Evatt: Politics and Justice*, "goes a long way towards doing justice to the most fascinating figure in the Australian labour movement since W.M. Hughes," according to a *Times Literary Supplement* reviewer, who singled out both Tennant's "control of complex material and events" and her "insight into Evatt's character." And in her 1959

children's book *All the Proud Tribesmen*, Tennant relates the lifestyles and history of Australia's Aborigines. P.D. Beard noted in *Library Journal* that Tennant's story "reveal[s] keen insight into the minds of a people and a fine sense of local atmosphere." Howard Boston likewise commented in *The New York Times Book Review* that in *All the Proud Tribesmen*, Tennant's "characterization is deft and sure, and she is adept at juggling several themes simultaneously." "The story's real strength, though," added Boston, "lies in its sensitive and appealing portrayal of the island folk."

Tennant's last novel, *Tantavallon*, published in 1983, displays the complexion of her earlier novels, offering a panorama of varied characters and situations. Featured in *Tantavallon*, notes Ken Goodwin in *A History of Australian Literature*, are "Vietnamese migrants mining uranium, a churchwarden attempting suicide in Sydney Harbour, a fire, a suburban street battle, a spectacular car accident, and a cancer scare." *Tantavallon* "illustrates well [Tennant's] belief that life in general is 'a thin layer of ice over a raging human volcano,' full of 'absurdity and chaos,'" according to Goodwin; however, as in Tennant's other novels, "there is always vigour, entertainment, and comedy in her depiction." The *Times* obituary writer comments on a lasting impression of Tennant's work: "Her often noted slapdash writing and lack of psychological penetration . . . are compensated for, in her best books, by her zest for life, humour and, above all, by her affection for the human race."

SOURCES AND SUGGESTED READING:

Dick, Margaret. *The Novels of Kylie Tennant*. Rigby, 1966.
Goodwin, Ken. *A History of Australian Literature*. St. Martin's, 1986.
Tennant, Kylie. *The Joyful Condemned*, reissued as *Tell Morning This*. Angus & Robertson, 1968.
———. *The Missing Heir: The Autobiography of Kylie Tennant*. Macmillan, 1986.

PERIODICALS:

Books. August 10, 1941.
Book Week. September 5, 1943, March 31, 1946.
Christian Science Monitor. November 5, 1953.
Commonweal. October 10, 1941.
Listener. March 23, 1943.
Meanjin Quarterly. No. 4, 1953.
New Republic. August 25, 1941.
New Statesman and Nation. January 25, 1941.
The New Yorker. August 28, 1943, March 30, 1946, October 2, 1954.
New York Herald Tribune Book Review. May 10, 1953.
The New York Times. August 10, 1941, November 8, 1941, February 14, 1943, September 12, 1943, April 7, 1946, May 10, 1953.
The New York Times Book Review. August 21, 1960.
Saturday Review. October 17, 1953.

Saturday Review of Literature. August 9, 1941, May 18, 1946.

Spectator. April 9, 1943.

Times Literary Supplement. January 4, 1941, March 20, 1943, February 27, 1953, June 26, 1953, February 8, 1968, July 30, 1971.

Weekly Book Review. April 4, 1943, September 12, 1943, March 31, 1946.

Yale Review. Autumn 1941.

COLLECTIONS:

Manuscripts at Australian National Library in Canberra.

Michael E. Mueller
for *Contemporary Authors* Online.
The Gale Group, 1999

Tennant, Margaret Mary

(1869–1946)

English social worker who became the first female factory inspector in England. Born Margaret Mary Edith Abraham in 1869; died in 1946; married Harold John Tennant (a politician), in 1896 (died 1946).

Born in 1869, Margaret Mary Tennant distinguished herself as a pioneer in the field of public reform. In 1893, she was the first woman in England to become a factory inspector, a position she held until 1896, the year she married Harold John Tennant, a Liberal member of Parliament. From 1914 until 1939, she served as a member of the Central Committee on Women's Employment. Named a Companion of Honor in 1917, she died in 1946.

SOURCES:

The Concise Dictionary of National Biography. Oxford: Oxford University Press, 1992.

Gloria Cooksey,
freelance writer,
Sacramento, California

Tennent, Madge Cook (1889–1972)

British-born artist and musician who devoted decades to painting the people and culture of Hawaii. Born Madeline Grace Cook on June 22, 1889, in Dulwich, England; died on February 5, 1972, in Hawaii; daughter of Arthur Cook (an architect) and Agnes Cook (a writer and publisher); educated at Academie Julian in Paris; studied with William Bouguereau; married Hugh Cowper Tennent (an accountant), in 1915 (died 1967); children: sons Arthur Hugh Cowper Tennent (b. June 11, 1916) and Valentine Leslie Tennent (b. April 5, 1919).

Served as headmistress of art at assorted schools in Capetown, South Africa; began exhibiting her works (early 1900s); established her own art school and gave piano recitals; appointed head instructor of the Government School of Art, New Zealand; devoted herself to artistic documentation of the Hawaiian culture (1923 on).

Born Madeline Grace Cook in Dulwich, England, on June 22, 1889, Madge Cook Tennent and her younger sibling **Violet Cook** were raised in a creative atmosphere. Their father Arthur Cook was an architect by profession, but he also painted seascapes and was an expert woodcarver. Their mother **Agnes Cook** was a writer and publisher. Interested in comparative religions and the occult, Tennent's parents were an artistic couple who were charitable as well, opening their home to anyone in need. In 1894, the family moved to South Africa and established residency near Capetown.

Other than her brief attendance at an English boarding school and a French convent, Tennent received little formal education. She learned to read and write at a young age and learned to play the piano from her mother. When she was 12, her parents sent her to the Capetown School of Art, where the curriculum was limited to drawing and portraiture. As Madge's artistic talents unfolded, her parents moved the family to Paris so that she might train at the Academie Julian and study the great works of art at the Louvre Museum. Considered a prodigy, Tennent studied with master artist William Bouguereau before financial necessity forced the family to return to South Africa in 1907.

Tennent began to exhibit her work by age 18 and supported herself by serving as the headmistress of art at various South African schools. Additionally, she performed piano recitals and established her own art school. After one of her recitals in July 1915, she became acquainted with an accountant, Hugh Cowper Tennent, and the two married in the fall of that year. Although Hugh was stationed in South Africa, the couple moved to his homeland of New Zealand and lived for a time in Woodville, where Madge gave birth to their first son, Arthur Hugh Cowper Tennent, in 1916. Tennent later moved to Invercargill, where she lived with her husband's parents while her husband worked in France. While Tennent was in New Zealand she accepted an appointment as the head instructor of the Government School of Art. After her husband was transferred to British Samoa, the Tennents remained in the South Pacific for six years. During that time, in 1919, their second son, Valentine Leslie Tennent, was born. In British Samoa, Tennent became absorbed with studying and painting the Polynesians, whose features she found classically beautiful.

The Tennents planned to move to England in 1923, but when their ship docked in Honolulu, the family became enamored with the people there and instead elected to remain in Hawaii, on Oahu. Tennent had a deep appreciation of the classic beauty of the Hawaiian people and developed an artistic vision that Hawaiian royalty had descended from gods—an image she sought to replicate in her art. Tennent studied the paintings of Paul Gauguin and, during her earliest years on the island, was highly influenced by his style. Her paintings also evince an admiration for Pierre Auguste Renoir and Pablo Picasso. Abetted by meticulous research of her subjects, she sought to document Hawaiian culture through her artwork. Tennent's personal style evolved over time as her paintings acquired a three-dimensional quality with exceptional fluidity and movement of design. She developed a unique artistic technique as she painted her subjects, especially the largely rotund and mature Hawaiians. Critics later characterized her work as "rhythm in the round." Bringing remarkable movement and grace to her paintings, Tennent sought to immortalize the beauty of the Hawaiian people. **Elaine Tennent** in *Notable Women of Hawaii* described Tennent's legacy as "inextricably woven into the tapestry of Hawaii's art history."

Madge Tennent's constitution began to fail sometime around 1950, and she suffered a series of heart attacks. Her husband also became ill with heart trouble. She was widowed on April 15, 1967. Herself in poor health, she remained at Maunalani Hospital until her death on February 5, 1972. Many of Tennent's paintings remain housed at the Tennent Art Foundation Gallery, a museum she and her husband established in 1954, located on the slope of Punchbowl Mountain on Oahu. Tennent also donated much of her work to friends and to charitable causes.

SOURCES:

Peterson, Barbara Bennett, ed. *Notable Women of Hawaii.* Honolulu, HI: University of Hawaii Press, 1984.

Gloria Cooksey,
freelance writer,
Sacramento, California

Tenney, Tabitha Gilman (1762–1837)

American author. Born Tabitha Gilman on April 7, 1762, in Exeter, New Hampshire; died on May 2, 1837, in Exeter; daughter of Samuel Gilman and Lydia Robinson (Giddinge) Gilman; education unknown; married Samuel Tenney (a surgeon and politician), in 1788 (died 1816).

Selected works: The New Pleasing Instructor *(1799); Female Quixotism: Exhibited in the Romantic Opinions and Extravagant Adventures of Dorcasina Sheldon (1801).*

Tabitha Gilman Tenney was born in 1762 in Exeter, New Hampshire. It is believed that she was the eldest of seven children of Samuel and **Lydia Giddinge Gilman**, whose early ancestors settled New England. Little is known of Tenney's formal education, though it is generally accepted that she was well schooled in the Puritan traditions by her mother. Tenney developed a passion for books and learning, which led to an adeptness in her writing and articulation skills.

In 1788, probably in September, she married Dr. Samuel Tenney, a surgeon in a Rhode Island regiment during the Revolutionary War who entered politics after the conflict. Tabitha Tenney published her first work of merit, *The New Pleasing Instructor*, a manual of poetry and classical selections for use in the education of young women, in 1799. She then traveled with her husband in 1800 to Washington, D.C., where the couple spent several seasons while Samuel Tenney served in Congress.

Tenney is best known for her fictional work, *Female Quixotism: Exhibited in the Romantic Opinions and Extravagant Adventures of Dorcasina Sheldon*, which was published in 1801. In two volumes, she follows a young and prosperous ingenue who is taken with romanticism, reverie, and reading romantic novels. The heroine and her handmaid Betty experience a variety of escapades at the hands of scoundrels and cads who purport to woo the young heiress. The book is widely viewed as a satirical admonition to foolish young women and is regarded as one of the best parodies of Cervantes' *Don Quixote*.

Returning to New Hampshire after the death of her husband in 1816, Tenney lived to the age of 75. She died in Exeter on May 2, 1837, after a short illness, and was buried in the Winter Street Graveyard there.

SOURCES:

Buck, Claire, ed. *The Bloomsbury Guide to Women's Literature.* NY: Prentice Hall, 1992.

Duyckinck, Evert A., and George L. Duyckinck. *Cyclopaedia of American Literature.* Philadelphia, PA: W.M. Rutter & Co., n.d. (reprinted Detroit, MI: Gale Research, 1965).

James, Edward T., ed. *Notable American Women, 1607–1950.* Cambridge, MA: The Belknap Press of Harvard University, 1971.

Gloria Cooksey,
freelance writer,
Sacramento, California

Tennyson, Emily (1813–1896)

Wife and amanuensis of English poet Alfred, Lord Tennyson. Name variations: Lady Tennyson; Baroness Tennyson; Emily Sellwood. Born Emily Sarah Sellwood in 1813 in England; died on August 10, 1896; the eldest daughter of Henry Sellwood (a solicitor); married Alfred, Lord Tennyson (1809–1892, the writer), on June 13, 1850; children: two sons, Hallam and Lionel.

The intelligent, well-read daughter of a Horncastle solicitor, Emily Sellwood first met poet Alfred, Lord Tennyson in 1830, thus beginning an on-again-off-again courtship that lasted for 20 years. They were first engaged in 1838, but Alfred broke it off two years later due to his unsteady financial situation. He proposed once more around 1847, but this time Emily refused, fearing Alfred's religious skepticism. It was not until 1850, after reading his poem *Elegies* (later titled *In Memoriam*), that she finally agreed to marriage. By all accounts, Emily and Alfred never wavered in their love for one another and suffered deeply during their various estrangements. H. Drummond Rawnsley, a cousin of Emily's, wrote that during their years apart they "ate out their hearts in secret," and Rawnsley's

Emily Tennyson

brother Willingham noted that while separated "each kept the sacred fire alight in their hearts." The wedding, which finally took place on June 13, 1850, may have been the most meaningful event in Alfred's life. James O. Hoge, editor of *Lady Tennyson's Journal*, writes: "Lonely, self-tormented, troubled by religious uncertainties and doubts about his own abilities, Tennyson probably exaggerated little when in 1845 he confessed to Aubrey DeVere 'that he must marry and find love and peace or die.'"

During her 42-year marriage to the poet, Emily managed several households (including the finances), cared for the couple's two sons, handled her husband's correspondence, copied his poems and helped to prepare them for publication, entertained visitors, and generally protected the poet from the distractions of daily life. "In short," writes Hoge, "Emily must be given paramount credit both for rescuing Tennyson from the tragic self-absorption that warped his youth and for managing his home and continuing to minister to his personal needs in a manner designed to promote his contentment and leave him free to write."

Plagued from childhood by a spinal disorder which rendered her physically frail, Emily nearly sacrificed her own health to provide for her family. "Do not throw away your life in the performance of imaginary duties which are really unimportant," advised family friend Benjamin Jowett, in 1861. Emily, however, did not heed her Jowett's advice, particularly as Alfred's fame increased, requiring more entertaining and the further censoring and answering of mail. In September 1874, finally pushed beyond endurance, Emily suffered a near-fatal breakdown, which caused her to temporarily give up serving as Alfred's secretary or his amanuensis. Within six months, however, she had recovered sufficiently to take over the household affairs and by 1877 had taken up correspondence once again, although she judiciously kept it within the family circle.

From the time of her marriage until her collapse in 1874, Emily kept a running journal of her life with Alfred, which Hoge, who edited and published the work in 1981, calls a "treasure trove" of invaluable information about the poet and the entire Tennyson family. "She periodically indicates his state of health, his mood, his plans for composition, revision, and publication, his reactions to praise or blame, his opinions on a host of topics, and (most important of all from her point of view) she describes Tennyson's relationship with herself and with their sons." The diary reveals great love and respect between husband and wife, which grew stronger with the years. Emily describes quiet evenings spent alone with Alfred, discussing poets and writers, or politics or religion. Alfred frequently read his work aloud, soliciting his wife's opinions and advice and usually acting upon her judgment. An accomplished pianist, Emily sometimes set her husband's poems to music, with the goal of providing an impression of the reading. Several were printed, including "The Song of the Alma River," "The City Child," and "Minnie and Winnie." In 1891, she gave permission to Polish pianist **Natalia Janotha** to perform several of her songs in concert at St. James's Hall.

Following Alfred's death in 1892, Emily assisted her son Hallam in the preparation of the Tennyson *Memoir*, which required the collecting and inspecting of hundreds of letters and other items related to the poet's life and works. She also prepared her own final Journal, recopying illegible sections and condensing where appropriate, although failing eyesight made the task quite difficult. As well, she spent time entertaining and caring for her five grandchildren. Even as she aged, Emily stayed involved in the world around her, retaining a clear grasp of the major issues of the day. In one of her last letters, she rejoices in the possibilities of women studying for the B.A. degree at Oxford, and in another she expresses concern about the possibility of war. She died on August 10, 1896. "Perhaps the desire that I could in any way influence [the world] according to what I believe to be right is more passionate than ever," she wrote in 1891. "If it were not so it would be hard indeed to go on living."

SOURCES:
Hoge, James O, ed. *Lady Tennyson's Journal*. Charlottesville, VA: University Press of Virginia, 1981.

Barbara Morgan,
Melrose, Massachusetts

Teotochi-Albrizzi, Isabella (1760–1836).

See Albrizzi, Isabella Teotochi, Contessa d'.

Teplova, Nadezhda Sergeevna (1814–1848)

Russian poet. Name variations: Nadezhda Sergeevna Teplóva. Born in 1814; died in 1848.

Nadezhda Sergeevna Teplova was born to a wealthy Russian family of merchants in 1814. She and her sister, **Serafima**, were well educated and encouraged in the art of poetry and are among the few recognized female poets associated with the Golden Age of Russia. Teplova's poetry is characterized by its introspective qualities and its fine lyricism. Her best-known works include "A Confession," "Advice," and "Spring." Teplova died in 1848, age 34.

SOURCES:
Buck, Claire, ed. *The Bloomsbury Guide to Women's Literature*. NY: Prentice Hall, 1992.

Gloria Cooksey,
freelance writer,
Sacramento, California

Terentia (fl. 69–45 BCE).

See Tullia for sidebar.

Teresa.

Variant of Theresa or Thérèse.

Teresa, Mother (c. 1766–1846)

Irish-born American religious leader and educator. Born Alice Lalor around 1766 in Ballyragget, County Kilkenny, Ireland (some sources cite County Queens, now County Laois); died on September 9, 1846, in Georgetown, District of Columbia; migrated to the United States, 1790s.

Established the oldest surviving school for girls in the original 13 colonies; founded the first Visitation convent in the United States, Georgetown, District of Columbia (1808).

Alice Lalor was born in Ireland about 1766. A deeply religious child, she wanted to join a community of Presentation nuns in Kilkenny but was dissuaded by her parents. Instead, she migrated to the United States with her elder sister in 1795 and settled in Philadelphia, Pennsylvania. Befriended on the journey by two widowed passengers, a Mrs. Sharpe and a Mrs. McDermott, Lalor established a religious community with them, guided by Father Leonard Neale, who assisted the three in founding a school for girls under the auspices of a religious order called the Pious Ladies. During a yellow fever epidemic in 1797 and 1798, Lalor and the others remained in the area to care for the sick. Although Lalor survived the epidemic, the two widows died.

When Neale accepted an appointment as the president of Georgetown College (now Georgetown University) in the District of Columbia in 1799, he invited Lalor and other Pious Ladies to join him in Georgetown. There, in 1804 or 1805, he acquired the deed to a convent abandoned by a community of Poor Clares. The Pious Ladies established a second school in Georgetown, and Lalor assumed title to the convent property in 1808. She embraced the lifestyle of the Visitation nuns of the Catholic Church and formally established the first American community of that order under the sanction of the pope. The community increased in numbers so much that by 1816 Lalor had assumed the position of the first mother superior of the cloister, after which she became known as Mother Teresa. Lalor held that position until 1819 and then resumed her work in relative anonymity. By the time of her death in 1846, the Visitation order in the United States had grown to include five convents throughout the country.

SOURCES:
Cyclopaedia of American Biography. Appleton, 1888.
McHenry, Robert, ed. *Famous American Women.* NY: Dover, 1980.
Twentieth Century Biographical Dictionary of Notable Americans. Boston, MA: The Biographical Society, 1904.

Gloria Cooksey,
freelance writer,
Sacramento, California

Teresa, Mother (1794–1861).

See Ball, Frances.

Teresa, Mother (1910–1997)

Albanian nun who founded the Missionaries of Charity and devoted her life to caring for the homeless and destitute population of Calcutta. Name variations: Agnes Bojaxhiu (1910–1931); Sister Teresa (1931–1950); Mother Teresa (1950–1997); Mother Teresa of Calcutta. Born Gonxha Agnes Bojaxhiu on August 27, 1910, in Skopje, Macedonia (then part of the Ottoman Empire); died of heart failure in Calcutta on September 5, 1997; daughter of Drana Bojaxhiu and Nikola Kole Bojaxhiu (both Albanians); educated in schools in Macedonia; never married; no children.

Joined Sisters of Loreto in Dublin (1928); sailed to India for novitiate (1929); adopted name Teresa with vows as a nun, and began work in St. Mary's School, Calcutta (1931); took final vows (1937); accorded exclaustration to begin work with the poor (1948); founded Missionaries of Charity (1950); opened Nirmal Hriday, home for the dying in Calcutta (1954); at her urging, Missionary Brothers of Charity founded (1963); awarded Nobel Peace Prize (1979).

Mother Teresa was the most famous nun in the world yet most of her work was done in India, a country with only a tiny Christian population. Her uncompromising dedication to the poor, the destitute, and the dying made her a Catholic celebrity throughout Europe and the Americas. After receiving the Nobel Peace Prize in 1979, she enjoyed the special favor and protection of Pope John Paul II who saw her as an exemplary figure of contemporary Catholicism.

She was born Agnes Bojaxhiu on August 27, 1910, in Skopje, Macedonia. Her father Drana Bojaxhiu was an Albanian merchant living in Macedonia under the rule of the Ottoman Empire. He had an Italian partner and traveled widely in Europe, was well educated, interested in progressive political movements, and an orthodox Catholic. The Albanian minority in that part of what later became Yugoslavia (and is now a republic) was Catholic, whereas the Macedonian majority belonged to the Greek Orthodox Church. A member of Skopje's town council, Drana Bojaxhiu was also part of an anti-Turkish independence movement. In 1912, when Agnes was only two, the Balkan provinces of the Turkish Empire waged a successful war of independence. It was followed almost immediately by the First World War (1914–18) which devastated parts of the region, and in which her father died, possibly the victim of poisoning by his political rivals. The family were impoverished by his death, but Agnes' mother **Nikola Bojaxhiu** was able to preserve her three children by working as a seamstress.

Agnes, a dedicated young Catholic, influenced by a charismatic Jesuit priest in Skopje, decided at the age of 12 that she had a vocation to the religious life, and in particular to service as a missionary in India. Her resolve hardened during her teens, and, at the age of 18, she joined the Sisters of Loreto, a missionary order which specialized in educating and evangelizing in India. India was then part of the British Empire, however, and Catholic organizations were obliged to work in collaboration with the imperial authorities. It was also an advantage to be able to speak English, the language of the administrators and, increasingly, the *lingua franca* of India itself. Saying goodbye to her mother and sister for the last time, she went first to Dublin, Ireland, to begin the study of English with the Loreto Sisters. Impressed by her rapid progress, they sent her to India after just six weeks. Her first destination there was Darjeeling, a pretty town in the Himalayan foothills, which was cooler and healthier than the city of Calcutta, in which most of her work would be done.

Agnes took her first vows as a nun in 1931 and adopted the religious name of Sister Teresa, in honor of **Thérèse of Lisieux, the 19th-century French nun and visionary. Mother Teresa's final vows, taken in 1937, bound her for life to the order, and included pledges of chastity, poverty, obedience, and enclosure. Her first job in Calcutta, following the Darjeeling novitiate, was to teach history and geography at St. Mary's, a girls' convent school belonging to the order. The convent was comfortable and the students came from prosperous families so Teresa, although she was aware of the horrific squalor around her, rarely came into immediate contact with it.

The 1930s and early 1940s, during which she proved herself an able teacher and administrator, rising to the position of school principal, were also the years of the Indian independence movement. Led by the inspirational Hindu advocate of non-violence, Mohandas K. Gandhi, the movement gained strength especially during the Second World War, and at the war's end, in 1945, Britain's new Labour Party government announced its intention to grant India independence in 1947. Members of the Muslim minority feared that Hindus would dominate the new nation and, despite Gandhi's pleas, communal violence broke out throughout the subcontinent. In Calcutta alone, religious street fighting caused 5,000 deaths. Communications broke down in the city and the Loreto convent found itself stranded and starving. Mother Teresa responded to the emergency by venturing onto the streets in search of food, finally getting some sacks of rice from British soldiers who escorted her back to the convent and warned her of the danger she faced.

The experience catalyzed her growing sense of restlessness at her work. Seeing unclaimed dead bodies scattered through the streets, in addition to the everyday miseries of Calcutta, convinced her that she should be working with Calcutta's poorest and most desperate people, rather than with the rich. Teresa asked her spiritual advisor and her bishop to release her from the vow of enclosure. For a time, it seemed as though she would be discharged as a nun altogether, which she did not want, but in 1948, after communication with Rome, the bishop acceded to her request for "exclaustration." "To leave Loreto" she wrote later, "was my greatest sacrifice, the most difficult thing I have ever done. It was much more difficult than to leave my family and country to enter religious life" because in Loreto "I had received my spiritual training. . . . I had given my life to Jesus in the Institute."

In the following months, she studied with the Medical Missionary Sisters, founded by another pioneering nun, Mother **Anna Dengel**, learning basic medical and nutritional techniques, how to deliver babies and how to set dislocated bones. The Medical Missionaries talked Teresa out of her original, impractical, idea of eating only the humblest diet of rice and salt, pointing out that she would soon die of tuberculosis or malnutrition. For the next two years, now wearing a white *sari* with a blue edge rather than her convent black, Sister Teresa tramped the slums of Calcutta's Motijhil district, setting up an ad hoc school for homeless children, giving first aid to the sick and wounded. In her diary, written as a form of religious meditation and as a way to stave off discouragement, she wrote: "God wants me to be a lonely nun, laden with the poverty of the Cross. Today I learned a good lesson. The poverty of the poor is so hard. When I was going and going until my legs and arms were paining, I was thinking how they have to suffer to get food and shelter. Then the comfort of Loreto came to tempt me. But God, out of love for you, and by my own free choice, I desire to do whatever be your holy will. Give me courage now, this moment." The solitude she felt in these early years of her work would not persist for long. Along with her self-sacrificing impulses, she possessed great organizational skill.

With the aid of the sympathetic Gomes family, who lived near Motijhil, she began to recruit helpers. The first two, **Subhasini Das** (Sister Agnes) and **Magdalena Gomes** (Sister Gertrude), and many subsequent volunteers, were graduates of the Loreto school where she had been a teacher. As the group increased, the Vatican granted it the constitution of a distinct order, the Missionaries of Charity, in 1950. Teresa, who had become an Indian citizen the previous year, was made its mother superior, and at an inaugural meeting she read out the sisters' duties, in particular: "seeking out in towns and villages all over the world even amid squalid surroundings the poorest, the abandoned, the sick, the infirm, the leprosy patients, the dying, the desperate, the lost, the outcasts." She added that the work must always be done cheerfully and for its own sake. They did not make Christian evangelization a priority and ensured that Muslim and Hindu patients in their hospitals would each have access to their own religious rites.

In 1954, as the order continued to grow, Mother Teresa persuaded the city authorities of Calcutta to give her an unused building which she converted into a hospice for the dying homeless. The center, the Nirmal Hriday, Place of the Immaculate Heart, became one center of her work. The next year, in a nearby building, she established the Nirmala Shishu Bhavan, an orphanage. The children were disproportionately girls rather than boys, because the widespread Indian preference for sons over daughters led to the abandonment of many baby girls. She also cared for abandoned or runaway teenaged girls, trying to forestall their descent into prostitution, and set up an ambitious program to aid the victims of leprosy, which included a rehabilitation center where leper families could learn crafts and become self-sufficient. Although the growing Catholic literature about her saintly work rarely stressed the point, Mother Teresa was in fact an extremely capable administrator and fund raiser, hard-nosed in negotiations with civic authorities when necessary, systematic in planning and organization, and able after a few years to command and direct a complicated system. As her Indian admirer B. Srinivasa Murthy wrote: "Mother Teresa has utilized practical entrepreneurial genius in setting up service centers around the world with astonishing success. . . . [She] must have splendid managerial capacity and prudential wisdom, for such achievements are impossible for theoretical idealists." She also had an iron constitution and showed little sign of slowing down either then, in her 40s, nor even 30 years later, in her 70s. The Indian government, unable to provide comprehensive welfare services to its massive population, recognized the value of her work and collaborated where possible with donations of land, buildings, and medical supplies, though the bulk of her funding came from charitable contributions made in the West. Air India, the national airline, helped out by giving her a lifetime free pass for all its flights.

It is Christ you tend in the poor. . . .
It is his wounds you bathe, his sores you clean, his limbs you bandage.

—**Mother Teresa**

She became a celebrity for American Catholics in 1960 when, on her first visit to the United States, she gave speeches in Las Vegas, New York, Washington, D.C., Milwaukee, and Peoria. On the same trip, she met *Dorothy Day, whose Catholic Worker Houses of Hospitality did the same kind of work among the destitute of New York that she was doing in Calcutta; the two women became mutual admirers. Although American homelessness and starvation were slight problems by Indian standards, Mother Teresa still saw much work to be done in America's cities. In a Milwaukee speech, she said:

> Right here in the United States, I'm sure you know better than I do, there are many poor people that need love and compassion. . . . People are not hungry just for bread; they are hungry for love. People are not naked only for a piece of cloth; they are naked for that human dignity. People are not only homeless for a room made of bricks; but

they are homeless—being rejected, unwanted, unloved. [In America] there is a terrible hunger of love, a terrible loneliness, a terrible rejection. That's a much greater hunger.

Mother Teresa also visited London and Rome, where she asked Pope John XXIII to take her organization under his special protection and permit it to spread beyond India to other parts of the world, where the same kind of work was needed. Vatican bureaucracy often moved slowly and four years were to pass before permission was granted. Despite repeated examples of clerical obstruction, Mother Teresa remained docile and submissive to male authority in the Church and never protested against intra-Catholic impediments to her schemes. Meanwhile, she encouraged a group of Catholic men who admired her work to set up a parallel organization, the Missionary Brothers of Charity, founded in 1963. And in 1969, with the aid of a British admirer and contributor, **Ann Blaikie**, she founded the International Association of the Co-Workers of Mother Teresa, a group of lay volunteers, donors, and publicists, who helped fund the missions.

The early 1960s, era of the Second Vatican Council, relaxed some of the rules governing religious orders and made it easier for a group like the Missionaries of Charity to expand their work. It also followed the lead of groups like hers in downplaying the role of evangelization and stressing the fraternity of all people, whatever their faith. John XXIII's successor, Pope Paul VI, took Mother Teresa's organization under his special protection in 1965, and it began its rapid international diversification. At first, it grew in the Third World, beginning with Venezuela and Tanzania, but at the pope's request it also established a mission in the gruesome slums of Rome itself. Paul VI also granted her a humanitarianism award in 1971, by which time she was becoming an international charity-celebrity. As often happens in such cases, she found, to her alarm, that she could do the most good for her order not by carrying on the daily work in the streets, her first love, but rather by traveling the world, making speeches, meeting politicians and donors. As a prominent Catholic in the Cold War era, she was lionized in the West but despised by the authorities of the Communist nations, including her parents' native Albania, which had suffered a severely repressive Communist regime since the Second World War. Despite her fame, Mother Teresa was unable to arrange exit visas for her mother and sister, both of whom died in the late 1960s without ever seeing her again.

Mother Teresa became controversial in the West when she spoke out against contraception

and abortion, in conformity with Catholic teaching. The 1960s and 1970s saw widespread concern about overpopulation—authors like the Stanford biologist Paul Ehrlich predicted that without severe population control measures the world faced an apocalyptic subsistence crisis.

Although she had battled for years in the overcrowded slums of Calcutta, Mother Teresa completely denied the validity of the "populationists'" proposed remedies. In her view, every life was sacred and beloved by God; she even declared that there could never possibly be too many people, each of whom embodied part of God's mystery. This difference in outlook between her and the secular scientific world was evident also in her attitude to suffering. For most scientists and doctors, pain was something to be avoided and alleviated at all costs. For Mother Teresa, by contrast, pain enabled people to get closer to Jesus and to share in the pain which he suffered to redeem mankind on the Cross. Pain, in her view, was a privilege as well as a burden. These views, expressed with clarity and simplicity in her books *A Gift for God* and *My Life for the Poor*, marked her remoteness from the scientific outlook of her times. She also tried hard to avoid politics and merely urged tyrants to emulate Christ. "The President of Mexico sent for me," she wrote in *My Life for the Poor*. "I told him that he had to become holy as a president: not as a Missionary of Charity, but as a president. He looked at me a bit surprised, but it is like that; we have to become holy, each of us, in the place where God has put us." She showed no interest in the politicized Liberation Theology movement which influenced Latin American Catholicism in the 1970s and 1980s and, to her detractors, she seemed like an advocate of the political status quo. And of course her outspoken opposition to abortion, which she made the centerpiece of her acceptance speech when she received the Nobel Peace Prize in 1979, marked her as an agent of the Catholic opposition to American and European pro-choice advocates.

Her work continued through the 1980s, with new establishments throughout the world. At the urging of Pope John Paul II, who held her in particularly high esteem, she went to Lebanon during the war of 1982 and tried to set up relief centers for the thousands of people displaced by the fighting. President Ronald Reagan awarded her the Presidential Medal of Freedom in 1985, and she continued to garner accolades, awards, honorary degrees, and large donations throughout the world, all of which she turned to good account in her expanding charitable empire.

Mother Teresa remained active throughout the early 1990s, slowed only somewhat by old age and increasingly poor health. Although she suffered from heart disease and was hospitalized periodically, she kept up a busy schedule of work and travel, speaking to large groups and heads of state and visiting the various branches of the Missionaries of Charity even after she stepped down as head of the order in March 1997. Succeeding her was her long-time aide Sister **Nirmala Joshi**, whose conversion in 1958 from Hinduism to Catholicism she had attended. Sister Nirmala, a university-trained political

scientist and lawyer, declined to take the title "mother," and Mother Teresa continued working. In June, by then wheelchair-bound, she visited Washington, D.C., where she was awarded the Congressional Gold Medal. Less than three months later, on September 6, 1997, Mother Teresa died of a heart attack at her mission in Calcutta. Her death came on the same day as the funeral for *****Diana**, princess of Wales (who had met with Mother Teresa at her mission in the South Bronx), and an extravagantly grieving world was further saddened, and perhaps sobered. Her body lay in state in one of Calcutta's largest churches for a week while some 60,000 people paid their respects each day. Thousands of dignitaries from church and state crowded that same church for her state funeral—only the second in India granted to a non-politician—while hundreds of thousands more akin to those she had loved and served waited in the streets. Her small coffin was then driven through the crowds in a carriage to the Mother House, where she was buried.

SOURCES:

Clucas, Joan G. *Mother Teresa*. NY: Chelsea House, 1988.

Egan, Eileen. *Such a vision of the Street*. NY: Doubleday, 1985.

Le Joly, Edward. *Mother Teresa of Calcutta*. San Francisco, CA: Harper and Row, 1977.

Muggeridge, Malcolm. *Something Beautiful for God*. London: Collins, 1971.

Murthy, B. Srinivasa. *Mother Teresa and India*. Long Beach, CA: Long Beach Publications, 1979.

Porter, David. *Mother Teresa, the Early Years*. Grand Rapids, MI: Eerdman, 1986.

Teresa, Mother. *My Life for the Poor*. San Francisco: Harper and Row, 1985.

SUGGESTED READING:

Sebba, Anne. *Mother Teresa: Beyond the Image*. NY: Doubleday, 1997.

Teresa, Mother. *Mother Teresa: A Simple Path*. NY: Ballantine, 1995.

———. *Mother Teresa: No Greater Love*. New World Library, 1997.

RELATED MEDIA:

Mother Teresa is the subject of at least ten television documentaries made in Britain, America, India, and Japan.

"Mother Teresa: In the Name of God's Poor" (2-hour cable-television movie), produced by Family Network, starred **Geraldine Chaplin**, 1997.

Patrick Allitt,
Assistant Professor of History,
Emory University, Atlanta, Georgia

Teresa Benedicta of the Cross
(1891–1942).

See Stein, Edith.

Teresa Cristina of Bourbon (1822–1889).

See Isabel of Brazil for sidebar.

Teresa de Cartagena (fl. 1400)

Spanish nun and writer. Flourished in 1400 in Cartagena, Spain; never married; no children.

Unfortunately almost nothing is known about Teresa de Cartagena, a Spanish nun and writer who had been born deaf. It is not certain whether she entered a convent because of her deafness, which made it unlikely that she would marry, or if only her piety led her there. It is clear that Teresa had an intense devotion to God, and experienced mystical trances and visions, which she wrote about for the enlightenment of others. She authored two books, in which she chronicles her own spiritual growth and gives guidance to others seeking the same path; she also wrote about physical deformities and handicaps, and created a cosmology in which the physically disabled could, by virtue of their suffering and unique experiences, play an important role in leading others to God.

SOURCES:
Echols, Anne, and Marty Williams. *An Annotated Index of Medieval Women.* NY: Markus Wiener, 1992.

Laura York,
Riverside, California

Teresa d'Entenza (fl. 1319)

*First wife of Alphonso IV. Name variations: Theresa de Entenza. Flourished around 1319; first wife of Alphonso IV, king of Aragon (r. 1327–1336); children: Jaime, count of Urgel; Pedro IV also known as Peter IV the Ceremonious (b. 1319), king of Aragon (r. 1336–1387). Alphonso's second wife was *Eleanor of Castile (1307–1359).*

Teresa of Aragon (1037–?)

*Princess of Aragon. Born in 1037; death date unknown; daughter of *Gilberga (d. 1054) and Ramiro I, king of Aragon (r. 1035–1069); married William VI, count of Provence.*

Teresa of Avila (1515–1582)

Spanish mystic and monastic reformer, influential writer on spirituality, founder of the Discalced Carmelite order of Roman Catholic nuns, and canonized saint, who was the first woman to be proclaimed a Doctor of the Church. Name variations: Teresa de Jesús; Santa Teresa; Teresa of Jesus; Teresa of Ávila; Theresa de Jesus des Carmes-Dechausses; Santa Teresa de Avila. Pronunciation: teh-REH-sah of AH-bee-lah. Born Teresa de Cepeda y Ahumada on March 28, 1515, at Avila, Spain; died on October 4, 1582, at Alba de Tormes, Spain; daughter of Alonso Sánchez de Cepeda and Beatriz de Ahumada; never married; no children.

Professed as a Carmelite sister (1537); experienced the Transverberation (1559); founded reformed convent of St. Joseph at Avila (1562); founded 16 additional reformed convents in other Spanish cities (1567–82); beatified (1614); canonized (1622); proclaimed Doctor of the Church (1970).

Works: El camino de la perfección *(The Way of Perfection);* El libro de su vida *(autobiography);* Las moradas, o el castillo interior *(The Dwelling Places, or the Interior Castle);* El libro de las fundaciones *(The Foundations);* Cuentas de conciencia *(Spiritual Testimonies).*

The woman whom Roman Catholics the world over would one day venerate as St. Teresa of Avila was born on March 28, 1515, the daughter of Alonso Sánchez de Cepeda and his second wife **Beatriz de Ahumada**. Traditionally, Teresa's birthplace is given as Avila, a walled city high on Spain's central plateau to the northwest of Madrid, but there is evidence that it was really the nearby village of Gotarrendura, location of the Ahumada family estate. In any case, it was in Avila that Teresa grew to womanhood and it was there that she spent most of her life, although during her later years she traveled extensively throughout Spain directing the work of her religious reform movement.

Founded in the 11th century, Avila was originally a fortress on the frontier between the Christian-controlled northern part of the Iberian peninsula and the Muslim-controlled southern part. As such, it played an important role in the Reconquista, the centuries-long war to restore all of Spain to Christian rule. The city's imposing system of defensive walls stands today as a reminder of its former strategic importance, but long before Teresa's time Avila was already in decline as a military center. By 1300, most of the south had been reconquered and incorporated into the two major Christian kingdoms, Castile and Aragon. The marriage in 1469 of *Isabella I, queen of Castile (r. 1474–1504), and Ferdinand II, king of Aragon (r. 1479–1516), known to history as the Catholic Monarchs, opened the way to the eventual political unification of Spain. Unification promised an era of internal peace, as did the completion in 1492 of the process of territorial consolidation when Ferdinand and Isabella captured the last remaining Muslim stronghold at Granada.

By the early 16th century, Avila's importance was no longer military but economic. The city's location in a principal sheep-raising area assured it a major role in the rapidly expanding woolens industry. Once a sleepy provincial town, Avila quickly emerged as a bustling center of trade and manufacture, attracting newcomers from less prosperous regions of the country. Many of these immigrant artisans and merchants were known at the time as *conversos*, or New Christians, meaning that they were former Jews who had converted to Christianity. Frequently, such conversions were made only for reasons of convenience, especially after 1492 when the Catholic Monarchs ordered the expulsion of Spain's Jewish population. Many *conversos* were sincerely devoted to their adoptive faith, but many more continued to practice Judaism in the privacy of their homes. All New Christians were subject to prejudice and legal disabilities, and all were vulnerable to accusations of apostasy, an offense which lay under the jurisdiction of the Spanish Inquisition, established in 1478 to impose religious unity on Spain's diverse population of Christians, Muslims, and Jews.

I look down upon the world as from above and care very little what people say or what is known about me.

—Teresa of Avila

One of the industrious New Christians attracted to Avila during the woolens boom was Teresa's father, Alonso Sánchez de Cepeda, who relocated from Toledo following a humiliating episode in 1485 when he and his father were convicted as secret Jews by the Inquisition and sentenced to perform a public penance. Sánchez de Cepeda was financially well off, but being a *converso* put him at a social and political disadvantage, even in the relatively forgiving atmosphere of worldly Avila. Many privileges in society, such as the holding of public office and entry into religious orders, were legally open only to Old Christians, whose blood was supposedly free of the "impurity" of Jewish or Muslim descent. Money had the power to cleanse, however, and, like many other wealthy *conversos*, Teresa's father purchased his way to acceptance and respectability. Recruiting witnesses to testify on his behalf, Sánchez de Cepeda won a suit to have himself declared a *hidalgo*, or noble, a legal status which entitled him to exemption from taxation and to be addressed by the honorific title "don." Also, by supplying generous dowries he took two wives in succession from noble Old Christian families, first **Catalina del Peso**, then after her death her cousin Beatriz de Ahumada, who became Teresa's mother.

The story of Teresa's Jewish ancestry has been known for some time. Traditional Catholic writers generally omit it, but it is important to any understanding of this remarkable woman, who, although endowed with great talent and intelligence, was born into a world in which she was doubly marginal. Teresa was a female in a male-dominated society, but she was also a social upstart in a city whose civil and ecclesiastical establishments were still dominated by an Old Christian aristocracy which traced its origin to the early days of the Reconquista. Her father's money and connections guaranteed Teresa access to the prestigious circles of Avila's high society, but as a young woman she must always have been aware of the precarious nature of her claim to social standing. Later, a rejection of snobbery and aristocratic pretense would become a central feature of Teresa's monastic reform program.

As a girl, Teresa was bright, impetuous, and strong-willed, and she was much influenced by tales of chivalry and the lives of saints, both of which were in her day common intellectual fare in conventional households. In her autobiography, Teresa tells us that the stories of holy martyrs so captivated her that, at the age of seven, she and her favorite brother Rodrigo dreamed of running away from home to invite beheading at the hands of imaginary Muslims in some unspecified neighboring province. According to some accounts, the children did actually depart on their gruesome errand but were intercepted on the road out of Avila by a relative, who returned them safely to the care of their parents.

In 1528, when Teresa was 13, Beatriz de Ahumada died, leaving her husband with ten children from two different marriages. In her autobiography, Teresa describes the loss of her mother with great emotion, telling us that she fell to her knees before an image of *Mary the Virgin to beseech the Mother of God to become her mother as well. Teresa is candid in her admission that this was no more than a routine response to personal tragedy, in keeping with the pious conventions of the day. In fact, as she matured into womanhood, the spiritual life was the furthest thing from her mind. By all accounts attractive and flirtatious, Teresa enjoyed the worldly company of other young people, especially some cousins of hers who lived nearby. At the age of 16, she began a clandestine romance with a man whose identity we do not know. Some writers state that during this period she lost her virginity, but the evidence is inconclusive. Teresa herself deals with the episode so circumspectly that it is clear only that her behavior,

Opposite page

Teresa of

Avila

had it become public knowledge, would have been an embarrassment to her and her family.

Moving decisively to contain the scandal, Don Alonso placed his lively daughter in the care of some Augustinian sisters who boarded the female children of noble families in their convent of Nuestra Señora de la Gracia just outside the city walls. Although Teresa tells us frankly that "at that time I had the greatest possible aversion from being a nun," she eventually settled into the monastic routine, remaining in the cloister for some 18 months until she became ill and was forced to return home for treatment. It is not clear at what point Teresa began to consider taking the religious state for life. Certainly her experience among the Augustinians had some influence, but it is also possible that becoming a nun seemed to her simply a fate preferable to spinsterhood, or to marriage to the kind of husband her father's money would be able to buy. With both her ancestry and her virginity open to question, and herself at 18 already past the customary age of matrimony, Teresa's stock would not have been high on Avila's marriage market.

Because her father initially opposed the idea, Teresa delayed taking the veil for some years, but in 1536 she finally became a novice at Avila's Carmelite convent of La Encarnación, where she made her final vows the following year. Rather typical of its time, La Encarnación was a loosely run community of approximately 100 sisters, most of whom were of aristocratic birth. The nuns were not cloistered and they were not expected to keep the rule of poverty, so they were free to come and go as they pleased and to enjoy private incomes and luxurious personal belongings. Rather than a genuine spiritual community, such a convent was in reality a genteel place of retirement for unmarried women of a certain social class and economic standing. Membership required not only an acceptable family tree, if only a partially fictive one as in Teresa's case, but also a dowry to provide for the new sister's maintenance. Religious life in the convent was limited largely to group vocal prayer for the souls of noble benefactors. These aristocrats provided generous endowments in return for the perpetuation of their proud family names through privileged places of burial in the convent chapel, ostentatious displays of their likenesses and armorial bearings, and the regular repetition of masses in their memory.

The Carmelite convent of La Encarnación was, in fact, a worldly, comfortable, and undemanding place to live. At first, Teresa appeared to thrive there. Known at this time as Doña

Teresa de Ahumada, because the aristocratic nuns she lived among preferred to retain their secular titles and identities rather than adopt religious names, she had a large, well-furnished apartment, and she enjoyed the company of a number of her female friends and relatives who were also sisters at La Encarnación. Allowing for frequent absences for various reasons, Teresa resided at the Carmelite convent off and on for about 20 years. During this period, however, she became increasingly dissatisfied with her surroundings. The mid-life transformation of Doña Teresa, contented aristocratic nun, into Teresa of Avila, gifted mystic and driven religious reformer, was not a sudden occurrence. Rather, it took place over a number of years and was marked by several crucial events, encounters, and conversion experiences.

In 1538, during a prolonged absence from the convent due to illness, Teresa received from a devout relative a copy of Francis of Osuna's *Abecedario espiritual* (Spiritual Alphabet, 1527). This book provided her introduction to the so-called Devotio Moderna, a movement for spiritual renewal within the Church which had its roots in Christian humanism. Associated with the figures of Thomas à Kempis (1380–1471) and Desiderius Erasmus (1466–1536), and, more radically, with Martin Luther (1483–1546), the new devotional style was particularly strong in Northern Europe, but in Teresa's time it also enjoyed widespread acceptance in Spain. Advocates of the Devotio Moderna criticized the empty formality of ritual observances, such as rote vocal prayer, which were the staple of Western religious life. Instead, they urged private reflection and mental prayer with the purpose of achieving a mystical union between the individual worshiper and God.

Impressed by her discovery, in the years that followed Teresa read heavily in the classics of Christian spiritual literature, but the atmosphere at La Encarnación was not congenial to her new interests. The other nuns were preoccupied with mundane daily concerns, and Teresa found it difficult to resist being caught up in them herself. What was worse, attempts to discuss her own spiritual growth with her confessors met with neither understanding nor sympathy. Teresa's sense of personal frustration must have been overwhelming. Sometime in the 1540s, she began to experience visions which she took at first to be divine revelations, although they sometimes frightened her, causing her to question whether they might not be the work of the devil instead. About 1555, these disquieting doubts led Teresa to entrust her spiritual welfare to two well-respected Avila clerics, Fathers Gaspar Daza and Francisco Salcedo, the latter of whom was related to her family by marriage.

Initially convinced that the troubled nun's case was indeed one of demonic possession, Daza and Salcedo turned for guidance to the fathers of the Society of Jesus, a decision which proved crucial for Teresa's future career. Founded in 1540 by the Spaniard Ignatius de Loyola (1491–1556), himself an enthusiast of the Devotio Moderna, the Jesuit order was a major force for spiritual renewal and reform within the Church. In Jesuit confessors such as Diego de Cetina and Baltasar Alvarez, Teresa at last found spiritual directors who were capable of helping her. Not only did they assure her that her gifts were of God, rather than of the devil, but also they encouraged her to continue her exploration of the life of the soul. Through them she was able to meet like-minded individuals, including two reformist clerics who became her defenders, the Franciscan Peter of Alcántara (1499–1562, canonized 1669) and the Jesuit Francis Borgia (1510–1572, canonized 1671).

Reassured by her new advisors, Teresa no longer resisted her mystical experiences. Recurring now more frequently, they were also increasingly dramatic, culminating about 1559 in the famous Transverberation, a powerful vision in which Teresa believed that an angel had pierced her through the heart with a fiery arrow. This episode is the subject of the most celebrated depiction of Teresa, Lorenzo Bernini's masterpiece in Rome's church of Santa Maria della Vittoria, in which the baroque sculptor blurs the distinction between erotic and religious experience.

In 1560 or 1561, Teresa became convinced that God was calling her to undertake a divine mission which transcended her own individual spiritual development. The result was her movement to reform the Carmelite order, which began in 1562 when she withdrew from La Encarnación with four young followers to found a separate house in Avila, that came to be known as the convent of San José, or St. Joseph. Teresa's monastic reform was part of the broader historical process known as the Counter Reformation, or Catholic Reformation, which was inspired by the contemporary spread of Protestantism in northern Europe. Convinced that the impoverishment of the individual soul in Catholic Europe had weakened the Church in the face of the Protestant threat, Teresa hoped to refortify the faithful spiritually, while at the same time contributing prayer in support of Rome's struggle for ascendancy over Western Christendom.

What Teresa disliked about aristocratic convents such as La Encarnación was the lax atmosphere which she traced to the abandonment in the late Middle Ages of the original ideals and rules of the Carmelite order. At San José, therefore, she sought to return to a purer and more primitive regime, which she modeled on Peter of Alcántara's so-called discalced (or barefoot) reform movement in the Franciscan order. Teresa's Discalced Carmelites did not literally go barefoot, but, as a sign of humility, they wore sandals without stockings. Their lives were to be devoted to silent prayer and spiritual discipline and growth, as well as to the performance of the daily menial chores necessary to sustain the community. Unlike the traditional, unreformed convents, there would be no servants or slaves for this purpose. Also, in order to ensure the community's freedom from worldly distractions and control by powerful patrons, Teresa insisted upon founding her new convent in complete poverty, that is, without an endowment. The nuns of the reform would live off the alms they collected from the general populace. No dowry would be required from entering novices and there would be no genealogical test for admission. Applicants would be judged on their aptitude for the rigorous spiritual life of the community, rather than on the economic status, nobility, or purity of blood of their families.

The Discalced Carmelite reform begun by Teresa had some powerful supporters, including Spain's King Philip II (1556–1598), but it also encountered a good deal of opposition. For example, the municipal authorities of Avila filed a lawsuit in an unsuccessful attempt to block the founding of San José without an endowment, because they feared that a convent which lacked its own independent financial base would become too great a burden on public charity. Other complaints came from Carmelite and other ecclesiastical authorities who feared the reform's implications for their own jurisdiction and prerogatives, from social conservatives who were alarmed by the movement's anti-aristocratic nature and by the enthusiasm shown for it by New Christians, and from theological conservatives who suspected affinities between Teresa's teachings and those of the Protestants, which shared common roots in the Devotio Moderna.

But Teresa of Jesus, as she now called herself, was neither a rebel nor a heretic. Always careful to proclaim her obedience and her orthodoxy, she was as opposed to Protestantism as were her conservative detractors. Through the force of her own strong personality, and taking advantage of her considerable rhetorical skills as well as the support of powerful friends, Teresa gradually won over or outmaneuvered the skeptics who tried to block her reform. In 1567, she won authorization to found more discalced convents in Spain and, between that year and her death in 1582, she would establish an additional 16, mostly in significant urban centers which had the population and the economic vitality to support communities of nuns who depended upon alms for their livelihood. During the same period, Teresa was active in promoting her reform in the male branch of the Carmelites as well. The first monastery of discalced friars was established in 1568 at Duruelo, and during Teresa's lifetime 13 more such houses would be founded. Teresa's collaborator in this effort was the renowned mystic and ascetic John of the Cross (Juan de Yepes, 1542–1591), who became her spiritual director and who, like Teresa, would be canonized after his death.

The rapid spread of reformed convents and monasteries is a tribute to Teresa of Avila's considerable gifts of leadership and organization. She was also a talented writer and, during her career, she found time to produce a number of works which have become classics of Western spiritual literature. The most important source on her own life and spiritual development, up to the establishment of the first discalced convent, is the *Libro de su vida*, or autobiography, composed at Avila between 1562 and 1565. Teresa's *El camino de la perfección* (The Way of Perfection), begun in 1565, was a practical manual of spiritual development through self-denial and prayer intended initially for the sisters at her new convent of San José. A work which occupied much of the rest of her life, being finished only shortly before her death in 1582, was the *Libro de las fundaciones* (Book of Foundations), in which Teresa recounted the history of the discalced reform.

By most accounts, Teresa of Avila's masterpiece is *Las moradas* (The Dwelling Places), also called *El castillo interior* (The Interior Castle). Begun in Toledo in 1577 at the order of her current confessor Jerónimo Gracián, *Las moradas* was intended to present a systematic exposition of Teresa's method of spiritual development through disciplined prayer. The book's title comes from the author's brilliant central metaphor, in which spiritual progress is conceived of as a series of seven rooms, or dwelling places, arrayed in concentric circles. Each room represents a different degree of prayer, and the goal of all prayer, union with God, lies at the center.

In 1580, Teresa's monastic reform, which had always enjoyed papal support, became fully institutionalized when Pope Gregory XIII decreed the formal separation of the Calced and Discalced Carmelite provinces in Spain. By this time, the years of work and struggle were beginning to show their effect on Teresa, a frail woman who had suffered poor health throughout her life, but who had stubbornly recovered from one serious illness after another. The same year as Pope Gregory's decree, Teresa, now 65 years of age, survived a severe bout with influenza, despite the fact that those around her had given her up for dead. Two years later, while on the road at Burgos, she fell ill again, but this time there would be no recovery. Refusing to abandon her travels on behalf of the order, she continued on to the discalced convent at Alba de Tormes and it was there, on October 4, 1582, that death overcame her.

By the time of her death, Teresa of Avila had developed a large popular following throughout Spain, and there was immediate talk of her being proposed for sainthood. Despite the stringent new requirements for canonization established recently by the Council of Trent, Teresa's case was rushed through the process. Beatified in 1614, she was declared a saint in 1622, only eight years later. More recently, in 1970, Pope Paul VI added another posthumous distinction to those already awarded to Teresa by Rome when he recognized her officially as a Doctor of the Church, a title reserved for saints of distinguished learning, whose ideas and writings have been particularly influential in the teaching of the faith. Teresa is the first female saint to be so honored. The tardiness of her formal acceptance, despite the power and appeal of her writings, is a reminder of the marginal role of women in the Church. Although for years Catholics referred to Teresa unofficially as a "doctor," Church authorities once held that she was unsuited to the dignity on grounds of gender, because the status of Doctor of the Church seemed closely related to the priesthood, which was open exclusively to males.

In the years since Teresa's time, there has been so much distortion of the facts of her life and career for both political and religious reasons that it is now difficult to discern the real woman behind the saint. Even so, her record of achievement as a reformer, builder, thinker, and teacher establishes her as one of the outstanding personalities of her time, and as a major presence in the history both of Spain and of Roman Catholicism.

SOURCES:
Bilinkoff, Jodi. *The Avila of St. Teresa: Religious Reform in a Sixteenth-Century City*. Ithaca, NY: Cornell University Press, 1989.

Lincoln, Victoria. *Teresa: A Woman: A Biography of Teresa of Avila*. Ed. by Elias Rivers and Antonio T. de Nicolás. Albany, NY: State University of New York Press, 1984.

Peers, E. Allison. *Mother of Carmel: A Portrait of St. Teresa of Jesus*. Wilton, CT: Morehouse-Barlow, 1944.

Teresa of Ávila. *The Life of Teresa of Jesus: The Autobiography of St. Teresa of Avila*. Trans. and ed. by E. Allison Peers. Image Books ed. Garden City, NY: Doubleday, 1960.

SUGGESTED READING:
Clissold, Stephen. *St. Teresa of Avila*. London: Sheldon Press, 1979.

Luti, J. Mary. *Teresa of Avila's Way*. Collegeville, MN: Liturgical Press, 1991.

Medwick, Cathleen. *Teresa of Avila: The Progress of a Soul*. NY: Knopf, 1999.

Teresa of Avila. *Teresa of Avila: The Interior Castle*. Trans. by Kieran Kavanaugh and Otilio Rodríguez. NY: Paulist Press, 1979.

Weber, Alison. *Teresa of Avila and the Rhetoric of Femininity*. Princeton, NJ: Princeton University Press, 1990.

Williams, Rowan. *Teresa of Avila*. Harrisburg, PA: Morehouse, 1991.

Stephen Webre,
Professor of History,
Louisiana Tech University,
Ruston, Louisiana

Teresa of Calcutta (1910–1997).

See Teresa, Mother.

Teresa of Castile (c. 1080–1130)

Countess of Portugal and queen regnant. Name variations: Theresa; Teresa of Portugal. Born around 1080 in Castile; died on November 1, 1130, in Portugal; daughter of Alphonso VI (Alfonso), king of Castile, and *Jimena Munoz (c. 1065–1128); married Henry, count of Burgundy, in 1095 (died 1112); married Fernando or Ferdinand, count of Trastamara, in 1124; children: (first marriage) *Urraca (c. 1096–1130); Sancha (b. around 1098, who married Fernando de Braganza); Teresa (b. around 1102, who married Sancho de Barbosa); Alphonso I Enriques or Henriques (c. 1110–1185), first king of Portugal (r. 1139–1185).

Teresa of Castile played a vital role in the establishment of the kingdom of Portugal. Born around 1080, she was the illegitimate daughter of King Alphonso VI of Castile and *Jimena Munoz, and the half-sister of *Urraca of Leon-Castile (c. 1079–1126). Despite Teresa's illegitimate status, her father used her for political purposes as he did his legitimate children; she was given the title countess of Portugal and married to Henry of Burgundy in 1095, to cement an alliance between Castile and Burgundy. Teresa had

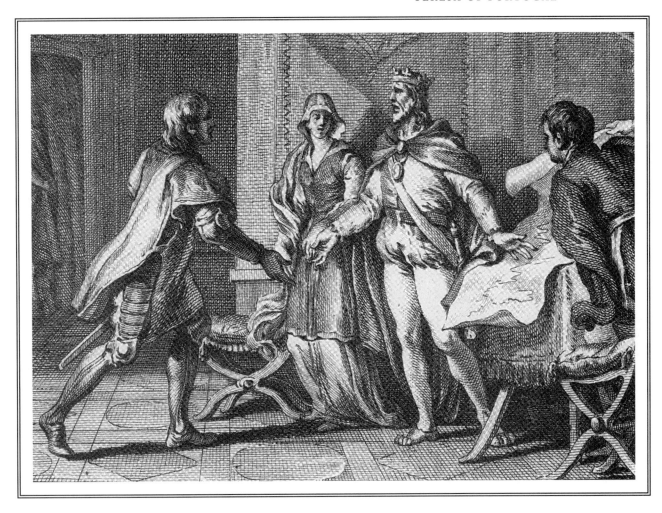

one son with Henry, Alphonso (I) Enriques, who inherited Burgundy when his father died in 1112. Teresa, acting as her son's regent, turned her attention to her holdings in Portugal, and spent the rest of her life working towards Portugal's independence from Spain. She was said to be a courageous ruler, openly ambitious and intelligent enough to recognize what resources Portugal needed to sustain itself.

Teresa made a campaign out of encouraging the Portuguese people to think of themselves as Portuguese, not a part of the Leon-Castile empire. She even led troops to force out the occupying soldiers of Castile, and encouraged urban development and capital investment to provide an economic base for sustainable independence. The countess enjoyed widespread popularity until her long-term affair with the noble Fernando Peres became public. Still her efforts focused on freeing Portugal until her now-adult son Alphonso forcibly removed her from the regency in 1128; she died two years later. However, Alphonso's debt to his mother's tireless efforts was incalculable, for only 13 years after her death Portugal won independence from Castile, and he became the first Portuguese king.

Laura York,
Riverside, California

Wedding of Teresa of Castile and Henry of Burgundy.

Teresa of Jesus (1515–1582).

See Teresa of Avila.

Teresa of Lisieux (1873–1897).

See Thérèse of Lisieux.

Teresa of Portugal (1157–1218)

*Portuguese princess. Born in 1157; drowned off Flanders on May 6, 1218; daughter of *Matilda of Maurienne (c. 1125–1157) and Alphonso I Henriques, also known as Alphonso I, king of Portugal (r. 1139–1185); sister of *Urraca of Portugal (c. 1151–1188), Sancho I, king of Portugal (r. 1185–1211), and *Matilda of Portugal (c. 1149–1173); married Philip the Great, count of Flanders and Artois, in 1183; married Eudes III, duke of Burgundy, in 1194 (divorced 1195).*

Teresa of Portugal (1793–1874)

*Princess of Beira and duchess of Molina. Born on April 29, 1793, in Queluz; died on January 17, 1874, in Trieste; daughter of *Carlota Joaquina (1775–1830) and John VI, king of Portugal; interred in Trieste Cathedral; married Pedro Carlos de Alcantra, on May 13, 1810; became second wife of Don Carlos also known as Charles (1788–1855), duke of Molina, on October 20, 1838. Teresa's sister *Francisca of Portugal was the first wife of Charles of Molina.*

Teresa of the Little Flower (1873–1897).

See Thérèse of Lisieux.

Teresa of Tuscany (1801–1855).

See Maria Theresa of Tuscany.

Tereshkova, Valentina (1937—)

Soviet cosmonaut, the world's tenth astronaut and first woman in space, who served as chair of the Committee of Soviet Women and a member of the Central Committee of the Communist Party. Name variations: Valya Nikolayeva-Tereshkova. Pronunciation: Ter-yesh-KOH-vah. Born Valentina Vladimirovna Tereshkova on March 6, 1937, in the village of Maslennikovo, near Yaroslavl, USSR; daughter of Vladimir Aksyonovich Tereshkov (a farmer) and Yelena (Fyodorovna) Tereshkova; finished secondary school, 1953; completed engineering course at textile technical institute, 1960; graduated from Zhukovsky Aviation Academy as military engineer, 1969; married Andrian Grigoryevich Nikolayev (a cosmonaut), in 1963 (divorced 1977); children: one daughter, Yelena (b. 1964).

Family moved to Yaroslavl (1945); started work at 16 in a tire factory; worked in textile factory (1955–60); joined airclub (1958); made first parachute jump (1960); selected as cosmonaut trainee (1962); joined Communist Party of the Soviet Union (1962); made spaceflight (1963); spoke at World Congress of Women in Moscow (1963); served as head of the Committee of Soviet Women (1968–87); elected member of the Central Committee (1971); became a member of Soviet Presidium (1974); elected chair of Union of Soviet Friendship Societies (1987). Awards: Hero of the Soviet Union; Order of Lenin; Hero of Socialist Labour (Czechoslovakia).

Valentina Tereshkova is a forthright person, even blunt. When an interviewer asked her to describe how she prepared for the "crucible day" of her spaceflight, Tereshkova replied, "Why do you call it a crucible? I do not see it like that. Cosmonauts in training did not think of death, danger or pain in the way you seem to think we did." When interviewers ask apologetically what her age is, Tereshkova responds with the precise date, commenting brusquely, "It is not correct to hide one's age." Until recently, however, Tereshkova's characteristic outspokenness has not extended to topics of political sensitivity, nor to comments on her own personal life and background, leading one writer to describe her as "a legend hidden in silence." Fortunately, since the advent of *glasnost* in 1987, and the subsequent demise of the Soviet Union, Tereshkova has finally felt free to speak more openly about a number of subjects on which she is able to shed interesting light.

The village of Maslennikovo, where Valentina Vladimirovna Tereshkova was born, lies about 200 miles northeast of Moscow, in the Yaroslavl region, a beautiful area of forests and meadows near the Volga River extolled in the verse of the 19th-century Russian poet Nikolai Nekrasov. At the time of her birth, in 1937, the village had not yet received electricity under the Five Year Plans of then Soviet ruler Joseph Stalin, and there was no running water. The effects of Stalin's brutal purges, however, which reached their peak that year, were felt in Tereshkova's village and home when a male cousin of hers who lived in the nearby city of Yaroslavl became one of many arrested without explanation. Released later in order to fight during the Second World War, he died in the conflict.

Tereshkova's father Vladimir Tereshkov was a tractor driver and mechanic on the local collective farm. Although he died when Valentina was less than three years old, she has often told interviewers that she felt a special closeness between them and often describes him as "young and handsome" and "popular and hard-working." Drafted in September 1939 to serve as a tank crewman in the Russo-Finnish War, he died in January 1940. Because the official notification did not state his place of burial, Valentina's mother **Yelena Tereshkova** hoped for many years that a mistake had been made and he would return. It was Valentina who eventually located in the military archives the burial record confirming his death.

Valentina grew up with an older sister, **Lyudmila Tereshkova**, and a younger brother, Vladimir Vladimirovich, born five months after their father's death. (Her mother also had earlier given birth to twins who died.) In their small village, food was relatively plentiful, but Yelena had no way of supporting her three children. In

June 1941, the Germans invaded the Soviet Union, and Valentina's memories of childhood are "completely involved in what happened during the war." Cryptically, she recalls herself as "one of the generation of war children without toys." Two of her father's brothers were killed in the war, and relatives of her mother in nearby Belorussia were executed during the Nazi occupation. At war's end, in 1945, Yelena took her children and moved in with her own mother in Yaroslavl, where she found work in a textile factory. The pay was poor, food was harder to obtain than it had been in the village, and Yelena never received the extra ration allotment due her as a soldier's widow.

Valentina finished her secondary education in 1953, at age 16. Her dream was to go to Leningrad and study to become a railroad engineer. Lyudmila was married and had started her own family, however, and when their mother became ill there was no one but Valentina to care for her. Partly due to misdiagnosis, Yelena's condition would deteriorate, and in 1956, at age 43, she suffered her first stroke, leaving her partially paralyzed for several months. Meanwhile in 1954, Valentina had taken her first job, at a Yaroslavl tire factory. From 1955 to 1960, she worked at the Yaroslavl textile factory, Krasny Perekop. Allergic to the omnipresent dust from the looms, she suffered reactions on her skin and face. She hated the work and continued to attend night school, graduating from the Textile Technical Institute as an engineer in 1960.

As well, in 1958 21-year-old Tereshkova had joined the local airclub. On May 21, 1959, she had made her first parachute jump. "I felt I wanted to do it every day," she said. She completed 160 parachute jumps and dreamed of becoming a pilot, knowing the dream was unattainable unless she left her family behind and moved to Moscow.

In April 1961, the Soviet Union's Yuri Gagarin became the first human to fly in space. With members of her airclub, Valentina eagerly followed the flight, and when she talked with her mother about the achievement, Yelena responded, "Now a man has flown in space; it is a woman's turn next." Strongly affected by her mother's remark, Tereshkova began to wonder whether the Soviet government might actually allow women into the cosmonaut program. She wrote to the group which sponsored Soviet airclubs, the Voluntary Organization for Cooperation with the Army, Air Force and Navy (DOSAAF), and volunteered for any future training program for female cosmonauts, un-

aware that the Soviet government was indeed preparing to put a woman into space. In December 1961, she was called to Moscow as one of several hundred women volunteers selected for preliminary medical screening. Early in 1962, she became one of the five women accepted for cosmonaut training. The program was conducted with such extreme secrecy that the women were not even allowed to inform their families they were preparing for space flight. Tereshkova told relatives she had been chosen for a special parachute team.

Early Soviet space capsules, unlike the cone-shaped capsules of American design, were hollow spheres, which Soviet designers believed would best withstand the heat and stress of reentry. But the falling ball was virtually impossible to "fly," spinning uncontrollably at times as it neared the ground. Soviet landings required the cosmonaut to eject from the capsule during the final stage of reentry, thus making qualification as a parachute jumper nearly as important as experience as a pilot or engineer.

As I saw the planet from space I realized how small Earth is, and how fragile, and that it could be destroyed very quickly.

—Valentina Tereshkova

In March 1962, Tereshkova moved to Star City, the cosmonaut training center about 45 miles from Moscow. The five women embarked on an 18-month training course, following the same strict regime as the men. They made an intense study of navigation and became familiar with the spacecraft's instruments, radios and cameras. Rigorous physical training, particularly in gymnastics, prepared them for conditions in space. Special aircraft flights simulated the weightless conditions of space, and centrifuge training tested their abilities to endure the high gravitational forces they would withstand during landing. To accustom them to the solitary confinement they would experience inside the space capsule, the trainees spent random periods of time, lasting from a few hours to several days, in an isolation chamber. The women were closely monitored for differences from the men in their responses to the various stresses of training. According to Tereshkova, they were not scheduled for centrifuge training during their menstrual periods.

Illness led to the removal of one woman, **Tatyana Kuznetsova,** from the program in 1962. Tereshkova continued with the three other remaining trainees, **Zhanna Yerkina**, **Valentina Ponomaryova** and **Irina Solovyova**. The Soviets prepared for the launch of two capsules, Vostok 5 and 6, one with a male cosmonaut and the other with a female, in June 1963. It was the usual Soviet practice at the time not to decide on the cosmonaut for any given flight until the last minute, taking advantage of the individual trainee's overall performance in training and medical fitness right up to the eve of the launch. In the case of the women, they would not be allowed to fly if they were menstruating.

On May 31, 1963, all four women were flown to the Baikonur cosmodrome, where, Tereshkova has noted, "no one knew which two girls would be chosen as the pilot and backup." That early June, Tereshkova proved lucky in the timing of her menstrual cycles. When Valery Bikovsky was named to pilot the Vostok 5, Tereshkova became pilot of the Vostok 6, with Solovyova as her backup.

The launch date for Vostok 6 was set for June 16. That morning, Tereshkova did some exercises, ate breakfast, then had an electrocardiograph test, and was wired with medical monitoring devices before donning her spacesuit and boots. Yuri Gagarin and Irina Solovyova accompanied her to the launch pad, where she was sealed into the capsule. Two hours later, Vostok 6 was launched into earth orbit, with Tereshkova in linked communication with Gagarin, her call sign *chaika* ("seagull").

"From space," Tereshkova later recalled, "the beauty of Earth was overwhelming. The blackness of the sky scattered with stars was impressive." Vostok 6 circled the Earth 114–144 miles above the surface, completing an orbit every 89 minutes. On board, Tereshkova performed a series of biological tests on plants and insects and took photographs and films for atmospheric studies, while also monitoring devices that recorded her responses to weightlessness and the progress of the capsule. Scheduled to orbit for 24 hours, with a possible 48-hour extension, Vostok 6 performed without technical difficulties the first day and was permitted to continue. On June 19, it was brought down after nearly 71 hours in orbit.

Landing over the Altai region, Tereshkova ejected from the capsule at around 23,000 feet and floated toward a field in her parachute. A strong wind made the landing fairly rough, and she bruised her face on the rim of her helmet. A quarter-mile from her capsule on the ground, Tereshkova radioed her position, changed into a jogging suit, and carried her spacesuit and para-

chute to the capsule to wait to be picked up. Farm workers helped her to carry the ejection seat to the capsule, then drove her to a telephone, where she notified Soviet Premier Nikolai Khrushchev of her successful landing before she returned to the field to meet her rescue plane.

The news of a woman cosmonaut orbiting the Earth had not been released until after the launch. Tereshkova's family learned from Soviet television that rather than training to jump from planes, Valentina was flying in space. According to Tereshkova, her mother "was very upset that I had deceived her and it took a long time for her to forgive me." In her flight, she had made 48 orbits, traveling 1.2 million miles. Khrushchev reveled in pointing out to the press that the flight had been longer than all four flights by American astronauts combined.

But Tereshkova was never assigned another flight, and many in the West viewed the launching as a ploy of pure propaganda, intended solely to give the Soviet Union the claim to being the first to send a woman into space. Lending support to this view is the fact that the selection of Tereshkova and the other women appears to have been based on quite different criteria than those applied to the men. While nearly all the men were both pilots and military officers, Tereshkova was only a worker in a textile factory, and some Western journalists have held that her job in the spaceflight therefore could not have been difficult.

Tereshkova rejects this assertion, pointing out that she completed the same training program, and was expected to perform the same functions while in orbit, as any of the men. Allowing that rivalry to be first in various aspects of space exploration clearly existed between the U.S. and the Soviet Union at the time, Tereshkova contends that if propaganda had been the only goal, a woman would have been included simply as a passenger, saving the Soviet government the time and effort in training five women for two years. She emphasizes that her flight was a solo one, and "needed the professional knowledge equal to that of a man." Westerners found the idea of a female cosmonaut so difficult to accept that rumors circulated declaring both that Tereshkova had never actually flown, and that she had become violently ill.

Tereshkova publicly claimed that there were no differences between the way the women and the men in training for space missions performed. Her colleague Kuznetsova, who left the mission, told an interviewer that Soviet doctors found that women performed better than men in some aspects of the training, including the centrifuge. Tereshkova denied any antagonism between the women and men, despite the women's lack of experience in certain areas (she admitted that "none of the women were qualified pilots, while the men were already professional, licensed pilots"). But, she pointed out, the women were all experienced as parachute jumpers, while many of the men were not.

One of the men Tereshkova met in training during 1962–63 was Andrian Nikolayev. In August 1962, Nikolayev became the third Soviet cosmonaut to complete a spaceflight, making 64 earth orbits. The following year, less than five months after Tereshkova's flight, she married Nikolayev, on November 3, 1963. The wedding was supposed to be secret, but word leaked out, and a huge crowd gathered around the Moscow marriage palace where the civil ceremony was held. Khrushchev was among the high-ranking guests. In her post-*glasnost* interviews with **Antonella Lothian**, Tereshkova related several instances when her mother had not approved of her actions, and added, "at my marriage she said, 'You must get your own life experience.' But she was not happy."

Valentina Tereshkova

Tereshkova, meanwhile, had become a Soviet international star, sent all over the world to make speeches and meet heads of state and world leaders, including the pope; she later claimed that Indian leader *Indira Gandhi had become a dear friend. Just a few days after her wedding, accompanied by Nikolayev, Tereshkova resumed her world tour of speaking engagements, ostensibly combining their honeymoon with her publicity duties. Within a few weeks, there were widespread rumors that Tereshkova was pregnant; seven months after the wedding, on June 10, 1964, their daughter was born by Caesarean section. Tereshkova has emphasized that premature births were common in her family, and that hers may have been induced partly by her fatiguing schedule of international travel combined with a heavy work load.

Since Tereshkova's marriage ended in 1977, she has been reluctant to discuss it. "I do not find it easy to speak about that period in my life," she said. "Husbands and wives should always be equal partners. Husbands who help their wives do exist and a few do not resent being outshone by their wives, but this is still too rare." She has also said that while love is the most important ingredient in marriage, respect, patience, and "a willingness to work together" are also critical.

In 1964, Tereshkova entered the Zhukovsky Air Force Engineering Academy, from which she graduated in 1969 with the rank of lieutenant colonel; she completed postgraduate work in 1976. The doubts cast in the West about her merits may have motivated her to seek the credentials of a military engineer, but Tereshkova emphasizes that it was her many years of work at the Cosmonaut Training Center which paid her salary, while her volunteer work, with the Committee of Soviet Women and as a member of the Soviet Central Committee, received greater attention.

Less than a week after her space flight, Tereshkova spoke at the 1963 World Congress of Women in Moscow. It was there, she said, "that I made my first appeal for international understanding. . . . My message was that we must protect Earth for future generations . . . I hoped Vostok 6 would be a bridge to unite the hearts of women in the world to achieve this aim." Tereshkova would be associated with women's issues for more than 20 years. She was named head of the Soviet government's Committee of Soviet Women in 1968, and in that position received thousands of letters from ordinary Soviet women detailing their problems with childcare, housing, working conditions, and pay. "It was

essential for the decision-makers firstly to admit that these problems existed, and then to provide solutions," she said, fully aware that when it came to women's rights, the Soviet government's policy was mostly talk and little action. In 1971, she was elected a member of the Central Committee. "I did my best to bring women's problems to the notice of the Politburo," she said, citing among her concrete results the addition to the Soviet constitution of Articles 35 and 53, providing for gender equality and family assistance. She was often disappointed, however, that recommendations she made were not implemented. Since *glasnost*, she has criticized the Soviet government for not practicing what it preached regarding equality of the sexes.

In the late 1970s, political scientist **Barbara Wolfe Jancar** described the limitations of Soviet committees, pointing out that Soviet citizens were not free to organize independently and that official committees were not truly representative. Moreover, according to Jancar, "I was told in Moscow . . . the Party leadership decides what should be done and then the committee undertakes the requisite research or performs the requested task. Representative of the nature of the women's committees is Soviet astronaut Valentina Tereshkova. Although chair of the Soviet National Women's Committee, she has never been identified as a specialist on women's problems. She is largely there as a figurehead." The committees primarily gave the Soviet Union the status of representation at international meetings, Jancar emphasized, while their effectiveness at home remained limited in scope. Undoubtedly, Tereshkova toed the official line. Her 1975 Women's Day speech shows her typical praise of the Soviet system: "The new way of life of women in the USSR and their new role in society are one of the most convincing arguments in favor of socialism." While she never admitted to any obstacles to women's equality in Soviet culture, even during the heavily pronatalist Stalin years, she seems also to have been genuinely dedicated to speaking out for world peace, and to doing what she could (however minor, given the situation) to improve women's lives.

In 1986, Tereshkova gained permission to hold a National Congress of Women, dedicated to public discussion of women's issues in the Soviet Union. She considers that event one of her biggest achievements. Others were more cynical; that same year, feminist dissident **Tatyana Mamonova** wrote: "Valentina Tereshkova, the celebrated spacewoman, remains a facade, for her position as president of the Committee of Soviet Women is used by the patriarchy against women; no ordinary woman has access to the president, and the Politburo dictates to the Committee of Soviet Women who may become delegates to international conferences and what statistics can be quoted there." After the congress, probably due to changes in the political mood under *perestroika*, Tereshkova failed to be reelected as head of the Committee of Soviet Women. When Gorbachev took power, her association with the past Soviet regimes of Khrushchev and Brezhnev diminished her popularity, although Tereshkova claims she left the committee because she was elected chair of the Union of Soviet Friendship Societies in 1987. She continued to promote international cooperation, espousing such concepts as "global morality," demilitarization, and the creation of a global rescue service or police force. This, she believed, could be used to provide international assistance during natural disasters, or as an international defense force in the event of extraterrestrial threats to the planet's security. After her space flight, she has said, "I saw my future as giving me the opportunity to bring people closer together, and to help different cultures and civilizations to see one world, as I had seen it."

Since the end of Soviet rule, Tereshkova has grown less reticent about commenting on the old Soviet system. In the Lothian interviews her bitterness surfaced, regarding the impact of the Stalinist purges on her own family. As children, she said, they had been told that her father's cousin was in prison, but it was not until the revelations of Khrushchev in 1956 that she began to understand the real scope of the past leader's repressions and executions. She called the Russo-Finnish War in which her father died "Stalin's whim," an unnecessary adventure in which the soldiers were not equipped for a winter war. "I resent very much what Stalin did to my father and other young Russian soldiers like him. I believe that Stalin took my father from me." At peace with herself today, Tereshkova loves opera and Russian poetry, and is able to recite long selections of her favorite poet, *Anna Akhmatova, by heart.

A biography of Tereshkova has yet to be written in the West. (Mitchell Sharpe wrote a brief work for juveniles in 1975, but the only information then available was secondhand, and some of the material in the book is erroneous.) The best source in English to date is Antonella Lothian's 1993 collection of transcribed postglasnost interviews, but the interviews, while interesting, avoid the difficult questions. A British journalist and activist for international women's issues, Lothian plans to write a full biography of

Tereshkova, which will perhaps address some of the thornier issues of her life and time.

SOURCES:

Clements, Barbara Evans. *Daughters of Revolution: A History of Women in the USSR.* Arlington Heights, IL: Harlan Davidson, 1994.

Jancar, Barbara Wolfe. *Women under Communism.* Baltimore, MD: Johns Hopkins University Press, 1978.

Lothian, Antonella. *Valentina, First Woman in Space: Conversations with A. Lothian.* Edinburgh: Pentland, 1993.

O'Neill, Bill. "Whatever became of Valentina Tereshkova?," in *New Scientist.* Vol. 14. August 1993, pp. 21–23.

Paulis, Pierre-Emmanual. "Valentina Ponomaryova's Story," in *Spaceflight.* Vol. 25, 1993, p. 41.

Reina Pennington, Ph.D. candidate
in military and women's history,
University of South Carolina,
Columbia, South Carolina

Teresia Benedicta of the Cross
(1891–1942).

See Stein, Edith.

Tergit, Gabrielle (1894–1982)

German writer and journalist. Born in 1894; died in 1982.

Selected works: Käsebier erobert den Kurfürstendamm *(novel, 1931);* Etwas Seltenes überhaupt, Erinnerungen *(posthumously published memoirs, 1983).*

Born in 1894 in Germany, reporter and novelist Gabrielle Tergit came to prominence during the 1920s as a reporter for the *Berliner Tageblatt* (Berlin Daily News), where she earned a reputation for her compelling renditions of court cases and courtroom activities. She published one novel *Käsebier erobert den Kurfürstendamm* (*Cheese and Beer Conquer the Kurfürstendamm*), in 1931. Tergit, of Jewish heritage, was forced underground during the Nazi rule of the 1930s and 1940s. She later wrote her memoirs before her death in 1982. *Etwas Seltenes überhaupt, Erinnerungen* (*Something Quite Special, Recollections*) was published in 1983 and is considered a respected historical reference about the fate of the Jews during the Nazi Holocaust.

SOURCES:

Bilsky, Lisa Anne. "Adrienne Thomas, Gertrud Isolani, and Gabriele Tergit: German Jewish Women Writers and the Experience of Exile." Ph.D. dissertation, University of Wisconsin, Madison, 1995.

"Gabriele Tergit's Novel on German Radio," in *AJR Information* [London]. Vol. 30, no. 4. April 1975, p. 7.

Tergit, Gabriele. *Käsebier erobert den Kurfürstendamm.* Berlin: Ernst Rowohlt, 1931.

Gloria Cooksey,
freelance writer,
Sacramento, California

Terhune, Mary Virginia

(1830–1922)

American novelist. Name variations: Mrs. E.P. Terhune; (pseudonym) Marion Harland. Born Mary Virginia Hawes on December 21, 1830, in Dennisville, Virginia; died on June 3, 1922, in New York, New York; daughter of Samuel Pierce Hawes (a merchant and magistrate) and Judith Anna (Smith) Hawes (direct descendant of Captain John Smith, the man who befriended *Pocahontas); married Edward Payson Terhune (a minister), on September 2, 1856 (died 1907); children: Edward Terhune (b. 1857); Christine Terhune Herrick (1859–1944, an author); Alice Terhune (b. 1863); Virginia Belle Terhune Van de Water (b. 1865, an author); Myrtle Terhune (b. 1869); Albert Payson Terhune (b. 1872, an author who married pianist Anice Morris Terhune).

Served as a copy editor for Home-Maker *(1888–90) and* Housekeeper's Weekly; *was a member of the Daughters of the American Revolution, the Association for the Preservation of Virginia Antiquities, and the Pocahontas Memorial Association.*

Selected writings under pseudonym Marion Harland: (novels) Alone; A Tale of Southern Life and Manners *(1854),* The Hidden Path *(1856),* Moss-Side *(1857),* Nemesis *(1860),* The Carringtons of High Hill *(1919); (domestic advice books)* Common Sense in the Household *(1871),* Dinner Year-Book *(1878),* Eve's Daughters *(1882),* Every Day Etiquette *(1905); also published three collections of short stories.*

Mary Virginia Terhune

Mary Virginia Terhune enjoyed a career as a home economics writer and novelist that spanned eight decades. She was born Mary Virginia Hawes in Amelia County, Virginia, in 1830, the third of nine children of Samuel Pierce Hawes and **Judith Smith Hawes**. Mary and her siblings received an excellent education from her father, a merchant who was related to Franklin Pierce, 14th president of the United States. He also hired tutors to give the children specialized instruction. Despite this encouragement, Judith Hawes did not approve of a woman pursuing a career and taught her girls to see homemaking as a woman's only proper role. In response to this position, Terhune kept secret from her parents the essays and short stories she composed.

In 1843, Terhune left home to attend classes in Prince Edward County, then spent a year at a Presbyterian girls' school in Richmond, Virginia. After her return home, she contributed stories anonymously to a weekly newspaper, but it was not until she was 23 years old that she earned any recognition for her work, when she won a prize offered by *Southern Era* for an article on temperance. At that point, Terhune enlisted the help of her father to privately publish her first full-length story, *Alone*, in 1854. It was sold to a New York publisher in 1856 to critical and popular acclaim (as was her second novel, *The Hidden Path*, which also appeared in 1856). Like most of Terhune's 25 novels, *Alone* was published under the name Marion Harland and concerned domestic life on a Southern plantation. Terhune's works were centered around female characters in their roles as wife and mother, and offered moral and religious lessons. New novels were published regularly between 1856 and 1873, and occasionally after that, making Marion Harland a household name among readers in the United States.

In 1856, Mary married a Presbyterian minister, Edward Payson Terhune, who was assigned to a local parish. It was a happy alliance, and Edward encouraged Mary's writing. The couple had two children before moving in 1859 to Newark, New Jersey, where four more children were born by 1872. Only three of the children survived to adulthood, all of them—***Christine Terhune Herrick**, **Virginia Van de Water**, and Albert Payson Terhune—eventually becoming writers as well.

As the wife of a parish minister, Mary Terhune had numerous responsibilities in addition to her obligations as a mother, yet she continued to publish frequently. While her earlier works were sentimental and romantic in tone, her later writings specifically attacked many of the goals of the emerging American woman's rights movement. Although Terhune did support a woman's right to higher education and thought women should be able to practice a profession if they had no husband or male family member to depend on, she maintained that marriage and motherhood were the ideal for all women.

Diagnosed with tuberculosis in the early 1870s, Terhune and her husband successfully sought a cure for the disease by traveling in Europe from 1876 to 1878. On their return to the East Coast, they settled first in Springfield, Massachusetts, then in Brooklyn, New York. At that time, Terhune began to concentrate on nonfiction, especially advice based on the new field of "domestic science," publishing books of domestic advice and household management for wives. Influenced by the immense cultural and social changes which followed the Civil War, Terhune tried to address the specific needs of professional women and those in the growing middle class. She also wrote magazine articles on homemaking, cooking, etiquette, and related topics.

In the 1880s, her consistently strong sales and common-sense advice led Terhune to accept the position of editor for two journals, *Housekeeper's Weekly* and *Home-maker*. In 1900, she began to write a syndicated column of domestic advice which appeared in 27 daily newspapers across the United States, including the *Chicago Tribune* (1911–17). Widowed in 1907, Terhune wrote on a variety of topics in her last years, among them travelogues based on her experiences in Europe, biographical sketches of famous American women, and Southern genealogy and history. She also composed a book of her personal philosophy, *Looking Westward*, which appeared in 1914. However, she remained best known for her domestic advice books. Mary Virginia Terhune died in her Brooklyn home in 1922, age 91. She was buried in Pompton, New Jersey.

SOURCES:
Duyckinck, Evert A., and George L. Duyckinck. *Cyclopedia of American Literature*. Vol. 2 (reprint). Detroit, MI: Gale Research, 1965.

Laura York, M.A. in History,
University of California,
Riverside, California

Terk, Sonia (1885–1979).
See Delaunay, Sonia.

Terk-Delaunay, Sonia (1885–1979).
See Delaunay, Sonia.

Ternan, Frances Eleanor
(c. 1803–1873)

*English actress and writer. Name variations: Frances Eleanor Trollope; Frances Eleanor Jarman; Mrs. Ternan. Born Frances Eleanor Jarman around 1803; died in 1873; second wife of Thomas Adolphus Trollope (1810–1892, a novelist); daughter-in-law of *Frances Milton Trollope (1779–1863).*

Frances Eleanor Ternan made her first stage appearance at Bath, England, in 1815. At Covent Garden in 1827–28, she appeared as Juliet to Charles Kemble's Romeo. Ternan accompanied her first husband on an American and Canadian tour in 1834–36. She appeared as Pauline in *The Winter's Tale* (1855) and as blind Alice in *The Bride of Lammermoor* (1866). Following her second marriage to Thomas Adolphus Trollope, Ternan left the stage, settled in Florence, and wrote *Aunt Margaret's Trouble* (1866), *Black Spirits and White* (1877), and *That Unfortunate Marriage* (1888). With her husband, she also published *Homes and Haunts of the Italian Poets* (1881).

Ternina, Milka (1863–1941)
Croatian operatic soprano who sang the title role in the first presentation of Puccini's Tosca *in London and New York. Born on December 19, 1863, in Vezišce, Croatia; died on May 18, 1941, in Zagreb, Croatia.*

Debuted in Zagreb, Croatia (1882); performed throughout Europe (1882–1906); performed in the United States (1896–1904); mastered a range of major roles, including Aïda, Tosca, Donna Anna, Kundry, Leonore, Isolde, Brünnhilde, and Elsa; retired from performing and began teaching (1906).

Born in 1863 in a small town outside of Zagreb, Croatia (then part of the Austro-Hungarian Empire), the soprano Milka Ternina was celebrated across Europe and the United States for her powerful voice and dramatic ability. Little is known of her family background. She studied voice first in the Croatian city of Zagreb under **Ida Winterberg**, then moved to Vienna to study with Joseph Gänsbacher at the Vienna Conservatory. Ternina debuted to strong acclaim at age 19 in Zagreb in the role of Amelia in *Ballo in Maschera*. She then enjoyed long contracts with opera companies in the German cities of Leipzig (1883–84), Graz (1884–86), and Bremen (1886–90).

From 1890 to 1906, Ternina performed regularly at the Munich Opera. In 1896, she traveled to the United States to make her American debut on the Boston stage with the Damrosch opera company. Her London debut followed in 1898 at Covent Garden, where she sang the role of Tosca in the first London performance of Puccini's opera; she would return to London in 1900 and 1906. Between 1899 and 1904, Ternina frequently made the long ocean journey between Germany and New York to maintain her engagements at the Munich Opera as well as at the Metropolitan Opera House in New York City. In those five years, she sang the title role in the first presentation of *Tosca* at the Metropolitan Opera on February 4, 1901, and performed 15 roles in 74 other productions; she also made sang on some of the earliest opera recordings.

In 1906, Ternina was struck with partial facial paralysis; unable to perform publicly, she retired to become an instructor. For several years, she taught American students at the Institute of Musical Art in New York, then Ternina returned to her native Zagreb as her health failed. The most renowned of her pupils was the soprano *Zinka Milanov.

SOURCES:

Hamilton, David. *The Metropolitan Opera Encyclopedia.* NY: Simon and Schuster, 1987.

Warrack, John, and Ewan West. *The Oxford Dictionary of Opera.* Oxford, UK: Oxford University Press, 1992.

Laura York, M.A. in History,
University of California,
Riverside, California

Terrell, Mary Church (1863–1954)

First president of the National Association of Colored Women, who championed causes including racial justice, woman's suffrage, and internationalism. Pronunciation: TER-el. Born Mary ("Mollie") Eliza Church on September 23, 1863, in Memphis, Tennessee; died of cancer at her home in Highland Beach, Maryland, on July 24, 1954; daughter of Robert Reed Church (a saloon owner who later became a millionaire) and Louisa (Ayers) Church (a hair store proprietor); attended Antioch College Model School; graduated from Oberlin College Academy, 1880; Oberlin College, B.A., 1884; married Robert Heberton Terrell, on October 28, 1891; children: Phyllis and Mary (adopted), and three who died in infancy.

Parents divorced (1869); enrolled in Antioch College Model School (1870); attended Oberlin College Academy (1875–80); attended Oberlin College (1880–84); taught at Wilberforce University (1885–87), and M Street Colored High School in Washington, D.C. (1887–88, 1890–91); was a member of the District of Columbia Board of Education (1895–1901, 1906–11); served as president of the National Association of Colored Women (1896–1901); was a founding member of the NAACP (1910); was a lecturer at the Brooklyn Institute of Arts and Science (1911–13); was a delegate to the founding conference of WILPF, Zurich (1919); appointed director of the Work among Colored Women in the East for the Republican National Committee (1920); wrote autobiography, A Colored Woman in a White World (1940); was the first African-American member of the American Association of University Women (1949); chaired the Coordinating Committee

for the Enforcement of the District of Columbia's Anti-Discrimination Laws (1949–53).

In September 1897, the newly elected president of the National Association of Colored Women (NACW) addressed its first annual conference in Nashville, Tennessee. In this stirring speech, Mary Church Terrell focused on the special role women should play in uplifting the plight of African-American children. She called for NACW activists to enter the home, "that sacred domain, to inculcate right principles of living and correct false views of life. Homes, more homes, purer homes, better homes, is the text upon which our sermons to the masses must be preached." She asked her audience, which included prominent, well-educated black women, to lead by example:

> Let us not only preach, but practice race unity, race pride, reverence, and respect for those capable of leading and advising us. Let the youth of the race be impressed about the dignity of labor and inspired with a desire to work. Let us do nothing to handicap children in the desperate struggle for existence in which their unfortunate condition in this country forces them to engage. Let us purify the atmosphere of our homes till it become so sweet that those who dwell in them will have a heritage more precious than great, more to be desired than silver or gold.

Mary Terrell's Nashville address was typical of the many talks she delivered around the turn of the 20th century, a time when the popular lecturer emerged as one of the most prominent African-American activists in the country. Her tone and ideas were generally conservative and consistent with prevailing notions about the proper role of women. They were also in line with her elite, sheltered upbringing. But Mary Terrell's ultimate goal was to accept nothing less than complete gender and racial equality. And as her disappointments mounted in both areas during the 20th century, she grew increasingly confrontational, battling segregation on picket lines and organizing sit-ins during the last years of her long life.

Mary Eliza Church was born in Memphis, Tennessee, on September 23, 1863, as the United States faced its greatest challenge, the Civil War. By 1860, Memphis was the sixth largest southern city, with a population of over 20,000, including about 4,000 blacks. Founded in 1819, the "Bluff city"—it stood on one of the Chickasaw Bluffs that rose over 100 feet above the Mississippi River—had grown from a rough frontier outpost to become the world's largest inland cotton market by the Civil War. During the rebellion, Memphis remained a prosperous commercial center. Occupied by Union forces, it nonetheless served as the center of illegal trade between the North and South.

The African-American population of Memphis expanded dramatically during the war, as refugees flooded the city. By 1870, the black population stood at over 15,000. The white population also increased during the period, but the rate of growth was only a third of that experienced by the African-American community. Thus Mary Church was born in an uncertain time in a place experiencing unsettling change, which created a period of both opportunity and danger for blacks. Her father Robert Reed Church, Sr., had been born a slave in 1839 in Holly Springs, Mississippi. His white father, Captain Charles B. Church, owned a fleet of Mississippi River boats. His mother, a house servant named **Emmeline**, had a limited impact on his upbringing because her owners moved from Holly Springs when Robert was young. Captain Church allowed his slave son to work as a dishwasher on his river boats, and later Robert became a steward in charge of purchasing. When the Union Navy gained control of the Mississippi River, putting the Captain's line out of business, father and son settled in Memphis. Robert, though technically still a slave, bought a saloon and hotel. He also began courting a local house servant, **Louisa Ayers**. Like the man she would marry, Louisa had never faced the harsh conditions a majority of slaves endured and, though not as light skinned as Robert, she could "pass" for white. Louisa had little experience with difficult physical labor and grew up as a close companion of her owner's daughter. She was well educated (even receiving French lessons) and well treated. When Robert and Louisa married, the Ayers family provided a trousseau from New York and an elaborate wedding reception.

The household where Bob and Louisa Church raised their young daughter Mollie, as Mary was usually called, was a sheltered, comfortable one. Terrell's house was a large, two-story home in the white section of town. Her friends were white, and she had no sense of having an inferior status based on race until she was five or six years old. She visited Captain Church on Sundays, though she did not know that the kindly man was actually her grandfather until she began to ask questions about his relationship to her father. Only when her maternal grandmother, **Eliza Ayers**, who was a great storyteller, began to relate some personal accounts of the horrors of slavery did young Terrell begin to appreciate her background. As the privileged girl would later note, "It nearly killed me to think that my dear grandmother, who I loved so devotedly, had once been a slave." Terrell was also greatly affected by an incident that took place when she was five years old. Traveling on a river boat with her father, who could pass for white whenever he wished, she was seated alone in the first-class car while her father went to the smoking car to socialize. As the conductor passed by he inquired, "Whose little nigger is this?," and pulled her from her seat. At this moment, her father returned to order the conductor to leave her alone. Her father consoled the frightened girl, but refused to explain the behavior of the conductor. Terrell's mother was equally reticent on the issue, which left the young girl confused and curious.

Robert and Louisa Church received their freedom on February 22, 1865, with the ratification of an amendment to the Tennessee state constitution abolishing slavery. Louisa had opened a successful "hair store" frequented by the wealthy women of Memphis, and Robert's saloon was thriving. But a year after the war ended, during the notorious Memphis Race Riot of May 1866, a group of policemen broke into Robert Church's saloon intent on robbing it. They shot him in the head and left him to die on the floor, but friends carried him home where he recovered from the wound. Robert Church would go on to make a fortune in Memphis real estate, build the largest theater for blacks in the country, and open a bank. By 1900, he was not only the richest African-American in Memphis, he may have been the nation's first black millionaire. He died in 1913, leaving daughter Mary with a considerable fortune.

Although she was certainly fortunate that her father recovered from the 1866 shooting, tragedy entered her young life in 1869 when her parents divorced. Louisa moved to New York where she started another successful hair business. In 1870, she enrolled her daughter in the integrated Antioch College Model School in Yellow Springs, Ohio. Here, Mary encountered little overt race discrimination, but she began to develop an appreciation of the history and present plight of others of her race. At the age of 12, she entered Oberlin College Academy, graduating in 1880. She then enrolled at Oberlin College, from which she graduated in 1884. Her academic achievements at both institutions were considerable. At Oberlin College, she pursued the rigorous classical course leading to the bachelor of arts degree, became freshman class poet, and edited the *Oberlin Review*. She was one of three black women who received the B.A. in the 1884 class. Though she encountered some discrimination because of her race, she later observed, "It would be difficult for a colored girl to go through a white school with fewer unpleasant experiences than I had."

Upon graduating in 1884, Mary Church told her father that she wished to return to Memphis to teach school. Appalled, Robert Church forbade his daughter to do so since "real ladies did not work." Instead, Mary took charge of his household for a year. But Robert Church remarried and Mary used this as an excuse to apply for teaching positions at black institutions. In spite of her father's threat of disinheritance, she accepted an offer to work at Wilberforce University in Ohio in 1885. Two years later, she moved to Washington, D.C., to teach Latin at one of the nation's leading black public schools, the M Street Colored High School.

A White Woman has only one handicap to overcome—a great one, true, her sex; a colored woman faces two—her sex and her race.

—**Mary Church Terrell**

In 1888, Robert Church convinced Mary to travel and study in Europe for two years. She learned French, Italian, and German at local schools, toured cultural and historic sites, and enjoyed an environment where her African ancestry mattered little. A German baron, along with other acquaintances, proposed marriage. But Mary Church decided to return home because she knew she "would be much happier trying to promote the welfare of my race . . . working under certain hard conditions, than I would be living in a foreign land where I could enjoy freedom from prejudice." No doubt, her feelings for the chair of the M Street High School language department, Robert Heberton Terrell, also played a role in the fateful decision. One of the first African-Americans to graduate from Harvard, Robert Terrell would later become the first black to serve as a municipal court judge in the District of Columbia. Mary married Robert in 1891 at her father's home in what the *New York Age* called "the most notable event in colored society for years."

Marriage forced Mary Church Terrell to give up her teaching career and turn her attention to domestic duties. Put simply, social convention forced her to abandon the role for which she was well trained in return for one for which she was poorly suited. But she did not remain tied to the home for very long. During the 1890s, she served on Washington's Board of Education, won election as the first president of the National Association of Colored Women, and

became a professional lecturer for the Slayton Lyceum Bureau. According to all accounts, Terrell was a superb speaker who traveled extensively to promote racial understanding. In talks such as "A Bright Side of a Dark Subject," she avoided discussions of the worst evils of racism. She hoped that by emphasizing the past accomplishments of prominent African-Americans and characterizing the future in a positive light she could better influence white audiences.

Terrell's non-confrontational lecturing style was certainly consistent with her training and elite status. But this is not the sole reason why she soft-pedaled her message. She saw herself as a publicist for racial cooperation and understanding which she assumed represented a prerequisite for achieving racial equality. She also possessed a tremendous faith in education. African-Americans could be "uplifted" through education, while whites would come to accept notions of racial equality if they only knew more about the black community. She especially hoped to reach white women because she believed "it is the women of the country who mould public opinion" and who teach values to the next generation. An ardent woman's suffragist, Terrell also predicted that when the time came "that trades and avocations shall not be closed against men and women on account of race or color, then the day of proscription and prejudice will darken to dawn no more."

Mary Terrell also reached thousands of Americans through her writings in the popular press and newspapers. As in the case of her lectures, she directed her message at a popular audience. She wrote about countless subjects, including aspects of African-American history. She condemned lynching, attacked the debt peonage system that kept many Southern black farmers in a state of bondage not unlike slavery, and promoted woman's suffrage. Her prose could be uncompromising, but she was careful to avoid offending white readers when possible.

In spite of her exhausting work schedule which included extensive travel, Mary remained active even after the birth of her daughter **Phyllis Terrell** (named after the black poet *****Phillis Wheatley**) in 1898. Mary had lost her first three children within days of their births, but Phyllis enjoyed good health from the beginning. In 1904, the Terrells adopted a niece, Mary, then ten years old, and raised her as if she were their biological daughter. When Terrell was away on extended lecture tours, her mother Louisa usually looked after the children. Robert Terrell, who earned a law degree by attending classes at night

during the 1890s, supported his wife's activism in every possible way.

Before the founding of the National Association for the Advancement of Colored People (NAACP) in 1910, Mary Church Terrell tended

to side with Booker T. Washington and the "Bookerites'" non-militant approach to achieving racial justice. But extensive exposure to Jim Crow laws in the South and the increasingly rigid segregation that overtook Washington, D.C., helped bring her to the founding meetings of the

NAACP. She served on the organization's executive board and increasingly involved herself in direct-action tactics. In some ways, her view of tactics designed to achieve racial equality came to mirror those of W.E.B. Du Bois, but her husband's close identification with the Bookerites restrained her actions somewhat. On the woman's suffrage issue, however, she joined *Alice Paul's militant Woman's Party to picket the White House in 1919. Terrell would be very disappointed when the former suffrage movement turned its back on black women during the 1920s.

As one of the nation's most prominent and popular African-American activists, Mary Church Terrell was often in demand as a speaker or organization participant during the first half of the 20th century. She continued to write extensively, including an autobiography, *A Colored Woman in a White World* (1940). She served on the executive board of the Women's International League for Peace and Freedom and was increasingly devoted to promoting internationalism. A lifelong Republican, in the 1920s and 1930s she worked for the Republican National Committee as director of Work among Colored Women in the East, and in other capacities. By the time she reached her 70s and 80s, she was honored at countless testimonials and given honorary doctorates.

Mary Terrell truly appreciated the admiration of a large number of Americans of all races, but she had no intention of resting on her laurels. Even at the age of 83, she was ready for new battles—maybe more ready than ever before. Her husband had died in 1925, her daughters were successful personally and professionally, and she had less and less to lose by making "public spectacles" of herself. So she addressed some new challenges. She applied for membership in the American Association of University Women and quickly received her expected rejection by this segregated organization. Noting that "I would be an arrant coward unless I opened the way for other colored women," she embarked on a three-year battle to break down the race barrier. After she succeeded in this campaign, she took on segregation in Washington eating establishments.

The District of Columbia had 1872 and 1873 laws on the books requiring "all eating-place proprietors to serve any respectable well-behaved person regardless of color." But the statutes had been illegally deleted from the District Code in the 1890s. A group of religious, social, and political leaders organized the Coordinating Committee for the Enforcement of the D.C. Anti-Discrimination Laws (CCEAD) in 1949, and asked Mary Church Terrell to become honorary chair. Not well suited to mere "honorary" positions, Mary came to lead the organization in a dramatic campaign to get the old laws reinstated. When local officials dragged their feet, the organization pressed on in court. It also used direct-action tactics. On February 28, 1950, three African-Americans and one white activist sat down at the food counter of the segregated Thompson's Restaurant. This group included 87-year-old Mary Church Terrell. After they were forbidden by a cashier from paying for food, they convinced the District commissioners to prosecute the restaurant owner, John Thompson. A three-year legal battle ensued.

During this time, Terrell led sit-ins and picketing to publicize the case of *District of Columbia* v. *John Thompson*. Kresge's, Hecht's, and Murphy's department stores all backed down and desegregated their lunch counters. The *Thompson* case went to the Supreme Court in the spring of 1953 and as Mary Terrell awaited the verdict, the 89-year-old advocate of racial justice received threatening phone calls and hate mail. But on June 8, Terrell was given the news of a great victory. Chief Justice William O. Douglas delivered the favorable verdict—segregated eating establishments were unconstitutional in Washington, D.C.

Two months later, a great celebration was held, including a reception at the White House, commemorating the 90th birthday of Mary Church Terrell. A new International Reading Room was dedicated in her name at Howard University. In a speech she gave on that day, Terrell told an audience of 1,500: "it shall be the happiest day of my life when our schools are integrated." It was thus only fitting that one of the nation's greatest champions of racial justice and harmony was alive to celebrate this monumental legal victory when, on May 17, 1954, the Supreme Court declared segregation unconstitutional in the *Brown* v. *Board of Education* decision. Alert and optimistic to the end, Mary Church Terrell died of cancer two months later at her summer home in Highland Beach, Maryland, on July 24, 1954.

SOURCES:

Jones, Beverly Washington. *Quest For Equality: The Life and Writings of Mary Eliza Church Terrell, 1863–1954*. Brooklyn, NY: Carlson, 1990.

Sterling, Dorothy. *Black Foremothers: Three Lives*. Old Westbury, NY: The Feminist Press, 1979.

Terrell, Mary Church. *A Colored Woman in a White World*. NY: Ransdell, 1940.

SUGGESTED READING:

Green, Constance. *The Secret City: A History of Race Relations in the Nation's Capital*. Princeton, NJ: Princeton University Press, 1969.

Sheppard, Gladys Byram. *Mary Church Terrell—Respectable Person.* Maryland: Human Relations Press, 1959.

COLLECTIONS:

Mary Church Terrell Papers, Library of Congress, Washington, D.C.

Mary Church Terrell Papers, Moorland Spingarn Collection, Howard University, Washington, D.C.

John M. Craig,
Professor of History,
Slippery Rock University, Slippery Rock, Pennsylvania,
author of *Lucia Ames Mead and the American Peace Movement*
and numerous articles on activist American women

Terriss, Ellaline (1871–1971)

British actress. Name variations: Ellaline Lewin; Lady Hicks. Born Ellaline Lewin on April 13, 1871, at the Ship Hotel, Stanley, Falkland Islands; died, age 100, on June 16, 1971, in England; daughter of William Terriss (an actor) and Amy (Fellowes) Terriss; sister of Tom Terriss (1874–1964, an actor); married Sir Seymour Hicks (an actor, writer, and impresario), in 1893 (died 1949); children: Betty Hicks (b. 1904) and one son (died in infancy).

Performed in amateur plays as a teenager; debuted professionally as Mary Herbert in Cupid's Messenger *(1888); signed with Charles Wyndham (1888); came to prominence in the role of Cinderella (1893); maintained an extensive repertoire, including* The Man in Dress Clothes, Sleeping Partners, *and* Bluebell in Fairyland; *wrote two books:* Ellaline Terriss, By Herself and With Others *(1928) and* Just a Little Bit of String *(1955).*

Selected filmography: Masks and Faces *(1917);* Blighty *(1927);* Land of Hope and Glory *(1927);* Atlantic *(1929);* A Man of Mayfair *(1931);* Glamour *(1931);* The Iron Duke *(1934);* The Royal Cavalcade *(1935);* The Four Just Men *(1939).*

A popular actress and singer, Ellaline Terriss appeared on the English stage for over 40 years. Born in the Ship Hotel in the Falkland Islands in 1871, she was the daughter of **Amy Fellowes Terriss** and William Terriss, a sheep farmer and aspiring actor. When she was very young the family moved to London, where William established himself in the theater. Although she received little formal education, Ellaline learned acting, singing, and dancing at home. After appearing in numerous amateur productions, she made her own debut as a professional actress at London's Haymarket Theater in *Cupid's Messenger* in 1888. Beautiful and demure with a strong, sweet voice, Terriss was hailed as a new talent; with her father's support, she was offered a three-year contract at the Criterion Theater

playing in musical comedies. When her father encouraged her to expand her repertoire with dramatic roles, Terriss left the Criterion in 1891 to perform in melodramas at the Princess Theater. In 1893, she married Seymour Hicks, a comedic actor and playwright; over the next 50 years, the couple would be one of the stage's most successful husband-and-wife teams.

Also in 1893 came Terriss' first major role, when she was offered the lead in the Lyceum's production of *Cinderella*, a role that brought her critical acclaim in the London press. This success led to Terriss' debut on the New York stage the following year in the same role. Hicks and Terriss signed on with the impresario George Edwardes of the Gaiety Theater on their return to London and often performed together. Terriss' most noted roles at the Gaiety were as the leads in *The Shopgirl, The Circus Girl,* as well as in *The Runaway Girl,* which ran for almost 600 performances. In 1897, Terriss gave birth to a son who survived only two days; soon after, she learned that her father, by then a star at the Adelphi Theater, had been murdered by a jealous colleague. Tragedy struck a third time a few months later with the death of her mother Amy. Despite her grief, Terriss returned to work at the Gaiety, then signed again with the Criterion in 1899. A short U.S. tour in 1900 was followed by several seasons at London's Vaudeville, which Hicks managed. Their daughter **Betty Hicks** was born in 1904.

In December 1905, Hicks and Terriss opened their first theater, The Aldwych. A second, the Hicks Theater, was opened in 1906; the couple starred in its most successful play, *The Beauty of Bath,* which ran for 341 performances. Terriss continued to perform in their own and other theaters across London as well as touring England in various productions until 1912, when she and Hicks went on a music-hall tour of South Africa. They were as popular as ever in London on their return home, but they now faced serious financial problems. With the outbreak of World War I in August 1914, theater attendance dropped off. This, combined with the costs of maintaining their theaters and their luxurious lifestyle, forced Terriss and Hicks to sell the theaters and jewelry to pay off their debts.

Their popularity among London theatergoers, however, allowed them to continue performing for other theater managers throughout the war. In 1917, Terriss was offered her first film role, in *Masks and Faces,* after which she returned to the London stage for several years. She toured Australia in 1924 in a production of *The Man in Dress Clothes,* returning in 1925 to London to perform in *Sleeping Partners*, one of her best-known roles. In addition to her many stage roles in the 1920s, Terriss made numerous gramophone recordings and appeared in the leading female role in her second movie, *Blighty* (1927), a World War I melodrama which also starred Hicks (he had appeared in films since 1913). Her third film, *Land of Hope and Glory*, was also released that year. In 1928, Terriss ventured into writing, publishing *Ellaline Terriss, by Herself and With Others*, an autobiographical work. In 1929, she made a third film, *Atlantic*, an early "talkie" about the sinking of the *Titanic*. She played in four more films in the early 1930s, including 1931's *Glamour*, directed by her husband, who also wrote screenplays for a number of other films.

In 1935, Seymour Hicks was honored with a knighthood and Terriss became Lady Hicks. In May 1935, at age 64, Terriss gave her final stage performance in a Victoria Theater production of *The Miracle Man*. Retired from theater, she made one last film, 1939's *The Four Just Men*. Hicks' memoirs, *Me and the Missus*, appeared that same year before the couple went on tour to entertain British troops in the Middle East. They then moved on to South Africa, but the unfolding events of World War II made ocean travel impossible and they were forced to remain there until 1946.

Sir Seymour Hicks died at age 78 in 1949, and Terriss retired from all public performances. In 1955, she published a second book of reminiscences, *Just a Little Bit of String*; the title was the name of a popular song she had performed in her early years. She died at age 100 in 1971.

SOURCES:
Morley, Sheridan. *The Great Stage Stars*. Australia: Angus & Robertson, 1986.
Terriss, Ellaline. *Just a Little Bit of String*. London: Hutchinson, 1955.

Laura York, M.A. in History,
University of California,
Riverside, California

Terry, Ellen (1847–1928)

Foremost English actress of the late 19th and early 20th centuries who is best remembered for her Shakespearean roles, in particular her interpretation of Portia in The Merchant of Venice. *Name variations: Mrs. George Frederic Watts (1864–78); Mrs. Charles Claverine Kelly (1878–85); Mrs. James Carew (1907–09); Dame Ellen Terry. Born Ellen Alice Terry on February 27, 1847 (and not in 1848 as found in her autobiography, which appears to have been an honest mistake); died on July 21, 1928; second daugh-*ter of Benjamin Terry (1818–1896, an actor) and Sarah Ballard Terry (1819–1892, an actress who performed as Miss Yerret); sister of Kate Terry (1844–1924), Marion Terry (1852–1930) and Florence Terry (1854–1896), all actresses; aunt of Phyllis Neilson-Terry (1892–1977) and **Beatrice Terry** (both actresses); great-aunt of John Gielgud, the actor; sister-in-law of Julia Neilson (1868–1957); had irregular education, trained as an actress by Mrs. Charles Kean [*Ellen Kean], whose husband managed a theater in London where Terry appeared as a child; married George Frederic Watts (a painter), in 1864 (divorced around 1878); married Charles Wardell (an actor who performed under the name Charles Kelly), in 1878 (divorced around 1885); married James Usselman (1876–1938, an American actor who performed under the name John Carew), in 1907 (divorced around 1909); children: (with Edward Godwin) Edith Craig (1869–1947, British actress, costume designer, stage director and suffragist); (Edward) Gordon Craig (b. 1872, world-famous stage designer).

*Awards: Golden Jubilee in the theater celebrated (1906); medal of the Founders of the New Theater (New York, 1910); LL.D., St. Andrew's University, Scotland (May 5, 1922); became the second actress (after *Genevieve Ward in 1921) to be created Dame Commander of the British Empire (1925).*

Having made her London debut (1856), teamed with Henry Irving (1878), becoming a great favorite with audiences in his lavish productions at the Lyceum Theater in London, and with whom she toured extensively, including appearances in the U.S., until his death (1905); was a great friend of the Anglo-Irish playwright George Bernard Shaw, and her extensive correspondence with him was published after her death; best remembered for the magnificent portrait in the role of Lady Macbeth, painted by John Singer Sargent, that hangs in the National Gallery in London.

Selected theater (unless otherwise noted, all appearances were in London): made debut as Mamillius in Charles Kean's production of The Winter's Tale at the Princess Theater (April 28, 1856); appeared as Puck in A Midsummer Night's Dream (1856), William Waddilove in To Parents and Guardians, Jacob Earwig in Boots at the Swan, the dual roles of Goldenstar and Dragonetta in The White Cat (1857), Karl in Faust and Marguerite, Prince Arthur in King John, Fleance in Macbeth, and the Genie of the Jewels in The King and the Castle (1858); appeared as Tiger Tim in If the Cap Fits, Hector Melrose in Home for the Holidays, Giles, Harry, James and other parts in Distant Relations (1859), Mabel Valecrusis in A Lesson for Life (1860), Puck in A Midsummer Night's

Dream, *Clementine in* Attar Gull, *Sophia Steinbach in* All in the Dark, *Rosetta in* A Stumping Legacy, *Letty Briggs in* The Governor's Wife, *Sophie Western in* Bamboozling, *Clara in* Matrimony, *Mabel in* A Lesson for Husbands, *Mrs. Brinstone in* A Nice Quiet Day *(1861); appeared as Florence in* A Chinese Honeymoon, *Louisa Drayton in* Grandfather Whitehead, *Clorinda in* A Family Failing, *Margot in* The Sergeant's Wife, *Sally Potts in* The Eton Boy, *Kate Mapleton in* Nine Points of the Law, *Cupid in* Endymion, *Alice in* Marriage at Any Price, *Dictys in* Perseus and Andromeda, *Marie in* The Marble Heart,

Marguerite de Stormberg in The Angel at Midnight, *Gertrude Howard in* The Little Treasure, *Hero in* Much Ado About Nothing, *Lady Touchwood in* The Belle's Stratagem, *Serena in* Conrad and Medera, *Fanny Fact in* Time Tries All *(1862); appeared as the Spirit of the Future in the opening ceremony of the Theater Royal in Bath, Titania in* A Midsummer Night's Dream, *Britannia in* Buckstone at Home, *Hero in* Much Ado About Nothing, *Lady Frances Touchwood in* The Belle's Stratagem, *Desdemona in* Othello, *Mary Ford in* A Lesson for Life, *Isabella in* A Game of Romps, *Flora in* The Duke's Motto, *Nerissa*

Ellen Terry

in The Merchant of Venice, *Constance Belmore in* One Touch of Nature, *Julia Melville in* The Rivals, *Sir Tristram in* King Arthur, *and Mary Merideth in* The American Cousin *(1863); appeared as Helen in* The Hunchback *(1866), Marion Vernon in* A Sister's Penance, *Margaret Wentworth in* Henry Dunbar, *Madeleine in* The Antipodes, *Kate Dalrymple in* The Little Savage, *Rose de Beaurepaire in* The Double Marriage, *Mrs. Mildmay in* Still Waters Run Deep, *Katherine in* Katharine and Petruccio *(1867); appeared as Kitty in* The Household Fairy *(1868), Philippa Chester in* The Wandering Heir, *Susan Merton in* It's Never too Late to Mend, *Helen Rolleston in* Our Seaman, *Volante in* The Honeymoon, *and Kate Hardcastle in* She Stoops to Conquer *(1874); appeared as Portia in* The Merchant of Venice, *Clara Douglas in* Money, *Mrs. Honeyton in* A Happy Pair, *Pauline in* The Lady of Lyons, *Mabel Vane in* Masks and Faces *(1875), Blanche Hayes in* Ours, *Kate Hungerford in* Brothers, *Lilian Vavasour in* New Men and Old Acres *(1876), Georgina Vesey in* Money, *Lady Teazle in* The School for Scandal, *Lady Juliet in* The House of Darnley *(1877), Mrs. Merryweather in* Victims, *title role in* Olivia, *Iris in* The Cynic's Defeat, *title role in* Dora *(1878); appeared as Ophelia in* Hamlet *(1878, Lyceum), Lady Anne in* Richard III, *Ruth Meadowes in* Eugene Aram, *Henrietta Maria in* Charles I, *and Frou-frou in* Butterfly *(1879); appeared in the title role in* Iolanthe *and as Beatrice in* Much Ado About Nothing *at Leeds (1880); appeared as Lilian Vavasour in* New Men and Old Acres, *Beatrice in* Much Ado About Nothing *(1880), Camma in* The Cup, *Letitia Hardy in* The Belle's Strategem *(1881), Desdemona in* Othello *(1881), Juliet in* Romeo and Juliet *(1882), Jeannette in* The Lyons Mail *and Clementine in* Robert Macaire *(1883), Viola in* Twelfth Night *(1884), Margaret in* Faust *(1885), Peggy in* Raising the Wind *(1886), Ellaline in* The Amber Heart, *Josephine in* Werner, *Mary Jane in* Wool-Gathering, *Lady Macbeth in* Macbeth *(1887), Catharine Duval in* The Dead Heart *(1889), Lucy Ashton in* Ravenswood *(1890), title role in* Nance Oldfield, *Queen Katharine in* Henry VIII *(1891), Cordelia in* King Lear, *Rosamund in* Becket *(1892), Lady Soupire in* Journeys End in Lovers' Meeting *(1894), *Guinevere in* King Arthur, *Yolande in* Godefroi and Yolande, *Imogen in* Cymbeline *(1895), Catharine in* Madame Sans-Gene *(1897), Catherine in* Peter the Great, *Sylvia Wynford in* The Medicine Man *(1898), Clarice in* Robespierre, *Mrs. Tresilian in* Variations *(1899), Volumnia in* Coriolanus *(1901), Mrs. Page in* The Merry Wives of Windsor *(1902), Hiordis in* The Vikings, *Evodia in* The Mistress of the Robes *(1903), Kniertje in* The Good Hope, *Brita in* Eriksson's Wife *(1904), Alice Grey in* Alice Sit-by-the-Fire *(1905), Lady Cicely Waynflete in* Captain Brassbound's Conversion, *Francisca in* Measure for Measure, *Hermione in* The Winter's Tale *(1906), Elizabeth of York in* Henry of Lancaster, *Aunt Imogen in* Pinky and the Fairies *(1908), Alexia Vane in* At a Junction, *Nance Oldfield in* A Pageant of Famous Women *(1909); toured with* Four Lectures on Shakespeare *(1910–21); toured the U.S. (1910); appeared as *Nell Gwynn in* The First Actress *(1911), the Abbess in* Paphnutius *(1914); toured Australia (1914–15); appeared as the Queen in* The Princess and the Pea, *Darling in* The Admirable Crichton *(1915); appeared in* The Lady of the Manor *(also known as* The Homecoming, *1916); appeared as Gran'Mere in* Ellen Terry's Bouquet *(1917), The Nurse in* Romeo and Juliet *(1919), Mrs. Long in* Pride and Prejudice *(1922); made final appearance on stage as Susan Wildersham in* Crossings *(1925).*

Filmography: Her Greatest Performance *(1916);* Pillars of Society *(1920);* The Bohemian Girl *(1921);* Potter's Clay *(1922).*

Ellen Terry was born in Coventry, England, on February 27, 1847, in a theatrical rooming house while her parents were on tour with Miss Acosta's acting troupe. Of mixed Irish and Scottish parentage, she appears to have had no English blood in her veins. She came from a theatrical family, and her life spanned the period between the days when actors were considered to be not quite respectable to the era when knighthoods were bestowed upon them. The founder of the family tradition was her father, Benjamin Terry, the son of an Irish innkeeper of Cork, who had come to Portsmouth as a young man and went on the stage at an early age. After his marriage to **Sarah Ballard Terry**, the daughter of a Scottish builder of Portsmouth, he induced his wife to follow the same profession and soon she was performing as Miss Yerret. Eleven children were born to this marriage: two died in infancy, but the rest entered the theater in one capacity or another. Three of the sons became theatrical managers; **Kate Terry** (1844–1924), the eldest daughter, went on the stage, as did her daughter **Mabel Gwynedd Terry-Lewis** (1872–1957). Two other sisters, **Marion Terry** (1852–1930) and **Florence Terry** (1854–1896), and a brother Fred Terry (1863–1933), were also in the theater as were Fred's children with actress **Julia Neilson**—Dennis Neilson-Terry and **Phyllis Neilson-Terry**. But it was the second daughter, Ellen Alice, who became the best-

Neilson, Julia.
See Braithwaite, Lilian for sidebar.

known member of the family, being hailed as the greatest English actress of her day.

Ellen Terry began her career as a child performer in London on April 28, 1856, appearing as Mamillius in Shakespeare's *The Winter's Tale*, the first performance of which inaugurated the Princess Theater in Oxford Street, with Queen *Victoria, Prince Albert and the princess royal *Victoria Adelaide in attendance. The production ran for 100 performances after which the child actress played in Shakespeare's *A Midsummer Night's Dream* at the Princess Theater, under the management of Charles Kean. There she received her first favorable notice: "Miss Ellen Terry played the merry goblin, Puck, a part that requires an old head on young shoulders, with restless, elfish animation, and an evident enjoyment of her own mischievous pranks." Thereafter, Terry played a great variety of roles, both male and female, occasionally appearing in two plays on the same evening. Her first striking success occurred on October 18, 1858, as Prince Arthur in Shakespeare's *King John*. The Kean management terminated in 1859, and Ellen Terry and her sister Kate then went on tour for several months in a drawing-room presentation; part one was called *Distant Relations* and part two *Home for the Holidays*. Returning to London, she appeared in *Atar Gull* and then went on to the Theater Royal in Bristol, where her parents and siblings had secured permanent positions with the local stock company, which, under the management of J.H. Chute, had become one of the finest ensembles in Britain. There, she again played various roles especially that of Cupid in *Endymion*, a lavish spectacle of the kind for which Chute was known. On March 4, 1863, Terry took part in the opening production of the new Theater Royal in Bath, playing the Spirit of the Future in the *Prologue* and Titania in *A Midsummer Night's Dream*. These years of repertory in Bristol and Bath allowed Terry to cut her teeth in a highly varied repertory of classic and recent plays, all of which enabled her to learn her craft. As her reputation grew, she was called back to London and on March 19, 1862, she appeared at the Haymarket Theater as the heroine opposite the distinguished E.H. Sothern (future husband of *Julia Marlowe) in *The Little Treasure*. The sincerity of her portrayal in this role greatly impressed audiences and made her name in London. She then appeared as Hero in *Much Ado About Nothing*, at which time one critic praised her as "graceful and winning," and then as Lady Touchwood in *The Belle's Stratagem*. Terry remained with the Haymarket Company until 1864, when she met the prominent painter George Frederic Watts, who had been engaged to render a portrait of her sister Kate; despite the fact that George was twice Ellen's age, she left the stage to marry him. Not quite 17, naive in regard to men and to life in "the real world," she was in love with the idea of love and marriage, and with the desire to become a part of Watts' milieu of artists and intellectuals. But Terry found herself completely lost in a world she was too ignorant and inexperienced to understand. An older man, lacking in patience, Watts soon realized that he had made a great mistake. Less than a year later, the exasperated artist sent her home to her family. His beautiful portrait of her, painted in 1864, survives to testify to the first months of their love.

At first all went well for Terry, for Watts gave her an allowance and her parents were content to let her stay at home, their ambitions for their children amply satisfied by the achievements of Kate, who was now a successful actress on the London stage. Only when Kate retired to marry in 1867 did the Terrys pin their

---

❧▶ **Neilson-Terry, Phyllis** (1892–1977)

*English actress. Name variations: Phyllis Terson. Born in London, England, on October 15, 1892; died in 1977; daughter of Fred Terry (an actor-manager) and Julia Neilson (1868–1957, an actress); niece of *Ellen Terry (1847–1928); educated at Westgate-on-Seas, Paris, and Royal Academy of Music; married Cecil King (died); married Heron Carvic.*

In 1909, Phyllis Neilson-Terry made her debut at the Opera House, Blackpool, as Marie de Belleforet in *Henry of Navarre*, under the stage name Phyllis Terson. She made her London debut in the same part at the New Theater in January 1910. That February, when her actress-mother *Julia Neilson took ill, Phyllis replaced her as Marguerite de Valois in the same play. In April, she played Viola in *Twelfth Night* at His Majesty's Theater, while her father Fred Terry played Sebastian. Neilson-Terry went on to play many of Shakespeare's women, including Juliet, Lady Macbeth, Desdemona, Rosalind, Katherine, and Portia. In November 1914, she made her first New York appearance, as Viola, at the Liberty Theater. After she played the title role in *Trilby*, she went on tour in America and Canada, returning to England in 1919, following the war.

In 1922, Neilson-Terry took up the management of the Apollo Theater and continued to act. Over the years, she was seen in numerous plays, including *Bella Donna*, *Craig's Wife*, *Sweet Nell of Old Drury*, and *Candida*. She also portrayed Elizabeth in *Elizabeth of England* and appeared in *Separate Tables*. Her movies include *Doctor in the House*, *Look Back in Anger*, and *Conspiracy of Hearts*.

---

hopes upon their second daughter and urge Ellen back upon the stage. In less than a year, however, the impulsive Ellen, now barely 21, suddenly and quietly left her home to live in a cottage in the country with the successful architect and stage designer Edward Godwin, a man 12 years her senior, whom she had known as a child when he was secretary of the Bristol Shakespeare Society. With the start of this new relationship, Terry again left the theater, this time for six years. Two children were born to Terry during this period, a daughter **Edith Craig** (1869) and a son Edward Gordon Craig (1872), neither of whom could be legitimized because their mother was still married to George Watts. In time, they chose the surname Craig, which both of them were to make famous. The country idyll with Godwin was not to endure. Beset with financial woes and losing interest in Terry, he turned to other matters, and the young mother found it necessary to return to work simply to support herself and her children.

I can pass swiftly from one effect to another, but I cannot fix one, and dwell on it, with that superb concentration which seems to me the special attribute of the tragic actress.

—Ellen Terry

It was through the urging of playwright Charles Reade that Terry returned to the stage in 1874, first as Philippa in his drama *The Wandering Heir* and as Katherine opposite Henry Irving's Petruchio in Shakespeare's *The Taming of the Shrew*. Despite her absence from the stage, she was so fine an actress that she again found herself immediately popular with audiences that seemed willing to overlook her decidedly un-Victorian escapade. During this period, she performed in a number of popular plays but especially as Portia in Shakespeare's *The Merchant of Venice*, a role that she would often repeat and which would eventually mark the height of her career. This engagement was the result of her having come into contact with the Bancrofts, who managed the Prince of Wales's Theater, and under whom Terry worked until late in 1876. After this, she appeared in a number of plays including *Ours*, in which George Bernard Shaw was to see her for the first time. In 1878, Terry, now safely divorced from Watts, suddenly married Charles Wardell, an actor who performed under the name Charles Kelly, but though he was good to her children, his jealous temper proved impossible to live with and, after securing a legal separation in 1881, Terry was once again on her own.

In 1878, Henry Irving took on the management of the Lyceum Theater in London's West End, and Terry was the first artist hired. He was 40; she was 31, and she would be his leading lady. Thus was begun the partnership that would last for years and become legendary in the annals of the London stage. Irving was then at the height of his career and powers. His Hamlet had created a sensation in 1874, and he knew that with his own theater he needed only a young actress of great promise to secure his position as the leading actor of Great Britain. Terry, aside from her successes as Portia and Olivia, was still poised at the threshold of her career and her greatest days lay before her. Their first performance at the Lyceum was in *Hamlet* with Terry as Ophelia, which opened the theater under Irving's management on December 30, 1878.

The Lyceum arrangement between Irving and Terry lasted for 24 years. During this time, she was to receive £200 per week (nearly $1,000), a handsome sum, which gave her financial security and the ability to raise and educate her children without worrying about the cost. Appearing as permanent leading lady at the Lyceum was a glorious position for Terry in the English theater. This was the late Victorian age, when Britain was at the height of its power and glory and the wealth and self-confidence of the country was at its peak, a time when those who reached the top found themselves at a very great height indeed. The Irving productions were lavish, the costumes, scenery, lighting and music the best that money could buy, and the receptions at the Lyceum drew members of the royal family, the nobility, the moneyed classes in general and the intellectual, artistic and cultural elite of the age. Each year, the company made a four-month tour of the provinces that was the event of the annual cultural life of much of the country, and on seven different occasions the company toured the United States. That Irving and Terry were lovers has never been proved, but all the evidence suggests that they were, and, in fact, in her old age she as much as admitted it. The dark side of the professional relationship, however, was that although her position at the Lyceum enabled Terry to shine in a number of great roles, especially Shakespearean ones, there were others that were denied her or early removed from the repertoire either because they had no suitable part for Irving or because for some reason or other Irving no longer chose to appear in them.

In 1883, Terry and Irving essayed their first American tour. Terry was then 35 years old, already an acclaimed actress and ready for the exposure in the New World that would enhance not only her reputation but her purse as well. Her first appearance on the New York stage was as Queen *Henrietta Maria (1609–1669) in W.G. Will's drama *Charles the First*. The *New York Tribune* was particularly enthusiastic about the young English artist:

> Miss Terry is spontaneous, unconventional, and positively individual, and will use all characters in the drama as vehicles for the expression of her own. Thus in Queen Henrietta Maria . . . Miss Terry's acting . . . proceeds essentially from the nervous system—from the soul. There were indications that her special vein is high comedy; but she was all the woman in the desolate farewell scene that ends the piece, and she melted every heart with her distress, even as she had charmed every eye with her uncommon loveliness.

From New York, the company moved on to Philadelphia, Boston, Baltimore, Brooklyn, Chicago, Cincinnati, and St. Louis, traveling in eight cars, enjoying the luxuries of American hotels but deploring the unpleasantness of early steam heat. Terry was to return to America again in 1884, 1887–88, 1893, 1907 (the first time without Irving), 1910 and 1915.

In his biography of Irving, Bram Stoker wrote of the positive aspects of the Irving-Terry relationship:

> Irving was only too glad to let her genius and her art have full swing. . . . In the studying of her own parts and the arranging of her own business of them she had always a free hand with Irving. At the Lyceum she was consulted on everything; and the dispositions of other persons and things were made to fit into her arrangements. . . . The advantages which both Irving and Ellen Terry gave to dramatic art will be even more marked in the future than it is at the present. . . . Naturally, the years that went into the doing of this fine art work threw the two players together in a remarkable way, and made for artistic comradeship which, so far as I know, has had no equal in their own branch of art. Her performance of Ophelia alone would have assured her a record of greatness; Irving never ceased expatiating on it.

Not everyone was enthusiastic about the Irving-Terry partnership. George Bernard Shaw writing 25 years after it ended said:

> To me Irving's years at the Lyceum, though a most imposing episode in the history of the English theater, were an exasperating waste of talent of the two artists who had seemed to me peculiarly fitted to lift the theater out of its old ruts and head it toward unexplored regions of drama. With Lyceum Shakespear [sic] I had no patience. Shakespear, even in his integrity, could not satisfy

the hungry minds whose spiritual and intellectual appetites had been whetted and even created by Ibsen.

On December 13, 1902, the Lyceum years came to an end with a performance at the Prince's Theater in Bristol. Tastes were changing, the company was earning increasingly less money, a fire destroyed much of their valuable scenery, and Irving's health began to give way. Meanwhile, in his private affections Irving had tired of Terry and had developed a new interest of an amorous nature. The pair acted together for the last time on July 14, 1903, at a benefit for the Actor's Association at the Drury Lane Theater, she playing Portia to his Shylock, after which they went their separate ways. Irving died in 1905.

In her appearance, Ellen Terry was a tall, handsome woman with blonde hair, gray eyes, and a strong, square jaw. A striking figure on stage, famed for her animation and grace in movement, she was a robust and, in her middle years, portly woman, considered, however, to be very attractive according to the taste of her day. Shaw insisted that every male theatergoer was in love with Terry but the remarkable fact about her was her ability to inspire the devotion of her own gender; she was extremely popular with female audiences in Britain and America alike. Despite her youthful indiscretions, the British public adored her as "our Ellen," and, though many people considered *Madge Kendal the greater artist, Terry was beyond any doubt the most popular actress on the stage in the late Victorian era—even more so than *Mrs. Patrick Campbell, who had a great vogue among theatergoers and critics alike but who never took her work seriously. As the leading lady of the English stage for some 25 years, Terry knew most of the major lights of her day—Shaw, Wilde, Tennyson, Browning and Ruskin—but remained a simple person, quite at home with ordinary people of every walk in life. A warm-hearted extrovert, she was a great favorite with artists; she posed for Rossetti and her painting in the role of Lady Macbeth (*Gruoch) by John Singer Sargent was the sensation of the year when it was first displayed at the New Gallery in 1888. Terry, troubled by the mixed reception her interpretation of the role had drawn, always felt that this portrait most clearly conveyed what she was aiming for.

When the Terry-Irving partnership came to an end, Terry undertook the management of the Imperial Theater, where she staged and appeared in *Much Ado About Nothing* and made a rare appearance in an Ibsen play, *The Vikings*. Two years later, in 1905, she played Alice Grey in James M. Barrie's *Alice Sit-by-the-Fire*. In 1906, she starred there as Lady Cicely in *Captain*

Brassbound's Conversion, a part especially written for her by Shaw. The same year marked the 50th anniversary of her first appearance on any stage, and it evoked a remarkable outpouring, not only from the luminaries of her own country but from her fellow artists both on the Continent and in America (*Sarah Bernhardt, *Eleonora Duse, *Adelaide Ristori, *Réjane, Coquelin, etc.). The jubilee banquet, which followed a matinee commemorative performance at the Drury Lane Theater and was attended by 22 members of her family, was presided over by the rising statesman Winston Churchill.

Terry is largely remembered as a Shakespearean actress, but her reputation as an interpreter of the Bard rested on a surprisingly few roles, most of which she undertook at an age when she was really too old to do them justice. Yet do them justice she did, enthralling her audiences as Portia in *The Merchant of Venice*, and as Beatrice, Juliet, Cordelia, Imogen and Hermione. Side by side with these roles, however, must be ranked the ones that she never undertook—Rosalind in *Twelfth Night*, Miranda in *The Tempest*, Perdita in *The Winter's Tale*, and Katherina in *The Taming of the Shrew*—and those in which she appeared with less than true success—Lady Macbeth and Volumnia in *Coriolanus*. The later post-Shakespearean classics she avoided, and the new drama of Ibsen she deliberately bypassed, an oddity when one considers that Ibsen reached Britain when she was in her prime and that she was in constant communication with George Bernard Shaw, one of Ibsen's greatest champions. Thus, in attempting to assess the greatness of Terry one must admit that the evidence was never fully in. Some observers considered her "restless and fidgety" on the stage but her grandnephew, John Gielgud, allowed in his memoirs that her restlessness on stage "was part of her glory," recalling that even in her old age "she moved with an extraordinary spontaneity and grace and crossed the stage with an unforgettable impression of swiftness." Shaw felt that she had a genius simply for standing still that contrasted strikingly with her bearing when she was in motion. For her part, Terry never once classed herself as a great actress though she took her work with the greatest seriousness.

But for all her devotion to her art, there remained until very late in life a streak of the devil-may-care in Terry's character, not the least of which lay in her relations with men. In 1907, at age 60, she allowed herself to be swept off into a third marriage, this time with American actor John Carew (né Usselman), a man 25 years younger than herself, whom she had met when he played in the production of *Captain Brassbound's Conversion*. The marriage lasted but two years, though Carew remained an occasional visitor even in her last years.

By 1913, it was clear that Terry had passed her prime and that her career was drawing to a close. Nevertheless, with the war raging in Europe, she undertook an exhausting tour of Australia with her readings in 1914–15. Beset by cataracts, she stopped in New York to have her eyes operated on in 1915, but she was close to blind thereafter and increasingly unable to remember lines. When she appeared as the Nurse in *Romeo and Juliet* in 1919, opposite **Doris Keane** and Basil Sydney in the title roles, she had to be aided by the actors who whispered cues to her. Unable to sustain the run of a play but badly in need of funds, she agreed to appear in films, but none of the five that she undertook between 1916 and 1922 amounted to anything that could be called artistic. She continued to give her readings until 1921, when she broke down on the stage of the Gaity Theater. Thereafter, ailing and not always fully lucid, she spent most of her time in her country home, Smallhythe, in Kent. In 1925, she was taken to Buckingham Palace to be created a Dame Commander of the British Empire (CBE), only the second actress to be so honored. Three and one-half years later, after suffering a stroke, she died peacefully at Smallhythe (now the Ellen Terry Museum) on July 21, 1928, with her daughter at her side.

Apart from her excellence as an actress, Terry was also a lady of letters. She published her autobiography, *The Story of My Life*, in 1908; kept a diary until the end of 1926; carried on a lengthy correspondence with **Audrey Campbell** (1887 to 1912), and an even lengthier one with Shaw (1892 to 1922) which was published after her death. It was Shaw who writing to her in 1918 observed: "I scan the rising generations of women for another Ellen; but Nature really seems to have broken the mould this time: nobody replaces you in my heart."

SOURCES:

Auerbach, Nina. *Ellen Terry Player in Her Time.* NY: London, 1987.

Manvell, Roger. *Ellen Terry.* London, 1968.

St. John, Christopher. *Ellen Terry and Bernard Shaw: A Correspondence.* NY, 1931.

Stoker, Bram. *Personal Reminiscences of Henry Irving.* London, 1906, repr. Westport, CT, 1970.

Terry, Ellen. *The Story of My Life.* London, 1908 (new ed. as *Ellen Terry's Memoirs with a Preface, Notes and Additional Biographical Chapters by Edith Craig and Christopher St. John*, London, 1932, repr. New York, 1969).

SUGGESTED READING:

Brereton, Austin. *The Life of Henry Irving.* London, 1908 (repr. 1969).

Craig, E.G. *Ellen Terry and Her Secret Self.* London, 1931.

Gielgud, John. *An Actor and His Time.* London, 1979.

Pemberton, T. Edgar. *Ellen Terry and her Sisters.* London, 1902.

Terry, Ellen. *Four Lectures on Shakespeare.* London, 1932.

Robert Hewsen,
Professor of History,
Rowan University,
Glassboro, New Jersey

Terry, Lucy (c. 1730–1821).

See Prince, Lucy Terry.

Terry, Rose (1827–1892).

See Cooke, Rose Terry.

Tervapää, Juhani (1886–1954).

See Wuolijoki, Hella.

Terzian, Alicia (1938—)

Argentine composer, conductor, musicologist, pianist, and lecturer who wrote numerous orchestral and vocal works as well as two ballets. Born in Córdoba on July 1, 1938.

Born in Córdoba in 1938, Alicia Terzian graduated from the National Conservatory in Buenos Aires in 1958 with a first prize and a gold medal. Her teachers were A. Ginastera, R. Gonzalez, R. Garcia Morillo, F. Ugarte, and G. Gilardi. Of Armenian descent, she specialized in 4th- to 12th-century medieval religious Armenian music. Terzian completed her studies in this subject in Venice under Padre Dr. Leoncio Dayan. The winner of several prizes, including the Outstanding Young Musician of Argentina Prize in 1970, Terzian directed many festivals of contemporary music in addition to composing.

John Haag,
Athens, Georgia

Tescon, Trinidad (1848–1928)

Philippine freedom fighter. Born in 1848 in San Miguel de Mayumo, Philippines; died in Manila in 1928; married Julian Alcantara.

Fought in the Philippine Revolution (from 1895); established a field hospital at Biak-na-Bota for injured soldiers; helped organize the Philippine Red Cross.

Trinidad Tescon is remembered as a hero of the Philippine Revolution. Little is known about her early years or family background except that she married Julian Alcantara, another Philippine nationalist. She was already an activist in the Masonic movement in the Philippines when, in 1895, she joined the Katipunan, a revolutionary nationalist army. She participated in battles against the Spanish army under generals Llanera, del Pilar, and Soliman, and was wounded several times. Among her many exploits were the theft of munitions from the Spaniards to supply her fellow troops. After one such daring act, Tescon was captured and interrogated for five days but managed to escape. While her husband and two others defended the fort of Biak-na-Bato in Bulacan, Tescon, from attack, Tescon turned her attention to nursing the wounded soldiers inside and set up a makeshift hospital. For this she was given the name "Mother of Biak-na-bato" by the soldiers. She went on to create nursing stations on the battle sites of the southern Philippine provinces, organizing and training nationalist women to serve in her hospitals. Her efforts were crucial in laying the groundwork for the expansion of the official Philippine Red Cross Society under the leadership of **Hilaria Aguinaldo** in 1899 (it had been established in 1863). After the Philippine-American war, Trinidad Tescon was honored by the American Red Cross for her nursing work. She died in Manila in 1928, and received a hero's burial in Manila's Tomb of the Veterans.

SOURCES:

Soriano, Rafaelita Hilario, ed. *Women in the Philippine Revolution.* Quezon City: Printon Press, 1995.

Uglow, Jennifer, ed. *The International Dictionary of Women's Biography.* NY: Continuum, 1985.

Laura York, M.A. in History,
University of California,
Riverside, California

Tess, Giulia (1889–1976)

Italian operatic soprano. Born on February 19, 1889, in Milan, Italy; died on March 17, 1976, in Milan; studied singing under Bottagisio; married Giacomo Armani (a conductor).

Giulia Tess, who was born in Milan, Italy, in 1889, achieved a noted career as an operatic soprano, beginning with her debut at Prato in 1904. During her earliest performances, she sang mezzo-soprano, but she retrained for several years and after 1922 successfully expanded her professional vocal range to that of a soprano. Her repertoire included the roles of Mignon, Salome, and Elektra. In 1909, she performed in Venice and in Prague. She also made appearances in Vienna and St. Petersburg.

Tess, who was married to the prominent conductor Giacomo Armani, retired from the stage in 1940 and devoted her time to opera production and to giving music lessons. Among her more memorable students were Tagliavini and *Fedora Barbieri. Tess died in Milan in 1976.

Gloria Cooksey,
freelance writer,
Sacramento, California

Tetberga (fl. 9th c.)

Queen of Lorraine. Name variations: Theutberga of Valois. Flourished in the 9th century in Lorraine, also known as Lotharingia; sister of Hubert, abbot of Saint-Maurice; married Lothar also known as Lothair II (c. 826–869), king of Lorraine (r. 855–869), in 855; no children.

The Frankish queen Tetberga was involved in a divorce case which altered the patterns of marriage in the Frankish empire. She had come from a politically important noble family and married King Lothair II of Lorraine. Yet after two years she had not given birth to any children, considered the first duty of any queen. Lothair's mistress *Waldrada had given birth to a child, however, which led Lothair to decide to rid himself of Tetberga and marry Waldrada. The king assumed he had enough power to dissolve his own marriage without any trouble, but the dissolution lasted several years and became known across Western Europe, for Tetberga was adamantly opposed to the divorce, as were most Church officials. Lothair had to take more drastic measures than simply casting his wife out.

He first accused his queen of incest with her brother Hubert, abbot of Saint-Maurice. Such a charge was one of the few acceptable reasons for an annulment. But Tetberga defiantly maintained her innocence, and even suffered through an ordeal by fire to prove it. She was imprisoned soon afterwards and possibly threatened with torture, until she claimed she wanted to join a convent. Lothair took her message to the Frankish bishops, but they still refused to end the union. Eventually the poor prisoner was forced to "confess" in public to incest, aborting a fetus, and various other sins.

Still the bishops supported her right to remain married; with their assistance, a desperate Tetberga wrote to Pope Nicholas for help. The pope agreed to aid her, but Lothair bribed the pope's legates and married Waldrada. In response, Nicholas called a synod, annulled Lothair's recent actions, and ordered Lothair to restore his lawful wife. Under immense political pressure, Lothair put Waldrada aside and brought Tetberga out from her prison cell and made her queen again.

Even this did not end Lothair's scheming; the issue had gone beyond this particular marriage and was now a power struggle between king and pope. In 866, Tetberga "requested" a divorce herself on grounds that she wanted to enter a convent; this request was almost certainly forced out of her, for there are no signs that the queen had given up hope of retaining her position, although the awkwardness and bitterness she must have felt are difficult to imagine. Pope Nicholas refused Tetberga's entreaty and declared that she could enter a monastery but Lothair was still bound to her as her husband and could never remarry. Since this would not serve Lothair's purposes, Tetberga remained at court, the question unresolved, until 869, when Lothair died just after receiving the permissions he needed to divorce Tetberga from Nicholas' successor, Pope Hadrian II.

This long, drawn-out legal and ecclesiastical battle had long-term implications for marriage in the Frankish Empire after Lothair's death. While the Church continued to deny divorce to petitioning husbands, marriages were ended through desertion and separation much more frequently than before; the Church was beginning to lose some of its authority over the laws and procedures of marriage.

SOURCES:

Klapisch-Zuber, Christiane, ed. *A History of Women in the West, vol. II: Silences of the Middle Ages.* Cambridge, MA: The Belknap Press of Harvard University, 1992.

Laura York, M.A. in History,
University of California,
Riverside, California

Tetrazzini, Eva (1862–1938)

Italian operatic soprano. Born in March 1862 in Milan, Italy; died on October 17, 1938, in Parma, Italy; sister of Luisa Tetrazzini (1871–1940) and Elvira Tetrazzini; studied under Ceccherini; married Cleofonte Campanini (a conductor).

Eva Tetrazzini, the lesser-known older sibling of soprano *Luisa Tetrazzini, made her debut as Marguerite in Florence, Italy, in 1882 after training with Ceccherini. She appeared in New York City in 1888 and 1908, and in London in 1890. Tetrazzini performed many roles, including Aïda, Valentine, Fedora, and Desdemona. She died at Salsomaggiore Terme in the province of Parma in northern Italy in 1938. Eva is not to be confused with her other sister, soprano **Elvira Tetrazzini**, who recorded under the name E. Tetrazzini.

Gloria Cooksey,
freelance writer,
Sacramento, California

Tetrazzini, Luisa (1871–1940)

Italian coloratura soprano. Born on June 29, 1871 (some sources cite 1874), in Florence, Italy; died on April 28, 1940, in Milan, Italy; sister of Eva Tetrazzini (1862–1938) and Elvira Tetrazzini; studied with Ceccherini at Liceo Musicale; married Giuseppe Scalaberni (an opera manager); married Pietro Vernati; married once more.

Debuted in Florence, Italy, as Inéz (1890); debuted in U.S. in San Francisco (1907), in Covent Garden, London (1907); with Enrico Caruso, published The Art of Singing *(1909); published autobiography,* My Life of Song *(1921); published* How To Sing *(1923); sang farewell concert (1933).*

Coloratura soprano Luisa Tetrazzini enjoyed a long career as an international opera star. She was born in 1871 into a family of Florentine musicians; her father, a military tailor, provided well for his children and had them tutored in music and singing. Luisa claimed that she started singing at age three. Her older sister *Eva Tetrazzini became a well-known opera singer, and Luisa determined to follow her. After marrying Giuseppe Scalaberni, owner of the Pagliano Theater in Florence, Tetrazzini began studying voice at the Liceo Musicale in Florence in 1890; only three months later she made an unusual professional debut as the lead in *L'Africaine* at the Pagliano. She was not originally cast in the production, but had attended the rehearsals with her husband and knew the role; when she learned that a performance was to be cancelled because the lead soprano was sick, Luisa offered to sing the role herself. Her flawless voice and remarkable range brought her critical praise, which led to a command performance of the role for *Margaret of Savoy, queen of Italy, in Rome. This was followed by an extended Italian tour.

Her sister Eva's husband Cleofonte Campanini, a well-respected conductor, then used his contacts to arrange engagements for Luisa abroad. By 1892, she was appearing in Buenos Aires and other South American cities, where she already commanded high fees. She traveled extensively during the 1890s, garnering fans in cities as far apart as Buenos Aires and St. Petersburg; she also toured in Spain, Portugal, and Mexico. In 1904, Tetrazzini made her North American debut in San Francisco, having traveled there from Buenos Aires in disguise with her lover, Giulio Rossi, in order to elude her husband. Later that year she went to New York, where she made several gramophone recordings.

But contract negotiations for a debut at the Metropolitan Opera faltered, and Tetrazzini returned to San Francisco amid controversy over whether she had signed with the Metropolitan Opera and was thus unable to perform elsewhere. This type of legal controversy would recur over the course of Tetrazzini's career.

In 1907, she made her London debut at Covent Garden, playing to sold-out houses. Her success in London confirmed her as a true international celebrity, and she was acclaimed for her dramatic and comedic skills as well as for her pure soprano voice. She was also praised for her personal warmth and kindness by students and fellow performers; a stout figure who heartily enjoyed the pleasures of dining, Tetrazzini was honored by numerous restaurant dishes invented and named in her honor.

In 1908, she accepted an invitation from the American Oscar Hammerstein for a contract with his Manhattan Opera House in New York, where she starred in productions from 1908 to 1910. She found time to work with another Italian opera great, Enrico Caruso, on an instruction manual for voice students, published in 1909 as *The Art of Singing*. However, when the Metropolitan Opera bought the Manhattan Opera, Tetrazzini found herself in new legal battles; Hammerstein argued that she was still contracted to sing exclusively under his management. As she had done six years before, Tetrazzini went back to San Francisco, despite Hammerstein's threat of a court injunction against her, declaring that she would sing in the streets if she had to.

On Christmas Eve 1910 she did just that, performing in front of the San Francisco Chronicle building for a crowd of about 250,000. She returned to New York for one season at the Metropolitan Opera (1911–12), then moved on to contracts in Chicago and Boston between 1912 and 1914. At the outbreak of World War I, Tetrazzini returned to Italy, where she raised money for wounded Italian soldiers and performed for the troops. Married and divorced a second time at the end of the war, she decided not to continue in opera roles but to focus on international solo concert tours instead. An autobiography, *My Life in Song*, appeared in 1921, followed by *How to Sing* in 1923.

Tetrazzini's concert career lasted until her retirement at age 64 in 1934, when she settled in Milan. Although she had been very highly paid for years, her extravagant lifestyle and the financial mismanagement of her third husband left her destitute by the mid-1930s, and she was forced to take on pupils to support herself. Luisa Tetrazzini died at age 68 in Milan following a stroke.

SOURCES:

Gattey, Charles Neilson. *Luisa Tetrazzini: The Florentine Nightingale*. Portland, OR: Amadeus Press, 1995.

Warrack, John, and Ewan West. *The Oxford Dictionary of Opera*. Oxford, UK: Oxford University Press, 1992.

Laura York, M.A. in History,
University of California,
Riverside, California

Teuta (c. 260–after 228 BCE)

Powerful queen of Illyria whose successful piracy and sieges in Greece were checked only by Roman military intervention. Born possibly around 260 BCE; died after 228 BCE; married Agron, king of the Illyrian tribe of the Ardiaioi.

Teuta was the wife of Agron, king of the Illyrian tribe of the Ardiaioi. Agron had unified the Adriatic coast from Istria (in modern Slovenia, just to the east of Italy) to Lissus (near where the modern Drin River enters the Adriatic in northern Albania) for the first time. His success came as a result of his skill in acquiring booty which was then used to reward the increasing number of followers who flocked to his banner. (In the 3rd century BCE, the Illyrians knew little of the settled social order long experienced by the urban peoples of the southern Balkans and Italy. Illyria was also poor and overpopulated at the time.) Agron's successful exploitation of local conditions, however, quickly posed a problem. After so many Illyrians came to acknowledge his hegemony, he both had a greater need than ever to acquire the booty essential to maintaining his followers' loyalty, and fewer opportunities to do so close to home since one-time victims were now allies. Instead of opting to range more widely by land, Agron sought to overcome his dilemma by exploiting sea-borne raiding, an innovation as far as the Illyrians were concerned. The sea—giving his raiders range and speed (it was always much faster to travel by ship than over land in antiquity)—made Agron a figure to be feared, especially among the Greeks who lived to the south of his expanded domain.

The Greeks were at the time especially susceptible to Illyrian attack because generations of conflict had left Greece hopelessly disunited and militarily feeble. Most significantly, in 233, just before Agron's power surged, the Molossian kingdom of Epirus (immediately abutting the realm of Agron on the south) was overthrown and replaced by a looser federation of tribes which was much weaker as a deterrent than had been the monarchy which preceded it. In addition, by 231 Macedonia (abutting Agron's kingdom to the east and southeast) was itself immersed in a bevy of political and military difficulties, not the least of which was the threat posed by the Dardanians, a people who lived to the north and northwest of Macedon (and thus, to the east and northeast of Agron). Therefore, two states which had long served to check Illyrian raiding to the south were not in a strong position to do so as Agron's power reached its acme.

Teuta's rise to fame beyond Illyria came as a result of the general disquiet then existing throughout Greece. In 231, the Aetolians, having for some time coveted the land of the Acarnanians which lay on the Adriatic just to the north of the Corinthian Gulf, attacked the Acarnanian city of Medeon. The Acarnanians had long been protected from such an assault by the Macedonians; however, when the Aetolians attacked, Macedonia was itself preparing for a Dardanian war. As a result, the Macedonian king, Demetrius II, paid Agron to send a relief force to counterattack the Aetolians. Agron sent 5,000 men in 100 ships to Medeon and successfully beat off the Aetolians. This force thereafter returned to Agron's court at Scodra with a significant amount of produce "liberated" from the Acarnanian countryside and a report about the easy pickings to be had for the taking in Greece. Agron took this news enthusiastically. In fact, during the celebration which followed his army's return, he ate and drank so much that he literally burst open and died.

Agron's heir, Pinnes, was underage at the time and, as a result, Teuta succeeded her husband. (Teuta was not Pinnes' mother, but clearly she was the dominant woman at Agron's court at the time of his death.) Teuta immediately exploited the news of Greek weakness by sending another fleet to ravage the countrysides of Elis and Messenia (south of Acarnania, along the west coast of the Peloponnesus). This operation was also very successful and proved to be a stimulus to even more extensive raiding. Over the winter of 231–30, Teuta, advised by a council which included two men of particular note—Scerdilaidas, and a Greek adventurer from Pharos named Demetrius—planned additional attacks.

These began in 230 with an Illyrian army approaching the Epirote city of Phoenice, supposedly seeking supplies to carry them farther south. Employed within Phoenice was a garrison of Gauls whose function was to protect the interests of the locals. When some Illyrians were admitted into the city, rather than purchasing supplies they offered the Gauls a lucrative reward in exchange for turning Phoenice over to the army just outside its gates. This the Gauls did, much to the shock of Greeks everywhere, for the seizure of a city (as opposed to the looting of the countryside) represented a radical escalation in the threat posed by the Illyrians. The Epirotes reacted by raising an army to relieve Phoenice, but at that moment Scerdilaidas with another force invaded northern Epirus by way of the Atiniania gorge. To meet the new threat, the Epirote army split in two and sent urgent requests for aid to the Aetolians and to the Achaeans (a federation of Peloponnesian cities). These states reacted quickly with help, but not before the half of the Epirote army that had remained at Phoenice was soundly defeated. Nevertheless, prodded by visions of armageddon, what remained of the Epirote army with its allies made ready to meet the Illyrian invaders in open battle. Just before a battle could be fought, however, an order from Teuta arrived in Scerdilaidas' camp, demanding his return home to deal with a rebellious Illyrian tribe which had made common cause with the Dardanians. The Illyrians extracted themselves from Epirus by agreeing to return Phoenice, but this was effected only after the Illyrians handily plundered the city.

Amid the violence which characterized the Illyrian occupation of Phoenice some resident Italian merchants were killed, a fact that would bode ill for Teuta, but not so in time to stem further aggression. In fact, even with the temporary retreat from Epirus, Teuta's raiding barely missed a beat. After quickly returning the Illyrian rebels to the fold, the queen renewed the offensive by personally leading an army and fleet to Issa, a small Greek colony which had been founded on an island of the same name off the central Illyrian coast. This was no hit-swiftly-and-flee operation, for the Issans had been on their guard against just such an assault and had defensively prepared their city against a siege. Before Issa, Illyrian attacks had been either sweeps across countrysides or, in the case of Phoenice, a ruse which won the city before effective resistance could be raised. Thus, the siege of Issa, which lasted for many months, represented another escalation in the threat posed by the Illyrians, for clearly they were organized for a long effort and confident of success.

This confidence, and the expectation that the Illyrians would soon return to where they had left off in Epirus, so unnerved the Epirotes that they attempted to forestall future attacks by forging an alliance with Teuta, in effect agreeing to aid and abet her efforts if she would only leave them alone. To ally with Teuta, of course, the Epirotes essentially had to double-cross the Aetolians and the Achaeans. They also were forced to cede to Teuta's control the Atintanian corridor linking Illyria with Epirus, thus providing the Illyrians with a land route into the heart of Epirus—useful, if Epirus failed to live up to Illyrian expectations. Clearly, Teuta was on a roll.

While Teuta was at Issa, two Roman envoys, brothers Gaius and Lucius Coruncanius, visited her. These were charged by the Senate to discover precisely what was going on in the Adriatic and to warn against any continuation of her disruptive campaigns. This delegation was certainly sparked by the loss of Italian life at Phoenice and probably also by a request from the Issans that the Romans intervene on their behalf—there being no other viable ally to turn to. The Romans, shocked by the magnitude of Teuta's power and the extent of its range, brusquely warned Teuta not to interfere with Roman interests, or with those of Rome's friends. Teuta displayed a cautious diplomacy in the face of Rome's frankness, replying that she would make sure that no Roman would henceforth be hurt by anyone associated with her "government," but that she did not have the right to stop "private" piracy. In reality, given the importance of raiding to the alleviation of Illyrian poverty, even if Teuta had been willing to bring law and order to her realm, she almost certainly would not have been able to do so. Not pleased with Teuta's response, Lucius Coruncanius shot back that if Teuta would not control her subjects, then the Romans would. Some Illyrian, perhaps even Teuta herself, was so offended by the Roman's arrogance—displayed without any evident means by which to carry out his threat—that Lucius' murder was planned, and carried out as the two brothers were making their way back to Rome.

The assassination of Lucius Coruncanius guaranteed Rome's intervention in the Adriatic. Even if Teuta suspected how quickly and with what force the Romans would react, however, that suspicion did not deter her from carrying on with her attacks upon Greeks. In 229, she both continued the assault on Issa and ordered Epidamnus and Corcyra to be put under siege. These newly attacked cities betray the extent of Teuta's ambition in 229, for they were two of the largest and most powerful Greek foundations in the Adriatic. Corcyra and Epidamnus responded (as did Apollonia, certain that it was next on the hit list) as the Epirotes had before their alliance with Teuta, by appealing to the Aetolians and the Achaeans. These latter states again responded, but the combined fleet sent to relieve the Greek northwest was soundly defeated by the Illyrians and their Acarnanian allies. Immediately thereafter, Corcyra fell to an Illyrian force led by Demetrius of Pharos. Clearly, things were quickly getting out of hand, for without some unforeseeable relief, all of Greece which had not struck a devil's bargain with the Illyrians would soon be subjected to their piracy.

At that moment, Rome appeared on the scene in the form of a large navy, commanded by Gnaeus Fulvius, and army (20,000 infantry and 2,000 cavalry strong), commanded by Aulus Postumius. This armada first made its way to Corcyra, where it overwhelmed the Illyrian garrison under Demetrius. So decisive was the Roman show of force (it must be remembered that by 229 the Romans had the Mediterranean's largest military establishment, Rome having both unified Italy and recently defeated the Carthaginians in the First Punic War), that Demetrius (Teuta's erstwhile adviser-general) immediately realized the futility of resistance and the advantage to be won by collaborating with Rome. Thereafter, Demetrius acted as Rome's guide in the war against Teuta. The campaign saw the Romans methodically proceed up the Adriatic coast, freeing one city and/or people after another from Illyrian control, thereafter to place each under Roman "protection," that is, without stationing any troops in the liberated areas the Romans made it clear that they would tolerate no attack on their new "friends."

The occasional minor setback did little to stem the Roman advance northward, so much more powerful were the Romans than the armies of the nascent Ardiain monarchy. It became painfully obvious to the Illyrians that, militarily speaking, the Romans were *not* to be compared with any contemporary Greek state. Within weeks, not only had the Romans relieved every region (including Issa) once threatened by Teuta, they had also destroyed the Illyrian unification so recently accomplished by Agron. Teuta herself fled to the fortified city of Rhizon and begged the Romans for peace. This she was granted upon the stipulation that she pay a stiff tribute to the Romans, that she surrender most of her Illyrian realm, and that she not sail beyond southern Illyria at any time with more than two ships. The Romans had fought this war strictly as a police action, and neither annexed any territory at its end nor kept any troops in the Balkans past the spring of 228. Clearly, Rome's intention was merely to bring peace to the region by the implicit threat of future violence if the locals did not behave. The lion's share of Teuta's realm the Romans gave over to Demetrius, with the explicit warning that he see to it that his subjects made a living from some occupation other than piracy. Thus ended the first Roman military intervention east of the Adriatic Sea. The second would occur ten years later, to chastise the traitorous Demetrius for failing to put an end to Illyrian raiding. What happened to Teuta after 228 is unknown. Presumably, she reigned over a fraction of her former realm from her seat at Rhizon, but we do not know how long she lived.

William S. Greenwalt,
Associate Professor of Classical History,
Santa Clara University,
Santa Clara, California

Tewdr, Nesta.

See Nesta Tewdr.

Tewdwr, Nesta (fl. 1090)

*Mistress of King Henry I. Flourished around 1090; daughter of Rhys ap Tewdwr, king of Deheubarth, and *Gladys (fl. 1075); mistress of Henry I, king of England (r. 1100–1135); children: Robert, 1st earl of Gloucester (c. 1090–1147).*

Texas Tessie (1897–1973).

See Douglas, Lizzie.

Tey, Josephine (1896–1952)

English writer best known for the eight mystery novels she wrote between 1929 and 1951, the first as Gordon Daviot and the rest as Josephine Tey, but who first achieved fame writing plays, all of them under the pseudonym Gordon Daviot. Name variations: Elizabeth Mackintosh; (pseudonym) Gordon Daviot. Born Elizabeth Mackintosh at Inverness in the Scottish highlands in 1896 (some sources cite 1897); died of cancer in London on February 13, 1952; daughter of Colin Mackintosh (a greengrocer) and Josephine Horne Mackintosh (a schoolteacher); educated at the Royal Academy in Inverness, 1903–15, and at the Anstey Physical Training College in Birmingham, England, 1915–18; never married; no children.

Began as a physical-training instructor at schools near Liverpool and at Tunbridge Wells in England; after mother's death (1926), abandoned teaching to care for her invalid father in Inverness; published first mystery novel The Man in the Queue *(under pseudonym Gordon Daviot) in London and New York (1929), followed that same year by the publication of the first of her four non-mystery novels,* Kif: An Unvarnished History, *also under name Gordon Daviot;*

turned attention to playwriting and achieved instant fame with Richard of Bordeaux, *which, with John Gielgud as actor and producer, ran for hundreds of performances in London (1932–33); had less success with play* Queen of Scots, *which ran for about 100 performances (1934); returned to mystery writing, and (1936) published her first crime novel as Josephine Tey,* A Shilling for Candles; *wrote little during World War II, but then completed a number of plays, six mystery novels and one historical novel (1946–52).*

Books: (as Gordon Daviot) The Man in the Queue *(London: Methuen, 1929, re-released under Josephine Tey, London: Davies, 1953, republished as* Killer in the Crowd, *NY: Mercury, 1954); (as Daviot)* Kif: An Unvarnished History *(London: Benn, 1929); (as Daviot)* The Expensive Halo *(London: Benn, 1931); (as Daviot)* Richard of Bordeaux *(London: Gollancz, 1933); (as Daviot)* The Laughing Woman *(London: Gollancz, 1934): (as Daviot)* Queen of Scots *(London: Gollancz, 1934); (as Tey)* A Shilling for Candles *(London: Methuen, 1936); (as Daviot)* Claverhouse *(London: Collins, 1937); (as Daviot)* The Stars Bow Down *(London: Duckworth, 1939); (as Daviot)* Leith Sands and Other Short Plays *(London: Duckworth, 1946); (as Tey)* Miss Pym Disposes *(London: Davies, 1946); (as Tey)* The Franchise Affair *(London: Davies, 1948); (as Tey)* Brat Farrar *(London: Davies, 1949, republished as* Come and Kill Me, *NY: Pocket, 1951); (as Tey)* To Love and Be Wise *(London: Davies, 1950); (as Tey)* The Daughter of Time *(London: Davies, 1951); (as Daviot)* The Privateer *(London: Davies, 1952); (as Tey)* The Singing Sands *(London: Davies, 1952); Plays, by Gordon Daviot (3 vols., London: Davies, 1953–54).*

Play productions: (as Daviot) Richard of Bordeaux *(London, Arts Theater Club, June 1932, revised version, London, New Theater, February 2, 1933); (as Daviot)* The Laughing Woman *(London, New Theater, April 7, 1934); (as Daviot)* Queen of Scots *(London, New Theater, June 8, 1934); (as Daviot)* The Little Dry Thorn *(Hammersmith, London, Lyric Theater, November 11, 1947); (as Daviot)* Valerius *(London, Saville Theater, October 3, 1948); (as Daviot)* The Stars Bow Down *(Malvern, Malvern Festival Theater, August 10, 1949); (as Daviot)* Dickon *(Salisbury, Salisbury Arts Theater, May 9, 1955).*

It would grieve Josephine Tey to know that almost 50 years after her death she is remembered primarily for her mysteries and not for any of her plays. Yet it was one of her plays, *Richard of Bordeaux*, which brought her sudden fame. As well, after her death a number of her plays were presented at drama festivals and on radio and television.

One might well ask why Tey wrote murder mysteries at all, given her pronounced preference for playwriting. The answer may simply be that between World War I and World War II and afterwards murder mysteries were extremely popular in both Great Britain and the United States, and while plays brought Tey fame, her mysteries brought her a moderate fortune.

She was born Elizabeth Mackintosh in 1896. From an early age she liked to write, and while studying at the Royal Academy in her hometown Inverness she wrote poems and short fiction. However, Tey gave up all thought of a writing career, as her parents Colin and **Josephine Mackintosh** could not support her indefinitely. Physical training, a relatively new discipline, guaranteed her a job, and during World War I she attended the Anstey Physical Training College in Birmingham, England. Between 1918 and 1926, Tey taught physical training at two girls' schools, one near Liverpool and the other at Tunbridge Wells. However, in 1926 her mother died and Tey gave up her teaching career and returned to Inverness to care for her invalid father. Except for short visits to London, she was to remain at Inverness until shortly before her death in 1952.

In 1929, her first mystery, *The Man in the Queue*, was published in London by Methuen and in New York by Dutton. That same year, her first non-mystery novel, *Kif: An Unvarnished History*, was published in London by Benn and in New York by Appleton. Both books appeared under the pseudonym Gordon Daviot, the pen name Tey was to use in the more than 25 plays she wrote between 1930 and 1952. The books were moderately successful, but from 1930 to 1936 Tey set aside novel writing and dedicated herself to playwriting. She had the great good fortune to attract the interest of John Gielgud, already a well-known name on the stage. In 1932, he appeared as Richard II in Tey's *Richard of Bordeaux*, which ran successfully for the remainder of that year. Gielgud then convinced Tey, whom he always called Gordon Daviot, to extensively revise the play, and the new version was a smashing success in 1933. In his autobiography *Early Stages* (1939), Gielgud noted that "people came thirty or forty times to see the play." He also wrote of "Daviot" that "in spite of her innate shyness, her dislike of staying in London for more than a few days at a time, Gordon is the most delightful author I have ever worked with in the theater." Gielgud was to remain her lifelong friend, writing that "it was to the brilliant inspiration and sympathy of Gordon Daviot that I owed the biggest personal success of my career."

Although John Gielgud was to remain a friend, in his foreword to a three-volume edition of *Plays by Gordon Daviot*, published after Tey's death from 1953 to 1955, he confessed: "I cannot claim ever to have known her very intimately." He added, "She never spoke to me of her youth or her ambitions. It was hard to draw her out. . . . She shunned photographers and publicity of all kinds, and gave no interviews to the Press."

Just about everyone who has written about Tey has noted that she was very reserved and reclusive, whether in Inverness or in London. **Mairi MacDonald**, in her *By the Banks of the Ness: Tales of Inverness and District* (1982), recalled that "strange as it may seem, few of us had ever known the real person. We had rubbed shoulders with her in our busy streets, admired her pretty home [Crown Cottage] and picturesque garden . . . yet no one enjoyed her companionship." No wonder MacDonald entitled chapter 18 of her work "The Enigma of Gordon Daviot." **Virginia B. Morris** noted that Tey's "private life is cloaked in mystery," while Robert Barnard, in his introduction to the "Scribner Paperback" series of the eight mysteries, wrote that Tey was "a writer who lives by her works alone. . . . Nobody seems to know anything much about her life." **Sandra Roy** notes that Tey "was remote and distant, having few if any friends and no one close to her."

*P*laywrights must lead blighted lives. Fifty to one, on an actuary's reckoning, against their play running more than three weeks; and then no one notices their name in the programme.

—Josephine Tey

Instead, scholars must turn to Tey's mystery novels for clues about her character, her interests, and her likes and dislikes. Inspector Alan Grant of Scotland Yard, the detective who appears in five of her eight mysteries, is clearly her alter ego. He is Scottish, and is a bachelor who, like his creator, viewed marriage as a loss of freedom. Roy notes that in Alan Grant, Tey presents "traits of honesty, sincerity, loneliness, sensitivity and occasional foolishness—traits which Tey must have seen somewhere in herself."

Tey seems to have been ambivalent about her own sex. In five of her eight mysteries, a woman is the criminal or would-be criminal. This was not unusual during the Golden Age of mystery writing (1920–50), as indicated by the title of **Jessica Mann**'s 1981 study *Deadlier Than the Male: Why Are Respectable English Women So Good at Murder?* In Tey's crime novels, the "bad woman," as well as the "bad man," is terribly vain and selfish. However, the "good woman" appears much more frequently than the bad. Among examples of good women in Tey's fiction are the kindly and sensible aunt or mother figure, the young ingenue who is sensitive and insightful, and the independent woman who is outspoken, talented, and content with her single state. The independent woman is often androgynous, and Tey herself appears to have recognized her own androgyny when she adopted the pen names of Gordon Daviot and Josephine Tey. No one who has written about Tey, however, has identified her as androgynous. For example, Morris argues that she adapted the Tey pseudonym only to "establish separate identities as playwright and as a mystery novelist."

Tey loved horseback riding, horse racing and fishing, and movies. Like the character of kindly Aunt Lin in *The Franchise Affair* (1948), she attended the movies twice a week in Inverness. She also had a deep love for the English countryside, as revealed in *Brat Farrar* (1949), and for the Scottish highlands and the Outer Hebrides, as is clear in her last mystery, *The Singing Sands* (1952). In her first mystery as Josephine Tey, *A Shilling for Candles* (1936), she has the murder victim, an English stage and film actress named Christine Clay, leave her "considerable fortune for the preservation of the beauty of England." This is exactly what Tey did 16 years later. In her will, she left the proceeds from her writings to the National Trust for Places of Historic Interest or Natural Beauty. It is calculated that the National Trust had received half a million dollars from Tey's estate by 1981.

Like most English writers of the Golden Age of mystery fiction, Tey was decidedly pro-English and in her writings she revealed her dislike of people from the Middle East, France, Spain, and Italy, as well as those Irish who were for the IRA and those Scots who were nationalists or Presbyterians. Contrary to one writer's assertion that Tey was anti-Semitic, no evidence is found in any of her mystery novels. Tey was, however, possibly homophobic. In *Miss Pym Disposes* (1941), same-sex relationships are viewed as abnormal, while in *To Love and Be Wise* (1950) the relationship of a male dancer and a male playwright is viewed as insane. It is impossible, as Shakespeare noted in *Troilus and Cressida* (Act II, Scene III) "to love and be wise." Homosexuality seems to have both attracted and repelled Tey. It is not surprising that she treated the subject, as she worked with a number of homosexuals in the theater, including her friend John Gielgud. In both Gielgud's memoir *Early Stages* and in his foreword to the 1953–54 edition of Tey's plays, he made particular mention of her devotion to the actress **Gwen Ffrangçon-Davies**, who was the leading actress in several of her plays. Other than that, we have no clues about Tey's sexual orientation or whether sex played any part in her life.

In *To Love and Be Wise*, Tey also deals with the theme of transvestism. The would-be murderer is a woman who leads a double life. As Leslie Searle, she masquerades as a male who travels widely and pursues a successful career as a photographer. As Lee Searle, a female, she is a promising artist with a studio in London. Both homosexuality and transvestism were rarely treated in crime novels of Tey's time.

Tey had a passion for history, as demonstrated by a number of her plays, one of her historical novels (*The Privateer*), a biography (*Claverhouse*), and her masterpiece (*The Daughter of Time*, 1951). In this mystery, published only months before her death, Inspector Grant, while recovering from a bad fall, investigates from his hospital bed the murder in the Tower of London of Edward IV's two sons in the 1480s. Grant complains to a sympathetic friend, "honestly I think historians are all mad." Near the end of *The Daughter of Time*, Grant asserts, "I'll never again believe anything I read in a history book." The hospitalized Grant, with the assistance of a young American researcher, Brent Carradine, comes to the conclusion that many historians over the centuries, beginning with Sir Thomas More, were dead wrong in concluding that Richard III (r. 1483–1485) was a monstrous and physically deformed man who ordered the murder of his two nephews during his brief reign. Inspector Grant concludes that Richard's usurper, Henry Tudor (Henry VII) had every reason in the world to order the murder of the young princes while Richard had no motive to do so.

Tey had first come to the defense of Richard III five years earlier. In her 1946 mystery, *Miss Pym Disposes*, which is set in an English physical training college for women, one of the teachers opines that Shakespeare's play *Richard the III* was "a criminal libel on a fine man, a blatant piece of political propaganda, and an extremely silly play." As Gordon Daviot, Tey wrote a play, *Dickon*, published posthumously in 1953, which also presents Richard III as a saintly leader. This seems to be the only instance in

Josephine Tey

which Tey wrote both a mystery and a play about the same subject.

Many historians who were incensed at Tey's attacks on the saintly Sir Thomas More and the immortal William Shakespeare dismissed her defense of Richard III as nonsense. However, in 1956 Paul Murray Kendall published a definitive study of the last Plantagenet monarch, *Richard the Third*, which made clear that while Richard was no saint, Tey was basically correct in her conclusions about him. Subsequent studies, such as Jeremy Potter's *Good King Richard? An Account of Richard III and his Reputation, 1483–1983* (1983), have also supported Tey's conclusions. Potter credits Tey's *The Daughter of Time* as being the largest single factor in the significant growth after 1952 of the English Richard III Society, originally founded in 1924. In addition, Potter notes that *The Daughter of Time* was reprinted 20 times between 1956 and 1980.

So little is known about Tey that we have no idea what she did during World War II, aside from caring for her father, who died in 1950. The only thing we know is that she seems to have published nothing between 1940 and 1945, so that perhaps she was busy aiding the war effort. Gielgud saw her in Edinburgh in 1942 and found her deeply depressed, but a visit with Gielgud and Gwen Ffrangçon-Davies cheered her up considerably.

After the war, Tey's creative powers reached their peak, and between 1946 and her death early in 1952 she wrote six mysteries, one historical novel, and a number of plays. Not long after her father's demise in 1950, she learned that she had cancer. In a race against death, Tey finished *To Love and Be Wise* and *The Daughter of Time*, which were published in 1950 and 1951, respectively. After she died on February 13, 1952, her last mystery, *The Singing Sands*, set in her beloved Scottish highlands and the Outer Hebrides, was discovered among her papers. It appeared in England before the end of 1952, and in New York the following year.

Tey was reclusive to the end. She told no one that she was dying of cancer. Although she had lived in Inverness most of her life, she chose to die in London. A host of actors who had worked with her, including Gielgud, Ffrangçon-Davies and *Edith Evans, attended her funeral. Gielgud concludes his foreword with "the theater is poorer for an unique talent, and I for a dearly valued friend."

In an essay, "The Guilty Vicarage," published in 1962, the late, great poet W.H. Auden confessed that he was addicted to detective stories, and that once he began one he could not work or sleep until he finished it. This is certainly true of Tey's mysteries, as they are masterpieces of suspense. However, Auden went on to note that he forgot the mystery as soon as he had finished it, and had no wish to read it again. Well, this writer first read Tey's classic, *The Daughter of Time*, 45 years ago and never forgot it. What distinguishes Josephine Tey among a host of mystery writers is that she was also a playwright. Because she was a dramatist, she makes excellent use of dialogue to delineate her interesting and memorable characters and to develop her always fascinating plots. Although she was herself a reserved person, she clearly cared about her readers and easily won their affection. Every one of her eight mysteries is in print. She would have preferred being remembered for her plays rather than for her crime novels, which she once referred to as her "yearly knitting." In *The Daughter of Time*, however, Grant's friend, the actress Marta Hallard, says, "There is nothing so soothing, I understand, as knitting. Isn't that so, nurse?"

SOURCES:

Gielgud, John. *Early Stages*. NY: Macmillan, 1939.
MacDonald, Mairi. *By the Banks of the Ness: Tales of Inverness and District.* Edinburgh: Paul Harris, 1982.

Mann, Jessica. *Deadlier Than the Male: Why Are Respectable English Women So Good at Murder?* NY: Macmillan, 1981.
Morris, Virginia B. "Josephine Tey," in *British Mystery Writers, 1920–1939*: Vol. 77, *Dictionary of Literary Biography.* Detroit, MI: Gale Research, 1989.
Roy, Sandra. *Josephine Tey.* Twayne's "English Authors" Series, 277. Boston, MA: Twayne, 1980.
Talburt, Nancy Ellen. "Josephine Tey," in Earl F. Bargainnier, ed., *Ten Women of Mystery.* Bowling Green, OH: Bowling Green State University Popular Press, 1981.

SUGGESTED READING:

Mackintosh, Elizabeth. *Plays by Gordon Daviot.* 3 vols. London: Davies, 1953–1955.

Anna Macías,
Professor Emerita of History,
Ohio Wesleyan University,
Delaware, Ohio

Teye (c. 1400–1340 BCE).

See Tiy.

Teyte, Maggie (1888–1976)

British operatic soprano. Name variations: Dame Maggie Teyte. Born Margaret Tate on April 17, 1888, in Wolverhampton, England; died on May 26, 1976, in England; daughter of Jacob James Tate (a hotel owner) and Maria (Doughty) Tate (a singer); attended Royal College of Music; studied with Jean de Reszke, Paris, 1904–06; married Eugène de Plùmon, on October 16, 1909 (divorced November 1915); married Walter Sherwin Cottingham, on March 12, 1921 (divorced May 1931); no children.

Debuted in Paris (1906); debuted in opera, Monte Carlo (1907); performed at the Opéra-Comique, Paris (1908–10); performed with Beecham Opera Company and British National Opera Company, London (1911–14, 1936–38); performed in the U.S. repeatedly (1911–19, 1940s); received the Croix de Lorraine (1943); retired after a farewell concert at Royal Festival Hall, London (1955); made a Chevalier of the Légion d'honneur (1957); made a Dame of the British Empire (1958); published autobiography, Star on the Door *(1958).*

Known in her day as the preeminent living interpreter of modern French songs, Maggie Teyte endeared herself to critics and connoisseurs on two continents during the Golden Age of Opera in the early 20th century. She came to prominence for her birdlike soprano and dramatic inflection, and her delicate physical beauty was said to enhance the romantic aura of her performances. Perhaps most beloved for her role in Claude Debussy's opera *Pelléas et Mélisande*, for which she trained personally

Opposite page
Maggie
Teyte

with Debussy, she was hailed by critics as the virtual embodiment of Mélisande, a heroine whose part she would play in over 30 performances during a career that spanned half a century. Among the many other great opera roles Teyte mastered were Zerlina, Blonde, Marguerite, Mimi, and Butterfly. At just over five feet tall and at the peak of her career reportedly weighing no more than six stone (84 pounds), she was called the "pocket diva" and "doll-sized magician."

She was born Margaret Tate in Wolverhampton, England, on April 17, 1888, the youngest of three daughters of Jacob James Tate and his second wife, **Maria Doughty Tate**. Jacob, a merchant and innkeeper, fathered ten children in all, of whom Maggie was the eighth. Although he was descended from Irish and Huguenot ancestors, he was a Scot by birth, and Maggie identified strongly with his Scottish origins. A strict Roman Catholic and stern father who ran his household with a firm hand, he was nonetheless considered extremely attentive to his children. Both Maggie's parents were musical. Her mother was a singer, and Jacob was an amateur pianist who once had studied under Theodor Leschetizky (a student of Austrian composer Karl Czerny) in Leipzig, Germany. Maggie attended St. Joseph's Convent School in Wolverhampton, and she was still of elementary school age when her father arranged for her to study at the Royal College of Music.

As she matured into her teens, she performed publicly on selected occasions and ultimately secured the backing of some wealthy patrons who sent her to Paris and sponsored her studies with Jean de Reszke. He became a mentor to Teyte, and she immersed herself in exhausting practice sessions. In 1906, she made a debut performance in Paris, and her operatic debut followed the next year at a Mozart Festival in Monte Carlo headed by Reynaldo Hahn. At some time during her early years of study in Paris, perhaps at de Reszke's suggestion, she changed the spelling of her last name from "Tate" to "Teyte," a traditional Scottish variation of the name, to assist French audiences with pronunciation.

Teyte sang successfully with the Opéra-Comique of Paris during the 1907–08 season, but then received the discouraging news from Albert Carré, the company's director, that she was to be released from employment at the end of the season. Shortly thereafter, however, Carré rescinded her release and offered her the

opportunity to sing the female lead in Debussy's *Pelléas et Mélisande* during the 1908–09 season. Exonerated, Teyte underwent a period of intensive study in preparation for the role of Mélisande. Still in her teens, she practiced for nine months under the direction of Debussy himself. Teyte debuted as Mélisande on June 13, 1908, to "rapturous" reviews. In all, she made 19 appearances in that role during the 1908–09 season alone. Over the years, Teyte would maintain contact with Debussy, whom she also came to regard as a mentor. During the following season, she performed with noted conductor Thomas Beecham in a Mozart series at His Majesty's Theater in London. Later in the same season, she appeared with Beecham at Covent Garden.

During the autumn in the 1910 season, Teyte and Beecham collaborated in the world premiere of the English adaptation of Eugen d'Albert's *Tiefland*. Teyte then signed with Andreas Dippell to perform in Chicago at the then-impressive price of $400 per performance for the 1911–12 season. She underwent preparations for an American debut with the Chicago-Philadelphia Opera Company and opened as Cherubino in Mozart's *Le Nozze di Figaro* at the Philadelphia Metropolitan Opera House on November 4, 1911. Campanini conducted the performance which also featured Gustave Huberdau and **Alice Zeppilli**. In November, Teyte performed a recital at Carnegie Hall, and in Chicago the same month created the role of Cinderella for the American premiere of Massenet's *Cendrillon*. Her performance met with such success that she received an invitation to reprise the role during the following season, and a painting of her as she appeared in *Cendrillon* was placed on permanent exhibition at the Art Institute of Chicago. Teyte also performed the role at the Metropolitan Opera House in New York City on February 20, 1912. Her other American performances included Lygia in *Quo Vadis*, Antonia in Offenbach's *Les Contes d'Hofmann*, and *Mignon*.

Teyte had married Eugène de Plumon, a Frenchman many years her senior, in 1909; by 1913, the marriage existed merely on paper. During the course of their relationship, Plùmon, who was adamantly opposed to fathering children, convinced Teyte to undergo the female sterilization surgery of tubal ligation. She naively believed that such an operation could be reversed if later she changed her mind. As it happened, she would regret the decision. According to her biographer and grandnephew Garry O'Connor, Teyte lost interest in Plùmon as her career soared, and

the couple became completely estranged. Following a summer tour of England and the Riviera in 1913, she returned to the United States that October for her third season with the Chicago-Philadelphia Orchestra (both 1915 and 1917 would see her again in the States). In November 1915, she divorced Plùmon, after which she reinstated her British citizenship.

After her return to England in 1915, Teyte appeared as Lady Mary Carlisle in *Monsieur Beaucaire* at London's Princess Theater. She followed this run with a series of light operas and also appeared in the lead role in *The Little Dutch Girl* by Emmerich Kalman at the Lyric Theater. In 1921, she married Walter Sherwin "Sher" Cottingham, heir to the Sherwin-Williams paint fortune, whom she had met aboard ship en route to Europe following her American tour in 1915. In contrast to her feelings for Plùmon, Teyte professed a deep love for her second husband. After their marriage, she withdrew from the stage and lived in relative isolation at Woolley, the Cottingham family estate at Maidenhead in England's Thames Valley, where Cottingham's father provided them with a house named Woolley Grange. For Teyte, the retreat to Woolley—the rural setting of which was not unlike the environment of the Tate homestead in Wolverhampton—was a badly needed respite from a hectic public life and a schedule of constant travel. At Woolley, she confined her singing to the privacy of the estate, her melodies falling almost exclusively on the ears of the many servants.

Teyte developed a great fondness for her father-in-law, Walter Cottingham, Sr. When he fell into ill health and became an invalid, she made frequent trips from the Grange to Woolley Hall to attend to his needs. During these years, she underwent repeated surgeries to reverse the sterilization procedure she had undergone earlier, but all failed. Her inability to conceive a child with Sher Cottingham, perhaps the greatest disappointment of her life, was a significant factor in the breakup of her second marriage. Following the death of his father in 1928, Teyte's husband took to extended absences, while she in turn cultivated a close emotional relationship with a neighbor from Maidenhead, **Gay Vernon**. The Cottingham marriage was dissolved in 1931. Under the terms of the divorce settlement, Teyte retained her residence at Woolley Grange. She remained in frequent contact with her ex-husband before his death from a cerebral hemorrhage in 1936.

As the Second World War threatened Europe in 1940, Teyte, now over 50, went to work as a truck driver for the Civil Defense Authority. Despite the end of Opera's Golden Age, she also returned to performing. Her professional life during the 1930s had revolved largely around the recording studio, but in June 1940, shortly before the German blitzkrieg hammered Europe, she performed in concert with the London Philharmonic at the National Gallery. By 1942, her career was fully revived. With Vernon, she had established a music-teaching partnership, the Teyte-Vernon School of Singing, which she neglected while performing throughout England in the midst of the war. Teyte also maintained a romantic liaison with conductor Beecham.

In 1945, after the war ended, she received an offer to record *Pelléas et Mélisande* with the New York Philharmonic. Two major U.S. broadcasting networks (NBC and CBS) vied to contract a performance by Teyte as well. Of the two, she elected to perform for NBC in a series of concerts for the "Bell Telephone Hour." In the U.S., she gave two performances at Town Hall in New York City and went on to tour in Philadelphia, San Francisco, Los Angeles, Portland, and Seattle. She also performed in Washington, D.C., for President Harry Truman, and in Toronto, Canada, for the opening of the War Loan drive. Teyte's presence in America followed an absence of more than 25 years, but critics declared that the passage of time had compromised neither the purity of her voice nor her youthful demeanor. Her American following was so awed by her energy and appearance that a rumor sprang up alleging that the real Maggie Teyte was dead and the woman on tour was in fact her daughter.

In 1948, at age 60, Teyte revived her role of the golden-haired Mélisande for the New York City Opera Company. The same year, she sang a Mozart concert at Carnegie Hall. She reached a financial settlement for a lump sum on her annuity from the Cottingham estate and used the money to relocate to New York City, where she rented a studio on East 55th Street. Her partner, Gay Vernon, also moved to New York City, and the pair continued to give music lessons under the auspices of the Teyte talent for the then-considerable sum of $50 per lesson. In 1951, Teyte made a trip to Vienna to study Schoenberg's twelve-tone method. During her absence, her confidante and business partner Gay Vernon remarried, which enraged Teyte. According to O'Connor, "Maggie never saw Gay again. Never forgot. Never forgave."

Teyte continued to perform in the United States until 1954, when she returned to England. There she culminated her 50-year career at a farewell concert on April 22, 1956, at the Royal Festival Hall. In 1957, she was named a Chevalier of the Légion d'honneur by the French cultural services, and in 1958 Queen *Elizabeth II named her a Dame of the British Empire. "Don't call me Dame," Teyte told the press. "I'm not going to be known as Dame."

Teyte's legacy includes a vast and diverse discography, with recordings dating back to 1907. Her final vocal recording, the soundtrack from a never-aired BBC program dated November 25, 1958, was released on EJS records; it includes two works by Reynaldo Hahn, "En sourdine" and "*Ciboulette*: Ce n'était pas la même chose." Her recordings from the 1930s and 1940s are the most plentiful, including many Debussy selections that she recorded for the Gramophone Company in London, with Alfred Cortot on piano. In 1958, she published her autobiography, *Star on the Door*. She served as a teacher to many aspiring opera singers, and in 1968 she founded the Maggie Teyte Prize for young women vocalists.

Although Teyte severed virtually all ties with her family early in her career, she had been assigned guardianship of her sister **Marie Odoli**'s daughter, **Rita Odoli-Tate** (later O'Connor), after Marie's death during World War I. Teyte took financial responsibility for Rita, put her through school, and spent time with her on occasion. For the most part, the young Rita was left in the care of a family nurse. Teyte enrolled her niece at the Royal College of Music, where Rita met her future husband, Cavan O'Connor. In the final years after her retirement, Teyte lived a reclusive existence, taught sporadically, and detached herself from friends and family, except for her niece Rita. She died of complications of old age on May 26, 1976. A funeral service was held on June 1 at the Carmelite Church on Kensington High Street, after which a rose tree was planted over her grave.

SOURCES:
Current Biography. NY: H.W. Wilson, 1945.
O'Connor, Garry. *The Pursuit of Perfection: A Life of Maggie Teyte*. NY: Atheneum, 1979.

Gloria Cooksey,
freelance writer,
Sacramento, California

Thacher, Edith (1910–1997).
See Hurd, Edith Thacher.

Thackeray, Anne (1837–1919).
See Ritchie, Anne Isabella.

Thackrey, Dorothy Schiff (1903–1989).
See Schiff, Dorothy.

Thaden, Louise (1905–1979)

American aviator. Born Iris Louise McPhetridge on November 12, 1905, in Bentonville, Arkansas; died on November 9, 1979, in High Point, North Carolina; daughter of Roy McPhetridge and Edna (Hobs) McPhetridge; married Herbert von Thaden, on July 21, 1928 (died 1969); children: Bill (b. 1930); Pat (b. 1933).

Set aviation records for consecutive flight, women's speed, and endurance (1928–32); won the first Powder Puff Derby (1929); won the Bendix Race (1936); received Claude B. Harmon Trophy (1936); published High, Wide, and Frightened *(1938).*

Louise Thaden was a celebrated pilot of the golden age of American aviation, as well known in her time as *Amelia Earhart. She was also an instructor and businesswoman, and advocated expanded opportunities for women pilots. Born in 1905 and raised in Bentonville, Arkansas, she attended public schools and then the University of Arkansas from 1921 to 1925, majoring in journalism and physical education. In her junior year, she left school to work for the Travel Air Corporation and moved to San Francisco. She began flying lessons in 1927; her solo pilot's license, signed by Orville Wright, was issued in 1928, making her one of the first women to achieve pilot status. In December 1928, Thaden, who had married army pilot and engineer Herbert von Thaden earlier that year, set a new world record for women's high altitude flying; this was followed by a short-lived endurance record for a 22-hour flight in March 1929. She also set a women's aviation speed record of 156 mph.

A few months later, Thaden went on to beat Amelia Earhart and win the first cross-country Women's Air Derby. The following year, she and Earhart co-founded the Ninety-Nines, an international association of women pilots. Thaden served as secretary and vice-president of the association between 1930 and 1936. In 1930, she moved to Pittsburgh, Pennsylvania, to work for Pittsburgh Aviation Industries and to serve as director of the women's division of the Pennsylvania School of Aeronautics. In 1935, she took a job with the Bureau of Air Service to promote the expansion of national airfields. The following year, Thaden and co-pilot **Blanche Noyes** became the first women to enter and to win the Bendix Cup Race, flying from New York to Los Angeles in a record-setting 14 hours, 54 minutes. This brought Thaden the coveted Claude B. Harmon Trophy as the most outstanding woman flyer of 1936. Throughout her career, Thaden was open about the skepticism of male pilots and the general public toward women aviators; in her memoirs she noted: "in an age where some men didn't think a woman should drive a horse and buggy, much less drive an automobile, it was a job to prove that females could fly." Changing the negative perception of women flyers was one of Thaden's lifelong goals.

After setting her last world speed record of 197 mph in 1937, Thaden decided to retire from competition to spend more time with her husband and two small children. She still found time to compose her memoirs, published as *High, Wide, and Frightened* (1938), and to work as a representative for Beech Aircraft (co-founded by *Olive Ann Beech). During World War II, Thaden served as a pilot in the Civilian Air Patrol, reaching the rank of lieutenant-colonel. She also worked for her husband's new company, Thaden Engineering, first as a purchasing agent, then in research and development for aviation materials. She remained involved in many aviation organizations in both the public and private sectors, including the Red Cross Motor Corps, the National Aeronautic Association, and the Department of Defense's Committee on Women in the Services. She was also very active in training new pilots and establishing programs for aviation instruction, especially for women, and contributed numerous articles to aviation magazines.

In 1955–56, Thaden was vice-president and director of the Thaden Molding Corporation, and became partner in Thaden Engineering in 1961. After Herbert von Thaden's death in 1969, Louise Thaden ran the company as sole owner until her own death from a heart attack at age 73 at her home in High Point, North Carolina.

Louise Thaden received many posthumous honors. Besides the renaming of the Louise Thaden Memorial Airfield in her native town of Bentonville, Arkansas, in 1991 her flying helmet was taken aboard NASA's Atlantis Space Shuttle mission. In 1999, she was inducted into the National Aviation Hall of Fame, and in 2000 was inducted into the Women in Aviation International's Pioneer Hall of Fame.

SOURCES:

Read, Phyllis J., and Bernard L. Witlieb. *The Book of Women's Firsts.* NY: Random House, 1992.
Williams, Nancy A., ed. *Arkansas Biography.* Fayetteville, AR: University of Arkansas Press, 2000.

Laura York, M.A. in History,
University of California,
Riverside, California

Thais (fl. 331 BCE)

Greek courtesan. Name variations: Thaïs. Flourished around 331 BCE; married Lagus (father of Ptolemy I Soter).

Thais accompanied Alexander III the Great on his 331 BCE campaign out of Egypt in his war with the Persians. After conquering Babylonia and Susa, his armies met with resistance at Persepolis. Thais is credited with persuading Alexander to set fire to the Persian palace and city. Though the authenticity of this account is doubtful, it is the subject of John Dryden's *Ode to Saint Cecilia's Day*. Thais eventually married Lagus, who with *Arsinoë (fl. 4th c. BCE) had sired Ptolemy I Soter, founder of the Ptolemaic line of Egypt. Numerous anecdotes and witticisms were attributed to Thais in *The Deipnosophists*, the 15 books of the Greek scholar Athenaeus.

Thalestris (fl. 334 BCE)

Legendary Amazon queen who is reported to have visited Alexander the Great in Hyrcania in order conceive a child with him. Name variations: Minythyia. Possibly flourished around in 334 BCE.

Thalestris (whose name is based on a Greek word meaning "the despoiler") was a legendary Amazon queen who is also known by the name of Minythyia. Justin (12.3.5–8) alleges that Thalestris visited Alexander III the Great in Hyrcania (northern Iran) as he was in the process of conquering the Persian Empire. She is reported to have traveled 25 days with 300 attendants through populous lands so as to meet the famous Macedonian king and conceive a child with him. Justin mentions that Alexander's retinue was astonished both by her military attire and the purpose of her visit. Further, Justin states that Alexander rested his army for 13 days so as to honor Thalestris' request, only renewing the attack upon Persia after Thalestris—convinced that she was pregnant by the famous conqueror—departed.

Justin's story is based on the discredited account of Onesicratus, a philosopher-pilot-writer who accompanied Alexander on his eastern expedition. Hoping to ingratiate himself with Lysimachus, one of Alexander's generals and political successors, after Alexander the Great's death, Onesicratus read to Lysimachus the passage from his book which detailed Thalestris' visit to Hyrcania, after which Lysimachus (who had been at Alexander's side when the great king had been in Hyrcania) sneeringly replied, "And where was I at the time?"

Although the episode is ahistorical, its fame as an anecdote grew, and in the process at least one version of the tale reported that Thalestris was an Illyrian. The repetition of Thalestris' story illuminates some important attitudes common to the Greeks in antiquity. First, the episode underscores the transcendence of Alexander's literary figure over his historical reality (a process which accelerated after the Roman conquest of Greece, but which had begun even before Alexander died). Alexander became a hero for whom nothing was impossible—he could journey to the bottom of the sea, travel to the moon, and even produce children by the semi-civilized queen of a primitive society of women when she came begging him to do so. As such, he became the archetypical Greek, capable of accomplishing anything and taming all lesser species.

Second, as an Amazon, Thalestris represented to the Greeks a perverse social order (one not embracing urban settlement) in which women not only dominated the culture, but actually assumed what were considered by the Greeks to be masculine social roles. Among other things, these included assuming the duties of a soldier and taking the initiative in sexual relations. The Amazons thus represented a threat to the Greek notion of ordered life. Alexander's ability to "tame" the queen of the Amazons functioned as proof that the Greek way of life was superior to exotic alternatives (just as Alexander's conquest of Persia "proved" that the Greeks were superior to the Persians).

Third, Thalestris' identification as an Illyrian could produce a similar result. Like the Amazons, the Illyrians posed a threat to Greek order, insofar as they all too frequently pillaged Greek lands (*see Teuta*). Also like the Amazons, the Illyrians did not live in cities. Since they "glorified" war without balancing that activity with the more humane pursuits thought available only in cities, they joined the Amazons in representing to the Greeks a more primitively organized society. This "inferiority" was reinforced in the Greek mind because Illyrian women were allowed greater freedoms than, it was thought, would ever be permitted in any polis (ironically, this was not so for the kingdom of Macedon, but by the time these stories circulated the more sophisticated Greeks of the city-state—having appropriated Alexander as one of their own—did not care to remember that he was not the product of the polis). We know, for example, that Illyrian women trained for war, participated in politics, and had greater sexual freedom than did Greek women. It is therefore not surprising that Thalestris became associated with an Illyrian background. Since this "Illyrian" had (in Onesicratus' story) acknowledged the superiority of the Greek Alexander by trekking to visit *him*, she provided yet another reaffirmation that Hellenic culture as personified by Alexander was superior to foreign alternatives—even though the foreigners in question could pose a very real threat to the health and well-being of historical Greeks.

SOURCES:
Plutarch. *Life of Alexander.*

William Greenwalt,
Associate Professor of Classical History,
Santa Clara University,
Santa Clara, California

Thamar.

Variant of Tamar.

Thamar (1160–1212).

See Tamara.

Thamaris.

See Timarete.

Thant, Mme

Burmese wife of the secretary-general of the United Nations during the Cold War era. Name variations: Daw Thein Tin; Ma Thein Tin. Born Ma Thein Tin in Mandalay, Burma (now Myanmar); daughter of U Khinn (a lawyer) and Daw Kye; married Maung Thant (U Thant), in November 1934; children: Maung Boh (b. 1936, died in infancy); Saw Lwin (adopted); Aye Aye; Maung Tin Maung (d. 1962); grandchildren: Thant Myint U (b. January 31, 1966).

Mme Thant, born Ma Thein Tin in Mandalay, Burma (now Myanmar), was the only daughter of **Daw Kye** and U Khinn, a prominent lawyer. After Khinn died while Ma Thein Tin was still in her teens, she moved with her mother to the house of her maternal grandparents in Pantanaw in lower Burma. Ma Thein Tin grew up there in a devout and conservative family environment. After graduating from high school, where she studied Pali, the Buddhist scriptural language, in 1934 she married Maung U Thant, the well-educated superintendent of Pantanaw schools and a journalist. Their first son was born two years later but died in infancy; the couple then adopted a boy, Saw Lwin. Ma Thein Tin later gave birth to two surviving children, a daughter **Aye-Aye** and a son Maung Tin Maung. The family settled in Rangoon after World War II, where U Thant joined the new Burmese independent government. He was given increasingly responsible positions and was frequently away from home, leaving Ma Thein Tin, who often suffered from ill health, to raise the three children alone.

In 1957, U Thant became Burma's representative to the United Nations and the family moved to New York City. Ma Thein Tin was unhappy in New York, but her husband's growing importance in international politics prevented her from returning to Burma. In 1961, U Thant became acting secretary-general of the UN after Dag Hammerskjöld died in an airplane crash; he was later elected to the post permanently, serving from 1962 to 1966. Ma Thein Tin's ill health was worsened by constant homesickness and the sudden death of her son Maung Tin Maung in 1962; he had fallen from a moving bus in Rangoon and suffered massive head injuries. Overwrought and unable to return to Burma, even for the funeral of her own son, Ma Thein Tin grew increasingly withdrawn. Although U Thant and Ma Thein Tin wanted to return to Burma when his term expired, U Thant was compelled to accept a second four-year term as secretary-general. Ma Thein Tin rarely attended official events with her husband, preferring to remain quietly at home, and received few visitors. U Thant retired in 1971, and died in November 1974 at their New York home.

SOURCES:
Frederick, Pauline. *Ten First Ladies of the World.* NY: Meredith Press, 1967.

Laura York, M.A. in History,
University of California,
Riverside, California

Tharpe, Rosetta (1915–1973)

American singer and guitarist whose music anticipated Chuck Berry and other rockers. Name variations: Sister Rosetta Tharpe. Born Rosetta Nubin on March 20, 1915, in Cotton Plant, Arkansas; died in Philadelphia, Pennsylvania, of a stroke on October 9, 1973; daughter of Kate Bell Nubin (a traveling gospel-bringer and old time shouter); married a pastor named Thorpe in 1934 (kept his name but changed the spelling); married Forrest Allen, 1940s; married Russell Morrison, in 1951.

Selected discography: Sister Rosetta Tharpe, Gospel, Blues, Jazz; Brighten the Corner Where You Are: Black and White Urban Hymnody; Gospel Train; Soul Sister; Sister Rosetta Tharpe.

Rosetta Tharpe grew up in the heart of gospel, the musical genre which spawned blues and rock. Her mother was **Kate Bell Nubin** a "traveling gospel-bringer, old-time shouter, pianist, and mandolinist," and Rosetta was raised in the Holiness Church where she learned how to make memorable music. Known as "Little Sister," she was only a child when she debuted in Chicago with her mother, singing "I Looked Down the Line and I Wondered" to a crowd of 1,000. At six, she began her professional touring career, singing most often to her own guitar playing and from time to time with her mother's accompaniment, traveling on the tent-meeting circuit with an evangelist. In Tharpe, the Holiness Church found a sanctified singer whose reputation developed widely during gospel music's early years. In addition to her mother's example, she was influenced by the blind pianist Arizona Dranes. Among her repertoire were **Lucie Campbell** and W.H. Brewster's gospel hymns as well as Thomas Andrew Dorsey's blues-touched gospels.

In 1934, Tharpe married a pastor named Thorpe in what was to be the first of three marriages (she would keep his name but alter the spelling to Tharpe). She came to national attention in 1938–39. That year, as the first gospel singer to sign with a major recording company, she contracted with Decca Records. "Rock Me," which was recorded with Lucky Millender, became a hit record, and Tharpe was the subject of a *Life* magazine feature. Her recordings document that Tharpe's guitar playing was years ahead of its time, a sound everyone in America would soon emulate. In addition to performing with the Cab Calloway Revue and appearing at the chic Café Society, Tharpe unleashed her talent in Carnegie Hall during the historic "Spirituals to Swing" concert (1938). As gospel became what Ellistine P. Holly notes as "the most important black music since early jazz" during the 1940s, Tharpe's hits popularized the gospel music to a wider audience, and in the following decade she was one among a handful of gospel prima donnas—including *Mahalia Jackson, *Willie Mae Ford Smith, **Sallie Martin**, and **Roberta Martin**—who spread the sound to the country.

In 1951, Tharpe married her third husband Russell Morrison, ex-manager of the Inkspots, at an outdoor ceremony with 25,000 paying guests. She took her music to Europe during the early 1950s (becoming the first gospel singer to engage in extensive European travel), toured England (1957), appeared at the Antibes Festival (1960), and performed at the Paris Jazz Festival (1968). At home, she lit the stage of New York's

Rosetta Tharpe, with Count Basie.

Apollo Theater (1960s) and the Newport Jazz Festival, and she received Grammy nominations.

Tharpe differed from most other gospels singers in what Holly has called her "flamboyant stage presence. . . . Even during the late sixties she would appear in her red-orange wig, blue jeans, high heels, and an elaborate feather boa." Her more secular style—begun as early as the 1930s—also set Tharpe apart from her gospel contemporaries. Notes Anthony Heilbut: "She could pick blues guitar like a Memphis Minnie [*Lizzie Douglas]. Her song style was filled with blues/inversion, and a resonating vibrato. She bent her notes like a horn player, and syncopated in swing band manner. And, starting in 1938, she scored as no gospel singer has done since."

As the first singer to bring gospel music to the secular stage, Tharpe popularized gospel at the expense of becoming what Heilbut called "*persona non grata* in the Sanctified church." This status endured, and Tharpe became a member of the Baptist Church in her later life. Her last years saw the deaths of her mother (1969) and her friend Mahalia Jackson (1972). While on tour in Europe during 1970, Tharpe had a stroke, and complications resulted in the amputation of her leg. She performed as late as early 1973 and died later that year following a second stroke. Tharpe's rise to prominence had gone hand in hand with the rise of gospel music.

SOURCES:

Sadie, Stanley, ed. *New Grove Dictionary of Jazz.* 2 vols. NY: Macmillan, 1986.

Smith, Jessie Carney, ed. *Notable Black American Women.* Detroit, MI: Gale Research, 1992.

Thatcher, Margaret (1925—)

Britain's first female Conservative Party leader and prime minister from 1979 until 1990. Name variations: Margaret Roberts; Mrs. Thatcher; Lady Thatcher. Born Margaret Roberts in Grantham, England, on October 13, 1925; daughter of Alfred Roberts (a shopkeeper and local politician) and Beatrice Roberts; attended Kesteven and Grantham Girls' School, 1936–43, Somerville College, Oxford, 1943–47; married Denis Thatcher (a London businessman), in December 1951; children: (twins) Carol and Mark (b. 1953).

Worked as a research chemist (1947–51); practiced law (1954–59); elected Conservative member of Parliament (1959); served as secretary of state for Education and Science (1970–74); elected Conservative Party leader (1975); elected prime minister (1979); re-elected prime minister (1983 and 1987); resigned as prime minister (1990); made Lady Thatcher (1992); published memoirs The Downing Street Years *(HarperCollins, 1993) and* The Path to Power *(HarperCollins, 1995).*

Margaret Thatcher, daughter of a provincial English grocer, rose to the heights of political power through hard work, ambition, and absolute single-mindedness. She won three consecutive general elections, which no British premier had done since the early 19th century, and dominated her party more completely than any other politician of the century. Contemptuous of feminism, she surrounded herself with strong and effective men but allowed none of them to rival her own power.

She was born Margaret Roberts in 1925 in Granthan, Lincolnshire. As a schoolgirl, she took elocution lessons, in which she began to learn the brittle, precise, and sometimes condescending tones of her adult oratory. She played field hockey, sang in the school choir, and studied hard, but had few close friends. Her father, an ambitious corner shopkeeper and Methodist lay preacher, became mayor of Grantham in 1943 and was chair of the board of Margaret's school. Finishing school with distinction in examinations, she

won a place at Somerville College, Oxford, one of the few women's colleges at the elite university. There she studied chemistry without great distinction but, showing an early political commitment, became president of the University's Conservative Association—the first woman to hold that office. The Conservatives suffered a stunning loss in the General Election of 1945 which ejected Britain's war leader, Winston Churchill, in favor of the Labour Party leader Clement Attlee. Thatcher's political convictions were already fully shaped although she was only 20, and she campaigned in Grantham that year for the unsuccessful Conservative candidate.

Graduating with a second class degree, she became a research and development chemist with a plastics firm near London but longed to get more directly involved in politics. She believed it would help her to become a lawyer, since scientists play a negligible role in British politics, but for the moment she could not afford the price of a judicial education. She first tried to win a seat in Parliament in 1950, in the strongly pro-Labour constituency of Dartford, Kent. Although she managed to erode the Labour MP's majority among the voters, she could not displace him.

In 1951, she married Denis Thatcher, a prosperous London business executive who, already well established, provided her with complete financial security for her future career and enabled her to turn to legal studies. As her career advanced, Denis Thatcher became a figure of fun in much of the British press, but he appears to have been an intelligent and capable man. He shared his wife's fierce conservative convictions from the start and provided a stable home environment, but was careful not to intervene in her political life. She gave birth to twins, **Carol** and Mark, in 1953, but when they were just one year old she passed the bar and began to practice as an attorney, concentrating on tax cases. It was unusual for well-to-do British wives to work during the 1950s, but Thatcher seems never to have doubted that she had a future in politics.

After several more unsuccessful bids for a parliamentary seat, she won the position of MP for Finchley (part of north London) in 1959, when the Conservatives were once more in power. Only two years later, Prime Minister Harold Macmillan appointed her junior minister in the Ministry of Pensions and National Insurance, where, despite her relative political inexperience, she was soon a dominant presence. Her senior, John Boyd-Carpenter, recalled: "Once she got there she very very quickly showed a grip on the highly technical matters of social security—and it's an extraordinarily technical, complex subject—and a capacity for hard work which she's shown ever since. It quite startled the civil servants and certainly startled me."

The Conservatives lost the General Election of 1964 and for the following six years Thatcher, now in her early and mid-40s, was parliamentary opposition speaker first on Pensions, then on Housing, Finance, Transport, and finally Education. In these years, she learned her way around many of the principal departments of government, experience which was to prove valuable later. Her Finchley seat was secure despite national Labour dominance, and she won it again in 1970, when the Conservatives returned to power under the leadership of Edward Heath.

Heath appointed Thatcher minister of Education and Science and at once she became a dominant—some said domineering—presence at the ministry. The British ministries are run by permanent staffs of civil servants who are expected to obey whichever party is in office. Thatcher suspected that, unless she watched them closely, her civil servants would go their own way rather than energetically enact her policies. Then and subsequently, she favored a confrontational style, making sure that everyone knew she was in charge, that all business passed through her hands, and that she would never be taken by surprise by events in her ministry. A prodigiously hard worker, she slept little, learned complex sets of facts and figures, was reluctant to delegate responsibility, and in parliamentary speeches could often overwhelm challengers with her mastery of detail.

For the first time, she became nationally famous when she decreed that, as part of an economy drive, government-run schools should no longer give free milk to every child (a policy enacted decades earlier when many urban children suffered from poor nutrition). A press campaign labeled her: "Thatcher, the milk snatcher," and she now had to endure heckling and public insults when she went to open new schools or give speeches in colleges. The National Union of Students, dominated by the radical left in the early 1970s, treated her with contempt when she tried to restrict its access to government subsidies. Local Labour councils opposed her plan to preserve selective grammar schools of the sort she had attended rather than hasten a nationwide change to universal "comprehensive" schools.

Edward Heath's premiership was marred by a long succession of bitter industrial strikes and a severe period of inflation. When he called a general election in 1974, hoping to increase his parliamentary majority, he lost, and Labour leader Harold Wilson became prime minister once more. Heath's defeat discredited him as Conservative Party leader and in the leadership struggle which followed Thatcher emerged as a prominent candidate. She was not widely liked by her fellow Conservatives. Many of them came from rich or aristocratic backgrounds, their party was notoriously snobbish, and she carried the stigma of being a provincial tradesman's daughter with an artificial accent and a frosty manner. On the other hand, she was fearless, decisive, and hard-working. One prominent Conservative leader, Airey Neave, a hero of World War II, pushed her candidacy against several male rivals and in the balloting of February 1975 she won.

In the following four years, Thatcher gained international prominence as an outspoken leader of the opposition. Like *Golda Meir in Israel and *Indira Gandhi in India, she gave no one the chance to rebuke her for feminine weakness. At the same time, she was contemptuous of the feminist movement and believed that any woman with energy to match her own could succeed. At the next general election, in May 1979, she benefited from Labour's economic crisis, won a resounding victory, and became prime minister, the first woman to hold Britain's highest political office. In the following decade, she carried out a conservative revolution even more dramatic than that of her American friend and counterpart President Ronald Reagan. From "milk snatcher," she graduated to a sterner nickname, "The Iron Lady," created by the Soviet press but soon picked up at home, which stayed with her for the next decade. Despite high levels of unemployment and the continued challenge of Britain's overmighty trade unions, she was to win re-election twice more and remain in power longer than any other 20th-century prime minister.

Since World War II, most of Britain's major industries, including coal, steel, railways, telephones, water, gas, and electricity, had been nationalized. Many of them ran at a loss, and were subsidized by heavy taxes. Thatcher, a dedicated free marketeer, was determined to end economic inefficiencies, and under her supervision these primary industries were, one by one, denationalized. Citizens were encouraged to become shareholders, and Thatcher warned management that if they could not turn a profit, they would have to face the vicissitudes of the marketplace like any other businessman. The National Health Service, however, had so much support from all sides that she did not seriously consider dismantling it. She also struck hard against the power of trade unions, organizing Acts of Parliament in 1980, 1982, and 1984 which curbed union power and outlawed the closed shop. Facing up to a yearlong coalminer's strike (March 1984–March 1985) in what the press dubbed the "Winter of Discontent," she won the affection of most middle-class voters but the undying hatred of union stalwarts.

A policy related to denationalization was Thatcher's decision to sell public-housing units (known in England as council houses) to their occupants. She believed that the government should do what it could to preside over the economy as judge and arbitrator rather than being itself a principal economic player. Selling council houses was politically beneficial too because it gave the purchasers the sense that, as property owners, they would be well served by voting Conservative from now on.

Thatcher dominated British politics and government in a fashion not witnessed since Churchill's leadership of Britain during World War II.

—E. Bruce Geelhoed

Shortly before her election victory she had told an interviewer that "as Prime Minister I couldn't waste time having any internal arguments." In the following years, she made good on that assertion, running Cabinet meetings briskly, moving quickly to prearranged decisions, and firing ministers who disagreed with her. Some ministers, notably Ian Gilmour, Francis Pym, and James Prior, favored conciliation and negotiated settlements with the trade unions. She called them the "wets" and got rid of them. She sometimes berated her associates, and as her power grew she tended increasingly to hector those who crossed her in matters both small and great. She was renowned for asking her closest associates, when a new candidate for office was under consideration, "Is he one of us?," meaning, ideologically and personally loyal to her.

The most dramatic event of Thatcher's first term of office, and one which did much to salvage her from economic and unemployment woes, was the Falkland Islands War. The corrupt Galtieri dictatorship of Argentina, hoping to distract the Argentine people from its domestic crises with a patriotic triumph, seized the South Atlantic Falkland Islands in April 1982. The islands had been a British colony for 150 years and, although they no longer had much strategic value for Britain, Thatcher took the view that Argentina could not be permitted to trample British sovereignty, especially when the population (of 1,800 farmers and fishermen) was also

loyal to Britain. She therefore ordered Britain's armed forces to prepare a counterattack.

Britain's NATO allies, particularly the Americans, had mixed feelings about this venture. They agreed with her that arbitrary invasion was deplorable, but did not want to see a large military effort so far from their main theater of concern, the Iron Curtain. The Americans were also afraid that inter-American relations would be damaged if they sided too openly with an old colonial power against Argentina. In the end, however, President Reagan stood by his ally, and the U.S. Navy and Air Force refuelled the British expeditionary force as it sailed south. The invading force suffered the loss of two ships sunk and twelve others damaged, and about 250 British military personnel were killed, but within a month of the landings, the war was over. Argentinean casualties were far higher—368 died in the sinking of one ship, the *General Belgrano*, alone—and the end of the war presaged the end of the Galtieri dictatorship.

Labour Party leader Michael Foot, convinced that Thatcher should have tried harder to make a negotiated settlement rather than fight a costly war for an irrelevant colony, led the parliamentary opposition to Thatcher and criticized her decision to visit the island in January 1983 at a cost of £200,000 (almost half a million dollars). British popular opinion, however, supported Thatcher and, on the strength of her new image as a successful war leader, she swept back into office in the General Election of June 1983. Her campaign was helped by the disarray inside the Labour Party, badly split between its moderate and militant sides, and by Labour's pledge of unilateral nuclear disarmament, which never had wide public support. She benefited from the professional advertising campaign mounted by the Saatchi and Saatchi company, which borrowed from and improved on American political advertising methods.

The next year, at the Conservative Party's annual conference, Thatcher was attacked by the Irish Republican Army (IRA), which detonated a bomb in Brighton's Grand Hotel where she and other party members were staying. The blast, coming at 2:30 in the early morning hours, killed 5 and injured 32, including her ministers John Wakeham and Norman Tebbitt. Thatcher survived; indeed, she was still awake and working on government papers and within minutes was able to appear before television cameras, outwardly calm, well dressed and composed, to denounce terrorism and reaffirm her government's Ireland policy. Her composure on this occasion fortified her reputation for inflexible determination,

Margaret
Thatcher

though terrorism must have been a source of constant anxiety—her friend and mentor Airey Neave had died in an IRA bomb attack in 1979.

When she won a third election in 1987, against a better-organized Labour Party under Neil Kinnock, Thatcher began to seem, to her friends and enemies, unassailable, and yet in this third administration she sowed the seeds of her downfall. First, she introduced a ruinously unpopular "poll tax," changing the local taxation structure and imposing the burden less progressively than hitherto. The tax turned out to be much higher for many taxpayers than previous local taxes had been, and by 1989 one of the plan's early supporters, Sir Rhodes Boyson, admitted ruefully that "the poll tax as it now stands is a Labour Party benevolent fund." Many members of her own party were uneasy about the reform, and a massive opposition to the tax led to underreporting, evasion, and protest events. The worst of these protests turned into the London riot of March 31, 1991—the most damaging political riot in 20th-century Britain—which hastened the end of the scheme (by which time Thatcher had resigned).

Second, Thatcher remained suspicious of Britain's role in the European Economic Community. Britain had joined it late, under her Conservative predecessor Edward Heath, and much of Britain's business community believed that closer economic and political ties with Europe would benefit the nation. Thatcher feared that closer ties, especially monetary union, would compromise British sovereignty and lead to German domination of the Community. In the early years of her premiership, she had made headlines by denouncing Community financing arrangements and winning a better deal for Britain, but now she seemed to be shirking obligations to which she had already assented. The issue rankled even some of her closest associates, among them Michael Heseltine (nicknamed "Tarzan"), a conservative maverick and spellbinding speechmaker who resigned from the Cabinet in 1987, partly over European differences.

In the following years, Heseltine became the rallying point for anti-Thatcher Conservatives, whose number grew steadily. Thatcher had now fired nearly all the senior Conservative men from their ministerial positions at one time or another, replacing them with younger (and sometimes more sycophantic) alternatives. A groundswell of opposition was building among Conservatives, and she was already widely hated by Labour, Liberal, and Social Democratic politicians. By late 1990, even her loyal supporter John Major, chancellor of the exchequer, was urging her to cooperate more fully in European monetary integration. That November, Thatcher's adversaries used her unpopularity in the polls (which showed she would lose an election held just then) to force an election for party leadership. In the balloting, her chief opponent Heseltine won 152 votes to her 204. Since her majority was not sufficient to fulfil party election rules, she faced the prospect of a second ballot. But to have lost so much support showed Thatcher that her long hold on power was finally coming to an end and that she

would be likely to lose later if not now, weakening the party as she did so. Accordingly she visited Queen *Elizabeth II, in line with protocol, then issued a statement of resignation, weeping a little at her last Cabinet meeting but otherwise keeping a close rein on her emotions.

John Major rather than Michael Heseltine succeeded her as party leader and went on to win another Conservative election victory two years later. Thatcher herself, elevated to a life peerage, became one of the elder chiefs of state of the Western world. Highly praised by conservatives overseas, and even by Mikhail Gorbachev and the leadership of China, she made successful speaking tours in America and Japan. Few commentators could doubt, however, that it was a source of bitter regret to her that she was no longer in a position of power and authority. She had made as strong a mark on British politics as any 20th-century prime minister. As Dennis Kavanagh wrote soon afterwards: "Mrs. Thatcher . . . has challenged certain long-established political assumptions: that a government could not be re-elected if it presided over a massive increase in unemployment; or that a government had to govern with the consent and co-operation of the major interests, particularly business and the unions. Mrs. Thatcher has successfully defied both beliefs." She left British politics a greatly changed arena, whose old rules no longer applied.

SOURCES:

Geelhoed, E. Bruce. *Margaret Thatcher: In Victory and Downfall*. NY: Prager, 1992.

Junor, Penny. *Margaret Thatcher: Wife, Mother, Politician*. London: Sidgwick & Jackson, 1983.

Kavanagh, Dennis. *Thatcherism and British Politics*. Oxford: Oxford University Press, 1990.

Skidelsky, Robert, ed. *Thatcherism*. London. Chatto & Windus, 1988.

Tebbitt, Norman. *Upwardly Mobile*. London: Weidenfeld & Nicholson, 1988.

Watkins, Alan. *A Conservative Coup: The Fall of Margaret Thatcher*. London: Duckworth, 1991.

Young, Hugo, and Anne Sloman. *The Thatcher Phenomenon*. London: British Broadcasting Corp., 1986.

SUGGESTED READING:

Abse, Leo. *Margaret, Daughter of Beatrice*. London: Jonathan Cape, 1989.

Thatcher, Margaret. *The Downing Street Years*. NY: HarperCollins, 1993.

———. *The Path to Power*. NY: HarperCollins, 1995.

COLLECTIONS:

Hansard, British Library, British newspaper archives.

Patrick Allitt,
Professor of History,
Emory University,
Atlanta, Georgia

Thaw, Evelyn Nesbit (1884–1967).

See Nesbit, Evelyn.

Celia
Laighton
Thaxter

Thaxter, Celia Laighton (1835–1894)

American poet. Born in Portsmouth, New Hampshire, on June 29, 1835; died on Appledore, one of the Isles of Shoals, off Portsmouth, on August 26, 1894; daughter of Thomas B. Laighton (a newspaper-man) and Eliza (Rymes) Laighton; married Levi Lincoln Thaxter, on September 30, 1851 (died 1884); children: Karl Thaxter; John Thaxter; Roland Thaxter (1858–1932, who would become a well-known botanist at Harvard, specializing in cryptogamic botany).

Celia Laighton Thaxter was born in Portsmouth, New Hampshire, in 1835, the daughter of Thomas B. Laighton and **Eliza Rymes Laighton**. Incensed by political associates and despairing of a political career in state government, Thomas retired to White Island, on the isolated Isles of Shoals, with Eliza and their three children in about 1841. For approximately ten years, he was keeper of the White Island lighthouse. These surroundings—about ten miles off the coast of Portsmouth—would serve to color the best of Celia Thaxter's later verse: the isolation of the winters, the sailing of a boat by ear in fog, the "tall, black-capped giant" of a lighthouse, the birds that flew violently against its lantern, the sound of the guns from the sinking brig *Pocahontas*, which went down with all hands lost.

In 1845, when her father built a summer hotel on Appledore Island, the first of its kind along the New England coast, many of the leading writers and artists of the period flocked to its doors. There 16-year-old Celia met her future husband Levi Thaxter, a lawyer and Harvard graduate who came as a missionary to preach to the fishermen on Star Island. They were married in 1851. Four years later, in 1855, Levi nearly lost his life in a sailboat accident while crossing to the mainland. He grew fearful of the sea and the islands, and the couple moved inland to Newtonville, Massachusetts, where they raised three sons. Much older than his wife and a retiring scholar by nature, Levi retreated into his books. Celia had an apposite nature. Following a serious illness, in 1868–69 Levi wintered in Florida with the two younger sons, the first in a series of long separations for the couple which eventually led to their living separate lives. Ostensibly a widow, Celia and her eldest son Karl (mentally ill since childhood) joined her brothers who had inherited the summer hotel on Appledore. There she became the center of a salon for the best minds of New England, including John Greenleaf Whittier, William Morris Hunt, and Edwin Arlington Robinson. "Though she never stood with the greatest," wrote **Laura Benét**, "her simple poems had both power and originality." Celia Thaxter died and was buried on Appledore at the age 59.

Her first printed poem, "Land-Locked," was published by James Russell Lowell in the *Atlantic Monthly*. Others verses followed. In lyrical form, her poems deal with storms at sea, shipwrecks, beacon lights, striped snails, rock flowers, and sandpipers. She also wrote prose sketches, including *Among the Isles of Shoals* (1873), *Driftweed*, a book about floriculture, *An Island Garden* (1894), and stories and poems for children while contributing articles to *St. Nicholas* magazine. A complete edition of her poems was edited by *Sarah Orne Jewett in 1896.

SOURCES:
Benét, Laura. *Famous American Poets*. NY: Dodd, Mead, 1950.

Thea (c. 165–121 BCE).

See Cleopatra Thea.

Theano (fl. 6th c. BCE)

Greek composer, poet, and philosopher. Name variations: Theano of Crotona. Flourished in the 6th centu-ry BCE; married Pythagoras (c. 582–c. 500 BCE, a Greek philosopher and mathematician who was devoted to the reformation of politics, morality, and society); children: daughters *Arignote, *Myia, and Damo; sons Telauges and Mnesarchus.

Although almost everyone knows about the Pythagorean theorem, created by Pythagoras, few realize the influence music had on this Greek mathematician's concepts. Pythagoras was married to Theano, who was a composer, poet, singer, and dancer. She taught him that the spheres and stars of heaven moved in eternal song and dance. She organized rites for her followers so that they could achieve inner harmony through movement to the music. This concept of natural harmonic movement was very influential in Greek thought. Other women flourished in the Pythagorean school, including **Aristoclea**, the teacher of Pythagoras at Delphi, *Damo, Theano and Pythagoras' daughter, and **Theoclea**, who became a high priestess.

John Haag,
Athens, Georgia

Theano II (fl. 5th c. BCE)

Poet. Flourished in the 5th century BCE.

There are no surviving works from the poet Theano II. She was a writer of lyric verse who was mentioned in the 10th-century *Suda* and Eustathius.

Thebom, Blanche (1918—)

American mezzo-soprano. Pronunciation: Ta'bom. Born in 1918 in Monessen, Pennsylvania; studied under Margarete Matzenmauer and Edyth Walker.

Debuted with the Metropolitan Opera (1944); appeared in musical sequence in the film When Irish Eyes Are Smiling *(1944); retired (1970).*

Born in Pennsylvania in 1918 and raised in Canton, Ohio, mezzo-soprano Blanche Thebom began to study piano and voice with her parents at age eight. She attended public schools in Canton and sang in school and church choirs. Although she hoped to go to college, the effects of the Depression made college impossible to afford, and Thebom instead enrolled in a vocational school to learn clerical skills. She had worked as a secretary for several years when her vocal talent was discovered during an impromptu concert onboard a ship bound for Sweden in 1938. A well-known concert pianist, Kosti Vehanen, was in the audience. Vehanen, renowned for his work as an accompanist to the great contralto *Marian Anderson, was so impressed by the strength and emotional range of Thebom's voice that he gave her a letter of introduction to a New York voice teacher. When Thebom's employer offered to pay her way, she moved to New York in 1939 with her parents' encouragement.

After two years of intensive study under *Edyth Walker, Thebom made her professional debut at a recital in Sheboygan, Wisconsin, in 1941. She then sang with the Philadelphia Orchestra as well as in countless small towns, followed by contracts with the Minneapolis Symphony in 1943 and New York's Town Hall in early 1944. Widely praised by critics, Thebom soon signed with the Twentieth Century-Fox studio to sing in the film *When Irish Eyes are Smiling*. She opened at the Metropolitan Opera House in December 1944 and played the 1944–45 season there. Throughout the 1960s, Thebom would perform regularly at the Metropolitan, usually in dramatic roles, to rave reviews. In 1948, she opened at the Philadelphia All-Star Concert Series. In addition to repeated appearances in San Francisco and Chicago, Thebom also made numerous recordings and was frequently featured on classical radio programs. She was also the first American to sing with the Bolshoi Opera in Moscow.

In the late 1960s, Thebom joined the music faculty of the University of Arkansas. In 1970, she retired from performing, and in 1973 was named director of the Hot Springs National Park Foundation for the Performing Arts. She then moved to San Francisco to teach privately. In 1988, she founded the Opera Arts Training Program in San Francisco and served as its director.

SOURCES:
"Blanche Thebom," in *Current Biography 1948*. NY: H.W. Wilson, 1948.
Morehead, Philip D. *The New International Dictionary of Music*. NY: Meridian, 1991.

Laura York, M.A. in History,
University of California,
Riverside, California

Thecla (fl. 1st c. CE)

Early Christian, follower of St. Paul and one of the best-known saints of the Greek Church, whose miraculous escapes from certain death became a famous legend. Name variations: Thecla of Seleucia. Flourished around the 1st century CE; born at Iconium, a small town in Cilicia (southern Anatolia); daughter of Theocleia.

Alleged to have been an early Christian who miraculously escaped martyrdom more than once, Thecla was originally linked to St. Paul in a late 2nd century CE apocryphal treatise entitled the *Acts of Paul and Thecla*, a work which can be characterized as a Christian romance. She does not appear in what eventually would become the canonical books of the Bible. Although mostly unhistorical, Thecla's story illustrates many of the ways in which 2nd century Christians perceived themselves to be at odds with the prevailing values of their contemporary imperial culture.

According to the *Acts of Paul and Thecla*, Thecla was born at Iconium, a small town in Cilicia (southern Anatolia) to which Paul once fled from Antioch with two sycophantic companions named Demas and Hermogenes. Demas and Hermogenes were more interested in the prestige to be accrued by associating with Paul than they were in his message. Paul was welcomed to Iconium by an admirer named Onesiphorus, in whose home Paul preached, especially emphasizing the virtues of a celibate life. The house of Thecla's parents lay close to that of Onesiphorus, so that although Thecla was not one of the women who initially came to Onesiphorus' house to hear Paul speak, she nevertheless had the opportunity to overhear Paul from a window in her own home. Although not previously inclined toward Christianity and betrothed before Paul's arrival, Thecla was so mesmerized by Paul's sermons, it is asserted, that she longed to sit at his feet and absorb both his voice and its message. For three days and nights, however, she meekly eavesdropped from her window-seat.

Thecla's mother **Theocleia** noted Paul's eerie hold over her daughter and despaired at its implications, for a daughter's celibacy meant no continuation of an earthly family—a great tragedy to most pagans, and even some Christians. Summoning Thamyris, Thecla's fiancé and Iconium's first citizen, Theocleia hoped to restore Thecla to her pre-Pauline state of mind, but although Thamyris added his appeals to those of Theocleia and the maidservants of the house, Thecla remained speechlessly transfixed by Paul's voice. Frustrated, Thamyris strode into the street to see who was entering and leaving the house of Onesiphorus. There he met Demas and Hermogenes, who were becoming extremely jealous of Paul's popularity, while none of the locals paid them any heed at all. Realizing an opportunity, Thamyris offered to pay Demas and Hermogenes to report what they knew about this "false" teacher encouraging celibacy. Initially they denied knowing Paul, but confirmed that his message was pro-celibacy and anti-marriage. A distressed Thamyris invited the duo to dinner, during which they traitorously suggested to their host that he ought to accuse Paul of propagating Christianity before the Roman governor of the region, one Castellius.

The next morning Thamyris and an armed crowd descended upon Onesiphorus' house to demand that Paul—as a "sorcerer" and "corruptor of wives"—be brought before Castellius. Interrogated by the Roman official, Paul affirmed that he had been preaching the will of God, but admitted to no wrong thereby. The governor, however, thought the matter worth greater deliberation and had Paul incarcerated. Learning of Paul's arrest, Thecla went to his prison at night and bribed her way into his cell to hear him preach. That night capped Thecla's conversion experience. After her family discovered Thecla at Paul's side, Thamyris and another hostile crowd again descended upon Castellius, howling for something to be done. Paul was brought before the gubernatorial throne while Thecla initially was left to her rapture in his cell. Eventually, however, she too was brought before Castellius. When the governor asked her why she now would not honor her pledge to marry Thamyris, Thecla remained mute, staring at Paul. Unable to bear the silence, Theocleia called out for her disobedient daughter's destruction as an example to the others who had fallen under Paul's anti-social spell. Castellius became greatly agitated at the situation but was unwilling to kill Paul, fearing the power of his "magic." Instead, Castellius ordered Paul's scourging and his removal from the city. Castellius then dealt even more harshly with Thecla: he ordered her immediate death by immolation in the town's theater. Looking to Paul for help, Thecla is said to have had a vision of Jesus in Paul's mein. Before this revelation ascended into heaven, it affirmed the truth of the message which had so entranced her. Preparations for Thecla's burning then proceeded. Stripped naked, she calmly made the sign of the cross and mounted the pyre. A fire was kindled and began to blaze, but it did not reach Thecla before a sudden downpour doused the flames. The throng which had bayed for Thecla's blood stood in awe of her and set her free.

Expelled from Iconium, Paul had made his way to Daphne. With him went the family of Onesiphorus, which had thought to divest itself of worldly possessions in order to follow Paul. Several days after Thecla's miraculous escape, this entourage was going without food for lack of the funds to procure it. When Onesiphorus' sons complained of hunger, Paul removed his outer garment and gave it to one of the children with instructions to sell it in a nearby village and buy some bread. The rest remained by the roadside near an open tomb where they had stopped

to fast. On his way to buy food the boy discovered Thecla and led her back to Paul. As she approached, Thecla found Paul by the open tomb in the act of praying for her salvation. (The open tomb, of course, making reference to the Resurrection of Jesus and Christian salvation.) A joyous reunion ensued, followed by a break in the group's fast. In the midst of this festive afternoon, Thecla proclaimed that she would henceforth demonstrate her embrace of celibacy by cutting her hair, after which she would follow Paul anywhere. She also sought baptism, but Paul demurred, arguing that the time was not yet ripe for her total commitment to Christianity, for Thecla was very beautiful and might yet fall prey to some future sexual temptation. And, as Paul posited, any succumbing to temptation after baptism would weigh far more heavily upon her soul than if she had yet to be baptized.

After his reunion with Thecla, Paul sent Onesiphorus and his family back to Iconium while he and his new traveling companion made for Antioch. Soon after they arrived there, Alexander, a prominent citizen of the town, was smitten by Thecla at first sight. Alexander assumed that Thecla was Paul's slave and tried to buy her, until Paul told him that she was not his to sell. When Alexander then shamelessly pawed at Thecla in public, she protested, making known her station and the reason for her expulsion from Iconium. She then physically defended herself against her molester and made of him a laughingstock. Alexander responded by bringing charges against Thecla before the local governor. When she admitted that she was guilty of leaving her physical mark upon Alexander, the local magistrate condemned her for the second time. Her punishment was to be thrown to the animals in the games Alexander was then sponsoring. Considering the fact that it was Alexander who had initiated their physical contact and that Thecla had only defended her honor, the women present when this verdict was handed down reviled it. Thecla, however, merely requested that her virginity be honored until she faced her new tribulation. Between sentencing and sentence, a rich local widow named **Tryphaena** (a woman with imperial connections, whose daughter had recently died) sheltered Thecla in her home.

When the time for Thecla's execution came, her tormentors lashed her to a lion in the hopes of inciting the animal to fury and paraded her through the streets. The attempt to goad the beast backfired, for far from enraging the lion, Thecla's presence mollified it to the point where it harmlessly began to lick her feet. Amazement arose, but the crowd's reaction was mixed. On the one

THECLA

hand, the authorities were disturbed and added a charge of sacrilege to the previous one of criminal assault. (For whatever good that was supposed to do: one can only be martyred once.) On the other hand, the women and children in attendance berated this additional condemnation and predicted that bad times would descend upon Antioch as a result of these injustices. Regardless, this episode caused a delay in Thecla's punishment, and she was again housed with Tryphaena. During this stay, Tryphaena had a dream in which her dead daughter appeared, exhorting her to treat Thecla as a second daughter in return for Thecla's prayers for the deceased's eternal salvation. When asked to pray for the departed, Thecla willingly did so, with the result that Tryphaena embraced her as a daughter newly discovered. Thus a Christian "family" was born, many times more significant to its members than any conceivable biological family could ever be.

When Alexander again came to claim Thecla for her destiny in the arena, Tryphaena intervened. The governor then sent soldiers, and although Tryphaena prayed to Thecla's God to protect her in her time of trial, she acquiesced to the authorities and accompanied Thecla to the stadium. As they proceeded, many women again made clear their opposition to the overly harsh sentence. At the arena, Thecla and Tryphaena parted, and Thecla was made ready for what was to come. Then came another miracle, for when a lioness and a bear were set loose on Thecla, the lioness protectively positioned itself between Thecla and the bear, much to the delight of the horde of discontented women in attendance. In the duel which followed, the lioness tore the bear apart. This feat was followed by the release of a specially trained lion, which the lioness also battled until both beasts died. Within a Christian context, femininity was asserting itself against an oppressive and impious male domination.

Thereafter many beasts were loosed against Thecla. She prayed for deliverance and, turning, discovered a body of water in which swam several watery nemeses. Thecla approached the water to the dismay of the audience and dove in so as to cleanse (baptize) herself spiritually. Far from being consumed by the monsters lurking therein, she was saved when a bolt of lightning appeared from nowhere and slew all of these creatures. Thecla was then enveloped in a cloud of fire. More beasts were unleashed, but these were overcome by sleep, so that nothing came near her. Alexander then requested of the governor that Thecla be torn asunder by bulls (the gender again is no accident in this context), and his request was granted. Thus, she was bound to

the legs of four bulls, who were incited to a frenzy by the placement of red-hot irons under their stomachs. The bulls leapt, but the same burning which aroused their panic destroyed the ropes which bound Thecla to them, freeing her.

All of these auspicious events caused Tryphaena to fall into a faint so profound that those around her thought she was dead. Everyone present was thoroughly alarmed by this portent, for Tryphaena was of high station: even the vindictive Alexander begged his superior to free Thecla, lest the wrath of the Roman emperor loosed at Tryphaena's loss raze the city. The governor concurred and summoned Thecla, wondering what kind of creature could survive all of her trials. She answered that she was but a follower of the "living" God and his Son. Thereafter, she humbly accepted her pardon. The governor acknowledged Thecla's piety, but this was overshadowed by the acclamation of Antioch's women, who praised the power of Thecla's God. Then Tryphaena revived to proclaim the salvation of her deceased daughter. She also acclaimed Thecla's God.

Thecla stayed with Tryphaena for a short time, but yearning for Paul, sought him out. Discovering him to be at Myra, Thecla proceeded there, attired as a man (the issue of gender remains a prominent theme). Paul was astonished at her arrival, and even more astonished after learning of the manner of her baptism. Paul then took Thecla's hand and led her into a meeting of the local faithful, there to retell her story. Paul's community marveled at the tale and prayed for Tryphaena. Thecla then announced her intention to return to Iconium, and Paul advised her to teach God's word. With Tryphaena's financial support, Thecla was able to serve the poor. Returning home, Thecla renewed herself with the house of Onesiphorus (conveniently restored to him) from which place Paul's voice had changed her life. She also returned to discover her ex-fiancé dead, but her mother alive. Thecla and Theocleia remained unreconciled. Thecla reproached her biological mother for valuing the things of the flesh over those of the spirit and implied that Tryphaena was now proven more her mother than was Theocleia. Having revisited Iconium and the places where she had been led to Christ, Thecla is said to have abandoned the city of her birth to live in a cave near a small town which would later be renamed Hagia Thecla (modern Meriamlik, near the more important ancient city of Seleucia) in her honor.

To whatever degree the *Acts of Paul and Thecla* are historical, Thecla's legend grew with time. A 5th-century tract credited her with miracles (including acts of healing and premonitions) and many good works which spread the word of God. This treatise avers that when she was 90, Thecla again faced persecution: this time at the hands of local pagan shamans, jealous of her healing powers. Yet, once again Thecla survived through felicitous support: as she fled her tormentors, the stone which rolled back and forth to permit or close off access to her cave is said to have autonomously opened to receive her, and closed behind her, before her adversaries could lay their hands on her.

Clearly, the legend of Thecla was developed in stages, initially to hearten Christian women during a time when the moral ethos of a burgeoning movement was at odds with that of the pagan culture in which they found themselves. Thecla's saga became widespread, as did her image in art. A sanctuary at Seleucia in her honor became a very popular site of pilgrimage during the Middle Ages and thereafter, and her purported accomplishments became institutionalized among Greek Orthodox Christians. September 24th is widely recognized as her feast day.

William Greenwalt,
Associate Professor of Classical History,
Santa Clara University,
Santa Clara, California

Thecla (c. 775–c. 823)

Byzantine empress. Name variations: Thekla. Born around 775; died around 823; daughter of a general; first wife of Michael II of Amorion, Byzantine emperor (r. 820–829); children: Theophilus I (r. 829–842). Michael's second wife was *Euphrosyne (c. 790–c. 840).

Thecla was the daughter of an unnamed general who was the chief military official of the Anatolian theme of the Byzantine Empire sometime during the late 8th century. As was common at that time (c. 795), Thecla's father patronized fortunetellers, one of whom predicted that two officers under his command, one named Michael (II) of Amorion (after the Phrygian village of his birth) and the other unnamed, would both one day become Byzantine emperors. As a result of this prophecy, Thecla's father arranged a banquet to which he invited the two officers. Michael was surprised by the invitation because of the humbleness of his birth, and was even more so when, in the course of the evening, the commander offered two of his daughters in marriage. Noting the differences in their respective social ranks, Michael and his colleague are initially said to have declined, but after their

commander pressed his proposition, they accepted the extraordinary alliances. Thus was the marriage of Thecla to Michael arranged, and the latter's rise to the imperial throne begun. (Michael's unnamed brother-in-law did not fare so well, thus calling into question the infallibility of the agent of Michael's ascent.)

Byzantium during Thecla's lifetime was a troubled state, beset as it was with foreign threats from every point of the compass (but especially from Bulgaria and the Arab world), and subject to the domestic turmoil brought on by the Iconoclastic Controversy. Between 717 and 867, the empire was deeply divided over the use of religious icons: one faction (primarily monastic) was devoted to their veneration, while another was equally bent on their destruction since it believed that it was the icon itself—and not the idea behind the icon—which was being adored by iconodules. One of the greatest of iconoclastic emperors, Constantine V (r. 741–775), was also one of the era's most successful generals against foreign enemies, a fact not lost upon many in the army who associated Constantine's military success with a divine favor bestowed as a result of his anti-icon religious policy. Only five years after Constantine's death, however, his son, Leo IV, also died. At the time, Leo's heir, Constantine VI, was still a minor, a fact which allowed Leo's iconodule widow *Irene of Athens to seize control of the empire, initially as her son's regent. In 784, Irene restored the veneration of icons, but the military's hostile reaction led to her ouster (790) and to the elevation of Constantine VI. Not a strong ruler, Constantine reappointed his mother to imperial status in 792, but in 797 the two had a complete falling out, at which time Irene dethroned her son, blinded him, and began to rule alone. Since Irene's reign saw military disaster after military disaster, the Byzantine army's bias against the veneration of icons was reinforced. After a palace coup toppled Irene (802), the emperors who served in her wake tended to favor the iconoclastic cause of the army yearning for the good old days of Constantine V. Growing up in a military household, Thecla was almost certainly an iconoclast, as was her husband, although when he ruled he would be somewhat moderate in his approach to iconodules.

Thecla's husband was an ambitious opportunist who exploited every chance to advance his career. After the overthrow of Irene by Nicephorus I, Michael supported the revolt of Bardanes Tourcus (803) against the new emperor, but Michael quickly abandoned that rebellion when it became evident that it would not succeed. Instead, when offered an olive branch by Nicephorus, Michael switched sides, for which treachery he was elevated in rank to the position of "Count of the Tent" and given a palace in Constantinople. A military disaster cut short Nicephorus' reign, but under the rule of Michael I Rangabe (r. 811–813), Michael of Amorion continued to advance under the patronage of Leo the Armenian, who himself engineered the coup which toppled Michael I. Under the newly ensconced Leo V (r. 813–820), Michael of Amorion again flourished, being regularly promoted and elevated into the patrician order. The relationship of Michael and Leo was as personal as it was professional: at some time Leo even stood as the godfather of one of Michael's and Thecla's sons (probably Theophilus, the later emperor). Michael's success, however, led him to conspire against Leo. Although Leo discovered Michael's treachery, had him arrested, and sentenced him to death on charges of treason, conspirators serving Michael's interest assassinated Leo and freed Michael. He was crowned emperor on December 25, 820, with Thecla at his side. In the spirit of the age, an ambitious former comrade-in-arms with Michael, Thomas the Slav, immediately rebelled against the new order, hoping to dislodge the new imperial claimant before Michael consolidated his power. After a three-year war, Michael overcame this threat to his personal authority.

It must be assumed that Thecla stood close by Michael's side as his fortunes rose, because when she died sometime during, or shortly after, Michael's war with Thomas, Michael mourned her deeply. Before her death, however, Thecla lived to see one of her sons, Theophilus, enthroned as Basileus and Augustus beside her husband, thus securing Michael's succession. Although it cannot be known for sure, it was probably Theophilus for whom Leo V acted as godfather. That, at least, would explain why immediately after Michael II's death in 829, Theophilus (an emperor who made the pursuit of justice one of his reign's central themes) executed the murderers of Leo, whose very deeds had saved Michael's life and ensured his own elevation to the throne.

Theophilus was enthroned on May 12, 821, on which day he was also married to *Theodora the Blessed, who had been selected by an imperial Bride Show probably run under the supervision of Thecla. If so, Thecla's military upbringing probably helped to shape imperial policy, for Theodora was from Paphlagonia and both her father and her uncle were officers in the army. Since Theophilus was succeeded on the throne by his son, Michael III, Michael II and Thecla es-

tablished a dynasty (the Amorion, or Phrygian), an accomplishment unmatched by Michael II's three imperial predecessors.

William S. Greenwalt,
Professor of Classical History,
Santa Clara University,
Santa Clara, California

Thecla (c. 810–c. 860).

See Theodora the Blessed.

Thecla (c. 823–c. 870)

Possible co-regent of the Byzantine Empire. Name variations: Saint Thecla. Born around 823; died around 870; daughter of Theophilus I, Byzantine emperor (r. 829–842), and Empress Theodora the Blessed (c. 810–c. 860); sister of Michael III the Drunkard (c. 836–867), Byzantine emperor (r. 842–867), and Mary (or Maria), Anna, Anastasia, and Pulcheria; mistress of Basil I, Byzantine emperor (r. 867–886).

Thecla was the daughter of Byzantine Emperor Theophilus I and Empress *Theodora the Blessed. Theophilus and Theodora were married on the day of Theophilus' accession (May 12, 821). Since **Maria** (one of Thecla's sisters) married an imperial colleague of Theophilus in 836, and since Maria's birth could not have come before 822 given the date of her parents' marriage, Thecla was probably her parents' second daughter. Maria died in 837; Thecla's other siblings included three more sisters (**Anna**, *Anastasia**, and **Pulcheria**) and two brothers (Constantine and Michael), the former of whom also predeceased Theophilus. Shortly before he died, Theophilus probably affianced Thecla to Louis II (the son of Lothair I, the grandson of Louis I, and the great-grandson of Charlemagne) of the newly created Holy Roman Empire. (The would-be bride is not named, but given her age at that time, and her subsequent status in Constantinople, it is likely that Thecla was the subject of these negotiations.) This marriage was arranged in the context of Arab advances which threatened Christians both East and West, and of a civil war which pitted Lothair against his brothers, after the death of their father in 840. This union, however, never materialized, because Lothair was defeated by his brothers at the Battle of Fontenoy in 841, Theophilus died in 842, and the Treaty of Verdun in 843 settled political conditions in the West for some time. In addition, since the Byzantine emperor Michael I had only begrudgingly acknowledged Charlemagne's assumption of the imperial title in 812 (12 years after Charlemagne was elevated to the rank by

Pope Leo III) in an attempt to consolidate his power against foreign and domestic rivals, the Eastern Empire was in no hurry to concede the status of equality to that great man's less-than-equally domineering great-grandson, which a marriage to Thecla would imply.

When Theophilus died, his heir Michael III was only three years old. As a result, Theodora the Blessed became the young emperor's regent, while Thecla was officially associated with the regime as an Augusta (a status apparently not conferred on Michael's other sisters). For political advice, Theodora relied most heavily on a Theoctistus, who had served Theophilus well. Conspicuously absent from Theodora's inner circle was her own brother, Bardas. This oversight apparently embittered Bardas to the point where in 856 he conspired with Michael, who, at 17, was now beginning to grow restless under the parsimony of his mother and her political allies. Bardas organized a plot which encouraged Michael to break free of the shackles which restrained him from fully enjoying the perquisites of imperial status. There followed the assassination of Theoctistus and the political eclipse of Theodora, whose influence over the young Augustus was replaced by that of Bardas.

Probably hoping to win over the embittered Theodora to new political realities, Michael and Bardas kept her at court for a while before consigning her to a convent at Gastria. Thecla, Anna, Anastasia, and Pulcheria preceded her there. How long the women of Michael's family remained cloistered we do not know, but at some time they were freed from their enforced religious incarceration.

Otherwise, for about a decade Bardas ran the empire well while Michael frolicked with a hand-chosen band of reprobates. Foremost among these was *Eudocia Ingerina, but eventually Basil (I) the Macedonian would rise to the top. Michael met the former while Theodora was still in power, and began an affair with her while he was still in his mid-teens. Theodora thought Eudocia Ingerina unsuitable as an imperial consort (perhaps because of her independent-mindedness), and in a Bride Show held shortly before her downfall, chose *Eudocia Decapolita (a daughter of one Decapolites) for Michael's bride. As much as anything else, the forced marriage to a woman whom Michael did not want precipitated Theodora's fall.

Basil was a problem of another sort altogether. Of humble birth and a one-time captive of the Bulgarians (who incarcerated him in their trans-Danubian territory [Macedonia]), Basil (an Armenian by birth) escaped to return to Byzantium and a remarkable career. Born about 810, Basil was a man of prodigious physical proportions who caught the attentions of an aristocratic patron who lived near Patras, and who used her infatuation with his physique to pave his way to Constantinople. There, after exploiting contacts, Basil had the good fortune to tame a horse deemed unbreakable by the emperor, who thereafter took Basil into his service and rapidly advanced his career. For a time content with playing the fool, Basil wheedled his way into an intimacy with Michael. Having won the emperor's confidence, Basil engineered the removal of Bardas (866) and his own designation as high chamberlain. Following these successes, he exploited his influence with Michael to the point that he was adopted by the childless emperor as the latter's son (even though Basil was around 29 years Michael's senior) and named co-emperor.

In 867, Basil completed his coup by assassinating Michael and ascending to the throne of the Byzantine Empire. But before these events transpired, others involving Thecla came into play. After Basil had been named high chamberlain, but before the murder of Michael, an interesting arrangement was mandated by Michael. Seeking a scintillating relationship with his favorite, Michael forced Basil to divorce his wife, so as to permit Basil's marriage to Eudocia Ingerina, Michael's longtime love. Michael remained married to Eudocia Decapolita who had been foisted upon him by his mother, and she retained the official dignity of her station. Nevertheless, Michael apparently used Basil's marriage to Eudocia Ingerina to mask his own continuing sexual relationship with Basil's "wife." (If Eudocia Ingerina truly maintained her fidelity to Michael during her marriage to Basil, then her son Leo VI, officially Basil's son and eventually his imperial heir, was not biologically his, but Michael's. This would mean that the Macedonian dynasty which Basil founded upon the murder of Michael was biologically, if not officially, an extension of the Amorion dynasty it replaced.) As a sop to this "liberated" arrangement, Michael offered Thecla to Basil as a mistress. For whatever reason, Thecla apparently consented to the offer, and served, beginning when she was about 43 years of age, as Basil's mistress. Long denied a marriage of her own (politics not having provided for an appropriate match since the missed opportunity offered in the person of Louis II), perhaps having something of Michael's lechery, and probably somewhat impressed by Basil's physical stature, Thecla thus indulged in the pleasures of collaborating with the powers-that-were.

Even so, things did not turn out well for The-cla. After the murderous accession of Basil, an apparently neglected Thecla became the mistress of one John Neatocometes. When Basil learned of this association, the enraged "cuckold" ordered the beating of John and his assignment to a monastery. Thecla, too, suffered beatings and the confiscation of her considerable property. She soon thereafter died bedridden and foresworn.

William S. Greenwalt,
Professor of Classical History,
Santa Clara University,
Santa Clara, California

Thekla.

Variant of Thecla.

Thekla (1815–1876).

See Düringsfeld, Ida von.

Theoctista (c. 740–c. 802)

Byzantine nun whose religious scruples helped to bring about the downfall of Emperor Constantine VI. Born around 740; died around 802; daughter of a Byzantine bureaucrat; married Photinus; children: three sons, Theodore, Joseph and Euthymius; one daughter (name unknown).

Born in Byzantium around 740, Theoctista was seven years old when her mother and her father, a Byzantine bureaucrat, died of plague. An uncle, an employee of the imperial treasury, raised Theoctista, her older brother Plato, and their sister (name unknown). Plato received the requisite education for a post in the civil service, and initially pursued such a career. He did not, however, remain a bureaucrat for long, preferring instead the monastic life. Theoctista and her sister received little formal schooling, but their uncle arranged suitable marriages for both. Theoctista's husband Photinus was a colleague of her uncle in the treasury. Their marriage produced three sons—Theodore, Joseph and Euthymius—and a daughter (name unknown). According to Theodore (who wrote his mother's eulogy at the time of her death), Theoctista was modest, virtuous, devout, ran a good house, took good care of her family, and never coveted material baubles. Theoctista was also generous to the underprivileged and to her servants, although when the latter broke the rules of the house, Theodore admitted, she could be excessively stern. Theodore also noted his mother's energy, willfulness, and ambitions for her children, especially her sons. Theoctista not only stressed the education of her children, she was

also personally involved in it after first educating herself. After raising her children, however, Theoctista fully embraced her spiritual side by convincing Photinus that they should henceforth live chastely, as if brother and sister instead of husband and wife.

Having always been pious, Theoctista was greatly affected by the Iconoclastic Controversy which raged throughout her entire lifetime. This dispute revolved around the use of icons as aids to religious education. In 726, the Byzantine emperor Leo III had proclaimed that all icons were really nothing more than idols which the religiously ignorant were physically worshiping. He then banned their use throughout his realm and encouraged their destruction. Icons, however, had their defenders, including popes in Rome and monks throughout the Byzantine east, so a struggle ensued over their use and even their continued existence. Despite the widespread unrest which Leo III's iconoclastic attitude created, his immediate successors continued to support that ban, including Leo IV (r. 775–780), even though that emperor was not as virulently iconoclastic as had been his father and grandfather. At least part of the reason why Leo IV began to soften the iconoclastic fervor of his predecessors was the fact that his wife and empress **Irene of Athens* was herself a devotee of icons and an ally of the monks who stood steadfast against the destruction of religious images. When Leo IV died, his and Irene's son, Constantine VI, was only ten. Irene became her son's regent, and was even recognized as his co-emperor. Her accession was challenged by an iconoclastic faction, but she suppressed the revolt which followed and pushed for the rehabilitation of icons. When she did this, many who had not been welcome in Constantinople when iconoclasm had been imperial policy returned to the capital and its court. One of these was Theoctista's brother Plato, by that time a monk of some standing.

The reunion with her brother energized Theoctista, whose house was thrown open to icon-venerating monks. Further, her entire family—upon her insistence—rededicated themselves to the devotion of God. As one (including even three of Photinus' brothers), the family renounced worldliness and embraced a religious life. Under Plato's influence, Theoctista sold most of the property she had inherited from her parents, as well as what she and Photinus had amassed together. The proceeds thus collected were mostly distributed to the poor. Theoctista then swore to live a religious life and retired with the rest of her family (except, notably, her sister) to an estate at Saccudium in Bithynia which had not been liquidated. There, under Plato's rule, a monastery was founded where all things feminine (including animals) were banned, except Theoctista, her daughter, and another female relative. Although these women were allowed to reside on the property under Plato's authority, they agreed to live somewhat apart from the others so as to intrude as little as possible upon the masculine enclave. After living for a while under such conditions, Theoctista decided to enter an established convent. She had difficulty with her fellow nuns, however, and was required to leave the convent, at which time she returned to the authority of her brother.

There she lived, until Constantine VI (now an adult in the process of trying to assert his authority against the continued influence of his mother) sought to divorce his first wife ◄❧ **Maria of Amnia** to marry *Theodota, both a woman of the court and a close relative of Theoctista. Since divorce was not religiously permitted unless there was grave cause, Constantine accused Maria of trying to poison him. The charge, however, was doubted by many, including the community at Saccudium which felt especially scandalized by the whole affair since the object of the emperor's passion was a member of Theoctista's family. Constantine initially attempted to placate the community, which was now led jointly by Theoctista's son Theodore and Plato, but when it proved adamant in its opposition to the marriage, the emperor had Plato arrested and Theodore (and others) beaten. In addition, the Saccudium community was dispersed, and its leaders sent to Thessaloniki in exile. Although she managed to stay with Plato and Theodore for awhile (against the imperial will) in order to console them, Theoctista was eventually forced to take up residence in Constantinople. There she did everything she could to raise opposition to Constantine and to maintain contact with her exiled family. Constantine imprisoned Theoctista for her continuing opposition, but by then her punishment only served to make a martyr of her in the eyes of the capital's masses. In 797, Irene of Athens staged a coup which toppled Constantine from the throne and ended the crisis.

Freed by Irene, Theoctista returned to Saccudium where she lived such an ascetic life that it even embarrassed her son Theodore. Nevertheless, she continued to care for her family and to use what little of her wealth remained to do good works. Theodore claimed that in her old age, Theoctista received the gift of prophecy—at least she is said to have correctly predicted that Photinus, Euthymius, and her daughter would all die before she did. Bereft of family when she

Maria of Amnia.

See Irene of Athens for sidebar.

perished (since Theodore was away on business), Theoctista died, probably in 802.

William Greenwalt,
Associate Professor of Classical History,
Santa Clara University,
Santa Clara, California

Theodelinda (568–628)

Queen of Lombardy who was instrumental in turning the Arian Lombards to the Roman Church. Name variations: Theodolinda; Theodelinde. Born in 568 in Bavaria; died in 628 in Lombardy; daughter of Garibald I; married Authari also known as Autarie, king of Lombardy (died); married Flavius Agiluphus of Pavia, also known as Ago (died); children: at least one son.

Theodelinda reigned as queen of Lombardy. She was born in 568 into the royal family of Bavaria, and as a young woman married King Autarie of Lombardy. Upon his death, she married Flavius Agiluphus of Pavia, but he also died young. Theodelinda did not marry again, instead choosing to hold the title queen-regent of Lombardy for her son alone. Theodelinda was both an excellent queen and a very devout woman. Among her works to aid the Lombards, she encouraged agriculture and instituted policies to increase Lombardy's economic stability. She also was responsible for the construction of many churches, monasteries, and nunneries. Through her popularity and religious influence, the queen successfully encouraged her subjects to turn back to orthodoxy from the spreading heresy of Arianism (whose members denied that Christ was divine). Theodelinda was known for her charitable work, and gained such a reputation for intelligence and faith that Pope Gregory I the Great dedicated one of his works, the *Dialogues*, to her. She died about age 60.

SOURCES:
Dunbar, Agnes. *Dictionary of Saintly Women, vol. I.* London: G. Bell & Sons, 1904.

Laura York, M.A. in History,
University of California,
Riverside, California

Theodelinde (1814–1857)

Countess of Wurttemberg. Name variations: Théodelinde; Theodelinda; Theolinde de Beauharnais. Born on April 13, 1814; died on April 1, 1857; daughter of *Amalie Auguste (1788–1851) and Eugene de Beauharnais (1781–1824), duke of Leuchtenburg; sister of *Josephine Beauharnais (1807–1876), queen of Sweden; married Count William of Württemberg, on February 8, 1841.

Theoderade.

See Theodorade.

Theodora (fl. 290s).

See Constantia for sidebar.

Theodora (d. 304)

Saint. Name variations: Saint Theodora. Died in 304.

Tradition has it that Theodora was a beautiful young Christian living in Alexandria (Egypt), when, at the height of the Great Persecution of Christians sanctioned ultimately by the Roman emperor Diocletian (303–311), she was arrested for her religion. Refusing to acknowledge the pagan gods, and thus proving herself guilty of impiety and treason, Theodora was sardonically sentenced to a life of prostitution in a common brothel. There she was discovered by a pagan named Didymus, who was so moved by the cruelty of this sentence that he determined both to convert to Christianity and to rescue Theodora from her debasement. The two, however, were discovered in their flight and martyred. Some authorities think that there may be some truth in this tale, others do not. Theodora has been recognized as a saint. Her feast day, which she shares with Didymus, is April 28.

William Greenwalt,
Associate Professor of Classical History,
Santa Clara University,
Santa Clara, California

Theodora (c. 500–548)

Byzantine empress, known for her courage and sharp political skills, who wielded enormous power as the wife of Justinian I and strongly influenced his policies and actions during their joint rule of the world's greatest existing empire. Pronunciation: Thee-oh-DOR-ah. Co-regent of Byzantium (r. 527–548). Born Theodora (meaning "The gift of God") on the island of Cyprus, or more likely in Syria, around 500 CE; died in 548; second of three daughters of Acacius (the keeper of the Green faction's bears in Constantinople's Hippodrome) and a mother of low status; sister of Comitona and Anastasia; married Justinian I, Byzantine emperor (r. 527–565); children: (before her marriage) two illegitimate children, a son John and a daughter whose name is unknown.

Theodora, probably the most powerful Byzantine woman ever, was born into humble circumstances about 500, probably in the province of Syria. Not long after Theodora's birth, her father Acacius landed a show-business position in the Byzantine Empire's capital, Constantinople. There he assumed the position of bear trainer for the "Greens" (an entertainment-political-religious faction)—an occupation which thrust his family into the hubbub of the Hippodrome, the focal point of all the sophisticated city's entertainment and vice. Unfortunately, Acacius died not much later, leaving an unnamed wife and three young daughters (✤➤ **Comitona**, Theodora and ✤➤ **Anastasia**), the oldest of whom (Comitona) was only six when she, her mother, and her sisters were faced with poverty and few respectable prospects. To keep her family afloat, the widow took up with another bear trainer and hoped to use her influence with the Greens to obtain Acacius' post for her new lover. As luck would have it, however, the Greens had another man in mind for the job. Nevertheless, Theodora's mother tried to bring pressure to bear on those in a position to secure her family's fortunes by adorning her young daughters as suppliants and having them petition the Greens on behalf of their "stepfather" in front of thousands of spectators. The crowd loved the girls and roared on their behalf, but the embarrassed Greens refused to reconsider their decision. As a result, they became the butt of the assembly. This provided an opportunity for the Greens' bitter rivals, the "Blues," whose bear trainer had also recently died. In order to make points with the masses, the Blues came to the rescue, offering Theodora's mother's friend their open position. Theodora never forgot the humiliation of the Greens' rejection (she *never* forgot a slight), holding it against them for the rest of her life.

And what a life hers was to be. Surrounded by the din, the excitement, and the vice of a Hippodrome childhood, Theodora and her sisters grew up on the busy streets of the world's greatest city. There they were exposed to all of the morality, material covetousness, and superstition of the gutter, and no matter how far they rose above the station of their birth much of this childhood world went along with them. This is not to say that the Byzantine elite shared none of the attitudes commonly found on the streets, for they frequently did. A good example of a common bond between rich and poor was a deep belief in the potency of magic—an art Theodora was associated with her entire life. Nevertheless, throughout her days, Theodora in particular exhibited an audacious sauciness which could only have been picked up in Constantinople's stews, and which frequently grated on the more refined sensibilities of those born to court life.

Soon after the aforementioned unsuccessful supplication, Theodora and her sisters were re-

Comitona and Anastasia. See joint entry under Anastasia and Comitona.

quired to contribute to their family's financial fortunes. When old enough to learn a few seductive dances, they were introduced to the stage at a time when the word *actress* was a synonym for *prostitute*. Unfortunately, even in this lowly profession Theodora was initially among the lowest, for she had no special training and merely sold "her attractions to anyone who came along." Her fortunes, however, rapidly improved, for her beauty, wit, intelligence, and manifest enthusiasm for her new occupation attracted the attention of the best heeled of Constantinople's pleasure-loving population. All indications suggest that the poor girl revelled in the attention, the fast-track partying, and the lucrative financial rewards which accompanied her willingness to share her sexual prowess with others. Yet, Theodora's career track had its drawbacks, for she gave birth to two illegitimate children (a son John and a daughter, name unknown) before she was 17. Theodora raised neither and, at least in the case of her son, gave custody to the father (who left Constantinople for Arabia, where the boy was raised).

For a time Theodora was the toast of the town, her apparent lack of modesty shocking even the most worldly. Before long, however, she realized that her moment in the spotlight would not last forever. Security demanded a more permanent liaison with someone of established station. Theodora found her opportunity in the person of Hecebolus, a middling bureaucrat of Tyrian extraction. When he was posted as the governor of Pentapolis (a region consisting of five cities in modern-day Libya), she accompanied him as his mistress. Yet this relationship proved short-lived, for once in Africa the two fell out for reasons unknown, and Theodora was unceremoniously sent packing with no resources to speak of. From Pentapolis, Theodora made her way to Alexandria, the second city of the Byzantine Empire. There she remained for a time, plying her trade. Nevertheless, it was also there that she became deeply involved with religiosity and religious issues—for the first time in her life as far as is known.

Alexandria supported one of the oldest and most respected Christian communities in the world, with its bishops and monks among the Church's most influential theologians and administrators. Although Christianity was about 500 years old when Theodora visited Alexandria, it by no means had become the monolithic institution which many imagine it to have been. Even before (but especially after) the legalization of Christianity in the 4th century, intense arguments had been waged within the Church con-

cerning a variety of issues. In this debate, regional differences had long been potent, and remained so in Theodora's time for two reasons. First, as populations converted to Christianity, they tended to interpret the Church's message in terms of their previous religious inclinations, which were frequently quite distinct in character. And second, these populations tended to support those (local) theologians who argued for their particular interpretations of sacred literature. As a result, well-developed and subtly divergent theological positions began to distinguish the beliefs of different Christian populations, and these then petrified into traditions. By the 6th century, these divergent traditions were already of some antiquity.

On the other hand, since the reign of Constantine I the Great (d. 337) there had been a tendency by the imperial government to merge the Church's organization into the existing political infrastructure of the empire to accomplish several goals, including the streamlining of bureaucratic administration. As a result, there existed imperial pressure for leaders of the Church to define *one* orthodoxy of belief—which could thereafter be imposed throughout the empire to help keep it all together and to help make it run smoothly. Just as there was to be one Roman Law and Government, there would be one Roman Christian Church, both to be ruled by the emperor, who would rely on bishops for theological advice and administrative assistance. Naturally, local and imperial notions of orthodoxy frequently clashed, with the unfortunate consequence that almost as long as there had been a legally recognized Christian Church, there had been imperial persecutions of those who, for one reason or another, refused to toe the "orthodox" line as it was at any one time defined by the emperor and those bishops who had his ear.

Since the 4th century, the Egyptian Church had been the source of many problems to those in Constantinople who would define orthodoxy. In Theodora's day, the main issue pitting Constantinople against Alexandria had to do with Christ's nature. As the orthodox forces in Constantinople understood Jesus, he was both God and Man. In Alexandria, however, there were many ecclesiastics (and many, many more everyday Christians) who believed that Jesus had but one nature, and that a divine one. Both sides argued from Scripture, but the religious establishment in Constantinople had the confidence of several emperors, who, as a result, denounced the Monophysites (as they were known) as heretics. When Theodora visited Alexandria, the Monophysites there led by one Timothy, who

Opposite page

𝒯heodora

(c. 500–548)

had a lasting effect on Theodora when the two personally met, were being persecuted. Whether she was won over by the kindness shown to a woman of suspect reputation, whether she embraced the arguments of the Monophysites, or whether she rallied to the cause of the underdog, we will never know, but Theodora came to favor the Monophysites, and later when in a position to do so became their patron, although politics frequently forced her to be discreet in her support. In the meantime, as if heeding an irresistible call, Theodora left Alexandria to make her way through the east from city to city "following an occupation which a man better not name," ultimately to return to her home in Constantinople. Perhaps the most important event during this phase of Theodora's life came in the Syrian city of Antioch where she met **Macedonia,** a dancing girl associated with the Blue faction of that city who was also reputed to be well versed in magic. Theodora befriended Macedonia, and the two thereafter remained close.

Once returned to the capital, Theodora seems not to have fully renewed her association with its elite. At least by day she modestly spun wool, and thus adopted a traditionally respectable feminine occupation. Shortly thereafter (c. 522), however, she met and probably seduced Justinian (I), about 15 years her senior. Jusintian, though a rising star at court, was still maneuvering against influential rivals to be named the heir of his uncle, Justin I, the reigning emperor of Byzantium. Whatever else might be said of their relationship in its early stages, it is clear that Theodora captivated the ambitious, arrogant, intelligent, vain, competent, and absolutist Justinian from the start. Whether Theodora was similarly smitten is unknowable, but, despite scurrilous gossip, it is clear that henceforth the one man in her life was Justinian. Emotional and physical considerations aside, however, this was a political coupling made in heaven: Justinian was well situated and had great potential; Theodora was a savvy manipulator whose talent for network building and intrigue would help Justinian secure his heart's desire—the imperial throne.

Justinian's infatuation with Theodora was manifestly displayed through lavish gifts which she appreciated with an intensity only those who have been destitute can ever know. Perhaps an even greater token of his love, however, was less material. Although he was very religious and intensely orthodox when Justinian learned of Theodora's Monophysite sympathies, he went out on a limb (considering both that the emperor was also orthodox and that Justinian had yet to

secure his status as heir-apparent) and persuaded Justin to curtail the existing persecution of that religious faction. (Later, however, when he was emperor, Justinian reinstituted the attacks on religious deviants, for he hoped to use orthodoxy to unify the empire and thus diminish existing opposition to his concurrent diplomatic and economic policies.) An invitation for Theodora to move into Justinian's palace and become his mistress followed, but before such a move could be possible socially there was a need to elevate her legal status, for nobody in the imperial inner circle could be an acknowledged intimate of anyone less than a Patrician. As a result, Theodora was officially enrolled as one of the empire's aristocracy. Justinian's subsequent desire to marry Theodora demanded even more maneuvering, for not only did there exist social prejudice against such a union (for example, Justin I's wife ⬅️ **Lupicinia-Euphemia** was appalled by the thought), there also existed a law which forbade any Senator from legally marrying a courtesan, no matter how much distance she had put between herself and her past. Not to be dissuaded, the increasingly influential Justinian (no doubt prodded by Theodora) was eventually able to convince his aging predecessor to grant him a special dispensation from this restriction, a request which was not granted as long as Justin's wife was alive, but which was accorded soon after her death in 523. Subsequently, Justinian and Theodora were legally married with full ecclesiastical approval and participation as soon as an appropriately splendid wedding could be planned. What the court thought of this development went unreported, but scarcely an eye blinked at Theodora's metamorphosis. The resulting reality, however, can be simply stated—Theodora had suddenly become the wife and confidante of the man who would soon be named heir to the most powerful state in the world. She had overcome her lowly birth.

⚜️ **Lupicinia-Euphemia** (d. 523)

Byzantine empress. Name variations: Lupicina-Euphemia. Died in 523; married Justin I (Flavius Justinus), Byzantine emperor (r. 518–527); children: adopted son Justinian I (a nephew of Justin's), Byzantine emperor (r. 527–565).

Before being purchased as a slave by Justin I, Lupicinia-Euphemia was a prisoner of war and camp cook. Justin legally married her long before he ascended to the throne as emperor of Byzantium in 518; by then, both were probably in their 60s. Lupicinia-Euphemia was known for her piety.

Thereafter, Justinian and Theodora expanded their dominance over the imperial court as virtual colleagues. Undoubtedly her street smarts, finely honed after years of living by her wits, proved a valuable resource amid the cutthroat realities of imperial politics. Although lacking the patina accompanying lofty social origin, Theodora was not all that much different from the narcissistic elite, a member of which she had become. For three years, Theodora helped Justinian ward off the vicious, if civilized, attacks of rivals, in the process learning the ins and outs of "Byzantine" politics. Among the skills she honed in this formative period were political blackmail and intimidation. She also seems to have ordered the occasional (necessary, of course) physical mutilation and political assassination. Theodora could be generous to a fault, or maliciously ruthless. Those loyal to her and her husband's interests were appropriately rewarded. Those who were not could experience the secret dungeons from which most who entered would never leave. Theodora was no sentimentalist and was capable of sacrificing even her own flesh and blood if circumstances seemed to demand it. Consider the example of her first born, her illegitimate son John, who had been reared by his father in Arabia. When John was in his teens, his father died, but not before revealing on his deathbed who John's mother was: by this time, Theodora was the empress of the Byzantines. The boy traveled to Constantinople, where in a private audience he presented himself to his mother. For whatever reason—perhaps Theodora feared Justinian's personal rejection if he learned of her son, or perhaps she feared that John would constitute an unwanted player in the future succession—John's audience with Theodora was the last anyone ever saw of him. His fate remains unknown, although the historian Procopius clearly hints that John was executed at the order of his mother. It should be realized, however, that Procopius was an unremittant enemy of Theodora.

Theodora and Justinian were well paired, both being political animals to the bone, and both with the talent to bring their ambitions to fruition. Acting in concert, the two systematically maneuvered to secure a formal declaration of his status as heir-apparent, and their efforts paid off when Justinian was so designated in 525. This victory elevated Justinian and Theodora to the positions respectively of Augustus and Augusta when Justin died two years later. Whatever ambitions Theodora might have aspired to, our sources emphasize her love of pleasure and physical comfort (she was even reported as going to the extreme of bathing every day), and whatever crimes she might have committed, she was neither more effete nor worse than her contemporaries—just more successful and therefore more envied.

Much of Theodora's success came as a result of making friends with the right people, and making sure that the right people were in the right places at the right time. In this sense, she was especially efficient in tapping the influence that women could bring to bear upon the imperial court. Before her success in this regard can be fully appreciated, however, power at the Byzantine court must be understood. Although the empire had a well-established legal tradition and an elaborate government whose very existence was vindicated insofar as it (theoretically) dispensed good justice, and although the emperor's authority was (theoretically) given to him by God so that he could oversee the apportioning of this good justice, the fact of the matter was that the empire was ruled by an autocrat whose word, just or unjust, was law. Power in this society, however allocated "constitutionally," was in reality a function of access to the official (always male—women remained legally barred from holding public office) in charge of any situation. Theodora realized that, as a result, any woman could in reality exert more influence than any male counterpart, if that woman could get closer to the wielder of power than any rival. Who was closer to the emperor than his bedmate? Who was closer to the emperor's most trusted administrators and generals than his wife?

Upon her arrival at court, Theodora seems immediately to have sensed the realities of power. As a result, she meticulously constructed a network of allies, mostly women, through whom she hoped to extend her influence. And Theodora's friends at court were carefully selected. On one level there were those, like Macedonia, who would do anything they were bidden and who were quite efficient in that capacity. Some from Theodora's past were also tapped. Such was the case of her sister Comitona, whom Theodora saw married to a Sittas, an old acquaintance of Justinian's and a competent general. Others of better birth, such as **Antonina**, an associate of Theodora's in magic as well as politics and the wife of the exalted general Belisarius, were in the long run less trustworthy. Theodora showered Antonina with honors and even helped to reconcile her with her alienated husband, but the obedience and feigned friendship lasted only as long as Theodora was alive; at the first opportunity, true colors were shown. Late in her life, Theodora arranged the marriage of her grandson (the son of her unnamed, illegitimate daughter—Theodora had no children with

Justinian) to the daughter of Antonina and Belisarius, seemingly to tie the two houses together and to align Belisarius' great wealth to her family. Although the young couple loved each other, at the first opportunity after Theodora's death, Antonina forced their divorce, objecting to the social origins of her daughter's husband, a blood relative of Theodora but not Justinian—and everyone who mattered knew the circumstances of his conception.

If you wish safety, my Lord, that is an easy matter. We are rich, and there is the sea, and yonder our ships. But consider whether if you reach safety you may not desire to exchange that safety for death. As for me, I like the old saying, that the purple is the noblest shroud.

—Theodora to Justinian, as he prepared to flee the city

Above and beyond Theodora's importance to Justinian as a political ally and intriguer—a status not to be under-appreciated given the factional rivalries which divided the imperial court—she played two great roles at Justinian's side. The first occurred in 532, shortly after a round of the recurrent Persian wars had been unsuccessfully concluded. Some background: Justinian was a truly great emperor who left his marks, both good and bad, on history. He, working closely with Theodora, had three great passions during his reign—a grandiose building campaign which culminated in the magnificent and still standing Hagia Sophia in Constantinople (modern-day Istanbul); an ambition to streamline and codify Roman law, resulting in the famous Code which exerted, and continues to exert, much influence on constitutional developments throughout Europe; and a wish to conquer the western Mediterranean from the Germans who then held it and thereby reconstitute the Roman Empire, a mission entrusted to Belisarius—whose work was of only limited and short-lived success. All of these interests were very costly, as was the maintenance of an increasingly glorious court. Expenses forced Justinian to engage in an unpopular financial policy of inventing new taxes, increasing old ones, and regularly absorbing private estates and their fortunes into the imperial fisc (treasury). As a result, he—and Theodora, whose love of high living was increasingly resented by those who had to pay for her extravagance—became unpopular among both rich and poor. This unpopularity was only increased by the emperor's attempts to introduce a number of oriental customs into court procedure which ritually emphasized the chasm of status between the Augustus and the Augusta, and the rest of society. For example, whereas Patricians before had approached the emperor as near equals, during Justinian's reign they received audience only after prostrating themselves on the floor with arms extended in suppliancy before their ruler. When in 532 the Persian war was less than satisfactorily concluded, the resentment of those who had been forced to pay more for failure boiled over into the Nika riot which almost cost Justinian his throne.

This civil disturbance involved a rare alliance between Constantinople's Blues and Greens, and as such, we must consider exactly what these factions had become. When Constantinople had been founded in the 4th century, the city had been divided into four wards. Each of these was given local leadership and to each of these ward governments was delegated certain civic and defense responsibilities. These wards were referred to by the colors "Blue," "Green," "Red," and "White." As time went on, the inhabitants of these four wards began to identify increasingly with their color, since the local organization had a neighborliness which the vastness of the imperial city as a whole did not. Constantinople's population thus split into four constituencies which vied among themselves for civic pride. Of course, there is only so much satisfaction gained by having the cleanest streets or best-maintained walls in the city. As a result, more exciting ways of vying with one another developed—especially in the fields of sport and entertainment. Each color began to sponsor its own circus and its own entries in the most popular sport of the day—chariot racing. Enormously popular spectacles evolved, with increasing amounts of money spent by each color to provide the best entertainments in the city. The desire to defeat the other colors, especially in the all-important chariot races run in the Hippodrome, caused the colors to begin recruitment programs for the best drivers and horses far beyond the capital. Associate clubs of similar colors began to spring up around the empire, with partisanship fed by the increasing numbers involved. Over time, the expenses became enormous, and since consistently the two most successful colors had been the Blues and the Greens, the Whites and the Reds threw in their respective towels. Actually, mergers were arranged, with the Whites joining the Blues and the Reds uniting with the Greens. This restructuring left only the Blues and Greens, but the new, simplified polarity only heightened the fanaticism of those involved. Just as World Cup soccer occasionally provides the opportunity for the violent expression of nationalism, so too did the dedication of the fans of the Blues and Greens spill over into occasional rioting.

Over time, this partisanship was fueled and made more complex by other social factors. For example, across the empire various professions tended to favor one color over the other. Sailors, for instance, gravitated to the Blues, as did farmers to the Greens—both groups seeing symbolic links between their vocations and their color. Also, the rivalries of the different approaches to Christianity tended to see their differences as associated with their preference of color. Justin and Justinian were both very orthodox in their beliefs and fanatic supporters of the Blues. It was only natural, therefore, for the Monophysites, when they were experiencing persecution, to root for the Greens. Add to these considerations the complexities of political opinion, and the importance of the Blues and the Greens to their contemporaries becomes more understandable. Unfortunately, open melees between the two were increasing in number during the 6th century, making the streets of Constantinople increasingly unsafe.

As for the events of 532, the failure against Persia and a simmering anger over increased taxes led to an explosion which temporarily united the Blues and the Greens. Everyone in power, but especially Justinian's finance ministers, became targets during the riots which swept the city. Justinian was so paralyzed with fear by the escalation of violence and looting which was even beginning to occur in and around the palace that he was just about to take the advice of some and flee the capital to save his own skin—a flight which might possibly have cost him his throne, for the mob had temporarily united behind the imperial claims of the nephew of Anastasius I (predecessor of Justin I). At a meeting of the Imperial Council on Sunday, January 18, Theodora sat silently listening to the men present debating whether or not Justinian should attempt to escape. Preparations were made, and a ship sat ready in the harbor to carry the emperor and empress to safety. Then Theodora rose and—as quoted in Browning's *Justinian and Theodora*—made what must be considered one of the greatest short speeches ever recorded:

> Whether or not a woman should give an example of courage to men, is neither here nor there. At a moment of desperate danger one must do what one can. I think that flight, even if it brings us to safety, is not in our interest. Every man born to see the light of day must die. But that one who has been emperor should become an exile I cannot bear. May I never be without the purple I wear, nor live to see the day when men do not call

me "Your Majesty." If you wish safety, my Lord, that is an easy matter. We are rich, and there is the sea, and yonder our ships. But consider whether if you reach safety you may not desire to exchange that safety for death. As for me, I like the old saying, that the purple is the noblest shroud.

Thus fortified by Theodora, Justinian ordered Belisarius, who commanded some troops near the city, to intercede. The general did so, taking to the streets with troops and rounding up the rioters in the Hippodrome. What followed was gruesome, for to reinstate order, Belisarius ordered the massacre of about 30,000 rioters. At this cost, Justinian retained his throne.

The second great service Theodora provided Justinian involved the law. During Theodora's lifetime, Justinian seldom issued a law which did not invoke the name of his wife, and it seems certain that Theodora was one of the important stimuli to Justinian's great recodification of Roman law. She appears to have been especially interested in the rights of women, paying special attention to access to property through inheritance, to the usufruct of dowries, and to the division of estates after divorce. As such, some of the traditional inequalities which had long put women at the economic disposal of men were redressed, and although it would be mistaken to think that equality reigned thereafter, it is clear that most women received more protection as a result of Theodora's influence over Justinian than they had enjoyed before.

Nevertheless, in the minds of the masses, Theodora's and Justinian's reputations suffered on account of the empire's increasing financial woes and the increase of taxes. She had no offspring with Justinian to honor her memory and to insist that others do so as well, and when she died in 548, Theodora's memory was soon blackened. The historian Procopius began the process when her wrote about her in a scandalous manner in his *Secret History*, composed in 550. Nevertheless, the fact that he deferred putting his thoughts on paper until two years after her death is a testimony to the power she wielded when she was alive. Justinian's greatest achievements were already behind him when Theodora died, although he lived and reigned for 17 more years. Nowhere is this seen more clearly than in his legal activity, which virtually dried up after his wife—who in her busy life had done much and seen just about every injustice there was to be seen—died.

SOURCES:

Evagrius. *A History of the Church.* Bohn's Ecclesiastical Library, 1861.

Procopius. *The Secret History.* Penguin, 1966.

SUGGESTED READING:

Bridge, A. *Theodora.* Chicago, IL: Academy Chicago, 1978.

Browning, R. *Justinian and Theodora.* Revised ed. London: Thames & Hudson, 1987.

Diehl, C. *Theodora: Empress of Byzantium.* Reprint. NY: Frederick Ungar, 1972.

Ostrogorsky, G. *History of the Byzantine State.* Oxford, 1968.

William S. Greenwalt,
Associate Professor of Classical History,
Santa Clara University,
Santa Clara, California

Theodora (fl. early 900s)

*Byzantine empress. Flourished in the early 900s; married Romanos I Lekapenus or Romanus I Lecapanus, emperor of Byzantium (r. 919–944); children: Christopher; Stephen; Constantine; Theophylact; *Helena Lekapena (c. 920–961).*

Theodora (fl. late 900s)

*Byzantine empress. Flourished in the late 900s; daughter of *Helena Lekapena (c. 920–961) and Constantine VII Porphyrogenetos (c. 906–959), Byzantine emperor (r. 913–959); sister of Romanus II, Byzantine emperor (r. 959-963); married John I Tzimisces, Byzantine emperor (r. 969–976).*

Theodora, Efua (1924–1996).

See Sutherland, Efua Theodora.

Theodora I of Rome (c. 875–c. 925).

See Theodora of Rome.

Theodora II of Rome (c. 900–c. 950).

See Theodora the Younger.

Theodora III of Rome (c. 875–c. 925).

See Theodora of Rome.

Theodora Batatzaina (fl. 1200s).

See Theodora Ducas.

Theodora Cantacuzene

*Byzantine princess. Daughter of *Irene Asen and John VI Cantacuzene, emperor of Nicaea (r. 1347–1354); married Orchan.*

Theodora Comnena (fl. 1080s)

*Byzantine princess. Flourished in the 1080s; daughter of Alexius I Comnenus, Byzantine emperor (r. 1081–1118) and *Irene Ducas (c. 1066–1133); sister of *Anna Comnena (1083–1153/55); married Constantine Angelus; children: John and Andronicus.*

Theodora Comnena (fl. 1140)

Byzantine royal. Flourished around 1140; daughter of Andronicus Comnenus (1104–1142); niece of Manuel I Comenus (c. 1120–1180), Byzantine emperor (r. 1143–1180); children: (with Manuel I) illegitimate son, Alexius Comnenus.

Theodora Comnena

(1145–after 1183)

Byzantine noblewoman, briefly queen of Jerusalem, who later was associated with Andronicus I Comnenus, future emperor of Byzantium. Born in 1145; died after 1183; daughter of Isaac Comnenus; granddaughter of the Byzantine emperor John II Comnenus (r. 1118–1143); niece of Manuel I Comnenus (c. 1120–1180), emperor of Byzantium (r. 1143–1180); married Baldwin III, king of Jerusalem (r. 1143–1162), in 1158; children: (with Andronicus I Comnenus) Alexius; Irene Comnena.

Theodora Comnena was the granddaughter of the Byzantine emperor John II Comnenus (r. 1118–1143), and niece of Emperor Manuel I Comnenus (r. 1143–1180). Theodora's father Isaac Comnenus, a *sebastokrator* (imperial agent), died a prisoner of the Vlachs when she was young. In 1157, the Crusader king of Jerusalem, Baldwin III (r. 1143–1162), sought an alliance and a wife from the Byzantine emperor Manuel. He did so for several reasons. First, ever since a Crusader army had won Jerusalem for Christendom in 1099 and made it the seat of one of several realms carved out of what had been Islamic territory, Baldwin's kingdom had been under the constant threat of a Muslim counterattack. This threat was made all the more palpable because of the disunity which had arisen amongst the second and third generations of Latin Christians in the east. Within the Kingdom of Jerusalem itself, Baldwin's father Fulk V of Anjou died when Baldwin was a minor. His mother *Melisande dominated the kingdom as regent until 1152, in which year Baldwin rebelled against her unwillingness to step aside in his favor. Baldwin won the civil war which followed, although in order to do so, he was forced to enhance the power of his nobility in order to overcome the faction which remained faithful to Melisande. This turmoil allowed the Islamic ruler of Syria, Nurredin, to seize Damascus, on the frontier of Baldwin's kingdom, and thus to reunite Syria (1154). Of course, the more the Islamic world was unified, the more it threatened Christian interests in the region.

Although he proved to be a good king, Baldwin needed a stalwart ally upon whom he could rely against foreign enemies and domestic rivals. In addition, Baldwin and Manuel had common enemies, both Christian and Muslim. Chief among these were two: the aforementioned Nurredin and Reynald of Chatillon, the prince of Antioch and Baldwin's nominal subordinate. This lord had recently ravaged Byzantine territories on Cyprus and had more than once tested Baldwin's feudal authority. In appealing to Manuel, Baldwin knew that the Byzantine Empire remained the most potent Christian power in the east, however much it might have declined over the centuries. Baldwin also recognized that Manuel sought to build bridges with the Latin west (although he did maintain some enmities there, especially with the Norman lords of Sicily), against the wishes of many of his subjects who believed that the growing military and commercial power of the west represented at least as much of a threat to Byzantine interests as did anything emanating from the Islamic world.

Manuel received Baldwin's marriage delegation well, and an alliance was arranged between Byzantium and Jerusalem. Securing this pact was Theodora Comnena, who went to Baldwin with a dowry of 100,000 hyperperi (gold coins), another 10,000 to pay for wedding expenses, and yet another 30,000 to be distributed as gifts. Baldwin endowed Theodora with the city of Acre and its revenues, to be her private possession if she outlived him and if he died childless. Both parties to this agreement promised military and political aid against Reynald and Nurredin. In 1158, the 13-year-old Theodora and her entourage came to Jerusalem where she was married to Baldwin by Aimery, the patriarch of Antioch. Theodora is said to have been very beautiful, and subsequent events suggest that this was so. As far as Baldwin was concerned, despite a wild youth, he settled down into a faithful marriage with Theodora. Nevertheless, in 1162, after a marriage of less than four years, Baldwin (age 33) died, childless, in Beirut after a short illness.

Thereafter, the Kingdom of Jerusalem was inherited by Baldwin's brother, Amalric I, formerly the count of Jaffa and Ascalon—an elevation which was ratified by the knights of his kingdom, although not without some disquiet. Theodora settled into her possession at Acre: a beautiful widow, who was still just 16 years old. For five years, she remained there. When she was 21, however, her 46-year-old second cousin, Andronicus I Comnenus, made his way to Acre.

Andronicus was a physically striking and charismatic member of the imperial family, whose potential assets were counter-balanced by his lusts for women and political ambition. His early career had been somewhat checkered, privately as well as publicly. In 1152, he had notably not distinguished himself as the governor of Cilicia when some Armenian chieftains based in the Taurus Mountains had descended upon the Byzantine lowlands and caught him unaware. Potentially more destructive to his career, however, were two issues: Andronicus' opposition to Manuel's overtures to the west, and his seduction of *Eudocia Comnena, the emperor's niece (and thus also a close relative of Andronicus). This latter escapade had especially antagonized the emperor, because Manuel had been eyeing Eudocia for himself. (Manuel is known to have had incestuous relations with another niece—a *Theodora Comnena [fl. 1140], the daughter of his brother Andronicus. The frequent repetition of names within families was not uncommon at the Byzantine court. Manuel's liaison with Andronicus' daughter produced a son, Alexius Comnenus, of whom more below.)

Despite the tensions which resulted from such nefarious episodes, Andronicus' charm worked well diplomatically, so when trouble broke out again in Cilicia in 1166, Manuel sent Andronicus there a second time to work toward a negotiated settlement. While there, official business took Andronicus to Antioch, ruled by the Crusader Bohemund III. Bohemund's sister, *Marie of Antioch, was Manuel's second wife, and she was a woman Andronicus especially despised, mostly because she was a Latin and symbolized the influence of the west on Manuel. The importance of Antioch to Manuel is additionally underscored by the fact that Bohemund's second wife, also named Theodora, was yet another relative of the Byzantine emperor. At Antioch, Andronicus met Bohemund's young sister, the princess *Philippa of Antioch. Lingering in the city far longer than he should have, Andronicus wooed and seduced Philippa, perhaps through scandal hoping to drive a wedge between Manuel and Bohemund, although Andronicus did not need an ulterior motive to court women. When Bohemund became cognizant of the relationship between Andronicus and Philippa, he angrily complained to Manuel, who, equally irked by Andronicus' improper behavior, demanded his immediate return to Constantinople. Andronicus, however, abandoned the empire and his Antiochene mistress (possibly wife) entirely, and, with a considerable percentage of the imperial revenues recently collected from Cilicia and Cyprus, made his way south to offer his services to Amalric of Jerusalem. Probably not knowing everything about Andronicus' recent activities, Amalric welcomed him to his realm and offered him Beirut, a fief then vacant.

Not long thereafter, Andronicus met Theodora Comnena at Acre. They perhaps knew each other when Theodora was a child, but now she was a stunning, mature beauty. Apparently, both fell in love, but they were far too closely related for legitimate ecclesiastical authorities even to consider the sanction of marriage. This did not keep them apart. Theodora abandoned Acre for Beirut, where she took up residence as Andronicus' mistress. When he learned about Andronicus' flight and his latest sexual conquest, Manuel became truly enraged. Orders were sent to ambassadors already at Jerusalem on other business, demanding that they secretly arrange for Andronicus' arrest and extradition. These orders, however, fell into Theodora's hands (as the one-time queen of the land, she still had friends in influential places) and she warned her lover. Knowing that Amalric could not afford to alienate Manuel by refusing to comply with his wishes and that Manuel intended to blind him as a punishment for treason, Andronicus arranged a flight with Theodora. Letting it be known that he was going to return to Byzantium so that Amalric would think that Manuel's purpose would be achieved without the king of Jerusalem suffering the embarrassment of having to remove a recently instated vassal, Andronicus returned to Beirut to settle local affairs. There he was met by Theodora, ostensibly come to say her last goodbye. Theodora, however, came with all of her movable wealth. To this Andronicus added his own, and the two surreptitiously slipped into Syria where Nurredin welcomed the renegades with hospitality as a gibe at both Manuel and Amalric. Acre reverted to Amalric.

The couple spent the next few years (excommunicated by Christian authorities) wandering around the Islamic middle east. Eventually they found refuge with Saltuq, the Turkish emir of Koloneia and Chaldia, regions abutting Byzantine Trebizond. Here they occupied an extremely well-located and fortified castle and went into the business of organized brigandage, although officially Andronicus held the rank of *toparch* (district governor) under the emir. Theodora gave birth to a son Alexius and a daughter **Irene Comnena**. In exile, Andronicus was joined by a legitimate son named John, who for a time helped Andronicus ward off the attempts by Manuel to arrest him. Eventually, however, Nicephorus Palaeologus, the governor of Trebizond, succeeded in kidnaping Theodora and her children, and they were held hostage against Andronicus' return to Byzantium. Loving his children and their mother, Andronicus surrendered to save their lives. When he returned to the empire of his birth (1180), Andronicus made such a show of contrition and so effectively groveled for amnesty that he moved Manuel to tears. Andronicus' theatrical display worked: he was "welcomed" home and was not blinded. (The fact that Andronicus maintained friendships with powerful figures within the empire certainly influenced how Manuel responded to his return.) He was, however, sent into internal exile at Oinaion, on the coast of the Black Sea, for his indiscretions were too great to be overlooked completely by Manuel. Regardless, Andronicus lacked for little at Oinaion, although there was never any question of Theodora, Alexius, or Irene joining him there. The period of intimacy which Andronicus and Theodora had enjoyed was over.

Theodora's historical role, however, was not quite complete. Not long after Andronicus returned to Byzantium, Manuel died, leaving behind as his heir the 11-year-old, Alexius II, under the regency of Marie of Antioch. Marie was not a popular figure among the Greeks at the imperial court (or indeed throughout much of the empire), and she relied heavily upon even more unpopular Latin support to secure her position. The prominence of Latins in her political entourage only exacerbated the antipathy of her Greek subjects. Andronicus saw an opportunity: riding the wave of anti-Westernism, he plotted a political comeback. Andronicus moved on Constantinople in 1182, proclaiming his intention to set Alexius II "free" from the undo influence of foreigners. Andronicus faced almost no opposition as he crossed Anatolia, and even when he established a camp at Chalcedon, Marie's faction found it impossible to mount an effective response to the challenge. Some of her former adherents, seeing the handwriting on the wall, even defected to Andronicus. Finally, incited by Andronicus' diatribes against Latins, a revolt broke out in Constantinople at the climax of which a mob massacred many, if not most, of the foreigners in the city; looting was rampant. Andronicus entered the capital and quickly executed his opponents. Even Marie was eliminated: Andronicus forced her imperial son to sign her death warrant with his own hand. In the fall of 1183, Andronicus deemed the time right to accede to the "wishes" of the court and church and to accept his elevation to the throne. For two months Andronicus played at co-emperorship. By the end of the year, however, Alexius II was murdered at Andronicus' command.

In order to tie the usurped authority of the new regime as much as possible to the one it had

ousted, Andronicus decided to engage in marriage politics: Andronicus, aged 65, married the 13-year-old widow of Alexius II, *Agnes-Anne of France. Andronicus may truly have once loved Theodora, and perhaps still did. Regardless, politics was politics. What made Andronicus' marriage to Agnes so deliciously ironic, however, was the fact that Agnes' father was Louis VII of France. Thus, she was a Latin and represented precisely the political influence against which Andronicus had so recently been raving.

Andronicus' years with Theodora were not yet forgotten, for he ordained a second marriage in order to associate his new authority even more closely to the memory of Manuel. What Andronicus had in mind was the marriage of his daughter Irene Comnena to Alexius Comnenus. Now this was an interesting proposal, for, of course, Irene's mother was Theodora. As such, Irene was both illegitimate and the product of an incestuous union as defined by the Church. Alexius' case (as briefly noted above) was even more extreme, for he was the son of Emperor Manuel and Manuel's niece, Theodora Comnena, daughter of Andronicus. Thus, not only was Alexius also a bastard, his parents were even more closely related biologically than were Andronicus and Theodora. As such, it is difficult to see how Andronicus expected to benefit from this union's consummation. As things stood, the proximity of Irene's and Alexius' kinship, although not legally recognized since they were both illegitimate, meant that Andronicus needed a special religious dispensation for the marriage to occur. He was able to bully and bribe an ecclesiastical synod to obtain this dispensation, but only over the very vocal outrage of such influential clerics as the patriarch of Constantinople, Theodosius Boradiotes. So mortified by the audacity of Andronicus' wheeling and dealing was Theodosius that, after it became apparent that Andronicus would have his way, he left Constantinople willingly and forfeited his see. Of course, Andronicus was able to fill the position with someone more to his liking (one Basilius II Camaterus), but the scandal of the whole affair did not bode well for Andronicus' continuing popularity.

To help offset the unpopularity of such episodes and to help consolidate his personal control over the empire, in addition to his attack on foreigners, Andronicus took up another cause which was popular in the capital and with the peasantry throughout the empire. When Manuel had been emperor, to bolster his support among the landed aristocracy, he had sanctioned the sale of political offices with lucrative financial perquisites for those who were buying. In the area of tax collecting, this had led to grave injustices against the poor, but it won Manuel aristocratic support that had been otherwise jeopardized by his pro-Western policies. Andronicus let it be known that he stood against such practices, and would work strenuously to clean up the system. What won Andronicus support among the many, however, cost him among the nobility, and, when the latter opposed his stand, Andronicus responded with such brutality that even members of his own family came to oppose his rule.

What Theodora thought about all of this is unknown, but she appears to have remained a partisan of her lover, at least for a time. This is suggested by the advice she gave to her nephew, Isaac (the son of a sister). Manuel had appointed this Isaac as the governor of Armenia and Tarsus, but he had been captured in battle by the Armenians and imprisoned by them for several years. After the death of Manuel, the Knights Templar ransomed him, but required to be repaid for their service. Theodora advised him to appeal to Andronicus for the money to repay the Knights. Other relatives and friends of Isaac urged Andronicus to pity this ex-exile and to help him. None of those who sought to bring Isaac into the party of Andronicus would have done so with any thought of success if their own loyalty to the reigning emperor were in question.

Isaac, however, rejected Theodora's advice and Andronicus' aid, seeking instead to rally the growing numbers of the discontented and oust Andronicus from power. Great landowners rallied to Isaac, who seized Cyprus, began minting coins (an imperial prerogative), and commandeered the imperial title. Henceforth, Cyprus would lie beyond the political control of Constantinople, a major loss to the empire. Because of mounting opposition, Andronicus could not amass the force to strike directly at Isaac. Instead, he vented his anger against those of Isaac's friends and family whom he caught in Constantinople. Among those who were so punished was Andronicus Ducas, a brother-in-law of Theodora's.

As domestic order disintegrated, other candidates for the throne were also raised. Among these was Alexius, the husband of Irene, whose marriage had cost Andronicus much moral authority among both ecclesiastics and lay people. Andronicus had Alexius blinded and imprisoned in a secure coastal fortress not far from Constantinople. So also was the fate of many of his sup-

porters. Even Irene, when forced by her father to choose between himself and her husband, chose to mourn the fall of Alexius, thus turning Andronicus' love to hate. She was banished from court. Whether Theodora and/or Alexius survived the banishment of Irene is unknown, for they fall from the historical record. (Indeed, since Alexius is not mentioned after the return of his father to Byzantium, it is possible that he had already died.)

Andronicus' fortunes rapidly declined. With widespread intrigue and open rebellion shattering the domestic peace of the Byzantine Empire, foreign enemies began to take advantage. Already the frontiers of the south and east were overshadowed by the rise of Saladin, who by the time of the reign of Andronicus controlled both Syria (having ousted Nurredin) and Egypt. In the face of increasing pressure on his southeastern frontier, Andronicus could not expect Western help, for he had been responsible for the loss of so many Western lives and so much Western property in the process of his elevation. In fact, in 1183 Bela III of Hungary proclaimed himself the avenger of the executed Empress Marie and took the opportunity afforded by Byzantium's disarray to raid and sack deeply into the empire's Balkan provinces. Most devastatingly, however, the Normans of Sicily renewed hostilities against the empire in 1185 and succeeded that year in conquering Dyrrachium, Corfu, Cephalonia, Zacynthus, and most significantly Thessalonica (Byzantium's second city). From Thessalonica, the Normans continued east toward Serres and Constantinople itself. In the capital, a great fear generated by domestic terror and the Norman advance exploded into violence: on September 12, 1185, Andronicus was torn to pieces in the streets. He was the last Comnenus to rule.

William Greenwalt,
Associate Professor of Classical History,
Santa Clara University,
Santa Clara, California

Theodora Crescentii the Elder
(c. 875–c. 925).

See Theodora of Rome.

Theodora Crescentii the Younger
(c. 900–c. 950).

See Theodora the Younger.

Theodora Ducas

Byzantine princess. Daughter of *Eudocia Macrembolitissa (1021–1096) and Constantine X Ducas (d. 1067), Byzantine emperor (r. 1059–1067).

Theodora Ducas (fl. 1200s)

*Byzantine empress. Name variations: Theodora Doukaina; Theodora Batatzaina. Flourished in the 1200s; daughter of John Ducas; married Michael VIII Paleologus (1224–1282), emperor of Nicaea (r. 1261–1282); children: *Irene Paleologina (fl. 1279–1280, who married Ivan Asen III of Bulgaria); Andronicus II (1259–1332), emperor of Nicaea (r. 1282–1328); Constantine; *Eudocia (c. 1260–?, who married John of Trebizond). Michael VIII also had an illegitimate daughter Euphrosyne (who married Nogaj).*

Theodora of Byzantium (c. 989–1056).

See Zoë Porphyrogenita for sidebar.

Theodora of Rome (c. 875–c. 925)

Roman woman who was influential in Italy and in Papal affairs. Name variations: Theodora the Elder; Theodora I the Elder of Rome; Theodora III; Theodora Crescentii; Theodora Crescentii the Elder; Theodora the Senatrix. Probably born in or near Rome around 875; died probably in or near Rome around 925; married Theophylactus from Tusculum (died c. 925), also known as Theophylact Crescentii and Theophylacte, governor of the Roman senate; children: Marozia Crescentii (885–938); Theodora the Younger (c. 900–950).

Theodora of Rome, probably born in or near Rome around 875, was the wife and political ally of Theophylacte from Tusculum, one of the most prominent Roman officials of his generation. Theophylacte held a number of important civic posts during his career, among them the offices of consul and vestararius. Theodora shared the public spotlight with her husband as is proven by contemporary documents in which she is noted as a vestaratrix. It is likely that she was of noble birth.

In the early 10th century, Rome was ruled by popes. Although these maintained that all Christians were subject to their political as well as religious authority (in fact, they claimed to be caesarpopes), in reality this was far from the truth. Other contemporary authorities, both ecclesiastical and laic, frequently overshadowed papal supremacy in the religious field as well as the secular. At the time, any pope's authority was a function of the relative strength of the Papal States in central Italy, the relative strength of his standing within those states, and what little moral authority he could muster abroad. Italy itself was politically divided and the papacy's interests were ever challenged by regional rivalries, German monarchs, Byzantine emperors, and Islamic incursions. It was a time when popes were very secular princes of a very besieged realm at least as much as they were religious authorities, but then again, it was an age when secular and religious power went hand in hand. Roman politics were intense, in part because (at least in theory) the papacy did not constitute a hereditary dynasty: for Rome's aristocrats the politics of the papal curia and succession were of critical interest, for it meant everything that a pope and his primary officials were either friends or (preferably) family.

Theophylacte and Theodora were close political allies of Pope Sergius III (r. 904–911). In 897, amid the extreme partisanship which followed the pontificate of Formosus (r. 891–896), Sergius made a play for the papal throne. Pope Formosus had generated much controversy by his vitriolic attitude toward the Eastern Church and the doctrines of Photius, the patriarch of Constantinople, over the objections of the strong factions which did not relish a break with Byzantium. Sergius did not, however, obtain his ambition until 904 (after which he secured his power by murdering the former pope Leo V [r. 903] and the anti-pope Christopher in prison). Sergius attempted to restore relations with the east, but his reversal of Formosus' policies and his support for the fourth marriage of the Byzantine emperor Leo VI weakened the papacy's influence in the east, while also antagonizing rivalries in Rome. Chief among Sergius' political allies in his struggles against Formosus and during his pontificate were Theophylacte and Theodora, but the pope's relationship with their family was probably not entirely political. At least, later reports allege that *Marozia Crescentii, the daughter of Theodora and her husband, was Sergius' mistress and that her son (Theodora's grandson, who later became Pope John XI [r. 931–935]) was fathered by the pontiff. In addition to this grandson, Theodora is known to have had two others by her daughter *Theodora the Younger: Pope John XIII and the noble Crescentius (*See Theodora the Younger*). Sergius rewarded the services of Theophylacte and his family by establishing Theophylacte as the first count of Tusculum, a sensitive march territory to the north of Rome. After the death of Sergius, Theophylacte and Theodora were instrumental in elevating John X (r. 914–928) to the papacy. One tradition has it that John's accession was fostered primarily because of a sexual liaison he maintained with Theodora, but this is unlikely. Whatever the truth about his accession, John X was eventually deposed, having aroused the hostility of Theodora's daughter Marozia.

As noted, Theodora maintained a prominent public status at the side of her husband. In fact, hers may have been the dominant personality in their marriage, for contemporary and posthumous accounts mention her more frequently than her husband, and more than one reference to the "monarchy of Theodora" is known. As such, her character was either vilified or extolled, depending upon the politics of several historical commentators. Even her supporters, however, admit that Theodora was excessively ambitious and perhaps a bit too avaricious for beatification.

Theodora of the Khazars (fl. 700s)

Byzantine empress. Name variations: Theodoar. Flourished in the 700s; sister of the khagan of the Khazars; second wife of Justinian II Rhinotmetos, Byzantine emperor (r. 685–695 and 705–711).

When Theodora of the Khazars became a Byzantine empress around 705 as the wife of Justinian II, she was Byzantium's first empress who hailed from a barbarian tribe outside the frontiers of the empire. Her husband Justinian twice ruled Byzantium, the first time without her. After coming to the throne at 16, he fell from power in a sudden coup d'etat, and Leontios became his successor. "Since no man with a serious physical defect was eligible to reign," notes *Byzantine Portraits*, Leontios had Justinian's nose cut off (a penalty known as *rhinokopia*). Banished to Cherson on the Black Sea, Justinian made his way to the barbarian tribe called the Khazars. He was well-received by the tribe's khagan, who provided his own sister to Justinian as a wife. She received the name Theodora from her new husband, "in memory of the first Justinian's empress" (*Theodora, c. 500–548).

Although the khagan pledged to help Justinian take back the empire, the promise of a reward for the ex-emperor led to the khagan's plans to betray him. It was Theodora of the Khazars who, upon hearing of the plan, warned Justinian, and her husband escaped the area. With aid from allies, in 705 Justinian marched on Constantinople, and Tiberius Apsimar, the reigning emperor, fled. Despite his disfigurement, Justinian resumed the throne, and it is said that a nose made of pure gold was worn by him to disguise the absence of his own. Theodora of the Khazars joined him in Byzantium as empress, for the two shared a deep devotion.

SOURCES:
Head, Constance. *Imperial Byzantine Portraits*. New Rochelle, NY: Caratzas Brothers, 1982.

Theodora Oldenburg (1906–1969)

*Margravine of Baden. Name variations: Théodora; Princess Mountbatten. Born on May 30, 1906, in Athens, Greece; died on October 16, 1969, in Budingen; daughter of *Alice of Battenberg (1885–1969) and Andrew, prince of Greece and Denmark; married Berthold Frederick William, margrave of Baden; children: *Margaret of Baden (b. 1932); Maximilian Andrew Frederick (b. 1933), margrave of Baden; Louis William George Ernest, prince (b. 1937).*

Theodora Paleologina (fl. 1200s)

*Matriarch of the Paleologi family. Name variations: Palaeologina. Flourished around the 1200s; daughter of *Irene and Alexius Paleologus; married Andronicus Paleologus; children: Michael VIII Paleologus, emperor of Nicaea (r. 1261–1282); John; Constantine; Maria Paleologina (who married Nicephorus Tarchaneiotes); *Eulogia Paleologina.*

Theodora Paleologina

*Byzantine princess. Daughter of Michael IX Paleologus (d. 1320), Byzantine emperor, co-emperor of Nicaea (r. 1295–1320) and *Maria of Armenia; married Theodore Svetoslav; married Michael Shishman or Sisman.*

Theodora Porphyrogenita (c. 989–1056).
See Zoë Porphyrogenita for sidebar.

Theodora the Blessed (c. 810–c. 860)

*Empress of Byzantium. Name variations: Thecla or Thekla; St. Theodora; Theodora of Paphlagonia; Theodora the Blessed. Born around 810 in Paphlagonia; died around 860 in Byzantium; sister of Bardas (Bardus); married Theophilus I, emperor of Byzantium, in 829 (died 842); children: Mary (or Maria); Thecla; Anna; *Anastasia (fl. 800s); Pulcheria; Constantine; Michael III (b. around 836), later known as Michael the Drunkard, emperor of Byzantium (r. 842–867).*

Theodora served as empress and regent of the Byzantine Empire and was made a saint by the Eastern Orthodox Church. She was born around 810, a princess of Paphlagonia, a region of the Byzantine empire situated on the Black Sea, and was chosen to be the wife of the emperor Theophilus I, whom she married around 830. Theophilus was an iconoclast and harsh on matters ecclesiastical; thus his marriage to Theodora was ironic, as she was an iconodule. Nonetheless, the marriage proved to be a wise decision for Theophilus, for the intelligent Theodora, noted for her courage and thoughtfulness, became quite popular. Though theirs was reputedly a happy marriage, the emperor was unaware that his wife and five daughters continued to venerate icons.

Empress Theodora was widowed in 842. Although her son Michael was proclaimed the new emperor as Michael III, he was still a young child, having been born around 836. Thus a regency was established to rule in his name until he came of age, and Theodora was chosen to act as regent. This was not surprising given that, unlike a stranger who might wield power for his own benefit, a mother could usually be trusted to act in her son's best interests, and Theodora had shown herself capable of handling the burden of rule in her years as Theophilus' empress-consort. (There is some indication that her eldest surviving daughter *Thecla might have shared the regency.)

Theodora's main achievement during her 14 years as regent was the restoration of religious orthodoxy. In previous years, various religious sects and heresies had been allowed to exist within the empire largely unchecked. Theodora, devoutly orthodox in her own beliefs, set to work at once to eliminate these threats to the Church. However, she showed considerable patience and moderation in doing so; she refused to sanction violence against the heretics as a means of stamping them out, and did not wish to incite fanatical hatred of them on the part of Orthodox citizens. Instead, she took cautious, slow steps to encourage all citizens to keep the Orthodox faith, and these efforts were rewarded by a decline in the popularity of such sects. She carried on the government with a firm and judicious hand, replenishing the treasury, and repelling the Bulgarians during an attempted invasion.

But when it came to her son, Theodora made some important mistakes which would ultimately end her reign. To ensure her power, she neglected her son's education, encouraged him to pursue a life of pleasure, and refused to allow him to co-rule with her, probably because she regarded herself as more qualified to reign. The licentious Michael resented her, despite the fact that she kept the empire peaceful and prosperous during her regency. Michael grew up under the influence of his uncle Bardas. Though Theodora tried in vain to counter her brother's authority, Bardas triumphed by murdering her advisor Theoctistus; he then had the senate proclaim Michael an independent ruler, ending Theodora's regency in 856. Convicted of intrigues, she was banished along with her daugh-

ters to a monastery. Theodora died about four years later, and was proclaimed a saint for her zeal on behalf of image-worship.

Laura York, M.A. in History,
University of California,
Riverside, California

Theodora the Elder (c. 875–c. 925).

See Theodora of Rome.

Theodora the Younger

(c. 900–c. 950)

Member of the influential Crescentii family and mother of Pope John XIII. Name variations: Theodora II of Rome; Theodora Crescentii the Younger. Born around 900; died around 950; daughter of Theophylactus from Tusculum (died c. 925), also known as Theophylact Crescentii and Theophylacte, governor of the Roman senate, and Theodora of Rome (c. 875–c. 925); sister of Marozia Crescentii; married John (a bishop); children: John (who was Pope John XIII from 965 to 972); Crescentius.

Theodora the Younger, born around 900, was the daughter of Theophylacte and *Theodora of Rome, the sister of *Marozia Crescentii, and the mother of Pope John XIII and Crescentius. Theodora married one John, who served Rome both as consul and duke and who late in life was made a bishop. Like her mother and sister, Theodora was an active partisan in the politics of Rome, but unlike both, she was not the target of sensationalist slander. John XIII was elevated to the papacy in 965 through the agency of the Holy Roman Emperor Otto I. Much of Rome's Patricians resented the influence of the German monarch (which would continue for generations), and John attempted to rein in their influence in the interests of his imperial patron. This generated open hostility, but helped by his brother and an imperial army, John retained his position. The loyalty of his brother Crescentius was rewarded by political preference in Rome. John XIII presided over the imperial accession of Otto II on Christmas day, 967. Despite the help he had given Otto I, Crescentius inaugurated a resistance to Otto II which culminated in a coup, giving him control of Rome (980). After his death (984), his son John Crescentius also maintained opposition to imperial intervention in Rome and controlled the papacy until he was captured and executed by Otto (998). John II Crescentius reinstated his family's control over Rome after Otto III's death (thus continuing its political dominance prominence into a fifth generation) and resurrected his fore-bears' anti-Germanism.

William Greenwalt,
Associate Professor of Classical History,
Santa Clara University,
Santa Clara, California

Theodorade

Queen of France. Name variations: Theoderade; Théodor-ade. Married Odo also known as Eudes (860–898), count of Paris and king of France (r. 888–898).

Théodore, Mlle (1760–1796).

See Crespé, Marie-Madeleine.

Theodoropoulou, Avra (1880–1963)

Greek musician, reformer, and critic. Born in 1880; died in 1963; married Agis Theros (a poet).

Founded School for Working Women (1911); founded Soldier's Sister (1918); founded and was president of Greek League for Women's Rights (1920–57).

Avra Theodoropoulou was a pianist and social reformer. Espousing the cause of women's rights, she founded the Greek League for Women's Rights in 1920 and for the next 37 years ran the league and served as its president, attending conferences on women and earning support and respect for the women's cause and other issues. Theodoropoulou was admired for her expertise and intelligence. Warm and compassionate, she helped to further other social and charitable institutions as well, founding the School for Working Women in 1911 and Soldier's Sister in 1918. In conjunction with her work at the League of Women's Rights, she also founded a number of orphanages and the Papastrateio School of Crafts for girls. For 52 years, Theodoropoulou supported herself by playing and teaching the piano. She was also a writer and a critic. Her husband Agis Theros was a well-known poet and a public figure in his own right. Avra Theodoropoulou died in 1963.

Gloria Cooksey,
freelance writer,
Sacramento, California

Theodosia.

Variant of Feodosia.

Theodosia (fl. 1220)

Russian princess. Flourished around 1220; daughter of Mystislav the Gallant, Prince of Novgorod, one of the greatest warriors of his day; married Yaroslav II, grand prince of Moscow and grand duke of Vladimir (r. 1238–1246); children: Andrew or Andrei II (c. 1220–1263), grand duke of Moscow (r. 1246–1252); Alexander Nevski, grand prince of Moscow (r. 1252–1263); Michael; Yaroslav III, prince of Tver and grand prince of Moscow (r. 1263–1272); Basil or Vasili Kostroma, grand prince of Moscow (r. 1272–1277); Michael Khorobrit.

Theodosia of Moscow (1475–1501)

Russian princess. Name variations: Feodosia. Born on May 29, 1475 (some sources cite 1488); died on February 19, 1501; daughter of *Sophia of Byzantium (1448–1503) and Ivan III the Great (1440–1505), grand prince of Moscow and tsar of Russia (r. 1462–1505); married Vassili, prince Cholinksi, on February 13, 1500.

Theodota (c. 775–early 800s)

Byzantine empress whose marriage prompted the coup that ended her husband's reign. Name variations: Theodote. Born around 775; died in early 800s; became second wife of Constantine VI Porphyrogenitus, Byzantine emperor (r. 780–797), in August 795. Constantine VI's first wife was Maria of Amnia.

Born around 775, Theodota was the second wife of the Byzantine emperor Constantine VI. Constantine was only ten when his father Leo IV died. As a result, his mother *Irene of Athens* was named his regent and co-emperor. Irene was a strong-willed woman at the time when the use of icons was a major religious and political issue within the Byzantine Empire. For a little over 50 years before the death of Leo, imperial policy towards icons was that they should never be used in the process of religious education and that those which existed should (in the best of all possible worlds) be destroyed. There was a strong pro-icon faction, however, which was led by monks and supported by Irene. After the death of her husband, Irene of Athens pursued a policy of restoring icons to a place of respect throughout the empire. Her sweeping about-face, however, was opposed by the numerous iconoclasts who continued to hold positions in the government and army.

The politics of icons was one major issue at the court of Irene; another developed when Constantine reached his majority, for he wanted Irene to surrender to himself all imperial power. This Irene would not do, and Constantine rebelled, soliciting iconoclastic support against his mother. Irene successfully suppressed this revolt (790), but her attempts to have the army swear an oath acknowledging her as its sole overlord generated another uprising in Anatolia. This time Irene was driven from Constantinople, and she remained in exile until her considerable support, especially among the general population, convinced Constantine to sanction her recall (792). Even with many placated by the return of Irene, Constantine was not a popular ruler among the masses and with some at court. For instance, an opposition faction also developed around his uncle, Nicephorus. Constantine crushed this threat, but he did so with such brutality that more unrest was spawned. Initially, this also was repressed, but it was done with such viciousness that Constantine's popularity among the general public—never high to begin with—plummeted.

After her recall, Irene awaited an opportunity to reassert her authority. This arose when Constantine became obsessed with Theodota, a beauty who served in Irene's courtly entourage. Irene cynically encouraged her son's passion (which should have made him wary), although he was already married to *Maria of Amnia. Constantine eventually decided to make Theodota his wife, but he had a problem: the divorce of Maria would create a scandal among the devout and most of the ecclesiastical infrastructure—and he needed no more enemies. Again, Irene encouraged her son to exploit his imperial position, knowing full well what would happen when he attempted to do so. Trying in advance to forestall opposition to his intentions, in 795 Constantine accused Maria of attempting to poison him. Many doubted this accusation (including Tarasius, the patriarch of Constantinople) and refused to acknowledge the legitimacy of what Constantine intended to do. Nevertheless, he divorced Maria and sent her off to a convent. Then, Constantine found a priest named Joseph who agreed to preside over his marriage to Theodota. The unpopularity of this union caused Constantine to overreact, both with the extravagance of the marriage festival and with the speed by which Theodota was hailed empress.

An explosion of public outrage followed, led by an especially strong monastic reaction. This latter was extremely embarrassing to Constantine and Theodota because the most vocal in their opposition were members of Theodota's own family: the monks Plato and Theodore and the nun *Theoctista. These labeled Constantine a new "Herod" and an adulterer. His and Theodota's initial attempts to placate their outrage failed, and soon the emperor's patience wore thin. Plato

and Theodore were banished after being physically beaten, but this only incensed public opinion all the more. Throughout the whole affair, Irene encouraged those who opposed the marriage. In 797, she engineered a successful coup, and toppled her son's regime. He was arrested, imprisoned in the Porphyry Chamber in which he had been born, and at Irene's order was blinded. Thereafter Constantine and Theodota lived out the rest of their days in obscurity.

The story did not quite end there, however. For reasons of factional politics, the later emperor, Nicephorus I, both reinstated (806) Joseph (who had been defrocked for his role in Theodota's marriage) and called a synod (809) to have the marriage of Constantine and Theodota officially recognized. These actions created a new controversy and fueled another round of court factionalism. They did not, however, bring either Constantine or Theodota out of their enforced retirement.

William Greenwalt,
Associate Professor of Classical History,
Santa Clara University,
Santa Clara, California

Theodrada (b. between 783 and 794)

*Abbess of Argenteuil. Name variations: Theodrada of Argenteuil. Born between 783 and 794; daughter of *Fastrada (d. 794) and Charles I also known as Charlemagne (742–814), king of the Franks (r. 768–814), and Holy Roman emperor (r. 800–814).*

Theophano (c. 866–c. 897)

*Byzantine empress and saint. Name variations: Saint Theophano. Born in Constantinople around 866 (some sources cite 865); died around 897 (some sources cite 893, 895 or 896); daughter of the patrician Constantine Martinacius; mother's name unknown; first of four wives of Leo VI the Wise, Byzantine emperor (co-ruled 870–886, r. 886–912); children: one daughter. Leo VI was also married to Zoë Zautzina, *Eudocia Baiane, and *Zoë Carbopsina.*

Born in Constantinople around 866, Theophano was the daughter of the patrician Constantine Martinacius. She was chosen as the first of four wives of Byzantine Emperor Leo VI by *Eudocia Ingerina (Leo's mother) at the imperial Bride Show, a kind of beauty contest, of 881–882. Leo co-ruled the Byzantine Empire from 870, and after his father Basil I's death, alone from 886 until 912. Leo was hailed as the "Wise" because of his legal and cultural interests (he took a philosophical interest in the law, wrote legal decrees, poems, sermons, orations, and even military treatises), but his talents were more scholarly than political, diplomatic or military. His foreign policy was a disaster, with critical losses to the Arabs in the west and to the Bulgarians in the north, and both enemies raided deeply into the Byzantine Empire. Leo's lackluster record and preference for negotiation over fighting, led to aristocratic unrest, and once, even to his incarceration. The court in Constantinople, however, tended to support Leo amid his tribulations.

Through all these troubles, Theophano supported Leo, but her extreme piety doomed the marriage. Preferring to spend her time in prayer and religious contemplation, she neglected the political side of her position, and seemed to prefer a chaste life to one which embraced the responsibility of providing for an imperial heir, though she did give birth to a daughter. As a result, although still married to Theophano, Leo came openly to live with his mistress, *Zoë Zautzina (the daughter of Stylianus Zaoutzes, one of Leo's most important political advisors), a situation which unsettled many of the pious. Theophano died young, still the legal wife of Leo. In death, she presented at least as much of a problem for Leo as she had in life, for her piety made her a popular symbol among the devout masses. Theophano was recognized as a saint soon after her demise, a fact which forced Leo to construct a sanctuary for her relics and to honor her holy memory lest her renown be appropriated entirely as a symbol by his political opposition. These relics were the objects of devotion for centuries.

William Greenwalt,
Associate Professor,
Santa Clara University,
Santa Clara, California

Theophano (c. 940–?)

Byzantine empress. Name variations: Theophano of Byzantium. Born around 940 (some sources cite 941) in Constantinople; died after 976; daughter of Anastaso (a publican); became second wife of Romanos or Romanus II, Byzantine emperor (r. 959–963), around 956; married Nicephorus II Phocas or Nikephoros II Phokas, Byzantine emperor (r. 963–969); children: (first marriage) Theophano of Byzantium (c. 955–991); Basil II (957–1025), Byzantine emperor (r. 976–1025); Constantine VIII (c. 960–1028), Byzantine emperor (r. 1025–1028); Anna of Byzantium (963–1011, who married Vladimir I, grand-duke of Kiev, around 989).

The daughter of an innkeeper, Theophano was beautiful enough to catch the eye of Ro-

manus II (the son of the Byzantine emperor, Constantine VII), whom she married about 955. It is alleged that Theophano persuaded Romanus to poison his father, so that he could ascend the throne. Theophano became the power behind Romanus, inciting him to place his five sisters (including Agatha and *Theodora [fl. late 900s]) in convents and to break with his mother *Helena Lekapena, so that she would face no opposition from the women of Romanus' family. Having established herself at court, Theophano is said to have lived a dissolute life. Romanus was an ineffective ruler who died in 963, but he had four children with Theophano: Basil (II), Constantine (VIII), *Theophano of Byzantium, and ❧➤ Anna of Byzantium.

Soon after the death of Romanus, Theophano married Nicephorus (II) Phocas and was germinal in his elevation to the imperial office. Nicephorus' accession was opposed (even though his previous military career had been very distinguished) by many who suspected that Theophano may have played an unsavory role in Romanus' passing. Nevertheless, she was officially established as the regent for her young sons, Basil and Constantine. Her new marriage is alleged to have disappointed Theophano, for Nicephorus was said to have lived too spartan a life for her lavish tastes. How much truth there was in these allegations cannot be determined, for they may be—at least in part—nothing more than the scurrilous smears of political enemies. It is reported that as a result of her frustrations, Theophano plotted the assassination of Nicephorus with John Tzimiskes (Nicephorus' cousin), a deed carried out in 969. Theophano is said to have offered John both marriage and the throne, but the intense opposition of the patriarch of Constantinople (Polyeuctus), who charged her with murder and adultery among other crimes, caused John both to repudiate her and to commit her to a convent. There Theophano remained until recalled to Constantinople in 976 in the midst of the contested accession of her son, Basil.

❧➤ **Anna of Byzantium** (963–1011)

*Grand-duchess of Kiev. Born on March 13, 963; died in 1011; daughter of *Theophano (c. 940–?) and Romanus II, Byzantine emperor (r. 959–963); sister of Constantine VIII (r. 1025–1028) and Basil II (r. 976–1025), both Byzantine emperors, and *Theophano of Byzantium (c. 955–991); married Vladimir I, grand-duke of Kiev, around 989; children: St. Gleb; St. Boris; and one daughter.*

Theophano's sons both ruled as Byzantine emperors. Basil II the Bulgar-slayer (d. 1025) was one of the Byzantine Empire's greatest rulers, although Constantine VIII (d. 1028) was somewhat more pleasure loving and far less noteworthy than his older brother. If Basil's vigor and skill were inherited from but one of his parents, it is certain that he owed a debt to Theophano rather than to Romanus. Theophano's daughters were shrewdly exploited to extend vastly the range of Byzantine influence: Theophano of Byzantium married the Holy Roman (in fact, German) emperor, Otto II, while Anna of Byzantium wed Vladimir I of Kiev, after he agreed to be baptized, thus expanding the range of Christianity farther east than ever before. Both of these unions helped to secure for a time Byzantium's northern frontier. When Theophano died is unknown, but it is likely that the last years of her life were spent with her reputation more or less officially intact.

William Greenwalt,
Associate Professor of Classical History,
Santa Clara University,
Santa Clara, California

Theophano of Athens (fl. 800s)

Byzantine empress. Born around 790; died probably much after 812; married Stavrakios or Stauracius, Byzantine emperor (r. 811); cousin of Irene of Athens (c. 752–803).

Theophano of Athens was a cousin of *Irene of Athens, the empress of the Byzantine Empire and a canonized saint who helped to restore the religious use of icons after they had been banned from the Byzantine Empire in 726. At issue was to what purpose were icons being used: those who approved of religious art, especially of anthropomorphic representations of God and the saints, argued that they were an expedient tool to educate the illiterate about—sometimes esoteric—points of orthodox doctrine; on the other hand, iconoclasts believed that icons did not serve this purpose, but rather, that the physical pieces of art were, themselves, actually *being* worshiped by the uneducated. Other issues were at hand in this controversy, but this was the central question of the debate.

In 807, Theophano of Athens was engaged and actually living with her betrothed, although not formally married, when the emperor Nicephorus I (r. 802–811) forced her to participate in a Bride Show (a contest through which a suitable wife was procured for a Byzantine emperor or his heir). Nicephorus had organized the show in order to find a wife for his son, Stauracius. Although Theophano was apparently not the most beautiful of the potential brides, she was chosen for Stauracius because of her kinship to Irene, with whose political and religious policies Nicephorus wished to be associated. Theophano's betrothal to Stauracius caused a scandal because of her earlier attachment, as did Stauracius' behavior during the several days of their wedding celebration, during which he openly consorted with two women he preferred physically to his new bride. Nevertheless, Theophano assumed the status of an Augusta.

As Stauracius' wife, Theophano was politically active, if not always in her husband's interests. (At least, it is reported that Theophano once acted as the political ally of *Prokopia, Stauracius' sister, in opposition to Stauracius. What was at issue is not recorded.) The marriage of Theophano and Stauracius produced no children before disaster struck. In 811, Nicephorus and Stauracius led an army against an invasion of their empire by the Bulgarian khan, Krum. In mountainous terrain to the northwest of Constantinople, however, Nicephorus was killed, Stauracius fatally wounded, and the Byzantine army virtually annihilated. Despite his wound, Stauracius reached the relative safety of Adrianople, where (after bitterly denigrating his father) Stauracius had his imperial status reconfirmed. Even so, since Stauracius was mortally wounded, since he had no children, and since the empire had an obvious need for a vigorous leader, voices were raised to the effect that a new emperor should be immediately selected. The leading candidate to succeed Stauracius was his brother-in-law, Michael Rhangabe, the husband of Prokopia, but Stauracius supported the ambitions of Theophano, who wanted to rule by herself, just as had her cousin, Irene of Athens, between 797 and 803. Making his way to Constantinople, Stauracius attempted to have Michael blinded and to relinquish the imperium to Theophano. Theophano's ambitions, however, caused several political rivals (including the patriarch of Constantinople—another Nicephorus—and a former supporter of Stauracius named Stephen) to overcome their differences and unite behind Michael. As a result, Stauracius was compelled to abdicate and Michael was acclaimed. Stauracius then retired to a monastery where he soon died. Also dethroned was Theophano, albeit to a kinder fate. Not wishing to exacerbate domestic rivalries amidst a crisis, Michael essentially bought Theophano off by providing her with a fine house at Hebraika and an endowment so as to enable her to become a nun with her own convent. Stauracius was buried in Theophano's new establishment, and she eventually died there.

William Greenwalt,
Associate Professor of Classical History,
Santa Clara University,
Santa Clara, California

Theophano of Byzantium

(c. 955–991)

Holy Roman empress and regent of Germany. Name variations: Theophanu. Born around 955 or 956 in Constantinople; died on June 15, 991; daughter of Romanus II, Byzantine emperor (r. 959–963), and Theophano (c. 940–?); sister of Constantine VIII (r. 1025–1028) and Basil II (r. 976–1025), both Byzantine emperors, and ❧▶ Anna of Byzantium (963–1011); married Otto II (955–983), Holy Roman emperor (r. 973–983), king of Germany (r. 973–983), on April 14, 972; children: Sophia of Gandersheim (c. 975–1039), abbess of Gandersheim; Otto III (980–1002), Holy Roman emperor (r. 983–1002); Adelaide of Quedlinburg (977–1045); Matilda of Saxony (978–1025); one who died young.

Theophano of Byzantium, the daughter of the Romanus II and *Theophano, was probably born before Romanus inherited the Byzantine throne from his father. Theophano's historical role unfolded somewhat to the west of Byzantium. In 962, after a series of military victories in Germany, Hungary and Italy, Otto I the Great (a German) was crowned the emperor of the resurgent Holy Roman Empire by Pope John XII in Rome (whom Otto deposed not long after). Otto's assumption of the title "Augustus" put him on a collision course with his Byzantine counterpart, for the eastern emperors had long held that their imperial authority had no earthly peer. Southern Italy arose as another bone of contention between East and West, for Otto was determined to add that region to his growing realm. The Italian south had long known turmoil, because although the Byzantine Empire claimed it as its own (and indeed, controlled a number of its cities), its countryside was steadily hounded by Arab (Islamic) raids launched primarily from Sicily. In 972, after some not very conclusive campaigning in the region, Otto managed to negotiate a peace with his Byzantine counterpart, John Tzimiskes (John was Theophano's uncle; her father was then dead). To cement this pact, the two emperors agreed to the marriage of Otto's son and heir, Otto II, to Theophano: southern Italy constituted a large part of her dowry.

There was some German opposition to the marriage, a fact which suggests that Theophano was not born "to the purple," that is, that she was born before her father became an emperor. If so, this significantly lessened her status in the eyes of her contemporaries. In fact, Theophano might have been sent to the West by John precisely because her status in Constantinople was not as high as other potential brides for Otto II. Clearly, the Germans sought a marriage tie with the Byzantine imperial family so as to reinforce the notion of the equality of the two imperial houses. Since the Germans were barbarians in John's eyes, however, he was loath to concede such an acknowledgment, even if he were at the time in no military or political position to reject a German alliance. Hence, the probable reason for the selection of Theophano: she was not so humble as to be insulting, but not so lofty as to cede symbolically Byzantium's claim of superiority over its western rival.

With whatever blessing from the east, Theophano met and married Otto II in Rome in 973, not long after the death of Otto I. Pope John XIII presided over the ceremony in St. Peter's. Although Otto II now technically ruled most of Italy, his more immediate political concerns lay in Germany where he managed to reduce a serious challenge to his authority (centered in Bavaria, strategically located across the trunk lines which linked the German and Italian portions of his realm) only in 978.

The Byzantine Empire which Theophano left behind when she took up residence in Germany was a highly sophisticated and cultured place: the German court to which she came was vastly less so in both cases. It is likely that Theophano found the cultural atmosphere of her adopted land galling, and that she encouraged her husband to patronize the kinds of theologians, scholars and artists who were fixtures at the court in Constantinople. Although there is no direct evidence that Theophano was behind the cultural quickening of Otto's court which occurred after her arrival, clearly emperors in the eastern sense were expected to surround themselves with the best minds and talents they could support. As the Holy Roman Empire strove to catch up to Byzantium in all things majestic, Theophano's personal knowledge of the cultural functioning of an imperial court doubtless influenced the cultural blossoming in Germany. Otto and Theophano had five children: three daughters, one son, and a child of unknown gender who died young. Two of the daughters, *Adelaide of Quedlinburg and *Sophia of Gandersheim, became abbesses. The third, *Matilda of

❧
Anna of Byzantium. *See Theopano (c. 940–?) for sidebar.*

Saxony, married and had ten children. Theophano's son, Otto III, was only three years old when his father died. Reared entirely under Theophano's influence, he became more Byzantine than German, a fact which was of significance to his reign.

In 980, buoyed by the successful repression of German rebels, Otto II and Theophano traveled to Italy where they received imperial coronations. When a renewed Arab assault threatened Theophano's territorial dowry two years later, Otto II, once again committed to Italian affairs, returned to Italy at the head of an army. Otto II, however, proved not to possess his father's outstanding military talent: before the end of 982 he was decisively defeated at the battle of Cotrone. Down but not completely out, Otto II began preparation for a second campaign, but before he could muster the necessary force, he died (983) in Rome, and was buried there. Although considerably less successful than he had hoped it would be, Otto's military intervention in Italy had the effect of benefiting Theophano's younger brother Basil II (who had overthrown John Tzimiskes and assumed the Byzantine throne) by preoccupying the Arabs who previously had been striking Byzantium. Basil made good use of his respite, enhancing the security of his empire. Otto II's positive (if incidental) benefit was somewhat ironic: Basil seems never to have cared overmuch for Theophano and surely had even less concern for the Holy Roman Empire which had with Theophano's dowry wrested away Byzantine-claimed land.

When Otto II died, Theophano became the regent for Otto III, a status which she maintained until she died eight years later, despite the ambitions of many, including especially that of a Bavarian noble, Henry the Quarrelsome. There were several reasons for this unrest beyond mere lust for power. The first was the already noted Byzantine upbringing of Otto III. The Holy Roman Empire was *not* the Byzantine Empire either in its culture or its political infrastructure. Thus, Otto's education was not preparing him to rule the empire he actually would inherit. Second, the Holy Roman Empire was feudally organized and not as secure from internal unrest as was the Byzantine Empire, making it difficult but not impossible for a woman to manage. And third, Theophano so inflamed Otto with visions of imperial grandeur that he eventually made it known that he intended to move his chief residence to Rome, far away from the militarily effective German aristocracy which constituted his real power base.

In 984, the disgruntled Bavarian, Henry, made an attempt on the throne, and actually kidnaped Otto III for a time. Henry's gambit failed to win the necessary support, however, and at an imperial diet held at Rohr, in Thuringia, he returned Otto III to Theophano and *Adelaide of Burgundy (Otto II's mother) and abandoned his ambitions for imperial power. Theophano was an effective regent and did everything necessary to demonstrate who was in control. In fact, she even adopted the masculine form of the title regent in legal documents to symbolize the strength of her rule. The business she oversaw, routine and otherwise, included guarding against foreign aggression (e.g., she foiled a French attempt to annex land at her expense); making political and religious appointments throughout her son's realm; overseeing Otto's education; and taking personal responsibility for ruling over Italy (after 988). During Theophano's regency, her relationship with her mother-in-law Adelaide of Burgundy deteriorated, but after Theophano's death in 991, Adelaide assumed the regency until Otto III came of age in 994.

Theophano died at Nimwegen, but not before her dreams had filled the head of her son with a burning desire to reconstitute the greatest empire Europe had seen since the end of antiquity. In this he bit off more than he could chew: by the time he died at age 21 (1002), Otto III had pushed his realm beyond what its resources could sustain.

William Greenwalt,
Associate Professor of Classical History,
Santa Clara University,
Santa Clara, California

Theophanu.

Variant of Theophano.

Théot, Catherine (d. 1794)

French visionary. Name variations: Catherine Theot. *Born at Barenton (Manche); died in prison on September 1, 1794.*

A French visionary, born at Barenton (Manche), Catherine Théot was a youthful victim of hallucinations. Following a long period of religious asceticism in the convent of the Miramiones in Paris, she suffered from dementia and was placed under restraint. After she was freed in 1782, her early delusions accelerated. Théot, convinced that she was chosen to be the mother of the new Messiah, described to her followers the coming of Paradise on earth. She was soon hailed as the "Mother of God." As the revolution in France began to ignite, the Théotists saw the redeemer of humankind in Robespierre. The enemies of Robespierre, resenting his theocratic aims, seized upon this news and saw in it a chance for revenge. When Théot was arrested and imprisoned, a letter to Robespierre was discovered in her house. In the Convention, M.G.A. Vadier advanced a conspiracy, asserting that Catherine Théot was a tool of England's William Pitt and that the mumblings of the Théotists only served to disguise clerical intrigue; he also insinuated that Robespierre was in favor of the schemes. The case was adjourned to the Revolutionary Tribunal and figured in the proceedings of the 9th Thermidor. Though the Théotists were ultimately acquitted, Catherine Théot died in prison on September 1, 1794.

Theoxena (fl. 315 BCE).
See Berenice I for sidebar.

Therbusch, Anna (1721–1782).
See Lisiewska, Anna.

Theresa (1767–1827)
Queen of Saxony. Name variations: Theresa Habsburg-Lotharingen; Maria Theresia. Born on January 14, 1767, in Florence; died on November 7, 1827, in Leipzig; daughter of ***Maria Louisa of Spain*** *(1745–1792) and Leopold II (1747–1792), count of Tuscany, ruler of Florence (r. 1765–1790), Holy Roman emperor (r. 1790–1792); married Anthony I Clement (1755–1836), king of Saxony (r. 1827–1836), on October 18, 1787. Anthony I Clement was also married to* ***Maria Charlotte of Sardinia*** *(c. 1761–c. 1786).*

Theresa, Saint (1515–1582).
See Teresa of Avila.

Theresa Henriques (c. 1176–1250)
Queen of Leon. Name variations: Teresa of Portugal; Theresa Enriques or Enriquez. Born around 1176; died on June 18, 1250, in Lorvano; daughter of Sancho I (1154–1211 or 1212), king of Portugal (r. 1185–1211 or 1212), and ***Douce of Aragon*** *(1160–1198); married Alfonso or Alphonso IX (1171–1230), king of Leon (r. 1188–1230), on February 15, 1191 (annulled 1198); children: Fernando (b. after 1192–1214); Sancha of Castile (b. after 1193–died before 1243); Dulce or Douce of Castile*

(b. 1194–died after 1243). Alphonso IX's first wife was ***Berengaria of Castile*** *(1180–1246).*

Theresa of Austria (1816–1867)
Queen of the Two Sicilies. Name variations: Marie Therese of Austria. Born on July 31, 1816; died on August 8, 1867; became second wife of Ferdinand II, king of the Two Sicilies (r. 1830–1859), on January 9, 1837; children: Louis, count of Trani (1838–1886); Albert (b. 1839); Alfonso (1841–1934), count of Caserta; ***Maria Annunziata*** *(1843–1871);* ***Maria Immaculata of Sicily*** *(1844–1899); Gaetano (1846–1871), count of Girgenti; Joseph of Sicily (b. 1848);* ***Pia of Sicily*** *(1849–1882); Vinzenz (b. 1851); Pascal (b. 1852), count of Bari; Louise of Sicily (1855–1874, who married Henry of Parma, count of Bardi); Gennaro of Sicily (b. 1857).*

Theresa of Avila (1515–1582).
See Teresa of Avila.

Theresa of Liechtenstein (1850–1938)
Princess of Liechenstein. Born on July 28, 1850; died on March 13, 1938; daughter of Aloysius II, prince of Liechtenstein; married Arnulf Wittelsbach (1852–1907), on April 12, 1882; children: Henry Wittelsbach (b. 1884).

Theresa of Modena (1801–1855).
See Maria Theresa of Tuscany.

Theresa of Savoy (1803–1879)
Duchess of Parma and Piacenza, queen of Etruria. Born on September 19, 1803; died on July 16, 1879; daughter of ***Maria Teresa of Austria*** *(1773–1832) and Victor Emmanuel I, king of Sardinia (r. 1802–1821); married Charles Louis also known as Charles II of Parma (1799–1883), duke of Parma and Piacenza, king of Etruria, on September 5, 1823; children: Louise (1821–1823); Charles III (b. 1823), duke of Parma.*

Theresa of Saxe-Altenburg (1836–1914)
Princess of Saxe-Altenburg. Born on December 21, 1836; died on November 9, 1914; daughter of Edward (b. 1804), prince of Saxe-Altenburg; married August Bernadotte (son of Oscar I, king of Sweden, and Josephine Beauharnais), on April 16, 1864.

Theresa of Saxony (1792–1854)

*Queen of Bavaria. Name variations: Princess Theresa of Saxe-Hildburghausen. Born on July 8, 1792, in Hildburghausen; died on October 26, 1854, in Munich; interred at St. Boniface Church in Munich; married Louis I Augustus also known as Ludwig (1786–1868), king of Bavaria (r. 1825–1848, abdicated), on October 12, 1810; children: Maximilian II (1811–1864), king of Bavaria (r. 1848–1864); Princess *Matilda (1813–1862, who married Louis III of Hesse-Darmstadt); Otto I (1815–1867), king of Greece (r. 1833–1862, deposed); Luitpold (1821–1912, regent [1886–1912]); Theodolinde (1816–1817); *Adelgunde of Bavaria (1823–1914); *Hildegarde of Bavaria (1825–1864); Adalbert (1828–1875).*

Theresa of Spain (1651–1673).

See Margaret Theresa of Spain.

Therese.

Variant of Teresa.

Therese of Austria (1801–1855).

See Maria Theresa of Tuscany.

Therese of Bourbon (1817–1886)

*Countess of Chambord. Name variations: Thérèse or Therese of Modena; Maria Theresia. Born on July 14, 1817, in Modena; died on March 25, 1886, in Gaz; eldest daughter of *Maria Beatrice of Sardinia (1792–1840) and Francis IV (1779–1846), duke of Modena (r. 1814–1846); married Henry V (1820–1883), count of Chambord, on November 16, 1846.*

Thérèse of Lisieux (1873–1897)

French Carmelite nun who, in her brief 24 years, left behind "the little path" for the devout to follow. Name variations: Saint Therese of Lisieux; Thérèse de Lisieux; Teresa of the Little Flower; The Little Flower of Jesus; St. Thérèse of the Child Jesus and of the Holy Face (Soeur Thérèse de l'Enfant Jésus et de la Sainte Face). Pronunciation: LEEZ-yair. Born Marie Françoise-Thérèse Martin in Alençon, Normandy, France, on January 2, 1873; died of tuberculosis at age 24 on September 30, 1897; seventh daughter of Louis Martin (a watchmaker) and Zélie (Guérin) Martin (a lacemaker).

Soon after the death of Thérèse of Lisieux, known as the Little Flower, many attested to spectral sightings of her—soldiers on the battlefield, those at the bedside of the seriously ill—and many cures were made in her name. Some claimed seeing white roses; others claimed an awareness of the flower's lingering fragrance. Though her corporal time on earth was brief, her impact was far-reaching. Her slight autobiography, *The Story of a Soul*, published in France in 1898, has undergone numerous translations and printings. In an unusually short interval for the Vatican, rare in the annals of the saints, Thérèse of Lisieux was beatified on April 29, 1923, and canonized on May 17, 1925. When she died, she was 24 years old.

Born on January 2, 1873, Thérèse of Lisieux was the seventh daughter of Louis and **Zélie Martin**. Louis, a religious man who loved to travel, wrote home often of his many pilgrimages. Coming from a military family, he relished duty and a sense of responsibility. Before he married, he had wanted to join the monastery of St. Bernard, high in the Swiss Alps, but was refused because of his lack of scholarly languages and poor health. Instead, he set out to live the life of a pious man in a secular world and apprenticed for seven years to learn the trade of a watchmaker. Following youthful travels, he set up shop in the town of Alençon in lower Normandy and eventually owned the house above his shop. Louis devoted his time to charity, continued pilgrimages, attended church all day Sunday, and took long walks in the forest; when he arrived home burdened with fish from sitting happily beside a stream for a day, he took his catch to the Convent of the Poor Clares in Alençon. It was not until Louis was 35 that he married Zélie Guérin.

Zélie had come from a parsimonious household—materially and emotionally. "My childhood and youth," she wrote her brother, "were shrouded in sadness, for if our mother spoiled you, to me . . . she was too severe. Good as she was, she did not know how to treat me, so that I suffered deeply." Well educated in Catholic academies, Zélie had also been thwarted from a religious calling and life in a convent. Accepting this reversal as the will of God, she too set out to live the life of a religious in the lay world; she took up lacemaking and after several years as an apprentice became so skilled that she opened a shop in her home in Alençon, a town famed for its Point d'Alençon lace. Zélie would design the work, acquire the inventory, and deal with the sales, while farming out assignments to homeworkers. Soon, Zélie's lace was considered the finest around, selling for 500 francs a meter (around 39 inches).

From 1853 to 1863, Zélie took orders from the Parisian firm of Pigache, at first with her sis-

WOMEN IN WORLD HISTORY

ter **Marie Louise Guérin,** "the soul of her soul," serving as business liaison. Marie Louise was also sternly religious, and so harsh on herself in her puritanical strivings that she suffered from ill health. Even so, in 1858 Marie Louise was accepted into the convent of the Visitation at Le Mans, taking the name Marie Dosithea.

Within three months after their initial meeting, Zélie and Louis were married at the Church of Notre Dame, on July 13, 1858. With Zélie's dowry of 5,000 francs, personal savings of 7,000 francés, Louis' properties, business, and savings of 22,000 francs, the couple started out in extremely comfortable circumstances. Eventually, Louis would abandon his watchmaking and join her in the lacemaking business. On their wedding day, however, when the couple visited Marie Louise in the convent, Zélie broke down in tears, longing for the path her sister had chosen. For the next few months, Zélie would visit her sister at the convent and know peace, only to return home to sadness. Because of his own longings, Louis understood.

At first, Louis proposed they remain celibate, and Zélie had agreed. After ten months, a confessor convinced the couple that marriage was not only for mutual support but also procreation and sanctity. When their children arrived, both parents began to experience some serenity. Their first was **Marie Louise**, followed by **Pauline, Léonie,** and Hélène who was farmed out to a wet nurse in 1865. In 1869, **Céline** was born and in 1870 Mélanie Thérèse, who was also handed over to a wet nurse. But the nurse was negligent, and during the parents' frantic search to find another, Mélanie Thérèse died. Their five-year-old daughter Hélène died around the same time. As well, two sons had died shortly after their births. Zélie mourned the losses greatly, but claimed that in her sorrow she found grace.

Throughout her life, Zélie was an ardent correspondent, writing to her daughters, brothers, sisters, and sister-in-law. (Zélie's brother Isidore had married a 19-year-old girl, also named Céline, and had started an apothecary in Lisieux.) All of Zélie's letters, which were saved, chronicle the joy found in her daughters, except for those to her sister Marie Louise.

In 1870, with the Franco-Prussian war at its height and the Prussians descending on Alençon, half of its population of 17,000 fled. The Martins remained, however, and Louis was conscripted to help hold the line, three miles out of town. When the city fell, nine Prussian soldiers were billeted with the Martins. Zélie wrote her sister of their demands, the threat of reprisals,

the loss of cattle for milk for her newborn: "In short, the business of the town is stopped. Everyone is weeping except myself." As soon as the war ended a year later, there was rioting in Paris, a class war over living and working conditions for the poor. Since the Catholic Church took the side of the monarchy, priests were murdered. Wrote a pregnant Zélie in 1874: "All that is happening in Paris fills my soul in sorrow. I have just learned of the Archbishop's death, and of the sixty-four priests shot yesterday by the Communards. I am utterly dismayed."

Thérèse of Lisieux

Zélie was over 40 when her daughter Thérèse was born in 1873, the ninth and final child. As with all her children, Zélie loved her dearly, but this one was different, even in the womb. "When I am singing, she sings with me," she wrote her sister-in-law. "I tell it to you in confidence. No one would believe it." But the newborn was ill with intestinal trouble following her birth. After the loss of so many of her children, Zélie became apprehensive. When a doctor recommended breast feeding, she set off one daybreak for a town six miles away to find "Little Rose," a peasant who had been a wet-nurse employed previously by the Martins. Initially, Rose was reluctant to leave her own four children but finally returned with Zélie to Alençon, to find the baby worse. Though Rose had little hope, she suckled the infant. Miraculously, Thérèse revived and was taken back to the home of Rose for 15 months.

Eight years before, in 1865, Zélie had discovered a lump in her breast. Now the lump was larger and painful. Consulting a doctor, she was given little hope. For consolation, she went to visit her beloved sister at the convent of the Visitation, but Marie Louise had contracted tuberculosis two years earlier and was gravely ill herself; she died one month later, in February 1877. Zélie than packed up Léonie, Marie, and Pauline and went on pilgrimage to Lourdes. Though it was an exhausting trip and no cure was forthcoming, she returned to Alençon at peace. After a few more months, Zélie died in great pain on

August 27, 1877, age 45. Amazingly, little Thérèse, four and a half years old at the time, would remember much of her years with her mother, as well as her mother's death, in detail.

The family moved to Lisieux to be near Isidore and Céline. Louis gave up his work and stayed home with the remaining children (Marie, the eldest, was now grown up). Outwardly, Thérèse was full of life. Before her mother's death, she had a happy nature, loved "far distances, wide spaces and trees," but by age three, "virtue began to appeal to her." Thérèse, who claimed that, for her, the age of reason arrived when she was two and a half, wrote that the saddest part of her life began after the death of her mother and lasted until she was 14. However, she loved their new house in Lisieux, loved growing flowers in the garden, decorating the little house altar, and taking walks with her father. She was a serious child and, like her sister Léonie, had enormous compassion when she encountered the poor.

Thérèse would always have a profound sense of guilt. She made her first confession at age five and then set about to ward off the attraction of worldly things. A pretty girl, she had to fight an awareness of it. "She was tempted to vanity and wept," writes *Dorothy Day, "and then wept because she had wept." Obsessed by scruples, she became convinced that life would be hard for her, but she felt such profound consolation in the thought that "suffering became my treasure."

Taught at home until age eight, Thérèse was then schooled by the Benedictines in Lisieux as a day student for the next four years. It was a sad time. Because she was first in her class, she suffered the enmity of some of the girls. Thérèse was so filled with love, she longed to find someone to bestow her affection on, but she was a little too pious for her classmates. Not many French girls of the time played "hermit" with their cousin, pretending to pray while the other tended the garden. Hungry for love, Thérèse longed for filial affection from the nuns but was clearly never a favorite. Then one day she was rebuffed by a friend. "I felt this very keenly," wrote Thérèse, "and I no longer sought an affection which had proved so inconstant." She would later write:

> Lucky for me that I had so little gift for making myself agreeable; it has preserved me from dangers. I shall always be grateful to our Lord for turning earthly friendships into bitterness for me, because, with a nature like mine, I could so easily have fallen into a snare and had my wings clipped. . . . It was only God's mercy that preserved me from giving myself up to the love of crea-

tures; without that, I might have fallen as low as St. *Mary Magdalen did.

Lonely at school, she found solace at home in the bosom of her close family. Thérèse adored her older sisters; Céline, the next in line, was her favorite. Céline was more docile than Thérèse and more easily controlled.

For five years, from age nine to fourteen, Thérèse went through mental agony. Huddled within the family, she became shy and touchy, often close to tears. At nine, though she continued her schooling, she had come down with a mysterious illness, accompanied by severe headaches. This occurrence seemed to be tied with the loss of Pauline who entered the Carmelite convent at Lisieux in 1882. When Thérèse heard that Pauline was going to be a nun, she decided that she too would be a nun and never veered from that decision. There would be other occasions for the headaches, generally times of sadness. In 1883, when an uncle discussed her dead mother, Thérèse had another attack so severe that she went through a period from October 1883 to May 1884 of being nursed by her sisters. At one point, the family held out little hope for recovery. Thérèse wrote in her autobiography:

> I do not know how to describe this extraordinary illness, I said things which I had never thought of; I acted as though I were forced to act in spite of myself; I seemed nearly always to be delirious; and yet I feel certain that I was never, for a minute, deprived of my reason. Sometimes I remained in a state of extreme exhaustion for two hours together, unable to make the least movement, and yet, in spite of this extraordinary torpor, hearing the least whisper. I remember it still. And what fears the devil inspired! I was afraid of everything. My bed seemed to be surrounded by frightful precipices; nails in the wall took the terrifying appearance of long fingers, shrivelled and blackened with fire, making me cry out in terror.

Thérèse was too ill to attend school, and Marie was in constant attendance. It was Marie's prayers and a smile from the statue of Our Lady in the sick room that Thérèse claims affected a cure. But when she told of the miracle to the nuns of the Carmelite convent at Lisieux, they gazed at the ten-year-old with such skepticism that she began to doubt what she thought she had seen and viewed herself with "contempt."

For more than a year the symptoms went away. At 11, she made her First Communion and prayed that God would make all things bitter for her, so that she would not want for the sweet things of this life. She wrote in her autobiography:

What comfort it brought to me, that first kiss our Lord imprinted on my soul! A lover's kiss; I knew that I was loved, and I, in my turn, told him that I loved him, and was giving myself to him for all eternity. It was a long time now since he had made any demands on me; there had been no struggles, no sacrifices; we exchanged looks, he and I, insignificant though I was, and we had understood one another. And now it wasn't a question of looks; something had melted away, and there were no longer two of us—Thérèse had simply disappeared, like a drop lost in the ocean; Jesus only was left, my Master, my King. Hadn't I begged him to take away my liberty, because I was so afraid of the use I might make of it.

At 12, an obsessive attack of scruples—called a "nervous, neurotic state" by Dorothy Day—made her wretched. The headaches recurred daily, and she was anxious and cried easily. At 13, Thérèse again left school, this time for good, to be tutored at home. Her father encouraged her governesses to bring her into contact with the outside world. "Visitors were often shown into the quaintly furnished room where I sat surrounded with my books," wrote Thérèse, "and though conversation was carried on, as far as possible, by my governess's mother, I did not succeed in learning much while the visits lasted. Though seemingly absorbed in my work, little escaped my attention, even of what it would have been far better I should not hear."

She had a love for reading and knew the *Imitation of Christ* by heart. In the convent, while still in her teens, she would read all the words of St. John of the Cross and St. *Teresa of Avila. The Bible, however, would be her only reading later on.

"I remained in this unhappy state for nearly two years. It is not possible for me to describe all the sufferings it entailed. . . . Every thought, every action, even the simplest, was a source of trouble and anguish." When her beloved Marie, at 26, entered the same Carmelite convent, "I made troubles out of everything. . . . If I unintentionally offended anyone, far from making the best of it, I fretted until I became quite ill, thus increasing my fault instead of repairing it." The episode ended as abruptly as it had begun, a week before her 14th birthday on Christmas eve, 1886. She called it the day of her conversion: "I have been happy ever since," she wrote.

Though she desired to be a saint, at 14 Thérèse gave up her dreams of doing noble deeds like *Joan of Arc who, at the time, had yet to be canonized. Thérèse was convinced that God was going to make her a great saint because

he wanted it. "Our Lord made me understand that the only true glory is the glory which lasts forever; and that to attain it there is no necessity to do brilliant deeds; rather should we hide our good works from the eyes of others, and even from ourselves, so that 'the left hand knows not what the right hand does.' Then, as I reflected that I was born for great things, and sought the means to attain them, it was made known to me interiorly that my personal glory would never reveal itself before the eyes of men, but would consist in becoming a saint."

Some months after her illness, on a stroll with her father in the garden, Thérèse told him she longed to join Pauline and Marie at the convent at Lisieux; she wanted to do penance and save souls and pray for priests. He reluctantly consented and stooped to pick a little white flower; noting it was fragile and complex, he compared her to it. "She took the flower and pressed it in her prayer book and since the roots had come up with the stem," wrote Day, "she thought of herself as being transplanted" to the Carmelite convent. "Later, when the stem broke, she took it as a sign that she was going to die young, as she did."

After my death I will let fall a shower of roses.

—Thérèse of Lisieux

The prioress at Lisieux, Mother **Marie de Gonzague**, was sympathetic, but the Canon Delatroette, a Carmelite superior, held that Thérèse could not enter the convent until she was 21, unless the bishop of Bayeux agreed. Accordingly, she wrote to the bishop, but received no reply. Accompanied by her father and Céline, Thérèse made a pilgrimage by train to Rome, intending to put forth her request to Pope Leo XIII. On Sunday morning, November 20, when it came time for the pilgrims to meet the pope, the vicar general of the Martins' diocese expressly forbade anyone to speak when called to come forward and kiss the pope's slipper. But when it was her turn, Thérèse, with the prompting of Céline, addressed the pope timidly, "Most Holy Father, I want to ask a great favor." After hearing her supplication, the pope left it to God and her superiors in France. Thérèse was grief-stricken, convinced that her mission had failed.

On her return, she again wrote the bishop. Her perseverance finally paid off. On April 9, 1888, at age 15, Thérèse Martin was welcomed into the cloistered walls of the Carmelite convent at Lisieux, where she and 20 other nuns shared little food, slept on beds made of planks, did the wash in stone washtubs outdoors in winter, and had no heat, save one stove in a communal room, during the harsh French winters. Though she was always called "little," Thérèse had grown quite tall and slender, and had great dignity for her years.

Finally in the convent, a peace passed over Thérèse that remained even throughout a demanding novitiate. The prioress Marie de Gonzague took the new postulant under her firm and moody wing and set about to prove the old saw that if virtue is to be virtue it must be tested. Thérèse, aware that Mother Marie was not popular with many of the nuns and suffered from their silent censure, determined to heal her wounds. Indeed, she once again fought within her a need to place her filial affection on the prioress.

During November–December 1891, an influenza epidemic took its toll on the convent, killing a former prioress, the infirmarian, and two other nuns. Since all the nuns had been felled by the disease, care of the sick was added to the formidable tasks of Thérèse, who had only a mild case. She did this and all else cheerfully. The life of a Carmelite nun is unceasing routine from 5:30 AM to 11 PM. Fatigue is the order of the day. The hardships of convent life were all endured without comment, save for the bone-chilling cold.

Outside the convent, there were other sad events. Her father, who had already endured a stroke, suffered a second, and in February 1889 he underwent recurring bouts of amnesia and a compulsion to run away and had to be put in the mental institution Bon Sauveur at Caen. Three years later, following another stroke which confined him to a wheelchair and made him incapable of running away, he was allowed to return to the home of Zélie's brother, Isidore Guérin.

Shortly thereafter, in February 1893, Pauline, now known as Mother Agnes of Jesus, was elected the new prioress at Lisieux, and Mother Marie de Gonzague was made novice mistress, with Thérèse as her assistant. That summer, Louis Martin died. Six weeks later, Céline entered the convent as one of Thérèse's postulants, and Thérèse set about to instruct her cherished sister. In 1896, Mother Marie de Gonzague was again elected prioress. That April, on the eve of Good Friday, Thérèse was undressing in the bitter cold in the dark of her cell when she began to cough, suffering a hemorrhage that soaked a handkerchief with her blood. At first, she was overjoyed at the prospect of a journey to "another and most beautiful country." Then for months she was "plunged in thickest gloom"; she had a heightened awareness of others who did not have faith and hope, others tortured by despair. "My God, if that table which they profane must be purified by one who loves Thee, I am willing to remain there alone to eat the bread of tears until the day when it shall please Thee to bring me to Thy kingdom of light." Informing Marie de Gonzague, she requested permission to continue working, despite the application of the usual remedies of her day, blistering, cupping, cauterizing. Thus, Thérèse went on washing windows and clothes and sewing, at all times sitting and standing straight, because a Carmelite leans on nothing but God.

Thérèse had long been a good storyteller. Before her illness, while Pauline was prioress, Thérèse was asked to regale the community with stories of her childhood. She was also told to put her narrations in writing, most especially to record what Thérèse called the "little way," a child-like spiritual path of total abandonment and confidence. By the time Pauline's term of three years was up, Thérèse had written eight chapters for her autobiographical *Story of a Soul*. After re-reading the chapters, and aware that her sister had not long to live, Pauline asked prioress Marie de Gonzague to order Thérèse to write something more serious, about her life in religion. It took Thérèse a month to write 50 pages. The last lines were written in pencil for, by then, she was too weak to endure the heft of a pen.

To the community, Thérèse seemed at peace, but her last writings tell a different story. In order to hide her suffering, she wrote poems of joy, but did not feel it:

> When I sing of Heaven's happiness, of what it is to possess God forever, I feel no joy. I simply sing *of what I want to believe.* Now and then, I must admit, a gleam of light shines through the dark night, to bring a moment's respite, but afterwards, its memory, instead of consoling me, only makes my night darker than ever. . . . Yet I realize as never before that the Lord is gentle and merciful; He did not send me this heavy cross until I could bear it. If He had sent it before, I am certain that it would have discouraged me, but now it merely takes away from me any natural satisfaction I might feel in longing for Heaven.

For more than a year from the onset of her illness, Thérèse kept the Carmelite routine. But she became gaunt, and gangrene set in, as well as tuberculosis of the intestines. When she could no longer keep up, she was put in the infirmary and wheeled out into the garden in summer, where she wrote the last chapters of her book. Since May, Pauline had been writing down the sayings of her sister, which would be published as *Novis-*

sima Verba. "I will spend my heaven doing good upon earth," Thérèse had said. "After my death I will let fall a shower of roses."

Hers was an agonizing death. Finally, on September 30, 1897, at 7 PM, Thérèse of Lisieux breathed her last. Wrote Pauline:

> During the long agony of St. Thérèse of the Child Jesus, a multitude of little birds took their station on a tree beside the wide open window of the Infirmary, where they continued to sing with all their might until her death. Never before had there been such a concert in the garden. I was rather depressed by the contrast between so much suffering within and the joyous notes without. . . . And although September 30, 1897, had been a dark and rainy day, nevertheless, towards seven o'clock in the evening, the clouds all dispersed with surpassing rapidity and soon the stars were shining in a bright, clear sky.

Thérèse was so successful in the outward show of ordinariness that her sisters were at first hard-pressed as to what to write of her life, for externally it seemed uneventful. Thérèse of Lisieux was determined to walk the ordinary path, to be an example to the world that piety was available to everyone, that the joys she knew in her spiritual life were joys that everyone could experience.

SOURCES:

Day, Dorothy. *Thérèse: A Life of Thérèse of Lisieux.* Springfield, IL: Templegate, 1960.

SUGGESTED READING:

Balthasar, Hans Urs von. *Thérèse of Lisieux.* NY: Sheed & Ward, 1954.

Gheon, Henri. *The Secret of the Little Flower.* NY: Sheed & Ward, 1944.

Görres, Ida. *The Hidden Face.* NY: Pantheon, 1958.

Petitot, O.P. *Sainte de Lisieux: A Spiritual Renascence.* London: Burns Oates.

Thérèse of Lisieux. *The Story of a Soul.*

Therese of Nassau (1815–1871)

Duchess of Oldenburg. Name variations: Therese von Nassau. Born on April 17, 1815; died on December 8, 1871; daughter of William George, duke of Nassau, and **Louise of Saxe-Altenburg** *(1794–1835); married Peter, duke of Oldenburg, on April 23, 1837; children:* ***Alexandra of Oldenburg*** *(1838–1900); Nikolaus (b. 1840); Cecilie (1842–1843); Alexander (b. 1844); Katharine (1846–1866); Georg (b. 1848); Konstantin (b. 1850);* **Therese of Oldenburg** *(1852–1883, who married Georg, duke of Leuchtenberg).*

Theresia.

Variant of Theresa.

Thermuthis (fl. 1500 BCE)

Egyptian pharaoh's daughter who raised the baby **Moses.** *Born and lived around 1500 BCE; daughter of Seti I or Ramses II; foster mother of Moses.*

The Egyptian princess Thermuthis is identified by Judeo-Christian scholars as the daughter of either the pharaoh Seti I or Ramses II. In the Old Testament she is recognized as the foster mother of Moses, a childless woman who rescued him as an infant and raised him as her own son in the pharaoh's palace.

Laura York, M.A. in History,
University of California, Riverside,
California

Théroigne de Méricourt, Anne-Josèphe (1762–1817)

Activist during the French Revolution, notably advocating equality for women, including the right to bear arms, who became the subject of numerous legends, and, tragically, a prominent figure in the history of insanity. Name variations: Theroigne de Mericourt; Mme Campinado. Pronunciation: AWN sho-SEFF tay-ROYN der MERRY-coor. Born Anne-Josèphe Terwagne on August 13, 1762, in Marcourt (Luxembourg), Belgium; died of pneumonia at the Salpêtrière Hospital in Paris on June 8, 1817, and was buried in the ditch of the hospital cemetery; daughter of Pierre Terwagne (1731–1786, a peasant proprietor) and Anne-Elisabeth Lahaye (1732–1767); had little (if any) formal education; never married; children: (with an unknown man) daughter, Françoise-Louise Septenville (d. 1788).

Met Mme Colbert and escaped a drudge's life (1778); had liaisons with an English officer (1782–87?), and the Marquis de Persan (c. 1784–c. 1793); went to Italy with the castrato Tenducci (1788–89); was in Paris during the fall of the Bastille and at Versailles during the October march of the women (1789); helped found Les Amis de la loi and spoke at the Cordeliers Club, but went to Belgium to avoid possible arrest (1790); abducted by French émigrés, imprisoned and questioned by Austrian authorities, but released in Vienna (1791); returned to France, became an activist advocating further revolution and the arming of women, and participated in the assault on the Tuileries (August 10) which overthrew the monarchy (1792); tried to preach political reconciliation but was whipped as a Girondin by a mob of Jacobin women (1793); arrested during the Great Terror but was certified as insane (1794); was confined in asylums, including the Hôtel-Dieu and La Salpêtrière (1795–1817).

When the French Revolution began in the spring of 1789, Anne-Josèphe Théroigne was in Paris, a still-young (aged 27) woman of means. Because the source of her money was unclear, she was suspected of being a kept woman. The truth was more complicated. During the Revolution, moreover, legends concerning her grew up and were embellished throughout much of the 19th century, legends which historical research has destroyed.

Anne-Josèphe Terwagne, born on August 13, 1762, was the eldest child of Pierre Terwagne, a prosperous peasant proprietor, and his first wife **Anne-Elisabeth Lahaye**. *Terwagne* was the Walloon spelling of a common name whose Frenchified version was *Théroigne*. The addition *de Méricourt*, which Anne never used, was invented by the royalist press during the Revolution and was a corruption of Marcourt, her native village, which lies on the Ourthe River in the Ardennes region about 50 miles south of Liège in the province of Luxembourg in present-day Belgium. When she was born, Marcourt belonged to the Bishopric of Liège, part of the Austrian Empire.

Anne's childhood was wretchedly unhappy. Her mother had two sons, Pierre-Joseph (b. 1764) and Nicolas-Joseph (b. 1767), but died after Nicolas' birth. Pierre remarried, while Anne was sent to an aunt in Liège, who put her in a convent for several years until it proved too expensive. The girl then shuttled among her aunt, stepmother, and paternal grandparents, all of whom mistreated or humiliated her. With her father sinking into ruin because of lawsuits, Anne ran away to Limbourg, where she was a cowherd for a year before becoming a governess in Liège. In 1778, her fortunes turned when she became a companion to a **Mme Colbert** in Antwerp. For four years, Anne lived and traveled with this gracious woman, who introduced her to high society, literature, and especially music. Ambitious and impulsive, dreaming of a career as a singer, and blessed with good looks—not truly beautiful, but pretty and petite, with chestnut hair, delicate hands and feet, and a slim-waisted figure—Anne was ripe for picking when in 1782 she met an English officer. He took her off to England with promises of marriage when he received his large inheritance.

Until Anne returned to Paris from Italy in May 1789, her life became a tangle typical of courtesans, which lent to her a certain air of mystery. The English officer soon came into an inheritance but refused to marry her, though he gave her a sizeable sum, 200,000 livres, which she invested in stocks and jewels. At some point she gave birth to a daughter, Françoise-Louise Septenville, who died in the spring of 1788; the officer refused to acknowledge paternity, and the name Septenville is a mystery. She also contracted syphilis, was cured (supposedly) by mercury, but complained thereafter of pains, digestive problems, and fatigue. In Paris in 1784 or 1785, she met Anne-Nicolas Doublet de Persan, marquis de Persan (b. 1728), a high official in the Ministry of Finance, with whom she deposited 50,000 livres in return for an annuity of 5,000 per year—probably a device to hide her expected status as a kept woman. Apparently, she gave the marquis little or no satisfaction; he complained that he had to pay her (which he did, with delays, until perhaps as late as 1793) while she ignored him to pursue other lovers and her musical ambitions. In the mid-1780s, she was known in society as Mme Campinado (a name in her mother's family) and drew attention by appearing in public alone and bejeweled without disclosing the source of her wealth.

Anne apparently sang on occasion in London, although probably not in Paris. Perhaps as early as 1785, she planned to go to Italy with the Italian tenor Giacomo Davide (1750–1830) for musical training. He backed out, but in 1788, possibly following her daughter's death, she visited her birthplace—where to save appearances she posed as the widow of an English colonel named Spinster—then went to Italy with the celebrated castrato Giusto Ferdinando Tenducci (c. 1735–1790), a rake, deeply in debt, who doubtless hoped to get his hands on her money. Though she successfully sued him for breach of contract, she stayed in Italy for a year, mostly in Genoa. Running short of money, she arrived in Paris on May 11, 1789.

Such was her unstable existence when it was taken over by the French Revolution. Théroigne fervently embraced the Revolution's promise of liberty, "For I have always been extremely humiliated by the servitude and prejudices under which the pride of men has held my oppressed sex." She began to frequent the Palais Royal arcades and gain a political education from the gossip there. In order to circulate more freely and "avoid the humiliation of being a woman," she took to dressing like a man, wearing a white, blue, or red riding habit and a round hat with a turned-up brim and a black feather. She did not help lead the July 14 storming of the Bastille, as legend later said, but heard of it at the Palais Royal; she donned the tricolor cockade and on the 17th marched with the throng escorting Louis XVI to Paris to make amends.

Utterly absorbed now by the revolutionary drama, on August 18 she took a room at Versailles near the palace in order to attend sittings of the National Assembly. Her self-education progressed as she realized that "here were the People confronted face to face with Privilege." She became a fixture in the visitors' gallery, every day in her riding habit, and made the acquaintance of Jérôme Pétion and François Beaulieu, the brother of Abbé Sieyès. On October 5, she watched the mob of women arrive from Paris seeking "the baker" (King Louis) and his wife (*Marie Antoinette). Théroigne again mingled as a spectator, although she may have urged nearby National Guards to arrest some of the aristocratic deputies. She did not follow the crowd and the king back to Paris on the 6th, but returned only when the Assembly moved there on the 19th.

None of her activities resembled the tales printed three months later by *Les Actes des apôtres*, a royalist newspaper, which said she had raised the October mob herself, distributing money from the Duc d'Orléans, and ridden ahead of it to Versailles and back on a horse (or astride a cannon), dressed in red, a sabre (or lance) in hand and pistols in her belt. Thomas Carlyle and other historians later seized on the image, Alphonse de Lamartine in particular romanticizing it past measure.

In Paris again, Théroigne continued to attend every Assembly session and began to conduct a salon. Numerous prominent figures were said to have attended—Pétion, Brissot, Camille Desmoulins, Marie-Joseph Chénier, Anacharsis Cloots, Fabre d'Églantine, Basire, Gorsas, Barnave, Saint-Just, Momoro—but the regulars were secondary types, such as Augustin Bosc d'Antic (a friend of *Mme Roland), Bernard Maret (the future Duc de Bassano), Méjean de Luc, François Beaulieu, and Gilbert Romme (1750–1794). A mathematician, political theorist, and future member of the Convention, Romme, like Théroigne, was awakened by the Revolution and wanted to play a role. She inspired him to found one of the first political clubs, Les Amis de la loi (The Friends of the Law), which intended to gather all possible information about the Assembly, push forward reform, and enlighten the masses about their new liberties.

The Amis at first met in Théroigne's rooms, beginning on January 10, 1790. She was the only female member and served as archivist until February 21. The club, which never surpassed about 20 members, held too many conflicting views and last met on March 17. (By then the Amis de la Constitution, the famous Jacobin

Club, had emerged with a similar program and was growing rapidly.) Théroigne, to her chagrin, found nobody save Romme (who presently let her down) favoring equal rights for women. The club also refused to admit her brother Pierre, on the specious ground that he (a Walloon) did not know French. And, finally, she failed to get the club to affiliate with the Cordeliers Club. Probably sensing the decline of the Amis, she had gone to the Cordeliers on February 20 to try to be admitted. Allowed to address the club, she delivered a passionate speech calling for the National Assembly to be housed in a Temple of Liberty erected on the site of the demolished Bastille. She won enthusiastic applause—and discovered her gift for oratory—but the project was buried in a committee and she was denied membership because of her sex. To cap these snubs and failures, her attempt to found a Club des droits de l'homme (Club of the Rights of Man) after the demise of the Amis fizzled out.

Meanwhile, Théroigne had become the butt of vicious attacks by royalist papers, starting on

Anne-Josèphe Théroigne de Méricourt

November 10, 1789, in *Les Actes des apôtres.* That "la Belle Liégeoise," as she had soon become known, was a vocal presence every day in the gallery of the Assembly, dressed flamboyantly, and conducted a salon attended by prominent revolutionaries sufficed to make her a target. The *Actes, Petit Gauthier, Sabbats Jacobites,* and *Apocalypse* slandered her mercilessly, accusing her of being the revolutionaries' whore, reveling in debauchery and blood lust. She joined *Germaine de Staël and Marie Antoinette, no less, as a favorite subject of scabrous stories, obscene cartoons, and even the text of a play in the *Actes* (*Théroigne et Populus ou le triomphe de la démocratie*, separately printed in 1791) recounting her "marriage" to a current deputy, Marie-Étienne Populus, whose name ("the People") suggested endless satirical possibilities. Ironically, she had in fact become quite resistant to the advances of the men around her.

*L*et us arm ourselves; we have the right by nature and even by the law. Let us show the men that we are not inferior to them, neither in virtues nor in courage.

—Théroigne de Méricourt

Discouraged and harassed, Théroigne was also running low on money, having pawned valuables since September 1789. The following spring, she changed her residence and name, perhaps upon learning that the Châtelet investigation of the October Days had heard a witness mention her. (Only 5 of some 400 did so.) By the end of May, she was back in Marcourt. "I left the French Revolution without too much regret," she said later. For a few months, she lived happily among her kinfolk in Marcourt and Xhoris and even sought to buy some land and settle down. The Revolution, however, still held her. In December 1790, she wrote her banker that she intended to return to Paris in ten months. While keeping a low profile—the Austrian Netherlands was bubbling due to spill-over from France—she did support some peasants' complaints and open her door to local patriots. Through her indiscretions, her presence became known to French émigré royalists nearby and thence to Austrian authorities up to Holy Roman Emperor Leopold II himself.

To save appearances, the Austrians arranged for her to be seized by French émigrés. On January 15, 1791, she was abducted at night from an inn at La Boverie (outside Liège) by two nobles and a former sergeant posing as friends. At Fribourg, they delivered her to the Austrians, who took her to Kufstein, the forbidding Tyrolean fortress-prison, arriving on March 9. Despite precautions, news of Théroigne's arrest leaked and briefly raised international tensions.

The Austrians, believing the royalist press, considered her a prize catch. They suspected she was a Jacobin spy sent to the Netherlands to raise rebellion, but above all they wanted her to reveal her role in the October Days (believing she had plotted to kill Marie Antoinette) and to inform them of the inner workings and personnel of the revolutionary movement. From May 29 to July 28, Aulic councillor François de Blanc interrogated her and also ordered her to write her autobiography. (It was first published in 1892 as her *Confessions*.) An honest, courageous official, he concluded she was no spy, the "confessions" she made to her abductors were fabrications, and the royalist press was totally unreliable. Ominously, a prominent physician called to examine her noted that her mental state "justifies every apprehension." She was taken to Vienna (arriving on August 14) and was interviewed by Imperial Chancellor Prince Kaunitz and, in great secrecy around October 25, by Leopold in an audience whose contents were never disclosed. The sagacious emperor decided to release her, probably hoping to dampen rising war talk in France and possibly thinking she might prove useful later because she, an Austrian subject, had never expressed any disloyalty or disrespect toward him. Having promised that she would not leave home without permission, Théroigne was freed on November 25 and arrived in Brussels on December 25.

Barely three weeks later, she was in Paris reviving her salon. No doubt the stifling atmosphere of Brussels and Liège, fostered by the failure of the revolution there and the authorities' surveillance of her, caused her to yearn for the free air of France. Moreover, the Châtelet's proceedings had been quashed on September 15, 1791. Her quick return, however, has always fed a suspicion that she was now an Austrian agent—yet more mystery—but no hard evidence supports it.

For the next eight months, Théroigne played her most active role during the Revolution. The constitutional monarchy set up in 1791 was already under siege. Théroigne sided with the rising Girondins (or Brissotins), moderate Jacobin republicans somewhat favorable to women's rights and pushing for a war abroad as a way to end the monarchy. The Montagnards, left-wing Jacobins heeding Robespierre, disagreed on both scores and were more frankly republican. On January 26, 1792, the Jacobin Club hailed her as a heroine of liberty and invited her to speak on February 1. Instead of relating her adventures, she issued an eloquent call in her Walloon-accented French for war on the émigrés and "despots" (though she never spoke ill of Leopold). She eagerly anticipated the liberation of her native land, assuring the Club that the Revolution had more supporters abroad than they imagined. She also launched an idea that had been heard now and then since 1789, namely, that legions of women soldiers ("amazons") should be formed.

The idea circulated during the fevered weeks leading to the declaration of war on Austria on April 20. On March 6, ❧▶ **Pauline Léon** and 300 others petitioned the Legislative Assembly (successor to the National Assembly) to allow women to arm themselves; and, on March 11, Théroigne summoned women to gather on the Champ de Mars for drill, but with little success. Meanwhile, she asked the Jacobins on March 4 to sponsor a patriotic demonstration to welcome the 40 amnestied soldiers of the Châteauvieux regiment who had been sent to the galleys in 1790 for mutiny against their royalist commanders at Nancy. The Jacobins voted it down, but on the 24th Théroigne petitioned the Paris city council, which approved it. The next day, she took part in a civic banquet on the Champs-Élysées followed by a march to the Jacobins and then to the hall of the Société fraternelle des Minimes on the rue Saint-Antoine, where she delivered a major speech on the amazon projects, advocating equality of the sexes and rejecting the view that women should be confined to care of the hearth: "Let us return to the days when the women of Gaul debated with men in the public assemblies and fought side by side with their husbands against the enemies of liberty."

Théroigne worked feverishly among the women of the faubourg Saint-Antoine to organize a political club and form a battalion of amazons. It was not to be. By some accounts, she was set upon by a crowd on April 12 and escaped a whipping only because authorities nearby snatched her away under armed escort. The next day at the Jacobin Club, a delegation from Saint-Antoine denounced her activities, saying she was luring women away from their domestic duties and that she had made unauthorized use of the names of Santerre, Collot d'Herbois, and Robespierre. Santerre mildly defended her but urged her to "desist from projects of this nature." Humiliated, she took no visible role in the Châteauvieux festival on the 15th—a massive demonstration by radical revolutionaries and a triumph for painter and pageant-master Jacques-Louis David. Her humiliation was crowned on April 23

at the Jacobin Club. Girondins and Montagnards were now coming to open war. Théroigne, who had outspokenly taken the Girondist side, was mocked by Montagnard Collot d'Herbois for presuming, as a woman, to have political opinions. Enraged by the derisive laughter, she vaulted the gallery railing and charged to the rostrum demanding to be heard. The president suspended the sitting during the ensuing tumult.

After this, Théroigne's activity became episodic. With invasion imminent, she probably helped organize the demonstration of June 20 ("The Visit to the King") urging a more radical war policy, but whether she was in—much less led—the mob which invaded the Tuileries is not known. Her presence in the August 10 assault which ended the monarchy, however, was widely noted. Clad in a blue riding habit, carrying pistols and a dagger, and in the grip of an intense excitement—behaving now the way her enemies had always depicted her—she urged on an already bloodthirsty crowd outside the Feuillants to kill the 22 royalist prisoners there. Eleven escaped; the nine who were slaughtered included François Suleau, a rabidly royalist editor at *Les Actes des apôtres*, who some accounts said, probably falsely, was stabbed by Théroigne herself. She then took a leading place in the final assault on the Tuileries and was one of the three women (with **"Queen" Audu** and *****Claire Lacombe**) decorated by the soldiers from Marseille (the *fédérés*) who headed the uprising. After August 10, Théroigne retired from the public scene, emerging only briefly, and tragically, in May 1793. She took no part in the September Massacres, legend again to the contrary. She probably frequented the clubs, kept a salon of sorts, attended the Convention, the new Republic's legislature, and may have tried to write her memoirs. It is certain that she was in financial distress; by January 1793, she was living in a room at 273 rue Saint-Honoré, perhaps aided by Abbé Sieyès, who lived there.

She resurfaced early in May as the author of a broadsheet calling for political conciliation in the face of rising domestic violence and a renewed threat of invasion. The Girondins, predominant since August 10, were fast losing out to the Montagnards; hence, her call for conciliation was bound to be dismissed as Girondist pleading. This manifesto, despite some troubling syntax and diffuse construction, contained a remarkably acute analysis of the current political and military situation. Interestingly, she warned of Austrian agents working for civil war. Her remedy for domestic turmoil, however, seemed chimerical at best, and contrasted dramatically

▶❧
Léon, Pauline.
See Lacombe, Claire for sidebar.

with her "military feminism" of a year ago. She called for election of six virtuous, wise women in each Paris *section* who, garbed in tricolor sashes, "would have the task of reconciling and uniting the men citizens" and monitoring their behavior in the *section* assemblies, where they would admonish miscreants. Not surprisingly, her proposal went nowhere.

Days later, on May 15, she received a wound from which she never fully recovered. A gang of women (*mégères*), led by the Jacobin sympathizer Claire Lacombe, was preventing their opponents access to the Convention's gallery. Théroigne, arriving as usual, was denounced as a "Brissotine" and mobbed by the women, who raised her skirts and whipped her savagely on her bare buttocks at the Convention's entrance. According to some accounts, Jean-Paul Marat, a Montagnard they revered, fortunately arrived and spirited her away. But her humiliation was profound—and had been inflicted by women.

After this sad affair, Théroigne withdrew from public life. She had long shown symptoms of mental illness, and in the following months she slowly sank toward a hopeless state. She likely worked on her memoirs until, on June 27, 1794, during the Great Terror, she was arrested on suspicion, probably for ill-considered words to neighbors. Her brother Nicolas, residing in Paris, had concurrently appealed to have her put in his custody. On July 26, the day before the fall of the Committee of Public Safety, she wrote a half-logical, half-delusional letter to Saint-Just, a powerful member, asking his aid. He was executed before he received it. On September 20, Théroigne was officially certified as insane, and, on December 11, she was released in her brother's care. Early in 1795, he had her committed to the madhouse of the faubourg Saint-Marceau. In 1797, she was known to be at the Hôtel-Dieu. On December 9, 1799, she was transferred to La Salpêtrière Hospital; on January 11, 1800, to the Petites-Maisons; and finally back to La Salpêtrière on December 7, 1807, where she died on June 8, 1817.

Théroigne's state in these last years was pitiable—locked up in hellish asylums, abandoned by her siblings, and fixated on the Revolution. She continually repeated words and slogans of the Revolution and would threaten others, "Moderates" and "Royalists," with arrest by the Committee of Public Safety. She complained of burning sensations, walked about naked, doused her person and bedclothes with cold water in winter or summer, crawled on all fours, and ate straw and feathers and excrement from the floor. Philippe Pinel's pupil and successor, Étienne Esquirol (1772–1840), carefully observed her from 1807 on, had an autopsy performed after her death, and described her case at length in *Des maladies mentales* (2 vols., 1838). It appears that her illness had no observable physical cause, notwithstanding her bout with syphilis. In current terminology, she would probably be described as afflicted with schizophrenia or manic-depressive psychosis.

Anne-Josèphe Théroigne's life was a tragedy. An ambitious, courageous woman who escaped from peasant drudgery only to fall into a life as a courtesan, she welcomed the French Revolution as a liberation. She longed to play a role and for all women to escape the oppression of their sex and be treated as equal to men in every way, including even the bearing of arms. The Revolution "transposed her repulsion at the idea of being a woman into a warrior feminism," writes **Elisabeth Roudinesco**. Sadly, because she was a déclassé woman of means and could not find acceptance among either middle-class or working women, she failed in almost everything she attempted. Paris organized no female legions, for example, although some were formed in the provinces. She was pilloried in the press, humiliated in public places, and by a terrible irony became famous (or infamous) for deeds she never did. Moreover, in later times, her insanity was taken, especially by conservatives, to symbolize the destiny of the Revolution itself. The Revolution certainly proved to be mostly a false dawn for her. The same was true for the women of France, who did not obtain the vote until 1944—150 years after Théroigne had disintegrated into madness.

SOURCES:
Dreyfous, Maurice. *Les Femmes de la Révolution française (1789–1795)*. Paris: Société française d'éditions d'art, 1903.

Erdman, David V. *Commerce des Lumières: John Oswald and the British in Paris, 1790–1793*. Columbia, MO: University of Missouri Press, 1986.

Ernst, Otto. *Théroigne de Méricourt, d'après des documents inédits ti're des Archives secrètes de la Maison d'Autriche*. Trans. by Lt. Col. P. Waechter. Paris: Payot, 1935.

Galante Garrone, Alessandro. *Gilbert Romme: Histoire d'un révolutionnaire (1750–1795)*. Trans. by Anne and Claude Manceron. Paris: Flammarion, 1971.

Gutwirth, Madelyn. *The Twilight of the Goddesses: Women and Representation in the French Revolutionary Era*. New Brunswick, NJ: Rutgers University Press, 1992.

Hamel, Frank [Fanny]. *A Woman of the Revolution: Théroigne de Méricourt*. NY: Brentano's, 1911.

Kelly, Linda. *Women of the French Revolution*. London: Hamish Hamilton, 1987.

Lacour, Léopold. *Trois femmes de la Révolution: *Olympe de Gouges*, Théroigne de Méricourt, Rose Lacombe*. Paris: Plon-Nourrit, 1900.

Rose, R.B. *The Making of the Sans-Culottes: Democratic Ideas and Institutions in Paris, 1789–92.* Manchester: Manchester University Press, 1983.

Roudinesco, Elisabeth. *Théroigne de Méricourt: A Melancholic Woman during the French Revolution.* Trans. by Martin Thom. London: Verso, 1991.

Villiers, Baron Marc de. *Histoire des clubs de femmes et des légions d'amazones, 1793–1848–1871.* Paris: Plon-Nourrit, 1910.

SUGGESTED READING:

Applewhite, Harriet B., and Darlene Levy, eds. *Women and Politics in the Age of the Democratic Revolution.* Ann Arbor, MI: University of Michigan Press, 1990.

Bosher, J.F. *The French Revolution.* NY: W.W. Norton, 1988.

Furet, François, and Denis Richet. *French Revolution.* Trans. by Stephen Hardman. NY: Macmillan, 1970.

Grubetzsch, Helga, Elisabeth Roudinesco, and Philippe Raxhon. *Les Femmes de la Révolution française.* Toulouse: Presses universitaires de Mirail, 1990.

Legros, Usmard. *Le Double Destin de Théroigne de Marcourt dite de Méricourt.* Hovine (Belg.): Marquain, 1969.

Levy, Darlene Gay, Harriet Branson Applewhite, and Mary Durham Johnson, eds. *Women in Revolutionary Paris, 1789–1795: Selected Documents.* Urbana, IL: University of Illinois Press, 1979.

Pellet, Marcellin. *Étude historique et biographique sur Théroigne de Méricourt.* Paris: Maison Quantin, 1886.

Schama, Simon. *Citizens: A Chronicle of the French Revolution.* NY: Alfred Knopf, 1989.

Strobl von Ravelsberg, Ferdinand. *Les Confessions de Théroigne de Méricourt, la fameuse amazone revolutionnaire. . . .* Paris: L. Westhausser, 1892.

David S. Newhall,
Professor Emeritus of History,
Centre College, author of
Clemenceau: A Life at War (Edwin Mellen, 1991)

Thessalonike (c. 345–297 BCE)

Macedonian queen. Born around 345 BCE; murdered in 297 BCE; daughter of Philip II, king of Macedonia, and Nicesipolis; married Cassander, king of Macedonia; children: three sons, Philip, Antipater (I), and Alexander (V).

Thessalonike was the daughter of Philip II of Macedon and **Nicesipolis**. It is not known precisely when Philip, who was polygamous, married Nicesipolis. One source suggests that they were wed early in Philip's reign, which began in 359, but it is more likely that they married in the 340s. Nicesipolis was the niece of Jason of Pherae, a tyrant and prominent player in politics of Thessaly, a land which lay directly to the south of Philip's realm. If Philip married Nicesipolis early in his rule, he did so to win powerful political allies and perhaps to open the door for involvement in Thessaly's affairs. If the union came later, Philip took Nicesipolis as part

of the settlement which made him Thessaly's overlord. Thessalonike almost certainly was not born until the 340s, because her name means "Victory in Thessaly"—a claim Philip could not make at the beginning of his reign. Apparently Nicesipolis experienced complications during Thessalonike's birth, because she died only 20 days after bringing her daughter into the world.

Thessalonike was almost certainly reared by *Olympias, Philip's chief wife and the mother of two of his children, Alexander III the Great and ❧▶ Cleopatra (b. 354 BCE), both of whom were older than Thessalonike. We know nothing about Thessalonike until 317–16 BCE, in the context of the civil wars which had arisen after Alexander's death near Babylon in June 323. Alexander had left behind no competent heir. Though his first wife *Roxane was pregnant, she was not due to deliver until the fall. Alexander's only living male relative was Philip's son with *Philinna, a mentally incompetent half-brother named Arrhidaeus. For over 300 years, Macedon had been ruled by the Argeads (Alexander's house), but the lack of even one suitable heir apparently had never been faced before; thus, there was no precedent for what the Macedonians should do, and the army which was with Alexander when he died was not in agreement about what should be done about the succession. After much consternation, a compromise was hammered out by which Arrhidaeus was acclaimed king immediately (under the throne name Philip III), with the understanding that if Roxane's child turned out to be a son, he would share the throne. In fact, Roxane delivered a son and he was hailed Alexander IV. This joint monarchy was thereafter put under a regency—with a general named Perdiccas initially appointed as the kings' primary guardian. It was assumed by almost everyone that Philip III, not being of sound mind, would never become a factor in future accessions and that one day the empire would be ruled by Alexander the Great's son. The joint kingship, however, proved unworkable because almost immediately the most ambitious generals began to plot in their own interest, not initially to establish their own kingdoms, but rather to prevail as first of the Macedonians under the kings. This created a spirit of distrust, into which *Eurydice (c. 337–317 BCE), Philip II's only granddaughter, thrust herself by demanding Philip III in marriage in the hopes of hijacking the succession from Alexander IV. When this union was realized it posed a threat to the eventual accession of Alexander IV. For a time this threat was kept in check, but by 317 Eurydice and Olympias, on behalf of Philip III

◀❧
Cleopatra. See
Olympia for
sidebar.

and Alexander IV respectively, were at war. Olympias seemed to have won this heavyweight bout when she captured and executed Eurydice and Philip, but before she died, Eurydice forged an alliance with Cassander, the son of Antipater (who when alive had been Olympias' single biggest political rival). Thessalonike was with Olympias, Roxane and Alexander IV, in the city of Pydna, when it came under attack by Cassander. After Cassander took Pydna, he had Olympias judicially executed, put Roxane and Alexander IV under "protective" custody (both would "mysteriously" die under his care, probably in 310), and married Thessalonike.

With one king dead and the other under house arrest, never to be set free, the Macedonian generals who were emerging as Alexander the Great's real heirs were in desperate need of some way to legitimize their authorities, for "might makes right" can only be carried so far before civil discord arises. Since marriage and politics had always gone hand in hand in Macedon, the more ambitious of these men sought to marry into the Argead house and thereafter father children who would be of half-royal ancestry. After 316, the only eligible Argead brides were Thessalonike and Cleopatra. The more highly desired of these was the latter, for she was the full sister of the great Alexander. Cleopatra was at the time a widow: her first husband, Alexander of Epirus, had died some years before while campaigning in Italy. Although she was the greater prize, none of the prospective suitors wanted her to marry anyone but himself. As a result, collectively they held her as a political hostage, until, when she did try to pick a husband in 309–08, she was murdered by another (Antigonus) whom she had not chosen. Thus, Cassander was the only successor of Alexander the Great to have any direct tie with the defunct Argead house, a fact which he hoped would make him more popular among the Macedonians at large. He was not able to rally Macedonian émigrés to his cause, but Thessalonike clearly was the primary reason why Cassander was able to rule Macedonia proper.

What Thessalonike thought about the demise of Olympias and her marriage is not known. Cassander, however, rendered her all due respect in public, as was only sensible in that his hopes to found a new royal dynasty relied heavily on her paternity. Yet, the sources are so curiously silent about Thessalonike after her marriage that is likely that Cassander did all that he could to keep her out of the public's eye so as to focus attention on himself. Nevertheless, Cassander did immortalize his bride by founding a city in her name (the modern Thessaloniki) which became one of the great cities of the ancient world and remains Greece's second largest city. His reason for doing so can be discerned. In Macedonia the founding and naming of cities was a royal prerogative. About the same time as Thessaloniki was established, Cassander founded another city named Cassandreia (a city which did not fare so well as Thessaloniki over time). Undoubtedly, the latter was created in order to set a precedent for Cassander doing something which, in his people's eyes, only a legitimate Macedonian king could do. Thessaloniki would thus have been added as a twin foundation to underscore his ties with the defunct Argead house and to mitigate any animosity which might arise as a result of his assuming a royal prerogative.

In 306, or about four years after the death of Alexander IV, which Cassander always insisted was not murder, Antigonus I in Asia became the first of the Macedonian successors to adopt formally the title of king. Thereafter, several rivals followed suit from their respective strongholds. Cassander was more circumspect in adoption of a royal title, because, since he alone ruled what was the ancestral homeland of the Macedonians, he had to be: nevertheless, he acted the part of a king without actually calling himself one, and, by the time of his death in 297 of consumption, Cassander had *de facto* established a new royal dynasty. Thessalonike and Cassander had three sons: Philip, Antipater, and Alexander—the first and third named to honor the two greatest Argead kings and the second to honor Cassander's father.

Philip (IV) succeeded his father, but very soon thereafter, died, probably also of consumption. Antipater and Alexander then became rivals for the vacant throne. It was at that moment that Thessalonike stepped out of the political shadows. Antipater seems to have been the older of her surviving sons (although neither was out of his teens), but Thessalonike apparently favored her youngest son. As a result, so as to leave Alexander some inheritance, Thessalonike attempted to divide the kingdom between the two. This act of "statesmanship" so enraged Antipater that he immediately murdered his mother. Amid the war which followed, both Antipater (I) and Alexander (V) claimed the kingship and sought alliances with Macedonians abroad: Antipater seeking the aid of his father-in-law, Lysimachus, and Alexander the help of Demetrius, the son of Antigonus I (and also the help of the Epirote, Pyrrhus). This was an age of treachery. Since both Lysimachus and Demetrius wanted to rule the homeland of their ancestors, each assassinated the son of Thessalonike who beseeched his help (in 294). Thus was Cassander's line eradicated, and with it, the last of the Macedonian kings to be biologically related to the Argead house. Demetrius (I) won the Macedonian stakes and became the country's king: his family ruled Macedon until the Romans conquered the realm and made it their first territorial province east of the Adriatic.

William Greenwalt,
Associate Professor of Classical History,
Santa Clara University,
Santa Clara, California

Theudesinda (fl. 700)

Wife of Grimoald. Married Grimoald II, mayor of Neustria and Austrasia (d. 714); children: Theudoald, mayor of Austrasia.

Theutberga (fl. 9th c.).

See Tetberga.

Thimig, Helene (1889–1974)

*Austrian actress, member of a great theatrical family and one of the leading actresses of Central Europe for half a century, whose career was closely linked for several decades to the achievements of her second husband Max Reinhardt. Name variations: Helene Thimig-Reinhardt; "Helene Werner." Born Ottilie Helene Thimig in Vienna, Austria, on June 5, 1889; died in Vienna on November 6, 1974; daughter of Hugo Thimig and Fanny (Hummel) Thimig; had brothers Fritz, Hans, and Hermann; married Paul Kalbeck; became second wife of Max Reinhardt (1873–1943, actor, manager, and stage director), in 1935; married Anton Edthofer. Max Reinhardt's first wife was **Else Heims**.*

Made English-language movies while in exile in the U.S.: The Hitler Gang (1944); None But the Lonely Heart (1944); Cloak and Dagger (1946); The Locket (1947).

An acclaimed theatrical star and a member of one of Central Europe's great acting families, Helene Thimig had a career that lasted more than six decades. She was born in 1889 in Vienna, the daughter of Hugo Thimig and **Fanny Hummel Thimig**. Hugo was not only a renowned actor but the director of Vienna's Burgtheater, the leading theater in German-speaking Central Europe. After studying with *Hedwig Bleibtreu, Helene Thimig made her debut in Baden bei Wien in 1907 and for the next several years was apprenticed with Germany's Meiningen Players, a troupe whose innovative

naturalistic style of acting was seen by Constantin Stanislavski who then went on to found the Moscow Arts Theater. By 1911, Thimig had moved to Berlin, where she caught the eye of the brilliant director and fellow Austrian Max Reinhardt. Soon, their relationship was much more than professional, but it would be many years before they married. In 1917, Thimig became one of the stars of Reinhardt's Deutsches Theater, Berlin's most innovative stage.

By the early 1920s, German critics were unanimous in their praise of Thimig in such roles as Gretchen in Goethe's *Faust*, Solveig in Ibsen's *Peer Gynt*, and Elisabeth in Schiller's *Maria Stuart*. From 1920 onward, she worked for Reinhardt at the Salzburg Festival, most memorably in the morality play *Jedermann* (Everyman), the annual festival production which she was to perform in until the early 1930s, and then help revive and once more star in for many years after World War II. Among the most exciting productions were those in which Thimig appeared on stage with members of her family. These included Schiller's *Kabale und Liebe* (Conspiracy and Love), in which her father Hugo appeared as stage father to her Luisa. In 1926, the Thimigs made stage history at Vien-

Helene Thimig

na's Theater in der Josefstadt, one of Max Reinhardt's newest theaters, when she appeared in a Nestroy farce with three members of her family: her father Hugo, as well as her brothers Hans and Hermann. This combination was to recur several times, most notably in a celebrated revival of Goldoni's *A Servant of Two Masters*, in which she shined as Smeralda. She and the other Thimigs also toured the United States during the 1927–28 season.

Along with Max Reinhardt, Helene Thimig was at the center of a circle of intellectuals and artists in interwar Berlin and Vienna. She created many roles in world premieres of plays, and among those written with her in mind were such important works as Hugo von Hofmannsthal's *Der Schwierige* and Max Mell's *Das Apostelspiel*. At the same time, Thimig insisted on continuing her appearances in the standard repertory, particularly in Shakespeare.

From 1933 through 1937, Thimig and Reinhardt lived in Austria; her close ties to Reinhardt, who was Jewish (she was not), had terminated her career in a now-Nazified Germany. Besides being featured on Viennese stages and at the Salzburg Festival, Thimig appeared in theaters in Prague. In 1935, while on an extended visit to the United States, Thimig and Reinhardt married in Nevada. In 1937, they immigrated to California. In 1939, she received special permission from Nazi leader Hermann Göring to make a brief visit to her aged father in Vienna. Although highly respected in America, Max was unable to earn the income to which he had been accustomed in Europe. Helene helped support him and herself by teaching at his Hollywood "Max Reinhardt Workshop for Stage, Screen and Radio," an actors' studio which was as luminous artistically as it was dismal financially. To pay bills, she appeared in many small roles in B-films, including *The Hitler Gang* (1944), in which she portrayed Adolf Hitler's half-sister **Angela Raubal**. Many of Thimig's California friends were Jewish refugee artists, among them *Salka Viertel, whose salon was a reminder of Central Europe in the alien world of southern California. Thimig appeared at several refugee benefits, including some sponsored by the Los Angeles refugee organization, the "Jewish Club of 1933."

Max Reinhardt died in New York City in October 1943. Three years later, Helene Thimig returned to Austria, where she immediately resumed her career both in Vienna's Burgtheater and at the revived Salzburg Festival, which the Nazi occupation had "Aryanized." She also taught acting both at Vienna's renowned

Hochschule für Musik und Darstellende Kunst (Academy of Music and Performing Arts) and at a revived version of the famous "Reinhardt Seminar" for aspiring actors in Salzburg's Schloss Leopoldskron that her late husband had founded and led half a century before. Profoundly respected, Helene Thimig died in Vienna on November 6, 1974.

SOURCES:

Adler, Gusti. *. . . aber vergessen Sie nicht die chinesischen Nachtigallen: Erinnerungen an Max Reinhardt.* Munich: Langen Müller, 1980.

Bier, Marcus, *et al. Schauspielportraits: 24 Schauspieler um Max Reinhardt.* Berlin: Verlag Hentrich, 1989.

Carter, Huntly. *The Theater of Max Reinhardt.* NY: Benjamin Blom, 1964.

Ebert, Gerhard. *Schauspieler werden in Berlin: Von Max Reinhardts Schauspielschule zur Hochschule für Schauspielkunst Ernst Busch.* Berlin: Berlin-Information, 1987.

Fetting, Hugo, ed. *Leben für das Theater: Briefe, Reden, Aufsätze, Interviews, Auszüge aus Regiebüchern [von Max Reinhardt].* Berlin: Argon, 1989.

Fiedler, Leonhard M. *Max Reinhardt in Selbstzeugnissen und Bilddokumenten.* Reinbek bei Hamburg: Ernst Rowohlt, 1975.

Fuhrich, Edda, and Gisela Prossnitz. *Max Reinhardt: ". . . ein Theater, das den Menschen wieder Freude gibt"—Eine Ausstellung der Max Reinhardt-Forschungsstätte, Salzburg.* Vienna: Österreichisches Theatermuseum, 1983.

"Helene Thimig," in *The Times* [London]. November 19, 1974, p. 17.

"Helene Thimig Dies; Viennese Actress," in *The New York Times Biographical Edition.* November 1974, p. 1635.

Hofmannsthal, Hugo von. *Prosa III.* Frankfurt am Main: S. Fischer, 1964.

Jacobs, Margaret, and John Warren, eds. *Max Reinhardt: The Oxford Symposium.* Oxford: Oxford Polytechnic, 1986.

Kaindl-Hönig, Max, ed. *Resonanz: 50 Jahre Kritik der Salzburger Festspiele.* Salzburg: SN/Salzburger Nachrichten, 1971.

Leisler, Edda, and Gisela Prossnitz, eds. *Max Reinhardt in Amerika.* Salzburg: Otto Müller, 1973.

New York Cultural Center. *Max Reinhardt, 1873–1973: An Exhibition Commemorating the Hundredth Anniversary of His Birth, June 7 through August 4, 1974.* Edited by Alfred G. Brooks. NY: New York Cultural Center, 1974.

"Register: Gestorben," in *Der Spiegel.* Vol. 28, no. 46. November 11, 1974, p. 204.

Reinhardt, Gottfried. *The Genius: A Memoir of Max Reinhardt.* NY: Alfred A. Knopf, 1979.

Sayler, Oliver M. *Max Reinhardt and His Theater.* Trans. by Mariele S. Gudernatsch and others. Rep. ed. NY: Benjamin Blom, 1968.

Schwiefert, Fritz. *Helene Thimig.* Berlin: Erich Reiss, 1923.

Steinberg, Michael P. *The Meaning of the Salzburg Festival: Austria as Theater and Ideology, 1890–1938.* Ithaca, NY: Cornell University Press, 1990.

Styan, J.L. *Max Reinhardt.* Cambridge: Cambridge University Press, 1982.

"Thimig, Helene," in Frithjof Trapp, *et al.*, eds. *Handbuch des deutschsprachigen Exiltheaters 1933–1945, Band 2: Biographisches Lexikon der Theaterkünstler, Teil 2, L–Z.* Munich: K.G. Saur, 1999, pp. 938–939.

Thimig-Reinhardt, Helene. *Wie Max Reinhardt lebte: Ein Handbreit über dem Boden.* Frankfurt am Main: Fischer, 1975.

Warren, John. "Max Reinhardt and the Viennese Theater of the Interwar Years," in *Maske und Kothurn.* Vol. 29, no. 1–4, 1983, pp. 123–136.

Wellwarth, George E. *et al.*, eds. *Max Reinhardt, 1873–1973: A Centennial Festschrift of Memorial Essays and Interviews on the One Hundredth Anniversary of His Birth.* Binghamton, NY: Max Reinhardt Archiv, 1973.

Wurm, Ernst. *Helene Thimig: Bildnis einer Persönlichkeit.* Vienna: Österreichischer Bundesverlag, 1969.

RELATED MEDIA:

Roszak, Jo. "Max Reinhardt: Mediator between Dream and Reality" (video), Cologne: Deutsche Welle TV, 1993.

"Von Fritz Kortner bis Curt Bois: Historische Aufnahmen der Reinhardt-Bühne, 2" (compact disc), original recordings, 1907–78, of performances of actors associated with Max Reinhardt, including Helene Thimig, Düsseldorf: Patmos PT 1255, 1999.

John Haag,
Associate Professor of History,
University of Georgia,
Athens, Georgia

Thirkell, Angela (1890–1961)

English novelist and short-story writer. Name variations: (pseudonym) Leslie Parker. Born Margaret Angela Mackail on January 30, 1890, in London, England; died on January 30, 1961, in Bramley, England; daughter of John W. Mackail (a professor of poetry); educated privately; married James Campbell McInnes (a singer), in 1911 (divorced 1917); married George Thirkell (in the military), in 1918 (divorced 1929); children: (first marriage) Graham, Colin, and one daughter (died); (second marriage) Lance.

Novels, except as noted: (memoirs) Three Houses *(Oxford University Press, 1931);* Ankle Deep *(Hamish Hamilton, 1933);* High Rising *(Hamish Hamilton, 1933);* Wild Strawberries *(Hamish Hamilton, 1933);* The Demon in the House *(Hamish Hamilton, 1934); (under pseudonym Leslie Parker)* Trooper to the Southern Cross *(Hamish Hamilton, 1934, republished under the name Angela Thirkell, Virago, 1985);* O These Men, These Men *(Hamish Hamilton, 1935);* The Grateful Sparrow *(Hamish Hamilton, 1935);* August Folly *(Hamish Hamilton, 1936);* Coronation Summer *(Oxford University Press, 1937);* Summer Half *(Hamish Hamilton, 1937);* Pomfret Towers *(Hamish Hamilton, 1938);* The Brandons *(Hamish Hamilton, 1939);* Before Lunch *(Hamish Hamilton, 1939);* Cheerfulness Breaks In *(Hamish Hamilton, 1940);* Marling Hall *(Hamish Hamilton, 1942);* The Headmistress *(Hamish Hamilton, 1944);* Northbridge Rectory *(Hamish Hamilton, 1944);* Miss Bunting *(Hamish Hamilton, 1945);* Peace Breaks Out *(Hamish Hamilton, 1947);* Private Enterprise *(Hamish Hamilton, 1947);* Love among Ruins *(Hamish Hamilton, 1948);* The Old Bank House *(Hamish Hamilton, 1949);* County Chronicle *(Hamish Hamilton, 1950);* The Duke's Daughter *(Hamish Hamilton, 1951);* Happy Returns *(Hamish Hamilton, 1952);* Jutland Cottage *(Hamish Hamilton, 1953);* What Did It Mean? *(Hamish Hamilton, 1954);* Enter Sir Robert *(Hamish Hamilton, 1955);* Never Too Late *(Hamish Hamilton, 1956);* A Double Affair *(Hamish Hamilton, 1957);* Close Quarters *(Hamish Hamilton, 1958);* Love at All Ages *(Hamish Hamilton, 1959);* Three Score and Ten *(Hamish Hamilton, 1961);* An Angela Thirkell Omnibus *(Hamish Hamilton, 1966);* A Second Angela Thirkell Omnibus *(Hamish Hamilton, 1967);* The Brandons, and Others *(Hamish Hamilton, 1968).*

Also author of The Fortunes of Harriette: The Surprising Career of Harriette Wilson *(1936). Contributor of short stories to periodicals in Australia and Great Britain.*

British author Angela Thirkell was a prolific novelist whose career spanned some three decades. Between the 1930s and 1950s, her books were popular with audiences in both Great Britain and the United States. For her settings, Thirkell borrowed 18th-century novelist Anthony Trollope's fictional Bartsetshire, but she wrote predominantly about characters in modern times. Nevertheless, critics often compared her gentle, humorous tone to that of another 18th-century novelist, *Jane Austen. Some of Thirkell's better-known novels include *Pomfret Towers, The Brandons* and *Marling Hall,* and several of her books remain in print. She is also well known for the memoir of her childhood, *Three Houses.*

Angela Thirkell was born Angela Margaret Mackail on January 30, 1890, in London, England. The daughter of a poetry professor, she was also the granddaughter of Pre-Raphaelite artist Edward Burne-Jones, who would draw pictures for her at her request during her childhood. Thirkell was also related to the famous British writer Rudyard Kipling, and spent a great deal of time with his daughter **Josephine Kipling**; the two girls were the trial audience for Kipling's *Just So Stories.* Thirkell recalls these and other experiences in detail in *Three Houses,* first published in 1931.

In 1911, Thirkell married a famed singer, James Campbell McInnes. Though the couple had three children—one of whom died in infancy—they were divorced in 1917. She married again the following year, to George Thirkell, an Australian military man. The Thirkells traveled to Australia in a troopship in 1920, an experience upon which Angela Thirkell would later base her 1934 novel *Trooper to the Southern Cross*. The couple lived for a while in Tasmania before settling in Melbourne, where Angela became a member of the higher social circles, friend to such Australian notables as Dame *Nellie Melba, Sir John Monash, and Thea Parker.

Partly because of a desire to write and partly because of a need to earn money, Thirkell began writing short stories while living in Melbourne. She managed to get some of her works published in periodicals in both Australia and England. Thirkell gave birth to another son in 1921, although her marriage was troubled. When her husband's business failed because of the Great Depression, she left him and returned to England in 1929.

Shortly after, Thirkell published her book of memoirs, *Three Houses*, which Dennis Drabelle later praised in the *Washington Post Book World* as "a genial exercise in nostalgia for a time when houses were enormous, children scampered through them in disregard of nannies and art popped up everywhere." In 1933, readers saw a virtual explosion of novels from Thirkell—*Ankle Deep*, *High Rising*, and *Wild Strawberries*, all published by Hamish Hamilton. She continued to publish one or more novels each year, with few exceptions, until her death in 1961. She did take some time off from her busy writing schedule in 1949, however, to travel to the United States and give lectures at Yale and Columbia universities.

SOURCES AND SUGGESTED READING:

McInnes, Graham. *The Road to Gundagai.* Hamish Hamilton, 1965.
Strickland, Margot. *Angela Thirkell, Portrait of a Lady Novelist.* Duckworth, 1977.
Washington Post Book World. February 8, 1987, p. 8.

Thiroux d'Arconville, Marie-Geneviève-Charlotte d'Arlus

(1720–1805).

See d'Arconville, Geneviève.

Thoburn, Isabella (1840–1901)

American Methodist evangelist, missionary, and educator. Born on March 29, 1840, near St. Clairsville, Ohio; died on September 1, 1901, in Lucknow, India; ninth of ten children of Matthew Thoburn (d. 1850, a farmer) and Jane Lyle (Crawford) Thoburn; educated at Wheeling Female Seminary in Wheeling, Virginia (now West Virginia); spent one year at Cincinnati Academy of Design.

Taught in several public and private schools; went to India as missionary (1869); began work in Lucknow (1870); opened the Lal Bagh Boarding School (1871); served as principal of girls' school in Cawnpore (1874); returned to the U.S. on furlough to travel and lecture on missionary work (1880–82); Lal Bagh became the Girls' High School and added collegiate department (1887); during second furlough, worked in Chicago with Lucy Meyer and taught at the Chicago Training School for City, Home, and Foreign Missions (1887–88); in Cincinnati, helped organize the Elizabeth Gamble Deaconess Home and Training School and helped direct Christ Hospital; returned to Lucknow and Lal Bagh (late 1890); helped establish the Wellesley School for girls in Naini Tal (1891); Lal Bagh added a teachers' course and kindergarten (1893); granted charter for Lucknow Woman's College (1895); made fund-raising tour of the United States (1899–1900); Lucknow Woman's College renamed Isabella Thoburn College (1903), and later became women's college of Lucknow University.

Isabella Thoburn's missionary work took her halfway around the world to the country of India, and she devoted most of her evangelical life there to opening up educational opportunities for girls and young women. Born in St. Clairsville, Ohio, in 1840 and raised a Methodist, she entered the Wheeling Female Seminary in Wheeling, Virginia (now West Virginia) at age 14. She completed the course and became a teacher in Ohio, then returned to the seminary for a self-directed course of study. She attended the Cincinnati Academy of Design for one year as an art student, then worked for several years as a teacher in Wheeling, Virginia, New Castle, Pennsylvania, and at Western Reserve Seminary, a Methodist school in West Farmington, Ohio.

In 1859, Thoburn's brother James went to India to work as a Methodist missionary. He became convinced that the church needed women missionaries to reach the women of India, and in 1866 wrote to Thoburn, who had joined the church when she was 19, suggesting that she join him. She was willing, but reluctant to come without formal authorization of the Methodist Church, which as yet had no agency to send out female missionaries. That changed in 1869 when the Women's Foreign Missionary Society of the Methodist Church was formed in Boston; one of its first undertakings was to send Thoburn to India. Accompanied by Dr. *Clara A. Swain, who was sent to provide medical help to the women of India, she sailed from New York City, arriving in Bombay on January 7, 1870. Thoburn was assigned to the city of Lucknow, where her brother had just been appointed presiding elder of the province of Oudh.

She began her evangelistic work in the women's quarters of private houses while looking for a place to start a school for girls. In April she opened her first school, in a small room rented in the middle of the bazaar, with six Christian girls, four of them Hindustanis. Two months later, her class had grown to 17 pupils, and by the end of the first year, the school required its own building. This was provided by the Women's Foreign Missionary Society in 1871, when it purchased a palatial seven-acre property named Lal Bagh, meaning Ruby Garden, that had once belonged to an official in the court of the last king of Oudh. This expanded space made it possible for Thoburn to accept boarding students, a new concept in missionary work at the time, and to provide education in a Christian environment to a larger number of girls. Located between the English and Hindustani Methodist churches, Lal Bagh became the headquarters of women's missionary work in Lucknow, a center for missionary families in the city and province, and a hostel for visiting church workers.

Along with directing Lal Bagh, Thoburn taught Sunday school classes for poor children, mostly Eurasian children of mixed European and Asian ancestry, and later for poor Hindu girls as well. She also directed a group of women evangelists known as "Bible Readers." In 1874, she added to this work the job of principal of a girls' school in Cawnpore, 45 miles from Lucknow. She not only evangelized, she practiced what she preached. Her students could come to her with any problem, and she would help and care for them. She consciously set an example for both the Christian workers under her directorship and the girls in Meyer's schools. Both friends and acquaintances were deeply impressed by her selfless service, and she emphasized Christian community to overcome the differences of caste and race.

In 1880, Thoburn suffered ill health and returned to the United States, ostensibly to recuperate. She had little rest, however, because she engaged in a speaking tour that took her all over the country. She returned to Lal Bagh in 1882 and resumed her role of principal, adding a "normal" class to prepare girls for evangelistic work. Her health began to fail again two years

later, and she was granted a second furlough in 1886 that lasted until 1890. During that time she became active in the new deaconess movement in the Methodist Church, which enlisted women for service in social institutions such as hospitals and orphanages. She worked for a year with *Lucy Meyer as a teacher in her Chicago Training School for City, Home, and Foreign Missions and as a chaperon for some of her recruits. In December 1888, she was called to Cincinnati, Ohio, to organize and superintend the new Elizabeth Gamble Deaconess Home and oversee its expansion to include Christ Hospital.

Late in 1890, Thoburn returned to Lucknow. In her absence, Lal Bagh had become the Girls' High School and had expanded to include more Eurasian and European students, as well as non-Christian students. In 1887, as a result of a suggestion made by Thoburn before her departure, a collegiate department had been added to meet the need for higher studies for girls. Although it started out with only three students and was slow to grow, it eventually became Lucknow Woman's College. When Thoburn returned, Lal Bagh had 160 pupils, including 96 boarders. Her responsibilities included developing the college, service in the local Hindustani Methodist church, helping to establish the Wellesley School for girls in Naini Tal in 1891, and editing a semimonthly Hindi-language paper for mothers and children called *Rafiq-i-Niswan* (Woman's Friend). In 1893, the school added a teachers' class and a kindergarten department.

The government granted the college a charter in 1895, and the new building required so much capital that Thoburn was sent to America in 1899 to raise funds. She traveled in the company of **Lilavati Singh**, one of her graduates and teachers, and toured the country, making a lasting impression on audiences. They returned to India and Lucknow in 1900. In the summer of 1901, Thoburn resumed her work but suffered a sudden attack of cholera shortly afterward and died at the school at age 61. Her burial in Lucknow cemetery drew a large crowd of mourners. In 1903, Lucknow Woman's College was renamed Isabella Thoburn College; it later became the women's college of Lucknow University.

SOURCES:

James, Edward T., ed. *Notable American Women, 1607–1950.* Cambridge, MA: The Belknap Press of Harvard University, 1971.

McHenry, Robert, ed. *Famous American Women.* NY: Dover, 1980.

Malinda Mayer,
writer and editor,
Falmouth, Massachusetts

Thoc-me-tony (1844–1891).

See Winnemucca, Sarah.

Thomas, Mrs. Albert (1900–1993).

See Thomas, Lera Millard.

Thomas, Alma (1891–1978)

African-American teacher and painter. Born on September 22, 1891, in Columbus, Georgia; died on February 25, 1978; daughter of John Harris Thomas (a businessman) and Amelia (Cantey) Thomas (a teacher); graduated from Miner Teachers Normal School; Howard University, B.S., 1924; graduated from Columbia University Graduate School, 1934.

Taught art classes at Shaw Junior High School, Washington, D.C. (1924–60); painted series of works, including Earth Paintings *and* Space Paintings; *held a solo exhibition, Du Pont Theater Art Gallery, Washington, D.C. (1960); exhibited at the Whitney Museum, New York City (1972).*

African-American visual artist Alma Thomas was born in 1891 to a middle-class family in Columbus, Georgia, the oldest of four girls. She grew up in rural Georgia, then moved with her family to Washington, D.C., in 1906. Thomas became interested in painting at Armstrong Technical High School, but planned a career in education and completed teacher preparation at Miner Teachers Normal School. She then taught art and theater at the Thomas Garrett Settlement House for several years in Wilmington, Delaware, before entering Howard University where she continued her studies in the visual arts under James Vernon Herring. She was the first graduate of Howard's art program in 1924. Her works from this period are realistic and brought her little critical recognition.

After graduating from Howard, Thomas became a teacher in Washington public schools, primarily teaching art at the elementary level. She completed a master's degree at Columbia University in 1934, and took additional courses in painting at American University in Washington, all the while continuing to teach. In the 1940s, Thomas became associated with the Barnett-Aden Gallery, an artistic center which played an important role in the development of African-American visual culture.

Thomas retired from teaching in 1960, and began to paint full time. In that year she was given her first solo exhibition, at the Du Pont Theater Art Gallery in Washington. While confined to her bedroom after developing severe arthritis, Thomas began to see the patterns of color and light in the gardens outside her window in new ways. This change in perception led to dramatic changes in her painting styles as she experimented with abstract artistic styles. Rather than trying to represent exactly what she saw, Thomas began to work with bright dabs and strokes of pigment reminiscent of the Impressionist school. Her new work brought considerable critical acclaim. In 1969 and 1970, she was invited to display her work in the Nixon White House in addition to many art gallery shows. In 1972, the Whitney Museum in New York mounted a solo exhibition of her paintings; after this exhibition Thomas was an undeniably important part of both Washington, D.C., and the national artistic community. Despite suffering from crippling arthritis, Thomas continued to paint regularly until her death in 1978, at age 86, following surgery.

SOURCES:

Bailey, Brooke. *The Remarkable Lives of 100 Women Artists.* Holbrook, MA: Bob Adams, 1994.

Smith, Jessie Carney, ed. *Notable Black American Women.* Detroit, MI: Gale Research, 1992.

Laura York, M.A. in History, University of California, Riverside, California

Thomas, Caitlin (1913–1994)

British poet. Born Caitlin Macnamara on December 8, 1913, in London, England; died on July 31, 1994, in Catania, Sicily, Italy; daughter of Francis Macnamara (an artist) and Yvonne (Majolier) Macnamara; married Dylan Thomas (the poet), on July 11, 1937 (died 1953); lived with or married Guiseppe Fazio (a film director); children: (with Dylan Thomas) Llewelyn (b. 1939), Aeronwyn (b. 1943), Colm (b. 1949); (with Giuseppe Fazio) Francesco Thomas (b. 1963).

Best known as the wife of poet Dylan Thomas but a poet in her own right, Caitlin Thomas was born in 1913 in London, the youngest child of **Yvonne Majolier Macnamara** and Irish artist Francis Macnamara. She grew up in Hampshire, England, after her father abandoned the family, although he remained in contact with his children. In her teens, Caitlin became an art model for her neighbor, the painter Augustus John, and the two had a brief affair. She also had a brief career as a dancer.

In 1936, she met the young Welsh poet Dylan Thomas, already a published writer at age 24 and gaining critical recognition. The couple married in 1937 and settled in Laugharne, Wales, where their first child, Llewelyn, was born in 1939. Two more children, daughter **Aeronwyn Thomas** and son Colm Thomas, followed in 1943 and 1949. The marriage of Caitlin and Dylan Thomas was stormy from the beginning, burdened by financial crises, a growing family, and their joint abuse of alcohol. Both Dylan and Caitlin had numerous extramarital affairs which, combined with other pressures, led to increasingly bitter arguments and periods of separation. Caitlin also wrote poetry, but resented her husband's fame and held him responsible for the fact that she was never recognized for her writing.

Although Dylan Thomas had steady employment with Strand Films during World War II and became more well known with the publication of each new collection of poetry or short stories, the Thomases continued to struggle with poverty and high debts, and the family was forced to move frequently. In the early 1950s, the marriage collapsed entirely, though they did not divorce. Dylan Thomas died unexpectedly (after downing 18 whiskies) while on a lecture tour in New York in November 1953; Caitlin, informed of his collapse, had landed in New York in time to see him before he died but there was no reconciliation, as she reveals in her memoirs.

Friends of the couple established a trust fund to manage the income from Thomas' royalties for the widow and her three minor children. With the rise in sales of Thomas' books after his death, the family was, for the first time, comfortably well off. In 1957, Caitlin moved to Catania, Sicily, where she began an affair with the Sicilian film director Giuseppe Fazio. That same year she published the first of her memoirs, *Left Over Life to Kill*, recalling her bitter memories of her marriage. A second book, *Not Quite Posthumous Letter to My Daughter*, was published in 1963; neither book was well received. Her son with Fazio, Francesco, was also born in 1963; Caitlin infuriated her lover by giving the boy the last name Thomas, which she herself had kept. Still battling alcoholism, Caitlin lived out the rest of her years in relative obscurity with Fazio in Sicily. A third book of memoirs, *Life With Dylan Thomas*, appeared in 1986. She died at age 80 in 1994. As she had wished, she was buried beside the grave of Dylan Thomas in Laugharne, Wales.

SOURCES:

Ferris, Paul. *Caitlin: The Life of Caitlin Thomas*. London: Pimlico, 1995.

FitzGibbon, Constantine. *The Life of Dylan Thomas*. London: J.M. Dent, 1965.

Laura York, M.A. in History, University of California, Riverside, California

Caitlin and Dylan Thomas

Thomas, Carey (1857–1935).

See Thomas, M. Carey.

Thomas, Debi (1967—)

Figure skater who was the first African-American to win a medal at any Winter Olympics. Born on March 25, 1967, in Poughkeepsie, New York; daughter of McKinley Thomas (a program manager) and Janice Thomas (a computer analyst); trained with Alex McGowan; Stanford University, B.A., 1991; attended Northwestern University Medical School; married Brian Vanden Hogen, on March 15, 1988 (divorced); married Christopher Bequette (an attorney), in 1997; children: (second marriage) Luc (b. 1997).

Won both U.S. and World championships (1986); won U.S. championship (1988); won bronze medal, Winter Olympics, Calgary, Canada (1988); won bronze medal, World Figure Skating championships, Budapest, Hungary (1988).

American figure skater Debi Thomas made history at Calgary Olympics in 1988 when her bronze-medal win made her the first African-American in history to medal at any Winter Games. As the first black athlete to skate at a level of world competition, she captured the national spotlight with a stunning combination of athleticism and grace. Unlike many skaters who go on from Olympic victories to lucrative careers in ice shows, Thomas then traded her sequins in for scrubs, becoming an aspiring orthopedic surgeon.

She was born on March 25, 1967, in Poughkeepsie, New York. Her mother **Janice Thomas**, a computer analyst, and her father McKinley Thomas, a program manager, divorced while Debi was still young. While raising her two children, Janice exposed them to opera, ballet, and ice shows. A clown performer on the ice caught Debi's attention, and at five she began taking skating lessons. Her first victory in competition, at age nine, solidified her passion for the sport. The Scottish coach Alex McGowan became her trainer the following year, and she made her first successful triple jump at age 11. After winning a silver medal in the novice class at 12, Thomas left school in order to train for the national junior championship. The year 1980 proved a disappointment, however, and she did not advance

Debi
Thomas

to the nationals. She made the decision to return to school, later telling *Time*, "I wasn't going to put the rest of my life on the line in front of some panel of judges who just might not like my yellow dress."

There were also financial realities which she had to confront. Notes Anne Janette Johnson: "Her family was not wealthy, and the considerable training costs—sometimes as much as $25,000 a year—put a burden on Janice Thomas especially. Often Debi would have to forego training in the summertime so her mother could catch up on the bills. Debi was also famous for making her own costumes, and for using worn-out skates until they crumbled." While she attended San Mateo High School, her mother drove her 150 miles a day so that she could practice at Redwood City Ice Lodge. "My mom made all the sacrifices that allowed me to reach my potential," said Thomas.

Thomas excelled not only in the rink but also in the classroom, earning acceptance to Stanford, Harvard, and Princeton. When asked

on her application to Stanford, the school she chose to attend, to provide a description of herself, Thomas wrote "invincible." In 1986, she was in the pre-med program at Stanford when she won the national championships. Thomas turned heads when she beat East Germany's *Katarina Witt to win the World championship six months later. Unwilling to stop her studies to train full time, Thomas proved unable to hold her titles in 1987 (the national title went to Jill Trenary; the world title to Witt). These losses prompted Thomas to take a year off from Stanford to begin practicing with her coach six days a week at the Olympic training facility in Boulder, Colorado. Among those with whom Thomas worked was the former Olympic champion *Peggy Fleming and the American Ballet Theater dancer George de la Pena, who had been sent by Mikhail Baryshnikov after Thomas went to Baryshnikov for advice. Regaining her national title in 1988, Thomas was one of the favorites going into the Winter Olympics.

The women's figure-skating finals in Calgary were to become known as the "battle of the Carmens," because, purely by coincidence, both Thomas and Witt skated to music based on the opera *Carmen* for their long programs. Witt, skating first, performed with her trademark artistry and landed all her jumps. Witt's jumps were conservative, however, opening the door to the gold medal for Thomas if she could land her more difficult jumps. Thomas, whom James Page called "[p]erhaps the most physically powerful performer ever seen in figure skating," fell out of a jump early in her program, landing on both feet, and after that, notes Johnson, "the heart seemed to go out of her performance." Witt took the gold, while Canada's Elizabeth Manley won the silver. A disappointed Thomas took home the bronze.

After four years of skating with Stars on Ice, Thomas turned in her skates so as to dedicate herself fully to medical school. Like winning an Olympic medal, becoming a doctor was a childhood ambition, and Thomas began studying orthopedic surgery at Northwestern University Medical School in Chicago. With a desire to specialize in sports medicine, she set her sights on having her own training complex, complete with ice rink, ballet room, weight room, and sports-medicine clinic. In 1997, she married attorney Christopher Bequette and had a son named Luc (Thomas' first marriage to Brian Vanden Hogen in 1988 had ended in divorce after three years). Showing continuing interest in perhaps pursuing yet another childhood dream, in 1995 Thomas made a visit to a NASA training center in consideration of becoming a candidate for astronaut training. "I tell people I'm too stupid to know what's impossible," she remarked to *Time* in 1996. "I had ridiculously large dreams, and half the time they came true."

SOURCES:

Johnson, Anne Janette. *Great Women in Sports*. Detroit, MI: Visible Ink, 1998.
Page, James A. *Black Olympian Medalists*. Libraries Unlimited, 1991.
Time. April 1, 1996, p. 25.
Tresniowski, Alex, and Luchina Fisher. "Spin Doctor," in *People Weekly*. September 16, 1996.

Thomas, Edith Matilda
(1854–1925)

American poet and translator. Born on August 12, 1854, in Chatham, Ohio; died on September 13, 1925, in New York City; daughter of Frederick Thomas and Jane (Sturges) Thomas; never married; no children.

Edith Thomas was one of the best-known American poets at the turn of the 20th century. Born in 1854 into a farming family in Chatham, Ohio, Thomas lost her father in 1861. Her mother raised Thomas and her sister in Bowling Green and Geneva, Ohio, where Thomas graduated from the Geneva Normal Institute in 1872. A dedicated student who excelled in classical literature, Thomas then briefly attended Oberlin College but dropped out to teach school.

She enjoyed writing even as a child, and with the support of her family she composed poetry for publication in local newspapers. Her uncle James Thomas took her in 1881 to New York, where she met the renowned poet *Helen Hunt Jackson; Jackson's public admiration for Thomas' verse helped Thomas secure publication in New York magazines and launched her professional career. Her poetry was first published in book form in 1885, in *A New Year's Masque*; subsequent collections, including *The Inverted Torch* (1890) and *The Guest at the Gate* (1909), would appear regularly over the next 30 years. In 1887, following her mother's death, Thomas moved to New York; she was much in demand by New York publishers for her verses, which were classic both in form and subject. Thomas looked to nature, to 19th-century European poets, and to classical Greek verse for inspiration. Her work was often published, most notably in *Century* and *Atlantic Monthly* among other literary periodicals, and she moved among New York's literary elite prior to World War I. She also composed poetry for children and prose on subjects ranging from nature to literary criticism to philosophy.

After the outbreak of the war, Thomas began editing work in addition to composition, editing *Harper's* magazine and the *Century Dictionary* until the time of her death in 1925. Consistently referred to by contemporary critics as one of America's finest living poets, Thomas suffered from ill health in her last years and her once-prolific output declined. She died from heart disease in her Harlem, New York, apartment in 1925, at age 71, and was buried in her hometown of Chatham.

SOURCES:

James, Edward T., ed. *Notable American Women, 1607–1950.* Cambridge, MA: The Belknap Press of Harvard University, 1971.

Rittenhouse, Jessie B., ed. *Selected Poems of Edith M. Thomas, edited with a memoir by Jessie B. Rittenhouse.* NY: Harper, 1926.

Laura York, M.A. in History,
University of California,
Riverside, California

Thomas, Edna (1886–1974)

African-American actress. Born Edna Lewis in 1886 in Lawrenceville, Virginia; died of heart disease on July 22, 1974, in New York City; married Lloyd Thomas.

Debuted in Turn to the Right, *Lafayette Players (1920); appeared as Lady Macbeth (1936); appeared in* Androcles and the Lion *with Dooley Wilson (1938), in* Harriet *with Helen Hayes (1944–45), in* Strange Fruit *(1945), and on Broadway and in the film* A Streetcar Named Desire *(1946).*

The stage and screen actress Edna Thomas made her name as part of the Harlem Renaissance. Little is known about her early life or education except that she was born in 1886 and raised in Virginia. She began performing in 1920 with the Lafayette Players, a touring dramatic troupe. She had moved to New York by the early 1920s, joining the resurgence of African-American literature, music, and drama known as the Harlem Renaissance. She performed in all-black theaters and vaudeville productions, perhaps most notably in *Comedy of Errors* in 1923 and *Porgy* in 1927. Like Langston Hughes and other figures of the Harlem Renaissance, Thomas enjoyed the support and friendship of the important white patron Carl Van Vechten, with whom she corresponded regularly. Opportunities for black actors fell drastically during the Depression, but Thomas' seasoned professionalism and reputation secured her roles in several productions in the early 1930s, including *Comedy of Errors, Lulu Belle*, and *Shuffle Along*, and leading roles in Hall Johnson's *Run, Little Chillun* (1933) and Paul Peters' *Stevedore* (1934). She also sang and performed in vaudeville.

Edna Thomas reached the height of her fame when she played Lady Macbeth in the Works Progress Administration (WPA)'s Federal Theater Project production of *Macbeth* in 1936–37. Directed by Orson Welles, the all-black cast received rave reviews in the New York press; Thomas' performance was hailed as "sensitive and magnificent." She went on to perform again with the Federal Theater Project in *Androcles and the Lion* with Dooley Wilson. The closing of the Project proved a hardship to Thomas and hundreds of other African-American actors; her next major role came in 1943 when she was cast in the Broadway play *Harriet*, about abolitionist *Harriet Beecher Stowe (portrayed by *Helen Hayes). Thomas appeared the following year on Broadway in *Strange Fruit*, an adaptation of *Lillian Smith's controversial novel about interracial relationships. In 1946, the light-skinned Thomas performed in her final Broadway production, playing a Mexican woman in *A Streetcar Named Desire*; she was also cast in the same role for the 1951 Hollywood film, her only movie credit. Thomas then retired from acting and spent her last years in New York, where she died at age 88 in 1974.

SOURCES:

Gill, Glenda E. *White Grease Paint on Black Performers: A Study of the Federal Theater, 1935–1939.* NY: P. Lang, 1988.

Smith, Jessie Carney, ed. *Notable Black American Women.* Detroit, MI: Gale Research, 1992.

Laura York, M.A. in History,
University of California,
Riverside, California

Thomas, Elizabeth (1675–1731)

British poet. Name variations: (pseudonym) Corinna. Born in 1675 (one source cites 1677) in England; died on February 5, 1731, in London, England; daughter of Emmanuel Thomas (a lawyer) and Elizabeth (Osborne) Thomas.

Selected writings (under pseudonym Corinna): Miscellany Poems on Several Subjects *(1722);* Codrus, or the Dunciad Dissected *(1729).*

British poet Elizabeth Thomas was born in 1675, the daughter of **Elizabeth Osborne Thomas** and Emmanuel Thomas, a respected lawyer. Emmanuel's death in 1677 left the family with few financial resources, and Elizabeth, though she did have some tutors, apparently was mostly self-taught in languages and literature. When she was a young adult, her middle-class birth allowed her to join a circle of London writers and to correspond with patrons and poets across England, including the feminist writers *Mary Lee Chudleigh and *Mary Astell, with whom she exchanged poems. At age 24, Thomas impressed the celebrated poet John Dryden when she sent him several verses, and they began a long correspondence. It was Dryden who suggested to Thomas the pen name "Corinna," which she would use the rest of her life. Her first published poems appeared in 1700 in *Luctus Britannici*, a collection of elegies on Dryden's death. Her other literary acquaintances included the poets Henry Cromwell and Alexander Pope. Thomas was published little during her life and was never financially successful, depending on gifts from admirers to support herself and her ailing mother. She never married, although she was engaged for many years to lawyer Richard Gwinnett of Gloucestershire. On his death in 1717, he bequeathed Thomas a small sum of money; she used the money, albeit ineffectively, to reduce some of the debt of her recently deceased mother.

In 1722, a book of her *Miscellany Poems on Several Subjects* was published. Four years later Henry Cromwell, who may have been her lover, gave Thomas some original letters written by Alexander Pope; she made the mistake of selling them to Pope's enemy, the libelous publisher Edmund Curll, who immediately published them. Pope was infuriated at Thomas; his enmity cost her much of her literary reputation in London, and she lost some patrons, even spending time in debtors' prison at Fleet in 1727. He also attacked her in his satirical *The Dunciad* the following year, and in response she published *Codrus; or The Dunciad Dissected* (1729) in which she and Curll in turn attacked Pope. In 1730, she published two new works, a fictionalized account of Dryden's death in Charles Wilson's *Memoirs of William Congreve* and *The Metamorphosis of the Town; or A View of the Present Fashions*. Elizabeth Thomas died in poverty and seclusion in February 1731, at age 55. Later that year, friends of Gwinnett and Thomas edited and published two volumes of their correspondence and poems under the title *Pylades and Corinna, or Memoirs of the lives, amours, and writings of Richard Gwinnett*, which included Thomas' partial autobiography, *The Life of Corinna, written by Herself*.

SOURCES:

Mack, Maynard. *Alexander Pope: a Life*. NY: W.W. Norton, 1985.

Shattock, Joanne. *The Oxford Guide to British Women Writers*. Oxford: Oxford University Press, 1993.

Laura York, M.A. in History, University of California, Riverside, California

Thomas, Elizabeth (1910–1963).

See Brousse, Amy.

Thomas, Helen (1920—)

American journalist. Born on August 4, 1920, in Winchester, Kentucky; daughter of George Thomas and Mary Thomas; Wayne State University, B.A., 1942; married Douglas B. Cornell (a journalist), October 11, 1971 (died 1982); no children.

Hired by United Press International (1956); was the first woman promoted to White House bureau chief (1974); awarded honorary L.L.D.s, Eastern Michigan University (1972) and Ferris State College (1978); awarded honorary L.H.D.s, Wayne State University (1974) and University of Detroit (1979); elected first woman president of the White House Correspondents Association (1975); elected first woman head of the Gridiron Club, Washington, D.C. (1975).

Journalist Helen Thomas covered the White House through eight presidential administrations and four decades, becoming one of the most respected members of the American press. She was born on August 4, 1920, in Winchester, Kentucky, one of nine children of George and **Mary Thomas**, illiterate Syrian grocers who had immigrated from the Middle East. After Thomas' birth the family moved to Michigan, and she grew up in the city of Detroit. Her parents were determined that their children be well educated, and despite their modest means and the effects of the Depression, they insisted that all of them go to college. An excellent student, Thomas was already interested in journalism before she entered Wayne State University in Detroit. Graduating with a degree in English in 1942, Thomas immediately moved to Washington, D.C., to pursue her dream of becoming a newspaper reporter.

Women were very rare in newsrooms in the 1940s, and paper after paper turned her down, believing, as Thomas reported later, that a woman employee would soon marry and quit working. However, with many men drafted into the army during World War II, Thomas found work as a "copy girl" with the Washington *Daily News*. Soon she was a radio news writer for the United Press' City News Service, primarily covering the events of the war. In 1955,

Thomas left the City News Service to work as a reporter; in 1956, she joined the national staff of United Press International (UPI) and began covering the Justice Department. By 1960, she had been promoted to White House correspondent, although as a woman she was mainly assigned to covering first lady *Jacqueline Kennedy rather than political news. She attributed her move to covering the president in part to the first lady's dislike of her tough questions and perceived intrusion into the president's daily life.

In the early 1960s, Thomas was given more "hard" news assignments, and in 1970 was named chief White House correspondent, one of American journalism's most coveted assignments. The following year, Thomas married a fellow journalist, Douglas Cornell, a White House correspondent for UPI's competitor, the Associated Press, but did not consider quitting work. She was the only print journalist to accompany Richard Nixon on his trip to China in 1972. In the early 1970s, during the heat of the Watergate scandal associated with Nixon's re-election campaign, Thomas successfully earned the confidence of *Martha Mitchell, wife of U.S. Attorney General John Mitchell, who had information about the high-profile scandal. Thomas, as a result, became privy for months to breaking news stories while the details of Watergate unfolded. In retrospect, Thomas expressed reproach for herself and other members of the elite White House Press Corps for their failure to perceive tell-tale irregularities that under further investigation might have exposed the Watergate affair much sooner. Syndicate executives were nonetheless pleased with her reporting, and in 1974 they promoted Thomas to the post of White House bureau chief for UPI. She was, in fact, the first woman ever to head the White House Bureau for a national wire service.

Over the course of many years at her post, Thomas' presence at White House Press Conferences became a matter of accepted routine. Presidents came and left the White House, while Helen Thomas outlasted each of them. In her 1975 publication Dateline: White House, she discussed the presidential administrations of Kennedy, Johnson, Nixon, and Ford, all of which she observed firsthand.

Besides serving as a model and inspiration for young journalists, Thomas was active in many professional press organizations. She was one of the leaders in the struggle of women journalists to open membership in the National Press Club and the Gridiron Club to women in the 1970s; she later served as the first woman officer of the National Press Club, as well as president of the Gridiron Club and of the White House Correspondents' Association.

Thomas remained chief correspondent until her retirement from the United Press (now UPI) in June 2000, the day after UPI was purchased by News World Communications, a company founded by the Reverend Sun Myung Moon. She offered no explanation for her departure after 57 years with UPI. Though she had had to struggle against the biases of male reporters, she earned the respect of her colleagues as well as of Washington politicians for her pointed questions and demands for straightforward answers from presidents and press secretaries. She once told **Bernice Mancewicz:** "There's no such thing as a news leak; a leak is legitimate news."

Helen Thomas remains outspoken against the discrimination still facing women in the press, and is a strong advocate of opportunities for women journalists. She is equally passionate about the special role of the press in preserving a democratic government by providing for an informed public. She has received many awards for outstanding writing and reporting and holds numerous honorary degrees. Her memoir, Front Row at the White House, was published in 1999.

SOURCES:

Gareffa, Peter M., ed. Newsmakers: The People Behind Today's Headlines. Detroit, MI: Gale Research, 1988.
Thomas, Helen. Front Row at the White House: My Life and Times. NY: Scribner, 1999.

Laura York, M.A. in History,
University of California,
Riverside, California

Thomas, Lera Millard (1900–1993)

American legislator who served in the U.S. House of Representatives, 89th Congress (1966–67). Name variations: Mrs. Albert Thomas. Born on August 3, 1900, in Nacogdoches, Texas; died on July 23, 1993, in Nacogdoches; attended Brenau College; attended University of Alabama; married Albert Thomas (a U.S. congressional representative), in 1922 (died 1966); children: Ann; Lera; and James.

Born in 1900 and raised in the small town of Nacogdoches in east Texas, congressional representative Lera Millard Thomas attended Brenau College in Georgia and the University of Alabama. She left college in 1922 to marry Albert Thomas, another Nacogdoches native and a law student at the University of Texas; the couple had three children. In 1930, they moved to Houston when Albert became assistant U.S. attorney. In 1936, he was elected to the House of Representatives, where he served as a Democrat until 1966. When Albert Thomas died in 1966, a special election was held to fill his seat; his widow, who had been active for years in Democratic causes and the League of Women Voters, easily won the election against a Republican candidate. She served in the House from March 26, 1966 to January 3, 1967. While in Congress, Lera Millard Thomas continued the efforts of her husband, particularly in support of NASA programs as well as Houston area economic initiatives. She also went to Vietnam in December 1966 to interview American soldiers as a correspondent for the *Houston Chronicle* and the armed services media. Thomas declined to run for re-election in 1967, and retired to Nacogdoches. There she was involved in historic preservation efforts, in particular the reconstruction of a 19th-century Texas village in Nacogdoches County. She died in 1993 at age 92.

SOURCES:

Office of the Historian, U.S. House of Representatives. *Women in Congress, 1917–1990.* Washington, DC: U.S. Government Printing Office, 1991.

Transcript, Mrs. Albert (Lera) Thomas Oral History Interview, 10/11/69, by David G. McComb, Lyndon B. Johnson Library.

Laura York, M.A. in History,
University of California,
Riverside, California

Thomas, Margaret Haig (1883–1958).

See Rhondda, Margaret.

Thomas, Mary Myers (1816–1888)

American physician and activist. Born Mary Frame Myers on October 28, 1816, in Bucks County, Pennsylvania; died of dysentery on August 19, 1888; daughter of Samuel Myers (a teacher and abolitionist) and Mary (Frame) Myers; Penn Medical University, M.D., 1856; married Owen Thomas (a physician), in 1839 (died 1886); children: Laura; Pauline Heald; Julia Josephine (Thomas) Irvine.

Practiced medicine in Richmond, Indiana (1856); served on the governor's Sanitary Commission, Indiana, during the Civil War; served on the city board of public health of Richmond, Indiana, for eight years; edited women's rights publications and resurrected Indiana Woman Suffrage Association (1869); was admitted to the Indiana State Medical Society, becoming first woman regular (1876); elected president of the American Woman Suffrage Association (1880); elected president of the Wayne County Medical Society (1887).

Mary Myers Thomas was born Mary Frame Myers, the second daughter of Quakers Samuel and **Mary Frame Myers**, on October 28, 1816, in Bucks County, Pennsylvania. Her mother died shortly after her birth, and in 1818 Samuel Myers married **Paulina Iden (Myers)**. Myers and Iden had seven more children together, five daughters and two sons. The family lived for a time in Silver Spring, Maryland, then moved to Washington, D.C.

Mary Myers Thomas was one of the first woman physicians in America and contributed to many social reform movements. She attended public schools and learned to value progressive causes from her father, an abolitionist. When she was 17, the Myers family moved to a Quaker colony in New Lisbon, Ohio, where Samuel Myers taught school and Mary married Owen Thomas, a medical student, in 1839. The couple had three daughters.

When her husband graduated and became a doctor, the family moved to Fort Wayne, Indiana, in 1849. Exposed to the nascent woman's rights movement in 1845, Mary Thomas decided to pursue a medical career as well. She began studying with her husband, and in 1853 she was accepted to study with the first class of women students at Penn Medical University in Philadelphia, where her half-sister *Hannah E. Longshore was teaching. Mary delayed her entrance when her oldest daughter became terminally ill, taking classes with her husband at Western Reserve College in Cleveland. After her daughter's death in 1855, Thomas began the medical program at Penn, graduating with an M.D. degree in July 1856. (Another half-sister would also become a physician in Pennsylvania.)

Thomas then opened a practice in Richmond, Indiana. During the Civil War, she served first as a nurse, then as an assistant surgeon to her husband in Nashville, Tennessee. The couple returned to Richmond after the war and reopened their separate practices. During her long years in private practice, Thomas combined her medical training with her Quaker upbringing to become active in many social causes. Perhaps her most important contributions were to the woman's rights movement in Indiana; primarily interested in female suffrage rights, she served as president of the Indiana Woman's Rights Society and edited two feminist newspapers, *The Mayflower* and *Amelia Bloomer's The Lily. In the 1870s, Thomas often spoke at suffrage conventions and even appeared twice before the Indiana state legislature on behalf of the suffragist cause. In the early 1880s, she served as president of both the American Woman Suffrage Association and the Indiana Woman Suffrage Association.

Mary Thomas' tireless activism extended to other causes as well. A Methodist by faith (despite her Quaker background), Thomas was a leader in the temperance movement, elected as an officer in the Woman's Christian Temperance Union. She also served on Richmond's public health board and was one of the first women admitted to the Wayne County Medical Society, the Indiana State Medical Society, and the American Medical Association; she later served as president of the Wayne County Medical Society. In all of these organizations Thomas was a strong voice for expanded opportunities and professional recognition for women physicians. She also demonstrated her personal convictions in her private practice, for example in caring for black patients in Richmond as well as serving as physician for the Home for Friendless Girls, an institution she had helped establish.

Thomas retired from practice and political work at age 69 due to poor health. Her husband died in 1886; Thomas herself died two years later, at age 72. Prior to her death, Thomas requested that six women bear the pall at her funeral, in representation of the Good Templars, the Woman's Christian Temperance Union, and the African Methodist Episcopal Church. The request was honored, and six women carried her casket to a burial at Maple Hill Cemetery in Hartford, Michigan, near her daughter's home.

SOURCES:

James, Edward T., ed. *Notable American Women, 1607–1950.* Cambridge, MA: The Belknap Press of Harvard University, 1971.

Laura York, M.A. in History,
University of California,
Riverside, California

Thomas, M. Carey (1857–1935)

President of Bryn Mawr College and advocate of higher education for women in the U.S. Name variations: Min or Minnie; Carey Thomas. Born Martha Carey Thomas on January 2, 1857, in Baltimore, Maryland; died in Philadelphia, Pennsylvania, of a coronary occlusion on December 2, 1935 (ashes placed in the cloisters of the Bryn Mawr library); oldest of ten children, eight of whom lived to adulthood, of James Carey Thomas (a doctor) and Mary Whitall Thomas; attended a Friends' school (Quaker) in Baltimore, and the Howland Institute, a Quaker boarding school, in Union Springs, New York; granted B.A., Cornell University; studied at Johns Hopkins University and Leipzig University; University of Zurich, Ph.D., 1882; lived with Mamie Gwinn (co-founder of Bryn Mawr) and Mary Garrett; never married: no children.

Awards: Ph.D. summa cum laude (first woman and first foreigner to be awarded the degree at Zurich).

Badly burned at age seven; spent two years at the Howland Institute (1872–74); spent two years at Cornell University (1877–89); co-founded and was board member of the Bryn Mawr School (1878); was appointed dean of Bryn Mawr (1884–94); made president of Bryn Mawr (1894–1922); was appointed first woman trustee, Cornell University (1897–1901); participated in Women's Medical School Fund, with Mary Garrett, which underwrote the Johns Hopkins University School of Medicine, open to both men and women; was active in the National American Woman Suffrage Association, the National College Equal Suffrage League, and the National Women's Party (1906–20); founded, with Mary Anderson (chief of the Women's Bureau) and Rose Schneiderman (head of the New York Women's Trade Union League), the Bryn Mawr Summer School for Women Workers (1921).

Selected publications: Education of Women (1900); "Should the Higher Education of Women Differ from That of Men?" in Educational Review XXI (1901); "Present Tendencies in Women's College and University Education," in Educational Review XXV (1906).

Helen Lefkowitz Horowitz, M. Carey Thomas' most recent biographer, maintains that Thomas ultimately "built better than she lived." Born in antebellum Baltimore during a time when few people expected women to achieve in scholarly circles, M. Carey Thomas lived to see higher education for women a commonplace in American culture. Her role in that transformation was an important one. She was co-founder of the Bryn Mawr School for girls, the first woman president of Bryn Mawr College and its primary architect for many years, and was instrumental in opening the Johns Hopkins Medical School to women. These public accomplishments would seem to be enough to ensure her inclusion in American educational history along with the other builders of American colleges and universities, yet she became obscured because of complexities in her private existence that seemed to be in direct conflict with this public image.

Nicknamed Minnie soon after birth, Martha Carey Thomas was born into a prominent family in Baltimore, Maryland, on January 2, 1857. Her father was a doctor and Quaker preacher, and her mother was a member of the Whitall family, well known for its strong Quaker women. Since **Mary Whitall Thomas** had suffered an earlier miscarriage, both parents were ecstatic over the arrival of their healthy baby girl. In addition, the new arrival would be doted on by her grandparents, particularly her maternal grandparents and her aunt ❧▸ **Hannah Whitall Smith**. These relatives delighted in Minnie's early "sturdy ways" and encouraged her in her voracious reading.

Despite the subsequent birth of nine other siblings, seven of whom survived to adulthood, the strong-willed Thomas would always be demanding of her mother's attention and resentful about diversions. This tendency was reenforced when, at seven years of age, she announced to her mother that she was going to be an "assistant cook" and went merrily downstairs. A few minutes later her horrified mother rushed to the head of the stairs to see her oldest child engulfed in flames. Her apron having caught on fire from the coals of the stove, Thomas rushed to her father's office but was unable to put out the flames. Her mother smothered the fire with blankets, but the burns were so severe that it would be months before Thomas would walk again. In later life, she suffered much pain because of the scar tissue that had formed around the burns and was forced to walk with a cane. During this crisis, Mary Thomas abandoned her other children to the care of others and stayed with Minnie constantly. Her devotion would never be forgotten, and the child craved her almost constant attention from this event until her mother's death in 1888.

By the time Thomas was 14, her aspirations to become an educated cultured woman were full-blown. The untimely death of her 18-year-old cousin, Frank Smith, with whom Thomas was quite smitten, released her to pursue this goal. She was, however, beginning to be aware how difficult her choice might be. She wrote in her diary: "I get perfectly enraged: how unjust—how narrow minded, how utterly incomprehensible to deny that women ought be educated. . . . If I ever live and grow up, my one aim and concentrated purpose shall be to show that a woman can learn, can reason, can compete with men in the grand fields of literature and science and conjecture."

In 1872, Thomas and her friend **Bessie King** were sent to the Howland School, a Quaker school in Union Springs, New York. While there, Thomas came under the influence of instructor **Jane Slocum** who encouraged her to become a scholar rather than a doctor. Slocum also

---

❧▸ **Smith, Hannah Whitall** (1832–1911)

*American religious leader and writer. Born Hannah Whitall in Philadelphia, Pennsylvania, on February 7, 1832; died on May 1, 1911, in Iffley, near Oxford, England; daughter of John M. Whitall (a wealthy glass manufacturer) and Mary (Tatum) Whitall; sister of Mary Whitall Thomas (mother of M. Carey Thomas); married Robert Pearsall Smith (brother of librarian Lloyd Pearsall Smith), in 1851 (died 1898); children: Nelly (died at age five); Logan Pearsall Smith (1865–1946, an English essayist); Franklin (died in 1872 at age 18 of typhoid); Rachel (died in 1879, age 11); Mary Berenson (who married Bernard Berenson); Alice or Alys Smith Russell (who married Bertrand Russell); grandmother of *Ray Strachey (1887–1940).*

Hannah Whitall Smith was born in Philadelphia, Pennsylvania, in 1832, the daughter of Quakers John M. Whitall, a wealthy glass manufacturer, and **Mary Tatum Whitall**. Hannah was the author of the religious classic *The Christian's Secret of a Happy Life* (1875). Married in 1851, she and her husband Robert Pearsall Smith lived in Germantown, Pennsylvania, then Millville, New Jersey, where both preached. In 1874, with Robert's health deteriorating, the family moved to England and continued their evangelical work. After returning to the United States in the late 1870s, Robert lost a fortune in worthless silver mines, money that had come from Hannah's family. In 1886, they settled permanently in England.

The couple had six children, including English essayist Logan Pearsall Smith and two daughters, *Mary Berenson and *Alys Smith Russell, who married powerful men: Bernard Berenson and Bertrand Russell, respectively. Hannah also wrote *The Record of a Happy Life: Being Memorials of Franklin Whitall Smith* (1873) and *The Unselfishness of God and How I Discovered It* (1903). Though her husband died a bitter fanatic in 1898, Hannah Smith took things in stride and spent her retirement at the home of her son Logan at Iffley, on the Thames in Sussex, England, where she wrote in 1907: "Although I am confined to my wheel chair and cannot get out much, yet the views out of our windows are so lovely, and the river is so shining, and the grass is so green, that I feel the lines have indeed fallen to me in a pleasant place. I often have a feeling as if I were living in a novel."

SOURCES:
Deen, Edith. *Great Women of the Christian Faith.* NY: Harper & Row, 1959.

convinced her that Cornell University would be the best place to go to school. Returning to Baltimore after graduation, Thomas spent a year preparing herself and her parents for Cornell. Initially opposed to his daughter going to a secular, coeducational institution, James Carey Thomas was eventually won over by the pleas (some sources say tears) of his wife and daughter. Entering Cornell as a junior, Thomas requested that people call her Carey and began to sign her name as M. Carey Thomas. One of 20 women in a class of 240, she lived in the new Sage College, a magnificent dormitory created for "coeds" (a word coined at Cornell University) and designed to increase revenues for the school. Swept up in the intellectual excitement of Cornell in the early years, Thomas excelled in advanced work in mathematics, science, Greek, Latin, literature, and philosophy. She did particularly well in Hiram Corson's courses in English literature and gradually she determined to become a scholar in languages and literature. Upon graduation in 1877, at age 20, however, she still feared that no woman would be able to hold a professorship in a "regular university unless the race of wise men dies out."

For the next two years, M. Carey Thomas suffered the lot of many of her college-educated peers. Women were, by the 1870s and 1880s, allowed limited access to colleges and universities. There were not, as yet, however, any career paths for women and few women were staunch enough, determined enough, and supported enough to obtain the necessary additional training to enter male-dominated fields. Thomas returned to Baltimore, "read" in philology under a

tutelage arrangement at Johns Hopkins University (where she was not allowed to obtain a graduate degree even though her father was on the board of trustees), and became increasingly depressed. She did form two close relationships with women who would remain her constant companions throughout much of the rest of her life, **Mamie Gwinn** and ◄❧ **Mary Elizabeth Garrett**. This threesome, along with two other friends, founded the Bryn Mawr School for Girls. At some point during this period, Thomas and Gwinn began to plan their escape to Europe for study despite considerable reluctance from both their families.

In 1882, M. Carey Thomas was able to return to Baltimore in triumph with a Ph.D., summa cum laude, from the University of Zurich. For more than three years, she and Gwinn had lived and studied in Germany and Switzerland and traveled throughout Europe. Emboldened by her new credentials and anxious to find a public arena for her new worldly cultural attainments, M. Carey Thomas asked, at age 26, to be named the president of the proposed Quaker college in Philadelphia, Bryn Mawr, where her uncle, James Whitall, was president of the board of trustees and her father was a member. Clearly, the presidency was an unrealistic goal for any woman at that time, and Thomas was eventually persuaded by her Aunt Hannah to consider the deanship of the new school. In March 1884, Thomas was named professor of English and dean of the faculty. For the next 18 months, she visited other women's colleges (Vassar, Smith, Wellesley), recruited faculty, planned curriculum, and generally prepared for the opening of what, for her, had to be the best college for women in the United States. Fifty years later, she characterized this period as a time when the men involved "set out to produce a well-behaved fowl . . . but found that they had hatched a soaring eagle instead."

❧► Garrett, Mary Elizabeth (1854–1915)

American philanthropist. Born Mary Elizabeth Garrett in Baltimore, Maryland, on March 5, 1854; died in Bryn Mawr, Pennsylvania, on April 3, 1915; daughter of John W. Garrett (president of the Baltimore & Ohio Railroad); never married; lived with M. Carey Thomas.

At her father's death in 1884, Mary E. Garrett inherited a third of his considerable fortune, and thereafter devoted her time and money to the advancement of medical education for women and to woman suffrage. During her lifetime, her benefactions amounted to a very large sum; for example, she raised $100,000 for Johns Hopkins medical school with the provision that women be admitted. When she died in 1915, Garrett bequeathed $15 million to *M. Carey Thomas, president of Bryn Mawr College, to be disposed of as she saw fit.

For the next ten years, Thomas busied herself with the educational details of the new school. She gathered a distinguished faculty which included a future president of the United States, Woodrow Wilson; she planned the construction of new academic buildings and dormitories; she supervised the curriculum; and she taught both large undergraduate courses and challenging graduate seminars. In the summers, she and her friend Mamie traveled to Europe where, despite her stated intentions to pursue her scholarship in philology, they reveled in the rich cultural life of late 19th-century Europe, attending plays, visiting museums, and dining with

M. Carey
Thomas

the literati of the continent. Clearly, Thomas was enjoying her busy and productive life.

In 1892, when President Rhoads of Bryn Mawr announced his desire to retire, he indicated to the board of trustees that he thought Dean Thomas should be his successor at the Quaker school. Some members of the board, concerned about the dean's secular lifestyle and what to them seemed like excessive independence, expressed reservations; approval for the appointment passed by only one vote. Thomas herself was not certain she should take the position, but take it she did; from 1894 on, she emerged as a major public voice for the higher education of women, advocating greater access and equal academic standards. Thomas achieved national stature after she gave a speech in 1899, at the Bryn Mawr Chapel, criticizing Charles Eliot, president of Harvard, for his opposition to coeducation. She remained as president of the college for 28 years until her retirement in 1922.

I think its cruel when a girl wants to go to college and learn and she can't . . . while a boy is made to go whether he wants to or not. I don't see why the world is made so unjust.

—From the diary of 14-year-old M. Carey Thomas, October 1, 1871

The years as president of Bryn Mawr were years of great accomplishment for Thomas, both at the college and as a speaker for women's rights in the larger society. She was the first president of the National College Women's Equal Suffrage League and worked for the National American Woman Suffrage Association. After the suffrage amendment passed, she joined the uncompromising National Women's Party led by *Alice Paul and opposed protective legislation for women. Thomas expressed in later years her belief in "sex solidarity." In 1921, she, along with labor activists *Mary Anderson and *Rose Schneiderman, founded the Bryn Mawr Summer School for Women Workers, an experiment in collaboration between academics and women workers that would be remarkably successful. In addition, Thomas was an exceptional fund raiser. She persuaded the notoriously close-fisted John D. Rockefeller to contribute matching funds for the construction of a dormitory named after him and, even though she often kept the college in debt, she created a campus that architecturally mirrored the high academic accomplishments of the Bryn Mawr students and faculty.

All was not serene during these busy years, however. Perceived as autocratic by the faculty, particularly the male faculty, Thomas was forced to capitulate when a crisis over governance occurred in the 1915–16 school year. She suddenly declared herself in favor of self-governance for faculty (a position she would deny in later years) and survived to serve as president for another six years. In addition, in 1904, her longtime companion Mamie Gwinn left the deanery (Thomas' extravagant residence on the Bryn Mawr campus where they both lived) and married one Alfred Hodder, a Bryn Mawr professor of questionable reputation. Furious about the marriage, Thomas never forgave

Gwinn and moved her other friend Mary Garrett, the railroad heiress who had often accompanied Thomas on trips and whose fortune had underwritten many of Thomas' professional and personal adventures, into the deanery. They lived together until Garrett's death in 1915. Finally, Thomas' increasingly virulent anti-Semitism and racism began to severely limit her effectiveness in working with broadly based women's groups.

Increasingly, after Garrett's death, Thomas absented herself from the Bryn Mawr campus. This was partially due to increasing disinterest in governance but more especially to the huge bequest she received in Garrett's will, which enabled her to indulge her taste for luxurious travel and fine things. In 1922, amid great accolades, she retired after ensuring that her successor would be a woman, **Marion Edwards Park**.

In retirement, Thomas traveled extensively, worked in a desultory fashion on her autobiography, and, whenever she was in residence at the deanery at Bryn Mawr, meddled in the affairs of the college. Her extravagant lifestyle (she had 15 servants) caught up with her in the 1930s, and she spent or lost virtually all of the fortune left her by Garrett. Thomas spoke at the 50th-anniversary celebration of Bryn Mawr College on November 2, 1935, and died a month later, on December 2, 1935.

SOURCES:
Cross, Barbara M., ed. *The Educated Woman in America: Selected Writings of *Catharine Beecher, *Margaret Fuller, and M. Carey Thomas*. NY: Teachers College Press, 1974.
Dobkin, Marjorie Housepian, ed. *The Making of a Feminist: Early Journals and Letters of M. Carey Thomas*. Kent, OH: Kent State University Press, 1979.
Finch, Edith. *Carey Thomas of Bryn Mawr*. NY: Harper and Row, 1947 (censored biography).
Horowitz, Helen Lefkowitz. *The Power and Passion of M. Carey Thomas*. NY: Alfred A. Knopf, 1994.
Veysey, Laurence R. "Martha Carey Thomas," in *Notable American Women, 1607–1950*. Cambridge, MA: The Belknap Press of Harvard University, 1971.

SUGGESTED READING:
Faderman, Lillian. *Odd Girls and Twilight Lovers*. NY: Columbia University Press, 1991.
Smith-Rosenberg, Carroll. *Disorderly Conduct: Visions of Gender in Victorian America*. NY: Alfred A. Knopf, 1985.
Solomon, Barbara Miller. *In the Company of Educated Women*. New Haven, CT: Yale University Press, 1985.

COLLECTIONS:
M. Carey Thomas Collection, Bryn Mawr College; Alan Mason Chesney Medical Archives, Johns Hopkins Medical School, Baltimore, Maryland; the Rockefeller Archive Center, North Tarrytown, New York.

Anne J. Russ,
Professor of Sociology,
Wells College,
Aurora, New York

Thomasse (fl. 1292)

Book illustrator and innkeeper of Paris. Flourished in 1292 in Paris.

Thomasse, a professional manuscript illuminator of Paris, was an exceptionally talented artist, well respected for her work. Very little is known about her, except that in addition to her career as a painter she also owned and managed a Parisian inn and tavern. Her life reveals the opportunities available to urban women, who were often forced to rely solely on themselves for support; this was especially true if they remained unmarried or were widowed, since governments and churches provided little in the way of welfare for these women.

Laura York,
Riverside, California

Thompson, Clara (1893–1958)

American psychiatrist. Born Clara Mabel Thompson on October 3, 1893, in Providence, Rhode Island; died of cancer on December 20, 1958, in New York City; daughter of T. Franklin Thompson (a tailor and salesman) and Clara (Medbery) Thompson; attended Pembroke College; graduated from Brown University, 1916; Johns Hopkins Medical School, M.D., 1920.

Worked at St. Elizabeth's Hospital, Washington, D.C.; established residency at Henry Phipps Psychiatric Clinic, John Hopkins (three years); maintained a private practice in Baltimore, Maryland; established the William Alanson White Institute of Psychiatry, Psychoanalysis, and Psychology in New York City.

A leading psychoanalyst for over a quarter century, Clara Mabel Thompson was born in 1893 and grew up in a devout Calvinist family of modest means in Providence, Rhode Island. An excellent student, she decided while in high school to become a medical missionary in India. After graduating from high school in 1912, she entered Pembroke College. Her exposure to intellectual life at Pembroke led Thompson to question the religious training of her youth, and she eventually abandoned her missionary career plans; instead she determined to become a practicing physician. In 1916, she became the first person in her family to graduate from college; she next entered Johns Hopkins Medical School.

While working one summer at a hospital in Washington, D.C., as part of her program, Thompson met psychiatrist William Alanson White, who was to have a major impact on her career. With his encouragement Thompson decid-

ed to specialize in psychiatry and psychoanalysis, and after completing her coursework and receiving her M.D. degree in 1920, she began a residency in the Henry Phipps Psychiatric Clinic at John Hopkins. However, she left the clinic before finishing her residency after a break with the clinic's director over Thompson's decision to undergo psychoanalysis in 1925. She then opened her own psychoanalytic practice in Baltimore and became an associate of analyst Harry Stack Sullivan.

In 1931, she moved to Budapest to study under Sandor Ferenczi, who was both teacher and analyst to her. Ferenczi criticized Freud and contemporary analysts for their devotion to theory and forming general formulas over clinical practice and the tangible benefits analysts could provide their patients. Deeply influenced by his ideas, Thompson returned home to open a new practice in New York City in 1933. Thompson became part of a small group of psychoanalysts known as the Zodiac Group. Comprised of analysts from the U.S. and Europe, the group also included Sullivan, *Karen Horney, and Erich Fromm, and met weekly to discuss the theory and practice of psychoanalysis. They also collaborated on publications; Thompson's first significant published paper was her "Notes on Female Sexuality," which appeared in Sullivan's text *Personal Psychopathology* in 1933.

Along with Horney, Thompson had become particularly interested in the psychology of women, and would devote most of her research over the next 20 years to questions about female sexuality and development. Horney and Thompson worked closely throughout the 1930s developing a feminist psychoanalytic theory; Horney's influence can be seen in the most well known of Thompson's papers, the article "'Penis Envy' in Women," published in 1943. In this controversial paper Thompson attacked Sigmund Freud's theory that there was a physiological basis for penis envy; instead she pointed to social and cultural discrimination against women, and argued that women did not wish unconsciously to become men, but wished to share in men's societal privileges.

In the late 1930s Thompson began a long relationship with Henry Major, a married Hungarian artist. The two lived together every summer at Thompson's summer home in Provincetown, Massachusetts; Major spent the rest of the year with his wife. Somewhat shy and reserved by nature, Thompson, who never married, had few other intimate relationships in her lifetime besides her personal and professional ties to Harry Stack Sullivan and Erich Fromm.

THOMPSON, CLARA

Differences in theoretical orientations led Thompson, along with Horney and Fromm, to leave the New York Psychoanalytic Institute in 1941. Horney then founded the American Institute of Psychoanalysis (AIP). However, Thompson left that group in 1943 after a conflict between Horney and Fromm over Fromm's membership in the AIP.

Thompson and Fromm, in conjunction with the Washington School of Psychiatry, then established their own psychiatric school in New York, which in 1945 was renamed the William Alanson White Institute of Psychiatry. Because of the earlier conflict with Horney's AIP, Thompson's school was soon censured by the American Psychoanalytic Association (APA), and her students were not allowed membership in the APA. Despite this lack of recognition from the largest American professional organization of psychoanalysts, Thompson's reputation flourished throughout the 1940s and 1950s. Besides activism in many other professional groups, she was an instructor at her own school, at Vassar College, and at the New York Psychoanalytic Institute. From 1946 on, she served as director of her Institute of Psychiatry.

By 1949, Major and Sullivan had both died, and Thompson became more withdrawn from social life, although she remained a dedicated teacher and mentor. In 1957, she was diagnosed with cancer and underwent unsuccessful treatments. Clara Thompson died December 1958 in her home in New York. As she requested, she was buried next to Henry Major in Provincetown. Today the White Institute which she founded remains a leading institution for psychoanalytic research and teaching.

SOURCES:
Sicherman, Barbara, and Carol Hurd Green, eds. *Notable American Women: The Modern Period.* Cambridge, MA: The Belknap Press of Harvard University, 1980.

Laura York, M.A. in History, University of California, Riverside, California

Thompson, Dorothy (1893–1961)

American foreign correspondent, columnist, and radio commentator who was the foremost woman journalist of her time. Born Dorothy Celène Thompson on July 9, 1893, in Lancaster, New York; died in Lisbon, Portugal, on January 30, 1961; daughter of Peter Thompson (a Methodist minister) and Margaret (Grierson) Thompson; attended Lewis Institute, Chicago, 1908–12, awarded A.A., 1912; attended Syracuse University, 1912–14, awarded B.A., 1914; did graduate study, University of Vienna; married

Josef Bard (unpublished writer), on April 26, 1923 (divorced 1927); married Sinclair Lewis (the novelist), on May 14, 1928 (divorced 1941); married Maxim Kopf (an artist), on June 16, 1943; children: (second marriage) Michael Lewis.

In early years, family lived in upstate New York villages: Clarence, Tonawanda, Hamburg, Gowanda, Spencerport; became foreign correspondent for Curtis-Martin newspapers, Philadelphia Public-Ledger *and* New York Evening Post *(1920–28); worked as columnist,* New York Herald Tribune *Syndicate (1936–41); also columnist for Bell newspaper syndicate (1941–58).*

Selected writings: The New Russia *(Holt, 1928);* "I Saw Hitler!" *(Farrar and Rinehart, 1932);* Refugees: Anarchy or Organization? *(Random House, 1938);* Dorothy Thompson's Political Guide: A Study of American Liberalism and Its Relationship to Modern Totalitarian States *(Stackpole, 1938);* Once on Christmas *(Oxford University Press, 1939);* Let the Record Speak *(Houghton Mifflin, 1939);* Listen, Hans *(Houghton Mifflin, 1942);* The Courage to Be Happy *(Houghton Mifflin, 1957).*

Late in 1931, Dorothy Thompson, then a correspondent for the American monthly *Cosmopolitan*, complained, "For seven years I have been trying to see Hitler." Now the time had come. She would be the first American newswoman to interview a man who, in little over a year, would be Germany's führer. She later recalled: "I was a little nervous. I considered taking smelling salts. And Hitler was late. An hour late." Yet when the interview took place, the journalist found herself measuring "the startling insignificance of this man who has set the world agog."

He is formless, almost faceless, a man whose countenance is a caricature, a man whose framework seems cartilaginous, without bones. He is inconsequent and voluble, ill-poised, insecure. He is the very prototype of the little man. The eyes alone are notable. Dark gray and hyperthyroid—they have the peculiar shine which often distinguishes geniuses, alcoholics, and hysterics.

Though Hitler addressed her as if he were speaking to a mass meeting, Thompson predicted that he would never gain power. Within a year, she wrote, "Oh Adolf! Adolf! You will be out of luck!"

On August 25, 1934, Adolf Hitler—now German chancellor—got his revenge on the author of the demeaning portrait. Indeed her articles exposing Nazi anti-Semitism, published in the *Jewish Daily Bulletin*, simply added to his fury. Thompson was expelled from Germany by the very "little man" she had found so insignificant. Having just finished breakfast in her room at Berlin's Hotel Adlon, she was visited by a Gestapo agent who gave her 24 hours to depart. In Western Europe, such orders were unprecedented, and nearly the entire American and British press corps saw her off. The event made headlines. Any banishment of Dorothy Thompson was front-page news.

Thompson was born in 1893 in Lancaster, New York, near Syracuse. Dorothy's father Peter Thompson was a Methodist minister who had immigrated from northern England. Throughout her youth, he held modest parishes in the industrial suburbs of Buffalo, and during one six-month period the family was so impoverished they survived on rice and apples. Her mother **Margaret Grierson Thompson**, the daughter of Scottish working-class immigrants, died when Dorothy was seven. Two years later, in 1903, her father married **Eliza Abbott**, parish pianist and rigid hypochondriac. Dorothy worshipped her father but despised her stepmother. As rebellious as she was intelligent, she was sent to Chicago, there to live with two aunts. In 1908, she began attending the Lewis Institution, a rigorous academy. Lack of money caused her to forego her dream of attending one of the Seven Sister colleges. Rather in 1912 she entered Syracuse University on a scholarship for children of Methodist clergy. Admitted as a junior, she completed all requirements within two years and graduated cum laude.

In September 1914, Thompson began work for the Buffalo headquarters of the New York State Woman Suffrage Party. Though she began as a clerk, stuffing envelopes at the salary of eight dollars a week, she soon became of one of the party's leading organizers, speaking and arranging promotional events throughout western New York. When, late in 1917, the state adopted women's suffrage, she moved to New York City. Here she worked for a religious publisher and an advertising agency. In the summer of 1918, she moved to Cincinnati, where she became publicity director for the National Social Unit Organization, a group fostering preventive medicine.

In July 1920, Thompson and a close friend, **Barbara De Porte**, moved to London, then to Paris. In part, she was escaping a romantic involvement with the Unit's director, Wilbur S. Phillips, a married man 18 years her senior. More important, she wanted to make her mark as a foreign correspondent. Almost immediately, she met with success, interviewing Zionist leaders, Irish nationalists, and Italian labor organizers. She was the last person to interview Terence MacSwiney, lord mayor of Cork, before he starved to death in a 73-day hunger strike. Her material was soon picked up by the *New York Evening Post*, the *Christian Science Monitor*, *Outlook* magazine, and the Hearst chain, though in Paris she usually had to support herself by writing publicity for the American Red Cross at a penny a line.

Finding the French capital saturated with shallow American expatriates, Thompson moved to Vienna, arriving early in 1921. She first wrote features for the *Philadelphia Public Ledger*, then went on to Budapest, where she continued Red Cross publicity work. She soon became a protegé of Marcel Fodor, the distinguished Hungarian-born correspondent of the *Manchester Guardian*. By May, the *Public Ledger* put her on a $50-a-week salary, in part because of her interviews of such European leaders as Czechoslovakia's Eduard Benes and Thomas Masaryk, Britain's Ramsay MacDonald, Germany's Gustav Stresemann, France's Aristide Briand, Turkey's Kemal Ataturk, Russia's Leon Trotsky, and Queen *Marie of Rumania. All southeastern Europe became her beat. In the summer of 1925, she was transferred to Berlin, in the process becoming, according to her biographer Peter Kurth, "the undisputed queen of the overseas press corps, the first woman to head a foreign news bureau of any importance." When the Ledger's foreign bureau merged with that of the *New York Evening Post*, both owned by Curtis Publishing, her audience became even wider.

All this time Thompson was ever on the move. In October 1921, she scooped the world by covering an abortive Habsburg coup in Hungary. To gain access to Empress *Zita of Parma and Emperor Charles I, grandnephew of the late Francis Joseph, Thompson disguised herself as a Red Cross nurse. Other feats included coverage of a uprising in Sofia, during which a machine gun peppered her balcony, and reporting a Polish rebellion in evening clothes and silk slippers. (She borrowed $500 for her trip to Warsaw from her friend Sigmund Freud, acting in the knowledge that the famous analyst was often paid in American dollars kept in an office safe.)

In the spring of 1922, Thompson entered into a love affair with Joseph Bard, a handsome Hungarian sophisticate of Jewish and Croatian background. After marriage, which took place in April 1923, Bard—supposedly a brilliant if unpublished writer—lived off her earnings while being openly unfaithful to her. Only in 1927, when Bard genuinely fell in love with a wealthy and beautiful British art student, did Thompson divorce him.

Soon she fell in love with Sinclair Lewis, America's most famous novelist, who would go on to win the Nobel Prize in 1930. Lewis' biographer Mark Schorer describes Thompson in the following terms:

> Her beauty was of herself rather than of her face alone, a shining expression of her warmth and vitality and intelligence. She had candid, hazel eyes, was fair and of imposing presence, with nothing petit or mincing in her gait, impulsive and generous, of a relaxed self-confidence that held no shred of self-importance.

Lewis proposed to Thompson within 48 hours after they met, then followed her when she covered the Soviet Union for the *New York Evening Post*. The couple lived near Naples, Italy, until Lewis' divorce was finalized. After their marriage in May 1928, they moved to "Twin Farms" in Barnard, Vermont, a 300-acre estate that served as an anchor amid their frequent moving. At first, the Lewises truly loved each other. Thompson (who always kept her maiden name) served as a genuine mother to Wells, Lewis' son by his first marriage, indeed far more so than to Michael, the child born to her and Lewis in 1930. She was the inspiration for Lewis' most successful novel of the 1930s, *It Can't Happen Here* (1935), which dealt with a fascist takeover in America. Once Lewis was so angered at Theodore Dreiser, who had plagiarized from Thompson's book *The New Russia* (1928), that he insulted the prominent novelist and got slapped for his pains.

*S*he was a voice of rare eloquence and courage.

—Marion K. Sanders

Yet Thompson found Lewis increasingly distant, demanding, and vituperative. Already facing a sharp waning of his talents, he was continually rude to her friends. She saw him wallowing in self-pity and literally drinking himself to death. She mocked his political apathy in columns entitled "Conversations with the Grouse." Lewis in turn became increasingly jealous of Thompson's fame and angered by her continual traveling and her crusading posture. Once he commented, "If I hear anything more about 'conditions' and 'situations' I'll shoot myself." He frequently said, "If I ever divorce Dorothy, I'll name Adolf Hitler as co-respondent." He revealed his hostility by thinly disguised portraits in the novels *Ann Vickers*

(1933) and *Gideon Plantish* (1943). By 1933, they rarely lived together. In 1937, they separated, though only in 1942 did she finally grant Lewis a divorce.

In 1931, Thompson had resumed reporting activities overseas, frequently contributing to the *Saturday Evening Post*. She also became a regular on the lecture circuit throughout the United States, beginning years of a grueling schedule. Moreover, she engaged in brief affairs with unidentified men. In 1932, she entered into a three-year intimate relationship with *Christa Winsloe, a beautiful sculptor who wrote the play *Gestern und Heute* (Yesterday and Today), which was the basis for the film *Mädchen in Uniform*.

On March 16, 1936, *Helen Rogers Reid, the de facto publisher of the *New York Herald Tribune*, hired Thompson to contribute a column, "On the Record," three times a week. By 1939, Thompson had 7.5 million readers in 196 newspapers. In the spring of 1937, she added a monthly column in the *Ladies' Home Journal*. Furthermore, thanks to a Monday night radio program over the National Broadcasting Company (NBC), she reached 5.5 million listeners. Thompson had definitely achieved celebrity status by 1939, when *Time* magazine found her second only to *Eleanor Roosevelt as America's most influential woman. Indeed, *Time* commented, "She can do more for any cause than any private citizen in the United States."

Because of her pronounced views and her intense personality, Thompson always made good press copy. Wrote editor Charles Angoff, with only slight exaggeration:

> She became sufficiently important for writers and cartoonists to satirize her. She was portrayed as giving advice to the Pope, to the President of the United States, to the Emperor of Ethiopia, to the President of the New York Stock Exchange, to the President of Harvard University. She became the Woman of the Year. She became the Woman of the Decade. She became the Woman of the Twentieth Century.

To her admirers, Thompson was the "blue-eyed tornado," "the first lady of American journalism," a cross between *Harriet Beecher Stowe and Nurse *Edith Cavell or between *Cassandra and *Joan of Arc. Correspondent John Gunther called her "the best journalist this generation has produced in any country." Critics labeled her a "blood-thirsty, breast-beating" *Boudica, a "wet nurse to destiny," the "Delilah of the Ink-Pot," the "*Molly Pitcher of the Maginot Line." Many on the left used such metaphors as the "*Florence

Nightingale of the wounded Tory intellect," and the "*Clara Barton of the plutocrat in pain."

As far as U.S. domestic policy was concerned, Thompson was strongly conservative. By 1935, she found the New Deal "on the rocks." To Thompson, seeds of fascism lay in such measures as large-scale relief, the Federal Writers Project, the Wagner Act, social security, and Supreme Court "packing." On December 3, 1938, she wrote, "I wish for us all, for the New Year, a Congress that is no longer willing to be a Nazi Reichstag." Franklin D. Roosevelt reciprocated by calling her "the oracle of Wall Street."

At the same time, she opposed "roughshod capitalism," which she defined as mindless accumulation at the expense of individual worth.

Always Thompson sought to alert Americans to the dangers of fascism. Although her 1932 prediction that Hitler would never rule often came back to haunt her, she soon found Germany an extremely dangerous power. Frequently predicting a general war, she often lambasted America's neutrality acts and Britain's appeasement policies. She wrote a preface to Austrian chancellor Kurt Schuschnigg's *My Austria* (1938), in which she said she would have given her life to save that country from Nazism. In February 1939, she "dropped in" on a meeting of the German-American Bund at Madison Square Garden. Wrote Kurth in *American Cassandra:*

> She was on her way that night to deliver a speech to a meeting of the Phi Beta Kappa Society, and her decision to take a detour to the Bund rally was not so casual as it appeared. She had been worrying a lot recently about the limitations of the First Amendment. She wondered to what extent free speech might need to be curtailed in the interest of its own protection. She had no answer to the problem. . . . She knew she would be on familiar territory in a sea of Nazi flags, and she arrived at Madison Square Garden with the express purpose of causing an uproar. She took her seat in the front row of the press gallery and commenced to interrupt the speakers with strident gales of raucous laughter, humiliating and infuriating the pride of American Nazism so deeply that after about ten minutes of this, while the Bundists shouted "Throw her out!," she was actually surrounded by a unit of Fritz Kuhn's "Storm Troopers" and muscled out the door. . . . It may have been her finest moment—the indelible dramatization of her promise to Hitler that she would not be muzzled by thugs.

Much of Thompson's attention was given to the plight of Europe's refugees, particularly Jews. She personally intervened on behalf of many stateless individuals, contributed financially to their welfare, and was often successful in finding them asylum. In November 1938, she defended the Jewish refugee Herschel Grynszspan, whose assassination of a German diplomat in Paris resulted in the horrors of Kristallnacht. A year and a half later, she collaborated on a play centering on refugees: *Another Sun*, written with a lover, Fritz Kortner. Because of a muddled plot, it closed on Broadway after a week's run.

When, on September 1, 1939, war broke out in Europe, Thompson immediately cabled British statesman Harold Nicolson, saying that the British Cabinet must engage "in mediation and prayer." Within days, however, she became a fervent interventionist. After the fall of France, she called for universal conscription. In May 1941, at a New York banquet of 3,000 held in her honor, she even started a small organization, the Ring of Freedom, which sought to put the United States on a war footing. On September 15, 1941, she called for an outright American declaration of war against Germany. No isolationist was safe from her attacks, and she particularly sought to label aviator Charles A. Lindbergh as "pro-Nazi." In turn, leading isolationist senators sought her investigation as a "British agent."

Although originally enthusiastic about Wendell Willkie, the Republican presidential standard-bearer in 1940, Thompson saw Roosevelt possessing the needed experience in foreign policy. She toyed with a bipartisan Roosevelt-Willkie ticket, but finally "jumped ship" in October by directly calling for Roosevelt's reelection. On October 14, in a speech at Buffalo, she claimed that Willkie was "a man supported by Axis agents, whatever his personal attitude toward them may be." (Once the election was over, she suggested that Willkie receive a Cabinet appointment.)

In March 1941, the strongly Republican *Herald Tribune*, angered by Thompson's endorsement of Roosevelt, failed to renew her contract. Her column was immediately picked up by the Bell syndicate, which distributed her column to over 200 papers, including the arch-liberal *New York Post*. During the early '40s, her prestige was at its height. She received so much mail that it had to be delivered in special trucks. Roosevelt occasionally used her as a speechwriter, and she also drafted material on Germany for the State Department and the Office of Strategic Services.

In June 1943, Thompson married Maxim Kopf, a German-Bohemian artist who was born in Vienna and raised in Prague. She had to bribe Kopf's third wife, actress **Lotte Stein**, to secure his divorce and the return of a damaging letter Thompson had written her.

During the war, Thompson defended the mass bombing of Germany. She was, however, horrified by Hiroshima, maintaining that the atomic strike had not been necessary to defeat Japan. In 1942, she made weekly shortwave broadcasts to Germany, calling upon Hitler's subjects to overthrow Nazi rule. Her scripts, which were anthologized in *Listen, Hans* (1942), took the form of messages to a non-Nazi German friend, in reality Resistance leader Helmuth von Moltke. She opposed the "barbaric" policy of unconditional surrender, claiming that it squelched "the forces in Germany that were anxious for peace." For the rest of her life, she was haunted by the belief that Wells Lewis, killed by a sniper's bullet in France in October 1944, would have remained alive had peace negotiations been opened. Appalled by the wartime conferences of Yalta and Potsdam and strongly anti-Communist, she hoped that Roosevelt would deal with the Russians when the war ended.

After the conflict, Thompson criticized the Nuremberg trials, saying major Nazi offenders should be summarily shot rather than be subject to what she saw as a travesty of the judicial process. She made marked comparisons of German treatment of the Jews and Allied treatment of German-speaking exiles from such areas as Poland, Silesia, and East Prussia. "It would have been more humane," she told an audience at New York's Town Hall, "to reopen the gas chambers for German children" than to permit mass starvation to continue.

In the immediate postwar period, Thompson foresaw an era of "endless minor wars" and "formless imperialism," an age of "lawlessness for the powerful and servitude for the weak." Hence, she sought international laws against rearmament and military conscription. By 1948, the once-militant interventionist was calling upon the United States to exercise caution in the world arena. She denied that the U.S. could serve as "world policeman," warned against continued dissipation of American troops and morale, feared "a hemorrhage of savings and income," and bemoaned the power of the military in American life. In the summer of 1950, she reluctantly endorsed American participation in the Korean War, finding it the product of "blind commitments" that must still be honored.

Critical of all power politics, in 1948 Thompson served as chair of the World Organization of Mothers of All Nations (WOMAN), a group seeking to revise the United Nations Charter by breaking the "monopoly" of the Security Council. Long-range goals included total disarmament of all nations and the abolition of "the right to wage international war." In 1951, under her direction, WOMAN sought to entrust the Society of Friends with the Korean truce negotiations. She maintained that the U.S., no less than the Soviets, menaced humanity by developing nuclear weapons. She had said four years earlier, "A corpse is neither a Communist nor a democrat."

Increasingly, Thompson found solutions lying in the realm of the spirit, not politics, and in November 1946 she called for a revival of a belief in "the absolute." American schools, she claimed, taught a dangerous relativism. In April 1949, she admitted she had unwittingly harbored a Soviet agent as a research assistant, writing an article for the *Saturday Evening Post* entitled "How I Was Duped by a Communist." Though she did not object in principle to congressional investigation of suspected subversives, she called McCarthyism "childish, and positively useful to the cause it seeks to injure."

In 1948, Thompson voted for the Socialist presidential candidate Norman Thomas on the grounds that the major parties lacked "serious ideas." In 1952, she originally sought to become

an adviser to the Democratic presidential candidate, Governor Adlai Stevenson of Illinois, but ended up voting for Dwight D. Eisenhower as a protest against "Truman and Trumanism."

Since she first covered the London Zionist Conference in 1920, Thompson had been a major voice for the movement, and during World War II she ardently supported Jewish immigration to Palestine. By July 1946, she was becoming a leading opponent of Jewish nationalism, calling it "an aggressive, chauvinist movement." She expressed strong sympathy for Arab refugees, opposed terrorist activities of the Stern gang and the Irgun, and called the nation-state of Israel "an expansionist power." Despite her long-standing effort on behalf of Jewish refugees, her early and militant opposition to Hitler, and the fact that husband Bard was half-Jewish, she was frequently labeled anti-Semitic.

In 1951, at the request of Rabbi Elmer Berger, executive director of the anti-Zionist American Council for Judaism, Thompson became president of American Friends of the Middle East (AFME), a group promoting Arab speakers in the U.S. and student exchange programs financed in part by the Central Intelligence Agency. In 1957, pressure from the Bell Syndicate caused her to resign this office, although she always remained a strong supporter of the organization.

Thompson's anti-Zionism led to her being dropped by the *New York Post* as early as March 1947, thereby depriving her of any outlet in the nation's largest city. Writes biographer Kurth:

> For the rest of her life she would function without a flagship paper, as an "independent" commentator, subject to cancellation without notice, censored regularly by local editors, and not knowing from one day to the next whether she would still be read by the thousands of people who wrote to praise or condemn her.

Her final years were anti-climatic. Thompson continued her lecture tours, sometimes for weeks at a time. Her husband Kopf, whom she deeply loved, died in July 1958, and at the end of August, weary and grieving, she gave up her column. Her son Michael was a strong disappointment, a heavy drinker whose marriage was in shambles and who was unable to keep a job. Overindulgence in food, amphetamines, and alcohol took its toll on Thompson herself, and moves to Hanover, New Hampshire, and Southern Pines, North Carolina, were simply occasions for boredom. On January 30, 1961, Dorothy Thompson died of a heart attack in Lisbon, Portugal, while visiting her daughter-in-law.

Thompson was by no means flawless. She, like Lewis, neglected any responsibility for raising her son, arbitrarily fired German nationals upon falsely hearing that they were "Nazi spies," overstated many issues, and personalized legitimate differences of opinion. There was a self-conscious showmanship that could degenerate into exhibitionism. On a deeper level, she lacked the kind of philosophical base that would have given cohesion to her often disparate opinions. Little wonder her eight books were all anthologies of speeches or columns. More important, however, she was a crack correspondent in a great age of frontline reporting, second to few in her knowledge of Central Europe, and always a woman of great courage and absolute integrity. In the history of American journalism, few individuals have been able to wield such influence in a period of immense crisis. What she did, said Winston Churchill, "can never be overestimated."

SOURCES:

Kurth, Peter. *American Cassandra: The Life of Dorothy Thompson.* Boston, MA: Little, Brown, 1990.

Sanders, Marion K. *Dorothy Thompson: A Legend in Her Time.* Boston, MA: Houghton Mifflin, 1973.

SUGGESTED READING:

Schorer, Mark. *Sinclair Lewis: An American Life.* NY: McGraw-Hill, 1961.

Sheean, Vincent. *Dorothy and Red.* Boston, MA: Houghton Mifflin, 1963.

COLLECTIONS:

The papers of Dorothy Thompson are located at Syracuse University.

Justus D. Doenecke,
Professor of History, New College,
University of South Florida, Sarasota, Florida

Thompson, Eliza (1816–1905)

American reformer who assisted in the founding of the National Woman's Christian Temperance Union. *Born Eliza Jane Trimble on August 24, 1816, in Hillsboro, Ohio; died on November 3, 1905, in Hillsboro; daughter of Allen Trimble (a governor of Ohio) and Rachel (Woodrow) Trimble; married James Henry Thompson (a lawyer), on September 21, 1837; children: Allen Trimble, Anna Porter, John Henry, Joseph Trimble, Maria Doiress, Mary McArthur, Henry Burton, John Burton.*

Born in 1816 and raised in a devout Methodist family, Eliza Jane Trimble grew up in rural Ohio. Her father Allen Trimble was already a prominent politician at the time of her birth; he would serve as acting governor and then governor of Ohio by the time she was ten years old. He was also a leader in the emerging temperance movement, and instilled in Eliza a belief in the evils of alcohol. Eliza was thus exposed to high-level state politics and to a devout and active Christian life from an early age, which influenced her later reformist efforts. She attended private schools in Cincinnati and at age 21 married a lawyer, James Henry Thompson. The couple settled in her hometown of Hillsboro, Ohio, in 1842. Over the next two decades, Thompson raised eight children. In 1873, she became involved in the temperance movement. The "crusade" against drinking which she launched in the town appealed both to her Methodist faith and its stress on an active life and to her belief in the importance of political action for the moral good. She led groups of women through Hillsboro, calling on saloon owners and druggists to stop selling alcohol, sometimes holding impromptu prayer meetings in these businesses until the owners obtained an injunction against Thompson's group for disturbing the peace. The Hillsboro women received considerable attention in newspapers, and their example inspired similar groups across the country. Momentum grew rapidly for a nationwide organization to guide the "Women's War," as it was dubbed. In November 1874, Thompson was a celebrity figure at the founding of the National Woman's Christian Temperance Union (WCTU) in Cleveland, Ohio, where the efforts of the Hillsboro temperance activists were hailed as the beginning of a new morality in American society. Now almost 60, Eliza Thompson did not continue her activism after the national movement began. She died at her Hillsboro home at age 89 in 1905.

SOURCES:

James, Edward T., ed. *Notable American Women, 1607–1950: A Biographical Dictionary.* Cambridge, MA: The Belknap Press of Harvard University, 1971.

Laura York, M.A. in History,
University of California,
Riverside, California

Thompson, Elizabeth Rowell (1821–1899)

American philanthropist. Born Elizabeth Rowell on February 21, 1821, in Lyndon, Vermont; died on July 20, 1899, in Littleton, New Hampshire; daughter of Samuel Rowell and Mary (Atwood) Rowell; married Thomas Thompson, in January 1844 (died 1869); no children.

Underwrote the Chicago-Colorado Colony of Longmont, Colorado (1871); enrolled as the first patron of the American Association for the Advancement of Science (1873); subsidized the establishment of the Yellow Fever Commission (1878); founded the Elizabeth Thompson Science Fund (1885).

A patron of the arts, scientific research, and women's political causes, Elizabeth Rowell Thompson was born in 1821 and grew up in a farming family of New Hampshire and Vermont. Intelligent and inquisitive, she attended public schools and worked as a maid in her teen years. Her life changed dramatically when, on a visit to Boston in 1843, at age 22, she happened to meet Thomas Thompson. Wealthy, well educated, and more than 20 years her senior, Thompson fell in love with Elizabeth, and they were married only a few weeks later. The couple lived in Boston and New York City, where they indulged their interests in collecting art and supporting charitable and political causes.

After her husband's death in 1869, Elizabeth Thompson, a very wealthy widow with no children, expanded her philanthropic activities. Perhaps her most important contributions were to organizations for scientific research. A professed Christian but not a member of any one church, she donated generously to organizations working in the natural sciences. Her gift of $1,000 to the new American Association for the Advancement of Science and her donation of over $25,000 to a start-up organization called the International Scientific Society were only two of the more significant gifts she made. The International Scientific Society soon folded, but its leaders later organized as the Elizabeth Thompson Science Fund.

Elizabeth Thompson was also an important patron of the campaigns for women's suffrage and the Christian temperance movement. In the 1870s, she also supported experiments in communitarian living. She provided the seed money for the Chicago-Colorado Colony in Longmont, Colorado, designed in 1871 to provide a cooperative, self-supporting community for residents of overpopulated urban areas.

Although the colony failed to attract the expected migrants from the East Coast, Thompson did not lose hope in such preplanned communities, and in 1879 she founded the Co-operative Colony Aid Association with clerics and the British utopian George Jacob Holyoake, who personally enjoyed Thompson's support for many years. Thompson was also the principal patron of the communal farm in Salina, Kansas, known as the Thompson Colony.

Elizabeth Thompson suffered partial paralysis after an apoplectic attack in 1890, and was forced to give up the active philanthropic life she had led for almost 50 years. Her last decade was spent being cared for by family in Connecticut. She died in Littleton, New Hampshire, at age 78,

in 1899. Her estate had an estimated worth of over $400,000 at her death, though she made no bequests for charitable causes in her will.

SOURCES:

James, Edward T., ed. *Notable American Women, 1607–1950: A Biographical Dictionary*. Cambridge, MA: The Belknap Press of Harvard University, 1971.

Read, Phyllis, and Bernard L. Witlieb. *The Book of Women's Firsts*. NY: Random House, 1992.

Laura York, M.A. in History,
University of California,
Riverside, California

Thompson, Elizabeth Southerden

(1846–1933).

See Butler, Elizabeth Thompson.

Thompson, Eloise Bibb

(1878–1928)

African-American writer and journalist. Born Eloise Bibb on June 29, 1878, in New Orleans, Louisiana; died on January 8, 1928; daughter of Charles H. Bibb (a customs inspector) and Catherine Adele Bibb; graduated from Teachers College of Howard University, 1908; married Noah Thompson (a historian and journalist), on August 4, 1911.

Published Poems *(1895); taught public school in Louisiana (1901–02); headed the Social Settlement at Howard University, Washington, D.C. (1908–11); wrote for the* Los Angeles Tribune *and* Morning Sun; *sold first work of drama,* A Reply to Clansmen *(1915); authored short fiction.*

African-American teacher, writer, and religious activist Eloise Bibb Thompson grew up in Louisiana, the only child of a devoutly Catholic middle-class couple. Educated in New Orleans public schools and drawn to writing from an early age, with her parents' support Eloise Bibb published her first book of poetry before she was 18. She entered Oberlin College Preparatory Academy in 1899, returning to teach in New Orleans in 1901. However, the following year she left Louisiana again to attend Howard University's Teachers College in Washington, D.C., graduating six years later. She remained in Washington as director of Howard's Social Settlement program until 1911, when she became the second wife of the respected African-American Catholic journalist Noah Thompson. The couple settled in Los Angeles, California.

Both devout, progressive Catholics wanting to help black Americans advance socially, the Thompsons worked together as writers, teachers, and church volunteers. Eloise Thompson became a contributor to the *Los Angeles Tribune* and the *Morning Sun*, and also wrote poetry and fiction for Catholic journals such as *The Tidings* and *Out West*. Her fiction and her plays often concerned racial issues and sometimes caused considerable controversy. She wrote four plays, three of which were produced in Los Angeles with black casts for black audiences—*Caught* (1920), *Africannus* (1922), and *Cooped Up* (1924). She also wrote numerous short stories on racial themes, including the critically acclaimed "Mademoiselle 'Tasie—A Story," published in 1925, which examined the issue of "passing" among Creoles, a theme Thompson returned to in later works.

It was during her early years in Los Angeles that Thompson, along with her husband, came to articulate a belief that the best way black Americans could help themselves and their race was not through political acts but through joining the church and performing good works which would bring meaning and peace to their lives. The crucial importance she gave to the role of religious faith becomes increasingly evident in Thompson's later plays, stories, and poems. In 1928, Eloise Thompson died at age 49 in Los Angeles.

SOURCES:

Smith, Jessie Carney, ed. *Notable Black American Women*. Detroit, MI: Gale Research, 1992.

Laura York, M.A. in History,
University of California,
Riverside, California

Thompson, Era Bell (1906–1986)

African-American journalist. Born on August 10, 1906, in Des Moines, Iowa; died on December 29, 1986, in Chicago, Illinois; daughter of Steward C. Thompson (a farmer and laborer) and Mary (Logan) Thompson; attended North Dakota State University; graduated from Morningside College, 1933; attended Medill School of Journalism, Northwestern University.

Contributed articles to the Chicago Defender; *won the Newbery fellowship (1945); published an autobiography,* American Daughter *(University of Chicago Press, 1946); won the Bread Loaf Writer's fellowship (1949); was managing editor of* Negro Digest *(1947–51); was managing editor, then promoted to international editor,* Ebony *(1951–86); given National Press Club citation (1961); named Outstanding Woman of the Year, Iota Phi Lambda (1965); granted honorary degrees from Morningside College (1965) and University of North Dakota (1969); inducted into the Iowa Hall of Fame (1978); member of Hull House, Urban League, Chicago Council on Foreign Relations, and the Chicago Press Club.*

A long-time editor for *Ebony* magazine, African-American writer Era Bell Thompson was born in 1906 and raised in Des Moines, Iowa, and Driscoll, North Dakota. Although her parents had little money and four children to support, Thompson entered North Dakota State University after graduating from a public high school in Driscoll. In college, she became a competitive athlete, a member of the track and basketball teams as well as an acrobat who dreamed of becoming a professional contortionist. During her junior year, she left North Dakota State University for Morningside College in Iowa. At Morningside, her teachers recognized her literary talent, but it took Thompson some time to decide to pursue a career in journalism.

She began to write for the *Chicago Defender*, first publishing articles in her own name, then, after causing some controversy for her political stands, publishing as the western cowboy "Dakota Dick." She graduated from Morningside in 1933 and studied for a time at Northwestern University's Medill School of Journalism. She then moved to Chicago hoping to find a job as a writer, but the impact of the Depression made work for African-American women writers impossible to find. She supported herself during these difficult years through a variety of skilled administrative jobs with the Works Progress Administration (WPA) and other government agencies, as well as with unskilled manual jobs, including work as a waitress and elevator operator.

Thompson was working for the Illinois State Employment Services in 1945 when she applied for and was awarded a Newbery writing fellowship. She used the money to write an autobiography, although she was only 41 years old. The book, published in 1946 as *American Daughter*, brought Thompson considerable critical acclaim, especially from members of the black literary community. One of those impressed by her work was John H. Johnson, publisher of the new journals *Negro Digest* and *Ebony*. He offered Thompson a job as managing editor of *Negro Digest*, a position she kept for four years before being named co-managing editor of *Ebony*, where she remained from 1951 to 1964. In 1954 her second book, *Africa, Land of My Fathers*, part travelogue and part history of African civilizations, was published. In 1964, Thompson was promoted to international editor of *Ebony*. She continued to work despite a diagnosis of breast cancer and a mastectomy while in her 60s.

Era Bell Thompson's work as a writer and editor for *Ebony* was recognized with numerous honors during her nearly 40-year career, including a National Press Club citation in 1949, honorary degrees from Morningside College (1965) and the University of North Dakota (1969), and induction into the Iowa Hall of Fame (1978). Radcliffe College also honored Thompson by including her in its Black Women Oral History Project (1978).

SOURCES:

Smith, Jessie Carney, ed. *Notable Black American Women*. Detroit, MI: Gale Research, 1992.

Laura York, M.A. in History, University of California, Riverside, California

Thompson, Estelle (1911–1979).

See Oberon, Merle.

Thompson, Flora (1876–1947)

English writer, unrecognized for much of her career, whose autobiographical trilogy about rural peasant life in the late 19th century is now treasured as a literary classic. Born Flora Jane Timms on December 5, 1876, at Juniper Hill, near Brackley, in the northeast corner of Oxfordshire, England; died at Brixham, England, on May 21, 1947; daughter of Albert Timms (a stonemason) and Emma (Lapper) Timms (a nursemaid prior to her marriage); attended a village school at Cottisford, Oxfordshire; married John Thompson (a post-office clerk); children: Basil, Winifred, and Peter.

Born at Juniper Hill, a hamlet on the boundary between Oxfordshire and Northamptonshire; educated at the school in the neighboring village of Cottisford; at age 14, left home to work as assistant to the post-office clerk in nearby Fringford; later worked in the post office at Grayshott in Hampshire; lived in Bournemouth (1903–16), where her two oldest children, Basil and Winifred, were born; began writing for magazines when her children grew beyond infancy; moved to Liphook (1916), where her son Peter was born; published Bog Myrtle and Peat, *a volume of verse (1921); moved to Dartmouth (1928); began to write sketches of her childhood (1937) that became the trilogy of rural life in the 1880s and 1890s,* Lark Rise to Candleford *(published 1945), which established her reputation as a writer.*

Selected writings: Bog Myrtle and Peat *(1921);* Lark Rise *(1939),* Over to Candleford *(1941), and* Candleford Green *(1943) were also published as the trilogy* Lark Rise to Candleford *(1945);* Still Glides the Stream *(1948).*

Flora Thompson's late blossoming as a writer is one of the most astonishing and unusual stories in English literature. It is also one of the least well-documented stories of a writer who lived in the 20th century. Although she later wrote, according to **Margaret Lane**, that she could not "remember the time when [she] did not wish and mean to write," and although she earned small sums as a professional writer most of her married life, she did not gain a reputation as a serious and established writer until she was in her 60s. Her slow development and emergence as a writer occurred against almost overwhelming odds: a background of rural poverty; scant formal education; lack of encouragement from her family; and the absence of a community of sympathetic readers and writers from whom she could draw inspiration, confidence, and support. Despite these disadvantages, she always regarded writing as central to her life and personal identity: "My brother and I used to make up verses and write stories and diaries from our earliest years, and I never left off writing essays for the pleasure of writing. No one saw them; there was no one likely to be interested."

By the time Flora Thompson had achieved a degree of fame and critical acclaim in her late 60s, she said that she was "too old to care much for the bubble reputation." Both she and her family were surprised by the late success that she had few years to enjoy. Since childhood she had lived on the fringes rather than at the center of the life around her, and her habit of solitude intensified as she grew older. She had always cherished what little privacy and leisure she could reserve from her obligations to her family and work to read voraciously, to take long walks through fields, heaths, and forests, and to retreat to the inner life she lived so intensely—an inner life nourished by memory, imagination, and an acute love of nature.

Flora's father Albert Timms was a stonemason, the son of a master builder from Oxford whose drinking and gambling led to the decline of fortune through which he became first a publican and later a builder's laborer. Albert was a skilled mason, proud of his stone-carving and hopeful of becoming a sculptor before drink and discontent took their toll on his early ambitions. In his 20s, he settled in Juniper Hill, a hamlet of about 30 cottages populated almost entirely by farm laborers, and for the next 35 years he walked three miles back and forth every day to work for a builder in Brackley. He resented the poverty he and his family endured throughout their lives, but seems to have done little to improve their lot. According to Lane, Flora remembered him as "a terrible spendthrift. . . . he never seemed to grasp the fact that he was responsible for our upbringing . . . . He had all of the bad qualities of genius and a few of the good ones."

Flora's mother, born Emma Lapper, from the nearby village of Ardley, was the daughter of an "eggler," an entrepreneurial intermediary of the period who collected eggs in his cart from farms and villages to sell at the nearby market town. Like most girls of the area, Emma went "into service" at age ten and had been nurse-maid at Fewcott Rectory before she married Timms. She gave birth to ten children between 1875 and 1898, six of whom lived beyond three years of age. **Emma Timms** was a great story-teller, and her memory was a storehouse of tradi-tional songs, games, and stories, with which she delighted her children.

Her mother's talent for evoking another world through story, and her father's youthful ambition to refine his talent for stone-carving beyond the workaday world of his trade, ac-count for the introspective, poetic temperament of the cottage child whose future was assumed to lie "in service." The distinctive quality of Flora Thompson's talent, however, was nurtured by the unlikely environment of Juniper Hill, the hamlet she describes in the first part of her trilo-gy, *Lark Rise:* "All around, from every quarter, the stiff, clayey soil of the arable fields crept up: bare, brown and windswept for eight months out of the twelve. . . . only for a few weeks in later summer had the landscape real beauty." In the 1880s, this community of poor farm labor-ers, who earned a standard wage of ten shillings a week that hardly provided for their basic needs, was barely touched by the Industrial Rev-olution that was transforming both the land-scape of England and the lives of its people. In *Lark Rise,* Thompson records that in Juniper Hill the women still "went to the well in all weathers, drawing up the buckets with a wind-lass and carting them home suspended from their shoulders by a yoke," and people rushed to their cottage doors to see "one of the old penny-farthing high bicycles" that passed through the hamlet at rare intervals.

Most of what is known about Flora Thomp-son's early years is recorded as thinly disguised autobiography in *Lark Rise* through the fiction-alized third person of Laura. Like Flora, Laura is the oldest child of a stonemason and his wife Emma. Flora's brother and closest companion, Edwin, a year and a half younger than she, ap-pears as Edmund in the book. Flora/Laura knew and was known to the inhabitants of every cot-tage in the hamlet, and she grew up with inti-mate knowledge of the natural world—the

fields, ditches, ponds, and hedgerows, the flow-ers and wild herbs, the birds and animals that she passed daily on her mile-and-a-half walk to the National School in the "mother village" of Cottisford, called Fordlow in the book.

Like the other children in the hamlet, Flora went to school from the age of five until twelve, when most girls went into service to earn their own living, as well as to make room in the cottage for the younger children. Her mother, expecting her to become a nursemaid, was disappointed to find her daughter more interested in reading and writing than in infants and wondered what would become of her quiet, reflective child. It appears that Flora, like Laura in *Over to Candleford,* found herself after leaving school "growing up . . . into a world that had no use for her." Then an old friend of her mother's, the postmistress of Fring-ford, a village eight miles from Juniper Hill, agreed to take Flora as an assistant, and she left home at 14 with a store of vivid memories that she would record some 50 years later.

When she went to work at the post office at Fringford in 1890, her responsibilities included selling stamps, sorting letters, and working the new telegraph machine. She lived with the post-mistress, and soon read every book in the cot-tage, including Shakespeare and the forbidden copy of Byron's *Don Juan.* She then took out a library ticket at the Mechanics Institute in a neighboring town and read the novels of Austen, Scott, Dickens, and Trollope. Though she never again suffered from the scarcity of books she felt at Juniper Hill, Thompson tells in *Candleford Green* how the young woman missed most in her new life "her old freedom of the fields . . . ; she longed to go alone far into the fields and hear the birds singing, the brooks tinkling, and the wind rustling through the corn, as she had when a child." This need was answered when she became a letter-carrier, a new responsibility that gave her the opportunity to walk each morning through the fields and woods she loved, delivering mail to outlying homes before return-ing to the daily routine at the post office.

For about five years, Flora Thompson re-mained in her job, until once again, as it had when she left school, the uncertainty of the fu-ture loomed before her. The world beyond Fringford beckoned, and she tried holiday-relief work at several other post offices before taking a position as postmaster's assistant in Grayshott, Hampshire. At Grayshott, she had access to li-braries and second-hand bookstores through which she continued her self-education. Besides her reading, she occupied her spare time writing

Flora
Thompson

stories and verses and keeping her diary, as she had since childhood. For the first time, she came in contact with living writers, for among those who came to the post office at Grayshott were Arthur Conan Doyle and George Bernard Shaw; they apparently did not notice the shy young postal assistant who closely but discreetly observed them as they came to post their mail. Thompson continued her habit of solitude, roaming the heaths and forests of the region and developing her naturalist's eye. She lived independently for the first time when she moved from lodgings with the Grayshott postmaster's family to her own bed-sitting room in 1901.

At 24, she married John Thompson, a post-office clerk from Aldershott, recently transferred to the main post office in Bournemouth, where she began her married life. She soon learned that her husband's family, influenced by the new middle-class suburban mass culture emerging in the early years of the 20th century, looked down upon her "cottage" origins and regarded her compulsion to read and write as an oddity and a waste of time. Her husband, too, disapproved of her writing, and since she soon had two children, Basil and **Winifred**, to care for, she had little leisure to pursue this pleasure. Nonetheless, Flora used the free library at Bournemouth to continue her reading, and when her children had grown beyond infancy began her writing again secretly.

She was surprised when an essay on *Jane Austen she had submitted for a competition in a women's newspaper won a prize. When she sent the paper another article and a short story which were accepted and for which she was paid, her husband had a change of heart about her writing. As long as it paid and did not interfere with her home duties, her writing was tolerated, if not valued and encouraged. Her writing, at this stage, assumed two different directions: she found she could easily write and sell what she called "small, sugared love stories" to earn enough to give her children a good education; and she wrote verse to please herself, for her secret ambition was to become a poet.

During this time, she made the one literary friendship of her life. For a contest, she submitted a critical essay on an ode published in *The Literary Monthly* about the *Titanic* disaster by Ronald Campbell Macfie, a Scottish physician and poet, who was so impressed with her winning entry that he wrote to her. A correspondence developed between them, and he encouraged her to continue her writing. Flora Thompson's friendship with Macfie continued until his death 20 years later. She remembered him as the only person who had given her encouragement and confidence to pursue her ambition to become a poet.

To be born in poverty is a terrible handicap to a writer. I often say to myself that it has taken one lifetime for me to prepare to make a start. If human life lasted two hundred years I might hope to accomplish something.

—Flora Thompson

The years of the First World War brought many changes to Thompson's life. In 1916, John Thompson was promoted to a subpostmastership at Liphook, in Hampshire, and the family moved. There, Flora helped the war effort by sorting extra mail and filling in at the post office for a clerk who had been drafted. She was devastated by grief when her brother Edwin, who played so large a part in her memories of childhood, was killed in action. Then, at 41, she gave birth to her last child, Peter. She had been unable to write since Edwin's death, but when the war was over and her older children were at good day schools as a result of her earnings, she began to write again. With Macfie's encouragement, she collected her verses and sent them to a publisher. The collection, *Bog Myrtle and Peat*, was dedicated to Dr. Macfie and published in 1921.

Although the book was favorably reviewed, it failed to sell, and Flora Thompson remained relatively unknown as a poet.

She was more successful with her prose: she sent several nature essays to *The Catholic Fireside*, which were so well received by readers that she continued the series for eight years; many of these pieces have been collected by Margaret Lane and published as *A Country Calendar*. Thompson also wrote occasional essays for *The Daily News* and various women's magazines. In 1924, she founded the Peveral Society, a round-robin postal club through which writers could find something of the kind of literary community she missed so much in her own life. Members circulated their work and wrote critiques of one another's efforts. She felt so strongly the importance of the Society in encouraging aspiring writers that she worked for it assiduously for the next 18 years.

In 1928, John Thompson was once again transferred, this time to Dartmouth, where Flora was to spend the next 12 years of her life in relative seclusion, her contacts with the outside world limited to members of the Peveral Society. She began to write several novels, but none satisfied her. One of them, "Heatherly," based on her years at Grayshott before her marriage, tells the story of Laura's young adulthood, but Thompson later decided not to offer it to her publishers. It is still unpublished. Then in the '30s, she began to write sketches of her childhood. "Old Queenie: A Memory" was published in *Lady* in 1937, and "An Oxfordshire Hamlet in the 'Eighties" and "May Day in the 'Eighties" were published in the *National Review* in 1937 and 1938. She was encouraged to send these and similar pieces to the Oxford University Press, where Sir Humphrey Milford urged her to expand the pieces to make a book.

Thompson worked steadily on what was to become *Lark Rise*. Her purpose, explained in an unpublished letter, was to give a "true picture of the people and time . . . to describe things exactly as they were, without sentimentalizing or dramatizing." A book that blurs the distinctions between fiction, autobiography, the personal essay, and social history, it presents what modern anthropologists would call "thick description" of a culture and way of life that had vanished by the time Thompson recorded it. Through her gift for portraiture, Thompson painted unforgettable characters like Old Sally and Dick, survivors of hard times through their labor and frugality, and Old Queenie, the lacemaker and beekeeper. These characters represent the last generation of the self-sufficient English peasantry, which suffered heavily but endured into the 19th century, after the Enclosure Acts had denied them use of "common" land for farming and grazing; as a class, they did not survive the Industrial Revolution. Thompson also describes the cottage interiors of the hamlet, inventories the belongings of the typical farm laborer's household, and recounts the activities in the ordinary day of the laborer and his family. She recalls childhood games and songs, and records in detail traditional folk celebrations such as May Day and Harvest Home, as well as new celebrations such as Queen *Victoria's Jubilee. When *Lark Rise* was published in 1939, it received universal praise in important reviews. At 63, Flora Thompson had realized her dream of being recognized as a writer.

She immediately began work on *Over to Candleford*, the second book in what was to become a trilogy, which places life at Juniper Hill in the context of a larger outside world and chronicles Laura's development as she moves beyond the hamlet to visit and spend summer holidays with relatives in the small market town of Candleford, where there are shops, pavements, and a railway station. As *Lark Rise* memorializes the vanishing peasantry, so *Over to Candleford* depicts another class on the verge of extinction, the artisans who make and sell their own products in small town shops. Laura's Uncle Tom, modeled on Flora's uncle Recab Holland, was a cobbler or "snob" in Buckingham, who liked to have his bookworm niece read to him from *Elizabeth Gaskell's *Cranford* as he cut and stitched away at the boots he made in his shop for the local gentry. *Over to Candleford* was published in 1941 and warmly received by the growing audience established by the popularity of *Lark Rise*.

In 1940, John Thompson retired, and the Thompsons moved to a cottage at Brixham. Their children were grown; Basil had left England to farm in Australia and Winifred was a nurse in Bristol. Flora was to suffer for a second time the numbing grief she felt after her brother Edwin was killed in World War I: her son Peter, who had joined the Merchant Navy, was killed in 1941 when his convoy ship was torpedoed in the Atlantic. She never fully recovered from this tragedy, but she forced herself to return to work and finished the last book of the trilogy, *Candleford Green*, published in 1943, which recounts Laura's life as assistant to the village postmistress from age 14 to about 20. In 1945, the three books based on her childhood and early youth were published in a single volume, the form in which they are usually read today.

With the publication of *Lark Rise*, Flora Thompson gained a small but enthusiastic and devoted readership. By the time her audience became curious enough to wish to know about the life of this "new" writer, Flora Thompson had died, at age 70, having had little opportunity to savor the literary achievement she had spent virtually her whole life preparing for, and apparently having little wish to share the details of the life she had lived for the last 50 years. Her last book, *Still Glides the Stream*, which she completed only weeks before her death, was published in 1948, a year after she died alone in her room at Brixton in May 1947. Since her death, *Lark Rise to Candleford* (in various editions) has been continuously in print, and appreciation of Flora Thompson's unique talent and achievement has grown. Her book has been used in England as a school text for both historical and literary classes, and in 1978, a study guide to *Lark Rise to Candleford* was published for students preparing for curriculum examinations in English schools. When the *Illustrated Lark Rise to Candleford* was published in 1983, it was on the *Times* bestseller list for 31 weeks. Flora Thompson's book, 60 years in the making, has remained both a popular success and a classic literary and historical work.

SOURCES:

English, Barbara. "Lark Rise and Juniper Hill: A Victorian Community in Literature and History," in *Victorian Studies*. Vol. 29. Autumn 1985, pp. 7–34.

Lane, Margaret. "Introduction" to *Flora Thompson: A Country Calendar and Other Writings*. Oxford: Oxford University Press, 1979.

Massingham, H.J. "Introduction" to *Lark Rise to Candleford: A Trilogy by Flora Thompson*. Hammondsworth: Penguin, 1973.

SUGGESTED READING:

Lindsay, Gillian. *Flora Thompson: The Story of the Lark Rise Writer*. Robert Hale, 1990.

Thompson, Flora. *A Country Calendar and Other Writings*. Oxford: Oxford University Press, 1979.

———. *Lark Rise to Candleford*. Hammondsworth: Penguin, 1973.

RELATED MEDIA:

Dewhurst, Keith, and the Albion Band. "Lark Rise to Candleford: A Country Tapestry" (Charisma Records, 1979).

Dewhurst, Keith. *Lark Rise to Candleford* (play script). London: Hutchinson, 1980.

Lane, Margaret. "Flora Thompson," radio script published in the *Periodical*. Vol. 31, 1956, pp. 209–214.

Patricia B. Heaman,
Professor of English, Wilkes University,
Wilkes-Barre, Pennsylvania

Thompson, Frank (1841–1898).

See Edmonds, Emma.

Thompson, Gertrude Caton (1888–1985).

See Caton-Thompson, Gertrude.

Thompson, Gertrude Hickman

(1877–1950)

American executive and philanthropist. Name variations: Mrs. William Boyce Thompson. Born Gertrude Hickman in 1877 in Virginia City, Montana; died on August 27, 1950, in Yonkers, New York; married William Boyce Thompson (died June 27, 1930).

Named chair of the board, Magma Arizona Railroad, and director of Newmont Mining Corporation (1930); established the Mrs. William Boyce Thompson Foundation.

Born in 1877 and raised in Montana, Gertrude Hickman married William Boyce Thompson, a wealthy railroad owner and president of the Magma Copper Company. After her husband's death in 1930, Gertrude Thompson was named chair of the board of the Bryce Thompson Institute for Plant Research in Yonkers, New York. She also became chair of the Magma Arizona Railroad and was named a director of her husband's Newmont Mining Corporation. Given control of these vast financial resources, Thompson became a philanthropist. She contributed money to help civilians in France, Belgium, and Italy during World War I, and during World War II established an organization to make and distribute clothing to Allied military personnel. Thompson also founded a clinic in Lille, France, to aid children with tuberculosis. She died about age 73 in Yonkers, New York.

SOURCES:
Read, Phyllis, and Bernard L. Witlieb. *The Book of Women's Firsts.* NY: Random House, 1992.

Laura York, M.A. in History, University of California, Riverside, California

Thompson, Grace Gallatin Seton

(1872–1959).

See Seton, Grace Gallatin.

Thompson, Helen (1908–1974)

American musician and orchestra manager. Born on June 1, 1908, in Greenville, Illinois; died of a heart attack on June 25, 1974, in Carmel, California; daughter of Jobe Herbert Mulford and Lena (Henry) Mulford; attended DePauw University, Indiana, 1926–27; graduated from University of Illinois, Phi Beta Kappa, 1932; married Carl Denison Thompson (a research chemist), on April 8, 1933; children: Charles Denison (b. 1940).

Played violin, Charleston Symphony (1940); earned affiliation with the American Symphony Or- *chestra League (ASOL, 1943–70); served as vice-president of ASOL (1963–70); was consultant to the Ford Foundation (1966); served as manager, New York Philharmonic (1970–73); authored various studies, including* The Community Symphony Orchestra: How to Organize and Develop It *(1952).*

Violinist and orchestra manager Helen Mulford Thompson was born in 1908 in the small town of Greeneville, Illinois. She began studying the violin at age six with the encouragement of her father, a pharmacist and clarinet player. Thompson played in her high school orchestra and studied music for one year at DePauw University in Indiana. She left college to work for a time, then in 1929 entered the University of Illinois, earning a degree in sociology and psychology. Following her graduation in 1932 she married a chemist, Carl Thompson. As her husband's job was relocated during the 1930s, Thompson worked for family welfare agencies in Illinois, Wisconsin, and New York. In 1940, the couple moved to Charleston, West Virginia, just before the birth of their only child, Charles.

Thompson did not return to social work after that but instead joined the Charleston Symphony, first as a violinist, then as manager, working to increase publicity and attendance for the new orchestra. She joined the Chicago-based American Symphony Orchestra League (ASOL) in 1943, serving as editor of its newsletter from 1948. The League's mission was to support and guide civic orchestras in issues of publicity, funding, repertoire, and management. Thompson's single-minded dedication to the organization led an anonymous donor in 1950 to make a grant to the League on condition that Thompson become the salaried executive secretary of the organization, its only paid staffmember. From then on, the League operated out of her home.

Thompson's activism on behalf of small orchestras sometimes took her into public view. Arguing that civic orchestras were important cultural institutions, Thompson in 1951 appealed in person to Congress to repeal a surcharge on symphony tickets. Under her leadership the League grew steadily, and by 1970 encompassed over 1,400 member orchestras across the country. She established training programs for conductors and orchestra managers, and wrote several works outlining her management guidelines. Thompson was serving as executive vice-president at the time of her retirement from the League in 1970 to accept the position of manager for the New York Philharmonic orchestra. There she was able to use her experience to publicize the Philharmonic and increase audience attendance. She was obliged to retire in 1973, when she turned 65, and moved to Carmel, California. There she opened a private consulting firm for performing arts organizations which she ran until her death the following year.

SOURCES:

Sicherman, Barbara, and Carol Hurd Green, eds. *Notable American Women: The Modern Period.* Cambridge, MA: The Belknap Press of Harvard University, 1980.

Laura York, M.A. in History,
University of California,
Riverside, California

Thompson, Jenny (1973—)

American Olympic swimmer. Born on February 26, 1973, in Georgetown, Massachusetts; graduated from Stanford University, 1995.

Trained at the Seacoast Swimming Association, Dover, New Hampshire; won a gold medal at the Pan American Games (1987); won 19 NCAA titles and 4 team titles in 4 years of college; set a world record in the 100-meter freestyle at the U.S. Olympic Trials (1992); earned two gold medals and one silver medal, Olympic Summer Games, Barcelona (1992); won six gold medals, Pan Pacific Games (1993); won five U.S. national titles (1993); named "U.S. Swimmer of the Year" (1993); won two gold medals, U.S. National championships (1994); won three individual and two relay events, NCAA championships (1995); contributed to three gold relay medals, Olympic Summer Games, Atlanta (1996); won two individual and two relay gold medals, World championships, Perth (1998); won three gold medals and one silver medal and set a world record, World Short Course championships (1999); won two gold medals and one silver medal and set one world record, World Short Course championships (2000); won three gold medals and one bronze, Olympic Games, Sydney (2000).

Olympic swimmer Jenny Thompson was born in Georgetown, Massachusetts, in 1973. Her parents separated when she was an infant, and Thompson was raised by her mother in Dover, New Hampshire. Drawn to athletics as a child, Thompson was encouraged to pursue competitive swimming despite her family's limited resources, and was soon recognized for her speed and agility. Before she was 13, she had already achieved world ranking in the 50-meter freestyle event. This was the beginning of a remarkable athletic career.

In addition to her many wins at high-school competitions, Thompson earned a gold medal at the 1987 Pan American Games at age 14, the youngest American swimmer to do so. She was an excellent student as well, and after graduating from high school in 1991 was admitted to Stanford University on an athletic scholarship. She led the Stanford women's swim team to national championships all four years she was in college, and won 19 NCAA individual titles, a record. As a sophomore, Thompson set a world record for the 100-meter freestyle event at the Olympic trials, and in the 1992 Summer Olympics in Barcelona she took home two gold medals in the 400-meter team relay events and a silver medal in the 100-meter individual freestyle competition. The following year, she won six Pan Pacific gold medals, five national titles, and five NCAA titles, and was named "1993 U.S. Swimmer of the Year."

In 1995, Thompson graduated from Stanford with a degree in human biology, planning to attend medical school and become a doctor. This goal did not prevent her from continuing to compete internationally. That year, she won three medals at the World championships, and went on to qualify for the 1996 Olympic team. In Atlanta at the Summer Games, she again helped the U.S. women's team to win gold medals in team relays for the 400-meter medley and freestyle events and the 800-meter freestyle. She competed in the World championships in Perth, Australia, in 1998, winning two individual gold medals in the 100-meter freestyle and 100-meter butterfly, and two gold medals for team relay events. Again she was named "U.S. Swimmer of the Year." The next year Thompson set a world record for the 100-meter individual medley event at the World Short Course championships.

Although she did not win an individual gold medal at the 2000 Summer Olympics in Sydney, Thompson did take home three gold medals for team relay events: the 100-meter freestyle, the 100-meter medley, and the 200-meter freestyle. She also won a bronze medal for the 100-meter freestyle. Though thwarted again in her goal to win a gold medal in a non-team event, Thompson currently holds the most gold medals won by any Olympic athlete and is the most decorated American swimmer. As of 2000, she ranked among the ten best swimmers in four events. In 2001, Thompson put her swimming career on hold to begin graduate work at Columbia University's medical program in New York City.

SOURCES:

Johnson, Anne Janette. *Great Women in Sports.* Detroit, MI: Visible Ink, 1998.

Laura York, M.A. in History,
University of California,
Riverside, California

Thompson, Kay (c. 1906–1998)

American entertainer and author who created the "Eloise" series of children's books. Born Kitty Fink around 1906, in St. Louis, Missouri; died in New York City on July 2, 1998; married and divorced twice; no children.

Kay Thompson is best remembered as the creator of four books featuring Eloise, the mischievous pint-sized denizen of the Plaza Hotel who first came to life in 1955 and, in the years since Thompson's death in 1998, has been rediscovered by a new generation. Thompson was also an acclaimed entertainer, a zany, multi-talented woman who viewed life as a banquet of opportunities. "Enthusiasm and imagination can carry you anywhere you want to go," she once proclaimed, "without Vuitton luggage."

Thompson, who would never divulge her age, was born Kitty Fink in St. Louis, Missouri, around 1906, the daughter of a local jeweler. A musical prodigy, she started piano lessons at age four and at sixteen played with the St. Louis Symphony. Shortly after, she became the featured singer with a local dance band. "I was a stage-struck kid," she recalled in an interview

with *Time* magazine (November 10, 1947), "and I got out of St. Louis fast." In 1929, Thompson went to California, where she landed a radio gig as a vocalist with the Mills Brothers. Then it was on to New York, to sing and arrange for the Fred Waring band. She later produced her own radio show, "Kay Thompson and Company," with Jim Backus. "We were an instantaneous flop," she said. "After this show I came to a serious decision. I had to be an actress and I had to be alone. So I went to Hollywood, where I was neither."

Unable to find work as a performer, Thompson signed on with MGM as an arranger and composer. After four years, she created her own night-club act, consisting of sophisticated songs, backed by the Williams Brothers— Richard, Robert, Donald, and Andrew. "The effect," said one reviewer, "was a combination of ballet, barber shop, roughhouse and penthouse that never for a moment got out of hand, but always seemed as if it might." The act opened at Ciro's in Hollywood in 1947 and toured for six years, before disbanding in the summer of 1953. Following the break-up, Thompson busied herself for a time designing trousers for tall women ("Kay Thompson Fancy Pants"), then created a one-woman show, which she opened at New York's Plaza Hotel in January 1954. In it, Thompson played an "outrageously blasé hostess" who entertained imaginary cocktail guests. The show was short-lived, but Eloise was waiting in the wings.

Thompson first dreamed up the irascible child back in the days with the Williams brothers. Priding herself on punctuality and expecting it from others, Thompson was late one day for rehearsal and apologized profusely to her colleagues in a high-pitched childish voice that she had never used before. One of the brothers jokingly asked her, "Who are you, little girl?" Thompson replied, "I am Eloise. I am 6." The others joined in, each assuming a different juvenile character, and the repartee became a regular pastime during rehearsals. Eloise was put aside when the night-club act ended, but reemerged shortly after Thompson began performing her solo show at the Plaza, when a friend introduced her to the artist Hilary Knight, thinking that he might be able to help bring Eloise to life through illustration. Knight sent Thompson the first rendering of Eloise on a Christmas card, and the two became collaborators a short time later.

Thompson took a three-month leave from her show to write the first Eloise book, *Eloise: A Book for Precocious Grown Ups*, which was

$\mathcal{K}$ay
$\mathcal{T}$hompson

published by Simon & Schuster in November 1955. By the time the first sequel, *Eloise in Paris*, was published in 1957, the initial book had sold 150,000 copies. The second volume sold 100,000 copies within a week and prompted a reviewer from *Publishers Weekly* (December 16, 1957) to explain the little girl to anyone who might still be in the dark. "Eloise is an overprivileged six-year-old, the terror of the Plaza Hotel in New York. She is also ill-mannered, ill-tempered and ugly. But she has her charm. She often means well, and her mother neglects her. Even though you know that you would do the same thing if she were yours, you can't help finding this appealing."

By the time Thompson's second book hit the shelves, Eloise had her own corporation, Eloise, Ltd., appropriately located at the Plaza Hotel. In 1963, the Plaza also established an Eloise room. Eloise merchandise included recordings, postcards, dolls, fashions, and an Emergency Hotel Kit for itinerant six-year-olds. Meanwhile, Thompson produced three additional sequels: *Eloise at Christmastime* (1958), *Eloise in Moscow* (1959), and *Eloise Takes a Bawth* (1964).

When not writing, Thompson continued to pursue her performing career, appearing with *Audrey Hepburn and Fred Astaire in the movie *Funny Face* (1956), and starring in her own television special, which, according to the *New York Herald Tribune* (October 16, 1957), was "an almost unqualified disaster." In 1970, she made another movie appearance in *Tell Me That You Love Me, Junie Moon*. That year, she abandoned Eloise to write *Miss Pooky Peckinpaugh and Her Secret Private Boyfriends Complete with Telephone Numbers*.

In her later years, Thompson, who was married and divorced twice and had no children, resided in Manhattan with her goddaughter **Liza Minnelli**. Her friendship with *Judy Garland and Vincente Minnelli dated back to her Hollywood days when she worked on the Minnelli-Garland movie *The Harvey Girls*. Before her death, Thompson had agreed to keep the original Eloise in print, but requested that the three sequels not be reprinted. After her death, her family allowed Simon & Schuster to reissue the unavailable titles, thus unleashing Eloise on a new crop of young, and not so young, readers. Also published was a new edition of the first book, retitled *Eloise: The Absolutely Essential Edition*, which included an 18-page scrapbook overview of Eloise's history by **Marie Brenner**, with assistance by Hilary Knight. Both declared the project "an act of love."

SOURCES:

"Blithe Spirit," in *People Weekly*. July 20, 1998.

Current Biography 1959. NY: H.W. Wilson, 1959.

Di Marzo, Cindi. "Kay Thompson's Eloise Makes a Comeback," in *Publishers Weekly*. April 5, 1999.

McHenry, Robert, ed. *Famous American Women*. NY: Dover, 1983.

"Obituary," in *The Boston Globe*. July 8, 1998.

"Obituary," in *The Day* [New London, CT]. July 7, 1998.

Barbara Morgan,
Melrose, Massachusetts

Thompson, Louise (1901–1999)

African-American educator, labor organizer, and social reformer. Name variations: Louise Patterson. Born Louise Alone Thompson on September 9, 1901, in Chicago, Illinois; died on August 27, 1999, in New York City; graduated from the University of California at Berkeley, 1923; married Wallace Thurman (a novelist and playwright), in August 1928 (separated 1929, died 1934); married William Patterson (a lawyer), in 1940 (died 1980); children: (second marriage) one daughter, Mary Louise Patterson (b. 1943).

A leading figure in the civil-rights and social-reform movements of the 1930s and 1940s, Louise Thompson was also associated with New York's Harlem Renaissance, mainly through her marriage to novelist and playwright Wallace Thurman, her first husband, and her long-time association with poet Langston Hughes, who dedicated his 1942 collection of poems, *Shakespeare in Harlem*, to her.

Thompson was born in 1901 in Chicago, Illinois, but spent her early years in a succession of small, predominantly white, towns across the Pacific Northwest, where her restless stepfather worked as a chef and her mother picked up jobs as a domestic. She and her mother, both light-skinned, frequently passed for white or Mexican as they moved from town to town, which helped overcome the racial alienation and isolation of their itinerant lives.

While attending the University of California at Berkeley, Thompson continued to alter her ethnic identity, finding most employment opportunities closed to black applicants. At Berkeley, however, she attended a lecture on racism by sociologist and historian W.E.B. Du Bois, whose uplifting message so motivated her that she became determined to move East and become part of the black literary renaissance he helped to inspire. It would be several years, however, before she would realize her goal.

After graduating in 1923 with a degree in business administration, Thompson spent a year teaching at a black college in Pine Bluff, Arkansas, then accepted a position at Hampton Institute in Virginia, a college with a black student body but a predominately white administration and faculty. Strongly opposing the subtly racist and paternalistic policies of the school, Thompson supported a student strike at Hampton before leaving for New York in 1928, to study at the New School for Social Research under a scholarship from the Urban League.

Thompson became part of the lively social circle of the Harlem Renaissance through her friendship with the painter Aaron Douglas and his wife **Alta Douglas**. Through them, she met writer Wallace Thurman, who hired her as a typist. Romance ensued and Thompson married Thurman in August 1928, overlooking his homosexuality and his chronic alcoholism and depression. They separated six months later, although the marriage was not terminated until Thurman's death in 1934. Meanwhile, Thompson became a secretary to Langston Hughes, whom she had first met when he gave a poetry reading at Hampton Institute. Having much in common, the two became close friends and often socialized together, although, contrary to rumors at the time, they were never romantically involved.

In 1932, after helping to form a Harlem branch of the Friends of the Soviet Union, Thompson was recruited by James W. Ford, the leading black American Communist of the day, to gather a group of black artists, writers, and intellectuals to travel to Moscow to make a Soviet-sponsored movie entitled "Black and White," about white supremacy in America. With much difficulty, Thompson assembled 22 participants for the project, including her friend Hughes, whom she recruited to help write the English dialogue for the screenplay. The project was canceled, however, shortly after the arrival of the group on Soviet soil. Ostensibly, the cancellation was blamed on an inefficient Soviet film company, although the true reason may have been the Soviet fear of negative American reaction. Despite the project's demise, Thompson was overwhelmed by the preferential treatment she received in the USSR. "For all of us who experienced discrimination based on color in our own land, it was strange to find our color a badge of honor, our key to the city, so to speak," she wrote in an article for *Freedomways* titled "With Langston Hughes in the USSR" (1968). Some in the group, however, saw Thompson as too trusting of her Russian hosts and took to calling her Madam Moscow.

Returning to the United States, Thompson became more politically radical than ever, organizing a march on Washington, D.C., to protest the Scottsboro case, which involved nine black youths who were wrongly accused of raping two white women, *Ruby Bates and **Victoria Price**, in a railroad car, and were sentenced to death. She later traveled to Spain to support the Republican cause in the Spanish Civil War. Throughout the 1930s, Thompson also ran a left-wing salon (Vanguard) from her Harlem apartment.

Through her association with the International Workers Order (IWO), a fraternal society affiliated with the Communist Party, Thompson arranged a series of lectures for Hughes entitled "A Negro Poet Looks at a Troubled World." She also persuaded the IWO to publish a collection of his radical poems, *A New Song*. In 1938, she and Hughes founded the Harlem Suitcase Theater, which was housed on the second floor of the IWO community center at West 125th Street. Among the agit-prop plays produced there was Hughes' musical play *Don't You Want to Be Free?*

In 1940, Thompson married William Patterson, a lawyer and the executive secretary of the International Labor Defense, which had defended the Scottsboro Nine. She moved with him to Chicago, where she continued to work for social causes and gave birth to a daughter Mary Louise in 1943. The couple eventually returned to New York, where Patterson died in 1980. Thompson died in a Manhattan nursing home in 1999, at age 97.

SOURCES:

Goldstein, Richard. "Obituaries," in *The New York Times*. September 2, 1999.

Smith, Jessie Carney, ed. *Notable Black American Women*. Detroit, MI: Gale Research, 1992.

SUGGESTED READING:

Berry, Faith. *Langston Hughes, Before and Beyond Harlem*. Westport, CT: Lawrence Hill, 1983.

Huggins, Nathan Irvin. *Harlem Renaissance*. NY: Oxford University Press, 1971.

Lewis, David Levering. *When Harlem Was in Vogue*. NY: Knopf, 1981.

Barbara Morgan,
Melrose, Massachusetts

Thompson, Lydia (1836–1908)

British actress. Born in England in 1836; died in 1908.

Actress Lydia Thompson's career lasted more than 30 years and spanned four continents. She made her debut in 1852 at Her Majesty's Theater in London. In 1864 and 1865, she performed at provincial theaters before also appearing in London at Drury Lane in 1865 and at the Prince of Wales Theater in 1866. Over the course of six years (1868–74), she toured three continents, stopping in America, Australia, and Asia (India). Afterward, on three separate occasions, she returned to the States. In London in 1874, she performed in a satire of *Bluebeard*; she also appeared in *The Sultan of Mocha* at London's Strand Theater in 1886.

Gloria Cooksey,
freelance writer,
Sacramento, California

Thompson, Mary Harris

(1829–1895)

American surgeon and professor. Born on April 15, 1829, in Washington County, New York; died of a cerebral hemorrhage on May 21, 1895; daughter of John Harris (a mine owner) and Calista (Corbin) Thompson; attended Ford Edward Collegiate Institute; graduated from New England Female Medical College, 1863; Chicago Medical College, M.D., 1870.

Helped to establish the Chicago Hospital for Women and Children (1865); cofounded and taught hygiene, obstetrics, and gynecology, Woman's Hospital Medical College (beginning 1870); founded a nurse training school (1874); elected vice-president, Chicago Medical Society (1881); elected to membership, American Medical Association (1886).

Mary Thompson, one of the first American women to become a professional surgeon, was born in Washington County in upstate New York, in 1829, the second oldest in a large family of an iron mine owner. After receiving tutoring at her home in Fort Ann, Thompson attended the Troy Conference Academy in West Poultney, Vermont. She went on to the Fort Edward Collegiate Institute in New York, working as a teacher to support herself through school after her father's iron mine gave out. She then enrolled in the New England Female Medical College in Boston to study physiology and anatomy under the direction of Dr. *Marie Zakrzewska, who soon inspired her to pursue a medical career. At the New York Infirmary for Women and Children, Thompson worked as an intern under both ☞ **Emily** and *Elizabeth Blackwell**, well-known doctors. Elizabeth Blackwell was the first American woman to earn a medical degree.

Thompson graduated with an M.D. degree in 1863 and opened a private practice in Chicago, because it had no other women doctors with whom she would need to compete. Never marrying, she would remain in Chicago the rest of her life as a specialist in abdominal and pelvic surgery

and the only female surgeon in the city. Thompson was also a general practitioner, instructor, and advocate for expanded opportunities for women doctors. Like all women doctors of the time, she faced personal and professional discrimination and ridicule from many male colleagues and the general public, who thought women were morally and intellectually unsuited to be doctors. However, her skill and dedication eventually won over enough colleagues to secure her election as vice-president of the Chicago Medical Society in 1881; she was also elected a member of the American Medical Association in 1886.

The first years of her practice passed during the Civil War. In this period, Thompson worked for the city's Sanitary Committee and led the effort to found a hospital to treat women and children exclusively. When the resulting Chicago Hospital for Women and Children opened in 1865, Thompson was made head of the medical staff. Hoping to obtain more specialized training, she began studying at the Chicago Medical School in 1869, the first year it allowed women students. She received a diploma the following year, immediately before the college shut its doors to women students once again; the other two female students she had studied with were forced to leave the school. At that time William Byford, a colleague and an instructor at Chicago Medical who supported women physicians, urged Thompson to open her own medical school. Byford served as the first director of Thompson's Woman's Hospital Medical College, where Thompson was an instructor in hygiene, gynecology, and obstetrics. The College implemented a training program for nurses in 1874. Renamed the Woman's Medical College in 1879, the school became part of Northwestern University in 1891.

Mary Thompson died after suffering a brain hemorrhage in 1895 at age 66. The Chicago Hospital for Women and Children which she had founded was renamed the Mary Thompson Hospital after her death. Thompson was buried in her native Fort Ann, New York.

SOURCES:

James, Edward T., ed. *Notable American Women, 1607–1950: A Biographical Dictionary.* Cambridge, MA: The Belknap Press of Harvard University, 1971.
Uglow, Jennifer, ed. *International Dictionary of Women's Biography.* NY: Continuum, 1985.

Laura York, M.A. in History,
University of California,
Riverside, California

Thompson, Ruth (1887–1970)

American judge and Republican congressional representative. Born on September 15, 1887, in Whitehall,

Blackwell, Emily.
See Blackwell,
Elizabeth for
sidebar.

Michigan; died on April 5, 1970, in Allegan County, Michigan; graduated from Muskegon Business College, 1905; studied law in night school.

Admitted to the bar of Michigan (1924); elected judge of Muskegon County Probate Court (1925–37); served as a representative, Michigan House of Representatives (1939–41); started private law practice in Michigan (1946); served as representative from Michigan's 9th District, 82nd through 84th Congresses (1951–57); became the first woman to sit on the U.S. House Judiciary Committee.

Born in 1887 in Whitehall, Michigan, Ruth Thompson served in the House of Representatives for six years. She attended public schools in Muskegon County before entering Muskegon Business College to prepare for a career as a court reporter. Thompson graduated in 1905 and went to work as a registrar for the Muskegon County Probate Court, where she would remain for 18 years. In 1918, she began taking law classes at night, and passed the Michigan bar examination in 1924, at age 37. She was then elected county probate judge, a post she held until 1937. At that time she ran successfully on a Republican ticket for the Michigan state legislature.

Thompson served in the legislature for two years before moving to Washington, D.C., for successive positions as an attorney in the Civil Service Commission, the Social Security Board, and the Department of Labor. She worked in the War Department during World War II; after the war, this led to 14 months in Frankfurt, Germany, working for the Adjutant General's office. From Germany, she was assigned to work in Copenhagen, Denmark, after which she returned to Michigan and opened a private law practice in 1946. In 1950, she ran as a Republican for the U.S. House of Representatives from Michigan's 9th District. That November, Thompson defeated two male candidates to become the first woman elected to Congress from Michigan, and began her first term in January 1951.

One of her first acts was to sign a petition seeking removal of Secretary of State Dean Acheson, whose foreign policy was criticized by many Republicans as insufficiently aggressive to the Communist threat in Asia. In her six years in Congress, Thompson served on the House Judiciary Committee, the first woman to do so, as well as on the Joint Committee on Immigration and Nationality Policy. On national issues, she consistently voted with conservative Republicans against the Truman administration, opposing domestic social programs and executive powers while supporting aid to non-Communist nations. In her home district, Thompson was active in many civic and professional organizations, including the prison commission, the State Bar Association, and the Governor's Advisory Board. After serving three terms, she lost the nomination for a fourth term due to delays and problems with a U.S. Air Force base being built in her district, and retired to Whitehall just before her 70th birthday in 1957. In failing health, Thompson entered the Plainwell Sanitorium in Allegan County, where she died in April 1970.

SOURCES:

Current Biography 1951. NY: H.W. Wilson, 1951.

Office of the Historian, U.S. House of Representatives. *Women in Congress, 1917–1990.* Washington, DC: U.S. Government Printing Office, 1991.

Laura York, M.A. in History,
University of California,
Riverside, California

Ruth Thompson

Thompson, Sada (1929—)

American actress. Born on September 27, 1929, in Des Moines, Iowa; daughter of Hugh Woodruff and Corlyss

Elizabeth (Gibson) Thompson; attended Carnegie Institute of Technology; married Donald E. Stewart.

Debuted professionally, University Playhouse, Mashpee, Massachusetts (1947); made New York debut (1953); won three Drama Desk Awards (1956–57, 1969–70, 1971–72); won two Obie (Off-Broadway) Awards (1964–65, 1969–70); won *Antoinette Perry ("Tony") Award for Best Actress, Drama (1972); nominated for five Emmy Awards (1976 [twice], 1980, 1991, 1995); nominated for three Golden Globe Awards for best TV Actress, Drama, for "Family" (1977, 1979–80); won Emmy Award for Outstanding Lead Actress in a Drama Series, for "Family" (1978).

Selected stage roles: appeared as Eliante in The Misanthrope *(1956), Valerie Barton in* The River Line *(1957), Dorine in* Tartuffe *(1965), Beatrice in* The Effect of Gamma Rays on Man-in-the-Moon Marigolds *(1970), Emily, Celia, Dorothy, and Ma in* Twigs *(1971); selected television roles: Mary Todd Lincoln in* "Sandburg's Lincoln" *(1975), Phoebe Rice in "The Entertainer" (1976), Kate Lawrence in "Family" (series, 1976–80), Mama Lozupone in "Cheers" episode (1991); Virginia McMartin in "Indictment: The McMartin Trial" (1995). Also appeared in the San Diego Globe production of Thornton Wilder's* The Skin of Our Teeth *which was broadcast live on PBS in December 1982.*

Actress Sada Thompson's career on stage and television has spanned over five decades and earned her numerous acting awards. She was born in Des Moines, Iowa, in 1929, the daughter of **Corlyss Gibson Thompson** and Hugh Woodruff Thompson. She was first drawn to acting while a student at the Carnegie Institute of Technology in Pittsburgh. She decided to pursue an acting career and made her professional debut on June 30, 1947, at the University Playhouse in Mashpee, Massachusetts, in the role of Harmony Blue-blossom in *The Beautiful People.* For the next five years, she performed regularly in a series of dramas at the Pittsburgh Playhouse and the Henrietta Hayloft Theater in Rochester, New York. In 1951, she made her first television appearance, on the "Goodyear Television Playhouse"; she would appear frequently in non-re-

Sada Thompson (center) in The Effect of Gamma Rays on Man-in-the-Moon Marigolds.

curring roles on television into the 1990s. Her New York City stage debut came in May 1953 at the Kaufmann Auditorium. The critical acclaim she received for her work in New York led to further stage roles over the next two decades in theaters and Shakespeare festivals from Phoenix to Connecticut to California to Wisconsin. Professional honors Thompson received during the 1950s and 1960s include two Obie Awards as well as Drama Desk Awards for her roles in *The River Line* and *The Misanthrope*.

In 1961, Thompson appeared in her first film, *You Are Not Alone*, then returned to the theater. In 1966, she signed a year-long contract with the American Conservatory Theater (ACT) in San Francisco where in 1974, she would portray Madam Ranevskaya in Chekhov's *The Cherry Orchard*. In 1970 at the Mercer-O'Casey Theater in New York, Thompson appeared in her best-known stage role, as Beatrice in Paul Zindel's Pulitzer Prize-winning *The Effect of Gamma Rays on Man-in-the-Moon Marigolds*. Her turn as a bitter, sarcastic woman who often submits her two daughters to emotional abuse earned her both a Drama Desk Award and an Obie Award, and led to her first Broadway role: a four-character part in 1971's *Twigs* at the Broadhurst Theater, in which she performed as Celia, Dorothy, Emily, and Ma. Her performance brought her a 1972 Tony Award for Best Actress. She subsequently took *Twigs* on tour for the 1972–73 season.

By the mid-1970s, Thompson began to concentrate on television roles. In 1975, she was cast as *Mary Todd Lincoln in the television miniseries "Sandburg's Lincoln," for which she was nominated for an Emmy in 1976; she also received a second Emmy nomination that same year for her performance in "The Entertainer." Also in 1976, Thompson began a regular role as matriarch Kate Lawrence in the acclaimed series "Family," garnering three Golden Globe nominations (1977, 1979, and 1980) and winning an Emmy Award for Outstanding Lead Actress in a Drama Series in 1978. Though she usually played in dramatic roles, Thompson also guest-starred on the comedy series "Cheers" in 1991, for which she was again nominated for an Emmy. Between 1977 and 1998, she starred in 15 made-for-television movies and miniseries, most notably in "Our Town" (1977), "The Adventures of Huckleberry Finn" (1981 and 1985), "Alex Haley's Queen" (1993), and "Any Mother's Son" (1997). Her appearance as accused child molester **Virginia McMartin** in "Indictment: The McMartin Trial" (1995) brought her her sixth Emmy Award nomination at age 66.

SOURCES:
Bair, Frank E., ed. *Biography News: January–February 1975*. Detroit, MI: Gale Research, 1975.
Herbert, Ian, ed. *Who's Who in the Theater*. Detroit, MI: Gale Research, 1977.

Laura York, M.A. in History, University of California, Riverside, California

Thompson, Sylvia (1902–1968)

English writer. Born on September 4, 1902, in Scotland; died on April 27, 1968; daughter of Norman Thompson; attended Somerville College, Oxford; married Theodore Luling (an artist), in 1926; children: three daughters.

Selected works: Rough Crossing (1921); The Hounds of Spring (1926); The Battle of the Horizons (1928); Breakfast in Bed (1934); (with Victor Cunard) Golden Arrow (play; 1935).

Sylvia Thompson was born in Scotland in 1902 and raised in Lyndhurst, Hampshire, England, in an upper-class family. She was well educated at Cheltenham, then entered Somerville College in Oxford. Drawn to writing at an early age, at 16 she published her first novel, *Rough Crossing* (1918), the story of a flapper. *A Lady in Green Gloves* appeared in 1924, the year after Thompson left Somerville without finishing a degree. Her third novel, *The Hounds of Spring* (1926), about a young woman whose fiancé turns up after being declared missing and presumably dead during World War I, was a bestseller. After its appearance, Thompson was confirmed as a new literary talent, although her works were written solely as entertaining escapism concerned with the private lives of the British elite.

In 1926, she married an American artist, Theodore D.P. Luling; the couple had three daughters and lived for a time in Venice, but returned to England shortly before World War II. Thompson had published new novels every year or two until the war. Her works were consistently popular with British readers and were praised by many critics for her characterizations and plot development, though they were also derided by some for a lack of substance. Her *Breakfast in Bed* (1934) did attempt a deeper commentary on the English class system, but the following work, *A Silver Rattle* (1935), returned to escapist plot formula as did most of her remaining books and her one play, *Golden Arrow* (1935). Written with Victor Cunard, the play was performed at London's Whitehall Theater, starring *Greer Garson and Laurence Olivier. Thompson wrote few new works after 1945, instead concentrating on raising her family. She died in England in 1968, at age 66.

SOURCES:

Kunitz, Stanley J., and Howard Haycraft, eds. *Twentieth Century Authors*. NY: H.W. Wilson, 1942.

Seymour-Smith, Martin, and Andrew C. Kimmens, eds. *World Authors, 1900–1950*. NY: H.W. Wilson, 1996.

Laura York, M.A. in History,
University of California,
Riverside, California

Thompson, Mrs. William Boyce
(1877–1950).

See Thompson, Gertrude Hickman.

Thoms, Adah B. (c. 1863–1943)

African-American nurse and activist. Name variations: Adah Belle Thoms; Adah Smith. Born Adah Belle Samuels in Richmond, Virginia, on January 12, around 1863 (some sources cite 1870); died in Harlem from a stroke on February 21, 1943, buried in New York's Woodlawn Cemetery under the name Adah Smith; daughter of Harry Samuels and Melvina Samuels; attended elementary public and normal school in Richmond; studied elocution and public speaking at the Cooper Union; graduated from the Woman's Infirmary and School of Therapeutic Massage in New York, 1900; graduated from the Lincoln Hospital and Home school of nursing in New York City, 1905; first marriage undocumented; married Henry Smith, in 1920s (died one year later).

Born in Richmond, Virginia, around 1863, Adah Thoms moved to Harlem, New York, in 1893. After graduating from a New York school of nursing in 1905, she was hired as an operating room nurse and supervisor of the surgical division at Lincoln Hospital. One year later, she was appointed assistant superintendent of nurses, remaining in that position for 18 years.

In 1908, she and *Martha Franklin helped organize the National Association of Colored Graduate Nurses (NACGN); Thoms served as president from 1916 to 1923. During World War I, she campaigned for acceptance of black nurses in the American Red Cross as well as the U.S. Army Nurse Corps. Despite her pioneering effort, black nurses with full rank and pay were not accepted into the Army Nurse Corps until December 1918. Once accepted, those 18 black nurses were then assigned to living quarters separate from the white nurses, in effect quarantined as carefully as were their patients suffering from highly contagious influenza. Thoms' book, *The Pathfinders*, explores their experiences.

In 1921, the assistant surgeon general of the Army appointed Thoms to serve on the Women's Advisory Council on Venereal Disease of the U.S. Public Health Service. In 1936, she became the first nurse to receive the *Mary Mahoney Award from the National Association of Colored Graduate Nurses.

Thomsen, Ellen Osiier (1890–1962).

See Mayer, Helene for sidebar on Ellen Osiier.

Thora (fl. 900s)

*Danish wife of Harald Bluetooth. Flourished in the 900s; one of three wives of Harald Bluetooth (c. 910–986), king of Denmark (r. 940–986). Harald was also married to *Gyrid and a Gunhilde.*

Thora (fl. 1100s)

Queen of Norway. Name variations: Thora Guthormsdottir. Flourished in the 1100s; married Harald IV Gille, also known as Harald IV Gilchrist, king of Norway (r. 1130–1136); children: Sigurd II Mund also known as Sigurd II Mouth (1133–1155), king of Norway (r. 1136–1155).

Thora (fl. 1100s)

A workwoman who had a liaison with Harald IV. Flourished in the 1100s; associated with Harald IV Gille, also known as Harald IV Gilchrist, king of Norway (r. 1130–1136); children: Haakon II the Broadshouldered (b. 1147), king of Norway (r. 1157–1162).

Thora Johnsdottir (fl. 1000s)

*Associated with two kings. Flourished in the 1000s; concubine or wife of Harald III Haardrade (1015–1066), king of Norway (r. 1047–1066); became second wife of Svend II Estridsen (d. 1076), also known as Sweyn Estridsen, king of Denmark (r. 1047–1074); children: (with Harald III) Magnus II Bareleg, king of Norway (r. 1066–1069); Olaf III Kyrri (the Peaceful), king of Norway (r. 1066–1093); (with Svend II) *Ingirid (fl. 1067, illeg.), queen of Norway.*

There are 16 children attributed to Svend II, who had four wives or paramours (Gunhild of Norway, *Gyde, *Elizabeth of Kiev, and Thora Johnsdottir). Any one of the four could be the mother of Svend's royal offspring: Harald Hén, king of Denmark (r. 1074–1080); St. Knud or Canute the Holy, king of Denmark (r. 1080–1086); and Oluf or Olaf Hunger, king of Denmark (r. 1086–1095).

Thorborg, Kerstin (1896–1970)

Swedish contralto. Born on May 19, 1896, in Hedemora, in northern Sweden; died on April 12, 1970, in Falun, Dalarna; daughter of a newspaper editor father and an amateur pianist mother; studied at the Royal Conservatory in Stockholm; married Gustav Bergman (general manager of the Gothenburg Opera).

Made debut at the Royal Theater, Stockholm (1924); sang in Prague, Berlin, Salzburg, and Vienna; debuted at Covent Garden (1936); debuted at New York's Metropolitan Opera as Fricka in Die Walküre *(1936), singing there until 1950; took part in radio broadcast Gluck's* Orfeo ed Eurydice; *taught voice in Stockholm after her retirement (1950).*

𝒦erstin 𝒯horborg

Born in 1896 in Hedmora, Sweden, Kerstin Thorborg was known as a singer who needed to be seen as well as heard. Wrote one critic, "It is difficult to say where singing, acting, costume, and makeup severally begin or end, so organically are they fused into one." Her stage career began when

she sang one performance of *Amneris* with another opera hopeful, a relatively obscure Norwegian soprano named *Kirsten Flagstad. The two would meet again on the stage of the Metropolitan Opera when they sang the first of many memorable *Walküres* together. (Kerstin is the Swedish spelling; Kirsten the Norwegian.) In 1936, Thorborg made a famous appearance in Vienna with Bruno Walter to perform Mahler's song-cycle *Das Lied von der Erde*, from which the first recording was made. This brought her to international prominence. In the early stages of her career, her voice was rich, pure, and steady. She was considered one of the great Orfeos in opera history. She performed at the Metropolitan Opera for 16 years before retiring to teach in Stockholm in 1950. Early recordings document the beautiful voice of this magnificent Swedish singer.

John Haag,
Athens, Georgia

Thoresen, Cecilie (1858–1911)

Norwegian pioneer in the campaign for women's rights. Name variations: Cecilie Krog; Ida Cecilie Thoresen. Born Ida Cecilie Thoresen in Eidsvoll, Norway, in 1858; died in 1911; married Fredrik Arentz Krog (1844–1923, a lawyer); children: son Helge Krog (1889–1962, the dramatist).

Cecilie Thoresen applied to enter the University of Oslo (then known as the University of Kristiania) in 1880, but was refused. Two years later, the Norwegian Parliament passed a law permitting women to sit the matriculation examination and the preliminary level of university examinations. That year, she also matriculated and became the first woman to study at Oslo University. She also studied science at the University of Copenhagen.

In 1883, Thoresen was voted to membership of the Norwegian Students' Union, again the first woman to be admitted. The same year, she founded a discussion group for "the advancement of the women's cause," and became a board member of other women's associations. The Norwegian branch of the International Federation of University Women (NKAL, founded 1920) owed much to these early women's organizations.

SOURCES:
Aschehoug & Glydendal's *Store Norske Leksikon*. Oslo: Kunnskapsforlag, 1992.
Lie & Rørslett, eds. *Alma Maters døtre* (Alma Mater's Daughters). Oslo: Pax, 1995.

Elizabeth Rokkan,
translator, formerly Associate Professor,
Department of English,
University of Bergen, Norway

Thorndike, Sybil (1882–1976)

English actress who, having made her debut in 1904, lived to become the last link between the glories of the Edwardian theater and those of the post-World War II "Age of Olivier." Name variations: Lady Lewis Casson; Dame Sybil Thorndike. Born Agnes Sybil Thorndike on October 24, 1882; died on June 6, 1976; daughter of Canon Arthur John Webster Thorndike and Agnes Macdonald (Bowers) Thorndike; sister of **Eileen Thorndike** *(1891–1954, a successful actress and principal of the Embassy School of Acting, 1933–39) and Russell Thorndike (1885–1972, a distinguished actor and playwright); attended the Guildhall School of Music; married Lewis Casson, in 1908; children: John, Christopher, Mary and Ann.*

Awards: Created Dame Commander of the British Empire (1931); Companion of Honour (1970); LL.D. from the universities of Manchester and Edinburgh, D.Litt from the universities of Southampton, Surrey, Oxford.

Selected roles: made debut as Phyllis in My Lord From Town *(June 18, 1904); toured the U.S. (1904) in a program of Shakespearean plays and classic comedies; made second American tour (1907); made London debut as Janet Morice in* The Marquis *(1908); appeared with Annie Horniman's company; appeared with Charles Frohman's company; appeared as Adrianna in* The Comedy of Errors, *Lady Macbeth in* Macbeth, *Portia in* The Merchant of Venice, *Viola in* Twelfth Night, *Constance in* King John, *Beatrice in* Much Ado About Nothing, *Imogen in* Cymbeline, *Prince Hal in* Henry IV (Part I), *Princess Catherine in* Henry V, *Queen Margaret in* Richard III, *Mistress Ford in* The Merry Wives of Windsor, *the Fool in* King Lear, *the title role in* Everyman, ***Peg Woffington** in* Masks and Faces *(late 1910s); Clara Bortswick in* The Great Day, *Anne Wickham in* Napoleon, *Hecuba in* The Trojan Women, *title role in* Sakuntala *(all 1919); appeared as Hecuba in* The Trojan Women, *title role in* Candida, *title role in* Medea, *Mary Hey in* Tom Trouble, *Beryl Napier in* The Showroom, *Louise in* The Old Woman, *the wife in* The Unseen *(all 1920); appeared at the Odéon in Paris as Lady Macbeth; appeared as Evadne in* The Maid's Tragedy, *title role in* Jane Clegg, *Charlotte Feriol in* The Scandal, *Beatrice in* The Cenci *(1922), April Mawne in* Advertising April, *Imogen in* Cymbeline, *Elinor Shale in* The Lie *(1923); appeared as title role in* Gruach, *Joan of Arc in* Saint Joan, *Sonia in* Man and the Masses, *Rosalind in* As You Like It *(1924); appeared as* Saint Joan, *Daisy Drennan in* The Round Table, *Elinor Shalke in* The Lie, *Queen Katherine in* Henry VIII *(1925), Beatrice in* The Cenci, *Duchesse de Crucy in* Israel, *Gertrude in* Hamlet, *Judith in* Granite, *Helen Stanley in* The Debit Account, *Lady Macbeth (1926); appeared at the Theater des Champs Élysees in* Saint Joan *and* Medea *(1927), at the Old Vic as Katherine, Portia, Beatrice, and the Princess in* Henry V *(1927–28); toured South Africa in* Jane Clegg, Henry V, Much Ado About Nothing, Macbeth, Saint Joan, *and as Mrs. Phelps in* The Silver Cord *(1928–29); appeared as Barbara Undershaft in* Major Barbara, *Lily Cobb in* The Mariners, *Lady Lassiter in* The Donkey's Nose, *and Madame de Beauvais in* Madame Plays Nap *(1929); appeared in the title role in* Phedre, *Sylvette in* The Fire in the Opera House, *Mrs. Alving in* Ghosts, *Emilia in* Othello *(1930); appeared as Monica Wilmot in* Dark Hester, *Eloise Fontaine in* Marriage by Purchase *(1931); in Australia appeared in* Saint Joan, Macbeth, Madame Plays Nap, Captain Brassbound's Conversion, Milestones, The Painted Veil, Advertising April, Granite *and other plays (1932); appeared as Evie Millward in* The Distaff Side, *title role in* Mrs. Siddons *(1933), Victoria Van Brett in* Double Door, *Nourmahal in* Aurengzebe, *the Passenger in* Village Wooing, *and Evie Millward in the New York production of* The Distaff Side *(1934); appeared as Blanche Oldham in* Grief Goes Over, *Lady Bucktroput in* Short Story, *Lisha Gerert in* Farm of the Three Echoes *(1935); toured in* My Son, My Son, Hands Across the Sea *and* Fumed Oak, Village Wooing, *and* Hippolytus *(1936); appeared in London as Ann Murray in* Yes, My Darling Daughter, *as Hecuba in* The Trojan Women *(1937); in New York as Mrs. Conway in* Time and the Conways, *in London as Volumnia in* Coriolanus, *and as Miss Moffat in* The Corn is Green *(1938); toured in mining towns of England and Wales with the Old Vic Company (1940–42); as Constance in* King John, *in title role in* Medea *(1941); toured with the Old Vic, then appeared in a special engagement as Mrs. Alving in* Ghosts, *Lady Cicely in* Captain Brassbound's Conversion *and Mrs. Hardcastle in* She Stoops to Conquer; *in Bristol as Lady Beatrice in* Queen Bee; *Mrs. Dundass in* Lottie Dundass, *in* The Rape of the Lock, *Queen of Hearts and as the Queen in* Alice in Wonderland *and* Through the Looking Glass *(1943); rejoined the Old Vic to play Aase in* Peer Gynt, *Catherine Petkoff in* Arms and the Man, *Queen Margaret in* Richard III, *at the Placa Theater; played in* Alice in Wonderland *(1944); toured with the Old Vic entertaining troops in Germany, Belgium and France and in Paris at the Comédie Française (1945), in London with the Old Vic played Mistress Quickly in* Henry IV, Parts I and II, *Jocasta in* Oedipus Rex *and the Justice's Lady in* The Critic *(1945–46); appeared as Clytemnestra in* Electra *(1946), Mrs. Whyte* *in* Waters of the Moon *(1951), Laura Anson in* A Day by the Sea *(1952); toured the Far East, New Zealand and India with Lewis Casson (1954); toured Australia and New Zealand (1955); appeared as the Grand Duchess in* The Sleeping Prince *and as Mrs. Railton-Bell in* Separate Tables *(1955); toured South Africa, North and South Rhodesia, Kenya, Israel and Turkey with Lewis Casson; appeared in London as Amy, Lady Monchensy in* The Family Reunion *and in New York as Mrs. Califer in* The Potting Shed *(1957); toured Australia and New Zealand (1957–58); as Mrs. St. Maugham in* The Chalk Garden *(1958); as Dame Sophia Carrell in* Eighty in the Shade; *toured England as Mrs. Kittredge in* The Sea Shell *(1959); as Lotta Bainbridge in* Waiting in the Wings *at the Dublin Festival and as St. Teresa in* Teresa of Avila *(1961) in London; toured Australia with Lewis Casson (1962); as Marina in* Uncle Vanya *in Chichester, as Lady Cuffe in* Queen B *in Windsor (1963); as the Dowager Countess of Lister in* The Reluctant Peer, *as Mrs. Stortch in* Season of Goodwill *(1964); as Mrs. Doris Tate in* Return Ticket *(1965); Abby Brewster in* Arsenic and Old Lace *(1966); in Guildford as Clair Ragond in* The Viaduct *and Mrs. Basil in* Cousin Jacky *(1967); toured as Mrs. Bramson in* Night Must Fall *(1968); as the Woman in* There Was an Old Woman *in Leatherhead (1969).*

Selected filmography (in Britain unless otherwise noted): Moth and Rust *(1921);* Tense Moments from Great Plays *(short, 1922);* *Edith Cavell *in* Dawn *(1928);* To What Red Hell *(1929);* Hindle Wakes *(1931);* A Gentleman of Paris *(1932);* Tudor Rose *(1936);* Major Barbara *(1941);* Nicholas Nickleby *(1947);* Britannia Mews *(US, 1948);* Stagefright *(1950);* Gone to Earth *(1950);* The Lady with the Lamp *(1951);* The Magic Box *(1951); Queen* *Victoria *in* Melba *(1953);* The Prince and the Showgirl *(1957);* Alive and Kicking *(1958);* Shake Hands with the Devil *(1959);* Hand in Hand *(1960). Made first television appearance in 1939.*

Unlike so many of her contemporaries in the British theater, Sybil Thorndike was not a Londoner nor was she raised there; rather, she came from Gainsborough, Lincolnshire, in the Midlands of England. Born on October 24, 1882, to a distinctly middle-class family, she was the daughter of Canon Arthur John Webster Thorndike of the Church of England and **Agnes Bowers Thorndike**, and all her life was a deeply religious adherent of the Anglican faith. She grew up in Rochester between London and Dover, where her father was an honorary canon of the local cathedral. She went on to the Guild-

ford School of Music in London to study for a musical career actually making some appearances as a pianist. An injury to her wrist thwarted her original goal, however, and she turned her artistic impulses toward the theater. Entering the Ben Greet academy, she made her debut in Oxford in a farce entitled *My Lord from Town* on June 18, 1904, at age 21. Not long after, she made her Shakespearean debut in *The Merry Wives of Windsor* with the same company. Before ever appearing in London, she spent four years (1904–08) touring the United States with the Ben Greet Company in a repertoire of Shakespearean and other classic English plays. During these years, Thorndike claimed to have played some 112 roles from leads to walk-ons to males parts, most of them Shakespearean and most of them in one-night stands throughout the country. In 1907, having damaged her voice through overuse, she returned home.

Once recovered, Thorndike at last made her London debut at the Scala Theater as Janet Morice in *The Marquise* on February 9, 1908; later that same year, she married the actor (later director) Lewis Casson, whom she had known since their days together with the Ben Greet Company. The couple had four children: John, Christopher, **Mary**, and **Ann Casson**. Lewis Casson was the son of a banker from North Wales and as a young man had intended to become an Anglican priest. Intensely religious, he was nevertheless devoted to the theater and, coming under the influence of Sir Harley Granville-Barker, he was especially drawn to what he considered to be its social and moral role in uplifting the public. Casson's ideas made a profound impression on Thorndike and helped shape her own vision of the role of the theater and the moral responsibilities of those within it. Casson was convinced that something had to be established to counter the commercial London theater, and he saw the expanding repertory companies of his day as the answer to fighting the "star system" and championing new playwrights. A moderate socialist on the order of George Bernard Shaw and the other Fabians, Casson gave a leftward color to Thorndike's own views for the rest of her life. Shortly after their marriage, the Cassons joined ***Annie Horniman**'s highly respected stock company in Manchester, where they gained valuable experience performing in both classic and modern plays, the latter including Shaw's *The Devil's Disciple*. In March 1910, the Cassons joined the London repertory company of the American impresario, Charles Frohman, after which he engaged them to come to America. There, they appeared with the cele-

brated actor John Drew in W. Somerset Maugham's *Smith* both in New York City and later on tour. Returning to London in 1912, Thorndike appeared as Beatrice Farrar in Stanley Houghton's popular Lancashire play, *Hindle Wakes*, for the first time under her husband's direction. Shortly thereafter, she appeared in the title role in Sir John Irvine's feminist play *Jane Clegg*, a part in which she scored a great success and one that she was to repeat often on tour in later years. That same year, she had a second success in Eden Phillpott's *The Shadow*. In these years, Thorndike played a number of "new woman" roles such as that of Clegg, whose prototype was Nora in Ibsen's *A Doll's House*, and Hedda in his *Hedda Gabler*.

With the outbreak of World War I, Lewis Casson joined the army, while Thorndike took a position with the struggling company at the Royal Victoria Hall then under the direction of *Lilian Baylis. Thorndike's four-year tenure with the Old Vic, as it was popularly known, coincided with the company's first attempt to mount all of the plays attributed to William Shakespeare, one after the other, a feat not attempted again until the 1950s (once more by the Old Vic). This was a remarkable period of growth for her as an actress, not only for the experience that it gave her but also for the exposure, night after night in role after role, before the most discriminating theatergoers in the English-speaking world. Until now, she had seemed to be drifting into becoming strictly an interpreter of modern roles, but at the Old Vic she soon appeared as Adrianna in *The Comedy of Errors*, Imogen in *Cymbeline*, Viola in *Twelfth Night*, Constance in *King John*, Beatrice, Rosalind, Portia and Lady Macbeth (*Gruoch) as well as Prince Hal, Puck, and the Fool in *King Lear*, which were just a few of the many roles both male and female, young and old, in which she appeared between the ages of 32 and 36. (The male roles were a necessary chore due to the departure of so many actors for military service.) Though the critics tended to neglect the performances at the Old Vic, in later years critic James Agate noted that it was here that Sybil Thorndike first became a great actress.

After the war and the return of Lewis Casson, Thorndike left the Old Vic and appeared in a number of plays elsewhere in London, the most important of which was *The Trojan Women* by Euripides, in which she played the all-important role of Queen Hecuba, thereby establishing herself as an interpreter of Greek tragedy. Then, over the years 1920–22, Thorndike and her husband appeared in some 30 plays with the seasons of Grand Guignol (horror dramas) at the Little Theater in London. The plays were hardly masterpieces of dramatic literature. Nevertheless, they were great favorites with audiences and wonderful experiences for the actors, who had a chance to let themselves go in a variety of flamboyant roles. All the while, however, with the profits from the commercially successful Grand Guignol productions, Thorndike continued to appear under her husband's direction in a series of matinees of Greek tragedy at the Old Vic, including *The Tro-jan Women, Medea,* and *Hippolytus*. In all of these, she dazzled the critics, who soon realized that in Sybil Thorndike, they were in the presence of a tragedian of the first rank. In fact, it would seem in retrospect that it was at this time of her life, when just past 40, that Thorndike was in her prime. Looking back, the critic W.A. Darlington wrote of her in 1960: "I saw her touch greatness, certainly as Hecuba, perhaps as Medea, and I hoped that these achievements were the prelude to others greater still—but they were not, they were her peak. Never again did I experience with her that sense of surrender which is the involuntary tribute that one pays to emotional acting at its highest pitch." Among her successes in these matinees was her performance as *Beatrice of Cenci in *The Cenci*, a lurid Renaissance-style tragedy by the Romantic poet Percy Shelley that had been banned for over a century in Britain.

In 1923, George Bernard Shaw, profoundly impressed with Thorndike's artistry, especially in the trial scene in *The Cenci*, undertook to write *Saint Joan* expressly for her. Although she was not the first to star in the play (the New York production with **Winifred Lenihan** had opened first), the London production starring Thorndike that opened in March 1924 has gone down in English theatrical history as the stuff of legend. Though at 41 she was admittedly somewhat old for the part of *Joan of Arc, Thorndike grasped immediately the intention of Shaw and, skillfully directed by her husband, was perhaps the only actress to play his Saint Joan as he interpreted her: a healthy, hearty, ebullient peasant girl. Even Tyrone Guthrie, a critic who thought her performance too boisterous for his taste, used the word "stupendous" to describe her in the trial scene. So greatly was she acclaimed in this role that she appeared in no less than twelve revivals of the play in six countries. The play was not only a great artistic success, but a financial one as well. Thorndike and Shaw together made some £30,000 (about $144,000) on the production, though she, with little interest in money, spent most of her share before her first tour of South Africa in 1928–29. *Saint Joan* established Sybil Thorndike as the leading tragic actress on the English stage. By 1929, critics, lamenting the decline of tragedy in the theater, were hailing her as the only inheritor of the great tradition of tragic acting that had characterized the Victorian and Edwardian eras. Role after role now came to her easily as the greatest playwrights of the day sought her out to interpret their works, but *Saint Joan* remained the summit of her career; she was never able to triumph in a play of equal stature.

In 1929, Thorndike appeared in a distinguished revival of Shaw's *Major Barbara* and, the following year, took part as Emilia in the now-famed production of *Othello* in which the American Paul Robeson became the first black actor to play the Moor and rising young *Peggy Ashcroft played Desdemona. This production resulted in the crowning of Thorndike's career with the title Dame Commander of the British Empire in 1931 at the early age of 49. The honor was followed by a trip to Egypt and Palestine, after which she and Casson sailed for Australia. There she toured in a repertory of varied plays including *Saint Joan, Macbeth, Captain Brassbound's Conversion* and *The Painted Veil.*

Upon her return to London, Dame Sybil appeared in one play after another, most notably as Evie Millward in *The Distaff Side*, a role she repeated in New York in 1934, as Volumnia in *Coriolanus*, as both Aphrodite and the Nurse in *Hippolytus* and again as Medea, Lady Macbeth, and Queen Hecuba in *The Trojan Women.* In 1936, she appeared as Mary Herries in *Kind Lady*, a suspense drama that starred her great American contemporary, *Ethel Barrymore, when it was transferred to the screen after World War II. Two years later, Thorndike gave one of her finest performances in the role of Miss Moffat in Emlyn Williams' *The Corn is Green*, in which she played an elderly spinster schoolteacher who discovers a genius among the children of Welsh miners in a village school. (Coincidentally, this was also Ethel Barrymore's last role on the stage, in the New York production of the same play; *Bette Davis would play Miss Moffat on the screen.) By now, Thorndike had given up her attempts to surpass *Saint Joan* and in the words of her son, John Casson, "had begun to come to terms" with the commercial theater, contenting herself with selecting roles that enabled her to advance a principle in which she firmly believed. Miss Moffat was one such role; Mrs. Linden in *The Linden Tree* was another one in later years, as was that of the widow in *Waters of the Moon.*

During the Second World War, Thorndike distinguished herself in a series of performances given throughout the English provinces, including a program of dramatic poetry readings in Scotland and the Orkney islands. When the Old Vic was bombed out of its quarters in 1944, Thorndike appeared with the company at its temporary quarters at the New Theater, first as Aase in Ibsen's *Peer Gynt* and then as Catherine Petkoff in *Arms and the Man* and as Queen Margaret in Shakespeare's *Richard III.* As the war drew to a close, she entertained the troops,

touring Belgium, France, and Germany with the Old Vic company, and taking time to appear at the Comédie Française in Paris. Returning to a ruined and deprived London in the summer of 1945, Thorndike appeared as Mistress Quickly in *Henry IV, Parts I and II* and then in the now near-legendary production of Sophocles' *Oedipus Rex*, playing Queen Jocasta to Laurence Olivier's Oedipus.

In the years following, Thorndike and Casson appeared in J.B. Priestley's much-appreciated *The Linden Tree* and then in a series of long-running plays that enabled audiences to enjoy her as a regular fixture upon the London stage: Farrell and Perry's *Treasure Hunt* (1949), N.C. Hunter's *Waters of the Moon* (1951) and *A Day by the Sea* (1953), and T.S. Eliot's *The Family Reunion* (1956). Reviewing her appearance in *Waters of the Moon*, American critic Moss Hart wrote in awe: "Sybil Thorndike is magical. For an act and a half she does almost nothing except sit and listen but never have I seen an actress . . . listen with such sly acuteness that the attention of the audience is riveted on her and on her alone. . . . [I]t is by no means a trick—it is acting of the purest sort and when she rises to her one scene at the end of the second act all the talent and artistry of years of classical playing are displayed . . . in a few magic moments."

*S*ybil Thorndike was surely the best-loved English actress since Ellen Terry, and these two great players shared many of the same fine qualities— generosity, diligence, modesty, simplicity.

—John Gielgud

Despite her advancing years, Thorndike spent much of the 1950s and early 1960s on rigorous foreign tours, giving audiences in various parts of the British Commonwealth and elsewhere the opportunity of seeing one of Britain's most distinguished actresses in the flesh. In 1954, she toured New Zealand and India; in 1955 and again in 1957–58, she was in New Zealand and Australia; in 1957, she made her last appearance in New York, as Mrs. Califer in *The Potting Shed.* As late as 1962, when she was 80, she toured Australia a third time, giving poetry recitals with her husband. In October 1959, she toured England as Mrs. Kittridge in *The Sea Shell*, and, as late as 1968, she toured the country again as Mrs. Bramson in *Night Must Fall.* In between these tours, she scarcely rested, taking time to repeat her stage role as the Grand Duchess in the film version of Terence Rattigan's 1955 comedy *The Sleeping Prince*, now titled

The Prince and the Showgirl and starring Laurence Olivier and *Marilyn Monroe. Those who expected fireworks between a grand dame of the theater and the little American movie queen were sorely disappointed. Wise in her years, Thorndike saw the best in Monroe and said later that she was always a darling and that everyone in the cast loved her—even though she was perpetually late on the set. Most important, she respected Monroe for her knowledge of her craft. Soon after, Dame Sybil appeared as Mrs. Railton-Bell in *Separate Tables* (1956), with *Margaret Leighton as her daughter; as Mrs. St. Maugham in *The Chalk Garden*; and as Dame Sophia Carrell in *Eighty in the Shade*, the last a play written for the Cassons by the popular British playwright *Clemence Dane to celebrate their golden wedding anniversary. Lewis Casson, knighted in 1945, died in 1969.

Dame Sybil Thorndike was never a beauty and in her photographs rarely looks young even when she was, yet she was a handsome woman and, though not at all tall, made an imposing impression on the stage largely through her magnificent carriage. Throughout her life, she remained the quintessential Englishwoman—cool, reserved and dignified. On stage, however, she was a passionate performer, who brought a hearty earnestness to her interpretation of Saint Joan and a terrifying intensity to the role of Medea. In her private life, she was a homebody, devoted to her husband, children and grandchildren. She was active in a number of causes, including the advancement of religious drama, the peace movement, trade unionism, women's rights, and the election of Socialist and Labour Party candidates for Parliament. In his memoirs, John Gielgud is unstinting in his praise for Thorndike, the woman, as he was for her as an artist:

> In her private life she managed somehow to retain a certain reserve and dignity, despite an ebullient facade. She had beautiful manners. Genuinely interested in everyone she met, strangers as well as friends, she could bounce and flounce without ever losing her modesty and basic humility. The moment you were lucky enough to work with her in the theater you knew she was a leader, but also a giver, not self-centered, professional to her fingertips, disciplined, punctual and kind.

Dame Sybil Thorndike always maintained that she never gave "a blessed hoot" about stardom and was willing to take on the humblest and most modest of roles if she felt that she could learn something from the part. As a result, in her long career she encompassed an enormous variety of roles, from the Greek classics through Shakespeare and Sheridan, and on to such modern playwrights as Ibsen, Chekhov, Maugham, Shaw, Priestly, Dane, Coward, Rattigan, Claudel, van Druten, and T.S. Eliot. She did not always succeed to the extent that she would have wished; she lacked sensuality in her performances, her acting could be over-emotional, her voice could be weak, her Lady Macbeth did not reach the heights, and she tended to be too heavy handed for comedy. Yet, she was counted by many as the finest English actress after *Ellen Terry and that, in itself, was a great achievement for an actress who was a contemporary, at least in her later years, of *Edith Evans, Peggy Ashcroft, and *Judith Anderson.

Thorndike's last appearance on the stage was as the Woman in *There Was an Old Woman*, the play which in October 1969 inaugurated the Sybil Thorndike Theater in Leatherhead, Surrey, just outside of London, and whose opening was attended by Princess *Margaret Rose and her then husband Lord Snowdon, along with Dame Sybil's relatives, friends, and colleagues from the theater. Interviewed at the time, she was in the best of spirits, regretting only what she called the deterioration of clear enunciation in the theater. The following year, she was made a Companion of Honour to Queen *Elizabeth II, who invested her with this dignity in a private ceremony. Thereafter, Thorndike began to fail, as her arthritis worsened and she grew deaf. Her last public appearance took place at the Old Vic Theater on the occasion of the closing of the old building prior to the reopening of the company in its new quarters by Waterloo Bridge. Arriving in the theater, the veteran and beloved actress was greeted with a standing ovation. Dame Sybil Thorndike died on June 6, 1976, her death an occasion of national mourning throughout Great Britain. On her passing, Sir Laurence Olivier, who was born three years after she made her debut, said of her: "She was one of the rarest and most blessed of women of whom this country could ever boast. The loss of her is incalculable." In his memoirs, Gielgud recalled that she was "blessed with immense talent, boundless energy, unremitting application and splendid health. . . . [S]he fought her way, helped by the devotion of a brilliant husband and loving family, to worldwide recognition."

SOURCES:
Casson, John. *Lewis and Sybil*. London, 1962.
Findlater, Richard. *The Player Queens*. NY, 1977.
Morley, Sheridan. *Sybil Thorndike: A Life in the Theater*. London, 1977.
Sprigges, Elizabeth. *Sybil Thorndike Casson*. London, 1971.
Thorndike, Russell. *Sybil Thorndike*. London, 1929, 2nd ed., 1970.
Trewin, J.C. *Sybil Thorndike*. London, 1955.

SUGGESTED READING:

Thorndike, Russell, and Sybil Thorndike. *Lilian Baylis.* London, 1938.

Thorndike, Sybil. *Religion and the Stage.* London, 1927.

Robert Hewsen,
Professor of History,
Rowan University,
Glassboro, New Jersey

Thorne, Florence (1877–1973)

American labor researcher and editor. Born Florence Calvert Thorne on July 28, 1877, in Hannibal, Missouri; died of pulmonary emboli on March 16, 1973, in Falls Church, Virginia; daughter of Stephen Thorne (a teacher and grocer) and Amanthis Belle (Mathews) Thorne; attended Oberlin College, 1896–99; University of Chicago, Ph.B., 1909.

Taught liberal arts (1899–1912); employed as a researcher, writer, and executive assistant to American Federation of Labor (AFL) president Samuel Gompers (1912–17); served on the Subcommittee on Women in Industry of the Advisory Committee of the Council of National Defense (1917); served as assistant director of the Working Conditions Service, War Labor Administration, U.S. Department of Labor (1918); director of research, AFL (1933–53); served as a delegate to the Federal Advisory Commission for Employment Security (World War II); served as adviser to the International Labor Organization; wrote Samuel Gompers, American Statesman *(1957).*

The labor organizer and editor Florence Thorne was born in Hannibal, Missouri, in 1877, the middle of three daughters of **Amanthis Belle Mathews**, a descendant of English aristocracy, and Stephen Thorne, a native of Georgia and a one-time Confederate soldier who later taught school before opening a grocery outlet. She was valedictorian of her high school class, graduating in 1896, and went on to Oberlin College in Ohio, where she majored in English and classical languages in preparation for a career as a schoolteacher. After three years at Oberlin, Thorne left to teach for a year in Georgia. In 1903, she returned to college, attending summer sessions at the University of Chicago for the next six years. During the school year, she supported herself by teaching high school in Hannibal. She finished her bachelor of philosophy degree in history and political science in 1909. Exposed to the trade-union movement by one of her courses, Thorne decided to pursue a graduate degree at Chicago in labor economics. While researching her thesis on the American Federation of Labor (AFL), Thorne met Samuel Gompers, president of the AFL and the man who would have the most impact on her career. Gompers was supportive of Thorne's research, and allowed her access to the AFL's files in Washington, D.C.

Although she had to leave her research to return to Hannibal to teach, Gompers had been so impressed by Thorne that in 1912 he offered to make her assistant editor of the AFL's publication, *The American Federationist.* This was the start of her 40-year professional association with Gompers and the AFL. Thorne became Gomper's assistant, speech writer, and confidante, in addition to her duties as the principal writer and editor of the *Federationist.* In the course of her first five years with the AFL, Thorne also conducted economic and political research to help the organization develop new political strategies. A supporter of American involvement in World War I, Thorne left the AFL in 1917 to work for the Advisory Committee of the Council of National Defense's Subcommittee on Women in Industry. She transferred to the Department of Labor in 1918, serving as assistant director of the Working Conditions Service of the War Labor Administration. With the end of the war, Thorne returned to work with Gompers, primarily as the researcher and ghostwriter of his autobiography, which she completed and published after his death in 1924 as *Seventy Years of Life and Labor: An Autobiography* (1925).

In 1925, Thorne again became editor of the AFL newsletter under the federation's new president, William Green. In 1933, she was made director of the AFL's new research department, which she had started as a volunteer effort in 1926 to collect vital statistics on unemployment among local unions. Throughout the Depression years, the research department interpreted New Deal programs to help local union leaders with labor negotiations. Thorne also directed many studies on topics such as unemployment and child labor. This type of research was soon to be used in the creation of the New Deal's protective labor legislation, which Thorne herself was politically opposed to; like Gompers, she believed that improvement in working conditions and economic equity through trade-union activism by workers themselves was preferable to government-imposed legislation.

During World War II, Thorne expanded her research function to include direct negotiations on AFL delegations. She also served as a consultant with the International Labor Organization and on the Federal Advisory Commission for Employment Security.

Florence Thorne retired from the AFL in 1953 at age 73. Never married, she shared a home in Falls Church, Virginia, with her longtime companion and AFL research associate **Margaret Scattergood**, whom she had met in 1928. In 1957, her biography of Gompers, *Samuel Gompers: American Statesman*, was published. Raised Baptist, she converted to Catholicism a short time before her death at age 95 in 1973.

SOURCES:

Sicherman, Barbara, and Carol Hurd Green, eds. *Notable American Women: The Modern Period*. Cambridge, MA: The Belknap Press of Harvard University, 1980.

Laura York, M.A. in History, University of California, Riverside, California

Thorne, Harriet V.S. (1843–1926)

American photographer. Name variations: Harriet van Schoonhoven Horne. Born Harriet Smith van Schoonhoven in 1843 in Troy, New York; died in 1926 in Bridgehampton, New York; great-grandmother of Rollie McKenna (b. 1918); married Jonathan Thorne (a businessman), in 1867 (died 1920); children: Josephine (b. 1869, died in infancy); Victor Corse (b. 1871); Samuel "Brink" Brinckerhof (b. 1873).

Photographed a variety of subjects, including Native Americans, architecture, wildlife, and flora; joined the New York Camera Club (1888–89); works exhibited posthumously, Yale University (1979).

Born in 1843 to an upper-class family in Troy, New York, photographer Harriet van Schoonhoven was privately educated. At age 24, she married a wealthy businessman, Jonathan Thorne, and began dividing her time between New York City and a summer estate, Schoonhoven, in Black Rock, Connecticut. She had three children between 1869 and 1873, two of whom survived to adulthood. At her summer home, Thorne experimented with the new artistic medium of photography, shooting and developing images in her own darkroom. She made portraits of family and friends in addition to interior scenes and images of Schoonhoven's extensive gardens and exotic wildlife. During the winters, Thorne also shot architectural scenes of New York. A member of the newly founded New York Camera Club in 1888, Thorne also worked on vacations to California and South Carolina, photographing Native Americans, botanical gardens, and wildlife.

Grief over the death of Jonathan Thorne in 1920, after 53 years of marriage, caused Harriet Thorne to give up photography and ask her sons to dispose of her equipment and negatives. She retired to Bridgehampton on Long Island, New York, where she died six years later.

Thorne's works might have been lost had it not been for the efforts of her descendants. In 1950, some negatives were discovered by **Therese Thorne McLane** and eventually were given to Harriet Thorne's great-granddaughter, the photographer *Rollie McKenna. McKenna collected other photographs and in 1979 mounted an exhibit of Harriet Thorne's work at the Yale University Art Gallery.

SOURCES:

Rosenblum, Naomi. *A History of Women Photographers*. NY: Abbeville Press, 1994.

Laura York, M.A. in History, University of California, Riverside, California

Thorne, Olive (1831–1918).

See Miller, Olive Thorne.

Thornton, Kathryn (b. 1952).

See Astronauts: Women in Space.

Thornton, Willie Mae (1926–1984)

African-American blues singer who had a hit with "Hound Dog" long before Elvis Presley recorded it. Name variations: Big Mama Thornton. Born on December 11, 1926, in Montgomery, Alabama; died in Los Angeles, California, on July 25, 1984.

Anyone who doubts the existence of racism in American music should study the life of Big Mama Thornton, who was the first to perform the song "Hound Dog." While Elvis Presley made millions off Thornton's creative work, she died in obscure poverty. Said Johnny Otis, "You have to understand that white people love the music but despise the people who created it." Black music and musicians were often exploited by whites.

Willie Mae Thornton was born in 1926 in Montgomery, Alabama. She learned music in church, where her father was a minister and her mother a member of the choir. Thornton began singing in amateur shows throughout the state and then stopped singing briefly when her mother died in 1939. In 1941, she toured the Gulf Coast with Sammy Green's Hot Harlem Revue. In 1948, she settled down in Houston, Texas, where she performed at the Eldorado Club. Her first recording was made in 1951 with E&W Records. After Johnny Otis spotted her, Thornton joined his Rhythm and Blues Caravan. It was Otis who gave her the nickname "Big Mama." Thornton also often performed with Johnny Ace until 1954, when he accidentally shot himself playing Russian roulette.

Big Mama Thornton's first hit was the song "Hound Dog." Written by Otis, with Jerry Lieber and Mike Stoller, the record was released in August 1952 and became the No. 1 rhythm and blues song of 1953. Thornton received only $500 for her performance. In 1956, Elvis Presley recorded this same song; his version sold over one million copies. Said Thornton, "I've been singing way before Elvis was born. And he jumps up and becomes a millionaire before me . . . off of something that I made popular. They gave him the right . . . now, why they do that. He makes a million and all this jive because his face is different from mine." Thornton faced prejudice in the concert hall as well, as did all black singers in the years before civil-rights legislation. "I had to play one night for the colored and the next night for the whites," said Thornton. "It was humiliating and it was the law of the South that you couldn't integrate audiences because there would be a cop waiting to lock you up. Sometimes we even had segregated audiences in the North."

Little is known about Willie Mae Thornton's private life, which she kept strictly to herself. Otis, who was closer to her than many, said:

> There was a guy around sometimes who was introduced as her husband, but I don't really think they were legally married. He was there as long as money was coming it. I could never get a handle on Willie Mae sexually and that's not a judgment. . . . People in the band heard these rumors that she was gay. She was a big woman and sometimes wore suits or masculine kinds of clothes, but that might not mean anything. All I can honestly say is that she was a good intelligent person. I personally never saw her with any men, but on the other hand, I never saw her with any women either. So all I know is that I don't know much about it.

By 1957, Thornton's career had begun to wind down. Peacock Records cheated her out of money so she quit and moved out to San Francisco, where she played with local clubs. She appeared at the Monterey Jazz Festival in 1964 and more appearances followed. Thornton toured with the American Folk Blues Festival in 1965 and re-recorded "Hound Dog." In 1967, the album *Big Mama Thornton with the Chicago Blues Band* was released. She also appeared on "The Dick Cavett Show," "The Della Reese Show," "The Midnight Special," and "Rock 1." Said Michael Erlewine, "Big Mama liked people. She'd look right at you and talk to you. She wasn't afraid of you, so there was nothing separating you and her. She included you in whatever was going on, but she wasn't catty. She was

real." "She was a big woman," he added, "but she could sing her ass off. *Janis Joplin learned most of her style from her. Everyone listened to Janis instead of Big Mama. I never quite understood that."

Big Mama Thornton kept working and kept winning fans into the 1980s, long after Joplin and Presley were dead. This was small consolation as she sunk deeper and deeper into poverty. Thornton had become an alcoholic. She had no royalties, not even from her reissues which were selling, and lived almost penniless in a Los Angeles boarding house. She died in Los Angeles on July 25, 1984. Said Otis: "It was Willie Mae, her sister, and a couple of friends sitting around drinking Jack Daniels or something. Willie Mae just put her head down on the table and never came up." She was 58.

Like many black performers, Thornton gained a place in death she had never enjoyed in life. Her records are still heard and her name is frequently mentioned in books and articles. She was a truly great performer.

SOURCES:
Carpenter, Bil. "Big Mama Thornton: 200 Pounds of Boogaloo," in *Living Blues*. No. 106. November–December 1992, pp. 26–32.
Santelli, Robert. *The Big Book of Blues: A Biographical Encyclopedia*. NY: Penguin, 1993.

John Haag,
Associate Professor of History,
University of Georgia, Athens,
Georgia

Thorpe, Elizabeth (1910–1963).

See Brousse, Amy.

Thorpe, Rose Hartwick
(1850–1939)

American poet. Born on July 18, 1850, in Mishawaka, Indiana; died of a heart attack on July 19, 1939, in San Diego, California; daughter of William Morris (a tailor) and Mary Louisa (Wight) Hartwick; married Edmund Carson Thorpe (a carriage maker), on September 11, 1871; children: Lulo May; Lillie Maud.

Penned the popular poem "Curfew Must Not Ring Tonight" (1870); wrote for St. Nicholas, Wide Awake, Youth's Companion, and Detroit Free Press; was employed as periodical editor for Temperance Tales, Well-Spring, and Words of Life; wrote five children's novels; published an anthology, The Poetical Works of Rose Hartwick Thorpe (1912).

The daughter of a tailor and pioneer settler, Rose Hartwick Thorpe was a popular poet and novelist. She was born Rose Alnora Hartwick in 1850 in Mishawaka, Indiana, the second of five children of William and **Louisa Hartwick**, and grew up in Indiana, Kansas, and Litchfield, Michigan. She attended public schools and became drawn to poetry and fiction as a child, enjoying the romantic works of writers such as Longfellow published in popular magazines, and imitating their flowery style in her own amateur verse. When she was 15, she wrote the poem for which she would become best known, "Curfew Must Not Ring Tonight." She developed it after reading in *Peterson's Magazine* a romantic short story, "Love and Loyalty," about a Cavalier heroine of the English Civil War who saved her lover's life. Thorpe rewrote the story in verse, and the poem was read by friends and family who encouraged her to continue writing. Some of her early poems were published by a Detroit newspaper, the *Commercial Advertiser*.

Thorpe graduated from high school in Litchfield in 1868. Two years later, "Curfew Must Not Ring Tonight" was published to immediate public acclaim by the *Commercial Advertiser*. Continually reprinted in newspapers and magazines across the country until the turn of the century, it quickly became one of the most popular sentimental poems of its time, used for poetry recitations in schools and translated for foreign publication. Rose Hartwick Thorpe's name became well known, though she did not hold a copyright on the poem and so did not benefit financially from its popularity. The year after its first publication she married amateur poet Edmund Thorpe, a carriage maker by trade; the couple had two daughters.

Throughout the 1870s and 1880s, Thorpe's short fiction and verse were frequently published in general interest and children's periodicals, including *Youth's Companion*, the *Detroit Free Press*, and *St. Nicholas*. Many of her stories and poems for children were written as religious instruction. The financial problems caused by the failure of Edmund Thorpe's business in 1881 led Rose to accept the position of editor and principal writer for a number of religious magazines published by Fleming H. Revell. She also began to publish full-length juvenile fiction in 1881, when *Fred's Dark Days* appeared. Four more juvenile books followed, her daughter **Lulo May Thorpe** providing the illustrations for some of them.

When Edmund Thorpe developed tuberculosis, the Thorpes moved from Michigan to San Antonio, Texas, for his health. Rose Thorpe's last well-known poem, "Remember the Alamo," was written in this period. They soon moved again to San Diego, California, in 1886, where she continued to contribute to literary magazines to support the family. A collection of her verse, *The Poetical Works of Rose Hartwick Thorpe*, was published in 1912. After Edmund Thorpe died in 1916, she volunteered with the Woman's Club of San Diego and the YWCA, and became involved in the movement for women's suffrage as well. She died at age 89 in 1939.

SOURCES:

James, Edward T., ed. *Notable American Women, 1607–1950*. Cambridge, MA: The Belknap Press of Harvard University, 1971.

McHenry, Robert. *Famous American Women*. NY: Dover, 1980.

Laura York, M.A. in History,
University of California,
Riverside, California

Thrale, Hester Lynch (1741–1821).

See Piozzi, Hester Lynch.

Three Marias, The

By writing and publishing The New Portuguese Letters *(1972), Maria Barreno, Maria Velho da Costa and Maria Teresa Horta led the modern feminist literary movement in Portugal and achieved notoriety because of the government's attempt to suppress their work.*

Maria Isabel Barreno (1939—). Born in Lisbon, Portugal, on July 10, 1939; granted degree in historic and philosophic sciences from the Lisbon Arts Faculty; employed in the National Institute of Industrial Research; participated in the writing of A Condicão da Mulher Portuguesa *(1968); published first novel,* De Noite as Arvores São Negras *(1968).*

Maria Teresa Horta (1937—). Born in Lisbon on May 20, 1937; studied at Lisbon Arts Faculty; published first volume of poetry, Espelho Inicial *(1960); published first novel,* Ambas as Mãos sobre o Corpo *(1970);* Minha Senhora de Mim *confiscated by censors (1971).*

Maria Velho da Costa (1938—). Born in Lisbon on June 26, 1938; granted degree in German philology from the University of London; high school teacher; employed in the National Institute of Industrial Research; co-author of Novas Cartas Portuguesas *(1972); her novel* Casas Pardas *won the City of Lisbon Prize (1977).*

In March 1971, a Portuguese printing house was typesetting *Novas Cartas Portuguesas*, written by Maria Isabel Barreno, Maria Velho da Costa, and Maria Teresa Horta, when an employee told the owner that the book was pornographic. He stopped production and spoke with Manuel Aquino, general secretary of the Estúdios Cor publishing house, which had hired the printer to produce the book. Aquino temporarily suspended the printing, but a few days later publisher Romeu de Melo authorized the printer to continue. The authors had reportedly worked with **Natália Correia**, the publisher's literary director, on revisions of some sections of the manuscript. Toward the end of April, after printing 2,000 copies, the printer sent one to the government censor. Meanwhile, Estúdios Cor distributed the new book for sale. By mid-December, however, the government arrested the authors and Melo on charges of pornography and offenses against public morality. Judicial proceedings commenced, with the accused free on bond. Thus began the case of "The Three Marias," as it became known internationally.

It unfolded in the waning days of the dictatorship that ruled Portugal for four decades. As minister of finances in 1932, António de Oliveira Salazar seized power and imposed a corporatist state (the *Estado Novo* or New State) on Portugal. He dominated Portugal through his National Union, the only legal political party, until 1968, when a stroke incapacitated him. President Américo Tomás then appointed Marcelo Caetano to head the Council of Ministers. A Salazar loyalist, Caetano nonetheless recognized the need for reforms. He allowed opposition candidates to stand for election to the National Assembly in November 1969 and generally maneuvered to win the support of middle-class liberals. He also attempted to modernize Portugal by bringing technocrats into the government as ministers. Salazar died in 1970, but the arch-conservatives (*Ultras*) of the ruling coalition forced Caetano toward the right. Even so, according to social scientists Ben Pimlott and Jean Seaton, Portugal witnessed "a growing awareness of a middle-class intelligentsia—expansive, outward-looking, and essentially liberal—steadily gaining confidence in an offensive against an anachronistic and traditional oligarchy whose institutional and corporate supporters were increasingly distracted and unsure, and which was moving toward its last stand."

The case of the Three Marias both reflected and helped shape the hope and the anxiety, the sense of emancipation and the final attempts at repression that characterized the expiring dictatorship. In their early to mid-30s at the time, Barreno, Velho da Costa, and Horta were university-educated, middle-class women. Aspiring writers with feminist inclinations, all three were wives and mothers. Although their case gained the most in-

ternational notoriety, several male writers also suffered the wrath of the dying regime. The Marias and their literary colleagues drew purpose from their nation's political crisis, and the regime's oppression grew more and more ineffectual.

When the Three Marias began writing *Novas Cartas Portuguesas* in 1971, each had already published literary works on her own. Maria Isabel Barreno provided the initial impetus for the undertaking. She knew that in early 1971, when Maria Teresa Horta published *Minha Senhora de Mim* (Milady of Me), a collection of poems that celebrated the female body, passion and love, officials had reacted harshly and confiscated unsold stocks of the book. Angry at the government's attack, Barreno suggested to Horta and Maria Velho da Costa that the three work together on a volume of feminist literature that would expose the abject conditions of Portuguese women and their sisters throughout the world, while at the same time censuring the dictatorship. From the beginning, they envisioned a political as well as literary work. Long-time friends, Barreno and Velho da Costa worked together in the Institute of Industrial Research, while Horta was a journalist who already enjoyed a reputation for her poetry and fiction.

Horta wondered, however, whether collaboration would interfere with her own creativity. When she finally agreed to go along, the women decided to meet twice each week. They gathered at a restaurant for a weekly lunch and the opportunity to discuss their own lives, radical politics, feminism, and literature. Meanwhile each wrote something to discuss at a private evening gathering. During the week, they also corresponded with each other. Their strategy was to date each piece of work but otherwise leave it anonymous. Their writings were consequently not conceived and executed in isolation. They were instead, as the three women later remarked, "the *written record* of a much broader, common, lived experience of creating a sisterhood through conflict, shared fun and sorrow, complicity and competition—an interplay not only of modes of writing but of modes of being, some of them conscious and some far less so, all of them shifting in the process."

It soon became obvious that they needed a unifying theme for their writings, and the *Lettres Portugaises* came to mind. Allegedly written in the 1660s by a Portuguese nun, *Mariana Alcoforado, these five love letters expressed her passion and anguish after being abandoned by her lover, the French military officer Noël Bouton, marquis of Chamilly. They created a sensation when published in Paris in 1669, in a French translation. Yet the Portuguese originals never surfaced, leading a number of scholars to argue that the *Lettres* were a fiction, written not by Alcoforado but by Gabriel Joseph de Lavergne, vicomte de Guilleragues. Be that as it may, the *Lettres* echoed with the tragic tones of a woman cast against her will into the celibate life of the convent.

The renown of Alcoforado and her letters in Portuguese literature made them a superb device for her literary descendants, the Three Marias. According to **Darlene J. Sadlier**, professor of Portuguese literature: "Whether or not these letters or ones like them were in fact written by Mariana Alcoforado is unimportant. For the three contemporary women writers, the letters became symbolic of the plight of all women who are confined, whether by an actual convent or by a reactionary political system." To Velho da Costa, Horta and Barreno, Portugal was a convent that imprisoned its unwilling female occupants. The patriarchy dominating Portuguese culture and society demanded that women remain at home, subservient to their fathers or husbands. An old Portuguese dictum held, for example, that a woman should leave home only twice: for her marriage and for her burial.

We three . . . will be regarded as peculiar creatures, and the courageous battles we wage will be dismissed as mere literary skirmishes, though their roots lie much deeper, the fruit of vines that have intertwined, grown, and been toughened as we have trained ourselves to be more conscious of ourselves as women, as something more than vineyards for men.

—The Three Marias

Between March and October 1971, the writings accumulated. By the authors' own reckoning, they ended up with poetry, letters written to each other, fictitious letters, essays, and fictional sketches. Several of the letters purport to be written by Mariana Alcoforado, her family, or friends. The women's work and family responsibilities, plus the requirement to complete something each week, meant that none of the items was more than a few pages long. Then they organized the pieces chronologically for the manuscript: "Things in it are presented as they came, with no other criteria for their arrangement save our belief in their own (our own) inner development and unity, each piece dated but unsigned, the THING pulsing with a life of its own."

While they understood they were challenging the regime with a book that would disturb many Portuguese, they did not anticipate their work's public impact nor the outpouring of national and international support once they were arrested. In fact, the legal proceedings against the Three Marias ripped away the mask of anonymity behind which nearly all Portuguese women lived and gave them each a public face. Barreno, Horta, and Velho da Costa became national figures, defended by prominent writers and international feminist organizations. European feminists went to Portugal to attend the court proceedings. Meanwhile, the Portuguese press hesitated. Fearful of the regime's ire, it made little mention of the Three Marias or other cases of Portuguese writers persecuted by the government.

During the legal proceedings, the government's behavior revealed its own internal weakness and lack of confidence. The accused gave depositions in mid-1972, denying the charges that their book was "immoral and pornographic." Barreno challenged the regime: "I mean that without those passages considered strongest the book would be amputated, as it is intended not only but very fundamentally to denounce the inferior situation of woman in Portuguese society and in all societies in general; it was necessary to denounce this situation not only on the economic, political, and social plane, but also on the sexual plane since relations between men and women concentrate all the laws of woman's inferiority."

The judge moved slowly, especially as international delegations of feminist organizations appeared in Lisbon to show their solidarity with the accused and to hold Portuguese justice up to the world's scrutiny. More than a year and a half passed without resolution of the case. Several notable Portuguese writers contributed strong depositions against the charges. Urbano Tavares Rodrigues asserted, for example, that two of Barreno's novels (*De Noite as Arvores São Negras* and *Os Outros Legítimos Superiores*) were among the most important works of Portuguese literature during the previous half century. He considered the controversial passages necessary to the structure of the book and in "no way pornographic." The accused also presented a letter of support written by José Gomes Ferreira, president of the Portuguese Writer's Association.

Several times the court scheduled the trial, only to postpone it, perhaps fearing the international protests that a conviction of the Three Marias would have caused. Probably out of sympathy for the accused, the state prosecutor refused to push the case. The dictatorship finally

The Three Marias (left to right): Maria Velho da Costa, Maria Isabel Barreno, and Maria Teresa Horta.

replaced him. Feminists from abroad complained of the regime's delaying tactics but continued their support. Eventually the judge scheduled a final judgment for mid-April 1974. He then delayed it once again, however, because of Portugal's deepening political crisis.

For Portugal had grown tired of the regime itself. After 1971, the Ultras forced Caetano to end his reforms and swing back to the right. Portugal's colonies were in open revolt. Young men resented the draft that carried them off to Africa to serve in futile imperialist wars. The Por-

THREE MARIAS, THE

tuguese military became restive, dismayed at the cost of the African campaigns and convinced the intransigent dictatorship would destroy the nation. On April 25, 1974, the armed forces overthrew the dictatorship and implemented a "bourgeois democratization of Portuguese society from above."

The Three Marias received almost immediate benefit from the Revolution of 1974. On May 7, the presiding judge, Dr. Acácio Artur Lopes Cardoso, rendered his verdict: "*Novas Cartas Portuguesas* is not pornographic nor is it immoral. To the contrary, it is a work of art, of a high level, in the sequence of other works of art that the authors have already produced." He praised the publishing house for providing a "service to culture," declared the authors innocent, and dismissed all charges against them.

Even before the judge made his ruling, translations of the *New Portuguese Letters* had been undertaken for the major European languages, and within a year after the trial, those editions began to appear. In October 1978, the theater of the University of Paris presented a dramatized version of the book, with the title of *La Clôture*. Barreno, Horta, and Velho da Costa built on the prestige won by their legal triumph. They published new novels and volumes of poetry. Velho da Costa's novel *Casas Pardas* won the City of Lisbon prize in 1977, and her *Lucialima* shared the D. Dinis Prize in 1983. More moderate in its feminism than the works of her two colleagues, Velho da Costa's writing showed the influence of French experimental linguistics. Barreno remained remarkably productive. She published a series of novels and short stories, including *Morte da Mãe* (1977); *Inventário de Ana* (1982); *Célia e Celina* (1985); *O Enviado* (1991); and *O Senhor das Ilhas* (1994). By temperament more sociological in perspective than the other two, Barreno also studied the Portuguese media's portrayal of women (*A Imagem da Mulher na Imprensa* [1976]) and sexual discrimination in education (*Falso Neutro: Um Estudo sobre a Discriminação no Ensino* [1985]). Probably the most prolific of the Three Marias prior to the trial, Horta continued to explore feminist themes in her later poetry and novels: *Os Anjos* (1983); *Ema* (1984); *Cristina* (1985); *Minha Mãe, Meu Amor* (1986); *Rosa Sangrenta* (1987); *Paixão Segundo Constança H* (1994). She also co-authored a work on abortion rights, *Aborto: Direito ao Nosso Corpo* (1975).

More than anything, however, *New Portuguese Letters* identified the Three Marias to international feminist and literary circles and served to raise the consciousness of Portuguese women. For Darlene Sadlier, it was a "pioneer work." According to **Maria Graciette Besse**, the book "functions as a symbol of all women, the archetype of alienation and feminine clausura in the breast of patriarchal society." Barreno, Velho da Costa, and Horta helped break down the walls that confined Portuguese women. Yet according to **Renata Wasserman**, their work was largely one of critique, exposing the nature of masculine oppression: "The contrast between the clarity of the portions that refer to the larger world, and the obscurity of the inner-directed ones exemplifies the emergence of private languages within powerless groups whose concerns are denied access to the language of power—but the expression of whose powerlessness must use the same language that resists their claims to empowerment." Their women suffer, often passively. When they strike back at men, they do so out of rage or desperation.

SOURCES:

Barreno, Maria Isabel, Maria Teresa Horta, and Maria Velho da Costa. *Novas Cartas Portuguesas*. Rev. ed. Lisbon: Moraes Editores, 1979.

———. *The Three Marias: New Portuguese Letters*. Trans. by Helen R. Lane. Garden City, NY: Doubleday, 1975.

Besse, Maria Graciete. "As *Novas Cartas Portuguesas* e o exercício da paixão," in *Letras & Letras* (Curitiba). Vol. 7, no. 110. July 1994, pp. 26–28.

Cabrita, António. "Maria Velho da Costa: 'Ha uma linguagem que nos escreve,'" in *Jornal de Letras, Artes & Ideias*. Vol. 8, no. 314. July 12–18, 1988, pp. 8–10.

Coelho, Nelly Novaes. "*Novas Cartas Portuguesas* e o Processo da Conscientização da Mulher—Século XX," in *Letras*. Vol. 23, 1975, pp. 165–171.

Dubois, E.T. "A Mulher e a Paixão: das *Lettres Portugaises* (1669) às *Novas Cartas Portuguesas* (1972)," in *Colóquio/Letras*. Vol. 102, 1988, pp. 35–43.

Figueiredo, Antonio de. "Portugal's Three Marias," in *The Nation*. Vol. 2. March 1974, pp. 268–269.

Pimlott, Ben, and Seaton, Jean. "Political Power and the Portuguese Media," in Lawrence S. Graham and Douglas L. Wheeler, eds. *In Search of Modern Portugal: The Revolution & Its Consequences*. Madison, WI: University of Wisconsin Press, 1983, pp. 43–57.

Sadlier, Darlene J. *The Question of How: Women Writers and New Portuguese Literature*. Contributions in Women's Studies, No. 109. NY: Greenwood Press, 1989.

Vidal, Duarte. *O Processo das Três Marias: Defesa de Maria Isabel Barreno*. Lisbon: Editorial Futura, 1974.

Wasserman, Renata. "The Absent Term: Private Unhappiness, Public Belief in the Fiction of M. Teresa Horta and Lya Luft," in Roberto Reis, ed., *Toward Socio-Criticism: Selected Proceedings of the Conference "Luso-Brazilian Literatures, a Socio-Critical Approach."* Tempe, AZ: Arizona State University, Center for Latin American Studies, 1991, pp. 125–134.

"Women Libbed," in *Economist*. April 13, 1974, p. 33.

SUGGESTED READING:

Almeida, Ana Nunes de, ed. *Bibliografia sobre a Família e a Mulher no Portugal do Século XX*. Lisbon: University of Lisbon, Institute of Social Sciences, 1987.

A Mulher na Sociedade Portuguesa: Visão Histórica e Perspectivas Actuais: Colóquio, 20–221 de Março de 1985: Actas. 2 vols. Coimbra: Instituto de Historia Económica e Social, University of Coimbra, 1986.

Kendall W. Brown,
Professor of History,
Brigham Young University, Provo, Utah

Thulin, Ingrid (1929—)

Swedish actress. Born on January 27, 1929, in Solleftea, Sweden; studied acting at the Royal Dramatic Theater, Stockholm; married Harry Schein (founder of the Swedish Film Institute).

Selected filmography, all Swedish except where noted: Where the Winds Blow *(1948);* Love Will Conquer *(1948);* Jack of Hearts *(1950);* Foreign Intrigue *(US, 1956);* Wild Strawberries *(1957);* Brink of Life *(1958);* The Magician *(1958);* The Judge *(1960);* The Four Horsemen of the Apocalypse *(US, 1962);* Winter Light *(1963);* The Silence *(1963);* Die Lady *(Games of Desire, Ger.-Fr., 1964);* Sextet *(Den., 1964);* Return from the Ashes *(US-UK, 1965);* La Guerre est finie *(Fr.-Sw., 1966);* Night Games *(1966);* Adélaide *(Fr-It., 1968);* Hour of the Wolf *(1968);* The Ritual *(1969);* La Caduta degli Dei *(Götterdämmerung or* The Damned, *It.-Ger., 1969);* Cries and Whispers *(1972);* A Handful of Love *(1974);* Devotion *(short, also dir., 1975);* La Cage *(Fr., 1975);* Moses *(UK-It. 1976);* Salon Kitty *(Madam Kitty, It.-Ger.-Fr., 1976);* The Cassandra Crossing *(US, 1977);* E Comincio il Viaggio nella Vertigini *(It., 1977);* One and One *(also co-dir., 1978);* Brusten Himmel *(Broken Sky, dir. only, 1982);* At the Rehearsal *(1984);* Il Giorno Prima *(Control, It.-Fr.-Can., 1987);* La Casa del Sorriso *(House of Smiles, It., 1991).*

One of Sweden's finest stage and screen actresses, Ingrid Thulin trained at Stockholm's Royal Dramatic Theater and studied pantomime with Etienne Decroux in Paris. Although she began her film career in 1948, it was her work with director Ingmar Bergman during the 1950s—both at the Malmö Municipal Theater and in films—that brought her international recognition. Known for her aloof blonde beauty and her intellectual approach to characterization, she has worked with other such acclaimed directors as France's Alain Resnais (*La Guerre est finie*) and Italy's Luchino Visconti (*The Damned*). She won the Best Actress award at the Cannes Film Festival in 1958, for her role in Bergman's *Brink of Life*. Thulin also directed several films,

including the short *Devotion* (1975), in which she also acted, and two features: *One and One* (1978) and *Brusten Himmel* (*Broken Sky*, 1982). The actress is married to Harry Schein, founder of the Swedish Film Institute.

Thumb, Mrs. Tom (1841–1919).

See Warren, Lavinia.

Thurber, Jeannette (1850–1946)

American music patron. Born on January 29, 1850, in New York City; died on January 2, 1946, in Bronxville, New York; daughter of Henry Meyer(s) and Anne Maria Coffin (Price) Meyer(s); married Francis Beattie Thurber (a merchant and attorney), on September 15, 1869; children: Jeannette M., Marianna Blakeman, Francis Beattie.

Lobbied for the establishment of the American School of Opera (1885); oversaw the establishment of the National Conservatory of Music (1891).

Jeannette Thurber

Jeannette Thurber was born into a well-to-do family in New York City on January 29, 1850, the daughter of Henry and Anne Meyer (some records list the family name as Meyers). Her father, who had immigrated to New York City from Copenhagen, Denmark, in 1837, was independently wealthy. Tutored privately in Paris and New York, Thurber was also taught music by her father, an amateur violinist. At age 19, she married Francis Beattie Thurber, a prosperous grocery wholesaler and later a lawyer. The couple had three children. With the financial resources of her family and husband, Thurber became a benefactor and patron of American classical music institutions. She was particularly interested in fostering music education, and donated money to allow American students to study in Europe. She also provided the financial backing for the first Wagner festival held in the U.S. and for free concerts for young people.

By the early 1880s, her ambitions grew to include a national music conservatory program. Thurber hoped to imitate the music education system in Western Europe, with private and government-funded conservatories around the country. In 1885, she obtained a charter from the state of New York to found the first National Conservatory of Music, which opened in New York City as the American School of Opera in December 1885. She also established a sister organization, the traveling American Opera Company, designed to employ conservatory graduates while exposing the American public to opera. It performed first in 1886 under the direction of Theodore Thomas, but despite high artistic standards and Thurber's dedicated efforts the company was dissolved the following year after failing to turn a profit and losing its wealthy patrons.

Disappointed, Thurber turned her attention to promoting the School of Opera, now called simply the National Conservatory of Music. With low tuition fees and an open-admissions policy, the school expanded beyond opera training to a range of music subjects. In 1891, Congress passed a bill to incorporate it, making it the only school of music in the country with the authority to confer diplomas and honorary degrees. The following year Thurber's efforts to find a world-renowned composer to head the school resulted in the appointment of Antonin Dvorak, who served as director from 1892 to 1895. Exposed to American folk music and especially African-American songs by Conservatory students, Dvorak, with Thurber's encouragement, composed several works incorporating these sources, including his celebrated Symphony No. 9, *From the New World*.

Yet despite Thurber's efforts as president and the prestige of the school's faculty and directors, the Conservatory, like the Opera Company, failed to attract the American public and continually suffered financial difficulties. By the early 1920s, the Conservatory had for all practical purposes ceased to function; President Woodrow Wilson attempted to revitalize it in 1921 by allowing it to establish other regional branches, but that too failed. Thurber, though remaining associated with the Conservatory, gave her time to other organizations in the 1920s and 1930s, particularly the YWCA, the Woman's Exchange, and the Woman's Art School of Cooper Union. She and Francis Thurber also founded the Onteora Club in the Catskill Mountains where they had a summer home. The National Conservatory of Music was officially closed in 1946, about the time of Thurber's death in Bronxville, New York, at age 95.

SOURCES:

James, Edward T., ed. *Notable American Women, 1607–1950*. Cambridge, MA: The Belknap Press of Harvard University, 1971.

McHenry, Robert, ed. *Famous American Women*. NY: Dover, 1980.

Read, Phyllis J., and Bernard L. Witlieb. *The Book of Women's Firsts*. NY: Random House, 1992.

Laura York, M.A. in History,
University of California,
Riverside, California

Thuringia, landgravine of.

See Elizabeth of Hungary for sidebar on Sophia (fl. 1211).

See Elizabeth of Hungary (1207–1231).

See Margaret of Germany (1237–1270).

Thurman, Sue (1903–1996)

African-American civic leader and religious worker.

Name variations: Sue Bailey Thurman. Born Sue Bailey on August 26, 1903, in Pine Bluff, Arkansas; died in San Francisco, California, on December 25, 1996; youngest of ten children of Isaac George Bailey (a minister and educator) and Susie (Ford) Bailey (an educator); graduated from Oberlin College, B.S., 1926; married Howard Thurman (a minister and theology professor), on June 12, 1932 (died 1981); children: (stepdaughter) Olive Thurman (b. 1932); Anne Thurman Chiarenza (b. 1933).

Met with Mohandas Gandhi in India (1936); founded and edited Aframerican Women's Journal (1940); cofounded the Church for the Fellowship of All Peoples, San Francisco (1944); established the Faculty Wives Hostess Committee for Service to International Students, Boston University (1953–64); edited International Cuisine, Kairos Press (1957); served as a board member of Boston University Women's Council, Harriet Tubman Community House, and South End Music Center; was honorary president of the Museum of Afro-American History, Boston; granted honorary doctorate, Livingstone College (1967).

The African-American spiritual and community leader Sue Thurman was born in 1903 in Pine Bluff, Arkansas, the daughter of educators and the granddaughter of former slaves. As well, Thurman's paternal grandmother was a Native American of the Cherokee tribe. Her father, a minister and Arkansas state legislator, founded a school for black children before his death in 1913. Thurman's mother also established educational facilities for black children and taught classes for women as well. Sue Bailey was sent to the *Nannie Burroughs School for Girls in Washington, D.C., and in 1916, at age 13, to Spelman Seminary (now Spelman College). She graduated in 1919, and moved to Ohio to study music at Oberlin College. Following her parents' example, she was active in student organizations, including serving as the first president of the Negro Student Forum as well as in the International Club and the World Fellowship Committee of the YWCA. Thurman became the first black student to receive a degree in music from Oberlin in 1926, and finished her liberal arts degree soon after. She took a job teaching music at Hampton Institute in Virginia, where she supported the student social protests in 1928. Reconsidering music education as a career, that summer she led a YWCA group to Europe. In 1930, she became traveling secretary of the national YWCA based in New York City, assisting women students at black colleges across the country.

Two years later she married Howard Thurman, whom she had known while a student at Spelman and who had recently been appointed professor of theology at Howard University. The couple had one child together, Anne, born in 1933; they raised Howard Thurman's child Olive from his previous marriage as well. After she married, Sue Thurman left the YWCA to coordinate the Howard University Faculty Wives organization, which assisted students and visitors to Howard. She also wrote and lectured on African-American history for the Howard University community.

In October 1935, as part of the Student Christian Federation effort to promote international friendship, the Thurmans began an eight-month trip to Burma (now Myanmar), Ceylon (now Sri Lanka), and India. Sue Thurman studied at the University of Santineeketan in Bengal, India, with the poet Rabindranath Tagore, and met privately with Mohandas Gandhi, with whom she discussed nonviolent resistance and spiritual leadership to effect social change. When she returned to the United States, Thurman began an ambitious lecture tour about Indian culture at American and Canadian colleges; the proceeds funded scholarships for black women to study in India.

Following the lecture tour, she founded a new magazine with the National Council of Negro Women (NCNW) in Washington, *Aframerican Women's Journal*. In the early 1940s, she was a leader in the NCNW, directing its library and museum collections. In 1944, however, the direction of her work changed when Howard Thurman took a leave from Howard University and they moved to San Fran-

cisco. Over the next decade, they were instrumental in the creation of the nation's first racially integrated and internationally oriented church, the Church for the Fellowship of All Peoples.

With the church strongly established, the Thurmans left San Francisco in 1953 for Boston University, where Howard Thurman became professor of theology and dean of Marsh Chapel. They remained in Boston until 1964. As she had done at Howard, Sue Thurman established a committee of faculty wives, again to promote international understanding and aid foreign scholars at Boston University. She arranged honors and testimonials for notable African-American artists, including poets *Phillis Wheatley and ✥ Georgia Douglas Johnson and the noted tenor Roland Hayes. Additionally, Thurman worked with her daughter, **Anne Thurman Chiarenza**, to create a map of the "Freedom Trails of Negro History in Boston." To raise money for loans to international students, Thurman edited a cookbook of international cuisine, published in 1957. Tireless in her volunteer efforts, Thurman was founder of the Museum of Afro-American History, as well as chair of the World Refugee Arts and Crafts program of Marsh Chapel, and board member of the Boston University Women's Council and the *Harriet Tubman Community House. She dedicated much of her time to teaching and promoting black history, and organizing events on campus to honor African-American heroes. One of these events was the 1957 exhibition of specially commissioned dolls, created by the black sculptor ✥ Meta Warrick Fuller to represent important African-American women of the 19th and 20th centuries. The exhibit traveled across the U.S. before the dolls were finally donated to Spelman College. The following year, Thurman edited *The Historical Cookbook of the American Negro*, published by the NCNW.

After her husband's retirement in 1964, the Thurmans traveled as missionaries and educators to Africa and East Asia before settling in San Francisco to resume their work with the Church for the Fellowship of All Peoples. Although they were not directly involved in the black civil-rights movement themselves, Thurman and her husband were friends and supporters of such civil-rights leaders as *Alberta Williams King—with whom she had attended school—her son Martin Luther King, Jr., and Jesse Jackson. In addition to founding international libraries at Arkansas State College, Spelman College, and Livingstone College in this period, Thurman also served as director of San

Johnson, Georgia Douglas. See *Women of the Harlem Renaissance*.

Fuller, Meta Warrick. See *Women of the Harlem Renaissance*.

Francisco's African American Historical and Cultural Society.

Howard Thurman died in 1981. Sue Thurman then became head of the Howard Thurman Educational Trust, which they had founded in 1964 to provide scholarships to black students as well as inspirational materials. She died in 1997, about age 94, in San Francisco.

SOURCES:

Smith, Jessie Carney, ed. *Notable Black American Women*. Detroit, MI: Gale Research, 1992.

Laura York, M.A. in History,
University of California,
Riverside, California

Thurn and Taxis, princess of.

See Helene of Bavaria (1834–1890).
See Margaret Clementine (1870–1955).

Thursby, Emma (1845–1931)

American concert singer. Born Emma Cecilia Thursby on February 21, 1845, in Williamsburg (now part of

Emma Thursby

Brooklyn), New York; died on July 4, 1931, in New York City; daughter of John Barnes Thursby (a manufacturer) and Jane Ann (Bennett) Thursby; studied singing with Julius Meyer, Achille Errani, Francesco Lamperti, Antonio Sangiovanni, and Erminia Mansfield-Rudersdorff.

Sang as a church soloist (1865–77); performed with Brooklyn Musical Association in Haydn's Creation (1868); toured with Patrick S. Gilmore's 22nd Regiment Band (1874); appeared in concert with Hans von Bülow (1875); toured California (1876); toured North America (1877–78); made London debut (1878), Paris debut (1879); went on a German tour (1880); received the medal of the Sociêtê des Concerts, Paris Conservatoire (1881); retired to teach (1895–1924); was a professor at the Institute of Musical Art (1905–11).

Born in Brooklyn, New York, on February 21, 1845, Emma Thursby was the daughter of Jane and John Thursby, descendants of Irish, French, and Dutch families. Included among Thursby's ancestors were a group of Huguenots who settled in Brooklyn in 1659. The Thursby family life revolved around the Old Bushwick Reformed Church in Williamsburg, where Thursby often sang, even as a child as young as five years old. Thursby's parents were well-to-do—her father was in the rope manufacturing business—and wholeheartedly encouraged her singing. After attending public schools, at age 12 she entered the Female Seminary in Bethlehem, Pennsylvania, where she studied music. Two years later, her father's terminal illness obliged her to return to New York. She attended a convent school briefly, but with her father's death her mother could no longer afford to pay for school. Instead Emma tutored other young people in music to support the family.

However, at age 20 she began to pursue a career as a professional vocalist in church choirs, including three years for the Reverend Henry Ward Beecher's Plymouth Church in Brooklyn and numerous concert appearances. In 1867, she began voice lessons with a New York tutor; in 1872, she commanded sufficiently high fees to be able to afford a year abroad in Milan, Italy, studying under Francesco Lamperti and Antonio Sangiovanni. After her return to New York, Thursby's fame continued to increase as concert audiences responded enthusiastically to her clear, powerful soprano and her remarkable two-and-a-half octave range. Through the 1870s she turned gradually from choir music to performing in classical music concerts in various

East Coast cities. She became especially well known for her interpretations of Mozart. Throughout her career, Thursby consistently refused to sing opera because of the dramatic skills required and the intense competition for roles. Reserved by nature and a devout member of the Dutch Reformed Church, she never married and shared little of her private life with the public.

Thursby's rise to national celebrity began with her 1874 appearance with Patrick Gilmore's 22nd Regiment Band at the Philadelphia Academy of Music. Critically and popularly acclaimed, Thursby toured with the Gilmore Band across the United States in 1875. By 1876, she was earning $3,000 a year as a soloist for the Broadway Tabernacle choir, the highest paid soloist in the country. One year later, she gave up church singing completely in order to concentrate on building a career as a concert vocalist. She signed a contract for $100,000 as principal vocalist in a North American concert series directed by Maurice Strakosch. Her European debut came in 1878 at St. James Hall in London, which led to an extended British tour. Thursby's French debut in 1879 and her German debut the following year were equally successful, and she enjoyed enormous popularity across western Europe. In 1881 she received the rare honor of a commemorative medal from the Paris Conservatoire. This was followed by concert tours in Holland, Spain, and Scandinavia.

Thursby curtailed her concert appearances in the late 1880s, after the death of her mother in June 1884 and that of her older sister the next January. After fulfilling a demanding performance schedule involving much travel for over a decade, she began to suffer from exhaustion and performed less and less frequently. A farewell concert in Chicago in December 1895 marked her final public performance, at age 50. Returning to New York, Thursby worked as a private voice instructor, and from 1905 to 1911 was a professor at the New York Institute of Musical Art. She continued to give music lessons until she suffered a partial paralysis in 1924, at age 79. Emma Thursby died of endocarditis and arteriosclerosis at her home in Gramercy Park, New York City, in 1931 and was buried in Brooklyn at the Cemetery of the Evergreens.

SOURCES:

James, Edward T., ed. *Notable American Women, 1607–1950.* Cambridge, MA: The Belknap Press of Harvard University, 1971.

McHenry, Robert, ed. *Famous American Women.* NY: Dover, 1980.

Laura York, M.A. in History,
University of California,
Riverside, California

Thurston, Katherine (1875–1911)

Anglo-Irish novelist. Born Katherine Cecil Madden on April 18, 1875, in County Cork, Ireland; died of asphyxia on September 5, 1911, in County Cork, Ireland; daughter of Paul Madden (a banker and mayor) and Catherine (Barry) Madden; married Ernest Charles Temple Thurston (a novelist), in 1901 (divorced 1910).

Selected works: The Circle *(1903);* The Masquerader *(published in England as* John Chilcote, M.P., *1904);* Mystics *(1907);* The Fly on the Wheel *(1908);* The Gambler *(1906);* Max *(1908).*

Novelist Katherine Thurston was born in 1875 in Wood's Gift, Cork, Ireland, the only child of **Catherine Madden** and Paul Madden, a prosperous Anglo-Irish banker and former mayor of Cork. She was well educated privately at their Cork County home, but did not show an inclination for writing until after her marriage at age 26 to an English novelist, Ernest Charles Temple Thurston. Two years later, she published her first novel, *The Circle* (1903), with little success. However, her popularity was assured with the serial publication in the American magazine *Harper's Bazaar* of her second work, *The Masquerader*. A tale of mistaken identity, *The Masquerader* (titled *John Chilcote, M.P.* in England) became a bestseller when it was published in the U.S. in book form in 1904. The novel was also turned into a popular play and was twice made into a film. Her third novel, *The Gambler*, appeared in *Harper's Bazaar* in serial form and was published as a book in 1906. Three more novels appeared to less acclaim between 1907 and 1910, but her previous successes made Thurston a popular literary figure in England and Ireland. She and her husband, who had no children, were divorced in 1910. Always in poor health, Katherine Thurston died at age 36 of asphyxia from a fainting fit at Moore's Hotel, Cork, in September 1911.

SOURCES:

Concise Dictionary of National Biography. Oxford: Oxford University Press, 1992.

Kunitz, Stanley J., and Howard Haycraft, eds. *Twentieth Century Authors.* NY: H.W. Wilson, 1942.

Laura York, M.A. in History,
University of California,
Riverside, California

Thurston, Lucy (1795–1876)

American Congregationalist missionary to Hawaii. Born Lucy Goodale on October 29, 1795, in Marlborough, Massachusetts; died on October 13, 1876, in Honolulu, Hawaii Territory; daughter of Abner Goodale (a farmer and deacon in the Congregational Church) and possibly Mary Howe (died after a brief illness in 1818); graduated from Bradford Academy in Massachusetts where she taught until her marriage; married Asa Thurston (a Congregationalist minister), on October 21, 1820 (died March 11, 1868); children: six, including Thomas G. Thurston and Persis G. Taylor.

Lucy Thurston was born Lucy Goodale in 1795 in Marlborough, Massachusetts, the daughter of Abner Goodale, a farmer and deacon in the Congregational Church, and possibly **Mary Howe** (little is known of Thurston's mother, who died after a brief illness in 1818). In 1820, she married Asa Thurston, a Congregationalist minister. That same year, the American Board of Commissioners for Foreign Missions (founded in 1810) called for a party of missionaries for the Pacific. Led by Asa and Hiram Bingham, the Thurstons sailed with 15 other missionaries to the Sandwich Islands (now Hawaii), landing in Kailua in 1821. There Lucy began her missionary work, spending the majority of her life in Kailua and returning to the United States only twice, once to enroll her daughters in finishing school and a second "to buy a pair of shoes."

In 1855, Thurston was diagnosed with breast cancer. Concern over her weak heart prevented use of topical or general anesthesia, and a complete mastectomy was performed while Thurston remained conscious. She maintained that she was buoyed by the grace and love of God. Thurston went on to live and work for another 21 years, moving to Honolulu only after retiring from missionary work in 1862. Asa died in Honolulu on March 11, 1868; Lucy died on October 13, 1876, 16 days before her 81st birthday. She left behind an autobiography, later edited and published by her daughter **Persis G. Taylor** and the Rev. Walter Freer as *The Life and Times of Mrs. Lucy G. Thurston* (Ann Arbor, 1876). Her son, Thomas G. Thurston, returned to Hawaii as a missionary after his graduation from Yale in 1862 and her grandson, Lorrin Andrews Thurston, become the minister of the interior in the new constitutional government of Hawaii, and later the envoy to the United States from Hawaii.

SOURCES:

Deen, Edith. *Great Woman of the Christian Faith*. NY: Harper, 1959.

Thurston, Lucy. *Life and Times of Mrs. Lucy G. Thurston, Wife of Rev. Asa Thurston, Pioneer Missionary to the Sandwich Islands, Gathered from Letters and Journals Extending Over a Period of More than Fifty Years*. Ann Arbor, MI: S.C. Andrews, 1934.

Amanda Carson Banks,
lecturer, Vanderbilt Divinity School,
Nashville, Tennessee

Thurston, Matilda (1875–1958)

American educator and missionary. Born Matilda Smyrell Calder on May 16, 1875, in Hartford, Connecticut; died of arteriosclerosis on April 18, 1958, in Auburndale, Massachusetts; daughter of George Calder (a carpenter) and Margery (Patterson) Calder; educated in Hartford public schools; Mt. Holyoke College, B.S., 1896; married John Lawrence Thurston (a missionary), in 1902 (died 1904).

Taught in Connecticut secondary schools (1896–1900); volunteered for foreign mission work (1900); taught at Central Turkey College for Girls, Marash, Turkey (1900–02); traveled to China with husband (1902); taught at Yale mission in Zhangsha, China (1903); returned to China with support from Presbyterian Board of Foreign Missions (1913); founded Ginling College for Women (1913) and served as school's first president (1913–28); served with relief organizations in China (1940–43); interned by Japanese (early 1940s); repatriated to Auburndale, Massachusetts (1943).

The eldest daughter of a Scottish immigrant father who worked as a carpenter and a northern Irish immigrant mother, Matilda Thurston was born in Hartford, Connecticut, on May 16, 1875. Both parents were staunch Presbyterians, and from them the young Matilda gained a respect for practicality, hard work, and faith. When she was 13, she joined the Presbyterian Church. Social life revolved around church and family, which included her younger sister **Helen Calder**, to whom she was very close, and her younger brother. She also very much enjoyed her education in the public schools of Hartford.

After graduating from high school, Thurston left home for the first time, to attend Mt. Holyoke College. A missionary delegation visited the campus during her senior year there, and she enrolled in a mission study class on India. Later, she joined the Student Volunteer Movement for Foreign Missions (SVM), and realized she had found her calling. After receiving a B.S. degree from Mt. Holyoke in 1896, Thurston embarked on a teaching career, spending four years in Connecticut public schools while attending SVM conferences at Northfield, Massachusetts, during the summers. These conferences heightened her desire to work as a missionary, and in 1900 she volunteered for service. Her first assignment was a two-year stint at Central Turkey College for Girls in Marash, Turkey. When she returned to America in 1902, she married John Lawrence Thurston, whom she had met during an SVM conference.

The son of a minister, Yale-educated John Thurston was a seminary student and co-founder of the Yale University Mission, for which the young couple would work in China. Not long after their marriage they sailed for China, where they spent their first months studying Chinese. They intended to find a location for what would become Yale-in-China, but John's tuberculosis forced them to return to the United States in August 1903. He died the following year in California.

Thurston continued to work for the SVM, spending two years as a field secretary before returning to China around 1906. In Zhangsha (Changsha), Hunan, she taught for five years at the boys' preparatory school at the Yale mission while also working in the mission hospital attached to the school. She was planning her departure for a trip home to America when the Chinese Revolution of 1911 erupted, forcing her to join the exodus of numerous Westerners from interior China. Anticipating expanded opportunities for women as a result of the revolution, refugee missionaries in Shanghai began to plan for a women's Christian college. While some two-year college programs already had been established, there was no four-year women's college in central China at that time.

Thurston returned to China in 1913, working under the aegis of the Presbyterian Board of Foreign Missions, one of five societies offering support for an interdenominational school for women. In November 1913, she was elected president of Ginling College for Women. As the college did not yet exist, her first charges were to locate a campus, hire a faculty, and publicize the new school. The college opened its doors with six faculty members and eight students in September 1915. Thurston established a close link with Smith College, one of the preeminent women's colleges in the U.S., and modeled the curriculum at Ginling after that of American liberal arts colleges. Both Smith and Mt. Holyoke provided teaching staff for short-term assignments. With its twin goals of furthering the Christian cause and helping women gain respect and independence, Ginling attracted the daughters both of well-to-do non-Christians and of less wealthy Christians, and its enrollment grew rapidly. Most classes were conducted in English, although Thurston frequently gave religious addresses in Chinese. In addition to handling administration of the school, she also taught astronomy, advanced mathematics, and religion, and conducted the choir. The school was known for its courses in the sciences, English, music, and physical education, and may well have been the first in China to award bachelor's degrees to women. Many of its graduates became middle-school teachers.

Thurston remained president of Ginling until 1928, when she turned the post over to one of the school's first graduates, **Wu Yi-fang**, in the face of continuing criticism of missionary-led schools by Chinese nationalists. She remained actively engaged at the school as an advisor, however, consulting on plans for building construction. From 1936 to 1939, Thurston lived in the United States, returning to China in 1939, after the start of World War II, to work with war and relief efforts. When the Japanese took over Nanjing (Nanking) in the early 1940s, Thurston was interned. Upon her release in 1943, she went to live with her sister Helen in Auburndale, Massachusetts. There, despite failing health from arteriosclerosis, she collaborated with **Ruth M. Chester** on a history of Ginling College that was published in 1955. Prior to its merger with several other schools in 1952, when the People's Republic of China brought all colleges and universities into a national system, the college had graduated about 1,000 students. Thurston died in 1958.

SOURCES:

Sicherman, Barbara, and Carol Hurd Green, eds. *Notable American Women: The Modern Period*. Cambridge, MA: The Belknap Press of Harvard University, 1980.

Lolly Ockerstrom,
freelance writer,
Washington, D.C.

Thusnelda (fl. 1st c. CE)

Germanic warrior and military advisor. Probably born at the end of the 1st century BCE; died early in the 1st century CE.

Known for her bravery, Thusnelda served as the key military advisor to Hermann of Germany (Arminius) during the first two decades of the 1st century. During their fight against the Romans, she was captured, put in chains, and taken to Rome. Thusnelda's bravery is celebrated in folktales.

Lolly Ockerstrom,
freelance writer,
Washington, D.C.

Thwaite, Lady Alice (1896–1953).

See Rawlings, Marjorie Kinnan.

Thynne, Frances (1699–1754).

See Seymour, Frances Thynne.

Thyra (fl. 891 or 936)

Queen of Denmark. Name variations: Thyri Klacksdottir. Flourished around 936 (some sources cite 891); daughter of Klack-Harald, king of Jutland; possibly the wife of Gorm the Old of Jutland, king of Denmark (r. c. 883–940) or possibly the wife of Harald Bluetooth; children: possibly Harald Bluetooth (c. 910–986), king of Denmark (r. 940–986); Knut "Danaást."

Gorm the Old was one of the first kings to rule over a united Danish kingdom. Thyra, queen of Denmark, was possibly his wife or she was the wife of his son Harald Bluetooth, who established Christianity in a consolidated Denmark and reigned from around 940 to his death in 985. Because of the constant incursions of Viking fleets during the summer months, the Danes had become masters of far-flung territories, including much of northeast Britain (present-day Scotland). While the men of Denmark were off raiding France, the British Isles, and the Low Countries, Queen Thyra was left to rule. Aware that Denmark was defenseless in the summer while the Vikings were away, the Germans continually invaded the unprotected southern border of Denmark and raided its great trading center at Slesvig. It is said that Thyra raised a great wall, parts of which are still extant, over a period of three years. Called the Danneverke, the wall served as a bastion of defense in the southern region for centuries to come.

Thyra (d. 1018)

Countess of Wessex. Name variations: Thyra Sveynsdottir. Born around 993; died in 1018; daughter of *Gunhilda of Poland (d. around 1015) and Sven or Sweyn I Forkbeard, king of Denmark (r. 985–1014) and king of England (r. 1014); first wife of Godwin of Wessex (d. 1053), earl of Wessex and Kent (r. 1018–1053). Godwin's second wife was *Gytha (fl. 1022–1042).

Thyra of Denmark (d. 1000)

Queen of Norway. Name variations: Thyre. Flourished around 999; died on September 18, 1000; daughter of Harald Bluetooth (c. 910–985), king of Denmark (r. 940–985), and *Gyrid; grandmother of *Gytha; sister of Sveyn or Sweyn I Forkbeard, king of Denmark (r. 986–1014), king of England (r. 1014); married Styrbjörn (son of Olaf, king of Sweden); betrothed to and possibly married King Burislaf of Wendland; married Olav I Tryggvason (968–1000), king of Norway, in 998 or 999; children: (first marriage) Thorgils Sprakalegg.

Thyra of Denmark was the daughter of Harald Bluetooth and sister of Sweyn Forkbeard, both kings of Denmark. She was first married to Styrbjörn, the son of Olaf of Sweden. Some sources suggest she was then betrothed to and possibly married King Burislaf of Wendland, an area of northern Germany occupied by a fierce Slavic people in the late 10th century. Burislaf was the father of *Geyra, first wife of Olaf I Tryggvason, king of Norway.

Thyra would become Olaf I's fourth wife in 998 or 999. While not all of the sources mention Olaf Tryggvason's four marriages, there seems to be general agreement on the details of his marriage to Thyra. She had fled from Wendland to Norway, appalled at the prospect of married life with an old, pagan king such as Burislaf. Olaf proposed and Thyra considered herself lucky "to marry so celebrated a man."

Soon after the wedding, she began to complain to Olaf of her relative poverty. She had left the dowry her brother Sweyn Forkbeard bestowed on her in Wendland; since Sweyn disapproved of her flight from old Burislaf, he refused to help her retrieve her dowry. Thyra begged Olaf Tryggvason to go to Burislaf to accomplish this task. Always keen for a foreign adventure, Olaf agreed to gather his warships for an expedition to Wendland. In the summer of 1000, he set out with a large number of warships and men. The reunion with his former father-in-law was a peaceful one, and Olaf was able to obtain Thyra's dowry.

Thyra of Denmark (1880–1945)

Danish princess. Born Thyra Louise Caroline Amelia in 1880; died on November 1, 1945; daughter of *Louise of Sweden (1851–1926) and Frederick VIII (1843–1912), duke of Schleswig-Holstein-Sonderburg-Augustenburg (r. 1869–1880), king of Denmark (r. 1906–1912); sister of Christian X, king of Denmark (r. 1912–1947).

Thyra Oldenburg (1853–1933)

Princess of Denmark and duchess of Cumberland. Name variations: Thyra, duchess of Cumberland and Teviotdale. Born Thyra Amelia Caroline Charlotte Anne on September 29, 1853, in Copenhagen, Denmark; died on February 26, 1933, in Gmunden, Austria; daughter of *Louise of Hesse-Cassel (1817–1898) and Christian IX (1818–1906), king of Denmark (r. 1863–1906); sister of *Marie Feodorovna and *Alexandra of Denmark; married Ernest Augustus, 3rd duke of Cumberland and Teviotdale, on De-

cember 21, 1878; children: *Marie Louise (1879–1948, who married Maximilian Alexander, prince of Baden); George William, earl of Armagh (1880–1912); *Alexandra Guelph (1882–1963); Olga (1884–1958); Christian (1885–1901); Ernest Augustus, duke of Brunswick-Luneburg (1887–1953).

Thyre.

Variant of Thyra.

Tibbetts, Margaret Joy (1919—)

American diplomat and ambassador to Norway. Born on August 26, 1919, in Bethel, Maine; daughter of Raymond R. Tibbetts (a physician) and Pearl (Ashby) Tibbetts (a nurse); Wheaton College, B.A., 1941; Bryn Mawr College, M.A., 1942, Ph.D. in history, 1944.

Was a research analyst for Office of Strategic Services (1944–45); was a research analyst with U.S. Department of State, Washington (1945–49); served as attaché to the American Embassy in London (1949–51 and 1951–54); served as officer in charge, U.S. consulate general of the Belgian Congo, Leopoldville (now Kinshasa, Congo, 1954–56); served as special assistant to the director, ICA (1959–61); served as 1st secretary at the American Embassy in Brussels, Belgium (1961–65); served as U.S. ambassador to Norway (1964–69); was deputy assistant secretary, Foreign Service, Bureau of European and Canadian Affairs (c. 1969–71); became a college professor (1970s).

Diplomat, researcher and scholar Margaret Joy Tibbetts served as a career foreign service officer in the U.S. Department of State during the 1950s and 1960s. In addition to assignments in England, Belgium, and the Belgian Congo, she served as ambassador to Norway from 1964 to 1969. She expressed a preference for political reporting and negotiations work over the social responsibilities attendant to representing the United States abroad, but was highly skilled in all dimensions of international diplomacy.

Tibbetts was born in Bethel, Maine, in 1919, one of three children of a country doctor and a nurse. The family had lived in Maine for 13 generations. A Phi Beta Kappa scholar at Wheaton College, she graduated summa cum laude in history in 1941. She then went to Bryn Mawr for graduate studies, receiving an M.A. (1942) and a Ph.D. in history (1944). Tibbetts' only brother had been killed in World War II, causing her to revise her plan of becoming a uni-

versity professor upon completion of her Ph.D. Instead, she entered the Office of Strategic Services (precursor to the Central Intelligence Agency) as a research analyst on Great Britain and the Commonwealth.

In London (1949–54), Tibbetts worked under **Frances Willis**, who in 1962 would become the first woman in the foreign service to be appointed a career ambassador. Highly respected and well connected in diplomatic circles, Willis mentored the younger officer through the initial years of her career. Tibbetts, articulate and unafraid to state her point of view, emerged unscathed in London in April 1952, after Senator Joseph McCarthy's representatives, Roy Cohn and David Schine, made a disruptive visit investigating "communistic tendencies" among foreign service officers. She was next posted to the Belgian Congo, working under a consul general who traveled a great deal. When inspectors came to the embassy and discovered that Tibbetts had been the officer in charge for more than three of the previous eight months, the re-

Margaret Joy Tibbetts

port that followed praised her leadership. She later pointed to this incident as having advanced her career; placed in charge by chance, she acquired more experience in political work than most women officers.

In 1964, Tibbetts was promoted from class 2 to class 1 in the foreign service. For a woman to receive such promotion was fairly rare, but also on the same promotional list were fellow foreign service officers **Katherine Bracken** and **Carol Laise**. This marked the first time that three women had been promoted simultaneously to class 1 by the Department of State. On April 28, 1964, Tibbetts, Bracken and Laise visited the White House to meet with President Lyndon Johnson, who used the "historically unique" occasion of their promotions to publicize the achievements of women in public service. Shortly thereafter, the president announced Tibbetts' appointment as ambassador to Norway. (Two other women, *****Florence Harriman** and Frances Willis, had previously served in that position.) During her first year as ambassador, Tibbetts escorted Martin Luther King, Jr., and *****Coretta Scott King** to the award ceremony in Oslo at which he received the Nobel Peace Prize. Tibbetts became fluent in Norwegian, putting herself in great demand when translation of sensitive documents was required. To avoid potential political problems with such translations all coming from one person, she also brought in *****Roz Ridgway** to assist her. Norwegian antipathy to American involvement in Vietnam was high during Tibbetts' tenure as ambassador, but her diplomatic strategy remained simple and straightforward; her own advice to foreign service officers and potential ambassadors was to remember that they were in someone else's country, and to avoid being overly aggressive.

Tibbetts described herself as a good executive but not an administrator, and somewhat less than enamored with the socializing that high diplomatic posts require. She once noted, "The question of a woman ambassador is not, 'Is she a good woman ambassador?' but, 'Is she a good ambassador?' And that's the only point that matters." Throughout her career, Tibbetts resisted the notion that women should be confined to particular assignments. When it was suggested in the State Department that certain diplomatic posts should be reserved for women, she reacted strongly, saying that such ideas were potentially damaging both for women per se and in the larger political sense. Although she did not identify herself as a feminist, she advocated for women's rights by example. In the mid-1990s, she said of the erstwhile Federal Woman's Award, "I always felt that was

an insult. You shouldn't nominate someone for being a good woman; you should nominate someone for being a good officer. The terrible thing is that most of the women who won the Federal Woman's Award were *outstanding*. They shouldn't have been given the Woman's Award; they should have been given the Medal of Freedom." She went on to note that the government "discontinued it about six or seven years ago because it is not consistent with the pattern of the times."

Following her term as ambassador to Norway, Tibbetts became the first woman assigned to the post of deputy assistant secretary in the Department of State, serving in the Bureau of European and Canadian Affairs beginning in 1969. Only two years later, at age 52, she offered her resignation in order to care for her ailing mother in Maine. At a time when male officers would have been offered a leave of absence without pay, female officers' only option was outright resignation. Tibbetts became a college professor after the death of her mother, and in 1973 began serving as the president of the historical society of her hometown of Bethel, Maine.

SOURCES:

Morin, Ann Miller. *Her Excellency: An Oral History of American Women Ambassadors.* NY: Twayne, 1995.

Lolly Ockerstrom,
freelance writer,
Washington, D.C.

Tibbles, Susette (1854–1902).

See La Flesche, Susette.

Tibors (b. around 1130)

European troubadour. Born around 1130 and grew up in the castle of Sarenom, known as Serignan, near Grasse in the Alpes Maritimes; daughter of a noble family; sister of troubadour Raimbuat d'Orange, or Rambaud of Orange; married Bertrand de Baux (assassinated 1181).

Women troubadours who emerged in medieval Europe were not unique, as their prototype had long existed in the Arabic world and even in ancient Egypt. As early as 2500 BCE, records exist of female singers in Egypt. This tradition continued and Arabic songstresses were some of the wealthiest and most powerful individuals in their culture. The Moors brought songstresses with them when they conquered Spain, and the custom of women singers spread to Southern France and then into Europe. Tibors was the sister of the troubadour Rambaud of Orange. Hers was a noble ancestry as her family held the castle of Sarenom, known as Serignan, near Grasse in the Alpes Maritimes. She married Bertrand de Baux, an important patron of the troubadours. He was assassinated in 1181 on the orders of Raymond V of Toulouse. Only one of Tibors' songs survives.

John Haag,
Athens, Georgia

Tickell, Mary (1758–1787).

See Linley, Mary.

Tickey, Bertha (1925—)

American softball player who pitched 757 winning games and lost 88. Born in Dinuba, California, on March 13, 1925.

Bertha Tickey was typical of the many talented women who left their mark on the game of softball. During her 23-year career, she pitched 757 winning games and lost only 88. For the 13 years she played for the Raybestos Brakettes, she never lost more than 13 games per season. "Blazing Bertha," as fans called her, was a member of 11 national championship teams—the Orange, California Lionettes (1950, 1951, 1952 and 1955) and the Raybestos Brakettes (1958, 1959, 1960, 1963, 1966, 1967, and 1968). She won the Most Valuable Player award eight times. In 1950, the first year Tickey played a national championship series, she won 65 of 73 games, struck out 795 batters, gave up 143 hits, and had 143 consecutive scoreless innings. Tickey's lifetime record as a pitcher was an incredible 162 no-hitters. In 1967, the year before she retired, she pitched a 13-inning no-hitter against Fresno. Bertha Tickey was named to the Connecticut Hall of Fame in 1973 and the National Softball Hall of Fame in 1972.

Karin Loewen Haag,
Athens, Georgia

Ticknor, Anna Eliot (b. 1823)

American educator who founded Boston's Society to Encourage Studies at Home. Born Anna Eliot Ticknor in Boston, Massachusetts, in 1823; eldest daughter and one of four children (two of whom died in childhood) of George Ticknor (b. 1791, first professor of modern languages at Harvard and founder of the Boston Public Library) and Anna Eliot Ticknor (Mrs. George Ticknor, who hosted a famous literary salon); cousin of historian Samuel Eliot; never married; no children.

Though Anna Ticknor was no educational revolutionary, writes **Jean Strouse**, she was "original in trying to interest all classes of women in her program; she saw education as an enhancing of life rather than as training for a particular career, and she had more in mind than book-learning." An early pioneer in distance education, Ticknor was born in 1823 in Boston, the eldest daughter of George Ticknor, the first professor of modern languages at Harvard and founder of the Boston Public Library, and **Anna Eliot**, who hosted a famous literary salon.

Anna Eliot Ticknor founded Boston's Society to Encourage Studies at Home in 1873. From her headquarters in the library of the family home at Nine Park Street in Boston, she enlisted the help of over 200 Boston women to assist with the enterprise, including *Elizabeth Cary Agassiz. The school offered instruction in 24 subjects organized within six departments: history, science, art, literature, French, and German. Many of her students were women, confined at home because of the conventions of a predominately patriarchal society. By the time the school closed down in 1887, it had taught 7,086 students from all social strata.

Ticknor, who never married, was a prolific letter writer and also authored the children's book *An American Family in Paris*, which was published anonymously in 1869. Additionally, she was instrumental in editing and publishing her father's letters and journals.

SOURCES:

Life, Letters, and Journals of George Ticknor. Vol. I. Boston, MA: James R. Osgood and Co., 1876.

Tyack, David B. *George Ticknor and the Boston Brahmins.* Cambridge, MA: Harvard University Press, 1967.

Tiedemann, Charlotte (1919–1979)

Duchess of Segovia. Born Charlotte Auguste Luise Tiedemann on January 2, 1919, in Konigsberg, Prussia; died on July 3, 1979, in Berlin, Germany; daughter of Otto Eugen Tiedemann and Luise Amalia Klein; married a man named Buchler; married a man named Hippler; married Jaime (1908–1975), duke of Segovia (renounced claim to the throne of Spain in 1939), on August 3, 1949.

Tiernan, Frances Fisher (1846–1920)

American author. Name variations: Frances Christine Fisher; (pseudonym) Christian Reid. Born Frances Christine Fisher on July 5, 1846, in Salisbury, North Carolina; died of pneumonia on March 24, 1920, in Salisbury; daughter of Charles Frederic Fisher (a newspaper editor and Civil War colonel) and Eliza-

beth Ruth (Caldwell) Fisher; educated at home and briefly attended St. Mary's School in Raleigh; married James Marquis Tiernan (a mineralogist), on December 29, 1887 (died 1898); no children.

Published first novel (1870); traveled to Europe (1879–80); lived in Mexico (1887–97); received University of Notre Dame's Laetare Medal (1909).

Major works (under pseudonym Christian Reid): Valerie Aylmer *(1870);* Morton House *(1871);* "The Land of the Sky"; or, Adventures in Mountain By-Ways *(1876);* Hearts of Steel *(1883);* Armine *(1884);* Carmela *(1891);* The Land of the Sun *(1894);* The Man of the Family *(1897);* The Chase of an Heiress *(1898);* Under the Southern Cross *(1900);* A Daughter of the Sierra *(1903);* Vera's Charge *(1907);* Princess Nadine *(1908);* The Light of the Vision *(1911);* The Wargrave Trust *(1912);* Daughter of a Star *(1913);* A Far-Away Princess *(1914);* The Secret Bequest *(1915).*

The author of 45 books with a deeply Catholic perspective, Frances Fisher Tiernan was born into privilege in Salisbury, North Carolina, on July 5, 1846. She was the eldest child of Charles Frederic Fisher, an influential editor and wealthy landowner, and **Elizabeth Caldwell Fisher**, who died while Frances was still young. Her father served as a colonel in the Confederate Army during the Civil War, and was killed in 1861 at the first battle of Bull Run. Reduced in financial circumstances (as were so many Southerners after the war) but not penniless, Frances and her sister **Annie** and brother Frederic were cared for by their aunt **Christine Fisher**. Aunt Christine, a convert to Roman Catholicism who was something of a recluse, also provided her niece with a home education. Frances was already possessed of a lively imagination, and would sometimes spin stories for her aunt, who then wrote them down. The children were very close and, following their aunt's example, all three converted to Roman Catholicism, Frances and her sister in 1868. This faith would later inform the content of her novels.

Although much of her early life was spent in Salisbury, Tiernan traveled to Baltimore and the North Carolina mountains with her family after the end of the Civil War. Later she managed to enroll in St. Mary's School in Raleigh, although she remained for only one semester. By now she was writing stories for amusement, most likely inspired by the experience of her limited travel and by her aunt, who also wrote occasionally. This literary pastime turned into a professional venture when she needed to earn money. A pseudonym was required to protect her modesty, and

Tiernan chose to use the name Christian Reid for its quiet dignity and gender ambiguity. Although she planned a novel on the Civil War for her first project, she quickly abandoned that idea for something more suitable to her talents. Her first novel, *Valerie Aylmer* (1870), featured a flirtatious heroine in the antebellum South.

Encouraged when the book unexpectedly sold 8,000 copies, Tiernan focused her energies on writing more novels. She published 13 books between 1871 and 1879, often writing at a pace of 20 pages a day. *Morton House* (1871) was among her favorites, along with a North Carolina travel novel, *"The Land of the Sky"; or Adventures in the Mountain By-Ways* (1876). Other novels from this early period include *A Daughter of Bohemia* (1874), *A Question of Honor* (1875), and *Bonny Kate* (1878). Tiernan wrote domestic fiction centered on family misunderstandings and romance, "period pieces" aimed at the genteel, middle-class women usually featured in her books. These same women regularly bought her novels, providing her with consistent income and respect as a writer, although her work holds little appeal for the modern reader. ("My purpose has always been to inculcate high standards of living, to influence none to do wrongly," she noted.)

Late in 1879, at age 33, Tiernan traveled to Europe in search of new experiences for her writing. Using funds she had saved from the proceeds of her novels, she visited England and Italy, but spent most of her time in Paris. Not surprisingly, her next novels, *Hearts of Steel* (1883) and *Armine* (1884), were set in Europe. Because of its consistent and heavy Catholic moralizing, her work was beginning to lose some of its popularity, but she nonetheless continued to publish regularly. In 1887, she met James Marquis Tiernan, a mineralogist and widower who had read her books and admired her from a distance. He pursued her avidly, and they were married in New Orleans late that December. James had mining interests in Mexico, and the couple spent the next ten years living there; both Tiernan's *Carmela* (1891) and *The Land of the Sun* (1894) were set in Mexico. A business trip to the West Indies with her husband provided background for two subsequent novels, *The Man of the Family* (1897), set in Haiti, and *The Chase of an Heiress* (1898), set in Santo Domingo.

James Tiernan fell ill in 1897, and the couple left Mexico for Frances' hometown of Salisbury, where James died early the next year. Tiernan continued to write for a few years, including *Under the Southern Cross* (1900), in which she finally essayed the Civil War (the heroine, a Southern belle, refuses on principle to marry the handsome Yankee). She then retired only to see the income from her husband's mines end in the early years of the new century, forcing her to begin writing again. In 1909, she received the Laetare Medal from the University of Notre Dame for her contributions as a lay Catholic to American life. Tiernan continued to publish until only a few years before her death from pneumonia in Salisbury in 1920, age 74.

SOURCES:

James, Edward T., ed. *Notable American Women, 1607–1950.* Cambridge, MA: The Belknap Press of Harvard University, 1971.

McHenry, Robert, ed. *Famous American Women.* NY: Dover, 1980.

Lolly Ockerstrom,
freelance writer,
Washington, D.C.

Tierney, Gene (1920–1991)

American actress who received an Oscar nomination for her performance in Leave Her to Heaven. *Name variations: Gene Lee. Born Gene Eliza Tierney on November 20 (one respected source cites the 19th), 1920, in Brooklyn, New York; died of emphysema in Houston, Texas, on November 6, 1991; one of three children (two girls and a boy) of Howard Tierney (an insurance broker) and Belle (Taylor) Tierney; attended St. Margaret's and Miss Porter's School in Connecticut, and Chateau Brilliantmont, in Lausanne, Switzerland; married Oleg Cassini (a fashion designer), on June 1, 1941 (divorced February 1952); married W. Howard Lee (an oil executive), in July 1960; children: (first marriage) two daughters,* Daria *and* Christina Cassini.

Theater: Molly O'Day in Mrs. O'Brien Entertains *(February 1939);* Peggy Carr in Ring Two *(November 1939);* Patricia Stanley in The Male Animal *(January 1940).*

Selected filmography: The Return of Jesse James *(1940);* Hudson's Bay *(1941);* Tobacco Road *(1941);* *Belle Starr *(1941);* Sundown *(1941);* The Shanghai Gesture *(1942);* Son of Fury *(1942);* Rings on Her Fingers *(1942);* Thunder Birds *(1942);* China Girl *(1943);* Heaven Can Wait *(1943);* Laura *(1944);* A Bell for Adano *(1945);* Leave Her to Heaven *(1945);* Dragonwyck *(1946);* The Razor's Edge *(1946);* The Ghost and Mrs. Muir *(1947);* The Iron Curtain *(1948);* That Wonderful Urge *(1948);* Whirlpool *(1950);* Night and the City *(1950);* Where the Sidewalk Ends *(1950);* The Mating Season *(1951);* On the Riviera *(1951);* The Secret of Convict Lake *(1951);* Close to My Heart *(1951);* Way of a Gaucho *(1952);* Plymouth Adventure *(1952);* Never Let Me Go *(1953);* Personal Affair *(UK, 1954);* Black Widow *(1954);* The Egyptian *(1954);* The Left Hand of God *(1955);* Advise and Consent *(1962);* Toys in the Attic *(1963);* The Pleasure Seekers *(1964).*

A tall brunette with chiseled cheekbones, slanted blue-green eyes, and famed overbite, Gene Tierney was wooed to Hollywood from a promising stage career, and was one of 20th Century-Fox's lineup of stars during the 1940s. Although she had roles in several box-office hits, she failed to win the acclaim of the critics, who consistently found her wooden. Sidetracked in the 1950s by her tumultuous personal life and a mental breakdown, she made a modest screen comeback in the 1960s.

Tierney was born in Brooklyn in 1920, the daughter of a wealthy Manhattan insurance broker, and attended private schools near the family estate in Connecticut, and in Switzerland. While she was still her teens, her emerging beauty brought offers from Hollywood, but her parents believed she should pursue the Broadway stage instead of movies. To that end, her father formed a family-owned corporation, Belle-Tier, to promote and manage her career. After small roles in two unsuccessful George Abbott productions—*Mrs. O'Brien Entertains* and *Ring Two* (both 1939)—she was enthusiastically received in the role of the kid sister of a college coed in *The Male Animal* (1940). Critics spoke of her beauty and animation and *Life* magazine included a four-page special feature on her. Although at the time Tierney told the press she was not ready for Hollywood, she was ultimately won over by Fox's Darryl F. Zanuck, who was looking to replace disgruntled star *Loretta Young. With the help of her father, Tierney negotiated a contract unique for the times. Not only did it allow her time off to return to Broadway each year, but it also stipulated that the studio would not color or cut her hair, or straighten her teeth.

Tierney's film debut as the female lead in *The Return of Jesse James* (1940) was bland and lackluster. A review in *The New York Times* calling her "singularly mannered and colorless" was just a hint at what was to come. Following her second screen appearance in *Hudson's Bay*, the *Harvard Lampoon* voted her one of the two worst film discoveries of 1940. While Tierney's film career floundered, her social life soared. She dated a number of Hollywood's most eligible men, including Howard Hughes, and was rumored for a short time to be on the brink of marriage to Robert Sterling. It came as quite a surprise then when, on June 1, 1941, she eloped with fashion designer

*Gene
Tierney*

Oleg Cassini. Her father was so incensed that he threatened to sue her on behalf of the corporation that had been formed to handle her business affairs. The feud was eventually resolved, although it is said to have contributed to the subsequent divorce of her parents.

Upon her return to moviemaking, Tierney arranged for her mother to be hired as a Fox press agent in Manhattan, and for her husband to design her movie wardrobes. Sadly, neither Cassini's clothes nor the full-screen Technicolor images of her remarkable face did much to advance her development as an actress in the eyes of the critics. For the press, only two roles stand out as high points in her career: the title role in Otto Pre-minger's sophisticated melodrama *Laura* (1944), and the role as the murderous Ellen Berent in *Leave Her to Heaven* (1945), for which she received her only Oscar nomination. Although both films were popular with audiences, as was the later *The Ghost and Mrs. Muir* (1947), they failed to bring the actress any critical acclaim.

Tierney's portrayal of the mysterious Laura in the Preminger film presented her with one of the most challenging entrances in movie history. "Laura is talked about for half an hour before she appears and that results in a very considerable build-up of anticipation in the audience," she recalled years later. "I was a bit leery in my first scene." Although the film was named one of the year's ten best pictures by *Film Daily* and garnered an Oscar nomination for Tierney's co-star Clifton Webb, most critics felt that Tierney failed to live up to the image that preceded her. "Pretty, indeed, but hardly the type of girl we had expected to meet," groused a reviewer for *The New York Times.* "For Miss Tierney plays at being a brilliant and sophisticated advertising executive with the wide-eyed innocence of a college junior." Although Tierney received an Oscar nomination for her performance in *Leave Her to Heaven* (1945), the critics were once again unmerciful. "No amount of strenuous plot trouble—or even a long fall down a flight of steps—seems to jar Gene Tierney's smooth deadpan," James Agee observed in *Time.*

Personal tragedy seemed to stalk Tierney. On October 15, 1943, Tierney gave birth to her first child, Daria, who was born blind, deaf, and developmentally challenged and was institutionalized. The child's birth defects were later traced to German measles, which Tierney had contracted late in her pregnancy. (A woman marine had broken quarantine to meet the film actress, who was entertaining soldiers at the Hollywood Canteen during her pregnancy.) The actress had a second child, Christina, in 1948, during one of many reconciliations she had with Cassini between their initial separation in 1947 and their divorce in 1952. She then began a romance with Aly Khan, but her hopes to marry him were dashed by the Aga Khan, who was wary of another movie star in the family. (Aly had formerly been married to *Rita Hayworth.) When the affair ended in 1954, Tierney finished work on *The Left Hand of God* (1955), but subsequently walked out on a television production of Ibsen's *A Doll's House* in which she was contracted to play Nora. Suffering a nervous breakdown, Tierney was hospitalized at the Institute of Living in Hartford, Connecticut, for 18 months, then released in her mother's custody. After a relapse, she received further treatment at the Menninger Clinic in Topeka, Kansas, and was released eight months later.

Returning to Hollywood in September 1958, Tierney was candid with the press. "My illness was a curable one, not cancer or something worse. It was something I was responsible for, not anyone else's fault. It was up to me to do something about it, and I did. Now I'm looking for a movie part. I want to go to work, and the doctors think that I should never give up acting." Unfortunately, work proved hard to find.

In 1960, Tierney married Houston oil millionaire W. Howard Lee, who had been married

to *Hedy Lamarr. The couple settled in Houston where Tierney wrote a column about her Hollywood days for the local newspaper and was active in fund-raising for cancer research, mental health, and the care of developmentally challenged children. In an interview at the time, she likened her new life to suddenly coming out of a dark tunnel into the light.

Tierney came out of retirement only occasionally, to play a character role in a film or to make a television appearance. In her autobiography, *Self-Portrait,* written with Mickey Herskowitz and published in 1979, the actress frankly discussed her past misfortunes and also revealed that she regularly dated John F. Kennedy during his Navy days. Tierney died of emphysema in 1991.

SOURCES:

Katz, Ephraim. *The Film Encyclopedia.* NY: Harper-Collins, 1994.

Lamparski, Richard. *Whatever Became of . . . ?* 5th series. NY: Crown, 1974.

Paris, James Robert. *The Fox Girls.* New Rochelle, NY: Arlington House, 1971.

Shields, Jonathan. "Gene Tierney," in *Films in Review.* November 1971.

Tierney, Gene, with Mickey Herskowitz. *Self-Portrait.* NY: Wyden, 1979.

Barbara Morgan, Melrose, Massachusetts

Tietjens, Eunice (1884–1944)

American poet, journalist, and writer. Born Eunice Strong Hammond on July 29, 1884, in Chicago, Illinois; died of cancer on September 6, 1944, in Chicago, Illinois; daughter of William Andrew Hammond (a banker) and Idea Louise (Strong) Hammond; educated in public schools in Evanston, Illinois, and in Europe; married Paul Tietjens (a composer), in May 1904 (divorced 1914); married Cloyd Head (a playwright and director), in February 1920; children: (first marriage) Idea (died in childhood), Janet Tietjens (b. 1907); (second marriage) Marshall (b. 1920), one daughter (died shortly after birth).

Went to Europe after the death of her father (c. 1897); began work with Harriet Monroe on Poetry *magazine (1913); traveled to China for six months (1916); served as war correspondent in France for the* Chicago Daily News *(1917); invited to MacDowell artists' colony, Peterborough, New Hampshire (1920s); lived in Tunisia (early 1920s); taught poetry at the University of Miami, Florida (1933–35); settled in Coconut Grove, Florida (late 1930s).*

Selected works: Profiles from China *(1917);* Body and Raiment *(1919);* Jake *(1921); (with husband Cloyd Head)* Arabesque *(play, 1925);* Boy of the

Desert *(1928); (editor)* Poetry of the Orient *(1928);* The Romance of Antar *(1929);* Leaves in Windy Weather *(1929); (with daughter Janet Tietjens)* The Jaw-Breaker's Alphabet of Prehistoric Animals *(1930);* Boy of the South Seas *(1931);* The World at My Shoulder *(autobiography, 1938).*

Eunice Tietjens—poet, war correspondent, and author of children's books—wrote with an international spirit derived from her travels to Asia, Europe, northern Africa, and the South Seas. Recognized for her expertise in Oriental poetry, she edited a highly successful anthology, *Poetry of the Orient*, in 1928 for Alfred A. Knopf and later went on to teach Asian poetry at the University of Miami. Largely through her work with *Harriet Monroe at *Poetry* magazine from 1913, Tietjens came into association with a number of important 20th-century poets, and her legacy in the literary world would be based more on her influence on other writers than on her own works.

She was born on July 29, 1884, in Chicago, Illinois, the eldest of four children of **Louise Strong Hammond** and banker William Andrew Hammond. Among her accomplished siblings

Eunice Tietjens

was her brother Laurens Hammond, who would become known for inventing the Hammond electronic organ. The family lived in Evanston, Illinois, where the children attended public schools until the death of William Hammond in 1897. Interested in painting and travel, Louise Hammond then took her four children to live in Europe. Eunice graduated from the Froebel Kindergarten Institute of Dresden and took courses at the University of Geneva, the College de France, and the Sorbonne. While in Paris during May 1904, she met and married Paul Tietjens, an American composer known for his score of L. Frank Baum's stage production of *The Wizard of Oz.*

The couple settled in New York City within weeks of their marriage, and had two daughters: Idea (who died in childhood) and **Janet Tietjens** (b. 1907). Although the Tietjenses separated in 1910 and would divorce in 1914, Eunice retained her married surname throughout her life. With her three-year-old daughter Janet, Tietjens returned to her native Chicago where she set up a French kindergarten for children of wealthy patrons. She quickly abandoned such efforts, however, so as to pursue a writing career. She was encouraged by her mother, as well as by a number of young writers from Chicago's literary circles, and got her first break when Harriet Monroe, founder and editor of the germinal *Poetry* magazine, accepted several of her poems for publication. Tietjens was in good company, as Ezra Pound, H.D. (*Hilda Doolittle), and T.S. Eliot were among the writers who were published by *Poetry* early in their careers. In 1913, she was offered a position on the *Poetry* staff and would remain associated with the influential publication for more than 25 years, eventually becoming an advisory editor. Through her contacts with the magazine, Tietjens formed close relationships with Monroe and a host of influential Midwestern poets, including Carl Sandburg, Edgar Lee Masters, Vachel Lindsay, and *Sara Teasdale.

The direction of Tietjens' poetry was steered by a trip to China in 1916, when she and her mother spent six months visiting her sister **Louise Hammond**, an Episcopalian missionary. Tietjens would later call the experience "one of the great influences of my life." Introduced to Asian thought by Edgar Lee Masters, who gave her a copy of the *Bhagavad-Gita*, she was affected by what she would term a mix of "sordidness, tragedy, beauty, and humor" which she found in China. Her impressions informed a collection of poetry that became her first book, *Profiles from China*, in 1917. The book represented what for Tietjens had been a defining moment of her life.

A year after her trip to China, she went to France to serve as war correspondent for the *Chicago Daily News*. Although her work focused on human-interest stories from Paris, Tietjens also traveled to the front lines and to areas that had been devastated by the fighting. She returned to Chicago two years later, in 1919, the same year a collection of her early poems was published as *Body and Raiment*. Tietjens was exhausted and emotionally drained from her war-time work experiences, and she took her daughter Janet, now 12, to live with her in a shack on the Indiana dunes along Lake Michigan. There, she wrote her first novel, *Jake* (1921), based on her observations during World War I. In February 1920, she married Cloyd Head, an American playwright, theater director, and publisher of medical texts, with whom she would have two children: a son, Marshall (b. 1920) and a daughter who died shortly after birth. Except for a visit to the MacDowell Artists' Colony in Peterborough, New Hampshire, she passed the next years largely dedicated to family life.

Tietjens was never content to remain still for long, however. During the 1920s, the family explored Paris, the Riviera, and Italy before settling in Hammamet, Tunisia. She and her husband worked together on *Arabesque*, a play concerning Arab life. Produced after their return to the States (1925), the play was unsuccessful. Following a second sojourn to North Africa, the family returned to Chicago in 1927, where Tietjens continued her writing and Head took a position as business manager for the Goodman Memorial Theater at the Art Institute. During this period, her anthology *Poetry of the Orient* (1928) was a great success, and she published two children's books based on her life in Africa, *Boy of the Desert* (1928) and *The Romance of Antar* (1929). A third volume of poetry, *Leaves in Windy Weather*, was published in 1929.

The 1930s found Tietjens and Head traveling again, this time to the Tahitian island of Moorea in the South Pacific. Her children's book *Boy of the South Seas* (1931) dates from this period. On the their return, they took up residence in Coconut Grove, Florida, and both joined the staff of the University of Miami, where Tietjens lectured in Asian poetry (1933–35) and Head taught in the speech department. In Florida, Tietjens began her final work, an autobiography entitled *The World at My Shoulder*. It was published in 1938, one year before Tietjens was diagnosed with cancer while traveling in Scandinavia. She died in Chicago on September 6, 1944, at the age of 60.

SOURCES:

James, Edward T., ed. *Notable American Women, 1607–1950*. Cambridge, MA: The Belknap Press of Harvard University, 1971.

Kunitz, Stanley, ed. *Twentieth Century Authors*. NY: H.W. Wilson, 1942.

Lolly Ockerstrom,
freelance writer,
Washington, D.C.

Tietjens, Therese (1831–1877)

German operatic soprano who achieved great success on the English stage. Name variations: surname sometimes spelled Titiens. Born Thérèse Johanne Alexandra Tietjens on July 17, 1831, in Hamburg, Germany; died on October 3, 1877, in London, England; studied music in Vienna, Austria.

Debuted in Hamburg, Germany, as Erma in Auber's Maçon (1848); debuted in title role of Donizetti's Lucrezia Borgia (1849); performed in Frankfurt, Germany, and Vienna, Austria; made London debut (1858).

A popular soprano on the London stage in the 19th century, Therese Tietjens was known for her velvety tone and significant dramatic ability. She was considered to be brilliant in concert and oratorio as well as in operatic productions.

Tietjens, born in Hamburg, Germany, in 1831, was thought to be of Hungarian parentage. Her training began in Hamburg, and she studied in Vienna with maestros Dellessie, Babing, and Proch. Tietjens debuted in Hamburg in 1848 and went on to success in the title role of Donizetti's tragic opera **Lucrezia Borgia*. Following her successful performance in London as Valentine in *Les Huguenots* (1858), England became her permanent home. Much loved by British opera fans for a magnetic presence and artistic skill, Tietjens further distinguished herself by performing in the provinces, an unusual effort for an internationally acclaimed prima donna.

From 1858 to 1869, she performed throughout Europe, appearing in opera houses in Vienna, London, Paris, and Naples. Among her most famous roles were Fidelio, Medea in Cherubini's opera, and Donna Anna in Mozart's *Don Giovanni*. Other roles included Elvira, Norma, Lucia, Ortud, and Leonore. Throughout her career, Tietjens was in great demand as a singer. Composer Richard Wagner pursued her with no success to sing Sieglinde and to create the role of Isolde. She displayed heroic resolve in her last performance, as Lucrezia, which she sang while suffering great pain due to cancer. She died in London on October 3, 1877.

Lolly Ockerstrom,
freelance writer,
Washington, D.C.

Tighe, Mary (1772–1810)

Irish poet. Born Mary Blachford in Dublin, Ireland, on October 9, 1772; died on March 24, 1810, at Woodstock, and buried at Inistioge; daughter of Reverend William Blachford and Theodosia (Tighe) Blachford; married Henry Tighe of Woodstock in 1793.

Left fatherless shortly after her birth, Mary Tighe received her education from her mother **Theodosia Tighe Blachford** who had participated in the Methodist movement in Ireland and was unusually well educated for a woman of her time. In 1793, the young Mary, admired for her beauty, contracted what proved to be an unhappy marriage with her cousin Henry Tighe, a member of the Irish Parliament, representing Inistioge, Kilkenny. To add to her growing depression and declining spirit, she also contracted consumption around 1803 or 1804.

Mary Tighe was the author of *Psyche, or the Legend of Love*, a poem of unusual merit which was privately printed in 1805 and published posthumously in 1811, along with some other poems. Originally completed in 1795 and circulated among her friends, it was founded on the story as told by Apuleius in *The Golden Ass* and written in the Spenserian stanza. The poem had many admirers, including Thomas Moore, *Felicia Hemans, and John Keats. In fact, a later study would show remarkable similarities between her poetry and that of Keats, while one of her sonnets would be misattributed to him. *Psyche* also won high praise in the *Quarterly Review* (May 1811) and was so successful with the public that it enabled Tighe to fund an addition to the orphan asylum in Wicklow, irresistibly known as the "Psyche Ward."

Tighe, Virginia (1923–1995)

American woman whose apparent recollection, while under hypnosis, of a past life fascinated the nation. Name variations: Bridey Murphy; Virginia Tighe Morrow. Born Virginia Tighe in Chicago, Illinois, in 1923; died of breast cancer on July 12, 1995; married.

In 1952, Morey Bernstein, a businessman and amateur hypnotist in Pueblo, Colorado, offered to hypnotize Virginia Tighe to relieve her allergies. Once under, Tighe spoke in a thick Irish brogue, claiming to have lived before as Bridey Murphy, a red-headed, 19th-century Irishwoman born in Cork 158 years previous. The story first appeared in a series of newspaper articles by William J. Barker in the *Denver Post*. Then Bernstein, who sold farm and mining equipment, went on to write *The Search for Bridey Murphy*, published in 1956. The book, No. 1 on the bestseller list for nonfiction, caused a national sensation, heaping notoriety on the head of the Colorado housewife. It also precipitated a national debate on reincarnation and an explosion of interest in the occult, long before the writings of **Shirley MacLaine**. Some 30,000 long-playing records were also sold in which Tighe was recorded as Bridey while in a trance. One 19-year-old boy in Shawnee, Oklahoma, killed himself, leaving a note saying that he was going to "investigate the theory in person."

What gave the story enormous authenticity was Tighe's ability to detail people, places, and customs with an accent and in words that seemed totally foreign to her. A few months later, an article in the Chicago *American* proposed that Tighe, during her girlhood in Chicago, subconsciously had ingested bits and pieces of background from another woman that eventually comprised the persona of Bridey. Reporters uncovered a **Mrs. Anthony Corkell**, nee Bridie Murphy, a 59-year-old mother of seven who had lived across the street from Tighe during her impressionable years. Tighe did not profit from the fame and successfully kept the press at bay for the remainder of her life.

Tii (c. 1400–1340 BCE).

See Tiy.

Tilberis, Liz (1947–1999)

British fashion magazine editor. Born Elizabeth Kelly on September 7, 1947, in Alderly Edge, England; died of ovarian cancer on April 21, 1999, in New York City; daughter of Thomas Stuart-Black Kelly (an eye surgeon) and Janet (Caldwell) Kelly; attended Jacob Kramer College of Art in Leeds; graduated from Leicester Polytechnic Art School with a degree in fashion design; married Andrew Tilberis (an artist), in 1971; children: (adopted) Robbie (born c. 1981) and Chris (born c. 1985).

Began working as an intern at British Vogue *(1969); became editor-in-chief of British* Vogue *(1989); became editor-in-chief of* Harper's Bazaar *(1992); received Editor of the Year citation from Ad-*

Liz
Tilberis

vertising Age *(1993); published memoir,* No Time to Die *(1998).*

Editor of two of the most influential maga-zines in the fashion industry, Liz Tilberis was known for her sharp eye for style and fashion photography. She was born in the home of her maternal grandfather in Alderly Edge, England, on September 7, 1947, the eldest of three chil-dren. Her father Thomas Stuart-Black Kelly was an eye surgeon who had served in the Royal Air Force during the Second World War, while her mother **Janet Caldwell Kelly** was a homemaker who encouraged her daughter's creativity. Growing up in Shirehampton, in the suburbs of the northwest industrial town of Manchester, Tilberis was drawn to fashion early on, and as a child industriously engaged in designing clothes for her dolls. Her passion for fabrics and clothing design led her to art school at the Leicester Polytechnic (from which she was expelled in 1965 for smuggling a boyfriend into her dormitory room). She spent a year at the Jacob Kramer College of Art in Leeds before returning to Leicester to finish her degree in fashion design.

Tilberis got her first break in the fashion world after winning an essay contest at British *Vogue*. Rewarded with a coveted internship on the *Vogue* staff during the summer of 1969, she became an assistant editor by 1971, when she was 23. That year she also married artist Andrew Tilberis, who had been one of her instructors at art school in Leeds. Within the cutting-edge pop culture scene of 1970s London, Tilberis scoured flea markets and bargain basements for clothing she could turn into fashion items on her meager starting salary of £900 a year. To earn extra money, she even repaired her colleagues' clothing, charging £1 to put in new zippers. Her career progressed steadily upwards as she advanced to fashion editor and to executive fashion editor, and she became a household name in the fashion industry. During this decade, unable to conceive and deeply desiring children, she also took fertility drugs and underwent in vitro fertilization nine times. These efforts proved ineffective, and she and her husband finally adopted two sons, Robbie and Chris. When **Anna Wintour**, the editor-in-chief of British *Vogue*, left to edit American *Vogue* in 1988, Tilberis was named to take her place. Among the many faces of fashion she brought to the pages of the magazine was that of her close friend *Diana, princess of Wales, whose portrait appeared on the cover in 1990. Tilberis remained at British *Vogue* until 1992, when *Harper's Bazaar* approached her to revitalize the sluggish 125-year-old periodical.

After secretly negotiating for six months with executives of *Harper's Bazaar*—archrival of *Vogue*—Tilberis accepted the post of editor-in-chief and moved with her family to Manhattan. She dove into the New York fashion world with characteristic vigor, and numbered among her friends such designers as Calvin Klein, Ralph Lauren, and **Donna Karan**. *Harper's Bazaar* experienced a renaissance; its design and photography departments began to reclaim influence in the fashion world, and the magazine won two National Magazine awards in the first year of her editorship. Her erstwhile boss Anna Wintour, still at the helm of *Vogue*, later called her a "formidable competitor." Tilberis was named Editor of the Year by the respected trade journal *Advertising Age* in 1993.

That December, at age 46, she was diagnosed with Stage 3 ovarian cancer. The morning after she hosted a gala holiday party for 250 guests at her Manhattan townhouse, Tilberis underwent surgery at Mt. Sinai Medical Center, where doctors confirmed the diagnosis. For the next six years, while she continued to edit *Harper's Bazaar* (often from her hospital bed), Tilberis underwent extensive treatments to stay the disease. At the same time, she began a campaign to educate women about ovarian cancer, a disease with a lower cure rate than breast cancer. She became president of the nonprofit Ovarian Cancer Research Fund, helping to raise money for the organization from the fashion world and traveling nationwide to talk with women about the disease. With **Aimee Lee Ball**, she wrote a memoir, *No Time to Die*, as part of her efforts to publicize the illness. Published in 1998, the book was simultaneously a narrative of glitter and glamour in the fast lane with the world's top fashion artists and headline makers and a tale of her bitter struggle with chemotherapy treatments and a bone-marrow transplant. It also detailed her conviction, despite the lack of scientific evidence, that the fertility drugs she had taken in the 1970s had increased her chances of developing the disease. Liz Tilberis, called "St. Liz" by her many admirers in the fashion world and beyond, died at age 51 in April 1999 of the ovarian cancer that had become her cause.

SOURCES:
The Boston Globe. April 22, 1999, p. F7.
The Day [New London, CT]. April 22, 1999.
Newsday. April 8, 1998, pp. B6–B8.
Newsweek. April 6, 1998, p. 58.
People Weekly. May 18, 1998, pp. 93–94, 96.
Publishers Weekly. March 2, 1998, p. 48.

Lolly Ockerstrom,
freelance writer,
Washington, D.C.

Tilley, Vesta (1864–1952)

English performer and male impersonator. Name variations: Lady de Freece; Great Little Tilley; Pocket Sims Reeves; London Idol. Born Matilda Alice Powles in 1864 in Worcester, England; died in 1952 in Monte Carlo; daughter of a variety-hall manager; married Sir Walter de Freece (a music-hall owner and member of Parliament), in 1890 (died 1935).

Debuted in Gloucester, England, at age 3 or 4; appeared on the London stage (1874–1920); appeared in Sinbad *(1882) and* Beauty and the Beast *(1890); toured America (after 1898).*

Vesta Tilley was the stage name of the popular English performer, singer, and male impersonator Matilda Alice Powles. She was born in Worcester, England, in 1864 and took to the stage before she was out of diapers. After making her professional debut at age three or four with the help of her father, who owned and managed a music hall in Gloucester, England, she appeared on stage in boy's clothing at age five and went on tour with her father under the marquee of "Harry Ball the Tramp Musician and the Great Little Tilley." When she was 10, Tilley made her first London appearance. By 16, she had been dubbed the "London Idol." In her signature top hat and tails, she anticipated 1920s cabarets, entertaining audiences with faultless performances in roles she researched herself.

Tilley frequently appeared in the principal boy's role in pantomimes and was seen in *Sinbad* (1882) and *Beauty and the Beast* (1890). After 1898, she toured the United States, earning critical acclaim in New York and Chicago. Among the songs for which she became known were "Burlington Bertie," "Jolly Good Luck to the Girl Who Loves a Soldier," "Following in Father's Footsteps," "After the Ball," "The Army of Today's All Right," and "Algy—The Piccadilly Johnny with the Little Glass Eye." In 1912, Tilley was featured in the first royal command performance of music-hall entertainers. A London stage presence for 50 years before retiring to the enthusiastic applause of well-wishers and loyal fans at the Coliseum, she helped to herald in the modern stage. Upon her retirement, actress *Ellen Terry presented her with a book containing the autographs of two million admirers.

Tilley was married in 1890 to Walter de Freece, a music-hall owner who was knighted (1919) and became a member of Parliament. After leaving the stage, she divided her time between England and the south of France. Nearing the age of 90, Tilley died in Monte Carlo during 1952.

SOURCES:

The Concise Dictionary of National Biography. Volume III. NY: Oxford University Press, 1992.

Uglow, Jennifer, ed. *The International Dictionary of Women's Biography*. NY: Continuum, 1985.

Lolly Ockerstrom,
freelance writer,
Washington, D.C.

Vesta Tilley

Tillion, Germaine (1907—)

Pioneering French ethnologist, a student of Algerian desert tribes, who was an early leader in the French Resistance during World War II, survived internment at the Ravensbrück concentration camp, wrote a germinal study of the camp system, and worked for peace during the Algerian War for Independence. Pronunciation: gher-MAYN TEE-YEE-OH. Born at Allègre (Haute-Loire) on May 30, 1907; daughter of Lucien Tillion (d. 1925, a magistrate) and Émilie (Cussac) Tillion (1875–1945, an art historian); educated at the Lycée Jeanne-d'Arc in Clermont-Ferrand and the Institut d'Ethnologie (Sorbonne).

Lived with a Berber tribe in southeastern Algeria (1934–40); joined the Resistance (1940); arrested and imprisoned (1942–43); interned at the Ravensbrück concentration camp (1943–45); published first edition of Ravensbrück *(1946); sent on a mission to Algeria and founded the Centres sociaux (1954–56); published* L'Algérie en 1957 *and had secret meetings with Algerian leaders (1957); organized education for pris-*

oners while at the Ministry of Education (1959–60); published Le Harem et les cousins, *a study of the treatment of women in Mediterranean cultures (1967); published revised edition of* Ravensbrück, *responding to revisionist theses on the camp system (1973); ended her teaching career at the École des Hautes Études en Sciences Sociales (1977); named president of the French Section of the Minority Rights Group (1978); published third edition (rev.) of* Ravensbrück *(1988).*

Major writings: Ravensbrück *(Paris: Éditions du Seuil, rev. and aug., 1973, also Eng. trans.);* Ravensbrück, *suivi de "Les Exterminations par gaz à Ravensbrück" par Anise Postel-Vinay et "Les Exterminations par gaz à Hartheim, Mathausen et Gusen" par Pierre-Serge Choumoff, nouvelle édition entièrement refondue (Paris: Éditions du Seuil, 1988);* L'Algérie en 1957 *(Paris: Éditions de Minuit, 1957, also Eng. trans.);* L'Afrique bascule vers l'avenir: l'Algérie en 1957 et autres textes *(Paris: Éditions de Minuit, 1960);* Les Ennemis complémentaires *(Paris: Éditions de Minuit, 1960, also Eng. trans.);* Le Harem et les cousins *(Paris: Éditions du Seuil, 1966, rev. ed., also Eng. trans., 1982);* La Traversée du mal: Entretiens avec Jean Lacouture *(Paris: Arléa, 1997);* Il était une fois l'ethnographie *(Paris: Éditions du Seuil, 2000).*

On June 17, 1940, as the German army rolled deep into France, **Émilie Tillion** and her daughter Germaine, a 33-year-old ethnologist just returned from six years in Algeria, inched their automobile along in an endless column of overladened vehicles crawling south from Paris in hopes of escaping the invaders. Word spread that an important announcement was coming from the government of Marshal Philippe Pétain, and the two women stopped and entered a house to hear it. At 12:30 PM, the aged soldier announced that France was asking for an armistice. Overwhelmed by anger and disgust, Germaine fled to the street and vomited. She did not hear General Charles de Gaulle's broadcast from London the next day proclaiming that no matter what the government might do, he and all who rallied to him would fight on until final victory. But Tillion did not need de Gaulle's summons to tell her where she would stand. She became a Resister from the first hour.

Germaine Tillion—she preferred the ancient pronunciation of the name, using a "yee" sound—was born in Allègre (Haute-Loire) in central France on May 30, 1907. A sister, **Françoise**, followed in 1909. Their father Lucien Tillion was a magistrate originally from Charolais (Saône-et-Loire). His family was fairly prosperous despite having had a spendthrift grandfather. It was Catholic but also Republican. Lucien boasted a broad general culture; he enjoyed archaeology, history, and photography, but especially music. He died in 1925, however, and it was her mother who had the greater influence. Germaine lovingly described her after her death in the Ravensbrück gas chamber as "a cherished model—unforgettable—of nobility of soul, understanding, and calm courage." Émilie Cussac Tillion (1875–1945) was from a family of prosperous landowners around Alleuze (Cantal) in central France. They were observant Catholics and Republicans like the Tillions, although more politically active, having furnished a line of "hereditary" mayors of the town since before the Revolution of 1789.

To avoid the influenza epidemic during the First World War, the Tillion sisters were sent in 1917 to live with relatives in Auvergne. They later graduated from the Lycée Jeanne-d'Arc in Clermont-Ferrand. Meanwhile, their parents moved after the war to Saint-Maur, a suburb of Paris. Neither parent tried to influence them unduly as to a career. Françoise enrolled at the École des Sciences politiques, one of few women to do so. Her mother being a historian of art, from childhood Germaine had heard talk of "old stones, of cathedrals, churches, and transepts." Her interests ranged so widely—psychology, Egyptology, pre-history, history of religions, Celtic culture—that she had trouble deciding. About 1930 she settled on ethnology, a branch of anthropology that analyzes the histories, similarities, and differences of cultures. It was fairly new in France, the Institut d'Ethnologie at the Sorbonne dating only from 1925. As she approached the time when she would do field work for her degree, she also attended courses at the École des Langues orientales.

At the Institut, Tillion was strongly influenced by two men, Marcel Mauss (1872–1950), the Institut's founder; and the Arabist-Islamisist Louis Massignon (1883–1962). Mauss, nephew of the sociologist Émile Durckheim, was a spellbinding polymath who specialized in the religion of "uncivilized" peoples. (He rejected the appellation.) He was an "armchair" scholar who nevertheless fervently preached the necessity of intensive field work, of living among peoples—preferably a single tribe, for example, over a long period of time—and observing everything possible. Tillion and several other students habitually escorted him around to his lectures at the Sorbonne and the Collège de France. It was at the Collège in 1932 that she met Massignon, a charismatic figure, ardent Catholic (friend of J.K.

Huysmans and Jacques Maritain), and France's leading student of the Arab-Islamic world. He had practiced ethnology and took a multi-disciplinary approach to his studies.

Tillion at first felt some chagrin over the choice of a locale for her field work. Instead of South America or some romantic isle in the South Pacific, she found that Mauss, via Paul Rivet—founder of the Musée de l'Homme (the Museum of Man), an affiliate of the Institut— had presented her name to the London-based Society of African Languages and Cultures. The Society was proposing to send two women to study the Berbers of the Aurès Massif in eastern Algeria—a daring venture for female investigators. Once she and **Thérèse Rivière** accepted, however, Tillion soon realized Mauss was not just throwing her a bone; this was a truly exciting project.

As luck would have it, Rivière fell ill soon after they reached Algeria in the spring of 1934, so Tillion was left to go on alone. Critically important to her was a skilled interpreter, which she was fortunate to find before leaving Arris,

the "capital" of the Aurès. She set off on horseback, accompanied by a dozen mules carrying her baggage and equipment, on a 14-hour, 40-mile (70 km.) trek to a Chaouïa-speaking tribe of Berbers, the Ah'Abderrahman, living in a district called l'Ahmar Khaddou. Tillion wanted to get well away from the few French at Arris in order to immerse herself completely in the native culture. She certainly succeeded, for none of the women of the tribe had ever seen a European; a few men had, but only because a French military doctor made an annual visit to vaccinate the children whom their fathers brought to him.

As described in her reading and by officials in Algiers, the inhabitants of the Aurès were little better than ignorant thieves and murderers— which only made her more sympathetic toward them. The tribe, about 800 in number, led a hard life. They were semi-nomadic, following their goats and sowing sparse crops of barley and coarse grain. Hunger was no stranger to them. Even so, she found herself welcome, helped by her dignified, calm, yet friendly demeanor. After several years, they gave her the title of *tamhurt*

Germaine Tillion

("the Old One"), the highest degree of respect. Never in the course of six years with them, she testified, did they threaten her physically or steal her property, which she left unlocked and unguarded. Such violence as these "murderers" inflicted reminded her of 16th-century European gentlemen because virtually the sole motive was affronts to honor.

She did not remain in the Aurès continuously, but took furloughs of several months in Paris in 1935, 1937, and 1939 to recuperate, consult with her advisers, and write up her notes. In 1937 the London society, at Mauss' suggestion, charged her with a complementary inquiry to allow her to finish her thesis. During her last two missions (1938–39, 1939–40), with the help of the National Center for Scientific Research (CNRS), she pursued the same work but also tried to look at the larger regional scene and Algeria as a whole. She became gravely concerned about the effects of poverty, population growth, and food scarcity. In a lecture in Paris during her 1937–38 winter layover, she spoke of growing instability in the country—a prophetic warning, it turned out.

*A*ll my life I have wanted to understand human nature, the world in which I live.

—Germaine Tillion

Tillion bade her Algerian Berber friends a final farewell on May 21, 1940. Not because of the Second World War (begun September 1, 1939), but because the spring of 1940 marked her scheduled terminal date. She did not learn of the German invasion of France (May 12) until she arrived in Arris. Anxious to join her mother, she finally reached Paris on June 9, five days before the German entry. At Saint-Maur, she found her mother stoical in the face of disaster. (Françoise was safe, having married an administrator now in Indochina.) They decided to leave Paris for the South, departing on June 13, and heard Pétain's call for an armistice on the 17th. Concluding that it was pointless to go on, they reentered Paris on June 24.

Germaine swiftly concluded that the government set up by Pétain at Vichy in the Unoccupied Zone was traitorous. She was no Germanophobe, but simply—quite simply, without thinking much about it—a patriot. She had stayed with a colleague in Königsberg, East Prussia, from December 1932 to February 1933, the very time that Hitler was coming to power. She observed the local Nazis and thought them "ridiculous." In 1938, she visited Bavaria for a week and was disturbed by the militarism and

aggressiveness on display. But she felt no hatred for Germans as such. Now, in June 1940, she concluded she must no longer ignore public affairs as she had for years. She wanted to "do something," but what "something" might be eluded her. Deciding she needed contacts and information, she went to the headquarters of the Red Cross. She entered but found the place deserted. While she was puzzling over this, another young woman came in from the street. After some conversation, the woman gave her the telephone number of a Colonel Paul Hauet, a retired 74-year-old officer of colonial troops who had offered himself as a hostage for Paris.

Tillion looked him up. They decided to use the moribund National Union of Colonial Combattants (UNCC) to establish contact with French colonial troops now POWs but still in France. The ostensible object was to find out who they were and arrange to send them letters and packages from sympathetic people. Secretly, the purpose was to aid escaped prisoners. For a headquarters, Tillion selected an apartment at 2, rue Bréguer, conveniently located between her Saint-Maur home and the Bibliothèque Nationale and the Musée de l'Homme, where she continued to work on her thesis. She stopped by the rue Bréguer daily to see Hauet, meet escapees and other fugitives, and furnish them with clothing, money, false papers, and information about routes and safe houses in order to reach the Unoccupied Zone. Hauet's group, which eventually numbered about 80, became involved mainly in aiding these fugitives, writing and distributing pamphlets, and (especially) gathering intelligence about the Germans. One of Hauet's key contacts was a fellow retired colonel, Charles du Theil de La Rochère, an intelligence specialist, around whom another group coalesced. Sending information to London posed continual problems. Hauet and La Rochère generally used a Captain d'Autrevaux of the Vichy army.

Tillion did not know more than a few of Hauet's contacts—she met La Rochère only once—and told few about her own at the Musée de l'Homme and the other museums at the Trocadéro and Chaillot palaces. Led by Boris Vildé, an escaped POW who was a linguist from the Baltic and a naturalized French citizen, Anatole Lewitsky, an anthropologist from Russia, and *Yvonne Oddon, a colleague and close friend of Tillion's, the museum Resisters initially were young left-wing intellectuals who had been opposing fascism since before the war. As the museum group expanded, however, it incorporated (as did Hauet's and La Rochère's) people from every walk of life. Many women were involved, both in ordinary and leadership roles. After the war, the government asked Tillion to document the composition and activities of these groups as part of a national effort to identify all Resistance organizations in order to award valid decorations and pensions; rather arbitrarily, she named the museum, Hauet, and La Rochère network after the Musée de l'Homme.

At its peak in early 1941, it numbered about 300 persons, with "cores" or "grouplets," as Tillion described them, scattered across the whole Occupied Zone. After the Allied invasion of French North Africa in November 1942, the Germans occupied all of France and the Vichy government became increasingly irrelevant. The Resistance grew far more structured and powerful, with a central direction imposed by de Gaulle's Free French movement. Tillion's experience of the Resistance was confined wholly to the pre-November 1942 period. She learned specifics about de Gaulle mostly after she was arrested and interned (August 1942). Before that she and her comrades knew him only as "our man," "the one who is right," who "agrees with us." While the vast majority of the French were not active in Resistance groups, Tillion found almost everyone willing to connive, so activists lived "like fish in the sea." As did *Simone Veil, a fellow survivor of the death camps, Tillion sharply criticized the famous postwar film about the Occupation, *La Chagrin et la Pitié* (1971), which portrayed the masses as mostly silent collaborators and the Resisters as *exaltés* or "boy scouts." The game was dangerous, certainly. Almost all who joined the Resistance in 1940 ended up arrested and either deported or shot. After the war, Tillion remarked that one had to be "very lucky" to have survived.

Misfortune struck the Musée de l'Homme network early on. Between mid-January and mid-April 1941, Vildé, Lewitsky, Oddon, and 16 others were arrested, betrayed by one Albert Gaveau, Vildé's right-hand man but a double agent. They were imprisoned and eventually, in February 1942, tried. Tillion escaped arrest because Gaveau did not know all of Vildé's contacts. But she did all she could to aid the prisoners, sending food and supplies and meeting almost daily with their lawyers and families. She even thought seriously of engineering an escape, but finally decided to try to persuade Monseigneur Baudrillart, rector of the Catholic Institute and member of the Académie Française, to intercede. She visited him on February 9 before the verdicts came down. He reluctantly signed a letter she had written to be sent to Hitler asking for clemency, a move suggested by Vildé's attorney. The verdicts, including

seven death sentences, were not set aside, and on February 23, 1942, Vildé, Lewitsky, and five others were shot. They were among the earliest martyrs of the Resistance.

More misfortune followed when Hauet and La Rochère were arrested on July 4–5, 1941. (Hauet was released but was arrested again 20 months later; both he and La Rochère died in deportation.) Tillion found herself in charge of what remained of their groups. She made new contacts, most important (in early 1942) with Jacques Legrand ("Bernard"), who headed "Gloria SMH," a British Intelligence network. This contact more or less solved the problem of regular communication with London. (It was in Gloria SMH that she first met Anise Girard, later **Anise Postel-Vinay**, called "Danielle," who was deported with her and became a lifelong friend.) Tillion may well have aroused suspicion, however, when on July 14 she organized the escape of a young Jew, **Juliette Tenine**, from a medical facility where she had been put temporarily after her arrest. Tenine was the sister of the Communist mayor of Ivry, who had been shot as a hostage just before her arrest. Assisted by Tillion, Tenine and her family went into hiding.

Tillion's arrest resulted from plans for another prison escape. Abbé Robert Alesch, vicar of the parish of La Varenne, had joined a group of young men in Saint-Maur and La Varenne plotting more escapes into the Unoccupied Zone, and they agreed to let him meet their "chief": Tillion. On August 13, 1942, Tillion had a rendezvous at the Gare de Lyon with Alesch and an Intelligence agent, Gilbert, a close friend of Legrand in Gloria SMH. Independent of the escape project, Tillion wanted very much to have some documents, concealed by Gilbert in a matchbox, taken by Alesch to a radio post in the Unoccupied Zone. Gilbert handed over the matchbox, and she told him to leave. She accompanied Alesch to the gate and saw him get his ticket punched. As he walked away into a crowd, a man tapped her shoulder and said, "German police. Follow me." She recalled that she replied in a half-ironic, half-aggressive tone, "You think perhaps I'm Jewish?" "No," he replied, "I knew right away that you're not. We only want to check your papers." Once this was done, three men bundled her into a car which sped off to the rue des Saussaies headquarters of the German military police (the Abwehr, not the Gestapo). Tillion's life in the Resistance was over.

She learned later that Gilbert also had been picked up. Alesch was in the Germans' pay, it turned out. He had penetrated Gloria SMH and had set the trap. Arrested by the Americans in 1944, he was tried and shot in 1948.

Tillion was questioned and then lodged in the Santé Prison until her transfer to Fresnes on October 13. She was interrogated at the rue de Saussaies on August 13, 14, 17, and 25, and October 9, 21, and 23. She was not tortured, but on one occasion she was told at nightfall that she would be shot in the morning. On October 23, she was formally charged with spying, terrorism, harboring an English parachutist, attempting to free prisoners from Fresnes, and aiding Germany's enemies. She denied everything. After some weeks of reflection, she asked for a pen and paper so she could address the tribunal. Her long letter, a sly masterpiece of irony, mockery, and injured innocence, again denied all charges. She never learned how her captors reacted, but it appears she earned a reputation as a hard case; Gestapo officers, it was said, would pound the table whenever her name was mentioned.

Although held incommunicado for five months, she exchanged news by corresponding with a friend on a piece of cloth which was then smuggled via the laundry in the lining of a dress furnished by the Red Cross. She learned to communicate with the cells immediately above and below her via the heating-duct opening. Eventually, the wardens relaxed her regime and allowed her to resume work on her thesis, which helped occupy her mind and fill the empty hours. In January 1943, the prison's chaplain passed on a gift from her mother, a tiny *Imitation of Christ* in which Germaine wrote notes about her captivity. He also relayed some appalling news: her mother had been arrested and was now in Fresnes. Tillion's arrest had inevitably led to her mother's. In Fresnes, they communicated secretly through letters, and once, on April 11, they caught sight of one another for a moment and exchanged smiles and signs. In August, however, her mother was sent to Romainville.

Tillion's projected trial never took place. By 1943, the Germans had neither the time, personnel, nor inclination to honor judicial norms. On October 21, she was put in a railroad coach with 24 other women. Four of them, whom she did not know, had been arrested, she learned, in the same round-up as she as a result of Alesch's betrayals. The papers of all 24 were marked with the mysterious letters "NN," for "*Nacht und Nebel*" (Night and Fog), a Hitlerian conceit used to label prisoners consigned to certain death. They were taken to Aachen, spent a week in a relatively comfortable prison, and then entrained to Fürstenberg, about 50 miles (80 km.)

north of Berlin. From there, on October 31, two trucks took them on the 20-minute ride to the concentration camp at Ravensbrück. Once inside the gates, the prisoners knew this place was like nothing they had known so far. The very air breathed death.

Ravensbrück was a labor camp, although in January 1945 it would acquire its own gas chamber. Worn-out prisoners who did not die on the premises from exhaustion, disease, beating, or shooting, were routinely shipped to extermination camps, mostly in Poland. The maximum number of prisoners was around 45,000, reached in the last months; when Tillion arrived in latter 1943 there were around 17,000 living in 32 "blocks" (barracks). Besides the thousands working inside the camp, more thousands were employed outside or loaned to a Siemens plant nearby or other factories. They were worked twelve hours per day and subjected to four roll calls, which could last for hours regardless of the weather. Practically all of the prisoners were women—Jehovah's Witnesses, Gypsies (Roma), Jews, common-law criminals, and "politicals" (mainly Resistance leaders, many of whom were Communists) from all over Europe, but principally Poland, Czechoslovakia, Austria, Germany, and France. Their social origins ranged from the aristocracy to the poorest peasantry. About a third of the French were Resisters, the rest criminals, prostitutes who had infected German occupiers, or merely the unlucky. Perhaps because they tended to be more uncooperative than the others, the French were picked upon more by the SS, starved more, and ranked at the bottom of the nationality groups. (Such, anyhow, was Tillion's perception of the matter.) German-speakers ranked at the top. Those designated NN were "living dead," subject to unlimited exploitation. There was also a category called *Verfügbar* (available), who could be used on any kind of job, especially the most vile. Tillion was both an NN and a *Verfügbar*. Prisoners were employed in virtually all capacities in the camp, including block warden, infirmary nurse, and (if German-speaking) secretary in the camp offices. Largely because of the office workers and transfers from other camps, news from the outside world circulated with remarkable speed. Within a week of her arrival, for example, Tillion learned from a Czech transfer from Auschwitz about the extermination of Jews there; and days in advance in 1944 she learned of Paris' imminent liberation.

Upon her arrival, her baggage—including her thesis—was confiscated and a red triangle, for "political," affixed to her, making her a special target of the SS guards. She was quarantined, came down with diphtheria, and was sent to the infirmary. When she got out, she was weak and barely able to walk. She had meanwhile resolved to avoid work altogether. For seven or eight months, she managed by cleverness and the complicity of friends to hide out in various blocks—a considerable exploit. Ironically, since she was a *Verfügbar*, she was in no particular authority's purview, which helped her to "fall through the cracks" and move about. She made many friends, among them (besides Anise Postel-Vinay) **Denise Jacob**, sister of Simone (Jacob) Veil; **Geneviève de Gaulle** (later Anthonioz), General de Gaulle's niece; and **Margarete Buber-Neumann*, a survivor of Stalin's Gulag. Tillion also made highly useful contacts among the mostly Austrian and Czech secretaries, whom she pumped for information. Luckily, the secretaries were "politicals," not common-law criminals as in most camps, and thus were apt to be more intelligent and inclined toward collaboration.

Eventually she was caught and set to unloading and classifying SS loot in freight cars from all over Europe. Her comrades, however, thought she was physically unsuited for this job, so they hid her in a packing case for a time. Found again, she was hitched to an iron roller used by the crew which maintained the camp's streets. Her health, excellent before her imprisonment, suffered greatly. At various times, Tillion contracted diphtheria, scurvy, bronchitis, and septicemia. Existing on a diet of rutabaga soup and bread, she once weighed as little as 65 lbs. (30 kg.). Her "capital discipline," which she used to keep herself going, was to groom and wash daily. The stench and cold and crowded quarters she could abide, but not the vermin. She would delicately pick them out of her clothing and give them to a neighbor to kill.

Tillion owed her survival, she wrote, "first—and most definitely—to chance, then to anger and the motivation to reveal the crimes I had witnessed, and finally to a union of friendship." Her comrades in suffering admired the pluck and guile which made her a kind of Robin Hood of the camp. She helped them in return, not least of all by keeping hope alive. Ever since the first days of the occupation of France, she was sure the Allies would win in the end. As for the chances of survival, Anise Postel-Vinay recalled her saying more than once, "My dear, in every human event, when all seems lost, there is still a 5 to 7 percent presence of the unknown, the unforeseen. It's a law of human societies." How astonishing it was that while hiding out in the packing case, no less, she wrote an operetta and read it to her 15 or 20 companions. It was a parody of Offenbach's *Orpheus in Hell* entitled *Le Verfügbar aux enfers, operette-revue en un prologue et 3 actes* (The *Verfügbar* in Hell). It took the form of a lecture describing a strange new animal, the *Verfügbar*, with comments offered by a Greek chorus singing well-known tunes. (The operetta, on 118 15x10 cm. pages, got by the SS, and made it to Paris after her release.)

On one occasion which became part of the camp's lore, she confronted an SS guard who had begun savagely beating a young girl for no reason. Prudently holding her glasses behind her back, she stepped forward, squinted up at him, and said simply, "Nein." He became so flustered that he stopped and wandered away. She then wrote a respectful letter to the commandant about the guard's "failing in his proper duties," got it translated, and sent it off with the signatures of several university-educated comrades. No reply was received and no reprisals followed.

Ever the professional observer of human behavior, Tillion constantly studied the camp's inhabitants and its rulers' "system." She took notes and hid them away. She was not thinking, surely, of writing a book, but of helping her comrades understand so they could protect themselves. She made a crucial discovery when she questioned a secretary who typed a daily report on the camp's income which was sent to the chief of the SS, Heinrich Himmler, and some others. This proved that the camp system was not only focused on extermination of Germany's enemies, but was also a vast, obscenely profitable economic enterprise. Terror and profit reinforced each other. As early as March 1944, five months after her arrival, she gave a "lecture" to her French compatriots about how it worked.

As time went on, she became ever more determined to bear witness should she survive. One piece of evidence, which won notoriety at the war-crimes trials, concerned medical experiments on some Polish girls from Lublin whose legs were deliberately cut and infected. (*See Oberheuser, Herta.*) In August 1944, thousands of Poles from Warsaw arrived. Some had contrived to steal a camera. Tillion and her friends used it to photograph the girls' mutilated legs. The plight of the "Rabbits," as they were dubbed, moved the camp deeply. In a remarkable feat, the prisoners managed at great risk to save them repeatedly from gassing by hiding them (with help from a majority of the wardens, most of whom were Poles) and exchanging or changing their numbers.

On February 3, 1944, Tillion's mother arrived from Compiègne with 958 other women packed in cattle cars. Germaine got word immediately through the grapevine and was devastated. Émilie Tillion, though still vigorous, was 69, and Germaine knew that anybody over 60 was doomed. Through various complicities, Germaine got her mother's age changed on the records to something under 60. Thereafter, "through a thousand ruses and a thousand risks," they were able to stay in the same block. By January 1945, however, Ravensbrück had its own gas chamber; "selections" for death multiplied. On March 1, Germaine went to the infirmary with a terribly painful abscessed jaw. That same day Émilie found herself in a targeted block. Germaine managed to rejoin her for the night. The next day, she returned for treatment to the infirmary—a very dangerous place during selections—but had to stay because a sudden general rollcall made leaving even riskier. When three SS doctors came in on a selection tour, her friend Grete Buber-Neumann, who lived there and was lying in bed, hid her under her legs covered by a blanket. Émilie Tillion was not so lucky. Her friends spirited her to another block, but she was selected anyway. She was gassed that day or the next. Tillion, utterly distraught, smuggled letters and tiny packages to her for a week. When they finally came back unopened, she had to accept the terrible truth.

On March 5, Tillion's jaw was operated on by a young prisoner-doctor unknown to her and "visibly terrified by the instruments in her hand." She developed septicemia; her temperature peaked on March 15 at 41°C (c. 106°F). Deeply depressed over her mother's death, she nearly gave up but finally rallied, deciding to live no matter what in order to defy her captors and bear witness against them.

Ironically, she was freed because of an absurd idea of Heinrich Himmler's. He wanted to succeed Hitler (who was still alive) by making an agreement with the Americans. On February 12, 1945, he met the Swedish diplomat Count Folke Bernadotte to persuade him to act as intermediary. Other meetings followed on April 2, 21, and 23. At the April 2 meeting, they agreed that French prisoners at Ravensbrück would be exchanged for Germans presently interned in liberated France. On April 8, 300 were freed by the Swiss Red Cross—but no NNs were included. By sheer luck and by flitting between her block and the infirmary or unobtrusively "joining" labor details, Tillion survived the escalating comb-outs, which especially targeted the sick and malingerers. At last, on April 23 pursuant to Bernadotte's deal, 20 Swedish Red Cross buses rolled into camp. Relief parcels were distributed and 800 French women, including Tillion, began boarding. Despite numerous searches by the guards, she and her friends smuggled out her notes, her *Imitation of Christ* with its notes, the operetta text, and (carried by Tillion) an empty Red Cross powdered-milk carton concealing the roll of film of the Rabbits' mutilations, which she had hidden for months in some rags in her pocket. After tense waiting into the night, while the gas chamber continued its work, the convoy left for Padbourg, Denmark, where "unforgettable" soup and beds awaited. The next day, April 24, after another long delay, a train took the survivors to Göteborg, Sweden, where they were immediately hospitalized. Five days later the Red Army liberated Ravensbrück.

Since March 1, when she began to think she had little chance of survival, Tillion had been taking more explicit notes. Her mother's death inspired her to "at least shed some light on her murder and on her murderers." Once in Sweden, she began a systematic questioning of the ex-prisoners. As a professional ethnologist, she seemed predestined to be a pioneer in the study of the concentration-camp system. Indeed, it was she and an Austrian ex-prisoner, Eugen Kogon (*Der SS-Staat*, 1946), who paved the way for serious study of it. During three months in Sweden, she gathered a remarkable body of continually cross-checked written and oral responses which comprised the foundation of her later publications. These demonstrated convincingly that the system linked extermination with the exploitation of slave labor, especially after 1942.

Upon her return to Paris, she attended the trial of Marshal Pétain, about whom she tempered her judgment somewhat. She found the 89-year-old soldier a pitiable figure. Afterward, friends sent her to Switzerland to recuperate. While there she wrote a 77-page essay, "À la recherche de la vérité" (In Search of the Truth), which was published in 1946 in a collective work, *Ravensbrück*, containing other (far shorter) essays by fellow deportees. This essay needed filling out, however. Once she was back in Paris, the CNRS proposed that she return to Algeria. Having lost most of her notes, she decided instead to turn from study of North African civilization to European "decivilization," as she put it—to try to "understand how a European people with a better-than-average education could have sunk into such a dementia." The CNRS agreed to support a study of the camp system. Tillion gave herself to this labor for eight years, until late 1954.

While at work on the project, she attended the Hamburg trial (November 1946–January

1947) of Ravensbrück criminals conducted by the British. At first they refused to allow deportees to attend; but the two associations of women deportees were finally allowed to send an observer, and they chose Tillion. She attended all sessions but did not testify; otherwise, she could not have attended until after testifying, as was the case with other deportees. The French trial of Ravensbrück war-crimes was held in Rastatt in 1950–51. She and Geneviève de Gaulle-Anthonioz were called in February 1950 to testify about charges made by a pair of deportees (very shady types, they discovered) who claimed two female guards had decapitated a French woman before the whole camp. They were anguished to have to testify because, while they did not know one of the accused, they knew the other as a brute; they also knew the charge was false. Fortunately, the accusers did not appear. Tillion and de Gaulle testified on general matters, and the attorneys chose not to press them.

During the trials, Tillion found herself feeling something akin to pity for the prisoners. They seemed so terribly ordinary, these men and women fallen from positions of absolute power over the lives of thousands. Their enormous crimes stood in such contrast to their shabby appearances and seamy attempts to deny their guilt.

She also sat on a jury, if an unofficial one. In November 1949, a former deportee, David Rousset, called upon the erstwhile Resistance deportees of Europe to form a commission (the CICRC) to investigate concentration-camp regimes. Tillion's Association des déportées et internées de la Résistance (ADIR) chose her to represent it. The CICRC conducted an investigation of the Soviet Union's Gulag. A former Soviet official, Viktor Kravtchenko, had published a book, *I Chose Liberty*, charging Stalin with running a vast camp regime. In May 1951 in Brussels, a CICRC jury, including Tillion, found Kravtchenko's charges justified—the first formal exposé and condemnation of the Gulag. When asked years later about comparisons between Hitler's and Stalin's camps, she noted that the Soviets didn't methodically kill children as did the SS and were not systematically racist; but in Ukraine, Stalin had unleashed genocide. In subsequent years the CICRC studied conditions in Greece, Franco's Spain, and Mao's China, among others. In 1957, Tillion represented it in an inquiry into the Algerian War prisons (see below).

Tillion's research included gathering data on the identities of all deported French women. She was able to list all the trains from France to Ravensbrück, often coach by coach, with names and numbers of the deportees, and especially to list the dead along with witnesses who had seen them die. The task involved combing vast files, e.g., of the war-crimes courts and the Gestapo and Abwehr, to corroborate the testimony obtained in Sweden in 1945. She also sent questionnaires to hundreds of former deportees or their families. In the summer of 1954, she went to the United States to examine the collections held by the American army. The McCarthy witch hunt was in full cry, but her service on the Brussels jury won her permission to consult the two librarians guarding the files. She and they presently became quite distressed to learn, however, that this trove was soon to be returned to Germany.

She turned the documentation over to the Ministry of Veterans, beginning in 1947, and the Comité d'histoire de la Deuxième Guerre mondiale. Ultimately, in 1995, they were deposited at Besançon in the Musée de la Résistance et de la Déportation (Fonds Germaine Tillion). When she finished in 1954, she also gave documents to her comrades in the Ravensbrück Society and the ADIR, which published *Les Françaises à Ravensbrück* (Gallimard, 1965). Tillion herself paid high respect to several women without whom the work of collecting and verifying information would have been "impossible": **Denise Vernay** and Anise Postel-Vinay; and three international friends: **Nina Iwanska** (Pole), Grete Buber-Neumann (German), and **Zdenka Nedvedova** (Czech). As far as Ravensbrück was concerned, "I thought I was done with it," she said. But as later events would prove, she was not.

In 1954, upon Tillion's return from the United States, her old mentor Louis Massignon asked her to accompany him to a meeting on November 25 with the current minister of the interior, François Mitterrand. A rising had begun on November 1 in Algeria in the Aurès. The place-name struck a chord with Massignon, who had immediately thought of Tillion. At the meeting, she accepted a mission to look into the situation of the populace in the region and elsewhere. Upon her arrival, she was shocked to learn of the rising and bloody repression at Sétif on May 8, 1945 (she was in Sweden), a town in "her" region. Although she had been apprehensive, in the 1930s the Aurès was still peaceful despite its increasing poverty. Her shock deepened as she viewed the misery into which all Algeria was now plunging. Medical progress had encouraged a population explosion resulting in a migration of masses of peasants to the cities, where they arrived without education or the social skills to adapt to urban life. Hunger ran rampant, families were disintegrating, and anger and hopelessness was festering.

While returning to Paris after three months, she stopped in Algiers and on February 22, 1955, met with the new governor-general Jacques Soustelle. A fellow ethnologist, he had once been a student with her at the Institut, associate director of the Musée de l'Homme in the late 1930s, and a militant Gaullist. Since he knew little about Algeria, he was glad to see her. She agreed to join his staff at once, in charge of social and educational affairs, asking only that she be allowed to protect her situation with the CNRS by taking a year's leave rather than resigning.

Soustelle, favoring enlightened, progressive measures, let her do as she saw fit. By far the most important action of her tenure was starting what she called "the great adventure of the Social Centers" (Centres sociaux). She believed that education of the displaced peasants was the key to Algeria's future. With the help of both French and Muslim teachers and social workers, beginning in March 1955 she set about creating a network of centers focused on education, professional training, and health, i.e., a scheme providing basic education for the illiterate masses while also growing a native élite. She directed the operation herself until she resigned in January 1956 upon Soustelle's recall. The centers eventually numbered several dozen with over 400 workers.

They operated in daunting circumstances. On August 20, 1955, a wave of killings (71 dead Europeans) and atrocities by the Algerian National Liberation Front (FLN) marked the start of outright civil war. Soustelle, profoundly shaken, began the brutal counter-offensive which the FLN had intended to provoke. (Even so, he officially sanctioned the Centres sociaux on October 27.) Tillion ploughed ahead, as did her successors. Many Algerians and even a fair number of settlers approved of the Centres. But to mix European and Algerian workers inevitably provoked suspicion and reprisals. The FLN tried to infiltrate the organization and intimidate the workers; three were murdered. As for the government, it resorted to judicial harassment. In 1957, 16 workers were arrested and tried, some after torture, by army authorities led by General Jacques Massu, a *para* charged with suppressing the rebellion. Most were acquitted but, in 1959, 20 more were arrested and tried, again with most being acquitted. "The great adventure" ended, to all intents and purposes, on March 15, 1962 (three days before signature of the Evian Accords ending the war) when the Secret Army Organization (OAS), comprised of French irreconcilables, assassinated six Centres sociaux leaders, including the director, Max Marchand, and the Muslim writer Mouloud Feraoun, both dear friends of Tillion's. The Centres sociaux had done much good and probably represented at that time the most constructive answer to Algeria's problems. But Tillion's project was a classic example of a grand idea which came too late.

Before returning to France after Soustelle's departure (February 2, 1956), Tillion spent three months with the Tuaregs studying family relations among the Berbers of the South and the Aurès. Once back in Paris, she found herself besieged by friends asking her to "explain" Algeria. The result was a concise book written from notes taken during her year there, published first in the Resisters' organ *Voix et Visage*, then as a pamphlet, finally by a major publisher, Éditions de Minuit, in 1957, under the misleading title *L'Algérie en 1957*. Misleading because it seemed to promise an account of events there now that the war was tearing France apart politically. Rather, it analyzed the social and economic reasons for the conflict. Informed, insightful, pithy, the book caught on immediately, making Tillion a major public figure. In describing Algeria's recent evolution, she coined a word which has become a standard term in describing the evolution of the Third World: *clochardisation*, literally "beggarization." She defined it in an interview years later as a process resulting from "the passage, without primary education leading to a skill, from the peasant condition (that is to say, natural) to the urban (that is to say, modern)."

Tillion contended that France and the settlers (mostly French and Italian) on the one hand and the Muslim Algerians on the other needed each other—were, as she put it, "complementary enemies." Without France, Algeria was condemned to economic regression and death. She pointed to how much France had done for Algeria—and how much more it had not done. Expulsion of the Europeans or partition of the country were neither feasible nor desirable. There was no simple solution. Relations between the opposing peoples must somehow move from colonialist exploitation into a regime of "collaboration." This was no endorsement of "Algérie française" (the cry of the settlers) nor "integration," i.e., simply "Frenchifying" Algeria. Still, "certainly in spite of me," as she later asserted, the settlers regarded her book as supporting both their contention that Algeria needed them (which it did) and their narrow views on the political future of the country—which it did not. She believed they must make an accommodation with Algerian self-determination.

Expert as she was in unraveling the socio-economic factors, she was not strong on their political and historical dimensions. Consequently, her book was praised and damned by all sides. Both the settlers and the FLN in 1957–58 rejected her thesis of "complementary enemies" (Lacouture). Sadly, the book, like the Centres sociaux scheme, came too late to help avert the worst. She seemed to have understood that, for by 1957 (when it became a bestseller) she was already moving well beyond her endorsement of Albert Camus' forlorn call (January 1956) for a "civil truce" and into open opposition to the government's policy.

It first became public in May 1957 when she (with Massignon and Jean-Paul Sartre) testified for the defense in the trial of Mohammad Ben Saddok, an assassin. She presented a photocopy of a bundle of compositions by Algerian school children who had been asked what they would do if they were invisible. Almost all said, "Kill a Frenchman." She thought those chilling replies should give the court pause in judging the conduct of this young product of the colonial system. (Saddok was spared execution and instead given life in solitary confinement.) Her testimony put her in the camp of those calling for a "war against the war."

The use of torture by the French was now, during Massu's offensive, becoming public knowledge. Evidence surfaced, in fact, that it had been employed since at least 1955. Tillion later admitted she had long been "simply unable to imagine" that France would stoop to such practices. When she finally learned the truth, she began to tell her friends, especially those in Rousset's CICRC and conscientious public figures, beginning with Charles de Gaulle. At the same time, however, she made no apologies for FLN terrorism, as did most leftist intellectuals, led by *Simone de Beauvoir and Jean-Paul Sartre. The survivor of Ravensbrück refused to excuse torture or murder or atrocities by anyone whomsoever. She had witnessed more than enough barbarism for one lifetime.

Under pressure, Premier Guy Mollet granted permission to the CICRC to inspect camps in Algeria where FLN prisoners were held. An international committee—one representative each from Belgium, Norway, and the Netherlands, plus two from France, including Tillion—arrived in June 1957. It found that torture had become commonplace and that, for good reason, both the French and the Muslims feared each other. The committee recommended creation of a permanent body to monitor respect for human rights. It was during this tour (June–August) that Tillion found herself involved in the most extraordinary episode of all her experience in Algeria.

In Algiers on July 3, 1957, a trembling Muslim woman friend told her that "they" wanted to see her. When her friend added she didn't know who "they" were, the Resistance veteran pricked up her ears; she suggested that she meet a man the next day at the bus stop near the hotel and follow him. It was agreed. On July 4 she was led by a roundabout route to a fine home in the Casbah where she was ushered into the presence of two young armed men—Yacef Saâdi (or Saâdi Yacef—he used it both ways), the FLN chief of the Algiers zone, and his adjunct, Ali la Pointe—and two young women, one of them **Zohra Drif**. Uncertain of what they wanted, Tillion began speaking at length, uninterrupted, about her ideas in *L'Algérie en 1957*, which they evidently had read. After a long time Saâdi asked her in an anxious tone how she thought it would all end. She replied that neither side could win definitively, that if France grew tired and withdrew, Algeria would fall into "bloody regression." The conversation became tense. In the course of it, she excoriated them for murdering innocent people. Suddenly, Saâdi said he would no longer harm the civilians. Tillion was "stupefied." She noticed that he kept drawing connections between terrorist acts and the government's executions of terrorists. She asked him if he would keep his promise about the civilians if the executions continued. He disclaimed responsibility for anything if that happened.

The meeting lasted five hours. At the door she turned to Ali la Pointe and gently shaking him by the shoulders said, "Have you really understood what I said: 'Innocent blood cries for vengeance'?" He responded with a subdued "Oui, m'dame." She had told them several times she would have to report the conversation to the government. They merely shrugged. Only after leaving did she begin to think that since terrorist acts responded to executions, then if the executions ceased and they stopped their reprisals, the two sides might at last find it possible to talk. She and Saâdi had struck no bargain, but one was implicit in what he had said. (Many years later she confessed she still did not know for certain why he had asked her to meet him.) In any event, of one thing she was by now convinced after this meeting and the CICRC investigation: the desire for outright independence was genuine and deep.

On July 6, two days after the meeting, she flew to Paris with the CICRC commission. On the 8th, she requested a meeting with André Boulloche, a Resister and deportee well known to her and currently chief of staff to the new premier, Maurice Bourgès-Maunoury. He complied the same day. To Boulloche and Louis Mangin, a childhood friend and Resister who was now head of the premier's military cabinet, she told of her meeting with Saâdi and proposed suspending executions in hopes he would carry out his promise to spare civilians. Boulloche and Mangin appeared sympathetic. In due course, Boulloche informed her that Bourgès-Maunoury (who had several other contacts at work) wanted her to return to Algiers to converse with one or several members of the FLN's executive council to find out their "real" point of view. (This may have been a stall.) She would, however, have to go at her own risk—which was not inconsiderable given that the government's "control" of Massu's forces and the Europeans in Algiers was a polite fiction.

On July 24, as she was preparing to leave, an embarrassed Mangin informed her that two executions were scheduled for the 25th. She got up, went out to the street, and cried. Once recovered, she decided to go ahead even though the mission appeared hopeless. On the 25th in Algiers she learned that there had been three executions. Eight bombs exploded on the 27th, one close to her—but nobody was killed. So she decided to push on. Circumstances resulted in her seeing Saâdi again instead of an executive council member. They met on August 9. Zohra Drif was present again and this time took part in the conversation. Saâdi, relaxed and smiling, claimed he had arranged for there to be no deaths in the recent bombings. He cautioned that he would need at least three days to institute a ceasefire if the executive council should order it.

Tillion purchased a ticket to return on the 11th, but on the 10th she learned from Muslim friends that there had been two executions the night before. Desperate, she sent word to Saâdi begging him to forgo any reprisal. He consented, not without complaints and a threat to resume if his two imprisoned sisters died. He kept his word; the truce held—until he and Zohra Drif were arrested by the army six weeks later (September 22). Within a week, terrorist killings resumed in full force. From this point on, the war only intensified, while the Fourth Republic slid inexorably toward its death and the coming to power of Charles de Gaulle (June 1, 1958).

Tillion spent October and November 1957 leading a campaign to get Saâdi transferred from the army's hands (where his fate was certain) to the civil jurisdiction. She besieged newspaper editors and prominent political figures, among the latter de Gaulle. Their meeting lasted two hours. He had read *L'Algérie en 1957* and praised it. What she now told him about conditions in Algeria was far more disturbing than what he was being told by people there trying to curry his favor. At one point she said France had a "magnificent" army, but later she described the terrible things it was doing, including the routine use of torture. In his inimitable manner, de Gaulle inquired, "And you call an army capable of what you have said a 'magnificent' army?"

The campaign succeeded, but a further effort, from late 1957 to the spring of 1958, to have Saâdi removed to France failed. Meanwhile, she composed a complete account of her meetings with him and submitted it to the authorities. Perhaps because of it—she liked to think so—the government put off trying and executing him forthwith. Finally, shortly after de Gaulle assumed office, Saâdi underwent three trials on three charges, on June 24, July 3, and August 25, 1958. Tillion was summoned to Algiers by the defense to testify in closed session on July 3 about her contacts with him and her impressions of him. When she finished, he rose and managed to hail the Resisters as "our models" before being silenced. She had to leave town immediately because of the danger posed by local fanatics and angry *paras*. A reliable *para* colonel volunteered to spirit her to the airport. On the way they noticed two men in a command car following them. When she reached the airport, she got out and called back to thank them for their "company." They covered their faces, spun around, and sped off.

Saâdi was condemned to death, but in 1959 de Gaulle pardoned him. Tillion remained active in trying to bring peace. Her Saint-Mandé apartment witnessed a parade of young Algerians, mainly students, who came and went, talked, ate, and slept over. Occasionally, officials privately sought her advice. She and Simone de Beauvoir, Simone Veil, and others collaborated with *Gisèle Halimi in 1960–61 in forcing a formal investigation of the torture of *Djamila Boupacha, a young woman accused of planting a bomb. (Hers was one of only two cases to win a full inquiry.) Tillion continued to write about the war. In 1960, she reissued *L'Algérie en 1957*, with added material and a new title, *L'Afrique bascule vers l'avenir* (Africa Teeters toward the Future). Also in 1960, she published *Les Ennemis complémentaires*, which included her account of the Saâdi meetings, parts of which had been leaked by *L'Express* on August 28, 1958.

Predictably, her revelations brought down a rain of praise and denunciation, including charges of "treason." (In his two books on the war, published in 1962 and 1982, Saâdi was silent on the meetings with Tillion and expressed no regrets about FLN atrocities.) In the book, she pleaded for open negotiations with the FLN and for the latter to cease trying to find in Washington or Moscow some alternative to sitting down with the French. Her name was invoked everywhere by advocates of independence for Algeria. Which in the end proved to be the case; after four years of tortuous maneuverings, de Gaulle and the Algerian leaders signed the Evian Accords on March 18, 1962.

In the meantime, while advocating measures to bring an honorable end to the war, Tillion accepted a position in de Gaulle's administration when André Boulloche, now minister of Education, asked her to join his staff. She stayed a year (1958–59). Her principal achievement was to get primary responsibility for the education of prisoners removed from the Bureau of Prisons (where Simone Veil also was promoting education) to the Ministry of Education. Consequently, a highly motivated prisoner could now conceivably advance from illiteracy to a doctorate. She took pride in reforming a system in which heretofore it had taken, as she put it, six months at least for a prisoner to receive—maybe—authorization for "a slate and a piece of chalk."

Apart from membership on the Boupacha Committee, after the Saâdi trials Tillion no longer intervened personally in Algerian affairs. For many years she continued to receive Algerian visitors at her apartment. During the war she had waxed optimistic about the appearance of "a natural, united Algerian consciousness" which was "not to be confused with opposition to France, membership in Islam, or tribal chauvinism." Sadly, after the war she witnessed instead an intensifying *clochardisation*, power struggles and corruption in the FLN, the growth of Muslim fundamentalism, and the onset of virtual civil war. About all she could do was plead for better treatment of the hundreds of thousands of Algerians now settled in France.

She resumed full-time professional life after 1960. She continued her connection with the CNRS (dating back to 1937) and was named in 1960 Director of Studies at the 6th Section of the École Practique des Hautes Études (after 1975 the École des Hautes Études en Sciences Sociales). As had Marcel Mauss, she attracted a group of 15 or so advanced students and taught in one-to-one or seminar settings. Her tapes-

tried, dossier-and-book-strewn apartment in Saint-Mandé overlooking the Parc de Vincennes was a favorite venue. Her particular interests ran to the study of the condition of women in the Mediterranean world and to the oral literature of North Africa. Under the auspices of the CNRS, the EPHE, and the World Health Organization at various times in the '60s and '70s, she travelled extensively—to Algeria (of course), Morocco, Tunisia, Egypt (a favorite destination), Libya, Syria, Jordan, Israel, Iraq, Iran, Pakistan, and India. Teams of researchers, many her students, usually accompanied her. Her only impediment was a chronic asthma, which she had contracted at Ravensbrück.

The principal fruit of her research was a controversial comparative study of women in the Mediterranean world, from the Greco-Latin north to the Arab-Berber south. Its provocative title alone—*Le Harem et les cousins* (1966)—elicited comment, as it seemed to promise a titillating excursion into Turkish seraglios and Muslim polygamy. Rather, it was an examination of the confining of females in all the Mediterranean cultures, of their enclosure in a family structure and set of attitudes and customs which, among other things, is both cause and result of a male sexual obsession with female virginity and leads, e.g., to crimes and blood feuds to protect the "honor" of the male or the family. Tillion contended that religion—Judaism, Christianity, even Islam—had far less to do with these characteristics than did the revolution wrought by the neolithic (late Stone Age) invention of settled agriculture, which encouraged endogamous marriage (i.e., within the tribe) in place of the custom of exogamous marriage practiced by hunter-gatherers.

With an assured food supply furnished by flocks and cultivated plants, the family or tribe found it advantageous to marry within itself, to "live from its own," build its population, crush external opposition by force, expand through warfare instead of seeking balance with its neighbors (as did the hunter-gatherers), and to urbanize, which required even stricter controls on women, such as cloistering and veiling. One of the most far-reaching measures was the prohibition of women from inheriting (despite Muhammad's commandment) because it would split the patrimony. Excluding women from inheriting and from many forms of social life resulted in a population of spoiled men and frustrated women. The latter accommodated themselves by "monopolizing" the children, notably creating a powerful tie between themselves and their eldest sons, the inheritors.

Tillion's work was groundbreaking. It was the first to propose a general theory explaining the origins of the subjugation of women in Mediterranean cultures and their neighbors to the east. By drawing attention to the neolithic agricultural revolution, she provoked a host of studies of these cultures which reexamined their origins, pushing them back to prehistoric times and relating them to the rise of endogamous marriage.

In 1968, **Olga Wormser-Migot** published a thesis, *Le Système concentrationnaire Nazi*. It was an early entry in a "revisionist" movement raising questions about the accepted accounts. She claimed there were no gas chambers in the Western camps, i.e., outside Eastern Europe, including Mauthausen and Ravensbrück. Tillion could not let such assertions go unanswered. The result was a second edition of *Ravensbrück*, in 1973, a revised and much-expanded version of the 1946 book. Given the notoriety she had won as author of *L'Algérie en 1957* and *Le Harem et les cousins*, the book received wide attention.

It contained a more nuanced version of the 1946 material along with some changes and reorganization. To this was added a scientific analysis of oral and written evidence concerning the fate of "the 27,000s," the convoy of 959 women (including Tillion's mother) of January 30, 1944, who were numbered in the 27,000s. A third part raised questions about the "routineness" of horror and the "ordinariness" of its perpetrators. By now she had come to believe that there was nothing specifically "German" about the horrors; no people is exempt from a collective moral disaster. A fourth section—far from the least important—discussed with impressive insight the problems historians confront in discovering the closest approximation one can have to the truth ("the Truth" being beyond recovery), especially the relative worths of written and oral materials. Several appendices, mainly by collaborators, presented incontrovertible proofs of the Western death operations. The book closed with a short, ironic, bitterly humorous piece by a friend, **Nelly Forget**, arrested and tortured in Algeria in 1956, who found a former SS member, now a Foreign Legionnaire, a more humane jailer than the French paratroopers (*paras*).

A third edition of *Ravensbrück*, in 1988, was provoked in part by further revisionist writing which even went so far as to deny the Holocaust altogether, calling the death camps "a fraud." The edition developed in a "more critical and more personal fashion the intuitions of 1945 and the analyses of 1973," wrote Pierre Vidal-Naquet. In the mass of books about the Nazi concentration camps, this final version, published by Tillion in her 81st year, will remain, like its predecessors, one of the truly germinal works on the camps and a testimony to its author's resourcefulness, critical acumen, and perseverance.

She also contributed regularly to *Voix et Visage*, and in 2000, responding to urging from friends, Tillion published a book based on notes she had taken while in the Aurès in the 1930s but had left behind in Paris, thus sparing them confiscation at Ravensbrück. Entitled *Il était une fois l'ethnographie* (Once Upon a Time There Was Ethnography), it also contained thoughts on the past and future of this discipline. She observed that some genres of it had become "outdated" because over the last 60 years societies had been fused by, especially, electronic inventions—the radio, the telephone, television, the Internet. Nevertheless, ethnology, "being a matter of patience, listening, courtesy, and time, can still serve for something, namely, teaching us how to live together." Looking ahead, she saw humanity confronting conditions which call into question the "sacrosanct neolithic [ideal of] growth." In the new millennium we must "invent something else."

Tillion retired from formal teaching in 1977. Well before then she had purchased a cottage on the south coast of Brittany at the village of Plouhinac (Morbihan), near the port of Lorient. Visitors, some complete strangers, continued to drop by as in Paris, many of them veterans of the war, the Resistance, and the deportation. In the early 1980s, she moved to another cottage nearby where she could plant trees and a garden. Thus, she divided her time between Paris and the coast.

Given her tireless energy, she of course remained engaged on several fronts. Politics was not one of them. She "explained" once that she belonged to "a generation of women born without the vote." More to the point, she remarked that she thought she had "more scientific curiosity than personal ambition." Although involved in selected public issues, she was an independent, unaffiliated with any party—save for one occasion. She harbored a profound admiration for Charles de Gaulle—although not for the constitution of his Fifth Republic, which she thought insufficiently democratic. On December 4, 1965, she sent a short letter to a Gaullist publication supporting his reelection. When he was forced into a runoff with Mitterrand, she spoke (as did other notables such as André Maurois, François Mauriac, and Maurice Schumann) at a

Gaullist rally on December 14 at the Sports Palace. Such was the extent of her political "career," excluding (as one should) two years' service on governmental staffs.

As for causes which interested her, from 1960 she was vice-president of the Association for the Development of World Law; spoke on demographic problems at a United Nations colloquy in 1965; spoke at a 1969 colloquy on international jurisprudence, where she dealt with the defense of public health from air, water, and noise pollution; was president of the Association Against Modern Slavery, allied with the venerable Anti-Slavery Society in London; and joined the Minority Rights Group in 1978, where she was president of the French Section. Concerning this last cause, she regarded the protection of minorities as the most troubling political problem around the world now that national frontiers were reasonably stable. Minorities drawing her particular interest included Native Americans, the Kurds, and the Tuaregs of the Sahara. She also spoke out, in 1996, on behalf of stateless persons, a chronic problem in a world generating a steady supply of refugees.

Among other broadly political concerns, she opposed Israel's invasion of Lebanon (1982), supported statehood for the Palestinians, and urged Israel to negotiate with the Palestine Liberation Organization. During the Gulf War, she joined in an appeal to the Western alliance made by several French friends of the Arabs to take seriously a semi-official statement from Iraq on February 15, 1991, about its willingness to evacuate Kuwait—to no avail, however. And in 1992 she was invited to Moscow by survivors of the Gulag to help them organize their first official meeting. As for women's issues, above all in the Third World, she was of course deeply interested. Not surprisingly in light of her conclusions in *Le Harem et les cousins*, she fought the subjugation of women and in particular assailed the practice of preventing females from inheriting. Female circumcision, an issue sharply dividing the West from many Eastern and African societies, found her opposed to the practice. She emphatically did not adopt the view of many anthropologists that just because a custom is ancient it is therefore right and good.

Germaine Tillion's personality combined a large physical presence with a smiling welcome, straightforward and attentive. She treated everyone with equal respect, from beggars to students to heads of state. She was genuinely interested in people, individually or collectively, never dismissive or patronizing. She was also clever, even crafty. These characteristics underlay her genius for drawing the truth from people. She was a born investigator. Besides being utterly courageous, physically and morally, she was highly intelligent. Students coveted the opportunity to work under her direction, but they confessed, too, that it took some time to get up to her speed and become accustomed to the peculiarities of her mental processes. She was naturally light-hearted and humorous—but about work entirely serious, wholly absorbed in the matter at hand.

In advanced old age she confessed that she remained an optimist *"une candide,"* about humanity. From prehistoric times to the present, it had survived every catastrophe and yet progressed. It gave her grounds for hope amidst all the evil she had witnessed and borne over a very long lifetime.

Her greatest joy was decades-old friendships. The closest were with her sister, Françoise; a niece Émilie; Geneviève de Gaulle-Anthonioz; Anise Postel-Vinay; Denise Vernay; **Jacqueline Fleury**; and two assistants, **Raphaëlle Anthonioz** (sister-in-law of Geneviève), her secretary through 40 years, and **Marlène Chamay**. So it is not surprising that when the French government honored Tillion on December 23, 1999, she preferred to have it done at her Saint-Mandé apartment, with Geneviève de Gaulle-Anthonioz standing in for the president of the Republic. The decoration was the highest that France bestows: the Grand Cross of the Legion of Honor.

Precious few men and a minuscule number of women have ever received this award. That Germaine Tillion was chosen to join them said all that was left to say about her.

SOURCES:

Les Françaises à Ravensbrück. Publié par l'Amicale de Ravensbrück et l'Association des Déportées et Internées de la Résistance. Paris: Gallimard, 1965.

Lacouture, Jean. *Le Témoignage est un combat: Une biographie de Germaine Tillion*. Paris: Éditions de Seuil, 2000 (indispensable).

Maran, Rita. *Torture: The Role of Ideology in the French Algerian War*. NY: Praeger, 1989.

Tillion, Germaine. "À la recherche de la verité," in *Ravensbrück*. Neuchatel: Éditions de la Baconnière, 1946, pp. 11–88.

———. *France and Algeria: Complementary Enemies*. Trans. by Richard Howard. NY: Alfred A. Knopf, 1961.

———. "Première résistance en zone occupée (Du côte du réseau 'Musée de l'Homme-Hauet-Vildé')," in *Revue d'histoire de la deuxième guerre mondiale*. Vol. 8, no. 30, 1958, pp. 6–22.

———. *Ravensbrück*. Trans. by Gerald Satterwhite. Garden City, NY: Doubleday, 1975.

———. *La Traversée du mal: Entretien avec Jean Lacouture*. Paris: Arléa, 1997.

Vidal-Naquet, Pierre. "Réflexions sur trois *Ravens-brück*," in *Réflexions sur la génocide*. Paris: Éditions La Découverte, 1995.

"Les Vies de Germaine Tillion," in *Esprit*. February 2000, pp. 82–170 (Tillion's article on the Resistance [see above] plus essays by friends and colleagues).

SUGGESTED READING:

Benamou, Georges-Marc. *C'était un temps déraisonnable: les premiers résistants*. Paris: Robert Laffont, 1989.

Blumenson, Martin. *Le Réseau du musée de l'Homme*. Paris: Éditions du Seuil, 1979.

Horne, Alistair. *A Savage War of Peace: Algeria 1954–1962*. NY: Viking Press, 1977.

Kogon, Eugen. *The Theory and Practice of Hell: The German Concentration Camps and the System Behind Them*. Trans. by Heinz Norden. NY: Farrar, Straus, 1949 (a translation and abridgement of *Der SS-Staat*, 3rd ed., 1949).

Noguerès, Henri, Jean-Louis Vigier, and Marcel Degliame-Fouché. *Histoire de la Résistance en France*. 5 vols. Paris: Robert Laffont, 1967–81.

Reudy, John. *Modern Algeria: The Origins and Development of a Nation*. Bloomington, IN: Indiana University Press, 1992.

COLLECTIONS:

Besançon, France: Fonds Germaine Tillion in the Musée de la Résistance et de la Déportation.

David S. Newhall,
Pottinger Distinguished Professor of History Emeritus,
Centre College, and author of
Clemenceau: A Life at War (1991)

Tillotson, Queena (1896–1951).

See Mario, Queena.

Tilly, Dorothy (1883–1970)

American civil-rights activist. Born Dorothy Eugenia Rogers on June 30, 1883, in Hampton, Georgia; died of respiratory arrest on March 16, 1970, in Atlanta, Georgia; daughter of Richard Wade Rogers (a Methodist minister) and Frances (Eubank) Rogers; graduated with honors from Reinhardt College, 1899; Wesleyan College in Macon, Georgia, A.B., 1901; married Milton Eben Tilly (a chemical distributor), on November 24, 1903 (died 1961); children: Eben Fletcher (b. 1904).

Served as secretary of children's work, Women's Missionary Society (1910s–20s); was director of summer leadership school at Paine College (1929); became member of executive committee, Association of Southern Women for the Prevention of Lynching (c. 1931); elected president of Georgia chapter of Committee on the Cause and Cure of War (1936); appointed member of Presidential Committee on Civil Rights (1945); served as director of women's work for Southern Regional Council (late 1940s); founded Fellowship of the Concerned (1949); was a delegate to Israel, American Christian Palestine Committee (1949).

During the 1920s, at his insistence, Georgia-born Dorothy Tilly accompanied her husband Milton Tilly on morning drives through the slums of Atlanta. In a wealthy section behind the posh Piedmont Hotel, she saw impoverished black children retrieving food from garbage cans. Shocked, she protested any further visits. Milton challenged her to let others know what she had witnessed, and promised financial assistance should she choose to work to alleviate the conditions of Southern African-Americans. This was the beginning of Dorothy Tilly's tireless crusade to eliminate poverty and racism. Outspoken on the moral dimensions of segregation, she would go on to publicly proclaim the need for integration in the South, including in the nation's capital.

Dorothy was born in Hampton, Georgia, on June 30, 1883, the fourth of eleven children, eight of whom survived infancy. Her father Richard Wade Rogers was a Methodist minister who would later serve as president of Reinhardt Junior College in Waleska, Georgia, and her mother **Frances Eubank Rogers** had graduated from Wesleyan College in Macon; both were descendants of early English settlers to Virginia. Her parents instilled in her a concern for social issues, and from an early age she was encouraged to value learning and to show compassion for others. Tilly graduated with honors from Reinhardt College in 1899, and received an A.B. from her mother's alma mater, Wesleyan College, in 1901. (She later served on the board of trustees of Wesleyan.) She married Milton Eben Tilly, a chemical distributor from Atlanta, in November 1903, and gave birth to their only son the following year.

Beginning in the 1910s, Tilly became active in the Women's Missionary Society of the Methodist Episcopal Church, North Georgia Conference, serving as secretary of children's work. After those car rides with her husband gave her energies new direction, in the late 1920s she directed the summer leadership school at Paine College in Augusta, Georgia, a program to train black Methodist women as community leaders. Early in the 1930s, Tilly joined the recently established Association of Southern Women for the Prevention of Lynching (ASWPL). As secretary of the group's Georgia chapter, she worked with *Jessie Daniel Ames, the ASWPL's founder, investigating and documenting lynchings in Georgia and trying to improve conditions for Southern blacks. She also became a member of the national executive committee of the ASWPL. Tilly joined the Commission on Interracial Cooperation (later the Southern Regional Council), serving as a field worker and director of the women's branch of the organization during the 1940s. At the same time, she also served as secretary of Christian social relations for the Women's Society of Christian Service in the southeast. Her work brought her national recognition, and in 1945 Harry S. Truman appointed her to the President's Committee on Civil Rights. One of only two Southerners on the committee and the only white woman, she counseled the other members not to view the South as the only region in which racial prejudice festered, but to learn to recognize its existence in all sections of the United States. She also campaigned against the Ku Klux Klan; in part because of her lobbying, the legislatures of Georgia and South Carolina passed antimask laws.

In September 1949, with the support of the Southern Regional Council, Tilly founded the Fellowship of the Concerned, an interracial and interfaith group, to carry forth the mission of the ASWPL, which had disbanded in 1942. An informal coalition of members from churches and synagogues from 12 southern states, the fellowship advocated for fair treatment of blacks in the courts. Tilly was convinced that defendants' civil rights would be less likely to be violated if prominent women attended trials, and urged group members to do so and report on what they had seen. As well, fellowship members accompanied registered black women voters to polling booths and campaigned to educate law enforcement officials on how to avert race riots and lynchings. Tilly also raised funds for the organization, which had more than 4,000 members by 1950. Among the projects the group sponsored were workshops to promote support for integrated schools, anticipating the 1954 *Brown* v. *Board of Education* Supreme Court decision.

Tilly was an advocate of peace as well as justice. Having served in 1936 as president of the Georgia chapter of the Committee on the Cause and Cure of War (founded by *Carrie Chapman Catt), she also supported formation of the League of Nations after World War II. Among the other groups to which she lent her energies were the Emergency Committee for Food Production (during the war), Americans for Democratic Action, the American Civil Liberties Union, and the American Christian Palestine Committee. In conjunction with the latter group, she had traveled to Israel in 1949 to study conditions in Jerusalem. Despite harassment by segregationist groups—in the 1950s a Ku Klux Klan plot to bomb her Atlanta home was uncovered—Tilly maintained her faith and her vision, continuing to work for peace, justice, and good race relations. Her response to threatening calls was to play a recording of the Lord's Prayer over the phone. Frail and

confined to a wheelchair, she attended meetings and spoke for civil rights well into the 1960s, as the civil-rights movement took hold throughout the country. Tilly lived long enough to mourn the assassination of Martin Luther King, Jr., dying of respiratory arrest in a nursing home in Atlanta, Georgia, on March 16, 1970.

SOURCES:

Sicherman, Barbara, and Carol Hurd Green, eds. *Notable American Women: The Modern Period.* Cambridge, MA: The Belknap Press of Harvard University, 1980.

Lolly Ockerstrom, freelance writer, Washington, D.C.

Tilney, Agnes (1476–1545).
See Tylney, Agnes.

Tilney, Elizabeth (d. 1497).
See Tylney, Elizabeth.

Tilton, Elizabeth (b. 1834)

American who was at the center of a storm of controversy for her liaison with Henry Ward Beecher. Name variations: Mrs. Theodore Tilton; Lib Tilton. Born in 1834; married Theodore Tilton (a journalist), in 1851; probably lived in Brooklyn, New York.

Elizabeth Tilton was at the center of a sensational six-month adultery trial that began in 1875. She was married to Theodore Tilton, a lecturer and journalist who was a friend of the well-known abolitionist preacher Henry Ward Beecher (brother of novelist *Harriet Beecher Stowe). One the most prominent public figures of his day, Beecher drew thousands to Brooklyn's Plymouth Congregational Church. Among those who came into his pastoral care was Elizabeth Tilton, with whom he conducted an affair which may have begun in October 1868. Their relationship remained unknown until 1870, when Elizabeth had a crisis of conscience and confessed to her husband Theodore.

Theodore accused his friend Henry of having seduced Elizabeth, and he pushed for legal action for "criminal conversation" with his devout wife. Although attempts were made prior to the trial to reach some kind of resolution between the two men, emotions escalated. Numerous inflammatory statements were exchanged between Henry and Theodore, and reconciliation could not be effected despite the involvement of a mutual friend, Frank Moulton. Much of what is known of the conflict is due to Moulton's carefully kept records of the pretrial statements, which reveal Henry Beecher's attempts to save face by changing his story: first confessing, then denying, any part in the adulterous liaison. Among other tactics, Henry characterized Elizabeth Tilton as mentally unbalanced—an accusation not uncommonly leveled against women of the day who embarrassed public figures.

Elizabeth, on the other hand, remained elusive and never presented a clear picture of events. Whereas prior to the trial she seemed to protect Beecher (claiming, according to Moulton's notes, that his behavior had simply consisted of "unhandsome advances"), after the trial she would declare herself an adulteress. Through the trial, she would never be permitted to testify.

In what became one of the foremost entertainment events of the period, the trial drew national and international attention. Required entry tickets to the proceedings were free but were in such great demand that they were scalped at the cost of $5 each. As many as 3,000 were turned away, and a carnival atmosphere developed, with vendors selling sandwiches and soft drinks and offering rented binoculars. Fans sent flowers to both Henry Beecher and Elizabeth Tilton.

Henry and Theodore, both testifying, made poor showings. Henry contradicted the testimony of the 95 witnesses who had appeared on his behalf and claimed a failure of memory 900 times. Theodore, meanwhile, failed to satisfactorily explain a brief association with feminist publisher and crusader *Victoria Woodhull, who, notes George Kohn, had "dared Beecher in print to have the courage of his adulterous predilections and 'fess up.' (Her letter caused Anthony Comstock to have her jailed for six months for using immoral language.)" When the trial finally ended in a hung jury (they were reportedly too confused to come to a verdict), the controversy remained. Nonetheless, Henry Ward Beecher's reputation as one of America's foremost ministers went untarnished. The same could not be said for Elizabeth Tilton.

SOURCES:

Kohn, George C. *Encyclopedia of American Scandal.* NY: Facts on File, 1989.

SUGGESTED READING:

Fox, Richard Wightman. *Trials of Intimacy: Love and Loss in the Beecher-Tilton Scandal.* Chicago, IL: University of Chicago Press, 1999.

> **Lolly Ockerstrom,**
> freelance writer,
> Washington, D.C.

Tilton, Martha (1915—)

American singer and actress. Born on November 14, 1915, in Corpus Christi, Texas; married an aerospace executive, in 1953; children: three.

Sang in Al Lippan's band; appeared on Benny Goodman's radio show (1940s); appeared in films Sunny *(1941),* Swing Hostess *(1944),* Crime, Inc. *(1945), and* The Benny Goodman Story *(1956); hosted "Liltin' Martha Tilton Time" on NBC Radio (c. 1948); appeared on series of radio shows (1950s and 1960s).*

Known as "Liltin' Miss Martha Tilton" during the Big Band era of the 1940s, Martha Tilton was the female singer on bandleader Benny Goodman's 1940s radio show. Her best-known hits were "And the Angels Sing," "Time After Time," "I'll Walk Alone," and "How Are Things in Glocca Mora."

Tilton was born in Corpus Christi, Texas, in 1915, but her family moved to Los Angeles when she was seven months old. Her piano-playing parents exposed their daughter to music early on. Then friends convinced the teenage Tilton to sing with a small band at a party. When that same band played at a local radio station, they asked her to come along. Tilton stayed on at the station as a regular performer without pay. Soon she was singing at the Coconut Grove with Al Lippan's band, a stint which was followed by a two-year tour with Hal Grayson's group. Tilton next became the "Miss" of "Three Hits and a Miss," which later evolved into the swing chorus for Benny Goodman's radio show.

Her break came when Goodman's lead female singer left the program, and Tilton was hired to fill the position. She spent the next three and a half years singing, recording, and appearing on radio programs. Despite a grueling performance schedule (she had one day off in a two-year period), she also appeared in four films: *Sunny* (1941), *Swing Hostess* (1944), *Crime, Inc.* (1945), and *The Benny Goodman Story* (1956).

In 1948, she began starring in her own NBC Radio program, "Liltin' Martha Tilton Time," which aired for several seasons. With Curt Massey, Tilton worked for eight years, starting in 1951, for Alka Selzer on CBS Radio. The two then continued performing together for another five years, with Country Washburn's Orchestra on NBC-TV. After NBC terminated the program in 1964, Tilton retired. The mother of three children, she later settled in the Mandeville Canyon section of West Los Angeles with her husband and daughter.

SOURCES:

Lamparski, Richard. *Whatever Became of . . . ?* 5th series. NY: Crown, 1974.

> **Lolly Ockerstrom,**
> freelance writer,
> Washington, D.C.

Timanoff, Vera (1855–1942)

Russian pianist. Born in 1855; died in 1942; studied with Anton Rubinstein, Carl Tausig, and Franz Liszt.

A prodigious talent, Vera Timanoff was a student of Anton Rubinstein, Carl Tausig and Franz Liszt. Tausig maintained that she played Chopin as well if not better than he could, while for Liszt her superb pianism made her *"la créme de la créme"* of all his students. She was clearly an extraordinary musician but never developed a significant concert career, perhaps because of stage fright. Returning to Russia, she became a teacher in St. Petersburg. The only tangible mementos of her talent are a few piano rolls she made early in the century, but they are considered important because of the prominence of her teachers.

John Haag,
Athens, Georgia

Timarete (fl. 3rd c. BCE)

Ancient Greek painter who painted a portrait of the goddess Artemis at Ephesus. Name variations: Timareta; Thamaris; Thamar. Pronunciation: teem-aret-AY. Probably born after the 90th Olympiad (420–417 BCE), perhaps in Syracuse in the 3rd century BCE; probably daughter of the artist Micon.

Timarete is the first woman painter in Pliny the Elder's list, which is given in reverse alphabetical order. His notice of her is limited to one sentence: "Timarete, daughter of Micon painted a very archaic panel-portrait of Diana at Ephesus." From elsewhere in the chapter (35.59) we know that Micon was also a painter, and thus we can group Timarete with two other women on the list, *Aristarete and *Irene, as daughters with famous artist fathers. It is perhaps curious to note, however, that Pliny does not explicitly say that Timarete learned to paint from her father, as he does of the other two.

If it is true that Irene painted a portrait of Persephone for Eleusis, then another similitude links her with Timarete. Diana, the Greek Artemis, was the city patron and chief attraction for pilgrims to Ephesus, and it is not inconceivable that a portrait of her, especially described in the terms that Pliny uses, was connected to aspects of the goddess' cult there. The fact that Pliny describes the portrait as "extremely archaic" (*antiquissimae*), however, also poses something of a problem for her dating. In 35.59, Pliny tells us that her father Micon was not identical with the famous artist of the same name who painted in Athens during the 5th century

BCE. Because Timarete's father was therefore known as Micon the Younger (*minor*), Pliny's reference to archaism must refer to the style of the work rather than its actual age. The reasons for this stylistic choice are unknown, and we do not know if it was characteristic of Timarete's work in general, or only of this particular portrait. Like Irene and *Iaia, Timarete (whom he calls "Thamaris") captured the attention of Boccaccio in his *De Mulieribus Claris* (*On Famous Women*). "Indeed, her work is worthy of much praise," he said. (*See also Aristarete.*)

SOURCES AND SUGGESTED READING:

Allgemeines Lexikon der Bildener Künstler von der Antike bis zur Gegenwart. Edited by Ulrich Thieme and Felix Becker. S.v. "Timarete." Leipzig: W. Engelmann, 1908–50.

Boccaccio, Giovanni. *Tutte le Opere.* Edited by Vittorio Zaccaria. Vol. 10: *De Mulieribus Claris.* 2nd ed. Verona: Arnoldo Mondadori, 1970, pp. 226–229.

Enciclopedia dell'Arte Antica Classica e Orientale. S.v. "Timarete." Rome: Instituto della Enciclopedia Italiana, 1958–66.

Peter H. O'Brien,
Instructor in English and Classics,
Boston University Academy,
Boston, Massachusetts

Timberlake, Margaret (c. 1799–1879).

See Eaton, Peggy.

Timmer, Marianne (1974—)

Dutch speedskater. Born in Sappemeer, the Netherlands, on October 3, 1974; daughter of Lucas Timmer; coached by Peter Mueller; works on her parents' sheep farm.

Marianne Timmer of the Netherlands won a gold medal in the 1,500 meters at Nagano in 1998 with a time of 1:57.58, setting a new world record. The silver was claimed by *Gunda Niemann, the bronze by *Chris Witty of the United States. In the women's 1,000 meters, Timmer beat out her friend, the heavily favored Witty, for another gold medal with a time of 1:16.51, breaking *Christa Rothenburger-Luding's previous Olympic record. *Catriona Le May Doan finished third.

Timoclea (c. 370–? BCE)

Woman of Thebes whose act of revenge against a marauding soldier won the respect of his commander Alexander the Great. Born around 370 BCE; sister of Theagenes of Thebes.

Timoclea was a prominent Theban and the sister of Theagenes, who commanded his city's army against Philip II of Macedon at the battle of Chaeronea (338 BCE) and died there. This defeat put Thebes, and most of the rest of Greece, under the political dominion of Macedon. After Philip's death and the accession of Alexander III the Great (336), Thebes lay uneasily under Macedon's yoke until the city openly rebelled in 335. This attempt to regain autonomy failed, however, after Alexander successfully stormed the city. Amid the looting which followed this event, a band of Alexander's Thracians broke into Timoclea's home seeking booty. Finding Timoclea, the leader of the Thracians raped her and then demanded that she reveal the hiding place of any valuables she might possess. She led him to her garden where she showed him a well into which she claimed to have thrown all of her gold and silver when it became obvious that the city was being taken. He peered into the recesses of the well, giving Timoclea the opportunity first to push him into its depths and then to stone him to death. His men arrived on the scene too late to save their leader, but thereafter bound Timoclea and led her to Alexander for punishment. She approached the conqueror haughtily. When Alexander asked her who she was, she proudly proclaimed her relationship to Theagenes and her anti-Macedonianism. Impressed by her spirit, Alexander not only declined to punish her, but gave her and her children their freedom—a remarkable fact, for the vast majority of the Thebans who were not killed in Alexander's assault or the subsequent pillaging, were sold by him into slavery, while their city was systematically razed to the ground.

William Greenwalt,
Associate Professor of Classical History,
Santa Clara University,
Santa Clara, California

Timothy, Ann (c. 1727–1792)

Colonial American newspaper publisher and printer.
Born Ann Donovan around 1727, probably in Charleston, South Carolina; died on September 11, 1792, in Charleston, South Carolina; thought to be a descendant of Daniel Donovan (a South Carolina settler); married Peter Timothy (a publisher), on December 8, 1745 (died 1783); children: possibly 15, including Peter (d. 1770); Sarah; Robert; Elizabeth Anne (who married Peter Valton); Frances Claudia (who married Benjamin Lewis Merchant); Benjamin Franklin; and seven who died in infancy.

Published the Gazette of the State of South Carolina *(1783–92); "Printer to the State" of South Carolina (1785–92).*

Ann Timothy was the second woman in South Carolina to become a newspaper publisher. The first was her mother-in-law *Elizabeth Timothy. Upon the deaths of their husbands, the Timothy women maintained the colony's first permanent newspaper, the *Gazette of the State of South Carolina*, keeping the venture in the family for three generations.

Probably born in Charleston, South Carolina, around 1727, Ann may have been related to Daniel Donovan, who had settled in the colony as early as 1687. Her marriage to Peter Timothy, in Charleston in 1745, would determine her later career. In 1746, Peter assumed full responsibility of what was then called the *South Carolina Gazette* from his mother Elizabeth, who had become publisher of the paper after the death of her husband Lewis Timothy. (When the paper was 12 months old, Lewis had taken it over in partnership with Benjamin Franklin.) During the ensuing years of marriage, Ann was often pregnant. Of her many children (possibly fifteen), seven died in infancy.

In 1777, Peter changed the name of the paper to the *Gazette of the State of South Carolina*, no doubt to emphasize states' rights. When the British occupied Charleston in 1781, Ann and her family were displaced to Philadelphia. The following year, Peter and two of the couple's daughters were lost at sea en route to Santo Domingo. Returning to Charleston and the *Gazette* in 1782, Ann assumed the role of publisher. With an assistant, E. Walsh, she continued the publication, which she renamed the *State Gazette of South Carolina* in 1785. Savvy in business, she also filled the post of "Printer to the State" from 1785 until her death in 1792, issuing at least 15 imprints. She died on September 11, 1792, whereupon her son Benjamin Franklin Timothy inherited the newspaper. He maintained it until his retirement in 1802, when the *Gazette* ceased publication.

SOURCES:

James, Edward T., ed. *Notable American Women, 1607–1950.* Cambridge, MA: The Belknap Press of Harvard University, 1971.

Lolly Ockerstrom,
freelance writer,
Washington, D.C.

Timothy, Elizabeth (d. 1757)

Colonial American newspaper publisher and printer.
Born in the Netherlands; died around May 1757 in Charleston, South Carolina; educated in the Netherlands; married Lewis Timothy (a publisher, died 1738); children: Peter (c. 1725–1782); Louisa (Mrs.

James Richards); Charles (d. September 1739); Mary Elizabeth (Mrs. Abraham Bourquin); Joseph (d. October 1739); Catherine (Mrs. Theodore Trezevant).

Immigrated to Philadelphia (1731); moved to Charleston, South Carolina (1733); was publisher of South-Carolina Gazette (1737–46); was proprietor of book and stationery shop (1747).

The first woman in America to publish a newspaper, Elizabeth Timothy published the *South-Carolina Gazette* following the December 1738 death of her husband Lewis Timothy. Before handing the paper over to her oldest son, she managed the paper singlehandedly for about two years. In his autobiography, Benjamin Franklin noted that Timothy had "manag'd the Business with such Success that she not only brought up reputably a Family of Children, but at the Expiration of the Term was able to purchase of me the Printing House and establish her Son in it."

Elizabeth Timothy was born and raised in the Netherlands, where she married Louis Timothée (who would change the spelling of his name in 1734). It is speculated that, like her husband, Timothy may have been a descendant of French Huguenots who had fled to Holland after the 1685 nullification of the Edict of Nantes brought religious and social persecution to France's Protestants. She was given a "Female Education" in Holland, including a grounding in accounting, which would serve her well in the management of the *Gazette*. In 1731, Elizabeth, her husband and their four young children emigrated from Rotterdam to Philadelphia. They remained there until 1733, when they moved to Charleston, South Carolina. Two more children were born in the colonies.

In Charleston, Lewis Timothy went into partnership with Benjamin Franklin and became the publisher of the weekly *South-Carolina Gazette*. Founded in 1732, the *Gazette* was the colony's first permanent newspaper. When Lewis died in an accident after five years of publishing the paper, Elizabeth Timothy stepped in as publisher without missing an issue. She maintained the paper in the name of her oldest son, Peter, who was about 14 at the time, until he was able to take sole control of the venture in 1746. While her first year as publisher was somewhat rocky, the paper steadily improved thereafter, and Timothy also published at least 20 books and pamphlets by other writers between the years 1739 and 1745.

After turning the *Gazette* over to her son, Timothy became owner of a small book and sta-

tioner's shop in 1747. She left Charleston in 1748, living elsewhere until her return in 1756. The following year, on April 12, 1757, she wrote a will disposing of her three houses, land, and eight slaves. Timothy died within a month, leaving behind a paper that ranked among the most prominent in the colonies and one of America's first newspaper dynasties. After the death in 1782 of her son Peter, the renamed *Gazette of the State of South Carolina* (later the *State Gazette of South Carolina*) was published by Peter's wife ***Ann Timothy** until her own death in 1792, when it was taken over by her son.

SOURCES:

James, Edward T., ed. *Notable American Women, 1607–1950.* Cambridge, MA: The Belknap Press of Harvard University, 1971.

Read, Phyllis J., and Bernard L. Witlieb. *The Book of Women's Firsts.* NY: Random House, 1992.

Lolly Ockerstrom,
freelance writer,
Washington, D.C.

Tinayre, Marcelle (c. 1870–1948)

French writer and journalist whose numerous novels dealt especially with the effects of love on women's freedom and development. Pronunciation: mar-SELL tee-NAIR. *Born Marguerite-Suzanne-Marcelle Chasteau at Tulle (Corrèze) in 1870 (or possibly 1871 or 1872); died at Grosrouvre, near Montfort-l'Amaury (Seine-et-Oise), on August 23, 1948, and was buried at the village church; eldest child of Chasteau Fourichon (a businessman [négociant]) and Louise Fourichon (c. 1850–1926, a teacher); educated at home, baccalaureate degree, 1889; daughter-in-law of Marguerite Tinayre (1831–?); married (Jean-)Julien Tinayre (1859–1923, an engraver), in 1889 (died 1923); children: Louise (b. 1890); Suzanne (1891–1896); Noël (b. 1896); Lucile (b. 1899).*

Sent a poem to Victor Hugo (1884); received the baccalaureate degree and married (1889); published Avant l'amour, *her first novel under her own name (1897); received a prize for* Hellé *and bought a country home (c. 1900); published her most praised work,* La Maison du péché *(1902); was denied the Legion of Honor after making some controversial remarks about it (1909); named to the Prix Flaubert jury (1923); named to the Prix Renée Vivien jury (1935); received the Prix Barthou (1938).*

Major writings (all published in Paris, most by Calmann-Lévy): Ménage d'artistes, *signed "Gilbert Doré" (1893);* Avant l'amour *(1897);* La Rançon *(1898);* Hellé *(1899);* L'Oiseau d'orage *(1900);* La Maison du péché *(1902);* La Vie amoureuse de François Barbazanges *(1904);* La Rebelle *(1905);* La

Consolatrice *(in* L'Illustration, *1907); L'Amour qui pleure (1908); Notes d'une voyageuse en Turquie (1909); L'Ombre de l'amour (1910); Le Paysage de Port-Royal (1910); Napoléon et la reine Hortense (1910); La Douceur de vivre (1911); Madeleine au miroir: Journal d'une femme (1912); La Veillée des armes: Le Départ (1914), translation of Au Pays des Pierres by Cécile Tormay (1914); Perséphone (1920); Les Lampes voilées: Laurence-Valentin (1921); Le Bouclier d'Alexandre (1922); Priscille Séverac (1922); L'Anneau de fer (1922); "La Legende de Duccio et d'Orsette," in* L'Illustration *(1923); La Vie amoureuse de Madame de Pompadour (1924); Un Drame de famille (1925); translation of* Scènes de la révolution communiste en Hongrie *by Cécile Tormay (1925); Figures dans la nuit (1926); "Saint Jean libérateur" in* L'Illustration *(1926); Une Provinciale en 1830 (1927); Terres étrangères: Norvège, Suéde, Hollande, Andalousie (1928); Josephine à Malmaison (1930); Vieilles chansons et vieux poèmes (1930); L'Ennemi intime (1931); La Femme et son secret (1933); Châteaux en Limousin (1934); Histoire de l'amour (1935); L'Affaire Lafarge (1935); Gérard et Delphine I: La Porte rouge (1936); Mariage (1937); "Sainte Marie du feu," in* L'Illustration *(1938); Gérard et Delphine II: Le Rendez-vous du soir (1938); Sainte-Marie du feu (1938); "Est-ce un miracle?" (1939); Châteaux disparus (1940); Madame du Barry (1940); Aventurine (1941); "Mémoires: Enfance et Adolescence," unpublished (1947);* Une Soirée chez Renée Vivien, 4 novembre 1908 *(1981).*

Journalism: collaborations of varying lengths; before World War I at La Vie populaire *and* Le Monde illustré, *where she published stories signed Gilbert Doré, short newsy items (échos) for* Le Gaulois *and* Gil Blas, *articles in* La Fronde *(1898–99),* Le Temps, La Revue de Paris, Fémina, Madame et Monsieur; *post-World War I at* Le Temps, La Vie heureuse, L'Européen, Le Journal de Marseille, La Pensée française, La Revue des deux mondes, La Revue de Paris, La Mode pratique, Madame et Monsieur, *and in 1933 editor of* La Nouvelle Revue féminine.

Marcelle Tinayre was one of France's most praised and popular novelists during the first two decades of the 20th century. Her favor declined thereafter, and at her death she was all but forgotten. When the feminist movement blossomed late in the century, however, she was rediscovered and the character and significance of her works reexamined.

No disagreement exists as regards her birthplace, the town of Tulle (Corrèze), in central southwestern France around 100 miles east of Bordeaux. As for her birth date, the most reliable current account of her personal life (by **Patricia Ferlin**) gives 1870, whereas her obituary says she was 76 in 1948. (Reference works and catalogs often give 1877, which is clearly erroneous.) Marcelle's father Chasteau Fourichon was a businessman of sorts (*négociant*) who found work as he could while his wife, a teacher, moved from post to post. Although her mother **Louise Fourichon** was the dominant figure in her youth, Marcelle described her father as "deeply artistic" and said she got her imagination, intellectual curiosity, and strong work ethic from him. Her mother, she said, was "remarkably intelligent," a powerful personality, and a born teacher. When not yet 30, Louise was appointed director of the women's teacher training school at Troyes. In 1880, she was named director of studies at the women's teacher training school at Fontenay-aux-Roses (Seine). She soon fell into disagreement with the inspector-general of education, however, and in May 1881 resigned from state service. The family—which also included Marcelle's younger sister, **Lucienne (Pelletan)**, future wife of a prominent publisher, Édouard Pelletan—then moved to Paris, where Louise taught in private schools and wrote for education reviews.

Marcelle was taught by her mother and, later on, tutors. She was petite, very fair-skinned, with dark hair and eyes, a remarkably bright child, perky and agreeable but also living an intense, concealed inner life fed by a fertile imagination. Her mother and maternal grandmother, who could recite reams of Hugo and Lamartine, read to her assiduously. She later said that the Bible and the *Odyssey* were important poetic influences on her; critics noted that her prose was marked by poetic traits. She began composing poems at about age nine, and in adolescence wrote a long poem about Christian missionaries in ancient Greece and a four-act play about François Villon. In 1884, at the urging of Eugène Hollande, a tutor, she sent a poem to Victor Hugo, who wrote an encouraging reply; Marcelle suspected he did so to everyone. "The idea of writing never occurred to me," she remarked in old age. "It just happened, that's all."

Recognizing her talent, her mother encouraged her to obtain the baccalaureate degree, which very few girls yet attempted. Her tutors were excellent, and the regime allowed her to take lessons for three hours a day and spend the rest "working for myself." She learned Latin from Hollande, a brother of a friend of her mother's. He was a fine scholar, befriended her, and later would see to the publication of her first novel, *Avant l'amour* (1897). Around 1885, during her studies, she discovered Blaise Pascal and contracted "a true religious fever" from the *Pensées*. It was then that the seeds of her novel *La Maison du péché* (The House of Sin, 1902), often considered her best, began germinating. Her sexual awakening accompanied, for a time, her religious "fever." She started going to parties and balls at 17 and enjoyed these diversions. When she took the baccalaureate examination at the Sorbonne in 1889, she was one of but three girls to attempt the written part and the only one to brave the oral part, winning the notation "Bien."

A few weeks later, aged 19 (or 17), she married a handsome, simple, shy, 30-year-old engraver, Julien Tinayre, son of an acquaintance of her mother's, *Marguerite Tinayre, a formidable woman who had been exiled for serving as an inspector of girls' schools during the Paris Commune revolt (1871). Marcelle's mother had feared that, given the social climate of the times, she soon would become hurt and disillusioned if she tried to carve out an independent career. Marcelle gave in to Louise's urgings to marry the son of a woman they both admired.

Julien was a good man, but Marcelle regretted the marriage from the start and rebelled against her mother's counsels of renunciation and submission. Matters worsened when she became pregnant almost immediately: "I became a mother too young and without having wished it." She never liked babies, although she did love children when they grew older. Forty years later she wrote in an unpublished memoir, "One must enter the reality of marriage by the golden door of illusion, without which no girl would commit the folly of enchaining herself." She soon ceased writing this memoir of her personal life, perhaps because it was redundant, for her novels had returned time and again to the theme of conflicts between women's full development and the constraints put upon them by marriage and motherhood.

Marcelle Tinayre had four children in short order: Louise (1890), Suzanne (1891–1896), Noël (1896), and Lucile (1899). Despite her maternal duties—or because of them—she began to write. She longed to "live life" but felt trapped. Besides, the household needed money, for photography was killing work for engravers. She got some short stories published as *Ménage d'artistes* (1893) in *La Vie populaire* and *Le Monde illustré* under the name "Gilbert Doré" and wrote short newsy pieces (*échos*) for *Le Gaulois* and *Gil Blas* for 5 francs each—a day's expense. And in 1898 she joined the staff of

Marcelle Tinayre

*Marguerite Durand's *La Fronde* (a daily newspaper written and printed entirely by women) as editor of the drama column for a time.

Meanwhile, she began to write novels— *Avant l'amour* (Before Love), *La Rançon* (The Ransom), and *L'Oiseau d'orage* (The Storm Bird)—which she put away in a drawer. Getting a first novel published at that time was exceedingly difficult, and she obviously had few hopes. But Eugène Hollande turned up and insisted on taking *Avant l'amour* (written under a male pseudonym) to *Juliette Adam, director of *La Nouvelle Revue*. Adam sent the manuscript to Jules Case and then Alphonse Daudet, a literary lion. Daudet replied that "the story displays inexperience, but you must publish it, for the young man [*sic*] will be someone." The *Nouvelle Revue* complied, and the *Mercure de France* followed with a hardback edition (1897). The book won enough notice to persuade Tinayre, who was astonished and delighted, to send *La Rançon* to *Le Temps*; the *Mercure* again issued it in hardback (1898). The uproar over the Dreyfus Affair might have drowned it out, but the editor of the *Revue de Paris*, Ganderax, was impressed. He opened the doors of the *Revue* and published *Hellé* (1899). The Académie Française awarded it a splendid prize of 5,000 francs. Tinayre was now fully launched, hailed by critics as one of the "new princesses" of literature.

Success brought affluence. With receipts from the prize, *L'Oiseau d'orage* (1900), *La Maison du péché* (1902), *La Vie amoureuse de François Babazanges* (1904), and *La Rebelle* (1905), she bought a dilapidated mansion at Grosrouvre (Seine-et-Oise) near Montfort l'Amaury, around 25 miles west of central Paris, and proceeded to renovate and enlarge it. She kept a Paris apartment but favored the country home, where she entertained visitors—notably Anatole France, Alphonse and Léon Daudet, René Doumic, Marcel Schwob, Fernand Gregh, Joseph Mardus and **Lucie Delarue-Mardrus**, and Abbé Arthur Mugnier. She kept a remarkably steady pace of about a novel per year until near the end of her life. She liked to travel, visiting England frequently, Italy, and in 1909 Turkey, under contract with the *Revue des deux mondes*, where she witnessed the climax of the revolt by the Young Turks, several of whom she had befriended in Paris.

Vivien, Renée.
See Barney,
Natalie Clifford
for sidebar.

Before and after the First World War she also lectured around France and Switzerland on literature and women, e.g., *George Sand (with whom some enthusiasts compared her). She wrote occasionally for periodicals, among them *Le Temps*, *La Vie heureuse*, *Madame et Monsieur*, *La Mode pratique*, *L'Européen*, *Le Journal de Marseille*, and *La Pensée française*, and often had her works published by the *Revue des deux mondes* or the *Revue de Paris* before they appeared in paperback. In 1933, she became the editor of *La Nouvelle Revue féminine*. She attracted an impressive list of contributors, including **Gabrielle Reval**, Lucie Delarue-Mardrus, Maurice Lavedan, Fernand Gregh, and François Mauriac, but it published only three issues.

In 1909, Tinayre provoked an uproar which occupied the press for some weeks. She had been nominated for the Legion of Honor, but when she wrote a letter to *Le Temps* joking clumsily about it—saying she wouldn't wear the ribbon because her 13-year-old son would think she had been an army canteen hostess (*cantinière*) back in the Franco-Prussian War—charges flew that she had insulted the Legion. When the final list appeared, her name was absent. Léon Blum, a supporter of women's rights (and a future premier), wrote tellingly in her defense that if a man

had written the letter, it would have been laughed off. The brouhaha upset her, and she went off on the trip to Turkey. In the end, however, she dismissed the snub with humor.

During the First World War, her husband was drafted for the duration despite his age, and in 1916 her son, Noël, volunteered and served at the front as a liaison agent to the end of the war. After the war, she continued writing novels but also some nonfiction potboilers—about *Pompadour and *Du Barry and extinct Parisian castles, a history of love, and so forth. She was falling out of fashion and becoming dated. None of her works dealt with, for example, independent, unmarried, "unsexed" career women, the "new" women. Love and marriage and their attendant problems remained the center of her universe. She produced some worthy pieces—e.g., *Perséphone* (1920), *Les Lampes voilées* (1922), *Le Bouclier d'Alexandre* (1922), *Un Drame de famille* (1925), *L'Ennemi intime* (1931), and *Gérard et Delphine* (2 vols., 1936–38)—but they have never drawn the attention of literary and social scholars largely because, unlike the case with her early works and the women's movement around 1900, they were not on the cutting edge. In 1923, nevertheless, she was named to the jury for the Prix Flaubert and in 1935 to the jury for the new prize for women poets named for the poet ◀ Renée Vivien (née Pauline Tarn, 1877–1909), whom she had strongly encouraged. In 1938, she received the Prix Barthou from the Académie Française.

Julien Tinayre faded to little more than a shadowy presence. He continued to live with her and had a workshop in the country home. In 1923, he died suddenly at age 63. In later life, she still divided her time between the retreat at Grosrouvre and an apartment on the rue de Lille. Frédéric Lefèvre visited her in 1931 and found her radiating a simple, elegant charm. Her surroundings exhibited a refined taste. She said she read a great deal of foreign and ancient literature. As for current authors, she preferred those different from her and highly praised Georges Bernanos, whom she regarded as "dominating" present literature. As the years advanced, she grew more contemplative and again interested in religion. Following the Second World War, she died on August 23, 1948, at her country home. She was given a private funeral and was buried at the village church.

Of Marcelle Tinayre's private life, little is known. In 1892 or 1893, while tending children and beginning to write seriously, she penned a long letter to her mother in which she said she needed the passion she no longer experienced in her marriage, and hinted that she would seek fulfillment elsewhere. Her mother replied, advising against infidelity as dangerous and rife with pain and sorrow. Their alienation dated from about this time. Her mother found her views too feminist, smacking of "anarchism," and refused to attend her lectures. Over the years Marcelle sought reconciliation at times, but without full success. When her mother died in 1926—Marcelle cared for her toward the end—she was left with painful regrets, for she sincerely admired her.

It seems all but certain she engaged in extramarital affairs, although when and with whom may become known only when her correspondence is opened in 2048. Her son, when interviewed after her death, said her books clearly reflected it. In her unpublished memoir, she spoke of a "double life," but without elaborating. To Frédéric Lefèvre she spoke of "duality," framing it as a personality trait. She said she loved youth and gaiety and good living, but that she had a "contained and ardent interior life" out of which came books with tragic themes. Her "double life," in short, appears composed of two elements: 1) a conventional marriage behind which she concealed infidelity, and 2) a personality showing to the world features quite different from what she experienced within her. A fairly obvious conclusion can be drawn, namely, that it was the effect of these contradictions working on a fervid imagination that made her so prolific a writer.

Tinayre was a daring feminist by the standards of the time, which in France were modest. She did not seriously challenge institutions and ideologies, although personally she favored socialism. Her audience being mainly women whose husbands might be looking over their shoulders, she had to be careful not to shock unduly lest she damage sales. (She sold well; in 1917 *La Rebelle* was in its 73rd edition.) The core and goal of her novels is the examination of love. She accepted the prevailing belief in her society regarding the nature of women, namely, that their aim in life is to love deeply and be loved well in return. She considered this simply stated proposition from many perspectives, however, dissecting its complexities, its ambiguities and pitfalls. Central to her writing is the tension between instinct and social convention, nature and nurture, an exploration of which reveals how complex are the choices forced upon women.

On the other hand, the theses (so to speak) that she advanced are fairly uncomplicated. She sought an end to the double standard in sexual matters. Women have a right to passion, just as do men. Here she violated a long-prevailing taboo in women's writing, i.e., the legitimizing and description (although not in her case graphically) of feminine sexual desires. Her heroines are legitimized because they believe that they have found true love. Error in love carries no shame. The ending of the double standard, however, is itself a product of the equalization of rights between men and women. Equalization is of paramount importance. There can be no true, honest existence for women unless they too, like men, may be educated and achieve autonomy, a full selfhood. Women will be emancipated only when love and autonomy are reconciled—no simple undertaking, as she demonstrated time and again. She wanted an end to suffering and renunciation as special female virtues: "The religion of human suffering is a snare." At the same time, she was quite conventional in holding that equality did not mean that men and women are identical. They have particular natures and proclivities and duties. What is needed is full, honest, mutual respect. Without it, women are doomed to continue to be treated as inferior creatures—a situation that is unfulfilling to *both* sexes.

The novelist is a haunted house.

—**Marcelle Tinayre**

Tinayre's style has been much praised. Like most female novelists of the time, she wrote to earn a living, not to dazzle, explore special techniques, or win prizes and election to the Académie. Consequently, her prose is direct and unpretentious. It carries one along, is seldom boring or unduly digressive. It is bold, virile, and combative but not violent. She also exhibits grace, lightness, ease of expression, a sense of proportion, and writes cadenced sentences appealing to the mind and ear. Plots are not complicated, although they tend to meander. The interest is in the characters, their psychology and reactions to situations. She was gifted with an eye for nature and life; some of her best work is set in the countryside of her native Corrèze.

When the feminist movement took wing in the latter 20th century, Tinayre's work drew renewed interest. In this context, probably the most commented-upon novel has been *La Rebelle* (1905), a depiction of self-realization. The heroine is an independent thinker who by sincerity and integrity raises herself and her lover to a higher plane of happiness when they achieve equality in their relationship. Feminism and social problems are dealt with in theses which are bold for their time albeit conventional by modern standards. In the public sphere, the heroine wins equality and autonomy, but within the home she freely accepts her husband's preeminence: "She has not the courage of her liberty. . . . Her one desire and her one regret is love." Jennifer Waelti-Walters notes that modern readers would find that she "relinquishes too much of her autonomy in the bedroom, but at least Josanne is allowed to be whole"—which was Tinayre's message to women of all degrees in the society of her day.

La Maison du péché (1902) secured Tinayre's reputation. The eminent critic Émile Faguet called it "almost incomparable." It is a tragic tale turning upon, as she put it, "rights of the flesh versus rights of the soul"—love versus religious duty, a time-honored theme in French literature. The heroine is a free-spirited, unreligious young widow, the hero a young man raised in the puritanical tradition of Jansenist Roman Catholicism. In the end he cannot overcome the conflict and commits suicide. When the French translation of James Joyce's *Critical Writings* appeared in 1966, *Le Figaro littéraire* was astonished to find that it was the only novel to which Joyce devoted a long review, and moreover, it was by far the most laudatory. As the editors point out, two elements drew Joyce's attention: 1) the plot resembles one he was developing for *Stephen Hero* and *A Portrait of the Artist as a Young Man*; and 2) the style conforms to what he believed it should be, namely, an expression of the subject, not the author. *Figaro* asked if it were not time for a reassessment of Tinayre. It proved to be a long time coming.

At her death, *Le Monde* called her "a classic writer," "a great novelist." Reflecting on her life in her unpublished memoir, she spoke in terms most writers of fiction can echo: "The novelist is a haunted house. The beings born of me and which no longer were of me, who were realized possibilities, transposed realities—[they] began to inhabit me. I freed myself from these phantoms. And that is all I did for my whole life."

SOURCES:

Duclaus, Mary. *Twentieth-Century French Writers (Reviews and Reminiscences)*. NY: Scribner, 1920.

Ferlin, Patricia. *Femmes d'encrier*. [Etrepilly]: Christian de Bartillat, 1995, pp. 145–185.

Holmes, Diana. *French Women's Writing, 1848–1994*. London: Althone, 1996.

Joyce, James. *The Critical Writings of James Joyce*. Ellsworth Mason and Richard Ellmann, eds. NY: Viking, 1959.

Lefèvre, Frédéric. *Une heure avec . . .* 6th ser. Paris: Ernest Flammarion, 1933.

"La Maison du péché," in *Dictionnaire des oeuvres de tous les temps et de tous les pays*. Laffont-Bompiane, ed. Paris: Société d'édition de dictionnaires et encyclopédias, 1953.

Martin-Mamy, Eugène. *Marcelle Tinayre*. "Les Célébrités d'aujourd'hui," vol. 6, pt. 1. Paris: E. Sansot, 1909.

"Mort de Marcelle Tinayre," in *Le Monde*. August 26, 1948.

Niderst, A. "Tinayre, Marcelle, née Chasteau," in *Dictionnaire des littératures de langue française*. J.P. Beaumarchais, Daniel Couty, and Alain B. Rey, eds. Paris: Bordas, 1984.

Rogers, Juliette M. "Tinayre, Marcelle (1877–1948)," in Eva Martin Sartori, ed., *The Feminist Encyclopedia of French Literature*. Westport, CT: Greenwood Press, 1999.

Stephens, Winifred [Whale]. *French Novelists of Today*. 2nd ser. NY: John Lane, 1915.

Waelti-Walters, Jennifer. *Feminist Novelists of the Belle Epoque: Love as a Lifestyle*. Bloomington, IN: Indiana University Press, 1990.

———. "Forgotten Women of France, 1900–1914," in *Atlantis* (Canada) Vol. 11, no. 1, 1985, pp. 1–6.

Woodbridge, Benjamin Matthew. "The Novels and the Ideas of Madame Marcelle Tinayre," in *Bulletin of the University of Texas*. January 25, 1915, pp. 3–24.

SUGGESTED READING:

Flat, Paul. *Nos femmes de lettres*. Paris: Perrin, 1909.

Tissot, Ernest. *Nouvelles Princesses de lettres*. Vol. 2. Paris: Fontemoing, 1911.

COLLECTIONS:

Paris: Dossier "Marcelle Tinayre," Bibliothèque Marguerite Durand.

Tulle (Corrèze): Fonds "Marcelle Tinayre," Archives départementales de la Corrèze.

David S. Newhall,
Pottinger Distinguished Professor of History Emeritus,
Centre College, and author of
Clemenceau: A Life at War (1991)

Tinayre, Marguerite (1831–?)

French educator and political radical who was condemned for her role in the Paris Commune (1871). Name variations: (pseudonym) Jules Paty. Pronunciation: mar-GREET tee-NAIR. Born Marguerite-Victoire Guerrier at Issoire (Puy-de-Dôme) on March 6, 1831, to a middle-class family; date and place of death unknown; married a notary's clerk named Tinayre (died 1871); children: one daughter and four sons, including engraver (Jean-)Julien (1859–1923, who married novelist Marcelle Tinayre), and painter (Jean-Paul-)Louis (b. 1861).

Licensed as an elementary teacher (1856); published two novels (1864–69?); founded the Société des Équitables de Paris (1867); was active in the Commune as a school inspector (1871); was in exile in Switzerland, Saxony, and Hungary as a governess and teacher (1871–79); condemned in absentia to deportation (1874); sentence remitted (1879); back in Paris (1880).

Marguerite-Victoire Guerrier was born on March 6, 1831, to a middle-class family in Issoire (Puy-de-Dôme) in central France. She adopted "advanced" ideas from her youth, doubtless stimulated by the hopes and disappointments of the Revolution of 1848. A good student, in 1856 at Lyons she received an elementary teacher's license. She married a self-effacing notary's clerk, Tinayre (d. 1871), and ran a private school (*école libre*) in Issoire for a time until they moved to Paris. There she organized private and "*protestante*" schools in the Paris suburbs of Neuilly, Bondy, Noisy-le-Sec, and Gentilly. Tinayre was reported to be a woman of good morals and "unusual energy and quickness," but a police note also cited her as "giving vent to her reckless imagination and having always professed advanced ideas." She shared these ideas with her brother Antoine-Ambroise Guerrier and a brother-in-law, Jules Babick, "a slightly crazy adherent of the Fusionist religion," writes historian **Edith Thomas**.

From the latter 1850s through the 1860s, Tinayre had a daughter and four sons. Under the pen name "Jules Paty" she also published two novels, *La Marguerite* (1864) and *Un Rêve de femme* (n.d.), turgid tearjerkers which were completely ignored. According to Thomas, *La Marguerite* was dedicated to *George Sand, who had encouraged Tinayre. It contained some good descriptions of Paris poverty and portrayed the Sisters of Saint Vincent de Paul as angels of mercy—an indication she was not clearly an anticlerical. Her story of peasants from Auvergne and Issoire struggling in Paris ends happily when they return to their villages. *Un Rêve de femme* (A Womanly Dream), a tragic tale of idealism, adultery, and suicide, forsook Sandian romanticism for realism, "if realism consists in seeking the ideal of art in the sincere imitation of nature," she wrote in her long-winded manner, "particularly if this inquiry into the physical order should lead to the discovery of harmonies and world balances of which religion and morality are merely formulas brought within the scope of a human understanding obscured by ignorance, tainted by passion, or atrophied by poverty." Tinayre revealed herself as a moralist skeptical about current morality and religion. Writes Thomas, she wanted to "put women on their guard against 'their pointless aspirations, their groundless worries,' and to draw their attention to the necessity of 'physical harmony' in marriage, a delicate subject that was scarcely spoken of in 1860." Tinayre expressed revolutionary sympathies while nevertheless mocking much of vintage 1848 revolutionary verbiage. She deplored the ignorance and selfishness of the masses yet expressed confidence that education

would triumph over them: "let the light shine into all darkened minds and you will see to what heights men can rise."

Like many of her generation, she looked to organization to help raise the masses, particularly mutual aid societies. In 1867, with some help from former Saint-Simonians, she founded a consumer cooperative, the Société des Équitables de Paris. Its meetings were held at the home of a shoemaker named Henry on the rue des Vieilles-Haudriettes. Tinayre got the society to join the Federation of Workers' Societies and Karl Marx's new International Workingmen's Association. In 1868, the police observed her speaking at meetings defending "socialist and anti-religious ideas." During the Franco-Prussian War and the siege of Paris (July 1870–January 1871), she continued advocating left-wing causes.

Not surprisingly, she joined the revolt (March–May 1871) of the Paris Commune against the government, currently headquartered at Versailles. The Communards believed Paris' sacrifices during the siege were unappreciated, and they feared the new Third Republic (1870–1940) would be swept away by the presently resurgent monarchists. The Commune's leaders thought secularization of education was critical to their cause. They named Marguerite Tinayre inspector of girls' schools in the 12th arrondissement. With public feeling running high against the Roman Catholic schools, in late March she informed the mother superior of the Corbes Passage School at Bercy that she must address all requests or complaints to her. Two weeks later, the mayor of the 12th accompanied by a dozen women expelled the nuns, who took refuge at Charenton. The Catholic schools' situation remained tense, and some violence by both sides occurred around the city.

When the Versailles troops broke into the city during Bloody Week, they arrested Tinayre on May 26 during a sweep of a rebel quarter and marched her in the rain to the Châtelet prison. Her husband, who had fought the Prussians but was opposed to the Commune, followed her there to try to defend her. She attempted to warn him off. The young officer and a corporal conducting a drumhead court-martial ignored all explanations, arrested him, and sent him away with others to be summarily shot. Marguerite, released the next day "miraculously" (as she later wrote), fled with her five children to Geneva. Her brother Antoine escaped to London, where he remained the rest of his life.

She continued her revolutionary activity, at least for a time. On March 5, 1873, *Le Pays* reported that she was seen presiding at a "civil baptism" and giving children names of revolutionaries: Danton, Millière, Flourens. From Geneva, she moved to Saxony, where she became a governess for a large family. In the meantime, on January 9, 1874, the Third Court-Martial convicted her *in absentia* of "having been in communication with the leaders of insurrectionary groups, and for having involved herself in public functions with no right to do so." It sentenced her to "deportation to a fortified place," meaning the prison colony at New Caledonia. Likewise, *André Léo, ◄⚜ Anna Jaclard, *Elizabeth Dmitrieff, and brother Antoine were condemned *in absentia* to deportation on similar charges.

Marguerite and her children eventually settled in Budapest, where she became a highly respected private teacher of girls. In 1879, she learned that women condemned by the extraordinary tribunals could return to France. She asked for a three months' residency in Paris but was denied on the grounds that the amnesty excluded her because in Geneva she had been involved in "socialistic and internationalistic intrigues." In reply, the French consul-general in Hungary, Comte de Bourgoing, wrote a laudatory letter saying her associations were exemplary and that "her bearing and irreproachable conduct have won her the respect of all." He admitted she was a convict, but one who had thoroughly amended her ways and hence should not be considered "a dangerous person."

Agonized by her situation, she wrote to *La Marseillaise* on October 15, 1879, putting her case before the public. She had made no secret that she had been "banished," but Budapest society had accepted that she was "a woman who had perhaps been led astray into extreme causes but definitely was a respectable woman." She still had two children to raise and two to support, while her eldest was working but would soon be drafted. She was a widow in fact but not in law since there was no formal documentation of her husband's death. If she were to ask for a pardon, it would be an admission of guilt: "And guilty I am not, nor can I desire to appear such before children to whom I owe the example of strength and constancy in the face of ill fortune." Moreover, if she returned, would she regain her civil rights, without which she could not teach?

Her eloquent plea crossed a slow mail from Paris bringing word that on September 3 the chief of the Sûreté Général had authorized her return for three months. Later she learned that

on November 27 her remaining sentence had been remitted.

Tinayre returned to France. On March 30, 1880, she wrote another appeal, to *La France*, explaining her plight. She was forbidden to teach, was in dire distress, and needed help to prove she was legally a widow so that her eldest son could be exempted from the draft in order to support the family. What then transpired is unknown, as there is no published account of her life thereafter. It is certain, however, that she was alive at least as late as 1889, when her son Julien married Marcelle Chasteau, who won fame as the novelist *Marcelle Tinayre**.

Marguerite Tinayre's life typified that of a significant cohort of her generation. Angered and disillusioned by the failure of the Revolution of 1848 to establish a permanent republic, and chafing under the surveillance of the Second Empire (1852–70), they sought to bring to revolutionary zeal a dose of "scientific" realism and organization. The doomed Paris Commune tried to establish an orderly, mildly socialistic regime but was still entranced, as 1848 had been, by the vision of revolution as the gateway to nearly instantaneous liberty, equality, and social peace. Its adherents, although long reviled by conservatives, left a memory of brave idealists who had suffered death, imprisonment, or exile for their beliefs, naïve as those beliefs may have appeared to their descendants.

SOURCES:
Dictionnaire biographique du mouvement ouvrier français, 1864–71. Sous la direction de Jean Maitron. Paris: Éditions Ouvrières, 1964—.
Pelletan, Camille. "Le Châtelet (Madame Tinayre)," in *La Semaine de mai.* Paris: Maurice Dreyfous, 1880, pp. 231–236.
Thomas, Edith. *The Woman Incendiaries.* Trans. James and Starr Atkinson. NY: George Braziller, 1966 (translation of *Les Pétroleuses.* Paris: Gallimard, 1963).

SUGGESTED READING:
Edwards, Stewart. *The Paris Commune 1871.* London: Eyre & Spottiswoode, 1976.
Horne, Alistair. *The Fall of Paris; The Siege and the Commune, 1870–71.* NY: St. Martin's Press, 1965.
Lissagaray, Prosper Olivier. *History of the Commune of 1871.* Trans. by *Eleanor Marx Aveling.* NY: Monthly Review Press, 1967 (1886).
Osmin, Léon. *Figures de jadis: Les Pionniers obscurs du socialisme.* Paris: Éditions "Nouveau Prométhée," 1934.
Tombs, Robert. *The War Against Paris 1871.* Cambridge: Cambridge University Press, 1981.
Zévaès, Alexandre. *Les Proscrits de la Commune.* Paris: Bureau d'éditions, 1936.

COLLECTIONS:
Paris: Archives nationales, BB 24/852, no. 732; Archives de la Ministère de la Guerre, 3e conseil, no. 1416.

David S. Newhall,
Pottinger Distinguished Professor of History Emeritus,
Centre College, and author of
Clemenceau: A Life at War (1991)

Jaclard, Anna.
See
Kovalevskaya,
Sophia for
sidebar.

Tingley, Katherine (1847–1929)

American theosophist leader. Name variations: Katherine Westcott; Katherine Westcott Tingley. Born Katherine Augusta Westcott on July 6, 1847, in New-bury, Massachusetts; died on July 11, 1929, in Vis-ingsö, Sweden; daughter of James P.L. Westcott (a merchant and hotelkeeper) and Susan Ordway (Chase) Westcott; attended public schools and briefly attended convent school in Montreal, Canada; married Richard Henry Cook (a printer), in 1867 (mar-riage dissolved after two months); married George W. Parent (a railroad investigator), around 1880 (di-vorced around 1887); married Philo Buchanan Tin-gley (a mechanical engineer), on April 25, 1888.

Founded Society for Mercy (1887); founded "Do-Good Mission" in Manhattan (1890s); was named Outer Head of Esoteric Section, Theosophical Society in America (1896); toured with Theosophical Society world crusade (1896); founded Point Loma Theosophical community in California (1897); found-ed International Brotherhood League (1897); formed War Relief Corps (1898).

Katherine Tingley was born in Newbury, Massachusetts, on July 6, 1847, the only daughter among three children of **Susan Chase Westcott** and James P.L. Westcott, who later gave up his lumber business to work as a hotelkeeper in near-by Newburyport. Katherine was educated in pub-lic schools in Massachusetts and Alexandria, Vir-ginia, where the family lived for a short time during the Civil War. She then briefly attended a convent school in Montreal, Canada, leaving it in 1867 to marry a printer named Richard Harry Cook. The marriage lasted less than two months. Her next years are poorly documented, but it is possible that for some period of time she traveled with a theatrical company. At some point she ar-rived in New York City, where around 1880 she married an investigator for the New York Elevat-ed Railway, George W. Parent. Around this time she also became drawn to charitable and spiritual-ist endeavors, and in 1887 founded the Society of Mercy to promote hospital and prison visitation. Her marriage to Parent ended sometime before April 25, 1888, when she married Philo Buchanan Tingley. Although Philo, a mechanical engineer who worked for a steamship company, would not figure prominently in her later public life, their union proved more lasting than her earlier efforts.

Tingley established the "Do-Good Mission" on the East Side of Manhattan early in the 1890s, and to support this charity and the Society of Mercy began giving occasional psychometric readings. Psychometrics experts, who along with mediums and séances became increasingly popu-lar during the late 19th and early 20th centuries, claimed that by touching something belonging to someone, or by being near a person, they could divine information about the subject. (On the other side of the Atlantic, poet W.B. Yeats en-gaged in similar spiritualist experiments.) In the winter of 1892–93, Tingley met William Quan Judge, who, with Madame *****Helena Blavatsky** and Henry Steel Olcott, had founded the Theo-sophical Society in 1875. The society, whose aim was the promotion of international solidarity and whose motto was "there is no higher religion than truth," mixed the occult, Buddhism and Hinduism in teachings Blavatsky claimed she had received telepathically from a secret Egyptian brotherhood. After Blavatsky's death in 1891, Judge attempted to wrest control of the Theo-sophical Society from her appointed successor, *****Annie Besant**. He lost this battle about a year after meeting Tingley. In 1895, he founded what he called the Theosophical Society in America, and she became one of his most ardent followers.

Katherine Tingley

Leadership of the Theosophical Society in America consisted not only of a presidential office but also of an "inner headship of the Esoteric Section" (supposedly a brotherhood of Tibetan holy men, although they were never seen) and an "outer headship of the Esoteric Section," which for obvious reasons was a more publicly powerful position, and exceeded in authority even the presidency of the society. Judge died in 1896, and certain passages he supposedly wrote in a secret diary, as well as her own receipt of messages from him from beyond the grave, pointed to Tingley as being his choice for Outer Head of the Esoteric Section. Duly appointed, Tingley soon embarked on a world tour to publicize and proselytize for the Theosophical Society in America (and to steal some thunder, converts, and credibility from Besant and her larger Theosophical Society). Along with five other renowned theosophists, she traveled in the British Isles, Europe, the Middle East, and Asia, visiting religious and occult sites including Kilarney Castle in Ireland and various temples in Greece. She claimed to have searched for and consulted with a mahatma while traveling in Tibet, an honor that strengthened her right to hold the outer headship of the Esoteric Section (which some in the society at home were debating). As well, these visits may have stimulated her own ideas for founding a theosophist community in the United States.

Upon her return to America, Tingley laid a cornerstone on February 24, 1897, at Point Loma, California, a dramatic site overlooking San Diego Bay. Later that year she founded the International Brotherhood League, which through a six-point program was intended to promote fellowship between the races and assist prisoners, the working class, and poor women thought to be "fallen." Among its first projects was a summer camp in New Jersey for children from tenements in New York City. In 1898, she wrote a new constitution for the Theosophical Society in America, one which merged it with the International Brotherhood League to create the Universal Brotherhood and Theosophical Society, of which, as "Leader and Official Head," she had complete control for life. Tingley directed the movement towards social causes as well; that year, she galvanized theosophist volunteers into a War Relief Corps to aid hospitalized Spanish-American War veterans at Point Montauk, Long Island. She was also active in antivivisection causes and opposed capital punishment, and later, when the First World War threatened, acted on her pacifist beliefs to try to prevent America from entering the war.

In 1900, Tingley officially established her headquarters at Point Loma. She concentrated on raising funds to support the Utopian community, which, with its exotic and eclectic architecture (generally wood painted white to resemble marble, leading to its frequent description as "the white city"), attracted both theosophist seekers and the curious from around the world. At the community's most popular time, some 600 people lived there. Interested in the arts as well as in social concerns, Tingley guided Point Loma's development as a cultural center. Among the many programs established were theater, music, and artist-in-residence programs; forestry and horticultural programs; and a print shop, which produced theosophical literature. (Tingley edited two theosophical publications, the weekly *Century Path* which became the *Theosophical Path* [1911–29], and *Raja Yoga Messenger*, a monthly periodical [1912–29].) Silk, school uniforms, and batik fabrics were created at the "Woman's Exchange and Mart." Perhaps best known, however, was the Raja Yoga school and college established at the community, a highly structured holistic educational venture that stressed a balance between spiritual, mental, and physical development. Three hundred children (including a number of impoverished Cuban children who were educated free of charge) lived at the school with about sixty teachers. Tingley attempted to establish similar schools in Germany, Sweden, Cuba, England, Massachusetts, and Minnesota, but none remained in existence long. She also set up the School for the Revival of the Lost Mysteries of Antiquity at Point Loma, which was later transferred to the community and in 1919 was chartered by the State of California as the Theosophical University at Point Loma.

She grew so focused on the Point Loma community that her leadership of the Universal Brotherhood and Theosophical Society suffered as a result, and in the early 1920s a number of her followers left either to rejoin Besant's group or to join a newly created, third theosophist organization. Tingley has also been described as possessing such an "overwhelming" personality that many of her close subordinates were unable to work with her for any lengthy period of time, and financial problems plagued Point Loma. Nonetheless, those who lived in communities around it were always highly supportive of its programs and of Tingley. In 1925, the wife of one of her followers successfully sued Tingley for alienation of affection, and she began spending much of her time in Europe. Severely injured in an automobile accident in Germany in 1929, she died on July 11, 1929, at the theosophist community at Visingsö, Sweden. (Some of her ashes were buried at Point Loma.) The Point Loma colony dwindled steadily for 13 more years, at which time its few remaining adherents moved to another site.

SOURCES:

James, Edward T., ed. *Notable American Women, 1607–1950*. Cambridge, MA: The Belknap Press of Harvard University, 1971.

McHenry, Robert, ed. *Famous American Women*. NY: Dover, 1980.

Lolly Ockerstrom,
freelance writer,
Washington, D.C.

Ting Ling (1904–1985).

See Ding Ling.

Tinker, Alice (1886–1968).

See McLean, Alice.

Tinné, Alexandrine (1839–1869)

Dutch explorer in Africa. Name variations: Alexandrine Tinne. Born Alexandrine Petronella Francina Tinné at The Hague, the Netherlands, on October 17, 1839; murdered on August 1, 1869; daughter of Philip F. Tinné (a merchant) and Baroness Van Steengracht-Capellan.

On October 17, 1839, Alexandrine Tinné was born at The Hague to Philip F. Tinné, a Dutch merchant, and the Dutch **Baroness Van Steengracht-Capellan**, daughter of Admiral van Capellan. With the passing of her father when she was five, Tinné became one of the richest heiresses in the country, with the prospects of a brilliant marriage and an enviable social position. Instead, when she turned 18, she decided to travel and left The Hague. She never returned. Tinné made journeys to Norway, Italy, and the East, and when in Egypt she ascended the Nile. A return trip to the Nile regions in 1861 was made in company with her mother and aunt. Her interest in African exploration, developed while she was in Egypt, fueled her resolve to devote her fortune and energies to the cause of geographical discovery, to report on the slave trade, and to help the oppressed people of the "dark continent."

The party departed Cairo on January 9, 1862, made a short stay at Khartum and then, notes one historian, "ascended the White Nile to a point above Gondokoro." After exploring a portion of the Sobat, they returned in November to Khartum. Joined by Dr. H. Steudner and Baron Theodor von Heuglin, the women headed for the Bahr-el-Ghazal during February 1863 to "explore that region and ascertain how far westward the Nile basin extended; also to investigate the reports of a vast lake in Central Africa eastwards of those already known—reports referring in all probability to the lake-like expanses of the middle Congo."

The journey, which took them to the borders of the Niam-Niam country, saw all travelers terribly ill with fever. After Steudner's death in April, Tinné lost her mother in June, followed by her aunt in Khartum, to which the party returned in July 1864. Tinné made her way back to Cairo, and the geographical and scientific results yielded by her expedition were of great importance in adding to the knowledge of remote regions. *Plantes Tinnéennes*, which detailed some of the plants Tinné had encountered, was published in 1867 by T. Kotschy and J. Peyritsch.

Tinné passed the following four years living in Cairo and making trips to Algeria, Tunisia, and additional locations of the Mediterranean. She began her last and fatal expedition in January 1869, departing with a caravan from Tripoli intending to reach the upper Nile. En route from Murzuk to Ghat on August 1, she and her three European attendants were murdered, the caravan plundered, and the bodies of the victims left unburied in the sands. She was killed "by Tuareg in league with her escort, who believed that her iron water tanks were filled with gold." Tinné would be remembered not only for her own voyages but for her generous assistance to other scientific travelers.

Tinsley, Pauline (1928—)

English operatic soprano. Born on March 23, 1928, in Wigan, England; studied in Manchester and at the London Opera Center.

Soprano Pauline Tinsley studied with Dillon in Manchester and with ***Joan Cross** at the London Opera Center, as well as with Keeler, Henderson, and Turner. She made her debut in London in Rossini's *Desdemona* in 1951. After joining the Welsh National Opera, Tinsley sang Elsa in Wagner's *Lohengrin*, Susanna in Mozart's *Le nozze di Figaro*, the title roles in *Aïda* and *Turandot*, and Lady Macbeth in Verdi's *Macbeth*. She joined the Sadler's Wells Opera in 1963, where she sang the Countess in *Figaro*, Fiordiligi in *Cosi fan tutte*, Donna Elvira in *Don Giovanni*, Queen Elizabeth in Donizetti's

Maria Stuarda, and Leonore in Beethoven's *Fidelio*. Tinsley toured widely, performing in Berlin, Hamburg, Amsterdam, Zurich, Verona, and the United States. She was considered particularly memorable as Lady Billows in Britten's *Albert Herring* at Covent Garden in 1989. Tinsley's other repertory roles include Queen of the Night, Anna Bolena, Leonora (in *Trovatore* and *Forza*), Brunnhilde, Zerlina, Donna Anna, Kundry, Kostelnicka, and Elektra.

Elizabeth Shostak, M.A.,
Cambridge, Massachusetts

Tipo, Maria (1931—)

Italian pianist known for her Romantic performances. Born in Naples in 1931.

Maria Tipo studied with her mother **Ersilia Cavallo**, a gifted pianist who had studied with Feruccio Buson and given the Naples premiere of the Tchaikovsky First Piano Concerto. At age 17, in 1948, Tipo won first prize in the Geneva Piano Competition. At the Queen Elizabeth competition in Brussels in 1952, she came in third but was heard by Artur Rubinstein who assured her that she would have a great career. Rubinstein arranged a recital for Tipo in Paris, where she was heard by the famous impresario Sol Hurok, who launched her American career. Her U.S. tour of 1955 was a great success, but she did not return to America until 1991. In Europe, she built up her reputation and repertoire with stylish performances of Mozart, Bach and Scarlatti. In an age of "authentic" period-instrument performances, her Romantic approach seemed anachronistic to some listeners and critics, but for many enthusiastic fans Tipo could do no wrong. Some went so far as to call her "the Neapolitan Horowitz."

SOURCES:

Kozinn, Allan. "Maria Tipo, Pianist," in *The New York Times*. November 9, 1991, p. 16.

Michener, Charles. "The Phantom of the Piano," in *New York*. Vol. 26, no. 38. September 27, 1993, pp. 50–54.

Schonberg, Harold C. "Maria Tipo is Back. Why Did She Dally?," in *The New York Times*. November 3, 1991, section 2, pp. 26, 40.

John Haag,
Athens, Georgia

Tipper, Constance (1894–1995)

English metallurgist. Born Constance Figg Elam in 1894; died on December 14, 1995, in Penrith, in northwest England; obtained doctorate from Cambridge University; married George Tipper (a geologist), in 1928 (died 1947).

During World War II, Britain began searching for a reason as to why some Liberty merchant vessels were cracking like glass while at sea. These vessels, used to replace American ships that had been sunk by the Nazis, were floating Russian roulette games. Some would sink, others would not, and there seemed to be no rhyme or reason. Members of the merchant marine were beginning to refuse to work on the ships. The military suspected the flaw was in the engineering design or the welding. Constance Tipper disagreed. The problem was brittle steel, she said, and set about to create the "Tipper test," a way to determine the brittleness of metal. As a researcher at Cambridge at the time, she was one of the few women working in the field of metallurgy. Because of Tipper, the British merchant marine's Liberty vessels remained afloat. She died in 1995 at age 101.

Tipton, Billy (1914–1989)

Cross-dressing American jazz pianist, saxophonist, and founder of the Billy Tipton Trio, whose sexual identity was not discovered until her death. Born Dorothy Lucille Tipton in Oklahoma City, Oklahoma, on December 29, 1914; died in Spokane, Washington, on January 21, 1989; daughter of George Tipton (an aviator) and Reggie Tipton; studied organ, piano, and saxophone in school; married at least five times, including Betty Cox and Kitty Kelly; children: (adopted three sons with Kitty Kelly) John, Scott, and William.

When Billy Tipton died, one obituary writer observed, "He gave up everything. There were certain rules and regulations in those days if you were going to be a musician." In fact, Billy Tipton had given up far more than any fellow musicians suspected. Notes Leslie Gourse, "There was an unwritten code in the jazz world, that women just didn't get hired." Tipton changed her name and her clothes, acquired a Social Security card as a man, and traded in a traditional life in order to play the music she loved. "To pass as a man," notes Dinitia Smith in *The New York Times*, "Dorothy bound her breasts with Ace bandages and wore a prosthetic device. Later she would tell people that she wore the bandages because of a childhood accident in which her ribs were broken." So well kept was Tipton's secret that the women he married maintained that they had no knowledge that their husband had not been born a man.

Born on December 29, 1914, Tipton grew up in Kansas City and loved jazz. She learned to play the piano, organ, and sax, but quickly concluded that a woman could never be successful in the jazz world. Assuming the persona of a man, Tipton added his tenor voice to a group known as the Banner Cavaliers. He performed with the Jack Teagarden, Russ Carlyle, and Scott Cameron bands.

In 1951, the musician formed the Billy Tipton Trio, performing as the group's leader with slicked-back hair and white dinner jacket. In a style which had tints of Benny Goodman's trio and quartet, the group played hits like "Exactly Like You," "All of Me," and "It's Only a Paper Moon." Two albums—*Sweet Georgia Brown* and *Billy Tipton Plays Hi-Fi on Piano*—were put out by the trio. One member of the group, singer and bass player Kenny Richards, would later note that he never had a clue that Tipton was anything but a man.

The women in Tipton's life were equally out of the know. Among them was 18-year-old **Betty Cox** whom Tipton met in 1946; they lived together as man and wife, complete with a sexual relationship, for seven years. Coming from a sheltered upbringing, Cox had never been exposed to discussions about sex. "Women didn't go around undressed," she noted. "You wore a robe. You didn't leave the lights on when you had sex." Tipton later met **Kitty Kelly** (now Kitty Oakes), a stripper, to whom he would write, "I love you with everything that is in me, and I only hope that I can make you happy for the rest of my life." They shared a home for many years and together adopted three sons. Writes Smith, "By all accounts, Tipton was an ideal father, a Scout master who loved to go on camping trips with his boys." When the couple separated due to growing tensions in the marriage, the boys went to live with Tipton. Following Billy's death, his son William would say, "He was the only father I ever knew. . . . He was there for us."

In his professional life, during 1958 Tipton turned down an opportunity for the big time—a recording contract and offer to open for Liberace in Reno. Diane Middlebrook, author of *Suits Me: The Double Life of Billy Tipton*, notes that Tipton may have been concerned that wider visibility might bring with it the threat of exposure. Settling in Spokane, he played jazz and was employed in a theatrical agency where he worked as a booker and met Kitty Kelly. By the time of the couple's separation in 1981, Smith notes that he was "suffering from arthritis, emphysema and ulcers. What Ms. Middlebrook calls his 'lifelong trait of avoidance' had prevented him from going to a doctor."

Tipton died at the age of 74 on January 21, 1989, of a perforated ulcer. Middlebrook writes that by the time of death Tipton had removed the sex-concealing measures used throughout life. The paramedics arriving on the scene ripped open Tipton's shirt and asked his son William, "Did your father ever have a sex change?" Notes Middlebrook: "Billy had prepared to emerge from behind his screen like the Wizard of Oz, to dissolve the magic into wisdom, revealing by her nakedness in death that 'the difference' between men and women is largely in the eye of the beholder."

SOURCES:

Sadie, Stanley, ed. *New Grove Dictionary of Music and Musicians*. 20 vols. NY: Macmillan, 1980.
Smith, Dinitia. "One False Note in a Musician's Life," in *The New York Times*. June 2, 1998.

SUGGESTED READING:

Middlebrook, Diane. *Suits Me: The Double Life of Billy Tipton*. 1998.

Tirconnell, queen of.

See MacDonald, Finula (fl. 1569–1592).

Tirol, countess of.

See Margaret Maultasch (1318–1369).

Tirzah

Biblical woman. The youngest of the five daughters of Zelophehad, of the Manasseh tribe; sister of Milcah, Mahlah, Noah and Hoglah.

When Zelophehad died without any male heirs, Tirzah and her four older sisters (*Mahlah, *Noah, Hoglah, and *Milcah) requested permission from Moses to inherit their father's property. Moses granted their request, stipulating only that the sisters marry within their father's tribe. Moses' judgment concerning the inheritance eventually became general law.

Tito, Jovanka Broz (1924—)

Croatian revolutionary fighter and first lady of Yugoslavia (1953–80). Name variations: Jovanka Broz; Jovanka Budisavljevic Broz; Jovanka Budisavljevic. Born Jovanka Budisavljevic on December 7, 1924, in rural Croatia near the Bosnian border; daughter of Miko Budisavljevic (a laborer); attended the University of Belgrade; became third wife of Josip Broz Tito (1892–1980, president of Yugoslavia), on April 25, 1952 (separated 1977).

Jovanka Broz Tito was born in a small village in Croatia, on the Balkan Peninsula, in

1924. The region was poor and its politics unstable. Jovanka's father Miko Budisavljevic sought work in the United States and hoped to be successful enough to be able to send for his wife and children. The Great Depression, however, ended his financial hopes, and he returned to his homeland in 1933. In 1935, Jovanka's mother died in childbirth, leaving the 11-year-old girl in charge of the household. Jovanka had to leave school in the fifth grade to work in the fields, cook, sew, and care for her younger siblings. Not until after her marriage in 1952 was she able to resume her education; she received a high school diploma and then studied literature and art at the University of Belgrade.

Jovanka, politicized at an early age, joined the Communist underground in 1940, when she was 16 years old. Inspired by the example of Stefan Matic, a young revolutionary who had died at the beginning of World War II, Jovanka wanted to help drive Nazi and Fascist powers from her homeland. She was also affected by ethnic conflicts in the region, including a massacre of 50 people at Pecane by Serbian troops. She became a private in the partisan army in 1942 and fought in guerilla campaigns in the mountains. One of only four survivors after her unit attacked an Ital-

Jovanka Broz Tito

ian post on the Dalmatian coast, Jovanka endured years of hardship, cold, and hunger with the army. Eventually she contracted typhus, and was brought to the field hospital at the headquarters of the commander in chief, Josip Broz Tito.

Tito, who was also born in Croatia, was leading the movement for Communist revolution in the Balkans. His forces resisted Nazi occupation during World War II and received support from the Soviet Union. At the end of the war, Tito helped to form the new country of Yugoslavia, a confederation of six Communist republics: Serbia, Montenegro, Croatia, Bosnia and Herzegovina, Macedonia, and Slovenia. Tito served as Yugoslavia's first prime minister in 1945. In 1948, however, with the backing of the United States and other Western countries, he broke with Soviet leader Joseph Stalin to impose his own brand of Communist rule. He became the first president of Yugoslavia in 1953 and remained in office until his death in 1980.

Jovanka first met Tito in 1944, at an assembly in a public square in Drarv. She was only 20 and still a private in the army; he was 52 and had been married twice, in January 1920 to **Pelagia Belousova** (or Belousnova), with whom he had had three children, and in 1937 to **Herta Hass**, with whom he had one child. A year later, Jovanka joined his staff in Belgrade, where she worked as a file clerk. She advanced in the army ranks to the level of major, but was demobilized after she married Tito in 1952. She became stepmother to one of Tito's sons, and two of his grandsons also lived with them.

Jovanka and Tito kept their marriage, which occurred on April 25, 1952, a state secret until the following September. Once the marriage was officially known, however, Jovanka was hailed as an attractive and elegant first lady. Foreign dignitaries admired her attractive features, her distinguished taste, and her vivacious personality. Jovanka traveled often with Tito and attended numerous public functions. Among the international heads of state she received with her husband were Prime Minister Jawaharlal Nehru of India, Premier Guy Mollet of France, Prime Minister Gamal Abdel Nasser of Egypt, Emperor Haile Selassie I of Ethiopia, and the king of Greece. Jovanka traveled with Tito to the United Nations when he addressed the General Assembly, and visited Washington, D.C., with him in 1963.

Though she had fought actively as a partisan, Jovanka assumed a more subordinate role after her marriage. "Of course, I am interested in politics, and I follow actively what is happening in the world and in the country and very often I discuss these events with my husband," she told reporters, "but I do not take an active part in it myself." She further explained: "I never attempt to interfere in [Tito's] business or to influence him. You might say I am his sounding board." Jovanka said that she enjoyed managing domestic affairs to please her husband, even choosing her own clothing to suit his personal tastes. She also appeared to enjoy the luxurious lifestyle to which Tito treated himself after assuming control of Yugoslavia. She was in charge of his numerous palatial residences and helped manage large staffs of gardeners, servants, and caretakers. Yet Jovanka also remained involved in larger affairs, in particular the issue of women's rights. She furthered her own interrupted education after becoming first lady, and supported her younger sisters' schooling as well. "Before the revolutionary war women had no rights whatsoever," she said. "Today, a Yugoslav woman is limited only by her talents in entering any field of work." In addition, Jovanka was credited with a movement to encourage toy manufacturers to make their designs more age-appropriate.

Yugoslavia remained under Tito's control until his death in 1980, although his last years in power were marked by political unrest as well as marital estrangement. He and Jovanka lived separately during the last three years of their marriage; some reports indicate he suspected her of involvement in a planned *coup d'etat*. When Tito died, the country became destabilized, and the president's vast estate was confiscated as the property of the people. Jovanka was prevented from inheriting his wealth, though she pressed her legal claim, as his widow, to millions of dollars of property said to include such items as a Rolls-Royce and a Cadillac, five motorboats, an orchard, and a vineyard. In the end, it appears, the family was left with only his personal belongings and the royalties to books he had written. She continued to live in Belgrade, receiving a government pension said to be $600 per month—five times the salary for an average Yugoslav worker. This apparently was decreased after Slobodan Milosevic came to power. In the 1990s, as his corrupt, war-mongering regime grew ever more unpopular with Yugoslavians, many began to remember Tito with increasing fondness. To prevent her from serving as a reminder of her husband, Milosevic kept Jovanka under virtual house arrest, watched by secret police and denied visitors. It was reported that his minions confiscated jewelry, clothes, and gifts she had been given while serving as first lady. He may have had other things to focus on in the

months after he was indicted in 1999 for war crimes in Kosovo, for on May 4, 2000, the 20th anniversary of Tito's death, Jovanka Tito attended a wreath-laying ceremony at the memorial to her husband in Belgrade.

SOURCES:

Chicago Tribune. June 26, 1986.

Frederick, Pauline. *Ten First Ladies of the World.* NY: Meredith Press, 1967.

U.S. News & World Report. October 27, 1986.

World Press Review. September 1999, p. 37.

Elizabeth Shostak, M.A.,
Cambridge, Massachusetts

Tituba.

See Witchcraft Trials in Salem Village.

Tiy (c. 1400–1340 BCE)

Queen of Egypt who was the highly influential wife of the pharaoh Amenhotep III, the world's most powerful monarch in the first half of the 14th century BCE, and mother of the enigmatic monotheistic pharaoh Akhenaten. Name variations: Taia, Teye, Tii, Tiye, and Tiyi. Pronunciation: Tee. Born around 1400 BCE; died in 1340 BCE; daughter of Tjuya and Yuya; common-born wife of the pharaoh Amenhotep III (Amenophis); children: four daughters and two sons, princesses Satamun, Isis, Henuttaneb, and Nebetah, and princes Thutmose (died young) and Amenhotep IV (known as Akhenaten).

Tiy, also transliterated as Teye and Tiye, was born about 1400 BCE to a leading family from Akhmim, a provincial town in Middle Egypt, and died around 1340 as the mother of the pharaoh of Egypt (and mother-in-law of *Nefertiti), possibly from a plague ravaging the Near East at that time. She was first buried at the new capital city of Akhetaten (Tell el-Amarna) which her son had built and dedicated to his sole god, the sun disk or Aten. Tiy was later reburied in the Valley of the Kings at Thebes, probably during the reign of Tutankhamun. The mummies of her parents survive because their burial, also in a tomb in the Valley of the Kings, was not disturbed until modern times. They reveal that her mother **Tjuya** was possibly of Nubian (Sudanese) extraction and that her father Yuya was of a completely different, possibly Asiatic lineage. His career as master of the royal stud farm and lieutenant general of royal charioteers suggests that he was descended from Western Asiatics, perhaps the Hyksos who had ruled the country two centuries before, and introduced the horse-drawn chariot to Egypt, and whose ouster or political defeat ushered in the Egyptian Empire period. Tiy's mother's titles included a high cultic rank in the temple of Min, the fertility god long associated with Akhmim, and also show her to have been the chief of female celebrants in the temple of Amun at Karnak, probably in accord with her son's high priestly position there. Somehow this couple became so influential at the royal court that they were able to have their daughter marry not only a prince, but the heir-apparent. It has been suggested that Yuya and Tjuya were actually the parents of the concubine who had won the favor of pharaoh Thutmose IV. This **Mutemwia** was the mother of his heir, Amenhotep III, for whom she ruled as regent until he was of age. Thus she would have been in a position to select his future wife from her own family circle, explaining the otherwise inexplicable influence wielded by this provincial family from Middle Egypt, whose one son, Anen, became Second Prophet at the great Karnak temple, cult place of Amun-Re, king of the gods, and whose other son, inheriting his father's positions, became the power behind the throne of the child-king Tutankhamun later in this 18th Dynasty and himself ruled Egypt briefly at its close.

The story of the common-born girl who became queen of the mightiest empire on earth and was even worshipped as a goddess with her own temples during her life has long fascinated students of ancient Egyptian history. While the portraits of Tiy, drawn from both art and written documents of her time, suggest a strong and shrewd personality, her story is not one of personal intervention with her fate but the accident of her birth as the daughter of a highly influential family. The rulers of Egypt's 18th Dynasty (1552–1295 BCE), which saw the creation of Egypt's greatest empire, beginning at least with King Thutmose III contracted marriages with foreign royal houses for political reasons. As important religious and government posts in Egypt were in control of the royal family, it was of course important within Egypt too for marriages to be contracted between the Palace and leading non-royal officials. Most likely, then, Tiy's marriage was arranged at an early age by Queen Mutemwia for her son and was not the passionate romance and "First Cinderella Story" that has sometimes been claimed. On the other hand, the marriage scarab's text, which was sent, like a press release, throughout the realm to commemorate the royal marriage (the only known occurrence of such publicity was Amenhotep III's series of five different commemoratives), was commissioned when Amenhotep was already

king (i.e. around 1389 BCE), so that, even though he was in his early teens, he may have acted with some autonomy in this personal matter. Together the royal couple had at least six children— four daughters and two sons: princesses **Satamun**, **Isis**, **Henuttaneb**, and **Nebetab**, and princes Thutmose, heir to the throne who died young, and Amenhotep, who ascended the throne as the fourth of this name but later changed his name to Akhenaten in order to honor his chosen god.

Amenhotep III and Tiy ruled over the most powerful empire the world had ever seen, established some 200 years before. Besides being the dominant political power of the ancient Near East, Egypt possessed vast gold reserves which formed the basis of her influence among the other great powers of the 14th century BCE, whose rulers sought friendly relations and royal gifts from Amenhotep, whose gold was "as plentiful as dust," or so they stated in their dealings with the Egyptian king. This wealth, at home in Egypt, supported ambitious building projects and exquisite decorative arts. Luxury, opulence, and sophistication were at their height under Amenhotep the Magnificent. Today his most impressive surviving monument is the huge but elegant temple of Luxor for which he was largely responsible. His great funerary temple, on the opposite bank of the river, now demolished, was once "wrought with gold and many costly stones"; "its floors adorned with silver and all its portals with fine gold." Before it stood two 50-foot statues of the seated king accompanied by smaller (but still over life-sized) sculptured images of his wife and mother. A huge tomb was hewn out of the cliff sides of the Western Valley, the first royal tomb alone in the majestic and awesomely quiet desolation of this lateral valley. To the venerable Karnak temple, seat of the king of the gods, he added a mighty pylon, but up and down the Nile the building of temples continued throughout his long and peaceful reign.

Amenhotep reigned for 39 years and all indications are that he and Tiy remained mutually supportive throughout their long marriage despite his huge harem and marriages with foreign princesses. Up to her time, no queen was so frequently depicted in art at the side of her husband, whether in sculptures he commissioned or in wall scenes in the tombs of private people who served in their court or government. Queen Tiy sits at her husband's side and is his equal in size in the gigantic sculptured group now dominating the central court of Cairo's Museum of Antiquities. No woman previously had ever been shown in such colossal dimensions. Also new are the portrayals in both private tomb scenes and on her own monuments of vigorous, even violent, images of the queen, portrayals previously only associated with kings. For instance, when the king and queen are depicted seated on thrones, Tiy's throne has on its side panels the queen shown as a female sphinx shaded by the symbolic fan which denotes kingly power, and as a sphinx she is depicted in more than one official's tomb as trampling enemies—female Africans and Asiatics—underfoot. Tiy is also shown wearing a special ceremonial necklace hitherto associated only with kings.

The importance of this queen, her involvement in the governing of her country, also jumps from the page of letters addressed by foreign rulers to the Egyptian court, which have remarkably survived to our time. Over a hundred years ago, in the 1880s, a peasant woman grubbing at the decaying brick walls of the abandoned city built by Tiy's son Akhenaten, now know by its Arabic name of Tell el-Amarna, came across a cache of inscribed bricks which, once scholars examined them, turned out to be tablets bearing official foreign-office correspondence written in Akkadian, the diplomatic language of the Near East at that time. Among the hundreds of letters from royal heads of state is one addressed directly to Queen Tiy and others referring to her, which leave no doubt that it was well known in official circles internationally that this queen of Egypt took a personal role in matters of state. She must have been present in the audience hall when ambassadors were received and privy to the correspondence which took place between her husband and foreign kings.

Tiy was the first queen to create out of the office of Royal Wife a position more powerful than that of King's Mother. Whether or not the dowager queen Mutemwia survived beyond the beginning of her son's marriage, she disappears from prominence and the records glorify only Tiy, who is called in official inscriptions "The Heiress, greatly praised," "Mistress of all lands," as well as "Mistress of Upper and Lower Egypt and Lady of the Two Lands." When Amenhotep III published and sent throughout the ancient world (from Cyprus to Syria) an entire series of large scarabs whose backs contain texts commemorating significant events in his reign, Tiy's name and titles are recorded on scarabs of all five events commemorated. Even when he announced his reception of the daughter of the king of Mitanni (northwest Syria) as his bride, he did not fail to repeat that Tiy was his principal or Great Royal Wife, no one would replace her in his esteem and affection.

One of the events commemorated in the scarab series occurred in Year 11 (the year following the marriage of Amenhotep with the princess from Mitanni), the digging of an enormous irrigation basin (sometimes viewed as a pleasure lake) measuring some 1,200 feet wide and over a mile in length, for Queen Tiy in the district which contained her hometown and was called Zerukha. Such an excavation would have greatly facilitated the agricultural production and thus prosperity of the region, and in turn rendered the revenues needed to support the local temple where a cult for Tiy as a divinity was established. A temple-town was also dedicated to Tiy in Nubia at Sedeinga, between the second and third cataract of the Nile, north of a temple dedicated to the cult of her husband as a divinity. Today the town's name, Adey, retains the elements of the ancient name of "Mansion of Tiy." Here, in the temple, she was closely identified with Hathor, the great goddess of love and consort of the sun god, while her husband the king was worshipped as a living manifestation of the sun. Numerous sculptured

Limestone fragment of statue of Queen Tiy.

portraits of Tiy exist showing her wearing the sun disk and horns headdress of the goddess Hathor. The walls of the Sedeinga temple also depict Tiy as a striding lioness, which perhaps is meant to equate her with the violent goddess Tefnut who is associated with the region in myth.

While the capital of Egypt was in the north of the country, not far from modern Cairo, at Memphis, Amenhotep built a palace in the warmer south, on the west bank at Thebes (modern Luxor). Here, just south of the great temple of Medinet Habu at a site today called Malkata, one may see the mounds of decaying brick walls denoting a large rambling palace whose walls, floors, and ceilings had been plastered and brightly painted with scenes taken from nature: plant, bird and animal life. Most likely Tiy and Amenhotep frequented this in the winter and moved back north in the summer, which brings very high temperatures to this region. The building of the Malkata palace necessitated as well the construction of a sizeable harbor on this side of the river to accommodate the many boats and barges bringing both visitors and supplies to the royal residence. It was here, in the last decade of his reign, that Amenhotep celebrated the age-old *sed* festival or royal jubilee that was intended to magically reinvigorate him and allow him to continue ruling forever. From the labels written on wine jars found in the ruins of the southern palace, it is known that three such jubilees were celebrated, and scenes from two of these are preserved in the nearby tomb of one of Queen Tiy's most trusted officials. This was her chief steward Kheruef who had one of the largest private tombs at Thebes. It was hewn into the limestone cliffs to the west of the cultivated land and was some 360-feet long and contained two large columned halls, reflecting the wealth and manpower at the disposal of the queen's servant. By the attention paid in such private monuments of the time to recording the *sed* festivals of Amenhotep III, one gains the impression that they were the most important events of the latter part of the king's reign and all took place at the new palace in Western Thebes. In the beautifully sculpted tomb of Kheruef, the queen stands behind the throne of the king, next to the great goddess Hathor, and assumes the role of the goddess Maat, partner to the king who is the living image of Re, the sun-god. In some of the art from the last years of his reign, both Amenhotep and Tiy are portrayed with juvenile features, as if to imply that they had undergone a mystical transformation and been reborn as solar deities, never to die. This indeed would have been the goal of the *sed* festivals and

apparently Tiy as well as the king benefited from their magical rites.

Even though Amenhotep would welcome to his harem many daughters of foreign royal families over the years, no princess ever took precedence over the strong-willed wife of his youth. Tiy has been universally deemed by scholars as energetic, bright, and imperious as well as beautiful. Her striking portrait in Cypriote yew wood, found at her palace in the north of the country at Ghurab and now in Berlin, and another stone portrait head found in Sinai and now in Cairo clearly show the same attractive but haughty face of an aging beauty accustomed to being obeyed, with similar lines around the down-turned and pouting mouth and with weary eyes. Towards the end of his life, Amenhotep III was often portrayed as obese and favoring the languid pose. He was not well, but attempted to find a cure for his ailments by appeasing the goddess of pestilence—Sekhmet of the lioness head—with more than 600 large stone statues of her set up in a magic circle around the sacred lake of the goddess Mut at Karnak. Also he received to his court the idol of the powerful Babylonian goddess Ishtar, lent him by a considerate colleague on the throne of that kingdom. The last carved scene from his reign is on a stone tablet from a private home and shows a fat and slouched Amenhotep seated next to Tiy, an arm thrown casually around her shoulders.

Tiy's power and presence at court did not end with the death of her husband, but continued well into the reign of her remarkable son. How much influence she had on her son and the religious revolution which he waged from the very beginning of his tenure is unknown. Her own brother had been Second Prophet of Amun-Re, and her first-born son, Prince Thutmose, had been a Chief Prophet in the temple of Ptah, the great state god of the capital city of Memphis, but her younger son had been educated under the tutelage of the priests of Re the sun god at Heliopolis who apparently encouraged his exclusive interest in the cult of the sun's disk. Although he eventually rejected most of the pantheon, closed the temples of other deities, and removed himself and his court to his new city in Middle Egypt, his mother did not abandon him, but visited and presumably spent much of her declining years within his family circle, enjoying her six granddaughters. Had she encouraged him in his independence and universalistic tendencies? Certainly she did not seem to have had success in limiting them, if in fact she would have so desired. Indeed, it would seem that her son was, in matters of religion, very independent of his mother because later generations did not obliterate her memory while they certainly persecuted his for the religious doctrine he had promoted in place of traditional beliefs. Perhaps her introspective and intellectual son had not approved of his parents' claims to divinity and seen the absurdity of the "rejuvenation" images in the official art during his father's last years. From the numerous anthropomorphic deities of the large Egyptian pantheon of gods, and especially the hidden god Amun, their leader, he turned away and embraced instead the visible sun's disk and its powers, recognizing it as the life-giving "father" of all nations and all beings, thus earning himself the appellation of "First Monotheist." Tiy's influence, however, continues to be seen in the queenly iconography of her famous daughter-in-law Nefertiti who also appeared in art as a sphinx trampling female foreign enemies and in other violent renditions, such as the smiting of foreign captives with a scimitar, just as a king might be portrayed. Nefertiti, like Tiy, in time took the role of primary woman in the reign of her husband, but before this happened, foreign heads of state were addressing Tiy along with her son as the rulers of Egypt.

Queen Tiy seems to have been an intelligent woman who took an active interest in matters of government. In a very long letter sent by the king of Mitanni (the Hurrian kingdom in Northern Syria and for decades Egypt's chief rival in the political world of the Near East) to her son, the young king Amenhotep IV (later Akhenaten), King Tushratta states that Tiy "knows all the words" that Amenhotep III had written in letters over the years: it is "your mother whom you must ask about all of them . . . the words that [your father] would speak with me over and over." In regard to presents of gold he expected to continue, as in the past, and the warm relationship that had existed between himself and Amenhotep III, Tushratta repeatedly urges the young king to ask his mother if the things that he says are not true. King Tushratta states that he had sincerely mourned at the news of the death of Amenhotep III and then states that he knows that Amenhotep IV *and* Tiy, his father's principal wife, were together exercising the kingship in the place of Amenhotep III. Obviously, the outside world had a strong impression that Tiy's power in the Egyptian Empire was unmatched and continued even after the death of her husband.

One of the surviving letters from this king makes reference to a letter (EA 26) that Queen Tiy must have sent to Tushratta herself. In it, she asked him to continue to send his embassies to her son and show friendship towards Egypt. Some historians have interpreted this appeal as reflecting her uncertainty about the policies her son would pursue.

However, even if Tiy played a role in the beginning of her son's administration, it is obvious that after only a few years her daughter-in-law assumed great prominence and must have possessed a personality that was an equal match to Tiy's. The dowager queen did live on, her last record being dated to year 12 of her son's reign, and she possessed an estate at the new capital city of Akhetaten and possibly died there.

When she died in her 50s, possibly in the pandemic that was sweeping the Near East at the time and that would claim other, younger lives within the royal family, Tiy was buried in a tomb prepared for her in the cliffs of the royal valley, east of the new capital city. The fragments of her stone sarcophagus have been found there. However, once this city was abandoned as a seat of government, the royal dead were removed to the age-old royal burial ground in Western Thebes. Tiy was laid to rest under a golden canopy in a tomb (number 55) in the Valley of the Kings along with another of her relations. However at some time, possibly centuries later in the 21st Dynasty, her body was moved once again by priests to a cache of royal mummies (in the tomb of Amenhotep II) where she was "reunited" with her husband, because his mummy too was deposited in the tomb of Amenhotep II for safe keeping. Her magnificently preserved mummified body, with one arm crossed over the breast as if to hold a scepter, was found outside of its coffin and was identified by archaeologists for years as simply "the elder lady." It has been identified now by using hair samples taken from it and matching these scientifically by an electron probe with a lock of hair placed in a small golden casket labeled with Tiy's name within the tomb of Tutankhamun. This heirloom, or family keepsake, indicates a blood relationship between Tiy and Tutankhamun, who was possibly her grandson. If indeed the identification is correct, the delicate and refined features of the queen's mummy are graced by luxuriant dark wavy hair, indicating that for most of her life, this regal lady had enjoyed good health and been truly an attractive woman.

SOURCES:

Blankenberg-Van Delden, C. *The Large Commemorative Scarabs of Amenhotep III.* Leiden: E.J. Brill, 1969.

Edwards, I.E.S. *Tutankhamun: his tomb and its treasures.* NY: Metropolitan Museum of Art and Alfred A. Knopf, 1976.

Grimal, Nicholas. *A History of Ancient Egypt.* Oxford: Blackwell, 1992.

Hayes, William C. "Amenhotep III's Display," in Chapter IX of *The Cambridge Ancient History.* 3rd ed. Edited by I.E.S. Edwards, *et al.* Cambridge: University Press, 1973. Vol. II, Part 1, pp. 338–346.

Kozloff, Arielle P., and Betsy M. Bryan, with Lawrence M. Berman. *Egypt's Dazzling Sun: Amenhotep III and his world.* Cleveland, OH: Cleveland Museum of Art, 1992.

Moran, William L. *The Amarna Letters.* Baltimore, MD: The Johns Hopkins University Press, 1992.

Morkot, Robert. "Violent Images of Queenship and the Royal cult," in *Wepwawet.* Vol. 2, 1986, pp. 1–9.

Partridge, Robert B. *Faces of Pharaohs: Royal Mummies and Coffins from Ancient Thebes.* London: Rubicon Press, 1996.

Redford, Donald B. *History and Chronology of the Eighteenth Dynasty of Egypt: seven studies.* Toronto: University of Toronto Press, 1967.

SUGGESTED READING:

Aldred, Cyril. *Akhenaten Pharaoh of Egypt: A New Study.* London: Thames and Hudson, 1988.

Arnold, Dorothea. *The Royal Women of Amarna: Images of Beauty from Ancient Egypt.* NY: Metropolitan Museum of Art, 1996.

Lesko, Barbara S. *The Remarkable Women of Ancient Egypt.* 3rd ed. Providence, RI: B.C. Scribe, 1996.

Redford, Donald B. *Akhenaten the Heretic King.* Princeton, NJ: Princeton University Press, 1984.

COLLECTIONS:

Sculptured portraits of Tiy are located in the Egyptian Museum of Antiquities, Cairo, Egypt; the Egyptian Museum, Turin, Italy; and the State Museum, Berlin, Germany. The painted limestone stela from a house shrine showing an old Amenhotep III and his Queen Tiy is in the British Museum, London, England.

Barbara S. Lesko,
Department of Egyptology,
Brown University,
Providence, Rhode Island

Tiye (c. 1400–1340 BCE).

See Tiy.

Tiyi (c. 1400–1340 BCE).

See Tiy.

Tizard, Catherine (1931—)

Lecturer in zoology at Auckland University who was the first woman to be elected mayor of Auckland and the first woman to be appointed governor-general of New Zealand. Name variations: Dame Cath Tizard. Born Catherine Anne Maclean on April 4, 1931; only child of Neil Maclean and Helen Maclean (both Scottish immigrants); educated at Waharoa Primary School, Matamata College, University of Auckland (BA); married Robert James Tizard, in 1951 (divorced 1983); children: Anne Francis, Linda Catherine, Judith Ngaire, Nigel Robert.

Grew up in a working-class community in New Zealand; met and became engaged to Robert (Bob) Tizard during the second year of her Arts Degree at Auckland University; married (1951) and had four children within six years; left in charge of home and family, while husband's political career flourished and he spent much of his time in Wellington (capital of New Zealand); returned to university and took courses in zoology (1961); eased herself into university teaching; took an interest in civic affairs; elected to the Auckland City Council (1971); made several television appearances and widely broadened her public-speaking experience; was elected mayor of Auckland, New Zealand's largest city—the first Labour mayor and the first woman to hold the post (1983); was re-elected twice and, during her third term of office, was offered the position of governor-general of New Zealand (1990), an appointment she held until March 1996.

Honors: Dame commander of the British Empire (DBE, 1985); Freedom of the City of London (1990); Dame Grand Cross of the Order of St. Michael and St. George (GCMG, 1990); Honorary Doctorate in Law, University of Auckland (1992); Suffrage Centenary Medal (1993); Dame Grand Cross of the Royal Victorian Order (GCVO, 1995); Companion of the Queen's Service Order (QSO, 1996).

It was a particular source of pride to Dame Catherine Tizard to be in office as governor-general during the 1993 centenary, when New Zealand celebrated being the first nation in the world where women won the vote. She felt, as she had on several occasions over her years in public office, that she represented the achievements of women of the past, present and future both at home and throughout the world.

Having been a young mother of four children under seven with an ambitious husband working away from home, she could always sympathize with the strain and exhaustion that the "average housewife" has to cope with. She took a full part in organizing what would now be called self-help and support groups in her neighborhood, joined and ran the PTA and then, when her husband lost his seat in the 1960 elections, returned to college to complete her own degree.

Her perception of her remarkable career is mainly that it has been a series of "happy accidents." For instance, her job in the zoology department at Auckland University came about, she says, because "the students, bless their unknowing little hearts, were pressing for more internal assessment, less cramming for exams." She was the perfect choice for tutoring and demonstrating because she "didn't mind the meniality of it and needed the money."

Similarly, Tizard joined the Auckland City Council when her husband put her name down because the Labour Party needed another candidate. To her astonishment, she was elected. She continued as a councillor and university lecturer until, after an unsuccessful first attempt, she won the Auckland mayoralty in 1983, a challenge that she had set for herself when her marriage began to disintegrate. She realized she would need a new direction. Tizard built her reputation for "good-humored, sensible politics" by speaking "just plain common sense," she said, or "what someone else is dying to say but just doesn't dare to." She went on to win two more mayoral elections. Her proudest achievements during this time were the building of Auckland's Aotea Center (used for conferences, civic functions and the performing arts) and the hosting of the 1990 Commonwealth Games—both of which were fraught with political and financial difficulties.

New Zealand is a member of the British Commonwealth, and the reigning monarch of Great Britain has to have a "local" representative to perform official duties at various functions. Though tipped to become the first woman governor-general, Dame Cath (as she then liked to be known) honestly thought she was too partisan and probably too outspoken for so diplomatic a role. But she was thrilled with the appointment. "I cannot ignore the fact that it is another male bastion that is crumbling," she said. "I don't think I did it by myself, but it's nice to think that a previously held male position is now open to both sexes." She brought her boundless energy, enthusiasm and charm into what had been a somewhat remote and starchy office. "I am going to have to start being dignified from now on!," she conceded. One of the first things she did was to employ a male housekeeper and female footmen at Government House in Wellington.

"I was born averagely intelligent, averagely healthy, averagely good-looking, and into an averagely sane family," said Tizard. "In many ways I feel I have lived an ordinary, typically New Zealand life, with nothing ostentatious or remarkable about it. Yet things have come together remarkably well for me."

SOURCES:
Material supplied by Government House, Wellington, New Zealand.

Bonnie Hurren,
freelance director, actor, lecturer,
Bristol, England

Tocco, Magdalena-Theodora
(fl. mid-1400s)

First wife of Constantine XI. Flourished in the mid-1400s; daughter of Leonardo Tocco; first wife of Con-

Catherine
Tizard

stantine XI Paleologus, emperor of Nicaea (r. 1448–1453).

Toc-me-to-ne (1844–1891).
See Winnemucca, Sarah.

Tod, Isabella (1836–1896)

Irish feminist campaigner and journalist. Born Isabella Maria Susan Tod in Edinburgh, Scotland, on May 18, 1836; died in Belfast, Ireland, on December 8, 1896; daughter of James Banks Tod and Maria Isabella (Waddell) Tod; educated at home; never married; no children.

Isabella Tod's biographer **Maria Luddy** observes that to write her life is to write the history of Irish feminism in the critical last four decades of the 19th century. She was "the outstanding advocate of women's rights during this period." Tod was born in 1836 in Scotland but the family moved to Belfast, in northern Ireland, in the

1860s. Tod's mother was Irish and encouraged her daughter to read widely. She also interested her in woman's affairs. Isabella was devoted to her mother who died in 1877.

Tod's name first came to public prominence in 1867 when the National Association for the Promotion of Social Science held its annual meeting in Belfast. Tod's primary interest at this time was women's education, and she wrote a paper for the meeting entitled "On advanced education for girls of the upper and middle classes." There were increasing demands for more participation by women in education, and in Belfast Tod's fellow campaigners included *Margaret Byers, headmistress of Victoria College, who became a close friend. In her paper, Tod argued that education was a complex process comprising three essential elements: moral and religious training; intellectual instruction; and mental discipline. She argued that if women were to take advantage of higher education, these elements had to be inculcated in school or college. Over the next decade, Tod and other campaigners in Belfast and Dublin lobbied and petitioned the government for reform. Their efforts were rewarded when the Irish University Act of 1879 opened degrees and scholarships to women. However, the educational facilities available to women were not addressed by the act and still lagged far behind those enjoyed by men. The following year, Tod was the main influence behind the establishment of the Ulster Head Schoolmistresses Association which worked closely with the Central Association for Irish Schoolmistresses. Both organizations were influential and worked throughout the 1880s and 1890s to advance the cause of women's education in Ireland.

Tod believed that education not only developed the intellectual and spiritual potential of women but served a profound social purpose as well. She was particularly critical of middle-class views of education for women. The middle classes expected their daughters to marry and to marry well, and they expected husbands to take active management of everything: "We shall not stop to discover whether such a state of things is even desirable. It is sufficient to point out that it does not and cannot exist." Tod became interested in the campaign to amend the Married Women's Property Act. As an active member of the Presbyterian Church, she regularly visited the poverty-stricken areas of Belfast and became aware of the economic exploitation of women whose earnings were appropriated by their husbands. She was the only woman who gave evidence in 1868 to the parliamentary select committee on the Married Women's Property Bill,

and she emphasized that women must not only be allowed to keep their wages but to have their property rights recognized as well.

It was through her campaigns on this act that Tod became acquainted with *Josephine Butler who was leading the movement to repeal the Contagious Diseases Act. In Ireland, there were three districts with large military garrisons where women could be detained and forcibly subjected to medical examination for venereal disease. In 1869, Butler founded the Ladies National Association to campaign for the repeal of the Contagious Diseases Act and by 1871 three branches had been established in Ireland. Along with *Anna Haslam, Tod was active in the movement, both in Britain and Ireland, from the beginning. Butler described Tod as "one of the ablest, and certainly the most eloquent, of our women workers." In a speech in 1883, Tod deplored the double standard, "that unspeakably wicked idea that most men may be expected so to sin, and that in them it is a venial offence." The acts were suspended that year and repealed in 1886.

Tod had a lifelong interest in temperance. In an 1893 interview, she noted that her visits to the poor had "soon taught me that drink is the main cause of poverty, and that yet in a larger measure it is the cause of domestic discord and misery." In 1874, she joined the committee of the Belfast Women's Temperance Association which opened refreshment houses and organized meals for women working in factories. Since women suffered most from intemperance they became the focus of the Association's work, as Margaret Byers, secretary of the BWTA, stressed. Temperance should be inculcated in the home which was women's sphere. The BWTA extended its work to helping women prisoners for, as Tod wrote in 1881, "the world is unspeakably harder to a woman who falls than a man, and doors of escape which stand open to him are closed to her." By 1889, the BWTA claimed to have about 40 branches in Ireland. Tod was also active in the British temperance movement and was vice-president of the British Women's Temperance Association from 1877 to 1892.

Tod's campaigns on all these issues convinced her that women's suffrage was a vital cause. Politics, she argued, were part and parcel of everyone's life and represented not only material and intellectual choices for women but moral ones as well. Like many suffragists of the time she favored a restricted, property-based franchise. She spoke at meetings up and down the country and produced a stream of articles for Irish newspapers and journals. Although the struggle for the parliamentary franchise was not won until after her death she lived to see women win the vote in municipal elections, a success in which she had played a major role.

In 1886, the British prime minister, W.E. Gladstone, introduced his first Home Rule Bill which was intended to give limited self-government to Ireland. Opposition was intense in northeast Ireland where opinion favored the maintenance of the union with Britain. Tod was a committed unionist and devoted the rest of her life to resisting Home Rule. This lost her many friends from her various campaigns who had Home Rule sympathies, but her dedication also affected her health. After her death in December 1896, two scholarships were instituted in her memory, the first at Victoria College and the second for the woman achieving the highest marks at the Royal University.

SOURCES:

Luddy, Maria. "Isabella M.S. Tod (1836–1896)," in *Women, Power and Consciousness in 19th Century Ireland: Eight Biographical Studies.* Edited by Mary Cullen and Maria Luddy. Dublin: Attic Press, 1984, pp. 197–230.

Deirdre McMahon,
lecturer in history at Mary Immaculate College,
University of Limerick,
Limerick, Ireland

Todd, Mabel Loomis (1858–1932).

See Dickinson, Emily for sidebar.

Todd, Marion Marsh

(1841–post 1913)

American lawyer, political activist, and writer. Born in March 1841 in Plymouth, Chenango County, New York; lived until at least 1914, with no record available of her death; daughter of Abner Kneeland Marsh (a Universalist preacher) and Dolly Adelia (Wales) Marsh; educated at Ypsilanti State Normal School (now Eastern Michigan University) and Hastings Law College, San Francisco; married Benjamin Todd (a reformist lawyer), in 1868 (died 1880); children: Lula.

Wrote political works, including Protective Tariff Delusions *(1886) and* Railways of Europe and America *(1893), and novels.*

A pioneer in women's rights and reformist politics, Marion Marsh Todd was born in 1841 in Plymouth, New York, one of seven children of **Dolly Wales Marsh** and Abner Kneeland Marsh. Her father, a Universalist preacher, taught Marion at home while she was young. In 1851, when the family moved to Eaton Rapids, Michigan,

she attended public school. She graduated from the Ypsilanti State Normal School at age 17, and began her career as a teacher. In 1868, she married Boston lawyer Benjamin Todd, who convinced her to join him in his work for women's rights. Marion gave up teaching to devote her time to public lectures on temperance, women's suffrage, and economic reform. During this period, she also gave birth to her only child, daughter **Lula Todd**.

In the late 1870s, the family moved to California to accommodate Benjamin's poor health. In 1879, Marion enrolled in the Hastings Law College in San Francisco, which activists ***Clara Shortridge Foltz** and ***Laura de Force Gordon** had recently convinced to begin admitting women students. There, Marion Todd concentrated in financial law, but was forced to leave without a degree after her husband's death. Nonetheless, she was admitted to the California bar in 1881 and opened a law practice in San Francisco. She also became active in political work. In September 1882, Todd attended the state convention of the Greenback Labor Party and was elected a member of the party's platform committee. She made significant contributions to the platform and received the party's nomination for state attorney general, making her one of the first women to run for statewide office. Though she received only 1,109 votes, she led the Greenback Party in the election.

Todd relinquished her law practice in 1883 to concentrate on work for the Greenback Party and other movements. She was instrumental in organizing the Anti-Monopoly Party in 1883, and campaigned widely for it and for the Greenback Party. In 1886, having moved back to Michigan, Todd was a state delegate to the General Assembly of the Knights of Labor in Richmond, Virginia. In 1887, with her friend **Sara E.V. Emery**, Todd organized the Union Labor Party, which focused on financial and railroad reform. She moved to Chicago in 1890 to become editor of the *Express*, a reformist weekly. The following year, she was a delegate to the Cincinnati conference at which the national People's (Populist) Party was formed.

Todd wrote eight published works, most of them on political themes. *Protective Tariff Delusions* (1886) denounced U.S. tariff laws that, in Todd's view, hurt American labor. Her 1890 campaign booklet, *Honest (?) John Sherman, or a Foul Record*, was widely used by the People's Party, and Todd later expanded it into a book, *Pizarro and John Sherman* (1891), that attacked Senator Sherman as an exploiter of his own people. Todd collected several pieces originally published in the *Express* in *Prof. Goldwin Smith and His Satellites in Congress* (1890), an assault on Smith's anti-women's suffrage position. In *Railways of Europe and America* (1893), considered her most ambitious work, Todd argued that the entire U.S. railway system needed to be restructured.

Todd also wrote three novels that protested capitalist exploitation, human profligacy, and religious hypocrisy. *Rachel's Pitiful History* (1895), *Phillip: A Romance* (1900), and *Claudia* (1902) were considered melodramatic vehicles for social protest, though the latter two were noted for their more positive views. Todd spent her last years in Eaton Rapids and then in Springport, Michigan, where she was reported living in 1914. No documentation on her death has been found.

SOURCES:

James, Edward T., ed. *Notable American Women, 1607–1950.* Cambridge, MA: The Belknap Press of Harvard University, 1971.

Elizabeth Shostak, M.A.,
Cambridge, Massachusetts

Todd, Mary (1818–1882).

See Lincoln, Mary Todd.

Thelma Todd

Todd, Olga Taussky (1906–1995).

See Noether, Emmy for sidebar.

Todd, Thelma (1905–1935)

American actress who died under mysterious circumstances at age 30. Born on July 29, 1905, in Lawrence, Massachusetts; died, possibly of carbon monoxide poisoning, on December 16, 1935.

Starred with the Marx Brothers in Monkey Business *(1931) and* Horse Feathers *(1932); also notable in comedy shorts and dramatic feature films.*

Selected film roles: Fascinating Youth *(1926);* Rubber Heels *(1927);* Nevada *(1927);* The Gay Defender *(1927);* The Noose *(1928);* Heart to Heart *(1928);* Vamping Venus *(1928);* The Crash *(1928);* The Haunted House *(1928);* Naughty Baby *(1929);* Seven Footprints to Satan *(1929);* Careers *(1929);* The House of Horror *(1929);* Command Performance *(1930);* Follow Thru *(1930);* The Hot Heiress *(1931);* Swanee River *(1931);* Aloha *(1931);* The Maltese Falcon *(1931);* Monkey Business *(1931);* Corsair *(1931);* This is the Night *(1932);* Horse Feathers *(1932);* Speak Easily *(1932);* Call Her Savage *(1932);* Klondike *(1932);* Cheating Blondes *(1933);* Fra Diavolo *(The Devil's Brother, 1933);* Son of a Sailor *(1933);* Sitting Pretty *(1933);* Counsellor-at-Law *(1933);* You Made Me Love You *(1933);* Hips Hips Hooray *(1934);* Palooka *(1934);* Bottoms Up *(1934);* Cockeyed Cavaliers *(1934);* Take the Stand *(1934);* Lightning Strikes Twice *(1935);* Two for Tonight *(1935);* The Bohemian Girl *(1936).*

Thelma Todd, an actress sometimes called the "Vamping Venus" or "The Hot Toddy," was born in 1905 in Lawrence, Massachusetts, and worked as a schoolteacher and part-time model before winning a beauty contest in the mid-1920s that initiated her film career. Considered talented as well as beautiful, she starred in short comedies opposite such actors as Charlie Chase, *ZaSu Pitts, and *Patsy Kelly, and in feature films with the Marx Brothers, Laurel and Hardy, Buster Keaton, and Bing Crosby. Todd was at the height of her career when she died under mysterious circumstances in 1935. After her body was found in her garage slumped over the steering wheel of her parked car, her death was ruled a suicide by carbon monoxide poisoning. But several details suggested foul play, including the fact that facial injuries indicated Todd had been in a struggle. A later inquest rejected the suicide ruling but found insufficient evidence to deem her death a murder.

Many suspected that Todd's lover, movie director Ronald West, may have had reason to want the actress out of his life. The couple owned a café and restaurant, and Todd had obtained for West considerable sums of money to run the business. In addition, she had recently embarked on a secret affair with a San Francisco businessman. On the night before Todd died, witnesses heard her and West in the midst of a bitter argument. Though West was never charged with murder, enduring suspicions against him destroyed his career. He never directed another film.

Also suspected in Todd's death was the gangster Charles "Lucky" Luciano. After Todd had refused to consent to his scheme to open an illegal gambling casino in the café she owned with West, the actress began to receive anonymous death threats. Some suggested that Luciano may have ordered a hit man to kill Todd. No evidence was found to prove this theory, however. Though it appears clear that Todd's death was a murder and not a suicide, the exact circumstances of her last moments have never been determined.

SOURCES:

Katz, Ephraim. *The Film Encyclopedia.* NY: Harper-Collins, 1994.

Kohn, George C. *Encyclopedia of American Scandal.* NY: Facts on File, 1989.

Elizabeth Shostak, M.A.,
Cambridge, Massachusetts

Todi, Luiza Rosa (1753–1833)

Portuguese mezzo-soprano. Born Luiza Rosa Aguiar in Setubal, Portugal, on January 9, 1753; died in Lisbon, Portugal, on October 1, 1833.

Luiza Todi was an actress at 15 before becoming a pupil of Lisbon conductor Davide Perez. She sang in London in 1772 and was extremely successful in Madrid in 1777. In 1780, Todi was a court singer in Berlin. Three years later, she provoked a famous rivalry with *Gertrud Mara.

Todora.

Variant of Theodora.

Tofana (1653–1723)

Italian poisoner. Name variations: La Toffania. Born in 1653; died in 1723.

Accounts of the life of notorious poisoner Tofana, sometimes called La Toffania, differ greatly. One source claims she was living in Palermo, Sicily, in the late 1600s; another indicates she lived in Naples. Little is known about her early life, and there is disagreement about the manner and date of her death. But it is agreed that Tofana had for many years supplied poison to high-born ladies who wished to get rid of unwanted husbands, facilitating as many as 600 deaths before she was discovered and tried by the authorities.

Tofana apparently operated by selling a substance she pretended was a medicine with near-miraculous healing powers. Called "Mana of St. Nicholas of Bari," it was in reality a powerful compound of arsenic. Reports indicate that this substance was much in demand among women of the region, and that Tofana sold it at high profits for many years. Not until authorities became suspicious at the unexplained increase in the death rate, however, were her crimes discovered. One account says she was exposed in 1659 when a secret society, run by a woman called La Spara (**Hieronyma Spara**), was discovered; though Spara and several others were executed, Tofana escaped to a convent. She remained there until 1709, when she was abducted and forced to confess to her part in the 600 deaths, though this could not be proved.

Another source suggests that Tofana's crimes were not discovered until 1719, when the viceroy of Naples ordered her arrested. After capturing her and obtaining her confession through torture, the viceroy ordered her strangled on the spot, and had her body tossed over the wall onto the grounds of the convent that had sheltered her. Though the date of Tofana's death is given as 1723, some sources cite 1720 and others suggest she may have lived until 1730. Her poison, which came to be known as "Aqua tofana," was later among those employed by Marquise *Marie de Brinvillers. Tofana was used as a model for the protagonist in *Sidonia the Sorceress.*

SOURCES:

Nash, Jay Robert. *Look for the Woman.* NY: M. Evans, 1981.

Uglow, Jennifer, ed. *The International Dictionary of Women's Biography.* NY: Continuum, 1985.

Elizabeth Shostak, M.A.,
Cambridge, Massachusetts

Tofts, Catherine (c. 1685–1756)

English operatic soprano. Name variations: Katherine Tofts. Born around 1685; died in 1756 in Venice; married John Smith (a British consul to Venice).

One of the earliest English prima donnas, Catherine Tofts began her career singing in concert from 1703 to 1704. The following year, she joined Drury Lane, London, where she sang until 1709, when she retired from the stage. Tofts, a rival of **Margherita de l'Épine**, was the first English-born singer to perform Italian opera in England, and her pleasant voice and graceful stage presence was admired by such critics as Cibber and Burney. She sang in *Arsinoe* (1705), *Rosamond*, *Love's Triumph*, and other operas, and also sang in such pasticcios as *Camilla*, *Thomyris*, and *Phyrrus and Demetrius*. Tofts earned a fortune during her career, and retired to Venice in 1709. There, she married British consul John Smith. Tofts lived until 1756, and reportedly died insane.

Elizabeth Shostak, M.A.,
Cambridge, Massachusetts

Toguri, Iva (1916—)

American-born woman of Japanese descent, known as Tokyo Rose, who broadcast over Tokyo Radio during World War II and later was wrongly convicted of treason to America. Name variations: Tokyo Rose; Ann; Orphan Annie; Iva Ikuko Toguri d'Aquino. Born Iva Ikuko Toguri in Los Angeles, California, on July 4, 1916; daughter of Jun Toguri (a shopkeeper and importer) and Fumi (Iimuro) Toguri; graduated from the University of California, Los Angeles, 1940; married Felipe d'Aquino, in Tokyo, in 1945; children: one (stillborn).

Worked as a translator and typist at Japanese news agency (1942–43); broadcast for Tokyo Radio (1943–45); was a prisoner of the U.S. government (1949–56); was a shopkeeper in Chicago (1956—).

During the Pacific War against Japan in the years 1941–45, American soldiers heard regular broadcasts by English-speaking women over Japanese short-wave radio stations. They nicknamed these broadcasters "Tokyo Rose" and imagined wily seductresses trying to sow discouragement in their ranks. When the war ended in August 1945, American journalists rushed to find "Tokyo Rose" and singled out Iva Ikuko Toguri, although she was only one among the 20 or more female English-speaking broadcasters. She was an American-born Nisei (second-generation immigrant) of Japanese descent and, after a long period of investigation, she was convicted in 1949 of treason against the United States.

Born on the 4th of July 1916, to Japanese immigrant parents, Toguri had been raised in Los Angeles. Her parents and her older, Japanese-born brother were *issei*, first-generation Japanese, who were denied American citizen-

ship. They ran a small general store and import business and lived in neighborhoods where most of their neighbors were white rather than clustering with other Japanese immigrants. The children went to public school, the whole family attended a Methodist church, and the English language dominated conversation in their home. In a later interview, Toguri denied that she had ever been the victim of anti-Asian prejudice, although it was widespread at that time and had led to a ban on Japanese immigration in 1924. She graduated from the University of California, Los Angeles, in the summer of 1940, being one of the less than ten percent of Japanese-American women to attend college in the depression decade of the 1930s. She hoped to become a doctor and took some pre-medical courses at UCLA the next year. Friends from her student days remembered her as a thoroughly assimilated woman, with an American rather than Japanese outlook and attitudes.

In the summer of 1941, Toguri responded to a Japanese aunt's invitation to visit the old country. Though she sailed when America and Japan were at peace, she was still there when the Japanese attack on Pearl Harbor that December began hostilities. Toguri had left America without a passport (it was legal to do so at that time) and found that she could only be evacuated via India at what was then the considerable sum of $425, which she could not afford. Instead, she was obliged to register as a foreign citizen. When the authorities refused her request to be imprisoned with other American nationals, she had to find work for the duration of the war. With news channels broken off, she was unaware that her parents, along with all other West-Coast Japanese-Americans, had been forcibly deported from Los Angeles to an internment camp in Arizona.

Toguri found it difficult to adjust to Japan. She disliked the food, which war and rationing had made scanty. Her command of Japanese was still so uncertain that she could not easily follow news broadcasts or newspaper stories, although she had signed on at a Japanese-language school early in her visit in an attempt to improve her fluency.

With the two countries at war, Toguri was pressured by the Japanese authorities to declare herself a Japanese citizen. She refused to do so (unlike many of the roughly 10,000 Nisei then in Japan) and had to suffer taunts from her aunt's neighbors that she was a spy. Policemen periodically visited the house and searched her possessions. To avoid embarrassing her relatives, she moved out and began to seek employment. She worked first at the Domei news agency as a translator of news stories picked up over the air on short-wave radio, a very ill-paying job. Poor diet and lack of vitamins led to her contracting scurvy and beriberi, and she was hospitalized for six weeks in the summer of 1943.

Later that year, she was recruited by Major Wallace Ince, an American, Lieutenant Norman Reyes, a Filipino, and Major Charles Cousens, an Australian, all of whom were prisoners of war, to work on a propaganda radio show with Tokyo Radio, where she had found an additional job as an English-language typist. Cousens, Reyes, and Ince insisted later that they were trying to *impede* the Japanese propaganda effort and offer news and solace to American troops in the Pacific. They claimed that they had deceived the Japanese into thinking that they were *helping* the Japanese war effort while actually hindering it. Toguri's job, they added, was to introduce music as a disc jockey, and her contributions had no anti-American propaganda content. Her voice was harsh rather than seductive: unlikely to fulfil the Japanese government's aim of inducing homesickness among the American troops. Cousens testified later:

> With the idea that I had in mind of making a complete burlesque of the program [her voice] was just what I wanted—rough. I hope I can say this without offense—a voice that I have described as a gin fog voice. It was rough, almost masculine, anything but a femininely seductive voice. It was a comedy voice that I needed for this particular job.

Her radio name was "Ann," later expanded to "Orphan Annie," and she told soldiers during her nightly broadcasts on a show named "Zero Hour" that she was their "favorite enemy."

In April 1945, Toguri converted from her original Methodism to Roman Catholicism, and married Felipe d'Aquino at the Jesuit mission church in Tokyo—the wedding reception was interrupted by an American bomber raid. D'Aquino was a linotype operator who also worked part time for Radio Tokyo and was half Japanese-half Portuguese. By virtue of the marriage, she gained Portuguese citizenship, although her husband, fluent in Japanese and English, could not speak any Portuguese. Like Toguri, he had been dismayed by the outbreak of the war and hoped for an Allied victory. They had both left the Domei news agency over this issue, and Toguri had found another temporary job as a typist at the Danish legation. Three months after their marriage, the atomic bombs at Hiroshima and Nagasaki brought the war to an end, and American occupation forces moved into the shattered ruins of Tokyo.

Contacted first by two journalists, Harry Brundidge and Clark Lee, who hid her in a hotel to protect their "scoop" and promised her $2,000 for her story, Toguri later spoke also to reporters from *Yank* magazine. It did not occur to her, apparently, that she might be in danger of prosecution. Instead, she enjoyed being in the company of Americans once more, and the offer of money in exchange for her story promised an end to the material privation she had suffered for the last four years. She admitted straight away that she was only one of several "Tokyo Roses." Following up on the news stories, the FBI sent an investigator to consider pressing treason charges against her, and imprisoned her in Tokyo's Sugamo Prison. The FBI and the Counter-Intelligence Corps, each of which investigated her, decided that a charge of treason could not be proved in court because her broadcast materials consisted of introductory remarks to light entertainment shows, all of which had been written by Major Cousens. Even so, she spent a full year at Sugamo.

Although the war was now over, Toguri decided to stay with her husband in Japan for the moment, and he urged her to avoid all possible press exposure in future. In 1947, when she was

Iva Toguri

pregnant, she applied for an American passport and declared her intention to return to the United States, perhaps because she wanted her child to be born on American ground. Her application set off a renewed flurry of interest in the American press, and she again, unwisely, spoke with reporters to declare her innocence. Harry Brundidge, whom she had earlier cheated of a scoop, and the inflammatory columnist and broadcaster Walter Winchell protested against letting her back into America, while the American Legion, a powerful veterans' organization, argued that she should be brought to justice as a traitor. The State and Justice departments were doubtful that a trial would lead to conviction, especially since Cousens and Ince, the prisoners of war who had hired Toguri, had been exonerated of possible treason charges.

Some said she was the wife of Saburo Kurusu, the last Japanese ambassador to Washington; others said she was General Tojo's mistress; or a hula dancer born in Maui; or a nisei woman born in Ottawa. . . . The most fascinating rumor of all was that Tokyo Rose might be Amelia Earhart, the famous woman pilot who disappeared in midflight over the Pacific in 1937.

—Masayo Duus

Toguri's child was stillborn. Under pressure from journalists and the American Legion, the attorney general's office decided to repatriate Toguri and prosecute her. It was an election year in 1948 and the Cold War was heating up. The Democratic administration of President Harry Truman was facing sharp Republican attacks for being "soft" on Communists and other "un-American" groups. Prosecuting Toguri must have seemed a tempting opportunity to Truman and his attorney general Tom Clark, especially once they found that FBI chief J. Edgar Hoover also favored pressing the case. Toguri was shipped to San Francisco in the fall of 1948 where a grand jury decided that there was sufficient evidence against her to warrant a trial. To help secure a conviction, the government transported 19 witnesses from Japan and paid them lavish expenses for the duration of their stay. Ironically, several of these witnesses were Nisei who had taken the easier wartime option of renouncing their American citizenship and had worked as Japanese loyalists at Tokyo Radio alongside the pro-American Toguri. The trial opened with great media fanfare. It was the first ever treason trial in San Francisco and it ran at the same time as the no-

torious Alger Hiss Communism and perjury trial back East in New York.

At that point, the government discovered that one of its principal witnesses, Hiromu Yagi, had lied about seeing Toguri broadcasting, and had done so at the urging of the journalist Brundidge. Nevertheless, the case went forward, beginning in July 1949 and featuring two other Nisei witnesses who had renounced their American citizenship. They said they had seen Toguri broadcasting news stories about American shipping losses, whose intent had been to discourage American soldiers. Her defense attorney, Wayne Collins, who had volunteered to work without payment, produced evidence that she had *avoided* giving "aid and comfort" to the enemy, and he managed to include in the court record evidence that some of the government's witnesses were involved in perjury and a cover-up. Collins, who already had a distinguished legal record on behalf of persecuted Japanese-Americans, also confirmed that she had tried to help American prisoners of war, and had cooperated with Cousens and Ince in their efforts to damage, rather than boost, Japanese propaganda.

The trial lasted three months and cost the government more than a half million dollars. Despite all the ambiguities of the case, an all-white jury, after four days of argument and frequent deadlock, convicted Toguri on one count of treason. Jury foreman John Mann admitted later that at first most jurors had wanted to find her not guilty but felt constrained by the judge's instructions. They reasoned that by finding her guilty on just one minor count they would satisfy the judge and that, since she had already been in custody for a total of two years, she would now be set free. To their horrified dismay the judge, Michael Roche, far from setting her free, sentenced her to ten years' imprisonment and a fine of $10,000.

An appeal failed and the Supreme Court refused to review the case. Accordingly, Toguri served a total of almost seven years in a women's prison in West Virginia. After her release in 1956, she went to live with her father, who, following the war, had built up a successful business in Chicago. To add to her burdens, she found on release that the government planned to deport her. But how could she be deported if she were a United States citizen, and how could she be a traitor if she had not been American to begin with? Bowing to this straightforward logic, the government never carried out the threat but continued to treat her as a stateless person and deny her the right to travel, in violation of the United Nations charter. A further hardship was that, during her trial, the government had permanently barred her husband d'Aquino from returning to America. This meant in effect that they were forcibly separated for their entire lives. As Catholics, they opposed divorce but under the circumstances agreed to a separation and never again met.

Toguri's friends and her attorney remained convinced that she had been wrongly accused and convicted. Most of her Japanese-American contemporaries had refused to concern themselves with her case because they were proud of their loyalty to the United States, even in the face of persecution, and saw her as an ugly exception to their otherwise spotless record. But a later generation of Japanese-Americans was more demanding. Not only did they pursue reparations for the injustice of internment; they also reopened the Toguri case and assembled overpowering evidence of her innocence. After years of efforts, they were finally able to get for Toguri a full pardon from President Gerald Ford on his last day in the White House, in January 1977. By then her lawyer was Wayne Collins, Jr., the son of her original defense attorney—she herself was 62 years old.

Historian Stanley Kutler sees Toguri as a scapegoat, who suffered in an atmosphere of Cold War paranoia. "Her acknowledged acts of broadcasting for the enemy took on a legendary mystique that heightened her importance far beyond the innocuous substance of her activities." Her biographer Masayo Duus, who saw the case as "one of the most egregious miscarriages of justice in American legal history," noted that other "political" trials of the era, notably those of Alger Hiss and Julius and *Ethel Rosenberg, became hotly contested public issues, whereas Toguri's did not. She "never became a cause celebre for anyone, not even for the Japanese American community, which regarded her indictment as a shameful blot on its otherwise unblemished record of wartime loyalty." In later life, she was, understandably, extremely reticent about meeting reporters or historians to discuss the events of her life. Instead, she devoted herself to running the Chicago business which her father had bequeathed to her at his death in 1973.

SOURCES AND SUGGESTED READING:

Duus, Masayo. *Tokyo Rose: Orphan of the Pacific*. Translated from Japanese by Peter Duus. NY: Harper and Row, 1979.

Howe, Russell Warren. *The Hunt for Tokyo Rose*. Lanham, MD: Madison, 1990.

Kutler, Stanley I. *The American Inquisition: Justice and Injustice in the Cold War*. NY: Hill and Wang, 1982.

COLLECTIONS:

Federal Bureau of Investigation "Tokyo Rose" files, and Counter Intelligence Corps of U.S. government "Tokyo Rose" files.

Patrick Allitt,
Professor of History,
Emory University,
Atlanta, Georgia

Toklas, Alice B. (1877–1967).

See Stein, Gertrude for sidebar.

Tokyo Rose (b. 1916).

See Toguri, Iva.

Tolstoi.

Variant of Tolstoy.

Tolstoy, Alexandra (1884–1979)

Daughter and secretary of Leo Tolstoy who tried to perpetuate his ideas through lectures, writing, and as president of the anti-Communist Tolstoy Foundation which aided Russian refugees coming to the United States. Name variations: Sasha Tolstoi or Tolstaya; Alexandra Tolstoj. Pronunciation: TOLE-stoye. Born Alexandra Lvovna Tolstoy on July 1, 1884, at the family estate, Yasnaya Polyana, in Russia; died at her Tolstoy Foundation estate, Reed Farm (an American Yasnaya Polyana), near Valley Cottage, New York, on September 26, 1979; daughter of Count Leo Nikolaevich Tolstoy (the author) and Sophia (Sonya) Andreyevna (Behrs) Tolstoy (1844–1919); aunt of **Vera Tolstoy** *(1903–1999, who worked with the Voice of America); mostly educated at parents' Moscow home; never married; no children.*

Secretary to Leo Tolstoy (1901–10); edited Tolstoy's posthumous works (1911–14); during World War I, served as nurse, Chief Medical Detachment (1914–17); founded Society for the Dissemination and Study of Tolstoy's Works (1918–28); became curator of Yasnaya Polyana Museum (1921–29); founded six schools (1921–29); arrested five times by Soviet government and spent one year in prison (1920–29); was a writer and lecturer in Japan (1929–31); entered U.S. (1931); served as president of the Tolstoy Foundation (1939–79).

Selected publications: Tragedy of Tolstoy *(Yale, 1933);* I Worked for the Soviet *(Yale, 1934);* Tolstoy: A Life of My Father *(Harper, 1953).*

Alexandra Tolstoy devoted her life to her father Leo Tolstoy and his literary career. Working as his secretary, she even refused marriage offers so that she could remain with him. When Tolstoy died in 1910, Alexandra realized that she had no life or interests that were purely her own. She had so idolized her father that his death left a deep void, an emptiness which she had no idea how to fill. She described the brief time between her father's death and the outbreak of World War I as the most difficult in her life. And yet, this remarkable woman served with distinction in wartime, openly opposed Communism, survived a prison camp, and immigrated to the United States where she established a humanitarian resettlement center for displaced persons and orphans.

Alexandra Tolstoy was the youngest daughter and 12th of 13 children of *Sonya Tolstoy and Count Leo Nikolaevich Tolstoy, the celebrated Russian author. She was born on July 1, 1883, at her parents' Russian estate, Yasnaya Polyana, in Tula province, about 130 miles south of Moscow. Shortly before her birth, Leo had almost stopped writing novels and had passionately turned to a study of religion and nonviolence. His writings described his search for God, his ideas about the Gospels, and the futility of war, and condemned the violent nature of the army, government, and Russian Orthodox Church. In one short novel, he even wrote of the immoral hatred that developed within marriage. In an already strained marriage, his efforts to put his religious theories into daily practice in his home led to a deep, emotional conflict within the Tolstoy family. As disciples, known as "Tolstoyans," came in steady streams to Yasnaya Polyana, Alexandra's mother Sonya remained loyal to the rituals and traditions of the Russian Orthodox Church. She never shared nor accepted his religious views.

Alexandra received most of her education at home from governesses who chided her for being a roughneck who loved nature and sports. With the exception of an Englishwoman, Miss Walsh, the other governess-teachers pulled her by the hair and gave her harsh penalties. Alexandra was in such despair that she once ran away with the intention of drowning herself in the Moscow River. Often ignored by her siblings, she was a plain little girl who grew closer to her eccentric father. She wrote that life was never easy in their family because they always had to choose between two lifestyles: either the life of an aristocrat or the life of a peasant who toiled on the land as her father advocated. Although she tried, she believed it was impossible to emulate those "peasant qualities" on a large estate, with sumptuous meals and 12 servants.

In 1901, Alexandra became a secretary to her father, chiefly copying his manuscripts and typing his correspondence. She was a rebellious young woman who defied her family's spiritual values by smoking, by slipping away to visit Gypsies (Roma), and by indiscriminately flirting. But nothing could keep her away from her father and quell her love for working on his manuscripts. Once he suggested that Alexandra marry a certain young man, but she refused, accusing him of offering her to a man of lesser quality. Leo warmly embraced her, and she swore to him that she would never put anyone in his place or marry. During those years, Alexandra also worked in a village clinic, a local school, and learned farming techniques. She blamed her mother for the depressing atmosphere of their home and wished to protect her aging father from the constant squabbles. Leo Tolstoy's death in a remote train station in 1910 resulted from pneumonia that he possibly contracted while, with Alexandra's help, he was attempting to flee from his wife and a sorrowful family life.

Under the terms of her father's will, Alexandra became the executor of his estate. In accordance with Leo's wishes, she prepared an edition of his unpublished works and negotiated an agreement for a complete edition of his writings. Also acting on his wishes, she used the proceeds of the literary contracts to purchase Yasnaya Polyana, which in the will had been divided among Tolstoy's widow and children, so that it could be transferred to the peasants. This transaction helped favorably settle Alexandra's relationship with her family. Her mother had blamed Alexandra for her complicity in Tolstoy's final trip, and she had been at odds with her brothers and sister Tatyana Tolstoy Sukhotina over Tolstoy's will.

In the difficult years following her father's death, Alexandra bought a farm, Novaya Polyana, about three miles from the Tolstoy estate. She obtained a herd of pedigree cattle and raised some purebred Orlov carriage horses. She studied and taught the peasants crop rotation and agronomy methods on the Tolstoy estate.

When her father was still alive, Alexandra had developed enough interest in medicine to study anatomy and physiology and to open a dispensary in the local peasant village. At the outbreak of World War I, she took short nursing courses and passed the nursing examinations while working at Zvenigorod Hospital near Moscow. Wishing to serve on the front, Alexandra became a nurse on a hospital train which provided emergency care while transporting wounded soldiers to hospitals. In 1914–15, she served in the All-Union Zemstvo Medical Service, a detachment of the Russian Red Cross, sent to fight an outbreak of typhus, typhoid, and malaria among the troops fighting the Turks on the Caucasian front. She was awarded the Medal of St. George, fourth class, for her service. After recovering from a bout with malaria, Alexandra served in an executive position running emergency schools and dining halls for thousands of children on the northwestern front. She then organized and commanded a military medical unit with three detachments. While establishing one of the detachments in Smorgon, Alexandra and her staff heroically treated thousands of soldiers while wearing gas masks during a chlorine gas attack. For her courage and valor, she was one of six to receive medals; hers was the Order of St. George, third class. She spent several months hospitalized while recovering from pyemia and recurring malaria and was released from the hospital shortly after the Russian Revolution in February 1917. Alexandra rejoined and reorganized the remnants of her medical unit which had been decimated by the war and lacked discipline as a result of the revolutionary collectivism being instilled by the new Communist government. She received a final medal of St. George for her efforts and her service against the Germans at the Battle of Krevo in 1917.

Alexandra
Tolstoy

When her service was completed, Alexandra returned to her home in Moscow in November 1917 and then went to Novaya Polyana, only to find that it had been confiscated as government property. She returned to Yasnaya Polyana where her mother and sister Tatyana were living. The Tolstoy estate had been spared because of the esteem the Russian people held for Leo Tolstoy. They struggled through the Russian famine of 1917–18 caused by the Red Communist Army's plundering during the Civil War. In 1918, the Yasnaya Polyana Society was formed by intellectuals in Tula to protect the Tolstoy estate and educate the estate peasants. When the society director became dictatorial and rude to the Tolstoy family living on the estate, Alexandra convinced the commissar of education, Anatoly Lunacharsky, to appoint her commissar of Yasnaya Polyana. She then fired the arrogant director and instituted a program transforming the estate into a national museum.

If you don't let me go, I shall have to telegraph Japan that you're frightened to let me go abroad.

—Alexandra Tolstoy to Soviet authorities

Alexandra spent most of her time at her home in Moscow and commuted to Yasnaya Polyana. In 1919, she was suddenly arrested and held for five days as a counter-revolutionary suspect. She was arrested again in March 1920 because she had permitted an organization, which unknown to her was made up of White Army subversives, to use the society office a year earlier. After two months in the notorious Lubyanka Prison, Alexandra was released along with several others until their trial. She was eventually sentenced to three years in the Novospasky Monastery, converted by the Communists into a prison camp. In the prison, she started a school and organized a chorus, astonishing her jailers with her spirit and her ability to adjust to the harsh conditions and common criminals incarcerated with her. After a year of imprisonment, she was released without explanation.

In late 1921, Alexandra was appointed curator of the national museum and educational center at Yasnaya Polyana. During her eight-year tenure, she founded a hospital, a clinic, a dispensary, four elementary schools, a nine-year agricultural high school and a seven-year industrial high school on the Tolstoy estate. Because no revolutionary politics were taught in schools, the Yasnaya Polyana estate was persecuted after 1924 by newspaper articles, government inspections, and critical evaluations. Communists from Tula began to influence the political and religious thinking of students, peasants, and employees of the estate. In desperation, Alexandra arranged to meet with Joseph Stalin in 1926 to enlist his support for a Tolstoy Jubilee in 1928 to celebrate the 100th anniversary of her father's birth. She hoped this would demonstrate the work and importance of the Yasnaya Polyana program. The Tolstoy Jubilee was held and foreign guests were impressed but only criticism appeared in Soviet newspapers. The Yasnaya Polyana complex was swept along in the wave of Stalin's reorganization program. As Communist doctrine and antireligious dogma filtered into the schools and teaching ranks, Alexandra resigned her position and, in October 1929, applied for government permission to travel to Japan to lecture on her father's literary career. Because of government opposition to granting her a passport, Alexandra threatened to telegraph Japan that the Soviets refused to let her travel abroad. She was then permitted to leave. For nearly two years, she lectured and wrote articles under the sponsorship of Japanese newspapers. In February 1931, she was ordered to return to the Soviet Union but chose instead to sever relations completely with her native land and embarked for the United States.

After spending some time in San Francisco, Alexandra traveled to Chicago where she stayed briefly with *Jane Addams at Hull House. She worked on a biography of her father and read to some of the elderly women there. Her time at Hull House was pleasant and restful, but she did not sympathize with Addams and her intellectual friends' academic views of Communism as social progress for the Russian people. When Alexandra expressed an interest in moving to New York, Addams recommended her to *Lillian Wald; thus, Alexandra stayed at the Henry Street Settlement House for a short time. She continued to write and to support herself with occasional lectures, and was also briefly reunited with her elder brother Ilya, who had been in the United States since 1916.

To support herself, Alexandra obtained a manager and went on the lecture circuit. Eventually, she was able to obtain a farm through the Neighborhood League at Newtown Square near Philadelphia. She and **Olga** and **Maria Kristyanovich**, who had accompanied Alexandra from Yasnaya Polyana to Japan and then to America, repaired and improved the dilapidated farm. Soon, Alexandra divided her time between lecturing about her father and anti-Communism and raising vegetables, chickens, and cows.

In 1933, Yale University accepted her biography of her father, *The Tragedy of Tolstoy*, for publication. (It had actually been published earlier in Japan and would eventually be published in several languages.) Though it was not her first book, it did establish her reputation in America. As the Great Depression deepened, Alexandra and her friends could not meet increased rental demands on the farm that they had worked so hard to improve. Just as things looked bleakest, **Jane Yarrow**, an American journalist who had met Alexandra in Armenia during World War I, appeared from nowhere to help. Yarrow had a friend with a small farm for sale in Haddam, Connecticut, for $1,000. With the $1,400 she received from *The Tragedy of Tolstoy*, Alexandra purchased the Haddam farm and moved there, accompanied by Olga and Maria.

Alexandra continued to speak to civic groups, women's clubs, forums and even the Society of Friends (Quakers) on the evils of Communism. She was disappointed in the lack of interest and faulty perception on the inhumane treatment of the Soviet people that pervaded the U.S. She even tried unsuccessfully in 1933 to interest President Franklin D. Roosevelt and Jane Addams in the human-rights issue.

In the meantime, the Russian émigrés lived happily and comfortably on the little farm in Haddam. Extra money was earned for incidentals during those Depression years by selling eggs at Wesleyan University fraternity houses in Middletown and at the Hamden farmers' cooperative. In 1933, she also spent time in New York City nursing her brother Ilya who died from cancer.

In 1934, Alexandra published *I Worked for the Soviet* which dramatically recounted the decade she spent in Russia following the Communist Revolution of 1917. On April 15, 1939, Alexandra, with the help of many Russian immigrants and prominent Americans, established the Tolstoy Foundation to assist victims of Soviet persecution. Among the foundation officers were aviator Boris V. Sergievsky, musician Sergei Rachmaninov, aviation pioneer Igor Sikorsky, Countess **Sophia V. Panin**, and historian Mikhail I. Rostovtsev. Former president Herbert Hoover served as honorary president. Alexandra, unanimously elected president of the foundation, sold the Connecticut farm, placed the proceeds in the foundation treasury, and opened an office in New York City. Initially, the organization sent food, clothing, and Bibles to the 50,000 Russian prisoners held in Finland following the Soviet Union's disastrous invasion of that country in 1939. In early 1941, the Tolstoy Foundation obtained Reed Farm, a former children's sanatorium with 74 acres near Valley Cottage, as a donation from the *Mary Stillman Harkness Foundation.

Under Alexandra's direction, Reed Farm became a temporary home for Russian exiles, displaced persons, and orphans trying to make a transition to a new life in America. She also built a hospital, dormitories, and a Russian Orthodox Church there. The Department of Immigration reported that the Tolstoy Foundation helped an estimated 3,500 people a year settle in the United States. Under Alexandra's guidance, the foundation sent assistance to displaced persons' camps in Germany, Austria, and Trieste. The foundation established branches in Chicago, Bridgeport, Washington, D.C., and on the West Coast. By 1953, it maintained 15 offices in Europe, primarily to assist people trying to escape from the Soviet Union. Under Alexandra's leadership, other offices were established in Brazil, Argentina, and Chile. Although it was primarily formed to aid Russian immigrants, Alexandra convinced the foundation to accept all refugees following the Hungarian revolution in 1956. Since that time, Reed Farm has aided Czechs, Tibetans, Himalayans, Ugandans, Kalmaks, Armenians, and even "boat people" from Indochina.

Alexandra Tolstoy, who became an American citizen in 1941, preferred no political associations but remained a staunch anti-Communist and a devout member of the Russian Orthodox Church. She lived at Reed Farm and remained active as the foundation's president and as a writer and lecturer. Though she suffered a stroke in 1977 that left her bedridden and nearly blind, she continued to dictate letters until shortly before her death on September 26, 1979, in the Tolstoy Foundation nursing home at Reed Farm. She was 95 years old. Following services at St. Sergius Russian Orthodox Church, she was buried in the Russian cemetery on the grounds of her beloved Tolstoy Foundation farm which she called the "American Yasnaya Polyana."

SOURCES:
Current Biography. NY: H.W. Wilson, 1953.
Edwards, Anne. *Sonya: The Life of Countess Tolstoy*. NY: Simon and Schuster, 1986.
The New York Times. September 27 and October 2, 1979.
Simmons, Ernest J. *Leo Tolstoy*. Boston, MA: Little, Brown, 1946.
Tolstoy, Alexandra. *I Worked for the Soviet*. Translated by Roberta Yerkes. New Haven, CT: Yale University Press, 1934.
————. *Out of the Past*. Edited by Katharine Strelsky and Catherine Wolkonsky. NY: Columbia University Press, 1981.
————. *Tolstoy, A Life of My Father*. Translated by Elizabeth Reynolds Hapgood. NY: Harper and Bros., 1953.

———. *The Tragedy of Tolstoy.* Translated by Elena Varneck. New Haven, CT: Yale University Press, 1933.

SUGGESTED READING:

Carroll, Sara Newton. *The Search: A Biography of Leo Tolstoy.* NY: Harper & Row, 1973.

Leon, Derrick. *Tolstoy: His Life and Work.* London: Routledge, 1946.

Tolstoy, Alexandra. *The Real Tolstoy.* Morristown, NJ: H.S. Evans, 1968.

Tolstoy, Nikolai. *The Tolstoys.* NY: William Morrow, 1983.

Troyat, Henri. *Tolstoy.* NY: Dell, 1967.

Phillip E. Koerper,
Professor of History,
Jacksonville State University,
Jacksonville, Alabama

Tolstoy, Sonya (1844–1919)

*Russian wife of Leo Tolstoy. Name variations: Countess Tolstoy or Tolstoi; Sonia, Sophie, Sofya, Sofia, Sofiya, Sofie Anreevna; Sophie Behrs. Born Sophia Andreyevna Behrs in 1844; died in 1919; daughter of Lyubov Alexandrovna Behrs (who was the illegitimate daughter of Princess Kozlovsky) and a Dr. Behrs; married Count Leo Nikolaevich Tolstoy (the novelist and social and moral philosopher), on September 23, 1862; children: thirteen (six died young), Sergei or Sergey Lvovich (1863–1947); **Tatyana Tolstoy Sukhotina** (1864–1950); Ilya (1866–1933, whose daughter **Vera Tolstoy** [1903–1999] worked for the Voice of America); Lev (1869–1945); Marya (1871–1906); Pyotr (1872–1873); Nikolai (1874–1875); Varvara (1875–1875); Andrei (1877–1916); Mikhail (1879–1944); Alexei (1881–1886); *Alexandra Tolstoy (1884–1979); Ivan (1888–1895).*

When 18-year-old Sonya Behrs wed Count Leo Tolstoy, he was almost twice her age and brought to the marriage a hard-lived soldier's past, one mistress, and an illegitimate son. They were both deeply in love, but, within two months of the ceremony, Sonya began to confide in a diary her inability to comprehend her moody husband and accept his previous life. "Today I suddenly felt that we would gradually drift apart and each live our own lives," she wrote on October 8, 1862, "that I would create my own sad world for myself, and he a world full of work and doubt. And this relationship struck me as vulgar. I have stopped believing in his love. When he kisses me, I think to myself: 'Well, I'm not the first woman.'" Bored, jealous, depressed, and longing for a deeper intimacy, Sonya was obsessed with Tolstoy and would remain obsessed. "When he is away or working, I always think of him, listening for his footsteps, and when he is here I keep watching his face."

She spent the first years of their lives together paying homage to his genius, copying his manuscripts, serving as his business manager, and bearing their children, and the last years begging to be recognized as her own person, with her own wants and needs. Thwarted in an attempt to become his literary companion, exhausted by the births of 13 children, Sonya became quarrelsome and self-pitying. The tension in the household grew worse when Leo turned away from fiction toward social and philosophical causes. With Sonya mystified by his new interests, the gap widened and their views polarized. His interest in Christianity sent her running to the arms of Russian Orthodoxy. Sonya found her husband's advocacy of asceticism and sexual abstinence hypocritical in light of his aristocratic existence and her continued pregnancies.

Sonya's need for her husband, and her need to understand and be understood by her husband, eventually took a toll on her mental health, though she often had enough clarity to assess her

$\mathcal{S}$onya
$\mathcal{T}$olstoy

own behavior. She wrote in December 1890: "It is sad that my emotional dependence on the man I love should have killed so much of my energy and ability; there was certainly once a great deal of energy in me." At age 82, in 1910, Leo fled Sonya and Yasnaya Polyana; ten days later, he died of pneumonia at an isolated railway station.

SOURCES:

Edwards, Anne. *Sonya: The Life of Countess Tolstoy.* NY: Simon and Schuster, 1986.

Shirer, William L. *Love and Hatred: The Troubled Marriage of Leo and Sonya Tolstoy.* NY: Simon & Schuster, 1994.

Tomaszewicz-Dobrska, Anna

(1854–1918)

Polish doctor. Name variations: Anna Tomaszewiczowna. Born in 1854 in Poland; died in 1918; educated in Zurich, Vienna, Berlin, and St. Petersburg; married a physician.

The first woman to practice medicine in Poland, Anna Tomaszewicz-Dobrska was born in 1854 into a family that did not encourage her career aspirations. She studied medicine in Zurich, and qualified as a doctor in Switzerland in 1878. Tomaszewicz-Dobrska then did graduate work briefly in Vienna, Berlin, and St. Petersburg, where she qualified to practice medicine in 1879. Returning to Warsaw, she married a physician and began working as a doctor. Despite objections from the medical establishment, she was made chief of Lying-In Hospital No. 2 in Warsaw, a facility for obstetric patients, and remained there until it closed in 1911. She also maintained a private practice. In 1896, Tomaszewicz-Dobrska was recognized by the Warsaw Medical Society. An advocate of women's rights, she participated in social work and was also a founding member of the Society of Polish Culture. She died in 1918.

Elizabeth Shostak, M.A.,
Cambridge, Massachusetts

Tomoe Gozen (fl. c. 12th c.)

Japan's legendary woman warrior, said to have been both beautiful and valiant, who displayed military prowess equal to that of any man during the Taira-Minamoto war (1180–1185). Pronunciation: Toemow-eh Go-zen. Flourished around the 12th century in Japan.

It is likely that Tomoe Gozen lived, but her story is more the stuff of romantic legend, having been recorded in war chronicles like *Heike Monogatari* (The Tale of the Heike), which were compiled from ballads sung by medieval traveling storytellers. Tomoe's story is linked with that of Kiso Yoshinaka, commander of the Minamoto forces in the clan wars of 1180–1185, who was described in the war chronicles as a "wild barbarian." Tomoe, his concubine, accompanied Yoshinaka into battle and was said to have personally commanded a force of 1,000 warriors. She was with him when he had to flee from his previous allies, who accused him of treachery and abuse of power, which appears to have been the case. Yoshinaka pleaded with Tomoe to leave him and thus spare her own life. She refused to flee, however, until she had taken the head of an enemy warrior to prove her military prowess. This she did, overpowering a great warrior in hand-to-hand combat. Yoshinaka committed suicide and Tomoe escaped. The chronicles say that Tomoe, who was then 28, became a Buddhist nun.

SOURCES:

Tyler, Royall. "Tomoe: the Woman Warrior," in *Heroic with Grace: Legendary Women of Japan.* Chieko Mulhern, ed. Armonk, NY: M.E. Sharpe, 1991, pp. 129–150.

Linda L. Johnson,
Professor of History,
Concordia College,
Moorhead, Minnesota

Tompkins, Sally Louisa

(1833–1916)

American military nurse who was the first woman commissioned as an officer in the Confederate Army. Born on November 9, 1833, in Poplar Grove, Mathews County, Virginia; died of chronic interstitial nephritis on July 25, 1916, in Richmond, Virginia; daughter of Christopher Tompkins (a justice of the peace, member of the militia, and state representative) and Maria Boothe (Patterson) Tompkins.

Sally Louisa Tompkins was born in 1833 in Mathews County, Virginia, where she spent her childhood as the youngest of four children in a family distinguished on both sides by political service. Her father, who became a justice of the peace and a militia member after an earlier career as a merchant mariner, was elected to the Virginia legislature. Her mother's father had fought in the Revolutionary War and been cited for bravery at the battle of Monmouth. The family was well known in Tidewater Virginia, and enjoyed a wide circle of friends. When Colonel Tompkins died shortly before the outbreak of the Civil War, the family moved to Richmond, Virginia, which became the capital of the Confederacy.

In Richmond, the Confederate Army opened many military hospitals to care for war casualties. Among the first was the 25-bed Robertson Hospital, operated by Tompkins (who financed most of the institution) and a group of socially prominent women she recruited as nurses. She had only a permanent staff of seven, including herself, two veterans unable to serve, and four slaves, but her hospital soon developed a reputation for the quality of its care. When the surgeon general of the Confederacy recommended that private hospitals in Richmond be closed, President Jefferson Davis did not want to lose the city's best facility. He commissioned Tompkins as a captain of cavalry—an unprecedented step—which enabled her to keep her hospital open as a military facility. She declined her captain's salary, however. From August 1, 1861, when it received its first patient, to June 13, 1865, when it discharged its last patient, the Robertson Hospital recorded only 73 deaths out of 1,333 admissions. This record was unmatched by any other hospital in either the North or the South, and was all the more outstanding because the most critical cases were often sent there. Tompkins' emphasis on sanitation may well have contributed to the success rate of her hospital. In addition, she was known to stress religion and to be effective in boosting the low morale of soldiers in her care.

After the war, Tompkins lived quietly in Richmond, engaging in local charity work. In 1905, after having exhausted most of her financial resources, she was invited by the board of managers of Richmond's Home for Confederate Women to live there as a guest, but she insisted on paying her own expenses. She remained there until her death in 1916, and was buried with full military honors.

SOURCES:
Griffin, Lynn, and Kelly McCann. *The Book of Women: 300 Notable Women History Passed By.* Holbrook, MA: Bob Adams, 1992.

James, Edward T., ed. *Notable American Women, 1607–1950.* Cambridge, MA: The Belknap Press of Harvard University, 1971.

McHenry, Robert, ed. *Famous American Women.* NY: Dover, 1980.

Read, Phyllis J., and Bernard L. Witlieb. *The Book of Women's Firsts.* NY: Random House, 1992.

Elizabeth Shostak, M.A.,
Cambridge, Massachusetts

Tomyris (fl. 550–530 BCE).

See Tamiris.

Tone, Matilda (c. 1769–1849)

Wife of Irish nationalist Wolfe Tone. Born Martha Witherington, exact date and place unknown, around 1769; *died on March 18, 1849, in Washington, D.C.; daughter of William Witherington and Catherine (Fanning) Witherington; married Theobald Wolfe Tone (the Irish nationalist), on July 21, 1785; married Thomas Wilson, on August 8, 1816; children: (first marriage) Maria Tone (1786–1803); William Tone (b. 1791); Frank Tone (b. 1793).*

Matilda Tone was born Martha Witherington around 1769. Her father William Witherington has been variously described as an English naval officer, a woolen draper, and a wine merchant. Her mother **Catherine Fanning Witherington** was the daughter of a wealthy Church of Ireland cleric, Edward Fanning, who was well-connected socially and politically. After the death of Catherine's mother, Catherine, William, and their two sons and four daughters went to live with Edward Fanning in Grafton Street, Dublin. It was there, one day at the beginning of 1785, that a young law student, Theobald Wolfe Tone, glimpsed Martha Witherington through a window of the house. "I soon grew passionately fond of her," he recalled, "and she was also much struck with me. . . . She was, at this time, not sixteen years and as beautiful as an angel." Tone soon insinuated himself into the family by making the acquaintance of Martha's brother Edward. After a courtship of a few months they eloped and were married in July 1785. As Tone's biographer **Marianne Elliott** notes, the elopement must have seemed like an appalling betrayal of trust to the Witheringtons, and, although there was a temporary rapprochement after the marriage, this did not last long. Relations between the two families, particularly between Tone and his brother-in-law Edward, deteriorated. Martha remained close only to her sister **Kitty Witherington**.

One of Tone's first actions after the marriage was to rename his wife Matilda. It was a bizarre yet eerily prescient gesture for Matilda would be a dramatic role played by **Eliza Martin** with whom Tone had been passionately in love before he met Martha. In the play *Douglas*, by John Home, Matilda was the virtuous widow of a fallen hero who remarried after his death but gave her new husband nothing more than companionship and respect. After their marriage, the Tones lived with his parents at their farm in County Kildare. Tone continued his university studies at Trinity College, Dublin, and graduated in February 1786. Their first child, **Maria Tone**, was born later that year. In October 1786, there was a violent robbery at the family home during which Matilda behaved with conspicuous bravery. "I can imagine no greater effort of courage," her husband wrote. There is little evidence about the early years of their marriage but what does exist indicates that it was uneasy. Tone spent long periods away from home (including two years pursuing his legal career in London between 1786 and 1788), leaving Matilda in Kildare. He also embarked on impetuous plans and projects without any consideration for what they would mean for her. One such example was his plan to set up a military colony in the Sandwich Islands. When this failed he considered in 1788 enlisting as a soldier with the East India Company. Elliott observes that while Tone criticized other men for neglecting their wives "he did so himself in the grandest of manners." When he returned from London in December 1788, Matilda was in poor health, but a gift of £500 from her grandfather eased their immediate financial problems. However, when her grandfather died a few years later they learned that Matilda had been cut out of his will, to the fury of her husband who blamed it on his brother-in-law's machinations.

The family spent the summer of 1790 at Irishtown, just south of Dublin city on the coast, and Tone remembered their sojourn there as the happiest days of his life. Their son William was born in April 1791, but Matilda saw little of her husband over the next year. He had become involved in a new radical group called the United Irishmen, who were inspired by the ideals of the French Revolution, and was spending most of his time in Dublin and Belfast. Matilda, still living in Kildare, sometimes accompanied him to Dublin, but she disliked large social gatherings. Another son, Frank, was born in 1793. In 1795, Tone's revolutionary activities led to him being exiled from Ireland. He, Matilda, their children and his sister **Mary Tone** left for America in June 1795 and made their way to Philadelphia. Their stay in America was unhappy. Tone hated America and Americans—"the most disgusting race, eaten up with the vice of commerce and that vilest of all pride, the pride of the purse." Matilda was in poor health and found their home near Princeton, New Jersey, inconvenient and uncomfortable. Tone did not want to bring up his children in America and longed to return to Ireland.

In February 1796, he went to France on a mission to persuade the French government to support an insurrection in Ireland. Matilda was pregnant again but did not tell him until he was about to leave so that he could not change his plans. Tone secured French help for an expedition to Ireland in December 1796, but the expedition collapsed due to severe storms and an ap-

athetic response in Ireland. Matilda, who had miscarried, left America with the children at the end of 1796 and arrived in Hamburg in January 1797, after a terrible Atlantic crossing. They lived happily outside Paris until September 1798, when Tone embarked on another expedition to Ireland. In her analysis of their correspondence before this event, Elliott concludes that both of them knew he would not come back, as the expedition was plagued by leaks of information, changes of plan and a lack of money. It was galling to Matilda to learn later that one of the leaks had come from Thomas Reynolds, husband of her sister **Harriet Witherington Reynolds**. Tone was captured when the expedition landed in Ireland, and on November 11 he learned that he was to be publicly hanged the following day. That night he slit his throat and died a week later. Suspicions of foul play were put forward at the time and since, but Matilda never doubted that it was suicide and wrote later: "he told me he knew his life was gone, but that executed he would never be."

Matilda's life after Tone's death was hard. Her brother Edward had promised Tone while he was in prison in Dublin that he would look after her but did not. She received some money from the French government, but the promised pension did not materialize until 1804 as a result of her personal appeals to Napoleon and Talleyrand. The pension was paid to her until her death by successive French governments. Her daughter Maria died of tuberculosis in 1803 and was followed three years later by her youngest child Frank, also of TB. This left only William who studied at the French military college at St. Germain and joined the French army. He fought in Napoleon's campaigns in 1813–14 and was awarded the Légion d'Honneur. He served under the brief Bourbon Restoration in 1814–15 but supported Napoleon during the Hundred Days in 1815.

Following Napoleon's defeat at Waterloo, Matilda and William applied for permission to return to Ireland, but the name Tone was still considered too dangerous for the authorities and they were refused. In August 1816, Matilda married an old friend of Tone's, Thomas Wilson, who was a Scottish doctor. The marriage would only last eight years until Wilson's death in 1824, but it was happy and gave Matilda much-needed stability and comfort. In 1817, she and Wilson joined William in America. In 1824, after Thomas Wilson's death, she and William started compiling a biography of Wolfe Tone based on his memoirs, journals and writings. The two-volume *Life of Theobald Wolfe Tone*, published in 1826 in Washington, was a work of great historical significance. However, Matilda and William made some key excisions: notably Tone's contemptuous comments on the Witheringtons; his criticisms of Americans and America (where his widow and son were now living happily); and Tone's references to other women and to such frivolous pursuits as theater, opera and ballet. The excised passages are included in Thomas Bartlett's 1998 edition of the *Life.*

William died of the family scourge, tuberculosis, in October 1828, leaving a daughter. Matilda stayed on in Washington, becoming something of a celebrity. A visitor from Ireland meeting her in 1836 noted that "both on the tongue and heart—her feelings are enthusiastically Irish." In the mid-1830s, R.R. Madden, who was writing his monumental history of the United Irishmen, arrived in America where many of the surviving exiles now lived. For some reason historians cannot explain, he never spoke to Matilda Tone and since she never wrote her memoirs ("a misfortune," as Frank MacDermot wrote in his 1939 biography of Wolfe Tone), Madden missed a major opportunity. When Matilda died in March 1849, in her 81st year, according to the obituaries, her funeral was attended by the French ambassador, French and American generals and a huge number of representatives from Irish-American societies.

SOURCES:

Curtin, Nancy J. "Matilda Tone and virtuous republican femininity," in *The Women of 1798.* Edited by Daire Keogh and Nicholas Furlong. Dublin: Four Courts Press, 1998, pp. 26–46.

Elliott, Marianne. *Wolfe Tone: Prophet of Irish Independence.* New Haven, CT: Yale University Press, 1989.

MacDermot, Frank. *Theobald Wolfe Tone: A Biographical Study.* London: Macmillan, 1939.

Reynolds, Thomas. *The Life of Thomas Reynolds, Esq. By his son.* London: Henry Hooper, 1839. 2 vols.

St. Mark, J.J. "Matilda and William Tone in Washington after 1798," in *Eire/Ireland.* Vol. 22, no. 4. Winter 1987, pp. 4–10.

Tone, William T.W. *Life of Theobald Wolfe Tone: Memoirs, Journals and Political Writings, compiled and arranged by William T.W. Tone, 1826.* Edited by Thomas Bartlett. Dublin: Lilliput Press, 1998.

SUGGESTED READING:

Jacob, Rosamond. *The Rebel's Wife* (novel). Tralee: The Kerryman, 1957.

Deirdre McMahon,
lecturer in history at Mary Immaculate College,
University of Limerick,
Limerick, Ireland

Tonga, queen of.
See Salote Topou III (1900–1965).

Tonnerre, countess of.
See Mahaut II de Dampierre (1234–1266).

See Yolande of Burgundy (1248–1280).
See Marguerite de Bourgogne (1250–1308).
See Jeanne of Chalon (1300–1333).

Toomey, Mary (b. 1940).
See Rand, Mary.

Toor, Frances (1890–1956)

American author, publisher, anthropologist and ethnographer whose books and journal Mexican Folkways *introduced Americans to the folk traditions and art of revolutionary Mexico. Name variations: Paca Toor; Panchita Toor. Born in Plattsburgh, New York, in 1890; died in New York City on June 16, 1956; had brothers Bernard, Elliott, Harold, and Herbert, and sisters Dorothy, Esther, and Mary; University of California, Berkeley, B.A. and M.A. degrees in anthropology; married J.L. Weinberger (a dentist, divorced early 1920s).*

Selected writings: Festivals and Folkways of Italy *(NY: Crown, 1953);* Frances Toor's Guide to Mexico, including Lower California *(8th ed. rev. and augmented by Fredericka Martin. NY: Crown, 1967);* The Golden Carnation, and Others Stories Told in Italy *(NY: Lothrop, Lee and Shepard, 1960);* Made in Italy *(NY: Alfred A. Knopf, 1957);* Spanish for Your Mexican Visit *(Mexico City: n.p., 1935);* The Three Worlds of Peru *(NY: Crown, 1949);* A Treasury of Mexican Folkways: The Customs, Myths, Folklore, Traditions, Beliefs, Fiestas, Dances and Songs of the Mexican People *(NY: Crown, 1947).*

Born in 1890 into a large Jewish family in upstate New York, Frances Toor moved west to study at the University of California at Berkeley, where she earned a B.A. and an M.A. in anthropology. In 1922, she went to Mexico along with her husband Dr. J.L. Weinberger, a dentist who headed the B'nai Brith office in Mexico City. Determined to become part of the intellectual life of the Mexican capital, Toor first attended courses for foreign students at the National University's summer school. Later, she taught English in government schools. In her leisure time, she visited local markets and shops and began to explore the nearby world of traditional peasant villages. What she found there, particularly folk art, music and dance, astonished her with its richness and colorful spontaneity. Like many foreigners, she fell in love with the Mexican people, whose passionate approach to life contrasted dramatically with the inhibited behavior deemed appropriate in the Anglo-Saxon world she had grown up in. The splendor of Mexico's folk art would change the course of her life: "The beauty of it was one of the motivating factors in my remaining. I wanted to know more of the country in which humble people could make such beautiful things."

Although she always remained somewhat quiet and reserved in manner, soon after her arrival in Mexico Toor divorced her husband and became part of a growing circle of artists and intellectuals, both American and Mexican. Her apartment was located in a building overlooking a shared courtyard, and her neighbors quickly became her close friends and colleagues. These included the radical journalist Carleton Beals and the Communists Bertram and **Ella Wolfe**. Known to her friends as either "Paca" or "Panchita" (the diminutive of Francisca, her name in Spanish), Toor could often be seen, a squat figure in khakis and boots, hoisting herself into the saddle of a horse or mule to scour the Mexican countryside for new treasures of folk and popular art untouched by commercialism and modernity. Seemingly indefatigable, she investigated backwater Mexico by bus, auto, train and plane. Of particular interest to her were the local fiestas, which she followed round the calendar. She joined in pilgrimages to shrines, feigned illness to be cured by Indian healers and witches, and questioned locals and aged storytellers. Back in her apartment, she would check for corroborating details in the centuries-old chronicles left by conquistadors and their padres.

In Mexico City itself, Toor became a supporter of the rapidly emerging mural movement associated with such artists as Diego Rivera, José Clemente Orozco, and Jean Charlot, a French painter of Mexican ancestry who after arriving in Mexico in 1920 was to play a crucial role in the revival of the fresco mural technique as well as the art of woodcuts. Toor also introduced the work of Carlos Mérida and David Alfaro Sequiros to art collectors in the United States. As a champion of the social reforms of the Mexican revolution, Toor hoped that her writings about the country's new artistic achievements, particularly the murals which defined the ideals of social progress, would be sympathetically received by American readers.

Convinced that Mexico's artistic Renaissance would be of permanent significance, not only for that revolution-racked nation but for the rest of the world as well, Toor decided to publish a magazine to disseminate these largely unknown cultural riches. With its first issue dated June–July 1925, *Mexican Folkways* appeared as a small bilingual journal with profuse illustrations. From its inception, *Mexican Folk-*

ways had an ambitious agenda; its purpose was to inform readers about Mexico's "legends, festivals, art, [and] archaeology." "Because of my own joy in the discovery of an art and civilization different from any that I had previously known," wrote Toor in the premiere issue, "I thought it would interest others as well." With a modest subsidy from the Mexican Department of Education, Toor was able to publish *Mexican Folkways* on a somewhat irregular basis from 1925 through 1937. Starting as a bimonthly, the journal became a quarterly in 1928, ceasing to publish entirely in 1931 due to a temporary but severe financial crunch and again for most of 1933. It was revived in 1934, being published again as of that year on an irregular basis, until the last issue finally appeared in July 1937.

Many of the subscribers to *Mexican Folkways* were convinced that in Mexico art and life had remained closely bonded. Critic Walter Pach celebrated the continuity modern Mexico had been able to maintain with its Indian past, particularly through its artifacts: "The millions of

Frances Toor

little earthen sculptures of heads that the soil contains, like the grand figures in stone, tell of people whose life was essentially that of today." *Mexican Folkways* contained articles on a great variety of subjects, including reproductions of the murals being painted by Toor's friend Diego Rivera, who for a number of years was a co-editor of the journal. Most of its contributors were also acquainted with its editor-publisher. For several years, Toor and *Tina Modotti were close friends, and in 1929 the journal published an article by Modotti on photography. Sociable and blunt, Toor was regarded by some as being scholarly and even pedantic, but despite such eccentricities she always found herself welcome in the convivial party scene of Mexico City's avant-garde artists and radical writers and journalists. For a number of years during the late 1920s, the conservative U.S. ambassador considered Toor to be a dangerous radical, his evidence being her close friendships with such subversive individuals as Modotti and, even more incriminating, with the Soviet ambassador to Mexico, *Alexandra Kollontai.

In the pages of *Mexican Folkways*, its readers were introduced to ephemeral or recently rediscovered aspects of Mexico's popular culture, ranging from folk songs and dances to *pulqueria* painting, children's art, and the woodcuts of José Guadalupe Posada. Posada (1852–1913) was an engraver of crude popular woodcuts whose ruthless social commentary easily matched that of the great French lithographer Honoré Daumier. With her sharp eye for cultural energy and quality, Toor brought the body of Posada's work to the attention of collectors and scholars, viewing his art as a forerunner of the mural movement of the 1920s, and "the stirring events of those days." Although subsequent scholarship on Posada has not always agreed with Toor's interpretations, her efforts on behalf of a deeper appreciation of his work—which in 1930 was crowned by the first publication of a book on his woodcuts—played an important role in bringing his art to the attention of the world.

By the early 1930s, the innocent enthusiasms of the previous decade were being changed by a new era of world economic depression and growing political rigidity. Some of Toor's friends, including Modotti, now became supporters of a Stalinist version of Communism. Toor's political enthusiasms had always been subordinated to her interest in art and folklore, and by the 1930s she had become strongly opposed to Stalinist ideas and practices. As a result, her friendship with Modotti collapsed.

Toor's other friendships sometimes suffered as well, probably because she had become so determined to succeed as an editor and publisher. For each negative evaluation, however, there were at least as many words of praise. In 1931, Tina Modotti's lover, the photographer Edward Weston, characterized Toor in his daybook as the "always generous and thoughtful Frances."

By the mid-1930s, Toor had become a successful entrepreneur. Her Frances Toor Studios published a highly popular series of tour guides, including *Frances Toor's Guide to Mexico*, which appeared in many editions, and language handbooks for tourists, including *Spanish for Your Mexican Visit*. Other popular books from her publishing firm included interpretive guides to the Orozco frescoes in Guadalajara and Diego Rivera's frescoes in Mexico City's Ministry of Education. These books brought Toor a measure of financial success which enabled her to enjoy a lifestyle of considerable affluence, moving from her modest apartment to a modern house designed by the noted architect Juan O'Gorman.

At least as important as material success to Toor, however, were her contributions to deeper cultural understanding between Mexico and the rest of the world, particularly the United States. In a letter of December 1932 to *Elsie Clews Parsons, Toor indicated that although she did not claim to be a scholar, "I'm more than content to have won the respect of people like you, Dr. [Franz] Boas, Dr. Paul Rivet and others for folkways." In 1947, Toor published *A Treasury of Mexican Folkways*, an encyclopedic reference work which has remained in print ever since and remains an important source of information not only for scholars but for the general reading public as well. For her achievements as a scholar and popularizer of Mexican cultural achievements abroad, Frances Toor was awarded one of the nation's highest honors, the Order of the Aztec Eagle.

In the 1940s, although she remained attached to Mexican culture and art, Toor's interests shifted considerably. She was now drawn to regions and cultures she had long wanted to visit and better understand. As a result of these extended travels, Toor published a number of books, including *The Three Worlds of Peru* (1949) which provides insights into that country's "three worlds," the coastal world, the sierra world, and the *montaña* world. She then decided to become acquainted with Italian folk traditions, producing after several years of intensive travel in that country a number of volumes that received positive reviews. Toor was pleased by the critical response received by her 1953 book *Festivals and Folkways of Italy*. The voluminous notes she had taken in Europe as well as her vivid memories allowed her to complete several more manuscripts during the next few years.

She did not, however, live to see their appearance in print. Frances Toor died in New York City on June 16, 1956. She had returned to the United States from Italy two weeks before and was planning to go to Mexico City in early July to give a course in Mexican folklore traditions at the National University. Instead, she became seriously ill and died of peritonitis in Manhattan's Mount Sinai Hospital. Frances Toor's last two books, *Made in Italy* (1957) and *The Golden Carnation, and Other Stories Told in Italy* (1960), appeared posthumously.

SOURCES:

Albers, Patricia. *Shadows, Fire, Snow: The Life of Tina Modotti*. NY: Clarkson Potter, 1999.

Britton, John A. *Carleton Beals: A Radical Journalist in Latin America*. Albuquerque, NM: University of New Mexico Press, 1987.

———. *Revolution and Ideology: Images of the Mexican Revolution in the United States*. Lexington, KY: University of Kentucky Press, 1995.

Brown, John. "Exuberancia México-Norteamericana, 1920–1940," in *Anglia* [Universidad Nacional Autónoma de México]. No. 1, 1968, pp. 95–122.

Delpar, Helen. *The Enormous Vogue of Things Mexican: Cultural Relations Between the United States and Mexico, 1920–1935*. Tuscaloosa, AL: University of Alabama Press, 1992.

"Diego Rivera," in *Mexican Folkways*. Vol. 6, no. 4, 1930, pp. 161–204.

Folgarait, Leonard. *Mural Painting and Social Revolution in Mexico, 1920–1940*. Cambridge: Cambridge University Press, 1998.

"Frances Toor, 66, Wrote on Mexico," in *The New York Times*. June 18, 1956, p. 25.

Frank, Patrick. *Posada's Broadsheets: Mexican Popular Imagery, 1890–1910*. Albuquerque, NM: University of New Mexico Press, 1998.

Mérida, Carlos, and Frances Toor. *Frescoes in Ministry of Education*. Mexico City: Frances Toor Studios, 1937.

———. *Modern Mexican Artists*. Mexico City: Frances Toor Studios, 1937.

———. *Orozco's Frescoes in Guadalajara*. Mexico City: Frances Toor Studios, 1940.

Schmidt, Henry C. "The American Intellectual Discovery of Mexico in the 1920's," in *The South Atlantic Quarterly*. Vol. 77, no. 3. Summer 1978, pp. 335–351.

Smoot, Sharene Lowery. "Frances Toor as an Authority on Mexican Folk Dance," M.A. thesis, East Carolina College, Greenville, NC, 1963.

Toor, Frances. "The Arts in Mexico," in *School Arts Magazine*. Vol. 31. February 1932, pp. 322–336.

———. "A Glimpse of Oaxaca," in *Mexican Folkways*. Vol. 2, no. 6, 1926, pp. 5–8.

———. "Máximo Pacheco: A Revolutionary Artist," in *Bulletin of the Pan American Union*. Vol. 62, no. 3. March 1928, pp. 286–290.

———. "Mexican Folk Dances," in Hubert Clinton Herring and Herbert Weinstock, eds., *Renascent Mexico*. NY: Covici, Friede, 1935, pp. 179–198.

———, et al., eds. *Monografia, Las Obras de José Guadalupe Posada, grabador Mexicano*. Reprint ed. Mexico City: Instituto Nacional de Bellas Artes-Instituto Cultural de Aguascalientes, 1991 (originally published by *Mexican Folkways* in 1930).

Werner, Michael S., ed. *Encyclopedia of Mexico: History, Society & Culture*. Chicago, IL: Fitzroy Dearborn, 1997.

COLLECTIONS:

Carleton Beals Collection, Mugar Memorial Library, Boston University.

Elsie Clews Parsons Papers, The American Philosophical Society, Philadelphia, Pennsylvania.

Frances Toor Papers, Department of Special Collections, University Research Library, University of California, Los Angeles.

Joseph Freeman Papers, Hoover Institution on War, Revolution, and Peace, Stanford, California.

John Haag,
Associate Professor of History,
University of Georgia,
Athens, Georgia

Toppan, Jane (1854–1938)

American mass murderer. Born Nora Kelley in 1854 in Boston, Massachusetts; died on August 17, 1938, in Taunton, Massachusetts; daughter of Peter Kelley (a tailor); attended nursing school in Cambridge, Massachusetts.

Jane Toppan shocked the country when it was discovered that the seemingly gentle private-duty nurse had for many years been poisoning the patients in her care. Toppan was born Nora Kelley in Boston in 1854, but after her father, a widower who worked as a tailor, was sent to an insane asylum for attempting to stitch his own eyelids, Jane and her three sisters went to live with their grandmother. They were then sent to an orphanage. Mr. and Mrs. Abner Toppan adopted Nora in 1859, when she was five, changed her name to Jane, and raised her in comfortable surroundings in Lowell, Massachusetts. Though Jane excelled in school and appeared to be happy, a hint of her darker side was revealed when her fiancé broke off their engagement. Jane hammered her engagement ring to pieces, refused to see friends, began to study dreams and clairvoyance, and twice attempted suicide. It was later reported that one of her sisters was eventually institutionalized for mental illness.

When she was 26, Toppan abruptly informed her parents that she intended to become a nurse. She studied at a hospital in Cambridge, Massachusetts, where she was energetic, enthusiastic, and popular. But in time, the nursing staff began to notice that Toppan's interest in autopsies seemed to exceed the bounds of normal curiosity. Then one of her patients, who had been rapidly recovering, suddenly died. Another death quickly followed. The chief surgeon of the hospital called Toppan in for questioning and, though he did not bring a specific charge against her, discharged her that day. She was then hired as a head nurse at another Cambridge hospital, but was fired when it was discovered that she had forged her graduate credentials.

From 1880 to 1901, Toppan served as a private nurse, telling her parents, "I will go to the old and the sick to comfort them in their neediest hour." She worked for scores of families throughout New England, earning their respect and trust. But in July 1901, after the death of Mrs. **Mattie Davis**, Toppan's crimes began to surface. Mattie was an old family friend whom Toppan had nursed during a sudden illness. Mattie's husband, Captain Davis, had begged Toppan to stay on after Mattie's funeral and care for his two married daughters, who had also been stricken by a mysterious illness. Within 45 days, both daughters and Captain Davis were dead. Captain Gibbs, the husband of one of the daughters, became suspicious after a cousin told him that his wife had acted scared of Toppan. He told police detective J.H. Whitney, who had Mrs. Gibbs' body exhumed for an autopsy. The results showed heavy concentrations of morphine. Medical specialists confirmed that all of Toppan's victims had showed signs of morphine poisoning, but did not exhibit constriction of the pupils, one of its telltale signs. Toppan later admitted she had masked this symptom by adding atropine, or belladonna, to the morphine she administered to her victims, to make their eyes appear normal.

Toppan was charged with murder and jailed, and detectives began exhuming dozens of bodies throughout New England. Autopsies showed they had all been poisoned with morphine and atropine. It was discovered that Toppan had been able to obtain large quantities of the narcotic by forging doctors' prescriptions. Though prominent families had at first defended Toppan, it soon became clear that she was guilty. Dr. Stedman, an alienist (psychiatrist) who visited Toppan, reported that she admitted to the killings. "I fooled them all," she told him. "I fooled the stupid doctors and the ignorant relatives. I've been fooling them for years and years." She also named 31 persons she claimed to have poisoned. At Toppan's murder trial, which began on June 25, 1902, Stedman testified that Toppan was incurably insane. She answered, "The alienist lies! I am not crazy! . . . I

know that I have done wrong! I understand right from wrong! That proves I am sane!" Toppan was sent to the Taunton State Asylum for the Criminally Insane, where she lived until her death in 1938. It was said that the old woman would occasionally call one of the nurses to her cell and whisper, "Get some morphine, dearie, and we'll go out in the ward. You and I will have a lot of fun seeing them die."

SOURCES:
Nash, Jay Robert. *Look for the Woman*. NY: M. Evans, 1981.

Elizabeth Shostak, M.A.,
Cambridge, Massachusetts

Torluemke, Judy (b. 1945).
See Rankin, Judy.

Tornabuoni, Lucrezia (1425–1482).
See Medici, Lucrezia de.

Torney, Lulu von Strauss und (1873–1956).
See Strauss und Torney, Lulu von.

Tornimparte, Alessandra (1916–1991).
See Ginzburg, Natalia.

Toro, Maria Teresa (d. 1803)

Wife of Simon Bolivar. Name variations: Maria Teresa Rodríguez del Toro. Born into a prominent family; died of yellow fever in 1803, six months after her marriage; married Simon Bolivar (1783–1830, liberator of Venezuela), in 1802.

Torrence, Gwen (1965—)

African-American track and field athlete. Born on June 12, 1965, in Atlanta, Georgia; attended the University of Georgia on an athletic scholarship, graduated 1987; married Manley Waller (a sprinter and coach); children: Manley Waller, Jr. (b. 1989).

Won gold medal and set meet record (6.57 seconds) in 55-meter dash, Millrose Games (1986); won NCAA championships in 55 meters, 100 meters, and 200 meters (1987); won gold medals in 100 and 200 meters, World University Games (1987); won the gold medal in 200 meters, U.S. outdoor championships (1991); won gold medals in 200-meter sprint and 4x100-meter relay, and silver medal in 4x400-meter relay, Barcelona Olympic Games (1992); won gold medals in 100 and 200 meters, U.S. outdoor championships (1995); won gold medal in 100 meters, World championships (1995); won gold medal in 4x100-meter relay, and bronze medal in 100-meter sprint, Atlanta Olympic Games (1996).

Born in 1965, Gwen Torrence was one of five children in a working-class family in Atlanta, Georgia. A shy girl, Torrence spent a quiet childhood, first in Atlanta, then in the nearby suburb of Decatur. At Columbia High School in Decatur, her physical education teacher, Ray Bonner, encouraged her to run track and field, but Torrence was hesitant. When she finally agreed to give running a try, she refused to wear spikes (running shoes) or shorts, embarrassed that they would attract too much attention to a body she considered "skinny." After setting an unofficial state record in the 220-yard dash during gym class, wearing low-heeled patent-leather pumps, Torrence gave in to her coach's insistence that she train in proper athletic clothing.

Torrence became a high school All American as well as a three-time state champion in the 100- and 200-meter events. During her senior year in high school, she won two gold medals in the TAC Junior Olympics and in 1984, at age 19, qualified for the U.S. Olympic trials. Lacking confidence in her ability, however, she declined to try out for the U.S. team. After high school, Torrence attended the University of Georgia on an athletic scholarship. Initially placed in remedial-level classes, she moved quickly into the standard curriculum and made the dean's list. In 1986, the year Torrence considers her turning point, she beat 1984 Olympic gold medalist *Evelyn Ashford in the 55-meter dash at the Millrose Games, setting a meet record of 6.57 seconds. The following year, she won NCAA championships at 55, 100, and 200 meters, and also took two gold medals at the World University Games in Zagreb, Yugoslavia.

In 1988, Torrence went to the Olympic Games in Seoul, South Korea, finishing fifth in the 100-meter finals and sixth in the 200-meter event. The next year, however, she experienced a setback when complications from her pregnancy kept her bedridden for three months. After her son was born in late 1989, Torrence had to work with great determination to regain strength, muscle tone, and endurance. Though she did not win a single race during 1990, she continued her disciplined training regimen, bolstered by her husband and coach Manley Waller, and in 1991 took home silver medals in the 100- and 200-meter World championship races. The woman who beat her, German athlete **Katrin Krabbe**, later tested positive for clenbuterol, a banned drug.

At the 1992 Olympics in Barcelona, Spain, Torrence finished a disappointing fourth in the 100-meter sprint, later commenting that she suspected her rivals of using performance-enhanc-

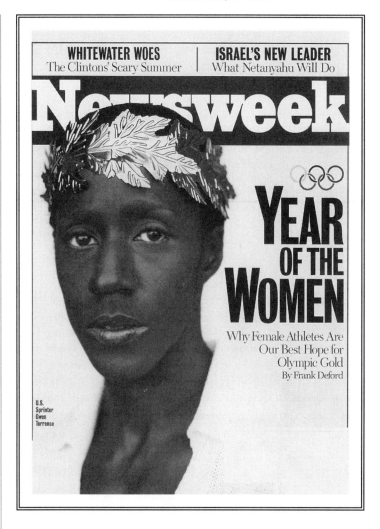

ing substances. When this remark was picked up by the media, it caused a scandal; although Torrence had not named names, she was vilified by the other runners and later issued a formal apology. Still at the center of the controversy, she went on to win a gold medal in the 200-meter sprint, another gold in the 4x100-meter relay, and a silver in the 4x400-meter relay. In 1993 and 1994, she won several U.S. and international meets, including the 100-meter races at the Grand Prix competitions.

In 1995, despite injuries to her right hamstring and knee, she won both the 100- and the 200-meter sprints at the U.S. outdoor championships. She almost repeated the feat at the World championships later that year, but although she easily won the 100, her winning time in the 200 was disqualified after replays showed she had stepped on the inside line of her lane. Torrence accepted the decision gracefully and prepared for her third Olympics. She entered the 1996 Olympic Games in Atlanta as a solid favorite in the sprints, but again injuries plagued

Gwen
Torrence

her. After disappointing heats in the 200, she did not make the finals. But Torrence did win a bronze in the 100, and anchored the USA's gold medal-winning 4x100-meter relay team.

One of her biggest inspirations, according to Torrence, is her older brother Charles, who was injured as a youth while playing street football and was paralyzed from the waist down. She hopes one day to have a career working with disabled children.

SOURCES:
Johnson, Anne Janette. *Great Women in Sports*. Detroit, MI: Visible Ink, 1998.

Elizabeth Shostak, M.A.,
Cambridge, Massachusetts

Torvill, Jayne (1957—)

British figure skater. Born in Nottingham, England, on October 7, 1957; daughter of a bicycle repairer.

Jayne Torvill and Christopher Dean.

With Michael Hutchinson, won British Pairs championship (1971); with Christopher Dean, won British Northern Ice Dance championship (1976),

British Ice Dance championships (1978–84), gold medals in European championships (1981, 1982, 1984, 1993) and World championships (1981, 1982, 1984), gold in World championship (1983); won Olympic gold medal in Sarajevo (1984), won the Olympic bronze medal in Lillehammer (1994).

She's the quiet one; he's emotionally explosive. He's the perfectionist; so is she. Together, they changed the world of ice dancing. Jayne Torvill, daughter of a bicycle repairer, and Christopher Dean, son of a coal-mining electrician, were first teamed on the ice in 1975. By 1980, with the help of a grant for training expenses from the Nottingham City Council, they quit their jobs and decided to "give it a go," to become the "best in the world." They finished 5th at the 1980 Olympics in Lake Placid.

On February 14, 1984, at the Sarajevo Olympics, they skated a slow, sensual, haunting dance to Maurice Ravel's sultry "Bolero" in blue flowing costumes. That night they were the first to use one piece of music through their entire free dance program, the first to create and sustain a mood, the first to start on their knees and end on their elbows. Said commentator Dick Button: "The world has expected everything from them and they have given it back." For artistic impression, the scores flashed across the board: 6.0, 6.0, 6.0, 6.0, 6.0, 6.0, 6.0, 6.0, 6.0. Three more 6.0s followed for technical merit. They had registered the highest scores ever recorded in an international ice dancing competition. Through the compulsories, which make up 30% of the scoring, the original set pattern, which makes up 20%, and the free skating (50%), they were awarded 19 perfect 6.0s. The previous best had been won by the same Torvill and Dean at the European championships that year. "They took ice dancing out of the ballroom," wrote *Newsweek*, "and skated it deliciously close to the back seat of a parked car."

T&D, as they are known in Britain, rehearsed to a fare-thee-well. Every detail was gone over thousands of times, but things still could go wrong. During the 1982 Nationals, for example, they had never skated in the costumes they were wearing, although the routine had been rehearsed over and over. "When we caught hands in the rock and roll routine," says Torvill, "my dress bobbed up in the air and Chris took both my hand and the dress. I knew that if he tried to release it, it would fall down, but in keeping hold, he might have ripped the dress." They had a split second where they just stared at each other in horror. "In the end he held on to everything and the dress slipped away, rather than tore."

The couple turned pro in 1985 and that should have been the end of their Olympic entries. But the world of ice dancing changed in the late 1980s: the ban on professionals was dropped by the International Skating Union. So they came back to Lillehammer, Norway, in 1994, the oldest skaters competing, and tried once again. After skating à la *Ginger Rogers and Fred Astaire to "Let's Face the Music and Dance," they were given a standing ovation. They'd "done everything by the book, just as they'd been told to do," wrote John Powers for the *Boston Globe*. "They worked up a ballroom dance and put it on ice. The crowd went wild. And the judges gave the Olympic title to a couple of Russian rock 'n' Rollers." Though the judges chose to hand the gold medals to **Maia Usova** and Aleksandr Zhulin and the silver to **Oksana Gritschuk** and Evgeni Platov, they could not take away from those who had watched Torvill and Dean skate their second gold-medal performance. In 1981, Queen *Elizabeth II** awarded T&D with the distinction of Members of the British Empire (MBE); in 2000, they were named Officers of the Order of the British Empire (OBE).

SOURCES:
Hemery, David. *The Pursuit of Sporting Excellence.* Champaign, IL: Human Kinetics, 1986.
Newsweek. February 21, 1994, p. 47.
Powers, John. "Torvill & Dean Face Music . . . ," in *Boston Globe.* February 22, 1994, p. 22.

Toselli, Louisa (1870–1947)

*Princess of Saxony. Name variations: Louise Antoinette; Louise of Habsburg-Lotharingen; Louise of Tuscany; Marie Louise; princess of Tuscany; countess Montignoso. Born Louisa or Louise Antoinette on September 2, 1870, in Salzburg, Austria; died on March 23, 1947, in Brussels, Belgium; second daughter of *Alicia of Parma (1849–1935) and Ferdinand IV (1835–1908), titular grand duke of Tuscany (r. 1859–1908); married Frederick Augustus III (1865–1932), king of Saxony (r. 1904–1918, abdicated in 1918), on November 21, 1891 (divorced 1903); married Enrico Toselli (a composer); children: (first marriage) George (b. 1893); Frederick Christian (b. 1893, who married *Elizabeth of Thurn and Taxis); Ernest Henry (b. 1896), prince of Saxony; Margaret; Maria; Anna.*

Toshiko, Princess (1740–1814).

See Go-Sakuramachi.

Toulouse, countess of.

See Elvira (fl. 1080s).
See Adelaide of Maurienne for sidebar on Constance Capet (c. 1128–1176).
See Joan of Toulouse (d. 1271).

Toumanova, Tamara (1919–1996)

Internationally known dancer, choreographer, and Hollywood film actress who, as one of the three "baby ballerinas" of the 1920s, became the personification of a Russian prima ballerina. Name variations: Tumanova; Tata. Born Tamara Vladimirovna Toumanova in Siberia, between Ekaterinburg and Tyumen, on March 2, 1919 (some sources cite 1917); died on May 29, 1996, at age 77, in a Santa Monica, California, hospital; daughter of Vladimir Toumanov (a colonel in the Russian Imperial Army) and Evgeniia Khacidovitch (who came from a noble Georgian family); attended school in Paris as well as studying ballet with Olga Preobrazhenska; married Casey Robinson (a movie producer), in 1943 (divorced 1953); no children.

Danced at polka at the Trocadero in Paris for her first public performance, having been selected for the role by the great ballerina Pavlova; debuted in Paris in L'Evantail de Jeanne, a children's ballet (1927); signed with the Ballet Russe de Monte Carlo (1932–38); appeared with the Original Ballet Russe and with the Ballet Theater (1940–45); danced with the Grand Ballet du Marquis de Cuevas (1949), with the Festival Ballet (1951–52 and 1956), and with the Paris Opera (1947–52 and 1956); became an American citizen and settled with her family in Southern California (1944); her father died (1963); her mother died (1988).

Ballets: L'Evantail de Jeanne (1927); Cotillon (1932); Concurrence (1932); Le Bourgeois Gentillhomme (1932); Jeux d'Enfants (1932); Mozartiana (1933); Songes (1933); Petrouchka (1934); Symphonie fantastique (1936); Firebird (1940); Spectre of the Rose (1940); Aurora's Wedding (1940); Les Sylphides (1940); Balustrade (1940–41); Swan Lake (1941); Magic Swan (1942); Giselle (1944–45); The Nutcracker (1944–45); Le Palais de Cristal (1947); Le Baiser de la Fee (1947); La legenda di Guiseppe (1951); Phedre (1952).

Filmography: Days of Glory (1944); Tonight We Sing (1953); Deep in My Heart (1954); Invitation to the Dance (1956); Torn Curtain (1966); The Private Life of Sherlock Holmes (1970).

According to most accounts, Tamara Toumanova was born on March 2, 1919, in Siberia, somewhere between Ekaterinburg and Tyumen, in a boxcar of the Trans-Siberian railroad then occupied by artillery horses belonging to the fleeing remnants of the defeated anti-Bolshevik White Army; her mother had become separated from her husband during the chaos of the retreat. The problem with this account is that in March 1919, far from retreating, the White Army was on the offensive, rapidly advancing towards Moscow. Its rout and subsequent retreat did not occur until July of that year.

*O*ne of the most glamorous stars of 20th-century dance.

—Jack Anderson

In any case, eight months later, while mother and daughter were staying in the Far Eastern port of Vladivostok, they were reunited with Tamara's father, Colonel Vladimir Toumanov of the Imperial Russian Army, through a fortuitous accident. Shortly thereafter, the family left Russia forever on a freighter bound for the Chinese city of Shanghai. A year later, they traveled to Cairo, and from there to Paris, where they began building a new life along with the thousands of other Russian refugees in similar circumstances. Vladimir Toumanov managed to eke out only a modest living doing whatever menial jobs were available. It was her mother **Evgeniia Toumanova**'s strong character that helped keep the family together. Her determination to give her daughter the best education possible led to Tamara's first dancing lessons from *Olga Preobrazhenska, a former ballerina. In later years, Toumanova remembered Olga as "the greatest guide and influence from the very beginning, my complete teacher."

Only a few months later, *Anna Pavlova, one of the great prima ballerinas of the era, while visiting her former colleague's studio, noticed Tamara dancing and selected her for a guest appearance—a polka—on her Red Cross benefit program at the Trocadero, in Paris. This was the beginning of Toumanova's spectacular dancing career. At 11, she danced the leading role in the children's ballet *L'Evantail de Jeanne* at the Paris Opera. The ballet critic Andrew Levinson was enthusiastic, but wrote: "It is astonishing; it is also terrifying. The human body will not support without grave danger such forced hot-house development." In 1929, the ballet, with Toumanova dancing, was once again presented at the Paris Opera, and Levinson again expressed his amazement at her technical competence.

The first months of 1932 laid the foundation for Toumanova's career. W. de Basil, a former Cossack colonel turned impresario, had just reorganized the famed Ballet Russe de Monte Carlo. During the next decade, his skillful management won worldwide acclaim for the company. One of his first acts was to hire George Balanchine as his new choreographer. It was Balanchine who convinced de Basil to sign Toumanova for several leading roles of the 1932 season, including the two new ballets that he had created, *Cotillon* and *Concurrence*. He also gave her the lead feminine role in *Le Bourgeois Gentillhomme*. Léonide Massine, another of de Basil's choreographers, created his ballet *Jeux d'Enfants* for her. The following year, Balanchine choreographed *Mozartiana* and *Songes* in which Toumanova danced.

It was probably Arnold Haskell, the well-known dance critic, who invented the expression "baby ballerinas" to describe the company's three young Russian girls who were then enthralling all of Paris: Toumanova age 14, ✤➤ **Irina Baronova** age 14, and ✤➤ **Tatiana Riabouchinska** age 17. Toumanova was generally considered to be the most gentle and least assertive of the trio, and it was she who embodied everyone's idea of what a Russian ballerina should be like. Exotic in appearance, with large dark eyes, raven hair and very white skin, she combined virtuosity with lyricism. She also had a grand manner which, coupled with youthful grace, was said to be truly magical. The three girls were close, despite their occasional rivalries over roles on stage, and also over the attentions of their partners. Through adolescence they had to work extremely hard in order to perfect their technical skills, their interpretations of numerous roles, as well as learning how to please their audiences. They danced almost every night, traveled all over Europe, attended social engagements, and gave frequent press interviews.

Balanchine's interlude with the Ballet Russe was a wonderful time for the young dancers. As he was attractive and easy to get along with, all three fell in love with him. Soon, however, he left the Ballet Russe Company and thereafter disappeared from their lives. Toumanova later spoke of him with great affection: he "taught me to understand what is beautiful in all arts and all people. He helped me to find the beauty of simplicity—and the simplicity of beauty." For his part, Balanchine emphasized the charm and flavor of her dancing, and revelled in her every pose and in her classic beauty.

The three young ballerinas also had to cope with their demanding mothers, women in their 30s, whose husbands were frequently unable to find work except that of military service. The mothers fought ferociously over every step of

❧ Baronova, Irina (1919—)

Russian ballerina. Born in Petrograd, Russia, in 1919; studied at College Victor-Hugo, Paris; studied ballet with *Olga Preobrazhenska in Paris; married German Sevastianov (divorced); married Cecil G. Tennant; children: three. Soloist at Paris Opéra (1930) and Théâtre Mogador (1931).

Discovered by George Balanchine while she attended the Preobrazhenska School in Paris, Irina Baronova became one of the three "baby ballerinas" of the Ballet Russe de Monte Carlo in 1932; she was 13. In addition to Baronova, the triumvirate included *Tatiana Riabouchinska and *Tamara Toumanova. Baronova created the roles of the princess in *The Hundred Kisses*, Passion in *Les Présages*, Josephina in *Choreartium*, Scuola di Ballo, Boulotte in *Bluebeard*, Helen in *Helen of Troy*, and First Hand in *Le Beau Danube*. She also danced *Aurora's Wedding, Swan Lake, Les Sylphides, Coq d'Or, Coppélia, La Fille Mal Gardée, Petrouchka, Le Spectre de la Rose*, and *Jeux d'Enfants*. Baronova danced in the films *Florian* (MGM, 1939) and *Yolanda* (Mexico, 1942), in the musical *Follow the Girls* (1944), with Léonide Massine's *Ballet Russe Highlights* (1945), and in the musical *Bullet in the Ballet* and the comedy *Black Eyes* (both in England in 1946). Retiring from the stage in 1946, she lived with her husband and three children in England where she was a member of the Technical Committee of the Royal Academy of Dancing and taught mime in the Teacher's Course of the Academy.

❧ Riabouchinska, Tatiana (1917–2000)

Russian ballerina. Name variations: Riabouchinskaia; Riabouchinskaya; Riabuchinskaya. Born in Moscow, Russia, in 1917; died on August 24, 2000, in Los Angeles, California; studied dance with *Olga Preobrazhenska and *Mathilda Kshesinskaia; married David Lichine (a choreographer and teacher), in 1943; children: daughter Tania Lichine Crawford.

A member of the "baby ballerina" triumvirate, Tatiana Riabouchinska made her debut at age 15 with Nikita Balieff's *Chauve-Souris* revue in Paris. She had arrived in Paris as an infant after her family managed to flee Russia during the early stages of the revolution; her father's erstwhile position as banker to Tsar Nicholas II had meant they were lucky to escape. George Balanchine saw Riabouchinska dancing, and she went from the *Chauve-Souris* revue to Colonel W. de Basil's Ballet Russe de Monte Carlo. She danced with the company from 1932 to 1941, creating Frivolity in *Les Présages*, the Daughter in *Le Beau Danube*, the Child in *Jeux d'Enfants*, Florentine Beauty in *Paganini*, Junior Girl in *Graduation Ball*, and the title roles in *Coq d'Or* and *Cinderella*. Considered among her best performances were those in Michel Fokine's *Les Sylphides* and *Le Spectre de la Rose*. She was known for the airiness and joy of her movements, and in 1940 she provided the model for the dancing hippopotamus in Walt Disney's classic *Fantasia*. Riabouchinska left the Ballet Russe de Monte Carlo the following year to work as a guest artist with companies including the London Festival Ballet and Ballet Theater. She married David Lichine, a choreographer and dancer from the Ballet Russe, in 1943. They had a daughter, and after their retirement from the stage in 1950 began teaching dance in Beverly Hills, California. Riabouchinska continued teaching until her death in November 2000, at age 83.

their daughter's careers. Of the three "ballet mothers," Evgeniia Toumanova was considered the most temperamental and acquired a reputation for passionate partisanship, as well as for shrewdness and eccentricity. But she was successful in advancing Tamara's career. Tamara was later to say, "What could be more beautiful and rewarding for a daughter than to have a friend in her own mother?" However, until December 1963 when he died, it was her father who was the dominant figure in their family. Only once did Toumanova interrupt her daily dance practice, or halt her professional activities, and that was after her father's death.

In 1933, when Balanchine left the Ballet Russe, Toumanova went with him, only to rejoin the company the following year and dance the title roles in *Firebird, Petrouchka* and *Aurora's Wedding*. It was then that Levinson pointed to Toumanova's "oriental languor," adding that in her technique she possessed a vigor and perfection that none of the Imperial Ballet sylphides of 1909 had. In 1934, Toumanova danced as the Puppet in *Petrouchka* which was staged in New York by Michel Fokine. In subsequent performances in London, Chicago, and Los Angeles, she danced in the role of the Ballerina under the baton of Igor Stravinsky.

The *Dancing Times* declared in 1935 that Toumanova had made more progress than any other member of her company; "she is rapidly developing into an ideal ballerina, both in appearance and technique." In 1936 all of London fell in love with de Basil's dancers and the Ballet

Juliana. See Wilhelmina for sidebar.

Russe repertoire. Massine presented Toumanova in Berlioz's *Symphonie fantastique*, in the central role as the Beloved. After seeing their performance, the critic Haskell proclaimed that there was now a "Massine School" of ballet and that Toumanova was its finest interpreter. During the winter of 1936–37, she shared the first part of the American tour with *Alexandra Danilova, but then, for reasons of health, and also in order to devote more time to her general education, she chose to remain in California.

When de Basil's dance company split in 1937, she joined Massine's Ballet Russe de Monte Carlo, and added *Giselle* to her repertoire. That year the noted ballet critic A.V. Coton, editor of *Dance Chronicle*, wrote that Toumanova was "surely the loveliest creature in history to dance" and that she "had attained the utmost skill of mime and bearing so that one was rarely aware of the individual behind the characterization."

At the height of World War II in 1940, Toumanova accompanied the Ballet Russe on its Australian tour. In Sydney, she danced *The Firebird, The Spectre of the Rose, Les Sylphides* as well as *Aurora's Wedding*. Australian critics spoke admiringly of her poise, her elegance, and her romantic appearance. The critic Basil Burdett wrote that Toumanova was a great dancer and a fine artist, even though she was inclined to be slightly uneven. But he added that it was probably inherent in her style, "which is at once extraordinarily controlled yet nervous and sensitive."

During the 1941–42 season in New York, Toumanova introduced another Stravinsky ballet, *Balustrade*. In October 1941, she danced the Black Swan (Odile) in *Swan Lake* at the Metropolitan Opera House. That winter, and in the spring of 1942, Igor Youskevitch and Andrew Eglevsky alternately partnered her in the *Magic Swan*, and when New Yorkers first saw Massine's *Le Tricorne*, it was Toumanova who danced the Miller's wife. "Working with Massine," Toumanova said, "is stirring. Soul-expanding. There is even more than his artistic mastery and precision. There is great power in his intensity, in his emotional depth and range." In 1944–45, she was a guest star at the Ballet Theater, partnered by Anton Dolin. The two danced together in *Giselle, The Nutcracker, Swan Lake*, and *Aurora's Wedding*. In 1945, she starred in *Bronislava Nijinska's *Harvest Time* and *Lesginka*.

Le Circle des Journalistes et Critiques de la Danse honored Toumanova in 1949 with Le Grand Prix de Giselle, a bronze sculpture whose replica was kept at her home in Southern California. That same year, she danced the role of Saint Saen's *Dying Swan* for Queen ◄ Juliana and Prince Bernard of Holland. She also danced *Giselle* for a de Basil Ballet post-performance gala at Covent Garden in 1952, in the presence of King George VI and Queen *Elizabeth Bowes-Lyon.

Toumanova was at La Scala, Milan, in 1951 and again in 1953. There, she created the ballet *La legenda di Guiseppe* for *Margarethe Wallmann, as well as *The Legend of St. Joseph, La Vita Del'uomo*, and *Setter Piccati*. She returned to Milan again in 1956 to choreograph Herbert von Karajan's presentation of Richard Strauss' *Salome*.

By official request of the French government in 1952, she danced the *Dying Swan* for President Vincent Auriole at the Château Chambord. This performance was attended by government leaders, as well as numerous prominent cultural figures. Saint-Saen's music was played by a string quartet, while Toumanova danced the solo on a priceless Gobelin tapestry that had been borrowed from the Louvre for the occasion. In 1958, she danced for three consecutive weeks with the Sadler's Wells Theater in London, and, in 1963, she recreated Phedre in the West Berlin Opera House with Serge Lifar's choreography. Of the Toumanova Phedre, ballet critic Leandre Vaillat wrote in his *La Danse de l'Opera de Paris* that if for Racine's Phedre one required a *Sarah Bernhardt, then the Phedre of Jean Cocteau called for a Toumanova.

In *Artists of the Dance*, **Lillian Moore** wrote of Toumanova:

> [She] has a quality that is rare among classic dancers: originality. There is nothing stereotyped about her talent. She is forceful and intense and sometimes haunting, but always distinctive, and always she is, quite simply, Toumanova. It is impossible to remain indifferent to her work. This essentially simple and sincere artist has been forced to live up to such dangerous and glamorous epithets as "the black swan" and the "black pearl of the Russian ballet."

Despite an almost universal admiration from ballet aficionados, Toumanova received occasional criticism including that, at times, she produced "a mannered caricature of the grand Russian style." In 1959, *Variety* was even harsher: "Though her arteries obviously haven't hardened at 40, it is evident that Toumanova's technique and artistic sense have become rusty. . . . She tends to be too orthodox."

Besides being an outstanding prima ballerina, Tamara Toumanova also had a successful acting career. She first played on Broadway with

Tamara
Toumanova

Jimmy Durante and *Ethel Merman in *Stars in Your Eyes* in 1938. Her initial film role was in the Warner Bros. production of *Capriccio Espagnol*. Then in 1944, she co-starred with Gregory Peck in *Days of Glory*. She portrayed Pavlova in *Tonight We Sing* (1953) and the French music-hall star *Gaby Deslys in MGM's *Deep in my Heart* (1954), opposite Paul Stewart, Walter Pidgeon, José Ferrer and *Merle Oberon. Gene Kelly cast Toumanova as a demimondaine in his *Invitation to the Dance* (1957), and Alfred Hitchcock turned her into a East

German police informer in *Torn Curtain* (1966). In Billy Wilder's film *The Private Life of Sherlock Holmes* (1970), Toumanova played Alexandra Petrova, a 19th-century prima ballerina, in which role she danced the pas-de-deux from Act II of *Swan Lake*. Toumanova married writer-producer Casey Robinson in 1944. During the ten years of their marriage, she continued her dancing and film careers.

At Sol Hurok's after-theater party on the roof of the St. Regis Hotel in New York City on May 8, 1966, Toumanova and her mother met William Como, editor of *Dance Magazine*, who became her close friend and "adopted brother." This party followed the Bolshoi Ballet presentation at the old Metropolitan Opera House building. The procession of guests was led by the Bolshoi's prima ballerina, *Maya Plisetskaya, followed by Toumanova, Dame *Alicia Markova, *Agnes de Mille and many other luminaries of the dance. Wrote Como:

> Toumanova is strikingly beautiful. Her pale and regular features framed by smooth, gleaming, black hair, are marvelously expressive. Her great dark eyes are sometimes ominously shadowed, and expressive. There was and has remained a sense of mystery about her. She is a private person; and as I have learned over the years, a warm and gracious woman.

In 1983, at its 99th Annual Banquet and Ball, the Dance Masters of America presented Toumanova with a special award for her extraordinary and long-running career in dance. Said Toumanova: "Throughout all the artistic excitement of career, through the turmoil and turbulence of life altogether, I thank God for my opportunities. Always I look forward. Never back. Dance is my constant inspiration, all the arts my master—my guiding star."

"Simplicity in art is a goal more difficult to attain than technical bravura," Toumanova once said. "But simplicity must reflect a choice growing out of ability, knowledge and understanding—applied with judgment and taste. It should not be a consequence of limitations. Nor does simplicity mean drabness. One cannot take away the glamour that is ballet's natural heritage. Elegance and clarity, sparkle and illusion—these are a part of ballet. In certain ways, the ballet is like a crystal chandelier. Through it, beautiful forms may shine. . . . Without faith we cannot enter this crystal world of beauty. . . . [A]n artist of the ballet must have a very humble and sensitive heart, a searching mind. Without these we cannot reach beyond the footlights to share with others the art we love."

SOURCES:

Anderson, Jack. "Toumanova," in *The New York Times*. May 31, 1996.

Como, William. "Editor's Log," in *Dance Magazine*. January 1979, December 1986.

Erni. "Tamara Toumanova," in *Variety*. Vol. 214, no. 79. April 22, 1959.

Koegler, Horst. *The Concise Oxford Dictionary of Ballet*. London: Oxford University Press, 1977.

Lifar, Serge. *Ma vie—From Kiev to Kiev*. NY: World, 1970.

Moore, Lillian. *Artists of the Dance*. Dance Horizons, 1979.

Reyna, Ferdinand. *Concise Encyclopedia of Ballet*. London: Collins, 1974.

Swinson, Cyril, ed. *Dancers and Critics*. London: A&C Black, 1950.

Swisher, Viola Hegyi. "Tamara Toumanova," in *Dance Magazine*. Vol. 44. September 1970, pp. 47–61.

———. "Toumanova in Hollywood," in *Dance Magazine*. March 1966, pp. 26–27.

Vaillat, Leandre. "Tamara Toumanova," in Cyril Swinson, ed., *Dancers and Critics*. London: A&C Black, 1950.

Vronskaya, Jeanne. *A Biographical Dictionary of the Soviet Union, 1917–1988*. London: K.G. Saur, 1989.

Walker, Kathrine Sorley. *De Basil's Ballet Russe*. London: Hutchinson, 1982.

Wilson, G.B.L. *A Dictionary of Ballet*. 3rd ed. London: A&C Black, 1974.

Dr. Boris Raymond,
Dalhousie University,
Halifax, Nova Scotia, Canada

Tour du Pin, Henriette de la
(1770–1853).

See La Tour du Pin, Henriette de.

Tourel, Jennie (1899–1973)

American operatic mezzo-soprano who was considered one of the best recitalists of her era. Born on June 22, 1899 (she claimed 1910), in Vitebsk, Russia (some sources cite Montreal, Canada); died of lung cancer on November 23, 1973, in New York City; daughter of Solomon Davidson (a banker) and Pauline (Schulkin) Davidson; studied music privately and with Anna El-Tour; married Bernhard Michlin (divorced); married Leo Michaelson (an artist, later divorced); married Harry Gross (a cardiac specialist), in 1955 (divorced 1957); naturalized U.S. citizen, 1946.

Debuted at the Opera-Russe, Paris (1931); performed as guest in title role of Carmen, *Paris Opéra-Comique (1933); sang under the baton of Arturo Toscanini in Hector Berlioz's* Roméo et Juliette *with New York Philharmonic Symphony (1942).*

Accounts of the early life of acclaimed mezzo-soprano Jennie Tourel differ widely. Tourel maintained that she was born in Montreal in 1910, while her Russian-Jewish parents were visiting that country. Other accounts, however, indicate that she was born in 1899 in the Russian city of Vitebsk. It is believed that she spent her earliest years in Russia and then moved with her parents to Paris. Though one account suggests Tourel moved there at the age of one, other reports indicate that the wealthy Davidson family fled to Paris in 1918 to escape the aftermath of the Russian Revolution.

From a very early age, Tourel enjoyed singing. Her mother, said to have had an appealing voice, sang to her in Russian, and by age two the girl was repeating many of these songs. When Tourel was six, she began formal lessons on flute and later studied piano. In 1926, Tourel began to study voice with Russian soprano **Anna El-Tour**, who had come to Paris to teach at the Eastern Conservatory and whose name the student adapted to use on the stage. Tourel remained with El-Tour for only two years, however, preferring to work with a coach on repertoire and to teach herself by listening to and imitating the best singers in Paris. She later named *Conchita Supervia** and **Marya Freund** as major influences, as well as **Madeleine Grey** and *Eva Gauthier**. Tourel made numerous concert appearances and by 1931 debuted at the Opéra-Russe. She first appeared in the United States with the Chicago Opera during the 1930–31 season, when she sang in Ernest Moret's *Lorenzaccio* and performed the role of Lola in Mascagni's *Cavelleria Rusticana*. She also appeared with *Mary Garden** in the world premiere of Hamilton Forrest's *Camille*.

In 1933, a member of the Paris Opéra-Comique heard Tourel singing at a party and suggested she audition for the company. The management was impressed with her ability, but did not give her a contract immediately because she lacked stage experience. Instead, they invited her to debut as a guest in the title role of *Carmen*. Tourel's performance elicited an ovation at the end of the second act, and she received a coveted contract for leading parts with the company. Among her roles were Charlotte in Massenet's *Werther* and the title roles in Rossini's *La Cenerentola* and Bizet's *Kjamileh*. She achieved particular success with her performances in *Carmen* and Thomas' *Mignon*.

Tourel's successful career was interrupted, however, when she abruptly fled Paris in June 1940, just two days ahead of the Nazi invasion. She escaped to Lisbon, where she became ill, and then had to wait in Havana, Cuba, before being allowed entry to the United States in January 1941. Hoping to resume her career by joining New York City's Metropolitan Opera, where she had sung Mignon and Carmen in 1937, Tourel found that all the roles for the season had already been assigned. The Metropolitan's conductor, Wilfred Pelletier, invited her to sing Carmen and Mignon under his direction in Montreal. Subsequently, she sang these and other roles on tour in Cuba and throughout the United States.

The event that launched Tourel's American career occurred the following year. In October 1942, she performed with Arturo Toscanini and the New York Philharmonic in *Roméo et Juliette*, a dramatic symphony by Berlioz. Critic Virgil Thomson, writing for the *New York Herald Tribune*, hailed her as a "singer in the great tradition" and noted, "Her voice is beautiful, her diction clear, her vocalism impeccable and her musicianship tops." Tourel, who told reporters that she had been "ecstatic" at the opportunity to perform under the baton of Toscanini, went on to perform with the Boston Symphony Orchestra under Serge Koussevitzky, with Leopold Stokowski and the NBC Symphony in the American premiere of Serge Prokofiev's *Alexander Nevsky Cantata* in March 1943, and with Stokowski again in Bach's *St. Matthew Passion* at the Metropolitan Opera House in April 1943. She made her New York City recital debut at Town Hall on November 13, 1943, prompting Virgil Thomson to enthuse: "Her musicianship in every domain is so thorough that from the whole technical and intellectual aspect her work belongs clearly with that of the great virtuosos of music."

Tourel's many performances of Berlioz and Mahler are thought to have led to the renewed popularity of those composers. She was also interested in avant-garde and contemporary music, in particular the works of Villa-Lobos, Stravinsky, Hindemith, Rorem, Poulenc, Debussy, Ravel, and Nin. She created the role of Baba the Turk in the Venice premiere of Stravinsky's *The Rake's Progress* in 1951, and became a close collaborator with Leonard Bernstein. Tourel sang in the premiere of his *Jeremiah* symphony in Pittsburgh in 1944; this was also the piece she chose for her last public appearance in Israel in 1973.

During the 1950s, Tourel performed with the American Opera Society in concert versions of less popular operas, such as Rossini's *Otello* and Offenbach's *La Grande Duchesse de Gerolstein*. She also started teaching during this period, and joined the faculty at the Juilliard School in 1964. She began offering public master classes at Carnegie Recital Hall in 1963, attracting many professionals and amateurs. In 1971,

Tourel appeared as the countess in a National Educational Television (NET) production of *Pique Dame*, and the following year she returned to the stage with the Seattle Opera in Pasatieri's *Black Widow*. Shortly before her death in 1973, Tourel appeared in the speaking role of the Duchess of Krakenthorp in the Chicago Lyric Opera's production of Donizetti's *La Fille du Régiment*.

Tourel became an American citizen in 1946. Fluent in a number of languages, including Russian, French, German, Italian, Spanish, Portuguese, Hebrew, and English, she was admired for the instinctive sensitivity with which she sang in each language. Wrote Thomson: "She moves around in each tongue as if it were a whole new landscape and climate, untranslated, untranslatable and unique." She was also admired for the technical skill and distinctive style she cultivated for her remarkable voice—a deep, rich contralto with a range from low G through high C. Tourel, who commented that she sang as an outlet for her "always burning"

Ludmila Tourischeva

emotions, was also considered a singer of extraordinary feeling.

Tourel had three marriages, all of which ended in divorce. Her first marriage, in Paris, was to businessman Bernhard Michlin. She later married artist Leo Michaelson. In 1955, she married cardiac specialist Dr. Harry Gross, but the couple divorced in 1957. In addition to music, Tourel enjoyed books, museums, paintings, theater, and film. She died of lung cancer in New York City on November 23, 1973.

SOURCES:

Current Biography. NY: H.W. Wilson, 1947.
Sicherman, Barbara, and Carol Hurd Green, eds. *Notable American Women: The Modern Period*. Cambridge, MA: The Belknap Press of Harvard University, 1980.

Elizabeth Shostak, M.A.,
Cambridge, Massachusetts

Tourischeva, Ludmila (1952—)

Russian gymnast who won ten Olympic medals. Name variations: Liudmila or Ludmilla or Lyudmila Turishcheva, Turischeva, or Turitscheva. Pronunciation: Lood-MEE-luh Too-REES-chuh-vuh. Born Ludmila Ivanovna Tourischeva on October 7, 1952, in Grozyni, USSR; married Valery Borzov.

USSR champion (1970–75); won USSR Cup (1967–74); World champion in the combined (1970, 1974), in the balance beam (1974), in the floor exercises (1970 and 1974); European champion (1971 and 1973); absolute USSR champion (1972 and 1974); World Cup winner (1975–76); won ten Olympic medals: team gold (1968, 1972, 1976), gold in individual combined (1972), gold in all-around (1972), silver in floor exercise (1972 and 1976), bronze in horse vault (1972 and 1976), bronze in all-around (1976); battled Nadia Comaneci and Olga Korbut for the spotlight toward the end of her career.

Americans became enthralled with women's gymnastics with the advent of *Olga Korbut, the Soviet gymnast who stole their hearts. Korbut was followed by Rumanian *Nadia Comaneci, whose Olympic scores won as much applause in the West as in the East. In fact, some might argue that the first thaw in the Cold War began with women's gymnastics. During the reign of these two stars, Ludmila Tourischeva was also a major competitor, winning ten Olympic medals.

Working hard since age ten under coach Vyacheslav Rastaratsky, Tourischeva became a heroine in Russia in 1967, when she won the USSR Gymnastics Cup. In 1968, she shared a team gold in Mexico City. When the Munich Olympics began in 1972, Tourischeva was world champion. She won a gold in the coveted all-around, a silver in floor exercises, and a bronze in vault. But all eyes were on a smiling pixie named Olga Korbut who took the floor exercise and the balance beam. By 1974, however, Tourischeva was the top woman gymnast in the world, winning three of the five individual first-place medals in the World championships at Varna, Bulgaria, including Korbut's specialties: the floor exercise and the balance beam. In 1975, in the first World Cup gymnastic competition held in London, Tourischeva won all five gold medals available.

The Soviet gymnast had been European champion five times and was trying for her sixth title when she was defeated by Nadia Comaneci in 1976. This would not be the last Tourischeva heard of the Rumanian who stole the show at the 1976 Montreal Olympics. Tourischeva was brilliant in Montreal, winning a team gold, a silver in floor exercises, a silver in vault, and a bronze in all-around. But the eyes of the world were on Comaneci who logged the first perfect score in the history of Olympic gymnastics, then followed that with six more. The largest crowd recorded for a gymnastics competition, approximately 18,000, packed the Forum in Montreal for the finals.

Tourischeva announced her retirement after the 1976 Olympics and married Valery Borzov, a track-and-field champion. In 1984, she was appointed head judge in balance beam at the Los Angeles Games, a well-deserved honor for an athlete who held ten Olympic medals.

SOURCES:

Golubev, V. *Liudmila Turishcheva*. Moscow, 1977.

Markel, Robert, Nancy Brooks, and Susan Markel. *For the Record: Women in Sports*. NY: World Almanac, 1985.

Karin Loewen Haag,
Athens, Georgia

Tourover, Denise (1903–1980).

See Ezekiel, Denise Tourover.

Toussaint, Anna Louisa (1812–1886).

See Bosboom-Toussaint, Anna.

Toussaint, Cheryl (1952—)

African-American track and field athlete. Born on December 16, 1952, in Brooklyn, New York; graduated from New York University, 1974.

Silver medalist, 4x400-meter relay (3:25.2), Munich Olympic Games (1972).

Cheryl Toussaint was born in 1952 in Brooklyn, New York, where she attended Erasmus High School and was a member of the Atoms Track Club. In 1970, Toussaint won the AAU 990-yard title, which she successfully defended the following year. In 1972, however, she lost the title to **Carol Hudson**. At the Olympic final trials that year, she lost the 990 to **Madeline Manning**. At the 1972 Olympic Games in Munich, Toussaint was eliminated in the 800-meter heats, but earned a spot on the U.S. relay team by placing fifth in the 400-meter final trials. In the heats, she ran the third leg in 51.3, helping the team to a new U.S. record of 3:22.8. The team won a silver medal in the 4x400-meter race with a time of 3:25.2. Toussaint won the AAU indoor 800 yards in both 1972 and 1973.

SOURCES:

Page, James A. *Black Olympian Medalists*. Englewood, CO: Libraries Unlimited, 1991.

Elizabeth Shostak, M.A.,
Cambridge, Massachusetts

Towle, Charlotte (1896–1966)

American social worker and educator. Born Charlotte Helen Towle on November 17, 1896, in Butte, Montana; died of a stroke on October 1, 1966, in North Conway, New Hampshire; daughter of Herman Augustus Towle (a jeweler) and Emily (Kelsey) Towle (a schoolteacher); graduated from Goucher College, 1919; graduate study at the New York School for Social Work (later the Columbia University School of Social Work), 1926–27.

Developed innovations in the field of psychiatric social work; wrote Social Case Records from Psychiatric Clinics *(1941),* Common Human Needs *(1945), and* The Learner in Education for the Professions *(1954).*

Charlotte Towle, the second of four children of Herman Augustus Towle and **Emily Kelsey Towle**, was born in 1896 and raised in Butte, Montana, where her father had a prosperous business as a jeweler. As a girl, Towle was exposed at home to discussions of political and social issues, including unemployment and labor-management problems—subjects that continued to interest her as an adult. After a year at a Virginia junior college, she began studies at Goucher College as an English major, but in her senior year enrolled in a program that enabled her to do field work with the Baltimore Prisoners' Aid Society and the American Red Cross. This experience convinced her to pursue a career in social work.

After graduating from Goucher in 1919, Towle was a caseworker for the Red Cross in

Baltimore, Denver, and Thermopolis, Wyoming. In 1922, she took a position with the U.S. Veterans Bureau in San Francisco, and in 1924 worked at the bureau's neuropsychiatric hospital in Tacoma, Washington. Towle was dissatisfied with the traditional casework method of her profession, and wished to develop a more psychiatric approach to the field. She obtained a Commonwealth Fund fellowship in 1926 to attend the New York School of Social Work (later part of Columbia University) to study psychoanalytic theory and develop her skills as a psychiatric social worker. In 1927, Towle took a position as a director of the Children's Aid Society in Philadelphia, where she served until 1928. She also taught at the Pennsylvania School of Social Work, where she met *Jessie Taft and Virginia P. Robinson, who were instrumental in developing the "functional school" of social work. Towle later accepted a position at the Institute for Child Guidance in New York City, where she supervised social-work students from the New York School and Smith College. From 1931 to 1932, Towle was a full-time field instructor for the New York School.

In 1932, *Edith Abbott, dean of the University of Chicago's School of Social Service Administration (SSA), persuaded Towle to develop a psychiatric casework program there. Though Towle was considered a leader in the diagnostic or psychosocial school of social work and the SSA's approach followed the social welfare policy tradition, Towle was able to work productively at the university. She became assistant professor in 1932, was promoted to associate professor in 1935, and became a full professor in 1944. At SSA, Towle developed new courses and wrote several important journal articles, as well as her first book, *Social Case Records from Psychiatric Clinics* (1941). Sensitive to the impact of social and economic adversity on personality, Towle insisted that all social workers needed thorough training in psychiatric theory, and instituted a curriculum that replaced separate courses with one generic course covering family, child welfare, medical, and psychiatric issues. This innovation was soon implemented by other schools as well, and in 1954 Towle was invited to help develop a similar program at the London School of Economics.

In addition to her teaching, Towle served as a consultant to many agencies. When she was asked in 1944 to develop a manual for workers at the U.S. Social Security Board Bureau of Public Assistance, who were responsible for helping their clients obtain old-age assistance, aid to the blind, and aid to dependent children, Towle ran into trouble. The manual she wrote, *Common Human Needs*, published by the U.S. Government Printing Office in 1945, argued that individuals had the inalienable right to food, shelter, and health care, and that public assistance workers had a duty to help clients prove they were eligible for such aid. This argument was branded "socialist" by journalists and members of the American Medical Association, who pressured the government to destroy the booklet. The director of the Federal Security Administration ordered it to be discontinued, but after several counterprotests by social workers and others, the American Association of Social Workers began publishing the book itself. *Common Human Needs* was translated into several languages, and was still in print in the late 1970s. Towle also attracted the government's suspicion when she signed a petition urging clemency for Julius and *Ethel Rosenberg, who had been sentenced to death for espionage.

Towle served on numerous committees and held significant advisory positions with the Veterans Administration (1946–48), the American Red Cross (1945–48), and the U.S. Public Health Service's Mental Health Division (1947–49 and 1953). She also served on the editorial board of the *Social Service Review*. She received several honorary degrees and in 1956 was honored with the Florina Lasker Award for distinguished service to the field of social work. She also received the Distinguished Service Award of the National Conference on Social Welfare in 1962.

Towle, who helped provide financial support for her parents and her other siblings, lived near the campus of the University of Chicago with her older sister and with social worker Mary Rall. She retired in 1962, but continued to do part-time teaching and also worked for the Scholarship and Guidance Association for two years. She died in 1966, after suffering a stroke while on vacation in North Conway, New Hampshire.

SOURCES:

Sicherman, Barbara, and Carol Hurd Green, eds. *Notable American Women: The Modern Period*. Cambridge, MA: The Belknap Press of Harvard University, 1980.

Elizabeth Shostak, M.A.,
Cambridge, Massachusetts

Towle, Katherine (1898–1986)

American educator and U.S. Marine Corps officer. Born Katherine Amelia Towle on April 30, 1898, in Towle, California; died in 1986; daughter of George Gould Towle and Katherine (Meister) Towle; graduated from University of California, Berkeley, B.A. (cum laude), 1920, M.A., 1935; graduate study at Columbia University, 1922–23.

Katherine Towle was born in 1898 in Towle, California, into a family whose American roots predated the Revolutionary War. She was valedictorian of her Berkeley, California, high school class, and in 1920 earned a B.A. *cum laude* in political science at the University of California, Berkeley. After working for a year as assistant admissions officer at Berkeley, Towle did graduate work at Columbia University, returning to administrative work at Berkeley the following year. In 1927, she became resident dean at a private girls' school in Piedmont, California, and two years later was named headmistress. In 1933, Towle returned to Berkeley to study for her M.A. in political science, which she completed in 1935. From 1935 to 1942, she was assistant to the manager and then senior editor of the University of California Press. She received a leave of absence from this position to accept a commission in the Women's Reserve of the U.S. Marine Corps in 1943, becoming one of the first women officers in that branch of the military service.

Towle was commissioned as a captain and called to active duty in February 1943. She served at corps headquarters in Washington, D.C., and at the women's training centers at Hunter College in New York City and Camp Lejeune in North Carolina. Towle was promoted to major in 1944 and named assistant director of the Women's Reserve. In March 1945, she was elevated to lieutenant colonel and in December was named a colonel and assigned to succeed *Ruth Cheney Streeter** as director of the Women's Reserve. In March 1946, Towle was awarded the U.S. Navy's Letter of Commendation, with Ribbon, for "meritorious service during the entire period of the growth and development of the United States Marine Corps, Women's Service." She also received the American Campaign Medal and the World War II Victory Medal.

In June 1946, the Women's Reserve was deactivated, and Towle returned to the University of California, where she became assistant dean of women in July 1947. When the Women's Armed Forces Integration Act of June 12, 1948, was passed, the Women's Reserve was integrated into the active line, and Towle resumed her position as director. She retired from this post in May 1953. From 1953 to 1962, she served as dean of women and associate dean of students at Berkeley. She became dean of students in 1962, a position she held until her retirement.

Towle was active in the American Association of University Women, the Women's Faculty Club of the University of California, the Town and Gown Club of Berkeley, the Sulgrave Club of Washington, and the national Association of Deans of Women. From 1946 to 1948, she was a member of the American Council on Education's national advisory committee on disabled veterans. Towle also served on the board of directors of the Berkeley chapter of the American Red Cross. She died in 1986.

SOURCES:

Current Biography. NY: H.W. Wilson, 1949.
McHenry, Robert, ed. *Famous American Women*. NY: Dover, 1980.

Elizabeth Shostak, M.A.,
Cambridge, Massachusetts

Towne, Laura Matilda (1825–1901)

American educator and abolitionist. Born on May 3, 1825, in Pittsburgh, Pennsylvania; died of influenza on February 22, 1901, on St. Helena Island, South Carolina; daughter of John Towne (a businessman) and Sarah (Robinson) Towne; educated in Boston and Philadelphia; studied homeopathic medicine privately and enrolled in the Penn Medical University (no record of degree).

Taught at charity schools and practiced medicine (1850s–61); became a teacher on the Sea Islands of South Carolina (1862); co-founded and taught at the Penn School (1862–1901).

Laura Matilda Towne was born in Pittsburgh, Pennsylvania, in 1825, the third daughter and fourth child of **Sarah Robinson Towne** and John Towne. Her mother came from Coventry, England, while her father was a descendant of William Towne, who had immigrated to the Massachusetts Bay Colony from England in the 1630s. John Towne was an immensely successful businessman with a wide range of interests, including trading cotton and sugar, growing fruit, and operating steamboats between Pittsburgh and New Orleans. An energetic and skilled businesswoman, Sarah partnered him in many of these ventures before her death in 1833, not long after the birth of the couple's seventh child. Laura was then eight.

John moved his family to Boston, where he was the superintendent of the city's gas works. Returning to Pennsylvania in 1840, the family settled in a house in Philadelphia and a country estate outside the city. Now a very wealthy man, John became one of Philadelphia's leading citizens and benefactors until his death in 1851. His son John Henry Towne, a respected engineer, continued his generous tradition, and the Towne School of Engineering at the University of Pennsylvania resulted from his large bequest.

Laura Towne was educated in Boston and Philadelphia, and by her 20s had become interested in both medicine and the abolition of slavery. She studied homeopathic medicine privately under the direction of Dr. Constantine Hering, who had founded homeopathic clinics in and around Philadelphia. Towne also enrolled at the Penn Medical University; there is no evidence, however, that she received a degree, and the institution itself had a short existence. Towne's family belonged to the First Unitarian Church of Philadelphia, where her interest in abolishing slavery took root. William Henry Furness, the church's minister, was a leading abolitionist in Philadelphia and clearly encouraged Towne.

From the late 1850s until the outbreak of the Civil War in 1861, Towne taught at several "charity schools" in the northeastern states. In Newport, Rhode Island, at the start of the war, she sought ways of serving the Union cause. In November 1861, Union troops captured and occupied the Sea Islands, a string of islands, including St. Helena and Port Royal, along the coast of South Carolina. These islands offered ideal conditions for the culture of long-staple cotton and thus had a large population of slaves. When their masters fled the advancing Union army, the slaves were abandoned without food, leadership, or organization; they quickly fell victim to disease and to the ill-treatment of soldiers. Over 10,000 former slaves had been abandoned in the Sea Islands alone. Salmon P. Chase, an abolitionist and secretary of the Treasury Department, sought solutions to the twin problems of helping them and saving the rich cotton crop. Chase appointed a young abolitionist from Boston named Edward L. Pierce to direct this relief effort, and Pierce quickly called for volunteers with skills in medicine, teaching, and the superintending of plantations. Laura Towne was one of the first to volunteer, and in April 1862, at age 36, she sailed to Port Royal with the backing of the Port Royal Relief Committee of Philadelphia.

The collection of volunteers at Port Royal set out to make the South Carolina Sea Islands an example of the benefits of emancipation and freedom, even though emancipation was not commonly accepted as one of the aims of the North early in the Civil War. Towne began her life on St. Helena Island as housekeeper and secretary to Pierce at his headquarters, but she expanded her duties to include practicing medicine, distributing clothing, and teaching school. She was described by Civil War veteran Thomas Wentworth Higginson as "the most energetic [person] in the department." Higginson observed her work while he recuperated from war wounds on the same plantation. She "prescribes for half the island & teaches the other half," he wrote, "besides keeping house beautifully & partly carrying on the plantation."

In 1862, **Ellen Murray**, a close friend of Towne's from Newport, joined her on St. Helena. That September, the two founded Penn School in a local Baptist church. One of the first schools for former slaves, it survived longer than most. By 1864, however, Towne's Unitarianism had alienated the Baptists, and Penn School moved into its own building. The new schoolhouse, prefabricated in Philadelphia by backers, was shipped in sections to the island.

A plain woman, Laura Towne was stout, short, and far from gentle. "I have the reputation of being able to look after my things pretty sharply," she said. She was well educated and chose a curriculum for her school founded on solid academics, including reading, writing, arithmetic, geography, and Greek and Latin. Other educational institutions that were established in the South during this period, such as the Hampton Institute and the Tuskegee Institute founded by Booker T. Washington, were fundamentally vocational schools. Towne's Penn School was not influenced by this leaning during her lifetime. By 1867, Towne found teaching more satisfying than practicing medicine, which she believed she did "badly and very inefficiently," and she was to devote the rest of her life to education. Unlike other Northerners, Towne was influenced by the rising spirit of independence of the ex-slaves she taught; she was pleased with the decline of the docile Southern attitude and the growth of independent thinking. Politically, Towne was a staunch Republican and a Northern sympathizer who had limited contact with the Southern white residents on the mainland.

In the decades following the end of the Civil War, Penn School provided the only secondary education available to the African-Americans who lived on the Sea Islands. By 1870, it included a normal school for training other teachers, who also worked on the islands. Towne took up other responsibilities besides teaching; she served as the local public health officer, an amateur legal adviser, and temperance leader. As a member of the Band of Hope, she was one of 1,500 who attempted to eliminate liquor. In her legal capacity, with no known training in the field, she helped the islanders to become the owners of the plantation lands they had worked all their lives. She also made the school a unifying force in the community by conducting annual graduation ceremonies that drew former pupils from throughout the islands. For almost 40 years, Towne volunteered her services; the "dowry money" bequeathed by her father and money inherited from her eldest brother after his death in 1875 were her sources of support. Penn School was endowed by several organizations: the Pennsylvania Freedmen's Relief Association, the Benezet Society of Germantown, Pennsylvania, and Towne's family.

In 1867, Towne purchased Frogmore, an abandoned plantation on St. Helena. After the house was renovated, she and Murray lived there for the rest of Towne's life. The women made occasional trips to the North and relaxed by gardening, surf bathing, and enjoying the companionship of a succession of dogs. Towne had attacks of malaria over a number of years, but on February 22, 1901, she succumbed to a bout of influenza at age 75. Her casket was carried by a simple mule cart to the Port Royal ferry, accompanied along the route by several hundred of the residents of the Sea Islands who sang the spirituals she had loved in life. Her body, returned to Philadelphia, was buried in the family plot in Laurel Hill Cemetery.

Ellen Murray retired from teaching soon after Towne's death, and their school was renamed the Penn Normal, Industrial, and Agricultural School. **Rossa B. Cooley**, a graduate of Vassar and a teacher at the Hampton Institute, assumed the leadership of the school and modified the curriculum to stress home economics for girls and agriculture for boys, in keeping with the practical education advocated by Booker T. Washington. A larger school building was constructed in 1904, and an industrial building was added in 1912. In 1948, the school was incorporated into the segregated public school system of the state of South Carolina. By the 1960s, it had become a community center providing civic activities and adult education.

SOURCES:

James, Edward T., ed. *Notable American Women, 1607–1950*. Cambridge, MA: The Belknap Press of Harvard University, 1971.

McHenry, Robert, ed. *Famous American Women*. NY: Dover, 1980.

Gillian S. Holmes,
freelance writer,
Hayward, California

Townsend Warner, Sylvia (1893–1978).

See Warner, Sylvia Townsend.

Towzey, Eleanor Stewart (1858–1931).

See Stewart, Nellie.

Toyen (1902–1980)

Czech painter and printmaker, her nation's leading Surrealist, who is generally regarded as the most important 20th-century woman artist from the Czech lands. Name variations: Marie Cermínová; Marie Cerminova. Born Marie Cermínová in Prague, Czechoslovakia, on September 21, 1902; lived in France from 1948 until her death in Paris on November 9, 1980; lived with Jindrich Styrsky (a leading Czech modernist artist).

Born in Prague in 1902, Marie Cermínová—who at an early age rejected this name for the assumed one of Toyen, which lacks gender designation—studied at her hometown's School of Fine Arts with Emanuel Dite from 1919 through 1922. She had already broken with her family in 1918 to live an independent life in radical political and artistic circles. In 1922, she met the painter Jindrich Styrsky, with whom she would live and collaborate artistically until his death in 1942. In these years, Toyen was already a vocal feminist, and politically she believed in anarchism, which in later years made her sympathetic to what she then thought were the liberating ideals of revolutionary Marxism. Artistically, her works of this period were strongly influenced by Cubism, followed for a brief period by naïve art. In 1923, Toyen and Styrsky joined the avantgarde Devetsil group (its name is a composite of the words "nine" and "forces"), which numbered among its members not only artists but photographers, writers and architects as well. From 1925 through 1929, the couple lived in Paris, where they announced that they had discovered their own alternative to both abstractionism and the emerging school of Surrealism. Naming their new approach Artificialism, which the couple defined in 1926 as a philosophy of creation that "makes identical the painter and poet," they were able after their return to Prague in 1929 to interest a number of young Czech artists in this style. Soon after, however, both Toyen and Styrsky found their work becoming ever more Surrealistic in content and spirit.

In her 1932 illustrations for a Czech translation of the Marquis de Sade's novel *Justine* (which appeared in Styrsky's *Edition 69*), Toyen signaled the beginning of an interest in the erotic that would inform her work. As early as 1929, she had begun to experiment with erotic themes as well as a new, rich language of psychological association. As a result of this breakthrough, throughout the 1930s Toyen was inspired to create a number of powerful works that combined eroded surfaces suggesting dreams and visions along with numerous hints of latent eroticism. Toyen started a formal organization of Czech Surrealists in 1934, and helped put together its first exhibition the following year. Strongly influenced by the "poeticist" aspect of the original Devetsil agenda, Czech Surrealism remained linked with developments in the world of literature.

In 1935, Toyen's deep ties to France were further strengthened when André Breton and Paul Eluard visited Prague and presented several lectures. The visitors were impressed with the activities of Toyen, Styrsky and the Prague Surrealist group. Prague appealed to Breton because of its surrealistic present but also because of its essentially magical, atmospheric past. Consequently, this 1935 visit can be viewed as the beginning of Breton's campaign for an international Surrealist movement. Both Toyen and Styrsky were now well-regarded Surrealist artists, and they were able to participate in all of the major Surrealist exhibitions of the latter part of the 1930s, including the ones held in London in 1936 and in Paris in 1938.

During the Nazi occupation of the historic Czech lands of Bohemia and Moravia, which began in March 1939, Toyen and Styrsky continued as underground artists. She was able to produce a striking series of book illustrations for the works of major authors, including Georg Büchner's *Lenz*, Queen *Margaret of Angoulême*'s *L'Heptaméron*, Guillaume Apollinaire's *Alcools* and selections of poems, Joseph Conrad's *Chance*, as well as Czech versions of books by *Pearl S. Buck* and Simonetta Buonaccini. In March 1942, Jindrich Styrsky died. His last major work, published illegally and at great risk the year before, was a small book of photographic sequences combined with verse which he and the poet Jindrich Heisler had created to voice their condemnation of the Hitler dictatorship that had swallowed up their small nation. After Styrsky's death, Toyen provided shelter in her apartment for Heisler who as both an antifascist and a Jew found himself in danger throughout the Nazi occupation.

By the end of World War II, Toyen's art had achieved full maturity. Her erotic works of Surrealism are gentler, more veiled and mysterious than those of Styrsky and other Czech male Surrealists. In her *Prometheus* (1934) and *The Abandoned Corset* (National Gallery, Prague, 1937), the sexual content of the piece is often suggested rather than explicit. The barbed wire that wraps a mummy-like form in *Prometheus* and the strident pink corset of *The Abandoned Corset* shock the viewer because of their alien-

ation and specificity. As art critic **Whitney Chadwick** notes: "They seem to intrude into the natural world as signifiers of menacing forms that are both present and absent. The anxious tension between what is whole and complete and what is not, between the visible and the invisible, roots the surrealist dialectic in a subjectivity of profound precariousness."

By 1948, when a Communist coup locked Czechoslovakia behind Stalin's Iron Curtain, Toyen had left her homeland for Paris, where she renounced her Czech citizenship and became a political refugee. Back in Prague, in 1951 her former Devetsil artistic colleague Karel Teige, having been declared "an enemy of the people," ended his life with poison when the police came to arrest him. In Paris, Toyen remained committed to the ideals of Surrealism, continuing to produce works of high quality. Solo exhibitions of her art took place there in 1960 and 1962. In 1966, she and Styrsky received belated recognition from a (partially) de-Stalinized Czechoslovakia when both were honored by an exhibition in the city of Brno. In 1968, Toyen was the subject of a retrospective show in Aquila, Italy. Even more important was the posthumous 1982 exhibition at Paris' Centre Georges Pompidou. By far the most important retrospective was the one held in Prague in 2000, which was accompanied by the publication of a high-quality catalogue of Toyen's artistic oeuvre totaling 360 pages.

Among Toyen's most memorable creations, her set of lithographs produced under Nazi occupation in 1939–40 entitled *Tir* (The Shooting Gallery) is arguably one of her most evocative works. It was published in Paris in 1973 as a limited edition (*livre-de-peintre*). Here the artist found it possible to redirect the personal grief over her homeland's loss of its freedom into a nightmare excursion, transforming the wonderland of Lewis Carroll's *Alice in Wonderland* and *Through the Looking Glass* into a Surrealistic view of the world as a shooting gallery. Toyen died in Paris on November 9, 1980. She is now being honored as one of the most innovative and sensitive members of the Surrealist movement and acclaimed as one of the most influential women within that branch of modern art. In November 1992, the Czechoslovak postal administration honored Toyen by depicting her great work of 1937, *The Abandoned Corset*, on an 8 crown postage stamp, this being one of the last issues released before the dissolution of the Czechoslovak Republic.

SOURCES:

Alexandrian, Sarane. *Surrealist Art*. Trans. by Gordon Clough. NY: Praeger, 1970.

Andel, Jaroslav. *Czech Modernism, 1900–1945*. Boston, MA: Museum of Fine Arts-Bulfinch Press, 1989.

El Arte de la vanguardia en Checoslovaquia, 1918–1938/ The Art of the Avant-Garde in Czechoslovakia, 1918–1938: IVAM Centre Julio González, 10 febrero/ 11 abril 1993. Valencia: IVAM Centre Julio González/ Generalitat Valenciana, Conselleria de Cultura, Educació, i Ciència, 1993.

Billeter, Erika, and José Pierre. *La Femme et le surréalisme*. Lausanne: Musée cantonal des beaux-arts, 1987.

Bischof, Rita, ed. *Toyen: Das malerische Werk*. Frankfurt am Main: Verlag Neue Kritik, 1987.

Bouyeure, Claude. "Europa, Europa, un siècle d'avant-garde en Europe de l'Est," in *L'Oeil*. No. 463. July–August 1994, pp. 60–67.

Breton, André. *Surrealism and Painting*. Trans. by Simon Watson Taylor. NY: Harper & Row, 1972.

Caws, Mary Ann, *et al.*, eds. *Surrealism and Women*. Cambridge, MA: MIT Press, 1991.

Chadwick, Whitney. "The Muse as Artist: Women in the Surrealist Movement," in *Art in America*. Vol. 73, no. 7. July 1985, pp. 120–129.

———. "Toyen: Toward a Revolutionary Art in Prague and Paris," in *Symposium: A Quarterly Journal in Modern Literatures*. Vol. 42, no. 4. Winter 1989, pp. 276–295.

———. *Women Artists and the Surrealist Movement*. Boston, MA: Little, Brown, 1985.

———, ed. *Mirror Images: Women, Surrealism, and Self-Representation*. Cambridge, MA: MIT Press, 1998.

Devetsil: Czech Avant-Garde Art, Architecture and Design of the 1920s and 1930s. Oxford: Museum of Modern Art-Design Museum, 1990.

Erotisme et surréalisme en Tchécoslovaquie: Emil Filla, Frantisek Ketzek, Rudolf Krajc, Vaclav Masek, Antonin Pelc, Jindrich Styrsky, Toyen, Alois Wachsmann, [exposition] novembre 1993, Galerie 1900–2000, Paris. Paris: Galerie 1900–2000, 1993.

French, Alfred. *The Poets of Prague: Czech Poetry between the Wars*. London: Oxford University Press, 1969.

Holten, Ragnar von. *Toyen: En surrealistisk visionär*. Köping: Lindfors, 1984.

Hubert, Renée Riese. *Magnifying Mirrors: Women, Surrealism, & Partnership*. Lincoln, NE: University of Nebraska Press, 1994.

Isvic, Radovan. *Toyen*. Paris: Editions Filipacchi, 1974.

Levinger, Esther. "Czech Avant-Garde Art: Poetry for the Five Senses," in *Art Bulletin*. Vol. 81, no. 3. September 1999, pp. 513–532.

Myers, John Bernard. "Surrealism's Elegant Imagination," in *Arts Magazine*. Vol. 49, no. 8, 1975, pp. 62–63.

Rosemont, Penelope, ed. *Surrealist Women: An International Anthology*. Austin, TX: University of Texas Press, 1998.

Seifert, Jaroslav. "Fräulein Toyen," in *Sinn und Form*. Vol. 37, no. 6. November–December 1985, pp. 1154–1162.

Smeral, Bohumir, *et al. Anthologie protifasistickych umelcu*. Prague: Odeon-Jan Fromek-Pavel Prokop, 1936.

Spector, Jack J. *Surrealist Art and Writing, 1919–1939*. Cambridge: Cambridge University Press, 1997.

Srp, Karel. *Toyen: City Gallery Prague, House of the Stone Bell, 12 May–6 August 2000*. Trans. by Karolina Vocadlo. Prague: Argo-City Gallery Prague, 2000.

Tschechische Kunst der 20er + 30er Jahre: Avantgarde und Tradition. Darmstadt: Mathildenhöhe, 1988.

Vlcek, Tomas. "Art between Social Crisis and Utopia: The Czech Contribution to the Development of the Avant-Garde Movement in East-Central Europe, 1910–30," in *Art Journal*. Vol. 49, no. 1. Spring 1990, pp. 28–35.

John Haag,
Associate Professor of History,
University of Georgia,
Athens, Georgia

Traba, Marta (1930–1983)

Argentinean novelist and critic. Born in 1930 in Argentina; died in 1983 in an airplane crash en route from Paris, France, to Bogotá, Colombia; daughter of Spanish immigrants to Argentina; graduated with a degree in philosophy and the history of art from the University of Buenos Aires; studied further in Chile on a scholarship; married second husband, Angel Rama (died 1983).

Moved to Colombia (1954); founded Prisma *magazine; founded the Museum of Modern Art, Bogotá (1965); taught art and literature at universities in Latin America and North America; wrote about Latin America in poetry, essays, novels, and critical works; opposed tyranny and corruption while advocating human rights, democracy, and women's rights; expelled from Colombia following anti-military protests (1967).*

Selected works: (poetry) Historia natural de la alegría *(Natural History of Happiness, 1951);* El museo vacío *(The Empty Museum, 1958);* Los cuatro monstruos cardinales *(The Four Cardinal Monsters, 1965); (novel)* Las ceremonias del verano *(Summer Ceremonies, 1966);* Premios de Casa *(House Prizes, 1966);* El son se quedó en Cuba *(The Sound Stayed in Cuba, 1966);* Los laberintos insolados *(Exposed Labyrinths, 1967);* Pasó así *(It Happened This Way, 1968);* La jugada del sexto día *(The Sixth Day's Play, 1969);* Dos décadas vulnerables en las artes plásticas latinoamericanas, 1950–1970 *(Two Vulnerable Decades in the Plastic Arts of Latin America, 1950–1970, 1973);* Homérica Latina *(Homeric Latin, 1979);* Conversación al sur *(Conversation to the South, 1981);* Siglo XX en las artes plásticas latinoamericanas: una guía *(Twentieth-century Plastic Arts in Latin America: A Guide, 1982–83);* En cualquier lugar *(In Any Place, 1984);* Marta Traba: selección de textos *(Marta Traba: Selected Texts, 1984); (essays)* Entrevista atemporal *(Atemporal Interview, 1984);* De la mañana a la noche *(From Morning to Night, 1986);* Casa sin fin *(Endless House, 1988).*

Marta Traba was born in 1930 to Spanish parents who had immigrated to Argentina. Her early education is undocumented, although it is presumed that she attended schools in Buenos Aires. She earned a degree in philosophy and the history of art from the University of Buenos Aires and was awarded a scholarship for further studies in Chile. Traba lived for a year in Italy from 1951 to 1952, and traveled extensively in the United States as well as in South and Central America.

In 1954, Traba moved to Bogotá, Colombia. She founded *Prisma* magazine there and also established, in 1965, the city's Museum of Modern Art. Teaching art and literature and writing in all manner of genres about Latin America were Traba's special interests, however. She taught at universities in Latin America and North America, where she also was outspoken in her political views in favor of democracy, feminism, and human rights and in opposition to corruption, military force, and tyranny in Latin America. In June 1967, following military occupation of the University of Bogotá, President Carlos Lleras expelled her from Colombia because of her political protest against the action. An example of her views is expressed in her critical essay, *Entrevista atemporal* (Atemporal Interview), published posthumously in 1984.

Traba wrote works of criticism, essays, poetry, and a number of novels. Her fiction often used the device of a personal odyssey to voice political opposition. In 1951, she published her first book of poems, *Historia natural de la alegría* (Natural History of Happiness). In 1966, her first novel, *Las ceremonias del verano* (Summer Ceremonies), met critical acclaim and was awarded the 1966 Casa de las Américas Prize; it concerns a woman whose life is spent traveling. In 1979, Traba became the first Latin American woman to voice opinions in novel form about the political kidnappings and torture of political prisoners in Latin America; these reactions were fictionalized in the novel *Homérica Latina* (Homeric Latin) and were based on her own odyssey, forced expatriation from Colombia. She also addressed these issues in the first two novels of a trilogy, *Conversación al sur* (Conversation to the South) and *En cualquier lugar* (In Any Place), published in 1981 and 1984, respectively. Her trilogy was to be completed with a book titled "Veinte años no es nada" (Twenty Years Is Nothing), but this work was still unfinished at the time of her death. In 1983, the year she became a Colombian citizen, she and her second husband Angel Rama were flying from Paris, France, to Bogotá, Colombia, to attend the First Spanish American Culture Conference. The plane was carrying a number of Spanish American writers when it crashed and all on board were killed. Traba left behind several other novels that were published after her death.

SOURCES:
Buck, Claire, ed. *The Bloomsbury Guide to Women's Literature.* NY: Prentice Hall, 1992.

Gillian S. Holmes,
freelance writer,
Hayward, California

Trafford, F.G. (1832–1906).
See Riddell, Charlotte.

Traill, Catherine Parr (1802–1899)

English-born Canadian author, botanist, and pioneer. Name variations: Catherine Strickland. Born Catherine Parr Strickland on January 9, 1802, in London, England; died on August 29, 1899, in Lakefield, Ontario, Canada; daughter of Thomas Strickland of Suffolk, England (a landowner and shipper) and Elizabeth (Homer) Strickland; sister of Susanna Moodie (1803–1885), Agnes Strickland (1796–1874), Elizabeth Strickland (1794–1875), Jane Margaret Strickland (1800–1888), and Samuel Stickland, all writers; educated privately at home; married Thomas Traill (a military officer), in 1832 (died 1859).

Authored her first book at age 16 in England; wrote over a dozen children's books and works on natural history before age 30 and contributed to various periodicals; emigrated to Upper Canada shortly after marriage; became recognized for authoritative works on Canadian natural history and the life of settlers in the wilderness.

Selected works: (as Catherine Strickland) The Tell Tale: An Original Collection of Moral and Amusing Stories *(1818),* The Young Emigrants: or, Pictures of Life in Canada *(1826); (as Catherine Parr Traill)* The Backwoods of Canada: Being Letters from the Wife of an Emigrant Officer; Illustrative of the Domestic Economy of British America *(1836),* The Canadian Crusoes *(1852, reprinted as* Lost in the Backwoods*),* The Female Emigrant's Guide, and Hints on Canadian Housekeeping *(1854, reprinted as* The Canadian Settler's Guide*),* Rambles in the Canadian Forest *(1859),* Canadian Wild Flowers *(1868),* Studies of Plant Life in Canada *(1885),* Pearls and Pebbles; or, Notes of an Old Naturalist *(1895).*

Catherine Parr Traill was born in London, England, on January 9, 1802, the daughter of Thomas Strickland, a landowner and shipper, and **Elizabeth Homer Strickland**. Shortly after her birth, Thomas retired, and the family moved from the city to the relative isolation of the

Waveney Valley of Suffolk County, England. Catherine had several sisters, and all were educated privately. Although their schooling was informal, it included not only sewing and embroidery but the classics, history, and literature. The girls and their brother also explored nature in the Waveney Valley, and Catherine became an expert in botany and natural history without formal training. The quiet rural life also encouraged the children to write; a number of her siblings were to become published authors, and she herself published *The Tell Tale: An Original Collection of Moral and Amusing Stories* in 1818 at age 16. Sisters *Elizabeth and *Agnes Strickland would go on to write several popular biographies, including *Lives of the Queens of England*, *Susanna Moodie achieved fame with *Roughing it in the Bush* in 1852, Samuel Strickland, like Catherine, wrote about natural history, and **Jane Margaret Strickland** was also a writer.

Traill wrote over a dozen natural history books and works for children before she married at age 30. She is also believed to have published articles in women's magazines and other periodicals, although the extent of her contributions is not known. Susanna's husband Dunbar Moodie introduced Catherine to Lieutenant Thomas Traill, and the two married in 1832. Shortly thereafter, they emigrated to Upper Canada to assume Thomas Traill's military land grant. They were to live in various places, primarily in Ontario, which was then a wilderness. (Curiously, Catherine's early writings had included *The Young Emigrants: or, Pictures of Life in Canada*, which was published in 1826.)

Despite the work she published in England before her migration, Traill is known as a Canadian author because of the books she wrote about the botany and natural history of her new homeland and the hardships of immigration and life in the wilderness. After living for three years in the bush, Traill published what was to become her best-known book, *The Backwoods of Canada: Being Letters from the Wife of an Emigrant Officer; Illustrative of the Domestic Economy of British America* (1836). She also wrote a number of children's stories and published sketches that were widely circulated. In 1854, Traill published *The Female Emigrant's Guide, and Hints on Canadian Housekeeping*, which was later retitled *The Canadian Settler's Guide* and printed in several editions. Traill seems to have epitomized the best of emigrants to the New World, and particularly to the wilds of Canada; her writings suggest that she rose to every challenge, faced all manner of hardships with pragmatism, and delighted in the differences Canada offered. *Margaret Lau-

rence, an important Canadian writer in the 20th century, drew upon Traill's life in her 1974 novel *The Diviners*.

Traill also published many nature studies and works about botany later in her life and received public acclaim for these as well. Her best-known naturalist works are *Canadian Wild Flowers* (1868), *Studies of Plant Life in Canada* (1885), and *Pearls and Pebbles; or, Notes of an Old Naturalist* (1895), published when she was in her 90s. After her husband's death in 1859, Traill built a house in Lakefield, Ontario, where she spent her remaining years. She died in 1899, at age 97.

SOURCES:

Buck, Claire, ed. *The Bloomsbury Guide to Women's Literature*. NY: Prentice Hall, 1992.

Kunitz, Stanley J., and Howard Haycraft. *British Authors of the 19th Century*. NY: H.W. Wilson, 1936.

Gillian S. Holmes,
freelance writer,
Hayward, California

Trani, countess of.
See Mathilde of Bavaria (1843–1925).

Tran Le Xuan (b. 1924).
See Nhu, Madame.

Trapani, Antonia von (b. 1851)

*Countess of Caserta. Born on March 16, 1851; daughter of Franz, count of Trapani; married Alphonse of Sicily (1841–1934), count of Caserta, on June 8, 1868; children: Ferdinand Pio, duke of Calabria (1869–1934); Charles or Carlos (1870–1949), prince of Bourbon-Sicily; Franz (1873–1876); Maria Immaculata (b. 1874, who married John George of Saxony); *Maria Cristina of Sicily (1877–1947); Maria Pia (b. 1878, who married Louis d'Eu); Maria Josephine (b. 1880); Gennaro (b. 1882); Reiner (1883–1973), duke of Castro; Philipp (b. 1885); Franz (1888–1914); Gabriel (b. 1897).*

Trapani, countess of.
See Maria Isabella (1834–1901).

Trapnel, Anna (fl. 1642–1661)

English prophet and writer. Birth date and place unknown; date of death unknown but evidence suggests she was still alive in 1661; daughter of William Trapnel (a shipwright); married, possibly in 1661.

Selected works: The Cry of a Stone; or a Relation of Something Spoken in Whitehall by Anna Trapnel . . . Uttered in Prayers and Spiritual Songs, by an Inspiration Extraordinary, and Full of Wonder *(1654); A*

Legacy for Saints: Being Several Experiences of the Dealings of God with Anna Trapnel (1654); Anna Trapnel's Report and Plea: or a Narrative of her Journey from London into Cornwall (1654); Strange and Wonderful Newes from White-hall (1654); A Voice for the King of Saints (1657).

Anna Trapnel's early history is unknown. She achieved some fame as a prophet during the period in which Oliver Cromwell (1599–1658) served as Lord Protector of England after the overthrow and execution of King Charles I. The Protectorate lasted from 1653 to 1658, and Trapnel uttered a number of politically charged prophecies during this time; she also published several works, including preachings and verse prophecies. Anna's mother died on December 31, 1641, and on New Year's Day of 1642, Anna was "seized with the spirit of the Lord" while John Simpson, a Baptist preacher, was delivering a sermon at St. Botolph's Church in Aldgate, London. This occasioned the start of Trapnel's career as a prophet; she began seeing visions and uttering prophecies that involved trances and periodically caused her to fall to the ground. She donated her possessions to the Parliamentarian Army and (possibly under Simpson's influence) joined the Fifth Monarchists. During the 1650s, this sect preached the imminent coming of the Kingdom of Christ on Earth, the downfall of Cromwell's government, and other radical political and religious views.

Trapnel attended the trial of Vavasour Powell, a Welsh Fifth Monarchist who had been arrested for foreseeing the end of the Protectorate. During the trial, she had another prophetic experience that lasted 12 days and involved singing, dancing, and uttering prophecies in verse and prose. Her first book, The Cry of a Stone; or a Relation of Something Spoken in Whitehall by Anna Trapnel . . . Uttered in Prayers and Spiritual Songs, by an Inspiration Extraordinary, and Full of Wonder, published in 1654, consists of the comprehensible verse prophecies that Trapnel spoke during this trance which were written down by an attendant. The book begins with a spiritual biography that contains virtually the only known biographical data about Trapnel.

Trapnel became a tool of the Fifth Monarchists as their propaganda campaign advanced out of the West Country. She called Cromwell the "little horn" on the head of the Beast, and was arrested and imprisoned in Plymouth, but she refused to stop prophesying in public. She wrote A Legacy for Saints: Being Several Experiences of the Dealings of God with Anna Trapnel while in prison in 1654 to describe her conversion. That year, she also wrote about her predictions and preachings prior to her imprisonment in Anna Trapnel's Report and Plea: or a Narrative of her Journey from London into Cornwall; she had been arrested on suspicion of witchcraft during her work in Cornwall. Trapnel maintained that the authorities apprehended her while she was in a prophetic trance. "They caused my eyelids to be pulled up," she wrote, "for they said I held them fast, because I would deceive the people. . . . One of the justices pinched me by the nose, and caused my pillow to be pulled from under my head, and kept pulling me, and calling me, but I heard none of this stir and bustle." Her interview with the justices and her second imprisonment, this time in Bridewell, are also dramatized; she depicts Cromwell as a bull and draws on passages from the Bible's Book of Daniel to describe political events.

Trapnel published her own account of her Whitehall trance in Strange and Wonderful Newes from White-hall in 1654. She experienced another trance in 1657 that lasted for ten months; it was documented in A Voice for the King of Saints, which, like The Cry of a Stone, was an account of her utterances, apparently printed with her approval. There are no records of any prophecies after 1658, and scant documentation of her life, although she may have married in 1661. That same year, the Fifth Monarchists staged an uprising, but it does not appear that Trapnel participated in the failed effort.

SOURCES:
Buck, Claire, ed. The Bloomsbury Guide to Women's Literature. NY: Prentice Hall, 1992.
Shattock, Joanne. The Oxford Guide to British Women Writers. Oxford: Oxford University Press, 1993.

Gillian S. Holmes,
freelance writer,
Hayward, California

Trapp, Maria von (1905–1987).

See Von Trapp, Maria.

Trask, Kate Nichols (1853–1922)

American writer and philanthropist who founded the Yaddo artists' colony. Name variations: Katrina Trask. Born on May 30, 1853, in Brooklyn, New York; died of bronchial pneumonia on January 8, 1922, at Yaddo, near Saratoga Springs, New York; daughter of George Little Nichols (an importer) and Christina Mary (Cole) Nichols; educated by tutors and in private schools; married Spencer Trask (a banker-financier), on November 12, 1874 (died 1909); married George Foster Peabody (a financier *and philanthropist), on February 6, 1921; children: (first marriage) Alan, Christina, Spencer, Katrina (none survived early childhood).*

Published first book after the deaths of her children (1892); planned Yaddo Artists' Colony (1913).

Selected works, under name Katrina Trask: Under King Constantine *(1892, first edition published anonymously, later editions published under Katrina Trask);* Sonnets and Lyrics *(1894);* White Satin and Homespun *(1896);* John Leighton, Jr. *(1898);* Christalan *(1903);* Free, Not Bound *(1903);* Night & Morning *(1907);* King Alfred's Jewel *(1908);* In the Vanguard *(1914);* The Mighty and the Lowly *(1915).*

Kate Nichols was born in 1853 in Brooklyn, New York, daughter of **Christina Cole Nichols** and George Little Nichols. Her maternal grandparents had emigrated to New York from Holland early in the 1800s and anglicized the family name from "Kool" to "Cole." Her father, of English ancestry, was a partner in a large importing company based in New York City and a politically active Republican. Trask, who grew up in an environment of wealth and social prominence, demonstrated literary talent from childhood. She was educated by a series of tutors at home, then in elite private schools. On November 12, 1874, she married Spencer Trask, a banker with a prominent Wall Street bank. His family had been established in New England for generations, and during the industrial expansion that followed the Civil War, he had become a wealthy financier, a member of the board of directors of several railroads, and president of New York's Edison Illuminating Company. In 1896, Spencer and others organized and financed the restructuring of *The New York Times* and placed Adolph Ochs at the newspaper's helm. Spencer became chair of the reorganized publishing company.

Despite her early literary leanings, Trask did not start writing seriously until late in life. She and Spencer had four children—Alan, Christina, Spencer, and Katrina—but all died in infancy or early childhood, the last in 1888. Trask, who experienced profound grief, illness, and despondency over their deaths, turned to writing for solace. In 1892, urged on by her husband, she anonymously published *Under King Constantine*, a trio of long love poems. The book was a success, with one critic praising Trask's writing for its "spiritual loveliness." For the second edition (there would be five), she agreed to use the name Katrina Trask on that and all subsequent works. Trask wrote poems, sonnets, novels, blank verse, and plays from 1892 to 1915. Her most notable works include the novel *Free, Not Bound* (1903); the

blank-verse narrative *Night & Morning* (1907); and *King Alfred's Jewel* (1908), a historical drama written in blank verse. A pacifist, Trask also wrote the antiwar play *In the Vanguard* (1914). First staged in the year preceding the start of World War I, it ran to eight editions, was performed widely for church groups and women's clubs, and became her best-known work.

Trask's works deal with love, marriage, spiritual strength and ethics, and romance. She was a conventionally religious woman whose style now seems sentimental; she employs emotional devices to represent her thoughts on social reform, pacifism, and morality. Her friends and literary associates were traditionalists like Henry van Dyke and Richard Henry Stoddard, who, at the turn of the 20th century, sought to preserve traditional values and cultural standards. The social crusader and editor of *Arena* magazine Benjamin O. Flower was also a friend of the Trasks. The couple entertained writers and artists at Yaddo, their 300-acre country estate near Saratoga Springs, New York. To Trask, Yaddo was an enchanted place, mystical and evocative.

Trask is also remembered for her philanthropy. The Trasks, who believed that the wealthy were obligated to improve society, supported many local charities over a number of years and established the St. Christina Hospital in Saratoga Springs for the care and treatment of crippled children. Ultimately, Yaddo itself became Trask's greatest accomplishment. In the summer of 1899, she experienced a mystical episode in which she envisioned the place as a wellspring of creativity for other artists. She saw her fellow artists making pilgrimages to Yaddo to "find the Sacred Fire, and light their torches at its flame." With no children to inherit the estate, the Trasks discussed the idea of making her vision a reality by converting the 55-room country home into an artists' colony after their deaths. In 1909, Spencer Trask perished in a railroad accident, and his wife began dedicating most of her efforts to the future of the estate. Four years later, in 1913, she made public the couple's plans for developing the property as an artists' residence. (The recently opened MacDowell Colony in New Hampshire, founded by ***Marion MacDowell**, offered artists a similar opportunity.) Also in 1913, Trask experienced a series of heart attacks that left her a semi-invalid. Confined physically to Yaddo, she focused on the financial development and future use of the estate.

On February 6, 1921, Trask married George Foster Peabody, a former business partner of Spencer Trask, who was a friend of long standing and fellow philanthropist. Less than a

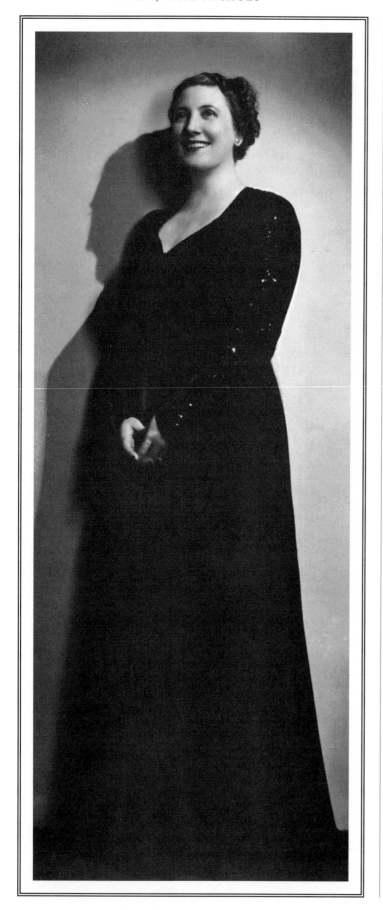

year later, on January 8, 1922, Trask died of bronchial pneumonia in her Yaddo home; she was buried on the grounds of the estate after a private Episcopal service. Yaddo was opened as an artists' colony four years later, in June 1926. The colony was designed so that artists could retreat there for periods of time, to work without being disturbed and without financial worry. The mansion, surrounded by woodlands, lakes, statuary, and rose gardens is the summer home of writers, artists, and composers every year as a living legacy of Kate Trask's patronage.

SOURCES:

James, Edward T., ed. *Notable American Women, 1607–1950.* Cambridge, MA: The Belknap Press of Harvard University, 1971.

McHenry, Robert, ed. *Famous American Women.* NY: Dover, 1980.

Gillian S. Holmes,
freelance writer,
Hayward, California

Trask, Katrina (1853–1922).

See Trask, Kate Nichols.

Trastamara, Eleanor (d. 1415).

See Joanna of Navarre for sidebar.

Traubel, Helen (1899–1972)

American soprano who dominated the Met in the 1940s and was one of America's greatest singers. Born in St. Louis, Missouri, on June 20, 1899; died in Santa Monica, California, on July 28, 1972; daughter of Clara Stuhr Traubel (a singer) and Otto Ferdinand Traubel (a druggist); married Louis Franklin Carpenter (a car salesman), in 1922 (divorced); married William L. Bass (her manager).

Helen Traubel's career was strange by any account. Blessed with a fabulous voice, she was little known until she reached 40 and became internationally famous. Traubel, who was talented in many fields, was determined to use her talents as she saw fit.

She was born in 1899 into a middle-class German family in St. Louis, Missouri, where love of music was considered natural. By the time she was 12, she had seen 30 operas. She began to sing in church choirs and took voice lessons with **Louise Vetta-Karst** in 1916. In 1922, she married Louis Carpenter, a car salesman, and two years later debuted with the St. Louis Symphony Orchestra. Traubel continued to sing locally until 1935 when Walter Damrosch, the American "Pope of Music," heard her sing and insisted that she come to New York. In the spring of 1937, she made her Metropolitan Opera debut appearing with *Kirsten Flagstad and Lauritz Melchior. She also began to sing on the radio with NBC and thus became more and more widely known throughout the United States.

In 1938, Traubel decided she should temporarily retire from the stage and study with Giuseppe Boghetti, *Marian Anderson's teacher. Finally she felt ready to appear in public again and debuted at New York's Town Hall on October 8, 1939. Two weeks later, she sang in Carnegie Hall and not long after at the Met. After Kirsten Flagstad returned to Norway in 1941, Traubel reigned supreme as the Met's "Queen of the German Wing." She was particularly known for her Wagnerian repertoire for which her large voice and big frame seemed ideally suited. She was the first entirely American-trained singer to do Isolde and all three Brünnhildes in a season. International tours followed, although Traubel remained essentially American.

During World War II, Traubel discovered that she enjoyed performing light music for the troops in USO concerts. With the advent of television, she appeared with Jimmy Durante, Red Skelton, Ed Sullivan and others. In the late 1940s, she began to write detective stories. (In her 1951 *The Metropolitan Opera Murders* a statuesque Wagnerian soprano solves a mystery.) In 1953, Traubel expanded her activities by appearing in nightclubs. This was the final straw for Rudolf Bing, the Met's very European director, who disdained her affinity for the popular media. Bing told Traubel she must choose between nightclubs and opera. Calling him a snob, Traubel ended her association with the Met and went to Hollywood to make three movies. She also made numerous recordings for RCA and Columbia and was the first singer to record with Arturo Toscanini and his NBC Symphony Orchestra. Recordings document what a fantastic voice this versatile performer possessed. Traubel died at 69, still greatly admired.

SOURCES:

Swan, John. "Traubel, Helen," in *Notable American Women, 1607–1950*. Cambridge, MA: The Belknap Press of Harvard University, 1971.

"Traubel, Great Soprano," in *The New York Times Biographical Edition*. July 1972, p. 1415.

SUGGESTED READING:

Traubel, Helen. *St. Louis Woman*. Duell, 1959.

John Haag,
Athens, Georgia

Trava, Teresa Fernandez de

(fl. 1170)

Queen of Leon. Flourished around 1170; became second wife of Fernando or Ferdinand II (1137–1188), *king of Leon (r. 1157–1188), before October 7, 1178; children: Fernando of Leon (born after 1179).*

Travell, Janet G. (1901–1997)

American physician, noted for her work in the field of neuromuscular pain, who was the first woman to serve as personal physician to a U.S. president. Name variations: Janet Powell. Born Janet Graeme Travell on December 17, 1901, in New York City; died on August 1, 1997, in Northampton, Massachusetts; daughter of Willard Travell (a physician) and Janet (Davidson) Travell; attended the Brearley School in New York City; Wellesley College, B.A., 1922; Cornell University Medical College, M.D., 1926; married John W.G. Powell (an investment counselor), in June 1929; children: Janet Powell McAlee; Virginia Powell Street.

Served as an ambulance surgeon while an intern and resident (1927–29); served as house physician at New York Hospital (1929–61); became expert in the use of digitalis to treat pneumonia, arterial disease, and pain; was an instructor, then associate professor in pharmacology, Cornell Medical College (1930–61); appointed to serve as personal physician to the president of the U.S. (1961–65); was known as a leader in the treatment and management of neuromuscular pain; published, with David G. Simons, Travell and Simons' Mysofascial Pain and Dysfunction: The Trigger Point Manual (2 vols., 1983, rep. 1998).

Known as a guiding light in the diagnosis and treatment of mysofascial pain, Janet G. Travell was born in 1901 in New York City, the daughter of Willard Travell, a physician, and **Janet Davidson Travell**. Willard specialized in relieving pain through physical medicine and in promoting exercise for good health, and his daughters **Virginia** and Janet followed his interests actively. He was to live to age 91, having practiced medicine for 60 years. Janet attended the Brearley School in New York City for both her primary and secondary education. She was an athlete who loved tennis and, during vacations at their summer home in Sheffield, Massachusetts, both Virginia and Janet caught turtles and frogs for informal anatomy lessons with their father. Virginia was later to become a pediatrician, practicing in Brooklyn. Their mother was a graduate of Wellesley College, and daughter Janet followed her there, winning three tennis championships and graduating Phi Beta Kappa in 1922. To study medicine, she returned to New York City and the Cornell University Medical College. She was granted an M.D. degree in 1926, was awarded the John Metcalf

Opposite page
Helen
Traubel

Polk Memorial Prize for academic excellence, and graduated at the top of her class.

Travell served her internship and residency from 1927 to 1929 at New York Hospital, an affiliate of the Cornell University Medical College. She also joined the New York City police force to serve as an ambulance surgeon. With the rank of lieutenant, she covered a rough area of the city that included the waterfront, subway stations on the West Side, and the area known as Hell's Kitchen. After completing her residency, she was named house physician at New York Hospital, where she was the only woman doctor on the staff. She remained with New York Hospital until 1961, except for a period in which she transferred to Bellevue Hospital for a special study of pneumonia patients. Travell won a fellowship enabling her to join specialists from Bellevue, Cornell, and the Rockefeller Institute in evaluating the common practice of giving digitalis to pneumonia patients. In an 18-month study, she tested 1,000 patients and concluded that the doses of digitalis should be smaller and given more selectively. As a result of this research, Cornell Medical College awarded her an instructorship in pharmacology in 1930. Her association with Cornell also continued until

Janet G. Travell

1961, and she achieved the rank of associate professor of clinical pharmacology in 1952.

Travell held several positions as visiting physician. From 1936 to 1945, she was visiting assistant (later associate) in cardiology at Sea View Hospital in Staten Island. Receiving a fellowship from the Josiah Macy, Jr., Foundation in 1939, she used it to study arterial disease from 1939 to 1941 at Beth Israel Hospital in New York City. This assignment introduced her to new methods of relieving pain, and she studied these techniques, becoming a pioneer in the field. She later joined the staff of Beth Israel and, by 1961, was an associate physician in the hospital's unit for cardiovascular research. From the 1930s to 1961, Travell also kept up a private practice in offices she shared with her father. Because both had begun their medical practices as general practitioners but had specialized in pain relief, their private patients included a number of athletes, prize fighters, and John F. Kennedy, who would become Travell's patient in 1955, when he was a senator. Following her studies of arterial disease and cardiology, Travell expanded her interest in pain relief to include chest pain, and, from there to the field of orthopedics, in which she specialized in musculoskeletal pain and its relief. She was one of the first to understand the contribution of muscle "trigger points" to pain syndromes, and to develop treatment to manage and alleviate chronic and acute pain.

By 1955, Senator Kennedy had had two operations on his spine and was suffering from severe back pain. His orthopedic surgeon, Dr. Philip D. Wilson, referred Kennedy to Travell. To relieve the muscle spasms causing his back pain, Travell injected low-strength procaine (a form of Novocaine) directly into the muscle, causing it to relax and receive a normal supply of blood. Travell also discovered that Kennedy's left leg was slightly shorter than the right, causing added strain to his lower back muscles. The simple addition of a quarter-inch lift to his left shoe helped eliminate this additional strain. On Kennedy's recommendation, other members of his family, including both his parents and his brother Robert F. Kennedy, also sought treatment from Travell. Travell had also recommended that Senator Kennedy use a rocking chair to provide mild muscular activity. Kennedy bought an old-fashioned rocker for $24.95 and, when he became president, had it stained mahogany and moved into the White House. Photos of the president in his rocking chair popularized the "Kennedy rocker," and the manufacturer of the chair saw its production increase several hundred percent.

On January 26, 1961, Travell's ministrations to John F. Kennedy put her in the record books when she became the first woman to serve as personal physician to the president and the first civilian to hold that post since Warren G. Harding's administration. On that date, she was appointed to succeed Major General Howard McC. Snyder, who had served President Dwight D. Eisenhower as the White House doctor. Her White House assignment forced Travell to stop her practice and "half a dozen full time jobs" to assume sole responsibility for the health of the president. A registered Republican before the 1960 presidential election, she had crossed party lines to support her patient and to work for the "Doctors for Kennedy" campaign; however, one of her other patients was Kennedy's opponent, Senator Barry M. Goldwater (whom Kennedy had referred to Travell when both men were senators). Travell described Kennedy's physical condition as excellent. As part of her job, she insisted on seeing the president every day for a brief period in the morning and in accompanying him on all trips. She also supervised the White House dispensary, open to the president's family and staff, which was staffed by a Navy captain, two corpsmen, and a nurse. Travell's recommendations to Kennedy included regular exercise suited to his previous training. Because the president was an excellent swimmer, she advocated swimming daily in the White House pool and supplementing this exercise with golf and tennis. She often joined him on the tennis court.

Travell's recommendation to the president for the rocking chair grew out of studies of muscle strain that made her an authority on all types of chairs and seating. She expressed the belief that chairs should be chosen for particular uses and to fit their occupants. Many firms, including the industrial designer Henry Dreyfuss, hired her as a consultant to help design more comfortable seats. Dreyfuss actually regretted having hired her at one point, because she suggested so many costly changes to the manufacture of seats for farm tractors. She also designed airplane seats, notably the tilt-back seat for the Lockheed Electra turbojet.

Travell wrote many technical articles and professional papers that were published in the *American Journal of Physical Medicine*, the *New York Journal of Medicine*, the *Journal of the American Medical Association*, and other medical journals. Her work on pain relief is cited extensively in the book *The Management of Pain*, which is considered a definitive work on the subject and was written by Dr. John J. Bonica in 1953. With Dr. David G. Simons, she wrote what is considered the bible of neuromuscular pain diagnosis and treatment, *Travell and Simons' Mysofascial Pain and Dysfunction: The Trigger Point Manual*, a two-volume set originally published in 1983 and reissued in 1998. She received grants for pain research from the National Heart Institute of the National Institutes of Health and the Lieutenant Joseph P. Kennedy, Jr., Foundation. Travell received an achievement award in August 1961 from the women's division of the Albert Einstein College of Medicine of Yeshiva University. Her memberships included the medical societies of New York City, New York State, Westchester, the American Medical Association, the New York Academy of Medicine, the American Geriatrics Society, the New York Academy of Sciences, and the American Association for the Advancement of Science. She was also a diplomate of the National Board of Medical Examiners.

Travell's personal life was equally full. A tall, trim woman with hazel eyes, she had married John W.G. Powell in June 1929. Powell, an investment counselor with Trainer Wortham & Company, had turned down contracts offered by three major league baseball teams to pursue a career in finance. The Powells had two daughters; **Janet Powell McAlee**, an operatic soprano, and **Virginia Powell Street**, a painter and sculptor whose works were displayed in Travell's White House office. Travell followed her own advice regarding exercise; she swam, skated, rode horseback, and chopped trees at the family's summer home in Sheffield, Massachusetts. She remained White House physician after Kennedy's assassination, serving until 1965, and continued to work extensively in the field of pain management in the following years. In 1996, the American Academy of Pain Management bestowed its first annual Janet G. Travell Soft Tissue Pain Management Award. She died the following year, having lived, like her father, past 90.

SOURCES:
Current Biography. NY: H.W. Wilson, 1961.
Read, Phyllis J., and Bernard L. Witlieb. *The Book of Women's Firsts*. NY: Random House, 1992.

Gillian S. Holmes,
freelance writer,
Hayward, California

Travers, Mary (1894–1941).

See Bolduc, Marie.

Travers, P.L. (1906–1996)

Australian-English theater and literary critic, writer on mythology and spirituality, who wrote the enor-

mously popular "Mary Poppins" books. Name variations: Pamela Lyndon Travers. Born Helen Goff Travers on August 9, 1906, in Queensland, Australia; died at her London home on April 23, 1996; daughter of Robert Travers and Margaret (Goff) Travers (Irish-Scottish ranchers); educated at home, then in Australian schools; never married; no children.

Was a writer, actress and dancer in Australia; freelance writer in England (1924–40); published Mary Poppins (1934); lived in America (1940–45), England (1945–65); was writer-in-residence at Radcliffe College, Massachusetts (1965–66), at Smith College, Massachusetts (1966–67), at Scripps College, California (1970); returned to England (1976).

I have long held that the secret of the successful children's book is that it is not written for children.

—P.L. Travers

Selected writings: author of twelve books for children and seven for adults, including Mary Poppins *(illustrated by Mary Shepard, Reynal & Hitchcock, 1934);* Mary Poppins Comes Back *(1935); (adult)* Moscow Excursion *(Reynal & Hitchcock, 1935);* Happy Ever After *(1940);* I Go by Sea, I Go by Land *(Harper, 1941); (adult)* Aunt Sass *(Reynal & Hitchcock, 1941);* Mary Poppins Opens the Door *(Reynal & Hitchcock, 1943);* Mary Poppins in the Park *(Harcourt, 1952); (adult)* In Search of the Hero: The Continuing Relevance of Myth and Fairy Tale *(Scripps College, 1970);* Friend Monkey *(Harcourt, 1971); (translator with Ruth Lewinnek)* Karlfried Montmartin's The Way of Transformation *(Allen & Unwin, 1971); (adult)* George Ivanovitch Gurdjieff *(Traditional Studies, 1973);* Two Pairs of Shoes *(Viking, 1980);* Mary Poppins in Cherry Tree Lane *(Delacorte, 1982).*

Pamela Travers, author of *Mary Poppins*, was a serious and prolific writer on mythology, legend, and spirituality, but the success of the Poppins books overshadowed her other literary accomplishments. Private, avoiding celebrity, and denying that she was a "children's writer," she lived in Australia, America, and England. She maintained an intense reserve on biographical questions and only a few fragments from her personal life are known to the many critics who have studied her. No more than occasional glimpses in her early poetry provide clues about her romantic life, her forms of support, or her motives for moving to England and America.

Travers was born in 1906 in Queensland, Australia, and grew up on a sugar cane plantation beside the Great Barrier Reef, to a family of mixed Scottish and Irish ancestry. Her parents

gave her no encouragement in her early experiments in storytelling, and let her spend long periods alone making "nests," sometimes for migrating birds and sometimes for herself. Her mother used to read romantic novels which as a child Travers found astonishingly dull: "The characters were all stationary figures; like waxworks they never did anything, never went anywhere, no teeth were ever brushed, no one was reminded to wash, and if they ever went to bed it was not explicitly stated." Much more exciting, in her view, was a book entitled *Twelve Deathbed Scenes* from her father's shelf. Designed to be edifying, it caused her "to long to die, on condition, of course, that I came alive again the next minute, to see if I, too, could pass away with equal misery and grandeur." She also loved the most gruesome stories from Grimm's fairy tales and from the Old Testament, once embarrassing her father with the question: "What is a concubine?"

In 1914, her father died. The seven-year-old Travers, along with her two younger sisters, went to live with her Aunt Christina in New South Wales, who later became the subject of her book *Aunt Sass* (1941). She first attended a local school and then a boarding school where she became an enthusiastic actress and playwright. Travers was offered a role on the Sydney stage at the age of ten but her mother forbade it. From earliest childhood, she had been writing stories, and directing and acting in her own plays. At the age of 16, possibly dissatisfied with home and school life where she was expected to shoulder burdens beyond her years, she joined a traveling company of dancers and actors, and soon began to work as a freelance writer of journalism and poetry. Saving her money from these assignments, she was able to immigrate to England in 1924, where she continued to sell work to magazines and newspapers. Early poems describe her search for love. In "The Plane Tree" (1927), she compares the unhappy ending of a love-affair to the falling of summer foliage which leaves nature starkly revealed:

> I know you now. Winter has laid you bare
> Of green falsehood and gold disguise.
> Farewell the traitor leaves and the soft drone
> Of cozening branches lying to the wind.

In Ireland, where she went in search of her father's relatives, she met the poet A.E. (George William Russell), who accepted her poetry for publication in his journal *The Irish Statesman*, introduced her to Indian mythology, and would take a keen interest in the ancestry of her fictional creation Mary Poppins. She nursed Russell in his last illness and was present at his death in Dublin in 1935. Biographer **Patricia Demers** thinks that much of her subsequent work was a playing out of themes introduced to her, or encouraged, by him during their close friendship. Russell also introduced her to William Butler Yeats, by then the grand old man of Irish literature, who encouraged her literary ambitions and shared a similar enthusiasm for fairy tales, legends, and magic. On a visit to see him, she gathered branches from rowan trees on the Isle of Innisfree, subject of one of his most famous poems.

Travers wrote *Mary Poppins* in an ancient thatched Sussex cottage, while recovering from an illness, and published it in 1934, but the character had been familiar to her since childhood. She had told her younger sister Mary Poppins stories when they were both children, and had written "M. Poppins" inside the cover of one of her own books when she was seven. The Banks family's nursemaid Mary Poppins is a magical being with a large fund of common sense, much less sentimental than her later personification in the movie, and imperious in her demands on the children she cares for. Having the outward appearance of an old-fashioned nanny, tall and thin, vain and prim, she flies through the air with the help of a parrot-headed umbrella, slides *up* the banisters, can whisk her charges around the world, or back in time, and resents receiving any instructions from her ostensible employers. She takes the children to the zoo one evening where they are lectured by a wise old snake, the Hamadryad. Mary Poppins refuses to explain her conduct or the nature of her magic. And she is always her own boss, coming or going as she pleases.

Mary Poppins, with illustrations by ✥➤ **Mary Shepard**, was an instant success—Travers claimed that she did not try to write for children, but just assumed that they would understand what she had written. "If you look at other so-called children's authors, you'll see they never wrote directly for children," she wrote. "Though Lewis Carroll dedicated his book to Alice, I feel it was an afterthought once the whole was already committed to paper. . . . And I think the same can be said of Milne or Tolkien or *Laura Ingalls Wilder*." Travers declined to explain to curious readers *how* Mary Poppins could work her magic or where she came from, though she did write five vastly popular sequels, elaborating the mystery. Much later, in 1981 she rewrote a section of the original book which included black children speaking in dialect, because black parents groups had protested it as racist and urged its removal from libraries and schools in San

Francisco. Travers was annoyed at having to submit to this pressure, arguing that children of all races enjoyed the book (it was already translated into 25 languages). "I wonder sometimes, how much disservice is done children by some individuals who occasionally offer, with good intentions, to serve as their spokesmen."

During the 1930s, Travers wrote regularly for a new magazine, the *New English Weekly*, and remained a faithful contributor until it folded in 1949. T.S. Eliot was one of its editorial advisors and she reviewed enthusiastically the first performances of several of his plays, including *Murder in the Cathedral*. She was a regular drama reviewer, willing to criticize the leading actors and directors of the era in London and Stratford and often expressing the opinion that British theater needed a transfusion of new blood. Theater, which she knew from both sides of the footlights, seemed to her a rich and expressive art. "The theater is the authentic link between person and person," she wrote in a 1937 review, "the common de-

P. L. Travers

See sidebar on the following page

Shepard, Mary (1909–2000)

English illustrator. Name variations: Mary Eleanor Jessie Knox. Born Mary Eleanor Jessie Shepard on December 25, 1909, in Surrey, England; died in London on September 4, 2000; daughter of Ernest H. Shepard (the illustrator) and Florence Eleanor (Chaplin) Shepard (an artist); attended Slade School of Art; married Edmund George Valpy Knox (an editor for Punch), on October 2, 1937 (died January 2, 1971); children: (stepdaughter) Penelope Knox (d. 1999) who under her married name of Penelope Fitzgerald wrote novels.

Mary Shepard was born on Christmas Day, 1909, in Surrey, England, the daughter of Ernest H. Shepard and **Florence Chaplin Shepard**, both artists. Florence died when her daughter was 17. Mary Shepard followed in the footsteps of her illustrious father who had illustrated A.A. Milne's "Winnie the Pooh" series, among others. In fact, in 1932 *P.L. Travers had first approached Ernest

to do the "Mary Poppins" series. When he had to beg off because of overwork, the assignment went to Mary.

In 1937, Mary married E.V. Knox, a widower and the editor of *Punch*. At the time, Mary was only seven years older than Knox's daughter Penelope, who would later be known as the author **Penelope Fitzgerald**. As Penelope grew older, she and Mary became like sisters, living near each other, and talking daily. Shepard, who spent her last years in a nursing home, died in September 2000. She was so modest, wrote Eden Ross Lipson, that she "did not wish to be buried with her husband in the pretty Hampstead cemetery because her name would add clutter to his stone." Rather, Penelope's children arranged for twin stones to be placed next to Knox's: one for their mother who had died in 1999 and one for Mary.

SOURCES:

Lipson, Eden Ross. "Mary Shepard Dies at 90," in *The New York Times*. October 2, 2000, B8.

---

nominator of humanity and the means by which the dramatic element in man is released and projected into actuality. We know ourselves not merely by inward but also by outward looking and the theater, of all the secondary arts, provides the greatest natural arena for the clash or contact of self with other." She contributed reviews of 17 Shakespeare plays in the 1930s, writing on at least one of the tragedies, *Hamlet*, five times.

Travers also wrote book reviews and travel pieces and in 1934 made a guided tour of the Soviet Union, which she commemorated in her second book *Moscow Excursion* (1934). She had no explicit political views to vindicate, unlike many literary pilgrims to the early Soviet Union, but she found the endless trumpeting of industrial and agricultural achievements rather hard to bear and much preferred seeing a Russian version of *Hamlet* in a Moscow theater. She also bristled at the knowing falsification of history presented to her by official guides and booklets, and by the disappointing realization that "the new State, wrested so nobly and with such heroism from chaos during the Ten Days, has developed merely into a new and more vigorous form of bourgeois bureaucracy. Looking for the New one is brought up rudely against the Old—garnished and prinked out in a new hat, of course, but recognizably the old." She added that in a world "rocking madly between Fascism and Communism" she would prefer the latter tyranny if forced to choose but that it

*Opposite page
From the movie
Mary Poppins,
starring Julie
Andrews.*

would be a "desolate alternative." She also recognized at once, with her mythopoeic outlook, that the idealized "Worker" and the mummified Lenin were the trappings of a parody religion rather than the alleged antithesis of all religion.

When the Second World War began, Travers was one of few British residents to welcome the nightly blackout, which most regarded as a terrible ordeal. It was, she wrote in 1939, an "ancient recreating fountain of darkness," in which London "swings now to earth's rhythm, goes with the sun and calmly obeys the law." A literary celebrity by 1940, she accepted an invitation from the Ministry of Education to visit the United States. Arriving by ship via Canada, she wrote a series of 12 "Letters from another world" for the *New English Weekly*, describing the American political scene in the days before American entry into the war. Another children's book, *I Go by Sea, I Go by Land* (1941), was based on her Atlantic voyage with a shipload of evacuees, but was seen through the eyes of an 11-year-old girl. Homesick for England but unable to return through the hazardous North Atlantic, she had the chance to visit a Navaho Indian reservation in New Mexico. She spoke about her writing to tribal meetings, bought native clothes, and received a secret initiation name from the tribe—events she frequently referred to in later interviews. She remained fascinated by the southwest and was an admirer of Carlos Castenada's novels about Mexican-Indian religion in the 1970s and 1980s.

Travers was back in London at the end of World War II, working once more for the *New English Weekly* and, following its failure in 1949, for several other English periodicals. In 1962, she published *The Fox at the Manger*, a tale of the animals which witnessed Christ's birth, which are joined by a fox, the wild animal that, she said, had been most harshly treated by earlier storytellers. Walt Disney made the musical film of Mary Poppins in 1963, starring **Julie Andrews** as Mary but mixing human and animated characters for the second time in Hollywood's history. Travers, now in her late 50s, was a consultant on the set and made Disney agree to certain stipulations, such as setting the film in the Edwardian era (rather than in the 1930s setting of the books) and *not* involving Mary Poppins in a romance. Even though it enriched her and pleased her in some ways, Travers said that the film was nothing like the books. She hoped it would stimulate a new interest in them rather than becoming their substitute. Later that year Travers posed for a statue of Mary Poppins being carved for New York's Central Park to stand beside the statues of Hans Christian Andersen and Alice in Wonderland, though due to planning and siting problems it was never installed.

In the mid- and late-1960s, she spent several years as writer-in-residence at American colleges—Radcliffe and Smith in Massachusetts and then Scripps College in Claremont, California. While working at Scripps, she published the text of a speech which summarizes many of her views, *In Search of the Hero: The Continuing Relevance of Myth and Fairy Tale* (1970), arguing against the demystification of life and literature and against the idea of a sharp separation between the thoughts and lives of children and adults. Reverting to this theme in a later article, she deplored the fact that "we grown-ups have become so timid that we bowdlerize, blot out, retell and gut the real stories for fear that truth, with its terrible beauty, should burst upon the children. Perhaps," she added "it is because we have lived through a period of such horror and violence that we tremble at the thought of inflicting truth upon the young. But children have strong stomachs. They need to know what is true." She gave an address to the Library of Congress in 1967 and became a familiar figure on the American literary landscape.

In this period, she also shared the widespread countercultural fascination with Eastern religion—a theme in her work ever since her friendship with George Russell. Now she wrote *George Ivanovitch Gurdjieff* (1973) about one of the gurus of the era, and spent several years studying with a master of Zen Buddhism. She

also contributed frequent articles to *Parabola*, a magazine of mythology and spirituality, and was one of its editors from its founding in 1976. In an early article, she discussed England's bronze age fortifications and stone circles with archaeologist Michael Dames. She showed that she did not allow her interest in these ancient places of worship to carry her off into the crackpot realm of latter-day Druids, but that she was emotionally gripped by the sense of continuity between ancient generations and her own. She compared crawling into an Irish burial mound with being born, adding: "I was overcome with the vibrations and the sense of power that was in this place. . . . One's whole body was vivified; it was almost unbearable." In later issues, she frequently contributed interpretations of fairy tales and folk-myths, and mythological short stories.

In the early 1970s, Travers was living in New York, where she wrote *Friend Monkey*, based on the Hindu monkey-god Hanuman who is both lively and sorrowful, and creates chaos wherever he goes at the time of Queen *Victoria's Diamond Jubilee in 1897. Neither it nor a retelling of the Sleeping Beauty myth were well received by critics, who saw them as heavy handed, didactic, and lacking the sharp edges which made *Mary Poppins* such a pleasure. Travers returned to England in 1976 to live in the affluent London district of Chelsea, in a terraced house with a pink front door, and published the last of the Mary Poppins books, *Mary Poppins and the House Next Door*, in 1988. She remained prolific and active through her 70s and 80s.

SOURCES:
Commire, Anne, ed. *Something About the Author*. Vol. 54. Detroit, MI: Gale Research, 1989, pp. 148–162.
Demers, Patricia. *P.L. Travers*. Boston, MA: Twayne, 1991.
Travers, Pamela. "I Never Wrote for Children," in *The New York Times Magazine*. July 2, 1978, pp. 10–12, 14.
———. "The Art of Fiction," in *Paris Review*. Vol. 86, Winter 1982, pp. 211–229.
———. *Moscow Excursion*. NY: Reynal and Hitchcock, 1934.
———, and Michael Dames. "If She's Not Gone She Still Lives There," in *Parabola*. Vol. 3, 1978, pp. 78–91.

RELATED MEDIA:
Mary Poppins, Walt Disney musical film, starring Julie Andrews, *Glynis Johns, and Dick Van Dyke, 1963 (for which Travers was a consultant).

Patrick Allitt,
Professor of History,
Emory University,
Atlanta, Georgia

Treble, Lillian M. (1854–1909)

Canadian philanthropist. Born Lillian Massey in 1854; died in 1909; daughter of H.A. Massey; married John Mill Treble.

Lillian M. Treble organized classes in domestic science which led to the adoption of a complete curriculum in household science in various women's colleges throughout Canada. She gave to Toronto University a handsome and spacious structure called the "Lillian Massey Household Science and Art Building," opened in 1913. In addition to numerous philanthropies in her lifetime, she bequeathed the greater part of a large fortune to charitable institutions.

Tree, Dolly (1909–1992)

American costume designer. Name variations: Dorothy Tree. Born in 1909; died in 1992.

Principal stage credits: Diamond Lil *(1927); various Paramount Circuit Stage Shows (1929); Capitol Stage Shows (1929).*

Principal film credits: Just Imagine *(1930);* Annabelle's Affairs *(1931);* Bad Girl *(1931);* Wicked *(1931);* Stepping Sisters *(1931);* Business and Pleasure *(1931);* Almost Married *(1932);* Meet the Baron *(1932);* The Prizefighter and the Lady *(1933);* The Chief *(1933);* Lazy River *(1934);* Viva, Villa *(1934);* Laughing Boy *(1934);* Manhattan Melodrama *(1934);* The Thin Man *(1934);* Stamboul Quest *(1934);* Hide-Out *(1934);* Straight Is the Way *(1934);* Evelyn Prentice *(1934);* The Gay Bride *(1934);* A Wicked Woman *(1934);* David Copperfield *(1934);* The Night is Young *(1934);* Vanessa, Her Story *(1934);* West Point of the Air *(1934);* The Casino Murder Case *(1934);* Times Square Lady *(1934);* Age of Indiscretion *(1935);* One New York Night *(1935);* Public Hero No. 1 *(1935);* Escapade *(1935);* The Flame Within *(1935);* Mad Love *(1935);* Woman Wanted *(1935);* The Bishop Misbehaves *(1935);* Here Comes the Band *(1935);* It's in the Air *(1935);* A Night at the Opera *(1935);* Ah, Wilderness! *(1935);* A Tale of Two Cities *(1935);* Riffraff *(1935);* Three Live Ghosts *(1935);* Exclusive Story *(1935);* Whipsaw *(1935);* The Garden Murder Case *(1935);* The Voice of Bugle Ann *(1935);* Wife Versus Secretary *(1935);* Moonlight Murder *(1935);* Petticoat Fever *(1935);* The Robin Hood of Eldorado *(1935);* Three Godfathers *(1935);* Absolute Quiet *(1936);* Small Town Girl *(1936);* The Unguarded Hour *(1936);* Fury *(1936);* Three Wise Guys *(1936);* We Went to College *(1936);* The Devil-Doll *(1936);* Suzy *(1936);* Sworn Enemy *(1936);* His Brother's Wife *(1936);* Piccadilly Jim *(1936);* Libeled Lady *(1936);* Mad Holiday *(1936);* Sinner Takes All *(1936);* After the Thin Man *(1936);* Dangerous Number *(1936);* The Good Earth *(1936);* Espionage *(1936);* Personal Property *(1936);* Good Old Soak *(1937);* Night Must Fall *(1937);* Mama Steps Out *(1937);*

Song of the City (1937); A Day at the Races (1937); Saratoga (1937); Live, Love and Learn (1937); My Dear Miss Aldrich (1937); Navy Blue and Gold (1937); Thoroughbreds Don't Cry (1937); Rosalie (1937); The Badman from Brimstone (1937); Man Proof (1937); Paradise for Three (1937); The First Hundred Years (1937); Of Human Hearts (1937); Big City (1937); Arsene Lupin Returns (1937); Four Girls in White (1938); The Girl Downstairs (1938); Stand Up and Fight (1938); Fast and Loose (1938); Let Freedom Ring (1938); Ice Follies of 1939 (1938); Test Pilot (1938); Hold That Kiss (1938); Yellow Jack (1938); Fast Company (1938); Lord Jeff (1938); Port of Seven Seas (1938); Woman against Woman (1938); The Chaser (1938); The Crowd Roars (1938); Rich Man, Poor Girl (1938); Too Hot to Handle (1938); Listen, Darling (1938); Spring Madness (1938); Young Tom Edison (1939); The Kid from Texas (1939); Society Lawyer (1939); Within the Law (1939); Bridal Suite (1939); Lucky Night (1939); Tell No Tales (1939); Maisie (1939); On Borrowed Time (1939); Six Thousand Enemies (1939); Stronger Than Desire (1939); Miracles For Sale (1939); These Glamour Girls (1939); They All Came Out (1939); Babes in Arms (1939); Blackmail (1939); Thunder Afloat (1939); Another Thin Man (1939); At the Circus (1939); Bad Little Angel (1939); Congo Maisie (1939); The Man from Dakota (1939); Forty Little Mothers (1939); Dancing Co-ed (1939); Twenty Mule Team (1940); Two Girls on Broadway (1940); Edison, The Man (1940); The Captain Is a Lady (1940); We Who Are Young (1940); Andy Hardy Meets Debutante (1940); I Love You Again (1940); Wyoming (1940); Dr. Kildare Goes Home (1940); Strike up the Band (1940); Gold Rush Maisie (1940); Hullabaloo (1940); Third Finger, Left Hand (1940); The Golden Fleecing (1940); Little Nellie Kelly (1940); Flight Command (1940); Go West (1940); The Penalty (1940); The Trial of Mary Dugan (1940); The Bad Man (1940); Sporting Blood (1940); Free and Easy (1941); Billy the Kid (1941); Wild Man of Borneo (1941); Two Gentlemen From West Point (1942); The Magnificent Dope (1942); The Loves of Edgar Allan Poe (1942); The Pied Piper (1942); Thunder Birds (1942); Tales of Manhattan (1942).

Dolly Tree's career began on Broadway in the 1920s, when she designed costumes and other aspects of Broadway musicals, revues, and plays. Most notably, she designed *Mae West's costumes for the original production of Diamond Lil, which was staged in New York. She was also a designer for the Capitol Stage and Paramount Circuit Shows in 1927. Two years later, she relocated to California and was signed by Winfield Sheehan as a "fashion creator" for Fox Studios. In 1932, she moved to Metro-Goldwyn-Mayer (MGM) Studios, where she designed costumes for hundreds of movies until 1942. Tree collaborated with many other leading lights of costume design, including **Sophie Wachner, Alice O'Neill,** Valles, Adrian, *Irene, and *Gwen Wakeling. Some of the more memorable movies in which her designs appeared were The Thin Man (1934) and Another Thin Man (1939), with William Powell and *Myrna Loy; the Marx Brothers' A Night at the Opera (1935), A Day at the Races (1937), and At the Circus (1939); the film versions of Eugene O'Neill's Ah, Wilderness! (1935), Charles Dickens' A Tale of Two Cities (1935), and *Pearl S. Buck's The Good Earth (1936); Babes in Arms (1939), with Mickey Rooney and *Judy Garland; and the star-studded (*Rita Hayworth, *Ginger Rogers, Charles Boyer and Henry Fonda, among others) Tales of Manhattan (1942), in which the plot revolves around a dress tailcoat.

SOURCES:

Leese, Elizabeth. Costume Design in the Movies. NY: Dover, 1991.

Gillian S. Holmes,
freelance writer,
Hayward, California

Tree, Ellen (1805–1880).

See Kean, Ellen.

Tree, Marietta (1917–1991)

American diplomat and social activist who was the first woman to serve as a chief U.S. delegate and a permanent ambassador to the UN. Born Mary Endicott Peabody on April 12, 1917, in Lawrence, Massachusetts; died on August 15, 1991, in New York City; daughter of Malcolm E. Peabody (a Episcopal bishop) and Mary (Parkman) Peabody; graduated from St. Timothy's girls' school in Catonsville, Maryland, 1934; attended finishing school at La Petite École Florentine, Florence, Italy; attended the University of Pennsylvania, 1936–39; married Desmond FitzGerald (a lawyer), on September 2, 1939 (divorced 1947); married Arthur Ronald Lambert Tree (an investment broker), on July 28, 1947; children: (first marriage) Frances FitzGerald (a journalist); (second marriage) Penelope Tree (a model).

Was a Democratic and civil-rights activist (beginning 1940s); worked on congressional and presidential election campaigns; appointed first woman to serve as chief U.S. delegate to the United Nations (1961); became ambassador to the UN on the Human

Rights Commission (1964) and served as member of the secretary general's staff (1966–67).

Marietta Tree was born Mary Endicott Peabody in Lawrence, Massachusetts, in 1917. The patrician Peabody family had long been a well-respected part of New England society; her paternal grandfather Endicott Peabody had founded the Groton School, and her father Malcolm E. Peabody was an Episcopal bishop and an overseer of Harvard University. Her maternal grandmother **Frances Parker Parkman**, a Boston hostess of some acclaim, had helped *Elizabeth Cary Agassiz found Radcliffe College, and her mother **Mary Parkman Peabody** was dedicated to community service. Mary Peabody was also an exemplar of the stern and frugal New Englander, and raised her children (apparently with little outward show of affection) to feel a sense of the duty to society inherent upon them because of their exalted station in life. Marietta had four younger brothers, all of whom would grow up to excel in their chosen fields of law, politics, education, and administration; Endicott "Chub" Peabody was governor of Massachusetts for two years. With her unquestioned intelligence, drive, background and charm, Marietta, in a later era, might well have become a U.S. senator, an ambition she announced to her grandparents when she was about ten years old. Instead, as she told friends when she was about 20, she decided to pin her ambitions on powerful men.

Tree was educated at St. Timothy's in Catonsville, Maryland, an exclusive girls' school where she was active in sports and the drama club. She was interested in social causes early on, thanks to her father's ministering among the families of the unemployed during the Depression. (She also claimed later that being the only daughter in a family with four boys made her aware of the challenges faced by minorities.) At age 15, she tested her political wings by campaigning for Herbert Hoover among her classmates. She was by then a beauty, blonde and well endowed, and by no means unaware of or unhappy with the effect she had on the opposite sex. After graduating from St. Timothy's in 1934, she spent a year at a finishing school in Florence, Italy. When she returned to the U.S., Tree told her father that she wanted to go to college to study political science. Surprised (despite his intention to pay his sons' way through college), Reverend Peabody agreed to provide her tuition on condition that she earn the money for her expenses. She attended the University of Pennsylvania for three years while working as a department store model in Philadelphia. After finishing her junior year, she left school to get married.

The wedding took place on September 2, 1939. Her new husband Desmond FitzGerald, a lawyer from a prominent family, joined the army in 1940, and until the end of the war they seldom saw each other. At the invitation of her friend Nelson A. Rockefeller, who at that time was Coordinator of Inter-American Affairs for the Department of State, Tree took a job as co-chair of the hospitality division of the Office of Inter-American Affairs. In this position she served as unofficial host for guests of the State Department who visited New York. From 1943 to 1945, she worked as a researcher for John K. Jessup, an editorial writer on the staff of *Life* magazine. Her research involved memorizing the voting records of all senators and the chairs of the House committees on major issues, and her experience made Tree an ardent supporter of the Democratic Party. She also became active in the cause of civil rights. In 1944, she had helped found Sydenham Hospital in New York City, the first voluntary interracial hospital in the United States. She served on the hospital's board, and was a director or board member of a number of other organizations, including the National Urban League, the Neighborhood Children's Center, the Puerto Rican Board of Guardians, the International Rescue Committee, the Franklin D. Roosevelt Foundation, and the National Conference of Christians and Jews.

Marietta and Desmond had a daughter **Frances FitzGerald**, but divorced in 1947. Motherhood did not slow her down, and she reportedly paid little attention to her first born, who would go on to study at Radcliffe College and later win the Pulitzer Prize for her book *Fire in the Lake*. In July 1947, Marietta married Ronald Tree, an investment broker who had been a Conservative member of the British Parliament for 13 years. According to biographer **Carolyn Seebohm**, this marriage was prompted at least in part by an affair with director John Huston she had had while her first husband was away during the war, the intensity of which had apparently startled her enough to make her seek calmer relations. The Trees relocated to Ronald's estate in England, Dytchley Park, which had been sumptuously decorated by his previous wife *Nancy Lancaster. They also had a summer home, Heron Bay, in Barbados (where Sir Winston Churchill and Lady *Clementine Churchill would visit them in 1960). One daughter would be born of the marriage, **Penelope Tree**, who also felt her mother's disinterest and later became famous as a model during London's Swinging '60s. In 1949, Tree and her husband sold Dytchley Park and returned to the U.S., where she took up interracial community work in New York City.

In 1952, Tree followed the advice of Earl Brown, an African-American member of the New York City Council and one of *Life* magazine's assistant editors, who suggested she take a more active role in the Democratic Party. She volunteered her time at the Democratic State Committee headquarters in New York as a researcher and speech writer, and joined the volunteers for Adlai Stevenson after attending the Democratic National Convention of 1952 in Chicago. "In politics, I can labor for a peaceful world for all children," she said, "a world that will give a better break to everyone. I am impelled by a feeling that I have so many blessings I must somehow try to pay for them in hard work for the community and in gratitude for being an American." She also had a longstanding affair with Stevenson.

During the congressional elections of 1954, Tree co-managed the campaign of Anthony B. Akers, who was a candidate for the House seat of New York's 17th District. She campaigned door-to-door, stuffed envelopes, and supervised volunteers, all in a losing cause. Tree also joined the Lexington Democratic Club, New York's largest and oldest Democratic reform club. That year, she succeeded *Dorothy Schiff, publisher of the New York *Post*, as a state committeewoman representing the 9th Assembly District. In 1955–56, Tree headed the New York branch of Volunteers for Stevenson, turning the drawing room of her home into a Democratic meeting place, but in this second campaign Stevenson was defeated again.

In 1958, Tree was recognized by the Modern Community Developers for her services as a member of the Fair Housing Practices Panel of New York City. She had joined the advisory council of the National Committee Against Discrimination in Housing because of her concern that adequate housing be made available to members of minority groups. In 1959, Mayor Robert F. Wagner appointed her to the Commission on Intergroup Relations (later the Commission on Human Rights), on which she served until 1961. She continued her work for the Democrats as well, and was named vice-chair of the New York Committee for special Democratic projects; in this capacity she raised funds for the advisory council of the Democratic National Committee. Tree also joined the advisory council's civil-rights committee, chaired by *Eleanor Roosevelt, and helped to draft the civil-rights plank of the Democratic platform for the 1960 National Convention in Los Angeles. (On her way home from the convention that year, she visited Huston on the set of

The Misfits, starring Clark Gable and *Marilyn Monroe, and at Gable's insistence made a brief appearance in an opening scene.) She served as deputy chair of the Citizens Committee for John F. Kennedy in the weeks leading up to the presidential election in November 1960; her drawing room, as well as her energy and abilities, were again devoted to the Democratic cause, and this time her candidate won.

Tree's service was rewarded by the newly elected president when, on February 16, 1961, Kennedy appointed her to represent the United States on the Human Rights Commission of the United Nations Economic and Social Council. She was also made chief U.S. delegate, the first woman ever so named. Tree initially was reluctant to accept the position, but she was sworn in on March 1, 1961. She had great faith in the United Nations; in 1964, she served on the UN's Trusteeship Council, becoming the first woman to hold the rank of permanent ambassador. From 1966 to 1967, she worked at the UN Secretariat as a member of the staff of Secretary General U Thant.

After she left the UN, Tree remained active in Democratic circles and civic groups as well as the social scene. She and her husband spent most

*Marietta
Tree*

of their time apart, although they remained married, and she had gentlemen friends into her 70s. In the 1980s, she crossed partisan lines to become friends with Henry Kissinger and his second wife **Nancy Maginnes Kissinger**, and in addition to throwing her own lavish, well-attended parties went to a number given for Republicans Ronald and *Nancy Reagan. Tree kept secret her diagnosis of breast cancer and her mastectomy, and it was a shock to many who knew her when she died of the disease in August 1991.

SOURCES:

Current Biography 1961. NY: H.W. Wilson, 1961.

Read, Phyllis J., and Bernard L. Witlieb. *The Book of Women's Firsts.* NY: Random House, 1992.

Seebohm, Caroline. *No Regrets: The Life of Marietta Tree.* NY: Simon & Schuster, 1998.

Gillian S. Holmes,
freelance writer,
Hayward, California

Tree, Nancy (1897–1994).

See Lancaster, Nancy.

Trefilova, Vera (1875–1943)

Russian ballerina and actress. Born in 1875, perhaps in St. Petersburg, Russia; died in 1943 in Paris, France; parentage and family history unknown; graduated from the St. Petersburg Imperial School of Ballet, 1894; married A.I. Butler (died); married N.V. Soloviev (died); married Valerian Svetlov (a ballet critic and author, died 1934).

Vera Trefilova

Prima ballerina of the Maryinsky Theater, St. Petersburg (1906–10); signature roles included Princess Aurora in The Sleeping Beauty *and Odette-Odile in* Swan Lake; *became dramatic stage actress (1915); returned to ballet with Diaghilev's Ballet Russe in Paris (1921).*

Vera Trefilova's early history is unknown, but she was born in 1875, presumably in St. Petersburg, because she trained there as a ballerina at the St. Petersburg Imperial School of Ballet. After graduating, she was accepted in the corps de ballet of the Maryinsky Theater of St. Petersburg. The talented dancer was limited to the back row of the corps de ballet for nearly two years because of intrigues and the machinations of other ballerinas. She was about to abandon her career when *Pierina Legnani, then the Maryinsky's prima ballerina, promised to help and took an interest in promoting her. Trefilova's strict adherence to classicism, virtuoso technique, and appearance caught the attention of the imperial court, the press and ballet critics, and the popular audience.

Trefilova became a ballerina in 1904, debuting as Princess Aurora in Tchaikovsky's *The Sleeping Beauty.* In 1906, she became the Maryinsky's prima ballerina. She took a leave of absence in 1907 to dance in Paris, where her performances received considerable acclaim. Returning to the Imperial Theater, Trefilova found she was still overwhelmed by backstage intrigue, and she resigned from the company in 1910 after a final appearance on the stage of the Maryinsky in Tchaikovsky's *Swan Lake.*

Trefilova left the world of dance and the theater completely for about five years. In 1915, she returned to the stage as a dramatic actress at the Imperial Mikhailovsky Theater in St. Petersburg. With the turmoil of the Russian Revolution in 1917, Trefilova left Russia and opened a ballet studio in Paris. In 1921, the great Russian ballet impresario Sergei Diaghilev (1872–1929), the founder of the Ballet Russe who is credited with reawakening interest in classical ballet, asked Trefilova to dance Princess Aurora in a full-length revival of his production of *The Sleeping Beauty* in London, England. She accepted and alternated nights in the role with ballerinas **Lyubov Egorova**, *Lydia Lopokova, and *Olga Spessivtzeva. These performances were the 46-year-old Trefilova's last appearances as a prima ballerina and on any stage.

Trefilova lived the rest of her life in Paris. Her first two marriages, to A.I. Butler and N.V. Soloviev, were cut short by their early deaths. Her third husband, Valerian Svetlov, was the leading Russian ballet critic of the day; among his best-known books was *Le Ballet Contemporain*, published in both French and Russian in 1911. Trefilova survived him by nine years, dying during the German occupation of Paris in 1943.

Gillian S. Holmes,
freelance writer,
Hayward, California

Trefusis, Violet (1894–1972)

English novelist, memoirist, and salon hostess. Born Violet Keppel in London, England, on June 6, 1894; died at the Villa l'Ombrellino in Florence, Italy, on

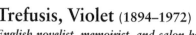

March 1, 1972; daughter of Colonel George Keppel (an army officer and brother of the earl of Albemarle) and Alice (Edmonstone) Keppel (1869–1947); sister of Sonia Keppel (1900–1986); married Denys Robert Trefusis (a cavalry officer with the Royal Horse Guards), on June 16, 1919, in London (died summer 1929); no children.

Had affair with Vita Sackville-West (April 1918–summer 1921); published first novel, Sortie de Secours (Emergency Exit) *(1929); awarded the Legion of Honor (France, 1950); published memoir* Don't Look Round *(1952); received the Order of Commendatore from Italian government (early 1960s).*

In her youth, Violet Keppel lived in a world of kings and castles, of nannies and governesses, a cosmopolitan world of elegance and charm. Violet's mother *Alice Keppel, a "regally beautiful" woman, was the acknowledged mistress of King Edward VII of England. Through her mother (née Edmonstone), Trefusis could claim descent from the Stuart dynasty. Likewise, the family of her handsome, "consummately tactful" father, Colonel George Keppel, had connections to English royalty as the "irregular descendants of King Charles II" through one of the king's several mistresses. Intelligent, effusive, scandalous, elegant, and eccentric, Violet loved poetry, travel (she spoke French, German, and Italian fluently), and gracious living; she shunned conventional morality, was ambiguous towards the male sex, and disliked children ("Violet was never young," her sister **Sonia Keppel** remarked).

In 1904, at age ten, Trefusis met the "grande passion" of her life, the aristocratic, equally eccentric *Vita Sackville-West, age twelve. They both attended Miss Wolff's exclusive school in London, shared common interests in their illustrious families and in books, and were avid Francophiles. Notes Philippe Jullian, Violet and Vita "were brought up by mothers with relaxed morals, but uncompromising manners." As a child, Violet was socially adept, amusing, and self-confident. King Edward VII "adored her" and wrote her notes signed "Kingy"; she accompanied her mother and the king to the French resort of Biarritz each year from 1905 until Edward's death in 1910. The Keppels spent summer holidays at Duntreath Castle, one of the largest castles in Scotland, which had been acquired by the Edmonstone family around 1434. With her French governess, Violet lived for months at a time in Paris and in Italy. Vita often joined them, since the girls had developed a "madly romantic" relationship. As Sackville-West

wrote later, "from the beginning I was utterly sure of her."

When Edward VII died in November 1910, his wife, Queen *Alexandra of Denmark, notified Alice Keppel of his demise. To avoid the prying eyes of the public and in deference to the royal family, the Keppels left London for Ceylon (now Sri Lanka). In 1911, Violet and Sonia left Ceylon to attend a finishing school in Munich, where Violet took painting lessons, attended operas, fell in love with a Bavarian prince, and developed a lifelong interest in Central and Eastern Europe.

A year later, Colonel and Alice Keppel purchased a sumptuous house in London on Grosvenor Square, the proper setting for entertaining royalty and the social elite of England and continental Europe; among their frequent guests were Prince Paul of Yugoslavia, Grand Duke Michael of Russia, the famous director of the Russian Ballet, Sergei Diaghilev, and Vaslav Nijinsky, the Russian dancer and choreographer. In letters to Vita, Violet signed herself "Lushka," and Vita called herself "Mitya," obviously influenced by the ballet's popularity among high society in London.

Trefusis' interest in literature led to her desire to become a writer; she had a few poems published and was working on a play in German. Alice Keppel was not pleased. She was readying Violet for her social debut, her "coming out," and was convinced that female intellectuals were not considered good marriage prospects. Equally worrisome was that Violet had a reputation for socializing in "fast" company such as the jazz-loving, unconventional debutante *Nancy Cunard and the gifted, but eccentric, composer and painter Lord Gerald Berners. Moreover, Violet was in love with Vita, a passionate, erotic attachment: at age 16, Trefusis had clearly revealed the depth of her feelings for Sackville-West: "I love in you what I know is also in me, that is, imagination, a gift for languages, taste, intuition, and a mass of other things. I love you, Vita, because I have seen your soul." As Sackville-West's son, Nigel Nicolson, later noted, "Marriage was nothing to this: marriage was only for husbands and wives." In similar fashion, Violet wrote to Vita, declaring, "Marriage is an institution that ought to be confined to temperamental old maids, weary prostitutes, and royalty."

Despite her antipathy towards marriage, Violet had several "suitable" admirers, including the future duke of Wellington, Gerald Wellesley, the poet and writer Sir Osbert Sitwell, and Julian Grenfell (son of Lord Desborough) who was killed early in World War I. However, both Violet and Vita believed that through marriage they would gain their freedom from parental control and public scrutiny of their lifestyles. Vita had married the British diplomat Harold Nicolson in October 1913, but Violet refused to commit herself to a formal engagement. A visit to the Nicolsons' home (Long Barn in Kent) in April 1918 launched the defining episode in Violet's life, a turbulent, torrid love affair with Vita that threatened to become a public scandal. A discreet adulterous affair was commonly accepted in upper-class society, but lesbianism was not. Alice Keppel and Vita's mother, Lady **Victoria Sackville-West**, were surprisingly reasonable about the situation, but were also determined to bring their daughters "back to the fold." The affair convinced Alice Keppel that Violet must marry, and that would "cure" her. But Violet wanted to live with Vita, "to pursue their ideals of freedom, beauty, and excitement."

Sackville-West's description of their love affair is found in her novel *Challenge*, begun in May 1918, and dedicated to Trefusis. It is, Nigel Nicolson claims, "Vita's defense of Violet, and of herself." As lovers, Violet assumed the "feminine" role, in fiction and in reality, and is called "Eve" in the novel. Vita appears as "Julian," and in fact, assumed a "masculine" persona when the lovers appeared together in public. The lovers' parents feared the scandalous depiction of their love affair would damage their daughters' reputations, and they urged Vita to withdraw her manuscript from the publisher. Vita complied with their wishes, much to Violet's disappointment, but the book appeared in the United States in 1924. Despite family pressures, the young women continued their liaison. From November 1918 to late March 1919, they traveled together in France. Vita's husband was convinced that Violet meant to wreck his marriage, and he wrote to his wife asking why "there is nothing between eloping with Violet and cooking my dinner?"

To Trefusis, love and marriage were not necessarily synonymous. Alice Keppel ignored Violet's nuanced distinction and was relieved when, on March 26, 1919, Violet became engaged to Major Denys Robert Trefusis of the prestigious Royal Horse Guards. Tall, handsome, charming, and "an accomplished sportsman," he came from an old family in Cornwall. As a young man, he had spent several years (1908–14) in Russia and was fluent in the language. During the First World War, he had commanded a company in France and was awarded the Military Cross for bravery in June 1919.

The couple were married in London on June 16, 1919. Vita was in France with her husband, furious that Violet had betrayed their commitment. As Vita had explained to Harold, "I feel that people like Violet can save me from a sort of intellectual stagnation, a bovine complacency." It has been suggested that Violet's marriage was never consummated, that Denys had agreed to this arrangement, and that he might have been impotent. Trefusis herself expressed no interest in sex with men, and **Victoria Glendinning** claimed that Violet had two obsessions, "chastity and the horror of male sexuality." Violet's marital status did not interfere with her affair with Vita for two more years, but in mid-1921, "the great adventure was over." Denys had threatened to divorce Violet, which would have meant a scandal if he had named Vita as co-respondent. Finally, Alice Keppel intervened; she would provide a generous allowance if the couple remained married and lived abroad.

In late 1921, Violet and Denys settled in Paris where they became part of Parisian high society. Through the Princesse Edmond de Polignac (the American heiress *Winnaretta Singer), an active patron of music in Paris, Violet was introduced to musicians and composers, and to poets and writers, including the Comtesse *Anna de Noailles and *Colette. Trefusis frequently traveled with Singer to North Africa, Greece, and Venice, often accompanied by Alice Keppel to avoid any hint of impropriety. In Paris, Violet avoided the company of well-known lesbians such as *Natalie Clifford Barney and *Gertrude Stein, but appeared to accept the wealthy, cultured princesse, a professed lesbian, whose husband was homosexual. Parisian café society did not appeal to Violet; it was "too bourgeois and contrived" for her taste. Her disdain for popular culture applied to America, too. In 1927, Violet and Denys visited the United States which they judged as philistine and boring. People drank too much and engaged in banal conversations. In Palm Beach, the millionaires displayed "a lack of any signs of intellectual life." The couple made a quick departure for Cuba.

At home in France, Trefusis presided over a salon that attracted well-known writers such as Jean Cocteau and Max Jacob, diplomats and politicians, including Paul Reynaud, the future prime minister of France, the famous couturiers Christian Dior and Pierre Balmain, and European royalty. A gracious host, Violet was also a gifted writer. Her fiction concerned the similarities and differences between England and France as seen in her first novel, *Sortie de Secours* (1929), which was a success. That same

Violet
Trefusis

year, Denys died of tuberculosis. In her memoir *Don't Look Round* (1952), Violet wrote of her husband, "We were both Europeans in the fullest sense of the term. . . . We quarrelled a lot, loved not a little. We were more to be envied than pitied."

As Trefusis assumed the rule of "international grande dame," she attracted the amorous attentions of a variety of aristocratic gentlemen, which she enjoyed. But literature and socializing interested her more than flirtatious affairs. Scotland was the setting of her next novel, *Echo* (1931), which became a bestseller and received good reviews. Two more well-regarded novels (*Tandem* and *Hunt the Slipper*) appeared during the 1930s. Her last work in French, *Les Causes Perdues* (*Lost Causes*), was published by Gallimard in German-occupied Paris in 1940. In her writing, Trefusis was credited with an "excellent gift of observation" and also a "talent for mimicry and flair for decor." These qualities are evident in her novels written in English and in French, and Violet is recognized as one of the few English writers to have written equally well in French. Her novels also reflect "a snobbery rather reminiscent of the turn-of-the-century attitudes," i.e., Edwardian, that had molded her worldly outlook.

Violet lived in Paris and at her country house, St. Loup de Naud, near Paris, which became a social center of high society for 15 years. She received, and rejected, numerous marriage proposals; of one suitor, she wrote, "I don't like his character, but I admire his faults." After age 40, Trefusis began to age rapidly, but she remained an active, fascinating, complex personality. In the 1930s, she took a small palace in Budapest and visited Russia, about which she wrote several articles for *Le Temps*. She also spent time at her parents' Villa dell'Ombrellino in Florence where she met Winston Churchill and the Italian dictator, Benito Mussolini. Trefusis was active but "rarely happy"; it has been remarked that her portraits exhibit the "wistfulness of exiles." England, and Vita, were never forgotten, however.

War broke out in Europe in 1939, and after France capitulated to the invading German forces in 1940, Violet closed St. Loup, hid her silver, and made plans to leave France. She moved to the Ritz Hotel in London with her parents and contacted Vita who informed Violet, "I don't want you to disrupt my life." While in England, Trefusis wrote short stories for *Horizon* magazine and broadcast for Radio Free France from London. Two months after the liberation of Paris, she obtained a visa and returned to France. Germans had taken over St. Loup during the occupation, and Trefusis set about repairing the damage and painting over graffiti on the walls. After the war, she became increasingly eccentric, but as Jullian observes, "Eccentricity is an impertinence which can flower fully only in an aristocratic society." And in Violet it came to full bloom. Now "a Paris dowager" with an "English flair," she resumed her lavish social life, hobnobbing with such celebrated exiles as the Duke and *Duchess of Windsor. In 1950, Trefusis was awarded the Legion of Honor in France, and in the early 1960s, the Order of Commendatore from the Italian government, seldom be-

stowed on women. She inherited l'Ombrellino from her parents and spent half of each year there. Like her home in Paris, the villa became an international social center. She even persuaded Vita and Harold Nicolson to visit her. With age, the women's ardor had cooled but not vanished, as Vita admitted to Violet, "There is a very odd thing between you and me, Lushka. There always was."

Despite declining health, Trefusis divided her time between London, Paris, and Florence. She had begun writing her memoirs in 1949, and in 1952, Vita corrected proofs of the book at Violet's villa in Florence. After Trefusis broke her hip a second time, she was still able to travel and to host lavish dinner parties. Her odd behavior manifested itself in the "myths and fantasies" with which she embroidered the realities of her life, and few friends dared question her: that Edward VII could have been her father, for example. However, Violet Trefusis was more than an eccentric dowager socialite; she was a distinguished writer, a woman of intelligence and wit. As Vita's son, Nigel Nicolson, observes, "She was always a bird of paradise, different, electric . . . a brilliant, exciting woman."

Trefusis died at l'Ombrellino in 1972, and was cremated and buried with her parents in Florence. A plaque at St. Loup is inscribed, "Violet Trefusis 1894–1972. Anglaise de naissance, Française de coeur" ("English by birth, French at heart").

SOURCES:
Glendinning, Victoria. *Vita: The Life of Vita Sackville-West*. Harmondsworth, England: Penguin, 1984.
Jullian, Philippe, and John Phillips. *The Other Woman: A Life of Violet Trefusis*. Boston, MA: Houghton Mifflin, 1976.
Nicolson, Nigel. *Portrait of a Marriage: V. Sackville-West and Harold Nicolson*. NY: Atheneum, 1980.

SUGGESTED READING:
Jullian, Philippe. *Violet Trefusis: Life and Letters*. London: Hamilton, 1976.
Keppel, Sonia. *Edwardian Daughter*. London: Hamilton, 1958.
The Last Edwardians: An Illustrated History of Violet Trefusis and Alice Keppel. Boston, MA: Boston Athenaeum, 1985.
Sharpe, Henrietta. *A Solitary Woman: A Life of Violet Trefusis*. London: Constable, 1981.
Souhami, Diana. *Mrs. Keppel and Her Daughter*. NY: St. Martin's Press, 1997.
Trefusis, Violet. *Don't Look Round*. London: Hutchinson, 1952, reprinted, Viking, 1992.

Jeanne A. Ojala, Professor Emerita, Department of History, University of Utah, Salt Lake City, Utah

Trelling, Ursula (b. 1901).

See Anderson, Regina M.

2

Trench, Melesina (1768–1827)

Irish writer best known for her journals and correspondence. Born Melesina Chenevix on March 22, 1768, in Dublin, Ireland; died on May 27, 1827, in Dublin; married Richard St. George (a colonel), in 1786 (died 1788); married Richard Trench (a barrister), in 1803; children: (first marriage) one son; (second marriage) three sons, including Francis Chenevix Trench (1806–1886) and Richard Chenevix Trench (1807–1886).

Principal works: Campaspe: An Historical Tale *(1815);* Thoughts of a Parent on Education *(1837);* Remains *(edited by Richard Chenevix Trench, 1862).*

Melesina Trench was born in Dublin, Ireland, on March 22, 1768, to parents of Huguenot descent. After their deaths early in her childhood, she was raised by her paternal grandfather, the bishop of Waterford. He died in 1779, and she was transferred to the care of her mother's father, Archdeacon Gervais, whose library provided the bulk of her education. Melesina was much celebrated as a beauty by 1786, the year she married Colonel Richard St. George. The couple had one son before Richard's death two years later. Beginning in 1797, Trench spent ten years living in Germany and in France, where she met leaders and prominent citizens from all over Europe, including Lord Horatio Nelson and Lady *Emma Hamilton. During this time, she wrote a series of journals and letters that are now hailed both as important historical documents and as literary achievements.

While in Europe, Melesina met Richard Trench, a barrister who was six years her junior. Shortly after their marriage in 1803, he was captured and imprisoned in France by Napoleon Bonaparte. Melesina petitioned Napoleon for her husband's release in 1806, and the following year they and their first son escaped from France and returned to Dublin. The marriage proved happy, and three of their sons would survive childhood. Two of these achieved fame in their own right as writers and theologians; Francis Chenevix Trench attended Oriel College at Oxford University and became rector of Islip and a well-known essayist, while Richard Chenevix Trench became a noted Irish philologist, poet, and theologian, and served as archbishop of Dublin from 1864 until his death in 1886. Trench lived the rest of her life in Dublin, writing novels, poetry, and essays until her death in 1827. None of these achieved the success of her posthumously published journals about her life and acquaintances in Europe during some of the years of Napoleon's reign, which her son Richard edited and released under the title *Remains* in 1862.

SOURCES:

The Concise Dictionary of National Biography. Oxford: Oxford University Press, 1992.
Kunitz, Stanley J., and Howard Haycraft, eds. *British Authors of the Nineteenth Century.* NY: H.W. Wilson, 1936.

Gillian S. Holmes, freelance writer, Hayward, California

Trevor, Claire (1909–2000)

American actress who received an Academy Award for her performance in Key Largo. *Born Claire Wemlinger on March 8, 1909, in New York City; died on April 8, 2000, in Newport Beach, California; attended George Washington High School, New York City; attended Columbia University and the American Academy of Dramatic Arts; married Clark Andrews (a producer), in 1938 (divorced 1942); married Cylos William Dunsmoore (divorced 1947); married Milton Bren (a producer), in 1948 (died 1979); children: (second marriage) Charles Dunsmoore (died 1978).*

Selected filmography: Life in the Raw *(1933);* The Last Trial *(1933);* The Mad Game *(1933);* Jimmy and Sally *(1933);* Hold That Girl *(1934);* Baby Take a Bow *(1934);* Wild Gold *(1934);* Black Sheep *(1925);* Dante's Inferno *(1935);* Navy Wife *(1935);* My Marriage *(1936);* Song and Dance Man *(1936);* Human Cargo *(1936);* To Mary—With Love *(1936);* Star for a Night *(1936);* 15 Maiden Lane *(1936);* Career Woman *(1936);* Time Out for Romance *(1937);* King of Gamblers *(1937);* One Mile from Heaven *(1937);* Dead End *(1937);* Second Honeymoon *(1937);* Big Town Girl *(1937);* Walking Down Broadway *(1938);* The Amazing Dr. Clitterhouse *(1938);* Valley of the Giants *(1938);* Five of a Kind *(1936);* Stagecoach *(1939);* I Stole a Million *(1939);* Allegheny Uprising *(1939);* Dark Command *(1940);* Honky Tonk *(1941);* Texas *(1941);* The Adventures of Martin Eden *(1942);* Crossroads *(1942);* Street of Chance *(1942);* The Desperadoes *(1943);* The Woman of the Town *(1943);* Murder My Sweet *(1944);* Johnny Angel *(1945);* Crack-Up *(1946);* The Bachelor's Daughters *(1946);* Born to Kill *(1947);* Raw Deal *(1948);* Key Largo *(1948);* The Babe Ruth Story *(1948);* The Velvet Touch *(1948);* The Lucky Stiff *(1949);* Borderline *(1950);* Hard Fast and Beautiful *(1951);* Best of the Badmen *(1951);* Hoodlum Empire *(1952);* My Man and I *(1952);* Stop—You're Killing Me *(1953);* The Stranger Wore a Gun *(1953);* The High and the Mighty *(1954);* Man Without a Star *(1955);* Lucy Gallant *(1955);* The Mountain *(1956);* Marjorie Morningstar *(1958)*; Two Weeks in Another Town *(1962)*; The Stripper *(1963)*; How to Murder Your Wife *(1965)*; The Cape Town Affair *(South Africa, 1967)*; Kiss Me Goodbye *(1982)*.

A veteran of over 100 films, blonde, sultry-voiced Claire Trevor was relegated to B movies for most of her career, but proved to be a highly accomplished actress when given the opportunity. Best remembered for her portrayal of the former singer and boozy mistress of gangster Edward G. Robinson in *Key Largo* (1948), for which she received an Academy Award as Best Supporting Actress, Trevor also received Oscar nominations for her roles in *Dead End* (1937) and *The High and the Mighty* (1954).

Trevor was born in 1909 in New York City, and attended Columbia University and the American Academy of Dramatic Arts. "From the time I was a child, the arts have played an important role in my life," she said. "I think using one's imagination to the fullest is necessary for a happy life, and one of the best ways to use one's imagination is by playacting."

From the movie Stagecoach, *starring Claire Trevor and John Wayne.*

She gained her early acting experience in stock and in a series of Vitaphone shorts, which were filmed in Brooklyn. In 1932, she made her Broadway debut opposite Edward Arnold in *Whistling in the Dark*, and launched her feature film career a year later, signing a five-year contract with Fox. Although usually typecast as a gangster moll, a prostitute, or a saloon floozy, Trevor never lost her respect for the old studio system. "You had to do a lot of work that you didn't want to do," she recalled in a 1995 interview, "that's true—a lot of crummy pictures. But they knew how to build a star and they knew what to do with you. They also taught you everything."

Also notable among her early films was the classic *Stagecoach* (1939), in which she played a frontier prostitute who is reformed by John Wayne. It was one of her favorite pictures because of John Ford's direction; she also liked *Key Largo* because of its outstanding cast, which included Robinson, Humphrey Bogart and **Lauren Bacall**. During filming, when she admitted to director John Huston that she was having trouble

playing the drunk scene, he told to think of herself as "all elbows." That solved it. "I could have stayed on that picture for the rest of my life," she said. "I adored it." She played opposite Robinson again in the later film *The Stripper* (1963), accepting the role as his harpy wife after it was turned down by *Jean Arthur. Her last film appearance was as **Sally Field**'s mother in *Kiss Me Goodbye*.

In the 1950s, when her film career began to slow, Trevor turned to television. In 1956, she won an Emmy Award for her television performance in "Dodsworth" on NBC's "Producers Showcase." She appeared on "The Love Boat" in 1977 and on "Murder She Wrote" in 1984. As late as 1987, she was seen in the television movie "Breaking Home Ties."

Trevor was married three times and had one son, Charles, who died in an airplane crash in 1978. Her last husband, producer Milton Bren, died the following year. The actress spent her later years in Newport Beach, California, where she died on April 6, 2000. "Claire was a special woman whose lifelong passion was to bring joy to others," said her stepson Donald Bren following her death. "Her legacy will be the many ways she touched people."

SOURCES
Katz, Ephraim. *The Film Encyclopedia*. NY: Harper-Collins, 1994.
"Obituary," in *The Boston Sunday Globe*. April 9, 2000.
"Obituary," in *The Washington Post*. April 9, 2000.
Shipman, David. *The Great Movie Stars: The Golden Years*. Boston, MA: Little, Brown, 1995.

Barbara Morgan, Melrose, Massachusetts

Trickey, Minnijean Brown (b. 1942).
See Bates, Daisy for sidebar.

Trieu, Lady (225–248 CE).
See Ba Trieu.

Trieu Au (225–248 CE).
See Ba Trieu.

Trieu Thi Chinh (225–248 CE).
See Ba Trieu.

Trieu Thi Trinh (225–248 CE).
See Ba Trieu.

Trieu Tring Nuong (225–248 CE).
See Ba Trieu.

Trigère, Pauline (1912—)

French-born American couturiere. Name variations: Pauline Trigere. Pronunciation: Tree-JAIR. Born on November 4, 1912, in Paris, France; daughter of Alexandre Trigère (a tailor) and Cécile (Coriene) Trigère; educated in Paris schools; attended Collège Jules Ferry; Collège Victor Hugo, B.A.; married Lazar Radley (a Russian-born tailor), in 1929 (separated 1941, eventually divorced); children: Jean-Pierre and Philippe.

Cofounded Trigère Inc. (1942); received numerous awards, including three Coty American Fashion Critics' Awards and induction into the Coty Fashion Hall of Fame (1959); named a chevalier of the Legion of Honor (2001).

The daughter of tailor Alexandre Trigère and **Cécile Coriene Trigère**, who often worked as a seamstress, Pauline Trigère was born in Paris on November 4, 1912. She and her family lived in quarters behind her father's tailoring business off Place Pigalle in the French capital. By age ten, Pauline had mastered the use of the family's Singer sewing machine, and she often helped her mother with custom tailoring jobs. Shortly after she entered her teens, she was making many of her own clothes, creating fashions that were much admired by her classmates.

After completing high school, Trigère studied for a time at Collège Jules Ferry and later at Collège Victor Hugo, from which she eventually earned a B.A. degree. She helped to finance these studies and herself after graduation by working in the Place Vendôme salon of Martial et Armand. There she learned the importance of construction and fabric choice, qualities that later would be the hallmarks of her designs.

Trigère married in 1929, a union that produced two sons, Jean-Pierre and Philippe, but was dissolved only a few years later. In 1937, she and her children joined her mother and brother in moving to the United States. For her first five years in New York, she worked for local fashion houses, including those of *Hattie Carnegie and Ben Gershel. In 1942, with the help of her brother Robert and three sewing machines, she launched her own clothing-design business in a New York City loft. Her first line of designer clothing, completed soon thereafter, consisted of 12 women's outfits. Her brother packed Trigère's creations into a large suitcase that he trundled across the country by bus to show to buyers at leading department stores. Retail executives quickly bought up the collection, and her designs were such a hit that buyers soon began to make the pilgrimage to her tiny loft to see what else she might have to offer. Lacking adequate space and facilities, the designer was forced to hang some of her dresses and other creations from light fixtures.

It was clear that Trigère had truly arrived on the American fashion scene when, in 1949, she was named winner of Coty's seventh annual American Fashion Critics' Award. The citation on the award read: "For her high and original talent in fashion design . . . and for her imaginative ideas which have set major trends." This first Coty fashion award was quickly followed in 1950 by a Neiman-Marcus Award and a Return Award and a second Coty a year later. The Coty award was particularly coveted among contemporary fashion designers because it reflected a decision by a jury made up of the most influential fashion editors in the country.

In 1944, Trigère became an American citizen, declaring that the United States had been "wonderfully kind to me," and that "Despite my love for France, I have found my niche here." She was active for years in Democratic politics and served on fund-raising committees for such charitable organizations as the Damon Runyon Fund, the Federation of Jewish Philanthropies, the Philharmonic Pension Fund, and the Visiting Nurses Service Association.

More recognition for Trigère's work came in 1959, when she won the Fashion Critics Award for the third time, making her eligible for induction into the Coty Fashion Hall of Fame. Only three other American designers—Norman Norell, *Claire McCardell, and John Galanos—previously had been so recognized. That same year, New York Mayor Robert F. Wagner presented her with the Cotton Award, the U.S. cotton industry's salute to the individual designer who has made the most innovative use of cotton during the previous year. "Cotton is a fabric to which you can talk," she said. "When it comes to designing, the fabric is my master. I can't draw, I can't paint, I can't even sew, but put a piece of fabric in my hands and magic happens." Trigère experiences "sheer joy from seeing something new coming out of a piece of material." One of her production assistants described Trigère's designing techniques: "She will put a bolt of material on a model and cut, just getting the feel of the cloth. I have never in my thirty-five years' experience seen another designer do this."

Although she is usually considered a conservative designer, noted especially for the reserved elegance of her clothes, Trigère is credited with the development of such fashion innovations as the sleeveless coat, the reversible coat, the mobile collar, and the spiral jacket. Only 16 years after its humble beginnings in a New York City loft, annual sales of Trigère Inc. had topped $2 million.

During the 1950s and 1960s, Trigère occupied a position at the forefront of American fashion, releasing some eighty outfits a year in four seasonal collections. Her views of matters of style and taste were closely followed by women throughout America and around the world. Although she made her fortune as a designer of clothes, she personally counseled women to buy fewer but longer-lasting garments. Every woman, she suggested, should have two suits, one black and one gray. Accessories, Trigère believed, were the key to expressing one's own individuality and personality. In line with the general air of restraint in her clothing, she recommended that fashion be approached with a degree of caution: "Just because a new hemline looks well on a model in a photograph," she observed, "there is no reason to think it will look well on you."

Fashion critics hailed as prophetic Trigère's 1960 collection, which included dresses and gowns with a pliant and distinctly medieval look. The following year, a number of the avant-garde designers, including Trigère, revived the high Empire bust line, marked by a sash or fabric band, which she called the "high-pitched" silhouette. She remained a significant presence on

Pauline Trigère

the American fashion scene in the 1970s, receiving the Silver Medal of the City of Paris in 1972, and in 1979 introduced an adaptation of the tuxedo for women's evening wear. In 1980, the designer showed she had lost none of her sense of humor over the years. At her spring show, she spoofed the revival of the mini-skirt by showing a collection of knee-baring designs which turned out to be Trigère designs from the 1960s. When the designer received a Lifetime Achievement Award from the Council of Fashion Designers of America in 1993, she had kept her design firm in business for over 50 years, a unique accomplishment. In May 2001, at age 92, she was named a chevalier of the Legion of Honor by the French government. A month later, Trigère attended the 20th annual American Fashion Awards in New York City, where she lives on Park Avenue.

SOURCES:

Current Biography 1960. NY: H.W. Wilson, 1960.

McHenry, Robert, ed. *Famous American Women.* NY: Dover, 1980.

The New York Times. June 17, 2001.

SUGGESTED READING:

"Ageless Chic," in *People Weekly.* April 23, 2001.

Don Amerman,
freelance writer, Saylorsburg, Pennsylvania

Trilling, Diana (1905–1996)

A trenchant observer of the New York City literary and cultural scene from the 1930s through the 1970s who emerged from the shadow of her husband to become a notable and iconoclastic critic in her own right. Pronunciation: TRIL-ing. Born Diana Rubin in New York City on July 21, 1905; died, age 91, in New York City on October 23, 1996; daughter of Joseph Rubin (a businessman) and Sadie Helene (Forbert) Rubin; had one sister and one brother; attended Erasmus Hall High School in Brooklyn; Radcliffe College, A.B., 1925; married Lionel Trilling (a critic and professor of English), on June 12, 1929 (died November 5, 1975); children: James Lionel Trilling.

Met Lionel Trilling (1927); worked as a fiction reviewer for The Nation *(1942–49); became freelance writer (1949); chaired the Committee for Cultural Freedom (1955–57); was recipient of a Guggenheim fellowship (1950–51); columnist for* New Leader *(1957–59); received grants from the National Endowment for the Humanities and the Rockefeller Foundation (1977–79); nominated for the Pulitzer Prize for her book* Mrs. Harris: The Death of the Scarsdale Diet Doctor *(1981).*

Selected writings: Claremont Essays *(Harcourt, 1964); (essays)* We Must March My Darlings: A Critical Decade *(Harcourt, 1977);* Reviewing the Forties *(fiction criticism, introduction by Paul Fussell, Harcourt, 1978);* Mrs. Harris: The Death of the Scarsdale Diet Doctor *(Harcourt, 1982);* The Beginning of the Journey: The Marriage of Diana and Lionel Trilling *(Harcourt, 1993).*

Editor: (and author of introduction) The Viking Portable D.H. Lawrence *(Viking 1947); (and author of introduction)* The Selected Letters of D.H. Lawrence *(Farrar, Straus, 1958); Lionel Trilling,* The Last Decade: Essays and Reviews, 1965–1975 *(1979); Lionel Trilling,* Prefaces to the Experience of Literature *(c. 1979); Lionel Trilling,* Of This Time, of That Place, and Other Stories *(1979);* The Uniform Edition of the Works of Lionel Trilling *(Harcourt, 1979); Lionel Trilling,* Speaking of Literature and Society *(1980).*

Other: (author of introduction) Mark Twain, Tom Sawyer *(Crowell-Collins, 1962). Contributor of essays and reviews on literary, sociological, and political subjects to numerous periodicals, including* Partisan Review, The New York Times, Harper's, Vogue, Esquire, Commentary, Newsweek, *and* Times Literary Supplement. *Member of editorial board,* American Scholar.

"I regard the whole of my adult life as having been lived in an anxious world," Diana Trilling wrote in a retrospective on her life and marriage. "This began with the economic breakdown of the thirties and has been steadily reinforced with the creation of the nuclear bomb and its threat to the survival of the planet." The great events and major writers of the 1930s through the 1970s—the era of the Depression, European dictators, World War II, and the Cold War—were the major topics in the essays and reviews of Trilling. Despite the fact that she did not begin her writing career until some ten years after her marriage to literary writer and critic Lionel Trilling, Diana Trilling established her own reputation as a perceptive and often witty cultural and literary critic.

Trilling's father Joseph Rubin was born in the Russian section of Poland and raised in the Warsaw ghetto; he came to the United States because he wanted to avoid serving in the armies of the tsar. Knowing only Yiddish, he sold macaroons on the Staten Island ferry during his first few months in his newly adopted country. As his English improved, he sold straw braid for women's millinery and eventually became owner of a plant which manufactured straw braid. Trilling's mother **Sadie Forbert Rubin**, who had been born in rural Poland some 50 miles from Warsaw, "left me a substantial legacy of determination," Trilling later wrote, adding that her mother was more "volatile and elusive" than her father.

Trilling traced her own outspokenness to both of her parents, noting that "the lust for honesty in my family was raving and incurable," even where "a touch of untruth would have been considerably more agreeable." After she had become a literary critic, Trilling noted that she could not remember her mother's reading a newspaper or her father's reading many books, although she did recall that one particular book, Victor Hugo's *Les Misérables*, had become her father's "secular Talmud."

"There was little religious observance in my childhood home," Trilling wrote; her mother had "grown to adulthood scarcely knowing that she was Jewish" and her father had "no religious upbringing." Saturday was not observed as a special day. "I had," said Trilling, "the childhood of an American who happened to be a Jew, and not that of a Jew who happened to be an American."

Trilling observed that unlike many Jewish émigrés to the United States in the late 19th and early 20th centuries, she and her future husband

Diana Trilling

"had our membership in the middle class secured for us by our parents," who, while not wealthy, were "comfortable." Until she was nine years old, the family lived in Westchester, first in Larchmont, where the family raised their own fruits and vegetables and kept chickens in their backyard, and then in New Rochelle. In 1914, Joseph Rubin had become prosperous enough that he decided to take his family on an extended trip to Europe. World War I broke out while the Rubins were on the European continent, and the ship that they had taken from New York, the French luxury liner *France*, was no longer available for a return trip. Although the family was able to book passage on a British liner instead, the return journey was tense, with the ship running without lights in order to escape the notice of submarines. That experience, plus the murder of a beloved neighborhood Portuguese woman, were the only real traumas that Trilling could remember from her childhood and youth.

Upon returning to the United States, the family moved to Brooklyn, where, as a student in Brooklyn's Erasmus Hall High School, Trilling helped a black student government candidate challenge the school's two-party system by creating a third party. After high school graduation, Sadie Rubin wanted her daughter to attend a college in Brooklyn. Trilling, who preferred to attend Radcliffe, was supported by Joseph. She did poorly in her first months at Radcliffe, a situation that she attributed to the fact that, since it had not been necessary for her study in high school, she chose not to attend most of her college classes and did not do the assigned readings. Shocked to receive solid "F's" on her first midterm grades, she was turned around by a series of stern warnings from her history teacher. Before graduation, she was elected to Phi Beta Kappa. She was not the first of her family to attend college—her brother Samuel had gone briefly to Cornell—but she was the first in her family to graduate.

Graduating during the decade following World War I, Trilling reported that she felt the social pressure that educated young women should "do something," but she concluded that she lacked the same "firm sense of goal" that drove her male colleagues to become directors of museums or "curators of our country." When a professor offered her jobs as either an assistant director of Harvard's Fogg Museum or as the founding member of a fine arts department at Mt. Holyoke College, she turned them down, preferring to work in New York City. Except for time spent in London and at Oxford University, New York would become her permanent residence.

Since Trilling's parents had moved during her college years from their Brooklyn home to an apartment on the Upper West Side of Manhattan, Trilling chose to apply for jobs at the Metropolitan Museum and at the new Frick Art Reference Library. Despite strong recommendations from the Harvard University art department, neither institution granted Trilling an interview, a situation she saw as her first real brush with anti-Semitism. "I was," she observed, "among the fortunate of this century in having little direct experience with anti-Semitism; the little that I experienced was concentrated into my first year back in New York after I graduated from college."

Trilling's mother died in 1926 after being bedridden at home for an extended period of time; an emergency blood transfusion, then a rarity, did not save her. After the death of their mother, Trilling and her sister **Cecilia Rubin** ran their father's home. Joseph began to indulge his love of travel, taking Diana and her sister with him on trips through Canada and the Midwest, Florida, Cuba, and South America. After their trip through South America, Trilling took a job with the National Broadcasting Company (NBC) as an assistant to the writer-producer of a children's radio serial. During a visit to one of the city's speakeasies, Clifton Fadiman and his first wife **Pauline Rush Fadiman**, a couple prominent in the city's literary circles, introduced her to aspiring writer Lionel Trilling. In 1929, Diana Rubin and Lionel Trilling decided that she would give up her NBC job and they would marry. They were wed on June 12, 1929, in her father's apartment, in a "traditional" Jewish wedding ceremony that, she reported, "did violence to our secularism, and certainly mine."

Joseph Rubin, who had taken out a substantial bank loan for his business shortly before the stock-market collapse of 1929, was deeply affected by the Depression. The bank that took over the business put her brother Samuel in charge. Although her father had scrupulously run a union shop, the bank required an open shop, and Trilling for many years claimed that she could still hear the boos from old union employees. Her father died in 1932.

The Trillings' first apartment was in Greenwich village. When Lionel began work as part-time editor and fiction writer for the *Menorah Journal*, Diana discovered that she was not enamored with his friends and associates. "With marriage I entered Lionel's world," she later wrote. "My career as a critic still lay in the future but unconsciously I may have been preparing for

it." She heard rumors that the staff of the *Menorah Journal* looked unfavorably on her manner of dress, on the furnishings she chose for their apartment, and on the general idea of "Lionel's marriage to a West End middle class girl." She found many intellectuals of the literary world overbearing and arrogant, and she believed that they took the natural "agreeableness" of the Trillings to be weakness or lack of depth. "They were not easy companions," she noted. "For an intellectual, the mind is primarily an instrument of speculation. It operates in the sphere where the consequences of thought are not necessarily put to the test of reality, as they would be, say, in a scientific laboratory or in politics."

> *In my view a liberal refuses to tolerate any form of totalitarianism, whether of the Right or Left. Democracy is my minimal demand. You cannot have dictatorship and at the same time have democracy, and you cannot have liberalism without democracy. There it is: the logic seems obvious to me, and yet it has been the most confused issue in the modern intellectual world.*
>
> —Diana Trilling

The Depression deeply affected the Trillings' early years as a married couple. "We foolishly supposed," she wrote, "that if we rejected the economic authority of society we were immune to its danger." Lionel's father lost his business, and both of Lionel's parents would come to rely on their son for financial support, which the Trillings provided from Lionel's teaching salary at Hunter College and subsequent fellowship from Columbia University for $1,800, followed by a salary of $2,400 as an instructor in the Columbia University English department. "We became the parents," Diana wrote. "They became the children."

Before their marriage, Diana had aspirations to become an opera singer, and she continued to "practice every day," even in their "honeymoon cabin." "My technique was disciplined but I was not," she observed; "not enough for a professional success." She was forced to abandon her hopes because of a thyroid operation which was performed in Boston shortly after her marriage.

In 1932, the same year that Lionel was made an instructor in the English department of Columbia University, she began to work for the National Committee for the Defense of Political Prisoners, acknowledging that her motivation was not "so much of a political impulse as a need to escape the fear of being alone." Although her husband also became a member, her work on the NCDPP proved to be a disillusioning experience. She argued openly with her colleagues over the committee's "exploitation" of African-American composer W.C. Handy, who was used to raise money for financial support of the "Scottsboro Boys," a group of nine young black males convicted of the rape of two white women (*Ruby Bates and **Victoria Price**) in Alabama. Eight were sentenced to death. Put in charge of a "subsidiary committee" entitled the Prisoners Relief Fund and told to sign her name to a fund-raising letter asking for contributions for the families of the "Scottsboro Boys," Trilling was stunned to learn that a government relief office was already providing such help. She became convinced that many of the funds raised by the committee were, instead, being used for political purposes by the Communist Party.

Trilling later wrote that the committee was essentially a "Communist front organization," as, she came to believe, were many organizations on the political Left during the 1930s. The Depression, she wrote, was not only a great "leveller" but made "Communists out of many Americans. . . . It was no longer a mark of moral superiority for writers and artists to stay aloof from politics; on the contrary it was imperative that they have political opinions and make them known."

Much of her writing during the 1930s and 1940s focused on such organizations. Trilling came to believe that the:

> proliferation of Communist front organizations was a significant political and cultural phenomenon of the 1930s and 1940s. With their imposing lists of sponsors—writers, artists, Hollywood and Broadway celebrities, lawyers, teachers, clerics—the Communist-front organizations were for two decades a formidable instrument of Communist propaganda in the western democracies.

She also asserted:

> In the universities and throughout the publishing and entertainment industries [there was] a chain of Communist command . . . in place to see that the preferences of the Soviet Union found their suitable cultural expression and that the supporters of Communism were justly rewarded.

Trilling traced her disillusionment, and her husband's disenchantment, with Communism to Stalin's foreign policy toward Hitler's Germany, reporting:

> All of us at the NCDPP . . . waited expectantly for the Communist Party and the Social Democratic party of Germany to unite in opposition to the Nazis. The fact that this union was never permitted and that the workers of Germany, even the most politically conscious of them, the Communists, did nothing to stop Hitler, significantly contributed to our suspicion of Stalin and thus to our impending break with the radical movement.

The Trillings caused a stir in New York City political and literary circles when they resigned from the Committee in 1933, and the controversy widened when they praised Stalin's great rival Leon Trotsky, who had been forced to flee the Soviet Union in 1929. "For a time," she reported, Lionel "and I came to admire Trotsky as a ready platform on which to launch our criticism of the official party." Lionel drew an unfavorable portrait of Stalin in his book *The Middle of the Journey*, and both Trillings became convinced that "Communism was not the fulfillment of an idea. It was itself a movement of power, and like all movements of power it was fed by ambition and self-interest."

When the writer *Mary McCarthy later referred to her as a "Trotskyist," Trilling replied, "Neither Lionel nor I was ever a Trotskyist . . . but as between Stalin and Trotsky, we for a long time took the side" of the latter. Yet the Trillings' insistence during the 1930s and 1940s that Stalinist influences permeated what they came to call the "radical movement" would involve them in controversy among New York City litterateurs for years to come.

Trilling was given an opportunity to publish many of her political opinions in 1941, when **Margaret Marshall**, literary editor of *The Nation*, telephoned Lionel and asked if he could recommend someone to write brief unsigned fiction notes for her magazine. At Diana's urging, he submitted her name. Diana Trilling had been a campus reporter for the *Boston Herald* as a freshman at Radcliffe, but she had only written some unpublished plays and stories out of boredom with the "life into which I had been catapulted by marriage." Thinking that her writing might be an embarrassment to her husband, some friends of the Trillings advised her to write under her maiden name, but her husband insisted that she write as his wife. Her work for *The Nation* required her to select, from up to 50 books a month which arrived at the magazine, which ones would be reviewed. Lacking an office, she worked at home, stacking books on her living-room table.

Trilling, who would be a fiction critic for *The Nation* for seven years, believed that *The Nation* was essentially "two magazines": a "front" and editorial section, which she believed was biased toward Communism, and the literary section in the rear, which came to reflect her branch of anti-Communism. While she reviewed the works of a plethora of literary figures—ranging from Jean-Paul Sartre to *Eudora Welty— she also mixed political commentary in the reviews. Despite pressure to give favorable treatment to "our Soviet ally during World War II," she argued that the "fine victories of the Soviet army" did not justify the "sins of Communism." "As a critic of *The Nation* in the 40s, I would write as an avowed anti-Communist," she recalled, "and as a free-lance writer after I left *The Nation* I frequently dealt with the issues of Communism and anti-Communism."

Many of her articles eventually appeared in her collections *Claremont Essays* (1964); *We Must March My Darlings: A Critical Decade* (1977); and *Reviewing the Forties* (1978). Although most of Trilling's articles were on political or literary topics, one, entitled "Lionel Trilling: A Jew at Columbia," was personal. It portrayed, in her words, a time when "Lionel came perilously close to losing his Columbia position, even though he did a substantial number of reviews, some literary essays, and spent much time on his dissertation." The article detailed, triumphantly, how he was able to reverse the decision. Trilling's independent mind—her iconoclasm—was evident in her insistence that anti-Semitism not be overrated as a reason for Lionel's troubles, even though he was told that "as a Jew, a Marxist and Freudian" he could not be "happy in his Columbia job and his appointment would not be renewed." Trilling's article attributed the reversal largely to the peculiarities of intellectuals—she was convinced that her husband's new assertiveness impressed colleagues who considered him too quiet—and to her husband's boldness in sending a copy of his latest book to the president of the university.

In 1950, no longer at *The Nation*, she began writing criticism for the *Partisan Review*, where she became known for her independent viewpoints. During the early years of *PR*, she noted, "Lionel and I had many fundamental disagreements with the positions it took. We had not for a long time been Communists. . . . We did not equate Churchill and Roosevelt with Hitler, as *PR* did, and far from supporting Chamberlain's appeasement of Hitler at Munich, were much opposed to it." She also commented, "We did not believe that the war against Hitler was war between rival imperalisms."

In subsequent years, she was a columnist for the magazine *New Leader* and wrote reviews and articles for a wide variety of literary-oriented journals and magazines, including *Commen-*

tary, American Scholar (on whose editorial board she served), *Harper's, Vogue,* and *Harper's Bazaar*, as well as such newspapers as *The New York Times* and *New York Herald Tribune*.

In the 1950s, she became a member of the executive board of the American Committee for Cultural Freedom, claiming that its parent organization, the Congress for Cultural Freedom, "was a long unacknowledged child of the CIA." She involved herself in the controversy over the case of Alger Hiss, a prominent State Department official who had been accused of espionage activities for the Soviet Union. Many American intellectuals regarded the charges as being part of an anti-Communist witchhunt, but Trilling refused to join in the outcry. She instead sided with one of Hiss' chief accusers, a former Communist named Whittaker Chambers. Chambers had unsuccessfully sought her help with his own pro-Soviet spy operation when she was a member of the NCDPP during the 1930s, she reported, but she believed that his accusations against Hiss were probably true. She defended Chambers' story that he had hidden secret microfilm in a hollowed-out pumpkin. When the writer and playwright *Lillian Hellman insisted that Chambers had to be lying, since a pumpkin "deteriorates," Trilling replied that the evidence was microfilm, and it was hidden "for only one day."

Trilling's anti-Communism and condemnation of "radicalism" made her unpopular in much of the New York City literary world, particularly during the 1950s, the era of the controversial, Communist-hunting tactics of Wisconsin Senator Joseph McCarthy and the House Un-American Activities Committee. She and Lionel wanted to be known as anti-Communist liberals during the McCarthy era. Trilling described her position on McCarthy in the *Partisan Review* and in the magazine *New Leader*, and many of her articles on Communism during the 1940s and 1950s appeared in *Claremont Essays* and *Reviewing the Forties*. "I was against both Communism and McCarthy," she reported in one of her articles. "Double positions of this kind are not popular," she conceded, "and it appears to be too much to ask of us that we hold two opposing ideas in our minds at the same time. Far from supporting McCarthy, I thought his procedures and those of the House Un-American Activities Committee were a serious threat to freedom and an offense to the democratic process." In Trilling's opinion, McCarthy had done the cause of anti-Communism a disservice, since he had taken "anti-Communism out of the realm of debate and by his example created for liberalism an automatic association between anti-Communism and reaction."

The fact that McCarthy used the anti-Communist ideas "solely for opportunist purposes," Trilling warned, "does not mean that Communism did not exist as a danger in the world or that the murderous Soviet regime lacked powerful support in America, particularly in the entertainment industry." She insisted that "intellectual seriousness" meant distinguishing between the "realities of a very faulty democracy" and the "sins" of Communism.

In light of her insistence that Communism remained a danger in the United States, Trilling's attitude toward Dr. Robert Oppenheimer, the director of the original American atomic bomb project, was a surprise. During the 1950s, Oppenheimer, who had opposed the construction of a more powerful hydrogen bomb, lost his security clearance. She observed that some of those who voted to remove his clearance had been, in fact, the instigators of an investigation against him; the prosecutors had become the judges and jurors. She defended Oppenheimer as a loyal American. "There was a time," she wrote in an essay on the Oppenheimer case, "before Dr. Oppenheimer had come to understand the true nature of the Soviet Union, when surely it was the gravest of risks to trust him with secrets which the Soviet Union wanted so badly. But he never told those secrets then, and to have granted him clearance at that time only to take it away from him now . . . seems to me to be tragic ineptitude."

By the 1950s, Trilling had gained sufficient recognition as a writer that *Look* magazine asked her to contribute an article on the topic, "The Case for the American Woman." Paid $3,000, she wrote a characteristically iconoclastic piece, arguing that American homes were mental hospitals in which the wives were the nurses and the husbands were the patients.

Her real interests in writing lay elsewhere. The Vietnam War, and widespread protests against the war in American universities, created a new target for Trilling's writings: the radical movement which arose during the war. Her observations about the "radical movement," particularly as it manifested itself in universities, were collected in her book *We Must March My Darlings* (the title was taken from a Walt Whitman poem). The book was an outgrowth of her return to Radcliffe College, where she and Lionel spent nine weeks on the campus while she interviewed students to try to find differences between "the present-day undergraduate and my own generation."

Reportedly, Little, Brown wanted to publish *We Must March My Darlings* but withdrew because of comments in the book that were critical of Hellman's *Scoundrel Time*, which the company had also published (Trilling's assertions, which included her characterization of Hellman's book as a "compendium of errors," were termed "stiffly courteous" and "reasoned" by one reviewer). Trilling refused to omit the comments and took the manuscript to Harcourt Brace Jovanovich, which published it.

We Must March My Darlings included her account of the student uprising at Columbia University during the Vietnam War ("On the Steps of Low Library"), in which Trilling wrote that "violence begets violence" and argued that both students and faculty had reacted too simplistically and thoughtlessly to the "ugliness of the police." She specifically criticized remarks made by the poet Robert Lowell and concluded, "those who welcome the Columbia uprising as a strenuous but nonetheless necessary occasion in the reform of our universities cling to liberal hopes that have no basis in political reality."

We Must March My Darlings also included Trilling's essay "The Prisoner of Sex" (1970), in which she admitted feeling no great sympathy for either side in a debate between novelist Norman Mailer and feminist writer **Germaine Greer**. She became annoyed when Mailer referred to her as a "lady" in what she thought to be a condescending way, but she added, "I have also had far too many pleasures and privileges in being a woman to think of myself as a victim in the way that feminist doctrine now seems to dictate. . . . I have been much more troubled by the petty superiorities which men assert over women than by the grand social injustices."

In a later essay, she added, "But men do have enough advantages in our culture, and I'd like those to be looked at" and corrected "where possible." She reported her disappointment, on a trip to Germany in 1967, when the host of their group, a Ruhr industrialist, would not let women join in a discussion of serious issues, and none of her male companions defended her right to participate. "I am no longer persuaded, as I may once have been," she wrote in "Female Biology in a Male Culture" (1970), "that a woman's willingness to cede power to men necessarily represents her wholesome acceptance of a biologically determined passivity; rather, I tend to see it as a cultural conformity or even an expediency or laziness."

The Trillings insisted that their condemnations of various forms of "radicalism" were not betrayals of liberal principles. Diana reported that in the summer of 1972 she received a call from the historian **Gertrude Himmelfarb**, asking the Trillings to add their names to a forthcoming *New York Times* advertisement sponsored by Democrats for Richard Nixon for President. "Although Lionel and I were uneasy about McGovern [the Democratic nominee], we refused to support Nixon," she reported. "In fact, the next year, when Lionel became the first recipient of the Jefferson Award in the Humanities, he sought reassurance that he would not be officially entertained in the Nixon White House."

In addition to publishing many of her essays from the 1940s through the 1970s, Trilling evinced a special interest in the British novelist D.H. Lawrence, publishing *The Portable D.H. Lawrence* (in the preparation of which she reported that she read every word that Lawrence wrote) and *The Selected Letters of D.H. Lawrence*.

In the summer of 1975, when the Trillings were on vacation in St. Andrews, Canada, Diana noted that Lionel seemed to tire easily during hikes. When the couple returned to New York, a medical examination revealed pancreatic cancer. He died in the fall of that year. Although Diana by that time had established her own identity and her own career as a literary writer, her book on their life together, *The Beginning of the Journey: The Marriage of Diana and Lionel Trilling* (1993), ends abruptly two pages after his death; there is no section entitled "Life after Lionel."

Diana Trilling did, however, subsequently spend time working on her late husband's papers, producing collections of his stories and essays, many previously unpublished. "By twentieth century standards," she noted, her husband had an "impressive [literary] productivity," an achievement made all the more impressive by the fact that writing was not easy for him and that he would "spend day after interminable day trying to write a single satisfactory sentence." *The Beginning of the Journey: The Marriage of Diana and Lionel Trilling* also became as much a tribute to her late husband as a chronicle of her growth as a writer. John F. Baker described *The Beginning of the Journey* as "partly an account of his life, partly of hers, but mostly of their life together; it is a riveting story of a marriage at the heart of New York literary and intellectual life, a relationship that also had extraordinary personal and financial strains." The book was written by dictation, since Trilling had by then lost most of her sight.

Trilling's work after the death of her husband included *Mrs. Harris: The Death of the Scarsdale Diet Doctor* (1982). Based on the fatal shooting of a physician who had become nationally prominent for his series of diet books, *Mrs. Harris* was begun only two days after his death. Until then, Trilling, although known in New York literary circles, was largely unknown to the public at large; *Mrs. Harris* promised both financial gain and a large popular audience. In what has been described as "riveting narrative," the book balanced "fact and emotion" to present a detailed analysis of the trial and of the "cultural and psychological motivation of the principals," including the "diet doctor," Dr. Hermann Tarnower, and **Jean Harris**, his lover and headmistress of a girls' school, who was on trial for his murder. While noting that many feminists had sympathized with Harris, who had learned that Tarnower had become involved with a younger woman, Trilling, in a detailed account of the trial, found some of Harris' testimony to be lacking in credibility, particularly her insistence that she was never angry with Tarnower. Nevertheless, Trilling concluded that Harris' conviction on second degree murder was an injustice because, she argued, the evidence did not clearly support the idea of an intention to kill with a gun.

Living in a cottage in Wellfleet, Massachusetts, with the help of several assistants, Trilling, despite health problems, remained active and firmly opinionated in her last years. As she approached her 90th birthday, she was debating a project on what she considered the scourge of political correctness. "I have spent my entire adult life trying to combat the influence in our culture of Stalinism, of communism," she said. "This began in the '30s and it didn't stop with the collapse of the Soviet Union. Where communism left off, political correctness has taken over. I think of political correctness as a continuation of Stalinist culture." Instead, her last book was "A Visit to Camelot," detailing an evening at the Kennedy White House, which she finished some months before her death on October 23, 1996.

Trilling established a reputation as a writer of what one reviewer has termed "incisive commentary on . . . cultural and political upheavals." Whether the topic was the poet Allen Ginsberg, the writer ***Virginia Woolf**, President John F. Kennedy, or ***Marilyn Monroe**, her writing was wide-ranging, thoughtful, and, above all, highly individualistic and provocative.

SOURCES:

Alter, Jonathan. "The End of the Journey," in *Newsweek*. November 4, 1996, p. 61.

Contemporary Authors. New Revision Series. Vol. 46. Detroit, MI: Gale Research, 1995.

"Diana Trilling" (obituary), in *The Day* [New London, CT]. October 26, 1996, p. B3.

Jacobs, Sally. "The Indomitable Diana Trilling," in *The Boston Globe*. September 19, 1995, pp. 51, 55.

Trilling, Diana. *The Beginning of the Journey: The Marriage of Diana and Lionel Trilling*. NY: Harcourt Brace, 1993.

———. *Claremont Essays*. NY: Harcourt Brace and World, 1964.

———. *Mrs. Harris: The Death of the Scarsdale Diet Doctor*. NY: Harcourt Brace Jovanovich, 1981.

———. *Reviewing the Forties*. NY: Harcourt Brace Jovanovich, 1978.

———. *We Must March My Darlings: A Critical Decade*. NY: Harcourt Brace Jovanovich, 1977.

SUGGESTED READING:

Hellman, Lillian. *Scoundrel Time*. Boston, MA: Little, Brown, 1976.

Podhoretz, Norman. *Ex-Friends: Falling Out with Allen Ginsberg, Lionel and Diana Trilling, Lillian Hellman, *Hannah Arendt, and Norman Mailer*. NY: Free Press, 1999.

COLLECTIONS:

Materials relating to Diana and Lionel Trilling are included in the Lionel Trilling Papers at Columbia University.

Niles Holt,
Professor of History,
Illinois State University, Normal, Illinois

Trimmer, Sarah (1741–1810)

English author. Name variations: Sarah Kirby. Born Sarah Kirby on January 6, 1741, in Ipswich, England; died on December 15, 1810, in London; daughter of John Joshua Kirby and Sarah (Bull) Kirby; married James Trimmer, in 1762; children: six daughters; six sons.

Sarah Trimmer, an author of popular children's stories and treatises on education, was born in Ipswich, England, in 1741, the daughter of John Joshua Kirby and **Sarah Bull Kirby**. Her father, an artist, encouraged Sarah to write and provided her with a good education in literature. After moving his family to London, John Kirby introduced Sarah to London's literary community, where she formed a friendship with Samuel Johnson. At age 21, Sarah married James Trimmer, a government bureaucrat of Kew who shared her literary interests. After settling in London, the couple had 12 children, who were educated by their mother at home. Trimmer did not approve of the educational texts available at the time, believing many of them to be frivolous or amoral, and she began writing her own lessons, combining them with stories of religious instruction. By 1780, her friends had convinced her to publish her stories as *Easy Introduction to the Knowledge of Nature*. The book went into numerous editions and was well received, encouraging Trimmer to publish more collections of stories throughout the 1780s, including her most popular book, *The History of the Robins*. Her works were pioneering in English children's literature in their use of illustrations as an aid in learning.

Trimmer also turned her pen to treatises on educational issues, and gradually emerged as an active proponent of widespread, religiously oriented popular education. Throughout the 1790s and early 1800s, she helped establish local schools to teach vocational subjects to the poor. With the assistance of her husband and older children, Trimmer then launched *Family Magazine*, stories and articles intended for adults to read with their children, which they produced between 1778 and 1789. This popular magazine was followed by *Guardian of Education*, a periodical review of new children's literature which was often deeply critical of other writers. Her teachers' guides were widely adopted in England, as was her illustrated *New and Comprehensive Lessons*, which was continuously in print until 1830.

Sarah Trimmer remained an active writer and publisher long after her children were grown. She died in 1810, at age 68.

SOURCES:

Shattock, Joanne. *The Oxford Guide to British Women Writers*. NY: Oxford University Press, 1993.

Yarde, D.M. *The Life and Works of Sarah Trimmer, a Lady of Brentford*. London: Hounslow History Society, 1971.

Laura York, M.A. in History,
University of California,
Riverside, California

Trintignant, Nadine (1934—)

French film director and screenwriter. Born Nadine Marquand on November 11, 1934, in Nice, France; became second wife of Jean-Louis Trintignant (an actor), in 1960.

Selected filmography: Fragilité—ton Nom est Femme *(1945);* Mon Amour mon Amour *(1967);* Le Voleur de Crimes *(1969);* Ça n'arrive qu'aux autres *(It Only Happens to Others, 1971);* Defense de savoir *(1973);* Le Voyage de Noces *(Jalousie, 1976);* Premier Voyage *(1979);* L'Ete Prochain *(Next Summer, 1984);* Le Maison de Jade *(1988).*

Pursuing an early interest in the cinema, French director and screenwriter Nadine Trintignant dropped out of school at age 15 to become an assistant in a film lab. She subsequently worked as an assistant editor and a script clerk before becoming the highly sought-after editor for such directors as Serge Bourguignon, Jacques Doniol-Valcroze, and Jean-Luc Godard. Trintignant launched her own directing career with a few shorts and a number of television productions, then undertook her first feature film in 1967. She wrote her own scripts which frequently starred her actor husband Jean-Louis Trintignant. Nadine Trintignant's brother Serge Marquand is an actor, while another brother Christian Marquand is an actor-director.

Triolet, Elsa (1896–1970)

French novelist, short-story writer, Communist sympathizer, and member of the French Resistance who was awarded the Prix Goncourt in 1945. Name variations: Mme Aragon. Born Elsa Yureyevna Kagan in Moscow, Russia, on September 24, 1896; died in Saint-Arnoult, France, on June 18, 1970; daughter of Yuri Alexandrovich Kagan (a Lithuanian Jew and lawyer) and Yelena (Borman) Kagan (a Latvian Jew); married Pierre-Marie-André Triolet, in 1918 (divorced 1939); married Louis Aragon (a poet and writer), on February 26, 1939 (died December 24, 1982); no children.

Met Vladimir Mayakovsky (1911); studied at the Institute of Architecture, Moscow (1913–17); left Russia (July 1918); journeyed to Tahiti (1919); separated from husband (1921); published first book, In Tahiti (Moscow, 1925); met Louis Aragon (November 1928); published first book in French, Goodnight, Thérèse (1938); German occupation of France (June 1940–August 1944); was a member of the French Resistance (1941–44); helped establish the National Committee of Writers (1941); awarded the Prix Goncourt (1945).

Elsa Triolet was a Russian, a Jew, and an ardent, lifelong supporter of Communism. She was an independent, seemingly innocent, promiscuous, and elusive woman who inhabited two worlds, her beloved Russia and her adopted country, France. Ever aware that she was an outsider, an alien, in France, Triolet realized: "To be a foreigner is not a question of a passport, it is to feel unwelcome." Adored by her poet-writer second husband Louis Aragon, who created a "cult of Elsa," she was not loved by everyone who knew this enigmatic couple. As she related in *Putting into Words* (1969): "I have a husband who is a Communist. And the *blame* lies with me that he is a Communist. I am a tool of the Soviets. . . . I am a lady and a slut. . . . I am a moralist and a frivolous being. . . . I am the muse and the curse of the poet. I am beautiful and I am repulsive." And because she was an excessively private, evasive figure, "People fill me up with thoughts and with feelings, as one stuffs a straw doll, while I have no hand in the matter at all." Elsa Triolet can be found in her novels and

short stories, in her ambiguous relationships with her husbands, her work with the French Resistance, and in her expressions of loneliness and exile. As one of her heroines lamented, "No one loves me"; Elsa feared this, too.

Born Ella Kagan in Moscow in 1896 to well-educated, talented, middle-class Jewish parents, Triolet enjoyed a privileged childhood. Her father Yuri Kagan was a lawyer and a judge who had comfortably assimilated into Russian and Western European culture, as had her mother **Yelena Kagan**, a German-speaking native of Latvia. Elsa and her sister **Lili Kagan Brik**, five years her senior, were independent, free-thinking mavericks; Elsa disliked being the younger sister and walked in Lili's shadow until she married and left Russia. Loyal servants, a house filled with music and culture, and travel outside of Russia with their mother provided the girls with a stable, comfortable lifestyle. Religion played no part in their lives; the Kagans did celebrate the "Christian festivals as a social conformity," not from any religious conviction. Elsa and Lili spoke Russian and German as their native languages, and learned French from their governess. In Triolet's first book, she recalls her happy childhood, her "snug and cozy" home, falling asleep listening to her mother playing the piano and her father "crumple the pages of his newspaper . . . sounds which, in my drowsy state, strike me as divine."

Triolet remained attached to the Kagan house; in her *Notebooks Buried Under a Peach Tree*, she admits "that even today I seem to look upon this Russian house as *the* house . . . something that is human, understanding and sunny which I never came across since." And Elsa respected and admired her parents, though their conventional lifestyle was not appealing. They were "genuinely good people" who finally gave up trying to make their uninhibited daughters fit into their middle-class milieu.

Triolet's love of poetry, especially the Russian symbolists, led to a close friendship with the poet Vladimir Mayakovsky whose bohemian dress and slovenly manners shocked her parents. Though polite to Mayakovsky, they disapproved of him, and Elsa broke off relations with the poet rather than upset her mother. There is no strong evidence that Triolet and Mayakovsky were lovers, but in the late 1950s she did admit that she had had an abortion, and it is likely that Mayakovsky was responsible for the pregnancy. At age 17, Elsa left secondary school with a gold medal and a diploma and enrolled in the Institute of Architecture, as had her sister Lili. They were fortunate to have been admitted, since Jewish students were subject to a 3% quota. Elsa also studied painting and music at the institute for four years.

When Yuri Kagan died in 1915, Elsa and her mother moved to Petrograd to be near Lili who had married Osip Maximovich Brik, a revolutionary Marxist. Mayakovsky came there to look for Elsa who introduced him to the Briks. This unkempt, "hulking, uncouth celebrity" fell in love with Lili, and for the next 15 years lived with the Briks in an amicable *ménage à trois*. Elsa refused to become a member of the group, and she and her mother returned to Moscow just as the revolution broke out in October 1917. Both Elsa and Lili were attractive young women, and Elsa was pursued by many admirers, but she was determined to finish her studies.

Nobody who knew [Triolet] ever thought she was a happy woman. Many wondered if they had ever really known her at all.

—Lachlan Mackinnon

During the winter of 1917–18, revolution, starvation, cold, and epidemics ravished Russia, and Elsa decided to leave the country, but only temporarily. She and her family supported the revolution "with enthusiasm. . . struck by the comradeship and great hopes which it brought about." Triolet had been converted to the Marxist ideology and became a passionate defender of the Soviet system. Her reasons for leaving Russia were personal, not political. It is thought that she met André Triolet at the French Embassy in Moscow in 1917. André was from a wealthy French landowning family, loved women and horses, and fell in love with Elsa. To the surprise of Elsa's family and friends, they married in 1918. She and André had nothing in common; Elsa, at age 21, had not yet had "a proper life of her own," she was "incompletely human," while André was a sophisticated, cultured "dandy." When he left Russia, Elsa remained to complete her education. However, as the country plunged into civil war, she and her mother applied for passports, leaving Lili, Osip, and Mayakovsky who were all firmly committed to the new Bolshevik regime.

Elsa met up with André again in London, from where they moved on to Paris. However, only a few months later this incongruous couple set out for Tahiti. André had survived four years of war, and in 1919, he just "wanted to forget both the living and the dead." Elsa, too, had escaped the turmoil afflicting her native land. Life in Tahiti was routine and tranquil. Typically, Elsa soon "yearned for another country, any ordinary country, a country which is like all countries." Consequently, she left André, and Tahiti, and returned to Paris. They were simply not suited to one another, but divorce was not contemplated at this time. André granted Elsa a monthly allowance so she would not need to work, and they remained on friendly terms even after she began her relationship with Louis Aragon. Life in Tahiti provided the material for Triolet's first published work, *In Tahiti*, published in Russia in 1925.

Restless and uncertain of her future, Elsa went to London, where her mother was working for the Soviet commercial bureau and her Uncle Borman owned a factory. For a short time, Elsa took a position with an architect but could not settle down. In 1922, she went to Berlin with her sister. Here she found an apartment and a variety of lovers among the large Russian expatriate colony. Russian artists and writers had established a thriving community and several publishing houses in Berlin. Mayakovsky was one of the prominent figures among these avant-garde Russians. However, Elsa was not interested in him any longer as an intimate friend; he gambled, drank, was socially inept, and was, after all, Lili's lover. Elsa Triolet had numerous brief liaisons, but Lachlan Mackinnon claims that her sexuality was held in check because "it may be that she feared the loss of self that sex entailed." Despite her reticence, Triolet attracted men throughout her life.

Victor Shklovsky was one of her admirers, but more important he helped launch her career as a writer. In his novel *Zoo*, he included some of Triolet's letters to him. Maxim Gorky, who was living near Berlin, read the manuscript, asked to meet Triolet, and encouraged her to write; "And that is how it all began," Elsa noted. In 1923, Elsa Triolet became a writer. By that autumn, the Russian community was dispersing, and Triolet returned to Paris. Max Adereth remarks that she did not choose to return to Russia or join her mother in London because "it mattered little where she was for she had by now grown accustomed to travelling inside [her] solitude." Elsa chose to reside in the Hotel Istria in the Montparnasse district of Paris; here she lived among the Surrealists and Dadaists, Fernand Léger, Man Ray, Francis Picabia and his wife **Gabrielle Buffet**, and Marcel Duchamp. Russian émigrés, such as Ilya Ehrenburg, met in the cafés in Montparnasse, and Triolet acquired a number of friends; "I was young, I was merry, loaded with lovers." She had found a familiar milieu which she described as "my family, the one which does not depend on blood-ties, and that one acquires in the course of life." Triolet completed *In Tahiti* and wrote *Wild Strawberry*, the latter based on childhood memories, her "attempt to rebuild a world which no longer existed." She made many French and Russian friends, but she also made enemies; the French police kept a dossier on Triolet and other Russians suspected of being Soviet agents. The creative energy that characterized the habitués of Montparnasse undoubtedly affected Elsa who continued to write. In July 1925, she went to Moscow where she remained for eight months.

Her two novels, published there before the end of the year, were well received but not financially successful. Back in Paris, Triolet began working on her third novel, *Camouflage*, which she brought with her during her next visit to Moscow in May 1927. Trouble with the Soviet censor delayed publication until November. This novel was not a success because, as Elsa noted, it was "too unhappy, its true subject being . . . the fear of life." The two women portrayed in the work reveal much about the author: "Lucile [a Frenchwoman] is the Elsa the world saw, Varvara [a Russian] her inner destitution." Disap-

Elsa Triolet

pointed over the negative reaction to the book, Triolet rejoined the Russian circle in Paris, decided to abandon writing, and contemplated going home permanently. And then she met Louis Aragon, which changed her life forever.

Aragon was a Parisian, a medical school graduate, decorated war hero, poet, womanizer, bisexual, a member of the French Communist Party (PCF), and active in the avant-garde movements which came out of the war experience of so many young people of France. Wrote one historian, "The first Dadists intended to mock and destroy the culture which was . . . busy killing their contemporaries." Surrealism, too, attracted the disaffected and disillusioned generation that rejected reality and set out to shock the banal bourgeoisie. Triolet did not share Aragon's enthusiasm for these movements, nor did she like Aragon's friends.

Elsa had read Aragon's novel *The Peasant of Paris*, and asked a mutual friend to introduce her to the author. They met at a café on November 6, 1928, and would remain together until Triolet's death in 1970. No one, including Elsa, believed their relationship would last, "especially because of my character, for I really have the temperament of an independent spinster," as she explained to Adereth. But for Triolet this unlikely liaison meant the end of being just another foreigner in France, "the end of aimless drifting." For Aragon, it was an all-consuming love that permeated his work from then on. He later acknowledged that it was Elsa "to whom I owe everything that I am, to whom I owe having found . . . the entrance to the real world where living and dying are worthwhile." In Aragon, Triolet had found "a kindred poetic soul," but denied that he ever had any direct influence on her writing; writers started with reality, she believed, and transformed it by imagination "to make us dream."

Shortly after their affair commenced, Triolet began separating Aragon from his Surrealist friends and forbade the mention of his former lovers in her presence. She brooked no rivals, male or female who might threaten her position. On the other hand, Elsa remained friends with André and his various mistresses. Triolet was the dominant partner, and she succeeded in creating for herself and Aragon a private life that "remained just that—private." Aragon usually acquiesced to Triolet, but he objected to her still receiving the monthly allowance from André. However, their combined incomes were inadequate even for their simple needs. A chance meeting in a Paris art gallery between Elsa and a

man from *Vogue* magazine in August 1929, opened up a new opportunity; Triolet began making necklaces, a kind of chic "junk jewelry" for the fashion houses of Paris. *Coco Chanel was not interested for she had "political suspicions about expatriate Russians." Aragon, too, was involved, peddling Elsa's handiwork to various customers. This business enterprise earned enough money for the couple to travel to Berlin to meet Lili and Mayakovsky (he would commit suicide in 1930).

In September 1930, Triolet, Aragon, and their friend Georges Sadoul set out for Russia to attend a congress of writers in Kharkov, Ukraine. On this, Aragon's first trip to the Soviet Union, he fervently expressed support for the Soviet system, ignoring the ruthless, repressive aspects of the regime. Elsa shared his Communist ideals, but her attachment "was largely of a sentimental nature" rather than political. Triolet has been blamed for Aragon's refusal to speak out in favor of creative freedom at the congress; he and Sadoul stated that they intended to adhere to the dictates of the Communist Party "to whose discipline and control we undertake to submit our literary activity." Mackinnon claims that Aragon's repudiation of freedom of expression "turned him into Elsa's creature" and against his Surrealist friends, which had been her objective all along. On subsequent visits to the Soviet Union in 1931 and 1932, neither Triolet nor Aragon had anything critical to say about the "totalitarian police state" that terrorized thinkers, writers, and political dissidents. They were fully aware of the situation "but they did not speak out," even when they returned to France.

In Paris, Aragon began to work as a journalist on the Communist daily *L'Humanité*, and Triolet turned to translating French novels for publication in Moscow. When the Russian publisher severely edited the translations without consulting her, Triolet said, "I gave up." Inexplicably, Aragon did not want Elsa to take up her own writing again, but Triolet ignored his wishes and produced her novel *Necklaces*, based on her brief venture in making and selling jewelry. After a portion of the book was published in a magazine in Moscow, it was banned without explanation, and it would not appear during her lifetime.

If she could not publish in her native country, Elsa would become a "French" writer. "Abandoning Russian," wrote her biographer, "she accepted her French destiny." Characteristically, she did not consult, or inform, Aragon when she was writing her first novel in French, *Goodnight, Thérèse*, in 1937. Triolet confessed in a public statement in 1964, addressed to Aragon, that she wanted to write "because everything prevented me. You could have helped by taking my side, by saying to me: *write!* But you weren't willing to say it, you knew nothing of what I was writing." Aragon eventually recognized and acknowledged that he had been excluded from an important part of Triolet's life; in his poem *Elsa* (1959), he wrote, "Beings were born of you whom I had not given you/ No one will ever know the violence/ The torture the jealousy/ The frenzy that came over me." Robert Denoël, Aragon's publisher, agreed to accept Triolet's novel "after reading only a few pages." It received favorable reviews, one by the French intellectual Jean-Paul Sartre.

Despite this success, the 1930s were largely devoted to "holding Aragon's fragile personality together," forcing Elsa into a subservient position in relation to him and his obligations to the French Communist Party (Triolet was never a member). It was "the most dispiriting decade of Elsa's life." However, she was active—though "an appendage" to Aragon—and they attended party meetings in France and writers' congresses in Spain, the Soviet Union, and the United States. It took the intervention of *Eleanor Roosevelt for them to enter the States in 1939; Aragon had stated on his visa application that he belonged to the Communist Party. While in New York, Paul Robeson, the African-American actor and singer, showed Triolet and Aragon around Harlem; Elsa was struck by capitalist American society, "an image which was to haunt her."

With war imminent in Europe, Aragon would undoubtedly be called to active military duty. Since he and Triolet had never married, she would not be permitted to have authorized contact with him. So, in February 1939, after her divorce from André was final, Triolet and Aragon were married in Paris. That August, the German-Soviet non-aggression pact was signed; this presented the couple with a dilemma and placed them in an awkward position. Elsa was afraid to criticize the agreement since Lili still lived in the Soviet Union. The French Communists had no hesitation, however, in supporting the pact. The French government quickly accused them of treason, and the following month declared the party illegal. Triolet and Aragon went into hiding in the Chilean embassy for several days. Aragon was called into service as a medical auxiliary and left Paris in early September. For Elsa, "by both origin and association," writes her biographer, "the war was to begin in ambiguity and end in disillusionment."

Aragon was actively involved in fighting in northern France and was awarded two medals for bravery before being evacuated at Dunkirk. France was defeated by the Germans in June 1940, and Triolet suffered along with her adopted compatriots: "in those moments," she recalled, "the supreme horror is not knowing where one's country is . . . or even if one has one." A year later, the Nazis attacked the Soviet Union, "a double defeat" for Triolet. After the French signed an armistice with the Germans, Aragon was discharged from the army. He and Elsa could have emigrated, but instead decided to remain in France and fight the German occupiers in any way they could. This would place them in danger; Triolet was a Russian Jew, Aragon was a Communist. They fled south to the unoccupied zone of France and joined the French Resistance.

In July 1940, members of the French Communist Party began to be arrested. Triolet and Aragon eluded the authorities by moving frequently from one town to another, to Carcassonne, to Avignon, Lyons, Nice, and several isolated villages. They began to organize a "literary Resistance" of writers and publishers in the south and in Paris. They also renewed contact with the outlawed Communist Party. In June or July 1941, Triolet and Aragon traveled to Paris, using false papers. They were detained by the Germans before reaching the city and spent ten days in prison. Elsa wrote of this experience in her story "It Was Only a Border Crossing," published in February 1945. She and Aragon were released and made their way unhindered to Paris where they met with other writers and founded the National Writers' Committee. Then they returned to the unoccupied zone to organize the Committee there.

War, occupation, arrests, and being constantly on the move seemed to stimulate Triolet's creativity. Her short stories reveal a new self-confidence; "The Beautiful Woman Grocer," "Personal Destiny," and "A Thousand Regrets" are critical of the "triviality and hypocrisy" of French society and depict marriage as "bogus." While living in Nice, Elsa worked on *The White Horse*, her most autobiographical work to date, written during "one of the happiest periods of her life," according to Mackinnon. The novel appeared in 1943, but only after the final sentence had been removed; Elsa made a reference to concentrations camps, and Denoël, the publisher, had to accommodate German censorship in Paris. Triolet's writing provided her with personal satisfaction and independence, a life separate from the stifling adoration of her husband. A local bookstore was the social center in Nice for people like the Aragons, "transients trying simply to survive." Triolet also became friends with the artist Henri Matisse whose work "spoke to and evoked something in Elsa herself."

In November 1942, Triolet and Aragon fled Nice as the Italians moved in to occupy the area; at the same time, the Germans took over the rest of France in response to the Allied landings in North Africa. Eager to continue their writing on behalf of the Resistance, the couple went to Lyons where they became part of a clandestine organization of intellectuals called "Les Étoiles" (The Stars), a "cell" of about five members who had implicit trust in one another. Their work in the Resistance movement created a personal crisis in 1943. Triolet informed Aragon she was going to leave him. Husbands and wives who were active in these closely knit cells were not to remain together. Elsa announced: "I cannot allow the idea that we shall get to the end of the war and when people ask me, 'And what did you do?' I shall have to say, 'Nothing.'" Not surprisingly, Triolet stayed, but on her own terms. **Dominique Desanti**, Elsa's French biographer, claims that Triolet actually wanted to leave Aragon permanently, that she was reacting against "having to play second fiddle to her male partner" as she had done during most of the 1930s.

While in Lyons, Elsa wrote a moving story that lends credence to Desanti's claim. Two lovers, Juliette and Célestin, who are involved in the Resistance, are forced to separate, and Juliette says, "I have always known that love was only a counterfeit and that there is no truth, only illusion. People do not love one another, nobody loves anybody." Triolet's "The Lovers of Avignon" was illegally published in October 1943, under the pseudonym Laurent Daniel. The story also includes allusions to the French Communists (the party was still forbidden in France) as "*le parti des fusillés*" (the party of those who were shot). After the Liberation of France, the French Communist Party took this expression as their own, to remind the nation that they had been among the most active resisters and that many of their members had been killed by the Nazis.

During the war, Triolet and Aragon continued to write and distribute an illegal newspaper; if caught, they would have been deported to a concentration camp or killed. As soon as Paris was liberated in August 1944, they returned to find their apartment had been requisitioned by the Germans. Amazingly, the four years of German occupation, of engaging in dangerous resistance activities, and constantly moving to evade capture was a time of great productivity for Elsa: "Writing was my freedom, my defiance, my luxury." Her collection of short stories, *The First Tear Costs Two Hundred Francs* (1944), won the prestigious Prix Goncourt in 1945; the title was taken from "a coded message to the Resistance on the eve of the Normandy landings." With the advent of peace came the Cold War, and Elsa's disillusionment is reflected in her novels *Nobody Loves Me, Armed Ghosts*, and *The Inspector of Ruins*. The "ruins" refer to "ruined men with nothing to go back to." Triolet was now a famous writer, and through Aragon's poems, especially *Elsa's Eyes* (1942), she became "an icon," a national symbol. But after the years of war and occupation, Triolet "would never live so intensely again."

Everyone in France wanted to forget the war, and Triolet and Aragon were quickly forgotten, too, "relegated to the [Communist] ghetto." They remained uncritical of the repressive Communist regimes in Eastern Europe where they traveled extensively. Their role in the "bloody and vindictive" purges of those who had collaborated with the Nazis in France, even former friends, "ensured . . . that Elsa and Aragon contracted a kind of intellectual leprosy." Most of Triolet's postwar novels and stories did not appeal to the war-weary French, and memories of the Resistance were fading. Both Triolet and Aragon were again contributing to the revived Communist newspapers in France; Triolet attended the Nuremberg trials and wrote "The Judges' Waltz" in which she stated that the public "feels a revulsion for the interminable judging of someone judged in advance by humanity" and did not need to be reminded of the camps of Dachau and Auschwitz. Her novel *The Red Horse* (1953) was practically ignored by the critics, which Triolet attributed to her Communist affiliation and to the fact that she was a woman and a foreigner.

Elsa Triolet was ever aware of her divided allegiance between her native and adopted lands. A poem by Mayakovsky describes her own feelings: "I would have loved to live and die in Paris/ If there had not been that land—Moscow!" Her novel *Where Strangers Meet* (1957) reflects these feelings for her two "homes." Triolet was not uncritical of Communism, as seen in *The Monument* (1957), the story of a sculptor in an unnamed Eastern European country who commits suicide because he believes his statue of Joseph Stalin is a failure. Based on an actual event, it drew sharp criticism from French Communists. Triolet defended her novel, saying "it was the duty of a socialist realist to tell the truth, no matter how unpleasant." Attacks by her political comrades left her "sick of it all. Sick of my own self, being as I was, obviously not meant for peace and quiet, sick of my personal feelings . . . sick of the scuffle." Although she won many French Communists over to her point of view, Triolet would try to avoid such controversy in the future. She began work on a trilogy, *The Age of Nylon*, which dealt with 20th-century issues such as modern technology, consumerism, and the position of women in modern society. Writing was "both pleasurable and painful" for Triolet, and she claimed she never had a specific conclusion in mind. In *The Grand Never* (1965), for example, the heroine leaves her lover, "and when she did," Elsa notes, "I asked myself: why on earth did she do that?"

During the last ten years of her life, she and Aragon were more financially secure which enabled them to live in an exclusive area of Paris and to purchase a small villa in the village of Saint-Arnoult. They also began to collaborate on a collection of their novels; these appeared in 40 volumes between 1964 and 1973, and "stand as the couple's best memorial." Since the early years of the war, Triolet had suffered from heart problems which led to her death in June 1970. She is buried in Saint-Arnoult where she died. Some years later, in tribute to Elsa, Aragon wrote, "My life. . . lasted forty-two years/ The rest. . . before, after/ The rest is only the rest/ Not even the remainder." He died on Christmas Eve 1982 and is buried next to Elsa.

SOURCES:

Adereth, Max. *Elsa Triolet and Louis Aragon: An Introduction to Their Interwoven Lives and Works.* Lewiston, NY: The Edwin Mellen Press, 1994.

Aragon: Poet of the French Resistance. Edited by Hannah Josephson and Malcolm Cowley. NY: Duell, Sloan, and Pearce, 1945.

Mackinnon, Lachlan. *The Lives of Elsa Triolet.* London: Chatto & Windus, 1992.

SUGGESTED READING:

Casey, Brenda Bruckner. "Elsa Triolet: A Study in Solitude," dissertation, Northwestern University, 1974.

Desanti, Dominique. *Elsa-Aragon: le couple ambiguous.* Paris: Belfond, 1994.

———. *Les Clés d'Elsa* (The Keys to Elsa). Ramsay, 1983.

Lottman, Herbert. *The Left Bank: Writers, Artists, and Politics from the Popular Front to the Cold War.* San Francisco, CA: Halo, 1991.

Oeuvres Romanesques croisées d'Elsa Triolet et Aragon. Paris: Robert Laffont, 1964–73.

Jeanne A. Ojala, Professor Emerita, Department of History, University of Utah, Salt Lake City, Utah

Tripoli, countess of.

See Hodierna of Jerusalem (c. 1115–after 1162).
See Lucia (r. 1288–1289).

Tristan, Flora (1803–1844)

French campaigner for women's rights and the rights of working people who attempted to found a "Universal Union of Working Men and Women." Born Flore-Célestine-Thérèse-Henriette Tristan Moscoso on April 7, 1803, in Paris, France; died in Bordeaux, France, probably of typhoid, on November 14, 1844; daughter of Mariano de Tristan y Moscoso (a Peruvian noble) and Anne-Pierre Laisnay; married André-François Chazal (a lithographer), on February 3, 1821 (separated 1824); children: a son (b. ca. 1822); Ernest-Camille (b. 1824); Aline-Marie Chazal (b. 1825, the mother of artist Paul Gauguin).

Married her employer at 17 (1820); left him at 21 (1824); traveled in Europe as a ladies' maid (1825–28); traveled to Peru to unsuccessfully seek inheritance (1833–34); began to campaign for women's rights (1835); was first linked with the French socialist movement (1835); attended feminist salons (1836); petitioned for the legalization of divorce (1837); seriously injured in a murder attempt by her husband (1838); petitioned for the abolition of capital punishment (1838); traveled to England to study social conditions (1839); devised a plan for a "workers' union" (1843); toured France to promote the workers' union (1844).

Major published works: Nécessité de faire un bon accueil aux femmes étrangères *(The need to extend a warm welcome to foreign women, Delaunay, 1835);* Pérégrinations d'une Paria 1833–1834 *(Arthus Bertrand, 1838, English translation:* Peregrinations of a Pariah 1833–1834, *Virago, 1986);* Méphis *(Ladvocat, 1838);* Promenades dans Londres *(Delloye, 1840, English translation:* The London Journal of Flora Tristan, *Virago, 1982);* L'Union ouvrière, chez tous les libraires *(1843, English translation:* The Workers' Union, *University of Illinois Press, 1983).*

At 2:30 PM on September 10, 1838, Flora Tristan was returning to her home in central Paris. Her estranged husband André Chazal had been seated in the wine bar opposite her apartment since 11:30 that morning, reading a geometry book and observing the passersby. When his wife appeared, Chazal left the bar and walked towards her along the street. She saw him approaching, the shape of two pistols clearly outlined in the pockets of his overcoat. He suddenly crossed the road and passed her, then crossed back and approached her from behind. As she turned to see what he was doing, he fired the first pistol at point-blank range, wounding her in the left side. Tristan crawled into a shop calling for help as Chazal prepared to fire the second pistol, but he hesitated in the crowd and confusion, afraid that he might wound a by-stander. Finally, hoping that one bullet might suffice to kill his wife, he handed over his pistols to a wine merchant. Meanwhile, Tristan was carried back to her apartment coughing blood, and slipping in and out of consciousness. It was several weeks before she was declared out of danger, though the bullet was never extracted.

The murder attempt was to prove a turning point in Flora Tristan's life. After several years of violent conflict with her estranged husband, his imprisonment for this crime finally freed her to live her own life and pursue the social causes which increasingly preoccupied her. It also threw into stark relief one of the most important of those causes: her struggle for the rights of women in her society.

Flora Tristan was of mixed Peruvian and French parentage. Her French mother **Anne-Pierre Laisnay** had sought refuge in Spain from the upheaval of the French Revolution. In Bilbao, she met Mariano de Tristan, the eldest son of a wealthy and powerful Peruvian family, and an officer in the Spanish army. They married in 1802, but their religious marriage was not formalized by the required civil ceremony when they returned to France later that year, so Flora and her younger brother were technically illegitimate. When Mariano died suddenly in 1807 without having made a will, Anne-Pierre had no legal right to his estate, and she was left to raise her four-year-old daughter and baby son as best she could. The family moved to L'Isle-Adam, north of Paris, and Flora grew up a country child.

Tristan and her mother returned to Paris shortly after the death of Flora's brother in 1817. Flora was nearly 15 at the time. She may have entertained hopes of making a good marriage, as befitted a daughter of the Tristan family, for although she appears to have received little formal education, she took dancing and painting lessons. However, her illegitimacy stood in the way of such an ambition, and in marrying André-François Chazal in 1821 she became the wife of a self-employed artisan. Chazal had been giving her lessons in painting, and employed her to color his engravings and lithographs. "She inspired in me a violent passion," he later declared. He persuaded her mother to support the marriage, and Tristan eventually succumbed to their combined influence. "I wish to become a perfect wife. . . . I want to treat my mother as I would like to be treated by my children," she wrote, but she would later insist that she had been forced into this marriage. The relationship was never happy, as financial pressures,

the speedy arrival of two children, and possibly Flora's discontent, took their toll. Divorce was illegal, but after four years of marriage the couple agreed to separate, and Chazal left Paris to escape his creditors.

Tristan, barely 21 and pregnant with her third child, was left with responsibility for her sons, but she found it difficult to find satisfactory employment. "The presence of my children prevented me from passing as a single woman," she wrote, "and I almost always introduced myself as a widow; but, living in the same town as my husband and my former acquaintances, it was very difficult to sustain a role which a host of circumstances could undermine." After several jobs in Paris had proved shortlived, Tristan placed her children in the guardianship of her mother and left Paris in an effort to find more reliable income. She was absent for nearly three years, and later reported that she had traveled in Switzerland, Italy, and England as a ladies' maid for two English women during this time. Her husband preferred to believe that she was really the mistress of a wealthy man, but no evidence remains to substantiate either case.

On her return to Paris in 1828, Tristan applied successfully to the courts for a separation of property, to prevent Chazal and his creditors from seizing control of her savings or income. In 1829, she was living in a boarding house with her daughter **Aline-Marie Chazal**, posing again as a widow, Madame Tristan. A ship's captain named Chabrié, who was also resident there, proceeded to tell her about the Tristans of Peru whom he had encountered in his voyages to that country. This meeting inspired her to try to reestablish contact with her Peruvian family, despite her mother's earlier lack of success. She wrote to her uncle Pío, introducing herself and outlining the circumstances of her birth: "As a military man, your brother needed the king's permission to get married: not wanting to seek it . . . he proposed to my mother that she marry him only in a religious ceremony (a marriage which has no standing in France). My mother, who felt that she could no longer live without him, consented to this proposal." In this honest but naïve sentence admitting her illegitimate status, Tristan unwittingly destroyed any chance of establishing a legal claim on her father's estate. Nevertheless, her uncle accepted her as the illegitimate daughter of his brother and sent her a small sum of money.

In 1831, Chazal reappeared and began to seek custody of his two surviving children. French law recognized a father's rights to the exclusion of those of the mother if children were legitimate, so Tristan's legal position was weak. Following a violent confrontation with Chazal at her uncle's place in March 1832, Tristan promised to surrender Ernest to Chazal's care. In return, he signed a declaration that he would agree to a divorce as soon as it became legal. But Tristan was determined to keep custody of her daughter Aline, who had been born after the couple had separated. Unsatisfied with not knowing even his daughter's whereabouts, Chazal tried to have Tristan arrested, since French law also required a wife to live in her husband's house. The

magistrate was unwilling to get involved on this occasion. However, convinced that Chazal would persist in his efforts to take Aline from her, Tristan left Paris again. After traveling in France for six months, she left Aline in boarding school in Angoulême and headed to Peru to try to pursue her inheritance claim.

Living aboard ship for four months with little privacy and 18 men for company proved a challenging experience. Tristan extended her education by reading with the officers, and practiced her Spanish with some of the passengers.

Flora
Tristan

Although she had already traveled within Europe, Tristan had never before encountered people and places so unfamiliar. She experienced the beauty and terror of the open sea; visited the coast of Africa where the slave trade was in operation; and, on reaching port, traveled by mule to the town of Arequipa, high in the Cordillera Mountains, where the ancestral Tristan estates were located. During her ten-month stay in Peru, Tristan visited sites of interest to the tourist, but she also witnessed a coup d'état and resulting civil war. She kept a detailed journal of her life, and later published a book which recounted her adventures and the lessons she had learned. It included observations on the political and economic systems of this slave-based society as well as on the situation of women, whom she discovered were "slaves everywhere."

While Tristan failed to persuade her uncle to recognize her full inheritance rights, he did pay her an allowance of 2,500 francs per annum, which she continued to receive until 1839. This income enabled her to establish herself as a writer, rather than needing to find more mundane employment. On her arrival back in France, Tristan was reunited with her daughter, and they returned to Paris in January 1835. An anonymous letter to Chazal in October informed him of his wife's whereabouts and said that she was rich. It suggested that he kidnap his daughter and hold her for ransom. "Once you have the little girl," his informant observed, "you will easily be able to get 15 or 20,000 francs out of her [mother] to make you agree to give her back." Chazal apparently took this advice, for shortly afterwards he abducted his daughter on her way to school. This was Aline's introduction to her father.

After discovering that Chazal had taken Aline to Versailles, Tristan went there to snatch her back on November 1. They managed to escape Chazal by paying a bonus to the coach driver, but now that he knew his wife's address he was able to take legal action against her. The court ruled that Aline should be placed in boarding school, at Tristan's expense, with both parents having access. Six months later, in July 1836, Chazal moved his daughter to a different school and restricted her contact with her mother. Aline responded by running away to her mother. Once again the court defended Chazal's paternal rights over Aline, and she was taken back to her father's place by the police in November. By this time Chazal's business had virtually failed. His apartment at Montmartre was sparsely furnished, and he and his two children slept in the one bed there. On April 1, 1837,

Tristan received a letter from Aline alleging that her father was sexually abusing her and, as Flora sought advice from her lawyer about what action to take, Aline arrived at her door. She had run away again. The judicial investigation resulted in charges being laid against Chazal, though these were later dismissed for lack of evidence. In March 1838, Tristan's petition for a full legal separation was upheld on the basis of these events, but they also motivated Chazal's decision to murder his wife. He began to plot her death, purchasing pistols, practicing firing them, and designing a headstone for her grave.

Chazal believed he had been denied justice at law. He was also enraged because his wife had begun to make her mark as a writer and public figure, challenging his male prerogatives in the process. She had published a pamphlet in 1835, and subsequently produced a number of newspaper articles. But the appearance of *Peregrinations of a Pariah* at the end of 1837 made her a minor celebrity. Her revelations about her marriage and her admission that, despite being a married woman, she was both attractive to and attracted by men she had met on her travels, were little short of scandalous. Tristan's behavior challenged social conventions, as well as Chazal's marital authority. The obituary Chazal wrote for his wife shortly before the shooting revealed his thinking: "You are fleeing justice which will not escape you. Sleep in peace to serve as an example to those sufficiently misguided to follow your immoral precepts."

Tristan's revelations in *Peregrinations of a Pariah* were meant to demonstrate the misfortunes of women shackled by the bonds of unhappy but indissoluble marriages, in which they had few legal rights. "It is not to myself personally that I wish to draw attention," she wrote, "but to all those women who are in the same position and whose number increases daily." In September 1838, during recuperation from her husband's attack, Tristan completed her second major work, the novel *Méphis*. Together with her first book, it sought to expose the inequalities faced by women in society. Women were deprived of education and rights, so they were forced to rely on relationships with men for their survival. Yet within marriage, Tristan argued, women became dependent creatures with no control over their own lives. They were raised for love, but rarely found it. Happiness and fulfillment remained elusive, although the socialization of girls numbed their sense of injustice and thus made their condition less painful. For those who rejected their fate, however, rebellion brought isolation and social condemnation. A separated wife, in particular, was a social outcast: "She is nothing more than an unfortunate Pariah, whom people believe they are treating indulgently if they spare her injury." Like many other feminists of that period, Tristan focused her demands on the reintroduction of divorce, female education, and the reform of the legal code which discriminated against women.

Flora Tristan had attended feminist salons in Paris in 1836, and she was also friendly with a number of feminists connected with the socialist movement. In the 1830s, the connections between feminism and socialism were strong, because reformers recognized that the creation of a world of justice and social equality could not be achieved while women remained in servitude. Similarly, many feminists believed that the position of women could not be improved unless a broader social transformation was achieved. Tristan may have encountered such ideas even before her voyage to Peru, since Saint-Simonian socialism (which had a strong feminist dimension) was at its height in Paris in the 1828–32 period. However, her first documented connections with other socialists date from 1835, and they extended not only to the various schools of French socialism but also to England, for the networks of feminists and socialists in these two countries were quite extensive in the 1830s and 1840s.

Socialism had been an important sub-theme in Tristan's earliest writings. The title of her novel *Méphis*, for instance, was also the name of its male hero, who described himself as "a man of the people . . . , one who is called today by the name of proletarian." The novel offered a vision of an ideal world transformed along both feminist and socialist lines. Tristan's growing consciousness of the plight of the "proletarian" stemmed not merely from reading socialist theory but from observation, for the world was changing significantly at that time. Urbanization was increasing, the workplace was being transformed by new methods of production, and the instabilities of early industrial capitalism saw repeated cycles of "boom and bust," the "busts" throwing enormous numbers out of work with nothing to fall back on but charity. Women workers, unable to support themselves at the best of times, were among the most vulnerable, and resorted to prostitution as a form of seasonal work. Philosophers and doctors decried the degeneration of the urban poor, whom they saw as a dangerous and insidious element in the midst of civilized society. For socialists, however, the poor were not so much dangerous as wronged, and their objective was to right that wrong.

Tristan's commitment to a broad vision of social transformation became particularly evident from the time of her trip to England in 1839. This was her fourth visit to that country, and she was struck by the growth of poverty and social unrest in what was then the world's most advanced industrial nation. Industrialization and poverty seemed to go together. While Tristan observed the lifestyle of the well-to-do, therefore, her focus was on the misery which pervaded "the monstrous city" of London. She visited its red-light district, its prisons, its squalid Irish quarter, and Bedlam insane asylum, as well as the industrial towns of Manchester and Sheffield. The account of this investigation, which Tristan published in 1840, was understandably bleak. It was relieved only by her admiration for the Chartists, fighting for a more democratic political system, and for the infant school system, which she believed would eventually imbue all children with cooperative values.

> *I* call for woman's rights because I am convinced that all the misfortunes of the world stem from the neglect and scorn shown until now for the natural and inalienable rights of woman.
> —Flora Tristan

Tristan believed that the publication of starkly realistic accounts like hers would alert people to the need for social reform. The fourth edition was dedicated "to the working classes": "Workers, it is to you, men and women, that I dedicate my book; I have written it to inform you about your position." She advised workers to educate themselves by reading the works of social reformers, and encouraged them to pursue their political rights. However, that was not enough: "You should consider political rights only as the means to put yourselves in a position to attack the evil at its source," she wrote. "You should concern yourselves with the social order, the base of the edifice."

At that time Tristan apparently had no mechanism in mind by which workers might tackle "the social order" and shape it in their interests. From 1840, however, she began to make contact with workers' organizations in France. The trade associations in which skilled workers were organized had given her an idea for a more general "union" of workers. Rather than being exclusive to a particular trade and strictly male-defined, her union would be a "universal union of working men and women." In 1843, she published *The Workers' Union*, in which she outlined her plan. If each worker contributed two francs per year, she argued, this union would raise sufficient capital to create communal establishments where children could be educated and the elderly retire in dignity. In addition, given the limited suffrage which prevailed in France, the workers could hire an official representative to lobby the government on their behalf, in order to pass legislation guaranteeing "the right to work" and the right to organize. This scheme was envisaged as a transitional one, offering a practical mechanism for moving from the oppressive present to the liberated future. With the newfound power which workers would exercise in society, they could begin to experiment with more far-reaching schemes for social reorganization.

Tristan's commitment to socialist politics from 1842 did not imply that her interest in feminist questions had disappeared. However, she believed that the questions of workers' rights and women's rights were inseparable, since the oppression of both was necessary to maintain the social privilege of wealthy men. Later generations of feminists would emphasize that women do not always have interests in common with each other. However, in the early 19th century this perspective was not widely held. Like many of her contemporaries, Tristan emphasized that all women were oppressed by men. However, while bourgeois women were oppressed by the men of their own class, working women suffered at the hands of both working men, imbued with notions of male superiority, and bourgeois men who exploited them as employers and seducers.

Tristan's aim in *The Workers' Union*, then, was to persuade working men that their own liberation depended upon the liberation of all women. She appealed to the principles of the French Revolution of 1789, on which those men based their own case for social justice:

> Are you beginning to understand, you men . . . why I demand rights for woman? Why I would like her placed in society on a footing of absolute equality with man, to enjoy the legal rights all human beings possess from birth? I call for woman's rights because I am convinced that all the misfortunes of the world stem from the neglect and scorn shown until now for the natural and inalienable rights of woman. . . . I call for woman's rights because it is the only way to obtain her rehabilitation before the church, the law, and society, and this rehabilitation is necessary before working men themselves can be rehabilitated.

Having developed her "saving idea," as she called it, Tristan threw her energies into promoting it among working people. Most of the 4,000 copies of the first edition of her book were given away free to workers. Three thousand brochures outlining the contents of the book were also distributed to workshops in Paris. Having organized a second edition of 10,000 copies, Tristan set out on a tour of France in April 1844 to promote her plan. She kept a detailed account of this trip, which was designed to provide the material for a later book on the "actual condition of the working class from the moral, intellectual and material perspectives." Tristan recorded her meetings with workers from Auxerre to Bordeaux, noting their wages and living conditions, their levels of literacy and politicalconsciousness. She took particular interest in the situation of working women, endeavoring to convince them that "politics reaches right to the hearth." Tristan observed the particularly outrageous working conditions endured by laundrywomen at Nîmes, and female porters at Marseille, recording in her diary at one point: "My sisters, I swear that I will deliver you." At Lyons, the stronghold of worker militancy in this period, Tristan began to groom a woman as her successor. **Eléonore Blanc** had the necessary qualification of passionate commitment to the cause, and Tristan became deeply attached to her.

Tristan's diary during this journey around France also recorded her deteriorating health. She had been suffering from stomach complaints and dysentery for several months before she reached Bordeaux on September 24, 1844. She was taken ill the following day, and treated for "cerebral congestion." However, after a brief improvement early in October, the typhoid-like symptoms grew steadily worse, perhaps aided by the constant doses of opium administered by her well-meaning nurses. She died at 10:00 PM on November 14, 1844, aged 41 years.

News of Tristan's death was circulated widely in the press, workers' newspapers paying tribute to her devotion to their cause, conservative papers understandably showing less regret. About 80 workers attended her funeral, along with a few radical members of the local bourgeoisie, and almost immediately they began raising funds to construct a monument. The project took four years to complete, and the monument was finally inaugurated in October 1848. Several thousand workers attended the ceremony, reading speeches and poems in Tristan's honor. A marble column surmounted by a sculptured book was inscribed: "In memory of Madame Flora Tristan, author of *The Workers' Union*, with the workers' gratitude. Liberty-Equality-Fraternity-Solidarity." Today that monument, in the Chartreuse Cemetery at Bordeaux, remains a place of commemoration for socialists and feminists alike.

SOURCES:

Caperon, Paulin. *Inauguration du Monument Elevé à Bordeaux à la Mémoire de Flora Tristan par les Travailleurs.* Bordeaux: Imprimerie de Causserouge, 1848.

Chazal jeune. *Mémoire à Consulter pour M. Chazal Contre Madame Chazal.* Montmartre: Imprimerie de Cosson, 1838.

———. "Pater Natae Suae Deflorationis Accusatus. Mémoire ayant pour but d'éclairer la Chambre de Conseil, adressé à Mes Juges pour être joint au dossier de l'affaire Chazal." Paris: manuscrit, 1837.

Le Droit. February 1 and 2, 1839.

Tristan, Flora. *Méphis.* Paris: Ladvocat, 1838.

———. *Pérégrinations d'une Paria 1833–1834.* Paris: Arthus Bertrand, 1838.

———. *Promenades dans Londres.* Edition établie et commentée par François Bédarida. Paris: François Maspéro, 1978.

———. *Le Tour de France.* Texte et notes établis par Jules-L. Puech. Paris: François Maspéro, 1980.

———. *L'Union ouvrière.* 3e édition. Paris: chez tous les libraires, 1844.

SUGGESTED READING:

Cross, Máire and Tim Gray. *The Feminism of Flora Tristan.* Oxford: Berg, 1992.

Grogan, Susan K. *French Socialism and Sexual Difference: Women and the New Society 1803–1844.* London: Macmillan, 1992.

Moses, Claire Goldberg. *French Feminism in the Nineteenth Century.* Albany, NY: State University Press of New York, 1984.

COLLECTIONS:

Correspondence, papers and memorabilia located in the Archives Nationales, the Bibliothèque *Marguerite Durand, the Bibliothèque Nationale and the Bibliothèque Historique de la Ville de Paris, all in Paris; in a number of provincial archives throughout France; and in the International Institute for Social History, Amsterdam, the Netherlands.

Susan Grogan, Senior Lecturer in History, Victoria University of Wellington, New Zealand, and author of *French Socialism and Sexual Difference: Women and the New Society 1803–1844*

Trivulzio, Cristina (1808–1871).

See Belgioso, Cristina.

Trocmé, Magda (1901–1996)

Italian-born French woman who, along with her husband and the entire village of Le Chambon, relied on nonviolent resistance to save 5,000 men, women and children from Nazi annihilation. Name variations: Magda Trocme. Born Magda Grilli in Florence, Italy, in 1901; died in Paris on October 10, 1996; daughter of an engineer; married André Trocmé; children: daughter Nelly; son Jacques.

On a cold, dark evening in France in 1940, Magda Trocmé, a Protestant minister's wife, heard a knock on the parsonage door. Seeking refuge was a German-Jewish woman escaping from an ever-tightening Nazi dragnet in France's German-occupied northern zone. The desperate woman was invited in with a simple, "Naturally, come in, and come in." This refugee from persecution would become the first of 5,000 endangered souls—70% of them Jewish—who would owe their survival not only to the kind woman who had opened the door, but to an entire village that opened its homes and hearts to provide refuge to those threatened by an evil tyranny. The town was Le Chambon-sur-Lignon, a small village in southcentral France, situated on a high plateau and surrounded by rugged mountains.

The "Good Samaritan of Le Chambon" was born Magda Grilli in 1901 in Florence, Italy. Magda's father, an engineer who had been a cavalry colonel, was Italian, but her mother was of Russian birth. Intelligent and independent, Magda asserted her independence early, rejecting the teachings of the Roman Catholic Church while a convent student, and embracing Protestantism in a land in which non-Catholics were scarce. While studying social work on a scholarship in New York City, in 1925 Magda met and fell in love with André Trocmé, a Frenchman and fellow Protestant who was a student at New York's Union Theological Seminary. André and Magda married in 1926 and returned to France. After his ordination, André began the search for a congregation that would accept him. This represented a challenge because of his radical views on major issues. For one thing, he was a committed pacifist, who had lived his unpopular beliefs as a conscientious objector during World War I. Regarded as a "difficult type" and a rebel within the French Protestant Church, André was not considered suitable for a normal pastorship.

In 1934, he was appointed pastor to the Reformed church in Le Chambon-sur-Lignon, situated in the remote department of Haut-Loire. Le Chambon's population of religious, hard-working peasants was almost totally descended from the Huguenots, French Protestants who had been persecuted in the 17th and 18th centuries and who had sought refuge in isolated places like Le Chambon. The Trocmés quickly became accepted by the villagers, who recognized that there were few contradictions between the Christian values they professed and the modest life they had chosen to live. Feeling they had found a true spiritual home, the Trocmés became rooted in Le Chambon, confidently raising their family in the austere but stable village. In 1938, they founded the Collège Cévenol, a private non-denominational secondary school whose mission would be to serve as an international center for peace and reconciliation.

The late 1930s was hardly a time to dream of peace, as a bloody civil war raged in nearby Spain and Nazi Germany and Fascist Italy increasingly menaced their neighbors. Both Trocmés had firsthand experiences with the darkening mood, since during vacations they would take turns visiting her relatives in Italy and his relatives in Germany (like his wife, André was of mixed nationality, his mother having been born a German). In both nations, they witnessed intolerance and militarism, while the inhumanity of Nazi Germany's anti-Semitism was spreading a moral stain impossible to ignore. Back in Le Chambon, the Trocmés began to alert their neighbors of the possibility of imminent war, he in his sermons and she as a teacher of Italian at the Collège Cévenol.

France was attacked by Nazi Germany on May 10, 1940, capitulating in less than six weeks' time. Numb with shock and disbelief, most French citizens passively went about their daily lives, accepting the foreign occupation. A large number of French collaborated with either the German occupiers or their French allies, the Vichy regime, which was granted a semi-sovereign status as a Nazi satellite state. At first, the Germans occupied only the north of France, and Le Chambon remained relatively free of interference. But from the start of the occupation, it was clear that a new and oppressive reality had taken hold of France. Even before the frantic woman had knocked on the Trocmés' door, refugees from defeated Republican Spain and French Jews had trickled into Le Chambon in search of sanctuary.

Setting the tone for the days ahead, André alerted his fellow parishioners of Le Chambon regarding the moral challenges they now faced every day: "The duty of Christians is to resist through the weapons of the spirit the violence that will be brought to bear on their consciences." After German forces occupied the south of France in late 1942, more and more frightened men, women, and children appeared in the town. Most were Jewish, but many sought safety because of their political beliefs or resistance activities. The peasants of Le Chambon now gave shelter to Jews and others whose lives would be worth nothing were they to fall into the hands of Vichy officials and their Nazi overlords. In protecting its vulnerable guests, Le Chambon acted as a single moral organism, carrying out every day what the townspeople called a "conspiracy of goodness" to protect fellow humans in peril. The Chambonnais never attempted to convert the Jews; rather, they helped to organize Jewish religious services whenever possible.

More than a generation later, when interviewed for Pierre Sauvage's documentary film, *Weapons of the Spirit*, many of the surviving villagers of Le Chambon found it difficult to understand why their deeds should be commemorated. "I helped simply because they needed to be helped," said an old woman. "What happened had a lot to do with people still believing in something." Another villager who had offered his home as shelter could only say, "When people came, if we could be of help . . . ," and then could not think of any other words of explanation. Other villagers offered succinct reasons for why they had acted as they had: "There was nothing admirable. It was merely logical," or, "Ours was a very solid faith which was put to the test, and was not found wanting." When asked to explain how the rescue efforts had been organized, an elderly woman shrugged off the idea that there had been any real plan, noting, "If we'd had one, we'd have failed." Another vil-

*M*agda *T*rocmé

lager, a pious old woman of granite-like fundamentalism, said of the Jews that she and the others had sheltered, "For us they were the people of God. That's what mattered."

When Magda Trocmé was asked why she had chosen to help Jews and others threatened by a seemingly all-powerful tyranny, she responded: "Those of us who received the first Jews did what we thought had to be done—nothing more complicated. . . . Sometimes people ask me, 'How did you make a decision?' There was no decision to make. The issue was: Do you think we are all brothers or not?" Much less a theologian or philosopher than her husband, Magda insisted that true religion had to be practical, or else it was little more than idle piety:

> I do not hunt around to find people to help. But I never close my door, never refuse to help somebody who comes to me and asks for something. This I think is my kind of religion. You see, it is a way of handling myself. When things happen, not things I plan, but things sent by God or by chance, when people come to my door, I feel responsible.

On one occasion during the Nazi occupation, the people at the Trocmés' door were French police who had come to arrest André. Since they had arrived around dinnertime, Magda invited the startled officers to eat with the family, later explaining to those who could not fathom it, "What are you talking about? It was dinnertime." Fortunately, André would be released from custody unharmed, immediately resuming his dangerous activities. Although both Trocmés survived the war years despite the key roles they played in saving thousands of people sought both by the Nazi and Vichy authorities, another member of their family was much less fortunate. André's cousin Daniel Trocmé, who directed the children's home Maison des Roches, was betrayed, most likely by a German officer staying at a military convalescent home in Le Chambon. Arrested on June 29, 1943, Daniel was taken to Moulins for interrogation and, after readily admitting his role in the rescue of Jewish children, was sent to the Buchenwald concentration camp near Weimar, Germany, where he perished in April 1944.

Le Chambon was liberated in the summer of 1944, and its guests soon returned to their homes in various parts of France or departed to the four corners of the world. Decades later, the inspiring story of the remote village "where goodness happened" was told in books by Philip Hallie and other authors, as well as in *Weapons of the Spirit*, a powerful documentary by Sauvage, who was born to Jewish parents in Le Chambon in 1943, thus owing his very life to this community. After the war, the Trocmés departed from Le Chambon when André became the European secretary for the Fellowship of Reconciliation (FOR), a universally respected United States-based pacifist organization. During the 1950s, the couple made several FOR fund-raising tours in North America. Later, André became pastor of a church in Geneva, Switzerland, where he died in 1971.

After his death, Magda moved to Paris to be closer to her son Jacques and some of her ten grandchildren (her daughter Nelly lives in the United States). Magda Trocmé died in Paris on October 10, 1996. Although she had been honored as one of the Righteous Gentiles by Yad Vashem, Israel's Martyrs' and Heroes' Memorial Authority, she never could comprehend why what she and her husband had done during the Holocaust had been in any way remarkable. Perhaps it was not an accident that Albert Camus had lived for a while in Le Chambon when he was writing *The Plague*, his novel-parable of the moral decay that was Hitlerism.

SOURCES:

Fogelman, Eva. *Conscience & Courage: Rescuers of Jews During the Holocaust*. NY: Doubleday, 1995.

Gushee, David P. "Learning from the Christian Rescuers: Lessons for the Churches," in *Annals of the American Academy of Political and Social Science* [*The Holocaust: Remembering for the Future*, Franklin H. Littell *et al.*, eds.]. Vol. 548. November 1996, pp. 138–155.

———. "Many Paths to Righteousness: An Assessment of Research on Why Righteous Gentiles Helped Jews," in *Holocaust and Genocide Studies*. Vol. 7, no. 3. Winter 1993, pp. 372–401.

Hallie, Philip P. *Lest Innocent Blood be Shed: The Story of the Village of Le Chambon and How Goodness Happened There*. NY: HarperPerennial, 1994.

Jostad, Karen Gail. "Area Jews Will Honor Heroes of Holocaust," in *The Star Tribune* [Minneapolis, MN]. November 30, 1996, p. 7B.

"Magda Trocmé, rescuer of French Jews, dies," in *The Christian Century*. Vol. 113, no. 33. November 13, 1996, p. 1106.

Paldiel, Mordecai. "Le Chambon-sur-Lignon," in Israel Gutman, ed., *Encyclopedia of the Holocaust*. Vol. 3. NY: Macmillan, 1990, pp. 859–860.

———. *The Path of the Righteous: Gentile Rescuers of Jews During the Holocaust*. Hoboken, NJ: KTAV-The Jewish Foundation for Christian Rescuers, 1993.

Rittner, Carol, and Sondra Myers, eds. *The Courage to Care: Rescuers of Jews During the Holocaust*. NY: New York University Press, 1986.

Rittner, Carol, and John K. Roth, eds. *Different Voices: Women and the Holocaust*. St. Paul, MN: Paragon House, 1993.

Silver, Eric. *The Book of the Just: The Unsung Heroes Who Rescued Jews from Hitler*. NY: Grove Press, 1992.

Thomas, Jr., Robert McG. "Magda Trocmé, 94, Is Dead; Sheltered Victims of Nazis," in *The New York Times*. October 19, 1996, section I, p. 52.

COLLECTIONS:

American Friends of the Collège Cévenol Papers, American Congregational Association Archives, Boston, Massachusetts.

André and Magda Trocmé Papers, Peace Collection, Swarthmore College Library, Swarthmore, Pennsylvania.

John Nevin Sayre Papers, Peace Collection, Swarthmore College Library, Swarthmore, Pennsylvania.

RELATED MEDIA:

Gardner, Robert, and Elie Wiesel. *The Courage to Care*, (video), Alexandria, VA: PBS Video, 1999.

Gossels, Lisa, and Dean Wetherel. *The Children of Chabannes* (video), NY: Perennial Pictures, 1999.

Sauvage, Pierre, and Bill D. Moyers. *Weapons of the Spirit* (video), Los Angeles: Friends of Le Chambon, 1994.

John Haag,
Associate Professor of History,
University of Georgia, Athens, Georgia

Troctula.

See Trotula.

Troll-Borostyani, Irma von

(1847–1912)

Austrian writer and women's rights activist. Name variations: Irma von Troll-Borostyáni; (pseudonym) Veritas Leo Bergen. Born Marie von Troll on March 31, 1847, in Salzburg, Austria; died after a stroke on February 10, 1912, in Salzburg; educated at monastery school and at home; married a man named Borostyani.

Selected writings: Die Mission unseres Jahrhunderts: Eine Studie über die Frauenfrage *(The Mission of Our Century: A Study on the Woman Question, 1878);* Die Gleichstellung der Geschlechter und die Reform der Jugenderziehung *(The Equality of the Sexes and Reform in Education, 1887);* Katechismus der Frauenbewegung *(The Catechism of the Women's Movement, 1903).*

Born Marie von Troll in 1847 in Salzburg, Austria, Irma von Troll-Borostyani was the fourth and last of her parents' children. Her mother and father enrolled her in a local monastery school, but her health was fragile, and she was eventually removed from classes there and educated at home.

Unhappy with the provincialism of her hometown, she moved in 1870 to the cosmopolitan Austrian capital of Vienna, where she hoped to become a concert pianist. Instead she began to write and became involved with women's rights. In 1878, she captured widespread attention with an essay published under the pseudonym Veritas Leo Bergen, *Die Mission unseres Jahrhunderts: Eine Studie über die Frauenfrage* (The Mission of Our Century: A

Study on the Woman Question). By the time she returned to Salzburg four years later to care for her dying mother, she had established herself as a writer and a champion of women's rights. She had also changed her first name from Marie to Irma and married a man with the Hungarian surname of Borostyani.

Troll-Borostyani found Salzburg much more receptive upon her return, and she and her sister **Wilhelmina von Troll** soon gathered about them a large coterie of similarly minded intellectuals. Irma continued to work aggressively for equal rights for women in Salzburg. Among the many essays she published were the pseudonymous collections *Die Gleichstellung der Geschlechter und die Reform der Jugenderziehung* (The Equality of the Sexes and Reform in Education, 1887) and *Katechismus der Frauenbewegung* (The Catechism of the Women's Movement, 1903).

Less than two months before her 65th birthday, Troll-Borostyani suffered a stroke in her Salzburg home and died shortly thereafter, on February 10, 1912. She was buried in Salzburg, where her headstone carries an inscription saluting her as "the courageous champion of the women's movement."

SOURCES:

Buck, Claire, ed. *The Bloomsbury Guide to Women's Literature.* NY: Prentice Hall, 1992.

Don Amerman,
freelance writer, Saylorsburg, Pennsylvania

Trollope, Eleanor (c. 1803–1873).

See Ternan, Frances Eleanor.

Trollope, Frances Eleanor (c. 1803–1873).

See Ternan, Frances Eleanor.

Trollope, Frances Milton

(c. 1779–1863)

English novelist and travel writer who began writing in middle age out of dire financial necessity and went on to enjoy wide popularity in a career that lasted over 20 years. Born on March 10, around 1779 (some sources cite 1778 or 1780), in Heckfield, near Bristol, England; died on October 6, 1863, in Florence, Italy; daughter of William Milton (a minister) and Frances (Gelsey) Milton; married Thomas Anthony Trollope, on May 23, 1809 (died 1835); children: Thomas Adolphus (1810–1892, a novelist who married Theodosia Garrow Trollope and *Frances Eleanor Ternan); Henry (1811–1834); Arthur (b. 1812); Emily (b. 1813, died in infancy); Anthony Trollope (1815–1882, a novelist); Cecilia Trollope Tilley (1816–1849, who wrote one novel); Emily Trollope (1818–1836).

First traveled to United States (1827); opened Trollope Bazaar (1828); published first book (1832); retired in Florence (1844); published last book (1856).

Selected works: Domestic Manners of the Americans (1832); The Refugee in America (1832); Jonathan Jefferson Whitlaw (1836); The Widow Barnaby (1839); Michael Armstrong (1839); The Widow Married (1840); The Barnabys in America (1843); Jessie Phillips (1843); Father Eustace (1847); Petticoat Government (1850); The Life and Adventures of a Clever Woman (1854); Fashionable Life (1856).

Frances Milton Trollope was an extremely prolific writer, publishing 34 novels and 6 travel books in her later life. She began writing seriously only in her 50s, after raising a large family. Born on March 10, around 1779, Frances Milton was the youngest daughter of **Frances Gelsey Milton** and William Milton, a well-to-do minister. Her mother died shortly after Frances' birth, leaving her father to raise her and her siblings alone. The Reverend Milton, an optimistic man educated at Oxford who took much pleasure in studying literature, science, and mathematics, seems to have given Frances and her sister **Mary Milton** the same classical education their older brother received. Had her mother been alive, it is most likely that Frances' education would have been aimed at fitting her for a domestic life as wife and mother. Instead, Frances and Mary took advantage of the reverend's extensive library and were tutored in French, Italian, and Latin, in addition to literature, art, and writing.

Frances thus grew up much better educated than most young Englishwomen of her time, a fact which prepared her for her future writing career. Along with her brother and sister, she inherited her father's cheerful, easy-going personality. As she would in later life, Frances traveled often in her youth; the family had homes in Heckfield and Bristol, and the children followed their father on his many trips to other parishes as well. Reverend Milton seems to have been in no hurry to have his daughters married, although most women at the time married young, and Frances was free to do much as she pleased.

In 1802, Reverend Milton remarried, an event which for the most part broke up the tight family unit. Frances and Mary moved to London the next year (their brother Henry already lived there), both to escape the awkwardness of living with their stepmother and for the cultural opportunities offered by the capital city. The three siblings shared a home, quickly becoming part of the social scene of London's gentry. They entertained often and were patrons of London's many museums, theaters, and other cultural attractions.

Frances was introduced to Thomas Anthony Trollope, a friend of her brother, in 1808. Trollope, a young lawyer, had broad intellectual interests and a quiet, serious demeanor. Despite the difference in their personalities—Frances being a fun-loving, high-spirited woman—they became interested in one another. After a brief engagement, they married on May 23, 1809. Frances was 30 years old, well past the usual age for women to marry. The newlyweds remained in London, leasing a home only a few houses from the one Frances had shared with her brother and sister.

Over the next seven years, Frances fulfilled the primary duty of a 19th-century English wife by giving birth to five children, four sons— Thomas, Henry, Arthur, and Anthony—and a daughter, Emily, who died in infancy. To accommodate this growing family, Thomas Anthony purchased a farm near Harrow in 1816. There, two more daughters were born, **Cecilia Trollope (Tilley)** in 1816, and a second **Emily** in 1818. Frances was clearly the dominant force in family life at Illots Farm. She taught all of her children herself, fostering in each a love of the same fields she had studied with her father, especially literature. Each child was encouraged to try his or her hand at writing; three of them excelled at it. Thomas went on to write historical romances, while Cecilia also composed novels. Anthony Trollope is by far the best known of Frances' children, the renown of his novels having earned him a place as one of England's finest 19th-century novelists. When they were not studying under their mother's tutelage, the children often acted as the entertainment at the Trollopes' parties, performing skits which Frances wrote for their guests.

As wife and mother, Frances often was forced to serve as the intermediary between her children and her husband. All six showed Frances' warm, open personality, which led them into conflict with Thomas, who became more reserved and less inclined to enjoy life's pleasures as the years passed. Frances tried to keep the household running smoothly while maintaining peace between its members.

During the years at Illots Farm, Thomas' law practice flourished, and the Trollopes enjoyed a high standard of living. However, this was to change unexpectedly. In 1820, the first of their economic troubles began. The family had moved in 1818 to a custom-built home called Julian Hill, in Harrow. Thomas had leased the farm as a temporary second residence for his family with plans to relocate to a large estate which he expected to inherit from an elderly uncle. However, after the lease was taken out on Julian Hill, he was disinherited when his uncle remarried in 1820. Since Thomas could not cancel the lease on the farm, the family was forced to rent out the new home they had built and move to an old farmhouse on the property, where they lived off Thomas' legal fees and the sale of farm produce. The Trollopes would remain there for several years. Despite a lower standard of living, the Trollopes initially were happy at Julian Hill. They continued to socialize with a wide circle of friends and often entertained guests.

In 1823, the entire family traveled to Paris. There they became acquainted with *Frances "Fanny" Wright, a radical utopian socialist with whom Frances Trollope became friends. During her stay in Paris, Trollope kept a journal of the people and places she encountered; it was her first substantial piece of writing, and its detailed observations reveal keen insight which would serve her well in her professional life. Back home at Julian Hill, the Trollopes' financial situation was worsening steadily. Thomas Trollope suffered from intense, recurring headaches (apparently caused by a brain tumor) which affected his ability to practice law. He alienated friends, family, and clients with his increasingly argumentative, irritable behavior. In 1827, fate struck the Trollopes another blow when a severe depression hit England. Thomas' practice failed completely, and the family could not make ends meet; they rented out Julian Hill and moved to a smaller home at Harrow Weald. Frances, sensing that their situation was not going to improve anytime soon, decided that drastic measures were needed to keep the family going.

Thus, she and the four children still living at home set sail in November 1827 for the United States. She had been invited by her friend Fanny Wright to join the work at Nashoba, Mississippi, a community of white social activists seeking to educate former slaves in an effort to push for the eradication of slavery. The project appealed to Frances Trollope for several reasons: she loved to travel, she wanted desperately to escape from her financial problems as well as from her embittered husband (who was opposed to the trip), and she believed in the abolitionist movement. However, she was totally unprepared for the harsh living conditions at Nashoba. There was little food, only primitive huts for sleeping in, an unhappy and demoralized population of ex-slaves, and rampant disease. The Trollopes remained there for only ten days, after which they fled north to

Cincinnati, Ohio—which Frances had heard described as the "Athens of the West"—having no money left to return to England.

After waiting in vain for money from her husband, who had ceased answering her letters, Frances realized that it was up to her to support herself and her four children. She had no job skills, but she did have her classical education, and so she proposed to a Cincinnati museum owner that she and her family put on exhibitions at his museum, for a share of the admission receipts. One attraction involved an unseen oracle (played by Frances' son Henry) who answered questions from the audience in five languages; the other involved mechanized wax figures representing scenes from Dante's *Inferno*. These attractions became fairly successful and enjoyed a long run.

The Cincinnati Bazaar was Frances' next enterprise, a much more costly and ambitious endeavor. Now called America's first mall, the Bazaar was Frances' original idea for a combination retail-residential-cultural building. It opened in 1828, after Frances culled the funds together from a variety of sources, including her husband, who had finally contacted her and had come to Cincinnati himself to bring her some money. The Bazaar included, in one building, apartments, retail shops, museums, concert halls, restaurants, a ballroom, and meeting spaces. Despite the imaginative concept and the extensive planning that went into its creation, the Bazaar failed for a number of reasons. Primarily it failed because Thomas Trollope, having gone back to England, declined to provide promised monies from Frances' inheritance from her father; as a result, Frances defaulted on her mortgage, and the building was foreclosed. Another reason was a lack of support from the citizens of Cincinnati, who felt that Frances was trying to alter American social customs which kept men and women in separated spheres of daily life; there was truth in this charge, for the Bazaar was advertised as a place for both sexes to mingle on equal terms, and for women to conduct business as men did. Frances found America's separation of the sexes and insistence on women's subordination culturally backward and frustrating, an opinion her books would comment on at length.

The closing of the Bazaar led to other troubles for Frances and her children: her furniture and other possessions were seized by debtors and they had to sleep at a neighbor's house. Destitute, without hope of aid from her husband, Frances made one last bid to support her family. She decided to write a memoir of her travels in America with the hope of getting it published.

Frances
Milton
Trollope

Thus out of desperate financial need she entered upon her new career.

In 1831, after touring more of the United States on borrowed money, the Trollopes returned to England, facing great debts. There Frances managed to find a publisher for her manuscript, a collection of notes on the people, events, and places she had encountered during her four-year stay, including her comparisons of America to England, in which England usually fared better. *Domestic Manners of the Americans*, with its pro-English viewpoint and fine quality of description and detail, became a bestseller in 1832, when its author was 53. The royalties allowed Frances to move her family back to their old farmhouse at Harrow and to provide her husband and children with the comforts they had done without for so long, such as candles and bed pillows. But Frances, realizing that eventually the royalties would cease and that Thomas, suffering from poor health, would never work again, resolved to continue writing regularly, hoping to sustain her good fortune. She made it a habit to begin her daily writing period every morning at four o'-clock, before her family awakened. With this strict regimen, which continued the rest of her career, she was able to complete full-length works in only a few months.

Her first novel, *The Refugee in America*, was published in late 1832 to positive reviews and good sales. A second novel, *The Abbess*, came out in 1833. Next Frances hoped to duplicate the success of her first travel book with one on Belgium and Germany. She made a long visit to those countries, taking note on everything from the character of the inhabitants to the landscape. The result, *Belgium and Western Germany*, was published to good reviews in 1834. However, the year 1834 was to see more tragedy than joy for Frances and her family. Despite strong sales of her books, the family's finances suffered from the depressed English economy. Thomas' health was deteriorating, and Frances' earnings were insufficient to care for him and the three children still at home, as well as to pay the educational expenses of her sons Thomas and Anthony away at college and to cover the high rents due on Julian Hill.

In spring 1834, the Trollopes' landlord foreclosed on their mortgage and seized most of their possessions in payment of their debts. Thomas and Frances fled to Belgium after a warrant was issued for Thomas' arrest; the children were sent to stay with relatives. The family managed to save only a few of their belongings by hiding them with friends. Frances and Thomas settled in Brussels, then brought the children over. However, their financial problems were soon compounded by the tragedy of death. Frances' second son Henry died in December 1834 at age 23, after a long bout with consumption. The next spring, his grieving mother visited Paris to gather material for her next travel book, *Paris and the Parisians*, published in 1835.

In October, her husband Thomas died as well, after many years of poor health; his son Anthony would later lament Thomas Trollope by noting in his *Autobiography* that his father was a good man who had suffered many misfortunes, his life "one long tragedy." Frances then returned to England, settling in Hadley. Only three months later, in February 1836, 18-year-old Emily died of consumption. Frances had nursed all three of them throughout their last months, continuing her pre-dawn writing periods both as a means of earning money and as an escape from her grief. Between Henry's death and Emily's death, Frances had completed three new books. The third of these, *Jonathan Jefferson Whitlaw*, was one of her best works, an antislavery novel set in America. It reflected Frances' belief in the need for social reform and was the first of her novels to explore the theme of emancipation, both for women and for slaves.

Later in 1836, Frances set off on her next foreign tour, to Austria and Italy, accompanied by her son Tom and daughter Cecilia. While they were still in Vienna, the trip had to be canceled when Cecilia's health began to fail. Back home in England, Frances moved to London in 1838, after the publication in 1837 of three new books: *Vienna and the Austrians*, *A Romance of Vienna*, and an anti-evangelical novel, *The Vicar of Wrexhill*. She spent the he following year in Manchester, researching her next novel, *Michael Armstrong, the Factory Boy*, which addressed the problems of child labor.

The years 1839 and 1840 saw the publication of the first two volumes of the "Widow Barnaby" series. These books garnered much attention, most of it negative, but enjoyed strong sales. They followed the life of the widowed Martha Barnaby, a strong-willed, educated woman who did not follow the conventional pattern for fictional heroines. Critics attacked the series for its portrayal of an aggressive, strong, "vulgar" woman who enjoyed being a widow, with the freedom and wealth it gave her, far more than she had being a wife. It appears that the Widow Barnaby was in many ways an autobiographical character; like Frances, the Widow enjoyed great personal autonomy, an improved financial situation, and the freedom to travel and indulge her intellect as much as she wished. In fact, most of Frances' novels could be termed antimarriage, as they centered around women suffering unhappy marriages.

Frances remained in England between 1836 and 1842, building a home in Penrith close to her daughter Cecilia and Cecilia's new husband. After the "Widow Barnaby" series, Frances completed three more novels in 1840. By this time, the woman who had begun to write only for money had attracted a strong and loyal following of readers and was enjoying a degree of fame. Frances would never gain critical acclaim from her Victorian-era male colleagues, however, despite the praise of her readers: her style was not lyrical, her characters were too "real," her themes were concerned with social realities, not philosophical ideas. Often the critics were ruthless in their condemnation of her novels and criticized the author as much as the work; the writer R.H. Horne charged in his book *The New Spirit of the Age*: "Nothing can exceed the vulgarity of Mrs. Trollope's mob of characters," who were "hideous and revolting," and referred to Frances' "constitutional coarseness." But Frances had faced too much real tragedy and hardship in her life to let the words of critics bother her; she took their attacks as proof that her books were worthy of critique and rejoiced in the admiration of her many devoted fans.

In 1842, Frances traveled to Italy with her eldest son Tom, who had left his job in Birmingham and moved back in with his mother, now in her 60s, to act as her companion. They were so taken with the beauty and culture of Italy, captured in *A Visit to Italy*, that they decided to remain in Florence indefinitely. The Trollopes became popular hosts in Florence, echoing earlier days at Julian Hill. Despite a busy social life, Frances continued to write as much as ever, completing 12 novels during her stay in Italy from 1842 to 1848. In 1847, Cecilia joined her mother and brother in an effort to cure the consumption which was beginning to destroy her health. The remedy was ineffective, and she returned home the next year; in 1849, word came from England that Cecilia was dying. Frances, as committed as ever to caring for her family, even at the age of 70, made the arduous journey back to England and nursed Cecilia through her last months.

She returned to Italy at the end of 1849. There she took up residence in Florence with Tom, his new wife ❧▸ **Theodosia Trollope**, and his father-in-law. For the next six years, Frances enjoyed fairly good health despite her advancing age and, as always, continued to publish novels on a regular basis, nine in all. In 1856, her last book, *Fashionable Life: or Paris and London*, appeared. She told her family that finally, at age 77, with 34 novels and 6 travel books behind her, she was putting down her pen for good. With both Anthony and Tom successfully publishing their own novels, she felt that it was time to slow down. Her range of activities was sharply curtailed after 1856, and she eventually slipped into senility. Frances Milton Trollope died at her home in Florence on October 6, 1863.

SOURCES:

Bigland, Eileen. *The Indomitable Mrs. Trollope*. NY: J.B. Lippincott, 1954.

Heineman, Helen. *Frances Trollope*. Boston, MA: Twayne, 1984.

———. *Mrs. Trollope: The Triumphant Feminine in the 19th Century*. Athens, OH: Ohio University Press, 1979.

SUGGESTED READING:

Neville-Sington, Pamela. *Fanny Trollope: The Life and Adventures of a Clever Woman*. NY: Viking, 1998.

Sadleir, Michael. *Trollope: A Commentary*. NY: Farrar, Straus, 1947.

Trollope, Anthony. *An Autobiography*. London: Oxford University Press, 1961.

Trollope, Frances. *Domestic Manners of the Americans*. NY: Alfred Knopf, 1949.

❧▸ **Trollope, Theodosia** (1825–1865)

English writer. Born Theodosia Garrow in 1825; died in 1865; married Thomas Adolphus Trollope (1810–1892, a novelist), in 1848; daughter-in-law of *Frances Milton Trollope (1779–1863).

Theodosia Trollope write on "Social Aspects of the Italian Revolution" for the *Athenaeum*; she also contributed to other periodicals and was the center of a salon in Florence.

COLLECTIONS:

Correspondence of Frances Milton Trollope, in the Garnett-Pertz Collection, Houghton Library, Harvard University, Cambridge, Massachusetts.

Correspondence of Frances Milton Trollope, in the Anthony Trollope Collection, University of Illinois Library, Urbana, Illinois.

Laura York, M.A. in History,
University of California,
Riverside, California

Trollope, Theodosia (1825–1865).

See Trollope, Frances Milton for sidebar.

Trot, Dame.

See Trotula.

Trotsky, Natalia Ivanovna

(1882–1962)

Russian revolutionary. Name variations: Natalia Ivanovna Sedova-Trotsky; Natalia Sedova; Natasha Trotsky. Born Natalia Ivanovna Sedova in Russia in 1882; died in 1962; became second wife of Lev Bronstein also known as Leon Trotsky (1879–1940, the Russian socialist and revolutionary), in 1903 (killed in Mexico City, August 21, 1940); children: Leon and Sergei.

For three years, Leon Trotsky was married to Marxist **Alexandra Sokolovskaya**. The couple founded the South Russia Workers' Union and distributed leaflets condemning terrible factory conditions. In 1898, the police closed in. Trotsky spent over a year in an Odessa prison and was sentenced to four years in Siberia. Because he and Alexandra married in jail in 1900, they were sent together beyond the Arctic Circle. Trotsky left his wife and risked escape with a fake passport. In late 1902, he reached London, where many socialist leaders lived. Trotsky's first duty was a fund-raising trip to émigré colonies around Europe for the newspaper *Iskra*. In Paris, he met Natalia Sedova, who became his second wife in 1903 and lifelong companion.

Trotsky's first wife and their two daughters, **Tina** and **Zina,** suffered imprisonment or death at Stalin's hands. Natalia, who had two sons, Leon and Sergei, was in Mexico City with her husband when a Soviet agent buried an ice axe in his skull on August 21, 1940. Natalia Trotsky was portrayed by **Valentina Cortese** in Joseph Losey's 1972 *The Assassination of Trotsky.*

Trotta (c. 1040s–1097).

See Trotula.

Trotter, Catharine (1679–1749).

See Cockburn, Catherine Trotter.

Trotula (c. 1040s–1097)

Professor of medicine at the University of Salerno, Italy, who wrote several works on medicine, including a text on obstetrics and gynecology that was used in Europe for at least six centuries. Name variations: *Troctula; Trotta; Dame Trot; Trotula Platearius.* Pronunciation: TROH-too-lah. *Born probably shortly before 1050, in Salerno; died in 1097; said to have been married to Giovanni Plateario (a fellow physician);*

children: said to have had two sons who became noted doctors.

Selected works: De mulierum passionibus *or* De passionibus mulierum *(On the diseases of women);* De ornatu mulierum *(On beautifying women);* De passionibus mulierum ante, in et post partum *(On the diseases of women before, during, and after birth).*

The idea that the education of women in the Middle Ages was abysmal is so universally accepted that the realization that some women not only received university instruction, but also acted as university professors, comes as a surprise. Yet the University of Salerno (on the west coast of the Italian peninsula, south of Naples), one of the oldest universities in Europe, had several women on its medical faculty in the Middle Ages. One such was Trotula, who specialized in obstetrics and gynecology. Said Trotula:

> Since . . . women are by nature weaker than men it is reasonable that sicknesses more often abound in them especially around the organs involved in the work of nature. Since these organs happen to be in a retired location, women on account of modesty and the fragility and delicacy of the state of these parts dare not reveal the difficulties of their sicknesses to a male doctor. Wherefore I, pitying their misfortunes and at the instigation of a certain matron, began to study carefully the sicknesses which most frequently trouble the female sex.

The University of Salerno, recognized as the leading institution of its kind in 12th-century Europe, was opened in the 9th century near the famous Benedictine abbey of Monte Cassino, founded by St. Benedict three centuries earlier. This order was interested in the medical arts, and it is possible that the university's medical school owed its creation, at least in part, to the need for the monastery to have trained physicians nearby. The entire area, in fact, was steeped in learning. The region had been conquered at various times by the Greeks and the Arabs, two cultures noted for their expertise in the sciences (including medicine), and, at the beginning of the 11th century, the Normans had conquered Sicily and much of the nearby peninsula, including Salerno, bringing yet another perspective and body of knowledge to the area.

Italy was a seat of learning for Europe, and, contrary to modern assumptions, women were accepted at nearly all southern European universities in this era. Though some areas of study were closed to them (they could not, for example, prepare for the priesthood), female students were given training in medicine alongside male

$\mathcal{T}$rotula

students. Salerno, aside from having women in the same classes with men, developed the Salernitan School for Women Physicians specifically for women to pursue medical studies. Many of the instructors were also female.

Indeed, women were needed as healers for several reasons. Of course, most midwives were female, and their expertise was useful to physicians attempting to treat women during pregnancy and in childbirth, but women also tended to have more experience in tending the sick, recognizing symptoms, and using herbal remedies for ailments. These abilities comprised what might be called the "folk" aspect of medicine. Surgical techniques were, in large part, learned from the Arabs. The scientific area of medieval medicine was derived mainly from Greek medical practice and required its students to know Latin and to have a grounding in alchemy and philosophy as well. One of the major tenets of this philosophy held that the human body was ruled by the balance or imbalance of the four humors: bile, black bile (or choler), spleen, and blood. These humors had qualities of heat and cold, dryness and moisture, associated with them. Health was achieved when the balance proper for each person was stuck through diet, herbal treatment, and other remedies.

The study of these humors and other "scientific" aspects of medicine was not for the uneducated. Attendance at a university was mandatory for those wishing to prescribe treatment for the ill; the punishment for the medieval equivalent of "practicing medicine without a license" was to be burned at the stake. That women were admitted to schools of medicine is evidenced not only by the names of women as faculty (the University of Bologna, for example, shows one ❧▸ **Allessandra Giliani**, the teacher of a physician known as Mondino, who was the first to teach anatomy through dissection), but also by laws defining what was and was not proper training for a physician. A French edict of 1311 forbade "unauthorized women" to practice surgery, recognizing their equal right to practice if they had been examined by a board of surgeons appointed by the city of Paris.

Some modern critics have assumed that women physicians specialized only in midwifery, but in fact women could specialize in any of a number of fields. One of Trotula's female colleagues, known as **Abella**, specialized in bodily fluids. Her two books, *On Black Bile* and *The Nature of Seminal Fluid*, show that women at Salerno were not trained exclusively in female health. ***Mercuriade of Salerno**, another of the

❧▸ **Giliani, Allessandra** (1307–1326)

Italian who pioneered anatomical dissection. Name variations: Alessandra. Born in 1307; died in 1326.

Salernitan School, wrote treatises entitled *On Crises in Pestilent Fever* and *The Cure of Wounds*, and **Rebecca Guarna** was the author of *On Fevers*, *On the Urine*, and *On the Embryo*. (The works of all these authors except Trotula's have been lost.)

Trotula's treatments reflect the best knowledge of her time period, and much of it appears strange to modern readers. Women were supposed to be composed mainly of cold and moist humors, and men of hot and dry humors (the opposition of these characteristics was assumed to draw them together, in an attempt to achieve a kind of equilibrium). A lack of balance in these humors could cause any number of ailments whose cure was to be effected by redressing the balance. Different herbs, minerals, and parts of animals (e.g., hooves or bones) also had different characteristics of moist and dry, hot and cold, and they could be used to offset an excess or lack of one of the humors. These ingredients were ingested in any number of ways: drunk in a tea, rubbed into the skin in an ointment, eaten, worn on the skin in a bag, inserted as a pessary or a suppository, or inhaled in smoke. In fact, some ailments of the uterus were to be treated by having the patient squat over a smoke made of certain herbs, having first taken the precaution to "anoint her vulva inside with cold ointments lest she be irritated."

Ingredients of some of the medications Trotula prescribed are familiar: carrots, eggs, clover, laurel, ginger, pennyroyal; some have qualities that are recognized as medications today: willow (related to the ingredient in aspirin), mint, sal ammoniac. Others have fallen into disfavor in the intervening centuries: weasel's testicles worn next to the skin (making sure that the weasel stayed alive through its surgery), eagle dung drunk in water, stag's horn mixed with ashes of a nettle, the womb of a virgin goat carried on the skin (to prevent conception).

It is likely that most of these "cures" derived from folk medicine, with infusions from the learning of the other cultures that held sway in Southern Europe. But where Trotula really left her mark was in her discussion of surgery. In speaking of childbirth, she emphasizes the importance of preventing tears to the perineum, instructing the attendant to press on the area with a folded-up linen cloth during delivery. If the perineum should tear nonetheless, Trotula provides detailed and precise instructions as to how to stitch up the area. This is the first written example of a perineorrhaphy in medical literature, and the technique described is not much different from modern practice.

I could find no one [in Salerno] practiced in medical arts but a certain very learned noblewoman.

—Rudolfus Malacorona

Given her specialty in obstetrics and gynecology, many of Trotula's treatments have to do with childbirth. Knowing that this was an extremely risky time for a woman, she writes, "In the first place and above all things when there is difficulty in childbirth one must have recourse to God. Descending then to lower means," and she briskly proceeds with more practical advice. She describes complications of labor and delivery, with instructions as to what intervention should be preformed, while admitting that in some cases, there is no treatment. A breech delivery is handled in much the same way as today; the midwife is to lubricate her "small and gentle hand" and attempt to turn the fetus. She also supplies several means of preventing conception, being careful to emphasize that they are to be used only by women who have fear of death in case of childbirth. There are no prescriptions for abortion in the text. Cures of light and heavy menstrual flow, choice of a wet-nurse, and ulcers of the womb are topics specific to women that she covered. She dealt as well with problems of conception, recognizing that it is often a problem with the man's reproductive system that causes difficulties.

Other of her writings concern more general health care (prevention of lice, sweetening of the breath, curing toothache), and recipes for cosmetics are included. Face powder, for example, is based upon a lead compound and is intended to be left on the skin for eight days. There are treatments for wrinkles, excessive paleness, and freckles.

Trotula's fame was such that when she died in 1097, her funeral train was said to have extended more than three kilometers. Her most important text, *On the diseases of women*, enjoyed great success in Europe and was translated into Irish, French, German, Old and Middle English, Flemish, and Catalan. An English version of 1545 enjoyed great popularity. Her name became a byword for a wise woman, especially a healer, and the "Dame Trot" encountered in several English nursery rhymes probably derives from Trotula.

It is perhaps due to the great success of the text and the obvious amount of learning evidenced in it that some scholars have refused to believe that it was written by a woman. Despite her declaration that she took up the practice of gynecology and obstetrics because women "dare not reveal the difficulties of their sicknesses to a male doctor," despite her feminine name, and despite the clear evidence of women doctors in southern Europe in her day, some scholars doubt the existence of a female physician and medical professor named Trotula, declaring that her books were written by a man (postulated to be named Trottus or Troctus). Ignoring the fact that the medical advice presented in the books was state of the art for the 11th century, and contradicting his praise of the surgical techniques described, Isaac Harvey Flack said in his *Eternal Eve* that the "*Trotula* were not very good books. . . . They covered all aspects of woman's life, ranging in rather Peeping Tom fashion from patchouli to parturition, and that they should have been wished on to a non-existent woman professor is not surprising." Other scholars, while not so condescending in tone, have also expressed doubts that a woman could have produced the works. James V. Ricci speculated in his *The Genealogy of Gynecology* that "Trotula" was probably a freedman of the Empress Julia, yet his text also lists five other Salernitan women physicians without mentioning any doubts as to their existence.

Elizabeth Mason-Hohl, who translated *De passionibus mulierum* in 1940, always argued for the case of her subject's actual existence. More recently, the debate seems to have cooled, and Trotula can once again take her place as an important figure in the history of Western medicine.

SOURCES:

Amt, Emilie, ed. *Women's Lives in Medieval Europe: A Sourcebook*. NY: Routledge, 1993.

Bertini, Ferruccio. "Trotula, il medico," in *Medioevo al femminile*. Rome: Laterza, 1989.

Flack, Isaac Harvey. *Eternal Eve*. NY: Doubleday, 1951.

Mason-Hohl, Elizabeth. "Trotula: 11th-Century Gynecologist," in *Medical Woman's Journal*. Vol. 47. December 1940, pp. 349–356.

Ricci, James V. *The Genealogy of Gynecology*. London: Blakiston, 1943.

Walsh, James Joseph. *Medieval Medicine*. London: A.&C. Black, 1920.

SUGGESTED READING:

Rowland, B. *A Medieval Woman's Guide to Health*. Kent, OH: Kent State Press, 1981.

Tuttle, E.F. "The *Trotula* and Old Dame Trot," in *Bulletin of the History of Medicine*. Vol. 50, 1976, pp. 62–65.

Tracy Barrett,
Senior Lecturer in Italian,
Vanderbilt University,
Nashville, Tennessee

Trotzig, Birgitta (1929—)

Swedish novelist and literary critic. Born Birgitta Kjellén in 1929 in Göteborg, Sweden; married Ulf Trotzig (an artist); children.

Selected writings: Ur de älskandes liv *(From the Lives of the Lovers, 1951);* Bilder *(Images, 1954);* De utsatta *(The Exposed, 1957);* En berättelse från kusten *(A Tale from the Coast, 1961);* Levande och döda *(The Living and the Dead, 1964);* Sveket *(The Betrayal, 1966);* Ordgränser *(Word Limits, 1968);* Sjukdomen *(The Sickness, 1972);* I kejsarens tid *(In the Time of the Emperor, 1975);* Berättelser *(Tales, 1977);* Jaget och världen *(The Ego and the World, 1977)* Dykungens dotter *(The Marsh King's Daughter, 1984).*

Born Birgitta Kjellén in Göteborg, Sweden, in 1929, Birgitta Trotzig studied literature and art history, and has worked as an art critic. She made her debut as a novelist at an early age, publishing *Ur de älskandes liv* (From the Lives of the Lovers) in 1951, when she was only 22. This first work of fiction was a collection of impressionistic sketches relating the loneliness of young girls. Although the book made clear Trotzig's unique sense of style, it in no way presaged the harsh depth of her later work.

Her next novel was *Bilder* (Images), published in 1954. Three years later, Trotzig's *De utsatta* (The Exposed) firmly established her as a novelist of exceptional ability. *Bilder* and *De utsatta*, along with *En berättelse från kusten* (A Tale from the Coast, 1961), are set during Scandinavia's Middle Ages. The first two of these novels take place in the southern Swedish province of Skåne, against a desolate backdrop of leaden skies and ceaseless salty winds from the sea. In *De utsatta*, a country pastor manages to hold onto his faith in God despite great adversity, including a period of confinement in an insane asylum where he is treated like an animal. This emerges as one of the central themes of Trotzig's fiction: the abiding presence of God, even in the face of utter despair.

For about 15 years, between 1954 and 1969, Trotzig lived with her husband, artist Ulf Trotzig, and their children in Paris. It was during this period that she converted from her childhood Protestantism to Catholicism, a turning point in view of her growing preoccupation with the spiritual well-being of characters in her later writing. Many literary critics classify Trotzig as a "Roman Catholic author" despite the fact that the world she creates within her fiction is one largely devoid of grace. Among the most obvious influences upon her work are Russian novelist Fyodor Dostoevsky and French novelist François Mauriac.

In 1964, Trotzig published *Levande och döda* (The Living and the Dead), a collection of three lengthy stories that explore the themes of love and life without love. She returned to the desolation of the southern Swedish landscape for her novels *Sveket* (The Betrayal, 1966) and *Sjukdomen* (The Sickness, 1972), although these are set in contemporary or near-contemporary times. The sickness to which the title of the latter novel refers is not just the mental retardation of its protagonist but also the sickness of life in a violent and selfish world.

In 1968's *Ordgränser* (Word Limits), a collection of essays, Trotzig questions the adequacy of language to adequately convey the pain and suffering so many experience in life. Another collection of essays, *Jaget och världen* (The Ego and the World, 1977), in which she relates the experiences in her earlier life that inspired much of her fiction, is essential reading for anyone seeking to fully understand Trotzig's writing.

SOURCES:

Buck, Claire, ed. *The Bloomsbury Guide to Women's Literature.* NY: Prentice Hall, 1992.

Columbia Dictionary of Modern European Literature. 2nd ed. NY: Columbia University Press, 1980.

Don Amerman,
freelance writer,
Saylorsburg, Pennsylvania

Troubetzkoy, Amélie (1863–1945).

See Rives, Amélie.

Troup, Augusta Lewis (c. 1848–1920)

American labor union executive. Name variations: Augusta Lewis. Born around 1848 in New York City; died on September 14, 1920, in New Haven, Connecticut; daughter of Charles Lewis and Elizabeth (Rowe) Lewis; educated by private tutors through high school level; attended Brooklyn Heights Seminary; graduated with honors from the convent school of the Sacred Heart in Manhattanville; married Alexander Troup (a newspaper publisher), on June 12, 1874 (died 1908); children: daughters Marie Grace, Augusta Lewis (died in infancy), Jessie (died in infancy), George Bernardine, and Elsie; sons Alexander and Philip.

Worked as a reporter for New York City newspapers; became an apprentice typesetter at the Era; *joined typesetting staff at the* World; *cofounded the New York Working Women's Association (1868); became founder and president, Women's Typographical Union No. 1, New York (1868); was elected corresponding secretary of the International Typographical*

*Union (1870), making her the first woman to be elect-
ed to an executive position in a national labor union.*

Born in New York City around 1848, Augusta Lewis Troup was the daughter of Charles
Lewis, an Englishman who had immigrated to
New York, and **Elizabeth Rowe Lewis**, a native
of New York. Both of her parents died while she
was still an infant, and Augusta, known affectionately as "Gussie," grew up in the home of
Brooklyn Heights broker and merchant Isaac
Baldwin Gager. Considered frail, she was educated at home by private tutors. She also lived
for a time in the home of one of her teachers in
Cold Spring, New York. Returning to the city,
she attended classes at the Brooklyn Heights
Seminary and later studied French, philosophy,
and the classics at the convent school of the Sacred Heart in Manhattanville, from which she
graduated with honors.

When the depression of 1866–67 forced her
to find a way to support herself, Troup, who as a
student had shown a gift for writing, took a job
as a reporter for the New York *Sun*. She also
earned additional money by selling articles to a
number of magazines, including the French-language *Courier des Etats-Unis*. In time, Troup was
drawn to the trade of typesetting, and after an apprenticeship at the *Era* joined the staff of the New
York *World*. She quickly became expert in her
newfound trade, although she continued to work
as a reporter as well. (In the latter role, she interviewed Charles Dickens when he visited New
York.) Troup soon became recognized as a leader
among the nonunionized women typesetters with
whom she worked. Late in 1867, the International Typographical Union (ITU) struck at the
World, but the women typesetters, none of whom
were members of the union, continued to work.
However, most of these women were promptly
sacked after the strike ended in the summer of
1868. To demonstrate her solidarity with the
women typesetters, Troup quit her job and took
what work she could find from printing companies which treated women workers equitably.

Convinced that women typesetters needed
to organize in order to protect their interests,
Troup joined with suffragists *Susan B. Anthony and *Elizabeth Cady Stanton, who published
the suffrage paper *The Revolution*, in forming
the New York Working Women's Association.
Proposing to "act for its members in the same
manner as the associations of workingmen now
regulate the wages, etc., of those belonging to
them," the organization was formally launched
on September 17, 1868, in the offices of *The
Revolution*. The founders of the association,
however, soon found themselves at odds. Stanton wanted the association to throw its support
behind the cause of women's suffrage, while
Troup feared that the very existence of the group
might be jeopardized if women new to organization had to shoulder this additional burden.
While Anthony sought the widest possible range
of employment opportunities for women, Troup
felt association members had to support union
loyalty at all costs, even when it meant turning
down a job. The underlying disagreement between the association's founders broke into the
open in 1869 when typesetters in New York
printing shops went on strike. Troup fought to
keep association members from scabbing, but
Anthony exhorted employers to replace striking
male typesetters with women. So acrimonious
was the discord between the two that Troup succeeded in blocking the seating of Anthony as a
delegate to the National Labor Union convention in Philadelphia in August 1869.

In the month after the formation of the Working Women's Association, Troup, with the support
of the ITU's New York Local 6, founded and became president of Women's Typographical Union
No. 1. Particularly supportive of the need for a
union for female typesetters was Alexander
Troup, corresponding secretary of ITU Local 6 as
well as the union's national secretary-treasurer,
who would later become her husband. In June
1869, Troup, accompanied by **Eva Howard**, who
served as treasurer of the women's local, appeared
before the national convention of the ITU to ask
for a charter for their union, a request that was
granted. However, the women's union never really
prospered, for a variety of reasons. Its members
steadfastly refused to serve as scabs for striking
male ITU members, and nonunion shops would
not hire union members. Also, because employers
refused to pay women wages equal to those
earned by their male counterparts, the presence of
these women typesetters working for lower pay
presented a significant threat to union scale. Given
the growing hostility of ITU members toward the
women typesetters, it is somewhat surprising that
the national convention of the union elected
Troup its corresponding secretary in 1870. During
her one-year term, she managed to bring many
nonunion women typesetters into the union.
About ten years after its formation, the Women's
Typographical Union No. 1 was disbanded, and
the ITU decided that it would no longer charter
women's unions. Before long, however, it began
admitting women as fully equal members.

Augusta married Alexander Troup, who had
abandoned labor activism to become publisher

of the *Union*, a labor-friendly newspaper in New Haven, Connecticut, on June 12, 1874, in Cold Spring, New York. Troup joined her husband in New Haven, where the couple had seven children, including two who died as infants. Alexander eventually became active in politics, serving as federal tax collector for Connecticut and Rhode Island, a member of the state legislature, and a member of Democratic National Committee. Troup contributed articles to the *Union* for the rest of her life, and was a strong advocate of women's suffrage. She was also active in local charities, in particular with programs to benefit New Haven's Italian community.

Suffering from heart valve disease, Troup died in New Haven on September 14, 1920. She was buried in the city's Evergreen Cemetery. Several years after her death, New Haven city officials built and named in her honor the Augusta Lewis Troup Junior High School.

SOURCES:

James, Edward T., ed. *Notable American Women, 1607–1950.* Cambridge, MA: The Belknap Press of Harvard University, 1971.

Read, Phyllis J., and Bernard L. Witlieb. *The Book of Women's Firsts.* NY: Random House, 1992.

Don Amerman,
freelance writer,
Saylorsburg, Pennsylvania

Troyanos, Tatiana (1938–1993)

American mezzo-soprano. Born on September 12, 1938, in New York; died of cancer on August 21, 1993, in New York City; daughter of Nickolas Troyanos and Hildagod (Langera) Troyanos; studied with Hans Heinz and at the Juilliard School of Music.

Debuted at New York City Opera (1963); was a member of the Hamburg State Opera (1965–75); debuted at Covent Garden (1969), Paris Opéra (1971), and Metropolitan Opera debut (1976).

Born in New York in 1938 and raised in Forest Hills, opera singer Tatiana Troyanos always identified with her father's Greek heritage and throughout her life described herself as Greek-American. Her early musical training was on the piano, although she also sang in school and in church choirs. As a teenager, she became enthralled with the recording of *Maria Callas (to whom she would later be compared) and began to attend opera performances at the Metropolitan as a standee. After deciding to study singing, Troyanos worked as a secretary at Random House while attending Juilliard, but left the prestigious music school when she was unable to study with the teacher of her choice, Hans

Heinz. She subsequently studied privately with Heinz for many years.

Troyanos did not have an easy time getting her career off the ground. She turned down small roles at the Met but fought hard for parts she wanted. When she was deemed too glamorous for a role as a nun in *The Sound of Music*, she returned in a disheveled state to audition a second time and landed the part. She got her first break in 1963, when she signed with the New York City Opera, debuting that year as Hippolyta in Benjamin Britten's *Midsummer Night's Dream* and also appearing as Jocasta in Stravinsky's *Oedipus Rex*. In 1965, Troyanos joined the Hamburg State Opera, where she sang a number of popular mezzo-soprano roles. She made her first major European debut in 1966, at Aix-en-Provence, as the Composer in Strauss's *Ariadne auf Naxos*. In 1969, she debuted at Covent Garden, singing Octavian in *Rosenkavalier*, a role she learned in a week's notice. It became a standard of her repertoire as did other "trouser roles," such as Cherubino in *Le Nozze di Figaro* and Romeo in Bellini's *I Capuletti e I Montecchi*.

Troyanos made her debut with New York's Metropolitan Opera in 1976, once again as Octavian, and subsequently became a regular on their roster. Among her many roles there were the Countess Geschwitz in Berg's *Lulu*, Sesto in Mozart's *Clemmenza di Tito*, Charlotte in *Werther*, and Adalgisa in *Norma*. Despite her preference for emotional and doomed heroines, Troyanos also became a noted Handel stylist and one of very few singers to take on the roles of both Cleopatra and Caesar in *Giulio Cesare*. She also had a flair for comedy and was said to be delightful as Dorabella in *Cosi fan tutte*. Just a year before she died from cancer at age 54, Troyanos performed at the Met, premiering the role of Queen Isabella in Philip Glass's new work, *Voyage*.

SOURCES:

Kozinn, Allan. "Obituary," in *The Day* [New London, CT]. August 23, 1993.

"Milestones," in *Time.* September 6, 1993.

Trubnikova, Mariia (1835–1897)

Leading 19th-century Russian philanthropist and feminist. Pronunciation: Troob-nih-KO-vah. Name variations: Maria Trubnikova; Marya Trubnikova. Born Mariia Vasil'evna Ivasheva on January 6, 1835, in Chita, eastern Siberia; died on April 28, 1897, in Tambov, Russia; daughter of V.V. Ivashev (an exiled Decembrist) and Camille LeDantieux; educated at home until age 16; married K.V. Trubnikov, in 1854;

children: seven, including daughter O.K. Bulanova-Trubnikova, and three who died in infancy.

Was active in Sunday School movement (1859–62); served as first chair of St. Petersburg's Society to Provide Cheap Lodgings for women (1861); co-founded women's Publishing Workshop (1863); was active in the establishment of the Vladimir Courses (1870) and Bestuzhev Courses (1878) for women.

During the winter of 1868–69, Mariia Trubnikova went out of her way to encounter Count Dmitrii Tolstoy at social gatherings in St. Petersburg. They made an odd pair—the reactionary, chauvinistic Minister of Education talking intimately with the much younger and progressive Russian feminist. Trubnikova, who for the past decade had been involved in various philanthropic activities, wanted to convince Tolstoy that women should be admitted to Russian universities. She hoped to impress upon him through her refined manner, proper dress and aristocratic background that women, especially educated ones such as herself, were not a threat to the social and male order of things and could even contribute to Russia's modernization. In an earlier visit to his office, however, she had sensed that he was more interested in her as a woman than in the ideas she was trying to advance. If a little flirting at balls and concerts would help the cause, then she was willing to play the role. This, plus her patience and tact, must have had the desired effect. In 1870, Tolstoy reluctantly agreed that professors could offer off-campus courses to prepare women for university-level work. Eight years later, women finally were given an opportunity to acquire a true higher education. This was probably the most important gain Russian women made in the 19th century.

In any place and under any circumstances, you need only two or three people of good will to accomplish something useful.

—Mariia Trubnikova

Mariia Trubnikova was born in the eastern Siberian city of Chita on January 6, 1835 (o.s.). Her father Vasilii Ivashev was of aristocratic origin and had been exiled to Siberia for his role in the Decembrist Revolt of 1825. Like many Decembrists, he was followed into exile by his wife, a Frenchwoman named **Camille LeDantieux**, who died during childbirth in 1839. A year later, after Ivashev himself had died of "grief and remorse," Mariia and her younger sister **Vera Ivasheva** moved to Samara where they were brought up by a wealthy aunt, Princess **Ekaterina Khovanskaia**. The home education Mariia received was much better than that normally accorded to aristocratic Russian women, and it was supplemented by travel and tutoring in Western Europe. By the time of her marriage in 1854 at age 19, she was attracted, according to her daughter **O.K. Bulanova-Trubnikova**, to a "vague evolutionary socialism." Her fiancé Konstantin Trubnikov fed this inclination and won her hand by reading passages to her from the forbidden works of Alexander Herzen. For a while she helped her husband edit his liberal newspaper *Birzhevye vedomosti* (The Stock Exchange News), and their St. Petersburg apartment soon became a meeting place for both men and women seeking change in Russian society. At the same time, she developed contacts with feminist groups in Western Europe and the United States as well as starting to write articles for various European journals.

The fact that in less than ten years she gave birth to seven children—only four of whom lived past infancy—took a physical toll on Trubnikova and may have stimulated her feminist thinking. Confined to her home, she spent much of the time reading and taking lessons in music and drawing. As **Ariadna Tyrkova** has surmised:

> The awareness of the possibilities of her own mind, the awareness that many men, less talented than her and less devoted to ideas, could so easily apply their ideas while she, as a woman, condemned to social inactivity, could not realize any of her dreams, gave a special passion to her femininity.

Among those attracted the Trubnikovs' apartment were *Nadezhda Stasova and Anna Filosofova. Led by Mariia, these three aristocratic women, who came to be known as the Triumvirate, sought ways of helping less fortunate women in the Russian capital. Out of their discussions emerged the Society to Provide Cheap Lodgings and Other Assistance to the Needy Population of St. Petersburg. This philanthropic enterprise, which Trubnikova chaired in 1861, bought a large house with a laundry and a communal kitchen. For 20 years, it offered clean accommodations at reasonable prices to impoverished middle-class women. As Trubnikova's daughter noted, it was "the only kind of social activity possible at that time." Trubnikova realized that, to be independent, women needed employment at a time when most respectable professions were closed to them. She was the driving force behind the Society for Women's Work which was to have provided both an employment exchange and a training center for women. Unfortunately, differences of opinion with more radical women never allowed this ambitious scheme to get off the ground. Trubnikova was more successful when she joined with Stasova to form a Publishing Workshop in 1863. This co-operative, which lasted until 1879, employed several dozen women as writers, translators, typesetters and binders.

These philanthropic activities and the government obstructionism which they encountered convinced the Triumvirate that lasting change could be achieved only if women were better educated. A petition was drawn up in Trubnikova's apartment, which was ultimately signed by 400 women, calling for the establishment of a women's university or at least the opening of courses at Russian universities to women. While Trubnikova was unable to convince the Minister of Education to go this far, Tolstoy did approve the offering of preparatory courses for women (the Vladimir Courses) in 1870 and then university-level instruction (the Bestuzhev Courses) in 1878. Trubnikova's moderation, her willingness to compromise, and her limited feminist agenda were all instrumental in achieving these advances.

These gains came at a high personal price. Trubnikova's husband resented her outside interests and perhaps her growing erudition. He became "a perfect despot at home" and at the same time managed to squander her considerable fortune through poor investments. Domestic troubles caused Trubnikova to have a nervous breakdown and in 1869 led to a separation from her husband. Several of her daughters, whose early education she had supervised and who would have benefited from the concessions she had won for all Russian women, felt that her objectives were too modest and joined the revolutionary movement over her protest. She nevertheless allowed her house to be used for illegal meetings and as a storage place for revolutionary literature. She also used her contacts in the government to work for the release of two of them after their arrests in 1881. In that same year Trubnikova's deteriorating mental health forced her to withdraw from further feminist activity. She died in a mental institution in Tambov at the age of 62 in 1897.

SOURCES:

Engel, Barbara Alpern. *Mothers and Daughters: Women of the Intelligentsia in Nineteenth-Century Russia.* Cambridge: Cambridge University Press, 1983.

Goldberg (Ruthchild), Rochelle Lois. "The Russian Women's Movement, 1859–1917," unpublished Ph.D. dissertation, University of Rochester, 1976.

Stites, Richard. *The Women's Liberation Movement in Russia: Feminism, Nihilism, and Bolshevism, 1860–1930.* Princeton, NJ: Princeton University Press, 1977.

SUGGESTED READING:

Bulanova-Trubnikova, O.K. *Tri pokoleniia* (Three Generations). Moscow, 1928.

R.C. Elwood,
Professor of History,
Carleton University,
Ottawa, Canada

Truganini (1812–1876)

Tasmanian Aborigine who lived through the white takeover of her homeland and the virtual extermination of her people. Name variations: Truccanini or Traucanini; also known as Trugernanner; "Lalla Rookh" or "Lallah Rookh." Born in 1812 (some sources cite 1803) at Recherche Bay, Tasmania; died on May 8, 1876, in Hobart, Tasmania; daughter of Mangerner (an Aboriginal elder); mother's name unknown; married Woorraddy (a member of the Nuenonne tribe), in July 1829.

Assisted George Augustus Robinson in relocating Tasmania's remaining Aborigines to a nearby island (1830–35); began to urge her fellow Aborigines to remain in Tasmania (1836); relocated to an abandoned

Australian postage stamp issued in honor of Truganini in 1975.

settlement at Oyster Cove on Tasmania (1847); became last of that group to survive and one of the last full-blooded Tasmanian Aborigines.

Truganini was born at Recherche Bay in Tasmania, an island off the tip of southeast Australia, in 1812. Nine years before her birth, the government of Great Britain had begun shipping convicts to Tasmania (then called Van Diemen's Land), which was established as a vast convict settlement. Land was cleared and farms were set up, and as more and more convicts—and the administrators and soldiers who controlled them, as well as a few free settlers—were imported, more and more land was occupied. For over 30,000 years, Tasmania had been the home of Aborigines; by the early 1800s, it has been estimated, they numbered between 4,000 and 20,000 (the lower number is probably closer to the mark). Bloody battles for land and life were fought between the Aborigines and the Europeans, the latter of whom had the advantage of firearms. Most of the Europeans considered Aborigines subhuman, a species distinct from and much lower than themselves; as well, many of the convicts were callous and vicious men, criminals further hardened by terrible experiences during their enforced sea voyages and their lives in the settlements. Inevitably, some of them escaped the settlements. Both the convicts and the prison troops acted with horrific brutality against the Aborigines of Tasmania. (Shooting "parties" and trapping are some of the mildest acts recorded.) In turn, Aborigines staged raids and murdered whites when they could.

This, then, was the world in which Truganini, the daughter of Mangerner, a Lyluequonny man and an elder of the southeast Aboriginal tribe, grew up. She spent her childhood near the front lines of the ongoing battles between her people and the white settlers, in which hundreds of lives were claimed on both sides. These battles began growing worse in the early 1820s, when non-convict Britons began moving to Tasmania and establishing their own settlements, frequently claiming what the Aborigines considered valuable hunting grounds. In late 1828, martial law was declared, and whites were permitted to kill on sight all Aborigines they saw near "settled" land. By the time Truganini and her father met secular missionary George Augustus Robinson in March 1829, much of her family had been decimated. Her mother had been slain by whalers, her uncle had been shot by a soldier, and her sister **Moorinna** had been kidnapped and shot by sealers. Her husband-to-be, Paraweena, was murdered by men who had come to the area to gather timber.

Truganini herself, described as a vibrant and attractive girl, had been raped by the timber gatherers. She had survived, however, and in July 1829, in a ceremony at the Bruny Island mission station, Truganini married Woorraddy, a member of the Nuenonne tribe from Bruny Island.

Robinson, a builder and untrained preacher, had been appointed by colonial authorities to mount a "friendly mission" to find the estimated 300 or so Aborigines believed still to be living in the Tasmanian hinterlands. Less than a year after Truganini married, so few Aborigines were left, and so many settlers had arrived (there would be some 40,000 by 1835), that the "black war" was over, and Aborigines were considered merely an irritant, less dangerous than the packs of wild dogs that roamed the streets of Tasmania's capital, Hobart Town. Robinson had been charged with the responsibility of relocating the Aborigines to a nearby island before they were all exterminated by the advancing British settlers. (This was not contrition or charity: they were generally expected to die out quietly there.) After meeting Truganini and her father, Robinson convinced them that he was their friend and would protect them. He further promised that if they came with him he would see that they were supplied with blankets, food, and shelter. Their customs would be respected, the missionary pledged. Truganini could see no way for her people to survive unless they accepted Robinson's offer.

Beginning in 1830, Truganini and her husband Woorraddy joined Robinson in his efforts to locate Tasmania's remaining Aboriginal people. The white missionary depended on Truganini and her family and friends to show him the way through the bush and to protect him. (In one instance, by 19th-century whites often blithely compared to the famous incident between *Poca-hontas* and John Smith, she is said to have saved his life by helping him float across a swift river on a log when he came under attack.) However, her biggest role was to convince other Aborigines that Robinson's relocation plan was their only hope for continued survival. Her efforts paid off, for by 1835 nearly all of Tasmania's Aborigines—that is, some 100 people—had been moved to nearby Flinders Island, a 40-mile island between Tasmania and Australia, where a settlement had been set up for them at Wybalenna.

In the settlement on Flinders Island, Robinson hoped to teach European customs and Christianity to the Aborigines. He and his "charges," however, had sharply contrasting perceptions of what the new settlement represented. The Aborigines felt that it was just a temporary home, where they would housed, fed, and protected until they could return to their ancestral homelands on Tasmania. Robinson and the colonial authorities saw the settlement as a permanent home for the Aborigines, and he separated children from parents and instituted a strict daily regimen of cleanliness inspections, Bible reading and the singing of hymns. Little fresh water was available at the settlement, and the diet provided to the Aborigines led to malnutrition.

A visit she made to Flinders Island in November 1835 proved to be an unsettling revelation for Truganini, for it became clear that she was expected to renounce her native culture and take on the mantle of a domestic servant. Robinson named her "Lalla Rookh," after the eponymous daughter of the emperor in the famous poem by Thomas Moore. The settlement had become, in effect, a virtual prison for the relocated Aborigines. Many fell ill and died. Truganini determined that Robinson's relocation plan was not a viable way to ensure the continued survival of her people. In March 1836, when she returned to Tasmania in the company of a handful of other "relocated" Aborigines to continue her quest for those who remained hidden, she began urging the few she found to stay where they were. She feared that if they followed the others who already had gone to Flinders Island, all of her people would soon be dead. Truganini returned to Flinders in July 1837 to find that even more Aborigines had died. Few babies were being born, and those that were usually died in infancy. She warned Robinson that all would probably be dead before the houses that were being built for them were ready for occupancy.

After Robinson was named protector of the Aborigines in Australia's Port Phillip district in 1839, Truganini and Wooraddy, along with 14 other Aborigines from Flinders, accompanied him to his new posting near Melbourne. A couple of years later, she escaped from the Port Phillip mission in the company of two Aboriginal men and two Aboriginal women. Near Western Port, the five went on a rampage, terrorizing a group of shepherds and shooting two whalers. (It has been speculated that one of the men shot may have been part of the group that earlier had killed Truganini's sister Moorinna.) For their crimes, the two men were hanged, and the three women were shipped back to Flinders Island. Accompanying them, Wooraddy died during the journey. Truganini remained on Flinders Island until October 1847, when the Aboriginal settlement, then consisting of about 46 people, was relocated to Oyster Bay, some 20 miles south of Hobart in Tasmania.

Although conditions at Oyster Bay were even more deplorable than those on Flinders Island, Truganini seemed to prosper now that she was back in her traditional homeland. She passed her days in such traditional pursuits as hunting in the bush, collecting shells, and revisiting childhood haunts. Few of the other Aborigines flourished, however, and by 1869 she was one of only three in the country known to remain alive. (One of those three, William Lanney, mockingly called "King Billy" in recognition of his status as the last full-blooded Aboriginal man, died that March. After his death, most of his body parts were removed and kept by surgeons and others as souvenirs.) In 1874, Oyster Bay was flooded, and Truganini was removed to the care of a white family—her "guardians"—in Hobart Town. She became a well-known figure there, wearing a bright red cap, her personal adaptation of the red gum tips or ochre her tribal group traditionally wore in their hair. In 1876, at age 64, Truganini died and was buried on the grounds of the women's prison in Hobart, denied her wish to be buried "behind the mountains." She was then believed to have been the last full-blooded Tasmanian Aborigine, although that claim has since been disputed. Her skeleton was exhumed two years later by scientists, with permission from the government on condition that it be kept from the public and seen only by "scientific men for scientific purposes." Ten years later her bones were displayed in Melbourne at the Centenary Exhibition. By 1904, they had been strung together in a full skeleton and placed on display at a Hobart museum, where they were for years the most visited exhibit. Public squeamishness caused the removal of the skeleton to a basement in 1947. As the years passed, Truganini became a symbol of the destruction of the Aborigines, interpreted in various ways and held up as a hero or a traitor by whites and Aborigines. Books and plays were written about her and her era, as well as poems and, in the later years of the 20th century, at least one film and a song by a hugely popular Australian band. An 1889 book, *Cassell's Picturesque Australia*, after noting her rescue of Robinson, stated: "She died at the age of sixty-five, and to the last was faithful to the whites. In every sense she was a heroine." In later years, she was at times vilified (often by whites) as a sort of *Malinche, delivering her people over to their murderers. Despite the steps begun by the Australian government in the late years of the 20th century to make some sort of reparation to all Aborigines, their treatment at the hands of whites, both in the early history of the colony and later, remains a controversial and still raw subject. Today, life expectancy of Aborigines is 20 years less than that of other Australians. In 1976, 100 years after her death, Truganini's remains were cremated, and Tasmanian Aborigines scattered the ashes on the waters of her tribal land.

SOURCES:

Bonwick, James. *The Last of the Tasmanians: Or the Black War of Van Diemen's Land* (originally published 1870). Adelaide, Australia: Australiana Facsimile Editions, 1969.

Radi, Heather, ed. *200 Australian Women: A Redress Anthology.* NSW, Australia: Women's Redress Press, 1988.

Turnbull, Clive. *Black War: The Extermination of the Tasmanian Aborigines.* Cheshire, UK: Lansdowne, 1965.

Wilde, William H., Joy Hooten, and Barry Andrews. *The Oxford Companion to Australian Literature.* Melbourne, Australia: Oxford, 1985.

Don Amerman,
freelance writer,
Saylorsburg, Pennsylvania

Truitt, Anne (1921—)

American sculptor, painter, and writer. Born Anne Dean on March 16, 1921, in Baltimore, Maryland; daughter of Duncan Witt Dean and Louisa Folsom (Williams) Dean; Bryn Mawr College, B.A., 1943; studied art at Institute of Contemporary Art, 1948–50, and with Alexander Giampetro, Kenneth Noland, and Octavo Medillin; married James McConnell Truitt (a journalist), on September 19, 1947; children: Alexandra; Mary; Samuel.

Selected works: (sculptures) Autumn Dryad *and* Spring Snow; *(published journals)* Daybook *(1982) and* Turn *(1986).*

A sculptor and painter of the minimalist school, Anne Truitt is perhaps better known within the art community than by the public at large. Despite her relatively low profile with the public, she has been a potent force in American art through several decades, helping to shape the modern era of abstract art. Art critic Tom Weisser, reviewing one of Truitt's shows for *ARTnews*, wrote that her trademark—"mostly monochromatic, rectangular pillars of color"—captures the attention of the viewer "with such esthetic economy that you edge closer in hopes of figuring out how and why this might be." Truitt's work has been shown at the Baltimore Museum of Art and New York City's Whitney Museum of American Art, among others.

She was born Anne Dean in 1921, the daughter of Duncan Witt Dean and **Louisa Williams Dean**, members of an affluent family in Baltimore, Maryland. After attending Baltimore schools, she enrolled at Bryn Mawr College in suburban Philadelphia. Graduating from Bryn Mawr in 1943 with a degree in psychology, Truitt moved to Boston, where she was involved for a time with psychological research at Massachusetts General Hospital. In 1945, she took an evening class in sculpture, which ignited what was to be a lifelong love of the arts.

On September 16, 1947, she married James McConnell Truitt, a journalist whose job frequently took him out of the country. For the next couple of decades, she worked on her art—both sculpture and painting—while the family shuttled around the United States and Japan. At the same time, she raised the couple's three children, Alexandra, Mary, and Samuel. During the course of her family's travels, Truitt managed to carve out enough time to study with teachers Alexander Giampetro and Kenneth Noland of the Institute of Contemporary Art in Washington, D.C., and Octavo Medillin at the Dallas Museum School.

Truitt's sculpture and paintings masquerading as sculpture were in the advance guard of the literalist-minimalist art movement that took a firm hold in the 1960s. Proponents of the movement rejected the use of all illusion, preferring to work instead with real forms and space. Typical of this movement were Andy Warhol's Brillo boxes and Jasper Johns' full-canvas painting of a flag. Some of the more notable Truitt creations from this literalist period were her painted boxes. The artist's boxes were neither representations nor abstractions of something else but instead were the thing itself. Truitt's boxes were among the first artworks from this period to be described by critics as "presences," objects that have the character of real entities. Another example of Truitt's art from this period is the sculpture *Autumn Dryad*. The sculpture at first glance appears to be little more than a wooden column to which multiple coats of paint have been applied. Art critic Peter Plagens, assessing the piece in a *Newsweek* article, observed that Truitt's unrelenting applications of paint to the column had the effect of making the wood disappear until "the sculpture looks like it's solid color, like butter is yellow all the way through." Although her painted wooden columns received at best a lukewarm reception when first shown, Plagens, for one, believes the work will stand the test of time: Truitt "doesn't whittle down material excess and then call a halt just before the sculpture disappears. She builds *up* from an emotion until she's made her poetic point, and then lets her objects stand there and sing. For those who choose to listen, it's more than enough."

Although Truitt's work is clearly linked with the minimalist school, she is more precisely a proponent of the Washington, D.C., art movement known as "Color Field." Writing in *Art in America* in 1991, Brooks Adams observed that Truitt's art suggests "many exhilarating alternatives to the macho canon of Minimalism." He further suggested that it belittles the full body of her work to consign Truitt to a single category of art. "What to do, for instance," Adams wrote, "with the fact that Truitt lived and worked from 1964 to '67 with her journalist husband in Japan (where she made aluminum pieces that have mostly been destroyed), or with the fact that she herself is a distinguished writer, having published two volumes of her journals? . . . In a sense, Truitt can write her own history; in another sense, her work subtly wrinkles the linear progress of art history."

It was in the nation's capital in the early 1960s that Truitt's distinctive artistic style matured. During a 1961 visit to New York City's Guggenheim Museum, the paintings of Barnett Newman and Ad Reinhardt inspired in Truitt a vision of color, space, and pure, uncluttered geometric form. Upon her return to Washington, she ordered the fabrication of tall vertical boxes, some as tall as 13 feet, made to her specifications. These she painted with striking bands of color. Critic Clement Greenberg was brought to see Truitt's painted minimalist boxes by Kenneth Noland, one of her former teachers. So impressed was Greenberg that he later wrote an article in which he suggested that the artist's boxes had changed the direction of American sculpture. He further praised her work's power to "move and affect." Truitt herself sees her trademark boxes as "three-dimensional paintings." To her, the boxes are metaphorical icons, each of which conveys a different mood. Analyzing her sculpture *Spring Snow*, she observed: "Icy green falls from the top of the sculpture through the tender air of early spring onto the warming earth below, which flattens itself to receive it."

In 1963, Truitt had her first one-woman show at the Andre Emmerich Gallery in New York City. She received a fellowship from the Guggenheim Museum in 1971 and had solo shows at New York's Whitney Museum in 1973 and at the Corcoran in Washington in 1974. Her work was also featured in the 1976 Whitney Bicentennial exhibition "200 Years of American Sculpture."

Writing in her journal (published as *Turn*) of the voyage of self-discovery that led to her own very distinctive brand of sculpture, Truitt recalled fondly a garden from her childhood. "The garden was bisected by a brick path. I noticed the pattern of its rectangles and then saw that they were repeated in the brick walls of the houses of Easton; their verticals and horizontals were also to be found in clapboard walls, in fences, and in lattices. In my passion (no other word will do for the ardor I felt) for something to love, I came to love these proportions—and years later, in 1961, when I was 40 years old, this love welled up in me and united with my training in sculpture to initiate and propel the work that has occupied me ever since."

SOURCES:
Art in America. October 1991.
ARTnews. May 1992.
Newsmakers 1993. Issue 1. Detroit, MI: Gale Research, 1993.
Newsweek. March 30, 1992.
Rubinstein, Charlotte Streifer. *American Women Artists.* Boston, MA: G.K. Hall, 1982.

Don Amerman, freelance writer, Saylorsburg, Pennsylvania

Truman, Bess (1885–1982)

American first lady from 1945 to 1953. Name variations: Bess Wallace. Born Elizabeth Virginia Wallace on February 13, 1885, in Independence, Missouri; died on October 18, 1982, in Independence; oldest of four children of David Willock Wallace (a merchant and politician) and Margaret Elizabeth (Gates) Wallace; attended Barstow School for Girls in Kansas City, Missouri; married Harry S. Truman (president of the United States), on June 28, 1919, in Independence, Missouri (died December 26, 1972); children: (Mary) Margaret Truman (b. 1924).

Although Harry S. Truman is now regarded by historians as one of the more esteemed presidents of the United States, Bess Truman remains one of the least-known first ladies in modern times. While he credited her as "a full partner in all my transactions—political and otherwise," he admittedly guarded her from public attention, because he did not want her to face the criticism so often leveled against presidents' wives. In his book *Mr. Citizen*, Truman wrote, "I hope some day someone will take time to evaluate the true role of the wife of a President, and to assess the many burdens she has to bear and the contributions she makes."

Elizabeth "Bess" Wallace was born in 1885 and grew up with Truman in Independence, Missouri, the privileged daughter of a well-to-do merchant. She was outgoing and athletic, easily the best tennis player in Independence, and not a bad third baseman. When she was 18, her life dramatically changed when her father committed suicide, after years of financial woes and bouts with alcoholism. Afterward, her mother became increasingly reclusive and dependent on her children, and lived at various times with Bess after she was married.

Bess was Harry's "first and only sweetheart," the girl he wooed for 30 years, through Sunday School, grammar school, and Independence High School. Shy and bookish, Harry later kidded that if he were allowed to carry her books, it was a big day. It was not until after high school, when he went to work in Kansas City, that he began commuting back to Independence to take Bess out on Saturday night. Though their engagement was announced in 1917, Harry postponed the marriage until after his service in World War I; he wanted to save her from possible widowhood. They married in 1919, when Bess was 34.

Bess Truman

Harry Truman's first business venture—the Truman & Jacobsen Haberdashery—floundered and then went bankrupt in 1922, with subsequent business attempts faring little better. His early political experience was gained under the auspices of the Pendergast brothers, who ran the powerful and corrupt Kansas City and Jackson County political machine during the war. After stints as a county judge and presiding judge of the county court, in 1934 Truman was offered support by the Pendergasts for a United States senatorial nomination.

During the early years, Bess Truman worked with her husband in his store and cared for their daughter *Margaret Truman, born in 1924 after a number of miscarriages. Though Bess usually took care to avoid the political arena, she was reluctantly drawn into his run for the Senate, working at campaign headquarters and advising on speeches. Harry called her a shrewd judge of character and relied on her intuition. When he won the Senate seat, she agreed to divide her year between Washington and Independence. Harry eventually put Bess on the payroll as secretary and researcher, at a yearly salary of $4,500, not an uncommon practice at the time. When *Clare Boothe Luce accused them of wrongdoing and leaked stories to the press referring to "Payroll Bess," Harry sent her a blistering letter and later banned her from White House social events.

Margaret Truman, who has written several biographies of her parents, recalls that when her father was selected as the running mate for Franklin Delano Roosevelt, Bess was "bitterly opposed." She watched the convention "looking tired and worried and as if she had been crying all night." Bess, along with the rest of the country, was no doubt aware that Roosevelt's ill health might prevent him from completing a fourth term. Already wary of the reporters and Secret Service men surrounding them, she is said to have asked her husband, "Are we going to have to go through this all the rest of our lives?"

When Harry Truman succeeded to the presidency after Roosevelt's death on April 12, 1945, less than three months into the term, Bess Truman entered the White House hesitantly, but determined to hang on to her privacy. Feeling that she was not elected to anything and that no one should be interested in what she had to say, in one of her first official acts she canceled the weekly press conference in favor of informal teas, held with the understanding that anything she said was off the record. If her public persona was practically non-existent, privately she was capable and efficient, accomplishing all of the duties that were customary or necessary to her position, and carrying out every protocol precedent set by her predecessors. With her daughter's welfare at heart, Bess made an enormous effort to maintain the quality of home life the Trumans had shared before coming to the White House. She oversaw household expenses, clipped coupons, played ping-pong with Margaret in the basement, addressed her own Christmas cards and drove herself around Washington, until the Secret Service complained that they could no longer keep track of her. She spent hours on the phone chatting to her bridge buddies back in Independence, and once got so lonely for them that she had them flown to Washington to visit her in what she called the "great white jail."

Bess Truman tempered her husband's "shoot from the hip" responses and his notorious public swearing. Once, when someone complained to her that he had used the word "manure" in public, Bess retorted that it had taken her some 20 years to get him to say manure. She also acted as his sounding board for some of the most important decisions in American history—whether to drop the A-bomb, the commitment of troops to Korea, the firing of General MacArthur, the Berlin blockade, and the Marshall Plan.

By 1948, Bess had had enough and was ready to retire to Independence. She agreed to another campaign, because she knew her husband wanted to finish what he had started—and probably because she believed, along with many others, that he could not possibly win reelection. Republican nominee Thomas E. Dewey was so sure of victory that he embarked on a campaign so low key as to be virtually nonexistent. Harry Truman undertook an ambitious family whistle-stop tour, winding up each speech by introducing Bess and his daughter as "The Boss" and "The Boss that Bosses the Boss." The crowds warmed to him, handing Harry S. the win in one of the major upsets in American political history.

Most of the Truman second term was spent in Blair House, the presidential guest house, due to extensive renovations to repair the "state of irreversible structural decay" of the White House. It was there in 1950 that an assassination attempt was made on the president by two Puerto Rican nationalists, who killed a guard and wounded another. When Harry decided he would not be a candidate for a third term, it was no wonder that Bess looked "the way you do when you draw four aces," said a friend.

They retired to Independence, where, after a European tour, Bess settled in to help edit and or-ganize her husband's memoirs and set up the Truman Library. She was a doting grandmother to her four grandsons, who visited often. In 1959, she underwent a mastectomy to treat breast cancer.

After her husband's death in 1972, Bess Truman lived quietly. She was honorary chair of the Thomas Eagleton 1972 Senate campaign. Her later years were plagued by arthritis and poor eyesight, but she was the longest surviving of any first lady. She died on January 20, 1982, age 97, and was buried next to her husband in the Truman Library courtyard. Harry Truman's final tribute to his wife's contributions was his order for her tombstone, which reads "First Lady, the United States of America, April 12, 1945–January 20, 1953."

SOURCES:

Healy, Diana Dixon. *America's First Ladies: Private Lives of the Presidential Wives*. NY: Atheneum, 1988.

Means, Marianne. *The Women in the White House*. NY: Signet, 1963.

Melick, Arden David. *Wives of the Presidents*. Maplewood, NJ: Hammond, 1977.

Paletta, LuAnn. *The World Almanac of First Ladies*. NY: World Almanac, 1990.

Barbara Morgan,
Boston, Massachusetts

Truman, Margaret (1924—)

American first daughter and writer. Name variations: Margaret Truman Daniel. Born Mary Margaret Truman in Independence, Missouri, on February 17, 1924; daughter of Harry S. Truman (president of the United States) and Bess Truman (1885–1982); attended Gunston Hall in Washington, D.C.; George Washington University, B.A., 1946; married (E.) Clifton Daniel (an award-winning foreign correspondent and managing editor of The New York Times; *died February 2000); children: Clifton Truman Daniel (b. around 1957); William Wallace Daniel (died on September 4, 2000, age 41); Harrison Gates Daniel; Thomas Washington Daniel.*

The much-desired, only child of *Bess Truman and Harry S. Truman, Margaret Truman was born in 1924, after Bess had suffered a number of miscarriages. Margaret attended public school in Independence until 1934, when her father was elected to the U.S. Senate, then transferred to Gunston Hall, a private school for girls in Washington. She received an associate's degree from George Washington University in 1944, the year her father was elected vice president, then went on to receive her B.A. degree from that institution in 1946. Her father, having succeeded to the presidency after the sudden death of Franklin D. Roosevelt in 1945, delivered the commencement address and presented her with her degree. Margaret viewed her brief residency in the White House as a mixed blessing; she enjoyed meeting interesting people, but deplored the lack of privacy.

A lover of music like her father, who played the piano, Margaret had studied voice from the age of 16, and following college, she embarked on a concert career. Truman made her professional singing debut with the Detroit Symphony Orchestra, on March 16, 1947, on its weekly network radio program, which her parents listened to from the "Little White House" in Key West, Florida. That August, she made her stage debut with Eugene Ormandy and the Hollywood Bowl Symphony, and then toured some 30 cities across the country. Because of the prominence of her family, Margaret found it difficult to obtain an objective evaluation of her talent; most reviewers tended to hedge on the side of kindness, although a few of the bolder among them questioned her proficiency.

In 1948, Margaret took a detour from singing to assist her father with his reelection campaign, then began performing again in 1949. Coached by Metropolitan Opera star *Helen Traubel, she made a television appearance on Ed Sullivan's "Toast of the Town" in 1950 and undertook another concert tour in 1951. A now-legendary exchange between Harry Truman and *Washington Post* music critic Paul Hume may have been instrumental in bringing the curtain down on Margaret's singing career, which ended shortly after her last tour. In a review of her concert in Washington, D.C., on December 5, 1950, Hume praised her personality but added that she "cannot sing very well" and "she is flat a good deal of the time." The president was incensed. "I have just read your lousy review," he wrote. "I never met you, but if I do you'll need a new nose."

After giving up singing, Margaret conducted her own radio show, "Authors in the News," for seven years, and also co-hosted the radio show "Weekday," with Mike Wallace. Allen Ludden, the producer, called her "a joy to work with, a nice, dignified, kind of square lady who was very good on the show." In 1955, substituting for Edward R. Murrow on his "Person to Person," she interviewed her parents.

On April 21, 1956, Margaret Truman married Clifton Daniel, then a foreign correspondent for *The New York Times* who would subsequently serve as its managing editor. Between 1957 and 1966, the couple had four sons: Clifton Truman, William Wallace, Harrison

Gates, and Thomas Washington. Having written her autobiography, *Margaret Truman's Own Story*, during her engagement, Margaret continued to write following her marriage, turning out biographies of her parents, *Harry S. Truman* (1973) and *Bess W. Truman* (1986), as well as a series of mystery novels, all set in Washington, D.C. The latest of the novels, 14 in all, came out in 1999. She also wrote a collective biography, *Women of Courage* (1976), which includes chapters on *Kate Barnard, *Prudence Crandall, *Elizabeth Blackwell, *Margaret Chase Smith, and *Mother Jones.

Margaret has served on the board of directors of the Harry S. Truman Library Institute, a non-profit corporation formed to support the library's educational activities, and was the secretary to the board of trustees of the Harry S. Truman Scholarship Foundation, which provides assistance to student pursuing careers in Government. In 1983 and 1984, she served on the Executive Committee of the Truman Centennial Committee, which planned the observance of the 100th anniversary of her father's birth. She was also the 1984 recipient of the Harry S. Truman Public Service Award, presented annually by the city of Independence to an outstanding American citizen.

Aside from a brief period in the 1970s, when Clifton was chief of *The New York Times'* Washington Bureau, the Daniels made their home in New York City, where Margaret still resides. Her husband died in February 2000, and later that year, on September 4, the couple's second son William, a well-respected social worker who worked with the mentally ill, died at age 41 after being struck by a taxi cab on Manhattan's Park Avenue. The Daniels' eldest son Clifton told an interviewer that although his mother was devastated by the deaths of her husband and son in such a short period of time, "she has her chin up."

SOURCES:

Moritz, Charles, ed. *Current Biography Yearbook 1987.* NY: H.W. Wilson, 1987.

"Private Citizen," in *People Weekly.* September 25, 2000.

Barbara Morgan,
Melrose, Massachusetts

Trumbull, Alice (1904–1971).

See Mason, Alice Trumbull.

Trung Sisters (d. 43 CE)

Two sisters, considered models and inspiration for centuries of Vietnamese resistance against foreign domination, who led the first Vietnamese insurrec-

tion against foreign occupation by the Chinese feudalists and ruled Vietnam for two years before being overthrown by the Chinese.

Trung Trac and Trung Nhi. Name variations: Hai Ba Trung (Two Ladies Trung); Trung Nu Vuong or Trung Vuong (She-king Trung); Truong sisters. Pronunciation: TCHUNG sisters. Born in village of Me Linh in Son Tay region in Vietnam (dates of birth unknown); died in 43 CE, committing suicide by throwing themselves into the river; daughters of a local chief and Ba Man Thien, reputed descendent of the Hung kings; Trung Trac married Thi Sach (a local chieftain assassinated by the Chinese); marital status of Trung Nhi unknown.

Led insurrection against Chinese rule (39 CE); commanded an army of 80,000 soldiers; defeated Chinese; liberated 65 fortresses and proclaimed themselves joint queens (40 CE); upon defeat by a Chinese general, threw themselves into the river (43 CE).

For 12 years the United States fought a bloody guerrilla war against Vietnam. Although America was many times richer and had far superior military might, Vietnam prevailed in the end, fueled by a desire to reunify the country, gain independence from foreign control, and preserve national dignity. It was not the first war of resistance to be fought by the Vietnamese people, nor would it be the last. The revolutionary spirit is a Vietnamese tradition that dates back many hundreds of years, launched by two heroic women in the 1st century CE. The story of the Trung sisters, who led Vietnam's very first war of resistance, is the story of Vietnam itself.

The earliest Vietnamese state was known as Van Lang, founded by the Hung (Hong) dynasty, possibly around 2800 BCE. The Hung Kingdom was made up of 15 tribes, the main one being Me Linh, northeast of current-day Hanoi. The Hung kings ruled through a system of civilian chiefs (*lac hau*), military chiefs (*lac tuong*), and lower-ranked officials (*bo chinh*). The capital was established in Me Linh. A succession of 18 Hung kings ruled until the 3rd century BCE, when Thuc Phan, king of Nam Cuong (now Cao Bang province and part of China's Kwangsi province), seized Van Lang and established the Kingdom of Au Lac. Thuc Phan proclaimed himself king under the name An Duong Vuong and established his capital at Co Loa (Shell Citadel). One can still view remains of the spiral-shaped citadel measuring some 8,000 meters near Hanoi, the present-day capital of Vietnam.

Vietnam's nascent years, however, would soon be dominated by its neighbor to the north, China. The Kingdom of Au Lac had successfully resisted troops sent by the Chinese Tsin Dynasty around the end of the 3rd century BCE. But in 180 BCE, Au Lac was overthrown by the Chinese general Trieu Da, who brought more territory under his control. His Nam Viet kingdom retained its independence for about a century, until 111 BCE, when it was overthrown by the Chinese Han emperor Wu Ti (Wudi). During the next ten centuries of Chinese occupation, Vietnam was in a constant struggle to safeguard its existence as a nation, to reclaim its independence, and to preserve its national culture.

It was during this time that the Han applied a policy of systematic assimilation, politically, culturally, and socially. They raised taxes and installed Chinese chiefs to rule the people. Before Chinese rule, women had possessed many of the same rights as men: they were allowed to inherit property and had legal rights within the family. But when the Chinese introduced Confucianism to Vietnamese society, women became subordinated to their husbands, who possessed all property rights and were permitted to take a second wife if the first failed to produce a son. Women were no longer allowed to serve in the bureaucracy, and they were banned from taking civil-service examinations.

Resentment of Chinese rule began to build as the Chinese administrators exacted more taxes and tried to increase their control over the Lac lords. (*Lac lords* is a term referring to the native Vietnamese who were landed aristocracy.) The Trung sisters were daughters of a Lac lord chief in the village of Me Linh. Their mother **Ba Man Thien** was reputed to be a descendant of the Hung kings, and the sisters were brought up in a "spirit of patriotism and love of military art." They were taught to be strong and independent. Trung Trac, the elder sister, killed a white tiger which had been known in the region for being invincible. This courageous act gained respect from people throughout the land.

Trung Trac married Thi Sach, son of a Lac lord from the nearby Chu Dien fortress. Even though they were married, they continued to live in their separate regions. (Vestiges of this tradition are still found in Vinh Phu, Ha Bac, and Ha Tay provinces.) Both Trung Trac and her husband were enraged by the Chinese governor's harsh rules and atrocities. When Thi Sach opposed the demands for more taxes and attempts to assimilate the Vietnamese, he was arrested, and the Chinese governor Su Ting ordered his execution. Although the Chinese hoped this action would stifle further opposition to their rule, it had the opposite effect.

The murder of her husband spurred Trung Trac into action to fight for her homeland. She put aside her grief, and without waiting for the funeral rites, removed her traditional mourning headdress. Along with her sister Trung Nhi, she rallied the other nobles and peasants, raising the flag of revolt. Trung Trac called her troops to battle with the oath:

> I swear, first, to avenge the nation;
> Second, to restore the Hungs' former position;
> Third, to have revenge for my husband;
> Fourth, to carry through to the end our common
>   task.

Before the military incursion, the young general Thieu Hoa begged Trung Trac to let the army wear mourning clothes. Trung Trac dismissed the idea, saying:

> This is a battle. If we presented ourselves in mourning, the spirit of fighting would diminish. I will wear my best armor to encourage our fighters and weaken our enemies. Not until I capture Lien Lau Citadel and Governor Su Ting, will I allow myself to salute the flags and begin the funeral.

Trung Trac donned her golden armor carved with a Me Linh bird; a belt was tightened around her waist, the buckle adorned with little bells. As legend has it, she was such a beautiful and awesome vision that the Chinese soldiers were stopped in their tracks by the sight of her. Flanked by the sisters' sides were women generals from the mountains of Thanh Thien and the plains in Bat Nan, Nguyet Thien, Nguyet Do, and Le Chan. One of the commanders was **Phung Thi Chinh**, the pregnant wife of a noble. She is said to have given birth in the middle of a battle but continued fighting with the newborn tied to her back. The Trung sisters attacked the home of Su Ting, forcing him to flee. Vietnamese still enjoy retelling how Su Ting had to cut his hair, shave his beard, and, in disguise, secretly leave the country through the sewage line.

In 40 CE, the Trung armies defeated the Chinese. The sisters installed themselves as queens of Nam Viet in their new capital of Me Linh. During their brief reign, they distributed Su Ting's wealth to the poor and liberated prisoners and soldiers who had been drafted into the Chinese army. But this period of independence was short-lived. Two years later, the Chinese emperor ordered preparations for the reconquest of the territory.

The veteran general Ma Yuan was sent to crush the insurgence. His troops met little resistance until they faced the Trung armies southwest of Me Linh. But Ma Yuan's troops proved superior, and the Trung sisters were defeated. Popular mythology claims that, following their defeat, the sisters killed themselves by drowning in the river Hat Giang at Cam Khe (above the Red River, at the border of Vinh Phu and Ha Tay provinces), rather than submit to Chinese rule. But some accounts say the sisters were caught by the invading Chinese forces and put to death.

Whatever their final end, the spirit of the Trung sisters lives on in the soul of the Vietnamese. In the "Record of Queen Trung," the Vietnamese showed their veneration of the women warriors:

> Fearing that because their ruler was a woman and would not be able to defeat the enemy, the mob scattered. Once more, a national government collapsed. Li Wen-hsiu said: "Trung Trac and Trung Nhi were women. Chiu-chen, Jih-nan and Ho-p'u, along with sixty-five cities south of the ranges, responded immediately to their call to arms. They created a nation, and took for themselves the title of Queen, as easily as turning their hands. We can see from this that circumstances among our people were at that time favourable enough to permit a centralized ruler. But alas, for more than a thousand years . . . the men of our country merely bowed their heads and kowtowed as slaves and servants of the men from the north. It can be said that their lack of shame in the face of the two Trung women was their self-destruction."

The sisters inspired generations of militant and courageous women fighters. In fact, the next major rebellion in Vietnamese history was also led by a woman, *Ba Trieu; she is sometimes referred to as the Vietnamese *Joan of Arc. A Vietnamese folk song celebrates her memory:

> Sleep my child, sleep
> Mother is fetching water to wash
>   the gilded seat of the elephant
> Let's climb the hill to watch Ba Trieu
>   on her elephant, beating the gong
> Let's fill the rose silk pouches
>   with betel leaves for our husbands
>   who are going to war

After the Trung sisters were defeated, the Chinese intensified their oppression of the Vietnamese. There were a few small uprisings, but nothing significant until 248 CE, when 19-year-old Ba Trieu, a noblewoman, and her brother, a headman in Quan An (Nong Cong, Nui Nua, Thanh Hoa), raised an army of 1,000 fighters to conduct guerrilla training. When Ba Trieu was advised that she should marry rather than stage a revolt, she replied:

> I want to ride the storm, tread the dangerous
>   waves,

Kill fierce sharks in the open sea, drive out the
Ngo aggressors,
Win back the Fatherland and break the yoke of
slavery.
I will not resign myself to the usual lot of women
I do not want to bow my head and be a servant
of man

When her brother died in battle, Ba Trieu took over the leadership, winning many victories and almost reclaiming all of Cuu Chan. She rode into battle atop an elephant, wearing golden armor, and her troops succeeded in killing the governor of the Giao Chau prefecture. The resistance carried on successfully for another six months before it was crushed by the Chinese. But though she was defeated, Ba Trieu inspired the awe and admiration of the Chinese soldiers:

Clad in a golden robe with a gold pin through
her hair, wearing ivory shoes, she was always
seen on her elephant, on the front line.
It is easy to handle a spear to attack a tiger, but
facing the Queen, how it is difficult to fight.

At the age of 23, Ba Trieu killed herself on Tung mountain, where her tomb and a temple in her honor still stand. Toward the end of the 20th century, a bronze sword was discovered on Mount Nua in Thanh Hoa province where the insurrection led by Ba Trieu took place. The carving on the handle showed a Vietnamese woman aristocrat wearing a turban and sumptuous clothing.

The exploits of the Trung sisters and Ba Trieu as related in popular mythology are a testament to the special status accorded women in Vietnamese society. Throughout history, Vietnamese women have enjoyed far greater rights and respect than their counterparts in other areas of the world, particularly elsewhere in Asia.

The Vietnamese continued to launch revolts against Chinese rule, but none succeeded until the 10th century, when Ngo Quyen vanquished the Chinese armies at the battle on the Bach Dang River. Thus ended 1,000 years of Chinese domination and ushered in a new era of independence for Vietnam. The first Westerners—Portuguese traders—began arriving in Vietnam in the 1500s, and by the 18th century French missionaries had gained a foothold. In the latter part of the 19th century, the French government began a more active involvement in Vietnam, leading to a period of colonial rule.

Once again, the spirit of nationalism rose up among the Vietnamese. Ho Chi Minh emerged as the leader of the independence drive. On May 7, 1954, the Viet Minh forces defeated the French troops in the battle at Dien Bien Phu. In subsequent peace negotiations, Vietnam was divided at the 17th Parallel, splitting the country into North and South. Elections were supposed to take place in 1956 to unify the country, but the vote was never held. Thus began the next battle for reunification and independence, with the United States intervening to keep the South from coming under the control of Ho Chi Minh and his Communist government.

Like their foremothers, women would again become an important part of the revolutionary movement. They were known as the "long haired" troops. Thousands of brave, dedicated women suffered years of war, brutal imprisonment, and separation from their families to fight for their political ideals. The walls of the Women's Museum in Ho Chi Minh City are lined with photographs of women who fought and died for the cause. The exhibit maintains that the women of Vietnam will never be subservient to anyone.

When the enemy comes, the women also should fight.
—Vietnamese proverb

The legacy of the Trung sisters is a nation of fierce nationalists, with strong and valiant women. The Trungs' memory is honored throughout Vietnam, with streets, schools, and hospitals bearing their name. On the southern outskirts of Hanoi sits the Den Hai Ba Trung (Trung Sisters Temple). It was built in 1142 and restored in the 19th and 20th centuries. It is said that every year the two sisters return for a stroll around the temple. A statue shows the sisters kneeling with their arms raised. Some say it portrays them as they prepare to drown themselves. Every year, with the return of spring, on the 16th day of the second moon, people in Vietnam celebrate the anniversary of the death of the Trung sisters. Schoolchildren still re-enact the battle of the Trung sisters and sing songs praising their heroic contribution to the fight for national dignity and independence.

SOURCES:

An Cuong. *Tieng Trong Me Linh.* Hanoi: Kim Dong, 1973.

Chesneaux, Jean. *The Vietnamese Nation.* Sydney: Current Book Distributors, 1966.

Hodgkin, Thomas. *Vietnam: The Revolutionary Path.* London: Macmillan, 1981.

Holmgren, Jennifer. *Chinese Colonisation of Northern Vietnam.* Canberra: Australian National University, 1980.

Le, Thi Nham Tuyet, and Thi Tu Mai. *Women in Viet Nam.* Hanoi: Foreign Languages Publishing House, 1978.

Nguyen, Khac Vien. *Vietnam: A Long History.* Hanoi: Foreign Languages Publishing House, 1987.

SarDesai, D.R. *Vietnam: Trials and Tribulations of a Nation.* New Delhi, India: Promilla, 1988.

Viet Nam, a Sketch. Hanoi: Foreign Languages Publishing House, 1971.

Doan Thi Nam Hau,
freelance writer, and
Willa Seidenberg, co-author of
A Matter of Conscience: GI Resistance During the Vietnam War

Truong Sisters (d. 43 CE).

See Trung Sisters.

Trusca, Gabriela (b. 1957).

See Comaneci, Nadia for sidebar.

Trussel, Elizabeth (1496–1527)

*Countess of Oxford. Name variations: Elizabeth de Vere. Born in 1496; died before July 1527; daughter of Edward Trussell and **Margaret Dun**; married John de Vere, 15th earl of Oxford, around 1508; children: *Frances de Vere (d. 1577); John de Vere (b. around 1516), 16th earl of Oxford; Aubrey de Vere; Robert de Vere; Geoffrey de Vere; **Elizabeth de Vere** (who associated with Thomas Darcy, 1st Lord Darcy); **Anne de Vere** (who associated with Edmund Sheffield, 1st Lord Sheffield, and John Brock).*

Truth, Sojourner (c. 1797–1883)

Former slave from New York who gained her freedom in 1827 and subsequently became a renowned religious reformer, public speaker, and activist on behalf of abolition and women's rights. Name variations: Isabella Bomefree or Isabella Baumfree; Isabella Van Wagener or Isabella Van Wagenen. Pronunciation: SO-jurn-er. Born Isabella Bomefree about 1797 in Ulster County, New York; died on November 26, 1883, at her home in Battle Creek, Michigan; daughter of Elizabeth and James Bomefree (both slaves of Colonel Johannes Hardenbergh); married Robert, a slave owned by a man named Catlin, sometime between 1810 and 1817 (relationship terminated by Catlin soon thereafter); married another fellow slave named Thomas about 1817; children: (first marriage) Diana (b. 1815); (second marriage) Peter, James, Elizabeth, and Sophia.

Upon the death of her second master, Charles Hardenbergh (1808), was sold away from her parents to a new owner, John Neely, also of Ulster County, New York; a few months later, was purchased by Martin Schryver, a local tavern-keeper; was sold again (1810), to John J. Dumont of New Paltz, New York; ran away from Dumont's plantation with her infant child (1826) and sought asylum with Maria and Isaac Van Wagener, who purchased her freedom from Du-

mont; went to court to reclaim her son Peter, who had been illegally sold to a Southern plantation (1828); joined a utopian religious commune called the Kingdom, led by self-styled prophet Robert Matthias (1832); after the Kingdom disintegrated, moved to New York City where she worked to support herself and her son; changed her name to Sojourner Truth and left New York City to become a traveling preacher (1843); in the winter of that year, entered a Massachusetts utopian community called the Northampton Association for Education and Industry, where she was introduced to the principles of feminism and abolitionism; gave her first speech on abolition (1844); spoke to the American Anti-Slavery Society in New York City (1845); dictated her life story to fellow Association member Olive Gilbert (1846) and had it printed by William Lloyd Garrison (1850); commenced formal association with the growing circuit of antislavery agitators in the Northeast and Midwest (1851); gave a speech on female equality at the Akron meeting of the Ohio Women's Rights Convention (May 1851); moved to Harmonia, a Progressive Friends (spiritualist) settlement near Battle Creek, Michigan (1857); upon the outbreak of the Civil War, made numerous speeches in support of the Union cause (1861); met Abraham Lincoln (1864); engaged in refugee relief work at the many camps established by the National Freedmen's Relief Association and the Freedmen's Bureau (1864–68); attended and spoke at the Equal Rights Association meeting in New York City (1867); undertook a petition campaign agitating for the federal government to provide western land grants to emancipated slaves (beginning 1868); suffered from several bouts of debilitating illness (early 1870s); had sufficiently recovered to embark on another lecture tour (1878); in the last years of her life, was cared for by her daughters Diana and Elizabeth in Battle Creek, where she died of a long illness at age 86.

During her lifetime, Sojourner Truth went from being a slave to a well-recognized speaker for the early women's rights and abolitionist movements. Nearly six feet tall, with a deep voice and dramatic persona, she convincingly presented her opinions about religion, slavery, and equality to captivated audiences throughout the North during the height of the anti-slavery movement of the 1850s.

Sojourner Truth was born a slave about 1797 near Rosendale, Ulster County, New York, on the farm of Colonel Johannes Hardenbergh. Her parents, James and **Elizabeth "Mau Mau Bett" Bomefree** (also spelled Baumfree), named her Isabella, by which name she went until she renamed herself at age 46. Because New York had originally been a colony of the Netherlands, many of the early settlers of the area were of Dutch descent, including Sojourner's owner. She, like the entire Hardenbergh family and all their slaves, spoke only Dutch.

Slavery in New York differed from that practiced on the plantations of Virginia or South Carolina. Although the state had the largest number of enslaved people in the North (early Dutch settlers had actively encouraged the importation of slaves), people of African descent still made up only 15% of the total population. Farmers and townspeople employed their slaves in a variety of tasks, including housework, field labor, and artisanal crafts like blacksmithing. Colonel Hardenbergh was a rather large slaveholder when viewed in this context; in 1790, he owned seven slaves, extensive farmland along the Wallkill River, and a grist mill. Sojourner's family lived as cottagers on Hardenbergh's land, which meant that they occupied a house unto themselves and, when not working at his behest, farmed a small plot of land for their own use. While their situation offered them a level of autonomy beyond that normally experienced by Southern slaves, bondage remained a painful and grueling existence for the Bomefrees. Sojourner's father had been married twice before, but both of his wives had been sold away from him. Moreover, although her mother had given birth to at least ten children before her, by the time Sojourner was born, Hardenbergh had sold all but one of her siblings, her brother Peter.

Sojourner's earliest memory was the end of her family's cottager life. When she was still quite small (about two years old), Colonel Hardenbergh died, leaving his slaves to his son, Charles. Shortly thereafter, Charles built a new house, which was to serve as a hotel, and moved his slaves out of their rural home into the basement of the establishment. As she recorded in the narrative of her life, Sojourner remembered the family's situation as "dismal," with all crowded together into the dank cellar, "its only lights consisting of a few panes of glass . . . and the space between the loose boards of the floor, and the uneven earth below . . . often filled with mud and water, the uncomfortable splashings of which were as annoying as its noxious vapors must have been chilling and fatal to health." Sojourner lived under these circumstances for the next seven years, until Charles Hardenbergh died and his heirs sold her to John Neely, along with a lot of sheep, for $100. When she later remembered this momentous event, Truth remarked with feeling, "Now the war begun." John Neely spoke no Dutch, but apparently understood it; his wife and family, however, were utterly unable to communicate with Sojourner, who neither spoke nor comprehended English, which provoked innumerable conflicts and great confusion for her. "If they sent me for a frying-pan, not knowing what they mean, perhaps I carried them the pot-hooks and trammels. Then, oh! how angry mistress would be with me!" Fierce beatings accompanied the anger of her owners, and one episode in particular scarred her for life. As she told the story later, her master once whipped her with "a bundle of rods, prepared in the embers, and bound together with cords." Neely's treatment awakened a renewed religious faith in Sojourner, and it became her habit to pray aloud whenever she was afraid or hurt. As a friend noted, "She had no idea God had any knowledge of her thoughts, save what she told him; or heard her prayers, unless they were spoken audibly." From this time forward, Truth found refuge in religion, frequently praying and speaking to God about her troubles and concerns.

When Sojourner had only been with the Neelys for a few months, her father visited, and while he was there, she begged him to help her get away. James Bomefree seems to have been able to intercede on her behalf, for soon thereafter a man named Martinus Schryver arrived at Neely's and paid him $105 for the girl, only later revealing to Sojourner that James Bomefree had suggested that he buy her. The Schryvers ran a tavern and a fishing business on their largely uncultivated farm. Truth remembered them as a rough crowd who spoke crudely and taught her to curse. While there, she "was expected to carry fish, to hoe corn, to bring roots and herbs from the wood for beers, to go to the Strand for a gallon of molasses or liquor, and 'browse around.'" She had a considerable amount of autonomy, and the life, although she later came to view it as morally backward, represented a safe haven from the brutality she had suffered with the Neelys.

Within a year and a half, however, Sojourner was again sold to a new master, John J. Dumont of New Paltz, New York. Dumont's farm was situated near the Hudson River, and on it he worked about four slaves and employed at least two white servants. Like her earlier owners, the Dumonts spoke only English; by this time, Sojourner had begun to learn the language but still struggled to communicate. She worked hard, both in the fields and the house, and seemed to gain a measure of respect from her master. However, she had an extremely difficult relationship with her mistress, who had not grown up in a slaveholding household and seemed, to Sojourner, to be unfamiliar with and resentful of slaves. Although Truth's memoirs describe Mrs. Dumont as unusually cruel and hateful, all except the most basic reasons for these troubles remain unexplained, "some from motives of delicacy, and others, because the relation of them might inflict undeserved pain of some now living," she wrote, "whom [I] remembers only with esteem and love."

Historians have contended that the unspeakable things to which the narrative refers included everything from sexual abuse, either by John Dumont or by Mrs. Dumont, to the daily humiliations of slavery. The fact remains that Sojourner offered little explanation for her choice to exclude certain aspects of her enslavement from her narrative. Moreover, Truth's description of her early adulthood as a slave differs significantly from the unmitigated opposition to slavery that characterized the abolition campaigns of former slaves *Harriet Tubman and Frederick Douglass. For instance, it is clear from her narrative that Sojourner had warm feelings for her master John Dumont, despite the fact that he beat her. As she later recalled, at the time she was Dumont's slave, she "firmly believed that slavery was right and honorable." Her memoirs do not offer an easy or uncomplicated reason for Sojourner's viewpoint at the time, except to demonstrate that as she matured, her feelings about slavery and her situation shifted markedly, to the point that she viewed her early feelings about Dumont "with utter astonishment."

That man over there says that women need to be helped into carriages, and lifted over ditches, and to have the best place everywhere. Nobody ever helps me into carriages, or over mud puddles, or gives me any best place, and ain't I a woman? . . . I have borne five children and seen most all sold off into slavery and when I cried out with a mother's grief, none but Jesus heard— and ain't I a woman?

—Sojourner Truth

One of the most important events in the evolution of her feelings about slavery occurred some years after she arrived at the Dumonts', when she fell in love with a slave named Robert, who lived on a neighboring farm. Robert's owner, Charles Catton, forbade them to continue in their relationship because he did not want Robert to have children with slaves Catton himself did not own. Despite this prohibition, Robert continued to visit Sojourner, which provoked Catton and his son to follow Robert to the Dumont farm and then beat him savagely

"with the heavy ends of their canes," writes Truth, "bruising and mangling his head and face in the most awful manner, and causing the blood, which streamed from his wounds, to cover him like a slaughtered beast." She watched in horror from her window as her lover was abused, bound, and led away. Robert never again visited Sojourner, but historians have suggested that her first child, **Diana** (born 1815), was in fact Robert's daughter and that Sojourner's pregnancy (not just the prospect of it) had inspired Catton to such violence.

Within a few years, Sojourner was married to another slave, Thomas, who lived on Dumont's farm. Throughout the United States, slave marriage, unlike civil marriage, was not an institution recognized either by law or by the church. Most slaves married one another either in ceremonies provided by their masters, or "after the slave fashion," in a ceremony officiated by the slaves themselves. It was in the latter manner that Sojourner and Thomas were united. By 1817, the state of New York enacted a law providing that slave marriage be recognized as legal, but only if the marriages were officially contracted. Such contracts were rarely employed, however, and Sojourner and Thomas did not have the benefit of an official marriage certificate. Between 1820 and 1826, Sojourner had four children: Peter, **Elizabeth**, **Sophia**, and James. James did not live to adulthood.

In 1799, New York State had made provisions for the gradual abolition of slavery, which was scheduled to occur on July 4, 1827. At some point during Sojourner's tenure with Dumont, he had promised to free her a full year before the state did, "if she would do well and be faithful." When July 1826 arrived, however, Dumont refused to fulfill his promise to her because he claimed that an injury to Sojourner's hand had made her less productive during the previous year and thus still liable for lost labor. Dumont's betrayal infuriated Sojourner, for her sense of fair play and duty had been a hallmark of her understanding of the master-slave relationship. "The slaveholders are TERRIBLE for promising to give you this or that, or such and such a privilege, if you will do thus and so; and when the time of fulfillment comes, and one claims the promise, they, forsooth, recollect nothing of the kind; and you are, like as not, taunted with being a LIAR; or at best, the slave is accused of not having performed his part or condition of the contract." Despite her great disappointment, Truth did not abandon her master without first making sure she had done enough labor to satisfy at least her sense of obligation to him. She de-

termined to spin 100 pounds of wool before she left, and after that, escaped before dawn one morning in 1826 with her infant daughter Sophia in her arms. "I did not run off, for I thought that wicked, but I walked off, believing that to be all right."

Even as she left, Truth had no clear idea of her destination. After wandering for much of the morning, praying constantly for direction, she arrived at the home of Isaac and **Maria Van Wagenen**, who happily gave her shelter and work. Within a few days, however, Dumont found her and insisted that she come back with him, which she refused to do. When he threatened to take her baby, Isaac Van Wagenen stepped in and offered to buy Sojourner's service for the remainder of the year, simply to keep her from returning to slavery. Agreeing, Dumont charged $20 and left Sojourner to her new owners, who refused to be called "master" and "mistress," but insisted instead that she call them by their given names. Although *Harriet Beecher Stowe later referred to the Van Wagenens as Quakers, there is no evidence that they were members of that faith, but simply that they "did not believe in slavery."

The next year of Sojourner's life was fraught with challenges, the first of which was her campaign to retrieve her young son, Peter. Shortly before she escaped, Dumont had leased the five-year-old to another slaveholder who had then illegally sent him out of New York to Alabama. Once free, Sojourner began a desperate attempt to get him back, appealing first to the Dumonts and then to the slaveholder's family, all to no avail. Finally, a friend put her in contact with a group of activist Quakers who directed her to the courthouse, where she could make an official complaint. After months of legal proceedings, her son was returned to her, covered with scars and full of stories about the abuse he received at the hand of his master.

During the time she was living with the Van Wagenens, Sojourner also had a life-changing religious experience, in which she became "overwhelmed with the greatness of the Divine presence" and was inspired to devote herself to preaching. Before this time, Sojourner's mother had been her sole source of religious instruction, her masters having never encouraged her to read or hear the Bible. She did not set foot into a church until she was nearly 30 years of age, but once involved, she attended the local Methodist church with devotion. Through her contact with local religious groups, Sojourner felt as though she had finally "found some work to do to benefit somebody," and in 1829 undertook her first foray into the world of religious reform, leaving Ulster County for New York City with a white evangelical teacher named **Miss Gear**. While in the city, she was introduced to numerous evangelicals and other activists, from whom she strove to learn as much about Christianity as she could. She quickly became known as a remarkable preacher whose "speaking was miraculous" in its influence on others.

It was at this time that she became acquainted with a man named Elijah Pierson, who, like other religious reformers of the early 1830s, advocated a strict adherence to Old Testament laws as the means to salvation. In his house, sometimes called the "Kingdom," he led a small circle of family members and fellow believers in an idiosyncratic search for religious truth. Sojourner began working as a housekeeper for Pierson, who invited her to become part of the group, treated her as a spiritual equal and encouraged her to preach to the other members. Shortly after she joined the Kingdom, a man named Robert Matthias arrived at the Pierson home, bringing with him stories of revelation and prophecy. As Sojourner's narrative notes, Matthias viewed himself as "God upon earth, because the spirit of God dwelt in him; while Pierson then understood that his mission was like that of John the Baptist." Eventually, Matthias gathered Pierson and the other followers together at the home of a wealthy New York merchant named Benjamin Folger, located near the town of Sing Sing. In all there were about 20 members, including Truth, who still worked as the group's housekeeper.

The affairs of the Kingdom appeared increasingly strange to the people outside of it. Matthias eschewed traditional marriage and mandated ritualized group cleansings, for which all the members were totally nude. He also claimed that only he could perform true marriages, through which he united "match spirits," or those people whom he determined, through divine revelation, were destined for one another. When legally married people began swapping spouses, scandalous rumors about the Kingdom spread like wildfire through the surrounding communities. In the midst of this excitement, Sojourner's first employer, Pierson, became seriously ill, but Matthias and Pierson refused to call a doctor. According to the doctrine of the Kingdom, all disease resulted from demonic possession, which only Matthias could remedy. When Pierson died in 1834, attended only by members of the Kingdom, his suspicious family and the neighboring community insisted that the coroner be allowed to examine the body. In the meantime, the group suffered serious financial difficulties, Matthias decided to relocate to the West, and his following began to unravel. Sojourner, however, remained stolidly loyal to Matthias and was the only member who decided to follow him on his journey.

Before Sojourner and Matthias left, however, the Folgers, whose home had been the center of the Kingdom, brought charges against both of them, accusing Matthias not only of stealing their money, but also of conspiring with Sojourner to poison Pierson. A witness at the time interpreted the Folgers' actions as an attempt to deflect their own public humiliation during the scandal onto the least socially important members of the group. The court exhumed Pierson's body and commenced a full-fledged investigation into Truth's role in his death. Despite the scrutiny she was under, she stood firm, asking for and receiving the public endorsement of her character from former employers. The charges against her never reached a courtroom, but Matthias was charged with Pierson's murder. Although Sojourner spoke on his behalf to the lawyers in the case, her testimony was never required at the trial. Upon being acquitted, Matthias left for the West, but Sojourner chose not to go with him as she had earlier planned.

Nearly all of Sojourner's life savings and material possessions had been squandered in the financial failures of the Kingdom, and after the affair came to a close, she not only felt betrayed, but was also very poor. Again living in New York City, she struggled to make ends meet but found that "for all her unwearied labors, she had nothing to show." As the city increasingly came to represent failure and demoralization in her mind, she resolved to leave it and make her way as a traveling preacher. On June 1, 1843 (the holy day of Pentecost), she took the name Sojourner Truth and informed her friends: "The Spirit calls me [East], and I must go." Although this marked the beginning of Truth's career as a public figure, she at first wandered in relative obscurity, depending on the kindness of fellow Christians for her food and shelter. As her narrative related, she meandered from religious meeting to religious meeting, "testifying of the hope that was in her"—exhorting the people to "embrace Jesus, and refrain from sin."

During her travels, Truth learned about the numerous "intentional communities" that reform-minded evangelicals had established around New England and the mid-Atlantic region during the 1830s and 1840s. Despite having been burned by the Matthias fiasco, she still found the principles and lifestyle of communitarian settlements attractive. Early in 1844, she visited the Northampton Association of Education and Industry in Massachusetts, which had been recommended to her as a moderate cooperative community. The Association was situated on 500 acres of farmland, where the members kept livestock, ran grist and saw mills, and operated a silk factory. Differing from most of the utopian efforts at the time, the Northampton group based their search for a simpler, more godly life in industrial pursuits, not farming.

Unlike Matthias' Kingdom, the Northampton Association had not been founded by a religious fanatic claiming to be God on earth. Instead, Samuel L. Hill and George Benson, both devoted abolitionists, established the Association in 1842 in order to provide a place where devoted individuals could retreat from the "frivolous occupations" and "vicious enjoyments" which characterized the lives of many, and turn instead to cooperative and productive labor. The community was strongly anti-slavery, religiously tolerant, pro-women's equality, and pacifist in its principles. When Truth arrived, she found about 210 members laboring together to support the community, for which they were paid a small wage. While there, she was introduced to the leaders of the anti-slavery movement at that time, including Frederick Douglass, David Ruggles, and William Lloyd Garrison. Through fellow members and illustrious visitors to the community, Truth was made aware of the great struggle against slavery and took it up as her own. Much later in life, she remembered the intellectually stimulating, reform-minded community with great fondness and respect. "I was with them heart and soul for anything concerning human right, and my belief is in me yet and can't get out."

Although its members had worked hard, the Association's silk-manufacturing business was simply not profitable enough to sustain the community, and in 1846, it disintegrated under a burden of debt. Sojourner took up lodging with the family of one of the founders, George Benson, who had since established a cotton mill. Within a few months, Truth began dictating her life story to a fellow Association member, **Olive Gilbert**, a white woman who shared some of Truth's evangelical experiences and beliefs. One of the more unusual facets of the narrative is that it ended with Truth proclaiming forgiveness of her old slave master, John Dumont. The occasion of the rapprochement was Truth's visit to see her ailing daughter, Diana, who had never left Dumont's household. Much to Truth's surprise, Dumont informed her that he had changed his views on slavery, saying that "it was the wickedest thing in the world, the greatest curse the earth had ever felt—that it was then very clear to his mind that it was so, though, while he was a slaveholder himself, he did not see it so, and thought it was as right as holding any other property."

Truth felt immense satisfaction at Dumont's change of heart: "Oh! how sweet to my mind was this confession! And what a confession for a master to make to a slave! A slaveholding master turned to a brother! Poor old man, may the Lord bless him, and all slaveholders partake of his spirit!" Truth's capacity for forgiveness makes her narrative somewhat unusual, for most slave autobiographies were composed as weapons against slavery and did not emphasize the humanity of the slaveholder. Truth's relationship with Dumont, like most in her life, had never been typical, however.

The *Narrative of Sojourner Truth* was privately printed by William Lloyd Garrison in 1850, when Sojourner was 57. The book opened up new avenues for Truth, providing her with the means to support herself while speaking on the anti-slavery lecture circuit, where she sold copies of the narrative to her eager audiences. In fact, her public career began in earnest only after the narrative was published, when she appeared before a large women's rights meeting in Worcester, Massachusetts, in October 1850. She was warmly received by the listeners, to whom she spoke for only a few minutes. As the *New York Herald* recorded it, "She said Woman set the world wrong by eating the forbidden fruit, and now she was going to set it right. She said Goodness never had any beginning; it was from everlasting, and could never die. But Evil had a beginning, and must have an end. She expressed great reverence for God, and faith that he will bring about his own purposes and plans."

Her next major public appearance occurred one month later at a meeting of the Rhode Island Anti-Slavery Society, which had been specially convened by Frederick Douglass and others to protest the passage of the Fugitive Slave Act. While most of the speakers spoke vehemently and passionately against the act, Truth seemed to have little to say on the subject. The New York-based *Anti-Slavery Standard* recorded her comments in this way: "She had been a slave, and was not now entirely free. She did not know anything about politics—could not read the newspapers—but thanked God that the law was made—that the worst had come to worst; but the best must come to best."

Despite her initial insecurity about speaking about politics, Truth continued to appear at the most important anti-slavery meetings of the day. In 1851, at William Lloyd Garrison's request, she joined the official antislavery feminist speaking circuit. While on the tour, she spoke to abolitionist audiences in Massachusetts, New York, and Ohio. In 1854, at the Ohio Woman's Rights Convention in Akron, led by feminist writer and activist *Frances D. Gage, Truth gave one of her most famous speeches. After listening to several clerics of various persuasions who declared that women were inferior to men and that God had not meant for women to have rights, Sojourner spoke directly to the men:

> That man over there says that women need to be helped into carriages, and lifted over ditches, and to have the best place everywhere. Nobody ever helps me into carriages, or over mud puddles, or gives me any best place, and ain't I a woman? . . . I have plowed, and planted, and gathered into barns, and no man could head me—and ain't I a woman? I could work as much and eat as much as a man (when I could get it), and bear the lash as well—and ain't I a woman? I have borne five children and seen most all sold off into slavery and when I cried out with a mother's grief, none but Jesus heard—and ain't I a woman?

Truth's speech was praised at the time for its straightforward, powerful language and the hints of humor within it. Throughout her lifetime, newspaper reporters and other observers consistently emphasized that Sojourner's combination of wit and honesty powerfully affected her audience, and often won support for her cause.

Throughout the 1850s, Truth continued to speak on behalf of women's rights and abolition. During the same period, she became involved in another popular religious movement, spiritualism, through a group known as Progressive Friends, an offshoot of the Quakers. The Progressive Friends believed in abolition, women's equality, and non-violence; they also espoused the practice of communicating with spirits. In 1857, Sojourner moved to Harmonia, Michigan, to be part of a Progressive Friends community. By 1860, however, she had left Harmonia for a new home in Battle Creek, for reasons that remain unclear.

During the Civil War, Truth agitated on behalf of the Union, enlistment of black troops in the army, and emancipation of Southern slaves. In 1864, she traveled to Virginia to work among the freed slaves who had arrived at a government refugee camp on Mason's Island. She described her feelings about her new work in a dictated letter to her friend **Amy Post**. "I do not know but what I shall stay here on the island all winter and go around among the freedmen's camps. They are all delighted to hear me talk. I think I am doing good." In November of that year, she met Abraham Lincoln in Washington, D.C. As she described it in a letter to a friend, "I must say, and I am proud to say, that I never was treated by any one with more kindness and cordiality than were shown to me by that great and good man." The president spoke with her about the war and emancipation, showed her a Bible given him by African-Americans from Baltimore, and signed a copy of her narrative. She said that upon leaving him, "I felt that I was in the presence of a friend, and I now thank God from the bottom of my heart that I always have advocated his cause, and have done it openly and boldly. I shall feel still more in duty bound to do so in time to come."

Truth's work after the war confirms her commitment to the cause of freedpeople. She continued her association with freedmen's relief agencies, and in 1867 began agitating for a plan she had devised to get the federal government to provide land grants in the West for newly freed slaves. For at least seven years, she campaigned on behalf of her idea but with little success. In 1879, much to her delight, Southern blacks began a westward and northward migration of their own accord. The Exodusters, as the emigrants were called, made Kansas their most popular destination. As Truth told reporters at the time, she had long prayed "that my people would go," because she believed African-Americans could "never be much in the South. They cannot get up. As long as the whites have the reins in their hands, how can the colored people get up there?" With great excitement, she traveled to Kansas to assist the refugees as they arrived, and spent a year speaking in white and black churches throughout the state in support of the Exodusters' efforts to build new lives for themselves.

The Kansas mission was to be the last campaign of Truth's life. She returned from it greatly debilitated and never truly recovered her health after that. She spent the final years of her life in Battle Creek, attended by her daughters Diana and Elizabeth. She died at home on November 26, 1883.

SOURCES:

Mabee, Carleton. *Sojourner Truth: Slave, Prophet, Legend.* NY: New York University Press, 1993.

Painter, Nell Irvin. *Sojourner Truth: A Life, A Symbol.* NY: W.W. Norton, 1996.

Stetson, Erlene, and Linda David. *Glorying in Tribulation: The Lifework of Sojourner Truth.* East Lansing, MI: Michigan State University Press, 1994.

Truth, Sojourner. *Narrative of Sojourner Truth; a Bondswoman of Olden Time, Emancipated by the New York Legislature in the Early Part of the Present Century with a History of her Labors and Correspondence, Drawn from Her Book of Life.* Battle Creek, MI: Published for the Author, 1878.

SUGGESTED READING:

Braude, Ann. *Radical Spirits: Spiritualism and Women's Rights in Nineteenth-Century America.* Boston, MA: Beacon Press, 1989.

Hooks, Bell. *Ain't I a Woman: Black Women and Feminism.* Boston, MA: South End, 1981.

Johnston, Paul E., and Sean Wilentz. *The Kingdom of Matthias.* NY: Oxford University Press, 1994.

Stewart, James Brewer. *Holy Warriors: The Abolitionists and American Slavery.* NY: Hill and Wang, 1976.

JUVENILE:

Adler, David A. *A Picture Book of Sojourner Truth.* Illus. by Gershom Griffith. NY: Holiday House, 1994.

Macht, Norman L. *Sojourner Truth: Crusader for Civil Rights.* Junior World Biographies. NY: Chelsea House, 1992.

McKissack, Patricia C., and Frederick McKissack. *Sojourner Truth: Ain't I a Woman?* (young adult). NY: Scholastic, 1992.

———. *Sojourner Truth: A Voice for Freedom.* Illus. by Michael Bryant. Hillside, NJ: Enslow, 1992.

Shumate, Jane. *Sojourner Truth and the Voice of Freedom.* Brookfield, CT: Millbrook Press, 1991.

COLLECTIONS:

Sojourner Truth Papers located at the Library of Congress, Washington, D.C.

Margaret M. Storey,
Assistant Professor of History,
DePaul University,
Chicago, Illinois

Truthgeba (700–779).

See Lioba.

Tsahai Haile Selassie (1919–1942)

Ethiopian princess and nurse. Name variations: Princess Tsahai Worq; Tsahaiwork; Tsehai. Born on October 13, 1919, in Addis Ababa, Ethiopia; died on August 17, 1942, in Lekemti, Ethiopia; youngest of six children of Tafari Makonnen, later Haile Selassie I (1892–1975), emperor of Ethiopia (r. 1930–1974), and Waizero Menen (1889–1962); attended schools in England and Switzerland; trained as a nurse at London's Great Ormond Street Hospital for Sick Children; graduated as a registered state children's nurse on August 25, 1939; married Colonel Abiye Ababa (a military officer), on April 26, 1942; no children.

The youngest daughter of *Menen and Emperor Haile Selassie of Ethiopia, Princess Tsahai was born in 1919, when her father, a distant cousin of the ruling empress *Zauditu, was still regent of Ethiopia and next in line for the throne. (Called "the garden of Africa," Ethiopia was at the time surrounded by colonial states, many of which were controlled by Italy.) As a young child, the princess lived with her six siblings in a compound known as the Little Gebbi (little palace), quite removed from the abject poverty of her country. From age eight, she attended school in England and Switzerland, and during vacations traveled with her royal relatives to France and Germany, learning each country's language as well as English. Even at her young age, the princess was impressed by the quality of life in Europe compared to the almost primitive conditions in her own nation.

Upon the death of Empress Zauditu in 1930 and the coronation of Haile Selassie as emperor, Tsahai's formal education was temporarily halted. She returned home and became involved in the royal activities of palace life. In the absence of her grown brothers and sisters, who had either married or were away at school, the princess became her father's close companion and confidante, accompanying him on official tours and frequently filling in for her mother at official dinners. Not yet a teenager, she was described at the time as possessing the dignity and grace of a mature woman.

By 1934, Haile Selassie had made great strides in reforming his country. Stone buildings were erected, foreign trade was increased, roads were widened, and schools and hospitals were built. In 1935, however, the emperor was sidetracked by Italy's attempt to absorb his country into its border colonies. A series of incidents in Ethiopia near the Italian frontiers deepened the threat of war, but when Haile Selassie appealed to the League of Nations to name Italy as an aggressor and impose sanctions, his plea fell on deaf ears. As her father prepared the country for battle, Tsahai convinced him to let her take an active role in the country's defense. In August 1935, under her sponsorship, the Ethiopian Women's Welfare Work Association (EWWWA) was formed, with a mission to expand health and welfare programs. With the threat of war, however, its members collected food and supplies for Ethiopian soldiers. The princess also worked with the new Ethiopian Red Cross, headed by **Geuta Herrouy**. Later, when the Italian army invaded, Tsahai worked as a volunteer with the first field ambulance of the emperor's army. As the war escalated, however, Ethiopia was crushed by Italian forces, and it became necessary for the emperor to send his wife and children to safety in England. As they were en route, Benito Mussolini announced the annexation of Ethiopia.

After another unsuccessful attempt to personally plead the cause of his country before the League of Nations in Geneva, Haile Selassie joined his family in Bath, England, where they lived in exile for the next five years. Welcomed as celebrities, the small group of Ethiopians was bombarded by journalists and news photographers. Princess Tsahai served as an interpreter for her mother and father and also became a spokesperson for her country, speaking before both large and small audiences about the plight of her people. The English were not only welcoming, but helpful to the Ethiopian cause. *Sylvia Pankhurst founded and edited the *New Times and Ethiopia News*, in hopes of spreading the truth about Ethiopia. Other Englishwomen organized the Friends of Abyssinia, dedicated to helping Ethiopian war victims.

At age 17, Tsahai decided that she wanted to become a nurse. Up until that time, no Ethiopian woman had ever trained as a nurse, and no woman of royal blood had ever worked at a profession. Her father, however, believing that in the long run his people would benefit, gave his consent. Another Englishwoman, **Lady Barton**, the wife of the former British minister to Ethiopia, arranged for the princess to interview with the Matron of London's Great Ormond Street Hospital for Sick Children, where she began training as a resident student nurse in August 1936.

Tsahai asked for no favors or special treatment, working alongside the other student nurses for the required 56 hours a week and earning a year's salary of £20. In August 1939, she graduated as a State Registered Children's Nurse, then received permission to continue her studies at London's Guy's Hospital, with the intention of becoming a State Registered General Trained Nurse. With the outbreak of World War II, the Probationers' School of Guy's had been moved to Pembury Hospital, some 29 miles southeast of London, and it was there that she enrolled in February 1940. The temporary housing for students was primitive, with no central heating and minimal sanitary facilities. The princess accepted a room with five other nurses, and when later offered an opportunity to move to a private nurses' home attached to the main hospital, turned it down. "I would not think of leaving the other nurses," she said. "I must be treated like everyone else."

After a year at Pembury, during which time the Nazis made their first mass air bombing on London, Tsahai was transferred to Farnborough, another base hospital. In March 1941, she was transferred again, to Guy's Hospital in London. On May 5, 1941, just months before she was to take her final state examinations, Haile Selassie made his state entry into the Ethiopian capital of Addis Ababa, to begin the process of liberation. The princess was ordered by her father to return home with her mother. Three British Red Cross Nurse volunteered to accompany the royal party to help her continue her nursing work in Ethiopia.

The journey home took three months, during which time the liberation was completed. Tsahai immediately went to work with the British Red Cross unit, setting up headquarters in the town of Dessie, which had suffered a massive air raid. They kept their London friends assessed of their progress through letters, one of which was published in the *Nursing Mirror*:

> We are running three large clinics: the largest is at Dessie, where we have an average of 150 patients. The second clinic is at Lake Haik, sixteen miles away—a most lovely place—and the third is at Bartie on the edge of the desert. . . .
>
> The Senior Political officer here at Dessie is quite sure the Unit has been the greatest thing done to help the people, for they were in grave distress. The Princess works in the morning very hard; we do the afternoons and evenings.

In conjunction with her work at Dessie, Tsahai also reactivated the Ethiopian Women's Welfare Work Association, which had been shut down during the occupation.

In April 1942, the princess married Colonel Abiye Ababa, a former member of the emperor's imperial guard, whom she had met in England. Before leaving to live in Lekemti, where Abiye was the newly appointed governor, she told an English woman journalist that she intended to carry on her work of establishing hospitals and medical service throughout her country.

Princess Tsahai did not have the opportunity to achieve her goals. Less than four months after her marriage, on August 17, 1942, she died of a hemorrhage suffered during a miscarriage. Ironically, it was believed that she might have survived had she received proper medical attention. To honor her memory, her friends in England later established Ethiopia's Princess Tsahai Memorial Hospital and nurses' training school, on a site donated by the emperor.

SOURCES:
McKown, Robin. *Heroic Nurses*. NY: Putnam, 1966.

Barbara Morgan,
Melrose, Massachusetts

Ts'ai Ch'ang (1900–1990).

See Cai Chang.

Ts'ai Yen (c. 162–239).

See Cai Yan.

Tschechowa, Olga (1897–1980)

Russian-born German film actress. Born on April 26, 1897, in Aleksandropol, Russia; died on March 9, 1980, in Munich, Germany; daughter of an engineer and a painter; studied sculpture and engraving in schools in Moscow and St. Petersburg; took acting lessons at Constantin Stanislavski's Moscow Art The- *ater school; married Michael Chekhov (an actor), around 1913 (marriage ended around 1916); children: daughter Ada.*

Selected filmography: Schloss Vogelöd *(Haunted Castle, 1921);* Liebe im Ring *(Love in the Ring, 1930);* Love on Command *(1931);* Liebelei *(Flirtation, 1933);* Der Choral von Leuthen *(The Hymn of Leuthen, 1933);* Maskerade *(Masquerade in Vienna, 1934);* Regine *(1934);* Die Welt ohne Maske *(The World Unmasked, 1934);* Burgtheater *(Town Theater, 1936);* Die gelbe Flagge *(The Yellow Flag, 1937);* Verliebtes Abenteuer *(Amorous Adventure, 1938);* Zwei Frauen *(Two Women, 1938);* Die unheimlichen Wünsche *(Sinister Desires, 1939);* Befreite Hände *(Unfettered Hands, 1939);* Gefährlicher Frühling *(Dangerous Spring, 1943).*

Born in Aleksandropol in the Caucasus Mountains of Russia in 1897, Olga Tschechowa was the daughter of a German-born father and a Russian mother. Her father, who came from Germany's Westphalia, was an engineer who served as minister of railways in tsarist Russia, while her mother was a painter. Her uncle was the famous Russian author and playwright Anton Chekhov; her aunt was the actress *Olga Knipper-Chekova.

It seemed preordained that Olga would find a life for herself somewhere in the arts, as had her mother, uncle, and grandmother who achieved fame as a singer. As a girl, she shuttled between schools in St. Petersburg and Moscow, where she studied sculpture and engraving. In her teens, she became interested in acting, and enrolled in classes at Constantin Stanislavski's Moscow Art Theater school. Tschechowa married her cousin Michael Chekhov, himself a well-established actor, when she was 16. The marriage ended just three years later, shortly after the birth of their daughter **Ada Chekhova**.

In the turmoil that followed Russia's Bolshevik Revolution, Tschechowa was persuaded in the early 1920s to leave her native Russia for the relative quiet of Berlin. There she worked designing posters until she was discovered by prominent German filmmakers Erich Pommer and F.W. Murnau. Murnau, one of the most influential German film directors of the period, cast Tschechowa in a leading role in his *Schloss Vogelöd* (Haunted Castle), and that single film launched her solidly on a career that would span three decades and earn her the epithet of the "Grand Dame of German film."

Tschechowa teamed with German boxing champion Max Schmeling in 1930 to star in *Liebe im Ring* (Love in the Ring). Three years later, she shared the screen with ***Magda Schnei-**

Olga
Tschechowa

der, Gustav Gründgens, *Luise Ullrich, and Paul Hörbiger in Max Ophuls' very successful *Liebelei* (Flirtation). In 1934, she appeared with newcomer *Paula Wessely in Willi Forst's masterpiece *Maskerade* (Masquerade in Vienna), a film that played her worldly sophistication off the innocence and naivete of her costar. Two years later, she costarred with Werner Krauss in *Burgtheater* (Town Theater).

These successes in German film soon took Tschechowa to film capitals through the world, including Paris, Prague, Rome, and Vienna. She visited Hollywood in 1931 to make *Love on Command*, the German adaptation of American director Mal St. Clair's *The Boudoir Diplomat*. After a decade in German film, the Russian émigré had acquired a sophistication and regal bearing that managed to keep autograph seekers and other admirers at bay. Her worldly image was enhanced by the traces of a Russian accent that she retained. When European casting agents of the day contemplated a role calling for an elegant woman of a certain age, beautiful and regal, Tschechowa was the first actress to spring to mind.

In 1933, as the Hitler regime was solidifying its hold on the German government, Tschechowa starred in *Der Choral von Leuthen* (The Hymn of Leuthen), in which she played a noblewoman who offered shelter within the walls of her castle to a Prussian platoon under the command of Frederick II the Great. The making of this film coincided with a call that went out from Berlin for propaganda films glorifying German history, particularly the days of Frederick the Great. Led by Joseph Goebbels, Hitler's propaganda apparatus called upon filmmakers to produce these "Fridericus-Filme" to depict the former German ruler as a widely popular hero who was devoted not only to his subjects but to traditional values. Nazi propagandists clearly hoped that, in these glamorous film portraits of the Hohenzollern king, German moviegoers of the early 1930s would see a striking resemblance to their current leader.

Despite the government edict calling for the production of German historical epics, Tschechowa herself clearly preferred working in such American-style comedies as *Die gelbe Flagge* (The Yellow Flag, 1937) and *Verliebtes Abenteuer* (Amorous Adventure, 1938). She was similarly disposed towards musicals and fantasy films, such as *Die Welt ohne Maske* (The World Unmasked, 1934) and *Die unheimlichen Wünsche* (Sinister Desires, 1939). In the latter film, Tschechowa's role was hardly a stretch. She portrayed a glamorous actress who seeks vengeance on a noble who spurns her in favor of a simple working girl.

The actress also enjoyed great success in roles that pitted her against younger and less worldly rivals for the affections of a man. Tschechowa's films of this type include *Zwei Frauen* (Two Women, 1938), in which she plays a woman who competes with her 18-year-old daughter for the affections of a pilot, as well as *Befreite Hände* (Unfettered Hands, 1939) and *Gefährlicher Frühling* (Dangerous Spring, 1943). In the latter film, she played a mature but still beautiful woman who manages to lure a professor away from her niece.

In the years following the end of World War II, Tschechowa launched her own film production company, an ill-fated venture that failed not long after it was begun. Much more successful was a cosmetics company that she founded in the early 1950s. Forty years later, the company boasted branches in Helsinki, Milan, Vienna, and the United States. Her stunning beauty on the silver screen and her success in later life as a cosmetics mogul prompted Tschechowa to write a number of beauty-care books, most of which received a warm reception from German readers. Less well received was her autobiography, *Meine Uhren gehen anders* (My Clocks Tell Different Times), despite the fact that it contained detailed instructions on how to create some of her secret beauty preparations.

In a November 1967 interview with the magazine *Sud-deutsche Zeitung*, she told a reporter: "I retired because I didn't want to spoil the illusions of all those people who admired me." Four years later, the actress emerged briefly from retirement to star in an episode of the German TV series "Duell zu dritt" (Duel for Three). Tschechowa died at her home in Munich on March 9, 1980, at the age of 82.

SOURCES:

Romani, Cinzia. *Tainted Goddesses: Female Film Stars of the Third Reich*. NY: Sarpedon, 1992.

Don Amerman,
freelance writer,
Saylorsburg, Pennsylvania

Tse-Hi or Tsu-Hsi (1835–1908).

See Cixi.

Tsu-mana (c. 1860–1942).

See Nampeyo.

Tsuru Aoki (1892–1961).

See Aoki, Tsuru.

Tsvetaeva, Marina (1892–1941)

Innovative Russian poet, long undervalued for political reasons, who is now generally recognized as a national treasure. Name variations: Marina Cvetaeva; Marina Tsvetayeva or Tsvétaieff; Marina Tsvetajewa-Efron. Pronunciation: Ma-PEE-na Tsve-TAH-ye-va. Born Marina Ivanovna Tsvetaeva in Moscow, Russia, on September 26, 1892 (according to the Julian calendar used then in Russia; the date would be October 6 "New Style" on the Gregorian calendar used in the West); committed suicide on August 31, 1941, in Yelabuga, USSR; daughter of Maria A. Meyn and Ivan

TSVETAEVA, MARINA

V. Tsvetaev; married Sergei Efron, in 1912; children: Ariadna Efron (b. 1912); Irina Efron (1917–1920); Georgii Efron (b. 1925).

Published first book (1910); emigrated from the Soviet Union (1922); returned to USSR (1939).

Selected books: Evening Album (Moscow, 1910); The Magic Lantern (Moscow, 1912); From Two Books (Moscow, 1913); Mileposts (Moscow, 1921 and 1922); Mileposts I (Moscow, 1922); The End of Casanova: A Dramatic Study (Moscow, 1922); Parting (Moscow-Berlin, 1922); Poems to Blok (Berlin, 1922); The Tsar-Maiden (Moscow, 1922 and Berlin, 1922); Psyche Romanticism (Berlin, 1923); The Swain (Prague, 1924); After Russia (Paris, 1928).

Major poems not in books: "Poem of the End" (Prague, 1926); "Poem of the Mountain" (Paris, 1926); "The Rat-Catcher" (Prague, 1926); "The Stairs" (Prague, 1926); "Attempt at a Room" (Prague, 1928); "From the Sea" (Paris, 1928); "New Year's Greeting" (Paris, 1928); "Poem of the Air" (Prague, 1930).

Major plays: Adventure (Prague, 1923); Phoenix (Prague, 1924); Theseus: A Tragedy (Paris, 1927); Phaedra (Paris, 1928).

One icy winter evening in 1921, Marina Tsvetaeva joined eight other women on stage for a poetry reading. Though the Civil War that followed the 1917 Bolshevik Revolution in Russia was drawing to a close, Moscow was hungry and cold. The audience, from the smell at least, was mainly Red Army soldiers, unfamiliar with "aristocratic" poetry. The poets were outfitted in nice dresses, furs and elegant shoes. But Tsvetaeva wore a man's coat and thick felt boots; she also wore a leather belt and carried a leather bag over her shoulder—the belt and field pouch of an officer in the tsar's army. These accessories declared her loyalty to the defeated royalist White Army, in which her husband had been an officer.

A prominent male poet introduced the readers, explaining that women could only write about love and passion. Tsvetaeva quickly leafed through her notebook, marking pages with matches. She then read seven rousing, risky poems about the White Army, against the new Bolshevik government. The audience applauded loudly, responding to the sounds rather than the meaning, while the moderator anxiously ushered her offstage. Political imprudence and artistic courage were typical of Tsvetaeva: she wrote poems about what she loved, regardless of political expediency. Her Romantic world-view convinced her that a poet's work and life could not be neatly separated, and that a poet must take certain risks.

Tsvetaeva's mother **Maria Alexandrovna Meyn** was a gifted pianist of Polish and German ancestry. Maria Alexandrovna's father, however, considered a concert career unsuitable for a decent young woman, so Maria performed only at home. At 22, she married Ivan Vladimirovich Tsvetaev, a 44-year-old widower with two small children. She soon concentrated her ambitions on the child she was expecting, sure it would be a son to name Alexander after her beloved, despotic father. Instead, the child was a girl, Marina, born on September 26, 1892. Sighed Maria Alexandrovna: "At least she will be a musician." A second girl—Marina's sister **Anastasia Tsvetaeva**, known as Asya—was born in 1894.

Ivan Tsvetaev was the son of a poor village priest. First educated at seminary, with hard work he became a university professor, museum director, and recognized authority on classical languages. His life's work was funding and building a museum of copies of ancient Greek sculpture, for poor Russian students to study. Tsvetaeva described her father as absorbed in his work, affectionate but inattentive to his children, and eternally mourning his beautiful first wife.

The household in old Moscow was complicated, between Ivan's older children and his second wife. Marina was a talented and difficult child who later recalled that her mother had favored her older half-brother and the younger, fragile Asya. Tsvetaeva had the musical talent, however, and her mother began teaching her to play piano when she was four. Throughout her childhood, she practiced every day, hating the metronome but never leaving the bench before her time was done. The children were educated by French and German governesses and tutors, and their mother read to them in French and German as well as in Russian: they grew up practically trilingual. It was a demanding childhood, full of mysterious hidden conflicts and burdensome expectations. Worst of all, her mother made fun of Marina's attempts at writing poetry (she began at the age of six). At the same time, this upbringing provided a rich cultural and literary background which Tsvetaeva would draw on all her life. She insisted that she learned everything important before the age of seven, and the important things included love, passion, longing, and the lure of forbidden fruit—mainly literary fruit, books her mother considered too adult for her.

In 1902, when Tsvetaeva was almost ten, her mother was diagnosed with tuberculosis of the lungs; she left for treatment in Italy, taking her two daughters along. Tsvetaeva and her sister spent the next three years in various émigré hotels and boarding schools, and their mother's absences forced them to become good friends. Their unusual closeness appears in Tsvetaeva's first published poems. In Italy, she met Russian anarchist revolutionaries and wrote poems in their honor. In a friendly boarding school in Switzerland, the Tsvetaeva sisters were drawn to Catholicism; later, in Germany, a less pleasant boarding school effectively soured that impression.

Trying to acclimate her lungs to colder climates, Maria Alexandrovna moved from Italy to Switzerland and then Germany. Instead, she caught a bad cold, and her illness returned, worse than ever. In 1905, she and her daughters went back to the Russian Empire, to the temperate southern climate of Yalta. Tsvetaeva was thrilled by reports of revolutionary activity; her mother, afraid that her passionate and headstrong children might give all their money to revolutionary organizations, wrote in her will that they would receive only the interest from the money she left them until they reached the age of 40. She died in 1906, saying, "I'm only sorry for music and the sun."

Maria Alexandrovna's death left Tsvetaeva motherless at 13. Her father, vague and preoccupied, was hardly able to guide her (he died in 1913), and no one else took on the task. Tsvetaeva attended a series of high schools: always a top student in Russian, French and German, always a miserable failure in mathematics. Her closest companions were her sister Asya and Asya's school friends. In time, Tsvetaeva stopped attending school regularly, hiding in the attic until her father left home in order to read or write in her room, living an intense and solitary life. She discovered the Romantic plays of the French writer Edmond Rostand (best known today for *Cyrano de Bergerac*) and fell in love with Napoleon and his ill-fated son. When her pious father discovered with horror that she had covered Saint Nikolai the Wonder-Worker in her bedroom icon with a painting of Napoleon, she refused to remove the painting.

Gradually, Tsvetaeva became aware of the literary excitement around her in Moscow. During her childhood and youth, poetry was the most important literary genre in Russia (following the decades of great novelists such as Dostoevsky and Tolstoy). Tsvetaeva's lifelong sense of being a poet, therefore, let her enter the country's cultural life on her own terms. She met a minor but fascinating Symbolist poet, who wrote under the pseudonym "Ellis," and she enjoyed a brief romance with his roommate. Through them, she came to Musaget, a society of writers and philosophers where many major poets discussed

their artistic theories. Tsvetaeva and her imitative sister cut their hair short (many years before this was fashionable), started smoking, wore high heels, and generally rebelled against the conservative background of their father's house.

After Ellis was accused of stealing from the museum Tsvetaeva's father directed, she was forbidden to see him. Though she had rejected proposals of marriage from both him and his roommate, she still missed them very much and decided to publish a book of poems to convey her feelings. At the time, nothing was easier for a well-off young Russian than publishing a book: she took her verses to a printer, chose the binding, and paid for an edition of 500 copies. Her first book, *The Evening Album*, appeared in 1910, the year she turned 18. The poems were well crafted but childish in content. Amazingly, three major Russian poet-critics wrote about the book, sensing the author's significant poetic gift. With one of these critics, Maximilian Voloshin, Tsvetaeva struck up a lasting friendship.

In order for the gods not to play with us, we must play with them!

—Marina Tsvetaeva

Voloshin invited Tsvetaeva to spend the summer of 1911 at his seaside house on the Black Sea. This was a kind of artists' colony where painters, actors and writers worked, joked and enjoyed walking over the sun-baked landscape. Tsvetaeva often told how she met a young man on the beach, which was covered with pretty pebbles, and thought, "If he brings me my favorite stone, I will marry him." Sergei Yakovlevich Efron, then 17 (a year younger than Tsvetaeva), found the carnelian bead she preferred, and the two immediately became inseparable. Efron was an orphan from a half-Jewish, half-Russian family and suffered from tuberculosis, a disease close to Tsvetaeva's heart. She protected and mothered him, encouraging him to write stories and to behave in a noble, suitably Romantic manner. The two married in January 1912, aged 19 and 18.

The first years of Tsvetaeva's married life were happy, the best of what a woman of her class could enjoy. She published her second book and Efron's first in 1912; the couple bought things they liked, spent time on the Black Sea, and paid servants to do the cooking and housekeeping. Their daughter **Ariadna Efron** (usually given the more Russian-sounding pet name Alya) was born in September 1912; Tsvetaeva first nursed her herself, then hired wet-nurses.

Tsvetaeva's poetry grew more mature, she won a Moscow literary prize, and occasionally published in journals or read at friends' houses. She published a selection from her first two books in 1913, but the next book would not appear until several years after the 1917 Revolution.

Tsvetaeva's poetry leaped in significance during her intense love affair with an older poet, *Sophia Parnok. Parnok matured slowly as an artist and would write her best poems, many of them beautiful evocations of a woman's love for a woman, in the 1920s and 1930s. Tsvetaeva was immediately attracted to Parnok, and the two traveled, read and wrote together, with frequent stormy quarrels, from the fall of 1914 until early 1916. Parnok encouraged Tsvetaeva to read 19th-century Russian women's poetry, took her on trips to the provinces, and helped her form connections in the publishing world. When the relationship ended, Tsvetaeva was becoming aware of other poets writing in Russia, meeting many personally. She turned to her native city, Moscow, in exploring her own poetic voice. It was a time of intense emotional, spiritual and artistic growth, as she began to write what is clearly great poetry. She also did not need to worry about making ends meet or taking care of her daughter if she were not in the mood; freedom from everyday cares let her consolidate a sense of herself as a serious artist.

The First World War left little mark on Tsvetaeva's poetry. But a month before her daughter Irina's birth, the February Revolution of 1917 forced the Russian tsar Nicholas II to abdicate. The often oppressive tsarist autocracy was replaced with unheard-of personal and political freedoms and an unwieldy Provisional Government (led by Alexander Kerensky). Most Russian artists and intellectuals welcomed this change, but it did not impress Tsvetaeva; she wrote gloomy poems about the faceless masses of soldiers, seeming to predict what was to follow. As the Bolsheviks opposed Kerensky's government, ongoing war and political agitation made it hard to continue the outwardly peaceful, inwardly turbulent life that Tsvetaeva had set up. October 1917 found her on the Black Sea, while Sergei Efron, now an officer in training, defended the Kremlin against Revolutionary forces. Tsvetaeva published an account of those days based on her journals: panic on the first train north to Moscow; fear that Efron had died in the fighting; their trip back south to her sister Asya and Voloshin; Voloshin's prophetic description of the Civil War ahead; her trip back to Moscow to collect the children; and, finally, realization that she could not leave Moscow, that she was isolated in a city gripped by revolution.

Toward the end of 1917, after a week of bloody fighting, Moscow fell to Lenin's followers, the Bolsheviks. In December, opponents of the Bolsheviks formed the first units of the White Volunteer Army to battle Lenin's "Reds." When Lenin was nearly assassinated in September 1918, his colleagues launched a "Red Terror," in which thousands of opponents were executed. By the close of 1918, Lenin's party, now renamed the Communists, had established a dictatorship. The White Army continued its opposition. These Civil War years in Moscow were both trying and triumphant for Tsvetaeva. She had no profession besides her poetry, was horribly nearsighted and was frightened of busy city streets. The new Communist government confiscated the money she would have inherited at 40. Her difficult childhood had not equipped her to meet all her children's physical and emotional needs, and selling books and furnishings did not bring much money. She chopped attic beams and furniture to feed the stove and used the fancy samovar to cook potatoes and porridge rather than tea. In late 1919, during the worst winter, friends convinced her to put her daughters into one of the new state-run children's homes in hopes they would be better fed there. On one visit, she found Alya sick and brought her home to take care of her. She then heard that Irina, stunted physically and mentally from malnourishment, had died of starvation before her third birthday.

At the same time, Tsvetaeva refused to cut back her work on poetry. Instead, she befriended young actors who were passionately excited about new artistic trends and freedoms, and she made her daughter Alya into a household helper and junior poet. Numerous love affairs and infatuations fueled wonderful poems. The hardships of this new life strengthened Marina's sense of artistic mission. She dressed in whatever she had, smoked whatever tobacco she could find, and defended her husband's and the White Army's fight to depose the new Bolshevik government. But in November 1920, the Whites were decisively defeated and forced to leave Russia. Many creative artists in the Soviet Union tried for years to understand the new Communist system, overlooking or rationalizing its flaws. Tsvetaeva liked many Communists personally, but she uncompromisingly rejected the political system which had presided over her daughter's starvation in the children's home. If she had stayed in the USSR, she would surely have been arrested long before the great Stalinist terror in the 1930s.

*Marina
Tsvetaeva, with
her daughter
Alya.*

Through a friend, Tsvetaeva learned that her husband was alive in the newly restored country of Czechoslovakia. It took more than a year to get money, permission for visas, and train tickets; in that time, she published two new books of poetry. In May 1922, she and Alya (al-most ten) left Russia. Tsvetaeva spent six weeks in the hectic literary climate of Berlin, where new publishers were flourishing, and managed to publish several more new books. Then she and Alya joined Efron in an almost rural suburb of Prague, and their émigré life began. The new government of Czechoslovakia wisely offered financial support to scholars and artists who had fled the Soviet Union; Efron studied literature at Charles University on scholarship, and Tsvetaeva received a subsidy as a poet.

Tsvetaeva remembered Prague fondly after leaving. She loved the landscape around the suburban villages, for walks and inspiration. The subsidy let her write a great deal—cycles of lyric poetry, a long folkloric poem, two long lyric poems based on an unhappy love affair, and a "lyrical satire" based on "The Pied Piper of Hamelin." The family combined resources to rent cheap rooms, where Tsvetaeva hauled water, scrubbed floors, cooked, washed, mended, and stoked the stove in winter. Efron, a student with tuberculosis, was never expected to do housework or find a paying job. After the birth of their third child, Georgii (with the pet name "Mur," after the cat in a story by E.T.A. Hoffmann), in February 1925, Tsvetaeva dreaded another bleak village winter, and she moved to Paris on November 1.

By 1925, Paris was the center of Russian émigré political and literary life. Journals and newspapers were run by various party groups, from leftist to moderate and right wing. Tsvetaeva at first published almost everywhere (except the right wing, she explained, because they lacked culture). She came to Paris a recognized poet, and her successful first reading earned praise and enough money for a holiday in Brittany. Soon, however, Tsvetaeva's pugnacious literary statements and flouting of convention made enemies among the émigré community. This made her life in Paris more interesting and difficult. In France, passportless Russian émigrés could not hold regular jobs, and Tsvetaeva, as always, was only qualified as a writer. The family lived in a series of grimy, working-class suburbs, often behind on their rent, and Tsvetaeva's earnings from publication and donations from admirers of her writing were the main source of income.

In France, Tsvetaeva enjoyed correspondence with Boris Pasternak, a great poet who remained in the Soviet Union, Rainer Maria Rilke, the Austrian poet who died at the end of 1926, and many less famous friends. She continued to write prolifically, short lyric poems and long narrative poems. Everyone agreed that she doted on her son Georgii, a brilliant child who grew into a self-centered, unpleasant adolescent. At the same time, her husband came to consider the White Army a terrible mistake and to favor the Soviet Union; young Alya adopted his opinions, at least partly to rebel against her mother's demands that she do housework and mind her little brother.

By the 1930s, economic depression made life precarious, and Tsvetaeva wrote more critical and autobiographical prose, which sold and paid better than poetry. Many of her stylistically innovative prose works are memoirs of writers she knew who had recently died; others examine the roots of her own poetry in childhood. Her uncompromising and unpopular political comments, combined with Efron's dubious political evolution, set editors against her. Right-wing publications objected to her "revolutionary" formal innovations, while left-wing publications did not want writing that presented the tsar or the White Army favorably.

In 1937, Alya returned to the Soviet Union; later the same year, Efron disappeared after a bungled political assassination and also left for the USSR. He turned out to have been working for years for the NKVD (the Soviet secret service), though it is unclear what Tsvetaeva knew about his activities. Left with her son, no longer a welcome contributor or friend, Tsvetaeva realized that she must return to the USSR as well, despite the problems she would face there. Boris Pasternak had often written that important Soviet literary figures valued her new work, so she may have expected more of a welcome than she would receive. She prepared slowly, assembling parts of her archive she could take with her, leaving them with dependable people. (Some of these writings survived the Second World War and are now in print.) Her last cycle of poems was a passionate protest against Hitler's occupation of Czechoslovakia; she must have worried about her son, with his Jewish last name, in a Europe menaced by Hitler. In June 1939, she left France with 14-year-old Georgii, who insisted that things in the USSR would be wonderful.

Of course, things were far from wonderful. Stalin's "Great Terror" reached its height between 1934 and 1939. Working to ferret out "traitors," Stalin and his secret police presided over a system which saw to it that millions of innocent people—including top party and government elites, army officers, artists, writers, scientists, ordinary citizens, and children—spent long years in forced labor camps or were killed. When Tsvetaeva arrived, she learned that her sister Asya was in a labor camp. For two months, the family lived together outside Moscow. In August, Tsvetaeva's daughter Alya, nearly 27, was arrested and disappeared into the Stalinist system of prisons and camps. In October, her husband Efron was arrested. Tsvetaeva would never see either of them again. She and her son were now homeless in a land where almost everyone shunned them as dangerous former émigrés. She found temporary places to live, and Pasternak helped her get work as a literary translator; Tsvetaeva, however, worked too conscientiously to make much money at translating. In 1940, she noted that she had been trying on the idea of death for a year—but there were no ceiling hooks, as chandeliers had all been replaced by electric bulbs.

Still, she lived, occasionally writing poems of her own, standing in lines to send packages to Efron and Alya in prison, until Hitler attacked the USSR in 1941. Tsvetaeva, protective as ever, was terrified that Georgii would get killed in German firebombing. She managed to get them evacuated southward with other writers, and they found a room in the small town of Yelabuga on the Kama River. People say that during her last days Tsvetaeva looked beaten and depressed, though she wanted to move to a town nearby where Georgii could attend school and be less bored. No one knows why she committed suicide on August 31, 1941, when everyone else was out of the house: quarrels with her son, fear of the advancing Germans, indignation at a supposed offer to collaborate with the secret police, or merely depressed exhaustion. She was buried in an unmarked grave in the Yelabuga cemetery.

Efron was evidently shot in 1941; Georgii was drafted into the Red Army and disappeared on the battlefield in 1944. Alya spent 17 years in prison, labor camps and exile for her nonexistent crimes. She was "rehabilitated" in 1955 and spent her last 20 years working to publish her mother's writings. At her request, Tsvetaeva's archive in Moscow was closed until the year 2000. Until the "thaw" after Stalin's death in 1953, Tsvetaeva remained a "non-person" in the Soviet Union. By the end of the 1970s, she was recognized as one of Russia's greatest 20th-century poets.

SOURCES:

Karlinsky, Simon. *Marina Tsvetaeva: The Woman, Her World and Her Poetry.* Cambridge: Cambridge University Press, 1986.

Schweitzer, Viktoria. *Tsvetaeva.* Trans. by Robert Chandler and H. T. Willetts, ed. by Angela Livingstone. London: HarperCollins, 1992.

SUGGESTED READING:

After Russia-Posle Rossii. (Bilingual edition.) Trans. by Michael Naydan. Ann Arbor, MI: Ardis, 1992.

Demesne of the Swans-Lebediny Stan. (Bilingual edition.) Trans. by Robin Kemball. Ann Arbor, MI: Ardis, 1980.

Pasternak, Yevgeny, Yelana Pasternak, and Konstantin Azadovsky, eds. *Letters Summer 1926: Correspondence Between Pasternak, Tsvetaeva and Rilke.* Oxford: Oxford University Press, 1985.

Selected Poems of Marina Tsvetayeva. Trans. by Elaine Feinstein. Oxford: Oxford University Press, 1971, rev. ed., London, 1986.

Taubman, Jane. *A Life Through Poetry: Marina Tsvetaeva's Lyric Diary.* Columbus, OH: Slavica, 1988.

Tsvetaeva, Marina. *Art in the Light of Conscience. Eight Essays on Poetry by Marina Tsvetaeva.* Trans. with intro. and notes by Angela Livingstone. Cambridge, MA: Harvard University Press, 1992.

———. *A Captive Spirit: Selected Prose.* Ed. and trans. by J. Marin King. Ann Arbor, MI: Ardis, 1980.

Tsvetaeva: A Pictorial Biography. Comp. by Mikhail Baltsvinik and Irma Kudrova. Ann Arbor, MI: Ardis, 1980.

Tsvetayeva, Marina: Selected Poems. Trans. by David McDuff. Newcastle-upon-Tyne: Bloodaxe Press, 1987.

Sibelan Forrester,
Assistant Professor of Russian,
Swarthmore College,
Swarthmore, Pennsylvania

Tsze Hsi An (1835–1908).

See Cixi.

Tubbs, Alice (1851–1930)

First and most successful woman professional gambler in the American West, who played at casinos from Oklahoma Territory to the Rocky Mountains in a career that spanned decades. Name variations: Poker Alice; Alice Ivers; Alice Huckert; Alice Duffield; Corduroy Alice. Born Alice Ivers on February 17, 1851, in Sudbury, England; died from a gall bladder condition on February 27, 1930, in Sturgis, South Dakota; only daughter of a schoolmaster and a housewife; moved with family to Virginia in late 1860s, then to Colorado; educated in a female seminary in southern United States; married Frank Duffield (a mining engineer), around 1870; married W.G. (George) Tubbs, in 1907; married George Huckert, after 1910; no children.

Began professional gambling in Lake City, Colorado (1876), as means of support after husband was killed in mine accident; traveled the West as gambler and ran roadhouses in Deadwood and Sturgis, South Dakota; retired (early 1920s).

Nearly $250,000 passed through the hands of Poker Alice during her career, but most of it went back into the faro and poker games she loved or to the down-on-their-luck compatriots who knew she was always good for a stake. Alice Ivers Duffield Huckert Tubbs was one of the first women professional gamblers in the American West. Eventually going by the moniker Poker Alice, she was certainly the most successful of the few women who made gambling an occupation.

Little is known about Alice Tubbs' childhood. She was born Alice Ivers in Sudbury, England, on February 17, 1851, the only daughter of a schoolmaster and a housewife. She was strictly brought up in the educational and religious ways of the 19th-century English middle class, and those values remained with her, even through her unorthodox career. In the late 1860s, the Ivers family left England for Virginia. Tubbs completed her education at a girls' school in the South, before the family moved to Colorado at the beginning of the silver boom.

A petite woman with blonde hair, pale blue eyes, and a clear English complexion, Alice was about 19 when she married Frank Duffield, a mining engineer. In 1875, they moved to the isolated mining camp of Lake City, Colorado. That spring, the settlement had had 3 log cabins and twice as many tents; by late summer when the Duffields arrived, the population was 500 and buildings numbered 67. By 1877, the population would hit 2,500, with 500 permanent buildings. Rapid growth and equally rapid decline was the norm for frontier mining camps.

Few women lived in the camp. Since Tubbs was not interested in sewing and chatting, there was little for her to do. Gambling was a major entertainment in mining communities, with all classes and professions represented. She became fascinated with the games. She would accompany Frank to the gambling halls and stand behind him while he played.

𝓘 enjoyed the game and never cared too much about the money part of it.

—Poker Alice

Then, in 1876, Frank was killed in a mining accident. Though Alice had enough education to teach, there was no school in Lake City. In fact, there were few occupations for Western widows outside of prostitution. So Tubbs took to gambling as a way to support herself, beginning a career that spanned 50 years.

Alice was one of only two or three women professionals for several years. In those days, professional gamblers wore clothing that set them off from other gamers. Men wore fashionable suits, including coats, vests, and hats. Most women gamblers wore ballroom fashions: gowns, gloves, slippers, and jewelry. Gamblers for the casinos worked in shifts, with tables opening at noon and closing at six o'clock the following morning. Tubbs, who was bright and skilled, quickly earned the respect of both amateur and professional gamblers. In the rough mining towns, she learned to protect herself; she began carrying a gun, later telling an interviewer that her father "had been an expert marksman. He taught me to shoot, and shoot well. I was never afraid."

Tubbs had to draw that gun more than once. There was the time she was playing faro and lost nearly $1,500. "I could not understand why I was always losing," she said, "so I began watching the dealer. . . . I detected a crooked maneuver, [and] watched him a second time and he very clumsily handled it in a crooked way. Then I drew my gun. I said, 'If you'd have done that cleverly I wouldn't kick. I could admire a clever crook, I'll admit that, but I have no use for a clumsy crook like yourself. Now before I pull the trigger, you give me back all the money I lost in your crooked dealing. I want all of it.'" She got her money back and left.

In the early days of the West, gambling was legal and took place in the same room as the bar, an entertainment for both players and observers. Tubbs maintained that most professionals were honest. When cheating occurred, a casino would get a reputation for dishonesty, and professionals would avoid the place until it was cleaned up, making the house lose a great deal of money. But when gambling was "forced into the rear of the saloons behind closed doors," said Tubbs, "honesty seemed to have left the tables." Consistent with her upbringing, Alice refused to gamble on Sunday, which cost her a bundle, since Sunday was often the biggest day in saloons. Miners, who worked a six-day week, came to town for entertainment on Saturday night and Sunday. But Alice believed in "resting on Sunday and working like hell for the devil the rest of the week."

In those early years, Tubbs was described as a refined, well-dressed woman with a hint of a British accent, smiling except at the gaming tables; there, she won or lost with the same expressionless face, speaking in monosyllables. When Lake City calmed after 1877, Tubbs moved to greener pastures, dealing games in several area mining towns. For about a year in 1878–79, she worked in Leadville, Colorado, during its rapid growth from a few hundred to 18,000 citizens in a few months.

In the early 1880s, Tubbs moved to Silver City, New Mexico. There, one evening, while playing faro, she kept winning until the dealer called out, "Bank's closed." Alice walked around the table and took the dealer's seat, an accepted practice for winners at faro in those days. She declared the bank open and "the sky's the limit." Faro is a complicated game, requiring close attention, alertness, and quick thinking from players and dealer alike. Usually the dealer has an assistant, but Alice worked alone that night. She won several thousand dollars. As word filtered out that a woman was winning so well, people sauntered in from the other casinos to watch. The next afternoon, Tubbs took her winnings and went to New York City, living high until the money ran out. She recalled in later years that her visit was mostly shows, suppers, and fine clothes, but made no mention of trying the city's elite gambling houses.

She returned to the West in 1889. A few other women had joined the gambling profession, but there were never many. According to Tubbs: "Women have too many nerves. . . . One must have a countenance that can remain immovable hour after hour." She noted the best known of the other women gamblers was **Eleonore Dumont**, known as Madame Mustache, who "was clever and had a great deal of charm. She was a good musician and a linguist. I often wondered why she began her career as a gambler. I've heard the same thing about myself—love or thrill of the game, that's enough." She also recalled **Kitty the Schemer**, who "called herself the 'Queen of California Gamblers' [and] didn't last long." **Faro Nell**, Alice reported, could shoot a whiskey glass out of a man's hand or the heel off his boot. "She did shoot a heel off occasionally." **Prairie Rose** was "a very pretty girl" who wagered she could walk naked down a Kansas street. "She won her bet," said Alice. "Rose picked a time when nearly everyone was off the streets. She walked down with a revolver in each hand to discourage any curious person. This gave her the name of 'Lady *Godiva of the Plains.'" Alice also knew **Airship Annie**, **China Mary**, **Haltershanks Eva**, **Bowlegged Mary**, and **Iowa Bull**, whom Tubbs described as "a robust, affectionate, quiet little woman."

Later in the year, Alice joined the homesteaders' run on newly released land in Oklahoma. She wasn't interested in land, but she knew there would be people who wanted to gamble. Tubbs drove from Caldwell, Kansas, into the Cherokee Strip, where she stayed for nearly two years before heading for Clifton, Arizona. Dealing at several casinos in Clifton, she received the nickname Corduroy Alice, for the suit she wore. Arizona was not friendly, however. An editorial in a local paper demanded that the law against women in saloons be strictly enforced, for such women "are of the lowest character and regular crime-breeders. . . . [They are] brazen-faced, blear-eyed, degenerate creatures." Since she was a professional gambler, not a prostitute, Tubbs did not consider herself "fallen." She was a woman doing what was considered man's work. "She met men on an equal basis . . . [taking] her booze straight, [smoking] cigars,

[packing a gun], and . . . cuss[ing] like a mule skinner," claimed one spectator.

Tubbs then moved to Creede, Colorado, where a silver boom had begun. Since she arrived just after the discovery was announced, she and **Mrs. Creede** were the only two women in a camp of seven people. After Alice cut and prepared the logs, neighbors helped with the construction of her cabin. In Creede, she was a dealer for Bob Ford, the former gang member who killed his pal Jesse James for reward money and amnesty for his crimes. Other women gamblers were attracted to Creede as well, including Calamity Jane (*Martha Jane Cannary*), **Kilarney Kate** and **Creede Lily**. None of these women gambled as well as Alice, and some reputedly resorted to prostitution occasionally. Tubbs stuck to her eight-hour shift at Ford's, every day but Sunday. While never wealthy, neither was she destitute, and unlucky gamblers knew she would advance them a bit of money.

As mining slowed, Tubbs left Creede. She worked in Bachelor City for a while, where it was not unusual for play to reach $30,000 a night. After Bachelor City, she drifted to Deadwood in the Black Hills of Dakota Territory.

Alice Tubbs

Though it was not the boomtown it had been in the 1870s, it still had a strong gambling contingent. But when Alice sought work in a saloon, the miners protested; they did not like to lose to a woman. So Alice put on her corduroy coat and a hat and stuck a cigar in her mouth. It was the first time she had smoked a cigar, and it was to become her trademark. Deadwood gamblers gave her the nickname Poker Alice and she became known as the toughest dealer in town.

At the next table was a dealer named George Tubbs. Alice and George became such rivals that eventually they refused to speak to each other. Then a drunken miner charged George with cheating and threatened him with a knife. As he backed George against the wall, Alice shot the miner through the arm. George proposed marriage shortly thereafter and Alice accepted.

The couple bought some land and left the gambling tables for homestead life. They worked hard and had few neighbors, but, said Tubbs, "It was the happiest part of my life with George." After three years, in the winter of 1910, George contracted pneumonia. He died during a raging blizzard. Unable to travel for several days, Alice preserved the body by freezing it. When the storm abated, she took off in the extreme cold and drove 48 miles into Sturgis, South Dakota. Having little money, she stopped en route and pawned her wedding ring to pay for the burial. There was no funeral parlor, so Alice convinced some men to dig a grave. After a few graveside words were said, she returned to town, entered a gambling hall, and asked for a job; she said she only had to earn $25. Later in the day, when the saloonkeeper told her she'd made her goal, Alice left, stopping on the way home to reclaim her wedding ring. She remained at the cabin for a while, grieving over her loss. Although she would marry again, George's name was the one she kept. She often said, "I was really in love with Tubbs and he was the only man I ever loved."

The homestead was too lonely, though, and Alice went back to the gaming tables, dealing faro in Sturgis for a short time before returning to Deadwood, where she reportedly opened a casino and dance hall. As was her long practice, the business was closed on Sunday. It was said that she taught Sunday School lessons to the women who worked at the house while their neighbors walked to church. Asked later about the dance hall girls she had met, Alice replied: "The life of a dance hall girl was what she cared to make it," she said. "It was entirely up to the woman to do what she pleased with her life— make it or wreck it."

As reformers began to force the closing of gambling halls and saloons, Tubbs went back to Sturgis and opened a roadhouse, providing liquor, gambling, and women primarily to soldiers from Fort Meade. She also had a sheep farm several miles from town and hired George Huckert to take care of the house and stock. She eventually married him, though it may have been largely a wedding of convenience. Apparently, Huckert had proposed marriage several times, but Alice always turned him down. Then, one day she figured up his back wages. "I owed him about $1,008," she said, "and all I had was about fifty dollars on hand, so I got to figuring it would be cheaper to marry him than pay him off." After Huckert died a few years later, Alice reverted to "Tubbs" as her last name.

The roadhouse near Fort Meade continued in operation despite moves for reform. One night some drunken soldiers created a ruckus. Two versions of the story exist—the official version and the one Tubbs told a friend. The official version said the soldiers had been turned away because the place was full. They tried to force their way in, battering on the door. Alice, in her 70s at the time, tried to persuade them to leave but again they refused. Still able to handle a gun, she shot through the door to frighten them, but a calvary trooper was killed.

Tubbs' version was that the soldiers were new to the fort, had been drinking, and wanted female companionship. She told them there was to be no roughhousing. Determined to show their toughness, however, the soldiers mistreated the women and, when Alice warned them, began tearing up the furniture. After repeated warnings, she finally threatened them with her revolver. One of the soldiers came at Alice apparently intending to kill her and, in self-defense, she shot him. She also had to injure another soldier before the group would leave. Tubbs was arrested and taken to jail where she read her Bible daily. When she stood trial, the jury acquitted her on grounds of self-defense. Elated, townspeople declared a holiday, while Alice returned to running her business.

But reformers eventually managed to have Tubbs arrested and charged with conducting a disorderly house. The business was shut down and Alice convicted of the charges; but friends appealed to the governor and she was pardoned. At this point, Alice Ivers Duffield Huckert Tubbs retired. She had saved money for her old age, but claimed that most of her life's winnings had gone to help those in need. "If I had all the money that I have passed out . . . , I would be rich," she said, "but there would be many haunting faces looking up at me from the past."

Alice was still a slight woman, her white hair pulled up in a bun and her blue eyes still bright. She spent her remaining years in Sturgis, wearing an army shirt and a black woolen skirt to work in her small garden or rock on her porch with a cigar clenched between toothless gums. A contemporary noted, "Any woman was welcome in her home and Poker Alice would see to it that she was protected from any and all advances or insults from any man."

Alice seemed to live mostly in the past after retirement, talking of days gone by and even of England. Soldiers left Fort Meade and the town changed. Tubbs became even more religious, joining the church and becoming involved in its activities. In Deadwood's annual "Days of '76" celebration, she would ride on a float in the parade, sitting behind a faro table and smoking her big black cigar. She appeared with Deadwood Dick (Richard Clark) at the Omaha (Nebraska) Diamond Jubilee when she was 78.

Many changes had occurred in Western life from Tubbs' early days in the mining camps, where there was "little regard for human life," to her final years, with modern developments like telephones. Despite many friends and acquaintances, Tubbs missed the old days and may have been lonely by herself. Once, a friend happened by and found her sitting with a gun, thinking about suicide. He managed to talk her out of it, but from that point on, friends made sure someone was with her at all times.

In 1930, at age 79, Alice Tubbs became ill with a gall bladder condition and needed surgery, but doctors said her chances of survival were poor. A gambler to the last, Alice replied, "Go ahead. I've bucked worse odds than that, and I've always hated a piker." When a concerned neighbor tried to persuade her against the surgery, Alice responded, "You know it's all in the draw."

Poker Alice died on February 27, 1930. Prior to her death, she had written that she wanted her tombstone to read "Alice Huckert Tubbs," honoring "the only man I ever loved." In her will, she disinherited any relatives "for the reason that they have not contributed to my welfare and happiness during the declining years of my life, nor have they made any effort to inquire as to my welfare for a great number of years." She left her chickens and the crop in her field to a neighbor, several individual items to other neighbors and friends, and the bulk of her estate to her friend David Keffeler.

Wherever her life had led her, Poker Alice died true to herself, her religious principles, and the code of the West. As directed in her will, she was given "a decent burial by the Church, consistent with [her] station in life," in the Catholic Cemetery at Sturgis, South Dakota.

SOURCES:

DeArment, Robert K. *Knights of the Green Cloth: The Saga of the Frontier Gamblers*. Norman, OK: University of Oklahoma Press, 1982.

Mumey, Nolie. *Poker Alice: Alice Ivers, Duffield, Tubbs, Huckert, 1851–1930: History of a Woman Gambler in the West*. Denver, CO: Artcraft Press, 1951.

SUGGESTED READING:

Horan, James D. *Desperate Women*. NY: Bonanza, 1952.

Ray, Grace Ernestine. *Wily Women of the West*. San Antonio, TX: Naylor, 1972.

COLLECTIONS:

More information about Alice Ivers Tubbs and other women who were professional gamblers in the American West may be found in the Denver (Colorado) Public Library's Western History Department.

RELATED MEDIA:

Poker Alice (television movie), starring *Elizabeth Taylor and produced by **Renee Valente**, released in 1987, was based on the life of Poker Alice in title only.

Margaret L. Meggs,
independent scholar,
Havre, Montana

Tubman, Harriet (1821–1913)

Legendary runaway slave from Maryland who, once free, returned to the South 19 times to guide as many as 300 enslaved African-Americans to freedom through the secret network known as the Underground Railroad. Name variations: Araminta "Minty" Ross; Harriet Ross. Pronunciation: TUB-mun. Born Araminta Ross in 1821 on the Edward Brodas plantation near Bucktown, Dorchester County, Maryland; died on March 10, 1913, in Auburn, New York; daughter of Harriet Greene and Benjamin Ross (slaves of Edward Brodas); married John Tubman, in 1844 (estranged 1848); married Nelson Davis, in 1869; no children.

Escaped from slavery (1849); planned and executed liberation excursions into slaveholding territory (1850s); settled in Auburn, New York (1858), after which she raised funds for John Brown's raid on Harper's Ferry, Virginia; moved to Beaufort, South Carolina (1862), where she worked for three years as a nurse, scout, and spy on behalf of the Union Army; Sarah Bradford published Scenes in the Life of Harriet Tubman *(1868); was a delegate to the National Association of Colored Women's first annual convention*

(1896); opened her house as the Harriet Tubman Home for Aged and Indigent Colored People.

Born in 1821, Araminta Ross—better known as Harriet Tubman—was the 11th child of **Harriet Greene** and Benjamin Ross. The family lived as slaves on Edward Brodas' plantation in Dorchester County on Maryland's Eastern Shore. Like most plantations of its time, the Brodas place was isolated, rural, and virtually self-sufficient. The nearest settlement, Bucktown, consisted merely of a cross-roads with a general store, a post office, a church, and eight or ten homes.

As was customary among slaveholders, Brodas both hired out and sold his slaves to other planters with some regularity. Tubman and her family did not escape the dislocation and cruelty of this practice. Two of her sisters were sold to plantations in the Deep South when Harriet was still quite young, and Tubman herself was first sent away from her family at age five. Forced to check muskrat traps in icy cold rivers, she quickly became too sick to work and was returned malnourished and suffering from exposure. Once she recovered, Brodas sent her to work as a house slave on a nearby plantation, where, despite her own youth, she worked as a nurse for the planter's infant child. It was here that Harriet, aged seven, first resisted the brutality of slavery. One morning, while standing by the breakfast table waiting to take the baby from its mother's arms, Harriet found her eyes wandering to a nearby bowl of sugar lumps. Just as she reached out to pinch a taste, her mistress turned and saw her. "The next minute she had the raw hide down: I give one jump out of the door, and I saw they came after me, but I just flew . . . I run, and I run, and I run." Although hunger forced her to return to her mistress, the episode marked the beginning of Tubman's lifelong opposition to slavery's dehumanization.

When she was 12, Tubman returned to work on her home plantation as a field slave. She continued to work in the fields for the rest of her teenaged years, and at one point sustained extensive physical injuries at the hands of an overseer, who dealt her such a blow to the head that she suffered from narcoleptic seizures for the rest of her life. Probably the most significant development at this time was the growth of her intense religious faith. Tubman described herself later as praying almost continuously about her soul, her work, and her family. As she matured, she began increasingly to identify the plight of slaves with that of the Israelites trapped in Egypt, waiting to be delivered into the land of Canaan. This religious sensibility fueled her desire for freedom.

When her master died in 1849, and she began to hear rumors that she and two of her brothers were to be sold to a chain gang, Tubman decided to act on her convictions. Many years later, she recalled walking through the slave quarters, singing a hymn to secretly enlighten her friends and family to her intentions. "When that old chariot comes/ I'm going to leave you/ I'm bound for the promised land/ Friends, I'm going to leave you." Late that same evening, she and her brothers crept away from the plantation, aware that at any moment their owner, or a slave patrol made up of local whites, might be alerted to their flight and pursue them. After a short distance, Tubman's brothers decided they could not take the risk and returned, leaving her to find her way alone. She traveled only at night, following the north star for days until she realized that she had crossed the border between the slaveholding and non-slaveholding states. "I looked at my hands," she recalled years later, "to see if I was the same person now I was free. There was such a glory over everything . . . and I felt like I was in heaven." Quickly, however, Tubman was overcome by the realization of how alone she was, in a strange land and separated from her family and friends. At that moment, she committed herself to freeing her family and making a home for them in the North.

After settling in Philadelphia, Tubman cooked, laundered, and scrubbed for a living, saving her money to finance her plans for rescuing her family. During her time in the city, she met members of Philadelphia's large and active antislavery organizations. One abolitionist whom she befriended was William Still, himself the son of escaped slaves and a leader in the Philadelphia Vigilance Committee. From Still, Tubman learned of the Underground Railroad and its secret networks of white and black abolitionists who aided escaped slaves as they made their way north. Like Tubman, many of these fugitives traveled up the Eastern Shore of the Chesapeake Bay, a peninsula noted for its complex system of waterways and marshes which afforded many places to hide. The towns north of the peninsula, like Philadelphia and Wilmington, Delaware, were populated in large part by supporters of the antislavery movement. Once there, fugitives found relief and assistance from former slaves, Methodists, Jews, Dunkers, Unitarians, and Roman Catholics as they moved through the countryside north to New York and eventually to Canada.

It was as a volunteer for the Underground Railroad that Tubman first returned to Mary-

Harriet
Tubman

land. Her mission was to lead her sister, **Mary (Bowley)**, and two nieces to Philadelphia from Baltimore. Mary's husband, a free black man named John Bowley, sent word through the Underground Railroad that his wife and daughters had been imprisoned in a slave pen in Cam- bridge, Maryland, and pled for help to get them out of Maryland. Bowley freed his family from the pen before they were sold, transported them to the house of a local Quaker, and then navigat- ed a boat up the Chesapeake Bay to Baltimore. By looking for light signals from the bank, the fugitives identified "conductors" who helped them disembark and led them to a farmhouse where Tubman herself was waiting. From that point, Tubman guided them along the Underground Railroad network until they came safely to Philadelphia.

> *There's two things I got a right to and these are Death and Liberty. One or the other I mean to have.*
>
> —Harriet Tubman

Emboldened by this success, Tubman returned to Maryland as many as 18 more times. As she was illiterate and her efforts were purposefully secret, it is difficult to document the specifics of these trips. What is clear, however, is how much her fellow Underground Railroad workers admired her courage and sacrifice. Thomas Garrett, an abolitionist of Wilmington, befriended Tubman, who often led her bands of fugitives to his station. On one such occasion, Garrett noted that she had arrived barefoot, having literally worn the shoes off her feet. She was, according to William Still, "a woman of no pretensions, indeed, a more ordinary specimen of humanity could hardly be found among the most unfortunate-looking farm hands of the South. Yet, in point of courage, shrewdness and disinterested exertions to rescue her fellow-men . . . she was without her equal."

During the decade preceding the Civil War, this "Moses of her people" garnered a reputation as an uncompromising and fearless foe of slavery. She carried a long rifle with her on her journeys and did not hesitate to aim it at those in her band whose courage faltered. As William Still noted, Tubman believed that "a live runaway could do great harm by going back, but a dead one could tell no secrets." Her name spread through slave quarters and abolitionist societies alike. Slaveholders in Maryland also took sharp notice and offered a $40,000 reward for her capture. Nevertheless, Tubman always evaded seizure and eventually rescued both her parents and settled them in a house she purchased from Senator William H. Seward in Auburn, New York.

Her ferocity on the escape route extended to even more aggressive efforts to overthrow slavery. In 1858 and 1859, Tubman joined forces with John Brown as he plotted a raid on Harper's Ferry, Virginia. Brown intended to seize the federal armory there, distribute weapons among the slaves, and instigate a widespread rebellion. According to historian Richard Hinton, while trying to raise money for his cause, Brown introduced Tubman to Boston abolitionist Wendell Phillips as "one of the best and bravest persons on this continent—General Tubman as we call

her." While she did not participate in the raid (although some historians suggest that she would have done so had she not become ill), Tubman met with Brown frequently and assisted him in his fund-raising efforts. When Brown's attempt failed and he was arrested and hanged, Tubman interpreted his fate in Biblical terms. She reportedly informed Franklin B. Sanborn, Brown's close friend and biographer, that after much thought she had decided "it wasn't John Brown that died on the gallows. When I think how he gave up his life for our people, and how he never flinched, but was so brave to the end; it's clear to me it wasn't mortal man, it was God in him." In one of the last interviews of her life (1912), Tubman still spoke of Brown as "my dearest friend."

During the Civil War, Tubman continued to find ways to attack and undermine slavery. In 1862, she moved to Beaufort, South Carolina (by that time occupied by the Union Army), with a group of missionary teachers. While there, she assisted hundreds of Sea Islander slaves through the transition from bondage to freedom. She was surprised, however, by the unexpected cultural differences between herself and the men and women she met. Tubman later recalled that when she tried to make a speech to them upon her arrival, "They laughed when they heard me talk, and I could not understand them, no how." The Sea Islanders spoke a dialect called Gullah, peculiar to the coastal regions of Georgia and South Carolina and born of a mixture of African languages and English. Slowly, however, Tubman learned to communicate, and she worked with them as a nurse, cook, and advisor.

While in Beaufort, she intermittently embarked on scouting and spying assignments for the army itself. Union Colonel James Montgomery, commanding the Second South Carolina Volunteers, a black regiment, called her "a most remarkable woman . . . invaluable as a scout." As well as locating slaves hoping to be liberated, Tubman identified potential targets for the Union Army, such as cotton stores and ammunition caches. The Boston Commonwealth described her efforts with the army in July 1863. "Col. Montgomery and his gallant band of 800 black soldiers, under the guidance of a black woman, dashed into the enemies' country . . . destroying millions of dollars worth of commissary stores, cotton and lordly dwellings, and striking terror to the heart of rebeldom, brought off near 800 slaves and thousands of dollars worth of property." In 1865, Tubman moved to Virginia where she cared for wounded black soldiers as the matron for the Colored Hospital at Fortress Monroe.

After the war, as before, Tubman continued to help African-Americans in need. Believing that she had been called by God to lead her people to freedom, she responded to the postwar world with characteristic fervor. She once said to an interviewer, "Now do you suppose he wanted me to do this just for a day, or a week? No! the Lord who told me to take care of my people meant me to do it just so long as I live, and so I do what he told me to do." She raised money for freedmen's schools, worked on behalf of destitute children, and continued to care for her aging parents. She also collaborated with **Sarah Bradford**, a white schoolteacher in Auburn, to write her autobiography, *Scenes in the Life of Harriet Tubman*, which was published in 1868 (and was later expanded and published as *Harriet Tubman: The Moses of Her People* in 1886). Shortly thereafter, she converted her family home in Auburn into the Home for Aged and Indigent Colored People. She continued to work closely with black churches, especially the African Methodist Episcopal Zion Church in Auburn, to which she had frequently brought fugitives in the 1850s and where Frederick Douglass had briefly published his famous abolitionist newspaper, *The North Star*. And, in the middle of this busy period, she took the time to marry a Civil War veteran named Nelson Davis, who had been a boarder at her house. Her first husband, John Tubman, to whom she was married in 1844, had refused to come to the North and had married another woman shortly after Tubman's escape.

Toward the end of the 19th century, Tubman undertook a new but related cause, women's suffrage. In 1896, she was a delegate to the National Association of Colored Women's first annual convention because she believed that political suffrage for women was vitally important to the preservation of their freedom. She was honored by the mostly middle-class and educated women in attendance, who extended every privilege and courtesy to her and asked her to speak to the gathering. Her topic was one close to her heart: "More Homes for our Aged."

Near the turn of the century, Tubman purchased 25 acres of land adjoining her home with money raised from various benefactors and speaking engagements. Shortly thereafter, she began arrangements for the home to be taken over by the A.M.E. Zion Church. Fittingly, in 1911, when Tubman herself became too sick to take care of herself, she was welcomed into the Harriet Tubman Home for Aged and Indigent Colored People. In a letter to Booker T. Washington asking for money to help support Tubman, Edward Brooks,

the superintendent of the home, wrote: "It is the desire of the Home management to give her every attention and comfort possible these last days." Many of the women with whom she had worked in the National Association of Colored Women and other women's organizations, upon hearing of her destitute condition, voted to provide her with a monthly pension of $25 for the rest of her life. When she died on March 14, 1913, these women also paid the costs of her funeral and a marble headstone for her grave. One year after her death, the city of Auburn commemorated Tubman with a service in which they dedicated a memorial tablet in her honor. It is located on the front entrance of the courthouse and reads:

> In memory of Harriet Tubman.
> Born a Slave in Maryland About 1821.
> Died in Auburn, N.Y., March 10, 1913.
> Called the Moses of her people, during the Civil War.
> With rare courage she led over three hundred negroes up from slavery to freedom, and rendered invaluable service as nurse and spy. With implicit trust in God, she braved every danger and overcame every obstacle. Withal she possessed extraordinary foresight and judgment so that she truthfully said
> "On my underground railroad
> I nebber run my train off de track
> an' I nebber los' a passenger."

As historian Benjamin Quarles has noted, Tubman garnered almost mythological status even during her lifetime. Friends and acquaintances were never at a loss for words of praise and respect. Despite her lack of formal education and impoverished state, she struggled continuously for the improvement of black life. Much of Tubman's appeal to her contemporaries and later generations had its source in the unremitting self-sacrifice of her day-to-day labors. Frederick Douglass once wrote to her with great appreciation of her humbleness and willingness to serve the poorest and most in need.

> The difference between us is very marked. Most that I have done and suffered in the service of our cause has been in public, and I have received much encouragement at every step of the way . . . while the most that you have done has been witnessed by a few trembling, scarred, and foot-sore bondmen and women, whom you have led out of the house of bondage, and whose heartfelt "God bless you" has been your only reward. The midnight sky and the silent stars have been the witnesses of your devotion to freedom and of your heroism. Excepting John Brown—of sacred memory—I know of no one who has willingly encountered more perils and hardships to serve our enslaved people than you have.

Like many abolitionists, Tubman approached her life's work with the conviction that slavery was an evil willed by man, not by God. What distinguished her was her unwavering belief that she was destined to lead her people out of the "jaws of hell" and into the land of freedom, or die in the effort.

SOURCES:

Blockson, Charles L. *Hippocrene Guide to the Underground Railroad.* NY: Hippocrene, 1994.

———. *The Underground Railroad: First Person Narratives of Escapes to Freedom in the North.* NY: Prentice Hall, 1987.

Bradford, Sarah. *Harriet Tubman: The Moses of Her People.* NY: Corinth Books, 1961 (reprint of second edition originally published in 1886).

Haskins, James. *Get on Board: The Story of the Underground Railroad.* NY: Scholastic, 1993.

Hinton, Richard J. *John Brown and His Men, with Some Account of the Roads they traveled to reach Harper's Ferry.* New York, 1894.

Quarles, Benjamin. "Harriet Tubman's Unlikely Leadership," in *Black Leaders of the Nineteenth Century.* Ed. by Leon Litwack and August Meier. Urbana, IL: University of Illinois Press, 1988.

Ripley, C. Peter, ed. *The Black Abolitionist Papers.* Volume 3: "The United States, 1830–1846" and Volume 5: "The United States, 1859–1865." 4 vols. Chapel Hill, NC: University of North Carolina Press, 1992.

Siebert, Wilbur H. *The Underground Railroad from Slavery to Freedom.* NY: Macmillan, 1898.

Sterling, Dorothy, ed. *We Are Your Sisters: Black Women in the Nineteenth Century.* NY: W.W. Norton, 1984.

Still, William. *Still's Underground Rail Road Records, Revised Edition, With a Life of the Author. Narrating the Hardships, Hairbreadth Escapes and Death Struggles of the Slaves in their Effort for Freedom.* Philadelphia, PA: William Still, Publisher, 1883.

SUGGESTED READING:

Douglass, Frederick. *Narrative of the Life of Frederick Douglass, an American Slave, Written by Himself.* Edited by William L. Andrews, and William S. McFeely. NY: W.W. Norton, 1997.

Franklin, John Hope. *From Slavery to Freedom.* NY: Alfred A. Knopf, 1967.

Genovese, Eugene. *Roll, Jordan, Roll: The World the Slaves Made.* NY: Pantheon, 1974.

Oates, Stephen B. *To Purge This Land with Blood: A Biography of John Brown.* Amherst, MA: University of Massachusetts Press, 1984.

JUVENILE:

Adler, David A., and Samuel Byrd, illustrator. *A Picture Book of Harriet Tubman.* NY: Holiday House, 1992.

Elish, Dan. *Harriet Tubman and the Underground Railroad.* Brookfield, CT: The Millbrook Press, 1993.

Lawrence, Jacob. *Harriet and the Promised Land.* NY: Simon and Schuster, 1968.

Schroeder, Alan, and Jerry Pinkney. *Minty: A Story of Young Harriet Tubman.* NY: Dial Books for Young Readers, 1996.

RELATED MEDIA:

"Roots of Resistance: A Story of the Underground Railroad" (video), produced and directed by Orlando Bagwell, written by Theodore Thomas, Alexandria, Virginia: Time-Life Video, 1990, distributed by PBS Video.

"The Underground Railroad" (video), Princeton, NJ: Films for the Humanities and Sciences, 1996.

HISTORIC SITES:

Harriet Tubman's Birthplace Marker, Bucktown, Maryland. Located eight miles south of U.S. 50 on Maryland Route 397.

The Harriet Tubman Home. Owned and operated by the A.M.E. Zion Church. Located at 180 South Street, Auburn, New York 13021. Telephone: 315-252-2081.

Margaret M. Storey,
Assistant Professor of History,
DePaul University,
Chicago, Illinois

Tuchman, Barbara (1912–1989)

American historian and two-time winner of the Pulitzer Prize whose writings have become popular bestsellers and are celebrated for their vivid style. Pronunciation: TUCK-man. Born Barbara Wertheim on January 30, 1912, in New York City; died of complications following a stroke on February 6, 1989, in Greenwich, Connecticut; daughter of Maurice Wertheim and Alma (Morgenthau) Wertheim; Radcliffe College, B.A., 1933; married Dr. Lester R. Tuchman, in 1940; children: Lucy, Jessica, Alma.

Served as research assistant, Institute of Public Relations, New York City and Tokyo (1934–35); worked as editorial assistant, The Nation, New York City (1936); stationed in Madrid to cover Spanish Civil War (1937); was staff writer, War in Spain, London (1937–38); served as American correspondent, New Statesman and Nation, London (1939); worked on Far East news desk, Office of War Information, New York City (1944–45); made trustee of Radcliffe College (1960); awarded Pulitzer Prize for The Guns of August (1962); awarded second Pulitzer for Stillwell and the American Experience in China (1971); served on Smithsonian Council (1971–89); decorated, Order of Leopold First Class (Belgium); fellow, American Academy of Arts and Letters (president, 1978–80); awarded AAAL Gold Medal for History (1978); served as treasurer of the Authors' Guild, on council of Authors' League, and as president of Society of American Historians (1971–73). Contributed to Foreign Affairs, Atlantic Monthly, American Heritage, Harper's, The New York Times, and other magazines and journals.

Selected writings: Bible and Sword: England and Palestine from the Bronze Age to Balfour *(NYU Press, 1956);* The Zimmerman Telegram *(Viking, 1958);* The Proud Tower: A Portrait of the World Before the War: 1890–1914 *(Macmillan, 1962);* The Guns of August

(Macmillan, 1962); Stillwell and the American Experience in China, 1911–45 (Macmillan, 1970); Practicing History: Selected Essays by Barbara W. Tuchman (Knopf, 1981); The March of Folly: From Troy to Vietnam (Knopf, 1984); A Distant Mirror: The Calamitous 14th Century (Knopf, 1984); The First Salute (Knopf, 1988).

Barbara Tuchman's reputation as a writer rests upon her ability to envelop the reader in vivid imagery and amazing detail. All of her works, produced between 1956 and 1988, became popular bestsellers; two of them, *The Guns of August* and *Stillwell and the American Experience in China*, were awarded the Pulitzer Prize. All rely on detailed research in primary sources. Throughout her career, Tuchman exemplified a philosophical school of history which has been all but eclipsed in the 20th century—a philosophy based upon the innate value of history for its own sake, which advocates the practice of history as an artistic, literary form. Her approach to writing history was idealistic and Olympian, yet rigorous and scholarly.

Tuchman's work bears the stamp of her earliest experiences in journalism. She received a bachelor's degree from Radcliffe in history and literature in 1933, but she never pursued a graduate degree. Instead, she developed her unique style through experience, beginning as a writer for the Office of War Information during World War II. Not content with the shallow nature of her journalistic assignments, she invested a great amount of time in doing background reading for her stories. In fact, she did so much historical research that her superior criticized her for clouding her judgment with too much knowledge.

When the war was over, Tuchman turned her attention to writing a full-blown historical monograph based on her research of relations between England and Palestine from ancient times to 1914. The result, entitled *Bible and Sword*, was published in 1956. She continued to write history for the rest of her career, and her books range in scope from Europe to the Middle East to America, examining events from ancient times to the mid-20th century. Her widest acclaim came from her work on recent European and American diplomacy.

Tuchman's first intention was always to produce objective, vivid, detailed accounts. She insisted that a historian should avoid expressing specific ideologies when writing history, and she proudly claimed that her "philosophy of history" was to rid herself of all "philosophies." She insist-

ed that "the material must precede the thesis." When the facts have been accurately reconstructed, according to Tuchman, truth will become evident both to the author and to the reader.

At the core of Tuchman's philosophy was a determination to portray "what really happened." She described the historian as a traveler who "gropes his way trying to recapture the truth of past events." Adhering to this goal is essential because it forces the historian to remain true to his sources. Even though the goal of relating "what really happened" will always remain just beyond our grasp, we must resist the urge to speculate, to fill in gaps, to use hindsight and put intentions that may not have been there to the actions of historical figures. She went so far as to define the first duty of the historian to be staying within the evidence.

Tuchman published on a wide variety of topics and dealt with many different ages in history. She considered it necessary to avoid judging past cultures through the perspective of hindsight. Her goal was to examine past events "in terms of what was known and believed at the time." Her treatment of the Middle Ages in *A Distant Mirror* is a clear example of her historical sympathy. She traced the chaotic 14th century through the vehicle of an actual medieval life, that of a Frenchman of the Second Estate, Enguerrand de Coucy VII (1340–1397). The view of the 14th century through the eyes of a typical representative of the period, she explained, required her to exercise "enforced obedience to reality," producing in the end "a truer version of the period than if I had imposed my own plan." The era, which she admits was perceived by many contemporaries as "a time . . . of Satan triumphant" was filled with contradictions that fly in the face of easy generalizations. "No age is tidy or made of whole cloth," she pointed out in her introduction, "and none is a more checkered fabric than the Middle Ages."

Tuchman can be compared to historians of the 19th-century Romantic period in her inclusive attitude towards historical evidence. In her introduction to *The Proud Tower*, she explained, "To probe for underlying causes and deeper forces one must operate within the framework of a whole society and try to discover what moved the people in it. I have tried to concentrate on society rather than the state." In *Bible and Sword*, Tuchman identified twin motives for man's actions: a cultural-moral motive and an imperial-material motive. The latter, which she also termed a "power motive," she described as the easiest to decipher, using "hard facts" like geography, dates, battles, and treaties. The other motive is more elusive, but just as important. It can be found only by a deeper examination of such evidence as myths, legends, traditions and ideas.

Writing is hard work. . . . But it brings a sense of excitement, almost of rapture; a moment on Olympus. In short, it is an act of creation.

—Barbara Tuchman

To Tuchman, history was primarily storytelling, the narration of true stories. For that reason, she placed prime importance on the selection and use of sources. She relied exclusively on primary sources in her own work, and mistrusted secondary sources, which she described as "helpful but pernicious." While secondary sources often contain helpful background information, she explained, the material in them has already been pre-selected, so the researcher cannot rely upon them when writing. She dealt with this quandary by reading secondary sources for background at the beginning of a project but never taking notes from them. Instead, she dedicated her research time to a careful examination of private letters, diaries, and the reports, orders and messages in government archives. She believed that important historical understanding could also come from researching the actual location of an event, so she traveled widely to the scene of the historical events she portrayed. All of these techniques allowed her to produce history with a vivid, intimate tone that draws the reader into the story with all the magnetism of a great novel.

Tuchman's secret for writing exciting, readable history was the use of corroborative detail. Any historical generalization, she insisted, should be supported by illustration. Narrative without fact is both dull and unconvincing, and is often inaccurate. Tuchman's great genius lay in her ability to weave detail with historical narrative in such a way as to make it both exciting and believable.

Tuchman's use of sources mirrored her intent to be open and sympathetic to all periods and all individuals. She examined all primary records, no matter how biased or inaccurate, insisting that by reading several versions of an event, the historian can correct for bias and extract the truth. Even a biased source, she noted, is valuable for its insight into the personality of the author. Even in *A Distant Mirror*, she relied heavily on contemporary chroniclers, using them to gain "a sense of the period and its attitudes."

Tuchman made a clear distinction between the historian and the contemporary chronicler. While contemporaries are the source of the raw material of history—letters, diaries, memoirs, newspapers and other documents—Tuchman believed that these eyewitness "compilers" cannot bring understanding or a balanced perspective to their accounts. She compared contemporary reports to "wine when the first pressing of the grapes is in hand. . . . [I]t has not fermented, and it has not aged." What these contemporaries lack, according to Tuchman, is perspective: "What he gains in intimacy through personal acquaintance . . . he sacrifices in detachment."

Tuchman defined history as an art, not a science. In doing so, she rebelled against the trend towards scientific history which has been ascendant since the mid-19th century. According to Tuchman, the historian should work in the same manner as the poet or novelist to create a work of art: "What his imagination is to the poet, facts are to the historian. His exercise of judgment comes in their selection, his art in their arrangement. His method is narrative. His subject is the story of man's past. His function is to make it known."

Tuchman also echoed George Trevelyan in her belief that history should be written for the general reader, not just for the specialist, and therefore, it must be both clear and interesting. She always considered herself to stand somewhere outside the professional "discipline" of history. To be an effective historian, according to Tuchman, one must first *distill* for the reader—"assemble the information, make sense of it, select the essential, discard the irrelevant"—and bring the material together into a dramatic narrative. In her opinion, to be a good historian, one must first be a good writer. A good writer will present his story using suspense. Therefore, the historian should always write "as of the time," without relying on hindsight or referring to events that lie ahead. Good writing also demands a high level of enthusiasm on the part of the author: "Belief in the grandeur of his theme" is essential to the creation of exciting history that will be worth reading.

Tuchman's suspicion of prefabricated systems placed her in direct conflict with the "systematizers" who dominated the field of history in academic circles through most of the 20th century. Tuchman criticized them for being "obsessed and oppressed by the need to find an explanation for history." She also took them to task for attempting to force historical events into a neat, prefabricated pattern. Their great mis-

Barbara
Tuchman

take, she claimed, was trying to deduce the "why" of history before examining the evidence:

> I believe it is safer to leave the "why" alone until after one has not only gathered the facts but arranged them in sequence; to be exact, in sentences, paragraphs, and chapters. The very process of transforming a collection of personalities, dates, gun calibers, letters, and speeches into a narrative eventually forces the "why" to the surface.

Too much influence on historical systems, Tuchman asserted, quickly leads to misuse of sources. The historian with a system in mind will use sources selectively, preferring the facts that suit his model best and glossing over or explaining away anomalies. She countered this system by insisting that "evidence is more important than interpretation." Tuchman believed strongly that historical events have intrinsic value independent of historical interpretation: "I mistrust history in gallon jugs whose purveyors are more concerned with establishing the meaning and purpose of history than with what really happened," she explained:

> Is it necessary to insist on a purpose? No one asks the novelist why he writes novels or the poet what is his purpose in writing poems. The lilies of the field, as I remember, were not required to have a purpose. Why cannot history be studied and written and read for its own sake, as the record of human behavior, the most fascinating subject of all? Insistence on a purpose turns the historian into a prophet—and that is another profession.

Tuchman also criticized professional historians for becoming too distanced from their subject matter. Because their efforts lack corroborative detail, they are too theoretical—not only dull, but inaccurate as well. In good history, Tuchman insisted, the writer allows the reader to become intimately acquainted with the characters of the narrative. She claimed that the reader of a historical work should be given opportunity to draw some of his own conclusions, saying that "the best book is a collaboration between author and reader."

Tuchman insisted that history must be readable by the wider public—research in and of itself is of little use if not communicated successfully. She warned professional historians against falling into elitist jargon and thus losing their audience among the wider public. She pointed to the disciplines of psychology and sociology, which she claimed had become unintelligible to all but the members of the disciplines themselves: "*They* know what they mean, but no one else does. . . . Their condition might be pitied if one did not suspect it was deliberate. Their retreat into the arcane is meant to set them apart from the great unlearned, to mark their possession of some unshared, unsharable expertise." Because of their exclusivity, Tuchman asserted, their greatest discoveries are useless to the world around them. It is because of this kind of elitism that non-academic historians produced more bestsellers in the 20th century than did academic historians. She claimed that the commercial success of non-academic historians comes from their emphasis on communication, on capturing

and holding the attention of their audience. Academic historians, she claimed, are becoming alienated from the reading public at large, primarily because the academic, who has a captive audience as a student then as a professor, seldom concerns himself with "keeping the reader turning the page."

Making history available to the public was a great concern to Tuchman because she had a definite idea of the ultimate purpose of history— to provide reassuring evidence to a troubled society, that mankind has experienced and survived dark ages before. In *A Distant Mirror*, Tuchman claimed that amidst the troubled years at the end of the 20th century, "it is reassuring to know that the human species has lived through worse before."

Despite her insistence on a greater purpose for history, Tuchman differed from the Romantics by defining history as cyclical rather than progressive. Whereas Romantic historians viewed the history of mankind as a single process of development from a beginning in savagery to an end in a perfectly rational and civilized society, Tuchman depicts the history of mankind as an unending process of muddling through. She agreed with John Adams' 18th-century assessment that government "is little better practiced now than three or four thousand years ago," and expressed small hope for improvement. The lot of man, according to Tuchman, is to make the best of the march through "patches of brilliance and decline, great endeavors and shadow." She depicted history as largely accidental and filled with contradictions and changing circumstances. Every era, as well as every individual, she claimed, contains certain amounts of both good and evil, crosscurrents and countercurrents.

Tuchman recognized the overwhelming unpredictability of history. No particular circumstances, she insisted, can predicate a particular outcome. For Tuchman, history was exciting and elusive, resisting confinement to any particular mold or pattern.

Although Tuchman achieved universal acclaim for her imaginative and dramatic prose, she also faced consistent criticism from the literary and scholarly community on various points. Many reviewers questioned her choice of material, and criticized her for making crucial omissions in her quest for dramatic effect. Another frequent criticism of her work was her lack of an organizing principle or ruling vision. Her work was too random, too narrative for many readers, who expressed the opinion that Tuchman's work did not portray a true and complete portrait. She was criticized for refusing to express a coherent theme in her works or to answer the significant questions raised by her research.

Tuchman's own principles seem occasionally contradictory. Throughout her career, she insisted upon avoiding preconceived ideas that skew the perspective of history. But she also admitted that no historian is completely free of bias. In fact, she insisted that a historian should make his opinions clear, claiming that the work of a "purely objective" historian would be unreadable—"like eating sawdust." In spite of her philosophy of simple narration, Tuchman made historical selections and judgments throughout her works, and used narrative to show cause and effect.

Tuchman's works have contributed greatly to the historical profession. Without exception, her books are thoroughly researched and vividly written. Her philosophy of history centered around producing history in its truest, most useful, and least contrived form. The result of her endeavors was a wide-ranging group of historical monographs that contain within them the spark of life.

SOURCES:

Tuchman, Barbara. *Bible and Sword: England and Palestine from the Bronze Age to Balfour.* NY: New York University Press, 1956.

———. *A Distant Mirror: The Calamitous 14th Century.* NY: Alfred A. Knopf, 1984.

———. *The First Salute.* NY: Alfred A. Knopf, 1988.

———. *The Guns of August.* NY: Macmillan, 1962.

———. *The March of Folly: From Troy to Vietnam.* NY: Alfred A. Knopf, 1984.

———. *Practicing History: Selected Essays by Barbara W. Tuchman.* NY: Alfred A. Knopf, 1981.

———. *The Proud Tower: A Portrait of the World Before the War: 1890–1914.* NY: Macmillan, 1962.

———. *Stillwell and the American Experience in China, 1911–45.* NY: Macmillan, 1970.

———. *The Zimmerman Telegram.* NY: Viking Press, 1958.

Kimberly Estep Spangler,
Assistant Professor of History and Chair,
Division of Religion and Humanities,
Friends University, Wichita, Kansas

Tucker, C. DeLores (1927—)

African-American politician and civil-rights activist. Born on October 4, 1927, in Philadelphia, Pennsylvania; daughter of Whitfield Nottage (a minister) and Captilda (Gardiner) Nottage (an entrepreneur); graduated from Philadelphia's Girls' High School; attended Temple University, Pennsylvania State University, and the University of Pennsylvania; married William J. Tucker (a real estate executive), in July 1951; no children.

Took part in the march from Selma to Montgomery, Alabama, and the White House Conference on Civil Rights (1965); served as secretary of the Commonwealth of Pennsylvania, becoming the highest-ranking black woman in any state government at the time (1971–77); was cofounder and chair, National Political Caucus of Black Women; was founding member, National Women's Caucus; served as vice-president, Pennsylvania chapter of the NAACP, and board member of NAACP's Special Contribution Fund; received honorary doctor of laws degrees from Villa Maria College and Morris College.

Born Cynthia DeLores Nottage on October 4, 1927, C. DeLores Tucker was one of eleven children of Reverend Whitfield Nottage and **Captilda Gardiner Nottage**, fundamentalist Christians who set down strict rules for their children and themselves. "We couldn't smoke, play cards, drink, dance, or listen to popular music," she later recalled. "No male company until I was 21. . . . We weren't taught to value material things. But we were taught that we were spiritual aristocracy, . . . [and] to place all our values in relationships—to heal the sick, to love everybody, to feed the poor, not to care about anything worldly." While her father refused to take payment for his ministry, preferring to rely on God, her mother ran a succession of small businesses to support the family.

The Nottages later moved to a farm in rural Montgomery County, outside Philadelphia. In her ninth-grade class, Tucker was the only African-American, earning her the hated nickname of "Black Beauty"—hardly a compliment, since it was originally the name of a fictional horse. Of her first day in the new school, she later recalled: "All the doors were open, all the children's heads were peepin' out, all the teachers' heads were above, and they were watching one little black girl come into that school."

Tucker graduated from Girls' High School in Philadelphia, an accomplishment for which her father rewarded her with an ocean voyage to the Bahamas. Told they would have to stay in special quarters because of their color, the rebellious Tucker balked, choosing to sleep instead in the damp air up on deck. This led to a lengthy illness that kept her from heading off to college in the fall as she had planned. Having spent a number of her summer vacations during high school working in hospitals, she had dreamed of one day becoming a doctor. Somehow this dream died when the illness delayed her college entry, although in later years she attended classes at Temple University, Pennsylvania State University, and the University of Pennsylvania. Instead,

Tucker became involved in Philadelphia real estate, a pursuit that soon brought her into contact with her future husband, successful real estate executive William J. Tucker. They were married two years later, in 1959.

Tucker had been active in the civil-rights movement in and around her native Philadelphia as well as elsewhere in the North, but as the battle for equality heated up in the South in the late 1950s and early 1960s, she longed to join the "real struggle." Although her husband was less than enthusiastic about the prospect of her risking danger on the front lines down South, Tucker flew down to march for the first time with nearly 100 ministers. During one of the civil-rights marches in which she participated, she related, "the heavens opened up; it poured torrents of rain. People shouted, 'Drown, you rats, drown'; you could feel their hate, they were spitting. It was very tense." Tucker marched with Dr. Martin Luther King, Jr., in the 1965 march from Selma to Montgomery, Alabama, and also served as a delegate to the White House Conference on Civil Rights.

Although she admits she grew up thinking politics was a "dirty word," she sees no better arena in which to work for meaningful change. "Politics affects everything we do, from birth certificate to death certificate, even from conception to resurrection." While still a teenager, Tucker entered the political fray as a worker in the campaign of Joseph Clark for the mayoralty of Philadelphia. She later became the first woman and first African-American member of the Philadelphia Zoning Board, and was a cofounder of the Black Women's Political Caucus and a founding member of the National Women's Caucus. Committed to feminism as well as to civil rights, Tucker noted in a 1974 interview that society tries to pigeonhole women and men from their earliest years: "For the blue blankets, the horizons are as big as all outdoors. But the pink blankets need not go much beyond their family doorstep. They need not go beyond winning the favor of the blue blankets and . . . keeping them feeling happy and proud." It was past time, she said, to stop debating "whether 53% of the people (women) or 23% (minority groups) should be involved" in running the country.

In 1971, Tucker attracted national attention when she was named Pennsylvania's commonwealth secretary under Governor Milton J. Shapp, a post roughly equivalent to secretary of state. Her appointment to the post made her the highest-ranking black woman in state government anywhere in the United States at the time.

During the six years she served as commonwealth secretary, Tucker often came under fire for concentrating more on promoting her own political image than on working at her job. Although she had been publicly chastised by Governor Shapp for accepting thousands of dollars in unreported honoraria, Tucker was reappointed to a second term as commonwealth secretary in 1975. The following year, she again came under fire when a state senator accused her of using her office to solicit funds for the New York congressional campaign of *Bella Abzug, a charge she vehemently denied. In 1977, Tucker was fired by Shapp after an investigation revealed she had used state employees to write speeches that she had delivered for fees exceeding $65,000.

Tucker remained active, however, serving on both state and national boards of the National Association for the Advancement of Colored People (NAACP). Having long been a colleague of *Coretta Scott King, she helped to found and served as president of the Philadelphia chapter of the Martin Luther King, Jr., Association. Tucker campaigned for her friend Jesse Jackson during his 1984 presidential campaign, and in 1987 was drafted by 150 organizational leaders into running for the post of Pennsylvania's lieutenant governor, although she did not win. In the 1990s, she joined in the campaign against rap music lyrics glorifying violence, drug use, and casual sex. Particularly critical about so-called gangsta rap, Tucker called for a halt to the sales of such music to children, charging that gangsta rap recording companies were "pimping pornography to the children for the almighty dollar."

SOURCES:
Bair, Frank E., ed. *Biography News*. Vol. 1, no. 8. Detroit, MI: Gale Research, 1974.
———. *Biography News*. Vol. 2, no. 4. Detroit, MI: Gale Research, 1975.
Smith, Jessie Carney, ed. *Notable Black American Women*. Detroit, MI: Gale Research, 1992.

Don Amerman,
freelance writer,
Saylorsburg, Pennsylvania

Tucker, Charlotte Maria

(1821–1893)

English children's writer and missionary. Name variations: (pseudonyms) A.L.O.E., A Lady of England. Born on May 8, 1821, in Barnet, England; died on December 2, 1893, in Amritsar, India; daughter of Henry St. George Tucker (a civil servant and financier) and Jane (Boswell) Tucker; educated privately in England; never married; no children.

Published first book (1852); published some 140 books for the young, and donated proceeds to charity; served as a Church of England missionary in India (1875–93).

Selected writings (under pseudonym A.L.O.E.): Claremont Tales; or Illustrations of the Beatitudes *(1852);* The Rambles of a Rat *(1854);* Wings and Stings *(1855);* Old Friends with New Faces *(1858);* The Story of a Needle; The Giant Killer *(1868);* Cyril Ashley *(1870).*

Born in Barnet, England, on May 8, 1821, Charlotte Maria Tucker was the sixth and last child of **Jane Boswell Tucker**, the Scottish-born daughter of an Edinburgh attorney who was related to James Boswell, biographer of Dr. Samuel Johnson, and Henry St. George Tucker, an expert on Indian finance who served as chair of the East India Company. Several generations of the Tucker family had been civil servants in the British colonies, including Bermuda and India.

When Tucker was only a year old, the family moved from Barnet to London, where she was educated privately in the family home. Her family's involvement in English politics made the Tucker house a popular gathering place for prominent political figures, including the duke of Wellington, and Tucker met many of these notables as they came and went while she did her lessons.

From the time she was young, Tucker spent much of her free time writing poetry and plays, although as she grew older she also became involved in charity work. Her father's opposition, however, kept her from pursuing her dream of publishing her writing until his death in 1851. Her first book, *Claremont Tales; or Illustrations of the Beatitudes*, published the following year, was a collection of morality tales aimed at children. It was well received, and she would go on to produce one to three books every year for the rest of her life. In all, Tucker wrote and published some 140 books; all were produced under the pseudonym A.L.O.E., short for "A Lady of England," and all the proceeds were donated to charity. She used her writings to convey moral lessons to young readers, employing allegory, homilies, adventure tales, and Bible stories to get her point across. Among the best known of her books are *The Rambles of a Rat, Wings and Stings, Old Friends with New Faces, The Story of a Needle*, and *The Giant Killer*.

Tucker lived with her mother until her mother's death in 1869, after which she made her home with a brother. A lifelong member of the Church of England, in 1875 she decided to travel to India

as a missionary in service of the church's Zenana Society. To prepare for this new challenge, she taught herself Hindi. Once in India, Tucker made her headquarters in Batala, north of Lahore. As part of her duties there, she visited high-caste Indian women who were kept in enforced seclusion and also focused on the education and conversion of Indian boys. To help spread the faith, she wrote a number of pamphlets that were later translated into local dialects.

In 1885, Tucker was laid low by a serious illness and never recovered her strength, although she continued to write. She died eight years later in the Indian city of Amritsar and was buried without a coffin, in accordance with her wishes that her funeral cost no more than five rupees, in her adopted city of Batala.

SOURCES:

Blain, Virginia, Pat Clements, and Isobel Grundy, eds. *The Feminist Companion to Literature in English.* New Haven, CT: Yale University Press, 1990.

The Concise Dictionary of National Biography. Oxford: Oxford University Press, 1992.

Kunitz, Stanley J., and Howard Haycraft, eds. *British Authors of the Nineteenth Century.* NY: H.W. Wilson, 1936.

Shattock, Joanne. *The Oxford Guide to British Women Writers.* Oxford: Oxford University Press, 1993.

Don Amerman,
freelance writer,
Saylorsburg, Pennsylvania

Tucker, Sophie (1884–1966)

American entertainer, the "Last of the Red Hot Mamas," whose career began in the days of vaudeville and ended only with her death in the 1960s. Born Sophia Kalish (later known as Sophia Abuza) on January 13, 1884, in Russia; died on February 9, 1966, in New York City; second of four children and the first of two girls of Charles Abuza (a restaurateur originally named Kalish) and Jennie (Yacha) Abuza (originally Kalish); attended Brown School in Hartford, Connecticut; married Louis Tuck (a beer-wagon driver), in 1903 (divorced 1913); married Frank Westphal (a pianist), in 1914 (divorced 1919); married Albert Lackey (a personal manager), in 1928 (divorced 1933); children: (first marriage) one son, Bert.

Theater includes: Ziegfeld Follies of 1909 *(1909);* Hello, Alexander *(1919);* Earl Carroll's Vanities of 1924 *(1924);* Leave It to Me *(1938);* The High Kickers *(1941). As a radio singer, had her own program, "Sophie Tucker and Her Show" (1938–39).*

Selected filmography: Honky Tonk *(1928);* Little Red Hot Schoolhouse *(1932);* Gay Love *(1934);* Broadway Highlights #1 *(1935);* Broadway Melody of 1928 *(1937);* Thoroughbreds Don't Cry *(1937);* Follow the Boys *(1944); The Joker is Wild (All the Way, 1957); The Heart of Show Business (1957).*

A show business legend, Sophie Tucker was born in Russia in 1884, began her career in vaudeville in 1906, and sang and kibitzed her way through the next six decades, performing at New York's Latin Quarter just four months before her death in 1966. The self-proclaimed "Last of the Red-Hot Mamas," Tucker created a flamboyant, frequently racy act that capitalized on her music-hall voice and rotund frame. Throughout her career, she altered her performance as time and circumstances dictated, believing that above everything, a performer must remain current. ("I'm the 3-D Mama with the Big Wide Screen," she bellowed to a new generation of fans late in her career.) Her appeal was universal and enduring; audiences flocked to see her even after she began losing her voice and had to "talk" her way through her songs.

Tucker was literally born on the road. Her mother **Jennie Kalish**, a Russian Jew, gave birth to her while traveling by truck across Poland to the Baltic, to join her husband in America. On his own journey to the United States, Tucker's father, on the lam from the Russian army, began calling himself Charles Abuza, a name he stole from an Italian traveling companion who died during the trip. "Don't ask me what the United States immigration officers made of an Italian who couldn't speak anything but Russian and Yiddish; but it was as 'Charles Abuza' that Papa got into the country, and found a job in Boston," Tucker wrote in her autobiography *Some of These Days.*

The "Abuzas" stayed in Boston for seven years, then moved to Hartford, Connecticut, when Charles bought a restaurant there. The enterprise involved all four of the Abuza children, and Tucker grudgingly served as dishwasher and waitress while she dreamed of a career in show business. She sometimes sang for the customers, receiving encouragement from some of the show-business regulars, who also wrote down new songs for her and occasionally took her to the theater. She would then try out the ideas she picked up from the shows at the amateur concerts in Riverside Park, although she was shy about getting up on stage because of her weight. "Gradually, at the concerts I began to hear calls for 'the fat girl,'" she recalls in her autobiography. "Then I would jump up from the piano stool, forgetting all about my size, and work to get all the laughs I could get."

At 16, to escape the drudgery of the kitchen more than anything else, Tucker eloped with Louis Tuck, a high school beau. After a year and the birth of son Bert, the couple encountered financial difficulties and moved back with the Abuzas. They subsequently separated, then divorced.

In 1906, Sophie left her son with her family and moved to New York to break into show business. Changing her name to Tucker, she sang in restaurants and haunted the offices of music publishers to make contacts and get new material. She got her first break in an amateur show, but it was costly. In her autobiography, she tells of her experience auditioning for the show at the 125th Street Theater. "This one's so big and ugly the crowd out front will razz her," the manager shouted. "Better get some cork and black her up." Tucker hated the idea of blackface, but was convinced she needed it because of her size and her plain features. She made her professional New York debut on December 9 of that year, at the 116th Street Music Hall, and then toured the vaudeville circuit for the next two years in blackface. One night, her luggage did not arrive in time for a performance, so she went on without the disguise. The audience loved her, and she never appeared in blackface again.

Tucker's career inched forward again in 1909, with a spot in the *Ziegfeld Follies*, starring *Nora Bayes, but she was fired during the run of the show when Bayes objected to Sophie's show-stopping number. After a brief dry spell, she had the good fortune to hook up with William Morris, who managed his own vaudeville circuit of American Music Halls across the country. Tucker began touring the circuit with great success, particularly in Chicago, where she was billed as "The *Mary Garden of Ragtime." It was during this period that she began to introduce songs filled with the double-entendre which came to be associated with her (tunes like "Nobody Loves a Fat Girl, But Oh How a Fat Girl Can Love" and "You've Got To See Mama Ev'ry Night"). "The innocents couldn't find a thing in it to object to," she said, "and the others would find a belly laugh in every line." In 1910, she struck a recording deal with Edison. One of her earliest recordings, the Sheldon Brooks song "Some of These Days," eventually became her theme song.

In August 1914, Tucker arrived at the pinnacle of her vaudeville career, playing the famed Palace Theater in New York, where according to one critic, "She just walked out and owned the place." Despite her success, she continued to alter her act, keeping up with the fashions and changes within her own life. As jazz began to replace ragtime, she organized a band, "The Five Kings of Syncopation" and performed as the

Sophie
Tucker

"Queen of Jazz." Around the time of her father's death, she began incorporating sentimental ballads into the act. To further enhance their messages, she started to dramatized the songs, introducing them with skits and monologues. Later, Tucker disbanded her jazz backup and began

performing with two piano players: Ted Shapiro and Jack Carol. Shapiro remained with her for the rest of her career.

By the mid 1920s, Tucker was at the peak of her popularity, both in the United States and in

England, where she first appeared in 1922 at the London Hippodrome in *Round in Fifty*. She continued to visit England frequently, particularly as vaudeville began to lose its foothold in the United States during the 1930s. (Tucker was never as popular on the Continent, and was once booed off the stage in Paris while singing one of her most popular numbers, "My Yiddishe Mama.") In New York, she owned a nightclub, Sophie Tucker's Playground, and headlined *Earl Carroll's Vanities of 1924*. In 1928, she added six Tivoli Girls to her vaudeville act, as well as her son Bert.

Between 1929 and 1945, Tucker also made eight movies (two in England) and appeared on Broadway in *Leave It to Me* (1931) and *The High Kickers* (1941). She was also active in radio, guesting on various shows and even hosting her own 15-minute series, "Sophie Tucker and Her Show" (1938–39). With the advent of television, she poured herself into spangled gowns and made the rounds of the variety shows like Ed Sullivan's "Toast of the Town." Tucker always preferred live performance over radio and television, however, objecting to censorship of her more risqué songs and banter. "I couldn't even say 'hell' or 'damn,'" she lamented about radio, "and nothing, honey, is more expressive than the way I say 'hell' or 'damn.'"

After divorcing Louis Tuck in 1913, Tucker married Frank Westphal, her pianist at the time, in 1914. That union ended in divorce, as did a third marriage to Al Lackey, a fan who became her personal manager. Early on, shortly after her first divorce, Tucker reached the conclusion that her difficulty with men stemmed from her independence, her ability to earn her own way in an age when women relied on men to provide for them. "Something happens to a women when she does that," she wrote. "She may kid herself that it's just temporary, only until the right man turns up, and then she'll throw her arms around his neck and be a clinging vine all the rest of her life. It doesn't work that way. Once you start on the independent circuit, you're committed for life."

In addition to supporting her husbands, her mother, and her son, Tucker was also generous to a number of philanthropic endeavors. In 1945, she established the Sophie Tucker Foundation and in 1955 endowed a chair in theater arts at Brandeis University. Profits from 1,500 deluxe $25 editions of her autobiography were split between theatrical and other charities. Tucker also gave of her time, becoming active in the American Federation of Actors (AFA) and serving as its president in 1938. (The AFA subsequently joined with Actors' Equity to form Equity's American Guild of Variety Artists.)

As late as the mid-1960s, Tucker embarked on a long and successful tour with Ted Lewis and George Jessel. In 1966, she had performed two nights of her four-week engagement at the Latin Quarter when she entered the hospital for treatment of an intestinal inflammation. She came home to recuperate, but died on February 9 of lung and kidney failure. The singer had never once given a thought to retiring from the profession she so adored. "Show business has been my life," she once said. "I wouldn't have had any other. It is the life I always wanted."

SOURCES:

Current Biography 1945. NY: H.W. Wilson, 1945.

McHenry, Robert, ed. *Famous American Women*. NY: Dover, 1980.

Parish, James Robert, and Michael R. Pitts. *Hollywood Songsters*. NY: Garland, 1991.

Sicherman, Barbara, and Carol Hurd Green, eds. *Notable American Women: The Modern Period*. Cambridge, MA: The Belknap Press of Harvard University, 1980.

Tucker, Sophie, with Dorothy Giles. *Some of These Days*, 1945.

Barbara Morgan,
Melrose, Massachusetts

Tuckwell, Gertrude (1861–1951).

See Bondfield, Margaret for sidebar.

Tuckwell, Patricia (b. 1926).

See Lascelles, Patricia.

Tudor, Elizabeth (1533–1603).

See Elizabeth I.

Tudor, Margaret.

See Beaufort, Margaret (1443–1509).
See Margaret Tudor (1489–1541).

Tudor, Mary.

See Mary Tudor (1496–1533).
See Mary I (1516–1558).

Tueting, Sarah (b. 1976).

See Team USA: Women's Ice Hockey at Nagano.

Tufty, Esther Van Wagoner
(1896–1986)

American journalist and war correspondent. Born Esther Van Wagoner on July 2, 1896, in Kingston, Michigan; died on May 4, 1986, in Alexandria, Virginia; daughter of James Van Wagoner and Florence (Loomis) Van Wagoner; attended Michigan State College, 1914–15; University of Wisconsin (Madison), B.A., 1921; married Harold Guilford Tufty, Sr. (an electrical engineer), on September 17, 1921 (divorced

1947); children: Harold Guilford Tufty, Jr. (b. 1922); James Van Wagoner Tufty (b. 1929).

Established the Tufty News Service in Washington, D.C. (1935); covered the Washington political scene, as well as Nazi air assaults on Britain, the Berlin airlift, and both the Korean and Vietnam wars (1935–85); worked as television and radio commentator (beginning 1952); served as president of the Women's National Press Club, American Newspaper Women's Club, and American Women in Radio and Television; became the first woman member of the National Press Club (1971).

Born in Kingston, Michigan, in 1896, Esther Van Wagoner Tufty was one of two distinguished siblings; her brother Murray Van Wagoner later served as governor of Michigan. Tufty got an early start in journalism, straight out of high school, going to work as assistant society editor of the *Pontiac Press* of Pontiac, Michigan, for $7.50 a week. She later attended the University of Wisconsin at Madison, from which she graduated with a bachelor's degree in journalism in 1921. Immediately after, she joined the reporting staff of the *Evanston* (Illinois) *News-Index*, working her way up to managing editor, a position few women achieved in those days. In September 1921, she also married electrical engineer Harold Guilford Tufty. They would have two sons, Harold Guilford Tufty Jr. (b. 1922) and James Tufty (b. 1929), before divorcing in 1947.

After several years working for newspapers in the Midwest, Tufty headed East to seek her fortune in the nation's capital. There in 1935, a year before her 40th birthday, she founded the Tufty News Service, for which she served in a trio of roles: as writer, editor, and president. Originally set up to serve 26 Michigan newspapers, over time Tufty's news agency came to feed reports to more than 300 U.S. newspapers. In the next few years, she concentrated on coverage of the administration of Franklin Delano Roosevelt, then in its first term, and other events on the domestic political scene. In the 50 years she spent at the helm of her news service, she covered every president from FDR to Ronald Reagan. With other pioneers, such as *Doris Fleeson and Sarah McClendon, she was one of the first women reporters to cover the White House. McClendon, the veteran Washington correspondent for a group of Texas newspapers, once recalled, perhaps a bit enviously: "I watched Esther Tufty, and she had everybody calling her 'the Duchess.' She was tall and statuesque and had beautiful, long braids. She had established this idea that she was very important and that she was the one to talk to and the one to invite to everything."

Beginning in 1952, Tufty began work as a television and radio commentator for the National Broadcasting Company (NBC), starting off at the 1952 Republican National Convention in Chicago. For a time she had her own radio program, "Tufty Topics," on a local Washington station. Tufty is the only woman to have served as president of Washington's top three press clubs for women: the Women's National Press Club (now the Washington Press Club), the American Newspaper Women's Club, and American Women in Radio and Television. In 1971, she became the first woman to join the National Press Club in Washington, which voted to admit women only two days after the Women's National Press Club agreed to accept men as members.

Being her own boss allowed Tufty to handpick her assignments, and when World War II broke out in Europe, she did not shy away from the perils that front-line coverage entailed. She traveled across the Atlantic to cover the war in Britain and in the years after the war flew into Berlin during the airlift sitting atop a load of coal. She also covered the wars in both Korea (when she was 55) and Vietnam (when she was 70). During the Vietnam War, a helicopter flying Tufty to visit a hospital was hit by enemy fire. Of the incident, she later recalled: "We were a sitting duck. It was an awful feeling. Then I reminded myself, 'You didn't have to come.'"

In 1983, Tufty's alma mater awarded her its Distinguished Service to Journalism Award, noting that when she graduated from the school of journalism, "Warren G. Harding was in the White House and a satellite was a falling star. Yet every weekday, there she is, pecking away at her typewriter in a cozily cluttered office in the National Press Building in Washington, D.C., still very much a newspaper reporter at the age of 86." And there she continued to work until she was felled by a massive stroke in 1985. She died the following year.

SOURCES:
Edwards, Julia. *Women of the World: The Great Foreign Correspondents.* Boston, MA: Houghton Mifflin, 1988.

Don Amerman, freelance writer, Saylorsburg, Pennsylvania

Tules, La (c. 1820–1852).
See Barcelo, Gertrudis.

Tuli, Felix (1886–1954).
See Wuolijoki, Hella.

Tullia
(fl. 535 BCE)

Tullia (fl. 535 BCE)

Infamous queen of Rome. Flourished around 535 BCE; daughter of Servius Tullius (578–535 BCE), the sixth king of Rome; married Tarquinius Superbus, the Etruscan king; children: Sextus Tarquinius (Tarquin); and others.

A byword for female villainy throughout Roman history, Tullia was a daughter of Servius Tullius, the sixth king of Rome. With her sister, also named Tullia, she was delivered in marriage as a sort of consolation gift to Lucius and Arruns, sons of Tarquin and *Tanaquil, after these sons were denied inheritance to the throne in favor of Servius Tullius. The first Tullia married Arruns, who was apparently more or less content with his unkingly lot, while her sister, said to be gentle and subservient, married Lucius. Impatient with her unambitious husband, the first Tullia approached her brother-in-law Lucius with a proposal: they should both kill their spouses and then themselves marry, the better to work together to achieve power. Lucius agreed, and the murders were done. Later, with the half-hearted agreement, if not blessing, of Servius Tullius (who did not know the true culprits in the deaths of his daughter and son-in-law), Lucius and the remaining Tullia were married.

Together, Roman chroniclers claim, they conspired to dispossess her father and seize the crown. In the struggle, Servius Tullius was killed, and Tullia, on her triumphant progress through Rome to greet her husband as king, drove over her father's dead body as it lay unburied in the street. The charioteer had hesitated at the sight of the corpse of the old man and would have negotiated his steeds around it, but Tullia told him, "Drive on!" The blood of her murdered parent stained her chariot wheels. Some five centuries later, according to Livy, that street was still known as "The Street of the Crime."

With her husband now king as Tarquinius Superbus, Tullia went on to gain an evil reputation among the citizens of Rome, both for the murder of her father and for (of course) the wanton lifestyle ascribed to her. The positions of power they had gained so bloodily would not last, however, for some years later, we are told, their son Sextus Tarquinius, accustomed, as son and heir of the king, to taking whatever he wanted, raped the noble Roman matron *Lucretia. As legend has it, her sense of honor drove her to kill herself after first informing her husband and father of the reason why, and these events proved to be the downfall for Tullia and her family. Rome rose up and overthrew Tarquinius Superbus, who with Tullia fled for safety to Etruria. (Their son fled too, but was later murdered.) So filled with contempt and disgust at the corrupt Etruscan dynasty were the Romans that they abolished the monarchy forever, leading to the establishment of the Roman Republic.

Tullia (c. 79–45 BCE)

Roman noblewoman. Born around 79 BCE; died in childbirth in 45 BCE; daughter of Terentia and Marcus Tullius Cicero (106–40 BCE), Roman orator and consul; married Calpurnius Piso; married second hus- band; married third husband Publius Cornelius Dolabella (consul, 44 BCE), in 50 BCE.

Born around 79 BCE, Tullia was the beloved daughter of ❧ Terentia and the noted orator and consul Cicero. When Tullia was around 12, her father arranged her first marriage, to Calpurnius Piso. A second marriage was also orchestrated by Cicero. However, in 50 BCE, under the auspices of her spirited mother, Tullia married the charming but dissolute Dolabella while Cicero was away. Though the marriage was legal, upon his return Cicero contemplated withholding dowry installments; instead, Dolabella reaped the political advancement he was after, serving as legate to Julius Caesar in the Civil War and becoming Roman consul in 44 BCE.

In 46, Cicero divorced Terentia, his wife of 30 years, allegedly for her disloyalty during the war of 49–48 BCE. Subsequently, he married the young and rich **Publilia**, whom he soon divorced (45) for her lack of sympathy over the passing of Tullia who died in childbirth. This tragedy devastated Cicero, as we know from the poignant letters (still extant) written shortly after his daughter's death.

Tully, Alice (1902–1993)

American opera singer and philanthropist. Born on September 11, 1902; died on December 10, 1993, in New York City; the daughter of a Corning heiress and a state senator; studied in Paris with Jean Perier and Miguel Fontecha.

Alice Tully was the maternal granddaughter of Amory Houghton, who founded the Corning Glass Works, and inherited his accumulated wealth. A trained singer, she was fairly successful as a mezzo-soprano and later as a dramatic soprano in opera and recitals from the late 1920s to the 1940s; she was also a specialist in French repertory. In the 1940s, Tully became interested in philanthropy: she contributed to museums, libraries, and the arts and was a patron, friend, and supporter of other singers, pianists, and composers. In 1958,

❧ **Terentia** (fl. 69–45 BCE)

*Roman noblewoman. Flourished around 69 to 45 BCE; married Marcus Tullius Cicero (106–40 BCE), Roman orator and consul, in 76 BCE (divorced 45 BCE); children: *Tullia (c. 79–45 BCE); Marcus.*

she received her inheritance on the death of her mother and expanded her philanthropic interests accordingly. She founded the Maya Corporation, which made anonymous gifts to the arts, until friends urged her to drop the anonymity. In the late 1960s, she was the main donor of finances for the $4.5 million Alice Tully Hall, a visually and acoustically impressive chamber-music concert hall that opened at Lincoln Center for the Performing Arts in 1969. She was particularly interested in what she called the hall's "creature comforts," and made sure it was luxuriously appointed. In addition to providing money for the hall, Tully also subsidized the formation of the hall's resident ensemble, the Chamber Music Society of Lincoln Center. She was a member of the boards of the Juilliard School of Music, the New York Philharmonic Orchestra, the Metropolitan Opera, and many other educational and arts institutions. She died at her Manhattan home in 1993.

Kelly Winters,
freelance writer

Tulu, Derartu (1972—)

Ethiopian runner. Born in Ethiopia on January 1, 1972.

Derartu Tulu became the first black African woman to win a gold medal at the Olympic Games when she won the 10,000-meter event at the 1992 Games in Barcelona, Spain. On the final lap of the race, she passed **Elana Meyer**, a white woman who was running for South Africa, a nation that had been banned from participation in the Olympics for 32 years because of its policy of racial apartheid. Tulu passed Meyer, winning wild cheers from the 60,000 spectators, but on the final lap of honor after the race, both women ran together, with Meyer holding Tulu's arm high. "We both ran for Africa," Meyer said. "I think we did that very well."

That year, 1992, was an incredible one for Tulu. Her winning time at the Olympics set a new African record. A few weeks before the Olympics, at the African Games, Tulu had won the 3,000 meters and 10,000 meters. Two months after winning in the Olympics, she competed at the World Cup in Havana, Cuba, where she became the first female distance runner to win two races: the 3,000 meters and the 10,000 meters. In that same year, she ran in only one road race, the Bob Hasan 10K in Jogjakarta, Indonesia, but she came in first in that race against a field of top women runners. For her performance in 1992, she received the Runner of the Year award.

Kelly Winters,
freelance writer

Tuqan, Fadwa (1917—)

Palestinian poet and feminist who is one of the Arab world's most distinguished poets. Born in 1917 in Nablus on the West Bank; studied with her brother, poet Ibrahim Tuqan.

Selected writings: Wahdi m'a al-Ayyam *(Alone with the Days, 1955);* Amam al-Bab al-Mughlaq *(Before the Closed Door, 1967);* al-Layl Wa-al Fursan *(Night and the Horsemen, 1969);* Ala Qimmat al-Dunya Wahidan *(Alone, at the Top of the World, 1973);* Kabus al-Layl Wa al-Nahar *(Nightmare in Daylight, 1974); (autobiography)* A Mountainous Journey *(trans. by Olive Kenny, 1990).*

Fadwa Tuqan was born during 1917 in Nablus on the West Bank into a middle-class family of soap manufacturers. She grew up in a large house with an extended family that ran the business collectively. In her autobiography, she describes the oppressive atmosphere of her youth in a culture which regarded women so lightly that her mother could not remember exactly when Tuqan was born. Simultaneously protected and ruled by her male relatives, she lived in a high-walled house under the omnipresent scrutiny of her relatives.

When she was 13, an admiring young boy followed Fadwa home from school one day and sent her a jasmine flower. Fearing a threat to her purity, her family promptly removed her from school. Although her brother Ibrahim Tuqan, a poet, could not release her from the seclusion the family had imposed, he brought her books and read with her. She ultimately committed 2,000 lines of classical verse to memory. Later, after Ibrahim married, he brought Fadwa to Jerusalem to live with him and his wife. There, she met and corresponded with many other writers. She was particularly influenced by the romantic poets of the period, including Ali Mahmud Taha, author of *Lost Sailor* (1934) and *Nights of the Lost Sailor* (1940).

When Fadwa's brother died in 1941, she had to return to the stifling house of her family. Because Ibrahim had been a political poet, her father asked that she also write political poetry. But Fadwa felt that being curtailed behind walls allowed for limited involvement in politics (in her youth she had been forbidden to even read the newspapers), and she at first refused. Tuqan changed her mind, however, when political turmoil erupted in Palestine in 1948 and women were released from their isolation. Fadwa joined factional and literary movements, and from then on she infused her poetry with politics.

The poetry written in her youth reflects the breadth of her reading, which included the *Qur'an*, the Bible, and Western European literature (with which she developed a deep familiarity). Her collected work shows a steady progression from romantic, introspective poetry to dynamic, liberated prose about the political plight of the Palestinian people. Translated by **Olive Kenny**, her autobiography *A Mountainous Journey* provided the English-speaking world with a woman's perspective of Arab culture as well as a look at the life of one of the Arab world's most distinguished poets.

SOURCES:

Buck, Claire, ed. *The Bloomsbury Guide to Women's Literature*. NY: Prentice Hall, 1992.

Kelly Winters,
freelance writer

Tureck, Rosalyn (1914—)

American pianist and musicologist. Born in Chicago, Illinois, on December 14, 1914; daughter of Samuel and Monya (Lipson) Tureck; studied with Sophia Brilliant-Liven, 1925–29, Jan Chiapasso, 1929–31, Leon Theremin, 1931–32; graduated cum laude from the Juilliard School of Music, 1935.

Conducted and taught at the Mannes School, the Juilliard School and elsewhere; known as the most convincing advocate of presenting Bach's works on the piano rather than the harpsichord or clavichord.

Recognized the world over as an authoritative interpreter of the music of Johann Sebastian Bach, American pianist Rosalyn Tureck has also played a significant role in bringing contemporary music to the concert stage. For Tureck, Bach serves as a springboard to contemporary composers. "The music of Bach is so universal in its human meaning and so all-embracing in its musical structures," said Tureck, "that for the receptive mind it illuminates all other music, including contemporary music. The artist need never feel limited with Bach as the fountainhead."

Rosalyn Tureck was born in 1914 in Chicago, Illinois, to parents of Russian and Turkish ancestry. She began her musical studies at age nine, under the tutelage of **Sophia Brilliant-Liven**. Tureck later characterized her first teacher as a hard taskmaster, whose only compliment in the four years they worked together, came after Tureck's performance in the semifinals of a piano competition. Brilliant-Liven told the 13-year-old prodigy: "If I had been listening from outside the auditorium, I would have sworn it was Anton Rubinstein himself play-

ing." Tureck went on to win the competition and still keeps a portrait of Rubinstein prominently displayed in her London home.

Tureck continued her studies with Dutch-Italian pianist and Bach specialist Jan Chiapusso. At 16, she received a four-year fellowship to the Juilliard School of Music in New York, where she studied with *Olga Samaroff, among others. After graduating *cum laude* in 1935, Tureck joined the faculty of the Philadelphia Conservatory of Music. That October, she also made her debut at New York's Carnegie Hall with the Philadelphia Orchestra, playing Brahm's Concerto in B-Flat.

In 1937, Tureck performed her first series of all-Bach recitals at New York's Town hall, executing the complete 48 preludes and fugues of the *Well-Tempered Clavier*, the "Goldberg Variations," and miscellaneous works. Since that time, she has devoted much of her concert career to Bach, becoming the most convincing advocate of the master and performing his works on the

Rosalyn Tureck

piano rather than the harpsichord or clavichord. "I aim to embrace a more holistic Bach," said Tureck. "You cannot imprison a mind such as his in any one medium. He himself did not. I also dispense with the static concept of 'the' piano, 'the' harpsichord. A harpsichord made in Northern Italy is different in sonority and texture from that of the Flemish or English. The piano also is far from being limited to a static, nineteenth century sonority and texture."

Tureck, who appears tall on stage, is only 5'2", and has small hands for a pianist. Her mastery of the works of Bach are the result of immense effort. She worked for 12 years before she felt prepared to publicly perform Bach's Chromatic Fantasy and Fugue, and the preparation included a detailed investigation of the 22 manuscripts from Bach's time that have survived, as well as 50 printed editions of the piece. The results of her research and performance experience were summed up in her three-volume study, *An Introduction to the Performance of Bach*. She has also recorded much of the master's music, including the 48 Preludes and Fugues (*Das wohltemperirte Clavier*).

Tureck refuses to be classified as exclusively a Bachian, however, and deplores narrowness of mind in all forms. "All my life, I've been interested in philosophy, the sciences, history and art besides work in music and the varied forms and styles of instrumental media," she said. "I've studied philosophy, history, religion, Asian music and art. A deeper understanding of all these fields enriches one's own concepts and performance." Her musical repertoire incorporates works of Liszt, Chopin, Weber, Tchaikovsky, Debussy, Albeniz, Ravel, and Rachmaninoff, as well as contemporary composers, such as American Paul Nordoff. She has been in the vanguard of contemporary and electronic music since the age of ten, when she heard and met Russian inventor Leon Theremin, with whom she later studied. In 1952, she presented the first program in the United States of tape and electronic music and has played Bach on the Moog synthesizer, performing in a 1971 concert, "Bach and Rock." In addition to her numerous world concert tours, Tureck has also made appearances as a soloist and conductor. In 1958, she was the first woman to conduct the New York Philharmonic. While directing an orchestra, she strives to capture the stylistic and emotional essence of the music, instead of emphasizing the instruments.

Tureck held her teaching post at the Philadelphia Conservatory of Music for seven years (1935–42) and subsequently taught at Juilliard (1943–55) and at the University of California,

San Diego (1966–72). She founded the International Bach Institute, New York, in 1966 and The Tureck Bach Research Foundation, Oxford, England, in 1993. Tureck has received five honorary degrees, including one from Oxford University, where she is an honorary Life Fellow at St. Hilda's. She was also granted the Commander's Cross of the Order of Merit from the government of the German Federal Republic in 1979. Since 1956, she has made her home in London.

SOURCES:

Current Biography. NY: H.W. Wilson, 1959.

Dubal, David. *The Art of the Piano.* NY: Summit, 1989.

Hinson Maurice. *Guide to the Pianist's Repertoire.* 2nd rev. ed. Bloomington, IN: Indiana University Press, 1987, p. 59.

Slonimsky, Nicolas, ed. *Baker's Biographical Dictionary of Musicians.* 8th ed. NY: Schirmer, 1992.

Tureck Bach Research Foundation.

Barbara Morgan,
Melrose, Massachusetts

Turell, Jane (1708–1735)

American poet. Born Jane Colman on February 25, 1708, in Boston, Massachusetts; died on March 26, 1735, in Medford, Massachusetts; daughter of Benjamin Colman (a pastor) and Jane (Clark) Colman; married Ebenezer Turell (a pastor), on August 11, 1726; children: three who died in infancy, and Samuel (who died in childhood).

Jane Turell was born in Boston in 1708, the oldest daughter and the second of three children of Benjamin and **Jane Clark Colman**. Her mother came from a wealthy Boston family, and her father was a pastor of the Church on Brattle Street. Known for his liberal views in church, at home he was a strict disciplinarian, filled with religious zeal and concern about his children's religious education. Jane was a physically frail child, but by the time she was two years old, she knew the alphabet and could speak clearly and relate many Bible stories to her father's satisfaction, as well as that of distinguished visitors such as Governor Joseph Dudley and what her father called "other Wise and Polite Gentlemen." Ola Elizabeth Winslow noted that this intensely religious upbringing "provides a key to understanding her limitations as a poet. She was a pulpit example almost from birth."

By the time she was four, Turell knew by heart most of the Assembly's catechism, many psalms, and several hundred lines of poetry, and could read aloud clearly and comment intelligently on what she had read. Her father taught her daily and counseled her to be aware of sin but to keep focused on godliness. Her mother augmented this teaching with similar spiritual advice and by praying with her. At age 11, Turell composed her first hymn, then went on to compose her own rhymed paraphrases of the psalms, as well as reverent meditations and prayers. By the time she was 18, she had exhausted the contents of her father's library.

In 1726, she married Ebenezer Turell, a young minister who had studied with her father. He had become a pastor in Medford, Massachusetts, two years earlier, and the couple moved there after their marriage. Jane continued to write to her father, who remained her mentor and spiritual advisor for the rest of her life. Although she occasionally wrote of her own down-to-earth life and of humble subjects, most of her poetry imitated the classics or the English poets, with lines about nightingales, "fragrant Zephyrs," and temples.

Turell's health, always frail, failed her at an early age. She died in Medford when she was 27 and was buried in the Salem Street Cemetery. In her short life, she had given birth to four children, three of whom died in infancy. The fourth, Samuel, lived only 18 months after his mother's death, dying at age six. After Turell's death, her husband published a biography of her, *Reliquiae Turellae et Lachrymae Paternal*, which includes several of her poems, letters, diary entries, and essays.

SOURCES:

Buck, Claire, ed. *The Bloomsbury Guide to Women's Literature*. NY: Prentice Hall, 1992.

Winslow, Ola Elizabeth. "Jane Turell," in *Notable American Women, 1607–1950*. Ed. by Edward T. James. Cambridge, MA: The Belknap Press of Harvard University, 1971.

Kelly Winters,
freelance writer

Turhan (1627–1683).

See Reign of Women for sidebar on Hadice Turhan.

Turnbo-Malone, Annie (1869–1957).

See Malone, Annie Turnbo.

Turnbull, Julia Anne (1822–1887)

American ballet dancer and actress. Born on June 18, 1822, in Montreal, Canada; died of tuberculosis on September 11, 1887, in Brooklyn, New York; daughter of John D. Turnbull (an actor and playwright) and his actress wife (name unknown); studied ballet with French dancer Mme LeComte and LeComte's brother, Jules Martin, and with James Sylvain.

Julia Anne Turnbull was born in 1822 in Montreal, Canada. Her Scottish father John D.

Turnbull was an actor and playwright, and her New York-born mother (name unknown) was also on the stage. When Julia was three years old, the family moved to Albany, New York, where she made her stage debut as an actress with her sisters **Emily** and **Caroline**. At age six, she appeared in *The Wandering Boys* in Albany, playing the part of Justin. In this important early performance, she shared the stage with *Louisa Lane Drew, who later became a celebrated actress. Turnbull became a regular player in the stock company at the Park Theater in New York City, simultaneously studying ballet with French dancer **Mme Le Comte** and LeComte's brother, Jules Martin. In June 1839, she debuted in her first leading dance role in *The Sisters* at the Bowery Theater, co-starring with **Mary Ann Lee** (c. 1824–1899), who was later the first American to dance *Giselle*.

In 1840, when the great Viennese ballet dancer *Fanny Elssler toured the United States, she chose Turnbull as a soloist in her company. Turnbull danced roles second only to Elssler's, and continued to study ballet with Elssler's partner, James Sylvain. When Elssler returned to Europe, Turnbull launched her own solo tour, returning to the Bowery Theater in 1847, where she joined the stock company and had a great hit as the star of *The Naiad Queen*. In the same year, she danced *Giselle*, for which she received rave reviews. Turnbull was one of the earliest American women to dance the classic title roles of *Giselle* and *Esmeralda*. During the 1840s, her popularity equaled or surpassed that of the European ballet stars who toured the United States.

In August 1848, a rivalry between Turnbull and Italian dancer **Giovanna Ciocca** resulted in a riot at the Bowery Theater. Although favored by the audience, Turnbull eventually left the company and continued to dance with great success, assuming more acting roles and earning accolades for these as well. She retired from the stage in 1857 and lived quietly in Brooklyn for the next 30 years. She did some dressmaking, and eventually died of tuberculosis and was buried in Greenwood Cemetery in Brooklyn.

SOURCES:

James, Edward T., ed. *Notable American Women, 1607–1950*. Cambridge, MA: The Belknap Press of Harvard University Press, 1971.

Kelly Winters,
freelance writer

Turner, Anne (1576–1615)

English murderer. Born in 1576; executed by hanging in 1615 in Tyburn, England; married George Turner.

Anne Turner, wife of George Turner, was a friend of the astrologer Simon Forman; she may actually have been Forman's daughter. In 1613, she helped *Frances Howard, countess of Somerset, to poison Sir Thomas Overbury, and in 1615 was hanged at Tyburn. Frances Howard, while later also sentenced to death, instead was pardoned by the king, James I, and merely confined in the Tower of London for six years.

Kelly Winters,
freelance writer

Turner, Elizabeth (1774–1846)

English children's writer. Name variations: Mrs. Turner. Born in 1774 in England; died in 1846 in Whitchurch, Salop, England.

Selected writings: The Daisy (1807); The Cowslip (1811); The Blue Bell (1838); The Crocus (1844).

Born in 1774 in England, Elizabeth Turner was one of the most popular children's book authors in the early and middle 19th century, but little is now known about her life. Her place and full date of birth, maiden name, education, marriages and children have not been recorded. Turner wrote many moral tales in verse, which she called "cautionary stories." The protagonists are flowers, and according to Stanley Kunitz, the verses, "though bald and unpoetic, are not without a certain quaint charm."

SOURCES:
Kunitz, Stanley J., and Howard Haycraft, eds. *British Authors of the Nineteenth Century.* NY: H.W. Wilson, 1936.

Kelly Winters,
freelance writer

Turner, Ethel (1872–1958)

Australian children's author and novelist. Born Ethel Burwell on January 24, 1872, in Doncaster, Yorkshire, England; died on April 8, 1958; daughter of G.W. Burwell; sister of Lilian Turner (1870–1956); attended Sydney Girls' High School; married Herbert Curlewis (a judge), in 1896; children: Jean.

Selected works: Seven Little Australians (1894); The Family at Misrule (1895); The Story of a Baby (1895); The Little Duchess (1896); The Little Larrikin (1896); Miss Bobbie (1897); The Camp at Wandinong (1898); Three Little Maids (1900); Gum Leaves (1900); The Wonder-Child (1901); Little Mother Meg (1902); Betty & Co. (1903); Mother's Little Girl (1904); A White Roof-Tree (1905); In the Mist of the Mountains (1906); The Stolen Voyage (1907); Happy Hearts (1908); That Girl (1908); Ethel Turner Birthday Book (1909); Fugitives from Fortune (1909); Fair

Ines (1910); The Raft in the Bush (1910); The Tiny House (1911); Fifteen and Fair (1911); The Apple of Happiness (1911); An Ogre Up-to-Date (1911); Ports and Happy Havens (1912); The Secret of the Sea (1913); Oh, Boys in Brown! (1914); Flower o' the Pine (1914); The Cub (1915); John of Daunt (1916); Captain Cub (1917); St. Tom and the Dragon (1918); (ed. with Bertram Stevens) Australian Soldiers' Gift Book (1918); Brigid and the Cub (1919); Laughing Water (1920); King Anne (1921); Jennifer J. (1922); Nicola Silver (1924); The Ungardeners (1925); Funny (1926); Judy and Punch (1928); (ed. with Jean Curlewis) The Sunshine Family: A Book of Nonsense for Girls and Boys (1923); excerpts from her diaries, compiled by her granddaughter, Philippa Poole, were published in 1979.

Ethel Turner was born in 1872 in Yorkshire, England, the second child of G.W. Burwell, who died two years later. Her mother then married Henry Turner, and Ethel and her sister **Lilian Turner** took his name. Like Burwell, he died young. In 1881, Turner's mother took the girls to Sydney, Australia, where she married her third husband Charles Cope, a clerk in the New South Wales public service.

Ethel Turner began writing at a young age, and during her teens she and her sister edited a magazine for schoolgirls, *Iris*, which was later renamed the *Parthenon*. Turner eventually became the editor of the children's column of the *Illustrated Sydney News* and began writing her own books. Following the tradition of domestic fiction, Turner wrote children's books similar to those of *Louisa May Alcott and *Charlotte Mary Yonge, but with characteristically Australian, middle-class settings and values. Her two best-known books, *Seven Little Australians* and *The Family at Misrule*, are concerned with the daily life of an army officer's family of seven children and their mischievous pranks, family relationships, and experiences in growing up.

In her books, which are more often set in the city than in the outback and which usually feature large families, the parents are frequently dead, absent, negligent or inadequate. Their inadequacy is compensated by the solidarity of the children and the family as a whole. The books particularly emphasize good taste, education, and manners. After World War I, however, Turner's perspective became more democratic, socialist, and patriotic; three novels written during this period—*The Cub, Captain Cub*, and *Brigid and the Cub*—emphasize the idea that people must sometimes make sacrifices for their country.

As suggested in *The Oxford Companion to Australian Literature*, although "Ethel Turner's range is limited and she has a tendency to lapse into sentimentality of melodrama . . . she has created some perennially authentic children." Moreover, her work is durable because of its "humor, empathy with children and the representative picture of Australian middle-class life of the early 20th century."

SOURCES:

Buck, Claire, ed. *The Bloomsbury Guide to Women's Literature*. NY: Prentice Hall, 1992.

Wilde, William H., Joy Hooton, and Barry Andrews. *The Oxford Companion to Australian Literature*. Melbourne, Australia: Oxford University Press, 1985.

Kelly Winters,
freelance writer

Turner, Eva (1892–1990)

English soprano. Name variations: Dame Eva Turner. Born on March 10, 1892, in Oldham, England; died on June 16, 1990, in London; studied with Dan Rootham, Giglia Levy, Edgardo Levy, Mary Wilson, and Albert Richards-Broad.

Debuted in London (1916), at Teatro alla Scala (1924), at Covent Garden (1928); taught at the University of Oklahoma (1949–59); joined the faculty at the Royal Academy of Music (1959); made a Dame Commander of the Order of the British Empire (1962).

Born in 1892 in Oldham, Lancashire, Eva Turner had to circumvent many odds to become an opera performer of note. Her father was a cotton mill engineer and her mother a housewife, but both considered music essential to their daughter's education. For her schooling, she went to Bristol, where she studied with Daniel Rootham, teacher of the renowned English singer Dame *Clara Butt. After five years of study at the Royal Academy of Music, Turner sang in the chorus of the Carl Rosa Opera Company in 1915. She continued singing lessons under Albert Richards-Broad and, with constant work, was able to establish herself as the prima donna of this provincial English touring company. One of Arturo Toscanini's assistants heard Turner sing in 1924 and urged her to audition at La Scala for the Maestro, who engaged her immediately. Turner was the only English opera singer to achieve international status during the interwar years.

Turner, who is especially remembered for her role of Turandot although her repertoire was enormous, used Richards-Broad as her manager, but he was not entirely a professional. In fact, many of her invitations to perform seem to have evolved from casual meetings rather than profes-

sional contacts. World War II curtailed Turner's career as she was confined to Great Britain, and after the war she was too old to continue in opera. She launched a successful teaching career at the University of Oklahoma, the Royal Academy, and as a private teacher; her students include **Amy Shaurd**, **Rita Hunter**, and ***Gwyneth Jones**. Turner's recordings, recently remastered on compact disks, testify to her abilities. She was made a Dame Commander of the British Empire in 1962 in recognition of her achievements.

John Haag,
Athens, Georgia

Turner, Florence E. (c. 1888–1946)

American actress, producer, and director. Born on January 6, around 1888, in New York City; died of cancer on August 28, 1946, in Los Angeles, California; daughter of William Clifton Turner (an artist) and Frances Louise (Bowles) Turner (an actress).

Selected filmography: How to Cure a Cold (1907); Francesca da Rimini (1910); Launcelot and

Florence E. Turner

Elaine *(1911)*; Jealousy *(1911)*; A Tale of Two Cities *(1911)*; Aunty's Romance *(1912)*; How Mr. Bullington Ran the Home *(1912)*; *(producer)* Through the Valley of the Shadows *(1914)*; *(producer)* A Welsh Singer *(1915)*; *(producer)* My Old Dutch *(1915)*; *(producer)* Film Favourites *(1924)*.

❧▶
Gish, Lillian. *See joint entry under Gish, Dorothy and Lillian.*

Florence E. Turner was born around 1888 in New York City. Her father died a year later, and she was raised in Brooklyn by her mother **Frances Bowles Turner** and grandmother, both actresses in local theaters there. When she was three, a stage manager convinced Frances Turner to allow her daughter a walk-on role in a production of *The Romany Rye*. Other roles followed until she enrolled at school at age 11. Four years later, without her mother's consent, Turner signed on as an extra in a Brooklyn theater, after which she ventured into musical comedy and a tour in vaudeville.

Unable to find stage work, Turner followed a friend's suggestion in May 1907 and turned her attention to motion pictures. She applied at the Vitagraph studios nearby and secured the lead in a short comedy, *How to Cure a Cold*. Turner was immediately popular with audiences, and when the Vitagraph Players were organized in October 1907, she became the first American film actor to receive a contract. At the time, the people they saw on screen were not known by name, so she was called "The Vitagraph Girl." By 1910, the public was becoming increasingly fascinated with film actors, and in May she was billed under her own name. Soon she was making personal appearances throughout New York City.

A skilled mime, "dark and magnetic" with "expressive eyes," Turner preferred comedy over romantic parts, and was often paired with Maurice Costello and Wallace Reid. After several successful films, she left Vitagraph in 1913 to form her own company, Turner Films, Ltd., in England, where she had long enjoyed acclaim. In 1915, a magazine poll determined that she was the most popular actress in England. Using the facilities of the Hepworth Company at Walton-on-Thames, she produced a small but well-received collection of films.

At the outset of World War I, inflation and other troubles associated with the war led her to close her company. Turner lost all her money in this venture, and by the time she returned to the United States, audiences there had forgotten her. Nevertheless, she worked regularly as an actor, writer, and director for Universal and Metro-Goldwyn-Mayer. In 1920, she returned to Eng-

Opposite page
ℒana
𝒥urner

land and appeared as the lead in several comedies produced by W.W. Jacobs before working a final time with the Hepworth Company to produce a two-reel comedy, *Film Favorites*, in 1924. In this film, she burlesqued dozens of famous actors, including Charlie Chaplin, Ben Turpin, *****Mae Murray**, and ◀❧ **Lillian Gish**; however, she was unable to secure distribution and her financial problems worsened. In 1925 her friend, actress *****Marion Davies**, who had her own company, offered her work back in the States. For the next two decades, Turner played character parts and comedy roles, and during the last ten years before her death she was a member of the MGM stock company.

Turner lived for most of her life with her mother and grandmother, and did not marry. She died of cancer at the Motion Picture Country House, an actors' home in Los Angeles, in 1946.

SOURCES:
James, Edward T., ed. *Notable American Women, 1607–1950.* Cambridge, MA: The Belknap Press of Harvard University Press, 1971.
McHenry, Robert, ed. *Famous American Women.* NY: Dover, 1980.
Read, Phyllis J., and Bernard L. Witlieb. *The Book of Women's Firsts.* NY: Random House, 1992.

Kelly Winters,
freelance writer

Turner, Mrs. G.D. (1882–1973).

See Wilson, Margaret W.

Turner, Mrs. Henry E. (1903–1961).

See Robertson, E. Arnot.

Turner, Lana (1921–1995)

American actress and World War II "pin-up" who was nominated for an Academy Award for her performance in **Peyton Place.** *Born Julia Jean Mildred Frances Turner on February 8, 1921, in Wallace, Idaho; died of throat cancer on June 29, 1995, in Los Angeles, California; only daughter of John Virgil Turner (a mine overseer) and Mildred (Cowan) Turner; attended the Convent of the Immaculate Conception in San Francisco and Hollywood High School in Los Angeles; married Artie Shaw (the bandleader), in 1940 (divorced 1941); married Stephen Crane (an actor turned restaurateur), in 1942 (annulled, then divorced 1943); married Bob Topping (a millionaire), in 1948 (divorced 1952); married Lex Barker (an actor), in 1953 (divorced 1957); married Fred May; married Robert Eaton; married Ronald Dante, also known as Ronald Peller (a hypnotist), in 1968; children: (second marriage) one daughter, Cheryl Crane (b. 1943).*

Selected filmography: A Star is Born *(bit, 1937);* They Won't Forget *(1937);* The Great Garrick *(1937);* The Adventures of Marco Polo *(1938);* Four's a Crowd *(1938);* Love Finds Andy Hardy *(1938);* The Chaser *(bit, 1938);* Rich Man Poor Girl *(1938);* Dramatic School *(1938);* Calling Dr. Kildare *(1939);* These Glamour Girls *(1939);* Dancing Co-Ed *(1939);* Two Girls on Broadway *(1940);* We Who Are Young *(1940);* Ziegfeld Girl *(1941);* Dr. Jekyll and Mr. Hyde *(1941);* Honky Tonk *(1941);* Johnny Eager *(1942);* Somewhere I'll Find You *(1942);* Slightly Dangerous *(1943);* The Youngest Profession *(1943);* DuBarry Was a Lady *(cameo, 1943);* Marriage Is a Private Affair *(1944);* Keep Your Powder Dry *(1945);* Week-End at the Waldorf *(1945);* The Postman Always Rings Twice *(1946);* Green Dolphin Street *(1947);* Cass Timberlane *(1947);* Homecoming *(1948);* The Three Musketeers *(1948);* A Life of Her Own *(1950);* Mr. Imperium *(1951);* The Merry Widow *(1952);* The Bad and the Beautiful *(1952);* Latin Lovers *(1953);* Flame and the Flesh *(1954);* Betrayed *(1954);* The Prodigal *(1955);* The Sea Chase *(1955);* The Rains of Ranchipur *(1955);* Diane *(1956);* Peyton Place *(1957);* The Lady Takes a Flyer *(1958);* Another Time Another Place *(1958);* Imitation of Life *(1959);* Portrait in Black *(1960);* By Love Possessed *(1962);* Bachelor in Paradise *(1961);* Who's Got the Action? *(1962);* Love Has Many Faces *(1965);* Madame X *(1966);* The Big Cube *(US-Mex., 1969);* Persecution *(*The Terror of Sheba *or* The Graveyard, *UK, 1974);* Bittersweet Love *(1976);* Witches' Brew *(1979).*

The Hollywood "Sweater Girl" who blossomed into one of the most glamorous, popular stars of the 1940s and 1950s, Lana Turner kept her career afloat through a tumultuous private life that included seven marriages and a scandal which involved her teenage daughter, a knife, and the death of a reputed gangster. A survivor in every sense of the word, Turner retained her star power well into the 1980s, when she played a recurring role in the popular prime-time soap-opera "Falcon Crest."

Lana Turner was born Julie Jean Mildred Frances Turner in 1921, in Wallace, Idaho, where her father John Virgil Turner worked as a mine overseer. When she was six, the family moved to California in search of a better life, but her father had difficulty finding work. Her parents eventually separated, and Turner spent time in several foster homes before she was permanently reunited with her mother **Mildred Cowan Turner**. John Turner would subsequently fall victim to a robbery-murder. Turner attended a

convent school in San Francisco and completed her education at Hollywood High in Los Angeles, where she and her mother moved in 1936.

One of Hollywood's great legends is how Turner got her start in films. The story that she was discovered as a teenager sitting at a soda fountain is true, but it was not at Schwab's Drugstore. Lana set the record straight in her memoir *Lana: The Lady, the Legend, the Truth.* "The Hollywood columnist Sidney Skolsky often ate lunch there. One day, as he sat at the fountain, a busty blonde came up and asked which stool was Lana Turner's. Skolsky simply picked one and pointed it out. Just like that, Schwab's became a mecca to thousands of would-be movie stars, and Hollywood gained another persistent myth." In reality, Turner had cut an afternoon typing class and was having a Coke at the Top Hat Café across from the high school. With the counter clerk serving as an intermediary, W.R. Wilkerson, editor of the motion-picture trade journal *Hollywood Reporter*, introduced himself and asked her if she wanted to be in the movies. "I don't know, I'll have to ask my mother," she replied. He then gave her his business card and told her to have her mother call him for a meeting.

Wilkerson subsequently hooked her up with the Zeppo Marx Agency, where agent Henry Wilson got her a walk-on in *A Star is Born* (1937). The agency then arranged a meeting for her with director Mervyn LeRoy at Warner Bros. "She was so nervous her hands were shaking," LeRoy later said about his first encounter with the actress. "She wasn't wearing any makeup, and she was so shy she could hardly look me in the face. Yet there was something so endearing about her that I knew she was the right girl. She had tremendous appeal, which I knew the audience would feel." LeRoy gave her an exotic new name and a contract, which she signed just days after her 16th birthday.

Turner's first small role in *They Won't Forget* (1937), however, did not exactly exploit her innocence. It included a shot of her character walking down the street in high heels, a tight sweater belted at the waist, and a contoured skirt. At the previews, the sight brought howls and cheers from the young men in the audience, and Lana Turner, the object of desire, was launched. After two additional pictures, one at Warners' (where Jack Warner predicted that she would not amount to anything) and one at MGM, Turner moved with LeRoy to MGM. There, she continued to play leads or second leads in minor productions, winning little acclaim from the critics, but receiving sacks of fanmail from admiring males.

Turner's next series of films, *We Who Are Young* (1940), *Ziegfeld Girl* (1941), *Dr. Jekyll and Mr. Hyde* (1941), and *Honky-Tonk* (1941), indicated that she had some potential as an actress, although the studio continued to exploit her sex appeal. Her popularity continued to soar during World War II, when she ranked among the nation's top "pin-up girls." In the postwar years, she was notable in *Green Dolphin Street* (1947), *Cass Timberlane* (1947), *The Three Musketeers* (1948), and *The Bad and the Beautiful* (1956), but turned in her most credible performance as the femme fatale Cora Smith, who convinces John Garfield to murder her elderly husband in the film version of James M. Cain's *The Postman Always Rings Twice* (1946). Turner received her only Oscar nomination, as Best Actress, for her portrayal of Constance MacKenzie in *Peyton Place* (1957), an adaptation of *Grace Metalious' scandalous bestseller. John Houseman, who produced *The Bad and the Beautiful*, felt Turner "was capable of brilliant individual scenes but seemed to lack the temperament or the training to sustain a full-length performance."

Turner's private life probably provided more melodrama than her movies and undoubtedly contributed to her screen mystique. Her name was linked to countless male stars, and she was purportedly once engaged to five different men at the same time. She was married seven times (or eight, if you count her two marriages to Stephen Crane), but all of the unions were brief. She met her first husband, bandleader Artie Shaw, on the set of *Dancing Coed* (1939), and they eloped to Las Vegas on their first date. Their tumultuous relationship endured for 4 months and 16 days, which the actress later referred to as her "college education." Turner also eloped with second husband Stephen Crane in 1942, after a whirlwind courtship of nine days. Crane's divorce from his first wife was not yet final at the time, so Turner had the marriage annulled. They later reconciled and married for a second time in March 1943, shortly before the birth of their daughter **Cheryl Crane**. That marriage also ended in divorce, as did subsequent unions with Bob Topping, Lex Barker, Fred May, Robert Eaton, and Robert Dante. In her autobiography, Turner addressed the subject of her many marriages, blaming herself for choosing men who took advantage of her; "takers," as she called them. "Something in me must have yelled 'patsy,'" she writes, "otherwise why would I have been taken advantage of again and again?"

One of her amours was with underworld hoodlum Johnny Stompanato. On April 5, 1958, when Turner attempted to end the relationship, Stompanato, who was frequently violent, threatened to kill her. He was hitting Turner in her Beverly Hills bedroom when Lana's 15-year-old daughter Cheryl burst into the room and stabbed him with an eight-inch kitchen knife. "I thought she hit him in the stomach," Turner later testified. "They came together and then they parted. I never saw the blade." Stompanato, whose kidney and aorta were punctured, died. The killing generated headlines worldwide; it was eventually pronounced a justifiable homicide on the grounds that Cheryl was protecting her mother from what she believed had been a threat to her life. (The court, however, ordered Cheryl to live with her grandmother Mildred.) The adverse publicity, which included the public airing of Turner's love letters to Stompanato, was agonizing for the actress. She became reclusive and uneasy about resuming her career, but Ross Hunter persuaded her to star in a remake of the 1934 film *Imitation of Life*, which had starred *Claudette Colbert. In his update, Ross had changed the main character from a successful businesswoman to a Broadway stage actress. The film turned out to be an enormous hit for Universal (perhaps due in part to a secondary plot line which involves the actress' troubled relationship with her teenage daughter), and Ross thereupon starred Turner in two follow-ups, *Portrait in Black* (1960) and *Madame X* (1966).

Turner continued in films throughout the next decade, but age was beginning to limit her choice of roles. She turned to television, starring in the short-lived series "The Survivors" (1970) and later playing the glamorous Jacqueline Perrault on the more successful "Falcon Crest" (1982–83). She also overcame her fear of audiences and toured in stage productions of *Forty Carats* and *Bell, Book, and Candle*, and opposite Louis Jourdan in *The Pleasure of His Company*.

In 1980, Turner suffered a period of ill health caused by alcohol and weight loss, but she emerged intact and ready to share her story. "I have come a long way since 1937," she wrote in the opening pages of her memoir, published in 1982. "I almost can't believe how far. I think it's because I've been so close to God these last two years. I wasn't born like this, the woman I am today. This new woman is no longer confused, she knows who she is." Turner died on June 25, 1995, after a battle with cancer, with her daughter Cheryl Crane at her side. "She never played The Star," said actress **Hope Lange**. "She had no sense of self-importance. There wasn't an ounce of condescension to her."

SOURCES:
"The Bad and the Beautiful," in *People Weekly*. July 17, 1995.
Current Biography 1943. NY: H.W. Wilson, 1943.
Current Biography 1995. NY: H.W. Wilson, 1995.
Katz, Ephraim. *The Film Encyclopedia*. NY: Harper-Collins, 1994.
Obituary. *Boston Globe*. July 1, 1995.
Shipman, David. *The Great Movie Stars: The Golden Years*. Boston, MA: Little, Brown, 1995.
Turner, Lana. *Lana: The Lady, the Legend, the Truth*. NY: E.P. Dutton, 1982.

SUGGESTED READING:
Crane, Cheryl, with Cliff Jahr. *Detour: A Hollywood Story*. Arbor House, 1988.

Barbara Morgan,
Melrose, Massachusetts

Turner, Lesley (1942—)

Australian tennis player. Born in 1942 in Sydney, Australia; married Bill Bowrey (a tennis player).

Lesley Turner was born in 1942 in Sydney into a well-known tennis family. In 1963, she was chosen as a member of Australia's inaugural Federation Cup team. In 1964 and 1967, she was runner-up for the Australian Open title. A stylish, strong, precise player, she eventually won 13 Grand Slam events, including two French singles titles in 1963 and 1965. With *Margaret Court, Turner won the 1964 Wimbledon ladies' doubles; the pair also took the French Open doubles title in 1964 and 1965. Turner captured the 1961 and 1964 mixed doubles titles at Wimbledon as well, partnering with Fred Stolle, and the women's doubles championship at the 1961 U.S. Open, teamed with *Darlene Hard. She married Bill Bowrey, a tennis player who won the Australian Open in 1968.

Kelly Winters,
freelance writer

Turner, Mary (d. 1918)

African-American woman whose lynching for "unwise remarks" galvanized efforts to pass federal anti-lynching legislation. Died on May 19, 1918, near Valdosta, Georgia; married Hayes Turner (died May 18, 1918).

Mary Turner was lynched at Folsom's Bridge over the Little River, in Brooks County, north of Valdosta, Georgia, on May 18, 1918, in order "to teach her a lesson," her offense being that she had made "unwise remarks" by suggesting that those who had lynched her husband Hayes Turner—a man innocent of any crime—should be brought to justice. Mary Turner's death turned the nation's attention to a savage tradition, serving to galvanize efforts to pass federal anti-lynching legislation, and her martyrdom has been commemorated and memorialized in African-American novels, poetry and works of art.

Although African-Americans were legally emancipated from slavery in the mid-1860s, by the end of the 19th century they had once again been reduced to a status of humiliation and bondage. Particularly in the Southern states of the former Confederacy, blacks lived under a regime of Jim Crow segregation that claimed to provide separate but equal opportunities but in reality relegated them to lives of poverty and fear. Soon after the Civil War, the Ku Klux Klan emerged in the states of the former Confederacy, quickly establishing a reign of terror over the recently emancipated blacks. Fear of various forms, including lynchings, kept this largely rural population under control so that they could be exploited as field hands and for other menial tasks, as did rural debt peonage and the convict lease system. Starting in 1882, scholars at the Tuskegee Institute began collecting data on lynching in the United States, including every known case of mob execution. African-Americans were not the only victims of lynch mobs; as late as 1892, of the total of 230 victims, 161 were African-Americans. From that year on, white victims of mob execution sharply and steadily decreased, while blacks in the South continued to be lynched in large numbers.

Between 1882 and 1968, 4,742 people were lynched in the United States. Of these, 3,445 or 73% were African-Americans. During the heyday of lynching, from 1889 to 1918, 3,224 were lynched, of whom 2,522, or 78%, were black. Typically, the victims were hanged or burned to death by vigilante mobs, frequently in front of thousands of spectators. In a carnival atmosphere, many of the onlookers would take pieces of the victim's body as "souvenirs" of their participation. Often, photographs were made of the victims, then later sold as grisly postcards and sent through the U.S. mails. In reporting lynchings, local newspapers customarily used sympathetic language in describing lynch mobs while reserving "callous damnation" for the victims. Often, the news stories provided moral, if not legal, justification for the mobs' acts. At the start of the 20th century, even important Southern newspapers like *The Atlanta Constitution* offered rewards for the capture of African-Americans alleged to have committed crimes, particularly rape, that virtually doomed them to death by lynching.

By the second decade of the 20th century, the South's business elites, including newspaper editors, began to realize that their region's reputation for racial violence brought nothing but scorn from the rest of the nation and the world. In Georgia, which had a horrendous record of lynchings, concern for the state's reputation and the desire to mollify critics motivated newspaper owners and editors to support efforts to suppress lawlessness. The 1915 lynching of Leo Frank (a Jew) gave Georgia a particularly bad name, and the state's economic elite realized the urgency of fostering a new spirit, that of "a New South" based on values of orderliness and social harmony (but not equality) that would encourage economic growth. By 1918, with the United States embarked on a great crusade during World War I to "make the world safe for democracy," several of Georgia's daily newspapers voiced their support for a state anti-lynching law.

Many Southerners justified vigilantism and lynching as a deterrent to the rape of white women by blacks. One Texan explained his position in a 1916 letter to *The Nation*: "It may be bad to lynch, but is it not far worse for a demonized fiend, swelling with bestial lust, to lay his cursed hands on a pure, defenceless woman to satisfy his animal nature?" In the South, demagogic politicians used these fears to enhance their popularity, as when Georgia's Thomas E. ("Tom") Watson bragged that he would lynch a Negro rapist as soon as he would shoot a dog. Mississippi governor James K. Vardaman's "humanitarian" impulses motivated him to criticize a lynch mob for burning rather than hanging an alleged black rapist, but he easily admitted that as a private citizen he would join a lynch mob, adding, "I haven't much respect for a white man who wouldn't." A 1918 editorial in a Little Rock newspaper observed that while disapproving Northerners "may [hold lynching to be] 'Southern brutality' . . . in polite circles, we call it Southern chivalry."

In the rural South, violence and lynching were methods of maintaining social control over an impoverished African-American population needed to work in cotton fields and small-town textile mills. Cheap black labor could only be maintained through a regime of oppression and terror, and it was this factor, rather than the oft-proclaimed white fear of unbridled African-American male sexuality, that played at least as important a role in maintaining the "hallowed tradition" of lynch justice.

Economic factors underlay much of the race hatreds that often exploded into lynchings. In the 1890s, the Populist movement had attempted to forge a "poor man's alliance" between

Southern whites and African-Americans, but not surprisingly the propertied white elements responded vigorously to defend their privileges, unleashing a campaign of white supremacy propaganda, violence, and hate-mongering to crush any potential unity between the exploited and propertyless classes of both races. This assault from all sides of the establishment succeeded in destroying the alliance between poor whites and blacks. As a result of the defeat of progressive forces, the South would remain for several more generations the most impoverished, backward, and violence-prone part of the United States.

Cotton planters, sheriffs, and other members of the rural elite did nothing to stop lynchings, and in fact often played key roles in the violence. Historian W. Fitzhugh Brundage has noted that lynchers were not "isolated deviants [but] representative . . . members of society." Those individuals most likely to be in a position to stop a lynching from taking place—pillars of the community, lawyers, sheriffs, jailers—were often a lynch mob's leaders. On countless occasions, the fact that "respectable" individuals were visible as members of a mob motivated local officials to release prisoners to its custody for "appropriate action."

The great majority of lynchings (more than 75%) were committed not in response to allegations of the rape of white women by black men, but in reaction to black acts of defiance against white abuse, both physical and economic. Although the overwhelming majority of lynching victims were male, in several dozen cases black women were put to death under terrible circumstances. Of the 460 lynching victims in Georgia between 1880 and 1930, 10 were black women (only 19 of the males were white). Outside the South, white women occasionally became victims of mob violence, as is attested to in the 1889 lynching in Wyoming of *Ellen Watson.

In May 1918, a veritable "holocaust of lynchings," writes Walter F. White, was unleashed in rural Brooks and Lowndes counties in southern Georgia. In mid-May, Hampton Smith, the white owner of a large plantation in Brooks County, was killed by one of his black employees, Sidney Johnson. Smith had long had a poor reputation in the area because of his harsh treatment of his African-American workers. Johnson, who had been assigned to Smith to work off a fine for gambling, did not show up one day. When Johnson told Smith he had been sick, the latter beat him despite his protestations. Several days later, while sitting in his home, Smith was killed instantly by two shots through the win-

dow; his wife was also shot but recovered. As soon as news of the murder reached the community, great crowds of men and boys from Brooks and Lowndes counties hurried to the Smith residence, forming posses.

As excitement rose, the posses searched for Sidney Johnson. There was also talk that there had been "a conspiracy" among a number of African-Americans against Hampton Smith, and that this group had allegedly met at the home of Hayes Turner, another black employee whom Smith had mistreated. Both Hayes and his wife Mary Turner had been beaten in the past by Smith. Hayes had previously served a term on the local chain gang for having threatened Smith after Smith had physically attacked Mary. At this point, frustrated by its inability to find Sidney Johnson, the mob was content to capture any "suspicious" black males they came across, "knowing full well that one Negro swinging from a tree will serve as well as another to terrorize the community," noted one contemporary black observer. On May 17, 1918, the mob captured Will Head and Will Thompson. The same evening, both men—although innocent of any crimes—were lynched near Troupeville, about five miles from Valdosta.

On May 18, Hayes Turner was captured and briefly placed in the Quitman jail. While en route to Moultrie, ostensibly a place where he would be safe from vigilante violence, he was taken out of the hands of the local sheriff by the mob. They lynched him near the fork of the Morven and Barney roads, with his hands fastened behind him. On Sunday, May 19, hundreds of sightseers—white men, women and children—came in automobiles, buggies, wagons and on foot to take a look at Hayes Turner's body hanging from a tree. It would remain there another full day.

On receiving the news of her husband's death, Mary Turner, who was then eight months' pregnant, claimed that he was innocent of the murder and that his lynching was unjust. She also said that if she knew the names of the persons who were in the mob that lynched her husband, she would have warrants sworn out against them and have them duly punished through the courts. Word of Mary Turner's response to her husband's death quickly reached the mob, which determined to "teach her a lesson." Captured at noon that same Sunday, the grief-stricken, terrified woman was taken "down a narrow road over which the trees touch at their tops, which, with the thick undergrowth on either side of the road, made a gloomy and appropriate spot for the lynching."

According to a contemporary account published in *The Daily Gazette* of nearby Tifton, Georgia, "the people in their indignant mood took exceptions to her remarks, as well as her attitude, and without waiting for nightfall, took her to the river where she was hanged and her body riddled with bullets." What actually happened that day was far more horrible than the local newspaper reported to its readers. After tying Mary Turner's ankles together, the mob hung her from a tree, head downward. Then the pregnant woman's clothes were doused with gasoline and motor oil, and she was set aflame, with her clothes soon burning off. While she was horribly burned but still alive, Mary Turner's abdomen was sliced open by a member of the mob using a knife ordinarily reserved for splitting hogs. An infant fell from her womb to the ground and emitted two feeble cries, whereupon a member of the assemblage crushed the baby's head beneath his heel. At this moment, hundreds of bullets were fired into Mary Turner's body. The rope was then cut, and her body tumbled into a shallow grave at the foot of the tree. Thoughtfully, the mob provided a "headstone" in the form of an empty whisky bottle, quart size, into whose neck was stuck a half-smoked cigar "which had saved the delicate nostrils of one member of the mob from the stench of burning human flesh."

Sidney Johnson, the man who had killed Hampton Smith, was found by a posse in Valdosta. A fusillade of bullets killed him in the house where he had sought refuge. Cheated of its prey, the mob vented its fury on Johnson's body, removing his genitals and throwing them into the street in front of the house. With a rope around his neck, Johnson's body was dragged by a car in open daylight down Patterson Street, one of Valdosta's main business thoroughfares, then out to a place near Barney and near the scene of the original crime. There, Johnson's mutilated corpse was tied to a tree and burned. By the end of the orgy of lynching, a total of 11 African-Americans, including MaryTurner, had been murdered in Brooks and Lowndes counties. In the weeks that followed, more than 500 blacks fled the Valdosta area, a wholesale migration that took place despite the threats of white planters, officials and property owners that any individuals who attempted to leave would indicate by this act alone that they must be implicated in one way or another in the Smith killing. Hundreds of acres of untilled, neglected farmland and dozens of deserted farmhouses gave mute testimony of the response of African-Americans to the lynchings.

Fuller, Meta Warrick. *See Women of the Harlem Renaissance.*

In the aftermath of the lynching of Mary Turner and many hundreds of other African-Americans in the particularly violent years of 1917–1919, many blacks were "discouraged and crushed by a spirit of humiliation and dread," as was the Toussaint L'Ouverture Branch of the Red Cross, a Savannah women's organization. Soon, however, a new mood of renewed assertiveness could be discerned among African-Americans and their white friends and allies. In 1920, Leonidas C. Dyer, a Missouri Republican representing a heavily black district on the south side of St. Louis, introduced a bill making lynching a federal crime. Strongly supported by the NAACP, the Dyer bill passed the House of Representatives in 1922, 1937, and 1940, but on each occasion Southern senators invoked filibusters that kept it from becoming the law of the land. The measure was thus defeated by a fatal mix of Southern racism and Northern indifference, and it would not be until 1968 that the U.S. Congress passed a law protecting citizens' civil rights that included de facto anti-lynching legislation.

◄❧ **Meta Warrick Fuller**, a prominent sculptor of the Harlem Renaissance, became one of the earliest visual artists to protest the horrors of lynching in her 1919 sculpture *Mary Turner (A Silent Protest)*, currently housed in Boston's Museum of African-American History. The same atrocity was the subject of no fewer than four short stories by ***Angelina Weld Grimké:** "Blackness," "The Creaking," "Goldie," and "The Waitin"; in 1916, Grimké had written a play, *Rachel*, which is believed to be the first full-length drama on the topic of lynching. Mary Turner's death was also the subject of a poem, "Little Mother (Upon the Lynching of Mary Turner)," by **Carrie Williams Clifford**, which appeared in her 1922 book *The Widening Light*. The extreme inhumanity represented by Mary Turner's lynching is recounted through the character of Mame Lamkins in *Cane*, a novel by Jean Toomer published in 1923. As can be experienced through a thought-provoking installation by **Kim Mayhorn**, "A Woman Was Lynched the Other Day" (exhibited at the HEREArt Gallery, in SoHo, Manhattan, 1998, and at The Beach Institute, Savannah, Georgia, 2001), the horror of Mary Turner's death remains a subject of deep concern for a nation that has not been able to banish racial hatred from contemporary life.

SOURCES:

Allen, James, Hilton Als, John Lewis, and Leon F. Litwack. *Without Sanctuary: Lynching Photography in America*. Santa Fe, NM: Twin Palms, 2000.

Brundage, W. Fitzhugh. *Lynching in the New South: Georgia and Virginia, 1880–1930*. Urbana, IL: University of Illinois Press, 1993.

———, ed. *Under Sentence of Death: Lynching in the South*. Chapel Hill, NC: University of North Carolina Press, 1997.

Clifford, Carrie W. *The Widening Light*. Boston, MA: Walter Reid, 1922.

Clarke, James W. "Without Fear or Shame: Lynching, Capital Punishment and the Subculture of Violence in the American South," in *British Journal of Political Science*. Vol. 28, part 2. April 1998, pp. 269–289.

Dittmer, John. *Black Georgia in the Progressive Era, 1900–1920*. Urbana, IL: University of Illinois Press, 1977.

Foley, Barbara. "'In the Land of Cotton': Economics and Violence in Jean Toomer's *Cane*," in *African American Review*. Vol. 32, no. 2. Summer 1998, pp. 181–198.

"Four Negroes Lynched," in *The Daily Gazette* [Tifton, Georgia]. May 20, 1918, p. 3.

Grimké, Angelina Weld. *Selected Works of Angelina Weld Grimké*. Edited by Carolivia Herron. NY: Oxford University Press, 1991.

Hall, Jacquelyn Dowd. *Revolt Against Chivalry: *Jessie Daniel Ames and the Women's Campaign Against Lynching*. Rev. ed. NY: Columbia University Press, 1993.

Hixson, William B., Jr. *Moorfield Storey and the Abolitionist Tradition*. NY: Oxford University Press, 1972.

Hull, Gloria. *Color, Sex, and Poetry: Three Women Writers of the Harlem Renaissance*. Bloomington, IN: Indiana University Press, 1987.

Lacayo, Richard. "Blood at the Root," in *Time*. Vol. 155, no. 14. April 10, 2000, pp. 122–123.

Litwack, Leon F. *Trouble in Mind: Black Southerners in the Age of Jim Crow*. NY: Alfred A. Knopf, 1998.

"The Looking Glass: Lynching," in *The Crisis*. Vol. 11, no. 6. April 1916, pp. 293–295.

National Association for the Advancement of Colored People. *Thirty Years of Lynching in the United States, 1889–1918*. Repr. ed. NY: Arno Press and The New York Times, 1969.

———. Papers of the NAACP, part 7, The Anti-Lynching Campaign, 1912–1953, series A, microfilm reel 1, press release dated May 22, 1918 [Frederick, MD: University Publications of America, 1986?].

Perkins, Kathy A., and Judith L. Stephens, eds. *Strange Fruit: Plays on Lynching by American Women*. Bloomington, IN: Indiana University Press, 1998.

Perloff, Richard M. "The Press and Lynchings of African Americans," in *Journal of Black Studies*. Vol. 30, no. 3. January 2000, pp. 315–330.

Rable, George C. "The South and the Politics of Antilynching Legislation, 1920–1940," in *The Journal of Southern History*. Vol. 51, no. 2. May 1985, pp. 201–220.

Raper, Arthur Franklin. *The Tragedy of Lynching*. NY: Negro Universities Press, 1969.

"The Shame of America," in *The Nation*. Vol. 109, no. 2820. July 19, 1919, p. 89.

"Thieving Negroes Murder and Loot," in *The Daily Gazette* [Tifton, Georgia]. May 18, 1918, p. 2.

Tolnay, Stewart Emory, and E.M. Beck. *A Festival of Violence: An Analysis of Southern Lynchings, 1882–1930*. Urbana, IL: University of Illinois Press, 1995.

Toomer, Jean. *Cane*. Repr. ed. NY: Liveright, 1969.

White, Walter. *Rope and Faggot: A Biography of Judge Lynch*. Repr. ed. NY: Arno Press and The New York Times, 1969.

White, Walter F. "The Work of a Mob," in *The Crisis*. Vol. 16, no. 5. September 1918, pp. 221–222.

Zangrando, Robert L. *The NAACP Crusade Against Lynching, 1909–1950*. Philadelphia, PA: Temple University Press, 1980.

RELATED MEDIA:

Fuller, Meta Vaux Warrick. *Mary Turner (A Silent Protest)*, sculpture, 1919, on exhibition at the Museum of Afro-American History, Boston.

Mayhorn, Kim. "A Woman Was Lynched the Other Day," installation exhibited at the HEREArt Gallery, SoHo, Manhattan, 1998, and at The Beach Institute, Savannah, Georgia, 2001.

John Haag,
Associate Professor of History,
University of Georgia,
Athens, Georgia

Turner, Tina (1938—)

Grammy-winning singer who, after years in a now famously abusive personal and professional relationship, went on to become one of the biggest rock 'n' roll stars of the 1980s and 1990s. Born Anna Mae Bullock on November 26, 1938, in Nut Bush, Tennessee; eldest daughter of Richard Bullock and Zelma Bullock; married musician Ike Turner (separated 1976, divorced 1978); companion of Erwin Bach (an EMI record company executive) for many years; children: (Raymond) Craig Turner; (with Ike Turner) Ronald Renelle Turner.

After meeting Ike Turner, began performing professionally while attending high school in St. Louis, Missouri; became the featured singer of the Ike and Tina Turner Revue; band reached its peak of popularity when it opened for the Rolling Stones during a U.S. tour (1969); appeared in film version of The Who's rock opera Tommy (1974); husband's abusive treatment led her to abandon both Turner and his band (1976); refused all compensation as part of their divorce; rebuilt career performing six nights a week in small nightclubs; after meeting an Australian manager who promoted her, won three Grammies for album Private Dancer (1984), and had soon far eclipsed whatever fame she had achieved previously with Turner's band; inducted into the Rock and Roll Hall of Fame (1991); went on tour which earned nearly $25 million (1997).

The congregation of Spring Hill Baptist Church never expected that Richard and **Zelma Bullock**'s eldest daughter would be such an addition to the choir. But little Anna Mae's voice, they said, was surely something to hear, rising clear and strong against the voices of the much older teens who made up the rest of the group. "She had a good voice, even then, oh, yes,"

Zelma once said of the daughter whom the world would come to know as Tina Turner. "She were somethin', all right."

Back then, however, the chances for a ten-year-old black girl from rural Tennessee didn't seem to extend much beyond the carefully tilled fields of Nut Bush, Tennessee, where Anna Mae Bullock was born on November 26, 1938. Nut Bush was little more than a crossroads, hidden away in the western part of the state and a long way from Knoxville or Memphis or Nashville. Her father Richard worked as a farm overseer for the most prominent white family in the area, spending his days supervising a large workforce of other African-Americans and his nights brawling with his wife Zelma. With their parents' frequent disputes the talk of Nut Bush, Anna Mae and her older sister **Alline Bullock (Selico)** sought comfort in each other's company and in the homes of various relatives. Then, too, there was the comforting domesticity surrounding the white family for whom her father worked. "There was segregation, of course," Turner once said, recalling early years marked by a polite separation from whites. "I don't know how it was for others, but for me, I remember the white people as being friendly then. There was a kind of harmony there." Music was another linchpin holding together a fragile childhood. Fifty years later, Turner still remembered a man named Mr. Bootsy, who would appear at picnics with his trombone and a drummer to play, and the joy of taking the lead in the most rousing numbers performed by the church choir.

With the coming of World War II, Richard took a higher-paying job at the government's new weapons development plant at Oak Ridge, near Knoxville, where he and Zelma moved. Anna Mae and Alline were left behind—Anna Mae with her paternal grandparents and Alline with Zelma's family—with only short visits to Knoxville, where Zelma was astonished to find that customers in some of the shops she frequented would offer Anna Mae money for singing to them. War's end brought her parents back home, but the family's reunion proved short-lived when Zelma deserted Richard unannounced and disappeared. "That's when it really hit me how much I loved my mother," Turner said years later, "and how much I hated her, too. I guess I was learning just how close love and hate can be." Richard's second marriage to a widow with her own two girls did little to alleviate the sense of loss, especially after he once again placed Anna Mae and Alline with relatives and gradually withdrew from their lives.

Anna Mae finally left Nut Bush and environs for good while she was still in high school and Zelma, who had settled in St. Louis after leaving her husband, sent for her daughters. Now, the rhythm and blues Turner had heard on the radio back in Tennessee became more of an influence. While country and western had been the norm back in Tennessee, East St. Louis, across the Mississippi River from its more strait-laced sister city, sported a number of all-night blues bars providing a tempting glimpse of another world to a teenaged country girl. When Anna Mae arrived in St. Louis, her older sister Alline was already working as a waitress at a St. Louis nightclub to supplement Zelma's income as a maid and traveling across the river after work to a decidedly less sophisticated place called the Manhattan Club. Anna Mae soon tagged along to hear the band everyone said was the best R&B group in the South, The Kings of Rhythm, led by a mesmerizing guitarist named Ike Turner. "There was something about him," Tina explained years later. "He got up on stage and picked up his guitar. And that joint started rocking. And I was just sitting there, amazed. I almost went into a trance just watching him."

Ike—born Izear Luster Turner and seven years older than Anna Mae—had grown up in Clarksdale, Mississippi, still considered a shrine of blues music by aficionados. His childhood had been considerably less comfortable than Anna Mae's. As a young boy, he had seen his father, a minister, fatally beaten by white thugs; and he had spent so much time playing pool when he should have been in high school that he never graduated. But his love of music and a talent for banging out rhythm and blues on the piano were his saviors. By the time he met Anna Mae Bullock, Ike had had his own radio show in Clarksdale, toured with a swing band called the Tophatters just after the war, and then formed The Kings of Rhythm when the Tophatters finally broke up. The band had gone through several permutations after recording with only moderate success when Ike stepped onto the stage at the Manhattan Club that night. He had already gone through two piano-playing wives as band members and was living in a vast, three-story brick house in East St. Louis that had earned the title "House of Thrills" from the blues *demimonde*, for the hard partying and womanizing that characterized the place. (Ike's nickname was The Weasel.)

"Each of the guys must have had ten girl-friends apiece," Turner said later, "and Ike had twenty. [But] there was tons of talent on that stage. I wanted to get up there so bad." And she

did, one night when her sister refused a microphone handed to her and Ike happened to be alone on the stage during a break, playing a B.B. King tune that Anna Mae recognized. Before long (and despite her mother's furious reaction and demands that she study to become a nurse), Turner had become the band's permanent girl singer, introduced by Ike as "Little Ann"—a diminutive title belying a voice that one band member said "could peel the wallpaper off the back wall of the room." Another compared her voice to that of the great blues queen *Bessie

Smith, cranked up to the higher energies of rhythm and blues. Ike, for his part, began to think that his discovery might provide the key to a larger audience and more lucrative gigs. Before long, "Little Ann" had become one of the many women inhabiting "The House of Thrills"; and although her relationship with Ike was strictly business at this point, she soon found herself pregnant by the band's saxophone player. Graduating from high school in the spring of 1958, Turner gave birth to a son in August of that year and moved with the child, named Raymond Craig, into a cheap apartment in a dilapidated section of St. Louis. She worked at a hospital as a maternity assistant by day, and sang with the band by night, to make ends meet. "I had to have the two jobs to take care of Craig," she later remembered. "I was a really good mother, I think—got him all the vitamins, the best clothes; made sure the baby sitter was one that would really care for him. And I was becoming my own little young woman, too." But the strain of nearly constant work proved too much. Soon, she had moved back into Ike's house with Craig, Ike promising to increase her salary to $25 a week— a generous offer considering Ike was at the moment being accused of involvement in a $20,000 robbery of a St. Louis bank. (He received a suspended sentence after a trial.)

I stood up for my life.

—Tina Turner, after her divorce from Ike Turner

"Little Ann" appeared on her first record with Ike's band in 1958, singing lead on a novelty song that got slight airplay; but there was little doubt that in live performances, it was Ike's new girl singer that was attracting the crowds. Before long, Ike and Anna Mae had become lovers; and by 1960, she was pregnant. The philandering Ike, however, had resumed a long-standing relationship with another woman, sending Anna Mae back into her own apartment in St. Louis; but that did not stop him from asking her to sing the lead on a demo for a new single, "A Fool in Love," which he had originally planned to record with a male singer who backed out at the last minute. The demo found its way to New York City and Henry "Juggy" Murray, one of the few African-Americans of the time to own a record label, which Murray had named Sue, after his mother. Murray soon arrived in St. Louis to sign Ike with a $25,000 advance. "That's where I met this Anna Mae Bullock," Juggy later recalled. "She was around—actually, she was wherever Ike wanted her to be. Along with his forty other women." It was Juggy's opinion that Little Ann's vocal on "A Fool in Love" was what made the

song; and it was his further opinion that Ike would never break out of St. Louis without making Little Ann the star of his band. Ike must have been listening, for when "A Fool in Love" was released nationally during the summer of 1960, it was credited not to Ike Turner and The Kings of Rhythm but to "Ike and Tina Turner." (Ike thought the name "Tina" was sexier than Ann, and the formality of marriage did not occur to him before he bestowed his last name on his new star.) The gritty, unsophisticated track, with Tina's wailing vocals backed up by three other girl singers, quickly moved off the R&B charts and onto white pop charts, then still dominated by much more prim acts like *Connie Francis and *Brenda Lee.

The newly christened Tina Turner had serious doubts about the song and her future with Ike. "I really didn't want to sing it—I didn't care for all that 'hey, hey, hey' stuff," Tina said; and Ike's miserly offer to pay her rent (keeping everything else the band made for himself) had little appeal for her. "I knew it could never work out between us," she later said. "So when he got the record deal, I went to talk with him. I told him I didn't want to get involved any further with him. And that was the first time he beat me up." Ike made sure there were no public appearances until her swollen face had returned to normal; and Tina, the mother of one child, about to give birth to a second, and terrified of Ike's angry fists, saw few alternatives to staying with him. "Singing with Ike was how I made my living," she said. "What was I going to do? I had to keep going forward."

Now six months' pregnant, Tina traveled with the band to Cincinnati, the first stop on a tour of the Eastern states, wearing a sack dress with plenty of chiffon to disguise her condition. The band opened in Cincinnati as the Ike and Tina Turner Revue; and within weeks was playing the Apollo in New York (where Tina electrified the crowd by jumping off the stage during one number) and appearing on Dick Clark's nationally broadcast "American Bandstand." Traveling west, the Revue played Las Vegas and had arrived in Los Angeles in October 1960 when Tina went into labor and gave birth to a second son whom she named Ronald Renelle. It didn't take long for Ike's common-law wife to notice the resemblance between the child and Ike, and even less time for her to pack up and leave for good. Ike gathered up his two children from the now defunct marriage, added Tina's first son and their own newborn, and set up house in Los Angeles. It was, Tina later said, a "shameful period" for her. "The whole thing was a public scandal, really embarrassing."

Although the Revue's releases during the next year brought the band an even wider, and increasingly white, audience, its backstage conflicts only worsened. Ike fired and hired band members at dizzying speed and kept Tina and the three backup girl singers (now called the Ikettes) in constant confusion, once docking the girls 25% of their pay after one performance because they hadn't looked happy enough on stage. Nor did the relationship between Tina and Ike improve. "In that first year of touring, fear moved into our relationship, and never left it," Tina said. While her extravagant wigs, flouncing costumes and earthy dance moves on stage packed houses from coast to coast, no one in the audience knew that Ike's physical abuse sometimes left her mouth so swollen that it was difficult for her to sing. She soon learned that the only way to avoid being beaten was to remain outwardly quiescent, even when Ike spirited her off to Mexico for a quick wedding in Tijuana as his affairs, many with whoever was the latest Ikette, multiplied. Then, too, there was the band's grueling tour schedule, with up to eight months of the year spent on the road, frustrated by the lack of a solid hit to follow up "A Fool in Love."

In 1965, the band's manager began weeks of delicate negotiations between Ike and teen-pop producer Phil Spector, who had made millions over the past five years with his famous "wall of sound" arrangements backing acts like **Darlene Love**, the **Ronettes** and the Righteous Brothers. Spector, who had seen the Turner Revue in Los Angeles, was looking for a girl singer who could handle a new song he'd co-written, "River Deep, Mountain High." Ike collected a reported $25,000 from Spector for the use of Tina's voice, along with Spector's agreement to promote the song as by "Ike and Tina Turner," and a reciprocal promise from Ike that he would stay away from all recording sessions for the number. "I loved that song," Turner later said of what became her most famous recording to date. "It wasn't just R&B, it had melody, it had structure." And it was the melody Spector wanted her to emphasize, not the vocal gymnastics Ike demanded. "He just wanted me to sing the song. It was my voice he liked, not the screaming." The 12-hour recording session at which Tina laid down the final vocals for the number, alone in the studio with just Spector, an engineer and management representatives, is still remembered with a sense of awe. "They go over it and over it and over it," the Turner Revue's manager Bob Krasnow remembered nearly 30 years later, "and Tina can't quite get it. Finally, she says, 'OK, Phil, one more time.' And she . . . gave a performance that . . . I mean, your hair was standing on end. It was like the whole room exploded. I'll never forget that as long as I live, man."

But because of Spector's deteriorating relationship with recording and broadcast executives, and the reported $20,000 he had spent on musicians and studio time to produce the record, "Mountain Deep" was not well received and reached only to No. 86 on the pop charts. It marked the effective end to Spector's reign as the music industry's *wunderkind*. Tina herself was of the opinion that the record "was too black for the pop stations, and too pop for the black stations"; but it provided an inkling of the kind of work she could do away from Ike's influence and would prove important to her later solo career. And, while the record sank into oblivion in America, it was wildly popular in Britain and soon brought an invitation from the Rolling Stones for the Revue to accompany them on a British tour in 1966, beginning at London's Royal Albert Hall. "There's no point in having some jerk band on before you," Mick Jagger pointed out. "You have to have somebody that'll make you top what they do. And Ike and Tina Turner certainly did that job admirably." The tour—raucous, exhausting and exhilarating all at once—was a huge success and, for Tina, another indication that she was good enough as a performer to survive without Ike.

In later years, Tina would characterize the times following the first Stones tour as "rock bottom." The Revue went without a hit during all of 1967, Ike using cocaine, a string of temporary "Ikettes," and what Tina came to call "a good whammin'" to deal with his frustration. By 1968, her trips to the emergency room of a hospital near the couple's south Los Angeles home had become so frequent that she was on a first-name basis with most of the staff. The four sons, too, were terrified of their father's unpredictable mood swings. "If Ike was home," one member of the Ike Turner organization later wrote, "the kids had to literally tiptoe through the house or he would explode." One night as she was packing to leave for a gig, Turner decided to take 50 Valium and, as she later put it, "die on stage." Found nearly unconscious in her dressing room just before the show and rushed to a hospital, she recovered, only to be forced back to work just days later by an angry Ike who accused her of trying to sabotage his career. "That's when I started to hate Ike Turner," she said.

Life with Ike remained a torment even when the Revue's 1969 version of the Otis Redding song "I've Been Loving You Too Long" became their first record to make it onto the pop charts in three years. But close observers noticed that the album from which the single was taken carried a producing credit for Tina and a song she herself had written, "I Am a Motherless Child," a sharp departure from the straight rhythm and blues numbers preferred by Ike. Its rock-tinged flavor was the first sign of Turner's increasing fascination with the fusion of white rock 'n' roll and black R&B she had heard firsthand during the Rolling Stones tour in England. The Stones' "Honky Tonk Woman" and the Beatles' "Come Together," she said, were inspirations for her. "Those bands were *interpreting* black music to begin with," she later said. "They touched on R&B, in a way, but it wasn't obvious. It wasn't the same old thing." As if to confirm her opinion, an invitation came from the Stones for the Revue to join their 1969 "Gimme Shelter" tour, along with blues legend B.B. King. The tour's date in Oakland is still considered by some the best rock concert in history, and not just because of the Stones. "In the context of today's show business, Tina Turner must be the most sensational female performer on stage," exclaimed *Rolling Stone*. "She comes on like a hurricane. Jagger ought to get a medal for courage in following . . . Tina Turner." Audiences were especially mesmerized by Turner's blatantly erotic rendition of "I've Been Loving You Too Long"—captured on film for the Stones documentary of the tour—during which *Rolling Stone* reported that she used the microphone "as if it were a high-tension erogenous zone" and *The New York Times* labeled her ministrations to that instrument as outright pornographic. "It's like acting," Tina protested. "I'm sure a lot of actors don't feel very comfortable with some of their parts, and I am an actress." The tour was the biggest thing to happen to the Revue in more than a decade, exposing the group to the Stones' millions of white fans and leading to a lucrative contract with United Artists. The result was several pop chart hits like "Got to Take You Higher" and "Bold Soul Sister." It would prove to be the band's peak, but the cost to Turner was a lengthy hospital stay after she was diagnosed with tuberculosis and forced into a long hospital convalescence.

Back on the road in 1970, Tina convinced Ike to let her record a version of John Fogerty's "Proud Mary," a big hit for Fogerty's band Creedence Clearwater Revival. The Revue's version proved to be the band's biggest hit when it reached No. 4 on the pop charts. "We made that song our own," Tina said, rather generously as it turned out, since only she was singled out for her first Grammy for Best R&B Vocal. By now,

the Revue was making so much money that Ike built and opened his own luxurious, state-of-the-art recording studio in Los Angeles, Bolic Sound, complete with a labyrinth of private "harem rooms," as Ike called them, a screening room and a full kitchen and dining room. But the band's increased exposure brought a cover story in *Rolling Stone*, in October 1971, detailing Ike's cocaine addiction and his abusive treatment of Tina and other women. Turner publicly denied involvement with any drug stronger than caffeine, and privately expressed horror at what was happening to Ike and the band. "They'd be walking around snorting and yapping, with that white stuff all over their faces, rocking back and forth," she said later. "They looked so silly, and they thought they were so cool." She would only come to the studio when Ike asked her to record, often bringing one of her sons as a reason for the band to behave itself and an excuse for leaving as soon as she had done what was required.

Ike's behavior grew worse as the band's fortunes declined during 1972, with none of its recordings breaking into the top 100 on the charts. Tina didn't dare point out that the band's only recent hits had been numbers outside its usual R&B repertoire, numbers like "Proud Mary" that she had convinced Ike to record. Now 34, sharing her children's terror of Ike Turner and watching the only life she had known disintegrate, Tina looked for solace and reassurance. It was at this point that she began to find comfort in a form of Buddhism taught her by a white friend whom she admired for having the courage to marry a black musician at a time when interracial marriages were rare. "Now I could feel the power deep inside me, stirring up after all these years," Turner said of her daily practice of chanting and meditation. She did not consider it a coincidence, therefore, when early in 1974 she received an offer from record and film producer Robert Stigwood to appear in a film of The Who's rock opera *Tommy*, to be directed by Ken Russell. She was offered the role of the Acid Queen, joining a cast including The Who, Elton John, **Ann-Margret**, and Eric Clapton. Ike grudgingly agreed to let Tina travel alone to London for the filming, and to stay on afterward to join Ann-Margret in a television special, later shown in the United States, in which she performed "Proud Mary" and "Honky Tonk Woman" for the first time in public without Ike. By now, Ike rarely ventured outside the studio, paralyzed by cocaine used in such quantities that one visitor claimed it had gotten inside the equipment and ruined the sound. More and more musicians refused to work with Ike. Nothing the Revue recorded from 1974 on proved successful, with 1975's "Baby Get It On" barely making it to No. 88.

But even when Turner's patience finally ran out, she at first could only find the courage to leave Ike for short periods—a few days here, two weeks there—before allowing herself to be dragged back to face his verbal and physical abuse. Ike knew the end was near, however, even if he still failed to understand why. "It just didn't make sense to him when all of a sudden his own wife says 'You can't treat me like that,'" a friend reported. "He was saying . . . that this was the way guys were. He just didn't get it." The end finally came in 1976, when Turner walked out during a tour stop in Dallas, after Ike had beaten her so severely she could barely talk, much less sing. Sneaking out of their room after Ike finally fell into a stuporous sleep, the front of her white dress covered in blood, she sought refuge in a nearby hotel with 38 cents and a credit card in her pocket, then called the band's attorney to come and rescue her.

Ike refused to provide money unless she returned, so for months afterward Tina Turner—who just a year before had been one of rock 'n' roll's most famous performers, who had toured twice with the Rolling Stones and who had appeared in a major feature film—was forced to live with generous friends and earn a living cleaning their houses. "It was the only way I could repay these people," she later said. "I didn't miss what you call the trappings of stardom at all. Because I finally had my freedom." Divorce proceedings stretched out over the next year and became so mired in wrangling over money that Turner eventually told her attorney to get a divorce agreement in place even if she received nothing from Ike in compensation. "She just gave it all away, over my objections," her lawyer said. "Tina walked out with what was on her back, essentially. But she said, 'My life's more important.'"

The divorce became final in March 1978 as Turner set about rebuilding a career from scratch. Again, friends she had made in the business during her years with Ike came to her rescue, helping her assemble a band and put together an act that she took on the road to small nightclubs and cabarets on the West Coast and Canada. Despite her name, the act failed to attract audiences of any size. An album released in 1978 was unsuccessful, and a contract she had signed with a financially troubled United Artists was not renewed. By 1979, Turner owed a reported $20,000 to her band's backers, along with $100,000 in back taxes to the IRS from her earn-

ings during the Revue years. She desperately needed a break; and it finally came from, of all people, **Olivia Newton-John**, the Australian pop star of the late 1970s and early 1980s, fresh from her starring film role opposite John Travolta in the movie version of *Grease*. Confessing to a lifelong admiration for Tina Turner's music, Newton-John invited her to appear on a television special in November 1978 and introduced Turner to a fellow Australian named Roger Davies.

Davies had seen Turner perform with the Revue in Australia before he had relocated to Los Angeles, and now traveled up to San Francisco to see her singing at the sedate, chandelier-laden ballroom of the venerable Fairmont Hotel. "She had so much energy, she blew me away," Davies later said, although he thought her act was still caught in the Revue mold and needed a good deal of polishing. "I mean, she did 'Disco Inferno' with smoke bombs, and the two male dancers ripped part of her dress away. It was bizarre." It was Davies' feeling that Turner's act should go further in the direction she had tried to push the Revue—that is, more toward rock and away from disco-themed rhythm and blues, the extravagant wigs, the silver lamé dresses. By the beginning of 1981, Davies had convinced Turner to fire her old band and the dress-rending dancers, and replace them with a simple, four-man group consisting of piano, guitar, drums and bass. Davies then proceeded to promote Turner by staging a comeback show at New York's Ritz, then the city's most popular night spot, and packed the audience with her friends and admirers from the old days. When the Rolling Stones played Los Angeles soon afterward, Davies made sure to bring Turner backstage for a reunion, the result of which was Tina's third tour with the Stones, during which she famously performed a duet of "Honky Tonk Woman" with Mick Jagger. After she made a second appearance at the Ritz, Capitol offered Turner a contract, under which she recorded in London her version of an earlier Al Green hit, "Let's Stay Together." With a lush string arrangement backing up Turner's sophisticated delivery, the record became an instant dance-club hit and sent Tina back into the studio to record her first album in nearly five years. It would include one of the biggest single releases of the mid-1980s, a song she initially didn't want to record because, she said, it was "too wimpy."

"I just thought it was some old pop song," she later said of "What's Love Got to Do With It," "and I didn't like it. I had just never thought of singing pop." Discovering that the song had been written especially for her by British composer Terry Britten, Turner relented after Britten responded to her complaint that the song wasn't "rough enough" by picking up an electric guitar and instantly producing an earthier sound for the tune. Davies brought Turner another number for the album he wanted to assemble for her, a song Dire Straits had left off their *Love Over Gold* album after deciding it was more suitable for a female vocalist. It was called "Private Dancer" and would lend its name to the album that rocketed up the charts on its release in 1984, led on the singles charts by "What's Love Got to Do With It." Turner's voice, said the *Los Angeles Times*, could "melt vinyl," while *Rolling Stone* awarded the album four stars. When "What's Love" hit No. 1, the magazine gave Turner an extensive cover story. Appearances on talk shows, a national "Private Dancer" tour, and even another movie role in George Miller's film *Mad Max—Beyond Thunderdome* (for which Turner also performed the film's title song, "We Don't Need Another Hero"), soon followed. At the 1984 Grammy Awards, fresh from a triumphant European tour, Tina was awarded Best Female Pop Vocal for "What's Love," while her work on the album *Better Be Good to Me* earned Best Female Rock Vocal and "What's Love" was named Best Record of the Year. Her rehabilitation was complete, detailed in the 1993 feature film *What's Love Got to Do With It?*, starring **Angela Bassett**, based on her autobiography *I, Tina*.

The inspiration and faith Turner found in her Buddhist practice during her most difficult years still informs her life. In 1991, she generously agreed to appear in public with Ike Turner for the first time in 20 years, when the two were inducted into the Rock 'n' Roll Hall of Fame; and despite those years with the Revue and her refusal to open for the new band Ike put together after 18 months in jail on drug-related charges, Turner still credits Ike with giving her a start in the music business. The price may have been high, but it brought with it a valuable lesson. "Sometimes, you've got to let everything go, purge yourself," Turner has said, "because you'll find when you're free, your true creativity, your true self comes out."

SOURCES:

Armani, Eddy. *The Real T*. London: Blake, 1998.

Bigelow, Barbara, ed. *Contemporary Black Biography*. Detroit, MI: Gale Research, 1994.

Turner, Tina, with Kurt Loder. *I, Tina: My Life Story*. NY: William Morrow, 1986.

Welch, Chris. *Take You Higher: The Tina Turner Experience*. London: W.H. Allen, 1986.

RELATED MEDIA:

What's Love Got to Do With It (118-min. film), based on the book *I, Tina*, starring Angela Bassett as Tina Turner and Laurence Fishburne as Ike, screenplay by **Kate Lanier**, directed by Brian Gibson, produced by Touchstone, 1993.

Norman Powers,
writer-producer, Chelsea Lane Productions,
New York, New York

Turpin, Luci Baines (b. 1947).

See Johnson, Luci Baines.

Turunku Bakwa (fl. 1530s)

Queen of Zaria. Name variations: Flourished in the 1530s as the queen of Zazzau (later Zaria) in central Nigeria; children: Amina (c. 1533–c. 1598) and Zaria (both would rule Zaria).

Turunku Bakwa was queen (*sarauniya*) of Zazzau, the large empire of the Hasau people that had come into existence by 1050. She was not originally Hasau, but was a Fulani who had moved into Macina, the eastern region of Niger. Some sources speculate that she came from the south, however, because she had guns that she had acquired from traders on the coast. Turunku Bakwa was a member of a warlike matriarchal clan. In 1536, she founded the city of Zaria in northcentral Nigeria, and named it after her younger daughter. Her two daughters, *Amina and Zaria, would rule after her death.

Kelly Winters,
freelance writer

Tusap, Srbuhi (1841–1901)

Armenian poet, novelist, and feminist. Born in 1841 in Constantinople; died in 1901; married Paul Tusap (a music teacher), in 1871; children: Dorine (d. 1890).

Selected writings: Mayda (1883); Siranoush (1885); Arak'sya kam Varjouhin (A. or the Teacher, 1887).

Srbuhi Tusap was born in 1841 in Constantinople, when the Ottoman Empire was in the midst of the Tanzimat Reform. Armenian writers and thinkers had already initiated a literary and social revival. Tusap was raised with a fluency in French, Italian, and Greek, and during her youth she mastered the works of Victor Hugo and *George Sand. At age 22, she met the Armenian poet Mkrtitch Peshikt'ashlian, who became her mentor. In 1871, she married her music teacher, Paul Tusap.

During the 1880s, Srbuhi Tusap gained recognition as a writer, social activist, and public speaker. She was the first Armenian feminist and woman writer, the leader of a literary salon, and a member of the group of writers known as the

"Renascence Generation." Her three novels, dozens of poems, and articles are significant as 19th-century examples of literature that championed feminist principles. She encouraged writers to use the Armenian language and wrote numerous articles about women's rights.

Tusap's first book, 1883's *Mayda*, influenced by her earlier reading of Rousseau, Goethe, and Sand, was the first novel in Armenian written by a woman, as well as the first to espouse women's rights. Written in the form of correspondence between two women, Siri and Mayda, it relates the stories of their lives. Although considered melodramatic and contrived, it advanced the idea that women were essentially slaves and needed to liberate themselves through education, work, and meaningful life choices. The book was criticized from all sides as an attack on Armenian family and social life. In Tusap's second novel, *Siranoush* (1885), the title character is coerced into an arranged marriage instead of marrying the man she loves and ends up being abused by her jealous, unfaithful husband. *Arak'sya kam Varjouhin* (A. or the Teacher, 1887), her third novel, features a schoolteacher whose lover is stolen by a more wealthy woman.

Tusap's daughter Dorine became ill with tuberculosis in 1889 and died the following year. Grief-stricken over this loss, Tusap never wrote again. She died in 1901.

SOURCES:
Pynsent, Robert B., ed. *Reader's Encyclopedia of Eastern European Literature*. NY: HarperCollins, 1993.

Kelly Winters,
freelance writer

Tuscany, countess of.

See Matilda of Tuscany (1046–1115).

Tuscany, grand duchess of.

See Joanna of Austria (1546–1578).
See Cappello, Bianca (1548–1587).
See Martelli, Camilla (fl. 1570s).
See Christine of Lorraine (c. 1571–1637).
See Maria Magdalena of Austria (1589–1631).
See Medici, Vittoria de (d. 1694).
See Marguerite Louise of Orleans (c. 1645–1721).
See Medici, Anna Maria de (d. 1741).
See Bonaparte, Elisa (1777–1820).

Tuscany, Matilda of (1046–1115).

See Matilda of Tuscany.

Tuscany, princess of.

See Toselli, Louisa (1870–1947).

Tussaud, Marie (1761–1850)

Wax modeler and entrepreneur who created one of London's most popular attractions, Madame Tussaud's. Name variations: known as Marie Grosholtz (1767–95), Marie Tussaud (1795–1850). Born Anna-Maria Grosholtz (also seen as Gresholtz) in Strasbourg, Germany, on December 7, 1761; died at age 90 in London, England, on April 15, 1850; daughter of Anna Maria (Walder) Grosholtz, of Strasbourg, and Johannes Grosholtz (a German officer from Frankfurt); married François Tussaud, on October 20, 1795; children: daughter (who died in infancy); two sons, Joseph Tussaud; François, known as Francis Tussaud (1800–1873).

Adopted by Dr. Philippe Guillaume Mathe Curtius of Berne; moved to Paris and tutored by Curtius (1767); hired to work with Madame Élisabeth of France (1781); modeled heads of guillotine victims (1792–93); inherited Curtius' fortune (1794); moved to England (1802); shipwrecked (1822); founded permanent exhibition in London (1835).

Madame Tussaud's, on the busy Marylebone Road, is a landmark for London visitors. Its founder was a talented artist in the unusual medium of dyed wax, and a far-sighted entrepreneur. After maneuvering through the hazards of the French Revolution, being close to all its central figures but avoiding their fate on the guillotine, Marie Tussaud started a new life in Britain at the age of 40 and made an even greater triumph there than she had in her native land.

Her father was a German officer in the service of General Count Dagobert de Wurmser, fighting for *Maria Theresa of Austria. Badly wounded in battle, Johannes Grosholtz returned to his young wife in Strasbourg, but died before their daughter was born. Tussaud's widowed mother **Anna Maria Grosholtz** moved to Berne in Switzerland almost at once and became cook and housekeeper to Philippe Curtius, a doctor who made anatomical models in wax. Some biographers speculate that Curtius and Anna Maria had been having an affair before her husband's death, and even that Curtius was Marie Tussaud's biological father.

Curtius graduated from making wax models of body parts (to help in medical education) to portraiture in wax, and opened a small museum of wax models in his Berne home. He was so successful with these models that he caught the eye of a traveling French noble, the Prince de Conti, who urged him to move to Paris. Conti was one of Rousseau's admirers and a leading patron of the intellectual opposition to the ancien regime. Curtius' three-dimensional likenesses—cleverly dressed, dyed, and painted—were even better than paintings in conveying a lifelike image, and he had no rival in this pre-photographic age. He became a favorite at court as well as among the intellectual opposition, and was soon summoned to model King Louis XV and Queen *Marie Leczinska. Trading on this and other successes with the court, Curtius opened a permanent exhibition, the Cabinet de Cire, which attracted visiting dignitaries from all over Europe. Among its sensations were a life-size recreation of the royal family eating dinner, and the "Chambre Des Grands Voleurs" (Chamber of Great Robbers), showing the recently condemned and executed criminals of Paris.

Tussaud and her mother, who had at first stayed behind in Berne, joined Curtius in 1767. Noticing Marie's interest, Curtius took her on as an apprentice. Tussaud called him her uncle and from him learned how to make plaster casts of a human face, alive or dead, and how to make the molds and mix the tinted wax to give the lifelike effect of human flesh. Of her education we know little because she did not write a diary or any letters that have survived, but we do know that by the time she was in her mid-teens she too had become an accomplished wax modeler. As a teenager, she made superb portraits of Benjamin Franklin (the young America's ambassador to France), Rousseau, and the octogenarian Voltaire. The bust of Franklin survives and is still on display in London.

In 1781, King Louis XVI's sister *Madame Elisabeth visited Curtius' Cabinet de Cire and met Marie. The princess was so impressed by the models she saw that she decided to try her hand at modeling too and engaged Marie, then aged 20, as her teacher. For the next eight years, Tussaud lived and worked with the princess, who was unmarried, at Versailles and Montreuil. In the spring of 1789, by which time Marie was a mature and accomplished wax-artist of 28, Curtius warned her to leave court and return to Paris. Influential and well connected with the Enlightenment intellectuals, he welcomed the onset of the Revolution and lent his models of unpopular ministers and princes to the Paris mob, which paraded them through the streets. He was present at the fall of the Bastille as a National Guard officer and made death-mask models of the Revolution's first victims, de Flesselles and Launay.

In the revolutionary years which followed, Curtius and Marie Tussaud were in demand to make models of the revolutionary heroes, representations of the republican virtues, and an imaginative Goddess of Liberty. Curtius was, besides, a friend and confidant of several leaders, Robespierre, Danton, Marat, and Sieyes, all of whom Marie Tussaud met at his house. The wax-workers made casts of former friends who were killed by the mob or the guillotine, including King Louis XVI himself, whom the Committee of Public Safety beheaded in January 1793, and his wife *Marie Antoinette. Later that year, Tussaud modeled the head of Jean-Paul Marat whom *Charlotte Corday had killed earlier on the same day. Her model was later used by the artist Jacques-Louis David in his famous painting of the incident. Two weeks later, Tussaud had the further job of modeling the severed head of Charlotte Corday after this young assassin in turn went to her death at the guillotine.

While the opportunistic Curtius, who profited steadily from the revolution and always stayed on good terms with the dominant party, was away on government business, Tussaud and her mother were denounced and arrested on a charge of Royalist sympathies. Within a week, they were suddenly released, however, thanks to the intervention of influential friends. After a short vacation to recover her nerve, Tussaud returned to work. The stay in prison introduced her to another condemned woman, soon to be reprieved, whom she would meet again, a few years later, as Napoleon's wife *Josephine. In 1794, Marie Tussaud was still making money from masks and models of guillotine victims, as Danton and Robespierre in their turn mounted the scaffold. In her memoirs, dictated 50 years after the event, Madame Tussaud recalled the gruesome death of Robespierre in July 1794:

> When he found that he had no means of escaping execution he endeavored with a pistol to blow out his brains, but only shattered his under jaw, which was obliged to be tied up when he was taken to the scaffold. The executioner when about to do his office, tore the dressing roughly away and Robespierre uttered a piercing shriek, as his lower jaw separated from the upper, whilst his blood flowed copiously. His head presented a dreadful spectacle; and immediately after death it was taken to the Madeleine.

There, Madame Tussaud took a cast of it. Still extant, the cast clearly shows the mutilated jaw.

Tussaud seems to have learned how to keep calm in the midst of danger, but we have no direct evidence of her emotional or political response to the revolution. The much later memoirs show her grieving for her many royal and

Marie
Tussaud

aristocratic friends (when it was safe to do so), but there is no sign of her having made any gesture on their behalf during the Terror.

Curtius died in September 1794, leaving everything to his 33-year-old pupil and "niece."

She supervised his funeral, took over his three houses, with their vast inventory of property, and realized that she was a rich woman. She kept the show open to paying customers and followed Curtius' policy of adjusting the exhibits to suit changes in the political wind, emphasizing different factions, and placing models of villains in her chamber of horrors, according to current trends. A year later, in the autumn of 1795, she married a civil engineer, François Tussaud, who was eight years her junior, and this union led to the birth of a daughter who died in infancy and two sons, Joseph and François, later known as Francis, who survived. In her marriage, as with many segments of her life, we have an abundance of her business records but no personal papers and know nothing of her first meetings with François or her decision to marry him. In any event, he lacked the business and artistic skills of her uncle, and she found she could not rely on him. To make matters worse, Madame Tussaud found, in the following years, that Parisians were beginning to lose interest in her waxworks, even those which showed France's rising star, Napoleon Bonaparte, and his generals.

$\mathcal{S}$he was among the first great career women, for although she never talked of feminist emancipation she created her own business and built up her own prestige without help from any man.

—Anita Leslie and Pauline Chapman

She had already sent exhibitions abroad, to Baden in Germany, to England, and to India, where they had enjoyed the success of spectacular novelties. In 1802, she resolved to move, and crossed the English Channel with a large part of the exhibition, leaving her husband behind. When her exhibition opened in a London theater, it became an instant success. Her skill with masks and wax carving, and her good connections, first at court and then with the revolutionaries, enabled English viewers to see the actual faces of Louis XVI, Marie Antoinette, Robespierre, Marat, and all the other larger-than-life figures who had transformed recent history. Despite stormy relations with her partner Paul de Philipstal, a French showman who had preceded her across the Channel with magic lanterns, a show of "ghosts," and optical illusions, she began to make money. The profits soared when she added models molded from the decapitated heads of English criminals, which she grouped under lurid blue light to emphasize their sinister nature. The most notable was an effigy of Edward Marcus Despard, an army officer who had conspired to kill the king and seize the Bank of England and the Tower of London before being arrested and executed. The success of such exhibits induced her to create a special section in all her shows, which developed into a permanent feature; it was referred to in publicity materials as "the separate room" and

one which was "not suitable for ladies." But as historian **Pauline Chapman** notes: "She was not interested in taking the likenesses of executed criminals just in order to introduce horror for horror's sake. Madame Tussaud was essentially a journalist in wax and she liked to point a historical or moral lesson too."

In 1803, she took the show to Edinburgh. Success there and in Glasgow partly compensated for the financial failures of her inept husband back in Paris. She also began to raise money from portraits. Just as her uncle Curtius had built up a noble group of clients in France, so Madame Tussaud found lords, members of Parliament, and minor royalty eager to sit for her in England, and she became a fashionable portraitist in wax. After a successful show in Dublin the following year, she managed to buy her independence from her troublesome partner Philipstal. She also wrote her husband that she had no intention of returning to Paris, adding "we can each go our own way." Though her mother and her younger son were still with him in Paris, from 1804 onwards she never again saw François Tussaud. This younger son, Francis, came to join her in 1822, and from then on both sons helped their mother with the traveling exhibition.

The year 1822 was also the year of King George IV's state visit to Ireland. Madame Tussaud decided that she, too, would visit Ireland and display her models of his coronation, which had made her a handsome profit in London. But her ship, the *Earl Moira*, was caught in a storm and wrecked soon after setting out from Liverpool. She managed to get into an open boat and with a handful of fellow survivors reached a deserted stretch of shore. Soaked and freezing, the survivors walked until they came to a house. The sympathetic owner, **Mrs. Ffarington**, took them all in, fed and dressed them in warm clothes, and set them back on their feet. By good luck, many of the wax models had not been on board ship—they were safe in storage back at Liverpool. According to a story written by one of her descendants, Mrs. Ffarington was so taken with Madame Tussaud that she gave her a collection of old dresses and lace with which to clothe the replacement models for those that had been lost. Another dangerous moment for the collection was the Bristol riots of 1831, which broke out while her show was on display there. The house in which Madame Tussaud was staying was set on fire, along with most others in the same street, and the Assembly Rooms themselves were about to go up in flames when she and her assistants arrived to rescue many of the models.

Tussaud's life in Britain settled into a steady routine of touring and exhibiting. She showed the same political dexterity that had served her well in France and was able to do business throughout the Napoleonic Wars despite being a French citizen. This was the time to emphasize her royalist connections and to minimize her former closeness to the revolutionaries and Napoleon. Packing the delicate models every few weeks required care and patience, but through frequent repetition she and her staff reduced it to a fine art. The heads and hands were modeled wax, the bodies made of wood and stuffed leather. With proper crating, everything could survive the buffeting journeys back and forth by road and sea. As time passed, her life models of the French monarchy and revolutionaries became increasingly valuable. She had little time to model new celebrities but managed portraits of local dignitaries in the counties she visited, and still made effigies of condemned criminals in nationally famous cases. The most successful were traitors and the culprits in gruesome murders. After the French wars, her models of Burke and Hare, two body-snatchers, became the chief draw. Burke and Hare had scandalized England in 1828 when evidence showed that they had lured the old and the poor to a boarding house, killed them, then sold their bodies in sacks for dissection in anatomy classes.

In 1834, Madame Tussaud returned from lengthy tours of the English provinces to mount her exhibition in London. Throughout her 32 years of traveling in Britain, the show had always used makeshift settings. But after a year of success in London, she decided to try putting it on a permanent basis, as Curtius had done in Paris. She rented large rooms in north London at the corner of Baker Street (later famous as Sherlock Holmes' address) in a building known as "the Bazaar." The next year, the display moved to a nearby building and from then on it settled down as a permanent part of the London entertainment landscape. *Punch* magazine nicknamed the more gruesome part of her work the "Chamber of Horrors" and said it contained "bloodshed and homicide in every variety." Charles Dickens used Madame Tussaud's as his model for "Mrs. Jarley's Waxworks" in *The Old Curiosity Shop* (1840), and it has since been featured in dozens of fictional representations of London. The Duke of Wellington, hero of Waterloo, whose effigy Tussaud sometimes placed alongside that of Napoleon, whom he had defeated, said that it was "the most entertaining place in London." Marie Tussaud was now 76

and her sons had reached responsible middle age so they were able to take over the daily running of the business. "She drummed her theories into their heads," says Chapman:

> The show must be kept both entertaining and instructive; past and present should be combined, so should the great and the humble, and, above all, they must always produce an atmosphere of glamour. When presenting human history in visual form, it was essential that the figures be accurate in every detail. These admonitions were accepted by her sons and they maintained the Exhibition's standards as she decreed.

Within a few months of the accession of Queen *Victoria in 1837, visitors could recapture the splendors of the Coronation and be certain that the models were absolutely true to life. Tussaud spent her declining years dictating her memoirs to a friend, Francis Herve, carefully excluding all personal matters. But we get a glimpse of her toughness from an 1841 exchange of letters between her sons, a mutual French friend, and her husband, who had traveled to England hoping for a reconciliation. Madame Tussaud and her sons absolutely refused to see him and said he had acted "scandalously," adding that he might find mercy from God but not from themselves. It is possible that he had been an adulterer, which had prompted her to leave him 40 years before, but it is not certain. So far as is known she had no close friends, did not go into society, and was regarded as a fascinating solitary by her large circle of London admirers.

Madame Tussaud died in her 90th year, 1850, having given full control and ownership of the waxworks to her sons, who had become British subjects in 1847. Passed down through the family, it has remained a successful venture up to the present, despite a ruinous fire in 1925 and German bombing in 1940. Always mixing scenes of historic interest with scenes of gruesome crimes and punishments, the exhibitors also include contemporary scenes of topical interest to increase visitors' enjoyments. Madame Tussaud was buried in the Catholic cemetery in Chelsea beside other revolution-era émigrés.

SOURCES:

Chapman, Pauline. *Madame Tussaud's Chamber of Horrors.* London: Constable, 1984.

———, and Anita Leslie. *Madame Tussaud: Waxworker Extraordinary.* London: Hutchinson, 1978.

Herve, Francis. *Madame Tussaud's Memoirs and Reminiscences of France.* London, 1838.

Tussaud, John Theodore. *The Romance of Madame Tussaud's.* London: Odhams, 1919.

SUGGESTED READING:

Pyke, E.J. *A Biographical Dictionary of Wax-Modellers.* Oxford: Blackwell, 1973.

COLLECTIONS:
Archives of Madame Tussaud's, Marylebone Road, London.
Victoria and Albert Museum, London.

Patrick Allitt,
Professor of History,
Emory University,
Atlanta, Georgia

Tuthill, Louisa Huggins (1799–1879)

American writer. Born Louisa Caroline Huggins on July 6, 1799, in New Haven, Connecticut; died on June 1, 1879, in Princeton, New Jersey; daughter of Ebenezer Huggins (a merchant) and Mary (Dickerman) Huggins; educated at seminaries for girls in New Haven and Litchfield, Connecticut; married Cornelius Tuthill (an editor), on August 6, 1817 (died 1825); children: Charles Henry (b. 1818); Cornelia Louisa (b. 1820); Mary Esther (b. 1822); Sarah Schoonmaker (b. 1824).

Selected writings: James Somers: The Pilgrim's Son *(published anonymously, 1827);* I Will Be a Lady: A Book for Girls *(1845);* I Will Be a Gentleman: A Book for Boys *(1847);* History of Architecture from the Earliest Times *(1848).*

The youngest of seven children of Ebenezer Huggins and **Mary Dickerman Huggins**, Louisa Huggins Tuthill was born in New Haven, Connecticut, in 1799. Her father was a successful merchant and her family descended from the city's founder, Theophilus Eaton. Attending local girls' seminaries, Louisa began writing as a child, but later burned her early work and determined not to be an author.

In 1817, she married Cornelius Tuthill who had graduated from Yale with plans to become a lawyer. However, following a religious experience, he studied for the ministry and received his license to preach. After an attack of typhus fever weakened him, he founded a literary magazine, *The Microscope*, in 1820, and Louisa was soon hosting literary gatherings in her home. Her husband, who encouraged her to write, published one of her manuscripts without her knowledge. It was well received, and helped to break down her resistance to writing. Six months after its inception, however, the magazine went out of business. Cornelius took a position as an editor and was elected to the state legislature, but his activities were increasingly limited by lung disease. After his death in 1825, Louisa was left with a meager estate of $131.62. She decided to take up writing.

In all, Tuthill wrote more than 30 books. Her first works, including *James Somers: The Pilgrim's Son* (1827), were published anonymously. She wrote several books providing guidance in moral living, manners, aesthetic and spiritual improvement, housekeeping, and child rearing. Later, she wrote *History of Architecture from the Earliest Times* (1848), which described buildings in the United States and Europe, and was the first history of architecture to be published in the United States. Tuthill also edited two collections of John Ruskin's work: *The True and the Beautiful in Nature, Art, Morals, and Religion* (1859) and *Precious Thoughts: Moral and Religious* (1866).

After the death of her mother in 1837, Tuthill embarked on a series of moves. While she was in Hartford, Connecticut, Hezekiah Huntington, a music publisher, encouraged her in her writing career; after his death, she relocated to Roxbury, Massachusetts, and in 1847 moved to Philadelphia, then to New York City, and finally to Princeton, New Jersey, where she died at age 79. She was buried next to her husband in Grove Street Cemetery in New Haven.

SOURCES:
James, Edward T., ed. *Notable American Women, 1607–1950.* Cambridge, MA: The Belknap Press of Harvard University, 1971.
Read, Phyllis J., and Bernard L. Witlieb. *The Book of Women's Firsts.* NY: Random House, 1992.

Kelly Winters,
freelance writer

Tutwiler, Julia Strudwick (1841–1916)

American educator and prison reformer. Born on August 15, 1841, in Tuscaloosa, Alabama; died on March 24, 1916, in Birmingham, Alabama; daughter of Henry Tutwiler (an educator and school administrator) and Julia (Ashe) Tutwiler; attended Madame Maroteau's boarding school (Philadelphia), Vassar College, and Deaconesses' Institute (Kaiserswerth, Germany).

Born in 1841 in Tuscaloosa, Alabama, Julia Strudwick Tutwiler was the third of eleven children of Henry Tutwiler, an educator and school administrator, and **Julia Ashe Tutwiler**. Her maternal grandfather Pascal Paoli Ashe was steward of the University of Alabama; her father was a member of the first graduating class of the University of Virginia and had known Thomas Jefferson. Henry founded the Greene Springs School near Havana, Alabama, and encouraged his daughter to pursue her educational interests.

These interests led Tutwiler to attend Madame Maroteau's boarding school in Philadelphia. With the onset of the Civil War, she returned home. She had wanted to be a nurse, but her father believed it was improper for an unmarried woman to nurse soldiers, so she taught in his school instead. In January 1866, she went north again, to attend Vassar College, but left after a semester and returned to teaching in Alabama. She studied Latin and Greek privately with professors at Washington and Lee University, then went to Europe, spending a year at the Deaconesses' Institute in Kaiswerswerth, Germany, a philanthropic institution that specialized in teacher training. Tutwiler was instructed by a Lutheran order of sisters of charity, and her experience there deepened her interest in helping others.

Tutwiler considered becoming a writer and contributed poems to several American newspapers and magazines during her stay in Germany, but by the time she returned to America, in 1876, she had decided to become a teacher. She joined the faculty of the Tuscaloosa Female College and taught modern languages and English literature for five years. She became well known as an educator and was appointed co-principal of the Livingston (Alabama) Female Academy in 1881. Through her urging, in 1883 the Alabama legislature approved an annual appropriation to establish the Alabama Normal College for Girls at Livingston Academy (later named Livingston Normal College). Tutwiler became principal of the college in 1890, a position she held for the next two decades. Elected president of the department of elementary education of the National Education Association (NEA) in 1891, Tutwiler persuaded the Alabama legislature to establish an industrial school for girls (later known as Alabama College at Montevallo). She also convinced the trustees at the University of Alabama to admit women at the sophomore level in 1893 and as freshmen in 1897.

Tutwiler also crusaded for better treatment of prisoners. In 1880, she organized the Tuscaloosa Benevolent Association, which worked toward prison reform. She sent a questionnaire to the jailers of every county in Alabama and publicized the results, which led to legislative reform of conditions in county jails. A few years later, she served as chair of the Woman's Christian Temperance Union's prison and jail work. Although she firmly supported the need for classification of offenders and regular state inspections of prisons and jails, she was unsuccessful in abolishing the practice of leasing convicts for labor. She believed strongly in the need for religious education in prisoner rehabilitation, and she conducted religious services and distributed Bibles to the prisoners, but she also continued to work toward legislative reform.

Tutwiler retired as president of Livingston Normal College in 1910, and died six years later in Birmingham. Her poem "Alabama," which she wrote in Germany in 1873, was later adopted as the state song.

SOURCES:

James, Edward T., ed. *Notable American Women, 1607–1950*. Cambridge, MA: The Belknap Press of Harvard University, 1971.

McHenry, Robert, ed. *Famous American Women*. NY: Dover, 1980.

Kelly Winters,
freelance writer

Tuyll, Isabella van (1740–1805).

See Charriere, Isabelle de.

Tweed, Blanche Oelrichs (1890–1950).

See Strange, Michael.

Tweedy, Hilda (1911—)

Irish feminist and consumer affairs campaigner. Born Hilda Anderson in Clones, County Monaghan, Ireland, on August 26, 1911; daughter of James Ferguson Anderson and Muriel Frances Victoria (Swayne) Anderson; educated at Alexandra School and College, Dublin, and at the University of London; married Robert Massy Tweedy, on July 18, 1936; children: one son, two daughters.

Awards: honorary doctorate, Trinity College, Dublin (1990).

Hilda Tweedy was born Hilda Anderson in 1911 in Clones, County Monaghan, but spent her childhood in Athlone, in the Irish midlands, where her father was a Church of Ireland cleric. After an education at Alexandra College in Dublin, in 1929 she joined her parents in Egypt where her father had become rector of St. Mark's Church at Alexandria. While there, she studied for an external degree in mathematics from the University of London, and she and her sister also started a small school for English-speaking pupils based on the PNEU system. (The Parents National Educational Union had been set up in England to devise courses for British children living abroad.) In 1936, following her marriage in Alexandria to Robert Tweedy, she came back to live in Ireland. She had applied for a teaching job but was turned down because she was married and "it would not be nice for the girls if you became pregnant." She did not complete her maths degree.

Although Ireland was neutral when war broke out in 1939, there were severe shortages of imported food items and fuel. These bore particularly heavily on the poor, and by 1941 malnutrition and poverty had increased. In that year, the situation was highlighted by Dublin pediatrician Robert Collis who began the Marrowbone Lane Fund with the aim of providing better food and housing for poor Dublin families. Tweedy made a list of friends who could help Collis and his Fund, but she was clear that she "did not want just another organization to alleviate conditions on the surface, but rather to get to the root of the matter, to attack the causes of such hardship." She and four friends—**Andrée Sheehy-Skeffington, Marguerite Skelton, Nancye Simmons** and **Sheila Mallagh**—decided to draw up a "housewives' petition" for presentation to the Irish government before Budget Day in May 1941. The petition urged government action on the production and distribution of food and fuel; fair prices; immediate and effective rationing; communal feeding schemes; and free milk for expectant mothers and children of the unemployed. The petition, which was signed by 640 women, had some success and rationing was introduced shortly afterwards.

Tweedy and the other women decided not to lose the momentum they had gained, and in May 1942 the Irish Housewives' Committee (IHC) was founded. Their immediate aims were price control, transport, school meals, and waste salvage. Each of these areas was investigated, and the reports were then sent to the relevant government departments. The IHC encountered some opposition; on school meals, for example, one cleric claimed that they would break up the sanctity of family life. After the war, in 1946, the IHC was reorganized as the Irish Housewives' Association (IHA) and drew up its first constitution. Its principal aims were (1) to unite housewives in order to ensure their right to play an active part in community planning; (2) to establish real equality of liberties, status and opportunity for everyone; and (3) to defend consumers' rights in the supply, distribution and price of essential commodities. In its early days the organization was largely dominated by Protestant women, although this soon changed. However, in her history of the IHA Tweedy acknowledged that the organization never managed to overcome its middle-class image, and this remained a weakness.

The membership of the IHA gradually built up by word of mouth, but in the late 1940s and early 1950s, two controversies emerged which created conflict in the organization. In 1949, the IHA was accused of Communist sympathies, when it sent a message of support for world peace to the Paris Peace Conference. This led to the resignation of two branches. In 1952, the IHA was again accused of Communist sympathies by a leading provincial newspaper. This time the IHA decided to institute proceedings for libel, a move which Tweedy opposed. She resigned from the IHA committee and from her position as secretary and concentrated instead on her work for the Lower Prices Council and for the producer-consumer market. She resumed her work for the IHA in 1961.

After its reorganization in 1946, the IHC forged links with other women's organizations both in Ireland and abroad. It became a member of the Joint Committee of Women's Societies and Social Workers in Ireland. The Irish Women Citizens' Association, a direct descendant of the Irish Women's Suffrage Association founded in 1874, amalgamated with the IHA in 1947, bringing into IHA ranks a group of new and able members. The following year, the IHA affiliated to the International Alliance of Women (IAW). Tweedy represented Ireland at IAW congresses between 1949 and 1986. At the first congress she attended in Amsterdam, she and the other Irish delegates were horrified by the extent of wartime destruction still visible in Holland. The 1961 Congress was held in Dublin and received the patronage of the Irish president, Eamon de Valera. The notoriously conservative Catholic archbishop of Dublin, J.C. McQuaid, lent them premises for Congress events.

In the 1960s, the IHA, along with other women's organizations, began to agitate for an end to the marriage bar and for women police and jurors. On the latter two aims they had some success. In 1967, the UN Commission on the Status of Women issued a directive to women's non-governmental organizations to examine the status of women in their respective countries. The IHA and other organizations decided to press the Irish government to set up a commission on the status of women to examine such issues as equal pay, employment discrimination, income tax, pensions, education and non-traditional jobs. After a long delay the government finally agreed to set up a commission at the end of 1969, but attempts to have the new commission chaired by a party political appointee were rejected by the women's organizations. The distinguished civil servant *Thekla Beere was appointed chair, and Tweedy represented the IHA on the commission. When the commission's report was published at the end of 1972, it was a major landmark in the advance of women's rights in Ireland. Tweedy became a founder member and the first chair of the Council for the Status of Women which was set up as a result of the commission's report. In 1990,

Trinity College, Dublin, awarded her an honorary doctorate of laws.

SOURCES:

Tweedy, Hilda. *A Link in the Chain: The Irish Housewives' Association 1942–1992.* Dublin: Attic Press, 1992.

Deirdre McMahon,
lecturer in history at Mary Immaculate College,
University of Limerick,
Limerick, Ireland

Twelvetrees, Helen (c. 1908–1958)

American actress. Born Helen Marie Jurgens on December 25, 1908 (some sources cite 1907), in Brooklyn, New York; died of a drug overdose on February 13, 1958, near Harrisburg, Pennsylvania; daughter of William Jurgens (in advertising) and Helen (Kelly) Jurgens; educated at Brooklyn Academy; trained for the stage at the American Academy of Dramatic Arts; married Clark Twelvetrees (an actor, divorced); married Jack Woody (a realtor, divorced 1936); married Conrad Payne (an Air Force officer), around 1946; children: (second marriage) Jack Bryan (b. 1932).

Selected filmography: The Ghost Talks *(1929);* Blue Skies *(1929);* Words and Music *(1929);* The Grand Parade *(1930);* Swing High *(1930);* Her Man *(1930);* The Cat Creeps *(1930);* The Painted Desert *(1931);* Millie *(1931);* A Woman of Experience *(1931);* Bad Company *(1931);* Panama Flo *(1932);* Young Bride *(originally titled* Love Starved, *1932);* State's Attorney *(1932);* Is My Face Red? *(1932);* Unashamed *(1932);* A Bedtime Story *(1933);* Disgraced *(1933);* My Woman *(1933);* King for a Night *(1933);* All Men Are Enemies *(1934);* Now I'll Tell *(1934);* She Was a Lady *(1934);* One Hour Late *(1934);* Times Square Lady *(1935);* She Gets Her Man *(1935);* The Spanish Cape Mystery *(1935);* Frisco Waterfront *(1935);* Thoroughbred *(1936);* Hollywood Roundup *(1937);* Persons in Hiding *(1939);* Unmarried *(1939).*

Helen Twelvetrees was born Helen Marie Jurgens on Christmas Day, probably in 1908 to a mother who encouraged her interest in music and art. When Helen decided she wanted to act after graduating from high school, her mother urged her to postpone that plan for a year to study drawing and painting at the Art Students' Union. She was chosen as a model by several well-known illustrators of magazine covers during that year, and ended it more resolved than ever to embark on an acting career.

Helen next spent three months at the American Academy of Dramatic Arts, where she met Clark Twelvetrees, a fellow student whom she married. They both appeared in one of the school plays and were offered jobs by Stuart Walker, owner of the Indianapolis Stock Company. The couple honeymooned by commuting between Indianapolis and Cincinnati, performing plays in Walker theaters—a period later described by Twelvetrees as the unhappiest of her life. They returned to New York after three months to look for work. Twelvetrees was chosen by Horace Liveright to play Sondra in an adaptation of Theodore Dreiser's *An American Tragedy*, then appeared in two unsuccessful plays, *Yen* by Charles Ray and *Roulette* by Leon DeCosta. While she was rehearsing for an adaptation of Sinclair Lewis' *Elmer Gantry*, a representative from Fox saw her and asked her to join the roster of new actors needed for movies with sound. She accepted the offer, leaving the *Elmer Gantry* cast before the play opened. At a party given in her honor by the cast members, her husband jumped or fell from a sixth-floor window, landing on the canvas top of a parked car below. Twelvetrees postponed her trip to California until he was well enough to come with her. However, their relationship deteriorated as her

Helen Twelvetrees

career blossomed and his declined. When she was signed by Fox, he left for New York, and they divorced soon after. The day the divorce was decreed, she married Jack Woody, a realtor, at Rio Del Mar, California. Their son, Jack Bryan Woody, was born in 1932.

Twelvetrees made only three undistinguished films for Fox before signing with Pathé, where her film career began to flourish, although her first two pictures were panned by critics. Her third film for Pathé, *Her Man*, began to establish her as a respected actress. According to Dion McGregor in *Film Fan Monthly*, the critics decided that "in this film she went a long way toward conquering her main fault: a tendency to exaggerate gestures." Based on the song "Frankie and Johnny," the film was set in a Havana waterfront dive and was the first in a series of what McGregor called "tart-with-a-heart" roles for Twelvetrees. *Her Man* was a box-office hit.

In *Millie*, the most important role of her career, she played a young, disillusioned woman who not only becomes a golddigger in order to support her daughter, but eventually kills the man who attempts to seduce that daughter. Her portrayal of Millie, from an innocent girl to a woman of the world in her 40s, was dramatic and convincing. Twelvetrees appeared in a number of Pathé films, usually as an innocent woman who is enticed into wrongdoing. In 1933, she moved to Paramount Studios, but also did films for Columbia, Universal, and Fox over the next several years. One of her more memorable roles during this period was opposite Spencer Tracy as a gentle, wronged wife in 1934's *Now I'll Tell*.

In 1936, Twelvetrees went to Australia, where her role in *Thoroughbred* made her the first American star of the "talkies" to film there. The attention she received in Australia was a welcome respite during a low point in her life, both professionally and personally. After she returned home, she divorced Woody, claiming that he was unemployed and living off her earnings. She filmed her last two pictures with Paramount in 1939, and then returned to the stage, where over the years she appeared in several plays, including *Arsenic and Old Lace*, *A Streetcar Named Desire*, and *The Man Who Came to Dinner*. It was during her European tour in the latter role that she met her third husband Conrad Payne, an Air Force officer.

Twelvetrees died in 1958, at the hospital at Olmstead Air Force Base near Harrisburg, Pennsylvania, of an overdose of sleeping pills; the death was ruled a suicide. She had been suspected of being an alcoholic for many years, and also

had a painful kidney ailment; according to McGregor, she may have taken the pills to find relief from her pain.

SOURCES:

Katz, Ephraim. *The Film Encyclopedia*. 3rd ed. NY: HarperPerennial, 1998.

McGregor, Dion. "Helen Twelvetrees," in *Film Fan Monthly*. January 1972, pp. 3–14.

Kelly Winters,
freelance writer

Twigg, Rebecca (1963—)

American cyclist. Born on March 26, 1963, in Honolulu, Hawaii; University of Washington, B.S. in biology, 1985; Colman College, San Diego, A.A. in computer science, 1989; attended graduate school at University of Colorado at Colorado Springs, 2000.

Four-time junior national champion; won national championship in individual pursuit (1981–82, 1984, 1986, 1992, 1995); won world championship in individual pursuit (1982, 1984–85, 1987, 1992, 1995); won national championship in individual time trial (1982, 1993–94); won national championship in kilometer time trial (1984, 1986, 1995); won silver medal, road race, Los Angeles Olympics (1984); named USCF Senior Female Athlete of the Year (1985, 1987, 1993, 1995); nominated for James E. Sullivan Award (1987, 1992, 1995); won bronze medal, individual pursuit, Barcelona Olympics (1992); sixteen-time Senior National champion.

Rebecca Twigg, a six-time world champion in the 3,000-meter individual pursuit bike race, began racing—and winning—while still in her teens, earning her first national championship at 18 and her first world title a year later. In heavy competition during the 1980s, Twigg earned national and world titles in events from road races to pursuit races to time trials. In the 1984 Los Angeles Olympics, she won a silver medal in the only women's cycling event—the road race. Although Twigg had planned to compete in the 1988 Summer Games, illness, crashes, and fatigue kept her from qualifying for the U.S. team that year.

With a bachelor's degree in biology granted in 1985 from the University of Washington, where she had taken classes since the age of 14, she went on to study computer science at Colman College. Working full-time as a computer programmer in San Diego, she trimmed her exercise routine to aerobics and weekend bike rides. When she heard that her best event—the women's 3,000-meter individual pursuit race—was being added to the program at the 1992 Olympics, Twigg called her old coach, Eddie Borysewicz, who believed in her chances. She returned to intensive training and found that her three years away had taken a toll. Wrote Anne Janette Johnson: "Her spin was gone, her muscles were leaden. But mind, dedication, and health she had, and after a month and a half of serious training, she began to recover her racing form." Her first year back, she again captured the U.S. pursuit title.

At the 1992 Barcelona Games, in the first Olympic women's pursuit race ever held, Twigg won the bronze medal. Soon after that, at the world championships in Hamar, Norway, she won the gold medal with a record time of 3:37.347, almost eight-tenths of a second faster than the previous world record. She won a dozen other victories in the same year, and was nominated for the James E. Sullivan Award as America's best athlete.

In 1993 and 1994, she earned two more national titles, but it was the following year that was particularly memorable. In 1995, she broke her collarbone two weeks before the World championships in Bogotá, Colombia, and chose to have a metal plate surgically implanted in her shoulder so that she would not miss the race. Immediately after this, she caught a cold, but decided to go to the competition and do her best anyway. She shattered her previous world record by almost a second, and won her sixth World championship. She was thrilled that the injury and cold had not slowed her time.

Prospects looked good for Twigg in 1996, as she prepared for the Olympic Games in Atlanta. Unfortunately, a conflict with the cycling team's coach, who criticized her after she performed poorly in the pursuit quarterfinals, caused her to leave the team before the end of the Games. She came under fire from teammates because she did not compete in the time trial event. Returning to Colorado Springs, Twigg camped and hiked in the Rockies while the controversy subsided. She has since returned to study multimedia computing and its applications at the graduate school at the University of Colorado at Colorado Springs.

SOURCES:

"Gone But Not Forgotten," in *Seattle Times*. December 29, 1996.

Johnson, Anne Janette. *Great Women in Sports*. Detroit, MI: Visible Ink Press, 1998.

Kelly Winters,
freelance writer

Twiggy (1946—)

British "Mod" fashion model, actress, and pop icon of the late 1960s. Born Lesley Hornby in 1946; mar-

ried second husband Leigh Lawson (a director), in 1988; children: (first marriage) daughter Carly.

In 1967, 21-year-old Lesley Hornby began modeling in Britain under the name Twiggy and became an icon for a fashion known as "Mod." Like **Kate Moss** of the 1990s, the aptly named Twiggy was razor thin, with large mascara-enhanced doe-like eyes. The ubiquitous model posed often for Richard Avedon and was seen on magazine cover after cover. With such face and name recognition, in 1971 she starred in Ken Russell's film of the Broadway musical hit *The Boyfriend*, a stage show that had given **Julie Andrews** her American start. *Pauline Kael noted that Twiggy sang admirably and danced even better, but under Russell's direction remained an "appealing blank." Retiring from modeling in the mid-1970s, Twiggy reappeared on the Broadway stage in 1983 as a star of the musical *My One and Only*, opposite dancer-director Tommy Tune. She subsequently co-starred with **Shirley MacLaine** in the film *Madame Sousatzka*

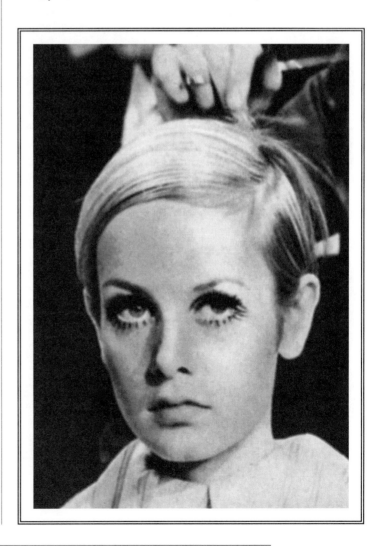

Twiggy

(1988) about which Kael was more enthusiastic, noting her "appealingly understated performance." Twiggy continues to appear in cameos for television and film. Her other movies include: *There Goes the Bride* (1980); *The Doctor and the Devils* (1985); *Club Paradise* (1986); "The Little Match Girl" (made for television, 1987); "The Diamond Trap" (made for television, 1988); *Young Charlie Chaplin* (1988); and *Istanbul* (1989). In 1999, she appeared off-Broadway in the musical *If Love Were All*.

Twomey, Mary (b. 1940).

See Rand, Mary.

Two "Mollies"

American revolutionaries who, during battle, manned artillery in the place of their fallen husbands—one at Fort Washington, November 16, 1776, and the other at the battle of Monmouth, June 28, 1778.

Corbin, Margaret Cochran (1751–c. 1800). Name variations: Captain Molly; Dirty Kate. Born Margaret Cochran on November 12, 1751, in what is now Franklin County, Pennsylvania; died in Highland Falls, New York, around 1800; daughter of Robert Cochran; married John Corbin, in 1772 (killed 1776); married a person unidentified, in 1782.

Father killed by Indians (1756) and mother made captive, never to return; accompanied husband John Corbin to the army; at Fort Washington, took over gunner's position in place of husband who was killed (November 16, 1776); received army pension and became a soldier in the Invalid Corps (1779), remaining in this capacity until the unit was disbanded (April 1783); lived in vicinity of West Point, drawing provisions from the army commissary; eventually settled in what is now Highland Falls, New York.

McCauley, Mary Ludwig Hays (1754–1832). Name variations: Molly Pitcher; Mary Hays; McAuley, M'Kolly, or McKolly. Born Mary Ludwig on October 13, 1754, near Trenton, New Jersey; died in Carlisle, Pennsylvania, on January 22, 1832; daughter of John George Ludwig; illiterate, signed her name with an "X"; married William Hays, probably on July 24, 1769 (died 1788); married John McCauley, in 1793 (died 1813); children (first marriage) John Ludwig Hays.

Worked as domestic servant for the family of Dr. William Irvine, Carlisle, Pennsylvania (1769–77); joined husband's military unit as "camp follower" (1778); at battle of Monmouth, took over husbands place as cannoneer when he was disabled (June 28, 1778); awarded army pension for life from state of Pennsylvania (1822); worked at odd jobs and as a domestic in Carlisle until her death (1832).

In the heat of battle, two heroines during the Revolutionary War assumed the duties of their fallen husbands as cannoneers. Certainly other women performed similar deeds. It was customary at the time for both the American and British armies to have large numbers of women "followers of the army," who served as nurses or performed menial tasks, such as cooking, mending, and laundering for the men in their lives, or simply hired on, with army pay and rations, as noncombatant workers. Many of the "camp followers," as they have often been called, found themselves in combat situations. Sometimes there were so many camp followers that General George Washington had to order that none should ride in wagons. The military women were subject to much of the same disciplinary code as the soldiers, deviation from which meant severe punishment, such as whipping or being "drummed" out of the army. Some of the army women had their children with them.

Women, at the time, of course, could not enlist into the regular ranks of the soldiers. But some women performed actual army duty in urgent situations, more likely so in artillery units, which involved crews operating guns distant from the enemy and interdependent skills. The two artillerist heroines—the two "Mollies"—learned the intricate steps of loading and firing from observing their husbands in gunnery drills.

Both had very similar careers, so much so that in the past they were often confused as one and the same. Each had a hardscrabble existence before and after the war, hailed from frontier Pennsylvania, and performed identical war feats. If record of their lives is otherwise sketchy, documentation bears out their individual identities and their exploits.

Margaret Corbin

Margaret Corbin and her family, like many Scots-Irish settlers, lived at Pennsylvania's far northwest frontier. At age five, when she and her brother were away from home for some reason, Indians descended on the farmstead, killing their father and taking away their mother. Margaret and her brother subsequently were raised by a maternal uncle. Nothing is known about Margaret's upbringing or education.

In 1772, she married John Corbin, who three years later enlisted as a matross (a private who assisted gunners in loading cannon), serving in Cap-

Mary McCauley at the Battle of Monmouth.

tain Thomas Proctor's first company of Pennsylvania artillery. Margaret accompanied her husband when he and a detachment were sent to Fort Washington (at present 183rd Street, New York City) overlooking the Hudson River. He was assigned to a two-gun battery at an outpost on Lau-

rel Hill, northeast of the fort on a ridge above the Harlem River. Each cannon shot a six-pound missile or its equivalent in grapeshot (a cluster of small iron balls used for a scatter effect). On November 16, 1776, John's battery withstood a heavy bombardment from the British frigate *Pearl* in the Hudson River, and from Hessian cannon across the Harlem River. When Hessian troops began an assault upon the ridge position, the American cannons proved ineffective because they could not be sufficiently lowered; John and his comrades then fired on the *Pearl*, striking the rigging and the hull. At this point, John was mortally wounded, and Margaret Corbin assumed her husband's duties. She received wounds from three British grapeshot; an arm was almost severed, and her breast was badly lacerated.

The British carried the day, and all Americans in defense of Fort Washington were made prisoners of war. Corbin, however, was an exception; because of her wounds, she was allowed to go to American-held Philadelphia for medical treatment.

The Executive Council of Pennsylvania, on June 29, 1779, granted Margaret Corbin $30 and recommended to the congressional Board of War that she receive a disability pension. Congress, on July 6, 1779, granted her a lifetime annuity of one-half monthly pay "drawn by a soldier in the service of these states." Later, Congress also provided that Corbin receive a suit of clothes annually or a dollar equivalent. Significantly, not only did Margaret Corbin become the first woman pensioner of the United States, but her award was for military service and not as the widow of a soldier.

Upon winning her pension in July 1779, Margaret Corbin was immediately enrolled for the duration of the war in the Corps of Invalids, whose members, despite their disabilities, performed guard or garrison duty. The Corps of Invalids was stationed at West Point. One of the obligations of the disabled was to instruct soldiers, and hence arose the idea that West Point would be suitable for this purpose in the future. Corbin was the only woman among the 286 "privates and others" who were discharged when the Invalid Corps was disbanded in April 1783.

By 1782, Corbin had remarried to a veteran artillerist who had served with her husband, but his name is unknown. Corbin felt discriminated against because she did not receive the full pay of a soldier and the allotted daily ration of rum. She appealed to Congress, which refused the pay request but accepted the claim for the spirits, thereby awarding her 257 gills of whisky (retroactive in relation to her military service) or the money equivalent. Known as a heavy drinker, Corbin might have opted for the whisky.

Margaret's new husband was apparently also one of the permanently impaired soldiers.

He either died shortly thereafter or the two separated, but both were too incapacitated to work. Like many disabled Revolutionary veterans, Corbin became unable to care for herself, and the military command at West Point made arrangements for households in the neighborhood to take her in. But even this was a problem. Corbin developed such a nasty temper and sharp tongue that she insulted everyone. A person coming face to face with her would salute her and call her "Captain Molly" but behind her back refer to her as "Dirty Kate." A commissary officer at West Point in 1786 wrote the secretary of war: "I am at a loss what to do with Captain Molly. She is such an offensive person that people are unwilling to take her in charge."

After leaving service, Margaret Corbin stayed close by West Point, from which she could draw rations. She died at Buttermilk Falls (now Highland Falls), New York, about three miles from West Point, and was buried in a private cemetery at Swimstown on a plot that became part of the J.P. Morgan estate. In 1926, in connection with the sesquicentennial of the Declaration of Independence, the New York State branch of the Daughters of the American Revolution (DAR) had Margaret Corbin's remains reinterred at the post cemetery at West Point.

Mary Ludwig Hays McCauley

Although her parentage has not been confirmed by historical research, it is believed that Mary Ludwig was born near Trenton, New Jersey, the daughter of John George Ludwig, who migrated from the Palatinate (a region in Germany) in 1749. Mary helped out on her father's dairy farm. At age 15, in 1769, she shows up as a domestic servant in Carlisle, Pennsylvania, in the household of Dr. William Irvine, who later became a general in the Continental army. She married William Hays, a barber, who had his shop in the same block as the Irvine home. The date of the event is uncertain. While the name of Mary's husband being William Hays is verified by later legal documents, the only mention of a Mary Ludwig being married in Carlisle during the immediate pre-Revolutionary period is a marriage bond of July 24, 1769, naming Caspar Hays as the husband. Be that as it may, it is well established that the Mary Ludwig who worked for the Irvines was the same person of "Molly Pitcher" fame.

William Hays, a native of Ireland, enlisted in the Pennsylvania artillery regiment of Colonel Thomas Proctor in May 1777 for three years; after discharge, he reenlisted in 1781. Mary

Ludwig Hays initially stayed on with the Irvines, but sometime in 1778, probably toward the end of the Valley Forge encampment, joined her husband as a camp follower of the army. When the British evacuated Philadelphia and headed toward the New Jersey coast on their way to New York City, General Washington gave pursuit. Intending at first only to harass the rear of the enemy force, Washington suddenly called for a full attack. As a result, there was confusion in forming a battle plan; General Henry Knox, chief of artillery for the American army, however, did manage to set up batteries of eight to ten guns at critical positions. The artillery cut gaping holes through the British ranks. William Hays, serving in the crew for one of the six-pounders, managed to fire two or more rounds of grapeshot per minute.

Temperatures at the battle of Monmouth on June 28, 1778, reached as high as nearly 100°. Soldiers were dropping from heat stroke. Mary Hays did the best she could to assist her husband and the other gunners. Finding a spring nearby, she carried water in buckets, sometimes called pitchers, to the thirsty soldiers. When her husband passed out because of the heat, Mary Hays immediately took over his role in the loading and firing of his assigned artillery piece. As Private Joseph Plumb Martin recorded the occasion:

> While in the act of reaching a cartridge and having one of her feet as far before the other as she could step, a cannon shot from the enemy passed directly between her legs, without doing any other damage than carrying away all the lower part of her petticoat. Looking at it with apparent unconcern, she observed that it was lucky it did not pass a little higher, for in that case it might have carried away something else, and continued her occupation.

Mary Hays returned to Carlisle, and so did her husband after the war. William Hays died in 1788, and, as his widow, Mary received 200 acres of land conferred as a veteran benefit from the state of Pennsylvania; she sold the land in 1807. In 1793, Mary married John McCauley, a veteran and friend of her first husband. He was lazy, and lived off money earned by his wife. He died in 1813; the two probably separated before that time.

Fortunately, Mary Hays McCauley did not have the total disability that plagued Margaret Corbin, and continued to work the rest of her life. She held a variety of jobs—domestic servant in different households, nursemaid, and charwoman. She was hired to wash and clean in the courthouse and other public buildings. Tradition

has it that she, for a time, cooked and washed for the soldiers at the Carlisle barracks that had been built by the Hessian prisoners from the battle of Trenton. Local tax records show that she and her two husbands owned a house on a half-acre lot, and usually one or two cows.

> [Molly Pitcher] immediately took up his gun and cartridges and like a Spartan heroine fought with astonishing bravery.
>
> —Dr. Albigence Waldo (July 3, 1778)

Unlike Margaret Corbin, Mary McCauley did not succeed in obtaining a federal pension. But the Pennsylvania legislature, on February 21, 1822, voted an annuity of $40, payable in half year installments, "for her services during the revolutionary war." Among her neighbors in Carlisle, Mary McCauley was often referred to as Molly Pitcher, as depositions from those who had known her attest. The name "Molly Pitcher," however, does not appear in print until the 1865 edition of Dr. James Thacher's Revolutionary War journal, 21 years after the author's death.

One soldier is said to have described "Molly Pitcher" as "rather stout and red" and a "coarse and uncouth looking female." In later years, neighbors remembered her fondly. **Harriet Foulke**, in whose home Mary McCauley worked, had childhood recollections of her:

> She was homely in appearance, not refined in manner or language, but ready to do a kind act for anyone. She was of average height, muscular, strong, and heavy-set. She was a busy talker. She wore a short gown, white or calico, a linsey-striped skirt, very short and full, woolen stockings, heavy brogans, and a broad white cap with wide flaring ruffles.

McCauley eventually became blind in one eye, caused by the intrusion of a piece of lime. By 1830, she was living in the household of her son, John Ludwig Hays, in Carlisle. She died there in 1832, her death being "hastened by a stubborn cutaneous disease," and was buried in the Old Graveyard in Carlisle, next to her first husband. A stone marker was erected in 1876. There are memorials to her at Carlisle and at the site of the battle of Monmouth. In 1905, a cannon and a masted flag were placed at her gravesite.

The two artillerywomen—"Captain Molly" and "Molly Pitcher"—performed feats of bravery and skill in the Revolutionary War. In so doing, they showed devotion to their fallen husbands and to their country. Their stories had great appeal as the nation a century later looked back to the glory in winning Independence. The two Mollies' rise to the pantheon of American heroes coincided with the gathering momentum of a women's movement seeking equal rights and the onset of a progressive era that sought to redefine America's past. Both Corbin and McCauley, after the war, were very much like old soldiers. Margaret Corbin, disabled and virtually homeless, struggled to make ends meet. Mary McCauley had the security of family and friends. Both women were known to be heavy drinkers and prone to swearing like troopers. McCauley relished in telling war stories. Supposedly she often told girls in Carlisle: "You should have been with me at Monmouth and learned how to load a cannon." If the American Revolution did not have a *Joan of Arc, it had two women, among many others, who demonstrated bravery in combat.

SOURCES:

Hall, Edward. *Margaret Corbin: Heroine of the Battle of Fort Washington, 16 November 1776.* NY: American Scenic and Historic Preservation Society, 1932.

Landis, John B. "Investigation into American Tradition of Woman Known as 'Molly Pitcher,'" in *Journal of American History.* Vol. V, 1911, pp. 83–96.

Perrine, William D. *Molly Pitcher of Monmouth County, New Jersey and Captain Molly of Fort Washington, New York, 1778–1937* [Leaflet]. Princeton Junction, NJ, 1937.

Smith, Samuel S. *A Molly Pitcher Chronology.* Monmouth Beach, NJ: Philip Freneau Press, 1972.

SUGGESTED READING:

Landis, John B. *A Short History of Molly Pitcher: The Heroine of the Battle of Monmouth.* Carlisle, PA: Cornman Printing, 1905.

Pierce, Grace M. "Three American Women Pensioned for Military Service," in *Daughters of the American Revolution Magazine.* Vol. LI, 1917, pp. 140–145, 222–228.

Whittier, John Greenleaf. *Moll Pitcher.* 1832.

COLLECTIONS:

The Molly Pitcher Papers, D.A.R., Cumberland County Chapter, Carlisle, Pennsylvania (includes photocopies of archival records).

Harry M. Ward,
Professor of History,
University of Richmond,
and author of 11 books on early American history

Two Sicilies, queen of.

See Maria Carolina (1752–1814).
See Maria Clementina of Austria (1777–1801).
See Migliaccio, Lucia (fl. 1810–1825).
See Christina of Sardinia (1812–1836).
See Theresa of Austria (1816–1867).
See Maria Sophia Amalia (1841–1925).

Twosret (c. 1220–1188 BCE).

See Tauseret.

Tyler, Alice S. (1859–1944)

American librarian and educator. Born Alice Sarah Tyler on April 27, 1859, in Decatur, Illinois; died on April 18, 1944, in Cleveland, Ohio; daughter of John William Tyler (a minister) and Sarah (Roney) Tyler; received professional certificate, Armour Institute Library School, 1895.

Alice Sarah Tyler was born in 1859, the youngest in a family of 14 children, and grew up on a farm five miles east of Decatur, Illinois, where her parents had pioneered as settlers. She went to local schools and stayed home with her elderly parents until their deaths. Interested in books, reading, and libraries as a young girl, she accepted a job in 1887 as an assistant in the Decatur public library. After her mother died in 1893, Tyler attended the library school at Armour Institute in Chicago and, at age 36, received her professional certificate. She then moved to Cleveland, Ohio, where she worked as head cataloguer in the public library. As the first professionally trained assistant to work there, she insisted on organization and quality, requesting that cataloguers be provided with typewriters to improve their work. She also taught at the summer school established at the library.

In 1900, she became secretary of the fledgling Iowa State Library Commission. Her position involved assisting all new libraries in the state, providing guidance to all libraries, and supporting the traveling library system. During her 13-year tenure, the number of public libraries in Iowa nearly tripled, and traveling book collections increased from less than 100 to more than 700. Tyler also served as director of a summer school for training librarians at the State University of Iowa from 1901 to 1912. She urged the use of local taxes to sponsor libraries and planned the development of libraries at all Iowa state hospitals. An expert in public relations, she was asked to speak at numerous engagements such as library dedications, conventions, and meetings. She also authored many articles for library publications and became editor of the Iowa Library Commission *Bulletin* in 1906. In addition, she worked as secretary of the first executive committee of the League of Library Commissions, founded in 1904, and served as its president from 1906 to 1907.

Tyler became director of the Library School at Western Reserve University in Cleveland in 1913. Under her leadership, the number of students in the school doubled. Previously, graduates of the course had received only a certificate, but in 1915 she instituted a combined four-year library science course that resulted in a bachelor's degree, and encouraged young men as well as young women to enroll. Tyler became dean of the school in 1925, receiving the title of professor of library science.

President of the Ohio Library Association from 1916 to 1917, and of the Association of Library Schools from 1918 to 1919, Tyler earned her greatest professional honor when she was elected president of the American Library Association in 1920, an office she held for one year. She was also founder and first president of the Cleveland Library Club from 1922 to 1923. After her retirement in 1929, Tyler continued to speak, to work as a library consultant, and to write for library periodicals until 1938, when a broken hip forced her to limit her activities. She died in 1944. "'The right books to the right person at the right time' is the slogan," she once said; "it seeks to make books vital factors in life."

SOURCES:

Danton, Emily Miller, ed. *Pioneering Leaders in Librarianship*. Boston, MA: Gregg Press, 1972, pp. 188–196.

James, Edward T., ed. *Notable American Women, 1607–1950*. Cambridge, MA: The Belknap Press of Harvard University, 1971.

Kelly Winters,
freelance writer

Tyler, Dorothy J. (b. 1920).

See Coachman, Alice for sidebar.

Tyler, Julia Gardiner (1820–1889)

American first lady (1844–45) who brought an air of royalty to the White House, provided outspoken support for her husband's Confederate views, and lobbied for pensions for presidential widows. Born on May 4, 1820, in Gardiner Island, New York; died on July 10, 1889, in Richmond, Virginia; third of four children of David Gardiner (a lawyer and state senator in New York) and Juliana (McLachlen) Gardiner (a daughter of a wealthy Scottish brewer of New York City); attended Chagaray Institute in New York City; became second wife of John Tyler (president of the United States), on June 26, 1844, in New York City; children: David Gardiner Tyler (b. 1846); John Alexander Tyler (b. 1848); Julia Gardiner Tyler (b. 1849); Lachlan Tyler (b. 1851); Lyon Gardiner Tyler (b. 1853, who became president of the College of William and Mary in Virginia); Robert Fitzwalter Tyler (b. 1856); Pearl Tyler (b. 1860).

The news that President John Tyler had married Julia Gardiner, "The Rose of Long Island," must have kept tongues wagging for days. The ceremony, held in New York City instead of Washington, had been kept a secret. The groom, at age 54, actually had children older than his 24-year-old bride. Finally, Julia, unlike John Tyler's dear first wife *Letitia Tyler, would certainly not be content to slip into the background of her husband's life.

Known for her raven hair, her hourglass figure, and a string of lovesick suitors, Julia Gardiner was born in 1820, the daughter of a prominent and wealthy New York family. Growing up in Long Island society, she was educated at the prestigious Chagaray Institute in New York City. A trend setter, even as a debutante, she created a fashion craze by wearing a diamond on her forehead held in place by a gold chain. At 19, she humiliated her conservative family by lending her likeness to a department store advertisement, an act which evidently resulted in a hastily arranged tour of Europe.

Julia's first visit to the capital during the winter social season of 1842–43 brought a flurry of marriage proposals, including one from John Tyler, a recent widower. During a return visit the following year, Julia and her family were invited with a number of other notable Washingtonians to sail on a test run of the first propeller-driven

Julia Gardiner Tyler

warship, the USS *Princeton*. The accidental misfiring of the ship's main gun on the upper deck resulted in the deaths of six men, including the secretary of state and Julia's father David. A stricken Julia fainted and was carried off the ship by the president, who provided fatherly comfort and guidance during the difficult weeks that followed. Romance blossomed, although many believe it was helped along by Julia's determination to marry into wealth and power. After the wedding on June 26, 1844, John Tyler's sons eagerly accepted Julia into the family fold. One, Robert, even served as best man. The president's daughters—**Mary Tyler** (b. 1815); **Letitia Tyler Semple** (b. 1821); **Elizabeth Tyler** (b. 1823); and **Alice Tyler** (b. 1827)—were less magnanimous.

Though technically still in mourning for her father, Julia filled her eight months as first lady with a flurry of social activities. She also hired a New York press agent, to insure favorable publicity. In a letter home, she wrote: "I have commenced my auspicious reign and am in quiet possession of the Presidential Mansion." Washington society could not help but be dazzled by the youthful new inhabitant of the White House, who entertained lavishly in the European court tradition. Greeting guests on a platform, flanked by young girls dressed in white, "Her Serene Loveliness," as one wag called her, wore a crownlike arrangement of diamonds and plumes in her hair.

If Julia reveled in her own popularity, she was also her husband's staunchest ally, lobbying openly for the annexation of Texas, which was enacted before the end of John Tyler's term in 1845. She would wear the gold pen with which he signed the Annexation Bill as a pendant. She is also reported to have taught the Marine band to play "Hail to the Chief" whenever her husband entered a room for official functions, and she referred to him as "the president" until the day he died.

At the end of his term, the couple moved to John Tyler's vast Virginia plantation, Sherwood Forest, and raised a second family. Julia had seven children—five sons and two daughters—the last of whom was born when her husband was over 70 years of age. (In all, John Tyler had 16 children.) He died of a heart attack in 1862, while attending a session of the Confederate Congress in Richmond. Although he was hailed by the Confederacy as a hero, the federal government did not acknowledge John Tyler's death, and Julia suffered a prolonged period of economic hardship. When the Tyler plantation

Letitia Tyler Semple. See *Tyler, Letitia* for sidebar.

was no longer safe from the Union army, Julia fled with her children to the Gardiner home in New York. She continued to support the Confederate causes of states' rights and the institution of slavery, which alienated some of her family beyond reconciliation.

After the war, Julia divided her time between New York and Sherwood Forest, finally managing to restore the ravaged plantation, pay off her debts, and educate her children. In the late 1870s, she took up residence in Washington, where she lobbied for federal pensions for widows. In December 1880, Congress voted her $1,200 a year. After James A. Garfield's assassination the following year, all presidents' widows were granted $5,000 a year, allowing Julia to live out her final years in style in Richmond. She died there in 1889, at age 69, and was buried beside her husband at Hollywood Cemetery.

SOURCES:
Healy, Diana Dixon. *America's First Ladies: Private Lives of the Presidential Wives.* NY: Atheneum, 1988.
James, Edward T., ed. *Notable American Women, 1607–1950.* Cambridge, MA: The Belknap Press of Harvard University Press, 1971.
Klapthor, Margaret Brown. *The First Ladies.* Washington, DC: White House Historical Association, 1979.
Melick, Arden David. *Wives of the Presidents.* Maplewood, NJ: Hammond, 1977.
Paletta, LuAnn. *The World Almanac of First Ladies.* NY: World Almanac, 1990.

SUGGESTED READING:
Seager, Robert II. *And Tyler Too: A Biography of John and Julia Gardiner Tyler,* 1963.

COLLECTIONS:
Gardiner Family Papers, Yale University, and John Tyler Papers, Library of Congress.

Barbara Morgan,
Melrose, Massachusetts

Tyler, Letitia (1790–1842)

American first lady (1841–42), who, crippled by a stroke in 1838, had a brief tenure in the White House, secluded in an upstairs room. Born Letitia Christian on November 12, 1790, in New Kent County, Virginia; died on September 10, 1842, in Washington, D.C. (the first wife of a president to die while her husband was in office); third daughter and one of nine children of Robert Christian (a planter) and Mary (Brown) Christian; became first wife of John Tyler (president of the United States), on March 29, 1813, in New Kent County, Virginia; children—nine, seven of whom survived infancy: Mary Tyler (b. 1815); Robert Tyler (b. 1816, who would later earn distinction as an Alabama newspaper editor and political figure); John Tyler (b. 1819); Letitia Tyler Semple (b. 1821); Elizabeth Tyler (b. 1823); Alice Tyler (b.

1827); *Tazewell Tyler (b. 1830). All three sons served the Confederacy during the Civil War, as did a son-in-law and several grandchildren. John Tyler also married *Julia Gardiner Tyler.*

After John Tyler became vice president under William Harrison ("Old Tippecanoe and Tyler Too") in the Whig campaign of 1840, he made plans to carry out the duties of his office from his home in Williamsburg, Virginia, so he could be near his ailing wife Letitia. But he received news of Harrison's sudden death after only a month in office, and had no choice but to move his family into the White House.

Little is known of Letitia Tyler except that she was devoted to her husband and children and appeared to find fulfillment in a life of simple domesticity. Described as a sweet-tempered Southern belle, she was born in 1790 and raised on a prosperous Virginia plantation with eight brothers and sisters. Her first encounter with John Tyler, at a neighborhood party, began a courtship that lasted for nearly five years. Although he wooed her with a shower of love letters and poetry, she is said to have allowed him only one kiss—on the hand—just three weeks shy of their wedding day. The pair married on March 29, 1813, after John had established his law practice.

Letitia gave birth to nine children over the course of the marriage, losing two in infancy. She was a dedicated mother, "content to sit gently by her child's cradle, reading, knitting or sewing." Although most of the tasks of the large household were carried out by family slaves, Letitia handled all the financial matters and attended to her beloved garden. As her husband's political career advanced, first in the Senate and then as governor of Virginia, Letitia remained in the background, appearing socially only when necessary. A crippling stroke in 1838, when she was 48, confined her to a wheelchair.

Letitia lived the last few years of her life in seclusion in the White House, appearing publicly only once, at the wedding of her daughter **Elizabeth Tyler** in January 1842. Social duties were assumed by her daughter-in-law, ***Priscilla Cooper Tyler**, and her daughter ❧▶ **Letitia Tyler Semple**. She succumbed to complications of her stroke in September 1842, the first wife of a president to die during her husband's term of office. She was buried at her childhood home of Cedar Grove, Virginia.

SOURCES:

Healy, Diana Dixon. *America's First Ladies: Private Lives of the Presidential Wives.* NY: Atheneum, 1988.

Melick, Arden David. *Wives of the Presidents.* Maplewood, NJ: Hammond, 1977.

Paletta, LuAnn. *The World Almanac of First Ladies.* NY: World Almanac, 1990.

Barbara Morgan,
Melrose, Massachusetts

Tyler, Priscilla Cooper

(1816–1889)

White House hostess. Born Elizabeth Priscilla Cooper on June 14, 1816, in New York City; died on December 29, 1889; third of nine children of Thomas Abthorpe Cooper (a British tragedian) and Mary (Fairlee) Cooper (a socialite); married Robert Tyler (son of Letitia Tyler and John Tyler), on September 12, 1839; children: Mary Fairlie Tyler (d. 1845); John Tyler (d. 1845); Letitia Christian Tyler (born in the White House); Grace Tyler; Thomas Cooper Tyler (died in infancy); Priscilla Tyler; Elizabeth Tyler; Julia Campbell Tyler; Robert Tyler.

ℒetitia Tyler

Priscilla Cooper Tyler was born in 1816 in New York City, the third of nine children of British tragedian Thomas Abthorpe Cooper and **Mary Fairlee Cooper**, a popular socialite. An actress, Priscilla made her debut at age three. She met Robert Tyler, son of ***Letitia Tyler** and future president John Tyler, when Robert was a

❧▶ **Semple, Letitia Tyler** (1821–1907)

White House hostess. Name variations: Letty Tyler. Born Letitia Tyler in 1821; died in 1907; fourth of nine children of John Tyler (president of the United States) and Letitia Tyler (1790–1842); married James Semple, in 1839; no children.

Little is known about the life of Letitia Tyler Semple, the fourth of nine children of John Tyler and his first wife ***Letitia Tyler**. During 1841 and 1842, she stood in for her invalid mother as White House hostess, along with her sister-in-law ***Priscilla Cooper Tyler**. Letitia had married James Semple in 1839, but had no children. Following her father's remarriage, she was resentful of her stepmother ***Julia Gardiner Tyler** (who was only one year her senior) and did not reconcile with her father for many years. She died in 1907 at the age of 89.

law student; they married in 1839. The couple had nine children (one daughter **Letitia Christian Tyler** was born at the White House). Because of the illness and subsequent death of first lady Letitia Tyler, Priscilla filled in at the White House. Quite beautiful, she made a charming and gracious hostess, but was happy to turn her duties over to ***Julia Gardiner Tyler** when her father-in-law remarried in 1844. Priscilla and her husband moved to Montgomery, Alabama, where Robert served as a Confederate treasury official, and later as editor of the *Montgomery Mail and Advertiser*. Priscilla died, at age 73, in Montgomery.

Tylicka, Justyna Budzynska (1876–1936).

See Budzynska-Tylicka, Justyna.

Tylney, Agnes (1476–1545)

Duchess of Norfolk and countess of Surrey. Name variations: Agnes Tilney; Agnes Howard. Born in 1476; died in May 1545; daughter of Hugh Tylney; married Thomas Howard (1443–1524), earl of Surrey and 2nd duke of Norfolk (r. 1514–1524), on August 17, 1497; children: William Howard, first Baron of Effingham (b. around 1510); Thomas Howard, Lord Howard; *Dorothy Howard, countess of Derby; *Anne Howard (d. 1559); Catherine Howard (related to Queen Catherine Howard); *Elizabeth Howard (d. 1534); step-grandmother of *Catherine Howard (who married Henry VIII).

Tylney, Elizabeth (d. 1497)

Countess of Surrey. Name variations: Elizabeth Tilney; Elizabeth Howard. Died on April 4, 1497; daughter of Frederick Tylney and Elizabeth Cheney; married Henry, also seen as Humphrey, Bourchier, 2nd baron Berners; married Thomas Howard (1443–1524), earl of Surrey and 2nd duke of Norfolk (r. 1514–1524), on April 30, 1472; children: (second marriage) Thomas Howard, 3rd duke of Norfolk (1473–1554); Edward Howard (c. 1477–1513), Lord High Admiral; Edmund Howard (c. 1478–1539); *Muriel Howard (who married John Grey, 2nd viscount L'Isle); *Elizabeth Howard (?–1538; mother of *Anne Boleyn); John Howard.

Tynan, Katharine (1861–1931)

Irish poet, novelist and author of five volumes of autobiography, which offer a valuable insight into late 19th- and early 20th-century Irish political and literary life. Name variations: Katharine Hinkson; Katharine Tynan-Hinkson. Born Katharine Tynan on January 23, 1861, in Dublin, Ireland; died in London, England, on April 2, 1931; daughter of Andrew Cullen Tynan (a farmer) and Elizabeth (O'Reilly) Tynan; attended Dominican Convent, Drogheda, 1871–74; married Henry Albert Hinkson (a barrister and author), in 1893; children: Theobald Henry Hinkson; Giles Aylmer Hinkson; Pamela Mary Hinkson.

Began to write poetry (1878); published Louise de la Valliere and Other Poems *(1885), the first of over 160 books which included novels, poetry and short stories; as a supporter of Parnell and a constitutional nationalist, was a member of the Ladies' Land League (1881–82); was also associated with the Irish literary renaissance (1880s–90s); moved to London on her marriage (1893) and continued writing career; returned to Ireland with family (1912) and lived for a number of years in County Mayo, where Henry Hinkson was a resident magistrate; after her husband's death (1919), traveled widely, living mainly in London, where she died (1931).*

Selected writings: Louise de la Valliere *(1885);* Shamrocks *(1887);* Ballads and Lyrics *(1891);* A Nun, Her Friends and Her Order *(1891);* The Way of a Maid *(1895);* A Lover's Breast-knot *(1896);* Innocencies *(1905);* Twenty-five Years: Reminiscences *(1913);* Flower of Youth: Poems in War Time *(1915);* The Holy War *(1916);* The Middle Years *(1916);* Herb O'Grace *(1918);* The Years of the Shadow *(1919);* The Wandering Years *(1922);* Evensong *(1922);* Memories *(1924);* Life in the Occupied Area *(1925);* Twilight Songs *(1927);* Collected Poems *(1930).*

Despite her own belief that she had been "born under a kind star" in Dublin in 1861, Katharine Tynan's life contained its fair share of sorrow. Indeed, her childhood, though in some ways idyllic, was marked by a period of sustained trauma, when for two years, as a result of eye disease arising from an attack of measles, she was threatened with total blindness. As she remembered in *Twenty-five Years*, her first volume of autobiography:

> From '67 to '69—approximately—there was darkness . . . and my only memory of that time is of a child sitting on a stool, her face buried in a chair—to avoid the light doubtless. A long dream of pain and shrinking from light were those days or months or years.

It was her father, impulsive, emotional and energetic, who took the situation in hand.

> He carried me from doctor to doctor. My sight was despaired of. He was told it was no use. At last he found the right man. . . . I remember the double hall doors of the house

that opened to receive us. I remember the wire blinds in the windows of the consulting-room, where the doctor's finger and thumb lifted the eyelids that it was a torture to keep open. Nothing more than that; but presently I was reading again and the darkness was a family tradition.

In fact, while Tynan's sight was restored, it remained imperfect, leaving her, in her own word, "purblind" for the rest of her life. The condition brought obvious inconveniences, but it is indicative of her optimistic nature and of her deep religious faith that she came to regard it ultimately as a blessing, as she insisted in her poem "The purblind praises the Lord":

I see the faces that are dear,
The others they may pass,
I thank my God I see not clear,
But dim, as in a glass.

A second probable legacy of this period was the very close bond which developed between Katharine and her father, which was to be central to Tynan's early life and writing career. It is her father who dominates Katharine's memories of childhood and young womanhood, in which neither her mother **Elizabeth O'Reilly Tynan** nor her siblings, with the exception of her adored older sister, **Mary Tynan**, feature to any great extent. "My father," she wrote, "was the big beneficent fairy godfather of my very little days. My mother was a large, placid, fair woman, who became an invalid at an early age and influenced my life scarcely at all."

The Tynans belonged to the Catholic middle class, which by the second half of the 19th century was rising in both fortune and influence in Ireland: Andrew Tynan was a "strong" or prosperous farmer, with an interest both in agricultural improvement and in literary and artistic matters. Katharine's early years were spent in Dublin, but in 1868 the family moved to Clondalkin, then a small village some miles outside the city. She fell instantly in love with this new home, with the "small cottage building with little windows under immense overhanging eaves of thatch," with its lawns, orchard and garden, and the surrounding countryside. "Think," she wrote of the first glorious summer there, "of a pack of children who had lived in the town and only had the country by snatches, turned loose a whole summer in this place packed with old-fashioned delights."

At age ten, Tynan was sent as a boarder to the Dominican Convent of St. *Catherine of Siena in Drogheda. She loved the serenity and security of life there, although she gained little in the academic sense, but three years later left without regret to return to the family home, re-

moved "wholly and solely, I believe, because my father wanted my society." Mary, who had been his favorite child, had died at the time of Katharine's illness, and now Katharine and her father, as she put it, "discovered each other." Sharing a love of nature, of reading and of the theater, they were continually in one another's company; Andrew Tynan encouraged his daughter's literary ambitions and, as she recalled in *Memories*, "he made a good many of my opinions during the years when I was pretty constantly his companion."

Another common interest was politics: both father and daughter were romantic nationalists and committed followers of Charles Stewart Parnell, and in 1881 Katharine joined the Ladies' Land League (founded by his sister *Anna Parnell), the female branch of the Land League, which had been established not long before by Parnell and Michael Davitt as a response to economic distress and agrarian unrest. She was present at the first meeting of the new body and became a regular worker in its Dublin office but, by her own admission, "was only one of the rank and file, and a frivolous one"—although her memoirs have since proved an invaluable source of information on the movement. Her loyalty to Parnell survived the suppression in 1882 of the Ladies' Land League, for which, she believed, he was primarily responsible, and later the O'Shea divorce scandal (See O'Shea, Katharine), which deprived him of political power and much of his popular support. When he died suddenly in October 1891, Tynan was one of the many thousands who attended his funeral, and in her poetry and her autobiography described the awe-inspiring moment of his burial, when "as earth touched earth . . . the most glorious meteor sailed across the clear space of the heavens and fell suddenly. He had omens and portents to the end."

I shall die young though many my years are—

For I was born under a kind star.

—Katharine Tynan

Meanwhile, however, Tynan had established her own reputation, not in the world of politics but of literature. She began writing poetry in about 1878, and went on to have pieces published in a number of Dublin newspapers and magazines. In 1885, her first collection of poems appeared, its publication financed by her father. *Louise de la Valliere* (*Louise de La Vallière) included a number of poems showing a Pre-Raphaelite influence, but others, such as "An answer," had a more distinctive note, displaying, in the words of Ernest Boyd, the first historian of

Ireland's literary renaissance, "something of the innocent tenderness, the devotional sensitiveness to external beauty which are associated with her best work." *Louise de la Valliere* was an immediate critical and financial success, and gave Tynan an acknowledged place in the literary worlds of London and Dublin. She continued to live at home, as she was to do until her marriage, and remained close to her father, but had an extremely active professional and social life. "From about 1884 onwards," she later remarked:

> I had really begun to live. I had found out what I could do and being regarded as an exceptional person at home and abroad, I had perfect freedom about my actions. I had as many masculine friends as I liked, and saw as much of them as I wished.

In fact, throughout her life, Tynan had a gift for friendship, with women as well as men. In London, her friends included the poet *Alice Meynell and her husband Wilfred, who helped to foster her career, and William and *Christina Rossetti. In Dublin, Tynan was one of a group of young intellectuals whose sympathies were broadly nationalist, and who were in the process of forging a literature which would reflect their own understanding of Ireland's past, and their aspirations for its future. They included Douglas Hyde, later to become a noted Gaelic scholar and the first president of an independent Ireland, the authors *Dora Sigerson and *Anna Johnston (MacManus), the artist *Sarah Purser, George Russell (AE), the writer and advocate of rural revival, and the young W.B Yeats, "at that time of our first meeting twenty years old . . . tall and lanky . . . all dreams and all gentleness," and already devoted to his art: Tynan remembered that when staying with the Yeats family, "I used to be awakened in the night by a steady, monotonous sound rising and falling. It was Willie chanting poetry to himself in the watches of the night."

Tynan and Yeats spent a good deal of time together during these years and corresponded regularly when apart; both favored home rule for Ireland and often attended political meetings "of a mild kind" together, at one of which Tynan "saw for the first time *Maud Gonne in her incomparable young beauty, easily the most beautiful woman I ever saw." They also commented on one another's work, Yeats sending Tynan a draft of his "Lake Isle of Innisfree" and offering qualified praise of her own poetry: her best work, he believed:

> Is always where you express your own affectionate nature, or your religious feeling, either directly or indirectly. Your worst . . . is where you allow your sense of colour to run

away with you, and make you merely a poet of the picturesque.

Inevitably, their nationalism was reflected in their writing: as Yeats wrote to Tynan in about 1888, "I feel more and more that we shall have a school of Irish poetry, founded on Irish myth and history." In fact, this influence was already apparent in Tynan's work: her first collection had included a number of poems on patriotic or national themes, such as "Waiting," which dealt with the legend of the Celtic hero Finn; her second volume of verse, *Shamrocks* (1887), included poems based on Gaelic legend such as "The pursuit of Diarmuid and Grainne" and "The fate of King Feargus," pre-dating Yeats' own *The Wanderings of Oisin*, which appeared in 1889, and justifying AE's claim that she was "the earliest singer in that awakening of our imagination which has been spoken of as the Irish Renaissance." The central element of this "awakening" was an awareness of Ireland's Celtic inheritance and of the existence of a specifically Celtic perspective, although definitions of what this implied in practice were far from unanimous. Tynan herself, writing in the journal *The Irish fireside* in 1886, struggled to identify the components of this "Irish note . . . the charm of which is so much easier to feel than to explain."

> Some of the parts which go to make up its whole are a simplicity which is naive—a freshness, an archness, a light touching of the chords as with fairy-finger tips; a shade of underlying melancholy as delicately evanescent as a breath upon glass, which yet gives its undertone and shadow to all; fatalism side by side with bouyant hopefulness; laughter with tears; love with hatred; a rainbow of all colours where none conflict; a gamut of all notes which join to make perfect harmony.

Tynan's third collection of poetry, *Ballads and Lyrics*, appeared in 1891, and included what was to be her most famous poem.

> All in the April evening,
> April airs were abroad,
> The sheep with their little lambs
> Passed me by on the road.

Like all her best work, "Sheep and lambs" combines a feeling for nature with a simple and deeply held religious faith. As Yeats wrote, Tynan "is happiest when she puts emotions that have the innocence of childhood into symbols and metaphors from the green world about her. She has . . . a devout tenderness like that of St. Francis for weak instinctive things." Boyd, too, noted that her verse "voices that naive faith, that complete surrender to the simpler emotions of wonder and pity which characterises the religious experiences of the plain man," but in his judgment the publication of *Ballads and Lyrics* marked the end of her development as a poet; she had, in his opinion, simply written too much "for one whose gift is manifestly of slender proportions." A more recent critic and biographer, **Ann Connerton Fallon**, suggests that by 1905, when *Innocencies* appeared, Tynan had begun "to narrow her field of endeavour in poetry," increasingly confining her subject matter to her favorite categories of "birds, children, nature, death, faith, and love." If this limited her range, it also allowed her to concentrate on those areas which best utilized her talent; as Fallon remarks, "when her feeling for nature combined itself with her religious sensibility, Tynan produced poems of simple and gentle beauty."

While Katharine continued to write poetry, she had also become a prolific journalist, producing regular pieces for newspapers and magazines in Ireland, England, and the United States. In 1890, she was commissioned by the Loreto Order to write the life of one of its members, Mother **Xaveria Fallon**. It was a task which should have been congenial, given her own strong Catholic faith and her sympathy for the religious life, but the publication in the following year of her first full-length prose work, *Life of a Nun,* coincided with the controversy about Parnell's leadership; consequently, according to Tynan, the work was "torn to rags and tatters" by the anti-Parnellite press.

In 1893, Tynan finally left her childhood home, her father, and Ireland, and in May of that year she married Henry Hinkson in London. Unlike Katharine, Hinkson was a Protestant, and at the time of their marriage, was still a student at Dublin's Trinity College; later he became a barrister and an author, although he apparently earned his living chiefly as a private tutor. While he makes only fleeting appearances in her memoirs, Tynan spoke more eloquently of her personal feelings in her poetry, and in "Annus mirabilis" she recorded her happiness at this time:

> That year the year was always May,
> Our year, in whose sweet close shall come
> No winter with a waning sky,
> Nor sad leaves fall, nor roses die;
> But roses, roses all the way,
> And never a nightingale be dumb.

For the next 20 years, the Hinksons were to live in England, although never losing touch with Ireland. Marriage, and later motherhood, as well as an active social life, made no difference to Tynan's own journalistic career. She produced a stream of articles and reviews; as she remarked in her autobiography, "I think at one time or anoth-

er I must have written for nearly every paper and magazine in London," and in one year, she had 50 poems in the *Pall Mall Gazette* alone. She also tried her hand at fiction; her first novel, *The Way of a Maid*, which appeared in 1885, dealt with the difficulties of religiously mixed marriages such as her own. As prolific in prose as she was in verse, she went on to produce more than 80 novels and collections of stories over the next 45 years: in 1911, as she recorded in her autobiography, she wrote *A Shameful Inheritance* "between the 6th of May and the 2nd of June, and had plenty of leisure for my friends"; on June 13, having corrected the typescript and "done some small literary chores," she began work on another novel, *Molly, My Heart's Delight*, which she finished on July 20.

In 1905, while on holiday in France, Tynan heard that her father had died. Writing of their parting before her marriage, she mused, "I often wondered afterwards how I could have left him," and their attachment had remained as strong as ever. He had visited her regularly during her early years in London, although in recent years, she wrote, "he had failed rapidly for one of his strong vitality and energy." Nevertheless, it was the memory of him in his prime, "strong, dominant, kind, fearless, true," which remained, and in one of many tributes which she paid to him she expressed her wish to recover the status of the adored and protected child:

> Over and over again I dream a dream;
> I am coming home to you in the starlit gleam;
> Long was the day from you and sweet 'twill
>   seem,
> The day is over and I am coming home.

In 1911, to Katharine's joy, the Hinksons were at last able to return to Ireland. In reality, the move apparently proved something of a disappointment, and, like many exiles, she felt that the country and its people had changed for the worse during her absence. Dublin at least offered the possibility of an active social life, but shortly after the outbreak of war in Europe, she and her husband moved to County Mayo, where he had been posted as a resident magistrate. Though Tynan faced this move, like all the others in her life, with "a high heart," she found that she disliked the harsh climate, the insularity and the isolation of the west. However, possibly because of the lack of distractions, her output actually increased over this period: in three and a half years, she recorded, she wrote ten novels, two volumes of memoirs, three volumes of poetry, and two schoolbooks, as well as numerous short stories, articles, and reviews. Some of this work, such as her widely popular poem "Flower of youth," was inspired by her feelings about the Great War. By 1916, both of her sons were in uniform and, though both were to return safely, she was constantly aware of their danger and witnessed the loss of many others whom she knew. Engrossed by news of the war in Europe, and far away from Dublin, she heard only rumors of the Easter Rising there; however, its aftermath, the outbreak of hostilities between England and Ireland, added to the unhappiness of these "years of the shadow."

In 1919, Henry Hinkson died suddenly. "Grief," she wrote, "had come to me at the end of the War as though the immunity of the boys had been bought with their father's life." The event is only obliquely recorded in her autobiography; again, it was in her poetry, in works such as "The first thrush," that she most eloquently and movingly expressed her sense of loss. As always, however, she was supported by her steady and unquestioning religious faith. As AE remarked:

> She has . . . that spiritual bravery which makes beauty out of death or sorrow. A friend passes and he is sped on his journey not with despair but with hope, almost with imaginative gaiety. . . . It is a great gift this, which on a sudden changes our gloom to glory, and only those have it who are born under a kind star.

Shortly after her husband's death, Tynan and her daughter, **Pamela Mary Hinkson**, left Mayo for Dublin. By now, however, Ireland was in turmoil, with the War of Independence being succeeded by civil war, and Tynan found herself increasingly out of sympathy with political developments there. As a moderate nationalist with many unionist friends, politically, she wrote, "we were in the unfortunate position of pleasing nobody." She spent more and more time out of Ireland, basing herself largely in London, and with Pamela, herself an author, traveled widely in England, Scotland, France, and Germany. Her husband's death had left her entirely dependent for financial support on her own efforts, and over the remaining decade of her life she maintained her very heavy workload, producing a great deal of journalism on her travels and on a mass of other subjects, as well as novels and poetry. Active almost to the end, she died in London on April 2, 1931, at the age of 70, and was buried there, beside her close friend Alice Meynell.

Writing of her own work, Tynan confessed:

> I am not especially proud of this facility of mine. It has produced a good deal of honest work, with of course, a good deal of necessary pot-boiling, and it has made some few people happy besides myself.

This characteristically modest assessment contains some truth. In the course of her writing career, Tynan produced over 160 books, and such a vast output must inevitably be of uneven quality. She had, in any case, a limited expectation of her own talent; as **Marilyn Gaddis Rose** remarks, "she set out to be a minor writer . . . [who] set too close a goal for herself" to enable her to equal the achievements of poets such as Christina Rossetti or *Elizabeth Barrett Browning. Her devout Catholicism, her love of beauty, and the innocence which she retained into maturity narrowed her vision and made her disinclined to come to grips with aspects of life which she regarded as peripheral or distasteful. As Rose puts it, she "could not in fact see far, and she restricts her spiritual vision analogously." Nevertheless, she was capable of writing directly and effectively on those subjects in which, as her friend AE declared, she was happy—"religion, friendship, children . . . beauty in gardens, flowers, in sky and clouds," on "normal humanity and its affections." Moreover, as Russell also noted in his foreword to her *Collected Poems*, "she has something which is rather rarer among poets than most people imagine, a natural gift for song. . . . What is common to Katharine Tynan's lyrics out of whatever mood she writes is a shapeliness in their architecture." This gift, applied to those topics on which she felt most deeply, marks her best work with a simple dignity, a lyricism and a charm which are distinctively her own.

> In a green land without hunger and drouth,
> God gave a gift of singing to my mouth,
> A little song and quiet that was heard
> Through the full choir of many a golden bird;
> As a little brook in grasses running sweet,
> Full of refreshment for the noontide heat.
> Some came and drank of me from near and far—
> I was born under a kind star.

SOURCES:

Fallon, Ann Connerton. *Katharine Tynan*. Boston, MA: Twayne, 1979.

Rose, Marilyn Gaddis. *Katharine Tynan*. London: Associated University Presses, 1974.

Tynan, Katharine. *Memories*. London: Everleigh Nash, 1924.

———. *The Middle Years*. London: Constable, 1916.

———. *Twenty-five Years: Reminiscences*. London: Smith, Elder, 1913.

———. *The Wandering Years*. London: Constable, 1922.

———. *The Years of the Shadow*. London: Constable, 1919.

SUGGESTED READING:

Coxhead, Elizabeth. *Daughters of Erin: Five Women of the Irish Renascence*. London: Secker and Warburg, 1965.

Fallis, Richard. *The Irish Renaissance: An Introduction to Anglo-Irish Literature*. Dublin: Gill and Macmillan, 1977.

Ward, Margaret. "The Ladies' Land League," in *Irish History Workshop*. Vol. 1, 1981, pp. 27–35.

Yeats, W.B. *Letters to Katharine Tynan*. Edited by Roger McHugh. Dublin: Clonmore and Reynolds, 1953.

Rosemary Raughter,
freelance writer in women's history,
Dublin, Ireland

Typhoid Mary (1867–1938).

See Mallon, Mary.

Tyrol, countess of.

See Margaret Maultasch (1318–1369).

Tyszkiewiczowa, Maria Anna (1904–1950).

See Ordonówna, Hanka.

Tyus, Wyomia (1945—)

African-American track-and-field sprinter who won three Olympic gold medals. Name variations: Wyomia Tyus Simberg. Born on August 29, 1945, in Griffin, Georgia; youngest of four children and only daughter of Willie Tyus and Marie Tyus; graduated from Tennessee State University; married in 1969; children: daughter Simone (b. 1970).

After excelling in high school track and field, trained at Tennessee State University before competing in her first Olympic Games in Tokyo (1964), where she captured the gold medal in the 100-meter dash and a silver medal in the 4x100-meter relay; in Mexico City Olympics, became the first athlete ever to win two consecutive gold medals in the same event by again winning the 100 meters (1968), also won a third gold in the 4x100-meter relay; won eight National AAU championships; elected to the National Track and Field Hall of Fame (1980) and the Women's Sports Hall of Fame (1981); inducted into the Olympic Hall of Fame (1985); was a founding member of the Women's Sports Association.

In the early spring of 1999, a small group gathered in Griffin, Georgia, to dedicate a new county park. The guest of honor had come all the way from Los Angeles to attend, for the new park bore her name in remembrance of the distinction Wyomia Tyus had brought to Griffin with her stunning Olympic triumphs in the late 1960s. Back then, when relations between Griffin's white and African-American communities had been more strained, the town had neglected to hold a parade in her honor; and many of Wyomia's contemporaries remembered the time the town had filled the municipal swimming pool with dirt to avoid civil-rights laws that

would require whites to share the pool with blacks. Now, 30 years later, Wyomia was finally receiving the recognition she had earned from her hometown.

Born on August 29, 1945, Wyomia Tyus was the only daughter and youngest of four children of Willie and **Marie Tyus**. Willie, who worked at a dairy farm, took care to instill in his children a realistic view of the challenges they would face as African-Americans, although the state of affairs was clear enough to any child growing up in the South during the 1950s. "The closest school to my house was within walking distance," said Tyus, "but it was whites-only. So each day, I had to ride an hour on a bus to get to school." Willie died in 1960, when Wyomia was just 15, but his warning kept her determination strong in the years that followed.

> *My* father used to tell us, "You will have to work twice as hard to get what you want."
> —Wyomia Tyus

Her three older brothers were all good basketball players, and by watching them play and then trying her own skills at the game, Tyus soon found herself on the girls' basketball team at Griffin's Fairmont High School. Track and field came almost as an afterthought, when an alert coach invited her to join the school's sprinting team after watching her on the basketball court. Wyomia's performance as a sprinter was impressive enough to bring an invitation to take part in a summer track-and-field program at Tennessee State University, which awarded her a partial scholarship on her graduation from high school in 1963.

She arrived at TSU at a propitious time for black athletes, for the school had gained a reputation for training some of the first African-American women to compete in international sports, especially in track-and-field competition. **Tydia Pickett** and **Louise Stokes** had been the first black women to compete in the Olympics, at the 1932 Games in Los Angeles, and were soon followed by TSU-trained *Alice Coachman, who won a gold medal in the high jump, and ✒ **Audrey Patterson**, who won a bronze in the 200-meter dash, both at the 1948 Olympics in London. By the time Wyomia arrived at Tennessee State, **Dorothy Richey** was entering her tenth year as the first African-American director of Olympic track-and-field events for the USOC.

The summer before beginning classes at TSU, Tyus traveled abroad for the first time in her life to take part in an international amateur

Patterson, Audrey. See Faggs, Mae for sidebar.

track-and-field competition in the Soviet Union, in which she won the 100-meter dash and anchored the winning 4x100-meter relay team. Further good fortune followed when she was assigned to TSU's respected track-and-field coach Ed Temple, joining future Olympians *Wilma Rudolph and *Edith McGuire. It took less than a year for Temple's coaching to show results. By early 1964, Tyus was among the top-ranked runners in the United States for the 100-meter dash; and that summer, she won the event at the National AAU Women's Outdoor Track and Field championships by equaling the world's record. Her victory qualified her, at age 19, for the 1964 Olympics in Tokyo, where she stunned the world by not only taking the gold medal in the 100-meter dash, setting a new Olympic and a world's record in the process, but by winning a silver medal as part of America's 4x100-meter relay team. Back home, Tyus set a new world's indoor record in the 70-yard dash in Louisville's Mason Dixon Games and came in second in the 100 meters at a Los Angeles meet between United States and Russian runners. She set two more

Wyomia Tyus crosses the finish line in the 100 meters in Tokyo, 1964.

world's records the following year—for the 100-yard dash at a meet in Kingston, Jamaica, and for the 440-yard dash at that year's Mason Dixon Games, where she also set a new indoor record for the event.

She won six more important races during 1966 in 100-meter and 100-yard dashes against American, Russian, and British rivals; and was a member of the 440-yard relay team at the AAU Senior Track and Field championships in Maryland that set a new indoor record. Now 21, Tyus had set four world records and captured Olympic gold and silver medals in just two years of top-level amateur competition. She added a Pan-American Games record in 1967 in her preliminary rounds for the 100 meters, as well as winning two events new to her growing repertoire—the 60-yard dash at the National AAU Indoor championships in Oakland and the 50-yard dash at the 1967 Maple Leaf Games in Toronto.

When Tyus equaled the 1968 world's record for the 100-yard dash at the Ohio AAU Track and Field Meet in Dayton and won the 100- and

200-yard dashes at the Olympic Development meet at Tennessee State, she qualified for her second time Olympics, at the 1968 competition in Mexico City. "I was 23 and people thought I was all washed up," Wyomia said later, but she quickly proved everyone wrong when she raced to a gold medal in the 100-meter dash, becoming the first woman to win two consecutive gold medals in the event, despite the fact that three of her competitors were world-record holders. When she crossed the finish line in a breathtaking 11 seconds, her victory was all the sweeter for setting both a new Olympic and a new world's record for the 100 meters. Two days later, Tyus captured a second gold medal as part of the American 4x100-meter relay team by running the anchor leg of the race in 42.8 seconds, setting yet another world's record. Spectators quickly learned, however, that Wyomia had more on her mind than winning medals. When her American teammates Tommie Smith and John Carlos were expelled from the Olympic Village for raising their fists in a show of solidarity with Black Power at the ceremony awarding them their medals, Tyus promptly announced she was dedicating her team gold from the relay to them. Sports had been a way for her to overcome generations of discrimination against blacks in America, and Tyus saw nothing wrong with expressing that sense of accomplishment and solidarity in the context of athletic competition. She made no statements to the press about her feelings; but at the conclusion of the 1968 Games, as her name was placed on the Olympic Committee's All-Time World List for the 100-meter dash, Tyus announced her retirement from amateur competition.

With multimillion-dollar endorsements and entertainment contracts years in the future, Tyus realized little economic security from her five years of competition. "Starting all over, it's kind of difficult saying where you want to go," she said at the time. "You go step by step, waiting and waiting and, I guess, being a sprinter, it's hard to wait." She put the degree in recreational education she received on her graduation from TSU to work in Los Angeles, where she took a job in the city's school system as a physical education coordinator. Although she was instrumental in the formation of the country's first professional track-and-field association and competed in its events during the mid-1970s (remaining, not surprisingly, undefeated), she found more satisfaction in supplementing her teaching by acting as a public relations administrator for track-and-field events and by serving on several track-and-field committees for the U.S. Olympic Committee. The political conscience she expressed at the 1968 Olympic Games was put to use at the Black Studies Center of the University of California and in her service as a Goodwill Ambassador for the United States to Africa. She found the most satisfaction, however, in the position she took in the mid-1990s at an outdoor skills education camp administered by the Los Angeles school system. By the time of her induction into the U.S. Olympic Hall of Fame in 1985, she had become known for her dedication to instilling a sense of self-confidence and pride in young people. In 1968, she had said little in public about the dedication of her gold medal to Tommie Smith and John Carlos, but she now admits it was an important turning point for her. "What I did was win a track event," Wyomia says. "What they did lasted a lifetime, and life is bigger than sport."

SOURCES:
Plowden, Martha Ward. *Olympic Black Women*. Gretna, LA: Pelican, 1996.

Norman Powers,
writer-producer, Chelsea Lane Productions,
New York, New York

Tzavella, Moscho (1760–1803)

Greek heroine. Born in 1760; died in 1803.

Known for her extreme bravery, Moscho Tzavella was born in 1760 and came from a family of Greek guerrilla fighters who had led insurgents against the Turkish conquerors. In her day, she commanded an uprising against Ali Pascha, the Albanian ruler of western Greece, who attacked her mountain village of Souli. Armed with sticks and stones, Tzavella and the women of her village forced the Pasha's army to retreat and abandon the campaign to capture her village. Tzavella, who was given the title of *capetanios* (captain), participated in the village councils of war and advised the guerrillas on military tactics.

Kelly Winters,
freelance writer

Tze Hsi (1835–1908).
See Cixi.

Tz'u-an (1837–1881).
See Cixi for sidebar.

Tzu Hsi, T'zu Hsi, or Tz'u-hsi
(1835–1908).
See Cixi.

U

Ubaida (fl. c. 830)

Arabian songstress and tunbur player who was considered the best instrumentalist of her time. Name variations: Ubayda; Obeidet. Flourished around 830.

Ubaida, a tunbur player and songstress during the golden age of classical Arabian culture, learned to play the tunbur (a skin-bellied stringed instrument) from Al-Zubaidi al-Tunburi who stayed in the family's house. She was considered an exceptional player; Ishaq al-Mausuli, then Islam's greatest musician and theorist, said: "In the art of tunbur playing, anyone who seeks to go beyond Ubaida makes mere noise." Masdud, the most celebrated tunbur player of that era, refused to enter a contest with her, fearing she might win. When her parents died, Ubaida became a public singer. Ali ibn al-Faraj al-Jajhi bought her, and she gave birth to his daughter. She also took a series of lovers who spent vast sums on her, leaving her a wealthy woman.

John Haag,
Athens, Georgia

Uchida, Yoshiko (1921–1992)

American writer. Name variations: Yohziko Uchida. Pronunciation: Oo-CHEE-dah. Born on November 24, 1921, in Alameda, California; died after a stroke on June 21, 1992, in Berkeley, California; daughter of Dwight Takashi Uchida (a businessman) and Iku (Umegaki) Uchida; University of California, Berkeley, A.B. (cum laude), 1942; Smith College, M.Ed., 1944.

Was an elementary school teacher in Japanese relocation center in Utah (1942–43); taught in Frankford Friends' School, Philadelphia, Pennsylvania (1944–45); was membership secretary, Institute of Pacific Relations (1946–47); was secretary, United Student Christian Council (1947–52); full-time writer (1952–57); was secretary, University of California, Berkeley (1957–62); full-time writer (1962–92).

Selected writings for children: The Dancing Kettle and Other Japanese Folk Tales *(illus. by Richard C. Jones, Harcourt, 1949);* New Friends for Susan *(illus. by Henry Sugimoto, Scribner, 1951); (self-illustrated)* The Magic Listening Cap—More Folk Tales from Japan *(Harcourt, 1955); (self-illustrated)* The Full Circle *(Friendship, 1957);* Takao and Grandfather's Sword *(illus. by William M. Hutchinson, Harcourt, 1958);* The Promised Year *(illus. by Hutchinson, Harcourt, 1959);* Mik and the Prowler *(illus. by Hutchinson, Harcourt, 1960);* Rokubei and the Thousand Rice Bowls *(illus. by Kazue Mizumura, Scribner, 1962);* The Forever Christmas Tree *(illus. by Mizumura, Scribner, 1963);* Sumi's Prize *(illus. by Mizumura, Scribner, 1964);* The Sea of Gold, and Other Tales from Japan *(illus. by Marianne Yamaguchi, Scribner, 1965);* Sumi's Special Happening *(illus. by Mizumura, Scribner, 1966);* In-Between Miya *(illus. by Susan Bennett, Scribner, 1967);* Hisako's Mysteries *(illus. by Bennett, Scribner, 1969);* Sumi and the Goat and the Tokyo Express *(illus. by Mizumura, Scribner, 1969);* Makoto, the Smallest Boy: A Story of Japan *(illus. by Akihito Shirawaka, Crowell, 1970);* Journey to Topaz: A Story of the Japanese-American Evacuation *(illus. by Donald Carrick, Scribner, 1971);* Samurai of Gold Hill *(illus. by Ati Forberg, Scribner, 1972);* The Birthday Visitor *(illus. by Charles Robinson, Scribner, 1975);* The Rooster Who Understood Japanese *(illus. by Robinson, Scribner, 1976);* Journey Home *(sequel to* Journey to Topaz, *illus. by Robinson, McElderry, 1978);* A Jar of Dreams *(McElderry, 1981);* The Best Bad Thing *(sequel to* A Jar of Dreams, *McElderry, 1983);* Tabi: Journey through Time, Stories of the Japanese in America *(United Methodist Publishing, 1984);* The Happiest Ending *(sequel to* The Best Bad Thing, *McElderry, 1985);* The Two Foolish Cats *(illus. by Margot Zemach, McElderry, 1987);* The Terrible Leak *(Creative Education, 1990);* The Magic Purse *(illus. by Keiko Narahashi, McElderry, 1993);* The Bracelet *(illus. by Joanna Yardley, Philomel, 1993);* The Wise Old Woman *(illus. by Martin Springett, McElderry, 1994).*

Selected writings for adults: We Do Not Work Alone: The Thoughts of Kanjiro Kawai *(Folk Art Society, Japan, 1953); (trans. of English portions)* Soetsu

Yanagi, ed., Shoji Hamada *(Asahi Shimbun Publishing, 1961);* The History of Sycamore Church *(Sycamore Congregational Church, 1974);* Desert Exile: The Uprooting of a Japanese-American Family *(University of Washington Press, 1982);* Picture Bride *(novel, Northland Press, 1987);* The Invisible Thread *(autobiography for young adults, J. Messner, 1991). Author of regular column, "Letter from San Francisco," in* Craft Horizons, *1958–61. Contributor of adult stories and articles to newspapers and periodicals, including* Woman's Day, Gourmet, Utah Historical Quarterly, Far East, *and* California Monthly.

Yoshiko Uchida's appreciation for her Japanese heritage inspired her to write many books on Japanese culture for readers of all ages. "In fiction, the graceful and lively books of Yoshiko Uchida have drawn upon the author's own childhood to document the Japanese-American experience for middle-grade readers," noted Patty Campbell in *The New York Times Book Review*. Among her nonfiction works for adults are studies of Japanese folk artists such as *We Do Not Work Alone: The Thoughts of Kanjiro Kawai*, as well as a memoir of wartime imprisonment, *Desert Exile: The Uprooting of a Japanese-American Family*.

After the bombing of Pearl Harbor, Americans of Japanese descent were incarcerated by order of the U.S. government. Uchida was a senior at the University of California, Berkeley, when her family was sent to Tanforan Racetracks, where thousands of Japanese-Americans lived in stables and barracks. After five months at Tanforan, they were moved to Topaz, a guarded camp in the Utah desert. Uchida taught in the elementary schools there until the spring of 1943, when she was released to accept a fellowship for graduate study at Smith College. Her parents were also released that year.

Uchida earned a master's degree in education, but because teaching limited her time for writing, she found a secretarial job that allowed her to write in the evenings. "I was writing short stories at the time," she said, "sending them to the *New Yorker, Atlantic Monthly* and *Harper's*—and routinely receiving printed rejection slips. After a time, however, the slips contained encouraging penciled notes and a *New Yorker* editor even met with me to suggest that I write about my concentration camp experiences. . . . And many of the short stories I wrote during those days were published eventually in literature anthologies for young people."

By the time *Woman's Day* accepted one of her stories, Uchida had found that writing for children promised more success. Her first book, *The Dancing Kettle and Other Japanese Folk Tales*, was well received upon its publication in 1949, and when a Ford Foundation grant enabled Uchida to visit Japan, she collected more traditional tales. In addition, she became fascinated with Japanese arts and crafts, and learned more about them from philosopher Soetsu Yanagi and other founders of the Folk Art Movement in Japan. But her most important gain from the visit, she wrote, was the awareness "of a new dimension of myself as a Japanese-American and [a] deepened . . . respect and admiration for the culture that had made my parents what they were."

The final children's books Uchida wrote before her death in 1992 reflect her interests not only in Japan but also in her Japanese-American heritage. *The Magic Purse*, for instance, offers a tale with many mythical Japanese elements. In the book, a poor farmer journeying through a swamp encounters a beautiful maiden held captive by the lord of the swamp. She persuades him to carry a letter for her to her parents in another swamp, giving him a magic purse as a reward for his efforts. The purse contains gold coins that forever multiply, and the coins make the farmer a rich man, even as he returns year after year to the swamp to make peace with the swamp lord and to remember the maiden. *The Bracelet*, meanwhile, is set in California during World War II and features a seven-year-old Japanese-American girl, Emi, who is being shipped off to an internment camp with her mother and sister; her father has already been taken to another camp. Once at the camp (Tanforan Racetracks, the same camp that the author lived in as a girl), Emi realizes that she has lost the gold bracelet that her best friend Laurie gave to her as a parting gift. Despite being despondent over the loss of the bracelet, Emi comes to understand that her memory of Laurie is something more precious than the bracelet, because the memory will stay with her forever. In *The Wise Old Woman*, Uchida's final children's book (published 46 years after her first), the author tells the story of a small village in medieval Japan in which the cruel young village lord has decreed that any person reaching 70 years of age must be taken into the mountains and left to die. A young farmer, unable to bear the thought of taking his mother away and letting her die, instead builds a secret room where she can hide. Later, a neighboring ruler comes to the village and declares that the village will be destroyed unless its citizens can carry out three seemingly impossible tasks. When the farmer's mother proves to be the only one capable of figuring out how to com-

Yoshiko Uchida

plete the tasks, the cruel young lord realizes the error of his ways and revokes the age decree.

The death of her mother in 1966 prompted Uchida to write a book for her parents "and the other first-generation Japanese (the Issei), who had endured so much." The result was *Journey to Topaz: A Story of the Japanese-American Evacuation.* Every book Uchida wrote after *Journey to Topaz* responded to the growing need for identity among third generation Japanese-Americans. "Through my books I hope to give young Asian-Americans a sense of their past and to reinforce their self-esteem and self-knowledge," she wrote. "At the same time, I want to dispel the stereotypic image still held by many non-Asians about the Japanese and write about them as real people. I hope to convey the strength of spirit and the sense of hope and purpose I have observed in many first-generation Japanese. Beyond that, I write to celebrate our common humanity, for the basic elements of humanity are present in all our strivings."

SOURCES AND SUGGESTED READING:

Children's Literature Review. Vol. 6. Detroit, MI: Gale Research, 1984.

Something about the Author Autobiography Series. Vol. 1. Detroit, MI: Gale Research, 1986.

Twentieth-Century Children's Writers. 3rd ed. Detroit, MI: St. James Press, 1989.

PERIODICALS:

Children's Book World. November 5, 1967.

Five Owls. January–February, 1994.

The New York Times Book Review. February 9, 1986; November 14, 1993, p. 21.

Publishers Weekly. October 24, 1994, p. 61.

School Library Journal. November 1993, p. 103; December 1993, p. 95; July 1995, p. 75.

Young Readers' Review. January 1967.

OBITUARY AND OTHER SOURCES:

Chicago Tribune. June 28, 1992, section 2, p. 6.

Los Angeles Times. June 27, 1992, p. A26.

The New York Times. June 24, 1992, p. A18.

School Library Journal. August 1992, p. 23.

COLLECTIONS:

The Kerlan Collection holds Uchida's manuscripts for *In-Between Miya* and *Mik and the Prowler*. Other manuscript collections are at the University of Oregon Library, Eugene, and the Bancroft Library, University of California, Berkeley.

Contemporary Authors, The Gale Group, 1999

Nadezhda Udaltsova

Udaltsova, Nadezhda (1885–1961)

Russian artist. Name variations: Nadezhda Andreevna Udaltsova. Born in 1885 in Orel, Russia; died in 1961; studied at Moscow School of Painting, at a school run by Konstantin Yuon, and with various artists in Paris and in Russia; married second husband Aleksandr Drevin (a painter), in 1920s (died 1938).

Nadezhda Udaltsova was born in the small town of Orel, Russia, in 1885. She and her three sisters grew up under the strict discipline of their military father and the tender care of their mother, who loved art and taught her daughters to draw. "Drawing was a second life to us," said Udaltsova. "We invented people and children and depicted them as if they were alive. We took the subjects from our own environment and from the books we read."

An introverted child, Udaltsova moved with her parents at the age of six to Moscow, where she attended school. After graduating from high school with distinction, she began training at the Moscow School of Painting, Sculpture, and Architecture. In 1906, she entered the school run by Konstantin Yuon in Moscow. Insecure about her art, Udaltsova believed it was inferior to that of the other students. One teacher in particular, Nikolai Ulyanov, was especially encouraging, however, and convinced her to commit herself to painting.

In the early 1900s, Russian art underwent a renaissance, and Udaltsova was spurred by artists and ideas from Western Europe. In 1908, she visited the Dresden Gallery and was inspired by the work of Tintoretto. Upon returning to Russia, she was offered the opportunity to study Sergei Shchukin's collection of works by Cézanne, Van Gogh, and Gauguin, which she viewed as "new, unprecedented forms, new visions of the world." A year later, Udaltsova began to study the principles of Cubist painting with Karol Kish. And in 1912, Udaltsova and *Liubov Popova went to Paris, where they studied with Cubist painters for a year. Nadezhda loved Paris. "My particular aspirations and endeavors began to define themselves," she wrote. "Cognition of the world of phenomena, clarity of construction, the composition of space, the correlation of masses—these were elements which I had sought long and importunately."

Upon her return to Russia in 1913, she began working with other artists who had also been influenced by Cubism. Udaltsova was involved with three major exhibitions and established herself as a prominent Cubist painter, and although this avant-garde art received a mixed critical reception, she published a persuasive essay defending the techniques and style of the movement. Despite executing a series of reliefs entitled *Painterly Constructions* for the State Tretyakov Gallery in 1915, Udaltsova did not follow other artists into Constructivism but remained interested in the use of color and texture on the canvas; she was, therefore, more aligned with Suprematism.

After the Russian Revolution in 1917, Udaltsova and her friends were on the side of the Soviets, whom they considered progressive, and her art received wide recognition by the new regime. She became an assistant at the Free State Studios and by 1920 had become a professor and senior lecturer at Vkhutemas, the former Higher Artistic and Technical Studios, where she would teach until 1934. She also became a member of the Institute of Artistic Culture (Inkhuk) in 1920. Deemed highly progressive during these years, Udaltsova was also implacable in her views on art. When the Inkhuk abandoned the concept of easel painting, she resigned.

During the 1920s, Udaltsova's style changed, with some critics labeling it regressive. According to M.N. Yablonskaya, "Udaltsova was theoretically astute, and seems to have understood that her non-objective art now needed the introduction of concrete natural impressions." Her art became more representational and included more landscapes. It was also around this time that she married her second husband, Aleksandr Drevin, a fellow painter with whom she often shared ideas. In the mid-1930s, they traveled across Russia, painting the Ural and Altai Mountains, Armenia, and Central Asia. Drevin died in a concentration camp in 1938. Udaltsova continued working after his death, despite an injury that had limited her mobility. Living on a small pension, she painted until her death in 1961.

SOURCES:

Yablonskaya, M.N. *Women Artists of Russia's New Age.* NY: Rizzoli, 1990.

Kelly Winters,
freelance writer

Udham Bai (fl. 1748–1754)

Queen and co-ruler of Mughal India. Flourished between 1748 and 1754; daughter of Farrukh-Siyar; married Muhammad Shah; children: Ahmad Shah Badahur (b. 1725).

Udham Bai married Muhammad Shah, the fourth in a line of weak rulers of the Mughal Empire, which was in serious decline. Under Muhammad's leadership, the empire lost the province of Kabul to Persian ruler Nadir Shah (c. 1741), lost the province of Katehr to the warrior Ruhela, and saw several other provinces become virtually independent. In 1725, Udham Bai had had a son, Ahmad Shah Badahur, who would prove to be no stronger than his father. Upon his father's death in 1748, 23-year-old Ahmad crowned himself king. Udham Bai, knowing he would not be an able ruler, manipulated his weakness and lack of responsibility and assumed de facto control of the rulership. Eventually this led to her downfall, as her son fled the invading Marathas rather than face them, thus abandoning her and the other women of the family and allowing them to be captured. He was nonetheless deposed and blinded by a joint force of Marathas and Doab Afghans in 1754.

Kelly Winters,
freelance writer

Ufford, Joan de (fl. 1300s).

See Montacute, Joan.

Ufford, Margaret de

Countess of Suffolk. Name variations: Baroness Ferrers of Groby. Married Robert de Ufford (1298–1369), 1st earl of Suffolk; married William Ferrers, 3rd baron Ferrers of Groby; children: Margaret Ferrers; Henry Ferrers (d. 1388), 4th baron Ferrers of Groby.

Ufford, Maud de (fl. 1360s).

See Vere, Maud de.

Uhde, Sonia (1885–1979).

See Delaunay, Sonia.

Uhl, Frida (1872–1943)

Austrian-born journalist and second wife of August Strindberg. Name variations: Frida Strindberg. Born in

Austria in 1872; died in 1943; daughter of Friedrich Uhl (a newspaper publisher and theater critic); married August Strindberg (1849–1912, the playwright), in 1893 (divorced 1895); children: (with Strindberg) one daughter; (with playwright Frank Wedekind) one child.

The daughter of Friedrich Uhl, the publisher of Austria's official government newspaper *Wiener Zeitung* and a respected theater critic, Frida Uhl once proclaimed that she "came into the world with ink in my veins." According to biographer **Monica Strauss**, Uhl was raised by her father to think of herself as a man, to seek her ambition to write, to speak her mind, and to align herself with men of talent. He did not, it would seem, prepare her to deal with the scorn of a society not yet equipped to deal with a woman of independence.

At age 20, while still a fledgling journalist, Uhl met and married playwright and novelist August Strindberg, who was 20 years her senior and had recently separated from his wife **Siri von Essen**. (He also had four children.) "His nerves are badly strained," Uhl wrote of Strindberg to her father, "but it is an inspired madness." In the course of their two-year union, which produced a daughter, Uhl subjugated herself to her husband's career, arranging for translations and productions of his work in England and managing the household and his business affairs. Strindberg, however, resented her meddling and was cruel and abusive to her. Jealous of her outside relationships and her translations of works other than his own, he accused her of being an unfit wife and mother. "Go your dirty way to the life you seek in the gutter," he once told her. Finally, with the emotional and financial help of her father, Uhl divorced Strindberg in 1895. (He would go on to marry actress *Harriet Bosse.)

The remainder of Uhl's life lacked focus. She had a second child with playwright Frank Wedekind who refused to marry her, adding yet another disgrace to her already compromised respectability. She left her children with her family, and took a job as the German agent for English publisher William Heinemann. Her work kept her on the fringe of the Viennese avant-garde writers whom she idolized and from whose midst she selected a series of lovers. Her behavior grew increasingly erratic, due in part, suggests Strauss, to "too many tranquilizing drugs." In 1905, she sued her most recent lover, writer Werner von Oesteren, for harassing a detective she had hired to investigate him. During the ensuing trial, it was revealed that she had previously threatened him twice with a revolver. A few years later, on New Year's Day, she fired a pistol in the Hotel Bristol, although it was not known whether the shot was meant for her latest paramour or for herself.

Uhl subsequently fled to England, setting herself up as an art dealer and opening a German-style cabaret theater, the Cave of the Golden Calf. She later sabotaged the venture by embezzling funds, and in 1914, turned up in the United States, where she was hired by Fox Film to develop Swedish and other European works for the screen. She became a frequent visitor to the New York Public Library. "My husband is there, complete now in 58 volumes," she explained. "My father, Friedrich Uhl, novelist, critic, connoisseur and editor, is also there." Having earlier hoped to promote Strindberg's work in a series of lectures, in 1937 she published a memoir of their years together, translated as *Marriage With Genius.*

SOURCES:
"Forecasts," in *Publishers Weekly.* June 26, 2000.

Strauss, Monica. *Cruel Banquet: The Life and Loves of Frida Strindberg,* 2000.

Wineapple, Brenda. "Scenes From a Hellish Marriage," in *The New York Times Book Review.* August 20, 2000.

Barbara Morgan,
Melrose, Massachusetts

Ukrainka, Lesya (1871–1913)

Prominent Ukrainian poet whose body of work presents both universal themes and a reflection of her homeland's struggle for greater freedom. Pronunciation: LESS-ya oo-CRYEN-ka. Name variations: Laryssa Kosach; Laryssa Kosach-Kvitka; Lesia or Lessya Ukrainka; Lesëiia Ukrainka; Lesja Ukrajinka; Lesia Ukraïnka; Lesya Ukrayinka. Born Laryssa Kosach on February 26 (sometimes given as February 25), 1871, in Zvyahel' in Volynia in northwestern Ukraine; died on August 15, 1913, in the Caucasus town of Surami near Tbilisi, of tuberculosis; daughter of Petro Antonovych Kosach (a lawyer and landowner) and Olha Petrivna Drahomaniv (a writer and political activist who wrote under the name Olena Pchilka); taught by private tutors; married Klyment Kvitka (an ethnographer and musicologist), in 1907.

With family, moved to Kovel (1878); after her aunt was arrested for political agitation, wrote first poem to protest the event (1879); afflicted with tuberculosis (1881); published first collection of poems (1893); journeyed to Bulgaria to visit Mykhailo Drahomaniv (1894); had first medical treatment in Berlin (1897); made first trip to Italy (1901–02); had further medical treatment in Berlin (1908); made first trip to Egypt (1909); returned to Egypt (1911).

Major works—poetry: Na krylakh pisen' *(On Wings of Song, 1892);* Nevilnychi pisni *(Songs of Slaves, 1893);* Dumy i mriyi *(Thoughts and Dreams, 1899);* Vidhuky *(Echoes, 1902).*

Dramas and dramatic poems: Blakytna troianda *(The Azure Rose, 1896);* Na ruinakh *(Upon the Ruins, 1903);* Vavylonskyi polon *(The Babylonian Captivity, 1903);* V domu roboty—v kraini nevoli *(In the House of Labor, In the House of Slavery, 1906);* Kassandra *(Cassandra, 1907);* Rufin i Pristsilla *(Rufinus and Priscilla, 1908);* Boiarina *(The Boyar Woman, 1910);* U pushchi *(In the Wilderness, 1910);* Lisova pisnia *(Song of the Forest, 1911);* Orhiya *(Orgy, 1913).*

Prose: Starodavnia istoriya skhidnykh narodiv *(Ancient History of Eastern Peoples, 1890–91).*

Translations: Knyha pisen' *(The Book of Songs, 1893).*

Laryssa Kosach, who wrote under the pseudonym Lesya Ukrainka, was an important Ukrainian writer at the turn of the 20th century. A prolific author of both poetry and plays, she is considered by many critics to be the greatest female poet in the Ukrainian language. Her literary name indicated the major theme of her writing since *Lesya Ukrainka* means *Lesya the Ukrainian woman.* In this, she followed other leading Ukrainian writers such as Taras Shevchenko who called himself *Kobzar* (the Bard) and Ivan Franko who called himself *Kamenyar* (Paver of the Way). She used a variety of poetic tools, and one critic has counted 20 different "verse forms" in her work.

Her writing embodies both nationalist themes and more universal elements. Soviet-era writers like Semen Shakhovsky have attempted to connect Ukrainka's nationalism with her supposed affinity for Marxist ideas. In contrast, George Grabowicz finds her best work, "Song of the Forest," to be rooted in her Ukrainian native tradition.

The poet's life and work were inevitably influenced by the linguistic and political status of her native Ukraine, which had been under Russian control since the middle of the 17th century. Led by the Romantic poet and painter Taras Shevchenko (1814–1861), many Ukrainians starting in the 1840s developed a heightened sense of national identity, a strong interest in the national language, and a feeling of political and cultural oppression at the hands of Russian authorities.

The Russian imperial administration grew increasingly alarmed, especially after the 1863 rebellion in Russia's Polish provinces. Leading Russian officials saw Ukraine as a borderland subject to the same separatist impulses that helped provoke the Polish uprising.

Starting in 1863, the Russian imperial government began an attack on the Ukrainian language, banning the publication of educational and religious books in that language.

Lesya Ukrainka

In 1876, when Lesya Ukrainka was still a young child, the restrictions became even more oppressive. It now became illegal to print any books in the Ukrainian language throughout the Russian Empire. Additional limitations were placed on the use of that language in plays, lectures, and even the words accompanying musical compositions. While imaginative Ukrainian writers and actors sought and found ways to circumvent these limits, the heavy hand of the Russian government severely constricted Ukrainian cultural freedom. Only after the Russian monarchy and government had been shaken by the Revolution of 1905 did Ukrainians regain the right to use their own language freely.

Modern literary Ukrainian had been founded by Shevchenko, who drew upon the folk songs and spoken tongue of the common people. Ukrainka represents one of the generations that built upon Shevchenko's accomplishments. By the close of the 19th century, Shevchenko's stress on folklore and Ukrainian history had given way to a second stage of literary accomplishment that historian Orest Subtelny labels "Ukrainian Realism." This movement sought to examine such questions as the social life of the Ukrainian peasant village and the impact of foreign cultures, drawn from Poland and Russia, on Ukrainian families.

Ukrainka represented a third group of writers who now departed from such Realism. As Subtelny notes, Ukrainka was part of "a new generation of authors [who] emerged by the turn of the century." They were writers who "attempted to go beyond the rigid, utilitarian strictures of Realism, to apply modernistic techniques, and to express individualistic perceptions." In his view, Lesya Ukrainka was at the center of this movement from Realism into the new and exciting genre of Modernism. By contrast, George Luckyj sees Ukrainka as a more transitional figure, "a major pre-modernist poet and dramatist," although he dubs her "the leading writer of her generation."

She was born Laryssa Kosach on February 26, 1871, in Volynia in the northwestern portion of Ukraine. Her father Petro Antonovych Kosach was a graduate of the law school at the University of Kiev and a district officer in the imperial administration. Soon after her birth, Petro Kosach became active in the Ukrainian nationalist movement, joining a secret social and cultural society and serving as an editor of a monthly literary journal. Her mother Olha Petrivna Drahomaniv Kosach was a distinguished Ukrainian writer, who wrote under the pseudonym **Olena Pchilka**. Olena was the sister of the Ukrainian activist Mykhailo Petrovych Drahomaniv.

Thus Ukrainka, like her five siblings, grew up in a home saturated with Ukrainian national sentiment. The family's sense of intense nationalism grew with Olena's decision to have her children educated by a number of private tutors rather than subjecting them to the public schools. This shielded them from a Russian-style education, and, in the case of Ukrainka, it also permitted the frail and bed-ridden child to become fully educated. Olena herself translated classic foreign literature, including the works of Hans Christian Andersen, into Ukrainian.

She belongs to the poets of the world not only for the wide range of her themes, but also for the great power of her poetic gift which we unqualifiedly call that of a genius.

—Maxim Rylsky

Her family connections gave Ukrainka access to leading figures on the cultural scene such as Ukrainian composer M. Lysenko, and she was also deeply immersed in the Ukrainian nationalist ideas of her uncle, Mykhailo Drahomaniv. He was a scholar from Kiev who had been driven into exile and now worked as a university professor in Sofia, Bulgaria. Drahomaniv's career as a Ukrainian nationalist also included a period of running a Ukrainian-language press in Geneva, Switzerland. The two did not see one another for decades but established a close relationship through their extensive correspondence.

Olena encouraged her children to become proficient in foreign languages, and Ukrainka was found to have a particular aptitude here. By the time she was an adult, she was proficient in a dozen tongues ranging from Ukrainian to English and Latin. Such an ability set the stage for the young woman to work as a translator and to absorb the full range of European literary works in their original languages.

Apparently due to her father's work, the family was uprooted on several occasions. When Ukrainka was seven, they moved to Lutsk and then to a town near Kovel. Despite the cultured nature of her family milieu, Ukrainka enjoyed playing with peasant children in Volhynia. From them, she learned much about rural culture. Eventually the Kosach family settled in Kiev.

Sadly, the poet was frail from birth, and her life was made especially hard when she contracted tuberculosis at the age of 12. "She was plagued by poor health, which never allowed her a painless, carefree day in her life," writes Subtelny. Physical affliction compelled her to spend many years in warm climates away from her homeland and would cause her death at a tragically early age.

Even in her youngest years, the girl began to write verse. Her first poem was a response, in 1879, to her shock upon hearing that a favorite aunt, **Aleksandra Kosach**, had been arrested by the tsarist police. The child's relative was one of several individuals implicated in an assassination attempt against a leading police official, and she was, as a consequence, exiled to Siberia. Typical of Lesya Ukrainka's later poetry, this early work reflected both her personal feelings as well as a sense of Ukrainian national pride.

The young girl, encouraged by her talented mother, began to submit her poetry for publication at the age of 12, under the pseudonym Lesya Ukrainka. Since Russian law barred the publication of writings in Ukrainian, her works for years to come had to be published in Lviv, a city across the border in Austria-Hungary. A significant portion of the Ukrainian population lived within the Austro-Hungarian Empire and enjoyed a degree of cultural freedom denied their compatriots in Russia. In Lviv, under the leadership of the Ukrainian historian Mykhailo Hrushevsky, a thriving center of Ukrainian scholarship and publishing had developed.

In 1881, the child began her struggle with tuberculosis, which first struck her bones, then, in later years, her lungs. The disease soon took a severe toll on her ambitions; as a talented pianist, she had dreamed of a career as a professional musician. Those hopes had to be abandoned. Nonetheless, she fought against the disease with surgery as well as prolonged sojourns in favorable climates. In the view of **Natalia Pazuniak**, "It was her enormous will power . . . that kept her alive for her beloved literature." The poet herself spoke at times of her "thirty years war" against the dread disease. Her individual tragedy was compounded when she married in 1907. Tuberculosis also afflicted her husband, a Ukrainian ethnographer and musician named Klyment Kvitka.

From her early teenage years, Ukrainka compensated for her physical ailment and its consequent restrictions on her movement by reading widely. The authors who influenced her and whose themes later appeared in her work ranged from the dramatists of ancient Greece to English Romantic poets of the 19th century. She also took up the task of translating foreign classics into Ukrainian, thereby stretching her own ability to write original verse in her native language.

In the early 1890s, she completed her own first volume of verse, *Na krylakh pisen'* (*On Wings of Song*). In 1893, she collaborated in a translation of the poetry of Heinrich Heine, published in Lviv as *Knyha pisen'* (*The Book of Songs*). Two years later, her collection of poetry, *Nevilnychi pisni* (*The Songs of Slaves*), expressed so ardent a sense of Ukrainian nationalism that it drew high praise from Ivan Franko, her noted Ukrainian literary contemporary. He had already greeted *Knyha pisen'* with the declaration that Ukrainka's reputation would come to match that of the great Taras Shevchenko. On Ukrainka's consistent concern with her native land, Pazuniak notes, "she never strays far from social themes; she is an integral part of Ukraine, and no personal experience can estrange her from the destiny of her fatherland." In a poem about the medieval king of Scotland Robert Bruce, written in 1893, Ukrainka maintained: "He is no poet who forgets the deep national wounds."

Ukrainka's poetry was also marked by a remarkable element of strength and optimism in the face of the tuberculosis that weakened her and added physical discomfort to daily life. Her courage was particularly evident in her poetry on the subject of hope. Here she wrote, on one occasion, that "through all my tears, I still will smile, Sing my songs though troubles round me loom." Coming from a family of means, Ukrainka was able to seek treatment for her medical needs with prolonged trips abroad. In 1897, she went to Berlin for surgery on her legs, but the tuberculosis now spread to her lungs, then her kidneys. Travel for her health sent her abroad to Italy and Egypt, and to such remote regions of the Russian Empire as the Crimea and the Caucasus.

She approached the task of promoting political freedom in an increasingly broad fashion by turning to a variety of themes concerning oppressed peoples of the past, especially the Jews. In *Vavylonski polon* (*The Babylonian Captivity*), she describes the struggles of the ancient Jews in their Babylonian exile. In *V domu roboty—v kraini nevoli* (*In the House of Labor, in the House of Slavery*), she takes up the subject of Jewish oppression in Egypt. Her growing interest in themes that transcended strictly Ukrainian topics became evident on the one hand in her practice of setting her work in such locales as ancient Greece and revolutionary France. It became clearer still as she took up such broad topics as the different kinds of love, and the tensions between a poet and society.

By 1907, the year of her marriage, doctors informed the young woman that her health was becoming increasingly precarious. In the face of this grim news, one of Ukrainka's poems of that year, *U pushchi* (*In the Wilderness*), stressed the need of the artist to follow his inspiration and produce works reflecting his own creative spirit. Her heightened sense of her own fragile mortality was expressed in such lines as "When will the angel of death call me? I have a premonition that he will come soon."

Her writing took a particularly strong and novel direction during the last several years of her life. Now, while continuing to produce lyric poetry of a high order, she focused most of her energies on poetic dramas. For example, her 1908 play *Rufin i Pristsilla* (*Rufinus and Priscilla*) is set in ancient Rome and reflects her longstanding interest in the history of early Christianity. In 1911, she wrote her most famous work, *Lisova pisnia* (*Song of the Forest*), in the space of three days. In telling the story of a forest nymph who falls in love with a human and who attempts to adopt human form, the poet eschewed politics to concern herself with the clash between an ideal world of nature and the harshness of human reality.

Nonetheless, much of her work still exuded an irrepressible nationalism. Her 1910 play, *Boiarina* (*The Boiar's Wife*), contained particularly harsh and explicit anti-Russian feeling. Set in the 17th century, it presented a young Ukrainian heroine who accompanies her husband to Moscow and encounters the indignities that Russian society placed on upper-class females. She experiences an even greater degree of despair when she realizes that the Russian tsar's government envisions only servitude for her homeland. The Communist government of Russia that came to power following the November 1917 revolution reacted to the vivid patriotism of *The Boiar's Wife* by forbidding its production. The play was banned from the stage and appeared only in print until 1989.

In his history of Ukrainian literature, modern critic Dmytro Chyzhevskyi notes that his predecessors in Ukrainka's own day failed to understand "the significance of the gigantic step the poetess had taken on to the field of world literature." They could not accept "a total absence of sumptuous costumes, song and dance, drinking and Cossack figures." Chyzhevskyi, by contrast, has nothing but praise for this effort as Lesya Ukrainka "raised Ukrainian literature to the level of a world literature . . . [treating] themes that are common and important to mankind as a whole." Said Natalia Pazuniak on the centennial of Ukrainka's birth, "Her works are truly universal."

The poet spent the last years of her life fighting off tuberculosis in Egypt and the Caucasus. She continued to write during her final year, and died at the age of 42 on August 15, 1913, in Surami near Tbilisi, in the Caucasus. Her body was returned to Kiev for burial.

At home, a statue in Kiev by **Halyna Kalchenko** commemorates Ukrainka's work. Following the mass emigration of Ukrainians after World War II, Ukrainians abroad honored her with monuments in the Garden of Culture, in Cleveland, Ohio, as well as in Toronto, Canada. Both were created by the Ukrainian sculptor Mykahilo Chereshniowskiy. Her stage plays have occupied a prominent role in the repertoire of such émigré companies as the Ukrainian Theater of America.

SOURCES:

Bida, Constantine. *Lesya Ukrainka: Life and Work*. Toronto: University of Toronto Press, 1968.

Chyzhevskyiy, Dmytro. *A History of Ukrainian Literature*. Trans. by Dolly Ferguson, Doreen Gorsline, and Ulana Petyk. Ed. by George S.N. Luckyj. Littleton, CO: Ukrainian Academic Press, 1975.

Grabowicz, George G. *Toward a History of Ukrainian Literature*. Cambridge, MA: Harvard University Press, 1981.

Luckyj, George S.N. *Ukrainian Literature in the Twentieth Century: A Reader's Guide*. Toronto: University of Toronto Press, 1992.

Pazuniak, Natalia I. "Lesya Ukrainka—Ukraine's Greatest Poetess," in *Ukrainian Quarterly*. Vol. 23, no. 3, 1971, pp. 237–252.

Rudnyckyj, Jaroslav B. *Egypt in [the] Life and Work of Lesya Ukrainka*. Slavistica No. 83. Cairo: [n.p.], 1938.

Shakhovsky, Semen. *Lesya Ukrainka: A Biographical Sketch*. Kiev: Dnipro, 1975.

Subtelny, Orest. *Ukraine: A History*. Toronto: University of Toronto Press, 1988.

Ukrainka, Lesya. *Spirit of Flame: A Collection of the Works of Lesya Ukrainka*. Trans. by Percival Cundy. Foreword by Clarence A. Manning. Ukrainian National Women's League of America, 1950 (reprinted 1971).

SUGGESTED READING:

Magocsi, Paul Robert. *A History of Ukraine*. Seattle, WA: University of Washington, 1996.

Petrenko, Halyna, ed. *Ukraine: A Concise Encyclopedia*. Clifton, NJ: Ukrainian Orthodox Church of the U.S.A, 1987.

Prymak, Thomas M. *Mykhailo Hrushevsky: The Politics of National Culture*. University of Toronto Press, 1987.

Neil M. Heyman,
Professor of History,
San Diego State University,
San Diego, California

Ulanova, Galina (1910–1998)

Prominent ballerina in the Soviet Union from the late 1920s to the early 1960s who flourished in both the classic and the newly composed propagandistic ballets that formed the repertoire of the Soviet dance world. Pronunciation: Ga-LEEN-ah oo-LAHN-ova. *Name variations: Galya. Born Galina Sergeievna Ulanova on January 10 (some sources cite January 8), 1910, in St. Petersburg; died at Moscow's Central Clinic Hospital on April 25, 1998, after a long illness; daughter of Sergei Nikolaevich Ulanov and Maria Fedorovna (Romanova) Ulanova (both professional dancers); attended Leningrad School of Choreography, 1919–28; married Vadim Rindin (chief set designer of the Bolshoi Theater); no children.*

Joined Leningrad State Theater (later Kirov Theater) of Opera and Ballet and debuted in The Sleeping Beauty *(1928); debuted as star dancer in* Swan Lake *(1929); took starring role in newly created* The Fountain of Bakhchisary *(1934); gave first guest performance with the Bolshoi Ballet (1935); awarded Order of Red Banner of Labor (1939); awarded Stalin Prize (1941); joined Bolshoi Ballet (1944); awarded Stalin Prize (1947); performed in Italy (1950); awarded title of People's Artist of the USSR (1951); performed in China (1952); made London debut (1956); awarded Lenin Prize (1957); toured the United States (1959); gave final performance with Bolshoi Theater (1960); retired and began career as teacher (1961); gala performance in her honor presented by Bolshoi Ballet, awarded title of Heroine of Soviet Labor (1974); gala performance by Bolshoi Ballet in honor of her 80th birthday (1990).*

Selected roles: title role in The Dying Swan; *title role in* Giselle; *Juliet in* Romeo and Juliet; *Masha in* The Nutcracker; *Odette-Odile in* Swan Lake; *Princess*

Aurora in The Sleeping Beauty; *Princess Maria in* The Fountain of Bakhchisary; *Tao Hoa in* The Red Poppy.

Galina Ulanova was the most prominent and widely hailed Soviet ballerina of her time. She was a member of the first generation to take their place in the Russian dance world in the decade after the Bolshevik Revolution, a group that included *Natalya Dudinskaya and *Olga Lepeshinskaya. Although some critics have found Ulanova's dancing technique limited, her abilities as an actress made her a star from the 1930s through the 1950s. Within the context of the propagandistic Soviet ballets of the Stalin era, in which choreographers often played down dance sequences in order to emphasize the role of mime, Ulanova had a place of unchallenged prominence.

In the 1950s, as the Soviet Union came in closer artistic contact with the non-Communist world, Ulanova became known to the West. She exhibited her talents in America and Western Europe with her starring role as a member of the Bolshoi Ballet. Performing with great success in the title role in *Giselle*, her favorite, she made an unforgettable impression on those who saw her. While her colleagues, like *Alla Shelest, had no chance to become known in the West, Ulanova, writes Gennady Smakov, "won fame for all of them."

Since the Bolshevik Revolution of November 1917, the Russian ballet has gone through sharp changes under the pressure of political ideology. A major influence was the loss—mainly through emigration—of almost half of the prominent dancers, teachers, and choreographers who had maintained the traditions of the pre-1917 Russian ballet. Notes ballet historian **Susan Au**: "A period of experimentation followed the 1917 Revolution" as the old fairy-tale themes established for an aristocratic audience "seemed out of touch with modern life and values." The art of dance had to be made "available as well as appealing to the masses." This could mean staging productions in circuses and outdoor theaters, using jazz bands to accompany the dancers, but in particular it meant creating political ballets. Thus, as early as 1924, choreographer Fedor Lopukhov created the ballet *Red Whirlwind* in which two groups of dancers showed how dissolute elements of society such as robbers and drunks were defeated by the workers. The political role of the ballet grew throughout the 1920s and continued for at least four decades. A high point of the development was the ballet *The Red Poppy*, first produced in Moscow in 1927. Its plot presents the sailors of a Soviet warship aiding the oppressed workers of the Chinese port where their ship is docked. Ulanova was to play the role of the work's Chinese heroine Tao Hoa on many occasions.

The emergence of Joseph Stalin's dictatorship, in which his artistic tastes took on deadly significance, reduced all of the arts to what **Mary Clarke** and Clement Crisp describe as "the dreadfully stultifying doctrine of 'socialist realism'" as "ballet in Russia now had to concern itself with large-scale dramas whose politically correct message was more significant than their artistic means." Even when choreographers had some success in decreasing the political content of their work, e.g., in *The Fountain of Bakhchisary*, in 1934, they remained bound to the need to present a clear-cut moral lesson to the audience. Here too Ulanova was a leading figure; her performance as Maria, that ballet's heroine, was one of her greatest roles.

Galina Ulanova was born on January 10, 1910, in St. Petersburg, soon to be renamed Leningrad. Her parents were both dancers at the distinguished Maryinsky Theater. Her father

Galina Ulanova

Sergei Ulanov, a member of the ballet corps, went on to become a ballet producer. Her mother ◄❧ **Maria Romanova**, before starting a career as a teacher, was a leading soloist in the company. These dance-minded parents introduced their daughter to the world of ballet at an early age. Her father took her to her first performance when she was only four. When she recognized her mother dancing one of the parts in *The Sleeping Beauty*, she startled the audience by shouting, "That's Mama, my Mama." Years later, she wrote, "even today the thought of *The Sleeping Beauty* never fails to call up the image of my mother as the Lilac Fairy." Her childhood memories also included the revolutionary year of 1917, the summer that the police searched her parents' apartment. But her more serene memories placed her backstage, taken to the theater with her parents when they were scheduled to perform and there was no one to care for her.

Ulanova's education began early, at the Maryinsky Ballet School in 1919. Her parents, once again, had a problem caring for her, and they placed the future star in the school largely so that she would have adult supervision. "My parents were terribly busy in those difficult early years" after the Revolution, said Ulanova, and she had to board at the school during her first two years of study. In the poverty-stricken Russia that was emerging from years of world war, revolution, and civil war, life was harsh, and Ulanova remembered freezing classrooms and dormitories, and meager rations. One of her teachers was her own mother, who left her career as a performer behind to take work as an instructor. After studying with Maria from 1918 to 1923, Galina spent five years in more advanced study with the renowned teacher *Agrip-

pina **Vaganova**. Ulanova's talent soon became evident at the school, and she graduated with honors in 1928. With the help of both her mother and Vaganova, she received a post immediately in the leading company in her native city.

A sign of the changing world in which Ulanova grew up was the shift in names in the dance institution in Leningrad that dominated her early years. Called the Maryinsky Imperial Theater before the revolution, it was subsequently named the State Theater of Opera and Ballet, the title it held when Ulanova joined it. In the 1930s, it finally took on the title of the Kirov, named after a leading Soviet politician.

The future star's debut came in October 1928 in a performance of *The Sleeping Beauty*. In a charming coincidence, she danced in the same ballet and the same theater where she had shouted out her greetings to her mother 14 years earlier. Moreover, her mother was present, "doubly anxious," said Ulanova, "because as my teacher she was thoroughly familiar with every difficult movement and with my weak points." Maria Romanova covered her face when Galina moved into some of the more difficult portions of her performance as Princess Florina. "My technique was by no means what I could have wished," said Ulanova. The following year, however, she made her debut in a starring role, Odette-Odile in *Swan Lake*.

As a young dancer, Ulanova suffered from what Léon Nemenschousky referred to vaguely as an "organic weakness." She spoke of it in her autobiography only as a "thoroughly prosaic illness." It was, nonetheless, serious enough to require treatment at the Essenkovsky spa in the Caucasus. In later years, the ballerina sometimes mentioned this problem as an influence on her lyrical style of dancing: "I tired too easily, did not like to move abruptly, did not care for running or jumping." "And," she suggested, "perhaps it was these things that made for the gentleness of movement and line which has often been counted to my credit."

A more critical view of her early years can be found in the account of Gennady Smakov. He notes how her personal timidity seemed to narrow the range of her dancing, as if she "had potential of which she did not want to make much use." Her physical limits, including a short neck and broad shoulders, also seemed likely to block her career from achieving distinction. Some roles such as Odette-Odile and Aurora reflected her technical limits. On the other hand, her restrained and lyrical style of dancing fit well into the title role in *Giselle*, and here she excelled for the rest of her career.

❧► **Romanova, Maria** (1886–1954)

Russian ballerina. Name variations: Maria Ulanova. Born Maria Fedorovna Romanova in 1886; died in 1954; married Sergei Nikolaevich Ulanov (1881–1950, a ballet dancer and regisseur of the Kirov ballet); children: Galina Ulanova (1910–1998).

Maria Romanova graduated from her theater school's corps de ballet in 1903. She toured abroad with *Anna Pavlova's company in 1911 and was a soloist with the former Maryinsky Ballet, then known as the State Theater of Opera and Ballet, until 1924. From 1917 on, Romanova taught at the Leningrad Ballet School and the School of Russian Ballet. For five years, one of her pupils was her daughter *Galina Ulanova; she also taught *Vera Volkova.

While being treated at Essenkovsky, the rising young ballerina began an important friendship with the actress **Elizaveta Ivanovna Timme**, a performer at Leningrad's Pushkin Theater. In her conversations with this figure from the Russian stage, Ulanova found guidelines for heightening the dramatic content of her dancing. Timme urged her "to feel the story of Odetta or of Giselle." Ulanova came to see that "however perfect its outward form, a role will be cold and empty unless filled with the fruit of thought."

She was also deeply influenced by the prevailing ideas of a revolutionary society. "Dances were staged now not for the sake of the charming waltz or gallop tune," she said, "but for the sake of expressing ideas and emotions." Despite her own talent and eminence, she wrote approvingly of the fact that, unlike the old Imperial Ballet with its focus on "the dancer of scintillating technique," the new ballet aimed at conveying ideas, notably "the basic idea of Soviet humanism, the idea of faith in man, in his strength, beauty, his will to fight for happiness."

The young star's performance in *Swan Lake* in 1933 made her a popular idol in the Soviet Union. The production, staged by her former teacher Agrippina Vaganova, had heavy political overtones, pointing to the barren role played in national life by the 19th-century aristocracy. Nonetheless, Ulanova's interpretation of her role, stressing her own femininity, went beyond the political message of the ballet. On the other hand, according to Smakov, her work was acceptable to the officials of the Soviet dictatorship because her lack of sexuality and her emotional restraint matched the propaganda image of the woman in 1930s Soviet art. "Ulanova's image happily satisfied the needs of both the Russian collective mind and Soviet propaganda," he wrote.

The mid-1930s saw Russian dance move increasingly toward the form Smakov calls "Soviet drama-ballet" or "Soviet ballet realism." In this genre, dance passages took second place to long sequences involving mime in ballets intended to convey a clear political message. Ulanova excelled in such work, making herself into "a dancing actress." She became the star of one such drama-ballet after another. She expressed distaste for ballets without plots and for other aspects of modern dance, and her strong defense of the Soviet dance tradition made her a noted favorite for Stalin and other political leaders of the time. Nonetheless, her acting abilities turned out to be restricted to the ballet stage; Sergei Eisenstein rejected her for the part of Anastasia in his film *Ivan the Terrible* after a failed screen test.

In her autobiography, Ulanova later recalled her role in the Kirov's 1934 production of *The Fountain of Bakhchisary*, one of these drama-ballets, as a crucial step forward in the progress of Soviet dance. Moving away from the abstraction and spectacle of the existing dance tradition, the leading characters, Maria (her role) and Zarema, now tried to express clear and changing emotions. This included what Ulanova called a "dialogue" with each other. According to Au, the ballet was a definitive point in Ulanova's artistic development, since the rising ballerina now incorporated the dramatic methods of Constantin Stanislavski in her performances.

> *I*f any one dancer typifies for Western audiences the artistry of Soviet ballet, it is Galina Ulanova.
>
> —Mary Clarke and Clement Crisp

During World War II, she and the other artists of the Kirov Theater left Leningrad and sought safety in the Urals. But she spent many months entertaining troops at the front or performing for those on leave in Moscow and Leningrad. She danced in Moscow at the Bolshoi during the dangerous months of September and October 1941 as German forces threatened to capture the city. In 1944, she formally joined the Bolshoi Ballet in Moscow as star ballerina, sharing the limelight only with *Maya Plisetskaya. One of the distinguished visitors before whom she performed was British Prime Minister Winston Churchill.

From the start of her career, Ulanova had paved the way for a smooth ascendancy to the top of her profession by enthusiastic expression of support for the achievements of the Russian Revolution. Starting in the 1930s, the Soviet ballet world presented two types of productions in which she took part: first, polished versions of 19th-century classics; second, newly commissioned works with a heavy political content. As dance historian **Mary Grace Swift** described ballet in the Soviet era, "the entire apparatus is state controlled. . . . [T]he state can easily decree the production of any type of ballet as simply as it can decree an increase in the production of cotton." Operating skillfully in this political milieu, Ulanova carefully avoided the offstage contact with Westerners that caused Soviet officials to see her rival Plisetskaya as politically suspect. In commenting on her trip to the People's Republic of China in 1950, Ulanova remarked on "the force of the Soviet people's example of creative work and labour heroism." She also claimed that she had received inspiration for her role as heroic martyr Tao Hoa, "the daughter of the people," in the propagandist ballet *Red Poppy* by her contact with the Chinese people, especially their "valiant and fearless" women. Her position as an ideologically correct ballerina was strengthened by her performance as a contemporary Soviet woman, Jeiran, in the propagandistic ballet *Life* in 1949. Here she played a young woman whose husband dies in the war, leading her to even greater devotion to her neighbors and their work in a collective farm.

Even in the darkest years of the Cold War, Ulanova's talent began to find a foreign audience. She was allowed to dance in Italy in 1951, receiving a tumultuous reception as *The Dying Swan* in Florence. But the politics of the era intervened in these early tours. Her performances in Italy were repeatedly postponed until the country's national elections had ended, and she returned to the Soviet Union to make public statements about the exploitation of artists in the Western world.

After Joseph Stalin's death in 1953, the political pressures lessened, and Ulanova became the outstanding star of the Bolshoi's extensive foreign tours. Her most notable performances abroad came in England in 1956 and in the United States in 1959. In these tours, she and other members of the Bolshoi undoubtedly benefited from the novelty of Soviet ballet for a Western audience as well as the softening political climate. In London, note Crisp and Clarke, the Bolshoi's "impact was as great as the Diaghilev ballet [at the start of the century], and Ulanova, no longer young, had the greatest triumph of all."

Ironically, Ulanova began to lose her popularity with Soviet observers in the same decade in which she became an international star. As she aged and the technical requirements of ballet became more difficult for her, Ulanova's dancing relied increasingly on her acting techniques. Meanwhile, under Nikita Khrushchev, closer contact with artists in the West now became possible. Thus, the influence of such innovative Western choreographers as George Balanchine produced a more sophisticated Soviet audience.

Acquaintances stress two features of Ulanova's personality. First, her personal shyness; second her fanatic, daily application to her art in the form of unending practice. Even among prima ballerinas, whose devotion to unending work is legendary, the Russian star's devotion was seen as beyond the ordinary. In her autobiography, she noted: "Dancing is an art that demands endless, unremitting toil." And, in speaking to Albert Kahn, she pointed to the goal she

sought to achieve: "Technical perfection should be such that the public should never notice, never suspect that any of the movements cost the dancer the least strain." Nemenschousky has described her working "with the tenacity of a workman at his lathe."

During the Bolshoi's extensive visit to the United States in 1959—its first—Ulanova danced in 30 out of the company's 60 performances. She was a remarkably unglamorous example of an international ballet star. Wearing no makeup and dressed in inconspicuous clothing, she seemed no more than an ordinary traveler when she stepped from airplanes in Paris and other major cities.

Although she received a heroine's reception from foreign audiences and stood as the darling of the Soviet establishment, critics of her artistic limitations spoke out both abroad and, somewhat more discreetly, back in the Soviet Union. The British-born Anatol Dolin disliked her prosaic version of *Giselle*, in which she used her unglamorous looks to portray the hapless peasant girl of the ballet's first act. At home, the noted poet *Anna Akhmatova dismissed her brutally: "As a ballerina she is no one. She is merely a mime of genius." Despite such criticism, Ulanova remained a member of her society's social and economic elite. She had been paid generously during her active career, and her salary was augmented by such bonuses as the monetary award that accompanied the Stalin Prize she won in 1941 and again in 1947. She retired with a pension greater than that given to a former prime minister, Nikolai Bulganin, who ended his career at the same time.

When Ulanova left her position as a preeminent dancer in the early 1960s, she took on a new role as teacher at the Bolshoi. She also served as a judge in prestigious international ballet competitions. But her withdrawal from the stage came at a time when new influences were at work in the Russian dance world. By the mid-1960s, for example, the new choreographer of the Bolshoi, Yuri Grigorovich, was deemphasizing the role of mime sequence in which Ulanova had excelled. Ulanova responded in a variety of ways to the shifting currents in the world of the arts. In 1962, she called for sweeping experiments in Soviet ballet based on increasing contact with non-Soviet dance companies. But she also endorsed Soviet leader Nikita Khrushchev's campaign against abstract art.

Ulanova remained an active and honored figure in her native country and abroad. In her role of ballet coach, she accompanied the Bolshoi on its tour to the United States in 1975. A high point of her visit was her meeting, in April of that year, with *Olga Spessivtzeva, an émigré dancer also famous for her playing the title role in *Giselle*. At age 79, Ulanova accompanied the Bolshoi to Great Britain, and, on the occasion of her 80th birthday, the Bolshoi presented a gala in her honor on January 8, 1990, but her failing health prevented her from attending. Galina Ulanova died on April 25, 1998, in Moscow after a lengthy illness.

SOURCES:

Au, Susan. *Ballet & Modern Dance*. London: Thames & Hudson, 1988.

Clarke, Mary, and Clement Crisp. *Ballerina: The Art of Women in Classical Ballet*. London: BBC Books, 1987.

———. *Ballet: An Illustrated History*. London: Hamish Hamilton, 1992.

Kahn, Albert E. *Days with Ulanova: An Intimate Portrait of the Legendary Russian Ballerina*. NY: Simon and Schuster, 1979.

Montague, Sarah. *The Ballerina; Famous Dancers and Rising Stars of Our Time*. NY: Universe, 1980.

Nemenschousky, Léon. *A Day with Galina Ulanova*. Trans. by Margaret McGregor. London: Cassell, 1960.

The New York Times. April–May, 1975.

Smakov, Gennady. *The Great Russian Dancers*. NY: Alfred A. Knopf, 1984.

Swift, Mary Grace. *The Art of Dance in the U.S.S.R.* Notre Dame, IN: University of Notre Dame Press, 1968.

Ulanova, Galina. *Autobiographical Notes and Commentary on Soviet Ballet*. London: Soviet News, 1956.

SUGGESTED READING:

Brinson, Peter, ed. *Ulanova, Moiseyev, & Zakharov on Soviet Ballet*. London: SCR, 1954.

Sizòva, M.I. *Ulanova: Her Childhood and Schooldays*. Trans. by Marie Rambert. London: Adam & Charles Black, 1962.

Neil M. Heyman,
Professor of History,
San Diego State University,
San Diego, California

Ulanova, Maria (1886–1954).

See Ulanova, Galina for sidebar on Maria Romanova.

Ulayya (fl. 800s)

*Arabian singer who became a leader of the Persian romantic music movement. Flourished in the 800s; daughter of Maknuna (a slave singer) and Caliph al-Mahdi (r. 775–785); half-sister of Harun al-Rashid, Ibrahim ibn al-Mahdi, and *Abassa; stepdaughter of *Khaizaran.*

Ulayya was the daughter of **Maknuna**, a slave songstress, and Caliph al-Mahdi (r. 775–785); he had paid 100,000 dirhem to obtain Maknuna, a fortune even for a caliph. Like her mother, Ulayya was a talented musician. Her half-brother, Ibrahim ibn al-Mahdi, became the leader of the Persian romantic music movement which sought to replace the classical conservative school led by Ishaq al-Mausuli. It was only natural then that Ulayya would share Ibrahim's interest in the Persian school, as did their half-brother Caliph Harun al-Rashid.

Ulayya was encouraged to perform with court musicians and wrote many songs which were sung by *Oraib, the preeminent songstress of the Persian school. Talented and beautiful like her mother, Ulayya spent a great deal of her time studying, writing, and praying, as she was quite religious. She preferred others to perform her work and did not live the exotic life of most Arabian songstresses. Ulayya used a fillet set with jewels to cover a blemish on her forehead. It became known as the fillet *à la Ulayya*, and was soon adopted by Muslims as the fashion of the day.

John Haag,
Athens, Georgia

Ulfeldt, Leonora Christina
(1621–1698)

Danish writer of A Monument to Suffering *which records her 22-year imprisonment in the Blue Tower of Copenhagen on the charge of conspiracy to treason. Name variations: Eleonora Ulfeldt; Leonora Ulfeld. Pronunciation: OOL-felt. Born Eleonora Christina on July 8, 1621, at the Castle of Frederiksborg in Hillerod, Denmark; died at Maribo Abbey, Denmark, on March 16, 1698; daughter of Christian IV, king of Denmark and Norway (r. 1588–1648), and his second wife Kirsten Munk (1598–1658); married Corfitz Ulfeldt, in 1636; children: presumably ten, of whom seven reached adulthood.*

Lived in exile with husband (1651–60) when both were arrested for treason and imprisoned at the island of Bornholm; released a year and a half later (1662); spent time in Denmark and abroad; was arrested and brought to the Blue Tower of Copenhagen (1663); released (1685); spent last 13 years at Maribo Abbey (1685–98); during prison term, wrote French Biography *and drafted a large part of* A Monument to Suffering *as well as a series of biographical sketches of women in history and mythology.*

Selected works: French Biography *(1673);* A Monument to Suffering *(published 1869);* The Ornament of Heroines *(only a fragment remains, published 1977).*

Although little known outside the borders of Denmark, Leonora Christina Ulfeldt has held her place among the illustrious names in Danish history for the past 300 years. As a person, she is hailed for her unfailing loyalty to her husband and the physical and intellectual courage with which she prevailed through 22 years of imprisonment. As a writer, she is acclaimed for the talent with which she orchestrated her autobiographical work *A Monument to Suffering*.

Daughter of King Christian IV of Denmark and his second wife ◀ᵇ **Kirsten Munk**, Leonora Christina was born at the magnificent baroque castle of Frederiksborg, north of Copenhagen, but she did not grow up there. As was the custom among nobility, she was given into the care of her maternal grandmother, who brought the child to her own home on the island of Funen immediately after Leonora's christening. She was joined there by other siblings, all of whom from the age of four were instructed in reading, writing, catechism and music. This daily routine of lessons was interrupted when their father's involvement in the Thirty Years' War necessitated his requisition of the nurseries for headquarters. Three children, including Leonora, were sent to Holland for safekeeping. They were to stay in the house of King Christian's niece, Princess **Sophie Hedwig**, who was married to Count Ernst Casimir of Nassau-Dietz. In *French Biography*, Leonora tells about her stay there, emphasizing a particular incident which speaks to her disposition for love and loyalty and dramatizes her earliest encounter with betrayal.

The object of her affection was the second-eldest son of the house, Mauritz, who had fallen

---

♘▶ Munk, Kirsten (1598–1658)

*Queen-consort of Christian IV. Name variations: Christine, countess of Schleswig-Holstein. Born on July 6, 1598; died on April 19, 1658, in Odense; daughter of Ludwig Munk, count of Schleswig-Holstein; married Christian IV (1577–1648), king of Denmark and Norway (r. 1588–1648), on December 31, 1615; children: 12, including *Leonora Christina Ulfeldt (1621–1698).*

In 1597, Christian IV, king of Denmark, married *Anna Catherina of Brandenburg**. Before she died in 1612, Anna gave birth to seven children, including a son and heir, the future King Frederick III. Three years later, Christian remarried, this time to a Danish woman named Kirsten Munk who would have 12 children. Christian eventually banished his second wife from the court for having committed adultery. Considering Christian's own reputation for promiscuity, this charge was, at the very least, incongruous.

---

in love with her on her arrival. He was 11 years old at the time; Leonora was 7. Mauritz talked her into believing that one day she would be his wife, and as a token of his affection he taught her to draw with chalk and shared his Latin vocabulary, a treasure traditionally preserved for boys. They spent their free time in one another's company until Leonora caught chickenpox. The attack was virulent, confining her to bed with blotches and blisters, too feverish to take account of her surroundings. She did not register that Mauritz' elder brother, Vilhelm, who had ridiculed their courtship, brought Mauritz to the door of his sweetheart's room so he might get a good look at her face and come to loathe her. Mauritz got "so agitated," reports Leonora, "that he immediately contracted the disease and nine days later he was dead."

When Leonora recovered and asked about him, she was told he was away on a trip with his mother. One day, however, her tutor took her to the room where the embalmed body of Mauritz was lying in a glass coffin. The tutor wanted "to see if she recognized it," so he lifted Leonora up for a better look. She immediately knew her beloved friend, and "a fright came upon her so great she fell into a swoon." Leonora was revived, but "because the dead boy held a wreath of rosemary, she never again would see those flowers without crying, and she took a loathing to their smell which is still with her."

Writing about her relationship with Mauritz, Leonora makes his death into a cataclysmic event with lifelong reverberations. The rosemary she mentions, which traditionally represents affection and remembrance, in her story takes on the connotation of betrayal as well. It is unlikely that the sight of Leonora's face caused Mauritz to become ill, as chickenpox has an incubation period of 14 to 21 days. But Leonora could not have known that, so Vilhelm's cruel joke involving her unknowing participation appeared to her as an act of treason against love itself for which she was partly responsible. The fact that the adults in her world had lied to her about Mauritz' death intensified her sense of loss.

This newly acquired knowledge of the world opened her eyes to the vulnerability of human relationships which confronted her on her return to Denmark. During the children's absence, King Christian had been forced to cede from the Thirty Years' War, a martial and marital loser. Outdistanced by Sweden's young king, Gustavus Adolphus, in their race to assume the Protestant leadership in the war against the German emperor and the Catholic League, and out-

---

performed in bed by one of his younger German officers, Christian had lost not only power and prestige but his usual confidence in his right to be loved. When finally he granted permission for his wife Kirsten Munk to leave his house, sending her illegitimate daughter after her like a parcel, he was a tired monarch who for the last 18 years of his reign would fight a losing battle to reconstitute his kingdom and his house.

Ranking high among his concerns was the education of his children. King Christian was fond of all of them, but he favored Leonora, who had inherited his physical energy, inquisitive mind, and artistic talents. Leonora gloried in her position as favorite but paid for it with the loneliness she experienced as the object of her siblings' jealousy. Consequently, she attached herself to the suitor her father selected for her: his most promising courtier, Corfitz Ulfeldt. Leonora was betrothed at the age of nine and spent the six years prior to her marriage in the "schools" her father provided in his palaces, presided over by carefully selected women of the aristocracy. To her early instruction in reading, writing, catechism and music were added lessons in German, French, and history. She and her siblings also learned to dance and participate in theatricals, and Leonora, especially, excelled in the art of embroidery. She took her education seriously and proudly asserted that she had an excellent memory; "she could memorize a hymn, copy another and pay attention to what was being said all at the same time."

Her marriage to Corfitz Ulfeldt in 1636 initiated a new stage in Leonora's life. For 12 years, from 1636 to 1648, the year of her father's death, she lived the life of adored wife and privileged daughter. She is exuberant in her characterization of Corfitz' married love: "[He] loved and honored her, and treated her like a lover not like a husband." Her phrasing shows her pleasure and surprise at this unconventional compatibility of love and marriage, which she made it her goal to perpetuate. She consequently invested her considerable intellectual and emotional powers in building a marriage which would gratify her need to give and receive love as well as honor the familial and societal demands placed on her in the roles of spouse and mother.

Leonora's view of marriage shows a departure from the conventional one held at the time in which she lived. The 17th century was a period of transition between the feudal society of previous centuries and the bourgeois regimes of future ones. One was dominated by the courtly love tradition; the other reflected the general shift towards greater individual freedom in matters of love and marriage. Courtly love was love for its own sake, unassociated with property and family (the primary concerns of marriage) and therefore focused on someone other than one's own wife. Leonora wanted Corfitz to remain her lover in the courting pattern of chivalry and at the same time make legitimate its illegitimate basis: he would love his spouse rather than another man's wife. The resulting progeny would make them a family resembling the bourgeois families of subsequent centuries, and property, rather than being the object of a marital liaison, would be its adjunct, acquired and amassed by joint effort.

That Leonora was successful in her endeavor was due partly to her own physical, emotional, and mental powers, and partly to the king's support of Corfitz' ambitious plans for promotion. Within seven years of their marriage, Corfitz became high steward, second in position only to the king, and Leonora held court as first lady of the city. She presided over their manor at Grey Friars' Square in Copenhagen and traveled abroad with her husband as appointed ambassador for Denmark. She also continued her educational pursuits, took painting lessons, practiced the flute, the viola da gamba, the guitar and, with her husband as tutor, added a knowledge of Dutch and Italian to her other languages. In his autobiography, their family doctor and friend Otto Sperling writes about those golden days on the Square. He praises Leonora's "considerable intellect and well developed judgement even though she was only in her sixteenth year. She was eager to know everything, also matters of medicine." Leonora herself was less satisfied with her progress under Sperling's tutorship. Her Latin suffered especially, due to her having so many irons in the fire, journeys to be made, and, as she wrote, every year she was in the habit of "lying-in, till the number of children totalled ten—in addition to other impediments."

Leonora's cavalier attitude towards "lying-in," which she perceived as just another "impediment," may be explained by her personal code which assigned her a role of equal partner in marriage rather than merely a breeder of children. Considering the high mortality rate of infants and women in childbirth during the 1600s, her statement furthermore measures the strength of her determination to be on equal terms with her husband. Leonora had ten living children and suffered at least three, possibly five, miscarriages between her 15th and 30th year. Yet she offers no complaints or remonstrances against the almost continuous pregnancies or the dangers of giving birth. Bearing children, she knew, was an inevitable consequence of married life, but offspring was not, by her standards, its *raison d'etre* and did not qualify as a reason to neglect individual accomplishments. To realize her goal of being equal, Leonora found it necessary to develop the skills Corfitz already possessed, preserve her feminine attributes to please him, and downplay the "impediments" which were the corollary of her success.

Their life on the square ended three years after Christian's death in 1648, when the rivalry between the Ulfeldts and the new king and queen—Leonora's stepbrother Frederick III and his wife *Sophie Amalie of Brunswick-Lüneberg—made staying in Denmark intolerable. In his effort to balance the state budget, King Frederick had demanded that Corfitz submit records of his financial transactions during his years as high steward, a request which Corfitz interpreted as not only an affront but a vote of no confidence. He refused to comply with Frederick's demands, and the result was renewed investigations which revealed misappropriations and graft extraordinary even by the standards of the 17th century. As a consequence, the Ulfeldts left Copenhagen in July 1651 to seek the support and protection of Queen *Christina of Sweden.

In exchange for considerable monetary concessions, Christina granted both these things, as well as a lease on her castle of Barth in Pomerania. From there, six years later, in 1657, Corfitz Ulfeldt joined Christina's successor, Charles X, in his war against Denmark. By then, the Ulfeldts had made several unsuccessful attempts at reconciliation with King Frederick, and Corfitz would wait no longer. He was willing to make war against his erstwhile king to regain his power and possessions in Denmark. Leonora followed him reluctantly but stood by him as the Swedes won the war and Corfitz, as Swedish counselor, negotiated a devastating treaty for the Danes. The Ulfeldts did not, however, return to Denmark. They chose to stay in Sweden in one of the manors Charles X had granted Corfitz for his valuable assistance in the downfall of his country. But Corfitz was not satisfied with his role as "Swedish" nobleman and overseer of Charles X's newly acquired Danish provinces in southern Sweden. He felt he had been slighted and let his dissatisfaction be known among the Danish nobles. His behavior drew the attention of the Swedish king, who sent first a warning and then an arrest on the charge of collaboration with Corfitz' fellow Danes to reclaim Sweden's Danish possessions for Denmark. Corfitz suffered a stroke, but Leonora defended him very skillfully in a trial held at their house. She conceded noth-

ing, and although the appointed court ruled that Corfitz was to forfeit life and property for treason against the Swedish king, their estates were not confiscated and the Ulfeldts were left in their manor without further interference. Charles X's hesitation to act enabled the Danish ambassador, who at the time was Leonora's brother-in-law, to negotiate their release. He was successful, but before he could relay the good news to his relatives, they had been alarmed by rumors about deportation to Finland. They therefore decided to flee. Corfitz was to go to Lübeck, Leonora to Copenhagen. Unfortunately, Corfitz changed his mind and went to Copenhagen where he contacted Frederick, who calmly awaited the arrival of Leonora. Frederick then confined the pair to the prison of Hammershus on the island of Bornholm in the Baltic Sea.

Their release after a year and a half cost them virtually all their possessions. They were allowed to reside at the manor of Ellensborg, on Funen, which Leonora had inherited after her grandmother. To leave Denmark, they had to secure the king's permission, which after a restless year at Ellensborg they obtained at the intercession of old friends. Once out of the country, Corfitz again started plotting against the Danish king, and Frederick charged him with high treason and sent out a warrant for his arrest. Corfitz fled—he died a year later as he was being rowed down the Rhine—but Leonora, who had gone to England to redeem a loan from Charles II, was apprehended in Dover and brought to Copenhagen for incarceration in the Blue Tower.

In the 22 years she spent there, she distilled all the powers of her being to produce the book she titled *A Monument to Suffering*. It records her inner struggle for mental and emotional balance and accounts for the transformation she would effect from outward loss to inward gain.

Deprived of her clothes and jewelry and dressed in the garments accorded her by the queen, her old rival, Leonora was questioned several times by the king's council who insisted she confess her complicity in her husband's treasonous plans. As she insisted on her ignorance, and remonstrated the unlikeliness of the existence of such plans, she was finally told that Corfitz had been sentenced without trial. Nothing she could say would change his fate; she might, however, be able to move the king to clemency if she would reveal all she knew. She denied any knowledge of treason, professing only to such support and loyalty as became a wife. The result was a political stalemate, and Leonora was left in her cell, unsentenced, to ponder her fate.

Opposite page

ℒeonora

𝒞hristina

𝒰lfeldt

716

Women in World History

Realizing that her good health denied her the death she wished for, she brought a series of accusations against God whom, she thought, was punishing her unjustly. She justified her past actions as those of a loving, loyal wife and after several days and nights of reckoning, she came to the realization that those God loves, He scourges. That enabled her to look at her imprisonment as a trial from which she could decide to emerge victorious. Her deceits notwithstanding, she knew she had been true and responsible in her relationship with Corfitz. She had not failed him—as she believed she had Mauritz—and on that conviction she would build a world in a cell six-by-seven paces.

As she explains to her children in the preface to *Monument*, she could have escaped from the Tower, but she was determined to stay until the king released her and thereby acknowledged the wrong committed against her. Only then could she be of help to them. *Monument to Suffering* shows the implementation of that decision in her turning away from reliance on external power and wealth to confidence in her own well-furnished mind and capable hands. Permitted nothing with which to while away the time, she invented tasks. The prick of a forgotten needle in her feather comforter made her ferret it out and put it to use with embroidery thread she obtained by unravelling her silk stockings. Ten years into her prison term, she wrote *French Biography*, relying on notes written on sugar wrappers with a quill made from a chicken wing dipped in soot and ale. By then, she had been permitted books and writing material, and she subsequently started a series of sketches of famous women. Her aim was to illustrate the equality of origin and performance of men and women. "Wisdom bides in the heart and reason resides in a well appointed brain . . . consequently both sexes have equal access to obtain and acquire [both]." She furthermore argues that "it is unjust to judge the deed by the doer rather then measure the doer by the deed" inasmuch as women are often as courageous as men, who do not always "match their actions to their titles," while "manly strength is often seen in weaker vessels."

Leonora's courage in adversity had proved a model of behavior for Danes even before they learned about her autobiographical *Monument*, which did not appear in print until 1869. With that she assured her fame, not as a saint but as a human being suffering losses and betrayals and prevailing by her ability to seek inspiration and find solace in even the bleakest of surroundings. Leonora's descriptions of the inmates of the Tower, the fleas that infested her floor, and the

projects she invented to stay occupied and alert are unsurpassed in Danish memoirs.

Leonora was 65 years old when King Frederick's son, Christian V, released her. She walked out of the Tower on an evening in May 1685, accompanied by her niece, and spent her last 13 years as head of her household at Maribo Abbey. There, she organized her days, as she had in prison, with reading, writing, and different kinds of handiwork. Most important, she was reunited with her three remaining children. When in March 1698 the old warrior laid down her quill and needle, she was given the spartan funeral she herself had planned in accordance with her philosophy that "no amount of finery will further our cause either here or beyond because, in the final reckoning, we have only ourselves to place in the wager."

SOURCES:

Dalager, Stig og Anne Marie. "Leonora Christina. Et forsvar for kvindekønnet," in *Danske kvindelige forfattere*. I, 35–65. Copenhagen: Gyldendal, 1982.

Historien om en Heltinde. Acta Jutlandica LVIII, Humanistisk Serie 57, Aarhus: Arkona, 1983.

Smith, S. Birket. *Leonora Christina Grevinde Ulfeldt Historie*. Copenhagen: Gyldendal, 1879–81.

———. *Leonora Christina Ulfeldt paa Maribo Kloster*. Copenhagen: Gyldendal, 1872.

Inga Wiehl,
a native of Denmark,
teaches at Yakima Valley Community College,
Yakima, Washington

Ulfhild (fl. 1112)

Queen of Sweden and Denmark. Name variations: Ulvhild. Flourished around 1112; married Inge (d. 1112), king of Sweden and co-regent (r. 1080–1112); became second wife of Niels, king of Denmark (r. 1104–1134); possibly mother of Magnus. Niels' first wife was Margarethe of Vastergotland.

Ulfhild was an important Christian founder in her capacity as queen of Sweden. A highly educated woman, she was a devout Catholic; when she read the sermons of the great Saint Bernard of Clairvaux, Ulfhild became interested in establishing religious houses devoted to Bernard's Cistercian rule. The Cistercian sect followed an ascetic lifestyle, its members wearing simple habits and living in isolated regions, spending their lives praying, fasting, and studying holy texts. Ulfhild succeeded in using her authority and influence to found several Cistercian houses in Sweden, both convents and monasteries. She was thus instrumental in the northward spread of the Cistercian order.

Laura York, M.A. in History,
University of California,
Riverside, California

Ulfhild of Denmark (d. before 1070)

*Duchess of Saxony. Died before 1070; daughter of *Ingigerd Haraldsdottir and Olaf I Hunger, king of Denmark (r. 1086–1095); married Ordulf, duke of Saxony, in 1042; children: Magnus, duke of Saxony (b. about 1045).*

Ulfsdatter, Merete (fl. 1320–1370).

See Margaret I of Denmark for sidebar.

Ulianova, Marie.

See Barkova, Anna for sidebar on Marie Ulyanova.

Ulion, Gretchen (b. 1972).

See Team USA: Women's Ice Hockey at Nagano.

Ullmann, Liv (1939—)

Internationally acclaimed Norwegian actress and director who is particularly known for her work with Ingmar Bergman. Born Liv Johanne Ullmann in Tokyo, Japan, on December 16, 1939; daughter of Viggo Ullmann (an aircraft engineer) and Janna (Lund) Ullmann; married Jappe Stang (a physician), in 1960 (divorced 1965); married Donald Saunders (a real-estate developer), in 1985 (divorced 1995, then reconciled, though not remarried); children: (with Ingmar Bergman) daughter Linn Ullmann (b. 1966, a writer).

Awards: Best Actress of the Year, National Society of Critics in America (1969, 1970, 1974); New York Film Critics' Award (1973, 1974); Hollywood Foreign Press Association's Golden Globe (1973); Best Actress of the Year, Swedish television (1973); Donatello Award (Italy, 1975); Bambi Award (Germany, 1975); nominated for Tony Award as Best Actress for her Broadway debut in A Doll's House *(1975); Los Angeles Film Critics' Award (1976); New York Film Critics' Award (1977); National Board of Review of Motion Pictures Award (1977); Peer Gynt Award (Norway, 1982); *Eleanor Roosevelt Award (1982); Roosevelt Freedom Medal (1984); Dag Hammarskjold Award (1986).*

Made theater debut in role of Anne Frank in the repertory company of Stavanger (1956); appeared in numerous movies and plays (1962–92); met Ingmar Bergman (1964); worked as goodwill ambassador for UNICEF (1980—); directed Sofie *(1992); directed* Kristen Lavransdatter, *a huge hit in Norway (1995); directed* Private Confessions *(Private Conversations) from a screenplay by Bergman (1996); directed* Faithless, *from a screenplay by Bergman (2001).*

Selected filmography: (as actress) Pan *(1965)*, Persona *(1966)*, The Hour of the Wolf *(1968)*, Shame *(1968)*, The Passion of Anna *(1969)*, The Night Visitor *(1971)*, The Emigrants *(1972)*, Cries and Whispers *(1972)*, Pope Joan *(1972)*, Lost Horizon *(1973)*, 40 Carats *(1973)*, The New Land *(1973)*, Zandy's Bride *(1973)*, Scenes from a Marriage *(1974)*, The Abdication *(1974)*, Face to Face *(1975)*, The Serpent's Egg *(1978)*, Autumn Sonata *(1978)*, Richard's Things *(1980)*, The Wild Duck *(1983)*, Love Streams *(1983)*, Baby Boy *(1984)*, Let's Hope It's a Girl *(1985)*, Dangerous Moves *(1985)*, Gaby Brimmer *(Gaby—A True Story, 1986)*, Moscow Adieu *(1986)*, Time of Indifference *(1987)*, La Amiga *(1987)*, The Rose Garden *(1989)*, Mindwalk *(1991)*, The Ox *(1991)*, The Long Shadow *(1992)*; *(as director)* Parting *(late 1970s)*, Sofie *(1992)*, Kristen Lavransdatter *(1995)*, Private Confessions *(Private Conversations, 1996)*, Faithless *(2001)*.

Selected plays: Brand *(1973)*; A Doll's House *(1975)*; Anna Christie *(1977)*; I Remember Mama *(1979)*; Ghosts *(1982)*; Old Times *(1985)*.

Selected writings: Forandringen *(Changes, 1976)*; Choices *(1984)*.

Liv Ullmann opens her autobiographical work *Changes* by recounting the memories of her mother **Janna Lund Ullmann** at the time of Liv's birth, on December 16, 1939, in Tokyo. A mouse ran across the floor, which she considered a sign of good luck; and a nurse bent over her, wondering in apologetic whispers whether the mother herself preferred to break the news to her husband that the child she had borne was another girl.

The Ullmanns would need all the luck a mouse could herald. Four months later, Hitler's troops invaded Norway. Rather than returning to their homeland, Liv's father Viggo Ullmann, an aircraft engineer then employed in Tokyo, opted to bring his wife and two daughters to Canada, where he could work in the displaced Norwegian Air Force. They joined the "Little Norway" colony of exiles outside Toronto, where they lived until 1943, when Viggo accidentally walked into a moving airplane propeller. A transfer to New York for treatment failed to save his life, and he died in a hospital just before the war's end. Two telegrams crossed the Atlantic on that occasion; one carrying the news of his death to relatives in Norway, the other bringing the message that Liv's grandfather had died in the German concentration camp at Dachau.

A few weeks later, Janna Ullmann sailed for Norway with Liv and her older sister on a pas-

senger-carrying freighter. She settled in the family home near Trondheim, where the girls could go to school and enjoy the proximity of relatives. Liv, a small, thin, awkward child, lonely and wild, was desperate to fit in with friends and classmates, but her primary accomplishment was a solitary activity: doing handstands on the handlebars of her bicycle. At dancing school, she was never asked to dance, and she spent her first ball in the ladies' room in her sister's hand-me-down pink silk dress. What she remembers most clearly is the feeling of being "outside," of being "different," a feeling she would battle throughout her life. "I lie in my bed at night and listen to the grownups talking and laughing in the living room," she writes in *Changes*, "and I think that when I grow up, I, too, will be a part of this wonderful world of ideas and laughter. But I am grown up and I am still outside."

She was at home, however, in the world of the imagination. Given to writing and directing plays and offering recitations, she would arrange theater performances in the high school gym. She wrote the plays, directed them, and cast herself in the best parts. Unconcerned about whether or not they had an audience, she and her friends explored the endless possibilities of "theater." At age 17, she announced to her family that she was finished with school and would not waste another day on the road to graduation. Instead, she would become an actress. Members of her father's family tried to dissuade her, appealing to her sense of obligation to the name of Ullmann. One even wrote her mother suggesting that it was fortunate Viggo had died before he learned about his daughter's failure to uphold their standards. (It would not help matters when her first film included a scene of her bathing naked.)

After she was denied admission to Oslo's National Theater School, Ullmann spent the money she had inherited from her father on a six months' stay in London, living at the local YWCA and hoping to gain entrance to the theater world there. Readings each morning with **Irene Brent**, an actress, were the closest she got to the stage. The rest of the day she would spend at the movies; ultimately, she was like other Norwegian women at the YWCA, who "improved their English a little and returned to Norway."

Back in Oslo, Ullmann failed the audition to the Theater School once more. She spent that evening walking the streets, convinced that her life would forever be like the balls where outsiders stood crying in the ladies' room in pink dresses. "In one night it was as if everything known and familiar had been torn away and I was in a place of transition." By morning, she had dimly perceived that her disappointment had a lesson in it, difficult but indispensable for growth: an individual must take responsibility for her life and be willing to accept grief as a stage in her development. She spent time at the library or did odd jobs, such as licking stamps or writing addresses, to make enough money to eat.

Ullmann's first break came with an offer from the repertory company at Stavanger to play the lead in *The Diary of Anne Frank*. Identifying completely with *Anne Frank, she gave a performance that caused critics to rave about her "letting Anne play Anne." "Each night's performance was real for me," she said. "I knew it was theater, but it was the reality of the theater. I felt the way I did as a child. I lived in the world of the imagination but I used real feelings and longings inside these fantasies." Ullmann stayed with the company for three years. On her return to Oslo, she obtained the coveted entry into Oslo's Theater School, where she would play Nora, Ophelia, and Juliet.

In Stavanger, she had experienced more than artistic success, for she had met Jappe Stang, a young doctor whom she married in 1960. Liv liked his courtly persona and romantic dreams, thinking them like her own. Their marriage lasted five years before foundering. "I was dependent and happy because he was the stronger and would protect me . . . [yet] from time to time we would experience a sudden hatred for one another because we felt a limitation we could not define. . . . [I]t was as if we never had occasion to really get to know one another. . . . I grieve above all about the many things we did not say."

The quiet, self-effacing young woman nonetheless was becoming an increasingly articulate actress. Ullmann was fortunate in having excellent directors early on. At the theater in Oslo, she worked with Peter Palitzsch, a former assistant director to Bertolt Brecht, who taught her to develop a balance between intuition and technique. He made her observe herself, constantly questioned her motivation for actions or gestures, and encouraged her to act not simply with her own emotions but with what she had learned about the character she was portraying.

World-renowned director Ingmar Bergman continued the process of development Palitzsch

had started. Ullmann and Bergman met in 1964 and made their first film together that summer. It was an enchanted season for both, artistically and personally. *Persona*, with **Bibi Andersson** and Liv Ullmann, was released to great international acclaim. Ullmann and Bergman also fell so deeply in love that both divorced their mates (his fourth) in anticipation of living together on the Baltic island of Farö, which had been the location of the film.

The second time Ullmann visited the island was to celebrate the raising of the roof on the house they were building for the life they were to share. It was winter, and the return to what had been the setting for a summer of incipient love proved a shock. The weather was cold beyond endurance, the ground was dry and stony, and not even the bottle of Champagne she broke against the rafters could bring back the splendor of the summer. Nevertheless, Bergman and Ullmann spent five years together in the island house, joined after her birth in 1966 by their daughter **Linn Ullmann**. Linn would later become one of Norway's leading journalists and literary critics and publish her first novel *Before You Sleep* in 2000. Reflecting on her relationship with Bergman, Ullmann notes, "We came into one another's life too early and too late. I sought total security, protection—and had a deep need to belong. He sought a mother's embrace: warm and without complications. Perhaps our violent love affair was based on an experience of loneliness both of us had had. . . . Our needs were beyond gratification." Bergman's jealousy became the ultimate corrodent in their relationship. He forbid her contact with friends and relatives, and their dry, barren island with its contorted pine trees became as if a prison for Ullmann; yet there were times she felt more alive there than ever. The short interludes of total happiness interspersed with long periods of pain and sorrow, she believes, helped to bring about the growth—the changes in herself—that she was seeking.

The island's isolated setting provided the backdrop for several other films, among them *The Hour of the Wolf* (1968). In that movie, Ullmann plays a pregnant wife drawn into the madness which is engulfing her husband, a gifted painter. Issues of individual growth and self assertion are further explored in *Shame* (1968) and *The Passion of Anna* (1969), which were also filmed on the island during Ullmann and Bergman's years together. Again, biographical material informs the films' stories, which suggest that the violence and cruelty of the action on screen are due to the characters' inability to see

Liv
Ullmann

themselves truthfully and to overcome their mutual isolation. For Ullmann's performance in *Shame*, considered one of Bergman's best films, movie critic Stanley Kauffmann gave her superior marks. "She now stands with Bibi Andersson and **Vanessa Redgrave** in the front rank of the world's young film actresses. She makes every moment crystalline, the quintessence of what it is about."

Bergman and Ullmann parted ways in 1969. The possible reason, said Ullmann, was that Ingmar seemed to need to view her as a woman "of one piece, with no neuroses." But the couple remained good friends and collaborators. "The best thing about him was how wonderful he was when it was over," she said. "I needed to talk to him every day, and he allowed me to do that. He never hung up on me. Most of them hang up. The terrible thing is when someone leaves you and you hear the door bang." Ullmann raised their daughter alone thereafter, without monetary support from Bergman (who was well able to afford it), although Linn did spend summers with her father. The close relationship between mother and daughter was complicated by Ullmann's many moves and busy work schedule over the years, and she would later express some bewilderment at the less than wholly complimentary portrait of the actress mother in Linn's semi-autobiographical first novel.

I never thought of myself as a muse.... I'm not sure what it is. If it's complimentary, then I want to be it. If it means being a pupil, then I don't want to be it.

—Liv Ullmann

In 1971, Ullmann joined other Bergman actors to film *Cries and Whispers*, an acknowledged and much-honored masterpiece. Ullmann gave a powerful performance as the beautiful and self-centered Maria, who comes to her sister's death bed bringing neither comfort nor compassion. "Liv Ullmann's Maria is a vacuous creative substance," wrote Jay Cocks, "a paradox which is one excellent measure of Bergman's talent and of Miss Ullmann's." *Pauline Kael was less satisfied by Ullmann's 1978 performance in *Autumn Sonata*. "That performance," wrote Kael, "doesn't have the beauty and clarity that her work had earlier. . . . There is a growing helplessness about her work for Bergman—a lack of shape, of completeness. . . . She enters into Ingmar Bergman's disturbed emotions and puts them on the screen, just as he desires; neither of them does the shaping job of an artist in *Autumn Sonata*—their collaboration has become a form of *folie à deux*." Kael, however, would laud Ullmann's 1973 performance in *The Emigrants* to the point of finding it almost beyond discussion. "There don't seem to be any performances. Ullmann and Von Sydow move in and out of frame, courting, marrying, having children. They belong to the region and the life there, and after a while you forget this is the same Liv Ullmann you've seen in the Bergman films."

Perhaps Ullmann herself felt that her inborn desire to please might prove a hindrance

McLean, Kathryn. See *Dunne, Irene* for sidebar.

to the development and exploration of her talent. During the filming of *Autumn Sonata*, *Ingrid Bergman** successfully challenged Ingmar Bergman on character interpretation, while Ullmann looked on with awe. "I used to sit in a corner and admire her," she said, "because this is the kind of woman I wanted to be." At any rate, Ullmann was now developing a repertoire of performances outside Bergman's territory. She had filmed in England, France, Denmark, Rumania, Sweden, and in America several times. Filming in the United States led her to consider living there, although she felt ambivalent about it: "I know that today people will invest in my talent and my personality, but what will happen when I grow too old? When I am no longer a commodity, a marketable article?" And yet, she found much to like in America: "a friendliness and generosity unlike anywhere else in the world. A love of work—a living film history—where one can still meet historical persons at a party, an atmosphere of earlier days which remains in the walls of the studios, in people's consciousness and their conversations." She found some of her best friends there as well.

Meanwhile, she was also successful as a stage actress. Ullmann's initial role was that of Nora in Ibsen's *A Doll's House*, a part she played first in Oslo, then on Broadway. Wrote Kauffmann, "This is the only Nora I have seen who seemed to me in genuine pain, under the smiling and skittering, from the very start: a woman who loves her husband insofar as she then understands him and the meaning of love, who loves her children and the idea of family life, but who is in a twofold anguish: fear of blackmail, for the forgery she committed out of love and discomfort with a society that has made her desperate action the only way she could act, that has emphasized her inferior position as woman." He called the last scene in which Nora leaves her husband and children "credible, courageous and lonely. . . . When she takes off her wedding ring and then holds out her hand for Torvald's ring, we have a performance that is a realized theatrical joy." Not surprisingly, Ullmann won a Tony Award for Best Actress for her performance.

In 1979, Ullmann returned to American theater as the lead in a musical version of *I Remember Mama*, based on ◆ Kathryn McLean's memoirs of growing up in America in a Norwegian immigrant family. Having already been panned for her singing and dancing in the 1973 movie musical *Lost Horizon*, she initially was wary of accepting the part. Upon meeting the play's composer Richard Rodgers, she told him she could neither sing nor dance. As she related, "[H]e said, 'Don't fear.' He was already sick and old and close to 80 at that time, and just sitting at his piano and he was so sweet and thin, and he said, 'Just sing Happy Birthday.' So I sang Happy Birthday and he aged 10 years, just like that." The show nonetheless ran for eight months. Toward the end of the run, Ullmann and other artists staged a campaign to collect money for Cambodian refugees. Moved by the refugees' plight, she traveled to the border of Cambodia and to refugee camps in Hong Kong and Macao, a journey which offered her "images that were never before part of my world." This first journey led to several; named the first female goodwill ambassador for UNICEF, she traveled to Asia, Africa, South America and Haiti.

The late 1970s offered another challenge, when Ullmann was asked to direct a film she had scripted many years earlier. *Parting* covers one morning in the life of an old man, a "guardian of love," as he visits his comatose wife in her hospital room. He feeds her, reads to her from the Bible, and before he leaves, "touches her tenderly." While Ullmann remained active as an actress over the next decade, it would be directing that finally claimed her full interest.

In 1992, she co-wrote and directed *Sofie*, a domestic drama set in Copenhagen late in the 19th century that many critics described as "Bergmanesque." Ullmann next wrote the screenplay for and directed the first screen adaptation of *Sigrid Undset*'s classic *Kristen Lavransdatter*, which after its release in Norway in 1995 became one of the most widely seen movies in that country's history; some half the population is estimated to have seen it during its theatrical run. The following year, Bergman gave her the screenplay for the final installment of his trilogy of films (begun with *Fanny and Alexander* and *Best Intentions*) about his parents' lives. *Private Conversations* (1996, released in the U.S. in 1999 as *Private Confessions*), starring **Pernilla August** and Max von Sydow, was widely acclaimed, and Ullmann received critical praise for both skillful directing and the film's fidelity to Bergman's trademark bleak vision.

Having overcome her earlier reservations, Ullmann now lives in the U.S., and when she is not traveling or working spends most of her time in Florida and Boston with her former husband Donald Saunders, with whom she was reconciled soon after they divorced in 1995. Her most recent movie also had a screenplay by Bergman, based on earlier events in his life; *Faithless* (2001), the story of a passionate affair that destroys a marriage and a family before itself being destroyed by the cruelty of one of the lovers, received glowing reviews for stars **Lena Endre** and Thomans Hanzon and for Ullmann's uncompromising direction. **Daphne Merkin** notes, "What is perhaps most interesting about the film. . . is its focus on the unforeseen harm done to children by the behavior of irresponsible adults." Many of the scenes in the film contain the mute presence of the daughter of one of the lovers, who, Merkin continues, "watches the breakup of her parents' marriage with enormous reproachful eyes." "The child was never in the script," Ullmann said. "Without changing any of [Bergman's] words, because he's very protective of his words, I put her in there, listening, vulnerable, desolate."

SOURCES:
The Guardian [Manchester, England]. January 23, 2001.
International Who's Who. London: Europa, 1993.
Kael, Pauline. *Reeling*. Boston, MA: Little, Brown, 1976.
———. *When the Lights Go Down*. NY: Holt, Rhinehart and Winston, 1980.
Kauffmann, Stanley. *Persons of the Drama*. NY: Harper and Row, 1976.
Merkin, Daphne. "An Independent Woman," in *The New York Times Magazine*. January 21, 2001.
Moritz, Charles, ed. *Current Biography 1973*. NY: H.W. Wilson, 1973.
Ullmann, Liv. *Forandringen*. Oslo: Helge Erichsens Forlag, 1976.
———. *Choices*. NY: Alfred A. Knopf, 1984.

Inga Wiehl,
Yakima Valley Community College,
Yakima, Washington

Ullrich, Luise (1911–1985)

Austrian actress. Born Aloisa Ullrich on October 31, 1911, in Vienna, Austria; died on January 22, 1985, in Munich, Germany; studied acting at the Vienna Theater-Akademie; married Wulf Diether, count of Castell-Rudenhausen (an airport director).

Selected filmography: Der Rebell *(The Rebel, 1932);* Liebelei *(Flirtation, 1933);* Versprich mir nichts! *(Promise Me Nothing!, 1937);* Ich liebe Dich *(I Love You, 1938);* Annelie *(1941);* Nora *(1944).*

Luise Ullrich was born Aloisa Ullrich in 1911 in Vienna, the daughter of a count who was a major in the Austro-Hungarian army, and she grew up in a strict, repressive household. Notes Cinzia Romani, perhaps this was what gave her "that well-bred manner that made her the ideal interpreter of so many stories of women living out lives of renunciation."

Ullrich studied acting at the Vienna Theater-Akademie while in high school, and as a teenager was offered a two-year contract with the Vienna Volkstheater. She also appeared in Richard Billinger's *Rauhnacht* (Brawly Night) at the Lessing-Theater in Berlin. In the audience one night was Luis Trenker, a former mountain guide who wrote, directed, and starred in his own mountain-climbing epics. He offered Ullrich the leading female part in a screenplay he was writing, released as *Der Rebell* (The Rebel) in 1932, in which she had little to do but cry on command and look beseechingly at the hero (Trenker).

Annelie: Die Geschichte eines Lebens (Annelie: The Story of a Life), which earned 6.5 million deutsche marks for its producers—a huge sum in 1941—is considered her best film. An intimate portrayal of an ordinary woman, it drew huge audiences of women eager to see a depiction on screen of a life so like their own. The film was also a piece of Nazi propaganda, showing how Annelie was devoted to the Fatherland, but as Romani noted, "There were also truly touching moments, as when Annelie, addressing her son, who is about to leave for the front, said, '*Im Leben übersteht man alles. Es ist nicht leicht, aber mit de Zeit lernt man's.*' (In this life one survives everything. It's not easy, but with time you learn.)"

The 1944 film *Nora* was a distorted version of Ibsen's *A Doll's House*, twisted to emphasize the importance of marriage rather than the stifling role it can impose on women. In the film, Ullrich plays a woman, writes Romani, who "seems to be modeled on the archetype of the woman who has learned to atone for sins that exist only in the mind of the one who condemns her."

After World War II ended, Ullrich continued to appear in television series and films. She published her memoirs, *Komm auf die Schaukel, Luise; Balance eines Lebens* (Come onto the Swing, Luise: Appraisal of a Life), in 1943. She also published a novel *Ricarda* in 1954, and several short stories, one of which appeared in the collection *The 56 Best Short Stories in the World*. Ullrich died in 1985 in Munich.

SOURCES:

Romani, Cinzia. *Tainted Goddesses: Film Stars of the Third Reich*. NY: Sarpedon, 1992.

Kelly Winters,
freelance writer

Ulmann, Doris (1882–1934)

American portrait photographer. Born in 1882 in New York City; died in 1934 in New York City; daughter of Bernard Ulmann and Gertrude (Maas) Ulmann; educated at public schools; studied with Lewis Hine at Ethical Culture School in New York; studied psychology and law at Columbia University; studied photography with Clarence White at Columbia University and at his school; married Charles H. Jaeger (a doctor), before 1917 (divorced 1925).

Doris Ulmann was born in 1882 and grew up in a prosperous household on Park Avenue in New York City. Her mother died when she was young, and she traveled abroad with her father, eventually learning to speak French, German, and Italian. As a child, she had a stomach ulcer; this was corrected by surgery, but she remained frail all her life and would endure several more operations.

From 1900 to 1903, Ulmann studied at the Ethical Culture School in New York with Lewis Hine, whose photographs of immigrants and laborers would shortly gain him fame and lead to changes in U.S. child-labor laws. For awhile, she was interested in psychology and law and took classes in those subjects at Columbia University. Around this time, however, Ulmann became seriously interested in photography, and in 1907 began studying the art with Clarence White (a contemporary of Alfred Stieglitz, who was also at Columbia). When White opened the Clarence H. White School of Photography in 1914, Ulmann became one of its students; a fellow classmate was *Laura Gilpin.

In the 1920s, Ulmann published her photographs in three books: *Portraits, College of Physicians and Surgeons* (1920), *Portraits, Medical Faculty, Johns Hopkins University* (1922), and *A Portrait Gallery of American Editors* (1925). In 1925, she began to shoot scenes of rural life, especially of people who lived in Dunkard, Mennonite, and Shaker communities in New York, Pennsylvania, Virginia, and New England. In 1927, she hired folk singer John Jacob Niles to travel with her by automobile while she photographed the people of Appalachia. In 1929 and 1930, she turned her attention to Gullah people on the islands of South Carolina and in 1933 published 70 of their portraits in *Roll, Jordan, Roll*, with text by *Julia Peterkin. That same year, she worked with Allen Henderson Eaton to photograph people engaged in traditional crafts in the Southern Highlands of the United States. Ulmann, who had contributed photographs to *Theatre Art Monthly, Bookman, Spur*, and *Vanity Fair*, died the following year in New York City.

Kelly Winters,
freelance writer

Ulpia Marciana (fl. 98–117 CE)

Roman noblewoman. Name variations: Marciana. Born Ulpia Marciana; daughter of M. Ulpius Traianus; sister of the Roman emperor Trajan; married C. Salonius Matidius Patruinus; children: Matidia I.

Ulrica Eleanora (1688–1741)

Queen of Sweden. Name variations: Ulrika Eleanor; Ulrika Eleanora; Ulrica Eleanora von Simmern; Ulrike Eleonore. Born on January 23, 1688, at Stockholm palace; died on November 24, 1741, in Stockholm; daughter of Carl XI or Charles XI (1655–1697), king of Sweden (r. 1660–1697), and Queen Ulrica Eleanora of Denmark (1656–1593); sister of Charles XII (1682–1718), king of Sweden (r. 1697–1718); married Frederick (1676–1751), landgrave of Hesse-Cassel, later Frederick I, king of Sweden (r. 1720–1751), on March 24, 1715; no children. Frederick's first wife was *Louise Dorothea of Brandenburg (1680–1705).

Ulrica Eleanora was one of three reigning queens in Swedish history, and was the last monarch of the Pfalz dynasty. A princess of the Swedish royal house of Pfalz, she was the daughter of King Charles XI and *Ulrica Eleanora of Denmark. Her brother became Charles XII on their father's death in 1697; by 1700, Sweden was embroiled in wars with Russia, Denmark, Poland, and Prussia. The burdens of the wars on the Swedish economy and people, coupled with the king's absence from the country since 1700, almost led to a coup d'etat in 1714. In that year, many members of the Estates voted to make Ulrica regent of the realm, as she indicated that she would bring immediate peace. However, royalist supporters of Charles XII won out in the political crisis which followed.

In 1715, Ulrica became the second wife of the German prince Frederick, landgrave of Hesse-Cassel (later Frederick I, king of Sweden). Together they formed the Hessian party at court, which pressed King Charles XII to name Ulrica heir to the throne since he was unmarried and had no legitimate children. The king refused to name any successor; when he was killed in battle in November 1718, Ulrica proclaimed herself queen. The Swedish senate would not recognize her claim to inherit because she was married, and her nephew the duke of Holstein-Gottorp also contested her right to reign. However, after negotiations between the senate and Ulrica's supporters, she was elected queen on January 23, 1719, her 31st birthday. In return, Ulrica

had to agree to relinquish much of the absolutist royal authority previously held by Swedish monarchs, and accept a new constitution establishing parliamentary government with authority over royal policy decisions. The period of her reign is known as the founding of the "Age of Liberty" because of the new limitations on royal power. She was crowned on March 17, 1719.

Queen Ulrica faced a very difficult political and social situation. Sweden was losing the war Charles XII had been fighting constantly for almost two decades, the treasury was depleted, the economy ruined, and the Swedish people wanted peace. Sweden's role as the great power of northern Europe ended when the senate and Queen Ulrica chose to bring peace at any cost and conceded defeat to Prussia, Denmark, and Russia, losing much of Sweden's continental territories to the victors.

Despite the limitations placed on her, the senate found Ulrica insufficiently submissive to their political authority, and in February 1720 it offered the crown to her husband and consort, Prince Frederick. Ulrica was forced to abdicate after only one year, the shortest reign in Swedish history. On her abdication, the senate passed a new constitution further restricting royal power. Her husband eagerly accepted the crown as King Frederick I, and Ulrica became queen-consort.

Ulrica was active as a patron of the arts, sciences, and literature during her 20 years as queen-consort. She died in Stockholm in 1741 at age 53; King Frederick died in 1751. Because Ulrica had had no children, Frederick was succeeded by her nephew and former political rival, Frederick of Holstein-Gottorp (Adolphus Frederick).

SOURCES:

Bain, R. Nisbet. *Charles XII*. NY: Putnam, 1895.
Jackson-Laufer, Guida M. *Women Who Ruled*. Santa Barbara, CA: ABC-CLIO, 1990.

Laura York, M.A. in History,
University of California,
Riverside, California

Ulrica Eleanora of Denmark (1656–1693)

Queen of Sweden. Name variations: Ulrica Eleanor the Elder; Ulrika Eleanor or Ulrika Eleanora. Born on September 11, 1656; died on August 6, 1693; daughter of Frederick III (1609–1670), king of Denmark and Norway (r. 1648–1670), and *Sophie Amalie of Brunswick-Lüneburg (1628–1685); married Carl XI or Charles XI (1655–1697), king of Sweden (r. 1660–1697); children: *Hedwig Sophia (1681–1708, who married Frederick IV of Holstein-Gottorp);

Charles XII (1682–1718), king of Sweden (r. 1697–1718); *Ulrica Eleanora (1688–1741), queen of Sweden (r. 1719–1720); Gustav (b. 1683); Ulrich (b. 1684); Frederick (b. 1685); Charles Gustav (b. 1686).

Ulrika or Ulrike.
Variant of Ulrica.

Ulster, countess of.
See Margaret de Burgh (d. 1303).
See Maud Plantagenet (c. 1310–c. 1377).
See Elizabeth de Burgh (1332–1363).
See Mortimer, Philippa (1355–1382).

Ultrogotte (fl. 558).
See Vultrogotha.

Ulvhild (fl. 1112).
See Ulfhild.

Ulyanova, Marie.
See Barkova, Anna for sidebar.

Uma no Naishi (fl. 10th c.).
See Murasaki Shikibu for sidebar.

Umeki, Miyoshi (1929—)
Japanese-born American actress who won an Academy Award for her performance in Sayonara. Born in 1929 in Otaru, Hokkaido, Japan.

Miyoshi Umeki began working as a radio and nightclub singer when she was still a teenager in Japan. In the 1950s, she came to the United States, where she first appeared on television. Her American breakthrough came with a role in *Sayonara* (1957), an adaptation of the James Michener novel set during the Korean War, starring Marlon Brando and **Miiko Taka**. Umeki won an Academy Award (Oscar) for Best Supporting Actress; she then appeared on Broadway in *Flower Drum Song*. The actress later returned to television in "The Courtship of Eddie's Father," and made a number of other films, including *Cry for Happy* (1961), *Flower Drum Song* (1961), *The Horizontal Lieutenant* (1962), and *A Girl Named Tamiko* (1963).

Kelly Winters,
freelance writer

Umilita or Umilta (1226–1310).
See Humilitas of Faenza.

Um Kalthum (c. 1898–1975)
Famous Arabic singer, a dominant force in the Arab world for several decades, whose recordings are still widely listened to, and whose political influence in Egypt was critical after the Israeli-Egyptian war in 1967. Name variations: Um Kalthoum; Oum Kalsoum; Umm Kulthum; Umm Thulum; Star of the East. Born Fatma el-Zahraa Ibrahim in the delta village of Tamay al-Zahirah (or Tammay al-Zahayrah) probably in 1898 but possibly in 1900; died of a cerebral hemorrhage on February 3, 1975; daughter of poor peasants; had one brother; other siblings unknown; married Dr. Hassan el-Hifnawi (a prosperous skin specialist), in 1954.

After World War I, went to Cairo and eventually gave public performances; took the stage name Um Kalthum, the name of one of the daughters of Mohammed; toured several Arabic countries (1932); gave the first broadcast for Radio Egypt (1934); awarded the highest decoration an Egyptian woman could receive, the Al-Kamal medal, from King Farouk (1944); gained influence in Gamal Abdel Nasser's government (1950s); married and had surgery for a goiter in U.S., both events of great importance in Egypt (1954); continued to give concerts until her death (1975).

For decades at 10 PM, on the first Thursday of each month, the Arab world came to a halt. Traffic slowed to a crawl; coffee shops emptied; wealthy Arabs left their bridge tables. Throughout the Muslim crescent, millions gathered around their radios to hear a woman sing. Many cried as they listened to the magical voice of the singer, who could hold a single note for 90 seconds. These concerts, which usually consisted of three songs, often lasted five hours, well into the night, but as Friday is the Muslim holy day, everyone could sleep late the next morning before going to the mosque. When the Nightingale of the Nile sang, all Arabs—rich or poor, female or male, religious or agnostic—were united. When she sang, she ruled the Arab world.

Um Kalthum was born in the Egyptian delta village of Tamay al-Zahirah, probably in 1898, the daughter of poor peasants. Her father frequently sang at religious ceremonies and led the local choir in Sebelawin, a small town northeast of Cairo. As he taught Um Kalthum and her brother to sing verses from the Koran, he soon noticed the unusual quality of his daughter's voice. Because women were not supposed to be seen in public, he dressed her in boys' clothes so that she could sing with the choir. Recognizing the girl's great talent, her father continued to coach her. She made her first professional appearance at age seven, earning 30¢ for performing at a village wedding. Within a month, her fee had been increased to $7.50, an enormous sum even in the modern world for Egypt's impoverished *fellahin*. For some years, she traveled with her father from village to village, on foot, by donkey, or, when they could afford it, on the wooden benches of a third-class train.

It has been said that no Westerner can really understand the Arab mind without understanding the singing of Um Kalthum. Her music seems repetitive and endless to Westerners whose popular songs tend to be three or four minutes long. Arab songs, on the other hand, last for hours. Quarter-tone intervals are important in Arabic music, while the short musical phrase dominates the West. In Arabic music, a melodic line is played by one instrument or several instruments in unison accompanied by percussion instruments, while polyphonic music performed by choruses and symphonies is more typical of the West. Rather than the eight-tone scale used in the West, Arabic music is built on maquamaat, modes or scales divided into seven steps; thus an octave can be divided into 24 quarter tones (though not every maquaam has quarter tones), while in Western music an octave would be di-

vided into 13 semitones. Progression in an Arabic melody does not move, except in rare cases. Unlike Western music, which was first developed for use in the church and thus reflects a certain sanctity, Arabic music and songs often originated in the homes of the wealthy and the palaces of kings, and can be more worldly and diverting.

Um Kalthum's music appealed largely to the poorer classes who refused to assimilate Western culture. Her music was from their world, rather than from the Western world which they did not understand. The upper strata of Egyptian society mimicked the West and enjoyed ballets, symphonies, and operas. The majority of Egyptians, however, never gave up their ancient cultural heritage. They remembered the stories of a glorious time when spices, silks, precious stones, and perfumes were sought by Europeans whose standards of living were vastly inferior to that enjoyed by those in the Arab world—a time when extensive contact with China and India brought luxuries undreamt of in Europe. Arabs had also been intellectually dominant; they invented Arabic numerals which allowed precise solution of

Um Kalthum

mathematical problems, and their libraries held priceless manuscripts from ancient Greece and Rome, which they used to advance their knowledge of science, medicine, and classical literature. Europeans were culturally inferior in the minds of most Arabs, a view which is still widely held.

After World War I, Um Kalthum moved to Cairo. One evening during Ramadan, the holy month of fasting, she and her troup performed before Sheik Abdul Ala Mohammed, the greatest singer of the time. At the end of the performance, the sheik offered to find her work in Cairo. Greatly excited by the prospect, she waited a year before a performance for a rich merchant was arranged. The experience was a disaster. The merchant treated her like a peasant, the money she earned was stolen, and she returned home. It was not until 1923 that supporters convinced her to sing in a Cairo theater. Still, she faced many barriers. Her father, who worried about her reputation, once placed a notice on the stage, "Do not touch." He also insisted that she be addressed as Mrs. Um Kalthum, in order to protect her good name.

Not before or since has there been a more popular singer in the Arab world. Um Kalthum sang of love and sorrow with such emotion that many people . . . cried. Her voice was magical, her prowess extraordinary.

—*Jehan Sadat

By the mid-1920s, she was no longer afraid of Cairo, which at the time was embracing the nationalistic ideas of the new prime minister Saad Zaglul and his Wafd party. After meeting the poet Ahmed Rami, who considered her a muse for his art, Um Kalthum sang his poems about absolute love that hovers between the sacred and the profane, the spirit and the flesh. She often used the word *habid* or *beloved*, which is also one of Allah's many names. When Um Kalthum became a star still in her early 20s, she made many changes in her performances. She added an orchestra, unbound her hair, exchanged her men's clothes for feminine Western dress, and clutched a silk scarf in her hand that became a trademark. As she sang, she would hypnotically tear the scarf into pieces. By the time Sheik Abdul died in 1927, she was choosing her own texts and having them set to music. In 1932, she toured Libya, Lebanon, Syria, and Paris. She then began performing on the radio, launching the station the "Voice of Cairo" with one of her songs. Radio Egypt began broadcasting her concerts in 1934.

"Egypt is a country overburdened with history and geography," writes one historian, "a history overwhelming yet inspiring, a geography restricting yet lifegiving." Um Kalthum's professional life reflected that rich heritage. Throughout her career, her influence was political as well as musical. Although nominally a part of the Turkish Empire until 1914, Egypt had been a British protectorate from the late 1870s until 1922, when (despite Britain's continued power in the country) it officially became a kingdom under the rule of King Farouk. Um Kalthum's singing had an enormous influence on the king and members of government. One premier, for example, dropped plans to arrest a powerful political enemy when she warned, "Don't do it; he's too popular." Like everyone else, King Farouk was besotted with her, and she was frequently a guest at the royal palaces. One day in 1944, apparently acting on impulse, he had himself driven to the National Sporting Club where Um Kalthum was singing and awarded her the highest decoration an Egyptian woman could receive—the Al-Kamal medal. Though the Egyptian upper crust took this as an affront (she was, after all, the daughter of poor peasants), the king's action was a hit with the general populace. It was "the most popular thing Farouk ever did," said one knowledgeable leader.

Um Kalthum could not separate herself from politics even if she wished; she personified the spirit of Egypt. Farouk's close association with the British and his free-spending ways made him increasingly unpopular throughout Egypt, and he was overthrown in 1952. Because the king had long supported Um Kalthum, some Egyptian revolutionaries felt it was time to oust her as well. She was forbidden to sing, and the new government's newspaper wrote that "only hashish-eaters listen to her." Gamal Abdel Nasser, the revolutionary leader whose government now ruled Egypt, was well aware that the singer had been one of his ardent supporters despite her long association with the former king. He immediately called the newspaper's editor to his office and growled, "Do you say I am a hashish-eater?" Like most Egyptians, Nasser listened regularly to Um Kalthum, and the ban on her singing was immediately rescinded. When Nasser announced the nationalization of the Suez Canal, his radio speech was preceded by one of her songs.

In 1954, Um Kalthum developed a goiter due to a hyperthyroid condition, a large growth in her throat that threatened to stop the Nightingale of the Nile from singing forever. Her illness created an international crisis; no Egyptian doctor would operate for fear of harming her vocal chords. Doctors in Europe were also reluctant to touch her throat. Egyptian newspapers reporting the dreadful news were framed in black, as they are after the death of someone important. Finally recognizing the value of a diplomatic gesture, the American ambassador to Egypt arranged for Um Kalthum to be treated at the U.S. Naval Hospital near Washington. One of the largest crowds in the history of Cairo saw her off at the airport. The Egyptian ambassador was a daily visitor at the hospital; the government issued communiqués about her medical progress. Fortunately, the operation was a success. In gratitude, Um Kalthum made a number of broadcasts on the Voice of America's Arab-language service.

That same year, at age 49, Um Kalthum married in the greatest secrecy. This was her second attempt at marriage. Six years later, she had announced her engagement to Mahmoud el-Sherif, a little-known musician, but the revelation had raised a storm of protest. Letters poured into newspapers, complaints were shouted at concerts, and strangers stopped her on the street. When King Farouk had forbidden the match, she bowed to public pressure. This time, however, she did not involve the public in her private life, and only two months after the ceremony had taken place was her marriage to Dr. Hassan el-Hifnawi, a prosperous skin specialist, announced. The Egyptian government carefully timed the disclosure so that as little tension as possible would be aroused among her many fans. Unlike the earlier liaison, this marriage caused no outcry whatsoever despite the fact that Dr. el-Hifnawi was a divorced father with two children.

When Egypt was defeated by Israel in 1967, Um Kalthum was around 70, not in good health, and rarely appeared outside Cairo. But she rallied to help her country. In the financial crisis which followed the war, she undertook a European tour to raise money for Egypt. In Paris, she sang for five hours, two evenings in a row, raising hundreds of thousands of francs. After returning to Egypt, she continued to tour Arab nations. Many at the time called her "Nasser's Bomb" and the "Nun of Islam," but as always her singing seemed to soothe millions and gradually the crisis waned.

When Um Kalthum died of a cerebral hemorrhage on February 3, 1975, millions mourned her passing. Even now her voice continues to dominate the Arab world. The Egyptian-born actor Omar Sharif noted that each morning she is reborn in the hearts of over 100 million Arabs. It is perhaps indicative of Western ignorance that so little is known about this woman whose cultural and political influence were so great. Wise in the use of power, she was a force for good in her lifetime and remains so today. "The legendary Um Kalthum was no mere singer," wrote a historian, "and her art, to millions of devotees throughout the Arab world, was no mere entertainment but an all-encompassing spiritual experience."

SOURCES:
"Egypt's Golden Voice," in *Newsweek*. Vol. 48, no. 4. July 23, 1956, p. 71.
"Egyptians Throng Funeral of Um Kalthoum, the Arabs' Acclaimed Singer," in *The New York Times*. February 6, 1975, p. 3.
El Araby, Kadri M.G. "Arabesque: The Legacy of Islamic Artistry in Europe," in *The Arab World*. Vol. 18, nos. 3–4. March–April 1972, pp. 10–17.
Gaskill, Gordon. "Mighty Voice of Um Kalthum," in *Life*. Vol. 52, no. 22. June 1, 1962, pp. 15–16.
Hopwood, Derek. *Egypt: Politics and Society 1945–1981*. London: George Allen & Unwin, 1982.
McErvin, Sabrina, and Carol Prumhuber. *Women: Around the World and Through the Ages*. Wilmington, DE: Atomium Books, 1991.
"The Middle East: Personalities of the Arab World," in *The Illustrated London News*. Vol. 247, no. 6587. October 30, 1965, p. 31.
Sadat, Jehan. *A Woman of Egypt*. NY: Simon and Schuster, 1987.
"Singer's death mourned by Arab world," in *The Times* (London). February 4, 1975, p. 8.
"Um Kalthoum, Egyptian Singer, A Favorite of Millions Is Dead," in *The New York Times*. February 4, 1975.

SUGGESTED READING:
Danielson, Virginia Louise. *"The Voice of Egypt": Umm Kulthum, Arabic Song, and Egyptian Society in the Twentieth Century*. Chicago, IL: University of Chicago Press, 1997.

RELATED MEDIA:
Umm Thulum: A Voice Like Egypt, documentary by Michal Goldman, Vanguard video, 1996 (English and Arabic with English subtitles).

John Haag,
Associate Professor of History,
University of Georgia,
Athens, Georgia

Umm al-Hakim (c. 590–c. 640).
See Zaynab bint Jahsh.

Umm al-Mu'minin (c. 613–678).
See A'ishah bint Abi Bakr.

Umm Kulthum (c. 1898–1975).
See Um Kalthum.

Umm Thulum (c. 1898–1975).
See Um Kalthum.

Under, Marie (1883–1980)
Acclaimed Estonian poet. Born in 1883 in Tallinn, Estonia; died in 1980; divorced first husband, 1917; married Artur Adson (a poet), in 1924.

Selected writings: Sonetid *(Sonnets, 1917);* Eeloitseng *(Budding, 1918);* Sinine puri *(Blue Sail, 1918);* Verivalla *(A Flowing of Blood, 1920);* Hääl varjust *(Voice from the Shadows, 1927);* Room Ühest ilusast päevast *(Delight in a Lovely Day, 1928);* Õnnevarjutus *(The Eclipse of Happiness, 1929);* Lageda taeva all *(Under the Open Sky, 1930);* Kivi südamelt *(A Stone from My Heart, 1935);* Ja liha sai Sonaks *(And the Flesh Became Word, 1936);* Mureliku suuga *(With Careworn Lips, 1942);* Sädemed tuhas *(Sparks in the Ashes, 1954);* Child of Man *(in English translation, 1955).*

Considered perhaps the finest poet in the Estonian language, Marie Under was born in 1883 in Tallinn, Estonia, the daughter of a teacher. She attended school in Germany and later worked as a governess, cashier, and clerk in a newspaper office. She then married and accompanied her husband to Russia, returning to Estonia in 1906. The marriage was an increasingly unhappy one, however, and Under began devoting more energy to literature and the company of other writers in Tallinn. In 1917, she divorced and published her first book, a collection of verse, *Sonetid* (Sonnets). The work's sensuality, spontaneity, and

Estonian postage stamp issued in honor of Marie Under in 1996.

passion were considered scandalous at the time. In 1924, she married Artur Adson, a poet.

Marie Under published *Eeloitseng* (Budding) and *Sinine puri* (Blue Sail) in 1918. In *Verivalla* (A Flowing of Blood) from 1920, she focuses on the "tragedy" of human life, and in the 1929 work *Onnevarjutus* (The Eclipse of Happiness) she attempts to modernize the ballad form.

In the 1930s and 1940s, Under turned to lyric verse, with *Lageda taeva all* (Under the Open Sky), published in 1930, and *Kivi südamelt* (A Stone from My Heart), in 1935. She expressed her feelings about her mother's death as well as the destruction brought about by World War II and the occupation of her country in *Mureliku suuga* (With Careworn Lips, 1942). In 1944, Under and her husband moved to Sweden, where she wrote more about the Soviet occupation of her homeland in *Sädemed tuhas* (Sparks in the Ashes, 1954). Much of her later work dwelt on similar themes.

As the *Columbia Dictionary of Modern European Literature* notes, Under "has been compared to both Goethe and Rainer Maria Rilke, yet she is unmistakably her own" with poems that encompass both fierce images of nature and human experience and metaphysics. She wrote for six decades, until her death in 1980.

SOURCES:
Columbia Dictionary of Modern European Literature. 2nd ed. NY: Columbia University Press, 1980.
Pynsent, Robert B., ed. *Reader's Encyclopedia of Eastern European Literature.* NY: HarperCollins, 1993.

Kelly Winters,
freelance writer

Underhill, Evelyn (1875–1941)

English poet, novelist, and writer on mysticism. Name variations: (pseudonym) John Cordelier. Born in December 1875 in Wolverhampton, England; died on June 15, 1941; daughter of Sir Arthur Underhill (a barrister) and Alice Lucy (Ironmonger) Underhill; educated privately and at King's College for Women, London; married Hubert Stuart Moore (a barrister), in 1907.

Selected writings: Grey World: A Novel *(1904);* The Lost Word *(1907);* Miracles of Our Lady St. Mary *(1908);* The Column of Dust *(1909);* Mysticism: A Study in the Nature and Development of Man's Spiritual Consciousness *(1911); (under pseudonym John Cordelier)* The Path of Eternal Wisdom *(1911); (as John Cordelier)* The Spiral Way *(1912);* Immanence: A Book of Verses *(1912);* The Mystic Way *(1913);* Practical Mysticism *(1914);* Ruysbroeck *(1915);* Theophanies: A Book of Verses *(1916);* Jaco-

pone da Todi *(1919);* The Essentials of Mysticism *(1920);* The Life of the Spirit and the Life of To-Day *(1922);* The Mystics of the Church *(1925);* Concerning the Inner Light *(1926);* Man and the Supernatural *(1927);* The House of the Soul *(1929);* The Golden Sequence *(1932);* Mixed Pasture: Twelve Essays and Addresses *(1933);* The School of Charity *(1934);* Worship *(1936);* The Spiritual Life: Four Broadcast Talks *(1937);* The Mystery of Sacrifice *(1938);* Abba *(1940);* Fruits of the Spirit *(1942).*

One of the leading writers on mysticism, Evelyn Underhill wrote numerous books on the subject, including two that are considered classics, *Mysticism* (1911) and *Worship* (1936). Although many members of her extended family were religious and her uncle was a priest, Underhill's immediate family members were not churchgoers. Her father, a barrister-at-law, preferred sailing on his yacht, and his only child became, like him, an excellent boat-racer. They often sailed with friends of the family, the Stuart Moores, and Underhill entered into what would prove to be a happy marriage with Hubert Stuart Moore in 1907. At about the same time, she experienced a religious conversion and began studying the lives of the mystics. She turned her upstairs study into a prayer room, where she wrote and prayed for at least an hour each day.

After 1900, Underhill published novels and light verse, but she came to prominence with *Mysticism* (1911), which has gone through a number of editions and is still in print. The book brought her to the attention of many prominent theologians and writers, including Baron von Hügel, who would be her mentor for the rest of his life. Upon his advice to balance intellect with action ("you badly want de-intellectualizing," he noted), she visited the poor and tried to assist them, which made her more aware of her own privileged position and grateful for the gifts in her life.

Underhill was well versed in the liturgical field. She lectured at Manchester College, Oxford, in 1921, and after 1924 became increasingly sought after to lecture and run retreats, an activity then fairly unusual for a woman in the Anglican Church. In addition to lecturing, she was a prolific writer, producing a book each year for 14 years. In 1927, Underhill became the first woman to be appointed an outside lecturer at Oxford University, when she was made a fellow of King's College. In the early 1940s, she began suffering from asthma and overwork. She died on June 15, 1941, and was buried at St. John's Parish Church in Hampstead.

SOURCES:
Deen, Edith. *Great Women of the Christian Faith.* NY: Harper & Row, 1959, pp. 389–392.
Kunitz, Stanley J., and Howard Haycraft, eds. *Twentieth Century Authors.* NY: H.W. Wilson, 1942.

Kelly Winters,
freelance writer

Underhill, Miriam O'Brien (1898–1976).

See O'Brien, Miriam.

Underwood, Agness Wilson
(1902–1984)

American journalist and first woman city editor of a major daily newspaper. Name variations: Aggie Underwood. Born Agness Wilson on December 17, 1902, in San Francisco, California; died of a heart attack on July 3, 1984, in Greeley, Colorado; daughter of Cliff Wilson and Mamie (Sullivan) Wilson; married and divorced; children: Mary Evelyn Underwood (who married William A. Weed); H. George M. Underwood.

Known as "Aggie," Agness Wilson Underwood began working as a reporter for the *Los Angeles Review* in 1931, after being with the paper for five years as a switchboard operator. She wrote for the paper for four years, and then served from 1935 to 1947 as a police beat reporter for the *Los Angeles Herald-Express* (which in 1962 became the *Los Angeles Herald-Examiner*). Underwood would go to great lengths to get a story, once hiding a murder suspect in her home for several hours in order to get an exclusive from the woman.

In 1947, Underwood became the paper's city editor, the first woman to hold that job at any major daily in the country. She also received a "headliner" award from Theta Sigma Phi, the National Women's Journalism fraternity, that year. In 1964, she was appointed assistant managing editor of the *Herald-Examiner*, a post she held until her retirement in 1968. Aggie Underwood was known to be tough, energetic, and imaginative; she wrote about her life experiences in her autobiography, *Newspaper Woman* (1949).

Kelly Winters,
freelance writer

Underwood, Sophie Kerr (1880–1965).

See Kerr, Sophie.

Undset, Sigrid (1882–1949)

Norwegian writer of novels, short stories and essays who was awarded the Nobel Prize for literature in

1928 and honored by her country with the Norwegian Grand Cross of the Order of Saint Olav in 1945. Born in Kalundborg, Denmark, on May 20, 1882; died at the hospital of Lillehammer on June 10, 1949; daughter of Ingwald Undset (a distinguished archaeologist) and (Anna) Charlotte (Gyth) Undset; married Anders Castus Svarstad (a painter), in 1913 (marriage annulled); children: son Anders (b. 1913); daughter Maren Charlotte (b. 1915); son Hans (b. 1919).

Converted to Catholicism (1924); received the Nobel Prize for Literature (1928) and the Grand Cross of the Order of Saint Olav (1945).

Selected works: Martha Oulie *(1907);* The Happy Age *(1908);* Gunnar's Daughter *(1909);* Jenny *(1911);* Four Stories *(1912);* Spring *(1914);* Tales of King Arthur and the Knights of the Round Table *(1914);* The Wise Virgins *(1918); "A Woman's Point of View" and "Postscript to the Fourth Commandment" (1919);* Kristin Lavransdatter *(1920–22); "Saint Hallvard's Life, Death and Miracles" and* Olav Audunsson in Hestviken *(1925);* Olav Audunsson and His Children *(1927);* Stages on the Road *and* The Wild Orchid *(1929);* The Burning Bush, *"Saint Olav, Norway's King" and "Sigurd and His Brave Companions" (1931);* Ida Elisabeth, *and "Christmas and Twelfth Night" (1932);* The Longest Years *and* Saga of Saints *(1934); "Progress, Race, Religion" (1935);* The Faithful Wife *(1936);* Men, Women and Places *(1938);* Madame Dorthea *(1939);* Happy Times in Norway *and* Return to the Future *(1942);* Articles and Tales from Wartime *(1952);* Catherine of Siena *(1954).*

Sigrid Undset, whose work was termed "an Iliad of the North," was the recipient of the Nobel Prize for Literature in 1928. This award was followed by the Grand Cross of the Order of Saint Olav in 1945, which was presented as much for her patriotic activities as for her writing. Although probably most well known for her *Kristin Lavransdatter,* published in 1920–22, Undset spent decades writing and exploring questions of morality, loyalty, sexuality, and spirituality with particular focus on the relationship between wife and husband. Her childhood exposure to history, and later meticulous research, made possible the powerful Middle Ages settings in which her most lauded works often found expression. An ardent patriot and anti-Nazi, Undset housed refugees during World War II, was a strong voice of opposition to Nazi aggression, and lost one of her sons to the war after the Nazis landed in Norway in 1940.

She was born in Kalundborg, Denmark, on May 20, 1882. Her mother **Charlotte Gyth Und**set was Danish, and her father Ingwald Undset was Norwegian. Ingwald, a distinguished archaeologist, has been considered perhaps the greatest influence in Undset's life, though he did not live to see her reach adolescence. His international reputation was achieved with *The Beginnings of the Iron Age in Northern Europe*, a book published in 1881. While he traveled a good deal for work, the family stayed with relatives until Ingwald received an appointment at the Museum of Antiquities which was associated with the University of Kristiania. Notes Olga S. Opfell of the young Sigrid's influences: "Almost before she could talk, the little girl babbled of 'blunt-butted axe' and 'shaft-hold axe' when her father showed her various implements. . . . When the museum was closed, Sigrid was allowed to run about the galleries. If she pointed at some fine things in the cabinets, they were lifted out, and she was decorated with necklaces and rings of gold and silver from the iron age."

While Ingwald provided his daughter with an early passion for archaeology and botany, her mother tutored her in both Norwegian and Danish history from the time Sigrid was five. Undset's grounding in early history would become intrinsic to her literature about life in northern Europe in the Middle Ages. In 1891, Sigrid, an independent-minded, precocious child, noted for her imagination, read *Njäl's Saga*, an Icelandic family saga which she would later credit as a turning point in her life.

The *History of Norwegian Literature* notes that Ingwald sensed that his death would come at a comparatively young age, and between the years of 1888 to 1892 he poured himself into efforts to complete as much of his work possible. During his last months, father and daughter read the Icelandic sagas in Danish together, with Ingwald occasionally requesting that his daughter read to him in Old Norse. After writing *From Akershus to the Acropolis*, Ingwald died in 1893 at the age of 40. Sigrid was 11 years old. Notes Opfell: "[He died] still hoping that Sigrid would devote herself to science and carry on his research."

The loss of Ingwald increased the family's financial difficulties. Sigrid and her two younger sisters, **Signe** and **Ragnhild Undset**, were able to stay at their school, run by Fru **Ragna Nielsen**, for free. Sigrid would later credit the school's liberal and progressive lines with prompting in her "an indelible distrust of enthusiasm for such beliefs." Ready to leave the school by age 14, she attended a commercial college. By the time she was 17 and took work as a secretary, Undset was in Opfell's words "a tall, slim, pretty girl

Sigrid
Undset

with deep, thoughtful eyes and long braided hair." She would spend ten years working in an electrical engineers' bureau office, remaining until her sisters were financially stable. Meanwhile, she wrote a draft of a novel set in 13th-century Norway. This was later to become the Olav Audunsson story which would contribute to her fame and to the Nobel committee's decision. For the time being, however, the story was not to see the light of day. After submitting the manuscript to Gyldendal publishers, she was told by them: "Don't try your hand at more historical novels. It's not your line. But you might, you know, try to write something modern."

Undset took this advice initially, and she wrote two contemporary works, *Martha Oulie* (1907) and *The Happy Age* (1908), which were received well enough to garner her a travel grant from the Norwegian government. *Martha Oulie* was written in diary form and set the theme which would pervade Undset's work, what Theodore Jorgenson called "the organic unity and the ideal power of marriage." *Jenny* appeared in 1911 and made her first success; its erotic descriptions caused a literary sensation. Opfell describes the novel's theme, which would reappear years later in *Kristin Lavransdatter*, as "love has its code of honor, and the cost of picking forbidden fruit is excessive." Notes Jorgenson of Undset's early works: "They are not optimistic books. Love is the key to the personalities of these girls, but society does not seem to be organized in such a manner that individual satisfaction is possible."

In her late 20s, Undset traveled to Rome where she fell in love with the married Anders Castus Svarstad, a painter whom Opfell describes as eccentric, "nervous and brusque, but keenly intelligent." She married him the following year (1912) in Belgium after he was divorced from his first wife. Undset wanted their first child to be born in Rome, where she had initially fallen in love, and there she gave birth to a son, Anders, in January 1913. Their living conditions were not good, however, so she and her son returned to Norway; her husband later joined them. Svarstad's three children by his earlier marriage stayed with the family for a time and later would come back for regular visits.

In 1915, their daughter Maren Charlotte (called Mosse) was born, and by the time the family relocated to Sinsen she was found to be severely retarded. Undset—described by her friend *Nini Roll Anker as once "strikingly beautiful, slim as a boy, and with a suggestion of classical perfection about her head which she seldom moved"—retained her elegant hands and feet as she became what Opfell calls "a heavyset housewife." Despite the difficulty of her life at the time, she is said to have had "an air of calm and great tranquility." By 1919, the Undset-Svarstad union was crumbling, and the couple separated in July of that year by mutual consent, three months before the birth of their second son, Hans. The marriage was later annulled.

Preferring a country environment in which to bring up her children, Undset moved her family to Lillehammer, where she purchased a farm which she named Bjerkebaek (the restored farm house dated from the year 1000). Despite her responsibilities as a mother and her own frequent ill health, several novels followed. "Meanwhile," writes Opfell, "the war was confirming her doubts about the beliefs she had been brought up with—feminism, socialism, liberalism, pacifism." In Undset's article "Some Reflections on the Suffragette Movement," she espoused woman's "fundamental position" in the domestic sphere, writing that "a woman can become nothing better than a good mother and nothing much worse than a bad one." It was her choice to keep Maren at home, and her attempts to secure medical assistance for her daughter were to no avail.

Undset's contemporary novels published before *Kristin Lavransdatter* were censured for their frank portrayals of female sexuality, demonstrating that a woman's need for sexual satisfaction, and right to it, is as justifiable as a man's. But the author also viewed women's responsibilities as different from men's. Sexual equality, she maintained, was guaranteed in the marriage vows, which, if they were taken seriously by both parties, secured the roles of husband and wife. These roles remained unchanged even if the male sought physical release outside the marriage. But a mother must be faithful; with her own chastity, she protected the welfare and continuance of the clan, which was her primary duty. For life to have meaning, wrote Undset, humans needed to uphold the "threadbare truths" of duty and responsibility, and women were especially obliged to preserve the day-to-day routines of life. Only a few—with demonstrably special gifts and as much physical energy as the author herself—would be able to sustain that responsibility and simultaneously fulfill their own needs, artistically or otherwise.

In Lillehammer, Undset produced the two works set in the Middle Ages which were to bring her international acclaim and the Nobel Prize. The first of these, *Kristin Lavransdatter*, offers readers particular insight into the author's concerns and her personal development. It depicts the relationship between the individual and the race or family, the power of human sexuality, and the consequences of passion. As a parable of a woman's journey from youth to responsible maturity to a devoutly religious old age, it can be seen to mirror Undset's own progression from young woman and writer searching for a man she can call master, to wife and mother holding home and life together for her children, to the converted Catholic she would become, exploring a human soul in relation to God.

Set in the 14th century, the novel is comprised of three sections—"The Bridal Wreath," "The Mistress of Husaby," and "The Cross"— each of which covers an epoch in the life of the protagonist. Jorgenson speculates: "She chooses the Catholic fourteenth century, because she feels that under the full power of the church of the Middle Ages, men had a moral earnestness and a religious zeal worthy of the stature of manhood and womanhood. Her charge against modern life is that it is a little of this and a little of that and not much of anything." "Wisely," writes Opfell, "Sigrid Undset chose a period without any great historical figures. Her main characters are purely fictitious. . . . Her primary sources, she noted, were old ballads and laws. Besides this impeccable scholarship, *Kristin Lavransdatter* shows great psychological depth. Its strong characters are not explained, but explain themselves."

In "The Bridal Wreath," 15-year-old Kristin falls passionately in love with the dashing Erlend Nikulausson, a warrior chief, for whom she abandons her responsibilities to her family and to Simon Darre, her betrothed. Pregnant at the time of her wedding to Erlend, Kristin can be seen to make a mockery of the bridal wreath she wears, symbolic of maidenhood; this leads to her parents Ragnhild and Lavrans confronting each other on her wedding night.

Ragnhild confesses that she had been another man's lover before her marriage to Lavrans. Throughout their married life, Ragnhild tells him, her guilt has made her feel that she has fed her husband mould for meat. Lavrans responds bitterly, "mayhap mould must be ground if meat shall grow." In his attempt to console her, Lavrans bespeaks his painful insight into the nature of sex, recognizing it as a life force, the power of which he, unlike his wife and daughter, has exempted himself. This view into the agony inherent in living a full life on earth while being God's servant foreshadows the last thoughts, many pages later, of Kristin before she dies. Lavrans and his daughter dramatize Undset's own contention that disloyalty and its consequences, which are frequently the price for sexual indulgence, are basic to the human condition; erotic passion is powerful and fulfilling enough to make people betray what they love the most. Writing *Kristin Lavransdatter* in the wake of her disintegrated marriage, Undset was fully aware of the power of human passion and the human desire for self gratification and rebellion against real or perceived authority. Asked by an interviewer if she liked Erlend Nikulausson—a character readers generally find as irresistible as Kristin does— the author answered in the negative.

Kristin bears eight male children, and the author's description of her Herculean efforts to build a home for them in the face of her husband Erlend's irresponsibility toward both property and progeny reflects her own fiercely maternal instincts. (Undset wrote her great novel during the quiet night hours, with coffee and cigarettes as boosters.)

Following publication of *Kristin Lavransdatter*, in 1924 Undset rejected the state religion of Lutheranism to become a convert to the Catholic Church. She had been for some time brooding intensely over the conflict of wills between God and man. Original sin, she reasoned, had obscured man's moral vision, which could only be made clear by the grace of God; man had to choose God, however, to be set free to become what God intended him to be, a creature made in His image. She argued that the only "thoroughly sane" people she had encountered in her readings of history were those that the Catholic Church calls saints. Only they seemed to know "the true explanation of man's undying hunger for happiness—his tragically insufficient love of peace, justice and goodwill to his fellowmen, his everlasting fall from grace."

I am one who has lived two thousand years in the land.

—Sigrid Undset

The other work in addition to the monumental *Kristin Lavransdatter* which was largely to influence Undset's receipt of the Nobel Prize was her tale of Olav Audunsson. This was originally published in two parts: *Olav Audunsson i Hestviken* and *Olav Audunsson og Hans Børn*. (When translated into English as *The Master of Hestviken*, it was published in one volume.) Notes Opfell, "When the first volume appeared, she burned her first draft, rejected twenty years earlier." Olav has been seen as a counterpart to Kristin, as both suffer estrangement from God and other misfortunes due to pride, but Olav's tale has a greater spiritual bent.

The Swedish Academy awarded Undset the Nobel Prize in 1928. Noted Per Hallström: "Sigrid Undset has received the Nobel Prize in Literature while still in her prime, an homage rendered to a poetic genius whose roots must be in a great and well-ordered spirit." Undset divided the prize money among the authors' society, families of children suffering from retardation like her own who wished to keep their children with them at home, and to Catholic children in financial need who were seeking enrollment in Catholic schools. A torchlight parade met her upon her return from Stockholm to Lillehammer. "It was one of the few times she came into contact with [her fellow citizens]," writes Opfell, "because, except for the company of her children and occasional visits from close relatives, she preferred to lead a rather solitary life."

Approaching age 50, Undset lived in her farm house at Lillehammer, where she presided as matriarch in the embroidered blouses and wool skirts recognized as Norway's native costume. She moved again to modern novels, producing such works as *The Wild Orchid*, *The Burning Bush*, and *The Faithful Wife*, as well as autobiographical essays. *Madame Dorthea* (1939), intended to be the first book of a trilogy, was instead her last novel.

By 1935, with Adolf Hitler coming to power, Undset's voice carried considerable weight when she became among the first to speak out against the regime in Germany, with a direct attack on Nazism. Declaring that lack of freedom was worse than "death and extinction," she confronted both Marxism and Nazism on moral grounds, alleging that they had sprung from the pride of Lucifer. Totalitarianism she opposed as self-worship and a path towards dissolution and death. In response, her books were banned in Germany, and the Norwegian Nazi newspaper denounced her as not only "foreign and offensive to us" but "hostile."

As Europe became embroiled in World War II, Undset fought against Germany's invasion of Norway with the powers she had at her disposal. Her writings during this period reflect her willingness to sacrifice the best she had, her art, on behalf of Norway. But well known as she was, she was in more danger than she realized. Once Norway was occupied, she was advised that as a famous writer and president of Norway's Society of Writers, she might be forced to make propaganda broadcasts or even be taken hostage. When nearby Finland was attacked by the Soviet Union, the author sold her Nobel medal to help the Finns and invited three refugee Finnish children—Elmi, Toimi, and Eira—into her house. Opfell notes that they would soon be joined by another refugee, "a German priest who had befriended some Jews. But Sigrid Undset's aversion to all things German was now so strong that he wore on her nerves. Quickly she arranged to have him sent over to Sweden." When the Germans neared Lillehammer, she relocated the Finnish children to a farm in a side valley to try to ensure their safety.

In May 1940—having recently lost both her mother and her daughter—she heeded the words of Norwegian authorities who encouraged her to flee. The day following her arrival in Sweden, she learned that her son Anders had been shot and killed defending a bridge outside Lillehammer. Her second son, Hans, escaped to Stockholm and flew with his mother to Moscow; from there, they went by Trans-Siberian Express across Russia to the port of Vladivostok, where they sailed for Kobe, Japan. The grueling journey challenged the writer's unflinching insistence on seeing and describing things the way they were. In Russia, she witnessed "indescribable filth, dilapidation, and wretchedness," and the cleanliness of Japan did not divert her from the "German trash, cheap and hideous" on display in store windows as she identified what she considered the common denominator of totalitarianism: a sure and steadily sinking standard of living and a regime which can only keep its promises to the people by annexing neighboring states.

Boarding the *President Cleveland* for San Francisco, Undset was to spend the next five years in the States. She traveled the country indefatigably, lecturing and writing articles in support of Norway's resistance movement, gathering news items for the Norwegian Information Service and reviewing books for *The New York Times*. With "nations like Germany attempting to destroy democracy completely," she saw the future of Western civilization at stake, but feared equally that, if the Allied countries acted on their current enemies with hatred and revenge, they might lose their souls in the process of making the world safe for democracy.

In 1945, with the war ended, Undset could return to Norway and Lillehammer. She sailed for home in July, and upon her arrival, writes Opfell, found that the "Nazi troops had rifled her extensive library, smashed her father's old desk at which she had written her great novels, and taken all her silver and linens." Photographs from this period show the toll of recent years. The writer was past 60, and despite her adherence to the principles of faith, hope and love, and her reliance on "our own . . . tireless, patient, and courageous exertion," noted in her *Return to the Future*, a light has gone out of her eyes. But she was deeply pleased to be honored that year with her country's Grand Cross of the Order of Saint Olav, in part for her writing, but equally for her soldiering and "efforts for Norway's cause during the war."

Her last creative effort, a biography of *Catherine of Siena, was rejected by Doubleday; it would be published posthumously. On June 10, 1949, Sigrid Undset was ill at the hospital of

Lillehammer. Sister Xavier, a Catholic nun who had kept a vigil with her through the night, was sent away by Undset so that the nun could rest. The writer died that day alone. In addition to *Catherine of Siena*, her *Articles and Tales from Wartime* was published posthumously.

SOURCES IN ENGLISH:

Bayerschmidt, Carl. *Sigrid Undset.* NY: Twayne, 1970.

Beyer, Harald. "Sigrid Undset," in *A History of Norwegian Literature*. Ed. by Einar Haugen. NY: New York University Press, 1956.

Brunsdale, Mitzi. "Sigrid Undset," in *A Critical Study of Long Fiction*. La Canada, CA: Salem Press, 1983.

———. *Sigrid Undset: Chronicler of Norway.* NY: St. Martin's Press, 1988.

Gustafson, Alrik. "Christian Ethics in a Pagan World: Sigrid Undset," in *Six Scandinavian Novelists*. Minneapolis, MN: Minnesota University Press, 1968.

Jorgenson, Theodore. *History of Norwegian Literature.* New York, NY: Macmillan, 1933.

Opfell, Olga. *The Lady Laureates.* Metuchen, NJ: Scarecrow Press, 1978.

Ruch, Velma. *Sigrid Undset's Kristin Lavransdatter: A Study of Its Literary Art and Its Reception in America, England and Scandinavia.* WI: University of Wisconsin, 1957.

Winsness, A.H. *Sigrid Undset: A Study in Christian Realism.* NY: Sheed and Ward, 1953.

Unger, Caroline (1803–1877)

Austrian operatic mezzo-soprano. Name variations: Karoline Unger; Caroline Unger-Sabatier. Born on October 28, 1803, in Stuhlweissenburg, Austria; died on March 23, 1877, in Florence, Italy; studied with Mozatti, Bassio, Lange, Vogl, and Ronconi; married François Sabatier (a writer).

Caroline Unger had an immense vocal range, from A to high D, and was known as one of the most outstanding and intelligent singers of her time. She studied in Vienna with Mozatti and Bassi, and later with others. She first appeared in Vienna in 1819, making her official debut in 1821, and sang there until 1824. In 1825 and 1826, she performed in Naples, and from 1827 to 1830 she appeared in Milan. She also sang in Paris in 1833 and again in Vienna from 1839 to 1840. Her last appearance on the opera stage was in Dresden in 1843, after which she retired, although she sang in concerts under her married name Caroline Unger-Sabatier.

Unger had a voice that was both forceful and flexible, and appeared in such roles as Zerlina, Rosina, and Isabella in *L'italiana*; she also created the roles of Isoletta in *La straniera*, Donizetti's Parisina, Maria di Rudenz, and Antonina in *Belisario*. In the premiere performance of Beethoven's Ninth Symphony, which was con-

ducted by the composer himself, she sang the alto solo. By this time, Beethoven was completely deaf. At the end of the symphony, it was Unger who turned Beethoven around so that he might see the impact of his music on the listeners.

Kelly Winters,
freelance writer

Unger, Mary Ann (1945–1998)

American sculptor. Born in 1945 in New York City; died of breast cancer on December 28, 1998, in New York City; daughter of William Unger and Dorothy Unger; Mt. Holyoke College, B.A., 1967; attended University of California, Berkeley; Columbia University, M.F.A., 1975; married Geoffrey Biddle (a photographer); children: Eve Biddle.

Began sculpting as a child; received B.A. in art (1967); received public commissions and exhibited at solo shows; work is held in collections of Hirschorn Museum and Sculpture Garden in Washington, D.C., the Brooklyn Museum of Art, and the Philadelphia Museum of Art.

Born in 1945, Mary Ann Unger exhibited her artistic talent as a young child when she began making sculptures in art classes at the Museum of Modern Art in New York City. One of two children and the only daughter of William and **Dorothy Unger**, she attended Mt. Holyoke College as an undergraduate; there she learned to weld, cast in bronze, and carve marble. After receiving her B.A. in art in 1967, she spent a year as a graduate student at the University of California at Berkeley, following that with several more years spent traveling around the world, including a trip to North Africa that she made alone. After returning to the United States, she completed her graduate degree at Columbia University in New York City. While there, she studied with George Sugarman and Ronald Bladen, receiving her M.F.A. in 1975. Critics noted that her works from the 1970s, with their lively, sinuous shapes, reflected the influence of Sugarman. These shapes evolved into tensile structures with repeating arcs, treelike forms that she used in her many public commissions.

In 1985, Unger was diagnosed with breast cancer. After this, her work became more expressionistic, making use of dark, sausage-shaped or beamlike shapes in an attempt to bring forth images of the body without actually showing it. Critics found these large-scale works, made of a lightweight plaster over steel frames, to be subtly expressive, with a sense of mythic power. When Unger died of breast cancer in December 1998, she had just completed a series of works for a solo show in the spring of 1999. Her sculptures are in the permanent collections of the Hirschorn Museum and Sculpture Garden in Washington, D.C., the Brooklyn Museum of Art, and the Philadelphia Museum of Art.

SOURCES:

"Mary Ann Unger, 53, a Noted Sculptor and Curator, Is Dead," in *The New York Times*. January 3, 1999, p. 29.

Malinda Mayer,
writer and editor,
Falmouth, Massachusetts

Ungureanu, Teodora (b. 1960).

See Comaneci, Nadia for sidebar.

Uno, Chiyo (1897–1996)

Japanese novelist. Born in 1897 in Yamaguchi prefecture, Japan; died of pneumonia on June 10, 1996, in Tokyo, Japan; married three times; children: one (died at birth).

Born in 1897, Chiyo Uno was a well-known Japanese writer who scandalized her country in the 1920s and 1930s. She was married three

times—she had only one child, who died hours after birth in 1920—and had several tumultuous love affairs with other writers and artists. One such was painter Seiji Togo, who had attempted suicide (by slashing his throat) with his previous lover. Uno was intrigued by this story, introduced herself, and the two lived together for many years. In 1927, she further shocked the conservative nation by cutting her hair short; this was such a radical move that when children saw her, they screamed and ran away.

Uno was known for her work as well as her lifestyle, however. In 1921, she won the Prize of Jijishinpo for *A Powdered Face*. Her 1935 novel *Confessions of Love* was based on Togo's love affairs and was set in Japan during the Roaring '20s. The following year, she and another lover, Kitahara Takeo, founded Japan's first fashion magazine, *Style*.

Uno's best-known work is *Ohan*, a story about the relationship between two women who share the same lover. The novel earned the author the Noma Prize for Literature in 1957. Her other novels include *A Dollmaker*, *Tenguya Hisakichi*, *A Cherry of Pale Pink*, and *To Stab*. Uno became a member of the Japanese Academy of Arts in 1972, and in 1982 was awarded the Kikuchi Kan Prize. Her memoir, *I Will Go On Living* (1983), became a Japanese bestseller and a television movie. Her advice columns for lovelorn young women were also collected in a book. Despite her scandalous past, Uno was recognized as a "person of cultural merit" by the Japanese government in 1990 and received a title from the emperor. She died of pneumonia in 1996, age 98.

SOURCES:

Buck, Claire, ed. *The Bloomsbury Guide to Women's Literature*. NY: Prentice Hall, 1992.

"Chiyo Uno" (obituary). *The Day* [New London, CT]. June 11, 1996.

Kelly Winters,
freelance writer

Unsoeld, Jolene (1931—)

U.S. congressional representative (January 3, 1989–January 3, 1995). Born Jolene Bishoprick on December 3, 1931, in Corvallis, Oregon; educated at primary schools in Shanghai, China, 1938–40, and public schools in Portland, Oregon; attended Oregon State University, Corvallis, 1949–51; married an educator.

Born in 1931 in Corvallis, Oregon, Jolene Unsoeld grew up in Oregon and the state of Washington but spent part of her childhood in Shanghai, China. With her husband, who was a mountain climber and educator, she lived in

Jolene Unsoeld

Kathmandu, Nepal, from 1962 to 1967. For two years during that time, she was director of the English Language Institute in Kathmandu.

Unsoeld's first experience in politics came in the 1970s and early 1980s, when, as a lobbyist in Olympia, Washington, she worked for campaign finance reform and environmental issues. From 1983 to 1988, she was a member of the Democratic National Committee, and meanwhile won election to the Washington House of Representatives in 1984, where she served until 1989. During her tenure in the state legislature, Unsoeld was known for her position on environmental issues, including a successful campaign to put an initiative on the ballot that would set more stringent guidelines for the cleanup of toxic waste sites in the state.

In 1988, Unsoeld won the Democratic nomination for Congress from the 3rd Congressional District in Washington state, and narrowly beat her Republican opponent to win the seat, which she held from the 101st Congress through the 103rd. She served on the Committee on Merchant Marine and Fisheries, the Committee on Education and Labor, and the Select Committee on Aging. After running unsuccessfully for reelection to the 104th Congress, Unsoeld retired to Olympia early in 1995.

SOURCES:

Women in Congress, 1917–1990. Washington, DC: U.S. Government Printing Office, 1991.

Kelly Winters,
freelance writer

Upton, Harriet Taylor (1853–1945)

American suffragist, political leader, and author. Name variations: Mrs. George Upton. Born on December 17, 1853, in Ravenna, Ohio; died of hypertensive heart disease on November 2, 1945, in Pasadena, California; daughter of Ezra Booth Taylor (a judge and legislator) and Harriet M. (Frazer) Taylor; married George Whitman Upton (a lawyer), on July 9, 1884 (died 1923).

Harriet Taylor Upton was born in 1853 in Ravenna, Ohio, and grew up in a political family. Her father Ezra Booth Taylor was a circuit court judge who later became a U.S. congressional representative and served as chair of the Judiciary Committee. The oldest child and only daughter, Upton was intrigued by politics and often accompanied her father on his speaking tours. She attended a two-room schoolhouse, and later went to Warren High School, where she was especially interested in science. Her father's opposition prevented her from attending

college; instead, she received a political education by traveling with him on his northern Ohio circuit and by serving as secretary of the Women's Christian Temperance Union of Trumbull County.

When Upton was in her late 20s, her mother **Harriet Frazer Taylor** died, and Upton accompanied her father to Washington, D.C., becoming his official hostess. As such, she met many national Republican leaders and became deeply familiar with American politics. In 1884, she married George Washington Upton, who became her father's law partner, and the newly married couple divided their time between Warren and Washington.

While still in her mid-20s, Upton had become aware of the issue of women's suffrage when *Susan B. **Anthony** spoke in Warren, Ohio. At that time, Upton did not support the suffrage movement because she disagreed with what she thought was its underlying implication that men were unjust to women. In 1888, Upton again met Anthony in Washington and also met *Elizabeth Cady Stanton, *Lucy Stone, and other women leaders. Although she liked Anthony, she was still opposed to suffrage, despite her father's support of it. In the process of researching an anti-suffrage article, however, she changed her mind and became an active supporter of the cause.

In 1890, she joined the National American Woman Suffrage Association (NAWSA) and began working for the movement. In 1893, she served on a committee that lobbied members of Congress for their opinions on suffrage. The following year, she began a 16-year term as treasurer of NAWSA, and from 1903 to 1909 she ran the association almost single-handedly from its headquarters in Warren. A skilled fund raiser and press agent and a tireless worker, Upton also edited reports of the national conventions, testified before Congressional hearings, oversaw the circulation of suffrage literature (including the group's monthly paper, *Progress*, which she edited from 1902 to 1910), and traveled to speak about the cause.

As well, she presided over the Ohio Woman Suffrage Association from 1899 to 1908 and from 1911 to 1920, organizing conventions and directing state referendum campaigns that ultimately resulted in securing municipal suffrage in the state. She also managed the campaign that led to the Ohio legislature's ratification of the 19th Amendment granting women the right to vote.

Upton wrote numerous political articles for newspapers and magazines, including *Woman's Home Companion, Harper's Bazaar*, and *Out-*

look. Many of her children's stories were published in such popular magazines as *St. Nicholas* and *Wide Awake*. She also wrote a history book, *Our Early Presidents: Their Wives and Children, from Washington to Jackson* (1892), as well as the local histories *A Twentieth Century History of Trumbull County, Ohio* (1909) and the three-volume *History of the Western Reserve* (1910). All her writing emphasized the role of women in history, something she thought had been minimized by historians.

After women gained the vote, Upton was appointed vice-chair of the Republican National Executive Committee when Warren G. Harding, who was also from Ohio, was running for president. She was one of the first women to hold such a high party post, and kept the position for four years. Upton used her influence to gain government appointments for women. A year after her husband died in 1923, 70-year-old Upton became an unsuccessful candidate for her father's old seat in Congress, losing in the primaries. In 1928, after serving as assistant state campaign manager for the Republican Party, she became liaison between Governor Myers Y. Cooper and the Ohio Department of Public Welfare. As liaison, she implemented reforms at the Madison Ohio Home for Soldiers' and Sailors' Widows and at the Girls' Industrial School at Delaware, Ohio. Upton retired to Pasadena, California, in 1931, and died there of heart disease in 1945.

SOURCES:

James, Edward T., ed. *Notable American Women, 1607–1950*. Cambridge, MA: The Belknap Press of Harvard University, 1971.

Kelly Winters,
freelance writer

Uraib (797–890).

See Oraib.

Urbino, duchess of.

See Sforza, Battista (1446–1472).
See Montefeltro, Elisabetta (1471–1526).
See Gonzaga, Eleonora (1493–1543).
See Madeleine de la Tour d'Auvergne (1501–1519).
See Este, Lucrezia d' (1535–1598).
See Medici, Vittoria (d. 1694).

Urbino, princess of.

See Medici, Claudia de (1604–1648).

Urraca (1033–1101)

Princess of Castile. Born in 1033; died in 1101; daughter of *Sancha of Leon (1013–1067) and Ferdinand I (c. 1017–1065), king of Castile (r. 1038–1065).

Urraca (c. 1079–1126)

Queen of Castile and Aragon who governed the Iberian kingdoms of Galicia, Leon and Castile, and through her marriage to Alphonso I of Aragon briefly united almost all of medieval Christian Spain. Recognized as queen of Leon-Castile in 1109. Born around 1079 (some sources cite 1081); died on March 8, 1126, in Saldaña; was the first surviving child of Queen Constance of Burgundy (c. 1046–c. 1093) and Alphonso VI (c. 1030–1109), king of Leon (r. 1065–1109), king of Castile (r. 1072–1109); married Raymond of Burgundy, in 1087 (died 1107); married Alphonso I the Battler (1073–1134), king of Aragon (r. 1104–1134), in 1109 (annulled in 1114); children: (first marriage) Princess Sancha (born by 1095–1159); Alphonso VII Raimúndez (1105–1157), king of Castile and Leon (r. 1126–1157); illegitimate children with Count Pedro González de Lara.

In 1079, Queen ⚜➤ **Constance of Burgundy**, the second wife of Alphonso VI (he had been married to ***Agnes of Poitou**), gave birth to a daughter christened Urraca. She was the first surviving child of the king of Leon and Castile. Medieval records and chronicles contain virtually nothing about the events of Urraca's childhood, her upbringing, or her physical appearance. She might have lived and died in relative anonymity had fate not denied her father a male heir to succeed him. As it turned out, however, Urraca not only acceded to her father's throne but ruled in her own right. She reigned longer than any other queen of a major Western European kingdom during the High Middle Ages.

Urraca's youth coincided with a tumultuous and momentous period in Iberian history. The great Caliphate of Cordoba, established after the Islamic invasion of the peninsula in 711, had splintered into petty kingdoms in 1035. With Moorish power thus weakened, the Christian kingdoms in the northern part of the peninsula began to expand south. In 1085, for example, Urraca's father Alphonso VI captured Toledo. Almoravid (*Murabit*) reinforcements from North Africa strengthened Islamic resistance but failed to reverse the Christian advance. Meanwhile, political power in the Christian kingdoms was also fragmented. Nobles resisted rulers' attempts to extend their authority. Christians battled among themselves nearly as much as they fought the Muslims. The period's most famous figure was not a monarch but Rodrigo Díaz de Vivar (El Cid), whose military exploits against Christians and Moors won undying fame.

Even a vigorous king such as Alphonso VI found it necessary to buy the support of powerful nobles through bequests and royal favors and to create alliances through strategic marriages. Urraca figured in one of the latter. Alphonso betrothed her to Count Raymond of Burgundy, probably in 1087, and the two may have been married shortly thereafter despite Urraca being younger than 12, the minimum age set by the Church. By 1090, Alphonso named Urraca and her husband the countess and count of Galicia and Portugal. Later, Raymond's cousin Henry, count of Burgundy, married Urraca's illegitimate half-sister *Teresa of Castile, further strengthening Alphonso's French alliance. Urraca's mother Constance died in 1093, and Alphonso still lacked a son to succeed him. His subsequent wives (including *Bertha of Burgundy [d. 1097]) likewise failed to produce the desired male heir, although his Moorish mistress *Zaida gave birth to an illegitimate son, Sancho, around 1093.

For her first three decades, Urraca's life held little to distinguish her from other medieval royal women. In fact, some sources assert that she had not displayed "prudence and steadiness," though gender made her an easy target for critics. Then, between 1107 and 1109, the deaths of Count Raymond, Sancho, and Alphonso propelled her to the throne of Leon and Castile. First to perish was her husband, in 1107, leaving Urraca with two children. The elder was Princess **Sancha**, born by 1095, followed by Alphonso (VII) Raimúndez, born in 1105. In 1107, Alphonso VI apparently recognized Sancho as his heir, despite his illegitimate birth. Nonetheless, he did not live to succeed the old king. Sancho died at the battle of Uclés in 1108, leaving Urraca as Alphonso's only viable heir. Almost immediately Alphonso sought a new husband for his daughter. She reportedly preferred Gómez González, the count of Candespina. But her father selected instead Alphonso I the Battler of neighboring Aragon. His fame as a warrior seemed to ensure that he could defend Urraca's authority, from both external threats and internal dissension. The marriage would also unite all the Christian realms of the peninsula except Catalonia. Before the wedding was celebrated, however, Alphonso VI died on June 30, 1109, at Toledo.

Castilian nobles swore fealty to Urraca as monarch, but her ability to retain power depended on their continued willingness to support a woman as ruler. Some of her vassals, especially in Galicia, preferred Urraca's young son, Alphonso Raimúndez. That he was too young to rule meant a period of weak royal power, attrac-

Constance of Burgundy (1046–c. 1093)

*Queen of Castile and Leon. Name variations: Constance Capet. Born in 1046; died in 1093 (some sources cite 1092); daughter of Robert I (b. 1011), duke of Burgundy, and *Helia de Semur; married Hugh II, count of Chalon-sur-Saone; became second wife of Alphonso VI, king of Leon (r. 1065–1109), king of Castile (r. 1072–1109), on May 8, 1081; children: *Urraca (c. 1079–1126), queen of Castile and Leon; Elvira (died young).*

tive to many aristocrats who resisted royal pretensions. Urraca's half-sister Teresa and her husband, Count Henry, also presented a challenge. Before Raymond's death, Count Henry had agreed to recognize his cousin's claim to the throne of Leon-Castile. In return, Urraca's husband allegedly promised, if he became king, to give Henry either the realm of Galicia or Toledo. But as Raymond had predeceased Alphonso VI, Henry found his ambitions frustrated. He and Teresa were willing to press their claims against Urraca through diplomatic or military means. Of course, Urraca also faced the Moorish threat from the south.

Pressed by her aristocratic allies, Urraca agreed to marry Alphonso the Battler, as her father had intended. The Almoravides were laying waste to the region around Toledo, and Alphonso seemed the only ruler capable of defending Christian Spain. The wedding occurred in October 1109 at Monzón. Urraca was about 30, her groom 36. Terms of the marriage determined the powers that each possessed in the other's realms and established the rules of succession. If either died, the other would rule in the deceased's kingdoms. Their son, should one be born, would inherit the united kingdoms. If no son were born and Alphonso died first, Urraca and Alphonso Raimúndez would inherit the Battler's realms. Should Alphonso outlive Urraca, Alphonso Raimúndez would rule his mother's kingdoms upon the death of his stepfather.

The union shortly ran into trouble. Neither found much attraction in the other. According to Alphonso's biographer, José María Lacarra, "Urraca had a true obsession to impose her will and a great fear that he might supplant her power, relegating her to the background. If the king was a man of energy, a decisive and good warrior, he in turn lacked the most elemental qualities to temporize with his wife." In fact, Alphonso had little inclination toward matrimony. Never married previously despite the pressing need to beget an heir, Alphonso was a warrior, crusader, and religious zealot. Urged by a comrade to secretly take a Moorish concubine from among his captives, Alphonso responded: "A true soldier must live with men and not with women." Possibly his sense of religious obligation caused him to marry Urraca: to defend the Christian kingdoms against the Almoravid onslaught and perhaps, through their marriage, to produce an heir capable of uniting Spanish Christianity against the infidel. Still, Alphonso seemed better suited to the role of knight Templar, a monkish warrior. Urraca later claimed that she had opposed the marriage all along and accused Alphonso of beating her.

It was the only time during the Spanish medieval period that a woman ruled in her own right for some seventeen years. That unprecedented event opened the possibility of the union of León-Castilla and Aragón by a marriage.

—Bernard F. Reilly

Key to the success of their marriage was the birth of an heir. Yet Urraca did not become pregnant. Meanwhile, the union had its foes, especially aristocrats who opposed a strong monarchy or the Aragonese alliance. Partisans of Alphonso Raimúndez feared the marriage might deprive him of his divinely ordained right to rule. The latter appealed to the papacy, asking that the marriage be invalidated on grounds of consanguinity because Urraca and Alphonso were both great-grandchildren of Sancho the Great of Navarre. By mid-1110, Pope Paschal II condemned the marriage, and open opposition flared against Urraca and Alphonso. In fact, led by Count Pedro Froilaz and the bishop of Santiago, Diego Gelmírez, Galicia had risen against the royal couple shortly after the wedding. Dissidents there feared a powerful Aragonese ruler might curb their rights and privileges. Galicia also rallied to the cause of Alphonso Raimúndez, Urraca's son with Count Raymond. Froilaz was the boy's guardian. The rebels found willing allies in nearby Portugal, where a rebellious Henry and Teresa took offense at Urraca's failure to surrender Toledo or Galicia.

Urraca and Alphonso moved quickly to deal with Galicia. Nonetheless, the latter proved so brutal in his punishment, summarily executing several of the rebel leaders, that Urraca turned away from him. Perhaps she recognized that Alphonso could not permanently subdue by force of arms all of Galicia, Leon, and Castile.

His cruelty antagonized the nobility and turned popular sentiment against the monarchs. Meanwhile, personal antipathy between the royal couple caused the separation in late 1110, with the queen staying on in Galicia. While Urraca reconciled with Froilaz and Gelmírez, her husband allied himself with Henry and Teresa against Urraca. In 1111, Alphonso captured Toledo, whereupon Henry, who desired it for himself, broke with the Aragonese king and temporarily supported Urraca.

The costly and destructive civil war continued, with alliances shifting whenever a faction became too strong. Urraca and her advisers managed to separate Alphonso and the Portuguese by promising Henry part of Castile. Then, the queen negotiated an alliance with Alphonso with the aim of expelling Henry from Castile. This ignited anti-Alphonso sentiment among the partisans of Alphonso Raimúndez, and Bishop Gelmírez crowned him king of Galicia on September 17, 1111. The boy's supporters proved no match for the army of Alphonso the Battler, however, and Alphonso Raimúndez took refuge with his mother. Under her immediate protection and control, Alphonso Raimúndez posed a less serious political threat to Urraca. She also perceived that she could placate her son and his supporters by acknowledging his rights as heir.

From 1112 to 1114, Alphonso the Battler held sizeable portions of Castile, but Urraca skillfully maneuvered to protect her crown and realms. Brief periods of marital reconciliation always gave way to personal dislike and papal pressure. In 1114, Alphonso publicly declared that he would not live with her any longer. Any pretense of marriage had ended, and neither showed an interest in resurrecting it. This left Urraca to rule personally over her kingdoms. Writes biographer Bernard F. Reilly, Urraca "seems always to have been more astute at diplomacy and politics than were her adversaries." Archbishop Bernardo of Toledo and Count Pedro González de Lara furnished loyal and shrewd guidance throughout nearly all her reign, but Urraca made the final decisions as an independent ruler. She benefited also from the decadence of Almoravid power to the south, which no longer challenged Castile as seriously as it had a few years earlier.

Having abandoned the marriage, Alphonso withdrew to Aragon and began the actions that culminated in his great conquest of Zaragoza (Saragossa). Meanwhile, Urraca tried to retake the parts of Castile held by her foes. She strengthened her authority in Galicia by working out a political settlement with her son. To curb the power and influence of Bishop Gelmírez, she divested him of the government of Santiago de Compostela in 1116 and turned it over to a commune of burghers. The following year, however, she changed her mind and restored Gelmírez's power. This caused a riot in Santiago. The bishop and queen took refuge in the cathedral's bell tower, which the rioters set afire. Historian Joseph F. O'Callaghan quotes a medieval Latin manuscript about the riot:

> the queen, urged by the bishop, accepted their guarantees, and came out of the tower; but when the rest of the mob saw her coming out, they made a rush upon her and seized her and knocked her to the ground in a muddy wallow; like wolves they attacked her and ripped off her clothes, leaving her body naked from her breasts on down; for a long time she lay shamefully on the ground in the presence of all. Many wanted to bury her under stones and one old lady of Compostela struck her harshly on the cheek with a stone.

Other townspeople finally saved her, however, and Alphonso Raimúndez's army intimidated the rebels into submission. At that point the queen apparently turned Galicia over to her son, appointing him to rule there and in Toledo while she governed Leon and Castile.

Turmoil still beset Urraca's reign, although relations with Alphonso the Battler calmed. He focused on breaking Moorish power in Zaragoza. With his forces occupied to the east, by 1117 Urraca reoccupied much of the Castilian territory previously held by the Aragonese. On December 18, 1118, Alphonso's armies captured the city of Zaragoza and doubled the size of his realm. More troublesome was Urraca's half-sister Teresa. Despite Count Henry's death in 1114, Teresa's ambition and her hatred for Urraca continued unabated. Having apparently given up hope of gaining the throne of Leon-Castile, Teresa began calling herself queen of Portugal. Effective establishment of the kingdom of Portugal would have to wait, however, until the reign of Teresa and Henry's son, Alphonso I Henriques.

Internal opposition also bedeviled Urraca. In early 1119, a palace coup at Leon nearly toppled her. It apparently resulted from aristocratic resentment of her favoritism showered on Pedro González de Lara. He was her lover, and she gave birth to their children. In Galicia, Bishop Gelmírez sometimes supported Urraca and other times defied her. She in turn made several attempts to confiscate parts of his vast holdings and even to seize his person. Her intermittent feud with Gelmírez failed to curb the prelate's power.

To counter Urraca's pressure, Gelmírez urged Pope Calixtus II to impose Urraca's abdication and the accession of Alphonso Raimúndez. This was no idle threat, as the pope was Count Raymond's brother and thus Alphonso's uncle. Urraca foiled these attempts but could not prevent Gelmírez's rise in power. In 1124, he secured the titles of archbishop and metropolitan, placing his stature and prestige beyond Urraca's reach.

By that time, however, Urraca's own position was more secure. She and Alphonso the Battler concentrated on their own realms, although he still claimed to be king of Castile. Alphonso Raimúndez ruled Galicia and Toledo, content to inherit the remainder of Urraca's kingdoms. Gradually the most powerful and ambitious courtiers began to leave Urraca's service and join her son. On May 25, 1124, in Santiago, 19-year-old Alphonso Raimúndez armed himself as a knight, a formal declaration that he was of age to rule. The queen's half-sister Teresa still held a few cities in Leon, but was no longer a grave threat to Urraca. Castilian and Leonese aristocrats sometimes grumbled and plotted, to little avail.

Queen Urraca died on March 8, 1126, in Saldaña. Her remains were buried in the church of San Isidoro at Leon. Contemporary chronicles said nothing about the nature of her death, but later reports alleged that she died in childbirth, apparently having continued her liaison with the count of Lara. The count reportedly hoped to marry Urraca. But strong-willed as ever, she refused to wed again and risk losing her power and freedom of action.

Over the centuries, Urraca has been a controversial figure in Spanish history. Aragonese writers have often criticized her while lauding Alphonso. Castilian scholars sometimes exaggerate her achievements. Historian Bernard Reilly has studied her reign closely and writes: "What is surprising, given the magnitude of the dynastic crisis that she inherited and the novelty of her own position as reigning queen, is the great extent to which she succeeded in these endeavors." She wisely perceived the need to make her son and his partisans active participants in her government. Although her marriage to Alphonso theoretically promised the unification of Christian Spain, Alphonso's inability, through impotence or sterility, to father an heir foreclosed that possibility. Furthermore, the northern kingdoms lacked centralized institutions on which to build that unity. While Urraca did not reconquer Portugal, neither did her male successor. Perhaps as Urraca's most important achievement, she bequeathed to her son Alphonso VII a stable and peaceful realm.

SOURCES:

Lacarra, José María. *Alfonso el Batallador.* Zaragoza: Guara Editorial, 1978.

Martín, José Luis. *La Península en la Edad Media.* 2 ed. Barcelona: Teide, 1980.

Miron, E.L. *The Queens of Aragon: Their Lives and Times.* NY: Brentano's, 1913.

O'Callaghan, Joseph F. *A History of Medieval Spain.* Ithaca, NY: Cornell University Press, 1975.

Reilly, Bernard F. *The Kingdom of León-Castilla under Queen Urraca, 1109–1126.* Princeton, NJ: Princeton University Press, 1982.

———. *The Medieval Spains.* NY: Cambridge University Press, 1993.

SUGGESTED READING:

Florez de Setien, Enrique. *Memorias de las reinas católicas de España.* 2 vols. Madrid: M. Aguilar, 1945.

Historia Compostellana. Trans. and ed. by Emma Falque Rey. Corpus Christianorum LXX. Turnhout: Brepols, 1988.

MacKay, Angus. *Spain in the Middle Ages: From Frontier to Empire, 1000–1500.* London: Macmillan, 1977.

Kendall W. Brown, Professor of History, Brigham Young University, Provo, Utah

Eleanor of Castile (1162–1214). See Blanche of Castile for sidebar.

Urraca (c. 1096–c. 1130)

*Countess of Trastamara. Born around 1096; died after 1130; daughter of *Teresa of Castile (c. 1080–1130) and Henry, count of Burgundy (r. 1093–1112); sister of Alphonso I Henriques, king of Portugal (r. 1139–1185); married Bermudo, count of Trastamara, before 1120.*

Urraca of Aragon

*Princess of Aragon. Daughter of *Gilberga (d. 1054) and Ramiro I, king of Aragon (r. 1035–1069); became a nun.*

Urraca of Castile (d. 1179)

*Queen of Navarre. Born after 1126; died on October 12, 1179 (some sources cite 1189), in Palencia; illegitimate daughter of Alfonso also known as Alphonso VII (1105–1157), king of Castile (r. 1126–1157), and Gontrada Perez; married Garcia Ramirez IV, king of Navarre (r. 1134–1150), on June 24, 1144; children: Sancha (who married Gaston V, vicomte of Bearn, and Peter, vicomte of Narbonne); Rodrigo, count of Montescaglioso. Garcia's first wife was *Marguerite de l'Aigle (d. 1141).*

Urraca of Castile (c. 1186–1220)

Queen of Portugal. Born in 1186 or 1187 in Castile; died in 1220; daughter of Alfonso or Alphonso VIII, also known as Alphonso III (1155–1214), king of Castile (r. 1158–1214), and Eleanor of Castile (1162–1214, daughter of Henry II of England and Eleanor of Aquitaine); sister of *Berengeria of Castile (1171–1246) and Blanche of Castile (1187–1252); married Alfonso or Alphonso II the Fat (1185–1223), king of Portugal (r. 1211–1223), in 1206; children: Sancho II (1207–1248), king of Portugal (r. 1223–1248); Alphonso III (1215–1279), king of Portugal (r. 1248–1279); *Leonor of Portugal (1211–1231); Fernando or Ferdinand (1217–1246, who married Sancha de Lara); Vicente (b. 1219, died young).*

Urraca of Castile was the daughter of Castilian King Alphonso VIII and Queen ◄ **Eleanor of Castile**. Her younger sister Blanca, or *Blanche of Castile, became one of medieval Europe's most powerful women as queen-regent of France. It had been expected that Urraca, as the older, more attractive daughter, would be chosen to marry the heir to the French throne. However, their grandmother, the English queen *Eleanor of Aquitaine, chose Blanche as the future queen of France. Her envoys, trying to justify the decision which had the Castilian court bewildered, explained that the French would have trouble pronouncing Urraca's name, but could easily pronounce Blanche's.

Alphonso eventually arranged a marriage between his older daughter and Alphonso (II), the heir of his powerful neighbor, the king of Portugal. Like Blanche, Urraca proved to be an excellent queen; she was popular among the people, pious, and a believer in the responsibilities inherent in kingship (or queenship). She involved herself in the daily functions of the administration, and presided over a large and intellectual court. She also used her own wealth to found hospitals and convents.

SOURCES:

Gies, Frances, and Joseph Gies. *Women in the Middle Ages.* NY: Harper and Row, 1978.

Laura York, M.A. in History, University of California, Riverside, California

Urraca of Portugal (c. 1151–1188)

*Queen of Leon. Born around 1151; died on October 16, 1188; daughter of *Matilda of Maurienne (c. 1125–1157) and Alphonso I Henriques, king of Portugal (r. 1139–1185); sister of Sancho I, king of Portugal (r. 1185–1211), *Matilda of Portugal (c. 1149–1173), and *Teresa of Portugal (1157–1218); became first wife of Fernando or Ferdinand II (1137–1188), king of Leon (r. 1157–1188), in 1165* *(divorced 1175); children: Alfonso or Alphonso IX (1171–1230), king of Leon (r. 1188–1230).*

Ursins, Marie Anne (c. 1642–1722).

See Marie-Anne de la Trémouille.

Ursins, Princess of the (c. 1642–1722).

See Marie-Anne de la Trémouille.

Ursinus, Sophie (1760–1836)

German murderer. *Born Sophie Charlotte Elizabeth Weingarten in 1760; died on April 4, 1836; daughter of an Austrian diplomat; married Ursinus of Berlin (a privy counselor), in 1779 (died 1800).*

Sophie Ursinus was born in 1760 and grew up in an affluent family, the daughter of an Austrian diplomat. In 1779, she married a wealthy elderly man, the privy counselor Ursinus of Berlin. He allowed her to have a younger lover, a Dutch officer named Rogay; the affair ended with Rogay's death. Doctors said he had suffered from tuberculosis. Ursinus' husband died on September 11, 1800.

More deaths followed the relatively young widow. Ursinus' aunt **Christina Regina Witte** died mysteriously on January 21, 1801. Later, it was determined that Ursinus had killed Witte, as well as the Dutch officer and her husband. Under police interrogation, Ursinus' servant, Benjamin Klein, said that Ursinus had given her husband arsenic because she did not want to be bothered with caring for an old man; she had poisoned Rogay because she suspected he would leave her. She had killed her aunt in order to inherit her estate. She also attempted to kill Klein, because he was planning to quit working for her and he knew too much. Although she gave him a dose of the poison, he recovered. Later, after she was convicted of murder, Ursinus gave him a generous pension.

Although Ursinus was suspected of all these murders, only the killing of her aunt could be proved against her. Sent to prison, she lived out her life in customarily grand style. She occupied a large suite of rooms on the top floor of the prison, a huge stone fortress at Glatz. She was allowed to have servants and fill the rooms with her own furniture. In addition to her fortune, inherited from her husband, she was also allowed to keep the money she had gained from the death of her murdered aunt. Ursinus gave parties in her suite that local aristocrats attended. Dressed in fine style, she was an attraction for many tourists curious about this upper-class

woman murderer who entertained them with stories of her innocence.

Ursinus died on April 4, 1836. Her lavish funeral was attended by hundreds of aristocrats. Members of the clergy praised her generosity to the poor, neglecting to mention the murders she had committed, while children sang hymns praising her.

SOURCES:
Nash, Jay Robert. *Look for the Woman.* NY: M. Evans, 1981.

Kelly Winters,
freelance writer

Urso, Camilla (1842–1902)

French violinist, widely acclaimed, who was the first female ever admitted to the Paris Conservatoire and one of the first female child prodigies to continue performing as an adult. Born in Nantes, France, on June 13, 1842; died in 1902; eldest child of Salvator Urso (an organist and flutist from Palermo, Italy) and Emilie Girouard (from Portugal).

One of the great virtuosi of her day, Camilla Urso was the first woman violinist to appear in concert in the United States. She also greatly influenced the development of high quality concert programming. Urso was born into an impoverished family in 1842 in Nantes, France. Her father Salvator Urso, an Italian musician, noted his daughter's early abilities and masterminded her career. As first flutist in the orchestra of the local opera, he carried his daughter to the theater almost every night. He was also organist at the Church of the Holy Cross.

At age six, Camilla stood listening at his side while the choir performed the mass of St. *Cecilia. In 1868, **Mary A. Betts** dramatically described the pivotal scene:

> Solemnly, slowly, the organ tones swelled and died. Clear voices of soprano and tenor rose upon the air with the saddening plaint of *Kyrie Eleison*. The orchestral harmonies interwove their pathetic or triumphant music. The dark-haired child . . . listened— not awed by the under-wave of the mighty organ . . . —but enchanted for life by the inarticulate passion and sorrow of the violin's changing vibrations. The last note of the mass floated into silence. . . . Her father's hand aroused her, and she walked home announcing in a firm tone . . . "I wish to learn the violin."

The following year, it was announced that the seven-year-old Urso would give her first concert, for the benefit of a widow. Friends came to applaud heartily, strangers came to laugh. The event was reported in a Nantes gazette:

> Never had violinist a *pose* more exact, firmer, and at the same time perfectly easy; never was bow guided with greater precision than by this little Urso, whose delivery made all the mothers smile. . . . [U]nder these fingers, which are yet often busied with dressing a doll, the instrument gives out a purity and sweetness of tone, with an expression most remarkable. Every light and shade is observed, and all the intentions of the composer are faithfully rendered. . . . Effects of double stopping, staccato, rapid arpeggios,—everything is executed with the same precision, the same purity, the same grace. It is impossible to describe the ovation that the child received. Repeatedly interrupted by applause and acclamations, she was saluted at the end by salvos of bravos and a shower of bouquets.

That same year, Salvator took Camilla to Paris in an attempt to gain her admittance to the prestigious Paris Conservatoire, where no female had been allowed to enter. The music world remained highly restricted to women. They were not supposed to perform in public and, when they did play in private, they were supposed to play "female" instruments like the piano. Urso's choice of the violin was in itself a proclamation of equality; at the time, the violin was a "masculine" instrument. The faculty found Signor Urso's request absurd: not only a woman, but too young, much too young. And the violin! But Salvator Urso pleaded. Possibly because the faculty was placating him, Camilla found herself playing before a panel of judges comprised of Rossini, Meyerbeer, Massart, and Auber, the school director. She was accepted unanimously: the first female allowed to enter the Paris Conservatoire.

Urso studied for three years, principally under Massart, practicing ten and twelve hours a day, learning harmony, solfeggi. To acquire a steadiness of position, she rehearsed with one foot in a saucer. Fear of breaking the dish kept her feet motionless.

During these years, her family was so poor that Camilla was allowed to concertize to support them, a special indulgence rarely granted by the conservatory. After she went on a three-month tour of Germany, the German public took her to its heart. She also appeared in public concerts in Paris. Wrote one critic: "She excels in that essential expression which comes wholly from the soul, and which the composer, from lack of means to note and write out, abandons to the discretion and intelligence of the executant."

At age ten, she was a sensation mainly because of her gender. Many were surprised to discover women (or girls) could play violins at all, much less extremely well. The child prodigy gave her first concert in New York, performing on the same bill with **Marietta Alboni** in Trippler Hall (1852). She then joined *Henriette **Sontag**'s U.S. tour in 1853. Sontag "was perfection," said Camilla Urso. "An angel, in talents, temper, and goodness. At fifty-two one would kneel to her,—what must she have been at twenty? She herself took the place of my mother, who was not in America. She plaited my hair, attended to my dresses, and cared for me in everything." They continued the tour in the South and Mexico to ecstatic audiences. When the tour broke up in March 1854, Salvator Urso took his daughter to Savannah, followed by more concertizing in the Southern states. When they returned to New York that May, they heard of the sudden death of Sontag from cholera. Urso was grief stricken. Losing her enthusiasm, she refused to give concerts. Her father, counting on a change of scene, took his daughter to Canada in 1856.

While in Canada in 1859, they learned that their New York apartment had been robbed and all her prized souvenirs taken. Then, on her return to New York, she received an overture from a **Mrs. McCready** to tour the West. At age 15, on her own for the first time, Urso left her father in New York and proceeded to Nashville to join McCready. But she was in the hands of a swindler: there was no contract, no tour and no money. Penniless, she enlisted the sympathy of Nashville citizens; a concert was scheduled and she raised $400. This was not, of course, Urso's first experience with those who fed off artists.

The series of losses had its effect. Urso retired from public life for the next five years and did not return to the concert hall until March 1863, at the Philharmonic in New York; she was now 21 and played better than ever. As a child, Urso had been a precocious novelty; now she was a mature artist. Her ability to draw large crowds was just as great. Though she performed with a grave and frequently sad expression, there was a playfulness in her; she capped one New Haven performance with "Yankee Doodle."

Reviews of the period reveal the innate sexism of the musical field, however. "Madame Urso's playing of the Mendelssohn Concerto was a marvel of art," wrote one authority. "The only qualification is that it was feminine; there was not of course the manly force, the . . . heroic onsweep of Carl Rosa's bow which carries all before it." Or, "Camilla Urso played the first movement of the Beethoven Concerto with such perfect purity of intonation, such fine and vital

Camilla Urso

quality of tone (though of course feminine and delicate rather than broad and manly)." The musicians of the orchestra of the Harvard Association, having heard her Mendelssohn, felt otherwise: "It is not enough to say that it was a wonderful performance for a woman; it was a consummate rendering, which probably few men living could improve upon." Sadly, the irrelevance of this discourse continues still. Urso, herself, did not consider such comments defamatory, since she capitalized on the fact that she was a woman.

Nineteenth-century concerts had a great deal in common with vaudeville in that they were not serious affairs. Their format had a number of variety acts; no concert was dedicated to any one artist. There were a large number of short selections and most were lightweight. Opera arias were particular favorites. When Camilla Urso began her career, she was one of many acts, a star because of her youth and gender. As she became an accomplished artist, Urso was more and more determined to change the concert format. She played fewer virtuosic showpieces and more substantial works from the classical repertoire. She often played Mendelssohn and Beethoven during a period when they were considered to be "modern" composers. She also devoted concerts to string quartets and chamber orchestras. Few soloists of the period were willing to become part of a group, but Urso enjoyed ensemble playing. She raised the level of concert playing to another tier and demonstrated that audiences would support the new programming.

Symphony orchestras of the period were all male. Because she was such an accomplished musician, members of the Philadelphia Philharmonic Society, an all-male organization, elected Urso an "honorary member." She had already appeared with the Paris Conservatoire orchestra in 1866, the first woman to do so. During her concert career, Urso became more and more convinced that women should have the opportunity to become regular orchestra players. She recognized that the male hierarchy of conductors, managers, boards of directors, and critics effectively discriminated against her sex. In the last years of her life, she was the honorary president of the Women's String Orchestra, one of the first female symphony orchestras. Urso believed, however, that women should be integrated into mainstream orchestras. It was not until well into the 20th century, when women demanded that musicians be auditioned behind curtains, that they were admitted into major symphony orchestras. The fact that they are now included is due, in part, to the remarkable violinist Camilla Urso.

SOURCES:

Barnard, Charles. *Camilla: A Tale of a Violin*. Boston, MA: Loring, 1874.

Betts, Mary A. "Camilla Urso," in *Eminent Women of the Age*. S.M. Betts, 1868.

Kagan, Susan. "Camilla Urso," in *The Strad*. Vol. 102, no. 1210. February 1991, pp. 150–152.

"Urso, Camilla," in *Dictionary of American Biography*. NY: Scribner, 1964.

"Urso, Camilla," in *Notable American Women, 1607–1950*. Cambridge, MA: The Belknap Press of Harvard University, 1971.

John Haag,
Associate Professor of History,
University of Georgia, Athens, Georgia

Ursula (fl. 3rd or 5th c.)

British princess, saint, and martyr. Birth date unknown; died in either 238, 283, or 451; daughter of a British prince.

A British princess, Saint Ursula is especially honored in Cologne, the place of her Christian martyrdom. One legend has it that while leading a group of virgins on a pilgrimage to Rome, she and her charges were massacred by the Huns at Cologne. Another version claims that she was fleeing Great Britain and the atrocities of the invading Saxons. The numbered dead is also in extremely wide dispute. Some sources assign the total of young girls martyred at 11,000, while others claim as few as 5. Omer Englebert, in his *Lives of the Saints*, suggest that 11 is more probable, and he offers the names Ursula, **Pinnosa**, **Martha**, **Saula**, **Brittica**, **Gregoria**, **Saturnina**, **Sabatia**, **Palladia**, **Sentia**, and **Saturia**. Early in the 12th century, the citizens of Cologne, while digging foundations across the cemetery of the old Roman settlement of Colonia Agrippina, found a number of bones. These were declared by the nun *****Elizabeth of Schönau** to be the relics of the virgins.

This 12th-century tale is found in the *Chronicle* of Sigebert of Gemblours and in the Bollandist *Acta Sanctorum*, and was popularized by Geoffrey of Monmouth. St. *****Catherine of Bologna** (1413–1463), a monastic woman artist, painted Ursula with an arrow in one hand while her cape protectively envelops some young girls. The feast day of Ursula, the patron saint of maidens, is celebrated on October 21.

Ursula of Brandenburg (1488–1510)

*Duchess of Mecklenburg. Born on October 17, 1488; died on September 18, 1510; daughter of *Margaret of Saxony (1449–1501) and Joachim I, elector of Brandenburg (r. 1486–1499); married Henry III, duke of Mecklenburg, on February 16, 1507; children: *Sophia of Mecklenburg (1508–1541); Magnus of Mecklenburg-Schwerin (b. 1509).*

Ursuleac, Viorica (1894–1985)

Rumanian soprano who created the leading soprano roles in several of Richard Strauss' operas. Born in Czernowitz on March 26, 1894; died in Ehrwald, Tyrol, on October 23, 1985; married Clemens Krauss (the conductor).

Viorica Ursuleac was born in 1894 in the Austro-Hungarian empire which collapsed at the end of World War I. Although she was Rumanian, culturally Ursuleac remained Austro-German. In the old empire, Vienna was the center of culture. It is not surprising then that the young singer trained in Vienna and by 1930 had moved there permanently. She created the leading soprano roles in several of Strauss' operas, in *Arabella* in Dresden in 1933, in *Friedenstag* in Munich in 1938, and in *Capriccio* in Munich in 1942. During her career, Ursuleac gave 506 performances in 12 Strauss roles. She was mainly a Central European performer and appeared only once at Covent Garden, in 1934, where she sang in the English premieres of *Arabella* and *Svanda the Bagpiper*. Ursuleac, who had 83 roles in her repertory over her long career, was a notable Tosca and Turandot as well as Senta and Sieglinde.

John Haag,
Athens, Georgia

Uta of Passau

Duchess of Carinthia. Daughter of Udalrich, count of Passau; married Ingelbert II, duke of Carinthia; children: Maud Carinthia (c. 1105–1160).

Utley, Freda (1898–1977)

English-American journalist, author, and ardent critic of the Soviet Union and the People's Republic of China. Born Freda Utley on January 23, 1898, in London, England; died of a stroke at Georgetown University Hospital in Washington, D.C., on January 21, 1977; daughter of Willie Herbert Utley (a journalist) and Emily (Williamson) Utley; educated at La Combe School, Geneva; Priors School, Surrey, England; King's College, London University, B.A. (first class honors), 1923; Westfield College, London University, M.A. (with distinction), 1925; research fellow, London School of Economics, 1926–27; doctorate, Russian Academy of Sciences, 1933; common-law marriage with Arcadi Berdichevsky, 1930; children: John (Jon) Basil.

Was a research fellow, London School of Economics (1926–28); worked as special correspondent, Manchester Guardian Commercial, in Japan (1928–29); employed in the Soviet Union by the Comintern, the Commissariat of Foreign Trade, the Commissariat of Light Industry, and the Institute of World Economy and Politics (1930–36); was special correspondent, London News-Chronicle, China war zone (1938); was an accredited correspondent, Reader's Digest, China (1945–46), Germany (1948); freelance writer.

Selected writings: An Illustrated History of the Russian Revolution *(International, 1928);* Lancashire

and the Far East *(G. Allen and Unwin, London, 1931);* Japan's Feet of Clay *(W.W. Norton, 1937);* Japan's Gamble in China *(Secker and Warburg, London, 1938);* China at War *(John Day, 1939);* The Dream We Lost: Soviet Russia Then and Now *(John Day, 1940);* Lost Illusion *(Fireside Press, 1948);* The High Cost of Vengeance *(Henry Regnery, 1949);* The China Story: How We Lost Four Hundred Million Allies *(Henry Regnery, 1951);* Will the Middle East Go West? *(Henry Regnery, 1957);* Odyssey of a Liberal: Memoirs *(Washington National Press, 1970).*

During the night of April 10, 1936, a couple living in a three-room flat in Moscow heard a knock at the door. "We have guests," Arcadi Berdichevsky told his common-law wife. Springing out of bed, Freda Utley saw a soldier in the hall. Two secret police agents in uniform entered the sitting room, followed by the building's janitor. Forbidding them to speak, the secret police meticulously searched the apartment. The couple possessed hundreds of books. Each one was systematically examined. Utley recalled that when her eyes met Arcadi's "we gave each other a smile and a look of confidence and calm. One must keep calm. Is it a dream? Has the end come to pass? Is this now happening to us which has happened to so many others? Will the nightmare pass, or is this the end of our love and our life?"

At 9 AM, the police led Berdichevsky away. After a parting kiss, Utley asked furtively, "To whom shall I go?" He shrugged. "No one can help," he said. Utley later recalled, "He passed out of my life on that lovely April morning in his old, Navy blue English flannel jacket, his black head hatless, a slight figure between the two stonefaced, khaki-clad police officers." Late in August 1936, Berdichevsky was sentenced without trial to five years at hard labor. Between that September and the following May, Utley received three postcards from him. Then all mail stopped, never to be resumed. Only on New Year's Eve of 1963 did she learn that her spouse had died on March 30, 1938, at Komi in the Arctic north.

Freda Utley's name would ever afterwards be linked with the strongest possible opposition to the Soviet Union and later to the People's Republic of China. In her books and articles, the British-born Utley fervently condemned Stalinist and Maoist rule and attacked any Westerners whom she perceived as favoring an accommodation to world communism. In her memoirs, she wrote, "It was I who had lured Arcadi to death or slavery in Soviet Russia by renewing his faith that God's kingdom on earth could be established by adhering to the godless faith of the Marxists."

Freda Utley was born on January 23, 1898, in London, England, to Willie Herbert Utley and **Emily Williamson Utley**. Both parents were Socialists, and indeed the couple had been introduced to each other by the son-in-law of Karl Marx. Willie was editorial writer and music critic for the *London Star*, contributed to British weeklies, and served as secretary of the Fabian Society. In Manchester, he had spoken from the same platform as Marx's collaborator Friedrich Engels. Emily, who had grown up in a radical Manchester family, was a trained nurse.

For a time, Willie was so prosperous that his daughter grew up in a large home in Hampstead full of servants and governesses. From ages five to nine, Freda and her brother Temple traveled in Switzerland and Italy. Then, for two years, Freda attended La Combe School in Geneva, where she was the only English pupil. The atmosphere, she remembered, was "studious, tolerant, kindly, and healthy," qualities she certainly did not find at her next school, Priors, located in Surrey, England. Claiming that Priors embodied a "frigid, mind-destroying atmosphere," she developed a strong hatred of what she called "the imperialist English bourgeoise." In 1915, she was forced to leave Priors' School, for her fa-

$Freda$
$Utley$

ther—already tubercular—had suffered heavy business losses. Her mother nursed her invalid husband under conditions of extreme poverty: the couple lived in a two-room cottage in Cornwall so primitive that Emily had to fetch water from a bucket. Suddenly Freda was experiencing a social system that, she later said, "could fling one into poverty from security, and prevent one from continuing one's education whatever the proof of one's mental qualifications."

Utley first taught in Manchester, living on bread, margarine, and marmalade, then in 1916 became a resident governess in Hampshire. Early the next year, she was hired as a clerk at the War Office, drawing a salary of $11 a week. She also served as branch secretary of a trade union, the Association of War Clerks and Secretaries, through which she obtained a scholarship to King's College, London University. In 1923, she received a B.A. degree, with first class honors in history. Two years later, after study at London University's Westfield College, she earned an M.A. degree, her thesis centering on trade guilds of the late Roman Empire. As a research fellow at the London School of Economics from 1926 to 1928, Utley studied the effect of Indian competition on the declining cotton industry of Lancashire. In the summer of 1926, she served as tutor to a son of philosopher Bertrand Russell, whom she later called "the greatest man I ever knew."

All this time, Utley was plunging into politics. She became secretary of the college's Socialist Society, then chair of the London University Labor Party. She joined the Independent Labor Party, a group more radical than the regular Labor Party. She also taught classes for the Workers' Educational Association, wrote book reviews for the London *Daily Herald*, and contributed articles to such journals as the *New Leader*, the *New Statesman*, *Labour Monthly*, and *Contemporary Review*. The General Strike of 1926 turned Utley to the extreme left as it convinced her of the reality of class war and the impossibility of any gradual approach towards socialism.

That year, while visiting a friend in Hampstead, Utley met Arcadi Berdichevsky, finance minister of the Soviet Trade Delegation in London. Never a Bolshevik, Berdichevsky had been a member of the Jewish Bund, a Social Democratic group in Russian Poland. Although always a dedicated Socialist, he had lived in England for six years and was ignorant of day-to-day life in the Soviet Union. Although Berdichevsky was already married, he and Utley were soon lovers.

In 1927, Utley visited the Soviet Union as vice president of the University Labor Federation, comprised of all the Labor and Socialist clubs in the British universities. Lenin's New Economic Policy was still in force and Leon Trotsky had not yet been exiled. Returning to England a true believer in the Russian experiment, Utley proclaimed her allegiance to British communism and addressed party meetings throughout the nation.

In the summer of 1928, when her London School fellowship ended, Freda joined Arcadi, who had moved to Moscow. "For him," she later wrote, "I was a symbol as well as the companion in the new life in socialist society which we both expected to lead." After brief employment as a translator, she went to China as a Comintern courier. Arriving in Shanghai, she met with leaders of the Communist underground. The couple spent 1929 in Tokyo, where she researched the textile industry and wrote for the *Manchester Guardian Commercial*, while Arcadi engaged in business activity for the Soviet government. By 1930, Utley had returned to Britain, where she served as a member of the party's Industrial Committee, wrote for Communist publications, and worked for the party among Lancashire textile workers.

Returning to Russia later that year, Utley entered into a common-law marriage with Berdichevsky. Arcadi worked for an economic agency, Promexport, which promoted the sale of Soviet manufactures overseas. Utley worked in turn for the Comintern, the Commissariat of Foreign Trade, the Commissariat of Light Industry, and the Institute of World Economy and Politics.

The couple lived a life of impoverishment, moving in Moscow from one primitive flat to another. At one point, they lived in a room with a single bed, a small table, and three hard chairs. Another time, they shared a bathroom with Berdichevsky's divorced wife and child and with another family of three. Moreover, the search for food became a daily struggle. Everywhere, Utley witnessed exploitation, starvation, gross incompetence, and a discriminatory reward system, with choice goods reserved for party functionaries. In 1933, she wrote her brother that Stalin was not a genuine Marxist and that she wished she could join Trotsky's exile movement. Soon she was disabused of Trotskyism as well.

Once her husband was arrested, Utley left Russia for England, for she feared her son might be in danger. Leaving her infant Jon in a nursery school in Ditching, Sussex, she returned to Russia where she daily joined the queue at the public prosecutor's office to discover her husband's fate. Whenever she was able to see an official,

she was told to return in a few days. Soon she started writing letters of appeal—to the prosecutor; to the assistant chief of the secret police, Nikolay Tezhov; and even to dictator Stalin himself. No one replied.

Finally in July 1936, Utley went back to England, where she thought she could exert greater pressure. For two years, she did not speak publicly, for she feared that an open protest would seal Berdichevsky's fate. Only in 1938 did she ask the British Foreign Office for aid. Although deserted by her former Communist associates, she was befriended by Bertrand and **Margery Spence Russell**, *Guardian* correspondent Malcolm Muggeridge (himself much disillusioned with the Soviet Union), and Socialist author H.N. Brailsford, all of whom petitioned the Soviet Union to release Berdichevsky. Playwright George Bernard Shaw first refused to cooperate, telling Utley that "imprisonment under the Soviet is not as bad as it is here in the west." After much cajoling by the Russells, he eventually joined the appeal.

Never in my life have I seen a woman in whose heart and mind every hope on earth has been slain as has hers.

—*Agnes Smedley

Already Utley was becoming known as an Asian specialist. In *Japan's Feet of Clay* (1937), she called Japanese expansion "the most brutal, oppressive and destructive of all Imperialisms." Yet, so she argued, Japan was "putting up a big bluff to the world," starting its military aggression with the scantiest of food and industrial resources. Indeed, she found social revolution imminent.

In 1938, as special correspondent for the *London News-Chronicle*, Utley covered the China war. Part of a small band of Westerners she named "Hankow (Hankou)'s Last Ditches," she remained at China's beleaguered wartime capital until it fell to Japan. At one point, she ventured to the front at Nanking (Nanjing). The press corps gave her the name "Clayfoot Utley," a spoof on the title of her latest book, but she won respect by her willingness to bear hardship.

While in China, Utley formed a dislike for *Song Meiling, commonly known as Mme Chiang Kai-shek, whom she found too egotistical and aloof from her people. Chiang Kai-shek himself, she believed, lacked vision and was insensitive to China's masses. At the same time, Utley welcomed courtship by China's Communists, whom she found agrarian reformers. Undoubtedly because of her strong opposition to

Japanese expansion, the Chinese Communist Party (CCP)—unlike its Russian counterpart—did not consider her an apostate. Zhou Enlai visited her quarters and the Eighth Route Army gave a reception in her honor. She in turn found Zhou a charming, intelligent, "most persuasive" human being and the CCP producing "a different breed" of Communist. The reds, she asserted, were China's "greatest realists" and its "most modern-minded element."

In 1938, Utley's book *Japan's Gamble in China* was published, with an introduction by the British political scientist Harold J. Laski. At this stage of her writing, she believed in the reality of a United Front between the Chinese Communists and the Guomindang (Kuomintang). In a letter to the British weekly *New Statesman and Nation* written in January 1939, she wrote, "there are no 'Bolsheviks' to-day in China; they have all become 'Mensheviks.'" In another book, *China at War* (1939), she gave credit to Chiang's forces fighting on the Yangtze (Yangtse) River. She still argued that "the Chinese Communist Party long ago abandoned the dream of establishing its own dictatorship."

While she was en route to the United States in 1939, there to engage in a lecture tour, Utley's ship docked in Yokohama. The Japanese government, far from pleased with her writings, placed an armed guard outside her cabin door. Once in America, Utley addressed audiences from coast to coast for six weeks, sometimes speaking twice a day. Her sponsor: the American Committee for Non-Participation in Japanese Aggression, a group that wanted to embargo U.S. export of war materials to Japan.

All this time, Utley feared the advent of another war between Germany and the West, claiming that Stalin would exploit the opportunity to overrun "an exhausted and ruined Europe." In 1938, she endorsed the Munich agreement. In March 1939, she suggested that a Russo-German alliance was imminent, a view that seemed so absurd that she could not get it published. Once war broke out on September 1, 1939, Utley urged the U.S. to remain aloof from the conflict.

When Utley had given up all hope that her husband was alive, she wrote a fullscale exposé of communism, *The Dream We Lost: Then and Now* (1940, revised and reprinted as *Lost Illusion* [1948], with foreword by novelist John P. Marquand). Much of the book described, in the bitterest of terms, her personal life in the Soviet Union. She condemned Germany's "mad course of conquest" as well as Hitler's "brutality, ruthlessness, and mysticism." Yet she argued that if

given economic opportunity and power, "the Germans may yet get rid of the brutal element now uppermost among the Nazis, and develop the progressive features of National Socialism: its Socialism as distinct from its rampant Nationalism." Indeed, she wrote of "the eventual democratization of the system." Furthermore, were the Germans to conquer the Soviet Union, the victory "would be a boon to the Russian masses" as Nazism ensured "the full development and utilization of resources." Continuing on this theme, Utley told a radio audience in July 1940: "The Russian brand of national socialism is even more oppressive, and far more destructive of life and material prosperity than the German."

In October 1941, Utley called for a negotiated peace, a proposal given national circulation in *Reader's Digest*. Here she claimed that the U.S. should place its power unequivocally behind any British efforts to reach an accommodation among equals. Such a truce, she conceded, would leave the European continent under German domination, but she found it the only way that Britain could preserve its trade and industrial plant. To Utley, any American invasion of the European continent would be folly, while wholesale bombing and economic blockade were counter-productive. Were such a peace made, there lay "the reasonable hope" that Germany would rid itself of "the gangsters that now rule her, and revert to civilized values."

By the end of 1939, Utley had decided to settle in the U.S., but she was unable to get citizenship until five years later. Her former Communist affiliations and extreme version of isolationism held up her application. Living in Baltimore, then in Greenwich Village, New York, she lectured and wrote in almost destitute conditions. Her contributions were usually to journals of small circulation, such as the *New Leader*, the *Progressive*, *Asia*, and *Common Sense* (where her plea for a negotiated peace originally appeared). In 1940, she became economic adviser to Starr, Park, and Freeman, Inc., an underwriting firm, where she worked until 1944. Her prediction in July 1941 that Japan would soon fight the U.S. saved the firm considerable funds.

In 1944, Utley moved to Washington, D.C., where she was consultant to the Chinese Supply Commission. She also gave confidential reports on China to the Office of Strategic Services, the U.S. wartime intelligence agency. Her enthusiasm for the Chinese Communists had chilled when Communist leader Mao Zedong rationalized Stalin's 1939 pact with Hitler. By 1941, she was portraying them as "under the aegis of a foreign power which is not the least interested in them, but only in the survival of the Stalinist bureaucracy." In an article in the *American Mercury* published in September 1944, Utley conceded that Chiang Kai-shek's ruling party, the Guomindang, possessed many shortcomings; it had, however, been making progress until Japan's attack in 1937.

In October 1945, *Reader's Digest* sent Utley to China as correspondent. During her stay, she visited Chongqing (Chungking), Shanghai, Yan'an (Yenan), and Beijing (Peking). Interviewing both Chiang and Communist leader Zhou Enlai, she claimed that the two might be "noble men." Still maintaining that the CCP was an instrument of the Soviet Union, she argued in her report, *Last Chance in China* (1947), that the U.S. should equip the Nationalist armies. At the same time, to insure lack of corruption, the U.S. should insist upon the installation of reformist officials to direct the nation's rehabilitation. Although the Guomindang would have to borrow money from the United States, it could raise additional funds by exporting to Japan's former markets in Asia. Utley went so far as to claim that the Guomindang was not tyrannical but—to the contrary—too weak. She wrote, "The main defect of the Chinese Government is not its dictatorial character but its failure to govern, the graft with which it is riddled and its inability to check abuses and carry out the reforms to which it is pledged." She continued, "The American demand for a strong *and* democratic China is totally unrealistic. China should not be expected to run before she can walk."

When, in 1949, the CCP took control of China, Utley blamed the United States. In *The China Story* (1951), she wrote, "We lost China by default and opened the way to the Communist conquest of the Far East." It was, she implied, a small clique of Communist sympathizers in America, epitomized by such figures as journalist Edgar Snow, who had deceived ordinary Americans into believing that Chinese Communists were merely agrarian reformers (her own former belief). Yet, noting that Chiang proclaimed a land-reform program in October 1950, when he established a rump regime on Taiwan, she wrote, "Sometimes a great disaster is required to awaken men to their fundamental errors."

In the immediate postwar years, much of Utley's attention was focused on Germany. In 1948, she covered events there for *Reader's Digest*, out of which emerged *The High Cost of Vengeance* (1949). She found the denazification proceedings unfair, the dismantling of industrial plants reckless. To Utley, the forced removals of German nationals from the Sudetenland and Silesia equaled "those crimes against humanity" (a term used in the Nuremberg indictment) committed by the Nazis. Indeed, so she claimed, for the women and children who perished on the forced march, "a quick death in a gas chamber would have been relatively merciful." Unlike many former isolationists, Utley endorsed the Truman Doctrine, Marshall Plan, Atlantic Pact, and U.S. entry into the Korean War.

When in 1950 Senator Joseph R. McCarthy (Rep.-Wis.) attacked Sinologist Owen Lattimore, Utley wrote one of McCarthy's speeches against the China specialist. Lattimore had befriended Utley in 1936 and Utley once used Lattimore as a character reference. Testifying before a Senate investigating committee, Utley denied McCarthy's charge that Lattimore was the top Kremlin agent in the U.S., but branded him "an out-and-out defender of the Soviet government," a man who had "done more than anyone else to have poisoned the wells of opinion with respect to China." She called Lattimore a "Judas cow," a stockyard animal that led others to the slaughter. "The Communist cancer," she said, "must be cut out if we are to survive as a free nation. Perhaps in this operation some healthy tissues on the fringe will be destroyed."

During 1952 and 1953, Utley was a correspondent in Europe for *Pathfinder* and the *Freeman*. Although she would write occasionally for *Commonweal* and the *Saturday Review of Literature*, she wrote most frequently for the *American Mercury*. When the Korean War ended in 1953, she claimed that President Dwight Eisenhower had delivered half of Korea to the aggressors. Eisenhower's efforts at détente always found her in opposition.

When William F. Buckley's conservative weekly, *National Review*, was first launched in 1956, Utley's name was briefly on the masthead. She was, however, never a woman of the extreme right. Indeed, when she first arrived in America, her circle tended to be more likely comprised of strongly anti-Communist Socialists than of staunch Republicans. Without the threat of totalitarianism, she mused, the capitalist system might never have been able to have "resolved its contradictions." She accused the anarcho-capitalist author *Ayn Rand of "believing in no god but Mammon." She served as ghostwriter for conservative General Albert Wedemeyer, whose modesty she had once praised, but ended up finding him too vain and equivocal.

During 1956, Utley visited India, Southeast Asia, and the Middle East. On her return, she praised American opposition to the joint English-French-Israeli attack on Suez. In her book *Will the Middle East Go West?* (1957), she asserted that the 1948 partition of Palestine had been unjust and claimed that Israel deserved Western protection. The Zionist state on its part, Utley said, should "accept definite boundaries and abandon her aim to ingather the Jews from everywhere in the world."

Utley wrote her memoirs, *Odyssey of a Liberal*, a spirited account as revealing of her politics as of her life, seven years before her death in Washington, D.C., on January 27, 1977. She chastised those conservatives who "fail to see the need for change," claimed that the Communist powers constituted a greater menace than Nazi Germany ever possessed, and endorsed an American victory in Vietnam. She justified calling herself a liberal by a quotation from British poet William Morris that she frequently cited:

> I pondered all these things and how men fight and lose the battle, and the thing they fought for comes about in spite of their defeat; and when it comes about it turns out not to be what they meant, and other men have to fight for what they meant under another name.

SOURCES:

Utley, Freda. *The Dream We Lost: Soviet Russia Then and Now.* NY: John Day, 1940.

———. *Lost Illusion.* Philadelphia, PA: Fireside Press, 1948.

———. *Odyssey of a Liberal: Memoirs.* Washington, DC: Washington National Press, 1970.

SUGGESTED READING:

Doenecke, Justus D. *Not to the Swift: The Old Isolationists in the Cold War Era.* Lewisburg, PA: Bucknell University Press, 1979.

Newnman, Robert P. *Owen Lattimore and the "Loss" of China.* Berkeley, CA: University of California Press, 1992.

Regnery, Henry. *Memoirs of a Dissident Publisher.* NY: Harcourt Brace Jovanovich, 1979.

Shewmaker, Kenneth E. *Americans and Chinese Communists: A Persuading Encounter, 1927–1945.* Ithaca, NY: Cornell University Press, 1971.

COLLECTIONS:

Papers of Freda Utley are located in the Hoover Institution of War, Revolution and Peace, Stanford, California.

Justus D. Doenecke,
Professor of History,
New College of the University of South Florida,
Sarasota, Florida

Utter, Suzanne (1865–1938).

See Valadon, Suzanne.

Uttley, Alison (1884–1976)

Prolific British writer who is primarily known for her "Little Grey Rabbit" series. Name variations: Alice

Jane Taylor Uttley. Born Alice Jane Taylor on December 17, 1884, in Cromford, Derbyshire, England; died on May 7, 1976, in High Wycombe, Buckinghamshire, England; daughter of Henry Taylor (a farmer) and Hannah (Dickens) Taylor; educated at Lady Manners Grammar School, Bakewell; graduated from Manchester University, B.Sc. (with honors), 1906; attended Ladies' Training College (later Hughes Hall), Cambridge, 1907; married James Arthur Uttley (a civil engineer), in 1911 (died 1930); children: one son John (1915–1978).

Selected novels: High Meadows *(1938);* When All Is Done *(1945).*

Selected nonfiction: The Country Child *(1931);* Ambush of Young Days *(1937);* The Farm on the Hill *(1941);* Ten Candlelight Tales *(1942);* Country Hoard *(1943);* Country Things *(1946);* Carts and Candlesticks *(1948);* (ed.) In Praise of Country Life *(1949);* Buckinghamshire *(1950);* Plowmen's Clocks *(1952);* The Stuff of Dreams *(1953);* Here's a New Day *(1956);* A Year in the Country *(1957);* The Swans Fly Over *(1959);* Something for Nothing *(1960);* Wild Honey *(1962);* Cuckoo in June *(1964);* A Peck of Gold *(1966);* Recipes from an Old Farmhouse *(1966);* The Button Box and Other Essays *(1968);* A Ten O'Clock Scholar and Other Essays *(1970);* Secret Places and Other Essays *(1972);* Country World: Memories of Childhood *(1984);* Our Village: Alison Uttley's Cromford *(1984).*

Selected writings for children: The Squirrel, the Hare and the Little Grey Rabbit *(1929);* How Little Grey Rabbit Got Back Her Tail *(1930);* The Great Adventure of Hare *(1931);* Moonshine and Magic *(1932);* The Story of Fuzzypeg the Hedgehog *(1932);* Squirrel Goes Skating *(1934);* Wise Owl's Story *(1935);* The Adventures of Peter and Judy in Bunnyland *(1935);* Candlelight Tales *(1936);* Little Grey Rabbit's Party *(1936);* The Adventures of No Ordinary Rabbit *(1937);* The Knot Squirrel Tied *(1937);* Fuzzypeg Goes to School *(1938);* Mustard, Pepper and Salt *(1938);* A Traveller in Time *(1939);* Tales of the Four Pigs and Brock the Badger *(1939);* Little Grey Rabbit's Christmas *(1939);* Moldy Warp, The Mole *(1940);* The Adventures of Sam Pig *(1940);* Six Tales of the Four Pigs *(1941);* Sam Pig Goes to Market *(1941);* Ten Tales of Tim Rabbit *(1941);* Six Tales of Brock the Badger *(1941);* Six Tales of Sam Pig *(1941);* Nine Starlight Tales *(1942);* Little Grey Rabbit's Washing-Day *(1942);* Sam Pig and Sally *(1942);* Hare Joins the Home Guard *(1942);* Water-Rat's Picnic *(1943);* Cuckoo Cherry-Tree *(1943);* Sam Pig at the Circus *(1943);* The Spice Woman's Basket and Other Tales *(1944);* Little Grey Rabbit's Birthday *(1944);* Mrs. Nimble and Mr. Bumble *(1944);* The

Weather Cock and Other Stories *(1945)*; The Speckledy Hen *(1945)*; Some Moonshine Tales *(1945)*; The Adventures of Tim Rabbit *(1945)*; Little Grey Rabbit to the Rescue *(play, 1946)*; The Washerwoman's Child: A Play on the Life and Stories of Hans Christian Andersen *(1946)*; Little Grey Rabbit and the Weasels *(1947)*; Grey Rabbit and the Wandering Hedgehog *(1948)*; Sam Pig in Trouble *(1948)*; John Barleycorn: Twelve Tales of Fairy and Magic *(1948)*; Macduff *(1950)*; Little Grey Rabbit Makes Lace *(1950)*; The Cobbler's Shop and Other Tales *(1950)*; Snug and Serena Pick Cowslips *(1950)*; Snug and Serena Meet a Queen *(1950)*; Going to the Fair *(1951)*; Toad's Castle *(1951)*; Yours Ever, Sam Pig *(1951)*; Hare and the Easter Eggs *(1952)*; Mrs. Mouse Spring-Cleans *(1952)*; Christmas at the Rose and Crown *(1952)*; The Gypsy Hedgehogs *(1953)*; Snug and the Chimney-Sweeper *(1953)*; Little Red Fox and the Wicked Uncle *(1954)*; Little Grey Rabbit Goes to the Sea *(1954)*; Sam Pig and the Singing Gate *(1955)*; The Flower Show *(1955)*; The Mouse Telegrams *(1955)*; Hare and Guy Fawkes *(1956)*; Little Red Fox and Cinderella *(1956)*; Magic in My Pocket: A Selection of Tales *(1957)*; Mrs. Stoat Walks In *(1957)*; Snug and the Silver Spoon *(1957)*; Little Red Fox and the Magic Moon *(1958)*; Little Grey Rabbit's Paint-Box *(1958)*; Snug and Serena Count Twelve *(1959)*; Tim Rabbit and Company *(1959)*; Grey Rabbit Finds a Shoe *(1960)*; John at the Old Farm *(1960)*; Sam Pig Goes to the Seaside: Sixteen Stories *(1960)*; Grey Rabbit and the Circus *(1961)*; Snug and Serena Go to Town *(1961)*; Three Little Grey Rabbit Plays *(1961)*; The Little Knife Who Did All the Work: Twelve Tales of Magic *(1962)*; Little Red Fox and the Unicorn *(1962)*; Grey Rabbit's May Day *(1963)*; Tim Rabbit's Dozen *(1964)*; Hare Goes Shopping *(1965)*; The Sam Pig Storybook *(1965)*; The Mouse, the Rabbit and the Little White Hen *(1966)*; Enchantment *(1966)*; Little Grey Rabbit's Pancake Day *(1967)*; Little Red Fox *(1967)*; The Little Red Fox and the Big Big Tree *(1968)*; Little Grey Rabbit's Valentine *(1969)*; Lavender Shoes: Eight Tales of Enchantment *(1970)*; Little Grey Rabbit Goes to the North Pole *(1970)*; The Sam Pig Storybook *(1971)*; The Brown Mouse Book: Magical Tales of Two Little Mice *(1971)*; Fuzzypeg's Brother *(1971)*; Little Grey Rabbit's Spring Cleaning Party *(1972)*; The Little Red Fox Book *(1972)*; Little Grey Rabbit and the Snow-Baby *(1973)*; Fairy Tales *(1975)*; Hare and the Rainbow *(1975)*; More Little Red Fox Stories *(1975)*; Stories for Christmas *(1977)*; Little Grey Rabbit's Storybook *(1977)*; From Spring to Spring: Stories of the Four Seasons *(1978)*; Tales of Little Grey Rabbit *(1980)*; Little Grey Rabbit's Second Storybook *(1981)*; Foxglove Tales *(1984)*.

Alice Jane Uttley, known as "Alison" to her friends and readers, was born in 1884 and grew up on remote Castle Top Farm in Derbyshire, England, which had been in the family for more than 200 years. She had a close child playmate in her brother George, although the two grew apart after she went off to school. Uttley's father was one of the earliest influences on her later writing career. Although he could not read, he had a remarkable skill for storytelling, and his "strange, grim stories," handed down by his ancestors, were fondly recalled by his daughter. In an essay in *Wild Honey* (1962), entitled "The Ladder to Writing," Uttley compares her father's stories to those of Thomas Hardy: "I found the life depicted in the books very similar to tales told by my father," she writes, "of his childhood in our farmhouse, with shepherds and ploughmen, guisers and fairs."

Uttley's mother, a devout Christian, but also a lover of literature and the arts, infused her daughter's early years with religion, but also sang and recited poetry to her and read aloud

Alison Uttley

from her husband's books. Many long winter nights were spent listening to Dickens, Defoe and Stevenson, a pastime shared by the entire family, including the servants. Uttley's reading was further enhanced by books brought by visitors or by the boarders the family took in during the summer months to supplement the farm income. Indiscriminate in her tastes, she would read whatever appeared on the parlor table, even an occasional history or philosophy book left behind by a vacationing professor.

Uttley was both an imaginative and highly sensitive child, characteristics that impacted her first school experience at Lea Board School, when she was seven. Like her later character Susan Garland in the autobiographical *The Farm on the Hill* (1941), she was frightened by her long walk to school through the woods, and imagined that while certain rocks were friendly, others were to be avoided at all costs. "Some stones must be trodden upon always, they demanded human companionship, and the touch of hand or foot. Others were inimical, sinister sharp-tongued, and cruel." Uttley would seek out a companion for her trek home from school by promising a story to anyone brave enough to join her.

Though attendance was sometimes a problem at Lea, Uttley received a scholarship to the Lady Manner School, where she flourished, particularly in science and mathematics. She won a second scholarship to Manchester University, earning a B.Sc. in physics, and in 1906 became the university's second woman honors graduate. After spending one year at a training college at Cambridge University, Uttley worked as a physics teacher at the Fulham Secondary School in London; there, she became interested in socialism and was active in the women's suffrage movement. Through her political involvement, she met with Ramsay Macdonald, who would later become prime minister as head of the Labour Party. In 1911, she married engineer James Uttley, whom she had met through his sister while studying at Manchester University. She married, quit her teaching job, and moved with her husband to Cheshire, where she gave birth to the couple's son, John, in 1915.

Uttley began writing after a chance encounter with philosophy Professor Samuel Alexander from her Manchester days, during which he confused her with another of his students and inquired as to whether she was still writing poetry. This provided the impetus for her to begin writing the story of her early years at Castle Top Farm, which later became *The Country Child*. Although it was her first written book,

it was not her first published. When she showed the manuscript to her husband, he declared it rubbish and threw it across the room, after which she locked it away. By Uttley's own account, her first published work, *The Squirrel, the Hare and the Little Grey Rabbit* (1929), was written for her son John, who had just left for boarding school. "Every day in our walks, in England, Wales and France, I told stories of hares and weasels, wolves and foxes, each one different and new," she recalled. "I was compelled by a strong urge to write down a tale and send it to him."

In 1930, after suffering from bouts of severe depression since his World War I service, James Uttley committed suicide, leaving his wife penniless. To support herself and her son, Uttley took up her pen in earnest, publishing *The Country Child* and producing over 100 books in the course of the next four decades. The "Little Grey Rabbit" series, which grew to include over 30 titles, are tales of anthropomorphic animals, a mode that Uttley used throughout her career. "There is a lot of Uttley herself in the character of Grey Rabbit: the resourceful countrywoman, the lover of tradition, customs and festivals, the sensitive observer who enjoyed all the signs and sounds and smells of the countryside," observes Peter du Sautoy in *Twentieth-Century Children's Writers*. The Grey Rabbit books, illustrated by **Margaret Tempest** and later by **Katherine Wigglesworth**, brought Uttley international recognition which grew with each regular addition to the series (often timed by the publisher for the Christmas market).

Uttley's other popular animal characters, Sam Pig, Tim Rabbit, Brock the Badger, and Fuzzypeg the Hedgehog, also inhabited a rural Victorian village similar to the one in which Uttley was raised. Although she was frequently compared with *Beatrix Potter in this regard, according to **Barbara Carman Garner**, Uttley maintained that "she did not write to escape the environment of her youth, as Beatrix Potter had done, but to enter more deeply into it and give it immortality."

Like her autobiographical *The Country Child*, Uttley also wrote a number of other nonfiction books directed at an adult readership, among them *Ambush of Young Days* (1937), *The Farm on the Hill*, and two unsuccessful novels, *High Meadows* (1938) and *When All is Done* (1945). Considered by some to be her best book for adults is *A Traveller in Time* (1939), a fantasy based on her childhood, but also drawing from a local plot to rescue *Mary Stuart, queen of Scots, in 1569.

In the course of her career, Uttley was critically compared to *Lucy Maud Montgomery and *Laura Ingalls Wilder. Noting that the women were essentially contemporaries, Garner writes, "Montgomery, Wilder, and Uttley were all interested in the same essential qualities that enrich life, and each wanted to record her own childhood experiences in her fiction for others to share." Like Montgomery, notes Garner, Uttley was also interested in dreams and recorded her own in her diary, which ultimately comprised more than 40 volumes. She published a collection of essays, *The Stuff of Dreams*, in 1953.

After her husband's death, Uttley made her home in Buckinghamshire, near Beaconsfield, where she lived for the rest of her life. Her strong and sometimes dominating personality made it difficult for her to get along with many of her relatives, but she was supported throughout her years by a few close women friends. Although she never remarried, she had two male friends who stood by her after her husband's suicide: Professor Samuel Alexander, who helped finance her son's education, and Walter de la Mare, who also became an adviser. Uttley, who was awarded an honorary doctorate from Manchester University in 1970, died in 1976, at age 91, in Buckinghamshire. Her son John, with whom she had an intense and later difficult relationship, committed suicide in 1978.

SOURCES:

Buck, Claire, ed. *The Bloomsbury Guide to Women's Literature*. NY: Prentice Hall, 1992.

The Concise Dictionary of National Biography. Oxford: Oxford University Press, 1992.

Contemporary Authors Online. Farmington Hills, MI: The Gale Group, 2000.

Garner, Barbara Carman. "Alison Uttley," in *Dictionary of Literary Biography*, Vol. 160: *British Children's Writers, 1914–1960*. Detroit, MI: The Gale Group, 1996, pp. 289–299.

Judd, Denis. *The Life of a Country Child (1884–1976): The Authorized Biography*. London: M. Joseph, 1986.

Saintsbury, Elizabeth. *The World of Alison Uttley: The Life and Times of One of the Best Loved Country Writers of Our Century*. London: Howard Baker, 1980.

Shattock, Joanne. *The Oxford Guide to British Women Writers*. Oxford: Oxford University Press, 1993.

Kelly Winters,
freelance writer

Uwilingiyimana, Agathe

(1953–1994)

Rwandan interim prime minister. Born in 1953 in Nyaruhengeri, Rwanda; assassinated by opposition soldiers on April 7, 1994; received master's degree in chemistry; married a university employee; children: five.

Agathe Uwilingiyimana was born in 1953 in the village of Nyaruhengeri, southeast of Rwanda's capital city of Kigali. Although a child of peasant farmers, she obtained an education, earning a master's degree in chemistry. Agathe, who remained in the countryside to teach science for ten years at the high school level, was eventually named to a government post as director for small- and medium-sized industries in the Ministry of Commerce of Industry.

Uwilingiyimana was a member of the moderate, multiethnic Rwandan Democratic Movement, and was also a member of the minority Tutsi tribe that had traditionally ruled the country before the majority Hutus took power in the 1960s. Rwanda had been shattered for years by tribal violence between the two groups. Uwilingiyimana, who had been named minister of higher education, was a strong advocate of equal educational opportunity for everyone, regardless of ethnic group. This view, as well as her Tutsi heritage, generated many enemies. In April 1993, assailants broke into her home and beat and raped her; she suspected that they had been sent by her political opponents.

When a tentative peace agreement was brokered, a coalition government dedicated to implementing it named Uwilingiyimana prime minister on July 18, 1993. However, political infighting in the coalition government led her party to expel Uwilingiyimana that same day; as a result, Rwanda's president Juvénal Habyarimana officially dismissed her from the post after less than a month. Since agreement between the country's many political parties was still tenuous, however, Uwilingiyimana remained in the post as a caretaker. She was to have given up power to a transitional government in March 1994, but one of the participating parties withdrew from the ceremonies, and she remained in the post.

In April 1994, Rwanda exploded into violence when a plane carrying President Habyarimana and President Cyprians Ntaryamira of neighboring Burundi—both Hutus—crashed under suspicious circumstances while returning from a conference dedicated to ending the Hutu-Tutsi conflict. While both Hutus and Tutsis had motives for the assassinations and could have fired the rockets that brought the plane down, Hutu soldiers used this as an excuse to begin reprisals against Tutsis and Hutu moderates, particularly those in government. When Uwilingiyimana prepared to address the nation, asking for calm after the president's death, Hutu soldiers surrounded her home. Ten Belgian soldiers, part of a 2,400-member United Nations peacekeeping force, helped her to leave. The Hutu guards followed, disarmed the U.N. guards, and killed Uwilingiyimana. The Belgians were tortured and killed, and three other Tutsi ministers in the government were shot. That same day soldiers went to her home and also murdered her husband in front of their five children, who survived but were forced to flee the country. The deaths of the president and the prime minister restarted the full-scale tribal conflict that Uwilingiyimana and her colleagues had tried so hard to resolve, leading to over 800,000 violent deaths that year.

During her brief tenure, women were encouraged by her progressive ideas. After her death, Uwilingiyimana was honored by the Forum for African Women Educationalists, a group to which she had belonged, by the establishment of the Agathe Uwilingiyimana Award, which honors innovative achievements in women's education. Subsequent Rwandan governments also announced the intent of building a shrine to the memory of the late prime minister and others killed in the violence.

SOURCES:

Hill, Kevin A. "Agathe Uwilingiyimana," in *Women and the Law*. Rebecca Mae Salokar and Mary L. Volcansek, eds. Westport, CT: Greenwood Press, 1996, pp. 323–328.

Masland, Tom, Joshua Hammer, Karen Breslau, and Jennifer Tanaka. "Corpses Everywhere," in *Newsweek*. April 18, 1994, p. 33.

Michaels, Marguerite. "Descent into Mayhem," in *Time*. April 18, 1994, p. 44.

Ms. July–August 1994, p. 13.

Kelly Winters,
freelance writer

Uzès, Anne, Duchesse d'

(1847–1933)

Immensely wealthy French aristocrat who, after failing to restore the monarchy by financing General Boulanger's political schemes, emerged as one of the most original women of her time—a sculptor, renowned hunter, generous supporter of charitable works, and an advocate and exemplar of the liberation of women. Name variations: Anne, duchess of Uzes; (pseudonym) Manuela. Pronunciation: AHN dew-SHESS dew-ZEH. Born (Marie-Adrienne) Anne-Victurnienne-Clémentine de Rochechouart-Mortemart on February 10, 1847, in Paris; died of pneumonia on February 3, 1933, at the Château de Dampierre (Seine-et-Oise) and was interred in the chapel of the Carmelites at Uzès (Gard); daughter and sole heir of (Anne-Victurnien-)Louis-Samuel de Rochechouart, Comte de Mortemart (1809–1873) and Marie-Clémentine Le Riche de Chevigné (1818–1877); educated by tutors; married (Amable-Antoine-Jacques-) Emmanuel de Crussol, 12th Duc d'Uzès (1840–1878), on May 11, 1867; children: Jacques, 13th Duc d'Uzès (b. 1868); **Simone, Duchesse de Luynes** (b. 1870); Louis-Emmanuel, 14th Duc d'Uzès (b. 1871); and **Mathilde-Renée, Duchesse de Brissac** (b. 1875).

Married to the Duc d'Uzès (1867–78); maintained the leading hunt in France, the Rallye Bonnelles (1880s–1933); received an honorable mention for sculpture at the Paris Salon (1887); involved in financing the political campaigns of General Georges Boulanger in hopes of restoring the monarchy (1888–89); was at the peak of her literary and sculpting activities (1890–1914); joined "L'Avant-Courrière" and began feminist activities (1894); became the first Frenchwoman to obtain an automobile driver's license (1898); helped launch La Française *and the* Union Française pour le Suffrage des Femmes *(1907–09); ran a hospital and nursed during World War I (1914–18); was the first woman made Wolf Lieutenant (1923); founded the Automobile-Club Féminin de France (1926); made vice-president of the Groupe Féminin de l'Aéro-Club (1932).*

Writings: Le Coeur et le sang *(three-act play, 1890);* Pauvre Petite *(novel, 1890);* Julien Masly *(novel, 1891);* Paillettes mauves *(poems, 1892);* L'Arrondissement de Rambouillet *(history, 1893);* Voyage de mon fils au Congo *(history, 1894);* Histoires de chasse *(stories, 1907);* Paillettes grises *(poems, 1909);* Une Saint-Hubert sous Louis XV *(one-act verse play, 1909);* Poèmes de la duchesse Anne *(selections from the* Paillettes, *1911);* La Chasse à courre *(history, 1912);* Le Suffrage féminin du point de vue historique *(brochure, 1913);* Souvenirs de la duchesse d'Uzès née Mortemart *(1934).*

Sculpture—principal works of "Manuela": Diane couchée; Diane debout; Diane surprise; Émile Augier *(Valence);* Galatée; Jeanne d'Arc *(Mehun-sur-Yèvre);* Jeanne d'Arc *(Pont-à-Mousson);* Nicolas Gilbert *(Fontenoy-le-Château);* Juliette Dodu *(Brièves);* *Madame de Sévigné *(Livry);* Notre-Dame-de-France *(Sainte-Clotilde church, Reims);* Notre-Dame-de Poissy *(Poissy);* Notre-Dame-des-Arts *(Pont-de-l'Arche);* Notre-Dame-du-Salve-Regina *(Pierrelongue);* Monument aux Morts *(Bonnelles);* Ophélie; Saint-Hubert *(Montmartre basilica);* Salomé *(Buenos Aires Museum);* Tombeau d'Henri de Pène.

In January 1933, a month before she died at 86, the Dowager Duchesse d'Uzès, vice-president of the Women's Group of the Aero Club of France, made her first airplane flight, piloted by her grandson—and accompanied by her confessor. Only 17 days before her death, she returned from her last stag hunt with yet another trophy to catalog and mount—No. 2056. Such behavior was in no way out of character, for this formidable lady had been devoting her tireless energy to an astonishing range of activities through 55 years of widowhood. What gave her activities a special distinction, however, was that her social position and wealth had put her under no personal obligation whatever (and in truth under no expectation from the world of her time) to do anything but give birth to an heir or two while spinning out a languid existence devoted to a high-society socializing whose frivolity might be redeemed by well-publicized patronizing now and then of some fashionable charities.

One of 19th-century France's very richest heiresses, Anne de Rochechouart-Mortemart surpassed them all in the distinction of her ancestry. The Rochechouarts and Mortemarts traced their lineages back well before the Crusades and also claimed descent from St. Louis IX (r. 1226–1270) through the female line and relations among the Bourbons. Moreover, marriages allied them with the great Montmorency clan, from whose tradition Anne derived her given name. On her mother's side she was a Chevigné and Chaffault, her maternal grandfather being Comte Louis de Chevigné (1793–1876), a minor poet. Ironically, it was her ancestry's least blue-blooded component that brought her the most money, for she was the sole direct heir of her great-grandmother Barbe-Nicole Clicquot-Ponsardin (1777–1866), the famed ✤➤ **Mme Clicquot** of the Champagne fortune. The climax of this relentless piling up of wealth and titles would come on May 11, 1867, when Anne arrived in a splendid carriage attended by bewigged footmen to marry the heir to the senior title (no less) in the French peerage: Emmanuel de Crussol, future 12th Duc d'Uzès. Despite appearances, it would be a love match.

As a child, Anne had led a somewhat lonely existence with few playmates. Her older and only siblings, Pauline and Paul, died at 10 and 16, the first of a long train of deaths in her immediate family that gave her spirit a lifelong note of melancholy. Fortunately, she was not stifled in Paris society but instead spent many months of the year at the family's country retreats, especially at the magnificent Château de Boursault (the Widow Clicquot's residence) and a small chateau at Villers-en-Prayères (Aisne). There she roamed freely and in her words, "studied the open book of Nature." She was educated by tutors, showing talent in drawing, painting, music, and modeling in wax. Both her

father and her maternal grandfather encouraged her to venture beyond the usual limits for females of her time; at 16, she took up Latin on her own initiative.

Anne's mother was a childlike woman who exerted little influence on her. Anne recalled her father as "goodness itself," tender, reserved, religious, and affable, though touched by melancholy. Appreciative of his surviving child's spirit, he once taught her how to handle a four-horse hitch; many years later, she set society agog in London when she took the reins of a carriage-and-four returning from the races and drove all the way to Rotten Row, a feat unheard of for any woman (much less a lady) to attempt.

Naturally, Anne's marriage was a major concern. Though no beauty, she was fairly attractive: petite, slender, with brown hair, a high forehead, very blue almond-shaped eyes, a straight, large nose, and firm mouth. She was naturally graceful but indifferent to fashion and not haughty or proud. Having grown up largely outside Paris society, she felt awkward at first and then chagrined, perceiving that interest after her debut centered solely on her name and fortune. Hence, it was her future husband's initial indifference to her that she noticed. Six months after they met, he was wounded in a hunting accident which scarred his face badly and cost him an eye. Anne went to his bedside to console him, love blossomed, and six months later they married.

Emmanuel de Crussol, seven years her senior with wealth and ancestry to match her own, had graduated without distinction from the Saint-Cyr military academy and left the army upon their marriage. He was a fine man—gracious, sincere, affectionate, and upright. He was elected to the

---

✤➤ **Clicquot, Mme** (1777–1866)

*French entrepreneur. Name variations: Barbe-Nicole Clicquot-Ponsardin; the Widow Clicquot. Born Barbe-Nicole Ponsardin in 1777; died in 1866; daughter of Baron Ponsardin; married François Clicquot (died); great-grandmother of *Anne, Duchesse d'Uzes.*

Barbe-Nicole Clicquot was the famed Widow Clicquot (Veuve Clicquot) of the Champagne fortune. This daughter of a mayor of Reims, whom Napoleon I had ennobled as Baron Ponsardin, married one François Clicquot but was widowed early. Blessed with brains and an uncommon business sense, she turned an inherited winery into the producer of the world's leading brand of Champagne, "Veuve Clicquot." She resided at Château de Boursault.

National Assembly in 1871 following France's defeat in the Franco-Prussian War and sat (to 1876) as a Legitimist, favoring the return of the Bourbon monarchy. On his father's death in 1872, he succeeded to the dukedom of Uzès and to properties all around France. The marriage meanwhile proved exceptionally happy. Anne had four children in eight years. But on November 28, 1878, Emmanuel died unexpectedly from effects of the lead shot he still carried in his head from the hunting accident. Anne mourned him for the rest of her life, never remarried or took a lover, and would be interred beside him "whose death shattered my life."

Although the tragedy inflicted a terrible private wound, it allowed her spirit's independence and daring to blossom. Her abundant energy enabled her to raise her children with care, oversee her vast properties, cultivate her artistic talents, support a host of charities, work to free women from legal and social discrimination, and indulge a passion for mounted hunting first awakened by her husband.

She gave time to her friends, money to the poor, and sat her horse like a field marshal riding sidesaddle. She will be unduplicated.

—*Janet Flanner

She was well launched in these activities (save the feminist cause) when, in March 1888, she embarked on a political venture which was to cost her much embarrassment and a huge amount of money. Impulsiveness was one of her traits; also, as she freely admitted, a certain naïveté—in this instance about politics. By family tradition she was a Legitimist. Upon the death of the childless Bourbon claimant, the Comte de Chambord, in 1883, she loyally obeyed his request to support the Comte de Paris, the Orleanist, not the Bourbon-Parma, heir. Her political ideas were fairly simple. She endorsed the basic liberties won in 1789 and an elected parliament of sorts but believed France needed strong leadership by a hereditary executive. Instead, the Third Republic (1870–1940), she held, was corrupt, leaderless, and (worst of all) bent upon a bigoted harassment of the Catholic Church. She was confident that the people, if given a chance, would support her views.

General Georges Boulanger (1837–1891), handsome and exuding a rough, soldierly charm, had risen rapidly in the army and in 1886 became minister of war. His talent for self-promotion soon made him wildly popular among the masses, who were feeling the pain of hard times, were fed up with the drab politicians, and wanted France's prestige restored to its pre-1870 luster. He was eased out of office after a year but, responding to noisy acclaim, began to intrigue with anyone and everyone to return. The government retired him from the army in the spring of 1888 when he let his name to be put up in by-elections for the Chamber of Deputies. He was being promoted by some Republican politicians who saw in him a way to get into power and cleanse the republic of its ills. The Royalists also latched onto his star, however. Their tactic was to use his vote-getting power to win enough seats in the Chamber to force a constitutional change which would bring the Comte de Paris to the throne. Boulanger, a gifted liar, repeatedly assured them of his monarchist sentiments while continuing to pose in public as a Republican.

Anne d'Uzès believed his assurances. She had first met him in 1886 and had found him, as had so many others, a fascinating specimen. When she was approached, in March 1888, by Royalist promoters during his first official by-election campaign, she gave 25,000 francs on the spot. A second solicitation transformed matters: after some thought, she replied on June 12 with an astonishing offer of 3 million francs. She had been told it might be within her means to restore the monarchy, an appeal she found irresistible. She acted out of pride and conviction, and (to her great credit) she expected nothing in return: "I have done my duty as the first peer of France; may the king do his." The Comte de Paris, amazed, but still uneasy about Boulanger, promised to repay her if he became king in fact. By accepting her gift, however, the Royalist chiefs found themselves fully committed to the risky tactic of using Boulanger as a stalking horse for the return of the monarchy.

Anne's money was the main financial source of Boulanger's string of successes from the triple-election triumph on August 19, 1888, in the Somme, Nord, and Charente-Inférieure through the spectacular Paris victory on January 27, 1889. She also opened doors to the general in Paris society. But on April 1, 1889, fearing arrest for conspiracy, he fled to Belgium. Disgusted, Anne threatened to withdraw support but was persuaded to use the 1.1 million left from her gift to try for victory in the fall general elections. For that effort, however, not she but a socially ambitious Jewish-Austrian financier, Baron Hirsch, gave the lion's share, some 5 million francs. She (in person) and others tried in vain to get Boulanger to return to France to campaign. The election sank Boulanger and ended any hope of a monarchial restoration.

Through the whole affair Anne, besides doling out allotments from the 3 million when requested by a steering committee, gave occasional, unwelcomed, advice, repeatedly holding Boulanger's and the politicians' feet to the fire whenever they hesitated. Her grit and selflessness lifted her above all other participants in the affair. When she became a principal source for the revelations by Mermeix (Gabriel Terrail) published in 1890 as *Les Coulisses du Boulangisme* (which first unveiled the true role of the Royalists and her money in the affair, to the private fury of the Comte de Paris), she did so naïvely, enjoying the notoriety but probably also the satisfaction of paying back the gutless politicians and (as she now called him) that "spineless weakling" Boulanger. Still, *noblesse oblige*, she twice visited him in exile after his defeat.

"I tried to do something through Boulanger," she remarked much later, "but he was a buffoon." She never entered electoral politics again. The 1890s saw Anne occupied instead in family affairs, literature, sculpture, and feminism. She suffered a cruel blow on June 20, 1893, when her oldest son, Jacques, died of fever at Cabinda after leading a failed expedition to reach the upper Nile from the Congo. He had been a playboy, with numerous liaisons, including one with the notorious ❧▸ Emilienne d'Alençon, and in 1890 Anne had taken legal steps to prevent his squandering the family's resources. Some said she had forced him to atone by undertaking this risky expedition; her version was that he had repented his ways and conceived a heroic project worthy of his ancestors which she felt she should encourage and finance despite her fears. In 1894, she memorialized him in a book, *Voyage de mon fils au Congo*. Since 1890, she also had published a play, two melodramatic novels, a respectable set of poems (*Paillettes mauves*), and a fine history of the district of Rambouillet, where she usually resided and hunted. She wrote not because of literary ambitions but because she felt the need. Her writings earned her membership in the Société des Gens de lettres and the Société des Auteurs dramatiques.

She was an excellent organist, but her true talent was for sculpting. Using the pseudonym "Manuela" (recalling her husband), she began to work seriously after his death: "The arts have sustained me greatly in my hours of bitterness. In my studio, thumbs in the clay and chisel in hand, I think of nothing else." Several eminent sculptors tutored her—especially Alexandre Falguière (1831–1900), but also Antonin Mercié (1845–1916), Auguste Cain (1822–1894), and Léon Gérome (1824–1904)—which they probably would not have done despite her wealth and prominence if they had not been convinced she had a gift. After an honorable mention at the 1887 Salon, she won a state contract in 1890 for a Virgin for the church at Poissy; other contracts followed, and she exhibited at the World's Columbian Exhibition in Chicago in 1893. She won the competition for a monument to the dramatist Émile Augier, but the 1895 Salon des Champs-Élysées rejected her model, apparently because the judges suspected that not all the five large figures were her work alone, an imputation she vigorously refuted. She defiantly displayed the model outside the Salon instead, and the finished monument was dedicated in 1897 at Valence with President Félix Faure attending. Her work on the whole has been described as that of a distinguished, talented amateur, by no means a "Sunday sculptor." It is well wrought but altogether conformist and academic, typical in every way of its era. For some reason, her daring did not carry over into either her writing or her art.

Anne's participation in the feminist movement surprised the public, for she not only was very conservative in her political loyalties but also a most devout Catholic and a leading light in High Society. She particularly associated with *Jeanne Schmahl, *Juliette Adam, *Sarah Monod, *Marguerite Durand, *Jane Misme, *Jeanne Chauvin (France's first female lawyer), *Maria Deraismes (despite her anticlericalism), and *Cécile Brunschvicg—personages distinctly superior to those she had dealt with in the Boulanger affair. Certainly her activities brought her far more applause from other feminists, because of the visibility she gave their cause, than from her social peers. But a part of her enjoyed stirring things up and savoring the resultant notoriety. She was a favorite of the press for her colorfulness and witty repartees.

She made her debut on January 18, 1894, when she, with Adam, became a principal spon-

---

❧▸ **Alençon, Emilienne d'** (fl. late 1800s)
French cicotte and liaison of Leopold of Belgium. Name variations: Emilienne d'Alencon. Flourished in the late 1800s.

Emilienne d'Alençon ran away from home at age 15 with a Gypsy (Roma) violinist. After managing to maneuver her way into the French Conservatoire, she quit and appeared at the Cirque d'Eté in an act with trained rabbits. One of her early "Protectors," along with Leopold II, king of the Belgians, was Jacques, Duc d'Uzès, until his mortified family shipped him off to a regiment in Africa where he died of dysentery at the age of 25.

sor of Schmahl's *L'Avant-Courrière* (The Advance Messenger), an organization advocating the equality of women with men in testifying in legal matters (gained in 1897) and in keeping and disposing of their own income (won in 1907 by the "Schmahl Law"). Anne had first met Schmahl in 1885 but had put off invitations to become involved in feminism. Schmahl's tactic of giving up left-wing political aims and provocative actions and instead seeking concrete legislative gains began to typify much of the second (post-1889) generation of French feminists, and it appealed to Anne. She was a doer and patron, not a theorizer. Her feminist "philosophy" was pretty well summed up in her impatient remark that "in these stupid discussions about whether men are superior to women or women superior to men we always forget that they are two halves of a whole called the human race!" She asked again the question put by the 18th-century philosophe Condorcet: "Can someone show me a difference between men and women which can legitimately establish a difference in their rights?" To her mind, the question answered itself.

For the rest of her life, she played a very visible part as a patron of feminist publications and organizations and occasionally as a public speaker (though she did not enjoy that role), but especially as an example of a woman who had no fear of doing things hitherto reserved to men. She was the first woman in France to earn an automobile driver's license (April 23, 1898)—and probably the first to get a speeding ticket (June 8, for exceeding Paris' 12 kph-8 mph limit); was president of the Union of Women Painters and Sculptors (from 1902); joined with Misme to found (1906) *La Française*, the official journal of the women's movement; and helped found (1907) and preside over (from 1908) the Lyceum Club of Paris, a female equivalent of a men's club, for women interested in art, science, and social works. In 1909, with Misme and Schmahl, she helped organize the French Union for Women's Suffrage (UFSF) and was the only aristocratic woman in the leadership of a cause which in pre-1914 France was regarded as extremely radical. After Schmahl died in 1913, Anne became inactive in the UFSF for a time but returned for good at the urging of Brunschvicg; her presence helped to defend Brunschvicg from attacks from Catholic quarters, attacks which Anne particularly resented. In 1926, she founded the Feminine Automobile Club of France, and led auto rallies around France and to Belgium, the Netherlands, and Italy; and in 1932 she was named vice-president of the Women's Group of the Aero Club. Along the way, she also saw to the admission of women to the École des Beaux-Arts and was a promoter of women's sports and president of the Gymnastic Society for Young Women.

Anne's numberless charitable activities swallowed oceans of time and money. She corresponded, cajoled, and wheedled, gave charity parties, and sat on an array of boards. Among her causes (a seemingly endless list) were Le Calvaire (for women cancer patients), Villepinte Sanatorium (for young women with tuberculosis), the League Against Cancer, the Blood Donors' Association, Day Nurseries of France, the Society for Protection of the Widows and Orphans of the Great War, several charities devoted to abandoned and orphaned children, a retirement home for women artists, and the building of a cathedral at Dakar to honor explorers of Africa.

It was because of her charities that she formed a surprising friendship with *Louise Michel, probably the most famous female anarchist of the time. Anne was not "playing revolutionary" and certainly disapproved of Michel's politics. Rather, the two shared a deep sympathy for suffering humanity. "If this woman had had religious faith," Anne wrote of Michel, "she would have donned a nun's habit and become a saint." They met in 1888 when Michel solicited her for widows of seamen, and they remained in touch until Michel's death in 1905. Michel repeatedly called upon Anne when she was faced with hard cases or was broke herself.

Likewise, Anne was not playacting when during the First World War she converted her Château de Bonnelles into an annex of the military hospital at Rambouillet and became—after duly passing the examination—a 67-year-old licensed nurse. Many society women found nursing a fashionable way to contribute to the cause. Most tired of the work and drifted away, but not Anne. She was also an inspector of nurses in hospitals at the front and organized workshops for Belgian refugees. On March 19, 1919, the Republic she had once tried to overthrow awarded her the Legion of Honor (although technically for her artistic work); she was decorated also by Belgium, Serbia, and the Holy See. In 1931, she was named an officer in the Legion.

Despite all these activities, Anne may have been best known to the masses as Europe's leading woman hunter, the autocratic chief of the Rallye Bonnelles, for whose Easter Monday hunt several thousand spectators, many coming by special train from Paris, would turn out to view the proceedings while newsreel cameras whirred. She began hunting in 1872 with her husband and later lived much of the year at Bonnelles (Seine-et-Oise), which

Opposite page

𝒜nne,

𝒟uchesse

𝒹'Uzès

boasted a magnificent 3,000-hectare (7,400-acre) park bordering on the vast state forest of Rambouillet, and a hunting lodge, "La Celle-les-Bordes," where she mounted her trophies. For decades, she hunted deer and sometimes boar on Tuesdays and Saturdays from October to April, rain, snow, or shine. (Spring and summer were given to riding, racing, and harness driving, sometimes at her Berder Island estate in Brittany, where she liked to take the wheel of her steam yacht, *Manuela*.) The cream of Europe's aristocracy, including royalty, prized invitations to these hunts. Anne—garbed always in silver-trimmed tricorne hat, black tunic (for mourning), blue skirt, sash, and boots, with whip at the ready—ruled like her ancestors of old and was fiercely determined always to be in at the kill, knife in hand. She wrote on hunting and lectured, bringing along buglers to sound the traditional calls. In 1923, she dared the government to appoint her as district Wolf Lieutenant (*lieutenant de louveterie*)—an ancient, largely ceremonial position carrying rights of a game warden and charged with enforcement of measures against wolves and varmints. The ministry complied, making her the first woman ever so honored—but only after she took the prescribed oath of loyalty to the Republic. She soon became honorary president of the Wolf Lieutenants' Association. She also participated in the Society of St. Hubert for patrons of hunting.

Active to the end, Anne died suddenly of pneumonia on February 3, 1933, while wintering at her surviving daughter's residence, the Château de Dampierre. She had outlived two of her children, Jacques (d. 1893) and Mathilde-Renée (d. 1908), two grandsons, two granddaughters, a son-in-law, and two sisters-in-law, all of whom were very close to her. She had prepared for death when she built for the Carmelites at Uzès a convent and chapel with burial niches (finished in 1888). She was placed there beside her husband after hugely attended funeral masses in Paris and Uzès.

Anne d'Uzès was an imposing yet attractive personage: witty, direct, unpretentious, courteous, quick, impulsive, naïve at times, absent-minded, curious, affable (except when hot in the hunt), and courageous. She also was deeply religious, attending mass every day and spending long hours in the night praying and reading devotional books. Yet, unlike so many pious aristocrats of her time, she was in no way bigoted, advocated separation of church and state, and counted friends among Protestants, Jews, and freethinkers alike. And she was generous, generous to a fault—so generous that by the 1920s her fortune was greatly depleted. Before and

after she died, vast amounts of goods and lands had to be sold, including Boursault, the Clicquot vineyards, and Bonnelles, which today is an international school. But she could face her Maker with a clear conscience, which was what she treasured above all else.

SOURCES:

Bidelman, Patrick K. *Pariahs Stand Up! The Founding of the Liberal Feminist Movement in France, 1858–1889*. Westport, CT: Greenwood Press, 1982.

Clement, Clara Erskine. *Women in the Fine Arts from the Seventh Century B.C. to the Twentieth Century A.D.* Boston, MA: Houghton Mifflin, 1905.

Dansette, Adrien. *Le Boulangisme*. Paris: Librairie Arthème Fayard, 1946.

Elliott, Maud H. *Art and Handicraft in the Woman's Building of the World's Columbian Exhibition*. NY: Goupil, 1893.

Gmeline, Patrick de. *La duchesse d'Uzès*. Paris: Librairie Perrin, 1986.

Hause, Stephen C., and Anne R. Kinney. "The Limits of Suffragist Behavior: Legalism and Militancy in France, 1876–1922," in *American Historical Review*. Vol. 86, no. 4. October 1981, pp. 781–806.

Irvine, William D. *The Boulanger Affair Reconsidered: Royalism, Boulangism, and the Origins of the Radical Right in France*. NY: Oxford University Press, 1989.

Lheureux, Simone. *Vies et passions d'Anne de Crussol, duchesse d'Uzès, 1847–1933*. Nîmes: C. Lacour, 1989.

Mermeix [pseud. Gabriel Terrail]. *Les Coulisses du Boulangisme*. Paris: Léopold Cerf, 1890.

Puget, Jean. *La duchesse d'Uzès née Mortemart*. Uzès: Éditions Henri Peladan, 1972.

Seager, Frederic H. *The Boulanger Affair: Political Crossroad of France, 1886–1889*. Ithaca, NY: Cornell University Press, 1969.

Uzès, Duchesse d' [Marie-Clèmentine de Rochechouart-Mortemart, duchesse d'Uzès]. *Souvenirs de la duchesse d'Uzès née Mortemart*. Paris: Librairie Plon, 1939.

SUGGESTED READING:

Brissac, Pierre, duc de. *La duchesse d'Uzès*. Paris: Gründ, 1950.

Brogan, Denis W. *The Development of Modern France (1870–1939)*. Rev. ed. London: Hamish Hamilton, 1967.

Harding, James. *The Astonishing Adventure of General Boulanger*. NY: Scribner, 1971.

Levillain, Philippe. *Boulanger, fossoyeur de la monarchie*. Paris: Flammarion, 1982.

Pisani-Ferry, Fresnette. *Le Général Boulanger*. Paris: Flammarion, 1969.

COLLECTIONS:

The principal repositories pertaining to Anne d'Uzès are the family archives in Uzès (Gard); and in Paris, the Archives nationales, the libraries of the École national d'équitation and the Jockey Club, and especially the Bibliothèque Marguerite Durand. Also consult the Société archéologique et historique de Bonnelles (Seine-et-Oise).

David S. Newhall,
Pottinger Distinguished Professor of History, Centre College, Danville, Kentucky, and author of *Clemenceau: A Life at War* (Edwin Mellen Press, 1991)

V (1801–1873).
See Clive, Caroline.

Vaa, Aslaug (1889–1965)

Norwegian poet and dramatist. Born in 1889 at Rauland in Telemark, Norway; died on November 28, 1965 (some sources cite 1967), in Oslo; daughter of a farmer; studied in Paris and Berlin, 1909; married Ola Raknes (a philologist and psychoanalyst), in 1911 (divorced 1938); children: five.

Selected writings: Nord i leite *(In the North Horizon, 1934);* Steinguden *(God of Stone, 1934);* Skuggen og strendan *(1935);* Villarkonn *(1936);* På vegakanten *(1938);* Tjugendagen *(1947);* Fotefar *(Footprints, 1947);* Munkeklokka *(The Monastery Bell, 1950);* Skjenkarsveinens visur *(The Innkeeper's Songs, 1954);* Bustader *(Living Quarters, 1963);* Dikt i utval *(1964);* Honningfuglen og leoparden *(1965);* Munkeklokka *(1966).*

Aslaug Vaa was born in 1889 and grew up in a rural region of southcentral Norway, the daughter of a farmer. She traveled to Paris and Berlin in 1909 to study literature, philosophy, art history, and theater at various universities. Two years later, she married Ola Raknes, a philologist and psychoanalyst. Following their divorce in 1938, she supported five children by working as a housekeeper and a translator. It was not until 1934, at age 45, that Vaa published her first work: a collection of poems, *Nord i leite*, and a play, *Steinguden.* However, she earned immediate

prominence in Norwegian literature, writing works influenced by William Blake, Cubism, Dadaism, and dramatic expressionism. She also drew from the folk life and art of her home region of Telemark, writing lyrical poems influenced by local ballads and folk songs. Her work, however, transcended regionalism, and the *Columbia Dictionary of Modern Literature* described her as "a visionary poet of universal themes."

She wrote seven poetry collections, four plays, and more than 150 articles and essays. In her early work, Vaa praised the virtues of rural life and traditions, imbuing her lyrical verse with the rhythms of traditional music. Later in her career, her work became more philosophically searching, filled with disaster, unrest, and yearning. In her plays, Vaa integrated realism and expressionism as well as lyricism. She was deeply influenced by old earth-honoring traditions, praising the earth as the source of all life and celebrating female power. According to Claire Buck, though, her work defies easy comprehension "as she writes a triple dialect of modernism, ecological feminism and a radical New-Norwegian dialect, *landsmål.*" Vaa died in Oslo on November 28, 1965.

SOURCES:

Buck, Claire, ed. *The Bloomsbury Guide to Women's Literature.* NY: Prentice Hall, 1992.
Columbia Dictionary of Modern European Literature. 2nd ed. NY: Columbia University Press, 1980.
Zuck, Virpi, ed. *Dictionary of Scandinavian Literature.* Chicago, IL: St. James Press, 1990.

Kelly Winters,
freelance writer

Vaganova, Agrippina (1879–1951)

Russian dancer and teacher who was the virtual founder of Soviet ballet, one of the greatest dance traditions of all time. Name variations: hailed in her youth by dance critics as "The Queen of Variations." Born Agrippina Yakovlevna Vaganova on June 26, 1879 (June 12 according to the Julian calendar in use in Russia at that time), in St. Petersburg, Russia; died in Leningrad on November 5, 1951; attended Ballet School (1889–97).

Awards: Granted the title Peoples' Artist of the Russian Soviet Federation (1934) and State Prize of the USSR (1946); Leningrad Choreographic School was renamed the Vaganova School in her honor (1957).

Soloist (1905); ballerina (1915); retired (1916); taught at the Miklos School, Petrograd (1917), at the Volynsky School of Russian Ballet (1920), and at the Theater School of Petrograd (1920–22); taught and coached at the State Academic Theater of Opera and Ballet (GATOB, later the Kirov Theater and Ballet, 1917–51); served as artistic director of the Kirov Bal-

let (1931–37); taught in the pedagogical departments of the Leningrad Ballet school (1934–41) and at the Leningrad Conservatory (1946–51).

Agrippina Vaganova was born in St. Petersburg in 1879, the daughter of an usher at the Maryinsky Theater, whose ballet school, one day to be named after her, she entered at the age of ten. There she studied under Lev Ivanov, Nicholas Legat, and **Ekaterina Vazem**, learning much from watching the classes of the legendary Enrico Cecchetti and later those of *Olga Preobrazhenska. Upon her graduation in 1897, Vaganova immediately entered the Maryinsky Company, performing such roles as Hebe in *The Awakening of Flora* (1900), The Chinese Doll in *The Fairy Doll* (1903), Thaw in *The Seasons* (1907), Mazurka in *Chopiniana*, and the principal dancer in *The Whisper of Flowers* (1910), Naila in *La Source* and the title role in *The Pearl* (1911), Odette-Odile in *Swan Lake* (1913), the Tsar-Maiden in *The Little Humpbacked Horse* (1915), and the title role in *Giselle* (1916).

Agrippina Vaganova

As a dancer Agrippina Vaganova was famous for her ballon and extension. A musical performer, she was known for her strong legs, her impetuousness in bravura pieces, and for her imperious attack. Her swift hovering flits across the stage when performing the mazurka are said to have received enormous applause.

Upon her retirement from the ballet in 1916, Vaganova, who was later to attain near-mythic status as a teacher and as the founder of Soviet ballet, was idle at first but soon turned her attention to the training of ballet students. Barely 40, she was far from teaching simply because she could no longer perform. Rather, after long years of dissatisfaction with the teaching of ballet in imperial Russia, she devoted much of her energy to the development of a new theory of dance instruction, one that would draw upon the best elements in the various systems taught at that time and in the past. Before the Revolution three traditions had existed in Russian dance: the French school with its soft, gentle and artificial manner of performance which made it difficult for a dancer to develop virtuosity, the Italian which emphasized strength and endurance at the expense of lyricism and harmony, and the Russian with its rich emotional and spiritual content. Vaganova's goal and what became her life's work was to consolidate the three traditions into one coordinated system that would nurture the best elements from each. In doing so, she drew upon the work of Cecchetti, and she revised Preobrazhenska's method extensively to better weave it into her own vision.

After teaching for a while at the Miklos Ballet School, in 1921 Vaganova joined the staff of the Volynsky School of Russian Ballet. Among her pupils there was *Vera Volkova, who studied with her for five years, learning the new techniques taught especially by Vaganova; in years to come, Volkova would be the first to bring the knowledge of these to the world of Western ballet.

In the years immediately after the Revolution, there were many in high positions who thought of the ballet, with its imperial patronage and its distance from everyday life, as something so associated with the previous regime, that it should be swept away like so much else of pre-revolutionary Russia. On the other hand, the suggestion that Vaganova's methods were revolutionary attracted the attention of other, more cultivated and imaginative Bolsheviks who thought that ballet, for all its apparent artificiality, might be salvageable under the new dispensation. Since anything new and supposedly revolutionary was warmly welcomed in the Soviet 1920s, Vaganova, aided by the support of the

Commissar for Education, Anatoli Lunacharsky, succeeded in her goal of establishing a distinctly Soviet classical dance system while retaining the elegance and brilliance of the old imperial ballet. Through her efforts and skill emerged three generations of astonishingly gifted and meticulously trained artists, who enabled the Russian ballet to remain in the forefront of the world's ballet tradition. This was important because the coming of the Revolution had seen the departure of most of the great dancers of the previous era, including such luminaries as *Matilda Kshesinskaia (1872–1971), *Anna Pavlova (1881–1931), *Tamara Karsavina (1885–1978), and Vaslav Nijinsky (1890–1950), as well as such eminent teachers as Cecchetti and Preobrazhenska.

Vaganova received continuous, strong support from the Soviet government, and it was under her tutelage that there emerged the first generation of Soviet dancers, including **Maria Semyonova** (b. 1908), *Galina Ulanova (1910–1998), *Olga Lepeshinskaya (b. 1916) and *Natalia Dudinskaya (b. 1912). Still later she trained **Tatiana Vecheslova** (b. 1915), the under-appreciated *Alla Shelest (b. 1919), **Alla Osipenko** (b. 1932), and, finally, her last pupil **Irina Kolpakova** (b. 1933), a dancer who, like Preobrazhenska, was more a product of hard work and good training than natural genius. Other noteworthy dancers who studied under Vaganova include *Nina Anisimova, **Feya Balabina, Yelena Gvaramadze, Olga Iordan, Natalia Kamkova, Olga Moiseyeva**, and **Olga Mungalova**.

As a teacher Vaganova was severe with her students, often raising her voice shrilly as she put them through their paces. But she was also kind and solicitous of their needs, and always available for help. She could be biased towards her favorites, for example holding back Alla Shelest for fear that she might draw luster away from Dudinskaya, but she was devoted to those upon whom she doted and used her influence to get Ulanova into the State company (before it was renamed the Kirov Ballet). Vaganova was a brilliant instructor, emphasizing strict carriage, the position of the back, the use of the hands, and the holding of the head and shoulders so as not to strain the muscles of the neck. Before the Revolution it was unusual for male dancers to engage in great leaps, but these were a part of Vaganova's teaching and such virtuoso movements became standard in Soviet ballet. On the other hand, she saw no point in sheer virtuosity for its own sake; the movements, however dazzling, must be a part of the overall artistic expression and be fully in keeping with the mood of the ballet and the character being portrayed. She was also adept at establishing precise methods to overcome specific shortcomings, and *Olga Spessivtzeva, who was already a noted dancer but whose work was regarded as too often slipshod and erratic, became a much more precise and disciplined performer after studying with Vaganova in 1919.

Spessivtzeva and Marina Semyonova were the first major products of Vaganova's instruction and the first proofs of the validity of her methods. On the basis of Semyonova's dazzling physical attributes, Vaganova reconstructed the ballerina roles in *La Bayadère, Swan Lake,* and *Sleeping Beauty* and thereby turned her favorite pupil into the greatest dancer of her generation. In 1934, Vaganova's technique of instruction, now fully evolved, was outlined, however incompletely, in her book *Fundamentals of Classical Dance,* which was translated into English almost immediately by Anatole Chujoy and published in New York in 1937. In time, this germinal work was translated into a number of other languages, including Czech, Georgian, German, Hungarian, and Spanish, thereby influencing the training of dancers in all of the then Communist countries. For all this, Vaganova herself did not personally stage many ballets, only *La Source* (1925), a famous production of *Swan Lake* (1933), *Esmeralda* (1935, new version, 1948), and *Chopiniana* after Fokine (1938). She did, however, choreograph a number of concert pieces and recital numbers, some of which are still performed.

> [H]er classes in Petrograd from 1920 were to be the proving ground of a new and vital extension of the old imperial ballet manner.
>
> —Mary Clarke

During World War II, the Kirov Company was evacuated from Leningrad before the German siege of the city, and Vaganova was able to continue her teaching, spending a year at the Bolshoi Theater in Moscow. One of her pupils during this period was the future prima ballerina *Maya Plisetskaya, who studied under Vaganova for only four months but later recalled her as a genius. In the 1930s, the Soviet government established two departments for the sole purpose of training ballet instructors, one at the Leningrad Ballet School which now bears Vaganova's name and where she taught from 1936 until 1951, and the other at the Leningrad Conservatory, where from 1946 until her death she occupied the chair of choreography and was honored with the title of professor.

Agrippina Vaganova continued to teach until her last year, dying on November 5, 1951, at the age of 72. To this day she is regarded as one of the greatest teachers of dance of all time, and her impact on the world of ballet both inside and outside of Russia may never be erased. In Leningrad, now renamed St. Petersburg, her bust stands in the rehearsal hall of the Vaganova School opposite that of the great choreographer of the tsarist period, Marius Petipa.

SOURCES:

Litvinoff, Valentina. "Vaganova," in *Dance Magazine.* July–August, 1964.

Music Collection, Free Library of Philadelphia.

Réné, Natalia. "She Linked the Generations," in *Dance and Dancers.* London. January 1962.

Smakov, Gennady. *The Great Russian Dancers.* New York, 1984.

SUGGESTED READING:

Krasovskaya, Vera. *Vaganova.* Leningrad, 1989.

Kremmshevskaya, G. *Agrippina Vaganova.* Leningrad, 1981.

Vaganova, Agrippina. *Fundamentals of Classical Dance.* New York, 1937.

Robert H. Hewsen,
Professor of History,
Rowan University,
Glassboro, New Jersey

Vail, Myrtle (1888–1978)

American actress who co-starred with her daughter on the long-running radio show "Myrt and Marge." Born on January 7, 1888, in Joliet, Illinois; died on September 18, 1978, in Kansas City, Missouri; married George Damerel (an actor), in 1907 (died 1936); children: Donna Damerel (1908–1941, an actress); George.

Selected roles: "Myrt and Marge" (radio serial, 1931–42); Bucket of Blood (1959); Little Shop of Horrors (1960).

Born in Joliet, Illinois, in 1888, Myrtle Vail became a screen, vaudeville, and radio actress. By age 17, she was already on stage as one of Ned Washburn's "broilers," another name for the chorus line that appeared in his show *The Umpire.* In 1907, Vail married George Damerel, a well-known actor who was the show's star. They had a daughter, **Donna Damerel**, the following year.

In 1924, the couple, known as "Damerel & Vail & Co.," changed the name of their act to "The Three of Us" when Donna joined her parents on stage. They traveled the Orpheum and Keith vaudeville circuits until 1925, when vaudeville began a sharp, irreversible decline and silent movies soared in popularity. They moved to Chicago where George entered real estate; but by 1929, when the stock market crashed, they were financially ruined.

The next summer, Vail devised the idea of a radio show about two show-business sisters and their backstage adventures. She would be the older sister, Myrt, a tough but good-hearted woman who watched over the well-being of her younger sister, Marge, played by Donna. Vail wrote ten scripts, showed them to sponsors from the Wrigley chewing gum company, and secured a deal for the show. With the strains of its theme song "Poor Butterfly," it debuted on November 2, 1931. "Myrt and Marge" was a hit, and became the most popular dramatic program on radio. The show ran opposite "Amos 'n' Andy" at 7 PM until 1937, when it was moved to daytime. For awhile, "Myrt and Marge" was so popular that it aired twice a day in order to cover the different time zones.

After Donna Damerel died in childbirth in 1941, **Helen Mack** played Marge for the rest of the season, but in 1942 the show was dropped despite outcries from loyal fans. In 1946, Vail brought it back in a syndicated version, but it lasted for less than a year. An unsuccessful television pilot was made in 1949, but did not sell. She later had bit parts in several films by B-movie king Roger Corman, including the beatnik horror-spoof *A Bucket of Blood* (1959) and the original, now-classic *Little Shop of Horrors* (1960), co-starring Audrey the flesh-eating plant. She died in Kansas City in 1978.

SOURCES:

DeLong, Thomas A. *Radio Stars.* Jefferson, NC: McFarland, 1966.

Lamparski, Richard. *Whatever Became of . . . ?* NY: Crown, 1970.

Truitt, Evelyn Mack. *Who Was Who on Screen.* 3rd ed. NY: R.R. Bowker, 1983.

Kelly Winters,
freelance writer

Vakalo, Eleni (1921—)

Greek poet and art critic. Born in 1921 in Athens, Greece; attended university and the Sorbonne, Paris; married a stage designer.

Eleni Vakalo was born in 1921 and grew up in Athens, where she attended the university and studied archaeology. Later, she was a student of art history at the Sorbonne in Paris. With her husband, she founded the School of Fine Arts in Athens in 1958, and she taught there for several years.

In addition to being a poet, Vakalo is one of the most well-known art critics in Greece, and has written extensively on this topic. Her works include numerous reviews and articles, as well as the verse collections *Themes and Variations* (1945) and *Recollections from a Nightmarish City* (1948). Her style is personal and nonlyrical, expressing alienation, and experimental, eschewing traditional forms. In *The Forest* (1954) and *Description of the Body* (1959), she displays her characteristically unsentimental but subjective writing. Vakalo feels an artistic kinship with the poet *Marianne Moore, and has translated Moore's poems into Greek. Translations of Vakalo's work have appeared in English, French, and Russian collections.

SOURCES:
Buck, Claire, ed. *The Bloomsbury Guide to Women's Literature.* NY: Prentice Hall, 1992.

Kelly Winters,
freelance writer

Valadon, Suzanne (1865–1938)

French artist's model who taught herself to paint, then produced still lifes, landscapes, and especially realistic views of women. Pronunciation: Va-la-DAWN. Name variations: Maria; Suzanne Utter. Born Marie-Clémentine Valadon on September 23, 1865, at Bessines-sur-Gartempe, France; died on April 7, 1938, in Paris of a stroke; daughter of Madeleine Valadon (an unmarried seamstress) and an unknown father; had an elementary education in convent school in Paris, 1870–74; married Paul Mousis (a Parisian businessman), in 1896 (divorced around 1909); married André Utter (a painter), in 1914; children: (possibly with Miguel Utrillo y Molins, a Spanish artist) illegitimate son, Maurice Utrillo (b. 1883, the artist).

With her mother, settled in the Montmartre section of Paris (1866); began work as an artist's model (c. 1881); completed first known works (1884); met with Degas (c. 1887); Miguel Utrillo formally adopts her son Maurice (1891); completed first paintings (1892); had love affair with Erik Satie (1893); had initial exhibition of her work (1894); Maurice committed for the first time to an insane asylum (1901); began her affair with André Utter and began to confine her work to painting (1909); had one-woman exhibition at Weill gallery in Paris (1915); had first joint exhibition with Utter and Utrillo (1917); signed lucrative contract with art dealer Bernheim (1924); marriage of her son (1935).

Major works: Adam and Eve *(Musée National d'Art Moderne, Paris, 1909);* Joy of Living *(Metropolitan Museum of Art, New York, 1911);* The Fortuneteller *(Petit Palais, Geneva, 1912);* Casting of the Net *(Musée National d'Art Moderne, Paris, 1914);* The Blue Room *(Musée National d'Art Moderne, Paris, 1923);* The Church of St. Bernard *(Musée National d'Art Moderne, Paris, 1929).*

Suzanne Valadon rose from an impoverished background as the illegitimate daughter of a seam-

stress to become a notable figure on the French art scene of the early 20th century. Distinguished by her lack of formal training, Valadon drew on her native talent, as well as her experiences as a model for some of France's most renowned painters, in producing her own body of work. Although she lived in an era in which European painting was dominated by such movements as Cubism, she went her own way and never became closely linked with them, although she may have been somewhat influenced by later trends in the artistic world, such as Post-Impressionism and Fauvism. Her work was characterized by its energy, realism verging on brutality, and rich color. As **Anne Sutherland Harris** and **Linda Nochlin** note: "She relied upon intuition rather than intellect and her canvases transmit the sensations of a highly charged, personal vision." Some critics, however, have pointed to the sometimes crude use of color and overly dramatic contrasts as the chief weakness in the work of this remarkable, intuitive artist.

Until the past decade or so, Valadon has been most famous for her colorful life as well as

Suzanne
Valadon

for being the mother of Maurice Utrillo, one of the great French painters of the first half of the 20th century. In the words of her biographer **Jeanine Warnod**, Valadon's "life was like a serial film—a mixture of poverty and melodrama . . . against the background of Montmartre." Similarly, **Germaine Greer** notes, "Boldness was her hallmark, boldness of conception, boldness of design and boldness of execution," and Valadon "lived with the same uncompromising boldness." Unfortunately, many details of Valadon's biography remain in dispute; these range from the extent of the injuries that forced her to give up her career as a circus acrobat to the dates when she first encountered various members of the French art world. She left no diary or other written record of her life, and the accounts of her experiences with which she entertained friends and acquaintances in her later years were an uncertain mixture of fact and imagination.

In recent years, feminist writers, such as **Whitney Chadwick**, Germaine Greer and **Patricia Mathews**, have examined Valadon's life and work from a different perspective. They see her as an example of female achievement in a conspicuously male-dominated part of French life. In particular, they laud the way in which she painted female nudes, her artistic specialty, from a woman's perspective. She presented her audience with images of both attractive and unattractive women, but all appeared with a lack of self-consciousness conspicuously different from traditional nudes offered to "the male gaze." Notes **Nancy Heller**, "There is an assertive sexuality in many of Valadon's figures; the nudes are unashamedly naked . . . . [S]he painted bodies that have obvious substance." For **Eleanor Tufts**, Valadon's style "is characterized by a consistency of fluid, elegant contours and an unlabored plasticity of form." In Chadwick's view, Valadon rejected a presentation of "the female body as a lush surface isolated and controlled by the male gaze." Instead, Valadon "emphasizes the awkward gestures of figures apparently in control of their own movements."

Suzanne Valadon was born in the village of Bessines outside the French city of Limoges on September 23, 1865. The child was illegitimate; her mother **Madeleine Valadon** was a seamstress from a peasant family employed in a local bourgeois household. Her father may have been a railroad engineer working in the Limoges region or a laborer in a local flour mill. Her mother gave her the name Marie-Clémentine. She would become known as Suzanne only at the age of 18 or 19, renamed by her lover, Henri Toulouse-Lautrec, who told her that Marie-Clé-

mentine was too pedestrian for someone who wanted to be a great artist.

Mother and daughter settled in Paris in 1866, apparently to escape the small-town scandal of the girl's illegitimate birth. They resided in Montmartre. Although this neighborhood was already a center of Parisian artistic life, Montmartre still had the character of a small, semi-rural community in the city's outskirts. Valadon spent the greater part of her life within this lively area which had formally become a part of Paris only a decade before their arrival.

Valadon had only a brief period of elementary education at the Convent of St. Vincent de Paul before she went out into the working world. Some authorities claim she got her first job at the age of nine; others say she was able to stay in school until she was eleven. According to biographer John Storm, Valadon spent much of her time as a barefoot and undisciplined street child. In later years, she claimed to have encountered and encouraged the young painter Auguste Renoir while he was at work on a Paris street scene. She was already beginning to draw, and she received beatings from her mother when Madeleine discovered the male and female nudes the child was sketching. She held a variety of jobs ranging from restaurant waitress to assistant in a millinery shop. At the age of 15 or 16, Valadon realized her childhood dream of becoming a circus performer. For about a year, she was an acrobat in a Parisian circus, a job she was forced to give up after an almost fatal accident.

From the early 1880s onward, Valadon was an artist's model. According to some sources, she first got to know some of the era's leading painters when she delivered the laundry which her mother had washed for them. Writes Tufts, "An appealing *gamine* with blue eyes and blonde hair, her supple body attracted the professional attention of the artists she liked to watch at work." She posed for some of the most brilliant painters of the era, including Henri Toulouse-Lautrec and Auguste Renoir. Her versatility as a model was evident in the year 1885 when Valadon appeared both as a jaded denizen of a Paris bar in Toulouse-Lautrec's *The Bar* and as a wholesome and attractive young woman in Renoir's *The Braid*.

An enthusiastic member of the bohemian circles of Montmartre, the pretty young model had a large number of sexual liaisons. She answered her mother's criticisms of her lifestyle by reminding Madeleine Valadon that she had given birth to an illegitimate daughter while respectably employed as a seamstress. When Suzanne gave birth to a son, Maurice, in December 1883, she herself seemed uncertain who the father was. She registered him at the local mayor's office as "Maurice Valadon." Eight years later, the Spanish journalist and amateur painter Miguel Utrillo legally accepted responsibility for fathering the child, and some students of Valadon's life now consider him to have been Maurice's actual parent.

According to some accounts, it was Henri Toulouse-Lautrec, her lover at the time, who rec-

ognized the young woman's remarkable innate talents. Other versions of her life say that her talent was first discovered by Renoir. In any case, from the early days in her modeling career Valadon had studied the skills of the artists who were painting her. Her initial works were self-portraits and images of her friends and family. At the urging of Toulouse-Lautrec, who was still in the early stages of his own career, she took samples of her work to Degas, probably in the year 1887. Already a distinguished painter, Degas was known for his generous attitude toward up-and-coming young artists. Toulouse-

Woman in White Stockings, *by Suzanne Valadon.*

Lautrec may also have wanted to contest Degas' long-held view that natural gifts without training and long study were an insufficient background for a real artist. Degas was immediately impressed with Valadon's work. The older artist "showered me with praise," she said. Their relationship was sufficiently close that "I dropped in at his studio every afternoon."

Initially, Valadon produced only drawings, but, starting in 1892, she began to paint as well. Meanwhile, she continued to do notable drawings, such as candidly nude depictions of her son as well as equally realistic portrayals of adolescent girls. These were everyday scenes, placed in her own apartment, of youngsters engaged in such acts as bathing or dressing. At Degas' insistence, she submitted five of her drawings to the Salon de la Nationale in 1894. Despite the obstacles for an unknown and untrained artist, she was nonetheless able to persuade the selection committee to exhibit her works that year. Degas continued to be a generous patron to the young woman in various ways, introducing her to art dealers, collectors, and other artists. He also gave her some formal instruction in making etchings. According to Warnod, this was "the only direct teaching she ever had." Valadon's early paintings included a portrait of the composer Erik Satie, her lover at the time.

On August 5, 1896, Suzanne Valadon's life took a new turn when she married the Parisian lawyer and businessman Paul Mousis and found herself in comfortable financial circumstances for the first time. She broadened her range of subjects once again, starting, in 1900, to produce still life paintings. A sadder theme, however, was her son's increasing alcoholism, which first became evident when he was only 13. At the beginning, she refused to recognize the problem. Nonetheless, starting in 1901, Maurice was sent off to the first in a series of institutions designed to deal with the mentally ill. In later years, Utrillo would describe Valadon as "a saintly woman whom I bless and venerate as one would a Goddess," and he would regret that his failure to follow his mother's advice meant that he "was dragged through the road of Vice . . . [to become] a repugnant drunkard."

During Maurice's confinement, Valadon diverted some of her despair into a new burst of activity. Although only a few drawings from this period have survived, Storm notes that she produced hundreds of nudes using herself as a model. They were, in his words, "deft, forceful, and supple, as nothing she had ever done up to that time had been." Female nudes became a cen-

tral subject for Valadon during the remainder of her career. Writes **Penny Dunford**: "Valadon worked against the voyeurism" that male artists brought to such scenes. Her "strong, dark, sinuous outlines and bold colours" were used to show her subjects "at moments not normally depicted in art because of an ungainly position, or because it is a moment exclusive to women." Valadon's images, notes Mathews, "are radical in their very lack of a controlling gaze, a lack that shifts them out of traditional categories of the female nude."

Upon Maurice's release, his mother became determined to interest him in painting. The idea originated with one of Valadon's neighbors, a Freudian psychologist who thought that such an activity would constitute a useful form of therapy for the troubled young man. At first, Maurice was unenthusiastic, but Suzanne persisted with daily lessons until the teenager's extraordinary gifts as an artist became evident even to him. Writes Storm, "In this first spate of painting he found sound health and security at last."

Maurice Utrillo's small circle of friends presented his mother with a new influence in the person of André Utter. A young artist of 24, Utter first made Valadon's acquaintance in 1909 when he brought an intoxicated Maurice home after an evening of heavy drinking. Despite the difference in their ages—Valadon was now well into her 40s—the two soon became lovers and set up housekeeping together. Her divorce from Paul Mousis followed in short order, and, in 1914, she married Utter at his insistence just before he left for service in World War I.

By now, Valadon was offering her work in one-woman shows. Some accounts of her life indicate such a solo exhibition as early as 1911. It is certain, however, that she put on a one-woman exhibit in 1915 at the Weill gallery in Paris. It received critical acclaim, and, according to some authorities, commercial success as well. In any case, now cut off from Mousis' financial support, Valadon was able to live on the proceeds from the sale of Maurice Utrillo's paintings. Starting in 1917, she, her son, and her husband presented the public with a series of joint exhibitions of their works.

Following the end of World War I, there was a boom in the sale of French paintings. Thus, even as her life was increasingly darkened with Maurice Utrillo's mental illness, Valadon saw her career and reputation flourish. Her works came to include group portraits, in the form of both drawings and paintings. Warnod has found a social basis for some of the new subjects Valadon now took up. Freed by time and artistic success from her humble origins, Valadon now "emphasized her new status by her portraits of respectable women" including the wives of government officials and art critics. The years with Utter also saw her increasingly interested in painting landscapes and urban scenes, and her work was widely exhibited. Sales brought her a substantial amount of wealth until the onset of the Depression. In the 1920s, money also flowed in from the sale of Maurice Utrillo's paintings. By now Utter had abandoned his own work as a painter to become the family's art dealer and business manager. During these years of prosperity, Valadon made up for her impoverished early life: she threw lavish parties, surrounded herself with flowers, and frequented the best Parisian restaurants. In one notably flamboyant gesture, she hired a taxi for a drive of 350 miles so that she could pick strawberries from her country garden. In flower stores, she sometimes responded to her indecision over what to buy by purchasing everything in the shop. But the alcoholism that had developed so strongly in her son also became a growing part of her own personality as she began to drink heavily.

In 1923, Valadon, her husband, and her son settled in a rundown medieval castle in the small town of Saint-Bernard in the Beaujolais region. In 1920, her son had been released from a mental institution only because she agreed to supervise him. But now Maurice, who continued to paint brilliantly, had gone beyond alcoholism to become suicidal, and Suzanne Valadon hoped a relocation to the countryside might help her nurse him back to health. The new locale became the inspiration for some of her notable landscapes, including *The Church of Saint-Bernard*, completed in 1929.

Valadon prided herself upon her ability to separate her reputation from that of other female artists. Starting in the 1920s, she exhibited her work merely as "Valadon," with the absence of a first name, indicating that she was now presenting her work in the normal fashion for a male artist. It was only under extreme financial pressure during the following decade that she reluctantly agreed to exhibit her work in all-female shows in the hope of boosting her meager sales.

In the 1920s and 1930s, Valadon grew increasing obsessed by the loss of her youthful beauty. For years, she had hidden her exact age from people, but now she flaunted the passage of time. A candid self-portrait done in the nude in 1932 graphically displayed her drooping breasts as well as her poorly fitting false teeth. By the early 1930s, her relationship with André

Utter ended with an informal separation. The two had become increasingly estranged as a result of Utter's love affairs, his drinking, and his violence toward her. Valadon's troubled son finally married in 1935, to a widow, **Lucie Pauwels**, but the end of Valadon's responsibility for caring for Maurice also brought her a deep sense of loneliness. She herself had a serious illness, the first in her life, in 1935 when she was hospitalized with a kidney infection.

The unique and energetic painter died of a stroke in Paris on April 7, 1938. She had been at work painting a still life with flowers and died en route to the hospital. The wild young artist's model had ended up as a pious woman who was a regular presence for mass at the local Catholic church. She was also the hostess to such prominent figures in French life as Prime Minister Edouard Herriot. Valadon's funeral was the occasion for a gathering of the Parisian art world, with such luminaries as Pablo Picasso, Georges Braque, and André Derain in attendance. The woman, whose first role in the Montmartre art scene had been as an impoverished model, was now recognized as a leading French artist. "I think maybe God," she once said, "has made *me* France's greatest woman painter."

SOURCES:

Chadwick, Whitney. *Women, Art, and Society*. London: Thames & Hudson, 1990.

Dunford, Penny. *A Biographical Dictionary of Women Artists in Europe and America Since 1850*. NY: Harvester Wheatsheaf, 1990.

Greer, Germaine. *The Obstacle Race*. NY: Farrar, Straus, and Giroux, 1979.

Harris, Anne Sutherland, and Linda Nochlin. *Women Artists, 1550–1950*. Los Angeles: Los Angeles County Museum of Art, 1976.

Lipton, Eunice. "Representing Sexuality in Women Artists' Biographies: the Cases of Suzanne Valadon and Victorine Meurent," in *The Journal of Sex Research*. Vol. 27, 1990, pp. 81–93.

Mathews, Patricia. "Returning the Gaze: Diverse Representations of the Nude in the Art of Suzanne Valadon," in *The Art Bulletin*. Vol. 73, 1991, pp. 415–430.

Mcmullen, Roy. *Degas: His Life, Times, and Work*. London: Secker and Warburg, 1985.

Storm, John. *The Valadon Drama: The Life of Suzanne Valadon*. NY: E.P. Dutton, 1959.

Tufts, Eleanor. *Our Hidden Heritage: Five Centuries of Women Artists*. NY: Paddington Press, 1974.

Warnod, Jeanine. *Suzanne Valadon*. NY: Crown, 1981.

SUGGESTED READING:

Baylis, Sarah. *Utrillo's Mother*. New Brunswick, NJ: Rutgers University Press, 1986.

Betterton, Rosemary, ed. *Looking On: Images of Femininity in the Visual Arts and Media*. London: Pandora, 1987.

Rose, June. *Suzanne Valadon: The Mistress of Montmartre*. St. Martin's, 1999.

Wallis, Brian, ed. *Art after Modernism: Rethinking Representation.* NY: New Museum of Contemporary Art, 1984.

Warnod, Jeanine. *Maurice Utrillo.* NY: Crown, 1983.

Neil M. Heyman,
Professor of History,
San Diego State University,
San Diego, California

Valasca (fl. 738)

Military leader of Bohemia. Name variations: Dlasta. Flourished around 738 in Bohemia.

A bold military leader, Valasca began her career as a soldier in the army of Queen *Libussa of Bohemia. Eventually she was made a general, and then became one of Libussa's most trusted aides. Around 738, Valasca led a coup d'etat against her queen, taking the throne for herself. It is reported that Valasca put women in high office and allowed only women to serve in her army, although these reports are almost certainly exaggerations. She was an aggressive queen and ruled a highly centralized government until her death.

Laura York, M.A. in History,
University of California,
Riverside, California

Valencia, duchess of.

See Leonora Telles for sidebar on Maria Telles (d. 1379).

Valentine, Lila (1865–1921)

American educational reformer and suffragist. Born Lila Hardaway Meade on February 4, 1865, in Richmond, Virginia; died after an operation for an intestinal obstruction on July 14, 1921, in Richmond; daughter of Richard Hardaway Meade (founder of a wholesale drug firm) and Kate (Fontaine) Meade; married Benjamin Batchelder Valentine (a banker), on October 28, 1886 (died 1919); children: one (stillborn).

Lila Valentine was born in 1865 into a wealthy family in Richmond, Virginia, where she was tutored at home and attended private schools. Dissatisfied, she undertook her own education, reading widely in her father's library, and became interested in the arts. In 1886, she married affluent banker Benjamin Batchelder Valentine, and two years later gave birth to a stillborn child, leaving her in frail health that would persist for the rest of her life. In 1892, her husband took her to England, hoping the change would help her migraine headaches and attacks of acute indigestion. Stimulated by the liberal climate in England, she returned to Virginia hoping to spread her progressive views, especially on universal education, in the South.

Convinced that everyone, regardless of race or gender, should receive an education, Valentine and several other women, including **Mary Branch Munford**, were inspired to found the Richmond Education Association after a visit to Richmond in April 1900 by a Boston advocate of kindergartens. Valentine served as president until 1904 of this association, which was dedicated to the improvement of public schools. In addition, as president of the Richmond Training School for Kindergartners, founded in 1901, she helped introduce kindergartens and vocational training into Richmond's schools and obtained a $600,000 city grant for a new high school. In 1902, Valentine attended the annual conference of the Southern Education Board, a regional group dedicated to the same goals. She succeeded in having the group convene in Richmond the following year, one of the first racially integrated meetings held in that city since the Civil War. Because of her work, she was appointed to the executive committee of the Co-operative Educational Association of Virginia, a citizens' organization devoted to raising the standards of schools in the state.

While working with the schools, Valentine recognized that many students were in poor health, and that the state needed public health facilities. With the aid of volunteer nurses, she founded the Instructive Visiting Nurse Association of Richmond. She also organized the Anti-Tuberculosis Auxiliary, which led the first major campaign against tuberculosis in Virginia. The auxiliary established a dispensary, clinics, and Pine Camp, a tuberculosis hospital.

In 1904, Valentine's own poor health required that she take a break from public life. The following year, she returned to England, where the active women's suffrage movement convinced her that because most political legislation affected women directly, they should have a voice in determining it. In 1909, the Equal Suffrage League of Virginia was formed, and Valentine became its president because she was, according to Lloyd C. Taylor, Jr., "the only woman who combined the requisite courage and intelligence" with "the inexhaustible patience of which victors and martyrs are made." She served as president of the organization for 11 years, during which time she worked tirelessly for the vote. In 1912 she addressed the Virginia House of Delegates, and in 1913 she gave more than 100 speeches throughout Virginia.

Valentine's opponents tried to discredit her because she supported education for African-

Americans, was active in groups such as the National Child Labor Committee and the American Association for Labor Legislation, and because she had spoken to the Central Labor Council of Richmond. She countered this by making unexpected appearances, on one occasion showing up at a meeting of the Virginia Road Builders' Association to assure its members that women knew the value of better roads and would vote for them given the opportunity. She was also active in the National American Woman Suffrage Association and served on its Congressional committee in 1916.

Valentine's husband, who had always been a strong supporter of her work, died in 1919, and Valentine moved to Maine and lived in seclusion with her two sisters for awhile. Early in 1920, realizing that the suffrage amendment would soon be ratified, she decided that women needed better political education in order to vote intelligently. In April 1920, the University of Virginia granted her request to hold a three-day conference on government. She also urged that public schools add civics to the curriculum. Her health was still poor, however, and she died on July 14, 1921, following surgery for an intestinal obstruction, at age 56. She was buried in Hollywood Cemetery in Richmond.

SOURCES:
Taylor, Lloyd C., Jr. "Lila Hardaway Meade Valentine," in *Notable American Women, 1607–1950*. Ed. by Edward T. James. Cambridge, MA: The Belknap Press of Harvard University, 1971.

Kelly Winters,
freelance writer

Valentine of Milan (1366–1408).
See Visconti, Valentina.

Valentino, Natacha (1897–1966).
See Rambova, Natacha.

Valentino, Mrs. Rudolph (1897–1966).
See Rambova, Natacha.

Valentinois, duchess of.
See Diane de Poitiers (1499–1566).

Valeria, Empress (c. 23–48 CE).
See Messalina, Valeria.

Valeria Messalina (c. 23–48 CE).
See Messalina, Valeria.

Valéry, Violetta (1824–1847).
See Plessis, Alphonsine.

Valeska, Countess (1786–1817).
See Walewska, Marie.

Valette, Aline (1850–1899)

French organizer, writer, and speaker who was a leading figure in the formative years of the French socialist movement. Pronunciation: ah-LEEN va-LET. *Born Alphonsine Goudeman in Lille (Nord), on October 4, 1850; died of tuberculosis at Arcachon (Gironde), on March 21, 1899, and was buried there; daughter of a railway worker and granddaughter of a college dean; educated to be a teacher; married to a lawyer, separated, and widowed; children: two sons.*

Elected secretary of the newly founded teacher's union (1878); joined the French Workers' Party (1879); published a widely circulated home economics text (1883); became a substitute inspector of child labor (1887); named secretary of the National Federation of Feminist Societies, and founded and directed L'Harmonie sociale (1892); elected to the National Council of the French Workers' Party and published Socialism and Sexualism *(1893); elected permanent secretary of the French Workers' Party (1896); contributed articles on women's labor to* La Fronde *(1897–98).*

Writings: La Journée de la petite ménagère *(Paris, 1883); with "Dr. Z." [Pierre Bonnier],* Socialisme et sexualisme, programme du Parti socialiste féminine *(Paris: Typographie A.M. Baudelot, 1893); articles for* L'Harmonie sociale *(Valette, ed.),* La Revue socialiste, La Petite République, Le Peuple *(Lyons),* La Revue féministe *(Clotilde Dissard),* Le Matin, *and* La Fronde *(Marguerite Durand).*

Aline Valette, with *Louise Michel, *Paule Mink, and *Eugénie Potonié-Pierre, was one of the most prominent women socialists in France in the late 19th century. More than the aforementioned, she was involved in party politics. She was the first woman to sit on the National Council of the French Workers' Party (POF), whose chief, Jules Guesde (1845–1922), the "Marxist pope," described her (rather archly) as "the sole woman who has understood socialism."

Valette, née Alphonsine Goudeman, born in Lille (Nord), on October 5, 1850, was a daughter of a railway worker and granddaughter of a college dean. She was trained as a teacher and taught in Paris in a private school in Montmartre, a working-class district, and then as a professor of the City of Paris in a teacher-training school on the rue Ganneron. In 1883, after she had married and left teaching, she published a highly successful textbook (34 editions in 10 years) on home economics for Paris schools which she later adapted for working women. *La Journée de la petite ménagère* (The Little Housewife's Day) included much data and advice on housekeeping, cooking, and good grooming. Later she wrote a column on "domestic working-class economy" for an independent socialist journal, offering, for example, recipes for 365 "soups of the year."

Valette became active in social, political, and feminist causes by the mid-1870s, doubtless stimulated by her childhood in a working-class family and observations of life in Paris. She was an early member of *Maria Deraismes' Society for the Amelioration of Women's Condition (1870, 1874—), was a delegate to the first Workers' Congress (rue d'Arras, 1876), and with Gustave Francolin, Camecasse, and **Maria Bonnevial** (b. 1841, a socialist teacher whose license was revoked by the Second Empire) founded France's first teachers' union, of which she was named secretary in 1878. It included both public and private lay teachers. Drawn to socialism by humanitarianism, she joined the POF at its birth in 1879 and probably the Union of Socialist Women, founded by Potonié-Pierre, *Marguerite Tinayre**, and **Léonide Rozade**, which during its brief life (1880–81) succeeded in getting women's issues included in future socialist party programs. At some point, she worked for the Charitable Society for Women Released from Saint-Lazare, which sought to integrate former prostitutes into society. In 1887(?), she also became an unpaid substitute child labor inspector, one of the first women so engaged. The conditions she witnessed helped persuade her to join a Guesdist study group, which she represented at the congress—the Marxist rather than the Possibilist version—which organized the Second International Workingmen's Association (1889). That year, she also attended the Second French International Congress for Women's Rights, but she came away disappointed by its narrow, moderate approach.

> The proletariat of the factories loved this woman of action, gentle and sickly—but how ardent in battle!
>
> —Léon Osmin

Valette's membership in the Eight-Hour League, an offspring of the Second International, brought her into Guesde's entourage, where she began a rapid rise in the POF. She had married a wealthy Paris lawyer some years ago and given birth to two sons. But the couple separated and he had died. As a comfortably well-off widow now, she was able to put to the full-time use of the party her first-class organizational skills and, it is said, excessively methodical ways. After Valette's election as permanent party secretary in 1896, her dining room in her spacious apartment at 12, rue de Notre-Dame de Lorette, became the party's office and meeting room for its executive committee. She was an altogether agreeable presence, lively in aspect, with a very expressive face, her blue eyes now sad, now twinkling in gaiety. Rather tall and slender, with blonde curly hair crowning a fine head which she carried high, she was graceful and gentle in manner, courageous in the face of difficulty or illness, and possessed an excellent mind. She was a talented public speaker and a capable, if too often rather dry, writer, well informed, especially in economic matters.

In 1891, Valette attended the Brussels congress of the Second International. Guesdist though she was, it was through feminism that she became a party leader. In November 1891, Potonié-Pierre launched the French Federation of Feminist Societies (FFSF), hoping through this umbrella organization eventually to replace the more moderate elements of the women's movement. Valette joined and assisted in organizing the Third French International Congress for Women's Rights (May 13–15, 1892). It attracted an amazingly broad range of participants, from Deraismes to the revolutionary Édouard Vaillant; as was all but inevitable, it failed to create much unity. It did endorse support of "the international proletariat's demands," however, and commissioned the drawing up of a "List of Feminine Grievances," which Valette eventually composed. Trouble soon arose in the FFSF, and on June 17 Potonié-Pierre resigned as secretary in a dispute with Valette over control of the organization. Valette succeeded her.

On October 15, 1892, the first issue of a weekly tabloid, *L'Harmonie sociale*, appeared, published and edited by Valette. While working on the List, she wanted to reach out to working women. The paper was the organ of a POF affiliate, the Feminine Socialist Party, and lasted until July 8, 1893. It tried to integrate the socialist and feminist causes through "sexualism" (see below). Valette's first article asserted that women had neglected their "natural role of reproducer" in favor of the "artificial role of producer"—a view which suggested that "sexualism" might have serious problems as a feminist theory. *L'Harmonie sociale*'s socialist intentions were sincere, but Valette tended to portray Guesde, the POF, and the International as more sympathetic to women's issues than they truly were. Probably the wish was father to the thought, notes Charles Sowerwine.

The FFSF passed the List on March 16, 1893, at its first and only general assembly. It was no radical document, being in essence "a bill of rights for middle-class women," writes Sowerwine, advocating, for example, access to all levels of education, professions, and public office, and abolition of all articles in the Napoleonic Code consecrating female inferiority. The FFSF circulated the List to all the district mayors of Paris and then disintegrated. Yet it was as secretary of the defunct federation that Valette attended the POF congress in October, one of only three women among the 92 delegates.

The congress elected her to the party's national council, the first woman in France to sit on any party's governing board. (Women did not obtain the vote in France until 1944.) Her elevation was somewhat fortuitous. Following a failure to recruit many female members at Lille, a labor stronghold, by supporting (as did Valette) a short-lived women's committee there working for a school-lunch program, the leadership decided they needed to reach out to women more visibly. Valette, to whom the party had entrusted a lecture mission in Roubaix in April, was ready at hand when it was decided to revamp the national council. She was considered the only woman in the party—only 2–3% of whose members were female—to have leadership potential.

As a member of the national council, Valette attended the annual party congresses from 1894 to 1897, after which illness intervened. In November 1896, she was elected permanent secretary of the party. A series of articles on women's labor conditions which she published in the party's official journal, *Le Socialiste*, from May 26, 1895, to January 5, 1896, formed the basis of a report she presented to the 1895 congress. The congress passed a resolution calling for the organization of women with male workers. At the 1897 congress, she sought approval of a program of women's rights which mostly repeated the usual bourgeois feminist demands—reform of the civil code, abolition of the legal power of husbands over wives, full political equality, the right to divorce, authorization of paternity suits, equalization of rights between legitimate and illegitimate children, and so forth. She stated that a "feminine program" was needed because "women's aptitudes and sexual burdens" create "a situation distinct from that of men." In effect, she was calling for the party to put theory into practice as regards women. The resolution passed, but then Guesde raised questions, so it was tabled for study until the next congress. By that time (1898), she was too ill to attend. Little came of the initiative.

Valette was engaged also in activities outside the party. Following the death of Deraismes, Valette was elected to the board of the French League for Women's Rights (LFDF). She also was a member of the Union of Socialist Writers, where she served on the study and propaganda committee. Aside from writing for *Le Socialiste* and *La Revue féministe* (1895—), her most prominent collaboration was at *La Fronde*, *Marguerite Durand*'s all-female-written-and-printed daily begun on December 9, 1897. It was a moderate journal on the whole, but a few radicals like Valette contributed because Durand was especially interested in women's labor unions. Valette wrote the "Labor Tribune" column, which contained detailed studies of women's working conditions, suggested reforms, encouraged women's unions, and supported strikes. Between December 15, 1897, and August 28, 1898, she produced some 25 articles on these subjects, after which illness forced her to hand over the column to her old friend Marie Bonnevial.

When Valette was reaching the peak of her powers, she was diagnosed with tuberculosis. During the winter of 1897–98, her coughing began to alarm her friends. In April, she went to take the cure at Arcachon (Gironde), south of Bordeaux. The warm climate and mineral waters did not avail. She continued to write until September 1898, convinced she was going to recover. The end came on March 21, 1899, six months shy of her 50th birthday. Guesde presided on January 31, 1900, at the dedication of a monument over her grave at Arcachon.

As a socialist and feminist, Valette has not fared well at the hands of critics. In 1892, she and Dr. Pierre Bonnier ("Dr. Z."), a gynecologist, published a brochure, *Socialisme et sexualisme*, setting forth ideas they had developed in articles in *L'Harmonie sociale*. (The brochure appears to have been mostly her product; Bonnier's role was perhaps to lend her scientific respectability.) Unfortunately, the work lacked intellectual rigor and organization. Briefly, in the brochure and articles (which were more influential) Valette argued that women have to wage two fights: social, as members of the working class, and sexual, as oppressed females. Men are producers of goods, women producers of the race. Capitalism owns what workers produce, and men own women, but "it is economic revolution [with the coming of socialism] which will set the absolute condition of human emancipation in its social form and in its sexual form." Once production is properly "organized" (a favorite socialist term), women can look forward to a "happy era when woman will be restored to her biological role of creator and educator of the species." In the meantime, until the Revolution women should organize unions and enter "the struggle of life" as the "ransom for their emancipation." Again, once emancipated, women would become free to leave the workplace and devote themselves fully to their maternal function.

Was such a program feminist? Valette did concern herself with the lot of working women, notably their low wages. And insofar as *some* feminists have always reserved a special place for women's maternal function, Valette was a feminist. On the other hand, so intent was she on emphasizing maternity that she did not even consider, for example, a community role in child-rearing, e.g., day-care centers, which was important in the widely read recent work of the eminent German socialist Auguste Bebel. Valette exemplifies the problem socialism, notably in France, was having—and for decades continued to have—with the place of women. It preached equality for all while at the same time preserving traditional sexual roles, which, in practice, meant female inferiority. It is instructive that Potonié-Pierre (who admittedly had a score to settle) was alone at the time in criticizing Valette's theory: "Sexualism is nonsense, a separatism, a hindrance to progress. It puts the man and the woman in different categories."

As usual, the Revolution would solve all social problems. Feminism, in Valette's formula, was to be incorporated into socialism as a means to improve the condition imposed upon women by capitalism—until the Revolution would solve the underlying problem for women, namely, writes **Marilyn Boxer**, "the self-serving individualism of men," by organizing men's work and making good socialists of them.

Ironically, Valette was no true revolutionary, a Paule Mink or Louise Michel, for example. Notwithstanding Guesde's accolade, she apparently did not tackle Marx's *Capital* until near the end of her life. It was not Marxism but humanitarianism and loving kindness which fueled her concern for the poor and downtrodden. Inevitably, however, she often found it difficult to communicate with the masses of still-unpoliticized working women because she herself had become a solidly middle-class woman. Class lines were painfully distinct. It is to her credit that she freely took to heart the suffering of others less fortunate than she. If the socialists never seriously accepted feminism and women did not join them en masse, she bore some of the responsibility. But these results were mostly due to causes far larger than the merits or faults of any individual however deeply dedicated—as Aline Valette most certainly was.

SOURCES:

Albistur, Maïté, and Daniel Armogathe, eds. *Le Grief des femmes*. Vol. 2: *Anthologie des textes féministes du second empire à nos jours*. Paris: Éditions Hier et Demain, 1978.

———. *Histoire du féminisme français, du moyen âge à nos jours*. Paris: Éditions du femme, 1977.

"Aline Valette," in *Le Mouvement socialiste*. April 1, 1899.

Bidelman, Patrick Kay. *Pariahs Stand Up! The Founding of the Liberal Feminist Movement in France, 1858–1889*. Westport, CT: Greenwood Press, 1982.

Bock, Gisela, and Pat Thane, eds. *Maternity and Gender Politics: Women and the Rise of the European Welfare State, 1880s–1950s*. NY: Routledge, 1991.

Boxer, Marilyn. "French Socialism, Feminism, and the Family," in *Third Republic-Troisième République*. Vol. 3, no. 4, 1977, pp. 128–167.

Dictionaire biographique du mouvement ouvrier français. Dir. Jean Maitron. Paris: Éditions ouvrières, 1969—. Part III (1871–1914).

Hause, Steven, and Anne Kenney. *Women's Suffrage and Social Politics in the French Third Republic*. Princeton, NJ: Princeton University Press, 1984.

Klejman, Laurence and Florence Rochefort. *L'Égalité en marche: Le Féminisme sous la Troisième République*. Paris: Presses de la Fondation nationale des sciences politiques-Éditions des Femmes, 1989.

Martz-Capgras, Andrée. "Pionnières: Aline Valette," in *Almanach populaire*, éditée par le Parti socialiste. Paris, 1939, pp. 152–154.

Osmin, Léon. "Aline Valette," in *Figures de jadis: Les Pionnières obscurs du socialisme*. Paris: Éditions "Nouveau Prométhée" [1934], pp. 84–87.

Rabaut, Jean. *Histoire des féminismes français*. Paris: Éditions Stock, 1978.

Sowerwine, Charles. *Sisters or Citizens? Women and Socialism in France since 1876*. Cambridge: Cambridge University Press, 1982.

Valette, Aline and Marcelle Capy. *Femmes et travail au XIXᵉ siècle: Enquêtes de La Fronde et La Bataille syndicaliste*. Présentation et commentaires par Marie-Hélène Zylberberg-Hocquard et Évelyne Diebolt. Paris: Syros [1984].

Verecque, Charles. *Dictionnaire du socialisme*. Paris: M. Giard & E. Brière, 1911.

SUGGESTED READING:

Boxer, Marilyn, and Jean H. Quateart, eds. *Socialist Women*. Boston, MA: Houghton Mifflin, 1978.

Historical Dictionary of the Third French Republic, 1870–1940. Patrick H. Hutton, ed. Westport, CT: Greenwood Press, 1986.

McMillan, James F. *Housewife or Harlot: The Place of Women in French Society*. NY: St. Martin's Press, 1981.

Noland, Aaron. *The Founding of the French Socialist Party (1893–1905)*. NY: H. Fertig, 1970 (1956).

Smith, Paul. *Feminism and the Third Republic*. Oxford: Clarendon Press, 1996.

Willard, Claude. *Les Guesdistes*. Paris: Éditions Sociales, 1965.

Wright, Gordon. *France in Modern Times*. 5th ed. NY: W.W. Norton, 1995.

COLLECTIONS:

Paris: Archives de la Préfecture de Police, B. a/1 1290; Bibliothèque Marguerite Durand, dossier Valette.

David S. Newhall,
Pottinger Distinguished Professor of History Emeritus,
Centre College, author of
Clemenceau: A Life at War (1991)

Valette Rachilde, Mme Alfred
(1860–1953).

> See Vallette, Marguerite.

Vallayer-Coster, Anne (1744–1818)

French still-life painter who was the first woman to become a member of France's Royal Academy. Name variations: Anna Vallayer-Coster. Born Anne Vallayer in France in 1744; died in 1818; daughter of a goldsmith; married Jean Pierre Coster (a lawyer), in 1781.

Anne Vallayer was born in 1744 and grew up in Gobelins, France, the daughter of a goldsmith who worked for the local tapestry factory. When she was ten, the family moved to Paris where her father opened his own shop. Upon his death, her mother continued to run the Paris workshop.

Little is known of the art training or earliest work of Anne Vallayer-Coster. Though Gabriel de Saint-Aubin was a family friend, it is doubtful that he ever became her teacher, and her first known painting was a portrait executed in 1762. Eight years later, in 1770, the 26-year-old Anne submitted her *Allegory of the Visual Arts* and *Allegory of Music* (now in the Louvre, Paris) to the Académie Royale and was unanimously elected a member. Denis Diderot admired her work, as did Royal Academy voting member Jean Georges Wille who noted: "I was absolutely enchanted by the talent of the likeable person, whom I saw for the first time and whose talent is truly that of a man perfected in this genre of painting representing still life."

Primarily a still-life painter greatly admired in her day, Vallayer-Coster was both versatile and resourceful and had many influential patrons; some 450 works are attributed to her brush, including portraits of flower arrangements, table settings, musical instruments, trophies, tureens of soup, kitchen utensils, tea services, bread, wine, hams, cheese, lobsters, and plums in a basket—all in simple or elaborate configurations. **Marie Antoinette* saw to it that Vallayer-Coster was assigned an apartment in the Louvre. Unlike **Elisabeth Vigée-Le Brun*, Vallayer-Coster did not leave Paris during the upheavals of the French Revolution, despite her royal connections, but she did very little painting after 1800.

Vallette, Marguerite (1860–1953)

French novelist and literary critic. Name variations: Mme Alfred Vallette or Valette; Mme Alfred Valette Rachilde; Marguerite Eymery; (pseudonym) Rachilde (pronounced RAH-sheeld). Born Marguerite Eymery on February 11, 1860, near Périgueux in southwest France; died in 1953; only child of a career army officer and a mother whose father was a newspaper editor; married Alfred Vallette (co-founder and editor of Mercure de France).

Wrote erotic novels; with husband Alfred Vallette, founded Le Mercure de France.

Selected works (under pseudonym Rachilde): Monsieur Vénus *(1884, which was banned in Belgium);* Nono *(1885);* Mme Adonis *(1888);* Les Hors Nature *(Nature's Outcasts, 1897);* L'Heure sexuelle *(The Sexual Hour, 1898);* La Tour d'Amour *(The Tower of Love, 1899);* La Jongleuse *(The Juggler, 1900);* La Souris japonaise *(The Japanese Mouse, 1912);* La Tour d'Amour *(1914);* La Maison Vierge *(1920);* Refaire l'Amour *(1928);* L'Homme au Bras de Feu *(1931);* Quand j'étais jeune *(When I Was Young, 1948).*

Born in France in 1860, Marguerite Vallette shocked the public of her time not only with her novels, which were considered "perverse," but with her personal appearance and outlook as well. During her adolescence she read widely, including the works of the Marquis de Sade. Her father, to whom she was devoted as a child, wanted a son and instilled in her feelings of worthlessness and contempt for her femininity. This is made clear in her autobiography, *Pourquoi je ne suis pas féministe* (Why I Am Not a Feminist, 1928). She wore men's clothing, a fashion among literary and artistic women of her day, referred to herself as a "man of letters," and wrote in the style of the Decadents, a highly misogynistic school of art inspired by the morbid, neurotic, and macabre.

Marguerite Vallette was a journalist before she began publishing works of fiction. Her first novel, *Monsieur Vénus*, was published in 1884 by Alfred Vallette, whom she later married; this work, produced under the pen name "Rachilde," launched Vallette upon a long literary career that would span some 60 works of fiction. A story of cross-dressing and gender role inversion, *Monsieur Vénus* was considered pornographic by many readers and was banned in Belgium, where it was first published. As is typical of *fin de siècle* erotic fiction, its focus on "perverse" activities seems very tame and inoffensive today. Rachilde's other novels continued along similar lines, with themes of incest (1897's *Les Hors Nature*), pedophilia (1912's *La Souris japonaise*), homoeroticism, and the complexities of the human mind. Her other titles include *Mme Adonis* (1888), *La Tour d'Amour* (The Tower of Love, 1899), *La Jongleuse* (The Juggler, 1900), in which the main character is in love with a Greek jar, and *L'Amazone rouge* (The Red Amazon).

Together with her husband, Vallette founded *Le Mercure de France*. It was one of the best-known literary review journals of the Symbolists, a primarily French literary movement of the late 19th century, in which ideas and emotions were expressed indirectly through symbols. Her memoirs, *Quand j'étais jeune* (When I Was Young, 1948), give an account of the world of the Symbolists.

SOURCES:

Buck, Claire, ed. *The Bloomsbury Guide to Women's Literature*. NY: Prentice Hall, 1992.

Harvey, Sir Paul, and J.E. Heseltine, eds. *The Oxford Companion to French Literature*. Oxford: Clarendon Press, 1959.

Malinda Mayer,
writer and editor,
Falmouth, Massachusetts

Valli, Alida (1921—)

Italian actress. Name variations: sometimes acted under the name Valli. Born Alida Maria Laura von Altenburger on May 3, 1921, in Pola, Italy; married Oscar de Mejo (a pianist-composer), in 1944 (separated).

Selected filmography: T'amerò sempre *(It., 1933)*; I Due Sergenti *(1936)*; L'Ultima Nemica *(1937)*; Ma

Alida Valli

l'Amor mio non muore *(1937)*; La Casa del Peccato *(1938)*; Assenza ingiustificata *(1939)*; Oltre L'Amore *(1940)*; Piccolo Mondo antico *(1941)*; L'Amante segreta *(1941)*; Ore 9–Lezione di Chimica *(Schoolgirl Diary, 1941)*; Le Due Orfanelle *(The Two Orphans, 1942)*; Noi Vivi *(Addio Kira, 1942)*; I Pagliacci *(Laugh Pagliacci, 1942)*; Apparizione *(1943)*; La Vita ricomincia *(Life Begins Anew, 1945)*; Il Canto della Vita *(1945)*; Eugenia Grandet *(1946)*; The Paradine Case *(US, 1948)*; The Miracle of the Bells *(US, 1948)*; The Third Man *(UK, 1949)*; The White Tower *(US, 1950)*; Walk Softly Stranger *(US, 1950)*; Les Miracles n'ont lieu qu'une fois *(Fr.-It., 1951)*; Ultimo Incontro *(1951)*; Les Amants de Tolede *(The Lovers of Toledo (Fr.-It.-Sp., 1953)*; Siamo Donne *(1953)*; La mano dello Straniero *(The Stranger's Hand, It.-UK, 1953)*; Senso *(The Wanton Contessa, 1954)*; Il Grido *(The Outcry, 1957)*; La Diga sul Pacifico *(This Angry Age or The Sea Wall, 1958)*; Les Bijoutiers du Clair de Lune *(The Night Heaven Fell, Fr.-It., 1958)*; Les Yeux sans Visage *(The Horror Chamber of Dr. Faustus, Fr., 1960)*; Les Dialogue des Carmélites *(Fr., 1960)*; Une aussi Longue Absence *(The Long Absence, Fr.-It., 1961)*; The Happy Thieves *(US, 1962)*; Aphelia *(Fr., 1962)*; El Vale de Las Spades *(The Castilian, Sp.-US, 1963)*; Edipo Re *(Oedipus Rex, 1967)*; Le Champignon *(Fr., 1970)*; La Strategia del Ragno *(The Spider's Stratagem, 1970)*; Le Prima Notte di Quiete *(1972)*; Tendre Dracula *(Tender Dracula, Fr., 1974)*; Ce Cher Victor *(Fr., 1975)*; 1900 *(1976)*; Le Jeu de Solitaire *(Fr., 1976)*; The Cassandra Crossing *(US, 1977)*; Berlinguer ti voglio bene *(1977)*; Suspiria *(1977)*; Un Cuore semplice *(1978)*; L'Anti Cristo *(The Tempter, 1978)*; La Luna *(Luna, Fr., 1979)*; Inferno *(1979)*; Aquella Casa En Las Afueras *(Sp., 1980)*; Puppenspiel mit toten Augen *(Ger.-It.-Sp., 1980)*; Aspern *(1982)*; Sogni Mostruosamente Proibiti *(It., 1983)*; Segreti Segreti *(It., 1984)*; Hitchcock *(1985)*; Il Brivido del Genio *(It., 1985)*; Le Jupon rouge *(Fr., 1987)*; A notre regrettable epoux *(Fr., 1988)*; Zitti e mosca *(The Party's Over, 1991)*; Il lungo silenzia *(1993)*; A Month By the Lake *(1994)*; The Seventh Room *(1994)*; Fotogrammi mortali *(Fatal Frames, It. 1996)*; Probably Love *(It.-Sw., 1998)*; Il dolce rumore della vita *(It., 1999)*; Semana Santa *(Eur.-US, 2000)*; La Grande strada azzura *(It., 2001)*.

Born in 1921 in Pola, Italy, to an Austrian journalist father and an Italian mother, Alida Valli briefly studied at Rome's Centro Sperimentale di Cinematografia and entered film at age 15. Although relegated to routine productions, her haunting beauty and natural charm soon made her a star, one of Italy's highest paid young actresses. During World War II, however, she refused to continue working for the Fascist film industry and was forced into hiding in order to avoid being arrested or executed. Her mother, ironically, was shot as a collaborator by anti-Fascists in 1945.

Following the war, Valli and her then-husband, pianist-composer Oscar de Mejo, went to Hollywood at the invitation of David O. Selznick. (Among de Mejo's musical credits is the seasonal classic "All I Want for Christmas is My Two Front Teeth.") Valli was quickly cast in two American films, *The Miracle of the Bells* (1948), in which she was lauded for her interpretation of a dying actress, and *The Paradine Case* (1948), a Hitchcock thriller which starred her as an accused murderer. It was her knock-out performance as the mysterious and alluring actress Anna Schmidt in the British spy thriller *The Third Man* (1949), however, that won Valli international acclaim. The film, which co-starred Joseph Cotten and Orson Welles and was based on the novel by Graham Greene, won the grand prize at Cannes in 1949 and is remembered not only for its intriguing plot and riveting performances, but also for its haunting theme song, "The Third Man Theme." Played on a zither by Anton Karas, it became an international hit, and, according to Selznick who co-financed the film, caused "The Third Man" to become a term relating to Cold War espionage.

Valli's success carried her through the next four decades, although she gradually moved from romantic roles to character parts. Her career suffered a brief setback during the 1950s, when she served as an alibi for one of the politicians implicated in a notorious illicit drugs and casual sex scandal surrounding the unsolved murder of Italian model *Wilma Montesi in April 1953.

SOURCES:

Katz, Ephraim. *The Film Encyclopedia*. NY: Harper-Collins, 1994.

Nash, Jay Robert, and Stanley Ralph Ross. *The Motion Picture Guide: L–M, 1927–1983*. Chicago, IL: Cinebooks, 1986.

Quinlan, David, ed. *The Film Lover's Companion*. Secaucus, NJ: Carol, 1997.

Sklar, Robert. *Film: An International History of the Medium*. NY: Harry N. Abrams, n.d.

Barbara Morgan,
Melrose, Massachusetts

Vallin, Ninon (1886–1961)

French soprano known especially for her recordings of 20th-century composers. Name variations: Nina Vallin. Born on September 8, 1886, in Montalieu-Vercieu, France; died on November 22, 1961, in Lyons; studied at the Lyons Conservatory.

Debuted in the premiere of Debussy's Le martyre de Saint Sébastien *(1911); sang with the Opéra-Comique (1912–16); debuted at the Teatro Colón in Buenos Aires (1916), Paris Opéra (1920); sang with the Teatro Colón (1916–36).*

Born in France in 1886, Nina Vallin possessed a voice of great beauty, with a superb sensual quality, though devoid of power. Her operatic career, which was centered in Paris and Buenos Aires, lasted 20 years. Vallin specialized in the work of composers who were alive during her lifetime—Massenet, Charpentier, Hahn, Nin, de Falla, Respighi, and Fauré. Many of the songs she recorded were accompanied by the composer at the piano. For example, while in her 50s, she made famous recordings of Charpentier's *Louise* supervised by him. When she was nearing 60, Vallin recorded the third-act aria of the Countess from *Le nozze di Figaro*. André Tubeuf wrote of her, "Ah Ninon! she could do nothing wrong, nor by halves. . . . Vallin was one of the very rare singers in this century who was

*Ninon
Vallin*

always not only the epitome of good singing but also of good taste."

John Haag,
Athens, Georgia

Valmore, Marceline (1785–1859).

See Desbordes-Valmore, Marceline.

Valois, countess of.

See Margaret of Anjou (c. 1272–1299).
See Jeanne of Burgundy (1293–1348).
See Catherine de Courtenay (d. 1307).
See Mahaut de Chatillon (d. 1358).

Valois, duchess of.

See Margaret of Valois (1553–1615).

Valois, Ninette de (1898–2001).

See de Valois, Ninette.

Van Alstyne, Frances (1820–1915).

See Crosby, Fanny.

Van Blarcom, Carolyn (1879–1960)

American nurse and midwife. Born Carolyn Conant Van Blarcom on June 12, 1879, in Alton, Illinois; died of bronchopneumonia on March 20, 1960, in Arcadia, California; daughter of William Dixon Van Blarcom (a financier) and Fanny (Conant) Van Blarcom (a linguist and pianist); graduated from Johns Hopkins Hospital Training School for Nurses, 1901.

Was an instructor of obstetrics and assistant superintendent of nurses, Johns Hopkins Hospital Training School (1901–05); served as director of sanitariums in Maryland and Massachusetts; served as secretary, New York Committee for the Prevention of Blindness (beginning 1909); became America's first licensed midwife (1913); helped establish a school for midwives (1914); published textbooks and popular health books.

Carolyn Van Blarcom was born in Alton, Illinois, in 1879, the fourth of six children in an affluent household. Although her father abandoned the family sometime before 1893, her mother **Fanny Van Blarcom**, a linguist and pianist, managed to raise the children in a middle-class atmosphere. Van Blarcom contracted rheumatic fever at age six, and this ailment eventually led to rheumatoid arthritis, leaving her weak and frail. For the rest of her life, she would have periods of illness that confined her to bed. Because of this, her early education took place at home, where her mother was her primary teacher.

Van Blarcom was 14 when her mother died, and she traveled East to live with her mother's father, the portrait painter Alban Jasper Conant. In 1898, despite her family's objections, she enrolled in the renowned three-year training program at the Johns Hopkins Hospital Training School for Nurses. Although her illness prevented her from studying for more than a year, she compensated for this and was invited to become a member of the faculty of the nursing school upon her graduation. She was an instructor in obstetrics for the next four years, and also served as assistant superintendent of nurses at the school.

In 1905, Van Blarcom left Johns Hopkins and went to St. Louis, where she reorganized a training school for nurses. For three years after that, an attack of rheumatoid arthritis curtailed her work. When her illness went into remission, she became director of the Maryland Tuberculosis Sanitarium at Sibillisville. Her success in that position led to the directorship of a sanatarium near New Bedford, Massachusetts, and under her leadership it was transformed from an underfunded, unequipped clinic to a state-of-the-art, highly regarded hospital.

In 1909, she was appointed secretary of the New York State Committee for the Prevention of Blindness, where she investigated the causes of blindness and educated the public about prevention and treatment. In 1916, she was elected secretary of the Illinois Society for the Prevention of Blindness. Van Blarcom discovered that among newborn babies, the leading cause of preventable blindness was an eye infection called ophthalmia neonatorum. This condition could easily be prevented by putting silver nitrate drops into newborns' eyes, but the treatment was not widely known or used by birth attendants. Van Blarcom's discovery of the appalling state of current midwifery practices led her to work with the New York State Committee and the Russell Sage Foundation to study midwifery practices in the United States, England, and 14 other countries. Through this research, she determined that the United States was the only developed country that did not provide for training and licensing of midwives. The results of the study were published in *The Midwife in England* (1913), her most important work. Van Blarcom was the first American nurse to become a licensed midwife, and her book established her as an authority in the field. Her articles appeared in medical and popular journals, she spoke at health conferences across the country, and she assisted in the establishment of a school for midwives, which was affiliated with Bellevue Hospital in New York City.

During World War I, Van Blarcom directed the Bureau of Nursing Services of the Atlantic

Division of the American Red Cross. In the 1920s, she devoted her energy to editing and writing, serving as health editor for the *Delineator* and also writing the textbook *Obstetrical Nursing* (1922). In addition, she wrote two popular books, *Getting Ready to Be a Mother* (1922) and *Building the Baby* (1929).

With the further deterioration of her own health in the 1930s, Van Blarcom retired, although she worked briefly during World War II, directing the nurses' aid training program of the American Red Cross chapter in Pasadena, California. After this, to her disappointment and dismay, her illness prevented her from working at all. She died of bronchopneumonia in Arcadia, California, on March 20, 1960, at age 80.

SOURCES:

Read, Phyllis J., and Bernard L. Witlieb. *The Book of Women's Firsts.* NY: Random House, 1992.

Sicherman, Barbara, and Carol Hurd Green, eds. *Notable American Women: The Modern Period.* Cambridge, MA: The Belknap Press of Harvard University, 1980.

Kelly Winters,
freelance writer

Vanbrugh, Irene (1872–1949)

English actress. Name variations: Irene Boucicault; Dame Irene Vanbrugh. Born Irene Barnes on December 2, 1872, in Exeter, England; died on November 30, 1949; daughter of Reginald H. Barnes (the vicar of Heavitree and prebendary of Exeter Cathedral) and Frances M.E. (Nation) Barnes; sister of Violet Vanbrugh (1867–1942); educated at Exeter High School and in London; studied acting with Sarah Thorne and John Toole; married Dion Boucicault the Younger (1859–1929, an actor), in 1901.

Dame Irene Vanbrugh was born Irene Barnes in 1872 in Exeter, England, one of six children. Her father Reginald H. Barnes was the vicar of Heavitree and prebendary (honorary canon) of Exeter Cathedral, and her mother **Frances M.E. Barnes** was the daughter of a barrister. Vanbrugh later said that her mother was a natural actress, although she never appeared on stage herself. She ensured that her children received a musical education at home and all of them became accomplished dancers. Each summer, they visited the theater in London, and in 1884 Vanbrugh's older sister Violet decided to go on the stage, choosing the stage name Vanbrugh. Irene joined her sister in looking for work in the London theater, and they spent much of their time at the Lyceum watching other actors and visiting agents. When *Violet Vanbrugh was hired for a stock season at the Theatre Royal, Irene went with her and

watched the rehearsals. After this she went to Paris, where another sister, **Angela Barnes**, was studying the violin. While there, Irene studied elocution at the Conservatoire.

She made her stage debut in a school production of *Beauty and the Beast*, drawing the attention of actress *Ellen Terry. Irene also took the name Vanbrugh and, on August 20, 1888, made her professional debut as Phoebe in *As You Like It* at **Sarah Thorne**'s Theatre Royal in Margate, where Violet was then a star performer. According to Eric Johns, "Any actress considered herself very lucky to be accepted by Miss Thorne. Even though it was a provincial playhouse one stood a chance of being seen there." And the Vanbrugh sisters showed sufficient promise to be admitted without paying the customary fees. That same season, Irene played Titania in *A Midsummer Night's Dream*, Arrah Meelish in *Arrah-na-Pogue*, and Rose in *Leah*. According to Johns, Thorne made Vanbrugh realize that she wanted to act more than anything else in the world.

Irene Vanbrugh

Vanbrugh's first London appearance was in December 1888 at the Olympic Theatre, playing the White Queen in *Alice in Wonderland*. In 1889, she appeared at the Strand, the Theatre Royal, and in numerous plays in London. In March 1890, she traveled to Australasia with John Toole's company, and returned to Toole's Theatre in London, where she played small parts for the next two years. In 1893, she decided it was time to try larger parts and opened at the Haymarket in September 1893 as the serving maid, Lettice, in Henry Arthur Jones' *The Tempter*. She also appeared in *Captain Swift, Six Persons*, and *The Charlatan*. In April 1894, Vanbrugh joined George Alexander's company at the St. James's Theatre, and appeared with the company for the next year. During this time she created the role of Gwendolyn Fairfax in Oscar Wilde's classic comedy *The Importance of Being Earnest*.

Vanbrugh's sister Violet had earlier married the actor-manager Arthur Bourchier, and in 1895 the couple assumed the management of the Royalty Theatre. Irene joined their company, and for the first time, the sisters appeared together. In 1896, the company traveled to America, where Irene made her New York debut as Dulcie in *The Chili Widow*. She returned to London in 1897, and for the next several years moved from company to company. Her roles during this time included the creation of Sophie Fullgarney in Pinero's *The Gay Lord Quex*. In 1901, she married another actor, Dion "Dot" Boucicault (the Younger), against her mother's wishes, and both became associated with Charles Frohman at the Duke of York's Theatre; this professional relationship lasted for the next 13 years. Vanbrugh appeared in numerous productions during this time, earning critical acclaim and leading roles, including the creation of Lady Mary Lasenby in J.M. Barrie's *The Admirable Crichton*.

In 1916, her husband became manager of the New Theatre, and Vanbrugh played major roles in several productions and spent some time working on an all-star film of *Masks and Faces*, which was being made by her brother Kenneth Barnes to benefit the Academy of Dramatic Art. Irene continued to appear in many plays in various theaters and on tours. Her husband became ill in 1921 and was confined to his bed for the next two years; following his recovery in 1923, the two traveled to Africa and Australasia for a repertory tour. In 1926, they returned to London, and Vanbrugh kept up her heavy performance schedule. In 1927, Dion became ill again; he eventually died in 1929. Several months later, Vanbrugh returned to the stage, touring and appearing at several theaters for many years.

Irene Vanbrugh was always careful in the roles she accepted and "prided herself on never having appeared in a cheap play," writes Johns. "She had lots of offers, even in old age, to appear in paltry thrillers and comedies by authors who hoped her name would lend distinction to their work and make it a box-office success. She always refused." On June 20, 1938, her golden jubilee on stage was celebrated with a charity matinee, attended by Queen *Elizabeth Bowes-Lyon at His Majesty's Theatre. Noel Coward gave the prologue, and Irene also performed. Created a Dame Commander of the British Empire in 1941, Vanbrugh continued to act and tour. She had appeared in movies since 1933, and her film credits include *Escape Me Never, Knight Without Armour, Wings of the Morning*, and *I Lived in Grosvenor Square*. She died in 1949 at the age of 76.

SOURCES:

The Concise Dictionary of National Biography: From Earliest Times to 1985. Oxford: Oxford University Press, 1992.

Johns, Eric. *Dames of the Theatre*. New Rochelle, NY: Arlington House, 1974, pp. 57–65.

Morley, Sheridan. *The Great Stage Stars*. Australia: Angus & Robertson, 1986, pp. 395–398.

Kelly Winters,
freelance writer

Vanbrugh, Violet (1867–1942)

English actress. Name variations: Dame Violet Vanbrugh. Born Violet Augusta Mary Barnes on June 11, 1867, in Exeter, England; died on November 10, 1942; daughter of Reginald H. Barnes (the vicar of Heavitree and prebendary of Exeter Cathedral) and Frances M.E. (Nation) Barnes; sister of Irene Vanbrugh (1872–1949); studied acting with Sarah Thorne; married Arthur Bourchier (an actor and theater manager), in 1894 (divorced 1917); children: Prudence Vanbrugh (b. 1902, an actress).

Dame Violet Vanbrugh was known as "Britain's greatest Shakespearean actress" during her lifetime, and played almost every important female part in the Bard's works. Born in 1867 in Exeter, she was one of six children in an affluent household. Her father Reginald H. Barnes was the vicar of Heavitree and prebendary (honorary canon) of Exeter Cathedral. Her mother **Frances M.E. Barnes**, the daughter of a barrister, loved the arts and ensured that her children received a musical education. Violet and her siblings became accomplished dancers, and visited the London theaters during the summer. In 1884 Violet decided to go on the stage and chose the name Vanbrugh, which was recommended to her by the noted actress *Ellen Terry.

Violet began looking for work in the London theater, and was soon followed by her younger sister, *Irene Vanbrugh, who would herself become a notable actress. The sisters spent hours at the Lyceum watching other actors and visiting agents. Violet was hired for a stock season at the Theatre Royal, and was later accepted at **Sarah Thorne**'s repertory company. She served with this group from 1886 to 1888, during which time she became a star player. She then toured the United States with W.H. Kendal and Dame *Madge Kendal from 1889 to 1891, and played *Anne Boleyn in Henry Irving's production of *Henry VIII* in 1892.

In 1894, she married Arthur Bourchier, an actor and stage manager. In 1895, the couple took over the management of the Royalty Theatre in London. Vanbrugh's sister Irene joined their company, and the two appeared together on the London stage for the first time, in the company's debut production *The Chili Widow*. Vanbrugh and her husband and sister then traveled to America on tour in 1896.

In addition to Shakespeare, Vanbrugh appeared in modern plays, often with her husband's company, although she divorced him in 1917. Some of her most notable roles include Queen Katherine in *Henry VIII* (1910) and Mistress Ford in *The Merry Wives of Windsor* (1911). She also appeared in a few films, including *Pygmalion*. Violet Vanbrugh made her last appearance on stage in a 1937 production of *The Merry Wives of Windsor*. She was created a Dame Commander of the British Empire before she died in November 1942.

SOURCES:

Concise Dictionary of National Biography: From Earliest Times to 1985. Oxford: Oxford University Press, 1992.

Current Biography 1943. NY: H.W. Wilson, 1943.

Kelly Winters,
freelance writer

Van Buren, Abigail (b. 1918).

See joint entry under Friedman, Esther Pauline and Pauline Esther.

Van Buren, Mrs. Abraham (1816–1878).

See Van Buren, Angelica.

Van Buren, Angelica (1816–1878)

*White House hostess. Name variations: Mrs. Abraham Van Buren; Angelica Singleton. Born Angelica Singleton in 1816; died in 1878; cousin of Dolley Madison (1768–1849); married Abraham Van Buren (son of Martin Van Buren, eighth president of the United States, and *Hannah Hoes Van Buren), in 1838.*

When the widower and newly elected U.S. president Martin Van Buren moved into the White House in 1837 with his four young sons, *Dolley Madison was convinced the country needed a hostess. So she married off her beautiful young cousin Angelica Singleton to Abraham, the eldest of the young Van Burens, the following year. While Abraham served as his father's secretary, Angelica was a gracious host. Her portrait, painted by Henry Inman in 1842, still hangs in the White House.

Van Buren, Hannah Hoes
(1783–1819)

Wife of Martin Van Buren, later U.S. president. Born on March 8, 1783, in Kinderhook, New York; died on February 5, 1819, in Albany, New York; daughter of John Dircksen Hoes and Maria (Quackenboss) Hoes; married Martin Van Buren (eighth president of the U.S.), on February 21, 1807, in Catskill, New York; children: five; four boys lived to adulthood, including the eldest Abraham.

Childhood sweethearts, Hannah Hoes and Martin "Matt" Van Buren grew up together in the Dutch settlement of Kinderhook, New York. Intent on establishing a law practice before marrying Hannah, Martin apprenticed himself to a lawyer at age 14, won his first case at 17, and went on to serve his clerkship in Manhattan. Hannah stayed home, tending to her dowry and devoting countless hours to church work, a practice that would continue throughout her life. The couple finally married in 1807, when they were both 24.

The newlyweds began married life in Kinderhook, but as Martin's career blossomed, they moved to Hudson and eventually Albany, where he served as state senator and then as New York State attorney general. Hannah would give birth to five boys, losing one in infancy. Their growing household is said to have bustled with the comings and goings of visiting relatives and, at one time, even included Martin's law partner and three apprentices. Apparently the marriage was a happy one.

Hannah fell ill with tuberculosis soon after the birth of her fifth child in 1817. She died just short of her 36th birthday, on February 5, 1819. Dedicated to the poor and needy even in illness, Hannah had asked that the customary mourning scarves be eliminated from her funeral ceremony, and the money given to charity. Recording her death, the Albany *Argus* called her "an ornament of the Christian faith." She was buried at the Second Presbyterian Church in Albany, but in 1855 was moved to the Kinderhook Cemetery.

Martin Van Buren never remarried, and although he often referred to Hannah's influence on his life, she is not mentioned in his rather lengthy autobiography. Historians speculate that this is because he believed that political and private lives should remain separate. He stayed unusually close to his sons, even in their adulthood. The eldest, Abraham, became his private secretary and later married Angelica Singleton (*Angelica Van Buren), who served as White House hostess during the Van Buren administration (1837–41).

SOURCES:

Klapthor, Margaret Brown. *The First Ladies*. Washington, DC: White House Historical Association, 1979.

Melick, Arden David. *Wives of the Presidents*. Maplewood, NJ: Hammond, 1977.

Paletta, LuAnn. *The World Almanac of First Ladies*. NY: World Almanac, 1990.

Barbara Morgan,
Melrose, Massachusetts

Van Buren, Mrs. Martin (1783–1819).

See Van Buren, Hannah Hoes.

Vance, Ethel (1896–1991).

See Stone, Grace Zaring.

Vance, Nina (1914–1980).

See Women of the Regional Theater Movement in America.

Vance, Vivian (1911–1979).

See Ball, Lucille for sidebar.

Van Cortlandt, Annettje Lockermans (c. 1620–after 1665)

Creator of the first paved street in America. Born around 1620 in the Netherlands; emigrated to the New Amsterdam colony in 1642; died sometime after 1665; married Oloff Van Cortlandt (a military officer); children: three.

Annettje Lockermans Van Cortlandt was an orphan when she came to the Dutch colony of New Amsterdam (later called New York City) in 1642. Soon after, she married a prosperous military officer, Captain Oloff Van Cortlandt, who built her a large and imposing house on Brower Street.

Van Cortlandt was known for her intelligence and forceful personality, and soon her house was a central gathering place for other strong-willed women of the colony, including her aunt *Annetje Jans. Although Van Cortlandt had a continuing campaign to get officials of the then-village of Manhattan to improve the filthy condition of the dirt road in front of her house, her complaints led to nothing. Realizing that she would have to solve the problem on her own, she instructed her servants to pave the road with cobblestones. Thus, in 1648, Brower Street became the first paved street in America. People came from miles around to see what they called the "stone street," and the thoroughfare is still there and still known by that name.

SOURCES:

Weatherford, Doris. *American Women's History*. NY: Prentice Hall, 1994.

Kelly Winters,
freelance writer

Van Cott, Margaret (1830–1914)

First female Methodist Episcopal evangelist in America. Name variations: Maggie Van Cott. Born Margaret Ann Newton on March 25, 1830, in New York City; died of cancer on August 29, 1914, in Catskill, New York; daughter of William K. Newton (a real estate broker) and Rachel A. (Primrose) Newton; married Peter P. Van Cott (a store owner and business-

man), on January 23, 1848 (died 1866); children: Rachel (died in infancy); Sarah Ellen Conselyea.

Margaret Van Cott, known as Maggie, was born in 1830 in New York City and grew up in an Episcopalian family. In 1857 or 1858, her spiritual convictions deepened after a conversion experience that drew her to prayer meetings at the Duane Street Methodist Episcopal Church in Manhattan. After her husband died in 1866, she joined the church. That same year she began to lead prayer meetings and Bible study classes at the nondenominational mission founded by *Phoebe Worrall Palmer in New York's Five Points slum area. Successful in winning converts, Van Cott accepted an invitation from a Methodist minister to hold revival meetings at his church in Durham, New York, in February 1868. Invitations from other pastors to speak to their congregations followed. Although Van Cott was initially reluctant to preach, she was encouraged by the number of people who converted after hearing her sermons. She received an Exhorter's License in 1868 and a Local Preacher's License in 1869, making her the first woman licensed to preach in the Methodist Episcopal Church in the United States.

Although many preachers and congregation members did not approve of women in the pulpit, her skills overcame their objections, and Van Cott preached at revivals for many denominations throughout the United States. She held special meetings for groups of mothers, veterans, and children, and specialized in "Praise Meetings," "Silent Meetings," and "Love Feasts." At the end of each revival, she organized the new converts into prayer bands with church members, so that their new faith could be maintained. For more than 30 years, she traveled up to 7,000 miles a year, converting over 2,000 people. By the time she retired in 1902, she had converted more than 75,000, half of whom joined the Methodist Episcopal Church. She derived her income from the small offerings received at the revivals, and $5,000 was raised from public contributions for her support in her old age. Although Van Cott lacked formal theological training, she was known for her dramatic flair and zeal. She died of cancer in 1914.

SOURCES:

James, Edward T., ed. *Notable American Women, 1607–1950.* Cambridge, MA: The Belknap Press of Harvard University, 1971.

Read, Phyllis J., and Bernard L. Witlieb. *The Book of Women's Firsts.* NY: Random House, 1992.

Kelly Winters,
freelance writer

Vandamm, Florence (1883–1966)

British portrait photographer. Born Florence Van Damm in 1883 in London, England; died in 1966 in New York City; married George R. Thomas (a photographer), in 1918 (died 1944); children: Robert.

Florence Vandamm was born Florence Van Damm in London in 1883. In 1908, she opened a photographic studio there, and also worked as a miniaturist and portrait painter. Her studio became an important meeting place for prominent painters, actors, musicians, and writers.

In 1917, she met George R. Thomas, an American photographer, and they were married the following year; their only son Robert would die during World War II. In 1919, Vandamm was elected a fellow of the Royal Photographic Society of Great Britain. That same year, she went into partnership with her husband, who would use the name Tommy Vandamm professionally. He specialized in "on-stage" photographs, while Florence specialized in studio portraits of actors.

Because of high unemployment in England in 1923, the couple moved to New York City, where they eked out a living until 1925, when their photographic talent was rediscovered by *Vogue* and *Vanity Fair*; they had previously done work for these magazines in London. They also became important photographers for the Theater Guild, and covered over 2,000 Broadway productions from 1925 to 1950. Their subjects included *Judith Anderson, *Ethel Barrymore, *Katharine Cornell, John Gielgud, *Helen Hayes, *Eva Le Gallienne, Alfred Lunt and *Lynn Fontanne, and Burgess Meredith. In 1944, Thomas died, and Vandamm, in addition to her studio work, began doing photographs on stage. In 1961, she donated her archives to the New York Public Library.

Kelly Winters,
freelance writer

Vandegrift, Frances (1840–1914).

See Stevenson, Fanny.

Van Deman, Esther (1862–1937)

American archaeologist who was the first woman to perform field work. Born Esther Boise Van Deman on October 1, 1862, in South Salem, Ohio; died of cancer on May 3, 1937, in Rome, Italy; daughter of Joseph Van Deman (a farmer) and Martha (Millspaugh) Van Deman; University of Michigan, A.B., 1891, A.M., 1892; graduate work at Bryn Mawr College, 1892–93; University of Chicago, Ph.D., 1898.

Esther Van Deman was the first woman field archaeologist, and her studies on early Roman architecture formed the basis for all later work in the area. She was born in 1862 in South Salem, Ohio, the youngest of six children. Her parents, who farmed land her paternal grandfather had received in return for his services in the Revolutionary War, believed in the value of education. While attending the South Salem Academy, she exhibited a talent for music, and her parents encouraged study in this area, which she thought might be her future career. However, in the 1870s, the family moved to Sterling, Kansas, and lived with Van Deman's married sister. In 1887, at age 24, she entered the University of Michigan, where she first developed her interest in the classical world. Although she left after her first year and did not return until 1889, she earned an A.B. degree in 1891 and an A.M. in 1892.

Van Deman continued her studies but also taught college between 1892 and 1906. Although she was a good teacher and enjoyed classroom time with her students, she preferred research to the paperwork and rules involved in teaching, which caused occasional conflicts with college administrators. She did graduate work at Bryn Mawr College (1892–93), taught Latin at Wellesley College (1893–95) and at Bryn Mawr School in Baltimore (1895–96), and then began graduate school at the University of Chicago, receiving a Ph.D. in 1898. Following this, she taught Latin at Mt. Holyoke College for three years.

In 1901, Van Deman won a fellowship to the American School of Classical Studies in Rome, returning to the U.S. in 1903 to work as associate professor of Latin and archaeology at Goucher College. In 1906, she was appointed a fellow of the Carnegie Institution of Washington and returned to Rome. Joining the staff of the Carnegie Institution in 1910, Van Deman remained in Rome for the rest of her life (although she returned briefly to the United States prior to World War I when a nervous condition required a stay at a sanatorium). Then from 1924 to 1925, she was the Charles Eliot Norton lecturer at the Archaeological Institute of America. She also became the Carnegie research professor of Roman archaeology at the University of Michigan from 1925 to 1930. And in 1936, she accepted an honorary degree from that university.

Van Deman's study of Roman buildings started in 1907. While listening to a lecture and looking at the walls of the Atrium Vestae in Rome, she noticed a difference between the bricks sealing a doorway and those of the surrounding wall. Believing that the size and material of bricks could indicate when they were made, she turned to written sources from the period, which confirmed her theory that different bricks were used at different points in Roman history. She applied her dating method to many buildings and works and wrote about her findings in *The Atrium Vestae* (1909). Van Deman then studied Roman aqueducts, a subject that had been previously neglected, and spent years writing an exhaustively detailed monograph that she completed only two years before her death. She had planned to perfect her brick-based dating method, but realized that she would not have time for this, so she organized her notes to allow her colleague **Marion E. Blake** to continue the work after her death.

During the 30 years that Van Deman spent in Rome, she became the leading authority on ancient Roman building methods. With relatively little change, the methodology she set forth in "Methods of Determining the Date of Roman Concrete Monuments" in 1912 remains the standard. She became ill in 1936 and died of cancer on May 3, 1937. She was buried in the Protestant Cemetery in Rome, where her grave site is marked by a mound of concrete and brick.

SOURCES:

James, Edward T., ed. *Notable American Women, 1607–1950.* Cambridge, MA: The Belknap Press of Harvard University, 1971.

McHenry, Robert, ed. *Famous American Women.* NY: Dover, 1980.

Kelly Winters,
freelance writer

Vandenhoeck, Anna (1709–1787)

Head of the most active academic publishing house in Germany, which prospered during the Enlightenment period under her guidance. Name variations: Anna Van den hoek; Anna van Hoeck. Pronunciation: fahn-den'hœk (German); fahn-den-hook (Dutch). Born Anna Parry on May 24, 1709, in London, England; died on March 5, 1787, in Göttingen, Germany; married Abraham Vandenhoeck, in 1720s; no children.

Moved with husband, Dutch bookseller and printer, to Hanover, Germany (1732); succeeded husband as head of the publishing house at the time of his death (1750); continued the book company for 37 years.

Selection of books published while Anna Vandenhoeck was head of the publishing house (1750–87):

Law:

Johann Stephan Pütter: Institutiones iuris publici Germanici, 1770. Der Büchernachdruck nach ächten Grundsätzen des Rechts geprüft, 1774.

Johann Jacob Schmauss: Historisches Jus Publicum des Teutschen Reichs, oder Auszug der vornehmsten Ma-

terialien der Reichs-Historie, welche zur Erkenntnis der Staatsverfassung unsers teutschen Reichs, von den ältesten Zeiten bis auf die heutige, dienen, *1752.*

Johann Heinrich Christian Selchow: Elementa iuris Germanici privati hodierni ex ipsis fontibus deducta *(7 imprints, 1757, 1762, 1766, 1771, 1775, 1779, 1787).*

History:

Johann Christoph Gatterer: Einleitung in die synchronistische Universalhistorie zur Erläuterung seiner synchronistischen Tabellen, *1771.* Weltgeschichte in ihrem ganzen Umfange, *Vol. 1 (Adam-Cyrus), 1785.*

August Ludwig Schlözer: Stats-Anzeigen, *19 vols., vols. 1–10, 1782–1787.* Briefwechsel meist historischen und politischen Inhalts, *10 vols., 1776–1782.*

Theology:

Gottfried Less: Christliche Religions-Theorie fürs gemeine Leben, oder Versuch einer praktischen Dogmatik, *2nd imprint 1780 (a "bestseller" with a run of 1,500 copies).*

Johann David Michaelis: Deutsche Übersetzung des Alten Testamentes mit Anmerkungen für Ungelehrte, *13 vols., 1769–1783, original imprints of vols. 1, 2, and 5 published by competitor Dieterich.* Einleitung in die göttlichen Schriften des Neuen Bundes, *vol. 1, 1750, vol. 2, 1777.*

Ludwig Timotheus Spittler: Grundriss der Geschichte der christlichen Kirche, *1782, reprinted 1785.*

Philosophy:

Samuel Christian Hollmann: Philosophiae naturalis primae liniae, *1753.*

Sciences:

Johann Beckmann: Physikalisch-ökonomische Bibliothek worinn von den neuesten Büchern, welche die Naturgeschichte, Naturlehre und die Land- und Stadtwirtschaft betreffen, zuverlässige und vollständige Nachrichten ertheilet werden, *11 vols., 1770–1781.*

Albrecht von Haller, ed.: Disputationum anatomaricum selectarum. *8 vols. 1743–1751.* Ed. *"Göttingische Gelehrte Anzeigen," published continuously since 1739.*

Carl von Linné: Systema naturae ex editione duodecima in epitomen redactum et praelectionibus academicis accomodatum . . . *(ed. J. Beckmann), Tomus I: Regnum animale, Tomus II: Regnum vegetabile, 2 vols., 1772.*

Johann Georg Roederer: Icones uteri humani observationibus illustratae, *1759.* Elementa Artis obstetricae in suum praelectionum academicarum, *3 imprints 1753, 1759, 1766.*

Philology:

Philip Pepin: The Man of Fortune's faithful Monitor: *translated from the French original, entitled* La véritable Politique des personnes des qualité *[by Caillere]. Published for the use of foreigners abroad who begin to study the English language, 1775.*

William Shakespeare: Julius Cesar. *A tragedy, selected from Dr. Johnson's and Mr. Steeven's commentaries, 1777.*

A common practice among immigrants, understandable if frustrating for the biographer, is their predilection for breaking ties to the past in order to focus more fully on the present in their chosen country. In the case of Anna and Abraham Vandenhoeck, it means that the information pertaining to their backgrounds before their immigration to Hamburg, Germany, in 1732, has to be reconstructed from scattered hints. When Anna Vandenhoeck died without children in 1787, she bequeathed certain personal objects—jewelry, silver, furniture—to various friends and confidants, but whatever clues to her that existed among memorabilia, personal correspondence or private papers have long since been lost. What we are therefore left to turn to, in the case of the 18th-century Englishwoman who took the helm of a failing business enterprise and turned it into one of Germany's most outstanding and longlived publishing houses, is a gleaning of the smallest details from the record of her business papers. A careful reading yields a personality of such generous proportions that it is possible to imagine that she appeared to her contemporaries as somewhat larger than life.

A glimmer of the early working style of Anna Vandenhoeck emerges in a letter of complaint, written by the royal deputy Gerlach Adolf Freiherr von Münchhausen, in 1753.

> We hear from various sources that Vandenhoeck's widow not only sells all books at a higher price than elsewhere but that she also rejects any publications offered to her, or at least knows to subjoin those which she accepts with the most difficult conditions.

The issue was business practices at "Abraham Vandenhoeck's Publishing House," being carried out under its new head, who had been put in charge following the death of her husband in 1750. The enterprise was affiliated with the university at Göttingen, and the complaint was provocative enough to elicit an investigation. But the response eventually received by Münchhausen suggests that the university found its interests allied with the publisher more than with the royal deputy, and was therefore willing to put up with some delays:

> Vandenhoeck's widow had gone away to the countryside. Further, when said person showed herself back here again, she time and again excused herself as indisposed, and finally declined personal appearance altogether. Thus, we found ourselves in the position of having to reveal those certain points to her store clerk, about which his principal, V., will have to explain herself.

A lady of the society on an overland journey, a lady excusing herself as indisposed—or a business professional choosing to disregard the usual complaints about books being too expensive and publishers too picky in their choice of manuscripts for publication? What the incident may show is that Anna Vandenhoeck, coming into her own as the first female entrepreneur in the university town, knew how to combine the advantages of both roles. In a later letter, when she rejected the same accusations in detail, her response was well received.

About the earlier life of the woman born Anna Parry, we know that she was born in London in 1709, but little else about her family background; her education was probably that of a woman expected to move in upper-class society. Although she may not have personally composed or dictated every letter sent out under her signature, correspondence signed by her in the archives of the publishing house she inherited suggest that she was competent in English, French, and German.

A contract dating from 1720 introduces the Dutch-born Abraham Vandenhoeck, then 20 years old, as a resident "of the parish of St. Mary London Strand and County bookseller." The Dutch led the world in the business of printing and publishing books, and Abraham had a brother, Isaac, in the same profession in the Netherlands. The change reflected in the spelling of Abraham's last name, from the Dutch form of van den Hoeck to a single word, was probably meant to facilitate doing business abroad. Sometime during the 1720s, a marriage took place between the Dutch bookseller and Anna Parry, who was nine years his junior (their marriage license has not been preserved); since the marriage remained childless, Anna Vandenhoeck may have assisted her husband in business matters from early on.

In 1732, possibly earlier, Abraham Vandenhoeck left his London business contracted out to a representative and emigrated with his wife to Hamburg, Germany, then an independent town in the Hanseatic League. It was there, probably, that Anna Vandenhoeck took advantage of Germany's greater religious freedom to change her church affiliation from the Anglican Church of England in which she had been baptized, raised and married, to join her husband in the Reformed Church, where she was to remain a faithful member until her death. The move was to have important implications for business.

As one historian of the firm has written about the period when the Vandenhoecks reached Hamburg, "All foreign things enjoyed appreciation in Germany, and everything British enjoyed particular appreciation in Göttingen and the Kingdom of Hanovar." In particular, the Dutch reputation for printing could open business doors, and the new Vandenhoeck firm quickly became recognized for producing books of distinguished quality. Two of its earliest works were an edition of the Bible using Martin Luther's translation "with useful summaries" and, in the Renaissance spirit of the times, a three-volume edition of the works of the pre-Christian Roman playwright Terence.

By 1734, when plans were under way to establish a new university at Göttingen, in the Kingdom of Hanover, the renown of the Vandenhoeck firm led the royal deputy Gerlach Adolf Freiherr von Münchhausen to inquire about "the Dutch printer in Hamburg." Along with the university, a publishing house was to be set up, as an independent enterprise but enjoying certain privileges and monetary grants from the government. The population of Göttingen was mostly Lutheran, and the theological faculty of the new university was to be the same, but a document of Münchhausen's dated 1733 stipulated that "freedom of conscience and tolerance" was to exist among the school's theologians.

A contract of February 13, 1735, verifies that Abraham Vandenhoeck had been chosen as the printer, publisher, and bookseller to be affiliated with the new university by this date; the school was set to open the following year. The first catalogue issued by the firm in Göttingen listed the Luther Bible and the Terence translation among its available books.

Support by the Hanoverian government did not keep the Vandenhoeck company from having to compete with other local printers, booksellers and publishers. Its heavy printing equipment also had to be brought from Hamburg to Göttingen, and to finance the move Anna Vandenhoeck's name was required along with her husband's on a surety-bond against advance payments. Meanwhile, she established a lasting friendship with the family of a Swiss university professor, Albrecht von Haller, who attended the local Reformed Church. Anna and Mrs. von Haller grew close, and Albrecht von Haller became one of the most productive authors of the publishing house. He was also the founding editor of *Göttingische Gelehrte Anzeigen*, now the oldest scholarly periodical in Germany, published continuously since 1739.

In August 1750, at a time when his company was in poor financial straits, Abraham Vandenhoeck died. It was a period of many difficulties for his widow. A letter of the time from her brother-in-law Isaac in the Netherlands begins with condolences to Anna, then conveys the news of her father's death, which he had learned about during a recent visit in London, before inquiring about payment for a box of books mailed earlier to Abraham. In reply, Vandenhoeck writes back that even though she is her husband's heiress, the authorities need Isaac's permission—presumably because he is the closest male relative—to probate her husband's will and testament, but acknowledges that the company is cash-strapped and she cannot cover his travel expenses to Göttingen. In a later letter, discussing terms of payment for the book shipment, an inquiry about any provisions in her favor in the will of a deceased cousin who had

promised to consider her, suggests the depths of her financial need.

In the letters concerning the fate of the business, however, a reader senses the trust felt within the royal government and the university about her experience and competence, confirmed when the loans and privileges necessary for the business to continue were extended to Anna Vandenhoeck. Nevertheless, a long and laborious business road lay ahead. A few months after her husband's death, she sold the printing plant, to concentrate her efforts on

Anna Vandenhoeck

publishing and book selling, and perhaps to raise necessary cash.

The real "capital" of any publishing house, of course, is its authors, and Vandenhoeck slowly increased her list of publications by building on her established contacts with the local professors and authors. She personally signed most contracts and kept in close touch with several writers and their families. In 1752, she took out a lease (the oldest existing document bearing her signature as head of the company) on a large storage room in Leipzig, then on its way to becoming the center of the book trade in Germany and the country's most important book fair. Booksellers and publishers from all over Germany and Europe came to those storage cellars to order and exchange bales of printed sheets, which were commonly bound by the final customer. (A trademark used in later years by the company shows two cherubs hurling such a bale, with Anna Vandenhoeck's tombstone in the background.)

The German book trade was hampered by an unwieldy system of commissions, cash payments and exchange. The business also suffered from the lack of universally accepted rules of copyright or legal means for collecting royalties from companies selling unauthorized reprints. In one outstanding example, Vandenhoeck's company issued a translation done by the theologian and linguist Johann David Michaelis of the highly popular early English novel by Samuel Richardson, *Clarissa Harlowe, or The History of a Young Lady*, published in seven volumes between 1748 and 1751. When a pirated edition was produced in Frankfurt, however, the company reaped no profits from its sale.

*C*urrently, all four local printing plants are busy with my work. Thus, they depend almost entirely on me for their livelihood. . . . Hardly any other book company in Germany achieves suchlike in six months.

—Anna Vandenhoeck

Book sales were also limited by the Seven Years' War, which involved most of Europe from 1756 to 1763. The company known under one of its imprints as "Abraham Vandenhoeck's Widow—Publishing House" was never forced to close its doors, partly because of its relationship with the university, although its sales suffered. In the town of Göttingen, however, Vandenhoeck's book store provided a welcome distraction from the security measures imposed by war, with its selection of foreign titles, mostly from France,

England, Italy, and the Netherlands. In his autobiography, the Göttingen law professor Johann Stephan Pütter wrote of his walks confined to the town limits, so that he frequently "took the way to Vandenhoeck's book store where one occasionally had the pleasure of meeting other friends at the same time for the same reason, and to have an agreeable conversation."

By the end of the war, the university at Göttingen was one of the most noted institutions teaching in the spirit of the period of critical Enlightenment, and its professors were providing a steady stream of new titles to Vandenhoeck's publishing house. Two of its outstanding Lutheran theological authors were Johan David Michaelis and Gottfried Less. In 1772, it brought out the two-volume work by the Swedish botanist Carl von Linné, or Linnaeus, that established the system of botanical classification still followed today.

In guiding the growth of the company, Vandenhoeck had help. Soon after the death of her husband, a store clerk named Schieck showed such competence that he came close to gaining the royal privilege of continuing the bookstore. At that time, Carl Friedrich Ruprecht was in his third year of apprenticeship, and Vandenhoeck soon bestowed on him the authority to represent the firm at book fairs; part of the reason may have been that travel at the time offered significant dangers to women. Ruprecht eventually rose to become manager of the publishing house, and letters between him and the owner when he was reporting to her from Leipzig, testify to a cordial relationship. While Ruprecht was still very young, Vandenhoeck had his portrait painted, possibly at the same time as hers.

In 1770, Anna Vandenhoeck shared in winning the lottery in Hanover with one other person, enjoying a substantial sum. By this time, her entrepreneurial sense had turned her company into one of the most flourishing and active publishing houses of the country. In a letter dated 1781, Georg Christoph Lichtenberg wrote of her as "the rich Madam Vandenhoeck."

At the time of her death, in 1787, Ruprecht wrote of his loss in a letter to Philip Erasmus Reich, co-owner of a bookstore in Leipzig and one of the most powerful people in the book business.

Most Noble Sir! With sincere and heartfelt sadness, I have to report the great loss which the Most Highest hath laid upon me: in his wise counsel and will, it pleased him to summon my foster mother and benefactress Mrs. Anna Vandenhoeck, after protracted weakening, on the 6th of this month out of this earthly life.

The last will and testament of Anna Vandenhoeck was typical in its display of charity, generosity and concern about the continuity of the business that had engaged much of her life. Dated 1778, it is in the handwriting of her pastor, friend and counselor, Lüder Kulenkamp. It allots generous sums of cash to domestic servants, store clerks, godchildren, two women close to her and a mentally retarded man in an institution. Personal items went to friends and her pastor, and Ruprecht, her manager, was named to carry on the publishing house, with part of the income allotted to a fund for widows of university professors, several of whom Vandenhoeck had counted among her friends. The will also provided a portion of the company income to the Reformed congregation. Though Ruprecht got a legal settlement which turned the continued payments into a single disbursement, the sum received by the church was enough to pay off the mortgage for the congregation's new building.

No other woman of the time or for many years to come, and few men, have achieved more in the book trade than Anna Vandenhoeck. More than 200 years later, the company is still one of Germany's academic publishing houses. To commemorate the bicentennial of her death, current owners and staff members of the publishing house gathered at her grave on a chilly spring day in 1987 and heard this author's grandfather, Günter Ruprecht, deliver a brief address in her honor. Then a yew tree, symbol of eternity, was planted on her grave.

When the streets for a new office and industrial park in the Göttingen suburb of Grone were being planned, District Mayor **Birgit Sterr** found no women on the list of proffered street names. Within a week of further research, enough information had been discovered about Göttingen's earliest woman entrepreneur to lead to the recommendation that she be honored, and in June 1993, the Göttingen town council voted unanimously to name the main circular road in the new district the "Anna-Vandenhoeck-Ring."

SOURCES:

Lösel, Barbara. *Die Frau als Persönlichkeit im Buchwesen: Dargestellt am Beispiel der Göttinger Verlegerin Anna Vandenhoeck (1709–1787)*. Wiesbaden: Otto Harrassowitz, 1991.

Ruprecht, Wilhelm. *Väter und Söhne. Zwei Jahrhunderte Buchhändler in einer deutschen Universitätsstadt*. Göttingen: Vandenhoeck & Ruprecht, 1935.

Sparn, Walter. "Vernünftiges Christentum. Über die geschichtliche Aufgabe der theologischen Aufklärung im 18. Jhd. in Deutschland," in ed. Rudolf Vierhaus. *Wissenschaften im Zeitalter der Aufklärung. Aus Anlass des 250 jährige Bestehens des Verlages Vandenhoeck & Ruprecht*. Göttingen: Vandenhoeck & Ruprecht, 1985.

SUGGESTED READING:

Goldfriedrich, Johann. *Geschichte des deutschen Buchhandels*. Volume 3: *Vom Beginn der klassischen Litteraturperiode bis zum Beginn der Fremdherrschaft (1740–1804)*. Leipzig: 1909.

Henze, Eberhard. *Kleine Geschichte des deutschen Buchwesens*. Düsseldorf: Verlag Buchhändler heute, 1983.

Wittmann, Reinhard. *Geschichte des deutschen Buchhandels*. München: C.H. Beck, 1991.

COLLECTIONS:

Correspondence, catalogues, some books, various papers, and two portraits located in the publishing house (now Vandenhoeck & Ruprecht) in Göttingen, Germany.

Most of the remaining original books and catalogues located in the library of the University of Göttingen.

Reinhilde Ruprecht,
freelance writer,
Federal Republic of Germany

Vanderbilt, Alice Gwynne

(1845–1934)

American socialite. Name variations: Mrs. Cornelius Vanderbilt II. Born Alice Claypoole Gwynne in 1845; died in 1934; married Cornelius Vanderbilt II (1843–1899, a banker, investor, and philanthropist); children: **Alice Gwynne Vanderbilt** *(1869–1874);* William Henry Vanderbilt II *(1872–1892);* Cornelius Vanderbilt III *(1873–1942);* Gertrude Vanderbilt Whitney *(1875–1942);* Alfred Gwynne Vanderbilt *(1877–1915, killed while on board the* Lusitania *when it was torpedoed and sunk);* Reginald Claypoole Vanderbilt *(1880–1925, father of* *Gloria Vanderbilt*);* and Gladys Moore Vanderbilt *(1886–1965, who married Count Laszlo Szechenyi).*

The formidable Alice Vanderbilt, along with her husband Cornelius Vanderbilt II, built The Breakers, a more-stately mansion overlooking Cliff Walk in Newport, Rhode Island, now on the tourist circuit. She thought of it as their summer cottage. The cottage, which had first appeared as a modest three-story affair of brick and wood on 11 acres, burned down in November 1892. Alice commissioned architect Richard Morris Hunt and, with her considerable input, the two replaced the burned-out shell with something more substantial: the new cottage had 70 rooms (33 held servants). Because of Newport's gusty ocean winds, Alice determined that rather than a center courtyard, she would have an interior courtyard, a center hall 45 feet high with a trompe l'oeil sky filled with billowing clouds on its ceiling. There was also a separate cottage for daughters *Gladys Moore Van-derbilt and *Gertrude Vanderbilt Whitney which came with its own butler and French chef. Alice, who became known as Alice of the Break-ers, had an arch-rival in opulence and fancy-dress-ball giving: her sister-in-law *Alva Smith Belmont, who was married to William K. Van-derbilt before she divorced and became Mrs O.H.P. Belmont.

Vanderbilt, Alva Smith (1853–1933).

> See Belmont, Alva Smith.

Vanderbilt, Amy (1908–1974)

American etiquette expert. Born on July 22, 1908, in Staten Island, New York; died in December 1974 in New York City; daughter of Joseph Mortimer Vander-bilt and Mary Estelle (Brooks) Vanderbilt; attended Institute Heubi, Lausanne, Switzerland, Packer Colle-giate Institute in Brooklyn, and special student in school of journalism, New York University, 1926–28; married Robert S. Brinkerhoff, in 1929; married Mor-ton G. Clark, in 1935; married Hans Knopf, in 1945; children: (second marriage) Lincoln Clark; (third mar-riage) Paul Vanderbilt Knopf; Stephen John Knopf.

Worked as society and feature writer for Staten Is-land Advance *(1927–29); was assistant advertising pub-licity director, H.R. Mallison Co. (1929–30); was an ad-vertising account executive, New York City (1930–33); was a columnist, International News Service, and busi-ness and literary manager of* American Spectator *(1933); worked as home service director, Tower maga-zines (1934); served as first vice president, Publicity Assos., New York City (1937–40), president (1940–45); was entertaining etiquette advisor, Royal Crest Sterling (1940–64); had a syndicated daily column, "Amy Van-derbilt's Etiquette," United Feature Syndicate (1954–74); was a television host on "It's Good Taste" (1954–56); consultant, Bristol Inc., New York City (1960–65). Author of many books on etiquette.*

Amy Vanderbilt wrote a syndicated column on good manners for two decades, from 1954 through 1974, challenging *Emily Post's domi-nant position in this field in the years after World War II. When Vanderbilt began writing her column, popular culture favored propriety and conservatism, but by the time she died, in 1974, the counterculture was dominant and there was less interest in conforming to "prop-er" standards. In addition to her syndicated col-umn, Vanderbilt wrote magazine articles and several books on manners. In the 1950s and

early 1960s, she also hosted a television show, "It's Good Taste."

Kelly Winters,
freelance writer

Vanderbilt, Consuelo (1877–1964)

American heiress and duchess of Marlborough. Name variations: Consuelo Churchill. Born on March 2, 1877, in New York; died in 1964; only daughter and one of three children of William Kissam Vanderbilt I (1849–1920) and Alva (Smith) Vanderbilt, later Alva Smith Belmont (1853–1933); educated privately at home; married Charles Richard Spencer Churchill (1871–1934), 9th duke of Marlborough, on Novem-ber 6, 1895 (separated 1905, divorced 1920); married (Louis) Jacques Balsan (1868–1956, a French lieu-tenant-colonel in the cavalry), on July 4, 1921; chil-dren: (first marriage) John Albert William (b. 1897); Ivor Charles (1898–1956).

Consuelo Vanderbilt, born in New York in 1877 into one of America's wealthiest families, was the only daughter and one of three children of William Kissam Vanderbilt I and *Alva Smith Belmont. Dominated by a mother she could not please, Consuelo was a precocious, introverted child, says biographer James Brough, "in the habit of searching her infant soul for faults and judging herself inadequate." Impeccably educat-ed and well traveled, Consuelo grew into a beau-tiful but melancholy young woman. In 1895, her mother arranged for her to wed the era's most el-igible bachelor, Charles Richard John Spencer Churchill ("Sunny"), the 9th duke of Marlbor-ough and a cousin and good friend of Winston Churchill. At the time Consuelo was deeply in love with Winthrop Rutherfurd, a wealthy play-boy lawyer, a fact she did not attempt to hide from Sunny. "I am sure that we shall both do our best to make the other happy, but there is something you must believe," Consuelo told Sunny on their wedding night. "Our marriage was my mother's idea, not mine. She insisted on it, even though there was another man who wanted me. She made me turn him away." Sunny barely looked up from the congratulatory telegrams he was reading. "Really? I take it he was an American. I don't see much point in dis-cussing it any farther."

The couple settled into Blenheim Palace in England, where Consuelo gave birth to two sons, John and Ivor, and fulfilled her official duties as duchess of Marlborough. Gossip about the prob-lems within the loveless marriage surfaced as early as 1901, and no one was surprised when the

Consuelo
Vanderbilt

couple separated after a decade together. It was at this time that Consuelo, anxious to find meaning in her life, became immersed in charity work, involving herself, writes biographer Brough, in "questions of sanitation affecting food supplies, milk, water, drains and ventilations, education of children, child and female labor, administration of relief to poor. . . . She corralled donors for the Young Women's Christian Association, and Sunderland House provided a center for a campaign to curb the traffic in women recruited as 'white slaves' for brothels overseas." Consuelo also supported women's suffrage (a cause her mother embraced fervently following the death of her second husband, Oliver Belmont) and the movement to improve the minimum wage for women factory workers. During World War I, she assisted the Red Cross and organized an employment service to help secure jobs for the 400,000 servants displaced when mansions were shut down or given over to the government.

Following her divorce from Churchill, on July 4, 1921, Consuelo married Jacques Balsan, a French lieutenant-colonel in the cavalry and a passionate balloonist. (She had her marriage to Churchill annulled in 1926, and married Balsan a second time in a Catholic ceremony.) The couple settled in France, dividing their time between Paris and a summer home on the Riviera. For a time, Consuelo gave up her many causes to oversee salons for a glittering set of writers, artists, diplomats and dignitaries, and when she grew restless, she renovated a château on the border of Normandy by the forest of Dreux. Slowly, she took up her charitable interests once more, this time focusing much of her attention on children. She began running a play school in the summer for the local children and later built a sanitarium on her property large enough to house 80 sick children. It was eventually expanded to include young tuberculosis patients.

At the outbreak of World War II, after learning that she was in danger of being captured as a hostage, Consuelo gave up her work with the Red Cross and returned to the United States, where she and Jacques lived in "quiet splendor," dividing their time between a home on New York's Sutton Place and another at Oyster Bay, on Long Island. In 1956, within two months of her husband's death, she also lost her estranged son Ivor, who died of a brain tumor. During her final years, Consuelo became close to her eldest grandchild Lady **Sarah Consuelo Churchill**, and it was to her that she left the bulk of her estate when she died in 1964. Income from family trusts were left to her remaining son and to Ivor's son Robert. Of the millions Consuelo had inherited from her father, only two million dollars remained.

SOURCES:

Brough, James. *Consuelo: Portrait of an American Heiress.* NY: Coward, McCann & Geoghegan, 1979.

Barbara Morgan,
Melrose, Massachusetts

Vanderbilt, Mrs. Cornelius.

See Vanderbilt, Sophia Johnson (1797–1868).
See Vanderbilt, Alice Gwynne (1845–1934).

Vanderbilt, Gertrude (1875–1942).

See Whitney, Gertrude Vanderbilt.

Vanderbilt, Gladys Moore
(1886–1965)

American socialite. Name variations: Countess Széchenyi. Born in 1886; died in 1965; daughter of Cornelius Vanderbilt II and *Alice Gwynne Vanderbilt (1845–1934); married Count Laszlo Szechenyani also seen as Lásló Széchenyi (Hungarian minister to U.S. and Britain); children: five daughters, including Alice Széchenyi (who also married a count).

Vanderbilt, Gloria (1924—)

American actress, artist, and designer who was a contested child in an infamous custody battle in the 1930s. Name variations: Gloria Vanderbilt-Cooper; Mrs. Wyatt E. Cooper. Born Gloria Laura Vanderbilt in New York City on February 20, 1924; daughter of Reginald Claypoole Vanderbilt (1880–1925) and Gloria Mercedes (Morgan) Vanderbilt (1904–1965); studied at private schools; married Pasquale (Pat) De Cicco (1909–1979, an actor's agent), in 1941 (divorced April 24, 1945); married Leopold Stokowski (1882–1977, the conductor), on April 25, 1945 (divorced October 1955); married Sidney Lumet (b. 1924, the movie director), on August 27, 1956 (divorced August 1963); married Wyatt E. Cooper, on December 24, 1963 (died January 5, 1978); children: (second marriage) Stanley and Christopher Stokowski; (fourth marriage) Carter Vanderbilt Cooper and Anderson H. Cooper.

Made first appearance on Broadway in Time of Your Life; *also appeared on numerous television shows; had solo shows as an artist at Barbara Shaeffer Gallery in New York (1954), Juster Gallery (1956), Hammer Gallery (1966); received the Neiman-Marcus fashion award (1969), the Fashion Hall of Fame award (1970), and the gold medal from the Society of Arts and Letters (1976); was also creative director of Gloria Vanderbilt Designs.*

Selected writings: Love Poems *(1955);* Gloria Vanderbilt Book of Collage *(1970);* Woman to Woman *(1979); (autobiography)* Once Upon a Time *(1985); (autobiography)* Black Knight, White Knight *(1987); (autobiography)* A Mother's Story *(1996).*

Heiress to the vast Vanderbilt fortune amassed by her great-grandfather Commodore Cornelius Vanderbilt, Gloria Vanderbilt was just one year old when her father Reginald Claypoole Vanderbilt died in 1925, leaving her a multimillion-dollar trust fund from which she received a monthly allotment. A further provision in Reggie's will provided for Gloria's beautiful 19-year-old mother **Gloria Morgan Vanderbilt**, as long as the child continued to live with her. The senior Gloria, however, did not totally adhere to her end of the agreement, continuing to live the life of an international socialite while leaving little Gloria in the care of her overprotective nurse **Emma Keislich**. When the child failed to thrive, her maternal grandmother **Laura Kilpatrick Morgan** became alarmed and shared her concern with Reggie's sister, ***Gertrude Vanderbilt Whitney**, herself the recent recipient of a large fortune. Whitney invited the child and her nurse to live with her at her Long Island estate, where Gloria blossomed and began attending a local school. In 1934, when Gloria was ten, Whitney sued for permanent custody of the child, charging that she had been neglected by her mother. The ensuing custody battle was one of the most publicized court cases of the 1930s, making headlines all over the world. As a result of Gloria's own testimony and that of her grandmother, the court ultimately granted custody to Whitney, while Gloria's mother was given visitation rights as well as a voice in the rearing of her daughter.

The years following the trial were lonely ones for Gloria. "The irony . . . was that as soon as my aunt was allowed to take charge of me, she lost interest," she said later. Whitney, who was 60 years old and in ill health by the end of the trial, saw to it that Gloria had everything she needed, but spent little time with her. Under her aunt's custody, Gloria attended the exclusive Mary C. Wheeler School in Providence, Rhode Island, and Miss (*Sarah) **Porter**'s School in Farmington, Connecticut. Whitney, a talented sculptor and a patron of the arts (she founded the Whitney Museum of American Art), also fostered Gloria's interest in art and the theater.

At 17, feeling overprotected by her aunt, Gloria quit school and went to live with her mother in California. "I was like a bird set free," she recalled, although the relationship with her mother would subsequently disintegrate. She began dating a variety of older men, and in 1941 married Pat De Cicco, an actor's agent, whom she divorced in 1945, shortly after coming of age and inheriting her sizable fortune. On April 25, 1945, the day after the divorce, she wed conductor Leopold Stokowski, a man 42 years her senior. Settling down to a life of relative obscurity as a wife and mother (the couple had two sons, Stanley and Christopher), Gloria turned her attention to poetry and painting. But her husband's career took precedence over any of her own ac-

tivities. While he toured, and she spent more and more time alone, she discovered her own ambition and her need to establish her own identity.

In 1948, under the name Glorya Stokowska, she gave a one-woman show at the Rabun Studio which included 14 oils and pastels that one critic called "directly in the Matisse-Picasso School of Paris tradition." In October 1953, she held a second one-woman exhibit at the Bertha Schaeffer Gallery, and in 1957, a third, at New York's Juster Gallery. The later show was made up primarily of paintings of children and animals, executed, said a critic for the *New York Herald Tribune*, "in the manner of half portraitist and half fantasist." Vanderbilt explained that she did not paint from life. "My work is filled with joy," she said, "a joy that springs from the pain of things that happened to me a long time ago, that I've spent my whole life working out. I'm now creating a joy that I never had in childhood, in recapturing something that never really happened."

Gloria was first lured into the theater by producer Gilbert Miller, who saw her perform at a charity ball and thought she had talent. She made her debut in 1953, in a summer stock production of Ferenc Molnar's *The Swan*, portraying Princess Alexandra. "Miss Vanderbilt reveals a personal theatricalism that is lovely to see," wrote a reviewer for *Variety* (August 18, 1954). "Her poise, savvy, expressive beauty, as well as her dignity and reserve all add up to a new personality to be reckoned with theatrically." Vanderbilt made her television debut a few months later in Noel Coward's *Tonight at 8:30*, which was followed in January 1955 by a small role in the New York City Center revival of William Saroyan's *The Time of Your Life*. That April, after taking acting lessons from Sanford Meisner, she played the female lead in a summer stock production of *Picnic*, directed by Sidney Lumet.

In 1955, Vanderbilt also published a volume of poetry, *Love Poems*, a collection of 27 verses drawn largely from her diary and focusing thematically on the search for love. The volume received a lukewarm reception, some reviewers feeling that its value lay more in the exploitation of the Vanderbilt name than in any artistic merit. She later wrote short stories and book reviews for magazines, and completed a full-length play, *Three by Two*, although she failed to get it produced.

Sidney Lumet became Gloria's third husband in 1956, after a very public divorce from Stokowski and a bitter custody battle over their children that rivaled the one over Gloria years earlier. Her marriage to Lumet lasted until 1963, during which time Vanderbilt continued to perform in summer stock and regional theater and on television. In 1959, Lumet directed her in a television dramatization of Tolstoy's *Family Happiness*, which was aired on the "U.S. Steel Hour."

Following her third divorce in 1963, Gloria married editor-writer Wyatt Emory Cooper, with whom she had two more sons, Carter and Anderson. With Cooper's support, she abandoned her performing and poetry, and began painting in earnest, working in her studio from early morning until late at night. Two one-woman shows at the Hammer Galleries in New York, the first in April 1966, at which she exhibited some 67 paintings executed in bright acrylic vinyls, and the second in April 1968, which included several large collages, were both successful, as were exhibits at the Washington Gallery of Art in 1967 and several subsequent one-woman shows across the country. In 1970, she published the *Gloria Vanderbilt Book of Collage*, written in collaboration with Alfred Allen Lewis. In it, she encouraged readers to make their own collages from fabric scraps, household items, and personal mementos.

In 1972, Vanderbilt began transferring the colorful motifs of her paintings to a line of products, including table linens, bathroom accessories, china, and wallpaper. She later brought out a line of cosmetics and began designing dresses, and in 1978 added to her business empire with a line of jeans carrying her signature logo, her name and a swan motif. "Sometimes I wonder, at fifty-two has success come too late?" she told an interviewer in 1976. "I needed it more in my 20's and 30's."

Vanderbilt's personal success, however, was accompanied by great personal tragedy. In 1978, her husband Wyatt died at the age of 50, following a series of heart attacks. In July 1988, as she watched helplessly, her son Carter, age 23, an editor at *American Heritage* and outwardly a well-adjusted young man, jumped to his death from the terrace of her Manhattan penthouse. It was a devastating blow and took her three long years before she was sure she could resolve her grief and move on. "I remember sitting in a restaurant one night and drinking a glass of water and feeling like a person," she said. "Until then, you feel you have no skin." Vanderbilt later attributed the suicide to Carter's use of a prescription allergy drug which had been known to cause psychotic episodes. One step in her recovery was her book *A Mother's Story* (1996), an account of her pain and loss and a companion piece to her earlier memoirs, *Once Upon a Time* (1985) and *Black Knight, White Knight* (1987).

SOURCES:

Goldsmith, Barbara. *Little Gloria . . . Happy at Last*. NY: Alfred A. Knopf, 1980.

Hubbard, Kim, and Anne Longley. "Living With Loss," in *People Weekly*. May 6, 1996.

Kohn, George C. *Encyclopedia of American Scandal*. NY: Facts on File, 1989.

Moritz, Charles, ed. *Current Biography 1972*. NY: H.W. Wilson, 1972.

O'Reilly, Jane. "Gloria Vanderbilt: everything's coming up roses," in *Home & Garden*. July 1976.

Vanderbilt, Gloria. *Black Knight, White Knight*. NY: Alfred A. Knopf, 1978.

RELATED MEDIA:

"Little Gloria . . . Happy at Last" (200 min. television film), starring *Bette Davis, Angela Lansbury, Christopher Plummer, and *Maureen Stapleton, first aired in 1982.

Barbara Morgan,
Melrose, Massachusetts

Vanderbilt, Maria (1821–1896)

American socialite. Name variations: Mrs. William Henry Vanderbilt I. Born Maria Louisa Kissam in 1821; died in 1896; married William Henry Vanderbilt I (1821–1885); children: nine, including Cornelius Vanderbilt II (1843–1899) and William Kissam Vanderbilt I (1849–1920).

Vanderbilt, Sophia Johnson (1797–1868)

American socialite. Name variations: Mrs. Cornelius Vanderbilt I. Born in 1797; died in 1868; married Cornelius Vanderbilt I, called the Commodore (1794–1877); children: 13, including William Henry Vanderbilt I (1821–1885). Cornelius' second wife was Frances Armstrong (Frank) Crawford (1839–1885), known as **Frances Vanderbilt**.

Vanderbilt, Mrs. William K. (1853–1933).

See Belmont, Alva Smith.

Vanderbilt I, Mrs. Cornelius (1797–1868).

See Vanderbilt, Sophia Johnson.

Vanderbilt II, Mrs. Cornelius (1845–1934).

See Vanderbilt, Alice Gwynne.

Vanderbilt-Cooper, Gloria (b. 1924).

See Vanderbilt, Gloria.

Van der Oosten, Gertrude (d. 1358).

See Gertrude of Ostend.

Vandeuil, Dame de (1573–1599).

See Estrées, Gabrielle d'.

van Deurs, Brigitte (1946—)

Duchess of Gloucester. Name variations: Bridget van Deurs. Born on June 20, 1946, in Odensee, Denmark; daughter of Asger Henriksen and Vivian van Deurs; married Richard Windsor (b. 1944), 2nd duke of Gloucester, on July 8, 1972; children: Alexander Windsor (b. 1974), earl of Ulster; Davina Windsor (b. 1977); Rose Windsor (b. 1980).

Van de Vate, Nancy (1930—)

American composer. Born in Plainfield, New Jersey, on December 30, 1930; received Rochester Prize scholarship and George Eastman scholarship to attend the Eastman School of Music; graduated with a degree in music theory from Wellesley College; master's degree in composition from the University of Mississippi; doctorate in music from Florida State University.

Awarded six American Society of Composers, Authors, and Publishers awards; premiered Six Etudes for Solo Vila *at Lincoln Center; challenged the granting procedures of the Rockefeller Foundation, the National Endowment for the Arts, and the John F. Kennedy Center for the Performing Arts, which she felt were biased against women; served as chair of the International League of Women Composers; was a professor of music at the University of Mississippi, Memphis State University, the University of Tennessee, and the University of Hawaii.*

"Most of the standard avenues for obtaining performances of their works have not been open to women," wrote Nancy Van de Vate. "In the past every city and town had its music club of genteel ladies who would listen to sentimental songs by women or works for solo piano. . . . But serious compositional aspirations have been about as welcome in women as beards and for the same reason." As a composer and active member of the League of Women Composers, Van de Vate sought to challenge musical stereotypes.

The birth of her child in 1955 led Van de Vate to composing; the constraints of time, energy, and financial resources made her realize that performance was no longer a feasible outlet for her ambitions. "I changed to composition, then became so totally engrossed in it that I never again wished to direct the major part of my time and energy to any other aspect of music." During the early part of her composing career, Van de Vate lived in the Southeast, which was also a

drawback. "Music composition is really an urban occupation, you must be where there are performers and audiences to hear your music. My own style was hampered by being in a rural environment. . . . There simply are few composers from places like South Dakota, North Dakota, Utah, Wyoming, Arkansas, and Nevada; it is just too rural." Despite the drawbacks of gender, location, and prejudice, Van de Vate continued to compose and gained increasing recognition for her work, which included pieces for chorus, orchestra, and chamber works, among others.

SOURCES:

Cohen, Aaron I. *International Encyclopedia of Women Composers.* 2 vols. NY: Books & Music (USA), 1987.

Morton, Brian and Pamela Collins. *Contemporary Composers.* Chicago, IL: St. James Press, 1981.

John Haag,
Athens, Georgia

Van Doren, Irita (1891–1966)

American editor. Born Irita Bradford in Birmingham, Alabama, on March 16, 1891; died on December 18, 1966; daughter of John Taylor Bradford (a merchant and owner of a sawmill) and Ida Henley (Brooks) Bradford (an accomplished musician); graduated from Florida State College for Women at Tallahassee, 1908; Columbia University, Ph.D.; married Carl Van Doren (literary critic and Pulitzer Prize-winning biographer), in August 1912 (divorced 1935); children: Anne Van Doren (b. 1915); Margaret Van Doren (b. 1917); Barbara Van Doren (b. 1920).

Irita Van Doren held the powerful position of editor of the weekly book review section of the New York *Herald Tribune*, starting in 1926. Graduating from Florida State College for Women at age 17, she went north to study at Columbia University where she met fellow graduate student Carl Van Doren. After their marriage in 1912, they bought an old farm in West Cornwall, Connecticut. During the early years, Van Doren helped Carl research his books. She then joined the editorial staff of *The Nation* (1919–22), becoming advertising manager (1922–23) and literary editor (1923–24). In 1924, she moved to the *Herald Tribune* as assistant to book editor Stuart P. Sherman; on his death, she succeeded him.

Van Duyn, Mona (1921—)

American poet laureate and Pulitzer Prize winner. Born on May 9, 1921, in Waterloo, Iowa; daughter of Earl George Van Duyn (a businessman) and Lora (Kramer) Van Duyn; University of Northern Iowa,

B.A., 1942; *University of Iowa, M.A., 1943; married Jarvis A. Thurston (a professor of English), on August 31, 1943.*

Selected works: Valentines to the Wide World *(1959);* A Time of Bees *(1964);* To See, To Take *(1970);* Bedtime Stories *(1972);* Merciful Disguises *(1973);* Letters from a Father, and Other Poems *(1982);* Near Changes *(1990);* If It Be Not I: Collected Poems 1959–1982 *(1994);* Firefall *(1994).*

Pulitzer Prize-winning poet laureate Mona Van Duyn began writing as a child. She was born in Waterloo, Iowa, in 1921 and grew up in Eldora, a small town where she spent much of her time in the public library. She kept notebooks full of poetry in elementary and junior high school and, in the second grade, had a poem published in a newspaper. Her early reading included formal poetry, but in college she began reading free verse and devoting herself more seriously to writing.

Alison Carb Sussman writes that Van Duyn is known for the "blend of formalism and colloquialism in her tough-minded, witty, and sometimes humorous work." Exploring the connections between life and art, she often uses domestic imagery to probe what lies beyond, which has caused some reviewers to describe her as a "domestic poet," a term she dislikes. She believes that she is thus labeled simply because she is a woman. Only about one-fourth of her poems are domestic, she said, adding, "I find my richest hunting ground for poems in that place where the undomesticated feelings, snapping and snarling, run round the domestic ring."

Praised for her "exceptionally crafted" and "polished and elegant" work as well as her "warmth and intellect," Van Duyn creates poems about love that are tempered with an equal amount of violence and destruction, often presenting women as victims of violence. She believes this emphasis may come from her upbringing: her father, a businessman who was not particularly interested in her, took books away from her and demanded she play outside instead. He also wanted her to marry a local boy and not go to college; however, she finally persuaded him to allow her to attend school on the scholarship she had won. His lack of approval or love, she believes, may have contributed to her view of love and struggle as intertwined.

After receiving her B.A. at the University of Northern Iowa, she earned an M.A. at the University of Iowa, where she met and married Jarvis A. Thurston, a professor of English. She taught English there and at the University of Louisville in Kentucky, where her husband was also hired. In 1947, they founded *Perspective: A Quarterly in Literature,* which Van Duyn edited from 1947 to 1967. From 1950 through 1967, she taught English at Washington University in St. Louis, Missouri. During the 1970s, she taught and lectured at various other universities in the United States and in Salzburg, Austria.

Van Duyn's impressive number of honors began accumulating with the 1956 *Eunice Tietjens Memorial Prize from *Poetry* magazine. In addition to several regional poetry awards in the 1960s, Van Duyn earned a grant from the National Endowment for the Arts in 1966, the *Harriet Monroe Memorial Prize from *Poetry* magazine, and the Hart Crane Memorial Award from American Weave Press, both in 1968. She won Yale University Library's Bollingen Prize in 1970, and in 1971 her book *To See, To Take,* a collection of verse from three of her previous volumes plus some uncollected work, won the National Book Award for Poetry. To her growing list of accolades, she added a Guggenheim fellowship in 1972 and the National Institute of Arts and Letters' Loines Prize in 1976. She became a member of the Academy of American Poets in 1981, and one of 12 chancellors for life in 1985. Cornell College in Iowa honored her with the Sandburg Prize in 1982, and the Poetry Society of American awarded her the Shelley Memorial Prize in 1987. Her finest recognition came in 1991 when, at age 70, she won the Pulitzer Prize for her poetry collection, *Near Changes.* In 1992, she became the first woman poet laureate (consultant in poetry) for the U.S. Library of Congress.

Van Duyn once told journalist Steve Paul: "There are writers, not just poets, who theoretically believe that words are more important than the world . . . that the world doesn't exist without the word. I think I am a little more oriented toward love of the actual world than many writers are. No poet has to give up the world for words. The words exist to praise the world, to define it and clarify it."

SOURCES:

Paul, Steve. *Kansas City Star.* May 26, 1991.

Sussman, Alison Carb. "Mona Van Duyn," in *Newsmakers 1993.* No. 2. Louise Mooney, ed. Detroit, MI: Gale Research, 1993.

COLLECTIONS:

The papers of Mona Van Duyn are collected at the Olin Library at Washington University in St. Louis, Missouri.

Kelly Winters,
freelance writer

Van Dyken, Amy (1973—)

American Olympic swimmer. Born on February 15, 1973, in Englewood, Colorado; attended the University of Arizona, 1992–94; graduated from Colorado State University, 1997; married Alan McDaniel, on October 14, 1995.

Won gold medal in 50-yard freestyle, NCAA championships (1994); won gold medal in 50-meter freestyle, U.S. National championships (1995); won gold medals in 50-meter freestyle, 100-meter butterfly, 4x100 freestyle relay, and 4x100 medley relay, Atlanta Olympics (1996); won gold medals in 50-meter freestyle, 4x100 freestyle relay, and 4x100 medley relay, World championships, Perth, Australia (1998); won a gold medal in the 4x100 freestyle relay in Sydney Olympics (2000).

Amy Van Dyken, the first American woman to win four gold medals in a single Olympics, suffered from severe asthma that was diagnosed when she was 18 months old. As a child, she was unable to run and play with other children because allergies aggravated her asthma. She carried an inhaler everywhere. When she was six, her doctor suggested that she take up swimming to increase her lung capacity. Unable to traverse the length of an Olympic-sized pool until she was 12 years old, she often came in last in meets, even when they included younger children. Despite her health problems and lack of success, she persevered. Van Dyken told journalist Melissa Murphy, "People can stomp you down and say, 'You really shouldn't be doing this, you're not very good at it.' But if you love something and keep pursuing it, good things can happen."

At age 13, Van Dyken began to improve, winning her first gold medal in a local swim meet. In high school, she became state champion and set records in the 50-meter butterfly and the 100-yard butterfly. She was named Colorado Swimmer of the Year twice. Van Dyken attended the University of Arizona on a swimming scholarship and won a silver medal in the 50-yard freestyle at the NCAA championships in 1993. The following year she transferred to Colorado State University, where, in 1994, she won a gold medal and set an American record in the 50-yard freestyle event at the NCAA meet and was named NCAA Swimmer of the Year. "This is something I've dreamed about for a long, long time," she said. "I try not to think about how fast it's happened, how far I've come, because if I think about it, I might not believe it's really happening." In 1995, she won a national title in the 50-meter freestyle, and set another American record in the event there and at the Pan Pacific Games.

Training without the medications that could have ameliorated her asthma because they are banned by the International Olympic Committee, Van Dyken nevertheless qualified for the U.S. Olympic swim team in 1996. She won four gold medals at the Olympic Games in Atlanta: as an individual in the 50-meter freestyle and the 100-meter butterfly, and as part of the 4x100-meter freestyle and medley relay teams. Perhaps because she had struggled for so many years, she became as well known for her personal warmth and generosity as for her swimming skills. Despite being deluged with requests from fans, she made efforts to accommodate those who wanted a photo taken with her after the Olympics.

Van Dyken was chosen from among 54 top women athletes to be named Sportswoman of the Year by the U.S. Olympic Committee in 1996. She was also featured on the cover of a Wheaties cereal box. In 1998, Van Dyken competed in the World championships in Perth, Australia, and won three gold medals: one in the 50-meter freestyle and two in the relay races. As of 2000, she was still ranked in the top eight in the 50-meter freestyle. A member of the Olympic team that competed in Sydney, Australia, Van Dyken won another gold medal as part of the 4x100 freestyle relay. Fluent in American Sign Language, Van Dyken hopes to teach high school or work with deaf children after she retires from swimming.

SOURCES:
Johnson, Anne Janette. *Great Women in Sports.* Detroit, MI: Visible Ink Press, 1998.
Murphy, Melissa. *The Day* [New London, CT]. October 27, 1996.

Kelly Winters,
freelance writer

Vane, Lady Frances Emily (d. 1899).

See Churchill, Jennie Jerome for sidebar on Fanny Churchill.

Van Fleet, Jo (1919–1996)

American character actress who won both an Academy Award and a Tony Award. Born on December 30, 1919, in Oakland, California; died on June 8, 1996, in New York City; daughter of Roy H. Van Fleet and Elizabeth (Gardner) Van Fleet; College of the Pacific, in Stockton, California, B.A.; attended the Neighborhood Playhouse School of the Theater; member of the Actors Studio; married William Bales (a dancer and choreographer who died in 1990); children: one son, Michael.

Selected theater: debuted as Miss Phipps in a touring production of Uncle Harry *(1945); debuted in New*

York as Dorcas in The Winter's Tale *(Cort Theater, January 15, 1946); appeared as Major Orlov in* The Whole World Over *(Biltmore Theater, 1947), Connie in* The Closing Door *(Empire Theater, 1949), Regan in* King Lear *(National Theater, 1950), Miss Foster in* Flight Into Egypt *(Music Box Theater, 1952), Marguerite Gautier in* Camino Real *(National Theater, 1953), Jessie Mae Watts in* The Trip to Bountiful *(Henry Miller Theater, 1953), Eliza Grant in* Look Homeward Angel *(Ethel Barrymore Theater, 1957), Madame Rosepettle in* Oh Dad, Poor Dad, Mama's Hung You in the Closet and I'm Feelin' So Sad *(Phoenix Theater, 1962), Amanda Wingfield in the 20th anniversary production of* The Glass Menagerie *(1965).*

Selected filmography: East of Eden *(1955);* The Rose Tattoo *(1955);* I'll Cry Tomorrow *(1955);* The King and Four Queens *(1956);* Gunfight at the O.K. Corral *(1957);* La Diga sul Pacifico *(This Angry Age or* The Sea Wall, *It.-Fr., 1958);* Wild River *(1950);* Cool Hand Luke *(1967);* I Love You Alice B. Toklas! *(1968);* 80 Steps to Jonah *(1969);* The Gang That Couldn't Shoot Straight *(1971);* Le Locataire *(The Tenant, Fr., 1976).*

A veteran of stage, screen, and television, Jo Van Fleet was acclaimed for her portrayals of tough, complex women, many of them years older than she. She was born in 1919 in Oakland, California, and began her theater studies at the College of the Pacific. After receiving her degree, she studied at the Neighborhood Playhouse with Sanford Meisner and at the Actors Studio with Elia Kazan, whom she later credited as a major influence in her career. She made her professional debut in 1945, in a touring production of *Uncle Harry*, and appeared in New York for the first time the following year, playing Dorcas in *The Winter's Tale*. In 1953, she won a Tony Award for her performance as Jessie Mae Watts in *The Trip to Bountiful* (1953), then two years later claimed an Academy Award as Best Supporting Actress for her role as James Dean's mother in *East of Eden* (1955), her first film. Elia Kazan, the film's director, later cast her as the 80-year-old matriarch Ella Garth in his film *Wild River* (1960). He also directed her on stage, in George Tabori's *Flight Into Egypt* (1952) and Tennessee Williams' *Camino Real* (1953).

Any review of Van Fleet's career reveals a gallery of diverse maternal roles beyond those in *East of Eden* and *Wild River*. On stage, she was Eliza Grant in *Look Homeward Angel* (1957), Amanda Wingfield in *The Glass Menagerie* (1959), and Madame Rosepettle in Arthur Kopit's absurdist comedy *Oh Dad, Poor Dad,*

Mama's Hung You in the Closet and I'm Feelin' So Sad (1962). In movies, she played the ambitious mother of *Lillian Roth (portrayed by *Susan Hayward) in *I'll Cry Tomorrow* (1955), for which she received the Motion Picture Exhibitors Award and the Film Daily Award, and Arletta, the ailing mother of Paul Newman in *Cool Hand Luke* (1967). She was also the wicked stepmother in the television revival of Rodgers and Hammerstein's *Cinderella* (1965).

In addition to Broadway, films, and television, Van Fleet also played off-Broadway and in summer stock. In the summer of 1961, she performed at the Festival of Two Worlds in Spoleto, Italy. The actress was married to dancer-choreographer William Bales, who died in 1990, and had one son, Michael. Van Fleet died in 1996, at the age of 81.

SOURCES:

Katz, Ephraim. *The Film Encyclopedia.* NY: HarperCollins, 1994.

McGill, Raymond, ed. *Notable Names in the Theater.* Clifton, NJ: James T. White, 1976.

"Obituary," in *The Day* [New London, CT]. June 11, 1996.

Barbara Morgan,
Melrose, Massachusetts

Van Gennip, Yvonne

Dutch speedskater. Born in the Netherlands.

Won three Olympic gold medals in Calgary: in the 1,000, 3,000 and 5,000 meters (1988).

In Calgary, Alberta, Canada, Yvonne Van Gennip put a screeching, single-handed halt to East Germany's domination over speedskating. Van Gennip took three gold medals: in the 1,500 meters over *Karin Kania-Enke, who was considered unbeatable; in the 3,000 meters, ahead of **Andrea Ehrig** and *Gabi Schönbrunn Zange; and in the 5,000 meters, once again in front of Ehrig and Zange.

Van Grippenberg, Alexandra
(1859–1913)

Finnish feminist and legislator. Name variations: Baroness Alexandra Van Grippenberg. Born in 1859; died in 1913.

Baroness Alexandra Van Grippenberg was a member of the temperance movement, and in 1884 was a founding member of the Finsk Kvinneførening (Finnish Women's Association). As a leader of the association, she headed an all-encompassing campaign for educational, professional, and political equality, and advocated feminist reforms of property rights, divorce laws, and the abolition of state-regulated prostitution. This broad-based campaign contrasted sharply with that of *Lucina Hagman, which focused solely on women's suffrage.

In 1883, Van Grippenberg attended the Women's Congress in Washington, D.C., that had been organized by *Susan B. Anthony. After the formation of the International Council of Women in 1889, Van Grippenberg became vice-president. She concentrated on educating women to be wise political participants after they won the vote in Finland in 1906.

In 1909, she was elected a member of the Finnish Diet, where she argued against legislation protecting women, on the grounds that total equality between the sexes would not be achieved if either of them received special protection. In 1912, she founded the Finnish National Council of Women and was elected its first president. She died one year later.

Kelly Winters,
freelance writer

van Hemessen, Caterina (c. 1528–c. 1587).

See Hemessen, Caterina van.

Van Hoosen, Bertha (1863–1952)

American surgeon, cofounder and first president of the American Medical Women's Association, who was the first woman to head a medical division of a coeducational university. Born on March 26, 1863, in Stony Creek, Michigan; died of a stroke on June 7, 1952, in Romeo, Michigan; daughter of Joshua Van Hoosen (a homesteader) and Sarah Ann (Taylor) Van Hoosen (a teacher); University of Michigan, A.B., 1884, medical degree, 1888; additional medical training in Detroit and Kalamazoo, Michigan, and in Boston.

Was an instructor of medicine, Women's Medical School of Northwestern University (1888–1902); established private practice in Chicago (1892); was a professor at University of Illinois College of Medicine (1902–12); became chief of gynecological staff of Cook County Hospital, Chicago (1913), then chief of obstetrical staff (1920); cofounded and was first president of the American Medical Women's Association (1915); was a professor and head of obstetrics, Loyola University (1918–37).

Bertha Van Hoosen was born on a farm in Michigan in 1863 and attended local schools there. She followed her older sister into litera-

ture studies at the University of Michigan, and after graduating decided to become a doctor. Her parents did not support her decision to go into medicine; her mother objected, and her father refused to finance her training. Undeterred, she paid her own way by doing obstetrical nursing, demonstrating classroom anatomy, and teaching. She received her medical training at the University of Michigan and, following graduation in 1888, spent four years in clinical residence at the Woman's Hospital in Detroit, the Kalamazoo (Michigan) State Hospital for the Insane, and the New England Hospital for Women and Children in Boston.

Van Hoosen opened a private practice in Chicago in 1892, which she kept afloat by teaching embryology and anatomy at the Woman's Medical School of Northwestern University. Her reputation as a skilled physician gradually overcame negative reactions to her gender, and within five years her practice was flourishing. She taught at the Illinois University Medical School from 1902 to 1912, despite the fact that many other professors objected to working with a woman. From 1918 to 1937, she was professor and head of obstetrics at Loyola University, making her the first woman to head a medical division of a coeducational university. An attending physician at several hospitals in Chicago, she became chief of gynecological staff at Cook County Hospital in 1913, the first time a woman physician received a civil-service appointment. In 1920, she became chief of the obstetrical staff there.

Throughout her life, Van Hoosen, who was particularly interested in women's health, treated mostly women and children. She worked to develop better methods of prenatal care and established the first human breast-milk bank in Chicago. Over the objections of male doctors who considered anaesthesia during childbirth unsafe, Van Hoosen pioneered the use of scopalamine-morphine, which allowed the patient to remain semiconscious. By 1908, she had delivered 2,000 healthy babies with minimal pain to their mothers. She published her research in three articles, including *Scopalamine-Morphine Anaesthesia* (1915). An excellent surgeon who often performed surgeries for other women physicians, Van Hoosen gained recognition in the mid-1940s for her ability to perform appendectomies through incisions less than a half-inch in length.

During her career, Van Hoosen trained more than 20 female surgeons, her "surgical daughters," many of whom later worked as missionaries in China. However, because of her gender, she was prohibited from joining the Chicago Gynecological and Obstetrical Society and was isolated at American Medical Association meetings. In response, she formed the American Medical Women's Association in 1915 and served as its first president. Although she fought for the right of women physicians to serve in the armed forces during World War I, she was unsuccessful in this campaign.

Van Hoosen wrote an autobiography, *Petticoat Surgeon*, in 1947. She performed her last operation at the age of 88 and practiced medicine nearly until her death from a stroke in 1952.

SOURCES:

Bailey, Brooke. *The Remarkable Lives of 100 Women Healers and Scientists.* Holbrook, MA: Bob Adams, 1994.

Read, Phyllis J., and Bernard L. Witlieb. *The Book of Women's Firsts.* NY: Random House, 1992.

Sicherman, Barbara, and Carol Hurd Green, eds. *Notable American Women: The Modern Period.* Cambridge, MA: The Belknap Press of Harvard University, 1980.

Kelly Winters,
freelance writer

Elizabeth Van Lew

Van Kleeck, Mary Abby (1883–1972).

See Anderson, Mary (1872–1964) for sidebar.

Van Lawick-Goodall, Jane (b. 1934).

See Goodall, Jane.

Van Lew, Elizabeth (1818–1900)

Virginia Unionist and Federal agent during the Civil War. Name variations: Crazy Bet. Born on October 17, 1818, in Richmond, Virginia; died on September 25, 1900, in Richmond; daughter of John Van Lew (a hardware merchant) and Elizabeth (Baker) Van Lew; educated in Philadelphia and at home.

A longtime opponent of slavery even before the Civil War began, Elizabeth Van Lew maintained loyalty to the Union despite her home state of Virginia's being a Confederate stronghold. She was born in Richmond in 1818; her father was a wealthy hardware merchant and her mother was the daughter of a former mayor of Philadelphia. The family enjoyed high social standing, entertaining Richmond's most distinguished figures in their home. While many of her friends and family conjectured that she had acquired her liberal views during her early schooling in Philadelphia, it was probably from her mother's teaching that she became an abolitionist. Though the Van Lews held slaves, she and her widowed mother liberated them in the 1850s, paying for the education of one former slave. They also bought members of their former slaves' families, who were owned by other households, and gave them their freedom.

When the Civil War began, Van Lew assisted inmates at Libby Prison, a confederate prison camp for federal officers. She and her mother brought food, books, and clothing to the prisoners, and smuggled their letters back to their families. They also helped more than 100 of them to escape, hiding them in a secret room in the Van Lew house. According to Frank Surge, Van Lew was also the Union's most valuable spy; she obtained Confederate military information at Libby, then passed it on to Union forces. Because Van Lew came from such a prominent Richmond family, she was trusted and allowed access to many places, including Jefferson Davis' Confederate White House, where, to gain even more information, she placed as a servant the former slave whose education she had sponsored, **Mary Elizabeth Bowser.**

One of Van Lew's best-known exploits was the surreptitious removal of the body of Colonel Ulric Dahlgren, who was killed during General

Hugh J. Kilpatrick's unsuccessful raid on Richmond in February 1864. The colonel had been ambushed and killed because the Confederates claimed he had been carrying papers proving that he was involved in a conspiracy to assassinate high-ranking members of the Confederate government and set fire to Richmond. Van Lew's agents found the desecrated and hastily buried body and removed it to a farm in the country, where it was respectfully reburied. Public opinion against Dahlgren was strong in Virginia, so Van Lew would have suffered serious consequences if this action had been discovered.

Late in 1864, when the Union Army was approaching Richmond and Van Lew and her family had received many serious threats, she began to dress and act peculiarly, which led people to believe she was insane and therefore incapable of spying. She was so successful at this ruse that she became known as "Crazy Bet." In this guise, she maintained several relay stations between the city of Richmond and the federal headquarters located down river. Surge writes that Van Lew devised a special code for her messages, which were delivered by her servants who carried baskets of eggs in which one hollow shell contained a message. Her servants also carried their missives in the soles of their shoes. As noted by Rae Foley, she also would work a code into the fabric of a dress, or carry a secret code in her watch.

When the Confederates evacuated Richmond in April 1865, Van Lew raised a huge American flag over her house—the first time the flag had flown in that city since 1861. She then went to the deserted government offices to collect Confederate documents for federal officials. General Ulysses S. Grant, head of the Union Army, thanked her in person for her efforts when his forces came to take over the city. When he was elected president, Grant appointed Van Lew postmistress of Richmond, an office she executed well, despite continuing hostility from fellow citizens. Her post ended in 1877 when President Rutherford B. Hayes took office. She then secured clerical work at the Post Office Department in Washington, D.C., although she ultimately resigned when the administration of President Grover Cleveland reassigned her.

Then in her late 60s, she returned to Richmond, impoverished because her family's estate had been exhausted by their wartime efforts. Still an outcast in Richmond society because of her Union sympathies, Van Lew lived in the family's old mansion with her niece and 40 cats. Financially destitute, she wrote a letter to the family of Colonel Paul Revere, a Bostonian and descendant of the Revolutionary War hero, whom she had aided at Libby Prison, borrowing a stamp to mail the letter. They quickly responded with an annuity for her subsistence. Van Lew spent the remainder of her life fighting for women's rights by protesting against paying her taxes, on the grounds that since women could not vote, they were enduring unconstitutional taxation without representation. After the death of her niece, she spent the remaining ten years of her life alone, dying on September 25, 1900. She was buried in Shockhoe Hill Cemetery in Richmond. Friends from Massachusetts, writes Foley, provided the bronze tablet engraved with the following inscription: "She risked everything that is dear to man—friends, fortune, comfort, health, life itself, all for the one absorbing desire of her heart—that slavery might be abolished and the Union preserved."

SOURCES:

Foley, Rae. "Elizabeth Van Lew, Grant's Spy in Richmond," in *Famous American Spies*. NY: Dodd, Mead, 1962, pp. 143–154.

Griffin, Lynne, and Kelly McCann. *The Book of Women: 300 Notable Women History Passed By*. Holbrook, MA: Bob Adams, 1992.

James, Edward T., ed. *Notable American Women, 1607–1950*. Cambridge, MA: The Belknap Press of Harvard University, 1971.

McHenry, Robert, ed. *Famous American Women*. NY: Dover, 1980.

Surge, Frank. *Famous Spies*. Minneapolis, MN: Lerner, 1969, pp. 41–46.

Weatherford, Doris. *American Women's History*. NY: Prentice Hall, 1994.

Kelly Winters,
freelance writer

van Oosterwyck, Maria (1630–1693).

See Oosterwyck, Maria van.

Vanozza, Rosa (1442–1518).

See Borgia, Lucrezia for sidebar on Vannozza Cattanei.

Vann, Jesse Matthews (c. 1890–1967)

African-American publisher. Born Jesse Ellen Matthews around 1890; died in 1967; married Robert Lee Vann (a publisher), in 1910 (died 1940).

Jesse Matthews Vann was one of the wealthiest African-American women during World War II, when she was publisher of the *Pittsburgh Courier*. In 1945, the paper was grossing about $2 million a year. Vann, who was described as so light-skinned that she could pass for white, declined to do so. Like her husband Robert Lee Vann, who was also light-skinned, she identified herself as black and chose to associate herself with black causes. The two met in 1908, when she was a kindergarten teacher and he was a law student. Robert joined the staff of the *Courier* a month after they were married in 1910.

Within ten years, the *Courier* had a circulation of 55,000, and in the early 1920s it began publishing a national edition. The paper had news bureaus nationwide and became a major source of information for African-Americans.

When Robert Vann died in 1940, Jesse Vann inherited the paper, and for the next two decades served as its publisher. The newspaper publicized the new opportunities for African-Americans that were created by World War II and, after the conflict, promoted the cause of civil rights. In the 1950s, when the American economy settled into a postwar regression, the *Courier*'s finances declined, and Vann's management was attacked by the board of directors. In 1965, two years after she retired, the members of the board realized that they could not do any better and sold the newspaper to the *Chicago Defender*. Vann died two years later, in 1967.

SOURCES:
Weatherford, Doris. *American Women's History.* NY: Prentice Hall, 1994.

Kelly Winters,
freelance writer

van Praagh, Peggy (1910–1990)

British ballet dancer who was largely responsible for the development of the Australian Ballet. Name variations: Dame Margaret van Praagh; Dame Peggy van Praagh; known professionally as Peggy van Praagh, despite the penchant for adopting exotic or at least dignified names among the ballerinas of her day. Born Margaret van Praagh on September 1, 1910, in London, England; died in Melbourne, Australia, on January 15, 1990, at age 79; daughter of a family doctor; educated at the King Alfred school in Hempstead and then trained under a series of dancers and dance teachers; received her diploma from the Cecchetti Society, in 1932.

Awards: Queen Elizabeth II Coronation Award (1953); Royal Academy of Dancing Award (1965); Commander of the Order of the British Empire (1966); Officer of the Order of the British Empire (1966); Dame Commander of the Order of the British Empire (1970); honorary doctorate, University of New England (1974); honorary doctorate of letters, University of New South Wales (1974); Distinguished Artist Award of the Australian Art Council (1975); honorary doctor of laws, Melbourne University (1981).

Made her debut at the London Coliseum (1929) opposite Anton Dolin in Revolution; *danced for the* Camargo Society (1930–33), *in ballets* Revolution *(1929) and* Adam and Eve *(1932); danced with Ballet Rambert (1933–38), in ballets* Mephisto Waltz *(1934), Valentine's Eve (1935), Circus Wives (1935), The Planets (1937), Dark Elegies (1937), Jardin aux Lilas (1938), and Gala Performance, Soirée Musicale; was co-director of the London Ballet with Maud Lloyd (1939–40); was a teacher and dancer with the Sadler's Wells Ballet (1941–46), for ballets* Coppélia, Les Patineurs; *was producer and ballet mistress with the same company (1946–52); was associate director of the company (1952–55); was a freelance producer and television dance director (1955–62); served as director, Borovansky Ballet, Melbourne (1960); was artistic director of the Australian Ballet (1963–74, 1978–79), with Robert Helpmann from 1965; retired (1979).*

Ballet dancer, teacher, and artistic director, Margaret van Praagh was born in London on September 1, 1910, the daughter of a family doctor of Dutch descent, and was educated at the King Alfred School in Hempstead. First exposed to dance when taken to a Christmas pantomime at the age of three, she began performing dance pieces for her family, relatives and guests. Encouraged by her parents, she was soon studying ballet under **Aimée Phipps** and **Margaret Craske** (1892–1990).

At the time that van Praagh began her studies, there was no native ballet in Great Britain, classical dance being regarded as a predominantly French, Italian, or Russian art. After the Russian Revolution, however, a number of ballerinas of the first rank settled abroad, including ****Matilda Kshesinskaia** in Paris and ****Tamara Karsavina** in London. Both began to teach. The great ****Anna Pavlova** also settled in London, and though she was almost constantly on tour, her repeated performances in Britain made a strong impression on a generation of young girls (and not a few boys), who went on to become members of the first generation of British classical dancers.

In classical ballet, Peggy van Praagh received her main training under Margaret Craske, the leading exponent in Britain of the teachings of the Italian ballet master Enrico Cecchetti (1850–1928), who had settled in London in 1918 and whose method of training for the classical ballet had a major influence on ballet in the Western world. Craske had studied directly under Cecchetti and then had danced with the brilliant and innovative Ballet Russe of Sergei Diaghilev. Van Praagh also trained later under the British dancer ****Lydia Sokolova** (1896–1974) and the Russian émigré ****Vera Volkova**

(1904–1975), and studied mime with Tamara Karsavina and modern dance with *Agnes de Mille (1905–1993).

Peggy van Praagh made her debut at the London Coliseum in 1929, in the ballet *Revolution*, in which she partnered Anton Dolin (1904–1983), who was one of the younger members of the Diaghilev troupe in its last years. Having made her debut, van Praagh thereupon began studying regularly with the Camargo Society under whose aegis she performed in Anthony Tudor's *Adam and Eve*.

The deaths of Sergei Diaghilev in 1929 and Anna Pavlova in 1931 had created a momentary crisis in the dance world of Britain, for upon the deaths of their founders, both of their companies immediately disbanded. On the other hand, these closings set free a number of important dancers who immediately began to generate creative activity on their own. The Camargo Society was an organization founded after the death of Diaghilev by *Ninette de Valois, Philip Richardson and Arnold C. Haskell for the production of ballets in Britain. The Society, in which Karsavina was also active, established a school of ballet at the Sadler's Wells theater in 1931, staged ballets there and at the Old Vic (becoming known as the Wells-Vic Ballet), and encouraged such new young British choreographers as Anthony Tudor (1909–1987) and Frederick Ashton (1904–1988).

Leaving the aegis of Camargo, van Praagh then danced as a soloist with the Ballet Rambert (1933–38), founded by *Marie Rambert, a dancer of Polish origin, who like Peggy van Praagh had studied with Craske, and had been teaching in London since 1913. By then, the Ballet Rambert had become a major force in the formation of British ballet. While dancing with the group, van Praagh created roles in several other ballets by Anthony Tudor, including that of Episode from His Past in *Jardin aux Lilas* (1936), Russian Ballerina in *Gala Performance*, Bolero in *Soirée Musicale*, and Mortal Under Mercury in *The Planets*. She also created both female roles in *Dark Elegies* (1937), works which became standards in the repertoires of British ballet companies. Her other roles included the Chatelaine-Bride in *La Fete étrange* and Venus in *The Judgment of Paris*.

Peggy van Praagh's performance in *Jardin aux Lilas* (also known by its English title *Lilac Garden*), a ritual of bereavement set to the music of Gustav Mahler's melancholy *Kindertotenlieder*, was particularly impressive and has been called the great breakthrough in her career as a dancer. Originally creating the role of Episode in this work, she later danced the part of the heroine Caroline. The ballet concerns a young woman, Caroline, about to be married to a man she does not love. At a party in her honor, she meets not only her former lover but also the woman (Episode) who has been the mistress of the man to whom she is about to be married. The ballet has been described as a continuous series of secret meetings, sudden interruptions and hasty partings, "the characters concealing their anguish behind a mask of upper class manners." The final irony of the ballet is that, "though all these people are well-to-do, their money and social positions actually hinder their search for personal happiness." With its heavy psychological overtones and generally dark mood, *Jardin aux Lilas* was considerably more weighty in theme and content than the typical stuff of ballet plots, and Peggy van Praagh triumphed in both roles that she undertook. *Lilac Garden* was probably the high point of her career as a dancer, and it was what brought her to the attention of everyone in the nascent British ballet world of that time.

In 1938, at age 28, van Praagh became one of the two principal dancers of Anthony Tudor's short-lived London Ballet, a position she held for two years. Tudor was arguably the first important English choreographer, and like Anton Dolin had been one of the younger members of the Diaghilev's Ballet Russe. In 1939, he left the London Ballet to go to America, and van Praagh and **Maud Lloyd** took over the direction of the company. Great things were expected of the London Ballet, but it lasted only until 1940. It was at this time, with the outbreak of the Second World War, that those unable to fight took it upon themselves to do whatever they could for the war effort. Van Praagh's contribution made a great impression at the time. With most of the theaters closed because of the fear of nighttime air raids, she introduced a series of afternoon performances at the Arts Theater called "Lunch-Hour Ballet," a much-appreciated booster to wartime morale.

The year after the dissolution of the London Ballet, van Praagh joined the Sadler's Wells Ballet of Ninette de Valois, later to become the Royal Ballet. Though engaged as a teacher with the company, she was soon performing as principal dancer in such roles as Swanilda in *Coppéllia*, Blue Girl in *Les Patineurs*. After the war ended in 1945, van Praagh, though only 35, retired from dancing but remained with the Sadler's Wells Theater Ballet in both a teaching and administrative capacity. Ninette de Valois, who with *Lillian Baylis had founded the school that evolved into the Sadler's Wells Ballet, was a dancer, choreographer, and teacher, as well as a first-rate administrator. The skills she saw in Peggy van Praagh would lead to van Praagh being endowed with the future responsibilities that would make her name on the international ballet scene.

Immediately following the war, the Sadler's Wells Ballet was invited to establish its home at the Royal Opera House at Covent Garden. This created a great deal of soul searching on the part of de Valois, partly because of the obligation to serve as the ballet for the operas staged at the Sadler's Wells Theater, and partly because of the increasing sense that the company had a responsibility to tour in the provinces. The solution settled upon was the establishment of a second, smaller company, averaging 30 dancers, that would remain at Sadler's Wells as the Sadler's Wells Ballet Theater and that would undertake the chores of touring. Though de Valois held the title of general director of the new company, van Praagh served as its ballet mistress from 1946 to 1952 and then as the company's artistic director from 1952 to 1955. In these roles she busied herself with the multifarious details of managing a large company while de Valois saw to the negotiations and planning that led to the establishment of the original Sadler's Wells company as the Royal Ballet. Between 1949 and 1958, van Praagh also staged several ballets for BBC television, serving as the organization's ballet producer. As a teacher, she nurtured such dancers as **Elaine Fifield, Maryon Lane** and David Blair. These instructional, administrative, directorial, and production experiences were to serve van Praagh well when she transferred her activities to Australia.

For all her success with the Sadler's Wells Ballet Theater, which with great diplomacy, tact and sympathy for her dancers, she had led through its formative years, and to which she had given a stamp of true independence and individuality, van Praagh never felt truly one of the company. While most of the members of the organization, slightly more than a decade old, had been with it from its inception, she had joined it not as a beginner but as someone entering from another company outside of it. She was particularly disappointed when the directorship of its touring company, which she had expected to be offered to her, was denied, and she resigned in 1955. Van Praagh then offered her services as a freelance artist which were immediately taken up. Traveling to Canada, West Germany, Norway, Sweden, Denmark, the United States, and France, where she staged various ballets by Ashton, de Valois, and Tudor, she brought considerable international luster to the reputation of British ballet. Among her various productions in

these years was *The Rake's Progress* for the Munich State Opera and *The Sleeping Beauty* for the Royal Swedish Ballet in 1956–57.

In 1957, Peggy van Praagh journeyed to Toronto, where she served as guest producer for the National Ballet of Canada. Ballet as a native art was then new to Canada, the company under the direction of *Celia Franca being then only five years old. At that time there was not only no government support for the arts in Canada but there was not even a national arts council. Thus, to raise funds, the ballet was forced to compete with other dance companies, symphony orchestras, and even medical research for such private donations as might be managed, all in a country with at that time fewer than 30 million people. Despite these drawbacks, Franca had put together a company of 36 dancers, 14 of them men, and had developed both a surprisingly large and varied repertoire and an ambitious schedule of touring around the vast country. Van Praagh worked for two months with the company's summer school, teaching the students Ashton's *Les Rendezvous*. She was a great inspiration not only to the company but also to Franca and to those who supported her work. Following her success in Toronto, van Praagh taught briefly at the Royal Ballet School in London in 1958, and the same year she also served as guest producer for the Norsk ballet in Oslo, Norway, and directed the resident company of the Edinburgh International Ballet in a production of *Ballet Premières* staged for the annual Edinburgh Festival. The following year, she was in the United States serving as a guest teacher at the prestigious Jacob's Pillow summer festival, the so-called "University of the Dance," then still under the direction of the renowned Ted Shawn.

In 1960, van Praagh made her first visit to Australia as the artistic director of the Borovansky Ballet, a company founded by the Czech dancer Edouard Borovansky who had died the year before. Borovansky, who had formerly danced with Pavlova, had struggled for some time to establish a permanent ballet company and school in Melbourne, which, without government support, had been drifting toward financial ruin. The call to take over his foundering company proved to be a turning point for both van Praagh and the development of serious dance in Australia. On her opening night, she made a curtain speech pressing for national support for a native ballet. Soon after, she made a plea to the Australian government to consider the establishment of a national ballet company. Surprisingly, her proposal fell upon sympathetic ears, and two years later she immigrated to Australia permanently, returning by government invitation to become the first artistic director of the new Australian Ballet (1963), a position she held until 1974, jointly with the Australian-born dancer Robert Helpmann for the last nine years (1965–74). The Borovansky Ballet, or what remained of it, was merged with the newly founded company and a permanent ballet presence in Australia was born.

During her Australian years, van Praagh devoted herself tirelessly to sowing the seeds of the British classical ballet tradition in the then not especially promising soil of a country devoted to athletics. Upon arriving in Australia in June 1963, she embarked on a tour of the Australian provinces, visiting every state to conduct auditions for the Australian Ballet. The summer was spent in planning, the company being formed and coming together for the first time on September 3. Eight weeks were spent in rehearsals in Melbourne, which became the central base of operations for the new formation.

At its inception, the Australian Ballet consisted of 44 members: a corps de ballet of 16

Peggy van Praagh, with Frederick Ashton.

women and 12 men, 12 soloists and 4 principals. Of these young people, 42 were native Australians, and two were especially imported, one, Caj Selling, as a principal dancer and the other, Karl Welander, as a senior soloist. The news of the formation of the Australian Ballet created a considerable stir both in Australia and abroad. No fewer than 11 of the dancers returned to their homeland to take part in the project and Ninette de Valois lent Ray Powell in the role of ballet-master to help van Praagh in the formation of her company, eventually extending the loan indefinitely. The remaining 31 dancers were students, some trained in the Royal Ballet School in London, some in Australian schools and some drawn from the Borovansky Company. The problems involved in developing a uniform style for a company whose members had been trained in such a variety of dance traditions were formidable but eventually were successfully overcome. The original repertory of the Australian Ballet consisted of standard classics (*Les Sylphides, Swan Lake, Coppelia*), revivals of British ballets (*Les Rendezvous, Lady and the Fool, One in Five*), and a few new works, including *Melbourne Cup*, choreographed by Rex Reid, *Just for Fun* (Ray Powell), and *The Night is a Sorceress* (Reid), which was actually a revival of a work earlier performed in Melbourne by the Victorian Ballet Guild. The company gave its first performance in Sydney on November 3 with **Sonia Arova** and the famous Danish *premier danseur* Erik Bruhn as guest artists, and there and in other Australian cities it had a most encouraging success.

By 1965, van Praagh felt sufficiently confident to take the Australian Ballet abroad to the International Festival of Dance in Paris, where she won a prize for her production of *Giselle*. Two years later, she took her company on a wider international tour, performing in London, Canada, China and elsewhere in the Far East. Everywhere, the Australian Ballet, so recently put together, was recognized as a company of international stature.

Apart from her teaching chores, van Praagh took on all of the major and ceaseless administrative burdens of running a ballet company. It was she who was responsible for the continuous efforts to raise money, lobby politicians, charm wealthy patrons, give interviews, and see to the publicity. Robert Helpmann, who had made a celebrated name for himself in London, was of inestimable service to her in this last regard simply by being the kind of attention-getting personality whose every activity caught the notice of the press. Her one regret as the increasing success of her company began to make itself felt was that she had been unable to find or develop in Australia a choreographer of the caliber of those such as John Cranko and Kenneth MacMillan, whom she had sponsored in Britain during her years with Sadler's Wells.

In 1970, van Praagh's distinctive achievement was recognized, and her career was crowned when she was created a Dame Commander of the British Empire by Queen *Elizabeth II, the female equivalent of a knighthood, one of eight ballerinas to have been so honored. The others were *Adeline Genée (1878–1970), Ninette de Valois (1898–2001), Marie Rambert (1888–1982), Alicia Markova (1910—), *Margot Fonteyn (1919–1991), *Beryl Grey (1927—) and Merle Park (1937—). Among her other activities, Dame Peggy van Praagh was an examiner and council member of the Cecchetti Society from 1935 and taught for the council in its summer seminars in the United States. She staged *Soirée Musicale* for the Robert Joffrey Ballet in America, and in 1961 was a guest teacher for the Ballet International du Marquis de Cuevas, during which time she gave lessons to Rudolf Nureyev upon his defection from Soviet Union. She was the author of two books, *How I Became a Dancer* (1954), written for children, and *The Choreographic Art* (1963) with Peter Brinson, a work which had a broad influence in its field.

In her later years, Dame Peggy, who had never married, was afflicted with serious arthritis and in 1974 was forced to retire for a time because of ill health following her third hip operation. After her recovery, however, she returned to teach at the Australian Ballet School (1975–82) of which she was a council member, and returned to the Australian Ballet as artistic director for two final years (1977–79), after which she retired definitively at the age of 69. Still suffering from arthritis, van Praagh was in poor health for the last decade of her life; she died in Melbourne on January 15, 1990, at the age of 79. A handsome, dark-haired woman, gifted with a warm and vivid personality and a keen intelligence, she was noted for her theatrical flair, musical sensibility, administrative and educational skills, and great zest for life. Her death was mourned internationally, above all in Australia where it was treated in the press and other media as an event of national importance.

Dame Peggy van Praagh was a fine dancer, whose strong technique and expressive dramatic range made her especially effective in semi-character roles, but she was not a great one and in the history of British ballet she has been overshadowed by her better-known contemporaries. She was, however, a great dance teacher and one who inspired enormous dedication in her students. One of her most significant achievements as an instructor was the manner in which she managed to reconcile the requirements of the traditional conservative ballet audience while at the same time deepening and satisfying the creative needs of a youthful and vigorous company through the undertaking of innovative and experimental ballets. A pioneer and a missionary, van Praagh devoted the last half of her professional life to sowing the seeds that would lead to the successful development of two national ballets of international stature, one in Canada and the other in Australia. To the extent that ballet has become an accepted and permanent feature of the cultural life of both of these large and increasingly important countries, she has earned her place in the history of world dance.

SOURCES:

Andrews, Deborah, ed. *The Annual of Obituary, 1990.* Chicago-London, 1991.

Music Department, Free Library of Philadelphia.

Sexton, Christopher. *Peggy van Praagh: A Life of Dance.* South Melbourne, 1985.

Van Praagh, Peggy. *How I Became a Dancer.* London, 1954.

———, and Peter Vincent. *The Choreographic Art.* London, 1963.

SUGGESTED READING:

Bland, Alexander. *The Royal Ballet: The First Fifty Years.* Garden City, NY, 1981.

White, Joan W., ed. *Twentieth Century Dance in Britain.* London, 1985.

Woodcock, Sarah C. *The Sadler's Wells Royal Ballet.* London, 1991.

Robert H. Hewsen,
Professor of History,
Rowan University,
Glassboro, New Jersey

Van Rensselaer, Catherine (1734–1803).

See Schuyler, Catherine Van Rensselaer.

Van Rensselaer, Maria Van Cortlandt (1645–c. 1688)

Colonial American administrator of the Dutch patroonship of Rensselaerswyck. Born Maria Van Cortlandt on July 20, 1645, in New Amsterdam (later New York City); died on January 24, 1688 or 1699, in Albany, New York; daughter of Oloffe Stevense Van Cortlandt (a merchant and city official) and Anna (Loockermans) Van Cortlandt; married Jeremias Van Rensselaer (first patroon, or proprietor, of Rensselaerswyck), on July 12, 1662 (died 1674); children: Kiliaen, Anna, Hendrick, Maria, Johannes, Jeremias.

Maria Van Cortlandt Van Rensselaer was born in 1645 into a wealthy family of New Amsterdam, the Dutch colonial settlement that later became New York City. The third of seven children of one of the city's wealthiest citizens, she married Jeremias Van Rensselaer, a son of another wealthy family, in 1662. Jeremias directed his family's large estate, Rensselaerswyck, near Albany, New York. When he died in 1674, the couple's four sons and two daughters were too young to administer the 24-square-mile property, so Maria took over, assisted by her brother, Stephanus Van Cortlandt.

Van Rensselaer soon proved that she was skilled in business and management. Colonial turmoil, however, led to difficulties with her gaining clear title to the property after the English conquest of the area in 1664, the Dutch reconquest in 1673, and the final English reconquest in 1674. In November 1685, she finally won clear title to the estate, but during this time she also dealt with a 1675 challenge from her husband's younger brother Nicholas, who arrived from the Netherlands, claiming that he, not Van Rensselaer, should be director. Eventually, he became director, Van Rensselaer became treasurer, and her brother Stephanus became bookkeeper.

In 1678, when Nicholas died and Stephanus was living far away in New York City, the work of running the estate again fell squarely on Van Rensselaer, who faced increasing debts. Although she had never regained her strength after the birth of her last child, she continued to run the estate and to fight the claims of others that they should receive a share of the property. In addition, she found homes and trades for most of her children, who had not been provided for in her husband's will. By the time she died at age 42 or 43, she had successfully secured title to the estate—the richest land patent in the colony—for her children.

SOURCES:

James, Edward T., ed. *Notable American Women, 1607–1950.* Cambridge, MA: The Belknap Press of Harvard University, 1971.

Kelly Winters,
freelance writer

Van Rensselaer, Mariana (1851–1934)

American author and first female professional art critic. Name variations: M.G. Van Rensselaer; Mrs. Schuyler Van Rensselaer. Born Mariana Alley Griswold on February 21, 1851, in New York City; died of arteriosclerosis on January 20, 1934, in New York City; daughter of George and Lydia (Alley) Griswold; educated privately and in Europe; married Schuyler

Van Rensselaer (an engineer), on April 14, 1873 (died 1884); children: George Griswold (b. 1875).

Selected works: Book of American Figure Painters *(1886);* American Etchers *(1886);* Henry Hobson Richardson and His Works *(1888);* Six Portraits *(1889);* English Cathedrals *(1892);* Art Out of Doors *(1893);* Shall We Ask for the Suffrage *(1894);* One Man Who Was Content *(stories, 1897);* History of the City of New York in the Seventeenth Century *(2 vols., 1909);* Poems *(1910);* Many Children *(children's poetry, 1921).*

The second of seven children, Mariana Van Rensselaer was born Mariana Griswold in 1851 into a wealthy New York family of long standing. She was tutored at home and studied in Dresden, Germany, where in 1873 she married Schuyler Van Rensselaer, an engineer and fellow New Yorker, and descendant of the patroons of Rensselaerswyck. They had one son, George, two years later. They resided in New Brunswick, New Jersey, traveling to Europe and throughout the United States.

Van Rensselaer began her writing career in 1876 with the publication of a poem in *Harper's Magazine* and an article on art in *American Architect and Building News*. She published other articles and reviews of art exhibitions in New York City after that. A devotee of pictorial realism, she published both *Book of American Figure Painters* and *American Etchers* in 1886.

Mariana Van Rensselaer

After her husband's death in 1884, Van Rensselaer moved to New York City to live with her mother. She also began writing her first important work in the field of architectural criticism, a series entitled "Recent American Architecture" in the *Century Magazine*. This led to the publication in 1888 of *Henry Hobson Richardson and His Works*, a study of the architect's work that is still a classic. She published studies of Renaissance and modern artists in *Six Portraits* in 1899, and was elected an honorary member of the American Institute of Architects a year later. In 1892, she published *English Cathe-*

drals, based on a series she had done for *Century Magazine*, followed by an introduction to landscape gardening, *Art Out of Doors*, in 1893. That same year, she became an honorary member of the Society of Landscape Artists.

Upon the sudden death of her son in 1894, Van Rensselaer became more interested in social issues. She taught literature at the University Settlement from 1894 to 1898 and was president of the women's auxiliary for two of those years. During this time, she wrote a collection of stories based in part on the slums of New York and their immigrant inhabitants, which she published as *One Man Who Was Content*. She was also a public school inspector for two years and served as president of the Public Education Association of New York City from 1899 to 1906. During her tenure, Van Rensselaer pressed to have reproductions of great art hung in every classroom. She also wrote a pamphlet arguing against women's suffrage entitled *Shall We Ask for the Suffrage*. Her opposition to the vote was based on her conviction that women, especially lower-class women, might be exploited by politicians and that they ought to concentrate instead on their families and the education of their children.

Interested in Colonial America, Van Rensselaer published a well-received two-volume *History of the City of New York in the Seventeenth Century* (1909). In 1910, Columbia University awarded her an honorary degree, and in 1923 she received a gold medal from the American Academy of Arts and Letters. Her other works include a book of romantic poetry and a volume of children's poetry. In a profile in *Notable American Women, 1607–1950*, John Early notes, "She always wrote for a general audience, and many of her books and articles depend heavily on the scholarship of others. But all her writings are shaped by her personal style and by her taste and intelligence." Van Rensselaer died in 1934.

SOURCES:

James, Edward T., ed. *Notable American Women, 1607–1950*. Cambridge, MA: The Belknap Press of Harvard University, 1971.

McHenry, Robert, ed. *Famous American Women*. NY: Dover, 1980.

Read, Phyllis J., and Bernard L. Witlieb. *The Book of Women's Firsts*. NY: Random House, 1992.

Kelly Winters,
freelance writer

Van Rensselaer, Martha
(1864–1932)

American home economist and educator. Born on June 21, 1864, in Randolph, New York; died of cancer on May 26, 1932, in New York City; daughter of

Henry Killian Van Rensselaer (a storekeeper and insurance agent) and Arvilla A. (Owen) Van Rensselaer (a schoolteacher and boardinghouse manager); educated at Chamberlain Institute; Cornell University, A.B., 1909.

Martha Van Rensselaer was born in 1864 in Randolph, New York, one of five children in a family of Dutch and Welsh ancestry. Her father was active in the Methodist Church and in politics, and her mother, a former schoolteacher who ran a boardinghouse, was also active in church and community affairs, including the women's suffrage movement. Although her parents were not wealthy, they were educated, and Van Rensselaer considered her home a source of gentility in the rural area in which they lived. From her parents, particularly her mother, Van Rensselaer learned that women possessed tremendous power in the home, but that they needed to be schooled to reach their full potential. Her education began at the coeducational Chamberlain Institute, a Methodist school where her father was a trustee. She graduated in 1884 and taught there as well as at other private schools for the next ten years.

Van Rensselaer also lectured at teachers' institutes, was active in women's clubs, and attended the Chautauqua Summer School, where she was secretary from 1894 to 1903 for the New York State Department of Public Instruction. In 1893, she switched from teaching to administration. She was nominated as one of two school commissioners of Cattaraugus County by a convention of the Women's Christian Temperance Union, and won the election. Although she was elected again in 1896, she failed in her bid for a third term in 1899.

As commissioner, she had assisted the efforts of the agricultural extension program at Cornell University, including *Anna Botsford Comstock's work using nature study to promote farming. When she realized from her visits to local farms that these educational efforts were failing to reach farm wives, Van Rensselaer accepted the invitation of Liberty Hyde Bailey, a professor of horticulture at Cornell, to organize an extension program for farmers' wives. This project involved her for the remainder of her life, and eventually evolved into the New York State College of Home Economics at Cornell University.

In January 1901, she published the first bulletin of the "Farmers' Wives' Reading Course." *Saving Steps* was originally distributed to 5,000 women who had signed up for the course; how-ever, within a few years there were 20,000 women enrolled and several local study groups had formed. The bulletins, which were published five times a year, addressed popular topics such as sanitation, interior decorating, nutrition, reading, dressmaking, and child care. Known as "Miss Van," Van Rensselaer also ran a boardinghouse in Ithaca for students and instructors.

Cornell University initiated resident, accredited home economics courses in 1903, when Bailey became dean of the College of Agriculture. He suggested to Van Rensselaer that she offer a class in homemaking, and in 1906 she began a more extensive course. The following year, a department of home economics was formed within the College of Agriculture, and Van Rensselaer was appointed co-chair with **Flora Rose**, a graduate of Kansas State Agricultural College.

In 1909, Van Rensselaer received her A.B. degree from Cornell, and in 1911 she and Rose became professors. Rose was in charge of resident teaching and research, while Van Rensselaer was involved with administration and extension work. By 1917, the program had expanded to include a four-year degree course in home economics, monthly bulletins, 200 Cornell Study Clubs, extension courses, work in the public schools, and Cornell's annual Home and Farm Week. In 1919, the department became a school within the College of Agriculture, and in 1925 it became the New York State College of Home Economics, with Van Rensselaer and Rose as co-directors. In 1929–30, the state allocated $1 million for the creation of a new home economics building, the Martha Van Rensselaer Hall at Cornell.

From 1914 to 1916, Van Rensselaer served as president of the American Home Economics Association, and also worked as homemaking editor for the journal *Delineator* from 1920 to 1926. During World War I, she directed the Home Conservation Division of the U.S. Food Administration, and in 1923 she served in Belgium with the American Relief Commission. She was also active in other home economics and health causes, including the White House Conference on Child Health and Protection, which met in 1930. Van Renssalaer died of cancer at St. Luke's Hospital in New York City in 1932, at age 68. She was buried in the Randolph Cemetery in New York.

SOURCES:

James, Edward T., ed. *Notable American Women, 1607–1950.* Cambridge, MA: The Belknap Press of Harvard University, 1971.

Kelly Winters,
freelance writer

Van Rensselaer, Mrs. Schuyler
(1851–1934).

See Van Rensselaer, Mariana.

van Schurmann, Anna Maria
(1607–1678)

Dutch scholar and artist. Name variations: Anna Maria van Schuurman or Schuurmann; van Schurman. Born on November 5, 1607, in Cologne, Germany; died on May 14, 1678, in Wieuwerd, Friesland; daughter of Frederik van Schurmann and Eva (von Harff) van Shurmann; never married; no children.

Writer, philosopher, theologian, and artist, Anna Maria van Schurmann was perhaps the most learned woman of 17th-century Europe. She was born in 1607, one of four children in a Calvinist family from the Dutch nobility, living in religious exile in Cologne. In 1610, the family returned to the Netherlands, settling in Utrecht. Van Schurmann was educated at home by her father. In accordance with Calvinist and Renaissance belief in the importance of education for women, van Schurmann, beginning at age two, received the same education as her brothers. By

Anna Maria van Schurmann

age eleven, she had demonstrated such a remarkable intellect that her parents decided to continue her classical training and forego instruction in the household skills other girls learned in preparation for marriage and motherhood. After Frederik van Schurmann's death in 1623, Anna Maria studied largely on her own. She mastered an extensive variety of subjects, including geography, astronomy, music, mathematics, and theology, the subject that would come to mean the most to her. She also composed poetry on religious issues in Dutch. Van Schurmann's accomplishments extended to the visual arts, where she excelled in painting, engraving, and embroidery. Numerous of her self-portraits survive, along with portraits done of family members and friends.

However, she was best known in her time for her exceptional knowledge of languages. Besides Dutch, she was fluent in French, German, Latin, Greek, and Hebrew. She also studied Eastern languages, including Turkish, Syrian, Arabic, and Ethiopian. This breadth of learning brought her early fame in the Netherlands and among the intellectual circles of Europe, where her astounding accomplishments as a scholar stimulated debate over the natural intelligence and capabilities of women.

Van Schurmann contributed to this debate as well. She became part of a wide network of learned men and women who contested philosophical and theological ideas through extensive correspondence. In the 1630s, she conducted one such debate with theologian André Rivet on the question of whether women should be educated. This debate was published as a *Dissertation* in 1641. In it, van Schurmann argues that not only do noblewoman have a right to devote themselves to scholarship, they are obligated to do so if they can, in order to find the path to salvation and virtue and so become better Christians. Throughout her writings defending women's education, this emphasis on its spiritual benefits brought van Schurmann the approval of many male scholars, who rejected as immoral the secular arguments for women's education.

In her late 20s, van Schurmann was allowed to attend lectures at the new university of Utrecht, the only woman given the privilege. Her former tutor in Greek and Hebrew, Gisbertus Voetius, was rector of the university and arranged a cubicle within which van Schurmann could hear lectures on theology and Asian languages without being seen by the male students. Under Voetius' influence, she began to turn away from poetry and painting as frivolous, and to concentrate more on spiritual matters.

On her mother's death in 1637, van Schurmann was left to care for two elderly aunts. This responsibility consumed much of her time, but she continued to correspond with philosophers and theologians across Europe. These included the French philosopher René Descartes, with whom she debated the nature of knowledge and reason. In 1648, she published a collection of these letters. In 1653, van Schurmann, her brother, and her aunts moved to Cologne to reclaim some family property, but by 1660 they had returned to the Netherlands and were living in a country estate outside Utrecht. By 1664, van Schurmann, age 57, resided alone, following the deaths of both aunts and her only surviving brother. This isolation, following a lifetime spent in the company of a devoted and supportive family, combined with her increasing religiosity, led van Schurmann to join a new Calvinist branch community in 1669. Its leader was Jean de Labadie, a Calvinist minister who broke from his church and established a Pietist community in Amsterdam. Van Schurmann was one of his earliest supporters; she followed him from Amsterdam to Westphalia, where the group sought asylum from persecution with her old friend *Elizabeth of Bohemia (1618–1680).

In 1673, van Schurmann published *Euklerion*, an autobiographical and spiritual work in which she explained her decision to join the Labadists as part of her spiritual path to God. The decision to join Labadie had cost van Schurmann the respect of many friends and colleagues; they were surprised and disappointed to learn that she was turning away from philosophy and the sciences to follow a small and unpopular sect of the Reformed Church. In *Euklerion*, she defended her choice and at the same time renounced much of her life's work. In particular, she rejected her *Dissertation*, claiming that spiritual fellowship and meditation on God was more important than learning; she thus rejected her own promotion of women's education. Written from the isolation of her small community, *Euklerion* served to sever most of van Schurmann's connections with her former friends and correspondents.

In 1675, the Labadists moved to Wieuwerd, in Friesland. There van Schurmann died at age 71 in 1678. Notwithstanding the loss of fame suffered in her final years, the "star of Utrecht" remained the model of the learned woman in Europe for decades after her death. Despite her later renunciation of her philosophical works, it is precisely these popular earlier works which have secured her reputation as part of the history of European philosophy, feminism, and Reformation theology.

SOURCES:

De Baar, Mirjam, *et al.*, eds. *Choosing the Better Part: Anna Maria van Schurman (1607–1678)*. Dordrecht, the Netherlands: Kluwer Academic, 1996.

Laura York, M.A. in History, University of California, Riverside, California

van Stockum, Hilda (b. 1908)

Dutch-born American writer and illustrator. Name variations: Hilda Van Stockum. Born on February 9, 1908 in Rotterdam, the Netherlands; daughter of Abraham John van Stockum and Olga (Boissevain) van Stockum; married Ervin Ross Marlin, on June 27, 1932; children: Olga; Brigid; Randal; Sheila; John; Elisabeth.

The career of children's writer Hilda van Stockum also includes book illustration, portrait painting, teaching, and translation. Born in the Netherlands, as a child van Stockum and her family traveled extensively with her father, a navy officer. After stays in Paris, the East Indies, and Switzerland, the family settled in Ireland, where van Stockum studied at the Dublin School of Art. She continued her education at the Amsterdam Academy of Art. Returning to Ireland in 1931, she worked as an art teacher and professional portrait painter, and also began illustrating children's books.

In 1932, she married E.R. Marlin, an American aviator, and moved to New York City, where she taught at a Montessori school. In 1934, van Stockum wrote and illustrated her first children's novel, *A Day on Skates: the Story of a Dutch Picnic*, which received the prestigious Newbery Honor Award in 1935. She then moved to Washington, D.C., and taught art and writing at the Institute of Lifetime Learning, while continuing to write herself. She became a U.S. citizen in 1936.

After a brief period of study at the Corcoran School of Art in 1937, van Stockum and her husband moved to Canada, where she concentrated on writing and illustrating her children's books, over 20 in all. Her books, set in Ireland, the U.S., and Holland, draw heavily on her childhood experiences as well as on her own children, and are recognized for their sensitive portrayal of her young characters. She also continued to illustrate for other authors, and translated numerous children's books into English. Van Stockum is also well known for her paintings, mainly still-life and portraiture, which were exhibited in one-woman shows from Dublin to the Netherlands to the U.S. from the 1950s to the 1970s. She and her husband returned to Washington in the 1960s, where she became president of the Children's Book Guild. In the 1980s, van Stockum retired to Hertfordshire, England.

SOURCES:

Chevalier, Tracy, ed. "Hilda van Stockum" in *Twentieth Century Children's Writers*. 3rd ed. Chicago, IL: St. James Press, 1989.

Commire, Anne, ed. "Hilda Van Stockum," in *Something About the Author*. Vol. 5. Detroit, MI: Gale Research, 1973.

Laura York, M.A. in History,
University of California,
Riverside, California

Van Vorst, Marie Louise

(1867–1936)

American author and reformer. Born on November 23, 1867, in New York City; died of pneumonia on December 16, 1936, in Florence, Italy; daughter of Hooper Cumming Van Vorst (a judge) and Josephine (Treat) Van Vorst; educated privately; married Count Gaetano Cagiati, on October 16, 1916; children: Frederick John (adopted).

Born in 1867, Marie Louise Van Vorst grew up in a prominent New York City family and was educated by private tutors. Although she had two brothers, she became closest to her brother John's wife, **Bessie McGinnis Van Vorst**. When Bessie was widowed around 1900, Marie joined her, and the two women went to France and began writing. Marie had already published poetry and prose in magazines, and Bessie had published letters in the *New York Evening Post*. Together, they wrote a light novel, *Bagsby's Daughter*, in 1901. Marie then wrote a more serious novel, perhaps as a result of her reading of *Mary E. Wilkins Freeman's 1901 book *The Portion of Labor*. Marie's next novel, *Philip Longstreth*, published in 1902, focused on a wealthy young man who is devoted to improving the lot of the poor, despite his family's opposition. Although this novel was technically flawed, the plot was well regarded by contemporaries.

The two women were by this time very interested in the plight of laborers, and decided that they needed practical experience of the working conditions of women factory employees. They returned to the United States and took aliases under which they secured jobs. Marie, as "Bell Ballard," worked in a shoe factory in Lynn, Massachusetts, and in cotton mills in the South; Bessie, as "Esther Kelly," worked in a pickle factory in Pittsburgh and a knitting mill near Buffalo. Drawing upon their experiences, they wrote *The Woman Who Toils; Being the Experiences of Two Ladies as Factory Girls* in 1903, an exposé of the poor living and working conditions faced by women and children. Prefaced with an introduction by President Theodore Roosevelt, the book represented a milestone in labor investigation and reporting, and attracted attention to the need for labor reform. The book was also notable for Marie Van Vorst's use of local dialect and dialogue, which added to its realism.

Of the two women, Marie became more widely known. After *The Woman Who Toils*, she wrote *Amanda of the Mill* (1905), a well-received novel set in a factory in the Blue Ridge Mountains. From 1906 to 1909, *Harper's Monthly* assigned Marie to write articles on "Rivers of the World," thus requiring her to travel to Europe and Africa. She also wrote poetry and fiction, including 15 more novels, which were not as well received as her earlier work.

During World War I, she became increasingly concerned about the situation in France, her adopted home, and volunteered to serve with the American Ambulance (field hospital) in Neuilly. Returning to the United States to lecture about her experiences and rally Americans to France's support, she also wrote *War Letters of an American Woman* (1916), a realistic account of life behind the front lines derived from letters written to friends and relatives.

In 1916, she married Count Gaetano Cagiati of Rome, in the Cathedral of Notre Dame in Paris. The couple adopted a son, but Marie did not allow her new-found family life to restrict her movement. In 1918, she became head of a commission that coordinated war relief for Italy. Four years later, she took up painting, exhibiting her work at the Sterner Galleries in New York City. She continued to work for women's rights until her death in 1936 in Florence, where she was buried.

SOURCES:

Edgerly, Lois Stiles, ed. and comp. *Give Her This Day*. Gardiner, ME: Tilbury House, 1990.

James, Edward T., ed. *Notable American Women, 1607–1950*. Cambridge, MA: The Belknap Press of Harvard University, 1971.

Kelly Winters,
freelance writer

Van Wagener, Isabella (c. 1797–1883).

See Truth, Sojourner.

Van Waters, Miriam (1887–1974)

American prison administrator, reformer, and social worker. Born on October 4, 1887, in Greensburg, Pennsylvania; died of pulmonary disease on January 17, 1974, in Framingham, Massachusetts; daughter of George Browne Van Waters (an Episcopalian minister) and Maude (Vosburg) Van Waters; University of Oregon, A.B., 1908, A.M., 1910; Clark University, Ph.D., 1913; children: Sarah Ann (adopted 1932).

A leader in women's corrections from the 1920s through the 1940s, Miriam Van Waters was born in Greensburg, Pennsylvania, in 1887. Her father was an Episcopal minister who believed in social responsibility, and in 1888 he moved the family to Portland, Oregon, where he began church colonization work. An adventurous child who enjoyed her new home, Van Waters once went with her father on a cougar hunt in the middle of the night. She was educated at home and then attended St. Helen's Hall, a local school founded by her father, from which she graduated in 1904. As a teenager, she assumed many domestic responsibilities because her father's pastoral career required him to travel frequently and her mother **Maude Vosburg Van Waters** often returned to Pennsylvania to be with her family. With the help of two uncles, Miriam managed the home and cared for her sisters, while administering to the needs of the rectory and visiting clergy.

Van Waters attended the University of Oregon, where she edited a literary magazine, wrote articles for the college newspaper, and acted in school plays. In 1908, she graduated with honors in philosophy and then earned an A.M. degree in psychology in 1910. She next applied for and won a fellowship at Clark University in Worcester, Massachusetts, where the psychology department was headed by G. Stanley Hall, and also studied with anthropologist Alexander Chamberlain. Van Waters earned her Ph.D. in 1913 with a dissertation on "The Adolescent Girl among Primitive Peoples," which recognized the validity of other cultures and showed an awareness of the power of female sexuality. In this, she anticipated the work of later anthropologists such as *Ruth Benedict and *Margaret Mead.

Van Waters was more interested in social reform than an academic career, however. In 1911, she visited the Boston Juvenile Court and noted the results of parental neglect and poor education. Two years later, she became an agent of the Boston Children's Aid Society and was placed in charge of young girls who were appearing before the court. She discovered that the girls charged with delinquency had also been suspected of unproven sexual offenses; not only were they considered "morally insane," they were deemed incapable of changing their behavior. Disagreeing with this assessment, Van Waters worked to improve court health-care services and to find foster homes for the girls. She became well known as a reformer, but the work exhausted her, and in 1914 she went back to Portland to run Frazer Hall, the county juvenile detention center. Soon after this, she was diagnosed with tuberculosis, and took three years off from work to recover.

In 1917, she passed a civil-service examination in Los Angeles, where she had gone to stay with friends. She was appointed superintendent of the county juvenile home, and successfully improved conditions there, leading to her appointment in 1919 to head El Retiro, another county home for delinquent girls that worked to prevent future delinquency. Van Waters tried to give the girls a sense of home and belonging and allowed them to govern themselves. Paying them wages, she also offered them a choice in their vocational training. She encouraged cultural activities, such as plays and poetry readings, and she saw that special occasions were celebrated. She opposed double standards that punished women more severely than men for sexual offenses and sought to validate and guide the young women's sexuality instead of repressing it. Her work at El Retiro attracted the attention of philanthropist **Ethel Sturges Dummer**, who funded Van Waters' national study of schools for delinquent girls, "Where Girls Go Right," published in 1922. Dummer provided additional aid as Van Waters wrote two other books, *Youth in Conflict* (1925) and *Parents on Probation* (1927), in which she found a correlation between the increasing mechanization of society and the increase in delinquency.

In 1920, Van Waters passed the California Bar Exam and was appointed referee of the Los Angeles Juvenile Court. She spoke at penal and social work conventions, and was invited by Justice Felix Frankfurter to examine juvenile facilities in Boston as part of the Harvard Law School Crime Survey. In 1929, she became a consultant to the National Commission on Law Enforcement, and prepared a study of juveniles who had broken federal laws. In *The Child Offender in the Federal System of Justice* (1932), she wrote about the failure of district courts to use juvenile court procedures or to supervise juvenile reformatories.

In 1932, Van Waters became superintendent of the Massachusetts Women's Reformatory in Framingham. She continued the liberal policies instituted by the previous superintendent, *Jessie Hodder, and increased medical and psychological services. She also organized clubs for inmates, whom she referred to as "students."

At the same time, as the mainstay of her family, Van Waters paid for her siblings' education and support when her father's investments failed, and gave jobs at Framingham to her brother and his wife. She did not marry, but in 1932, she adopted a ten-year-old girl, Sarah Ann, whom she had met when the child was seven and a ward of the Los Angeles Juvenile Court.

On November 10, 1947, when a prisoner committed suicide at Framingham. Van Waters' methods of governing the prison were investigated by political opponents, and she was charged with condoning lesbianism, illegally hiring former inmates as employees at the prison, and failing to supervise indenture for day work or adult education. In January 1949, she was fired, but the decision was reversed by a special governor's commission. Friends and supporters rallied to her defense, and she was cleared of most of the charges at a final hearing. Van Waters returned to work at Framingham and was welcomed emotionally by the inmates. She served as superintendent until 1957, earning praise for her liberal principles and receiving several honorary degrees. She lived near the prison until 1974, when she died of pulmonary disease.

SOURCES:
Freedman, Estelle B. *Maternal Justice: Miriam Van Waters and the Female Reform Tradition, 1887–1974.* Chicago, IL: University of Chicago Press, 1996.
Sicherman, Barbara, and Carol Hurd Green, eds. *Notable American Women: The Modern Period.* Cambridge, MA: The Belknap Press of Harvard University, 1980.

Kelly Winters,
freelance writer

Van Zandt, Marie (1858–1919)

American opera singer. Born on October 8, 1858, in New York City; died on December 31, 1919, in Cannes, France; daughter of James Rose Van Zandt (a clerk) and Jennie Van Zandt (a concert singer); studied singing with her mother, Adelina Patti, and Francesco Lamperti; married Mikhail Petrovitch de Tscherinoff (a Russian state councilor and professor), on April 27, 1898.

Marie Van Zandt was born in New York City in 1858, to a father who was a clerk and a mother who was a successful concert singer in Brooklyn. Under the stage name Madame Vanzini, **Jennie Van Zandt** undertook an operatic career that took her to Paris, Milan, and London, and throughout America. Marie accompanied her mother to Europe, where she was briefly educated in a convent school. She was first coached in singing by her mother, who ended her public career in order to teach her. Later, Marie studied with *Adelina Patti and Francesco Lamperti in Milan.

Van Zandt debuted in Turin in early 1879 at age 20, performing the role of Zerlina in *Don Giovanni*. In May 1879, she made her first appearance in London, singing Amina in *La Sonnambula*. The following year, she sang in Paris, and her performance in *Mignon* led to a five-year contract with the Opéra-Comique; with that company, she rapidly achieved fame. Van Zandt's best-known role, however, was the title character in Léo Delibes' *Lakmé*, an opera said to be written specifically for her.

In 1884, she experienced a disaster when she lost her voice during a performance of *Il Barbiere di Siviglia* (*The Barber of Seville*) and was unable to finish. She was replaced by **Cécile Mézeray**. Although her friends attributed the cause to overwork, others maintained incorrectly that she was drunk, and her reputation suffered. When she returned to the stage after three months, there were riots against her that were probably politically motivated. She requested to be released from her contract, and this was promptly granted.

Van Zandt then went to St. Petersburg, where she was welcomed by the Russians. She also sang at London's Covent Garden and in various venues in America, including the Metropolitan Opera House, before spending the remainder of her career in Europe. She enjoyed a successful season at the Opéra-Comique in 1896–97 before her 1898 marriage to Mikhail Petrovitch de Tscherinoff, a Russian state councilor and professor at the Imperial Academy of Moscow. She then retired from the stage and spent several years residing in Moscow. Following the Russian Revolution, she made her home in Cannes, France, where she died in 1919.

SOURCES:
James, Edward T., ed. *Notable American Women, 1607–1950.* Cambridge, MA: The Belknap Press of Harvard University Press, 1971.
McHenry, Robert, ed. *Famous American Women.* NY: Dover, 1980.

Kelly Winters,
freelance writer

Varano, Costanza (fl. 1445).

See Sforza, Costanza.

Varda, Agnes (1928—)

Award-winning French filmmaker whose films, a creative mixture of both fictional and documentary *styles, anticipated the French New Wave school of filmmaking. Name variations: Agnès Varda. Born in Ixelles, Belgium, on May 30, 1928, but raised in France; daughter of Eugène Jean Varda (an engineer) and Christiane (Pasquet) Varda; studied art history before pursuing a career in photography; married Jacques Demy (a French filmmaker), on January 8, 1962 (died 1990); children: **Rosalie Demy**; Mathieu Demy.*

Working in Paris as official photographer of the Théâtre National Populaire when she made her first film, La Pointe-Courte (1954), considered to be a major influence on the French cinema movement of the 1960s known as the New Wave; after a series of shorts, released second feature-length film, Cleo from 5 to 7, which brought international attention and was her first commercial success (1961); has since written and directed feature-length and short films in Europe and the U.S. which are known for their blend of personal history, social commentary, and dramatic intensity seen from a feminist perspective.

Filmography: La Pointe-Courte *(1954);* O saisons, ô châteaux *(Oh Seasons, Oh Chateaux, short, 1957);* L'Opéra-Mouffe *(short);* Du côté de la d'côte *(short, 1958);* Cléo de cinq à sept *(Cleo from 5 to 7, 1961);* Salut les Cubains *(Salute the Cubans, short, 1963);* Le Bonheur *(Happiness, 1964);* Les Créatures *(The Creatures, 1966);* Elsa *(short, 1967),* Loin du Vietnam *(filmed essay, co-director, 1967);* Uncle Yanko *(short, 1968);* The Black Panthers *(short, 1968);* Lion's Love *(1969);* Nausicaa *(television documentary, 1970);* Daguerreotypes *(1975);* Réponses de femmes *(film essay, 1975);* Plaisir d'amour en Iran *(1976);* L'une chante, l'autre pas *(One Sings, the Other Doesn't, 1976);* Mur Murs *(1980);* Documenteur *(1980);* Une minute pour une image *(One Minute for One Image, 1982);* Ulysse *(1982);* Le Dites-Caryatides *(The So-called Cariatids, 1984);* 7P., cuis., S. de B . . . *(7 rooms, kitchen, bath, 1984);* Sans toit ni loi *(Without Roof or Law, also called* Vagabond, *1985);* T'as de beaux escaliers, tu sais *(1986);* Le Petit Amour *(1987);* Kung Fu Master *(1987);* Jane B. par Agnès V *(1988);* Jacquot de Nantes *(1990);* Les demoiselles on eu 25 ans *(1992);* L'Univers de Jacques Demy *(The Universe of Jacques Demy, 1993);* Les 101 nuits *(The One Hundred and One Nights, 1994);* Les glaneurs et la glaneuse *(The Gleaners and I, 1999).*

Agnes Varda remembers her initial hint of the cinema revolution she helped create. It came in 1954 as she was editing her first film, *La Pointe-Courte,* when her editor mentioned that her picture reminded him of Luchino Visconti's 1948 Italian neo-realist film *La Terra Trema.*

"Who's Visconti?," she wanted to know. Years later, long after she had been called "the Grandmother of the New Wave," Varda admitted that she made that first film, at 25 years of age, "without having seen twenty-five films. Not even ten."

She had, in fact, been intent on a career in photography when she discovered the creative possibilities of movies. She was born, one of five children, on May 30, 1928, in suburban Brussels, Belgium. Her mother was French and her father was Greek. Varda moved with her family to France when she was a child and came of age during World War II in Montpellier, in the south of France, where her parents had moved to escape the Nazi occupation in the north. Not far away from Montpellier was a fishing village perched on the Mediterranean coast which would lend its name to her first picture, but it was to Paris that Varda traveled after the war to enroll in classical studies at the Lycée Victor-Duruy and the Sorbonne. Sculpture and painting proved especially interesting to her, and she transferred to a four-year course of study at the school of the Louvre Museum, specializing in art history. She planned to become a museum curator. But she was soon bored by the heavy load of art theory her courses required, and in an effort to find a more practical means of making a living, she began taking night courses at the Vaugirard school of photography. By 1951, she had been named the official photographer for the Théâtre National Populaire, an organization founded in post-World War II France with the goal of creating popular interest in serious theatrical works. She would not relinquish the post until she had made her second feature-length film in 1961. Her work with the theater exposed her to the creative energies of postwar Paris and the new, innovative and sometimes controversial work for which the TNP was known; and two of its actors would take the leading roles in the film she began shooting during 1953—a film that was later hailed by one critic as "the first bell in an immense concert of bells."

The idea for *La Pointe-Courte* came to her when she shot some 8-millimeter footage of the fishing village near her family home for a childhood friend who had become terminally ill. While still photography had provided her with a good living, Varda soon realized that the effect of a moving image on a viewer provoked stronger and more immediate reactions, both emotional and intellectual, while at the same time capturing a sense of place as no single photograph could. "I believe that people are made not only of the places where they were brought up," she once said, "but of those they love." *La Pointe-Courte,* which she wrote after friends encouraged her to explore this idea on film, tells the story of a recently married couple who return to the village where the husband spent his childhood. The wife, however, is a cosmopolitan Parisienne who comes to loathe the very different lifestyle of the village—a lifestyle carefully laid out in the scenes of village life which are interwoven with the couple's story. While Varda cast her leads with two actors from the TNP, she used actual villagers in actual situations for the other part of the story—a daring mixture of fiction and real life never before seen in French cinema. It was so daring, in fact, that the film galvanized a group of young filmmakers and writers that included François Truffaut, Eric Rohmer, Jean-Luc Godard and Claude Chabrol, the front line of what would become a style of filmmaking so different from anything that had come before in France that it came to be called *la nouvelle vague*, or the New Wave. Varda's use of real locations rather than studio sets, a hand-held camera, natural lighting and an unrehearsed atmosphere in the scenes she captured in *La Pointe-Courte* so excited these neophyte directors that Varda could barely follow their enthusiastic reactions at a screening of the film for the bible of the New Wave, the magazine *Cahiers du Cinéma*. "They referred to a thousand films," Varda said, admitting she knew none of the titles, "all speaking quickly, arguing with animation. I was nobody, ignorant, the only girl among the men of the New Wave."

She would, in fact, remain outside the New Wave's inner circle; and in histories of the New Wave, she is often relegated to a more intellectually and politically oriented "Left Bank Group" of filmmakers. Indeed, she would not make another feature film for seven years, turning instead to short subjects and documentaries after the modest success of *La Pointe-Courte*. She also returned to her career as a still photographer, shooting photographs for magazines until the French Government Tourist Office gave her a commission to make two short travel films. The resulting films, *O saisons, ô châteaux* (*Oh Seasons, Oh Chateaux*, 1957) and *Du côté de la d'côte* (1958), both in color, proved to be very unconventional travel films. Varda did not admire the lavish houses and private beaches of the rich, a fact made clear in both films. In place of the expected melange of tourist sites, she produced films that made playful fun of aspects of modern life in France, contrasting, for example, the elaborate clothing of French models with the older and sometimes rundown buildings they posed against, or comparing the beaches available for public use with the lavish recreational preserves of the wealthy. Some of her other short works, like her

first film, were just as intensely personal and just as tightly bound to a strong sense of place. The 1958 documentary *L'Opéra-Mouffe*, for example, recorded how her reactions to a familiar neighborhood changed when she was pregnant with her first child, examining through her eyes a number of residents of the Left Bank's rue de Mouffetard. Her pregnancy was a result of her relationship with the great French director Jacques Demy (best known for *The Umbrellas of Cherbourg*), whom she had met at the Toulouse Film Festival, where one of her short films had been entered; the two would marry in 1962, but not before Varda made the film that brought her international attention, *Cléo de cinq à sept* (*Cleo from 5 to 7*).

The film examines 90 minutes in the life of a Parisian singer (played by another of Varda's actor friends from the TNP) who fears she has developed stomach cancer and is awaiting the results of the medical tests she undergoes at the beginning of the picture. Agnes used the story to examine another of her favorite themes, how the passage of time affects what she called "the wounds of the soul." Most of the film is centered around a long walk that Cleo takes through the city of Paris, observing party revellers and talking to a young soldier who, under normal circumstances, she might have ignored. It becomes a walk of self-realization and spiritual development. At the beginning of the movie, Cleo makes the comment that "being ugly is like being dead." Accustomed to being the object of looks from others, she begins, in her journey through Paris, to become a "subject who looks." In contrast to her lavish lifestyle in a fashionable apartment, Cleo encounters scenes of suffering on the streets of Paris that make her own life seem trivial and superficial. (Varda told an interviewer in the late 1990s that she would like to modernize the story with a remake starring **Madonna**, and replacing cancer with AIDS.) The film was an instant success in France and was the first of Varda's films to be shown in mainstream American theaters rather than in the small art houses in which *La Pointe-Courte* had found a home.

Varda defied predictions that her marriage to Demy would cut short her career by creating a second major full-length feature (*Le Bonheur*) and two documentaries during the first years of the union. She had complained that *Cléo* threatened to stereotype her as a director of films about "dying blond singers," and she chose a very different subject for *Le Bonheur* (*Happiness*, 1964). In writing the scenario, Varda claimed that she was influenced by old photographs which recalled memories of happy times, particularly vacations, and by looking at Impressionist paintings. She called it a story "told in the content and style of Impressionist painters." While *Le Bonheur*'s idyllic settings—lush and sunny natural visuals, summer picnics, and vivid colors—helped to make it one of her best-known films, it also contains a jolting plot. A youthful carpenter from the Parisian suburbs, seemingly happily married and with children, falls in love with a young woman working at the nearby post office. He suggests to his wife that the postal worker move in with the family, in what he thinks is a quite "natural" combination. The carpenter is shocked when his wife refuses—he thinks it shows that she is too possessive—and then is stunned when she drowns herself.

Some writers believe that the major point of the film is that there is no genuine line between the "real" world and the world of film, a viewpoint reinforced by the fact that the actors were all actual family members—the French television actor Jean Claude Drouet, his wife **Claire Drouet**, and their children. And Varda, who has said that she enjoys playing with colors in many of her films, uses colors which do not reinforce the mood of particular scenes but, instead, actually seem to clash with what is happening on screen. In her view, it is a technique likely to cause viewers to become more than "voyeurs" or passive spectators. Although some of Varda's admirers were put off by the film, regarding it as an attempt at a fantasy rather than her usual reality-based documentary style (she herself called it "a beautiful fruit that tastes of cruelty"), it won a number of awards, including the Silver Bear at the Berlin film festival and the David Selznick award.

A similar theme pervaded Varda's *Les Créatures* (*The Creatures*, 1966). Photographed in black and white but including sections tinted in color, the film explored the relationship between illusion and reality. *Les Créatures* portrays the visit of a married couple to an island in Britanny. Both are recovering from injuries suffered in an automobile accident; the wife is unable to speak and the husband, a writer of science fiction, is recovering from both physical and emotional injuries. During the time that couple spend on the island, the husband works on a new book he is writing, incorporating into the story actual people he meets there. In another Varda juxtaposition of "fiction" and reality, he even plays chess with the "creatures" in the book in a successful bid to destroy forces that he believes are threatening to them. *Les Créatures* was not a financial success, and from 1966 and 1975 Varda would be unable to obtain outside financing for making films.

When Demy was offered a three-year contract with Columbia Pictures in 1967, Varda settled easily into the creative life of Hollywood and into America's political left by making several documentaries for French television about, among other subjects, the Black Panthers and the anti-Vietnam War movement. She was fascinated by San Francisco and in 1969 produced, in color, an homage to hippie culture entitled *Lion's Love*, a film which also lampooned some of her experiences in Hollywood. But like Demy, who directed only one picture in Hollywood, Varda found it difficult to find a place in the studio-dominated atmosphere of American filmmaking. During these years, she later said, she was "at a standstill. Not of inspiration, but of courage," and she would later record her frustrations in two documentaries about Hollywood, *Mur Murs* and *Documenteur*. A question raised in both short films is the nature of reality: is it "objective" (the literal picture that the camera sees) or "subjective" (what those on screen see)? In fact, the title of the second film, *Documenteur*, is a kind of pun, a combination of the French words for "documentary" and "liar." In effect, Varda seems to be raising the questions of whether documentaries contain fiction, as well as how much truth is in "fictional" films. Of the two films, *Mur Murs* gathered the most critical

Agnes Varda

praise, winning the Josef von Sternberg prize at the Mannheim festival and the grand prize at the Florence film festival.

Demy and Varda remained in California until the early 1970s, by which time Varda had given birth to a second child. She returned to Paris and to familiar territory with her 1974 documentary *Daguerreotypes*, about the street where she had set up her first photography studio, the rue Daguerre (where she still lives); and by turning her increasing interest in the feminist movement into a filmed essay called *Réponses de femmes* in 1974. She had been active in the feminist movement since the 1950s, when she had joined a group of politically liberal French women to protest the anti-contraceptive policies of the country's Communist Party; and later, in the 1960s, she had publicly supported a group of prominent French women, including the actress *Jeanne Moreau and the novelist *Marguerite Duras, who challenged the government to arrest them under the then-current law for having had abortions.

I'm more loved than well-known.

—Agnes Varda

The struggle for women's rights was reflected in Varda's next feature film, *L'une chant, l'autre pas (One Sings, the Other Doesn't)*, released in 1976. It was the story of two women, friends since childhood, whose lives take very different courses, which they relate to each other in a series of letters and postcards over a ten-year period. Pomme is a protest singer active in leftist causes who takes up with an Iranian boyfriend, suffers under the repressive anti-feminist laws of Iran when she moves there with him, and moves back to France with her children, where she is able to retake control of her life. Suzanne, on the other hand, finds herself married to an emotionally troubled man who commits suicide, forcing her to move back to her home village with her two children, where she is ostracized to such a degree for being unable to attract another husband that she marries a man whom she doesn't love. At the end of the film, the two women reunite and discuss how their lives might have been different had they enjoyed the freedom to make different choices.

L'une chante became one of Varda's most popular films and won a Grand Prix at the Taormina film festival The film is unique in the sense that it is Varda's only film dealing directly with the women's movement. The legal right to an abortion had recently been established in France; early in the film, Pomme helps Suzanne obtain an abortion. Part of the film is a recreation of the Bobigny trial, a trial in France in

1972 of four women accused of obtaining an abortion for the daughter of one of them; included in this section of the film is a lawyer who was actually involved in the trial.

By now, Varda had developed a style of film making she referred to as *cinécriture* (film-writing), a reference to her opinion that making a good film is similar to writing a good novel. "A well-written film is equally a well-made film," she said. "The rhythm of the direction and editing have been felt and thought like the choices a writer makes—dense phrases or not, the kinds of words, the frequency of adverbs, parentheses, chapters which continue the story or go against it." She told one interviewer, for example, that at least part of the inspiration for the way she constructed and shot *La Pointe-Courte* had been taken from the novel *Wild Palms* by one of her favorite authors, William Faulkner.

She refined her *cinécriture* even further with 1985's *Sans Toit ni Loi*, released in English as *Vagabond*. The film is a marvel of careful construction, drawing the viewer into the mystery surrounding the death of a "wandering character," a teenage drifter named Mona, whose body is discovered in a ditch at the beginning of the film. The young woman's story is told in a series of flashbacks (narrated by Varda) and in interviews with people who came in contact with her—a truck driver, an old woman, an immigrant worker, and others—each of whom offers a different view of her. Just as she had explored in *La Pointe-Courte* the way in which her characters' backgrounds influence how they view their surroundings, Varda examined in *Vagabond* how that influence extends to how we perceive other people. She herself claims that she did not understand Mona—there is something about Mona, she noted, that "both attracts and repels me"—lending credence to rumors that Mona was based on an actual "street person."

Although Varda began *Vagabond* with only a two-page scenario, by this time she had gained enough of a national reputation that she was able to secure financing from French television and the French minister of culture, among others. Like many of her films, *Vagabond* mixes nonprofessionals—a variety of mechanics, workers, and some real drifters—with professional actors. The theme of people's alienation from other people, apparent in Varda's other films, appears again: Mona, the character most alienated, seems to be unreached by the other characters, although all of the other characters turn out to be interconnected (often to know each other casually) in some way. The film appears to be edited to cause the audience to be concerned about Mona's unreachability, and some critics believe the ending—Mona's death—is intended to produce a sense of relief rather than grief. Varda commented that she hoped the film would cause viewers to question how they would have reacted to Mona personally. Would they, she asked, have given Mona a ride if she were a hitchhiker?

Uncharacteristically, Varda test-marketed the film, giving test showings to focus groups whose responses became a basis for editing the preliminary version of more than 140 minutes down to slightly less than two hours. The film was well received by critics—some of whom were intrigued by the fact that it pretends to be a documentary but is, in fact, a fictional film. Critics also praised the film highly for its sense of authenticity, its lyrical structure, and the striking imagery used in the film. It won a Cesar for actress **Sandrine Bonnaire**, who played Mona, and won the Golden Lion. "It's perfectly evident why this film won the Golden Lion at the 1985 Venice Film Festival," film critic *****Pauline Kael** told her *New Yorker* readers on the film's American release in 1986. "It's the work of a visual artist." And Roger Ebert wondered after seeing the film, "Although many have shared our time, how many have truly known us?"

The 1980s saw the release of two more films for which Varda was much praised. Her friendship with the French actress **Jane Birkin** resulted in the documentary *Jane B. par Agnès V.* in 1986; and the feature film *Kung Fu Master*, released in 1987, was a dark-tinged coming-of-age story in which Varda cast her son, Mathieu, and Birkin's daughter **Charlotte Gainsbourg** as the love interests. All the while she was working on yet a third picture, a tender mixture of documentary and imagined biography about her husband, who had become terminally ill and who died in 1990, the same year Varda's tribute to him, *Jacquot de Nantes*, was released in France. Again blurring the line between fiction and fact, Varda told Demy's life story using actual interviews with Demy and those who had known him interspersed with fictional recreations of episodes from his life. Agnes called the film an "evocation" of Demy's life, and still photographs of Demy are prominent in it. Parts of the film are playful: the main character, Jacques, appears early and demands that the credits appear immediately, instead of at the end. In what appears to be another Varda device to remind the audience that they are only watching a story, the credits promptly appear. Varda would produce a second, more traditional documentary, *The Universe of Jacques Demy*, in 1993.

Varda turned to more light-hearted material in 1994 with *Les 101 Nuits* (*The One Hundred and One Nights*), which she made to mark the centenary of the French film industry. It was her first outright comedy, and she stuffed it with as many celebrities as she could talk into appearing in it, from **Catherine Deneuve** to Robert De Niro, all of whom materialize while the film's 101-year-old "Mr. Cinema" (played by the French actor Michel Piccoli) reminisces about the favorite films of his long life. "The whole thing was an opportunity to make some references to films I love and to have visitors, because on a first level, cinema is about stars," she said. "Whatever we love—the auteur theory, the directors—what people see is faces on the screen." It was a remarkable statement from the woman who, nearly 30 years earlier, had never heard of Luchino Visconti.

As she entered her fifth decade of making films, the motivation for her filmmaking came under her scrutiny. Taking Millet's famous painting *The Gleaners* for her inspiration, Varda spent seven months in the French countryside with a digital video camera and a small crew to make *Les glaneurs and la glaneuse* (released in English as *The Gleaners and I*), ostensibly a documentary about scavengers of rural fields, lonely beaches and urban trash cans but equally about her own career of picking through the lives of her characters on screen to arrive at basic truths about the human condition. Varda herself appears frequently on camera in the picture, discussing everything from the wrinkle patterns on the backs of her hands to a collection of discarded, heart-shaped potatoes she gathered during her seven months of scavenging. She turned 72 as *The Gleaners and I* premiered at the 2000 New York Film Festival. "I'm somewhat of a leftover myself," she joked at the time, pointing out that she had three grandchildren to occupy her, "so you don't do movies like a machine." No one could ever accuse Agnes Varda of that particular method of filmmaking in her idiosyncratic career, and the observations she has collected on film over the years remain fresh and piquant for all to share.

SOURCES:

Flitterman-Lewis, Sandy. *To Desire Differently: Feminism and the French Cinema.* Urbana, IL: University of Illinois Press, 1990.

Heyward, Susan, and Ginette Vincendeau, eds. *French Film: Text and Contexts.* London: Routledge, 1990.

Pallister, Janis. *French-Speaking Women Film Directors.* Teaneck, NJ: Fairleigh Dickinson University Press, 1997.

Smith, Alison. *Agnes Varda.* NY: St. Martin's Press, 1998.

Varda, Agnes. "Agnes Varda: A Conversation with Barbara Quart," in *Film Quarterly.* Vol. 40, no. 2. Winter 1986–87, pp. 3–10.

———. *Varda par Agnes.* Paris: Cahiers du Cinéma, 1994.

SUGGESTED READING:

Acker, Ally. *Reel Women.* NY: Continuum, 1991.

Arnes, Roy. *French Cinema since 1946.* Cranburg, NJ: Barnes, 1970.

Bandy, Mary Lea, ed. *Rediscovering French Film.* NY: Museum of Modern Art, 1983.

Buss, Robin. *The French through their Films.* NY: Ungar, 1988.

Foster, Gwendolyn Audrey. *Women Film Directors: An International Bio-Critical Dictionary.* Westport, CT: Greenwood Press, 1995.

Hayward, Susan. *French National Cinema.* London: Routledge, 1993.

COLLECTIONS:

Varda's films are held by her company, Cine-Tamaris, and her films are still studied at film institutes such as the Cinema Studies Institute of New York University or the Centre Universitaire Americain du Cinema et de la Critique in Paris.

Norman Powers,
writer-producer, Chelsea Lane Productions,
New York, New York, and **Niles Holt**,
Professor of History,
Illinois State University, Normal, Illinois

Vare, Glenna Collett (1903–1989)

American golfer who won more amateur golf championships than any other athlete and brought a new power and accuracy to the game. Name variations: Glenna Collett. Born in Providence, Rhode Island, on June 20, 1903; died on February 3, 1989, in Gulfstream, Florida; daughter of Ada Collett and George Collett; married Edward Vare, in 1931.

Even today many women are forced to leave a sport when their amateur status ends. That this is not the case in golf is due in part to Glenna Collett Vare. Over her long career, she won numerous championships in an era when only amateur competition existed. Her career was so remarkable that she attracted the attention of many sportswriters. Gradually it became accepted that golf was a sport for women as well as men and that they, too, could become professionals. Before Glenna Collett Vare, one sportswriter's comments were typical of most, "The women swing at the ball as though they were beating off purse-snatchers with an umbrella." When Vare came on the course, such comments ceased.

Vare was born Glenna Collett in Providence, Rhode Island, in 1903, the daughter of George and **Ada Collett**. Athletics were important in the Collett family. Glenna, who played baseball and tennis with her brother, was also an outstanding swimmer and diver. Her interest in athletics coincided with the "Golden Age of Sports" in the 1920s, when sports celebrities and participating in new sports were the rage. George Collett took his daughter to the Metaco-

ment Golf Course in East Providence when she was 13, and she added golf to her expanding list. Her enthusiasm grew two years later when she watched famed golfer Bobby Jones in an exhibition match. Vare began to work daily with Alex Smith, a Scottish golfer, to develop her powerful swing. She won the Berthellyn Cup in Philadelphia in 1921 and for the next decade was virtually unbeatable.

The public believed that a woman playing golf would be weak and inaccurate, but Vare soon proved that assumption wrong. She once drove a ball 307 yards off the tee. Her long, powerful drives were accurate as well, attracting the attention of journalists who wrote of her exploits. In 1922, Vare won the U.S. Women's Amateur championship, the first of six. A year later, she took the Canadian Women's Amateur. In 1924, probably her best year, Vare won 59 out of the 60 events she entered.

Although the Curtis Cup, featuring American and English women, had been established in 1905, the United States Golf Association (USGA) did not agree to make it a regular event until Vare arranged for a group of American women to play in Great Britain in 1930.

After Vare married in 1931, her playing dropped off for the next few years. In 1935, she was back on the course. Over 15,000 spectators came to watch her compete against *Patty Berg, when Vare won her sixth U.S. Women's Amateur championship. She then began to play less frequently, but never totally set aside her clubs. At age 56, she won the Rhode Island State championship. At 83, she was still on the course, participating in her 62nd straight Rhode Island Invitational Tournament, at Pointe Judith.

SOURCES:

Collett, Glenna. *Ladies in the Rough.* NY: Alfred A. Knopf, 1928.

Condon, Robert J. *Great Women Athletes of the 20th Century.* Jefferson, NC: McFarland, 1991.

Harvin, Al. "Glenna Collett Vare, 85, Golfer," in *The New York Times Biographical Service.* February 1989, p. 135.

Hollander, Phyllis. *100 Greatest Women in Sports.* NY: Grosset & Dunlap, 1976.

Sonderberg, Paul, and Helen Washington, eds. *The Big Book of Halls of Fame in the United States and Canada.* NY: R.R. Bowker, 1977.

Woolum, Janet. *Outstanding Women Athletes.* Phoenix, AZ: Oryx Press, 1992.

Karin L. Haag,
freelance writer,
Athens, Georgia

Varley, Isabella (1821–1887).

See Banks, Isabella.

Várnay, Astrid (1918—)

Swedish-born American operatic soprano. Name variations: Astrid Varnay. Born Ibolyka Astrid Várnay on April 25, 1918, in Stockholm, Sweden; came to the United States, 1923, became a naturalized citizen, 1943; *daughter of Alexander Várnay (a tenor and stage director) and Maria (Yavor) Várnay (an operatic soprano); studied voice with her mother, and later with Weigert; married Hermann O. Weigert (a conductor), in 1944.*

Astrid Várnay was born in 1918, the daughter of Alexander Várnay and **Maria Yavor Várnay**. Her mother was a coloratura soprano in the European opera, and her father, a tenor, later became a stage director. They were both of Hungarian ancestry and were working for the Royal Opera in Stockholm, Sweden, when she was born. Five years later, the Várnays moved to South America, where they worked in the opera houses in Rio de Janeiro and Buenos Aires. Astrid accompanied them to work, and the colorful atmosphere of the opera filled her earliest memories.

Soon after the family moved to the United States in 1923, Alexander died. Astrid and Maria lived in Brooklyn, then in Jersey City, where Várnay began studying the piano at age 11. Planning to become a concert pianist, she continued these studies throughout high school, and sang at her high school graduation. Her classmates, impressed by her talent, predicted that she would become a member of the Metropolitan Opera by 1950. However, Várnay, who still assumed that she would become a pianist and not a singer, realized that she would also have to obtain practical job skills in order to make a living. She had studied commercial subjects in high school, and after graduation secured a job as a typist, and

Astrid Várnay

then worked in a bookstore. Eventually she realized that her piano technique would never be good enough for her to succeed as a concert pianist, and in 1938 she stopped studying piano and began voice training with her mother. Várnay studied for a year and a half, learning not just her own parts, but entire operas. The two would spend summer evenings sitting together as she sang an opera and her mother tapped out the orchestral rhythms. Throughout her singing career, she continued this habit of studying the full opera, and considered it an essential practice for any opera singer.

In 1939, Maria Várnay sought out a more advanced teacher for her daughter. Hermann O. Weigert, assistant conductor for the Metropolitan Opera, offered to train Astrid, and by the end of a year she had learned 13 solo parts in Wagnerian operas. In 1941, she earned a contract to sing with the Metropolitan Opera for the 1941–42 season, and made her debut in *Die Walküre*, in which she sang the part of Sieglinde when *Lotte Lehmann became ill. Appearing in a hastily made costume, with no rehearsal, she impressed both critics and audience alike. Várnay continued to sing with the Met for the rest of her career. She became an American citizen in 1943, and the following year married Weigert. In 1946, she repeated her feat of 1941, appearing in a performance of *Tristan und Isolde* on short notice with no rehearsal.

Known for her interpretations not only of Wagner but also of Richard Strauss, especially the roles of Herodias and Klytemnestra in *Salome* and *Elektra*, Várnay also added Italian roles from *Aïda*, *La Gioconda*, and *Otello* to her repertoire. By the end of the 1950–51 season, she had sung 13 of the 14 soprano parts in Richard Wagner's operas and had made acclaimed recordings of the *Ring* cycle. Várnay began singing mezzo-soprano roles after 1962. Having appeared at major opera houses in Bayreuth, Milan, London, and Buenos Aires, she retired to Munich in 1979.

SOURCES:
Current Biography, 1951. NY: H.W. Wilson, 1951.
Harrap's Illustrated Dictionary of Music and Musicians. NY: Harrap's, 1989.
Morehead, Philip D., and Anne MacNeil. *The New International Dictionary of Music.* Meridian, 1991.
Warrack, John, and Ewan West, eds. *The Oxford Dictionary of Opera.* Oxford: Oxford University Press, 1992.

Kelly Winters,
freelance writer

Varnhagen, Rahel (1771–1833)

Jewish-German salonnière and letter writer whose Berlin salons (1789–1806 and 1819–33) attracted many well-known personages—men and women—of various social classes, religions, and occupations. Name variations: Rahel Levin changed to Rahel Robert in 1810, baptized Antonie Friederike in 1814, married name Rahel Varnhagen or Rahel Varnhagen von Ense. Pronunciation: RA-hell VARN-ha-gen. Born Rahel Levin on May 19, 1771, in Berlin, Germany; died in Berlin in 1833; daughter of Chaie Levin and Markus Levin (a Jewish Berlin banker); converted from Judaism to Christianity in 1814; married Karl August Varnhagen von Ense, in 1814; no children.

Published some of her letters anonymously in Cotta's "Morgenblatt für die gebildete Stände" (1812) and in various journals until her death; best known for her salons and extensive correspondence, which continued until her death (1833).

Works: anonymous publications of selected letters in "Morgenblatt für gebildete Stände" (1812); Schweizerisches Museum (1816); Die Wage (1821); Der Gesellschafter oder Blätter für Geist und Herz (1821); Eos (1826); Berlinische Blätter für Deutsche Frauen (1829); posthumous collection of her letters, edited by Karl Varnhagen von Ense, Rahel: Ein Buch des Andenkens für ihre Freunde (1833); posthumous collections of her letters with various people, including David Veit (1861), Karl Varnhagen von Ense (1874–75), Karoline von Humboldt (1896), Alexander von der Marwitz (1925), Pauline Wiesel (1982), and Rebecca Friedländer (1988).

To read the correspondence of Rahel Varnhagen is to experience life, with all its joys and sorrows, its contemplations and whims, its questions and complexities. Likewise, to have visited her salon in the Jägerstrasse in Berlin at its apex in the 1790s would have been to see life in its widest diversity, with aristocrats and intellectuals, actresses and professors, Jews and Christians gathering out of pure delight for stimulating conversation and company. Indeed, to follow Rahel Varnhagen's life and writings is an exercise in social and intellectual history that very few other writers provide us to any comparable extent.

In many ways, Rahel's life epitomizes that of other Jewish women living in Berlin at the turn of the 19th century—*Dorothea Mendelssohn and *Henriette Herz, to name two famous contemporaries. All seized the opportunities that opened up to them as Jews following the reforms of Moses Mendelssohn and Gotthold Ephraim Lessing in that all three women became centers of an intellectual life that seemed ready to break barriers of religion and gender. All, however, were also caught within the contradictions that

the enlightened despotism of Frederick II the Great brought. While Frederick the Great eased certain laws that restricted the Jews' freedom of movement and expression, mostly to help build the militaristic Prussian state, Jews still faced long-standing anti-Semitism and legal inequalities. For all three women, conversion to Christianity became a part of the process of assimilation, although certainly not a foolproof solution. And as Jewish women, they were hindered doubly by the contradictions that promoted education for both sexes while refusing to establish institutional policies to enact such measures.

Rahel, the name by which her friends and then scholars called her, was born to **Chaie Levin** and the banker Markus Levin on May 19, 1771. The exact date is one that biographers have had to ascertain from Rahel's own assertions that all she knew about her birthday was that she was born on Whitsunday in 1771, for her father would allow no birthdays to be kept in the family. That family rule was among many that the domineering, strict father established in the household of five children, of which Rahel was the eldest. Frail and sickly as a child, Rahel received no formal education. In spite of these disadvantages, she soon amazed guests to the Levin home with her brilliance and wit.

With her father's death in 1789, Rahel acquired more freedom, and she began her earliest salon, at first an informal gathering of intellectuals in the garret of her home, where she served weak tea. To the evenings of the first salon came such writers and philosophers as August Wilhelm Schlegel, Friedrich Schlegel, Alexander von Humboldt, Wilhelm von Humboldt, Ludwig Tieck, Friedrich Schleiermacher, Johann G. Fichte, Friedrich de la Motte Fouqué, and Heinrich von Kleist; such aristocrats as Prince Louis Ferdinand and Prince de Ligne; and women who would become close friends, such as **Pauline Wiesel** and **Rebecca Friedländer**. Comments from those who frequented the salon attest to Rahel's talent of elevating conversation to a true art form. She was an "explorer of souls" whose profound expressions of thought and feeling "illuminated far wider expanses than sheets of dissertations," as Johann Wolfgang Goethe described her. To visit her salon must have been as stimulating and entertaining as an evening at the best theater in the city. Gustav von Brinckmann describes how her wit and frankness succeeded "in gradually collecting about her a numerous social circle, which was beyond comparison the most delightful and gifted in the whole of Berlin."

Salon guests began arriving at five o'clock to the modest garret in Jägerstrasse. There were no special invitations; everyone felt welcome. Rahel made no formal speeches, but rather continually interjected comments that tied together the threads of conversation or that energized reaction. If there were a lull in the conversation, there was music on the piano, with either Rahel, who was an accomplished pianist, or another guest performing a well-practiced piece or improvising. There also could be a spontaneous performance of a theater piece or a reading of a letter or literary work out loud. The group began to break up about nine o'clock, when the conversation and performances had reached their height.

Besides turning conversation into art, the first salon years also inspired the art of letter-writing. Rahel had always written letters to her childhood friends. Most of these early friends belonged to economically privileged Jewish families living in the neighborhood. Notes about theater performances and literary readings were commonplace in these early epistles. The full extent of these early relationships are still being explored by **Barbara Hahn**, who is working on a new edition of Rahel's letters, which will include previously unpublished childhood letters, many of them written in Hebrew script. Rahel's most famous letters have come down from the posthumous collection of letters that her husband Karl Varnhagen von Ense edited and published just after her death. In that collection one finds lively correspondence with her siblings, including her younger sister **Rose**, with the Jewish doctor David Veit, and with friends Friedrich von Gentz, Karl Gustav von Brinckmann, Alexander von der Marwitz, and August Karl von Finckenstein, in which Rahel lays out the philosophies of her life, speaking on the value of truth, friendship, nature, and letter writing. Rahel's success at corresponding lay in her ability to bring art to life and life to art. "Everything is thus, as it is—and only trivialities, small moments of eternity exist for me," she writes to Rebecca Friedländer. To Brinckmann, she conveys her appreciation of his letters: "At least believe me, dear friend, that no word in your four heavenly letters became lost; fun, seriousness, sorrow, everything to its place in my soul." Rahel elevated the reading and writing of letters to a literary sensation; she writes to Brinckmann: "even in a literary sense no one can appreciate, judge, and enjoy your letters better than I." Very few topics escaped Rahel's pen, including gender equality. At one point, she advises her sister to travel and visit new places, stressing: "We women need this doubly. . . . It's ignorance of human nature when people imagine our intellect to be different, constituted for other needs, and that we could live, for example, totally off the lives of our husbands or sons. This demand arises solely from the supposition that a woman's soul knows nothing higher than the demands and expectations of her husband, or the talents and desires of her children."

It was in the first salon that Rahel befriended Pauline Wiesel as well, who would become her lifelong correspondent. In the correspondence with Wiesel, which spanned over 25 years, the women formed a bond outside of a society that they felt excluded them. Wiesel's extramarital love affair with Prince Louis Ferdinand and her eventual divorce ostracized her from Berlin society. In Rahel's salon, Pauline Wiesel found the comfort of a neutral meeting ground for people of diverse backgrounds and opinions. Rahel and Pauline quickly established a friendship in which one complemented the other: "Such people as you should have had my musings, my circumspection, my rationality!" Rahel wrote, "Such people as I your courage, and your beauty. Otherwise we have completely what makes a talented human nature. Sense, senses, intellect, humor, sensitive heart, sense for art and nature—that means in our language, 'we love greenness.'" With Pauline, she refused to submit to the binding norms of society that force one to be untrue, opting instead to live on the margins: "The daggers in my poor, tender heart I want to bear: the lie I cannot bear: it must always come out again, as often as the course of life washes it ashore."

The later years of the first salon also inspired the correspondence between Rahel and another Jewish woman, Rebecca Friedländer (1783–1850), lasting from the years 1805 to 1810. Friedländer was a writer of romantic novels, turning to the profession after she had divorced. Like Pauline Wiesel, she felt isolated from society and her family due to her stormy personal history, and thus she found in Rahel and her salon a comforting tolerance. Considering that Rebecca asked for her letters back after Rahel's death, indicating that she wanted to burn them, readers only have Rahel's letters to Rebecca. Like those to Pauline Wiesel, they are rich in philosophy, literary comment, and social history. The relationship came to an end, however, after Rebecca published her novel *Schmerz der Liebe* in 1810, in which Rahel appeared as a character portrayed not in a totally favorable light. In letters, Rahel seems less concerned about the nature of the portrayal than about Rebecca's decision to reify her life and thoughts in a published form: "What should I really say after you have cited my own words to me 'that only a cook and an equipage stir me!' with what trust can I speak when you interpret me in such a way, not out of malice, but in seriousness." Despite the eventual falling out between the women, which also brought the end of the correspondence, in Rahel's letters to Rebecca, with all their unusual punctuation, orthography, and vocabulary, with their streams of thoughts and aphorisms, mixed with stories from the day and reports on the weather, readers can imagine how much the lively salon conversations must have resembled the letters and vice versa.

The first salon ended in 1806, after Napoleon's defeat of Prussia in Jena and the burgeoning anti-Semitism that Prussia's nationalism incurred. The French occupation of Berlin brought also financial hardship to Rahel's family. Rahel closed her salon but continued to remain in contact with other intellectuals by attending lectures such as those by the philosopher Ludwig Fichte. In 1809, her mother died; Rahel had cared for until her death. She also met Karl Varnhagen von Ense, her future husband, in 1808, who visited her daily in Charlottenburg. Karl was 23, Rahel 37, when the two first met.

Rahel
Varnhagen

Rahel had had two stormy love affairs, the first from 1796 to 1800 with the Count August Karl von Finckenstein, who had severed the relationship due to his family's unwillingness to accept the class differences between him and Rahel, and the second from 1802 to 1804 with the Spanish diplomat Raphael d'Urquijo, whose extreme jealousy and volatility became incompatible with Rahel's nature. Rahel was frank with Karl about these affairs and tolerant of Karl's own on-going affair with **Fanny Herz** in Hamburg. Rahel shared her letters with her previous lovers with Karl, who showed great interest in collecting and preserving them. The two shared many passions, including conversation, reading, theater, and letter writing.

Everything is thus, as it is—and only trivialities, small moments of eternity exist for me.

—Rahel Varnhagen

In fact, in 1812, Karl published Rahel's correspondence, anonymously, but with her consent, in Cotta's "Morgenblatt für gebildete Stände." These letters reveal Rahel's passion for Goethe, one that continued throughout her life. With their publication began the first outward signs that Rahel did indeed perceive her letters as literature that deserved a wider audience. Several publications of her correspondence would follow, often anonymously or under a pseudonym. Both Karl and Rahel also gathered one of the most extensive collections of 19th-century private documents and manuscripts of German cultural figures that exists. The Varnhagen Collection, housed in the Jagiellonska University Library in Krakow, Poland, contains Rahel's extensive correspondence, and is a particular storehouse of wealth for letters and manuscripts by and about other women of the time.

In 1813, Prussia declared war on France and thus began the anti-Napoleon "Befreiungskriege," or "Liberation Wars." Karl Varnhagen von Ense began diplomatic services with Russia. Out of fear for the warlike conditions, Rahel and her family fled in May from Berlin to Breslau. On May 30, she met up with her brother Ludwig Robert in Prague and began staying there with the actress **August Brede**. Distraught by the many wounded soldiers in the city, Rahel began to act energetically on their behalf. She wrote to friends in Berlin and garnered funds from them to support the efforts to help the wounded. She helped cook meals and gather clothing and supplies for the several hospitals and cloisters that were housing the sick. Her room in Prague became a kind of charity office where she organized funds and continued to meet with friends and intellectuals of the day. The war with France ended on May 30, 1814, and Rahel returned to Berlin.

On September 23, 1814, Rahel converted to Christianity at her bother Moritz's house in Berlin. Four days later, she married Karl Varnhagen von Ense. Conversion to Christianity was not uncommon, especially for Jewish women who married men not raised in Jewish households. Still, the motives behind such an act and the depth to which women such as Rahel were conscious of their Jewish heritage remain topics of scholarly inquiry. Clearly, several of Rahel's close friendships and her most profound correspondences were with Jewish men and women. If one looks closely at Rahel's letters, one finds scattered comments about her Jewishness, both pride and resentment. She writes to David Veit, "I have such a fantasy; as if an extraterrestrial being, as I am forced into this world, had stabbed me with these words like a dagger into the heart at the moment of my entrance: 'Yes, have feelings, see the world, as few see it, be great and noble, I cannot even take away your eternal thoughts, one thing has been forgotten, however; be a Jew!' In contrast to this seeming regret to have been born Jewish, on her deathbed, she remarked: "What for such a long time of my life was the greatest disgrace, the harshest sorrow and misfortune, to have been born a Jew, I would not like to forego it now at any price."

Between 1815 and 1819, Rahel lived in Vienna, Frankfurt am Main, and Karlsruhe, following the diplomatic career of her husband, who was involved in peace talks following Napoleon's defeat at Waterloo and then was appointed business correspondent for Prussia in Baden. Due to his democratic beliefs, however, Karl Varnhagen von Ense was asked to resign his post in 1819. Along with anti-democratic sentiments throughout Germany came also anti-Semitic outbreaks, such as the so-called "Hep-hep Stürme." Rahel and Karl returned to Berlin in 1819, when Rahel also began her second salon there.

Rahel's second salon was frequented by intellectuals such as Leopold Ranke, Georg Hegel, Alexander von Humboldt, and Fürst Pückler, and then later Heinrich Heine and *Bettina von Arnim. It did not have the same dynamic, unconventional qualities of the first salon, although Rahel's wit and intellect did attract visitors until her death in 1833. Salon visitors showed enthusiastic support for the July Revolution in 1830 in

France. They also lived through the devastation of the cholera epidemic in Berlin in summer 1831 as well as Goethe's death in March 1832.

Following Rahel's death, Karl Varnhagen von Ense's collection of her letters appeared in 1834. The edition met with great success and is still widely read. Scholars have in the meantime found shortcomings with Karl Varnhagen von Ense's editing methods and thus have issued new and more complete editions of Rahel's individual correspondences. With each new publication of her letters, readers stand in awe at the philosophical insights and at the breadth of human emotion, knowledge, and perception they hold. A letter from her, as Rahel herself wrote to Karl, "gives the past life, and the present shape," revealing her as "a marvel of nature, a comer-person in nature's concept of humanity."

SOURCES:

*Arendt, Hannah. *Rahel Varnhagen: The Life of a Jewish Woman*. Rev. ed. NY: Harcourt Brace Jovanovich, 1974.

Hahn, Barbara. *"Antworten Sie mir!" Rahel Levin Varnhagens Briefwechsel* (*"Answer me!" Rahel Levin Varnhagen's Correspondence*). Basel, Frankfurt am. Main: Stroemfeld/ Roter Stern, 1990.

*Key, Ellen. *Rahel Varnhagen: A Portrait*. Translated by Arthur G. Chater, with an introduction by Havelock Ellis. NY: Putnam, 1913.

Rahel Varnhagen: Eine jüdische Frau in der Berliner Romantik: 1771–1833. Ausstellung zum 160. Todestag (*Rahel Varnhagen: A Jewish Woman in Berlin Romanticism: 1771–1833. Exhibition for the 160th Anniversary of Her Death*). Berlin: Beratungsstelle für Frauen und Familien Berlin, 1993.

Rahel Varnhagen. Jeder Wunsch wird Frivolität genannt. Briefe und Tagebücher. Ed. by Marlis Gerhardt. Darmstadt: Luchterhand, 1983.

"Rahel Varnhagen: Translation of Selected Letters," in *Bitter Healing: German Women Writers 1700–1830*. Introduction, bibliography, and translation by Katherine R. Goodman. Ed. by Jeannine Blackwell and Susanne Zantop. Lincoln, NE: University of Nebraska Press, 1990, pp. 401–416.

Rebecca Friedländer: Briefe an eine Freundin. Rahel Varnhagen an Rebecca Friedländer. Ed. by Deborah Hertz. Cologne: Kiepenheuer & Witsch, 1988.

Scurla, Herbert. *Rahel Varnhagen. Die grosse Frauengestalt der deutschen Romantik*. Berlin: Verlag der Nation, 1962.

Stern, Carola. *Der Text meines Herzens: Das Leben der Rahel Varnhagen* (*The Text of My Heart: The Life of Rahel Varnhagen*). Reinbek bei Hamburg: Rowohlt, 1994.

Tewarson, Heidi Thomann. *Rahel Levin Varnhagen. Mit Selbstzeugnissen und Bilddokumenten* (*Rahel Levin Varnhagen. With Personal Testimonials and Pictorial Documents*). Reinbek: Rowohlt Taschenbuch, 1988.

Varnhagen, Rahel. *Gesammelte Werke*. Ed. by Konrad Feilchenfeldt, Uwe Schweikert, and Rahel E. Steiner. Munich: Matthes & Seitz, 1983 (contains a reprint of the original correspondence that Karl Varnhagen von Ense published posthumously in 1834, entitled *Rahel: Ein Buch des Andenkens für ihre Freunde*).

SUGGESTED READING:

Goodman, Katherine R. "The Cases of Varnhagen and Arnim," in *Dis/Closures: Women's Autobiography in Germany between 1790–1914*. NY: Peter Lang, 1986, pp. 73–120.

———. "The Impact of Rahel Varnhagen on Women in the Nineteenth Century," in *Gestaltet und gestaltend: Frauen in der deutschen Literatur*. Ed. by Marianne Burkhard. Amsterdam: Rodopi, 1981, pp. 125–153.

———. "Poesis and Praxis in Rahel Varnhagen's Letters," in *New German Critique*. Vol. 27, Fall 1982, pp. 123–139.

Hertz, Deborah. "Inside Assimilation: Rebecca Friedländer's Rahel Varnhagen," in *German Women in the Eighteenth and Nineteenth Centuries: A Social and Literary History*. Edited by Ruth-Ellen B. Joeres and Mary Jo Maynes. Bloomington, IN: Indiana University Press, 1986, pp. 271–288.

———. *Jewish High Society in Old Regime Berlin*. New Haven, CT: Yale University Press, 1988.

Tewarson, Heidi Thomann. *Rachel Levin Varnhagen: The Life and Work of a German Jewish Intellectual*. Lincoln, NE: University of Nebraska Press, 1999.

Weissberg, Liliane. "Turns of Emancipation: On Rahel Varnhagen's Letters," in *In the Shadow of Olympus: German Women Writers Around 1800*. Edited by Katherine R. Goodman and Edith Waldstein. Albany, NY: State University of New York Press, 1992, pp. 53–70.

———. "Writing on the Wall: The Letters of Rahel Varnhagen," in *New German Critique*. Vol. 36. Fall 1985, pp. 157–173.

COLLECTIONS:

Most of Rahel's original correspondence and manuscripts are in the Varnhagen Collection in the Jagiellonska University Library in Krakow, Poland.

Lorely French,
Professor of German and
Chair of the Humanities Division
at Pacific University,
Forest Grove, Oregon

Varo, Remedios (1906–1963)

Twentieth-century Surrealist painter in Spain and Mexico. Name variations: Maria de los Remedios Varo y Uranga. Born Maria de los Remedios Varo y Uranga on December 16, 1906, in Anglés, Spain; died on October 8, 1963; daughter of Rodrigo Varo y Zejalbo and Ignacia Uranga y Bergareche; married Gerardo Lizárraga, in 1930; married Benjamin Péret, in 1942; married Walter Gruen, around 1952.

Born in 1906 in Anglés, Spain, Remedios Varo was the daughter of Rodrigo Varo y Zejalbo and **Ignacia Uranga y Bergareche**. At an early age, she displayed a talent for drawing and painting and a fascination with a magical world that would later infuse her Surrealism. Varo also rebelled against the conservative Catholicism of her mother. Having settled in Madrid, her parents arranged for her to attend art and graphics schools, and by 15 she had gained admittance to the Academy of San Fernando, the most important art school in the Spanish capital. She received a broad and rigorous training in the graphic arts, met fellow student Salvador Dali, and in 1930 married another student, Gerardo Lizárraga.

Influenced by Surrealism, the young couple moved to Paris but returned to Spain in 1932, settling in Barcelona where the cultural and political climate was more liberating than in Madrid. A bohemian nonconformist, Varo began an affair with Esteban Francés while still living with Lizárraga. When the Spanish Civil War broke out in 1936, she also began a liaison with the French Surrealist poet Benjamin Péret, who had arrived in Barcelona to join the International Brigades. In 1937, Varo, Péret, and Francés went to Paris, with Lizárraga remaining behind to fight. Varo and Péret, who had no regular income, lived from odd jobs and whatever they could earn from their paintings and poetry. Varo earned some money through imitating Giorgio de Chirico paintings.

The Spanish Civil War ended in 1939, but Varo could not return home, because the Franco government had sealed the border to leftist exiles. Then World War II began, and ideological strife tore at France. Early in 1940, the police arrested Varo and held her in prison for several traumatic months. The Germans overran France about the time she was released. Varo and her leftist friends managed to escape France, helped by the Emergency Rescue Committee. From Marseilles, they went to Morocco and then to Mexico.

She and Péret joined a large contingent of other political refugees in Mexico. When he returned to France in 1947, Varo stayed in the Americas, with a new lover, Jean Nicolle. They lived in Venezuela for a couple of years, visiting members of her family who had immigrated there. In 1949, Varo and Nicolle returned to Mexico, and it became her homeland. Leaving Nicolle, she took up with Walter Gruen, whom she eventually married. He provided basic financial security, and Varo dedicated her energies to her art. Over the next decade, she painted prolifically, her works evolving from the Surrealism of the 1930s. Although her paintings were still infused with dream-like images drawn from the magical world of her imagination, Varo planned her canvases and techniques rather than allowing her subconscious to control the process. The influence of Hieronymus Bosch, El Greco, and Goya appears in some of her paintings. In 1958, she met her mother in France but could not enter Spain on her old Spanish Republic passport.

Remedios Varos was still productive and her fame increasing when she died of a heart attack on October 8, 1963. In Mexico City, the Palace of Fine Arts and the Museum of Modern Art held major retrospective exhibitions of her paintings, to great popular acclaim, in 1964, 1971, and 1983.

SOURCES:

Chadwick, Whitney. *Women Artists and the Surrealist Movement*. Boston, MA: New York Graphic Society, 1985.

Kaplan, Janet A. *Unexpected Journeys: The Art and Life of Remedios Varo*. NY: Abbeville Press, 1988.

Kendall W. Brown,
Professor of History,
Brigham Young University,
Provo, Utah

Varst (1894–1958).

See Stepanova, Varvara.

Vasconcellos, Karoline Michaëlis de (1851–1925)

Portuguese university professor and scholar. Name variations: Carolina Michaëlis de Vasconcelos. Born Karoline Wilhelmina Michaëlis in 1851 in Germany; died in 1925; married Joaquim de Vasconcellos (a historian), in 1876.

Karoline Michaëlis de Vasconcellos was born in Germany in 1851 but became a Portuguese citizen in 1876 when she married her husband, a Portuguese historian. She was known for her broad scholarship in the philology of Romance languages, and in 1911 became the first woman appointed to a university chair in Portugal. She is best known for her two-volume work *Cancioneiro da Ajuda* (1904), which discusses the role of women in the creation of early Portuguese poetry. She is also known for her 1902 work *A Infanta Dona Maria de Portugal e as Suas Damas* (The Infanta Dona Maria of Portugal and Her Ladies).

Vasconcellos believed in the necessity for education for women and for educational reform, and wrote extensively on the subject, particularly in *O Movimiento Feminista em Portugal* (The Feminist Movement in Portugal, 1901). When asked about this essay at the time, however, she commented that it was too early for a feminist movement to exist in Portugal, and that in order for feminism to take root, more Portuguese women needed to be educated and economically independent.

SOURCES:

Buck, Claire, ed. *The Bloomsbury Guide to Women's Literature.* NY: Prentice Hall, 1992.

Kelly Winters,
freelance writer

Vasey, Jessie (1897–1966)

Australian social reformer. Born Jessie Mary Halbert on October 19, 1897, in Roma, Queensland, Australia; died from a stroke on September 22, 1966; daughter of Joseph Halbert (a pastoralist) and Jessie (Dobbin) Halbert; University of Melbourne, B.A., 1921; married George Alan Vasey (an army officer), early 1920s (died 1945); children: George Alan (b. 1925), Robert (b. 1932).

Was a founding member of the Australian Imperial Forces Women's Association; established the War Widows' Craft Guild to improve plight of Australia's war widows (1946).

Jessie Vasey was born in Australia in 1897 and began her early education at Moreton Bay Girls' High School, where she boarded until 1911, when her family moved to the property known as "Tarcombe," near Aurel, Victoria. She then transferred to Lauriston Girls' School and continued her secondary education at Methodist Ladies' College in Kew. She earned a B.A. from the University of Melbourne in 1921, and also pursued interests she shared with her father, including his love of the bush and horses and his engagement in real estate.

Jessie married army officer George Alan Vasey in the early 1920s, and their son George was born in 1925. The family was posted to India in 1928, where they stayed until 1930. Returning home, Vasey gave birth to a second son, Robert, in 1932, and then lived again in India with her family from 1934 to 1936. During their stays, Vasey pursued an interest in Indian tapestry and antiques.

While living at the "Wantirna" estate in the Dandenongs during World War II, Vasey worked with the Australian Comforts Funds and was a founding member of the Australian Imperial Forces Women's Association. After her husband, then a major general, was killed in a plane crash near Cairns on March 5, 1945, she wrote to every war widow in Victoria and proposed that they form a craft guild to improve the plight of Australia's war widows. Following the inaugural meeting in November, the War Widows' Craft Guild was officially established on February 21, 1946, and Vasey was elected its first president.

Although Vasey was never able to persuade the Australian legislature to raise widows' pensions, she did gain improvements in their pensions and benefits under the Repatriation Health Scheme. She also proved adept at raising funds for her organization beyond government assistance, turning to donations from wealthy friends and proceeds from raffles to finance the Guild's projects. In this way, for instance, the Guild founded Caroline House, a home for eight elderly widows who concurrently served as resident caretakers of a ground-floor museum. In 1958, the Guild further formed the Vasey Housing Auxiliary, which by 1965 was housing 200 widows in Victoria alone. Jessie Vasey was named an Officer of the British Empire in 1950 and a Commander of the British Empire in 1963. She died three years later at the age of 68.

SOURCES:

Radi, Heather. *200 Australian Women.* NSW, Australia: Women's Redress Press, 1988.

Lisa S. Weitzman,
freelance writer,
Cleveland, Ohio

Vashti (fl. 5th c. BCE)

Queen of Persia in the Biblical story of Esther who, by defying her husband, was deposed and replaced by the compliant Esther. Name variations: Astin; Vastis; Vasthi; Wasti. Pronunciation: (Hebrew) wasti; (English) Vashti. What is known about Vashti is contained in the scroll of Esther, one of the writings in the Hebrew Scriptures. Her brief, but significant, story comprises the first 27 verses of this "early Jewish novella." Vashti was the wife of King Xerxes I (Ahasuerus in the Biblical text), and she may have been associated with Persian nobility (though the wives of Persian kings were required to come from specific Persian noble families, this was not always the case).

The story of Esther has traditionally enjoyed historical status. However, modern critics consider the major plot to be improbable, and many allow for only a kernel of historicity. Numerous features of the novella are collaborated by other historical sources, including the reign and personality of Ahasuerus, identified as Xerxes I, who was renowned for building great palaces, giving lavish parties, and displaying a bellicose temper. However, other details are either incompatible with known facts or considered too fantastical. The fact that Amestris, rather than Vashti, is recorded as Xerxes' queen during the period under study has raised questions about Vashti's historicity. However, given the numerous concubines and mistresses the king enjoyed, it is not implausible for him to have had more than one queen. Scholars today find study of the literary themes of the story to reveal important aspects of world history, even if not actual events. In terms of its inclusion in the Hebrew scriptures, the story of Esther provides an explanation for the origins of Purim, a Jewish festival. The core of the book dates to the period of Persian dominance (539–332 BCE), and its final form probably took shape in the 2nd century BCE.

Mentioned briefly in the Book of *Esther*, Vashti was a queen whose claim to fame is that she refused to be paraded in front of a group of men and then faded ignobly from the dramatic narrative. She was replaced in the king's harem by *Esther, who takes center stage as the heroine of the tale. In the annual enactment of this story during the Jewish festival of Purim, young girls abjure from playing Vashti and yearn to play Esther. The audience may even "boo" Vashti's entrance, identifying her as a rebellious and undesirable creature. However, even the anger fades quickly and Vashti is soon sidelined and forgotten.

Yet, Vashti actually plays a key role in the story of Esther and in the history of women. The unlikeliness that a queen would exhibit such courage as to go against the king's command (even an unreasonable one) is one argument given as evidence against the historicity of this story. Vashti is usually dismissed as a literary device for paving the way for Esther's entrance into the drama. Yet the narrative itself, and current interpretations of its meaning, allow us to let the spotlight linger on Vashti long enough to see in her an important character. Whether or not she actually was a historical personage, she is a figure in world history; and she is a predecessor to those who have made—or will make—history against the tide of cultural role expectations. But few are aware of her heroic legacy.

Though we know little about this woman, we do know some things about the setting in which we find her. We can infer from historical sources, as well as from the description of the young women in this story, that one such as Vashti would have been groomed for submission to male authority, obeisance to the king, obedience to the law, training in feminine grace and appeal, and perhaps intensive beauty treatments. There were exceptions to this. Historian Herodotus, who wrote an engaging history of Persia in the 5th century BCE, relates how *Artemisia I, upon her husband's death, served in a military expedition against the Greeks with "manliness." In fact, tales of her exploits were used by the king to humiliate his "womanly" men into greater bravery. Artemisia earned respect for her cunning and was even sought out

to give advice to Xerxes. Significantly, on one occasion, when Xerxes is pleased with Artemisia's counsel, he sends her off to take care of his bastard children as a reward.

Under Xerxes' rule, crossing the king could at times lead to unexpected clemency; however, the general expectation was that even mere disagreement with the king would end in death. When one of Xerxes' loyal subjects asked that the eldest of his five sons be spared from battle so that one might live to carry on the family responsibilities, the enraged king not only refused his request but cut that son in two and set each half on either side of the road as trail markers for the army to march through. As if to spoof his own nature, the impulsive king is reputed to have lashed and fettered the stormy sea as punishment for "wronging" him. In the Persian Empire thusly ruled, young maidens could be rounded up for the king's harem, young boys could be conscripted into service as eunuchs, and children of nobility were on occasion buried alive as a sacrifice to the gods. Such is the historical backdrop into which the tale of Vashti is spun.

The story of *Esther* opens with King Ahasuerus hosting a long and opulent house party (180 days). For the final, week-long repast, "drinking was by flagons, without restraint; for the king had given orders to all the officials of his palace to do as each desired." This lavish feast (literally "drinking bout") apparently was for men only, as Queen Vashti gave a separate, sparely described, banquet for the women. The implied reason for the king's six-month extravaganza is to allow the monarch to "display the great wealth of his kingdom and the splendor and pomp of his majesty." As a climax to this exhibition, Ahasuerus, "merry with wine," plans to show off the "crown" of his possessions. His wife Queen Vashti is ordered to appear with crown to display her beauty before his officials.

Incredibly, Vashti refuses to come at the king's command. Though the author gives no explanation for Vashti's momentous defiance, its setting in the midst of a drunken court, occupied for the moment only by men, suggests personal reserve and integrity to be the motive. It may also be possible that this woman, though groomed for compliance, is simply exerting her will. However, given the inviolability of the command of the king (a recurring theme in the story), it is questionable that Vashti would risk her life on a whim. Whether out of modesty or whim, the queen imposes a restraint on the king—whose will is tantamount to law.

Such brazenness from the queen stirs up a furor in the court. Burning with anger at this defiance, Ahasuerus consults his legal counselors for a course of action. The king's advisor, afraid that other wives will follow suit, recommends that Vashti be deposed as queen. In a twist on Vashti's own intentions, she is ordered "never again to come before King Ahasuerus." Her royal position is to be given to one "better than she" (i.e. more obedient). To quell any further rebellion, a law is to be set in motion that declares every man should be master in his own house, and every woman should honor and obey her husband. The full panoply of Persian law, administration, and communications systems is deployed in a frantic effort to restore and ensure order in the kingdom.

However, there is a hint that the exertion of power is not full consolation for a now lonely king. Though he appears to have second thoughts about the harsh edict he imposed on Vashti, the immutability of the law binds the autocrat to his own decree. To forestall further regret, the king's servants suggest that all the young virgins in the kingdom be gathered to the palace to vie for Vashti's vacated place in the harem. The girls are so gathered, and among them is Esther, a young "Jewess" who keeps her heritage a secret. Each girl receives 12 months of cosmetic and perfume treatment, which leads to an all-determining night spent in the king's bed. Only those who delight the king are invited back. Esther finds favor with the king, and he sets the royal crown on her head, making her queen "instead of Vashti." With a good excuse for celebration, the king gives another lavish banquet in Esther's honor. Vashti is now completely out of the picture. The drama moves on and weaves around an evil plot against the Jews, pitting Esther and her cousin Mordecai against the king's chief vizier, Haman.

Some interpreters identify Vashti's plunge into oblivion as a thinly veiled warning to brazen women. *Esther* may reflect a period of social turmoil when upper-class Israelite women were beginning to chafe at traditional societal expectations and constraints. If so, posits **Alice Laffey**, then "the details of this 'fiction' are meant to be didactic: do not mess with the sys-

Vashti

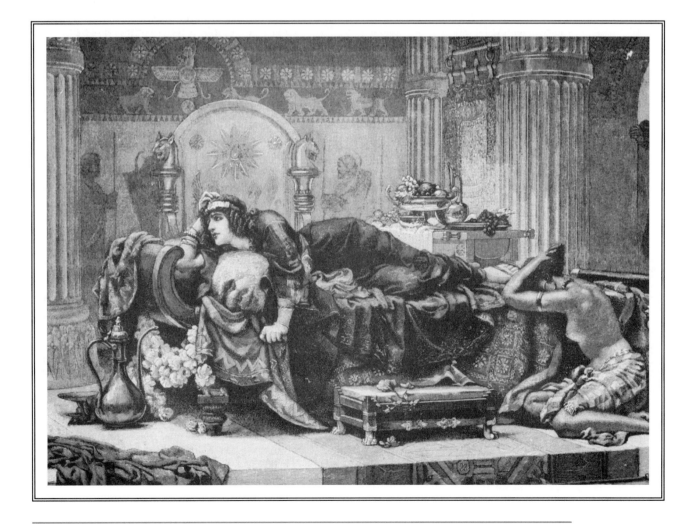

tem, or you too will be rejected." The joining of Vashti's downfall with Esther's triumph through compliance is seen as an attempt to reinforce stereotypic feminine behavior. While this interpretation may explain how the story has functioned in tradition, there are some literary features of the text that support an alternate reading of the author's intention.

In the introductory narrative, told for comedic effect, the king is portrayed as a partier and boaster, having to rely on and exert external power. Vashti, on the other hand, appears as proudly dignified, upheld by inner valor. While Ahasuerus can dispatch a law to force homage, the necessity of such a desperate measure reveals his personal ineffectiveness. Vashti has no strings to pull and no power-brokers to defend her, and yet she earns silent honor. To be sure, Vashti suffers the consequences of refusing to ingratiate the men, but it is the latter's foolishness that is put into relief in the story. The author's expansive and farcical account of the king's excessive behavior stands in striking contrast to the sparse and serious reporting of the queen's resolute deportment. Michael V. Fox claims that the author portrays the king as a "buffoon," "weak-willed, fickle, and self-centered." He and his advisers are "a twittery, silly-headed, cowardly lot who need to hide behind a law to reinforce their status in their homes." The author is making a crucial point here: outward success is not equal to inner worth. The king's elaborate palace and supreme power are facades; Vashti is the truly regal one. This implicit message was perhaps some solace to the majority of people in western Asia, whose dire poverty was mocked by such royal extravagance.

$\mathcal{I}$ propose that Vashti be reinstated on the throne along with her sister Esther, together to rule and guide the psyches and actions of women.

—Mary Gendler

Even if he is sympathetic, the author does not romanticize Vashti's actions. "The girl who pleases the king" was put in her stead, and Vashti was put in her place. She broke out of the pattern expected of women, and she paid a great cost for doing it. But this does not necessarily imply that the author condemns Vashti's actions. In fact, the story line develops so that, what Vashti sows, Esther reaps. Vashti's cause does not die with her banishment, it merely goes sub rosa. Though she could not fully blaze the trail, she enabled her successor, Esther, to have a foothold.

In fact, Esther is no less rebellious. Though Vashti would not come forth when summoned, Esther will come to the king without summons as the story unfolds. Upon discovering that Ahasuerus, encouraged by Haman, has sanctioned a pogrom (organized massacre) against all Jews, Esther risks her life to convince the king to rescind his murderous edict. Though entering the king's presence without a summons is punishable by death, retractable only if the monarch extends his scepter and welcomes the visitor, Esther takes the chance. Bedecked in her royal robes, the beautiful queen humbly seeks audience with the king; unpredictably, she is received. She dazzles and pleases Ahasuerus and Haman through a series of banquets. While the royal guard is lowered, this seemingly subservient queen persuades her husband to pronounce a counter-edict which implicates Haman and offsets the danger to the Jews. First Vashti would not lend her beauty to satisfy the king's boastful whims, and subsequently Esther uses her beauty to overturn his capricious laws. A woman's right to possess her own beauty has finally been vindicated.

The novella as a whole is replete with such "reversals of expectation," including episodes in which "the villain suffers the fate of his intended victim," writes **Katheryn Darr**. After Vashti's martyrdom, it is as if her spirit is resurrected; insubordinates gain full reign. Mordecai, who refuses to bow down to the imperious Haman, affronts the man in a way that is parallel to Vashti's provocation of Ahasuerus. As Vashti is deposed and women in general ordered to submit to their husbands, Mordecai is sentenced to be hanged and Jews in general massacred. However, as the Hebrew text announces, this time "the opposite happened." Interestingly, while in Vashti's case, there is no male defender to come to her rescue, in Mordecai's case, the female champion Esther brings deliverance. The villain Haman receives a twist on the elevation he sought. He is literally hoist on his own petard as the gallows he erected for his victim are employed for his own death.

Though at the end of the tale the surviving males (Ahasuerus and Mordecai) are paid token tribute, they are completely upstaged by the women protagonists. The first scene of the drama portrays the ruler's desperate attempt to ensure that the queen listen to the king; the climax of the story has the king taking orders from the queen. The cracks in the facade of male dominance, despite attempts to seal them up, now run all the way to the foundation of the court. As Fox states: "The king and his nobility are the butt of some rather broad irony. The world-ruler banishes a wife he cannot control, only to take on later a new one who controls him completely." In a world where the deadliest insult was to call a man worse than a woman, the author leaves open the possibility that women are wiser than men. Indeed, some commentators have conjectured that Vashti's name is a derivative of the Avestan word "vahista," which means "the best."

As Darr notes, it turns out that Esther, as well as Vashti, is "more than just a pretty face." These two women, through bravery and wit, together drive the course of events in this tragi-comedy. The tale as a whole announces that women are not just created by history, but they also are creators of history. Commentators who consider the teller of this story to be a "proto-feminist" have some basis for such a claim, especially given the context in which it was written.

Though deposed in the narrative, Vashti is rising to importance in women's history. Some early commentators on this defiant queen were so indignant at her lack of compliance that they deemed her "the wicked queen" and concocted for her a villainous pedigree of deeds and relations. Others more sympathetic to her cause considered her tactics unrealistic and foolish. However, contemporary feminists laud Vashti's "damn the consequences" heroism in openly defying authority and find in her forthright activism a model superior to Esther's stereotypic use of feminine wiles. Artist and writer **Marjory Zoet Bankson** celebrates that Vashti's "reckless strength," though it is costly, "meets a longing" in herself to refuse violation and exploitation.

We need not pit Vashti and Esther against one another. Those who shape the course of history are not of one mold. Vashti, though clearly cooperative on many matters (such as being a beautiful and gracious hostess for the women's banquet), comes to a point of uncompromising insistence on what she sees as right. Esther, after a history of compliance, continues to work within the status quo. Yet, despite her careful use of sexual tactics, Esther too reaches a point at which she throws role expectations to the wind. Though she was successful, that success was not predictable.

Because Vashti's actions are not personally triumphal, her story is either misinterpreted as a warning or ignored altogether. Certainly there is a realism to Vashti's harsh fate that we cannot deny, and many women will justifiably prefer more tempered approaches to promoting change. Nevertheless, Vashti's "failure" does not gainsay her efforts. As Esther's triumph is indebted to her forerunner, so have others gained from the likes of Vashti. Vashti not only stands with those who are condemned for their costly steps, but she also

walks before those who have succeeded in making positive strides. It was in her refusal to parade her beauty that Vashti's regal beauty was displayed for all the world to see.

PRIMARY SOURCE:
Esther (contained in *The New Oxford Annotated Bible*). New rev. standard version. NY: Oxford University Press, 1991.

SUPPLEMENTARY SOURCES AND SUGGESTED READING:

Baldwin, Joyce G. *Esther: An Introduction and Commentary.* Downer's Grove, IL: Intervarsity Press, 1984.
Bankson, Marjory Zoet. *Braided Streams: Esther and a Woman's Way of Growing.* San Diego, CA: Lura-Media, 1985.
Darr, Katheryn Pfisterer. *Far More Precious than Jewels: Perspectives on Biblical Women.* Louisville, KY: Westminster-John Knox, 1991.
Fox, Michael V. *Character and Ideology in the Book of Esther.* Columbia, SC: University of South Carolina Press, 1991.
Gendler, Mary. "The Restoration of Vashti," in Koltun's *The Jewish Woman.* NY: Schocken, 1976.
Herodotus. *The History.* Trans. by David Grene. Chicago, IL: University of Chicago Press, 1987.
Laffey, Alice. *An Introduction to the Old Testament: A Feminist Perspective.* Philadelphia, PA: Fortress Press, 1988.
Moore, Carey A. *The Anchor Bible: Esther.* NY: Doubleday, 1971.
Weems, Renita J. *Just a Sister Away.* San Diego, CA: LuraMedia, 1988.

Carol Lakey Hess
teaches at Princeton Theological Seminary
and is working on issues relating
to theology and gender

Vassiltschikov, Anna

Russian empress. Fifth wife of Ivan IV, tsar of Russia. Ivan IV also married *Anastasia Romanova (d. 1560) in February 1547; *Maria of Circassia (d. 1569) in August 1561; Marta Sobakin (d. 1571) in October 1571; Anna Koltoskaia (d. 1626) in April 1572 (divorced 1574); *Maria Nagaia (d. 1612); and Vassilissa Malentieva around 1576 (divorced 1577).

Vastis (fl. 5th c. BCE).

See Vashti.

Vaucher, Yvette (1929—)

Swiss mountaineer. Born Yvette Pilliard in Vallorbe, northeast of Geneva, Switzerland, in 1929; married Michel Vaucher (a mountaineer), in 1962.

Made first direct ascent of North Face of Dent Blanche (1966); made first female ascent of North Face of the Matterhorn.

Yvette Vaucher joined the disastrous 1971 International Everest Expedition during which one man died of exposure. Reports of squabbling sullied many reputations unfairly, including that of Vaucher. In 1951, she began rock climbing at the Salève. Four years later, she moved to Neuchâtel, took up free-fall parachuting, and made over 100 descents. Then, she formed a climbing team with Michel Vaucher. Yvette made many important climbs: the North Faces of the Matterhorn, Piz Badile, Triolet, Drus, Dent Blanche, Eiger, and Grandes Jorasses. She also climbed Ninagougo in Zaire and the West Ridge of Mt. McKinley in Alaska.

SOURCES:
Birkett, Bill, and Bill Peascod. *Women Climbing: 200 Years of Achievement.* London: A.&C. Black, 1989.

Vaughan, Helen Gwynne- (1879–1967).
See Gwynne-Vaughan, Helen.

Vaughan, Kate (c. 1852–1903).
See Fuller, Loïe for sidebar.

Vaughan, Sarah (1924–1990)

Grammy Award-winning African-American singer known for her unique combination of jazz, pop, and classical styles. Name variations: (nicknames) "Sassy" Sarah Vaughan; the Divine One; the Divine Miss Sarah. Born Sarah Vaughan on March 27, 1924, in Newark, New Jersey; died of lung cancer in California on April 4, 1990; only child of Ada Vaughan and Asbury "Jake" Vaughan; educated through junior year of high school; married George Treadwell, in 1946 (divorced 1958); married Clyde B. Atkins, in 1958 (divorced 1962); married Waymon Reed, in 1978 (divorced 1981); children: (adopted) daughter, Debra, known professionally as Paris Vaughan.

Sang and played piano and organ as a child in her family's Baptist church in Newark; by early teens, played and sang at local nightclubs and ballrooms; was hired by Earl Hines to sing with his band (1943), then with Billy Eckstine's band (1944), before striking out as a solo artist; gained international reputation under guidance of first husband and manager, and began a nearly 50-year career as a progressive jazz artist, pop singer, and concert performer, culminating in two Grammy awards; inducted into the Jazz Hall of Fame (1988).

One day in 1939, a stranger came to call on Jake and **Ada Vaughan** at their home in the "Down Neck" section of Newark, New Jersey, near the railroad station. He said he ran a nightclub in a less-than-genteel part of town and had been admiring the way their daughter Sarah played the piano and sang for his customers; so much so, that he wanted to give Sarah a full-time job playing every night. That was how the Vaughans found out what their 15-year-old daughter had been up to, why she was so tired during the day, and why her bedroom window was oddly open in the morning, even in the middle of winter. Although everyone knew that Sarah liked to sing and play, her parents were the last to find out how deeply she was committed to music.

Sarah Vaughan had been playing the organ and the piano at the New Zion Baptist Church every Sunday for as long as anyone could remember—practically, it seemed, since she was born in 1924. Both parents were musically inclined, Ada playing the piano and "Asbury" Jake strumming the guitar and singing some of the country and blues songs he'd learned in his native Virginia. Sarah was known both at church and at school for her musical talents, especially her singing. Even in grammar school, she was in the house by 5:15 every weekday to hear Bob Howard's program from the CBS station in New York, and would imitate his singing and playing style for her friends.

By the time she was in her teens, Vaughan and her friends were sneaking out at night to local ballrooms and clubs to hear the big bands that played Newark's night spots, especially the Adams Theater, where Earl "Fatha" Hines and his band would perform frequently, with Billy Eckstine handling the vocals. Then there was always The Mosque, The Picadilly, and any number of more than 60 vaudeville, burlesque, and movie houses that catered to a music scene nearly as lively as Manhattan's, just across the Hudson River. "Everybody wanted to become a star," remembered Gil Fuller, who grew up with Sarah and went on to become a composer and arranger for Dizzy Gillespie. Fuller also remembered Ada and Jake Vaughan. "They were the sort of people who didn't even want their children to go to dances," he recalled, pinpointing the source of years of friction between Sarah and her parents, especially when Vaughan dropped out of high school in her junior year and announced she was going to be a star. "I want it! I like it! And I'm going to hit!" she defiantly told a fuming Jake.

By her late teens, Vaughan was an all-night fixture at clubs around town, singing requests whenever anyone would ask her and enjoying the company of musicians. Her high-volume cigarette habit was already established, sometimes more than two packs a day, and she had already

Sarah Vaughan

developed a taste for gin with a splash of water and a twist. She loved loud music, crowds of people, and the hazy blue atmosphere of a nightclub in the early morning hours; and she quickly gained a reputation for her sharp repartée and fluent profanity. "Whatever she had to say," a friend remembered from those days, "she would say it right out. She didn't hold things back." The men in the various bands Vaughan befriended started calling her "No 'Count Sarah," because she held no one to account for her welfare except herself.

Like that of so many other singers of her generation, Vaughan's career began at Harlem's Apollo Theater, where she sang "Body and Soul" one amateur night in 1942 and won first prize. The master of ceremonies, who almost kept her from performing because she arrived so late, was in awe of her ability to vocalize changes around the melody: "She jumped octaves like she owned them." Beside the ten-dollar first prize, Vaughan walked away with a promise of a week's work at the Apollo, which didn't materialize until the spring of 1943, when she appeared on a bill headed by *Ella Fitzgerald—another discovery of Apollo's amateur night. Fitzgerald was the only singer in later years who could challenge Vaughan for the title of leading female jazz vocalist. The rivalry between the two was always friendly, with Ella protecting Sarah after the Apollo show from booking agents who swarmed around her. Many years later, Fitzgerald would generously call Vaughan "the greatest singing talent in the world." Also in the house that night at the Apollo were Earl Hines and Billy Eckstine, both later laying claim to "discovering" Sarah. Three weeks later, Vaughan had her first full-time paying job in the music business with the Hines band, singing duets with Eckstine and playing second piano with Hines.

The band was Vaughan's home, family, and music school for the next year, and she couldn't have found better. In addition to Eckstine, from whom she learned much about phrasing, interpretation, and stage presence, the band included two men who would usher in the age of "progressive" jazz—trumpeter Dizzy Gillespie and saxophonist Charlie Parker. "What was so exciting about the Hines band," Vaughan later recalled, "was that they were playing harmonies and complex rhythms and textures that I already knew from classical music. This was a whole new age of jazz." Gillespie was quick to realize Vaughan's ability to follow the fast, complex changes and harmonies of what he came to call *bebop*, with its choppy rhythm patterns and unusual note sequences. (A more musically conservative Cab Calloway called it "Chinese music.") "Sarah can sing notes that other people can't even hear," Gillespie said.

Unlike most women singers, who spent their time before and after shows in their hotel rooms, Vaughan spent her off-stage time with the band members, drinking, smoking and cursing with the best of them. It was probably during this time that she acquired the taste for cocaine that would plague her for much of her life; but no matter what habits she indulged in or how few hours of sleep she managed, her voice just got better as time went on. Her versions of "He's Funny That Way," "Once in a While," and "Sweet and Lovely," delivered in a rich, vibrato voice that was often described as smoky, became the definitive treatments for those pop standards. Her voice, with its astounding range, became as much an instrument of the band as Gillespie's trumpet or Parker's alto sax, and one reviewer noted that she could be "delicate and sweet as a violin at the top of her range, sonorous as an organ at the bottom, with all the suppleness of a trumpet in between."

In 1943, Billy Eckstine left Hines' band to form his own group, taking Gillespie and Parker with him. A year later, Vaughan followed. Now that the group was free of Hines' insistence on pop standards, Sarah found new challenges and had to integrate her voice even more tightly into the ensemble. "You had to know a little about music or have a hell of a good ear to stand before that band," Vaughan later said; but added, "I loved it, I loved it!" In 1944, she made her first recording, "I'll Wait and Pray," released that December, and picked up the nickname that would stay with her the rest of her life—"Sassy," given to her by Eckstine's pianist, John Malachi, who liked to needle her just to produce a sharp and salty retort. Later that year, when Gillespie left Eckstine's band to set up his a purely bebop ensemble, Vaughan decided to try it on her own as a solo act. She played all the 52nd Street clubs in New York—the Famous Door, the Onyx, the Three Deuces, sometimes backed by Charlie Parker, sometimes joined by Eckstine, who was often playing nearby. Although the time between gigs sometimes forced her to return home to Newark for weeks at a time, her reputation as a unique jazz stylist grew, especially when influential critic Leonard Feather wrote of her in his jazz encyclopedia for 1944: "Sarah Vaughan's voice . . . brought to jazz an unprecedented combination of . . . a beautifully controlled tone and vibrato; an ear for the chord structure of songs . . . [and] a coy, sometimes archly naïve quality alternating with a great sense of sophistication." He was so impressed with her that he helped get Vaughan her first recording contract with a small label called Continental, under which she released four recordings in 1944, at $20 a song. Among them was "East of the Sun, West of the Moon," which became one of her most requested numbers. The next year, she recorded "Lover Man" with Dizzy, generally considered the first widely accepted "progressive" jazz release.

Still, not everyone was ready for her sound. Her trademark vibrato was often criticized, and she was accused of being overstylized, with too many deliberate vocal fireworks—"wandering and amateurish," one reviewer put it; and *Time* compared her voice to a kazoo, although the magazine later printed an explanation that the kazoo was one of the few instruments that could handle half notes and quarter tones the way Vaughan could, and that the comparison had actually been meant as a compliment. Her next memorable recording, as if to prove her versatility, was as far away from bebop as she could get, a version of "The Lord's Prayer," released for the 1950 Christmas season by Musicraft, with whom Vaughan had signed after leaving Continental. It was so successful that contralto *Marian Anderson, whose version until then had been the standard, sent her a congratulatory note. Even Vaughan's father, who had nearly disowned her over her career choice, began to think it hadn't been such a bad idea after all.

By the late 1940s, the stage was set for Vaughan's emergence as an international talent, and the catalyst was the man she married in September 1946, George Treadwell. Treadwell played the trumpet for a Harlem band, and traveled down to Greenwich Village one night, to a club called Café Society, to hear the new singer everyone was talking about. He fell in love—first, he said, with the music and, second, with the woman. In a pattern Vaughan would repeat throughout her life, the man she married also became her manager. Treadwell put every aspect of Sarah's career under his control—from the clothes she wore, to the vocabulary she used, to the songs she sang—with great success. Some of her best recordings for Musicraft were done under his guidance, including her first jazz recording to cross over to the pop charts, "Tenderly," released in 1947, and "It's Magic," which stayed at number 11 on the charts for nearly three months. When he met her at Café Society in 1946, she was being paid $250 a week; when she played the same club three years later, she received over $2,000 a week, plus a percentage of the door. Treadwell secured interviews for her on radio, in magazines and newspapers, and made sure her records received plenty of airplay. *Esquire* gave her its New Star award in 1947, and *Down Beat* named her most popular female vocalist for five years running. Treadwell took care of everything, including handling the money, for Vaughan freely admitted she was a spendthrift. "He can count good," she said of her husband in 1947, "and he likes chili and so do I." Treadwell organized her first national tour, with appearances from Miami to Los Angeles to Chicago, where radio personality

Dave Garroway became such a fan that he put her on his live midnight show from the Sherman Hotel and played Vaughan's version of "Don't Blame Me" so often that it became his theme song. It was Garroway who dubbed Sarah "The Divine One," a title with which, by 1948, few felt inclined to argue. *Metronome* noted that "not since *Billie Holiday has a singer hit other singers so hard."

After a contract dispute with Musicraft, Vaughan signed with Columbia in 1949, where she recorded another jazz-pop crossover tune, "Make Believe," and her first pure pop standard, "I Cried for You." By now, Treadwell was promoting her as a pop stylist, rather than a jazz singer, and the transformation was apparent to *The New York Times*' jazz critic John Wilson, who noted that she had moved from being an "esoterically appreciated singer into a showman who can hold her own with those select few who roost up on the top rung."

I sing. I just sing.

—Sarah Vaughan

In 1951, Vaughan embarked on the first of many European tours, where jazz fans in London, Paris, and Munich flocked to hear the new American phenomenon. Friends remembered that first trip as one long party for Sarah, and again expressed amazement that the alcohol, cigarettes, and drugs only seemed to improve her voice. They also noted that relations between Vaughan and Treadwell were becoming strained, so much so that George often stayed in New York to run their management business while Sarah was touring. Now earning close to $200,000 a year, with soldout appearances at Carnegie Hall and guest spots on major network television shows, Vaughan had seen her career explode under Treadwell's eye, but she missed her jazz roots and resented Treadwell's emphasis on pop. She left Columbia and signed with Mercury in a deal that allowed her to record mainstream music under their main label and more experimental jazz under a subsidiary label, EmArcy. "My contract with Mercury is for pops," she said, "and my contract with EmArcy is for *me*." Her last recording under Treadwell's guidance was "Broken-Hearted Melody," a love ballad Sarah disliked and called "corny," but it was her first million seller and was nominated for a Grammy in 1959, the first of seven such nominations. But by then, George and Sarah had divorced, with George revealing that of the $150 million Vaughan had supposedly made on royalties, only $16,000 remained. There were never any public explanations of where the rest had gone, but even so, Sarah always admitted that she owed much of her success to George.

Shortly after the divorce was finalized, Vaughan announced her marriage to Clyde B. ("C.B.") Atkins, a shadowy Chicago businessman who claimed to own a fleet of taxicabs and to have been a professional football player. Although he knew nothing about the music business, Sarah turned the running of The Devine [sic] One, her new management company, over to her new husband. She went back to work by leaving Mercury and signing a new contract with Roulette Records, and left again for Europe to sing at the Brussels World Fair in 1958 at the invitation of the State Department. C.B. and Sarah adopted a daughter, Debra, in 1961, and Vaughan portrayed herself publicly as a happily married woman. But friends knew differently. C.B. jealously kept her at home when she wasn't performing, spent much of his time gambling with her money, and abused her physically. Claiming C.B. threatened her life, Vaughan filed for divorce in 1962, only to discover that C.B. had left her $150,000 in debt. The IRS seized her home in Newark for non-payment of taxes, and Sarah and Debra eventually moved in with John "Preacher" Wells, a childhood friend, who, not unexpectedly, became Vaughan's manager and lover. Wells sorted out Sarah's finances, even opened her first official checking account, and helped get her life back on track.

Even with Wells' help, however, Vaughan found it hard to give up the all-night hours and habits to which she was accustomed. Roy McClure, who played bass for her group for a time, claimed she would "gorge herself on drugs, alcohol, and cigarettes" before a performance, and then sing like a bird. Sarah's voice just seemed to get deeper and richer, but by the late '60s, rock 'n' roll was replacing jazz as the alternative to pop, and her recordings of the '40s and '50s were now being played as oldies on the radio. Searching for new ways to use her voice, Vaughan recorded "The Messiah" with a 40-voice chorus for Quincy Jones, which formed part of the soundtrack for the 1969 film *Bob and Carol and Ted and Alice*, and even expressed a desire to sing opera. But from 1967 to 1970, she made no recordings and had no contract with a major label. Vaughan broke up with Wells, moved with Debra to a rented house in Los Angeles, and tried to remain active by appearing at "event" concerts and jazz festivals, often sharing the bill with old friends from the Harlem days, like Billy Eckstine, Fitzgerald, and *Carmen McRae*.

Finally, Sarah met the person who would do for her in the 1970s what George Treadwell had done for her in the 1950s. Marshall Fisher, a successful Chicago restaurateur, had been a fan since the Sherman Hotel days and introduced himself one night after Sarah's performance at a jazz festival in California. Although he was a white man, the love affair that followed seemed to friends to be just the thing for their Sassy. Fisher "hustled her music, not her money," as one of them said. "He fit right in. The racial difference didn't mean a thing to Sassy or to any of us." Fisher, like Treadwell before him, made sure Vaughan wore the right clothes, chose the right songs, and was seen with the right people—even going so far as to convince her to move with him to a luxurious home in an exclusive Los Angeles community, Hidden Hills. Although they never married, the press always referred to Marshall as Vaughan's husband, which he was in all but the legal sense until Sarah took a new lover six years later. She legally married 38-year-old Waymon Reed, a trumpeter for the Count Basie band, in 1978, when she was 54. But Reed's drinking and psychological problems brought a divorce in 1981.

Despite the turmoil in her personal life, Vaughan kept up a nearly constant touring schedule, and, by the late 1970s, she had been discovered by a new generation, helped by a series of all-Gershwin concerts she sang with the young composer and conductor, Michael Tilson Thomas, and which brought her her first Grammy Award in 1982 for the Gershwin album they recorded together. Further appearances with the Philadelphia Symphony, the Washington National Symphony, and the classical orchestras of other cities from Denver to Kansas City underscored her astounding range and versatility with everything from "America, the Beautiful" to "The Man I Love." She sang at the White House for visiting dignitaries, was praised in Congress where she was honored for her many appearances on behalf of American cultural programs abroad, and won an Emmy Award for one of the Gershwin concerts that had been presented on PBS. In 1988, she was made a member of the Jazz Hall of Fame, and in 1989 was awarded a second, special Grammy for lifetime achievement.

By 1989, however, Vaughan's health began to trouble her. She was often short of breath, and suffered from arthritis in her hands. She was forced to cancel several appearances that year, including part of an engagement at The Blue Note in New York, during which she learned she had lung cancer. She underwent chemotherapy and recovered enough to plan a new album with Quincy Jones, swearing she'd get it done "even if I have to sing it right from this bed." But on a July evening in 1990, while watching a television film in which Debra, known professionally as **Paris Vaughan**, was starring, she quietly passed away.

The reach of Sarah Vaughan's influence can be gauged by the variety of artists who attended the many memorial services in her honor— *Rosemary Clooney, Nell Carter, *Joni Mitchell, opera diva *Leontyne Price, who said that Vaughan "had gone to the place the music comes from," and a frail Billy Eckstine, who remarked to reporters that "God must have needed a lead singer." Vaughan would have been pleased, having once confessed to Leonard Feather, "It's a nice feeling to know that people will remember you after you've gone; that you'll manage to be a little bit of history."

SOURCES:
Gourse, Leslie. "Sarah Vaughan" (interview), in *Down Beat.* July 27, 1967.
———. *Sassy: The Life of Sarah Vaughan.* NY: Scribner, 1993.
———. "The Wondrous Warble of Sarah Vaughan" (obituary), in *U.S. News and World Report.* Vol. 108, no. 15. April 16, 1990.

Norman Powers,
writer-producer, Chelsea Lane Productions,
New York, New York

Vaux, Anne (fl. 1605–1635)

British radical. Flourished between 1605 and 1635; third daughter of William Vaux, 3rd Baron Vaux.

A strong-minded British woman, Anne Vaux often taunted the ecumenical and secular laws of her time. For instance, under the name of Mrs. Perkins, she sheltered the Jesuit Henry Garnett and was imprisoned at Hindlip in 1606 when Garnett was arrested at her home. Ultimately, she was deemed a recusant, a term most commonly associated with Roman Catholics who refused to accept or obey the established authority of the Church of England, including attending church services. So powerful was the Church of England at this time that such behavior was deemed a statutory offense. Vaux also held company with gunpowder plotters, who gathered at her home in Wandsworth in 1604 and in Enfield in 1605. Having established a school for Roman Catholic youth near Derby, she was forced by the Privy Council to close it in 1635.

SUGGESTED READING:
Fraser, Antonia. *Faith and Treason.* NY: Doubleday, 1999.

Lisa S. Weitzman,
freelance writer,
Cleveland, Ohio

Vaux, Clotilde de (1815–1846)

French writer and muse of Auguste Comte. Born in Paris on April 3, 1815; died of tuberculosis in Paris on April 5, 1846; first child of Captain Joseph Marie and Countess Henriette-Josephine de Ficquelmont; educated at home by her mother; married Amenee de Vaux; beloved by philosopher Auguste Comte.

Selected works: several essays; Lucie, *a novel published in the journal* The National; Wilhelmine, *an unfinished novel.*

Clotilde de Vaux was born in Paris in 1815, the first child of Captain Joseph Marie and **Henriette-Josephine de Ficquelmont**. Clotilde's mother was a countess belonging to a long aristocratic line, de Ficquelmont of Lorraine, who had lost their fortune during the French Revolution. The countess was well educated, with a particular interest in the arts and philosophy, and schooled her daughter well. Clotilde's father was a retired sea captain, now working as a tax collector for the District of Oise. He was dictatorial, as well as being suspicious of his wife's artistic bent and aristocratic unbringing, although she followed the liberal ideals of the time.

Clotilde married Amenee de Vaux, a friend of her mother's and a protegé of the marquis de Mornay, to gain independence from her father, whom she hated. Amenee replaced Clotilde's father as tax collector upon his retirement. But Amenee did not take his job or home responsibilities seriously. He frequently went off to Paris to gamble, without Clotilde, and eventually disappeared after embezzling 15,000 francs and burning the records.

Amenee wrote to Clotilde from Liege, Belgium, and pleaded with her to forgive him and join him. She wrote back in refusal, and remained officially married but without the financial or social benefits of wedlock. Clotilde continued to live in a small apartment, the rent paid by her uncle and meals provided by her brother. Despite her poverty, she enjoyed her independence and concentrated on writing, publishing several essays, and a novel *Lucie*

Clotilde de Vaux

Eva-Maria Veigel, with husband David Garrick.

pains and a constant cough. Her affection for him was genuine, if not romantic, and their friendship intensified as her illness progressed. But there was no hope of their marriage; even if Auguste could have divorced his wife **Caroline Massin**, Clotilde could not divorce her husband. There is little indication that they were ever lovers; if so, it would have been only once, near the end of her life.

Clotilde received poor medical treatment, even for the time, which probably hastened her death on April 5, 1846. Because Cherest's therapy of digitalis (for a weak heart) offered no relief and worsened her symptoms, Clotilde switched to Comte's doctor, Grandchamp. However, Grandchamp just prescribed more severe medication which made her violently ill. Comte could see that the treatment was a disaster, but he was jealous of the handsome Cherest and enjoyed Clotilde's dependency on him. When her family took charge of her, in her final days, she had to insist that they allow her to have Auguste's company. He was the only one in the room when she died.

After her death, Comte's devotion to her became religious, involving prayers and commemorations. He had adopted her as a model of saintly womanhood, holding her to be his muse like Dante's *Beatrice Portinari. He credited her with having inspired his new religious philosophy, the "Religion of Humanity," a religion of science modeled on the Catholic Church, in which the idolatry of de Vaux replaced that of *Mary the Virgin. His belief that he would be reunited with her lessened the suffering before his death on September 4, 1857. He made sure to be buried holding a lock of her hair; and an inscription on his tombstone reads "Clotilde de Vaux, the eternal companion of Auguste Comte, born April 3, 1815, in Paris, and deceased April 5, 1846, in Paris."

SOURCES:

Sokoloff, Boris. *The "Mad" Philosopher Auguste Comte.* Westport, CT: Greenwood Press, 1961.
Standley, Arline Reilein. *Auguste Comte.* Boston, MI: Twayne, 1981.

Catherine Hundleby, M.A. Philosophy,
University of Guelph,
Guelph, Ontario, Canada

in the journal *The National*. Her family discouraged her literary career, as they felt her great beauty—she was petite with blonde hair and blue eyes—could easily gain her another husband to support her.

Clotilde met the philosopher Auguste Comte in August 1844 through their mutual friend Maximilien Marie, a professor at the Sorbonne. Comte was immediately impressed and made nervous by her beauty, although she found him ridiculous and unattractive at first. She had difficulty keeping him at a distance when he fell in love with her. His infatuation led him to believe that she returned his sentiments, while she enjoyed his intellectual companionship and respect, which inspired and flattered her.

She was particularly grateful for his attention as she was lonely, receiving little notice from her family—in part because of their growing jealousy as she became close to Comte. His friendship also offered her comfort when she became ill with tuberculosis, suffering chest

Vega, Elvira de la (fl. late 1300s)

Mistress of the king of Castile. Born Elvira Iniguez de la Vega; mistress of Henry II of Trastamara, king of Castile (r. 1369–1379); children: Constanza (who married John, duke of Valencia); Juana (who married Denis, count of Villar-Dompardo).

Veigel, Eva-Maria (1724–1822)

Italian-born English dancer, actress, and Bluestocking. Name variations: Eva Maria Veigel; Eva-Maria Garrick; Eva Maria Violetti; (stage name) La Violette. Born in 1724 in Vienna; died in 1822 in London; married David Garrick (the actor), in London, on June 22, 1749; no children.

Little is known about Eva-Maria Veigel's family or childhood. She was born in Vienna in 1724 and in 1746 moved to London, where she worked as a dancer at the Haymarket Opera House. Her stage name was La Violette, so she was also known as Eva Maria Violetti. In 1747, she met David Garrick, London's most celebrated actor and manager of the popular Drury Lane theater. She declined his offer to dance at the theater, but agreed to marry him and retire from performing in 1749; her aristocratic supporters, the earl and countess of Burlington, provided a substantial sum of £6,000 to her as a dowry. It was a happy marriage and the Garricks became well known among London's high society. In 1763, they left England for a sightseeing tour of the European continent, visiting France, Italy, and Germany, before their return two years later. Garrick retired in 1775, and the couple became regulars in the literary clubs flourishing in London, often reciting scenes to amuse their audience. After Garrick's death in 1779, the grieving Veigel shared a home with *Hannah More, the poet, playwright, and religious writer who had been a longtime intimate of the Garricks; Veigel referred to More as her "chaplain."

When she came out of mourning in 1781, Veigel again joined in the salons of London's Bluestockings, a group of women who gathered weekly to discuss literature and other scholarly topics. Although she was not well educated like most of the other women, such as her close friend the host and poet *Elizabeth Montagu, Veigel was a respected member of these informal societies. Eva-Maria Veigel outlived all of her companions, dying in London in 1822, at age 98.

SOURCES:
Barton, Margaret. *Garrick*. London: Faber and Faber, 1948.
Kendall, Alan. *David Garrick: A Biography*. NY: St. Martin's Press, 1985.

Laura York, M.A. in History,
University of California,
Riverside, California

Veil, Simone (1927—)

Most important female politician in France in the 20th century, the first woman minister of the Fifth Republic, who saw to passage of the laws on adoption and abortion (the loi Veil) and was the first president of the European Parliament after it became elected by popular vote. Pronunciation: see-MOHN VAY, the L is sounded but truncated. Born Simone-Annie-Liline Jacob in Nice, France, on July 13, 1927; daughter of André Jacob (1890–c. 1944, an architect) and Yvonne Steinmetz Jacob (1900–1945); sister of Denise Jacob; educated at the Lycée de Nice, the Institut d'Études Politiques, and the Faculty of Law (Sorbonne); married Antoine Veil (b. 1926), in 1946; children: Jean (b. 1947); Claude-Nicolas (b. 1949); François-Pierre (b. 1954).

Deported to Auschwitz and Bergen-Belsen (1944–45); received diploma from the Institut d'Études Politiques and law license from the Faculty of Law (Sorbonne, 1948); qualified as a magistrate (1956); was attaché at the Ministry of Justice with the Administration of Prisons (1957–64); at the Ministry of Justice's Office of Civil Affairs (1964–68); passage of the Adoption Law (1966); served as secretary-general of the Conseil Supérieur de la Magistrature (1970–79); was minister of Health in Jacques Chirac's cabinet (1974–76); passage of the Abortion Law (1974–75); was minister of Health and Social Security in Raymond Barre's cabinet (1976–79); was a member of the European Parliament (1979–93); was president of the European Parliament (1979–82); chaired the Legal Affairs Committee of the European Parliament (1982–84); chaired the Liberal and Democratic and Reforming Group of the European Parliament (1984–89); was minister of Health, Social Affairs, and Urban Affairs in Édouard Balladur's cabinet (1993–95); signed the Manifesto of Ten (1996); member of the Conseil Constitutionnel (1998—).

Writings: (with Clément Launay and Michel Soulé) L'Adoption: Données médicales, psychologiques, et sociales (Paris: Éditions Sociales français, 1968).

On Sunday, March 30, 1944, the Gestapo arrested Simone Jacob, aged 16, during a roundup of Jews in Nice, France. The memory of that moment haunted her ever afterward—even more, if possible, than the horrific experiences which followed at Auschwitz and Bergen-Belsen.

Simone Veil was the youngest of four children—**Madeleine "Milou" Jacob** (b. 1923), **Denise Jacob** (b. 1924), Jean Jacob (b. 1925), and Simone—born to André Jacob and **Yvonne Steinmetz Jacob**. In 1924, André moved his family from Paris to Nice, where Simone was born on July 13, 1927. The son of a gas-company bookkeeper, he had graduated from the École des Beaux-Arts, spent most of the World War I as a prisoner of war in Germany, and became an architect, winning second prize in the Prix de Rome competition. Yvonne was the daughter of a Paris furrier and had trained as a chemist. To Yvonne's disappointment, André demanded that she give up her dream of becoming a research scientist. The move to Nice also hurt her, for she was a Parisienne to the fingertips. André, rigid, upright, and old-fashioned, tyrannized his family. Yvonne was a beautiful woman physically and morally, beloved by all who knew her, and very protective of her children. Beneath the charming exterior, however, Simone sensed a note of deep melancholy. The memory of her mother's situation was a critical stimulant to her later outspoken advocacy of married women's right to work outside the home. It fired her determination to practice her profession once her children were past infancy.

Simone clung to her mother until adolescence. Much more than her sisters, she stood up to her father. She wanted a closer relationship with him, but he believed in maintaining a "proper distance" between parent and child. Although their personalities differed, she and her two sisters were extremely close and well known and admired outside the home. André prospered, and the family lived a comfortable existence. By 1931, however, the Great Depression took hold in France, and commissions for villas on the Côte d'Azur began to dry up. The children were denied nothing important, but expenses had to be curtailed and the vacation home sold.

The Jacobses were determined to have their children well educated and cultured. They were reared on the classics; Simone retained a lifelong love of reading, Proust, Balzac, and Henry James being favorites. The only neglected cultural area was music, which André despised as an inferior diversion. Simone entered the Nice lycée for girls and pursued the classical curriculum (Greek, Latin, philosophy) to prepare for the baccalaureate examination, gateway to a university. She was intelligent enough but somewhat undisciplined. Quick to anger and to tenderness, she was at once sunny and serious, expansive and fragile. Like her sisters, she was active in scouting, which seems to have contributed significantly to her maturation.

Religion played no part in their lives. "My family was totally detached from Judaism," said Veil; she first heard the phrase "next year in Jerusalem" while at Auschwitz. French, and proud of it, the Jacobses were wholly assimilated. They did not deny their Jewish ancestry; they simply ignored it.

André disbelieved that the rise of the Nazis in Germany endangered Europe and Jews, much less patriotic French citizens. France's defeat in June 1940 came as a terrible shock and humiliation to him. A vague plan to escape to England via Spain died stillborn due to its complications. The family remained in Nice, which for now was in the Unoccupied Zone and thus out of the Germans' reach. Nice became a major destination for Jewish refugees. Things began to change when on October 3, 1940, the collaborationist regime set up at Vichy under Marshal Pétain began issuing anti-Jewish legislation. Amazingly, André continued to believe his family was in no real danger. Simone always thought otherwise. Matters turned grave after a decree (September 24, 1941) forbade Jews professional employment, thus depriving André of his living. When the Allies invaded North Africa in November 1942, the Germans and Italians occupied the rest of France. Nice fell into Italy's small zone. The Italian authorities showed no interest in cooperating with Germany's persecution of the Jews, although, as Veil later put it, their occupation was "no operetta." Life became extremely difficult as food and fuel dried up; day-long lines had to be endured to keep alive.

The last stage began after Italy's surrender on September 8, 1943. The Germans rapidly moved into the Italian zone and began roundups of Jews. Even André now felt menaced. The family dispersed in town, while Denise joined the Resistance. A **Mme de Villeroy**, professor of classical studies at the lycée, sheltered Simone. On November 12, the directress of the lycée told Simone she must no longer attend school because it would implicate everyone. She stubbornly continued to prepare for the examination, with students passing her material and professors grading her papers. Many years later, Veil harshly criticized a famous film about the occupation, *Le Chagrin et la Pitié* (1971), which implied that almost everybody was a collaborator—thus implying, too, that nobody was *really* guilty. On the contrary, she emphasized how many people in her experience took grave risks to shelter Jews, and how few were truly "*salauds*" (scoundrels).

The trap closed on March 30, 1944. While unwisely walking in public with a boyfriend two days after passing the baccalaureate examination, she was stopped by a Gestapo squad. Her false identity card read "Jacquier." "Jacquier, that's Jacob," said one. The boyfriend foolishly ran to Mme de Villeroy's to warn the family. He was followed, of course, and within hours all were in custody save André, who was found a dozen days later. How little most Jews knew even as late as 1944 is illustrated by the fact that

Simone and her family felt a momentary sense of relief, thinking they would be sent to a camp somewhere merely to wait out the war. Yvonne even asked a friend to bring her a long list of items for the camp stay, including works by Racine, Molière, and Pascal.

From the Excelsior Hotel lockup in Nice, Simone, her sister Milou, and Yvonne were sent up to the Drancy depot at Paris. On April 13, they left Drancy in a cattle car on a train carrying 646 men and 834 women and children to Auschwitz, two nights and three days without food or water. (Jean and his father left Drancy on May 15 for Kovno and Reval and disappeared forever; Denise was arrested in June and sent to Ravensbrück, where she survived the war.) When they clambered from the train, an unknown woman whispered to Simone, "Say you're eighteen." Since all children under eighteen went straight to the gas chambers, the advice saved her life; her mature beauty fooled the officials.

The three were sent to the Birkenau camp—Auschwitz was a 20-square-mile complex—where they waited for two months before being selected for a work section rather than the gas chambers. The number 78651 was tattooed on Veil's arm. (She has never had it removed.) The labor was brutal, often pointless, 12-hour days digging ditches and building roads and railway lines. Food, clothing, and shelter were abominable. In July there was a request for eight or nine women to work in a Siemens plant, newly opened at Bobrek (another part of the complex), which made equipment for aircraft. A female Polish capo (Jewish guard) recommended Veil, telling her that a girl like her did not deserve to die. Simone insisted they include Yvonne and Milou; amazingly, she got her wish. For three months, they worked hauling soil, then as masons, and finally in the plant, which at least had a roof and heat.

Appalling as life was in Birkenau and Bobrek, worse followed. On January 17, 1945, with the Russians closing in, the Germans began moving their prisoners in hopes of continuing to use their labor. Some 31,894 (including 236 at Bobrek) began a 63-mile (102-km.) death march in bitter cold to Gleiwitz, where open coal cars awaited for a trip through Czechoslovakia, Austria, and Germany to the Bergen-Belsen camp outside Hamburg. The survivors arrived some time in February. Conditions at Belsen were beyond description: a giant mortuary where starvation and disease raged unchecked. Yvonne, Milou, and Simone fell ill with typhus. Around March 25, Yvonne, who

Simone Veil

had endured with a fortitude and gentleness which awed all who knew her, died in Milou's arms. Three weeks later, on April 14, British soldiers arrived. Struck dumb by what they saw, they instantly quarantined the place for a month. Simone, working outside the wire at the moment, was not allowed in to join her sister and thus missed celebrating the liberation with her. It seemed to her like the last insult.

When asked once how she survived, Veil replied simply, "Luck." (Of the 75,000 Jews shipped from Drancy, only 2,500 returned.) Miraculously, the three had stayed together through the entire ordeal. Without mutual support, they probably would have perished. Surely Yvonne and Milou would have; they were too "good," too easily taken advantage of by others. Simone, the toughest, did things about which she later felt pangs of remorse: "To survive you had to have a certain aggressiveness." To her great anger, it was often hinted that female survivors had traded sex for favors. She denied it, adding that such accusations show no understanding of what the camps were really like.

"Those who have not lived through the deportation cannot truly understand it, no matter how earnestly they try," she said. She found portrayals like *Sophie's Choice* or the American documentary *Holocaust* (1979) "prettied up," sentimentalized, with selfless prisoners tenderly taking care of each other. "In truth we had become veritable beasts," she said. The worst aspect of the camps was the destruction of the dignity of all involved, both prisoners and guards. Psychological conditioning and fear had turned them into "robots."

Veil claimed she had been "marked" but not warped: "[I] assimilated it and integrated it into my life." It made her more perceptive about people individually and collectively; they can be by turns saints or beasts, and nobody is exempt. It fed both pessimism and optimism—pessimism because of the depravity she had witnessed, optimism because of the resources of "generosity, love, and vitality" she found in humans. The experience also made her fully conscious of her Jewish inheritance. She did not try to leave it behind. Also, as she observed among many survivors, it made her more "European" in outlook, readier to seek transnational ways to prevent such a tragedy from ever happening again.

Simone arrived back in Paris on May 23, 1945. Ill physically and psychologically, she felt like a stranger: "Every day was a burden." She missed her mother terribly and clung to Milou, who had nearly died of typhus and debilitation. No welcome awaited in France. Liberation, the Resistance, and Charles de Gaulle were cheered to the skies. Denise was treated like a hero and invited everywhere, but not Simone and Milou. Simone acquired a certain permanent distaste for Gaullism because the general never made the least gesture to recognize the Jewish martyrs. Denise got Simone a month's stay in a Swiss recovery facility, but results were disappointing. Veil bore much pent-up anger which exploded now and then. A psychiatrist later noted, however, that unlike so many deportees, she could speak frankly and precisely about her experiences. Most of the time she showed an impassive front. People who had known her in Nice found her changed, "a veritable block of ice," according to one.

Despite these trials, Veil was determined to build a new life without delay. From early adolescence, she had dreamed of a career in law. In October 1945, she enrolled at the Faculty of Law at the Sorbonne and, not feeling fully occupied by legal studies, at the Institut d'Études Politiques. Behind her beauty and a distant air, people detected a touching sadness and vulnerability. A mutual friend brought her in touch with Antoine Veil, a fellow student at Law and the In-

stitut. A year older than she, he was from a well-to-do non-practicing Jewish family in textile manufacture in Grenoble. In December 1943, he had crawled under the wire into Switzerland. After the Liberation, he returned to join the army and was demobilized on October 1, 1945.

Simone and Antoine were married on October 26, 1946, in a civil ceremony in Paris. She described him as someone with "a great serenity and a solid character. He was charming, impulsive, composed, but also rigid and intransigent . . . a passionate fighter." Like her father, he was possessive of her, a trait which often caused problems. A friend of Simone's described her as a marvelous companion but admitted, too, that it would be difficult to be her husband. Still, despite tensions, they fashioned a solid marriage, invariably consulting each other on all important matters.

Simone wanted children quickly to reconstruct a family. Jean was born on November 26, 1947, and Claude-Nicolas arrived in 1948, shortly after she and Antoine received their certificates from the Institut and their law licenses. Like Yvonne, she was an exceptionally devoted mother. She gave herself unreservedly to her children and shielded them when necessary from Antoine, who could be overly stern—again, much like her own father. Antoine moved ahead rapidly. On January 20, 1947, a leading minister, Pierre-Henri Teitgen, of the Christian socialist Popular Republican Movement (MRP), hired Antoine as a parliamentary attaché. When Teitgen left office in September 1948, Antoine joined the staff of another leading politician, Alain Poher (MRP), secretary of state at the Budget bureau. Poher in turn got him appointed as third officer at the consulate in Wiesbaden, Germany, starting January 1, 1950.

That Simone agreed to live in Germany astonished everybody, including Antoine. But her decision was in character. She could never pardon Germany (whatever that might mean), much less forget (or let anyone else forget) the Holocaust. But she believed that, for the sake of the children, France and Germany simply had no other choice now but to learn to live together. It was time to turn a page, time for constructive action. She preferred life to death.

The Veils lived in Wiesbaden in 1950–51 and then in Stuttgart in 1952. Antoine loved social life. Simone felt distinctly awkward early in their marriage, but at Wiesbaden she blossomed as a hostess in the rounds of entertaining expected in the consular service. Meanwhile, Antoine decided to try for admission to the new École National d'Administration (ENA), designed to be the crown jewel of the preparatory system for the highest State posts. He failed on his first try but passed on his second, in 1952.

Shortly before Antoine's success, Simone suffered a cruel blow. At Meaux, while returning to Paris on August 14, 1952, from a visit to the Veils in Stuttgart, Milou (who was now a psychologist) and her young son, Luc, died in an automobile accident. Veil could only say, "It's unjust." It took all her strength to climb out of this darkness. She could never speak of Milou again except to her closest friends, and always with tears.

Simone went with Antoine to Safi, Morocco, in 1953 for his six-month stage as civil comptroller, and then for six months at the prefecture in Châteauroux. In March 1954, their third child, Pierre-François, arrived, the same year that Antoine graduated a splendid sixth from the ENA. He chose the Valhalla of the French bureaucracy, the Inspectorate of Finance, and began a brilliant career in State service and then in the private sector. His positions furnished the couple with a host of connections to the country's elite.

Simone herself did internships in an attorney's office and then at the Paris prosecutor's office (the *parquet*). She wanted to be a trial lawyer, but Antoine would not hear of it. The issue caused the only serious battle between them, she said later. She was determined not to share her mother's fate as a frustrated professional. Antoine finally relented, suggesting she might become a judge, a newly opened occupation for women. She could still defend the weak, which she had dreamed of doing. At length she gave way, set to work, and in 1956 passed the examination for the magistracy.

Because of family considerations, she did not want a posting to the provinces, where junior judges usually started. Antoine pulled some strings; she remained in Paris, but at an unprestigious branch of the Justice ministry, the Administration of Prisons. Given her background, the choice seemed foreordained. From 1957 to 1964, she inspected prisons and made recommendations regarding prisoners' rights, sentencing, and parole. Her tours took her all over the country; she later said she had probably seen more prisons than anyone in France. She often found conditions appalling and the mindset of the administration antediluvian, "worthy of Dachau or Buchenwald." She believed in punishment but rejected automatic sentences unfitted to individual cases. She was strict, however—some even said harsh—about parole: good behavior alone was insufficient if the release posed any credible

threat to society. At the same time, she adamantly insisted that prison was meant to be only a deprivation of freedom, not an injury to one's fundamental dignity. She fought for equal treatment of men and women. (Women habitually were subjected to needless humiliations.) With tuberculosis rates running high, she got a mobile X-ray unit instituted. She also helped establish psychiatric services. She was charged, too, with starting educational programs for young prisoners, and after a long fight with the Old Guard she got a librarian's position approved.

One of the great figures of France and Europe today.

—Sir Michael Jay

Veil worked under trying conditions. She felt the strain on her family, where much of her children's care fell to maids. She was a doting mother when she was at home, but provincial tours and evening social engagements took a toll. The boys were treated as adults from an early age and could be hard to handle. At work, she found herself the only woman (save for typists) in the central administration, with all that implied in the way of cold receptions and male condescension in a notoriously misogynous service. Go to lunch with a colleague twice, she remarked wryly, and he thought you were ready to go to bed with him. In time, she won sincere respect by her competence and willingness to assume responsibilities. Her colleagues discovered that her being a woman did not mean she was a hand-wringing "bleeding heart." Notably, she exhibited traits which remained in the years to come: humane but strict, a reformer while also respectful of traditional structures and authority.

The vicious war for Algerian independence (1954–62) drew her in when the ethnologist *Germaine Tillion recommended to de Gaulle's minister of Justice, the able, humane Edmond Michelet, that Simone Veil would be an excellent choice to inspect the prisons in Algeria and address the problem of what to do about some 600 prisoners condemned to death for "terrorism." Veil sent back a confidential report to Michelet roundly condemning prison conditions, which included use of torture. She worked to get the cases converted from criminal to political offenses, hence not subject to the death penalty, and took charge of a risky mission to transfer some noted female detainees to safer confinement in France. Among them was *Djamila Boupacha, a 22-year-old woman accused of planting a bomb, whose case had been made into a cause célèbre by *Simone de Beauvoir. Veil's experiences converted her to the cause of Algerian independence, but she never countenanced violent opposition to the war.

After Jean Foyer succeeded Michelet at Justice, a turn to tougher policies in the prisons left Veil in mounting distress. She finally took Antoine's advice and asked for a transfer. In 1964, she was assigned to the Department of Civil Affairs and assigned to a committee writing a new law on adoptions. Existing legislation, based on a 1939 statute, was a hopeless tangle. Veil became the main drafter of the Adoption Law of 1966, which she regarded as one of her life's proudest achievements. President Charles de Gaulle and Premier Georges Pompidou were interested in this legislation, so she spent much time shuttling between the ministry, the Élysée Palace, and the Hôtel Matignon. When the bill went before Parliament, she sat with the minister as technical counsellor. Also, with pediatrician Dr. Michel Soulé and Professor Clément Launay, Veil authored a book on the subject.

The law—which became a model elsewhere, notably in Belgium and Italy, where she and Soulé later conducted seminars—put the child's interests first and gave adopted children the same rights as natural children. A key provision dealt with abandonment. Once a specified delay expired, the child could not be reclaimed from adoption. The law also opened the way later for dealing with children conceived artificially. While completing this huge labor, Veil showed herself to be a shrewd pragmatist. When de Gaulle flatly insisted that couples with legitimate children not be allowed to adopt, she inserted a provision granting a right of dispensation—to the president alone. She could settle for half a loaf, as she would show when she drafted the abortion law some years later.

Because of her interest in judicial reform, Veil joined the Magistrates' Union during the May uprising of 1968. She had already belonged to an informal society of like-minded reformers, the Association Vendôme, where she was noted as a moderate, careful thinker, and she found the uprising rather exciting. (The Veils lived in the student quarter.) Antoine, in big-business administration since 1964, took a dim view of it. Simone left the Union after a few months, put off by violence and its politicization and frivolous thinking.

Simone Veil was becoming known, as was her husband. They were seen in "Tout Paris" circles and became close friends of Marcel Bleustein-Blanchet, the father of modern advertising in France, at whose estate on the Côte d'Azur they spent some vacations. When René Pleven, whom she greatly respected, became minister of Justice in 1969 under the new president, Pompidou, he appointed her to his personal staff as a technical counsellor. She had general oversight of staff functions, handled press relations, and prepared the amnesty law. But the hours proved long, and her youngest son was feeling abandoned. After nine months, she asked for a reassignment, e.g., as director of Prisons. Pleven made counteroffers. Finally, on March 14, 1970, he named her secretary-general of the Conseil Supérieur de la Magistrature. The Council supervises the judges, rules on promotions, gives the president legal advice, and, before the death sentence was abolished, handled death-sentence appeals. Veil found preparing agendas and minutes and sitting in meetings dull work despite the position's prestige. (She was the first woman to hold it.) But it gave her a perch from which to observe even more of the workings of France's huge central bureaucracy. She filled out her time by serving on several committees, including those on women's labor and the women's information center, the joint committee of the press and Justice on secrecy of pretrial examinations (*instruction*), and (from 1972) the board of the Office of French Radio and Television (ORTF).

On May 27, 1974, while dining out with friends, she received a telephone call from the new premier-designate, Jacques Chirac, asking her to become minister of Health. She accepted the next day, becoming the first woman to be a full minister (not just a secretary of state) since **Germaine Poinso-Chapuis** headed the Ministry of Public Health and Population in 1947–48. Despite having been proposed by a women's magazine, *Marie-Claire* (February 1973), as premier in an all-female "dream" cabinet, Veil was unknown to the public at large. Because of her prior positions, her knowledge of Parliament's ways and personnel was far more extensive than often realized. Still, to many deputies and senators she was merely a name. She had been put up for the position, in fact, as a result of complicated maneuverings amongst the various factions of the government preparing for the introduction of reform to the antique, largely unenforced law of 1920 banning abortion. (A bill to this effect had died in Parliament in 1973, but new president Valéry Giscard d'Estaing, sincerely impressed by the feminist movement, was resolved to change the law.) Apparently, a stunned Veil knew nothing of these palavers before the phone call. She had never seriously thought of being a minister. Antoine urged her to accept, asking only that she try to see that protocol rules did not condemn him to the company of the "second fiddles" at State functions. She kept the promise and succeeded more often than not, making it a rule to be seen to defer to him when in public.

In some ways she was an ideal choice to deal with an abortion bill, being a woman and a judge, not a member of Parliament with political baggage and constituents to please. On the other hand, she was Jewish (a handicap in dealing with Catholics on a religiously sensitive issue) and had no prior experience as a minister. Nor was she especially conversant with the Health ministry, although she had dealt with it regarding adoption, children's services, and psychiatric care. Anyhow, given the importance of the impending abortion struggle, the ministry's day-to-day functioning would fall to the professional staff for now. The bill consumed her first six months in office and provoked arguably the most wrenching purely legislative battle France had seen since the Second World War. It also fixed her public image permanently.

Abortion—which distressed Veil personally—had ballooned into a major issue by the early 1970s. On April 5, 1971, *Delphine Seyrig, Françoise Fabian, Simone de Beauvoir, *Christiane Rochefort, and 339 other prominent women stated in a manifesto that they had undergone abortions. Some 330 physicians published a manifesto on February 3, 1973, saying they had performed abortions. Several high-profile court cases agitated public opinion, notably a trial in Grenôble in May 1973 of Dr. **Annie Feray-Martin** for performing an abortion on a minor. Estimates of the number of abortions in France ranged from 300,000 to 500,000 annually, with about 300 women dying. The 1920 law was in tatters, derided in all quarters. Nobody, observed Giscard, really would imprison a woman for having an abortion. Yet opposition was fervent among conservatives (who held a parliamentary majority) and among many Catholics of all political persuasions. Moreover, radical feminists wanted no law at all, claiming women should control their bodies absolutely as a matter of right. Most of the Left in Parliament, while favoring a new law, did not want to support a Right-led government. Chirac, in tight quarters, agreed to support a bill only after Veil assured him it would "respect life." When Giscard said in his first news conference (July 22, 1974) that it was high time to revise the 1920 law, the war was on.

Veil set to work. Unlike the radical feminists, she believed abortion should be legally regulated because the door otherwise would remain open to abortion mills, scams, and "angel makers"—all of which threatened women's health. The emphasis on health would win support. It also made her ministry, rather than Justice, the logical drafter of the bill. Giscard thoroughly agreed. Veil believed the final decision must rest with the woman, but with provisions to ensure the decision would be well informed and thoughtful. Her fundamental purpose was to help women in distress. She rejected, however, a proposal to have a doctor sign a certificate of distress because "distress" could not be clearly defined in law; conscience would have to rule. She refused to advocate the Left's "unsellable" idea (as she saw it) that a woman may decide to abort because a pregnancy is inconvenient. To her, a bill asserting a woman's right to control her body invited defeat; her only request of Giscard and Chirac was to keep *Françoise Giroud, the secretary of state for the Condition of Women—and an outspoken feminist who had published an article in L'Express in 1972 advocating "free abortion"—off the scene. In short, she refused to be drawn into theological or theoretical issues, e.g., about when a human life begins. She would rest the case on pragmatic considerations focused on women's health.

The original bill contained the following provisions: (1) it would be voted on again after a five-year trial; (2) a woman in distress could ask for an abortion before the end of the tenth week; (3) the decision would be the woman's alone but only after two preliminary consultations with a physician and a social worker; (4) abortion could not be used as a birth-control measure; (5) it could be performed only by a physician in a hospital; (6) a physician could not be compelled to perform one (the "conscience clause"); (7) it could not be paid for by public health insurance; and (8) implementation would fall to State health officers, not municipal commissions. Veil inserted the "conscience clause" in an unsuccessful attempt to mollify the archbishop of Paris, who had issued a scathing denunciation (October 9). As for non-reimbursement, she regretted it but knew the public would be shocked if abortions were paid for when some other procedures and drugs were not. But she made provision to regulate the expense strictly.

Prospects brightened when a bill on contraceptives, which expanded access and information and treated the Pill like any other drug, breezed through (the law of December 4, 1974). Abortion-bill lobbying became intense. Veil entertained every member of the majority at lunch or dinner at the ministry and, as did Chirac and Michel Poniatowski, the powerful minister of the

Interior-designate who had pushed for her appointment, put aides to work buttonholing deputies. She appeared in a television interview; although nervous and sometimes groping for words, she made a favorable impression as a sincere, well-informed, and unpretentious woman—in the public's eyes not a "typical" politician, male or female. (It took her quite some time to overcome a fear of committing a gaffe which could force her into an embarrassing resignation.)

The first hurdle was the committee that would report the bill to the National Assembly. Veil proved she could be a clever tactician. She and her supporters in the committee wanted Dr. Henry Berger elected *rapporteur* (floor manager for the committee's version). But he was such an outspoken partisan of the bill that pushing him forward would look like a taunt to the committee's hostile minority. So she quietly sent word to her supporters to stay away when the *rapporteur* was elected. She then remained silent when the opposition chose one of theirs, Alexandre Bolo, who promptly presented seven hostile amendments. Veil's supporters now showed up and defeated them all. Bolo felt obliged to resign. They then elected Berger. Veil later admitted, "I've always loved ruses, foreseeing moves in advance."

She appeared before the committee on November 19, unruffled, master of the subject, impossible to bait. To ease passage, she accepted two amendments: husbands could be "associated" in the decision, and minors must have parental consent. She did not like doing it. It was part of her contradictory nature to be a moderate consensus-seeker while resenting having to compromise. The committee approved the bill 22 to 11 with 2 abstentions. (Members of the government's majority voted 13 to 7 against; the socialists and communists furnished 15 of the 22 favorable votes.)

Floor debate in the Assembly began on November 26. At the entrances to the Palais-Bourbon, bands of opponents from "Let Them Live," led by priests, distributed graphic literature, waved prayer books, and hurled insults. Debate lasted three days and two nights, thirty hours in all. Seventy-seven speakers held forth after Veil's opening speech. She spoke for an hour, calmly if sometimes awkwardly. She made a sympathetic image: a small woman alone at the rostrum before an almost wholly male audience (barely a dozen of the 490 members were women), stating her case with a touching sincerity.

It is the disorder [in the law] that must be ended. It is the injustice which we must agree to end. I say this with all my convic-

tion: abortion should remain the exception, the last recourse for situations with no way out. I would like to share with you a woman's conviction—excuse me for doing so before this Assembly composed almost exclusively of men: no woman resorts to abortion with a light heart. It is enough to listen to women. It is a drama and remains a drama.

Chirac, despite his reservations, supported her with a steady presence. The famously shrewd president of the Assembly, Edgar Faure, garbed in formal attire to underscore the importance of the occasion, also lent support by foiling obstructive tactics and moving expeditiously through 170 amendments.

Speeches ran the gamut from reasoned essays to passionate harangues. The French National Assembly is one of the world's most testing venues for a debater. Simone Veil stood her ground, answering coolly or with heat as needed. A number of opposition speakers alluded to Nazi doctors, torture, euthanasia, and vivisection. "Abortion is legal genocide!" thundered René Feit. Veil lost her composure only once, when Jean-Marie Daillet spoke of tossing embryos into garbage cans and crematories (*sic*). Tears welled in her eyes and she dropped her head, silently sobbing. After she recovered, she made only a short reply. (Daillet later privately apologized . . . saying he didn't know she had been a deportee.) Denouncing such tactics on another occasion, she retorted, "Guilt by association is a technique of intellectual terrorism which has no place in a debate where each finds himself facing his conscience and his responsibility."

Three incidents threatened to defeat the bill. She accepted an amendment saying abortions could take place in private (mostly Catholic) hospitals only if the director had not refused such interventions. In effect, this meant that physicians willing to perform abortions could not do so in Catholic hospitals. The Left howled in protest and threatened to sink the bill. During a quick recess, Veil persuaded Gaston Defferre, the Socialist leader, that it was necessary to appease the bishops in this manner or risk defeat. The amendment passed, 294–105. Another close call came when a deputy slyly noted the absence from the ministerial bench of Jean Lecanuet, minister of Justice-designate and leader of the Catholic Centrists who had quietly agreed not to oppose the bill. Smelling trouble, Veil instantly went to the rostrum to inform the Assembly that he was in Brussels on official business. The next day he returned and, amidst shouts of "Traitor!" from the opposition, delivered an eloquent speech in favor of the bill. Lecanuet's support swung critical undecided votes in the Center, especially among moderate Catholics. The final crisis came on Jean Foyer's amendment, the only one of the 170 which threatened the whole bill and was thus put to a ballot, not raised hands. It was defeated, 286 to 178. Final passage thus became a formality. On November 29 at 3:40 AM the bill passed, 284 to 189, with solid support from the Left and enough from the government's majority. With Poniatowski and Lecanuet lobbying hard, the Senate, to some surprise, passed the bill two weeks later without much ado. Final votes came on December 20. On January 17, 1975, the *loi Veil* (as it was quickly dubbed) was promulgated.

When Simone Veil returned home after the National Assembly victory, a magnificent bouquet from Chirac greeted her. During the preceding weeks she had received flowers and encouraging letters from around the country. But these were drowned in a flood of letters and phone calls, most of them anonymous and soaked in anti-Semitism. Graffiti defaced her hallway walls, and when she arrived at the Palais-Bourbon she was greeted by jostling crowds waving prayer books to "exorcise" her. She kept her sanity through the ordeal, and she had won. Poniatowski declared that no *man* could have gotten the bill through. Said Giscard, "She passed the unpassable" in making France the first Catholic country to legalize abortion. *France-Soir* spoke for the bulk of the press when it concluded, "This woman is a rock."

The *loi Veil* came back for review in 1979 and was passed again after noisy debates. In 1983, insurance reimbursement was added. Simone Veil disliked the law's nickname; she found personal identification with something as repellent as abortion disagreeable. But she was helpless to prevent her name and image from being fixed in the public's consciousness by her first six months in office. Writes Michel Sarazin, she "retained all her reasons to please: she appeared beautiful but not provocative, competent but not a technocrat, tolerant but not hesitant, honest but not naïve, courageous but not belligerent, touching but not weepy." It was an image any politician could envy. Yet it also stereotyped her as an icon, the people's "platonic love" (as someone put it), too far above most politicians to make her seem a credible participant in the rough-and-tumble fights for high office.

Veil served as minister of Health for five consecutive years in the cabinets of Chirac and Raymond Barre, an unusually long tenure in the same post. In 1977, the Social Security Adminis-

tration was added to her responsibilities. Thus, almost the entire task of directing France's mammoth program of social services fell to her. She did not shirk her duties; indeed, she was a workhorse (and expected as much from subordinates). But by the spring of 1979 she was worn out. Her task had been made more onerous by the spiraling expense of the programs due mainly to a great surge of inflation by the mid-1970s. The Right resented her criticism of powerful interests, privileges, and wasteful spending, while the Left called her a "*réactionnaire*" for reining in benefits. She often found herself at odds, too, with the bigwigs of medicine about priorities. She said once she had not appreciated how strenuous a minister's job is, how intense the pressure of unending responsibility. At the same time, a close acquaintance noted she had little by little acquired a certain taste for power and a growing discomfort with jokes at the expense of people exercising it.

To the mantra "Health has no price" she was the first minister to reply "Health has a cost." She cut back the purchase of heavy equipment and instituted tighter accounting in medical administration to combat an "always more" psychology. With huge hospital-building programs devouring budgets while the length of stays was declining, she put a lid on expansion of the number of beds. Convinced that continued rapid growth of the number of physicians would increase demands for services, reduce their incomes, and lower the quality of service, she slightly lowered medical school acceptances each year and introduced a "needs of the nation" clause in the budget which remained after she left office. The hospitals and doctors howled, of course, given all the vested interests involved. She also sought to slow the rise of drug prices by hacking at waste and preaching restraint. It took years of wars with three other ministries to bring drugs under a single authority. On the other hand, she increased budgets for medical research and bailed out the Pasteur Institute. She improved conditions for the aged, sick, and handicapped. Probably her most appreciated reforms were a systematic abolition of hospital wards (where conditions were notoriously bad) and a general improvement of hospital surroundings. And for nurses, who were resorting to strikes because of low pay and understaffing, she increased nursing schools and pay scales and instituted a bonus (still called the *prime Veil*).

One of her most noticed initiatives was France's first campaign to reduce tobacco use despite the fact that the State's tobacco monopoly is a major source of revenue. Ironically, she was herself a three-pack-a-day smoker. (A celebrated photo showed her, cigarette stuck in her mouth, receiving a light from Chirac.) She reduced her consumption to one pack per day and ceased smoking in public. She pushed another *loi Veil*, this one restricting advertising, extending no-smoking areas (including the cabinet room at the Élysée), and educating the public about tobacco's effects. In arguing her case, she was not naive about life's risks: "Knowing what one risks is essential to true liberty [of choice]." The budget for prevention shot from 1 million francs in 1975 to 19 million in 1978. The results, however, proved mixed at best.

A cabinet reshuffle in 1977 brought the direction of Social Security to her portfolio. Not until after the legislative elections of 1978 was the Social Security deficit addressed despite Chirac's promise to do so in 1975. It remained a puzzle, practical and political. She tried or advocated several expedients, raising this tax or lowering that. But for 1979 the deficit rocketed to 6 billion, not the projected 2.2 billion. Just before she left office she instituted a Commission of Accounts for Social Security which would report annually to Parliament. Illustrative of her quandary is the fact that among other things she expanded family benefits, lengthened maternity leaves, increased prenatal care, and improved the plight of single mothers—all praiseworthy causes almost impossible to square with deficit reduction. The succeeding minister blamed her for the problem. She had been the first to attack it but lacked enough time. Her measures were basically continued.

Veil's political activity during her tenure reflected both her dislike of party politics and her standing at the top of the polls, which at its peak (1977) reached an astonishing 70%. Her relations with Giscard, Chirac, and Barre were never easy. Toward Giscard she was loyal, never criticizing him publicly. She admired his mental powers but found it impossible to communicate with him. Nor did he ever understand her. In all her time in office, he never telephoned her more than about once a year. It was said he feared her, partly because she would sometimes drop mordant, unexpected remarks in cabinet meetings. She concluded that his "reforming" phase had petered out by 1976 and wondered sometimes why she was staying on. Chirac's was a different case. They felt a genuine mutual affection, but they grated on each other when it came to politics. She regarded him as a fine chap but too much the politician, a weak man easily tempted by demagoguery. Even so, his resignation, on August 25, 1976, pained her. As for Barre, his successor, Antoine Veil described their relations as "complicated." She admired his competence but chafed at his smugness. Yet when she found herself for the first time in flat opposition to Giscard—on restriction of immigration by using quotas (a word which horrified her)—Barre, with principle at stake, proved a firm ally.

Her most striking political involvement concerned her "candidacy" to be the first popularly elected mayor of Paris (March 20, 1977). Rumors said she was a prospect for mayor in Bourges, Orléans, Belfort, and elsewhere. (In France, politicians often combine a mayorship with another office such as deputy or senator.) Nice was the only one which could interest her, but its mayor was very popular. The only one, that is, except for the greatest prize: Paris. Giscard instituted popular election for the office and, of course, wanted one of "his own" elected. To make an excessively complicated story short, in the struggle between Giscard and Chirac over control of Paris, Veil's name surfaced as a possible compromise. She was interested—enough, indeed, to make quiet preparations to run even though Antoine would have to resign his seat on the Paris Municipal Council. But did Giscard really want her? In any event, she refused to go to him in the fall of 1976 to state her intentions or probe his. Evidence suggests that he was only using her name in his chess match with Chirac. She later claimed this was the case. In the end, Chirac himself ran against a Giscardien and won.

As an administrator, Veil was a hands-on type, criticized sometimes for doing too much herself. She retorted that if she didn't do it, things just didn't move along. Her staff, diversely composed, stayed fiercely loyal and almost unchanged despite her hard-driving ways and occasional explosions of temper. Disrespectful of protocol, she cultivated good relations with the ministry's minor employees, who loved her. She could be too slow to decide but was helped by her training as a judge. She was a stout defender of her "turf" and of the rights of women. Too many women in government, she maintained, are not tough enough in dealing with men, especially their "crafty" paternalism, which she would not tolerate. Women must combat the popular notion that their decisions are mostly the product of emotion, caprice, or guile. At the same time, she took care to present a chic feminine image, invariably stylishly garbed in dresses or suits loaned to her by Chanel. In short, she proved to be on the whole an effective, highly presentable administrator, certainly not to be trifled with. She set an important example for both

France and Europe of what a woman could do in high office.

Given her popularity, Chirac and Barre wanted to use her in the 1978 Assembly elections. She declined Chirac's invitation to join the Rally for the Republic (RPR), his version of the old Gaullist party. She consented, however, to open and close the campaign with television appeals on behalf of Giscard's and Barre's Union for French Democracy (UDF). But she would do no more. This aggravated Barre, and their relations deteriorated. As noted, by 1979 she was tired and ready to quit. As she remarked once, "I'm ill-at-ease everywhere, as much with the moralistic right as with the sectarian left, as much with the rich as with the poor." As André Rousselet put it, "Simone has consented to be an accident."

Providentially, by the spring of 1979, when she was poised to resign at the first suitable opportunity, an ideal prospect presented itself. The European Parliament, a body chosen by the parliaments of the (then) nine members of the European Community (which includes the Common Market), was being doubled in size (to 410 members) and election changed to direct popular vote. Giscard, ever alert to seize an advantage in the feud with Chirac, decided to emphasize "Europe." He needed someone to head his UDF-based list of candidates, a deeply committed "European" but not too involved in party politics. Simone Veil, still a poll-leader, fitted the bill wonderfully. She accepted his offer on the spot.

Suddenly launched now into her first personal campaign, she conducted herself well, even though she dreaded large public meetings and was uncomfortable on television, if less so with journalists. After a disastrous attempt at reading a fuzzy typescript in Marseille, she memorized speeches. She spoke in a level tone, seriously, attempting no oratorical flights, and held her own in debates with other candidates. Typically, she refused at first to allow her poster to include a photo of her. She finally relented under urgent pleas; the one chosen, an informal picture of her on vacation, proved a hit, embellishing her image as a straight-talking, unpretentious, sincere, "ordinary" woman, "*la petite mère Veil.*" On June 10, 1979, her Union for France in Europe (UFE) list drew 27.5% of the votes, topping Mitterrand's Socialists (23.5%), Georges Marchais' Communists (20.5%), and Chirac's RPR, a distant fourth (16.2%).

Giscard was not done yet. He now wanted her elected as the Parliament's first president. This would symbolize his estimate of France's deserved place in the new Europe and confirm the Franco-German axis he was promoting through his close ties with the German chancellor, Helmut Schmidt. In Parliament, the conservatives held the majority—a combination of Liberals (in the European sense, i.e., capitalist free-traders and social moderates), British Conservatives, and Christian Democrats/Socialists. As an unpartisan, politically moderate Jewish woman and Auschwitz survivor, Veil had great symbolic appeal for European unity. But she was also "the Abortionist," making her a hard sell among Christian Democrats. A month of feverish lobbying produced a deal which included Veil's election as a Liberal to half the five-year term, a German Christian Democrat to succeed her for the remainder, with lesser posts and committee chairs spread around to pacify sundry blocs. In a critical move, she won the support of a key Italian—the Italians were outspokenly unhappy with talk of a Franco-German axis— Massimo Silvestro, secretary-general of the Liberal group, thus torpedoing the candidacy of Luxemburg's Gaston Thorn, president of the Federation of Liberal European Parties. At the last moment, however, Chirac's RPR put forward one of theirs, Christian de La Marlène, offering a tortured explanation that since the conservatives had a majority, the RPR did not want to be blamed if Veil lost, the ballot being secret. On July 17, Veil was opposed by La Marlène and three Italian leftists. She fell nine votes short of the required absolute majority. On the second ballot, after La Marlène and one Italian had dropped out, she won an absolute majority by three votes.

In her inaugural speech the next day, Veil vowed to be the president of "the whole assembly." She pleaded for a Europe "of solidarity, independence, and cooperation" which would address the three most pressing issues: peace, freedom, and economic well-being (unemployment was high). It was a highly charged moment for her. In an interview given to the Associated Press in October, she dissected its meaning:

> As a Jew, as a concentration camp survivor, as a woman, you feel very much that you belong to a minority that has been bullied for a long time. As for the deportation, what remains with you most is the memory of humiliation, and that's a feeling many women have, too, of trampled dignity. . . . If this Parliament has a Jew, a woman, for its president, it means everyone has the same rights.

Her term got off to a rocky start. She could be undiplomatic, had obstructive opponents, and lacked a solid group of supporters, even from France, where Giscard inexplicably now ignored her. At the outset, she did not know all the intricacies of the European Community, whose operations were directed simultaneously from Brussels, Luxemburg, and Strasbourg. Fortunately, she was a fast learner. She found the bureaucracy even more frustrating than France's, if that were possible, and blew up enough to confirm the stories preceding her arrival. Fluent in no foreign language, she suffered further annoyance in the translation delays caused by seven official languages. Her most substantive frustration stemmed from the limited powers the Parliament could exercise. It could amend and even reject the Community's budget, but it had no legislative powers equal to conventional parliaments. Its main duties were (1) to supervise the European Commission (the top executive body, appointed not by it but by the governments) and force it (but only by a two-thirds vote) to resign if things ever came to such a pass; and (2) to provide a forum for the airing of general European concerns. From the beginning she worked to expand these powers and revise the body's rules so that very small numbers of members could not obstruct business. She obtained rule changes but never could get the Parliament's prerogatives extended. Yet by the end of her term she had succeeded through great labor in transforming a "club" into a genuine assembly. Unfortunately, her immediate successor lost most of the ground she had gained.

Veil led a busy, sometimes exhilarating life. There was the hard work of presiding over the Parliament (at which she got better), chairing meetings, and conferring with dignitaries. And there was travel, a great deal of it, not just around Europe but in the world at large, where she was greeted as "Madame Europe." She had always enjoyed travel. Among her destinations were Venezuela, Africa, Japan, Israel, Egypt, Australia, and China. In January 1980, she visited the United States, where she caused a flap back in France by stoutly supporting President Jimmy Carter's boycott of the Moscow Olympics because of the Soviet Union's actions in Afghanistan: "Politicians [e.g., Carter] must take responsibility. Actions of this kind are not neutral, they commit those who make decisions. And I believe the games cannot be considered separate from political life." She thought the affair might help teach young people "what responsibility really is."

Honors rained down. In 1975, Princeton had awarded her an honorary degree; likewise the Weizmann Institute in 1976. While president she received degrees in 1980 from Bar Ilan, Yale, Cambridge, and Edinburgh and in 1981 Georgetown and Urbino. More followed in succeeding

years. Likewise with prizes: the Onassis Foundation Athena Prize (1980) and the Charlemagne and *Louise Weiss Foundation prizes in 1981. She also was invited into numerous organizations, her most satisfying being the UN commission on humanitarian issues.

Her speeches and conversations constantly promoted European institutional integration and common action on problems of the environment, employment, and women's rights. She wanted the Community to extend its powers and was hostile to the veto rights held by particular nations. She especially emphasized Europe as a haven of democratic values and rich culture. She wanted to make it a useful counterweight in the Cold War between the U.S. and the Soviet Union. She also encouraged greater French participation in the Common Market and promoted economic unity to make Europe competitive with the United States and Japan.

According to the deal struck in 1979, Veil's half-term would end in January 1982. It was clear, however, that Egon Klepsch, the "designated" German Christian-Democrat successor, had lost ground among the right-wing majority. Veil's name came up as a compromise. But Chirac's RPR continued to support Klepsch. On January 19, the first two ballots yielded no winner. (If one were thinking ahead, on a fourth ballot only a plurality would be needed.) When emissaries appeared urging her to put up her name, she hesitated. It is alleged that she warned the RPR floor leader that a leftist, the Dutch Socialist Pieter Dankert, would win but that she could beat him. The RPR, however, stayed with Klepsch. Moreover, Martin Bangemann, president of the Liberal group (of which she was a member), appealed to her not to run. So she remained silent. To general surprise, Dankert won on the third ballot.

Once more, she had passed up an opportunity to win if she had made a strong effort. Why? Pride, again, it would seem—not wanting to risk a rejection. And a distaste for behaving like other politicians. Her candidacy would have been caused by disunion, whereas she had always preached unity. Furthermore, she would have had to accept some votes from the Left, even the Communists. The "betrayal" by the RPR hurt, too, practically and personally. Because of the RPR's attitude, she had never had the support of a united French delegation. Giscard and Barre, too, had failed to aid her during her term for reasons never made clear. Not until 1981, after Mitterrand succeeded Giscard as president, did she receive an invitation to a full-dress dinner at the Élysée, an honor accorded her in every other capital.

The Parliament applauded her warmly when she stepped down, a contrast to its rather cool reception in 1979. She returned to the ranks now as an ordinary member, but much sought after. She became president of the Legal Affairs Committee (1982–84), which did important work on human rights. She was freer now to be a player in domestic politics, but she assumed the role with her usual caution. In 1981, she had consented, reluctantly, to write an article supporting Giscard against Mitterrand in the presidential election. It was tepid at best. She later said she had become convinced Giscard would lose.

While strongly opposed to Mitterrand as a person and sharply critical of many of his policies, she also gave measured support to many others. She was, as she put it, a "reformist" rather than a conservative. She backed the government rather than the Right in both keeping basic social services and cutting costs in the social security administration; allowing more flexible working hours (a boon to women); ending capital punishment; reimbursing abortion expenses; putting more money into research and culture; supporting plans for the steel industry and for funding the "euromissile"; and opposing any drastic curbing of the role of the State in industry. (She approved of *Margaret Thatcher's industrial policy in Britain but thought it "too tough" for France.) On the other hand, she despised "ideological" reforms in education, the press, and hospitals, and scorned class-war talk. She flayed the anti-inflation policy as incoherent. As for the Cold War, she was hawkish, believing France (and Europe) should support the United States and President Reagan more consistently, e.g., in the Grenada affair. In general, especially in domestic affairs, she thought the Left was too sectarian, too rigid, nursing a "religious war" mentality: "There is a kind of pretention to a monopoly of virtue which is altogether insupportable."

The Right had its problems. On July 9, 1983, a ten-year-old Muslim boy, Tafik Ouannes, died when an overwrought neighbor fired a gun into a noisy Ramadan celebration. Chirac used the tragedy to denounce clandestine immigration. This aroused Veil's fears that the Right was becoming polluted by Jean-Marie Le Pen's immigrant-hating National Front (FN), a proto-fascist party. (FN thugs had attacked one of her election meetings back in 1979; afterward she had marched over to the party's headquarters and denounced them as a pack of "small-bore SS" types who didn't scare her because she

had known the real thing.) Thus, when in September 1983 in a by-election at Dreux (Eure-et-Loir) the RPR and UDF agreed to accept the support of the FN in a runoff, she excoriated the decision and said if she were a voter there she would abstain and let the Left win. A national uproar ensued, with many celebrities coming to her support. But not the Right's bigwigs. In the end she lost her fight and the RPR-UDF-FN won—a bitter disappointment to her.

The Dreux affair became the prologue to what she would regard as the one political act she truly regretted: her agreement to allow Robert Hersant a place on her list in the European Parliament election in 1984. By herself she had persuaded the UDF and the RPR to offer a union list. Chirac was in a "European" mode, while the UDF knew it couldn't win much without her. Besides, the move would help prepare the ground for the legislative elections in 1986. Veil thus headed the 81-member union list, but her partners took "revenge" by letting her pick only one co-lister and insisting that Robert Hersant be included and placed 23rd, thus quite likely to be elected. Hersant had become the Fifth Republic's most powerful press lord, e.g., owner of *Le Figaro*, which Giscard and Chirac had helped him buy in 1977. But he had a Vichyite past, having written for a Pétainist paper articles with anti-Semitic connotations. The Liberation nevertheless had whitewashed him, saying he had "aided" the Resistance. Veil objected vehemently to Hersant's inclusion, but she stopped short of handing Chirac and Barre an ultimatum. It might have worked since her partners dearly wanted her name at the top. Instead, she spent many uncomfortable hours during the campaign explaining to the media and outraged leftists how she could stomach Hersant. She served up lame arguments to the effect that she shouldn't be expected to be more moral than others on the list, or that President Mitterrand himself also had some links with Vichy. For the first time in a decade, Antoine felt obliged to speak out in public to help her.

The UDF was as usual disorganized, and the RPR did not provide the support she expected. She was disappointed on June 17, 1984, that the list did not pull 50% of the electorate, winning only 43%. Still, it ran first and got 41 of the 82 seats in the French delegation. This success proved larger than any the coalition would win thereafter. She had strengthened the Right's ties to "Europe," achieved an entente among the French delegates of the Right at Strasbourg, and administered a serious check to the Left which would help in 1986. But Chirac never did thank her.

To her chagrin, the Hersant affair made her appear far more rightist than she really was. She also was disturbed that Le Pen's list got 11%, a breakthrough. She had decided to ignore him during the campaign, perhaps because of lingering bitterness over her failure at Dreux; but this appeared now to be a mistake. Her warnings to the Right about Le Pen, however, began sounding prophetic. Chirac and Barre came around to her view, but not soon enough to prevent Mitterrand's reelection in 1988. Too many centrists had drifted toward the Left in the wake of Dreux and Robert Hersant.

After her reelection to the European Parliament in 1984, she was named deputy president. She also chaired (to 1989) the Parliament's Liberal, Democratic, and Reforming Group and traveled widely to recruit members, notably in Spain and Portugal after they joined the Common Market. In 1985 she retired as a magistrate. With parliamentary elections looming for 1986, Mitterrand anticipated that the UDF and RPR would win. Probably wanting to send a message to Giscard and Chirac, he made soundings about naming Veil premier, notwithstanding their mutual dislike. The situation resembled Giscard's whispering about her in 1978 as the next premier. It is hard to believe Mitterrand was serious, although Chirac took some precautions. In the end, the Right won its expected victory. The UDF supported Chirac, who became premier (1986–88). Some years later he said he regretted he had not included Veil in his cabinet as she "would have done some good."

All attention turned now to the presidential election of 1988. Mitterrand would oppose either Chirac or Barre. Veil supported Barre as more "tolerant" and less "monopolistic" in his attitude toward power. Chirac beat Barre, however, only to be roundly defeated by Mitterrand, who named a Socialist, Michel Rocard, as premier. At least twice Rocard invited Veil to join his government, offering the prestigious ministry of Justice. But the circumstances suggested that he and Mitterrand wanted her as a "hostage," profiting from her high poll standings while keeping her isolated from her centrist and rightist supporters. She would not bite. In order to counter the rising threat from the Le Pen side, she wanted proportional representation adopted and opposed new parliamentary elections. Rocard disagreed and withdrew the offers. Personally, she regretted that "the Opening," which sought to unite centrists enough to make the Left more receptive to the Right and vice versa, failed to materialize. Rocard, in fact, had shown interest in it and attended some meetings of the infor-

mal Club Vauban, at the Veils', which was promoting the idea.

Meanwhile, she continued to serve France and Europe, in 1987 being named president of the French Committee for the Year of Europe and the Environment and in 1988 president of the European Committee for the Year of Europe of Cinema and Television. On June 18, 1989, she was reelected to the European Parliament, heading a small centrist list which won a respectable 8.4% of the vote. The Assembly election of March 1993, however, suddenly opened a door to her when the UDF and RPR won a crushing victory.

Mitterrand named Édouard Balladur (RPR) premier. Even though she had been interviewed frequently on television as if it were certain she would return to office, she seemed surprised by Balladur's offer of Justice and the prestigious rank of minister of State. She hesitated because of her age (66) and the stress and fatigue involved. Yet Balladur had impressed her immensely by his discretion, frankness, honesty, and courtesy. At a journalists' luncheon she astonished them by flatly asserting that Balladur "is the only one who can rid us of the accursed pair Chirac-Giscard. To carry out this labor of public cleansing, the French are going to rally to him [*plébisciter*] and install him in the Élysée." After the usual parleys, she accepted the ministry of Health, Social Affairs, and Urban Affairs with minister of State rank. (In 1994 she added the department of Women's Affairs. She and **Michèle Alliot-Marie** at Youth and Sports were the only female ministers.) She had taken on a charge dealing with virtually every major problem except the economy and defense—a huge responsibility. She explained, "As for me, I want to undertake humanitarian action in France and concern myself with people's daily life."

To repeat in 1993 the overall success she had won in 1974–79 was probably impossible. Unemployment rose in 1993 to an appalling 12% by November. Homelessness and urban decay, especially in immigrant neighborhoods, ignited strikes and riots. The Budget, drained by unceasing social security outlays, ran rivers of red ink, while a spate of corruption scandals fed public cynicism. Balladur described the situation, somewhat grandly, as the "worst" in France since 1945.

It was obvious that the government, taking a hard line on immigration, hoped Veil's presence would reassure the country that it was committed to humane social programs in order to reduce tensions in the immigrant ghettos. When, for example, Minister of the Interior Charles Pasqua proposed an "ethnic profiling" scheme for police stops, she got it withdrawn by threatening to resign, sensitive as she was to anything smacking of racism. Her approach deemphasized repression. She believed mothers could lead the way to integration of immigrants, so she fostered State aid to non-religious associations offering them education and job training. In the main, she confirmed preexisting socialist innovations while pushing reforms which would reduce their cost.

Reflationary measures brought some recovery by mid-1994. But unemployment stayed unchanged, the stock market was feeble, investment low, and housing starts the lowest in 30 years. The only bright spot was inflation, which remained below 2%. Nothing promised resolution of the social problems Veil was trying to tame. How intractable the situation was is illustrated by what happened when the next ministry (Alain Juppé's) merely announced—not implemented—reform projects in social security and health, cuts in pensions for State employees, and austerity for the French National Railways. Strikes, beginning on the railways, all but paralyzed the country for over two weeks. As for the health front, finding matters no better financially than when she had left in 1979, she pressed for budget constraints. The most dramatic problem was the spread of AIDS, partly as a result of a scandalous contamination of the blood supply which had brought trials of officials, including a former premier. In 1994, she initiated a 42-nation summit meeting in Paris to mark World AIDS Day.

On the international scene, she aided Balladur's support of the European Community. A wave of xenophobia ("Euroscepticism") surged up in many countries, with protection for agriculture a particularly thorny issue. On a happier note, her reputed status as the No. 2 person in the cabinet was underscored when she stood beside *Elizabeth II as France's representative at ceremonies marking the 50th anniversary of D-Day (June 1994).

Despite all, Balladur, a cautious man, remained quite popular in the polls. Nor did Veil lose much ground. He had said when he became premier that he would not seek the presidency in 1995. After he reversed himself and declared his candidacy in January, he began losing ground to Chirac, who campaigned non-stop. Needless to say, Veil, as did most of the UDF, supported Balladur. On April 23, he ran third behind Socialist Lionel Jospin and Chirac. He withdrew and Chirac then defeated Jospin soundly in the May

7 runoff. Balladur resigned and Juppé replaced him. Veil was out.

It seemed all but certain that whatever chances she might have had to become a minister again, to say nothing of premier or (as some whisperings always went) president, were now dead. She did not leave political life altogether. In 1996, she strongly criticized Chirac for reneging on promises he made in 1995 about poverty and the homeless. She also lambasted Juppé for doing too little to boost women's presence in politics. She and nine other female ex-ministers signed the Manifesto of Ten (December 1996), which led to pressure resulting in an ongoing debate about proposed male-female quotas for elective office.

Throughout the '80s and '90s, Veil received a host of honors, including degrees, international prizes, and decorations from several countries, among them Germany, Brazil, Senegal, Greece, and Spain. France made her a chevalier in the Ordre National du Mérite. In September 1997, the British government at the insistence of the Foreign Office made her the first French woman to receive an honorary dameship in the Order of the British Empire, an extremely rare distinction for a foreign national. The British ambassador cited her as "one of the great figures of France and of Europe today." More or less topping off her career, in 1998 she was named to a blue-ribbon UN fact-finding committee sent to examine the civil war in Algeria. She also was appointed to a nine-year term on the Conseil Constitutionel, which serves as the watchdog over the French constitution.

Simone Veil's relations with Judaism and feminism deserve a word. Her Jewishness was neither religious—she was an agnostic, though in the 1970s she began visiting a synagogue on Yom Kippur—nor militant: "Jews should not let anything get by, but they shouldn't dramatize things either." On the other hand, she became discouraged with trying to make people understand the realities of the camps and the Holocaust's true nature. It was partly on this point that she took issue with the war-crimes trials in the '80s and '90s of Klaus Barbie, René Bousquet, and Paul Touvrier. These criminals should be denounced, she said, but that should be all. Any sentence they received would appear derisory beside the crimes they committed; such trials, too, encourage people to think that the Holocaust has been "dealt with." She did say once on television that she wouldn't have minded if someone had "bumped off" Barbie in Bolivia—a comment that raised some eyebrows.

She was prey to a lurking fear that anti-Semitism would swell and genocide return. She was quick to denounce it in words or acts, e.g., when she led a protest march in 1980 on the Champs-Élysées after the bombing of a synagogue on the rue Copernik in Paris. National unity, she believed, was the best defense against anti-Semitism. The Six-Day War (1967) shook her with fear of a return to extermination and then vast relief when Israel won. She regularly visited Israel from 1971 on, but her attachment was sentimental, not religious or political. While in office, she viewed Israel objectively and regarded a Palestinian state as a just solution.

As a woman who continually had to combat ingrained prejudices to succeed in the overwhelmingly male world of politics, Veil was a symbol of achievement to millions of women. She stood up for women's progress and issues yet did not let herself be "ghettoized" into dealing only with women's problems. At the same time, being a woman helped her when "they" were looking for one; the prospect of being the only woman on the scene did not stop her from accepting responsibilities. She used the rights women had gained—and criticized the mass of women for too often not doing likewise. She worried that young women seemed to think that all the battles had been won. On the other hand, she was uncomfortable with militant feminism. As in the abortion struggle, she approached women's issues in a pragmatic way. Feminist theory left her cold, and she thought feminist intellectuals often do not understand the real problems of most women.

She carried herself with pride, conscious of her worth. Yet she knew her limitations. Not conventionally ambitious, she was clear about what was possible and what she wanted whenever she was offered a position. She focused well on getting useful things done, not on basking in public acclaim. Her approach fitted her political stance, which was center-left, so to speak, "the politics of reason." She confessed to being at heart a "democratic socialist," but she rejected left-wing ideology and coolly considered the cost of programs. She remarked cogently that people want both security and less regulation, a contradiction which encourages politicians to resort to ambiguities and unfulfillable promises. In social philosophy, she was conservative. The role of the government "is not in my opinion to curtail or augment the chances of one or another, but to give maximum chances to all."

Simone Veil forged an extraordinary political career by being "an independent personali-ty," as she put it. She participated to some degree in party affairs through the UDF but was never comfortable there. She won a unique place in French politics and public opinion as someone free of ordinary political ties. It was one of the ironies of the life of this complicated woman that with all her success she remained shy. Although she liked wielding power, she did not seek notoriety. As she told a *Washington Post* reporter in 1980, "I don't understand why I have this life. I didn't look for it. . . . Yes, perhaps I'm timid. It's terrible for me to be what we call '*vedette*' in French—yes, that's it, 'star.' It's terrible being in the limelight. If I could I would go under that table." So spoke the president of the European Parliament.

SOURCES:

Biographical Dictionary of French Political Leaders since 1870. David S. Bell, Douglas Johnson, Peter Morris, eds. NY: Simon & Schuster, 1990.

Current Biography Yearbook 1980. Charles Moritz, ed. NY: H.W. Wilson, 1980.

Encyclopaedia Britannica Book of the Year, 1976, 1980, 1993, 1994, 1995, 1996. Chicago, IL: Encyclopaedia Britannica, 1976, 1980, 1993–96.

Historical Dictionary of the French Fourth and Fifth Republics, 1946–1991. Wayne Northcutt, ed. Westport, CT: Greenwood Press, 1992.

International Who's Who 2000. London: Europa, 1999.

Press: *The Washington Post*, Jan. 30, 1980; *The Herald* (Glasgow), April 27, 1993; *The Guardian* (London), April 28, 1993; *The Daily Telegraph* (London), June 9, 1994; *The Jerusalem Post*, Nov. 21, 1995; *The Irish Times* (Dublin), Sept. 5, 1996; *Agence France Presse*, March 26, Sept. 11, 1997; *The New York Times*, July 28, 1998; *Le Monde* (Paris), Nov. 29, 1999.

Sarazin, Michel. *Une femme Simone Veil.* Paris: Robert Laffont, 1987.

Szafran, Maurice. *Simone Veil: Destin.* Paris: Flammarion, 1994.

Who's Who in France: Qui est qui en France. 31st ed. Paris: Jacques Lafitte, 2000.

SUGGESTED READING:

Agulhon, Maurice. *The French Republic, 1879–1992.* Tr. by Antonia Nevill. Oxford: Basil Blackwell, 1993.

Allwood, Gill, and Khursheed Wadia. *Women and Politics in France, 1958–2000.* NY: Routledge, 2000.

Freers, J.R. *France in the Giscard Presidency.* London: George Allen & Unwin, 1981.

Popkin, Jeremy D. *A History of Modern France.* Englewood Cliffs, NJ: Prentice Hall, 1994.

Wright, Gordon. *France in Modern Times.* 5th ed. NY: W.W. Norton, 1995.

David S. Newhall,
Pottinger Distinguished Professor of History Emeritus,
Centre College, and author of
Clemenceau: A Life at War (1991)

Vejjabul, Pierra (b. 1909)

Thai physician. Name variations: Dr. Pierra. Born Kunying Pierra Hoontrakul on November 27, 1909, in Lampang, Siam (now Thailand); daughter of Thongkich Hoontrakul (a teak merchant) and Phon He Hoontrakul; Sorbonne, Paris, M.B., 1934, M.D. with Silver Medal, diploma of hygiene, 1936.

Born Kunying Pierra Hoontrakul in Lampang, Thailand, in 1909 to the third wife of a successful teak merchant, Pierra Vejjabul (or Dr. Pierra, as she is known) fought tradition by pursuing a medical career. She was inspired by a French doctor who had saved the life of her mother, and her resolve to become a physician was further fortified when an unwed mother committed suicide and died in her arms. These experiences provided the cornerstone of her lifelong commitment to the women of Thailand and their children.

Although her father agreed to pay for expensive French boarding schools in Thailand, he refused to subsidize her proposed medical training. Denied admission into the American-operated medical schools in Bangkok because of her gender, she fled to Saigon, South Vietnam, when she was only 16, to further her education. Her father, however, soon insisted that she return home. Undaunted, Pierra convinced her father to allow her to travel to London as the governess for a Thai prince's family. She then sold her valuables and used the blank check he had given her to run away to Paris, thereby financing her early training at the Sorbonne School of Medicine. She earned an M.B. in 1934 and an M.D. in 1936 from the French Academy, graduating with honors.

Following the completion of her medical studies, Pierra returned to Bangkok in 1937 and began working as a medical officer in the division of venereal diseases at the Hospital of the Ministry of Public Health. She instituted the practice of using blood tests to determine the presence of syphilis among factory workers and government employees and was eventually appointed acting director of the division. She also introduced a dual study of venereal diseases from the perspective of medicine as well as sociology, and worked to educate the public on the issue.

From the beginning of her career, Pierra crusaded tirelessly for women's rights. Repeatedly working to improve the unhygienic practices in child care, she also opposed other Thai traditions that were detrimental to women, including polygamy and prostitution, despite threats to her own life. Through the Ministry and later through her own Pierra Maternity and Child Welfare Foundation, she further joined in the international effort to solve global medical and social welfare problems. In 1950, she also helped found the Association of Women Physicians in Thailand.

Willing to embrace sensitive subjects, she was particularly concerned with the problem of prostitutes in Thailand, and she pioneered a study on their rehabilitation. During the late 1930s, Pierra worked for the Ministry of the Interior in fighting venereal diseases. When the Ministry of Public Health appointed her as the overseer of licensed prostitution, she began a project in 1938 to cure venereal diseases among prostitutes. Concurrently, she founded the Institute for Social Welfare for Women, an organization dedicated to rehabilitating prostitutes. She later took a leading position with the National Research on Prostitution in Thailand and in 1960 played a pivotal role in securing the enactment of legislation that abolished legal prostitution. After that time, she focused on creating halfway homes that emphasized vocational retraining for prostitutes. She also devoted substantial energy to studying the rise in Thai rates of divorce and juvenile delinquency, the issue of homosexuality, and the appearance of venereal diseases among teens.

The Pierra Maternity and Child Welfare Foundation, founded by Pierra in 1938, provided free medical care and lodging to needy mothers. She also taught mothers the best psychological and hygienic methods for rearing children as a

Pierra
Vejjabul

means of raising the living standard of the family as a whole. Toward this same end, she published *Mother and Child Magazine* and gave weekly radio talks on child care, child guidance, the protection of children, and venereal diseases. Through the Pierra Foundation, she also legally adopted children whose parents were unable to provide for them. By 1963, she had fostered 660 children, 77 of whom were still living with her. When the Hoontrakul family objected to having all of these children bear their name, Thai Premier Luang Pibul Songram bestowed her with the name "Vejjabul," which means "complete doctor."

In 1956, she joined the governing body of the International Family Planning Association and helped found the Thai Family Planning Association, for which Vejjabul also served as vice-president. In 1957, she also served on the executive committee of the International Union Against Venereal Diseases and Treponematosis, and in 1960, she joined the British Eugenics Society. For her lifelong efforts, Vejjabul received the Thai government's Order of the Crown of Siam and the Order of the White Elephant, as well as the Silver Order of the Thai Red Cross Society. The French government decorated her as a Commander of the Legion of Honor, and in 1963 the United States presented her with the prestigious Albert Einstein Award for humanitarian efforts.

SOURCES:
Current Biography 1964. NY: H.W. Wilson, 1964.

Lisa S. Weitzman,
freelance writer,
Cleveland, Ohio

Velarde, Pablita (1918—)

Native American artist. Name variations: Tse Tsan (Golden Dawn). Born in September 1918 at Santa Clara Pueblo, New Mexico; daughter of Herman and Marianita Velarde; married Herbert Hardin, in 1942 (divorced 1959); children: Helen Bagshaw Hardin (1943–1984, an artist); Herbert Hardin, Jr. (b. 1944).

Awards: grand prize, Philbrook Art Center's Annual Indian Art Show (1948); awarded Ordre des Palmes Académiques, Government of France (1954); grand prize, Inter-Tribal Indian Ceremonial, Gallup, New Mexico (1955); Western Book of the Year citation (1960); Philbrook Special Trophy, Outstanding Contributions to Indian Art, the first woman to receive this honor (1968); New Mexico Governor's Award for Outstanding Achievement in the Arts (1977); honor award, National Women's Caucus for Art.

Selected works: Koshares of Taos (1947); The Betrothal (1953); Old Father (1955); The Green Corn Dance (1956); The Herd Dance (1970s).

One of the most prominent Tewa painters from the Santa Clara Pueblo in New Mexico, Pablita Velarde was born on a September morning in 1918; at a naming ceremony four days later, she was called Tse Tsan (Golden Dawn) by her paternal grandmother **Qualupita**, a medicine woman. Pablita, as she was later known, was only three years old when her mother died from tuberculosis, leaving her father to raise three daughters plus a new baby. Shortly thereafter, both Velarde and the infant contracted a disease that caused them to lose their eyesight. After she was treated by her father, Velarde's eyesight, although weak, eventually returned two years later. She grew up watching the ceremonial dances of the Pueblo, especially impressed by the elaborate costumes and masks.

After attending a local day school, in 1924, Velarde and her two older sisters enrolled in St. Catherine's Indian School in Santa Fe. When the girls returned to the pueblo during the summers, Velarde frequently stayed with her grandmother. From her, Velarde learned traditional Pueblo customs and arts, including the art of pottery, while her father, a respected storyteller, would weave together traditional myths and legends for her amusement. She also eagerly studied the petroglyphs as she played among the Puye Ruins, gaining an appreciation for ancestral designs.

In 1932, Velarde continued her studies at the Bureau of Indian Affairs' Santa Fe Indian School. Under the tutelage of art teacher **Dorothy Dunn**, a pioneer in the revival of Indian art and the founder of the first Indian art school in the United States, Velarde began to paint from her tribal experience and to master the tribal symbols. Dunn taught Velarde the basics of color and brush handling and how to express action from memory. Under Dunn's guidance, Velarde was initially drawn to painting Santa Clara women involved in their daily rituals. She then turned her artistic attention to Native ceremonials, capturing them with photographic detail. Velarde's talents were quickly recognized. In 1933, at age 15, she was selected to work with artist **Olive Rush** on murals for the Chicago World's Fair.

Velarde's success, however, created distracting tensions at home. First, her art was not for Indians but rather only told about them. Even more important, painting was traditionally viewed as the domain of men, and thus Velarde was viewed as a rebel. Her father, in fact, attempted to coerce her to forsake her painting and learn typing instead. At his insistence, she returned to Santa Clara, entered a nearby high school, and enrolled in a business course. After a year, however, she returned to the government school in Santa Fe and graduated from there in 1936, the first in her family to earn a high school diploma.

After teaching arts and crafts at the Santa Clara Day School and touring the Midwest and East with Ernest Thompson Seton and his second wife **Julia Buttree Seton**, Velarde returned to New Mexico and resumed her artistic efforts. At first, she pursued further collaboration with Rush. For instance, in 1938, under the auspices of the Federal Art Project, they completed an impressive mural depicting home activities of the Santa Clara Pueblo for the facade of the Maisel Trading Post in Albuquerque. In 1939, the Park Service employed Velarde to paint archaeological and ethnological murals for the Bandelier National Monument Visitors' Center, murals which reconstructed the life of her ancestors in Frijoles Canyon. At the conclusion of this project, Velarde returned to Santa Clara, where she built her own studio and continued to paint for several years before moving to Albuquerque.

Upon arriving there, Velarde first found employment as a switchboard operator for the Bureau of Indian Affairs. While greatly disliking this job for its obvious lack of creative outlets, she did meet Herbert Hardin, a non-Indian night watchman at the Bureau, and they were married in 1942. She continued to work until her husband was drafted for military service and sent to Texas. Velarde followed him there but, unable to find adequate housing, she returned to Albuquerque to live with her husband's family. She then rejoined Hardin following his transfer to Pennsylvania but went back to Santa Clara with their two young children when he was stationed in California. After finishing his tour of duty, Herbert remained in California to complete his education, while health reasons forced Velarde and the children to remain in Santa Clara. With Herbert in school, the family desperately needed income, and Velarde once again began to paint. During this period, she produced some of her finest work. Ironically, when Herbert eventually returned to Albuquerque, he was disturbed by the extent to which Velarde's art had consumed her energies. They eventually divorced in 1959. Their daughter, **Helen Bagshaw Hardin**, also became a distinguished artist.

Although centered around the rich cultural heritage of the Pueblos, Velarde's work continued to evolve in many directions. For instance, in 1960 she wrote and illustrated *Old Father, Story Teller*, a book of Tewa tribal legends, which resulted from the time she spent listening to and recording the stories of her father. She also began a project to record and preserve the traditions and customs of the Pueblos as remembered by the older members of her community. After some months of work, however, she began to sense hostile feelings and ultimately abandoned the project. In the 1970s, she completed four panels for the Museum of New Mexico under a grant from the National Endowment for Humanities and a large acrylic mural, *The Herd Dance*, for the new Indian Pueblo Cultural Center in Albuquerque.

Velarde's career has spanned more than 50 years. She has exhibited widely and has received many accolades for her work, including the Philbrook Art Center's Grand Prize in 1948 and a special trophy for Outstanding Contributions to Indian Art in 1968, which made her the first woman to be so honored. In 1954, she received the Ordre des Palmes Académiques from the French government, and in 1977, the governor of New Mexico presented her with the Award for Outstanding Achievement in the Arts for her book *Old Father, Story Teller*. In 1990, Velarde received the Women's Caucus for the Arts Award for Life Achievement. One of her paintings was presented by President Lyn-

Pablita
Velarde

don Johnson to the prime minister of Denmark, and in 1993 a retrospective of her work, "Woman's Work: The Art of Pablita Velarde," was held at the Wheelwright Museum in Santa Fe. Steeped in the fundamentals of the "traditional style" of the Santa Fe School, while meticulously detailing Indian crafts, ceremonies, myths, and daily life in her many paintings and murals, Velarde's work is imbued with historical scholarship, ethnographic research, and a clear sense of passion for her subjects. It is thereby valued on an anthropological as well as an aesthetic level, particularly for her insight into the lives of the Pueblo Indians of the Rio Grande area.

SOURCES:

Bataille, Gretchen M., ed. *Native American Women*. NY: Garland, 1993.

Gridley, Marion E. *American Indian Women*. NY: Hawthorne, 1974, pp. 94–104.

Rubinstein, Charlotte Streifer. *American Women Artists: From Early Indian Times to the Present*. Avon, 1982.

Lisa S. Weitzman,
freelance writer,
Cleveland, Ohio

Loreta Velásquez

Velásquez, Loreta (1842–1897)

Cuban-born American Confederate soldier. Name variations: Loreta Janeta Velasquez; Loretta Velasquez; Loreta Velazquez. Born in 1842 in Cuba; died in 1897; married an American Confederate Army officer.

Loreta Velásquez was born in 1842 in Cuba and educated in Louisiana. After she married a Confederate Army officer, she was determined to accompany him into battle, so she disguised herself as a man, complete with a false mustache and a wire-based chemise that minimized her waist and breasts. Under the assumed name of Harry T. Buford or Burford, she enlisted with a group of independent volunteer scouts.

Velásquez fought valiantly at the Battle of Bull Run in 1861 and several times penetrated Northern lines as a spy and blockade runner. Even the death of her husband in battle did not dampen her fighting spirit. She remained in active combat and earned praise for her efforts from General Stonewall Jackson, who never discovered her true identity. Later arrested by her own forces as a federal spy, she was able to talk her way out of imprisonment. At this point, she joined the 21st Louisiana Regiment, engaging in guerrilla warfare before she was wounded. Some say it was at this time that she was forced to confess her gender; other accounts claim that her sex remained hidden until her wire encasement fell apart. In the end, Confederate officers fined her $10 and sentenced her to ten days in jail for her misrepresentations.

Following the war, Velásquez joined an expedition to Venezuela and eventually returned to live in the southwestern United States. There she dabbled in gold mining and traveled on the women's lecture circuit. She ultimately published her story in 1876 as *The Woman in Battle: A Narrative of the Exploits, Adventures, and Travels of Madame Loreta Velásquez*. She died in 1897.

SOURCES:

Felton, Bruce, and Mark Fowler. *Famous Americans You Never Knew Existed*. NY: Stein and Day, 1979.

Macksey, Joan, and Kenneth Macksey. *The Book of Women's Achievements*. NY: Stein and Day, 1976.

Weatherford, Doris. *American Women's History*. NY: Prentice Hall, 1994.

Lisa S. Weitzman,
freelance writer,
Cleveland, Ohio

Veley, Margaret (1843–1887)

British novelist and poet. Born on May 12, 1843, in Braintree, Essex, England; died on December 7, 1887; educated at home.

A Victorian novelist and poet whose output was slender but well regarded, Margaret Veley was born in the English town of Braintree on May 12, 1843. Her schooling took place at home. In 1870, she began to contribute prose and poetry to some of the leading literary magazines of the day, and by 1878 she had completed her first novel, *For Percival*. The book, which had a strong element of humor, remained the best known from Veley's works, and two years after its publication she moved to London. Notable prose works of Veley's London years include *Mitchelhurst Place* (1884) and *A Garden of Memories* (1887). Veley, who never married, died at the age of 44 in 1887. After her death, her poetry was collected and published under the title *A Marriage of Shadows*. The poem that gave the volume its name had aspects of fantasy; another important poem, "A Japanese Fan," was described by the critic George Saintsbury as "something of a positive masterpiece of quiet ironic passion." Although she did not live to learn of the high opinions bestowed upon it, Veley's poetry made perhaps a stronger impression on later chroniclers than did her prose works.

SOURCES:

Kunitz, Stanley J., and Howard Haycraft, eds. *British Authors of the Nineteenth Century.* NY: H.W. Wilson, 1936.

James M. Manheim,
freelance writer,
Ann Arbor, Michigan

Velez, Lupe (1908–1944)

Mexican-American actress. Born Maria Guadalupe Velez de Villalobos on July 18, 1908, in San Luis Potosí, Mexico; committed suicide in late 1944; educated in a convent in San Antonio, Texas; married Johnny Weissmuller (an actor and swimmer), in 1933 (divorced 1938); no children.

Selected filmography: Sailors Beware *(1927);* The Gaucho *(1927);* Stand and Deliver *(1928);* Wolf Song *(1929);* Lady of the Pavements *(1929);* Where East Is East *(1929);* Tiger Rose *(1929);* Hell Harbor *(1930);* The Storm *(1930);* East Is West *(1930);* Resurrection *(1931);* The Cuban Love Song *(1931);* The Squaw Man *(1931);* The Broken Wing *(1932);* Kongo *(1932);* Hot Pepper *(1933);* Palooka *(1934);* Strictly Dynamite *(1934);* Laughing Boy *(1934);* Gypsy Melody *(1936);* Mad About Money *(1938);* The Girl from Mexico *(1939);* Mexican Spitfire *(1940);* Six Lessons from Madame La Zonga *(1941);* Playmates *(1941);* Honolulu Lu *(1941);* Ladies' Day *(1943);* Redhead from Manhattan *(1943);* Nana *(1944).*

An actress who led an uninhibited life and came to a sad end, Lupe Velez was known as "The Mexican Spitfire" in recognition of her personal magnetism, flamboyant ways, and sharp temper. Her youth was a binational one: she was born Maria Guadalupe Velez de Villalobos in 1908 in San Luis Potosí, Mexico, but received her education at a Catholic convent in San Antonio, Texas. She performed as a dancer in both Mexico and Hollywood during her teenage years, and broke into the movies when she was hired in 1926 for a group of comedy shorts directed by Hal Roach; the following year, she appeared with Laurel and Hardy in *Sailors Beware*.

A leading role opposite actor Douglas Fairbanks, Sr., in *The Gaucho* that same year put her in the minds of moviegoers for good. That film launched a period of stardom during which Velez played a series of passionate women onscreen, and lived an equally passionate existence in real life. She had affairs with actors John Gilbert and Gary Cooper (whom she met on the set of the 1929 Western *Wolf Song*) before marrying Olympic swimmer and *Tarzan* star Johnny Weissmuller in 1933. The marriage was a stormy one, enduring a series of separations that were splashed across the pages of the scandal-oriented press. Velez and Weissmuller divorced in 1938.

Lupe Velez

Despite her personal problems, Lupe was riding high as an actress through much of the 1930s. Winning starring roles not only in the United States but also in Britain, Velez became wealthy and purchased a Spanish-style mansion in Beverly Hills. She became known as something of a party animal. After her divorce from Weissmuller, however, Velez suffered a decline in popularity. In the early 1940s she found work only in a succession of low-grade comedies, and her personal life also ran into trouble. Beset by mounting debts, she endured several failed love affairs. In 1944, she was linked with 27-year-old actor Harold Ramond, and in November of that year, still a practicing Catholic, she discovered that she was pregnant. Ramond agreed only to a paper marriage, and even that engagement was soon broken off, but religious considerations dissuaded Velez from having an abortion.

Instead she planned an elaborately theatrical suicide. After filling her mansion with flowers and enjoying a last supper with two female friends, Velez swallowed a huge overdose of Seconal. She wrote to Ramond in her suicide note that she would rather kill herself and her baby than bring shame to the child. She then arranged herself attractively on her bed and waited to die. However, the combination of spicy food, alcohol and some 75 pills made her ill, and during the night she staggered drugged and vomiting to the bathroom, where she slipped, struck her head and drowned in the water in the toilet bowl. Lupe Velez was 36 years old when she died; the unfortunate manner of her death is now generally remembered more than the fact that it was a suicide.

SOURCES:
Katz, Ephraim. *The Film Encyclopedia*. 3rd ed. NY: HarperCollins, 1998.
Kohn, George C. *Encyclopedia of American Scandal*. NY: Facts on File, 1989.

SUGGESTED READING:
Conner, Floyd. *Lupe Velez and Her Lovers*. Barricade, 1993.

James M. Manheim,
freelance writer,
Ann Arbor, Michigan

Velho de Costa, Maria (b. 1938).
See The Three Marias.

Veltman, Vera (1905–1973).
See Panova, Vera.

Vendôme, countess of.
See Euphrosine (d. 1102).
See Jeanne de Castile (r. 1366–1374).
See Catherine of Vendôme (r. 1374–1412).
See Marie of Luxembourg (d. 1546).

Vendôme, duchess of.
See Henrietta of Belgium (1870–1948).

Vengerova, Isabelle (1877–1956)

Russian pianist known for her teaching at the Curtis Institute. Name variations: Izabelle Vengérova. Born Isabella Afanasievna in Minsk, Russia, on March 1, 1877; died in 1956; sister of *Zinaida Vengerova (1867–1941).

Born in Minsk in 1877, Isabelle Vengerova studied at the Vienna Conservatory with Joseph Dachs, and privately with Theodor Leschetizky. Returning to Russia, she completed her musical education with *Annette Essipova, then began teaching at the St. Petersburg Conservatory in 1906. Vengerova left Russia in 1920, first touring Europe and then settling in the United States in 1923. She joined the faculty of the Curtis Institute in Philadelphia when that illustrious school was founded in 1924. Her best-known Curtis students were Leonard Bernstein, Samuel Barber, *Lilian Kallir, Gary Graffman, Leonard Pennario and Lukas Foss.

SUGGESTED READING:
Graffman, Gary. *I Really Should be Practicing*. Garden City, NY: Doubleday, 1981.

John Haag,
Athens, Georgia

Vengerova, Zinaida (1867–1941)

Russian literary critic. Name variations: Zinaida Vengérova; Zinaida Afanas'evna Vengérova. Born in 1867 in Russia; died in 1941; sister of Isabelle Vengerova (1877–1956); educated at universities in Russia and England and at the Sorbonne in Paris; married N.M. Minskii (a poet and critic), in 1925 (died 1937).

Zinaida Vengerova was a literary critic and translator who built bridges between the Russian and Western European modernist literary and artistic worlds. Born in Russia in 1867, she was active in the last decades of the 19th century and at the beginning of the 20th century. Vengerova translated the latest and most advanced writings from Western Europe into Russian; she also wrote essays on such influential figures as Norwegian dramatist Henrik Ibsen, French poets Paul Verlaine and Arthur Rimbaud, German dramatist Gerhard Hauptmann, and, from England, science-fiction writer H.G. Wells and poet Ezra Pound. She lectured on Russian writers abroad, and allied herself with a characteristically Russian feminism that avoided affiliation with wider feminist movements, instead locating the forefront of women's advances with modern Russian women themselves.

Vengerova was better educated than all but a very few women of her time, undertaking university-level literary studies not only in Russia but also, between 1887 and 1891, at the Sorbonne in Paris and at various English universities. For 15 years, she wrote a column on European literature for the Russian periodical *The Herald of Europe*. Living in St. Petersburg, she exchanged ideas with other leading Russian minds of the time, such as those who surrounded the ballet impresario Sergei Diaghilev. For many years she was a widely published critic in Russia; her essays filled a three-volume collection, *Literary Characteristics*, published between 1897 and 1910. Her *English Writers of the 19th Century* was published separately in 1913. Vengerova spent the years of the First World War in England, where she frequently lectured and gave interviews on culture and literature in her homeland, as well as on the status of Russian women. She returned to Russia following the Communist Bolshevik takeover in 1917. However, she left Russia for good in 1921, moving first to Berlin and then to London, where she married the writer N.M. Minskii in 1925. The couple moved to France, and following Minskii's death there in 1937 Vengerova lived out the rest of her life in New York City with her sister *Isabelle Vengerova, a pianist. She died in 1941.

SOURCES:
Buck, Claire, ed. *The Bloomsbury Guide to Women's Literature.* NY: Prentice Hall, 1992.

James M. Manheim,
freelance writer,
Ann Arbor, Michigan

Venier-Baffo, Cecelia (1525–1583).

See Reign of Women for sidebar on Nurbanu.

Vera Constantinovna (1854–1912)

*Duchess of Wurttemberg. Name variations: Vera Romanov. Born on February 4, 1854; died on April 11, 1912; daughter of *Alexandra of Saxe-Altenburg (1830–1911) and Constantine Nicholaevitch (son of Nicholas I of Russia and *Charlotte of Prussia); married Eugene, duke of Wurttemberg, on May 8, 1874.*

Vera-Ellen (1926–1981)

American dancer and actress. Born Vera-Ellen Westmeyer Rohe on February 16, 1926, in Cincinnati, Ohio; died of cancer on August 30, 1981, in Los An- geles, California; daughter of Martin F. Rohe (a piano tuner) and Alma (Westmeyer) Rohe; married Robert Hightower (a dancer; marriage ended); married Victor Rothschild (an oilman), on November 19, 1954 (divorced 1966).

Appeared as a Rockette at Radio City Music Hall (1930s); made stage debut in Very Warm for May *(1939); signed to MGM and made film debut in* The Wonder Man *(1945); danced opposite leading stars Gene Kelly, Fred Astaire, and others in series of musicals (1940s–1950s); retired from film (1957).*

Selected filmography: Wonder Man *(1945);* The Kid from Brooklyn *(1946);* Three Little Girls in Blue *(1946);* Carnival in Costa Rica *(1947);* Words and Music *(1948);* On the Town *(1949);* Love Happy *(1950);* Three Little Words *(1950);* Happy Go Lucky *(1951);* The Belle of New York *(1952);* Call Me Madam *(1953);* The Big Leaguer *(1953);* White Christmas *(1954);* Let's Be Happy *(1957).*

Appearing in leading roles over a 12-year film career as dance partner to Gene Kelly, Fred Astaire, and other leading stars of musical film, Vera-Ellen received consistently high marks for her abilities. Adept in all the varied styles used in cinematic dance, including tap, toe, acrobatic, and dramatic dancing, she appeared in 14 screen musicals and a number of Broadway stage productions.

Vera-Ellen was born Vera-Ellen Rohe in Cincinnati, Ohio, in 1926; her mother had dreamed of the name a few nights before her birth. Suffering from poor health, at age ten she began taking dance lessons to strengthen her constitution. She studied dance at a local studio and in high school in Cincinnati, and did so well that she was sent to a Dancing Teachers of America convention in New York City. While in New York, she tried out for a touring revue and was accepted. She talked her mother into moving to New York with her, and though she was still in her early teens, stage work began to come her way. One of her early jobs was as a Rockette at Radio City Music Hall.

Vera-Ellen made her stage musical debut in 1939 in a show called *Very Warm for May* and appeared in several more shows during the World War II years. A 1943 performance in a revival of the musical *A Connecticut Yankee* caught the eye of Samuel Goldwyn, the legendary movie executive and co-founder of the Metro-Goldwyn-Mayer (MGM) studio. Goldwyn signed her to a movie contract, and Vera-Ellen's career was launched in 1945 with an appearance opposite Danny Kaye in *The Wonder Man.* Critics lauded the work of the young unknown.

Vera-Ellen had made four films for Gold-wyn and for Twentieth Century-Fox by 1947, but that year, after the failure of the film *Carnival in Costa Rica*, she found herself without a contract, despite the positive reviews her own performance had received. Rededicating herself to her craft, she undertook new studies in dance, singing, and dramatics, and was planning to return to New York City when her studies paid off in 1948. She was signed to perform in the "Slaughter on Tenth Avenue" ballet segment of the Gene Kelly film *Words and Music*, and her performance gained her a new seven-year contract with MGM.

The dancer appeared as a co-star with Kelly in 1949's *On the Town*, an ambitious undertaking that featured music by the young composer Leonard Bernstein. She was teamed with the three Marx Brothers in *Love Happy* the following year, and with Fred Astaire in *Three Little Words* (1950) and *The Belle of New York* (1952). Her 1950s films, several of them British, continued to receive stellar notices. In 1953, she appeared in the film version of Irving Berlin's *Call Me Madam*, starring *Ethel Merman and based on the life of Washington hostess and ambassador *Perle Mesta, and in 1954 she was featured in the perennial holiday chestnut *White Christmas*, co-starring Bing Crosby and *Rosemary Clooney. Vera-Ellen married and divorced twice. Her last film was the British-made *Let's Be Happy*, in 1957, although she occasionally appeared on television after that. Following her divorce from Victor Rothschild in 1966, she lived in seclusion until her death from cancer in 1981.

SOURCES:
Current Biography 1959. NY: H.W. Wilson, 1959.
Katz, Ephraim. *The Film Encyclopedia.* 3rd ed. NY: HarperCollins, 1998.

James M. Manheim,
freelance writer,
Ann Arbor, Michigan

Verbruggen, Susanna (c. 1667–1703)

English actress. Born around 1667; died in 1703; daughter of an actor named Percival; married William Mountfort (an English actor and playwright), in 1686 (died 1692); married John Verbruggen (fl. 1688–c. 1707, an actor).

Susanna Verbruggen's first recorded stage appearance was in 1681 in D'Urfey's *Sir Barnaby Whig*. She then played at Dorset Garden and the Theatre Royal. By 1690, Verbruggen was one of the leading actresses in Thomas Betterton's company. About a year after her actor-playwright husband William Mountfort was stabbed to death by a jealous suitor of *Anne Bracegirdle (at the urging of Lord Mohun, who was acquitted by his peers), in 1692, she married John Verbruggen, also an actor of considerable ability.

Vercheres, Madeleine de (1678–1747)

Canadian national hero. Name variations: Madeleine Jarrett Tarieu. Born Madeleine Jarrett Tarieu in 1678 in Canada; died in 1747.

Sometimes referred to as the Canadian *Joan of Arc, Madeleine de Vercheres, whose real name was Madeleine Jarrett Tarieu, grew up on family lands in Vercheres, not far from present-day Montreal. She often went hunting with her family and became an accomplished markswoman. Madeleine was just 14 years old when Iroquois braves attacked the French-held fort of Vercheres in the early 1690s, during the long conflict that raged between native peoples and the French in what is now Quebec. She had been left alone while the soldiers of the fort were away on a mission, but instead of submitting to what seemed the inevitable she rose to the occasion, loading guns that were scattered around the fortification and firing them in random patterns so that the attackers could not tell from where the next shot might come. In the end, she repulsed the entire Iroquois force in this way. She is also said to have helped to beat back another attack, this time by changing her clothes repeatedly so that the Iroquois believed that a large number of defenders were present. She died in 1747.

James M. Manheim,
freelance writer,
Ann Arbor, Michigan

Verde.

Variant of Virida.

Verdon, Gwen (1925–2000)

American dancer, singer, and actress whose string of hits included Damn Yankees *and* Sweet Charity. *Born Gwyneth Evelyn Verdon on January 13, 1925, in Los Angeles, California; died on October 18, 2000, in Woodstock, Vermont; daughter of William Verdon (a gardener) and Gertrude (Strandring) Verdon (a dancer); attended Hamilton High School in Los Angeles; married James Henaghan (a Hollywood journalist), in 1942 (divorced 1947); married Bob Fosse (a dancer-choreographer), in April 1960 (legally separated 1971,*

Opposite page
Gwen
Verdon

Women in World History

died 1987); children: (first marriage) one son, James, Jr.; (second marriage) one daughter, Nicole Fosse.

Selected theater: Broadway debut in Alive and Kicking *(1950); Claudine in* Can-Can *(1953); Lola in* Damn Yankees *(1955); Anna in* New Girl in Town *(1957); Essie Whimple in* Redhead *(1959); Charity Valentine in* Sweet Charity *(1966); Roxie Hart in* Chicago *(1975).*

Selected filmography: On the Riviera *(1951);* David and Bathsheba *(1951);* Meet Me After the Show *(1951);* The Mississippi Gambler *(1953);* The Farmer Takes a Wife *(1953);* Damn Yankees *(1958);* The Cotton Club *(1984);* Cocoon *(1985);* Nadine *(1987);* Cocoon: The Return *(1988);* Alice *(1990);* Marvin's Room *(1996).*

An irrepressible redhead whose high kicks and crackling voice won her four Tony Awards, Gwen Verdon was once described by critic Brooks Atkinson as having everything anyone could want in a musical performer. "She can portray character like a full licensed dramatic actress," he wrote in 1959. "She can sing in a russet-colored voice that is mighty pleasant to hear. . . . And Miss Verdon can dance with so much grace and gaiety that her other accomplishments seem to be frosting on the cake."

Gwyneth Evelyn Verdon was born in 1925, in Los Angeles, the daughter of British expatriates. Her father Joseph Verdon was a stage electrician at MGM and her mother **Gertrude Strandring Verdon** had been a member of the influential Denishawn modern-dance troupe (founded by ***Ruth St. Denis** and Ted Shawn). Throughout her childhood, Verdon wore knee-high orthopedic boots to strengthen legs which had been weakened by several early illnesses. Still, her determined mother dragged her to dancing lessons from the age of two. At four, she appeared in her first dance recital and at six was billed at the Loew's State Theater as the "world's fastest tapper." During her teenage years, Verdon modeled and danced in the chorus at various night clubs.

Verdon's career was just getting off the ground when she eloped with Hollywood journalist James Henaghan, with whom she subsequently had a son, James, Jr. (Jimmy). When the marriage ended five years later, Verdon left her child with her parents and went back to work, joining the troupe of the talented and notoriously difficult choreographer Jack Cole. She made her Broadway debut in Cole's short-lived musical *Alive and Kicking* (1950), and through his connection with the Hollywood studios, obtained

some small dancing roles in several films. She also worked as a movement coach for such stars as *Lana Turner, *Betty Grable, and *Jane Russell.

In 1953, at the suggestion of choreographer Michael Kidd, Verdon auditioned for the musical *Can-Can*, and won a part as a featured dancer. The show starred the temperamental French actress-singer Lilo, who was so threatened by Gwen's talent that she had Verdon's numbers whittled down in out-of-town tryouts. However, on opening night, Verdon's Apache dance brought the audience to their feet. They remained standing and chanting her name even after the dancer had exited to her dressing room for a costume change, and one of the producers had to fetch her back on stage for a curtain call before the show could continue. It was thus, at age 28, Verdon won her first Tony Award and made her presence known on the musical stage.

Verdon's next Broadway role was Lola, the devil's beguiling assistant, in the Adler and Ross musical *Damn Yankees* (1955), based on Douglass Wallop's novel *The Year the Yankees Lost the Pennant*. Verdon, still stinging from her first Broadway experience, signed on mainly for the opportunity to work with the bright new choreographer Bob Fosse. As it turned out, dancer and choreographer forged not only an artistic collaboration but a love match. Years later, Fosse told the *Los Angeles Times*, "People ask if I created Gwen and I say, 'She was hot when I met her. That alabaster skin, those eyes, that bantam-rooster walk. Her in the leotard I will never forget.'" For Verdon, Fosse provided the direction she needed. "Bob choreographs down to the second joint of your little finger," she once said.

Verdon won a second Tony for her portrayal of Lola, bringing the house down with her rendition of "Whatever Lola Wants," a locker-room seduction scene in which she danced a seductive but playful striptease. "She was absolutely magic onstage," said Ray Walston, who portrayed the cunning, lovable devil. "I would glance into the first five or six rows, and all eyes were glued on Gwen." Verdon later reprised the role of Lola in the 1968 movie, stipulating before signing the film contract that no part of her performance would be cut without her permission.

Verdon won two subsequent Tonys for her roles in *New Girl in Town* (1957) and *Redhead* (1959), both of which were directed and choreographed by Fosse. In the former, an unlikely musical adaptation of Eugene O'Neill's bleak waterfront tale *Anna Christie*, Verdon had as much of an opportunity to act as dance, and she proved capable of the challenge. "The finest thing in *New Girl in Town* is Miss Verdon's reticent, moving performance as Anna," wrote Brooks Atkinson about her portrayal of the unhappy ex-prostitute who is redeemed by love. "There is nothing hackneyed or superficial about [her] acting. It is an illuminating portrait of a wretched inarticulate creature." *Redhead*, the story of Essie Whimple, an English spinster transformed into a music-hall performer, also gave Verdon ample opportunity to emote, but it was the Fosse dances, everything from tangos to ragtime, that stole the show. "The amount of physical activity in which this frail-seeming creature indulges is perfectly flabbergasting," wrote Kenneth Tynan in *The New Yorker*, "spinning, prancing, leaping, curvetting, she is seldom out of sight and never out of breath. Yet beneath the athletic ebullience is something more rarified— an unfailing delicacy of spirit."

After her marriage to Fosse in 1960, Verdon retired from performing, giving birth to their only child Nicole Fosse in 1963. It would be six years before she would return to the stage to play a dancer in *Sweet Charity* (1966), a show developed especially for her and again both directed and choreographed by her husband. Despite lukewarm reviews, the show ran for 600 performances, although Verdon was forced by fatigue to surrender the lead to Helen Gallagher before the end of the run. In the later film version of the show, Verdon lost out to the younger Shirley MacLaine.

Meanwhile, Verdon's marriage was in trouble, due to Fosse's numerous affairs. In 1971, the couple separated, although they never divorced. Verdon starred in the original production of Fosse's *Chicago* in 1975, sharing the stage with Chita Rivera and Jerry Orbach in what Clive Barnes called "three superlative, knock-em-in-the aisles performances by three stars who glitter like gold dust all evening." It was, however, Verdon's farewell Broadway performance; Ann Reinking, Fosse's paramour at the time, succeeded her in the role and also restaged Fosse's choreography for a later revival of the show.

Despite their marital woes and separation, Verdon and Fosse continued their working collaboration. Verdon served as supervisor of his 1978 musical *Dancin'*, and also worked on his 1979 autobiographical film *All That Jazz*. She was with him in 1987 when he suffered a fatal heart attack on a Washington street shortly after the opening of the revival of *Sweet Charity*. Following his death, she was instrumental in helping to preserve his remarkable dance legacy, in which she had played such an important part.

Verdon's later work included the made-for-television movie "Legs" (1983) and several films, notably *Cocoon* (1985), *Cocoon: The Return* (1988), and *Marvin's Room* (1996). In August 2000, the dancer moved to Vermont to help her daughter, the mother of three, whose husband had been killed by a drunk driver. Verdon died there in her sleep on October 18, at age 75. That evening, the League of American Theaters and Producers arranged for the lights of Broadway's marquees to be dimmed at eight o'clock in her memory.

SOURCES:

Charles, Nick, Lucia Green, and Lorenzo Benet. "Show Stopper," in *People Weekly*. November 6, 2000.

Current Biography 1960. NY: H.W. Wilson, 1960.

Katz, Ephraim. *The Film Encyclopedia*. NY: Harper-Collins, 1994.

"Obituary," in *The New York Times*. October 19, 2000.

Barbara Morgan,
Melrose, Massachusetts

Verdun, Maud de (fl. 1200s).

See Fitzalan, Maud.

Vere, Diana de (d. 1742)

English aristocrat. Name variations: Lady Diana de Vere; Lady Diana Beauclerk. Died in 1742; only child of Aubrey de Vere, 20th earl of Oxford, and Diana Kirke (d. 1719); married Charles Beauclerk (1670–1726), 1st duke of St. Albans (and son of *Nell Gwynn), on April 13, 1694; children: Charles Beauclerk, 2nd duke of St. Albans (b. 1696); William, Lord Beauclerk (b. 1698); Baron Vere Beauclerk of Hanworth (b. 1699); Col. Henry Beauclerk (b. 1701); James Beauclerk, Lord Bishop of Hereford (b. 1702); Sidney Beauclerk (b. 1703, vice-chamberlain and MP); Lt. Gen George Beauclerk (b. 1704); Cmdr. Aubrey Beauclerk (b. 1711).

Vere, Elizabeth de.

See Howard, Elizabeth (c. 1410–1475).
See Trussel, Elizabeth (1496–1527).

Vere, Frances de (d. 1577)

Countess of Surrey. Name variations: Frances Howard. Died on June 30, 1577; daughter of John de Vere, 15th earl of Oxford, and *Elizabeth Trussel (1496–1527); married Henry Howard (1517–1547), earl of Surrey; married Thomas Staynings; children: (first marriage) Thomas Howard (b. 1537), 4th duke of Norfolk; *Catherine Howard (d. 1596); Henry Howard, earl of Northampton; *Jane Howard (d.

1593); Margaret Howard (d. 1592, who married Henry, Lord Scrope of Bolton).

Vere, Margaret de

Baroness Beaumont. Name variations: Margaret Beaumont. Daughter of John de Vere, 7th earl of Oxford, and *Maud Badlesmere (d. 1366); married Henry Beaumont (1340–1369), 3rd baron Beaumont; children: John Beaumont (b. 1361), 4th baron Beaumont; Eleanor Beaumont (who married Richard de Molines).

Vere, Maud de (d. 1366).

See Badlesmere, Maud.

Vere, Maud de (fl. 1360s)

Countess of Oxford. Name variations: Maud de Ufford. Born Maud de Ufford; daughter of *Maud Plantagenet (c. 1310–c. 1377) and Ralph de Ufford; married Thomas de Vere (1337–1371), 8th earl of Oxford; children: Robert de Vere, 9th earl of Oxford and duke of Ireland (1362–1392).

Vered, Ilana (1939—)

Israeli pianist who concertized widely in America and Europe. Born in Tel Aviv on December 6, 1939.

Ilana Vered was born in 1939 into a musical family; her mother was a concert pianist, her father a violinist. Her mother taught her until she was 13, when a government grant enabled Vered to continue her studies at the Paris Conservatoire with Vlado Perlemuter and *Jeanne-Marie Darré. Subsequently, she studied with *Rosina Lhévinne and *Nadia Reisenberg at the Juilliard School in New York. A 1969 grant from the *Martha Baird Rockefeller Foundation made a major tour of Europe possible. By the 1970s, she had established a solid career with tours in Europe and the United States. Vered was not afraid of behaving like an old-fashioned virtuoso, yet at the same time could tame her spirits for the more delicate world of Mozart and Chopin.

John Haag,
Athens, Georgia

Vergilia (late 6th c.–mid-5th c. BCE).

See joint entry under Veturia and Volumnia.

Vergniaud Pierre-Noël, Loïs M. (1905–1998).

See Jones, Loïs Mailou.

Verina (fl. 437–483).

See Ariadne for sidebar.

Verne, Mathilde (1865–1936)

English pianist who was especially known for her chamber concert performances. Born Mathilde Wurm on May 25, 1865, in Southampton, England; died in London on June 4, 1936; daughter of Bavarian music teachers; sister of Alice Verne Bredt (1868–1958) and Adela Verne (1877–1952); cousin of the artist Sir Hubert von Herkomer; studied with Franklin Taylor and Clara Schumann.

Born in Southampton, England, in 1865, Mathilde Verne studied first with her parents and then with *Clara Schumann in Frankfurt am Main. Verne had a successful career in England, and from 1907 until her death gave a series of chamber music concerts. In 1909, she established her own school, which produced many excellent pianists. Her sisters **Alice Verne Bredt** and **Adela Verne** gained considerable fame as teachers and concert performers. On June 4, 1936, while celebrating the publication of her memoirs *Chords of Remembrance*, about 100 of her pupils and friends gathered at a party at the Savoy Hotel in London. After she played a Schumann concerto with her sister Adela, while one of her students began to sing the "Ave Maria," Mathilde Verne collapsed and died.

SUGGESTED READING:

Verne, Mathilde. *Chords of Remembrance.* London: Hutchinson, 1936.

John Haag,
Athens, Georgia

Verneuil, Marquise de (1579–1633).

See Medici, Marie de for sidebar on Henriette d'Entragues.

Verney, Margaret Maria (1844–1930)

British historical writer. Name variations: Lady Verney. Born Margaret Maria Williams in 1844; died in 1930; married E.H. Verney (a naval officer and baronet), in 1868.

Margaret Maria Verney, a historical writer, chronicled the long history of her husband's family and investigated the small-town life and the educational system that surrounded her in the regions of Anglesey, Wales, and Buckinghamshire, England. Born Margaret Maria Williams in 1844, she married Captain E.H. Verney in 1868, becoming a member of the English nobility, and gaining the designation of Lady Verney when her husband received the title of 3rd baronet. She planned and executed a series of *Memoirs of the Verney Family* that eventually ran to six volumes. She completed the first two in 1892, the third and fourth (which she published herself) in 1894 and 1899, and two supplementary volumes, dealing with the life of the family in the 18th century, before her death in 1930.

James M. Manheim,
freelance writer,
Ann Arbor, Michigan

Vernon, Barbara (1916–1978)

Australian writer and broadcaster. Born Barbara Mary Vernon on July 25, 1916, in Invernell, New South Wales, Australia; died of a heart attack in April 1978 in Sydney, Australia; daughter of Murray Menzies Vernon (a doctor) and Constance Emma (Barling) Vernon; attended the University of Queensland; never married; no children.

Australian screenwriter, dramatist, broadcaster, and novelist Barbara Vernon was born in Invernell, New South Wales, Australia, on July 25, 1916. The last of four children of a doctor, she received a fine official education at a girls' school. She served in the Australian Women's Auxiliary Air Force during World War II, and afterwards attended the University of Queensland, where she studied psychology. Her unofficial education consisted of reading and writing every time she got the chance, with particular emphasis on the *Brontë sisters, H. Rider Haggard, and Rudyard Kipling.

For much of her life Vernon worked in radio and television, both as a scriptwriter and as an on-air personality. She began her broadcast career at the radio station 2NZ in her hometown, where she organized a children's hour and helped its participants stage several plays. Two of these, *The Multi-Coloured Umbrella* and *The Passionate Pianist*, were her own works, and both would later be performed on television. She moved with her mother to Sydney in 1959, finding success when the national Australian Broadcasting Corporation produced a serial radio play she had written about the life of writer *George Sand. Several of her stage plays also found producers. Many of her stage dramas were published or anthologized, and *The Multi-Coloured Umbrella* earned second prize in a drama competition sponsored by the Sydney Journalists' Club, and thereafter was given a number of stage productions. Vernon was best known for creating a long-running television series of the 1960s and 1970s, "Bellbird," the inspiration for which came from her own small-town background. She later wrote two novels, *Bellbird: The Story of a Country Town* (1970) and *A Big Day at Bellbird* (1972), the latter of which was made into the film *Country Town*. She wrote many other stage plays, some of them for children. Vernon retired to a spacious property near Cassilis and died of a heart attack in April 1978, during a visit to Sydney.

SOURCES:

Radi, Heather, ed. *200 Australian Women: A Redress Anthology.* NSW, Australia: Women's Redress Press, 1988.

Wilde, William H., Joy Hooten, and Barry Andrews. *The Oxford Companion to Australian Literature.* Melbourne: Oxford University Press, 1985.

James M. Manheim,
freelance writer,
Ann Arbor, Michigan

Vernon, Mabel (1883–1975)

American suffragist and peace advocate. Born on September 10, 1883, in Wilmington, Delaware; died of heart disease on September 2, 1975, in Washington, D.C.; daughter of George Washington Vernon (a newspaper publisher) and Mary (Hooten) Vernon; graduated from Wilmington Friends' School, 1901; Swarthmore College, B.A., 1906; Columbia University, M.A. in political science, 1924.

Worked as an organizer and sometimes militant activist in cause of women's suffrage (1913–early 1920s); interrupted speech by President Woodrow Wilson (1916); joined Women's International League for Peace and Freedom (1930); present as inter-American committee delegate at founding of the United Nations (1945).

A key figure in both the women's suffrage movement and the pacifist movement, Mabel Vernon devoted her life's work to social change. She did not shy away from civil disobedience in the struggle for the right to vote, and was one of the first suffrage activists to spend time in jail for the cause.

The youngest of seven children, Vernon was born in 1883 in Wilmington, Delaware. Although the family belonged to a local Presbyterian church, the Quaker faith also played a role in her development; her father, a newspaper publisher, came from a Quaker background, and Mabel attended the Wilmington Friends School, graduating in 1901. The Quakers had (and still have) a long tradition of pacifism and social ac-

tivism, and this spirit was to inspire Vernon throughout her career. She earned a bachelor's degree from Swarthmore College, near Philadelphia, in 1906, and then supported herself by teaching German and Latin.

*Alice Paul, with whom she had become friends in college, sparked Vernon's interest in the growing women's rights movement, and in 1912 she attended the convention in Philadelphia of the National American Woman Suffrage Association (NAWSA) as an usher. Paul also encouraged her to quit teaching and take a job as a suffrage organizer, at meager wages, in 1913. Vernon, a verbally oriented woman who had excelled as a debater in college, took naturally to the work. Soon she became an organizer at the national level for the Congressional Union for Woman Suffrage, a militant suffrage group that had split from NAWSA and would later become a component of the National Woman's Party (NWP). Vernon traveled around America, successfully working with *Anne Henrietta Martin to enact a suffrage law in the state of Nevada in 1914 and organizing a cross-country suffrage auto caravan for ☙ Sara Bard Field.

On July 4, 1916, Vernon interrupted a speech by President Woodrow Wilson in Washington, D.C., an act that signaled a new boldness in the efforts of suffragists. As part of a group she met personally with Wilson in May 1917 to press the cause, but embarked on a course of civil disobedience again later in the year when she picketed the White House, was arrested, and spent three days in jail. Undaunted, she toured the country after her release on an NWP speaking tour.

After the 19th Amendment to the U.S. Constitution was passed by Congress in 1919, Vernon worked to promote its ratification. When this task was successfully completed in 1920, granting women the right to vote, she spoke in support of women candidates for office, but also took time out to recharge herself philosophically for new challenges. She lectured on feminism and returned to school, earning a master's degree in political science from Columbia University in New York City in 1924.

The new effort that would absorb Vernon's attention for the rest of her long life was the cause of world peace and disarmament. She joined the Women's International League for Peace and Freedom (WILPF) in 1930, immediately putting her organizational skills to work and helping to launch the WILPF on a trajectory that has made it among the most durable of pacifist societies. As she had done in her suffragist days, she organized a transcontinental caravan.

Field, Sara Bard.
See Bryant,
Louise for
sidebar.

She represented the U.S. WILPF chapter at international conferences, and at a 1936 meeting in Buenos Aires, Argentina, began to develop a specific interest in Latin American countries. In 1945, in the capacity of representative of an inter-American delegation, Vernon was present at the founding of the United Nations in San Francisco. The organization that had sent her to Buenos Aires, the Peoples Mandate Committee for Inter-American Peace and Cooperation, made her its director in the 1940s and then its chair, a position she held until her retirement in 1955.

Vernon was recognized as an activist who excelled both in the spotlight and behind the scenes. An orator whose speeches helped achieve women's suffrage, she was equally gifted as a fund raiser and as what today would be called a lobbyist. In 1972 and 1973, approaching her 90th year, Vernon recounted to oral historians at the University of California at Berkeley the events in her life, which stood at the center of monumental changes in action and attitude. She died in 1975 of heart disease.

SOURCES:

Sicherman, Barbara, and Carol Hurd Green, eds. *Notable American Women: The Modern Period.* Cambridge, MA: The Belknap Press of Harvard University, 1980.

James M. Manheim,
freelance writer,
Ann Arbor, Michigan

Vérone, Maria (1874–1938)

First woman lawyer in France to plead in the criminal courts, who was a journalist, lecturer, and a leader in the struggle for equal rights for women. Pronunciation: mah-REE-ah vay-ROHN. Born in Paris, France, on June 20, 1874; died in Paris of hepatitis on May 24, 1938; daughter of an accountant and a shop clerk; educated at the École Primaire supérieur Sophie Germain and other public schools and at the Faculty of Law (Sorbonne); married and divorced; married Georges Lhermitte (an attorney), in 1908; children: (first marriage) two.

Worked as a substitute teacher in Paris (1894–97); wrote for La Fronde *(1897–1902); named secretary-general of the French League for Women's Rights (LFDF, 1904); helped reestablish* Le Droit des femmes *and became its editor (1906–38); admitted to the Paris bar (1907); sponsored Jeanne Laloë's candidacy for the Paris Municipal Council (1908); author of a report to the National Council of French Women (CNFF) which formed the basis for the women's suffrage bill (1909); left the Socialist Party (1912); served as president of the Suffrage Section of the CNFF (1913–20); involved with the Jeanne Halbwachs trial*

and the Condorcet demonstration (1914); served as president of the LFDF (1918–38); was a columnist for L'Oeuvre *(1918–35); named president of the Legal Section of the CNFF (1921); when Senate defeated the women's suffrage bill, became "Madame Quand-même" (1922); was convener of the Suffrage Section of the International Council of Women (1927–36); arrested in a suffragist demonstration (1928); wrote an Open Letter to Premier André Tardieu, and was a founder of Open Door International (1929); represented the CNFF at The Hague Conference on Codification of Law (1930); was a founder of the Sexological Educational and Studies Association (1931); assisted* La Femme Nouvelle *(1934–36); opposed Blum's project of a National Feminist Council (1936); final passage of the Renoult Law on women's civil rights (1938).*

Publications (from M. Hamburger): Le Suffrage des femmes en pratique: Documents réunis par Chrystal Macmillan, Marie Stritt, Maria Vérone, préface de ***Carrie Chapman Catt** (Paris: L'Alliance international pour le suffrage des femmes, 1913);* La Femme et la loi *(Paris: Librairie Larousse, 1920);* Pourquoi les femmes veulent elles voter *(Paris, 1922);* La Séparation et ses conséquences *(with Georges Lhermitte);* Résultat du suffrage des femmes; La Femme et la loi autour du monde; La Situation juridique des enfants naturels; La Livre de la jeune fille *(collaboration, crowned by the Académie des Sciences Morales et Politiques).*

Journalism: La Fronde *(1897–1902);* La Paix *(1897–1900);* Le Droit des femmes *(1906–38);* La Bataille syndicaliste *(1911–12);* La France libre *(1916–18);* L'Oeuvre *(1918–35); contributed to other newspapers and reviews.*

Maria Vérone was a leading trial lawyer in France in a time when female attorneys were exceedingly rare and almost never appeared in open court. Nevertheless, she was best known to the public as an advocate of women's rights, especially the right to vote.

She was born on June 20, 1874, in Levallois, a working-class suburb of Paris. Her father was an accountant, her mother a shop clerk. They were Voltairian agnostics involved in freemasonry and influenced her toward left-wing politics. Precociously bright, at 15 Vérone served as secretary at the International Congress of Freethinkers and at 18 was one of its lecturers. Her performance as a student won her a scholarship to an upper-level school in Paris, where she intended to pursue a career in mathematics. But her father died, so she had to help support the family. She and her mother worked as *plumassières*, making ornaments and artificial flowers and feathers for women's clothing. Still, she continued her education somehow, for in 1894 she was appointed a traveling substitute teacher.

In 1897, she was dismissed without her final two months' pay because of her political opinions and unionizing activities among teachers and found herself reduced to singing in a chorus line at a small theater. She married a young journalist and joined him on the staff of Georges Clemenceau's *L'Aurore*. In December 1897, she came aboard ***Marguerite Durand**'s new all-female-operated newspaper, *La Fronde*, where until 1902 Vérone wrote a regular column (signed "Themis") on legal and judicial matters. She and **Martha Meliot** (financial affairs) challenged exclusively male institutions such as the stock exchange and forced them for the first time to accredit female journalists. Her experiences led her to decide to become a lawyer.

This was a very tall order, because by now she was divorced and supporting two small children. She had to learn enough Greek and Latin to pass the baccalaureate examination in order to gain admission to the Faculty of Law. She carried it all off and in 1907 became only the fifth woman in French history to be admitted to the bar. (***Jeanne Chauvin** and **Olga Petit** in 1900 were the first.) Unlike the others, Vérone at once entered courtroom practice. Two months after becoming a probationary attorney, she pled before the Court of Assizes, the first woman to do so. More firsts followed, including pleas before the Council of War and the High Court of Appeals (*Cour de Cessation*). Small, alert, fearless, she spoke at the bar in a clear, distinct voice with great eloquence but without oratorical flights. Her forte was a remorseless logic that could shred an opponent's case in minutes.

Vérone accepted many kinds of cases, notably fraud and medical and pharmacological malpractice, but her specialty was juvenile justice. She was a major figure in establishing it as a distinct branch of the law. One result was laws on prostitution by minors (1908), juvenile courts (1912), and child vagrancy (1921). While working to create juvenile courts, she drew attention to anomalies permitting children as young as seven to be tried in regular courts even though the fault usually lay with the family. As early as 1911, after only four years in practice, she was being cited in Parliament as an expert. She also conducted an inquiry on these subjects in Budapest at an international congress. Moreover, in 1908 she was the first attorney to win a case in

which the *puissance paternelle*—the father's exclusive legal power over his children, redefined in 1907—was granted to a woman because of the interests of the child, thus setting a precedent.

Her competence and character—good humored, frank and open, ardent, charming, cultivated, full of panache—made her one of the ornaments of the French bar and a distinguished member of a score of professional organizations. At various times she was a professor of law at the Philotechnical Association, a member of the Defense Committee for Prosecuted Children, the Organization Commission of the Children's Tribunal of the Department of the Seine, the Extra-Parliamentary Commission for the Editing of the Children's Code (1914), *rapporteur* (floor manager and spokesperson) for the Superior Consultative Commissions on Rentals (*loyers*, 1914), and secretary-general of its Housing Section. She was also founder and president of the National Union of French Lawyers and of the Union of Women Lawyers, president of the League of Nations' International Women's Committee on the Nationality of Women, and a corresponding member of the American Institute of Comparative Law and Legislation of Mexico.

Maria Vérone was one of the premier female public speakers of her time, and not just in the courts. She lectured widely on women's issues and legal topics, but additionally she revealed her cultural range and sophistication by holding forth on such subjects as "In the Days of the Courts of Love," "Woman and Love in the Old French Chanson," "The Court of Louis XV before ***Madame de Pompadour**," "The Rehabilitation of Madame de Pompadour," "The Household of Victor Hugo," "The French Woman and the Novel," "In Algeria: Manners, Customs, and Costumes," "Impressions of the East: The New Turkey," "A Traveler in the Kabyle" (Algeria and Tunisia), and others.

Long live the Republic just the same!
—Maria Vérone, 1922, upon the Senate's defeat of women's suffrage

As if these labors were not enough, during the *La Fronde* years, especially as a result of her involvement in 1900 with Durand in the Fifth International Congress on the Condition and Rights of Women, she had become active in the women's movement. She had also joined socialist organizations. In 1900, she was a delegate to the founding congress of the Social Cooperatives' Exchanges and was a member of its central committee for several years. She joined the new Feminine Socialist Group, founded in 1895 by

Louise Saumoneau; but it faded by 1905—which did not displease her altogether because Saumoneau emphasized preparation for the Revolution rather than women's issues as such. She then joined the Unified Socialist Party (SFIO, 1905) but soon found it likewise rather tone-deaf to women's concerns.

The French League for Women's Rights (LFDF, 1882) suited her better. It was friendlier to left-leaning ideas than most women's organizations, tended to appeal to well-educated and (increasingly numerous) professional women, and unlike many feminist organizations cultivated relations with prominent men favoring feminism. When **Maria Bonnevial** became president of the LFDF in 1904 following **Maria Pognon** (1894–1904), Vérone became secretary-general, from which position over the next several years she almost single-handedly revived this once-important organization and made the suffrage its main concern. She also helped re-establish (in 1906) the rather highbrow monthly *Le Droit des femmes* (1869), editing it with the aid of attorney Georges Lhermitte, whom she married in 1908, and **Andrée Lehmann**, vice presidents of the LFDF. Ensconced in the LFDF and *Le Droit des femmes*, Vérone occupied "an extremely important position in the evolution of French suffragist tactics," that is, the middle ground between militants like *Hubertine Auclert and *Madeleine Pelletier, who contemplated violence on the model of the English "suffragettes," and the great mass of moderates, who opposed all street action. She could be confrontational toward authority and sympathetic to calls for direct action, but her temperament and training led her to prefer working within and through the law: "For the decade before World War I, Vérone sought a careful compromise of legalism and militancy that could attract moderate feminists to more active suffragism," writes Steven Hause.

An early—arguably decisive—showdown over tactics occurred during the municipal elections of 1908. Initially as a circulation stunt, *Le Matin* persuaded one of its young reporters, **Jeanne Laloë**, to run for the Paris City Council in the 9th arrondissement. Vérone took up her cause, gave her legal advice, and urged her to run seriously since the Municipal Elections Law of 1884 did not explicitly bar women candidates. She secured Laloë a school hall for a meeting—the first time such legal recognition had been afforded a woman. Over 2,000 people came out, including some 20 news photographers. Hecklers, however, turned the affair to derision. Auclert and Pelletier spoke but came away disillusioned and calling for forceful mea-

sures. On election day, Auclert smashed a voting urn and was arrested. When police prevented Vérone and Laloë from entering a polling place to witness the ballot counting, Vérone argued that the police were acting illegally. More police arrived. At this critical moment, she retreated rather than imitate Auclert, whose actions had shocked almost all the suffragists. Instead, she brought a suit (soon dismissed) over the counting and the denial of entry. Estimates of Laloë's illegal tally ran to 987 votes, or about 22% of the votes cast, a figure hailed by most feminists as a great victory. The more profound result was a defeat for the radicals' forlorn attempt to turn the French suffragists toward the English model of violent activism. For this outcome Vérone, for better or worse, bore considerable responsibility.

The movement forged ahead, exuding optimism. The important League of the Rights of Man and Citizen affiliated with the LFDF in 1908 (Vérone joined its central committee in 1910), and a national feminist congress endorsed the suffrage. In 1909, the National Council of French Women (CNFF, 1901), a federation of all types of women's organizations including the LFDF, asked her to write a report on the pending Dussaussoy Bill (1906), which granted women municipal suffrage. Her lengthy report was approved and sent to Ferdinand Buisson, who relied upon it heavily in his 400-page report submitted (July 16) to the Chamber of Deputies favoring full women's suffrage—the first formal endorsement of the idea the Chamber had received. It was not until 1919, however, that the suffrage question reached the floor, the First World War (1914–18) accounting for much of the delay.

For the parliamentary elections in 1910, Vérone launched an ambitious effort to run female candidates all over Paris. She organized a meeting in March which drew over 2,000 people, with hundreds more turned away. She favored big meetings such as were held in other countries, but the CNFF and the moderate, recently founded French Union for Women's Suffrage (UFSF, 1909) would not go along, leaving her to rely on smaller organizations and sympathetic politicians. The March meeting promised well, but in the end only 9 of 20 candidates registered and only 4 actively campaigned.

Despite disappointments and confusion, the suffrage seemed on the verge of victory before the war—although Vérone, for one, took a less sanguine view of its prospects than most women. She joined the Socialist Women's Group (GdSF), founded in 1912 by **Marianne Rauze** to promote the suffrage, and sat on the executive committee. She also became president (1913) of the Suffrage Section of the CNFF. The Section, founded in 1906 as a study body, was becoming more action-oriented. But that same year Vérone left the Unified Socialist Party over the Couriau affair, when the party failed to support women trying to join a trade union; and in the winter of 1913–14, Louise Saumoneau took over the GdSF in a coup and forced her off the board. Trying to link socialist politics with women's causes only earned her frustration. She concluded women needed some kind of autonomous political identity, although their own party, as in America, seemed out of the question. She spoke of "a new course," "a new place" in the struggle, but groped to define it. Non-violent activism seemed its closest equivalent. In December 1913, the LFDF opened a "suffragist kiosk" on the fashionable boulevard de Sébastopol. It distributed small Christmas gifts wrapped in feminist literature. It is indicative of the moderation of the women's movement as a whole that this timid example of "street action" drew considerable comment.

The success of the kiosk persuaded her and the LFDF in January 1914 to sponsor women's voter registration for the parliamentary elections that year. The object was to force the issue into the courts. Officials reacted cautiously, but finally the prefecture of the Seine refused all female registration. Vérone and Georges Lhermitte brought suits in five districts, basing them on contradictory interpretations of "French" and "citizen" in the law. The case of a socialist student **Jeanne Halbwachs** (later a prominent pacifist as Halbwachs-Alexandre) drew the most attention. The trial judge and the High Court of Appeals ruled that men alone can be "citizens"; women remain "françaises" only and hence cannot exercise political rights. The blunt verdict effectively ended all the cases.

The year 1914 marked the apogee of the women's movement to date and arguably its most hopeful moment ever. The National League for the Vote for Women (LNVF) was formed, a more militant organization than the LFDF and most others. Vérone joined and gave lectures but grew uncomfortable with its tone. She, as did almost all the feminist leagues, refused to participate in a demonstration in late March (the Carrefour Feydeau affair—a dismal failure) sponsored by the LNVF to protest the Halbwachs verdict. She disliked the unauthorized use of her name and didn't want to denounce the courts, where she had cases pending. She served, however, on the committee, adroitly led by the great journalist *Séverine, which put together a

demonstration (July 5) at the statue of Condorcet, an 18th-century philosophe sympathetic to women's rights. It drew 5–6,000 participants from all the major women's organizations, making it the largest demonstration that French suffragists ever staged. But fate intervened less than a month later when France went to war. The catastrophe crippled the movement at the moment it had at last seemed on the verge of success.

After the war began in August 1914, Vérone directed, under the auspices of the LFDF, a clothing warehouse for refugees and some 13 workshops for needy women, subsidized by the National Aid. She also founded an organization (Marrainage de Guerre) of some 400 women who served as "godmothers" to soldiers, writing to them, sending packages, and receiving them in their homes.

The suffrage issue began to revive in 1917 when Pierre-Étienne Flandin presented a report to the Chamber's committee on universal suffrage which revived the Dussaussoy municipal-vote project. Vérone, Durand, and others regarded it as far too moderate and told him so. Action was postponed to the end of the war, by which time Vérone was again in full stride.

She succeeded the late Maria Bonnevial in 1918 as president of the LFDF, remaining there until her death in 1938. Wanting to make it a national federation and thus pressure the much larger UFSF from the left, she undertook lecture tours which spread LFDF chapters to 23 departments by 1920, with about 1,000 members. (By 1927, the figure had risen to 27,000.) She also began a collaboration with Gustave Téry's *L'Oeuvre* in 1918. She wrote more than 500 articles for the paper until she resigned in January 1935 because of differences with editor Marcel Déat over his support of the Laval-Mussolini accords. In 1920, **Elisabeth Fonsèque** succeeded her as president of the Suffrage Section of the CNFF, but in 1921 Vérone returned as president of the Legislative Section. She was also named head of the Legislative Section of the International Council of Women and in 1927–36 convener of its Suffrage Section. In politics, she rejected Bolshevism, left the Unified Socialist Party again, in 1920, as a result of the schism which produced the Communist Party, and (with Durand) joined the small, moderate Republican Socialist Party. The LFDF, which welcomed support from all parties, was probably closer to the Republican Socialists than to others, but that party's "anti-suffragist tendencies coupled with Maria Vérone's determination not to become identified with any one party made any closer collaboration quite impossible," writes Paul Smith. Nevertheless, in a report to the CNFF in 1926 she urged women to join parties in order to get their issues put on the agendas.

In response to the brave and economically vital performance of women during the war, women's suffrage came to the fore from 1919 to 1922. On May 20, 1919, the Chamber of Deputies passed a bill by a 395–329 margin (with numerous abstentions) and sent it to the Senate. Vérone worked to influence the parliamentary elections due in November 1919. She tried to organize a demonstration similar to the Condorcet rally of 1914, but police pressure—the Clemenceau government feared disturbances of any kind might harm France's position at the ongoing Paris Peace Conference—plus the fragmentation of the women's movement frustrated the project. Likewise, a mock election for women sponsored by L'Oeuvre in October fizzled when only 12,688 voted. Police surveillance in 1918–19 particularly galled her. She hinted that violence was a possibility, although she plainly preferred to stay within legal channels.

Vérone continued to focus the LFDF's activities heavily on the suffrage, convinced that it was vital to progress on all other women's issues. The Senate procrastinated, while women's organizations failed to coordinate their efforts. Vérone floated an interesting idea of starting a national chain letter to inundate the Senate, but she couldn't carry it out. She did, however, organize two banquets that attracted large crowds and much press attention. In March 1921, the LFDF held a 50th-anniversary banquet at the Trocadero Palace which drew several thousand, and in December a "Feminist Festival" at the Trocadero featured a speech by former president of the Republic Raymond Poincaré, who was returning to the Senate and was shortly to become premier. The banquet was a huge success, but Poincaré never delivered on his promise to use his full influence in the Senate to get the suffrage bill passed.

In the meantime, an alternative, the "family vote," a proposal floating around since the 1870s, gathered support among politicians wary of granting women equal voting power with men. It would give women a vote and men a vote plus one for each child in the family. Writing in Le Droit des femmes and L'Oeuvre, Vérone and Lhermitte adamantly opposed this peculiar scheme, which many women supported as at least a start. They attacked any two-class voting system and had no difficulty pointing out the inevitable complications, practical and legal,

e.g., how to count children in cases of divorce or illegitimacy or abandonment. Nevertheless, the idea in various versions remained strong for years. By the mid-1930s, Vérone would eventually decide to support it in alliance with Catholic women as a stopgap means of insuring that, if it passed, married women could vote and not have their votes delegated to their husbands.

After innumerable delays, the suffrage bill reached the Senate floor in November 1922. The debate lasted two weeks, at the end of which the bill was returned to committee on a 156–134 vote (November 21). From the packed, stunned gallery, Vérone called out, "Vive la République quand-même!" (Long live the Republic just the same!) It was a cry of anguish, not of acquiescence; from that time on, however, she bore the ambiguous nickname, "Madame Quand-même."

The 1922 disaster would prove irretrievable, a source of deep resentment for Vérone until her death 16 years later. "If only we had a fraction of the funds the British or Americans have," she moaned in 1922. Time and again she threatened to resort to illegal direct action. (She once also proposed, apparently seriously, that women embarrass senators by publicizing names of those observed patronizing brothels.) In April 1925, the Chamber passed a bill granting women the vote in municipal and cantonal elections. Vérone criticized the Chamber for appearing to back away from its 1919 position of equal suffrage rights across the board. Still, while the Senate stalled, officials allowed women to stand for local offices, 80 in Paris alone. Only 10 were elected, all in the provinces and mostly Communists, but Vérone hailed it as a "feminist victory." The Council of State, however, nullified these elections.

Feminists worked hard during the 1928 Chamber elections, with some success. The Senate remained obdurate. When it at last took up the municipal franchise bill, in June 1928, it refused full floor discussion by a 166–116 vote. This second Senate defeat so infuriated Vérone that she summoned women to imitate their English sisters ("En avant les suffragettes," L'Oeuvre, June 20). A week later the LFDF, CNFF, and some other organizations called for a mass demonstration outside the Palais Luxembourg (Senate). The authorities cancelled it, citing a recently enacted law (1927) forbidding marches. In reply, Vérone warned in Le Droit des femmes: "Feminist organizations are in agreement in declaring that they will stop short of nothing in order to win the vote."

No such agreement existed, as the lack of a truly forceful response made painfully clear. The vast majority of women and their organizations (including Vérone's own) harbored too many reservations about what she was calling upon them to do, wedded as they were to moderation and "proper" deportment.

In Angers, at the 1928 congress of the Radical Republican Party—actually anticlerical moderates, dominant in the Senate, who feared women's suffrage would endanger the Republic, especially (as they expected) by increasing the political power of the Roman Catholic Church—she organized a series of demonstrations to disrupt meetings and also to discomfit *Cécile Brunschvicg, a feminist prominent in Radical party affairs. The climax of the campaign came on November 6, 1928, when at the opening of the fall session of Parliament a number of women wearing rosettes and carrying placards arrived at the Luxembourg in taxis decorated with feminist slogans. Over-zealous police moved in and arrested 28, Vérone among them. They were released after a night in jail. Further arrests of women in suffragist garb ensued outside the Senate in the days following. Vérone filed a complaint, but the suit was eventually dismissed for lack of evidence. In March 1929, the Senate refused to revive the municipal franchise bill, 164–120. (The question returned in 1931 and 1935 with similar results.) "Monsieur Véto [Louis XVI] has been resurrected in the guise of a Radical senator," was Vérone's acid verdict.

During the 1928–32 legislature, constitutional revision, e.g., proportional representation, no runoff elections, and halving the size of the Chamber, began to affect the suffrage cause. It split the feminists. Vérone thought revision could open the door for the suffrage; she would support whomever supported the vote. On November 13, 1929, she published an Open Letter to Premier André Tardieu urging him to include women's suffrage with his revisionist proposals. Because revision tended to be supported by many moderates and the Right, however, Radicals and Socialists began to fear it. As the Great Depression deepened and the fascist threat mounted in Europe, even in France (e.g., the rioting on February 6, 1934), suffragists faced a tougher fight with the Radical-dominated Senate, now more determined than ever to hold the line on innovations they believed might threaten the Republic's survival. Vérone took the opposite view, writing that February 6 proved the government had grave faults and needed sweeping reforms such as abolition of the Senate or its election by popular vote (senators were chosen by members of local governing bodies) and the recognition of women as full citizens. Such mea-sures would strengthen, not weaken, the Republic. In this context, the fact that the Left took to calling pro-revision feminists "fascists" contributed to her decision (noted above) to resign from *L'Oeuvre* in January 1935 when its editor supported the Laval-Mussolini accords.

Women's suffrage limped on. The Chamber added it as an amendment to an election reform bill (February 12, 1932), but the Senate detached it and postponed discussion. At the end of the 1932 session (March 31), the Chamber reaffirmed women's suffrage, 463–68, and urged the Senate to act; but in June, when Senator René Renoult introduced a bill to reform women's civil status (see below), the Senate used this as an excuse to put off the suffrage bill once more. In December 1933, the Senate again adjourned the bill, 155–114—its last vote on the suffrage, it turned out, before the Third Republic collapsed during Hitler's conquest in 1940. Not that the suffragists had given up. The 1933 setback led to the birth of La Femme Nouvelle (The New Woman), a movement founded by *Louise Weiss, a journalist heretofore not active in the feminist movement. Vérone gave a "sparkling" speech (according to Weiss) at the founding rally on October 6, 1934. La Femme Nouvelle went on to stage a series of highly publicized demonstrations and stunts—women chaining themselves together at the Place de Bastille monument or interrupting the running of the Grand Prix de Longchamps. Vérone limited her help, perhaps fearing a loss of LFDF members and feeling some pangs of jealousy.

The LFDF helped sponsor a large rally on March 19, 1935, which supported yet another pro-suffrage vote in the Chamber (although the bill was returned to committee) and backed female candidates for the municipal elections in June. It also helped set up a broadly leftist Committee for the Defense of the Rights of Women, which played a role in getting the coming Popular Front government of 1936 to guarantee women the right to work. Feminists won some success in the municipal elections. Returns from the Senate elections in November prompted *Le Droit des femmes* to proclaim "Feminism has won," but the results actually were inconclusive.

The year 1936 was charged with drama. The Popular Front coalition of Communists, Socialists, and Radicals led by Socialist Léon Blum swept to victory in April and swiftly enacted a number of important social reforms. Women's issues, however, were treated with promises and then postponed because other matters seemed more pressing and because of their perceived linkage to constitutional reform and hence too often to the Right. Blum made a widely noted gesture by appointing three women to his cabinet, a historical first, as under-secretaries of state—Cécile Brunschvicg, *Suzanne Lacore, and *Irène Joliot-Curie. Vérone and Weiss could not fathom why they (Brunschvicg in particular) would accept Cabinet posts with no firm assurances on the suffrage. When in June Blum proposed a National Feminist Council to deal with women's issues, Vérone and the editors of La Française persuaded him to scrap the idea; they said they appreciated the thought but preferred the vote.

Although the Chamber voted yet again (July 30, 1936) for full political equality for women, the bill languished because of the government's reluctance to push this divisive issue in the face of current domestic and foreign crises. As for a bill reserving a certain number of seats for women on municipal councils, Vérone opposed it as just another timid gesture. In short, to Vérone the Popular Front (1936–37) proved to be a cruel disappointment—hardly assuaged by her receipt of the Legion of Honor, of which she nevertheless was justly proud.

Important, even consuming, as the suffrage was to Vérone, it was far from her only preoccupation. The First World War forced a reexamination of the civil rights of women, especially married women. Napoleon's Civil Code of 1804, which had undergone only minor revisions in this regard, made a married woman a legal minor, equivalent to a child, criminal, or mental defective, totally subject to her husband, unable to acquire or dispose of property or raise her children without his authorization. The war had left women to run their households unsupervised or work outside the home, and a postwar influx of immigrants to fill jobs left by fallen soldiers led to marriages with French women who therewith lost their French nationality. On this latter point, Vérone, who had pled the Halbwachs case in 1914, was a major advocate in obtaining passage of a law (1927) allowing married women to keep their nationality, with certain limitations, upon marriage to a foreigner. She welcomed the law as a progressive step but continued to argue for an unrestricted right.

On the broader question of civil rights, she and the LFDF campaigned for a reform to end the "slavery" of women. She thought France should follow Italy's example (1919) and simply abolish all legal distinctions between men and women at one stroke with a single amendment. The government, however, decided to examine and alter the Code line by line, arguing that this method would make the abolition more secure by leaving less to judicial interpretation. Most feminists in the early 1920s thought that the suffrage was nearly won and that new legislation would soon finish the job. But the suffrage stalled in the Senate. The government nevertheless went ahead on women's rights and in 1925 appointed an Extra-Parliamentary Commission on the Revision of the Rights of Women. (Neither Vérone nor Catholic representatives were named to it, i.e., the Left and Right were in effect shut out.) The commission's report (May 20, 1928) favored abolition of married women's civil incapacity and rewriting the Code as regards marriage contracts. Despite its omissions, Vérone, as president of the CNFF's Legislative Section, defended the report before the Estates-General of Feminism—a large affair drawing wide attention—in February 1929. But she added that the puissance paternelle should be abolished, and the Estates-General agreed. She repeated similar views when she represented the CNFF at The Hague in 1930 at the International Conference on the Codification of Law.

The 1928 report formed the basis for the bill presented to the Senate on June 23, 1932, by Minister of Justice René Renoult, late president of the Extra-Parliamentary Commission. The Renoult bill, sent to committee, made substantial revisions in the Code but, to Vérone's disappointment, kept hands off the puissance paternelle. Still, prospects looked good—the Senate's Radicals disliked the suffrage but favored civil rights—until Renoult suddenly announced (June 24, 1933) that issues concerning marriage contracts and the conseil de famille—a council of a man's relatives which assumed his puissance paternelle after his death, his widow being excluded—would be dealt with later in other bills. Vérone and most of the non-Catholic ("secular") feminists were outraged, suspecting (rightly) that this mutilation of the original bill was a maneuver to help the Senate ignore the suffrage bill. She pointed out that the division gutted any attempt to grant married women full civil capacity: "In his haste," she wrote sarcastically, "the rapporteur [Renoult] forgot to propose the abolition of certain articles of the Code which will effectively nullify the reform proposed by M. René Renoult." Marriage contracts must be reformed and the conseil de famille ended, otherwise "the vast majority of married women would not be capacitated in practice." What Vérone wanted was simple legal equality within marriage. Unlike a *Nelly Roussel or Madeleine Pelletier, however, she was no radical prepared to consider abolition of marriage or dissolution of the family.

Bad luck stalked the civil-rights movement. By the time the Renoult bill reached the Senate floor (December 1936), a backlash in France and elsewhere in defense of the traditional male-dominated family was in full swing, fed by the crises attendant upon the Great Depression and the darkening international scene. In the end, the bill which passed the Senate (March 19, 1937) had evolved from one liberating women into one protecting the family. Nevertheless, most feminists, Vérone included, wanted the Chamber of Deputies to pass it (which it did, on February 18, 1938) so they could move on to reforming marriage contracts and getting the suffrage. The Renoult Law was at best a gingerly step in the right direction. The whole business had confirmed Vérone's dictum that "parliament only votes laws for those who vote for parliament." Not even she, unillusioned as she was by now, would have imagined that comprehensive reforms of marriage contracts and mothers' rights over their children would wait until 1965 and 1970, two decades after a world war had brought the enfranchisement of women.

There was one other area of special concern to Vérone: sex education, motherhood, and France's low birthrate. The last-named had worried prewar France, and the immense loss of young men in the war made it during the 1920s and 1930s a matter of grave concern about the country's economic and military future. "Natalism" (so-called) and the Family Movement (its participants, the "*familiaux*," emphasizing traditional moral values and large, traditionally structured families) sought to meet the challenge and were most influential in the years 1919–23 and 1934–40. Vérone supported natalism. She praised motherhood as "a rare enough sport" and pleaded that it "ought not to be seen solely as a burden but also a joy, and above all never a source of shame" (*L'Oeuvre*, November 29, 1923). She also believed that celibacy in women often causes "nervous illnesses, such as anemia and neurasthenia," although she stopped short of advocating sexual activity for single women. She couldn't, however, resist tweaking the government for awarding medals to mothers of large families, saying women would prefer the vote in exchange for doing their "patriotic duty." At the same time, nevertheless, she opposed laws against advertising or supplying contraceptives (1920) and forbidding abortion (1923). "To prevent abortion," she wrote, "we must respect motherhood" and concentrate instead on positive steps to ease the conditions women face.

Not surprisingly, Vérone and other secular feminists found themselves by the mid-1920s quite out of tune with the increasingly reactionary tone of most *natalistes* and *familiaux*. (She took to calling them *lapinistes*—"rabbiteers.") She and her feminist cohorts—most notably Cécile Brunschvicg, **Germaine Montreuil-Strauss, Marcelle Kraemer-Bach, Suzanne Schreiber-Crémieux,** and **Yvonne Netter**—were more interested than they in the new science of pediatrics and the latest advances in obstetrics and gynecology and were also impressed by the ideas of Havelock Ellis and *Marie Stopes and others in England and the United States promoting sexual reform and education. Such subjects along with a revived interest in eugenics (which intrigued Vérone) grew quite fashionable by the late 1920s. In 1931, she became a founder and vice-president of the Sexological Education and Studies Association (AEES). In 1929 (in Berlin) she had also helped found Open Door International to oppose the mounting calls for women to confine themselves to their homes and children; and in 1935, she was named honorary president of the newly founded branch in France. Her point of view regarding the general situation of women was well stated in her Open Letter to Tardieu (Nov. 13, 1929), translated by Paul Smith:

> We are forever hearing about the needs of large families, but before you get to the twelfth child, you have to start with the first. The State must take steps to protect the life of every being conceived either in or out of wedlock. Things would be very different if you had to present your program to an assembly of women.

Opinions such as these fueled her opposition to the family-vote schemes, which enjoyed a considerable vogue in the interwar years. The *natalistes* and *familiaux* in turn generally took a dim view of feminism, blaming it for promoting a "selfish individualism" to which they attributed the decline of the birthrate. At a meeting of the LFDF (January 23, 1935), she vented her anger over the frustrations the feminists were experiencing in trying to make any progress whatever on the suffrage, civil rights, the promotion of sex education, and the protection of mothers. Men, she said, because of the double standard, are responsible for the destruction of the family: "Marriage is no longer safe for women. There are women today who prefer to live in free unions, because that way a woman, the mother, keeps her rights." Clearly her tone on this subject had changed since the early 1920s. Certainly, she was less optimistic about women's imminent attainment of equality and security than she had been. In those hopeful days, even the new fashions for women had promised a brighter future—short hair, non-constricting clothing more suited to outdoor and professional activity: "The women who had preceded us," she wrote, "gave us examples of false hair, false sentiments, marriage without love." No doubt changes for the better had occurred, but in her last years Vérone was having trouble seeing them as harbingers of dramatic improvements in women's lives any time soon.

By 1937, her health was failing. She stayed the course as best she could. Quite in character, during her last three months she took great interest in Louise Weiss' new (February 7, 1938) Union of French Women Decorated with the Legion of Honor. It sought to strengthen the country through non-partisan efforts to improve civil rights and lobby on questions of general interest, especially public morals and health.

Maria Vérone succumbed to hepatitis on May 24, 1938, at age 64, six years shy of General Charles de Gaulle's grant to women of the right to vote. She was survived by her husband, children, and several grandchildren. (Andrée Lehmann, a long-time associate, succeeded her as president of the LFDF.) Visitors to her deathbed viewed a tiny, white-haired lady with diaphanous skin, the Legion of Honor pinned over her heart. Decorating an attorney, journalist, lecturer, and tireless activist and organizer serving the causes she believed in, the red-ribboned medal was well placed. Few if any women of her generation owned better title to it.

SOURCES:

Bard, Christine. *Les Filles de Marianne: Histoire des féminismes, 1914–1940.* Paris: Fayard, 1995.

Dictionnaire biographique du movement ouvrier français. Jean Maitron, dir. Paris: Éditions Ouvrières, 1964—.

Française, La. June 4, 1938. Obituary by Suzanne Grinberg.

Hamburger, Maurice. "Maître Maria Vérone," in *La Robe noire, ou la tradition libérale de l'ordre des avocats.* Paris: Les Éditions des Presses modernes, 1937, pp. 170–176.

Hause, Steven, with Anne Kennedy. *Women's Suffrage and Social Politics in the French Third Republic.* Princeton, NJ: Princeton University Press, 1984.

Hesse, Raymond Gaston, and Lionel Nastorg. *Leur manière . . . Plaidoiries à la façon de . . . Maria Vérone [et al.].* Paris: B. Grasset, 1925, pp. 25–35.

Historical Dictionary of the Third French Republic, 1870–1940. 2 vols. Patrick H. Hutton, ed. NY: Greenwood Press, 1986. Esp. K.M. Offen, "Women: Movement for Political Rights," 2:1077–9; P.K. Bidelman, "Feminism," 1:369–73.

Klejman, Laurence, and Florence Rochefort. *L'Égalité en marche: Le féminisme sous la Troisième République.* Paris: Presses de la Fondation nationale des sciences politiques-Éditions des femmes, 1989.

Rabaut, Jean. *Féministes à la Belle Époque.* Paris: Éditions France Empire, 1985.

Roberts, Mary Louise. *Civilization Without Sexes: Reconstructing Gender in Postwar France, 1917–1927.* Chicago, IL: University of Chicago Press, 1994.

Smith, Paul. *Feminism in the Third Republic.* Oxford: Clarendon Press, 1996.

Temps, Le [obituary]. May 25, 1938.

Weiss, Louise. *Mémoires d'une européene.* Vol. 3: *Combats pour les femmes.* Paris: Albin Michel, 1971–80.

SUGGESTED READING:

Agulhon, Maurice. *The French Republic, 1879–1992.* Tr. by Antonia Nevill. Oxford: Basil Blackwell, 1993.

Cooperateur de France, Le. June 4, 1938. Obituary by Jean Gaumont.

Droit des femmes, La. Memorial issue. June 1938, esp. pp. 83–86.

Weber, Eugen. *The Hollow Years: France in the 1930s.* NY: W.W. Norton, 1994.

Wright, Gordon. *France in Modern Times: From the Enlightenment to the Present.* 5th ed. NY: W.W. Norton, 1995.

COLLECTIONS:

Paris: Vérone dossiers in the Bibliothèque Marguerite Durand and the Fonds Marie-Louise Bouglé, Bibliothèque Historique de la Ville de Paris.

RELATED MEDIA:

The Blaze of Day (sound disc), includes "Le Féminisme, Maître Maria Vérone, speaker," Wedhurst, East Sussex, England: Pearl, 1992.

David S. Newhall,
Pottinger Distinguished Professor of History Emeritus, Centre College, and author of *Clemenceau: A Life at War* (1991)

Veronica (fl. 1st c. CE?)

Saint. Name variations: Berenice or Bernice; Berenike or Beronike. Possibly flourished around the 1st century CE. Feast Day is on July 12.

Acknowledged as a saint, Veronica allegedly met Jesus on the day of his crucifixion as he agonized his way to Calvary. Feeling compassion for his pain and predicament, she is said to have wiped his face with a cloth upon which thereafter was left a permanent likeness. There is no record of this episode in the canonical Gospels, although both Mark 15.40–41 and Luke 23.27–29 mention unnamed women-in-mourning among those in Jesus' train. A medieval version of the *Acts of Pilate* identified Veronica with the anonymous woman found in Matthew 9.20–22 whom Jesus is portrayed as having miraculously cured. (Variants of the same tale, however, call this woman "Bernice." The *Acts of Pilate* is an apocryphal work probably dating in its most complete form to the 4th century, although episodes incorporated in the better-developed version seem to have been referred to by Justin Martyr in the 2nd century.) Veronica's story as it now stands is no earlier than the 14th century, but it is possible that she is to be associated with a veil (called the Veronica Cloth or Veronica's Veil) bearing a hallowed visage which has been housed in Rome perhaps since the 8th

Opposite page

Shirley Verrett

century, and in Saint Peter's since the late 13th century. The name Veronica is derived from words meaning "true image," so it is possible—perhaps even probable—that Veronica as she now stands was invented to give a human touch to the existence of a holy relic which many believed to be a portrait of the living Jesus.

William Greenwalt,
Associate Professor of Classical History,
Santa Clara University,
Santa Clara, California

Veronica of Correggio (1485–1550).

See Gambara, Veronica.

Verrett, Shirley (1931—)

American soprano. Name variations: known professionally as Shirley Verrett-Carter until 1963. Born on May 31, 1931, in New Orleans, Louisiana; one of the six children (two girls and four boys) of Leon Verrett (a building contractor) and Elvira (Harris) Verrett; attended primary and secondary school in Oxnard, California; received an Associate in Arts degree from Ventura (California) College, in 1951; studied with Anna Fitziu and Hall Johnson; studied with Marian Szekely-Freschl at Juilliard School of Music, New York City, graduating in 1961; married second husband Louis Frank LoMonaco (a painter and illustrator), on December 10, 1963; no children.

Debuted in Britten's The Rape of Lucretia *in Yellow Springs, Ohio (1957); made New York debut as Irina in Weill's* Lost in the Stars *(1958); appeared as Athaliah, Queen of Judea, in world premiere at Lincoln Center (1964); Teatro alla Scala debut (1966); debuted at Metropolitan (1968) where she continued to sing.*

Hailed by music critic Alan Rich as one of the foremost singers of her time, mezzo-soprano Shirley Verrett is acclaimed as a recitalist and orchestra soloist and as an opera star. Since her professional debut in 1958, she has performed concerts in the major musical capitals of the world and has graced the stages of the world's foremost opera houses, including the Metropolitan Opera in New York, La Scala in Milan, and the Bolshoi in Moscow. In 1996, after nearly four decades, Verrett gave up performing and joined the faculty at the University of Michigan as the James Earl Jones Distinguished University Professor of Music.

Born in 1931 in New Orleans, Louisiana, Verrett was part of a large and musical family; all five of her siblings either sang or played instruments. Her father, the choirmaster at the Sev-

enth-Day Adventist church in New Orleans, provided her early training. Later, after the family had moved to California, Verrett began more formal voice lessons. Despite her obvious talent, she was convinced by her father to pursue a less precarious career in business. At his urging, she received a business degree at Ventura College and then opened a real estate office in Los Angeles. Although the business prospered during its first year, Verrett was still drawn to music and began voice training with Metropolitan Opera soprano **Anna Fitziu**. In 1955, Verrett made an appearance on Arthur Godfrey's "Talent Scouts," a television show for young performers, singing an aria from *Samson and Delilah*. Her performance caught the attention of **Marian Szekely-Freschl**, who was at the time teaching voice at New York's Juilliard School of Music. Verrett subsequently became a student of Szekely-Fresch's at the prestigious school and remained there for six years, receiving financial assistance through various awards and scholarships.

In 1957, while still a student, Verrett made her operatic debut at the Antioch College Shakespearean Festival in Yellow Springs, Ohio, singing featured roles in Benjamin Britten's *The Rape of Lucretia* and Kurt Weill's *Lost in the Stars*. She also sang Weill for her professional operatic debut at New York City Opera in 1958. That year as well, she performed in her first recital at New York's Town Hall, singing arias by Handel, Bach, and Mozart, as well as works by Chausson, Brahms, Purcell, and Persichetti. A critic for the *New York Herald Tribune* found the performance promising and Verrett's voice refreshingly free of some of the mannerisms typical of the mezzo range.

Although Verrett would become known for her interpretation of Carmen in the well-known Bizet opera, it took some time for her to win over the critics. Her first performance in the role, at the Festival of Two Worlds in Spoleto, Italy, in July 1962, was criticized as too intellectual, with not enough exuberance. However, a performance at Moscow's Bolshoi Theater in 1963 was greeted with a 20-minute ovation. When she finally sang the role of Carmen with the New York City Opera Company at City Center in October 1964, critic Louis Biancolli, of the New York *World-Telegram and Sun*, proclaimed it "one of the most seductive Carmens I have ever seen, and one of the best vocally and artistically. Miss Verrett didn't portray the role, she was the role."

In 1966, Verrett sang Carmen for her debut at Milan's La Scala and performed Ulrica in Verdi's *Un Ballo in Maschera* for her first appearance at London's Covent Garden, where she was cheered. On September 21, 1968, she debuted at the Metropolitan Opera House in New York, again as Carmen. She continued to sing at the Met regularly for more than two decades and made musical history when she sang both Cassandra and Dido at the opening night of the Metropolitan Opera's new production of Berlioz's *Les Troyens*. Verrett also appeared at the Metropolitan as both Norma and Azucena in Bellini's *Norma*, and as Tosca, Eboli, Lady Macbeth, Ammeris, and Azucena.

Shirley Verrett has been particularly acclaimed for her ability as a singing actress, and for her unique and varied repertoire, which embraces some of the most demanding roles for a dramatic soprano, such as Norma, Lady Macbeth, Medea, Tosca, Aïda, Desdemona, and Leonore in Beethoven's *Fidelio*. The singer, however, was slow to add to her operatic repertory. "The real danger in any kind of music is learning and singing too quickly," she told Eric Salzman in an interview for the New York *Herald Tribune* in 1963. "I try to work slowly and get inside the music. I want the notes to come easily and naturally; to be in *gola*, in the throat. When the notes are firmly in the throat, then I can get inside the style or the character of the part. The point is, I don't just want to sing beautiful tones; I want them to make musical sense; I want to find out and project what the tones mean."

Since 1964, Verrett has recorded a number of albums, the first of which was a selection of hymns, *How Great Thou Art, Precious Lord*. Another interesting departure from her usual repertoire was her 1965 album, *Seven Popular Spanish Songs*, and a 1966 release of folk and protest songs, *Singin' in the Storm*, which Howard Klein of *The New York Times* called "powerful stuff." Verrett did not record Carmen, however, or some of her other more popular operatic roles.

Verrett ventured to Broadway in 1994, to perform the role of Nettie Fowler in Rodgers and Hammerstein's *Carousel* at New York's Lincoln Center. The production won five Tony Awards and garnered Verrett a nomination for the Outer Critics Circle Award. Her busy performing schedule did not prevent her from devoting time to a number of charitable and humanitarian activities. Verrett is a life member of the NAACP and performed a benefit concert for the organization in Carnegie Hall. In 1989, she and Placido Domingo sang a benefit concert for UNESCO in Paris to aid refugee children in Asia, Africa, and Latin America. She has also sung benefit concerts to raise money for AIDS research.

In her more recent position as a professor of voice at the University of Michigan School of Music, Verrett encourages her music students to concentrate on becoming fully educated. "I have now come to believe that specializing too early is counter-productive and can stunt your growth," she told a group of entering freshmen in 1997. "I have heard many a voice professor talk about 'the voice' as if it were detached from the physical body, the emotions, and especially the mind. Of course, nothing could be further from the truth. Your mind is your greatest asset."

SOURCES:

Moritz, Charles, ed. *Current Biography 1967*. NY: The H. W. Wilson, Co., 1967.

Slonimsky, Nicolas, ed. *Baker's Biographical Dictionary of Musicians*. 8th ed. NY: Schirmer, 1992.

Barbara Morgan,
Melrose, Massachusetts

Versois, Odile (1930–1980)

French actress. Born Katiana de Poliakoff-Baidaroff on June 14, 1930, in Paris, France; died in 1980; daughter of a painter; sister of actresses Hélène Vallier (Militza de Poliakoff-Baidaroff) and Marina Vlady.

An actress whose popularity crossed many national boundaries, Odile Versois was a European film star of the mid-20th century. She was born Katiana de Poliakoff-Baidaroff in Paris in 1930, the daughter of an artist. Her sisters **Hélène Vallier** and **Marina Vlady** both became actresses as well. Versois took to the stage as a child, winning a place in the ballet troupe of the Paris Opera. Her film debut came at the age of 16. For much of her career she played leads, usually in gentle, optimistic roles. She appeared in films not only in her native France (*Dernières Vacances*, 1948, *Fantômas contre Fantômas*, 1949, *Mademoiselle Josette ma Femme*, 1951, *Belle Amour*, 1951, *Le Rendez-vous*, 1961, and *Le Dernier Tiercé*, 1964, among others), but in Britain (*A Day to Remember*, 1953, *The Young Lovers*, 1954, *To Paris with Love*, 1955, *Passport to Shame*, 1959, and more), Germany (*Herrscher ohne Krone*, 1957), and Italy (*Paolo e Francesca*, 1950). She died in 1980.

James M. Manheim,
freelance writer,
Ann Arbor, Michigan

Vesaas, Halldis Moren (1907–1995)

Norwegian poet, prose writer and translator. Born Halldis Moren in 1907 in Trysil, Norway; died on August 9, 1995, in Oslo, Norway; daughter of Sven Moren (1871–1938, a writer); graduated from a teachers' college; married Tarjei Vesaas (the Norwegian novelist, poet and Nordic prizewinner), in 1934; children: son Olav Vesaas; daughter **Guri Vesaas**.

One of the first strong female voices in the modern poetry of Norway, Halldis Moren Vesaas was born in Trysil, in southeastern Norway, in 1907. The daughter of a writer, she attended a teachers' college and worked as a teacher in Oslo, Norway, and Geneva, Switzerland. She also worked for the Norwegian consulate in Vevey, Switzerland. Her knowledge of languages led to her work as a translator of such widely different plays for the Norwegian stage as those by Shakespeare, Racine, and Claudel, and to published works such as *The Threepenny Opera* and A.A. Milne's *Winnie the Pooh*. Vesaas claimed that bringing literature to a wider public through the theater had satisfied her most.

In 1934, she married the novelist and poet Tarjei Vesaas, who became Norway's leading writer of the mid-20th century. Her numerous prose writings include biographies of her father and of her life with Tarjei, and essays on a wide variety of subjects, many in a warm, conversational style. People, books and nature, she stated, were the most significant things in her life, not necessarily in that order.

However, it is for Vesaas' many volumes of lyric poetry, influenced by poet *Edith Södergran and spanning more than 60 years, that she will perhaps best be remembered in Norway. Her first collection, *Harpe og dolk* (Harp and Dagger, 1929), attracted attention because of its openness at a time when it was unusual for Norwegian women to publish poetry. She also often expressed faith in the creative power of nature, even as she turned toward bleak subjects such as World War II-era life in Norway and the postwar threat of nuclear annihilation. One of her many nature themes is that of the tree as a symbol of life, reflecting the significance of the traditional courtyard tree to be found on Norwegian farms. Her verse forms were essentially traditional, but later in life she turned more often toward modern experiments. Vesaas' readership was wide. Some of her other important collections were *Morgonen* (Morning, 1930), *Tung tids tale* (The Voice of Tragic Times, 1945), *Treet* (The Tree, 1947), and *I ein annan skog* (In a Different Forest, 1955).

Vesaas read from her last volume, *Livshus* (House of Life), on its publication only a few days before she died. By then, she had made an

*S*imonetta
*V*espucci

immensely significant contribution to the literature of Norway written in New Norwegian, not only with the amount and breadth of her writing and the charm of her personality, but also through public service on a number of literary and cultural committees, and her collaboration on an anthology of literature for schools. Halldis Moren Vesaas received many literary prizes, and the accolade of Commander of the Order of St. Olav for her services to literature.

SOURCES:

Beyer, E., ed. *Norges Litteraturhistorie* (A History of Norwegian Literature). Oslo: Cappelen, 1975.

Buck, Claire, ed. *The Bloomsbury Guide to Women's Literature.* NY: Prentice Hall, 1992.

Columbia Dictionary of Modern European Literature. 2nd ed. NY: Columbia University Press, 1980.

Vesaas, H. Moren. *I Midtbøs bakkar* (On Midtbøs Hillsides). Oslo: Aschehoug. 1974.

Vesaas, O. *En bok om Tarjei Vesaas* (A Book about Tarjei Vesaas). Oslo: Cappelen, 1995.

Elizabeth Rokkan,
formerly Associate Professor, Department of English,
University of Bergen, Norway,
and **James M. Manheim**, freelance writer,
Ann Arbor, Michigan

Vesey, Elizabeth (c. 1715–1791)

Irish writer and Bluestocking. Name variations: Elizabeth Vessey. Born Elizabeth Vesey around 1715 in Ireland; died in 1791 in London, England; daughter of Bishop Sir Thomas Vesey and Mary (Muschamp) Vesey; married William Handcock, around 1730; married Agmondesham Vesey (an Irish MP and member of Dr. Johnson's club), in 1746; no children.

Elizabeth Vesey was a prominent social hostess and member of the Bluestockings' literary circle of London. Born around 1715 in Ireland into a prosperous family of ecclesiastics and property holders, Vesey was the second daughter of the bishop of Ossory. Little is known about her childhood, except that her parents provided their children with a thorough classical education. Around 1730, she married a member of Parliament, William Handcock. The marriage did not last, however, and in 1746 she was married again, this time to her Irish cousin Agmondesham Vesey. He was a wealthy member of Parliament, later appointed accountant-general of Ireland. After their marriage, the couple divided their time between their estates in Ireland and a home in London.

The Veseys' arrival in London corresponds to the emergence in the later 18th century of a new form of aristocratic social life. This was the salon, an informal gathering of literary and political figures in the homes of educated aristocratic women. Through her husband's political and social ties, and through her friendship with leading hostess *Elizabeth Montagu, Vesey gradually became acquainted with the literary elite of London. Soon she was well enough established in London to emerge as a leading host in her own right. Her parties brought together London's female intellectuals with members of "The Club," a circle of prominent male writers, scholars, and philosophers, including Horace Walpole, Samuel Johnson, and her husband Agmondesham.

The Bluestockings, a literary club of highly educated women who shared ideas and debated issues at weekly parties, emerged in the 1760s as a female counterpart to "The Club." Vesey's friends admired her wit, vivacity, and artful conversation. She was also a prolific correspondent. Her imaginative letters reveal the joy she took in poetry and in playing with language. They also reveal her frequent bouts of depression and her constant ill health, which declined rapidly after the death of Agmondesham in 1785. Although he had been supportive of his wife's social and literary activities, Agmondesham had never been a faithful husband. Elizabeth was deeply grieved to discover that he had left her very little of his fortune for her support as a widow. Instead he provided a large yearly income for his longtime mistress, with most of the rest of his property going to a nephew.

After this, Vesey, about age 70, ended her weekly parties and withdrew into retirement. She became increasingly senile over the next few years, and died in her London home in 1791.

SOURCES:

Carter, Elizabeth. *A series of letters between Mrs. Elizabeth Carter and Miss Catherine Talbot . . . [with] Letters from Mrs. Elizabeth Carter to Mrs. Vesey.* NY: AMS Press, 1975.

Scott, Walter S. *The Bluestocking Ladies.* London: J. Green, 1947.

Laura York, M.A. in History, University of California, Riverside, California

Vespasia Polla (fl. 50 CE)

Mother of Vespasian. Married T. Flavius Sabinus; children: Flavius Sabinus (who married **Arretina***); Vespasian, Roman emperor (r. 69–79 CE).*

Vespucci, Simonetta (d. 1476)

Italian beauty who was the inspiration for Botticelli's **The Birth of Venus.** *Name variations: Simonetta de' Vespucci; Simonetta de Vespucci; Simonetta Cattaneo. Born Simonetta Cattaneo in Genoa, Italy, in 1453; died on April 26, 1476, in Florence; daughter of Gasparo Cattaneo; married Marco Vespucci, in 1469; no children.*

Famous in her own time as "la Bella Simonetta," Simonetta Vespucci was long thought to have been the model for Sandro Botticelli's famous painting *The Birth of Venus.* Though this theory is now discredited, it is still thought that she served as his inspiration for Venus. She was born in Genoa in 1453, to a respectable non-aristocratic family. At age 16, she married the Florentine Marco Vespucci. Her husband was a follower of the dominant Medici family party of Florence, allowing Simonetta to move among the Florentine elite. Tall and blonde-haired, Simonetta was considered by many the most beautiful woman in Florence, and numerous court poets and writers, including Poliziano, wrote works in praise of her beauty and charm. Soon Simonetta became the mistress of the powerful Giuliano di Piero de Medici. It was this connection which brought her to the attention of painter Sandro Botticelli, who was at the time working for the Medici. His studio produced a portrait of her in profile, now at the Pitti Gallery in Florence.

Simonetta Vespucci died suddenly of tuberculosis in April 1476, at age 23. Her admirers, from Poliziano to Florence's ruler Lorenzo de Medici, composed Latin elegies and sonnets in her memory. Said Lorenzo: "It seemed impossible that she was loved by so many men without any jealous and praised by so many women without envy." She was buried in the Church of Ognissanti in Florence. Botticelli's *The Birth of Venus* was completed four years later. Painter Piero di Cosimo also portrayed her, with a snake around her throat to symbolize the consumption that killed her.

SOURCES:

Ady, Julia Mary Cartwright. *The Life and Art of Sandro Botticelli.* London: Duckworth, 1904.

Lightbown, Ronald. *Sandro Botticelli.* Berkeley, CA: University of California Press, 1978.

Laura York, M.A. in History, University of California, Riverside, California

Vestris, Lucia (1797–1856)

English actress, singer and theatrical manager who had a great influence on the development of stagecraft, insisting on realism in scenery and furnishings and historical accuracy in costume. Name variations: Mrs. Armand Vestris; Eliza or Elizabeth Vestris; Madame Vestris; Mrs. Charles Mathews or Matthews; Lucia Elizabeth Mathews; known as Lucy to her family but preferring Elizabeth or Eliza on the stage. Born Lucia Elizabetta Bartolozzi on March 3, 1797, in London, England; died in London on August 8, 1856; granddaughter of the famous engraver Francesco Bartolozzi; daughter of Gaetano Stefano Bartolozzi (a music teacher) and Theresa Janssen Bartolozzi (a German musician and music teacher); married Armand Vestris (1787–1825, a dancer and ballet master), in 1813; married Charles James Mathews, Jr. (1803–1878, an actor and son of the actor Charles Mathews, sometimes seen as Charles James Matthews), in 1838; no children. Lucia Vestris is not to be confused with another Madame Vestris, the French actress Françoise-Rose Gourgaud (1743–1804) who was married to Angelo Vestris (né Vestri), a relation of Lucia Vestris' first husband, and had migrated from Italy to Paris in 1747.

Made first stage appearance in the title role in von Winter's opera Il Ratto di Proserpina *(1815); subsequently appeared in such productions as* The Siege of Belgrade, The Haunted Tower, Artaxerxes, Harlequin's Invasion, Giovanni in London, *and* The Beggar's Opera *(all 1820);* Tom and Jerry, or Life in London *(1821),* The School For Scandal, The Poor

Soldier, and as Ophelia in Hamlet (all 1822); La Gazza Ladra, Dirce, La Donna del Lago, Ricciardo e Zoraide, Matilde de Shabran, The Merry Wives of Windsor, and The Comedy of Errors (all 1823); Zelmira, and The Barber of Seville (both 1824); Paul Pry and Oberon (both 1825); Pong Wong (1826); The National Guard and Hofer, or Tell of the Tyrol (both 1829); appeared at the Olympic in Mary Queen of Scots, The Grenadier, Duke for a Day, My Great Aunt, Chaste Salute, Olympic Revels, The Love Spell, The Widow, or my Uncle's Will, Dumb Belle, and Olympic Devils or Orpheus and Eurydice (all 1831), My Eleventh Day, The Young Hopeful, Olympic Devils, The Court of Queen's Bench, The Conquering Game, and The Paphian Bower, or Venus and Adonis (all 1832), A Match in the Dark, High, Low, Jack, and the Game, Beulah Spa, The Welch Girl, and Deep, Deep Sea, or Perseus and Andromeda (all 1833), Loan of a Lover, The Retort Courteous, How to Get Off, and Telemachus or the Isle of Calypso (all 1834), A New Farce, Why Don't She Marry?, Hearts and Diamonds, The Court Beauties, Love in a Cottage, The Two Queens, or Politics in Petticoats, The Beau Ideal, and Olympic Picnic (all 1835), One Hour, or the Carnival Ball, A Handsome Husband, Court Favour, or Private and Confidential, Olympic Devils, Barrack Room, The Two Figaros, and Riquet with Tuft (all 1836), The Sentinal, The Rape of the Lock, Country Squire, Hugo Bambino, A Dream of the Future, The Ladder of Love, and Puss in Boots (all 1837), The Black Domino, You Can't Marry Your Grandmother, The Drama's Levee, or Peep at the Past, A Hasty Conclusion, and Naval Engagements (all 1838), Blue Beard, Our Cousin German, or I Did it for the Best, Faint Heart Never Won Fair Lady, Izaac Walton, and Meet Me by Moonlight (all 1839); appeared at Covent Garden in The Fortunate Isles (1840), London Assurance (1841), The Confederates, A Match for a King, Don Cesar de Bazan and London Assurance (1844), Medea and Time Works Wonders (both 1845); appeared at the Lyceum in a variety of burlettas and comedies (1847–56).

The exact date of the birth of Lucia Elizabetta Bartolozzi, later known as Lucia Vestris, is uncertain; 1797 is the year given in most sources. The place was the Marylebone district of London. Records were poorly kept at the turn of the 18th century, and as an actress she had good reason to keep her age to herself. Vestris was of mixed Italian and German descent. Her father Gaetano Bartolozzi, a penurious music and fencing teacher, was the son of the celebrated Florentine engraver and bon vivant Francesco

Bartolozzi, who had migrated to England in 1764, where he was later joined by his son and future daughter-in-law, Lucia's parents. Her mother **Theresa Janssen Bartolozzi** was an accomplished German musician and music teacher whom Gaetano had met in Aachen (Aix-la-Chapelle). They were married in London on May 16, 1795, at St. James Church, Piccadilly. In 1797, Gaetano moved to Paris, where Theresa, finding him unable to provide for his family, left him and returned to London. There she supported herself and her two daughters, Lucia and **Josephine Bartolozzi** (1807–1848), by giving music lessons. Lucia was educated at Manor Hall School, where she studied music under Dr. Jay and Domenico Corri. A precocious child, she early showed a talent for music, learned to play the piano, and mastered both French and Italian. In 1811, Lucia entered the school at Her Majesty's Theater, where she studied dance and appeared in the ballet there for a season. That winter, she was sent to Paris to study at the Académie, returning to London to study dance for one year under the celebrated dancer and ballet master Armand Vestris. Lucia's upbringing was relaxed and liberal, her mother taking her to the theater regularly and allowing her to attend operas, concerts and balls as soon as she was old enough to do so.

At age 16, Lucia married Armand in London on January 28, 1813, at the church of St. Martin-in-the-Fields. Armand, ten years older than his bride, came from a family of dancers, who had originated in Italy and whose Italian name was Vestri. Armand was connected with the English theater through his father, Auguste Vestris (1770–1842), who had fled the French Revolution and who had become associated with the King's Theater in London. Taking Eliza as her Christian name, Vestris used her husband's surname professionally for the rest of her life, even though after her marriage to Charles Mathews, she tried unsuccessfully to substitute his name in its place. Despite the fact that she had been trained as a dancer under his tutelage, Armand was impressed more by his bride's rich contralto than by her terpsichorean talents, and arranged for her debut as an opera singer at the King's Theater, on July 20, 1815. Remarkably, she was given the title role in von Winter's now forgotten opus Il Ratto di Proserpina and scored an immediate success. This was followed by another success as Susanna in Mozart's Le Nozze di Figaro and then by an appearance in Zaira. Meanwhile, Armand had gone bankrupt and soon after took his young wife to Paris where, through her connection with the Vestris family,

Lucia Vestris

she was able to perform at the Comédie Française for the next three years (1816–19). There she appeared in both comedy and tragedy with the celebrated French tragedian François Joseph Talma (1763–1826), who had begun his career as a dentist in London and who spoke fluent English. From Talma, Lucia learned the importance of realism in scenery and costumes, and from him she imbibed the idea of the need for realism upon the stage. Talma deplored the turgidity of the classical stage with its artificial acting and pompous declamation, and called for a greater naturalism in acting and staging, sentiments already being expressed in London by the prominent actor John Kemble, and which Vestris never forgot.

Armand and Lucia Vestris were poorly matched and two years after their arrival in Paris were separated when he left for Naples with another woman. Lucia never saw him again. A drinker, gambler and philanderer in his youth, he grew increasingly dissolute over the years, dying at 37 in Vienna in 1825. The successes of Lucia Vestris in post-Napoleonic Paris, including occasional roles in Italian opera, were such that upon that her return to London by September 1819 she was easily able to secure engagements on her own terms. Her first success came at the Drury Lane Theater in the 1820 revival of Montcrief's *Giovanni in London*, a satire on Mozart's opera *Don Giovanni* first staged in 1817. Such satires, known as burlettas or burlesques, were common in the London theater of the day and Mme Vestris not only appeared in many such productions in her career but eventually became noted for having advanced this particular theatrical form. Already, in the role of Giovanni, which had played to a packed house at the Drury Lane Theater and had catapulted her to stardom, she showed herself to be an actress of subtlety and refinement whose naturalistic approach to comedy was at the time something quite new. Contemporary critical estimates of her qualities as a singer vary, but her soft, contralto voice pleased the audiences of her day, as did her vivacious personality and comic sense, although the rumors of her private life in Paris also did much to spread her name.

Vestris continued her career as a singer-actress on her own for several seasons under the management of Robert William Elliston and John Ebers, alternating between elevated singing parts at the King's Theater and comic male roles or "breeches parts" as they were then known. Despite her excellent singing voice, which easily would have qualified her for an operatic career had she chosen to follow one, she preferred to be seen in burlesques and light comedies and in these productions dominated the light theater of London for nearly 30 years, the display of her shapely legs in Giovanni having contributed no small part to her success in the role. In the comic *Tom and Jerry or Life in London* (1821), based on a popular novel of the day, Vestris again delighted audiences in a play noteworthy for dealing with real London types, some of them speaking a London slang now virtually unintelligible to a modern audience and at that time taken for the height of realism. In 1823, she performed in musical versions of two of Shakespeare's plays, *The Merry Wives of Windsor* and *The Comedy of Errors*. When she appeared in the burlesque *Paul Pry* in 1825, her rendition of the ballad "Cherry Ripe" is said to have created a considerable stir and ever afterwards the song was associated with her name. As a singer, Vestris did not hesitate to alter a lyric to suit herself, and later as a manager thought nothing of inserting songs from one burletta into another or dropping a song entirely. Gifted with exquisite taste, she was equally cavalier with costumes, dressing for roles to suit herself.

In her youth, Lucia Vestris specialized as what was known then as a "singing soubrette," a performer described decades later as an actress who "possessed a good voice, could sing by ear,

and had a saucy way of tossing her head that was half-boyish, half hoydenish, and wholly captivating." Long after Vestris' time, this character would evolve into the saucy and sexy characterization of *Anna Held and *Gaby Deslys. In her day, she became highly popular as a singer of ballads and a comedian in light opera specializing in male roles. One of her most popular parts was that of Macheath in John Gay's *The Beggar's Opera*. This excursion into what was then known as travesty (Italian: cross-dressing) was common in the theater and remained so throughout the 19th century, when a woman's legs were still carefully concealed offstage and any excuse to display them was utilized as a device to draw male audiences into the theater. Unlike male actors, who cross-dressed for comic effect—usually parodying elderly, plain or otherwise sexless women—actresses engaged in travesty as a mode of sexual attraction. Dressing as a man enabled a woman to show her legs—in trousers, if she were cautious; in tights, if she decided to throw caution to the winds. Charles Mathews' comic Mrs. Tulip is an example of male travesty accepted by Victorian audiences; Mme Vestris as Don Giovanni, Don Felix, and Macheath are examples of the latter. Of her performance in *The Beggar's Opera*, the *European Magazine* for November 1820 reported:

> Drury Lane, November 7, 1920. This evening "The Beggar's Opera" was performed with the novelty of Madame Vestris as Macheath. . . . Macheath was received with great applause, and as an exhibition of female versatility there was some interest in Madame Vestris' adroit representation of the gay highwayman. She sang with a bold plainness that was not unsuitable to the dashing spirit of the robber; and her acting was appropriate and animated.

From their first appearance on the English stage in the late 17th century until well into the 20th, women of the theater dwelled in a strange half-world outside the limits of conventional society, limits, it may be added, that together with their exceptions, were thoroughly defined by men. For one thing, actresses came from all social classes and, according to whether they appeared in large patent theaters or as entertainers in cheap saloons, they worked on every social level. Some, like Lucia Vestris, were highly paid and lived well; others lived little better than the parlor maids or factory girls who so envied them. Actresses in Vestris' day were often married more than once, were frequently childless, and were presumed to be of easy morals if not worse. In the pulpit, it was assumed that they were sinners destined, after a brief flash of glory, for a destitute old age, and for hellfire thereafter. Nevertheless, despite the poverty, squalor, hardships and sexual exploitation that faced actresses on its lowest levels, the theater was one of the few outlets available to women of independent natures, active minds, and a certain amount of talent, beauty or captivating personality. The theatrical world was anything but dull. The liveliest minds of the day—writers, artists, designers, musicians, composers, intellectuals—circulated around it, and the wealthiest and most influential men patronized its ladies and showered the better-favored ones with gifts of clothes, jewels, carriages, and cash. Successful and famous actresses wore the latest fashions, appeared on stage with handsome matinee idols, and had, or were presumed to have, innumerable lovers. They worked when they pleased, traveled freely, slept late, and when offstage spent their business hours in long and involved discussions with managers, producers, directors, costumers, set designers, music arrangers, and choreographers, or in the company of fawning and flattering hairdressers, wigmakers, voice coaches, and dancing masters.

Lucia Vestris reached the highest levels of her profession appearing with the finest actors. In 1828, she took part in a benefit for the actor John Fawcett at Covent Garden in which the famed Edmund Kean appeared in the third act of *Richard II*, Charles Kemble in the last act of *Romeo and Juliet* and she, herself, appeared as Macheath. On February 14, 1840, she presented *The Fortunate Isles* to commemorate the marriage of Queen *Victoria to Prince Albert, the royal couple honoring the occasion by their presence. Above all, Vestris was extraordinarily popular with the theatergoing public, "London's Goddess of Joy." In 1832, *The London Tatler* described her archly, saying:

Madame Vestris is the best actress that ever sang and decidedly the best singer that ever acted. She was born to fascinate the world and she has a world of fascination. A man might be satisfied with the charms of her mind, if could avoid minding her charms. With talent to transcend beauty, she has beauty as transcendent as her talent. Those most ready to frame faults can find no fault with her frame. . . . Her lips are severed cherries imbued with their own dew; and the commentary they form on Horn's song "Cherry Ripe" gave to that song its popularity . . . she will never grow old, for time that flies with others stands to gaze at her; his wings are idle while he is loitering at hers.

In her private life, Vestris was a child of the 18th century flourishing in an early 19th century milieu that had little time for the prudishness

that one has come to associate with the Victorian era. A lover of men and of intrigue, she created a mild scandal in her youth. Until her father's death in 1821, she had lived at home with her parents and sister, but by late 1822 she had taken her own apartment in Curzon Street, where she soon reigned as "The Belle of Mayfair." A star ever since her appearance in the revival of *Giovanni in London,* she was courted by many of the beaux and dandies of the day, the so-called "Vestry-men," often coyly negotiating her love affairs through the use of intermediaries and anonymous letters. With her extravagant tastes in clothes and jewels, her lavish entertainments, and her need to support her mother and younger sister, Vestris freely accepted annuities and diamonds and the pampering and protection of rich admirers. The most popular ballad singer in London by 1826, she also accepted payment from composers for the promotion of their songs. Surrounded by gossip and the subject of scurrilous verses, Vestris knew the value of publicity, and even the suit she brought against the publisher of a scandalous "memoir" attributed to her pen was perhaps motivated by the desire to keep her name in the papers.

As a singer-actress in the years 1820–31, Vestris appeared in an astonishing number of roles and took part in a grueling number of performances annually. In 1825 alone, she gave no fewer than 114 performances in the enormously successful *Paul Pry,* then offered a series of concerts at Vauxhall. The following year, she appeared in Dublin and upon her return gave 76 performances at Covent Garden in 18 different roles. On tour, she offered managers a choice of 15 productions in which she was prepared to appear. A woman of prodigious energy, she regularly went on tours of the English provinces, appearing as far afield as Edinburgh and in Dublin and other Irish towns. Despite the looseness of her private life, by all accounts she took her professional work with the greatest seriousness. Personally extravagant and self-indulgent, she was a conscientious, disciplined, and dedicated artist. Her sister Josephine, some ten years her junior, hankered after a theatrical career of her own, and Vestris, devoted to her, did her best to launch her on the stage. She took her with her company on her tour of the provinces in 1829, but the girl failed to achieve any success and seems to have lived her life not being Mme Vestris.

The career of Lucia Vestris spanned a new and most important period in the history of the London stage, and she, herself, was very much a part of it. In the early 19th century, the London theatrical scene was dominated by two theaters, the Haymarket, opened in 1705, and Covent Garden (1732) which alone had "patents" (permits) to produce serious drama. The only other theaters permitted to operate were the so-called minor theaters, which were required by law to limit themselves to musical satires. Theaters such as these were rented by large repertory companies sponsored by either wealthy patrons or a small group of investors whose funds supported a theatrical family, or, in the case of Vestris and her second husband Charles Mathews, by a star performer or acting team. Otherwise, a repertory company would tour the provinces playing at strings of theaters owned and operated by an individual or a family who offered seasonal contracts. The custom of having touring companies offering "road productions of London successes" belongs to a later period. This situation of two patent theaters and several minor ones, though often challenged in bills set before Parliament, continued until 1848, when the Theater Regulation Act granted full freedom to the management of theaters and to the production of plays. Thereafter, theaters proliferated and spread throughout the country, competition between managements increased and so did opportunities for employment, especially in the provinces and on the increasingly lively touring circuits where the new railroads made travel so much less arduous. Women performers in particular benefited from the new system; whereas only 310 actresses were recorded in England and Wales in the census of 1841 as opposed to 1,153 actors (26.89%), by 1851, there were 643 actresses against 1,398 actors, women having now risen to 46% of the profession.

By enhancing the physical and existential distance between the stage and the auditorium, she fundamentally altered the playhouse dynamics.

—T.C. Davis

Before this happened, however, the move toward a more realistic staging and performance of plays had already been initiated by the actor-manager David Garrick (1717–1779) and this continued to be developed into the new century. The formality and bombast of 18th-century classical actors, such as John Philip Kendle (1757–1823), and *Sarah Siddons (1755–1831) were being replaced by a more emotional style better suited to the new Romantic drama. Vestris, dissatisfied with current production methods, became intrigued with the bold and novel idea for a woman, of leasing and managing her own theater. It was as the lessee and operator of such a theater that Lucia Vestris made her mark in English theatrical history. In 1831, she

rented Covent Garden in conjunction with the playwright J.R. Planché assembling a company that included such well-known performers of the day as *Julia Glover, J. Vining, F. Mathews, John Liston, and *Maria Foote. The venture was an immediate success and soon after, Vestris took a five-year lease on the Olympic Theater in London, which at her own expense she had redecorated and which she reopened as a "minor" theater, managing it herself for almost a decade. There she introduced realism in scenery and abandoned the grotesque costumes and acting styles long associated with burlettas. The active years of Mme Vestris also saw a slow but steady rise in the status of the acting profession, which increasingly came to be seen as a middle-class occupation, a rise which culminated in the offer of a knighthood to Henry Irving in 1883, an honor that he declined to accept until 1895.

Vestris was an excellent theatrical manager, and, ruling her company with an iron hand, introduced some notable reforms into both the business of running a theater and the staging of plays. At the Olympic, she was aided not only by her excellent company (now augmented by the engagement of **Mary Ann Orger** and **Anne Humby**) but above all by the advice of Planché, who wrote and staged a series of magnificent burlettas for which the Olympic became famous. Lavishly mounted, with elaborate sets and the richest costumes, these productions made use of the latest advances in theatrical machinery and technical developments, especially in the new gas lighting first utilized for footlights in the season of 1817–18. She rehearsed her company before each production, thereby ending the wildly improvisatory acting that was then common, and when not performing herself, she often sat in a box and took notes to correct her cast before the next performance. Recalling his Olympic association years later, Planché described the theater under Vestris' management as "a confectioner's shop, where, although one could not absolutely make a dinner, one might enjoy most agreeable refection, consisting of jellies, cheesecakes, custards and such trifles, 'light as air,' served upon the best Dresden china in the most elegant style."

Lucia Vestris is said to have made a breakthrough in theatrical presentation in 1832, when she staged a play with an interior setting consisting of a ceiling and three connected walls (a rear wall with two flanking walls on either side), the three-walled room with a missing fourth wall that dominated stage settings until the 1920s and which has survived to a great extent ever since. With this, she is credited with adding the first ceiling used in a stage setting. Only the proscenium arch was needed to complete the enclosed, room-with-a-missing-fourth-wall effect; this, however, was not to come until after Vestris' time at the hands of Squire Bancroft (1841–1926) and his wife Marie Winton, known as **Lady Bancroft** (1839–1921). There is some dispute among historians of the theater as to whether or not these innovations should be attributed to Vestris. Some say the first boxed set was not used by her until 1841 in the play *London Assurance* at Covent Garden. Others say she did not invent it at all. Nevertheless, she was certainly one of the first managers to use historically correct costumes and was responsible for introducing the use of real props on the stage rather than facsimiles of wood or cardboard. In the words of T.C. Davis, "She achieved artistic notoriety by setting performances within box sets, making herself seem less approachable within a domestic, scenic framework. By enhancing the physical and existential distance between the stage and the auditorium, she fundamentally altered the playhouse dynamics. Within the closed domestic scenic interior, Vestris seemed to restore the proper demarcation of public and private realms, or at least achieved a partial illusion of having done so."

At the Olympic, Vestris not only produced and appeared in both burlesques and farces but also staged Shakespearean comedies in which she devoted great attention to historical accuracy in both settings and costumes. This was the era of romanticism in literature, drama, and in every other branch of the arts, a movement that rejected the cold, formal, intellectual approach to life and art that had its source in an 18th-century understanding of Greece and Rome, an intellectual interpretation that saw everything through the prism of reason. In its place, or at least by its side, the romantics would put the emotional and spiritual side of human nature, rejecting sheer reason and logic for intuition, and calculation for spontaneity. Though the modern drama of Henrik Ibsen lay in the future, the theater of Vestris' day was dazzled by the new romantic drama of Victor Hugo, Alexandre Dumas *père*, and Charles Gordon (Lord Byron), as well as, of course, by the gloriously romantic dramas of William Shakespeare—as originally written rather than in the sentimentalized 18th-century versions in which, for example, *Romeo and Juliet* was endowed with a happy ending. Hugo rejected the classical unities of time and place that stipulated that the action of a play must take place in a single locale and not exceed the time span encompassed by the play itself.

Shakespeare, though never losing his popularity, was considered by many in the 18th century to have been brilliant but uncultivated. By the romantics, however, he was regarded as a native, spontaneous genius, who had produced his masterpieces through the outpouring of emotional passion unfettered by classical rules.

The same forces that were producing a new tragic acting were also at work in comedy, and at the Olympic Vestris was aided by the playwright J.R. Planché in developing her own natural style of acting which created humor through its contrast with the extravagant words and action of the burlesques that he either wrote for her, himself, or translated from the French. In 1835, Vestris and Planché were joined at the Olympic by the actor Charles Mathews, whose depiction of the elegant English gentleman with neither irony nor exaggeration was much esteemed by critics and audiences alike. In 1850, George Henry Lewis described Vestris and Mathews in a performance together as "a lady or gentleman such as one meets in drawing rooms, graceful, quiet, well-bred, perfectly dressed, perfectly oblivious to the footlights." This was a new style of acting that was to be raised to a perfection by Squire Bancroft at the Prince of Wales Theater, which he managed from 1865 to 1880.

On July 17, 1838, Mme Vestris and Charles Mathews were married, an event that led to the emergence of a famous though probably apocryphal anecdote that swept London at the time. Three members of her company were discussing the impending nuptials. Mrs. Humby said that she had heard that, before agreeing to marry, Mme Vestris had made a complete confession of her previous affairs to her intended husband. "What a touching confidence," added Humby, to which Mrs. Orger replied, "What endless trouble!," to which Mrs. Glover replied, "What a memory!" At the time of their wedding, Vestris was about 40 and Mathews 34. Genuinely in love and thoroughly devoted to one another, the couple remained together for 18 years, through good times and bad, and the rest of Vestris' career was completely interwoven with that of her husband.

One week after their marriage, the team of Mathews and Vestris embarked for an American engagement for which they had been promised $100,000 for a year of performances. In New York, they opened at the Park Theater on September 17 in *The Drama's Levee,* but soon ran afoul of the New York newspapers, first because of Lucia's unwillingness to mingle with the other guests at her Catskill hotel to which she had repaired to escape a New York heat wave that was in full force when she arrived, second for some disparaging remarks that she had made in regard to certain popular New York actors, and third because of the rumors that had begun to circulate concerning her supposedly scandalous private life in London. English artists had not been welcome on the American stage for decades after the American Revolution and only in 1822 did the beauty and charm of the young *Fanny Kemble so captivate her New World audiences that the way was cleared for Vestris and Mathews to appear in the United States without prejudice. Unfortunately, Vestris' lack of sensitivity and a bad press caused her American tour to end a failure. Audiences too, having heard of her mildly scandalous reputation and expecting a glamorous coquette, were disappointed to find before them a woman no longer young. Originally scheduled for 36 performances at the Chestnut Street Theater in Philadelphia, the Mathews-Vestris engagement was cut to 12 (October 8–12) and the manager of the theater where they were to appear in Baltimore canceled their engagement entirely. Their final appearances back in New York drew better audiences, but Mathews alone managed to salvage some personal success of his own. Upon returning to England, the couple found that they had realized but £1,750 instead of the £20,000 they had expected to bring home.

In 1841, Vestris and Mathews, having given up the Olympic, now leased the theater known as Covent Garden (1839–42). There they opened in *London Assurance*, the first play by Dion Boucicault the Elder (1822–1890), a 19-year-old actor and playwright of Irish extraction, who later immigrated to the United States where he enjoyed a highly successful career. Of this production, *The Theatrical Observer* reported: "The squire's house, opening on to a green lawn, the drawing room so magnificently furnished, with the most costly articles of decoration—not stage properties, but *bona fide* realities—were such as were never before seen beyond the pale of fashionable life, and could only have been imitated by one used to that society." Though this production was a great success, things did not always go well financially for Vestris and Mathews. Mounting plays and managing a theater were risky undertakings in early Victorian London as, indeed, they remain. Twice they were forced into bankruptcy and once in 1847 they were both imprisoned for a short time for debt. Released, Mme Vestris quickly took control of the Lyceum Theater, which she managed for eight years (1847–55). There, she staged French plays that she and Mathews introduced to London in English translation and continued to stage the lavish

musical productions for which they had become famous. Charles Mathews the Elder, Lucy's famed father-in-law, had been celebrated for his solo performances known as "At Homes" in which he impersonated one character after another, and in time, his son and Mme Vestris demonstrated their versatility as performers by presenting a similar entertainment titled "Mr. and Mrs. Mathews at Home," a series of brief sketches in which the two likewise played a number of different characters.

Throughout the Lyceum years, Vestris and Mathews suffered many financial crises. The expense of their lavish productions made it very difficult to return a profit. Their lifestyle, moreover, with its elegant carriages, expensive jewels, and the latest fashions for both of them, though justified by their position in the theatrical world, was more the result of their own extravagant temperaments and kept them continually on the verge of bankruptcy. Many of their tours were necessitated by the need to raise cash to pay their creditors. Generous to a fault and childless, Vestris supported her mother until she died in 1843, and took in her sister's children after Josephine's death from tuberculosis in 1848.

As the years passed, Lucia Vestris appeared less and less frequently on the stage, though she was always available for benefits held for her fellow performers, who, together with her unfailingly faithful public, held her in high regard. Forced to retire in 1855 for reasons of failing health, she made her last appearance on the stage at the Lyceum in 1856 and died of cancer of the uterus on August 8, 1857. Her husband, in debtors' prison in Lancaster at the time, was released to enable him to attend the funeral. Lucia Vestris was buried at Kindle Green, where her grave now lies untended with the inscription on the tombstone completely worn away. Charles Matthews continued to act until his death in 1878.

Though photography did not exist until 1839, engravings made in Mme Vestris' youth show a fair woman with a long oval face, long rounded chin, slender graceful neck, large eyes, dark hair, and a broad forehead. She did not have the type of features that aged well, but she kept her figure, retained her voice, her wit, and her charm, and, as an entertainer, was said to have been at the height of her career when she retired. Vestris was neither a great actress nor a great beauty but through her personality and wit, she dominated the "light" theater of London and delighted audiences for over 30 years. Not all that skilled in straight comedy, she excelled as a singer-actress, especially in musical extravaganzas in which her acting was said to have been characterized by skill, grace and finesse. Her real importance, however, lies partly in the fact that she was the first woman ever to operate her own theater, a feat not duplicated in the United States until *Louisa Lane Drew took control of the Arch Street Theater in Philadelphia a generation later, but more because of the real and permanent advances that she made in the staging of plays and the development of set, scenery, and costume design. Passionate and energetic, she led a rich and exciting life, and as both an actress and a personality she stood alone on the English stage in the second quarter of the 19th century.

SOURCES:

Appleton, A.A. *Madame Vestris and the London Stage*, 1974.

The Free Library of Philadelphia, Theater Collection.

Geisinger, Marion. *Plays, Players and Playwrights*. New York, 1971.

Gilder, Rosamond. *Enter the Actress*. New York, 1931.

Mullen, Donald, comp., ed. *Victorian Actresses in Review . . . 1837 to 1901*. London, 1983.

Pearce, Charles. *Madame Vestris and her Times*. London, 1923 (at least two spurious autobiographies of Mme Vestris appeared in the 19th century; both were sensational and designed to make money through the use of her name and somewhat scandalous reputation; Pearce's biography draws too heavily on these to be reliable).

Watson, Ernest Bradlee. "Vestris an Actress-Manager of 1830," in *Theater Arts*. November 1928.

SUGGESTED READING:

Confessions of Mme. Vestris; in a Series of Letters to Handsome Jack. n.p.: New Villon Society, 1891.

Davis, Tracy C. *Actresses as Working Women: Their Social Identity in Victorian Culture*. London-New York, 1991.

Hewitt, Bernard. *History of the Theater from 1800 to the Present*. New York, 1970.

Memoirs of the Life of Madame Vestris of the Theaters Royal, Drury Lane and Covent Garden. Privately printed. London, 1830 [actually c. 1840].

Robert H. Hewsen,
Professor of History,
Rowan University,
Glassboro, New Jersey

Vestris, Madame (1797–1856).

See Vestris, Lucia.

Vestris, Thérèse (1726–1808)

French-Italian ballerina. Name variations: Therese Vestris. Born in 1726; died at age 82 in 1808; sister of Gäetan Vestris (a ballet dancer) and Angelo Vestris (a dancer).

The list of Thérèse Vestris' lovers runs half a page in Migel's *The Ballerinas*: counts, dukes, ministers, soldiers, ballet masters and husbands, all men of power, all once tidily recorded by the Paris secret police. At age 21, she arrived in Paris with her mother and five of her eight siblings (1747). Her father and three other siblings stayed in Italy. Gaetan, Thérèse and Angelo Vestris were soon employed with the Opera. **Violante Vestris** sang in concerts at court, and Jean-Baptiste Vestris became a housekeeper for the others.

With his enormous talent, Gaetan's star ascended. Thérèse, who shared his arrogance but not his talent, had an affair with the Opera's ballet master Lany and focused her competitive energy on **Mlle Puvigny**, who had replaced *Marie-Anne Cupis de Camargo and *Marie Sallé as premiere danseuse. Eventually, the directors grew tired of her scheming and forced her out. From then on, she used her skills as a courtesan; her only loyalty was to her family. Gaetan, Thérèse, and Angelo all died within a few months of each other.

Veto, Madame (1755–1793).

See Marie Antoinette.

Vetsera, Marie (1871–1889)

Austrian baroness who died at Mayerling. Name variations: Marie Alexandrine; Baroness Mary Vetsera. Born on March 19, 1871, in Vienna, Austria; died on January 29, 1889, at Mayerling, near Vienna; daughter of Baron Albin Vetsera and Helene Baltazzi Vetsera; never married; no children.

The short and tragic life of Marie Vetsera began in 1871 in Vienna. She was the eldest daughter in a prosperous Austrian family. Her mother was **Helene Baltazzi Vetsera**; her father Albin Vetsera was a career diplomat in the Austro-Hungarian Empire who was made a baron in 1870. Marie spent most of her childhood traveling with her parents on the baron's assignments; she was not well educated, preferring horses and fashion to her studies. She was particularly fond of horse racing, a very popular sport in Austria at the time. It was at one race in around 1885 that the Vetseras met the future King Edward VII of England. Edward subsequently introduced them to the Austrian crown prince Rudolf (1858–1889), son of *Elizabeth of Bavaria (1837–1898) and Emperor Franz Joseph. Marie's parents, eager to have their daughter marry into the high aristocracy, approved of her new circle of friends. But Marie became infatuated with the unstable prince Rudolf, who was

13 years her senior, married to *Stephanie of Belgium, and suffered from very poor mental and physical health, probably due to syphilis. At age 17, Marie became one of Rudolf's numerous mistresses, visiting him frequently but covertly at the emperor's palace in Vienna. Her parents, suspecting an intimate relationship, tried unsuccessfully to prevent their meetings.

As Rudolf's mental state deteriorated, he became deeply depressed, and late in 1888, considered suicide. Marie, whose romantic nature led her to believe she truly loved the prince, agreed to die with him. Together they planned for the fatal event, which would occur at Rudolf's isolated hunting lodge of Mayerling, outside Vienna. Marie wrote her will on January 18; and on January 28 the couple drove to Mayerling. Rudolf's aides found them on January 30; Marie had been shot by Rudolf, who then shot himself. (Not surprisingly, there have been rumors that they were murdered, possibly because Rudolf sympathized with Hungarian nationalists.) The tragic and scandalous event, which the imperial

house tried desperately to conceal, shocked Austria and Europe. The crown prince was the emperor's only son; his death, and his murder of a 17-year-old baroness who was his lover, was seen as a sign of the empire's imminent moral and political collapse. The emperor refused to allow Marie Vetsera's body to be buried in Vienna, despite her family's protests. She instead was buried quietly in Heiligenkreuz, near Mayerling, while her lover received a state funeral in Vienna. The tragedy has been the subject of numerous plays, books, and films. The 1936 film classic *Mayerling*, based on the novel *Idyl's End* by Claude Anet, starred Charles Boyer and *Danielle Darrieux. Other versions featured Omar Sharif and Catherine Deneuve and Mel Ferrer and *Audrey Hepburn.

SOURCES:

Judtmann, Franz. *Mayerling: The Facts Behind the Legend.* Trans. by Ewald Osers. London: George G. Harrap, 1971.
Markus, Georg. *Crime at Mayerling: the Life and Death of Mary Vetsera.* Trans. by Carvel de Bussy. Riverside, CA: Ariadne Press, 1995.

RELATED MEDIA:

Mayerling (96 min. film), starring Charles Boyer and Danielle Darrieux, with *Gabrielle Dorziat as Elizabeth of Bavaria, directed by Anatole Litvak, Concordea, 1937.
Mayerling (140 min. film), starring Omar Sharif and Catherine Deneuve, with *Ava Gardner as Elizabeth of Bavaria, directed by Terence Young, MGM, 1968.
"Mayerling" (90-minute special for "Producer's Showcase"), starring Audrey Hepburn and Mel Ferrer, NBC, 1958.
Mayerling to Sarajevo (French film), 1940.

Laura York, M.A. in History,
University of California,
Riverside, California

Marie Vetsera

Veturia and Volumnia

(late 6th c.–mid-5th c. BCE)

Patrician mother and wife of Gnaeus Marcius Coriolanus who convinced him not to fight with Rome.

Veturia. Name variations: Volumnia. Mother of Coriolanus.

Volumnia. Name variations: Vergilia or Virgilia. Married Gnaeus Marcius Coriolanus. (In William Shakespeare's Coriolanus, *first presented around 1609, the character of Volumnia is the mother of Coriolanus; the character of Virgilia is the wife.)*

Veturia was the mother of Gnaeus Marcius Coriolanus; Volumnia was his wife (although a less likely tradition names them Volumnia and Vergilia, respectively). Veturia raised her son by herself since her husband died when the boy was young. Gnaeus Marcius (his birth name) grew to become very conservative in his politics (being a patrician at the time, he was by status a member of the political elite) and was much opposed to making any concessions to the hard-pressed plebeians of his day as they began to agitate for basic securities against patrician exploitation. (The political activism of the plebeians at this time inaugurated the so-called "Conflict of the Orders," a struggle which pit plebeians against patricians for about 200 years, ending with the plebeians attaining the securities they wanted.) Although his political views were reactionary, for a while Gnaeus Marcius retained his prominence thanks to the fact that he was a noteworthy soldier at a time when Rome was threatened by many neighbors and not particularly strong. Among Rome's rivals were the Volsci, against whom a war was waged in 493. During this conflict, Gnaeus Marcius fought bravely and was the main reason the Romans were able to wrest the city called Corioli from the Volsci. After this success, his fellow citizens attempted to honor Gnaeus Marcius for his martial prowess with substantial material rewards. However, he is reported to have accepted no special honor for his services except the distinction of having "Coriolanus" added to his name.

Attempting to exploit his new renown, Coriolanus ran for the consulship but failed to win. However much he was appreciated as a soldier, Coriolanus' politics were simply too reactionary for the majority of his contemporaries to vote him into Rome's highest annually elected office. Embittered by this failure, Coriolanus became even more set in his ways. When a famine struck Rome in 491, necessitating the import of grain from abroad and driving up its cost, Coriolanus stunned his fellow Senators and outraged the plebeians by speaking forcefully against the distribution of grain to the starving poor at below market value prices. His stand against such a policy nearly embroiled the state in open civil war, and did cause him to be exiled from his native land, for even his peers came to deem him a danger to the domestic peace.

Irate at Rome's rejection of what he stood for, Coriolanus made straight for the Volsci and Attius Tullius, one of their leaders. At Tullius' hearth, he both sought sanctuary and offered his

Coriolanus receives the delegation of Roman matrons led by his mother Veturia and his wife Volumnia.

services against Rome. Although Tullius had been one of Coriolanus' bitterest rivals, Coriolanus convinced Tullius of his sincere lust for vengeance against Rome. Once persuaded, Tullius induced his fellow citizens to exploit Coriolanus' skill in war. Thus, in 490 Coriolanus became the commander of a Volscian army with which he ravaged the Roman countryside and its smaller cities. Coriolanus was so successful against his former comrades-in-arms that several embassies were sent to him to negotiate for peace. Coriolanus' terms (including a demand that Rome return to the Volsci that territory which Coriolanus had helped to conquer), however, were rejected by the Romans as being too severe. Unable to come to terms, Coriolanus continued his assault until he came upon Rome itself.

Then, realizing that their men were not up to the task of defending against Coriolanus, the women of Rome came to the aid of their city. Urged on by one **Valeria**, Veturia and Volumnia were beseeched to intervene with Coriolanus. This the mother and wife of Coriolanus agreed to do, and with Coriolanus' young children in tow (all dressed in tatters) they traveled forth into the camp of the enemy, now commanded by their son and husband. Their arrival moved Coriolanus greatly and he embraced all, beginning with Veturia. However, whatever Coriolanus imagined brought his family to his camp (at first he probably thought that they either had been expelled from Rome or voluntarily intended to join him), he was shocked to learn what their real motive was. Far from taking his side in the current dispute, Veturia especially berated her son for his attack on Rome, and declared that he would advance further only over her dead body. She understood the dilemma with which they posed him, for she knew that if Coriolanus, for them, quit the war, that he would betray the faith of the Volsci. Still, Veturia remained adamant that Coriolanus would only proceed by killing her, the woman who had given him birth and who had raised him alone.

Stunned, Coriolanus backed down and led his Volscian army back to their homeland, but only after returning his family—upon its patriotic insistence—back to Rome. What happened to Coriolanus is disputed. Most sources agree that he was executed by the Volsci when he returned to their land, but a variant tradition had it that he lived to an old age. What happened to Veturia and Volumnia, however, is agreed upon. Hurt very much economically by the permanent loss of Coriolanus, they nevertheless willingly added to their loss. Asked by the state how it could honor them for their role in turning aside Coriolanus'

invasion, Veturia and Volumnia requested the construction of a temple in honor of "Women's Fortune." Although the state agreed to shoulder the expense of this project, much money toward its erection was also donated by the two women most closely associated with Coriolanus.

Although this episode is of disputed historicity (the early years of the Roman Republic are shrouded in mist), there is no reason not to believe in its essential truth. Historical or not, the characters of Veturia and Volumnia had a large impact upon Roman values, for they came to personify the degree to which patriotic Roman women were expected selflessly to honor the state over family.

William S. Greenwalt,
Associate Professor of Classical History,
Santa Clara University,
Santa Clara, California

Veysberg, Yuliya (1878–1942)

Russian composer. Name variations: Yuliya Weissberg; Yuliya Rimskaya-Korsakova. Born Yuliya Lazarevna Veysberg in Orenburg on December 23, 1878; died in Leningrad (now St. Petersburg) on March 1, 1942; married Andrei Rimsky-Korsakov (son of the composer).

Yuliya Veysberg's compositions were often tinged with exoticism, and when writing her music she was probably influenced by memories of her youth in Orenburg, at the time a semi-Asiatic town. Veysberg was born in 1878 and attended the St. Petersburg Conservatory where she studied under Nikolai Rimsky-Korsakov and Alexander Glazunov. The latter composer greatly influenced her composing style, and she is considered to be the composer most like Glazunov. Like many young Russians of the period, Veysberg was politically liberal, and she was expelled from the Conservatory for taking part in a demonstration against its director during the revolutionary upheavals of 1905. She lived in Germany from 1907 to 1912, completing her musical education, before returning to St. Petersburg where she married Andrei Rimsky-Korsakov, son of the great composer. Her abilities as a composer were quickly recognized. Leonid Sabanayeff, a contemporary Russian music critic, claimed that she was "a master in the full sense of the word, and in this respect she stands above all other women composers." One of her most successful pieces was written in 1923 to Alexander Blok's poem "The Twelve." Exotic and dramatic works greatly interested Veysberg, who was drawn to subjects like the

Arabian Nights. She wrote numerous works for children, including operas, a cantata, partsongs, and songs. Her translation of the musical writings of Romain Rolland appeared in print in Moscow in 1938. Veysberg died in the Siege of Leningrad, during World War II.

SOURCES:

Sabaneyeff, Leonid. *Modern Russian Composers.* Trans. by Judah A. Joffe. NY: International, 1927.
Sadie, Stanley, ed. *New Grove Dictionary of Music and Musicians.* 20 vols. NY: Macmillan, 1980.

John Haag,
Athens, Georgia

Vezin, Jane Elizabeth (1827–1902)

British actress. Name variations: Mrs. Charles Young. Born Jane Elizabeth Thompson in 1827; died in 1902; married Charles Frederick Young (a comedian), in 1846 (divorced 1862); married Hermann Vezin (an actor), in 1863.

An important Shakespearean actress and woman of the stage through the third quarter of the 19th century, Jane Elizabeth Vezin was born in 1827. By age eight, she had appeared on stage as a singer and dancer. She married young, in 1846, to a comedian named Charles Frederick Young. In 1855, she toured Australia with a theatrical company; she had already visited that growing British colony with her parents when she was a child.

Her London stage debut came in 1857, and over the next several years she took several leading roles in Shakespeare's plays; an 1860 appearance opposite the rising American-born actor Hermann Vezin (at the Sadler's Wells theater) resulted in her divorce from Young in 1862 and marriage to Vezin the following year. She played Desdemona in Shakespeare's *Othello* in 1864, and continued to earn marquee roles for most of the next two decades; in 1880 and 1881, she appeared opposite the stage idol Edwin Booth. Jane Vezin died in 1902.

James M. Manheim,
freelance writer,
Ann Arbor, Michigan

Viardot, Louise (1841–1918).

See Viardot, Pauline for sidebar.

Viardot, Pauline (1821–1910)

French-born singer of Spanish parentage, one of history's greatest opera stars, who was also a composer, teacher, and for 40 years the intimate friend of the Russian writer Turgenev. Name variations: Pauline

Garcia; Pauline Viardot-Garcia or Viardot-García. Pronunciation: paw-LEEN VEE-AR-DOH gar-SEE-ah. Born Louise-Ferdinande-Michelle-Pauline Garcia in Paris, France, on July 18, 1821; died of heart failure in Paris on May 18, 1910; buried in Montmartre Cemetery; daughter of Manuel del Popolo Vincente Rodriguez Garcia (1775–1832, an opera singer and teacher) and (Maria) Joaquina Stiches di Mendi (1780–1862, a singer); sister of Maria Malibran (1808–1836); educated privately; married Louis Viardot (1800–1883, a critic, director, and author), in April 1840; children: Louise Viardot (1841–1918); Claudie Viardot Chamerot (1852–1914); Marianne Viardot Duvernoy (1854–?); Paul-Louis-Joachim Viardot (1857–1941).

Was with her family in New York and Mexico City (1825–29); sister Maria Malibran died (1836); debuted in concert in Brussels (1837); made opera debut in London in Rossini's Otello (1839); met George Sand (1839); gave up in Paris and went to Central Europe (1843); made first Russian tour and met Turgenev (1843–44); made second Russian tour (1844–45); had highly acclaimed seasons in Berlin and London (1846–49); debuted at the Paris Opéra in Meyerbeer's Le Prophète (1849); Gounod's Sapho a semi-failure (1851); Turgenev left for Russia, beginning a six-year separation (1850); made third and last Russian tour (1853–54); Turgenev back in Paris, but a sudden change in relations occurred (1856); Ary Scheffer died and a correspondence opened with Julius Rietz (1858–59); debuted in Gluck's Orphée, her artistic summit (1859); debuted in Gluck's Alceste (1861); retired from the Paris opera stage (1863); lived in Baden-Baden (1863–70); fled to London, then returned to Paris (1870–71); ended public career (c. 1875); husband and Turgenev died (1883); went into retirement in Paris but continued to teach (1883–1910).

Operatic repertoire: Beethoven's Leonore (Fidelio); Bellini's Romeo (I Capuleti ed i Montechi), Norma (Norma), Amina (La Sonnambula); Cimerosa's Orazio (Gli Orazi ed i Curiazi), Fidalma (Il Matrimonio Segreto); Donizetti's Alina (Alina, Regina de Golconda), Norma (Don Pasquale), Adina (L'Elisir d'amore), Leonore (La Favorita), Lucia (Lucia di Lammermoor), Mafio Orsini (Lucrezia Borgia), Maria (Maria de Rohan); Flotow's Martha, Lady Harriet (Martha); Gluck's Alceste (Alceste), Orphée (Orphée), Iphigénie (Iphigénie en Tauride); Gounod's Sapho (Sapho); Halévy's Rachel (La Juive); Meyerbeer's Valentine (Les Huguenots), Fidès (Le Prophète), Alice, Isabelle (Robert le Diable); Mozart's Zerlina, Donna Anna, Donna Elvira (Don Giovanni), Papagena, Pamina (Die Zauberflötte); Rossini's Rosina (Il Barbieri di

Siviglia), Cenerentola (La Cenerentola), Malcolm Groen (La Donna del lago), Ninette (La Gazza ladra), Desdemona (Otello), Arsace (Semiramide), Tancredi (Tancredi); Verdi's Lady Macbeth (Macbeth), Azucena (Il Trovatore).

First performances, concert repertoire: soloist, Rossini, Stabat Mater (1841); Brahms, Alto Rhapsody, Op. 53 (1870); title role in Massenet, Marie-Magdeleine, sacred oratorio (1873).

Selected compositions: 96 songs, 16 chamber and ensemble works; 32 piano pieces; 14 arrangements; Cendrillon, opéra comique (1904); operettas: Trop de femmes (1867), L'Ogre (1868), Le Dernier Sorcier (1869), Le Conte de fées (1879); stage music for a pantomime, Au Japon, and Racine's Andromaque, Phèdre, and Athalie (post-1871).

Writings: Ecole classique du chant (Paris, 1861); An Hour of Study: Exercises for the Voice (2 vols.).

Pauline Viardot was born into a household drenched in music and frequented by prominent musicians. "It was my father who taught me music," she recalled. "When I don't know, for I cannot remember a time when I did not know it." Manuel del Popolo Vincente Garcia, who was a leading tenor of his day, and **Joaquina Stiches di Mendi**, his second wife, sired one of the most remarkable family of musicians of modern times. They had three children: Manuel Patricio Rodriguez Garcia (1805–1906), *Maria Malibran* (1808–1836), and, much the youngest, Pauline. Manuel, who emigrated to England, is generally regarded as the greatest singing teacher of the 19th century. Maria, who married a French-born American businessman, Eugène Malibran—hence her nickname, "La Malibran"—became almost instantly a legendary opera singer until her untimely death at age 28 from effects of a fall from a horse. Pauline likewise became a brilliant opera star before retiring to become one of the most influential teachers of her time. Manuel and Joaquina's six grandchildren included three singers and a violinist; nine great-grandchildren included two singers and two pianists, and a great-great-granddaughter became a singer.

Viardot was born Pauline Garcia in Paris on July 18, 1821, 14 years after her parents moved there from Spain. (Once in France they had adopted the French spelling of their names, Garcia dropping the accent and Stiches becoming Stichès.) Her mother, from a socially prominent family, probably sang and acted under the name Briones or Brianes until her marriage. She was a calm, good-natured, determined woman, a de-

vout Catholic, and played the organ. Pauline loved her dearly and sheltered her until her death in 1862. But it was her father who exercised paramount influence over her even though he died when she was only 11.

Manuel Garcia was a remarkable man. Born in Seville, he did not know his father but believed him to be a Gypsy (Roma); others thought he was a Jew or Moor. He worked in Madrid as a tenor, producer, director, composer, and teacher until he moved to Paris in 1807 to expand his opportunities, Spain being an operatic backwater. By 1808, he was signed by the Théâtre-Italien and thereafter was its leading tenor, its "soul," until his voice began to decline by the mid-1820s. Meanwhile, he composed at an incredible pace—symphonies, masses, quartets, songs, and at least 43 operas and operettas. In 1811, he went to Italy to study with a master teacher of bel canto style, Giovanni Ansani (?), whom he worshipped. His own teaching, to which he turned increasingly in his last years, would extend Ansani's influence into the 20th century. While in Italy, he also met Rossini, who, much impressed, wrote the role of Count Almaviva for him in *The Barber of Seville*, which he debuted in 1816.

Manuel was handsome, passionate, charming, and seemingly able to do anything he set out to do. "He believed neither in God nor the Devil," Viardot remembered. "His own religion was *life*, with all its most ardent passions!" But there was a vulgar side to him and at times a brutality. Rossini once told Pauline, "If your father had had as much sense of tact as he had of musical sense, he would have been the foremost musician of the age." He frequently hit Maria while teaching her to sing, although she later said, "If my father had not been so severe with me, I should never have been very good. I was lazy and intractable." Only once did he slap Pauline, for failing to concentrate. He doted on her; Maria called her "the model of studious girls."

Pauline inherited her father's energy, wide interests, love of travel, and drive: "When I want to do something, I do it in spite of water, fire, society, the whole world." Her industriousness earned a family nickname, "the Ant." Like her father, she was also gay and sociable and liked tricks and games. Unlike him she was self-controlled, calm, and needed periods of solitude. Highly intellectual and, like her mother, aristocratic in bearing, she had none of her father's rough edges. She was precociously bright. By age six, she could speak Spanish, French, Italian,

Pauline
Viardot

and English. Later she added German, Russian, Polish, and Swedish, and by age 28 Greek and Latin. At age six, as a student of Maricos Vega, organist of the cathedral of Mexico City, she took first prizes in recitals. At age eight, she was accompanying her father's pupils on the piano.

Her education essentially began between her fourth and eighth years while she and her family were introducing Italian opera to New York and Mexico City (1825–29). The Garcias and several accompanying singers did everything in mounting their operas. Thus, Pauline found herself utterly immersed in the world of opera at a very early age. She listened to the lessons her father gave her brother and sister and began to receive some herself. While in America, Maria married against her father's will, probably to escape his relentless pressure, and remained largely alienated from him until his death. It is possible that the seriousness of marriage was impressed upon Pauline by her father's rage when Maria shamed the family by bearing a child out of wedlock with the violinist Charles de Bériot. (Maria later married him.) The episode likely affected Pauline's own complex marital life.

She later said she was not born with a good voice but made it good by working hard under her parents' instruction. Her father wrote exercises for her which she used all her life. Maria early recognized her talent and predicted she would "eclipse us all." Maria was devoted to her musical education, but her own meteoric career prevented frequent contact. In old age, Pauline remarked, "I hardly knew my sister. She did not live with us, and was always away." But she idolized Maria all the same, even though she learned that being the sister of "La Malibran" set for herself cruelly high expectations.

She confronted one other obstacle. The French opera stage valued beauty, whereas Viardot was famously homely. Her large black eyes bulged from under heavy, hooded lids, her neck was unusually long, her mouth was much too big and toothy, and her lower lip was extraordinarily large besides. On the other hand, her inborn majesty and grace of movement struck all observers and also made her appear taller than her medium height. She was slender and well proportioned. Her hair was a shining raven-black, and her complexion was smooth. She looked healthy and was always elegantly turned out. Her expression was ordinarily elevated, spiritual; her gaze bright with intelligence.

Viardot never expressed regret over her looks. To the contrary: her father had adored her and that settled the case for her. Her features, in fact, lent an air of exoticism which many people—notably a troop of prominent men—found powerfully attractive. A famous sketch of her by the German poet Heinrich Heine reads in part:

> She is ugly but with a kind of ugliness which is noble, I should almost say beautiful. . . . Indeed the Garcia recalls less the civilized beauty and tame gracefulness of our European homelands than she does the terrifying magnificence of some exotic and wild country. . . . At times, when she opens wide her large mouth with its blinding white teeth and smiles her cruel sweet smile, which at times frightens and charms us, we begin to feel as if the most monstrous vegetation and species of beasts from India and Africa are about to appear before us.

Said Ary Scheffer (1795–1858), an artist and dear friend, "She is terribly ugly, but if I saw her again, I'd fall madly in love with her."

Pauline's mother took charge of her voice training after her father's death. She was knowledgeable and stern but not cruel. Concurrently, Pauline took intensive piano lessons from Meysenberg—and Franz Liszt. About ten years her senior, he was already acclaimed by many as the greatest pianist of the age. She suffered the pangs of puppy love for him and even late in life called him "a most attractive man." There is no evidence he ever considered her more than a dear friend. Her talent impressed him when she played the two volumes of Bach's *Well-Tempered Clavier*—from memory. She transcribed Beethoven and Bach and Italian opera pieces for him, and he wrote exercises for her. But on her 15th birthday (1836), her mother had her sing a Rossini aria and then announced, "Good, I've made up my mind. Close the piano. From now on you are going to sing." Dutiful daughter that she was, she bowed to Joaquina's pronunciamento, but with anguish. Viardot remained a first-class pianist. Chopin delighted in playing with her, while Camille Saint-Saëns described her and the virtuoso *Clara Schumann (1819–1896), who was her friend for 60 years, as peers.

Pauline's first concert experience had been at age 13 as piano accompanist for a tour by her sister and Bériot in 1834. On September 23, 1836, only two months after Joaquina's decision, Maria died, to immense public shock. Pauline did not venture a debut until December 13, 1837: a charity concert with Bériot in Brussels in the presence of Leopold I and *Louise d'Orleans, king and queen of the Belgians. It was a grand success. Pauline followed with a concert in Louvain and a tour of Germany with Bériot and her mother in the spring of 1838—Frankfort, Salzburg, Dresden, Leipzig, Berlin—which established her as a coming artist. The queen of Prussia, **Auguste von Harrach**, gave her emeralds, and the tsar and tsarina jewels and art works. Most significantly, she moved the tough Berlin critic Ludwig Rellstab, not so much by her voice, which he found unremarkable (not yet 17, she was still developing) as by "a soul, a spirit, or if you will, a physiognomy." It was a prescient observation, for she would always be acclaimed more for her interpretation and musicianship than for her purely vocal gifts.

In late 1838 after the German tour, she sang in a concert or two in Paris drawing rooms filled with important connoisseurs, among them the young (28) but already famous poet and critic Alfred de Musset. The Théâtre de la Renaissance witnessed her formal debut, a recital on December 15. Hector Berlioz was not overly impressed (for now), but Musset and poet Théophile Gautier wrote glowing reviews in important journals. Her opera debut followed on May 9, 1839, at Her Majesty's Theatre in London as Desdemona in Rossini's *Otello*. A critic called it a "thundering success." H.F. Chorley, who was to be one of her greatest admirers, picked at her voice and other matters in the prestigious *Atheneum* but concluded, "There could be no doubt with anyone who saw that Desdemona on that night that another great career was begun." She followed with a number of concerts and salon recitals, twice for young Queen *Victoria. Reigning stars felt threatened, particularly the beautiful *Giulia Grisi (1811–1869), who began a long-running vendetta. The Paris opera debut finally arrived, on October 9 at the Théâtre-Italien, again in *Otello*. Once more, Pauline scored a triumph.

A most impressive feature was her artistic integrity. She researched her roles, reading Shakespeare for *Otello* and Beaumarchais for *The Barber of Seville*, and designed her own costumes throughout her career, being skilled at drawing and well informed on historical settings. In her London debut, she refused to repeat arias, as was the custom, because it would break the flow of the performance. For an 18-year-old debuting singer to take such a liberty was startling. Moreover, she did not merely repeat conventional interpretations or, above all, simply copy La Malibran, which audiences half-expected. Malibran's Desdemona, for example, was an Amazon, boldly expressing love, anger, terror; Viardot's was a naïve, loving young woman, brave only at the moment of her death. Her Rosina (*The Barber of Seville*) was a playfully mischievous, unspoiled girl, not the currently popular bawdy, deceitful wench. In short, she established her own artistic identity—an important step for the younger sister of the already mythic Malibran.

Not content merely to praise Pauline in print, Musset began to court her. He dreamed of her and the new actress *Rachel (1821–1858), whom he also pursued, as the inaugurators of a renaissance of the arts in France. Viardot remained cool, which frustrated him, for he had a reputation as a lothario. The affair grew complicated when *George Sand (1804–1876), famed novelist and recently Musset's mistress, weighed

in to oppose his suit and counter the effects of his flattering attentions to Joaquina.

Mutual friends, possibly Louis Viardot, had introduced Pauline to Sand (and her current lover Chopin) some time after mid-October 1839. Sand (aged 36) was bowled over by the young singer's artistry, intellectual force, and appearance. "I am fond of genius," she wrote, "but when it is coupled with goodness, I bow before it." In a word, she fell in love with her, "the only woman I have loved with an unmixed enthusiasm," she confided to her diary. In an important article in the *Revue des Deux Mondes*, February 14, 1840, Sand sounded some of the same themes as Musset: "The appearance of Mlle. Garcia will be a striking fact in the role women have played in the history of art. . . . It is a prodigy. . . . This voice comes from the soul and goes to the soul. . . . [She] enters the mind of the composers; she is alone with them in her thoughts."

The most gifted woman I have known.
—Clara Schumann

Sand did not rest content with warnings about Musset, who probably had proposed. She found another candidate, a friend, Louis Viardot, who had known Pauline since childhood. Sand probably saw in him both a husband and, what Pauline needed now, a manager. He was a wealthy, 40-year-old critic, director of the Théâtre-Italien, author of works on foreign literature, European museums, the Moors in Spain, and an excellent translation of *Don Quixote*, and was a passionate radical republican. His knowledge and connections would be of inestimable help to Pauline, who knew it. On the other hand, he lacked "the child-like element, freshness of mind," as she put it, was far from colorful, was, in short, on the boring side. He also had three older unmarried sisters who could (and did) make life difficult for her. Pauline took awhile deciding to marry him once her mother had succumbed to Sand's warnings against "that libertine" Musset. Louis, for his part, loved her profoundly: a selfless love which never wavered for the rest of his life.

Louis Viardot and Pauline Garcia married on April 18, 1840, in a civil ceremony. (His anticlericalism ruled out a church wedding.) She felt true affection for him—she called him "Papa"—but confessed 20 years later that despite her best efforts she had never been able to match his love by anything beyond warm friendship. As for Musset, he brooded about her for several years. She probably hurt him more than she realized and did not sufficiently appreciate his importance to her, for his artistic judgment was sound and his opinions carried weight. Privately, he dubbed her "Pauline the Ungrateful."

Following her marriage, Pauline Viardot experienced much frustration in building a career. Louis, exceedingly scrupulous, felt obliged to resign as director of the Théâtre-Italien because his marriage posed a possible conflict of interest. His successors, pressured by the Grisi cabal, refused to sign her. At the Opéra, the prima donna, **Rosine Stoltz** (1815–1903), blocked her. The Grisi cabal also kept her out of London until the spring of 1841, when she was given secondary or trouser roles—Tancredi and Arsace (Rossini) and Romeo (Bellini), in which she played to Grisi's Juliet. (Women in male roles were by no means unusual, and her great vocal range made them possible for her.) She appeared occasionally in concerts: soloist in Mozart's *Requiem* for the interment of Napoleon at the Invalides, December 15, 1840; charity concerts in England in 1841; the debut of Rossini's *Stabat Mater*, October 31, 1841; and February 20 and 21, 1842, at the Conservatoire and with Chopin.

Between these engagements, on December 14, 1841, she gave birth to ◄⚜ **Louise Viardot**. Talented in her own right, Louise became an unhappy, difficult person who claimed her mother had "abandoned" her at birth. The charge was unjust, but it was true that Pauline seldom put her career in second place.

Friendships were immensely important to Viardot. Visits to Sand at Nohant brought her contact with Chopin and Eugène Delacroix (who was much impressed by her drawings). Through 1841–42, Sand wrote a long novel, *Consuelo*, whose title character is a singer closely modeled on Viardot. Ary Scheffer, a prominent painter, entered her life via Louis, his biographer, and became a mentor and father-confessor. He fell in love with her but did not tell her until shortly before he died.

Frustrated in Paris, Pauline toured Spain with Louis from mid-April to August 1842 to revive Italian opera by using local professionals and amateurs. It was there that she first sang in Bellini's *Norma*, which she regarded as the supreme test. Although she was happy, at Sand's urging she returned for a "re-debut" in Paris. It did not work out well; again, she got only secondary roles, save one, and on December 1 Sand's enemies attacked her in the *Revue des Deux Mondes*. So in 1843, after publishing an album of six songs, illustrated by Scheffer, Viardot quit Paris for central Europe. Her debut in Vienna on April 19, 1843, as Rosina was sensational and was followed by similar successes in operas and concerts in Prague and the Germanies until her return to Paris and Nohant in mid-August. In Berlin, she met Mendelssohn, of whose vocal music she became a great interpreter; but also, above all, she met Giacomo Meyerbeer, the current king of opera composers, who was so enthralled that he forbade the Paris Opéra to perform any new work of his until she could sing there. Meyerbeer's support was a major help for her at this critical time. Back in France, she signed on for a season in St. Petersburg. The German and Russian tours marked the turning point in her career—and her life, for in Russia she met a budding writer, Ivan Sergeyevich Turgenev (1818–1883).

In her peak years, Viardot was a natural mezzo-soprano who by "immense effort and skill" extended her range to contralto and soprano. Estimates differ, but her range at its best, around 1843–53 (aged 22–32), was three octaves plus two to four notes beyond (e.g., D below middle C to F above high C). To land the top roles one had to be a soprano. In time, Viardot lost on the high end, and by age 40, when most singers are reaching their prime, her voice was obviously fading. As she told her pupils after retiring, "Don't do as I did. I wanted to sing everything and spoiled my voice." To achieve the effects she did, she displayed a variety of timbres. Gounod thought her intermediate octaves, her chest voice, extraordinarily suave and sonorous. Over the whole range there was a continuity from chest to head voice, a smooth transition, with tones round and clear. "Freshness" and "vibrant warmth" were often noted, but one finds disagreement as regards tone, some saying "silvery," others (e.g., Saint-Saëns) noting a harshness, not velvet or crystal, still others some "Spanish" combination of harshness and sweetness (Musset). Many just gave up

⚜► **Viardot, Louise** (1841–1918)

French contralto. Name variations: Louise Héritte-Viardot or Louise Heritte-Viardot. Born Louise-Pauline-Marie on December 14, 1841; daughter of Pauline Viardot (1821–1910) and Louis Viardot; died in 1918; married a diplomat; children.

Louise Viardot married a diplomat, then separated from him and became a professor at the St. Petersburg School of Music and later at Frankfurt, Berlin, and Heidelburg. In 1864, she made her 43-year-old mother *Pauline Viardot a grandmother.

SUGGESTED READING:

Héritte-Viardot, Louise. *Une Famille de grands musiciens: Memoirs de Louise Héritte-Viardot*. Paris: Stock, 1923.

and spoke of it as "a voice à la Viardot." Most admitted that it grew on one, whatever its imperfections, and was above all *moving*.

There was no dispute about her mastery of bel canto technique—learned from her father, who greatly admired the art of the 18th-century castrati. Bel canto requires a light, fluid, effortless delivery with equal tone through the range. Viardot had full command of its demands: trills, arpeggios, leaps, and runs like strings of pearls. Some thought her bravura passages too florid; in any event they were original and informed by musicianship. No technical challenge daunted her.

The voice alone comprised, if anything, less than half of Viardot's art. As noted before, she projected deep feeling, a "soul." Wrote Musset, "She possesses . . . the great secret of artists: before expressing something, she feels it." As she matured, she became more the actress-singer than the singer-actress. To say she was the originator of character acting in the bel canto tradition would be a disservice to *Giuditta Pasta (1797–1865), *Wilhelmine Schröder-Devrient (1804–1860), and Malibran. But she brought it to its peak, paving the way for the "realistic" style, musical and dramatic, developed by Verdi and Wagner which succeeded bel canto as the dominant mode. Her original interpretations became models for her successors. She once compared her mind to a little theater, where her roles, as it were, "unfolded," making it unnecessary to practice them before a mirror. So much the actress was she that she admitted she gave recitals mostly because they paid well. Baritone Sir Charles Santley, a pupil of her brother's, said simply, "[N]o woman in my day has ever approached her as a dramatic singer." Among later singers, *Maria Callas (1923–1977) has most often been compared with her: "unclassifiable," with some vocal imperfections, but using even these to bring to bel canto roles dramatic intensity of the highest order.

Viardot was near the best she would ever be in high soprano roles when she arrived in Russia in October 1843. Italian opera in Italian had been missing from St. Petersburg for a generation; only a German company singing it in German and a mediocre Russian company performing it in Russian were on the scene. When the great tenor Giovanni Battista Rubini scored a major success in concerts there early in 1843, he was asked to return in the fall with a company. He chose reigning baritone Antonio Tamburini and Viardot to star with him. The public, on the brink of a new cultural awakening, greeted them with feverish anticipation. She debuted on No-

vember 3 as Rosina to roaring applause and nine curtain calls. It only built from there: Desdemona, *Lucia di Lammermoor* (Donizetti), and her greatest triumph, *La Sonnambula* (Bellini), which drew some 15 curtain calls, Empress *Charlotte of Prussia (against regulations) throwing her a bouquet after the 7th. The single most emotional moment came on November 27 when as Rosina Viardot sang a Russian song—with flawless pronunciation—in the music-lesson scene. She was the first foreigner to sing Russian music in Russian. The house exploded; Tsar Nicholas I was observed cheering "like a madman." Night after night the theater was packed; crowds hailed her in the streets. As if she needed more to do, she also gave 20 concerts in 21 days to benefit retired Russian singers.

Perhaps no singer has ever had a season of triumphs to equal Viardot's first in Russia. Years later a contemporary recalled, "She was an extraordinary phenomenon upon our stage; she aroused us from our lethargy, brought to life new artistic perceptions, tuned us to an elevated pitch, and set our nerves a-tingling. Her name . . . should be inscribed in gold in the annals of our opera."

Viardot first met Turgenev at her St. Petersburg residence on November 13. She paid no particular attention, but for him it was love—a lifelong love, an obsession—at first sight. She later said he was introduced to her as "a young Russian landowner, a good shot, an agreeable conversationalist, and a bad poet." He was an aristocrat, a handsome, blue-eyed, chestnut-haired giant with an odd, squeaky voice. At 25, three years her senior, he was only beginning to write seriously while vegetating in a minor government job. He was intelligent, cultured, highly imaginative, unpredictable, a neurotic and hypochondriac, extremely kind and generous, a mesmerizing raconteur, but something still of a young, snobbish show-off. His high artistic sensibility responded above all to music: even in old age, Viardot's singing could drive him to such a state of excitement that he would jump up from his seat humming and gesticulating.

Viardot had a covey of male admirers, which left Turgenev frustrated. He incessantly proclaimed his love to one and all, making himself ridiculous and annoying her. So ardent was he, however, that she could not help but take an interest in this strange fellow. Rivers of ink have flowed describing their ensuing relationship, "one of the most enigmatic *ménages à trois* in literary and musical history," writes Henry Pleasants. For the next 40 years, Turgenev lived near or with her or corresponded, often daily, while

Louis played the understanding, self-effacing husband to a point beyond imagining. Astonishingly, the two men remained friends, spending countless hours conversing or hunting. (Both were passionate hunters, Louis madly so.) Did Viardot and Turgenev ever have sexual relations? Probably, although some authorities have denied it given the absence of conclusive proof. Turgenev had numerous sexual encounters throughout his life; he could separate sex from love, but not love from sex or at least the desire for it.

What he beheld in Viardot was not a mistress but the embodiment of the Beautiful, which he revered. Love is never fully requited and happiness never fully attained, his works proclaim, but, as he wrote to her early in their relationship, "Beauty is the only imperishable thing . . . [and] nowhere does it shine with such power as in the human personality: it is here that it speaks most clearly to the human mind, and that is why I always prefer a great musical talent served by an imperfect voice to a good voice which is stupid, the beauty of which is only material." Notes Richard Freeborn, Viardot also embodied "the glamour of things European, the epitome of civilization and culture and a living symbol of the free flight of music, detached and remote from terrestrial cares, which was to be the poetic ideal of his art."

Viardot's attraction to Turgenev is harder to decipher. She always needed close friends to whom she could confide her deepest thoughts and feelings: "I love my friends with the sacred flame of passion, and could not live without them." His all-too-obvious devotion coupled with his profound understanding of human beings and music encouraged her to find in him a soulmate. She never returned all his passion. She was too independent, too disciplined, too ambitious to surrender her life to him, much less marry him. She dominated the man she had married and risked losing control if she were to become Turgenev's wife, given all that 19th-century law and custom conferred on husbands. Moreover, she was a bit strait-laced and in her sister's example (and her father's anger) had learned a lesson in the pains and scandal of infidelity. "If you want to be an artist," she once told a pupil, "try to be indifferent to everything except your art." She sought to live by the maxim, obviously not always successfully. Reflecting on her struggles, she once characterized love as a destructive force: "Love kills when it cannot inflame." If it does burn, "it dies out only with time, inflicting on its victim the daily torture of a terrible agony."

The first Russian season finished, Viardot returned to France. For several years she sang only abroad, the Opéra "lockout" continuing. In October 1844, she returned to Russia and stayed until early May. After the opera season in St. Petersburg, she gave concerts there and in Moscow. The season was a fine success but, inevitably, could hardly match the first. Audiences were becoming more discriminating, and Viardot found a pretty and competent rival in **Jeanne Castellan (1819–1858)**. After singing in a festival in Coblenz in August 1845 organized by Mendelssohn and Meyerbeer to honor Victoria and Albert and the king of Prussia, she arrived in October in Russia once again. By now the vogue was over, abetted by managers who overbooked and overcharged. She appeared in only three of eight operas mounted, and her voice showed signs of strain. She and daughter Louise fell ill with whooping cough and Louis with cholera, which won her permission to leave early, on February 24. In the fall and winter of 1846–47, Viardot was in Berlin for a highly successful season, following up with performances elsewhere in Germany and in London. She returned to Germany for the 1847–48 season in Dresden, Hamburg, and Berlin.

In 1844, she and Louis had bought a château, Courtavenel, near Paris at Rozay-en-Brie (Seine-et-Marne). Dating from the 16th century, complete with towers, moat, and drawbridge, it was Viardot's first real home of her own, although she was often away. They converted a large room into a miniature theater, and the place became a magnet for guests from the artistic world. She proved a splendid host—simple, friendly, gracious, and attending to quality in all things.

Her private life experienced some serious strains in these years. She hurt Sand's feelings by putting off invitations to Nohant. She was more independent now, and Sand probably felt she was slipping away. Sand's problems with her children and her painful breakup with Chopin contributed to the stress. Viardot tried, unsuccessfully, to mediate between Sand and Chopin. To top it off, Sand's young (21) son Maurice Dudevant fell in love with her. How tempted she was by him is unclear.

Meanwhile, Viardot's relations with Turgenev followed a meandering course, in the long run tending to tighten. After the second Russian season, during which he continued her Russian lessons begun the year before, he resigned his post to follow the Viardots west. He spent a short stay at Courtavenel in the summer of 1845, "the happiest time of all my life," he later called it. He simply adored her in her surroundings, asking for nothing more. During her third Russian season, they saw a good deal of each other and on New Year's Eve exchanged a kiss, a serious matter. He remained behind, however, when she left in February 1846. He wrote to her continually, always asking if she would return. She, probably fighting her feelings, did not resume corresponding until her German tour of 1846–47. Already he had begun submitting drafts of his work to her for approval, which he did for the rest of his life. In return, she sought his advice on music. He joined her in Berlin by early February, followed her to Paris, spent the summer of 1847 at Courtavenel, and remained now in France until June 1850.

During the Paris and London seasons of 1848–49, Viardot at last received the acclaim she had experienced elsewhere. Audiences seemed more accepting of her "intellectual" approach to her work. She had arrived at full artistic maturity. The London season of 1848 witnessed a three-way "war" between *Jenny Lind (1820–1887) at Her Majesty's Theatre and Viardot and her rivals at Covent Garden. Grisi persuaded two tenors (including the great Mario, her lover) to report "ill" for Viardot's debut in Les Huguenots. She had to settle for a singer who knew only the French version (the work was being sung in Italian). She learned that version backstage and astounded the audience by shifting into French during the performance. Grisi's ploy had failed, but she repeated it and again in 1850. Also at the Garden were *Marietta Alboni (1823–1894) and Fanny Persiani (1812–1867), formidable rivals. Bur Viardot more than held her own. She gave several concerts, too, including in them her own transcriptions of some Chopin mazurkas, which he warmly approved. She later published 15 of them. Sadly, a year after the London engagements she would be singing a solo from Mozart's Requiem at his funeral (October 30, 1849).

Eighteen forty-nine was the year of Le Prophète. Meyerbeer, hugely popular in Paris for a quarter century, had not produced a new opera in 13 years. Nevertheless, he stood by his vow to force the Opéra to accept Viardot. He was obliged, in fact, to reshape the opera around her rather than the title role because the tenor could not handle it. She had a great deal to do with both the writing and production of this work, which required 52 rehearsals before its heralded debut on April 16, 1849. She sang Fidès, a mother who must renounce her son in order to save his life. The role is infamously demanding vocally and dramatically, combining bel canto style and a huge range with the forceful, sus-

tained singing being introduced by Verdi. The dramatic range of acting is likewise daunting. (The difficulties of the role, in fact, contributed greatly to the opera's disappearance from the standard repertoire after a few years.) The critics gave the work mixed reviews but lauded Viardot to the skies. She sent a note to Sand: "VICTOIRE!" Fidès became a signature role for her for a few years; she sang it over 200 times, in French, German, and Italian. In St. Petersburg in 1853, she earned a phenomenal 21 curtain calls. When Berlioz heard it in Berlin, he wrote: "Madame Viardot is one of the greatest artists . . . in the past and present history of music."

Charles Gounod's Sapho proved a different story. She had met him briefly in Rome in 1840 on her honeymoon. In 1849, he was contemplating taking Holy Orders when she "discovered" him. She was not easily impressed, as a rule, but his talent and charm dazzled her, leading her in a letter to Sand to put him in "the same elevated sphere" as Mozart, no less. She encouraged him to write an opera and promised to perform it. She opened doors at the Opéra for him while he wrote passionate letters to her. It appears unlikely they became lovers, but when he and Turgenev spent several months alone together at Courtavenel in the spring of 1850, the latter understandably grew morose because she wrote to Gounod but not to him. Sapho debuted on April 16, 1851, but ran only a mediocre nine performances. The London run in August likewise proved disappointing. The critics praised Viardot, but Gounod blamed her for the failure. A year later, in May 1852, they broke off after he treated her in an insulting manner in connection with his marriage. His behavior reeked of "selfishness and vanity and calculation," she wrote to Sand. The estrangement lasted until 1870.

From 1848 to 1850, her relationship with Turgenev underwent severe strains. She and Louis built a house at 48, rue de Douai, Place Vintimille, on the (then) outskirts of Paris. Turgenev, seldom far away, took rooms nearby. Despite ups and downs, they very probably became lovers on or soon after June 26, 1849. She was evidently torn and so was he, for differing reasons. Finally, he left for Russia in late June 1850, beginning a six-year separation. Why he went remains a matter of dispute. The most obvious reason was that his dying mother had called him home. He also probably felt a need to reconnect with Russia for the sake of his writing. Had there been a scene with Louis? Had she told him to go? (He wrote promising to return only if she called him.) It is clear, however, that she underwent a crisis. It was Scheffer who helped her through. Years later she wrote, "without Ary Scheffer I would have committed a great crime—for I had lost my willpower—I recovered it in time to *break my heart* and do my duty. . . . I did not commit a sin." Scheffer, she wrote, had given her strength by showing her "Art in its most consoling, its most divine aspect. . . . I almost went mad, but his great wisdom restored the balance of my distracted mind."

She left the "great sin" unexplained. It might have been to forsake her art and career for love. The separation did not mean that ties were broken. She lamented the absence of "so precious a friend." Most revealing is a surprising sequel. When Turgenev returned home he found that his mother had been coldly mistreating his eight-year-old illegitimate daughter, **Pelageya Turgenev**, whom he had fathered a year before he met Viardot. He now wrote to her revealing the child's existence, and she replied with an offer to take her into her home as a daughter. In October 1850, he shed tears of joy and sent "Paulinette," as he renamed her, to Paris, instructing her to look upon Viardot as her mother now. All but inevitably, the child came to hate her with a passion, and joined Louise as an unhappy, ungovernable presence in the household. She grew up there, supported financially by her father.

Viardot settled into a smoother domestic life. Louis, ever faithful, stood by her. On May 21, 1852, she gave birth to Claudie ("Didie," later Mme. Chamerot)—a "reconciliation child"? Temperamentally, Didie proved to be Louise's opposite: a happy person. Turgenev, meanwhile, had numerous sexual encounters, corresponded with other women, and considered marrying a kinswoman, **Olga Turgenev**. But he wrote to Viardot almost daily. She sent friendly replies now and then. His longing haunted him: "Oh God! I wish I could spend my whole life, like a carpet, under your dear feet, which I kiss a thousand times." And his torture: In his play *A Month in the Country*, written in 1849–50, a character says, "You will learn what it means to belong to a skirt, what it means to be enslaved, infected—and how shameful and oppressive this slavery is."

Viardot's career suffered a setback when in August 1851 her Opéra contract was cancelled. Politics had always figured in her troubles there, for Louis was an outspoken republican. He (and she) rejoiced at the founding of the Second Republic during the Revolution of 1848, but by 1851 the political climate had changed, with President Louis-Napoleon Bonaparte (Napoleon III) preparing the coup which in December effectively ended the republic and paved the way to the proclamation of the Second Empire a year later. Consequently, until the Third Republic arrived in 1870–71, her principal engagements usually were outside France. In the autumn of 1851, in fact, their home was searched for subversive materials. They went off to spend the winter in Scotland, where she at least did some composing.

After a year mostly of domesticity, including Claudie's birth, Viardot returned to Russia, opening in St. Petersburg on January 15, 1853, as Rosina, to great acclaim. Soon Mario again tried to sabotage her by pleading "illness." Rather than cancel, she appeared—without rehearsal—in *La Cenerentola*, which she had not sung in at least seven years, and triumphed once again. After that she experienced no further trouble from Grisi and Mario. She went on to Moscow and an even bigger success.

While she was in Moscow, Turgenev slipped from his estate, Spasskoye, some time between April 3 and 12 to be with her. (Louis had had to leave Russia because of illness.) He had been arrested for political libel in April 1852 and exiled to Spasskoye, where he would remain until December 1853. What transpired in Moscow is not known, but after the tryst the relationship again appeared past rescue.

She returned to St. Petersburg for concerts which included music by Russian composers Glinka and Dargomyzhski. She also began a long friendship with pianist Anton Rubenstein. For the rest of the century, Viardot served as one of the most important agents in making Russian composers known in Western Europe, among them Borodin, Rimsky-Korsakov, and Tchaikovsky. She was, however, never to return to Russia after the 1853 tour.

During the London season of 1853, she gave 36 concerts in 42 days, and then returned to Paris to await the birth of a third daughter, Marianne (later Mme. Duvernoy), on March 15, 1854. From June 8 to August 10, she appeared at Covent Garden, and again the next year when on May 10 she sang the part of Azucena, a Gypsy mother, in the first London performance of Verdi's *Il Trovatore*. She went on as a substitute with only three days and one rehearsal to learn the role—another astonishing feat. (Her Fidès is said to have helped inspire Verdi to use a tragic-mother figure as a principal.)

Between tours abroad and public and private recitals in Paris, she and Louis hosted frequent dinner parties for a crowd of prominent artists, writers, musicians, foreign visitors (notably Charles Dickens), and left-wing politicians and exiles. Many were invited to Courtavenel for meals, hunting, and amateur theatricals, usually plays by Racine, Molière, and Beaumarchais. Sand was still a close friend, but they saw little of each other, leading separate lives. Scheffer was often present, although he had married a widow in 1850. Hector Berlioz began spending time at Courtavenel; besides music, they shared similar literary tastes—Shakespeare, Goethe, Virgil, and (her favorite) Homer. Rossini, her father's old friend, long retired in Paris, came by sometimes, and she visited him frequently. He regularly marked scores and gave advice. One memorable day he fell on his knees and kissed Mozart's manuscript of *Don Giovanni*, which she had just acquired. *Constanze Mozart had sold the score in 1799 to the André d'Offenbach family. When museums in Berlin, Vienna, and London judged it too expensive, Viardot sold her best jewels and bought it. (On July 6, 1893, she gave it to the Paris Conservatoire on condition that it never leave the premises—and there it remains.)

Relations with Turgenev went their usual tortuous way. They waned or waxed solely at her discretion. Their correspondence had been fitful from 1852 to 1856. She confided in Scheffer, while Turgenev confided in **Countess Lambert,** the middle-aged wife of an aide-de-camp of the tsar. When, however, he told Pauline about his aborted marriage project to Olga Turgenev, she showed some jealousy. In July 1856, he suddenly turned up in Paris, having against his better judgment left Russia and hope of a settled, married life there. He went to Courtavenel in the fall and was never happier. He adored Didie, sent angry Paulinette off to a boarding school, and got along as usual with Louis. But in November came a sharp change. Pauline had conceived again and now shut him out once more, throwing him into a spiritual crisis from which he emerged into his most productive years as a writer. He told Tolstoy he loved her "more than ever," but the affair was now conducted like a passionless friendship.

At the news of her son Paul's birth in July 21, 1857, Turgenev wrote a letter overflowing with hurrahs, and in August and September he was back at Courtavenel for a calm stay. Was he Paul's father? He may have thought so at first, but he was quoted at least twice later as regretfully denying he had any children with Pauline. Paul himself—tall like Turgenev, not short like the Viardots—several times told his son he was uncertain. The weight of scholarly opinion rests uneasily with Louis as the father, and much more decisively in Didie's case, which has also been mooted.

Turgenev traveled a good deal in 1857–58 before settling in Russia from June 1858 until April 1859. Relations with Viardot continued cool at brief encounters in Leipzig and London in 1858—although, interestingly, she began (unsuccessful) negotiations for another Russian tour. She suffered a great shock when Scheffer died on June 15, 1858. She needed a new psychiatrist (so to speak) and by the end of the year found Julius Rietz (1812–1877), a German conductor, minor composer, and musicologist. Almost daily for a year she wrote long, passionate, revealing letters, although the correspondence petered out by 1864. Turgenev meanwhile was unburdening himself to Countess Lambert, not Viardot.

Viardot reached the artistic pinnacle of her career in 1859–61 in productions of Gluck's *Orphée* and *Alceste*. During another strenuous tour of the English provinces (50 concerts) and Dublin (3 weeks of opera with Grisi and Mario) in February and March 1859, she sang Lady Macbeth (*Gruoch) in the English debut of Verdi's *Macbeth*, with great success. Returning to Paris, she won such acclaim at the Théâtre-Lyrique singing extracts from *Le Prophète* and *Otello* that the manager proposed reviving Gluck's *Orphée*. She loved Gluck and found this opportunity to end her eight-year absence from the Paris opera stage tempting. She accepted, scarcely dreaming that a hoped-for *succès d'estime* would become a towering popular success. To do this with an opera as dated, serious, and static as *Orphée* constituted an artistic tour de force.

Berlioz, long a friend, became much involved with her in these years. On August 4, 1859, she and a tenor, Lefort, gave the first performance of extracts from his *Les Troyans*, a work in progress which greatly impressed her. He promised her a lead in it. (He would break this promise some four years later, believing her voice no longer up to the part; crushed, she would sever their relations permanently.) By the end of August, when they were at the Baden-Baden festival, where he directed, she discovered he was in love with her. She smoothly kept him at bay until he finally realized his love was hopeless. Nevertheless, they remained collaborators through the revival of *Alceste* in 1861. She gave him her moral support (he was intensely unhappy and ill) and worked so closely with him on *Les Troyans* that he referred to it as "our opera."

Orphée, also starring ***Marie Constance Sass** (1834–1907) as Eurydice, debuted at the Théâtre-Lyrique on November 18, 1859. Berlioz, the conductor, had transposed Orpheus from a tenor (originally a castrato) to a contralto role. Young Camille Saint-Saëns also assisted. Despite a throat condition which robbed her of some power and quality, she scored an immense success. Wrote George Sand, "This is, no doubt, the purest and most perfect artistic expression that we have seen for half a century, this Orpheus of hers—understood, clothed, played, mimed, sung, spoken, and wept through in the way that she interprets it." Of the bravura aria ending Act I, Chorley wrote, "The torrent of roulades, the chain of notes, unmeaning in themselves, were flung out with such exactness, limitless volubility, and majesty as to convert what is essentially a commonplace piece of parade into one of displays of passionate enthusiasm to which nothing less florid could give scope." And so it went. The crown jewel aria, "J'ai perdu mon Eurydice," provoked an ovation lasting a full two minutes. By June 21, 1860, Viardot had sung the role 121 times and in three years some 150 times. Her daughter Louise testified she heard it 34 times and "was deeply moved each time. Her Orpheus was never the same twice running, there was always some new and unexpected touch."

While continuing *Orphée* in 1860—amazingly, fighting bronchitis through most of the run—she gave 11 performances as Leonore in Beethoven's *Fidelio*—not a good choice, as the role was too high for her now. She performed *Orphée* privately in London in July, sang at the Baden-Baden Festival in August, then toured England, with *Orphée* excerpts much in demand. In 1861, she "warmed up" at the Opéra with *Le Prophète*, *Les Huguenots*, and *Il Trovatore*, and then debuted in *Alceste* on October 21, Berlioz conducting. It was her last triumph on the grand stage. Inevitably, it could not match *Orphée*. On May 12, 1862, Viardot sang her last *Alceste* at the Opéra but continued in *Orphée* at the Théâtre-Lyrique until, on April 24, 1863 (although she had to repeat the performance), she deliberately bade farewell to the Paris opera stage. She would continue for many years to give concerts and, in provincial cities, perform in some operas. But she was wise enough to know when her voice no longer had the quality for premier venues.

She continued to play the host in these crowded years of her greatest celebrity, and to encourage others. In February 1860, Richard Wagner (whom she had met in 1839) came to her home to give his patron, **Mme Kalergis**, a preview of Act II of *Tristan und Isolde*, then in preparation. Berlioz and a pianist were the only others present. Viardot and Wagner sang the parts. Her sight-reading and perfect German left him awe-struck. He later asked her to be an adviser for the Bayreuth festivals, but she declined because of her summer teaching demands. Given his titanic ego, his praise of her as "the greatest artist and musician of the century" is arresting, to say the least. He is said to have told singers, "Go to Viardot and learn how to sing Mozart. Then you will be able, without harm to your voice, to sing my operas." In contrast, although she greatly respected his musicianship, for years her opinion of his music was not high, but as she aged she came to appreciate it, beginning with *Die Meistersinger* (1868).

On the whole, her relations with Turgenev from 1859 to 1863 were at their most distant. Not, of course, by his choice. He *had* none save to admit that his dream of happiness would not be fulfilled, that he would, as he aptly put it, spend his life "perched on the edge of another man's nest." Depression dogged him: "I just go on existing," he wrote to Countess Lambert in January 1861. In July and August 1859, he stayed at Courtavenel, and after a year returned from Spasskoye to live in Paris from May 1860 to May 1861, with visits to Courtavenel in July and September 1860. Often while he was there, she was away. They met in Paris a few times, and he did some hunting and translating with Louis. Concerns with Paulinette, who no longer lived with the Viardots, gave him excuses to stay in touch. Correspondence, however, nearly ceased. But when son Paul nearly died of bronchial pneumonia early in 1860, Viardot called him from Russia to help her in her distress. He obeyed the "command," only to find her cool once he arrived. Still, the relationship changed once again when in late 1863 the Viardots moved to Germany, to Baden-Baden.

Since 1862 they had been building a Swiss chalet there on three acres near the Black Forest. Louis could no longer stomach Napoleon III's regime; she had never liked Paris and its constant intrigues and had always found the Germans more attentive and informed about music than most Parisians, among whom Offenbach was now the rage. Their property eventually included a small concert hall with an organ (which she loved to play) and a Temple of Art to display their collection—Velázquez and Dutch masters, including Rembrandt. Louis was wealthy, while she commanded top fees. Some accused her of greed, noting that she even charged 2,000 francs for singing at Chopin's funeral. She viewed the matter differently, once telling a pupil, "Never sing for nothing! You are not going to make yourself into an artist just for pleasure. I hope that it will give you pleasure, but you must also earn your living." In recompense, she gave large sums to charities and needy fellow artists.

Save for an interlude (1868–70) in Karlsruhe for the children's education, they lived in Baden-Baden until October 1870, with infrequent short visits to Paris. When the Franco-Prussian War (1870–71) erupted, Viardot helped briefly in German women's auxiliary services; but with Napoleon III's fall and the proclaiming of the Third Republic, their patriotic sentiments finally led them to decamp to London. The Baden-Baden years had proved quite happy on all counts. She gave concerts in Strasbourg, Karlsruhe, Vienna, Breslau, Berlin, *et al.*, recitals in homes, and occasional opera performances. She composed and taught a great deal, attracting pupils from all over Europe, notably Russia, including *Désirée Artôt (1835–1907) before the Baden years, and **Anna Aglaia Orgeni** (1843–1926), *Marianne Brandt (1842–1921), and **Antoinette Sterling** (1843–1904). Viardot was demanding but warm and generous, giving students a weekly dinner party and encouraging them to develop their own selves and not merely imitate her.

Composition had always attracted her. As a girl, she studied under Antoine Reicha at the Conservatoire (as did Berlioz). She published several song collections in St. Petersburg and Leipzig in the 1860s and early 1870s, e.g., *Twelve Poems by Pushkin, Fet and Turgenev* (1864). Turgenev, unbeknown to her, subsidized some and importuned embarrassed friends to promote them. Her music won praise from Liszt, Clara Schumann, Anton Rubenstein, and important critics but did not sell well. Sometimes in recitals she would slyly announce one of her own songs as written by "Mozart," at which, to her amusement, the audience would beam. With Turgenev furnishing the librettos (to the dismay of his Russian worshippers), she also wrote four operettas for performance by her children and pupils. Liszt helped get *Le Dernier Sorcier* performed professionally at Weimar on April 8 and 11, 1869, before the king and queen of Prussia, but it earned mixed reviews. She learned that long compositions strained her capabilities.

Her entertaining continued apace, with "at homes" on Saturdays becoming an institution among the elite and crowned heads at this famous resort. She was gay, lively, and always interesting, but Louis had become a virtual recluse. Clara Schumann visited often. Despite temperamental differences (Latin vs. German), they remained fairly good friends while admiring each other's talents unreservedly. Brahms became a casual friend and a huge admirer, calling her a "most remarkable and superior woman and the greatest artist of the century." He once wrote a serenade for her birthday, and on March 3, 1870, at Jena she premiered his great *Alto Rhapsody*.

As for her family, Didie was talented in painting and Marianne in singing, while little Paul was already on his way to becoming a concert violinist. Louise became a professor at the St. Petersburg School of Music. In 1864, to Viardot's great sorrow, her mother died in Brussels, where she had gone after the move to Baden-Baden. They had always been close and affectionate, and Turgenev likewise was very devoted to her.

The relationship with Turgenev experienced its most settled phase in these years. He had already considered moving to Germany and was only too glad to take rooms in Baden-Baden for four years while building a villa next door to the Viardots. Her attitude toward him softened. When he returned to Russia at intervals, he wrote daily and passionately and she warmly and almost as often. They appeared to have reached a kind of *modus vivendi* now that they were, as he put it, tied up "to the pier of old age" (old age being here a relative term). During a chance encounter in Berlin in 1867, they were blissfully happy. As usual, happiness only made him more pessimistic than ever about life. She, on the other hand, while since childhood not a practicing Catholic, believed in the immortality of the soul, "a divine spark in us which never perishes, and which will end by being part of the great light." As for Louis, gossip about the two perturbed him enough to cause her to continue to guard appearances and treat her husband with more open affection. Meanwhile, Turgenev's Russian foes and friends blamed him more strongly than ever for becoming her "toady," and her for "seducing" him away from the Motherland.

Upon their flight to London in 1870, the Viardots took residence in a fine Georgian house at 30 Devonshire Place, with Turgenev nearby. But cash was low. Although she sang in concerts and oratorios, especially in the provinces, bronchitis limited her success. So she had to accept as students all who applied. Her brother Manuel, long settled in London and a famous teacher, was a welcome presence. Not wanting to leave her family for seven months a year, she turned down offers wangled by Turgenev from the Moscow and St. Petersburg conservatories. In July 1871, with the war over, they moved back to Paris. The harsh terms levied on France had made them very anti-Prussian now. Besides, France again was a republic.

They lived at the 48, rue de Douai house until 1874, when they moved to a larger place at number 50. In both houses Turgenev took rooms upstairs; keeping up appearances no longer seemed important. He rigged a long tube to the downstairs so he could hear her sing. Courtavenel having been demolished after they had moved to Baden-Baden, Turgenev in October 1874 financed purchase of a villa, "Les Frênes" (The Ash Trees), overlooking the Seine at Bougival, an hour or so from central Paris. Rich and famous now, he built a Swiss chalet for himself on the grounds. Thereafter they spent summers in Bougival, winters in Paris.

It was too late for her to rejoin the Opéra, but she contracted with the Conservatoire, where she taught until October 13, 1875. She also gave lessons privately. A fine teacher but not in love with the profession, she found too many pupils preferred comic opera to high tragedy, and she disliked sharing them with other teachers. Her own voice returned for a time, although less bright. She sang in popular concert-series at the Cirque d'Hiver and in recitals at soirées. Gluck, Pergolesi, Marcello, Paisiello, Schubert, Schumann, Rimsky-Korsakov, Tchaikovsky, and Spanish songs were standbys. She took a lively interest in young Jules Massenet and gave his career a boost at a critical juncture when she sang the lead in his oratorio *Marie-Magdeleine* at the Odéon on April 11, 1873. It was her last premiere performance. Saint-Saëns wrote *Samson et Delila* for her but took so long composing that she could no longer handle it. To his delight, however, in August 1874 she (as Delila and playing the piano), her pupils, and others performed the first two acts for him with homemade costumes and scenery. (The Opéra finally mounted it in 1892.)

By 1875, her public career was over. In private life, she reserved Thursdays for a strictly musical gathering featuring performances by her children and pupils and new talents. Sunday soirées were for family and old friends, with games, music, and conversation. Didie, the apple of Turgenev's eye, married a master printer in 1874. In 1876, Viardot nursed Louise back to health and a (temporary) reconciliation after a railway accident. As for Marianne, Gabriel Fauré, aided by Viardot, became engaged to her. To his intense shock, she broke off to marry a second-rank composer, Alphonse Duvernoy. Viardot herself suffered a shock with the death on June 8, 1876, of her closest woman friend, George Sand.

Her relations with Turgenev entered their final chapter. The two were happy, if less so than at Baden-Baden. She spent hours in his apartment. He would read to her in the mornings, and she would help with criticism, proofreading, and translation. He would join the family for dinner and evening pastimes.

Passion had subsided, even on his side. His fame drew crowds of friends, refugees, and favor-seekers. The Russians in particular could be a noisy nuisance. She had to act as gatekeeper, for he was never organized. Caring for two aging men now, she felt the strain, becoming more domineering, difficult, and bad-tempered. Louis, nearing 80, was slowly failing. Turgenev had always been hard to cope with: forgetful, unpunctual, superstitious, neurotic, often depressed, and a hypochondriac with increasing real ailments. She compared him to a child who constantly needs a nanny. His decline shocked his friends, who blamed her for it. His condition, however, did not prevent him from returning to Russia regularly and from ridiculous infatuations, unconsummated, with Baroness **Julia Vrevskaya** (1841–1878) and actress **Maria Savina** (1854–1915). They could only be might-have-beens for him now. The attraction Viardot exerted did not fade, but he felt a bitterness over what it had cost him. Savina said he wrote a poem he never published, "To Her," with the line, "You have plucked all my flowers and you won't come to visit my grave."

In early March 1882, Louis suffered a stroke, and in April Turgenev fell ill with cancer of the spine. Viardot gave up teaching momentarily after Louis' stroke, but that alarmed him so much about his condition that she resumed. For 18 months, she nursed and taught, a grinding existence. Fortunately, Didie and Marianne were there to help. Louis died on May 5, 1883, leaving, Viardot said, "a great void in my existence." She could not have asked for a more upright, unselfish, wise, and capable husband, and she knew it. Turgenev's last months were terrible. Pain devoured him. His mind often became unhinged; in a rage he once threw an inkwell at her. At news of his illness, visitors came by in droves. She usually had to send them away because he was too sick. The Russians in particular resented her for it. His last words to her were touching: "Here comes the Queen of Queens! How much good she has done!" He died on September 3, 1883. Didie and Marianne accompanied his funeral train to St. Petersburg, where huge crowds attended the rites. Viardot stayed behind because he had asked her not to visit his grave but instead to read now and then a few pages which had been dear to them and think of him. Viardot suffered Turgenev's loss greatly. She told friend Ludwig Pietsch, "I am just like a grain of sand in the sea! So lonely, so sad, so unhappy. So endlessly alone!"

Turgenev left everything to Viardot except for 100,000 francs to Paulinette. Years of legal wrangling followed. Paulinette's estranged husband sued but lost. Viardot inherited the Bougival chalet and all its contents. In Russia, the court ruled that his estates were "patrimonial" and hence could not be held outside the family; they went to distant relatives. He left her all papers and literary rights, but shortly before his death he had sold the copyrights. Not all the money had been paid, however. Eventually, she received at most c. 85,000 rubles—less lawyers' fees. As for the papers, she destroyed his diary as he had requested. He had named Pavel Annenkov his literary executor. Viardot turned over papers to him but probably destroyed most of her letters to Turgenev, or else they have been retained by her descendants unseen. After Annenkov finished examining the huge mass of papers, some of which he published, he returned them to her, and she destroyed some, both unimportant and important. The tale of his letters to her is exceedingly tangled. Suffice it to say, she probably destroyed all post-1870 letters, but there remained some 150 which she had left behind at Baden-Baden in 1870 and which came into other hands. A few were stolen. She allowed publication of some during her lifetime after she had expurgated them, and apparently gave permission for publication in entirety after her death. After partial publications between 1898 and 1912, the complete known surviving correspondence was published in 1972.

Viardot lived for 27 years after Turgenev's death. She spent them well despite the loneliness that would overtake her at the loss of friends. Clara Schumann, her last remaining girlhood friend, died in 1896, and her brother, Manuel, in 1906 at age 101. Saint-Saëns was about the only intimate from her glory years who survived her. In 1884, she sold the rue de Douai and Bougival homes and moved into a fine apartment at 243, boulevard Saint-Germain, with views of the Palais-Bourbon and the Place de la Concorde. She continued to teach for many years, giving free lessons to those who could not pay. One of her pupils was **Anna Eugénie Schoen-René** (1864–1942), later a professor at the Juilliard School in New York and teacher of *Risë Stevens (b. 1913), **Margaret Harshaw** (1909–1997), **Thelma Votipka** (1906–1972), Charles Kullman, and Paul Robeson. She also composed, including the libretto and music for a comic opera, *Cendrillon* (1904), which was revived at Newport in 1971, and stage music for a pantomime, *Au Japon*, and Racine's *Andromaque*, *Phèdre*, and *Athalie*. Viardot won critical esteem but little popularity. The growing popularity of Russian music pleased her since she had had much to do with it. When not teaching or composing, she drew and painted and traveled, especially to Switzerland. Her health flourished for many years, and her hair turned gray only very late in life. When Tchaikovsky visited her in 1886 and 1889, he emerged marvelling at her vitality. In time, most of her visitors were not musicians but journalists and writers seeking information about Turgenev and other famous people she had known. Experience taught her caution in dealing with them.

Her sight and then her hearing started to fade around 1900. From 1906 on, she was nearly blind from cataracts, and bronchial and kidney ailments recurred. She began to fail seriously around Christmas 1909. On May 16, 1910, two months shy of her 89th birthday, she announced to her startled intimates that she had two days to live. She fell asleep in an armchair and died without waking at about 3:00 AM on May 18. Her last spoken word was "Norma"—the role she had always considered her greatest challenge. That she spoke not of her family or Turgenev but of her profession reveals much about how she viewed her life.

Her funeral on May 20 was buried in the press by the funeral of England's Edward VII the same day. The rites were held at the Basilica of Sainte-Clotilde. Soloists sang Carissimi's *O vulnera doris* and Fauré's *Pie Jésu*. Saint-Saëns, Massenet, and a government representative spoke. (She had received the Legion of Honor in 1901.) Burial followed at the Montmartre Cemetery. Fauré wrote a fine tribute in *Le Figaro*; but she had been off the stage for 40 years and could have been at best a dim memory for most people.

Extravagant praise was the norm when contemporaries spoke of Pauline Viardot's skill as a singer and actress. She herself, nevertheless, was modest and praised and encouraged others. Needless to say, she had a very acute sensibility. She described herself once: "My romantic soul expressed in my Southern temperament perhaps is wrongly understood in the cooler atmosphere of the North, but in my Southern land the heart beats quicker and emotions mingle with the warmth of the character." Before she went on stage her heart would pound and she would turn pale and lose her breath: "I feel the presence of the enemy." Professionally, writes Pleasants, she established "the prototype of the modern mezzo-soprano." In Richard Mohr's words, she "lifted the mezzo-soprano in opera from the handmaiden to prima donna rank." Arguably, no singer before Callas infused bel canto roles with such emotional power and believability. She could clothe the pyrotechnics with dramatic meaning; display pieces were never simply displays. Moreover, her service to Russian music was huge. As Alexander Herzen wrote, "After Liszt and Berlioz, no foreigner did more valuable work for [our] Russian music than Pauline Viardot."

Her relationship with Turgenev will provide fodder for scholars forever. She poured into friendships all the characteristics of love. Because she was so sensitive, she often forced herself to be cold and indifferent to protect herself. She described her will as "the insuperable sister" of her conscience. She also protected her career. Love threatened it. Fearing the loss of her career and self-esteem if she wholly surrendered, she took refuge in passionate friendships. Turgenev helped her career greatly: by encouraging her at every step, by introducing her to literature which would enhance her interpretations, and by being a perceptive, informed critic.

His debt to her was enormous, beginning with the encouragement she gave him to be a professional writer. In 1867, he wrote to her, "[Y]ou are the sovereign judge and umpire. . . . I don't know what success my [latest] work will have in Russia, but I have success—the only kind I aspire to: your approval." In 1876, she spoke to a visitor about this "saddest of men," as she once called him: "Not a single line of Turgenev has appeared in print for a very long time without his first acquainting me with it. You Russians don't really know how much you are indebted to me that Turgenev goes on writing and working." Lacking in self-confidence, he needed the support of strong personalities. Her specific influence on plots and characters will be debated endlessly, but it is clear that his repeated use of strong women and weak men owed much to his relationship with her. He also owed her a great debt in matters of style and imagery. More than anyone or anything, she helped "fuse" his life and works. And not least of all, it was through her that he completed his Westernization, putting him in contact with artists and writers outside Russia.

Viardot's memory, sad to say, survives almost wholly through her connection with Turgenev. Such is the fate of performers before the invention of the phonograph and the motion picture: their art vanishes in an instant, discernible now only dimly in yellowing, crumbling reviews and memoirs. By contrast, in both senses of the word, Turgenev's works are immortal.

SOURCES:

Barry, Nicole. *Pauline Viardot, l'égérie de Sand et Tourguéniev*. Paris: Flammarion, 1990.

Cofer, Angela Faith. "Pauline Viardot-Garcia: The Influence of the Performer on Nineteenth-Century Opera." Ph.D. diss., University of Cincinnati, 1988.

Desternes, Suzanne, and Antoinette Chandet. *La Malibran et Pauline Viardot, avec la collaboration d'Alice Viardot*. Paris: Fayard, 1969.

FitzLyon, April. *The Price of Genius: A Life of Pauline Viardot*. London: John Calder, 1964.

Freeborn, Richard. *Turgenev: The Novelist's Novelist—A Study*. London: Oxford University Press, 1963.

Knowles, A.V. *Ivan Turgenev*. Boston, MA: Twayne, 1988.

Magarshack, David. *Turgenev*. NY: Grove Press, 1954.

Pahlen, Kurt. *Great Singers: From the Seventeenth Century to the Present Day*. Trans. by Oliver Coburn. NY: Stein & Day, 1974.

Pleasants, Henry. *The Great Singers: From the Dawn of Opera to Our Own Time*. NY: Simon & Schuster, 1966.

Rogers, Francis. *Some Famous Singers of the Nineteenth Century*. NY: H.W. Gray, 1977.

Schapiro, Leonard. *Turgenev: His Life and Times*. NY: Random House, 1978.

Waddington, Patrick. "Turgenev and Pauline Viardot: An Unofficial Marriage," in *Canadian Slavonic Papers*. Vol. 26, no. 1, 1984, pp. 42–64.

Yarmolinsky, Avrahm. *Turgenev: The Man, His Art, and His Age*. NY: Century, 1926.

SUGGESTED READING:

Baker, T., trans. "Pauline Viardot-Garcia to Julius Rietz (Letters of Friendship)," in *Musical Quarterly*. Vol. 1, 1915, pp. 350–80, 526–559; Vol. 2, 1916, pp. 32–60.

Blanchard, Roger, and Roland de Candé. *Dieux et divas de l'Opéra*. Paris: Plon, 1987.

Dulong, Gustave. *Pauline Viardot, tragédienne lyrique*. Paris: Association des amis d'Ivan Tourguéniev, Pauline Viardot, Maria Malibran, 1987.

Héritte-Viardot, Louise. *Une Famille de grands musiciens: Memoirs de Louise Héritte-Viardot*. Paris: Stock, 1923.

Malvern, Gladys. *The Great Garcias*. NY: Longmans, Green, 1958.

Rozonov, Aleksandr S. *Polina Viardo-Garsia*. Leningrad: "Muzyka," 1982.

Sand, George. *Correspondance*. Ed. George Lubin. Paris: Garnier frères, 1980.

———. *Lettres inédites de George Sand et de Pauline Viardot, 1838–1849*. Ed. Thérèse Marix-Spire. Paris: Nouvelles Éditions Latines, 1959.

Schoen-René, Anna Eugénie. *America's Musical Inheritance: Memories and Reminiscences*. NY: Putnam, 1941.

Tourguéniev, Ivan. *Lettres inédites de Tourguéniev à Pauline Viardot et à sa famille*. Ed. H. Grandjard and A. Zviguilsky. Lausanne: Éditions de L'Age d'homme, 1972.

Turgenev, Ivan. *The Dodillon Copies of Letters by Turgenev to Pauline Viardot and Louis Viardot*. Ed. by Patrick Waddington. Belfast: Queen's University of Belfast, 1970.

Viardot, Paul. *Souvenirs d'un artiste*. Paris: Fischbacher, 1910.

Waddington, Patrick. "Turgenev's Last Will and Testament," in *New Zealand Slavonic Journal*. Vol. 2, 1974, pp. 39–64.

David S. Newhall,
Pottinger Distinguished Professor of History Emeritus,
Centre College, and author of
Clemenceau: A Life at War (1991)

Vibia Aurelia Sabina (b. 166).

See Faustina II for sidebar.

Vibia Perpetua (181–203).

See joint entry under Perpetua and Felicitas.

Vibia Sabina (88–136 CE).

See Sabina.

Viborada (d. 925)

Frankish recluse and saint. Died in 925 in France; never married; no children.

Viborada lived as a recluse and was made a saint a century after her death. She was born into a petty noble family of France, and lived in monastic austerity even as a girl. When her brother joined the monastery at St. Gall to study for the priesthood, Viborada also began working there in the scriptorium, primarily designing and executing handsome leather and metal book covers. On her brother's ordination, the two left St. Gall and opened their house as a hospital which received people of any means. After a pilgrimage to Rome, Viborada had a cell built for her at a nearby church. Her piety and mysticism gained her many followers who frequently sent her gifts and provided donations for her support. As an ascetic, Viborada kept only the barest supplies she needed to maintain life, and gave the rest to the poor.

After a few years of receiving visitors and consulting people of all ranks on spiritual matters, Viborada wanted to shut herself into total isolation. Thus about 891, she moved to another cell at a more remote church. She no longer received visitors and spoke to almost no one, but made an important exception for a young woman named **Rachilda**, who was suffering from an undiagnosed disease and could not be cured. Viborada requested that Rachilda be brought to her, and insisted that she would be healed if she remained as a recluse with her. The woman's parents agreed, and Rachilda remained with Viborada in her tiny rooms until Viborada's death over 30 years later. Rachilda was indeed cured by the treatment and prayers of the holy woman, a phenomenon which served to increase Viborada's already widespread renown.

About 925, Hungarian troops at war with the Franks invaded that country. The local bishop offered Viborada refuge at a nearby fortress, but the aged holy woman refused to leave her cell or to let Rachilda leave. The enemy troops burned the church and, it is reported, burned the roof off of the recluses' cell. Unable to find any valuables in their looting, they killed Viborada, who would not run. Rachilda survived her spiritual mentor for over 20 years. In 1047, Pope Clement II canonized Viborada.

SOURCES:

Dunbar, Agnes. *Dictionary of Saintly Women, vol. I*. London: G. Bell and Sons, 1904.

Laura York, M.A. in History,
University of California,
Riverside, California

Vicario, Leona (1789–1842)

Mexican revolutionary, born in an age of upheaval in Europe and the Americas, who became the most notable woman of wealth and privilege to join the struggle for Mexican independence from 1810 to 1821. Born María de la Soledad Leona Camila Vicario Fernández de San Salvador (but from childhood known simply as Leona Vicario) on April 10, 1789, in Mexico City; died at home in Mexico City on August 21, 1842; daughter of Gaspar Martín Vicario (a wealthy merchant born in Spain) and Camila Fernández de San Salvador y Montiel (of a distinguished family of Toluca, Mexico); educated at home in religion, Spanish and French, history, painting, sketching and music; married Andrés Quintana Roo (the future statesman), in 1813; children, Genoveva (b. 1817); María Dolores (b. 1820).

Orphaned and an heiress at 18 (1807); learned of French occupation of Spain (mid-1808); sympathized with educated Mexicans' efforts (late 1808) to establish a national congress; deplored Spaniards' violent removal of viceroy from office (September 15, 1808) for supporting Mexicans' desire for a voice in their government; after independence movement began (September 16, 1810), contacted and aided the revolutionaries (1811–13); detected (February 28, 1813); fled Mexico but was recaptured and imprisoned in a convent in Mexico (March 11, 1813); freed by patriots (late April 1813); joined insurgents and married Andrés Quintana Roo, one of the intellectual lights of Mexican independence (late 1813); with husband, suffered incredible hardships eluding enemy for four years; first child born in a hovel (1817); accepted pardon (1818); returned to Mexico City (early 1820) where second child was born; after independence was achieved (1821), her husband served in cabinet, legislature, and supreme court while she retired to private life.

Writings: her letters in defense of her role in the Mexican independence movement appeared in the newspaper El Federalista Mexicano *(February–March 1831).*

Leona Vicario, born into a society characterized by extreme male dominance, was a wealthy woman of independent mind and resolute will. In an age when middle- and upper-class women occupied themselves exclusively with domestic affairs, Vicario took a great interest in the public sphere. And at a time when well-off Mexican women seldom left their homes unchaperoned, during the Mexican revolution for independence she traveled hundreds of miles from home. Her companions were mostly men who, like her, were bent on independence from Spain. During the 1810–21 struggle, she challenged most of the stereotypes concerning "the weaker sex" and "woman's sphere." In her day, Leona Vicario was admired by patriots and scorned by traditionalists. Since her death and for over 150 years, she has been an icon of Mexican history.

Leona Vicario had a conventional and pious upbringing as the only child of a self-made Spanish immigrant and a Mexican-born mother of Spanish origin. Her father Gaspar Martín Vicario, born near Palencia in Old Castile, was one of tens of thousands of impoverished Spaniards, going back to the Conquest, who went to Mexico in search of wealth and social position. As was true of most *gachupines*, as Spaniards were derisively called by Mexican *criollos* (whites born in Mexico), Gaspar worked and possessed such good business sense that when he chose Doña **Camila Fernández de San Salvador y Montiel** as his second wife in 1787, he had amassed a considerable fortune as a merchant. Camila, whose father died when she was a child, brought no dowry to her marriage, but she did bring class to her union with Gaspar. At the time she married him, all three of her brothers had attained high positions in the judiciary, in the university, and in the revenue service.

If they were educated at all, women of the wealthy class were educated at home. As an only child, Leona's parents lavished their attention on her schooling, especially her religious education. However, Leona also learned to speak and to write with grace and eloquence, and to paint and sketch well. She learned French well enough to try her hand at translating into Spanish one of the great works of the early French Enlightenment, Archbishop Fénélon's *The Adventures of Telemachus*. As well, Vicario studied music, but insisted that she sang badly.

What distinguished Leona from most young women of her social class was her interest in serious literature, as shown by her reading of Fénélon. She also read the works of the 18th-century Spanish polymath Friar Feijoó, which is of interest, as Feijoó was a champion of both women's education and of the *criollos* of America. It disturbed Feijoó that *criollos* were systematically excluded from all but the lower to middling positions in the Spanish colonial government. Vicario was also acquainted with Buffon's works on natural history, and read the learned Spanish Jesuit Hervas y Panduro's *Idea of the Universe*. She read some fiction, as the German Joachim-Henrich Campe's *The New Robinson* and Samuel Richardson's *Clarissa*, but her tastes tended toward works on history, politics, art and the sciences.

From Fénélon, Vicario learned that in governing, those who rule should avoid absolutism, war, luxury, adulation and corruption. Rulers should keep the taxes low, Fénélon reminded a future king of France, and be always mindful of the public good. Leona, like many other educated *criollos*, was aware that Spanish absolutism had increased rather than diminished since the start of the French Revolution. In addition, luxury, adulation, and corruption were pervasive in the Spanish court. And, to pay for Spain's wars against France and England, by 1808 taxes and forced loans were at very high levels in the Spanish colonies.

Vicario's life changed drastically in 1807, when first her father and then her mother died. Camila left her only daughter a considerable fortune of over 100,000 pesos. To help the 18-year-old Leona administer the inheritance prudently, Camila appointed her eldest brother, who was also Leona's godfather, to serve as his niece's legal guardian. Agustín Pomposo Fernández de San Salvador y Montiel was one of Mexico's most distinguished lawyers and was past rector of the capital's Royal and Pontifical University. He was scrupulous in his administration of his dear niece's fortune. Aware of her independent will but need for protection, he arranged to rent a mansion for Leona in which he and his family occupied a separate wing.

After her mother's death, Vicario was for months engrossed in repairing and furnishing her part of the mansion her uncle had rented. However, given her interest in public issues, she had to be aware of the political drama that was unfolding in Mexico City. Early in 1808, Napoleon Bonaparte occupied Spain and deposed King Charles III and then his heir Prince

Ferdinand (I), later king of the Two Sicilies. When Napoleon installed his brother Joseph on the Spanish throne, all of the Spanish colonies were thrown into turmoil. In many colonial cities, the *criollos* seized the opportunity to establish either a *junta* or a congress which they hoped would eventually be the vehicle for separation from Spain. In Mexico, Viceroy Iturrigaray, an undistinguished and corrupt executive, gave into the demands of the *criollos* for a national congress, which native-born Mexicans would clearly dominate. In Mexico in 1808, there were only some 70,000 Spaniards out of a total population of about 7 million.

To prevent the Congress from meeting in Mexico City, on the night of September 16, 1808, some 300 well-armed Spaniards deposed the viceroy and imprisoned the most prominent advocates of a national congress. For the next 12 years, Mexico was to endure harsh military rule and a bloody revolution which took the lives of over 500,000 Mexicans.

We do not know Vicario's initial reaction to the unprecedented events of 1808. Mindful that her kind uncle Agustín was publishing pamphlet after pamphlet in defense of the colonial system, she probably kept her own counsel. She must have felt extremely ambivalent about the crisis at hand. On the one hand, she was the daughter of a Spanish father, but on the other she was also the daughter of a Mexican mother and a woman of liberal ideas. Her loyalty toward her Spanish heritage was demonstrated by her devotion to the Virgin of Remedios, who was associated with the success of the Spanish conquest. However, Vicario was also devoted to the Virgin of Guadalupe, the patron of the conquered. Guadalupe became the symbol of Mexican nationhood after a parish priest, Miguel Hidalgo, began the long revolt against Spanish rule in September 1810.

Father Hidalgo was captured and executed early in 1811, but the rebellion continued in the western and southern provinces. Sometime that year Vicario chose sides, for by early 1812 she was corresponding with the followers of Hidalgo's successor, the lawyer Ignacio Rayón. To protect her correspondents and herself, she devised elaborate ciphers and used literary pseudonyms. She also became associated with the "Guadalupes," a secret society of *criollos* who favored the insurgents, as the proponents of independence were called.

While Agustín was fulminating against the rebellion, his cousin Juan Bautista Raz y Guzmán was leading the Guadalupes. The society engaged in espionage and transmitted information on troop movements to the badly outnumbered insurgents. They also supplied the insurgent leader Rayón with monetary aid and, most important, a printing press. Until the press arrived at Rayón's headquarters in late 1811, the insurgents lacked the means to counter royalist propaganda. Three female relatives of Leona, including Raz y Guzmán's wife, were able to get the press out of Mexico City by concealing it in their coach. The women were chosen for the dangerous mission precisely because it would have been unthinkable to search upper-class women or their coach. Later, in April 1813, when Vicario fled the capital to join the insurgents she took with her printer's ink and other accessories for the press.

During 1812 and until early 1813, Vicario provided the insurgents with funds for badly needed food, clothing, arms and ammunition. She also came to the financial aid of the wives and children of captured or deceased insurgents. One question that has not been addressed by biographers of Leona Vicario is how she was able to aid the insurgents while living adjacent to her pro-royalist uncle Agustín. There is no evidence that, up to March 2, 1813, Agustín was aware of his niece's activities on behalf of the insurgents or of the involvement of other relatives in the Guadalupe Society. In fact, not until 1815, when the revolution was moribund for a time, were Raz y Guzmán and his associates placed under arrest for aiding and abetting the insurrection.

It is not love alone that determines the actions of women. . . . The desire for the glory and liberty of their homeland are sentiments not unknown to them.

—Leona Vicario

Vicario escaped detection until February 27, 1813, when one of her servants, who was carrying her letters, some clothing, and two watches to the insurgents, was intercepted by the royalists. Threatened with death, he revealed her identity. On learning of her danger, on March 1 Leona precipitously left Mexico City in the company of three female companions, ostensibly to attend a country picnic. For the next ten days, from March 1 to 11, Vicario sought vainly to elude capture. She endured the first physical hardships she had ever experienced in her life. Ill due to exposure, lack of food, and polluted water, Leona was persuaded by her anguished uncle Agustín to return to Mexico and accept an *indulto*, or royal pardon. The authorities assured him that his niece could return to her house and that she would not be harassed by the dreaded Junta of Security and Order.

However, the duplicity of the royalists was notorious. On March 11, 1813, she was taken by force to the Convent of Belén where for weeks she was interrogated relentlessly about her pro-insurgent activities. Her interrogators were unable to break her will, and she steadfastly refused to implicate anyone but herself. Informed of her situation in April 1813, Rayón dispatched three insurgent officers to Mexico City to enter the convent by a ruse and free Vicario from her captors. Dressed in rags and with a coal-blackened face to escape detection, the once elegant heiress traveled hundreds of miles to insurgent territory in the west. There she joined her first cousin, Manuel (eldest son of her hapless uncle Agustín) and Andrés Quintana Roo, the young man she had fallen in love with two years before.

Andrés Quintana Roo was a gifted poet, writer and law student from Yucatan, who, by 1810, had come under the wing of Leona's uncle Agustín in Mexico City. As Agustín's legal assistant, Quintana Roo saw a great deal of Leona, which distressed her uncle. Earlier, Agustín had arranged for her engagement to a promising and wealthy young man who was abroad at the time Leona met Andrés, serving as an American delegate to Spain's first parliament in modern history. Agustín also became increasingly suspicious of the young Andrés' political leanings and discouraged contact between Andrés and his niece.

Early in 1812, Andrés decided to throw in his lot with the insurgents, and left Mexico City for Tlalpujahua in western Mexico with Agustín's eldest son, Manuel. Agustín must have been stunned on learning of his son's defection. Once among the insurgents, Andrés began publishing one of the most distinguished newspapers of the insurgency, the *Despertador Americano*, or the *American Awakener*.

After Leona's reunion with Andrés and before the end of 1813, they were married in a rural parish in Tlalpujahua. Within months, however, and by early 1814, the insurgents led by generals Morelos and Rayón had been decisively defeated and only the most stalwart revolutionaries refused to give up.

Among the stalwarts were Leona and Andrés, who, despite incredible physical hardships, refused to seek a pardon until early 1818, a year after the birth of their first daughter, **Genoveva**. By 1818, most of the insurgent leaders were either dead or had accepted a royal pardon. The young family was ordered to leave the country for Spain, but they were unable to do so because the same royal government refused to return any of Leona's seized property. For two years Leona, Andrés and their child lived in seclusion in Toluca, some 80 miles from Mexico. They were finally permitted to return to the capital early in 1820. In that year, Andrés received his law degree from the Royal College of Lawyers and Leona gave birth to their second and last child, **María Dolores**. After independence was achieved in 1821 and until his death in 1851, Quintana Roo served successively as under secretary of State, member of Congress, government mediator, and, finally, justice of the Mexican Supreme Court.

From 1818 until her death in 1842, Vicario retired to the domestic sphere, speaking on public issues only when attacked in print by the ultra-conservative enemies of her husband. While her husband pursued an active career in the government and as a journalist, Vicario devoted her time and energies to managing a large household and educating her two daughters, Genoveva and María Dolores. She also devoted considerable time to administering the urban and rural properties she had been awarded by the Republic in 1824 in compensation for the total loss of her fortune in service to her country. By the time of her death in August 1842, she was widely revered as the "strong woman of Mexican independence." The then president of the Republic, General Antonio López de Santa Anna, an old acquaintance despite his political differences with Leona and her husband, led the enormous funeral procession to the cemetery of Nuestra Señora de los Ángeles in Mexico City. Nine years later, her husband was laid to rest at her side. In 1910, their ashes were interred in the Independence Column on the broad avenue of the Reforma in Mexico City, joining the remains of other outstanding heroes of Mexican independence.

SOURCES:

Echánove Trujillo, Carlos A. *Leona Vicario: La mujer fuerte de la independencia*. México: Ediciones Xochitl, 1945.

García, Genaro. *Leona Vicario: Heroína insurgente*. México: Editorial Innovación, 1985.

González Cosío D., Bertha. *Los Sepulcros de Santo Domingo y Cocheres: Una casa en el centro histórico de la Ciudad de México*. México: INBA, 1993.

Sosa, Francisco. *Biografías de Mexicanos Distinguidos*. México: Oficina Tipografica de la Secretaría de Fomento, 1884.

SUGGESTED READING:

Staples, Anne. *Leona Vicario*. México: Departamento Editorial de la Secretaría de la Presidencia, 1976.

Anna Macías,
Professor Emerita of History,
Ohio Wesleyan University,
Delaware, Ohio

$\mathcal{A}$CKNOWLEDGMENTS

Photographs and illustrations appearing in *Women in World History, Volume 15,* were received from the following sources:

Photo by Ernest A. Bachrach, **p.** 57; Painting by Jacques-Emile Blanche, **p.** 557; Photo by Marcus Blechman, **p.** 553; Photo by Robert Capa, **p.** 177; Courtesy of Capitol Records, photo by Ken Veeder, **p.** 709; Photo by Barron Claiborne, **p.** 521; From a painting by Benjamin Constant, **p.** 349; Painting by Piero di Cosimo, **p.** 886; From a painting by De la Perche, **p.** 481; Detail of a painting by Carolus Duran, **p.** 795; Courtesy of the Arab Republic of Egypt, **p.** 233; Photo by Gisèle Freund, **p.** 573; Photo by Gilda Grillo, **p.** 437; Courtesy of Hadassah, the Women's Zionist Organization of America, **p.** 81; Painting by William Hogarth, **p.** 844; Photo by Horst, **p.** 427; Painting by Henry Inman, **p.** 785; Photo by J.R. Jameson, **p.** 194; Photo by Christie Jenkins, **p.** 522; Photo by Gene Komman, **p.** 452; Courtesy of the Learning Corporation of America, **p.** 560; Courtesy of the Library of Congress, **pp.** 15, 65, 94, 169, 305, 633, 683, 727, 733; Courtesy of Longman International Education, Essex, **p.** 31; Courtesy of the Margaret Thatcher Foundation, **p.** 335; Photo by Angus McBean, **p.** 323; Photo by John Miehle, **p.** 780; Photo by Jack Mitchell, **p.** 151; Photo by Tina Modotti, **p.** 516; Courtesy of Det Nationalhistoriske Museum på Frederiksborg, Hillerød, **p.** 717; Painting by Ernst Normand, **p.** 835; © Paramount, 1950, **p.** 59; Photo by Man Ray, **p.** 161; Photo by A.L. Schafer, **p.** 199; Photo by Arthur Ochs Sulzberger, **p.** 9; Photo by Patrick Demarchelier, **p.** 457; Courtesy of Helen Suzman, **p.** 51; Painting by Isaac Taylor, **p.** 190; Courtesy of the University of Tennessee, **p.** 13; Courtesy of the Tolstoy Foundation at Valley Cottage, New York, **p.** 509; Portrait study by John T. Tussaud, **p.** 673; Courtesy of the U.S. House of Representatives. **pp.** 4, 420, 738; Courtesy of the U.S. State Department, **p.** 447; Courtesy of the United Nations, **p.** 492; Courtesy of USA Hockey, Inc., **p.** 243; © Walt Disney, 1964, **p.** 547; © Warner Bros, 1990, **p.** 157; © WNBA Enterprises, LLC, photo by Bill Baptist, **p.** 73.

ISBN 0-7876-4074-3

90000